BLED (p719)
A lake, an island, a mountaintop castle as a backdrop – it doesn't get more picturesque
DUBROVNIK (p163)
MOSTAR (p92)
The Balkans' most iconic bridge unites Hercegovina's enthralling, magical city
KOTOR (p583)
Brooding mountains tower over labyrinthine lanes and castle ruins in Montenegro's fjord town
BERAT (p59)
Set in rugged mountains, 'the town of a thousand windows' is an Ottoman gem
İSTANBUL (p861)
East meets West in this vast, teeming city, a roiling cauldron of human activity
GOZO (p567)
A relaxed, peaceful place, Malta's little sister boasts delightful scenery and great diving
ATHENS (p351)
For once 'mythical' is right – Athens' major sight, the Acropolis, is arguably the greatest monument in the Western world
KARPAS PENINSULA (p197)
Pad around virgin sand dunes and spy on nesting turtles in this remote haven
SWEDEN
ESTONIA
LATVIA
LITHUANIA
RUSSIA
Russia
POLAND
BELARUS
CZECH REPUBLIC
SLOVAKIA
UKRAINE
MOLDOVA
AUSTRIA
HUNGARY
ROMANIA
SLOVENIA
CROATIA
BOSNIA & HERCEGOVINA
SERBIA
MONTENEGRO
KOSOVO
MACEDONIA
BULGARIA
ALBANIA
GREECE
TURKEY
CYPRUS
LEBANON
ISRAEL & the Palestinian Territories
EGYPT
LIBYA
MALTA
BALTIC SEA
BLACK SEA
ADRIATIC SEA
AEGEAN SEA
IONIAN SEA
MEDITERRANEAN SEA
Sea of Marmara
Sea of Crete
CARPATHIAN MOUNTAINS
APENNINES

Mediterranean Europe Highlights

Mediterranean Europe is a mesmerising mix of ancient wonders, modern masterpieces and natural treasures. Iconic monuments and grand ruins litter the landscape, tropical waters lap at dreamy beaches, and great swaths of forest carpet remote, rugged mountains. There are highlights at every turn.

IZZET KERI

1 COASTAL TURKEY

For the bluest of blue water head to the lagoon of Ölüdeniz (p897) or take a boat trip to Butterfly Valley. A short distance away in the hills are the poignantly ruined houses of Kayaköy (p895), home now only to wild poppies and dragonflies.

Will Gourlay, Traveller

HVAR ISLAND, CROATIA

The island of Hvar (p158) off the Dalmatian coast claims more sunshine per year than anywhere else in Europe. I don't know if that's true, but something in the air on Hvar invites profound laziness. Eat, swim, sleep…and repeat. A short bus trip across the island from Hvar Town is Jelsa. So this is where the people live. A tranquil harbour village, Jelsa features original stone buildings, farmhouses and cobbled laneways that were made to wander through.

Željko Basić, Lonely Planet Staff

2

ANDREW BURKE

TAORMINA, ITALY

We ended a fortnight-long Sicilian adventure with the high point of Taormina (p535), which seamlessly combines all of Italy's best offers: stunning Amalfi-esque scenery, antipasto to feast on, majestic Etna, stylish Italians enjoying the *passeggiata* (traditional evening stroll), a coastal amphitheatre and some of the best gelato on the planet.

Shona Gold, Lonely Planet Staff

3

BETHUNE CARMICHAEL

OLIVIER CIRENDINI

4

BONIFACIO, CORSICA

The beauty of Bonifacio (p332) seems to attract the bold and brazen. A locus for Homer's *Odyssey*, Vandals, Moors, Ostrogoths and more recently foreign legionnaires, Bonifacio's history and legends are epic, and so too is its scenery. Precipitous limestone cliffs and secluded grottoes gradually cede to the force of winds and unruly ultramarine seas; it seems everything and everyone here eventually succumbs to the elements. Sail out into the bay for an experience you'll long remember and views you'll never forget.

Debra Herrmann, Lonely Planet Staff

TARA RIVER, MONTENEGRO

The Tara River (p596) slices deeply through the Durmitor range, creating one of the world's most dramatic rafting routes and the nation's most popular active attraction.

Peter Dragicevich, Lonely Planet Author

5

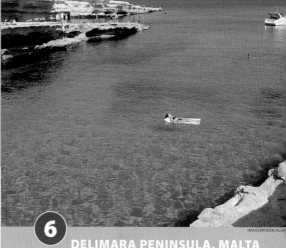

DIOMEDIA/ALAMY

IMAGEBROKER/ALAI

6

DELIMARA PENINSULA, MALTA

The best tip I can give anybody going to Malta is to hire a car and escape the large touristy resorts. We headed southeast (p566) down to Delimara Peninsula and the natural lido called Peter's Pool – it's hard to find but worth it. With only a few local kids to keep you company, it's great to laze around on the smooth, sun-drenched rocks and dive into the clear blue sea to cool off. We finished the afternoon with a freshly caught fish platter at one of the many small family-owned restaurants in Marsaxlokk and a carafe or two of Maltese wine.

Louise Vicente, Lonely Planet Staff

RUSSELL MOUNTFOI

7

THE BEST MEAL IN SICILY, ITALY

We arrived in Sicily (p529) at lunchtime on a stinking hot day in September. By chance, we walked into a little restaurant off a cobbled street and had the most amazing meal of our lives. Salty cheese drizzled in honey, anchovies, prosciutto, cherry tomatoes and fresh bread. This was followed by grilled fish and squid and a simple pasta with the freshest tomatoes. 'No more,' we cried. But then there was dessert. Succulent figs washed down with a complimentary glass of *limoncello* (lemon liqueur) at the bar.

Diana Steicke, Traveller

LATE-AFTERNOON LIGHT IN VALLETTA, MALTA

Crossing from modern, bustling Sliema by ferry to Valletta (p557) in the late afternoon is an unforgettable sight – the limestone buildings all richly luminous in the waning light, the churches of the city cresting above uniform houses and defensive walls as the Maltese capital falls quiet for the evening. Once there, wander through the tranquil, hilly streets to Trabuxu for a glass of local red wine before continuing to fabulous Rubino for dinner – that's pretty much an unbeatable Mediterranean evening for me.

Tom Masters, Lonely Planet Author

8

JOHN ELK III

ROCK PINNACLES & WONDER-OF-THE-WORLD MONASTERIES, GREECE

The ochre and russet rock spires of Meteora (p373) stunned us with their austere beauty. And then to see the elaborate stone monasteries painstakingly built on the top of these isolated outcroppings just blew us away. We happened to be some of just a few visitors that day, so the serenity of the monasteries and the gorgeous vistas surrounded us completely.

Alexis Averbuck, Lonely Planet Author

9

ANTHONY PIDGEON

DOUG MCKINLA

10 SARAJEVO, BOSNIA & HERCEGOVINA

Sarajevo (p78) was the place where WWI got started when Gavrilo Princip assassinated Archduke Franz Ferdinand in 1914, and seeing the spot where it happened was the whole reason we first visited 25 years ago. Back then concrete 'footprints' marked the spot from which Princip had pounced. Returning in 2008 I found that those footprints had been removed (as has the traffic from the now pedestrianised Latin Bridge opposite), but there's now a great little museum there that tells the whole story.

Mark Elliott, Lonely Planet Author

WAYNE WALTON

11 WALKING THE CLIFFTOPS OF SANTORINI, GREECE

The startling sight of the submerged caldera of Santorini (p388) grabbed our attention and wouldn't let go as we wandered along the path to Oia, the northern village famed for its picture-postcard sunsets. Recovering from our exertions in a caldera-facing taverna, we sank ice-cold Mythos beer and wondered at the seeming impermanence and precariousness of our spectacular surroundings.

Craig McLachlan, Lonely Planet Author

DJEMMA EL-FNA, MOROCCO

If you ever needed definitive proof that Morocco is a whole continent away from Europe, you'll find it at the Djemma el-Fna in Marrakesh (p644). When the sun dips, this huge square comes alive with steaming food stalls, acrobats, musicians, storytellers and snake charmers. It's *1001 Nights* come to life, and one of Morocco's truly unmissable experiences.

Paul Clammer, Lonely Planet Author

12

DOUG MCKINLAY

OLIVER STREWE

13

DOURO, PORTUGAL

Exploring the impossibly scenic vineyards along the Douro (p695), a Unesco World Heritage site with wine estates clinging to steep hillsides above the meandering Douro River, is truly a highlight.

Regis St Louis, Lonely Planet Author

WAYNE WALTON

14

MLJET ISLAND, CROATIA

Seventy percent of Mljet (p162) is a natural park; there are three salt lakes in the middle of the island, remote sandy beaches and only one conventional hotel; and the food – consisting of fresh fish, octopus and goat, all baked under hot coals – is magnificent. Need I say more?

Vesna Maric, Lonely Planet Author

PETER PTSCHELINZEV

15 AMASYA, TURKEY

Wandering Amasya (p912), a truly stunning representative of Turkey's Ottoman revival, is like stumbling upon a fairy-tale kingdom. Pontic tombs are carved into the wrinkly cliff faces beneath the citadel's lofty perch, with a tunnel worming between them like an ancient log flume. The half-timbered Ottoman mansions bulge over the Yeşilırmak River, their balconies gazing across the water at Amasya's minarets and *medreses* (Islamic seminaries). There's even a local Romeo and Juliet–style folk tale about a humble craftsman, Ferhat, who carved a channel through the mountains to woo the royal Şirin. The outside world only intrudes when a train chugs between the old town and the castle rock.

James Bainbridge, Lonely Planet Author

CALA GONONE, SARDINIA

Everyone had told me how beautiful Sardinia was but nothing, not even seven years of travelling in Italy, had prepared me for the spectacular landscape around Cala Gonone (p541). Impenetrable granite peaks brooding over wooded valleys, forbidding gorges gashed out of grey rock, tropical waters lapping at hidden beaches – it really is nature at its most imperious. Driving down from Dorgali, the road plummets through a series of second-gear hairpin bends to Cala Gonone, nestled snugly in her own quiet corner of paradise.

Duncan Garwood, Lonely Planet Author

16

ANDREW PEACOCK

JEAN-BERNARD CARILLET

17

MARSEILLE, FRANCE

The ancient port of Marseille (p307) has been described as the most North African of European cities. When you're sipping coffee by the water's edge of the Vieux Port, it's hard not to be carried away by the illusion that you're in Algiers, Tunis or even Beirut.

Anpl, Traveller

TONY WHEELER

18

ALBANIA'S CASTLES

Being spooked in castles ain't unusual in Albania (p39); Robert Carver wrote about it years ago in *The Accursed Mountains*. Being on your own with practically unrestricted access to isolated historical monuments does bring up some 'skin crawl' moments, but just emphasises how fresh to tourism this country is.

Jayne D'Arcy, Lonely Planet Author

KARPAS PENINSULA, CYPRUS

For travellers wanting to experience a different Cyprus, the uniqueness and beauty of the Karpas (also known in Turkish as Kırpaşa) Peninsula (p197) cannot be overrated. The 'end' of Cyprus really feels like the world's end, far from the urban and tourist bustle. It has miles of rolling fields, endless beaches, wildlife, and fantastic swimming, cycling and hiking.

Vesna Maric, Lonely Planet Author

19

DAVID ROBERTSON/ALAMY

CRAIG PERSHO

20

VRŠIČ PASS, SLOVENIA

More often than not, even serial visitors to Slovenia like myself just stop and stare, mesmerised by the sheer beauty of this land. With so much splendour strewn across the country, it's nigh on to impossible to choose a *številka ena* (that's No 1 to you) absolute favourite top place. OK, OK, it's the Vršič Pass (p724), which stands (literally) head and shoulders above the rest, and leads me past Mt Triglav, and down to sunny Primorska province and the bluer-than-blue Soča River in a hair-raising, spine-tingling hour.

Steve Fallon, Lonely Planet Author

HOLGER LE

21

STROMBOLI, ITALY

Visiting this island (p533) on an organised trek to climb a live volcano at night is one of the most magical things I have ever done. It is terrifying being at the top when it starts to rumble and bubble, but worth it for the adrenalin rush of being able to look right into the crater when it is blowing out fire and pumice.

Phillipa Blitz, Lonely Planet Staff

Contents

Regional Map Contents

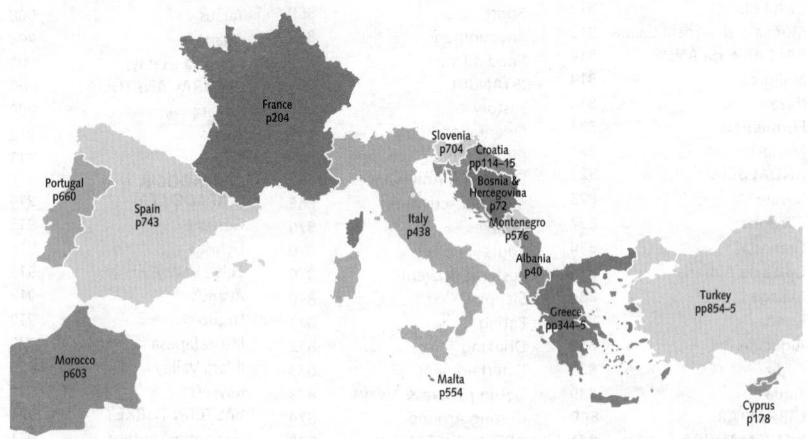

Destination Mediterranean Europe

Golden beaches lapped by azure waters, the feel of sun on your skin and sand under your feet, ancient ruins rising out of parched rocks, stunning seascapes, great art, awe-inspiring architecture – Mediterranean Europe is all these things. But, more than just the snapshots, what makes this region so endlessly fascinating is the reality behind the gloss, the struggles, passions and politics of its 300 million inhabitants.

The Mediterranean has long been a byword for sun and southern sensuality, and it is today the world's top tourist destination. Of the planet's 10 most visited nations, four are Mediterranean countries (France, Spain, Italy and Turkey), and every year close to 200 million people pour into the region.

The reasons why are no secret. The Mediterranean boasts Europe's best beaches, and a long, varied coastline that stretches from Portugal's windswept western seaboard to Turkey's 'Turquoise Coast'. Along this stretch the scenery is compelling and the food is magnificent.

The region's cultural legacy is without rival. Classical ruins testify to the power and ambition of ancient empires; Islamic art tells of Moorish sophistication and Ottoman vision; and Gothic cathedrals, Renaissance palaces and baroque facades record the great artistic movements of history. A roll-call of Mediterranean artists reveals names such as Michelangelo, da Vinci, Goya, Monet, Dalí and Picasso.

While the region is steeped in history, however, it is not stuck in it. Mediterranean countries might be conservative by northern European standards – traditions are respected and religion remains an influential social arbiter – but they have enthusiastically embraced modern life. The result is a mesmerising tableau of juxtapositions – packed commuter buses rattle past the Colosseum in Rome; Prada-clad locals sip Starbucks coffee amid minarets in İstanbul; camera-toting tourists snap away in Fez' medieval medina.

In terms of politics, the Mediterranean map is currently a tepid shade of blue. Right-wing governments call the shots in Albania, Croatia, France, Greece, Italy, Morocco and Portugal. A high-profile exception is Spain, where the socialist leader, José Luis Rodríguez Zapatero, has polarised opinion with his commitment to progressive, often controversial, social policy. Since assuming power, he has legalised gay marriage (making Spain only the third country in the world to do so), passed laws on women's rights and approved legislation against domestic violence. He's also signed an amnesty granting residency to 700,000 illegal immigrants.

Migration has long been an issue for Mediterranean countries, although until relatively recently it was emigration rather than immigration that was the main concern. Many of the migrants who poured into North America in the early 1900s came from southern and Eastern Europe. Today, however, the Mediterranean is an important destination in itself, and the main gateway into Europe. Policing of the key routes into the region – from North Africa to Spain, Italy and Malta, and from Iran across Turkey and into Greece – has increased in recent years, but still large-scale immigration persists.

Public and political opinion remains sharply divided on the subject. Supporters claim that immigration is necessary to compensate for Europe's ageing population and low birth rates, while opponents assert that it merely exacerbates unemployment and leads to increased crime. National governments are similarly divided in their approach. Nevertheless, agreement was reached in 2008 on the need for a European-wide response, and the 27 member states of the EU signed the European Pact on Immigration and Asylum, calling for a system of targeted immigration and common asylum procedures.

At the time of writing, Mediterranean Europe, like the rest of the world, had been hit hard by the global recession. The most obvious indicator of this has been an increase in unemployment across the region. The effect the recession will have on Mediterranean tourism remains to be seen, but commentators are predicting hard times for countries reliant on foreign tourists, such as Spain and Greece. The continued growth of the Eastern European and Balkan destinations is also likely to slow down. In recent years, these countries have been actively focusing on tourism, attracting travellers with offers of unspoilt countryside and adrenalin-charged adventure sports. And while they are well placed to continue growing – they're affordable, and exotic enough to excite without being intimidating – competition for tourist revenue has never been tougher.

One of the challenges currently facing Mediterranean Europe is how to promote tourism while simultaneously safeguarding the environment. The Mediterranean's natural resources are considerable – it's home to an estimated 25,000 species of flora and some 6% of the world's marine species – but these resources are increasingly under attack from a long list of enemies, including climate change, pollution, overfishing, desertification and coastal erosion. Spearheading the environmental cause is the WWF, whose Rome-based Mediterranean Programme Office is involved with projects across the region. These include efforts to preserve the Mediterranean's cork forests, to save the bluefin tuna from extinction, and to conserve fresh water in North Africa and the western Balkans.

In many respects, the issues affecting Mediterranean Europe mirror those faced elsewhere in the Western world, yet the region remains unique. Located on the crossroads of east and west, north and south, it boasts an unparalleled cultural and geographic make-up. Its myths, its spectacular coasts and snow-capped mountains, its heady cities, its world-class sights and its gourmet pleasures have survived more than 3000 years of tumultuous history, and chances are they'll survive for some time yet.

Getting Started

Mediterranean Europe is not a difficult destination to make your way around: travellers have been passing through for thousands of years and the region is well set up for visitors. Accommodation runs the gamut from backpacker crash pads to luxurious five-star palaces; transport is efficient and reasonably priced; and there are any number of eating options. English is widely spoken in the main tourist centres, but attempts to speak the local language will generally elicit a friendly response. In the region's rocky hinterland you might encounter some language difficulties, but they'll rarely prove insurmountable.

How much you plan in advance largely depends on what you want to do and when. For much of the year you can pretty well make it up as you go along, but if you're hoping to spend two weeks on the beach in August, you'd do well to book ahead. Similarly, you'd be advised to plan ahead over Easter, Christmas and New Year.

WHEN TO GO

Any time's good but the best periods are spring (April through to mid-June) and early autumn (September and October). In these periods, the weather is sunny without being stifling (it's generally hot enough for the beach in June and September), crowds are bearable and prices are not at summer peaks. If you want to travel in summer, try to avoid August. Everyone in France, Spain and Italy takes their beach holidays in this month, which means that prices are sky-high, accommodation is fully booked and the major resorts are packed. It can also get uncomfortably hot with temperatures regularly topping 40°C in some parts. That said, if you can bear the heat, you'll sometimes find savings to be made in the big cities as hoteliers drop their rates to lure punters away from the coast.

For the low-down on the region's current affairs, log onto www.southeuropenews.com. You'll find articles on everything from politics to finance, fashion and sport.

Summer is the best time of the year to catch a festival; hundreds are staged between June and September – for listings see the Events Calendar, p29. Easter is another big festival period, marked by processions, parades and passion plays across the region.

Ski resorts begin operating in late November/early December and move into full swing after the New Year, closing down when the snow begins to melt in late March or April. Expect to pay high-season rates between Christmas and the first week in January and then from late January through to late March. Away from the ski resorts and major cities, winter (December through to March) is the region's downtime. The weather, if not cold by northern standards, is often grey and wet, and many resorts simply shut up shop until the next season.

See Climate Charts (p944) for more weather information.

For country-specific weather information, see the Climate & When to Go sections in individual chapters. As a general rule, the Mediterranean coast is hotter and drier than the Atlantic seaboard, with most rain falling in autumn and winter (roughly November to March). In most places, bank on high season prices between May and September, at Easter, and over Christmas and New Year. Low season generally runs from October through to March or April.

COSTS & MONEY

Europe is not cheap, but as a general rule the further south and east you go, the cheaper it gets. Of the countries covered in this guide, Morocco, Turkey and the Balkan nations are cheaper than France, Italy and Spain.

DON'T LEAVE HOME WITHOUT...

- ID card or passport and visa if required (see p955).
- Travel insurance (see p948) – make sure it covers the countries you're visiting and any activities you might be doing (diving, bungee jumping etc).
- Your driving licence and, if necessary, International Driving Permit if you're planning to hire a car (see p965).
- Your ATM/credit card PIN number in figures not letters.
- Photocopies of all important documents.
- Plug adaptor, power transformer and mobile-phone recharger (see p947).
- A torch.
- A smart 'going-out' set of clothes.
- Sandals/thongs for showers and pebbly beaches.
- A penknife with a corkscrew for those impromptu picnics.
- Solar batteries.

Of all your expenses, accommodation is by far the greatest cost. Whether you stay in youth hostels (roughly €10 to €30 for a dorm bed), budget pensions (up to about €55 for a double) or midrange hotels (from about €80), your accommodation will probably amount to between a half and two-thirds of your daily expenditure. Needless to say, prices drop considerably outside of the main tourist centres and in the low season, sometimes by as much as 40%. For details of accommodation options, see p938.

Eating can be as cheap or as expensive as you like. Grab a bite from a roadside snack bar and you could pay as little as €1.50. Alternatively, sit down to a restaurant meal and you should reckon on at least €25.

XE (www.xe.com) is an up-to-the-second online currency-exchange calculator. Find out the rates for Mediterranean European currencies, and see exactly how much your trip is going to cost you.

Public transport throughout the region is largely efficient. Buses and long-distance coaches are generally cheaper than trains, especially for cross-border travel, and ferry travel is reasonably priced. Car hire is expensive, typically from about €30 per day, plus fuel (also expensive).

As a rough guide, a backpacker cutting all the corners – sticking to youth hostels, snacking at noon and travelling slowly – should reckon on €25 to €50 per day. Midrange travellers staying in budget hotels, eating in modest restaurants and visiting one or two sights a day, can expect to pay anything from €50 to €150. At the top end of the scale, staying in resort hotels and eating full-course restaurant meals could easily cost from €200 per day.

To save money there are a number of things to look out for. If you're travelling with kids, note that some hotels don't charge for toddlers who bunk up with mum and dad, and that many state museums in EU countries are free to under 18s (and over 65s). Discount cards, city and transport passes will often save you a bob or two – see individual country chapters and the Regional Directory (p946) for further details. When eating out, try ordering set lunchtime menus and drinking the local wine as opposed to expensive bottled beer. Note also that where hotel breakfasts are charged as extra, you'll often save money (and eat better) by grabbing something at a nearby bar or cafe.

Compare prices on everything from travel insurance to car hire, airport parking and credit cards on www.moneysupermarket.com.

The best way to access your money on the road is to use an ATM card. ATMs are widely available throughout the region. It's always a good idea, however, to have a little spare cash for emergencies, both in the local currency and in an easily exchanged currency such as US dollars. About €150 should be sufficient. For further details on money matters, see p949 and individual country chapters.

TRAVELLING RESPONSIBLY

On a global scale, your individual journey might not seem particularly environmentally significant, but consider tourism's impact on the Mediterranean. The region is the world's biggest tourist destination, receiving about 200 million visitors each year. And with this figure set to rise – the UN's World Tourism Organisation estimates that Mediterranean tourist arrivals will reach 346 million by 2020 – the strain on the area's already stretched natural resources is only going to get worse.

So what can you do to reduce your environmental footprint?

Getting There & Away

Budget airlines are here to stay and they bring in a large percentage of visitors to the region. This is good news for tourism in the region but less so for the environment as air travel is a major contributor to climate change. Mile for mile, the amount of carbon dioxide emitted for one person driving a car is much the same as for one passenger on a plane, but with flying the carbon and other greenhouse gases are spewed out at much higher altitudes and this has a significantly greater effect on climate change.

Check out the region's best beaches on www.blueflag.org. Spain has 442 beaches with the prestigious Blue Flag rating; Greece has 416 and Turkey 258.

To alleviate the impact of your carbon emissions, there are a number of carbon offset schemes that enable you to calculate your emissions and offset them by contributing to renewable energy schemes and reforestation projects. For further information, check out the website of **Climate Careout** (www.jpmorganclimatecare.com), a leading British carbon offset organisation.

There are alternatives to flying into Mediterranean Europe. If you're coming from northern Europe or the UK it's perfectly possible to get to the region by train, bus and/or ferry. See p957 for details on the various forms of transport.

Slow Travel

Train travel is making a comeback as the concept of slow travel (fly less, stay longer) catches on. Mediterranean Europe is covered by an extensive train, bus and boat network, and with enough patience you can easily travel from one end of the region to the other without ever setting foot on a plane. Overland (and over-water) travel is not necessarily cheaper than flying – although overnight journeys will save you the cost of a night's accommodation – but it allows you to see far more of the region and is often more relaxing than jumping in and out of planes.

Within individual countries, the quality of public transport varies. A hire car can be useful for exploring remote rural areas, but it can also be a major headache in city centres where parking is impossible and traffic chaotic. Many of the region's major cities suffer from the choking effects of traffic smog and while attempts are being made to curb the flow of cars, they tend to be half-hearted. If you've got the legs for it, cycling is a wonderfully green alternative. Scooters, like jet-skis and other vehicles with two-stroke engines, are heavy polluters.

The Mediterranean is the world's third-largest sea after the South China Sea and the Caribbean. It measures 3900km at its longest point and 1600km at its widest.

Accommodation & Food

The choice of where you sleep and eat can impact on the local economy, as well as the environment. If possible always try to stay in locally owned establishments, rather than international chain hotels. By staying in an Italian *agriturismo*, a Portuguese *Turihab* property, a Cypriot *agrotourism*, or a family-run B&B, you're ensuring your money stays local.

In terms of environmental credentials, it can be difficult to distinguish genuinely eco-friendly accommodation options from opportunists trying to cash in on the trend for all things green. Look out for places bearing the EU's

CONDUCT IN MEDITERRANEAN EUROPE

Most Mediterranean countries are fundamentally conservative and attach a great deal of importance to appearance, so your clothes may well have a bearing on how you're treated, especially in Spain, Portugal, Italy and Greece. By all means dress casually, but keep your clothes clean and ensure sufficient body cover (trousers or a knee-length dress) if your sightseeing includes churches, monasteries, mosques or synagogues. Also keep in mind that in most Muslim countries, Westerners in shorts or sleeveless shirts are virtually in their underwear in the eyes of traditional locals.

On the beach, nude bathing is generally limited to particular areas, but topless bathing is common in many areas. As a rule, if nobody else seems to be doing it, you shouldn't do it either.

European Ecolabel or carrying certification from accredited bodies, such as Legambiente in Italy, WWF France, or the Malta Tourism Authority.

Eating locally produced food make sense. Most countries in the Mediterranean produce delicious fruit, veg, meat and seafood, so keeping it local shouldn't really be a problem. Let's face it, there are worse ways of doing your bit than eating paella in Valencia, pizza in Naples or a kebap in İstanbul. The same goes for drinking – why order an expensive New World wine when you're in the Burgundy Valley? There are plenty of local beers and wines with which to slake your thirst.

Water is a precious commodity in the Mediterranean, particularly in Malta and Cyprus where consumption outweighs regeneration rates, and you should try to save every last drop. Bottled mineral water gives rise to its own problems, most obviously in the form of the plastic bottles it's sold in. If possible, try to refill water bottles rather than throwing them away – if the tap water is not drinkable, try public drinking fountains.

Responsible Travel Organisations

There are many green travel organisations out there:

Responsible Travel (www.responsibletravel.com) A British travel agency offering everything from gap-year trips to honeymoon packages and worldwide accommodation.

Ethical Escape (www.ethicalescape.com) Ecofriendly travel advice with links to accommodation providers throughout the Mediterranean.

Save Our Snow (www.saveoursnow.com) Has news on what ski resorts are doing to clean up their act and has listings of green accommodation and tour operators.

Walks Worldwide (www.walksworldwide.com) A travel agency specialising in international walking holidays.

TRAVEL LITERATURE

For as long as people have been travelling in the Mediterranean, authors have been writing about them. Way back in the 8th century BC, Homer penned *The Odyssey*, his epic tale of Odysseus' attempts to return home to Ithaca (modern-day Ithaki – see p416) after the Trojan War. Almost a millennium later, in the 2nd century AD, historian and geographer Pausanius wrote the world's first travel guide, the 10-book *Description of Greece*.

Whet your appetite for the Mediterranean with Elizabeth David's classic cookbook *A Book of Mediterranean Food*, a passionately written homage to the region and its food, smells and tastes.

Two of the greatest Mediterranean travel writers, however, sought their fame elsewhere. The great Moroccan explorer Abu Abdullah Muhammed Ibn Battuta (1304–69) is said to have covered some 120,000km in 30 years of travel in Asia and the eastern Mediterranean, while Venetian adventurer Marco Polo (1254–1324) thrilled with his tales of Asian exotica.

But as home-grown authors have left, so too northern authors have sought solace in the southern sun. Goethe and Stendhal, Byron, Dickens and DH Lawrence all travelled to the region seeking inspiration.

To get you into the mood for a Mediterranean odyssey:

- *Francesco's Mediterranean Voyage: A Cultural Journey Through the Mediterranean from Venice to Istanbul* (Francesco Da Mosta) An elegant read, this glossy coffee-table book follows TV architect and historian Francesco Da Mosta as he cruises the eastern Med.
- *On the Shores of the Mediterranean* (Eric Newby) The ideal travelling companion, Newby turns his sparkling eye to the Italian mafia, Arabian harems and communist Albania as he wanders the length of the Med.
- *Mediterranean Winter: The Pleasures of History and Landscape in Tunisia, Sicily, Dalmatia and Greece* (Robert Kaplan) In recounting a trip through low-season Mediterranean, Kaplan vividly recalls the history behind the area's great landscapes.
- *Labels: A Mediterranean Journal* (Evelyn Waugh) From Malta to Morocco, Waugh cuts a swath through the Mediterranean with his pointed pen and irreverent wit. It's as much about the people he meets as the famous sites, and it's a great read.
- *Route 66: On the Trail of Ancient Roman Tourists* (Tony Perrottet) A light read, this is one of the better 'follow-in-the-footsteps-of-the-ancients' books. Perrottet combines classical references, modern jokes and amusing anecdotes.
- *Pillars of Hercules* (Paul Theroux) With his usual caustic wit and languid style, veteran traveller Theroux leads the reader along the shores of Spain to the French Riviera, Sardinia and Sicily.
- *We Followed Odysseus* (Hal Roth) Join Roth in his boat as he retraces Odysseus's legendary 10-year journey. If you're not going to read *The Odyssey,* this is the next best thing.
- *The Seventh Wonder* (Juan Villar) Part travelogue, part guidebook, this is the entertaining account of Villar's attempt to visit each of the Seven Wonders of the Ancient World on a three-week holiday.

INTERNET RESOURCES

Cheap Flights (www.flycheapo.com) Get the low-down on budget airlines and the routes they serve.

Ferry To (www.aferry.to) Book your ferries on this comprehensive site detailing routes, rates, operators and ports.

Lonely Planet (www.lonelyplanet.com) Read up on destinations, book hotels and exchange thoughts on the Thorn Tree forum.

Michelin (www.viamichelin.com) A great planning tool for drivers – get directions, check weather forecasts and peruse maps.

Seat 61 (www.seat61.com) Encyclopaedic site detailing everything you'll ever need to know about international train travel.

Visit Europe (www.visiteurope.com) A massive online A to Z of European travel with tons of practical travel advice and links to national tourist authorities.

MUST-SEE MOVIES

Here's a selection of celluloid teasers to put you in the Mediterranean mood:

- *Vicky Cristina Barcelona* (2008; Woody Allen) Woody Allen gives Barcelona (p777) star billing in this ironic, off-beat comedy. Passions run high as Penelope Cruz turns up to haunt ex-husband Javier Bardem and his latest lover, Scarlett Johansson.
- *Mamma Mia!* (2008; Phyllida Lloyd) All you need to know about this mega-grossing musical is that the music is Abba, the Greek island (p412) setting is gorgeous and it's all obscenely OTT.

The French film *Le Graine et le Mulet,* known to international audiences as *Couscous* or *The Secret of the Grain,* is an engaging study of a North African immigrant family in France.

- *The Talented Mr Ripley* (1999; Anthony Minghella) Set in sexy *dolce vita* Italy, this is an unsettling drama of murder and stolen identity. Matt Damon stars as a bespectacled sociopath giving free rein to his inner demons.
- *Travels with My Aunt* (1972; George Cukor) Based on a Graham Greene novel, this classic comedy caper features a tour de force from Brit actress Maggie Smith and some stunning scenery in Italy, Morocco, Spain and Turkey.
- *Karaula* (2006; Rajko Grlic) A coproduction involving all the former-Yugoslav republics, this bittersweet comedy tells of love, syphilis and a state of emergency in a 1980s mountain-top outpost.

Events Calendar

Mediterranean Europe's great festivals are noisy, colourful, passionate and anarchic. Ranging from solemn religious processions to wild street parties, costumed balls and glitzy film festivals, they showcase the region's passionate nature and its spiritual character. Here we highlight Mediterranean Europe's biggest and best events.

JANUARY–FEBRUARY

INTERNATIONAL CIRCUS FESTIVAL OF MONACO mid–late Jan
Cheer the world's circus elite as they perform under Monte Carlo's big top (p326).

FESTIVIDAD DE SAN SEBASTIÁN 20 Jan
Drums provide the backbeat for costumed celebrations and prolonged feasting at this festival (p846) in San Sebastián, Spain.

FANTASPORTO late Feb
The annual film festival in Porto (Portugal; p690) screens everything from blockbusters to sci-fi and fantasy flicks.

CARNIVAL Feb-early Mar
In the build-up to Lent, look out for Carnevale in Venice (Italy; p487), Kurentovanje in Ptuj (Slovenia; p735), and Karneval in Rijeka (Croatia; p141).

MARCH–APRIL

LAS FALLAS mid-Mar
Pyrotechnic wizardry lights up Valencia's party marathon (p809) in Spain for the week leading up to 19 March.

EASTER Mar/Apr
Easter week in Italy is celebrated with parades, processions and passion plays. On Easter Sunday, the pope blesses the faithful in St Peter's Square, Rome. See p458.

ZAGREB BIENNALE Apr
World-class musicians perform at Croatia's most important musical event (p128), taking place in odd-numbered years.

MAGGIO MUSICALE FIORENTINO Apr-Jun
The curtain goes up on opera, classical music and ballet at Florence's prestigious music festival. See p502.

FESTIVAL OF SUFI CULTURE mid-Apr
Blow your mind on Sufi culture and music in Fez, Morocco's spiritual capital. See p636 for more.

FERIA DE ABRIL late Apr
Gorge on folklore, flamenco, tapas and sherry at Seville's week-long jamboree (p825), Spain.

QUEER ZAGREB FM FESTIVAL late Apr-early May
Stick around in Croatia for Zagreb's exuberant festival of gay-themed films and concerts (p128).

MAY

MAY DAY 1 May
On the first day of May the French give each other *muguets* (lilies of the valley; see p335); Greeks gather wildflowers (p420); and Italians rock at a vast open-air concert (p458).

FESTA DI SANT'EFISIO 1-4 May
Crowds of costumed townsfolk flock to Italy's Cagliari for its high-spirited annual parade (p540).

FESTAS DAS CRUZES 3 May
Portugal's medieval town of Barcelos stages grand processions, concerts and performances on and around 3 May (p699).

FESTA DI SAN GENNARO 1st Sun in May
In Italy, Neapolitans honour their patron saint and pray for the miraculous liquefying of his blood (p518); also celebrated on 19 September and 16 December.

QUEIMA DAS FITAS mid-May
Students of the Portuguese town of Coimbra raucously celebrate the end of the academic year for a week following the first Thursday in May (p687).

CANNES FILM FESTIVAL mid-May
Cannes (p321) rolls out the red carpet for the film world's finest.

FIESTA DE SAN ISIDRO 15 May
Madrid celebrates its patron saint with street parties and bullfights among other things (p756) in Spain on and around 15 May.

DRUGA GODBA late May-early Jun
Ljubljana's flamboyant festival of alternative and world music features everything from new jazz to contemporary folk (p713).

KATAKLYSMOS 50 days after Easter
Cypriots hit the wet stuff in commemoration of the biblical flood (p199).

JUNE

FEZ FESTIVAL OF WORLD SACRED MUSIC Jun
With an international cast of top performers, this is one of the Med's most popular world-music festivals (p636), held in Fez, Morocco.

PALIO DELLE QUATTRO ANTICHE REPUBBLICHE MARINARE Jun
Historic rivalries are rekindled in Italy during boat races between Pisa, Genoa, Amalfi and Venice (p547). In 2011 the event is held in Venice.

INTERNATIONAL İSTANBUL MUSIC FESTIVAL Jun-Jul
Catch a concert in a sultan's palace or a 4th-century church in İstanbul, Turkey (p870).

ESTATE ROMANA Jun-Sep
The summer sees thousands of events, ranging from book fairs to raves and gay parties (p458) in Rome, Italy.

VENICE BIENNALE Jun-Nov
A major exhibition of international art with the accent on contemporary works (p487), held in odd-numbered years in Italy.

VIP INMUSIC FESTIVAL 3-4 Jun
In Croatia, headline acts at Zagreb's two-day music festival have included Nick Cage and the Prodigy (p128).

FESTA DE SANTO ANTÓNIO 12-13 Jun
Lisbon's annual shindig involves parades, street parties and unfeasible quantities of Portuguese grilled sardines (p669).

RAVENNA FESTIVAL mid-Jun–mid-Jul
A month-long music festival with the accent on classical music takes place in the Italian town of Ravenna (p495).

HELLENIC FESTIVAL mid-Jun–Aug
Athens' major cultural event boasts music, dance and theatre performances (p358), Greece.

GNAOUA & WORLD MUSIC FESTIVAL 3rd weekend Jun
Essaouira hosts this four-day extravaganza of Moroccan Gnaoua music (p654).

FÊTE DE LA MUSIQUE 21 Jun
The curtain goes up on concerts across France (p335) for this music festival.

FESTA DE SÃO JOÃO 23-24 Jun
Revellers flock to beach parties at Porto's big street bash (p690), Portugal.

FESTA DI SAN GIOVANNI 24 Jun
Florentines dress up and play footie to commemorate patron saint St John (p502), in Italy.

FESTA DEI SANTI PIETRO E PAOLO 29 Jun
In Italy, Romans celebrate patron saints Peter and Paul (p458) with events centred on St Peter's Basilica.

LENT INTERNATIONAL SUMMER FESTIVAL late Jun-early Jul
A cultural cocktail of folklore, music, theatre, dance and sport (p734) in Maribor, Slovenia.

ROCK OTOČEC late Jun-early Jul
Dust down the denim and head to Novo Mesto for Slovenia's biggest open-air rock concert (p737).

FESTIVAL D'AIX-EN-PROVENCE late Jun-Jul
Enjoy a month of top-class music, opera and ballet (p336) in France's Aix-en-Provence.

OIL-WRESTLING CHAMPIONSHIP late Jun-Jul
Greased-up geezers entertain huge crowds at Kırkpınar (p930) in Turkey.

JULY

BAŠČARŠIJSKE NOĆI Jul
Dance, music and street theatre are performed throughout the month at Baščaršija (p84), Bosnia.

FESTIVAL D'AVIGNON Jul
Avignon, France, hosts a month-long bonanza of drama, music, dance and poetry (p314).

MARRAKESH POPULAR ARTS FESTIVAL Jul
Get into the swing at this celebration of traditional Moroccan music (p654).

ZAGREB SUMMER EVENINGS Jul
Zagreb's Upper Town hosts its summer festival, a cycle of classical music concerts and theatre performances (p128), in Croatia.

NATIONAL FESTIVAL OF BERBER CULTURE early Jul
Fez showcases Amazigh (Berber) culture with music events, poetry readings and exhibitions (p636).

ORTIGUEIRA INTERNATIONAL CELTIC MUSIC FESTIVAL early Jul
Learn to tell your bagpipes from your *bombos* (big drums) at this four-day homage to Galician music (p805), in Spain.

LJUBLJANA FESTIVAL early Jul-late Aug
Thousands flock to Slovenia's capital for world-class music, theatre and dance (p713).

IL PALIO 2 Jul & 16 Aug
Bareback jockeys ride for glory at Siena's legendary horse race (p547).

SANFERMINES 6-14 Jul
In Spain, Pamplona's annual bull running (p801) is not for the faint-hearted. Or the sane.

BASTILLE DAY 14 Jul
Patriotic crowds salute the military parade on Paris' Champs-Élysées on France's national day (p336).

NICE JAZZ FESTIVAL mid-Jul
France's Côte d'Azur swings to the sounds of jazz (p317).

UMBRIA JAZZ mid-Jul
Top jazz musicians lead the party in the medieval town of Perugia, Italy (p511).

DUBROVNIK SUMMER FESTIVAL mid-Jul–mid-Aug
Croatia's headline festival boasts international artists and over 100 performances in the Old Town (p167).

SPLIT SUMMER FESTIVAL mid-Jul–mid-Aug
Drama and music enjoy top billing at Split's annual culture fest (p154), in Croatia.

FESTA DEL REDENTORE 3rd weekend in Jul
Gondola regattas serve as the build-up to a spectacular fireworks display in Venice (p487), Italy.

IKARI BRIDGE JUMPING late Jul
In Bosnia and Hercegovina, daredevil divers leap off Mostar's iconic bridge, Stari Most (p94), into the Neretva River 21m below.

AUGUST

ETHNOAMBIENT early Aug
Musicians from all corners of the world descend on the Croatian town of Solin (p156) for this homage to world music.

SEMANA GRANDE 1st half of Aug
Towns on Spain's northern coast celebrate their Basque heritage with a week-long frenzy of bullfighting, boozing and spectacular fireworks (p846).

FEAST OF THE ASSUMPTION 15 Aug
Celebrated across Mediterranean Europe – shops shut and crowds swarm to the beaches.

FESTAS DE NOSSA SENHORA DA AGONIA weekend nearest to 20 Aug
Three days of spectacular merrymaking, folk arts, parades and fireworks in Viana do Castelo, Portugal (p699).

SARAJEVO FILM FESTIVAL mid-Aug
Bosnia and Hercegovina hosts one of Europe's largest film festivals (p85), screening commercial and art-house movies, almost all with English subtitles.

MOSTRA DEL CINEMA DI VENEZIA late Aug-early Sep
Movie-world A-listers alight at Venice for the world's oldest film festival (p487), in Italy.

SEPTEMBER

BIENAL DE FLAMENCO Sep
Give yourself up to the passion of Spain's largest flamenco festival (p825), held in Seville every even-numbered year.

BRADERIE DE LILLE 1st weekend in Sep

A mecca for bargain hunters, the annual flea market in Lille (p242), France, is one of the largest in Europe, attracting up to two million visitors. Stalls sell everything from books to stuffed animals, while restaurants compete to serve the most mussels.

REGATA STORICA 1st Sunday in Sep

Gondolas are swathed in 15th-century finery and raced down Venice's Grand Canal (p487), in Italy.

COWS' BALL early–mid-Sep

Folkloristic revelry in Bohinj greets the return of Slovenia's cows from their high pastures to the valleys (p723).

FESTES DE LA MERCÈ around 24 Sep

In Spain, eight-storey human towers lord it over Barcelona's exuberant annual bash (p785).

MOUSSEM OF MOULAY IDRISS II Sep/Oct

Jubilant festivities honour Moulay Idriss, Morocco's most revered saint, in the holy streets of Fez (p636).

INTERNATIONAL WOMEN'S FESTIVAL mid-Sep

Women from all over converge on the Greek island of Lesvos for a two-week festival of workshops, concerts, sport and herstory writing (p409).

ROMAEUROPA late Sep-Nov

Rome's premier cultural fest salutes the best international music, dance and theatre (p459), in Italy.

OCTOBER–NOVEMBER

ADVENTURE RACE MONTENEGRO early Oct

Montenegro's two-day challenge involves 27km of kayaking, a 40km cycle and a 25km run (p598).

FESTIVAL INTERNAZIONALE DEL FILM DI ROMA mid-Oct

Hollywood transfers to the Eternal City for Rome's film festival (p459).

OHI (NO) DAY 28 Oct

Celebrated throughout Greece, Ohi Day sees parades, folk dancing and much furious feasting (p420).

INTERNATIONAL JAZZ FESTIVAL early Nov

Sarajevo's internationally acclaimed jazz fest showcases local and international performers (p85), in Bosnia and Hercegovina.

DECEMBER

FÊTE DES LUMIÈRES 8 Dec

In France, Lyon's spectacular Festival of Lights (p336) illuminates the city's historic centre.

CHRISTMAS 25 Dec

Festive highlights include Alsace's historic markets (p336), in France, and Naples' elaborate *presepi* (nativity scenes; p547), in Italy.

Itineraries

CLASSIC ROUTES

A TALE OF TWO CONTINENTS

One Month / Lisbon to Barcelona

Kick off in **Lisbon** (p664), Portugal's laid-back capital, before heading down to the beaches at **Lagos** (p681). From here, make a beeline to sexy **Seville** (p823), famous for its full-blooded lifestyle. Continue on to **Tarifa** (p839), where you can catch a ferry to **Tangier** (p606). Push on down the Moroccan coast to cosmopolitan **Casablanca** (p624) and the hip resort of **Essaouira** (p627). Next, venture inland to **Marrakesh** (p641), one of Morocco's highlights. Watch the sun set on the blood-red walls before pressing on to **Fez** (p631) and its labyrinthine medina (old city). Once you've found your way out of the maze, head back to Spain via **Melilla** (p617) and **Málaga** (p834). As you head north take time to admire the Alhambra in **Granada** (p830) and the Mezquita in **Córdoba** (p827), two of Spain's most celebrated Moorish marvels. Stop off at **Toledo** (p774), renowned for its stunning cathedral, before hitting **Madrid** (p748), Spain's thumping capital. Overdose on culture and clubbing before moving on to **Barcelona** (p777) to feast on Gaudí's madcap architecture.

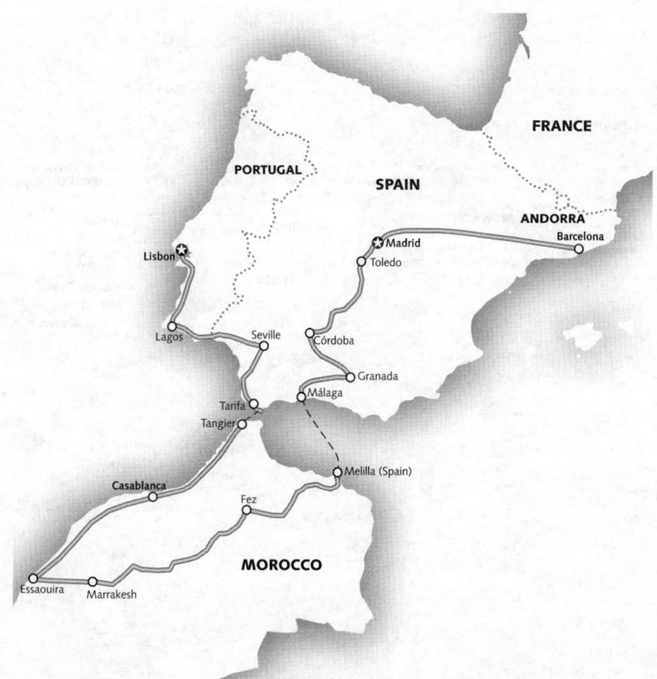

Marvel at amazing architecture, get lost in Moroccan medinas, kick back on Atlantic beaches, party in legendary clubs – this 3200km intercontinental trip caters to most tastes. Give yourself a month for a comfortable ride.

A COASTAL JAUNT

One Month / Marseille to Split

Passing through the French Riviera, several Unesco-listed national parks and a number of full-blooded Mediterranean ports, this three-country route takes in some of the region's finest coastal scenery.

Start in **Marseille** (p307), France's edgy, multiethnic Mediterranean port. Dine on bouillabaisse and enjoy the atmosphere before heading east. Top up your tan at **St-Tropez** (p323) and catch a film at **Cannes** (p321) as you wend your way along the Riviera to **Nice** (p315), the Côte d'Azur's busy, cosmopolitan capital.

From Nice, take a train to **Genoa** (p469), where you can eyeball sharks in Europe's largest aquarium. For more sea thrills head down to the **Cinque Terre** (p471), one of Italy's most spectacular stretches of coastline.

The road now leads to **Rome** (p443), as all eventually do. Take in the highlights before continuing south to manic, in-your-face **Naples** (p514). Don't miss the nearby ruins of **Pompeii** (p521) en route to the **Amalfi Coast** (p524), a dreamy stretch of shimmering seascapes and plunging cliffs.

From the Mediterranean coast, cross over to the Adriatic port of **Bari** (p527) and catch a ferry to **Dubrovnik** (p163), star of Croatia's Dalmatian coast. Once you've marvelled at the city's marble streets and baroque buildings, jump on a boat for some island hopping. Nearby, peaceful **Mljet Island** (p162) is a seductive mix of forests, vineyards and small villages, while further north **Hvar Island** (p158) boasts sunshine, beaches and a vibrant nightlife. From Hvar, it's a short ferry ride to **Split** (p150), Croatia's second city and home to the Unesco-listed Diocletian's Palace.

From the chic resorts of the Côte d'Azur to the splendours of Italy's Amalfi Coast and Croatia's craggy seaboard, this 1700km voyage is a sea lover's dream tour. Allow a month to do it justice, although you can easily break it down into shorter segments.

AEGEAN ISLAND HOPPING

Three Weeks / Athens to Knossos

With their beautiful beaches, ancient ruins and hedonistic pleasures, the Greek Islands have been seducing sailors for millennia. Today they are connected by a comprehensive ferry network, making an island-hopping tour both feasible and fun.

The obvious starting point is **Athens** (p351). Here, among the traffic and modern mayhem, you'll find some of Europe's most iconic monuments. From nearby **Piraeus** (p365), jump on a ferry for **Mykonos** (p381), one of Greece's top island destinations. A hedonistic hot spot, it boasts action-packed beaches and a pretty whitewashed town. Before leaving, take time for a day trip to **Delos** (p383), the mythical birthplace of the god Apollo. Explore the Sanctuary of Apollo and climb Mt Kynthos for sensational views.

From Mykonos, sail south to **Naxos** (p385), the largest and greenest of the Cyclades islands. With its enticing main town and striking interior, it's much more than a beach stop and is well worth exploring. From Naxos, it's a quick ferry ride to laid-back **Paros** (p383) and the popular beaches of **Antiparos** (p383).

Continuing southwards, you come to **Santorini** (p388), one of the Aegean's most impressive islands. The sight of its volcanic cliffs sheering up from the limpid blue water with whitewashed villages perched precariously on the rock is one you won't forget in a hurry.

Greece's most southerly island, Crete makes a fitting finale. Just southwest of the main city **Iraklio** (p392) is **Knossos** (p393), the ancient capital of Minoan Crete where the mythical Minotaur is supposed to have lived.

Starting in Athens, this 349km hop around Greece's islands takes in some of the Aegean's most popular destinations. With ferry routes reduced in winter, it's a trip best undertaken in summer.

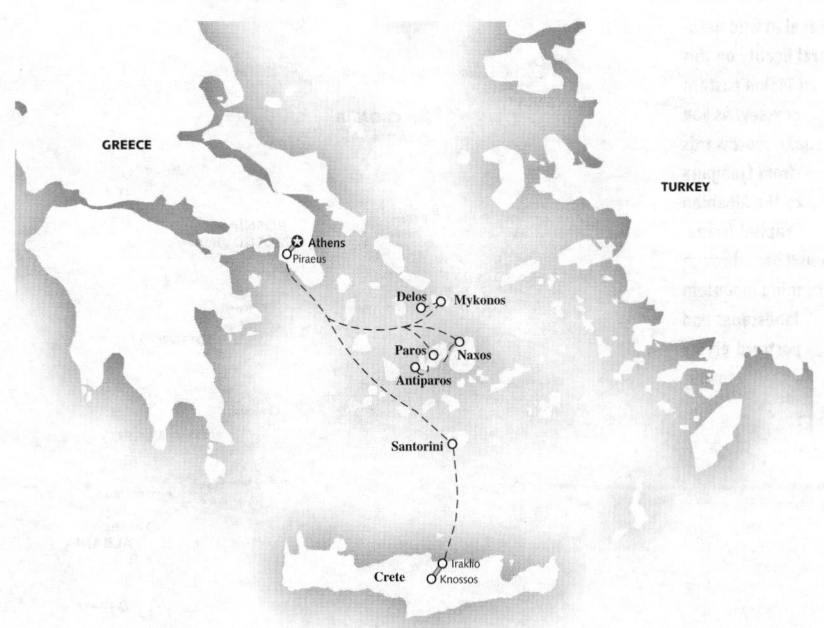

ROADS LESS TRAVELLED

CASTLES, LAKES & MOUNTAINS

One Month / Ljubljana to Tirana

Mountainous and covered in great swaths of forest, Slovenia and the Balkan countries present the tougher, more rugged side of the Mediterranean landscape. Starting in Slovenia's cultured capital, **Ljubljana** (p707), the first leg of the tour leads northwest to the lakeside town of **Bled** (p719). A gorgeous spot in its own right, Bled makes a great base for exploring the Julian Alps.

From Bled double back to Ljubljana to pick up a bus to the Croatian capital, **Zagreb** (p122). Hang around for a coffee or two in the Upper Town before pushing on to **Bihać** (p106), a pretty staging post on the road to **Sarajevo** (p78). Before reaching the Bosnian capital, take time to stop off in **Jajce** (p103), famous for its catacombs, citadel and waterfall, and **Travnik** (p102), home to some impressive castle ruins.

After a few days enjoying Sarajevo's hip vibe, continue south to **Mostar** (p92), whose Stari Most bridge stages a spectacular diving competition every July. From Mostar, take a bus to **Herceg Novi** (p581), an attractive walled town on Montenegro's eastern coast. Nearby, the dramatic **Kotor** (p581) sits wedged between dark mountains at the head of southern Europe's deepest fjord. The road here turns inland, via Montenegro's former capital **Cetinje** (p590), on to **Podgorica** (p593), the nation's modern capital. About 65km from Podgorica on the southeastern tip of Lake Shkodra, ancient **Shkodra** (p53) provides a good introduction to Albania with its smattering of interesting sights. From here the last stretch takes you south to **Tirana** (p46), once a model of drab Soviet-style urban blandness, now a crazy, colourful, buzzing city.

Revel in wild natural beauty on this 1045km eastern odyssey. As you snake southwards from Ljubljana to the Albanian capital Tirana, you'll pass through stunning mountain landscapes and postcard-pretty towns.

TURKISH DELIGHTS

Two Weeks / İstanbul to Göreme

Bridging the gap between East and West, Turkey is a compelling cauldron of culture and style. A modern secular state with a Muslim past, it's a country where mosques stand next to churches and headscarves are as likely as halter tops.

Nowhere are Turkey's contradictions more visible than in **İstanbul** (p861), whose highlights include the Topkapı Palace, Aya Sofya and the Blue Mosque. Further round the Aegean coast **Çanakkale** (p879) is a popular base for visiting nearby **Gallipoli** (p878), scene of vicious WWI fighting, and the legendary town of **Troy** (p880).

Following the coast around to the southeast, you arrive at **Bergama** (p881), celebrated for its ravishing ruins of ancient Pergamum, once a powerful Middle Eastern kingdom. More classical treasures await at **Ephesus** (p886), Turkey's version of Pompeii, near **Selçuk** (p884), itself home to one of the Seven Wonders of the Ancient World.

From Selçuk, push on to **Patara** (p898), where you can share a magnificent 20km-long beach with breeding turtles. Tanned up, spend a day or two hanging out in a tree house in **Olympos** (p901) before heading on to **Antalya** (p903), a modern town with an interesting Ottoman core. At this point head inland. A six-hour bus ride away, **Konya** (p913) boasts some fine Seljuk architecture and gave birth to the 13th-century whirling dervishes. Further northeast, the eerie, rocky landscape around **Göreme** (p915) is one of Turkey's most incredible sights.

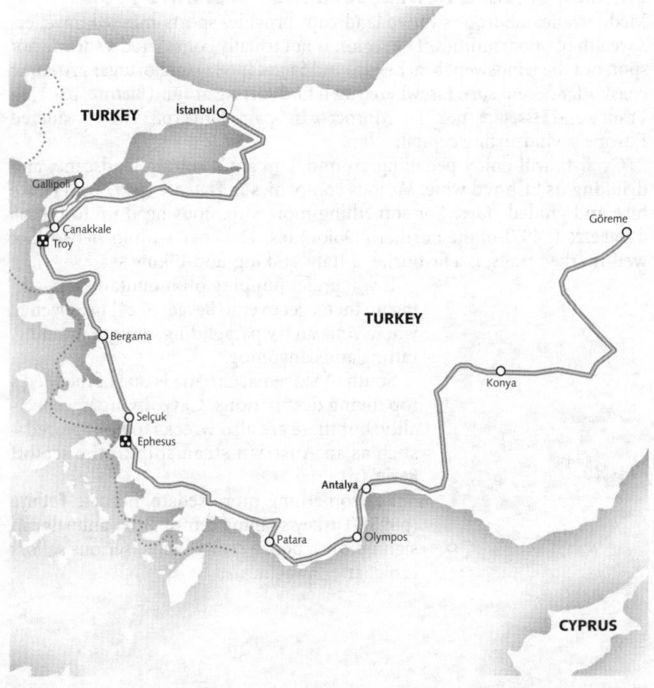

There's something for everyone on this two-week, 1100km tour of Turkey's delights. Bazaars, battlefields and some of the Med's most beautiful beaches line the land that the ancients knew as Asia Minor.

TAILORED TRIPS

THE MED ON A PLATE

To whet your appetite, start with a few days in **Paris** (p211), dining at neighbourhood bistros and lingering over streetside coffees. Warmed up and ready to go, make for Burgundy and serious wine country. Stop off at **Dijon** (p273), at the **Côte d'Or Vineyards** (p276) and at **Lyon** (p278), a cultural and gastronomic centre par excellence. Down on the south coast, **Marseille** (p307) is the place to try bouillabaisse, a staple of Provence fishing folk for centuries.

Over the Alps in Italy, **Bologna** (p492) is considered by many to be the nation's culinary capital. Home of bolognese sauce (known to Italians as *ragù*), it also gifted the world tortellini, lasagne and mortadella (Bologna sausage). Italy also means pizza, and pizza means **Naples** (p514). It was here in 1889 that the *margherita* (tomato, mozzarella and basil) was invented and pizza was propelled to the gastronomic big league.

Over the pond in Spain, **Valencia** (p807) is the place to go for a steaming plate of paella. To the north, in the Basque seaside town of **San Sebastián** (p797), you'll be spoiled for choice as you stumble from one tapas bar to the next.

THRILLS, SPILLS & BUNGEE JUMPING – A SPORTS TOUR

Mediterranean Europe's varied landscape provides sports-minded travellers a wealth of opportunities. The region is not usually considered a surfing hot spot, but the windswept beaches around **Sagres** (p682) on Portugal's Atlantic coast offer decent surf. Elsewhere you'll find surfing around **Biarritz** (p301) in France and **Essaouira** (p627) in Morocco. In Spain, **Tarifa** (p839) is considered Europe's windsurfing capital.

Cyclists will enjoy pedalling around Tuscany's rolling landscape, and drinking its lush red wine. Various companies in **Florence** (p497) offer bike hire and guided rides. For something more strenuous head up to **Cortina d'Ampezzo** (p497) in the northern Dolomites. The area, with its network of well-marked trails, is a favourite of Italy's hiking-and-biking set.

If you prefer jumping off mountains to walking up them, get over to **Bovec** (p724) in Slovenia, where you can try paragliding, bungee jumping, rafting and canyoning.

South of Slovenia, Croatia is one of the Med's top diving destinations. Cave diving is a speciality, but there are also wrecks to be explored – such as an Austrian steamship in the sea off **Rovinj** (p135).

For something more sedate, head to **Fethiye** (p895), Turkey's sailing centre. Party animals can sign up for a booze cruise, while serious sailors can charter a yacht.

Albania

Alps sprout in the background, vast plains and lakes surround the central mountain ranges, and coastal areas provide the traveller to Albania (or Shqipëria, as the locals call it) with a huge variety of experiences in this country of dramatically different cultural and geographical landscapes. Head up into the isolated mountains, stay in luxury accommodation on peaceful beaches, or visit historic homes in equally historic towns where the main streets are lined with Roman pillars. City slickers can down coffee after coffee in busy, always surprising Tirana before heading out to an exhibition, free art-house cinema night or a buzzing nightclub.

Albanians, after years of government-enforced isolation, welcome travellers with sincere hospitality. There are signs of a lack of infrastructure, though the upgraded roads that swirl past new houses and bar/restaurant/hotel developments is evidence of newfound prosperity.

Summer, particularly August, sees quiet seaside spots morph into loud disco-laden towns where every day is a thumping weekend. In contrast, head north and you'll find locals in traditional dress and shepherds guiding flocks in the otherwise inhospitable mountains.

The unique sights of Albania are hard to forget: donkeys tethered to concrete bunkers, houses crawling up each other to reach the top of hills in the Unesco World Heritage–listed Ottoman towns of Berat and Gjirokastra, and pockets of isolated beaches.

Like a good meat-and-three-veg dish, Albania is affordable, filling and ready to eat.

FAST FACTS

- **Area** 28,748 sq km
- **Capital** Tirana
- **Currency** lekë; €1 = 131 lekë; US$1 = 96 lekë; UK£1 = 140 lekë; A$1 = 67 lekë; ¥100 = 101 lekë; NZ$1 = 54 lekë
- **Famous for** cool flag, concrete bunkers, international diaspora
- **Official language** Albanian
- **Phrases** *miredita* (hello/good day); *lamtumirë* (goodbye); *ju lutem* (please); *ju falem nderit* (thank you); *më fal* (excuse me/sorry)
- **Population** 3.62 million
- **Telephone codes** country code ☎ 355; international access code ☎ 00
- **Visas** no visa needed for citizens of the EU, Australia, New Zealand, the US and Canada; see p68

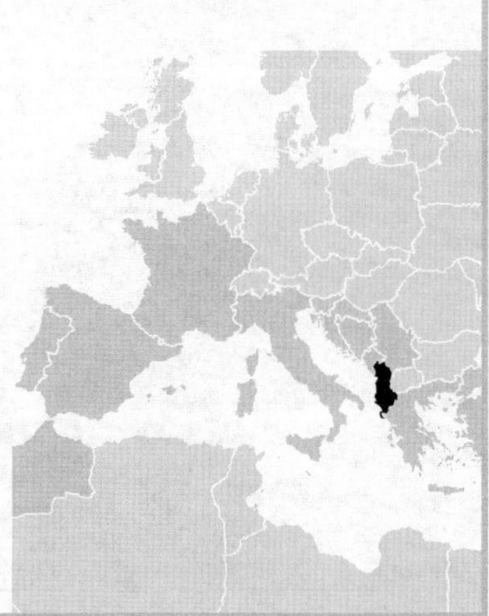

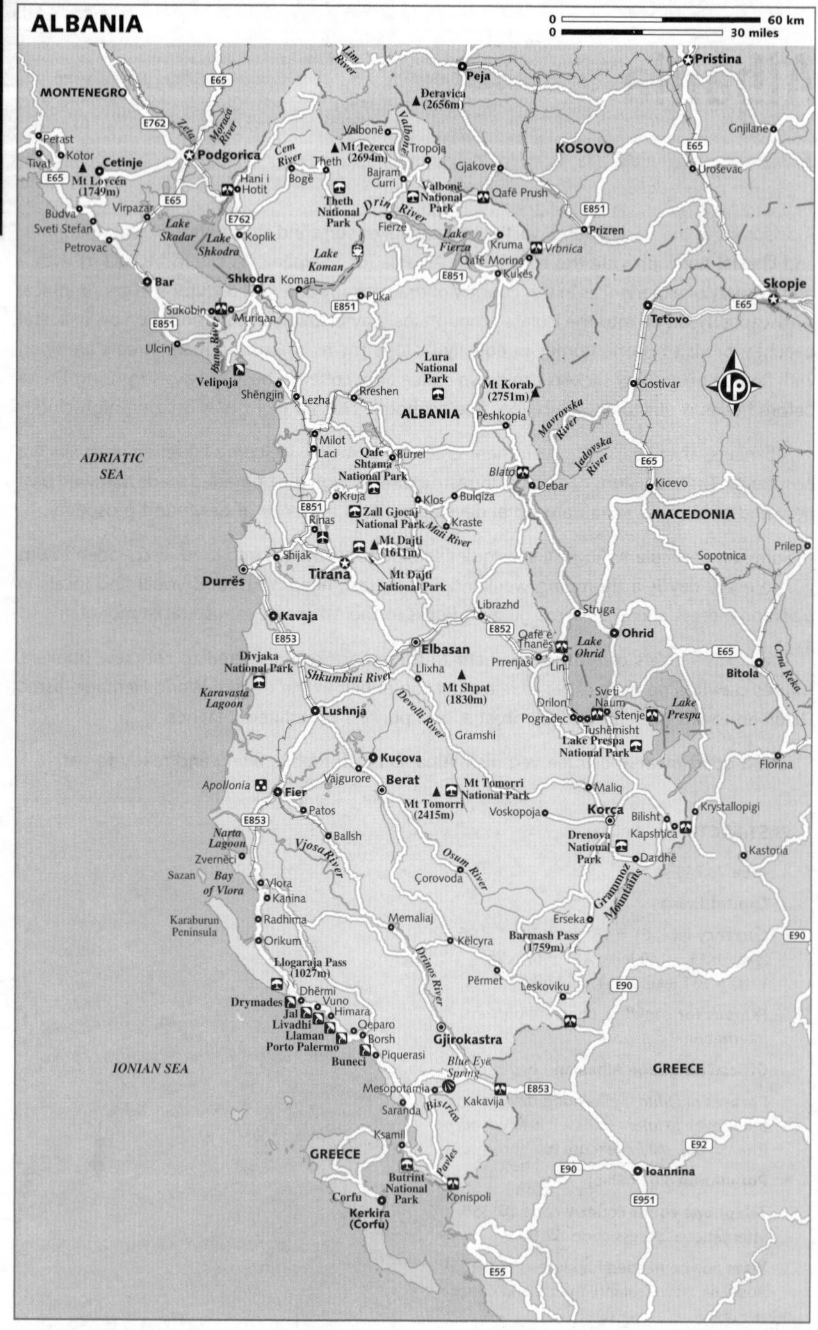
ALBANIA
0 60 km
0 30 miles
MONTENEGRO
KOSOVO
ALBANIA
MACEDONIA
GREECE
ADRIATIC SEA
IONIAN SEA
Podgorica
Cetinje
Mt Lovćen (1749m)
Perast
Kotor
Tivat
Budva
Sveti Stefan
Petrovac
Virpazar
Bar
Sukobin
Ulcinj
Peja
Đeravica (2656m)
Pristina
Gnjilane
Uroševac
Gjakove
Prizren
Skopje
Tetovo
Gostivar
Kicevo
Prilep
Sopotnica
Ohrid
Struga
Bitola
Florina
Kastoria
Krystallopigi
Ioannina
Kerkira (Corfu)
Corfu
Shkodra
Koman
Koplik
Hani i Hotit
Lake Skadar
Lake Shkodra
Lake Koman
Lake Fierza
Theth
Theth National Park
Bogë
Mt Jezerca (2694m)
Valbonë
Tropoja
Bajram Curri
Valbonë National Park
Fierzë
Qafë Prush
Kruma
Vrbnica
Qafë Morina
Kukës
Puka
Muriqan
Velipoja
Shëngjin
Lezha
Rreshen
Lura National Park
Mt Korab (2751m)
Peshkopia
Milot
Laci
Qafe Shtama National Park
Burrel
Kruja
Klos
Bulqiza
Blato
Debar
Zall Gjocaj National Park
Kraste
Rinas
Mt Dajti (1611m)
Mt Dajti National Park
Shijak
Tirana
Durrës
Kavaja
Librazhd
Elbasan
Qafe e Thanës
Prrenjasi
Lin
Lake Ohrid
Divjaka National Park
Karavasta Lagoon
Llixha
Mt Shpat (1830m)
Lushnja
Drilon
Pogradec
Sveti Naum
Tushemisht
Stenje
Lake Prespa
Lake Prespa National Park
Gramshi
Kuçova
Vajgurore
Berat
Mt Tomorri National Park
Mt Tomorri (2415m)
Maliq
Apollonia
Fier
Patos
Voskopoja
Korça
Bilisht
Kapshtica
Drenova National Park
Dardhë
Ballsh
Narta Lagoon
Zvernëci
Sazan
Bay of Vlora
Vlora
Kanina
Çorovoda
Grammoz Mountains
Karaburun Peninsula
Radhima
Orikum
Memaliaj
Këlcyra
Erseka
Barmash Pass (1759m)
Llogaraja Pass (1027m)
Përmet
Leskoviku
Dhërmi
Vuno
Drymades
Jal
Himara
Livadhi
Llaman
Qeparo
Borsh
Porto Palermo
Buneci
Piquerasi
Gjirokastra
Blue Eye Spring
Mesopotamia
Kakavija
Saranda
Ksamil
Butrint National Park
Konispoli
Lim River
Zeta
Moraca River
Cem River
Valbona
Drin River
Buna River
Mati River
Mavrovska River
Jadovska River
Shkumbini River
Devolli River
Osum River
Vjosa River
Drinos River
Bistrica
Pavles
Crna Reka
E65
E762
E851
E852
E853
E90
E92
E951
E55

HIGHLIGHTS

- Feast your eyes on the wild colour schemes and experience the hip Blloku cafe culture in **Tirana** (p46).
- Explore the Unesco World Heritage-listed museum cities of calm **Berat** (p59) and slate-roofed **Gjirokastra** (p65).
- Catch some sun along the south's dramatic Ionian Coast and its wonderful beaches, including **Dhërmi** (p62).
- Travel back in time to the ruins of **Butrint** (p64), hidden in the depths of the forest in a serene lakeside setting.
- Make your way to the hard-to-reach village of **Theth** (p55), high in the northern Alps.

ITINERARIES

- **Three days** Drink frappé at Tirana's trendy Blloku cafes, then spend the night dancing in nightclubs and get some morning mountain time on the Djati Express before heading to the Ottoman-era town of Berat to explore the town's old quarters. Kruja is a good airport detour; check out one of the country's best ethnographic museums and buy your souvenirs in its authentic little bazaar.
- **One week** Spend two days in Tirana then trek south via the scenic Llogaraja Pass. Take on beachside Dhërmi before making a pit stop at Saranda to prepare for a stroll around Butrint's ruins. Pause at the Blue Eye Spring en route to the Ottoman-era town of Gjirokastra.

CLIMATE & WHEN TO GO

Coastal Albania has a pleasant Mediterranean climate. Summer is the peak tourist season, when people from the sweltering interior escape temperatures that can reach the high 30s in July. In August, the temperature is high, accommodation is very tight in coastal regions and most hotels will only take bookings for stays of one week or more. The high mountains can experience heavy snow between November and March, and the road to Theth can be blocked as late as June. The best time to visit Albania is spring or autumn.

HISTORY

Albanians call their country Shqipëria, and trace their roots to the ancient Illyrian tribes. Their language is descended from Illyrian, making it a rare survivor of the Roman and Slavic influxes and a European linguistic oddity on a par with Basque. The Illyrians occupied the western Balkans during the 2nd millennium BC. They built substantial fortified cities, mastered silver and copper mining and became adept at sailing the Mediterranean. The Greeks arrived in the 7th century BC to establish self-governing colonies at Epidamnos (now Durrës), Apollonia and Butrint. They traded peacefully with the Illyrians, who formed tribal states in the 4th century BC.

Roman, Byzantine & Ottoman Rule

Inevitably the expanding Illyrian kingdom of the Ardiaei, based at Shkodra, came into conflict with Rome, which sent a fleet of 200 vessels against Queen Teuta in 229 BC. A long war resulted in the extension of Roman control over the entire Balkan area by 167 BC.

Under the Romans, Illyria enjoyed peace and prosperity, though the large agricultural estates were worked by slaves. The Illyrians preserved their own language and traditions despite Roman rule. Over time the populace slowly replaced their old gods with the new Christian faith championed by Emperor Constantine. The main trade route between Rome and Constantinople, the Via Egnatia, ran from the port at Durrës.

When the Roman Empire was divided in AD 395, Illyria fell within the Eastern Empire, later known as the Byzantine Empire. Three early Byzantine emperors (Anastasius I, Justin I and Justinian I) were of Illyrian origin. Invasions by migrating peoples (Visigoths,

CONNECTIONS: MOVING ON FROM ALBANIA

Albania is a mere hop from Greece's Corfu, and there are daily ferries heading each way (p64). It's a longer journey to Italy (up to 12 hours) and ferries leave from Vlora (p62) and Durrës (p58) frequently. Mainland Greece is easily reached via bus from almost every town in Albania and especially from the southern coast. Travel via the Koman River ferry (p55) to Kosovo is popular, as is simply walking to the Macedonian border near Pogradec. Shkodra (p55) has daily buses to Montenegro, and Tirana (p52) has buses to Kosovo and Macedonia.

HOW MUCH?

- **Shot of mulberry raki** 100 lekë
- **Bottle of good Albanian wine** 600 lekë
- **Short taxi ride** 300 lekë
- **English translation of an Ismail Kadare novel** 1800 lekë
- **Pizza** 300 lekë

LONELY PLANET INDEX

- **1L petrol** 120 lekë
- **1L bottled water** 50 lekë
- **Beer (Tirana)** 150 lekë
- **Souvenir T-shirt** 800 lekë
- **Street snack (byrek)** 30 lekë

Huns, Ostrogoths and Slavs) continued through the 5th and 6th centuries.

In 1344 Albania was annexed by Serbia, but after the defeat of Serbia by the Turks in 1389 the whole region was open to Ottoman attack. The Venetians occupied some coastal towns, and from 1443 to 1468 the national hero Skanderbeg (Gjergj Kastrioti) led Albanian resistance to the Turks from his castle at Kruja. Skanderbeg won all 25 battles he fought against the Turks, and even Sultan Mehmet-Fatih, the conqueror of Constantinople, could not take Kruja. After Skanderbeg's death the Ottomans overwhelmed Albanian resistance, taking control of the country in 1479, 26 years after Constantinople fell.

Ottoman rule lasted 400 years. Muslim citizens were favoured and were exempted from the janizary system, whereby Christian households had to give up one of their sons to convert to Islam and serve in the army. Consequently many Albanians embraced the new faith.

Independent Albania

In 1878 the Albanian League at Prizren (in present-day Kosovo) began a struggle for autonomy that the Turkish army put down in 1881. Further uprisings between 1910 and 1912 culminated in a proclamation of independence and the formation of a provisional government led by Ismail Qemali at Vlora in 1912. These achievements were severely compromised when Kosovo, roughly one-third of Albania, was ceded to Serbia in 1913. The Great Powers tried to install a young German prince, Wilhelm of Wied, as ruler, but he wasn't accepted and returned home after six months. With the outbreak of WWI, Albania was occupied in succession by the armies of Greece, Serbia, France, Italy and Austria-Hungary.

In 1920 the capital city was moved from Durrës to less vulnerable Tirana. A republican government under the Orthodox priest Fan Noli helped to stabilise the country, but in 1924 it was overthrown by the interior minister, Ahmed Bey Zogu. A northern warlord, he declared himself King Zogu I in 1928, but his close collaboration with Italy backfired in April 1939 when Mussolini ordered an invasion of Albania. Zogu fled to Britain with his young wife, Geraldine, and newborn son, Leka, and used gold looted from the Albanian treasury to rent a floor at London's Ritz Hotel.

On 8 November 1941 the Albanian Communist Party was founded with Enver Hoxha as first secretary, a position he held until his death in April 1985. The communists led the resistance against the Italians and, after 1943, against the Germans.

The Rise of Communism

In January 1946 the People's Republic of Albania was proclaimed, with Hoxha as president and 'Supreme Comrade'.

In September 1948 Albania broke off relations with Yugoslavia, which had hoped to incorporate the country into the Yugoslav Federation. Instead, it allied itself with Stalin's USSR and put into effect a series of Soviet-style economic plans – raising the ire of the USA and Britain, which made an ill-fated attempt to overthrow the government.

Albania collaborated closely with the USSR until 1960, when a heavy-handed Khrushchev demanded that a submarine base be set up at Vlora. Breaking off diplomatic relations with the USSR in 1961, the country reoriented itself towards the People's Republic of China.

From 1966 to 1967 Albania experienced a Chinese-style cultural revolution. Administrative workers were suddenly transferred to remote areas and younger cadres were placed in leading positions. The collectivisation of agriculture was completed and organised religion banned.

Following the Soviet invasion of Czechoslovakia in 1968, Albania left the

Warsaw Pact and embarked on a self-reliant defence policy. Some 60,000 igloo-shaped concrete bunkers (see p44) serve as a reminder of this policy. Under the communists, some malarial swamps were drained, hydroelectric schemes and railway lines were built, and the literacy level was raised.

With the death of Mao Zedong in 1976 and the changes that followed in China after 1978, Albania's unique relationship with China also came to an end, and the country was left isolated and without allies. The economy was devastated and food shortages became more common.

Post-Hoxha

Hoxha died in April 1985 and his associate Ramiz Alia took over the leadership. Restrictions loosened but people no longer bothered to work on the collective farms, leading to food shortages in the cities. Industries began to fail and Tirana's population tripled as people took advantage of being able to freely move to the city.

In June 1990, inspired by the changes that were occurring elsewhere in Eastern Europe, around 4500 Albanians took refuge in Western embassies in Tirana. After a brief confrontation with the police and the Sigurimi (secret police), these people were allowed to board ships for Brindisi in Italy, where they were granted political asylum.

Following student demonstrations in December 1990, the government agreed to allow opposition parties, and the Democratic Party, led by heart surgeon Sali Berisha, was formed.

The March 1992 elections ended 47 years of communist rule, with parliament electing Sali Berisha president. Former president Alia was later placed under house arrest for writing articles critical of the Democratic government, and the leader of the Socialist Party, Fatos Nano, was also arrested on corruption charges.

During this time Albania switched from a tightly controlled communist regime to a rambunctious free-market free-for-all. A huge smuggling racket sprang up, in which stolen Mercedes-Benzes were brought into the country and the port of Vlora became a major crossing point for illegal immigrants from Asia and the Middle East into Italy.

In 1996, 70% of Albanians lost their savings when private pyramid-investment schemes, believed to have been supported by the government, collapsed. Riots ensued, elections were called, and the victorious Socialist Party under Nano – who had been freed from prison by a rampaging mob – was able to restore some degree of security and investor confidence.

In 1999 a different type of crisis struck when 465,000 Kosovars fled to Albania as a result of a Serbian ethnic-cleansing campaign. The influx had a positive effect on Albania's economy, and strengthened the relationship between Albania and Kosovo, which has historically been close. In 2008, songs sung by Albanian pop stars celebrating Kosovo's independence hit the top of the charts in both countries.

Since 2002 Albania has found itself in a kind of miniboom, with much money being poured into construction projects and infrastructure renewal. The general election of 2005 saw a return of Berisha's Democratic Party to government, and since then Albanian politics and the economy have been stable; however, work still has to be done to ensure that there is an end to electricity shortages and other infrastructure deficiencies that plague the country.

Albania signed NATO accession protocols in 2008, and EU membership beckons.

PEOPLE

In July 2008 the population was estimated to be 3.62 million, of which approximately 95% is Albanian, 3% Greek and 2% 'other' – comprising Vlachs, Roma, Serbs, Macedonians and Bulgarians.

Albanians are generally kind, helpful and generous. If you ask for directions, don't be surprised if you're guided all the way to your destination. The majority of young people speak some English, but speaking a few words of Albanian will be useful. Italian and Greek speakers are also widespread.

Albanians shake their heads sideways to say yes *(po)* and usually nod and 'tsk' to say no *(jo)*. Albanians working with tourists usually take on the nod-for-yes way, which is even more confusing.

The Ghegs in the north and the Tosks in the south have different dialects, music, dress and the usual jokes about each other's weaknesses.

RELIGION

Albanians are nominally 70% Muslim, 20% Christian Orthodox and 10% Catholic, but

BUNKER LOVE

On the hillsides, beaches and generally most surfaces in Albania, you will notice small concrete domes with their rectangular slits. Meet the bunkers: Enver Hoxha's concrete legacy, built from 1950 to 1985. Weighing in at five tonnes of concrete and iron, these little mushrooms are almost impossible to destroy. They were built to repel an invasion and can resist full tank assault – a fact proved by their chief engineer, who vouched for his creation's strength by standing inside one while it was bombarded by a tank. The shell-shocked engineer emerged unscathed, and tens of thousands were built. Some are creatively painted, but most are just eyesores with no further use; that said, quite a few Albanians will admit to losing their virginity in the security of one, and the bunkers also seem to make handy public toilets.

more realistic statistics estimate that up to 75% of Albanians are nonreligious. Religion was ruthlessly stamped out by the 1967 cultural revolution, when all mosques and churches were taken over by the state. By 1990 only about 5% of Albania's religious buildings were left intact. The rest had been turned into cinemas, army stores or were destroyed. Albania remains a very secular society, and it is difficult to assess how many followers each faith has.

The Muslim faith has a branch called 'Bektashism', similar to Sufism, and its world headquarters were in Albania from 1925 to 1945. Bektashi followers go to *teqe* (temple-like buildings without a minaret), which are usually found on hilltops in towns where those of the faith fled persecution. Most Bektashis live in the southern half of the country.

ARTS

Literature

One Albanian writer who is widely read outside Albania is Ismail Kadare (1936–). In 2005 he won the inaugural Booker International Prize for his body of work. His books are a great source of information on Albanian traditions, history and social events, and exquisitely capture the atmosphere of the country's towns, as in the lyrical descriptions of Kadare's birthplace, Gjirokastra, in *Chronicle in Stone* (1971). *Broken April* (1990), set in the northern highlands before the 1939 Italian invasion, describes the life of a village boy who is next in line in a desperate cycle of blood vendettas.

There is no substantial body of Albanian literature before the 19th century besides some Catholic religious works. Poetry that drew on the great tradition of oral epic poetry was the most popular literary form during the period leading up to Albanian independence in 1912. A group of romantic patriotic writers at Shkodra, including Migjeni (1911–38) and Martin Çamaj (1925–92), wrote epics and historical novels.

Perhaps the most interesting writer of the interwar period was Fan Noli (1880–1965). Educated as a priest in the US, Noli became premier of Albania's Democratic government until it was overthrown in 1924, when he returned to head the Albanian Orthodox Church in the US. Although many of his books have religious themes, the introductions he wrote to his own translations of Cervantes, Ibsen, Omar Khayyám and Shakespeare established him as Albania's foremost literary critic.

Cinema

During Albania's isolationist years the only Western actor approved by Hoxha was UK actor Sir Norman Wisdom (he became quite a cult hero). However, with so few international movies to choose from, the local film industry had a captive audience. While much of its output was propagandist, by the 1980s this little country was turning out an extraordinary 14 films a year. Despite a general lack of funds, two movies have gone on to win awards at international film festivals. Gjergj Xhuvani's comedy *Slogans* (2001) is a warm and touching account of life during communist times. This was followed in 2002 by *Tirana Year Zero,* Fatmir Koci's bleak look at the pressures on the young to emigrate.

Another film worth seeing is *Lamerica* (1995), a brilliant and stark look at Albania around 1991. Woven loosely around a plot about a couple of Italian scam artists and Albanians seeking to escape to Italy, the essence of the film is the unshakeable dignity of the ordinary Albanian in the face of adversity.

Vdekja e Kalit (1995) covers the harrowing 1980s and the change of regime in 1992, and is the only film that includes Albania's Roma.

Renowned Brazilian director Walter Salles *(Central Station)* adapted Ismail Kadare's novel *Broken April*: keeping the novel's main theme, he moved the action to Brazil in *Behind the Sun* (2001).

Music

There's pop aplenty in Albania, and artists like Sinan Hoxha manage to merge traditional instrumental polyphony with new beats. Others you may hear include the band The Dream, and Erion Korini.

Polyphony, the blending of several independent vocal or instrumental parts, is a southern Albanian tradition dating from ancient Illyrian times. Choirs perform in a variety of styles, and the songs, usually with an epic-lyrical or historical theme, may be dramatic to the point of yodelling, or slow and sober, with alternate male and female voices combining in harmony. Instrumental polyphonic *kabas* (a sedate style, led by a clarinet or violin alongside accordions and lutes) are played by small Roma ensembles. One well-known group that often tours outside Albania is the Lela Family of Përmet (www.kabarecords.com).

Visual Arts

The art scene in Albania is on the rise. One of the first signs are the multicoloured buildings of Tirana, a project organised by the capital's mayor, Edi Rama, himself an artist. The building's residents don't get a say in the colour or design, but some of the more inventive work includes paintings of silhouettes of laundry hanging to dry under windowsills.

Remnants of socialist realism still adorn the walls and gardens of some galleries and museums, although most were destroyed after the fall of the communist government in protest against against the old regime.

One of the most delicious Albanian art treats is to be found in Berat's Onufri Museum (p60). Onufri was the most outstanding Albanian icon painter of the 16th and 17th centuries, and his work is noted for its unique intensity of colour, derived from natural dyes that are as fresh now as the day he painted with them.

Churches around the country also feature amazing and original frescos.

ENVIRONMENT

The Land

The diversity of Albania's land is visually stunning; the country consists of 30% vast interior plains, over 300km of coastal region and the mountainous spine that runs its length. Mt Korab, at 2764m, is Albania's highest peak. Forest covers just under 40% of Albania, with Mediterranean shrubs at up to 600m, an oak forest belt between 600m and 1000m, and beech and pine forests between 1000m and 1600m.

The country's large and beautiful lakes include the Balkans' biggest, Lake Shkodra, which borders Montenegro in the north, and the ancient Lake Ohrid in the east (one-third Albanian, two-thirds Macedonian). Albania's longest river is the Drin (280km), which originates in Kosovo and is fed by melting snow from mountains in Albania's north and east. Hydroelectricity has changed Albania's landscape: Lake Koman was once a river, and the blue water from the Blue Eye Spring near Saranda travels to the coast in open concrete channels via a hydroelectricity plant. Agriculture makes up a small percentage of land use, but citrus and olive trees spice up the coastal plains while most rural householders grow their own food.

Wildlife

Snakes, turtles, bats, toads and a huge variety of birds are easy to spot all over Albania, but for those after something more glamorous, the northern Alps impress with its collection of brown bear, wolf, otter, marten, wild cat, wild boar and deer. Falcons and grouse are also alpine favourites, and birdwatchers can also flock to the country's wetlands at Lake Butrint, Karavasta Lagoon and Lake Shkodra (though the wetlands aren't pristine).

Lake Ohrid's trout is endangered (but still eaten), and endangered loggerhead turtles nest on the Ionian Coast and on the Karaburun Peninsula, where there have also been sightings of critically endangered Mediterranean monk seals.

National Parks

The number of national parks in Albania has risen from six to 15 since 1966 and include Mt Dajti, Butrint, Mt Tomorri, Valbone and Theth. Most are protected only by their remoteness, and tree-felling and hunting still take place. Hiking maps of the national parks are available, though they can be hard to find, and more guest houses and camping grounds are popping up. Llogaraja Pass has an established accommodation scene and is suitable for shorter hikes. Mt Tomorri near Berat is becoming popular with hikers; local organisations in Berat operate guided tours, and plenty of experienced hikers are taking on the Valbone–Theth route with the assistance of local guides. The Karaburun Peninsula near Vlora is a nature reserve protected largely, again, by its isolation.

Independent camping is not advisable as the mountains are almost completely uninhabited and have no cellphone coverage; in case of an injury, help would be impossible to find.

Environmental Issues

During communism, there were around 2000 cars in the country; the number of roaring automobiles has since risen to Western European levels. Many of them are old diesel Mercedes-Benzes stolen from Western Europe. As a consequence of the explosion, air pollution levels in Tirana are five to 10 times higher than in Western European countries.

Illegal logging and fishing reached epidemic proportions during the 1990s, and there are signs of it today; fishing for the endangered *koran* trout in Lake Ohrid continues, as does fishing with dynamite along the coast.

Badly maintained oilfields around Fier continue to leak sludge into the surrounding environment, and plans for an oil pipeline and hydrocarbon terminal are opposed by local environmentalists. Several coastal regions discharge raw sewage into seas and rivers. The rapid development of beach areas has compounded the issue, though projects are in place to improve waste disposal in sensitive environmental areas, including Lake Ohrid.

There is rubbish everywhere. Albania was practically litter-free until the late '90s; everything was reused or recycled. The change seems to be a result of both novelties like nonbiodegradable plastic bags and a reaction against the harsh communist-era rules on littering. Even household garbage is an issue: walk around the outside of a picturesque hotel and you are likely to come across its very unpicturesque dumping ground. Some Albanians are doing their bit to improve these conditions, and there is considerable Western investment in aiding this process. The **Organic Agriculture Association** (www.organic.org.al) is one group trying to make a difference.

FOOD & DRINK

Foodwise, the only thing you're likely to be lacking in Albania is *mëngjes* (breakfast), which tends to consist of a shot of the spirit raki or an espresso. If you're desperate, most shops sell packet croissants, or ask your hotel for some *bukë* and *mjaltë* (bread and honey) to go with your espresso. Albanians make excellent coffee and bread, and the local honey (usually sold by the side of the road) is delicious.

Patate të skuqura (potato chips) are served everywhere, and all meals come with bread. In coastal areas the calamari, mussels and fish will knock your socks off, while mountain areas like Llogaraja have roast lamb worth climbing a mountain for.

Offal is popular; *fërgesë Tiranë* is a traditional Tirana dish of offal, eggs and tomatoes cooked in an earthenware pot. If the *biftek* (beef) you ordered looks suspiciously like veal, take heart that it's likely to have been reared in a more humane way than it is elsewhere.

Italian influences mean vegetarians will probably become vegitalians, and most restaurants serve pizza, pasta or grilled vegetables.

Raki is very popular. The two main types are grape raki (the most common) and *mani raki* (mulberry raki). Ask for homemade if possible *(raki ë bërë në shtëpi)*. If raki is not your cup of tea, try a glass of wine from the Rilindja region, which produces a sweet white and a medium-bodied red. Wine aficionados should seek out the Çobo winery near Berat. Local beers include Tirana, Norga (from Vlora) and Korça.

Restaurants, cafes and bars are usually open from 8am and stay open until midnight or later. Most restaurants allow smoking, though some may have designated nonsmoking areas.

TIRANA

☎04 / pop 600,000

Lively, colourful Tirana has changed beyond belief in the last decade from the dull, grey city it once was (see the old Albanian movies for evidence). It's amazing what a lick of paint can do – it covers one ugly tower block with horizontal orange and red stripes, another with concentric pink and purple circles, and plants perspective-fooling cubes on its neighbour.

Trendy Blloku buzzes with the well-dressed nouvelle bourgeoisie hanging out in bars or zipping between boutiques. Quite where their money comes from is the subject of much speculation in this economically deprived nation, but thankfully you don't need much of it to have a fun night out in the city's many bars and clubs.

The city's grand central boulevards are lined with fascinating relics of its Ottoman, Italian and communist past – from delicate minarets to socialist murals – guarded by bored-looking soldiers with serious automatic weaponry. The traffic does daily battle with both itself and pedestrians in a constant scene of unmitigated chaos.

Loud, crazy, colourful, dusty – Tirana is simply fascinating.

ORIENTATION

Running through Tirana is Blvd Zogu I, which becomes Dëshmorët e Kombit as it crosses the Lana River. At its northern end is Tirana train station, and the south section ends at Tirana University. The main sites of interest are on or very close to this large blvd, including, roughly halfway along, the orientation point of Sheshi Skënderbej (Skanderbeg Square).

Most of the eating and drinking action is at Blloku, a square of 10 blocks of shops, restaurants, cafes and hotels situated one block west of Dëshmorët and along the Lana River in south Tirana. Mt Dajti (1612m) rises in the distant east.

Incoming buses will probably drop you off at the bus and train station at the north end of Blvd Zogu I, a five-minute walk from Sheshi Skënderbej. *Furgons* (shared minibuses) can also drop you at various points around the city, and it's easy and reasonably cheap to catch a waiting taxi to your destination.

INFORMATION

Bookshops

Adrion International Bookshop (☎ 2235 242; Palace of Culture, Sheshi Skënderbej; 🕑 9am-9pm Mon-Sat) Stocks Penguin classics, maps of Tirana and Albania, foreign magazines and newspapers and an excellent selection of books on the region.

Internet Access

More and more of Tirana's Blloku cafes offer free wi-fi to go with your frappé, but if you didn't bring your own laptop expect to pay 100 lekë per hour.

Internet Café (Rr Presidenti George W Bush; 🕑 9am-11pm)

Top Net (Rr Vasco Pasha; 🕑 8.30am-11pm) In the thick of Blloku.

Laundry

Drycleaner and laundry (☎ 068 216 8268; Rr Hoxha Tahsim; 🕑 8am-8pm Mon-Sat, 9am-1pm Sun) Charges 200 lekë per kilo of washing.

Medical Services

ABC Clinic (☎ 2234 105; Rr Qemal Stafa 260; 🕑 9am-1pm Mon-Fri) Has English-speaking doctors and a range of services, including regular (€50) and emergency (€80) consultations.

Money

Tirana has plenty of ATMs linked to international networks. The main ATM chains are Alpha Bank, Tirana Bank, Pro Credit Bank, Raiffeisen Bank and the American Bank of Albania.

Independent money exchangers operate directly in front of the main post office and on Sheshi Skënderbej and offer the same rates as the banks. Changing money here is not illegal or dangerous, but do count the money you receive before handing yours over. Travellers cheques are near impossible to exchange outside Tirana, so if you're relying on them (our advice is, don't), try one of the following:

American Bank of Albania (☎ 2276 000; Rr Ismail Qemali 27; 🕑 9.30am-3.30pm Mon-Fri) A reliable, secure place to cash your travellers cheques (2% commission). Also an Amex representative.

National Savings Bank (☎ 2235 035; Blvd Dëshmorët e Kombit; 🕑 10.30am-5pm Mon-Fri) Located in the Rogner Hotel Europapark Tirana, it offers MasterCard advances and currency exchange and cashes US-dollar, euro and sterling travellers cheques for 1% commission.

Post

DHL (☎ 2227 667; fax 2233 934; Rr Ded Gjo Luli 6).

Main post office (☎ 2228 262; Rr Çameria; 🕑 8am-8pm) On a street jutting west from Sheshi Skënderbej. There's an Albtelecom office next door.

Tourist Information

Tirana does not have an official tourist office, but travel agencies can help. *Tirana in Your Pocket* (www.inyourpocket.com) lists what's going on and can be downloaded free or bought at bookshops, hotels and some of the larger kiosks for 400 lekë.

TIRANA

0 — 500 m
0 — 0.3 miles

INFORMATION

ABC Clinic 1 D3
Adrion International Bookshop .... (see 30)
American Bank of Albania 2 C6
Avis .... (see 43)
DHL 3 C4
Drycleaner & Laundry 4 D4
Dutch Embassy 5 D6
French Embassy 6 B4
German Embassy 7 B4
Greek Embassy 8 B4
Internet Café 9 D5
Italian Embassy 10 C6
Macedonian Embassy 11 B4
Main Post Office 12 C5
National Savings Bank .... (see 43)
Serbian Embassy 13 C6
Top Net 14 C6
UK Embassy 15 B4
US Embassy 16 D6

SIGHTS & ACTIVITIES

Albanian Experience 17 C6
Archaeological Museum 18 C6
Clock Tower 19 C4
Congress Building 20 C6
Equestrian Statue of Skanderbeg 21 C4
Et'hem Bey Mosque 22 C4
Former Residence of Enver Hoxha 23 C6
Fortress of Justinian 24 C5
Lincoln Centre 25 C6
Luna Park 26 D5
National Art Gallery 27 C5
National Museum of History 28 C4
Outdoor Albania 29 B5
Palace of Culture 30 C4
Prime Minister's Residence 31 C6
Pyramid 32 C5
Statue of the Unknown Partisan 33 C4
Tanners' Bridge 34 D5

SLEEPING

Firenze Hotel 35 C4
Freddy's Hostel 36 C4
Hotel Endri 37 C6
Hotel Nirvana 38 B4
Hotel Nobel 39 C4
Lana River's Last House Standing 40 A6
Luna Hotel 41 C6
Pension Andrea 42 D5
Rogner Hotel Europapark Tirana 43 C6
Tirana Backpacker Hostel 44 D5

EATING

Anais 45 B6
Era 46 B6
Green House 47 C5
Pasticeri Française 48 C5
Villa Ambassador/Chocolate 49 D6

DRINKING

Buda Bar 50 B6
Charl's 51 C6
Sky Club Bar 52 C5

ENTERTAINMENT

Academy of Arts 53 C6
Kinema Millennium 2 .... 54 C5
Living Room 55 C4
Theatre of Opera & Ballet 56 C4

SHOPPING

National Museum of History .... (see 28)
Natyral & Organik 57 C6

TRANSPORT

Bus Stand 58 C3
Buses to Airport 59 C4
Drita Travel & Tours 60 C4
Europcar 61 A3
Hertz 62 C4
Pollogu Travel Agency 63 C3
Sixt 64 B4

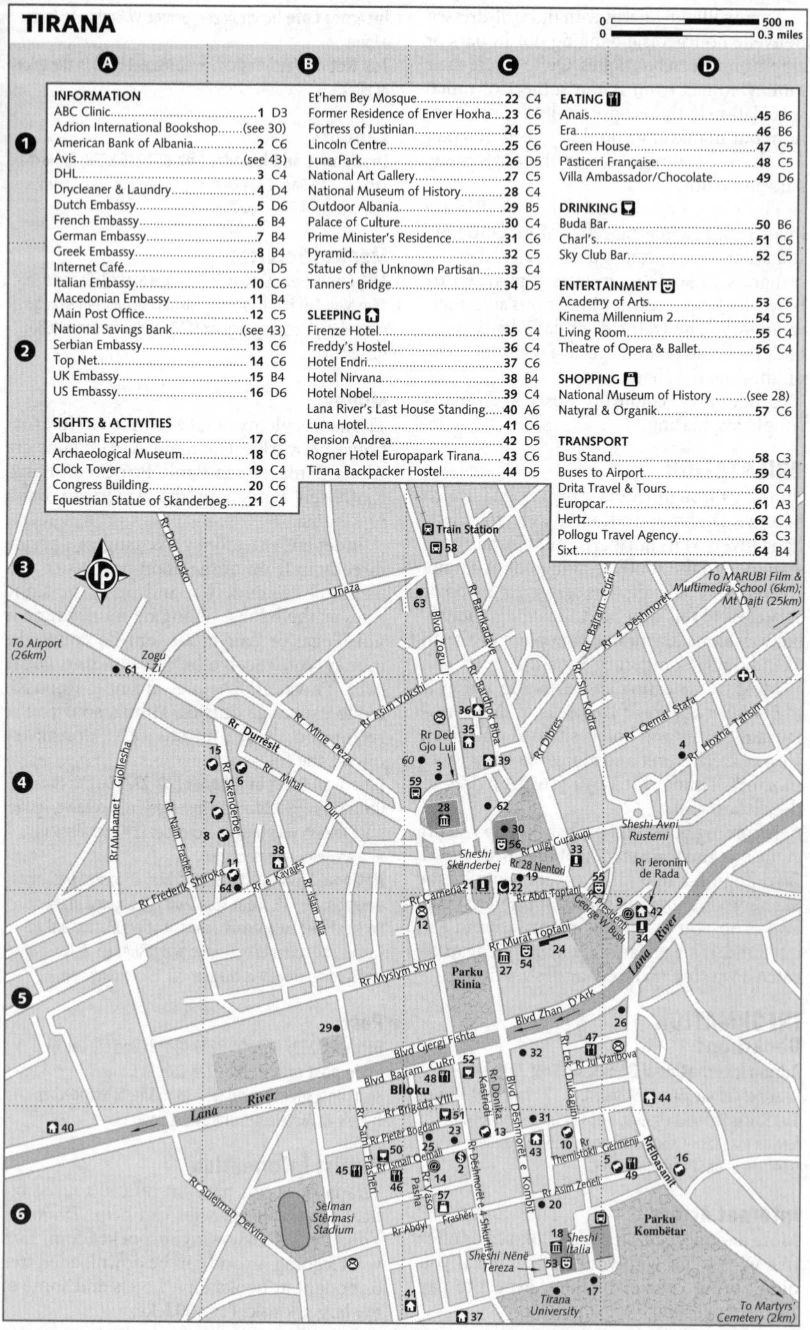

TIRANA IN TWO DAYS

Start your day with croissants in **Pasticeri Française** (p51) and stroll up to **Sheshi Skënderbej** (below) to explore the **National Museum of History** (right). Look around **Et'hem Bey Mosque** (below) and march down to the **National Art Gallery** (right). Admire the stunning views of Tirana at sunset as you have a beer, wine or sundae at the **Sky Club Bar** (p51). Drink and party the night away in the trendy **Blloku** (p50) area.

On day two catch a lbus up to the **Martyrs' Cemetery** (p50), then dine at **Villa Ambassador/Chocolate** (p51) for a mouth-watering meal in regal surrounds.

Travel Agencies

Travel agencies and airlines of all descriptions and destinations abound on Rr Mine Peza northwest of Sheshi Skënderbej. Nearly all sell tickets to leave Albania.

DANGERS & ANNOYANCES

Tirana is a very safe city with little petty crime. The streets are badly lit and there are a few massive potholes, though, so mind your step and arm yourself with a pocket torch at night to light your way. There are occasional power cuts in the city so the torch idea stretches further. Crossing the street is not for the faint-hearted – don't assume the traffic automatically stops at a red light.

SIGHTS

North of the River

Sheshi Skënderbej is the best place to start witnessing the daily goings-on. Until it was pulled down by an angry mob in 1991, a 10m-high bronze statue of Enver Hoxha stood here, watching over a mainly carless square. Now only the **equestrian statue of Skanderbeg** remains, deaf to the cacophony of screeching horns as cars four lanes deep try to shove their way through the battlefield below.

If you stop to examine Skanderbeg's emblematic goat's-head helmet, the minaret of the 1789–1823 **Et'hem Bey Mosque** will catch your eye. The small and elegant mosque is one of the oldest buildings left in the city, spared from destruction during the atheism campaign of the late '60s because of its status as a cultural monument. Take your shoes off to look inside at the beautifully painted dome.

Behind the mosque is the tall **Clock Tower** (Kulla e Sahatit; Rr Luigi Gurakqi; admission 50 lekë; 🕒 9am-1pm Mon, 9am-1pm & 4-6pm Thu), which you can climb for views of the square. Further on, the socialist realist **Statue of the Unknown Partisan** attracts day labourers waiting for work, some with their own jackhammers – a fitting image of the precarious position of the postcommunist Albanian worker.

To the east of Sheshi Skënderbej is the white stone **Palace of Culture** (Pallate Kulturës; Sheshi Skënderbej), which has a theatre, shops and art galleries. Construction of the palace began as a gift from the Soviet people in 1960 and was completed in 1966, years after the 1961 Soviet-Albanian split. The entrance to the National Library is on the south side of the building.

On the northwestern side of the square, beside the 15-storey Tirana International Hotel, is the **National Museum of History** (Muzeu Historik Kombëtar; Sheshi Skënderbej; admission 300 lekë; 🕒 9am-1pm & 4-7pm Tue-Sat, 9am-noon Sun). This, the largest museum in Albania, holds most of the country's archaeological treasures and a replica of Skanderbeg's massive sword. The fantastic mosaic mural entitled *Albania* adorning the museum's facade shows Albanians victorious and proud from Illyrian times through to WWII. In case you thought everyone had erased the Hoxha era from their minds, a sombre gallery devoted to its miseries is on the top floor. Its walls are covered with the names of those killed from 1941 to 1985 – and there are many, many names. Even the guides seem to find the exhibit confronting. The museum's better with a guide (around 100 lekë), and they speak English, French and Italian. There's a good souvenir shop on site. Note that you won't be let in if you arrive half an hour or less before closing time.

Stroll down the spacious tree-lined Blvd Dëshmorët e Kombit to Tirana's **National Art Gallery** (Galeria Kombëtare e Arteve; Blvd Dëshmorët e Kombit; admission 100 lekë; 🕒 9am-1pm & 5-8pm Tue-Sun), whose garden is adorned with statues of proud partisans. See the astonishing exhibition of icons inside by Onufri, the renowned 16th-century master of colour. If you're lucky you'll catch some modern work by Albanian-born artists in the ground-floor temporary exhibition area.

If you turn up Rr Murat Toptani, you'll pass the 6m-high walls of the **Fortress of Justinian**

FREE THRILLS

There are plenty of look-see free thrills in Tirana:

- Check out the **Lana River's last house standing**, a few kilometres west of the centre – surrounding houses were demolished in a clean-up attempt in 2002, but this one was protected thanks to a long-lasting blood feud. The men stay in here, in fear of their lives, while Tirana's business goes on around them.
- See free art-house movies on Thursdays during the school term at **MARUBI Film & Multimedia School** (p52).
- Take a jump on the trampolines at Tirana's mini **Luna Park** on Rr Elbasanit.
- Stroll with the masses on the evening **xhiro** (walk).
- Admire the innovative artwork on Tirana's **apartment blocks** (p45).

(Rr Murat Toptani), the last remnants of a Byzantine-era castle. Strangely, half a cinema overflows over the top. East from here, on the corner of Rr Presidenti George W Bush and the Lana River is **Tanners' Bridge**, a small 19th-century slippery-when-wet stone bridge.

South of the River

It's hard not to notice the sloping white-marble and glass walls of the 1988 **Pyramid** (Blvd Dëshmorët e Kombit), formerly the Enver Hoxha Museum, designed by Hoxha's daughter and son-in-law. Now used as a disco and conference centre, the building never really took off as a museum, but makes a good slide. Nearby is the **Prime Minister's Residence** (Blvd Dëshmorët e Kombit), where Enver Hoxha and cronies would stand and view military parades from the balcony.

Another creation of the dictator's daughter and son-in-law is the square **Congress Building** (Blvd Dëshmorët e Kombit), just a little down the blvd. Follow Rr Ismail Qemali two streets north of the Congress Building and enter the once totally forbidden but now totally trendy **Blloku** area. This former communist party elite hang-out was opened to the general public for the first time in 1991. Security still guards the **former residence of Enver Hoxha** (cnr Rr Dëshmorët e 4 Shkurtit & Rr Ismail Qemali).

The **Archaeological Museum** (Muzeu Arkeologik; Sheshi Nënë Tereza; admission 200 lekë; 10.30am-2.30pm Mon-Fri) houses an extensive collection close to Tirana University. The foyer displays maps and information about current archaeological digs in Albania.

At the top of Rr Elbasanit is the **Martyrs' Cemetery**, where some 900 partisans who died in WWII are buried. The views over the city and surrounding mountains (including Mt Dajti to the east) are excellent, as is the sight of the immense, beautiful and strangely androgynous Mother Albania statue (1972). Hoxha was buried here in 1985, but was exhumed in 1992 and interred in an ordinary graveyard on the other side of town. Catch any municipal bus heading up Rr Elbasanit; the grand driveway is on your left.

TOURS

Get off the beaten track or discover Albania's tourist attractions with the following Tirana-based tour companies:

Albanian Experience (☎ 2266 389; Sheraton Hotel, Sheshi Italia; 8.30am-7pm Mon-Fri, 8.30am-5pm Sat) Organises tours of Albania with knowledgeable guides.

Outdoor Albania (☎ 069 218 8845, 2227 121; www.outdooralbania.com; Metropol Bldg, Rr Sami Frashëri; 8am-8pm Mon-Fri) Excellent trailblazing adventure tour agency offering trekking, rafting, ski touring, sea and white-water kayaking and, in summer, hikes through the Alps.

SLEEPING

Budget

our pick Tirana Backpacker Hostel (☎ 068 216 7357; www.tiranahostel.com; Rr Elbasanit 85; dm €12) Albania's first hostel opened in 2005 in a 70-year-old villa close to the city centre. The 25 beds are spread over four rooms with shared bathrooms. It has big balconies, a great garden with a cosy outdoor kitchen, a summer cinema in the basement and friendly, helpful young managers. Head east along Rr Ismail Qemali until it meets Rr Elbasanit; it's over the road on your left.

Freddy's Hostel (☎ 068 203 5261; www.freddyshostel.com; Rr Bardhok Biba 75; dm/r €12/30) Freddy's has a bunch of clean, basic rooms in different configurations and in two different buildings in the same area. To find the main apartment block, walk north of Tirana International Hotel and look for the suburban street parallel to Blvd Zogu I. The hostel is past Hestia restaurant (a great place for a snack and a beer), on the left.

Pension Andrea (☎ 069 290 4915; Rr Jeronim de Rada 103; s/d €20/30) Gina runs this homey, quiet pension. All rooms have TVs and a couple also have air-con. There's a safe storage area for bicycles. On Rr Jeronim de Rada take the first right down the court; it's on your right.

Hotel Endri (☎ 2244 168, 2229 334; Rr Vaso Pasha 27; r €30; ❄) The Endri is good value and located south of Blloku, where all the action is. The 'hotel' is basically a couple of clean rooms in a building next to owner Petrit Alikaj's apartment. It's on the left at the end of Rr Vaso Pasha, but call Petrit for directions.

Midrange

Hotel Nobel (☎ 2256 444; www.hotelnobeltirana.com; Blvd Zogu I; s/d €40/50; ❄) Albania's two Nobel Peace Prize winners are Mother Teresa and Prof Ferid Murad, the inventor of Viagra. It's good to see a hotel getting into the spirit of things, and charismatic owner Edmond has done a great job giving his hotel some Nobel personality (although the stick of dynamite in his drawer is curious). The six rooms are clean and bright, there's wi-fi and an Italian restaurant downstairs, and it's central (next to VEVE Business Centre).

Luna Hotel (☎ 2272 950; www.hotels-tirana.com; Rr Sami Frashëri 4; s/d €50/60; ❄) Just south of Blloku, off Sami Frasheri, this modern hotel has had the power of Zen through its rooms and bathrooms. Gigantic stencilled flowers decorate the hall's lime-green walls, and everything's been thought of, down to hairdriers in the bathrooms.

Firenze Hotel (☎ 2249 099; firenzehotel@albaniaonline.net; Blvd Zogu I 72; s/d €50/70; ❄) This cheerful and colourful little hotel between the railway station and Sheshi Skënderbej has seven cosy, clean rooms with TV and minibar and a great 'magazine corner' in the breakfast room.

Hotel Nirvana (☎ 2235 270; Rr e Kavajës 96/2; s/d €60/80; ❄) With its ostentatious marble staircase and walls dripping in art (apparently this is nothing compared with the owner's house), this hotel may have delusions of grandeur, but thankfully the price remains reasonably humble and the staff friendly and helpful.

Top End

Rogner Hotel Europapark Tirana (☎ 2235 035; www.hotel-europapark.com; Blvd Dëshmorët e Kombit; s €210-240, d €250-290, ste €320-350; ❄ 💻 🏊) With an unbeatable location in the heart of the city, the Rogner is a peaceful oasis with a huge garden, tennis court, free wi-fi in the lobby, banks, car rental and travel agencies. The rooms are spacious and comfortable and have flat-screen TVs.

EATING

If you thought that cuisine in Tirana's restaurants might be monotonous or that eating out would be a downmarket experience, you were wrong.

Era (☎ 2266 662; Rr Ismail Qemali; mains from 200 lekë; 🕑 11am-midnight) Serves traditional Albanian and Italian fare in the heart of Blloku. Be warned: it's hard to move on once you've eaten here. Also does delivery and takeaway.

Pasticeri Française (☎ 2251 336; Rr Dëshmorët e 4 Shkurtit 1; breakfasts from 300 lekë; 🕑 8am-10pm) One of the few breakfast spots in Tirana, this French-owned cafe has red walls, high ceilings and a huge selection of sweet pastries.

Green House (☎ 2222 632; Rr Jul Varibova 6; mains from 700 lekë; 🕑 9am-11pm) This quite formal restaurant is a modern and friendly expat hangout with a varied menu (including non-Albanian fare like gnocchi gorgonzola) and a huge wine list. It offers boutique-style accommodation (single/double €100/110) upstairs, too.

Villa Ambassador/Chocolate (☎ 069 206 6257; Rr Asim Zeneli 2; mains 700-1500 lekë; 🕑 8am-midnight) Located in the former Romanian Ambassador's residence, this well-regarded restaurant has a great team creating and serving up tasty Albanian dishes for carnivores and vegetarians alike. Crêpes and pastries make it a good spot for breakfast, too.

Anais (☎ 2246 624; Rr Sami Frashëri 20; mains 1000-1200 lekë; 🕑 11am-11pm) Quite expensive by local standards, the Ottoman cuisine served here by a chef who worked in Turkey is utterly superb. The selection of mezes is tremendous: puréed eggplant, spicy beans and mushrooms and rich kebabs.

DRINKING

Most of Tirana's nightspots let you party on to the wee hours.

Sky Club Bar (☎ 2221 666; Sky Tower, Rr Dëshmorët e 4 Shkurtit; 🕑 8am-midnight) Start your night here for spectacular city views from the revolving bar on top of one of the highest buildings in town. If you're just going up for a look, it's cheaper to buy a beer up there than pay the 250-lekë charge that reception may request.

Living Room (☎ 2274 837; Rr Presidenti George W Bush 16; 🕑 7.30pm-late) This is the hippest place to drink and dance in Tirana, with eclectic DJs, a good crowd, cool lampshades and '70s sofas for you to lounge on when you're danced (or drunk) off your feet. The terrace is airy and fun.

Charl's (☎ 2253 754; Rr Pjetër Bogdani 36; 🕑 8am-late) Charl's is a consistently popular bar with Tirana's students because of its ever-varying live music, with bands coming from places as diverse as Cuba and Serbia. The relaxed vibe is enhanced by the bar's open-air garden.

Buda Bar (☎ 068 205 8825; Rr Ismail Qemali; 🕑 4.30pm-late) This place is all about a relaxed atmosphere, with subdued lighting, incense burning, chaise longues and armchairs abounding with cushions.

ENTERTAINMENT

There is a good choice of entertainment options in Tirana, in the form of bars, clubs, cinema, performances, exhibitions and even ten-pin bowling. For the low-down on events and exhibitions, check out the free fortnightly *Planet Albania* (www.planet-albania.com) guide as well as the monthly leaflet *ARTirana* (a free supplement in *Gazeta Shqiptare*) and the weekly *Tirana Times*.

MARUBI Film & Multimedia School (www.afmm.edu.al; Rr Aleksander Moisiu 76; admission free; 🕑 7pm Thu) shows free art-house movies during the semester. It's near the last Kino Studio bus stop in the city's northeast.

Kinema Millennium 2 (☎ 2253 654; www.ida-millennium.com; Rr Murat Toptani; tickets 200-500 lekë) Current-release movies that are cheaper the earlier in the day you go.

Theatre of Opera & Ballet (☎ 2224 753; Sheshi Skënderbej; tickets from 300 lekë; 🕑 performances from 7pm, from 6pm winter) Check the listings and posters outside this theatre for performances. You can buy tickets half an hour before the show for 200 lekë.

Academy of Arts (☎ 2257 237; Sheshi Nënë Tereza) Classical music and other performances take place throughout the year in either the large indoor theatre or the small open-air faux-classical amphitheatre; both are part of the university. Prices vary according to the program.

SHOPPING

Natyral & Organik (☎ 2250 575; Rr Vaso Pasha) This wonderful store in Blloku not only supports small village producers by stocking organic olive oil, honey, herbs, tea, eggs, spices, raki and cognac (these make great gifts, but be aware of customs regulations in the countries you're travelling through); it's also a centre for environmental activism.

Find souvenir shops on Rr Durrësit and Blvd Zogu I or try the National Museum of History (p49). They all sell the same things: red Albanian flags, red T-shirts, red lighters, bunker ashtrays and lively traditional textiles.

GETTING THERE & AWAY

Air

Nënë Tereza International Airport (Mother Teresa Airport, Rinas airport) is at Rinas, 26km northwest of Tirana. Its new passenger terminal opened in 2006. There's a €10 entry fee to enter Albania by air.

For a list of airlines flying to Albania, see p69.

Bus

You have the option of buses or *furgons* (minibuses). Since there are few actual bus stations in Tirana, it's impossible to pin down where the buses and *furgons* actually leave from. It's best to jump in a taxi and say '*Dua të shkoj në...*', meaning 'I want to go to...'. Taxi drivers always know the latest departure points and, given Albania's unique attitude to assisting travellers, will often secure the next part of the trip for you as well.

See below for costs, distances and durations of domestic departures from Tirana. *Furgons* are usually 20% to 30% more expensive than buses.

Buses for Pristina (€30, 10 hours, 343km, three daily) leave from behind the museum

BUSES FROM TIRANA

Destination	Cost	Duration	Distance
Berat	400 lekë	2½hr	122km
Durrës	100 lekë	1hr	38km
Elbasan	300 lekë	1½hr	54km
Fier	300 lekë	2hr	113km
Gjirokastra	1000 lekë	7hr	232km
Korça	800 lekë	4hr	181km
Kruja	200 lekë	30min	32km
Pogradec	700 lekë	3½hr	150km
Saranda	1200 lekë	8hr	284km
Shkodra	400 lekë	2hr	116km
Vlora	500 lekë	3hr	147km

near Sheshi Skënderbej. To Macedonia, there are buses via Struga (€10, five hours) to Tetovo (€15, seven to eight hours), and Skopje (€25, eight hours). If you're heading to Greece, buses go daily to Thessaloniki (11 hours) and Athens (17 hours).

The **Pollogu travel agency** (☎ 2235 000, 069 209 4906; Pall 103 Blvd Zogu I) sells tickets for the Macedonian bus company Polet, which has services at 9am and 9pm daily from the train station. The Pollogu office is upstairs in a modern apartment building at the top end of Zogu I. **Drita Travel and Tours** (☎ 2251 277; www.dritatravel.com) has offices at the train station and behind the museum, and runs an evening service to Skopje.

Train

The run-down train station is at the northern end of Blvd Zogu I. Albania's trains range from sort of OK to very decrepit. Albanians travel by train if they can't afford to travel by bus. Six trains daily go to Durrës (70 lekë, one hour, 36km). Trains also depart for Elbasan (190 lekë, four hours, two daily), Pogradec (2km out of town; 295 lekë, seven hours, once a day at 5.55am), Shkodra (150 lekë, 3½ hours, once a day at 1.15pm) and Vlora (250 lekë, 5½ hours, once a day at 2.50pm). Check timetables at the station the day before travelling. You can't buy tickets in advance, however; purchase them just before hopping on the train.

GETTING AROUND

To/From the Airport

The Rinas airport bus operates an hourly (6am to 6pm) service from the western side of the National Museum at Sheshi Skënderbej for 250 lekë. The going taxi rate is €20. It usually takes 20 to 25 minutes to get to or from the airport, but plan for traffic delays.

Car & Motorcycle

Driving around Albania is not as hard as it once was, although there are bound to be hair-raising moments.

Major car-hire companies in Tirana include the following:

Avis (☎ 2235 011; Rogner Hotel Europapark, Blvd Dëshmorët e Kombit)
Europcar (☎ 2227 888; Rr Durrësit 61)
Hertz (☎ 2255 028; Tirana Hotel International, Sheshi Skënderbej)
Sixt (☎ 2259 020; Rr e Kavajës 116)

Taxi

Taxi stands dot the city, and taxis charge 400 lekë for a ride inside Tirana and 600 lekë at night and to destinations outside the CBD area. Make sure you reach an agreement with the driver before setting off. **Radio Taxi** (☎ 377 777), with 24-hour service, is particularly reliable.

AROUND TIRANA

Just 25km east of Tirana is **Mt Dajti National Park** (1611m). It is the most accessible mountain in the country, and many Tiranans go there to escape the city rush and have a spit-roast lamb lunch. A cable car, **Dajti Express** (www.dajtiekspres.com; 500 lekë return), plies the route, cutting the time it takes to chug up the hill down to 15 minutes. Check first if it's operating.

If you're driving, there's a checkpoint where you pay a park admission fee of 200 lekë per car. Put your sturdy shoes on for a gentle hike in the lovely, shady beech and pine forests and then have a coffee and enjoy the spectacular views from the wide terrace of the **Panorama Restaurant** (☎ 361 124; meals 800 lekë; 🕒 9am-11pm).

To get to the Dajti Express departure point, take the public bus from outside Tirana's Clock Tower to 'Porcelain' (20 lekë), then walk uphill, following the signs, for around 10 minutes. Taxis seem to charge what they want to the Express, but the 6km trip should only cost 600 lekë. A taxi from the city to the top takes about 45 minutes, and you can arrange to phone the driver to pick you up when you want to go back. The road to the park starts on Tirana's Rr Qemal Stafa.

NORTHERN ALBANIA

The northern Albanian landscape has rich wildlife, swamps and lagoons around Shkodra and Lezha and high mountains around Theth in the northeast (named the Accursed Mountains, Bjeshkët e Namuna, in Albanian). Blood feuds may occupy the locals' minds, but pose little risk to tourists (see p54).

SHKODRA

☎ 022 / pop 91,300

Shkodra (Shkodër), the traditional centre of the Gheg cultural region, is one of the oldest cities in Europe. Rozafa Fortress is beautiful, and the Marubi permanent photography exhibition is small but fascinating. A section of town (between the mosque and cathedral) has benefited from sensitive renovations of most of its older houses and storefronts, and Shkodra's locals are more likely to ride a bicycle than drive a car. Out of the centre, tatty grey apartment buildings lend it a rather sombre air.

Travellers pass through here on the way between Tirana and Ulcinj in Montenegro, but more are beginning to use the town as a base for forays into the alpine area of Theth and the isolated wonder of Lake Koman.

As the Ottoman Empire declined in the late 18th century, Shkodra became the centre of a semi-independent *pashalik* (region governed by a pasha, an Ottoman high official), which led to a blossoming of commerce and crafts. In 1913 Montenegro attempted to annex Shkodra (it succeeded in taking Ulcinj), a move not approved of by the international community, and the town changed hands often during WWI. Badly damaged by an earthquake in 1979, Shkodra was subsequently repaired and is Albania's fourth-largest town. The communist-era Hotel Rozafa in the town centre does little to welcome guests, but it makes a good landmark: restaurants, transport to Montenegro, and most of the town's sights are close by.

Sights

Three kilometres southwest of Shkodra, near the southern end of Lake Shkodra, is the **Rozafa Fortress** (admission 200 lekë; 🕒 8am-10pm), founded by the Illyrians in antiquity and rebuilt much later by the Venetians and Turks. The fortress derives its name from a woman named Rozafa, who was allegedly walled into the ramparts as an offering to the gods so that the construction would stand. The story goes that Rozafa asked that two holes be left in the stonework so that she could continue to breastfeed her baby. There's a spectacular wall sculpture of her near the entrance of the castle's **museum** (admission 150 lekë; 🕒 8am-7pm). Some nursing women come to the fortress to smear their breasts with the milky water that seeps from the wall and appears annually in January and February. A return (with waiting time) taxi from Shkodra is 800 lekë, or, if you're up for a steep walk through a poor part of town, municipal buses stop near the turn-off to the castle.

Hidden behind a building that looks like a block of flats, the **Marubi Permanent Photo Exhibition** (Rr Muhamet Gjollesha; admission 100 lekë; 🕒 8am-4pm Mon-Fri) has fantastic photography by the Marubi 'dynasty', Albania's first and foremost photographers. The first-ever photograph taken in Albania is here, taken by Pjetër Marubi in 1858. The exhibition shows fascinating portraits, places and events. Not only is this a rare insight into what things looked like in old Albania, it is also a small collection of mighty fine photographs. To get here, go northeast of the clock tower to Rr Çlirimi; Rr Muhamet Gjollesha darts off to the right. The exhibition is on the left in an unmarked building, but locals will help you find it if you ask. Postcards of some of the images are for sale for 100 lekë.

FAMILY FEUD WITH BLOOD AS THE PRIZE

The *Kanun* (Code) was formalised in the 15th century by powerful northern chieftain Lekë Dukagjin. It consists of 1262 articles covering every aspect of daily life: work, marriage, family, property, hospitality, economy and so on. Although the *Kanun* was suppressed by the communists, there has been a revival of its strict precepts in northern Albania. How much so is uncertain, as dramatic incidents may have been overplayed by the media.

According to the *Kanun*, the most important things in life are honour and hospitality. If a member of a family (or one of their guests) is murdered, it becomes the duty of the male members of that clan to claim their blood debt by murdering a male member of the murderer's clan. This sparks an endless cycle of killing that doesn't end until either all the male members of one of the families are dead, or reconciliation is brokered through respected village elders.

Hospitality is so important in these parts of Albania that the guest takes on a godlike status. There are 38 articles giving instructions on how to treat a guest – an abundance of food, drink and comfort is at his or her disposal, and it is also the host's duty to avenge the murder of his guest, should this happen during their visit.

WORTH THE TRIP: THETH

Heading north to Theth is truly heading into Albania's unknown. Wooden watermills, fast-flowing rivers, great hiking trails and lock-in towers (where men waited, protected, during a blood feud) are features of this small town and, with foreign nongovernment investment assisting the locals to move into the B&B industry, the three-hour hair-raising journey is rewarded with fully catered homestay accommodation. Theth's snowed out much of the year (outside June to September).

Petrit Imeraj (☎ 069 206 5205) is a Shkodra-based mountain man who offers a variety of tours around the region.

Harusha Family Home (☎ 069 277 0294; per person 2500 lekë) is a friendly homestay in Theth's 'centre'. The Harushas are the biggest family in the village, so look out for a bunch of (English-speaking) children and you're close. The house is on the left, over the bridge.

A *furgon* (shared minibus; 500 lekë, three hours) is supposed to make a daily trip, departing at 7am from outside Shkodra's Café Rusi.

Sleeping & Eating

Hotel Kaduku (HK; ☎ 42 216; Sheshi 5 Heronjtë; r €30) This popular and clean hotel is behind Raiffeisen Bank on the roundabout near Hotel Rozafa. The two wings have been renovated, and staff and other guests are great information providers. Breakfast is an extra €4.

Piazza Park (Rr 13 Dhjetori; mains 250-1000 lekë) Where the locals return to, night after night, day after day. Once you get past security, people-watch (or be watched) next to the fountains.

G&T Tradita (tradita Gegë dhe Toskë; Rr Skenderbeu; meals 1100 lekë) Serves great food (fresh fish is a speciality) in what could be an ethnographic museum. You can watch grills and pita being cooked on the huge hearth. It's really dim inside, but no doubt that's part of the Gheg and Tosk's atmosphere.

Getting There & Away

There are frequent *furgons* to and from Tirana (350 lekë, 2½ hours). From Shkodra, *furgons* depart from Radio Shkodra near Hotel Rozafa. The train station is a fair walk away, but *furgons* meet arriving trains.

Furgons to Ulcinj and Bar in Montenegro leave at 9am and 3pm (500 lekë) from outside the Hotel Rozafa. They fill quickly, so get in early. Taxis to Han i Hotit on the way to Podgorica charge about 2500 lekë; you can also catch a *furgon* to Koplik (the turn-off to Theth) and a taxi from there.

Buses also depart Shkodra for Lake Koman (400 lekë, two hours, 6.30am and 9.30am), dropping you at the ferry terminal for the wonderful ferry trip across the lake to Fierza (400 lekë), located near the border with Kosovo.

CENTRAL ALBANIA

Central Albania crams it all in. Just an hour or two from Tirana and you can be Ottoman house-hopping in brilliantly alive Berat, or musing over ancient ruins in deserted Apollonia or bubbly beachside Durrës. Don't forget to bargain for antiques under the gaze of Skanderbeg in Kruja, and to take time out on the cable car to Mt Dajti National Park.

KRUJA

☎ 0511 / pop 20,000

From the road below, Kruja's houses appear to sit in the lap of a mountain. An ancient castle juts out to one side, and the massive Skanderbeg Museum juts out of the castle itself. The local plaster industry is going strong, so, sadly, expect visibility-reducing plumes of smoke to cloud views of the Atlantic.

Kruja is Skanderbeg's town. Yes, Albania's hero was born here, and although it was over 500 years ago, there's still a great deal of pride in the fact that he and his forces defended Kruja until his death. As soon as you get off the *furgon* you're face to knee with a statue of Skanderbeg wielding his mighty sword with one hand, and it just gets more Skanderdelic after that.

At a young age Kastrioti, the son of an Albanian prince, was handed over as a hostage to the Turks, who converted him to Islam and gave him a military education at Edirne in Turkey. There he became known as Iskander (after Alexander the Great) and Sultan Murat II promoted him to the rank of *bey* (governor), thus the name Skanderbeg.

In 1443 the Turks suffered a defeat at the hands of the Hungarians at Niš in present-day

Serbia, and nationally minded Skanderbeg took the opportunity to abandon the Ottoman army and Islam and rally his fellow Albanians against the Turks. Skanderbeg made Kruja his seat of government between 1443 and 1468. Among the 13 Turkish invasions he subsequently repulsed was that led by his former commander Murat II. Pope Calixtus III named Skanderbeg the 'captain general of the Holy See' and Venice formed an alliance with him. The Turks besieged Kruja four times. Though beaten back in 1450, 1466 and 1467, they took control of Kruja in 1478 (after Skanderbeg's death).

Kruja's sights can be covered in a few hours, making this an ideal town to visit en route to Tirana's international airport, which is only 16km away. The main sight in Kruja is the **castle** (admission 100 lekë; 24hr) and its peculiar **Skanderbeg Museum** (admission 200 lekë; 9am-1pm & 4-7pm Tue-Sun). Designed by Enver Hoxha's daughter and son-in-law, it opened in 1982, and its spacious seven-level interior displays replicas of armour and paintings depicting Skanderbeg's struggle against the Ottomans. The museum is something of a secular shrine, and takes itself very seriously indeed, with giant statues and dramatic battle murals.

The **Ethnographic Museum** (admission 100 lekë; 9am-7pm) in the castle complex below the Skanderbeg Museum is one of the best in the country. Set in an original 19th-century Ottoman house that belonged to the affluent Toptani family, this museum shows the level of luxury and self-sufficiency the household maintained by producing its own food, drink, leather and weapons. They even had their very own mini-*hammam* (Turkish bath) and watermill. The walls are lined with original frescos from 1764. The English-speaking guide's detailed explanations are excellent; offer a tip if you can.

A short scramble down the cobblestone lane are the remains of a small *hammam* as well as a functioning *teqe* – a small place of worship for those practising the Bektashi branch of Islam. This beautifully decorated *teqe* has been maintained by successive generations of the Dollma family since 1789. Skanderbeg himself reputedly planted the knotted and ancient olive tree in front.

The bazaar is the country's best place for souvenir shopping and has WWII medical kits, antique gems and quality traditional ware, including beautifully embroidered tablecloths, copper coffee pots and plates. You can watch women using looms to make *kilims* (rugs) and purchase the results.

Kruja is 32km from Tirana. A cab from Tirana to Kruja and back with two hours' waiting time costs around 4000 lekë, while a *furgon* one way costs 200 lekë. It is very easy to reach the airport (100 lekë, 30 minutes) by *furgon* or taxi from here, and there are direct links by bus and *furgon* to Durrës (200 lekë, one hour).

DURRËS

☎ 052 / pop 114,000

Durrës is an ancient city and was, until 1920, Albania's capital. Its 10km-long beach begins a few kilometres southeast of the city (past the port and tangle of overpasses and roundabouts). Here families take up position under rented umbrellas and sun lounges, and the brave cool down in its shallow, and frequently red-flagged, section of the Adriatic Sea. The beaches are something of a lesson in unplanned development; hundreds of hotels stand side by side, barely giving breathing space to the beach and contributing to the urban waste problem that has caused outbreaks of skin infections in swimmers.

Away from the beach, Durrës is a relaxed, amiable city with some gracious early-20th-century buildings, centrally located ancient ruins, a unique museum and an abundance of fun waterfront eating options.

Orientation

The town centre is easily covered on foot. The **Great Mosque** (Xhamia e Madhe Durrës; Sheshi i Lirisë) serves as a point of orientation: the archaeological attractions are immediately around it, and the train and bus stations are a kilometre to the northeast. The former palace of King Zogu I and the lighthouse are to the west, on the ridge.

Information

There are plenty of ATMs near the station, on Rr Tregtare, and a branch of the American Bank of Albania is on Sheshi Mujo Ulqinaku.

Century 91 Internet (Rr Tregtare; per hr 60 lekë; 1pm-midnight) Down a lane near the Great Mosque.

Dea Lines (☎ 30 386; dealines@dealines.com; Rr Tregtare 102; 8.30am-8pm) Trustworthy travel agency that will help you find up-to-date information on ferries and flights.

Post office (Blvd Kryesor) One block west of the train and bus stations.

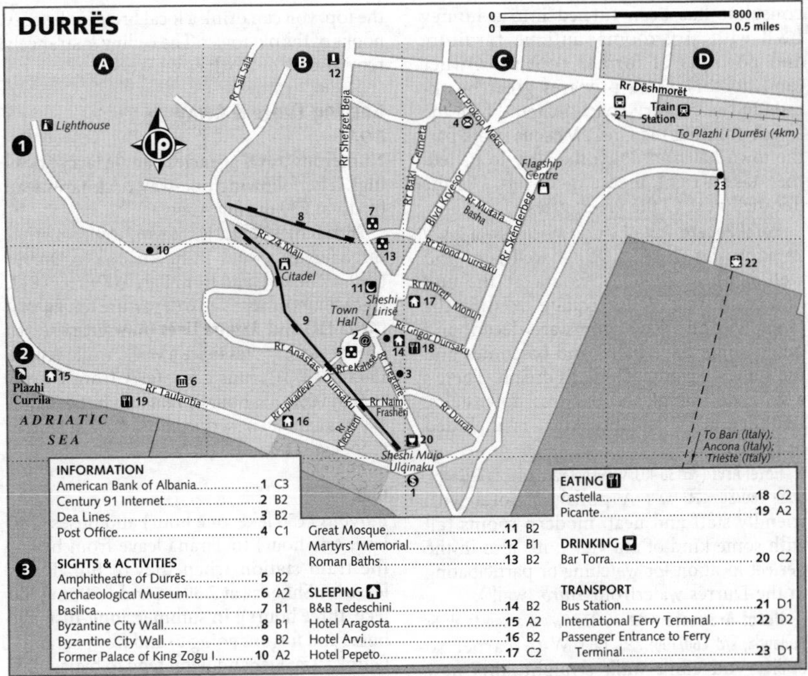

Sights

The **Archaeological Museum** (Muzeu Arkeologik; Rr Taulantia; admission 200 lekë; 9am-3pm Tue-Sun), on the waterfront, is well laid out and has an impressive collection of artefacts from the Greek, Hellenistic and Roman periods. Highlights include engraved Roman funeral stelae and some big carved-stone sarcophagi. Back in the day when it was called Epidamnos, Durrës was a centre for the worship of Venus, and the museum has a cabinet full of little busts of the love goddess.

North of the museum, beginning at the Torra and following Rr Anastas Durrsaku, are the 6th-century **Byzantine city walls**, built after the Visigoth invasion of AD 481 and supplemented by round Venetian towers in the 14th century.

The **Amphitheatre of Durrës** (Rr e Kalasë; admission 500 lekë; 8am-7pm) was built on the hillside inside the city walls in the early 2nd century AD. In its prime it had the capacity to seat 15,000 spectators, but these days a few inhabited houses occupy the stage, a reminder of its recent rediscovery and excavation. The Byzantine chapel in the amphitheatre has several mosaics.

Ruins of **Roman baths** are just off the main square at the back of the Alexandër Moisiu Theatre. Across the road a large circular **basilica** still has some columns standing. Also intriguing are the Roman columns located in front of the shopfronts, palm trees and road lights on Rr Tregtare.

Durrës' attractions are not all ancient. There are some fine socialist-realist monuments, including the **Martyrs' Memorial** (Rr Shefqet Beja) by the waterfront.

On the hilltop west of the amphitheatre stands the decaying **former palace of King Zogu I** (Rr Anastas Durrsaku). It's a 15-minute climb up from the town centre to what was a grand palace (marble staircases, carved wooden ceilings and the like), but it's slightly derelict now and closed to the public.

Sleeping

Durrës has a variety of accommodation options in the city itself, but most line the beach to the east.

our pick **B&B Tedeschini** (☎ 24 343, 068 224 6303; ipmcrsp@icc.al.eu.org; Rr Dom Nikoll Kaçorri 5; s/d €15/30) This gracious 19th-century former Italian consulate has been turned into a homey B&B with airy rooms, antique furniture and portraits of former consuls. Owner (and doctor) Alma prepares great breakfasts in the country-style kitchen. From the square fronting the Great Mosque, walk past the town hall and down the alley to its left, then take a right, then a quick left. Use the doorbell next to the green gates.

Hotel Pepeto (☎ 24 190; Rr Mbreti Monun 3; s/d/ste incl breakfast €20/30/50; ❄) A well-run (and well-signposted) guest house at the end of a court, just off the square fronting the Great Mosque. The rooms are decent and quiet, some have baths and balconies and the suite is an attic-dweller's dream. There's a spacious lounge and bar area downstairs. Laundry is €5 and breakfast is included in rates.

Hotel Arvi (☎ 30 403; www.hotelarvi.com; Rr Taulantia; d/ste €60/80; ❄ 💻) A polished hotel with friendly staff and neat, modern rooms (all with some kind of sea view), it's also in the perfect location for watching or participating in the Durrës waterfront *xhiro* (walk).

Hotel Aragosta (☎ 26 477; www.aragosta.al; Rr Taulantia; s/d €60/100; ❄ 💻) With carpet so cushy you can't walk straight, this new beachfront hotel is close to good restaurants and has one of its own, while staff boast that its private beach is the cleanest beach in town. Its name means 'lobster' and you can guess the colour scheme of the modern rooms (some with wonderful spa baths). Totally nonsmoking – and proud of it.

Eating & Drinking

Castella (Rr Grigor Durrsaku; mains 200-400 lekë; ⏲ 10am-4pm Mon-Sat) Popular with locals who prefer a good feed rather than being seen, this casual restaurant has bargain-priced homestyle lunches.

Picante (Rr Taulantia; mains 700-4000 lekë) Upping the trendiness ante is this stark white restaurant on the promenade. The red-chilli motif may indicate how hot this place is; it's certainly where the young locals are spending their disposable income. The music's good, the furniture is white and minimalist, and the meals are priced to stretch the budget.

Bar Torra (Sheshi Mujo Ulqinaku) Housed inside a fortified Venetian tower at the beginning of the city walls, this was one of the first private cafes in Albania, opened by a team of local artists. After you've had a peek at the view from the top, you can drink a local brew in the cosy nooks of the old tower. The ceiling is strangely reminiscent of Hoxha's bunkers.

Getting There & Away

BOAT

Numerous travel agencies handle ferry bookings. The following one-way deck fares leap by up to €30 during August.

Adria Ferries (☎ 220 105; booking@adriaferries.al) has three ferries a week from Ancona to Durrës (€90, 17 hours), and from Bari to Durrës (€42, eight hours); there's a €6 departure fee. **Agemar** (☎ 25 154) and **Azzurra Lines** (www.azzurraline.com) ply the same routes twice a week, while **Venezia Lines** (☎ 30 383) runs a fast ferry from Durrës to Bari (€60, 3½ hours). **Ventouris Ferries** (☎ 25 338) has a frequent service from Bari to Durrës (€56, eight hours).

BUS

Furgons (150 lekë, one hour) and buses (100 lekë, one hour) to Tirana leave from beside the train station when they're full. Buses leave for Shkodra at 7.30am and 1.30pm (300 lekë, three hours). In summer, long-distance buses and *furgons* going to and from Saranda, Gjirokastra, Fier and Berat tend to bypass this station, picking up and dropping off passengers at the end of Plazhi i Durrësi, to the far east of the harbour. A taxi there costs 500 lekë, or catch the orange municipal bus to 'Plepa' for 20 lekë (10 minutes).

In July and August there are additional services to ethnic Albanian towns in Macedonia.

TRAIN

Albania's 720km railway network centres on Durrës. There are six trains a day to Tirana (70 lekë, one hour), one to Shkodra at 1pm (160 lekë, 3¾ hours) via Lezha, one to Pogradec at 7.07am (300 lekë, 5½ hours) via Elbasan (2½ hours), and one to Vlora at 4.05pm (260 lekë, four hours) via Fier. Times and services change, so check the station noticeboard beforehand to confirm. They sometimes depart slightly before schedule. If your train plans fall through, there are plenty of buses at the adjacent bus station.

APOLLONIA

The ruined city of ancient **Apollonia** (admission 700 lekë; ⏲ 9am-5pm) is 12km west of Fier, which is 90km south of Durrës. Apollonia is set on rolling hills among olive groves, and the plains below stretch for miles. Apollonia (named after the God Apollo) was founded by Greeks from Corinth and Corfu in 588 BC and quickly grew into an important city-state, which minted its own currency and benefited from a robust slave trade. Under the Romans (from 229 BC) the city became a great cultural centre with a famous school of philosophy.

Julius Caesar rewarded Apollonia with the title 'free city' for supporting him against Gnaeus Pompeius Magnus (Pompey the Great) during the civil war in the 1st century BC, and sent his nephew Octavius, the future Emperor Augustus, to complete his studies here.

After a series of military and natural disasters (including an earthquake in the 3rd century AD that turned the river into a malarial swamp), the population moved southward into present-day Vlora, and by the 5th century AD only a small village with its own bishop remained at Apollonia.

There is far less to see at Apollonia than there is at Butrint, but there are some picturesque ruins within the 4km of city walls, including a small original theatre and the elegant pillars on the restored facade of the city's 2nd-century-AD administrative centre. The 3rd-century-BC House of Mosaics is closed off to the public, and its mosaics have been covered with sand to protect them from the elements.

Inside the Museum of Apollonia complex is the Byzantine monastery and church of St Mary, which has fascinating gargoyles on the outside pillars. Many of the rooms inside the complex are not open for display yet, but interesting and ancient statues are displayed in the church garden and cloisters and labelled in Albanian. Much of the site remains to be excavated, but more recent discoveries include a necropolis outside the castle walls with graves from the Bronze and Iron Ages.

Apollonia is best visited on a day trip from Tirana, Durrës, Vlora or Berat, as there's nothing of interest in the nearby industrial centre of Fier. From Fier, *furgons* head to Durrës (200 lekë, 1½ hours), Tirana (300 lekë, two hours), Berat (500 lekë, one hour) and Vlora (200 lekë, one hour). The train from Tirana (175 lekë, 4½ hours) comes via Durrës. Once in Fier there's no public transport to the site, so expect to pay around 2500 lekë for a return taxi journey (15 minutes each way, including an hour's waiting time.)

BERAT

☎ 032 / pop 45,500

A highlight of any trip to Albania is a visit to beautiful Berat. Its most striking feature is the collection of white Ottoman houses climbing up the hill to its castle, earning it the title of 'town of a thousand windows' and helping it join Gjirokastra on the list of Unesco World Heritage sites in 2008. Its rugged mountain setting is particularly evocative when the clouds swirl around the tops of the minarets, or break up to show the icy top of Mt Tomorri.

The old quarters are lovely ensembles of whitewashed walls, tile roofs and old stone walls guarding grapevine-shaded courtyards. Surrounding the town, olive and cherry trees decorate the gentler slopes, while pine woods stand on the steeper inclines. In true Albanian style, an elegant mosque with a pencil minaret is partnered on the main square by a large new Orthodox church. The centre of town and the newer outlying areas along the river flats are less attractive ensembles of rectilinear concrete housing blocks, but the Osum River and its bridges (especially the 1780 seven-arched stone footbridge) help redeem it.

In the 3rd century BC an Illyrian fortress called Antipatrea was built here on the site of an earlier settlement. The Byzantines strengthened the hilltop fortifications in the 5th and 6th centuries, as did the Bulgarians 400 years later. The Serbs, who occupied the citadel in 1345, renamed it Beligrad, or 'White City'. In 1450 the Ottoman Turks took the town. After a period of decline, in the 18th and 19th centuries the town began to thrive as a crafts centre specialising in woodcarving.

For a brief time in 1944 Berat was the capital of liberated Albania.

Sights

Berat is in the midst of a tourism transformation: audioguides to the sights are available for hire from the **Medieval Centre** (behind the King's Mosque).

KALA

Start by taking a 15-minute walk up to the impressive 14th-century **Kalasa** (Citadel; admission 100 lekë; ⏲ 24hr). The neighbourhood inside the walls, Kala, still lives and breathes; you'll see old Mercedes-Benz cars struggling to get up the cobblestone roads to return locals home. If you walk around this busy, ancient neighbourhood for long enough you'll invariably stumble into someone's courtyard thinking it's a church or ruin (no one seems to mind, though). In spring and summer the fragrance of chamomile is in the air (and underfoot), and other wildflowers seem to burst from every gap between the stones.

Kala was traditionally a Christian neighbourhood, but fewer than a dozen of the 20 churches remain. The quarter's biggest church, **Church of the Dormition of St Mary** (Kisha Fjetja e Shën Mërisë), is the site of the **Onufri Museum** (Muzeu Onufri; ☎ 32 248; admission 200 lekë; ⏰ 9am-1pm & 4pm-7pm Apr-Sep, 9am-4pm Oct-Mar, closed Mon). The church itself dates from 1797 and was built on the foundations of a 10th-century church. Onufri's spectacular 16th-century artworks are displayed on the ground level along with a beautifully gilded iconostasis.

Ask at the Onufri Museum if you can see the other churches and tiny chapels in Kala, including **St Theodore** (Shën Todher), close to the citadel gates; the substantial and picturesque **Church of the Holy Trinity** (Kisha Shën Triades), below the upper fortress; and the little chapels of **St Mary Blachernae** (Shën Mëri Vllaherna) and **St Nicholas** (Shënkolli). Some of the churches date back to the 13th century. Also keep an eye out for the **Red Mosque**, which was the first in Berat and dates back to the 15th century.

The rest of Berat and the Osum valley look quite spectacular from Kala. The highest point of the citadel is occupied by the **Inner Fortress**, where ruined stairs lead to a Tolkien-esque water reservoir (take a torch). Perched on a cliff ledge below the citadel is the artfully positioned little chapel of **St Michael** (Shën Mihell), best viewed from the Gorica quarter.

Down from the castle is Berat's **Ethnographic Museum** (Muzeu Etnografik; ☎ 32 224; admission 200 lekë; ⏰ 9am-1pm & 4-7pm Tue-Sat, 9am-2pm Sun Apr-Sep, 9am-4pm Tue-Sat, 9am-2pm Sun Oct-Mar). It's in an 18th-century Ottoman house that is as interesting as the exhibits. The ground floor has displays of traditional clothes and the tools used by silversmiths and weavers, while the upper storey has kitchens, bedrooms and guest rooms decked out in traditional style. Check out the *mafil*, a kind of mezzanine looking into the lounge where the women of the house could keep an eye on male guests (and see when their cups needed to be filled). Brochures are available, but to get the most out of it, ask for a guided tour and give a tip.

MANGALEM

Down in the traditionally Muslim Mangalem quarter, there are three grand mosques. The 16th-century **Sultan's Mosque** (Xhamia e Mbretit) is one of the oldest in Albania. The **Helveti teqe** behind the mosque has a beautiful carved ceiling and was specially designed with acoustic holes to improve the quality of sound during meetings. The Helveti, like the Bektashi, are a dervish order, or brotherhood, of Muslim mystics. Staff at the neighbouring Medieval Centre should have the keys.

The big mosque on the town square is the 16th-century **Lead Mosque** (Xhamia e Plumbit), so named because of the lead coating its sphere-shaped domes. The 19th-century **Bachelors' Mosque** (Xhamia e Beqarëvet) is down by the Osum River; look for the enchanting paintings on its external walls. This mosque was built for unmarried shop assistants and junior craftsmen and is perched between some fine Ottoman-era shopfronts.

GORICA

Gorica has tremendous views of the Kala and the Mangalem quarter. It's tucked under a steep hillside and never sees the sun in the winter (it's also one of the coolest places to be in summer). It's a tough, unmarked walk up to the negligible remains of an old **Illyrian fortress** in the woods above Gorica.

Sleeping

Berat Backpackers (☎ 069 306 4429; www.beratbackpackers.com; Gorica; dm €12; ⏰ summer) This English-run hostel with dorm rooms and camping spots (€6) is next to the Monastery of St Spyridon and has wonderful views of Berat's thousand windows and castle.

Hotel Mangalemi (☎ 32 093, 068 242 9803; Rr e Kalasë; s/d €17/25) Tomi Mio (the hotel is known locally as Hotel Tomi) and his family run a great hotel in a sprawling Ottoman house with a restaurant on the ground floor and a clutch of warm, cosy rooms upstairs, plus a terrace with great views across Berat over to Mt Tomorri. It's on the street that runs from the main square up to Kala.

Getting There & Away

Buses and *furgons* run between Tirana and Berat (400 lekë, 2½ hours) hourly until 4pm. From Tirana, buses leave from the 'Kombinati' station (catch the municipal bus from Sheshi Skënderbej to Kombinati for 30 lekë). In Berat, all buses depart from and arrive at the bus station next to the Lead Mosque. From Berat there are buses to Vlora (300 lekë, 2½ hours, nine daily), Saranda via Gjirokastra (1000 lekë, six hours, three daily at 8am, 9.30am and 1.30pm) and Gjirokastra (700 lekë, five hours, one daily).

SOUTHERN COAST

With rough mountains falling headfirst into bright blue seas, this area is wild and ready for exploration. Some of the beaches are jam-packed in August, yet there's plenty of space, peace and happy-to-see-you faces in low season. With careful government planning, the southern coast could shine. In the meantime, if the rubbish lying next to you on the beach gets you down, you only have to bend your neck a bit to see the snowcapped mountain peaks and wide green valleys zigzagged by rivers around you. There are still untouched beaches here.

VLORA

☎ 033 / pop 124,000

It's here in sunny Vlora (the ancient Aulon) that the Adriatic Sea meets the Ionian. The beaches are muddy and grubby, but it's a bustling little port city. A long (1.5km) palm-lined avenue runs through the centre of town from the port and Independence Museum, ending at the mosque, bus station and grand Independence Monument. The outstanding museums deserve a few hours' exploration, and a quick hike up the hill to Kuzum Babai behind the bus station is rewarded with good views. The road out to Zvernëci passes through some of the Vlora neighbourhoods that harboured illegal immigrants during the 1990s – speedboats laded with Kurds, Chinese and marijuana used to zip across the 75km Straits of Otranto to Italy almost nightly. The 1997 revolution after the collapse of the pyramid schemes started here, and it took several years for the authorities to crack down on local gangs.

Information

Everything you'll need in Vlora is on Rr Sadik Zotaj, including ATMs, the post office and telephone centre. The best place to get online is **Internet Café Studenti** (Rr Kullat Skele 2; per hr 100 lekë; ⌚ 7am-midnight), just off Rr Sadik Zotaj.

The helpful **Colombo Travel Agency** (☎ 27 659; www.colomboalb.com; Hotel Sazani, Sheshi i Flamurit; ⌚ 8am-7pm), on Hotel Sazani's ground floor (near Muradi Mosque), runs tours and sells ferry tickets to Italy.

Sights

Start at **Sheshi i Flamurit** (Flag Square), near the top of Sadik Zotaj. The magnificent socialist-realist **Independence Monument** stands proud against the sky with the flag bearer hoisting the double-headed eagle into the blue. Near the base of the monument lies the grave of local Ismail Qemali, the country's first prime minister.

On the other side of the avenue is the **Muzeu Historik** (History Museum; Sheshi i Flamurit; admission 100 lekë; ⌚ 8am-2pm & 5-8pm), displaying a collection of items dating from the 4th century BC up to WWII. Opposite, behind an inconspicuous metal fence, is the home that houses the excellent **Ethnographic Museum** (Sheshi i Flamurit; admission 100 lekë; ⌚ 9am-2pm Mon-Sat).

Walk down towards the 16th-century **Muradi Mosque**, a small elegant structure made of red and white stone and with a modest minaret; its exquisite design is attributed to one of the greatest Ottoman architects, Albanian-born Sinan Pasha. Overlooking the town is the Bektashi shrine of Kuzum Baba. Walk up the steps behind Hotel Alpin to see the well-kept gardens, bars and restaurants and take in the great views over the Bay of Vlora. Narta Lagoon is in the distance.

Down by the harbour the **National Museum of Independence** (admission 200 lekë; ⌚ 9am-1pm & 5-8pm Mon-Sat, 9am-noon & 5-8pm Sun) is housed in the villa that became the headquarters of Albania's first government in 1912. If you're lucky you'll get a passionate pro-independence guided tour; otherwise the preserved offices, historic photographs and famous balcony still make it an interesting place to learn about Albania's short-lived, but long-remembered, 1912 independence.

Vlora's main beaches stretch south from the harbour, and the further south you go, the better they get. Turn left before the harbour to reach Plazhi i Ri, a long public beach that can get quite crowded. Apparently new sand is trucked in each year. A good 2km walk away, **Uji i Ftohtë** (meaning 'cold water') is a better beach choice. It has open-air bars and discos during summer, and plenty of private beaches (ie someone actually picks up the rubbish). You'll need to hire a sunbed and umbrella for 200 lekë per person. Orange municipal buses run from Sadik Zotaj to the Uji i Ftohtë post office (20 lekë, 10 minutes, every 15 minutes from 7am to 9pm).

Sleeping & Eating

Hotel Konomi (☎ 29 320; Rr e Uji i Ftohtë; r 2000 lekë) Set on top of a hill with views of the party end of town, this stark former workers' camp is good for the socialist idealism experience. It's a short hike up from the last bus stop along the beach road.

Hotel Alpin (☎ 069 224 1198; r 2500 lekë) This new hotel next to the bus station is named after its owner's passion: climbing Albania's Alps. The rooms are spotless and modern, with large bathrooms and excellent beds.

Hotel Vlora International (☎ 24 408; www.vlorainternational.com; Rr Sadik Zotaj; s/d €50/60;) Perched by the port, this luxury hotel has modern, comfortable rooms with flat-screen TVs, a fitness centre, indoor pool and restaurant.

Xhokla (Plazhi i Ri; mains 200-1000 lekë) Attentive staff, great Italian food and a good variety of wines make this the best restaurant in town. Being on Vlora's beachfront *xhiro* route makes for great people-watching, too.

Getting There & Away

Buses (500 lekë, three hours) and *furgons* (600 lekë, two hours) to Tirana and to Durrës (bus/*furgon* 500 lekë, three hours) whiz back and forth in the morning hours. Buses to Saranda (1000 lekë, six hours) and on to Gjirokastra (1300 lekë, seven hours) leave at 5am, 7am, 1pm and 2pm. There are nine buses a day to Berat (300 lekë, two hours).

Buses leave from Rr Rakip Malilaj, although departures to Athens (€40) and all major cities in Italy (€60 to €80) leave from near the Muradi Mosque.

There's one train a day from Tirana to Vlora at 2.50pm and from Vlora to Tirana at 5.40am (250 lekë, five hours).

Ferries from Vlora to Brindisi, Italy, take around six hours. From Monday to Saturday, there are departures from Brindisi at 11pm and Vlora at noon (deck tickets €35 to €70). Buy tickets at Colombo Travel Agency (p61).

LLOGARAJA PASS NATIONAL PARK

Reaching the pine-tree-clad Llogaraja Pass National Park (1025m) is one of the special moments of Albanian travel. If you've been soaking up the sun on the southern coast's beaches, it seems impossible that after a steep hairpin-bend climb you're up in the mountains tucking into spit-roasted lamb and homemade wine. There's great scenery up here, including the *pisha flamur* (flag pine) – a tree resembling the eagle design on the Albanian flag. Watch clouds descending onto the mountain, shepherds on the plains guiding their herds, and thick forests where deer, wild boar and wolves roam. Check out the resident deer at the Tourist Village before heading across the road to the cute family-run cabins at **Hotel Andoni** (☎ 068 240 0929; cabins 4000 lekë). The family do a wonderful lamb roast (800 lekë) here, too.

DHËRMI & DRYMADES

As you zigzag down the mountain from the Llogaraja Pass National Park, the white crescent-shape beaches and azure waters lure you from below. **Dhërmi** (Dhërmiu) is under the tourist trance and ferryloads of Italians arrive in the beach town almost daily in summer, while Tirana-based Albanians and expats pack the beaches, bars and restaurants on the weekends.

Just after the beginning of the walk down to Dhërmi beach is the dirt road to **Drymades beach**. Turn right, and a 45-minute walk through olive groves brings you to **Drymades Hotel** (☎ 068 228 5637; sites 500 lekë, cabins 4000 lekë), a quiet accommodation option where a white virgin beach (albeit with bunkers) stretches before you. A constellation of cabins and rooms under the shade of pine trees is just a step away from the blue sea. You can stay indoors, camp or simply sleep under the stars on the beach. There's a bar, restaurant and shaded playground, plus a classic beach bar with a straw roof.

The best place to stay and eat is **Hotel Luciano** (☎ 069 209 1431; Dhërmi Beach; r per person 1000 lekë;). The water is metres away, the views are sublime, rooms simple but comfortable and staff busy but helpful. There's a popular waterfront restaurant here too, with plenty of pasta choices and good wood-fired pizzas (300 lekë). To get here, turn left at the bottom of the hill.

Hotel Riviera (☎ 068 263 3333; Dhërmi Beach; d €40-60;) has had a leopard-skin-curtain makeover and is now truly focussed on too-cool-for-school, with orange, lime green and brown walls. The new futon-style beds and flat-screen TVs make it all acceptable. An ubercool bar is perched on the water's edge.

The beach is about 2km below the Vlora–Saranda road, so ask the conductor to stop at the turn-off on the Llogaraja side of the village. From here it's an easy 10-minute walk downhill (not so easy on the way back though).

HIMARA

☎ 0393 / pop 4500

This sleepy town has fine beaches, a couple of great Greek seafood tavernas, some hi-tech, good-looking hotels and an interesting Old Town high on the hill. Most of the ethnic Greek population left in the 1990s, but many have returned. The lower town comprises three easily accessible rocky beaches, the town's hotels and restaurants. The main Vlora–Saranda road passes the entrance to the hilltop castle and, like the one in Berat, many residents still call it home. A taxi there from Himara costs 300 lekë. From the top you can take in the superb views of Livadhi beach and check out some frescos in the old churches. Try Albania's best top-end resort, **Rapos Resort** (☎ 22 856; www.raposresorthotel.com; d €65-90;), or the very cool **Manolo** (☎ 22 375; d €50) near the port.

Buses towards Saranda and Vlora pass through town in the morning only; check with locals exactly when.

SARANDA

☎ 0852 / pop 32,000

Skeletal high-rises crowd around the horseshoe shape of Saranda, a result of the past few years' astounding level of development. Barring blackouts, a night view of the town shows just how few of the buildings are actually occupied. Despite this massive development, Saranda is still a really pleasant town that is increasingly drawing mostly Albanian tourists into its sea. To make things interesting, a daily stream of Corfu holidaymakers take the 45-minute ferry trip to Albania, add the Albanian stamp to their passports and hit Butrint and Blue Eye Spring before heading back.

The town's name comes from Ayii Saranda, an early monastery dedicated to 40 saints; its bombed remains (including some preserved frescos) are still high on the hill above the town. The town was called Porto Edda for a period in the 1940s, after Mussolini's daughter.

Saranda's stony beaches are quite decent for a town of this size, and the section near the port even has built-in starting blocks and lanes for swimmers. Apart from the beach, Saranda has other attractions: a well-preserved mosaic floor bizarrely housed in what looks like an office complex on Rr Flamurit, as well as a central 5th-century synagogue. The other sights are a bus or taxi trip out of the town itself: the mesmerising ancient archaeological site of Butrint and the hypnotic Blue Eye Spring. Between Saranda and Butrint, the lovely beaches and islands of Ksamil are perfect for a dip after a day of exploring.

Orientation & Information

Four main streets arc around Saranda's bay, including the waterfront promenade that becomes prime *xhiro* territory in the evening. There are six banks with ATMs along the sea road (Rr 1 Maji) and the next street inland (Rr Skënderbeu). The incredibly helpful **information centre** (ZIT; Rr Skënderbeu; 8am-4pm Mon-Fri) provides bus timetables and maps. **Sipa Tours** (☎ 66 75; Rr 1 Maji; www.sipatours.com) arranges tours to Butrint for around €30.

Sleeping & Eating

Hairy Lemon (☎ 069 355 9317; dm €13) This backpackers hostel is in an orange-and-yellow apartment block. It's a 10-minute walk from the port (turn left as you exit).

Hotel Palma (☎ 22 929; Rr Mithat Hoxha; s/d/apt incl breakfast €20/30/120;) Right next to the port, this hotel has carpets that don't fit, but some rooms have great views with large balconies and the location is handy. If you're up for it, guests get free entry into the on-site disco. Breakfast and wi-fi are free.

Hotel Republica (☎ 22 240; Rr 1 Maji; s/d €25/30) This is a central hotel with character, and the restaurant on the top floor (there's a lift with a view) comes to life in summer. The bar underneath will bemuse history lovers; you drink coffee at tables wedged between the ruins of the town's ancient walls.

Hotel Grand (☎ 25 574; Rr Saranda-Butrint 1; d incl breakfast €40;) This hotel takes up a fair whack of Saranda's eastern foreshore with its swimming pool, playground, bar and restaurant. Rooms are spacious and rates include wi-fi access and breakfast.

Castle of Lekursi (Kalaja e Lëkurësit; ☎ 25 555; mains 250-1200 lekë; 11am-midnight) This restaurant sits inside the reconstructed castle above Saranda and serves traditional Albanian cuisine (grills and fish) plus Italian dishes. Sit back on the wrought-iron thrones and check out the tremendous views of Saranda and

Butrint lagoon. A taxi costs about 1000 lekë return; arrange a time for the driver to pick you up. The cheaper Piceri Lekursi (pizza restaurant) operates from the castle's lower tier between May and September.

Pupi (Rr Saranda-Butrint; seafood dishes around 650 lekë; 9am-midnight) Pupi has an unfortunate name but serves good seafood dishes in a terrace setting with pine trees. It's about 50m from Hotel Grand towards Butrint. Check out the great wall mosaic inside, and in summer take a swim at its private beach.

Getting There & Away

In a stroke of genius, the information centre gives out up-to-date bus timetables. The main bus station is uphill from the synagogue on Rr Vangjel Pando, and taxis wait for customers here and opposite Central Park on Rr Skënderbeu.

Nine regular municipal buses go to Butrint via Ksamil (100 lekë, about 40 minutes), leaving from the information centre and opposite Hotel Butrinti.

Buses to Tirana (1200 lekë, eight hours) leave at 5am, 6.30am, 8.30am, 9.30am and 10.30am, and buses to Gjirokastra (300 lekë, 1½ hours) depart at 6am, 8am, 11am and 1pm; there's one bus to Durrës (900 lekë, seven hours) at 7.30am. Buses to Himara leave at 5.30am, 6am and 2pm, and daily services to Korça leave at 5.30am (1200 lekë, eight hours).

Furgons to Gjirokastra (300 lekë, one hour) and Vlora (via Himara; 600 lekë, six hours) usually leave between 5.30am and 10am.

A taxi to the Greek border at Kakavija will cost 4000 lekë, while a cab to the border near Konispoli will cost around 5000 lekë.

Finikas (☎ 60 57; finikaslines@yahoo.com; Rr Mithat Hoxha) has two boats a day, at 10.30am and 4pm, to Corfu (one way €17.50, including the €2.50 port tax). From Corfu it's €15 for the 90-minute boat trip to Saranda, which leaves at 9am. **Ionian Cruises** (www.ionian-cruises.com) operates a faster, Dolphin boat that departs Corfu at the same time (€17.50, 45 minutes). There's a one-hour time difference between Greece and Albania.

AROUND SARANDA

Butrint

The ancient ruins of **Butrint** (www.butrint.org; admission 700 lekë; 8am-dusk), 18km south of Saranda, are renowned for their size, beauty and tranquillity. They're in a fantastic natural setting and are part of a 29-sq-km national park. Set aside at least three hours to lose yourself and explore this fascinating place.

Although the site had been inhabited long before, Greeks from Corfu settled on the hill in Butrint (Buthrotum) in the 6th century BC. Within a century Butrint had become a fortified trading city with an acropolis. The lower town began to develop in the 3rd century BC, and many large stone buildings had already been built by the time the Romans took over in 167 BC. Butrint's prosperity continued throughout the Roman period, and the Byzantines made it an ecclesiastical centre. The city subsequently went into decline and was abandoned until 1927, when Italian archaeologists arrived. These days Lord Rothschild's UK-based Butrint Foundation helps maintain the site.

As you enter the site the path leads to the right, to Butrint's 3rd-century-BC **Greek theatre**, secluded in the forest below the acropolis. Also in use during the Roman period, the theatre could seat about 2500 people. Close by are the small **public baths**, whose geometric mosaics are buried under a layer of mesh and sand to protect them from the elements.

Deeper in the forest is a wall covered with crisp Greek inscriptions, and the 6th-century palaeo-Christian **baptistery** decorated with colourful mosaics of animals and birds, again under the sand. Beyond are the impressive arches of the 6th-century **basilica**, built over many years. A massive **Cyclopean wall** dating back to the 4th century BC is further on. Over one gate is a relief of a lion killing a bull, symbolic of a protective force vanquishing assailants.

The top of the hill is where the **acropolis** once was. There's now a castle here, housing an informative **museum** (8am-4pm). The views from the museum's courtyard give you a good idea of the city's layout, and you can see the Vivari Channel connecting Lake Butrint to the Straits of Corfu. There's a community-run shop inside the gates where you can buy locally produced souvenirs.

The local bus from Saranda to Butrint costs 100 lekë. A taxi to Butrint from Saranda will cost around 2000 lekë, and you can usually negotiate to get there and back and see the Blue Eye Spring for 4000 lekë. Saranda-based **Sipa Tours** (☎ 66 75; Rr 1 Maji; www.sipatours.com) arranges local tours for around €30 and can include a

WORTH THE TRIP: GJIROKASTRA

Like something from a vampire movie, it's hard to imagine a creepier setting than the stone city of Gjirokastra, shrouded in clouds on its rocky perch and surrounded by savage mountains. Above it all a gloomy, dark castle with a blood-chilling history watches over everything, perpetually guarded by black crows. It's the sort of place where dictators are raised (Enver Hoxha) and young boys dream up dramatic stories and become famous writers (Ismail Kadare, whose *Chronicle in Stone* is set here). In short, it's a thrilling place to spend a day absorbing the life of its steep cobbled streets, where the pace is slow and suspended in the past.

our pick **Hotel Kalemi** (☎ 63 724; draguak@yahoo.com; Lagjia Palorto; r 4000 lekë) is the spot to go an authentic experience of Ottoman Albania. It's a cross between a hotel and an ethnographic museum, with original carved wooden ceilings and stone fireplaces.

Gjirokastra is located 70km northeast of Saranda; the bus here takes 90 minutes and costs 300 lekë.

translator, which is useful to get the whole gist of Butrint. Make sure you pick up a written guide to the site from the ticket booth.

Ksamil

Ksamil, 17km south of Saranda, has three small, dreamy islands within swimming distance and dozens of beachside bars and restaurants that open in the summer. To get to the beach, head past the church and take the second right, then first left. You'll pass **Hotel Jon** (☎ 069 209 1554; s/d 1000/1500 lekë) near the roundabout, which is the bar and hotel of choice.

Blue Eye Spring

About 25km east of Saranda, the **Blue Eye Spring** (Syri i Kaltër; admission 50 lekë) is a hypnotic pool of deep-blue water surrounded by electric-blue edges like the iris of an eye. It feeds the Bistrica River and its depth is still unknown. It's a pleasant spot; blue dragonflies dash around the water, and the surrounding shady oak trees make a good picnic spot. If you don't mind a 3km walk, any bus heading between Saranda and Gjirokastra can drop you off at the turn-off to Blue Eye Spring. Otherwise it's only accessible by taxi or on a private tour.

ALBANIA DIRECTORY

ACCOMMODATION

Albania's budget accommodation (doubles €15 to €50) is usually decent and clean; breakfast is sometimes included in the price. Finding people who've partly converted their homes into private accommodation is possible, and backpacker-style hostels are sprouting up in Tirana, Saranda and Berat. Midrange hotels (doubles €50 to €100) are a notch up, with wi-fi, telephones and evidence of attempts to spruce up the rooms. Top-end hotels (doubles €100 to €270) are mostly on a par with modern European hotels in terms of price, comfort and facilities, and offer fitness centres, satellite TV, internet access and swimming pools.

Hotels line the beaches in Saranda, Durrës and Vlora, while homestays abound in Theth. Most towns have at least a few good hotel or B&B options in most price categories. The local hotel booking company **Albania-hotel .com** (www.albania-hotel.com) is a reliable resource for new lodgings.Camping is possible in the south and sometimes on deserted beaches.

Prices given in this chapter include private bathroom unless otherwise stated.

ACTIVITIES

The further south you get, the better the swimming is. South of Vlora the sandy Adriatic gives it up for its rockier Ionian counterpart, but it's much more picturesque. You can go birdwatching around Lezha, Velipoja and the Drin delta and hiking in Mt Dajti National Park. For challenging hiking, find a local guide and try Theth. Hiking and adventure sports are in their infancy in Albania, and the leaders are the team at Outdoor Albania (p50). A few Berat operatives run hiking tours to Mt Tomorri National Park. Cyclists: get motivated. There are more than a few two-wheeled adventurers carving up the countryside.

BOOKS

For a helpful list of Albanian words and phrases, check out the *Mediterranean Europe Phrasebook* from Lonely Planet. *Colloquial*

Albanian (2007) by Isa Zymberi is a good teach-yourself language course accompanied by a CD.

The Albanians: A Modern History (1999), by Miranda Vickers, is a comprehensive and very readable history of Albania from the time of Ottoman rule to the restoration of democracy after 1990.

James Pettifer's *Albania and Kosovo Blue Guide* (2001) is a thoroughly informed source for Albanian history and a good guide of things to see.

Albania: From Anarchy to a Balkan Identity (1999) by Miranda Vickers and James Pettifer covers the tumultuous 1990s in great detail, while managing to convey a sense of the confusion Albania faced as it shed its communist past.

Biografi (1993) by New Zealander Lloyd Jones (also author of *Mr Pip*) is a rather arresting story set in post-1990 Albania: a semi-factual account of the writer's quest to find the alleged double of former communist dictator Enver Hoxha.

Rumpalla: Rummaging Through Albania (2002) by Peter Lucas is a personal account of Albania before and after the revolution by this American journalist of Albanian descent.

The Best of Albanian Cooking (1999) by Klementina Hysa and R John Hysa is one of scant few books on Albanian cuisine and contains a wide range of family recipes.

High Albania (published in 1909 and reprinted in 2000), written by Albania's 'honorary citizen' Edith Durham, recounts the author's experiences in northern Albania in the early 20th century.

The Accursed Mountains (1999) is written by a seemingly miserable Robert Carver, who doesn't have many nice things to say about his journey through Albania in 1996.

Black Lambs and Grey Falcons (1991; edited by John B Allcock and Antonia Young) is a collection of stories by women writers who travelled through the Balkans.

BUSINESS HOURS

Most offices open at 8am and close around 5pm. Shops usually open at 8am and close around 7pm, though some close for a siesta from noon to 4pm, and then stay open till 8pm. Banking hours are shorter (generally 9am to 3.30pm). Restaurants, cafes and bars are usually open from 8am and stay open until midnight or later.

COURSES

The **Lincoln Centre** (Map p48; ☎ 2230 880; www.lincoln-intl.org; Rr Qemal Stafa 184, Tirana) runs Albanian language courses. Private tutorial is another way of picking up the language, so if you're keen, stop by the secretariat office of the University of Europe on the Lana River and ask for students who can teach Albanian.

DANGERS & ANNOYANCES

Albania is a relatively safe country to travel around, although locals suggest it's best to travel with a local guide to Bajram Curri and Tropoja in the far north, and in the area around Theth. There are still landmines near the northern border with Kosovo, though these are being removed.

There isn't a hard-core drinking culture here so it's almost unheard of to be bailed up by drunks after dark. Take the usual precautions of avoiding rowdy demonstrations, and beware of pickpockets on crowded city buses. The most serious risk is on the roads – Albania has a high traffic accident rate. Other dangers are the ripped-up pavements, ditches and missing manhole covers – watch your step! Packs of dogs are an issue; take particular care around castles.

To avoid being overcharged, travellers who've just entered Albania from Montenegro should know the real price for a *furgon* trip to Tirana is 400 lekë. Sometimes it pays to show taxi drivers how much you will pay, as mysterious things can happen with the number '0', and a taxi ride may cost 3000 instead of the 300 you thought you had negotiated (and even, perhaps, written down).

As Albania was closed off for so long, black travellers may encounter some curious stares; in fact, most visitors to Albania can expect a certain amount of curiosity.

There are risks in drinking tap water and local milk; plenty of bottled water and imported UHT milk is available. The standard of health care in Albania is variable: local hospitals and clinics are understaffed and underfunded, but pharmacies are good.

EMBASSIES & CONSULATES

There are no Australian, New Zealand or Irish embassies in Albania. The following embassies and consulates are in Tirana (Map p48; area code ☎ 042):

France (☎ 2234 054; ambafrance.tr@adanet.com.al; Rr Skënderbej 14)

Germany (☎ 2274 505; www.tirana.diplo.de; Rr Skënderbej 8)
Greece (☎ 2274 670; gremb.tir@mfa.gr; Rr Frederik Shiroka 3)
Italy (☎ 2275 900; www.ambtirana.esteri.it; Rr Lek Dukagjini 2)
Macedonia (☎ 2230 909; makambas@albnet.net; Rr e Kavajës 116)
Netherlands (☎ 2240 828; www.mfa.nl/tir; Rr Asim Zeneli 10)
Serbia (☎ 2232 091; www.tirana.mfa.gov.yu; Rr Donika Kastrioti 9/1)
UK (☎ 2234 973; www.uk.al; Rr Skënderbej 12)
USA (☎ 2247 285; http://tirana.usembassy.gov; Rr Elbasanit 103)

GAY & LESBIAN TRAVELLERS

Gay and lesbian life in Albania is alive and well but is not yet organised into out clubs or organisations. It's no problem to be foreign and affectionate with your same-sex partner in the street, but keep in mind that no couples are overly demonstrative in public in Albania so any public sexual behaviour beyond holding hands and kissing will be a spectacle. Gaydar will serve gay and lesbian visitors well here: you'll have to ask on the street where the parties are. The alternative music and party scene is queer friendly.

HOLIDAYS

New Year's Day 1 January
Summer Day 14 March
Nevruz 22 March
Catholic Easter March or April
Orthodox Easter March or April
May Day 1 May
Bajram i Madh September
Mother Teresa Day 19 October
Bajram i Vogël November
Independence Day 28 November
Liberation Day 29 November
Christmas Day 25 December

MEDIA

A diverse range of newspapers is printed in Tirana; *Shekulli* is the largest daily paper.

The *Albanian Daily News* is a fairly dry English-language publication that has useful information on happenings around Albania. It's generally available from major hotels for 300 lekë.

The weekly *Tirana Times* is 350 lekë from central street kiosks. Despite many of the articles being about the same topic (with a different perspective), it has some interesting features.

Foreign newspapers and magazines, including the *Times*, the *International Herald Tribune* and the *Economist*, are sold at most major hotels and some central street kiosks, though they tend to be a few days old.

The BBC World Service can be picked up in and around Tirana on 103.9FM, while the Voice of America's mainly music program is on 107.4FM.

MONEY

ATMs

A variety of ATMs can be found in most towns and cities, except for villages like Theth and Dhërmi. ATMs frequently offer currency in euros or lekë. The main networks are Alpha Bank, Raiffeisen Bank, American Bank of Albania, Pro Credit Bank and Tirana Bank.

Credit Cards

Credit cards are accepted only in the larger hotels and travel agencies, and in only a handful of establishments outside Tirana. Major banks can offer credit-card advances.

Currency

Albanian banknotes come in denominations of 100, 200, 500, 1000 and 5000 lekë. There are five, 10, 20, 50 and 100 lekë coins. In 1964 the currency was revalued 10 times; prices on occasion may still be quoted at the old rate (3000 lekë instead of 300). Happily, if you hand over 3000 lekë you will probably be handed 2700 lekë in change.

Everything in Albania can be paid for with lekë, but most of the hotel prices are quoted in euros. Day trippers from Corfu can rely on euros, though they won't get a good exchange rate.

You will not be able to change Albanian lekë outside of the country, so exchange them or spend them before you leave.

Moneychangers

Every town has its free-currency market, which usually operates on the street in front of the main post office or state bank. Such transactions are not dangerous or illegal and it all takes place quite openly, but make sure you count the money twice before tendering yours. The advantages are that you get a good rate and avoid the 1% bank commission. Currency-exchange businesses in major towns are usually open 8am to 6pm and closed on Sundays.

Travellers Cheques

Travellers cheques are about as practical and useful here as a dead albatross, though you can change them at Rogner Hotel Europapark Tirana and at major banks in Tirana. Some banks will change US-dollar travellers cheques into US cash without commission. Travellers cheques (euro and US dollar) can be used at a few top-end hotels, but cash (euro or lekë) is preferred everywhere.

POST

Outside of main towns there are few public postboxes, but there is an increasing number of post offices around the country where you can hand in your mail directly (whether they have stamps is another matter). Sending a postcard overseas costs around 60 lekë, while a letter costs 80 to 160 lekë. The postal system is fairly rudimentary – there are no postcodes, for example – and it does not enjoy a reputation for efficiency. Don't rely on sending or receiving parcels through Albapost.

RESPONSIBLE TRAVEL

You'll get fed up with the amount of active littering that you'll see, and litter you have to negotiate around, whether on the beach or walking down the street. Lead by example. Lake Ohrid trout is endangered, and travellers should resist buying it. Buying locally produced beer and wine supports the local economy.

TELEPHONE & FAX

Long-distance telephone calls made from main post offices (Albtelecom) are cheap, costing about 90 lekë a minute to Italy. Calls to the USA cost 230 lekë per minute. Calls from private phone offices are horribly expensive, though – 800 lekë per minute to Australia, for example. Albania's country phone code is ☎ 355. For domestic directory enquiries call ☎ 124; international directory assistance is ☎ 12. Faxing can be done from the main post office in Tirana for the same cost as phone calls, or from major hotels, though they will charge more.

Mobile Phones

The three established mobile-phone providers are Vodafone, AMC and Eagle, and a fourth licence has been promised. Nearly all populated areas of the country are covered, though the networks can become congested. Prepaid SIM cards cost around 1000 lekë and usually include credit. Mobile tariffs are roughly 45 to 60 lekë a minute nationally, and 200 to 245 lekë a minute to Zone 4 areas (including USA, Australia and Japan). International texts are 20 lekë. You can also check to see if a roaming agreement exists with your home service provider. Numbers begin with ☎ 067, ☎ 068 or ☎ 069. To call an Albanian mobile number from abroad, dial ☎ 355 then either ☎ 67, ☎ 68 or ☎ 69 (ie drop the 0).

EMERGENCY NUMBERS

- Ambulance ☎ 127
- Fire ☎ 128
- Police ☎ 129

TOILETS

Carry toilet paper with you and expect the occasional squat toilet.

TOURIST INFORMATION

Tourist information offices operate in Saranda, Gjirokastra, Berat and Korça, and hotel reception or travel agencies also assist with information. You can buy city maps of Tirana in bookshops, and maps of Vlora, Saranda, Gjirokastra, Durrës and Shkodra from the respective town's travel agencies or hotels.

TRAVELLERS WITH DISABILITIES

There are few special facilities for travellers in wheelchairs, and footpaths are not wheelchair friendly. Tirana's top hotels cater to people with disabilities, however. The roads and castle entrances in Gjirokastra, Berat and Kruja are cobblestone, although taxis can get reasonably close to the action.

VISAS

No visa is required by citizens of EU countries or nationals of Australia, Canada, New Zealand, Japan, South Korea, Norway, South Africa or the USA. Travellers from other countries should check www.mfa.gov.al. Citizens of all countries – even those entering visa-free – will be required to pay €1 to enter the country, or €10 if arriving at Tirana Airport. Israeli citizens pay €30.

WOMEN TRAVELLERS

Albania is quite a safe country for women travellers, but outside Tirana it is mainly men who go out and sit in bars and cafes in the evenings. While they are not threatening, it may feel strange to be the only woman in a bar. It's extremely unlikely that you'll be involved, but be aware that Albania is a source country for people trafficking.

TRANSPORT IN ALBANIA

GETTING THERE & AWAY

Air

Albania's international airport is the recently renovated **Nënë Tereza International Airport** (Mother Teresa Airport or Rinas airport), 26km northwest of Tirana. There are no domestic flights within Albania. The following airlines fly to and from Albania:

Adria Airways (JP; ☎ 04-2272 666; www.adri.si)
Bulgaria Air (FB; ☎ 04-2230 410; www.air.bg)
Jat Airways (JU; ☎ 04-2251 033; www.jat.com)
Malév Hungarian Airlines (MA; ☎ 04-2234 163; www.malev.hu)

Land

There are no passenger trains into Albania, so your border-crossing options are buses, *furgons*, taxis or walking to a border and picking up transport on the other side.

BUSES

From Tirana, regular buses head to Pristina, Kosovo; to Struga, Tetovo and Skopje in Macedonia; and to Athens and Thessaloniki in Greece (p52). *Furgons* and buses leave Shkodra (p55) for Montenegro and Kosovo, and buses head to ethnic Albanian towns in Macedonia from Durrës and southern coastal towns in July and August. Buses travel to Greece from most Albanian towns; buses to Italy leave from Vlora (p62).

CAR & MOTORCYCLE

To enter Albania, you'll need a Green Card (proof of third-party insurance, issued by your insurer); check that your insurance covers Albania.

The two main crossings between Albania and Kosovo are at Qafë Morina between Kukës and Prizren, and Qafë Prush. The popularity of the Lake Koman car ferry means you're unlikely to be alone on the drive to Qafë Prush.

For Macedonia, the two best crossings are on either side of Lake Ohrid. The southern crossing is at Tushëmisht/Sveti Naum, 29km south of Ohrid; the northern crossing is at Qafë e Thanës, between Struga and Pogradec. However, there are sometimes delays at Qafë e Thanës due to trucks.

At the time of writing there are two border crossings between Albania and Macedonia, one at Han i Hotit (between Shkodra and Podgorica) and another at Muriqan (between Ulcinj and Shkodra).

TAXI

Heading to Macedonia, taxis from Pogradec will drop you off just before the border at Tushëmisht/Sveti Naum. Alternatively, it's an easy 4km to the border from Pogradec.

Sea

A few ferries a day ply the route between Saranda and Corfu (p64), and frequent ferries leave for Italy from Vlora (p62) and Durrës (p58).

GETTING AROUND

Bicycle

Cycling in Albania is tough but certainly doable. Expect lousy road conditions including open drains, some abysmal driving from fellow road-sharers and roads that are not really roads (eg the road to Theth). Organised groups head north for mountain biking, and cyclists are even spotted cycling the long and tough Korça–Gjirokastra road. Shkodra is one of the few places you'll see the locals embracing the two-wheeled beast.

Bus

Albanians travel around their country in private minivans called *furgons* or in buses. These run fairly frequently throughout the day, though peak time is in the morning, and services are usually a distant memory by 2pm. Buses to Tirana depart from towns all around Albania at the crack of dawn. The fares are low (eg Tirana–Durrës costs 150 lekë), and you pay the conductor on board (don't expect a ticket).

Municipal buses operate in Tirana, Durrës, Shkodra and Vlora, and trips usually cost 30 lekë. Watch your possessions.

Car & Motorcycle

Albania's drivers are not the best in the world, mostly due to the communist era, when car ownership required a permit from the government, and only two were issued to nonparty members. As a result, the government didn't invest in new roads, and most Albanians were inexperienced motorists. Nowadays the road infrastructure is improving, especially on the routes from the Macedonian border to Dhërmi; from Durrës to Korça, and on the stretch from Fier to Gjirokastra.

If you're keen to drive, spend a few hours in a taxi first so you can see what conditions to expect. Off the main routes a 4WD is a good idea. Driving at night is particularly hazardous, and driving on mountain 'roads' at any time is a whole new field of extreme sport. Cars, *furgons,* trucks and buses *do* go off the edge.

There is no national automobile association in Albania as yet.

DRIVING LICENCE

Foreign driving licences are permitted, but it is recommended to have an International Driving Permit as well. Car-hire agencies usually require that you have held a full licence for one year.

FUEL & SPARE PARTS

There are plenty of petrol stations in the cities and increasing numbers in the country. Unleaded fuel is available along all major highways, but fill up before driving into the mountainous regions. A litre of unleaded petrol costs 170 lekë, while diesel costs 160 lekë. There isn't yet a highly developed network of mechanics and repair shops capable of sourcing parts for all types of vehicles, but if you're driving an old Mercedes-Benz there will be parts galore.

HIRE

There are four car-hire companies operating out of Tirana: Avis, Europcar, Hertz and Sixt (see p53). Hiring a small car costs from €35 per day.

ROAD RULES

Drinking and driving is forbidden, and there is zero tolerance for blood-alcohol readings. Both motorcyclists and passengers must wear helmets. Speed limits are as low as 30km per hour in built-up areas and 35km per hour on the edges. Keep your car's papers with you as police are active paper-checkers.

Train

Albanians prefer bus and *furgon* travel, and when you see the speed and the state of the (barely) existing trains, you'll know why. However, the trains are dirt cheap and travelling on them is an adventure. Daily passenger trains leave Tirana (p53) for Durrës, Shkodra, Fier, Vlora, Elbasan and a few kilometres out of Pogradec. Check timetables at the station in person, and buy your ticket 10 minutes before departure.

Bosnia & Hercegovina

Bosnia and Hercegovina (BiH) describes itself as the 'heart-shaped land'. Geographically the allusion is surprisingly anatomically accurate. Emotionally too, the deep yet unimposing human warmth of this craggily beautiful land fits the bill. And despite some lingering scars, the heartbreaking societal haemorrhaging of the 1990s has been completely stemmed (if not forgotten). The BiH of today has regained its once-famed religious tolerance. Rebuilt churches, mosques and synagogues huddle closely, rekindling that intriguing East-meets-West atmosphere born of Bosnia's fascinatingly blended Ottoman and Austro-Hungarian histories.

Socialist urban planning and war damage still combine to give certain post-industrial cityscapes all the charm of a Molvanian nightmare. But such scenes are surprisingly rare blots on a beautiful, largely rural landscape. Meanwhile the reincarnated Austro-Ottoman centres of Sarajevo and especially Mostar are unexpected delights. And the majority of Bosnian towns are lovably small, wrapped around medieval castles and surrounded by mountain ridges, verdant hills or merrily cascading river canyons. Few places in Europe offer better rafting or such accessible and excellent-value skiing.

Fashionable bars and wi-fi-equipped cafes abound but employment concerns remain as the fledgling state finally comes to terms with postcommunist realities that were masked for years by more pressing war worries. Roads remain slow and winding but they're extremely scenic, mostly well surfaced and relatively quiet, making for delightful random adventures, especially if you're driving. Indeed, however you travel, BiH offers a great sense of discovery, of real personal interaction and of very fair value for money that's all too rare in the heart of 21st-century Europe.

FAST FACTS

- **Area** 51,129 sq km
- **Capital** Sarajevo
- **Currency** convertible mark (KM, BAM); €1 = 1.96KM; US$1= 1.43KM; UK£1 = 2.08KM; A$1 = 0.99KM; ¥100 = 1.50KM; NZ$1 = 0.80KM
- **Famous for** 1984 Sarajevo Winter Olympics, the bridge at Mostar
- **Official languages** Bosnian, Croatian, Serbian
- **Phrases** *zdravo* (hello); *hvala* (thanks); *molim* (please)
- **Population** 4 million (estimate)
- **Telephone codes** country code ☎ 387; international access code ☎ 00
- **Visas** not required for most visitors, see p110

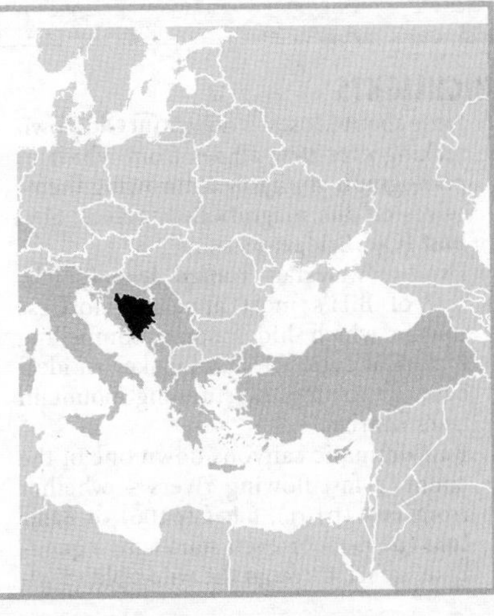

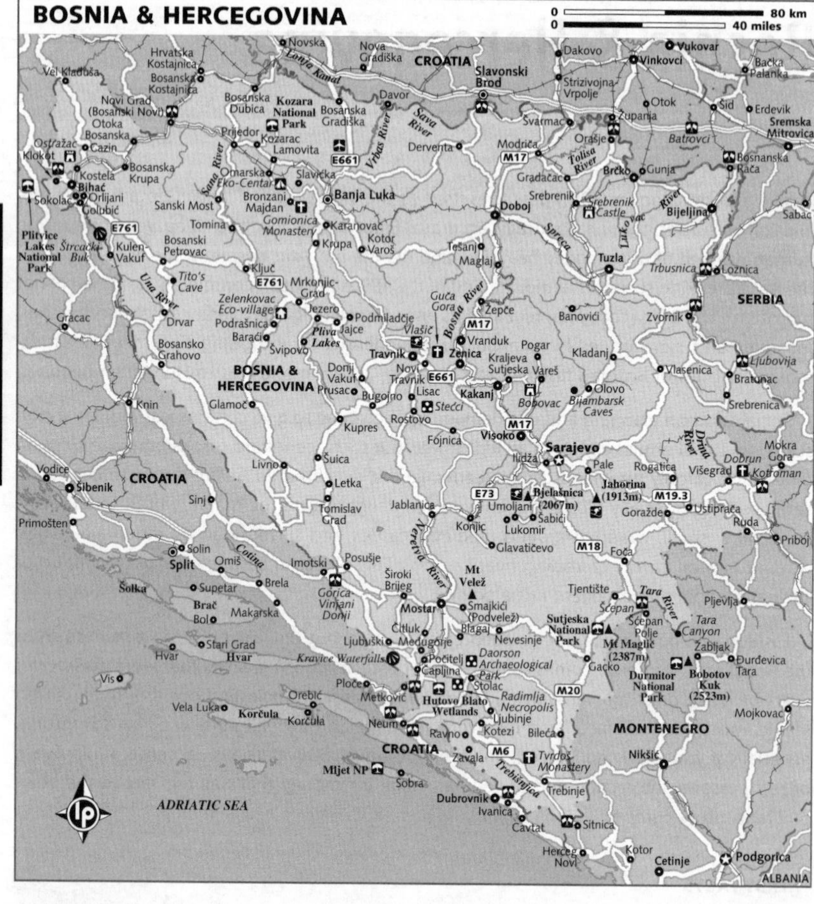

HIGHLIGHTS

- Nose about Mostar's delightful Old Town seeking ever-new angles from which to photograph young men throwing themselves off the magnificently rebuilt **Stari Most** (Old Bridge; p94).
- Explore waterfall-fronted **Jajce** (p103), one of BiH's most appealing fortress towns, which hides some compelling historical curiosities and makes an ideal base for visiting the stunning mountain lakes nearby.
- Raft dramatic canyons down one of the county's fast-flowing rivers – whether from **Foča** (p101), **Bihać** (p106) or **Banja Luka** (p105) – or even start with a quad-bike 'safari' through the wild upland villages behind the ski resort of **Bjelašnica** (p91).
- Potter around the timeless Turkish- and Austrian-era pedestrian lanes of **Sarajevo** (p78), sample its fashionable cafes and eclectic nightlife or gaze down on the mosque-dotted, red-roofed cityscape from the Park Prinčeva restaurant.

ITINERARIES

- **Six days** Arriving from Dubrovnik (coastal Croatia), roam Mostar's Old Town and join a day-tour visiting Počitelj, Blagaj and Kravice Waterfalls. After two days in Sarajevo head for Jajce then bus down to Split (Croatia). Or visit Višegrad en route to Mokra Gora and Belgrade (Serbia).

CONNECTIONS: MOVING ON FROM BOSNIA & HERCEGOVINA

Regular buses link the Croatian coast to Mostar (p98) and Sarajevo (p90), and there's also one little-publicised Trebinje–Dubrovnik bus (p100). A new Sarajevo–Zagreb sleeper train (p89) offers an inexpensive and comfortable westward exit. Connections to Serbia and Montenegro are easiest from the Republika Srpska, with a direct night train from Banja Luka to Belgrade (p106) and various useful bus links from Višegrad (p101) and Trebinje (p100). Connecting to Hungary is now limited to one poorly timed all-day train from Sarajevo (p89).

- **Two weeks** As above, but add quaint Trebinje and historic Stolac between Dubrovnik and Mostar, ski or go quad-biking around Bjelašnica near Sarajevo, visit the controversial Visoko pyramid and old-town Travnik en route to Jajce, and consider adding in some high-adrenaline rafting from Banja Luka, Bihać or Foča.

CLIMATE & WHEN TO GO

Winters are cold and snowy, albeit milder in Hercegovina, where summers are baking hot. On spring nights you'll need a light sweater but days are gently warm with dazzling blossoms and lush meadow greenery. Rafting in April is high-adrenaline, world-quality stuff but by July white water calms down, making rivers less taxing for novices.

In spring and autumn tourists are rare but in summer accommodation can be stretched in Sarajevo and Mostar as diaspora Bosnians come 'home'. The peak ski season is mid-December to mid-March but prices fall considerably in later March if you're prepared to gamble on snow conditions (often excellent but much less predictable at that time).

HISTORY

Be aware that much of BiH's 'history' remains highly controversial and is seen very differently according to one's ethno-religious viewpoint.

In AD 9 ancient Illyrian Bosnia was conquered by the Romans. Slavs arrived from the late 6th century and were dominant by 1180, when Bosnia first emerged as an independent entity under former Byzantine governor Ban Kulina. BiH had a patchy 'golden age' between 1180 and 1463, especially in the late 1370s when Bosnia's King Tvtko gained Hum (future Hercegovina) and controlled much of Dalmatia.

But for the next 80 years Turkish raids whittled away at the country. By the 1460s most of Bosnia was under Ottoman control. Within a few generations, Islam became dominant among townspeople and landowners, though a sizeable proportion of the serfs *(rayah)* remained Christian. Bosnians also became particularly prized soldiers in the Ottoman army, many rising eventually to high rank with the imperial court. The broad-minded early Ottoman era also produced great advances in infrastructure, with fine mosques and bridges built by charitable bequests. However, the Ottomans failed to follow the West's Industrial Revolution.

By the 19th century the empire's economy was archaic, and all attempts to modernise the feudal system in BiH were strenuously resisted by the entrenched Bosnian-Muslim elite. In 1873 İstanbul's banking system collapsed under the weight of the high-living sultan's debts. To pay these debts the sultan demanded added taxes. But in 1874 BiH's harvests failed, so paying those taxes would have meant starving. With nothing left to lose the mostly Christian Bosnian peasants kicked off a wave of revolts that snowballed into a tangle of pan-Balkan wars.

HOW MUCH?

- **Short taxi ride** 5KM
- **Internet access per hour** 1.50KM to 3KM
- **Espresso coffee** 0.50KM to 2KM
- **Shot of šljia (plum brandy)** 1.50KM
- **Movie ticket** 3KM to 5KM

LONELY PLANET INDEX

- **1L petrol** 1.51KM
- **1L bottled water** 0.90KM
- **500mL beer (in a bar)** 3KM
- **Souvenir T-shirt** 15KM
- **Street snack (burek)** 2KM

Austro-Hungarian Rule

These pan-Balkan wars ended with the farcical 1878 Congress of Berlin, at which the Western powers carved up the western Ottoman lands. Austria-Hungary was 'invited' to occupy BiH, which was treated like a colony even though theoretically remaining Ottoman under sovereignty. An unprecedented period of development followed. Roads, railways and bridges were built and coal mining and forestry became booming industries. Education encouraged a new generation of Bosnians to look increasingly towards Vienna.

But new nationalist feelings were simmering: Bosnian Catholics increasingly identified with neighbouring Croatia (itself within Austria-Hungary) while Orthodox Bosnians sympathised with recently independent Serbia's dreams of a greater Serbian homeland. In between lay Bosnia's Muslims (40%), who belatedly started to develop a distinct Bosniak 'ethnic' consciousness.

While Turkey was busy with the 1908 Young Turk revolution, Austria-Hungary annexed BiH. This was a slap in the face for all those who dreamed of a pan-Slavic or greater Serbian future. The resultant scramble for the last remainders of Ottoman Europe kicked off the Balkan Wars of 1912 and 1913. No sooner had these been (unsatisfactorarily) resolved than the heir to the Austrian throne was shot dead while visiting Sarajevo. One month later Austria declared war on Serbia and WWI swiftly followed.

World Wars, Communism & Political Tension

WWI killed an astonishing 15% of the Bosnian population. It also brought down both the Turkish and Austro-Hungarian empires, leaving BiH to be absorbed into proto-Yugoslavia.

During WWII BiH was occupied partly by Italy, partly by Germany, then absorbed into the newly created fascist state of Croatia. Croatia's Ustaše decimated Bosnia's Jewish population, and they also persecuted Serbs and Muslims. Meanwhile a pro-Nazi group of Bosnian Muslims committed their own atrocities against Bosnian Serbs while Serb Četniks and Tito's Communist Partizans put up some stalwart resistance to the Germans (as well as fighting each other). The BiH mountains proved ideal territory for Tito's flexible guerrilla army, whose greatest victories are still locally commemorated with vast memorials. At Jajce (p104) in 1943, Tito's antifascist council famously formulated a constitution for an inclusive postwar, socialist Yugoslavia.

After WWII, BiH was granted republic status within Tito's initially anti-religious Yugoslavia. After Tito fell out with the USSR in 1954 and became prominent in the 'non-aligned movement', Yugoslavia's alliances with countries like Egypt meant that having 'token' Muslim Bosnians on the diplomatic staff suddenly became a useful cachet. However, up until 1971, 'Muslim' was not considered an 'ethnic group' so Bosniaks had had to register as Croat, Serb or 'Other/Yugoslav'.

Despite considerable mining development in the northeast and the economic boost of the 1984 Sarajevo Winter Olympics, Bosnia remained one of the least developed Yugoslav republics.

The 1990s Conflict

In the post-Tito era, as Yugoslavia imploded, 'ethnic' tensions were ratcheted up by the ultranationalist Serb leader Slobodan Milošević and equally radical Croat leader Franjo Tuđman. Although these two leaders were at war by spring 1991, they reputedly came up with a de facto agreement in which they

WHAT'S IN A NAME?

Geographically Bosnia and Hercegovina (BiH) comprises Bosnia (in the north) and Hercegovina (pronounced Her-tse-GO-vina, in the south), although the term 'Bosnian' refers to anyone from BiH, not just from Bosnia-proper. Politically, however, BiH is divided into two entirely different political entities. Southwest and central BiH falls mostly within the Federation of Bosnia and Hercegovina, usually shortened to 'the Federation'. Meanwhile most areas bordering Serbia, Montenegro and the northern arm of Croatia are within the Serb-dominated Republika Srpska (abbreviated RS). The entities were once at war, but these days you'll sometimes struggle to know which one you're in. The biggest giveaway is the use of the Cyrillic alphabet in the RS, but a few minor practicalities are also different, notably stamps and phonecards.

planned to divide BiH between breakaway Croatia and rump Yugoslavia.

Under president Alija Izetbegović, BiH declared independence from Yugoslavia on 15 October 1991. Bosnian Serb parliamentarians wanted none of this and withdrew to set up their own government at Pale, 20km east of Sarajevo. BiH was recognised internationally as an independent state on 6 April 1992 but Sarajevo was already under siege both by Serb paramilitaries and by parts of the Yugoslav army (JNA).

Over the next three years a brutal and extraordinarily complex civil war raged. Best-known is the campaign of ethnic cleansing in northern and eastern BiH creating the 300km 'pure'-Serb Republika Srpska (RS). But '*there were terrible criminals on our side too*' as locals of each religion will readily admit. In western Hercegovina the Croat population armed itself with the help of neighbouring Croatia, eventually ejecting Serbs from their villages in a less-reported but similarly brutal war.

Perhaps unaware of the secret Tuđman–Milošević understanding, Izetbegović had signed a formal military alliance with Croatia in June 1992. But by early 1993 fighting had broken out between Muslims and Croats, creating another war front. Croats attacked Muslims in Stolac and Mostar, bombarding their historic monuments and blasting Mostar's famous medieval bridge into the river. Muslim troops, including a small foreign mujahedin force, desecrated churches and attacked Croat villages, notably around Travnik.

With atrocities on all sides, the West's reaction was confused and erratic. In August 1992, pictures of concentration-camp and rape-camp victims (mostly Muslim) found in northern Bosnia spurred the UN to send a Protection Force (Unprofor) of 7500 peacekeeping troops. They secured the neutrality of Sarajevo airport well enough to allow the delivery of humanitarian aid, but overall proved notoriously impotent.

Ethnic cleansing of Muslims from Foča and Višegrad led the UN to declare 'safe zones' around the Muslim-majority towns of Srebrenica, Župa, and Goražde. But rarely has the term 'safe' been so misused. When NATO belatedly authorised air strikes to protect these areas, the Serbs responded by capturing 300 Unprofor peacekeepers and chaining them to potential targets to keep the planes away.

In July 1995 Dutch peacekeepers could only watch as the starving, supposedly 'safe area' of Srebrenica fell to a Bosnian Serb force led by the infamous Ratko Mladić. An estimated 8000 Muslim men were slaughtered in Europe's worst mass killings since WWII. Somewhat miraculously, Goražde held out, albeit in ruins, thanks to sporadically available UN food supplies.

By this stage, Croatia had renewed its own internal offensive, expelling Serbs from the Krajina region of Croatia in August 1995. At least 150,000 of these dispossessed people then moved to the Serb-held areas of northern Bosnia.

Finally, another murderous Serb mortar attack on Sarajevo's Markale Market kick-started a shift in UN and NATO politics. An ultimatum to end the Serbs' siege of Sarajevo was made more persuasive through two weeks of NATO air strikes in September 1995. US president Bill Clinton's proposal for a peace conference in Dayton, Ohio was accepted soon after.

The Dayton Agreement

While maintaining BiH's pre-war external boundaries, Dayton divided the country into today's pair of roughly equally sized 'entities' (see the boxed text, opposite), each with limited autonomy. Finalising the border between the Federation of Bosnia & Hercegovina (the Muslim and Croat portion including central Sarajevo) and the Republika Srpska (RS; the Serb part) required considerable political and cartographic creativity. The process was only finally completed in 1999 when the last sticking point, Brčko, was belatedly given a special self-governing status all of its own. Meanwhile BiH's curious rotating tripartite overall presidency has been kept in check by the EU's powerful 'High Representative' (www.ohr.int).

For refugees (1.2 million abroad, and a million displaced within BiH), the Dayton Agreement emphasised the right to return to (or to sell) their pre-war homes. International agencies donated very considerable funding to restore BiH's infrastructure, housing stock and historical monuments.

An embarrassing problem post-Dayton was the failure to find and try as war criminals Ratko Mladić and the Bosnian Serb leader Radovan Karadžić (president of the RS until July 1996). Despite $5 million dollar rewards offered for their arrest, Karadžić was only apprehended in 2008, while Mladić remains at large, probably protected by supporters who perceive him to be an honest patriot.

Bosnia & Hercegovina Today

Nonnationalist politicians now run the RS, while under EU and American pressure BiH has centralised considerably in a movement away from the original Dayton 'separate powers' concept. BiH now has a unified army and common passports. Both entities now have indistinguishable car licence plates and use the same currency, albeit with banknotes in two somewhat different designs. Many (though by no means all) refugees have returned and rebuilt their pre-war homes.

Today it's economics more than nationalism that is the great concern for most Bosnians. Those few socialist-era factories that weren't destroyed in the 1990s conflicts have downsized to fit tough 21st-century global realities. New 'business-friendly' government initiatives, including a recent wave of privatisations, are eyed with suspicion; the populace fears growing corruption. People assume that one day BiH will join the EU, though for many, nearby Slovenia's experience suggests that EU membership will just push up prices and make life harder. 'Life's tough' one war-widowed homestay hostess told us, 'but at least there's peace'.

PEOPLE

Bosniaks (Bosnian Muslims), Bosnian Serbs (Orthodox) and Bosnian Croats (Catholics) are all Southern Slavs. Physically they are indistinguishable. The pre-war population was mixed, with intermarriage common in the cities. Stronger divisions have inevitably appeared since the 'ethnic cleansing' of the 1990s. The war resulted in massive population shifts, changing the size and linguistic balance of many cities. Notably the population of Banja Luka grew by over 100,000 as it absorbed Serb refugees from Croatia.

Bosniaks now predominate in Sarajevo and central BiH, Bosnian Croats in western and southern Hercegovina, and Bosnian Serbs in the RS, which includes Istochno (East) Sarajevo. Relations between the three groups have virtually normalised on a human level, though politically contacts remain limited.

RELIGION

Blurring the borderline between Europe's Catholic west and Orthodox east, sparsely populated medieval Bosnia had its own independent church. This remains the source of many historical myths, but the long-popular idea that it was 'infected' by the Bulgarian Bogomil heresy is now largely discounted.

Following their conquest by the Ottoman Turks, many Bosnians converted to the easy-going Ottoman brand of Sufi-inspired Islam, as much to gain civil privileges as for spiritual enlightenment. The Ottoman Empire was much more religiously open minded than Western Europe at that time and offered refuge to the Sephardic Jews evicted en masse from Spain in 1492. While conditions varied, Bosnian Jews mostly prospered up until WWII, when most of the 14,000-strong community fled or were murdered by Nazis.

Bosnian Muslims also suffered horribly during WWII, with at least 756 mosques destroyed. Postwar Yugoslavia's Stalinist initially anti-religious line softened when Tito repositioned the country as a 'nonaligned' state, resulting in the growing status of Islam within 1950s Yugoslavia.

Today, about 40% of the population is Muslim, 31% is Orthodox (mostly Bosnian Serbs), 15% Roman Catholic (mostly Bosnian Croats) and 4% Protestant. There are around 500 Jews. Religion is taken seriously as a badge of ethnicity but spiritually most people are fairly secular.

ARTS

Bosnia's best-known writer, Ivo Andrić (1892–1975) won the 1961 Nobel Prize in

Literature. With astonishing psychological agility, his epic novel, the classic *Bridge over the Drina,* retells 350 years of Bosnian history as seen through the eyes of unsophisticated townsfolk in Višegrad. His *Travnik Chronicles* (aka Bosnian Chronicle) is also rich with human insight, though its portrayal of Bosnia is through the eyes of somewhat jaded 19th-century foreign consuls in Travnik.

Many thought-provoking essays, short stories and poems explore the prickly subject of the 1990s conflict, often contrasting horrors against the victims' enduring humanity. Quality varies greatly but recommended collections include Miljenko Jergović's *Sarajevo Marlboro* and Semezdin Mehmedinović's *Sarajevo Blues.*

The relationship between two soldiers, one Muslim, one Serb, caught alone in the same trench during the Sarajevo siege was the theme for Danis Tanović's Oscar-winning 2002 film *No Man's Land.* The movie *Go West* takes on the deep taboo of homosexuality as a wartime Serb-Bosniak gay couple become latter-day Romeo and Juliet. *Gori Vatra* (aka Fuse) is an irony-packed dark comedy set in the pretty Bosnian castle town of Tešanj just after the war, parodying efforts to hide corruption and create a facade of ethnic reintegration for the sake of a proposed visit by US President Bill Clinton.

Sevdah (traditional Bosnian music) typically uses heart-wrenching vocals to recount tales of unhappy amours. Meanwhile Sarajevo has an annual jazz festival (p85) and the post-industrial city of Tuzla has vibrant rap and metal scenes.

Medieval Bosnian craftsmen created unique oversized gravestones called *stećci* (singular *stećak*). The best-known examples are found at Radimlja near Stolac (p99). However, those collected outside Sarajevo's National Museum (p84) are finer, while a group near Umoljani (p92) has a much more visually satisfying setting.

BiH crafts from *kilims* (woollen flat-weaves) to copperware and decoratively re-purposed bullet casings are widely sold in Mostar's Kujundžiluk (p97) and Sarajevo's Baščaršija (p89).

ENVIRONMENT

BiH is predominantly mountainous. Some 30 peaks rise between 1700m and 2386m, while only 8% of BiH's 51,129 sq km are below 150m. Just a toe of land tickles the Adriatic Sea at Neum. The arid south (Hercegovina) gives way to limestone uplands carved with grey craggy caves and deep canyons. The mountain core then descends again through green rolling hills further north, finally flattening out altogether but only in the very northeasternmost corner.

BiH's highest mountains are divided by breathtaking canyons, waterfalls and alpine valleys in the magnificent Sutjeska National Park.

Hercegovina's Hutovo Blato wetlands provide a prime sanctuary for migratory birds.

Environmental worries include landmines, wrecked building-stock and unexploded ordnance still left over from the 1990s war, plus rubbish disposal difficulties and air pollution from metallurgical plants.

FOOD & DRINK

Popular all across the Balkans, Bosnia's archetypal dishes are made of grilled minced meat formed into cylindrical little *ćevapi (ćevapčići)* or patty-shaped *pljeskavica.* Either are typically served in spongy *somun* bread, ideally with an added scoop of *kajmak* (local curd-butter). *Čevabdžinica* are *ćevapi* specialist-eateries but almost all restaurants serve them along with *šnicla* (steak/schnitzel), *kotleti* (normally veal), *ražnijići* (shish kebab), *pastrmka* (trout) and *ligne* (squid). Pizza and pasta are also ubiquitous.

Aščinica (usually downmarket local canteens) are most likely to serve pre-prepared traditional dishes like *dolme* (cabbage leaves or vegetables stuffed with minced meat) and hearty stews including *bosanski ionac* (cabbage and meat hotpot).

Buregdžinica eateries serve *burek* (meat stuffed filo pastry) or equivalent meat-free *sirnica* (filled with cheese), *krompiruša* (with potato) or *zeljanica* (with spinach). Pre-cooked versions of the same dishes are sold by weight at many a *pekara* (bakery shop).

Vegetarians might also consider side dishes of stewed beans or courgettes (zucchinis), though meaty traces can't be discounted.

Typical desserts include sugar-soaked baklava, excellent stuffed *palačinci* (pancakes), *hurmastica* (syrup-soaked sponge fingers) and *tufahije* (baked apple stuffed with walnut paste and topped with whipped cream). Bosnian cakes and ice creams are divine.

Tap water is almost always drinkable. Alcohol is readily available in both Muslim and Christian areas. Hercegovina produces some excellent wines. Good local beers cost as little as 1.50KM per 300ml glass. Shots *(pića)* of *šljiva* (plum brandy) or *loza* (local grappa) make great aperitifs or digestives.

Coffee *(kava)* is the main social lubricant. Traditional *bosanski* coffee is served, grinds-and-all, in a *džezva* (small long-handled brass pot) then carefully decanted into thimble-sized cups *(fildžan)*. Excellent espressos are widely available.

Cafes open from around 9am and restaurants from around 11.30am; they generally close around midnight if there's custom, and much earlier when there isn't.

SARAJEVO

☎ 033 / pop 737,000

In the 1990s Sarajevo was on the edge of annihilation. Today it's a cosy, vibrant capital whose humanity, wonderful cafe scene, attractive contours and East-meets-West ambience are increasingly making it a favourite summer traveller destination. Meanwhile in winter it's brilliantly handy for some of Europe's best-value skiing.

HISTORY

Romans had bathed at Ilidža's sulphur springs a millennium earlier, but Sarajevo was officially 'founded' by 15th-century Turks. It rapidly grew wealthy as a silk-importing entrepôt and developed considerably during the 1530s when Ottoman governor Gazi-Husrevbey lavished the city with mosques and built the covered bazaar that still bears his name (see p80). In 1697 the city was burnt by Eugene of Savoy's Austrian army. When rebuilt, Sarajevo cautiously enclosed its upper flank in a large, fortified citadel whose remnants still dominate the Vratnik area.

The Austro-Hungarians were back more permanently in 1878 and erected many sturdy central European–style buildings. However their rule was put on notice by Gavrilo Princip's fatal 1914 pistol shot that killed Archduke Franz Ferdinand, plunging the world into WWI.

Seventy years later, Sarajevo hosted the 1984 Winter Olympics. Then from 1992 to 1995 the infamous siege of the city grabbed headlines and horrified the world. Sarajevo's heritage of six centuries was pounded into rubble and its only access to the outside world was via a metre-wide, 800m-long tunnel under the airport (p84). Over 10,500 Sarajevans died and 50,000 were wounded by Bosnian Serb shelling and sniper fire. Endless white-stoned graveyards on Kovači (Map pp82–3) and up near Koševo Stadium (Map p79) are a moving testimony to those terrible years.

ORIENTATION

Sarajevo is tightly wedged into the steep, narrow valley of the modest Miljacka River. Attractive Austro-Hungarian era avenues Maršala Tita/Ferhadija and Obala Kulina Bana converge at the very atmospheric Baščaršija 'Turkish Town'. North, east and south a pretty fuzz of red-roofed Bosnian houses dotted with uncountable minarets climbs the valley sides towards remarkably rural green-mountain ridges. Westward, however, Sarajevo sprawls for over 10km through Novo Sarajevo and dreary Dobrinja past contrastingly dismal ranks of bullet-scarred apartment blocks. Park-filled Ilidža, beyond the airport, marks the end of the city's tramway spine with a parkland flourish.

INFORMATION

Bookshops

For maps, guidebooks, magazines and English-language books on ex-Yugoslavia try:

BuyBook (Map pp82-3; ☎ 716450; www.buybook.ba; Radićeva 4; ⏰ 9am-10pm Mon-Sat, 10am-6pm Sun)

Šahinpašić (Map pp82-3; ☎ 667210; www.btcsahinpasic.com; Vladislava Skarića 8; ⏰ 9am-8pm Mon-Sat)

Sejtarija (Map pp82-3; ☎ 205233; www.sejtarija.com; Maršala Tita 19; ⏰ 9am-8pm Mon-Sat)

Internet Access

Click (Map pp82-3; Kundurdžiluk 1a; per hr 3KM; ⏰ 9am-11pm) Nonsmoking.

Cyber (Map pp82-3; Pehlivanuša 2; per hr 3KM; ⏰ 10am-11pm Mon-Sat, noon-7pm Sun)

Internet Caffe Baščaršija (Map pp82-3; Aščiluk bb; per hr 1.5KM; ⏰ 24hr) Take the steps marked Sultan Caffe.

Laundry

Askos Laundry (Map pp82-3; Halilbašića 2; ⏰ 9am-5pm Mon-Fri, 9am-3pm Sat)

Left Luggage

Luggage can be left at the main bus station (p89) It costs 2KM for the first hour and then 1KM for subsequent hours.

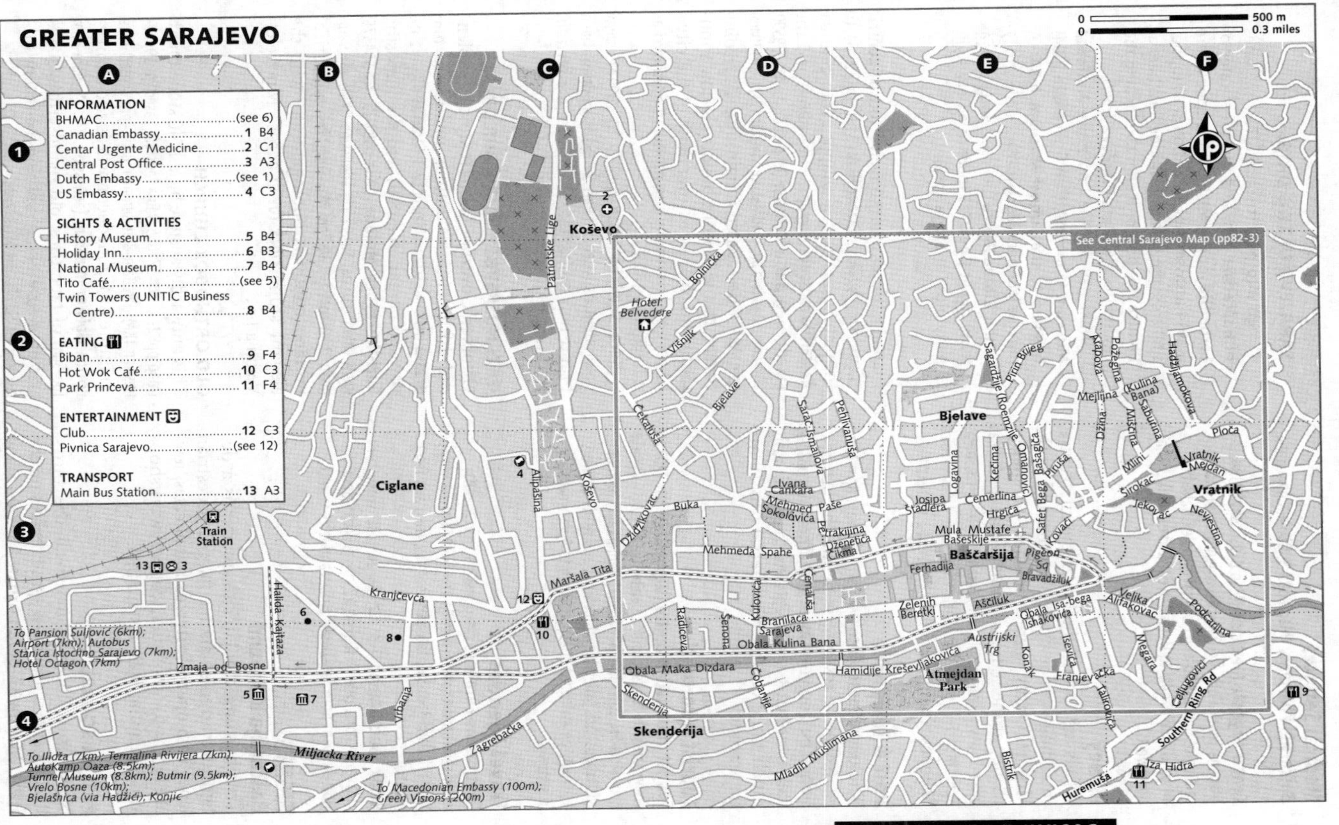
GREATER SARAJEVO
INFORMATION
BHMAC (see 6)
Canadian Embassy 1 B4
Centar Urgente Medicine 2 C1
Central Post Office 3 A3
Dutch Embassy (see 1)
US Embassy 4 C3
SIGHTS & ACTIVITIES
History Museum 5 B4
Holiday Inn 6 B3
National Museum 7 B4
Tito Café (see 5)
Twin Towers (UNITIC Business Centre) 8 B4
EATING
Biban 9 F4
Hot Wok Café 10 C3
Park Prinčeva 11 F4
ENTERTAINMENT
Club 12 C3
Pivnica Sarajevo (see 12)
TRANSPORT
Main Bus Station 13 A3
0 500 m
0 0.3 miles
See Central Sarajevo Map (pp82-3)
Train Station
Hotel Belvedere
Ciglane
Koševo
Bjelave
Vratnik
Baščaršija
Pigeon Sq
Atmejdan Park
Skenderija
Miljacka River
Southern Ring Rd
To Pansion Šuljović (6km); Airport (7km); Autobus Stanica Istočno Sarajevo (7km); Hotel Octagon (7km)
To Ilidža (7km); Termalina Rivijera (7km); AutoKamp Oaza (8.5km); Tunnel Museum (8.8km); Butmir (9.5km); Vrelo Bosne (10km); Bjelašnica (via Hadžići); Konjic
To Macedonian Embassy (100m); Green Visions (200m)

Medical Services

Baščaršija Pharmacy (Map pp82-3; Obala Kulina Bana 40; 24hr)

Centar Urgente Medicine (Map p79; ☎ 297330; Stepana Tomića bb; 24hr) Emergency assistance section of the vast Koševo Hospital complex. Take bus 14 from Dom Armije to Hotel Belvedere then walk 300m northwest.

Money

ATMs are sprinkled all over the city centre, including outside the bus station and in the airport. Oddly there's nowhere to change money at the stations. **Turkish Ziraat Bank** (Map pp82-3; www.ziraatbosnia.com; Ferhadija 10; 8.30am-8pm Mon-Fri, 9am-3pm Sat) cashes travellers cheques if you show the original receipt.

Post & Telephone

The **central post office** (Map p79; 7am-8pm Mon-Sat) for poste restante is beside the bus station. The gorgeous **main post office** (Map pp82-3; Obala Kulina Bana 8; 7am-8pm Mon-Sat) is actually much more central. Counters 17 to 19 are for stamps.

Tourist Information

Tourist information centre (Map pp82-3; ☎ 220724; www.sarajevo-tourism.com; Zelenih Beretki 22a; 9am-6pm Mon-Fri, 9am-3pm Sat & Sun) Remarkably helpful with maps, bus timetables, brochures and ready answers for many an awkward question. Open to 9pm weekdays in summer.

Travel Agencies

Centrotrans-Eurolines (Map pp82-3; ☎ 205481; www.centrotrans.com; Ferhadija 16; 8.30am-8.30pm Mon-Fri, 9am-3pm Sat) International bus, train and ferry tickets.

Relax Tours (Map pp82-3; ☎ /fax 263 330; www.relaxtours.com; Zelenih Beretki 22; 8.30am-8pm Mon-Fri, 9am-5pm Sat) Books airline and ferry tickets.

SIGHTS

Baščaršija & Around

This bustling old Turkish quarter is a delightful warren of marble-flagged pedestrian lanes with open courtyards full of cafes, jewellery shops, mosques, copper workshops and charming little restaurants.

PIGEON SQUARE

Nicknamed Pigeon Sq for all the birds, Baščaršija's central open space centres on the **Sebilj** (Map pp82–3), an ornate 1891 drinking fountain. It leads past the lively if tourist-centric coppersmith alley, **Kazandžiluk** (Map pp82–3), to the picturesque garden-wrapped 16th-century **Baščaršija mosque** (Map pp82-3; Bravadžiluk) and the six-domed **Bursa Bezistan** (Map pp82-3; ☎ 239590; www.muzejsarajeva.ba; Abadžiluk 10; admission 2KM; 10am-6pm Mon-Fri, 10am-3pm Sat). Originally a silk trading bazaar, this 1551 stone building is now a museum with bite-sized overviews of the city's history and a compelling model of Sarajevo as it looked in 1878.

Kuća Sevdaha (Map pp82-3; ☎ 239943; www.artkucasevdaha.ba/en/; Halači 5; 10am-6pm) is a brand-new multimedia showcase for *sevdah*, traditional Bosnian music.

SARAJEVO IN TWO DAYS

Plunge into pedestrianised 'Turkish' lanes of **Baščaršija** (left) and the street cafes of **Ferhadija** (opposite). From the spot where a 1914 assassination kicked off WWI (opposite) cross the cute Latin Bridge for a beer at **Pivnica HS** (p88) or dinner overlooking the city rooftops at **Park Prinčeva** (p87).

Next day see the impressive **National Museum** (opposite), then from **Ilidža** (p84) bus-hop to the **Tunnel Museum** (p84). A drink at laid-back **Mash** (p88) or delightfully Gothic **Zlatna Ribica** (p88) sets you up for a feisty gig at **Bock/FIS** (p88) or an old-style party night at **Sloga** (p88).

GAZI-HUSREVBEY VAKUF BUILDINGS

Ottoman Governor Gazi-Husrevbey's splendid 16th-century complex includes a **madrassa** (religious school; Map pp82-3; Sarači 33-49), a fine covered bazaar (see p89) and the imposing **Gazi-Husrevbey Mosque** (Map pp82-3; ☎ 534375; www.vakuf-gazi.ba; Sarači 18; admission 2KM; 9am-noon, 2.30-4pm & 5.30-7pm May-Sep). Its cylindrical minaret contrasts photogenically with the elegant stone **clock tower** across Mudželeti Veliki alley.

OLD ORTHODOX CHURCH

This outwardly austere little 1740 stone **church** (Map pp82-3; ☎ 571065; Mula Mustafe Bašeskije 59; admission 1KM; 8am-8pm summer, 8am-4pm winter) has an impressive gilded iconostasis and a three-room **cloister-museum** (admission 2KM; 9am-3pm Tue-Sun) of tapestries, old manuscripts, icons and photo-alerts highlighting the recent suffering of Serbs in Kosovo.

Bjelave & Vratnik

These lived-in neighbourhoods have their share of dreary apartment blocks but also feature a few intimidating Catholic edifices like **Vrhbosnanska Bogoslovija Seminary** (Map pp82-3; Josipa Štadlera bb) and Moorish masterpieces like the fabulous **Islamic Science Faculty building** (Map pp82-3; Ćemerlina 54). Of several traditionally Turkish-styled houses retaining courtyards and *doksat* (overhanging box-windows), the most impressive example is the brilliantly restored 18th-century **Svrzo House** (Svrzina Kuća; Map pp82-3; ☎ 535264; Glođina 8; admission 2KM; 🕑 10am-6pm Mon-Fri, 10am-3pm Sat). For great views over town continue up towards the once-vast **Vratnik Citadel** (Map pp82–3), built in the 1720s and reinforced in 1816. Its **Kula Ploče tower** (Map pp82-3; Ploča bb; admission free; 🕑 10am-6pm Mon-Fri, 10am-3pm Sat) houses a fascinating little museum to BiH's first president, Alija Izetbegović. But the best panoramas are from the grassy-topped **Yellow Bastion** (Map pp82-3; Žuta Tabija; Jekovac bb). Minibus 55 runs to Vratnik.

Ferhadija & Around

Summer street-cafes fill every open space around pedestrianised Ferhadija, lined with the city's Austro-Hungarian era main thoroughfare. The city's harmonious pre-1990s past is illustrated by the close proximity of three places of worship. The 1889 neo-Gothic **Catholic Cathedral** (Katedrala; Map pp82-3; Trg Fra Grge Martića 2; 🕑 9am-4pm) is where Pope John Paul II served mass during his 1997 visit. The large 1872 **Orthodox Cathedral** (Saborna Crkva; Map pp82-3; Trg Oslobođenja), built in Byzantine-Serb style, is artfully lit at night. And the atmospheric 1581 Sephardic Synagogue is still active at Rosh Hashana (Jewish New Year), though otherwise doubles as the interesting **Jewish Museum** (Map pp82-3; ☎ 535688; Mula Mustafe Baśveskije 40; admission 2KM; 🕑 10am-6pm Mon-Fri, 10am-1pm Sun).

Further west, several fine if somewhat triumphalist early-20th-century architecture lines Maršala Tita beyond an **eternal flame** (Vječna vatra; Map pp82-3; Maršala Tita 62) that commemorates victims of WWII.

The Riverbank

Intricately decorated with story-book Moorish arched balconies, Bosnia's once-glorious **National Library** (Map pp82–3) started life as the 1892 City Hall. In 1992 it was deliberately hit by a Serb incendiary shell and its unique collection of Bosnian books and irreplaceable manuscripts was destroyed. Restoration work has stalled and the building remains a stabilised partial-ruin.

The **Sarajevo 1878–1918 Museum** (Map pp82-3; ☎ 533288; Zelenih Beretki 2; admission 2KM; 🕑 10am-6pm Mon-Fri, 10am-3pm Sat) is a one-room exhibition on Sarajevo's Austro-Hungarian era focusing on the infamous 1914 assassination of Franz Ferdinand that happened right outside (ultimately triggering WWI). Further west, Obala Kulina Bana is patchily flanked with fine Austro-Hungarian era buildings. The grand **main post office** (Map pp82-3; Obala Kulina Bana 8; 🕑 7am-8pm Mon-Sat) has a soaring interior and old-fashioned brass counter-dividers. Next door, the **University Rectorate** (Map pp82-3; Obala Kulina Bana 7) is similarly grand. Across the river the splendid Gothic Revival style **Academy of Arts** (Map pp82-3; www.unsa.ba/eng/pregled.php; Obala Maka Dizdara) looks like a miniature version of Budapest's magnificent national parliament building.

Novo Sarajevo

During the 1992–95 siege, the wide road in from the airport (Zmaja od Bosne) was dubbed 'sniper alley' because Serb gunmen in surrounding hills could pick off civilians as they tried to cross it. The distinctive, custard-and-pudding-coloured **Holiday Inn** (Map p79; ☎ 288000; www.holidayinn.com/sarajevo; Zmaja Od Bosne 4) famously housed most of the embattled journalists covering the war and Sarajevo's **Twin Towers** next door spent much of the post-civil-war period as burnt-out wrecks, a sad symbol of the city's devastation. Today they're gleamingly reconstructed as the UNITIC Business Centre.

NATIONAL MUSEUM

Large and very impressive, the **National Museum** (Zemaljski Muzej Bosne-i-Hercegovine; Map p79; ☎ 668026; www.zemaljskimuzej.ba; Zmaja od Bosne 3; adult/student 5/1KM; 🕑 10am-5pm Tue-Fri, 10am-2pm Sat & Sun) is a quadrangle of four splendid neoclassical buildings purpose-built in 1913. The ancient history section displays fine Illyrian and Roman carvings in a room that looks dressed for a toga party. Upstairs, peep through the locked, high-security glass door of room 37 to glimpse the world-famous **Sarajevo Haggadah**, a 14th century Jewish codex estimated to be worth around a billion US dollars. Geraldine

CENTRAL SARAJEVO

INFORMATION

Askos Laundry	1	F4
Australian Consulate	2	C6
Baščaršija Pharmacy	3	E5
BuyBook	4	A6
Centrotrans-Eurolines	5	D5
Click	6	E5
Croatian Embassy	7	B4
Cyber	8	D4
French Embassy	9	A4
German Embassy	10	B4
Internet Caffe Baščaršija	11	E5
Japanese Embassy	12	E6
Main Post Office	13	B6
Montenegrin Embassy	14	F5
Relax Tours	15	D5
Šahinpašić	16	C5
Sartour	17	E4
Sejtarija	18	B5
Serbian Embassy	19	A6
Slovenian Embassy	20	G5
Tourist Information Centre	21	D5
Turkish Ziraat Bank	22	D5
UK Consulate	23	C4

SIGHTS & ACTIVITIES

Academy of Arts	24	A6
Baščaršija Mosque	25	F5
Bursa Bezistan	26	E5
Catholic Cathedral	27	D5
Clock Tower	28	E5
Eternal Flame	29	C5
Gazi-Husrevbey Madrassa	30	E5
Gazi-Husrevbey Mosque	31	E5
Islamic Science Faculty Building	32	F4
Jewish Museum	33	E4
Kazandžiluk	34	F5
Kula Ploče Tower	35	G3
Kuća Sevdaha	36	F5
Ljubičica	37	F4
National Library	38	F5
Old Orthodox Church	39	E4
Orthodox Cathedral	40	D5
Sarajevo 1878-1918 Museum	41	E5
Sebilj	42	F5
Svrzo House	43	E3
University Rectorate	44	B6
Vratnik Citadel	45	H4
Vrhbosnanska Bogoslovija Seminary	46	D4
Yellow Bastion	47	H4

SLEEPING

Ada Hotel	48	F4
Guest House Halvat	49	F4
Hecco Deluxe	50	C5
Hostel City Center	51	D5
Hostel Marko Polo	52	E4
Hostel Posillipo	53	E4
Hostel Sebilj	54	F5
Hotel Astra	55	D5
Hotel Europa Garni	56	D5
Hotel Gaj	57	A6
Hotel Hecco	58	F2
Hotel Michele	59	C4
Hotel Safir	60	F4
Hotel Unica	61	B6
Identico	62	F5
Kod Keme	63	E5
Ljubičica Hostel	(see 37)	
Motel Sokak	64	D4
Pansion Lion	65	F5
Pansion Stari Grad	66	F4
Pansion Vijećnica	67	F5
Sartour Hostel	68	G3
Villa Wien	69	E5

EATING

Amko	70	B5
Bosanska Kuća	71	F5
Butik-Badem	72	E5
Ćevabdžinica Petica	73	F5
DM	74	D5
Dveri	75	E5
Gradska Tržnica	76	C5
Hoše	77	B4
Inat Kuća	78	G5
Karuzo	79	C4
Konsum	80	F4
Markale Market	81	C4
Metropolis	82	B5
Michele	83	D5
Pekara Edin	84	F4
Pekara Nina	85	C5
Sara	86	F5
To Be ~~or Not~~ to Be	87	E5
Urban Grill	88	B4
Vinoteka	89	A6
Željo 1	90	E5
Željo 2	91	E5

Hadži-Sulejmanova
Sarač Ismailova
Pehlivanuša
Nikole Kašikovića
Ivana Cankara
Mejtaš
Buka
Mehmed Paše Sokolovića
Josipa Štadlera
Petrakijina
Mulabdića
Dženetića Čikma
Mula Mustafe Bašeskije
Mehmeda Spahe
Dalmatinska
Kaptol
Trg Fra Grge Martića
Jelića
Ferhadija
Štrosmajerova
Saliha Muvekita
Čemaluša
Muhameda Kantardžića
Trg Oslobođenja
Kulovića
Radićeva
Šenona
Zelenih Beretki
Cumurija
Branilaca Sarajeva
Despićeva
Gimnazijska
Čobanija
Obala Maka Dizdara
Ashkenazi Synagogue
Viewpoint
Hamidije Kreševljakovića
Skenderija

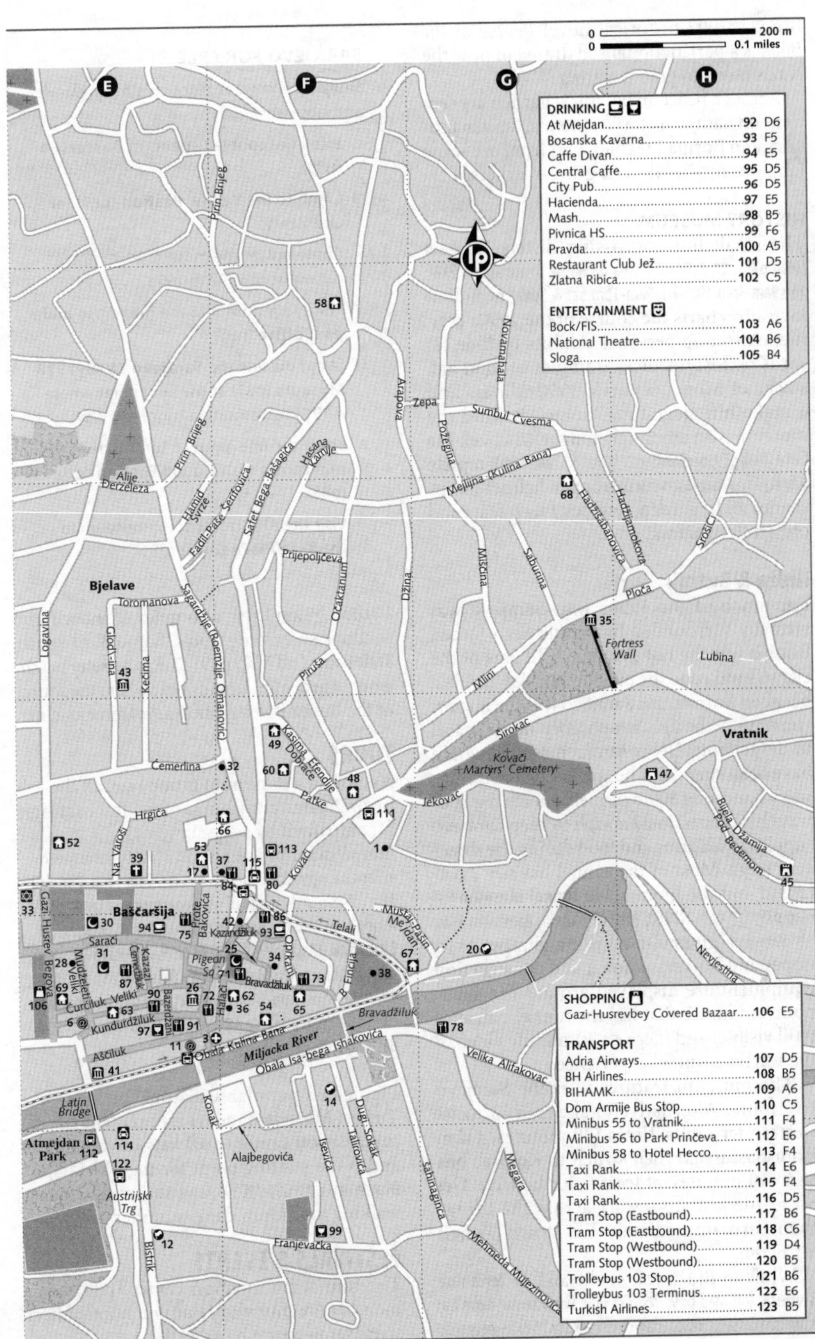
0 200 m
0 0.1 miles
E
F
G
H
DRINKING
At Mejdan.......92 D6
Bosanska Kavarna.......93 F5
Caffe Divan.......94 E5
Central Caffe.......95 D5
City Pub.......96 D5
Hacienda.......97 E5
Mash.......98 B5
Pivnica HS.......99 F6
Pravda.......100 A5
Restaurant Club Jež.......101 D5
Zlatna Ribica.......102 C5
ENTERTAINMENT
Bock/FIS.......103 A6
National Theatre.......104 B6
Sloga.......105 B4
SHOPPING
Gazi-Husrevbey Covered Bazaar.....106 E5
TRANSPORT
Adria Airways.......107 D5
BH Airlines.......108 B5
BIHAMK.......109 A6
Dom Armije Bus Stop.......110 C5
Minibus 55 to Vratnik.......111 F4
Minibus 56 to Park Prinčeva.......112 E6
Minibus 58 to Hotel Hecco.......113 F4
Taxi Rank.......114 E6
Taxi Rank.......115 F4
Taxi Rank.......116 D5
Tram Stop (Eastbound).......117 B6
Tram Stop (Eastbound).......118 C6
Tram Stop (Westbound).......119 D4
Tram Stop (Westbound).......120 B5
Trolleybus 103 Stop.......121 B6
Trolleybus 103 Terminus.......122 E6
Turkish Airlines.......123 B5
Pirin Brijeg
Novamahala
Arapova
Žepa
Sumbul Čvesma
Požegina
Mejlijna (Kulina Bana)
Hasana Kamije
Safet Bega Bašagića
Fadil-Paše Šerifovića
Hamid Svrze
Alije Đerzeleza
Hadžisabanovića
Hadžijamokova
Sirošići
Prijepoljčeva
Očaktanum
Džina
Miščina
Saburina
Ploča
Bjelave
Toromanova
Sagardžije (Roemzije Omanovići)
Logavina
Clodt-ina
Kečima
Fortress Wall
Lubina
Mlini
Pirušа
Širokac
Vratnik
Kovači Martyrs' Cemetery
Jekovac
Kasima Efendije Dobrače
Patke
Čemerlina
Hrgića
Na Varoši
Kovači
Bijela Džamija
Pod Bedemom
Baščaršija
Gazi Husrev Begova
Saraći
Mudželeti Veliki
Kazazi
Ćemedžiluk
Prote Bakovića
Kazandžiluk
Telali
Mustaj Pašin Mejdan
Oprkanj
Pigeon Sq
Bravadžiluk
B Fincija
Čurčiluk Veliki
Bazerdžani
Halači
Kundurdžiluk
Ašćiluk
Obala Kulina Bana
Miljacka River
Obala Isa-bega Ishakovića
Nevjestina
Velika Alifakovac
Latin Bridge
Atmejdan Park
Austrijski Trg
Konak
Alajbegovića
Dugi Sokak
Tahirovića
Isevića
Šahinagića
Megara
Mehmeda Mujezinovića
Franjevačka
Bistrik

Brooks' 2007 historical novel *People of the Book* is a part-fictionalised drama of how the Nazis failed to grab it during WWII.

Across a peaceful botanical garden are sections on natural history, minerals, Roman mosaics and Bosnian textiles. Out front are some fabulous medieval *stećci* grave-markers.

HISTORY MUSEUM

The small but engrossing **History Museum** (Map p79; ☎ 210418; Zmaja od Bosne 5; admission 2KM; 9am-4pm Mon-Fri, 9am-1pm Sat & Sun) 'nonideologically' charts the course of the 1990s conflict. Affecting personal exhibits include ID cards of 'lost' medics, examples of food aid, stacks of Monopoly-style 1990s dinars and a makeshift siege-time 'home'. Behind the museum is an amusingly tongue-in-cheek **Tito Café** (Map p79; beer/coffee 2/1KM; 7am-3am), replete with Tito busts, stormtrooper-helmet lampshades and a garden-terrace of Jeep seats and old artillery pieces.

Ilidža & Butmir

For much of the 1990s war, Sarajevo was virtually surrounded by hostile Serb forces. Butmir was the last Bosniak-held part of the city still linked to the outside world. However, between Butmir and Sarajevo was the airport runway. Although supposedly neutral and under tenuous UN control, crossing it would have been suicidal. The solution, in extremis, was a hand-dug 800m tunnel beneath the runway that proved just enough to keep Sarajevo supplied with arms and food during the three-year siege. Most of the tunnel has since collapsed, but the unmissable **Tunnel Museum** (off Map p79; ☎ 061-213760; Tuneli 1, Butmir; admission 5KM; 9am-4pm) gives visitors just a glimpse of its hopes and horrors. Photos and construction equipment are displayed around the shell-pounded house that hid the tunnel entrance (still visible) and there's a 20-minute video of the wartime tunnel experience.

The museum features in many Sarajevo city tours. Alternatively take tram 3 to its western terminus, Ilidža (30 minutes, 11km from Baščaršija) then switch to Kotorac bus 68A (10 minutes, at least twice-hourly). Get off at the last stop, walk across the bridge then turn immediately left down Tuneli for 600m.

While in Ilidža you could soak at **Termalna Rivijera** (off Map p79; ☎ 771 000; www.terme-ilidza.ba; Butmirska Cesta 18, Ilidža; adult/child weekday 10/8KM, weekends 14/12KM; 9am-10pm), a complex of indoor and outdoor swimming pools. Some 3km south, **Vrelo Bosne** (off Map p79) park is a pretty patchwork of lush mini-islands near where the source of the Bosna River gushes out of a rocky cliff.

SARAJEVO FOR FREE

Sarajevo is a great place to simply wander and observe:

- Stroll the cobbled streets of **Baščaršija** (p80).
- Climb to the **Yellow Bastion** (p81) for city views .
- Contemplate the massed white graves dating from 1992 to 1995.
- Poke your nose into the grandiose **main post office** (p81).
- Stand outside the **Sarajevo 1878–1918 Museum** (p81) at the very point where a 1914 assassination triggered WWI.
- Enjoy the free lump of Turkish delight that comes with a good Bosnian coffee (p88).
- Visit the Alija Izetbegović museum in the **Kula Ploče tower** (p81).

TOURS

Assuming a minimum group size, all the following offer city tours, often fascinatingly accompanied by siege survivors:

Green Visions (off Map p79; ☎ 717290; www.greenvisions.ba; opposite Radnička 66; 9am-5pm Mon-Fri) Also offers a wide range of set-departure and tailor-made hiking trips into the Bosnian mountains and villages.

Ljubičica (Map pp82-3; ☎ 232109, 061-131813; www.hostelljubicica.net; Mula Mustafe Bašeskije 65; 8am-10pm Oct-Apr, 7am-11pm May-Sep) Helpful and popular.

Sartour (Map pp82-3; ☎ 238680; Mula Mustafe Bašeskije 63; 9am-7pm)

Ljubičica's popular €15 tour includes the Tunnel Museum (and transport). The tourist information centre (p80) lists private guides and is the starting point for the €10 **Sarajevo Discovery** (☎ 061-190591; www.sarajevo-discovery.com) walking tour (3pm daily, summer only).

FESTIVALS & EVENTS

The tourist information centre (p80) has a monthly *Programme of Cultural Events*; check www.sarajevoarts.ba as well.

Baščaršijske Noći (Baščaršija Nights; www.bascarsijske noci.ba) A whole range of international events in July covering dance, music and street theatre performed at various open-air stages around town.
Futura (October) Electronic music.
International Jazz Festival (www.jazzfest.ba) Week-long event in November showcasing local and international performers.
Sarajevo Film Festival (☎ 209411; www.sff.ba; Zelenih Beretki 12/1; tickets 3-6KM) Globally acclaimed festival held in August screening commercial and art-house movies, almost all with English subtitles.

SLEEPING

Budget

Tour agencies (p80) can arrange hostel and homestay accommodation. Beware that many budget hostels have much less central 'overflow' locations.

AutoKamp Oaza (off Map p79; ☎ 636141; www.hotel iilidza.ba/site/oaza; sites per person 10KM, per tent/car/camper-van 7/8/12KM) Tree-shaded camping and caravan hook-ups (electricity 3KM extra) tucked behind the Hotel Izmit, 1.5km west of Ilidža terminus (ie 12km from Baščaršija). Youthful, international vibe.

Sartour Hostel (Map pp82-3; ☎ office 238680; www.sartour-hostel-sarajevo.ba; Hadžisabanovića 15; dm €7-13, tw €24-30) Obliging Sartour (opposite) acts as agent for various homestays, *pansions* and hostels but also has its own house-hostel with a pleasant if sloping garden (camping from €5) and fine views from some windows. Linen costs €3 extra per person so bring your own sleeping bag. Lockout is between 11am and 5pm.

Ljubičica Hostel (Map pp82-3; ☎ 232109; Mula Mustafe Bašeskije 65; dm/homestay/apt from €10/15/20; 🕑 8am-10pm winter, 7am-11pm summer) The mixed bag of simple homestay rooms here can be decent value if you score a relatively central one. The hostel is contrastingly dingy, with tight-packed bunk-beds and battered old bathrooms, but it's superbly central and free transfers from the stations ensure a steady flow of takers.

Hostel City Center (HCC; Map pp82-3; ☎ 503294; www.hcc.ba; 3rd fl, Saliha Muvekita 2; dm/s/d/tr/q €12/18/32/45/54) Head and shoulders above most Bosnian hostels, the brand new HCC has new bunk rooms, an appealing chill-out space, kitchen and free internet access. Ring the bell marked HCC at a doorway beyond downmarket shot-bar Bife Velež.

Hostel Posillipo (Map pp82-3; ☎ 061-778603; amassko@hotmail.com; Besarina Čikma 5; s/d from €15/30) Tucked away up a tiny lane in central Baščaršija, the three small, clean rooms here share a decent bathroom. The three-bed apartment (€20 per person) has a bar area, leather sofas and its own bathroom. The overflow sister building is close by. The helpful if slightly chaotic owners speak good English.

Hostel Sebilj (Map pp82-3; ☎ 573500; www.pansion sebilj.com.ba; Bravadžiluk bb; dm/s/d/tr from €15/15/30/45) Around a decent-sized if unsophisticated barn-like sitting area, most rooms at this hostel share his-or-hers bathrooms, though the €20 four-bed dorms have private facilities.

Kod Keme (Map pp82-3; ☎ 531140; Mali Ćurčiluk 15; s/d from €20/40) This place has neat, unfussy rooms, two of which are surreally pierced by a Corinthian column. Most share bathrooms. Nera, the charming Bosnian-Aussie owner, will soon open a full hotel at Mali Ćurčiluk 11.

Pansion Lion (Map pp82-3; ☎ 236137, 061-268150; www.lion.co.ba; Bravadžiluk 30; dm/s/d/tr/q 30/50/100/120/200KM) Warm antique effects, teddies on some beds, dried flowers and hairdriers in bathrooms all take this 10-room *pansion* up a notch above most hostels, though the five- and eight-bed dorms are windowless and less cutesy. No real lounge area.

Other options:

Hostel Marko Polo (Map pp82-3; ☎ 535000, 061-245620; www.hostel-markopolo.com; 1st fl, Logavina 6; dm/d €10/30) Unexceptional but decently located family flat-hostel with tight-packed beds and no common area. Emina speaks minimal English.
Identico (Map pp82-3; ☎ 233310; Halači 3; dm/s/d with shared bathroom from €15/15/20, s/d with private bathroom €20/40) Unspectacular rooms, minuscule shower booths but perfect old-city location.
Motel Sokak (Map pp82-3; ☎ 570355; www.sokak-motel.com; Mula Mustafe Bašeskije 24; s/d/tr €42/68/93) The 11 fairly plain rooms have limited natural light but there's a decent communal sitting area.

Midrange

Pansion Suljović (off Map p79; ☎ 627670; www.suljovic.com; Kurta Schorka 22; s/d 50/90KM) Functional rooms above a pizzeria beside the EP petrol station, 1.5km from the airport, 10 minutes' (unpleasant) walk from Stup tram stop. Cheaper budget rooms (35KM per person) share bathrooms.

Pansion Vijećnica (Map pp82-3; ☎ 233433; www.pansionvijecnica.co.ba; Mustaj-Pašin Mejdan 5; s/d €30/50) This four-bedroom mini-hotel has period furniture, suave little lobby, attractive lilac interiors and excellent private showers.

It's slightly more sophisticated than sister-property Pansion Stari Grad (Map pp82–3; ☎ 239898; www.sgpansion.co.ba; Bjelina Čikma 4; singles/doubles from €35/50).

Hotel Hecco (Map pp82-3; ☎ 273730; www.hotel-hecco.net; Medresa 1; s/tw/d/tr 80/110/130/150KM; 💻) Twenty-nine bright, airy modern rooms with strong rectilinear lines lead off an artfully designed warren of corridors dotted with armchairs, pot plants and even a weight-training machine. Staff are delightful but there's no lift and only the top floor has air-con. Minibus 58 stops outside.

Guest House Halvat (Map pp82-3; ☎/fax 237714; www.halvat.com.ba; Kasima Efendije Dobraće 5; s/d/tr 90/121/152KM; 💻) Homely, five-room family-run guest house with a friendly, super-talkative hostess still mourning her beloved Dalmatian.

Ada Hotel (Map pp82-3; ☎ 475870; www.adahotel.ba; Abdesthana 8; s/d/tr/apt 90/140/170/200KM) Popular with embassy guests, this eight-room hideaway has lots of loveable touches. Corridor surprises include a fake fireplace that opens to reveal secret cabinets. Old teapots and a guitar await in the attractive breakfast room. Rooms in peach or pastel green are a little less characterful but pleasant and calm.

Hotel Safir (Map pp82-3; ☎ 475040; www.hotel safir.ba; Jagodića 3; s/d 98/140KM) The ultrawhite rooms have artistic flashes in sunny colours, stylish conical basins and a kitchenette. Great value.

Hotel Gaj (Map p79; ☎ 445200; www.hotel-gaj.co.ba; Skenderija 14; s/d/apt €60/90/120) The bright, modern-coloured rooms here have polished wood floors and some have antique-style bedsteads and gilt-framed pictures. All have great clean shower booths. Take breakfast in the half-timbered restaurant or on the garden verandah.

Hotel Octagon (off Map p79; ☎ 471105; www.hotel-octagon.com; Akifa Šeremeta 48; s/d 120/150KM) This place tries overly hard to look upmarket but staff are friendly and it's just a short stroll from the airport, albeit well hidden.

Top End

Villa Orient (Map pp82-3; ☎ 232702; http://hotel-villa-orient.com; Oprkanj 6; s/d 153/206KM; 💻) The great location, neo-Ottoman exterior and soothing modern water features in the stylish lobby set expectations high, so the very ordinary rooms and worn carpets prove sadly disappointing. However, when occupancy is low, significant discounts are possible.

Hotel Astra (Map pp82-3; ☎ 252100; www.hotel-astra.com.ba; Zelenih Beretki 9; s/d 153/206KM) Behind a striking Austro-Hungarian era facade, the minimalist reception booth is hidden within a '40s-retro cafe. Rooms are impressively spacious and elegantly trendy, sporting over-bed 'flying' drapes. Three rooms have jacuzzi-showers.

Hotel Unica (Map pp82-3; ☎ 555225; www.hotel-unica.ba; Hamdije Kreševljakovića 42; s/d 156/195KM) Tan and brown tones of boutiquey Modernisme are reflected even in the receptionists' suits. The stylish breakfast room has reverse ceiling beams, 1940s-style square seats and walls partly decorated with old newspapers.

Hotel Europa Garni (Map pp82-3; ☎ 232855; www.europa-garni.ba; Ferhadija 30a; s/d/apt 183/236/306KM) Behind a discordantly uninteresting facade, this invitingly modern, supercentral hotel has warm peach-toned rooms with polished pine floors draped in Persian rugs. Some have computers. Ask about the Villa Wein annexe (Ćurčiluk Veliki 3), which is cosier and more stylish yet slightly cheaper.

Hecco Deluxe (Map pp82-3; www.hotel-hecco.net/deluxe.html; 9th-12th fl, Ferhadije 2; s/d/tr 195/254/279KM) Plonked atop a misleadingly scraggy apartment block, the 12 oddly shaped but stylishly appointed modern rooms have unsurpassed views of the city centre.

our pick **Hotel Michele** (Map pp82-3; ☎ 560310; www.hotelmichele.ba; Ivana Cankara 27; d/apt €100/150) Looking at the building's unrefined contemporary exterior, nothing prepares you for the eccentric, lavish luxury of this marvellously offbeat boutique hotel. Most rooms are vast, exotically furnished apartments. Celebrity guests have included Bono and Richard Gere.

EATING

There's plenty of choice, but some of Sarajevo's real gems are so small that you might need to book ahead.

Restaurants

Bosanska Kuća (Map pp82-3; Bravadžiluk 3; mains 6-9KM; 🕑 24hr) Colour-picture menus make choosing a meal here easy and among the Bosnian standards are a couple of vegie options.

Biban (Map p79; ☎ 232026; Hošin Brijeg 95a; grills 6-12KM, wine from 20KM per litre) The comparatively rustic Biban offers superbly panoramic views similar to those from Park Prinčeva, without the latter's scurrying army of waistcoated waiters. Walk 600m uphill from Park Prinčeva and turn left after Nalina 15.

Karuzo (Map pp82-3; ☎ 444647; Dženetića Čikma 2; mains 6-18KM; ⏲ noon-3pm & 6-11pm Mon-Fri, 6-11pm Sat) This tiny, friendly one-man (ie slow service) restaurant is styled like a yacht's interior. Some dishes, like the Indian-influenced vegetarian chickpea pockets, are successful – however, the strange 'sushi' uses 'tuna' that tastes more like watery beef than *maguro*.

Inat Kuća (Spite House; Map pp82-3; ☎ 447867; Velika Alifakovac 1; mains 7-12KM, steaks 18KM) This Sarajevo institution is a veritable museum-piece, an Ottoman house with great views of the National Library from a perfect riverside terrace. The menu tells its odd history but much of the typical Bosnian food (stews, *dolme*) is pre-prepared and slightly lacklustre. The *sirnica* (cheese pie) is fresh and might suit vegetarians. Beer costs 4KM to 6KM.

Hot Wok Café (Map p79; ☎ 203322; Maršala Tita 12; meals 10-15KM; ⏲ 8am-midnight) Hot Wok's puntastic menu of southeast-Asian fusion meals is full of unexpected flavour combinations that confuse the palate but leave you wanting to lick the plate. Stylish decor recalls a scene from *Kill Bill*. High stool–seating puts fashion before comfort.

Dveri (Map pp82-3; ☎ 537020; www.dveri.co.ba; Prote Bakovića 10; meals 10-16KM; ⏲ 11am-11pm Mon-Fri, 8am-11pm Sat & Sun; ⊠) This charming 'country cottage' is hung with loops of garlic and corn cobs, and dotted with gingham-curtained windows. Inky risottos, vegie-stuffed eggplant or plum goulash all wash down a treat with 5KM glasses of the house red, a truly excellent Hercegovinian Blatina. But beware when offered 'homemade bread': it's good but costs 5KM extra.

To Be or Not to Be (Map pp82-3; ☎ 233205; Čizmedžiluk 5; meals 10-22KM; ⏲ noon-11pm) Arched metal shutters creak open to reveal a tiny two-table room lovably decorated in traditional Bosnian style. Try the daring, tongue-tickling steak in chilli chocolate (18KM). The name's crossed-out 'or Not' bit dates from the war years when not surviving was not an option.

Park Prinčeva (Map p79; ☎ 222708; www.parkprinceva.ba; Iza Hidra 7; meals 12-23KM; ⏲ 9am-late) Like Bono and Bill Clinton before you, gaze down from this picture-perfect ridge-top perch for fabulous views of Sarajevo's rooftops, mosques and twinkling lights. Wine starts at 30KM a bottle. Get there by minibus 56 from Latin Bridge.

Vinoteka (Map pp82-3; ☎ 214996; Skenderija 12; mains 18-32KM; ⏲ 11am-3pm & 7-11pm Mon-Sat, wine bar 7pm-1am) This expat favourite has an appealing rafter room up top, a mini rainforest effect on the ground floor, and a basement wine bar. The menu changes weekly and includes such delights as venison in forest fruits and John Dory with roast vegies.

Quick Eats

BAKERIES

Inexpensive bakeries with sit-in tables include **Pekara Edin** (Map pp82-3; Mula Mustafe Bašeskije 69; ⏲ 5am-midnight) facing the Sebilj, and the unremarkable but all-night **Pekara Nina** (Map pp82-3; Mula Mustafe Bašeskije; ⏲ 24hr).

CAKE-SHOP CAFES

Indulgent coffee-and-cake paradises include fashionably relaxed **Metropolis** (Map pp82-3; Maršala Tita 21; cakes 3.50KM; ⏲ 8am-11pm Mon-Fri, 9am-11pm Sat, 11am-10pm Sun), the supercentral **Sara** (Map pp82-3; Baščaršija 22; cakes from 1.50KM) and the ever popular **Michele** (Map pp82-3; ☎ 444484; Ferhadija 15; coffee 2KM, cakes 3KM, pizzas 7-11KM; ⏲ 8am-10.30pm) with its period drawing-room interior, Arabian Nights basement and great people-watching street-terrace.

ĆEVABDŽINICAS

Željo (Map pp82-3; ☎ 441200; ćevapi 3-7KM; ⏲ 8am-10pm) Željo 1 (Kundurdžiluk 17); Željo 2 (Kundurdžiluk 20) These twin eateries are not as sexy as many surrounding restaurants but they're veritable institutions famous for offering Sarajevo's best *ćevapi*. They deliver too, and at sensible prices. Don't shirk on the 1KM dollop of *kajmak*.

For similar fare in a more stylish, contemporary setting try **Ćevabdžinica Petica** (Bravadžiluk 29; ćevapi 3-6KM) or **Urban Grill** (www.urbangrill.ba; Pruščakova 8; ćevapi 3.50-5.50KM).

Self-Catering

Markale market (Map pp82-3; Mula Mustafe Bašeskije; ⏲ 7am-5pm Mon-Sat, 7am-2pm Sun) Facing off across a busy road, Markale comprises a huddle of vegetable stalls and the covered 1894 Gradska Tržnica (Map pp82–3) market hall selling meat and dairy goods. Market-goers were massacred here on several occasions by Serb mortar attacks in the 1990s, including a 1995 assault that proved a 'last straw', triggering NATO air strikes against the forces besieging Sarajevo.

Butik-Badem (Map pp82-3; Abadžiluk 12) This super little health-food shop sells caramelised nuts, luscious Turkish delight and a variety of tempting snack foods by weight. There's another branch at Maršala Tita 34.

Handy central supermarkets include **Konsum** (Map pp82-3; Safvet Basagica; 7am-10pm), **DM** (Map pp82-3; Ferhadija 25; 9am-9pm Mon-Sat), **Amko** (Map pp82-3; Maršala Tita; 7am-10pm Mon-Sat, 8am-6pm Sun) and **Hoše** (Map pp82-3; Mejtaš 5; 7am-10pm Mon-Sat, 7am-3pm Sun).

DRINKING

As chilly April melts into sunny May, street-terraces blossom and central Sarajevo becomes one great cafe.

Bars

Pivnica HS (Map pp82-3; Franjevačka 15; 10am-1am) This fabulous Willy Wonka–meets–Las Vegas beer hall is the only place to be sure of finding excellent Sarajevskaya dark beer: it's brewed next door! Superb food too (mains 12MK to 22KM).

Mash (Map pp82-3; 1st fl, Branilaca Sarajeva 20; beer 2KM; 8am-1am Mon-Thu, 9am-3am Fri & Sat, 10am-midnight Sun) Within an outwardly unpromising 1970s concrete building, Mash offers a brilliantly chaotic stylistic mishmash of colours, old furniture and bric-a-brac attracting a studenty clientele.

Hacienda (Map pp82-3; www.placetobe.ba; Bazerdzani 3; 10am-very late) The not-quite Mexican food could be spicier. Not so the ambience at 2am, by which time this cosy, cane-ceilinged cantina has metamorphosed into one of the Old Town's most happening nightspots.

our pick **Zlatna Ribica** (Map pp82-3; Kaptol 5; 9am-late) This marvellously Gothic cafe-bar serves wine in delightful little potion-bottle carafes with complimentary nibbles and dried figs. The uniquely stocked toilet will have you laughing out loud. Unmissable.

City Pub (Map pp82-3; Despićeva bb; 8am-late) Despite a could-be-anywhere pub interior, this friendly place is a very popular meeting point, with occasional live music.

Restaurant Club Jež (Map pp82-3; ☎ 650312; Zelenih Beretki 14; 6pm-late) Atmospheric, under-lit, pseudo-olde basement bar that's a packed-full late-night hot spot with a varying program of themed events and parties.

Cafes

The choice in Sarajevo is simply phenomenal.

Bosanska Kavarna (Map pp82-3; Oprkanj 9; coffee 0.50KM; 8.30am-6pm Mon-Sat) Copper bra-pad lamps, tick-tocking wall-clocks and not-so-saucy Islamic pin-ups adorn this down-market, very authentic coffee house whose primary clientele are wizened old local men.

Caffe Divan (Map pp82-3; Morića Han, Saraći 77; coffee 1.50-3KM; 8am-10pm) Relax in wicker chairs beneath the wooden beams of a gorgeous *caravanserai* (inn) courtyard whose stables now contain a fine Iranian carpet shop.

Pravda (Map pp82-3; www.pravdasarajevo.com; Radićeva 4c; coffee 2-5KM, cocktails 7-14KM; 8am-midnight) Choose from marigold-patterned chill-out sofas or angular perch-stools, then strike your pose amid Sarajevo's gilded youth. Oh no, don't say they've all gone next door to the Nivea?!

Central Caffe (Map pp82-3; Strosmayerova 1; 7.30am-3am) Pure '70s retro with beam-me-up-Scottie ceiling effects and hip youthful clientele. The whole street outside becomes one long cafe in summer.

At Mejdan (Map pp82-3; Atmejdan Park; coffee 3KM, beer 3-5KM; 9am-11pm Mon-Sat, 10am-11pm Sun) Like a Middle Eastern pagoda, this open-sided wooden pavilion has curls of communal sofa seating upstairs and oodles of upmarket summer terrace-space. Fresh fruit juices and wines are served, but there's no food.

ENTERTAINMENT

Nightclubs & Live Music

Sloga (Map pp82-3; Mehmeda Spahe 20; beer from 2.50KM) Downstairs the taverna-style bar Club Gandeamus (open 7pm to midnight) has live Bosnian folk music on Thursday nights around 10pm. Upstairs, much bigger blood-red Seljo-Sloga (open 8pm to 4am) is a cavernous 1990s-style concert/disco/music bar drawing an excitable, predominantly student crowd.

Bock/FIS (Map pp82-3; ☎ 063-943431; www.bock.ba; Musala bb; 6pm-2am) There's no easy-to-spot sign for this wonderfully intimate zebra-striped venue for live alternative and 'urban' music. Uncompromisingly real. Dress in black.

Behind gruffly humourless bouncers, the subterranean trio of stone cavern rooms called **Club** (Map p79; ☎ 550550; www.theclub.ba; Maršala Tita 7; beer 4KM; 10am-late) contains a highly esteemed DJ bar (live concerts too), a plush chill-out space and a surprisingly decent late-night restaurant. If you arrive too early, the **Pivnica Sarajevo** (Map p79; coffee/beer 2/2.50KM; 8am-midnight) behind the same building also offers alternative cavern rooms, plus a plushly cushioned garden terrace.

Performing Arts

National Theatre (Narodno Pozorište; Map pp82-3; ☎ 221682; www.nps.ba; Obala Kulina Bana 9; tickets from 10KM; ⏰ box office 9am-noon & 4pm-7.30pm) Classically adorned with fiddly gilt mouldings, this proscenium-arched theatre hosts a ballet, opera, play or philharmonic concert (www.sarf.com.ba) virtually every night in season (mid-September to mid-June).

SHOPPING

Baščaršija's pedestrian lanes are full of jewellery stalls and wooden-shuttered souvenir shops flogging slippers, Bosnian flags, carpets, archetypal copperware and wooden spoons, though if you're heading to Mostar, you might find prices better there. The attractive, one-street, stone-domed **Gazi-Husrevbey Covered Bazaar** (Map pp82-3; ☎ 534375; www.vakuf-gazi.ba; ⏰ 8am-8pm Mon-Fri, 9am-2pm Sat) sells relatively inexpensive souvenirs, fake bags and sunglasses (from 5KM).

CDs of highly suspect legality cost 3KM from stalls filling a hidden yard behind the Hecco Deluxe hotel (p86).

GETTING THERE & AWAY

Air

Sarajevo's modest international **airport** (off Map p79; ☎ 234841; www.sarajevo-airport.ba; Kurta Šchorka 36) is about 12km southwest of Baščaršija. For flight details see p110.

Bus

Sarajevo's **main bus station** (Map p79; ☎ 213100; Put Života 8) primarily serves locations in the Federation, Croatia and Western Europe, while most services to the RS and Serbia leave from the **Autobus Stanica Istochno Sarajevo** (Аутобус Станица Источно Сарајево; off Map p79; ☎ 057-317377; Nikole Tesle bb). It's commonly, if misleadingly, nicknamed 'Lukavica bus station', and lies way out in the Dobrinja suburb, 400m beyond the western terminus of trolleybus 103. Buses to some destinations – Banja Luka, Belgrade, Pale, Srebrenica – leave from both stations.

Buses to the mountain villages of Bjelašnica and to Butmir start from behind the Ilidža tram terminus.

The 10pm bus to Novi Pazar (€15, eight hours) 'secretly' continues to Pristina (around 12 hours) and Prizren in Kosovo, for which you'll pay an extra €5 fare once you reach Novi Pazar.

For services to Serbia, Croatia and Montenegro, see p90. Other international destinations include Amsterdam (206KM, four weekly), Berlin (167KM, three weekly), Brussels (206KM, Sunday), Dortmund (209KM, Saturday to Thursday), Cologne (235KM, Saturday to Thursday), Ljubljana (74KM, four weekly), Munich (190KM, daily), Paris (260KM, Thursday), Stockholm (280KM, daily) and Vienna (92KM, twice daily).

Train

The **train station** (Map p79; ☎ 655330; Put Života 2) is close to the main bus station. Two daily services connect Ploče (on the Croatian coast) via Mostar (9.90KM, three hours) at 6.45am and 6.18pm. Both either continue on to Zagreb or connect with trains heading there. The overnight Sarajevo–Zagreb section (56.60KM, 9½ hours, 9.20pm) has one carriage of comfortable six-berth couchettes (19.60KM supplement).

The Budapest train (96KM, 12 hours) leaves Sarajevo at 7.14am, routed via Doboj, Šamac and Osijek (Croatia). It returns from Budapest-Keleti at 9.25am.

From Sarajevo to Belgrade (46KM, nine hours), take the Budapest train, changing in Strizivojna-Vrpolje (Croatia) with 1½ hours' wait. Or take the 9.20pm Zagreb-bound service and change at Doboj (13.60KM) around midnight; that will get you onto the Banja Luka–Belgrade train (eight hours), which runs overnight eastbound (departing Banja Luka at 10.30pm).

GETTING AROUND

To/From the Airport

There's no direct airport–centre bus. Blue bus 36 departs from directly opposite the terminal to Nedžarići on the Ilidža–Baščaršija tram line, but it only runs twice an hour. Much more frequent is trolleybus 103, which picks up around 700m away. To find the stop turn right out of the airport then take the first left. Shimmy right/left/right past the Hotel Octagon, then turn right at the Panda car wash (Braće Mulića 17). Just before the Mercator Hypermarket (Mimar Sinana 1) cross the road and take the bus going back the way you've just come.

Metered airport taxis charge around 7KM to Ilidža and 25KM to Baščaršija.

BUSES FROM SARAJEVO

Destination	Station	Price (KM)	Duration (hr)	Departures
Banja Luka (via Jajce)	M	29	5	5am, 7.45am, 9.15am, 2.30pm, 3.30pm & 4.30pm
	L	31	5	9.30am & 11.30am
Bihać	M	41	6½	7.30am, 1.30pm & 10pm
Belgrade (via Zvornik)	M	55	10	6am
	L	55	10-11	6.15am, 8am, 9.45am, 11am, 12.30pm, 3pm & 10pm
Dubrovnik	M	30-44	5-7	7.15am & 10am (plus 2.30pm & 10.30pm summer)
Foča	L	9	1½	11am, 4.35pm & 6.25pm; Trebinje & Višegrad services also stop here
Goražde	M	11	2¼	six daily, four Sunday
Gradačac (via Srebrenik)	M	31	4¼	8.30am & 5pm
Herceg Novi	M	38	7½	11am year-round, 10.30pm summer only
Jahorina (in ski season)	M	10	1	9am Fri, Sat & Sun
Mostar	M	16	2½	15 daily
Niš	L	40	11	8.40am & 6pm
Novi Pazar	M	30	7-8	9am, 3pm, 6pm, 9pm & 10pm
Pale	L	3.50	40min	14 daily Mon-Fri (but 3.15pm only weekends)
	M	4	25min	7am, 10am, 2pm
Podgorica	L	31	6	8.15am & 2pm
Split (via Čapljina)	M	41	7½	10am & 9pm
Split (via Livno)			7¼	6am & 11pm
Split (via Imotski)			6¾	2.30pm
Srebrenica	M	32	3½	7.10am
	L	27.50	3¾	8.40am & 3.30pm
Tešanj	M	23	3	7am, 1.15pm & 5.15pm
Travnik	M	15	2	nine daily
Trebinje (via Sutjeska National Park)	L	23	5	7.45am, 1pm & 4.05pm
Tuzla	M	20	3¼	hourly 10am-4pm plus 6.50pm
Visoko	M	5.70	50min	at least hourly by Kakanj bus
Zagreb	M	54	9½	6.30am, 9.30am, 12.30pm & 10pm

Note: M = main bus station, L = Autobus Stanica Istochno Sarajevo

Car

Sarajevo is not driver-friendly. One-way systems are awkward and Baščaršija is largely pedestrianised with minimal parking. However, renting a car makes it much easier to reach the surrounding mountain areas. Most major car-hire agencies have offices at Sarajevo airport including **Budget** (☎ 766670), **Hertz** (☎ 235050), **Avis** (☎ 469933), **Sixt** (☎ 622200) and **National** (☎ 267590), but booking ahead (online) is advisable.

Public Transport

Tram 3 runs every four to seven minutes from Ilidža, passing the Holiday Inn then looping anticlockwise around Baščaršija. Tram 1 (every eight to 20 minutes) does the same but starting from the main bus station (but note that it's only seven minutes' walk from the Tram 3 line to the stations).

Handy for the Lukovica bus station and the airport, usefully frequent trolleybus 103 runs along the southern side of the city from Austrijski Trg to Dobrinja (30 minutes), with stops near Hotel Unica, the Skenderija Center and Green Visions en route.

From Dom Armije, bus 16B runs past the US embassy to the Koševo area.

Many lines (including tram 3, trolley 103, minibus 56) operate 6am to 11pm daily, but some stop after 7pm, and all have reduced services on Sundays. Full timetables are available in Bosnian on www.gras.co.ba. Click 'Redove Voznje' then select mode of transport.

Single-ride tickets cost 1.60/1.80KM from kiosks/drivers and must be stamped in a special machine once aboard the bus/tram; inspectors have no mercy on 'ignorant foreigners'. Some major kiosks (with red-on-yellow signs) sell good-value 5.30KM day passes, valid for almost all trams, buses and trolleybuses.

Taxi

Charges usually start at 2KM plus about 1KM per kilometre. While all of Sarajevo's taxis have meters, **Žuti Taxis** (Yellow Cab; ☎ 663555) actually turn them on.

There are handy central taxi ranks near Latin Bridge, Hotel Kovači and outside Zelenih Beretki 5.

AROUND SARAJEVO

Tempting moutains rise straight up behind the city, making access to winter skiing or summer rambles in the highland villages very convenient. But don't forget the dangers of landmines – stick to well-used paths.

JAHORINA ЈАХОРИНА

☎ 057

This purpose-built **ski resort** (ski pass per day 30KM, ski rentals per day 24-50KM) offers world-class pistes designed for the 1984 Winter Olympics. In summer there's mountain biking, hiking and **AeroKlub Trebević** (☎ 065-350201; per hr €25; 🕑 Jun-Sep) offers paragliding.

Jahorina's single main road wiggles 2.5km up from a little seasonal shopping 'village' where cheaper pansions open only during the ski season. It passes the Termag Hotel (300m), s-bending past the Dva Javora (1.5km), the post office and the still-ruined Hotel Jahorina, tunnelling beneath Rajska Vrata before dead-ending at the top of the long Skočine Lift.

Sleeping & Eating

All accommodation is within 300m of one of Jahorina's six main ski lifts. Beware that most hotels won't take bookings for less than seven-day stays. You can always turn up hoping for a cancellation. Lowest (summer) and highest (New Year) prices are quoted but several shoulder pricings exist within the main December to March ski season.

Pansion Sport (☎ 270333; s/d 80/160KM; 🕑 20 Dec-10 Apr) Pleasant Swiss chalet-style guest house at the bottom 'village area' of the resort.

Hotel Club Dva Javora (☎ 270481; www.dvajavora.com; s/d/apt 47.50/65/125KM, peak season 118/150/300KM) Above a seasonal shopping centre, the refreshingly modern lobby bar feels like a trendy London coffee house. Rooms are less hip but very presentable.

Hotel Bistrica (☎ 270020; www.oc-jahorina.com; s/d with half-board 71.50/123KM, peak season 160/214KM; 🍴) This vast, unsophisticated 1984 resort complex feels somewhat dated but there are lovely views and many family-style facilities in season. It's set back 300m from the Dva Javora.

Termag Hotel (☎ 270422; www.termaghotel.com; per person from 96KM Apr-Nov, 132KM Dec-Mar; ❄ 💻 🍴) Within an oversized mansion built in Scooby Doo Gothic style, the Termag is a beautifully designed fashion statement where traditional ideas and open fireplaces are given a stylish, Modernisme twist. Sumptuous rooms have glowing bedside tables and high headboards.

Rajska Vrata (☎ 272020; www.jahorina-rajskavrata.com; beer 2.50-3.50KM, mains 7-14KM) Beside the longest piste, this perfect alpine ski-in cafe-restaurant has rustic sheepskin benches around a centrally flued real fire. In summer, lovely fully equipped bedrooms (doubles/triples €50/75) are available.

Getting There & Away

Ski-season-only buses depart from Pale (3KM, 25 minutes) at 6.15am, 2.15pm and 8pm, returning 7am, 3.15pm and 11pm. From Sarajevo's main bus station there's a direct bus on winter Fridays, Saturdays and Sundays at 9am, returning at 3.45pm. There are no summer buses. A taxi from Pale costs 30KM.

BJELAŠNICA

☎ 033

Sarajevo's second Olympic ski field has only one hotel (as yet) but **Eko Planet** (☎ 579035; www.touristbiro.ba) can organise year-round apartment rental (100KM to 200KM) and offers exciting summer quad-bike trips that can take you cross country through bracing upland scenery to **Lukomir**, Bosnia's most traditional surviving mountain village. Sarajevo's ecotourism outfit Green Visions (p84) organises hikes in this lovely area.

Fronted by what looks like a giant Plexiglas pencil, the aging **Hotel Maršal** (☎ 279100;

> **WARNING**
>
> Stay on the groomed ski runs and hiking paths around Jahorina and Bjelašnica as there are mines in the vicinity of both resorts.

WORTH THE TRIP: UMOLJANI

If you're driving consider driving randomly to the web of villages tucked away in the grassy uplands above Bjelašnica. All suffered severely in the war, so traditional architecture is very limited, but the settings are truly lovely. **Umoljani village** (16km from Bjelašnica) is a particularly interesting choice with *stećci* above the beautiful approach lane and more in **Šabići** (11km), a junction village you'll pass part way. In Šabići, there's cheap accommodation at the very rustic **Hojta Hostel** (☎ 437874; emina2708@yahoo.com; Šabići Village; dm 20KM, dinner 6KM), run by a gruff, Bosnian Basil Fawlty. Its front room forms the de facto village pub attracting a wonderfully genuine cross-section of farming folk for a beer and a chat. No English is spoken.

www.hotel-marsal.ba; s/d €46/62, s/d winter €59/78; 💻) is very friendly but haphazardly patched-up and somewhat lacklustre. In season seven-day minimum bookings apply.

Minibus 85 from Ilidža bound for Sinanovići runs just four times a week and drives via Bjelašnica and Šabići. Consider renting a car to come up here.

HERCEGOVINA

Hercegovina is the part of BiH that no one in the West ever mentions, if only because they can't pronounce its name. Its arid, Mediterranean landscape has a distinctive beauty punctuated with barren mountain ridges and photogenic river valleys. Famed for its fine wines and sun-packed fruits, Hercegovina is sparsely populated, but it has several intriguing historic towns and the Adriatic coast is just a short drive away.

MOSTAR

☎ 036 / pop 94,000

At dusk the lights of numerous mill-house restaurants twinkle delightfully across gushing streamlets. The impossibly quaint Kujundžiluk 'gold alley' bustles joyously with trinket sellers. And in between, the Balkans' most celebrated bridge forms a truly majestic stone arc between reincarnated medieval towers. It's a magical scene.

Meanwhile, behind the delightful cobbled lanes of the attractively restored Ottoman quarter, a less palatable but equally unforgettable 'attraction' lies in observing the devastating urban scars that still recall the brutal 1990s conflict all too vividly.

Add in a selection of fascinating day trips for which Mostar makes an ideal base and it's not surprising that this fascinating little city is starting to attract a growing throng of summer visitors. Visit in low season and you'll have it much to yourself.

History

Mostar means 'bridge-keeper' and the crossing of the Neretva River here has always been its raison d'être. In the mid-16th century, Mostar boomed as a key transport gateway within the powerful, expanding Ottoman Empire. Some 30 *esnafi* (craft guilds) included the tanners for whom the Tabahana was built, and goldsmiths (hence Kujundžiluk, 'gold alley'). In 1557, Suleyman the Magnificent ordered a fine stone arch to replace the suspension bridge whose wobbling had previously terrified tradesmen as they gingerly crossed the fast-flowing Neretva River. The beautiful Stari Most (Old Bridge) that resulted was finished in 1566 and came to be appreciated as one of the world's engineering marvels. It survived the Italian occupation of WWII, but after standing for 427 years the bridge was destroyed in November 1993 by Bosnian Croat artillery. That was one of the most poignant, pointless and depressing moments of the whole Yugoslav civil war.

Ironically Muslims and Croats had initially fought together against Serb and Montenegrin forces who had started bombarding Mostar in April 1992. However on 9 May 1993 a bitter conflict erupted between the former allies. Bosnian Croat forces expelled many Bosniaks from their homes: some were taken to detention camps, others fled to the very relative 'safety' of the Muslim east bank of the Neretva. For two years the two sides swapped artillery fire and the city was pummelled into rubble.

By 1995 Mostar resembled Dresden after WWII with all its bridges destroyed and all but one of its 27 Ottoman-era mosques utterly ruined. Vast international assistance efforts have since rebuilt almost all of the Unesco-listed old city core. By 2004 the Stari Most had been painstakingly reconstructed using

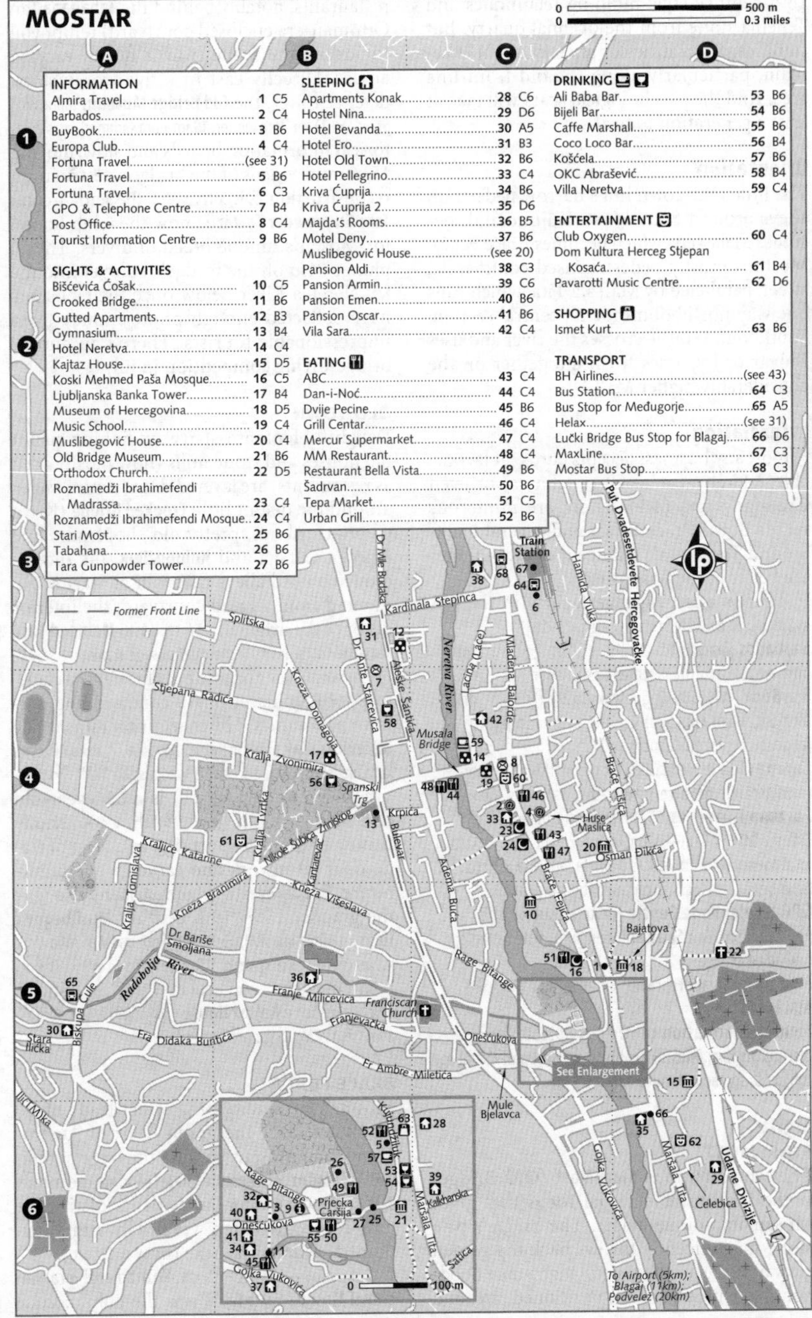
MOSTAR
0 500 m
0 0.3 miles
INFORMATION
Almira Travel 1 C5
Barbados 2 C4
BuyBook 3 B6
Europa Club 4 C4
Fortuna Travel (see 31)
Fortuna Travel 5 B6
Fortuna Travel 6 C3
GPO & Telephone Centre 7 B4
Post Office 8 C4
Tourist Information Centre 9 B6
SIGHTS & ACTIVITIES
Bišćevića Ćošak 10 C5
Crooked Bridge 11 B6
Gutted Apartments 12 B3
Gymnasium 13 B4
Hotel Neretva 14 C4
Kajtaz House 15 D5
Koski Mehmed Paša Mosque 16 C5
Ljubljanska Banka Tower 17 B4
Museum of Hercegovina 18 D5
Music School 19 C4
Muslibegović House 20 C4
Old Bridge Museum 21 B6
Orthodox Church 22 D5
Roznamedži Ibrahimefendi Madrassa 23 C4
Roznamedži Ibrahimefendi Mosque 24 C4
Stari Most 25 B6
Tabahana 26 B6
Tara Gunpowder Tower 27 B6
SLEEPING
Apartments Konak 28 C6
Hostel Nina 29 D6
Hotel Bevanda 30 A5
Hotel Ero 31 B3
Hotel Old Town 32 B6
Hotel Pellegrino 33 C4
Kriva Ćuprija 34 B6
Kriva Ćuprija 2 35 D6
Majda's Rooms 36 B5
Motel Deny 37 B6
Muslibegović House (see 20)
Pansion Aldi 38 C3
Pansion Armin 39 C6
Pansion Emen 40 B6
Pansion Oscar 41 B6
Vila Sara 42 C4
EATING
ABC 43 C4
Dan-i-Noć 44 C4
Dvije Pecine 45 B6
Grill Centar 46 C4
Mercur Supermarket 47 C4
MM Restaurant 48 C4
Restaurant Bella Vista 49 B6
Šadrvan 50 B6
Tepa Market 51 C5
Urban Grill 52 B6
DRINKING
Ali Baba Bar 53 B6
Bijeli Bar 54 B6
Caffe Marshall 55 B6
Coco Loco Bar 56 B4
Košćela 57 B6
OKC Abrašević 58 B4
Villa Neretva 59 C4
ENTERTAINMENT
Club Oxygen 60 C4
Dom Kultura Herceg Stjepan Kosaća 61 B4
Pavarotti Music Centre 62 D6
SHOPPING
Ismet Kurt 63 B6
TRANSPORT
BH Airlines (see 43)
Bus Station 64 C3
Bus Stop for Međugorje 65 A5
Helax (see 31)
Lučki Bridge Bus Stop for Blagaj 66 D6
MaxLine 67 C3
Mostar Bus Stop 68 C3
Former Front Line
Train Station
Splitska
Kardinala Stepinca
Stjepana Radića
Kralja Zvonimira
Spanski Trg
Krpića
Kraljice Katarine
Kneza Branimira
Kneza Višeslava
Dr Bariše Smoljana
Radobolja River
Franje Milicevica
Franciscan Church
Franjevačka
Fra Didaka Buntića
Fr Ambre Miletića
Onešćukova
Mule Bjelavca
Neretva River
Musala Bridge
Rage Bitange
Bajatova
Osman Đikća
Huse Maslića
Brace Fejića
Adema Buća
Bulevar
Dr Mile Budaka
Dr Ante Starčevića
Aleske Šantića
Kneza Domagoja
Kralja Tvrtka
Kralja Tomislava
Biskupa Čule
Stara Ilička
Lacina (Laće)
Mladena Balorde
Hamida Vuka
Put Dvadesetdevete Hercegovačke
Braće Ćišića
Gojka Vukovića
Maršala Tita
Udarne Divizije
Čelebica
See Enlargement
To Airport (5km); Blagaj (11km); Podvelež (20km)
Kujundžiluk
Priecka Čaršija
Kalkhanska
Onešćukova
Gojka Vukovića
Maršala Tita
Šatića
0 100 m

16th-century-style building techniques and Tenelija stone from the original quarry. But significant quantities of ghostlike rubble remain, particularly along the old front-line area. And the psychological scars will take at least a generation to heal.

Orientation

The little Old Town hugs narrow pedestrian alleys around Stari Most. Kujundžiluk becomes Mala Tepa which becomes Braće Fejića, Mostar's mostly pedestrianised commercial street, paralleled by Maršala Tita, which runs one way northbound for its central section. Southbound traffic crosses the river and uses Bulvar or bypasses town altogether on the considerably higher M17.

Information

Almost any business accepts euros (at favourable 2:1 rates for small purchases) or even Croatian kuna (4:1). There are numerous ATMs down Braće Fejića and several banks around Trg Musala change money, but rates are better at the post office.

There's a left-luggage facility in the bus station; it's 2KM per item per day.

Barbados (Braće Fejića 26; per hr 2KM; 9am-11pm) Internet access; upstairs, enter by side door.

BuyBook (558810; Onešćukova 24; 9am-9pm Mon-Sat, 10am-6pm Sun) A useful array of English-language books, guidebooks and CDs.

Europa Club (Huse Maslića 10; per hr 1KM; 7am-midnight) Internet access; beneath a stationery shop.

Fortuna Travel (552197; www.fortuna.ba; Rade Bitange 34; 8am-4.30pm Mon-Fri, 9am-1pm Sat) Major local agency with sub-offices on Mala Tepa and at Hotel Ero. Arranges guided tours, accommodation and car hire.

GPO & Telephone Centre (Dr Ante Starčevića bb; 7am-7pm Mon-Sat, 8am-noon Sun) Poste restante; bureau de change.

Post office (Braće Fejića bb; 8am-8pm Mon-Sat) ATM outside.

Tourist information centre (397350; www.hercegovina.ba; Onešćukova bb; 9am-9pm) Useful but subject to sporadic closures out of season.

Sights

STARI MOST

The world-famous **Stari Most** (Old Bridge) is the indisputable visual focus that gives Mostar its unique magic. The bridge's pale stone magnificently throws back the golden glow of sunset or the tasteful night-time floodlighting. Numerous well-positioned cafes and restaurants, notably behind the **Tabahana** (an Ottoman-era enclosed courtyard) tempt you to admire the scene from a dozen varying angles. Directly east in a five-storey stone defence tower, the **Old Bridge Museum** (admission 5KM; 11am-2pm winter, 10am-6pm summer) has historical information boards and slow-moving 15-minute videos of the bridge's destruction/reconstruction. Directly west, the semicircular **Tara Gunpowder Tower** is now the 'club house' for Mostar's unique breed of divers. They'll plunge 21m off the bridge's parapet into the icy Neretva River below once their hustlers have collected enough photo money from impressionable tourists. There's an annual bridge-diving competition in July.

OLD TOWN

Delightful footpath-stairways linking quaint old houses and stone mills (now mostly used as restaurants) are layered down a mini-valley around the quaint little **Crooked Bridge** (Kriva Ćuprija). Above, pretty old shopfronts line Prječka Čaršija and **Kujundžiluk**, the picturesque cobbled alleys that join at Stari Most. Entered from a gated courtyard, the interior decor of the originally 1618 **Koski Mehmed Paša Mosque** (Mala Tepa 16; mosque/mosque & minaret 3/5KM; 9am-6pm) lacks finesse but climbing its claustrophobic minaret offers commanding old-town panoramas. The charmingly ramshackle **Bišćevića Ćošak** (Turkish House; 550677; www.biscevicakuca.bravehost.com; Bišćevića 13; admission 2KM; 9am-3pm Nov-Feb, 8am-8pm Mar-Oct) is a 350-year-old Ottoman-Bosnian home with a colourfully furnished interior sporting a selection of traditional metalwork and carved wooden furniture. For interesting comparisons also visit the grander 18th-/19th-century **Muslibegović House** (admission 3KM; 10am-8pm mid-Apr–mid-Oct), where you can spend the night (see p96) if you really like what you see, and the less-central, 16th-century **Kajtaz House** (550913; Gaše Ilića 21; admission 2KM; unpredictable).

BRAĆE FEJIĆA

Mostar's main shopping street leads up to **Trg Musala**, once the grand heart of Austro-Hungarian Mostar, passing the large, rebuilt 1557 **Karađozbeg Mosque** (Braće Fejića; mosque/minaret 3/2KM; 9am-6pm Sat-Thu) with its distinctive lead-roofed wooden verandah and four-domed madrassa annexe (now a clinic).

The early-17th-century **Roznamedži Ibrahimefendi Mosque** (Braće Fejića) was the only mosque to survive the 1993–95 shelling relatively unscathed. Its associated **madrassa** has just been rebuilt, the original having been demolished in 1960.

BAJATOVA

The little **Museum of Hercegovina** (☎ 551602; Bajatova 4; admission 1.50KM; 9am-2pm Mon-Fri, 10am-noon Sat) is housed in the former home of Džemal Bijedić, an ex-head of the Yugoslav government who died in mysterious circumstances in 1978. A well-paced 10-minute film features pre- and post-1992 bridge-diving plus war footage that shows the moment Stari Most was blown apart.

Stairway-lane Bajatova climbs on towards the M17 with an underpass leading towards the site of a once imposing **Orthodox church** almost totally destroyed by Croat shelling in 1993. From amidst the rubble there are superb city views.

WAR DAMAGE

Along the thought-provoking and intensely moving **former front line**, many buildings remain shockingly burned-out wrecks, including the once-stately 1896 **Gymnasium** (High School; Spanski Trg), now under slow reconstruction; the once-beautiful 1898 **Hotel Neretva** (www.cinv.co.ba/en/neretva.htm); and the 1920s **Music School**. The bombed-out nine-storey former **Ljubljanska Banka Tower** (Kralja Zvonimira bb) and the **gutted apartments** on Aleske Šantića seem even more heart-rendingly poignant being so comparatively modern.

Tours

With French- and English-speaking guides, **Almira Travel** (☎ /fax 551873; www.almira-travel.ba; Mala Tepa 9; 9am-5pm Mon-Sat, later in season) offers a vast range of imaginative tour options including wine-tasting tours. It can arrange guided tours, accommodation and car hire, and sells decent BiH–Croatia maps (€7).

Homestay owners can also organise tours, and the trips organised through Madja's Rooms (right) are particularly good value.

Sleeping

If you're stumped for accommodation the tourist information centre (opposite) and travel agencies can help you find a bed. Almira Travel (above) also offers rural village homestays. Note that mid-summer prices can rise 20% to 50%.

BUDGET

All places listed are effectively glorified homestays. None have full-time receptionists so calling ahead is wise, especially in low season when some are virtually dormant (and unheated). At such times you'll probably get a whole room for the dorm price. All but the Armin have shared bathrooms.

Hostel Nina (☎ 061-382743; www.hostelnina.ba; Čelebica 18; dm/s/d with shared bathroom €10/15/20;) Good-value homestay-style accommodation with three rooms per neat bathroom run by a very obliging English-speaking lady. Her overflow-annexe is out near the Rondo.

Pansion Oscar (☎ 061-823649; Oneščukova 33; per person €10-20, breakfast €5;) Six very presentable rooms, some with balconies, share two bathrooms in a truly unbeatable location near the Stari Most. Seid speaks good English, and washing machines are available (€5 per load), but there's no communal sitting area.

Vila Sara (☎ 555940; www.villasara-mostar.com; Sasarogina 4; dm/s/d/tr with shared bathroom 20/30/40/60KM) Crammed-together new beds with fresh duvets share a decent kitchen and cramped but piping-hot showers. Phone ahead in low season. Checkout is a yawny 10am.

Pansion Aldi (☎ 552185, 061-273457; www.pansion-aldi.com; Laćina 69a; dm/d/apt with shared bathroom €10/20/42) This no-frills hostel has 13 beds in five spacious if simple rooms (two air-conditioned) sharing a kitchenette and riverside garden terrace but only one shower and two squat toilets. It's unmarked but very handy for the bus station. No heating, limited English.

Majda's Rooms (☎ 061-382940; 1st fl, Franje Milicevica 39; dm/d with shared bathroom €11/24;) By sheer force of personality, and a very human awareness of traveller needs, sharp-witted Bata and his surreally delightful mother have turned a once-dreary tower-block apartment into Mostar's cult hostel. Most rooms are eight-bed dorms. Bata's regional tours are superb value.

Pansion Armin (☎ 552700; Kalkhanska 3; s/d from €15/30) Excellent-value en suite rooms in a bright-yellow new house with trellis frontage facing the eerie ruin of a bombed-out school.

MIDRANGE & TOP END

Apartments Konak (☎ 551105; http://apartmani-konak.com/; Maršala Tita 125; d/tr/q €30/45/60;) Good-value homely apartments, central and fairly well set back from the noisy main road up a little stairway.

BOSNIA & HERCEGOVINA

Motel Deny (☎ 578317; www.mdmostar.com; Kapetanovina 1; s/d 53/86KM, high season 63/106;) This modern mini-hotel overlooks the mill area of the Old Town and has a charming lobby decked out with flickering candles. Rooms are slightly plain in comparison but well furnished and clean.

Pansion Emen (☎ 581120, 061-848734; www.motel-emen.com; Oneščukova 32; ; s/d/tr from €30/50/60;) More a fashionable mini-hotel than a pansion, the Emen is one of old Mostar's most prized addresses, with understated chic and a remarkably reasonable price tag. It features wonderful sitting areas, two shared internet computers and angular bath fittings straight from a design magazine.

Kriva Ćuprija (☎ 550953; www.motel-mostar.ba; s/d/apt from €30/55/65;) Soothe yourself with the sounds of gushing streams in new, impeccably furnished (if not necessarily large) rooms ranged above this charming stone mill-house restaurant overlooking the Crooked Bridge. Don't be palmed off to Kriva Ćuprija 2, a new annexe on the main road across Lučki Bridge.

our pick **Muslibegović House** (☎ 551379; Osman Đikća 41; www.muslibegovichouse.com; s/d €40/70;) In summer tourists pay to visit this superbly restored 18th-century Ottoman courtyard house (p94). But it's simultaneously an extremely convivial 15-room homestay-hotel. Room sizes and styles vary significantly, mixing excellent modern bathrooms with elements of traditional Bosnian-Turkish design. Room 2 is especially atmospheric.

Hotel Pellegrino (☎ 061-480784; Faladjica 1c; www.hotel-pellegrino.ba; s/d/tr 90/130/150KM;) Above a surprisingly spacious neo-Tuscan restaurant/lounge, expansive rooms have excellent anti-allergenic bedding and kitchenette. Each room has its own oddity, be it a giant black lacquer vase, a bundle-of-twigs lamp or a whole-cow mat.

Hotel Old Town (☎ 558877; www.oldtown.ba; Onešvćukova 30; d/tr/ste from €90/120/150) This delightful supercentral boutique hotel is full of specially designed handmade furniture, uses energy-saving waste-burning furnaces for water-heating and has ecofriendly air-circulation to save on air-conditioning wastage.

Hotel Ero (☎ 386777; www.ero.ba; Dr Ante Starčevića bb; s/d/apt 99/166/215KM;) The 165 solidly renovated rooms have balconies and peachy-cream new decor, though rickety doors and abandoned floor-lady areas faintly recall its previous Tito-era incarnation.

Hotel Bevanda (☎ 332332; www.hotelbevanda.com; Stara Ilićka 1; s/d/ste 199/255/425KM;) The over-shiny little atrium does little to support the Bevanda's illusions of grandeur, though rooms are perfectly comfortable and the very plush suites come with a waiting decanter of brandy.

Eating

Cafes and restaurants with divine views of the river cluster along the western riverbank near Stari Most. Although unapologetically tourist-oriented, their meal prices are only a *maraka* or two more than any ordinary dive, though wine can get comparatively costly.

Šadrvan (☎ 579057; Jusovina 11; dishes 6-17KM) On a quaint corner where the pedestrian lane from Stari Most divides, this appealing, gently upmarket restaurant has tables set around a trickling fountain made of old Turkish-style metalwork, shaded by the spreading tentacles of a kiwi-fruit vine. The menu covers all Bosnian bases. Several other streamside mill-restaurants nearby are every bit as good: simply pick the atmosphere that suits.

Restaurant Bella Vista (☎ 061-656421; Tabahana; pizzas 7-10KM, mains 7-17KM) Along with the almost indistinguishable Restaurants Babilon and Teatr next door, the Bella Vista has stupendous terrace views across the river to the Old Town and Stari Most. The food is less impressive than the views, but some of the set 'tourist menus' are excellent value.

ABC (☎ 194656; Braće Fejića 45; pizza & pasta 6-9KM, mains 12-15KM; 8am-11pm Mon-Sat, noon-11pm Sun) Downstairs is Mostar's most popular cake shop and a narrow see-and-be-seen pavement cafe. Upstairs is a relaxed pastel-toned Italian restaurant. Pizzas are rather bready but the plate-lickingly creamy Aurora tortellini comes with an extra bucketful of parmesan.

Also recommended:

Urban Grill (www.urbangrill.ba; Mala Tepa; ćevapi 3.50-5.50KM) Can *ćevapi* ever be cool? They think so here.

Grill Centar (Braće Fejića 13; grills 5KM; 8am-11pm) Unsophisticated *ćevadžinica* attached to an old Bosnian courtyard house.

MM Restaurant (Mostarskog Bataljona 11; meals 6-12KM; 8am-10pm Mon-Sat) Easy to use buffet-style feeding station.

For self-caterers, **Mercur Supermarket** (Braće Fejića 51; 7am-10pm) is a sizeable, central grocery store, while **Dan-i-Noć** (Mostarskog Bataljona 8; 24hr) is an all-night bakery.

Some of the gnarled characters working at **Tepa market** (Braće Fejića bb; 6.30am-2pm), a modest fruit-and-veg market, look like they've been here for centuries. Great views from the parapet behind.

Drinking

Ali Baba Bar (Kujundžiluk; summer only) Remarkable, seasonal bar-club tucked into the cliff-face that looms directly above Kujundžiluk.

our pick **OKC Abrašević** (561107; www.okcabrasevic.org; Alekse Šantića 25; beer 2KM; variable) This uncompromising yet understatedly intellectual bar offers Mostar's most vibrantly alternative 'scene', and has an attached venue for offbeat gigs. You'll need the guts to seek it out, as it's hidden away between the prison and the city's most daunting burnt-out war ruins.

Bijeli Bar (Stari Most 2; coffee 2KM, beer 4KM; 7am-11pm) The ubercool main bar zaps you with a wicked white-on-white Clockwork Orange decor. Meanwhile, around the corner the same bar owns an utterly spectacular perch-terrace from which the old bridge and towers appear from altogether new angles. The latter is entered from Maršala Tita, through a wrought-iron gate marked Atelje Novalić: cross the Japanese-style garden and climb the stone roof-steps.

Košćela (Kujundžiluk; coffee 2KM; 10am-7pm) Bridge views are almost as perfect as from the Bijeli Bar terrace and Bosnian coffee (2KM) comes in full traditional copper regalia, complete with Turkish delight. Light grill-meals are served but there's no alcohol.

Caffe Marshall (Oneščukova bb; beer 3KM; 8am-midnight) Minuscule but appealing box-bar draped with musical instruments.

Villa Neretva (Trg Musala; 7am-11pm) This spacious, modern cafe attracts a calm, literate crowd, while the attached Monkey Bar has a livelier music vibe that pumps harder as the evening progresses.

Coco Loco Bar (Kralja Zvonimira bb; 8am-late) With minimal decor and wafting, questionable vapours, this place is nonetheless packed to the gunnels at weekends for deafening DJ-parties.

Entertainment

Club Oxygen (512244; www.biosphere.ba/biosfere-stranice-oxigen-en.html; Braće Fejića bb; variable) Oxygen has movie nights, DJ-discos and Mostar's top live gigs. In summer its rooftop SkyBar takes over as the place to party.

Dom Kultura Herceg Stjepan Kosaća (323501; Rondo; variable) Large cultural centre offering diverse shows, concerts and exhibitions. Visiting opera, ballet and theatre companies from Croatia show up occasionally.

OKC Abrašević (left) and the **Pavarotti Music Centre** (550750; Maršala Tita 179) also host occasional concerts.

Shopping

The stone-roofed shop-houses of Kujundžiluk throw open metal shutters to sell agreeably colourful, inexpensive if somewhat trashy Turkish souvenirs from amulets to glittery velveteen slippers (€7), pashmina-style wraps (from €5), fezzes (€5), *boncuk* (evil-eye) pendants and Russian-style nested dolls. Many stalls sell pens fashioned from old bullets, while master coppersmith **Ismet Kurt** (550017; Kujundžiluk 5) hammers old mortar-shell casings into works of art while you watch.

Getting There & Away

AIR

Mostar airport (OMO; 350992) is 6km south of town off the Čapljina road. **BH Airlines** (551820; Braće Fejića 45; 9am-5pm Mon-Fri) flies to İstanbul on Sunday mornings for €180.

BUS

From the main **bus station** (552025; Trg Ivana Krndelja), tickets for most services are pre-sold through **Autoprevoz-bus** (551900). See p98 for details of services.

Yellow **Mostar Bus** (552250; www.mostarbus.ba/linije.asp) services to Blagaj and Podvelež depart from opposite the station and also pick up from the Lučki Most stop.

For Međugorje (4KM, 45 minutes) buses pick up outside the Bevanda Hotel at 6.30am, 11.30am, 1.10pm, 2.30pm, 3.30pm, 6.10pm and 7.30pm on weekdays. The 6.30am, 11.30am, 6.10pm and 7.30pm services operate on Saturdays, and only the 7.30pm bus runs on Sundays.

CAR

Vehicle rentals are available at travel agencies, from **Helax** (382114; Hotel Ero, Dr Ante Starčevića bb; from 490KM per week; 8am-5pm Mon-Fri, 8am-noon Sat) and **MaxLine** (551525; www.maxline.ba; Station Sq; from €45/245 per day/week; 8am-6pm Mon-Fri, 9am-3pm Sat).

BUSES FROM MOSTAR

Destination	Price (KM)	Duration (hr)	Departures
Banja Luka (via Jajce)	25	6	1.30pm
Belgrade	48	11	7.30pm
Čapljina	6	40min	twice-hourly weekdays, only six daily Sun
Dubrovnik	27	3½	7am, 10.15am & 2.30pm
Sarajevo	16	2½-3	hourly 6am-3pm plus 6.15pm & 8.30pm
Split	25	4½	9.30am, 10.45am, 12.50pm, 5.30pm & midnight
Stolac	4	1	6.15am, 3.30pm & 8.15pm
Tešanj	34	6	5.30pm
Trebinje (via Nevesinje)	19	3	5.30pm
Trebinje (via Stolac)	19	3	6.15am & 3.30pm
Visoko	20	3¾	6.30pm
Zagreb	43	9½	9am

TRAIN

The **train station** (☎ 552198) is beside the bus station. Two daily services run to Sarajevo (9.90KM, 2¾ hours) at 7.38am and 6.40pm, puffing alongside fish farms in the pea-green Neretva River's magnificent dammed gorge before struggling up a series of switchbacks behind Konjic to reach Sarajevo after 65 tunnels.

AROUND MOSTAR

By joining a tour or sharing a hire-car you can combine into a single day visits to Blagaj, Počitelj, Međugorje and the brilliant but awkward-to-reach Kravice Waterfalls. Maybe visit a winery or two en route: look for the white-on-brown Vinska Cesta road-signs or consult www.wine route.ba.

Blagaj

☎ 036 / pop 4000

Pretty Blagaj village culminates at the very picturesque, half-timbered **Tekija** (Dervish monastery; ☎ 573221; admission 3KM; ⏲ 8am-10pm), whose charmingly wobbly carved wooden interior entombs two Tajik 15th-century dervishes. Outside, the green Buna River gushes out of a gaping cave backed by soaring cliffs topped way above by the **Herceg Stjepan Fortress** ruins.

Walking to the Tekija takes 10 minutes from the seasonal **tourist information booth** (⏲ 10am-7pm in season), passing the delightful **Oriental House** (Velagomed, Velagic House; ☎ 572712; www.velagomed.ba; Velagicevina bb; admission 2KM; ⏲ 10am-7pm), an artistically appointed 18th-century Ottoman ensemble with fabulous island-meadow gardens and even a couple of simple rooms to rent (double €30). Near the 1892 octagonal **Sultan Sulejman Mosque**, the friendly unmarked **Kayan Pansion** (☎ 572299; nevresakajan@yahoo.com; tw €20) offers well-kept homestay rooms and Merima (☎ 061-346969) speaks English.

Mostar Bus lines 10, 11 and 12 run patchily to or near Blagaj (1.80KM, 30 minutes), but check www.mostarbus.ba/linije.asp for the frequently changing schedule. There's no public transport from Blagaj to Podvelež or Počitelj.

Međugorje

☎ 036 / pop 4300

Since the Holy Virgin spoke to six local teenagers on 24 June 1981, **Međugorje** (www.medjugorje.hr) has been transformed from poor winemaking backwater to BiH's pilgrim central. The odd blend of honest faith and cash-in tackiness is reminiscent of Lourdes (France) or Fatima (Portugal). Pilgrim numbers just keep growing, even though the Catholic Church has not officially acknowledged the visions' legitimacy.

There are countless hotels and *pansions*, but for many nonpilgrims a two-hour visit often proves plenty long enough to get the idea. The town's focus is double-towered 1969 **St James' Church** (Župna Crkva), 200m behind which is the mesmerising **Resurrected Saviour** (Uskrsli Spasitej). This masterpiece of Modernisme sculpture shows a gaunt 5m-tall metallic Christ standing crucified yet cross-less, his manhood wrapped in scripture. Erected in 1998, the statue 'miraculously' weeps a colourless liquid from its right knee, with pilgrims queuing to dab a drop of this holy fluid onto specially inscribed pads.

A 3km (5KM) taxi ride away is **Podbrdo** village from which streams of faithful climb **Brdo Ukazanja** (Apparition Hill) to a white statue of the Virgin Mary at the site of the original 1981 visions. The red-earth paths are studded with sharp stones and some pilgrims make the 15-minute walk barefoot in deliberately painful acts of penitence.

Download artist's-eye town maps from the **tourist association** (www.tel.net.ba/tzm-medjugorje/1%20karta100.jpg).

Počitelj

☎ 036 / pop 350

This stepped Ottoman-era fortress village is one of the most picture-perfect architectural ensembles in BiH. Cupped in a steep rocky amphitheatre, it was systematically despoiled in the 1990s conflicts but its finest 16th-century buildings are now rebuilt, including the **Šišman Ibrahim Madrassa**, the 1563 **Hadži Alijna Mosque** and the 16m **tower** (Sahat Kula). The upper village culminates in the still part-ruined **Gavrakapetan Tower**.

There's a basic cafe but no accommodation. Počitelj is right beside the main Split–Mostar road, 5km north of Čapljina. Mostar–Split and Mostar–Čapljina buses pass by, but southbound only the latter (roughly hourly on weekdays) will usually accept Počitelj-bound passengers. In summer arrive early to avoid the heat and the Croatian tour groups.

Kravice Waterfalls

In spring this stunning mini-Niagara of **25m cascades** pounds itself into a dramatic, steamy fury. In summer the falls themselves are less impressive but surrounding pools become shallow enough for swimming. The site is 4km down a dead-end road that turns off the Čapljina–Ljubuški road at km42.5. There's no public transport.

NEUM

Driving between Split and Dubrovnik, don't forget your passport, as you'll pass through BiH's tiny toe-hold of Adriatic coastline. The one resort here, **Neum** (www.neum.ba), is crammed with concrete apartment-hotels for holidaying locals and the water isn't as inviting as in parts of neighbouring Croatia. For most travellers the brief refreshment break taken on the Neum bypass by Split–Dubrovnik buses is ample.

STOLAC

☎ 036 / pop 12,000

Guarding an impressive craggy canyon, the attractive castle town of Stolac was the site of Roman Diluntum (3rd century AD), then a prominent 15th-century citadel. Stolac suffered serious conflict in 1993 but the displaced population has returned and reconstruction of the shattered town continues apace. From the bus station, cross the river to the pretty main street, Hrvatske-Brante (aka Ada), which arcs around the base of overgrown **Vidoški Grad** (the castle hill). After 600m in the town centre, the fine 1735 **Šarić House** faces memorable mural-fronted **Čaršija Mosque**, rebuilt to look just like the 1519 original. Upstream are several delightfully picturesque if partly ruined 17th-century stone **mill-races**. Beside the Mostar road 3km west of Stolac, **Radimlja Necropolis** is a famous if somewhat disappointing collection of around 110 *stećci* grave-markers (see p76). Stolac's only hotel, **Villa Ragusa** (☎ 853700; s/d/tr 35/70/105KM), offers worn if mostly clean rooms across a small bridge from the town centre.

Weekday buses run approximately hourly to Čapljina (5KM, 45 minutes, last departure at 5pm), with five services on Saturdays and none on Sunday. Weekdays only, buses run to Mostar at 6.30am and 12.30pm. Mostar–Trebinje buses pass through twice daily but oddly bypass Stolac's bus station.

EASTERN BOSNIA & HERCEGOVINA

To get quickly yet relatively easily off the main tourist trail, try linking Sarajevo or Mostar to Dubrovnik via Trenbinje, possibly visiting the gorgeous Sujeska National Park. You'll pass through the 'other half' of BiH, the Republika Srpska, where's it's fascinating to hear about the nation's traumas from the 'other side'.

TREBINJE ТРЕБИЊЕ

☎ 059 / pop 36,000

A beguiling quick stop between Dubrovnik (28km) and Višegrad (or Mostar), Trebinje has a small, walled **Old Town** (Stari Grad) where inviting, unpretentious cafes offer a fascinating opportunity to meet friendly local residents and hear Serb viewpoints on divisive recent history. Old-town ramparts

BOSNIA & HERCEGOVINA

back onto the riverside near a 19th-century former Austro-Hungarian barracks which now houses the eclectic **Hercegovina Museum** (Музеј Херцеговине; ☎ 271060; Stari Grad 59; admission 1KM; ⌚ 8.30am-2pm). Lovely stone-flagged **Trg Svobode** is ringed with chestnut trees, street cafes and old buildings with wrought-iron overhangs. It's reminiscent of rural France and hosts a lively Saturday market.

Trebinje's 1574 **Arslanagić Bridge** (Perovića Most) is a unique, double-backed structure sadly let down by the unexotic suburban location (700m northeast of Hotel Leotar) to which it was moved in the 1970s.

For phenomenal views take the 2km winding lane leading east of Motel Etage to hilltop **Hercegovacka Gracanica**, where the compact but eye-catching **Presvete Bogorodice Church** was erected in 2000 to rehouse the bones of local hero Jovan Dučić. Its design is based on the 1321 Gračanica monastery in Kosovo, a building that's symbolically sacred to many Serbs.

For town maps visit www.trebinje.info/trebinje/mape or the **tourist office** (☎ 273122; www.trebinjeturizam.com; Preobraženska 10; ⌚ 8am-3pm Mon-Fri). The latter is hidden in an unlikely apartment building behind the very central **Balkan Investment Bank** (☎ Preobraženska 6; ⌚ 8am-4pm Mon-Fri), which changes money and has an ATM.

Sleeping

Hotel Leotar (☎ 261086; www.hotelleotar.com; Obala Luke Vukalovića bb; old s/d 51.50/83KM, deluxe 81.50/113KM) This growling four-storey socialist-era remnant faces the old-town ramparts across the river. So far 35 deluxe rooms have been attractively upgraded, but twice that many are sorry old affairs with all the glamour of a 1960s hospital ward.

Motel Etage (☎ 261443; Dušanova 9; s/d/tr incl breakfast €30/45/55) Bright, colourful but not overlarge rooms with a decent buffet breakfast included. Cross the river east of the tourist office then turn left at the T-junction.

Motel Viv (☎ 273500; www.hotelviv-trebinje.com; Dušanova 11; s/d/tr 60/90/120KM) Slightly more prone to road noise, this joint is marginally smarter than its next-door neighbour Motel Etage.

Hotel Platani (☎ 225134; www.hotelplatani.com; Trg Svobode; s/d/tr 79/115/135KM; ⌘) Perfectly located above the town's top street-cafe, this cosy 12-room hotel is gently upmarket but the tiny reception can take a bit of finding.

Eating & Drinking

Pizza Castello (☎ 223192; Trg Travunije 3; pizzas 6.50-7.50KM; ⌚ 7.30am-midnight) Castello's three-table terrace is great for people-watching. Jovial host Snezhan speaks great English and the thin-crust pizza is excellent. Several other relatively downmarket eateries share this same Old Town square.

Galerija Veritas (Stari Grad 17; beer 2.50KM; ⌚ 9am-11pm) This eccentric brick-domed cavern cafe is dotted with antique TV sets. Check out the beamed upper level. It's hidden on an alley between the museum and Kameni Bridge.

Azzovo (Stari Grad 114; beer 2KM; ⌚ 8am-11pm Mon-Sat, 10am-11pm Sun) Cosy, Old Town blues-oriented bar with ceilings of bamboo and vine-stems. Nearby several others have similarly great summer terraces, while Kafe Serbia and Bajica Caffe are built right into the old-town ramparts.

Getting There & Away

Since 2007, the '**bus station**' (Vojvode Stepe Stepanovića) is an unmarked parking area west of the centre through the park behind large Saborna church.

BUSES FROM TRENBINJE

Destination	Price (KM)	Duration (hr)	Departures
Belgrade (via Foča & Višegrad)	40	11	8am & 6pm
Dubrovnik	5	¾	10am Mon-Sat (returns at 1.30pm)
Herceg Novi (via Risan)	13	1¾	6am
Ljubinje	9	1½	2.10pm Mon-Fri, 7pm daily
Mostar (via Nevesinje)			10am
Mostar (via Stolac)	19	3	6.15am & 2.30pm
Pale (via Foča)	22	4½	5am
Podgorica (via Nikšič)	20	3½	8.30am, 3pm & 4.30pm
Sarajevo (via Foča)	20	4	5am, 7.30.am &11am

TREBINJE TO VIŠEGRAD

Trebinje–Belgrade and Trebinje–Sarajevo buses pass through the glorious **Sutjeska National Park** (www.npsutjeska.srbinje.net in Bosnian), where magnificent wooded canyon-lands open out near an impressively vast concrete **Partizans' Memorial** commemorating the classic WWII battle of **Tjentište**. Further north, war-battered **Foča** is a centre for world-class **rafting** on the Tara River that cascades out of Europe's deepest canyon (across the Montenegrin border) then thunders over 21 rapids (class III to class IV in summer, class IV to class V in April). Foča's very professional extreme sports outfit **Encijan** (☎ 211220; www.pkencijan.com; Kraljapetra-I 1; 9am-5pm) can organise everything.

VIŠEGRAD ВИШЕГРАД

☎ 058 / pop 20,000

Višegrad is internationally famous for its 10-arch 1571 **Mehmet Paša Sokolović Bridge** (www.pbase.com/vmarinkovic/the_bridge_on_the_drina) immortalised in Andrić's classic *Bridge on the Drina*. In early July there's a very popular Mostar-style **bridge-diving competition** from this Unesco World Heritage Site. The town is otherwise architecturally unexotic, but it's set between some of Bosnia's most impressive river canyons. The ultrahelpful **tourist office** (☎ 620821; www.visegradturizam.com; Užičkog 11; 8am-3pm Mon-Fri) operates a summer-only information kiosk right by the south end of the old bridge. Its website has a town map.

The central, garishly coloured **Hotel Višegrad** (☎ 620378) is under reconstruction. Until it reopens, the best accommodation is **Motel Aura** (☎ 631021; auravgd@teol.net; Kraljapetpui bb; s/d from 45/65KM) behind the AutoGas LPG station, 1km northeast of the old bridge. Adequate but lacking style, **Motel Okuka** (☎ 065-998761; s/d/tr 50/80/120KM) is a similar distance upstream but on the other bank. Many longer-distance buses conveniently stop outside. Useful departures include Sarajevo (8am), Mostar (4am), Foča (7am) and Trebinje (10am) via Foča and Sutjeska National Park. Buses to Belgrade (9.30am and 1.30pm) and to Užice (7.30am, 11.30am and 6pm) pass the historic **Dobrun Monastery** (11km east) and Mokra Gora (Serbia). From 2009 a newly reconstructed narrow-gauge railway should start operating from Dobrun to Mokra Gora, connecting with Serbia's popular **Šargan 8 tourist train** (www.zeleznicesrbije.com). The Dobrun–Višegrad section is slated to open in 2010.

CENTRAL & WESTERN BOSNIA

West of Sarajevo lies a series of gently historic towns, green wooded hills, rocky crags and dramatic rafting canyons. The area offers ample opportunities for exploration and adrenaline-rush activities.

VISOKO

☎ 032 / pop 17,000

Once the capital of medieval Bosnia and the spiritual centre of the controversial Bosnian Church, this unremarkable leather-tanning town had been largely forgotten in the 20th century. Then, Bosnian archaeologist Semir Osmanagic hatched a bold theory that Visoko's 250m high Visočica Hill is in fact the **World's Greatest Pyramid** (Sun Pyramid; www.piramidasunca.ba), built around 12,000 years ago by a long disappeared superculture. Initial **archaeological excavations** (admission free) have revealed what seem to be 'paving' and 'tunnel entrances' and tourists have flocked here to take a look. The forested hill does indeed have a remarkably perfect pyramidal shape when viewed from some angles. However, a long ridge at the back rather spoils the idea.

The site is 15 minutes' walk from Visoko bus station. Cross the river towards the Motel Piramida-Sunca tower, turn immediately left down Visoko's relatively attractive main street, passing the **museum** (Alije Izetbegovića 29), **tourist office** (☎ 733189; Alije Izetbegovića 29; 9am-4pm Mon-Fri) and **post office** (Čaršijska 75; 8am-8pm Mon-Fri, 8am-3pm Sat). Then after the bazaar merge left into Tvrtka/Mule Hodžić. Opposite Mule Hodžić 25 climb steeply up winding Pertac, then turn left at the top.

Sleeping & Eating

Motel Piramida-Sunca (☎ 731460; www.motelpiramidasunca.co.ba; 6th fl, Musala 1; s/d/tr/q 50/80/100/120KM;) Good, unfussy new rooms aren't nearly as wacky as you'd expect from the triangular key-fobs, crazy nozzle lamps and acid-trip colours in the corridors.

our pick **Hotel Centar** (☎ 730030; www.hotelcentar.ba; Alaudina 1; d/apt 156/206KM;) This design-book, high-fashion boutique hotel has dark-wood

BOSNIA & HERCEGOVINA

interiors, top quality linens and an excellent, city-centre location above Volksbank (Alije Izetbegovića 37). Apartment 301 has pyramid views and the remarkable basement restaurant is designed like an old Bosnian village courtyard.

Caffe Fashion (Čaršijska 14; coffee 1KM, beer 2.50KM; 7am-10pm) Curious little multilevel cafe near the bazaar with unexplained stove-doors, token beams and a ribbon-wrapped piano.

Getting There & Away

Buses stop here twice hourly until 8.30pm, running between Sarajevo (5.50KM, 50 minutes) and Kakanj (4.40KM, 35 minutes). For Travnik (10.50KM, 1¼ hours) buses leave at 8.10am, 9.50am, 2.10pm, 4.10pm and 10.30pm, or change in Zenica (14 buses on weekdays).

TRAVNIK

☎ 030 / pop 27,500

Once the seat of Bosnia's Turkish viziers (Ottoman governors), Travnik's sizeable castle ruin and patchily attractive old architecture makes it a good half-day stop between Sarajevo and Jajce. The town wiggles along the deep Lavša Valley, the M5 highway roughly paralleled by main street Bosanska. From the **bus station** (☎ 792761), west of the centre, exit through the yellow fencing and walk past the **post office** (☎ 547102; Prnjavor) to emerge on Bosanska near the Lipa Hotel. Here, the **Viziers' turbe** is the best known of several Travnik tombs. Turn right for the **tourist office** (☎ 511588; www.tzsbk.com; Bosanska 75; 8am-4pm Mon-Fri). Or turn left and walk 400m east to reach the mural-fronted **Many Coloured Mosque** (Bosanska 203), remarkable for the *bezistan* (mini-bazaar) built into the arches beneath the main prayerhouse.

Readers who enjoyed *Bosnian Chronicle* should visit the **Ivo Andrić museum** (☎ 518140; Zenjak 19; admission 2KM; 10.30am-5pm Thu-Tue) in an old-style house designed to simulate Andrić's birthplace. Labels are in Bosnian but the enthusiastic curator speaks English. The museum is one block off Bosanska (between 171 and 169). If it's locked, request the key from the somewhat stuffy **Regional Museum** (Zavičajni Muzej Travnik; ☎ 518140; adult/child 1.50/1KM; 9am-3pm Mon-Fri, 10am-2pm Sat & Sun) opposite Bosanska 145.

Using a pedestrian underpass beneath the M5, climb up Varoš to reach the impressive **medieval castle ruins** (Stari Grad; admission 2KM; 9am-6pm Oct-Apr, 8am-8pm May-Sep) then descend further east at **Plava Voda** (Blue Water), where a rushing mountain stream is criss-crossed by small stone bridges and overlooked by several delightful restaurants.

Sleeping

Central hotels suffer somewhat from road noise. There are six other motels within 10km along the eastbound M5.

Motel Aba (☎ 511462; www.aba.ba; Šumeća 166a; s/d/tr/q 30/40/50/70KM) Central Travnik's best yet cheapest option offers highly acceptable, unfussy en suite rooms at excellent prices; breakfast costs 10KM. But it's not really a motel: getting a car to this area near Plava Voda can prove modestly challenging given the one-way system.

Hotel Lipa (☎ 511604; Lažajeva 116; s/d 52/84KM) Entering from Bosanska, the Lipa's zinc-wrap retro-trendy cafe creates a misleadingly hip image. In fact its renovated rooms are uninspired and the corridors dingy. But at least the showers are good and the location's handy.

Motel Consul (☎ 514195; www.consultravnik.20fr.com; s/d 52/84KM) With a private orchard, sepia photos of Old Travnik, big double beds and an art-filled dining-room, this peaceful new eight-room retreat is the town's most comfortable option. However it's inconveniently situated 1.5km west of the centre, overlooking the industrial zone.

CASTLE CAPERS

Dotted among the faceless industrial towns of virtually untouristed north-eastern Bosnia are several very photogenic medieval castle ruins.

- **Srebrenik** Truly dramatic crag-top setting 6km east of Srebrenik town.
- **Vranduk** Small ruins set in BiH's most idyllic castle village, around 10km north of Zenica.
- **Tešanj** Powerful ruins rise above a loveable Old Town square.
- **Doboj** The city is an ugly railway junction but the castle hosts costumed festivals and there's a great little cafe-tower.
- **Gradačac** Dominating Gradačac town centre, the partly reconstructed castle now hosts a unique hotel (www.zebed.com.ba).

BUSES FROM TRAVNIK

Destination	Price (KM)	Duration (hr)	Departures
Bihać	28-31	6	6.50am, 9.30am, 3.30pm, 4.20pm & 11.50pm
Guča Gora	2.30	30min	approx hourly, weekdays only (Maline bus)
Jajce	8-12	1½	nine daily
Sarajevo	15	2	hourly in morning, plus 3.40pm, 6.20pm & 7.10pm
Split	28-36	4½	up to six daily via Bugojno
Vranduk	7.50	1¼	8.40am, noon or 3.30pm (Tuzla bus)
Zenica	4.50-7	1	25 daily

Eating

Along Bosanska self-caterers will find supermarkets, bakeries, a decent market and several shops selling Travnik's trademark white cheese.

Ćevabdžinica Asko (ćevapi 3.50-6KM; ⌚ 7am-10pm) Just 30m south of the Many Coloured Mosque, Asko's streamside terrace is the best central cheapy for warm sitting-out evenings.

Restaurant Divan (☎ 061-786471; Zenjak 19; meals 5-17KM; ⌚ 8am-11pm) Dine on fish, squid or Bosnian grills around the piano in thick-walled, timber-beamed rooms beneath the Ivo Andrić museum.

Konoba Plava Voda (☎ 512171; Šumeće bb; meals 5.50-12KM) Three restaurants, all called Plava Voda, each have lovely summer terraces overlooking the attractive springs area.

Getting There & Away

Travnik's **bus station** (☎ 792761) is off Sehida (the M5 highway), set back one block behind Bosanska. For bus services, see above.

AROUND TRAVNIK

Three-lift ski resort **Vlašić** (www.babanovac.net; ski passes 26KM; ⌚ lifts 9am-4pm in season) at **Babanovac Village** has a wide selection of accommodation. The homely **Hotel Central** (☎ 540165; www.hotel-central-vlasic.net; s/d 35/70KM, peak season 70/140KM), facing the ski jump, is rare for not demanding five-day minimum stays. Buses from Travnik (4KM, 40 minutes) leave at 10am and 3.10pm in summer, or at 7.15am, 11.30am and 6pm in winter, returning around 90 minutes later.

JAJCE

☎ 030 / pop 30,000

Above an impressive waterfall, Jajce's fortified Old Town climbs a steep rocky knoll to the powerful, ruined castle where Bosnia's medieval kings were once crowned. The surrounding array of glorious mountains, lakes and canyons make Jajce a great exploration base, while curious catacombs and a Mithraic temple will intrigue fans of mysterious 'lost' religions.

Information

Several central, moneychanging banks also have ATMs.

Eko Kuća (Eco House; ☎ 654100; www.plivatourism.ba; Pijavice bb; ⌚ 8am-3pm Mon-Fri, 8am-1pm Sat) Regional ecotourism and rural self-help group selling local biological produce.

Kantonal tourist office (1st fl, Sadije Softića 1; ⌚ 8am-3pm Mon-Fri, 8am-1pm Sat) Within the historic Omirbegović House. Brochures but minimal English spoken.

Network Internet (Trg Jajačkih Branitelja; per hr 1.50KM; ⌚ 9am-midnight)

Tourist information kiosk (☎ 065-323782; ⌚ 9am-8pm with various breaks May-Sep) Helpful Alida arranges homestay accommodation and has the key for closed attractions.

Sights

Old-town Jajce's attractions can be seen in a two-hour ramble, assuming you can locate the sites' various key-holders: the tourist booth can help.

CATACOMBS

Built around 1400, the **catacombs** (Svetog Luke bb; admission 1KM) are unique for their boldly sculpted interior featuring a sun and crescent moon design considered one of the best surviving memorials to the independent Bosnian Church. Tito is said to have hidden here during 1943 and the small, half-lit subterranean space is very atmospheric. Request the key from the little cafe/hairdresser opposite, built onto the side of the sturdy round **Bear Tower** (Medvjed Kula).

Other attractive buildings on Svetog Luke (Ademovića) include an 1880 **schoolhouse** and the fine, 15th-century campanile **Tower of St Luke**.

FORTRESS

From the Tower of St Luke, a stairway leads past the small **Dizdar Mosque** (Women's Mosque) to the stone **fortress entry portal** of the sturdy main **fortress** (Tvrđava; admission 1KM), whose ramparts enclose mostly bard grass but offer sweeping views of surrounding valleys and crags. Get the key from Mediha at the second house on the right before the entry portal.

From the **Velika Tabija** (Gornja Mahala) descend a further section of citadel wall to the **Midway Tower** (Mala Tabija) facing the attractively renovated **Old Kršlak House**.

WATERFALLS

Jajce's impressive 21m-high **waterfalls** mark the confluence of the Pliva and Vrbas Rivers. For the classic tourist-brochure-view photo, cross the big Vrbas bridge and turn left on the Banja Luka road. After walking 500m, at the third lay-by on the left climb over the low crash-barrier and double back 150m down a footpath through the pine-woods to the viewpoint.

AVNOJ MUSEUM

In 1943 the second congress of AVNOJ (Antifascist Council of the People's Liberation of Yugoslavia) formulated Yugoslavia's post-war socialist constitution in a building that's now the small **AVNOJ-a Museum** (☎ 657712; admission 2KM; 🕒 8am-6pm). Peep in to see a large brooding statue of partisan Tito in gold-painted polystyrene.

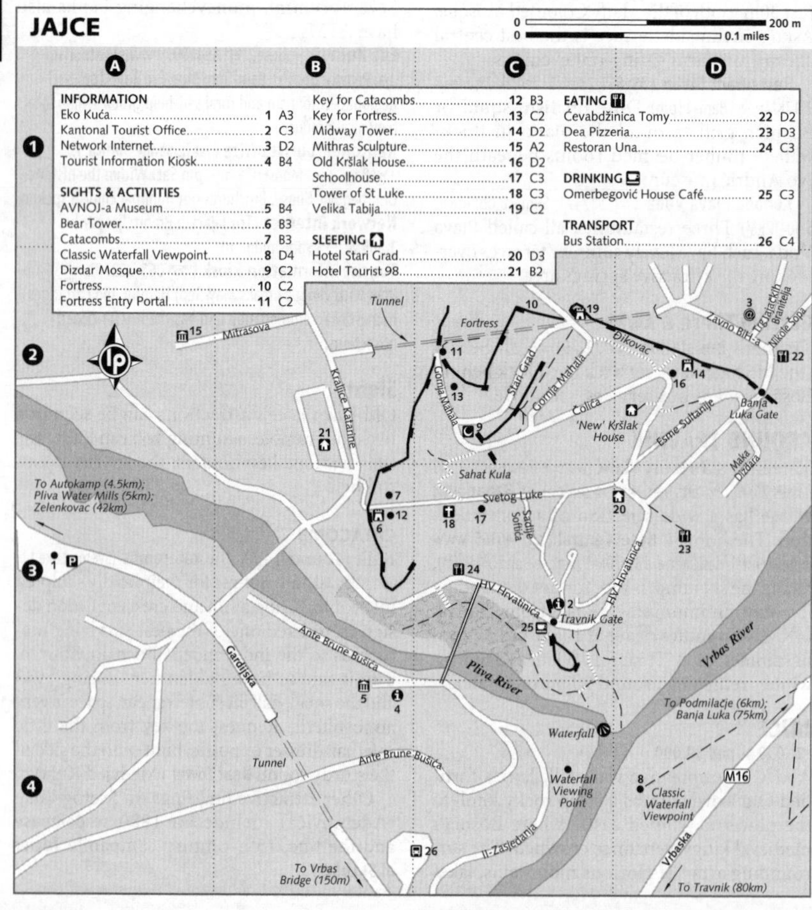

BUSES FROM JAJCE

Destination	Price (KM)	Duration (hr)	Departures
Banja Luka	9.50	1½	7.30am, 9.15am, 1pm, 4.40pm & 5.30pm
Bihać	23.50	3½	8.30am, 11.15am, 12.40pm & 5.25pm
Jezero	2.50	¼	nine daily, last return at 5.30pm
Mostar	18.50	3	2.20pm
Sarajevo	23.50	3½	7am, 9.15am, 10.20am & 5.20pm
Split	30.50	4½	6am (from Split departs at 12.30pm)
Zenica	14	2¼	8.15am, 1.45pm & 3.15pm

MITHRAS SCULPTURE

In an unassumingly house-like building, remnants of a 4th-century **sculpture** (Mitrasova 12; admission 1KM) feature Mithras fighting a bull for an audience of ladies and centurions. Once worshipped in a now-mysterious, forgotten religion, Mithras was a pre-Zoroastrian Persian sun God 'rediscovered' by mystical Romans. You can get the key from the tourist booth.

Sleeping

The tourist booth can arrange old-city **homestays** (s/d 30/50KM), while Eko Kuća can find rooms in rural village homes from 30KM per person.

Hotel Stari Grad (☎ 654006; hotel.stari.grad@tel.net.ba; Svetog Luke 3; s/d/apt 55/80/160KM; ❄) Although it's not actually old, beams, wood-panelling and a heraldic fireplace give this comfortable little hotel a look of suavely modernised antiquity. Unbeatably central, it's the ideal address as long as you can manage the stairs. An added curiosity is the lobby restaurant's glass floor beneath, which are the excavations of an Ottoman-era *hammam* (Turkish bath).

Hotel Tourist 98 (☎ 658151; Kraljice Katerine bb; s/d/tr/q/apt 57/84/106/135/120KM; ❄) This bright-red box beside Jajce's big hypermarket offers new, very straightforward rooms that are clean and mostly spacious.

For lakeside alternatives see right.

Eating & Drinking

The Hotel Stari Grad serves decent Bosnian and Italian food in its appealing little lobby **restaurant** (mains 9-14KM; 🕑 7am-9pm). Several potentially intriguing cafe-bars are cut out of the cliff-face on HV Hrvatnica. However, only the lovably incompetent **Restoran Una** (mains 4-12KM; 🕑 10am-9pm) serves full meals and even here most items were unavailable when we tried to dine. **Dea Pizzeria** (☎ 657173; pizzas 6-8KM; 🕑 8am-11pm) opposite the Hotel Stari Grad bakes acceptable pizzas. **Ćevabdžinica Tomy** (grills from 3KM; 🕑 8am-3pm Mon-Sat) offers fast(ish) food from a cube of an ancient stone building.

The unpretentiously local **Omerbegović House Café** (coffee/beer 0.50/2KM; 🕑 7am-11pm) is intriguingly hidden in the bare stone former guard house of the medieval Travnik Gate. Enter via the stairway of the Kantonal tourist office.

Getting There & Away

See above for services from the **bus station** (☎ 659202; II-Zasjedanja AVNOJ-a).

For Travnik (8KM to 12KM) take Zenica or Sarajevo buses.

AROUND JAJCE

Wooded mountains reflect idyllically in the two picture-perfect **Pliva Lakes** (Plivsko Jezero) and a park between the two contains a superquaint collection of 17 miniature **watermills**. Take Jezero-bound buses to km92 on the M5 (4km from Jajce), then walk 800m via the **Autokamp** (per child/adult 5/10KM, site without/with electricity 8/12KM; 🕑 mid-Apr–Sep). A kilometre beyond, the lakeside lane rejoins the M5 beside waterfront **Plaža Motel** (☎ 647200; s/d 40/70KM) and the plusher **Hotel Plivsko Jezero** (☎ 654090; www.hoteljajce.bet.net.ba; s/d/tr/q/apt 57/84/106/135/120KM).

BANJA LUKA БАЊА ЛУКА

☎ 051 / pop 232,000

Probably Europe's least-known 'capital' (of the Republik Srpska since 1998), Banja Luka was devastated by a 1969 earthquake and its 15 mosques were subsequently dynamited during the civil war. Today just two blocks of impressive old architecture remain around the iconic **Orthodox Church of Christ Saviour** (Crkva Hrista Spasitelja), whose brick bell tower looks like a Moroccan minaret on Viagra. It's 300m north up the main thoroughfare, Kralja Petra,

BOSNIA & HERCEGOVINA

BUSES FROM BANJA LUKA

Destination	Price (KM)	Duration (hr)	Departures
Belgrade	35	7	15 daily
Bihać	20	3	5.30am, 7.30am (Mon-Sat only), 1pm & 2pm
Jajce	11.50	1½	6.40am, 7.45 (Mon-Sat only), 2.25pm, 1pm, 2pm & 4pm
Sarajevo	31	5	6.30am, 7.45am, 2.30pm, 4pm, 5pm & midnight
Zagreb	24	7	8.45am, 9.10am, 4.10pm & 5.30pm

from the **tourist office** (☎ 232760; www.banjaluka-tourism.com; Kralja Petra 87; 8.30am-5.45pm Mon-Fri, 9am-2pm Sat). Directly southeast of the tourist office the chunky walls of a large, squat 16th-century **castle** (Kaštel) enclose riverside parkland where in summer there's a well-reputed arts festival that encompasses open-air plays, Thursday-night folklore displays and the **Demofest** (www.demofest.org), at which up-and-coming raw garage bands blare out their new music.

Sleeping & Eating

Prenoćište vl Marija C (☎ 218673; Solunska 21; s/d with shared bathroom 27/54KM) Four slightly spartan rooms share a decent bathroom in this inexpensive family homestay. Turn diagonally right at the south end of Kralja Petra and enter from the rear.

Hotel Palace (Хотел Палас; ☎ 218723; Kralja Petra 60; www.hotelpalasbl.com; s/d/tr/ste from 63.50/117/130.50/147KM;) Almost elegant behind its copious street cafe, the Palace's 1933 building's lobby uses hypnotic new art deco–inspired design. Rooms are straightforward, mid-range international standard, while cheaper singles are small and built into the sloping roof.

Vila Vrbas (☎ 433840; Brace Potkonjaka 1; s/d/ste 70/110/120KM) Excellent-value boutique hotel peering through the plane trees at the castle ramparts from across the river. Some rooms have a computer, internet access and a wraparound shower pod. For dining, the Sur Sedra next door has a terrace that's cheaper and less pretentious than the Vila Vrbas' well-known restaurant.

Running parallel to Kralja Petra, Veselina Maslaše offers a wide range of tempting street-cafes, bars, pastry shops and ice-cream vendors.

Getting There & Away

The **main bus station** (☎ 315555; Prote N Kostića 38) and train station are together, 3km north by buses 6, 8 or 10 from near Hotel Palace.

Useful rail connections include Zagreb (4¼ hours, 3.30pm) and Sarajevo (five hours, 1.15pm). The Banja Luka–Belgrade train (eight hours) runs overnight eastbound (departing 10.30pm) but don't expect much sleep: you'll be woken twice for both Croatian and Serbian border crossings. The westbound train returns by day, departing Belgrade at 1.20pm.

AROUND BANJA LUKA

Vrbas Canyons

Between Jajce and Banja Luka the Vrbas River descends in a wonderful series of lakes and gorges that together form one of BiH's foremost adventure-sport playgrounds. Based at Ada, near Karanovac, **Kanjon Rafting** (☎ 065-420000; www.kanjonraft.com) is a reliable, well-organised adventure outfit offering guided canyoning (€25, no minimum group number) and rafting (€25 per person for three hours including transport, four person minimum). At **Krupa** (26km), a pretty set of cascades tumbles down between little wooden mill-huts, mountaineers scale the canyon sides nearby and limestone grottoes attract cavers. The canyon beyond offers top-class rafting and the Jajce road winds steeply on past a high dam into the long, beautiful Bočac Reservoir gorge.

BIHAĆ

☎ 037 / pop 80,000

A closely clumped **church tower**, **turbe** and 16th-century stone **tower-museum** (☎ 223214; admission 2KM; 9am-4pm Mon-Fri, 9am-2pm Sat) look very photogenic viewed across gushing rapids in central Bihać. But that's about all there is to see here apart from nearby **Fethija Mosque**, converted from a rose-windowed medieval church in 1595. If you're driving, Bihać could make a decent staging post for reaching the marvellous Plitvice Lakes (p150) in Croatia, 30km away. Otherwise grab a map-brochure from Bihać's **tourist booth** (Bosanska 1; 8am-4pm) then head out into the lovely Una Valley, preferably on a raft!

WARNING

The Bihać area was mined during the war so stick to paths and concreted areas.

Sights & Activities

In the **Una Valley**, the adorable **Una River** gushes through lush green gorges, over widely fanned rapids and down pounding cascades most dramatically at **Kostela** and **Štrcački Buk**. There are lovely watermill restaurants at **Otoka Bosanska** and **Bosanski Krupa** and spookily Gothic **Ostrožac Fortress** (☎ 061-236641; www.ostrozac.com; admission 1KM; ⏲ 8am-6pm by phoning caretaker) is the most inspiring of several castle ruins.

Several adventure-sports companies offer rafting (€25 to €40, six person minimum), kayaking and climbing. Each has its own campsites and provides transfers from Bihać. Try **Una Kiro Rafting** (☎ /fax 223760; www.una-kiro-rafting.com; Golubic), **Sport Bjeli** (☎ 388555; www.una-rafting.ba; Klokot) or **Limit** (☎ 061-144248; www.limit.co.ba; Džanića Mahala 7, Bihać). The **Una Regatta** in late July is festive but very busy, with hundreds of kayaks and rafts following a three-day course from Kulen-Vakuf to Bosanska Krupa, via Bihać.

Sleeping & Eating

CENTRAL BIHAĆ

Villa Una (☎ /fax 311393; Bihaćkih Branilaca 20; s/d/tr 50/70/90KM) This friendly homestay-style *pansion* behind a jewellery shop, halfway between the bus station and the Una Bridge, suffers somewhat from road noise.

Hotel Park (☎ 226394; www.aduna.ba; ul 5-Korpusa bb; s/d/apt 69/125/160KM; ❄) This very central hotel looks dated but thoroughly renovated rooms have good new bathrooms and wheelchair access. Singles are pretty small. Reception can help with information if the nearby tourist info booth is closed.

Restaurant River Una (☎ 310014; Džemala Bijedića 12; mains 7-15KM, beer 2KM; ⏲ 7am-11pm) Of several riverside eateries facing central Bihać's pretty rapids, River Una has the most appealing wooden-rustic interior, with stone platforms, giant hooks and 'flying' fish.

UNA VALLEY

Motel Estrada (☎ 531320; Ostrožac; s/d 30/60KM) Homely en suite rooms in the fifth unmarked house on the left up the Prečići road; 300m southwest of the castle.

Pansion Kostelski Buk (☎ 302340; www.kostelski-buk.co.ba; M14 hwy, Kostela; s/d 60/90KM; ❄) Lavishly equipped great-value rooms and an excellent-view-restaurant overlooking some dramatic waterfall-rapids. It's 9km from Bihać towards Banja Luka.

Getting There & Away

Bihać's **bus station** (☎ 311939) is 1km west of the centre, just off Bihaćkih Branilaća. Buses run to Zagreb (25KM, 2½ hours, 4.45am, 10.20am, 2pm and 4.45pm) and Banja Luka (20KM, three hours, 5.30am, 7.30am, 1pm and 3pm) via Bosanska Krupa and Otoka Bosanska. Sarajevo buses (40.50KM, seven hours, 12.45am, 7.30am, 2.30pm and 10pm) drive via Travnik. Cazin-bound buses (5.50KM, 11 daily except Sundays) pass through Kostela (10 minutes) and Ostražac (25 minutes). **Super-Matrix** (☎ 061-257098; Zagreb Hwy) rents cars.

BOSNIA & HERCEGOVINA DIRECTORY

ACCOMMODATION

Prices quoted are for the low season, which is October to May generally, but April to November in ski resorts. In Mostar and Sarajevo summer prices rise 20% to 50% and touts appear at the bus stations. These cities also have a wide selection of home-hostels bookable via international hostel-booking sites.

Pansions range from glorified homestays to sophisticated little boutique hotels. Very widespread new suburban motels are ideal for those with cars, though occasionally the term 'motel' is confusingly used to simply imply a lower midrange hotel. Don't assume there's parking.

Many hotels inhabit the husk of old Tito-era concrete monsters. Although some of these have been elegantly remodelled, others remain gloomy and a little forbidding.

Slip-on shoes and plentiful clean socks are a boon if you're sleeping in homestays, since it's normal courtesy to remove shoes on entering a private house. Hosts will provide slippers.

Breakfast is usually included for *pansions*, motels and hotels. Unless stated, all rooms have private bathroom (except in hostels).

ACTIVITIES

BiH is an outdoor wonderland. For inexpensive yet world-class skiing visit Jahorina (p91), Bjelašnica (p91) or Vlašić (p103). Superb rafting reaches terrifyingly difficult class V in April/May but is more suitable for beginners in summer. Top spots are around Foča (p101), Bihać (p107) and Banja Luka (p106).

Hiking and mountain biking have been compromised since the 1990s by the presence of landmines, but many upland areas and national parks now have safe, marked trails. Expat-run ecotourism organisation Green Visions (p84) offers regular hiking excursions from Sarajevo.

BOOKS

Noel Malcolm's very readable *Bosnia: A Short History* is a great introduction to the complexities of Bosnian history. Joe Sacco's deeply humane comic-strip books give moving, personal insights into the sufferings of the 1990s. Nobel Prize–winning Ivo Andrić's epic historical-fiction *Bridge over the Drina* is a must-read, especially if you go to Višegrad. Time Out publishes the excellent, annual *Sarajevo and Bosnia-Herzegovina for Visitors* magazine-guide (15KM), available locally. Babić and Bozja's *Mountaineering Tourist Guide* (35KM) is a great resource for hikers with detailed topographic maps and many photos. **BuyBook** (www.buybook.ba) produce several regional guides.

Tim Clancy's photo-book *Bosnia and Hercegovina: People and Places* makes a great gift for people back home. Some Sarajevo bookshops (p78) still stock the darkly humorous *Sarajevo Survival Guide* (23KM), originally published during the 1992–93 siege.

BUSINESS HOURS

Official hours are 8am to 4pm Monday to Friday; banks open Saturday mornings. Shops open longer, usually 8am to 6pm, including Sundays. Restaurants typically serve food from 11.30am till around 10.30pm in winter, 11.30pm in summer, but whatever their signs say, actual closing time depends more on cusom than fixed schedules. Note that restaurants that claim to open in the morning usually operate as a cafe till 11.30am or noon, only starting to serve food from lunchtime.

DANGERS & ANNOYANCES

An estimated million landmines and fragments of unexploded ordnance are spread over around 4% of BiH's area, causing around 40 mine casualties per year. That's only a twentieth of the number in Cambodia, but caution remains the key. Stick to asphalt/concrete surfaces or well-worn paths and don't enter war-damaged buildings. Sarajevo's Mine Action Centre, **BHMAC** (Map p79; ☎ 033-209762; www.bhmac.org; Zmaja od Bosne 8; 🕑 8am-4pm Mon-Fri) has more information.

EMBASSIES & CONSULATES

The nearest embassies for Ireland and New Zealand are found in Ljubljana (p707) and Rome respectively. Representation in Sarajevo:

Australia (Map pp82-3; ☎ 033-206167; Obala Kulina Bana 15/1) Honorary Consulate.
Canada (Map p79; ☎ 033-222033; Grbavička 4/2)
Croatia (Map pp82-3; ☎ 033-444331; Mehmeda Spahe 16)
France (Map p79; ☎ 033-282050; Mehmed-bega Kapetanovica Ljubusaka 18)
Germany (Map pp82-3; ☎ 033-275000; Buka bb)
Hungary (☎ 033-208353; www.hungemb.ba; Splitska 2)
Japan (Map pp82-3; ☎ 033-209580; Bistrik 2)
Macedonia (off Map p79; ☎ 033-206004; Splitska 57)
Montenegro (Map pp82-3; ☎ 033-239925; Talirovića 4)
Netherlands (Map p79; ☎ 033-562600; www.netherlandsembassy.ba; Grbavička 4/1)
Serbia (Map pp82-3; ☎ 033-260080; Obala Maka Dizdara 3a)
Slovenia (Map pp82-3; ☎ 033-271251; Bentbaša 7)
UK (Map pp82-3; ☎ 033-208229; Petrakijina 11)
USA Sarajevo (Map p79; ☎ 033-445700; Alipašina 43); Banja Luka (☎ 051-211500; Jovana Dučića 5)

GAY & LESBIAN TRAVELLERS

Although homosexuality was decriminalised per se in 1998 (2000 in the RS), attitudes are very conservative. **Logos** (www.logos.org.ba/cont) focuses on combating discrimination against sexual minorities, while **Association Q** (www.queer.ba) attempts to empower the self-reliance of the gay community in BiH. The English-language **Gay Romeo** (www.gayromeo.com) chat site reportedly has around 400 Sarajevo members and www.queer.ba (in Bosnian) organises occasional local meet-ups.

HOLIDAYS

Major Islamic festivals are observed in parts of the Federation, their dates changing annually according to the Muslim lunar calendar. The Feast of Sacrifice is known locally as Kurban Bajram, while the end of Ramadan celebration is called Ramazanski Bajram. Orthodox Easter (variable) and Christmas (6 January) are observed in the RS. Western Easter (variable) and Christmas (25 December) are celebrated in the Federation. The following are national holidays celebrated across the whole of BiH:

New Year's Day 1 January
Independence Day 1 March
May Day 1 May
National Statehood Day 25 November

INTERNET RESOURCES

BiH Ministry of Foreign Affairs (www.mvp.gov.ba) Visa and embassy details.
BiH Tourism (www.bhtourism.ba)
Bosnian Institute (www.bosnia.org.uk) Bosnian cultural affairs.
Grad Sarajevo (www.sarajevo.ba) City site.
Herceg-Bosna (www.hercegbosna.org) BiH seen from a Croat angle.
Hidden Bosnia (www.hiddenbosnia.com) Useful if commercial overview.
InsideBosnia (www.insidebosnia.com) Events and interesting links.
Office of the High Representative (www.ohr.int) BiH's EU overseers.

LANGUAGE

Notwithstanding different dialects, the people of BiH basically speak the same language. However, it's referred to as 'Bosnian' (Bosanski) in Muslim parts, 'Croatian' (Hrvatski) in Croat-controlled areas and 'Serbian' (Српски) in the RS. The Federation uses the Latin alphabet. The RS uses predominantly Cyrillic (ћирилица) but Latin (Latinica) is gaining wider parallel usage there too. Brčko uses both alphabets equally.

MAPS

Freytag & Berndt's very useful 1:250,000 BiH road map costs 12KM in Sarajevo bookshops (p78). City maps are patchily available from bookshops, kiosks or tourist information centres. Many cities post town plans on their .ba websites.

MONEY

Bosnia's convertible mark (KM or BAM) is pronounced *kai-em* or *maraka* and divided into 100 fenig. It's tied to the euro at approximately €1=1.96KM. Many establishments (shops, restaurants and especially hotels) unblinkingly accept euros though this is slightly rarer in the RS. In Mostar even Croatian kuna are also accepted without fuss. ATMs accepting Visa and MasterCard brands are ubiquitous.

Travellers cheques can be readily changed at Raiffeisen and Zagrebačka Banks but you'll usually need to show the original purchase receipt.

POST

Post and telephone offices are usually combined. Poste restante is available for a small fee but only at main cities' central post offices. BiH's complex postal history makes it fascinating for philatelists and three postal organisations still issue their own stamps. The Cyrillic lettering makes RS **Srpske Poste** (www.filatelija.rs.ba) stamps obviously distinctive. Those from Mostar-based **HP Post** (www.post.ba) and Sarajevo's **BH Post** (www.bhp.ba) have their own designs but are both marked 'Bosnia i Hercegovina' in Latin.

TELEPHONE

BiH's country code is ☎ 387. Of the three mobile-phone companies here, BH Mobile (☎ 061- and ☎ 062-) is most widely used in the Federation. Its prepaid 'Ultra' SIM cards cost 15KM including 10KM credit. Alternatives are ☎ 063- (HT/EroNet), and ☎ 065- (M-Tel), with marginally cheaper call costs. All have virtually nationwide coverage.

Phonecards for public telephones can be purchased at post offices or from some street kiosks for 10KM but beware that different cards are required for the Federation and for RS.

Dial ☎ 1201 for the international operator, ☎ 1188 for local directory information.

EMERGENCY NUMBERS

- Ambulance ☎ 124
- Fire ☎ 123
- Police ☎ 122
- Roadside assistance ☎ 1282, 1288

BOSNIA & HERCEGOVINA

TOURIST INFORMATION

All BiH cities and many smaller towns have tourist offices. The typically underemployed staff are generally delighted to see travellers, dispensing maps, brochures and advice and sometimes helping with accommodation. However, don't be surprised by unexplained office closures.

TRAVELLERS WITH DISABILITIES

Most of Bosnia's most appealing town- and village-cores are based around steep, rough streets and stairways. It's visually charming but very awkward if you're disabled. A few places have wheelchair ramps in response to all the war-wounded, but smaller hotels won't have lifts and disabled toilets are still extremely rare.

VISAS

EU nationals don't need visas. Nor do citizens of Andorra, Australia, Brunei, Canada, Croatia, Japan, Kuwait, Liechtenstein, Macedonia, Malaysia, Monaco, Montenegro, New Zealand, Norway, Qatar, Russia, San Marino, Serbia, Switzerland, the Vatican, Turkey and the USA.

For other nationals, single-/multi-entry visas cost from €31/57. Visa applications must be accompanied by one photograph and either a letter of invitation or a tourist agency voucher. For full details see www.mvp.gov.ba.

TRANSPORT IN BOSNIA & HERCEGOVINA

GETTING THERE & AWAY

Air

Even BiH's main airport, **Međunarodni Aerodrom Sarajevo** (SJJ; ☎ 033-289100; www.sarajevo-airport.ba) is decidedly modest, served by just the following airlines:

Adria Airways (JP; Map pp82-3; ☎ 033-232125; www.adria-airways.com; Ferhadija 23)
Austrian Airlines (OS; ☎ 033-202059; www.aua.com)
BH Airlines (JA; Map pp82-3; ☎ 033-218605; www.bhairlines.ba; Branilaca Sarajeva 15; 9am-5pm Mon-Fri, 9am-2pm Sat)
British Airways (BA; www.ba.com)
Croatia Airlines (OU; ☎ 033-666123; www.croatiaairlines.hr)
JAT (JU; ☎ 033-259750; www.jat.come)
Lufthansa (LH; ☎ 033-278590; www.lufthansa.com; Mula Mustafe Bašeskije 2)
Malév Hungarian Airlines (MA; ☎ 473200; www.malev.hu)
Turkish Airlines (TK; Map pp82-3; ☎ 033-666092; www.thy.com; Branilaca Sarajeva)

Between them, all of BiH's other airports have only seven scheduled flights a week on three routes: Mostar–İstanbul (p97), Banja Luka–Zürich and Banja Luka–Belgrade.

The national carrier, BH (pronounced 'Bay-Ha') Airlines flies inexpensively from Sarajevo to Frankfurt, Cologne/Bonn, İstanbul, Skopje, Stuttgart and Zürich. Phone in reservations then pay at the airport immediately before departure.

If prices to Sarajevo seem high, consider taking budget flights to Dubrovnik, Split or Zagreb in Croatia, then connecting to BiH by bus or train.

Land

Crossing borders is generally hassle free. By bus or train just wait: either a border guard gets on board to check documents or the driver collects passports and takes them to the guard post. Don't panic, this is normal.

When driving simply queue up and flash your passport and car documents.

BUS

Most towns in the Federation have daily buses to Zagreb and/or Split (Croatia). RS towns usually have links to Serbia and Montenegro. Most bigger BiH cities have weekly services to Germany/Scandinavia. See p89 for details on Sarajevo's international bus services.

CAR & MOTORCYCLE

Drivers need to ensure that they have Green Card insurance for their vehicle and an EU or International Driving Permit. Petrol (95 and 98 octane) and diesel are readily available in any town, though many service stations close between 11pm and 7am.

TRAIN

Two daily services connect Ploče (on the Croatian coast) via Mostar to Sarajevo. There are also services from Banja Luka to Belgrade and Sarajevo–Belgrade. A service from Sarajevo to Budapest goes via Doboj, Šamac and Osijek (Croatia); see p89 for details.

GETTING AROUND

Bicycle

Roads are very hilly, but for tough cyclists BiH's calm secondary routes can prove a delight. Several mountain areas now have suggested off-road trails for mountain bikers but beware of straying off-route into minefields (see p108).

Bus

Slow if usually on time, BiH's buses can be annoyingly infrequent. At weekends local shorter-hop buses drastically reduce services, often stopping altogether on Sundays. Bus stations pre-sell tickets but it's normally easy enough to wave down any bus en route. Advance reservations might be necessary for overnight routes or during peak holiday times.

Fares vary between different companies but average around 7KM per hour travelled. A return ticket is usually significantly cheaper than two singles, but inconveniently limits you to a specific company. Add 2KM per stowed bag.

Car & Motorcycle

Given the minimal transport to BiH's most spectacular remote areas, having wheels can really transform your trip. Bosnian roads are winding, lightly trafficked and almost unanimously beautiful, a delight for driving as long as you aren't in a hurry. Flowers and graves litter sharper bends where haste proved fatal. Luckily most local drivers are reasonably calm and the main frustration can be getting past slow trucks, tractors or occasional horse-carts. Some country roads are not asphalted.

EU or International Driving Permits are accepted.

AUTOMOBILE ASSOCIATIONS

BIHAMK (Automobile Association of Bosnia & Hercegovina; Map pp82-3; ☎ 033-212771; www.bihamk.ba; Skenderija 23, Sarajevo; annual membership 25KM; 8am-4.30pm Mon-Fri, 9am-noon Sat) offers road assistance and towing services for members.

HIRE

Most bigger towns in BiH offer car hire starting at around €43/245 per day/week with unlimited mileage and basic insurance. Before signing, check car condition, insurance excess and whether the 17% VAT costs extra.

ROAD RULES

Driving is on the right, seatbelts must be worn and headlights must be kept on day and night. The maximum tolerated blood-alcohol level is 0.05% (roughly 0.5g/l). Speed limits are 80km/h for rural roads, dropping to 60km/h or less in town, often without reminder signs for many kilometres. Police spot-checks are very common. Parking is awkward in Mostar and Sarajevo, where tow-away trucks are ruthless. However, elsewhere parking is usually contrastingly easy; in town centres expect to pay 1KM per hour to an attendant.

Train

Trains depart much less frequently than buses but they're generally 30% cheaper. **RS Railways** (www.zrs-rs.com/red_voznje.php?pageNum_vozovi=4&totalRows_vozovi=105) has full, up-to-date timetables.

Croatia

Touted as the 'new this' and the 'new that' for years since its re-emergence on the world tourism scene, it is now clear that Croatia is a unique destination that can hold its own and then some: this is a country with a glorious 1778km-long coast and a staggering 1185 islands. The Adriatic coast is a knockout: its limpid sapphirine waters draw visitors to remote islands, hidden coves and traditional fishing villages, all while touting the glitzy beach and yacht scene. Istria is captivating, thanks to its gastronomic delights and wines, and the bars, clubs and festivals of Zagreb, Zadar and Split remain little-explored gems. Eight national parks protect pristine forests, karstic mountains, rivers, lakes and waterfalls in a landscape of primeval beauty. Punctuate all this with breathtaking Dubrovnik in the south and a country couldn't wish for a better finale.

Sitting on a see-saw between the Balkans and central Europe, Croatia has suffered from having something of a love-hate-love affair with the European Union. Statistics show that the support for joining the vast EU – once palpable – is lately hovering around the 50% mark, thanks to the already seemingly elusive joining date (Is it 2010? Or 2011? Or even 2012?) becoming snagged on a number of hurdles. Developers and investors are increasing by the year, but despite this the country has, with few exceptions, managed to keep (massive) development at bay and maintain the extraordinary beauty of the coast – the very thing that keeps the punters coming back for more.

FAST FACTS

- **Area** 56,538 sq km
- **Capital** Zagreb
- **Currency** kuna (KN); €1 = 7.42KN; US$1 = 5.44KN; UK£1 = 7.87KN; A$1 = 3.76KN; ¥100 = 5.66KN; NZ$1 = 3.05KN
- **Famous for** neckties, Slaven Bilić, Tito
- **Official language** Croatian
- **Phrases** *bog* (hello); *doviđenja* (goodbye); *hvala* (thanks); *pardon* (sorry)
- **Population** 4.5 million
- **Telephone codes** country code ☎ 385; international access code ☎ 00
- **Visas** unnecessary for citizens of the EU, USA, Australia and Canada; see p172 for details

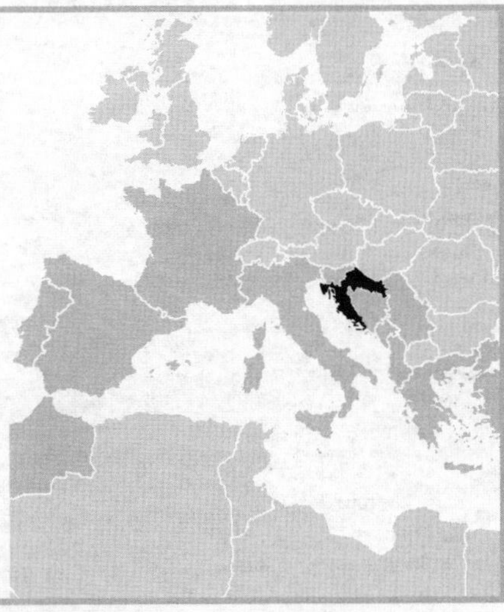

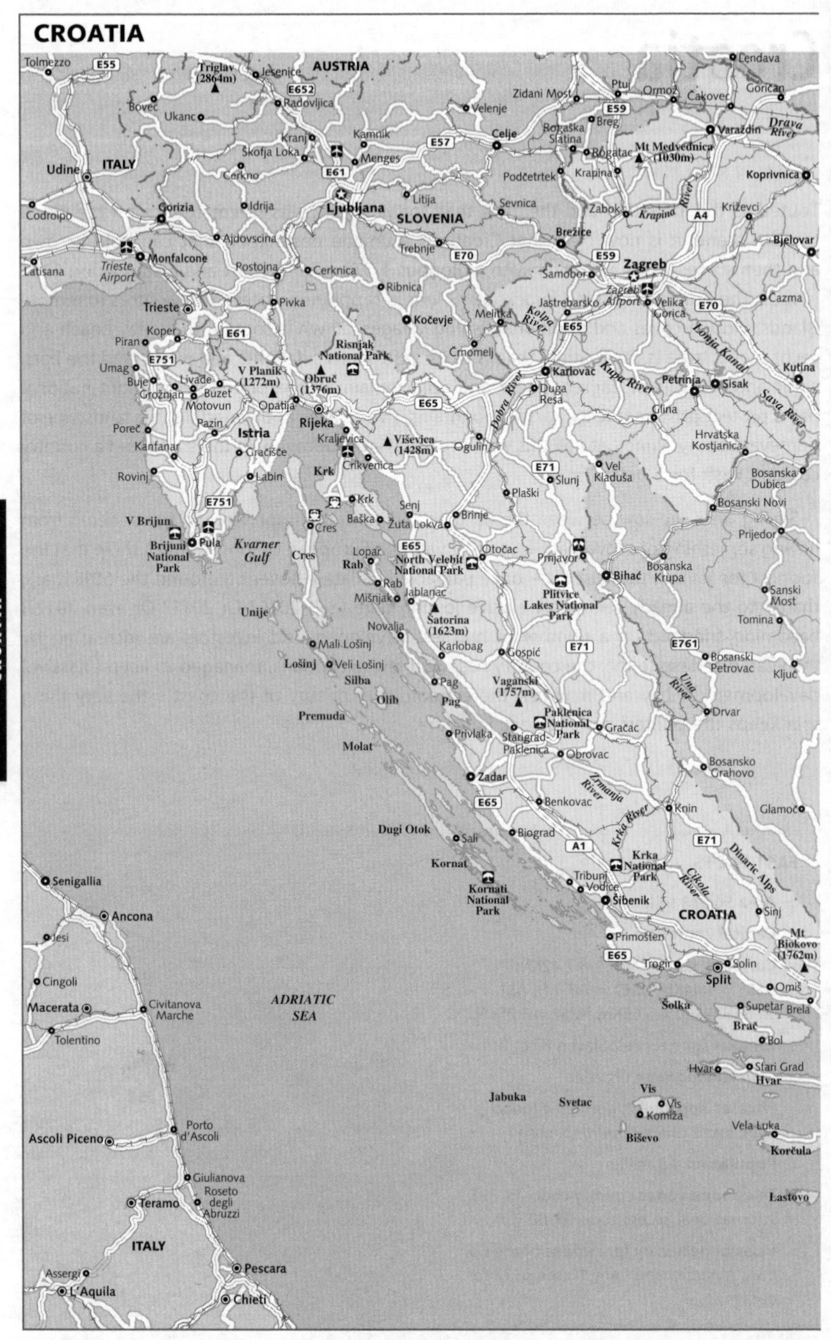
CROATIA
Tolmezzo
E55
Triglav (2864m)
Jesenice
AUSTRIA
E652
Radovljica
Bovec
Ukanc
Velenje
Zidani Most
Ptuj
Ormož
Čakovec
Lendava
Goričan
E59
Breg
Rogaška Slatina
Varaždin
Drava River
Kranj
Kamnik
E57
Celje
Škofja Loka
Menges
Rogatac
Mt Medvednica (1030m)
Udine
ITALY
Cerkno
E61
Podčetrtek
Krapina
Koprivnica
Ljubljana
Litija
Sevnica
Krapina River
Križevci
Codroipo
Gorizia
Idrija
SLOVENIA
Zabok
A4
Ajdovscina
Brežice
Bjelovar
Monfalcone
Trebnje
E70
E59
Zagreb
Latisana
Trieste Airport
Postojna
Cerknica
Samobor
Ribnica
Zagreb Airport
Velika Gorica
E70
Čazma
Trieste
Pivka
Jastrebarsko
Kočevje
Melitka
Kolpa River
Koper
E61
E65
Lonja Kanal
Piran
Risnjak National Park
Črnomelj
E751
Karlovac
Kupa River
Kutina
Umag
V Planik (1272m)
Obruč (1376m)
Duga Resa
Petrinja
Sisak
Buje
Livade
Dobra River
Grožnjan
Buzet
Sava River
Motovun
Opatija
E65
Rijeka
Glina
Poreč
Pazin
Istria
Kraljevica
Višević (1428m)
Ogulin
Hrvatska Kostjanica
Kanfanar
Gračišće
Crikvenica
Krk
E71
Vel Kladuša
Rovinj
Labin
Slunj
Bosanska Dubica
Plaški
E751
Krk
Senj
Bosanski Novi
V Brijun
Baška
Žuta Lokva
Brinje
Cres
Prijedor
Brijuni National Park
Pula
Kvarner Gulf
Cres
E65
Otočac
Lopar
North Velebit National Park
Prnjavor
Bihać
Bosanska Krupa
Rab
Rab
Plitvice Lakes National Park
Sanski Most
Mišnjak
Jablanac
Unije
Šatorina (1623m)
Tomina
Novalja
Mali Lošinj
Karlobag
E761
Gospić
E71
Bosanski Petrovac
Lošinj
Veli Lošinj
Ključ
Silba
Pag
Vaganski (1757m)
Una River
Olib
Pag
Premuda
Paklenica National Park
Drvar
Privlaka
Starigrad Paklenica
Gračac
Molat
Obrovac
Bosansko Grahovo
Zadar
Zrmanja River
E65
Benkovac
Glamoč
Krka River
Knin
Dugi Otok
Sali
Biograd
A1
E71
Kornat
Krka National Park
Dinaric Alps
Tribunj
Vodice
Cikola River
Senigallia
Kornati National Park
Šibenik
CROATIA
Sinj
Ancona
Primošten
Mt Biokovo (1762m)
Jesi
E65
Trogir
Solin
Cingoli
Split
Omiš
ADRIATIC SEA
Macerata
Civitanova Marche
Šolka
Supetar
Brela
Brač
Tolentino
Bol
Hvar
Stari Grad
Hvar
Vis
Jabuka
Svetac
Vis
Komiža
Porto d'Ascoli
Vela Luka
Ascoli Piceno
Biševo
Korčula
Giulianova
Lastovo
Teramo
Roseto degli Abruzzi
ITALY
Pescara
Assergi
L'Aquila
Chieti

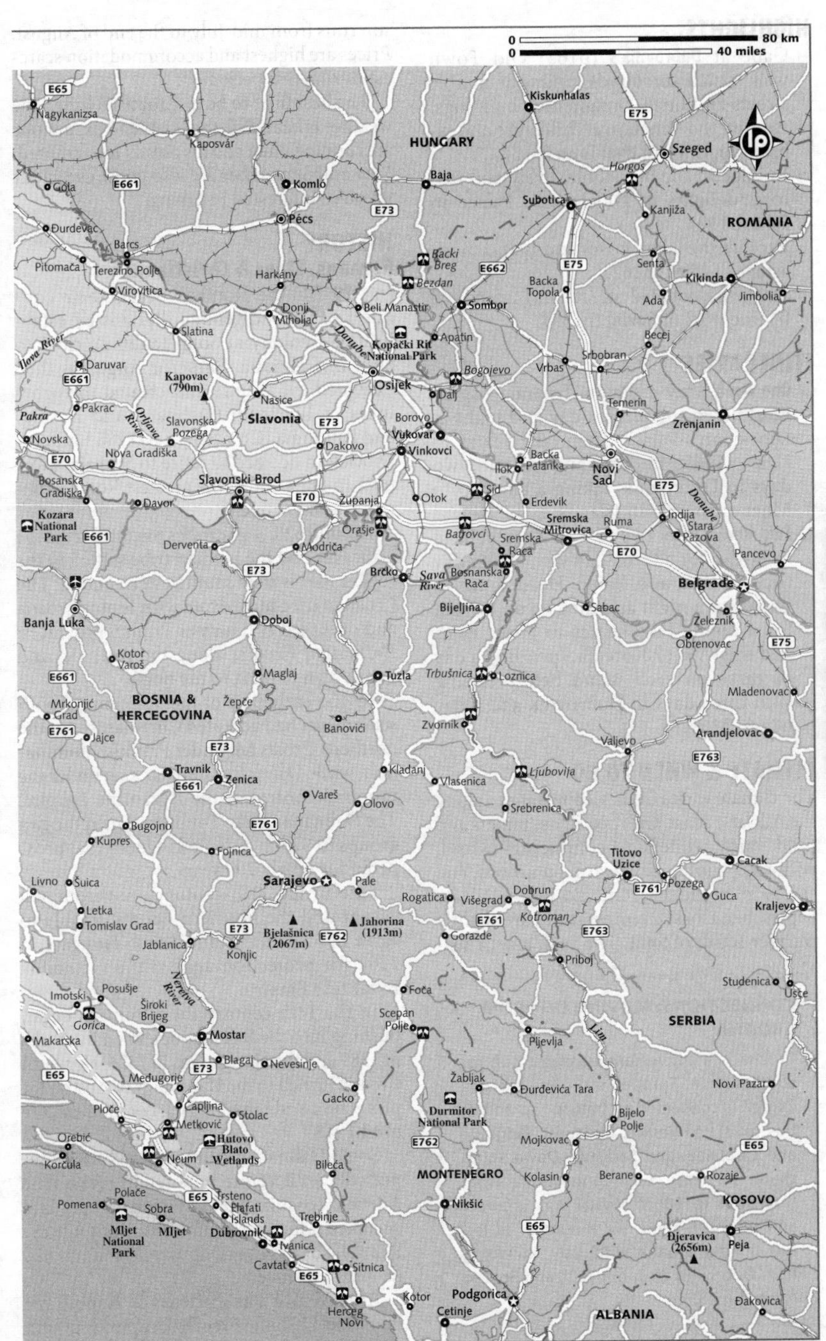
0 80 km
0 40 miles
HUNGARY
ROMANIA
BOSNIA & HERCEGOVINA
SERBIA
MONTENEGRO
KOSOVO
ALBANIA
Slavonia
Kiskunhalas
Szeged
Nagykanizsa
Kaposvár
Baja
Komló
Pécs
Subotica
Horgos
Kanjiža
Senta
Kikinda
Jimbolia
Gola
Đurdevac
Barcs
Pitomača
Terezino Polje
Virovitica
Harkány
Backi Breg
Bezdan
Backa Topola
Ada
Sombor
Beli Manastir
Donji Miholjac
Slatina
Apatin
Kopački Rit National Park
Danube
Ilova River
Daruvar
Kapovac (790m)
Osijek
Bogojevo
Vrbas
Srbobran
Becej
Dalj
Pakrac
Pakra
Nasice
Orljava River
Slavonska Pozega
Temerin
Zrenjanin
Novska
Borovo
Vukovar
Vinkovci
Dakovo
Nova Gradiška
Backa Palanka
Ilok
Novi Sad
Bosanska Gradiška
Slavonski Brod
Županja
Otok
Šid
Erdevik
Davor
Kozara National Park
Orašje
Batrovci
Sremska Mitrovica
Ruma
Indija
Stara Pazova
Derventa
Modriča
Sremska Raca
Pancevo
Brčko
Sava River
Bosnanska Rača
Belgrade
Bijeljina
Sabac
Banja Luka
Doboj
Zeleznik
Obrenovac
Kotor Varoš
Maglaj
Tuzla
Trbušnica
Loznica
Mladenovac
Mrkonjić Grad
Žepče
Banovići
Zvornik
Arandjelovac
Valjevo
Jajce
Travnik
Zenica
Kladanj
Vlasenica
Ljubovija
Vareš
Olovo
Srebrenica
Bugojno
Kupres
Fojnica
Titovo Uzice
Cacak
Livno
Šuica
Sarajevo
Pale
Pozega
Guca
Rogatica
Višegrad
Dobrun
Kotroman
Kraljevo
Letka
Tomislav Grad
Bjelašnica (2067m)
Jahorina (1913m)
Gorazde
Jablanica
Konjic
Priboj
Neretva River
Posušje
Imotski
Gorica
Široki Brijeg
Foča
Studenica
Usce
Scepan Polje
Lim
Makarska
Mostar
Pljevlja
Blagaj
Nevesinje
Međugorje
Žabljak
Đurđevića Tara
Novi Pazar
Gacko
Čapljina
Ploče
Stolac
Metković
Durmitor National Park
Bijelo Polje
Orebić
Hutovo Blato Wetlands
Mojkovac
Korčula
Neum
Bileća
Kolasin
Berane
Rozaje
Polače
Pomena
Sobra
Trsteno
Elafati Islands
Nikšić
Mljet National Park
Mljet
Trebinje
Dubrovnik
Ivanica
Djeravica (2656m)
Peja
Cavtat
Sitnica
Herceg Novi
Kotor
Podgorica
Cetinje
Đakovica
E65
E661
E73
E75
E662
E70
E761
E762
E763

CROATIA

HIGHLIGHTS

- Gape at **Dubrovnik's** (p163) Old Town wall, which surrounds luminous marble streets and finely ornamented buildings.
- Admire the Venetian architecture and vibrant nightlife of **Hvar Town** (p158).
- Indulge in the incredible, lively and historic delights of Diocletian's Palace in **Split** (p150).
- Explore the lakes, coves and island monastery of **Mljet** (p162).
- Stroll the cobbled streets and unspoiled fishing port of **Rovinj** (p135).

ITINERARIES

- **One week** After a day in dynamic Zagreb head down to Split for day and night at Diocletian's Palace. Then take a ferry to Hvar, windsurf in Brač and end with two days in Dubrovnik, taking a day trip to Mljet or the Elafiti Islands.
- **Two weeks** After two days in Zagreb, head to Rovinj for a three-day stay, taking day trips to Pula and Poreč. Head south to Zadar for a night and then go on to Split for a night. Take ferries to Hvar, Brač, and then Vis or Korčula, spending a day or three on each island before ending with three days in Dubrovnik and a day trip to Mljet.

CLIMATE & WHEN TO GO

The climate varies from Mediterranean along the Adriatic coast, with hot, dry summers and mild, rainy winters, to continental inland, with cold winters and warm summers. You can swim in the sea from mid-June until late September. Coastal temperatures are slightly warmer south of Split. The peak tourist season runs from mid-July to the end of August. Prices are highest and accommodation scarcest during this period.

The best time to be in Croatia is June. The weather is beautiful, the boats and excursions are running often and it's not yet too crowded. May and September are also good, especially if you're interested in hiking.

CONNECTIONS: MOVING ON FROM CROATIA

Croatia is a convenient transport hub for southeastern Europe and the Adriatic. Zagreb is connected by train (p131) and/or bus (p131) to Venice, Budapest, Belgrade and Ljubljana, and Sarajevo. Down south there are easy bus connections from Dubrovnik (p168) to Mostar and Sarajevo, and to Kotor. There are a number of ferries linking Croatia with Italy, including from Dubrovnik to Bari (p168), and Split to Ancona (p155).

HISTORY

Romans, Slavs & Christianity

In 229 BC the Romans began their conquest of the indigenous Illyrians by establishing a colony at Solin (Salona), close to Split in Dalmatia. Emperor Augustus then extended the empire and created the provinces of Illyricum (Dalmatia and Bosnia) and Pannonia (Croatia). In AD 285 Emperor Diocletian decided to retire to his palace fortress in Split, today the greatest Roman ruin in Eastern Europe.

Around 625, Slavic tribes migrated from the Caucasus and the Serbian tribe settled in the region that is now southwestern Serbia. The Croatian tribe moved into what is now Croatia and occupied two former Roman provinces: Dalmatian Croatia along the Adriatic, and Pannonian Croatia to the north.

By the early part of the 9th century both settlements had accepted Christianity but the northern Croats fell under Frankish domination, while Dalmatian Croats came under the nominal control of the Byzantine Empire. The Dalmatian duke Tomislav united the two groups in 925 in a single kingdom that prospered for nearly 200 years.

Late in the 11th century the throne fell vacant and the northern Croats, unable to agree upon a ruler, united with Hungary in 1102 for protection against the Orthodox Byzantine Empire.

In the 14th century the Ottomans began pushing into the Balkans, defeating the Serbs in 1389 and the Hungarians in 1526. Northern Croatia turned to the Hapsburgs of Austria for protection and remained part of their empire until 1918.

Some Dalmatian cities changed hands repeatedly until Venice imposed its rule on the Adriatic coast in the early 15th century and occupied it for nearly four centuries. Only the Republic of Ragusa (Dubrovnik) maintained its independence.

After Venice was shattered by Napoleonic France in 1797, the French occupied southern

Croatia, abolishing the Republic of Ragusa in 1808. Napoleon merged Dalmatia, Istria and Slovenia into the 'Illyrian Provinces', but following his defeat at Waterloo in 1815, Austria-Hungary occupied the coast.

Push for Independence

It wasn't long before Croatia began itching for independence from the Austrian empire and for the unification of Dalmatia and Slavonia. When an uprising in Hungary threatened Austrian rule, Croatia seized the opportunity to intervene in return for greater autonomy. The Croatian commander Josip Jelačić set out to fight the rebels but his campaign was unsuccessful and Croatian hopes were crushed. Disillusionment spread after 1848, and deepened when the monarchy placed Croatia and Slavonia within the Hungarian administration, while Dalmatia remained within Austria.

The river of discontent running through late-19th-century Croatia forked into two streams that dominated the political landscape for the next century. On the one side was Bishop Josif Juraf Strossmayer, who believed that *Jugoslavenstvo* (south-Slavic unity), unified by a common language, was the only way forward for the aspirations of the southern Slavs. His opponent, the militantly anti-Serb Ante Starčević, envisaged an independent Croatia made up of Slavonia, Dalmatia, the Krajina, Slovenia, Istria and part of Bosnia and Hercegovina.

South Slavic Unity

The first organised resistance against the Austro-Hungarian empire formed in Dalmatia. Croat representatives in Rijeka and Serb representatives in Zadar joined together in 1905 to demand the unification of Dalmatia and Slavonia with a formal guarantee of Serbian equality as a nation. The spirit of unity mushroomed, and by 1906 Croat-Serb coalitions had taken over local government in Dalmatia and Slavonia, forming a serious threat to the Hungarian power structure.

Similar resistance was going on in the neighbouring Bosnia and Hercegovina (BiH) and with the outbreak of WWI, the idea that only Slavic unity could check Great Power ambitions in the region was cemented. With the collapse of the Austro-Hungarian empire in 1918, the Kingdom of Serbs, Croats and Slovenes was established. Italy seized Pula, Rijeka and Zadar in November 1918.

HOW MUCH?

- **Short taxi ride** 60KN
- **Plate of fish stew** 50KN
- **Loaf of bread** 4KN
- **Bottle of house white** 40KN
- **Newspaper** 8KN

LONELY PLANET INDEX

- **1L petrol** 7KN
- **1L bottled water** 10KN
- **33cL beer (Karlovačko)** 12KN
- **Souvenir T-shirt** 90KN
- **Street snack (slice of burek)** 10KN

Problems with the kingdom began almost immediately, with the abolishment of Croatia's Sabor (Parliament) and the centralisation of power in Belgrade. The new electoral districts under-represented the Croats and the new government gave away Istria, Zadar and a number of islands to Italy.

One of the main opposition leaders was Stjepan Radić, who, together with Svetozar Pribićević, advocated a federal democracy within the Kingdom and tried to promote the idea of an egalitarian state. He formed HSS (The Croatian Peasant Party), a political party that remains influential to this day. Following a number of heated debates in the parliament, Radić was assassinated, along with two other party members. Exploiting fears of civil war, on 6 January 1929 King Aleksandar in Belgrade proclaimed a royal dictatorship, abolished political parties and suspended parliamentary government.

Ustaše, Chetniks & Partisans

One day after the coup d'état, a Bosnian Croat, Ante Pavelić, set up the Ustaše Croatian Liberation Movement in Zagreb with the stated aim of establishing an independent state by force if necessary. Fearing arrest, he fled to Sofia in Bulgaria and then to Italy. There, he established training camps for his organisation, favoured by Mussolini. Pavelić succeeded in assassinating King Aleksandar in Marseilles in 1934 and Italy responded by closing down the training camps and imprisoning Pavelić and many of his followers.

When Germany invaded Yugoslavia on 6 April 1941, the Nazis installed the exiled Ustaše with the support of the Italians. In return, Pavelić agreed to cede a good part of Dalmatia to Italy, which left him with the Lika region southwest of Zagreb and western Hercegovina as his political base.

Within days the Independent State of Croatia (NDH), headed by Pavelić, issued a range of decrees designed to persecute and eliminate Serbs, Jews, Roma and antifascist Croats. Villages conducted their own personal pogroms against Serbs and extermination camps were set up, most notoriously at Jasenovac (south of Zagreb). The extermination program was carried out with appalling brutality. The exact number of Serb victims is uncertain and controversial, with Croatian historians tending to minimise the figures and Serbian historians tending to maximise them. The number of Serb deaths range from 60,000 to 600,000, but the most reliable estimates settle somewhere between 80,000 to 120,000. Whatever the number, it's clear that the NDH and its supporters made a diligent effort to eliminate the entire Serb population.

Armed resistance to the regime took the form of Serbian 'Chetniks' led by General Draža Mihajlović, which began as an antifascist rebellion but soon degenerated into massacres of Croats in eastern Croatia and Bosnia.

In the meantime, Josip Broz, himself of Croat-Slovene parentage, the leader of the outlawed Yugoslavian Communist Party, fronted the partisans, who consisted of left-wing Yugoslav intellectuals, Croats disgusted with Chetnik massacres, Serbs disgusted with Ustaše massacres, and antifascists of all kinds.

Although the Allies initially backed the Serbian Chetniks, it became apparent that the partisans were waging a far more focused and determined fight against the Germans. On 20 October 1944 Tito entered Belgrade with the Red Army and was made prime minister. When Germany surrendered in 1945, Pavelić and the Ustaše fled and the partisans entered Zagreb.

The remnants of the NDH army, desperate to avoid falling into the hands of the partisans, attempted to cross into Austria at Bleiburg. A small British contingent met the 50,000 troops and promised to intern them outside Yugoslavia in exchange for their surrender. Tricked, the troops were forced into trains that headed back into Yugoslavia where the partisans claimed the lives of at least 30,000 men (although the exact number is in doubt).

Tito's Yugoslavia

Tito's attempt to retain control of the Italian city of Trieste and parts of southern Austria faltered in the face of Allied opposition, but Dalmatia and most of Istria were made a permanent part of postwar Yugoslavia. Tito was determined to create a state in which no ethnic group dominated the political landscape. Croatia became one of six republics – Macedonia, Serbia, Montenegro, BiH and Slovenia – in a tightly configured federation. Tito effected this delicate balance by creating a one-party state and stamping out opposition.

During the 1960s, the concentration of power in Belgrade became an increasingly testy issue as it became apparent that money from the more prosperous republics of Slovenia and Croatia was being distributed to the poorer regions, such as BiH, Kosovo and Montenegro. Serbs in Croatia were over-represented in the government, armed forces and the police – this was, allegedly, partly because state service offered financial certainty and career opportunities among the poorer Yugoslavs.

The dissatisfaction with Tito's government manifested itself in many student and other demonstrations across Yugoslavia during the late '60s, but Croatia's unrest reached a crescendo in 1971, during the 'Croatian Spring'. Led by reformers within the Communist Party of Croatia, intellectuals and students first called for greater economic autonomy and then constitutional reform to loosen Croatia's ties to Yugoslavia. Tito's crackdown meant that leaders of the movement were either jailed or expelled from the party. Serbs viewed the movement as the Ustaše reborn, and jailed reformers blamed the Serbs for their troubles. The stage was set for the later rise of nationalism and war that followed Tito's death in 1980, even though his 1974 constitution afforded the republics more autonomy.

Independence

After Tito's death, Yugoslavia was left with a large external debt. The country was unable to service the interest on its loans and inflation soared. The authority of the central government sank along with the economy, and mistrust among Yugoslavia's ethnic groups resurfaced.

In 1989 the repression of the Albanian majority in Serbia's Kosovo province sparked renewed fears of Serbian hegemony and heralded the end of the Yugoslav Federation. With political changes sweeping Eastern Europe, many Croats felt the time had come to separate from Yugoslavia and the elections of April 1990 saw the victory of Franjo Tuđman's Croatian Democratic Union (HDZ; Hrvatska Demokratska Zajednica). On 22 December 1990 a new Croatian constitution was promulgated, changing the status of Serbs in Croatia from that of a 'constituent nation' to a national minority.

The constitution's failure to guarantee minority rights, and mass dismissals of Serbs from the public service, stimulated the 600,000-strong ethnic Serb community within Croatia to demand autonomy. In early 1991 Serb extremists within Croatia staged provocations designed to force federal military intervention. A May 1991 referendum (boycotted by the Serbs) produced a 93% vote in favour of independence, but when Croatia declared independence on 25 June 1991, the Serbian enclave of Krajina proclaimed its independence from Croatia.

War & Peace

Under pressure from the EC (now EU), Croatia declared a three-month moratorium on its independence, but heavy fighting broke out in Krajina, Baranja (the area north of the Drava River opposite Osijek) and Slavonia. The Serb-dominated Yugoslav People's Army intervened in support of Serbian irregulars, under the pretext of halting ethnic violence.

When the Croatian government ordered a blockade of 32 federal military installations in the republic, the Yugoslav navy blockaded the Adriatic coast and laid siege to the strategic town of Vukovar on the Danube. During the summer of 1991, a quarter of Croatia fell to Serbian militias and the Yugoslav People's Army.

In early October 1991 the federal army and Montenegrin militia moved against Dubrovnik to protest the blockade of their garrisons in Croatia, and on 7 October the presidential palace in Zagreb was hit by rockets fired by Yugoslav air-force jets in an unsuccessful assassination attempt on President Tuđman. When the three-month moratorium on independence ended, Croatia declared full independence. On 19 November the city of Vukovar fell after a bloody three-month siege. During six months of fighting in Croatia 10,000 people died, hundreds of thousands fled and tens of thousands of homes were destroyed.

To fulfil a condition for EC recognition, in December the Croatian Sabor (which was re-established under Tito) belatedly amended its constitution to protect minority groups and human rights. A UN-brokered ceasefire from 3 January 1992 generally held. The federal army was allowed to withdraw from its bases inside Croatia and tensions diminished. In January 1992 the EC, succumbing to strong pressure from Germany, recognised Croatia. This was followed three months later by US recognition and in May 1992 Croatia was admitted to the UN.

In January 1993 the Croatian army launched an offensive in southern Krajina, pushing the Serbs back and recapturing strategic points. In June 1993 the Krajina Serbs voted overwhelmingly to join the Bosnian Serbs (and eventually Greater Serbia). Meanwhile, continued 'ethnic cleansing' left only about 900 Croats in Krajina out of an original population of 44,000.

On 1 May 1995 the Croatian army and police entered occupied western Slavonia, east of Zagreb, and seized control of the region within days. The Krajina Serbs responded by shelling Zagreb in an attack that left seven people dead and 130 wounded. As the Croatian military consolidated its hold in western Slavonia, some 15,000 Serbs fled the region, despite assurances from the Croatian government that they were safe from retribution.

Belgrade's silence throughout this campaign showed that the Krajina Serbs had lost the support of their Serbian allies, encouraging Croats to forge ahead. On 4 August the military launched a massive assault on the rebel Serb capital of Knin and, vastly outnumbered, the Serb army fled towards northern Bosnia and into Serbia. An estimated 150,000 civilians fled and many were murdered. The military operation ended in days, but was followed by months of terror. Widespread looting and burning of Serb villages, and attacks upon the remaining Serbs cemented the huge population shift. The Dayton Accord signed in

Paris in December 1995 recognised Croatia's traditional borders and provided for the return of eastern Slavonia, which was effected in January 1998. The transition proceeded relatively smoothly, but the two populations still regard each other with suspicion.

Although the central government in Zagreb has made the return of Serb refugees a priority in accordance with the demands of the international community, its efforts have been less than successful. Serbs intending to reclaim their property face an array of legal impediments.

Franjo Tuđman's combination of authoritarianism and media control, and tendency to be influenced by the far Right, no longer appealed to the postwar Croatian populace. By 1999 opposition parties united to work against Tuđman and the HDZ. Tuđman was hospitalised and died suddenly in late 1999, and planned elections were postponed until January 2000. Still, voters turned out in favour of a centre-left coalition, ousting the HDZ and voting the centrist Stipe Mesić into the presidency.

The country gradually began welcoming foreign tourists again, and the economy opened up to foreign competition. General Mirko Norac turned himself in to the Hague in 2001 and General Ante Gotovina was arrested in 2005 for crimes against the Krajina's Serb population. Gotovina's handover was one of the conditions for the EU to start discussing Croatia's eventual membership. The arrests of both men were accompanied with some nationalist protest. A spate of suspected mafia-related murders in late 2008 – of 26-year-old Ivana Hodak, the daughter of a prominent Croat lawyer, and Ivo Pukanic, editor of political weekly *Nacional* – triggered nationwide protests and a political crackdown, as well as further doubts over the date of Croatia joining the EU. The discussions with the EU have been slowed down by various hurdles and the proposed joining date is anywhere between 2010 and 2012.

PEOPLE

Croatia has a population of roughly 4.5 million people. Before the war Croatia had a population of nearly five million, of which 78% were Croats and 12% were Serbs. Bosnians and Hercegovinians, Hungarians, Italians, Czechs, Roma and Albanians made up the remaining 10%. Today Croats constitute 89% of the population and slightly less than 5% of the populations are Serb, followed by 0.5% Bosnians and about 0.4% each of Hungarians and Italians. Most Serbs live in eastern Croatia (Slavonia). The largest cities in Croatia are Zagreb (780,000), Split (188,700), Rijeka (144,000), Osijek (114,600) and Zadar (72,700).

RELIGION

Croats are overwhelmingly Roman Catholic, while the Serbs belong to the Orthodox Church. Catholicism is undergoing a strong resurgence in Croatia. Pope John Paul II visited Croatia several times before his death, though Benedict XVI had not visited at the time of writing. Muslims make up 1.2% of the population and Protestants 0.4%, with a small Jewish population in Zagreb.

ARTS

Literature

Croatia's towering literary figure is 20th-century novelist and playwright Miroslav Krleža (1893–1981). His most popular novels include *The Return of Philip Latinovicz* (1932), which has been translated into English.

Some contemporary writers worth reading are expat writer Dubravka Ugrešić (www.dubravkaugresic.com), best known for her novels *The Culture of Lies* and *The Ministry of Pain*. Slavenka Drakulić's *Café Europa – Life After Communism* is an excellent read, while Miljenko Jergović's *Sarajevo Marlboro* and *Mama Leone* powerfully conjure up the atmosphere and the life in pre-war Yugoslavia.

Music

Although Croatia has produced many fine classical musicians and composers, its most original musical contribution lies in its rich tradition of folk music. The instrument most often used in Croatian folk music is the *tamburica,* a three- or five-string mandolin that is plucked or strummed. Translated as 'group of people', *klapa* is an outgrowth of church-choir singing. The form is most popular in rural Dalmatia and can involve up to 10 voices singing in harmony.

There's a wealth of homegrown talent on Croatia's pop and rock music scene. Some of the most prominent pop, fusion and hip-hop bands are *Hladno Pivo* (Cold Beer), *Pips Chips & Videoclips, TBF, Edo Maajka, Vještice* (The Witches), *Gustafi* and the deliciously insane *Let 3*.

Visual Arts

Vlaho Bukovac (1855–1922) was the most notable Croatian painter in the late 19th century. Important early-20th-century painters include Miroslav Kraljević (1885–1913) and Josip Račić (1885–1908). Post-WWII artists experimented with abstract expressionism but this period is best remembered for the naive art that was typified by Ivan Generalić (1914–92). Recent trends have included minimalism, conceptual art and pop art. Contemporary art that is attracting notice include the multimedia works of Andreja Kulunči and the installations of Sandra Sterle.

ENVIRONMENT

The Land

Croatia is half the size of both Serbia and Montenegro in area and population. The republic swings around like a boomerang from the Pannonian plains of Slavonia between the Sava, Drava and Danube Rivers, across hilly central Croatia to the Istrian Peninsula, then south through Dalmatia along the rugged Adriatic coast.

The narrow Croatian coastal belt at the foot of the Dinaric Alps is only about 600km long as the crow flies, but it's so indented that the actual length is 1778km. If the 4012km of coastline around the offshore islands is added to the total, the length becomes 5790km. Most of the 'beaches' along this jagged coast consist of slabs of rock sprinkled with naturists. Don't come expecting to find sand, but the waters are sparkling clean, even around large towns.

Croatia's offshore islands are every bit as beautiful as those off the coast of Greece. There are 1185 islands and islets along the tectonically submerged Adriatic coastline, 66 inhabited.

Wildlife

Deer are plentiful in the dense forests of Risnjak, as well as brown bears, wild cats and *ris* (lynx). Occasionally a wolf or wild boar may appear, but only rarely. Plitvice Lakes National Park, however, is an important refuge for wolves. A rare sea otter is also protected in Plitvice, as well as in Krka National Park.

The griffon vulture, with a wing span of 2.6m, has a permanent colony on Cres Island, and Paklenica National Park is rich in peregrine falcons, goshawks, sparrow hawks, buzzards and owls. Krka National Park is an important migration route and winter habitat for marsh birds such as herons, wild duck, geese, cranes, rare golden eagles and short-toed eagles.

National Parks

The eight national parks occupy nearly 10% of the country. Brijuni near Pula is the most carefully cultivated park, with well-preserved Mediterranean holm oak forests. The mountainous Risnjak National Park near Delnice, east of Rijeka, is named after one of its inhabitants – the *ris*.

Dense forests of beech and black pine in the Paklenica National Park near Zadar are home to a number of endemic insects, reptiles and birds. The abundant plant and animal life, including bears, wolves and deer, in the Plitvice Lakes National Park between Zagreb and Zadar has warranted its inclusion on Unesco's list of World Natural Heritage sites. Both Plitvice Lakes and Krka National Parks (near Šibenik) feature a dramatic series of cascades and incredible turquoise lakes.

Environmental Issues

The lack of heavy industry in Croatia has left the country largely free of industrial pollution, but its forests are under threat from acid rain from neighbouring countries. The dry summers and brisk *maestral* winds pose substantial fire hazards along the coast. Waste disposal is a pressing problem in Croatia, with insufficient and poorly regulated disposal sites.

FOOD & DRINK

Croatian food is a savoury smorgasbord of taste, echoing the varied cultures that have influenced the country over the course of its history. You'll find a sharp divide between the Italian-style cuisine along the coast and the flavours of Hungary, Austria and Turkey in the continental parts.

Staples & Specialities

Zagreb and northwestern Croatia favour the kind of hearty meat dishes you might find in Vienna. Juicy spit-roasted and baked meat features *janjetina* (lamb), *svinjetina* (pork) and *patka* (duck), often accompanied by *mlinci* (baked noodles) or *pečeni krumpir* (roast potatoes).

Coastal cuisine is typically Mediterranean, using a lot of olive oil, garlic, fresh fish and shellfish, and herbs. Along the coast, look for lightly breaded and fried *lignje* (squid) as a main course. For a special appetiser, try *paški sir*, a pungent hard cheese from the island of Pag. Dalmatian *brodet* (stewed mixed fish served with polenta; also known as *brodetto*) is another regional treat, but it's often only available in two-person portions.

Istrian cuisine has been attracting international foodies for its long gastronomic tradition, fresh foodstuffs and unique specialities. Typical dishes include *maneštra*, a thick vegetable-and-bean soup, *fuži*, hand-rolled pasta often served with truffles or game meat, and *fritaja* (omelette often served with seasonal vegies). Istrian wines and olive oil are highly rated.

It's customary to have a small glass of brandy before a meal and to accompany the food with one of Croatia's many wines. Croatians often mix their wine with water, calling it *bevanda*. *Rakija* (brandy) comes in different flavours. The most commonly drunk are *loza* (grape brandy), *šljivovica* (plum brandy) and *travarica* (herbal brandy).

Zagreb's Ožujsko *pivo* (beer) is very good but Karlovačko *pivo* from Karlovac is even better. You'll probably want to practise saying *živjeli!* (cheers!).

CROATIA

Where to Eat & Drink

Most restaurants cluster in the middle of the price spectrum – few are unbelievably cheap and few are exorbitantly expensive. A restaurant *(restauracija* or *restoran)* is at the top of the food chain, generally presenting a more formal dining experience. A *gostionica* or *konoba* is usually a traditional family-run tavern. A *pivnica* is more like a pub, with a wide choice of beer. A *kavana* is a cafe. Self-service cafeterias are quick, easy and inexpensive, though the quality of the food tends to vary.

Restaurants are open long hours, often noon to midnight, with Sunday closings outside of peak season.

Smoking is a widespread activity in Croatia, and nonsmoking establishments are few and far between. You'll find bars and nightclubs permanently clouded in smoke, while some restaurants have nonsmoking sections.

Vegetarians & Vegans

Outside of major cities like Zagreb, Rijeka, Split and Dubrovnik, vegetarian restaurants are few but Croatia's vegetables are usually locally grown and quite tasty. *Blitva* (swiss chard) is a nutritious side dish often served with potatoes. The hearty *štrukli* (baked cheese dumplings) are a good alternative too.

ZAGREB

☎ 01 / pop 780,000

Everyone knows about Croatia, its coast, beaches and islands, but a mention of the country's capital still draws confused questions of whether it's nice or worth going to for a weekend. Well, here it is, once and for all: yes, Zagreb is a great destination, weekend or week-long. There's lots of culture, arts, music, architecture, nightlife, gastronomy and all the other things that make a quality capital. Admittedly, it doesn't register highly on a nightlife Richter scale, but it does have an ever-developing art and music scene and a growing influx of fun-seeking travellers.

Zagreb is made for strolling, drinking coffee in almost permanently full cafes, popping into museums and galleries and enjoying theatres, concerts, cinema and music. It's a year-round outdoor city; in spring and summer everyone scurries to Lake Jarun in the southwest to swim, boat or dance the night away in a lakeside disco, and in autumn and winter the Zagrebians go skiing at Mt Medvednica, only a tram ride away, or hiking in nearby Samobor.

HISTORY

Medieval Zagreb developed from the 11th to the 13th centuries in the twin villages of Kaptol and Gradec, which make up the city's hilly Old Town. Kaptol grew around St Stephen's Cathedral (now renamed the Cathedral of the Assumption of the Blessed Virgin Mary) and Gradec centred on St Mark's Church. The two hilltop administrations were bitter and often warring rivals until a common threat in the form of Turkish invaders emerged in the 15th century. The two communities merged and became Zagreb, capital of the small portion of Croatia that hadn't fallen to the Turks in the 16th century. As the Turkish threat receded in the 18th century, the town expanded and the population grew. It was the centre of intellectual and political life under the Austro-Hungarian empire and became capital of the Independent State of Croatia in 1941 after the German invasion. The 'independent state' was in fact a Nazi puppet regime in the hands of Ante Pavelić and the Ustaša movement, even though most Zagrebians supported Tito's partisans.

In postwar Yugoslavia, Zagreb took second place to Belgrade but continued expanding. The area south of the Sava River developed into a new district, Novi Zagreb, replete with the glum residential blocks that were a hallmark of postwar Eastern European architecture. Zagreb has been capital of Croatia since 1991, when the country became independent.

ORIENTATION

The city is divided into Lower Zagreb, where most shops, restaurants, hotels and businesses are located, and Upper Zagreb, defined by the two hills of Kaptol and Gradec. As you come out of the train station, you'll see a series of parks and pavilions directly in front of you and the twin neo-Gothic towers of the cathedral in Kaptol in the distance. Trg Jelačića, beyond the northern end of the parks, is the main city square of Lower Zagreb. There is a bus that runs from the airport to the bus station (see p132). The bus station is 1km east of the train station. Trams 2 and 6 run from the bus station to the train station, with tram 6 continuing to Trg Jelačića.

INFORMATION

Bookshops

Algoritam (Gajeva 1; ⌚ 8am-7pm Mon-Fri, 9am-5pm Sat) A wide selection of books and magazines to choose from in English, French, German, Italian and Croatian.

Discount Cards

Zagreb Card (www.zagrebcard.fivestars.hr/page_hr_on linecatalogue.htm; 24/72hr 60/90KN) Provides free travel on all public transport, a 50% discount on museum and gallery entries, plus discounts in some bars and restaurants, car rental etc. The card is sold at the main tourist office and many hostels, hotels, bars and shops.

Emergency

Police station (☎ 45 63 311; Petrinjska 30) Assists foreigners with visa problems.

Internet Access

Sublink (☎ 48 11 329; Teslina 12; per hr 15KN; ⌚ 9am-10pm Mon-Sat, 3-10pm Sun) It was the city's first cybercafe and it remains its best.

Laundry

If you're staying in private accommodation you can usually arrange with the owner to do your laundry, which would be cheaper than the two options listed below. Expect to pay about 65KN to do 5kg of laundry.

Petecin (☎ 48 14 802; Kaptol 11; ⌚ 8am-8pm Mon-Fri)
Predom (☎ 46 12 990; Draškovićeva 31; ⌚ 7am-7pm Mon-Fri)

Left Luggage

Garderoba bus station (per hr 1.20KN; ⌚ 5am-10pm Mon-Sat, 6am-10pm Sun); train station (per hr 1.20KN; ⌚ 24hr)

Medical Services

Dental Emergency (☎ 48 28 488; Perkovčeva 3; ⌚ 24hr)
KBC Rebro (☎ 23 88 888; Kišpatićeva 12; ⌚ 24hr) East of the city, it provides emergency aid.
Pharmacy (☎ 48 16 159; Trg Jelačića 2; ⌚ 24hr)

Money

There are ATMs at the bus and train stations and the airport, as well as numerous locations around town. Exchange offices at the

ZAGREB IN TWO DAYS

Start your day with a stroll through Strossmayerov Trg, Zagreb's oasis of greenery. While you're there, take a look at the **Strossmayer Gallery of Old Masters** (p127) and then walk to Trg Josipa Jelačića, the city's centre. Head up to **Kaptol** (p126) for a look at the **Cathedral of the Assumption of the Blessed Virgin Mary** (p127), the centre of Zagreb's (and Croatia's) spiritual life. While you're in the Upper Town, pick up some fruit at the **Dolac fruit and vegetable market** (p126). Then, get to know the work of Croatia's best sculptor at **Meštrović Atelier** (p127) and take in a contemporary art exhibition at **Galerija Klovićevi Dvori** (p127). See the lay of the city from the top of **Lotrščak Tower** (p127). Enjoy a drink at **Škola** (p130) or bar-crawling along **Tkalčićeva** (p130).

On the second day, tour the Lower Town museums, reserving a good two hours for the **Museum Mimara** (p127), then have lunch at **Tip Top** (p130). Early evening is best at **Trg Petra Preradovića** (p130) before dining at one of the **Lower Town restaurants** (p129) and sampling some of Zagreb's nightlife.

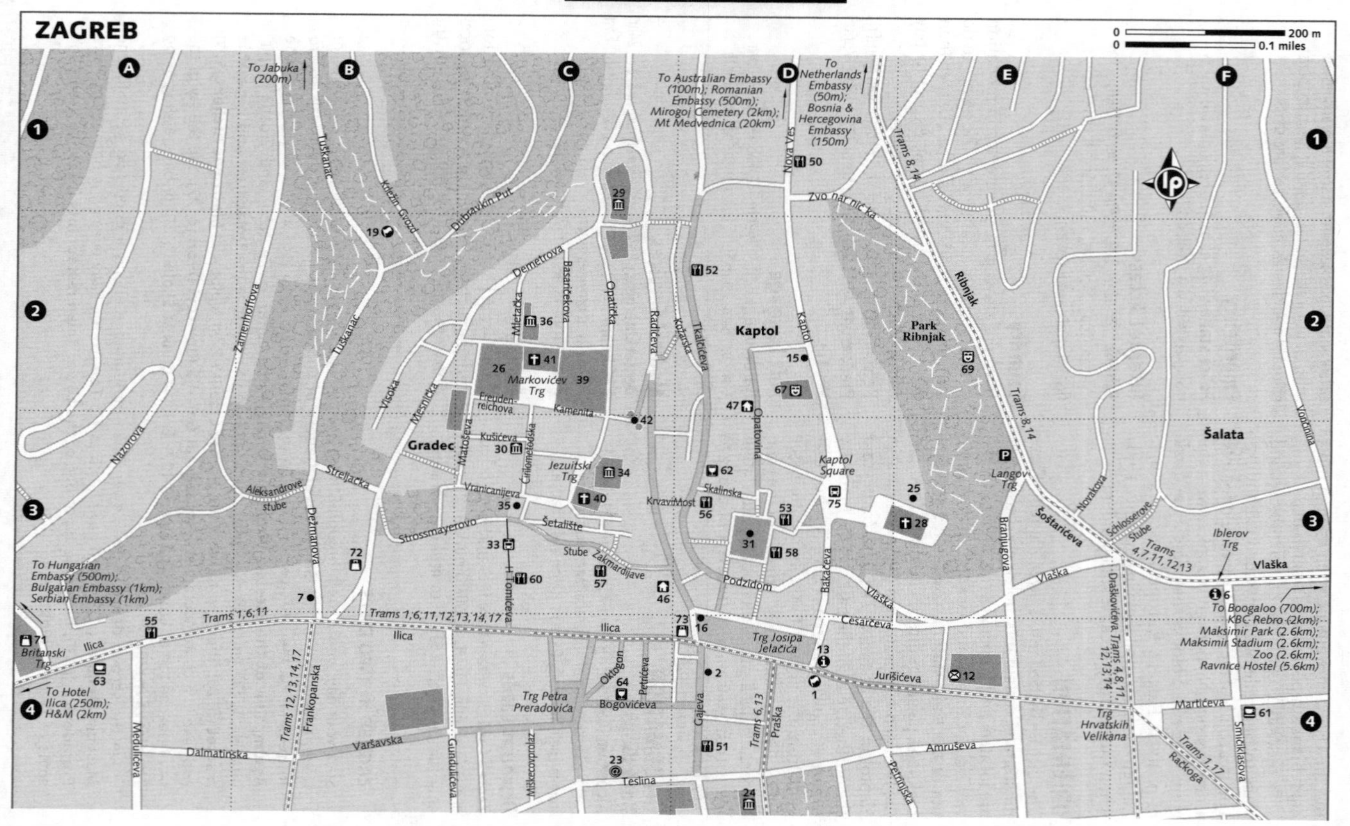
ZAGREB
0 200 m
0 0.1 miles
To Jabuka (200m)
To Australian Embassy (100m); Romanian Embassy (500m); Mirogoj Cemetery (2km); Mt Medvednica (20km)
To Netherlands Embassy (50m); Bosnia & Hercegovina Embassy (150m)
Nova Ves
Zvonarnička
Trams 8,14
Ribnjak
Park Ribnjak
Šalata
Vončinina
Tuškanac
Krležin Gvozd
Dubravkin Put
Demetrova
Mletačka
Basaričekova
Opatička
Radićeva
Kožarska
Tkalčićeva
Kaptol
Zamenhoffova
Markovićev Trg
Freudenreichova
Kamenita
Visoka
Mesnička
Matoševa
Gradec
Kušićeva
Ćirilometodska
Jezuitski Trg
Opatovina
Kaptol Square
Langov Trg
Novakova
Schlosserove Stube
Šoštarićeva
Nazorova
Strelјačka
Aleksandrove stube
Vranicanijeva
Skalinska
Krvavi Most
Branjugova
Strossmayerovo
Šetalište
Stube Zakmardijeve
Dežmanova
Tomićeva
Podzidom
Bakačeva
Vlaška
Iblerov Trg
Trams 4,7,11,12,13
Vlaška
To Hungarian Embassy (500m); Bulgarian Embassy (1km); Serbian Embassy (1km)
Trams 1,6,11
Trams 1,6,11,12,13,14,17
Ilica
Trg Josipa Jelačića
Cesarčeva
Draškovićeva Trams 4,8,11,12,13,14
To Boogaloo (700m); KBC Rebro (2km); Maksimir Park (2.6km); Maksimir Stadium (2.6km); Zoo (2.6km); Ravnice Hostel (5.6km)
Britanski Trg
Ilica
To Hotel Ilica (250m); H&M (2km)
Oktogon
Petrićeva
Jurišićeva
Trg Petra Preradovića
Bogovićeva
Gajeva
Trams 6,13
Praška
Martićeva
Trg Hrvatskih Velikana
Trams 12,13,14,17
Frankopanska
Medulićeva
Dalmatinska
Varšavska
Gundulićeva
Miškecovprolaz
Teslina
Amruševa
Petrinjska
Trams 1,17
Račkoga
Smičiklasova
A B C D E F
1 2 3 4

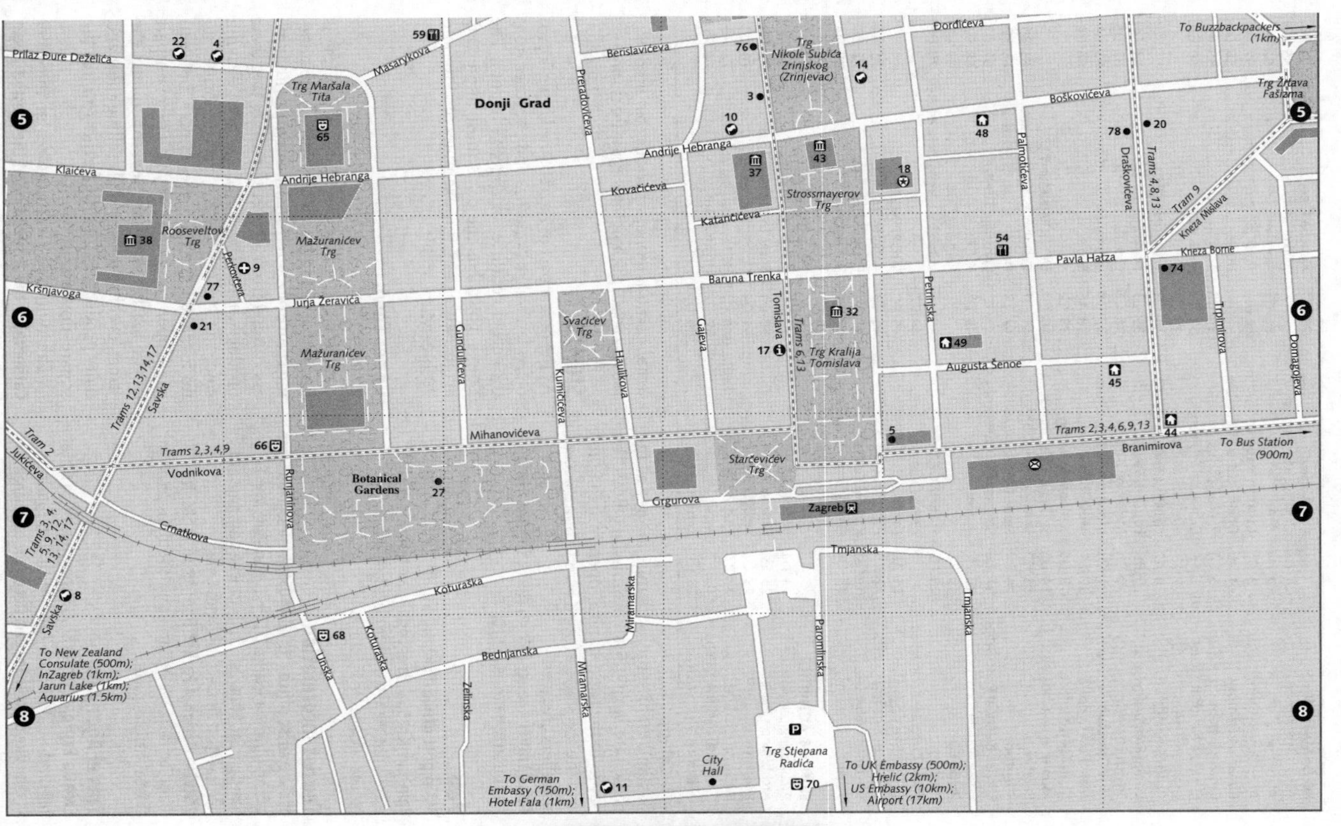
To Buzzbackpackers (1km)
Trg Žrtava Fašizma
Đorđićeva
Prilaz Đure Deželića
Masarykova
Berislavićeva
Trg Nikole Subića Zrinjskog (Zrinjevac)
Boškovićeva
Trg Maršala Tita
Donji Grad
Preradovićeva
Andrije Hebranga
Klaićeva
Kovačićeva
Strossmayerov Trg
Palmotićeva
Draškovićeva
Trams 4,8,13
Tram 9
Kneza Mislava
Katančićeva
Rooseveltov Trg
Mažuranićev Trg
Perkovčeva
Kneza Borne
Pavla Hatza
Baruna Trenka
Kršnjavoga
Jurja Žeravića
Svačićev Trg
Gundulićeva
Gajeva
Tomislava
Trams 6,13
Trg Kralja Tomislava
Petrinjska
Trpimirova
Domagojeva
Trams 12,13,14,17
Savska
Kumičićeva
Haulikova
Augusta Šenoe
Trams 2,3,4,6,9,13
Mihanovićeva
Tram 2
Jukićeva
Trams 2,3,4,9
Vodnikova
Runjaninova
Botanical Gardens
Starčevićev Trg
Branimirova
To Bus Station (900m)
Grgurova
Zagreb
Crnatkova
Trams 3,4,5,9,12,13,14,17
Tmjanska
Koturaška
Miramarska
Paromlinska
Unska
Bednjanska
Zelinska
To New Zealand Consulate (500m); InZagreb (1km); Jarun Lake (1km); Aquarius (1.5km)
Trg Stjepana Radića
City Hall
To German Embassy (150m); Hotel Fala (1km)
To UK Embassy (500m); Hrelić (2km); US Embassy (10km); Airport (17km)

CROATIA

INFORMATION
Albanian Embassy ... **1** D4
Algoritam ... **2** D4
Atlas Travel Agency ... **3** D5
Canadian Embassy ... **4** A5
Croatia Express ... **5** E7
Croatian National Tourist Board ... **6** F3
Croatian YHA ... **7** B3
Czech Embassy ... **8** A7
Dental Emergency ... **9** B6
French Embassy ... **10** D5
Irish Consulate ... **11** C8
Main Post Office ... **12** E4
Main Tourist Office ... **13** D4
Montenegrin Embassy ... **14** D5
Petecin ... **15** D2
Pharmacy ... **16** D4
Plitvice National Park Office ... **17** D6
Police Station ... **18** E5
Polish Embassy ... **19** B2
Predom ... **20** F5
Savez Organizacija Invalida Hrvatske ... **21** A6
Slovakian Embassy ... **22** A5
Slovenian Embassy ... (see 8)
Sublink ... **23** C4

SIGHTS & ACTIVITIES
Archaeological Museum ... **24** D4
Archbishop's Palace ... **25** E3
Banski Dvori ... **26** C2
Botanical Gardens ... **27** B7
Cathedral of the Assumption of the Blessed Virgin Mary ... **28** E3
City Museum ... **29** C1
Croatian Museum of Naïve Art ... **30** C3
Croatian National Theatre ... (see 65)
Dolac Fruit & Vegetable Market ... **31** D3
Exhibition Pavilion ... **32** D6
Funicular Railway ... **33** C3
Galerija Klovićevi Dvori ... **34** C3
Lotrščak Tower ... **35** C3
Meštrović Atelier ... **36** C2
Modern Gallery ... **37** D5
Museum Mimara ... **38** A6
National Assembly ... **39** C2
St Catherine's Church ... **40** C3
St Mark's Church ... **41** C2
Stone Gate ... **42** C3
Strossmayer Gallery of Old Masters ... **43** D5

SLEEPING
Arcotel Allegra ... **44** F7
Evistas ... **45** F6
Fulir Hostel ... **46** C3
Krovovi Grada ... **47** D2
Nemoj Stati/Never Stop ... **48** E5
Omladinski Hostel ... **49** E6

EATING
Baltazar ... **50** D1
Boban ... **51** D4
Fruit & Vegetable Market ... (see 71)
Ivica i Marica ... **52** D2
Kerempuh ... **53** D3
Konoba Čiho ... **54** E6
Makronova ... **55** A4
Nocturno ... **56** D3
Pod Gričkom Topom ... **57** C3
Rubelj ... **58** D3
Tip Top ... **59** B5
Vallis Aurea ... **60** C3

DRINKING
Booksa ... **61** F4
Cica ... **62** D3
Eli's Café ... **63** A4
Škola ... **64** C4

ENTERTAINMENT
Croatian National Theatre ... **65** B5
David ... **66** B7
Komedija Theatre ... **67** D2
KSET ... **68** B8
Purgeraj ... **69** E2
Vatroslav Lisinski Concert Hall ... **70** D8

SHOPPING
Antiques Market ... **71** A4
Prostor ... **72** B3
Rukotvorine ... **73** D4

TRANSPORT
Budget Rent-a-Car ... **74** F6
Buses to Mirogoj ... **75** D3
Croatia Airlines ... **76** D5
Hertz ... **77** A6
Hrvatski Autoklub ... **78** F5

bus and train stations change money at the bank rate with 1.5% commission. Both the banks in the train station (open 7am to 9pm) and the bus station (open 6am to 8pm) accept travellers cheques.

Atlas Travel Agency (☎ 48 13 933; Zrinjevac 17) The Amex representative in Zagreb.

Post

Main post office (Branimirova 4; 24hr Mon-Sat, 1pm-midnight Sun) Holds poste-restante mail. This post office is also the best place to make long-distance telephone calls and send packages.

Tourist Information

Main tourist office (☎ 48 14 051; www.zagreb-touristinfo.hr; Trg Josipa Jelačića 11; 8.30am-8pm Mon-Fri, 9am-5pm Sat, 10am-2pm Sun) Distributes city maps and free leaflets. It also sells the Zagreb Card.

Plitvice National Park Office (☎ 46 13 586; Trg Kralja Tomislava 19; 9am-5pm Mon-Fri) Has details on Croatia's national parks.

Travel Agencies

Croatia Express (☎ 49 22 237; www.zug.hr; Trg Kralja Tomislava 17; 9.30am-7pm Mon-Fri, 9am-3pm Sat) At this office opposite the train station you can change money, make train reservations, rent cars, buy air tickets and ferry tickets, plus book hotels around the country.

SIGHTS

As the oldest part of Zagreb, the Upper Town offers landmark buildings and churches from the earlier centuries of Zagreb's history. The Lower Town has the city's most interesting art museums and fine examples of 19th- and 20th-century architecture.

Upper Town

KAPTOL

Zagreb's colourful **Dolac** (Market; 6am-3pm) is just north of Trg Josipa Jelačića. It's the buzzing centre of Zagreb's daily activity, with traders coming from all over Croatia to flog their products here. The Dolac has been heaving since the 1930s when the city authorities set up a market space on the 'border' between the Upper and Lower towns. The main part of the market is on an elevated square; the street level has indoor stalls selling meat and dairy products and a little further towards the square, flower stands.

The twin neo-Gothic spires of the 1899 **Cathedral of the Assumption of the Blessed Virgin**

Mary (Katedrala Marijina Uznešenja; formerly known as St Stephen's Cathedral) are nearby. Elements of the medieval cathedral on this site, destroyed by an earthquake in 1880, can be seen inside, including 13th-century frescos, Renaissance pews, marble altars and a baroque pulpit. The baroque **Archbishop's Palace** surrounds the cathedral, as do 16th-century fortifications constructed when Zagreb was threatened by the Turks.

GRADEC

From Radićeva 5, off Trg Jelačića, a pedestrian walkway called stube Ivana Zakmardija leads to the **Lotrščak Tower** (Kula Lotrščak; ☎ 48 51 768; admission 10KN; 🕑 11am-7pm Tue-Sun) and a **funicular railway** (one way 3KN; 🕑 6.30am-9pm) built in 1888, which connects the Lower and Upper Towns. The tower has a sweeping 360-degree view of the city. To the east is the baroque **St Catherine's Church** (Crkva Svete Katarine), with Jezuitski trg beyond. The **Galerija Klovićevi Dvori** (☎ 48 51 926; Jezuitski trg 4; adult/student 40/20KN; 🕑 11am-7pm Tue-Sun) is Zagreb's premier exhibition hall, where superb art shows are staged. Further north and to the east is the 13th-century **Stone Gate**, with a painting of the Virgin, which escaped the devastating fire of 1731.

Gothic **St Mark's Church** (Crkva Svetog Marka; ☎ 48 51 611; Markovićev trg; 🕑 11am-4pm & 5.30-7pm) marks the centre of Gradec. Inside are works by Ivan Meštrović, Croatia's most famous modern sculptor. On the eastern side of St Mark's is the Croatia's 1908 **National Assembly** (Sabor).

West of the church is the 18th-century **Banski Dvori**, the presidential palace, with guards at the door in red ceremonial uniform. Between April and September there is a changing of the guard ceremony at noon at the weekend.

Not far from the palace is the former **Meštrović Atelier** (☎ 48 51 123; Mletačka 8; adult/concession 30/15KN; 🕑 10am-6pm Tue-Fri, to 2pm Sat), now housing an excellent collection of some 100 sculptures, drawings, lithographs and furniture created by the artist. There are several other museums nearby. The best is the **City Museum** (Muzej Grada Zagreba; ☎ 48 51 364; Opatička 20; adult/concession 20/10KN; 🕑 10am-6pm Tue-Fri, to 1pm Sat & Sun), with a scale model of old Gradec, atmospheric background music and interactive exhibits that fascinate kids. Summaries in English and German are in each room of the museum, which is in the former Convent of St Claire (1650). There's also the lively and colourful **Croatian Museum of Naive Art** (Hrvatski Muzej Naivne Umjetnosti; ☎ 48 51 911; Ćirilometodska 3; adult/concession 10/5KN; 🕑 10am-6pm Tue-Fri, to 1pm Sat & Sun).

FREE THRILLS

Though you'll have to pay to get into most of Zagreb's galleries and museums, there are some gorgeous parks and markets to be enjoyed for nowt – and there's always window shopping!

- Taste bits of food for free at **Dolac** (opposite) – but don't be too cheeky!
- Smell the herbs at the **Botanical Gardens** (p128).
- Enjoy the long walks around **Maksimir Park** (p128).
- See the magnificent **Mirogoj cemetery** (p128).
- Pop inside the gorgeous baroque **St Catherine's Church** (above) and the ever-renovated **cathedral** (above).

Lower Town

Zagreb really is a city of museums. There are four in the parks between the train station and Trg Jelačića. The yellow **exhibition pavilion** (1897) across the park from the station presents changing contemporary art exhibitions. The second building north, also in the park, houses the **Strossmayer Gallery of Old Masters** (Strossmayerova Galerija Starih Majstora; ☎ 48 95 115; www.mdc.hr/strossmayer; Zrinjevac 11; adult/concession 10/5KN; 🕑 10am-1pm & 5-7pm Tue, 10am-1pm Wed-Sun). When it's closed you can still enter the interior courtyard to see the Baška Slab (1102) from the island of Krk, one of the oldest inscriptions in the Croatian language.

The fascinating **Archaeological Museum** (Arheološki Muzej; ☎ 48 73 101; www.amz.hr; Trg Nikole Šubića Zrinjskog 19; adult/concession 20/10KN; 🕑 10am-5pm Tue-Fri, to 1pm Sat & Sun) has a wide-ranging display of artefacts from prehistoric times through to the medieval period. Behind the museum is a garden of Roman sculpture that is turned into a pleasant open-air cafe in the summer.

The **Modern Gallery** (Moderna Galerija; ☎ 49 22 368; Andrije Hebranga 1; adult/concession 20/10KN; 10am-6pm Tue-Sat, to 1pm Sun) presents temporary exhibitions that offer an excellent chance to catch up with the latest in Croatian painting.

The **Museum Mimara** (Muzej Mimara; ☎ 48 28 100; Rooseveltov trg 5; adult/concession 20/15KN; 🕑 10am-5pm

Tue, Wed, Fri & Sat, to 7pm Thu, to 2pm Sun) houses a diverse collection amassed by Ante Topić Mimara and donated to Croatia. Housed in a neo-Renaissance palace, the collection includes icons, glassware, sculpture, Oriental art and works by renowned painters such as Rembrandt, Velázquez, Raphael and Degas.

The neobaroque **Croatian National Theatre** (☎ 48 28 532; Trg Maršala Tita 15; 🕒 box office 10am-1pm & 5-7.30pm Mon-Fri, to 1pm Sat, 30min before performances Sun) dates from 1895 and has Ivan Meštrović's sculpture *Fountain of Life* (1905) in front. The **Botanical Gardens** (Mihanovićeva; admission free; 🕒 9am-7pm Tue-Sun), laid out in 1890, has 10,000 species of plant, including 1800 tropical flora specimens. The landscaping has created restful corners and paths that seem a world away from bustling Zagreb.

Out of Town

A 20-minute ride north of the city centre on bus 106 from the cathedral takes you to **Mirogoj** (Medvednica; 🕒 6am-10pm), one of the most beautiful cemeteries in Europe. The cemetery was designed in 1876 by one of Croatia's finest architects, Herman Bollé, who also created numerous buildings around Zagreb. The sculpted and artfully designed tombs lie beyond a majestic arcade topped by a string of cupolas.

Another suburban delight is **Maksimir Park** (Maksimirska; 🕒 9am-dusk), a peaceful wooded enclave covering 18 hectares; it is easily accessible by trams 4, 7, 11 and 12. Opened to the public in 1794, it was the first public promenade in southeastern Europe. There's also a modest **zoo** (adult/child under 8yr, 20/10KN; 🕒 9am-8pm).

TOURS

The main tourist office sells tickets for two-hour walking tours (95KN) that operate Monday through Thursday, leaving from Trg Jelačića, as well as three-hour bus and walking tours (150KN) that operate Friday through Sunday, leaving from the Arcotel Allegra hotel.

FESTIVALS & EVENTS

During odd-numbered years in April there's the **Zagreb Biennale** (www.biennale-zagreb.hr), Croatia's most important classical music event. Zagreb also hosts the gay **Queer Zagreb FM Festival** (www.queerzagreb.org). Zagreb's highest profile music event is **Vip INmusic Festival** (www.vipinmusicfestival.com), a two-day extravaganza on 3 and 4 June, taking place on Jarun Lake's island. In July and August the **Zagreb Summer Festival** presents a cycle of concerts and theatre performances on open stages in the upper town. For a complete listing of Zagreb events, see www.zagreb-convention.hr.

SLEEPING

Zagreb's accommodation scene has been undergoing a small but noticeable change with the arrival of some of Europe's budget airlines: the budget end of the market (so far rather fledgling) has started to get a pulse. Although the new hostels cater mainly to the backpacker crowd, it's a good beginning. For midrangers and those wanting more privacy and a homely feel, there are private rooms and apartments, arranged through agencies.

Prices stay the same in all seasons, but be prepared for a 20% surcharge if you arrive during a festival, especially the autumn business fair (16 to 21 September).

If you intend to stay in a private house or apartment, try not to arrive on Sunday, because most of the agencies will be closed. Prices for doubles run from about 300KN and apartments start at 400KN per night for a studio. Some agencies:

Evistas (☎ 48 39 554; evistas@zg.htnet.hr; Augusta Šenoe 28; s from 200KN, d 250KN, 🕒 9am-1.30pm & 3-8pm Mon-Fri, 9.30am-5pm Sat) Recommended by the tourist office.

InZagreb (☎ 65 23 201; www.inzagreb.com; Remetinečka 13; apts from €65-86) Great, centrally located apartments with a minimum two-night stay. The price includes bike rental and pick-up and drop-off from the train and/or bus station.

Nemoj Stati/Never Stop (☎ 48 73 225; www.nest.hr; Boškovićeva 7a; 🕒 9am-5pm Mon-Fri) Has apartments in the centre of town, but note the minimum three-night stay. Contact for prices.

Fulir Hostel (☎ 48 30 882; www.fulir-hostel.com; Radićeva 3a; dm 100-140KN; 💻) Right in the centre of town and seconds away from the bustle of Jelačića and bars on Tkalčićeva, the Fulir has 16 beds, friendly owners, self-catering facilities (perfect for its proximity to Dolac market), a DVD-packed common room, satellite TV and free internet. Opened in summer 2006, it's a popular spot for shoestring travellers, so book in advance.

Omladinski Hostel (☎ 48 41 261; www.hfhs.hr; Petrinjska 77; 6-/3-bed dm per person 103/113KN, s/d 193/256KN) A bit of a sad place, which, although recently refurbished, maintains the old gloomy feel. The rooms are sparse and clean, it's relatively central and the cheapest in town.

Buzzbackpackers (☎ 23 20 267; www.buzzbackpackers.com; Babukićeva 1b; dm from 120KN; d from 400KN;) More slick and bright than Fulir, but a bit further out, Buzzbackpackers is another great-value newcomer. It's clean, the rooms are bright, there's wi-fi access, free internet, a shiny kitchen, laundry service (for a fee), and a BBQ area for the summer months. Take tram 4 or 9 from the main train station to Heinzelova stop, it's a short walk from there (check the website for detailed directions).

Krovovi Grada (☎ 48 14 189; Opatovina 33; s/d/tr 200/300/400KN) Possibly the most charming of Zagreb's central options, this place is right in the Upper Town. The restored old house is set back from the street and has creaky-floor rooms with pieces of vintage furniture and grandma blankets. There are two large apartments with shared bathrooms that can sleep eight.

Hotel Ilica (☎ 37 77 522; www.hotel-ilica.hr; Ilica 102; s/d/tr/apt 399/499/599/849KN;) A great central option, with rooms ranging from super kitsch to lushly decorous – there are gilded motifs, plush beds, wall-long paintings and lots of reds. The bathrooms are well-equipped and the setting is quiet. Trams 6, 11 and 12 stop right outside the entrance, or walk down buzzy Ilica for 15 minutes.

our pick **Arcotel Allegra** (☎ 46 96 000; www.arcotel.at/allegra; Branimirova 29; d €152-162;) The Arcotel Allegra is Zagreb's first designer hotel, with airy, elegant rooms and a plush, marble-and-exotic-fish reception. The bed linen is covetable and soft and the bed throws are printed with the faces of Kafka, Kahlo, Freud, Lorca and numerous other iconic personalities. There's a DVD player in each room and the hotel has movies you can borrow. The top floor has a gym, sauna and great views of the city. The on-site Radicchio restaurant is good and Joe's Bar's hot on Latino music.

EATING

You'll have to love Croatian and (below par) Italian food to enjoy Zagreb's restaurants, but new places are branching out to include Japanese and other world cuisines. The biggest move is towards elegantly presented haute cuisine at haute prices.

Upper Town

Rubelj (☎ 48 18 777; www.rubelj-grill.hr; Tržnica Mala Terasa; mains from 25KN) One of the many Rubeljs across town, this Dolac branch is a great place for a quick portion of *ćevapi* (spicy beef or pork meatballs). And though none are as tasty as those in neighbouring Bosnia and Hercegovina (the spiritual home of the *ćevap*), these are Zagreb's best.

Vallis Aurea (☎ 48 31 305; Tomićeva 4; mains from 30KN) This is a true local eatery that has some of the best home cooking you'll find in town, so it's no wonder that it's chock-a-block at lunchtimes. Taste the Dalmatian staple, the *pašticada* (beef stew) or the slightly spicy beans, and accompany either with some house red. Right by the lower end of the funicular.

Ivica i Marica (☎ 48 17 321; Tkalčićeva 70; mains from 40KN) Based on the Brothers Grimm story of Hansel and Gretel, this little restaurant–cake shop is made to look like the 'food house' from the tale, with waiting staff clad in traditional costume. It's not exactly vegie, but it does have a decent range of vegie and fish dishes plus meatier fare. The ice creams and cakes are good too.

our pick **Kerempuh** (☎ 48 19 000; Kaptol 3; mains 50-70KN) Overlooking Dolac market, this is a fabulous place to taste a) Croatian cuisine cooked well and simply, and b) the market's ingredients on your plate. The daily set menu changes, well, daily, and the dishes are decided in the morning, when the chef gets that day's freshest ingredients from Dolac. Get an outside table and enjoy the excellent food and market views.

Pod Gričkim Topom (☎ 48 33 607; Zakmardijeve Stube 5; mains from 90KN) Tucked away by a leafy path below the Upper Town, this restaurant has a somewhat self-conscious charm, but it has an outdoor terrace and good Croatian meat-based specialities. It's a great place to hole up on a snowy winter evening or dine under the stars in the summer months.

Baltazar (☎ 46 66 999; www.restoran-baltazar.hr; Nova Ves 4; mains from 120KN; Mon-Sat) Meat – duck, lamb, pork, beef and turkey – is grilled and prepared the Zagorje and Slavonia way in this upmarket old-timer with a good choice of local wines. The summer terrace is a great place to dine under the stars.

You can pick up excellent fresh produce at Dolac market (p126).

Lower Town

Nocturno (☎ 48 13 394; Skalinska 4; mains 20-50KN) Right on the sloping street underneath the Cathedral, this place is very popular for its

Italian menu and lively outdoor terrace. There are all the usual pizzas, plus some good salads, which will gladden vegetarian hearts. The risottos are pretty huge, so order one of those if you're starving.

our pick **Tip Top** (☎ 48 30 349; Gundulićeva 18; mains from 35KN) Oh, how we love Tip Top and its wait staff, who still sport old Socialist uniforms and scowling faces that eventually turn to smiles. But how we mostly love the excellent Dalmatian food. Every day has its own set menu (in addition to à la carte) but Thursdays are particularly delicious, with the octopus *brodet* (octopus stewed in red wine, garlic and herbs). Owned and run by Korčulans, you'll find that island's wines on offer – the wines that were no doubt enjoyed by Tin Ujević, Tip Top's once most loyal customer.

Boban (☎ 48 11 549; Gajeva 9; mains 40-60KN) Italian is the name of the game in this cellar restaurant that's owned by the Croatian World Cup star Zvonimir Boban. Devised by an Italian chef (who hasn't quite instilled the concept of *pasta al dente* into the local chefs), the menu is a robust range of pastas, salads and meats. It's a popular lunch and dinner spot; the upstairs cafe's terrace attracts Zagreb's youngsters.

Konoba Čiho (☎ 48 17 060; Pavla Hatza 15; mains from 55KN; Mon-Sat) Another old-school Dalmatian *konoba*, where downstairs you can get fish and seafood grilled or stewed just the way the regulars like it. Try the wide range of *rakija*.

Makronova (☎ 48 47 115; www.makronova.com; Ilica 72; mains 80-120KN; Mon-Sat) This macrobiotic restaurant is elegant and peaceful and more than welcoming for those of the vegan persuasion. It's part of a whole healthy emporium – there's a health-food shop downstairs, shiatsu treatment, yoga classes and feng-shui courses.

There's also a **fruit and vegetable market** (7am-3pm) on Britanski Trg.

DRINKING

In the Upper Town, the chic Tkalčićeva is throbbing with bars. In the Lower Town, Trg Petra Preradovića is the most popular spot for street performers and occasional bands in mild weather. One of the nicest ways to see Zagreb is to join in on the *špica* – the Saturday morning and pre-lunch coffee drinking on the many terraces along Preradovićeva and Tkalčićeva.

our pick **Booksa** (☎ 46 16 124; www.booksa.hr; Martićeva 14D; 9am-11pm Tue-Sun) Bookworms and poets, writers and performers, oddballs and artists, and anyone on the creative side of things in Zagreb come to chat and drink coffee, buy books and hear readings at this lovely bookshop. There are English-language readings here too, so check the website.

Eli's Café (☎ 091 527 9990; www.eliscaffe.com; Ilica 63; 8am-9pm Mon-Sat, 9am-3pm Sun) You'll see why this tiny place was awarded the 'Best Coffee in Croatia' in 2008, when you try the excellent espresso or smooth cappuccino. There are also breakfast pastries for dipping.

our pick **Škola** (☎ 48 28 197; www.skolaloungebar.com; Bogovićeva 7) This has to be the best designed bar in the whole of Zagreb with its huge, differently themed rooms, lounge sofas, an olive tree in the middle of the main room, and notebook-style menus (it's called School, you see?). There are DJ nights, various 'after-school' parties and it's packed with the trendiest of people (and, of course, students).

Cica (Tkalčićeva 18) It's the size of an East London bedsit, with a similar vibe to match: an underground place with a massive choice of *rakija* in all flavours – herbal, nutty, fruity – you think it, they have it. Lovers of hedonistic pleasures, Cica is your place.

ENTERTAINMENT

Zagreb is definitely a happening city. Its theatres and concert halls present a great variety of programs throughout the year. Many (but not all) are listed in the monthly brochure *Zagreb Events & Performances*, which is available from the main tourist office.

Nightclubs

The dress code is relaxed in most Zagreb clubs. It doesn't get lively until near midnight.

KSET (☎ 61 29 999; www.kset.org; Unska 3; 8pm-midnight Mon-Fri, to 3am Sat) Zagreb's best music venue, with everyone who's anyone performing here.

Aquarius (☎ 36 40 231; Jarun Lake) A truly fab place to party, this enormously popular spot has a series of rooms that open onto a huge terrace on the lake.

Boogaloo (☎ 63 13 021; www.boogaloo.hr; OTV Dom, Vukovarska 68) A great venue that hosts DJ nights and live music.

Purgeraj (☎ 48 14 734; Park Ribnjak) Live rock, blues, rock-blues, blues-rock, country rock and avant-garde jazz.

CROATIA

Jabuka (☎ 48 34 397; Jabukovac 28) An old-time favourite, with 1980s hits played to a thirty-something crowd that reminisces about the good old days.

Gay & Lesbian Venues

The gay and lesbian scene in Zagreb is finally becoming more open than it had previously been, although 'free-wheeling' it isn't. Many gays discreetly cruise the south beach around Jarun Lake and are welcome in most discos. **David** (☎ 091 533 7757; Marulićev Trg 3) is a sauna, bar and video room, popular on Zagreb's gay scene.

Sport

Football (soccer) games are held every Sunday afternoon at the **Maksimir Stadium** (Maksimirska 128), on the eastern side of Zagreb; catch tram 4, 7, 11 or 12 to Bukovačka. If you arrive too early for the game, Zagreb's zoo is just across the street.

Performing Arts

It's worth making the rounds of the theatres in person to check their programs. Tickets are usually available for performances, even for the best shows. A small office marked 'Kazalište Komedija' (look out for the posters) also sells theatre tickets; it's in the Oktogon, a passage connecting Trg Petra Preradovića to Ilica 3.

The neobaroque Croatian National Theatre (p128) was established in 1895. It stages opera and ballet performances.

Komedija Theatre (☎ 48 14 566; Kaptol 9) Near the cathedral, the Komedija Theatre stages operettas and musicals.

Vatroslav Lisinski Concert Hall (☎ ticket office 61 21 166; Trg Stjepana Radića 4; 9am-8pm Mon-Fri, to 2pm Sat) Just south of the train station, this concert hall is a prestigious venue where symphony concerts are held regularly.

SHOPPING

Ilica is Zagreb's main shopping street.

our pick **Prostor** (☎ 48 46 016; www.multiracionalnakompanija.com; Mesnička 5; noon-8pm Mon-Fri; 10am-3pm Sat) A fantastic little shop that's an art gallery and a clothes shop at the same time, featuring some of the city's best independent artists and young designers.

Rukotvorine (☎ 48 31 303; Trg Josipa Jelačića 7) Sells traditional Croatian handicrafts such as dolls, pottery and red-and-white embroidered tablecloths.

MARKET DAYS

The Sunday **antiques market** (9am-2pm) on Britanski Trg is one of central Zagreb's joys, but to see a flea market that's unmatched in the whole of Croatia, you have to make it to **Hrelić** (7am-3pm). It's a huge space that's packed with anything – and we mean anything – from car parts, cars, antique furniture to clothes, records, kitchenware, you name it. Apart from the shopping it's a great place to experience the truly Balkan part and chaotic fun of Zagreb – Roma, music, bartering, grilled meat smoke and general gusto. If you're going in the summer months, take a hat and put on some sunscreen – there's no shade. Take bus 295 to Sajam Jakuševac from behind the train station.

GETTING THERE & AWAY

Air

For information about international flights to and from Croatia, see p172.

Bus

Zagreb's big, modern **bus station** (☎ 61 57 983; www.akz.hr, in Croatian) has a large waiting room and a number of shops. You can buy most international tickets at windows 17 to 20.

Buses depart from Zagreb for most parts of Croatia, Slovenia and places beyond; see p132 for domestic services. There is a service between Sarajevo (BiH) and Zagreb (€18, eight hours, three daily), as well as a service from Zagreb to Belgrade (€20, six hours, six daily; at Bajakovo on the border, a Serbian bus takes you on to Belgrade). There are buses from Ljubljana (Slovenia) to Zagreb (110KN, three hours, two daily).

Train

Domestic trains depart from **Zagreb train station** (☎ 060 33 34 44; www.hznet.hr); see p132 for services. All daily trains to Zadar stop at Knin. Reservations are required on fast InterCity (IC) trains and there's a supplement of 5KN to 15KN for fast or express trains.

For destinations outside Croatia, there's a daily train service to Zagreb from Sarajevo (BiH) each morning (260KN, eight hours), five daily trains between Zagreb and Belgrade (Serbia; €25, seven hours), and up to 11 trains daily between Zagreb and Ljubljana

BUSES FROM ZAGREB

Destination	Fare (KN)	Duration (hr)	Daily services
Dubrovnik	250	11	7-8
Korčula	224	11	1
Krk	160-190	4-5	4
Mali Lošinj	260-280	6½	2
Osijek	125-160	4	8
Plitvice	80	2½	19
Poreč	170-210	5	6
Pula	170-230	4-5	6
Rab	195	5	2
Rijeka	125-150	2½-3	14
Rovinj	170-190	5-8	8
Šibenik	165	6½	15
Split	195	5-9	27
Zadar	120-140	3½-5	20

(Slovenia; €16, 2¼ hours). There are also four daily trains from Zagreb to Budapest (€60, 5½ to 7½ hours). Between Venice and Zagreb (€60, 6½ to 7½ hours) there are two daily direct connections and several more that run through Ljubljana.

GETTING AROUND

Zagreb is a fairly easy city to navigate, whether by car or public transport. Traffic isn't bad, there's sufficient parking and the efficient tram system should be a model for other polluted, traffic-clogged European capitals.

To/From the Airport

The Croatia Airlines bus to Pleso airport leaves from the bus station every half-hour or hour from about 4am to 8.30pm, depending on flights, and returns from the airport on about the same schedule (50KN one way). A taxi would cost about 300KN.

Car

Of the major car-hire companies, you could try **Budget Rent-a-Car** (☎ 45 54 936; Kneza Borne 2) in the Hotel Sheraton and **Hertz** (☎ 48 46 777; Vukotinovićeva 4). Prices start at 300KN per day. Bear in mind that local companies will usually have the lower rates. Try **H&M** (☎ 37 04 535; www.hm-rentacar.hr; Grahorova 11), which also has an office at the airport.

Zagreb is relatively easy to navigate by car, but remember that the streets around Trg Jelačića and up through Kaptol and Gradec are pedestrian only. Watch out for trams sneaking up on you.

The **Hravatski Autoklu** (HAK, Croatian Autoclub; ☎ 46 40 800; Derenćinova 20) information centre helps motorists in need. It's just east of the centre.

Public Transport

Public transport is based on an efficient network of trams, though the city centre is compact enough to make them unnecessary. Buy tickets at newspaper kiosks for 8KN. Each ticket must be stamped when you board. You can use your ticket for transfers within 90 minutes but only in one direction.

A *dnevna karta* (day ticket), valid on all public transport until 4am the next morning, is 25KN at most Vjesnik or Tisak news outlets. (See p123 for details of the Zagreb Card.) Controls are frequent on the tram system, with substantial fines for not having the proper ticket.

Taxi

Zagreb's taxis ring up 8KN per kilometre after a flag fall of 25KN. On Sunday and during the hours of 10pm to 5am there's a 20% surcharge.

TRAINS FROM ZAGREB

Destination	Fare (KN)	Duration (hr)	Daily services
Osijek	113	4	5
Pula	131	6½	2
Rijeka	96	5	5
Šibenik	149	6½-10	3
Split	160	6-8½	6
Zadar	156	7-9¾	5

ISTRIA

☎ 052

Continental Croatia meets the Adriatic in Istria (Istra to Croatians), the heart-shaped 3600-sq-km peninsula just south of Trieste in Italy. While the bucolic interior of rolling hills and fertile plains has been attracting artists and visitors to its hilltop villages, rural hotels and farmhouse restaurants, the verdant indented coastline is enormously popular with the sun 'n' sea set. Vast hotel complexes line much of the coast and its rocky beaches are not Croatia's best, but the facilities are wide-ranging, the sea is clean and secluded spots still aplenty.

The northern part of the peninsula belongs to Slovenia. Just across the water is Italy, but the pervasive Italian influence makes it seem much closer. Italian is, in fact, a second language in Istria, many Istrians have Italian passports, and each town name has an Italian counterpart. Perhaps they dream of the days when the string of Istrian resorts belonged to Italy. Italy seized Istria from Austria-Hungary in 1918, then gave it up to Yugoslavia in 1947. Tito wanted Trieste (Trst) as part of Yugoslavia too, but in 1954 the Anglo-American occupiers returned the city to Italy so that it wouldn't fall into the hands of the 'communists'.

Visit Poreč, Rovinj and Pula on the coast and then move on to the interior, known for its hilltop towns and acclaimed gastronomy, starring prime truffles, wild asparagus, top olive oil and award-winning wines.

POREČ

pop 17,000

Poreč (Parenzo in Italian) sits on a low, narrow peninsula halfway down the western coast of Istria. The ancient Roman town is the centrepiece of a vast system of resorts that stretch north and south, entirely devoted to summer tourism. While this is not the place for a quiet getaway (unless you come out of season), there is a World Heritage–listed basilica, well-developed tourist infrastructure, a strip of rocky beaches nearby and the pristine Istrian interior within easy reach.

Orientation

The compact Old Town, called Parentium by the Romans, is based on a rectangular street plan. The ancient Decumanus with its polished stones is still the main street running through the peninsula's middle, lined with shops and restaurants. Hotels, travel agencies and excursion boats are on the quay, Obala Maršala Tita, which runs from the small-boat harbour to the tip of the peninsula. The bus station is just outside the Old Town, behind Rade Končara.

Information

You can change money at any of the many travel agencies or banks. There are ATMs all around town.

Atlas Travel Agency (☎ 434 933; www.atlas-croatia.com; Eufrazijeva 63; 🕙 9am-2pm & 6-9pm) Books excursions.

CyberM@c (☎ 427 075; Mire Grahalića 1; per hr 42KN; 🕙 8am-10pm) A full-service computer centre.

Di Tours (☎ 432 100; www.di-tours.hr; Prvomajska 2; 🕙 9am-10pm Jul & Aug, to 9pm Jun & Sep) Finds private accommodation.

Garderoba (per day 22KN; 🕙 7am-9pm daily) Left-luggage facilities at the bus station.

Main post office (Trg Slobode 14; 🕙 8am-noon & 6-8pm Mon-Sat)

Poreč Medical Centre (☎ 451 611; Maura Gioseffija 2)

Sunny Way (☎ 452 021; Alda Negrija 1; sunnyway@pu.t-com.hr; 🕙 9am-9pm Jul & Aug) Specialises in boat tickets and excursions to Italy and around Croatia.

Tourist office (☎ 451 293; www.to-porec.com; Zagrebačka 9; 🕙 8am-10pm Mon-Sat, 9am-1pm & 6-10pm Sun Jul & Aug, 8am-4pm Mon-Sat rest of the year)

Sights

The main reason to visit Poreč is the 6th-century **Euphrasian Basilica** (☎ 431 635; Eufrazijeva bb; admission free, belfry 10KN; 🕙 7am-8pm Apr–mid-Oct or by appointment), one of Europe's finest intact examples of Byzantine art. What packs in the crowds are the glittering wall mosaics in the apse, veritable masterpieces featuring biblical scenes, archangels and martyrs. The belfry affords an invigorating view of the Old Town. Worth a visit is the adjacent **Bishop's Palace** (admission 10KN; 🕙 9am-7pm Apr–mid-Oct or by appointment) which contains a display of ancient stone sculptures, religious paintings and 4th-century mosaics from the original oratory.

The numerous historic sites in the Old Town include the ruins of two **Roman temples**, between Trg Marafor, once the site of the Roman forum, and the western end of the peninsula. There's also a medley of Gothic and Romanesque buildings to look out for, as well as the baroque Sinčić Palace, which houses the

Regional Museum (Decumanus 9; www.muzejporec.hr), under renovation at the time of research but due to re-open at the end of 2009.

From May to October there are passenger boats (15KN) travelling to **Sveti Nikola**, the small island that lies opposite Poreč harbour. They depart every 30 minutes to an hour from the wharf on Obala Maršala Tita.

Activities

Nearly every activity you might want to enjoy is outside the town in either Plava Laguna or Zelena Laguna. For details, pick up the yearly *Poreč Info* booklet from the tourist office, which lists all the recreational facilities in the area.

From March to early October a tourist train operates regularly from Šetalište Antuna Štifanića by the marina to Plava Laguna (10KN) and Zelena Laguna (15KN). There's an hourly passenger boat that makes the same run from the ferry landing (25KN).

The well-marked paths make **cycling** and **hiking** a prime way to explore the region. The tourist office issues a free map of roads and trails. You can rent a bike at many places around town; try the outlet just below the **Hotel Poreč** (☎ 098 335 838) for 70KN per day.

There is good diving in and around shoals and sandbanks in the area, as well as to the nearby *Coriolanus*, a British Royal Navy warship sunk in 1945. At **Plava Laguna Diving Center** (☎ 098 367 619; www.plava-laguna-diving.hr) boat dives start at 100KN (more for caves or wrecks).

Sleeping

Accommodation in Poreč is plentiful but gets booked ahead of time, so advance reservations are essential if you come in July or August.

If you want to find private accommodation consult Poreč's travel agencies (see p133). Expect to pay between 200KN and 250KN for a double room in high season (up to 350KN for a two-person apartment), plus a 30% surcharge for stays of less than four nights. There are a limited number of rooms in the Old Town, where there's no parking. Look for the *Domus Bonus* certificate of quality in private accommodation.

Camp Zelena Laguna (☎ 410 700; www.plavalaguna.hr; per adult/site 55/75KN; Apr-Sep) Well equipped for sports, and with access to many beaches, this camping ground is only 5km from the Old Town.

Camp Bijela Uvala (☎ 410 551; www.plavalaguna.hr; per adult/site 55/75KN; Apr-Sep) It can be crowded, as it houses up to 6000, but there are two outdoor pools and the facilities of Zelena Laguna a stone's throw away.

Hotel Poreč (☎ /fax 451 811; www.hotelporec.com; Rade Končara 1; s 285-495KN, d 395-730KN;) While the rooms inside this concrete box have uninspiring views over the bus station, they're acceptable and an easy walk from the Old Town. It's open all year.

our pick **Hotel Hostin** (☎ 408 800; www.hostin.hr; Rade Končara 4; s 300-650KN, d 395-920KN;) Each of the well-equipped rooms comes with balconies, in verdant parkland. An indoor swimming pool, fitness room, Turkish bath and sauna are nice perks, as is the pebble beach 70m away.

Eating

A large supermarket and department store are situated next to Hotel Poreč, near the bus station.

Nono (☎ 435 088; Zagrebačka 4; pizzas 45-80KN) Nono serves the best pizza in town, with puffy crust and toppings such as truffles. Other dishes are tasty too.

Barilla (☎ 452 742; Eufrazijeva 26; mains from 45KN) Comforting Italian concoctions in all shapes and forms. There are tables on the square and a quieter patio in the back. Try the spaghetti with seashells (170KN for two).

our pick **Dva Ferala** (☎ 433 416; Obala Maršala Tita 13a; mains from 50KN) Savour well-prepared Istrian specialties, such as Istarski Tris for two – a copious trio of homemade pastas (110KN) – on the terrace of this pleasant *konoba*.

Drinking

Lapidarium (Svetog Maura 10) Gorgeous bar with a large courtyard in the back of the regional museum and a series of antique-filled inner rooms. Wednesday is jazz night in the summer, with alfresco live music.

Torre Rotonda (Narodni Trg 3a) Take the steep stairs to the top of the historic Round Tower and grab a table at the open-air cafe to watch the action on the quays.

Entertainment

Byblos (www.byblos.hr; Zelena Laguna bb) Celeb guest DJs like David Morales and Eric Morillo crank out house tunes at this humongous open-air club, one of Croatia's hottest places to party.

Getting There & Away

There are daily buses from the **bus station** (☎ 432 153; Rade Končara 1) to Rovinj (38KN, 40 minutes, seven daily), Zagreb (217KN, five hours, seven daily), Rijeka (81KN, two hours, 11 daily) and Pula (50KN, one to 1½ hours, 11 daily).

The nearest train station is at Pazin, 37km to the east. There are about 10 buses daily from Poreč (34KN, 30 minutes).

Sunny Way (☎ 452 021; sunnyway@pu.t-com.hr; Alda Negrija 1; 9am-9pm Jul & Aug) runs a fast catamaran to Venice daily in season (one way/return 430/520KN). **Ustica Lines** (www.usticalines.it) has ferries to Trieste (one way/return 150/280KN, two hours), which run daily except Monday.

ROVINJ

pop 14,200

Rovinj (Rovigno in Italian) is coastal Istria's star attraction. While it can get over-run with tourists in the summer months and residents are developing a sharp eye for maximising their profits (by upgrading the hotels and restaurants to four-star status), it remains one of the last true Mediterranean fishing ports. Fishermen haul their catch into the harbour in the early morning, followed by a horde of squawking gulls, and mend their nets before lunch. The massive Cathedral of St Euphemia, with its 60m-high tower, punctuates the peninsula. Wooded hills and low-rise hotels surround the Old Town webbed by steep, cobbled streets and piazzas. The 13 green, offshore islands of the Rovinj archipelago make for a pleasant afternoon away, and you can swim from the rocks in the sparkling water below the Old Town.

Orientation

The Old Town of Rovinj is contained within an egg-shaped peninsula, with the bus station just to the southeast. There are two harbours – the northern open harbour and the small, protected harbour to the south.

Information

There's an ATM next to the bus station entrance, and banks all around town. Most travel agencies will change money.

Futura Travel (☎ 817 281; www.futura-travel.hr; Matteo Benussi 2; 8.30am-9pm Mon-Sat, 8.30am-1pm & 5-9pm Sun May-Sep) Private accommodation, excursions and transfers.

Garderoba (per hr 1.40KN; 6.30am-8.15pm Mon-Fri, 7.45am-7.30pm Sat & Sun) Left luggage at bus station. Note the three 30-minute breaks, at 9.15am, 1.30pm and 4.30pm.

Globtour (☎ 814 130; www.globtour-turizam.hr; Alda Rismonda 2; 9am-10pm Jul & Aug, reduced hr rest of year) Excursions, private accommodation and bike rental (60KN per day).

Kompas (☎ 813 211; www.kompas-travel.com; Trg Maršala Tita 5; 9am-10pm Jul & Aug, reduced hr rest of year) Daily excursions.

Main post office (Matteo Benussi 4; 7am-8pm Mon-Fri, to 2pm Sat)

Medical Centre (☎ 813 004; Istarska bb)

Planet (☎ 840 494; Svetog Križa 1; per 10min 6KN; 9am-10pm Mon-Sat, 9am-1pm & 5-9pm Sun) Travel agency with an internet terminal.

Tourist office (☎ 811 566; www.tzgrovinj.hr; Pina Budicina 12; 8am-10pm Jul & Aug, to 9pm Sep & Jun) Just off Trg Maršala Tita, it has plenty of brochures, maps and materials.

Sights

The town's showcase is the imposing **Church of St Euphemia** (Sveta Eufemija; ☎ 815 615; Petra Stankovića; 10am-6m Jul & Aug, 11am-3pm Sep-Jun) that dominates the Old Town from its hilltop location. Built in 1736, it's the largest baroque building in Istria, reflecting the period during the 18th century when Rovinj was its most populous town, an important fishing centre and the bulwark of the Venetian fleet.

Inside the church behind the right-hand altar, don't miss the marble tomb of St Euphemia, Rovinj's patron saint martyred in AD 304, whose body mysteriously appeared in Rovinj according to legend. On the anniversary of her martyrdom (16 September), devotees congregate here. The mighty 60m tower is topped by a copper statue of St Euphemia, which shows the direction of the wind by turning on a spindle. You can climb it for 10KN.

The **Heritage Museum** (☎ 816 720; www.muzej-rovinj.hr; Trg Maršala Tita 11; adult/concession 15/10KN; 9am-3pm & 7-10pm Tue-Fri, 9am-2pm & 7-10pm Sat & Sun mid-Jun–mid-Sep, 9am-3pm Tue-Sat rest of year) in a baroque palace contains a collection of contemporary art and old masters from Croatia and Rovinj, as well as archaeological finds and a maritime section.

Nearby is the elaborate **Balbi Arch**, built in 1679 on the location of the former town gate. The cobbled street of **Grisia** leads uphill from behind the arch to St Euphemia, lined with galleries where local artists sell their work. On the second Sunday in August each year, narrow Grisia becomes an open-air **art exhibition** with anyone from children to professional

CROATIA

painters displaying their work. The winding narrow backstreets that spread around Grisia are an attraction in themselves. Windows, balconies, portals and squares are a pleasant confusion of styles – Gothic, Renaissance, baroque and neoclassical.

On the harbour, **Batana House** (☎ 812 593; www.batana.org; Pina Budicina 2; admission free, with guide 15KN; 10am-1pm & 7-10pm Tue-Sun May-Sep, 10am-1pm Tue-Sun rest of year) is a multimedia museum dedicated to the *batana*, a flat-bottomed fishing boat that stands as a symbol of Rovinj's seafaring and fishing tradition.

When you've seen enough of the town, follow the waterfront on foot or by bike past Hotel Park to the verdant **Golden Cape Forest Park** (Zlatni Rt, or Punta Corrente) about 1.5km south. Covered in oak and pine groves and boasting 10 species of cypress, the park was established in 1890 by Baron Hütterott, an Austrian admiral who kept a villa on Crveni Otok. Here you can swim off the rocks or just sit and admire the offshore islands.

CROATIA

Activities

Most people hop aboard a boat for swimming, snorkelling and sunbathing. A trip to Crveni Otok or Sveti Katarina is easily arranged. In summer, there are 18 boats daily to Sveta Katarina (15KN, five minutes) and on to Crveni Otok (15KN return, 15 minutes). They leave from just opposite Hotel Adriatic and also from the Delphin ferry dock near Hotel Park.

Diver Sport Center (☎ 816 648; www.diver.hr; Villas Rubin) is the largest operation in Rovinj, offering boat dives from 210KN, with equipment rental. The main dive attraction is the wreck of the *Baron Gautsch*, an Austrian passenger-steamer sunk in 1914 by a mine.

Biking around Rovinj and the Golden Cape Park is a superb way to spend an afternoon. You can rent bicycles at many agencies around town, from 60KN per day. The cheapest bike rental (5KN per hour) is at the town entrance, by the Valdibora parking lot and the market.

Tours

Most travel agencies (p135) sell day trips to Venice (450KN to 520KN), Plitvice (580KN) and Brijuni (380KN to 420KN). There are also fish picnics (250KN), panoramic cruises (100KN) and trips to Limska Draga Fjord (150KN). These trips can be slightly cheaper if booked through one of the independent operators that line the waterfront; **Delfin** (☎ 813 266) is reliable.

Sleeping

Rovinj has become Istria's destination of choice for hordes of summertime tourists, so reserving in advance is strongly recommended.

If you want to stay in private accommodation, there is little available in the Old Town, plus there is no parking and the cost is higher. Double rooms start at 180KN in the high season, with a small discount for single occupancy; two-person apartments start at 380KN. You can book directly through www.inforovinj.com or one of the listed agencies.

The surcharge for a stay of less than three nights is 50% and guests who stay only one night are punished with a 100% surcharge. Outside summer months, you should be able to bargain the surcharge away.

Except a few private options, most hotels and camping grounds in the area are managed by **Maistra** (www.maistra.com).

Porton Biondi (☎ 813 557; www.portonbiondi.hr; per person/tent 40/23KN; Apr-Oct) This camping ground that sleeps 1200 is about 700m from the Old Town.

Vila Lili (☎ 840 940; www.hotel-vilalili.hr; Mohorovičića 16; s 333-385KN, d 505-730KN;) Bright rooms with all the three-star perks, including air-con and minibars in a small modern house a short walk out of town.

Hotel Adriatic (☎ 815 088; www.maistra.hr; Pina Budicina bb; s 392-589KN, d 522-784KN;) The location right on the harbour is excellent and the rooms spick-and-span and well equipped, albeit on the kitschy side. The sea-view rooms are more spacious.

our pick **Casa Garzotto** (☎ 811 884; www.casa-garzotto.com; Via Garzotto 8; s 510-760KN, d 650-1015KN;) Each of the four nicely outfitted studio apartments have original detail, a stylish touch and up-to-the-minute amenities. The historic townhouse can't be better placed. Bikes are complimentary.

Hotel Villa Angelo D'Oro (☎ 840 502; www.angelodoro.hr; Vladimira Švalbe 38-42; s 619-990KN, d 1005-1762KN;) In a renovated Venetian townhouse, the 24 plush rooms and (pricier) suites of this boutique hotel have lots of antiques plus mod perks aplenty. There's sauna, jacuzzi and a lush interior terrace, a great place for a drink amid ancient stone.

Eating

Most of the restaurants that line the harbour offer the standard fish and meat mainstays at similar prices. For a more gourmet experience, you'll need to bypass the water vistas. Note that many restaurants shut their doors between lunch and dinner. For an evening snack of local cheese, cured meats and tasty small bites, head to **Ulika** (Vladimira Švalbe 34; dinner only), a tiny tavern a few doors down from Angelo d'Oro.

Veli Jože (816 337; Svetog Križa 3; mains from 35KN) Graze on good Istrian standards, either in the eclectic interior crammed with knick-knacks or on the outdoor tables with water views.

Trattoria Dream (830 613; Joakima Rakovca 18; mains from 75KN) Tucked away in the maze of narrow streets, with its two earthy-coloured outdoor terraces, this stylish trattoria does flavourful dishes such as salt-baked sea bass and some global favourites such as chilli con carne and chicken curry.

La Puntuleina (813 186; Svetog Križa 38; mains 100-160KN) Sample creative Med cuisine on three alfresco terraces – from traditional recipes like *žgvacet* (a sauce made from chicken, beef and venison, and served with pasta) to revamped ones like truffle-topped fish fillet. Pastas are more affordable (from 55KN). At night, grab a cushion and sip a cocktail on the rocks below this converted townhouse. Reservations recommended.

Picnickers can get supplies at the supermarket next to the bus station or at one of the Konzum stores around town.

Drinking

Havana (Aldo Negri bb) Tropical cocktails, Cuban cigars, straw parasols and the shade of tall pine trees make this open-air cocktail bar a popular spot to chill and watch the ships go by.

Zanzibar (813 206; Pina Budicina bb) Indonesian wood, palms, wicker lounge chairs and subdued lighting on the huge outdoor terrace of this cocktail bar create a tropical and definitely upscale vibe.

Getting There & Away

Eurostar Travel (813 144; Pina Budicina 1; 9am-9pm Mon-Sat, 9am-1pm & 5-8pm Sun) has schedules and tickets for boats to Venice and Trieste.

There are buses from Rovinj to Pula (35KN, 40 minutes, 13 daily), Dubrovnik (593KN, 16 hours, one daily), Poreč (37KN, one hour, eight daily), Rijeka (112KN, 3½ hours, four daily), Zagreb (173KN to 255KN, five hours, four daily) and Split (417KN, 11 hours, one daily). For Slovenia, there is one weekday bus that runs between Rovinj and Koper (87KN, three hours) stopping at Piran, Poreč and Portorož (41KN, 1½ hours), as well as a daily bus from Rovinj to Ljubljana (94KN, 5½ hours).

The closest train station is at Kanfanar, 20km away on the Pula–Divača line.

PULA

pop 65,000

The wealth of Roman architecture makes the otherwise workaday Pula (ancient Polensium) a standout among Croatia's larger cities. The star of the Roman show is the remarkably well-preserved Roman amphitheatre, which dominates the streetscape and doubles as a venue for summer concerts and performances. Historical attractions aside, Pula is a busy commercial city on the sea that has managed to retain a friendly small-town appeal. A series of beaches and good nightlife are just a short bus ride away at the resorts that occupy the Verudela Peninsula to the south. Further south along the indented shoreline, the Premantura Peninsula hides a spectacular nature area, the protected cape of Kamenjak.

Orientation

The oldest part of the city follows the ancient Roman plan of streets circling the central citadel. Most businesses are clustered in and around the Old Town, as well as on Giardini, Carrarina, Istarska and Riva, which runs along the harbour. The bus station is 500m northeast of the town centre. The harbour is west of the bus station. The train station is near the sea, less than a kilometre north of town.

Information

You can exchange money in travel agencies, banks or at the post offices. There are numerous ATMs around town.

Arenaturist (529 400; www.arenaturist.hr; Splitska 1a; 8am-8pm Mon-Fri, to 6pm Sat) In the Hotel Riviera, it books rooms in the network of hotels it manages. It also offers guide services and excursions.

Garderoba (per hr 2.20KN; 4am-10.30pm Mon-Sat, 5am-10.30pm Sun) Left luggage at bus station.

Hospital (376 548; Zagrebačka 34)

Istra Way (214 868; www.istraway.hr; Riva 14; 9am-9pm Jul–mid-Sep) On the harbour, it books private accommodation, offers excursions to Brijuni, Rovinj and Lim and has bikes for rent (100KN per day).

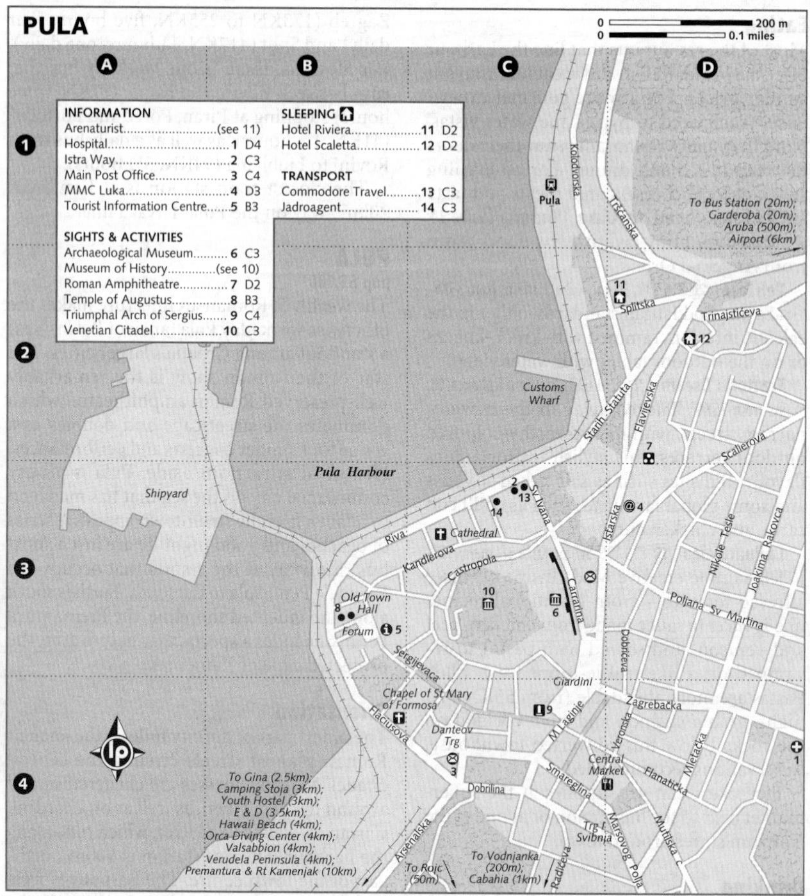

Main post office (Danteov Trg 4; ⌚ 7.30am-7pm Mon-Fri, to 2.30pm Sat) You can make long-distance calls here. Check out the cool staircase inside!

MMC Luka (☎ 224 316; Istarska 30; per hr 20KN; ⌚ 8am-midnight Mon-Fri, to 3pm Sat) Internet access.

Tourist information centre (☎ 212 987; www.pulainfo.hr; Forum 3; ⌚ 8am-9pm Mon-Fri, 9am-9pm Sat & Sun summer, 8am-7pm Mon-Fri, 9am-7pm Sat, 10am-4pm Sun winter) Knowledgeable and friendly, it provides heaps of maps and brochures. Pick up the useful *Domus Bonus* booklet, which lists the best-quality private accommodation in Istria.

Sights

ROMAN RUINS

Pula's most imposing sight is the 1st-century **Roman amphitheatre** (☎ 219 028; Flavijevska bb; adult/concession 40/20KN; ⌚ 8am-9pm summer, 9am-8pm spring & autumn, 9am-5pm winter) overlooking the harbour. Built entirely from local limestone, the amphitheatre, with seating for up to 20,000 spectators, was designed to host gladiatorial contests. In the chambers downstairs is a small museum with a display of ancient olive oil equipment. Every summer, Pula Film Festival is held here, as are pop and classical concerts.

The **Archaeological Museum** (Arheološki Muzej; ☎ 218 603; Carrarina 3; adult/concession 20/10KN; ⌚ 9am-8pm Mon-Sat, 10am-3pm Sun May-Sep, 9am-2pm Mon-Fri Oct-Apr) presents archaeological finds from all over Istria. Even if you don't enter the museum, be sure to visit the large sculpture garden around it, and the **Roman theatre** behind. The garden, entered through 2nd-century twin gates, is the site of concerts in summer.

Along Carrarina are **Roman walls**, which mark the eastern boundary of old Pula. Follow these walls south and continue down Giardini to the **Triumphal Arch of Sergius** (27 BC). The street beyond the arch winds right around old Pula, changing names several times. Follow it to the ancient **Temple of Augustus** (☎ 218 603; Forum; adult/concession 10/5KN; 🕑 9am-8pm Mon-Fri, 10am-3pm Sat & Sun summer, by appointment otherwise), erected from 2 BC to AD 14 and now housing a small historical museum with captions in English.

BEACHES

Pula is surrounded by a half-circle of rocky beaches, each one with its own fan club. The most tourist-packed are undoubtedly those surrounding the hotel complex on the **Verudela Peninsula** although some locals will dare to be seen at the small turquoise-coloured **Hawaii Beach** near the Hotel Park.

For more seclusion, head out to the wild **Rt Kamenjak** (www.kamenjak.hr, in Croatian; pedestrians & cyclists free, cars 20KN, scooters 10KN; 🕑 7am-10pm) on the Premantura Peninsula 10km south of town. Istria's southernmost point, this gorgeous, entirely uninhabited cape has wild flowers, including 30 species of orchid, 30km of virgin beaches and coves, and a delightful beach bar, **Safari** (snacks 25-50KN; 🕑 Easter-Sep), half-hidden in the bushes near the beach. Watch out for strong currents if swimming off the southern cape. Take city bus 26 (15KN) from Pula to Premantura and rent a bike to get inside the park from **Windsurf Bar** (☎ 091 512 3646; Camping Village Stupice; www.windsurfing.hr) near the bus top (50KN to 100KN per day).

OTHER SIGHTS

The 17th-century **Venetian citadel**, on a high hill in the centre of the Old Town, is worth the climb for the view if not for the meagre maritime-related exhibits in the tiny **Museum of History** (Povijesni Muzej Istre; ☎ 211 566; Gradinski Uspon 6; adult/concession 15/7KN; 🕑 8am-9pm Jun-Sep, 9am-5pm Oct-May) inside.

Activities

There are several diving centres around Pula. At **Orca Diving Center** (☎ 224 422; www.orcadiving.hr; Hotel Histria) on the Verudela Peninsula you can arrange for boat dives, wreck dives and introductory dives.

In addition to windsurfing courses, Windsurf Bar (above) in Premantura offers biking (250KN) and kayaking (300KN) excursions.

Sleeping

Pula's peak tourist season runs from the second week of July to the end of August. During this period it's wise to make advance reservations. The tip of the Verudela Peninsula, 4km southwest of the city centre, has been turned into a vast tourist complex, replete with hotels and apartments.

Any travel agency can give you information and book you into one of the hotels, or you can contact Arenaturist (p137). The travel agencies listed find private accommodation but there is little available in the town centre. Count on paying from 250KN to 490KN for a double room (up to 535KN for a two-person apartment).

Camping Stoja (☎ 387 144; www.arenaturist.hr; Stoja 37; per person/tent 52/30KN; 🕑 Apr-Oct) The closest camping ground to Pula, 3km southwest of the centre, has lots of space on the shady promontory, with a restaurant, diving centre and swimming possible off the rocks. Take bus 1 to Stoja.

Youth Hostel (☎ 391 133; www.hfhs.hr; Valsaline 4; dm 85-114KN, mobile home 103-134KN; 💻) This hostel overlooks a beach in Valsaline bay, 3km south of central Pula. There are dorms and mobile homes split into two tiny four-bed units, each with bathroom and air-con on request (15KN per day). There's bike rental (80KN per day) and camp sites (per person/tent 70/15KN). Take bus 2 or 3 to the 'Piramida' stop, walk back to the first street, then turn left and look for the sign.

Hotel Riviera (☎ 211 166; www.arenaturist.hr; Splitska 1; s 283-354KN, d 464-600KN) There's plenty of old-world elegance at this grand 19th-century building but the rooms need a thorough overhaul and the carpets a serious scrub. On the plus side, it's in the centre and the front rooms have water views.

our pick **Hotel Scaletta** (☎ 541 599; www.hotel-scaletta.com; Flavijevska 26; s 398-498KN, d 598-718KN) There's a friendly family vibe, the rooms have tasteful decor and a bagful of trimmings, such as minibars, plus the restaurant serves good food. It's just a hop from town.

Eating

There are a number of decent eating places in the city centre, although most locals head out of town for better value and fewer tourists.

Vodnjanka (☎ 210 655; Vitezića 4; mains from 30KN; ⌚ closed Sun & dinner Sat) Locals swear by the home cooking here. It's cheap, casual, cash-only and has a small menu that concentrates on simple Istrian dishes. To get here, walk south on Radićeva to Vitezića.

our pick **Gina** (☎ 387 943; Stoja 23; mains from 60KN) Istrian mainstays like *maneštra* and *fritaja* are prepared with care, pastas are handmade, and vegies picked from the garden. This stylish but low-key eatery near Camping Stoja draws in a local crowd. Try the semifreddo with a hot sauce of figs, pine nuts and lavender.

Valsabbion (☎ 218 033; www.valsabbion.hr; Pješčana Uvala IX/26; mains 95-175KN) The creative Croatian cuisine conjured up at this award-winning restaurant, one of Croatia's best, is an epicurean delight. The decor is showy but stunning and the menu gimmicky in its descriptions but the food is tops. Sampling menus range from 395KN to 555KN. It doubles as a plush 10-room hotel (doubles 860KN) with a top-floor spa. It's in upscale Pješčana Uvala, south of the city.

Drinking

Although most of the nightlife is out of the town centre, in mild weather the cafes on the Forum and along the pedestrian streets, Kandlerova, Flanatička and Sergijevaca, are lively people-watching spots.

our pick **Cabahia** (Širolina 4) An artsy hideaway in Veruda, with cosy wood-beamed interior, eclectic decor of old objects, dim lighting, South American flair and a great garden terrace in the back. It hosts concerts and gets packed on weekends.

E&D (☎ 894 2015; Verudela 22) Lounge just above Umbrella beach on Verudela, on the lush outdoor terrace with several levels of straw-chair seating interspersed with small pools and waterfalls. The sunset views are great and weekend nights spiced with live DJ tunes.

Entertainment

You should definitely try to catch a concert in the spectacular amphitheatre; the tourist office has schedules.

For the most underground experience, check the program at **Rojc** (Gajeva 3; www.rojcnet.hr), a converted army barracks that now houses a multimedia art centre and art studios with occasional concerts, exhibits and other events.

Getting There & Away

BOAT

Jadroagent (☎ 210 431; www.jadroagent.hr; Riva 14; ⌚ 7am-3pm Mon-Fri) has schedules and tickets for boats connecting Istria with Italy and the islands. They also represent Jadrolinija.

Commodore Travel (☎ 211 631; www.commodore-travel.hr; Riva 14, ⌚ 8am-8pm Jun-Sep) sells tickets for a catamaran between Pula and Zadar that runs five times weekly from July through early September (100KN, five hours) and twice weekly in June and September. There's a weekly boat to Venice between June and September (370KN, 3½ hours).

BUS

From the Pula **bus station** (☎ 500 012; Trg 1 Istarske Brigade bb) there are buses heading to Rijeka almost hourly (86KN to 91KN, two hours). In summer, reserve a seat a day in advance and be sure to sit on the right-hand side of the bus for a stunning view of the Kvarner Gulf.

Other destinations you can reach by bus include: Rovinj (35KN, 45 minutes, 15 daily), Poreč (54KN to 65KN, one to 1½ hours, 13 daily), Zagreb (210KN, four to five hours, 18 daily), Zadar (249KN to 257KN, seven hours, three daily), Split (360KN to 396KN, 10 hours, three daily) and Dubrovnik (568KN, 10½ hours, one daily).

TRAIN

There are two daily trains to Ljubljana, with a change in Buzet (133KN, two hours), and four to Zagreb (125KN to 148KN, 6½ hours), but you must board a bus for part of the trip, from Lupoglav to Rijeka.

Getting Around

The city buses of use to visitors are bus 1, which runs to the Autocamp Stoja, and bus 2 and 3 to Verudela. Tickets are sold at *tisak* (newsstands) for 6KN, or 10KN from the driver.

KVARNER REGION

☎ 051

The Kvarner Gulf (Quarnero in Italian) covers 3300 sq km between Rijeka and Pag Island in the south, protected by the Velebit Range in the southeast, the Gorski Kotar in the east and the Učka massif in the northwest. Covered with luxuriant forests, lined with beaches and dotted with islands, the region has a mild gentle climate and a wealth of vegetation.

The metropolitan focus is the busy commercial port of Rijeka, Croatia's third-largest city, only a few kilometres from the aristocratic Opatija Riviera. The islands of Krk, Rab, Cres and Lošinj offer picture-perfect old towns just a ferry ride away, as well as plenty of beaches for scenic swimming.

RIJEKA

pop 147,700

While Rijeka (Fiume in Italian) doesn't quite fit the bill as a tourist destination, it does offer an insightful glimpse into the workaday life of Croatia's largest port. Most people rush through en route to the islands or Dalmatia but for those who pause, a few assets await. Blend in with the coffee-sipping locals on the bustling Korzo pedestrian strip, stroll along the tree-lined promenade that fronts the harbour, and visit the imposing hilltop fortress of Trsat. Rijeka also boasts a burgeoning nightlife, and every year it hosts Croatia's biggest and most colourful Carnival celebration.

Much of the centre contains the ornate, imposing public buildings you would expect to find in Vienna or Budapest, evidence of the strong Austro-Hungarian influence. The industrial aspect is evident from the boats, cargo and cranes that line the waterfront but there's a seedy beauty to it. As one of Croatia's most important transportation hubs, Rijeka has buses, trains and ferries that connect Istria and Dalmatia with Zagreb.

Orientation

Korzo runs through the city centre, roughly parallel to Riva (seafront), towards the Rječina River in the east. The intercity bus station is at the western edge of Riva. The train station is a five-minute walk west of the intercity bus station, along Krešimirova.

Information

There are two ATMs at the train station and a number of them along Korzo and around the city centre. The exchange offices adjacent to the train and bus stations keep long hours.

There's free wireless internet access along Korzo and in parts of Trsat.

Blitz (Krešimirova 3a; small load 51KN; ⌚ 7am-8pm Mon-Fri, to 2pm Sat) Laundry facilities.

Cont (☎ 371 630; Andrije Kačića Miošića 1; per hr 15KN; ⌚ 7am-10pm) This cafe inside Hotel Continental has a full bank of computers.

Hospital (☎ 658 111; Krešimirova 42)

Garderoba intercity bus station (per day 13KN; ⌚ 5.30am-10.30pm); train station (per day in locker 15KN; ⌚ 4.30am-10.30pm) The bus station left-luggage facility is at the cafe next door to the ticket office.

Main post office (Korzo 13; ⌚ 7am-8pm Mon-Fri, to 2pm Sat) Has a telephone centre and an exchange office.

Tourist information centre (☎ 335 882; www.tz-rijeka.hr; Korzo 33a; ⌚ 8am-8pm Mon-Sat, 9am-2pm Sun summer, 8am-8pm Mon-Fri, 8am-2pm Sat rest of year) This spiffy centre has plentiful free materials and info about private accommodation.

Sights

Rijeka's main orientation point is the distinctive yellow **City Tower** (Korzo), originally a gate from the seafront to the city and one of the few monuments to have survived the devastating earthquake of 1750.

Just up from the Korzo on the 2nd floor of the University Library is the **Museum of Modern & Contemporary Art** (Muzej Moderne i Suvremene Umjetnosti; ☎ 334 280; www.mmsu.hr; Dolac 1; adult/student 10/5KN; ⌚ 10am-1pm & 6-9pm Tue-Sun summer, 10am-1pm & 5-8pm rest of year) in an L-shaped space that puts on rotating shows. The **Maritime & History Museum** (Pomorski i Povijesni Muzej Hrvatskog Primorja; ☎ 553 666; www.ppmhp.hr; Muzejski Trg 1; adult/student 10/5KN; ⌚ 9am-8pm Tue-Fri, to 1pm Sat) gives a vivid picture of life among seafarers, with model ships, sea charts, navigation instruments and portraits of captains. A five-minute walk to the east is the **Natural History Museum** (Prirodoslovni Muzej; ☎ 553 669; Lorenzov Prolaz 1; adult/student 10/5KN; ⌚ 9am-7pm Mon-Sat, to 3pm Sun), devoted to the geology and botany of the Adriatic, inside a 19th-century villa.

Also worth a visit is the **Trsat Castle** (☎ 217 714; adult/student 15/5KN; ⌚ 9am-8pm May-Oct, to 5pm Nov-Apr), a 13th-century hill fortress that houses two galleries and great vistas from the open-air cafe. During the summer, the fortress features concerts, theatre performances and fashion shows. The other hill highlight is the **Church of Our Lady of Trsat** (Crkva Gospe Trsatske; ☎ 452 900; Frankopanski Trg; ⌚ by appointment only), a centuries-old magnet for believers that showcases an apparently miraculous icon of Virgin Mary.

Festivals & Events

The **Rijeka Carnival** (www.ri-karneval.com.hr) is the largest and most elaborate in Croatia, with two weeks of partying that involves pageants, street dances, concerts, masked balls, exhibitions and an international parade. Check out

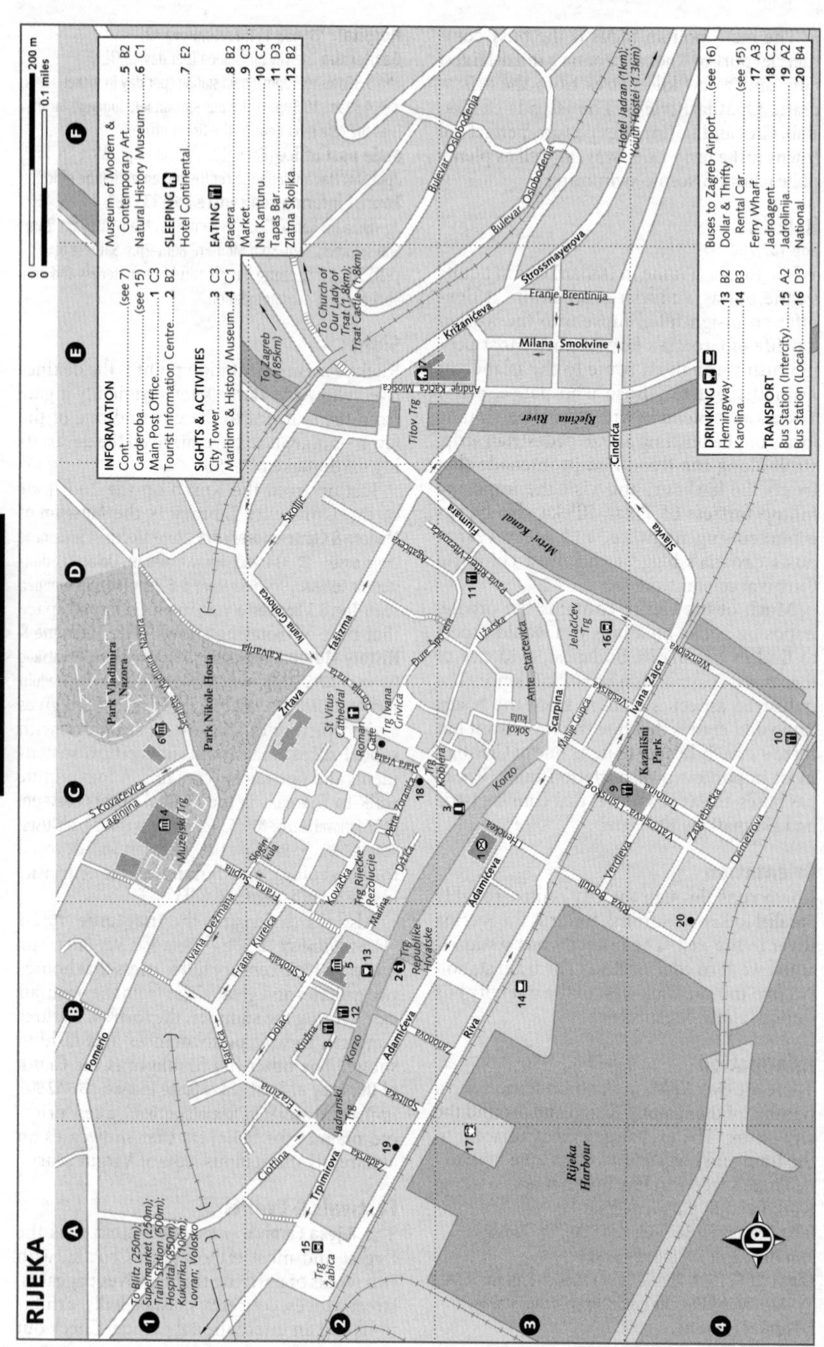
RIJEKA
0 200 m
0 0.1 miles
INFORMATION
Cont. (see 7)
Garderoba (see 15)
Main Post Office 1 C3
Tourist Information Centre 2 B2
SIGHTS & ACTIVITIES
City Tower 3 C3
Maritime & History Museum 4 C1
Museum of Modern & Contemporary Art 5 B2
Natural History Museum 6 C1
SLEEPING
Hotel Continental 7 E2
EATING
Bracera 8 B2
Market 9 C3
Na Kantunu 10 C4
Tapas Bar 11 D3
Zlatna Školjka 12 B2
DRINKING
Hemingway 13 B2
Karolina 14 B3
TRANSPORT
Bus Station (Intercity) 15 A2
Bus Station (Local) 16 D3
Buses to Zagreb Airport (see 16)
Dollar & Thrifty Rental Car (see 15)
Ferry Wharf 17 A3
Jadroagent 18 C2
Jadrolinija 19 A2
National 20 B4
To Blitz (250m); Supermarket (250m); Train Station (500m); Hospital (850m); Kukuriku (10km); Lovran; Volosko
To Zagreb (185km)
To Church of Our Lady of Trsat (1.8km); Trsat Castle (1.8km)
To Hotel Jadran (1km); Youth Hostel (1.3km)
Park Vladimira Nazora
Park Nikole Hosta
Muzejski Trg
St Vitus Cathedral
Roman Gate
Trg Ivana Grivica
Trg Rijecke Rezolucije
Trg Republike Hrvatske
Jadranski Trg
Trg Žabica
Titov Trg
Jelačićev Trg
Kazališni Park
Rječina River
Mrtvi Kanal
Rijeka Harbour
Korzo
Riva
Adamićeva
Bulevar Oslobođenja
Strossmayerova
Križanićeva
Fiumara
Žrtava Fašizma

the *zvončari,* masked men clad in animal skins who dance and ring loud bells to frighten off evil spirits. The festivities take place anywhere between late January and early March, depending on when Easter falls.

Sleeping

Prices in Rijeka hotels generally stay the same year-round, except at popular Carnival time, when you can expect to pay a surcharge. There are few private rooms in Rijeka itself; the tourist office lists these on its website. Opatija (see p145) is a much better choice for accommodation.

Youth Hostel (☎ 406 420; rijeka@hfhs.hr; Šetalište XIII Divizije 23; dm/s/d 130/235/310KN; 💻) Five bus stops east of the centre (bus 2) in the leafy residential area of Pečine, this renovated 19th-century villa has clean and snug units and a communal TV room. Breakfast is available (15KN) and reservations advisable in the summer.

Hotel Continental (☎ 372 008; www.jadran-hoteli.hr; Andrije Kačića Miošića 1; s/d 384/449KN; 💻) At the time of writing, more than half of the rooms inside this grand building were being revamped. Once they're primped up, the rating will go up to three stars and the prices by 15%. The location is prime, just northeast of the centre.

our pick **Hotel Jadran** (☎ 216 600; www.jadran-hoteli.hr; Šetalište XIII Divizije 46; s/d 672/793KN; ❄ 💻) The four-star upgrade of this long-standing hotel produced airy rooms with huge glass windows or balconies offering sea vistas. Perks include a restaurant, a small gym and a private beach below. Worth the 1km trip east of the city centre.

Eating

If you want a meal on a Sunday, you'll be relegated to either fast food, pizza or a hotel restaurant, as nearly every other place in Rijeka is closed.

Tapas Bar (☎ 315 313; Pavla Rittera Vitezovićia 5; tapas around 25KN) This small and stylish spot churns out Croatian-inspired tapas. Delicious *bruschette* are topped with anchovies, truffles, fresh tuna…at 9KN per piece. Portions are small and the bill adds up.

our pick **Na Kantunu** (☎ 313 271; Demetrova 2; mains from 35KN) If you're lucky enough to grab a table at this tiny lunchtime spot on an industrial stretch of the port, you'll be treated to a superlative daily catch.

Zlatna Školjka (☎ 213 782; Kružna 12; mains 65-95KN) Savour the superbly prepared seafood and choice Croatian wines at this classy maritime-themed restaurant. The mixed fish starter Conco d'Oro is pricey (100KN) but worth it.

The adjacent Bracera, by the same owners, serves crusty pizza, even on Sunday.

Kukuriku (☎ 691 417; Trg Matka Laginje 1a, Kastav; 6-course meal 370-510KN; 🕑 closed Mon winter) Among the pioneers of the slow-food movement in Croatia, this gastronomic destination in the Old Town of Kastav, Rijeka's hilltop suburb, offers delectable meals amid lots of rooster-themed decoration. It's worth the splurge and the trek on bus 18.

For self-caterers, there's a large supermarket between the bus and train stations, and a **city market** (btwn Vatroslava Lisinskog & Trninina) open till 2pm daily (till noon Sunday).

Drinking

With several recent openings, Rijeka's nightlife got a boost of energy. Bar-hoppers cruise the bars and cafes along Riva and Korzo for the liveliest social hubbub. Many of the bars double as clubs on weekends.

Hemingway (☎ 211 696; Korzo 28) This stylish venue for coffee-sipping, cocktail-drinking and people-watching pays homage to the bar's namesake, with the hero's large black and white photos and eponymous drinks. It's part of a fashionable chain.

Karolina (☎ 211 447; Gat Karoline Riječke bb) Trendy but not self-conscious about it, this waterfront bar-cafe is a relaxed place for a daytime coffee. At night, crowds spill out onto the wharf in a huge outdoor party.

Getting There & Away

BOAT

Jadrolinija (☎ 211 444; www.jadrolinija.hr; Riva 16; 🕑 8am-8pm Mon-Fri, 9am-5pm Sat & Sun) sells tickets for the large coastal ferries that run all year between Rijeka and Dubrovnik on their way to Bari in Italy, via Split, Hvar and Korčula. Other ferry lines include Rijeka–Cres–Mali Lošinj and Rijeka–Rab–Pag. All ferries depart from Rijeka's **wharf** (Adamićev Gat).

Jadroagent (☎ 211 626; www.jadroagent.hr; Trg Ivana Koblera 2) has information on all boats around Croatia.

BUS

If you fly into Zagreb, there is a Croatia Airlines van directly from Zagreb airport to Rijeka (145KN, two hours, 3.30pm and 9pm) and back from Rijeka (5am and 11am).

BUSES FROM RIJEKA

Destination	Fare (KN)	Duration (hr)	Daily services
Baška	71	2¼	4-8
Dubrovnik	340-485	12-13	2-3
Krk	50	1-2	14
Poreč	72-114	1-3	7-11
Pula	78-88	2¼	8-10
Rab	125	3	2
Rovinj	81-112	2-3	4-5
Split	241-327	8	6-7
Zadar	153-202	4-5	6-7
Zagreb	95-174	2½-3	13-17

There are six daily buses from the **intercity bus station** (☎ 060 302 010; Trg Žabica 1) to Trieste (Italy; 60KN, 2½ hours) and one daily bus to Plitvice, with a change in Otočac (130KN, four hours). There's a service between Sarajevo (BiH) and Rijeka too (€35, 10 hours, daily) and a bus between Ljubljana (Slovenia) and Rijeka (84KN, 2½ hours, one daily).

See above for popular domestic routes.

CROATIA

CAR

Dollar & Thrifty Rental Car (☎ 325 900; www.subrosa.hr) with a booth inside the intercity bus station has rental cars from 466KN per day (2500KN per week) with unlimited kilometres. You can also try **National** (☎ 212 452; www.nationalcar.hr; Demetrova 18b).

TRAIN

The **train station** (☎ 213 333; Krešimirova 5) is a five-minute walk from the city centre. Seven trains daily run to Zagreb (96KN, 3½ to five hours). There's a daily train to Split that changes at Ogulin, where you wait for two hours (160KN, 10 hours). Reservations are compulsory on some *poslovni* (executive) trains. For Slovenia, there are four trains daily between Rijeka and Ljubljana (93KN, three hours).

OPATIJA

pop 9070

Opatija stretches along the coast, just 13km west of Rijeka, its forested hills sloping down to the sparkling sea. It was this breathtaking location and the agreeable all-year climate that made Opatija the most fashionable seaside resort for the Viennese elite during the Austro-Hungarian empire. The grand residences of the wealthy have since been revamped and turned into upscale hotels, with a particular accent on spa and health holidays. Foodies have been flocking from afar too, for the clutch of fantastic restaurants in the nearby fishing village of Volosko.

Orientation & Information

Opatija sits on a narrow strip of land sandwiched between the sea and the foothills of Mt Učka. Ulica Maršala Tita is the main road that runs through town; it's lined with travel agencies, ATMs, restaurants, shops and hotels.

Da Riva (☎ 272 990; www.da-riva.hr; Ulica Maršala Tita 170; 🕑 8am-8pm Jun–mid-Sep, reduced hr rest of year) Finds private accommodation and offers excursions around Croatia.

Linea Verde (☎ 701 107; www.lineaverde-croatia.com; Andrije Štangera 42, Volosko; 🕑 8am-10pm Mon-Sat, to 9pm Sun summer, to 4pm Mon-Sat rest of year) Hiking excursions to Risnjak, gourmet tours to Istria and shepherd's picnics to Učka.

Tourist office (☎ 271 310; www.opatija-tourism.hr; Ulica Maršala Tita 101; 🕑 8am-10pm Mon-Sat, 5-9pm Sun Jul & Aug, 8am-7pm Mon-Sat Apr-Jun & Sep, 8am-4pm Mon-Sat Mar & Oct) Distributes maps, leaflets and brochures.

Sights & Activities

Visit the exquisite **Villa Angiolina** (Park Angiolina 1), which houses the **Croatian Museum of Tourism** (admission free; 🕑 9am-1pm & 4.30-9.30pm Tue-Sun summer, reduced hr rest of year) with the collection of old photographs, postcards, brochures and posters tracing the history of travel. Admission was free at the time of research, but due to increase to 20KN later. Don't miss a stroll around the park, overgrowing with gingko trees, sequoias, holm oaks and Japanese camellia, Opatija's symbol.

The pretty **Lungomare** is the region's showcase. Lined with plush villas and ample gardens, this shady promenade winds along the sea for 12km, from Volosko to Lovran. Along the way are innumerable rocky outgrowths on which to throw down a towel and jump into the sea from – a better option than Opatija's concrete beach.

Opatija and the surrounding region offer some wonderful opportunities for hiking and biking around the **Učka** mountain range (the tourist office has maps and information).

Sleeping & Eating

There are no real budget hotels in Opatija, but the midrange and top-end places offer surprisingly good value for money considering Opatija's overall air of chic. Maršala Tita is lined with serviceable restaurants that offer pizza, grilled meat and fish. The better restaurants are away from the main strip.

Private rooms are abundant and reasonably priced. The travel agencies listed opposite find private accommodation. In high season, rooms cost between 80KN and 115KN per person, depending on the amenities. A 30% surcharge applies for stays under three nights.

Camping Opatija (☎ 704 836; www.rivijera-opatija.hr; Liburnijska 46, Ičići; per adult/site 36/27KN; Apr-Oct) In a pine forest 5km south of town before you reach Lovran.

Hotel Residenz (☎ 271 399; www.liburnia.hr; Ulica Maršala Tita 133; s 293-524KN, d 354-816KN) While rooms boast no frills – unless you pay extra for a unit with a balcony – the building is a classic right on the seafront, with a private beach below.

Hotel Mozart (☎ 718 260; www.hotel-mozart.hr; Ulica Maršala Tita 138; s 660-920KN, d 1095-1530KN) Light-flooded rooms feature old-school style and Secessionist furniture, the stars add up to five, and the spiffy new spa offers saunas and steam baths. Most rooms come with sea-facing balconies.

Istranka (☎ 271 835; Bože Milanovića 2; mains from 45KN) Graze on flavourful Istrian mainstays like *maneštra* and *fuži* at this rustic-themed tavern in a small street just up from Maršala Tita.

Bevanda (☎ 493 888; Zert 8; mains from 80KN) It recently switched the ownership that built its reputation but this elegant restaurant on the Lido still delivers terrific fresh fish and shellfish. Get a table at the all-white terrace right on the sea.

Entertainment

An **open air-cinema** (Park Angiolina) screens films nightly and presents occasional concerts at 9.30pm from May to September. There are some bars around the harbour, although Rijeka has a much more dynamic scene.

Getting There & Away

Bus 32 stops in front of the train station in Rijeka (15KN, 20km) and runs along the Opatija Riviera west of Rijeka to Lovran every 20 minutes until late in the evening.

KRK ISLAND

pop 16,400

Croatia's largest island, 409-sq-km Krk (Veglia in Italian) is also one of the busiest in the summer. It may not be the most beautiful or lush island in Croatia – in fact, it's largely over-developed and stomped over – but its decades of experience in tourism make it an easy place to visit, with good transport connections and a well-organised infrastructure.

GETTING THERE & AROUND

The Krk toll bridge links the northern part of the island with the mainland, and a regular car ferry links Valbiska with Merag on Cres (17KN/113KN passenger/car, 30 minutes). Another ferry by Split Tours operates between Valbiska and Lopar (37KN, 1½ hours) on Rab four times daily.

Krk is also home to **Rijeka airport** (www.rijeka-airport.hr), the main hub for flights to the Kvarner region, which consist mostly of low-cost and charter flights during summer.

About 14 buses per weekday travel between Rijeka and Krk Town (50KN, one to two hours). There are 10 daily buses to Baška from Krk Town (27KN, 45 minutes). All services are reduced on weekends.

Six daily buses run from Zagreb to Krk Town (163KN to 183KN, three to four hours). Note that some bus lines are more direct than others, which will stop in every village en route.

Krk Town

The picturesque Krk Town makes a good base for exploring the island. Baška, on a wide sandy bay at the foot of a scenic mountain range, is the island's prime beach destination. It clusters around a medieval walled centre and, spreading out into the surrounding coves and hills, a modern development that includes a port, beaches, camping grounds and hotels. From the 12th to 15th centuries, Krk Town and the surrounding region remained semi-independent under the Frankopan Dukes of Krk, an indigenous Croatian dynasty, at a time when much of the Adriatic was controlled by Venice. This history explains the various medieval sights in Krk Town, the ducal seat.

ORIENTATION & INFORMATION

The **seasonal tourist office** (☎ 220 226; www.tz-krk.hr, in Croatian; Obala Hrvatske Mornarice bb; 🕑 8am-9pm Jun-Sep) distributes brochures and materials, including a map of hiking paths. Out of season, go to the **main tourist office** (☎ 220 226; Vela Placa 1; 🕑 8am-3pm Mon-Fri) nearby. You can change money at any travel agency (there are 13 in town) and there are numerous ATMs around town.

The bus from Baška and Rijeka stops at the station (no left-luggage office) by the harbour, a few minutes' walk from the Old Town.

SIGHTS

Sights include the Romanesque **Cathedral of the Assumption** and the fortified **Kaštel** (Trg Kamplin) facing the seafront on the northern edge of the Old Town. The narrow cobbled streets that make up the pretty old quarter are worth a wander.

SLEEPING & EATING

There is a range of accommodation in and around Krk, but many hotels only open between April and October. Private rooms can be organised through any of the agencies, including **Autotrans** (☎ 222 661; www.autotrans-turizam.com; Šetalište Svetog Bernardina 3; 🕑 8am-9pm Mon-Sat, 9am-1.30pm & 6-9pm Sun) in the bus station. You can expect to pay between 210KN and 250KN for a double room in the high season.

Autocamp Ježevac (☎ 221 081; camping@valamar.com; Plavnička bb; per adult/site 44/56KN; 🕑 mid-Apr–mid-Oct) The beachfront ground offers shady sites and places to swim. It's the closest camping ground to town, a 10-minute walk southwest.

Bor (☎/fax 220 200; www.hotelbor.hr; Šetalište Dražica 5; s 152-369KN, d 231-564KN) The rooms are modest and without trimmings at this low-key hotel, but the seafront location amid pine forests makes it a worthwhile stay.

Marina (☎ 221 357; www.hotelikrk.hr; Obala Hrvatske Mornarice 6; s 760KN, d 1168KN; ❄ 💻) The most recent overhaul boosted this Old Town hotel to four-star. Now each of the 10 deluxe units sports sea vistas and modern trappings like LCD TV.

Konoba Nono (☎ 222 221; Krčkih Iseljenika 8; mains from 40KN) Savour local specialities like *šurlice* (homemade noodles) topped with goulash or scampi, just a hop and a skip from the Old Town.

Casa del Padrone (Šetalište Svetog Bernardina bb) Krk partygoers crowd the two floors of this faux-Renaissance bar-club, which hosts DJs on summer weekends. Daytime fun consists of lounging on the seaside tables as you nibble on cakes and sip espresso.

Baška

At the southern end of Krk Island, Baška has its most beautiful beach, a 2km-long crescent set below a dramatic, barren range of mountains. There's one caveat should you visit in summer – tourists are spread towel-to-towel and what's otherwise a pretty pebble beach turns into a fight for your place under the sun. The 16th-century core of Venetian townhouses is pleasant enough for a stroll but what surrounds it is a bland tourist development of apartment blocks and restaurants.

The bus stops at the top of a hill on the edge of the Old Town, between the beach and the harbour. The main street is Zvonimirova, which overlooks the harbour; the beach begins at the western end of the harbour, continuing southwards past a big sprawling hotel complex. The **tourist office** (☎ 856 817; www.tz-baska.hr; Zvonimirova 114; 🕑 7am-9pm Mon-Sat, 8am-1pm Sun Jun–mid-Sep, 8am-3pm Mon-Fri mid-Sep–May) is just down the street from the bus station.

Popular trails include an 8km walk to **Stara Baška**, a restful little village on a bay surrounded by stark, salt-washed limestone hills.

Most hotels and the two camps are managed by **Hoteli Baška** (☎ 656 111; www.hotelibaska.hr). Private accommodation can be arranged by most agencies in town, such as **PDM Guliver** (☎/fax 856 004; www.pdm-guliver.hr; Zvonimirova 98; 🕑 7am-9pm Mon-Sat, 8am-1pm Sun Jun–mid-Sep, reduced hr rest of year). There's a four-night minimum stay in summer (or a hefty surcharge).

DALMATIA

Roman ruins, spectacular beaches, old fishing ports, medieval architecture and unspoilt offshore islands make a trip to Dalmatia (Dalmacija) unforgettable. Occupying the central 375km of Croatia's Adriatic coast, Dalmatia offers a matchless combination of hedonism and historical discovery. The jagged coast is speckled with lush offshore islands and dotted with historic cities.

Split is the largest city in the region and a hub for bus and boat connections along the Adriatic, as well as home to the late-Roman Diocletian's Palace. Nearby are the early Roman ruins in Solin (Salona). Zadar has yet more Roman ruins and a wealth of churches. The architecture of Hvar and Korčula recalls the days when these places were outposts of the Venetian empire. None can rival majestic Dubrovnik, a cultural and aesthetic jewel.

ZADAR

☎ 023 / pop 72,700

It's hard to decipher the mystery of why Zadar (ancient Zara), the main city of northern Dalmatia, is an under-rated tourist destination. Is it because it has a compact, marble, traffic-free Old Town that follows the old Roman street plan and contains Roman ruins and medieval churches? Or could it be that it's recently been dubbed as Croatia's 'city of cool' for its clubs, bars and festivals run by international music stars?

Zadar is a city to behold on the Dalmatian coast – its cultural and entertainment offers are growing by the year, and with one of Europe's biggest budget airlines (Ryanair) starting to fly into its airport, it's safe to say that Zadar is not going to remain off-the-beaten track for much longer.

History

In the past 2000 years Zadar has escaped few wars. Its strategic position on the Adriatic coast made it a target for the Romans, the Byzantine, Venetian and Austro-Hungarian empires and Italy. Although it was damaged by Allied bombing raids in 1943–44 and Yugoslav rockets in 1991, this resilient city has been rebuilt and restored, retaining much of its old flavour. Don't forget to sample Zadar's famous maraschino-cherry liqueur.

Orientation

The train station and the bus station are adjacent and are 1km southeast of the harbour and Old Town. From the stations, Zrinsko-Frankopanska leads northwest to the town and harbour. Buses marked 'Poluotok' run from the bus station to the harbour. Narodni trg is the heart of Zadar.

Information

Aquarius Travel Agency (☎/fax 212 919; www.jureskoaquarius.hr; Nova Vrata bb) Books accommodation and excursions.

Garderoba (per day 15KN) bus station (🕑 7am-9pm Mon-Fri); Jadrolinija dock (🕑 7am-8pm Mon-Fri, to 3pm Sat); train station (🕑 24hr)

Hospital (☎ 315 677; Bože Peričića 5) Emergency services are available 24 hours.

Main post office (Poljana Pape Aleksandra III) You can make phone calls here.

Miatours (☎/fax 212 788; www.miatours.hr; Vrata Sveti Krševana) Books accommodation and excursions. Vrata Sveti Krševana is an extremely tiny passage through the walls that contains little more than the travel agency.

Internet Spot (Varoška 3; per hr 30KN)

Tourist office (☎ 316 166; www.tzzadar.hr; Mihe Klaića 5; 🕑 8am-8pm Mon-Sat, to 1pm Sun Jun-Sep, to 6pm Mon-Sat Oct-May)

Sights & Activities

Most attractions are near **St Donatus Church** (Sveti Donat; ☎ 250 516; Šimuna Kožičića Benje; admission 10KN; 🕑 9.30am-1pm & 4-6pm Mar-Oct), a circular 9th-century Byzantine structure built over the Roman forum. Slabs for the ancient forum are visible in the church and there is a pillar from the Roman era on the northwestern side. In summer, ask about the musical evenings here (featuring Renaissance and early baroque music). The outstanding **Museum of Church Art** (Trg Opatice Čike bb; adult/student 20/10KN; 🕑 10am-12.30pm daily, 6-8pm Mon-Sat), in the Benedictine monastery opposite St Donatus, offers three floors of elaborate gold and silver reliquaries, religious paintings, icons and local lacework.

The 13th-century Romanesque **Cathedral of St Anastasia** (Katedrala Svete Stošije; Trg Svete Stošije; 🕑 Mass only) has some fine Venetian carvings in the 15th-century choir stalls. The **Franciscan Monastery** (Franjevački Samostan; Zadarskog Mira 1358; admission free; 🕑 7.30am-noon & 4.30-6pm) is the oldest Gothic church in Dalmatia (consecrated in 1280), with lovely interior Renaissance features and a large Romanesque cross in the treasury, behind the sacristy.

The most interesting museum is the **Archaeological Museum** (Arheološki Muzej; Trg Opatice Čike 1; adult/student 10/5KN; 🕑 9am-1pm & 6-9pm Mon-Fri, 9am-1pm Sat), across from St Donatus, with an extensive collection of artefacts, from the Neolithic period through the Roman occupation to the development of Croatian culture under the Byzantines. Some captions are in

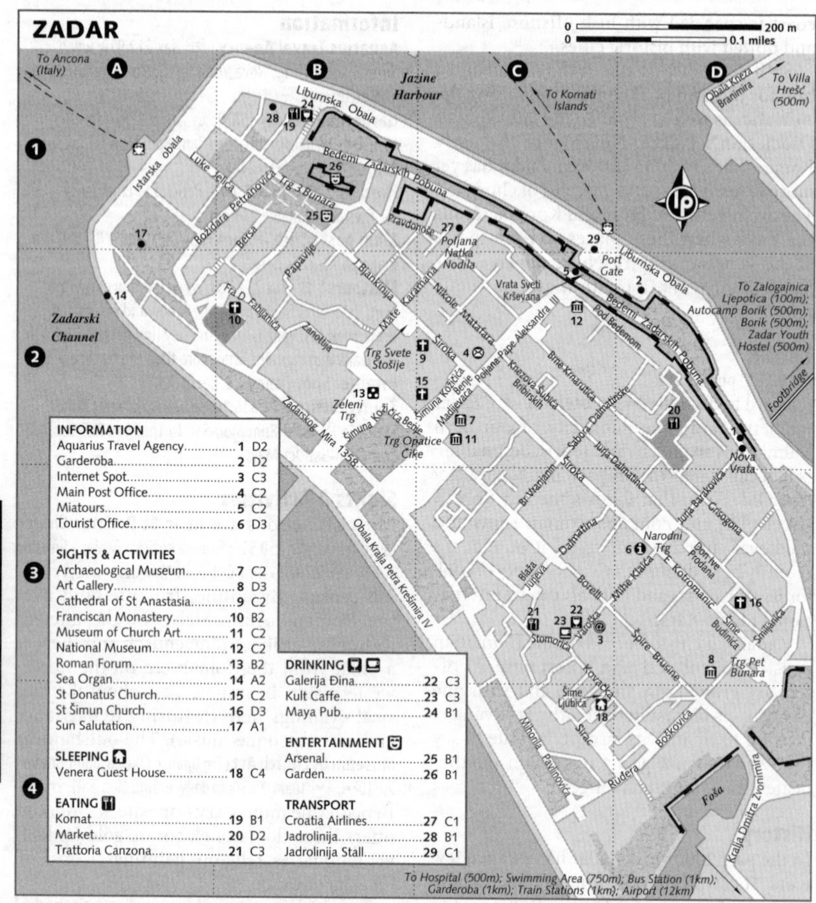

English and you are handed a leaflet in English when you buy your ticket.

Less interesting is the **National Museum** (Narodni Muzej; Poljana Pape Aleksandra III; admission 10KN; 9am-1pm & 5-7pm Mon-Fri), just inside the sea gate, featuring photos of Zadar from different periods, and old paintings and engravings of many coastal cities. The same admission ticket will get you into the **Art Gallery** (Galerija; Smiljanića; 9am-noon & 5-8pm Mon-Fri, 9am-1pm Sat). One church worth a visit is **St Šimun Church** (Crkva Svetog Šime; Šime Budinića; 8am-1pm & 6-8pm Jun-Sep), which has a 14th-century gold chest.

Zadar's incredible (and world's only) **Sea Organ** (Morske Orgulje), designed by local architect Nikola Bašić, is bound to be one of the more memorable sights you'll see in Croatia. Set within the perforated stone stairs that descend into the sea is a system of pipes and whistles that exudes wistful sighs when the movement of the sea pushes air through the pipes.

Right next to it is the newly built **Sun Salutation** (Pozdrav Suncu), another wacky and wonderful Bašić creation. It's a 22m circle, cut into the pavement and filled with 300 multilayered glass plates that collect the sun's energy during the day and, powered by the same wave energy that makes the sound of the Sea Organ, produces a trippy light show from sunset to sunrise, meant to simulate the solar system.

You can swim from the steps off the promenade and listen to the sound of the Sea Organ. There's a **swimming area** with diving boards, a small park and a cafe on the coastal promenade off Zvonimira. Bordered by pine trees and parks, the promenade takes you to a beach in front of Hotel Kolovare and then winds on for about a kilometre up the coast.

Tours

Any of the many travel agencies around town can supply information on tourist cruises to the beautiful **Kornati Islands** (Kornati Islands National Park is an archipelago of 147 mostly uninhabited islands), river-rafting and half-day excursions to the Krka waterfalls.

Sleeping

Most visitors head out to the 'tourist settlement' at Borik, 3km northwest of Zadar, on the Puntamika bus (6KN, every 20 minutes from the bus station). Here there are hotels, a hostel, a camping ground, big swimming pools, sporting opportunities and numerous *sobe* (rooms) signs; you can arrange a private room through a travel agency in town. Expect to pay from €22 to €50 for a room, depending on the facilities.

Autocamp Borik (☎ 332 074; camp sites per adult 36-53KN, per site low/high season 90/135KN; ⌚ May-Oct) Steps away from Borik beach, this camping ground is shaded by tall pines and has decent facilities.

Zadar Youth Hostel (☎ 331 145; zadar@hfhs.hr; Obala Kneza Trpimira 76; dm €13; 💻) A great option for backpackers, with plain but clean rooms – some have wooden floors that creak comfortingly. Borik beach is minutes away. There's internet access at 5KN for 15 minutes.

Venera Guest House (☎ 214 098; www.hotel-venera-zd.hr; Šime Ljubića 4a; d 300-450KN) Venera – also known as the Jović Guesthouse – is the centre's only option. Although the rooms are miniscule, have oversized wardrobes and no numbers on the doors, all have private bathrooms, the beds are good and the atmosphere is pretty relaxed.

our pick **Villa Hrešć** (☎ 337 570; www.villa-hresc.hr; Obala Kneza Trpimira 28; s 550-650KN, d 750-850KN; ❄ 🏊) Zadar's plushest choice is in a cheery pink building on a bay. The stylish rooms are in pastel colours, the beds are luxurious dreaming spots, and as you lounge by the swimming pool you can admire views of the Old Town.

Eating

Zalogajnica Ljepotica (☎ 311 288; Obala Kneza Branimira 4b; mains from 35KN) The cheapest place in town prepares three to four dishes a day at knock-out prices in a setting that would fit well in a Kaurismaki movie – you know, a rugged, lonesome diner and a pot-bellied chef/waiter who brings you a steaming dish with a somnolent look on his face. The food is great and home cooked, and the dishes are usually squid-ink risotto, tomato and seafood pasta, plus something meaty.

Trattoria Canzona (☎ 212 081; Stomorića 8; mains 40KN) A great little trattoria in the Old Town, with red-and-white chequered tablecloths, friendly waiters and tons of locals who love the menu of daily specials. Try the delicious *pašticada* that comes with a bunch of juicy gnocchi, and accompany it with a crunchy green salad.

our pick **Kornat** (☎ 254 501; Liburnska Obala 6; mains from 80KN) This is without a doubt Zadar's best restaurant. It's elegant, with wooden floors and modern furnishings, and the service is excellent, but it's the food that's the real knockout. There's the smooth Istrian truffle monkfish, a creamy squid and salmon risotto (70KN), and the fresh fish (around 350KN per kilogram) is prepared with simple ingredients to maximum deliciousness.

Zadar's morning **market** (⌚ 6am-3pm) is one of Croatia's best.

Entertainment

In summer the many cafes along Varoška and Klaića place their tables on the street; it's great for people-watching.

Arsenal (☎ 253 833; www.arsenalzadar.com; Trg Tri Bunara 1) A large renovated shipping warehouse now hosts this brilliant cultural centre, with a large lounge bar-restaurant–concert hall in the centre, that has a small stage for live music and shows.

our pick **Garden** (☎ 450 907; www.thegardenzadar.com; Bedemi Zadarskih Pobuna; ⌚ late May-Oct) One of the reasons many of Croatia's youngsters rate Zadar as 'a really cool place' is basically because it has the Garden. It's owned and run by UB40's producer Nick Colgan and drummer James Brown. Daytime here is relaxed, while night-time is when the fun really begins. Don't miss it if you're in town.

Getting There & Away

AIR

Zadar's airport, 12km east of the city, is served by **Croatia Airlines** (☎ 250 101; Poljana Natka Nodila 7) and **Ryanair** (www.ryanair.com). A Croatia Airlines bus meets all flights and costs 15KN; a taxi into town costs around 175KN.

WORTH THE TRIP: PLITVICE LAKES NATIONAL PARK

Midway between Zagreb and Zadar, **Plitvice Lakes National Park** (☎ 053 751 015; www.np-plitvicka-jezera.hr; adult/student Apr-Oct 110/50KN, Nov-Mar 70/35KN; 🕑 7am-8pm) is 19.5 hectares of wooded hills and 16 turquoise lakes, all connected by a series of waterfalls and cascades. The mineral-rich waters carve new paths through the rock, depositing tufa (new porous rock) in continually changing formations. Wooden footbridges follow the lakes and streams over, under and across the rumbling water for an exhilaratingly damp 18km. Swimming is not allowed. Your park admission (prices vary by season) is valid for the entire stay and also includes the boats and buses you need to use to see the lakes. There is hotel accommodation only on-site, and private accommodation just outside the park. Check the options with the National Parks information office in Zagreb (see p126).

The Zagreb–Zadar buses that don't use the new motorway road (ie the ones that drive between Zagreb and Zadar in over three hours) stop at Plitvice (check www.akz.hr for more details). The journey takes three hours from Zadar (80KN) and 2½ hours from Zagreb (60KN). Luggage can be left at the **tourist information centres** (☎ 053 751 015; www.np-plitvice.com; 🕑 7am-8pm), located at each entrance to the park.

BOAT

The office of **Jadrolinija** (☎ 254 800; www.jadrolinija.hr) is on the harbour and has tickets for all local ferries, or you can buy ferry tickets from the Jadrolinija stall on Liburnska Obala. The company runs car ferries from Ancona, Italy (€49.50, six to eight hours, daily). Ferries are less frequent during winter months.

BUS

The **bus station** (☎ 211 035; www.liburnija-zadar.hr, in Croatian) is a 10-minute walk from the centre and has daily buses to Zagreb (100KN to 140KN, 3½ to seven hours, 20 daily).

TRAIN

The **train station** (☎ 212 555; www.hznet.hr; Ante Starčevića 3) is adjacent to the bus station. There are five daily trains to Zagreb: two fast trains (150KN, seven hours) and three slower ones (134KN, 9¾ hours).

SPLIT

☎ 021 / pop 188,700

The second-largest city in Croatia, Split (Spalato in Italian), is a great place to see Dalmatian life as it's really lived. Free of mass tourism and always buzzing, this is a city with just the right balance of tradition and modernity. Just step inside Diocletian's Palace – a Unesco World Heritage site and one of the world's most impressive Roman monuments – and you'll see dozens of bars, restaurants and shops thriving amid the atmospheric old walls where Split life has been going on for thousands of years. Split's unique setting and exuberant nature make it one of the most delectable cities in Europe. The dramatic coastal mountains are the perfect backdrop to the turquoise waters of the Adriatic and you'll get a chance to appreciate the gorgeous Split cityscape when making a ferry journey to or from the city.

History

Split achieved fame when Roman emperor Diocletian (AD 245–313) had his retirement palace built here from 295 to 305. After his death the great stone palace continued to be used as a retreat by Roman rulers. When the neighbouring colony of Salona was abandoned in the 7th century, many of the Romanised inhabitants fled to Split and barricaded themselves behind the high palace walls, where their descendants continue to live to this day.

Orientation

The bus, train and ferry terminals are adjacent on the eastern side of the harbour, a short walk from the Old Town. The seafront promenade, Obala Hrvatskog Narodnog Preporoda, better known as Riva, is the best central reference point.

Information

BOOKSHOPS

Algoritam (Map p152; Bajamontijeva 2) A good English-language bookshop.

DISCOUNT CARDS

Split Card (1 day 36KN) Not a bad deal at all – get the Split Card for one day and you can use it for three days without

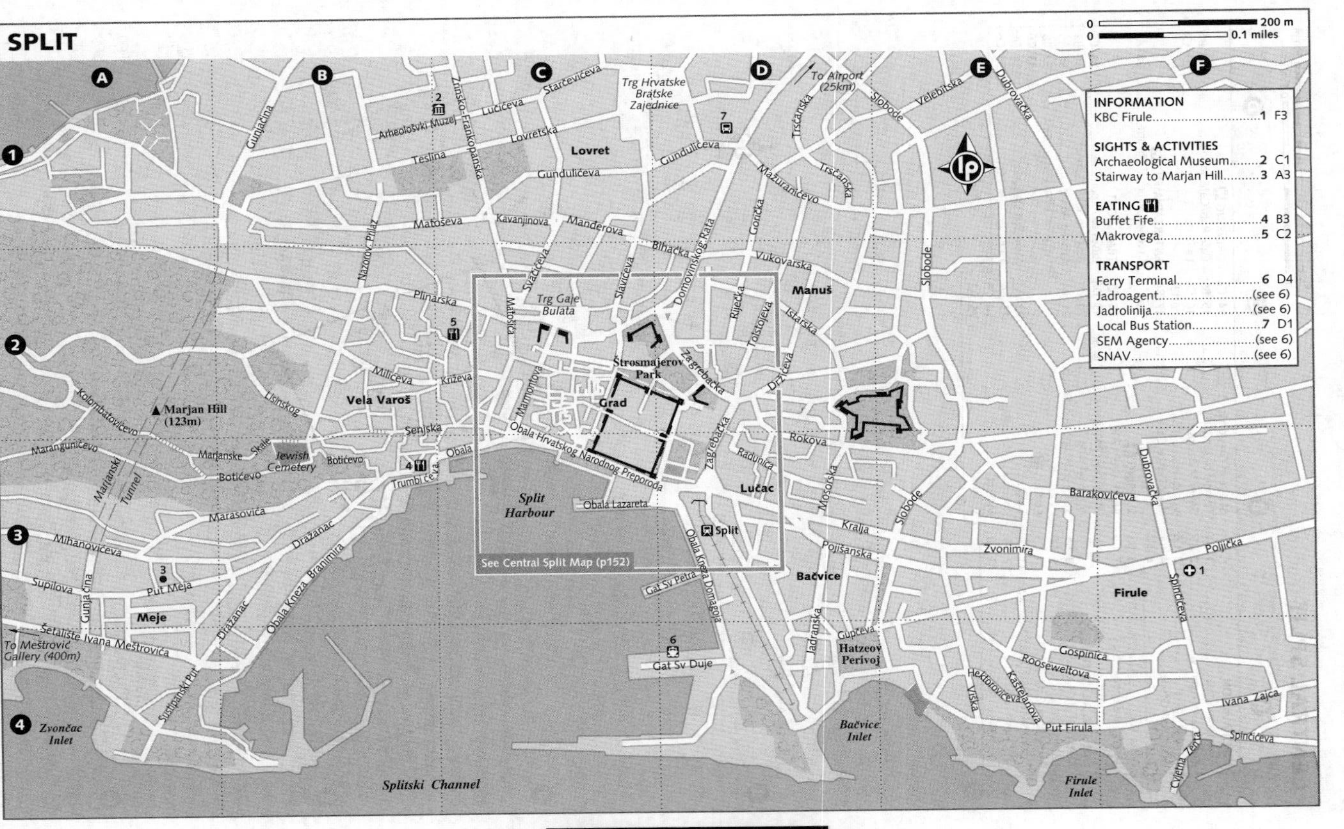
SPLIT
0 200 m
0 0.1 miles
INFORMATION
KBC Firule 1 F3
SIGHTS & ACTIVITIES
Archaeological Museum 2 C1
Stairway to Marjan Hill 3 A3
EATING
Buffet Fife 4 B3
Makrovega 5 C2
TRANSPORT
Ferry Terminal 6 D4
Jadroagent (see 6)
Jadrolinija (see 6)
Local Bus Station 7 D1
SEM Agency (see 6)
SNAV (see 6)
See Central Split Map (p152)
To Airport (25km)
To Meštrović Gallery (400m)
Marjan Hill (123m)
Split Harbour
Splitski Channel
Bačvice Inlet
Firule Inlet
Zvončac Inlet
Jewish Cemetery
Štrosmajerov Park
Trg Gaje Bulata
Trg Hrvatske Bratske Zajednice
Hatzeov Perivoj
Grad
Lovret
Manuš
Lučac
Bačvice
Firule
Vela Varoš
Meje

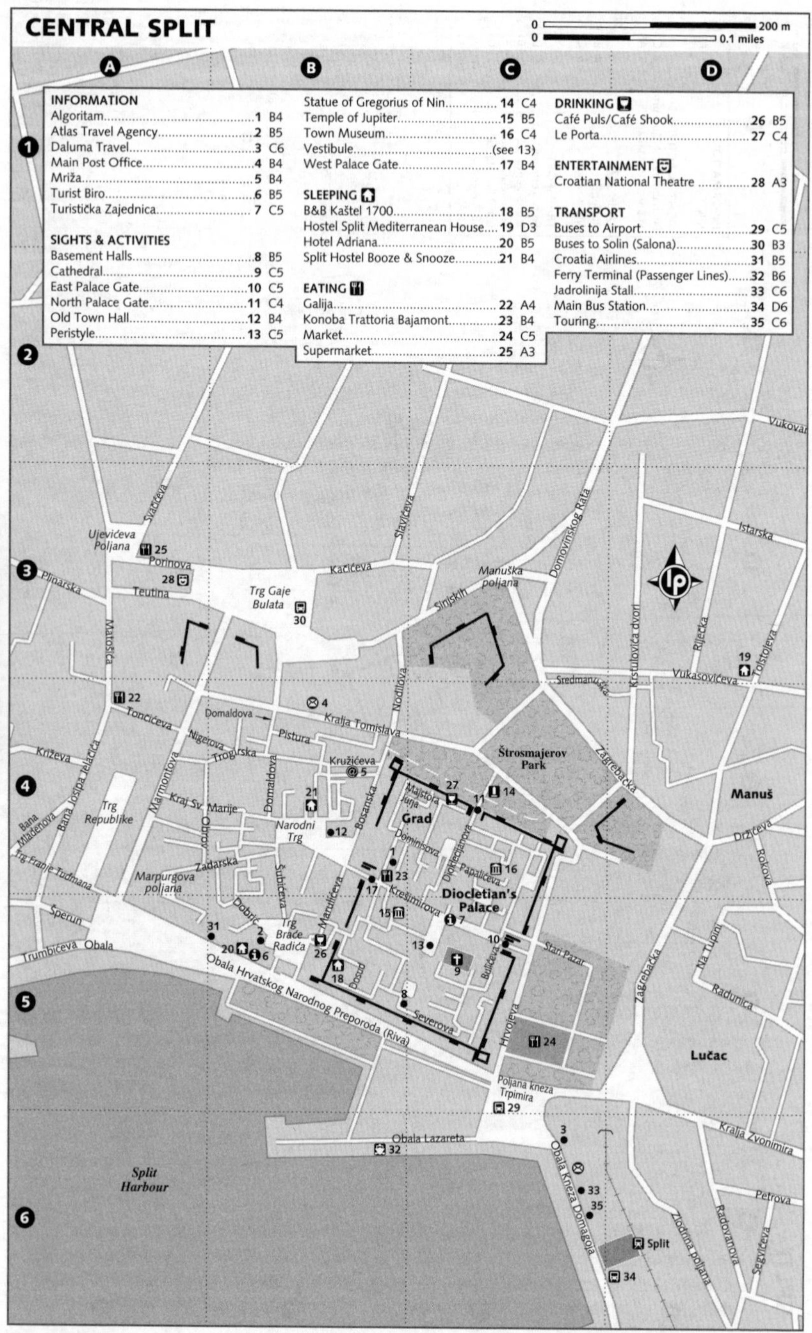
CENTRAL SPLIT
0 200 m
0 0.1 miles
A
B
C
D
1
2
3
4
5
6
INFORMATION
Algoritam 1 B4
Atlas Travel Agency 2 B5
Daluma Travel 3 C6
Main Post Office 4 B4
Mriža 5 B4
Turist Biro 6 B5
Turistička Zajednica 7 C5
SIGHTS & ACTIVITIES
Basement Halls 8 B5
Cathedral 9 C5
East Palace Gate 10 C5
North Palace Gate 11 C4
Old Town Hall 12 B4
Peristyle 13 C5
Statue of Gregorius of Nin 14 C4
Temple of Jupiter 15 B5
Town Museum 16 C4
Vestibule (see 13)
West Palace Gate 17 B4
SLEEPING
B&B Kaštel 1700 18 B5
Hostel Split Mediterranean House 19 D3
Hotel Adriana 20 B5
Split Hostel Booze & Snooze 21 B4
EATING
Galija 22 A4
Konoba Trattoria Bajamont 23 B4
Market 24 C5
Supermarket 25 A3
DRINKING
Café Puls/Café Shook 26 B5
Le Porta 27 C4
ENTERTAINMENT
Croatian National Theatre 28 A3
TRANSPORT
Buses to Airport 29 C5
Buses to Solin (Salona) 30 B3
Croatia Airlines 31 B5
Ferry Terminal (Passenger Lines) 32 B6
Jadrolinija Stall 33 C6
Main Bus Station 34 D6
Touring 35 C6
Vukovar
Svačićeva
Slavićeva
Domovinskog Rata
Istarska
Ujevićeva Poljana
Porinova
Kačićeva
Manuška poljana
Plinarska
Teutina
Trg Gaje Bulata
Sinjskih
Matošića
Kristulovića dvori
Rijećka
Tolstojeva
Sredmanuška
Vukasovićeva
Nodilova
Domaldova
Kralja Tomislava
Tončićeva
Nigerova
Pistura
Trogirska
Križeva
Kružićeva
Štrosmajerov Park
Zagrebačka
Marmontova
Majstora Jurja
Grad
Manuš
Bana Josipa Jelačića
Bana Mladenova
Trg Republike
Kraj Sv Marije
Bosanska
Narodni Trg
Dominisova
Diokleцijanova
Držićeva
Obrov
Zadarska
Papalićeva
Rokova
Trg Franje Tuđmana
Marpurgova poljana
Kresimirova
Diocletian's Palace
Šubićeva
Marulićeva
Dobrić
Šperun
Trg Braće Radića
Stari Pazar
Na Tupini
Trumbićeva Obala
Bulićeva
Obala Hrvatskog Narodnog Preporoda (Riva)
Dosud
Severova
Radunica
Hrvojeva
Lučac
Poljana kneza Trpimira
Kralja Zvonimira
Obala Lazareta
Obala Kneza Domagoja
Split Harbour
Petrova
Zlodrina poljana
Radovanova
Šegvićeva
Split

paying anything extra. You get free access to most of the city museums, half-price discounts to many galleries, and tons of discounts on car rental, restaurants, shops and hotels.

INTERNET ACCESS

Mriža (Map p152; ☎ 321 320; Kružićeva 3; per hr 20KN)

LEFT LUGGAGE

Garderoba (per hr/day 2.20/20KN) bus station (⏲ 6am-10pm); train station (Obala Kneza Domagoja 6; ⏲ 7am-9pm) The train station's left-luggage office is about 50m north of the station.

MEDICAL SERVICES

KBC Firule (Map p151; ☎ 556 111; Spinčićeva 1) Split's hospital. Emergency services are available 24 hours.

MONEY

Change money at travel agencies or the post office. You'll find ATMs around the bus and train stations.

POST

Main post office (Map p152; Kralja Tomislava 9; ⏲ 7.30am-7pm Mon-Fri, 8am-noon Sat) There's also a telephone centre (open 7am to 9pm Monday to Saturday) here.

TOURIST INFORMATION

Turist Biro (Map p152; ☎ /fax 342 142; turist-biro-split@st.t-com.hr; Obala Hrvatskog Narodnog Preporoda 12) This office arranges private accommodation and sells guidebooks and the Split Card (€5, offers free and discounted admission to Split attractions).

Turistička Zajednica (Map p152; ☎ /fax 342 606; www.visitsplit.com; Peristile; ⏲ 9am-8.30pm Mon-Sat, 8am-1pm Sun) Has information on Split; sells the Split Card.

TRAVEL AGENCIES

Atlas Travel Agency (Map p152; ☎ 343 055; Nepotova 4) The town's Amex representative.

Daluma Travel (Map p152; ☎ /fax 338 484; www.daluma.hr; Obala Kneza Domagoja 1) Finds private accommodation and has information on boat schedules.

Sights

DIOCLETIAN'S PALACE

The Old Town is a vast open-air museum and the new information signs at the important sights explain a great deal of Split's history. **Diocletian's Palace** (Map p152; entrance Obala Hrvatskog Narodnog Preporoda 22), facing the harbour, is one of the most imposing Roman ruins in existence. It was built as a strong rectangular fortress, with walls measuring 215m from east to west, 181m wide at the southernmost point and reinforced by square corner towers. The imperial residence, mausoleum and temples were south of the main street, now called Krešimirova, connecting the east and west palace gates.

Enter through the central ground floor of the palace. On the left are the excavated **Basement Halls** (Map p152; ⏲ 10am-6pm), which are empty but impressive. Go through the passage to the **Peristyle** (Map p152), a picturesque colonnaded square, with a neo-Romanesque cathedral tower rising above. The **Vestibule** (Map p152), an open dome above the ground-floor passageway at the southern end of the peristyle, is overpoweringly grand and cavernous. A lane off the peristyle opposite the cathedral leads to the **Temple of Jupiter** (Map p152), which is now a baptistry.

On the eastern side of the peristyle is the **Cathedral** (Map p152), originally Diocletian's mausoleum. The only reminder of Diocletian in the cathedral is a sculpture of his head in a circular stone wreath, below the dome which is directly above the baroque white-marble altar. The Romanesque wooden doors (1214) and stone pulpit are notable. For a small fee you can climb the tower.

In the Middle Ages the nobility and rich merchants built their residences within the old palace walls; the Papalic Palace is now the **Town Museum** (Gradski Muzej; Map p152; ☎ 341 240; Papalićeva ul 5; adult/concession 10/5KN; ⏲ 9am-noon & 5-8pm Tue-Fri, 10am-noon Sat & Sun Jun-Sep, 10am-5pm Tue-Fri, 10am-noon Sat & Sun Oct-May). It has a tidy collection of artefacts, paintings, furniture and clothes from Split; captions are in Croatian.

OUTSIDE THE PALACE WALLS

The **East Palace Gate** (Map p152) leads to the market area. The **West Palace Gate** (Map p152) opens onto medieval Narodni Trg, dominated by the 15th-century Venetian Gothic **Old Town Hall** (Map p152).

Go through the **North Palace Gate** (Map p152) to see Ivan Meštrović's powerful 1929 **statue of Gregorius of Nin** (Map p152), a 10th-century Slavic religious leader who fought for the right to perform Mass in Croatian. Notice that his big toe has been polished to a shine; it's said that touching it brings good luck.

OUTSIDE CENTRAL SPLIT

The **Archaeological Museum** (Arheološki Muzej; Map p151; ☎ 318 720; Zrinjsko-Frankopanska 25; adult/student 20/10KN; ⏲ 9am-2pm Tue-Fri, to 1pm Sat & Sun), north of town, is a fascinating supplement to your walk around Diocletian's Palace, and to the site of ancient Salona. The history of Split is traced from Illyrian times to the Middle Ages, in chronological order, with explanations in English.

The finest art museum in Split is **Meštrović Gallery** (Galerija Meštrović; ☎ 358 450; Šetalište Ivana Meštrovića 46; adult/student 30/15KN; 9am-9pm Tue-Sun Jun-Sep, 9am-4pm Tue-Sat, 10am-3pm Sun Oct-May). You'll see a comprehensive, well-arranged collection of works by Ivan Meštrović, Croatia's premier modern sculptor.

From the Meštrović Gallery it's possible to hike straight up **Marjan Hill** (Map p151). Go up Tonča Petrasova Marovića on the western side of the gallery and continue straight up the stairway to Put Meja. Turn left and walk west to Put Meja 76. The trail begins on the western side of this building. Marjan Hill offers trails through the forest to lookouts and old chapels.

Festivals & Events

February Carnival This traditional carnival is presented in the Old Town.

Feast of St Duje 7 May.

Split Summer Festival Mid-July to mid-August. Features open-air opera, ballet, drama and musical concerts.

Sleeping

Split is quite thin on the ground when it comes to good budget accommodation, unless you're looking to sleep in dorms. Private accommodation is again the best option and in the summer you may be deluged at the bus station by women offering *sobe* (rooms available). Make sure you are clear about the exact location of the room or you may find yourself several bus rides from the town centre. The best thing to do is to book through the **Turist Biro** (Map p152; ☎/fax 342 142; www.turistbiro-split.hr; Obala Hrvatskog Narodnog Preporoda 12; 9am-7pm Mon-Fri, to 4pm Sat). Expect to pay between 145KN to 220KN for a double room where you will probably share the bathroom with the proprietor.

Hostel Split Mediterranean House (Map p152; ☎ 098 987 1312; www.hostel-split.com; Vukasovićeva 21; dm from 100KN;) It's a 10-minute walk from the Northern Gate to this friendly, family-run hostel set in a lovely old stone building. There are two six-bed dorms and some newer en-suite three-bed dorms.

Split Hostel Booze & Snooze (Map p152; ☎ 342 787; www.splithostel.com; Narodni Trg 8; dm 110-180KN;) A great new addition to Split's backpacker scene, this hostel is run by Aussie Croats and does exactly what it says on the tin – it's a party place, with 23 beds to snooze in, a nice terrace and it's right in the centre of town.

our pick **B&B Kaštel 1700** (Map p152; ☎ 343 912; www.kastelsplit.com; Mihovilova Širina 5; s 290-510KN, d 400-660KN;) Among Split's best value for money places, it's near the bars, overlooks Radićev Trg and has sweet and tidy rooms and friendly, efficient service.

Hotel Adriana (Map p152; ☎ 340 000; www.hotel-adriana.com; Obala Hrvatskog Narodnog Preporoda (Riva) 9; s 550-650KN, d 750-900KN;) Good value, excellent location. The rooms are not massively exciting, with their navy curtains and beige furniture, but some have sea views, which is a real bonus in Split's Old Town.

Eating

Galija (Map p152; Tončićeva 12; pizzas from 26KN) Galija has been the most popular place on Split's pizza scene for several decades now. It's the sort of joint that the locals take you to for an unfussy but good lunch or dinner, and where everyone relaxes on the wooden benches with the leftovers of a *quattro staggioni* or a *margharita* in front of them.

Makrovega (Map p151; ☎ 394 440; www.makrovega.hr; Leština 2; mains from 40KN; 9am-7pm Mon-Fri, to 4pm Sat) A meat-free haven with a clean, spacious (nonsmoking!) interior and delicious buffet and à la carte food that alternates between macrobiotic and vegetarian.

Buffet Fife (Map p151; ☎ 345 223; Trumbićeva Obala 11; mains around 40KN) Dragomir presides over a motley crew of sailors and misfits who drop in for the simple, home-cooking (especially the *pašticada*) and his own brand of grumpy but loving hospitality.

our pick **Konoba Trattoria Bajamont** (Map p152; ☎ 091 253 7441; Bajamontijeva 3; mains from 50KN) A one-room joint with four or five tables on one side and a heavily leaned-on bar on the other; there's no sign above the door and the menu is written out in marker pen and stuck in an inconspicuous spot by the entrance. The food is excellent and the menu usually features things such as small fried fish, squid-ink risotto, *brujet* (fish/seafood stew with wine, onions and herbs, served with polenta) and octopus salad.

The delicatessen at the **supermarket** (Map p152; Svačićeva 1) has a wide selection of meat and cheese for sandwiches. The **market** (Map p152; ⏲ 6am-2pm), outside the east palace gate, has a wide array of fresh local produce.

Drinking

Split is great for nightlife, especially (or more so) in the spring and summer months. The palace walls are generally throbbing with loud music on Friday and Saturday nights.

Le Porta (Map p152; Majstora Jurja) Next door to Teak Caffe, Le Porta is renowned for its cocktails. On the same square – Majstora Jurja – are Kala, Dante, Whisky Bar and Na Kantunu, all of which end up merging into one when the night gets busy.

Café Puls (Map p152; Mihovilova Širina) and **Café Shook** (Map p152; Mihovilova Širina) are pretty much indistinguishable late on Friday or Saturday night, when the dozen steps that link these two bars are chock-a-block with youngsters.

Entertainment

Croatian National Theatre (Map p152; Trg Gaje Bulata; best seats about 60KN) During winter, opera and ballet are presented here. Erected in 1891, the theatre was fully restored in 1979 in its original style; it's worth attending a performance for the architecture alone.

Getting There & Away

AIR

The country's national air carrier, **Croatia Airlines** (Map p152; ☎ 062-777 777; Obala Hrvatskog Narodnog Preporoda 8), operates flights between Zagreb and Split (170KN to 350KN, 45 minutes) up to four times every day. Rates are lower if you book in advance. There's also **easyJet** (www.easyjet.com).

BOAT

The following companies have ferries to/from Italy:

Jadrolinija (www.jadrolinija.hr) Croatia's national boat line runs car ferries from Ancona to Split (€51, nine or 10 hours, six weekly), as well as a route from Bari to Dubrovnik (€51, eight hours, six weekly), which continues on to Rijeka, Stari Grad and Split. Ferries are less frequent during winter months.

SNAV (Map p151; ☎ 322 252; www.snav.com) Has a fast car ferry that travels from Ancona to Split (4½ hours, daily), and another from Pescara to Hvar (3½ hours, daily) and on to Split (6½ hours).

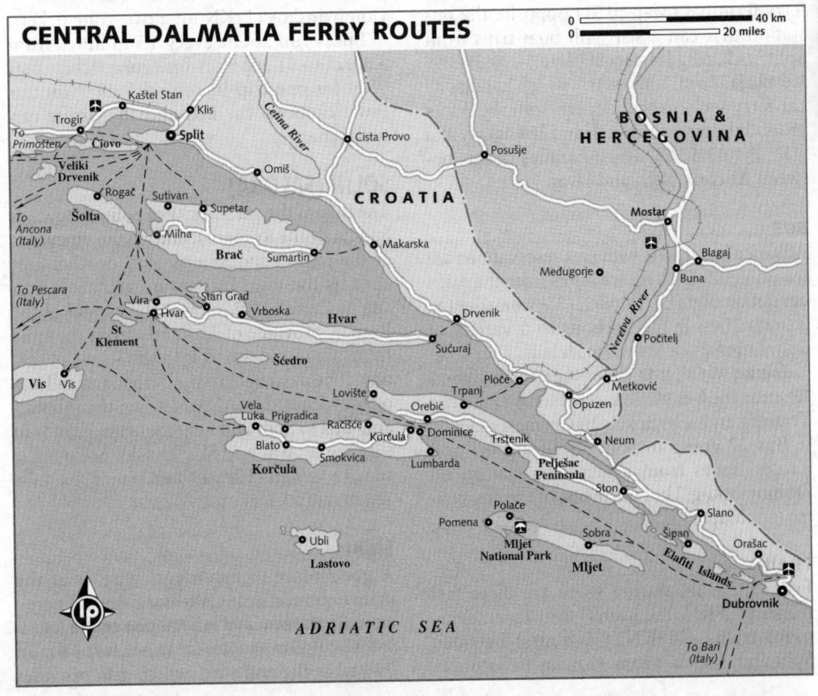

BUSES FROM SPLIT

Destination	Fare (KN)	Duration (hr)	Daily services
Dubrovnik	105-166	4½	12
Ljubljana*	310	10½	1
Makarska	60	1½	every 30min
Međugorje**	120	3	5
Mostar**	120	2-4	4
Pula	331	10	1
Rijeka	250-380	7½	10
Sarajevo**	200	7	5
Zadar	120	3	8
Zagreb	195	5-9	27

*Slovenia
**Bosnia & Hercegovina

Split Tours (www.splittours.hr) Connects Ancona and Split (nine hours), continuing on to Stari Grad (Hvar, 12 hours). In summer, ferries leave twice daily Saturday to Monday and daily on other days. In winter, they travel three times a week, and only as far as Split.

You can buy tickets for passenger ferries at the **Jadrolinija stall** (Map p152; Obala Kneza Domagoja). There are also several agents in the large ferry terminal (Map p151) opposite the bus station that can assist with boat trips from Split, including **Jadroagent** (Map p151; ☎ 338 335); **Jadrolinija** (Map p151; ☎ 338 333), which handles all car-ferry services that depart from the docks around the ferry terminal; and **SEM agency** (Map p151; ☎ 060 325 523), which handles tickets between Ancona, Split and Hvar.

BUS

Advance bus tickets with seat reservations are recommended. There are buses from the main **bus station** (Map p152; ☎ 060 327 327; www.ak-split.hr, in Croatian) beside the harbour to a variety of destinations; see above for details.

Touring (Map p152; ☎ 338 503; Obala Kneza Domagojeva 10), near the bus station, represents Deutsche Touring and sells tickets to German cities.

Bus 37 going to Solin, Split airport and Trogir leaves from a local bus station on Domovinskog, 1km northeast of the city centre (see Map p151).

TRAIN

From the train station there are three fast trains (138KN, six hours) and three overnight trains (138KN, 8½ hours) between Split and Zagreb. From Monday to Saturday there are six trains a day between Šibenik and Split (33KN, two hours) and four trains on Sunday.

Getting Around

There's an airport bus stop at Obala Lazareta 3 (Map p152). The bus (30KN, 30 minutes) leaves about 90 minutes before flight times, or you can take bus 37 from the bus station on Domovinskog (11KN for a two-zone ticket).

Buses run about every 15 minutes from 5.30am to 11.30pm. A one-zone ticket costs 9KN for one trip in central Split. You can buy tickets on the bus and the driver can make change.

SOLIN (SALONA)

The ruin of the ancient city of Solin (known as Salona by the Romans), among the vineyards at the foot of mountains 5km northeast of Split, is the most interesting archaeological site in Croatia. Salona was the capital of the Roman province of Dalmatia from the time Julius Caesar elevated it to the status of colony. It held out against the barbarians and was only evacuated in AD 614 when the inhabitants fled to Split and neighbouring islands in the face of Avar and Slav attacks. Solin is the site of a summer **Ethnoambient** (www.ethnoambient.net) music festival each August.

Sights

A good place to begin your visit is at the main entrance, near Caffe Bar Salona. There's a small **museum and information centre** (admission 10KN; 🕒 9am-6pm Mon-Sat Jun-Sep, to 1pm Mon-Sat Oct-May) at the entrance, which also provides a helpful map and some literature about the complex.

Manastirine, the fenced area behind the car park, was a burial place for early Christian martyrs before the legalisation of Christianity. Excavated remains of the cemetery and the 5th-century basilica are highlights, although this area was outside the ancient city itself. Overlooking Manastirine is **Tusculum**, with interesting sculptures embedded in the walls and in the garden.

The Manastirine-Tusculum complex is part of an archaeological reserve that can be freely entered. A path bordered by cypress trees runs south towards the northern **city wall** of Salona. Note the **covered aqueduct** along the inside base of the wall. The ruins in front of you as you stand on the wall were the early Christian cult centre, which include the three-aisled, 5th-century **cathedral** and a small **baptistry** with inner columns. **Public baths** adjoin the cathedral on the eastern side.

Southwest of the cathedral is the 1st-century east city gate, **Porta Caesarea**, later engulfed by the growth of Salona in all directions. Grooves in the stone road left by ancient chariots can be seen at this gate.

Walk west along the city wall for about 500m to **Kapljuč Basilica** on the right, another martyrs' burial place. At the western end of Salona you'll find the huge 2nd-century **amphitheatre**, which was destroyed in the 17th century by the Venetians to prevent it from being used as a refuge by Turkish raiders.

Getting There & Away

The ruins are easily accessible on Split city bus 1 direct to Solin every half-hour from the city bus stop at Trg Gaje Bulata.

From the amphitheatre at Solin it's easy to continue to Trogir by catching a westbound bus 37 from the nearby stop on the adjacent new highway. If, on the other hand, you want to return to Split, use the underpass to cross the highway and catch an eastbound bus 37 (buy a four-zone ticket in Split if you plan to do this).

Alternatively, you can catch most Sinj-bound buses (15KN, 10 daily) from Split's main bus station to take you to Solin.

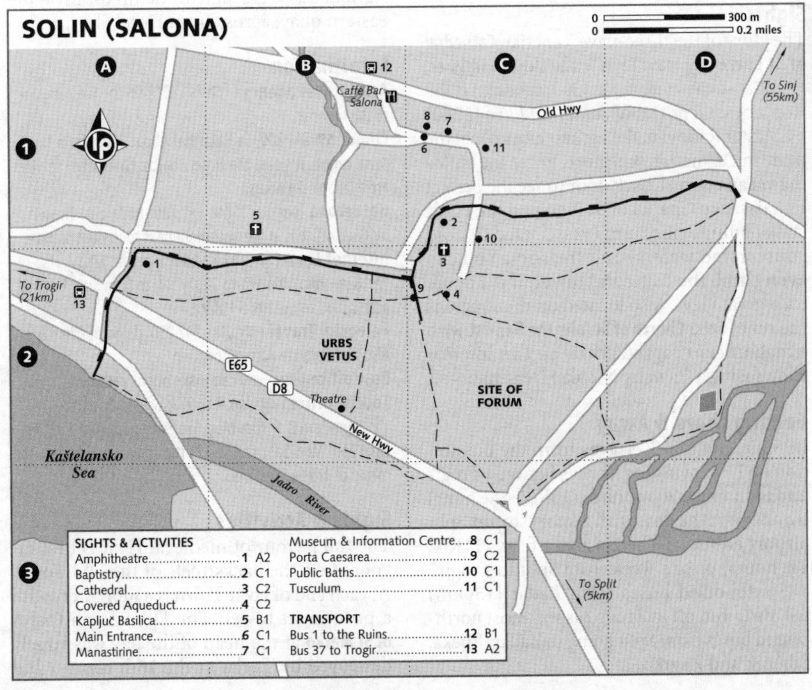

TROGIR

☎ 021 / pop 600

Gorgeous and tiny Trogir (formerly Trau) is beautifully set within medieval walls, its streets knotted and maze-like. It's fronted by a wide seaside promenade lined with bars and cafes and luxurious yachts docking in the summer. Trogir is unique among Dalmatian towns for its profuse collection of Romanesque and Renaissance architecture (which flourished under Venetian rule), and this, along with its magnificent cathedral, earned it the status as a World Heritage site in 1997.

Trogir is an easy day trip from Split and a relaxing place to spend a few days, taking a trip or two to nearby islands.

Orientation & Information

The heart of the Old Town is a few minutes' walk from the bus station. After crossing the small bridge near the station, go through the north gate. Trogir's finest sights are around Narodni Trg to the southeast.

Atlas travel agency (☎ 881 374; www.atlas-trogir.com; Zvonimira 10) finds private accommodation, books hotels and runs excursions.

Sights

The glory of the three-nave Venetian **Cathedral of St Lovre** (Trg Ivana Pavla II; adult/child 15KN/free; 9.30am-noon year-round, plus 4.30-7pm summer) is the Romanesque portal of *Adam and Eve* (1240) by Master Radovan, the earliest example of the nude in Dalmatian sculpture. Enter the building via an obscure back door to see the perfect Renaissance Chapel of St Ivan and the choir stalls, pulpit, ciborium (vessel used to hold consecrated wafers) and treasury. You can even climb the cathedral tower, if it's open, for a great view. Also located on the square is the renovated **Church of St John the Baptist** with a magnificent carved portal and an interior showcasing a *Pietá* by Nicola Firentinac.

Getting There & Away

In Split, city bus 37 leaves from the bus station on Domovinskog. It runs between Trogir and Split every 20 minutes (15KN, one hour) throughout the day, with a short stop at Split airport en route. There's also a ferry (11KN, 2½ hours) once a week from Split to Trogir.

Southbound buses from Zadar (130km) will drop you off in Trogir, as will most northbound buses from Split going to Zadar, Rijeka, Šibenik and Zagreb.

HVAR ISLAND

☎ 021 / pop 12,600

Hvar is the number-one carrier of Croatia's superlatives: it's the most luxurious island, the sunniest place in the country (2724 sunny hours each year) and, along with Dubrovnik, the most popular tourist destination. Hvar is also famed for its verdancy and its lilac lavender fields, as well as other aromatic herbs such as rosemary and heather.

The island's hub and busiest destination is Hvar Town, estimated to draw around 30,000 people a day in the high season. It's odd that they can all fit in the small bay town, but fit they do. Visitors wander along the main square, explore the sights on the winding stone streets, swim on the numerous beaches or pop off to nudist Pakleni Islands. There are several good restaurants and a number of great hotels, as well as a couple of hostels.

Orientation

Car ferries from Split deposit you in Stari Grad but local buses meet most ferries in summer for the trip to Hvar Town. The town centre is Trg Sv Stjepana, 100m west of the bus station. Passenger ferries tie up on Riva, the eastern quay, across from Hotel Slavija.

Information

Atlas travel agency (☎ 741 670) On the western side of the harbour.

Clinic (☎ 741 300; Sv Katarina) About 200m from the town centre, it's past the Hotel Pharos. Emergency services are available 24 hours.

Garderoba (per day 15KN; 7am-midnight) The left-luggage office is in the bathroom next to the bus station.

Internet Leon (☎ 741 824; Riva; per hr 42KN; 8am-9pm Mon-Fri, to 10pm Sat, to 6pm Sun) Internet access next to the Hotel Palace.

Pelegrini Travel (☎ /fax 742 250; pelegrini@inet.hr) Also finds private accommodation.

Post office (Riva) You can make phone calls here.

Tourist office (☎ /fax 742 977; www.tzhvar.hr; 8am-1pm & 5-9pm Mon-Sat, 9am-noon Sun Jun-Sep, 8am-2pm Mon-Sat Oct-May) In the arsenal building on the corner of Trg Sv Stjepana.

Sights & Activities

The full flavour of medieval Hvar is best savoured on the backstreets of the Old Town. At each end of Hvar Town is a monastery with a prominent tower. The Dominican **Church of St Marko** at the head of the bay was largely destroyed by Turks in the 16th century but you can visit the local **Archaeological Museum** (admission 10KN; ⌚ 10am-noon Jun-Sep) in the ruins. If it is closed you'll still get a good view of the ruins from the road just above, which leads up to a stone cross on a hilltop offering a picture-postcard view of Hvar.

At the southeastern end of Hvar you'll find the 15th-century Renaissance **Franciscan Monastery** (⌚ 10am-noon & 5-7pm Jun-Sep, Christmas week & Holy Week), with a wonderful collection of Venetian paintings in the church and adjacent **museum** (admission 15KN; ⌚ 10am-noon & 5-7pm Mon-Sat Jun-Sep), including *The Last Supper* by Matteo Ingoli.

Smack in the middle of Hvar Town is the imposing Gothic **arsenal**, and upstairs is Hvar's prize, the first **municipal theatre** in Europe (1612) – both under extensive renovations at the time of research. On the hill high above Hvar Town is a **Venetian fortress** (1551), and it's worth the climb up to appreciate the lovely, sweeping panoramic views. The fort was built to defend Hvar from the Turks, who sacked the town in 1539 and 1571.

Sleeping

Accommodation in Hvar Town is extremely tight in July and August: a reservation is highly recommended. For private accommodation, try Pelegrini Travel (see opposite). Expect to pay from 160/280KN per single/double with bathroom in the town centre.

Green Lizard Hostel (☎ 742 560; www.greenlizard.hr; Lučića bb; dm 110KN, d per person 135KN; ⌚ Apr-Nov) This privately run hostel is a welcome and most necessary budget option on Hvar. Rooms are simple and immaculately clean, there's a communal kitchen and a few doubles with private and shared facilities.

Jagoda & Ante Bracanović Guesthouse (☎ 741 416, 091 520 3796; www.geocities.com/virgilye/hvar-jagoda.html; Poviše Škole; s 100-120KN, d 190-220KN) The Bracanović family has turned a traditional stone building into a small *pensione*. Rooms come with balconies, private bathrooms and access to a kitchen, and the family goes out of its way for guests.

Hotel Croatia (☎ 742 400; www.hotelcroatia.net; Majerovica bb; per person 245-575KN;) Only a few steps from the sea, this medium-size, rambling 1930s building is among gorgeous, peaceful gardens. The rooms are simple and fresh, many with balconies overlooking the gardens and the sea.

our pick **Hotel Riva** (☎ 750 750; www.suncanihvar.hr; Riva bb; s €176-380, d €187-391; ❄ 💻) Now the luxury veteran on the Hvar Town hotel scene, the Riva is a 100-year-old hotel that's a picture of modernity. The location is right on the harbour, perfect for watching the yachts glide up and away.

Eating

Konoba Menego (☎ 742 036; mains from 70KN) This is a rustic old house where everything is decked out in Hvar antiques and the staff wears traditional outfits. Try the cheeses and vegetables, prepared the old-fashioned Dalmatian way.

Luna (☎ 741 400; mains from 70KN) Climb the 'stairway to heaven' (you have to guffaw) to the rooftop terrace. Luna has dishes such as gnocchi with truffles, and seafood and wine pasta.

Yakša (☎ 277 0770; www.yaksahvar.com; mains from 80KN) A top-end restaurant where many come not just for the food but also for its reputation as the place to be seen in Hvar. There is a lovely garden at the back and the food is excellent, with lobster being a popular choice (250KN).

The pizzerias along the harbour offer predictable but inexpensive eating. The **grocery store** (Trg Sv Stjepana) is a viable restaurant alternative, and there's a morning market next to the bus station.

Drinking

Hvar has some of the best nightlife on the Adriatic coast, and it's mainly famous for **Carpe Diem** (☎ 742 369; www.carpe-diem-hvar.com; Riva), the mother of all Dalmatian clubs. The music is smooth, the drinks aplenty and there's lots of dancing on the tables in bikinis.

Veneranda (⌚ from 9.30pm), a former fortress on the slope above Hotel Delfin, alternates star DJs with live bands while the punters dance on a dance floor surrounded by a pool.

Getting There & Away

The Jadrolinija ferries between Rijeka and Dubrovnik stop in Stari Grad before continuing to Korčula. The Jadrolinija agency sells boat tickets. Car ferries from Split call at Stari Grad (42KN, one hour) three times daily (five daily in July and August). The speedy catamaran goes five times a day between Split and Hvar Town in the summer months (22KN, one hour). The **Jadrolinija agency** (☎ 741 132; www.jadrolinija.hr; Riva) is beside the landing in Stari

Grad. There are at least 10 shuttle ferries (less in the low season) running from Drvenik, on the mainland, to Sućuraj on the tip of Hvar island (13KN, 25 minutes).

It's possible to visit Hvar on a (hectic) day trip from Split by catching the morning Jadrolinija ferry to Stari Grad, a bus to Hvar town, then the last ferry from Stari Grad directly back to Split.

Ferries to/from Italy:

Jadrolinija (www.jadrolinija.hr) Runs car ferries from Bari to Dubrovnik (€51, eight hours, six weekly), continuing on to Rijeka, Stari Grad and Split.

SNAV (www.snav.com) Has a car ferry that travels from Pescara to Hvar (3½ hours, daily) and on to Split (6½ hours).

Split Tours (www.splittours.hr) Connects Ancona to Split (nine hours) and Stari Grad (12 hours). In summer, ferries leave twice daily Saturday to Monday and daily on other days.

Getting Around

Buses meet most ferries that dock at Stari Grad in July and August, but if you come in the low season it's best to check at the tourist office or at Pelegrini to make sure the bus is running. A taxi costs from 150KN to 200KN. **Radio Taxi Tihi** (☎ 098 338 824) is cheaper if there are a number of passengers to fill up the minivan. It's easy to recognise with the photo of Hvar painted on the side.

CROATIA

KORČULA ISLAND

☎ 020 / pop 16,200

Rich in vineyards and olive trees, the island of Korčula was named Korkyra Melaina (Black Korčula) by the original Greek settlers because of its dense woods and plant life. As the largest island in an archipelago of 48, it provides plenty of opportunities for scenic drives, particularly along the southern coast.

Swimming opportunities abound in the many quiet coves and secluded beaches, while the interior produces some of Croatia's finest wine, especially dessert wines made from the *grk* grape cultivated around Lumbarda. Local olive oil is another product worth seeking out.

On a hilly peninsula jutting into the Adriatic sits Korčula Town, a striking walled town of round defensive towers and red-roofed houses. Resembling a miniature Dubrovnik, the gated, walled Old Town is criss-crossed by narrow stone streets designed to protect its inhabitants from the winds swirling around the peninsula.

Orientation

The big Jadrolinija car ferry drops you off either in the west harbour next to the Hotel Korčula or the east harbour next to Marko Polo Tours. The Old Town lies between the two harbours. The large hotels and main beach lie south of the east harbour, and the residential neighbourhood Sveti Nikola (with a smaller beach) is southwest of the west harbour. The town bus station is 100m south of the Old Town centre.

Information

There are ATMs in the town centre at HVB Splitska Banka and Dubrovačka Banka. You can change money there, at the post office or at any of the travel agencies. The post office is hidden next to the stairway up to the Old Town. The post office also has telephones.

Atlas travel agency (☎ 711 231; Trg Kralja Tomislava) Represents Amex, runs excursions and finds private accommodation. There's another office nearby.

Eterna (☎ 716 538; eterno.doo@du.t-com.hr; Put Sv. Nikola bb) Finds private accommodation and offers internet access (per hour 25KN).

Hospital (☎ 711 137; Ul 59, Kalac) It's south of the Old Town, about 1km past the Hotel Marko Polo. Emergency services are available 24 hours.

Marko Polo Tours (☎ 715 400; marko-polo-tours@du.t-com.hr; Biline 5) Finds private accommodation and organises excursions.

Tino's Internet (☎ 091 50 91 182; ul Tri Sulara; per hr 30KN) Tino's other outlet is at the ACI Marina; both are open long hours.

Tourist office (☎ 715 701; tzg-korcule@du.t-com.hr; Obala Franje Tudjmana bb; 🕑 8am-3pm & 5-9pm Mon-Sat, 8am-3pm Sun Jun-Sep, 8am-1pm & 5-9pm Mon-Sat Oct-May) An excellent source of information, located on the west harbour.

Sights

Other than following the circuit of the former city walls or walking along the shore, sightseeing in Korčula centres on Trg Sv Marka. The Gothic **St Mark's Cathedral** (Katedrala Svetog Marka; 🕑 10am-noon & 5-7pm Jul & Aug, Mass only rest of year) features two paintings by Tintoretto (*Three Saints* on the altar and *Annunciation* to one side).

The **Town Museum** (Gradski Muzej; ☎ 711 420; Trg Sv Marka Statuta; admission 10KN; 🕑 10am-1pm Nov-Mar, 10am-2pm Apr & May, 10am-2pm & 7-9pm Jun & Oct, 10am-9pm Jul & Aug) in the 15th-century Gabriellis Palace opposite the cathedral has exhibits of Greek pottery, Roman ceramics and home furnishings, all with English captions. The **treasury** (☎ 711 049; Trg Sv Marka; admission 15KN; 9am-2pm & 5-8pm May-Oct), in the 14th-century Abbey Palace next to the cathedral is also worth a look. It's said that Marco Polo was born in Korčula in 1254; you can visit what is believed to have been his **house** (Depolo; admission 10KN; 10am-1pm & 5-7pm Mon-Sat Jul & Aug) and climb the tower.

There's also an **Icon Museum** (Trg Svih Svetih; admission 7.50KN; 9am-2pm & 5-8pm May-Oct) in the Old Town. It isn't much of a museum, but visitors are let into the beautiful old **All Saints Church**.

In the high summer season, water taxis at the east harbour collect passengers to visit various points on the island, as well as to **Badija Island**, which features an historic 15th-century Franciscan Monastery in the process of reconstruction, plus **Orebić** and the nearby village of **Lumbarda**, which both have sandy beaches.

Tours

Both Atlas travel agency and Marko Polo Tours offer a variety of boat tours and island excursions.

Sleeping & Eating

The big hotels in Korčula are overpriced, but there are a wealth of guest houses that offer clean, attractive rooms and friendly service. Atlas and Marko Polo Tours arrange private rooms, charging from 200KN to 220KN for a room with a bathroom, and starting at about 400KN for an apartment. Or you could try one of the following options.

Autocamp Kalac (☎ 711 182; fax 711 146; per person/site €5.40/8.20) This attractive camping ground is behind Hotel Bon Repos, about 4km from the west harbour, in a dense pine grove near the beach.

Pansion Marinka (☎ 712 007, 098 344 712; marinka.milina-bire@du.t-com.hr; d 150-230KN) This is a working farm and winery situated in Lumbarda, in a beautiful setting within walking distance of the beach. The owners turn out excellent wines and liqueurs, catch and smoke their own fish and are happy to explain the processes to their guests.

Villa DePolo (☎/fax 711 621; tereza.depolo@du.t-com.hr; d 240/290KN;) In the residential neighbourhood close to the Old Town and 100m west of the bus station, this guest house has four modern, clean rooms, some with sea views. Note that there is a 30% extra charge for one-night stays.

Fresh (☎ 091 799.2086; www.igotfresh.com; 1 Kod Kina Liburne; snacks from 20KN) Right across from the bus station, Fresh is fab for breakfast smoothies, lunch wraps or beers and cocktails in the evening.

Planjak (☎ 711 015; Plokata 19 Travnja; mains from 50KN) Meat lovers should head here for the mixed grill and proper Balkan dishes, served on a covered terrace.

Konoba Marinero (☎ 711 170; Marka Andrijića; mains from 50KN) Right in the heart of the medieval Old Town, the family-run and marine-themed Marinero has the sons catch the fish and the parents prepare it according to a variety of traditional recipes.

Konoba Maslina (☎ 711 720; Lumbarajska cesta bb; mains from 50KN) It's well worth the walk out here for the authentic Korčulan home-cooking. The multibean soup is a standout. It's about a kilometre past the Hotel Marko Polo on the road to Lumbarda, but you can often arrange to be picked up or dropped off in town.

Entertainment

Between June and October there's **moreška sword dancing** (tickets 100KN; show 9pm Thu) by the Old Town gate; performances are more frequent during July and August. The clash of swords and the graceful movements of the dancers/fighters make an exciting show. Atlas, the tourist office and Marko Polo Tours sell tickets.

Getting There & Away

Transport connections to Korčula are good. There's one bus every day to Dubrovnik (87KN, three hours), one to Zagreb (195KN, 12 hours), and one a week to Sarajevo (165KN, eight hours).

There's a **Jadrolinija office** (☎ 715 410) about 25m up from the west harbour.

There's a regular afternoon car ferry between Split and Vela Luka (35KN, three hours), on the island's western end, that stops at Hvar most days. Six daily buses link Korčula town to Vela Luka (28KN, one hour), but services from Vela Luka are reduced at the weekend.

The daily fast boat running from Split to Hvar and Korčula is great for locals working in Split but not so great for tourists who find themselves leaving Korčula at 6am. Nevertheless, you can go quickly from Korčula to Hvar (33KN, 1½ hours) and to Split (55KN, 2¾ hours). Get tickets at Marko Polo.

WORTH THE TRIP: OREBIĆ

Orebić, on the southern coast of the Pelješac Peninsula between Korčula and Ploče, offers better beaches than those found at Korčula, 2.5km across the water. The easy access by ferry from Korčula makes it the perfect place to go for the day. The best beach in Orebić is Trstenica cove, a 15-minute walk east along the shore from the port.

In Orebić the ferry terminal and the bus station are adjacent to each other. Korčula buses to Dubrovnik, Zagreb and Sarajevo stop at Orebić.

From Orebić, look for the passenger launch (15KN, 15 minutes, at least five times daily on weekdays), which will drop you off near Hotel Korčula. There's also a car ferry to Dominče (10KN, 15 minutes), which stops near the Hotel Bon Repos, where you can pick up the bus from Lumbarda (10KN) a few times a day or a water taxi to Korčula town.

Next to Marko Polo, **Rent a Đir** (☎ 711 908; www.korcula-rent.com) hires autos, scooters and small boats.

CROATIA

MLJET ISLAND

☎ 020 / pop 1110

Of all the Adriatic islands, Mljet (Meleda in Italian) may be the most seductive. Over 72% of the island is covered by forests and the rest is dotted by fields, vineyards and villages. Created in 1960, Mljet National Park occupies the western third of the island and surrounds two saltwater lakes, Malo Jezero and Veliko Jezero. Most people visit the island on excursions from Korčula or Dubrovnik, but it is now possible to take a passenger boat from Dubrovnik or come on the regular ferry from Dubrovnik and stay a few days for hiking, cycling and boating.

Orientation & Information

The island is 37km long, and has an average width of about 3km. The main points of entry are Pomena and Polače, two tiny towns about 5km apart. Tour boats from Korčula and the Dubrovnik catamarans arrive at Polače wharf in the high season. Pomena is the site of the island's only conventional hotel, Hotel Odisej. There's a good map of the island posted at the wharf. Jadrolinija ferries stop only at Sobra but catamarans from Dubrovnik and Korčula stop at Polače.

Goveđari, the national park's entry point, is just between Pomena and Polače. The **national park** (adult/concession 90/30KN) measures 54 sq km and the entry price includes a bus and boat transfer to the Benedictine monastery. If you stay overnight on the island you only pay the park admission once.

The **tourist office** (☎ 744 186; www.mljet.hr; 🕑 8am-8pm Mon-Sat, 8am-1pm Sun Jun-Sep, 8am-1pm & 5-8pm Mon-Fri Oct-May) is in Polače and there is an ATM next door. There's another ATM at the Hotel Odisej in Pomena.

The administrative centre of the island is at Babino Polje, 18km east of Polače, where there is another **tourist office** (☎ /fax 745 125; www.mljet.hr; 🕑 9am-5pm Mon-Fri) and a post office.

Sights & Activities

From Pomena it's a 15-minute walk to a jetty on **Veliko Jezero**, the larger of the two lakes. Here you can board a boat to a small lake islet and have lunch at a 12th-century **Benedictine monastery**, which now houses a restaurant.

You can catch an early boat back to the main island and spend a couple of hours walking along the lakeshore before taking the late-afternoon excursion boat back to Korčula or Dubrovnik. There's a small landing on the main island opposite the monastery where the boat operator drops off passengers upon request. It's not possible to walk right around Veliko Jezero because there's no bridge over the channel that connects the lakes to the sea.

Mljet is good for cycling; several restaurants along the dock in Polače and the Odisej Hotel in Pomena hire bicycles (10/100KN per hour/day). If you plan to cycle between Pomena and Polače be aware that the two towns are separated by a steep mountain. The bike path along Veliko Jezero is an easier pedal but it doesn't link the two towns.

The island offers some unusual opportunities for **diving**. There's a Roman wreck dating from the 3rd century in relatively shallow water. The remains of the ship, including amphorae, have calcified over the centuries and this has protected them from pillaging. There's also a German torpedo boat from WWII and several walls to dive. Contact **Kronmar diving** (☎ 744 022; Hotel Odisej).

Sleeping & Eating

The Polače tourist office arranges private accommodation at 200KN per double room in summer but it is essential to make arrangements before arrival in peak season. There are more *sobe* signs around Pomena than Polače, but practically none at all in Sobra.

Stermasi (☎ 098 939 0362; Saplunara; per apt €30-45;) An excellent choice for those wanting to self-cater and get away from it all – seven well-equipped, bright apartments sleep two to four people. Saplunara is pretty isolated, though, on the eastern side of the island, but you are near the only sandy beaches on Mljet. There's a good restaurant here too.

Soline 6 (☎ 744 024; www.soline6.com; Soline; d €45-75) This is the only accommodation within the national park and is designed with waterless toilets, solar heating and organic waste composting. You'll have to do without electricity though.

Odisej (☎ 744 022; Pomena; s/d from €62/88;) Rooms are pleasant enough here, plus you are right on the port and can hire bicycles, snorkelling equipment etc.

Melita (☎ 744 145; www.mljet-restoranmelita.com; St Mary's Island, Veliko Jezero; mains from 60KN) A more romantic (and touristy) spot can't be found on the island – this is the restaurant attached to the church on the little island in the middle of the big lake.

Getting There & Away

Jadrolinija ferries stop only at Sobra (32KN, two hours) but the **Melita catamaran** (☎ 313 119; www.gv-line.hr; Vukovarska 34) goes to Polače (70KN) after Sobra (50KN) in the summer months, leaving Dubrovnik at 9.45am daily and returning from Polače at 4.55pm, making it ideal for a day trip from Dubrovnik. From Sobra, you can get to Pomena on a bus (1½ hours) and from Polače you can either cycle or walk there.

Tickets are sold in the **tourist office** (Map p164; ☎ 417 983; Obala Stjepana Radića 27) in Gruž or on board, but it's wise to buy in advance as the boat fills up quickly.

DUBROVNIK

☎ 020 / pop 43,800

No matter whether you are visiting Dubrovnik for the first time or if you're returning again and again to this marvellous city, the sense of awe and beauty when you set eyes on the Stradun never fades. It's hard to imagine anyone, even the city's inhabitants, becoming jaded by its marble streets and baroque buildings, or failing to be inspired by a walk along the ancient city walls that once protected a civilised, sophisticated republic for five centuries and that now look out onto the endless shimmer of the peaceful Adriatic.

History

Founded 1300 years ago by refugees from Epidaurus in Greece, medieval Dubrovnik (Ragusa until 1918) shook off Venetian control in the 14th century, becoming an independent republic and one of Venice's more important maritime rivals, trading with Egypt, Syria, Sicily, Spain, France and later Turkey. The double blow of an earthquake in 1667 and the opening of new trade routes to the east sent Ragusa into a slow decline, ending with Napoleon's conquest of the town in 1806.

The deliberate shelling of Dubrovnik by the Yugoslav army in 1991 sent shockwaves through the international community but, when the smoke cleared in 1992, traumatised residents cleared the rubble and set about repairing the damage. Reconstruction has been extraordinarily skilful.

After a steep postwar decline in tourism, Dubrovnik has become a major tourist destination once again.

Orientation

The Jadrolinija ferry terminal and the bus station are next to each other at Gruž, several kilometres northwest of the Old Town, which is closed to cars. The main street in the Old Town is Placa (better known as Stradun). Most accommodation is on the leafy Lapad Peninsula, west of the bus station.

Information

You can change money at any travel agency or post office. There are numerous ATMs in town, near the bus station and near the ferry terminal.

Algoritam (Map p166; Placa) Bookshop with a good selection of English-language books, including guidebooks.

Atlas Travel Agency Obala Papa Ivana Pavla II (Map p164; ☎ 418 001; Obala Papa Ivana Pavla II 1); Sv Đurđa (Map p164; ☎ 442 574; Sv Đurđa 1) In convenient locations, this agency is extremely helpful for general information, as well as finding private accommodation. All excursions are run by Atlas.

Garderoba (Map p164; 5.30am-9pm) Left luggage; at the bus station.

Hospital (Map p164; ☎ 431 777; Dr Roka Mišetića bb) Emergency services are available 24 hours.

Lapad post office (Map p164; Šetalište Kralja Zvonimira 21)

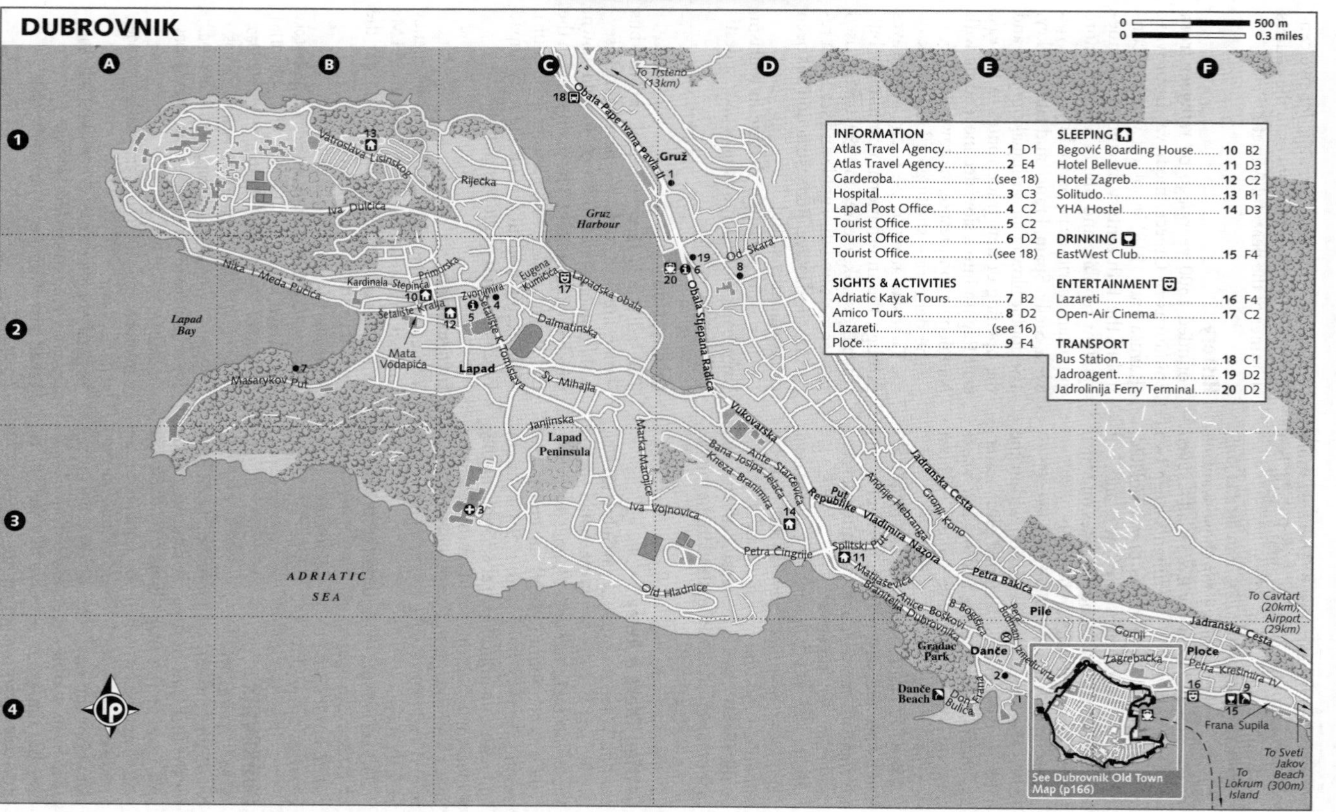

DUBROVNIK
0 500 m
0 0.3 miles
INFORMATION
Atlas Travel Agency 1 D1
Atlas Travel Agency 2 E4
Garderoba (see 18)
Hospital 3 C3
Lapad Post Office 4 C2
Tourist Office 5 C2
Tourist Office 6 D2
Tourist Office (see 18)
SIGHTS & ACTIVITIES
Adriatic Kayak Tours 7 B2
Amico Tours 8 D2
Lazareti (see 16)
Ploče 9 F4
SLEEPING
Begović Boarding House 10 B2
Hotel Bellevue 11 D3
Hotel Zagreb 12 C2
Solitudo 13 B1
YHA Hostel 14 D3
DRINKING
EastWest Club 15 F4
ENTERTAINMENT
Lazareti 16 F4
Open-Air Cinema 17 C2
TRANSPORT
Bus Station 18 C1
Jadroagent 19 D2
Jadrolinija Ferry Terminal 20 D2
To Trsteno (13km)
Gruž
Gruz Harbour
Obala Pape Ivana Pavla II
Obala Stjepana Radića
Od Skara
Vukovarska
Jadranska Cesta
Andrije Hebranga
Gronji Kono
Put Republike
Vladimira Nazora
Petra Bakića
Pile
Ploče
Danče
Gradac Park
Danče Beach
Don Bulića
Lapad
Lapad Peninsula
Lapad Bay
ADRIATIC SEA
Masarykov Put
Nika i Meda Pucića
Iva Dulčića
Riječka
Vatroslava Lisinskog
Primorska
Kardinala Stepinca
Šetalište Kralja Zvonimira
Šetalište K Tomislava
Eugena Kumičića
Lapadska obala
Mata Vodopića
Sv Mihajla
Dalmatinska
Janjinska
Marka Marojice
Iva Vojnovića
Petra Čingrije
Splitski Put
Kneza Branimira
Bana Josipa Jelačića
Ante Starčevića
Matijaševića
Anice Boškovi
Branitelja Dubrovnika
B Bogišića
Pera Budmani
Između vrta
Old Hladnice
Gornji
Zagrebačka
Frana Supila
Petra Krešimira IV
To Cavtart (20km); Airport (29km)
To Sveti Jakov Beach (300m)
To Lokrum Island
See Dubrovnik Old Town Map (p166)

Main post office (Map p166; cnr Široka & Od Puča)

Netcafé (Map p166; ☎ 321 125; www.netcafe.hr; Prijeko 21; per hr 30KN; 9am-11pm) A wonderfully friendly cafe with a fast connection and good services.

Tourist office (www.tzdubrovnik.hr) Bus Station (Map p164; ☎ 417 581; Obala Pape Ivana Pavla II 24; 8am-8pm Jun-Sep, 8am-3pm Mon-Fri, 9am-2pm Sat, closed Sun Oct-May); Gruž Harbour (Map p164; ☎ 417 983; Obala Stjepana Radića 27; 8am-8pm daily Jun-Sep, 8am-3pm Mon-Fri, 9am-2pm Sat, closed Sun Oct-May); Lapad (Map p164; ☎ 437 460; Šetalište Kralja Zvonimira 25; 8am-8pm daily Jun-Sep, 8am-3pm Mon-Fri, 9am-2pm Sat, closed Sun Oct-May); Old Town (Map p166; ☎ 323 587; Široka 1; 8am-8pm daily Jun-Sep, 8am-3pm Mon-Fri, 9am-2pm Sat, closed Sun Oct-May); Pile Gate (Map p164; ☎ 427 591; Dubrovačkih Branitelja 7; 8am-8pm daily Jun-Sep, 8am-3pm Mon-Fri, 9am-2pm Sat, closed Sun Oct-May) Maps, information and the indispensable *Dubrovnik Riviera* guide.

Sights

OLD TOWN

You will probably begin your visit of Dubrovnik's World Heritage–listed Old Town at the city bus stop outside **Pile Gate** (Map p166). As you enter the city, Dubrovnik's wonderful pedestrian promenade, Placa, extends before you all the way to the **clock tower** (Map p166) at the other end of town.

Just inside Pile Gate is the huge 1438 **Onofrio Fountain** (Map p166) and **Franciscan Monastery** (Muzej Franjevačkog Samostana; Map p166; ☎ 321 410; Placa 2; adult/concession 20/10KN; 9am-6pm) with a splendid cloister and the third-oldest functioning **pharmacy** (Map p166; 9am-5pm) in Europe; it's been operating since 1391. The **church** (Map p166; 7am-7pm) has recently undergone a long and expensive restoration to startling effect. The **monastery museum** (Map p166; adult/concession 20/10KN, 9am-5pm) has a collection of liturgical objects, paintings and pharmacy equipment.

In front of the clock tower at the eastern end of Placa (on the square called Luža) is the 1419 **Orlando Column** (Map p166) – a favourite meeting place. On opposite sides of the column are the 16th-century **Sponza Palace** (Map p166) – originally a customs house, later a bank, and which now houses the **State Archives** (Državni Arhiv u Dubrovniku; ☎ 321 032; admission 15KN; 8am-3pm Mon-Fri, 8am-1pm Sat) – and **St Blaise's Church** (Map p166), a lovely Italian baroque building built in 1715 to replace an earlier church destroyed in the 1667 earthquake. At the end of Pred Dvorom, the wide street beside St Blaise, is the baroque **Cathedral of the Assumption of the Virgin** (Map p166). Located between the two churches, the 1441 Gothic **Rector's Palace** (Map p166; ☎ 321 437; Pred Dvorom 3; adult/student 35/15KN, audio guide 30KN; 9am-6pm) houses a museum with furnished rooms, baroque paintings and historical exhibits. The elected rector was not permitted to leave the building during his one-month term without the permission of the senate. The narrow street opposite opens onto Gundulićeva Poljana, a bustling **morning market** (Map p166). Up the stairs south of the square is the 1725 **Jesuit Monastery** (Map p166; Poljana Ruđera Boškovića).

As you proceed up Placa, make a detour to the **Museum of the Orthodox Church** (Muzej Pravoslavne Crkve; Map p166; ☎ 323 283; Od Puča 8; adult/concession 10/5KN; 9am-2pm Mon-Sat) for a look at a fascinating collection of 15th- to 19th-century icons.

By now you'll be ready for a leisurely walk around the **city walls** (Gradske Zidine; Map p166; adult/child 50/20KN; 9am-7.30pm Apr-Oct, 10am-3.30pm Nov-Mar), which has entrances just inside Pile Gate, across from the Dominican monastery and near Fort St John. Built between the 13th and 16th centuries, these powerful walls are the finest in the world and Dubrovnik's main claim to fame. They enclose the entire city in a protective veil over 2km long and up to 25m high, with two round and 14 square towers, two corner fortifications and a large fortress. The views over the town and sea are great – this walk could be the high point of your visit.

Whichever way you go, you'll notice the 14th-century **Dominican Monastery** (Muzej Dominikanskog Samostana; Map p166; ☎ 322 200; off Svetog Dominika 4; adult/child 20/10KN; 9am-5pm) in the northeastern corner of the city, whose forbidding fortress-like exterior shelters a rich trove of paintings from Dubrovnik's finest 15th- and 16th-century artists.

Dubrovnik has many other sights, such as the unmarked **synagogue** (Sinagoga; Map p166; ☎ 321 028; Žudioska 5; admission 10KN; 9am-3pm Mon-Fri Oct-May, 10am-8pm daily Jun-Sep) near the clock tower, which is the second-oldest synagogue in Europe. The uppermost streets of the Old Town below the north and south walls are pleasant to wander along.

One of the better photography galleries you're likely to come across, **War Photo Limited** (Map p166; ☎ 326 166; www.warphotoltd.com; Antuninska 6;

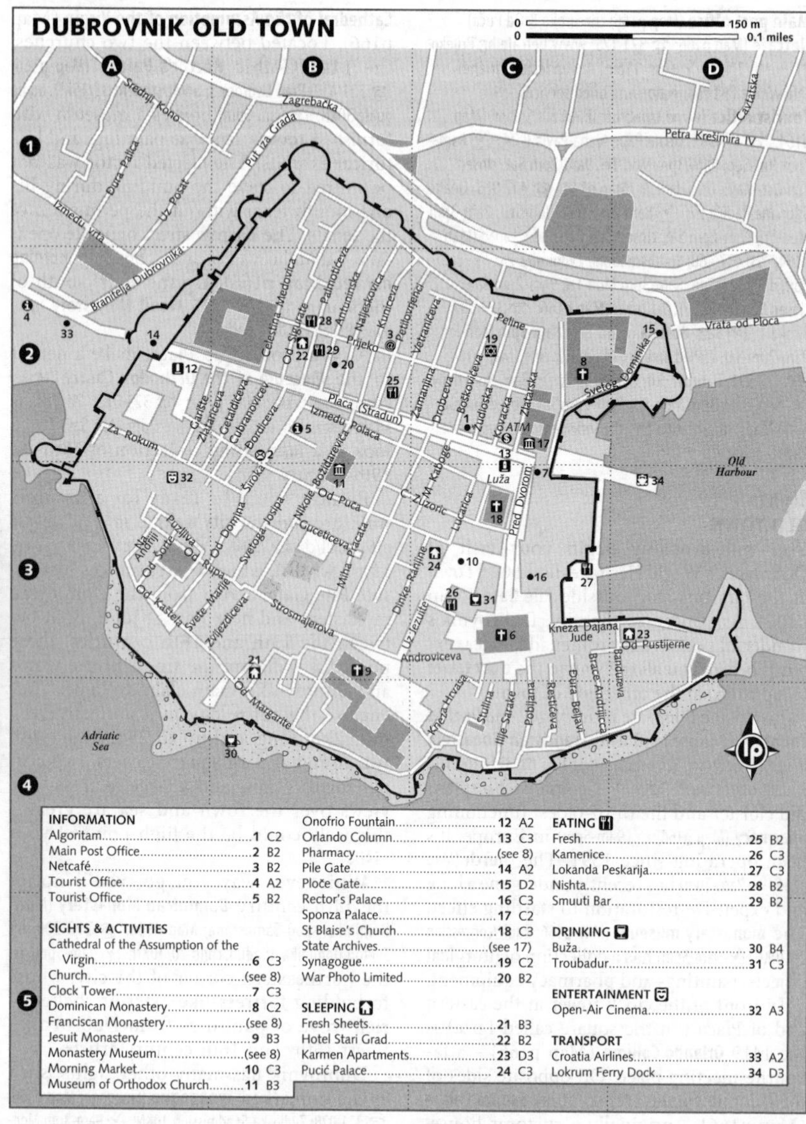

admission 30KN; ⏰ 9am-9pm daily May-Sep, 10am-4pm Tue-Sat, 10am-2pm Sun Oct & Apr, closed Nov-Apr) has changing exhibitions that are curated by the gallery owner and former photojournalist Wade Goddard. It's open summer only, and has up to three exhibitions over that period, relating to the subject of war and seen from various perspectives.

BEACHES

Ploče (Map p164), the closest beach to the Old Town, is just beyond the 17th-century **Lazareti** (Map p164; a former quarantine station) outside **Ploče Gate** (Map p166). Another nearby, good, local beach is **Sveti Jakov**, a 20-minute walk down Vlaho Bukovac or a quick ride on bus 5 or 8 from the northern end of the Old

Town. There are also hotel beaches along the **Lapad Peninsula** (Map p164), which you are able to use without a problem.

An even better option is to take the ferry that shuttles half-hourly in summer to lush **Lokrum Island** (return 40KN), a national park with a rocky nudist beach (marked FKK), a botanical garden and the ruins of a medieval Benedictine monastery.

Activities

Adriatic Kayak Tours (Map p164; ☎ 312 770; www.kayakcroatia.com; Frankopanska 6) offers a great series of kayak tours for experienced and beginner kayakers.

Tours

Amico Tours (Map p164; ☎ 418 248; www.amico-tours.com; Od Skara 1) offers day trips to Mostar and Međugorje (390KN), Montenegro (390KN), Albania (990KN), Korčula and Pelješac (390KN), and the Elafiti Islands (250KN), as well as numerous kayaking, rafting and jeep safari day trips (590KN).

Festivals & Events

Feast of St Blaise 3 February
Carnival February
Dubrovnik Summer Festival Mid-July to mid-August. A major cultural event, with over 100 performances at different venues in the Old Town.

Sleeping

Private accommodation is generally the best option in Dubrovnik, but beware of the scramble of private owners at the bus station or Jadrolinija wharf. Some offer what they say they offer, others are rip-off artists. Expect to pay about €28 to €50 a room in high season.

OLD TOWN

Fresh Sheets (Map p166; ☎ 091 799 2086; beds@igotfresh.com; Sv Šimuna 15; per person €25; 💻) A brand new place, this is a collection of four individually decorated apartments – Lavender, Rainforest, Sunshine, Heaven – each sleeping two to four people (plus a sofa), and one double room. The location is excellent – in the heart of Old Town – you get free internet and wi-fi and, when the Fresh bar's kitchen is open, a free smoothie.

our pick Karmen Apartments (Map p166; ☎ 323 433, 098 619 282; www.karmendu.com; Bandureva 1; apt €55-145; ❄) Set inside an old stone house in the middle of the Old Town, the four apartments are beautifully decorated with original artwork and imaginative use of recycled materials. There are small, one- to two-person apartments, as well as two for three and four people. Book well in advance because it all gets snapped up by June.

Hotel Stari Grad (Map p166; ☎ 322 244; www.hotelstarigrad.com; Palmotićeva; s 650-1180KN, d 920KN-1580KN; ❄) Staying in the heart of the Old Town in a lovingly restored stone building is an unmatchable experience. The eight rooms are elegantly and tastefully furnished to feel simple and luxurious at the same time.

Pucić Palace (Map p166; ☎ 326 222; www.thepucicpalace.com; Od Puča 1; s €206-315, d €290-505; ❄) Right in the heart of the Old Town and inside what was once a nobleman's mansion, this five-star hotel is Dubrovnik's most exclusive and hottest property. There are only 19 rooms, all exquisitely decorated and featuring Italian mosaics, Egyptian-cotton linen and baroque beds.

OUTSIDE THE OLD TOWN

Solitudo (Map p164; ☎ 448 200; Vatroslava Lisinskog 17; per person/site €5.40/10.20) This pretty and renovated camping ground is within walking distance of the beach.

YHA Hostel (Map p164; ☎ 423 241; dubrovnik@hfhs.hr; Vinka Sagrestana 3; B&B per person 85-120KN) Basic in decor, the YHA Hostel is clean and, as travellers report, a lot of fun. The best dorms are rooms 31 and 32, for their 'secret' roof terrace.

Begović Boarding House (Map p164; ☎ 435 191; http://begovic-boarding-house.com; Primorska 17; dm €14-19, s €25-32, d €32-40) A long-time favourite with our readers, this friendly place in Lapad has three rooms with shared bathroom and three apartments. There's a terrace out the back with a good view. Breakfast is an additional 30KN.

Hotel Zagreb (Map p164; ☎ 430 930; www.hotels-sumratin.com; Šetalište Kralja Zvonimira 27; s 400-660KN, d 700-1060KN; ❄) Under the same ownership as Hotel Sumratin, Hotel Zagreb is a more stylish sister, set inside a lovely, salmon-coloured 19th-century building. The rooms are large, with marine motifs and large bathrooms.

our pick Hotel Bellevue (Map p164; ☎ 330 000; www.hotel-bellevue.hr; Petra Čingrije 7; d from €250; ❄ 💻 🏊) Although not within the borders of the Old Town, but a five-minute walk west from Pile Gate, Hotel Bellevue's location – on a cliff that overlooks the open sea and the lovely bay underneath – is pretty much divine. The rooms are beautifully designed, and the balconies overlook the said sea and bay.

Eating

Weed out tourist traps and choose carefully, and you'll find fabulous food in the Old Town.

Smuuti Bar (Map p166; ☎ 091 896 7509; Palmotićeva 5; smoothies 18-25KN) Perfect for breakfast smoothies and nice big mugs of coffee (at a bargain 10KN).

Fresh (Map p166; ☎ 091 896 7509; www.igotfresh.com; Vetranićeva 4; wraps from 20KN) A mecca for young travellers who gather here for the smoothies, wraps and other healthy snacks, as well as drinks and music in the evening.

Nishta (Map p166; ☎ 091 896 7509; Prijeko 30; mains from 30KN) Head here for a refreshing gazpacho, a heart-warming miso soup, thai curries, vegies and noodles, and many more vegie delights.

Kamenice (Map p166; ☎ 421 499; Gundulićeva Poljana 8; mains from 40KN) It's been here since the 1970s and not much has changed: the socialist-style waiting uniforms, the simple interior, the massive portions of mussels, grilled or fried squid and griddled anchovies, and *kamenice* – oysters – too.

our pick **Lokanda Peskarija** (Map p166; ☎ 324 750; Ribarnica bb; mains from 40KN) Located on the Old Harbour right next to the fish market, this is undoubtedly one of Dubrovnik's best eateries. The quality of the seafood dishes is unfaltering, the prices are good, and the location is gorgeous.

Drinking

our pick **Buža** (Map p166; Ilije Sarake) The Buža is just a simple place on the outside of the city walls, facing out onto the open sea, with simple drinks and blissful punters.

EastWest Club (Map p164; ☎ 412 220; Frana Supila bb) By day this outfit on Banje Beach rents out beach chairs and umbrellas and serves drinks to the bathers. When the rays lengthen, the cocktail bar opens.

Troubadur (Map p166; ☎ 412 154; Bunićeva Poljana 2) A legendary Dubrovnik venue; come here for live jazz concerts in the summer.

Entertainment

Lazareti (Map p164; ☎ 324 633; www.lazareti.du-hr.net; Frana Supila 8) Dubrovnik's best art and music centre, Lazareti hosts cinema nights, club nights, live music, masses of concerts and pretty much all the best things in town.

Open-Air Cinema (Lapad Map p164; Kumičića; Old Town Map p166; Za Rokom) In two locations, it is open nightly in July and August with screenings starting after sundown (9pm or 9.30pm); ask at Sloboda Cinema for the schedule.

Getting There & Away

AIR

Daily flights to/from Zagreb are operated by **Croatia Airlines** (Map p166; ☎ 413 777; Brsalje 9). The fare runs from 400KN one way, higher in peak season; the trip takes about an hour.

There are also nonstop flights to Rome, London and Manchester between April and October.

BOAT

In addition to the **Jadrolinija** (Map p164; ☎ 418 000; Gruž) coastal ferry north to Hvar, Split and Rijeka (Rijeka–Split 12½ hours, Split–Hvar 1¾ hours, Hvar–Korčula 3¾ hours, Korčula–Dubrovnik 3¼ hours), there's a local ferry that leaves from Dubrovnik for Sobra on Mljet Island (50KN, 2½ hours) throughout the year. There are several ferries a day year-round to the outlying islands of Šipanska, Suđurađ, Lopud and Koločep. See also the Central Dalmatia Ferry Routes map (p155).

Jadroagent (Map p164; ☎ 419 009; fax 419 029; Radića 32) handles ticketing for most international boats from Croatia.

For international connections:

Azzurra Lines (www.azzurraline.com) Sails from Bari, Italy to Dubrovnik (€65).

Jadrolinija (www.jadrolinija.hr) Runs car ferries from Bari to Dubrovnik (€51, eight hours, six weekly), which continue on to Rijeka, Stari Grad and Split. Ferries are less frequent during winter months.

BUS

In a busy summer season and at weekends buses out of Dubrovnik can be crowded, so book a ticket well before the scheduled departure time.

Internationally there are daily bus connections from Sarajevo (€18, five hours, daily), Međugorje (€18, three hours, two daily) and Mostar (€15, three hours, two daily) in Bosnia and Hercegovina to Dubrovnik, plus a daily bus from Kotor (Montenegro) to Dubrovnik (120KN, 2½ hours) that starts at Bar and stops at Herceg Novi.

BUSES FROM DUBROVNIK

Destination	Fare (KN)	Duration (hr)	Daily services
Korčula	95	3	1
Orebić	80	2½	1
Rijeka	400	13	2
Split	120	4½	14
Zadar	250	8	7
Zagreb	250	11	7-8

Getting Around

Čilipi international airport is 24km southeast of Dubrovnik. The Croatia Airlines airport buses (25KN, 45 minutes) leave from the main **bus station** (Map p164; ☎ 357 088) 1½ hours before flight times. Buses meet Croatia Airlines flights but not all others. A taxi costs around 200KN.

Dubrovnik's buses run frequently and generally on time. The fare is 10KN if you buy from the driver but only 8KN if you buy a ticket at a kiosk.

CROATIA DIRECTORY

ACCOMMODATION

Budget accommdation in this chapter includes camping grounds, hostels and some guest houses, and costs up to 500KN (€70) for a double. Midrange accommodation costs 500KN to 900KN (€125) a double, while top-end places start at 900KN and can go as high as 4000KN (€550) a double. Unless otherwise stated, all rooms in this chapter include private bathroom.

Accommodation listings in this guide have been arranged in order of price. Many hotels, rooms and camping grounds issue their prices in euros but some places to stay have stuck with the kuna. Although you can usually pay with either currency, we have listed the primary currency the establishment uses in setting its prices.

Along the Croatian coast accommodation is priced according to three seasons, which tend to vary from place to place. Generally October to May are the cheapest months, June and September are mid-priced, but count on paying top price for the peak season, which runs for a six-week period in July and August. Price ranges quoted in this chapter are from the cheapest to the most expensive (ie low to high season) and do not include 'residence tax' (7.50KN per person per night). Note that prices for rooms in Zagreb are pretty much constant all year and that many hotels on the coast close in winter. Some places offer half-board, which is bed and two meals a day, usually breakfast and one other meal.

Most hotels have smoking and nonsmoking rooms.

Camping

Nearly 100 camping grounds are scattered along the Croatian coast. Opening times of camping grounds generally run from mid-April to September, give or take a few weeks. The exact times change from year to year, so it's wise to call in advance if you're arriving at either end of the season.

Nudist camping grounds (marked FKK) are among the best, as their secluded locations ensure peace and quiet. However, bear in mind that freelance camping is officially prohibited. A good site for camping information is www.camping.hr.

Hostels

The **Croatian YHA** (Map pp124-5; ☎ 01-48 47 472; www.hfhs.hr; Dežmanova 9, Zagreb) operates youth hostels in Dubrovnik, Zadar, Zagreb and Pula. Nonmembers pay an additional 10KN daily for a stamp on a welcome card; six stamps entitles you to a membership. Prices in this chapter are for high season during July and August; prices fall the rest of the year. The Croatian YHA can also provide information about private youth hostels in Krk, Zadar, Dubrovnik and Zagreb.

Hotels

Hotels are ranked from one to five stars with most in the two- and three-star range. Features, such as satellite TV, direct-dial phones, high-tech bathrooms, minibars and air-con, are standard in four- and five-star hotels, and one-star hotels have at least a bathroom in the room. Many two- and three-star hotels offer satellite TV but you'll find better decor in the higher categories. In August, some hotels may demand a surcharge for stays of less than four nights, but this is usually waived during the rest of the year, when prices drop steeply. In Zagreb prices are the same all year.

Breakfast is included in the prices quoted for hotels in this chapter, unless stated otherwise.

Private Rooms

Private rooms or apartments are the best accommodation in Croatia. Service is excellent and the rooms are usually extremely well kept. You may very well be greeted by offers of *sobe* as you step off your bus and boat, but rooms are most often arranged by travel agencies or the local tourist office. Booking through an agency will ensure that the place you're staying in is officially registered and has insurance.

It makes little sense to price-shop from agency to agency, since prices are fixed by the local tourist association. Whether you deal with the owner directly or book through an agency, you'll pay a 30% surcharge for stays of less than four nights and sometimes 50% or even 100% more for a one-night stay, although you may be able to get them to waive the surcharge if you arrive in the low season. Prices for private rooms in this chapter are for a four-night stay in peak season.

ACTIVITIES

The clear waters and varied underwater life of the Adriatic have led to a flourishing dive industry along the coast. Cave diving is the real speciality in Croatia; night diving and wreck diving are also offered and there are coral reefs in some places, but they are in rather deep water. Most of the coastal resorts mentioned in this chapter have dive shops. See **Diving Croatia** (www.diving-hrs.hr) for contact information.

If you're interested in hiking, Risnjak National Park at Crni Lug, 12km west of Delnice between Zagreb and Rijeka, is a good area in summer. Hiking is advisable only from late spring to early autumn.

There are countless possibilities for anyone carrying a folding sea kayak, especially among the Elafiti and Kornati Islands. Lopud makes a good launch point from which to explore the Elafiti Islands; there's a daily ferry from Dubrovnik.

BOOKS

Lonely Planet's *Croatia* is a comprehensive guide to the country.

As Croatia emerges from the shadow of the former Yugoslavia, several writers of Croatian origin have taken the opportunity to rediscover their roots. *Plum Brandy: Croatian Journeys* by Josip Novakovich is a sensitive exploration of his family's Croatian background. *Croatia: Travels in Undiscovered Country* by Tony Fabijančić recounts the life of rural folks in a new Croatia.

BUSINESS HOURS

Banking and post office hours are 7.30am to 7pm on weekdays and 8am to noon on Saturday. Many shops are open 8am to 7pm on weekdays and until 2pm on Saturday. Along the coast life is more relaxed; shops and offices frequently close around noon for an afternoon break and reopen around 4pm. Restaurants are open long hours, often noon to midnight, with Sunday closings outside of peak season.

EMBASSIES & CONSULATES

The following addresses are in Zagreb (area code ☎ 01):

Albania (Map pp124-5; ☎ 48 10 679; Jurišićeva 2a)
Australia (off Map pp124-5; ☎ 48 91 200; www.auembassy.hr; Kaptol Centar, Nova Ves 11) North of the centre.
Bosnia & Hercegovina (off Map pp124-5; ☎ 46 83 761; Torbarova 9) Northwest of the centre.
Bulgaria (off Map pp124-5; ☎ 48 23 336; Novi Goljak 25) Northwest of the centre.
Canada (Map pp124-5; ☎ 48 81 200; zagreb@dfait-maeci.gc.ca; Prilaz Đure Deželića 4)
Czech Republic (Map pp124-5; ☎ 61 77 239; Savska 41)
France (Map pp124-5; 48 93 680; consulat@ambafrance.hr; Hebrangova 2)
Germany (off Map pp124-5; ☎ 61 58 105; www.deutschebotschaft-zag reb.hr in German; ul grada Vukovara 64) South of the centre.
Hungary (off Map pp124-5; ☎ 48 22 051; Pantovčak 128/I) Northwest of the centre.
Ireland (Map pp124-5; ☎ 66 74 455; Turinina 3)
Netherlands (off Map pp124-5;Map pp124-5; ☎ 46 84 880; nlgovzag@zg.t-com.hr; Medveščak 56)
New Zealand (off Map pp124-5; ☎ 61 51 382; Trg Stjepana Radića 3) Southwest of the centre.
Poland (Map pp124-5; ☎ 48 99 444; Krležin Gvozd 3)
Romania (off Map pp124-5; ☎ 45 77 550; roamb@zg.t-com.hr; Mlinarska ul 43) North of the centre.
Serbia (off Map pp124-5; ☎ 45 79 067; Pantovčak 245) Northwest of the centre.
Slovakia (Map pp124-5; ☎ 48 48 941; Prilaz Đure Deželića 10)
Slovenia (Map pp124-5; ☎ 63 11 000; Savska 41)
UK (off Map pp124-5; ☎ 60 09 100; I Lučića 4)
USA (off Map pp124-5; ☎ 66 12 200; www.usembassy.hr; Ul Thomasa Jeffersona 2) South of the centre.

FESTIVALS & EVENTS

In July and August there are summer festivals in Dubrovnik, Split, Pula and Zagreb.

Dubrovnik's summer music festival emphasises classical music, with concerts in churches around town, while Pula hosts a variety of pop and classical stars in the Roman amphitheatre and also hosts a film festival. Mardi Gras celebrations have recently been revived in many towns with attendant parades and festivities, but nowhere is it celebrated with more verve than in Rijeka.

GAY & LESBIAN TRAVELLERS

Homosexuality has been legal in Croatia since 1977 and is tolerated, but public displays of affection between members of the same sex may be met with hostility, especially outside major cities. Exclusively gay clubs are a rarity outside Zagreb, but many of the large discos attract a mixed crowd.

On the coast, gays gravitate to Rovinj, Hvar, Split and Dubrovnik and tend to frequent naturist beaches. In Zagreb, the last Saturday in June is Gay Pride Zagreb day, an excellent opportunity to connect with the local gay scene.

Most Croatian websites devoted to the gay scene are in Croatian only, but a good starting point is the English-language www.touristinfo.gay.hr which has articles on the gay scene and links to other relevant websites.

HOLIDAYS

New Year's Day 1 January
Epiphany 6 January
Easter Monday March/April
Labour Day 1 May
Corpus Christi 10 June
Day of Antifascist Resistance 22 June; marks the outbreak of resistance in 1941
Statehood Day 25 June
Victory Day and National Thanksgiving Day 5 August
Feast of the Assumption 15 August
Independence Day 8 October
All Saints' Day 1 November
Christmas 25 and 26 December

INTERNET RESOURCES

Croatia Homepage (www.hr.hr) Hundreds of links to everything you want to know about Croatia.
Croatia Traveller (www.croatiatraveller.com) All ferry schedules, flights, forums, accommodation, sightseeing and travel planning.
Dalmatia Travel Guide (www.dalmacija.net) All about Dalmatia, including reservations for private accommodation.

MONEY

Credit Cards

Amex, MasterCard, Visa and Diners Club cards are widely accepted in large hotels, stores and many restaurants, but don't count on cards to pay for private accommodation or meals in small restaurants. You'll find ATMs accepting MasterCard, Maestro, Cirrus, Plus and Visa in most bus and train stations, airports, all major cities and most small towns. Many branches of Privredna Banka have ATMs that allow cash withdrawals on an Amex card.

Currency

The currency is the kuna. Banknotes are in denominations of 500, 200, 100, 50, 20, 10 and five. Each kuna is divided into 100 lipa in coins of 50, 20 and 10. Many places exchange money, all with similar rates.

Tax

A 22% VAT is imposed upon most purchases and services, and is included in the price. If your purchases exceed 500KN in one shop you can claim a refund upon leaving the country. Ask the merchant for the paperwork, but don't be surprised if they don't have it.

Tipping

If you're served well at a restaurant, you should round up the bill, but a service charge is always included. Bar bills and taxi fares can also be rounded up. Tour guides on day excursions expect to be tipped.

POST

Mail sent to Poste Restante, 10000 Zagreb, Croatia, is held at the **main post office** (Branimirova 4; 24hr Mon-Sat, 1pm-midnight Sun) next to the Zagreb train station. A good coastal address to use is c/o Poste Restante, Main Post Office, 21000 Split, Croatia. If you have an Amex card, most Atlas travel agencies will hold your mail.

TELEPHONE

Mobile Phones

Croatia uses GSM 900/1800. If your mobile is unlocked, SIM cards are widely available.

Phone Codes

To call Croatia from abroad, dial your international access code, ☎ 385 (Croatia's country code), the area code (without the initial zero) and the local number. When calling from one

CROATIA

region to another within Croatia, use the initial zero. Phone numbers with the prefix 060 are sometimes free and other times charged at a premium rate, while numbers that begin with 09 are mobile numbers (and are quite expensive). When in Croatia, dial ☎ 00 to speak to the international operator.

Phonecards

To make a phone call from Croatia, go to the town's main post office. You'll need a phonecard to use public telephones, but calls using a phonecard are about 50% more expensive. Phonecards are sold according to *impulsa* (units), and you can buy cards of 25 (15KN), 50 (30KN), 100 (50KN) and 200 (100KN) units. These can be purchased at any post office and most tobacco shops and newspaper kiosks.

TOURIST INFORMATION

The **Croatian National Tourist Board** (Map pp124-5; ☎ 45 56 455; www.htz.hr; Iblerov Trg 10, Importanne Gallerija, 10000 Zagreb) is a good source of information with an excellent website. There are regional tourist offices that supervise tourist development and municipal tourist offices that have free brochures and good information on local events. Some arrange private accommodation.

TRAVELLERS WITH DISABILITIES

Because of the number of wounded war veterans, more attention is being paid to the needs of disabled travellers. Public toilets at bus stations, train stations, airports and large public venues are usually wheelchair accessible. Large hotels are wheelchair accessible but very little private accommodation is. The bus and train stations in Zagreb, Zadar, Rijeka, Split and Dubrovnik are wheelchair accessible but the local Jadrolinija ferries are not. Note that the steep streets in the Old Towns, such as in Dubrovnik, are restrictive for travellers with walking difficulties and those in wheelchairs. For further information, get in touch with **Savez Organizacija Invalida Hrvatske** (☎ /fax 01-48 29 394; Savska cesta 3, 10000 Zagreb).

VISAS

Visitors from Australia, Canada, New Zealand, the EU and the USA do not require a visa for stays of less than 90 days. For other nationalities, visas are issued free of charge at Croatian consulates.

EMERGENCY NUMBERS

- Ambulance ☎ 94
- Fire ☎ 93
- Police ☎ 92
- Roadside Assistance ☎ 987

TRANSPORT IN CROATIA

GETTING THERE & AWAY

Connections into Croatia are in a constant state of flux, with new air and boat routes opening every season. Following is an overview of the major connections into Croatia.

Air

The major airports in the country are as follows:

Dubrovnik (☎ 020-773 377; www.airport-dubrovnik.hr)
Pula (☎ 052-530 105; www.airport-pula.com)
Rijeka (☎ 051-842 132; www.rijeka-airport.hr)
Split (☎ 021-203 506; www.split-airport.hr)
Zadar (☎ 023-313 311; www.zadar-airport.hr)
Zagreb (☎ 01-62 65 222; www.zagreb-airport.hr)

The following airlines fly to Croatia:

Adria Airways (JD; ☎ 01-48 10 011; www.adria-airways.com)
Aeroflot (SU; ☎ 01-48 72 055; www.aeroflot.ru)
Air Canada (AC; ☎ 01-48 22 033; www.aircanada.ca)
Air France (AF; ☎ 01-48 37 100; www.airfrance.com)
Alitalia (AZ; ☎ 01-48 10 413; www.alitalia.it)
Austrian Airlines (OS; ☎ 062 65 900; www.aua.com)
British Airways (BA; www.british-airways.com)
Croatia Airlines (OU; ☎ 01-48 19 633; www.croatiaairlines.hr; Zrinjevac 17, Zagreb)
ČSA (OK; ☎ 01-48 73 301; www.csa.cz)
Delta Airlines (DL; ☎ 01-48 78 760; www.delta.com)
Easyjet (EZY; www.easyjet.com)
Germanwings (GWI; www.germanwings.com)
Hapag Lloyd Express (HLX; www.hlx.com)
KLM-Northwest (KL; ☎ 01-48 78 601; www.klm.com)
LOT Polish Airlines (LO; ☎ 01 48 37 500; www.lot.com)
Lufthansa (LH; ☎ 01-48 73 121; www.lufthansa.com)
Malév Hungarian Airlines (MA; ☎ 01-48 36 935; www.malev.hu)
SNBrussels (SN; www.flysn.com)
Turkish Airlines (TK; ☎ 01-49 21 854; www.turkishairlines.com)
Wizzair (W6; www.wizzair.com)

CROATIA

Land

BUS

Bosnia & Hercegovina

See p168 for details on transport between Dubrovnik and Sarajevo, Međugorje and Mostar. See p156 for details on connections between Sarajevo and Split (via Mostar); p131 for buses between Sarajevo and Zagreb; and p144 for buses between Sarajevo and Rijeka.

Italy

There are bus connections between Rijeka and Trieste (p144).

Montenegro

The border between Montenegro and Croatia is open to visitors, allowing Americans, Australians, Canadians and Brits to enter visa-free. See p168 for details of the bus between Kotor and Dubrovnik.

Serbia

See p131 for details of the bus between Zagreb and Belgrade.

Slovenia

Slovenia is well connected with the Istrian coast; see p137 for details on connections with Rovinj. There are also connections between Ljubljana and Zagreb (p131), Rijeka (p144) and Split (p156).

CAR & MOTORCYCLE

The main highway entry/exit points between Croatia and Hungary are Goričan (between Nagykanisza and Varaždin), Gola (23km east of Koprivnica), Terezino Polje (opposite Barcs) and Donji Miholjac (7km south of Harkány). There are dozens of crossing points to/from Slovenia, too many to list here. There are 23 border crossings into Bosnia and Hercegovina and 10 into Serbia and Montenegro, including the main Zagreb to Belgrade highway. Major destinations in Bosnia and Hercegovina, such as Sarajevo, Mostar and Međugorje, are accessible from Zagreb, Split and Dubrovnik.

Motorists require vehicle registration papers and the green insurance card to enter Croatia. Bear in mind that if you hire a car in Italy, many insurance companies will not insure you for a trip into Croatia. Border officials know this and may refuse you entry unless permission to drive into Croatia is clearly marked on the insurance documents. Most car-hire companies in Trieste and Venice are familiar with this requirement and will furnish you with the stamp. Otherwise, you must make specific inquiries.

See p174 for road rules and further information.

TRAIN

Bosnia & Hercegovina

See p131 for details on connections between Sarajevo and Zagreb. There's also a daily train to Osijek (113KN, 8½ hours), and a daily service to Ploče (310KN, 10 hours), near Dubrovnik via Mostar, Sarajevo and Banja Luka.

Hungary

There are services from Budapest to Zagreb; see p132.

Italy

Trains run between Venice and Zagreb; see p132.

Serbia

See p131 for details on connections between Belgrade and Zagreb.

Slovenia

See p131 for details on connections between Ljubljana and Zagreb, and p144 for details on trains between Rijeka and Ljubljana.

Sea

Regular boats from several companies connect Croatia with Italy from towns including Poreč (p135), Pula (p140), Rijeka (p143), Zadar (p150), Split (p155), Stari Grad (p160) on Hvar Island, and Dubrovnik (p168).

GETTING AROUND

Air

Croatia Airlines is the one and only carrier for flights within Croatia. The price of flights depends on the season and you get better deals if you book ahead. Seniors and people aged under 26 get discounts.

Bicycle

Cycling is a great way to see the islands, and bikes are fairly easy to hire in most tourist spots. Many tourist offices have helpful maps of cycling routes. However, bike lanes are nearly unknown in Croatia; you'll need to exercise extreme caution on the many narrow two-lane roads.

Boat

Year-round Jadrolinija car ferries operate along the Bari–Rijeka–Dubrovnik coastal route, stopping at Zadar, Split and the islands of Hvar, Korčula and Mljet. Services are less frequent in winter. The most scenic section is Split to Dubrovnik, which all Jadrolinija ferries cover during the day. Ferries are a lot more comfortable than buses, though somewhat more expensive. From Rijeka to Dubrovnik the deck fare is €26/31 in low/high season, with high season running from about the end of June to the end of August; there's a 20% reduction on the return portion of a return ticket. With a through ticket, deck passengers can stop at any port for up to a week, provided they notify the purser beforehand and have their ticket validated. This is much cheaper than buying individual sector tickets but is only good for one stopover. Cabins should be booked a week ahead, but deck space is usually available on all sailings.

Deck passage on Jadrolinija is just that: *poltrone* (reclining seats) are about €6 extra and four-berth cabins (if available) begin at €48.50/58 in low/high season from Rijeka to Dubrovnik. You must buy tickets in advance at an agency or the Jadrolinija office, as they are not sold on board. Cabins can be arranged at the reservation counter aboard the ship, but advance bookings are recommended if you want to be sure of a place. Bringing a car means checking in at least two hours in advance, more in the summer.

Bus

Bus services are excellent and relatively inexpensive. There are often a number of different companies handling each route so prices can vary substantially, but the prices in this book should give you an idea of costs (and unless otherwise noted, all bus prices are for one-way fares). Generally, the cheaper fares are on overnight buses.

It's generally best to call or visit the bus station to get the complete schedule but the following companies are among the largest:

Autotrans (☎ 051-660 360; www.autotrans.hr) Based in Rijeka with connections to Istria, Zagreb, Varaždin and Kvarner.

Brioni Pula (☎ 052-502 997; www.brioni.hr, in Croatian) Based in Pula with connections to Istria, Trieste, Padua, Split and Zagreb.

Contus (☎ 023-315 315; www.contus.hr) Based in Zadar with connections to Split and Zagreb.

> **FLIGHT-FREE TRAVEL**
>
> To learn how to get to Zagreb from London without having to fly, log on to www.seat61.com and search 'Croatia'. You'll get instructions on how to get to Zagreb from the UK capital via bus and rails (it gives you departure times and all!).

At large stations bus tickets must be purchased at the office; book ahead to be sure of a seat. Tickets for buses that arrive from somewhere else are usually purchased from the conductor. Buy a one-way ticket only or you'll be locked into one company's schedule for the return

On schedules, *vozi svaki dan* means 'every day' and *ne vozi nedjeljom ni praznikom* means 'not Sunday and public holidays'. Check www.akz.hr (in Croatian) for information on schedules and fares to and from Zagreb.

Car & Motorcycle

You have to pay tolls on the motorways around Zagreb, to use the Učka tunnel between Rijeka and Istria, the bridge to Krk Island, as well as the road from Rijeka to Delnice and from Zagreb to Split. Tolls can be paid in foreign currencies. The motorway connecting Zagreb and Split has cut travel time to the coast to around four hours. Tolls add up to about 160KN. Over the next few years, look for completion of the final leg running from Split to Dubrovnik. For general news on Croatia's motorways and tolls, see www.hac.hr.

DRIVING LICENCE

Any valid driving licence is sufficient to legally drive and hire a car; an International Driving Permit is not necessary. **Hrvatski Autoklub** (HAK; Croatian Auto Club; www.hak.hr) offers help and advice, plus there's the nationwide **HAK road assistance** (vučna služba; ☎ 987).

FUEL

Petrol stations are generally open 7am to 7pm and often until 10pm in summer. Petrol is Eurosuper 95, Super 98, normal or diesel. See www.ina.hr for up-to-date fuel prices.

HIRE

The large car-hire chains represented in Croatia are Avis, Budget, Europcar and Hertz. Throughout Croatia, Avis is allied with the Autotehna company, while Hertz is often represented by Kompas.

Independent local companies are often much cheaper than the international chains, but Avis, Budget, Europcar and Hertz have the big advantage of offering one-way rentals that allow you to drop the car off at any one of their many stations in Croatia free of charge.

Prices at local companies begin at around €40 a day with unlimited kilometres.

ROAD RULES

Unless otherwise posted, the speed limits for cars and motorcycles are 50km/h in the urban zones, 90km outside urban zones, 110km/h on main highways and 130km/h on motorways. The maximum permitted amount of alcohol in the blood is – none at all! It is also forbidden to use a mobile phone while driving.

Hitching

Hitching is never entirely safe, and we don't recommend it. Hitchhiking in Croatia is unreliable. You'll have better luck on the islands, but in the interior cars are small and usually full.

Local Transport

Zagreb has a well-developed tram system as well as local buses, but in the rest of the country you'll only find buses. In major cities such as Rijeka, Split, Zadar and Dubrovnik buses run about every 20 minutes, and less often on Sunday.

Taxis are available in all cities and towns, but they must be called or boarded at a taxi stand. Prices are rather high (meters start at 25KN).

Train

Train travel is about 15% cheaper than bus travel and often more comfortable, although slower. The main lines run from Zagreb to Rijeka, Zadar and Split and east to Osijek. There are no trains along the coast. Local trains usually have only unreserved 2nd-class seats. Reservations may be required on express trains. 'Executive' trains have only 1st-class seats and are 40% more expensive than local trains.

On posted timetables in Croatia, the word for arrivals is *dolazak* and for departures it's *odlazak* or *polazak*. For train information check out **Croatian Railway** (www.hzn et.hr).

Cyprus Κύπρος

Cyprus is a kaleidoscopic blend: despite its economic and political proximity to Europe, the island's character is stirred (and sometimes shaken) by its physical propinquity to Asia and the Middle East. Cyprus' location has bequeathed it with invaluable archaeological remains and a cuisine that mixes up many influences with originality and gusto. But it's the Mediterranean that is at the core of Cyprus' character. Whether you know it as the 'island of sin' (or 'fun') thanks to wild stories from Agia Napa or, as tourist brochures love to point out, 'the island of Aphrodite', Cyprus confirms and confounds the stereotypes. It's a place that can be both rewarding and repelling, and visitors need to exercise discernment to get the best out of the island.

Avoid overdeveloped, tourist-swamped places such as Kato Pafos, Agia Napa, and the tourist strips of Lemesos, Larnaka and Protaras; concentrate on exploring agrotourism and eco options in the villages on the Akamas and Karpas Peninsulas, while taking advantage of their lovely beaches. Alternatively, head for the peaks of the Troodos – where more wonderful agrotourism accommodation awaits – and Kyrenia (Girne), for medieval churches, castles and hiking. Finally, dive into the urbanity of Lefkosia, where you can see the merging of modern and traditional Cyprus. Most importantly, visit both sides of the island – you'll get a fuller picture of the complex and fractured Cypriot identity.

The last few years have seen a sea change in Cypriot politics. Travellers cross between the Greek south and the Turkish north just by showing their passports at the border. A four-year stalemate on peace and unification talks was revived in 2008, so watch this space.

FAST FACTS

- **Area** 9250 sq km
- **Capital** Republic: Lefkosia; North Cyprus: Lefkoşa.
- **Currency** Republic: euro (€); North Cyprus: Turkish lira (TL); €1 = TL2.08; UK£1 = €1.13/TL2.35; US$1 = €0.73/TL1.53; A$1 = €0.56/TL1.17; ¥100 = €0.76/TL1.59; NZ$1 = €0.44/TL0.91
- **Famous for** beaches, mezes, mosaics
- **Official languages** Republic: Greek; North Cyprus: Turkish
- **Phrases** Republic: *yasas* (hello); North Cyprus: *merhaba* (hello)
- **Population** 792,600
- **Telephone codes** ☎ Republic 357, North Cyprus 90 392
- **Visas** not needed for EU citizens; see p200

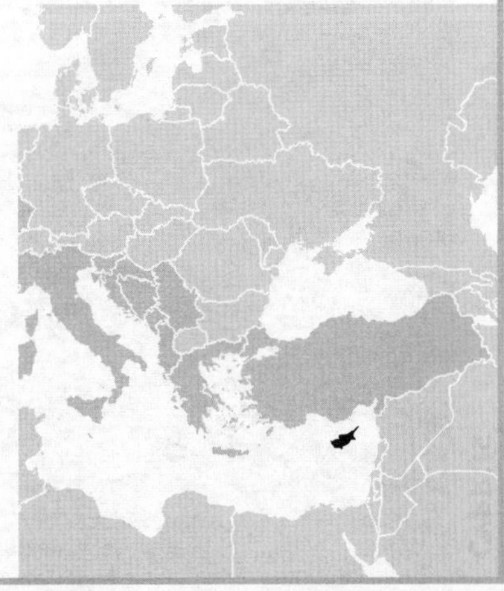

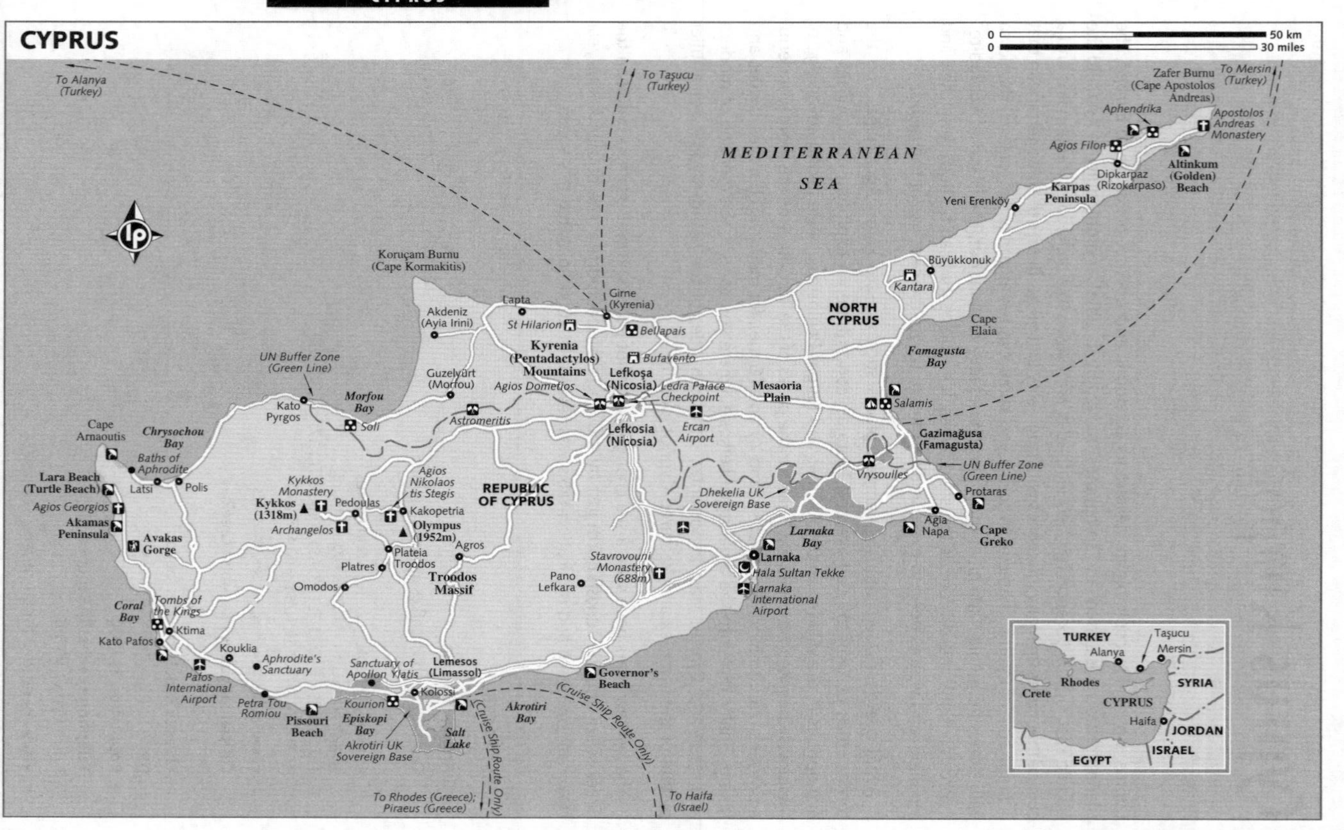
CYPRUS
0 50 km
0 30 miles
To Alanya (Turkey)
To Taşucu (Turkey)
To Mersin (Turkey)
Zafer Burnu (Cape Apostolos Andreas)
Aphendrika
Apostolos Andreas Monastery
Agios Filon
Altinkum (Golden) Beach
Dipkarpaz (Rizokarpaso)
Karpas Peninsula
Yeni Erenköy
MEDITERRANEAN SEA
Büyükkonuk
Kantara
NORTH CYPRUS
Cape Elaia
Famagusta Bay
Salamis
Gazimağusa (Famagusta)
UN Buffer Zone (Green Line)
Vrysoulles
Protaras
Agia Napa
Cape Greko
Koruçam Burnu (Cape Kormakitis)
Lapta
Girne (Kyrenia)
Akdeniz (Ayia Irini)
St Hilarion
Bellapais
Bufavento
Kyrenia (Pentadactylos) Mountains
Lefkoşa (Nicosia)
Ledra Palace Checkpoint
Mesaoria Plain
Guzelyürt (Morfou)
Agios Dometios
Ercan Airport
Lefkosia (Nicosia)
UN Buffer Zone (Green Line)
Morfou Bay
Kato Pyrgos
Soli
Astromeritis
Cape Arnaoutis
Chrysochou Bay
Baths of Aphrodite
Latsi
Polis
Lara Beach (Turtle Beach)
Agios Georgios
Akamas Peninsula
Avakas Gorge
Kykkos Monastery
Kykkos (1318m)
Archangelos
Pedoulas
Agios Nikolaos tis Stegis
Kakopetria
Olympus (1952m)
REPUBLIC OF CYPRUS
Dhekelia UK Sovereign Base
Larnaka Bay
Larnaka
Hala Sultan Tekke
Larnaka International Airport
Plateia Troodos
Agros
Platres
Troodos Massif
Omodos
Stavrovouni Monastery (688m)
Pano Lefkara
Coral Bay
Tombs of the Kings
Ktima
Kato Pafos
Kouklia
Aphrodite's Sanctuary
Pafos International Airport
Petra Tou Romiou
Pissouri Beach
Sanctuary of Apollon Ylatis
Kourion
Episkopi Bay
Akrotiri UK Sovereign Base
Kolossi
Lemesos (Limassol)
Salt Lake
Akrotiri Bay
Governor's Beach
(Cruise Ship Route Only)
(Cruise Ship Route Only)
To Rhodes (Greece); Piraeus (Greece)
To Haifa (Israel)
TURKEY
Taşucu
Mersin
Alanya
Rhodes
Crete
CYPRUS
SYRIA
Haifa
JORDAN
ISRAEL
EGYPT

HIGHLIGHTS

- Be king of the castle at the Crusader fortresses of **Kolossi** (p189), **Kantara** (p197) and **St Hilarion** (p195).
- Bring history to life at the fabulous Graeco-Roman ruins of **Pafos** (p191), **Kourion** (p189) and **Salamis** (p196).
- Step back to Byzantine times in the **Troodos Massif** (p190), home to stone villages, medieval monasteries and rugged mountain trails.
- Trek the wild trails of the **Akamas Peninsula** (p193), the last untamed wilderness in southern Cyprus.
- Walk along beaches untouched by human footprints in the splendidly isolated **Karpas Peninsula** (p197).

ITINERARIES

- **One week** With just a week in Cyprus, head to the capital to explore north and south Lefkosia. Cross the border for an overnight trip to Girne, then head south to Lemesos and Pafos for the island's best Graeco-Roman ruins, with a stop in the scenic Troodos Massif.
- **Two weeks** With more time, hire a car and explore Frankish ruins in Gazimağusa and drive up to the wild Karpas region. If you're up for some more untamed nature, head to the rugged Akamas Peninsula and Polis. Then visit Larnaka to pay your respects at the grave of Lazaros.

CLIMATE & WHEN TO GO

Cyprus has a typical Mediterranean climate: cool and dry in winter, hot and dry in summer. The peak season is from June to August, but the island really cooks during these months and you can go from pasty white to lobster red in minutes. April to May and September to October offer warm sunny days and pleasantly balmy nights – perfect for walking in the hills. See Climate Charts for more info, p944.

HISTORY

Blessed with natural resources but cursed by a strategic location, Cyprus has been a pawn in the games of empires since ancient times. Greek culture arrived in 1400 BC with the Mycenaeans, but the ancient Greek cities at Pafos, Salamis and Kourion were massively expanded by the Romans, who converted the island to Christianity.

As Roman influence declined, Cyprus was incorporated into the Byzantine Empire, and Orthodox Christianity became the dominant religion. King Richard the Lionheart of England annexed Cyprus on his way to the Third Crusade in 1191, and the island then passed to the castle-building Knights Templar, then to the Catholic Franks, and then to the Venetians, who built huge walls around Lefkosia and Gazimağusa to protect themselves from Arab marauders. This failed to stop the Ottomans from invading in 1570 and dominating Cyprus for the next 300 years.

In 1878 Turkey sold Cyprus to Britain, but the majority Greek Cypriot population demanded *enosis* (independence from foreign rule and union with Greece). In response, the British created a Turkish Cypriot police force to subdue the Greek Cypriots. Such 'divide and rule' politics paved the way for civil war.

Over the next 60 years, ripples of violence spread across the island, spearheaded by the National Organisation of Freedom Fighters (EOKA) and the Turkish Defence Organisation (TMT), which aimed to divide Greek and Turkish Cypriot populations as a stepping stone towards *taksim* – the partition of Cyprus. Britain finally granted independence to Cyprus in August 1960, but the violence continued.

Forces from mainland Greece launched a coup against the government of Archbishop Makarios III on 15 July 1974, killing dozens of Turkish Cypriots. In response, Turkish forces occupied the northern third of the island, driving 180,000 Greek Cypriots from their homes and killing 8000 more. Some 65,000 Turkish Cypriots were displaced in the opposite direction before the island was partitioned into Greek and Turkish states.

Over the following decades, all traces of Greek culture were removed from the north.

CONNECTIONS: MOVING ON FROM CYPRUS

The main place to get to and from Cyprus by boat is Turkey – go between Girne and Taşucu in summer, and Gazimağusa to Mersin overnight (for details, see p201). Lemesos' old harbour is having a facelift costing some hefty millions (see p189), and new ferry and boat routes should be running to and from the Republic by 2011.

The area was flooded with thousands of illegal settlers from mainland Turkey and hundreds of churches, monasteries and archaeological sites were plundered of their treasures. Despite a series of international resolutions, Cyprus remains a divided island. The Turkish Republic of Northern Cyprus, created by Turkish Cypriot leader Rauf Denktash in 1983, is recognised only by Turkey. There have been moves, however, towards reunification.

The Green Line (the ceasefire line that divides Cyprus into two, cutting through the capital) was opened in 2003 to allow refugees from both sides to revisit their homes, and in 2004 the two communities held a referendum on UN proposals for reunification. Unfortunately, the UN plan was heavily skewed in favour of Turkey – it was accepted by 65% of Turkish Cypriots and rejected by 75% of Greek Cypriots.

As a result, the southern Republic of Cyprus entered the EU alone in May 2004. Since then, border restrictions have eased, allowing easy travel between the two sides, but wounds are still fresh. A four-year stalemate on peace and unification talks was revived when the Republic's left-wing president Demetris Christofias (elected in February 2008) met with the Turkish-Cypriot leader Mehmet Ali Talat in September 2008 for new peace talks. It is unclear how long the talks will go on for since no time limit was imposed, but it's clear that they will take at least a good part of a year to bear any fruit, since progress has been repeatedly stalled. The most difficult, pressing and perennial issues for the two leaders to resolve are power-sharing and land ownership.

HOW MUCH?

- **Meze meal from** €8 in the Republic/TL12 in North Cyprus
- **Budget hotel room** €50/UK£35
- **Intercity bus ride** €7/TL6
- **Museum admission** €1 to €3.50/TL7 to TL12
- **2kg bag of oranges** €3/TL5

LONELY PLANET INDEX

- **1L** €1.10 in the Republic; TL1.5 in the North
- **1L** €1.50/TL2
- **Local beer** €2/TL3
- **Souvenir T-shirt** €10/TL20
- **Street snack (kebab)** €4/TL6

PEOPLE

Since partition, the vast majority of Greek Cypriots live in the Republic, but a few hundred Greek Cypriot farmers cling on in the remote Karpas Peninsula (p197). In the north, the Turkish Cypriot population is now heavily outnumbered by Anatolian settlers from the Turkish mainland.

Cypriots on both sides of the line are friendly, honest and law-abiding, if nationalistic. Family life, marriage and children still play a central role in society, as does religion. The population of the Republic has recently become much more diverse with the arrival of large numbers of migrant workers from southeast Asia and the Indian subcontinent.

RELIGION

More than 99% of the North Cyprus population is Sunni Muslim, while the Republic is 94% Greek Orthodox, with small but growing communities of Maronites, Roman Catholics, Hindus and Muslims. You should wear clothing that covers the legs and shoulders when visiting churches and monasteries, and remove your shoes before entering mosques.

ARTS

The definitive art of Cyprus is the production of icons – the paintings of saints that grace Greek Orthodox churches. You can see examples dating back to the Byzantine period in many churches and monasteries. Performing arts have been big in Cyprus since ancient times, and several Roman amphitheatres are still used for performances. Relics of Cyprus' architectural heritage can be seen all over the island, from stone-age settlements to vast Roman cities and Frankish cathedrals.

ENVIRONMENT

Cyprus is divided by two mountain ranges: the Kyrenia (Pentadactylos) Mountains in North Cyprus and the Troodos Massif in the centre of the Republic. The most important nature reserves in the Republic are the Troodos National Forest Park (see p190) and Akamas Peninsula (p193). The north has just one reserve in the Karpas.

GREEN TRAVEL TOP TIPS

- If using batteries, take advantage of Cyprus' many hours of sunshine and get a solar powered battery charger for cameras, iPods or GPS devices to avoid wasting batteries.
- Refill your water bottle whenever possible, instead of buying a new one, to prevent landfills of plastic bottles.
- Save water in Cyprus – water shortages are an ever-present issue on the island.
- Walk or cycle wherever possible. Cyprus has some gorgeous hiking and cycling routes, and its villages, towns and cities are best discovered on foot.
- Stay at agrotourism ventures and local B&Bs – you'll help out the local economy and hopefully make some great local friends.
- Eat local food – thanks to its fantastic climate, Cyprus has some of the freshest, most delicious fruit and vegetables in the Mediterranean. Seek out small, village tavernas where things are made from scratch, and enjoy a homemade meal.
- Don't pick the wildflowers in spring; others may want to enjoy them too.
- Spread your spending money around, and support small businesses and local artists.

On both sides of the divide, the construction of tourist villas is putting a huge strain on natural resources – as long as expats continue to buy holiday homes, the concrete jungle will keep on growing. Tourism is the island's main polluter, but urbanisation and hunting are affecting wildlife populations, including the rare mouflon (wild sheep).

FOOD & DRINK

Cypriot food is a combination of Greek, Turkish and Middle Eastern cuisines, based primarily on meat, vegetables and bread. Popular Cypriot dishes include *souvlakia* (pork kebabs), *seftalia* (pork rissoles), *kleftiko ofto* (lamb baked in a sealed oven), *afelia* (pork stew with wine and coriander), *stifado* (beef and onion stew), *koupepia* (stuffed vine leaves) and *yemista* (vegetables stuffed with rice and mince). These dishes are often served together in a huge meal known as a meze.

The north relies on Anatolian cuisine, with numerous variations on the kebab theme. Vegetarians can rely on meat-free dishes in meze, as well as beans and other pulses, often stewed alone, with olive oil, lemon and herbs. For a quick picnic anywhere in Cyprus, grab some bread, halloumi (firm, salty white cheese), olives, juicy Cypriot tomatoes and some fresh figs or a hefty watermelon.

The wine from the Troodos Massif mountain range is decent – sweet *komandaria* is the traditional wine, while *zivania* (a strong spirit distilled from grape pressings) is the local firewater.

Smoking in restaurants is widespread and only a few have nonsmoking areas.

Most restaurants in Cyprus are open for lunch and dinner daily, but the smaller places are usually closed on Sundays.

THE REPUBLIC OF CYPRUS

Covering the southern 63% of the island, the Republic of Cyprus has the lion's share of the beaches and historical treasures. Development is rampant at the main beach resorts, but head inland and you'll find pretty stone villages that have hardly changed for centuries.

LEFKOSIA (SOUTH NICOSIA) ΛΕΥΚΩΣΙΑ

pop 213,500

Lefkosia is an attractive, enticing city and the country's cultural heart; it's ideal for experiencing what modern Cyprus is all about. The ancient walls, glitzy bars, traditional eateries and a growing multicultural core are a showcase of the city's basic make-up. The country's best museum is here, housing an extensive archaeological collection. The Old City's narrow streets are a labyrinth, hiding churches, mosques, arty bars and beautiful, often dilapidated, colonial houses. The city has been labelled with the beaten cliché of 'the last divided capital', a reality that,

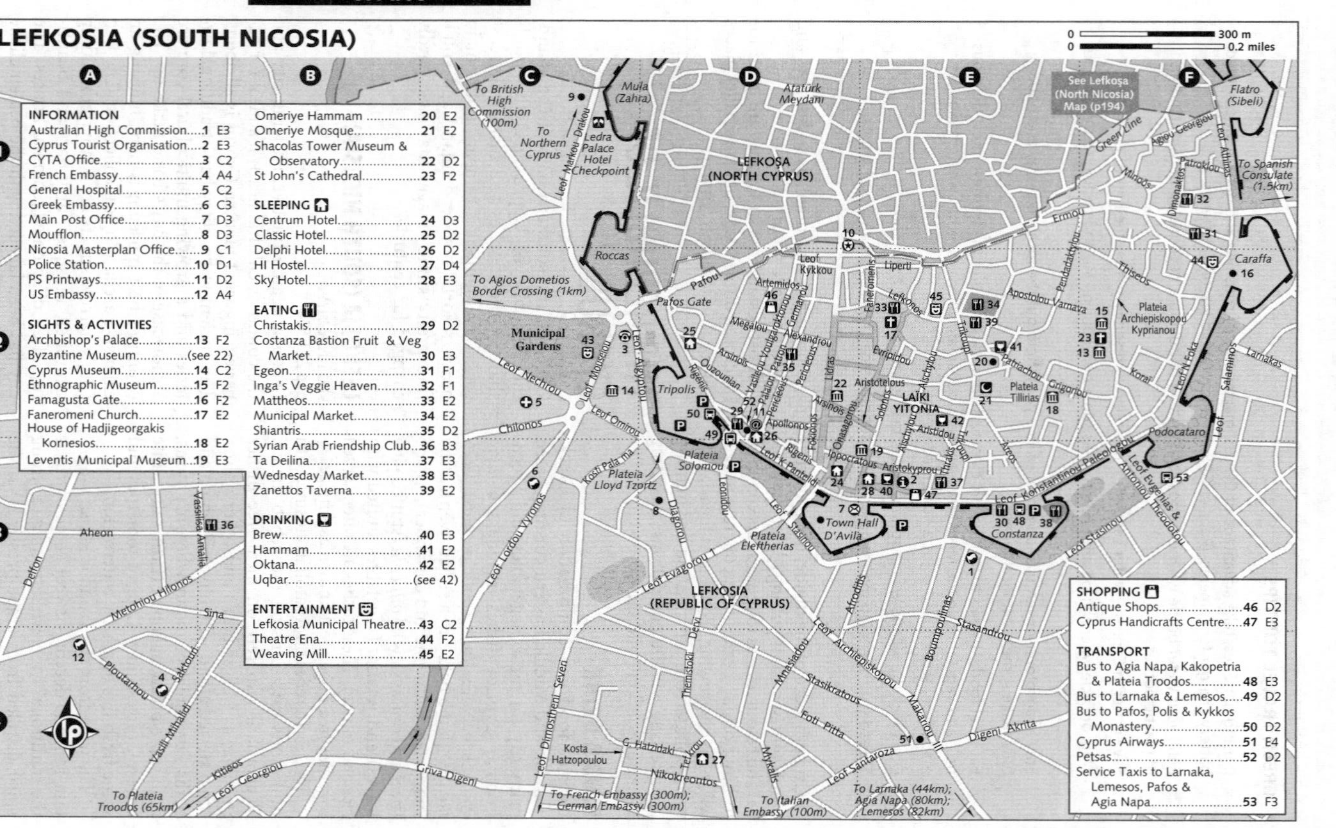
LEFKOSIA (SOUTH NICOSIA)
0 300 m
0 0.2 miles
INFORMATION
Australian High Commission 1 E3
Cyprus Tourist Organisation 2 E3
CYTA Office 3 C2
French Embassy 4 A4
General Hospital 5 C2
Greek Embassy 6 C3
Main Post Office 7 D3
Moufflon 8 D3
Nicosia Masterplan Office 9 C1
Police Station 10 D1
PS Printways 11 D2
US Embassy 12 A4
SIGHTS & ACTIVITIES
Archbishop's Palace 13 F2
Byzantine Museum (see 22)
Cyprus Museum 14 C2
Ethnographic Museum 15 F2
Famagusta Gate 16 F2
Faneromeni Church 17 E2
House of Hadjigeorgakis Kornesios 18 E2
Leventis Municipal Museum 19 E3
Omeriye Hammam 20 E2
Omeriye Mosque 21 E2
Shacolas Tower Museum & Observatory 22 D2
St John's Cathedral 23 F2
SLEEPING
Centrum Hotel 24 D3
Classic Hotel 25 D2
Delphi Hotel 26 D2
HI Hostel 27 D4
Sky Hotel 28 E3
EATING
Christakis 29 D2
Costanza Bastion Fruit & Veg Market 30 E3
Egeon 31 F1
Inga's Veggie Heaven 32 F1
Mattheos 33 E2
Municipal Market 34 E2
Shiantris 35 D2
Syrian Arab Friendship Club 36 B3
Ta Deilina 37 E3
Wednesday Market 38 E3
Zanettos Taverna 39 E2
DRINKING
Brew 40 E3
Hammam 41 E2
Oktana 42 E2
Uqbar (see 42)
ENTERTAINMENT
Lefkosia Municipal Theatre 43 C2
Theatre Ena 44 F2
Weaving Mill 45 E2
SHOPPING
Antique Shops 46 D2
Cyprus Handicrafts Centre 47 E3
TRANSPORT
Bus to Agia Napa, Kakopetria & Plateia Troodos 48 E3
Bus to Larnaka & Lemesos 49 D2
Bus to Pafos, Polis & Kykkos Monastery 50 D2
Cyprus Airways 51 E4
Petsas 52 D2
Service Taxis to Larnaka, Lemesos, Pafos & Agia Napa 53 F3
LEFKOŞA (NORTH CYPRUS)
LEFKOSIA (REPUBLIC OF CYPRUS)
See Lefkoşa (North Nicosia) Map (p194)
LAIKI YITONIA
Municipal Gardens
To British High Commission (100m)
To Northern Cyprus
Ledra Palace Hotel Checkpoint
To Agios Dometios Border Crossing (1km)
To Spanish Consulate (1.5km)
To Plateia Troodos (65km)
To French Embassy (300m); German Embassy (300m)
To Italian Embassy (100m)
To Larnaka (44km); Agia Napa (80km); Lemesos (82km)
Pafos Gate
Tripolis
Roccas
Mula (Zahra)
Flatro (Sibeli)
Caraffa
Podocataro
Constanza
Town Hall
D'Avila
Plateia Solomou
Plateia Eleftherias
Plateia Lloyd Tzortz
Plateia Archiepiskopou Kyprianou
Plateia Tillirias
Green Line

LEFKOSIA IN ONE DAY

Start your day after breakfast by popping into **Faneromeni Church** (below). Take a couple of hours to explore the **Venetian walls** (p184), the city's guardians for centuries, and go to **Famagusta Gate**, where concerts and other events are often held. The best part of the day is spent simply wandering around the streets of the Old City and checking out the old colonial houses, now falling into decay. Trace the Green Line and have lunch at **Shiantris** (p185), where you can have a real Cypriot meal alongside the city's working men. After lunch, go to the **Cyprus Museum** (below), where the oldest artefact dates back to 8000 BC. Have a luxurious Turkish bath in the **Omeriye Hammam** (below) and then prepare to eat some of the finest meze on the island at **Egeon** (p185). Finish with some drinks at **Hammam** (p185).

although still present, is slowly changing thanks to 24-hour checkpoints crossing into its northern half, Lefkoşa. This is especially so with the recently opened Ledra St crossing, which allows pedestrians to hop back and forth between the two parts of town. It's now possible to see Lefkosia as one city, though it may be years still until it's truly that way.

See p193 for details on Lefkoşa (Nicosia) in North Cyprus.

Orientation

Almost everything of interest lies inside the city walls. From Plateia Eleftherias (Eleftheria Sq), Lidras St runs north to the Green Line, but most of the tourist attractions are tucked away in the nearby alleys of Laiki Yeitonia or around the Archbishop's Palace on Plateia Archiepiskopou Kyprianou.

Buses and shared taxis leave from Plateia Solomou and several smaller stands around the walls. The rest of Lefkosia is a sprawling mass of superstores and tower blocks, less interesting but busier than the Old Town.

Information

Plateia Eleftherias has banks with foreign-exchange desks and ATMs.

Cyprus Tourist Organisation (CTO; ☎ 2267 4264; cytour@cto.org.cy; Aristokyprou, Laïki Yitonia; 🕑 8.30am-4pm Mon-Fri, to 2pm Sat) Close to Plateia Eleftherias and has complimentary maps for the Republic. Free walking tours leave the office at 10am on Mondays, Thursdays and Fridays.

CYTA office (cnr Mouseiou & Aigyptou; 🕑 7.30am-5.15pm Mon, Tue, Thu & Fri, to 1.30pm Wed, to 1pm Sat) The main city call centre, near Pafos Gate.

General Hospital (☎ 2280 1400; Nechrou) English-speaking staff.

Main post office (D'Avila Bastion, Konstantinou Palaiologou; 🕑 7.30am-1.30pm & 3-6pm Mon-Fri, 8.30-10.30am Sat) No afternoon service Wednesdays.

Moufflon (☎ 2266 5155; Sofouli 1) The best-stocked bookshop in town is just south of Plateia Solomou.

Police station (☎ 2267 1434; Lidras)

PS Printways (☎ 2266 1628; Rigainis 63b; per hr €2; 🕑 8am-midnight) The best of several internet cafes near Plateia Solomou.

Sights & Activities

Located near the old Pafos Gate, the **Cyprus Museum** (☎ 2286 5888; Leoforos Mouseiou 1; admission €4; 🕑 9am-5pm Mon-Sat, 10am-1pm Sun) houses an incredible collection of pots, statues and tomb offerings, including the famous Aphrodite statue from Soloi. Arrive here early to beat the crowds.

Most other attractions are inside the city walls. Just off Lidras St, the intriguing **Leventis Municipal Museum** (☎ 2266 1475; Ippokratous 17; admission free; 🕑 10am-4.30pm Tue-Sun) traces the history of Lefkosia from prehistoric times. The nearby **Shacolas Tower Museum & Observatory** (☎ 2267 9396; 11th fl, Shakolas Tower, cnr Ledra & Arsinois; admission €0.85; 🕑 10am-6.30pm), offers stupendous views over the city, including across the Green Line. Nearby, the appealing sandstone **Faneromeni Church** is full of 17th-century icons.

A little deeper in the Old Town on Plateia Tillirias are the recently restored **Omeriye Mosque** and upmarket **Omeriye Hammam** (Ömeriye Hamam; ☎ 2275 0550; www.hamambaths.com; Plateia Tyllirias 8; admission & Turkish bath €20 for 2hrs, traditional body peeling €20 for 20 mins, massage €40-50; 🕑 9am-9pm). The *hammam* is open to men only on Tuesdays, Thursdays and Saturdays, and women only on Wednesdays, Fridays and Sundays; there are tours only from 11am to 5pm Mondays. One block east of these, the well-preserved **House of Hatzigeorgakis Kornesios** (☎ 2230 5316; Patriarchou Grigoriou 20; admission €1.70; 🕑 8am-2pm Mon-Fri, 9am-1pm Sat) is fully decked out with original Ottoman furnishings.

There are three museums in the **Archbishop's Palace** compound on Plateia Archiepiskopou Kyprianou. **St John's Cathedral** (9am-1pm Mon-Sat, 2-4pm Mon-Fri) has stunning frescos from 1662; the **Ethnographic Museum** (2243 2578; Plateia Arhiepiskopou Kyprianou; admission €1.70; 9am-5pm Mon-Fri, 10am-1pm Sat) displays traditional Cypriot folk art; and the **Byzantine Museum** (2243 0008; Plateia Arhiepiskopou Kyprianou; admission €1.70; 9am-4.30pm Mon-Fri, to 1pm Sat) has a superb collection of ancient icons and frescos rescued after 1974.

Lefkosia has many more art galleries and museums – contact CTO or follow the brown signs.

Tours

The **CTO** (p183) runs free guided walks on Mondays, Thursdays and Fridays, all starting at 10am, from the CTO office in the Old City. 'Chrysaliniotissa & Kaimakli: the Past Restored' is a bus and walking guided tour that runs on Mondays; on Thursdays it's a walk through Old Lefkosia; and Friday's 'Nicosia – Outside the Walls' is a bus and walking guided tour. All walks last two hours and 45 minutes, and have a 30 minute break in the middle. Alternatively, pick up a CTO walking-tours brochure.

Sleeping

HI Hostel (9943 8360; Tefkrou 5; dm €10-15) About 1.5km from the city walls, just off Themistokli Dervi, this brightly painted hostel has a guest kitchen, fan-cooled dorms and resident cats.

Delphi Hotel (2266 5211; Leoforos Kostaki Pantelidi 24; s/d from €40/55;) Close to Plateia Solomou bus stand, the Delphi has inviting, angular rooms that are better than you'd expect for the price. Some have balconies with views of the Old Town.

Sky Hotel (2266 6880; www.skyhotel.ws; Solonos 7c; s/d €43/60;) The best budget place in Lefkosia, Sky is bang in the centre of the Old Town, with good, spacious rooms, most of which have large balconies overlooking the surrounding rooftops. The blue paintwork isn't the top of style, but the place is relaxing and the staff is friendly. Breakfast is included.

Centrum Hotel (2245 6444; www.centrumhotel.net; Pasikratous 15; r €92;) A fairly stylish hotel that's a crossover between a boutique and business hotel, the Centrum offers spacious rooms with balconies (though not in all), decked out in blushes and salmon colours; some have baths too, so state your preference when booking. The hotel is within seconds of Plateia Eleftherias. The business facilities are excellent.

CITY WITH A PLAN

In an effort to bring North Cyprus and the Republic closer together, more than 80 Ottoman, Frankish and Byzantine buildings in Lefkosia have been faithfully restored with funding from the UN and EU. The **Nicosia Masterplan** covers churches and mosques, *hammams* (Turkish baths) and tombs, mansions and monuments, museums and cultural centres – the aim is to promote understanding of the shared history between the two sides. Close to the Ledra Palace Hotel checkpoint, the **Masterplan office** (2266 8864; 8am-6pm Mon-Fri, 9am-5pm Sat & Sun) has full listings of the restored buildings in a handy, free guide.

PREPARING A NEW SQUARE

A massive reconstruction project has been obstructing much of Lefkosia's Plateia Eleftherias for a few years now. But it's for a noble cause: a sweeping, floor-lit design is intended to paint the capital's main attraction, the **Venetian walls**, in sharp relief, while remaining in harmony with its ancient surroundings. The architect is Zaha Hadid, a top contemporary designer renowned for her socially aware projects. Hadid's impressive CV includes the Strasbourg tram station, a housing project for IBA-Block 2 in Berlin, and the Mind Zone in London's Millennium Dome. Together with her Cypriot associate, Christos Passos, Hadid plans to construct a green belt along the moat that surrounds the walls at present, turning the area within into Lefkosia's central park, encircled by a palm-tree-lined pedestrian walkway. She calls the design an 'urban intervention'. There has been some controversy – and what's a grand architectural work without controversy? – with local opponents complaining of too little public consultation on the project and voicing concerns about the impact a large concrete structure will have on the ancient walls. Work started in 2008 and the estimated time to finish the square is two years.

our pick **Classic Hotel** (☎ 2266 4006; www.classic.com.cy; Rigenis 94; s/d €80/97;) This three-star hotel, close to Pafos Gate, is a member of the 'Small Luxury Hotels of the World' group, and you can see why. Everything, from the reception to the rooms, is done up in relaxing creamy, wood colours; the design is minimalist; and the rooms are smart and comfortable. The 59 Knives restaurant, part of the hotel, specialises in haute cuisine, adding its own contribution to the Classic's luxuries.

Eating

Shiantris (☎ 2267 1549; Pericleous 21; mains from €6; lunch) One of Lefkosia's hidden delights, Shiantris is named after its vociferous owner who cooks up a fantastic array of seasonal beans with lemon, parsley and olive oil, and, for carnivores, meat dishes such as *afelia* and baked lamb. A great place to immerse yourself in local life and cuisine. At the time of writing, the restaurant was moving to a new and bigger space across the road.

Mattheos (☎ 2275 5846; Plateia 28 Oktovriou 6; mains from €6; lunch) Another simple local lunch place; decked out in chequered table cloths, this place is superatmospheric. The food is not as good as Shiantris, but Mattheos does have the most gorgeous outside eating space, right behind the little mosque, next to Faneromeni Church. The food is Cypriot, with *kleftiko*, *stifado* and stuffed vegetables on the menu.

Zanettos Taverna (☎ 2276 5501; Trikoupi 65; mains from €7) This place has a great reputation in the city, as it is allegedly one of the oldest traditional taverns. The locals flock here in their dozens, and it's definitely worth joining them. A great place for meze, it's hidden away in a slightly shady part of town, where the painted ladies sit in their doorways waiting for business.

Inga's Veggie Heaven (☎ 2234 4674; Chrisaliniotissa Crafts Centre, Dimonaktos 2; mains €8-10; 9am-5pm) Recently opened, Inga's is an invaluable addition to Lefkosia's eating scene. It's a simple, neat and elegant eatery, with half a dozen tables sitting under the tall eaves of the old roof. Inga is a friendly Icelandic chef who prepares two fresh dishes of the day, such as aubergine lasagne or a delicious kidney-bean burger, always served with a salad and homemade bread. There's a small terrace outside, too.

our pick **Egeon** (☎ 2243 3297; Ektoros 40; meze from €15; dinner) The ever-so-discreet yet very popular Egeon draws a faithful following of mainly local devotees. The food, basically meze, is divine. Order some courgettes scrambled with egg or potent and rich garlicky yoghurt, before you move onto the fantastic vegetable and meat dishes – the *sheftalia* (lamb meatball) is fresh and aromatic. You'll dine in the courtyard of the atmospheric old house in the summer, and inside the house in the winter. Bookings are essential.

Syrian Arab Friendship Club (SAFC; ☎ 2277 6246; Vassilisa Amalia 17; meze from €15; 11am-midnight) In addition to being one of the best places to eat in Lefkosia, this is the ideal place for vegetarians. The meze is massive, so approach it with respect, and if you come for lunch, you won't be eating dinner that night. Offerings include green beans, chickpeas, *tabouleh* (bulgur-wheat and parsley salad) and plenty of meat, too. Try the delicious *mahalabia* (a light rice custard, which is served cold) for dessert and, once you're so stuffed you can't move, puff on a *nargileh* (water pipe).

There are several workers cafes that sell rustic village meals of *seftalias* and *souvlakia* for less than €5 – try **Christakis** (☎ 2266 8537; Plateia Solomou; Mon-Sat) by the bus stand or **Ta Deilina** (☎ 2275 8287; Thermopylon; dinner Mon-Sat) just off Xanthis Xenierou.

On Wednesdays each week there's a fantastic **fruit & veg market** set up in the Constanza bastion. Alternatively, drop in on the **municipal market** (Plateia Dimarchias; Mon-Sat) in the Old Town.

Drinking & Entertainment

Hammam (☎ 2276 6202; Soutsou 9) This place is right behind Omeriye Hammam. Located inside a heavenly old colonial house with a grand arched door and beautifully tiled floors, it is the perfect place for sitting under the stars and sipping a cocktail beneath an aromatic fig tree. It's superpopular and always packed.

our pick **Oktana** (☎ 2276 0099; Aristidou 6) Located in the Old City, Oktana serves just as well as a cafe, though it's at its most packed in the evening. There is a fantastic garden at the back, a bookshop and an interior seating area in the old house where Oktana is set, and a wide range of board games that are happily utilised by the Lefkosians. The interior basement space, Uqbar, is favoured by the *nargileh* smokers.

Brew (☎ 2210 0133; Ippocratous 30) Another gorgeous space, Brew stretches through the ground floor of an old mansion. It's an airy, spacious place, with good music, painted white wood furniture and lots of tea, cocktails and food.

There are several cinemas that show international films (the *Cyprus Mail* has full listings). Art-house movies are shown at the bohemian **Weaving Mill** (☎ 2276 2275; www.ifantourgio.org.cy; Lefkonos 67-71) in the Old Town.

Classical theatre is showcased at the **Lefkosia Municipal Theatre** (☎ 2266 4028; Mouseiou), while **Theatre Ena** (☎ 2234 8203; Athinas 4) is the leading venue for off-beat productions. Contact CTO (p183) for information on performances.

Shopping

Two places worth checking out are the **Cyprus Handicrafts Centre** (☎ 2230 5024; Athalassis 186; ⌚ 7.30am-2.30pm Mon-Fri, 3-6pm Thu), where you can get Cypriot lace and embroideries at decent prices, as well as leatherware, mosaics, ceramics and pottery. For antiques, visit two very dusty and very fun **antique shops** (☎ 99 66 47 22; Vasileou Voulgaroktonou 5 & 6) on opposite sides of the street (you might very well have to ring the owner to come down for you to browse). You'll find lots of great stuff, from retro bits and pieces, to lovely ceramics, paintings, ornaments and so on.

Getting There & Around

Private taxis loiter around Plateia Eleftherias. For car hire, try **Petsas** (☎ 7777 1515; Kostaki Pantelidi 24; per day from €25) near Plateia Solomou.

Buses leave from several stands around the old city walls; there are no Sunday services. **Nicosia Buses** (☎ 2266 5814; www.nicosiabuses.com.cy) to the suburbs leave from Plateia Solomou.

From the main stand at Plateia Solomou, **Intercity** (Green Bus; ☎ 2464 3492; www.intercitybuses.com) runs to Larnaka (€10, 45 minutes, six a day Monday to Friday, two on Saturday), while **Alepa** (☎ 2266 4636) and **LLL Bus** (☎ 2266 5814) run to Lemesos (€15, one hour, four to nine daily). Alepa also has a bus from Tripolis Bastion to Pafos (€20, 2½ hours) at 2.45pm daily (12.45pm Wednesday and Saturday).

Solis (☎ 9943 1363) and **Lysos** (☎ 9941 4777) have daily minibuses from Tripolis Bastion to Polis (€25, 3½ hours), leaving around 11.30am. **Eman** (☎ 2372 1321; www.emantravel.com) goes from Constanza Bastion to Agia Napa (€10, 1½ hours) at 3pm.

For towns in the Troodos, **Clarios** (☎ 2275 3234; Constanza Bastion) has around 10 daily buses to Kakopetria (€7, one hour) – the 10.20am weekday and 11.30am Saturday services continue to Plateia Troodos (€12, 1½ hours), where you can pick up buses to Platres. There are also one or two daily services to Pedoulas (€10, 1½ hours).

From Tripolis Bastion, **Kambos** (☎ 9962 3604) has a daily bus to Kykkos Monastery (€7, two hours) at 11.30am, returning at 6am the next day.

Close to Podocataro Bastion, **Travel & Express** (☎ 7777 7474; www.travelexpress.com.cy; Salaminos) has half-hourly service taxis to Larnaka (€9, one hour) and Lemesos (€12, one hour), with connections to Pafos (€22, 1½ hours) and Agia Napa (€18, one hour).

LARNAKA ΛΑΡΝΑΚΑ

pop 73,200

Calmer and friendlier than the other coastal resorts, Larnaka is famous as the final resting place of Agios Lazaros, who rose from the dead in the Bible. There's a busy waterfront strip with a modest beach and a quieter Old Town and Turkish quarter. The Republic's main airport is 5km south of town, near the salt lake.

The **CTO** (☎ 2465 4322; Plateia Vasileos Pavlou; ⌚ 8.15am-2.30pm & 3-6.15pm Mon-Fri, 8.15am-1pm Sat, closed Wed afternoon) has the usual maps and brochures. Free walking tours of the city leave the CTO office at 10am on Wednesdays and Larnaka Castle on Fridays.

The main post office and banks are on Zinonos Kitieos, near the CTO.

Check your mail at **Replay** (☎ 2462 1588; Leoforos Athinon; per hr €3; ⌚ 10am-1am) on the seafront promenade.

Sights & Activities

The Old Town is dominated by the stately Byzantine-era **Agios Lazaros Church** (Agiou Lazarou; ⌚ 8am-12.30pm & 3.30-6.30pm), which contains fabulous icons and the tomb of the esteemed Lazaros. There's also a small **museum** (☎ 2465 2498; admission €1; ⌚ 8.30am-1pm & 3-5.30pm Mon, Tue, Thu, Fri & Sun, 8.30am-1pm Wed & Sat) with ancient icons.

Down on the waterfront, **Larnaka Castle** (☎ 2463 0576; Leoforos Athinon; admission €1; ⌚ fort & museum 9am-7pm Mon-Fri) has Crusader grave slabs, and displays on ancient architecture and ceramics.

Opposite the tourist office, the excellent **Pierides Museum** (☎ 2481 4555; Zinonos Kitieos 4; admission €2; 9am-4pm Mon-Thu, 9am-1pm Fri & Sat), has an amazing collection of ceramics, maps and folk art amassed by the Pierides family. There are more antiquities in the town's **Archaeological Museum** (☎ 2463 0169; Kalogreon; admission €2; 9am-2.30pm Mon-Fri, 3-5pm Thu Sep-Jun).

Islamic monuments include the **Büyük Mosque** (Büyük Cami) in old Larnaka and the **Hala Sultan Tekke** (admission by donation; 9am-7.30pm May-Sep, 9am-5pm Oct-Apr) near the airport, containing the mausoleum of Hala Sultan, the foster-aunt of the prophet Mohammed. Büyük Mosque reluctantly accepts visitors (you'll be refused altogether during prayer times); you may be able to climb its minaret for a small fee.

About 30km west of Larnaka, the monastery of **Stavrovouni** (☎ 2253 3630; admission free; 6am-noon & 3-6pm) is perched atop a 688m buttress with panoramic views over the island – unfortunately for women, only men can enter.

Sleeping & Eating

HI Hostel (☎ 2462 8811; Nikolaou Rossou 27; dm €10) Upstairs by the Bekir Pasa mosque, the hostel is old and creaky but OK for the money. Dorms are single-sex and family rooms sleep four.

our pick **Les Palmiers Beach Hotel** (☎ 2462 7200; www.lespalmierscityhotel.com; Leoforos Athinon 12; s/d €60/78;) What was once the grimmest hotel in town has been turned into a knockout boutique hotel that has great prices and friendly service to boot. Decorated simply and tastefully, with elegant camel-coloured rooms, Les Palmiers is the town's best option. Low season prices drop as low as €42/60 for singles/doubles.

Prasino Amaxoudi (☎ 2462 2939; Agias Faneromenis; mains €5; noon-10pm) If you like a good, no-frills kebab, this is the top place in Larnaka. The supertasty grilled *helimi* (halloumi) in hot pitta has salad erupting from the middle. The tender chicken kebabs are equally scrumptious. It's just by the Grand Mosque in the old Turkish quarter.

our pick **1900 Art Cafe** (☎ 2462 3730; Stasinou 6; mains from €8; 6pm-midnight Wed-Mon) A wonderfully atmospheric place on two floors, with art-exhibition posters and paintings covering the walls. It serves both vegetarian and meat dishes. Open for dinner only.

Militzis Restaurant (☎ 2465 5867; Piale Pasia 42; mains €9-15) A Larnaka institution, Militzis offers fabulous *kleftiko ofto* fresh from the clay oven.

Getting There & Around

From the airport to central Larnaka, you have the choice of taxis (€10, 20 minutes) or local buses 22 and 24 (€1, 30 minutes, Monday to Saturday). Buses in the opposite direction stop on Ermou, near the junction with Vasilou Evagorou.

The bus stop is on the waterfront, opposite the old Four Lanterns Hotel. **Eman** (☎ 2372 1321) and **Intercity** (☎ 2462 3492) have regular daily buses to Agia Napa (€4, one hour), except on Sunday. Intercity also runs to Lefkosia (€5, one hour, seven daily) and Lemesos (€7, one hour, four daily); two services run on each route on Saturday.

Travel & Express (☎ 7777 7474; www.travelexpress.com.cy; Papakyriakou) operates service taxis every half-hour to Lemesos (€11, one hour) and Lefkosia (€9, one hour).

AGIA NAPA (AYIA NAPA)

Two generations of runaway development have transformed the quiet monastery of Agia Napa into Cyprus' answer to Spain's Costa del Sol. Sunbathing, clubbing and binge-drinking are the main attractions – some love it, others are happy to leave it well alone.

The beautifully cloistered **Monastery of Agia Napa** (Plateia Seferi; admission free; 9am-6pm) is incongruously sited next to the pub-and-club centre of the adjoining square. Best visited in the early morning, after the revellers have gone to bed, the monastery is an oasis of calm amid the crass commercialism of Agia Napa's entertainment scene.

As well as the busy beach, you can visit the new **Thalassa Museum** (☎ 2381 6366; Leoforos Kryou Nerou 14; adult/child €3/1; 9am-1pm & 6-10pm Wed-Sun & 6-10pm Tue May-Oct, 9am-5pm Wed-Sun & 1-5pm Tue Nov-Apr), dedicated to the maritime history of Cyprus.

The **CTO** (☎ 2372 1796; Kyrou Nerou 12; 8.30am-2.30pm & 3-6pm Mon-Fri, closed Wed afternoon) has information on tours to North Cyprus and other touristy activities.

You'll find more package-holiday resorts at **Protaras** on the other side of the cape.

Sleeping & Eating

There are loads of holiday apartments for rent in the area.

Green Bungalows (☎ 2372 1511; www.greenbungalows.com; Katalymata 19; 2-person apt from €50; ⏲ Apr-Oct) A superior B-class apartment hotel. This place offers cosy apartments and breakfast from €4.

Faros (☎ 2372 3838; www.faroshotel.com.cy; Leoforos Arhiepiskopou Makariou III; r per person €60;) A rather swanky place very close to the harbour, with sleek, bright rooms and a great pool surrounded by bungalows. Note that there is a four-night minimum stay in July and August. Low-season rates can cost as little as €34 per person.

our pick Xylino (☎ 2396 2403; Vrysoulles; meze €14) Situated outside of Agia Napa, in the village of Vrysoulles, Xylino excels in the art of meze. It is worth seeking out for this very reason, and for its low prices. It's easily spotted once you're in the village (it's opposite the church) and it draws a loyal local crowd – and few tourists.

Tsambra (☎ 2372 2513; Dionysiou Solomou 9; mains €10-15) For a change in style, try the shaded courtyard of this Lebanese–Cypriot restaurant. Tsambra serves up good shish kebabs, barbecued lamb, *tabouleh* and, for dessert, *mahalabia*.

Entertainment

As the clubbing capital of Cyprus, Agia Napa is packed with flamboyant bars and clubs. **Freedom Reggae Bar** (☎ 2372 2801; Ari Velouhioti; ⏲ 9am-2am) is a bar with a difference in that it opens for breakfast, when clubbed-out punters head here for the exceptionally chilled-out atmosphere. Freedom even serves an early Sunday roast.

Bedrock Inn (☎ 2372 2951; Agias Mavris) is a grotesque Fred Flintstone and Barney Rubble–style karaoke palace, extremely popular with the tourists.

Getting There & Around

From Monday through to Saturday, **Eman** (☎ 2372 1321) and **Intercity** (☎ 2464 3492) have regular buses travelling to Larnaka (€4, one hour), stopping south of the monastery on Archiepiskopou Makarios III. Eman also has a single bus at 8am to Lefkosia (€10, 1½ hours) and regular shuttle buses to Protaras (€1.40, 20 minutes).

Service taxis between Paralimni and Larnaka pick up and drop off in Agia Napa – contact **Travel & Express** (☎ 7777 7474; www.travelexpress.com.cy).

Dozens of places in town rent out mopeds, cars and jeeps for around €30 per day.

LEMESOS (LIMASSOL) ΛΕΜΕΣΟΣ

pop 163,400

Part beach resort, part economic hub, Lemesos is the second-largest town in Cyprus. Some see it mainly as an industrial and commercial centre with little to recommend it. But if you like a city that's rough around the edges, with great places to eat and drink, plus several spots for beach parties and fantastic sights, then pay a visit to Lemesos.

The town rose to prominence after Richard the Lionheart married Berengaria of Navarre here in 1191, but most visiting package tourists skip the historic town centre for the string of bland beach resorts running west along the coast.

Orientation & Information

The main shopping street is Agiou Andreou, one street back from the waterfront near the old port. The new port, 2km west of the centre, is mainly used by freight and cruise ships.

The **CTO** (☎ 2536 2756; cnr Spyros Araouzou & Dimitriou Nikolaidi; ⏲ 8.15am-2.30pm & 3-6.15pm Mon-Fri, to 1.30pm Sat, closed Wed afternoon) is on the waterfront, a few blocks east of the old harbour.

There are banks all over town and a post office on Archiepiskopou Kyprianos. Check your mail at **CyberNet** (Eleftherias 79; per hr €2.50; ⏲ 1-11pm Mon-Fri, 10am-11pm Sat & Sun), a convenient Old City location.

Sights

With the closure of the Time Elevator, the main attraction in Lemesos is the solid-looking **Lemesos Castle Medieval Museum** (☎ 2530 5419; Eirinis; admission free; ⏲ 9am-5pm Mon-Sat, 10am-1pm Sun). Inside you can see Crusader gravestones and lots of Byzantine sgraffito pottery.

In the same area are the **Jami Kebir mosque** (Genethliou Mitella) and the restored unisex **Turkish baths** (☎ 9947 4251; Loutron 3; steam bath & sauna/massage €15; ⏲ 2-10pm). The district **Archaeological Museum** (☎ 2533 0157; cnr Vyronos & Kaningos; admission €1.70; ⏲ 9am-5pm Mon-Sat, 10am-1pm Sun) is also worth a trip.

The villages around Lemesos are famous for arts and crafts. All are very touristy, however, and you'll need a hire car to explore the area. Probably the best known is the lacemaking village of **Lefkara**, which lies about 30km northeast of town.

A MARINA LIKE NO OTHER

If you get to visit Lemesos in 2011, chances are it'll be a very different place from what it was when the decrepit Old Harbour greeted visitors with a neglected, shabby face and a smile full of broken teeth. All that is going to change: the harbour is about to embark on a €270 million facelift. The competition for the new **Limassol Passenger Terminal** was won by Cyprus' own Nicosia-based architects Dickon Irwin and Margarita Kritioti at Irwin & Kritioti Architects (www.irwinkritioti.com) in 2007. The company already has Nicosia's new Town Hall and the new National Archive for Cyprus under its belt, and their innovative and lush idea for Lemesos' marina sees the harbour's shape mimic the sea with a series of steel wavelike oval shapes, giving it a postcard-perfect look. But aside from its impressive aesthetics, the marina is meant to bring life back to the city centre year-round, so when the high tourist season wanes in the early winter months, the harbour will turn into a conference and lecture centre.

All this is estimated to take three years to build. The marina is expected to be the most luxurious place on the island and is so far the only Cypriot project of its size. It will hold 1000 yachts, there'll be living spaces, shops, bars, restaurants and cafes, wi-fi internet access, and a number of other, superexclusive areas. A park will encircle the marina and the buildings inside the new space will all cohere with traditional Lemesos architecture.

Check out the flashy website www.limassolmarina.com and the more informative www.marinalimassol.com. And make sure you bring your yacht.

The old coast road to Pafos is dotted with sites linked to Aphrodite, the Greek goddess of love. About 26km towards Pafos, **Petra tou Romiou** is the legendary birthplace of the goddess – it's a scenic spot with huge, white-marble boulders on a pebble beach with great skimming stones. Nearby **Pissouri Beach** is nicer and less developed than the main tourist beach at Lemesos, but you need your own vehicle to get here.

A few kilometres east, the Graeco-Roman site at **Kourion** (☎ 2599 5048; admission €1.70; 🕒 8am-7.30pm Jul & Aug, 7.30am-5pm Sep-Jun) has Roman baths, an *agora* (public forum) and a famous amphitheatre backed by the setting sun. Get here before 10am to beat the crowds, or arrive in the afternoon to appreciate the sunset (though it might be a bit busier).

Nearby are the partly restored remains of the **Sanctuary of Apollon Ylatis** (☎ 2599 5049; admission €1.70; 🕒 9am-7.30pm May-Sep, 9am-5.30pm Oct-Apr), sacred to a cult of Apollo worshippers in Graeco-Roman times. Closer to Lemesos is the robust keep of **Kolossi Castle** (☎ 2593 4907; admission €1.70; 🕒 9am-7.30pm Jul-Aug, 9am-5pm Sep-Jun), built in Crusader times.

Sleeping

There are a few old-fashioned guest houses in between the lace shops on Agiou Andreou.

Luxor Guest House (☎ 2536 2265; Agiou Andreou 101; dm €11, r per person €13; 💻) The Luxor is the only place in the city, and possibly in the country, that has a real backpacking atmosphere. The rooms are airy, with painted wood-board ceilings and little balconies. The bathrooms are mostly shared – there is one en suite double (€29) – and there is a small (outdoor) breakfast kitchen.

Metropole (☎ 2536 2330; www.metropole.com.cy; Ifigenias 6; s/d €29/43; ❄) You may get a pretty unwelcoming reception if you walk into the Metropole off the street, but this is by far the best budget option in the centre and it has to be mentioned. It's a comfortable three-star place with a rather classic decor where navy bed quilts match the curtains. The bathrooms are en suite. The hotel's location is supercentral, so it's very convenient if you want to be in the Old City.

our pick **Chrielka** (☎ 2535 8366; www.chrielka.com.cy; Olympion 7; 2-person ste €60-100; ❄ 🏊) Chrielka is a great, quality self-catering option: the 33 apartments vary in size and level of 'luxury', but all are tastefully decorated and include a balcony, kitchenette and satellite TV. The beds are comfortable; you can breakfast on the balcony – some apartments overlook the Municipal Gardens; and you're close to the beach, the Old Town and the tourist area. It has a nice swimming pool, too.

Eating & Drinking

our pick **127** (☎ 2534 3990; Eleni Paleologinas 5; salad/sandwiches from €5) The people in this place know how to make a salad (and how to make your mouth water): the seafood salad is swamped with succulent prawns, thin slices of salmon and bits of squid, all drizzled with balsamic vinegar to bring out the taste. Meat eaters can tuck into grilled meats. The decor is all vintage furniture and exposed-brick walls painted in vibrant colours.

Dino Art Café (☎ 2576 2030; Irinis 62-66; mains from €7) Dino's has a great reputation and many a follower among Cypriots thanks to its smart decor, friendly boss and great food. The (massive) salads (€12) are fantastic, with the duck and orange salad holding a special place in our hearts (and bellies). There's a good sandwich selection and some delicate sushi, too. Book in advance.

Draught Microbrewery (☎ 2582 0470; Vasilissis) The first microbrewery on the island, this boisterous nightspot serves a full range of lagers, ales and wheat beers.

Getting There & Around

Intercity (☎ 2266 5814; cnr Enoseos & Irinis) runs nine daily bus services to Lefkosia (€6, one hour) from its bus stop north of the castle.

Buses to Larnaka (€5, 45 minutes) run from the Old Fishing Harbour or from outside the CTO office. Both **Alepa** (☎ 9962 5027) and **Nea Amoroza** (☎ 2693 6822) have daily buses to Pafos (€6, 45 minutes). Alepa leaves from the Panikos kiosk on the promenade, while Nea Amoroza leaves from the Old Fishing Harbour.

A bus to Platres (€5, one hour) leaves from the Municipal Market every day at 9.30am.

Travel & Express (☎ 7777 7474; www.travelexpress.com.cy; Thessalonikis 21) has regular service taxis to Lefkosia (€12, 1½ hours), Larnaka (€11, one hour) and Pafos (€10.50, one hour). They will also drop you off at Larnaka airport (€13.50) and Pafos airport (€12.50) but do allow extra time for your check-in. Another taxi option is **Acropolis Service Taxis** (☎ 2536 6766; Spyrou Araouzou 65), which departs regularly for the same destinations.

Local buses, to Germasogeia and back, are basically cans on wheels, and they run every 20 minutes from the City Bus Station (€1, 30 minutes). The last one leaves the centre at 6pm.

TROODOS MASSIF (TROODOS)
ΤΡΟΟΔΟΣ

The last great wilderness in the Republic, the Troodos Massif mountain range is a haven for walkers and nature buffs. Dotted among the black pines are small wine-making villages and Unesco World Heritage–listed Byzantine monasteries. The highest point is Mt Olympus (1952m), crowned by NATO radar beacons. The former colonial government had its summer headquarters in Plateia Troodos (Troodos Sq) – most visitors these days stay in Platres, about 7km south.

Information

Platres has banks, a post office and **CTO** (☎ 2542 1316; 🕓 8.30am-4pm Mon-Fri).

Just south of Plateia Troodos is the **Troodos Visitor Centre** (☎ 2542 0144; admission €0.85; 🕓 10am-4pm) with a nature museum, video show and information leaflets. For skiing information, contact the **Cyprus Ski Federation** (www.cypru sski.com).

Sights & Activities

The most famous monastery in the Troodos is **Kykkos Monastery**, about 20km west of Pedoulas. The stone-walled compound is full of shimmering, contemporary mosaics and frescos, and there's a distillery producing *komandaria* and *zivania*. The **museum** (☎ 2294 2736; www.kykkos-museum.cy.net; admission €3.40; 🕓 10am-6pm Jun-Sep, 10am-4pm Nov-May) is full of relic cases and other intriguing bits of religious paraphernalia. With advance notification, you may be able to stay in the **pilgrim's quarters** (☎ 2294 2435; donation requested). Archbishop Makarios III is buried in a guarded mausoleum, about 2km uphill.

Nearby Pedoulas has a small **icon museum** (☎ 2295 3636; admission free, but donations expected; 🕓 10am-1pm & 2.30-5pm). It also holds the key to the teeny stone **Church of Archangelos**, which contains hellfire-and-brimstone frescos that date from 1474. Near Kakopetria, **Agios Nikolaos tis Stegis** (admission by donation; 🕓 9am-4pm Tue-Sat, 11am-4pm Sun) has even older frescos depicting stern-looking saints and dating from the 12th century.

About 30km south of Pedoulas, **Omodos** is a village of perfect stone houses, set around the **Timios Stavros Monastery** (admission by donation; 🕓 8am-4pm). Local women make lace, while local men prepare *komandaria*. The **House of Socrates** (Linou; admission free; 🕓 9am-8pm) has a small, eccentric wine-making museum.

The mountains are criss-crossed by walking trails, and walkers can pick up walking-trail brochures from the Troodos Visitor Centre.

One of the most popular walks is the 1km hike from Platres to pretty **Kaledonia Falls**.

Sleeping & Eating

PLATRES

Platres is the most popular place to stay and half a dozen tavernas offer inexpensive Cypriot grills and stews.

Petit Palais Hotel (☎ 2542 1723; www.petitpalaishotel.com; s/d €45/65) A palace it may have been once, but it's pretty sad and tired now, with slightly dingy rooms. On the upside, there are two balconies in each room, and you get en suite bathrooms, TVs and odd-looking space-age telephones. Low-season rates drop to €35/55 for singles/doubles.

our pick **Skylight** (☎ 2542 2244; mains from €8; 9am-6pm) A fabulous combination of a restaurant and a large swimming pool (admission per day €5), Skylight has some good grills and the usual Cypriot dishes on offer, which you can eat between swimming and lounging on the sunny terrace.

PLATEIA TROODOS

Plateia Troodos is a one-street town with no real year-round population. Services are aimed at visitors who come for the walking in summer and skiing in winter. It has several simple restaurants on the main road offering Anglicised Cypriot meals.

Troodos camping ground (☎ 2242 1624; camp sites €4; May-Oct) Below town on the Lefkosia road, the camping ground has plenty of pines for shade and a small cafe.

our pick **Jubilee Hotel** (☎ 2542 0107; jubilee@cytanet.com.cy; s/d €60/98) A stylish and elegant hotel, 350m from the village along the Prodromos road. Outside the hotel there are deck chairs for you to recline in and enjoy the fresh air. Inside is a soothing lounge in dark wood, decorated with shadow puppets and furnished with inviting armchairs. The rooms are comfortable and cosy, and there is central heating in winter. Low-season rates drop to €35/60 for singles/doubles; kids ages six to 12 years stay half-price and kids under six stay for free.

PEDOULAS

This is a quieter alternative to Platres, with lots of historic treasures.

Two Flowers (☎ 2295 2372; r per person €25, August €50 full board only) A lovely little B&B with 19 simple, clean and bright rooms, five of which sit in an old house that overlooks the valley. The rest of the rooms are in the main building (where the restaurant is, too), each with a private bathroom. The owners are friendly and, outside of the more expensive month of August, it's great value.

our pick **Platanos** (☎ 2295 2518; mains €8) Platanos offers a real slice of rural life – there's a furious backgammon game going on in the corner at all times of the day and the shade of the *platano* (plane tree) offers atmospheric seating. You can get good Cypriot dishes such as moussaka and *afelia* as well as some juicy kebabs.

Getting There & Around

Villages in the Troodos are widely spaced so a rental car is the best way to get around. From Monday to Friday, **Troodos Mountain Bus** (☎ 2555 2220) has a daily bus from Plateia Troodos to Lemesos (€10, 1¾ hours) via Platres (€4, 20 minutes). See p186 for information on buses from the capital.

Rural taxis in Platres can ferry you around the monasteries. A taxi from Lemesos to Platres will cost around €40.

PAFOS ΠΑΦΟΣ

pop 48,300

The former capital of Cyprus, Pafos is packed with historical relics…and tourists. If you find the beach strip at Kato Pafos too developed, head up to quieter Ktima on the hillside. More beach resorts are strung out west along the coast towards Agios Georgios. To escape the crowds, rent a car and head for the wonderfully untouched Akamas Peninsula (see p193).

The **CTO** (☎ 2693 2841; Gladstonos 3; 8.15am-2.30pm & 3-6.15pm Mon-Fri, 8.15am-1.30pm Sat, closed Wed afternoon) office is just down from Ktima's main square. There's a second office on Poseidonos in Kato Pafos.

There are banks and post offices in Ktima and along the Kato Pafos tourist strip. **Maroushia Internet** (per hr €3; 10am-11pm Mon-Sat, 3-10pm Sun) has branches in both Kato Pafos (☎ 2691 0657; Poisidonos) and Ktima (☎ 2694 7240; Plateia Kennedy 6).

Sights

The **Tombs of the Kings** (☎ 2694 0295; admission €1.70; 8.30am-7.30pm May-Sep, 8.30am-5pm Oct-Apr) is a Unesco World Heritage site and Pafos' main attraction. The site contains a set of well-preserved underground tombs and chambers

CYPRUS

used by residents of Nea Pafos from the 3rd century BC to the 3rd century AD, during the Hellenistic and Roman periods. It's about 2km north of Kato Pafos.

It's worth braving the crowds to see **Pafos Archaeological Site** (☎ 2694 0217; admission €3.40; 🕑 8am-7.30pm), with its astounding Roman mosaics, many featuring the rambunctious exploits of Dionysos, the god of wine. Within the same compound are the ruins of a castle and amphitheatre. There's another castle on the harbour and more Roman ruins in the grounds of the **Chrysopolitissa church** (Agias Kriakis; 🕑 dawn-dusk).

There's more intriguing history uphill in Ktima at the **Byzantine Museum** (☎ 2693 1393; Andrea Ioannou 5; admission €1.70; 🕑 9am-4pm Mon-Fri, 9am-1pm Sat) and the **Ethnographic Museum** (☎ 2693 2010; Exo Vrysis 1; admission €1.70; 🕑 9am-6pm Mon-Sat, 9am-1pm Sun).

Sleeping & Eating

Ktima has the best hotels for walk-ins.

Axiothea Hotel (☎ 2693 2866; www.axiotheahotel.com; Ivis Mallioti 2, Ktima; s/d €40/80; ❄) This hotel, on the high ground to the south of the CTO office, has a glass-fronted bar and reception with wonderful views of the sea – perfect for watching the sunset. It's a two-star place that is a reasonable budget option. In low season, you can pick up singles/doubles for €40/52.

Kiniras (☎ 2694 1604; www.kiniras.cy.net; Arhiepiskopou Makariou III 91, Ktima; s €45-60, d €60-85; ❄) Bang in the centre of Ktima, Kiniras is passionately run by its house-proud owner. The rooms are decorated in dark red wood, and have telephone, radio, TV, fridge and safe box. The hotel's downstairs restaurant, Kiniras Garden, is a good place to eat.

our pick **Pyramos Hotel** (☎ 2693 0222; www.pyramos-hotel.com; Agias Anastasias 4, Kato Pafos; s/d €45/55) A marvellous change from the old Pyramos, the newly refurbished hotel is gleaming, tasteful and well equipped. The 21 rooms are simple but just right, with orange bed throws and stylishly tiled modern showers. One of the best small hotels in Kato Pafos.

Kiniras Garden (☎ 2694 1604; Arhiepiskopou Makariou III 91, Ktima; mains €8-30; 🕑 dinner) The owner demands booking in advance, as he gets his ingredients fresh according to the number of diners booked. *Kleftiko* is a house speciality and worth coming for. There are homemade desserts, and the wine list has good wines from the Pafos area (€15 to €30).

Fetta's (☎ 2693 7822; Ioanni Agroti 33, Ktima; mains €9-17; 🕑 dinner) Often proclaimed as one of Cyprus' best traditional restaurants, Fetta's is a real treat. A *yaya* (grandma) prepares a fantastic meze (€16) and grilled meat, dishing them out onto a low, smoky window on the side of the house, while efficient waiters dart between the kitchen and the pavement or a little park, where the tables are sprawled.

Getting There & Around

Nea Amoroza Transport Co (☎ 2693 6822; Leoforos Evagora Pallikaridi 79, Ktima) and **Kemek Transport** (☎ 2693 6822; Leoforos Evagora Pallikaridi 79, Ktima) operate buses to Polis, Lemesos and Lefkosia. Buses leave from the main bus station in Ktima. There are two services per day to Lemesos (€7, one hour) and Lefkosia (€10, 1½ hours), and around 10 buses a day to Polis (€5, 50 minutes). There are also three buses daily (except Sundays) to Pomos village (€6, one hour), northeast of Polis.

Service taxis are operated by **Travel & Express** (☎ 0777 7474; www.travelexpress.com.cy; Leoforos Evagora Pallikaridi 9) in Ktima. Rates are €10 to Lemesos (one hour), €20 to Larnaka (change at Lemesos, 1½ hours) and €22 to Lefkosia (change at Lemesos, 1½ hours).

POLIS ΠΟΛΙΣ

pop 1800

Built over the ruins of ancient Marion, Polis is the Mediterranean everyone remembers – orange groves above a pretty beach and small tavernas clustered around the village square. Pedestrianised Griva Digeni is the main street and the beach is a 15-minute walk downhill along Verginas.

The **CTO** (☎ 2632 2468; Vasileos Stasioikou 2; 🕑 9am-1.30pm Mon-Fri, 9am-2pm Sat) office is on the road to Prodromi. There are several banks and a post office around Griva Digeni.

Sights

As well as the beach, there are some interesting old churches and a small **Archaeological Museum** (☎ 2632 2955; Leoforos Makariou; admission €1; 🕑 8am-2pm Mon-Wed & Fri, 8am-6pm Thu, 9am-5pm Sat), which has treasures excavated from Marion.

About 5km west along the coast are the **Baths of Aphrodite**, natural springs where the goddess is said to have bathed to restore her virginity. You can't try this out for yourself, but the baths are a great starting point for hikes into the **Akamas Peninsula**. This stunning natural wilderness is protected as a national park and the hills are criss-crossed by dirt tracks and walking trails – pick up CTO's *European Long Distance Path* brochure. **Avakas Gorge** on the west side of the cape is a particularly rewarding hike.

There are also some wild, isolated beaches here – gorgeous **Lara Beach** has a turtle research station operating from June to September, accessible by car from Agios Georgios.

Sleeping & Eating

Polis camping ground (☎ 2681 5080; camp sites per tent/person €3.50/3) Hidden in a grove of eucalyptus trees down on the beach, there is a beach cafe for day trippers.

Bougainvillea Hotel Apartments (☎ 2632 2201; fax 2632 2203; Verginas 13; studio/1-bed apt €50/65;) On the beach road, Bougainvillea offers quiet and roomy split-level apartments beside a decent-sized pool.

For meals, there are half a dozen tavernas clustered together on the main square, serving Cypriot standards such as halloumi pittas and *keftedes*. **Savvas** (☎ 2632 1081; Griva Digeni) is usually the busiest.

Getting There & Around

Hourly **Nea Amoroza** (☎ 2632 1114; Kyproleontos) buses to Pafos (€5, 45 minutes, Monday to Saturday) leave from near the CTO. There are also three buses on weekdays to the Baths of Aphrodite (€1, 20 minutes).

NORTH CYPRUS

Growing numbers of tourists are exploring the Turkish Republic of Northern Cyprus (TRNC), but the state is recognised only by mainland Turkey. Historic ruins abound, beaches are breathtaking and locals are friendly, but the legacy of 1974 casts a long shadow in the form of looted churches and neglected national treasures.

LEFKOŞA (NORTH NICOSIA)

pop 46,600

The northern half of Lefkosia is lost in time. Life moves at a snail's pace and the dusty streets are lined with ancient mosques and Frankish ruins. With the relaxing of border restrictions, many people take a day trip across from the Republic (and vice versa) via the Ledra Palace checkpoint, but there are few tourist facilities – just a handful of small hotels and kebab houses.

See p181 for details on Lefkosia in the Republic of Cyprus.

Orientation & Information

The well-preserved Kyrenia Gate on the north side of the city wall contains the **tourist office** (☎ 227 2994; 9am-4pm Mon-Fri, to 1pm Sat & Sun), which has free maps and brochures. From here, Girne Caddesi runs south to Atatürk Meydani (the main square) and the historic Selimiye Mosque. **Rustem Bookshop** (☎ 228 3506; Girne Caddesi 22) sells more-detailed city maps.

For foreign exchange, try the banks on Girne Caddesi or **Denizati Döviz** (☎ 228 2623; Girne Caddesi 17; 8am-5pm Mon-Fri, to 1pm Sat) by the Saray Hotel.

There's a **post office** (8am-12.30pm & 1.30-5pm Mon-Fri) on Sarayönü Sokak, and **Orbit Internet Café** (☎ 229 1787; Girne Caddesi; per hr TL2.5; 24hr) has reasonably fast connections.

Sights & Activities

Just inside the walls, the **Mevlevi Shrine Museum** (Mevlevi Tekke Müzesi; Girne Caddesi; adult/child 5/3TL; 9am-12.30pm & 1.30-4.45pm Jun–mid-Sep, 9am-2pm mid-Sep–May) is dedicated to the whirling Sufi dervishes (Muslim mystics), who were based here until the 1950s. Traditional *sema* (devotional dances) take place during the Shebu Arus celebrations in December.

The Selimiye quarter is dominated by the **Selimiye Mosque** (Selimiye Camii; Selimiye Meydanı; admission free), built as a cathedral between 1209 and 1326. A major restoration project is underway at the nearby **Bedesten** (Selimiye Meydanı), another grand Frankish church formerly used as an Ottoman bazaar.

A few blocks west, **Büyük Han** (Tarihi Büyük Hamam, Great Baths; Irfan Bey Sokak 9) is an old Ottoman inn that now contains a crafts market. Many more ancient monuments are being restored by the UN – pick up a copy of the *Nicosia Trail* brochure from the tourist office or visit the Nicosia Masterplan headquarters at the Ledra Palace Hotel (see the boxed text, p184).

Sleeping & Eating

Accommodation in Lefkoşa is limited and the few budget options available are not recommended for lone female travellers.

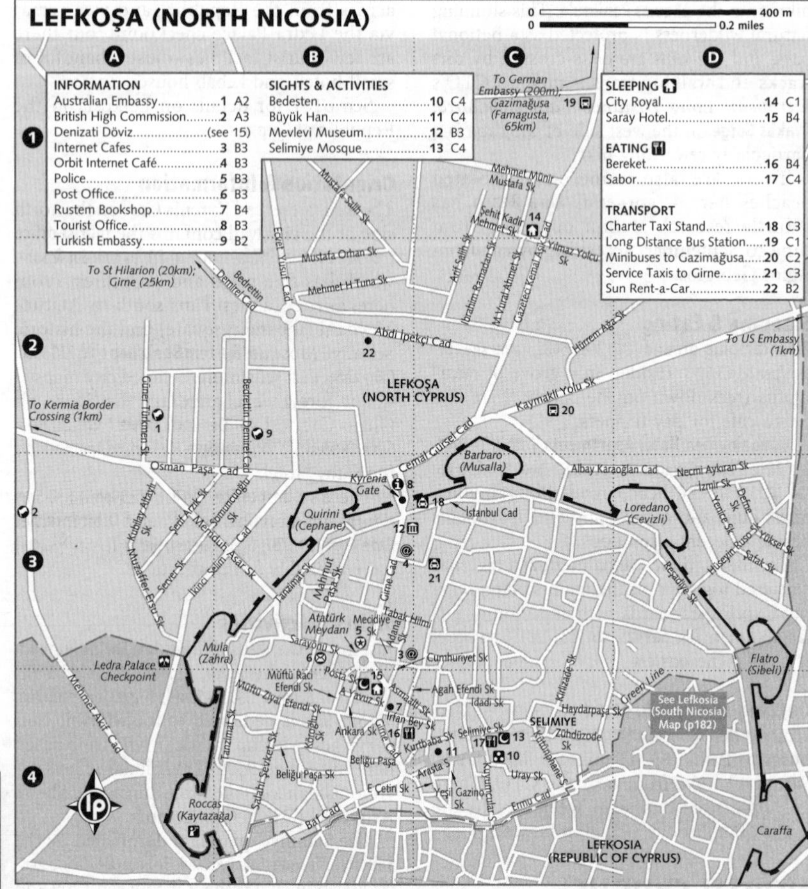

Saray Hotel (☎ 228 3115; saray@northcyprus.net; Atatürk Meydanı; s/d UK£43/70; ❄) Once a star on the Lefkoşa hotel scene, this has a sense of faded glory to it. The rooms are spacious and resemble a '70s interiors ad, and the beds are soft and pretty uncomfortable for a price so high. It is right in the centre of the Old City, on Atatürk Meydanı.

City Royal (☎ 228 7621; crhotel@kktc.net; Gazeteci Kemal Aşik Caddesi; r from UK£50; ❄ 🏊) A much more upmarket place, it's popular with travellers on business and with casino lovers. All rooms are fully serviced and have minibar, phone, satellite TV, and even a phone in the bathroom. There is also a swimming pool and a gym.

Bereket (☎ 227 1166; Irfan Bey Sokak; pide & lahmacun 7-10TL; 🕑 lunch) It's not really a restaurant, but more of a kiosk, with a few tables on the pavement under a parasol, just a few metres away from the grand Büyük Han. Bereket is run by Ahmet, who makes the best pide and *lahmacun* (Turkish-style pizza, topped with minced lamb and parsley) in town, in his stone oven.

our pick **Sabor** (☎ 228 8322; Selimiye Meydanı 29; mains around 10TL) Right next to Selimiye Mosque, this is decidedly Lefkoşa's trendiest and loveliest restaurant. Its excellent Italian and Spanish food is especially good for those days when you can't take another kebab – there are fantastic seafood salads, the portions are generous, the staff is friendly and the prices are low.

Getting There & Away

The long-distance bus station is a 15-minute walk north along Gazeteci Kemal Aşik

CYPRUS

Caddesi. **Girneliler Seyahat** (☎ 228 1018) has very regular minibuses to Girne (TL4, 30 minutes), while **Akva/Ulusoy** (☎ 227 2524) goes frequently to Güzelyurt (TL5.50, 45 minutes). **Itimat** (☎ 227 1617) minibuses to Gazimağusa (TL4, one hour) leave half-hourly from Kaymakli Yolu Sokak, just east of Kyrenia Gate.

Kombos (☎ 227 2929) service taxis to Girne (TL5, 30 minutes) run from Mevlevi Tekke Sokak in the Old City. A private taxi (departing from the charter taxi stand) to Ercan airport will cost TL30 (40 minutes).

For car hire, your best bet is **Sun Rent-a-Car** (☎ 227 2303; www.sunrentacar.com; Abdi Ipekci Caddesi 10; per day from UK£20).

GIRNE (KYRENIA)

pop 19,300

This is the Mediterranean as it used to be – a picturesque stone harbour, ending abruptly at a looming Byzantine castle. The old part of Girne is delightful, but in the surrounding hills, hundreds of British expats are living the dream of owning a holiday villa in a housing estate overlooking a building site. Visit now before the whole area vanishes under a sea of holiday homes.

Most things in Girne are sandwiched between the harbour and Ramadan Cemil Meydani, the main roundabout. The **tourist office** (☎ 815 2145; ⌚ 9am-5pm) is by the water at the west end of the harbour.

There are banks and foreign-exchange offices on Ziya Rifki Caddesi and the post office is on Mustafa Çağatay Caddesi. For internet access, try **Café Net** (☎ 815 9259; Efeler Sokak; per hr 3TL; ⌚ 10am-midnight) between Ramadan Cemil Meydani and the waterfront.

Sights & Activities

Dominating the harbour is Girne's main attraction, the **Kyrenia Castle & Shipwreck Museum** (Girne Kalesi; adult/child 12/3TL; ⌚ 9am-12.30pm & 1.30-4.45pm mid-Sep–May, 9am-8pm Jun–mid Sep), an impressively preserved castle with spooky dungeons and the remains of Cyprus' oldest shipwreck – thought to have sunk in a storm around 3000 BC. Just uphill is Girne's main mosque, **Aga Cafer Paşa Cami**. The tourist office has details of other museums in town.

A TL10 taxi ride from Girne gets you to the late-Byzantine abbey ruins at **Bellapais** (admission adult/child 9/3TL; ⌚ 9am-12.30pm & 1.30-4.45pm mid-Sep–May, 9am-8pm Jun–mid-Sep), the setting for Lawrence Durrell's *Bitter Lemons*. Minibuses run from the main roundabout to the pretty hill village of **Lapta**, a popular retirement spot for British expats.

Draped along the highest, rockiest ridge above Kyrenia, **St Hilarion Castle** (☎ 0533 161 276; adult/child 7/3TL; ⌚ 9am-12.30pm & 1.30-4.45pm mid-Sep–May, 9am-6.30pm Jun–mid-Sep) is an archetypal Crusader castle. Views are stupendous, but it sits in the middle of an army base, so the only way in is by hire car or taxi (TL25 return from Girne). On a 4WD track off the Girne–Gazimağusa road, the remote Crusader castle of **Buffavento** offers more breathtaking views.

Various adventure activities are possible at the harbour, including diving, paragliding and boating. Half-day boat trips cost UK£25 per person, including a barbecue lunch.

Sleeping & Eating

Sidelya Hotel (☎ 815 6051; fax 815 6052; Nasır Güneş Sokak 7; s/d UK£12/17) This is a good budget option, with some spacious basic rooms and views of the sea and the lighthouse on the pier.

Nostalgia Hotel (☎ 815 3079; fax 815 1376; Cafer Paşa Sokak 7; r per person from UK£20; ❄) The rooms are decorated in an old-fashioned style. If you are after some luxury, the Venus Suite, with its four-poster bed, is gorgeous. All rooms have TV, phone and air-con.

our pick **White Pearl Hotel** (☎ 815 4677; www.whitepearlhotel.com; Girne Limanı; s/d UK£40/55; ❄) The nine rooms in this boutique hotel are very good value. Individually decorated and bearing names of important Northern Cypriot towns, such as Salamis or Bellapais, they exude cleanliness and understated style. There are lovely views of the harbour.

For a romantic dinner, whisk your date into the alleys behind the harbour. **Set Restorante Italiano** (☎ 815 6008; Aga Cafér Sokak; mains from TL20) serves authentic Italian food in a Romanesque stone courtyard.

The waterfront has dozens of expensive tourist restaurants serving kebabs and Anatolian interpretations of a Greek meze. There's a cluster of cheaper kebab houses just west of Ramadan Cemil Meydani.

Getting There & Away

Buses and service taxis stop near the main roundabout. **Girneliler Seyahat** (☎ 866 1068) has regular minibuses to Lefkoşa (TL4, 30 minutes). Hourly **Virgo Trans/Göçmen** (☎ 815 7287) minibuses to Gazimağusa (TL6, one hour) leave from an office on the south side of Ramadan Cemil Meydani.

Kombos (☎ 815 1872; Ramadan Cemil Meydani) has service taxis to Lefkoşa (TL5, 30 minutes) and Gazimağusa (TL8, one hour).

The ferry terminal is a TL6 taxi ride from town – see p201 for boats to Turkey.

GÜZELYURT (MORFOU)

A backwater, even by Cyprus standards, Güzelyurt is a faded, citrus-producing town, close to a rugged, rocky coast. Few tourists come here, but the **Museum of Archaeology & Nature** (☎ 714 2202; Ecevit Caddesi; admission TL7; 8am-4.30pm) has the only collection of any size in the North. Nearby, lovely **Ayios Mamas Church** (Ecevit Caddesi) has been preserved in its original condition, largely through the efforts of the exiled bishop of Morfou. The restored amphitheatre at **Soli** (Soli Harabeleri; adult/child TL7/3; 9am-12.30pm & 1.30-4.45pm Jun–mid-Sep, 9am-7pm mid-Sep–May) is accessible by chartered taxi.

There's nowhere to stay, but Güzelyurt is an easy day trip from Lefkoşa by bus (TL4, 45 minutes) or service taxi (TL7, one hour).

GAZIMAĞUSA (FAMAGUSTA)
ΑΜΜΟΧΩΣΤΟΣ

pop 36,400

Despite burgeoning villa developments along the coast, Gazimağusa still feels medieval. Bound by mighty Venetian walls, the city was one of the last places to fall in the Ottoman invasion and little has changed here in centuries. The Old Town is dotted with Frankish and Venetian ruins and ferries run to Mersin on mainland Turkey.

Orientation & Information

There are three entrances through the city walls, two by the waterfront and one near the main roundabout. From the inland gate, İstiklal Caddesi runs down to Kemal Meydani (the main square), lined with shops, banks and foreign-exchange offices. The **tourist office** (☎ 366 2864; 7.30am-4pm Mon-Fri, 9am-6pm Sat & Sun) is housed in the Akkule Bastion at the south end of İstiklal Caddesi.

Sights

Gazimağusa is awash with Frankish ruins, and several medieval churches have been converted into mosques, including the famous **Lala Mustafa Paşa** (Erenler Sokak; adult/child TL7/3; outside prayer times) where the Frankish kings were crowned – it's probably the finest example of Gothic architecture in Cyprus.

Right on the city walls, **Othello's Tower** (Othello Kalesi; adult/child TL7/3; 9am-12.30pm & 1.30-4.45pm mid-Sep–May, 9am-8pm Jun–mid-Sep) is where the Venetian governor Cristofo Moro is said to have killed his wife Desdemona in a fit of jealous rage. The incident inspired Shakespeare's *Othello,* but the bard mistakenly assumed that Cristofo was a Moor, thereby adding an unexpected racial twist to the tale.

About 9km north of Gazimağusa are the impressive but poorly maintained Graeco-Roman ruins of **Salamis** (Salamis Harabeleri; adult/child TL9/5; 9am-12.30pm & 1.30-4.45pm mid-Sep–May, 9am-8pm Jun–mid-Sep). You can see mosaics, columns and a huge amphitheatre, and there's a gorgeous sandy beach here with interesting snorkelling. A return taxi from Gazimağusa will cost TL35.

Across the highway is the intriguing **Salamis Necropolis** (Salamis Mezarlık Alanı; ☎ 378 8331; adult/child TL5/3; 9am-12.30pm & 1.30-4.45pm mid-Sep–May, 9am-8pm Jun–mid-Sep), famous for its horse-chariot burials. Nearby, the **Monastery of St Barnabas** (☎ 378 8331; church & museum adult/child TL7/3; 9am-12.30pm & 1.30-4.45pm mid-Sep–May, 9am-8pm Jun–mid-Sep) has been opened as an 'icon museum', but most of the valuable treasures from the area vanished after 1974.

Sleeping & Eating

The camping ground near the ruins at Salamis is open to tourists intermittently – check with the tourist office.

Altun Tabya Hotel (☎ 366 2585; cnr Altun Tabya & Kizilkule Sokak; d TL50-60;) Tucked inside the city walls, this family-owned place has a collection of simple, spotless rooms. To get here, turn right after you pass through the inland gate.

Golden Set Pansiyon (☎ 0533 879 9052; Yeşil Deniz Sokak; s/d with air-con TL40/70;) Overlooking Othello's Tower, this old arched house has chintzy but comfortable rooms with cooking facilities. The owners are friendly but they don't speak much English.

Petek (☎ 366 7104; Yeşil Deniz Sokak 1; snacks & sweets from TL5) This is an Aladdin's Cave of a cake shop, selling sweet and savoury pastries, cakes, Turkish delight, and strong, sweet Turkish coffee.

Half a dozen pavement restaurants on the main square serve pizzas, burgers and other

WORTH THE TRIP: BÜYÜKKONUK ECOVILLAGE

Büyükkonuk is a small settlement at the bottom end of the Karpas Peninsula. Cyprus' first ecovillage, Büyükkonuk was selected to try and start up a fashion for sustainable development, agrotourism and an ecofriendly lifestyle. So far the village's 800 residents have used €1.8 million from USAID (United States Agency for International Development), the UN and Turkey since the beginning of the project to renovate a number of traditional buildings. The most notable is the **Old Olive Mill** (8am-8pm daily, admission free), on the main road through the village. Restored in 2007, the mill is an example of traditional local architecture that aims to revive and highlight the role of olive farming as the epicentre of Cypriot agricultural life. If you want to experience life in the village, you can stay at **Lois & Ismail Cemal's B&B** (www.ecotourismcyprus.com; r per person UK£16), where the decor is simple but activities are plentiful: you can learn how to make traditional food, explore one of the local walking trails or go birdwatching in spring. The Canadian–Cypriot couple also runs a traditional craft shop, where you can pick up some lovely souvenirs.

Anglo-American meals. For homestyle kebabs and halloumi pittas, there are several *salonus* (diners) on Liman Yolu, just north of the mosque.

Getting There & Away

İtimat (☎ 366 6666) minibuses to Lefkoşa (TL6, one hour) leave every half-hour from the main roundabout. **Virgo Trans/Göçmen** (☎ 366 4313) minibuses to Girne (TL5, one hour) leave hourly from Gazi Mustafa Kemal Bulvari.

Kombos (☎ 365 2623) run share taxis to Girne (TL6, one hour), leaving from Eşref Bitlis Caddesi, about 500m northwest of the ciy walls.

The ferry terminal is about 500m southeast of the centre – see p201 for information on ferries to Turkey. **KT Denizcilik** (☎ 366 5786) has an office on Bülent Ecevit Bulvarı.

KARPAS (KIRPAŞA) PENINSULA

For a taste of what Cyprus was like before partition, hire a car and head to the remote Karpas Peninsula. This wild area has barely been touched by tourism, but the tiny **tourist office** (☎ 374 4984; 9am-5pm) in the post office in Yeni Erenköy can point you towards archaic tombs and basilicas.

At the west end of the Karpas, reached via a winding, bumpy road, the swooningly romantic Crusader-era castle of **Kantara** (Kantara Kalesi; adult/child TL5/3; 9am-12.30pm & 1.30-4.45pm Jun–mid-Sep, 9am-5pm mid-Sep–May) hovers above the Mesaoria plain.

Over on the south coast, **Altinkum Beach** (aka Golden Beach or Turtle Beach) is a sea of golden dunes with hardly a human footprint on the sand. Turtles nest here from June to August. On the north coast, there's another nice beach and a ruined Roman/Byzantine basilica at **Ayios Filon**, and more ruined basilicas and beaches at **Aphendrika**.

Ayios Filon has the friendly **Oasis at Ayfilon** (☎ 0533 840 5082; www.oasishotelkarpas.com; s/d with shared bathroom UK£24/32, with private bathroom UK£32/38), a homely restaurant and guest house, right on the water beside the basilica.

The enclaved Greek Cypriot population here was able to protect some of the churches and monasteries after 1974, and you can see ancient icons in the slightly forlorn-looking monastery of **Apostolos Andreas** at the tip of the peninsula.

CYPRUS DIRECTORY

ACCOMMODATION

Double rooms in hotels or guest houses cost up to €50 (in the Republic) and up to UK£35 (in the North). En suite bathrooms and breakfast are included in the price, unless otherwise stated. There are Hostelling International (HI) affiliated hostels in Lefkosia (p184) and Larnaka (p187), but none in North Cyprus.

The Republic has six licensed camping grounds, including good sites at Polis, Plateia Troodos and Governor's Beach (near Lemesos) – expect to pay from €4 for two people and a tent. The four official camping grounds in the North are often closed, but wild camping is popular in the Karpas.

Accommodation prices are listed for the high season (August).

Smoking is widespread and few places have nonsmoking areas, though hotels have nonsmoking rooms, available upon request.

ACTIVITIES

All the seaside resorts offer water sports such as banana-boat rides, scuba dives, boat trips and paragliding. The Akamas Peninsula and Troodos Massif in the Republic and the Karpas Peninsula and Kyrenia Mountains in North Cyprus offer fantastic hiking and mountain biking. The European Long Distance path from Pafos to Larnaka connects with similar trails across Europe – pick up the *European Long Distance Path* brochure from a CTO office or the visitor centre in Plateia Troodos.

See p201 for information on mountain biking in Cyprus.

BOOKS

To understand the glory that was undivided Cyprus, read Colin Thubron's *Journey into Cyprus* or Lawrence Durrell's *Bitter Lemons,* set around Bellapais. Brendan O'Malley and Ian Craig's *The Cyprus Conspiracy* explores American collusion in the partition of Cyprus. Reconciliation and understanding is explored in *Echoes from the Dead Zone,* by Yiannis Papadakis, describing the author's first journey across the divide.

BUSINESS HOURS

Banks are generally open from 8.30am to 12.30pm Monday to Friday, plus 3.15pm to 4.45pm on Monday afternoons in the Republic. Government offices are open from 7.30am to 2.30pm on weekdays and 3pm to 6pm on Thursday afternoons (or Monday afternoons in North Cyprus). Shops close early on Wednesdays and Saturdays, and many places close at lunchtime in summer in both the Republic and North Cyprus. Almost all restaurants are open for lunch and dinner daily, but smaller places close on Sundays. Throughout Cyprus, restaurants are open from 11am to 2pm and from 7.30pm to 11pm daily.

CHILDREN

Most attractions in Cyprus offer discounts for children, and hotels can arrange extra beds in rooms for a small additional charge. The coastal resorts have the most to offer children – Agia Napa (p187) and Pafos (p191) are packed with family-friendly attractions and activities.

CUSTOMS REGULATIONS

The Republic joined the EU in 2004; see the Regional Directory, p945, for standard EU allowances. In North Cyprus you can bring in 500g of tobacco or 400 cigarettes, plus 1L of spirits or wine and 100mL of perfume duty free.

ELECTRICITY

The electricity supply in Cyprus is 240V at 50Hz. Most places use mainly British three-pin plugs.

EMBASSIES & CONSULATES

The Republic of Cyprus is represented worldwide, while North Cyprus has just a few overseas offices. See p200 for visa information.

Countries with diplomatic representation in Lefkosia in the Republic of Cyprus include the following:

Australia (Map p182; ☎ 2275 3001/3; Leoforos Stasinou & Annis Komninis 4, 2nd fl)
France (Map p182; ☎ 2258 5300; Saktouri 14-16, Agiou Omologites)
Germany (off Map p182; ☎ 2245 1145; Nikitara 10)
Greece (Map p182; ☎ 2244 5111; Leoforos Lordou Vyronos 8-10)
Italy (off Map p182; ☎ 2235 7635; 25th Martiou 11, Egkomi)
Spain (off Map p182; ☎ 2245 0410; Strovolou 32, Strovolos)
UK (off Map p182; ☎ 2286 1100; Alexandrou Palli)
USA (Map p182; ☎ 2239 3939; Gonia Metochiou & Ploutarchou, Egkomi)

Countries with diplomatic representation in Lefkoşa in North Cyprus include:

Australia (Map p194; ☎ 227 7332; Güner Türkmen Sokak 20)
Germany (off Map p194; ☎ 227 5161; 28 Kasım Sokak 15)
Turkey (Map p194; ☎ 227 2314; Bedreddin Demirel Caddesi)
UK (Map p194; ☎ 227 4938; Mehmet Akif Caddesi 23)
USA (off Map p194; ☎ 227 8295; Saran Sokak 6, K Kaymakli)

FESTIVALS & EVENTS

The Republic celebrates numerous festivals, and Christian feast days are also celebrated with aplomb. The useful *List of Events* brochure is available from CTO offices and it's well worth picking up. Events that are held every year in the Republic include the following:

Epiphany (6 January) Priests bless houses with holy water, and a sacred cross is thrown into the sea by the archbishop and retrieved by local youths everywhere in the Republic.
Apokreo (2nd week of February) Two weeks of pre-Lenten feasting all over Cyprus and a big carnival in Lemesos (p188).
Easter (March/April) Huge Holy Week celebrations with special meals, religious processions and bonfires for the symbolic burning of Judas.
Kataklysmos (50 days after Easter) Coastal towns commemorate the biblical flood by throwing water around, feasting and singing improvised songs.
Ancient Greek Drama Festival (July/August) Open-air performances of Greek dramas at Kourion (p189) and other amphitheatres.

The main celebrations in North Cyprus are linked to Muslim holidays.

HOLIDAYS

Holidays in the Republic are the same as those in Greece (p832), with the addition of **Greek Cypriot Day** (1 April) and **Cyprus Independence Day** (1 October).

North Cyprus has a three-day holiday to celebrate the end of Ramazan, starting on 21 September 2009, 11 August 2010 and 1 August 2011. There is also a four-day holiday for the Muslim festival of Kurban, starting on 27 November in 2009, 16 November 2010 and 6 November 2011. Annual holidays:

National Sovereignty/Children's Day 23 April (Republic)
Labour Day 1 May (Republic and North Cyprus)
Youth & Sport Day 19 May (Republic and North Cyprus)
Peace & Freedom Day 20 July (Republic and North Cyprus)
TMT Day 1 August (North Cyprus)
Victory Day 30 August (North Cyprus)
Turkish Republic Day 29 October (North Cyprus)
Proclamation of the Turkish Republic of Northern Cyprus Day 15 November (North Cyprus)

INTERNET RESOURCES

As well as the tourist department sites, useful resources include www.traveltocyprus.com.cy and www.kypros.org for the Republic, and www.cypnet.co.uk/cyradise/index.html and www.northcyprus.net for North Cyprus.

MEDIA

English-language newspapers in the Republic include **Cyprus Weekly** (www.cyprusweekly.com.cy) and **Cyprus Mail** (www.cyprus-mail.com). *Cyprus Today* and the **Turkish Daily News** (www.turkishdailynews.com) are the main English-language newspapers in North Cyprus. Numerous radio stations on both sides of the line play international pop music with English-language news broadcasts. In the Republic, you can see English TV news on CYBC2 at 9pm daily.

MONEY

The Republic's currency is the euro (€). Foreign exchange is mainly handled by banks, except in the coastal resorts. Most currencies and travellers cheques are accepted and almost all banks have ATMs that take international cards.

The unit of currency in North Cyprus is the revalued Turkish lira (TL), but UK pounds and euros are widely accepted. Banks have exchange facilities and ATMs, and private foreign-exchange offices (*döviz*) can be found in all towns.

TELEPHONE

In the Republic (country code ☎357), phone booths use CYTA phonecards, which are available from shops. Calling abroad with these cards costs €0.0621 per minute to a landline and €0.15 per minute to mobile phones. For more info, see www.cyta.com.cy.

In North Cyprus, pay phones take KKTC Telekomünikasyon phonecards, which are available from shops – calls cost TL0.80 per minute to Europe and TL1.50 to the USA. To call North Cyprus from abroad, first dial ☎90 (the country code for Turkey), then the regional code ☎392, and then the number.

Roaming GSM phones can be used all over Cyprus. Prepaid phone SIM packs are available from shops and phone offices.

To call North Cyprus from the Republic, dial its country code followed by the local number. To call the Republic from North Cyprus, call its country code followed by the local number. Regional area codes form part of the phone number throughout Cyprus.

EMERGENCY NUMBERS

- Ambulance ☎Republic 199, North Cyprus 112
- Fire ☎Republic 199, North Cyprus 199
- Police ☎Republic 199, North Cyprus 155

CYPRUS

CROSSING THE LINE

Border restrictions in Cyprus were further relaxed in 2005, allowing overnight trips across the Green Line. In theory foreign tourists are permitted to cross from south to north (or vice versa) and stay for up to three months, but it's not currently possible to enter Cyprus on one side of the line and leave from the other. Pedestrian crossings are at Ledra St and Ledra Palace Hotel in Lefkosia. Cars can cross at Agios Dometios/Kermia (near Lefkosia), Vrysoulles (near Agia Napa) and Astrometiris/Zohdia (near Güzelyurt). Temporary car insurance is available at the border. Hire cars can only be taken from south to north, not the other way. The situation is volatile, so check locally before attempting to cross.

TOURIST INFORMATION

The **Cyprus Tourism Organisation** (CTO; www.visitcyprus.org.cy) has offices at Larnaka and Pafos airport and in all major towns in the Republic, with excellent maps and information leaflets.

North Cyprus Tourism (www.holidayinnorthcyprus.com) has offices in Lefkoşa, Gazimağusa, Girne, Ercan airport and Yeni Erenköy, with limited brochures and information.

VISAS

Nationals of Australia, New Zealand, the US, Canada, Japan and all European Economic Area countries can enter and stay in either the Republic or North Cyprus for up to three months without a visa. Citizens of Greece, the Republic of Cyprus and Armenia need a visa for North Cyprus, and Turkish citizens need a visa for the Republic.

With the thawing of political relations, tourists are now allowed to cross the Green Line and stay on the opposite side. No special visa is required and immigration stamps are made on a separate piece of paper to avoid future problems entering the Republic – see the boxed text, above, for more information.

CYPRUS

TRANSPORT IN CYPRUS

Cyprus is a convenient gateway between Europe and the Middle East. There are air connections to major cities in Europe and the Middle East, and ferries between North Cyprus and Turkey. It has recently become much easier to travel between the Republic of Cyprus and North Cyprus, but you must enter and leave Cyprus from the same side of the Green Line. See the boxed text, left, for more information.

GETTING THERE & AWAY

Ferry services to the Republic are currently suspended, so almost all travellers arrive by air. Departure tax varies with the destination and is always included in the ticket price.

Air

The Republic's international airports are at Larnaka and Pafos. The main airport in North Cyprus is Ercan, but flights sometimes land at Geçitkale.

TO/FROM REPUBLIC OF CYPRUS

There are budget, scheduled and charter flights from major cities throughout Europe and the Middle East with Cyprus Airways as well as other carriers – fares from London to Cyprus cost between UK£80 and £200, depending on the season. As well as the following scheduled airlines, budget carriers **easyJet** (U2; ☎ +44 871 244 2366; www.easyjet.com), **Aegean Airlines** (A3; ☎ 2265 4000; www.aegeanair.com), **Monarch** (ZB; ☎ 800 95242; http://flights.monarch.co.uk) and **Eurocypria** (UI; ☎ 8000 0809; www.eurocypria.com) have discount flights to Larnaka from the UK, Greece and central Europe.

Airlines flying to the Republic:

British Airways (BA; ☎ 2276 1166; www.britishairways.com)
Cyprus Airways (CY; ☎ 2266 3054; www.cyprusairways.com)
Egypt Air (MS; ☎ 2250 9000; www.egyptair.com.eg)
El Al Israel Airlines (LY; ☎ 2557 4180; www.elal.co.il)
Emirates (EK; ☎ 2281 7816; www.emirates.com)
Gulf Air (GF; ☎ 2237 4064; www.gulfairco.com)
KLM (KL; ☎ 2267 1616; www.klm.com)
Lufthansa (LH; ☎ 2287 3330; www.lufthansa.com)
Olympic Airlines (OA; ☎ 2271 6500; www.olympicairlines.com)

TO/FROM NORTH CYPRUS

Flights to Ercan airport in North Cyprus start in Turkey so you must fly there first. Fares from London to Ercan (via İstanbul) start at UK£250. A return ticket to Ercan from İstanbul costs around US$150.

Airlines flying to North Cyprus:

Atlasjet (KK; ☎ 231 4188; www.atl asjet.com)

Cyprus Turkish Airlines (YK; ☎ 227 3820; www.kthy.net)
Turkish Airlines (TK; ☎ 227 1061; www.thy.com)

Sea

Services to the Republic's main port at Lemesos are currently suspended. If they start up again, contact **Salamis Shipping** (☎ 2589 9999) and **Louis Cruise Lines** (☎ 7777 8555).

There are several ferry routes to mainland Turkey from North Cyprus. **KT Denizcilik** (Cyprus Turkish Shipping; ☎ 366 5786) sails from Gazimağusa to Mersin (one-way TL65, 12 hours) on Tuesdays, Thursdays and Sundays, returning the following day.

Fergün (☎ 815 4993) and **Akgünler** (☎ 815 6002) both have daily fast passenger ferries and slow car ferries between Girne and Taşucu (TL60 to TL71 per person, two to five hours). In summer there's also a twice-weekly ferry between Girne and Alanya (TL75, four to five hours) on Wednesdays and Sundays.

GETTING AROUND

Bicycle

Cyprus has loads of quiet back roads for cyclists, and the Troodos Massif, Kyrenia Mountains and the Karpas and Akamas Peninsulas are perfectly suited for mountain biking. The CTO produces the occasionally inaccurate *Cycling Routes* booklet or you can contact the **Cyprus Cycling Federation** (☎ 2266 3344; Kimonos 1, Egkomi, Lefkosia) for information.

Mountain bikes can be rented in Plateia Troodos and Polis and in many coastal resorts.

Bus

Inexpensive buses and minibuses are operated by various private companies on both sides of the Green Line – contact details for bus companies are listed under individual towns. Buses link all major cities and many villages. The last daily service on most routes leaves around 5pm. Note that few buses run on Sundays in the Republic.

Car & Motorcycle

You can hire cars and motorbikes in most towns, and rates start at around €25 per day for cars and €10 per day for mopeds and motorcycles. Most car and motorcycle licences are valid in the Republic, but only British and international licences are accepted in North Cyprus. The minimum age for hiring a car is 21; drivers under 25 pay extra insurance fees. You must be 17 or over to ride a motorcycle (18 or over for engines bigger than 50cc); these restrictions apply in both the Republic and North Cyprus.

Cars hired in the Republic can be temporarily insured for travel within North Cyprus at the border, but hire cars cannot be taken in the opposite direction. If you travel with your car to Cyprus on the ferry from Turkey, you are eligible to obtain a three-month duty waiver and local insurance upon your arrival.

For assistance, contact **Cyprus Automobile Association** (☎ 22 31 32 33; www.cyprusaa.org)

Taxi

Service taxis run between major towns, leaving when they have seven passengers. All service taxis in the Republic are run by **Travel & Express** (☎ 7777 7474; www.travelexpress.com.cy) – you can go directly to the depots or call ahead to arrange a pick-up. In the north, **Kombos** (☎ 227 2929) connects Lefkoşa, Girne and Gazimağusa.

There are urban taxis in all large towns, and rural taxis connect rural villages.

France

Few countries in Europe provoke such a passionate panoply of responses as La Belle France. Love it or loathe it, everyone seems to have their own opinion about this Gallic goliath. Snooty, sexy, superior, chic, infuriating, arrogant, officious and inspired in equal measures, the French have long lived according to their own idiosyncratic rules, and if the rest of the world doesn't always see eye to eye with them, well, *tant pis* (too bad) – that's just the price you pay for being a culinary trendsetter, artistic pioneer and all-round cultural icon.

If ever there was a country of contradictions, this is it. In many ways France is a deeply traditional place: castles, chateaux and ancient churches litter the landscape, centuries-old principles of rich food, fine wine and joie de vivre underpin everyday life, and any decision to meddle with the status quo is guaranteed to bring out half the nation in a placard-waving protest.

But it's also a place that never seems content to rest on its historic laurels. France has one of the most multicultural make-ups of any European country, not to mention a well-deserved reputation for artistic experimentation and architectural invention (just take a look at the futuristic Viaduc de Millau or the superfast new AGV *(automotrice grande vitesse)* trains. And with their vertically challenged, personality-driven, supermodel-marrying new president Nicolas Sarkozy advocating the need for profound social and industrial change in years to come, there are bound to be a few French fireworks on the horizon. Time to join the party.

FAST FACTS

- **Area** 551,000 sq km
- **Capital** Paris
- **Currency** euro (€); US$1 = €0.73; UK£1 = €1.06; A$1 = €0.50; ¥100 = €0.76; NZ$1 = €0.41
- **Famous for** croissants, cheese, food, wine, the Eiffel Tower, the Alps, bad driving, the Gallic shrug
- **Official language** French
- **Phrases** *s'il vous plaît* (please), *merci* (thank you), *parlez-vous Anglais?* (do you speak English?), *excusez-moi* (excuse me), *ou est?* (where is?)
- **Population** 63.4 million
- **Telephone codes** country code ☎ 33; international access code ☎ 00
- **Visas** not needed for citizens of the EU, Australia, the US, Japan and most other Western nations; see p337

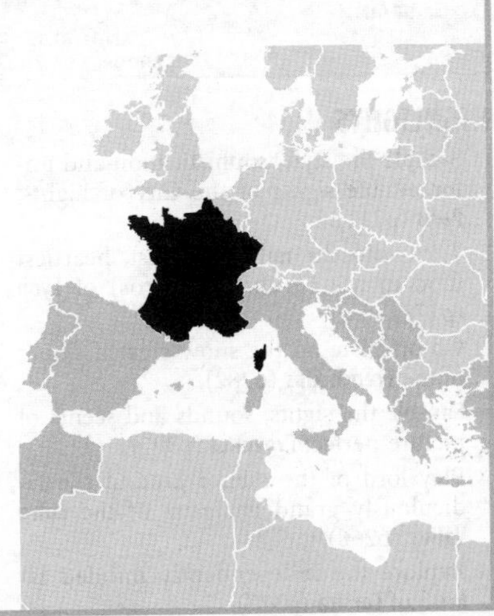

FRANCE

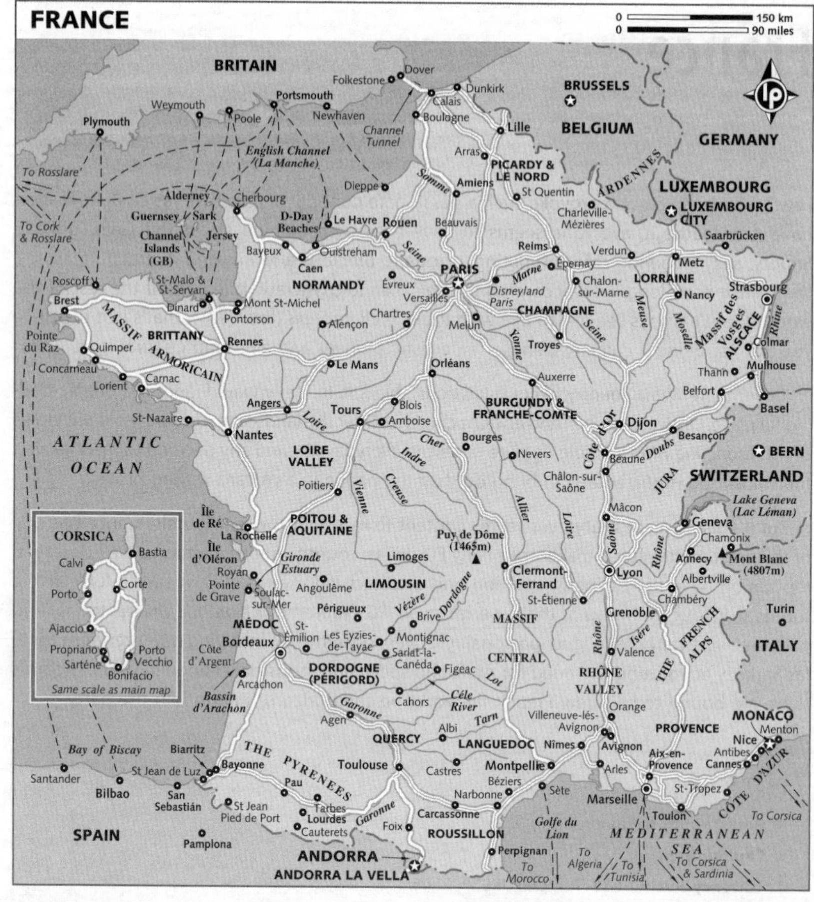

HIGHLIGHTS

- Sample the style, sophistication and unforgettable sights of the City of Lights, **Paris** (p211).
- Tuck into the nation's halest, heartiest food in the *bouchons* (bistros) of **Lyon** (p278).
- Go off-piste on the snow-crested slopes of the **French Alps** (p282).
- Sample the sights, sounds and scents of picture-perfect **Provence** (p307).
- Play lord of the manor around the ridiculously grand chateaux of the **Loire Valley** (p266).
- Explore the independently minded island of **Corsica** (p327).

ITINERARIES

- **One week** Every French adventure has to begin with a few days exploring the capital city of Paris. There are enough sights and attractions to fill a lifetime of visits, but in a week you'll have enough time to visit the Louvre, the Eiffel Tower, the Musée d'Orsay, Notre Dame, Montmartre and a boat trip along the Seine, with just enough time left over for a field trip to Normandy, Monet's garden at Giverny, and Versailles.
- **Two weeks** Once you've ticked off Paris, your best bet is to concentrate on exploring one region rather than trying to do everything in a whistlestop dash. High-speed TGV *(train à grande vitesse)*

trains zip from Paris to practically every province: for prehistoric interest, head for the Dordogne; for architectural splendour, you can't top the Loire Valley; for typical French atmosphere, try the quiet villages of Provence; and for sunshine and seafood, the Côte d'Azur is the only place to be.

CLIMATE & WHEN TO GO

France's climate is generally temperate and mild except in mountainous areas. The Atlantic brings rain and wind to the northwest. The pleasant Mediterranean climate extends from the southern coast as far inland as the southern Alps, the Massif Central and the eastern Pyrenees, but the mistral winds can sometimes bring sudden storms and heavy showers.

France is at its best in spring. Summer can be baking hot, especially in the south away from the coast. Even Paris can swelter in July and August. It can also be a crowded, traffic-choked and expensive time to travel, especially around the Mediterranean. Autumn by contrast is mellow and pleasant everywhere, and swimming and sunbathing are often viable until October. Winter provides excellent winter sport opportunities in the mountains.

See p23 and p944 for general information about the region's climate.

CONNECTIONS: MOVING ON FROM FRANCE

France is well connected to practically everywhere in Western and Mediterranean Europe. High-speed trains travel from Paris to many major European cities, including Milan, Brussels, Cologne, Amsterdam, Frankfurt and Zürich, as well as London via the Channel Tunnel/Eurostar service. Ferry links from Cherbourg, St-Malo, Calais and other north-coast ports travel to England and Ireland, while ferries from Marseille, Nice and Toulon provide regular links with seaside towns in Corsica, Italy and North Africa. Regular bus and rail links cross the French–Spanish border via the Pyrenees, and the French–Italian border via the Alps and the southern Mediterranean coast. For more information, see p337.

HISTORY

Prehistory

Neanderthals were the first to live in France (about 90,000 to 40,000 BC). Cro-Magnons followed 35,000 years ago and left behind cave paintings and engravings, especially around the Vézère Valley (see the boxed text, p294). Neolithic people (about 7500 to 4000 years ago) created France's incredible menhirs (standing stones) and dolmens (megalithic tombs), especially in Brittany (p253).

The Celtic Gauls arrived between 1500 and 500 BC. They were superseded by the Romans for around five centuries after Julius Caesar took control around 52 BC, until the Franks and Alemanii overran the country.

The Frankish Merovingian and Carolingian dynasties ruled from the 5th to the 10th century AD. In 732 Charles Martel defeated the Moors, preventing France from falling under Muslim rule. Martel's grandson, Charlemagne (742–814), extended the power and boundaries of the kingdom and was crowned Holy Roman Emperor in 800.

The Early French Kings

The tale of William the Conqueror's invasion of England in 1066 is recorded in the Bayeux Tapestry (p248), sowing the seeds for a fierce rivalry between France and England that lasted three centuries, reaching its height during the Hundred Years War (1337–1453).

Following the occupation of Paris by the English-allied dukes of Burgundy, John Plantagenet was made regent of France on behalf of England's King Henry VI in 1422. Less than a decade later he was crowned king at Paris' Notre Dame cathedral (p221). Luckily for the French, a 17-year-old warrior called Jeanne d'Arc (Joan of Arc) came along in 1429. She persuaded Charles VII that she had a divine mission from God to expel the English from France. Following her capture by the Burgundians and subsequent sale to the English in 1430, Joan was convicted of witchcraft and heresy and burned at the stake in Rouen, on the site now marked by the city's cathedral (p246).

The arrival of Italian Renaissance culture during the reign of François I (r 1515–47) saw the construction of some of France's finest chateaux, especially in the Loire Valley.

The 30-year period from 1562 to 1598 was one of the bloodiest periods in French history. Ideological disagreement between

HOW MUCH?

- **Bottle of table wine** €5
- **Baguette sandwich** €3.50 to €6
- **Two-course lunch menu** €12 to €15
- **Espresso** €0.90
- **Public transport ticket** €1.50

LONELY PLANET INDEX

- **1L petrol** €1.14
- **1L bottled water** €0.90
- **Beer (25cL, at a bar)** €3 to €3.50
- **Souvenir T-shirt** €10
- **Street snack (crêpe)** €2 to €4

the Huguenots (French Protestants) and the Catholic monarchy escalated into full-scale war – a conflict known as the French Wars of Religion.

The Sun King

Louis XIV, Le Roi Soleil (the Sun King), ascended the throne in 1643, and spent the next 60 years in a series of bloody wars. He also constructed the fabulous palace at Versailles.

Louis XV ascended to the throne in 1715 and shifted the royal court back to Paris. As the 18th century progressed, the ancien régime became increasingly out of step with the needs of the country. Antiestablishment and anticlerical ideas expressed by Voltaire, Rousseau and Montesquieu further threatened the royal regime.

Revolution to Republic

Social and economic crisis marked the 18th century. The general mood of discontent among the French populace flared into violence when a Parisian mob stormed the prison at Bastille (now a roundabout). France was declared a constitutional monarchy, but before long the moderate republican Girondins lost power to the radical Jacobins. Louis XVI was publicly guillotined in January 1793 on Paris' place de la Concorde.

The Reign of Terror between September 1793 and July 1794 saw religious freedoms revoked, churches closed, cathedrals turned into 'Temples of Reason' and thousands beheaded. In the chaos a dashing young Corsican general named Napoleon Bonaparte (1769–1821) stepped from the shadows.

In 1799 Napoleon assumed power and in 1804 he was crowned emperor of France at Notre Dame. Napoleon waged several wars in which France gained control over most of Europe. Two years later, Allied armies entered Paris, exiled Napoleon to Elba and restored the French throne at the Congress of Vienna (1814–15).

In 1815 Napoleon escaped, entering Paris on 20 May. His glorious 'Hundred Days' back in power ended with the Battle of Waterloo and his exile to the island of St Helena, where he died in 1821.

Second Republic to Second Empire

The subsequent years were marked by civil strife and political unrest, with monarchists and revolutionaries vying for power. Louis-Philippe (r 1830–48), a constitutional monarch, was chosen by parliament but ousted by the 1848 Revolution. The Second Republic was established and Napoleon's nephew, Louis Napoleon Bonaparte, was elected president. But in 1851 Louis Napoleon led a coup d'état and proclaimed himself Emperor Napoleon III of the Second Empire (1852–70).

France enjoyed significant economic growth. Paris was transformed under urban planner Baron Haussmann (1809–91), who created the 12 huge boulevards radiating from the Arc de Triomphe (p223). But Napoleon III embroiled France in various catastrophic conflicts, including the Crimean War (1853–56) and the Franco-Prussian War (1870–71), which ended with Prussia taking the emperor prisoner. Upon hearing the news, defiant Parisian masses took to the streets demanding that a republic be declared – the Third Republic.

The World Wars

The 20th century was marked by two of the bloodiest conflicts in the nation's history, beginning with the Great War (WWI). The northeastern part of France bore the brunt of the devastating trench warfare between Allied and German forces: 1.3 million French soldiers were killed and almost one million injured, and the battlefields of the Somme (see the boxed text, p245) have become powerful symbols of the unimaginable costs and ultimate futility of modern warfare.

Following the end of the war, the Treaty of Versailles imposed heavy reparations on the defeated nations, including the return of Alsace-Lorraine, which the French had lost to Germany in 1871. These punitive terms sowed the seeds for future unrest, when the fanatic leader Adolf Hitler rose to power and promised to restore the German nation's pride, power and territory. Despite constructing a lavish series of defences (the so-called Maginot Line) along its German border, France was rapidly overrun and surrendered in June 1940. The occupying Germans divided France into an Occupied Zone (in the north and west) and a puppet state in the south, centring on the spa town of Vichy.

The British Army was driven from France during the Battle of Dunkirk (p245) in 1940. Four years later, on 6 June 1944, Allied forces stormed the coastline of Normandy (p250) in the D-Day landings. The bloody Battle of Normandy followed and Paris was liberated on 25 August.

The Fourth Republic

In the first postwar election in 1945, the wartime leader of the Free French, Général Charles de Gaulle, was appointed head of the government, but quickly sensed that the tide was turning against him and in 1946 he resigned.

Progress rebuilding France's shattered economy and infrastructure was slow. By 1947 France was forced to turn to the USA for loans as part of the Marshall Plan to rebuild Europe. The economy gathered steam in the 1950s but the decade marked the end of French colonialism in Vietnam and in Algeria. The Algerian war of independence (1954–62) was particularly brutal, characterised by torture and massacre meted out to nationalist Algerians.

The Modern Era

De Gaulle assumed the presidency again in 1958, followed by his prime minister Georges Pompidou (1911–74) in 1969, Valéry Giscard d'Estaing (in power 1969–74), François Mitterrand (in power 1981–95), and the centre-right president Jacques Chirac, who (among other things) oversaw the country's adoption of the euro in 1999, and remained in power until 2007.

In October and November 2005, France was rocked by several weeks of running battles, sparked off by the deaths of two North African teenagers who were electrocuted while attempting to hide from the police. The following year, huge student demonstrations hit the streets in protest against a law designed to shake up France's labour market, forcing the government into an embarrassing legislative U-turn.

The presidential race in 2007 was contested by socialist Ségolène Royal (the first female presidential candidate) and the dynamic and highly ambitious Nicolas Sarkozy of Chirac's centre-right UMP (Union pour un Mouvement Populaire; Union for a Popular Movement) party. Sarko (as he was quickly dubbed by the popular press) eventually won, with 53% of votes compared with Royal's 47%. Sarkozy's first period in office has been dogged by controversy, especially thanks to his infamous split with his second wife in order to marry the sexy chanteuse and supermodel Carla Bruni.

But beyond Sarkozy's high-profile private life, there have been some major political developments too, including the banning of smoking in public places in 2007, and the ratification of a new EU treaty in 2008.

PEOPLE

France is not very densely populated – 107 people inhabit every square kilometre (compared with 235 in Germany, 240 in the UK and 116 in the EU), although 20% of the national population is packed into Paris' greater metropolitan area.

In keeping with European trends, France's overall population is ageing: on 1 January 2006 almost 22% of the population was aged 60 or older (compared with 16% in 1950, 17% in 1980 and 19% in 1990). This demographic phenomenon is less marked in urban areas like Paris and Lyon and on the Mediterranean coast.

Of the country's 4.3 million foreign residents, 13% are Algerian, 13% Portuguese, 12% Moroccan and 9% Italian. Only one-third has French citizenship, which is not conferred at birth but is subject to various administrative requirements.

RELIGION

Since the Revolution, secular France has maintained a rigid distinction between Church and State. Some 55% of French people identify themselves as Catholic, but no more than 10% attend church regularly. Another one million are Protestant, while France's Muslim community is around 5 million (12% of the country's population). Over half of France's 600,000-strong Jewish population (Europe's largest) lives in and around Paris.

ARTS

Literature

France has made huge contributions to European literature. The philosophical work of Voltaire (1694–1778) and Jean-Jacques Rousseau dominated the 18th century. A century later the poems and novels of Victor Hugo – *Les Misérables* and *Notre Dame de Paris* (The Hunchback of Notre Dame) among them – became landmarks of French Romanticism.

In 1857 two literary landmarks were published: *Madame Bovary* by Gustave Flaubert (1821–80) and Charles Baudelaire's collection of poems, *Les Fleurs du Mal* (The Flowers of Evil). Émile Zola (1840–1902) meanwhile strove to convert novel-writing from an art to a science in his series *Les Rougon-Macquart*.

Symbolists Paul Verlaine (1844–96) and Stéphane Mallarmé (1842–98) aimed to express mental states through their poetry. Verlaine's poems, with those of Arthur Rimbaud (1854–91), are seen as French literature's first modern poems.

After WWII, the existentialist movement developed around the lively debates of Jean-Paul Sartre (1905–80), Simone de Beauvoir (1908–86) and Albert Camus (1913–60) over coffee and cigarettes in Paris' Left Bank cafes.

Contemporary authors include Françoise Sagan, Pascal Quignard, Anna Gavalda, Emmanuel Carrère, Stéphane Bourguignon and Martin Page, whose novel *Comment Je Suis Devenu Stupide* (How I Became Stupid) explores a 25-year-old Sorbonne student's methodical attempt to become stupid.

Cinema

Cinematographic pioneers the Lumière brothers shot the world's first-ever motion picture in March 1895 and French film flourished in the following decades. The post-WWII nouvelle vague (new wave) filmmakers, such as Claude Chabrol, Jean-Luc Godard and François Truffaut, pioneered the advent of modern cinema, using fractured narratives, documentary camerawork and highly personal subjects.

Big-name stars, slick production values and nostalgia were the dominant motifs in the 1980s, as filmmakers switched to costume dramas, comedies and 'heritage movies'. Claude Berri's depiction of prewar Provence in *Jean de Florette* (1986), Jean-Paul Rappeneau's *Cyrano de Bergerac* (1990) and *Bon Voyage* (2003), set in 1940s Paris – all starring France's best-known (and biggest-nosed) actor, Gérard Depardieu – found huge audiences in France and abroad.

La Haine (1995) directed by Mathieu Kassovitz, documented the bleak reality of life in the Parisian suburbs, and looks even more relevant in the wake of recent ethnic riots. At the other end of the spectrum, *Le Fabuleux Destin de Amélie Poulain* (*Amélie;* 2001) is a feel-good story about a Parisian do-gooder, directed by Jean-Pierre Jeunet, and was a massive international hit.

One of the biggest box-office hits of recent years was *Bienvenue chez les Ch'tis* (2008), which debunks grim stereotypes about the industrialised regions of the north of France with high jinks and hilarity.

Music

French musical luminaries – such as Charles Gounod (1818–93), César Franck (1822–90) and *Carmen* creator Georges Bizet (1838–75) among them – were a dime a dozen in the 19th century. Claude Debussy (1862–1918) revolutionised classical music with *Prélude à l'Après-Midi d'un Faune* (Prelude to the Afternoon of a Faun); while Maurice Ravel (1875–1937) peppered his work, including *Boléro,* with sensuousness and tonal colour.

Jazz hit 1920s Paris, which post-WWI hoisted the likes of Sidney Bechet, Kenny Clarke, Bud Powell and Dexter Gordon.

The *chanson française* (a tradition dating from medieval troubadours) was revived in the 1930s by Edith Piaf and Charles Trenet. In the 1950s the Left Bank cabarets nurtured *chansonniers* (cabaret singers) such as Léo Ferré, Georges Brassens, Claude Nougaro, Jacques Brel and Serge Gainsbourg.

French pop music has evolved massively since the 1960s *yéyé* (imitative rock) days of Johnny Hallyday. Particularly strong is world music, from Algerian *rai* and other North African music (artists include Natacha Atlas) to Senegalese *mbalax* (Youssou N'Dour) and West Indian zouk (Kassav, Zouk Machine). One musician who combines many of these elements is Paris-born Manu Chao (www.manuchao.net).

Electronic music from Daft Punk and Air has found a global following, while French rap continues to break new ground: pioneered in the 1990s by MC Solaar and continued by young French rappers such as Disiz La Peste, Monsieur R, Rohff (www.roh2f.com), the trio Malekal Morte and Marseille's hugely successful home-grown IAM (www.iam.tm.fr).

Architecture

Southern France is the place to find France's Gallo-Roman legacy, especially at the Pont du Gard (p305), and the amphitheatres in Nîmes (p304) and Arles (see the boxed text, p314).

Several centuries later, architects adopted Gallo-Roman motifs in roman (Romanesque) masterpieces such as Poitier's Église Notre Dame la Grande (p297).

Impressive 12th-century Gothic structures include Avignon's pontifical palace (p314), Chartres' cathedral (p241), and of course, Notre Dame in Paris (p221).

Art nouveau (1850–1910) combined iron, brick, glass and ceramics in new ways. See it for yourself at Paris' metro entrances and in the Musée d'Orsay (p216).

Contemporary buildings to look out for include the once-reviled (but now much-revered) Centre Pompidou (p223) and IM Pei's glass pyramid (p222) at the Louvre. In the provinces, notable buildings include Strasbourg's European Parliament, a 1920s art deco swimming pool–turned–art museum in Lille (p242) and the stunning new Musée des Confluences in Lyon (p280).

Painting

An extraordinary flowering of artistic talent occurred in 19th- and 20th-century France. The Impressionists, who endeavoured to capture the ever-changing aspects of reflected light, included Edouard Manet, Claude Monet, Edgar Degas, Camille Pisarro, and Pierre-Auguste Renoir. They were followed by the likes of Paul Cézanne (who lived in Aix-en-Provence; see p311) and Paul Gauguin, as well as the fauvist Henry Matisse (a Niçois resident; see p315) and cubists including Spanish-born Pablo Picasso and Georges Braque (1882–1963).

ENVIRONMENT

The Land

Hexagon-shaped France is the largest country in Europe after Russia and Ukraine. The country's 3200km-long coastline ranges from chalk cliffs (Normandy) to fine sand (Atlantic coast) and pebbly beaches (Mediterranean coast).

Europe's highest peak, Mont Blanc (4807m), crowns the French Alps along France's eastern border, while the rugged Pyrenees define France's 450km-long border with Spain, peaking at 3404m. The country's major river systems include the Garonne, Rhône, Seine, and France's longest river, the Loire.

Wildlife

France has more mammals (around 110) than any other country in Europe. Couple this with 363 bird species, 30 types of amphibian, 36 varieties of reptile and 72 kinds of fish, and wildlife-watchers are in paradise. Several distinctive animals can still be found in the Alps and Pyrenees, including the marmot, chamois (mountain antelope), *bouquetin* (Alpine ibex) and mouflon (wild mountain sheep), introduced in the 1950s. The *loup* (wolf) disappeared from France in the 1930s, but was reintroduced to the Parc National du Mercantour in 1992. The *aigle royal* (golden eagle) is a rare but hugely rewarding sight in the French mountain parks.

National Parks

The proportion of land protected in France is low relative to the country's size: six small *parcs nationaux* (national parks) fully protect just 0.8% of the country. Another 7% is protected by 42 *parcs naturals régionaux* (regional parks) and a further 0.4% by 136 smaller *réserves naturelles* (nature reserves).

Environmental Issues

Summer forest fires are an annual hazard. Wetlands, essential for the survival of a great number of species, are shrinking. More than two million hectares – 3% of French territory – are considered important wetlands, but only 4% of this land is protected.

France generates around 80% of its electricity from nuclear power stations – the highest ratio in the world – with the rest coming from carbon-fuelled power stations and renewable resources (mainly wind farms and hydroelectric dams).

FOOD & DRINK

Staples & Specialities

If there's one thing the French are known for, it's their food. Every region has its distinctive cuisine, from the rich, classic dishes of Burgundy, Périgord, Lyon and Normandy, to the Mediterranean flavours of Provence, Languedoc and Corsica. Broadly speaking, the hot south tends to favour olive oil, garlic and tomatoes, while the cooler north favours cream and butter. Coastal areas specialise in mussels, oysters and saltwater fish. Wherever you choose to eat, one thing's for sure – you won't go hungry.

Nothing is more French than *pain* (bread). More than 80% of all French people eat it at every meal. The classic French bread is the long, thin baguette (and the similar but fatter *flûtes*), but there are countless other varieties.

France has nearly 500 varieties of *fromage* (cheese). The choice on offer at a *fromagerie* (cheese shop) can be overwhelming, but *fromagers* (cheese merchants) always allow you to sample and are usually happy to advise.

Traditionally charcuterie is made only from pork, though a number of other meats – from beef and veal to chicken and goose – are used in making sausages, blood puddings, hams and other cured meats. Pâtés, terrines and rillettes (potted meats) are prepared in many different ways.

The traditional French breakfast is usually coffee, French bread and jam, occasionally accompanied by a croissant or a *pain au chocolat* (chocolate croissant). Meats, yoghurts, cereals and fresh fruit are often eaten at breakfast.

There are dozens of wine-producing regions throughout France, but the principal regions are Alsace, Bordeaux, Burgundy, Champagne, Languedoc-Roussillon, the Loire region and the Rhône. Areas such as Burgundy comprise many well-known districts, including Chablis, Beaujolais and Mâcon, while Bordeaux encompasses Médoc, St-Émilion and Sauternes among many others.

The *bière à la pression* (draught beer) is served by the *demi* (about 33cL). Northern France and Alsace produce some excellent local beers.

The most popular nonalcoholic beverages consumed in France are coffee and mineral water. If you prefer tap water rather than bottled water, ask for *une carafe d'eau* (a jug of water).

The most common coffee is espresso. A small espresso, served without milk, is called *un café noir, un express* or simply *un café*. *Café crème* is espresso with steamed milk or cream.

Where to Eat & Drink

BISTROS & BRASSERIES

A bistro (often spelled *bistrot*) can be simply a pub or bar with snacks and light meals, or a fully fledged restaurant. Brasseries – which can look very much like cafes – serve full meals, drinks and coffee from morning till late at night.

RESTAURANTS

Restaurants generally specialise in a particular style of food – regional, traditional, ethnic etc – and nearly always have a *carte* (menu) posted outside. Most offer at least one fixed-price, multicourse meal, known as a *menu* or *menu du jour* (daily *menu*). This usually offers an entrée, such as salad, pâté or soup; a main dish, including the *plat du jour* (daily special); and a final course (cheese or dessert).

Boissons (drinks) cost extra unless the *menu* says *boisson comprise* (drink included), in which case you may get a beer or a glass of mineral water. If the *menu* has *vin compris* (wine included), you'll probably be served a 25cL *pichet* (jug) of house wine.

Restaurants generally serve lunch from noon or 12.30pm to 2pm or 2.30pm and dinner from 7pm or 7.30pm until 9.30pm or 10pm; they are often closed one or two days of the week (generally Sunday or Monday). Cafes are usually open all day long, while bars open in the early evening and close at 1am or 2am.

NO SMOKING

As of 2007 smoking in all public spaces has been banned in France. This includes airports, stations, shops and offices, as well as hotels and restaurants. Much to everyone's surprise, the French seem to have been pretty sanguine about accepting the controversial new law – although there are inevitably a few pockets of Gallic resistance, smoking inside is a rare sight indeed in France these days. Quel change!

Vegetarians & Vegans

Vegetarians and vegans will have a tough time in many parts of France. Specialist vegetarian restaurants are few and far between, and most menus are still very meat-heavy, although vegetarian choices and *produits biologiques* (organic products) are becoming more common.

PARIS

pop 2.15 million

What can be said about the sexy, sophisticated City of Lights that hasn't already been said a thousand times before? Quite simply, this is one of the world's great metropolises, a trendsetter, market leader and cultural capital for over a thousand years and still going strong. This is the place that gave the world the cancan and the cinematograph, a city that reinvented itself during the Renaissance, bopped to the beat of the jazz age and positively glittered during the belle époque (literally, 'beautiful era'). As you might expect, Paris is strewn with historic architecture, glorious galleries and cultural treasures galore, but the modern-day city is much more than just a museum piece. It's a heady hotchpotch of cultures and ideas – a place to stroll the boulevards, shop till you drop or just do as the Parisians do and watch the world buzz by from a streetside cafe. Savour every moment.

PARIS IN TWO DAYS

You'll barely scratch the surface of Paris in two days – but if that's all the time you've got, you'll have to strip things down to the key sights: **Notre Dame** (p221), the **Louvre** (p222), the **Eiffel Tower** (p216) and the **Arc de Triomphe** (p223). Head up to lively **Montmartre** (p233) for dinner.

On day two swing by the **Musée d'Orsay** (p216), **Ste-Chapelle & the Conciergerie** (p221) and the **Musée Rodin** (p217). Take a romantic **river cruise** (p226) in the early evening before checking out the bistros and nightlife of the **Marais** (p230).

HISTORY

The Parisii, a tribe of Celtic Gauls, settled the Île de la Cité in the 3rd century BC. Paris prospered during the Middle Ages and flourished during the Renaissance, when many of the city's most famous buildings were erected.

The excesses of Louis XVI and his queen, Marie-Antoinette, led to an uprising of Parisians on 14 July 1789, and the storming of the Bastille prison – kick-starting the French Revolution.

In 1851 Emperor Napoleon III oversaw the construction of a more modern Paris, complete with wide boulevards, sculptured parks and a sewer system. Following the disastrous Franco-Prussian War and the establishment of the Third Republic, Paris entered its most resplendent period, the belle époque, famed for its art nouveau architecture and artistic and scientific advances. By the beginning of the 1930s, Paris had become a centre for the artistic avant-garde until the Nazi occupation of 1940–44.

The compact city centre is surrounded by the *banlieue*, a network of sprawling suburbs mostly occupied by Paris' ethnic communities. In late 2005 the city was rocked by violent clashes between police and angry youths from the *banlieue;* the violence spread to many French cities and took several weeks to bring under control.

ORIENTATION

Central Paris is quite small: around 9.5km (north to south) by 11km (east to west). Excluding the Bois de Boulogne and the Bois de Vincennes, its total area is 105 sq km. The Seine River flows east–west through the city; the Rive Droite (Right Bank) is north of the river, while the Rive Gauche (Left Bank) is to the south.

Paris is divided into 20 *arrondissements* (districts), which spiral clockwise from the centre. City addresses always include the number of the arrondissement.

The city has 372 metro stations and there is almost always one within 500m of where you need to go.

INFORMATION

Bookshops

Librairie Ulysse (Map pp218-19; ☎ 01 43 25 17 35; www.ulysse.fr; 26 rue St-Louis en l'Île, 4e; ⌚ 2-8pm Tue-Fri; Ⓜ Pont Marie) Travel guides, maps and more than 20,000 back issues of *National Geographic.*

PARIS

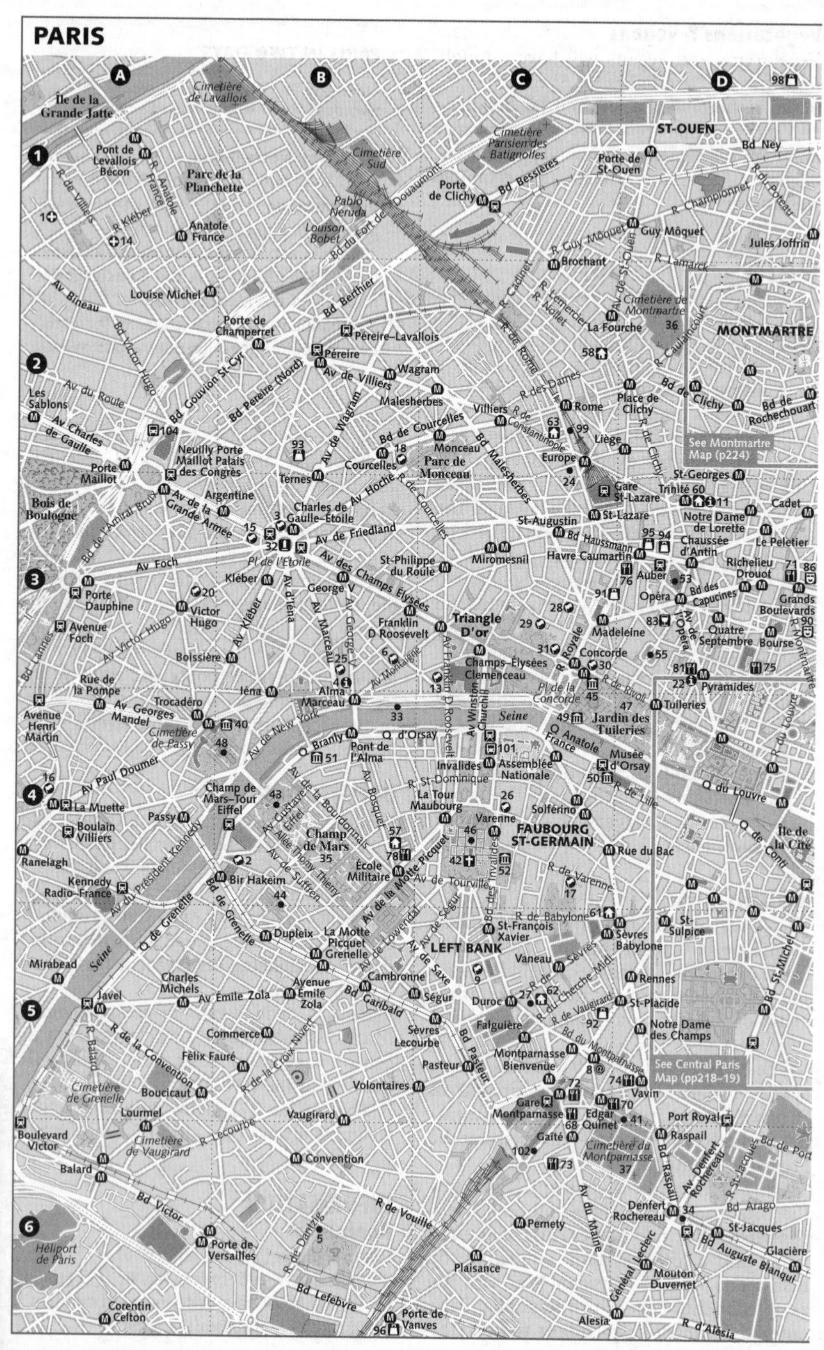

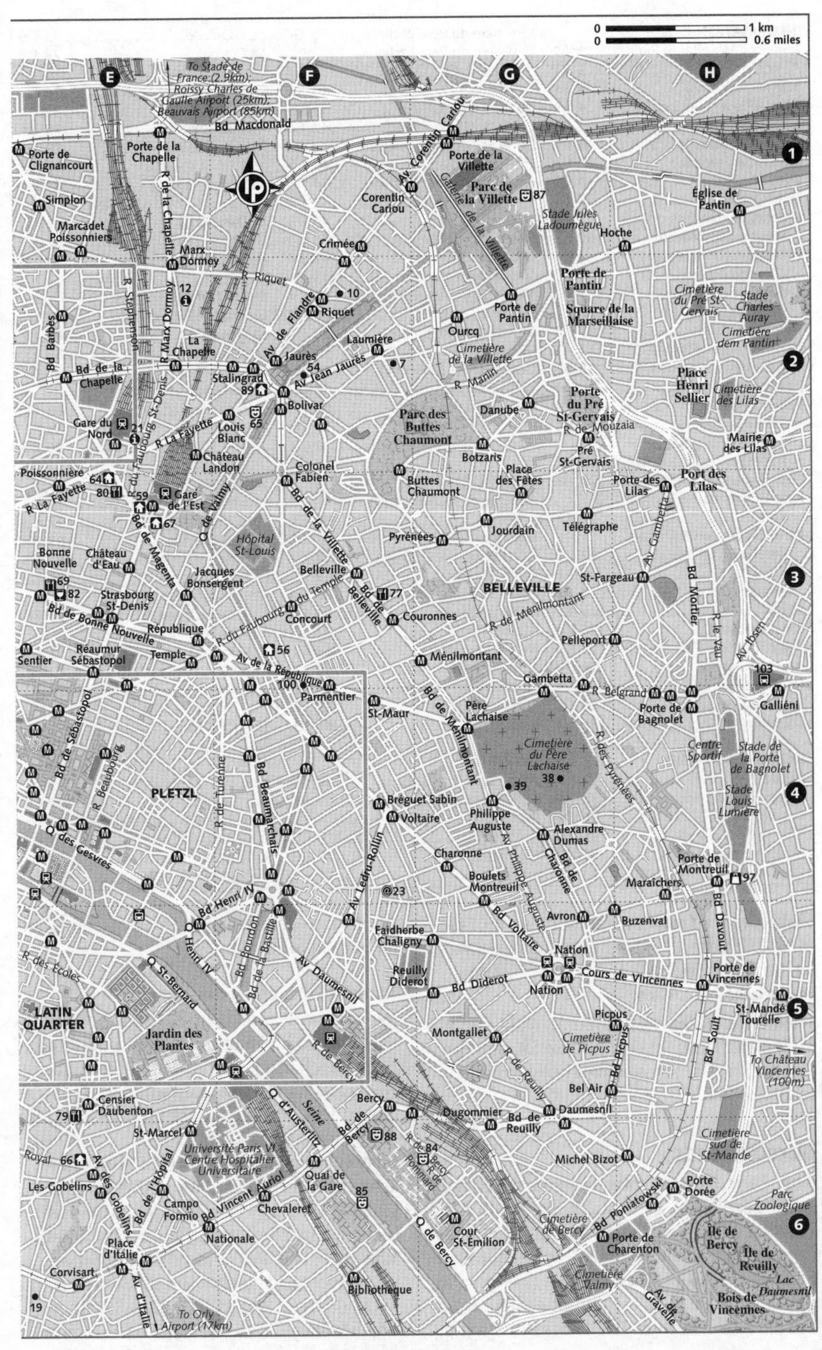

0 1 km
0 0.6 miles
E
F
G
H
To Stade de France (2.9km); Roissy Charles de Gaulle Airport (25km); Beauvais Airport (85km)
Bd Macdonald
Porte de Clignancourt
Porte de la Chapelle
Av Corentin Cariou
Porte de la Villette
Parc de la Villette
87
Galerie de la Villette
Simplon
R de la Chapelle
Corentin Cariou
Stade Jules Ladoumègue
Église de Pantin
Marcadet Poissonniers
Crimée
Hoche
Marx Dormoy
R Riquet
R Stephenson
R Marx Dormoy
12
10
Riquet
Porte de Pantin
Porte de Pantin
Square de la Marseillaise
Cimetière du Pré St-Gervais
Stade Charles Auray
Cimetière dem Pantin
Av de Flandre
Ourcq
Barbès
La Chapelle
Laumière
Cimetière de la Villette
Jaurès
54
Bd de la Chapelle
Stalingrad
Av Jean Jaurès
7
R Manin
89
Place Henri Sellier
Cimetière des Lilas
Bd Barbès
Porte du Pré St-Gervais
Bolivar
Danube
Parc des Buttes Chaumont
R de Mouzaia
Gare du Nord
21
R du Faubourg St-Denis
Louis Blanc
65
R La Fayette
Mairie des Lilas
Botzaris
Pré St-Gervais
Château Landon
Colonel Fabien
Place des Fêtes
Port des Lilas
Porte des Lilas
Poissonnière
64
80
59
Gare de l'Est
Buttes Chaumont
R La Fayette
Bd de Magenta
67
Q de Valmy
Bd de la Villette
Télégraphe
Hôpital St-Louis
Jourdain
Av Gambetta
Pyrénées
Bonne Nouvelle
Château d'Eau
Jacques Bonsergent
Belleville
St-Fargeau
69
82
77
BELLEVILLE
Strasbourg St-Denis
Bd de Belleville
Bd Mortier
R le Vau
Bd de Bonne Nouvelle
R du Faubourg du Temple
Concourt
Couronnes
R de Ménilmontant
République
Pelleport
Réaumur Sébastopol
Sentier
Temple
56
Av Ibsen
Ménilmontant
Av de la République
103
100
Parmentier
Gambetta
R Belgrand
Gallieni
St-Maur
Porte de Bagnolet
Père Lachaise
Bd de Sébastopol
Bd de Ménilmontant
Cimetière du Père Lachaise
Centre Sportif
Stade de la Porte de Bagnolet
R Beaubourg
38
R de Turenne
Bd Beaumarchais
R des Pyrénées
PLETZL
39
Stade Louis Lumière
Bréguet Sabin
Philippe Auguste
Voltaire
Alexandre Dumas
Q des Gesvres
Charonne
Bd de Charonne
Av Philippe Auguste
Porte de Montreuil
97
Av Ledru-Rollin
Boulets Montreuil
Maraîchers
23
Bd Davout
Bd Henri IV
Avron
Buzenval
Bd Voltaire
Bd Bourdon
Bd de la Bastille
Q Henri IV
Faidherbe Chaligny
Nation
R des Écoles
Reuilly Diderot
Cours de Vincennes
Porte de Vincennes
Q St-Bernard
Av Daumesnil
Bd Diderot
Nation
St-Mandé Tourelle
LATIN QUARTER
Picpus
Jardin des Plantes
Montgallet
Cimetière de Picpus
Bd Picpus
R de Reuilly
R de Bercy
To Château Vincennes (100m)
Bd Soult
Bel Air
Censier Daubenton
79
Q d'Austerlitz
Seine
Bercy
Dugommier
Daumesnil
St-Marcel
Bd de Bercy
88
Bd de Reuilly
Cimetière sud de St-Mandé
R de Bercy
84
R de Pommard
Université Paris VI Centre Hospitalier Universitaire
Royal
66
Av des Gobelins
Quai de la Gare
Michel Bizot
Les Gobelins
Bd de l'Hôpital
Bd Vincent Auriol
85
Porte Dorée
Campo Formio
Chevaleret
Bd Poniatowski
Parc Zoologique
Nationale
Cour St-Émilion
Q de Bercy
Cimetière de Bercy
Porte de Charenton
Île de Bercy
Île de Reuilly
Place d'Italie
Corvisart
Cimetière Valmy
Lac Daumesnil
Av de Gravelle
Bibliothèque
Bois de Vincennes
19
To Orly Airport (17km)
Av d'Italie
1
2
3
4
5
6

FRANCE

INFORMATION
American Hospital of Paris......1 A1
Australian Embassy......2 B4
Belgian Embassy......3 B3
Bienvenue à la Ferme......4 B3
Bureau des Objets Trouvés......5 B6
Canadian Embassy......6 B3
Club Alpin Française......7 F2
Cyber Cube......8 C5
Dutch Embassy......9 C5
Federation Française de la Randonnée Pédestre......10 F2
Fédération Nationale des Gîtes de France......11 D3
Fédération Unie des Auberges de Jeunesse (FUAJ)......12 E2
German Embassy......13 C3
Hertford British Hospital......14 A1
Irish Embassy & Trade Office......15 B3
Italian Consulate......16 A4
Italian Embassy......17 C4
Japanese Embassy......18 B2
Ligue Française pour les Auberges de la Jeunesse......19 E6
New Zealand Embassy......20 A3
Paris Convention & Visitors Bureau......21 E2
Paris Convention & Visitors Bureau (Main Branch)......22 D3
Phon'net......23 F4
Ski France......24 C2
Spanish Embassy......25 B3
Swiss Embassy......26 C4
Tea & Tattered Pages......27 C5
UK Consulate......28 C3
UK Embassy......29 C3
US Consulate......30 C3
US Embassy......31 C3

SIGHTS & ACTIVITIES
Arc de Triomphe......32 B3
Bateaux Mouches......33 B4
Catacombes......34 D6
Champ de Mars......35 B4
Cimetière de Montmartre......36 D2
Cimetière du Montparnasse......37 C6
Cimetière du Père Lachaise......38 G4
Cimetière du Père Lachaise Conservation Office......39 G4
CineAqua......40 B4
Conservation Office......41 D5
Église du Dôme......42 C4
Église St-Louis des Invalides......(see 46)
Eiffel Tower......43 B4
Fat Tire Bike Tours Office......44 B4
Galerie National du Jeu de Paume......45 C3
Hôtel des Invalides......46 C4
Jardin des Tuileries......47 D4
Jardins du Trocadéro......48 B4
Musée de l'Orangerie......49 C4
Musée d'Orsay......50 C4
Musée du Quai Branly......51 B4
Musée Rodin......52 C4
Opera House Museum......(see 53)
Palais Garnier......53 D3
Paris Canal Croisières......54 F2
Place Vendôme......55 D3
Tombeau de Napoléon 1er......(see 42)

SLEEPING
Auberge de Jeunesse Jules Ferry......56 F3
Hôtel du Champ-de-Mars......57 B4
Hôtel Eldorado......58 C2
Hôtel Français......59 E3
Hôtel Langlois......60 D3
Hôtel Lindbergh......61 D4
Mayet Hôtel......62 C5
New Orient Hôtel......63 C2
Nord-Est Hôtel......64 E3
Peace & Love Hostel......65 F2
Port Royal Hôtel......66 E6
Sibour Hôtel......67 E3

EATING
Atac......68 C5
Aux Deux Canards......69 E3
Boulevard Edgar Quinet Food Market......70 C5
Chartier......71 D3
Inno......72 C5
La Cagouille......73 C6
La Coupole......74 D5
Le Grand Colbert......75 D3
Le Roi du Pot au Feu......76 D3
Marché Belleville......77 F3
Marché Rue Cler......78 B4
Marché Rue Mouffetard......79 E5
Marché St-Quentin......80 E3
Monoprix Opéra......81 D3

DRINKING
De La Ville Café......82 E3
Harry's New York Bar......83 D3

ENTERTAINMENT
Cinémathèque Française......84 G6
La Dame de Canton......85 F6
Le Limonaire......86 E3
Le Zénith......87 G1
Palais Omnisports de Paris-Bercy......88 F6
Point Éphémère......89 F2
Social Club......90 D3

SHOPPING
Fauchon......91 D3
Fnac Montparnasse......92 C5
Fromagerie Alléosse......93 B2
Galeries Lafayette......94 D3
Le Printemps......95 D3
Marché aux Puces de la Porte de Vanves......96 B6
Marché aux Puces de Montreuil......97 H4
Marché aux Puces de St-Ouen......98 D1

TRANSPORT
ADA......99 C2
ADA......100 F3
Aérogare des Invalides......101 C4
easyCar......102 C6
Gare Routière Internationale de Paris-Galliéni......103 H3
Parking Pershing Express Bus......104 A2

Shakespeare & Company (Map pp218-19; ☎ 01 43 26 96 50; 37 rue de la Bûcherie, 5e; ⏲ 10am-11pm Mon-Sat, 11am-11pm Sun; Ⓜ St-Michel) Paris' most famous English-language bookshop.

Tea & Tattered Pages (Map pp212-13; ☎ 01 40 65 94 35; 24 rue Mayet, 6e; ⏲ 11am-7pm Mon-Sat, noon-6pm Sun; Ⓜ Duroc) The best secondhand English-language bookshop in Paris.

Discount Cards

The **Paris Museum Pass** (www.parismuseumpass.fr; 2/4/6 days €30/45/60) is valid for around 38 Parisian sights – including the Louvre, Centre Pompidou and the Musée d'Orsay, plus the St-Denis basilica, parts of Versailles and Fontainebleau. You can buy it online, from the Paris Convention & Visitors Bureau (opposite), Fnac outlets, major metro stations and all participating venues.

Internet Access

Wi-fi is widespread in Parisian hotels (although you'll sometimes have to pay a connection charge). For a list of free-access wi-fi cafes, visit www.cafes-wifi.com. If you're laptop-less, Paris is awash in internet cafes with computers:

Cyber Cube (Map pp212-13; ☎ 01 56 80 08 08; www.cybercube.fr; 9 rue d'Odessa, 14e; per 15/30min €1/2, per 5/10hr €30/40; ⏲ 10am-10pm; Ⓜ Montparnasse Bienvenüe) Expensive, but handy for Gare Montparnasse.

Milk (☎ 08 20 00 10 00; www.milklub.com; daytime per 1/2/3/5hr €4/7/9/12, night-time per 3/10hr €6/13; ⏲ 24hr) Panthéon (Map pp218-19; 17 rue Soufflot, 5e; Ⓜ Luxembourg); Les Halles (Map pp218-19; 31 blvd de

Sébastopol, 1er; Ⓜ Les Halles) This chain of seven internet cafes is bright, buzzy and open round the clock.
Phon'net (Map pp212-13; ☎ 01 42 05 10 73; 74 rue de Charonne, 11e; per 1/5/15/30hr €5/16/30/45; ⏲ 10am-midnight; Ⓜ Charonne or Ledru Rollin)
Web 46 (Map pp218-19; ☎ 01 40 27 02 89; 46 rue du Roi de Sicile, 4e; per 15/30/60min €2.50/4/7, 5hr €29; ⏲ 10am-11pm Mon-Fri, 10am-9pm Sat, noon-11pm Sun; Ⓜ St-Paul) Cybercafe in the heart of the Marais.

Internet Resources

Go Go Paris! Culture! (www.gogoparis.com) All things cultural: clubs, art, gigs, food and drink.
Mairie de Paris (www.paris.fr) Comprehensive Paris info from opening times to city stats.
Paris Convention & Visitors Bureau (www.parisinfo.com) Official tourist office site.
Paris Pages (www.paris.org) Mainly museums and cultural events.

Laundry

There's a *laverie libre-service* (self-service laundrette) on every corner in Paris; your hotel or hostel can point you to one.

Medical Services

Major 24-hour hospitals:
American Hospital of Paris (Map pp212-13; ☎ 01 46 41 25 25; www.american-hospital.org; 63 blvd Victor Hugo, 92200 Neuilly-sur-Seine; Ⓜ Pont de Levallois Bécon)
Hertford British Hospital (Map pp212-13; ☎ 01 46 39 22 22; www.british-hospital.org; 3 rue Barbès, 92300 Levallois-Perret; Ⓜ Anatole France)
Hôpital Hôtel Dieu (Map pp218-19; ☎ 01 42 34 82 34; www.aphp.fr; 1 place du Parvis Notre Dame, 4e; Ⓜ Cité) One of the city's main government-run public hospitals; after 8pm use the emergency entrance on rue de la Cité, 4e.

Money

Post offices with a Banque Postale offer the best exchange rates in Paris, and accept banknotes (commission €4.50) as well as travellers cheques issued by Amex (no commission) or Visa (1.5%, minimum €4.50). Bureaux de change are faster and easier, open longer hours and give better rates than commercial banks.

Post

Most *bureaux de poste* (post offices) in Paris are open from 8am to 7pm weekdays and 8am or 9am till noon on Saturday. *Tabacs* (tobacconists) usually sell postage stamps.
Main post office (Map pp218-19; ☎ 01 40 28 76 00; 52 rue du Louvre, 1er; ⏲ 24hr; Ⓜ Sentier or Les Halles) Open round the clock for letters and poste restante mail. Other services, including currency exchange, operate during regular business hours.

Toilets

The public toilets in Paris are signposted *toilettes* or *WC*. The tan-coloured, self-cleaning toilets you see on Parisian pavements are open 24 hours and are free of charge. *Libre* means 'free'; *occupé* means 'occupied'.

Tourist Information

The main branch of the **Paris Convention & Visitors Bureau** (Office de Tourisme et de Congrès de Paris; Map pp212-13; ☎ 08 92 68 30 00; www.parisinfo.com; 25-27 rue des Pyramides, 1er; ⏲ 9am-7pm Jun-Oct, 10am-7pm Mon-Sat & 11am-7pm Sun Nov-May, closed 1 May; Ⓜ Pyramides) is 500m northwest of the Louvre. There are also branches at **Anvers** (Map p224; opp 72 blvd de Rochechouart, 18e; ⏲ 10am-6pm, closed Christmas Day, New Year's Day & 1 May; Ⓜ Anvers), **Gare de Lyon** (Map pp218-19; Hall d'Arrivée, 20 blvd Diderot, 12e; ⏲ 8am-6pm Mon-Sat, closed Sun & 1 May; Ⓜ Gare de Lyon) and **Gare du Nord** (Map pp212-13; 18 rue de Dunkerque, 10e; ⏲ 8am-6pm, closed Christmas Day, New Year's Day & 1 May; Ⓜ Gare du Nord).

Syndicat d'Initiative de Montmartre (Map p224; ☎ 01 42 62 21 21; 21 place du Tertre, 18e; ⏲ 10am-7pm; Ⓜ Abbesses) is in Montmartre's prettiest square.

DANGERS & ANNOYANCES

Paris is generally a safe city, but as always it makes sense to keep your wits about you. Take extra care on the metro after dark, and if you can it's best to steer clear of the stations at Châtelet-Les Halles. Château Rouge in Montmartre; Gare du Nord; Strasbourg St-Denis; Réaumur Sébastopol; and Montparnasse Bienvenüe.

Two problems you're much more likely to encounter are pickpocketing and the ever-present scourge of Parisian streets, dog poo. Thefts from handbags and rucksacks are a particular problem around Montmartre, Pigalle, Forum des Halles, the Latin Quarter, the Eiffel Tower, and on the metro during rush hour. Meanwhile stepping into something nasty is a problem practically anywhere you walk in Paris: the capital's dogs produce up to 16 tonnes of excrement every single day, and only 60% of dog owners admit to cleaning up after their pooches.

Lost Property

All objects found in Paris (except those picked up on the trains or in train stations) – are brought to the **Bureau des Objets Trouvés** (Lost Property Office; Map pp212-13; ☎ 08 21 00 25 25; www.prefecture-police-paris.interieur.gouv.fr/demarches/article/service_objets_trouves.htm; 36 rue des Morillons, 15e; 8.30am-5pm Mon-Thu, 8.30am-4.30pm Fri; Ⓜ Convention). Telephone inquiries are impossible, so if you've lost something, you'll just have to go down and fill out the forms and hope it turns up.

Items lost on the **metro** (☎ 3246; 7am-9pm Mon-Fri, 9am-5pm Sat & Sun) are held at the station before being sent to the Bureau des Objets Trouvés, while lost property on trains is taken to the lost-property office of the relevant station.

SIGHTS

Left Bank

EIFFEL TOWER

It's impossible now to imagine Paris (or France, for that matter) without La Tour Eiffel, the **Eiffel Tower** (Map pp212-13; ☎ 01 44 11 23 23; www.tour-eiffel.fr; lifts to level 1 adult/child €4.80/2.50, level 2 €7.80/4.30, top level €12/6.70; lifts 9am-midnight mid-Jun–Aug, 9.30am-11pm Sep–mid-Jun, stairs 9am-midnight mid-Jun–Aug, 9.30am-6pm Sep–mid-Jun; Ⓜ Champ de Mars-Tour Eiffel or Bir Hakeim), but the 'metal asparagus', as some Parisians snidely called it, faced fierce opposition from Paris' artistic elite when it was built for the 1889 Exposition Universelle (World Fair). The tower was almost torn down in 1909, and was only saved by the new science of radiotelegraphy (it provided an ideal spot for transmitting antennas). The city should be thankful it's still standing – some 6.9 million people make the 324m trek up to the top each year, and it's as synonymous with France these days as fine cooking and smelly cheese. If you're feeling steely legged and sturdy-lunged, you can dodge the lift fees by taking the stairs (€4/3.10 over/under 25 years old) to the 1st and 2nd platforms, but be warned: it's steep. Really, really steep. So don't blame us if you run out of puff halfway up.

Since the millennium, the tower has been lit up every hour after dusk by a spectacular flashing light display, but it's recently been announced that the city has decided to halve the time the bulbs are left on in an effort to reduce the electricity bill – and with over 20,000 bulbs to power, you can't really blame them.

> **FREE THRILLS**
>
> Paris is far from cheap, but a visit to the City of Lights doesn't have to blow your budget. Here are a few of our favourite free treats:
>
> - Turn up some treasures at the **Marché aux Puces de St-Ouen** (see the boxed text, p236)
> - Pack a picnic for the **Jardin du Luxembourg** (opposite)
> - Wander the celebrity gravestones at the **Cimetière du Père Lachaise** (p225)
> - Marvel at the architectural ambition of the **Cathédrale de Notre Dame** (p221)
> - Watch the painters and portraitists at work on **Place du Tertre** (p224) in Montmartre

Spreading out around the Eiffel Tower are the **Jardins du Trocadéro** (Map pp212-13; Ⓜ Trocadéro), whose fountains and statue garden are grandly illuminated at night. On the eastern side of the gardens is **CineAqua** (Map pp212-13; ☎ 01 40 69 23 23; www.cineaqua.com; 2 av des Nations Unies, 16e; adult/under 3yr/3-12yr/13-17yr €19.50/free/12.50/15.50; 10am-8pm), a huge new aquarium housing more than 500 species of underwater life in 3500 sq metres of space.

MUSÉE D'ORSAY

The **Musée d'Orsay** (Map pp212-13; ☎ 01 40 49 48 14; www.musee-orsay.fr; 62 rue de Lille, 7e; adult/under 18yr/18-30yr €8/free/5.50, 1st Sun of month free; 9.30am-6pm Tue, Wed & Fri-Sun, 9.30am-9.45pm Thu; Ⓜ Musée d'Orsay or Solférino), housed in a turn-of-the-century train station overlooking the Seine, displays France's national collection of paintings, sculptures and artwork produced between the 1840s and 1914. The museum is especially renowned for its Impressionist and art nouveau collections: the upper level contains a celebrated collection of Impressionist paintings by Monet, Pissarro, Renoir, Sisley, Degas and Manet, plus post-Impressionist works by Cézanne, Van Gogh, Seurat and Matisse. Art nouveau aficionados will want to linger on the middle level, while on the ground floor, look out for early works by Manet, Monet, Renoir and Pissarro.

Tickets are valid all day, so you can come and go as you please. The reduced entrance fee of €5.50 applies to everyone after 4.15pm (6pm on Thursday). A combined ticket including the Musée Rodin costs €12.

PANTHÉON

The domed landmark now known as the **Panthéon** (Map pp218-19; ☎ 01 44 32 18 00; www.monuments-nationaux.fr; place du Panthéon, 5e; adult/under 18yr/18-25yr €7.50/free/4.80, 1st Sun of month Oct-Mar free; 10am-6.30pm Apr-Sep, to 6.15pm Oct-Mar; M Luxembourg) was commissioned around 1750 as an abbey church, but because of financial and structural problems it wasn't completed until 1789 (not a good year for opening churches in France). The crypt houses the tombs of Voltaire, Jean-Jacques Rousseau, Victor Hugo, Émile Zola, Jean Moulin and Nobel Prize winner Marie Curie, among many others. Inside the gloomy Panthéon itself a working model of Foucault's Pendulum demonstrates the rotation of the earth; it wowed the scientific establishment when it was presented here in 1851.

MUSÉE RODIN

The **Musée Rodin** (Map pp212-13; ☎ 01 44 18 61 10; www.musee-rodin.fr; 79 rue de Varenne, 7e; adult/18-25yr permanent or temporary exhibition plus garden €6/4, both exhibitions plus garden €9/7, garden only €1, under 18yr free, 1st Sun of month free; 9.30am-5.45pm Tue-Sun Apr-Sep, 9.30am-4.45pm Tue-Sun Oct-Mar; M Varenne) is both a sublime museum and one of the most relaxing spots in the city, with a lovely sculpture garden in which to rest. The 18th-century house displays some of Rodin's most famous works, including *The Burghers of Calais (Les Bourgeois de Calais), Cathedral, The Thinker (Le Penseur)* and *The Kiss (Le Baiser)*.

HÔTEL DES INVALIDES

The **Hôtel des Invalides** (Map pp212-13; M Varenne or La Tour Maubourg) was constructed in the 1670s by Louis XIV as housing for 4000 *invalides* (disabled war veterans). On 14 July 1789, a mob forced its way into the building and seized 28,000 rifles before heading to the prison at Bastille, starting the French Revolution.

To the south are the **Église St-Louis des Invalides** (Map pp212–13), once used by soldiers, and the **Église du Dôme** (Map pp212–13), which contains the extraordinarily extravagant **Tombeau de Napoléon 1er** (Napoleon I's Tomb; 10am-6pm Apr-Sep, 10am-5pm Oct-Mar, closed 1st Mon of month).

MUSÉE DU QUAI BRANLY

It's been a long time coming, but the **Musée du Quai Branly** (Map pp212-13; ☎ 01 56 61 70 00; www.quaibranly.fr; 37 quai Branly, 7e; adult/under 18yr/student & 18-25yr €8.50/free/6, admission free for 18-25yr after 6pm Sat, 1st Sun of month free for all; 11am-7pm Tue, Wed & Sun, to 9pm Thu-Sat; M Pont de l'Alma or Alma-Marceau) has finally been installed in a fantabulous glass, wood and turf structure beside the Seine, designed by renowned architect Jean Nouvel. It's an immersive experience, closer to an artwork than a museum, making use of video, music, audio and ambitious displays exploring the cultures of Africa, Oceania, Asia and the Americas.

JARDIN DU LUXEMBOURG

When the weather is fine Parisians flock to the terraces and chestnut groves of the 23-hectare **Jardin du Luxembourg** (Map pp218-19; 7am-9.30pm Apr-Oct, 8am-sunset Nov-Mar; M Luxembourg) to relax and sunbathe.

CATACOMBES

There are few spookier sights in Paris than the **Catacombes** (Map pp212-13; ☎ 01 43 22 47 63; www.catacombes.paris.fr, in French; 1 av Colonel Henri Roi-Tanguy, 14e; adult/under 14yr/14-26yr €7/free/3.50; 10am-5pm Tue-Sun; M Denfert Rochereau), one of three underground cemeteries created in the late 18th century to solve the problems posed by Paris' overflowing cemeteries. Twenty metres below street level, the catacombs consist of 1.6km of winding tunnels stacked from floor to ceiling with the bones and skulls of millions of Parisians – guaranteed to send a shiver down your spine.

If you haven't had your ghoulish fix, you can check out lots more famous graves at the **Cimetière du Montparnasse** (Map pp212-13; cnr blvd Edgar Quinet & rue Froidevaux, 14e; 8am-6pm Mon-Fri, 8.30am-6pm Sat, 9am-6pm Sun mid-Mar–early Nov, 8am-5.30pm Mon-Fri, 8.30am-5.30pm Sat, 9am-5.30pm Sun early Nov–mid-Mar; M Edgar Quinet or Raspail), including the poet Charles Baudelaire, writer Guy de Maupassant, playwright Samuel Beckett, photographer Man Ray, industrialist André Citroën, philosopher Jean-Paul Sartre and the crooner Serge Gainsbourg. Maps are available from the **conservation office** (Map pp212-13; ☎ 01 44 10 86 50; 3 blvd Edgar Quinet, 14e).

CENTRAL PARIS

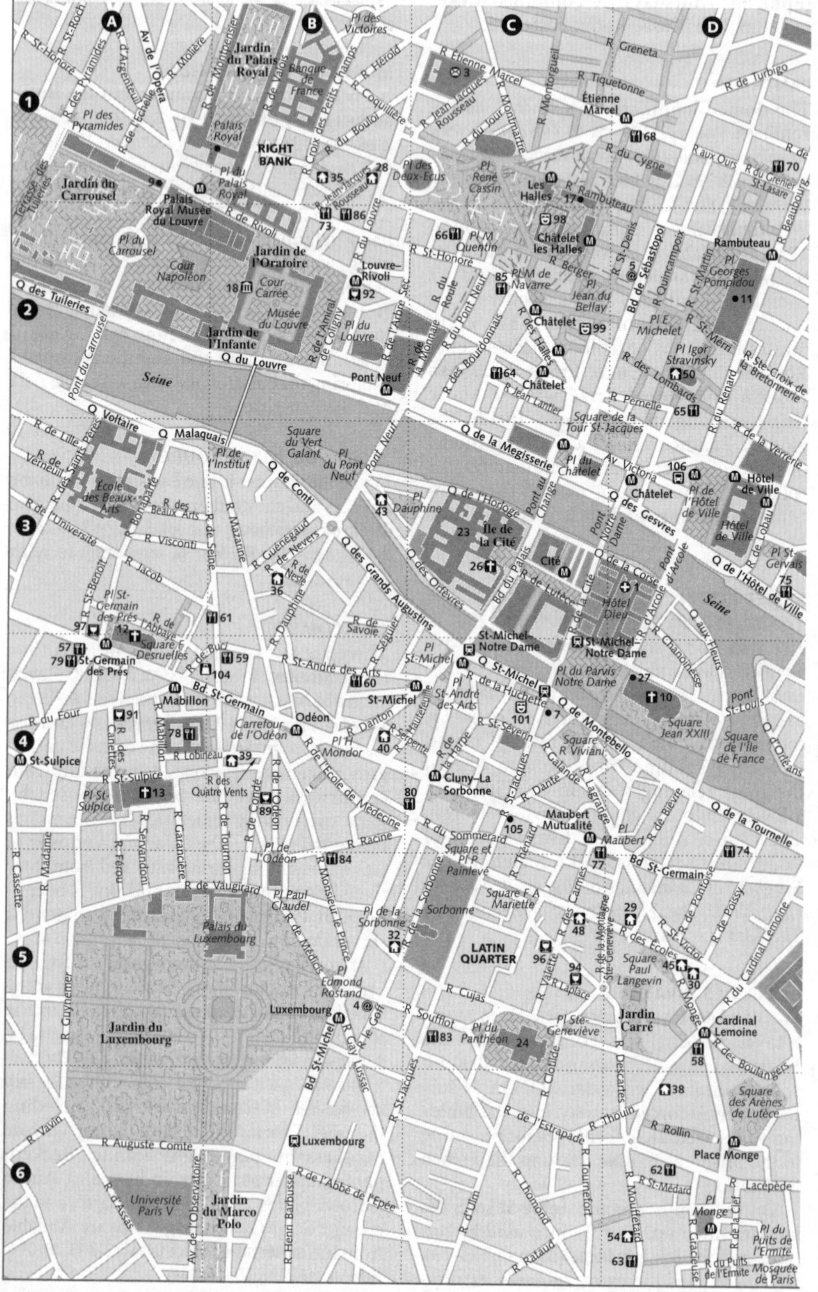

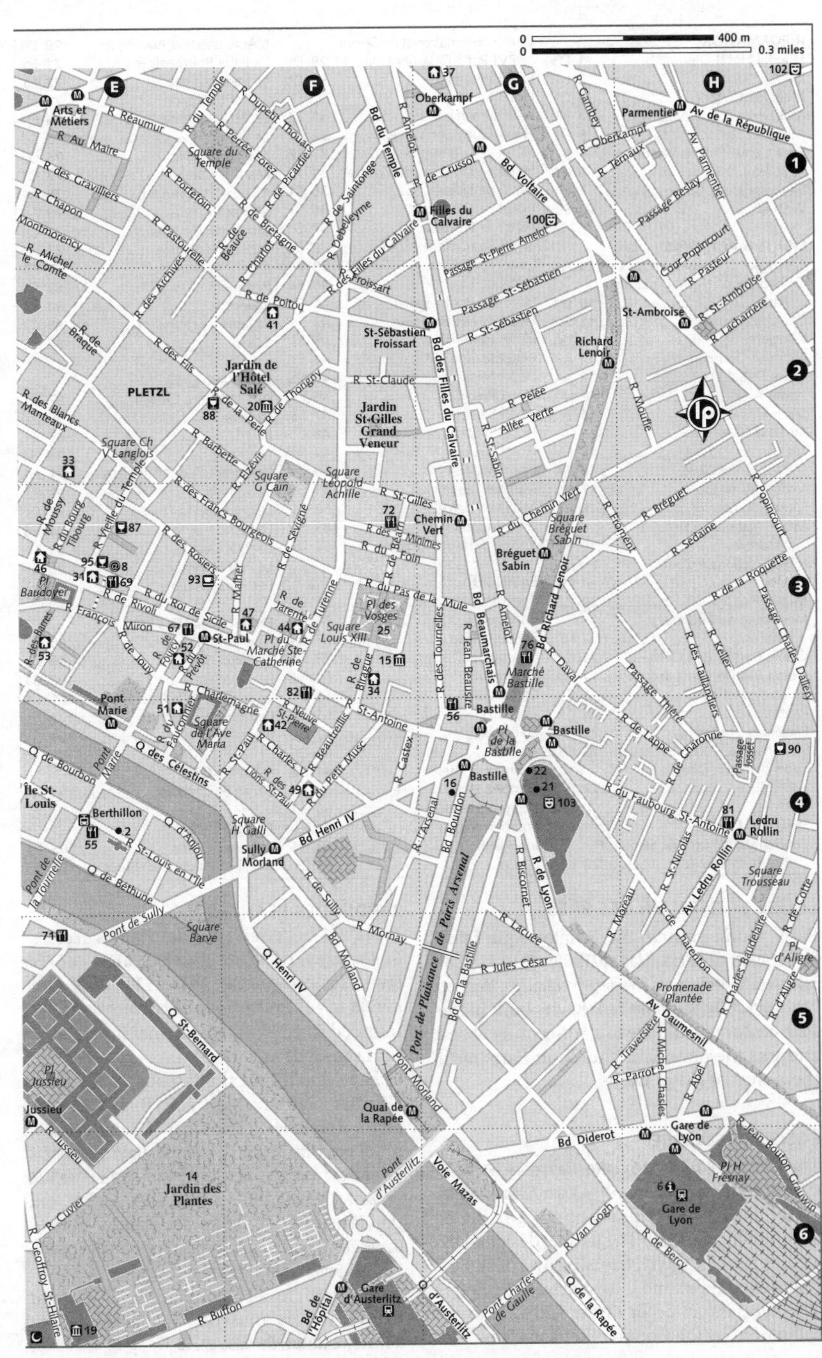
0 400 m
0 0.3 miles
Arts et Métiers
Oberkampf
Parmentier
Av de la République
Bd du Temple
Bd Voltaire
Filles du Calvaire
Square du Temple
St-Sébastien Froissart
St-Ambroise
Richard Lenoir
Jardin de l'Hôtel Salé
PLETZL
Jardin St-Gilles Grand Veneur
Square Léopold Achille
Chemin Vert
Bréguet Sabin
Square Bréguet Sabin
Pl des Vosges
Square Louis XIII
St-Paul
Pl du Marché Ste-Catherine
Pont Marie
Square de l'Ave Maria
Bastille
Pl de la Bastille
Marché Bastille
Ledru Rollin
Square Trousseau
Île St-Louis
Berthillon
Sully Morland
Square H Galli
Square Barve
Port de Plaisance de Paris Arsenal
Promenade Plantée
Quai de la Rapée
Gare de Lyon
Pl H Fresnay
Jussieu
Pl Jussieu
Jardin des Plantes
Gare d'Austerlitz
Pont d'Austerlitz
Pont Charles de Gaulle
Bd Diderot
Voie Mazas
Q de la Rapée
R de Bercy
R de Lyon
Av Daumesnil
Av Ledru Rollin
R du Faubourg St-Antoine
R St-Antoine
R de Rivoli
Bd Henri IV
Q Henri IV
Q St-Bernard
Q des Célestins
Q de Bourbon
Q d'Anjou
Q de Béthune
Pont de Sully
Pont de la Tournelle
Pont Morland
R Buffon
R Cuvier
R Geoffroy St-Hilaire
R Jussieu
Bd de l'Hôpital
Bd Beaumarchais
Bd Richard Lenoir
Bd des Filles du Calvaire
Bd Bourdon
Bd de la Bastille
Bd Morland
FRANCE

INFORMATION
Hôpital Hôtel-Dieu 1 D3
Librairie Ulysse 2 E4
Main Post Office 3 C1
Milk 4 B5
Milk 5 D2
Paris Convention & Visitors Bureau 6 H6
Shakespeare & Company 7 C4
Web 46 8 E3

SIGHTS & ACTIVITIES
Carrousel du Louvre Entrance 9 A1
Cathédrale de Notre Dame de Paris 10 D4
Centre Pompidou 11 D2
Conciergerie (see 23)
Église St-Germain des Prés 12 A3
Église St-Sulpice 13 A4
Jardin Alpin (see 14)
Jardin des Plantes 14 E6
Jardin d'Hiver (see 14)
Maison de Victor Hugo 15 F3
Maison Roue Libre 16 G4
Maison Roue Libre 17 C1
Musée du Louvre 18 B2
Musée National d'Histoire Naturelle 19 E6
Musée Nationale d'Art Moderne (see 11)
Musée Picasso 20 F2
Ménagerie du Jardin des Plantes (see 14)
Opéra Bastille Box Office 21 G4
Opéra Bastille Tours Entrance 22 G4
Palais de Justice 23 C3
Panthéon 24 C5
Place des Vosges 25 F3
Ste-Chapelle 26 C3
Tours de Notre Dame Entrance 27 D4

SLEEPING
Centre International de Séjour BVJ Paris-Louvre 28 B1
Centre International de Séjour BVJ Paris-Quartier Latin 29 D5
Familia Hôtel 30 D5
Hôtel Caron de Beaumarchais 31 E3
Hôtel Cluny Sorbonne 32 B5
Hôtel de la Bretonnerie 33 E2
Hôtel de la Place des Vosges 34 F3
Hôtel de Lille 35 B1
Hôtel de Nesle 36 B3
Hôtel de Nevers 37 G1
Hôtel des Grandes Écoles 38 D6
Hôtel du Globe 39 B4
Hôtel du Lys 40 B4
Hôtel du Petit Moulin 41 F2
Hôtel du Septième Art 42 F4
Hôtel Henri IV 43 B3
Hôtel Jeanne d'Arc 44 F3
Hôtel Minerve 45 D5
Hôtel Rivoli 46 E3
Hôtel Sévigné 47 F3
Hôtel St-Jacques 48 C5
Hôtel St-Louis Marais 49 F4
Hôtel St-Merry 50 D2
MIJE Le Fauconnier 51 E4
MIJE Le Fourcy 52 E3
MIJE Maubuisson 53 E3
Young & Happy Hostel 54 D6

EATING
Berthillon 55 E4
Bofinger 56 G4
Brasserie Lipp 57 A4
Champion 58 D5
Champion 59 B4
Chez Allard 60 B4
Cosi 61 B3
Ed l'Épicier 62 D6
Franprix 63 D6
Franprix Châtelet 64 C2
Franprix Hôtel de Ville 65 D2
Franprix Les Halles 66 C2
Franprix Marais 67 E3
Joe Allen 68 D1
L'Alivi 69 E3
L'Ambassade d'Auvergne 70 D1
La Baba Bourgeois 71 E5
Le Petit Marché 72 F3
Le Petit Mâchon 73 B2
Le Petit Pontoise 74 D4
Le Trumilou 75 D3
Marché Bastille 76 G3
Marché Maubert 77 C4
Marché St-Germain 78 A4
Monoprix 79 A4
Monoprix (St-Michel) 80 C4
Monoprix Bastille 81 H4
Monoprix Marais 82 F3
Perraudin 83 C5
Polidor 84 B5
Saveurs Végét'halles 85 C2
Scoop 86 B2

DRINKING
Au Petit Fer à Cheval 87 E3
La Perle 88 E2
Le 10 89 B4
Le Bistrot du Peintre 90 H4
Le Comptoir des Canettes 91 A4
Le Fumoir 92 B2
Le Loir dans la Théière 93 E3
Le Piano Vache 94 C5
Le Pick Clops 95 E3
Le Pub St-Hilaire 96 C5
Les Deux Magots 97 A3

ENTERTAINMENT
Fnac Forum des Halles 98 C2
Le Baiser Salé 99 C2
Le Bataclan 100 G1
Le Caveau de la Huchette 101 C4
Le Nouveau Casino 102 H1
Opéra Bastille 103 G4

SHOPPING
Cacao et Chocolat 104 A4

TRANSPORT
Eurolines Office 105 C4
Noctilien (Night Bus) Stops 106 D3

ÉGLISE ST-GERMAIN DES PRÉS

Paris' oldest church, the Romanesque **Église St-Germain des Prés** (Map pp218-19; ☎ 01 55 42 81 33; 3 place St-Germain des Prés, 6e; 8am-7pm Mon-Sat, 9am-8pm Sun; Ⓜ St-Germain des Prés) was built in the 11th century on the site of a 6th-century abbey and was the dominant church in Paris until the arrival of Notre Dame.

ÉGLISE ST-SULPICE

The Italianate **Église St-Sulpice** (Map pp218-19; ☎ 01 46 33 21 78; place St-Sulpice, 6e; 7.30am-7.30pm; Ⓜ St-Sulpice), lined with 21 side chapels, was built between 1646 and 1780. The facade, designed by a Florentine architect, has two rows of superimposed columns and is topped by two towers. The neoclassical decor of the vast interior is influenced by the Counter-Reformation.

JARDIN DES PLANTES

Paris' 24-hectare **Jardin des Plantes** (Botanical Garden; Map pp218-19; ☎ 01 40 79 56 01/54 79; 57 rue Cuvier & 3 quai St-Bernard, 5e; 8am-5.30pm, to 8pm summer; Ⓜ Gare d'Austerlitz, Censier Daubenton or Jussieu) was founded in 1626 as a medicinal herb garden for Louis XIII.

Here you'll find the famous **Jardin d'Hiver** (Winter Garden; Map pp218–19) and the **Serres Tropicales** (Tropical Greenhouses), renovated in 2008; the **Jardin Alpin** (Map pp218-19; weekend admission adult/under 4yr/4-15yr €1/free/0.50; 8am-4.30pm Mon-Fri, 1-5pm Sat & Sun Apr-Oct), and the **Ménagerie du Jardin des Plantes** (Botanical Garden Zoo; Map pp218-19; adult/under 4yr/4-15yr €7/free/5; 9am-5pm), a historic zoo founded in 1794.

The gardens also contain the city's main natural history museum, the **Musée National d'Histoire Naturelle** (Map pp218-19; ☎ 01 40 79 30 00;

www.mnhn.fr, in French; 57 rue Cuvier, 5e; 10am-5pm Wed-Mon; M Censier Daubenton or Gare d'Austerlitz), with several galleries covering evolution, geology, palaeontology and the history of human evolution. You can buy individual tickets, but the two-day combo ticket is much better value at €20/15 adult/child.

OPÉRA & GRANDS BOULEVARDS

Place de l'Opéra is the site of Paris' world-famous (and original) opera house, the **Palais Garnier** (Map pp212-13; 08 92 89 90 90; place de l'Opéra, 9e; M Opéra). Around the opera house are the eight contiguous 'Great Boulevards' – Madeleine, Capucines, Italiens, Montmartre, Poissonnière, Bonne Nouvelle, St-Denis and St-Martin – laid out in the 17th century, and later the cultural hub of the city during the belle époque. Blvd Haussmann is the heart of the city's commercial district and boasts many famous department stores, including Galeries Lafayette and Le Printemps (p236).

If you fancy taking a look inside the opera house, guided **tours** (08 25 05 44 05; http://visites.operadeparis.fr; adult/10-25yr/senior €12/6/10; 11.30am & 2.30pm daily Jul & Aug, 11.30am & 2.30pm Wed, Sat & Sun Sep-Jun) run in summer, or you can check out three centuries' worth of operatic costumes, backdrops and scenery at the **opera house museum** (Map pp212-13; 08 92 89 90 90, 01 40 01 24 93; adult/under 10yr/senior, student & 10-25yr €8/free/5; 10am-5pm Sep-Jun, to 6pm Jul & Aug).

The Islands

ÎLE ST-LOUIS

The smaller of the Seine's twin islands, **Île St-Louis** (Map pp218-19; M Pont Marie) is just downstream from the Île de la Cité. The streets and quays of Île St-Louis are lined with 17th-century houses, art galleries and upmarket shops, and it feels a world away from the hustle of the rest of the city. The area around **Pont St-Louis**, the bridge across to the Île de la Cité, and **Pont Louis Philippe**, the bridge to the Marais, is one of the most romantic spots in Paris.

ÎLE DE LA CITÉ

The site of the first settlement in Paris around the 3rd century BC and later the Roman town of Lutèce (Lutetia), the **Île de la Cité** (Map pp218–19) remained the centre of royal and ecclesiastical power throughout the Middle Ages. The seven decorated arches of Paris' oldest bridge, **Pont Neuf** (Map pp218-19; M Pont Neuf) have linked the Île de la Cité with both banks of the Seine since 1607.

CATHÉDRALE DE NOTRE DAME DE PARIS

The **Cathédrale de Notre Dame de Paris** (Map pp218-19; 01 42 34 56 10; www.cathedraledeparis.com; place du Parvis Notre Dame, 4e; audio guide €5; 7.45am-6.45pm; M Cité) is the true heart of Paris; in fact, distances from Paris to all parts of metropolitan France are measured from **place du Parvis Notre Dame**, the square in front of Notre Dame.

Notre Dame is one of the masterpieces of French Gothic architecture, famed for its stunning stained-glass rose windows, leering gargoyles and elegant flying buttresses, as well as a monumental 7800-pipe organ. Constructed on a site occupied by earlier churches (and, a millennium before that, a Gallo-Roman temple), it was begun in 1163 and completed by the mid-14th century, before being heavily restored by the 19th-century architect Viollet-le-Duc. The interior is 130m long, 48m wide and 35m high and can hold 6000 worshippers. Free tours in English run at noon on Wednesday and Thursday and at 2.30pm on Saturday.

The entrance to the famous **tours de Notre Dame** (Map pp218-19; 01 53 10 07 02; rue du Cloître Notre Dame; adult/under 18yr/18-25yr €7.50/free/4.80, 1st Sun of month Oct-Mar free; 10am-6.30pm daily Apr-Jun & Sep, 9am-7.30pm Mon-Fri, 9am-11pm Sat & Sun Jul & Aug, 10am-5.30pm daily Oct-Mar) is from the North Tower. The 422 spiralling steps take you to the top of the west facade for face-to-face views of countless gargoyles, the massive 13-tonne 'Emmanuel' bell in the South Tower and an unforgettable bird's-eye view of Paris. No hunchbacks, though, despite what you may have heard from Victor Hugo.

STE-CHAPELLE & THE CONCIERGERIE

Paris' most exquisite Gothic monument is **Ste-Chapelle** (Holy Chapel; Map pp218-19; 01 53 40 60 97; www.monuments-nationaux.fr; 4 blvd du Palais, 1er; adult/under 18yr/18-25yr €6.50/free/4.50, 1st Sun of month Oct-Mar free; 9.30am-6pm Mar-Oct, 9am-5pm Nov-Feb; M Cité), tucked within the Palais de Justice (Law Courts). Built in just under three years, Ste-Chapelle was consecrated in 1248. The chapel was conceived by Louis IX to house his sacred relics, now kept in the treasury of Notre Dame.

Nearby, the 14th-century palace known as the **Conciergerie** (Map pp218-19; 01 53 40 60 97; www.monuments-nationaux.fr; 2 blvd du Palais, 1er; adult/

under 18yr/18-25yr €8/free/6, 1st Sun of month Oct-Mar free; 9.30am-6pm Mar-Oct, 9am-5pm Nov-Feb; M Cité) became the city's main prison during the Reign of Terror (1793–94). Many famous inmates were incarcerated here before meeting their eventual fate beneath the guillotine, including Marie Antoinette, the radicals Danton, Robespierre and, finally, the Tribunal judges themselves. You can also visit Europe's largest surviving medieval hall, the **Salle des Gens d'Armes** (Cavalrymen's Hall). A joint ticket with Ste-Chapelle costs €11.50/9 adult/18 to 25 years.

Right Bank

MUSÉE DU LOUVRE

The vast Palais du Louvre was constructed as a fortress by Philippe-Auguste in the 13th century and rebuilt in the mid-16th century for use as a royal residence. In 1793 the Revolutionary Convention transformed it into the **Musée du Louvre** (Map pp218-19; ☎ 01 40 20 53 17; www.louvre.fr; admission permanent collections/permanent collections & temporary exhibits €9/13, after 6pm Wed & Fri €6/11, permanent collections free for under 18yr & after 6pm Fri for under 26yr, 1st Sun of month free; 9am-6pm Mon, Thu, Sat & Sun, 9am-10pm Wed & Fri; M Palais Royal-Musée du Louvre), the nation's first (and foremost) national museum.

There are four main sections: the Sully, Denon and Richelieu Wings, and the Hall Napoléon, collectively housing a staggering 35,000 exhibits. It's been estimated that you'd need about nine months to see everything, so trying to pack it all into a single afternoon isn't a terribly good idea: you'll get much more out if it by concentrating on a single section or period that interests you.

The collection is mind-bogglingly diverse, ranging from Islamic artworks and Egyptian artefacts through to a fabulous collection of Greek and Roman antiquities (including the *Venus de Milo* and the *Winged Victory of Samothrace*). But it's the celebrated paintings that draw most visitors; highlights include signature works by Raphael, Botticelli, Delacroix, Titian, Géricault and of course Leonardo da Vinci's slyly smiling *La Joconde*, better known as the *Mona Lisa*. If you have time, don't miss the section devoted to objets d'art, which houses a series of fabulously extravagant salons, including the apartments of Napoleon III's Minister of State, a collection of priceless Sèvres porcelain and the crown jewels of Louis XV.

The gallery's main entrance and ticket windows in the Cour Napoléon are covered by the iconic 21m-high **Pyramide du Louvre**, a glass pyramid designed by the Chinese-American architect IM Pei. You can avoid the queues outside the pyramid or the Porte des Lions entrance by entering via the Carrousel du Louvre shopping centre, at 99 rue de Rivoli, or by following the 'Musée du Louvre' exit from the Palais Royal-Musée du Louvre metro. Machines in the Carrousel du Louvre sell advance tickets, or for an extra €1.10 you can buy online (www.louvre.fr), from Fnac ticket offices, or by ringing ☎ 08 92 68 36 22 or 08 25 34 63 46. Tickets remain valid for the whole day.

Free maps are available at the circular information desk in the centre of the Hall Napoléon, and multilingual audio guides (€5) can be hired at the entrance to each wing. 1½-hour **guided tours** (☎ 01 40 20 52 63; tours €5) in English leave from under the Pyramide du Louvre at 11am, 2pm and (sometimes) 3.45pm Monday to Saturday.

JARDIN DES TUILERIES

Joggers and picnickers congregate in the 28-hectare **Jardin des Tuileries** (Map pp212-13; ☎ 01 40 20 90 43; 7am-9pm daily Apr, May & Sep, 7am-11pm Jun-Aug, 7.30am-7.30pm Oct-Mar; M Tuileries or Concorde), laid out in the mid-17th century by André Le Nôtre, designer of the gardens at Versailles (p240).

The stately palace that once stood beside the gardens, the Palais des Tuileries, was largely razed during the Revolution, but two of its buildings still remain and have now been converted for use as museums. In the northwestern corner is the **Galerie Nationale du Jeu de Paume** (Map pp212-13; ☎ 01 47 03 12 50; www.jeudepaume.org; 1 place de la Concorde, 1er; adult/under 13yr/senior, student & 13-18yr €6/free/3; noon-9pm Tue, noon-7pm Wed-Fri, 10am-7pm Sat & Sun; M Concorde), housed in a mid-19th-century building designed for playing 'real' tennis, now used for contemporary art exhibitions.

In the gardens' southwestern corner is the **Musée de l'Orangerie** (Map pp212-13; ☎ 01 44 77 80 07; www.musee-orangerie.fr; Jardin des Tuileries, 1er; adult/senior, student & 13-18yr €6.50/4.50, 1st Sun of month free; 12.30-7pm Wed, Thu & Sat-Mon, 12.30-9pm Fri; M Concorde), which exhibits some important Impressionist works, including a series of Monet's *Water Lilies*), as well as works by Cézanne, Matisse, Picasso, Renoir, Sisley and Utrillo.

ARC DE TRIOMPHE

The **Arc de Triomphe** (Map pp212-13; ☎ 01 55 37 73 77; www.monuments-nationaux.fr; viewing platform adult/under 18yr/18-25yr €9/free/6.50, 1st Sun of month Nov-Mar free; ⏰ 10am-11pm daily Apr-Sep, to 10.30pm Oct-Mar; Ⓜ Charles de Gaulle-Étoile) stands in the middle of the world's largest traffic roundabout, **place de l'Étoile** (Map pp212-13; Ⓜ Charles de Gaulle Étoile), officially known as place Charles de Gaulle. The 'triumphal arch' was commissioned in 1806 by Napoleon to commemorate his victories, but remained unfinished when he started losing battles, and wasn't completed until 1836. Since 1920, the body of an **unknown soldier** from WWI has lain beneath the arch; a memorial flame is rekindled each evening around 6.30pm.

The **viewing platform** affords wonderful views of the dozen avenues that radiate out from the arch, many of which are named after Napoleonic generals. **Av Foch** is Paris' widest boulevard, while **av des Champs Élysées** leads south to **place de la Concorde** and its famous 3300-year-old pink granite obelisk, which once stood in the Temple of Ramses at Thebes (present-day Luxor).

PLACE VENDÔME

The octagonal **place Vendôme** (Map pp212-13; Ⓜ Tuileries or Opéra) has long been one of the city's smartest addresses, famous for its 18th-century architecture, exclusive boutiques and the superposh Hôtel Ritz-Paris. The 43.5m-tall **Colonne Vendôme** was fashioned from cannons captured by Napoleon at the Battle of Austerlitz in 1805; the general stands on top of the column dressed in suitably imperial garb.

CENTRE POMPIDOU

Opened in 1977, the **Centre National d'Art et de Culture Georges Pompidou** (Map pp218-19; ☎ 01 44 78 12 33; www.centrepompidou.fr; place Georges Pompidou, 4e; Ⓜ Rambuteau) – Centre Pompidou for short, and also known as the Centre Beaubourg – is one of central Paris' most iconic modern buildings; it was one of the first structures to have its 'insides' turned out. It's now a huge cultural and artistic centre; the main attraction is the **Musée National d'Art Moderne** (MNAM, Map pp218-19; adult €10-12, senior & 18-25yr €8-10, under 18yr free, free 6-9pm Wed for 18-25yr, 1st Sun of month free for all; ⏰ 11am-9pm Wed-Mon), on the 4th and 5th floors, which contains France's national collection of post-1905 art, with surrealists, cubists, fauvists and pop artists all amply represented.

Elsewhere you'll find temporary art exhibitions, cinemas, a library, and a museum devoted to the Romanian sculptor Brancusi (1876–1957), while outside, buskers and street artists congregate around lively place Georges Pompidou, and nearby place Igor Stravinsky is famous for its fanciful mechanical fountains of lips, skeletons and treble clef.

HÔTEL DE VILLE

After having been gutted during the Paris Commune of 1871, Paris' **Hôtel de Ville** (Map pp218-19; ☎ 39 75; www.paris.fr; place de l'Hôtel de Ville, 4e; Ⓜ Hôtel de Ville) was rebuilt in the neo-Renaissance style (1874–82). The ornate facade is decorated with 108 statues of noteworthy Parisians. There's a **Salon d'Accueil** (Reception Hall; 29 rue de Rivoli, 4e; ⏰ 10am-7pm Mon-Sat), which dispenses copious amounts of information and brochures and is used for temporary exhibitions, usually with a Paris theme.

PLACE DES VOSGES

The Marais, the area of the Right Bank north of Île St-Louis in the 3e and 4e, was originally a marsh before it was transformed into one of the city's most fashionable districts by Henri IV, who constructed the elegant *hôtels particuliers* around place Royale – today known as the **Place des Vosges** (Map pp218-19; Ⓜ St-Paul or Bastille).

The novelist Victor Hugo lived here from 1832 to 1848, and the **Maison de Victor Hugo** (Map pp218-19; ☎ 01 42 72 10 16; www.musee-hugo.paris.fr, in French; permanent collections admission free, temporary exhibitions adult/under 14yr/senior & student/14-26yr €7.50/free/3.50/5.50; ⏰ 10am-6pm Tue-Sun) now houses drawings, paintings and memorabilia relating to the author.

MUSÉE PICASSO

The **Musée Picasso** (Map pp218-19; ☎ 01 42 71 25 21; www.musee-picasso.fr, in French; 5 rue de Thorigny, 3e; adult/under 18yr/18-25yr €7.70/free/5.70, 1st Sun of month free; ⏰ 9.30am-6pm Wed-Mon Apr-Sep, 9.30am-5.30pm Wed-Mon Oct-Mar; Ⓜ St-Paul or Chemin Vert) contains more than 3500 of the *grand maître*'s engravings, paintings, ceramics and sculptures, as well as works from his own art collection by Braque, Cézanne, Matisse, Modigliani, Degas and Rousseau.

PLACE DE LA BASTILLE

The Bastille is the most famous monument in Paris that no longer exists; the notorious prison was demolished by a Revolutionary mob on 14 July 1789, and the **place de la Bastille** (Map pp218-19; Ⓜ Bastille) where the prison once stood is now a busy traffic roundabout. The 52m-high **Colonne de Juillet** (July Column) was erected in memory of Parisians killed during the July Revolution of 1830.

Just south of the square is Paris' 'second' opera house, the **Opéra Bastille** (Map pp218-19; ☎ 08 92 89 90 90; www.opera-de-paris.fr, in French; 2-6 place de la Bastille, 12e; Ⓜ Bastille), inaugurated on 14 July 1989 to mark the 200th anniversary of the storming of the Bastille. There are 1¼-hour **guided tours** (☎ 01 40 01 19 70; adult/under 11yr/senior, student & 11-25yr €11/6/9), which usually depart at 1.15pm Monday to Saturday. Tickets go on sale 10 minutes before departure at the **box office** (130 rue de Lyon, 12e; 🕑 10.30am-6.30pm Mon-Sat).

MONTMARTRE & PIGALLE

During the late 19th and early 20th centuries, bohemian Montmartre attracted a number of important writers and artists, including Picasso, who lived at the studio called **Bateau Lavoir** (Map p224; 11bis place Émile Goudeau; Ⓜ Abbesses) from 1908 to 1912. Although the activity shifted to Montparnasse after WWI, Montmartre retains an upbeat ambience that all the tourists in the world couldn't spoil.

Montmartre's most famous landmark is the **Basilique du Sacré Cœur** (Map p224; ☎ 01 53 41 89 00; www.sacre-coeur-montmartre.com; place du Parvis du Sacré Cœur, 18e; 🕑 6am-10.30pm; Ⓜ Anvers), whose gleaming white **dome** (admission €5; 🕑 9am-7pm daily Apr-Sep, 9am-6pm Oct-Mar) has one of the most spectacular city panoramas anywhere in Paris.

Nearby **place du Tertre** (Map p224; Ⓜ Abbesses) was once the main square of the village of Montmartre; these days it's filled with cafes, restaurants, endless tourists and a concentrated cluster of caricaturists and painters – if you want to get your portrait painted in Paris, this is definitely the place.

Only a few blocks southwest of the tranquil residential streets of Montmartre is lively, neon-lit Pigalle (9e and 18e), one of Paris' two main sex districts. It's connected to the top

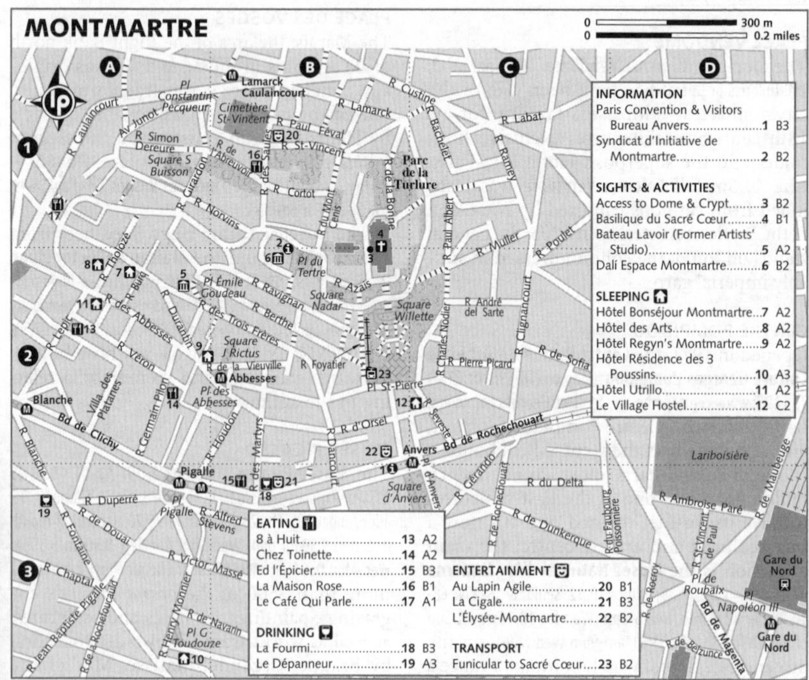

BOIS DE BOULOGNE & VINCENNES

The so-called 'lungs' of Paris, the **Bois de Vincennes** and the **Bois de Boulogne** make ideal places for picnicking, sunbathing and generally escaping the city hustle.

The 845-hectare **Bois de Boulogne** (Map pp212-13; blvd Maillot, 16e; Ⓜ Porte Maillot), on the western edge of Paris, was inspired by Hyde Park in London. Attractions include formal gardens, a kids' amusement park and the 1775 **Château de Bagatelle** (Map pp212-13; ☎ 01 40 67 97 00; route de Sèvres à Neuilly, 16e; adult/under 7yr/student & 7-18yr €3/free/1.50; 🕑 9am-6pm Apr-Sep, 9am-5pm Oct-Mar). It's best to steer clear after dark, as the Bois de Boulogne is a well-known zone for unsavoury types.

On the southeast edge of the city, the 995-hectare **Bois de Vincennes** (Map pp212-13; blvd Poniatowski, 12e; Ⓜ Porte de Charenton or Porte Dorée) encompasses its own fortified castle, the **Château de Vincennes** (off Map pp212-13; ☎ 01 48 08 31 20; www.chateau-vincennes.fr; av de Paris, 12e; 🕑 10am-6pm May-Aug, 10am-5pm Sep-Apr; Ⓜ Château de Vincennes); it's free to explore the grounds, but the keep and royal chapel can only be visited on a guided **tour** (adult/under 18yr/18-25yr €7.50/free/4.80). Nearby there's a huge floral park, zoo and aquarium.

of Butte de Montmartre (Montmartre Hill) by a funicular.

CIMETIÈRE DE MONTMARTRE

Established in 1798, **Cimetière de Montmartre** (Map pp212-13; 🕑 8am-6pm Mon-Fri, 8.30am-6pm Sat, 9am-6pm Sun mid-Mar–early Nov, 8am-5.30pm Mon-Fri, 8.30am-5.30pm Sat, 9am-5.30pm Sun early Nov–mid-Mar; Ⓜ Place de Clichy) is the most famous cemetery in Paris after Père Lachaise (below). It contains the graves of writers Émile Zola, Alexandre Dumas and Stendhal, composer Jacques Offenbach, artist Edgar Degas, film director François Truffaut and dancer Vaslav Nijinsky – among others. Maps are available free from the **conservation office** (☎ 01 53 42 36 30; 20 av Rachel, 18e).

DALÍ ESPACE MONTMARTRE

More than 300 works by Salvador Dalí (1904–89), the flamboyant Catalan surrealist printmaker, painter, sculptor and self-promoter, are on display at the **Dalí Espace Montmartre** (Map p224; ☎ 01 42 64 40 10; www.daliparis.com; 11 rue Poulbot, 18e; adult/under 8yr/student & 8-26yr/senior €10/free/6/7; 🕑 10am-6.30pm; Ⓜ Abbesses), a surrealist-style basement museum west of place du Tertre. The collection includes reproductions of Dalí's strange sculptures, lithographs, illustrations and furniture (including the 'lips' sofa).

CIMETIÈRE DU PÈRE LACHAISE

The world's most-visited graveyard, **Cimetière du Père Lachaise** (Map pp212-13; ☎ 01 55 25 82 10; admission free; 🕑 8am-6pm Mon-Fri, 8.30am-6pm Sat, 9am-6pm Sun mid-Mar–early Nov, 8am-5.30pm Mon-Fri, 8.30am-5.30pm Sat, 9am-5.30pm Sun early Nov–mid-Mar; Ⓜ Philippe Auguste, Gambetta or Père Lachaise) opened its one-way doors in 1804. Among the 800,000 people buried here are Chopin, Molière, Balzac, Proust, Gertrude Stein, Colette, Pissarro, Seurat, Modigliani, Sarah Bernhardt, Yves Montand, Delacroix, Édith Piaf and even the 12th-century lovers Abélard and Héloïse. The graves of **Oscar Wilde** (Division 89) and **Jim Morrison** (Division 6) are perennially popular. Free maps are available from the **conservation office** (Map pp212-13; 16 rue du Repos, 20e).

ACTIVITIES

Cycling

Paris is a lot more bike-friendly these days, with 370km of dedicated cycle lanes running through the city. Get hold of the free booklet *Paris à Vélo* (Paris by Bicycle), published by the Mairie de Paris. For bike hire, try **Maison Roue Libre** (☎ 08 10 44 15 34; www.rouelibre.fr; 🕑 9am-7pm daily Feb-Oct, 10am-6pm Wed-Sun Nov & Jan; Forum des Halles Map pp218-19; Forum des Halles, 1 passage Mondétour, 1er; Ⓜ Les Halles; Bastille Map pp218-19; 37 blvd Bourdon, 4e; Ⓜ Bastille), sponsored by RATP, the city's public transport system. Bicycles cost €4/10/15/28 per hour/half-day/day/weekend (plus €150 deposit) and include insurance, helmet and baby seat.

For guided tours, contact **Fat Tire Bike Tours** (Map pp212-13; ☎ 01 56 58 10 54; www.fattirebiketoursparis.com; 24 rue Edgar Faure, 15e; 🕑 office 9am-6pm; Ⓜ La Motte Picquet Grenelle), which runs a daily spin around the city (adult/student €24/22) at 11am daily, plus 3pm from April to October. Night tours (adult/student €28/26) depart at 7pm daily from mid-March to October, and on Tuesday, Thursday, Saturday and Sunday in winter.

Tours start near the Eiffel Tower's south pillar. Bike hire and rain gear are included.

Boat Trips

There's no finer way to appreciate the City of Lights than a cruise on the River Seine. The most famous riverboat company is **Bateaux Mouches** (Map pp212-13; ☎ 01 42 25 96 10; www.bateauxmouches.com, in French; Port de la Conférence, 8e; adult/under 4yr/senior & 4-12yr €9/free/4; mid-Mar–mid-Nov; Ⓜ Alma Marceau), based just east of the Pont de l'Alma. From April to September, 1000-seater cruises (70 minutes) depart eight times daily between 10.15am and 3.15pm and then every 20 minutes till 11pm. They depart 10 times a day between 10.15am and 9pm the rest of the year. Commentary is in French and English.

Alternatively, **Paris Canal Croisières** (Map pp212-13; ☎ 01 42 40 96 97; www.pariscanal.com; Bassin de la Villette, 19-21 quai de la Loire, 19e; adult/under 4yr/4-11yr/senior & 12-25yr €17/free/10/14; Ⓜ Jaurès) has daily 2½-hour cruises via the charming Canal St-Martin and Canal de l'Ourcq. Departures are at 9.30am from quai Anatole France and at 2.30pm from Bassin de la Villette.

Walking

Paris Walks (☎ 01 48 09 21 40; www.paris-walks.com; adult/under 15yr/student under 21yr from €10/5/8) has English-language tours of several different districts, including Montmartre at 10.30am on Sunday and Wednesday (leaving from Abbesses metro station, Map p224) and the Marais at 10.30am on Tuesday and at 2.30pm on Sunday (departing from St-Paul metro station, Map pp218–19). There are other tours focusing on themes including Hemingway, medieval Paris, the Latin Quarter, fashion, the French Revolution and even chocolate.

SLEEPING

The Paris Convention & Visitors Bureau (p215) can nearly always find you a room and doesn't charge for reservations, although you'll need a credit card, and queues can be horrendously long in high season. For B&B rooms, contact **Alcôve & Agapes** (☎ 01 44 85 06 05; www.bed-and-breakfast-in-paris.com) and **Good Morning Paris** (☎ 01 47 07 44 45; www.goodmorningparis.fr).

Louvre & Les Halles

Centre International de Séjour BVJ Paris–Louvre (Map pp218-19; ☎ 01 53 00 90 90; www.bvjhotel.com; 20 rue Jean-Jacques Rousseau, 1er; dm/d €28/60; Ⓜ Louvre-Rivoli;) Modern 200-bed hostel run by the Bureau des Voyages de la Jeunesse (Youth Travel Bureau), with bunks in single-sex dorms for the 18 to 35 crowd. There's no kitchen, but there's usually space even in summer, so pitch up early.

Hôtel de Lille (Map pp218-19; ☎ 01 42 33 33 42; 8 rue du Pélican, 1er; s €35-38, d €43-50, tr €65-75; Ⓜ Palais Royal-Musée du Louvre) This old-fashioned but spotlessly clean 13-room hotel is down a quiet side street in a 17th-century building. Some rooms have just washbasin and bidet (communal showers cost €3),while the rest have showers too.

Marais & Bastille

BUDGET

Auberge de Jeunesse Jules Ferry (Map pp212-13; ☎ 01 43 57 55 60; www.fuaj.fr; 8 blvd Jules Ferry, 11e; dm/d €21/42; Ⓜ République or Goncourt;) This 'official' hostel is institutional but the atmosphere's relaxed. The 99 beds are in two- to six-person rooms, all locked between 10.30am and 2pm for housekeeping, but there's no curfew. HI cards buy a discount of €2.90 per night.

Hôtel Rivoli (Map pp218-19; ☎ 01 42 72 08 41; 44 rue de Rivoli or 2 rue des Mauvais Garçons, 4e; s €35-55, d €44-55, tr €70; Ⓜ Hôtel de Ville) Long an LP favourite, the Rivoli is forever cheery but not as dirt cheap as it once was, with 20 basic, noisy rooms. The cheaper singles and doubles have washbasins only but showers are free. The front door is locked from 2am to 7am.

Maison Internationale de la Jeunesse et des Étudiants (MIJE; Map pp218-19; ☎ 01 42 74 23 45; www.mije.com; dm/s/d/tr €29/47/68/90;) The MIJE runs three hostels in renovated 17th- and 18th-century *hôtels particuliers* (private mansions) in the heart of the Marais, and it's difficult to think of a better budget deal in Paris. Costs are the same for all three; there are single-sex, shower-equipped dorms, as well as singles, doubles/twins and triples. The curfew is 1am to 7am, and the maximum stay is seven nights. You can make reservations by calling the central switchboard or emailing; they'll hold you a bed till noon.

Hôtel de Nevers (Map pp218-19; ☎ 01 47 00 56 18; www.hoteldenevers.com; 53 rue de Malte, 11e; s €39, d €45-55, tr €75-87;; Ⓜ Oberkampf;) This 32-room budget hotel is handy for the Marais nightlife. Cheaper rooms share bathing facilities, and if you like cats you'll be dead happy – there are three in-house moggies to greet prospective guests.

MIJE Le Fauconnier (Map pp218-19; 11 rue du Fauconnier, 4e; Ⓜ St-Paul or Pont Marie) A 125-bed hostel two blocks south of MIJE Le Fourcy.

FRANCE

MIJE Le Fourcy (Map pp218-19; 6 rue de Fourcy, 4e; M St-Paul) The largest of the three branches, with 180 beds. The three-course *menu* is a bargain at €10.50.

MIJE Maubuisson (Map pp218-19; 12 rue des Barres, 4e; M Hôtel de Ville or Pont Marie) The pick of the three, this 99-bed place is half a block south of the local *mairie* (city hall).

MIDRANGE & TOP END

Hôtel Jeanne d'Arc (Map pp218-19; ☎ 01 48 87 62 11; www.hoteljeannedarc.com; 3 rue de Jarente, 4e; s €60-97, d €84-97, tr/q €116/146; M St-Paul; 💻) This cosy, 36-room hotel near place du Marché Ste-Catherine almost has a country feel and is a great little base for exploring the Marais. Sadly, it's far from a well-kept secret these days, so book ahead. Wheelchair access available.

our pick **Hôtel du Septième Art** (Map pp218-19; ☎ 01 44 54 85 00; www.paris-hotel-7art.com; 20 rue St-Paul, 4e; s €65, d €90-145; M St-Paul; 💻) Filmic fun place for cinema buffs (*le septième art*, or 'the seventh art', is what the French call cinema), with a black-and-white-movie theme throughout the 23 rooms, right down to the tiled floors and bathrooms.

Hôtel Sévigné (Map pp218-19; ☎ 01 42 72 76 17; www.le-sevigne.com; 2 rue Malher, 4e; s €67, d & tw €80-91, tr €107; M St-Paul; ❄) Named after the celebrated 17th-century writer the Marquise de Sévigné, and offering an excellent price:location ratio. The hotel's 29 rooms, spread over six lift-accessible floors, are basic but comfortably furnished.

Hôtel de la Place des Vosges (Map pp218-19; ☎ 01 42 72 60 46; www.hotelplacedesvosges.com; 12 rue de Birague, 4e; r €90-95, ste €150; M Bastille; 💻) This superbly situated 17-room hotel is an oasis of tranquillity near sublime place des Vosges. The public areas are impressive and the rooms warm and cosy – floors one to four have a lift, but beyond that it's stairs only. Go for the top-floor suite for fab views.

Hôtel St-Louis Marais (Map pp218-19; ☎ 01 48 87 87 04; www.saintlouismarais.com; 1 rue Charles V, 4e; s €99, d & tw €115-140, tr €150, ste €160; 💻) Charming hotel in a converted 17th-century convent (more Bastille than Marais). Wooden beams, terracotta tiles and heavy drapes tend to darken the 19 rooms but certainly do add to the atmosphere.

Hôtel de la Bretonnerie (Map pp218-19; ☎ 01 48 87 77 63; www.bretonnerie.com; 22 rue Ste-Croix de la Bretonnerie, 4e; r €125-160, ste €185-210; M Hôtel de Ville; 💻) With 17th-century architecture, a central Marais location, and a smattering of four-poster and canopy beds, this hotel is a real find. Three 'duplex' suites can easily accommodate three or four people.

our pick **Hôtel Caron de Beaumarchais** (Map pp218-19; ☎ 01 42 72 34 12; www.carondebeaumarchais.com; 12 rue Vieille du Temple, 4e; r €125-162; M St-Paul; ❄ 💻) Decorated as an 18th-century private house, this is an ostentatious little gem. An 18th-century pianoforte, gaming tables, gilded mirrors, and candelabras, set the tone in the palatial lobby, but the 19 rooms are smallish and the welcome's rather frosty.

our pick **Hôtel St-Merry** (Map pp218-19; ☎ 01 42 78 14 15; www.hotelmarais.com; 78 rue de la Verrerie, 4e; d & tw €160-230, tr €205-275, ste €335-407; M Châtelet; 💻) Beamed ceilings, church pews and wrought-iron candelabra make this a goth's dream (or should that be nightmare?) come true. Standing side by side with next-door Église St-Merry, the 11 rooms and single suite are crammed with Gothic character, but there's no lift or air-con.

Hôtel du Petit Moulin (Map pp218-19; ☎ 01 42 74 10 10; www.hoteldupetitmoulin.com; 29-31 rue de Poitou, 3e; r €180-280, ste €350; M Filles du Calvaire; ❄ 💻) Scrumptious boutique hotel designed from top to bottom by Christian Lacroix. Its 17 rooms, named after Parisian neighbourhoods, range from medieval and rococo Marais to more modern *quartier* with contemporary murals and heart-shaped mirrors.

The Islands

Hôtel Henri IV (Map pp218-19; ☎ 01 43 54 44 53; 25 place Dauphine, 1er; s & d €52-76, tr €76; M Pont Neuf or Cité) This dowdy old place, with 15 worn rooms, is worth the nod solely for its location, location, location on the tip of the Île de la Cité. It's romantic and dead cheap, but a little threadbare round the edges. Book well in advance.

Latin Quarter

The Latin Quarter offers the best value on Paris' Left Bank, especially compared with the sky-high prices of the hotels in the neighbouring 6e.

Young & Happy Hostel (Map pp218-19; ☎ 01 47 07 47 07; www.youngandhappy.fr; 80 rue Mouffetard, 5e; dm/d €23/52; M Place Monge; 💻) Frayed but friendly spot in the centre of the Latin Quarter, popular with a slightly older crowd nowadays. Beds are in cramped rooms for two to eight people with washbasins. Turn up pre-8am if you want to bag a bed in summer.

Centre International de Séjour BVJ Paris–Quartier Latin (Map pp218-19; ☎ 01 43 29 34 80; www.bvjhotel.com;

44 rue des Bernardins, 5e; dm/s/d €28/42/64; Ⓜ Maubert Mutualité; 💻) This Left Bank hostel is a sister branch of the Centre International BVJ Paris–Louvre (p226). It has 100 beds in singles, doubles and single-sex dorms for four to 10 people – all with showers and telephones.

Port Royal Hôtel (Map pp212-13; ☎ 01 43 31 70 06; www.hotelportroyal.fr; 8 blvd de Port Royal, 5e; s €41-89, d €52.50-89; Ⓜ Les Gobelins) It's hard to imagine that this 46-room hotel, owned and managed by the same family for three generations, still only bears one star. The spotless, quiet rooms overlook a glassed-in courtyard (eg No 15) or the street (No 14), but we especially like room 11, with its colourful bed frame and pretty bathroom.

Hôtel Cluny Sorbonne (Map pp218-19; ☎ 01 43 54 66 66; www.hotel-cluny.fr; 8 rue Victor Cousin, 5e; d €70-95, q €130-150; Ⓜ Luxembourg; 💻) Surrounded by the prestigious buildings of the Sorbonne University, this hotel has literary cachet (Rimbaud dallied here in 1872). Its 23 rooms are showing their age, but the cheery staff make up for its shortfalls: ask for room 63, for memorable views of the college and the Panthéon.

Familia Hôtel (Map pp218-19; ☎ 01 43 54 55 27; www.familiahotel.com; 11 rue des Écoles, 5e; s €86, d & tw €103-124, tr €161-173, q €184; Ⓜ Cardinal Lemoine; ❄ 💻) Family-run hotel with sepia-tinted murals of Paris' landmarks in 21 of its 30 rooms. Eight have balconies with distant glimpses of Notre Dame. By far the choicest rooms are Nos 61, 62 and 65 (with four-poster bed), and we love the flowery windows, parquet floors and complimentary buffet breakfast.

Hôtel Minerve (Map pp218-19; ☎ 01 43 26 26 04; www.parishotelminerve.com; 13 rue des Écoles, 5e; s €90-125, d €106-136, tr €156-158, all incl breakfast; Ⓜ Cardinal Lemoine; ❄ 💻) Run by the owners of the Familia, this two-building hotel is decked out in oriental carpets, antique books, frescoes of French monuments and reproduction 18th-century wallpapers. Aim for a Notre Dame view, or ask for one of the courtyard rooms for that extra-romantic touch.

Hôtel St-Jacques (Map pp218-19; ☎ 01 44 07 45 45; www.hotel-saintjacques.com; 35 rue des Écoles, 5e; s €92, d €105-137, tr €168; Ⓜ Maubert Mutualité; ❄ 💻) Stylish 38-room hotel overlooking the Panthéon. Audrey Hepburn and Cary Grant, who filmed *Charade* here in the 1960s, would appreciate the mod cons that now complement the trompe l'œil ceilings and iron staircase.

our pick **Hôtel des Grandes Écoles** (Map pp218-19; ☎ 01 43 26 79 23; www.hotel-grandes-ecoles.com; 75 rue du Cardinal Lemoine, 5e; d €110-135, tr €125-155; Ⓜ Cardinal Lemoine or Place Monge) Wonderful hotel with one of the loveliest situations in the Latin Quarter, tucked away off a medieval street around its own courtyard. There are three buildings: our favourite is the garden annexe, with five rooms (Nos 29 to 33) leading directly onto the terrace.

St-Germain, Odéon & Luxembourg

The well-heeled St-Germain des Prés is the quintessential place to stay in central Paris, but you'll need to bring your spare change – budget places just don't exist in this part of town.

Hôtel de Nesle (Map pp218-19; ☎ 01 43 54 62 41; www.hoteldenesleparis.com; 7 rue de Nesle, 6e; s €55-85, d €75-100; Ⓜ Odéon or Mabillon) The Nesle is a relaxed, colourful place with 20 rooms, half of which are painted with murals taken from classic literature. Pathways, trellises and a small fountain are dotted around the delightful rear garden; room 12 has the nicest aspect.

Hôtel du Globe (Map pp218-19; ☎ 01 43 26 35 50; www.hotel-du-globe.fr; 15 rue des Quatre Vents, 6e; s €95-140, d €115-150, ste €180; Ⓜ Odéon; 💻) The Globe is an eclectic caravanserai with 14 small but completely renovated rooms just south of the blvd St-Germain. Some rooms verge on the minuscule, and there is no lift. Still, we're suckers for armour – there are at least two full sets here – and canopy beds (go for room 43).

Hôtel du Lys (Map pp218-19; ☎ 01 43 26 97 57; www.hoteldulys.com; 23 rue Serpente, 6e; s/d/tr €100/120/140; Ⓜ Odéon) This 22-room hotel is situated in a former 17th-century *hôtel particulier*. Beamed ceiling and chinoiserie wallpaper in the lobby, and a tempting choice of rooms including blue-toned No 13 and terracotta-themed No 14.

Faubourg St-Denis & Invalides

The 7e is a lovely arrondissement in which to stay, but it's a little removed from the action.

Hôtel du Champ-de-Mars (Map pp212-13; ☎ 01 45 51 52 30; www.hotelduchampdemars.com; 7 rue du Champ de Mars, 7e; s/d/tw/tr €84/90/94/112; Ⓜ École Militaire; 💻) This charming 25-room hotel in the shadow of the Eiffel Tower is on everyone's wish list, so book a good month in advance. The shopfront entrance leads to a colourful lobby done up in yellow and charcoal. Lower rooms are cupboard-like – go higher for a glimpse of Mademoiselle Eiffel.

Mayet Hôtel (Map pp212-13; ☎ 01 47 83 21 35; www.mayet.com; 3 rue Mayet, 6e; s incl breakfast €95-120, d €120-140, tr €160; Ⓜ Duroc; 💻) Light-hearted and loads of fun, this 23-room boutique hotel has a penchant for oversize clocks and primary colours, plus good-sized rooms and complimentary breakfasts.

Hôtel Lindbergh (Map pp212-13; ☎ 01 45 48 35 53; www.paris-hotel-lindbergh.com; 5 rue Chomel, 7e; d €98-160, tr €156-180, q €166-190; Ⓜ Sèvres Babylone; 💻) We're not quite sure why this place has kitted itself out in Charles Lindbergh memorabilia, but it works. The Parisian landmark room-plates, ample-sized bathrooms and friendly staff make this a terrific option.

Clichy & Gare St-Lazare

This area is a good choice for midrange hotels, with the better deals set away from Gare St-Lazare.

Hôtel Eldorado (Map pp212-13; ☎ 01 45 22 35 21; www.eldoradohotel.fr; 18 rue des Dames, 17e; s €35-57, d & tw €68-80, tr €80-90; Ⓜ Place de Clichy) This bohemian place is one of Paris' great finds: a welcoming, well-run place with 23 colourfully decorated rooms divided between a quiet main building and a garden-backed annexe. Cheaper-category singles have washbasin only.

New Orient Hôtel (Map pp212-13; ☎ 01 45 22 21 64; www.hotelneworient.com; 16 rue de Constantinople, 8e; s €89-115, d €106-115, tw €115-140, tr & q €150; Ⓜ Europe; ❄ 💻) This 30-room hotel surrounded by music shops has a lot of personality, especially in the common areas. Some rooms (eg twin room 7 and double 8) have balconies.

Hôtel Langlois (Map pp212-13; ☎ 01 48 74 78 24; www.hotel-langlois.com; 63 rue St-Lazare, 9e; s €105-120, d & tw €120-140, ste €180; Ⓜ Trinité; ❄ 💻) Built in 1870, this 27-room hotel has retained its belle époque feel. The hotel's rooms and suites (eg Nos 11 and 15) are large for a cheapish Parisian hotel in Paris: room 64 has wonderful views of Montmartre's rooftops.

Gare du Nord, Gare de l'Est & République

The areas around the Gare du Nord and Gare de l'Est are far from the prettiest parts of Paris, but you will find plenty of decent-value hotels here.

Peace & Love Hostel (Map pp212-13; ☎ 01 46 07 65 11; www.paris-hostels.com; 245 rue La Fayette, 10e; dm/d €25/60; Ⓜ Jaurès or Louis Blanc; 💻) This modern-day hippy hang-out is a groovy though chronically crowded hostel with beds in 21 smallish, shower-equipped rooms for two to four people. There's a great kitchen and eating area, and the ground-floor bar stays open till 2am.

Sibour Hôtel (Map pp212-13; ☎ 01 46 07 20 74; www.hotel-sibour.com; 4 rue Sibour, 10e; s €40-55, d €45-65, tr/q €80/110; Ⓜ Gare de l'Est) This friendly place has 45 well-kept rooms, including some old-fashioned ones – the cheapest singles and doubles – that only have washbasins. Hall showers cost €3. Some of the rooms look down on to pretty Église de St-Laurent.

Nord-Est Hôtel (Map pp212-13; ☎ 01 47 70 07 18; hotel.nord.est@wanadoo.fr; 12 rue des Petits Hôtels, 10e; s/d/tr/q €65/75/110/145; Ⓜ Poissonnière; 💻) This 30-room hotel, charmingly located on the 'Street of Little Hotels', is set away from the street and fronted by a small terrace. It's convenient to both the Gare du Nord and the Gare de l'Est, but net access is extortionate: €8/12 for 30/60 minutes.

Hôtel Français (Map pp212-13; ☎ 01 40 35 94 14; www.hotelfrancais.com; 13 rue du 8 Mai 1945, 10e; s €94-101, d €99-106, tr €134-141; Ⓜ Gare de l'Est; ❄ 💻) This two-star hotel facing the Gare de l'Est has 72 attractive, almost luxurious and very quiet rooms, some with balconies. The place has recently been freshened up; we love the new mock-cafe breakfast area.

Montmartre & Pigalle

Montmartre is one of the most charming neighbourhoods in Paris, with a clutch of midrange and top-end hotels. The area east of Sacré Cœur can be rough; it might be prudent to avoid Château Rouge metro station at night.

Le Village Hostel (Map p224; ☎ 01 42 64 22 02; www.villagehostel.fr; 20 rue d'Orsel, 18e; dm/d/tr €24/60/81; Ⓜ Anvers; 💻) A fine 25-room hostel with beamed ceilings and views of Sacré Cœur. Dorms all have showers and toilets. Kitchen facilities are available, and there's a popular bar too (no curfew).

Hôtel Bonséjour Montmartre (Map p224; ☎ 01 42 54 22 53; www.hotel-bonsejour-montmartre.fr; 11 rue Burq, 18e; s €33-40, d €44-55, tr €58-65; Ⓜ Abbesses; 💻) The 'Good Stay' is a perennial budget favourite. It's a simple place – hall showers, no lift – but welcoming and comfortable. Some rooms (Nos 14, 23, 33, 43 and 53) have little balconies, and at least one room (No 55) offers a fleeting glimpse of Sacré Cœur.

Hôtel Utrillo (Map p224; ☎ 01 42 58 13 44; www.hotel-paris-utrillo.com; 7 rue Aristide Bruant, 18e; s €73, d & tw €83-88, tr €105; Ⓜ Abbesses or Blanche; 💻) This friendly 30-room hotel, named for the 'painter of Montmartre', Maurice Utrillo (1883–1955), and decorated in primary colours, has a few extras such as a little leafy courtyard out back and a small sauna. Wheelchair access available.

Hôtel des Arts (Map p224; ☎ 01 46 06 30 52; www.arts-hotel-paris.com; 5 rue Tholozé, 18e; s €75-95, d & tw €95-105, tr €160; Ⓜ Abbesses or Blanche; 💻) The 'Arts Hotel' is a friendly and attractive 50-room place convenient to both place Pigalle and Montmartre. Towering over it is the old-style windmill Moulin de la Galette. The resident canine is very friendly.

Hôtel Regyn's Montmartre (Map p224; ☎ 01 42 54 45 21; www.hotel-regyns-paris.com; 18 place des Abbesses, 18e; s €79-89, d & tw €91-111, tr €117-131; Ⓜ Abbesses; 💻) This 22-room hotel is a good choice if you want to stay in old Montmartre and not break the bank. It's just opposite the Abbesses metro station, and some of the rooms have views out over Paris.

our pick **Hôtel Résidence des 3 Poussins** (Map p224; ☎ 01 53 32 81 81; www.les3poussins.com; 15 rue Clauzel, 9e; s/d €137/152, 1- or 2-person studio €187, 3- or 4-person studio €222; Ⓜ Pigalle or St-Georges; ❄ 💻) The 'Hotel of the Three Chicks' is a lovely property due south of place Pigalle, with 40 rooms, half of them small studios with their own cooking facilities. This place positively exudes style, and the rear patio is a lovely spot for summer lounging.

EATING

When it comes to food, Paris has everything… and nothing. As the culinary centre of the most aggressively gastronomic country in the world, the city has more 'generic French', regional, and ethnic restaurants than any other place in France.

Louvre & Les Halles

Saveurs Végét'halles (Map pp218-19; ☎ 01 40 41 93 95; 41 rue des Bourdonnais, 1er; starters & salads €4.80-9.80, mains €11.20-17.20, lunch menus €9.80-15.30, dinner menus €15.30; 🕑 lunch & dinner Mon-Sat; Ⓜ Châtelet) Strictly vegan eatery offering mock-meat dishes such as *poulet végétal aux champignons* ('chicken' with mushrooms) and *escalope de seitan* (wheat gluten 'escalope'). No booze.

Le Petit Mâchon (Map pp218-19; ☎ 01 42 60 08 06; 158 rue St-Honoré, 1er; starters €7-12.50, mains €14-22; 🕑 lunch & dinner Tue-Sun; Ⓜ Palais Royal-Musée du Louvre) An upbeat bistro with Lyon-inspired specialities. Try the *saucisson de Lyon* (Lyon sausage) studded with pistachios.

Joe Allen (Map pp218-19; ☎ 01 42 36 70 13; 30 rue Pierre Lescot, 1er; starters €7.50-10.30, mains €15.50-26, lunch menus €13.90-22.50, dinner menus €18-22.50; 🕑 noon-1am; Ⓜ Étienne Marcel) An institution in Paris since 1972, Joe Allen is a little bit of New York in Paris. There's an excellent brunch (€19.50 to €23.50) from noon to 4pm at the weekend.

Le Grand Colbert (Map pp212-13; ☎ 01 42 86 87 88; 2-4 rue Vivienne, 2e; starters €10-21.50, mains €19.50-30, lunch menus €32-39, dinner menus €39; 🕑 noon-3am; Ⓜ Pyramides) This former workers' *cafétéria* transformed into a fin de siècle showcase is a convenient spot for lunch when visiting the nearby *passages couverts* (covered arcades).

Scoop (Map pp218-19; ☎ 01 42 60 31 84; 154 rue St-Honoré, 1er; dishes €10.90-16.90; 🕑 11am-7pm; Ⓜ Palais Royal-Musée du Louvre) This American-style ice-cream parlour has been making quite a splash for its wraps, burgers, tarts and soups and central, trendy location. Sunday brunch (11.30am to 4pm) includes pancakes with maple syrup.

Supermarkets around Forum des Halles include **Franprix Les Halles** (Map pp218-19; 35 rue Berger, 1er; 🕑 8.30am-9.50pm Mon-Sat; Ⓜ Châtelet) and **Franprix Châtelet** (Map pp218-19; 16 rue Bertin Poirée, 1er; 🕑 8.30am-8pm Mon-Sat; Ⓜ Châtelet).

Marais & Bastille

The Marais, filled with small restaurants of every imaginable type, is one of Paris' premier neighbourhoods for eating out.

Le Trumilou (Map pp218-19; ☎ 01 42 77 63 98; 84 quai de l'Hôtel de Ville, 4e; starters €4.50-13, mains €15-22, menus €16.50 & €19.50; 🕑 lunch & dinner; Ⓜ Hôtel de Ville) This no-frills bistro is a Parisian institution known for its classic French cooking: try *confit aux pruneaux* (duck with prunes) and the *ris de veau grand-mère* (veal sweetbreads in mushroom cream sauce).

Le Petit Marché (Map pp218-19; ☎ 01 42 72 06 67; 9 rue de Béarn, 3e; starters €8-11, mains €15-25, lunch menus €14; 🕑 lunch & dinner; Ⓜ Chemin Vert) This great little bistro just up from place des Vosges attracts a mixed crowd with its hearty cooking and friendly service. The salad starters are popular, as is the *brochette d'agneau aux épices doux* (spicy lamb brochette).

our pick **L'Ambassade d'Auvergne** (Map pp218-19; ☎ 01 42 72 31 22; 22 rue du Grenier St-Lazare, 3e; starters €8-16, mains €14-22, lunch menus €20-28, dinner menus €28;

THE GOURMET GLACIER

our pick Berthillon (Map pp218-19; ☎ 01 43 54 31 61; 31 rue St-Louis en l'Île, 4e; ice creams €2-5.40; 🕑 10am-8pm Wed-Sun; Ⓜ Pont Marie) on Île St-Louis is the place to head to for Paris' finest ice cream. There are 70 flavours to choose from, ranging from fruity cassis to chocolate, coffee, *marrons glacés* (candied chestnuts), *Agenaise* (Armagnac and prunes), *noisette* (hazelnut) and *nougat au miel* (honey nougat). One just won't be enough…

🕑 lunch & dinner; Ⓜ Rambuteau) The 100-year-old 'Auvergne Embassy' is the place to go if you're hungry; the sausages and hams of this region are among the best in France. The house special is clafoutis, a custard-and-cherry tart baked upside down like a *tarte Tatin* (caramelised apple pie).

Bofinger (Map pp218-19; ☎ 01 42 72 87 82; 5-7 rue de la Bastille, 4e; starters €8-18.50, mains €15.50-31.50, lunch menus €24-31.50, dinner menus €31.50; 🕑 lunch & dinner to 12.30am; Ⓜ Bastille) Glimmering in art nouveau brass and polished mirrors, Bofinger is reputedly the oldest brasserie in Paris (founded in 1864). Specialities include *choucroute* (sauerkraut; €18 to €20) and seafood.

L'Alivi (Map pp218-19; ☎ 01 48 87 90 20; 27 rue du Roi de Sicile, 4e; starters €9-16, mains €15-23, lunch menus €17-29, dinner menus €25-29; 🕑 lunch & dinner; Ⓜ St-Paul or Bastille) Corsican food in downtown Paris, with *brocciu* cheese, charcuterie and basil featuring strongly on the menu.

For all-round atmosphere, check out the incomparable **Marché Bastille** (see the boxed text, p232). For general supplies:

Franprix Marais (Map pp218-19; 135 rue St- Antoine, 4e; 🕑 9am-9pm Mon-Sat; Ⓜ St-Paul); Hôtel de Ville (Map pp218-19; 87 rue de la Verrerie, 4ex; 🕑 9.30am-9pm Mon-Sat; Ⓜ Hôtel de Ville)

Monoprix Marais (Map pp218-19; 71 rue St- Antoine, 4e; 🕑 9am-9pm Mon-Sat; Ⓜ St-Paul); Bastille (Map pp218-19; 97 rue du Faubourg St-Antoine, 11e; 🕑 9am-9.45pm Mon-Sat; Ⓜ Ledru Rollin)

Latin Quarter & Jardin des Plantes

From cheap-eat student haunts to chandelier-lit palaces, the 5e has something to suit every budget and culinary taste.

Le Petit Pontoise (Map pp218-19; ☎ 01 43 29 25 20; 9 rue de Pontoise, 5e; starters €8-13.50, mains €15-25; 🕑 lunch & dinner; Ⓜ Maubert Mutualité) This charming bistro offers a blackboard menu of seasonal delights: *rognons de veau à l'ancienne* (calf's kidneys), *boudin campagnard* (black pudding) and roast quail with dates.

Perraudin (Map pp218-19; ☎ 01 46 33 15 75; 157 rue St-Jacques, 5e; starters €10-20, mains €15-30, lunch menus €19-29, dinner menus €29; 🕑 lunch & dinner Mon-Fri; Ⓜ Luxembourg) Ubertraditional Perraudin has barely changed since it first opened in 1910 – if you're after classic French dishes such as boeuf bourguignon (beef stew) and *gigot d'agneau* (leg of lamb), this frayed old place is tough to top.

Le Baba Bourgeois (Map pp218-19; ☎ 01 44 07 46 75; 5 quai de la Tournelle, 5e; mains €15-20; 🕑 lunch & dinner Wed-Sat, 11.30am-5pm Sun; Ⓜ Cardinal Lemoine) Contemporary dining on the Seine in a former architect's studio. Its *tartines* (open-face sandwiches), terrines, *tartes salées* (savoury tarts) and salads are delicious, and there's an all-you-can-eat Sunday buffet.

Place Maubert becomes the lively food market **Marché Maubert** on Tuesday, Thursday and Saturday mornings, while **rue Mouffetard** (see the boxed text, p232) and **place Monge** (Map pp218-19; place Monge, 5e; 🕑 7am-2pm Wed, Fri & Sun; Ⓜ Place Monge) both have their own street markets.

Supermarkets:

Ed l'Épicier (Map pp218-19; 37 rue Lacépède, 5e; 🕑 9am-1pm & 3-7.30pm Mon-Fri, 9am-7.30pm Sat; Ⓜ Place Monge)

Franprix (Map pp218-19; 82 rue Mouffetard, 5e; 🕑 8.30am-8.50pm Mon-Sat; Ⓜ Censier Daubenton or Place Monge)

Monoprix (St-Michel) (Map pp218-19; 24 blvd St-Michel, 5e; 🕑 9am-midnight Mon-Sat; Ⓜ St-Michel)

St-Germain, Odéon & Luxembourg

Polidor (Map pp218-19; ☎ 01 43 26 95 34; 41 rue Monsieur le Prince, 6e; starters €4.50-17, mains €11-22, menus €22-32; 🕑 lunch & dinner to 12.30am Mon-Sat, to 11pm Sun; Ⓜ Odéon) A meal at this quintessentially Parisian bistro is like taking a quick trip back to Victor Hugo's Paris – the restaurant and its decor date from 1845 – but everyone knows about it and it's pretty touristy.

our pick Chez Allard (Map pp218-19; ☎ 01 43 26 48 23; 41 rue St-André des Arts; starters €8-20, mains €25, menus €25-34; 🕑 lunch & dinner Mon-Sat; Ⓜ St-Michel) One of our favourite Left Bank eateries, always busy and always superb. Try 12 snails, some *cuisses de grenouilles* (frogs' legs) or *un poulet de Bresse* (France's most legendary chicken, from Burgundy) for two.

TO MARKET, TO MARKET

Paris counts about 70 *marchés découverts* (open-air markets) held two or three times a week and another dozen or so *marchés couverts* (covered markets), which keep more-regular hours: generally 8am to 1pm and 3.30pm or 4pm to 7pm or 7.30pm from Tuesday to Saturday (till lunchtime on Sunday). Here are some of our favourites:

Marché Bastille (Map pp218-19; blvd Richard Lenoir, 11e; 7am-2.30pm Tue & Sun; M Bastille or Richard Lenoir) Arguably the best open-air market in Paris.

Marché Belleville (Map pp212-13; blvd de Belleville, 11e & 20e; 7am-2.30pm Tue & Fri; M Belleville or Couronnes) Large ethnic market popular with the African, Asian and Middle Eastern immigrants of the *quartiers de l'est* (eastern neighbourhoods). Between rue Jean-Pierre Timbaud and rue du Faubourg du Temple.

Marché St-Quentin (Map pp212-13; 85 blvd de Magenta, 10e; 8am-1pm & 3.30-7.30pm Tue-Sat, 8.30am-1pm Sun; M Gare de l'Est) Iron-and-glass covered market built in 1866 lined with gourmet food stalls.

Rue Cler (Map pp212-13; rue Cler, 7e; 8am-7pm Tue-Sat, 8am-noon Sun; M École Militaire) Commercial street market in the sometimes-stuffy 7e, with an almost party-like atmosphere on weekends.

Rue Mouffetard (Map pp212-13; rue Mouffetard; 8am-7.30pm Tue-Sat, 8am-noon Sun; M Censier Daubenton) Rue Mouffetard is the city's most photogenic market street – the place where Parisians send tourists (travellers go to Marché Bastille). The market takes place around rue de l'Arbalète.

Cosi (Map pp218-19; ☎ 01 46 33 35 36; 54 rue de Seine, 6e; sandwich menus €9-11; noon-11pm; M Odéon) With sandwich names like Stonker, Tom Dooley and Naked Willi, Cosi could easily run for Paris' most imaginative sandwich maker. Classical music and homemade Italian bread add to the appeal.

Brasserie Lipp (Map pp218-19; ☎ 01 45 48 53 91; 151 bd St-Germain, 6e; starters €10-15, mains €15.50-25; noon-2am; M St-Germain des Prés) Expect politicians, celebs, media moguls and plenty of waistcoated waiters at the lovely Lipp, one of Paris' most beloved of brasseries.

With the Jardin du Luxembourg nearby, this is the perfect area for putting together a picnic. There is a large cluster of food shops on **rue de Seine** and **rue de Buci** (Map pp218-19, M Mabillon), 6e. The renovated and covered **Marché St-Germain** (Map pp218-19; 4-8 rue Lobineau, 6e; 8.30am-1pm & 4-7.30pm Tue-Sat, 8.30am-1pm Sun; M Mabillon), just north of the eastern end of Église St-Sulpice, has a huge array of produce and prepared food. Nearby supermarkets include the following:

Champion (Map pp218-19; 79 rue de Seine, 6e; 1-9pm Mon, 8.40am-9pm Tue-Sat, 9am-1pm Sun; M Mabillon)

Monoprix St-Germain des Prés (Map pp218-19; 50 rue de Rennes, 6e; 9am-10pm Mon-Sat; M St-Germain des Prés)

Montparnasse

Since the 1920s the area around blvd du Montparnasse has been one of the city's premier avenues for enjoying that most Parisian of pastimes: sitting in a cafe and checking out the scenery on two legs.

La Coupole (Map pp212-13; ☎ 01 43 20 14 20; 102 blvd du Montparnasse, 14e; starters €6.50-20, mains €12.50-35, lunch menus €24.50-31.50, dinner menus €31.50; 8am-1am Sun-Thu, to 1.30am Fri & Sat; M Vavin) This 450-seat brasserie, which opened in 1927, has mural-covered columns painted by such artists as Brancusi and Chagall. Its dark-wood panelling and indirect lighting have hardly changed since the days of Sartre, Soutine, Man Ray and Josephine Baker. You can book for lunch, but you'll have to queue for dinner.

our pick **La Cagouille** (Map pp212-13; ☎ 01 43 22 09 01; 10 place Constantin Brancusi, 14e; starters €11-15, mains €18-33, menus €26-42; lunch & dinner; M Gaîté) Chef Gérard Allemandou, one of the best seafood cooks (and cookbook writers) in Paris, gets rave reviews for his fish and shellfish. The *menus* here are exceptionally good value.

Opposite the Tour Montparnasse there's the outdoor **Boulevard Edgar Quinet Food Market** (Map pp212-13; blvd Edgar Quinet; 7am-2pm Wed & Sat; M Edgar Quinet). Supermarkets:

Atac (Map pp212-13; 55 av du Maine, 14e; 9am-10pm Mon-Sat; M Gaîté)

Inno (Map pp212-13; 29-31 rue du Départ, 14e; 9am-9.50pm Mon-Fri, 9am-8.50pm Sat; M Montparnasse Bienvenüe)

Opéra & Grands Boulevards

The neon-lit area around blvd Montmartre forms one of the Right Bank's most animated cafe and dining districts.

Chartier (Map pp212-13; ☎ 01 47 70 86 29; 7 rue du Faubourg Montmartre, 9e; starters €2.20-12.40, mains €6.50-16, menus incl wine €20; ⏲ lunch & dinner; Ⓜ Grands Boulevards) Chartier is a real gem for the budget traveller, justifiably famous for its 330-seat belle époque dining room and its excellent-value menu. Reservations are not accepted and lone diners will have to share a table.

Le Roi du Pot au Feu (Map pp212-13; ☎ 01 47 42 37 10; 34 rue Vignon, 9e; starters €5-7, mains €17-20, menus €24-29; ⏲ noon-10.30pm Mon-Sat; Ⓜ Havre Caumartin) The typical Parisian bistro atmosphere adds immensely to the charm of the 'King of Hotpots', where the dish of the day is always *pot au feu*, a stewed stockpot of beef, root vegetables and herbs. No bookings.

Aux Deux Canards (Map pp212-13; ☎ 01 47 70 03 23; 8 rue du Faubourg Poissonnière, 10e; starters €5-14.50, mains €16-25, lunch menus €20; ⏲ lunch Tue-Fri, dinner Mon-Sat; Ⓜ Bonne Nouvelle) The name of this bistro – 'At the Two Ducks' – reflects the duck-focused menu; it comes in varieties from foie gras to *à l'orange*.

Both av de l'Opéra and rue de Richelieu have several supermarkets, including the large **Monoprix Opéra** (Map pp212-13; 21 av de l'Opéra, 2e; ⏲ 9am-10pm Mon-Fri, 9am-9pm Sat; Ⓜ Pyramides).

Montmartre & Pigalle

You'll still find some decent eateries in Montmartre, but beware the tourist traps.

Chez Toinette (Map p224; ☎ 01 42 54 44 36; 20 rue Germain Pilon, 18e; starters €6-9, mains €15-20; ⏲ dinner Tue-Sat; Ⓜ Abbesses) This convivial French restaurant has somehow managed to keep alive the tradition of old Montmartre in one of the capital's most touristy neighbourhoods.

Le Café Qui Parle (Map p224; ☎ 01 46 06 06 88; 24 rue Caulaincourt, 18e; starters €7-14, mains €13.50-20, menus €12.50-17; ⏲ lunch & dinner Thu-Tue; Ⓜ Lamarck Caulaincourt or Blanche) 'The Talking Cafe' offers inventive, reasonably priced dishes prepared by owner-chef Damian Mœuf. We love the art on the walls. Brunch (€15) is served from 10am on Saturday and Sunday.

La Maison Rose (Map p224; ☎ 01 42 57 66 75; 2 rue de l'Abreuvoir, 18e; starters €7.20-13, mains €14.50-16.50, menus €16.50; ⏲ lunch & dinner daily Mar-Oct, lunch & dinner to 9pm Thu-Mon Nov-Feb; Ⓜ Lamarck Caulaincourt) Looking for the quintessential Montmartre bistro that featured in a Maurice Utrillo lithograph? Head for the tiny 'Pink House' just north of place du Tertre. It's not so much about food but rather location, location, location.

Towards place Pigalle there are lots of grocery stores, many of them open until late at night; try the side streets leading off blvd de Clichy (eg rue Lepic). For supermarkets: **8 à Huit** (Map p224; 24 rue Lepic, 18e; ⏲ 8.30am-10.30pm Mon-Sat; Ⓜ Abbesses)

Ed l'Épicier (Map p224; 6 blvd de Clichy, 18e; ⏲ 9am-9pm Mon-Sat; Ⓜ Pigalle)

DRINKING

Paris is justly famous for its cafe culture, but these days there's a huge range of drinking establishments, especially in the Marais and along the Grands Boulevards. Bear in mind that drinking in Paris means paying the rent for the space you are occupying – it costs more sitting at tables than standing, more on a fancy square than a backstreet, more in the 8e than the 18e.

Louvre & Les Halles

Le Fumoir (Map pp218-19; ☎ 01 42 92 00 24; 6 rue de l'Amiral Coligny, 1er; ⏲ 11am-2am; Ⓜ Louvre-Rivoli) The 'Smoking Room' is a huge, stylish colonial-style bar-cafe opposite the Louvre. It's a fine place to sip top-notch gin while nibbling on olives; during happy hour (6pm to 8pm) cocktails, usually €8.50 to €11, drop to €6.

Marais & Bastille

Au Petit Fer à Cheval (Map pp218-19; ☎ 01 42 72 47 47; 30 rue Vieille du Temple, 4e; ⏲ 9am-2am; Ⓜ Hôtel de Ville or St-Paul) The original horseshoe-shaped zinc counter (1903) leaves little room for much else at this genial bar, but nobody seems to mind.

La Perle (Map pp218-19; ☎ 01 42 72 69 93; 78 rue Vieille du Temple, 3e; ⏲ 6am-2am Mon-Fri, 8am-2am Sat & Sun; Ⓜ St-Paul or Chemin Vert) This is where *bobos* (bohemian bourgeois types) come to slum it over *un rouge* (glass of red wine) until the DJ arrives and things liven up.

Le Bistrot du Peintre (Map pp218-19; ☎ 01 47 00 34 39; 116 av Ledru-Rollin, 11e; ⏲ 8am-2am; Ⓜ Bastille) Lovely belle époque bistro and wine bar, with a 1902 art nouveau bar, elegant terrace and spot-on service.

our pick **Le Loir dans la Théière** (Map pp218-19; ☎ 01 42 72 90 61; 3 rue des Rosiers, 4e; ⏲ 9.30am-7pm; Ⓜ St-Paul) The 'Dormouse in the Teapot' is filled with retro toys and comfy couches, while scenes of *Through the Looking Glass* decorate the walls. It serves sandwiches, sticky puddings and a dozen teas, plus stronger stuff after dark.

Le Pick Clops (Map pp218-19; ☎ 01 40 29 02 18; 16 rue Vieille du Temple, 4e; 7am-2am Mon-Sat, 8am-2am Sun; M Hôtel de Ville or St-Paul) Retro neon-lit cafe-bar with formica tables, ancient bar stools and mirrors. Try the rum punch.

Latin Quarter & Jardin des Plantes

Le Piano Vache (Map pp218-19; ☎ 01 46 33 75 03; 8 rue Laplace, 5e; noon-2am Mon-Fri, 9pm-2am Sat & Sun; M Maubert Mutualité) Just downhill from the Panthéon, the 'Mean Piano' is effortlessly underground and a huge favourite with students, with bands and DJs playing mainly rock, plus some goth, reggae and pop.

Le Pub St-Hilaire (Map pp218-19; www.pubsthilaire.com; 2 rue Valette, 5e; 11am-2am Mon-Thu, 11am-4am Fri, 4pm-4am Sat, 3pm-midnight Sun; M Maubert Mutualité) 'Buzzing' fails to do justice to this student-loved pub. Happy hours last forever, while pool tables, board games, and music on two floors keep the punters happy.

St-Germain, Odéon & Luxembourg

Le 10 (Map pp218-19; ☎ 01 43 26 66 83; 10 rue de l'Odéon, 6e; 5.30pm-2am; M Odéon) A local institution, this cellar pub groans with students, smoky ambience and cheap sangria. Posters adorn the walls, and an eclectic jukebox jumps from jazz and the Doors to *chansons françaises* (traditional French songs).

Le Comptoir des Canettes (Map pp218-19; ☎ 01 43 26 79 15; 11 rue des Canettes, 6e; noon-2am Tue-Sat; M Mabillon) A faithful local following pours into this basement bar, draped with red tablecloths, melting candles and nostalgic photos of musicians.

Les Deux Magots (Map pp218-19; ☎ 01 45 48 55 25; www.lesdeuxmagots.fr; 170 blvd St-Germain, 6e; 7am-1am; M St-Germain des Prés) The favoured hangout of Sartre, Hemingway, Picasso and André Breton. Everyone has to sit on the terrace here at least once and have a coffee or the famous hot chocolate served in porcelain jugs.

Opéra & Grands Boulevards

De la Ville Café (Map pp212-13; ☎ 01 48 24 48 09; 34 blvd de Bonne Nouvelle, 10e; 11am-2.30am; M Bonne Nouvelle) This one-time brothel has an alluring mix of restored history and modern design. DJs play most nights, so it's popular with the preclub crowd.

our pick **Harry's New York Bar** (Map pp212-13; ☎ 01 42 61 71 14; 5 rue Daunou, 2e; 10.30am-4am; M Opéra) One of the most popular American-style bars in the interwar years, Harry's manages to evoke a golden past without feeling like a museum piece. Lean upon the bar where F Scott Fitzgerald and Ernest Hemingway drank and gossiped, while white-smocked waiters mix killer martinis and Bloody Marys.

Montmartre & Pigalle

La Fourmi (Map p224; ☎ 01 42 64 70 35; 74 rue des Martyrs, 18e; 8am-2am Mon-Thu, 8am-4am Fri & Sat, 10am-2am Sun; M Pigalle) A Pigalle stayer, 'The Ant' always hits the mark: hip but not snobby, with a laid-back crowd and a rock-orientated playlist.

Le Dépanneur (Map p224; ☎ 01 44 53 03 78; 27 rue Pierre Fontaine, 9e; 10am-2am Mon-Thu, 24hr Fri-Sun; M Blanche) An American-style diner-cum-bar open (almost) round the clock, 'The Repairman' specialises in tequila and fancy cocktails (€7.50) and DJs after 11pm from Thursday to Saturday.

ENTERTAINMENT

It's impossible to sample Paris' entertainment scene without first studying *Pariscope* (€0.40) or *Officiel des Spectacles* (€0.35), both published every Wednesday. For more general info check out *Les Inrockuptibles* (www.lesinrocks.com, in French; €3), a national music zine with a strong Paris bias, or the freebies such as *À Nous Paris* (www.anous.fr/paris, in French) and the pocket-sized *LYLO* (short for *Les Yeux, Les Oreilles,* meaning 'eyes and ears'; www.lylo.fr, in French), both widely available at bars and cafes.

Tickets for concerts, theatre performances and events are sold at *billeteries* (ticket offices) in **Fnac** (☎ 08 92 68 36 22; www.fnacspectacles.com, in French) or **Virgin Megastores** (☎ 08 25 12 91 39; www.virginmega.fr, in French).

Cinemas

Going to the cinema in Paris is not cheap: expect to pay up to €10 for a first-run film. Students, under 18s, and over 60s get discounted tickets (usually just under €6), except Friday night, all day Saturday and on Sunday matinees. Wednesday yields discounts for everyone.

Cinémathèque Française (Map pp212-13; ☎ 01 71 19 33 33; www.cinemathequefrancaise.com; 51 rue de Bercy, 12e; adult/under 12yr/student €6/3/5; box office noon-7pm Mon, Wed, Fri & Sat, noon-10pm Thu, 10am-8pm Sun; M Bercy) This national institution is a veritable temple to the 'seventh art', and always screens its foreign offerings in their original language.

Live Music

ROCK & POP

The city's big gig venues are the **Palais Omnisports de Paris-Bercy** (Map pp212-13; ☎ 08 92 39 01 00; www.bercy.fr, in French; 8 blvd de Bercy, 12e; Ⓜ Bercy) in Bercy; the **Stade de France** (off Map pp212-13; ☎ 08 92 70 09 00; www.stadedefrance.fr, in French; rue Francis de Pressensé, ZAC du Cornillon Nord, St-Denis La Plaine; Ⓜ St-Denis-Porte de Paris) in St-Denis; and **Le Zénith** (Map pp212-13; ☎ 08 90 71 02 07; www.le-zenith.com, in French; 211 av Jean Jaurès, 19e; Ⓜ Porte de Pantin).

For smaller acts, head along to **La Cigale** (Map p224; ☎ 01 49 25 89 99; www.lacigale.fr; 120 blvd de Rochechouart, 18e; admission €25-60; Ⓜ Anvers or Pigalle), a music hall dating from 1887 that prides itself on its avant-garde program, and **L'Élysée-Montmartre** (Map p224; ☎ 01 44 92 45 47; www.elyseemontmartre.com; 72 blvd de Rochechouart, 18e; admission €15-45; Ⓜ Anvers), another old music hall that specialises in one-off rock and indie concerts.

Meanwhile, **Le Bataclan** (Map pp218-19; ☎ 01 43 14 00 30; www.bataclan.fr, in French; 50 blvd Voltaire, 11e; admission €20-45; Ⓜ Oberkampf or St-Ambroise) was Maurice Chevalier's debut venue in 1910 and today draws some French and international acts.

JAZZ & BLUES

Le Baiser Salé (Map pp218-19; ☎ 01 42 33 37 71; www.lebaisersale.com, in French; 58 rue des Lombards, 1er; admission free €20; Ⓜ Châtelet) 'The Salty Kiss' is one of several jazz clubs on the same street. The *salle de jazz* (jazz hall) on the 1st floor has concerts of trad jazz, Afro and Latin, jazz fusion and breaking acts.

Le Caveau de la Huchette (Map pp218-19; ☎ 01 43 26 65 05; www.caveaudelahuchette.fr; 5 rue de la Huchette, 5e; admission Sun-Thu/Fri & Sat €11/13; 🕑 9.30pm-2.30am Sun-Wed, to 4am Thu-Sat; Ⓜ St-Michel) Housed in a *caveau* (cellar) used as a courtroom and torture chamber during the Revolution, this club has hosted all the jazz greats. It's touristy, but the atmosphere's a lot more lively than the more serious jazz clubs.

FRENCH CHANSONS

French music has come a long way since the days of Édith Piaf, Jacques Brel and Georges Brassens, but you'll still find traditional *chansons* at lots of Parisian venues.

Au Lapin Agile (Map p224; ☎ 01 46 06 85 87; www.au-lapin-agile.com; 22 rue des Saules, 18e; adult €24, student except Sat €17; 🕑 9pm-2am Tue-Sun; Ⓜ Lamarck Caulaincourt) This historic cabaret venue in Montmartre still hosts *chansons* and poetry readings. Admission includes one drink.

Le Limonaire (Map pp212-13; ☎ 01 45 23 33 33; http://limonaire.free.fr; 18 cité Bergère, 9e; admission free; 🕑 7pm-midnight Mon, 6pm-midnight Tue-Sun; Ⓜ Grands Boulevards) This wine bar is one of the best places to listen to traditional French bistro music. Singers perform on the small stage nightly, starting at 7pm on Sunday, 8.30pm on Monday and at 10pm Tuesday to Saturday.

> **DIGITAL CLUBBING**
>
> Track tomorrow's hot 'n' happening soirée with these Parisian nightlife links.
>
> - www.gogoparis.com (in English)
> - www.lemonsound.com
> - www.novaplanet.com
> - www.parisbouge.com
> - www.parissi.com
> - www.radiofg.com
> - www.tribudenuit.com

Clubs

Paris's clubbing scene changes fast – the internet's usually the best place to find out where the action's at. Admission costs anything from €5 to €20 and often includes a drink; admission is usually cheaper before 1am and men can't always get in unaccompanied by a woman.

La Dame de Canton (Map pp212-13; ☎ 01 53 61 08 49, 06 10 41 02 29; www.damedecanton.com, in French; opp 11 quai François Mauriac, 13e; admission €10; 🕑 7pm-2am Tue-Thu, 7pm-dawn Fri & Sat; Ⓜ Quai de la Gare or Bibliothèque) This floating *boîte* (club) aboard a three-masted Chinese junk hosts DJs and concerts (8.30pm) ranging from pop and indie to electro, hip hop and rock.

Le Nouveau Casino (Map pp218-19; ☎ 01 43 57 57 40; www.nouveaucasino.net, in French; 109 rue Oberkampf, 11e; club admission €5-10, concerts €15-22; 🕑 7.30pm-midnight or 2am Sun-Thu, to 5am Fri & Sat; Ⓜ Parmentier) 'The New Casino' has an eclectic program – electro, pop, deep house, rock – with live music concerts and top DJs.

Point Éphemère (Map pp212-13; ☎ 01 40 34 02 48; www.pointephemere.org; 200 quai de Valmy, 10e; admission free-€14; 🕑 10am-2pm; Ⓜ Louis Blanc) A new arrival by the Canal St-Martin, with some of the best electronic music nights in town. Once this self-proclaimed 'centre for dynamic artists' gets in gear, '*on y danse, on danse*' (you'll dance your arse off).

Social Club (Map pp212-13; ☎ 01 40 28 05 55; www.myspace.com/parissocialclub; 142 rue Montmartre, 2e; admission free-€20; 🕑 11pm-3am Wed & Sun, to 6am Thu-Sat; Ⓜ Grands Boulevards) Once known as Triptyque, this vast club occupies three underground rooms, with a serious sound system pumping out electro, hip hop and funk, as well as jazz and live acts.

SHOPPING

Department Stores

Paris' *grands magasins* (department stores) include the vast **Galeries Lafayette** (Map pp212-13; ☎ 01 42 82 34 56; 40 blvd Haussmann, 9e; 🕑 9.30am-7.30pm Mon-Wed, Fri & Sat, 9.30am-9pm Thu; Ⓜ Auber or Chaussée d'Antin) and **Le Printemps** (Map pp212-13; ☎ 01 42 82 57 87; 64 blvd Haussmann, 9e; 🕑 9.35am-7pm Mon-Wed, Fri & Sat, 9.35am-10pm Thu; Ⓜ Havre Caumartin). Le Printemps, 'The Spring' (as in the season), is actually three separate stores: one for women's fashion, one for men and one for beauty and household goods.

Food

Cacao et Chocolat (Map pp218-19; ☎ 01 46 33 77 63; 29 rue du Buci, 6e; 🕑 10.30am-7.30pm Mon-Sat, 11am-7pm Sun; Ⓜ Mabillon) This place is a contemporary take on chocolate, showcasing the cocoa bean in all its guises.

Fauchon (Map pp212-13; ☎ 01 70 39 38 00; 26 & 30 place de la Madeleine, 8e; 🕑 8.30am-7pm Mon-Sat; Ⓜ Madeleine) Paris' most famous caterer has a half-dozen departments in two buildings selling the most incredibly mouth-watering delicacies from pâté de foie gras and truffles to *confitures* (jams).

Fromagerie Alléosse (Map pp212-13; ☎ 01 46 22 50 45; 13 rue Poncelet, 17e; 🕑 9.30am-1pm & 4-7pm Tue-Thu, 9am-1pm & 3.30-7pm Fri & Sat, 9am-1pm Sun; Ⓜ Ternes) The best cheese shop in Paris, bar none.

GETTING THERE & AWAY

Air

AÉROPORT D'ORLY

Orly (ORY; off Map pp212-13; ☎ 3950, 01 70 36 39 50; www.aeroportsdeparis.fr), the older and smaller of Paris' two major airports, is 18km south of the city.

AÉROPORT ROISSY CHARLES DE GAULLE

Roissy Charles de Gaulle airport (CDG; off Map pp212-13; ☎ 3950, 01 70 36 39 50; www.aeroportsdeparis.fr), 30km northeast of Paris, consists of three terminal complexes and two train stations, linked to the TGV network.

AÉROPORT PARIS-BEAUVAIS

The international airport at **Beauvais** (BVA; off Map pp212-13; ☎ 08 92 68 20 66, 03 44 11 46 86; www.aeroportbeauvais.com), 80km north of Paris, is used by charter companies as well as Ryanair, Central Wings and other budget airlines.

Bus

DOMESTIC

France's intercity bus system is practically nonexistent – for domestic destinations, you're much better off travelling by train; see p341.

INTERNATIONAL

Eurolines links Paris with most parts of Western and central Europe, Scandinavia and Morocco. The central **Eurolines office** (Map

FLEA MARKETS

Even the most chichi Parisians aren't above a bit of digging in the city's wonderful *marchés aux puces* (flea markets).

The largest is **Marché aux Puces de St-Ouen** (Map pp212-13; rue des Rosiers, av Michelet, rue Voltaire, rue Paul Bert & rue Jean-Henri Fabre, 18e; 🕑 9am-6pm Sat, 10am-6pm Sun, 11am-5pm Mon; Ⓜ Porte de Clignancourt), with some 2500 stalls grouped into 10 *marchés* (market areas), each with its own speciality (eg Marché Serpette and Marché Biron for antiques, Marché Malik for secondhand clothing).

Marché aux Puces de la Porte de Vanves (Map pp212-13; av Georges Lafenestre & av Marc Sangnier, 14e; 🕑 7am-6pm or later Sat & Sun; Ⓜ Porte de Vanves) is the smallest and friendliest of the big three flea markets, with everything from designer curios to handbags and household goods.

Marché aux Puces de Montreuil (Map pp212-13; av du Professeur André Lemière, 20e; 🕑 8am-7.30pm Sat-Mon; Ⓜ Porte de Montreuil) Established in the 19th century, this flea market is renowned for its secondhand clothing, jewellery and designer seconds.

pp218-19; ☎ 01 43 54 11 99; www.eurolines.fr; 55 rue St-Jacques, 5e; 🕑 9.30am-6.30pm Mon-Fri, 10am-1pm & 2-5pm Sat; Ⓜ Cluny-La Sorbonne) takes reservations and sells tickets. The **Gare Routière Internationale de Paris-Galliéni** (Map pp212-13; ☎ 08 92 89 90 91; 28 av du Général de Gaulle; Ⓜ Galliéni), the city's international bus terminal, is in the eastern suburb of Bagnolet.

Train

Paris has six major train stations, each handling passenger traffic to different parts of France and Europe.

Gare d'Austerlitz (Map pp218-19; blvd de l'Hôpital, 13e; Ⓜ Gare d'Austerlitz) Spain and Portugal; Loire Valley and non-TGV trains to southwestern France.

Gare de l'Est (Map pp212-13; blvd de Strasbourg, 10e; Ⓜ Gare de l'Est) Luxembourg, parts of Switzerland (Basel, Lucerne, Zürich), southern Germany (Frankfurt, Munich) and points further east; regular and TGV Est trains to areas of France east of Paris (Champagne, Alsace and Lorraine), and Luxembourg.

Gare de Lyon (Map pp218-19; blvd Diderot, 12e; Ⓜ Gare de Lyon) Parts of Switzerland (eg Bern, Geneva, Lausanne), Italy and points beyond; regular and TGV Sud-Est and TGV Midi-Méditerranée trains to areas southeast of Paris, including Dijon, Lyon, Provence, the Côte d'Azur and the Alps.

Gare Montparnasse (Map pp212-13; av du Maine & blvd de Vaugirard, 15e; Ⓜ Montparnasse Bienvenüe) Brittany and places en route from Paris (eg Chartres, Angers, Nantes); TGV Atlantique Ouest and TGV Atlantique Sud-Ouest trains to Tours, Nantes, Bordeaux and other destinations in southwestern France.

Gare du Nord (Map p224; rue de Dunkerque, 10e; Ⓜ Gare du Nord) UK, Belgium, northern Germany, Scandinavia etc (terminus of the high-speed Thalys trains to/from Amsterdam, Brussels and Cologne and Eurostar to London); trains to northern France, including TGV Nord trains to Lille and Calais.

Gare St-Lazare (Map pp212-13; rue St-Lazare & rue d'Amsterdam, 8e; Ⓜ St-Lazare) Normandy (eg Dieppe, Le Havre, Cherbourg).

GETTING AROUND

To/From the Airports

AÉROPORT D'ORLY

There are loads of public transport options to and from Orly airport. Apart from RATP bus 183, all services call at both terminals. Tickets are sold on board.

Air France bus 1 (☎ 08 92 35 08 20; www.cars-airfrance.com; one way/return €9/14; 🕑 from Orly 6am-11.30pm, from Invalides 5.45am-11pm) This shuttle bus runs every 15 minutes to/from the eastern side of Gare Montparnasse (Map pp212-13; rue du Commandant René Mouchotte, 15e; Ⓜ Montparnasse Bienvenüe) as well as Aérogare des Invalides (Map pp212-13; Ⓜ Invalides) in the 7e. Request stops include metro stations Porte d'Orléans or Duroc. It takes 30 to 45 minutes.

Jetbus (☎ 01 69 01 00 09; adult/under 5yr €5.70/free; 🕑 from Orly 6.20am-11.10pm, from Paris 6.15am-10.30pm) Jetbus runs every 15 to 25 minutes to/from metro Villejuif Louis Aragon (Map pp212-13) on the city's southern fringe; it takes 55 minutes From there a regular metro/bus ticket will get you into the centre of Paris.

Noctilien bus 31 (☎ 08 92 68 77 14, in English 08 92 68 41 14; adult/4-9yr €6/3; 🕑 12.30am-5.30pm) Part of the RATP night service, Noctilien bus 31 runs once an hour, linking Gare de Lyon, Place d'Italie and Gare d'Austerlitz with Orly-Sud. It takes 45 minutes.

Orlybus (☎ 08 92 68 77 14; adult/4-11yr €6.10/3.05; 🕑 from Orly 6am-11.50pm, from Paris 5.35am-11.25pm) This RATP bus runs every 15 to 20 minutes to/from metro Denfert Rochereau (Map pp212-13) and stops in the eastern 14e. It takes 30 minutes.

Orlyval (☎ 08 92 68 77 14; adult/4-10yr €9.30/4.65; 🕑 6am-11pm) This RATP service links Orly with the city centre via a shuttle train and the RER. An automated shuttle train (every 4 to 12 minutes) runs between the airport and Antony RER station (eight minutes) on RER line B, from where it's an easy journey into the city; to get to Antony from the city (26 minutes), take line B4 towards St-Rémy-lès-Chevreuse. Orlyval tickets are valid for travel on the RER and metro.

RATP bus 183 (☎ 08 92 68 77 14; adult/4-9yr €1.50/0.75 or 1 metro/bus ticket; 1hr; 🕑 5.35am-8.35pm) Cheap but very slow public bus that links Orly-Sud (only) with metro Porte de Choisy (Map pp212-13). It runs every 35 minutes.

RER C (☎ 08 90 36 10 10; adult/4-10yr €6/4.25; 🕑 5.30am-11.50pm) An Aéroports de Paris (ADP) shuttle bus links the airport with RER line C at Pont de Rungis-Aéroport d'Orly RER station every 15 to 30 minutes; the trip takes 50 minutes. From the city, take a C2 train towards Pont de Rungis or Massy-Palaiseau.

AÉROPORT ROISSY CHARLES DE GAULLE

Roissy Charles de Gaulle has two train stations: Aéroport Charles de Gaulle 1 (CDG1) and the sleek Aéroport Charles de Gaulle 2 (CDG2). Both are served by RER line B3. A free shuttle bus links the terminals with the train stations.

Air France bus 2 (☎ 08 92 35 08 20; www.cars-airfrance.com; one way/return €13/18; 🕑 5.45am-11pm) Links the airport with two locations on the Right Bank every 15 minutes: near the Arc de Triomphe just outside 2 av Carnot, 17e (Map pp212-13; Ⓜ Charles de Gaulle-Étoile) and the Palais des Congrès de Paris (Map pp212-13; blvd Gouvion St-Cyr, 17e; Ⓜ Porte Maillot). The trip takes 35 to 50 minutes.

DOOR-TO-DOOR TRANSPORT

If you want to get into (or out of) the city in a hurry, you could catch a **taxi** (around €40 to €50 between central Paris and Orly; €40 to €60 to/from Roissy Charles de Gaulle; €110 to €150 to/from Beauvais; and about €60 between Orly and Roissy Charles de Gaulle) or a private minibus such as **Allô Shuttle** (☎ 01 34 29 00 80; www.alloshuttle.com), **Paris Airports Service** (☎ 01 55 98 10 80; www.parisairportservice.com) or **PariShuttle** (☎ 01 53 39 18 18; www.parishuttle.com). Count on around €25 per person (€40 between 8pm and 6am) for Orly or Roissy Charles de Gaulle and €150 for one to four people to/from Beauvais. Book ahead and allow extra time for pick-ups and drop-offs.

Air France bus 4 (☎ 08 92 35 08 20; www.cars-airfrance.com; one way/return €14/22; 7am-9pm from Roissy Charles de Gaulle, 6.30am-9.30pm from Paris) Air France bus 4 links the airport with Gare de Lyon (Map pp218-19; 20bis blvd Diderot, 12e; M Gare de Lyon) and Gare Montparnasse (Map pp212-13; rue du Commandant René Mouchotte, 15e; M Montparnasse Bienvenüe) every 30 minutes; it takes 45 to 55 minutes.

Noctilien buses 120, 121 & 140 (☎ 08 92 68 77 14, in English 08 92 68 41 14; adult/4-9yr €7.50/3.75; 12.30am-5.30pm) Noctilien buses 120 and 121 link Montparnasse, Châtelet and Gare du Nord with Roissy Charles de Gaulle, and bus 140 links Gare du Nord and Gare de l'Est with the airport. They run once an hour.

RATP bus 350 (☎ 08 92 68 77 14; adult/4-9yr €4.50/2.25 or 3 metro/bus tickets; 1hr; every 30min 5.45am-7pm) This public bus links Aérogares 1 & 2 with Gare de l'Est (Map pp212-13; rue du 8 Mai 1945, 10e; M Gare de l'Est) and with Gare du Nord (Map p224; 184 rue du Faubourg St-Denis, 10e; M Gare du Nord).

RATP bus 351 (☎ 08 92 68 77 14; adult/4-9yr €4.50/2.25 or 3 metro/bus tickets; 7am-9.30pm from Roissy Charles de Gaulle, 8.30am-8.20pm from Paris) Links place de la Nation (Map pp212-13; av du Trône, 11e; M Nation) with the airport every 30 minutes (1 hour).

RER B (☎ 08 90 36 10 10; adult/4-11yr €8.20/5.80; 5am-midnight) RER line B3 links CDG1 and CDG2 with the city every 10 to 15 minutes (30 minutes). To get to the airport, take any RER line B train whose four-letter destination code begins with E (eg EIRE), and a shuttle bus (every five to eight minutes) will ferry you to the appropriate terminal. Regular ticket windows can't always sell RER tickets as far as the airport so you may have to buy one at the RER station where you board.

Roissybus (☎ 08 92 68 77 14; €8.60; 45-60min; every 15min 5.45am-11pm) This direct public bus (every 15 minutes) links both terminals with rue Scribe (Map pp212–13; M Opéra) behind the Palais Garnier in the 9e (45 to 60 minutes).

AÉROPORT PARIS-BEAUVAIS

The special **Express Bus** (☎ 08 92 68 20 64; €13; 8.05am-10.40pm from Beauvais, 5.45am-8.05pm from Paris) leaves **Parking Pershing** (Map pp212-13; 1 blvd Pershing, 17e; M Porte Maillot), just west of Palais des Congrès de Paris, three hours before Ryanair departures (you can board up to 15 minutes before a flight) and leaves the airport 20 to 30 minutes after each arrival, dropping off just south of Palais des Congrès on Place de la Porte Maillot. Tickets can be purchased online (http://ticket.aeroportbeauvais.com), at the airport from Ryanair (☎ 03 44 11 41 41), or at a car-park kiosk. The trip takes one to 1¼ hours.

Car & Motorcycle

If there's one sure-fire way of turning your Parisian getaway into a nonstop nightmare, it's bringing the car. Even if the city's drivers don't send you over the edge, trying to find a parking spot will. If you really have to drive, you'll find all the main rental companies at the airports and main train stations.

Avis (☎ 08 02 05 05 05; www.avis.fr, in French)
Budget (☎ 08 25 00 35 64; www.budget.fr, in French)
Europcar (☎ 08 25 35 83 58; www.europcar.fr, in French)
Hertz (☎ 08 25 88 92 65; www.hertz.fr)
National Citer (☎ 08 25 16 12 12; www.citer.fr)
Sixt (☎ 08 20 00 74 98; www.sixt.fr, in French)

Smaller agencies often offer attractive deals; check the *Yellow Pages* (www.pagesjaunes.fr) under 'Location d'Automobiles: Tourisme et Utilitaires'.

ADA (☎ 08 25 16 91 69; www.ada.fr, in French) 8e arrondissement (Map pp212-13; ☎ 01 42 93 65 13; 72 rue de Rome; M Rome); 11e arrondissement (Map pp212-13; ☎ 01 48 06 58 13; 34 av de la République; M Parmentier)

easyCar (www.easycar.com) Montparnasse (Map pp212-13; Parking Gaîté, 33 rue du Commandant René Mouchotte, 15e; M Gaîté) Britain's budget car-rental agency hires cars at train stations and underground car parks. The system is fully automated, and you have to book in advance.

Public Transport

Paris' public transit system, operated by the **RATP** (Régie Autonome des Transports Parisiens; ☎ 32 46,

08 92 69 32 46; www.ratp.fr; ⌚ 7am-9pm Mon-Fri, 9am-5pm Sat & Sun), is one of the most efficient in the Western world.

The same RATP tickets are valid on the metro, the RER, buses, the Montmartre funicular and Paris' three tramlines. A single ticket costs €1.50; a *carnet* (book) of 10 is €11.10 (€5.55 for children aged four to 11 years). Tickets and transport maps are available from all metro stations.

One metro/bus ticket lets you travel between any two metro stations (no return journeys) for a period of 1½ hours, regardless of the number of transfers; you can also transfer between buses and between buses and trams, but not from the metro to bus or vice versa. Always keep your ticket until you leave the station; you may be stopped by a *contrôleur* (ticket inspector) and will have to pay a fine (€25 to €45 on the spot) if you can't produce a valid ticket.

BUS

Paris' bus system runs between 5.45am and 12.30am Monday to Saturday. Services are drastically reduced on Sunday and public holidays (when buses run from 7am to 8.30pm) and from 8.30pm to 12.30am daily when a *service en soirée* (evening service) of 20 buses runs, followed by **Noctilien** (www.noctilien.fr) night buses, departing every hour between 12.30am and 5.30am. There are two circular lines (the N01 and N02) linking the four main stations – St-Lazare, Gare de l'Est, Gare de Lyon and Montparnasse – plus popular nightspots such as Bastille, the Champs-Élysées, Pigalle and St-Germain. Look for blue *N* or 'Noctilien' signs.

Short bus rides (ie rides in one or two bus zones) cost one metro/bus ticket (€1.50); longer rides require two. Remember to cancel *(oblitérer)* single-journey tickets in the *composteur* (cancelling machine) next to the driver.

METRO & RER NETWORK

Paris' underground network consists of two interlinked systems: the Métropolitain (metro), with 14 lines and 372 stations; and the RER (Réseau Express Régional), a network of suburban train lines.

Each metro train is known by the name of its terminus. On lines that split into several branches (such as lines 3, 7 and 13), the terminus is indicated on the cars with backlit panels, and often on electronic signs on the station platforms. The last metro train on each line begins sometime between 12.35am and 1.04am, before starting up again around 5.30am.

The RER is faster than the metro, but the stops are further apart. Some of Paris' attractions, particularly those on the Left Bank, can be reached more easily by the RER than by metro. RER lines are known by an alphanumeric combination – the letter (A to E) refers to the line, the number to the spur it will follow to the suburbs.

TOURIST PASSES

The Mobilis card allows unlimited travel for one day in two to six zones (€5.60 to €15.90; €4.55 to €13.70 for children aged four to 11 years), while the Paris Visite pass allows unlimited travel (including to/from airports) plus discounted entry to museums and activities. The version covering one to three zones costs €8.50/14/19/27.50 for one/two/three/five days. Children aged four to 11 years pay €4.25/7/9.50/13.75. Both passes are valid on the metro, the RER, buses, trams and the Montmartre funicular.

TRAVEL PASSES

If you're staying for a while, a combined travel pass might be a good investment. The **Navigo system** (www.navigo.fr, in French), similar to London's Oyster or Hong Kong's Octopus cards, consists of a weekly, monthly or yearly pass that can be recharged at Navigo machines in metro stations; you simply swipe the card across the electronic panel as you go through the turnstiles. The Navigo Découverte costs €5 and can be recharged for one week or more; you'll need a passport photo.

Otherwise, weekly tickets *(coupon hebdomadaire)* cost €16.30 for zones 1 and 2 and remain valid from Monday to Sunday, while the monthly ticket (*coupon mensuel;* €53.50 for zones 1 and 2) runs from the first day of the month.

Taxi

The *prise en charge* (flag-fall) in a Parisian taxi is €2.10. Within the city limits, it costs €0.82 per kilometre between 10am and 5pm Monday to Saturday (Tarif A; white light on meter), and €1.10 per kilometre from 5pm to 10am, all day Sunday, and public holidays (Tarif B; orange light on meter).

The first piece of baggage is free; additional pieces over 5kg cost €1 extra, as do pick-ups from SNCF mainline stations. Most drivers won't carry more than three people, for insurance reasons.

To order a taxi, call Paris' **central taxi switchboard** (☎ 01 45 30 30 30, passengers with reduced mobility 01 47 39 00 91; 🕐 24hrs).

Alpha Taxis (☎ 01 45 85 85 85; www.alphataxis.com)
Taxis Bleus (☎ 01 49 36 29 48, 08 91 70 10 10; www.taxis-bleus.com)
Taxis G7 (☎ 01 47 39 47 39; www.taxisg7.fr, in French).

AROUND PARIS

Bordered by five rivers – the Epte, Aisne, Eure, Yonne and Marne – the area around Paris is rather like a giant island, which explains why it's often referred to as the Île de France. In past centuries, this was where you'd find the country retreats of the French kings – most notably at the extravagant chateaux of Versailles and Fontainebleau. These days the royal castles have been joined by a kingdom of a rather more magic kind.

DISNEYLAND PARIS

In 1992, Mickey Mouse, Snow White and chums set up shop on reclaimed sugar-beet fields 32km east of Paris at a cost of €4.6 billion. Though not quite as over-the-top as its American cousins, **Disneyland Paris** (☎ 01 60 30 60 30; www.disneylandparis.com) is still capable of packing in the crowds – some 12 million visitors strolled through its gates in 2008.

The main **Disneyland Park** (🕐 9am-11pm daily mid-Jul–Aug, 10am-8pm Mon-Fri, 9am-8pm Sat & Sun Sep-Mar, 9am-8pm daily Apr–early May, 10am-8pm Mon-Fri, 9am-8pm Sat & Sun early May–mid-Jun, 9am-8pm daily mid-Jun–early Jul) is divided into five *pays* (lands), including an idealised version of an American **Main St**, a recreation of the American Wild West in **Frontierland**, futuristic **Discoveryland**, and the exotic-themed **Adventureland**, complete with *Indiana Jones* and *Pirates of the Carribean* connections. Unsurprisingly, the candy-coated heart of the park is **Fantasyland**, where you'll come face-to-face with fairy-tale characters such as Sleeping Beauty, Pinocchio, Peter Pan and Snow White.

Meanwhile, the adjacent **Walt Disney Studios Park** (adult/under 3yr/3-11yr €46/free/38; 🕐 9am-6pm daily Jul-Sep, 10am-6pm Mon-Fri, 9am-6pm Sat & Sun Oct-Mar, 10am-6pm Apr-Jun) has a sound stage, backlot and animation studios illustrating how films, TV programs and cartoons are produced.

Standard **admission fees** (adult/under 3yr/3-11yr €46/free/38) only cover one park – to visit both you'll need a **Passe-Partout** (adult/under 3yr/3-11yr €56/free/48) ticket, or the two-/three-day **Hopper Ticket** (adult €103/128, child €84/105) if you want to spread your visit.

Marne-la-Vallée/Chessy, Disneyland's RER station, is served by line A4; trains run every 15 minutes or so from central Paris (€7.50, 35 to 40 minutes). The last train back to Paris leaves just after midnight.

VERSAILLES

pop 85,300

The leafy, oh-so-bourgeois suburb of Versailles, 21km southwest of Paris, is the site of France's grandest and most famous chateau. It served as the kingdom's political capital for more than a century, from 1682 to 1789 – the year Revolutionary mobs massacred the palace guard and dragged Louis XVI and Marie Antoinette back to Paris, where they eventually had their heads separated from their shoulders. It's an enormously popular spot – you can usually dodge the worst crowds in the early morning or late afternoon, and buying your ticket in advance: either online (www.chateauversailles.fr), from Fnac or any SNCF train station or office.

Sights

The **Château de Versailles** (☎ 08 10 81 16 14; www.chateauversailles.fr; adult/under 18yr €13.50/free, from 4pm/3pm in low/high season €10/free; 🕐 9am-6.30pm Tue-Sun Apr-Oct, to 5.30pm Tue-Sun Nov-Mar) was built in the mid-17th century by Louis XIV – the Roi Soleil (Sun King) – to project the absolute power of the French monarchy. Jointly designed by the architect Louis Le Vau (later replaced by Jules Hardouin-Mansart), the painter and interior designer Charles Le Brun, and the landscape artist André Le Nôtre, it's a fabulous monument to the wealth and ambition of the French aristocracy.

The 580m-long palace itself is split into several wings, each with its own astonishing array of grand halls, wood-panelled corridors and sumptuous bedchambers, including the **Grand Appartement du Roi** (King's Suite) and the **Galerie des Glaces** (Hall of Mirrors), a 75m-long ballroom with 17 huge mirrors on one side. Outside the main palace are the vast **landscaped gardens**, filled with canals, pools and neatly trimmed box hedges, and two outbuildings, the **Grand Trianon** and the **Petit Trianon**.

The basic ticket includes an English-language audio guide and entry to the state apartments, the chapel, the **Appartements du Dauphin et de la Dauphine** and various galleries. The so-called **Passeport** (adult/under 18yr €20/free Tue-Fri & €25/free Sat & Sun Apr-Oct, €16/free Nov-Mar) includes the same, as well as the Grand Trianon and, in high season, the Grandes Eaux Musicales fountain displays. Enter the palace through Entrée A with a palace ticket; Entrée C with a Passeport.

Guided tours (☎ 08 10 81 16 14; adult with/without palace ticket, Passeport or ticket to the Domaine de Marie-Antoinette €7.50/14.50, under 18yr €5.50; 🕑 9.45am-3.45pm Tue-Sun) explore several themes – life at court, classical music, 'Versailles splendours', the private apartments of Louis XV and Louis XI – although only a few are in English.

Versailles is currently undergoing an enormous €370 million restoration program, so at least one part of the palace is likely to be clad in scaffolding until 2020.

Getting There & Away

RER line C5 (€2.80, every 15 minutes) goes from Paris' Left Bank RER stations to Versailles-Rive Gauche, 700m southeast of the chateau.

SNCF operates up to 70 trains daily from Paris' Gare St-Lazare (€2.80) to Versailles-Rive Droite, 1.2km from the chateau. Versailles-Chantiers is served by half-hourly SNCF trains daily from Gare Montparnasse (€2.80); trains continue to Chartres (€10.90, 45 to 60 minutes). An SNCF package *(forfait loisir)* covering the metro, return train journey to/from Versailles and chateau admission costs €19.20.

CHARTRES

pop 40,250

The magnificent 13th-century cathedral of Chartres, crowned by two very different spires – one Gothic, the other Romanesque – rises from rich farmland 88km southwest of Paris and dominates the medieval town. With its astonishing blue stained glass and other treasures, the cathedral at Chartres, France's best-preserved medieval basilica, is a must-see.

Information

Office de Tourisme de Chartres (☎ 02 37 18 26 26; www.chartres-tourisme.com; place de la Cathédrale; 🕑 9am-7pm Mon-Sat, 9.30am-5.30pm Sun Apr-Sep, 10am-6pm Mon-Sat, 10am-1pm & 2.30-4.30pm Sun Oct-Mar) The tourist office rents audio guides (for one/two people €5.50/8.50; 1½ hours) around the medieval city.

Post office (3 blvd Maurice Violette)

Sights

In a nation of spectacular cathedrals, the 130m-long **Cathédrale Notre Dame de Chartres** (☎ 02 37 21 22 07; www.diocese-chartres.com, in French; place de la Cathédrale; 🕑 8.30am-7.30pm) still manages to take your breath away. The original Romanesque cathedral was devastated in a fire in 1194, but remnants of it remain in the **Portail Royal** (Royal Portal) and the 103m-high **Clocher Vieux** (Old Bell Tower, also known as the South Tower). The rest of the cathedral predominantly dates from the 13th century, including many of the 172 glorious **stained-glass windows**, which are renowned for the depth and intensity of their 'Chartres blue' tones.

A platform emerges some 70m up the 112m-high **Clocher Neuf** (new bell tower; adult/under 18yr/18-25yr €6.50/free/4.50, 1st Sun of certain months free; 🕑 9.30am-noon & 2-5.30pm Mon-Sat, 2-5.30pm Sun May-Aug, 9.30am-noon & 2-4.30pm Mon-Sat, 2-4.30pm Sun Sep-Apr), with superb views of the cathedral's three-tiered flying buttresses and 19th-century copper roof.

Eating

Café Serpente (☎ 02 37 21 68 81; 2 Cloître Notre Dame; starters €6-14.80, mains €15-20; 🕑 10am-11pm) Its location slap-bang opposite the cathedral ensures this atmospheric brasserie and *salon de thé* (tearoom) is always full. Cuisine is traditional, and its chef constructs well-filled sandwiches (€3.80 to €5.80).

Maison du Saumon et de la Truie qui File (☎ 02 37 36 28 00; 10-14 rue de la Poissonnerie; menus €29.80-32.90; 🕑 lunch Tue-Sun, dinner to 11.30pm Tue-Sat) Inhabiting Chartres' most photographed half-timbered building, this medieval landmark cooks up a bit of everything, ranging from Polish stuffed-cabbage rolls to Alsatian *choucroute* and Moroccan *tajines* (stews; €18.50).

Food shops surround the **covered market** (place Billard; 🕑 7am-1pm Wed & Sat), just off rue des Changes south of the cathedral.

Getting There & Away

More than 30 SNCF trains a day (20 on Sunday) link Paris' Gare Montparnasse (€12.90, 70 minutes) with Chartres via Versailles-Chantiers (€10.90, 45 minutes to one hour).

FAR NORTHERN FRANCE

It's grim up north – or so the stereotype goes. But while France's northernmost corner is certainly one of the most densely populated and heavy industrialised areas of the country, there's still plenty to see – including the Flemish-style city of Lille, the cross-Channel shopping centre of Calais and the moving battlefields and cemeteries of WWI.

LILLE

pop 224,900

Lille (Rijsel in Flemish) may be the country's most underrated major city. In recent decades this once-grimy industrial metropolis (which has a population of one million in the wider metro area) has transformed itself – with generous government help – into a glittering and self-confident cultural and commercial hub. Highlights of the city include an attractive Old Town with a strong Flemish accent, three renowned art museums, and a cutting-edge, student-driven nightlife.

Orientation

Place du Général de Gaulle (also called the Grand' Place) separates Lille's main shopping precinct (around pedestrianised rue Neuve), to the south, from the narrow streets of Vieux Lille (Old Lille), to the north. Lille's two main train stations, old-fashioned Gare Lille-Flandres and ultramodern Gare Lille-Europe, are 400m apart on the eastern edge of the city.

Information

4 Players (☎ 03 20 07 43 18; 9 rue Maertens; per 10min/hr prepaid €0.50/3; ⏰ 11am-10.30pm Mon-Fri, 10am-11.30pm Sat, 2-10pm Sun; Ⓜ République Beaux Arts) Yes, it's pronounced 'foreplayers'.

Laundrette (4 rue Ovigneur; ⏰ 7am-8pm; Ⓜ République Beaux Arts)

Main post office (8 place de la République; Ⓜ République Beaux Arts) Changes money.

Net Arena (☎ 03 28 38 09 20; 10 rue des Bouchers; per hr €3; ⏰ 10am-10pm Mon-Sat, 2-8pm Sun) Thirty internet-access computers.

Tourist office (☎ from abroad 03 59 57 94 00, in France 08 91 56 20 04; www.lilletourism.com; place Rihour; ⏰ 9.30am-6.30pm Mon-Sat, 10am-noon & 2-5pm Sun & holidays; Ⓜ Rihour) Sells the Lille City Pass (one-/two-/three-day €18/30/45) covering Lille's museums and public transport.

Sights

Vieux Lille (Old Lille), which begins just north of place du Général de Gaulle, is justly proud of its restored 17th- and 18th-century houses. The old brick residences along **rue de la Monnaie** were all but abandoned by the 1970s, but they now house the city's chicest boutiques, as well as the **Hospice Comtesse Museum** (☎ 03 28 36 84 00; 32 rue de la Monnaie; adult/under 12yr/student €3/free/2; ⏰ 10am-12.30pm & 2-6pm, closed Mon morning & Tue), featuring mainly religious art.

Nearby, the 1652 **Vieille Bourse** (Old Stock Exchange; place du Général de Gaulle; Ⓜ Rihour) consists of 24 houses decorated with caryatids and cornucopia.

Lille's world-renowned **Fine Arts Museum** (☎ 03 20 06 78 00; www.pba-lille.fr; place de la République; adult/under 12yr/12-25yr €5/free/3.50; ⏰ 2-6pm Mon, 10am-6pm Wed-Sun; Ⓜ République Beaux Arts) has a truly first-rate collection of 15th- to 20th-century paintings, including works by Rubens, Van Dyck and Manet.

Housed in an art deco swimming pool (built 1927–32), **La Piscine Musée d'Art et d'Industrie** (☎ 03 20 69 23 60; www.roubaix-lapiscine.com; 23 rue de l'Espérance, Roubaix; adult/under 18yr €3.50/free; ⏰ 11am-6pm Tue-Thu, 11am-8pm Fri, 1-6pm Sat & Sun; Ⓜ Gare Jean Lebas), 12km northeast of Gare Lille-Europe, showcases fine arts and sculpture.

Sleeping

Auberge de Jeunesse (☎ 03 20 57 08 94; www.hihostels.com; 12 rue Malpart; dm incl breakfast €16.85, d €33.70; ⏰ closed 23 Dec–mid-Jan; Ⓜ Mairie de Lille; 💻) This former maternity hospital has 165 beds (two to eight per room), hall showers, kitchen facilities and a rather spartan atmosphere.

Hôtel Kanaï (☎ 03 20 57 14 78; www.hotelkanai.com; 10 rue de Béthune; d Mon-Thu €75-95, Fri-Sun €60-65, festival period €105; Ⓜ Rihour; ❄) Completely renovated in 2007, the 31 rooms at this supercentral hotel have clean, minimalist lines; top-floor rooms have views, but there's no lift.

Hôtel Brueghel (☎ 03 20 06 06 69; www.hotel-brueghel.com; 5 parvis St-Maurice; s/d from €78/84; Ⓜ Gare Lille-Flandres) The 65 two-star rooms here are a mix of modern styling (eg the bathrooms) and antique furnishing, though they don't have nearly as much Flemish charm as the lobby.

Grand Hôtel Bellevue (☎ 03 20 57 45 64; www.grandhotelbellevue.com; 5 rue Jean Roisin; d €135-165; Ⓜ Rihour; ❄) Mixing Best Western trappings with turn-of-the-century style, this smart establishment features a charmingly creaky belle époque lift and 60 spacious rooms with high ceilings, antique-style French furnishings and flat-screen TVs.

Eating

The *estaminets* (traditional eateries) of Lille, especially Vieux Lille, specialise in Flemish dishes such as *carbonnade* (beef stewed with beer and brown sugar).

Estaminet 'T Rijsel (☎ 03 20 15 01 59; 25 rue de Gand; mains €9.90-19.90; ⏰ noon-1.30pm & 7.30-9.30pm, to 10 or 10.30pm Fri & Sat, closed Mon lunch & Sun) This homey, unpretentious eatery serves up local specialities such as *carbonnade* (€9.90), *pot'je vleesch* (a cold meat terrine; €11.90) and *poulet au Maroilles* (chicken with Maroilles cheese).

Tous Les Jours Dimanche (☎ 03 28 36 05 92; 13 rue Masurel; menus €15.50-16.50; ⏰ restaurant noon-2.30pm, salon de thé noon-6.30pm, closed Mon, also closed Sun May-Sep) Surrounded by antique furniture and objets d'art, lunch here feels like hanging out in an arty friend's living room. Specialities include salads, sandwiches (€11) and quiche-like *tartes*.

our pick À l'Huîtrière (☎ 03 20 55 43 41; www.huitriere.fr, in French; 3 rue des Chats Bossus; lunch menus €45, other menus €100-140; ⏰ noon-2pm & 7-9.30pm, closed dinner Sun & late Jul–late Aug) On the 'Street of the Hunchback Cats', this sophisticated restaurant is almost as well known for its art deco trappings as for its fabulous seafood – weekend bookings are essential.

Lille's beloved **Wazemmes food market** (place de la Nouvelle Aventure; ⏰ 8am-2pm Tue-Thu, 8am-8pm Fri & Sat, 8am-3pm Sun & holidays; Ⓜ Gambetta) is in the ethnically mixed Wazemmes district, about 1.5km southwest of the tourist office. The city's largest **outdoor market** (⏰ 7am-1.30pm or 2pm Tue, Thu & Sun) takes place outside on Sunday morning.

The city's largest supermarket is **Carrefour** (Euralille shopping mall; ⏰ 9am-9.30pm Mon-Sat; Ⓜ Gare Lille-Europe).

Drinking

Lille has two main nightlife zones: the small, chic bars of Vieux Lille, and the student-orientated bars around rue Masséna and rue Solférino.

Meert (☎ 03 20 57 07 44; www.meert.fr; 27 rue Esquermoise; ⏰ 9.30am-7.30pm Tue-Fri, 9am-7.30pm Sat, 9am-1pm & 3-7pm Sun; Ⓜ Rihour) Vanilla-flavoured *gaufres* (waffles; €2.30 each) are the speciality of Meert, a luxury tearoom-cum-pastry-and-sweets-shop in business since 1761.

L'Illustration Café (☎ 03 20 12 00 90; www.bar-lillustration.com, in French; 18 rue Royale; ⏰ 12.30pm-3am Mon-Sat, 2pm-3am Sun) Quintessentially French cafe, adorned with art nouveau woodwork and frequented by an intellectual crowd.

Le Balatum (☎ 03 20 57 41 81; www.myspace.com/balatum; 13 rue de la Barre; ⏰ 4pm-3am Sun-Fri, 2pm-3am Sat) Funky, dimly lit place favoured by a *branché* (in-the-know) crowd, with weekend gigs and DJs.

Café Le Relax (48 place de la Nouvelle Aventure; ⏰ 9am-midnight Tue, Thu & Sun, 10.30am-midnight Mon & Wed, 10.30am-1am Fri, to 2am Sat; Ⓜ Gambetta) A genuine, ungentrified *café de quartier* (neighbourhood cafe) where locals drop in for an espresso or a strong Belgian beer and to run into friends.

Getting There & Away

Eurolines (☎ 03 20 78 18 88; 23 parvis St-Maurice; ⏰ 9.30am-6pm Mon-Fri, 10am-noon & 1-6pm Sat; Ⓜ Gare Lille-Flandres) serves cities such as Brussels (€15, 1½ to two hours), Amsterdam (€30, five hours) and London (€34, 5½ hours). Buses depart from blvd de Leeds, to the left of Gare Lille-Europe.

The city has two train stations. Gare Lille-Flandres is used by regional services and by TGVs travelling to Paris' Gare du Nord (€37.60 to €52.20, one hour, 14 to 18 daily), while the ultramodern Gare Lille-Europe handles all other trains, including the Eurostar services to London, TGVs/Eurostars to Brussels-Nord (Monday to Friday/weekend €25.20/16.30, 35 minutes, 12 daily), and TGVs to Nice (€110 to €132.70, 7½ hours, two direct daily).

Getting Around

Lille's two speedy metro lines, two tramways and bus lines are run by **Transpole** (☎ 08 20 42 40 40), which has an **information window** (⏰ closed Sun) in Gare Lille-Flandres and its metro station. Tickets (€1.25) are sold on buses but must be purchased (and validated in the orange posts) *before* boarding a metro or tram. A Pass Journée (all-day pass) costs €3.50.

CALAIS

pop 74,200

As Churchill might have put it, 'never in the field of human tourism have so many travellers passed through a place and so few stopped to visit'. Over 15 million people pass through

Calais en route to the cross-Channel ferries, but precious few take the time to explore the town itself – and while Calais is far from the most fascinating town in France, it's worth a stop for Rodin's famous sculpture, *The Burghers of Calais*.

Orientation & Information

Gare Calais-Ville (the train station) is 650m south of the main square, place d'Armes. The car-ferry terminal is 1.5km northeast of place d'Armes (by car the distance is double that). The Channel Tunnel's vehicle-loading area is 6km southwest of the town centre. The **tourist office** (☎ 03 21 96 62 40; www.calais-cotedopale.com; 12 blvd Georges Clemenceau; ⏲ 10am-1pm & 2-6.30pm Mon-Sat year-round, 10am-1pm Sun Jul & Aug) is a short walk north across the river from the station along blvd Georges Clemenceau.

Sights

Calais' Flemish Renaissance–style **town hall** (1911–25) houses the town's main sight – Rodin's *Les Bourgeois de Calais* (The Burghers of Calais; 1895), honouring six local citizens who, in 1347, held off the besieging English forces for more than eight months. Edward III was so impressed by their efforts he ultimately spared the Calaisiens and their six leaders.

WWII artefacts fill the **Musée de la Seconde Guerre Mondiale** (☎ 03 21 34 21 57; adult/student/family of 5 incl audio guide €6/5/14; ⏲ 10am-6pm May-Sep, 11am-5pm Wed-Mon Feb-Apr & Oct-Nov), housed in a concrete bunker once used as a German naval headquarters. In spring 2009, a brand-new museum dedicated to Calais' lace-making legacy, the **Musée de la Dentelle et de la Mode** (rue Sambor), is set to open in a 19th-century lace factory.

Sleeping

Lots of two-star hotels can be found along rue Royale.

Auberge de Jeunesse (☎ 03 21 34 70 20; www.auberge-jeunesse-calais.com; av Maréchal de Lattre de Tassigny; s €24, dm in double r €18, incl breakfast; ⏲ 24hr) Modern, well equipped and just 200m from the beach, this 162-bed hostel is served by buses 3 and 9.

Hôtel Victoria (☎ 03 21 34 38 32; hotelvictoriacalais@wanadoo.fr; 8 rue du Commandant Bonningue; d €42, with washbasin €30) A hotel so ordinary that it could be described as 'extraordinarily ordinary'. The 14 two-star rooms are clean, comfortable and in good repair.

Hôtel La Sole Meunière (☎ 03 21 96 83 66; www.solemeuniere.com; 53 rue de la Mer; s/d/q €49/59/89) A family-run two-star place named after the ground-floor restaurant, which – you guessed it – specialises in butter-sautéed sole. There are 18 attractive, pastel rooms, some with port views.

Hôtel Richelieu (☎ 03 21 34 61 60; www.hotelrichelieu-calais.com; 17 rue Richelieu; d/2-room q €57/116) At this welcoming two-star place, the 15 cheery rooms, each one unique, are lovingly maintained and outfitted with antique furniture redeemed by the owner from local flea markets.

Eating

Tonnerre de Brest (☎ 03 21 96 95 35; 16 place d'Armes; weekday lunch menus €10.50-18.50; ⏲ closed Mon except Jul & Aug) At this rustic eatery run by two sisters, you can tuck into 28 savoury galettes or 31 sweet crêpes washed down with local cider.

Histoire Ancienne (☎ 03 21 34 11 20; www.histoire-ancienne.com; 20 rue Royale; menus du jour from noon-1pm & 6-8pm €11.50, 2-/3-/5-course menus €18/25.50/35.50; ⏲ closed Sun & dinner Mon) Specialising in French and regional dishes, some grilled over an open wood fire, this 1930s Paris-style bistro has treats such as *escargots à l'ail* (garlic snails).

Aux Mouettes (☎ 03 21 34 67 59; 10 rue Jean Pierre Avron; menus €16-34; ⏲ closed dinner Wed, dinner Sun & Mon) Fisherfolk sell their daily catch across the street at the quay, so you can count on the freshest seafood, including locally caught sole (€22).

Au Cadre Vert (☎ 03 21 34 69 44; 3 rue André Gerschell; menus incl wine €18.50; ⏲ closed Sun, lunch Sat & lunch Wed) A family-run restaurant known for specialities such as *magret de canard* (duck breast fillet; €14) and *pièce de bœuf sauce pleurotte* (beefsteak in mushroom sauce).

Getting There & Around

BOAT

Every day, 35 to 52 car ferries from Dover dock at Calais' bustling car-ferry terminal.

P&O Ferries Calais town centre (41 place d'Armes); car-ferry terminal (☎ 03 21 46 10 18; ⏲ 6am-10pm); car-ferry car park (⏲ 24hr)

SeaFrance Calais town centre (2 place d'Armes); car-ferry terminal (☎ 03 21 46 80 05; 🕑 7.30am-7.30pm); car-ferry car park (🕑 24hr)

Shuttle buses (€1.50 or UK£1, roughly hourly from about 10am to 7pm or 7.40pm) link Gare Calais-Ville and place d'Armes with the car-ferry terminal.

BUS

Ligne BCD (☎ 08 00 62 00 59) is an express service linking Calais' train station with Dunkirk (€7.70, 45 minutes, 11 daily Monday to Friday, three on Saturday) and Boulogne (€7.20, 40 minutes, five daily Monday to Friday, two on Saturday).

CAR & MOTORCYCLE

To reach the Channel Tunnel's vehicle-loading area at Coquelles, follow the road signs on the A16 to 'Tunnel Sous La Manche' and get off at exit 42.

TRAIN

Calais has two train stations: central Gare Calais-Ville, and Gare Calais-Fréthun, a TGV station 10km southwest of town near the Channel Tunnel entrance. They are linked by trains and shuttle buses. Gare Calais-Ville serves Amiens (€22.10, 2½ to 3½ hours, six to eight daily), Boulogne (€7.20, 30 minutes, 15 to 18 daily Monday to Saturday, eight on Sunday), Dunkirk (€7.70, 50 minutes, two to five Monday to Saturday) and Lille-Flandres (€15.30, 1¼ hours, seven to 11 daily). Gare Calais-Fréthun is served by TGVs to Paris' Gare du Nord (€39.60 to €54.60, 1½ hours, six daily Monday to Saturday, three on Sunday) as well as Eurostars to London (one hour, three daily).

DUNKIRK

pop 209,000

Dunkirk (Dunkerque), made famous and flattened almost simultaneously in 1940, was rebuilt during one of the most uninspired periods in Western architecture. Charming it may not be, but the port city has two worthwhile museums, a mellow beach and several colourful pre-Lent carnivals.

Dunkirk's **tourist office** (☎ 03 28 66 79 21; www.lesdunesdeflandre.fr; rue de l'Amiral Ronarc'h; 🕑 9.30am-12.30pm & 1.30-6.30pm Mon-Sat, 10am-noon & 2-4pm Sun & holidays, no midday closure Jul & Aug) is housed in a 58m-high belfry (adult €2.80) with spectacular views.

The **Musée Portuaire** (Harbour Museum; ☎ 03 28 63 33 39; www.museeportuaire.com; 9 quai de la Citadelle; adult/student/family €4/3/10; 🕑 10am-12.45pm & 1.30-6pm Wed-Mon, also open Tue & no midday closure Jul & Aug) will delight ship-model lovers of all ages. Forty-five-minute **guided tours** (adult/student/family €7.50/6/18, incl the museum €9/7.50/22) take visitors aboard a lighthouse ship, a *peniche* (barge) and the *Duchesse Anne*, a three-masted training ship built for the German merchant marine in 1901.

The faded seaside resort of **Malo-les-Bains** is 2km northeast of Dunkirk's city centre. Its promenade-lined beach, **Plage des Alliés**, is named in honour of the Allied troops evacuated from here in 1940. The **British Memorial** (route de Furnes), honouring more than 4500 British and Commonwealth soldiers missing in action from 1940, is 1.5km southeast of the tourist office.

Most trains from Dunkirk's train station, 1km southwest of the tourist office, stop at Gare Lille-Flandres (€12.70, 30 to 80 minutes, 30 daily Monday to Friday, 11 to 15 daily weekends). For bus details, see left.

BATTLE OF THE SOMME MEMORIALS

The Battle of the Somme, a WWI Allied offensive waged northeast of Amiens, was designed to relieve pressure on the beleaguered French troops at Verdun. On 1 July 1916, British, Commonwealth and French troops went 'over the top' in a massive assault along a 34km front. But German positions proved virtually unbreachable, and on the first day alone 21,392 Allied troops were killed and another 35,492 were wounded.

By the time the offensive was called off in mid-November, some 1.2 million lives had been lost: the British had advanced just 12km, the French 8km. The Battle of the Somme has since become a symbol of the meaningless slaughter of war and its killing fields and cemeteries have since become a site of pilgrimage (see www.somme-battlefields.co.uk); the tourist offices in **Amiens** (☎ 03 22 71 60 50; www.amiens.com/tourisme) and **Arras** (☎ 03 21 51 26 95; www.ot-arras.fr) can supply maps, guides and minibus tours.

NORMANDY

Famous for cows, cider and Camembert, the largely rural region of Normandy (www.normandie-tourisme.fr) is one of the most traditional areas of France, home to the historic D-Day beaches, the otherworldy spires of Mont St-Michel and the half-timbered houses and Gothic cathedral of Rouen, as well as the world's largest comic-strip – the Bayeux Tapestry.

ROUEN

pop 108,800

With its elegant spires, beautifully restored medieval quarter and soaring Gothic cathedral, the ancient city of Rouen is one of Normandy's highlights. Devastated several times during the Middle Ages by fire and plague, the city was later badly damaged by WWII bombing raids, but has been meticulously rebuilt over the last six decades, and the city makes an ideal base for exploring the northern Normandy coast.

Orientation

The main train station (Gare Rouen-Rive Droite) is at the northern end of rue Jeanne d'Arc, the main thoroughfare running south to the Seine. The old city is centred around rue du Gros Horloge between the place du Vieux Marché and the cathedral.

Information

Cybernet (☎ 02 35 07 73 02; 47 place du Vieux Marché; per hr €4; ⏲ 10am-8pm Mon-Sat, 2-7pm Sun) Internet access.

Laundrette rue Cauchoise (56 rue Cauchoise; ⏲ 7am-9pm); rue d'Amiens (55 rue d'Amiens; ⏲ 7am- 9pm)

PlaceNet (☎ 02 77 76 90 21; 37 rue de la République; per 15min/hr €1/3; ⏲ 2.30pm-12.30am Sun & Mon, 10.30am-12.30am Tue-Thu, 10.30am-3am Fri & Sat) Internet access.

Post office (45 rue Jeanne d'Arc) Changes foreign currency.

Tourist office (☎ 02 32 08 32 40; www.rouentourisme.com; 25 place de la Cathédrale; ⏲ 9am-7pm Mon-Sat, 9.30am-12.30pm & 2-6pm Sun & holidays May-Sep, 9.30am-12.30pm & 1.30-6pm Mon-Sat, 2-6pm Sun & holidays Oct-Apr) Opposite the cathedral.

Sights

The old city's main thoroughfare, rue du Gros Horloge, runs from the cathedral west to **place du Vieux Marché**, where 19-year-old Joan of Arc was executed for heresy in 1431. Dedicated in 1979, the modernist **Église Jeanne d'Arc** (⏲ 10am-noon & 2-6pm Apr-Oct, to 5.30pm Nov-Mar) marks the spot where Joan was burned at the stake.

Rouen's stunning Gothic **Cathédrale Notre Dame** (⏲ 8am-6pm Tue-Sun, 2-6pm Mon) is the famous subject of a series of paintings by Monet, although the great man would hardly recognise the place these days – an ongoing restoration project has polished up the soot-blackened stone to its original brilliant-white colour.

Inside a desanctified 16th-century church, the riveting **Musée Le Secq des Tournelles** (☎ 02 35 88 42 92; 2 rue Jacques Villon; adult/under 18yr/student €2.30/free/1.55; ⏲ 10am-1pm & 2-6pm Wed-Mon) is devoted to the blacksmith's craft, with some 5000 wrought-iron items ranging from shop signs to an elaborate choir grille from 1202.

The **Musée des Beaux-Arts** (☎ 02 35 71 28 40; esplanade Marcel Duchamp; adult/under 18yr/student €3/free2/; ⏲ 10am-6pm Wed-Mon), housed in a grand structure erected in 1870, features canvases by Caravaggio, Rubens, Modigliani, Pissarro, Renoir, Sisley (lots) and (of course) several works by Monet, including a study of Rouen's cathedral (in room 2.33).

Sleeping

Hôtel Le Palais (☎ 02 35 71 41 40; 12 rue du Tambour; s/d €36/42, with hall shower €24/30) The rooms are basic and not all have private bathrooms, but this old-school cheapie is bang in the middle of the old city.

Hôtel Le Cardinal (☎ 02 35 70 24 42; www.cardinal-hotel.fr; 1 place de la Cathédrale; s €47-59, d €58-72, q €96) In a supercentral spot facing the cathedral, this postwar hotel has 18 simply furnished rooms with lots of natural light; 4th-floor rooms have private terraces overlooking the square.

Hôtel des Carmes (☎ 02 35 71 92 31; www.hoteldescarmes.com, in French; 33 place des Carmes; d €49-65, tr €67-77; 💻) This sweet little hotel has 12 rooms decked out with patchwork quilts and vibrant colours; some even have cerulean-blue cloudscapes painted on the ceilings.

Le Vieux Carré (☎ 02 35 71 67 70; www.vieux-carre.fr; 34 rue Ganterie; d €58-62) Set around a cute little garden courtyard, this quiet half-timbered hotel has a delightfully old-fashioned *salon de thé* and 13 smallish rooms decorated with old postcard blowups and threadbare rugs.

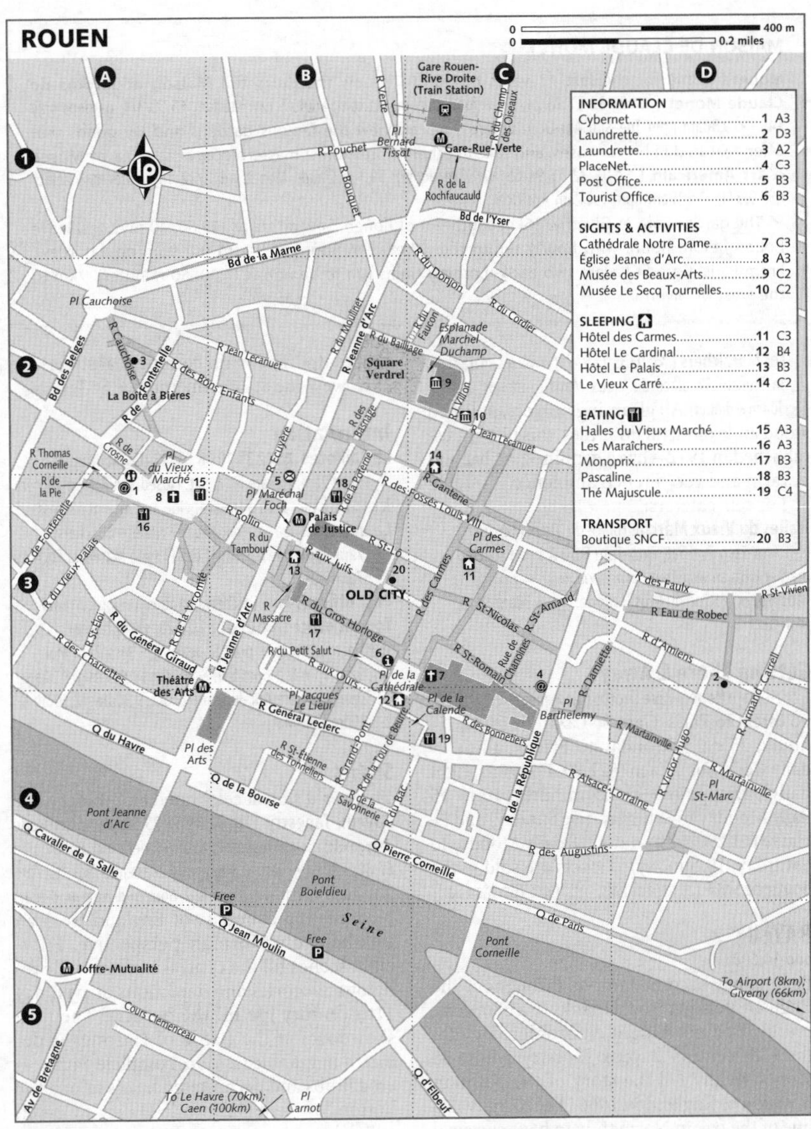

Eating

Thé Majuscule (☎ 02 35 71 15 66; 8 place de la Calende; plats du jour €10.50; 🕑 restaurant noon-2pm Mon-Sat, salon de thé 2.30-6.30pm Mon-Sat) Downstairs it's a typically chaotic French secondhand bookshop, upstairs a homey tearoom with homemade *tartes,* salads, cakes and exotic teas (€3.30).

Pascaline (☎ 02 35 89 67 44; 5 rue de la Poterne; menus €14.90-26.90; 🕑 lunch & dinner) A top spot for a great-value *formule midi* (lunchtime menu), this bustling bistro serves up French cuisine in typically Parisian surroundings – think net curtains, white tablecloths and chuffing coffee machines.

MAISON DE CLAUDE MONET

Monet's home for the last 43 years of his life is now the delightful **Maison et Jardins de Claude Monet** (☎ 02 32 51 28 21; www.fondation-monet.com; adult/7-12yr/student €5.50/3/4, gardens only €4; 9.30am-6pm Tue-Sun Apr-Oct), where you can view the famous gardens and lily ponds that often featured in his canvases, and take in other Impressionist masterpieces at the nearby **Musée d'Art Américain** (☎ 02 32 51 94 65; www.maag.org; 99 rue Claude Monet; adult/12-18yr/student & senior €5.50/3/4; 10am-6pm Tue-Sun Apr-Oct).

The gardens are in Giverny, 66km southeast of Rouen. Several trains (€9.60, 40 minutes) leave Rouen before noon; with hourly return trains between 5pm and 10pm (till 9pm on Saturday). From Paris' Gare St-Lazare two early-morning trains run to Vernon (€11.90, 50 minutes), 7km to the west of Giverny.

Les Maraîchers (☎ 02 35 71 57 73; www.les-maraichers.fr, in French; 37 place du Vieux Marché; menus €16-25; lunch & dinner) All gleaming mirrors, polished wood and colourful floor tiles, this bistro – established in 1912 – has a genuine zinc bar and a warm and very French ambience.

For self-caterers:

Halles du Vieux Marché (place du Vieux Marché; 7am-7pm Tue-Sat, 7am-1pm Sun) A small covered market with an excellent *fromagerie*.

Monoprix (65 rue du Gros Horloge; 8.30am-9pm Mon-Sat)

Getting There & Away

From **Gare Rouen-Rive Droite** (rue Jeanne d'Arc), trains go direct to Paris' Gare St-Lazare (€19.30, 1¼ hours, 25 daily Monday to Friday, 14 to 19 daily weekends), Caen (€21.80, 1½ hours, eight daily), Dieppe (€9.90, 45 minutes, 10 to 15 daily Monday to Saturday, five Sunday) and Le Havre (€12.90, 50 minutes, 18 daily Monday to Saturday, 10 Sunday). Tickets are sold at the **Boutique SNCF** (20 rue aux Juifs; 10am-7pm Mon-Sat).

BAYEUX

pop 14,600

Bayeux has become famous throughout the English-speaking world thanks to a 68m-long piece of painstakingly embroidered cloth: the 11th-century Bayeux Tapestry, whose 58 scenes vividly tell the story of the Norman invasion of England in 1066. The town is also one of the few in Normandy to have survived WWII practically unscathed, with a centre crammed with 13th- to 18th-century buildings, wooden-framed Norman-style houses, and a fine Gothic cathedral.

Orientation

The cathedral, 1km northwest of the train station, is the most visible landmark in the city centre. The main commercial streets are east–west rue St-Martin and rue St-Jean.

Information

La Paillote (☎ 02 31 10 08 73; 25 rue Montfiquet; 5pm-2am, to 3am Fri & Sat, closed Sun & Mon winter) A laid-back pub with a tropical vibe and internet access.

Laundrettes rue des Bouchers (67 rue des Bouchers; 7am-9pm); rue Maréchal Foch (13 rue Maréchal Foch; 7am-9pm)

Post office (14 rue Larcher) Changes foreign currency.

Tourist office (☎ 02 31 51 28 28; www.bayeux-bessin-tourism.com; pont St-Jean; 9am-7pm Mon-Sat, 9am-1pm & 2-6pm Sun & holidays Jul & Aug, 9.30am-12.30pm & 2-6pm Apr-Jun, Sep & Oct, 9.30am-12.30pm & 2-5.30pm Nov-Mar)

Sights

The world's most celebrated embroidery, the **Bayeux Tapestry** (☎ 02 31 51 25 50; www.tapisserie-bayeux.fr; rue de Nesmond; adult/student incl audio guide €7.80/3.80; 9am-6.30pm mid-Mar–mid-Nov, to 7pm May-Aug, 9.30am-12.30pm & 2-6pm mid-Nov–mid-Mar) recounts the conquest of England from an unashamedly Norman perspective. Fifty-eight scenes fill the central canvas, while religious allegories and depictions of everyday 11th-century life fill the borders. The final showdown at the Battle of Hastings is depicted in graphic fashion, complete with severed limbs and decapitated heads (along the bottom of scene 52), while Halley's Comet, which blazed across the sky in 1066, appears in scene 32. Scholars believe that the 68.3m-long tapestry was commissioned by Bishop Odo of Bayeux, William the Conquerer's half-brother, for the opening of Bayeux' cathedral in 1077.

Bayeux was the first Normandy town liberated after D-Day, and the **Memorial Museum** (☎ 02 31 51 46 90; blvd Fabien Ware; adult/student

€6.50/3.80; 9.30am-6.30pm May-Sep, 10am-12.30pm & 2-6pm Oct-Apr) on the edge of town explores the major events using photos, personal accounts, dioramas and wartime objects. Nearby, the **Bayeux war cemetery** (☎ 02 21 21 77 00; blvd Fabien Ware) contains the graves of 4848 soldiers from the UK and 10 other countries (including Germany). Some 1800 other Commonweath soldiers whose bodies were never found are commemorated on the memorial across the road.

Most of Bayeux' spectacular Norman Gothic **Cathédrale Notre Dame** (rue du Bienvenu; 8.30am-7pm Jul-Sep, 8.30am-6pm Apr-Jun & Oct, 9am-5pm Nov-Mar) dates from the 13th century, though some parts are 11th-century Romanesque.

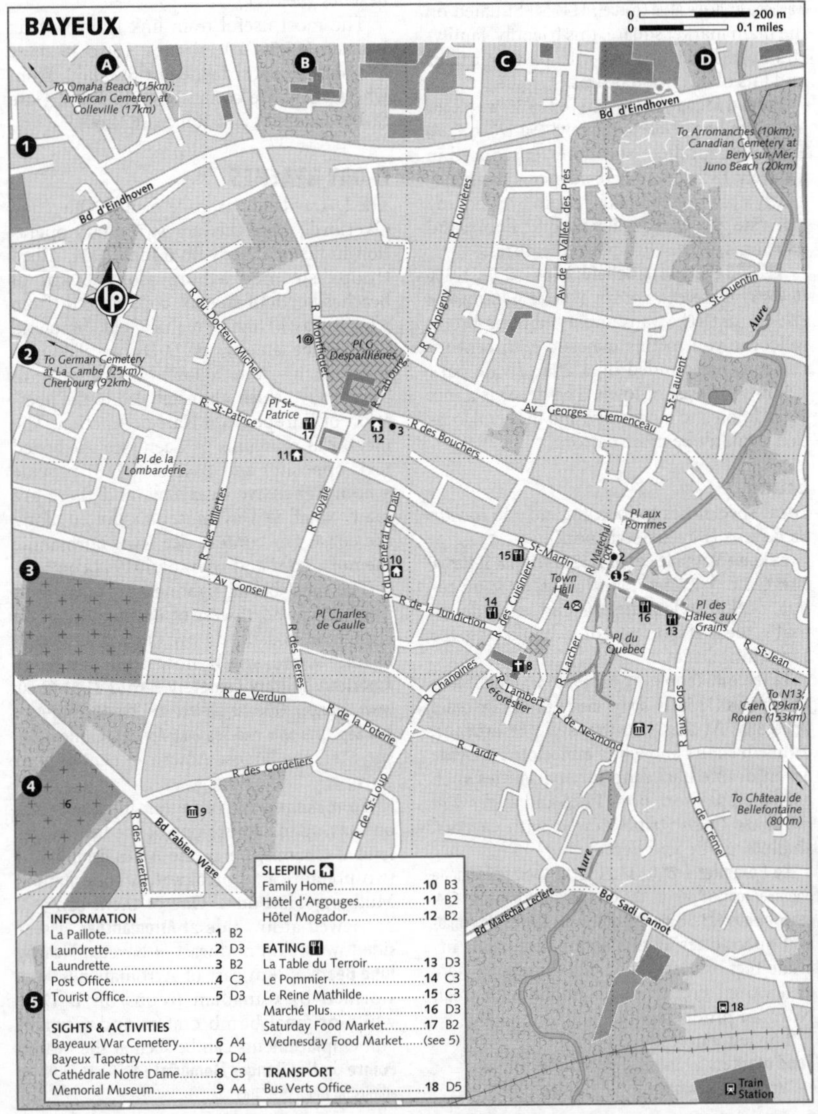

Sleeping

Family Home (☎ 02 31 92 15 22; www.fuaj.org; 39 rue Général de Dais; dm/s €19/30) One of France's most charming youth hostels, this place sports a 17th-century dining room, a delightful 16th-century courtyard, and 80 beds in rooms for one to four people. If reception isn't staffed, phone and someone will pop by.

Hôtel Mogador (☎ 02 31 92 24 58; hotel.mogador@wanadoo.fr; 20 rue Alain Chartier; d €44-54) Situated on the main market square, this friendly, family-run hotel has 14 rooms with pastel curtains and lots of old wood beams.

Hôtel d'Argouges (☎ 02 31 92 88 86; www.hotel-dargouges.com; 21 rue St-Patrice; d €90-120, q €280) This graceful three-star hotel, ensconced in a stately 18th-century residence, has an elegantly decorated breakfast room overlooking a private garden; squeaky parquet floors; and 28 rooms, some with period features.

our pick **Château de Bellefontaine** (☎ 02 31 22 00 10; www.hotel-bellefontaine.com; 49 rue de Bellefontaine; d €125-140, ste €160) Swans and a bubbling brook welcome you to this majestic 18th-century chateau, surrounded by a 2ha private park 1.5km southeast of town. The decor is a mix of tradition and modernity, and the rural location couldn't be more pastoral.

Eating

Local specialities to look for include *cochon de Bayeux* (Bayeux-style pork).

La Reine Mathilde (☎ 02 31 92 00 59; 47 rue St-Martin; cakes €2.30; ⏲ 8.30am-7.30pm Tue-Sun) A sumptuous, c 1900-style *pâtisserie* and *salon de thé* that's ideal if you've got a hankering for something sweet.

La Table du Terroir (☎ 02 31 92 05 53; 42 rue St-Jean; lunch menus €12.50-14, dinner menus €21-28; ⏲ closed dinner Sun) At this country-style restaurant, crimson chairs and white tablecloths provide an enjoyable backdrop for specialities such as grilled salmon, pork fillet and *tripes à la mode de Caen* (tripe stewed with carrots, shallots, garlic and herbs).

Le Pommier (☎ 02 31 21 52 10; www.restaurantlepommier.com; 38-40 rue des Cuisiniers; lunch menus €14, other menus €23-36.25; ⏲ closed Tue & Wed Nov–mid-Mar) Specialities at this smart restaurant include filet of roast duck, *filet mignon de porc* and varied French dishes made with fresh Norman products.

For self-caterers:

Food markets rue St-Jean (⏲ Wed morning); place St-Patrice (⏲ Sat morning)

Marché Plus (16 rue St-Jean; ⏲ 7am-9pm Mon-Sat, 8.30am-12.30pm Sun)

Getting There & Away

Bus Verts (☎ 08 10 21 42 14; www.busverts.fr) runs to Caen (bus 30; €4, one hour, three or four daily Monday to Friday except holidays) and provides regular buses to the D-Day beaches (below).

The most useful train link from Bayeux is Caen (€5.50, 20 minutes, 13 to 19 daily Monday to Saturday, eight Sunday), from where there are connections to Paris' Gare St-Lazare (€32) and Rouen (€24.60).

D-DAY BEACHES

The D-Day landings, code-named 'Operation Overlord', were the largest military operation in history. Early on 6 June 1944, Allied troops stormed ashore along 80km of beaches north of Bayeux, code-named (from west to east) Utah, Omaha, Gold, Juno and Sword. The landings on D-Day – called Jour J in French – were followed by the Battle of Normandy, which ultimately led to the liberation of Europe from Nazi occupation. The memorial museums in Caen (see the boxed text, opposite) and Bayeux (p248) provide a comprehensive overview, and there are many small D-Day museums dotted along the coast. For context, see www.normandiememoire.com and www.6juin1944.com.

The most brutal fighting on D-Day took place 15km northwest of Bayeux along the stretch of coastline now known as **Omaha Beach**, where you'll now find the huge **American Military Cemetery** (☎ 02 31 51 62 00; www.abmc.gov; Colleville-sur-Mer; ⏲ 9am-6pm mid-Apr–mid-Sep, 9am-5pm mid-Sep–mid-Apr) at Colleville-sur-Mer, the largest American cemetery in Europe.

To make it possible to unload cargo without having to capture one of the heavily defended Channel ports, the Allies established two prefabricated breakwaters code-named Mulberry Harbours. One of them can still be viewed at low tide at **Arromanches**, a seaside town 10km northeast of Bayeux. Nearby **Juno Beach**, 12km east of Arromanches, was stormed by Canadian troops on D-Day, while original bomb craters and German gun emplacements can be seen at the nearby **Pointe du Hoc Ranger Memorial** (☎ 02 31 51 90 70; admission free; ⏲ 24hr).

CAEN MÉMORIAL

Caen's hi-tech museum, **Mémorial – Un Musée pour la Paix** (Memorial – A Museum for Peace; ☎ 02 31 06 06 45; www.memorial-caen.fr; esplanade Général Eisenhower; adult/under 10yr & war veteran/student €16/free/15; 9am-7pm Mar-Oct, 9.30am-6pm Nov-Feb, closed last 3 weeks Jan) uses sound, lighting, film, animation and lots of exhibits to explore the events of WWII, the D-Day landings and the ensuing Cold War. Tickets remain valid for 24 hours. The museum also runs tours (below) of the D-Day beaches.

Tours

Caen Mémorial (☎ 02 31 06 06 45; www.memorial-caen.fr; adult/under 18yr €69/55; tours 1pm Oct-Mar, 9am & 2pm Apr-Sep) Excellent four- to five-hour minibus tours around the landing beaches. The price includes entry to Mémorial (see the boxed text, above).

Normandy Sightseeing Tours (☎ 02 31 51 70 52; www.normandywebguide.com) From May to October (and on request the rest of the year), this experienced outfit offers morning (adult/under 10 years/student €40/25/35) and afternoon tours (€45/30/40) of various beaches and cemeteries. These can be combined into an all-day excursion (€75/45/65).

Normandy Tours (☎ 02 31 92 10 70; www.normandy-tours-hotel.com; 26 place de la Gare; adult/student €41/36; year-round) Bayeux-based operator offering four- or five-hour tours of the main sites at 8.15am and 1.15pm.

Getting There & Away

Bus Verts (☎ 08 10 21 42 14; www.busverts.fr, in French) bus 70 (two or three daily Monday to Saturday, extra buses in summer) goes northwest from Bayeux to Colleville-sur-Mer and Omaha Beach (€2, 35 minutes), Pointe du Hoc (€4) and Grandcamp-Maisy. Bus 74 (bus 75 in summer; three or four daily Monday to Saturday, extra buses in summer) links Bayeux with Arromanches (€2, 30 minutes), Gold and Juno Beaches, and Courseulles (€3, one hour).

MONT ST-MICHEL

On a rocky island opposite the coastal town of Pontorson, connected to the mainland by a narrow causeway, the sky-scraping turrets of the abbey of **Mont St-Michel** (☎ 02 33 89 80 00; www.monuments-nationaux.fr; adult/under 18yr/18-25yr incl guided tour €8.50/free/5; 9am-7pm May-Aug, 9.30am-6pm Sep-Apr, last entry 1hr before closing) provide one of France's iconic sights. The surrounding bay is notorious for its fast-rising tides: at low tide the Mont is surrounded by bare sand for miles around, but at high tide, barely six hours later, the bay, causeway and nearby car parks can be submerged.

At the base of the mount, just inside Porte de l'Avancée as you enter the abbey, the **Mont St-Michel tourist office** (☎ 02 33 60 14 30; www.ot-montsaintmichel.com; 9am-7pm Jul & Aug, 9am-12.30pm & 2-6.30pm Mon-Sat, 9am-noon & 2-6pm Sun Apr-Jun & Sep, 9am-noon & 2-6pm Mon-Sat, 10am-noon & 2-5pm Sun Oct-Mar) sells detailed visitor maps (€3). From here, a winding cobbled street leads up to the **Église Abbatiale** (Abbey Church), incorporating elements of both Norman and Gothic architecture. Other notable sights include the arched **cloître** (cloister), the barrel-roofed **réfectoire** (dining hall), and the Gothic **Salle des Hôtes** (Guest Hall), dating from 1213. A one-hour tour is included in the ticket price: English tours are run twice a day (11am and 3pm) in winter, hourly in summer. From Monday to Saturday in July and August, there are illuminated *nocturnes* (night-time visits) with music from 7pm to 10pm.

Les Couriers Bretons (☎ 02 99 19 70 80) links Pontorson with St-Malo (1¼ hours, one round-trip daily). Trains from Pontorson include Bayeux (€19.60, 1¾ hours, two or three direct daily), Cherbourg (€24.50, 2¼ hours, two daily) and Rennes (€11.90, 1¾ hours, two or three daily).

BRITTANY

Thrust out into the Atlantic, France's westernmost promontory might be called Finistère, meaning 'land's end', but its Breton name, *Penn ar Bed*, translates as 'head of the world'. It's long considered itself a separate nation from the rest of France, with its own history, customs and Breton language; chuck in some scenic coastline, windswept islands and the eeriest stone circles this side of Stonehenge, and you'll discover one of France's most fascinating corners.

QUIMPER

pop 64,900

Small enough to feel like a village – with its slanted half-timbered houses and narrow cobbled streets – and large enough to buzz as the troubadour of Breton culture, Quimper (pronounced *kam-pair*) is Finistère's thriving capital.

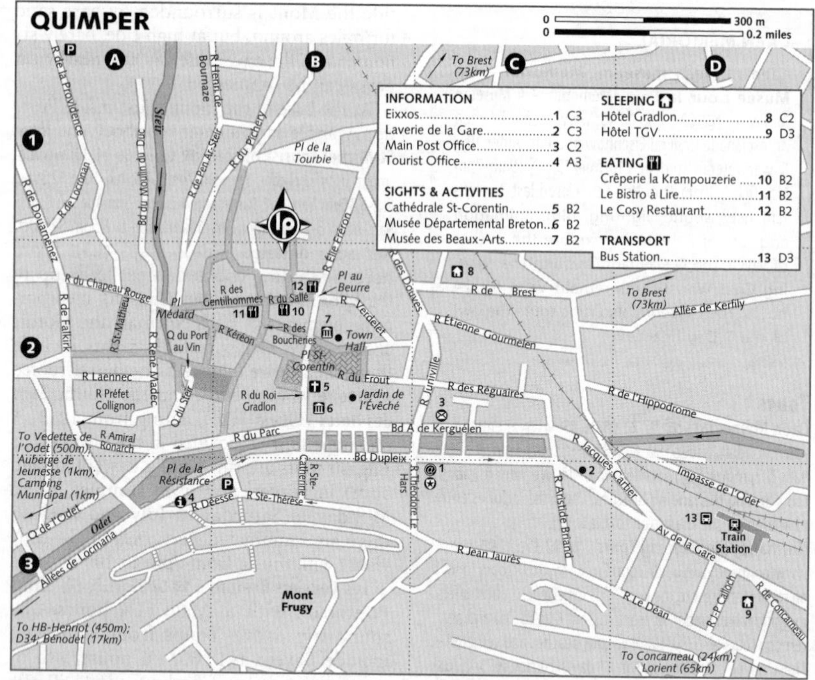

Orientation

The mainly pedestrianised old city clusters around the cathedral on the north bank of the River Odet, overlooked by Mont Frugy on the south bank. Most of Quimper's historic architecture is concentrated in the tight triangle that is formed by place Médard, rue Kéréon, rue des Gentilhommes and its continuation, rue du Sallé, to place au Beurre.

Information

Eixxos (☎ 02 98 64 40 56; 12 blvd Dupleix; per hr €3.50; 🕑 11am-10pm Mon-Thu, 11am-1am Fri & Sat, 2-10pm Sun) Internet access.

Laverie de la Gare (4 av de la Gare; 🕑 8am-8pm) Laundry.

Main post office (blvd Amiral de Kerguélen)

Tourist office (☎ 02 98 53 04 05; www.quimper-tourisme.com, in French; place de la Résistance; 🕑 9am-7pm Mon-Sat, 10am-12.45pm & 3-5.45pm Sun Jul & Aug, 9.30am-12.30pm & 1.30-6pm or 6.30pm Mon-Sat Sep-Jun, 10am-12.45pm Sun Jun & 1-15 Sep) Runs weekly 1½-hour guided city tours in English (€5.20) in July and August, and sells the Pass' Quimper (€13) to four attractions/tours.

Sights

Quimper's **Cathédral St-Corentin** (🕑 9.30am-noon & 1.30-6.30pm Mon-Sat, 1.30-6.30pm Sun May-Oct, 9am-noon & 1.30-6.30pm Mon-Sat, 1.30-6.30pm Sun Nov-Apr) has a distinctive kink, said by some to symbolise Christ's inclined head as he was dying on the cross. Though construction began in 1239, the cathedral's dramatic twin spires weren't added until the 19th century. High on the west facade, look out for an equestrian statue of King Gradlon, the city's mythical 5th-century founder.

The **Musée des Beaux-Arts** (☎ 02 98 95 45 20; 40 place St-Corentin; adult/child €4.50/2.50; 🕑 10am-7pm daily Jul & Aug, 10am-noon & 2-6pm Wed-Mon Apr-Jun, Sep-Oct, 10am-noon & 2-6pm Wed-Sat & Mon, 2-6pm Sun Nov-Mar) is a mite gloomy, although the upper levels are brightened up by Picasso sketches and a room dedicated to Quimper-born poet Max Jacob.

Recessed behind a magnificent stone courtyard beside the cathedral, the **Musée Départemental Breton** (☎ 02 98 95 21 60; 1 rue du Roi Gradlon; adult/child €4/2.50; 🕑 9am-6pm daily Jun-Sep, 9am-noon & 2-5pm Tue-Sat, 2-5pm Sun Oct-May) showcases Breton history, furniture, costumes, crafts and archaeology. Adjoining the museum is the **Jardin de l'Évêché** (admission free; 9am-5pm or 6pm).

Sleeping

Auberge de Jeunesse (02 98 64 97 97; quimper@fuaj.org; 6 av des Oiseaux; camp sites €6, dm incl breakfast €15.20; Apr-Sep) Quimper's seasonal youth hostel has self-catering facilities. Sheets cost €2.80.

Hôtel TGV (02 98 90 54 00; www.hoteltgv.com; 4 rue de Concarneau; s/d €36/38) The cheapest and best value of several hotels around the train station, 800m from the old city, the TGV has 22 small but bright en-suite rooms. Light sleepers will find the top-floor rooms quieter. Wi-fi's free.

Hôtel Gradlon (02 98 95 04 39; www.hotel-gradlon.com; 30 rue de Brest; r €82-160; closed mid-Dec–mid-Jan) Quimper's most charming hotel is this former 19th-century coach house. Recently renovated with floral and checked fabrics, its 22 rooms include three elegant suites set around a rose-garden courtyard.

Eating

Crêpes are king in Quimper, but fine-diners won't be disappointed either.

our pick **Crêperie la Krampouzerie** (02 98 95 13 08; 9 rue du Sallé; galettes €3.50-7.70; lunch & dinner Tue-Sat) The best crêpes in town, made from organic flours and regional ingredients like *algues d'Ouessant* (seaweed), Roscoff onions and homemade ginger caramel.

Le Bistro à Lire (02 98 95 30 86; 18 rue des Boucheries; snacks around €4.50, mains €7.80; lunch Tue-Sat, salon de thé 9am-7pm Tue-Sat, plus Mon afternoon Jul & Aug) Amid the shelves at this bookshop–*salon de thé*, you can tuck into lasagne and the *gâteau du jour* (cake of the day) for €5.50.

Le Cosy Restaurant (02 98 95 23 65; 2 rue du Sallé; mains €11.50-15; lunch & dinner Tue-Sat Jul & Aug, lunch Tue-Sat, dinner Fri & Sat Sep-Jun) *Pas de crêpes!* (No crêpes!) the blackboard menu proudly proclaims. Make your way through the well-stocked *épicerie* (specialist grocer) and climb the stairs to the dining room for top-quality gratins and *tartines*.

Getting There & Away

CAT/Connex Tourisme (02 98 90 68 40) bus destinations include Brest (€6, 1¼ hours), while **Le Coeur** (02 98 54 40 15) runs to Concarneau (€2, 45 minutes, seven to 10 daily).

There are frequent trains heading to Brest (€14, 1¼ hours, up to 10 daily), Rennes (€30.10, 2½ hours, five daily) and Paris (Gare Montparnasse; €68.20, 4¾ hours, eight daily).

THE MORBIHAN MEGALITHS

Predating Stonehenge by 100 years, **Carnac** (Garnag in Breton) comprises the world's greatest concentration of megalithic sites. There are more than 3000 of these upright stones scattered across the countryside between **Carnac-Ville** and the village of **Locmariaquer**, mostly erected between 5000 BC and 3500 BC. No one's quite sure what purpose these sites served, although theories abound. A sacred site? Phallic fertility cult? Or maybe a celestial calendar? Even more mysterious is the question of their construction – no one really has the foggiest idea how the builders hacked and hauled these vast granite blocks several millennia before the wheel arrived in Brittany, let alone mechanical diggers.

Because of severe erosion, the sites are usually fenced off to allow the vegetation to regrow. **Guided tours** (€4) run in French year-round and in English at 3pm Wednesday, Thursday and Friday from early July to late August. Sign up for guided visits at the **Maison des Mégalithes** (02 97 52 89 99; rte des Alignements; admission free; 9am-8pm Jul & Aug, to 5.15pm Sep-Apr, to 7pm May & Jun).

Opposite the Maison des Mégalithes, the largest menhir field – with no less than 1099 stones – is the **Alignements du Ménec**, 1km north of Carnac-Ville. From here, the D196 heads northeast for about 1.5km to the **Alignements de Kermario**. Climb the stone observation tower midway along the site to see the alignment from above. Another 500m further on are the **Alignements de Kerlescan**, while the **Tumulus St-Michel**, 400m northeast of the Carnac-Ville tourist office, dates back to at least 5000 BC. For more background, the **Musée de Préhistoire** (02 97 52 22 04; 10 place de la Chapelle, Carnac-Ville; adult/child €5/2.50; 10am-6pm Jul & Aug, 10am-12.30pm & 2-6pm Wed-Mon Apr, May, Jun & Sep, 10am-12.30pm & 2-5pm Wed-Mon Oct-Mar) chronicles life from the Palaeolithic and neolithic eras to the Middle Ages.

ST-MALO

pop 49,600

The pretty port of St-Malo is inextricably tied up with the briny blue: the town became a key harbour during the 17th and 18th centuries as a base for merchant ships and government-sanctioned privateers, and these days it's a busy cross-Channel ferry-port and summertime getaway. The St-Malo conurbation consists of the harbour towns of St-Malo and St-Servan plus the modern suburbs of Paramé and Rothéneuf to the east.

Orientation

The old walled city of St-Malo is known as Intra-Muros ('within the walls') or Ville Close. From the train station, it's a 15-minute walk westwards along av Louis Martin.

Information

Cyberm@lo (☎ 02 99 56 07 78; 68 chaussée du Sillon; per 15 min/hr €1.50/4; 🕑 10am-1am Mon-Sat, 11am-11pm Sun mid-Jun–mid-Sep, 11am-9pm Tue-Thu, 11am-11pm Fri & Sat, 3-8pm Sun mid-Sep–mid-Jun) Internet access along the seafront.

Main post office (1 blvd de la République)

Tourist office (☎ 08 25 13 52 00, 02 99 56 64 43; www.saint-malo-tourisme.com; esplanade St-Vincent; 🕑 9am-7.30pm Mon-Sat, 10am-6pm Sun Jul & Aug, 9am-12.30pm & 1.30-6pm or 6.30pm Mon-Sat Sep-Jun, 10am-12.30pm & 2.30-6pm Sun Easter-Jun & Sep)

Sights

The city's sturdy ramparts were constructed at the end of the 17th century by the military architect Vauban, and afford fine views of the old walled city – you can access them from all of the main city *portes* (gates). From their northern stretch, you'll see the remains of the former prison, the **Fort National** (adult/child €4/2; 🕑 Jun-Sep), and the rocky islet of **Île du Grand Bé**, where the great St-Malo–born 18th-century writer Chateaubriand is buried. You can walk across at low tide, but check the tide times with the tourist office.

The battle to liberate St-Malo destroyed around 80% of the old city during August 1944; damage to the **Cathédrale St-Vincent** (place Jean de Châtillon; 🕑 9.30am-6pm except during Mass) was particularly severe.

Within **Château de St-Malo**, built by the dukes of Brittany in the 15th and 16th centuries, is the **Musée du Château** (☎ 02 99 40 71 57; adult/child €5.20/2.60; 🕑 10am-noon & 2-6pm daily Apr-Sep, Tue-Sun Oct-Mar). The museum's most interesting exhibits – the history of cod fishing and photos of St-Malo after WWII – are in the Tour Générale.

The attractions at the fantastic **Grand Aquarium** (☎ 02 99 21 19 00; av Général Patton; adult/child €14/10; 🕑 at least 10am-6pm Feb-Dec, to 8pm Jul & Aug) include a minisubmarine descent and a *bassin tactile* (touch pool), where you can fondle rays, turbot – even a baby shark. The aquarium is 4km south of the city; bus C1 travels from the train station every half-hour.

If you're hardy enough to brave the Atlantic swells, there are also several pleasant **beaches** around St-Malo.

Sleeping

Camping Aleth (☎ 02 99 81 60 91; camping@ville-saint-malo.fr; allée Gaston Buy, St-Servan; camp sites €12; 🕑 May-Sep) Perched on a peninsula, Camping Aleth (also spelt Alet) has panoramic 360-degree views and is close to beaches and some lively bars.

Auberge de Jeunesse Éthic Étapes (☎ 02 99 40 29 80; www.centrevarangot.com; 37 av du Père Umbricht; dm incl breakfast €15.50-18.70; 💻) This efficient place has a self-catering kitchen as well as free sports facilities. Take bus C1 from the train station.

Hôtel San Pedro (☎ 02 99 40 88 57; www.sanpedro-hotel.com; 1 rue Ste-Anne; s €46-48, d €53-70; 🕑 Feb-Nov; 💻) Tucked at the back of the old city, the San Pedro has cool, crisp, neutral-toned decor with subtle splashes of colour, friendly service and superb sea views.

Hôtel de l'Univers (☎ 02 99 40 89 52; www.hotel-univers-saintmalo.com, in French; place Chateaubriand; s €48-78, d €63-95) Right beside Porte St-Vincent, this cream-coloured two-starrer is perfectly poised for St-Malo's attractions and boasts its own maritime-themed bar.

Eating

Le Biniou (☎ 02 99 56 47 57; 3 place de la Croix du Fief; crêpes €2-8, menus around €10; 🕑 10am-1am summer, closed Thu winter) St-Malo has no shortage of crêperies, but this one – with cute little illustrations of Breton *biniou* (bagpipes) – is a time-honoured fave. Savour 100 galettes and crêpes, including the house speciality: apples flambéed in Calvados.

Crêperie Margaux (☎ 02 99 20 26 02; 3 place du Marché aux Légumes; crêpes €7.50-13; 🕑 closed Tue & Wed, daily during school holidays) The owner of this wonderful crêperie makes traditional crêpes by hand (her motto: 'if you're in a hurry,

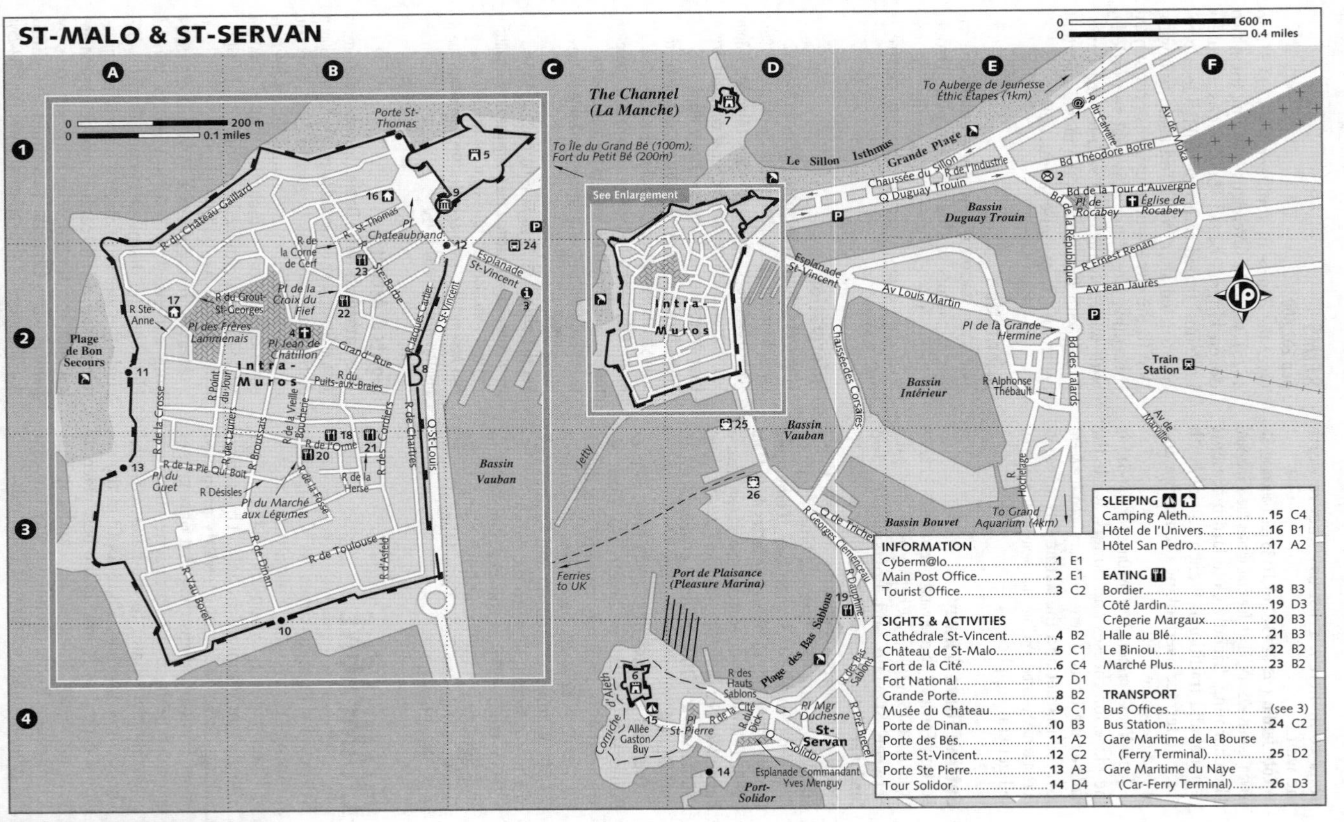
ST-MALO & ST-SERVAN
0 600 m
0 0.4 miles
0 200 m
0 0.1 miles
The Channel (La Manche)
To Île du Grand Bé (100m); Fort du Petit Bé (200m)
To Auberge de Jeunesse Éthic Étapes (1km)
To Grand Aquarium (4km)
See Enlargement
Intra-Muros
Porte St-Thomas
R du Château Gaillard
Pl Chateaubriand
R St-Thomas
R de la Corne de Cerf
Ste-Barbe
Pl de la Croix du Fief
R du Grout-St-Georges
Pl des Frères Lammenais
R Ste-Anne
Pl Jean de Châtillon
Grand' Rue
R du Puits-aux-Braies
R Jacques Cartier
Q St-Vincent
Q St-Louis
R de Chartres
R des Cordiers
R de la Vieille Boucherie
R de l'Orme
R de la Herse
R de la Fosse
Pl du Marché aux Légumes
R Désisles
R de la Pie Qui Boit
Pl du Guet
R de la Crosse
R Point du Jour
R des Lauriers
R Broussais
R de Dinan
R de Toulouse
R d'Asfeld
R Vau Borel
Plage de Bon Secours
Esplanade St-Vincent
Bassin Vauban
Jetty
Ferries to UK
Port de Plaisance (Pleasure Marina)
Plage des Bas Sablons
R des Hauts Sablons
R de la Cité
R du Dick
Pl St-Pierre
Allée Gaston Buy
Corniche d'Aleth
Pl Mgr Duchesne
St-Servan
Solidor
Esplanade Commandant Yves Menguy
Port-Solidor
R des Bas Sablons
R Pré Brecel
R Dauphine
R Georges Clemenceau
Q de Trichet
Bassin Bouvet
R Hochelage
Chausséedes Corsaires
Bassin Intérieur
R Alphonse Thébault
Av Louis Martin
Pl de la Grande Hermine
Bd des Talards
Le Sillon Isthmus
Grande Plage
Chaussée du Sillon
R de l'Industrie
Q Duguay Trouin
Bassin Duguay Trouin
Bd de la République
Bd Théodore Botrel
R du Calvaire
Av de Moka
Bd de la Tour d'Auvergne
Pl de Rocabey
Église de Rocabey
R Ernest Renan
Av Jean Jaurès
Train Station
Av de Marville
A B C D E F
1 2 3 4
INFORMATION
Cyberm@lo 1 E1
Main Post Office 2 E1
Tourist Office 3 C2
SIGHTS & ACTIVITIES
Cathédrale St-Vincent 4 B2
Château de St-Malo 5 C1
Fort de la Cité 6 C4
Fort National 7 D1
Grande Porte 8 B2
Musée du Château 9 C1
Porte de Dinan 10 B3
Porte des Bés 11 A2
Porte St-Vincent 12 C2
Porte Ste Pierre 13 A3
Tour Solidor 14 D4
SLEEPING
Camping Aleth 15 C4
Hôtel de l'Univers 16 B1
Hôtel San Pedro 17 A2
EATING
Bordier 18 B3
Côté Jardin 19 D3
Crêperie Margaux 20 B3
Halle au Blé 21 B3
Le Biniou 22 B2
Marché Plus 23 B2
TRANSPORT
Bus Offices (see 3)
Bus Station 24 C2
Gare Maritime de la Bourse (Ferry Terminal) 25 D2
Gare Maritime du Naye (Car-Ferry Terminal) 26 D3

don't come here'). Trust us – they're worth the wait.

Côté Jardin (☎ 02 99 81 63 11; 36 rue Dauphine, St-Servan; menus €25; ⌚ lunch Tue-Sun, dinner Tue & Thu-Sun) The charming, friendly Côté Jardin presents regional and traditional French cuisine, with a scenic terrace overlooking the marina and St-Malo's walled city.

Jean-Yves **Bordier** (9 rue de l'Orme; ⌚ Tue-Sat) is the place for cheeses and butters, while the **Halle au Blé** (rue de la Herse; ⌚ 8am-noon Tue & Fri) covered market and the **Marché Plus** (cnr rue St-Vincent & rue St-Barbe; ⌚ 7am-9pm Mon-Sat, to noon Sun) sell general supplies.

Getting There & Away

Brittany Ferries (☎ reservations in France 08 25 82 88 28, in UK 0870 556 1600; www.brittany-ferries.com) sails between St-Malo and Portsmouth, and **Condor Ferries** (☎ France 08 25 13 51 35, UK 0870 243 5140; www.condorferries.co.uk) runs to/from Poole and Weymouth via Jersey or Guernsey.

From April to September, **Compagnie Corsaire** (☎ 08 25 13 80 35) and **Vedettes de St-Malo** (☎ 02 23 18 41 08; www.vedettes-saint-malo.com) run a **Bus de Mer** (Sea Bus; adult/child return €6/4; ⌚ hourly) shuttle service (10 minutes) between St-Malo and Dinard.

Courriers Bretons (☎ 02 99 19 70 80) serves Pontorson (€2.50, one hour) and Mont St-Michel (€4.30, 1½ hours, three to four daily). **TIV** (☎ 02 99 82 26 26) has buses to Dinard (€1.50, 30 minutes, hourly) and Rennes (€3, one to 1½ hours, three to six daily).

TGV train services run between St-Malo and Rennes (€11.60, one hour), and there are direct trains to Paris' Gare Montparnasse (€58, three hours).

CHAMPAGNE

Known in Roman times as Campania, meaning 'plain', the agricultural region of Champagne is synonymous these days with its world-famous bubbly. This multi-million-dollar industry is strictly protected under French law, ensuring that only grapes grown in designated Champagne vineyards can truly lay a claim to the hallowed title. The town of Épernay, 30km south of the regional capital of Reims, is the best place to head for *dégustation* (tasting), and a special 'Champagne Route' wends its way through the region's most celebrated vineyards.

REIMS

pop 202,600

Over the course of a millennium (AD 816 to 1825), some 34 sovereigns – among them two dozen kings – began their reigns as rulers in Reims' famed cathedral. Meticulously reconstructed after WWI and again following WWII, the city – whose name is pronounced something like 'rance' – is neat and orderly, with wide avenues and well-tended parks. Along with Épernay, it's the most important centre of Champagne production.

Orientation

The train station is 1km northwest of the cathedral, across sq Colbert from place Drouet d'Erlon, the city's major nightlife centre. Virtually every street in the city centre is one way.

Information

Clique et Croque Cyberspace (☎ 03 26 86 93 92; www.cliqueetcroque.com; 19 rue Chanzy; per min/hr/5h/10hr €0.07/4/18/30; ⌚ 10am-midnight Mon-Sat, 2-8pm Sun) Internet access opposite the Musée des Beaux-Arts.

Laundrette (59 rue Chanzy; ⌚ 7am-9.30pm)

Post office (2 rue Cérès; ⌚ 8.30am-6pm Mon-Fri, to noon Sat) On the eastern corner of place Royale.

Reims City Card (€14) Includes a Champagne-house tour, an all-day bus ticket, entry to the municipal museums and a guided tour of the cathedral. Sold by the tourist office.

Tourist office (☎ 03 26 77 45 00, 08 92 70 13 51; www.reims-tourisme.com; 2 rue Guillaume de Machault; ⌚ 9am-7pm Mon-Sat, 10am-6pm Sun & holidays mid-Apr–mid-Oct, 10am-6pm Mon-Sat, 11am-4pm Sun & holidays mid-Oct–mid-Apr)

Sights & Activities

The **Cathédrale Notre Dame** (www.cathedrale-reims.com, in French; place du Cardinal Luçon; ⌚ 7.30am-7.30pm, closed Sun morning) was begun in 1211 and for centuries served as the venue for all French royal coronations – including that of Charles VII, who was crowned here on 17 July 1429, with Joan of Arc at his side.

Heavily restored since WWI, the 138m-long cathedral is now a Unesco World Heritage site. Its most famous features include the western facade's 12-petalled **great rose window**, a 15th-century wooden **astronomical clock** and several decorative windows by painter Marc Chagall. You could also climb the 250 steps of the **cathedral tower** (adult/12-25yr

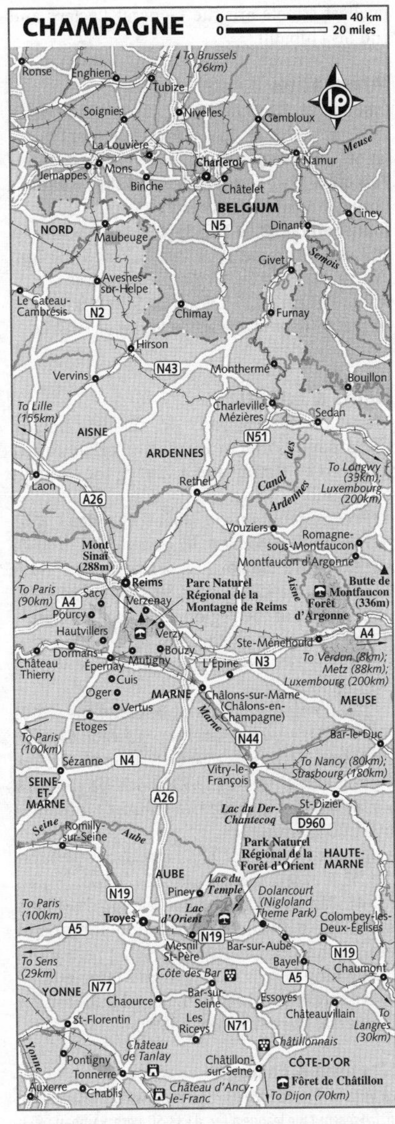

€6.50/4.50; ⌚ Tue-Sat & afternoon Sun early May–early Sep, Sat & afternoon Sun mid-Mar–early May & early Sep–Oct).

Next door, the 17th-century **Palais du Tau** (☎ 03 26 47 81 79; www.palais-du-tau.fr, in French; 2 place du Cardinal Luçon; adult/under 18yr/student €6.50/free/4.50; ⌚ 9.30am-6.30pm Tue-Sun early May–early Sep, 9.30am-12.30pm & 2-5.30pm Tue-Sun early Sep–early May) was where French princes stayed before their coronations, and now serves as a museum housing statuary and liturgical objects.

Some of the most celebrated names in Champagne production have their base in Reims, complete with *caves* (cellars) and tasting tours. **Mumm** (☎ 03 26 49 59 70; www.mumm.com; 34 rue du Champ de Mars; tours adult/under 12yr €8/free; ⌚ tours 9am-11am & 2-5pm Mar-Oct, Sat Nov-Feb), pronounced 'moom', is the only *maison* in central Reims. Founded in 1827, it is now the world's third-largest producer (eight million bottles a year), offering edifying one-hour tours of cellars stocked with over 25 million bottles.

Pommery (☎ 03 26 61 62 55; www.pommery.fr; 5 place du Général Gouraud; tours adult/under 12yr/student & 12-17yr €10/free/7; ⌚ tours 9.30am-7pm Apr–mid-Nov, 10am-6pm Sat & Sun mid-Nov-Mar) occupies an Elizabethan-style hilltop campus (built 1868–78) 1.8km southeast of the cathedral. Cellar tours venture 30m underground to Gallo-Roman quarries and 25 million bottles of bubbly. Take the E or V bus to the Gouraud stop.

One-hour tours at **Taittinger** (☎ 03 26 85 84 33; www.taittinger.com; 9 place St-Niçaise; tours adult/under 12yr €10/free; ⌚ tours 9.30am-noon & 2pm-4.30pm, closed Sat & Sun mid-Nov–mid-Mar) explore everything from *remuage* (bottle turning) to *dégorgement* (sediment removal at -25°C). The site's 1.5km southeast of the cathedral; take the Citadine 1 or 2 bus to the St-Nicaise stop.

Sleeping

Centre International de Séjour (CIS; ☎ 03 26 40 52 60; www.cis-reims.com; chaussée Bocquaine; bed in s/d/q per person €40.60/24.90/18.90, with shared toilet €26.90/18.20/16.40; ⌚ 24hr; 💻) The 85 bright rooms are utterly devoid of charm but the price is right and it's near the canal. To get there, take bus B, K, M or N to the Comédie stop or bus H to the Pont de Gaulle stop.

Latino Hôtel (☎ 03 26 47 48 89; www.latinocafe.fr, in French; 33 place Drouet d'Erlon; s & d €54-74, apt €130; ❄ 💻) Neo-boutique hotel above a buzzy musical cafe, with a dozen fruity guest rooms (cherry, pumpkin and aubergine). Look out for quotes from the great and the good (Gandhi, Boris Vian) graffitied on the hall walls.

Hôtel de la Cathédrale (☎ 03 26 47 28 46; www.hotel-cathedrale-reims.fr; 20 rue Libergier; s/d/q €54/62/78; 💻) Charm, graciousness and a resident Yorkshire terrier greet guests at this hostelry run by a music-loving couple. The 17 tasteful rooms are smallish but pleasingly chintzy.

Eating & Drinking

Côté Cuisine (☎ 03 26 83 93 68; 43 blvd Foch; starters €6-21, mains €11.80-22.50, weekday lunch menus €13.50-16.90, dinner menus €32.50; lunch & dinner Mon-Sat) A spacious, modern place with well-regarded traditional French cuisine. Try to get a table overlooking Sq Colbert.

Brasserie Le Boulingrin (☎ 03 26 40 96 22; www.boulingrin.fr; 48 rue de Mars; starters €6.50-14, mains €13-24, menus €18-25; Mon-Sat) This place offers a minitrip back in time, with original decor and fittings, including an old-time zinc bar dating to 1925. The culinary focus is *fruits de mer* (seafood).

L'Apostrophe (☎ 03 26 79 19 89; 59 place Drouet d'Erlon; starters €6.50-15.10, mains €14.50-25, weekday lunch menus €14; lunch & dinner) This stylish (and sprawling) cafe-brasserie dispenses some mean *piscines* (enormous cocktails for several people) along with its French and international cuisine.

Self-caterers should try the **Marché du Boulingrin** (place du Boulingrin; 5am-3pm Sat) food market, or the food shops along the south side of place du Forum. There's also a **Monoprix** (21 rue de Chativesle; 9am-9pm Mon-Sat).

Getting There & Away

Direct trains link Reims with Épernay (€5.70, 22 to 38 minutes, 23 daily weekdays, 14 daily weekends), Laon (€8.50, 35 to 55 minutes, eight daily Monday to Friday, six on Saturday, two on Sunday) and Paris' Gare de l'Est (€22.70, 1¾ hours, 10 to 15 daily), half of which are TGVs (€28, 45 minutes). Tickets can be bought at the city-centre **Boutique SNCF** (1 cours Jean-Baptiste Langlet; 9am-7pm Mon-Fri, 10am-6pm Sat).

ÉPERNAY

pop 24,500

Prosperous Épernay, the self-proclaimed *capitale du champagne* and home to many of the world's most celebrated Champagne houses, is the best place in Champagne for touring cellars and sampling bubbly. Beneath the town's streets, some 200 million of bottles of Champagne are slowly being aged, just waiting around to be popped open for some fizz-fuelled celebration.

Orientation

Av de Champagne, where many of Épernay's Champagne houses are based, stretches east from the town's commercial heart, whose liveliest streets are rue Général Leclerc and rue St-Thibault.

Information

Cybermania (☎ 03 26 52 26 26; 11 place des Arcades; per 30min/hr €2/3; 2pm-midnight Mon, from 11am Tue-Sat, 2-8pm Sun)

Post office (place Hugues Plomb; 8.30am-6.30pm Mon-Fri, to noon Sat) Has currency exchange.

Tourist office (☎ 03 26 53 33 00; www.ot-epernay.fr; 7 av de Champagne; 9.30am-12.30pm & 1.30-7pm Mon-Sat, 11am-4pm Sun & holidays mid-Apr–mid-Oct, 9.30am-12.30pm & 1.30-5.30pm Mon-Sat mid-Oct–mid-Apr) Has details on cellar visits, car touring, and walking and cycling options.

Sights & Activities

Many of the *maisons* on or near av de Champagne offer informative cellar tours, followed by tasting and a visit to the factory-outlet bubbly shop.

Prestigious *maison* **Moët & Chandon** (☎ 03 26 51 20 20; www.moet.com; 1/2 glasses adult €11/18, 10-18yr €6.70, under 10yr free; 20 av de Champagne; tours 9.30-11.30am & 2-4.30pm, closed Sat & Sun mid-Nov–Mar) offers some of the region's best cellar tours – if you're feeling flush, pick up a 6L methuselah of 1995 Dom Pérignon at a smidgen over €6000.

The 45-minute tours of **De Castellane** (☎ 03 26 51 19 11; www.castellane.com, in French; 64 av de Champagne; 1/2/3 glasses adult €7/12/18, under 10yr free; tours 10.30-11.15am & 2.30-5.15pm mid-Mar–Dec, Sat & Sun Jan–mid-Mar) include the *maison*'s informative bubbly museum.

Mercier (☎ 03 26 51 22 22; www.champagnemercier.com; 68-70 av de Champagne; adult/12-17yr €7/3; tours 9.30-11.30am & 2-4.30pm mid-Mar–late Nov, closed Tue & Wed late Nov–mid-Mar), the most popular brand in France, has long thrived on self-promotion. Everything here is flashy, from a laser-guided tourist train to a 160,000L barrel built for the Universal Exposition of 1889.

Sleeping & Eating

La Villa St-Pierre (☎ 03 26 54 40 80; www.villasaintpierre.fr, in French; 1 rue Jeanne d'Arc; d €33-50, with washbasin €23;) In an early-20th-century mansion that has hardly changed in half a century, this homey one-starrer has 15 simple rooms that retain the charm and atmosphere of yesteryear.

Hôtel de la Cloche (☎ 03 26 55 15 15; hotel-de-la-cloche.c.prin@wanadoo.fr; 5 place Mendès France; d from €48;) This rather snooty place has two stars, and 19 cheerful rooms with bright, compact bathrooms. Some rooms have park views. The attached restaurant gets rave reviews.

Le Clos Raymi (☎ 03 26 51 00 58; www.closraymi-hotel.com; 3 rue Joseph de Venoge; d from €100, ste €160; 💻) Staying at this delightful three-star place is like being a personal guest of Monsieur Chandon himself, who occupied this luxurious home over a century ago. The seven romantic rooms have giant beds, 3.7m-high ceilings, ornate mouldings and parquet floors.

L'Ancêtre (☎ 03 26 55 57 56; 20 rue de la Fauvette; starters €8.30-12, mains €13-22, menus €15.50-29; 🕒 closed Mon & lunch Wed) A rustic eatery specialising in traditional French cuisine. Book ahead.

Le 7 (☎ 03 26 55 28 84; Hôtel Les Berceaux, 13 rue des Berceaux; starters €9-15, mains €19-27, menus €17.50 & €24; 🕒 closed Mon & Tue) This bistro at the Hôtel Les Berceaux (it also has a more formal restaurant) has traditional French fare and a relaxed vibe.

La Cave à Champagne (☎ 03 26 55 50 70; 16 rue Gambetta; starters €9-15, mains €12-16, menus €16.50 & €32; 🕒 closed Tue & Wed) 'The Champagne Cellar' is a locals' favourite for Champenois cuisine, including *potée à la champenoise* (poultry and pork oven-baked with cabbage; €14).

Getting There & Around

Direct trains link Nancy (€26.40, two hours, five or six daily), Reims (€5.70, 23 to 32 minutes, 23 daily weekdays, 14 daily weekends) and Paris' Gare de l'Est (€19.40, 1¼ hours, eight to 13 daily).

TROYES

pop 60,500

Troyes – like Reims, one of the historic capitals of Champagne – has a lively old centre that's graced with some of France's finest medieval and Renaissance half-timbered buildings. It is one of the best places in France to get a sense of what Europe looked like back when Molière was penning his finest plays and the Three Musketeers were swashbuckling.

Orientation & Information

Cyber Café Viardin Micro (8 rue Viardin; per 1/10/20hr €2/6/14; 🕒 2-7pm Mon, 9.30am-noon & 2-7pm Tue, to midnight Wed-Sat) Internet access.

Post office (38 rue Louis Ulbach; 🕒 8am-7pm Mon-Fri, 9am-noon Sat)

Tourist office (www.tourisme-troyes.com) train station (☎ 03 25 82 62 70; 16 blvd Carnot; 🕒 9am-12.30pm & 2-6.30pm Mon-Sat year-round except holidays, 10am-1pm Sun & holidays Nov-Mar); city centre (☎ 03 25 73 36 88; rue Mignard; 🕒 10am-7pm daily Jul–mid-Sep, 9am-12.30pm & 2-6.30pm Mon-Sat, 10am-noon & 2-5pm Sun & holidays Apr-Jun & mid-Sep-Oct, closed Nov-Mar) Pass' Troyes (€12) includes entry to the city's museums, a Champagne tasting session, a tour of the old city and a horse-drawn carriage ride (July and August).

Sights

Half-timbered houses line the old centre, rebuilt after a devastating fire in 1524. Lanes worth exploring include **rue Paillot de Montabert**, **rue Champeaux**, **rue de Vauluisant**, **rue de la Pierre** and **rue Général Saussier**, while tiny **ruelle des Chats** (Alley of the Cats) feels like stepping back into the Middle Ages.

Sometimes known as *la ville aux 10 églises* (the town with 10 churches), Troyes' most important ecclesiastical landmark is **Cathédrale St-Pierre et St-Paul** (place St-Pierre; 🕒 10am-7pm daily Jul & Aug, 10am-1pm & 2-6pm Mon-Sat, to 5pm Sun & holidays Sep-Jun, closed Mon Nov-Mar) is a hotchpotch of Champenois Gothic architecture, with medieval **stained-glass windows**, a fantastical 18th-century baroque **organ** and a tiny **treasury** (🕒 Jul & Aug) with Meuse enamels. Back in 1429, Joan of Arc and Charles VII stopped here en route to his coronation in Reims.

The town's museums include the **Maison de l'Outil et de la Pensée Ouvrière** (Museum of Tools & Crafts; ☎ 03 25 73 28 26; www.maison-de-l-outil.com; 7 rue de la Trinité; adult/under 18yr/student & 12-18yr €6.50/free/3, 1st Sun of month free; 🕒 10am-6pm), exploring traditional crafts made obsolete by the Industrial Revolution.

The **Musée d'Art Moderne** (☎ 03 25 76 26 80; place St-Pierre; adult/student under 25yr, under 18yr & 1st Sun of month €5/free; 🕒 10am-1pm & 2-6pm Tue-Sun) focuses on ceramics and French painting (including lots of fauvist works) created between 1850 and 1950. Featured artists include Derain, Dufy, Matisse, Modigliani, Picasso and Soutine.

Musée St-Loup (☎ 03 25 76 21 68; 1 rue Chrestie de Troyes; adult/student under 25yr, under 18yr & 1st Sun of month €4/free; 🕒 9am-noon & 1-5pm Tue-Sun), opposite the cathedral, has a wide-ranging collection of medieval sculpture, enamel, archaeology and natural history.

If you come down with an old-fashioned malady – scurvy, perhaps, or unbalanced humours – the place to go is the **Apothicaire de l'Hôtel-Dieu-le-Comte** (☎ 03 25 80 98 97; quai des Comtes de Champagne; adult/student under 25yr, under 18yr & 1st Sun of month €2/free; 🕒 9am-noon & 1-5pm Tue-Sun), a fully outfitted, wood-panelled pharmacy from 1721.

Sleeping

Hôtel Le Trianon (☎ 03 25 73 18 52; 2 rue Pithou; d with washbasin/shower €25/34, tr/q €72/82; reception 11am-8pm Mon, 6.30am-8pm Tue-Sat, 9am-1pm Sun) At this gay-owned establishment, the rainbow flag flies proudly from the balcony. The eight rooms, above a jaunty yellow bar, are spacious but ordinary, though most have fireplaces.

Hôtel Les Comtes de Champagne (☎ 03 25 73 11 70; www.comtesdechampagne.com; 56 rue de la Monnaie; d/q from €50/70, d with washbasin €33;) For centuries, the same massive wooden beams have kept this superwelcoming place from collapsing into a pile of toothpicks. We love the bright courtyard lobby, flower boxes and huge, romantic doubles.

our pick Hôtel Arlequin (☎ 03 25 83 12 70; www.hotelarlequin.com; 50 rue de Turenne; d with shower/shower & toilet from €41/58; reception 8am-12.30pm & 2-10pm Mon-Sat, 7am-12.30pm & 6.30-10pm Sun & holidays;) The 22 cheerful rooms at this charming two-star hostelry come with antique furnishings, high ceilings and *commedia dell'arte* playfulness. The whole place is lovingly kept, from the smart custard facade to the lemony breakfast room.

Eating

The people of Troyes are enormously proud of the local speciality, *andouillette de Troyes* (pork or veal tripe sausage), but it's something of an acquired taste.

Le Grenier du Trappeur (☎ 03 25 73 21 86; 24 rue Louis Ulbach; starters €4.50-12, mains €9.50-18, menus €11-16; lunch & dinner to 9.30-10pm Mon-Sat) Pancake-flat Champagne is a long way from the mountains but this Savoyard restaurant with its chalet decor will whisk you back to the Alps with its all-you-can-eat *raclette* (€18).

L'Aquarelle (☎ 03 25 73 87 82; 24 rue Georges Clemenceau; lunch menus €12.50; noon-late, closed dinner Mon & Sun Nov-Mar) Delicious savoury galettes (€3.30 to €7.80), sweet crêpes (€2.80 to €6.50), and local Pays de l'Othe *cidre*.

Valentino (☎ 03 25 73 14 14; 35 rue Paillot de Montabert; starters €15-22, mains €24-34, menus €22-50; Tue-Sat) Modern restaurant with a *fusionista* approach, combining classic French ingredients and savoir faire with East Asian spices and textures. It's in a quiet medieval courtyard.

our pick La Mignardise (☎ 03 25 73 15 30; 1 ruelle des Chats; starters €18-28.50, mains €27.50-32, menus €26-53; closed dinner Sun & Mon) Traditional French cuisine served beneath ancient wooden beams, 19th-century mouldings and ultramodern halogen lamps. More than half of the 15 mains on offer come from the briny deep.

For self-caterers:

Covered market (place de la Halle; 8am-12.45pm & 3.30-7pm Mon-Thu, 7am-7pm Fri & Sat, 9am-12.30pm Sun)

Monoprix (1st fl, 71 rue Émile Zola; 8.30am-8pm Mon-Sat)

Getting There & Away

The **bus station office** (☎ 03 25 71 28 42; 8.30am-12.30pm & 2-6.30pm Mon-Fri), run by Courriers de l'Aube, is in a corner of the train station building. Troyes is on train line linking Basel (Bâle; €40.20, four hours) and Mulhouse (€37.50, three hours) in Alsace with Paris's Gare de l'Est (€22.20, 1½ hours, 12 to 15 daily).

ALSACE & LORRAINE

Teetering on the tempestuous frontier between France and Germany, the neighbouring regions of Alsace and Lorraine are where the worlds of Gallic and Germanic culture collide. Half-timbered houses, lush vineyards and forest-clad mountains hint at Alsace's Teutonic leanings, while nearby Lorraine is indisputably Francophile.

STRASBOURG

pop 427,000

Prosperous, cosmopolitan Strasbourg (City of the Roads) is the intellectual and cultural capital of Alsace, as well as the unofficial seat of European power – the European Parliament, the Council of Europe and the European Court of Human Rights are all based here. The city's most famous landmark is its pink sandstone cathedral, towering above the restaurants, *winstubs* (traditional Alsatian eateries) and pubs of the lively old city.

Orientation

The train station is 400m west of the Grande Île (Big Island), the core of ancient and modern Strasbourg, whose main squares are place Kléber, place Broglie (*broag*-lee), place Gutenberg and place du Château. The quaint Petite France area, on the Grande Île's southwestern corner, is subdivided by canals.

Information

Laundrettes Grand' Rue (29 Grand' Rue; 7.30am-8pm; Alt Winmärik); rue de la Nuée Bleue (8 rue de la Nuée Bleue; 7am-9pm; Broglie); rue des Veaux (15 rue des Veaux; 7am-9pm)

FRANCE

L'Utopie (☎ 03 88 23 89 21; 21-23 rue du Fossé des Tanneurs; per 1/20hr €3/20; 7am-11.30pm; Homme de Fer) Cybercafe with free wi-fi.

Main post office (5 av de la Marseillaise; République) Exchange services.

Main tourist office (☎ 03 88 52 28 28; www.otstrasbourg.fr; 17 place de la Cathédrale; 9am-7pm; Langstross Grand' Rue) A city-centre walking map costs €1, and the Strasbourg Pass (adult/four to 18 years €11.40/5.70) will save you some sightseeing cash.

Milk (☎ 03 88 32 06 02; 32-34 rue du Vieux Marché aux Vins; per hr €4; 24hr; Homme de Fer) Has 100 internet-access computers. Discounts are available.

Tourist office annexe (☎ 03 88 32 51 49; 9am-7pm; Gare Centrale) In the train station's southern wing.

Sights & Activities

With its bustling squares and upmarket shopping streets, the Grande Île – Unesco-listed since 1988 – is a paradise for the aimless ambler. The narrow streets of the **old city** are especially enchanting at night, while the half-timbered buildings and flowery canals around **Petite France** are fairy-tale pretty. The romantic **Terrasse Panoramique** (admission free; 9am-7.30pm) on top of **Barrage Vauban** (7.30am-7.30pm), a dam built to resist river raids, affords the best views.

Strasbourg's lacy, candy-coloured Gothic **Cathédrale Notre Dame** (admission free; 7am-7pm) is one of the marvels of European architecture. The west facade was completed in 1284, but the 142m spire wasn't finished till 1439. The 30m-high contraption inside the southern entrance is the 16th-century *horloge astronomique* (astronomical clock), which strikes solar noon at 12.30pm. The 66m-high **platform** (☎ 03 88 43 60 40; adult/student & under 18yr €3/1.50; 9am-5pm Mon-Fri, 10am-5pm Sat & Sun Apr-Oct, to 4.30pm Nov-Mar) provides a stork's-eye view of Strasbourg.

The world-renowned **Musée de l'Œuvre Notre-Dame** (☎ 03 88 32 88 17; 3 place du Château; adult/under 18yr/student under 25yr & senior incl audio guide €4/free/2; noon-6pm Tue-Sun; Langstross Grand' Rue) has one of Europe's premier collections of Romanesque, Gothic and Renaissance sculptures, 15th-century paintings and stained glass.

The **Musée d'Art Moderne et Contemporain** (MAMC; ☎ 03 88 23 31 31; place Hans Jean Arp; adult/under 18yr/student under 25yr & senior €5/free/2.50; noon-7pm Tue, Wed & Fri, noon-9pm Thu, 10am-6pm Sat & Sun; Musée d'Art Moderne) has pieces from practically every major art movement from Impressionism to cubism and surrealism.

The **Palais Rohan** (☎ 03 88 52 50 00; 2 place du Château; for whole complex adult/under 18yr/student under 25yr & senior €6/free/3, for each museum €4/free/2; noon-6pm Mon & Wed-Fri, 10am-6pm Sat & Sun) was built between 1732 and 1742 as a residence for Strasbourg's bishops. It houses several museums including the **Musée Archéologique**, which has exhibits from the Palaeolithic period to AD 800.

BREWERY TOURS

As well as being the seat of the great European project, Strasbourg is also the home of two of the continent's favourite lagers, found at **Brasseries Heineken** (☎ 03 88 19 57 55; annabelle.ferry@exirys.com; 4 rue St-Charles; admission free; tours Mon-Fri) and **Brasseries Kronenbourg** (☎ 03 88 27 41 59; siege.visites@kronenbourg-fr.com; 68 rte d'Oberhausbergen; adult/12-18yr/family €5/3/14; tours approx hourly Mon-Sat, closed Jan; Ducs d'Alsace). Both breweries are based north of the city centre and run guided tours of their facilities (sometimes in English); ask nicely and they might even throw in a beer-tasting session.

Tours

Batorama (☎ 03 88 84 13 13; www.batorama.fr, in French; 9 rue de Nantes; adult/student 25yr & under €7.60/3.80; excursions begin at 10.30am, 1pm, 2.30pm & 4pm Nov & Jan-Mar, to 9pm or 10pm Apr-Oct; Porte de l'Hôpital) runs scenic boat excursions in nine languages, taking in Petite France and the European institutions.

Sleeping

CIARUS (☎ 03 88 15 27 88; www.ciarus.com; 7 rue Finkmatt; dm in 8-/4-/2-bed room incl breakfast €21.50/25.50/28, s €44.50;) Hostels don't get more stylish than this 295-bed place; dorms all have industrial-strength furniture, toilets and showers. By bus, take bus 2, 4 or 10 to the place de Pierre stop.

Hôtel Patricia (☎ 03 88 32 14 60; www.hotelpatricia.fr; 1a rue du Puits; d €43-45, s with washbasin €28; reception 8-11am & 2-8pm Mon-Sat, 8-11am Sun; Langstross Grand' Rue) Dark, rustic interior and Vosges sandstone floors hint at the building's former incarnation as a convent. The 22 rooms are simply furnished but immaculate and spacious; some (eg rooms 3 and 6) have great views.

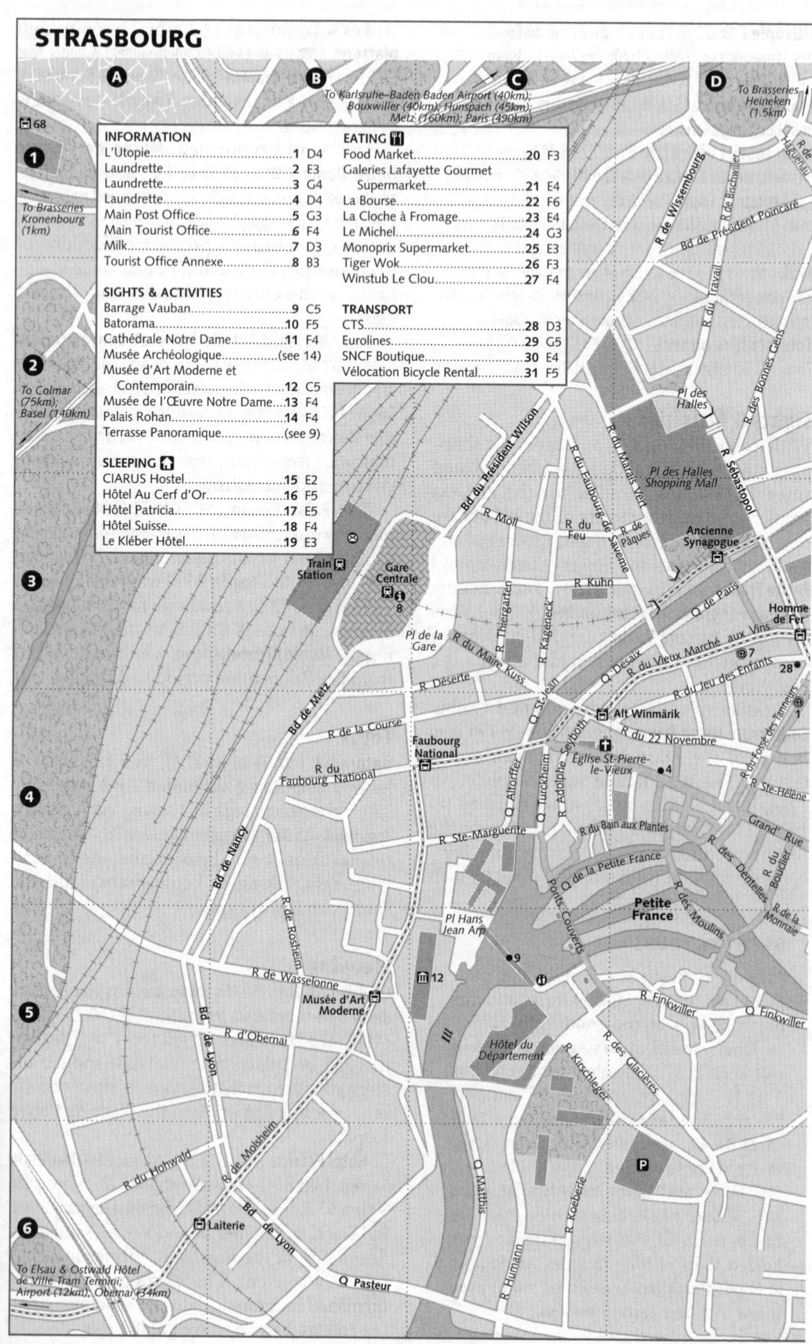
STRASBOURG
INFORMATION
L'Utopie 1 D4
Laundrette 2 E3
Laundrette 3 G4
Laundrette 4 D4
Main Post Office 5 G3
Main Tourist Office 6 F4
Milk 7 D3
Tourist Office Annexe 8 B3
SIGHTS & ACTIVITIES
Barrage Vauban 9 C5
Batorama 10 F5
Cathédrale Notre Dame 11 F4
Musée Archéologique (see 14)
Musée d'Art Moderne et Contemporain 12 C5
Musée de l'Œuvre Notre Dame 13 F4
Palais Rohan 14 F4
Terrasse Panoramique (see 9)
SLEEPING
CIARUS Hostel 15 E2
Hôtel Au Cerf d'Or 16 F5
Hôtel Patricia 17 E5
Hôtel Suisse 18 F4
Le Kléber Hôtel 19 E3
EATING
Food Market 20 F3
Galeries Lafayette Gourmet Supermarket 21 E4
La Bourse 22 F6
La Cloche à Fromage 23 E4
Le Michel 24 G3
Monoprix Supermarket 25 E3
Tiger Wok 26 F3
Winstub Le Clou 27 F4
TRANSPORT
CTS 28 D3
Eurolines 29 G5
SNCF Boutique 30 E4
Vélocation Bicycle Rental 31 F5
To Karlsruhe–Baden Baden Airport (40km); Bouxwiller (40km); Hunspach (45km); Metz (160km); Paris (490km)
To Brasseries Heineken (1.5km)
To Brasseries Kronenbourg (1km)
To Colmar (75km); Basel (140km)
To Elsau & Ostwald Hôtel de Ville Tram Termini; Airport (12km); Obernai (34km)
R de Wissembourg
R de Bischwiller
R de Haguenau
Bd de Président Poincaré
R du Travail
R des Bonnes Gens
Pl des Halles
Pl des Halles Shopping Mall
R Sébastopol
R du Marais Vert
R du Faubourg de Saverne
Bd du Président Wilson
R Moll
R du Feu
R de Pâques
Ancienne Synagogue
Train Station
Gare Centrale
R Kuhn
R Thiergarten
R Kageneck
Q de Paris
Homme de Fer
Pl de la Gare
R du Maire Kuss
Q Desaix
R du Vieux Marché aux Vins
R du Jeu des Enfants
R Déserte
Q St-Jean
Alt Winmärik
R du Fossé des Tanneurs
Bd de Metz
R de la Course
Faubourg National
R du 22 Novembre
R du Faubourg National
Église St-Pierre-le-Vieux
R Seyboth
R Adolphe
Q Altorffer
Q Turckheim
R Ste-Hélène
Grand' Rue
R du Bain aux Plantes
R Ste-Marguerite
Bd de Nancy
Q de la Petite France
R des Dentelles
R du Bouclier
Ponts Couverts
Petite France
R des Moulins
R de la Monnaie
R de Rosheim
Pl Hans Jean Arp
R de Wasselonne
Musée d'Art Moderne
R Finkwiller
Q Finkwiller
Ill
Bd de Lyon
R d'Obernai
Hôtel du Département
R des Glacières
R Kirschleger
R du Hohwald
R de Molsheim
Q Matthis
R Koeberlé
Laiterie
R Humann
Q Pasteur

FRANCE

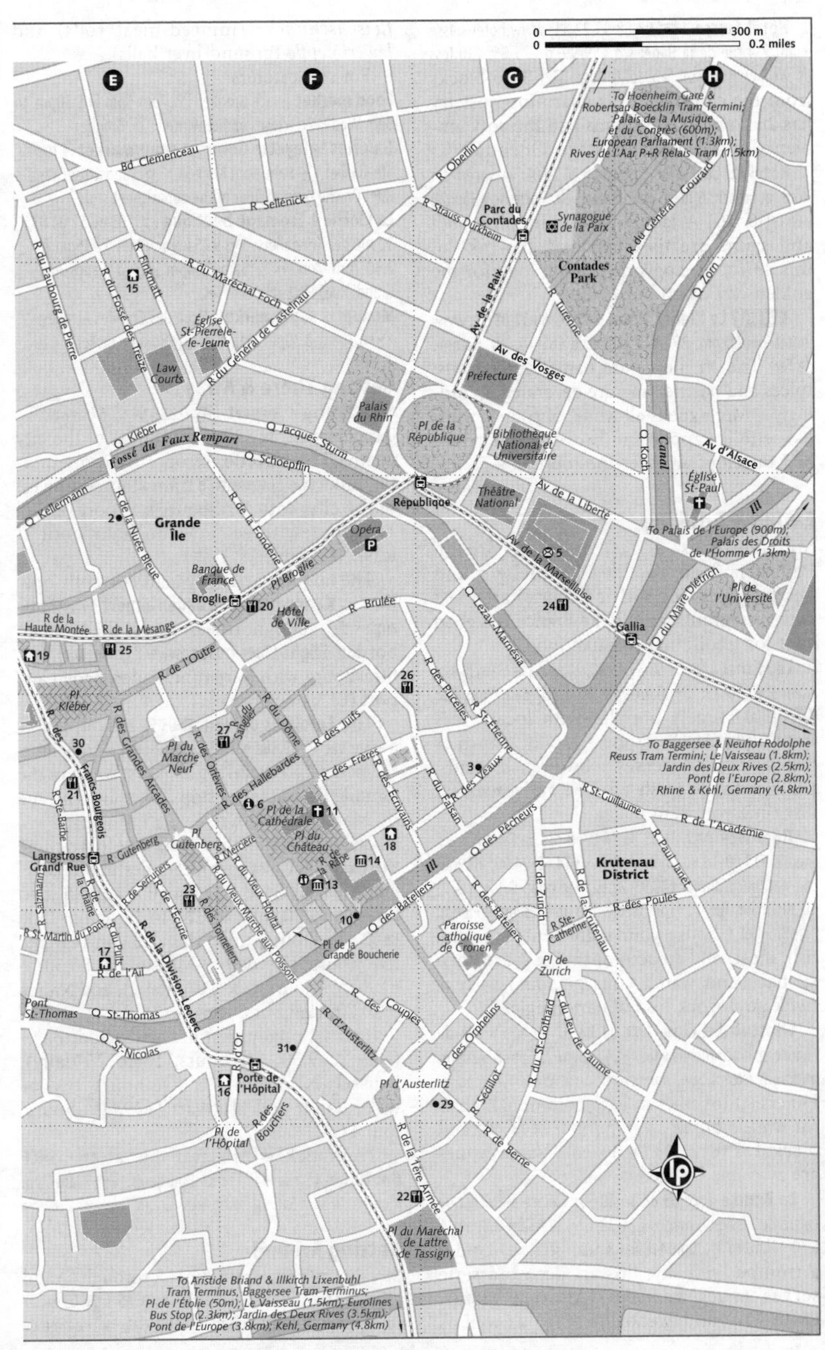
0 300 m
0 0.2 miles
E
F
G
H
To Hoenheim Gare & Robertsau Boecklin Tram Termini; Palais de la Musique et du Congrès (600m); European Parliament (1.3km); Rives de l'Aar P+R Relais Tram (1.5km)
Bd Clemenceau
R Oberlin
R Sellénick
R Strauss Durkheim
Parc du Contades
Synagogue de la Paix
R du Général Gourard
Contades Park
Q Zorn
R du Faubourg de Pierre
R du Fossé des Treize
R Finkmatt
15
R du Maréchal Foch
Église St-Pierre-le-Jeune
R du Général de Castelnau
Av de la Paix
R Turenne
Law Courts
Av des Vosges
Préfecture
Palais du Rhin
Pl de la République
Bibliothèque National et Universitaire
Q Kléber
Fossé du Faux Rempart
Q Jacques Sturm
Q Schoepflin
Q Koch
Canal
Av d'Alsace
Église St-Paul
Q Kellermann
République
Théâtre National
Av de la Liberté
Ill
2
Grande Île
R de la Nuée Bleue
R de la Fonderie
Opéra
To Palais de l'Europe (900m); Palais des Droits de l'Homme (1.3km)
Banque de France
Pl Broglie
Av de la Marseillaise
5
Broglie
20
Hôtel de Ville
R Brulée
Q Lezay-Marnésia
24
Pl de l'Université
Q du Maire Dietrich
R de la Haute Montée
R de la Mésange
Gallia
19
25
R de l'Outre
26
R des Pucelles
Pl Kléber
R des Grandes Arcades
R du Sanglier
R du Dôme
R des Juifs
R St-Étienne
To Baggersee & Neuhof Rodolphe Reuss Tram Termini; Le Vaisseau (1.8km); Jardin des Deux Rives (2.5km); Pont de l'Europe (2.8km); Rhine & Kehl, Germany (4.8km)
30
R des Francs-Bourgeois
27
Pl du Marché Neuf
R des Orfèvres
R des Frères
R des Écrivains
3
R des Veaux
R du Faisan
R des Hallebardes
R St-Guillaume
21
6
Pl de la Cathédrale
11
R de l'Académie
R Ste-Barbe
Pl Gutenberg
Pl du Château
18
R des Pêcheurs
R Paul Janet
Langstross Grand' Rue
R Gutenberg
R Mercière
R de la Râpe
14
R de Zurich
Krutenau District
R de Serruriers
R du Vieux Marché aux Poissons
13
R des Bateliers
R de la Krutenau
R Salzmann
R de la Chaîne
R de l'Écurie
23
R des Tonneliers
10
Q des Bateliers
R des Poules
R St-Martin du Pont
R du Puits
R Ste-Catherine
Pl de la Grande Boucherie
Paroisse Catholique de Cronen
17
R de l'Ail
R de la Division Leclerc
Pl de Zurich
Pont St-Thomas
Q St-Thomas
R des Couples
R d'Austerlitz
R des Orphelins
R du St-Gothard
R du Jeu de Paume
Q St-Nicolas
31
R d'Or
Porte de l'Hôpital
16
Pl d'Austerlitz
R Sédillot
29
R des Bouchers
Pl de l'Hôpital
R de la 1ère Armée
R de Berne
22
Pl du Maréchal de Lattre de Tassigny
To Aristide Briand & Illkirch Lixenbuhl Tram Terminus, Baggersee Tram Terminus; Pl de l'Étolie (50m); Le Vaisseau (1.5km); Eurolines Bus Stop (2.3km); Jardin des Deux Rives (3.5km); Pont de l'Europe (3.8km); Kehl, Germany (4.8km)

FRANCE

Hôtel Suisse (03 88 35 22 11; www.hotel-suisse.com; 2-4 rue de la Râpe; s/q €59/99, d €75-85, €10 less on weekends in Jan, Feb, Jul & Aug;) Two blocks from the cathedral, this charming hostelry has 26 comfortable rooms and the cosy ambience of an Alsatian cottage. Often full.

Hôtel Au Cerf d'Or (03 88 36 20 05; www.cerf-dor.com, in French; 6 place de l'Hôpital; Porte de l'Hôpital; r €61-110;) A Jacuzzi, 5m swimming pool and sauna are the cherry on the cake of this 43-room, Logis de France; look for the golden *cerf* (stag) out front.

ourpick **Le Kléber Hôtel** (03 88 32 09 53; www.hotel-kleber.com; 29 place Kléber; d €65-78; Homme de Fer) The 30 rooms are named after fruits, spices and pastries and are decorated accordingly – Meringue is all white, of course, while Noisette is cappuccino-brown and Pavlova or Kougelopf are over-the-top treats.

Eating & Drinking

Strasbourg is a gastronome's dream. Pedestrianised rue des Tonneliers and nearby streets (eg rue de l'Écurie) are lined with restaurants, and Petite France is a good spot for traditional Alsatian food.

Le Michel (03 88 35 45 40; 20 av de la Marseillaise; menus €9.50-15; 6am-9pm Mon-Fri, 6am-7pm Sat; Gallia) Hugely popular with locals, this Paris-style cafe-brasserie – locally known as Snack Michel – serves solid French mains, pastries made fresh all day, and breakfast any time you want it.

Tiger Wok (03 88 36 44 87; 8 rue du Faisan; lunch menus €13.60-16.60, dinner menus €14.60-24.90, all-you-can-eat lunch/dinner €20.95/22.92; noon-2.15pm & 7-10.30pm Sun-Tue, to 11pm Wed & Thu, to 11.30pm Fri & Sat; Broglie) Choose your ingredients (veggies, fish, meat) and an accompanying sauce, then sit back and watch your personal *wokeur* (wok guy) work his culinary magic.

Winstub Le Clou (03 88 32 11 67; 3 rue du Chaudron; lunch menus €15; 11.45am-2.15pm & 5.30pm-midnight except Sun, holidays & lunch Wed; Broglie) Diners sit together at long communal tables for *wädele braisé au pinot noir* (€16.40) and *bibeleskäs* (€12.20). A dozen Alsatian wines are available by the glass.

La Bourse (03 88 36 40 53; 1 place Maréchal de Lattre de Tassigny; menus €24-32; 11.45am-2.30pm & 6.30-11pm, to 11.30pm Fri, Sat & Sun; Étoile) Under a trompe l'œil sky, this art deco brasserie serves *tartes flambées* (Alsatian pizzas; €8 to €10) and *bæckeoffe* (€18) as well as *fleischschnäcke* (minced-meat rolls) and *lewerknepfle* (ground-liver balls).

For self-caterers:

Food market (place Broglie; 7am-5pm or 5.30pm, to 6pm Wed & Fri, closes earlier winter; Broglie)

Galeries Lafayette Gourmet supermarket (4 rue Ste-Barbe; 9am-8pm Mon-Sat; Langstross Grand' Rue) On the ground floor of the department store.

La Cloche à Fromage boutique (03 88 52 04 03; 32 rue des Tonneliers; 9.15am or 10am-12.15pm & 2.30-7pm Mon-Fri, 8.15am-6.30pm Sat; Langstross Grand' Rue) First-rate cheeses.

Monoprix supermarket (5 rue des Grandes Arcades; 8.30am-8.30pm Mon-Sat; Homme de Fer)

Getting There & Away

Strasbourg's **airport** (03 88 64 67 67; www.strasbourg.aeroport.fr) is 12km southwest of the city centre. The Navette Aéroport (airport shuttle) links the Baggersee tram stop, southwest of the city, with Strasbourg's airport (€5.20, 15 minutes, three times an hour until at least 10.20pm).

The budget carrier Ryanair currently only flies to **Karlsruhe/Baden Baden airport** (www.badenairpark.de), 40km northeast across the German border. **Flight Liner buses** (www.flightliner.de) link Strasbourg with Karlsruhe/Baden Baden airport (€17, one hour).

The **Eurolines office** (03 90 22 14 60; 6d place d'Austerlitz; 9.30am-12.30pm & 2-6pm Mon-Fri, 10am-12.30pm Sat; Porte de l'Hôpital) is just south of the Grande Île, but buses stop 2.5km away on rue du Maréchal Lefèbvre.

The train station has had a refit to welcome the new TGV Est Européen; destinations include Paris' Gare de l'Est (€55 to €86, two hours and 20 minutes, 13 to 17 daily), Lille (€52, 3½ hours, three daily), Lyon (€48.30, five hours, five daily), Marseille (€80.50 to €100, 6½ hours, one TGV daily), and Nancy (€20.70, 1½ hours, seven to 12 daily).

Internationally, destinations include Basel (Bâle; €19.30, 1¼ hours, 16 to 25 daily), Brussels-Nord (€61.70, five hours, two or three daily) and Stuttgart (€39, 1¼ hours, four TGVs daily).

Train tickets are available at the **SNCF Boutique** (5 rue des Francs-Bourgeois; 10am-7pm Mon-Fri, to 5pm Sat; Langstross Grand' Rue).

Getting Around

Strasbourg's five tramlines (A through E) and city-centre buses are run by **CTS** (03 88 77 70 70; www.cts-strasbourg.fr; Mon-Sat; Homme de

WORTH THE TRIP: MASSIF DES VOSGES

The sublime **Parc Naturel Régional des Ballons des Vosges** covers 3000 sq km in the southern Vosges range. In the warm months, the gentle, rounded mountains, deep forests, glacial lakes and rolling pastureland are a walker's paradise, with an astounding 10,000km of marked trails and cycle routes, and in winter you'll discover three dozen inexpensive skiing areas.

For information on the park, contact the **Maison du Parc Naturel Régional des Ballons des Vosges** (☎ 03 89 77 90 34; www.parc-ballons-vosges.fr, in French; 1 cour de l'Abbaye, Munster; 🕑 10am-noon & 2-6pm Tue-Sun mid-Jun–Sep, 2-6pm Mon-Fri Oct–mid-Jun, plus 2-6pm Sat & Sun Dec).

Fer). The main hub is at place de l'Homme de Fer; trams operate until midnight or 12.30am, while buses run until about 11pm. Tickets (valid on both buses and trams) cost €1.30, or there's a 24-hour ticket for €3.50.

The city is ultra bike-friendly: the **Vélocation** (www.velocation.net) system rents single-speed bikes (per half-/full day €5/8, Monday to Friday €12, deposit €100 to €200) from various locations:

City Centre (☎ 03 88 24 05 61; 10 rue des Bouchers; 🕑 9.30am-12.30pm & 1.30-7pm Easter–mid-Oct, 9.30am-12.30pm & 1-5pm mid-Oct–Easter; 🚊 Porte de l'Hôpital)

Train Station (☎ 03 88 23 56 75; 🕑 7am-8pm Mon-Fri, 9.30am-12.30pm & 1.30-7pm Sat & Sun Easter–mid-Oct, 7am-8pm Mon-Fri, 9.30am-12.30pm & 1.30-5.30pm Sat mid-Oct–Easter; 🚊 Gare Centrale)

NANCY

pop 331,000

Delightful Nancy has an air of refinement found nowhere else in Lorraine. With a magnificent central square, several fine museums and sparkling shop windows, the former capital of the dukes of Lorraine seems as opulent today as it was in the 16th to 18th centuries, when much of the city centre was built.

Orientation

Pedestrians-only place Stanislas connects the medieval Vieille Ville (Old Town), centred on the Grande Rue, with the 16th-century Ville Neuve (New Town) to the south. The train station is 800m southwest of place Stanislas.

Information

E-café Cyber Café (☎ 03 83 35 47 34; 11 rue des Quatre Églises; per min/hr €0.09/5.40; 🕑 11am-9pm Mon & Sat, 9am-9pm Tue-Fri, 2-8pm Sun) Proper cybercafe with qwerty keyboards.

Laundrette (124 rue St-Dizier; 🕑 7.45am-9.30pm)

Post office (10 rue St-Dizier; 🚊 Point Central) Currency exchange.

Tourist office (☎ 03 83 35 22 41; www.ot-nancy.fr; place Stanislas; 🕑 9am-7pm Mon-Sat, 10am-5pm Sun & holidays Apr-Oct, 9am-6pm Mon-Sat, 10am-1pm Sun & holidays Nov-Mar) Inside the Hôtel de Ville.

Sights

Neoclassical **place Stanislas** (🚊 Cathédrale), laid out in the 1750s, is one of the most dazzling public spaces in Europe. The rococo fountains, gilded gateways and opulent buildings form one of France's finest ensembles of 18th-century architecture.

Two kilometres southwest of the city centre, the brilliant **Musée de l'École de Nancy** (☎ 03 83 40 14 86; 36-38 rue du Sergent Blandan; adult/student & senior incl audio guide €6/4, students free Wed; 🕑 10am-6pm Wed-Sun) collects furnished rooms and curvaceous glass produced by the turn-of-the-20th-century art nouveau (Jugendstil) movement. Catch buses 122, 126, 134 or 135 to the Painlevé stop.

Star attractions at the **Musée des Beaux-Arts** (☎ 03 83 85 30 72; 3 place Stanislas; adult/student & senior incl audio guide €6/4; 🕑 10am-6pm Wed-Mon) include a superb collection of art nouveau glass and paintings from the 14th to 18th centuries.

The 16th-century Palais Ducal, former residence of the dukes of Lorraine, now houses the **Musée Historique Lorrain** (☎ 03 83 32 18 74; 64 & 66 Grande Rue; adult/student & senior for both sections €5.50/3.50, students free Wed; 🕑 10am-12.30pm & 2-6pm Wed-Mon), dedicated to fine arts and folklore.

Sleeping

Hôtel de l'Académie (☎ 03 83 35 52 31; fax 03 83 32 55 78; http://academie-hotel.com; 7bis rue des Michottes; d €32-36, q €49, s/d with shower €25/30) This offbeat, 29-room, one-star place has a tacky fountain that tinkles like a broken urinal and very simply furnished rooms with acoustic tile ceilings and plastic shower pods.

Hôtel des Portes d'Or (☎ 03 83 35 42 34; www.hotel-lesportesdor.com; 21 rue Stanislas; d €55-65) This two-star hostelry, situated just metres from place Stanislas, has 20 comfortable but uninspiring rooms with upholstered doors. It's often full, so call ahead.

Hôtel de Guise (☎ 03 83 32 24 68; www.hoteldeguise.com; 18 rue de Guise; d €64-100;) A grand stone staircase leads to extra-wide hallways and 48 bright, spacious, two-star rooms. The bathrooms are as modern as the 18th-century hardwood floors are creaky.

Hôtel des Prélats (☎ 03 83 30 20 20; www.hoteldesprelats.com; 56 place Monseigneur Ruch; d €104; Cathédrale;) In a grand building that's been a hotel since 1906, this three-star place offers 41 rooms with parquet floors, antique-style furnishings and creative tile bathrooms.

Eating & Drinking

Aux Délices du Palais (☎ 03 83 30 44 19; 69 Grande Rue; starters €5, mains €9, desserts €4; Mon-Fri & dinner Sat) Billing itself as *bistronomique* (whatever that means), takes in everything from chicken *tajine* (North African–style stew) to beef fajitas to endive *tartes*.

Brasserie Excelsior (☎ 03 83 35 24 57; 50 rue Henri Poincaré; after-10pm menus €18.90, other menus €30.50; 8am-12.30am Mon-Sat, 8am-11pm Sun, meals served noon-3pm & 7pm-closing time; Nancy Gare) Built in 1910, this brasserie mixes a shiny art deco interior with similarly polished food, including *choucroute à trois poissons* (sauerkraut with salmon, haddock and monkfish).

Le Gastrolâtre (Chez Tanésy; ☎ 03 83 35 51 94; 23 Grande Rue; lunch menus €25, other menus €42; Tue-Sat) Homey, intimate bistro specialising in mouth-watering Lorraine- and Provence-inspired cuisine.

For self-caterers:

Aux Croustillants (10 rue des Maréchaux; 24hr except from 8pm Sun to 5.30am Tue) An almost-24/7 *boulangerie-pâtisserie*.

Au Vieux Gourmet (26 rue St-Georges; 9am-8pm Mon-Fri, 9am-7.30pm Sat, 9.30am-12.30pm Sun; Cathédrale) A grocery since 1889, this place carries luxury products (Fauchon, Hédiard) as well as staples.

Covered market (place Henri Mengin; 7am-6pm Tue-Thu, 7am-6.30pm Fri & Sat; Point Central)

Monoprix supermarket (rue des Ponts; 8.30am-8.30pm Mon-Sat) Deep inside the St-Sébastien shopping mall.

Getting There & Away

The **train station** (place Thiers; Nancy Gare) is on the line linking Paris' Gare de l'Est (€50.50 by TGV, 1½ hours, eight to 10 direct daily) with Strasbourg (€20.70, 1½ hours, seven to 12 daily). Beat the ticket queues at the **SNCF office** (18 place St-Epvre; 12.30-6pm Mon, 9.30am-1pm & 2-6pm Tue-Fri).

THE LOIRE VALLEY

One step removed from the French capital and poised on the frontier between northern and southern France, the Loire was historically the place where princes, dukes and notable nobles established their country getaways, and the countryside is littered with some of the most extravagant architecture outside Versailles.

BLOIS

pop 49,200

Blois' historic chateau was the feudal seat of the powerful counts of Blois, and its grand halls, spiral staircases and sweeping courtyards provide a whistlestop tour through the key periods of French architecture. Sadly for chocoholics, the town's historic chocolate factory, Poulain, is off-limits to visitors.

Orientation & Information

Blois, on the northern bank of the Loire, is a compact town – almost everything is within 10 minutes' walk of the train station. The old city is southeast and east of the chateau, which towers over place Victor Hugo.

Post office (rue Gallois) Changes money.

Tourist office (☎ 02 54 90 41 41; www.bloispaysdechambord.com; 23 place du Château; 9am-7pm Mon-Sat, 10am-7pm Sun Apr-Sep, 9.30am-12.30pm & 2-6pm Mon-Sat, 10am-4pm Sun Oct-Mar)

Sights

Blois' old city, heavily damaged by German attacks in 1940, retains its steep, twisting medieval streets. The **Château Royal de Blois** (☎ 02 54 90 33 32; place du Château; adult/6-17yr/student €7.50/3/5; 9am-7pm Jul & Aug, 9am-6.30pm Apr-Jun & Sep, 9am-12.30pm & 1.30-5.30pm Oct-Mar) makes an excellent introduction to the chateaux of the Loire Valley, with elements of Gothic (13th century); Flamboyant Gothic (1498–1503), early Renaissance (1515–24) and classical (1630s) architecture in its four grand wings.

Opposite the chateau is the former home of watchmaker, inventor and conjurer Jean Eugène Robert-Houdin (1805–71), after whom the great Houdini named himself. It's now the **Maison de la Magie** (☎ 02 54 55 26 26;

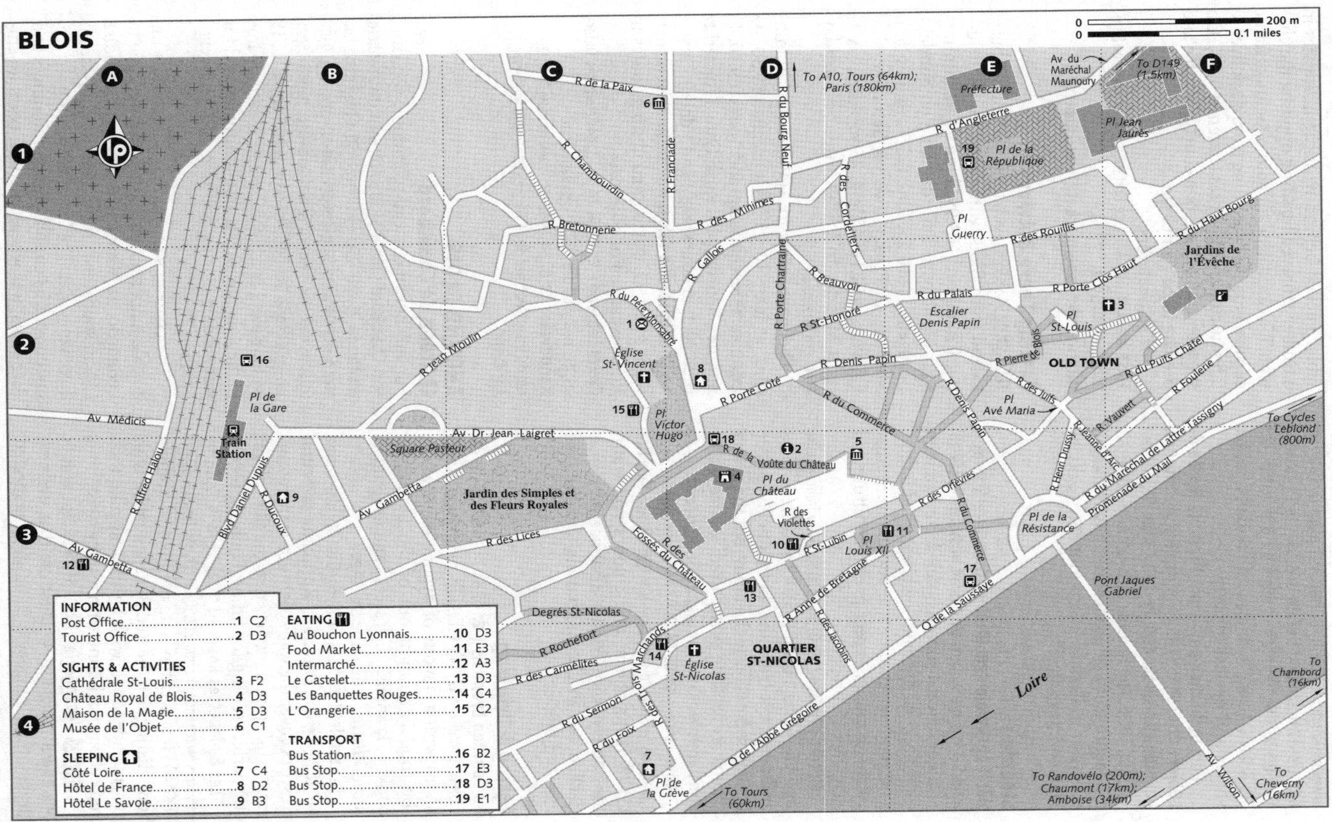
BLOIS
0 200 m
0 0.1 miles
INFORMATION
Post Office 1 C2
Tourist Office 2 D3
SIGHTS & ACTIVITIES
Cathédrale St-Louis 3 F2
Château Royal de Blois 4 D3
Maison de la Magie 5 D3
Musée de l'Objet 6 C1
SLEEPING
Côté Loire 7 C4
Hôtel de France 8 D2
Hôtel Le Savoie 9 B3
EATING
Au Bouchon Lyonnais 10 D3
Food Market 11 E3
Intermarché 12 A3
Le Castelet 13 D3
Les Banquettes Rouges 14 C4
L'Orangerie 15 C2
TRANSPORT
Bus Station 16 B2
Bus Stop 17 E3
Bus Stop 18 D3
Bus Stop 19 E1
To A10, Tours (64km); Paris (180km)
To D149 (1.5km)
Av du Maréchal Maunoury
Préfecture
Pl Jean Jaurès
Pl de la République
R d'Angleterre
R de la Paix
R Chambourdin
R Franciade
R du Bourg Neuf
R des Minimes
R Bretonnerie
R des Cordeliers
Pl Guerry
R des Rouillis
R du Haut Bourg
Jardins de l'Évêche
R Porte Clos Haut
R Gallois
R Beauvoir
R du Palais
R Porte Chartraine
R du Père Monsabré
R St-Honoré
Escalier Denis Papin
Pl St-Louis
OLD TOWN
R Pierre de Blois
R du Puits Châtel
R Foulerie
R Jean Moulin
Église St-Vincent
R Denis Papin
R des Juifs
Pl Avé Maria
R Vauvert
R Jeanne d'Arc
R Henri Drussy
R du Maréchal de Lattre Tassigny
Promenade du Mail
To Cycles Leblond (800m)
Pl de la Gare
Train Station
Av Médicis
Pl Victor Hugo
R Porte Coté
R du Commerce
Av Dr Jean Laigret
Square Pasteur
R de la Voûte du Château
Pl du Château
R des Orfèvres
R Alfred Halou
Blvd Daniel Dupuis
R Ducoux
Av Gambetta
Jardin des Simples et des Fleurs Royales
R des Violettes
R St-Lubin
Pl Louis XII
Pl de la Résistance
R des Lices
R des Fossés du Château
Q de la Saussaye
Pont Jaques Gabriel
Degrés St-Nicolas
R Anne de Bretagne
R des Jacobins
R Rochefort
R des Carmélites
R des Trois Marchands
Église St-Nicolas
QUARTIER ST-NICOLAS
Loire
R du Sermon
R du Foix
Pl de la Grève
Q de l'Abbé Grégoire
To Tours (60km)
To Randovélo (200m); Chaumont (17km); Amboise (34km)
Av Wilson
To Chambord (16km)
To Cheverny (16km)

FRANCE

www.maisondelamagie.fr, in French; 1 place du Château; adult/6-17yr/student €7.50/5/6.50, incl château €12.50/5.50/8.50; 10am-12.30pm & 2-6.30pm Mar–late Sep & late Oct–early Nov), and offers daily magic shows and optical trickery.

The brilliant (and very French) **Musée de l'Objet** (02 54 55 37 45; www.museedelobjet.org; 6 rue Franciade; adult/student €4/2; 1.30-6.30pm Wed-Sun late Jun–Aug, 1.30-6.30pm Fri-Sun late Feb–late Jun & Sep-Dec) is a treasure trove of modern art based around everyday materials – look out for works by Dalí and Man Ray.

Sleeping

Hôtel Le Savoie (02 54 74 32 21; hotel.le.savoie@wanadoo.fr; 6 rue Ducoux; s/d €45/54, with shower €41/48) Straightforward station hotel, decorated with multinational flags and a whitewashed facade. The modern chain-style rooms are hardly award-winning: expect prefab furniture and easy-clean fabrics.

Hôtel de France (02 54 78 00 53; www.franceetguise.com; 3 rue Gallois; s €45, d 49-53) Chandeliers, glass and brass left from this hotel's belle époque heyday still decorate the lobby, but the musty rooms are looking pretty tired: ask for a balcony overlooking the Église St-Vincent.

Côté Loire (02 54 78 07 86; www.coteloire.com; 2 place de la Grève; d early Nov-Mar €48-67, Apr-early Nov €53-72) If it's charm and colours you want, the homely Loire Coast has haphazard rooms decked out in checks, pastels and the odd exposed brick.

Eating & Drinking

Au Bouchon Lyonnais (02 54 74 12 87; 25 rue des Violettes; mains €12-14) Classic neighbourhood bistro with a flavour of bygone days, where the food is straight out of the Lyonnaise cookbook: snails, duck steaks and *la veritable andouillette* (true tripe sausage).

Le Castelet (02 54 74 66 09; 40 rue St-Lubin; menus €17-28.20; closed Wed & Sun) Rusticana and rural frescoes cover the walls of this country restaurant, while piped medieval music fills the air: the perfect setting for filling Touraine food.

Les Banquettes Rouges (02 54 78 74 92; 16 rue des Trois Marchands; menus €22.50/28.50; lunch & dinner Tue-Sat) Handwritten slate menus and homely food distinguish the Red Benches: rabbit with marmalade, duck with lentils and pike with red cabbage, all done with a spicy twist.

our pick **L'Orangerie** (02 54 78 05 36; 1 av du Dr Jean Laigret; menus €32-74) Dust off that evening dress – the Orangery is Blois' most respected table. Tucked behind wrought-iron gates in a timber-storeyed building opposite the chateau, it's cloud nine for connoisseurs of haute cuisine – expect everything from duck liver to langoustine and foie gras (fattened liver). On summer nights, opt for a courtyard table and prepare to be pampered.

For self-caterers:

Food market (rue Anne de Bretagne; 7.30am or 8am-1pm Tue, Thu & Sat)

Intermarché supermarket (16 av Gambetta)

Getting There & Away

TLC (02 54 58 55 44; www.tlcinfo.net) handles buses to and from Blois, with destinations including Chambord (€3.99, Line 2, 40 minutes, four Monday to Saturday, one on Sunday), Beaugency (€10.55, Line 1, 55 minutes, four Monday to Friday, two on Saturday) and Cheverny (€1.10, Line 4, 45 minutes, six to eight Monday to Friday, three on Saturday, two on Sunday).

There are trains to Amboise (€6, 20 minutes, at least 10 daily), Orléans (€9.30, 45 minutes, at least hourly) and Tours (€9.10, 40 minutes, hourly), plus Paris' Gare d'Austerlitz (€23.30, two hours, eight to 13 daily).

The **Châteaux à Vélo** (www.chateauxavelo.com) network offers 11 waymarked cycling routes in the Blois area. For bike hire:

Cycles Leblond (02 54 74 30 13; 44 Levée des Tuileries; per half-/full day €9/12; 9am-9pm)

Randovélo (02 54 78 62 52; www.randovelo.fr; 29 rue du Puits Neuf; per day €14; 9am-6pm Mon-Fri Apr-Oct)

AROUND BLOIS

Château de Chambord

For full-blown chateau splendour, you can't top **Chambord** (02 54 50 50 20; www.chambord.org; adult/under 18yr/18-25yr €9.50/free/7.50, €1 reduction Jan-Mar & Oct-Dec; 9am-7.30pm mid-Jul–mid-Aug, 9am-6.15pm mid-Mar–mid-Jul & mid-Aug–Sep, 9am-5.15pm, Jan–mid-Mar & Oct-Dec), constructed from 1519 by François I as a lavish base for hunting game in the Sologne forests, but eventually used for just 42 days during the king's 32-year reign (1515–47).

The chateau's most famous feature is the double-helix staircase, attributed by some to Leonardo da Vinci, who lived in Amboise (34km southwest) from 1516 until his death three years later. The Italianate rooftop terrace, surrounded by cupolas, domes, chimneys and slate roofs, was where the royal court assembled to watch military exercises and hunting parties returning at the end of the day.

Several times daily there are 1½-hour **guided tours** (€4) in English. Free *son et lumière* (sound and light) shows, known as **Les Clairs de Lune**, are projected onto the chateau's facade nightly from July to mid-September.

Chambord is 16km east of Blois, 45km southwest of Orléans and 17km northeast of Cheverny. For details on public transport options see opposite.

Château de Cheverny

Thought by many to be the most perfectly proportioned chateau of all, **Cheverny** (☎ 02 54 79 96 29; www.chateau-cheverny.fr; adult/7-14yr €7/3.40; 9.15am-6.45pm Jul & Aug, 9.15am-6.15pm Apr-Jun & Sep, 9.45am-5.30pm Oct, 9.45am-5pm Nov-Mar) has hardly been altered since its construction between 1625 and 1634 by Jacques Hurault, an intendant to Louis XII. Inside you'll find a formal dining room, bridal chamber and children's playroom (complete with Napoleon III–era toys), as well as a guards' room full of pikestaffs, claymores and suits of armour.

Behind the chateau is the 18th-century **Orangerie**, where many priceless artworks (including the *Mona Lisa*) were stashed during WWII. Hérgé used the castle as a model for Moulinsart (Marlinspike) Hall, the ancestral home of Tintin's sidekick, Captain Haddock. **Les Secrets de Moulinsart** (combined ticket with chateau adult/7-14yr €11.80/6.80) explores the Tintin connections.

Cheverny is 16km southeast of Blois and 17km southwest of Chambord. For information on the bus from Blois see opposite.

Château de Chaumont

It's a brisk climb up to **Château de Chaumont-sur-Loire** (☎ 02 54 51 26 26; adult/6-12yr/12-18yr €7.50/free/5; 10am-6pm mid-May–mid-Sep, 10.30am-5.30pm Apr–mid-May & mid-Sep–end Sep, 10am-5pm Oct-Mar) is set on a bluff overlooking the Loire. The entrance, across a wooden drawbridge between two wide towers, opens onto an inner courtyard from where there are stunning views. Opposite the main entrance are the luxurious stables, built in 1877.

Chaumont-sur-Loire is 17km southwest of Blois and 20km northeast of Amboise. Onzain, an easyish walk from Chaumont across the Loire, has trains to Blois (€3, 10 minutes, 10 to 14 daily) and Tours (€7.20, 35 minutes).

TOURS

pop 298,000

Hovering somewhere between the style of Paris and the conservative sturdiness of central France, Tours is one of the principal cities of the Loire Valley. It's a smart, solidly bourgeois kind of place, filled with wide 18th-century boulevards, parks and imposing public buildings, as well as a busy university of some 25,000 students.

Orientation & Information

The central hub of place Jean Jaurès connects the main thoroughfares – west–east blvd Béranger and blvd Heurteloup, and north–south rue Nationale and av de Grammont. The old city encircles place Plumereau, 400m west of rue Nationale.

Emega Cyberstation (43 rue du Grand Marché; per hr €2; noon-midnight Mon-Sat, 2-11pm Sun) Internet access.

Post office (1 blvd Béranger) Currency exchange.

Tourist office (☎ 02 47 70 37 37; www.ligeris.com; 78-82 rue Bernard Palissy; 8.30am-7pm Mon-Sat, 10am-12.30pm & 2.30-5pm Sun mid-Apr–mid-Oct; 9am-12.30pm & 1.30-6pm Mon-Sat, 10am-1pm Sun mid-Oct–mid-Apr)

Sights

Arranged around the courtyard of the former archbishop's palace, the **Musée des Beaux-Arts** (☎ 02 47 05 68 73; 18 place François Sicard; adult/under 13yr/student €4/free/2; 9am-12.45pm & 2-6pm Wed-Mon) is a fine example of a French provincial arts museum – look out for works by Delacroix, Degas and Monet, as well as a rare Rembrandt miniature and a Rubens portrait of the Virgin Mary.

With its twin towers and Gothic arches, buttresses and gargoyles, the **Cathédrale St-Gatien** (place de la Cathédrale; 9am-7pm) is a show-stopper. It's particularly known for its stained glass; the interior dates from the 13th to 16th centuries, and the domed tops of the 70m-high **towers** date from the Renaissance.

France's skilled labourers, including pastry chefs, coopers and locksmiths, are celebrated at the **Musée du Compagnonnage** (☎ 02 47 61 07 93; 8 rue Nationale; adult/under 12yr/student €5/free/3; 9am-12.30pm & 2-6pm daily mid-Jun–mid-Sep, 9am-noon & 2-6pm Wed-Mon mid-Sep–mid-Jun), where displays range from handmade clogs to booby-trapped locks, vintage barrels and cakes.

Tours has several public parks, including the 19th-century **Jardin Botanique** (blvd Tonnelle; admission free; 7.45am-sunset), a five-hectare

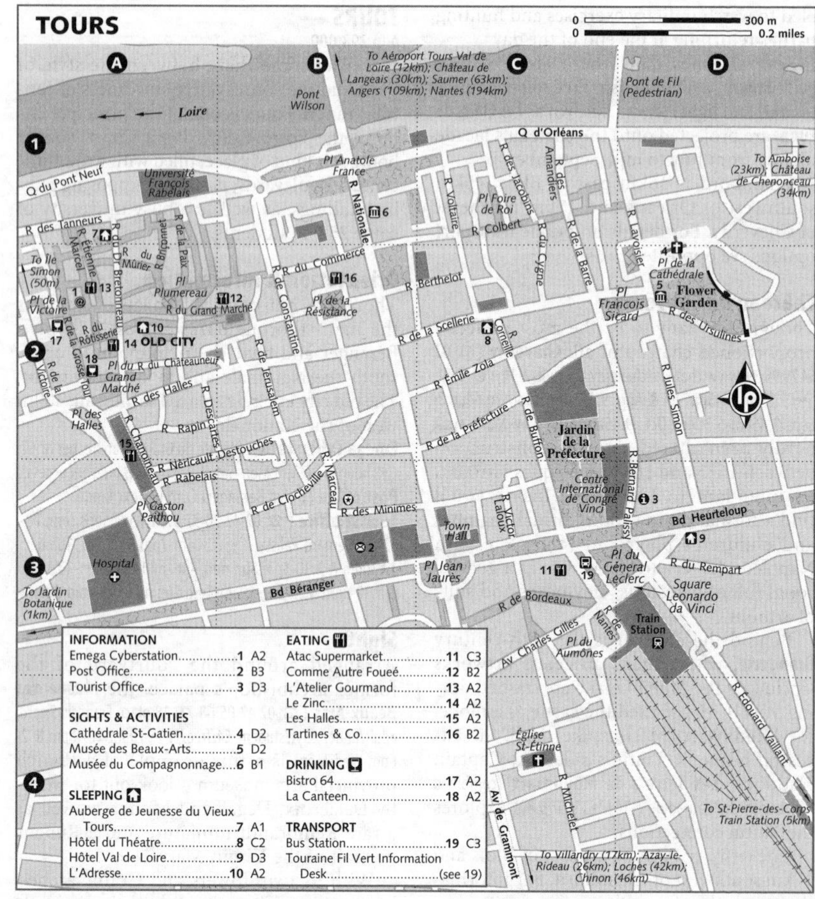

landscaped park with a tropical greenhouse, medicinal herb garden and petting zoo. The park is 1.6km west of place Jean Jaurès; bus 4 along blvd Béranger stops nearby.

Sleeping

Auberge de Jeunesse du Vieux Tours (☎ 02 47 37 81 58; www.ajtours.org; 5 rue du Dr Bretonneau; dm €17.40; reception 8am-noon & 6-11pm;) Friendly, bustling hostel with a large foreign-student and young-worker contingent; there are lots of kitchens (mostly small) and lounges to hang out in, but no en-suite bathrooms.

Hôtel Val de Loire (☎ 02 47 05 37 86; hotel.val.de.loire@club-Internet.fr; 33 blvd Heurteloup; s €30-40, d €40-50) Higgledy-piggledy rooms spread around an 1870 town house, with period features including parquet floors, faded rugs and scruffy furniture, as well as wi-fi and double glazing to shut out the road noise.

our pick **L'Adresse** (☎ 02 47 20 85 76; www.hotel-ladresse.com; 12 rue de la Rôtisserie; s €50, d €70-90) Looking for Parisian style in provincial Tours? Then you're in luck – 'The Address' is a boutique bonanza, with rooms finished in sleek slates and ochres, topped off with wi-fi, flat-screen TVs and designer sinks.

Hôtel du Théâtre (☎ 02 47 05 31 29; www.hotel-du-theatre37.com; 57 rue de la Scellerie; s €51-56, d €56-62) This hotel's near the city theatre. A spiral staircase reaches up a timber-framed courtyard to the 1st-floor lobby; the rooms are old-fashioned in a comfy way. There's wi-fi and a beamed dining room in which to breakfast.

Eating

In the old city, place Plumereau, rue du Grand Marché and rue de la Rôtisserie are loaded with restaurants and cafes.

Tartines & Co (☎ 02 47 20 50 60; 6 rue des Fusillés; mains from €8.50, lunch menus €13.20; ⏲ 10am-5pm) Snazzy little bistro that reinvents the traditional *croque* (toasted sandwich). Choose your topping – gourmet chicken, roasted veg, carpaccio beef – and it's served on toasted artisan bread.

Comme Autre Fouée (☎ 02 47 05 94 78; 11 rue de la Monnaie; lunch menus €10, other menus €16-19.50; ⏲ lunch Sat & Sun, dinner Tue-Sat, also lunch Tue-Thu mid-May–mid-Sep) For local flavour, you can't top this place, which churns out the house speciality of *fouées*, a pitta-like disc of dough stuffed with pork rillettes, *haricots blancs* (white beans) or goat's cheese.

L'Atelier Gourmand (☎ 02 47 38 59 87; 37 rue Étienne Marcel; menus €20; ⏲ closed Mon) You might not love the eighties-style decor, but there's no quibbling with the food – hunks of roast lamb, green-pepper duck and authentic bouillabaisse (fish chowder), delivered with a modern spin.

Le Zinc (☎ 02 47 20 29 00; 27 place du Grand Marché; menus €20.50-25.50; ⏲ closed Wed & lunch Sun) Simple staples and market-fresh ingredients underpin this buzzy bistro – expect duck breast, beef fillet, river fish served up in a buzzy terracotta-floored dining room.

For all your picnicking needs:

Atac supermarket place du Général Leclerc (5 place du Général Leclerc; ⏲ 7.30am-8pm Mon-Sat); place Jean Jaurès (19 place Jean Jaurès; ⏲ 9am-7.30pm Mon-Sat) The place Jean Jaurès branch is inside the shopping centre.

Les Halles (covered market; place Gaston Pailhou; ⏲ 7am-7pm)

Drinking

Place Plumereau and the surrounding streets are plastered in grungy bars and drinking dens.

Bistro 64 (64 rue du Grand Marché; ⏲ 11am-2am Mon-Sat) Cosy neighbourhood that's one step removed from the place Plumereau hustle. Scuffed-up decor, jazz combos and plenty of house beers keep the local crowd happy.

La Canteen (☎ 02 34 74 10 30; 10 rue de la Grosse Tour; ⏲ noon-2.30pm & 7.30-11pm Mon-Sat) Rough stone walls sit alongside leather sofas and chrome artworks at this designer bar. Loads of wines by the glass, including Loire vintages.

Getting There & Away

Aéroport Tours Val de Loire (☎ 02 47 49 37 00; www.tours-aeroport.com), about 5km northeast of Tours, is linked to London's Stansted and Dublin by Ryanair. A shuttle bus (€5) leaves the bus station two hours before and half an hour after each Ryanair flight.

Touraine Fil Vert (☎ 02 47 47 17 18; www.touraine-filvert.com, in French) runs buses to Amboise (35 minutes, 12 daily Monday to Saturday) and Chenonceaux (1¼ hours, two daily). Single-journey tickets cost a flat-rate €1.50. The bus station has an **information desk** (☎ 02 47 05 30 49; place du Général Leclerc; ⏲ 7am-7pm Mon-Sat).

Tours is the Loire's main rail hub. The train station is linked to St-Pierre-des-Corps, Tours' TGV train station, by frequent shuttle trains. Trains run at least hourly between Tours and Orléans (€16.60, one to 1½ hours), stopping at Amboise (€4.60, 20 minutes) and Blois (€9.10, 40 minutes). High-speed TGVs rocket to Paris-Gare Montparnasse (€39.10 to €55.10, 1¼ hours, around 15 daily), Bordeaux (€45, 2¾ hours), Poitiers (€18.50 to €20.40, one hour) and Nantes (€25 to €26.90, 1½ hours).

AROUND TOURS

Tours is an excellent base for exploring the nearby chateaux – contact the tourist office for details of *son et lumières* and other summer spectacles.

The 16th-century **Château de Chenonceau** (☎ 02 47 23 90 07; www.chenonceau.com; adult/student & 7-18yr €10/7.50, incl audio guide €14/11.50; ⏲ 9am-8pm Jul-Aug, 9am-7.30pm Jun & Sep, 9am-7pm Apr & May, 9.30am-5pm or 6pm rest of year) is one of the most architecturally attractive (and busiest) of the Loire chateaux, surrounded by a glassy moat and sweeping gardens, and topped by turrets and towers. The highlight is the stunning 60m-long Grande Gallerie spanning the Cher River.

Built in the 1500s on an island in the River Indre, **Azay-le-Rideau** (☎ 02 47 45 42 04; adult/18-25yr €7.50/4.80; ⏲ 9.30am-7pm Jul & Aug, 9.30am-6pm Apr-Jun & Sep, 10am-12.30pm & 2-5.30pm Oct-Mar) is another moat-ringed wonder, decorated with geometric windows, ordered turrets and decorative stonework, as well as a famous loggia staircase.

For medieval atmosphere, head for **Château de Langeais** (☎ 02 47 96 72 60; adult/under 10yr/10-17yr €7.50/free/4; ⏲ 9.30am-7pm Jul & Aug, to 6.30pm Feb-Jun & Sep–mid-Nov, 10am-5pm mid-Nov-Jan), complete with its own working drawbridge, crenellated battlements and ruined 10th-century donjon (keep), thought to be the oldest in France.

CHATEAUX TOURS

If you're visiting several chateaux, the **Pass'-Châteaux** is available from local tourist offices in several combinations: sample prices include Chambord–Cheverny–Blois for €19, while Blois–Cheverny–Chaumont–Chambord is €25.20.

If you're short on time, several operators also offer minibus trips: half-day trips cost between €18 and €33; full-day trips range from €40 to €50 including lunch (chateau admission is usually extra).

Acco-Dispo (☎ 06 82 00 64 51; www.accodispo-tours.com)
Alienor (☎ 02 47 61 22 23, 06 10 85 35 39; www.locationdevelos.com)
Quart de Tours (☎ 06 85 72 16 22; www.quartdetours.com)
St-Eloi Excursions (☎ 02 47 37 08 04; www.saint-eloi.com)

AMBOISE

pop 11,500

The childhood home of Charles VIII and the final resting place of the great Leonardo da Vinci, upmarket Amboise is an elegant provincial town, perched along the Loire and overlooked by its fortified 15th-century chateau. Da Vinci whiled away his last three years under the patronage of François I; you can view his former home and many of his wackiest contraptions at the mansion of Clos Lucé.

Information

Laundrette (7 allée du Sergent Turpin; 🕑 7am-8pm)
Playconnect (119 rue Nationale; per hr €3; 🕑 3-10pm Sun & Mon, 10am-10pm Tue-Sat) Internet access.
Post office (20 quai du Général de Gaulle)
Tourist office (☎ 02 47 57 09 28; www.amboise-valdeloire.com; 🕑 9am-8pm Mon-Sat & 10am-6pm Sun Jul & Aug, 10am-1pm & 2-6pm Mon-Sat, 10am-1pm Sun Apr-Jun & Sep, 10am-1pm & 2-6pm Mon-Sat Oct-Mar) Sells walking and cycling maps and a discount ticket for the chateau and Clos Lucé.

Sights

The **Château Royal d'Amboise** (☎ 02 47 57 00 98; place Michel Debré; adult/7-14yr/15-25yr €9/5.30/7.50; 🕑 9am-7pm Jul & Aug, 9am-6.30pm Apr-Jun, 9am-6pm Sep & Oct, 9am-5.30pm Mar & early Nov, 9am-12.30pm Jan, Feb & mid-Nov–Dec) sprawls on a rocky bluff above town. Charles VIII (r 1483–98) was born and brought up here, and was responsible for the chateau's Italianate remodelling in 1492. Today, just a few of the original 15th- and 16th-century structures survive, notably the **Flamboyant Gothic wing** and the **Chapelle St-Hubert**, believed to be the final resting place of da Vinci. The circular **Tour Hurtault** features an ingenious sloping spiral ramp designed for easy carriage access.

Leonardo da Vinci installed himself at nearby **Clos Lucé** (☎ 02 47 57 00 73; www.vinci-closluce.com; 2 rue du Clos Lucé; adult/6-15yr/student Mar–mid-Nov €12.50/7/9.50, mid-Nov–Mar €9.50/6/7; 🕑 9am-8pm Jul-Aug, 9am-7pm Feb-Jun & Sep-Oct, 9am-6pm Nov-Jan) in 1516 on the invitation of François I. The house and landscaped grounds feature scale models of many of his inventions, including a protoautomobile, tank, parachute, hydraulic turbine and even a primitive helicopter.

Sleeping

Camping Municipal de l'Île d'Or (☎ 02 47 57 23 37; Île d'Or; camp sites adult €2.45-2.50, tent €3.25-3.30; 🕑 mid-Mar–early Oct; 🏊) Pleasant camping ground on a peaceful river island, with tennis courts, ping pong and canoe hire.

Centre Charles Péguy-Auberge de Jeunesse (☎ 02 47 30 60 90; www.mjcamboise.fr; Île d'Or; dm €12; 🕑 reception 2-8pm Mon-Fri, 5-8pm weekend; 💻) Efficient boarding school–style hostel on the Île d'Or, with 72 beds mostly in three- or four-bed dorms, and treats including table football and bike hire.

Hotel Blason (☎ 02 47 23 22 41; www.leblason.fr; 11 place Richelieu; d €44-58, tr €66-68; 💻) Quirky, creaky budget hotel, on a quiet square in a wood-fronted building that previously served as a convent school, laundry and blacksmith's. The 25 higgledy-piggledy rooms are titchy, flowery and timber-beamed.

Villa Mary (☎ 02 47 23 03 31; www.villa-mary.fr; 14 rue de la Concorde; d €60-120) Four tip-top rooms in an impeccably furnished 18th-century town house, crammed with beeswaxed antiques, glittering chandeliers and antique rugs. Choose from red, violet, pink and blue rooms, all with period pieces and patterned wallpaper.

Eating

Café des Arts (☎/fax 02 47 57 25 04; 32 rue Victor Hugo; meals €4-12) Spit-and-sawdust local's bar, dishing up beer and bar snacks near the chateau's old gate.

Bigot (☎ 02 47 57 59 32; 2 rue Nationale; 9am-7.30pm Tue-Fri, 8.30am-7.30pm Sat & Sun) Since 1913 this award-winning chocolatier and *pâtisserie* has been whipping up some of the Loire's creamiest cakes and gooiest treats: multicoloured *macarrons*, buttery biscuits and handmade *petits fours*.

Chez Bruno (☎ 02 47 57 73 49; place Michel Debré; 2-/3-course menus €11/15; lunch Wed-Sun, dinner Fri & Sat) Amboise's new boy uncorks a host of local vintages in a coolly contemporary setting (white tablecloths, big gleaming glasses, snazzy artwork), accompanied by honest regional cooking.

L'Épicerie (☎ 02 47 57 08 94; 46 place Michel Debré; menus €20.90-30.90; Wed-Sun) At the Grocery, rich wood and neo-Renaissance decor is matched by filling fare such as *cuisse de lapin* (rabbit leg) and *tournedos de canard* (duck fillet).

Amboise's excellent outdoor **food market** (8am-1pm Fri & Sun) fills the riverbank car parks west of the tourist office. There's also a **Marché Plus** (5 quai du Général de Gaulle; 7am-9pm Mon-Sat, 10am-2pm Sun).

Getting There & Away

Touraine Fil Vert's line C1 links Amboise's post office with Tours (€1.50, 45 minutes, nine daily Monday to Saturday). One bus continues on to Chenonceaux (15 minutes) from Monday to Saturday, with an extra afternoon bus in the summer.

The **train station** (blvd Gambetta) is served by trains from Paris' Gare d'Austerlitz (€24.20, 2¼ to three hours, 11 daily), Blois (€5.60, 20 minutes, 10 to 20 daily) and Tours (€4.50, 15 minutes, 10 to 20 daily).

Hire mountain bikes at **Cycles Richard** (☎ 02 47 57 01 79; 2 rue de Nazelles; per day €15; 9am-noon & 2.30-7pm Tue-Sat).

BURGUNDY & THE RHÔNE VALLEY

If there's one place in France where you're really going to find out what makes the nation tick, it's Burgundy. Two of the country's enduring passions – food and wine – come together in this gorgeously rural region, and if you're a sucker for hearty food and the fruits of the vine, you'll be in seventh heaven.

DIJON

pop 230,000

Filled with elegant medieval and Renaissance buildings, dashing Dijon is the region's lively capital, as well as the spiritual home of French mustard. The city makes an excellent launch pad for exploring wider Burgundy, and a population of some 25,000 students keeps the nightlife snappy.

Orientation

Dijon's main thoroughfare, known for much of its length as rue de la Liberté, stretches from the train station eastwards to the Palais des Ducs and Église St-Michel. The main shopping precinct is around rue de la Liberté and perpendicular rue du Bourg. The focal point of the Old Town is place François Rude.

Information

Cyberbisey (☎ 03 80 30 95 41; 53 rue Berbisey; per hr €3; 10am-8pm Mon-Fri, noon-8pm Sat) Internet access.

Cyberspace 21 (☎ 03 80 30 57 43; 46 rue Monge; per hr €4; 11am-midnight Mon-Sat, 2pm-midnight Sun & holidays) Internet access.

Laundrettes rue Auguste Comte (41 rue Auguste Comte; 6am-9pm); 28 rue Berbisey (28 rue Berbisey; 6am-9pm); rue Berbisey (55 rue Berbisey; 7am-8.30pm); place de la Banque (8 place de la Banque; 7am-8.30pm)

Main post office (place Grangier) Exchanges foreign currency.

Tourist office (☎ 08 92 70 05 58; www.dijon-tourism.com; 11 rue des Forges; 9am-7pm Mon-Sat, 9am-12.30pm & 2.30-5pm Sun & holidays May-Oct, 10am-noon & 2-6pm Mon-Sat, 2.30-5.30pm Sun & holidays Nov-Apr). *The Owl's Trail* (€2.50), available in 11 languages, details a self-guided city-centre walking tour (follow the bronze triangles). The Dijon Côte de Nuits Pass (one/two/three days €18/32/48) saves some cash.

Tourist office annexe (place Darcy; 9am-12.30pm & 2.30-6pm Mon-Sat, 2-6pm Sun & holidays May-Oct, 10am-12.30pm & 2.30-6pm Mon-Sat Nov-Apr)

Sights & Activities

MEDIEVAL & RENAISSANCE ARCHITECTURE

Once home to the region's rulers, the elaborate **Palais des Ducs et des États de Bourgogne** complex lies at the heart of old Dijon. The eastern wing houses the Musée des Beaux-Arts. The 15th-century **Tour Philippe le Bon** (☎ 03 80 74 52 71; adult/under 12yr/student & over 65yr €2.30/free/1.20; accompanied climbs every 45min 9am-noon & 1.45-5.30pm Easter–late Nov, 9-11am & 1.30-3.30pm Wed afternoon, Sat & Sun late Nov-Easter) affords fantastic views over the city from the top of the tower.

FRANCE

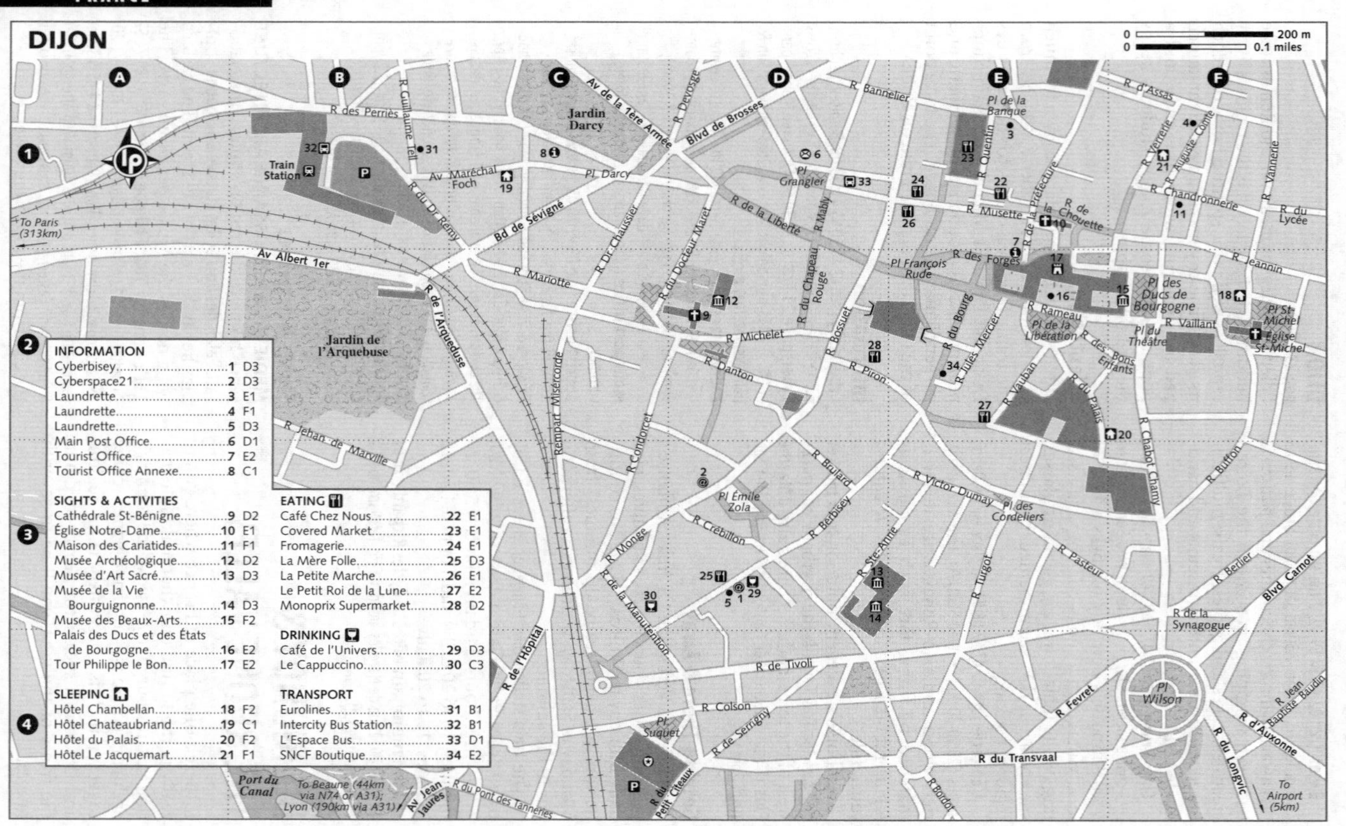
DIJON
0 200 m
0 0.1 miles
INFORMATION
Cyberbisey 1 D3
Cyberspace21 2 D3
Laundrette 3 E1
Laundrette 4 F1
Laundrette 5 D3
Main Post Office 6 D1
Tourist Office 7 E2
Tourist Office Annexe 8 C1
SIGHTS & ACTIVITIES
Cathédrale St-Bénigne 9 D2
Église Notre-Dame 10 E1
Maison des Cariatides 11 F1
Musée Archéologique 12 D2
Musée d'Art Sacré 13 D3
Musée de la Vie Bourguignonne 14 D3
Musée des Beaux-Arts 15 F2
Palais des Ducs et des États de Bourgogne 16 E2
Tour Philippe le Bon 17 E2
SLEEPING
Hôtel Chambellan 18 F2
Hôtel Chateaubriand 19 C1
Hôtel du Palais 20 F2
Hôtel Le Jacquemart 21 F1
EATING
Café Chez Nous 22 E1
Covered Market 23 E1
Fromagerie 24 E1
La Mère Folle 25 D3
La Petite Marche 26 E1
Le Petit Roi de la Lune 27 E2
Monoprix Supermarket 28 D2
DRINKING
Café de l'Univers 29 D3
Le Cappuccino 30 C3
TRANSPORT
Eurolines 31 B1
Intercity Bus Station 32 B1
L'Espace Bus 33 D1
SNCF Boutique 34 E2
To Paris (313km)
Train Station
Jardin Darcy
Jardin de l'Arquebuse
Pl Darcy
Pl Grangier
Pl Émile Zola
Pl François Rude
Pl de la Libération
Pl des Ducs de Bourgogne
Pl du Théâtre
Pl St-Michel
Église St-Michel
Pl de la Banque
Pl des Cordeliers
Pl Wilson
Pl Suquet
Port du Canal
To Beaune (44km via N74 or A31); Lyon (190km via A31)
To Airport (5km)
Av Albert 1er
R de l'Arquebuse
Bd de Sévigné
Av Maréchal Foch
R du Dr Remy
R Guillaume Tell
R des Perriès
Av de la 1ère Armée
Blvd de Brosses
R Devosge
R de la Liberté
R du Docteur Maret
R Dr Chaussier
R Mariotte
R Michelet
R Danton
R Condorcet
Rempart Miséricorde
R Jehan de Marville
R de l'Hôpital
R Monge
R de la Manutention
R Crébillon
R Berbisey
R Brulard
R Victor Dumay
R Ste-Anne
R Piron
R Bossuet
R du Chapeau Rouge
R Mably
R Bannelier
R Musette
R Quentin
R de la Préfecture
R de la Chouette
R des Forges
R Jules Mercier
R du Bourg
R Vauban
R Rameau
R des Bons Enfants
R du Palais
R Chabot Chamy
R Vaillant
R Jeannin
R Chandronnerie
R Verrerie
R Auguste Comte
R d'Assas
R Vannerie
R du Lycée
R Buffon
Blvd Carnot
R Berlier
R de la Synagogue
R Pasteur
R Turgot
R Fevret
R du Transvaal
R Bordot
R de Tivoli
R Colson
R de Serrigny
R du Petit Cîteaux
R du Longvic
R d'Auxonne
R Jean Baptiste Baudin
Av Jean Jaurès
R du Pont des Tanneries

Many of Dijon's finest **hôtels particuliers** are situated north of the Palais des Ducs on and around rues Verrerie, Vannerie and des Forges. The 17th-century **Maison des Cariatides** (28 rue Chandronnerie) is particularly impressive.

CHURCHES

A little way north of the Palais des Ducs, the decorative **Église Notre-Dame** was built between 1220 and 1240. The facade's three tiers are decorated with leering gargoyles and an elaborate clock, the **Horloge à Jacquemart**. Outside, rue de la Chouette is named after the small stone *chouette* (owl) carved into the north wall of the church, said to grant happiness and wisdom to those who stroke it.

Built over the tomb of St Benignus (believed to have brought Christianity to Burgundy in the 2nd century), Dijon's Burgundian Gothic-style **Cathédrale St-Bénigne** (9am-7pm) was built around 1300 as an abbey church.

All of Dijon's major churches are open from 8am to 7pm.

MUSEUMS

Dijon's municipal museums are free except during special exhibitions.

Housed in the Palais des Ducs, the **Musée des Beaux-Arts** (03 80 74 52 09; audio guide €3.90; 9.30am-6pm Wed-Mon May-Oct, 10am-5pm Wed-Mon Nov-Apr) has an enormously varied collection ranging from medieval paintings to sculptures by the Dijon-born artist François Rude (1784–1855) and a modern section (closed 11.30am–1.45pm) featuring Manet and Monet. You can also visit the **ducal kitchens** and the wood-panelled **Salle des Gardes** (Guards' Room), containing the medieval sepulchres of two Valois dukes.

The **Musée Archéologique** (03 80 30 88 54; 5 rue du Dr Maret; 9am-12.30pm & 1.30-6pm Wed-Sun, also open Mon mid-May–Sep) displays Celtic, Roman and Merovingian artefacts, including a 1st-century bronze of the goddess Sequana standing on a boat.

The **Musée de la Vie Bourguignonne** (03 80 44 12 69; 17 rue Ste-Anne; 9am-noon & 2-6pm Wed-Mon) explores village and town life in Burgundy in centuries gone by. Nearby, the **Musée d'Art Sacré** (03 80 44 12 69; 15 rue Ste-Anne; 9am-noon & 2-6pm Wed-Mon) displays ritual objects from the 12th to 19th centuries inside the convent's copper-domed chapel (1709).

PARKS

Dijon has plenty of green spaces including **Jardin de l'Arquebuse**, whose stream, pond and formal gardens are across the tracks from the train station.

Sleeping

Hôtel Chambellan (03 80 67 12 67; www.hotel-chambellan.com; 92 rue Vannerie; s/d with washbasin €29/32, with private bathroom from €43/48) Built in 1730, this two-star place has a vaguely medieval feel. Most rooms, decorated in cheerful tones of red, orange, pink and white, have courtyard views.

Hôtel Le Jacquemart (03 80 60 09 60; www.hotel-lejacquemart.fr; 32 rue Verrerie; s/d with washbasin €29/32, d with private bathroom €52-62;) In the heart of old Dijon, this two-star hotel has tidy, comfortable rooms; the pricier ones come with fireplaces.

Hôtel Chateaubriand (03 80 41 42 18; www.hotelchateaubriand.fr, in French; 3 av Maréchal Foch; d with washbasin €36, with private bathroom €41-46) An old-style cheapie, this 23-room place has the air of a well-worn dive but has far more character than the sterile chain hotels down the block.

Hôtel du Palais (03 80 67 16 26; www.hoteldupalais-dijon.com; 23 rue du Palais; d €44-68, q €83) A two-star place in a 17th-century *hôtel particulier*. The 13 rooms are spacious and welcoming and the public spaces exude old-fashioned charm. The breakfast room has an 18th-century painted coffered ceiling.

Eating

Café Chez Nous (03 80 50 12 98; impasse Quentin; lunch noon-2pm, bar 10am-2am, closed Mon to 2pm & Sun) Quintessentially French *bar du coin* (neighbourhood bar) down an alleyway from the market. The decor's scruffy, the grub's solid, and fine wine's served by the glass. On Monday evenings a customer sometimes cooks dinner for everyone – sign up on the chalkboard.

La Mère Folle (03 80 50 19 76; 102 rue Berbisey; lunch menus €10, other menus €15-23; closed Tue, lunch Sat & lunch Wed) This Burgundian bistro is crammed with character, from the gilded wall mirrors to the pineapple-shaped table lamps. Specialities include *magret de canard au miel, thym et mirabelles* (fillet of duck with honey, thyme and cherry plums; €13).

La Petite Marche (03 80 30 15 10; 27-29 rue Musette; menus €10.50-14; lunch Mon-Sat) An organic restaurant with loads of salads and veggie options, which make a welcome change from heavy Burgundian classics.

WORTH THE TRIP: CÔTE D'OR VINEYARDS

Burgundy's most renowned vintages come from the Côte d'Or (Golden Hillside), a range of hills made of limestone, flint and clay that runs south from Dijon for about 60km. The northern section, the **Côte de Nuits**, stretches from Marsannay-la-Côte south to Corgoloin and produces reds known for their robust, full-bodied character. The southern section, the **Côte de Beaune**, lies between Ladoix-Serrigny and Santenay and produces great reds and great whites.

Tourist offices can provide local brochures: *The Burgundy Wine Road*, an excellent free booklet published by the Burgundy Tourist Board (www.bourgogne-tourisme.com); and a useful map, *Roadmap to the Wines of Burgundy* (€0.50). There's also the **Route des Grands Crus** (www.road-of-the-fine-burgundy-wines.com), a signposted road route of some of the most celebrated Côte de Nuits vineyards.

Wine & Voyages (☎ 03 80 61 15 15; www.wineandvoyages.com; 2-/3hr tours €55/65; ⏰ Mon-Sat Mar–mid-Dec) runs minibus tours in English; reserve online or at the Dijon tourist office. Reservations for **Safari Tours** (www.burgundy-tourism-safaritours.com) and **Vinea Tours** (www.vineatours.com) are handled by the Beaune Tourist Office – tours cost €34 to €43.

our pick **Le Petit Roi de la Lune** (☎ 03 80 49 89 93; 28 rue Amiral Roussin; lunch menus €13.80; ⏰ closed Sun & lunch Mon) 'The Little King of the Moon' specialises in reinvented French cuisine – expect imaginative dishes such as *Camembert frit avec gelée de mûre* (breadcrumbed Camembert served with blackberry jelly; €9.80) and the bizarrely brilliant *aiguillettes de canard au Coca Cola* (duck strips in a Coca-Cola sauce; €14.90).

For self-caterers:

Covered Market (Halles du Marché; rue Quentin; ⏰ 7am-1pm, Tue & Thu-Sat) A huge market on Fridays and Saturdays, with a smaller version on Tuesdays and Thursdays.

Fromagerie (28 rue Musette; ⏰ 6am or 7am-12.30pm or 1pm & 2.30-7pm, no midday closure Fri & Sat, closed Mon morning & Sun) A friendly, top-quality cheese shop.

Monoprix supermarket (11-13 rue Piron; ⏰ 9am-8.45pm Mon-Sat)

Drinking & Entertainment

For the latest on Dijon's cultural scene, pick up the free zine *Spectacles*. Dijon's club scene centres on place de la République, and there are wall-to-wall bars along rue Berbisey.

Le Cappuccino (☎ 03 80 41 06 35; 132 rue Berbisey; ⏰ 5pm-2am Mon-Sat) Previously a coffee bar, this nightspot now focuses on wine by the glass and a varied selection of 80 beers, including Mandubienne, Dijon's local brew.

Café de l'Univers (☎ 03 80 30 98 29; 47 rue Berbisey; ⏰ 5pm-2am) Mirrors and beer ads cover the walls of this ground-floor bar. There's live music between 9pm and 1am on Friday and Saturday.

Getting There & Away

Dijon-Bourgogne airport (☎ 03 80 67 67 67; www.dijon.aeroport.fr), 5km southeast of the city centre, is currently only used by domestic flights.

Trains run from Dijon to Paris' Gare de Lyon (€43.40 to €54.10 by TGV, 1¾ hours, 10 to 14 daily, most frequent in the early morning and evening), Lyon–Part Dieu (€25.10, two hours, 11 to 19 daily), Nice (€79.10 to €91.30 by TGV, 6¼ hours, two direct daily) and Strasbourg (€38.90, 3½ hours, three or four nondirect daily). There's a city-centre **SNCF Boutique** (55 rue du Bourg; ⏰ 12.30-7pm Mon, 10am-7pm Tue-Sat).

Buses run from outside the train station. An **information and ticket counter** (⏰ 5.45am-9pm Sun-Thu, to 9.30pm Fri, 8pm Sat) deals with TER trains and regional Transco buses: bus 60 (18 to 21 daily Monday to Friday, 10 Saturday, two Sunday) links Dijon with the northern Côte de Nuits wine villages. Other Transco buses travel to various destinations around Burgundy.

International bus travel is handled by **Eurolines** (☎ 03 80 68 20 44; 53 rue Guillaume Tell; ⏰ Mon-Fri & Sat morning).

Getting Around

Details on Dijon's bus network, operated by Divia, are available at **L'Espace Bus** (☎ 08 00 10 20 04; www.divia.fr, in French; place Grangier; ⏰ 7.30am-6.45pm Mon-Fri, 8.30am-6.30pm Sat). Single tickets cost €0.95 and are valid for an hour; a Forfait Journée ticket (€3.20) is available from the tourist office or L'Espace Bus.

The tourist office rents mountain bikes year-round for €12/18 per half-/full day, €50 for three days, or you can rent city bikes from 33 automated sites, run by **Velodi** (☎ 08 00 20 03 05; www.velodi.net, in French), around town.

BEAUNE

pop 21,300

Beaune (pronounced 'bone'), 44km south of Dijon, is the unofficial capital of the Côte d'Or. This thriving town's raison d'être is wine – making it, tasting it, selling it, but most of all, drinking it. Consequently Beaune is one of the best places in all of France for wine tasting. The jewel of Beaune's old city is the magnificent Hôtel-Dieu, France's most splendiferous medieval charity hospital.

Orientation

The old city, enclosed by ramparts and a stream, is encircled by a one-way boulevard with seven names. The tourist office and the commercial centre are about 1km west of the train station.

Information

Laundrettes rue du Faubourg St-Jean (19 rue du Faubourg St-Jean; 🕑 6am-9pm); rue de Lorraine (63 rue de Lorraine; 🕑 7am-9pm)

Le Clos Carnot (☎ 03 80 22 73 43; 34 place Carnot; per hr €3; 🕑 8am-midnight) A cafe-brasserie with two internet computers.

Post office (7 blvd St-Jacques) Currency exchange.

Tourist office (☎ 03 80 26 21 30; www.beaune-burgundy.com; 6 blvd Perpreuil; 🕑 9am-7pm Mon-Sat, 9am-6pm Sun Easter–mid-Nov, 9am-12.30pm & 1.30-6pm Mon-Sat, 10am-12.30pm & 1.30-5pm Sun mid-Nov–Easter) Has an internet computer (per 15 minutes €1.50) and sells the Pass Beaune, offering discounts on local attractions.

Sights & Activities

Founded in 1443, the celebrated Gothic **Hôtel-Dieu des Hospices de Beaune** (☎ 03 80 24 45 00; rue de l'Hôtel-Dieu; adult/under 18yr/student €6/2.80/4.80; 🕑 tickets sold 9am-6.30pm Easter–mid-Nov, 9am-11.30am & 2-5.30pm mid-Nov–Easter, interior closes 1hr later) is topped by ornate turrets and pitched rooftops covered in multicoloured tiles. Interior highlights include the barrel-vaulted **Grande Salle**; an 18th-century **pharmacy** lined with flasks once filled with powders such as *beurre d'antimoine* (antimony butter) and *poudre de cloportes* (woodlouse powder); and the brilliant **Polyptych of the Last Judgement** by the Flemish painter Roger van der Weyden, depicting Judgment Day in glorious technicolour.

Underneath Beaune's streets, millions of dusty bottles of wine are being aged to perfection in cool, dark, cobweb-lined cellars. You can visit several local cellars on a wine tour, including the **Marché aux Vins** (☎ 03 80 25 08 20; www.marcheauxvins.com, in French; 2 rue Nicolas Rolin; admission €10; 🕑 9.30-11.30am & 2-5.30pm, no midday closure mid-Jun–Aug), where you'll taste 15 wines from a special *tastevin* cup, and **Patriarche Père et Fils** (☎ 03 80 24 53 78; www.patriarche.com; 5 rue du Collège; audio guide tours €10; 🕑 9.30-11.30am & 2-5.30pm), the largest cellars in Burgundy, lined with 3 million to 5 million bottles of wine.

Sleeping

Campground (☎ 03 80 22 03 91; campinglescentvignes@mairie-beaune.fr; 10 rue Auguste Dubois; camp sites per adult/tent €3.60/4.35; 🕑 mid-Mar–Oct) A flowery, four-star camping ground 700m north of the centre.

Hôtel Rousseau (☎ 03 80 22 13 59; 11 place Madeleine; s/d with washbasin from €30/38, d with private bathroom €55, all incl breakfast) An endearingly old-fashioned, 12-room hotel run since 1959 by a friendly lady *d'un certain âge*. Reception occasionally shuts without warning so she can go shopping. A hall shower costs €3.

Hôtel de la Cloche (☎ 03 80 24 66 33; www.hotel-cloche-beaune.com; 40-42 rue du Faubourg Madeleine; d €57-98; ❄) The 32 rooms at this veteran three-star establishment mix classic decor with contemporary comfort.

Abbaye de Maizières (☎ 03 80 24 74 64; www.beaune-abbaye-maizieres.com; 19 rue Maizières; d €77-107, ste €133-149) An idiosyncratic hotel inside a 12th-century abbey whose 13 tastefully converted rooms feature old brickwork and ancient wooden beams.

Hôtel des Remparts (☎ 03 80 24 94 94; www.hotel-remparts-beaune.com; 48 rue Thiers; d €92-108, low season €79-95, ste €116-150; ❄ 💻) Set around two courtyards, this 17th-century town house has 22 rooms with red-tile floors, antique furniture and luxurious bathrooms.

Eating

Cafes and restaurants surround place Carnot, place Félix Ziem and place Madeleine.

Caves Madeleine (☎ 03 80 22 93 30; 8 rue du Faubourg Madeleine; menus €12-22; 🕑 closed Thu, Sun & lunch Fri) A convivial Burgundian restaurant, where locals share tables for regional classics such as boeuf bourguignon, *cassolette d'escargots* (snail casserole) and *jambon persillé* (jellied ham).

Le Bistrot Bourguignon (☎ 03 80 22 23 24; www.restaurant-lebistrotbourguignon.com; 8 rue Monge; lunch menus €12.90; closed Sun & Mon) A cosy bistro-style restaurant that serves good-value cuisine billed as *régionale et originale* and 17 Burgundies by the glass (€2.60 to €7).

Le P'tit Paradis (☎ 03 80 24 91 00; 25 rue Paradis; lunch menus €18, other menus €27-35; closed Sun & Mon) An intimate restaurant on a medieval street, known for *cuisine elaborée* (creative cuisine) made with local products.

Ma Cuisine (☎ 03 80 22 30 22; passage Ste-Hélène; menus €22; 12.15-1.30pm & 7.30-9pm Mon, Tue, Thu & Fri, closed Aug) A low-key, 13-table place hidden down an alley. The traditional French and Burgundian dishes include *pigeon de Bresse entier rôti au jus* (whole Bresse pigeon; €32). The wine list includes 850 vintages (€18 to €830).

The covered market hall at place de la Halle hosts a **food market** (to 12.30pm Sat) and a much smaller **marché gourmand** (gourmet market; Wed morning).

Alain Hess Fromager (7 place Carnot; 9am-12.15pm & 2.30-7.15pm Mon-Sat, plus 10am-1pm Sun Easter–Dec) Fine cheeses.

Casino supermarket (28 rue du Faubourg Madeleine; 8.30am-7.30pm Mon-Sat, 9am-noon Sun) Through an archway on rue du Faubourg Madeleine.

Getting There & Away

Bus 44, run by **Transco** (☎ 08 00 10 20 04) travels to Dijon (€6.30, one hour, seven Monday to Friday, six Saturday, two Sunday and holidays), stopping at Côte d'Or wine-growing villages such as Vougeot, Nuits-St-Georges and Aloxe-Corton. Some line 44 buses also serve villages south of Beaune, including Pommard, Volnay, Meursault and La Rochepot.

Beaune has frequent trains to Dijon (€6.50, 25 minutes, 25 to 40 daily) via Nuits-St-Georges (€3, 10 minutes), Paris' Gare de Lyon (€50.50 to €62.40, two direct TGVs daily) and Lyon–Part Dieu (€21.60, 1¾ hours, 11 to 17 daily).

LYON

pop 467,400

Gourmets, eat your heart out: Lyon is *the* gastronomic capital of France, with a lavish table of piggy-driven dishes and delicacies to savour. The city has been a commercial, industrial and banking powerhouse for the past 500 years, and is still France's second-largest conurbation, with outstanding art museums, a dynamic nightlife, green parks and a Unesco-listed Old Town.

Information

AOC Exchange (20 rue Gasparin, 2e; 9.30am-6.30pm Mon-Sat; M Bellecour) Currency exchange.

Laverie de la Fresque (1 rue de la Martinière, 1er; 6am-10pm; M Hôtel de Ville)

Post office (10 place Antonin Poncet, 2e; M Bellecour)

Raconte-Moi La Terre (☎ 04 78 92 60 22; www.raconte-moi.com; 38 rue Thomassin, 2e; per hr €4; 10am-7.30pm Mon-Sat; M Cordeliers) Stylish surfing in the 1st-floor cafe of a travel bookshop.

Tourist office (☎ 04 72 77 69 69; www.lyon-france.com; place Bellecour, 2e; 9am-6pm; M Bellecour)

Sights

VIEUX LYON

Old Lyon, with its cobblestone streets and **medieval and Renaissance houses** below Fourvière hill, is divided into three quarters: St-Paul at the northern end, St-Jean in the middle and St-Georges in the south. Lovely old buildings languish on **rue du Bœuf**, **rue St-Jean** and **rue des Trois Maries**. The partly Romanesque **Cathédrale St-Jean** (place St-Jean, 5e; 8am-noon & 2-7.30pm Mon-Fri, 8am-noon & 2-7pm Sat & Sun; M Vieux Lyon), seat of Lyon's 133rd bishop, was built from the late 11th to the early 16th centuries. The **astronomical clock** chimes at noon, 2pm, 3pm and 4pm.

FOURVIÈRE

Over two millennia ago, the Romans built the city of Lugdunum on the slopes of Fourvière. Today, Lyon's 'hill of prayer' – topped by a basilica and the **Tour Métallique**, an Eiffel Tower–like structure built in 1893 and used as a TV transmitter – affords spectacular views of the city and its two rivers. Footpaths wind uphill but the funicular departing from place Édouard Commette is the least taxing way up; a return ticket costs €2.20.

Crowning the hill is the 27m-high **Basilique Notre Dame de Fourvière** (☎ 04 78 25 86 19; www.fourviere.org; 7am-7pm), a superb example of exaggerated 19th-century ecclesiastical architecture. **Rooftop tours** (adult/under 12yr €5/3; 2.30pm & 4pm daily Jun-Sep, 2.30pm & 4pm Wed & Sun Apr, May & Oct, 2.30pm & 3.30pm Wed & Sun Nov) climax on the stone-sculpted roof, although the **Tour de l'Observatoire** (Observatory Tower) is closed for a €5m restoration.

Sacred treasures are showcased in the **Musée d'Art Religieux** (☎ 04 78 25 13 01; 8 place de Fourvière, 5e; adult/under 26yr €6/4; 10am-12.30pm & 2-5.30pm daily; M Fourvière funicular station), while Gallo-Roman artefacts take centre stage at

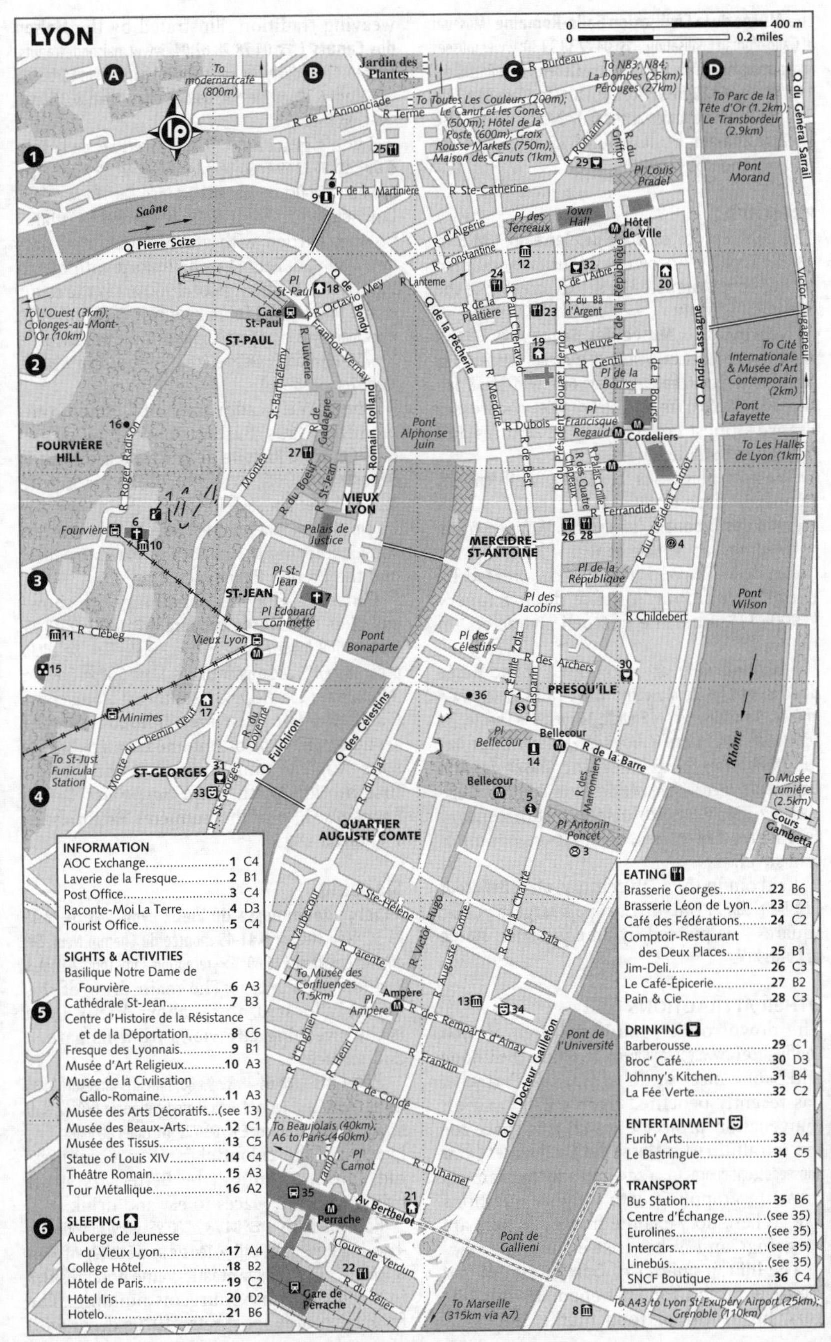
LYON
0 400 m
0 0.2 miles
A
B
C
D
1
2
3
4
5
6
Jardin des Plantes
To modernartcafé (800m)
R Burdeau
To NB3; N84; La Dombes (25km); Pérouges (27km)
To Parc de la Tête d'Or (1.2km); Le Transbordeur (2.9km)
Q du Général Sarrail
R de L'Annonciade
R Terme
To Toutes Les Couleurs (200m); Le Canut et les Gones (500m); Hôtel de la Poste (600m); Croix Rousse Markets (750m); Maison des Canuts (1km)
R Romarin
R du Griffon
Pl Louis Pradel
Pont Morand
R de la Martinière
R Ste-Catherine
Saône
Q Pierre Scize
Pl des Terreaux
Town Hall
Hôtel de Ville
R d'Algérie
R Constantine
R Lanterne
R de l'Arbre
Pl St-Paul
Gare St-Paul
R Octavio Mey
Q de Bondy
Q de la Pêcherie
R de la Platière
R Paul Chenavard
R du Bât d'Argent
R de la République
Victor Augagneur
To L'Ouest (3km); Colonges-au-Mont-D'Or (10km)
ST-PAUL
R Juiverie
Franhois Vernay
R Neuve
R Gentil
Pl de la Bourse
R de la Bourse
Q André Lassagne
To Cité Internationale & Musée d'Art Contemporain (2km)
R St-Barthélemy
R de Gadagne
Q Romain Rolland
Pont Alphonse Juin
R Mercière
R Dubois
R du Président Édouard Herriot
Pl Francisque Regaud
Cordeliers
Pont Lafayette
To Les Halles de Lyon (1km)
FOURVIÈRE HILL
R Roger Radisson
Montée
R du Boeuf
R St-Jean
VIEUX LYON
R de Brest
R des Quatre Chapeaux
R Palais Grillet
R Ferrandière
R du Président Carnot
Fourvière
Palais de Justice
MERCIDRE-ST-ANTOINE
Pl de la République
Pl St-Jean
ST-JEAN
Pl Édouard Commette
Pl des Jacobins
R Childebert
Pont Wilson
R Clébeg
Vieux Lyon
Pont Bonaparte
Pl des Célestins
R Émile Zola
R des Archers
R Gasparin
PRESQU'ÎLE
Minimes
Monte du Chemin Neuf
R du Doyenné
Q Fulchiron
Q des Célestins
Pl Bellecour
Bellecour
R de la Barre
Rhône
To St-Just Funicular Station
ST-GEORGES
R St-Georges
R du Plat
R des Marronniers
To Musée Lumière (2.5km)
Cours Gambetta
QUARTIER AUGUSTE COMTE
Pl Antonin Poncet
R Ste-Hélène
R Sala
R Vaubecour
R Jarente
R Victor Hugo
R Auguste Comte
R de la Charité
To Musée des Confluences (1.5km)
Pl Ampère
Ampère
R des Remparts d'Ainay
Pont de l'Université
R d'Enghien
R Henri IV
R Franklin
R de Condé
Q du Docteur Gailleton
To Beaujolais (40km); A6 to Paris (460km)
Pl Carnot
R Duhamel
Perrache
Av Berthelot
Pont de Gallieni
Cours de Verdun
R du Bélier
Gare de Perrache
To Marseille (315km via A7)
To A43 to Lyon St-Exupéry Airport (25km); Grenoble (110km)
INFORMATION
AOC Exchange....1 C4
Laverie de la Fresque....2 B1
Post Office....3 C4
Raconte-Moi La Terre....4 D3
Tourist Office....5 C4
SIGHTS & ACTIVITIES
Basilique Notre Dame de Fourvière....6 A3
Cathédrale St-Jean....7 B3
Centre d'Histoire de la Résistance et de la Déportation....8 C6
Fresque des Lyonnais....9 B1
Musée d'Art Religieux....10 A3
Musée de la Civilisation Gallo-Romaine....11 A3
Musée des Arts Décoratifs....(see 13)
Musée des Beaux-Arts....12 C1
Musée des Tissus....13 C5
Statue of Louis XIV....14 C4
Théâtre Romain....15 A3
Tour Métallique....16 A2
SLEEPING
Auberge de Jeunesse du Vieux Lyon....17 A4
Collège Hôtel....18 B2
Hôtel de Paris....19 C2
Hôtel Iris....20 D2
Hotelo....21 B6
EATING
Brasserie Georges....22 B6
Brasserie Léon de Lyon....23 C2
Café des Fédérations....24 C2
Comptoir-Restaurant des Deux Places....25 B1
Jim-Deli....26 C3
Le Café-Épicerie....27 B2
Pain & Cie....28 C3
DRINKING
Barberousse....29 C1
Broc' Café....30 D3
Johnny's Kitchen....31 B4
La Fée Verte....32 C2
ENTERTAINMENT
Furib' Arts....33 A4
Le Bastringue....34 C5
TRANSPORT
Bus Station....35 B6
Centre d'Échange....(see 35)
Eurolines....(see 35)
Intercars....(see 35)
Linebús....(see 35)
SNCF Boutique....36 C4

the **Musée de la Civilisation Gallo-Romaine** (Museum of Gallo-Roman Civilisation; ☎ 04 72 38 39 30; www.musees-gallo-romains.com, in French; 17 rue Cléberg, 5e; adult/under 18yr/18-25yr €3.80/free/2.30, free Thu; 10am-6pm Tue-Sun; M Fourvière funicular station). Next door, the **Théâtre Romain**, built around 15 BC, once sat an audience of 10,000.

PRESQU'ÎLE

The centrepiece of **place des Terreaux** (M Hôtel de Ville) is the 19th-century fountain sculpted by Frédéric-Auguste Bartholdi, creator of the Statue of Liberty.

Nearby, the **Musée des Beaux-Arts** (☎ 04 72 10 17 40; www.mba-lyon.fr; 20 place des Terreaux, 1er; adult/under 18yr €6/free; 10am-6pm Wed, Thu & Sat-Mon, 10.30am-6pm Fri; M Hôtel de Ville) showcases France's finest collection of sculptures and paintings outside Paris.

West of place des Terreaux, well-known Lyonnais peer out from the seven-storey **Fresque des Lyonnais** (cnr rue de la Martinière & quai de la Pêcherie, 1er; M Hôtel de Ville) – look out for the yellow-haired Little Prince, created by Lyon-born author Antoine de St-Exupéry (1900–44), amid the frescoed characters on the wall.

Lyonnais silks are showcased at the **Musée des Tissus** (Textile Museum; ☎ 04 78 38 42 00; www.musee-des-tissus.com, in French; 34 rue de la Charité, 2e; adult/under 16yr/16-25yr €6/free/3.50; 10am-5.30pm Tue-Sun; M Ampère). Next door, the **Musée des Arts Décoratifs** (free with Musée des Tissus ticket; 10am-noon & 2-5.30pm Tue-Sun) displays 18th-century furniture, tapestries, wallpaper, ceramics and silver.

Laid out in the 17th century, **place Bellecour** (M Bellecour) – one of Europe's largest public squares – is pierced by an equestrian **statue of Louis XIV**.

OTHER ATTRACTIONS

The downtrodden industrial area of **Lyon Confluence** (www.lyon-confluence.fr), where the Rhône and Saône meet south of Gare de Perrache, has recently benefited from a €780 million rejuvenation project – watch this space for the ultrafuturistic **Musée des Confluences** (www.museedesconfluences.fr), a science-and-humanities museum grappling with weighty questions like 'Where do we come from?', 'Where are we going?' and 'What are we doing?'.

The hilltop quarter of **Croix Rousse** (M Croix Rousse) is famed for its bohemian inhabitants, lush outdoor food market and silk-weaving tradition, illustrated by the **Maison des Canuts** (☎ 04 78 28 62 04; www.maisondescanuts.com; 10-12 rue d'Ivry, 4e; adult/under 12yr/student €6/free/3; 10am-6.30pm Tue-Sat, guided tours 11am & 3.30pm; M Croix Rousse).

Lyon's graceful 117-hectare **Parc de la Tête d'Or** (☎ 04 72 69 47 60; blvd des Belges, 6e; 6am-11pm mid-Apr–mid-Oct, to 9pm mid-Oct–mid-Apr; M Masséna), landscaped in the 1860s, is graced by a lake, botanic garden with greenhouses, rose garden and zoo. Bus 41 or 47 links it with metro Part-Dieu. Nearby, post-1960 art is the focus of the **Musée d'Art Contemporain** (☎ 04 72 69 17 17; www.moca-lyon.org; 81 quai Charles de Gaulle, 6e; adult/under 18yr/18-25yr/family €8/free/6/10; noon-7pm Wed-Fri, 10am-7pm Sat & Sun).

The WWII headquarters of Gestapo commander Klaus Barbie houses the evocative **Centre d'Histoire de la Résistance et de la Déportation** (CHRD; ☎ 04 78 72 23 11; 14 av Berthelot, 7e; adult/under 18yr/student €4/free/2; 9am-noon & 2-5.30pm Wed-Fri, 9am-6pm Sat & Sun; M Perrache or Jean Macé), exploring the history of Nazi atrocities and the French Resistance.

Cinema's glorious beginnings are showcased at the **Musée Lumière** (☎ 04 78 78 18 95; www.institut-lumiere.org; 25 rue du Premier Film, 8e; adult/under 18yr €6/5, audio guide €3; 11am-6.30pm Tue-Sun; M Monplaisir-Lumière), 3km southeast along cours Gambetta. The museum is housed inside the art nouveau home of Antoine Lumière, whose sons Auguste and Louis shot the world's first motion picture, *La Sortie des Usines Lumières* (Exit of the Lumières Factories) in 19 March 1895.

Sleeping

Auberge de Jeunesse du Vieux Lyon (☎ 04 78 15 05 50; lyon@fuaj.org; 41-45 montée du Chemin Neuf, 5e; dm incl breakfast €16.60; reception 7am-1pm, 2-8pm & 9pm-1am; M Vieux Lyon) The main draw of this superbly located hostel above Vieux Lyon is the sweeping city views from its garden and terrace.

Hôtel Iris (☎ 04 78 39 93 80; hoteliris@freesurf.fr; 36 rue de l'Arbre Sec, 1er; s/d with shared bathroom €40/42, s/d/tr with private bathroom €50/60/72; M Hôtel de Ville) The location of this colourful dame in a centuries-old convent couldn't be better: its street brims with hip places to eat and drink.

Hôtel de Paris (☎ 04 78 28 00 95; www.hoteldeparis-lyon.com; 16 rue de la Platière, 1er; s/d from €48/62; M Hôtel de Ville;) This fantastic-value hotel resides in a 19th-century bourgeois building. The funkiest rooms sport retro 1970s decor with chocolate-and-turquoise or candyfloss-pink colour scheme.

Hotelo (☎ 04 78 37 39 03; www.hotelo-lyon.com; 37 cours de Verdun, 2e; s/d/tr from €79/90/97; M Perrache) Our hot choice around Gare de Perrache, this striking newbie with a refreshingly contemporary design. Studios have a kitchenette and one room is perfectly fitted out for travellers with disabilities.

our pick Collège Hotel (☎ 04 72 10 05 05; www.college-hotel.com; 5 place St-Paul, 5e; d €110-140; M Vieux Lyon;) Superstylish hotel, although those with a dislike of white might not appreciate it. Reception is decked out in warm, ochre tones, while the white minimalism of the bedrooms is dazzling. Enjoy a balcony breakfast, savour the schoolroom-style breakfast room, or lounge on the roof-garden.

Eating

Memorable dining in Lyon is guaranteed, with everything from fast food to fusion cuisine. The traditional place to eat is the *bouchon* (literally meaning 'bottle stopper' or 'traffic jam', but in Lyon a small, friendly bistro).

RESTAURANTS

Le Canut et Les Gones (☎ 04 78 29 17 23; 29 rue de Belfort, 4e; plats du jour €9, lunch/dinner menus €15/35; lunch & dinner Tue-Sat; M Croix Rousse) The culinary experience at this retro bistro attracts a hip, local crowd, and the food is a creative mix of local and French.

Toutes les Couleurs (☎ 04 72 00 03 95; 26 rue Imbert Colomès, 1er; plats du jour €9.50, 2-course menus €13 & €16.50, 3-course menus €18, €21 & €25; lunch Tue-Fri, lunch & dinner Fri & Sat; M Croix-Paquet) Vegetarians in France for a while will be in seventh heaven at this 100% authentic *restaurant bio*. Its exclusively vegetarian, season-driven menu includes *végétalien* (no eggs or dairy products) and gluten-free dishes.

Brasserie Georges (☎ 04 72 56 54 54; www.brasseriegeorges.com; 30 cours de Verdun, 2e; breakfasts €11.50-14, menus €20-25, seafood platters €36.50-66; 8am-11.15pm Sun-Thu, 8am-12.15am Fri & Sat; M Perrache) At this huge art deco brasserie, up to 2000 punters tuck into hearty portions of onion soup, mussels, sauerkraut and seafood.

Brasserie Léon de Lyon (☎ 04 72 10 11 12; www.leondelyon.com; 1 rue Pléney, 1er; plats du jour €15, 2-/3-course menus du jour €23/26; lunch & dinner Mon-Sun; M Hôtel de Ville) Legendary Lyonnais chef Jean-Paul Lacombe has turned his Michelin-starred gastronomic restaurant into a soulful brasserie – same 1904 decor, similar culinary products, more-affordable prices.

Comptoir-Restaurant des Deux Places (☎ 04 78 28 95 10; 5 place Fernand Rey, 1er; lunch/dinner menus €15/28; lunch & dinner Tue-Sat; M Hôtel de Ville) Red-and-white checked curtains, an old-world interior and a menu scribed in black ink contribute to the overwhelmingly traditional feel here. Its tree-shaded pavement terrace is particularly idyllic.

Café des Fédérations (☎ 04 78 28 26 00; www.lesfedeslyon.com, in French; 8 rue Major Martin, 1er; lunch/dinner menus €19.50/24; lunch & dinner Mon-Fri; M Hôtel de Ville) B&W photos of old Lyon speckle the wood-panelled walls of the city's best-known *bouchon*. Feast on *caviar de la Croix Rousse* (lentils in creamy sauce), followed perhaps by an *andouillette* (tripe sausage).

QUICK EATS

Pain & Cie (☎ 04 78 38 29 84; 13-15 rue des Quatre Chapeaux, 2e; salads €3.50-14.50; 7am-10.30pm Mon-Sat, 7am-7pm Sun; M Bellecour) Join the crowds for a well-topped *tartine* (thick toast with topping) or weekend brunch (€9 to €21).

Jim-Deli (☎ 04 78 38 31 67; 14 rue des Quatre Chapeaux, 2e; starters/pasta €8/15; lunch & dinner Mon-Sat; M Bellecour) Half of this Italian duo serves panini to take away; the other half carpaccio, pasta, salads and other Italian dishes.

Le Café Épicerie (☎ 04 72 77 44 40; 6 rue du Bœuf, 5e; lunch & dinner Thu-Mon; M Vieux Lyon) Trendy eating space attached to one of the city's most romantic hotels, doubling as one of old Lyon's most stylish lunch spots.

SELF-CATERING

Lyon has two superb **outdoor food markets** Presqu'île (quai St-Antoine, 2e; Tue-Sun morning; M Bellecour or Cordeliers); Croix Rousse (blvd de la Croix Rousse, 4e; Tue-Sun morning; M Croix Rousse), as well as a legendary indoor market, **Les Halles de Lyon** (102 cours Lafayette, 3e; 8am-7pm Tue-Sat, 8am-2pm Sun; M Part-Dieu).

Drinking

The bounty of cafe terraces on place des Terreaux buzz with all-hours drinkers.

Barberousse (☎ 04 72 00 80 53; 18 rue Terrailles, 1er; 7pm-3am Tue-Sat; M Hôtel de Ville) Student-loved shooter bar on the buzzy back-alley of rue Terrailles. Its flavoured rums include cinnamon, chestnut and rhubarb and caramel.

Broc' Café (☎ 04 72 40 46 01; 2 place de l'Hôpital, 2e; 8am-1am Mon-Sat; M Bellecour) This laid-back cafe-bar is stocked with jumble-sale furniture and its student crowd oozes street cred.

Johnny's Kitchen (☎ 04 78 37 94 13; www.myspace.com/johnnyskitchen; 48 rue St-Georges, 5e; noon-1am daily; M Vieux Lyon) Busy pub in St-Georges where Johnny dishes up burger-shaped world cuisine and bands jam in the cellar.

La Fée Verte (☎ 04 78 28 32 35; www.lafeeverte.fr, in French; 4 rue Pizay, 1er; 9am-2am Mon-Wed, 9am-3am Thu & Fri, 10am-1am Sat & Sun; M Hôtel de Ville) Hit the Green Fairy for a drink in a steely setting, and live bands after dusk.

modernartcafé (☎ 04 72 87 06 82; www.modernartcafe.net; 65 blvd de la Croix Rousse, 4e; 11.50am-1.50am Mon-Fri, 3.30pm-2am Sat, 11am-2am Sun, shorter hr winter & rain; M Croix Rousse) Retro furnishings, artworks, free wi-fi and even a pocket-sized beach make Croix Rousse's art bar one cool place to be.

Entertainment

The cultural scene is dynamic. Listings guides include weekly **Lyon Poche** (www.lyonpoche.com, in French; €1 at newsagents) and the free **Le Petit Bulletin** (www.petit-bulletin.fr, in French), available on street corners.

Lyon's top gig venues include grungy **Furib' Arts** (☎ 04 72 00 26 41; www.myspace.com/lefuribart; 60 rue St-Georges, 5e; admission free-€4; 3pm-1am Tue-Sat; M Vieux Lyon) and **Le Bastringue** (☎ 06 70 15 81 39; http://lebastringue.free.fr, in French; 14 rue Laurencin, 2e; 8pm-1am Tue-Sat; M Ampère), while touring bands head for **Le Transbordeur** (☎ 04 78 93 08 33; www.transbordeur.fr, in French; 3 blvd de Stalingrad, Villeurbanne). Take bus 59 from metro Part-Dieu to Cité Inter Transbordeur stop.

For the hottest clubs, check out the www.lyonclubbing.com, www.lyon2night.com and www.night4lyon.com (all in French).

Getting There & Away

Flights to/from European cities land at **Lyon St-Exupéry airport** (☎ 08 26 80 08 26; www.lyon.aeroport.fr), 25km east of the city. **Satobus** (☎ 04 72 68 72 17; www.satobus.com) runs city-centre shuttles (single/return €8.60/15.20) every 20 minutes between 5am or 6am and midnight.

In the Perrache complex, **Eurolines** (☎ 04 72 56 95 30), **Intercars** (☎ 04 78 37 20 80) and Spain-oriented **Linebús** (☎ 04 72 41 72 27) have offices on the bus-station level of the Centre d'Échange.

Lyon has two mainline train stations: **Gare de Perrache** (M Perrache) and **Gare de la Part-Dieu** (M Part-Dieu), which mainly handles long-haul trains. Tickets are sold at the **SNCF Boutique** (2 place Bellecour, 2e; 9am-6.45pm Mon-Fri, 10am-6.30pm Sat; M Bellecour).

TGV destinations include Paris' Gare de Lyon (€61, two hours, every 30 to 60 minutes), Lille-Europe (€80.20, 3¼ hours, nine daily), Nantes (€89.20, 4½ hours, five daily), Dijon (€28.50, 2¾ hours, at least 12 daily) and Strasbourg (€52.80, 5¼ hours, five daily).

Getting Around

Buses, trams, a four-line metro and two funiculars linking Vieux Lyon to Fourvière are run by **TCL** (☎ 08 20 42 70 00; www.tcl.fr, in French; 5 rue de la République, 1er; 7.30am-6.30pm Mon-Fri, 9am-noon & 1.30-5pm Sat; M Bellecour). Public transport runs from around 5am to midnight. Tickets for all forms of public transport cost €1.50/12.50 for one/carnet of 10. Remember to time-stamp your ticket.

Public bikes are available from 200-odd bike stations around the city thanks to **vélo'v** (☎ 08 00 08 35 68; www.velov.grandlyon.com; first 30min free, first/subsequent hr €1/2).

THE FRENCH ALPS & JURA

Whether it's paragliding among the peaks, hiking the trails or hurtling down a mountainside strapped to a pair of glorified toothpicks, the French Alps is the undisputed centre of adventure sports in France. Under Mont Blanc's 4807m of raw wilderness lies the country's most spectacular outdoor playground, and if the seasonal crowds get too much, you can always take refuge in the little-visited Jura, a region of dark wooded hills and granite plateaux stretching for 360km along the French–Swiss border.

CHAMONIX

pop 9086 / elev 1037m

Supercharged Chamonix is the mecca of French mountaineering, and its knife-edge peaks, plunging slopes and massive glaciers have enthralled generations of adventurers and thrill-seekers (not to mention thousands of holidaying French and Brits). It's renowned for its pumping après-ski scene, and adventurous souls can brave the world's highest (and most terrifying) cable car.

Information

Laverie Automatique (174 av de l'Aiguille du Midi; 7/16kg wash €5.50/10; ⌚ 8am-10pm)
Mojo (21 place Balmat; sandwiches €5-6; ⌚ 9am-8pm) Cafe with internet-connected computers.
PGHM (Peloton de Gendarmerie de Haute-Montagne; ☎ 04 50 53 16 89; 69 rue de la Mollard) Mountain rescue service.
Post office (89 place Balmat)
Shop 74 (☎ 04 50 90 73 17; impasse du Bartavel; per hr €6; ⌚ 10am-8pm) Internet access.
Tourist office (☎ 04 50 53 00 24; www.chamonix.com; 85 place du Triangle de l'Amitié; ⌚ 8.30am-7.30pm Dec-Apr, 9am-12.30pm & 2-6.30pm Mon-Sat, 9am-12.30pm Sun May-Nov) Accommodation and activity information, plus ski passes and free wi-fi.

Sights

AIGUILLE DU MIDI

A jagged pinnacle of rock 8km from the domed summit of Mont Blanc, the **Aiguille du Midi** (3842m) is one of Chamonix' iconic landmarks. If you can handle the height, the panoramic views from the summit are unforgettable.

The **Téléphérique du l'Aiguille du Midi** (Aiguille du Midi Cable Car; ☎ 04 50 53 30 80, advance reservations 24hr 04 50 53 22 75; 100 place de l'Aiguille du Midi; adult/4-15yr/family return €38/30.40/114, adult/4-15yr return to midstation Plan de l'Aiguille €21/16.80; ⌚ 6.30am-6pm Jul & Aug, 8.30am-4.30pm late-Dec–Mar, hr vary rest of year) links Chamonix with the Aiguille du Midi; be prepared for long queues, and bring warm clothes – the temperature at the top rarely rises above -10°C.

Between mid-May and mid-September the **Télécabine Panoramic Mont Blanc** (cable car; ☎ 04 50 53 30 80; adult/4-15yr return from Chamonix €54/44; ⌚ 8.50am-4pm mid-May–Jun & Sep, 8.15am-4.30pm Jul & Aug) to **Pointe Helbronner** (3466m) continues for another 30 minutes over the French–Italian border, affording views of glaciers, snowfields and seracs.

LE BRÉVENT

The highest peak on the western side of the valley, **Le Brévent** (2525m) has fabulous views of the Mont Blanc massif and is reached via the **Télécabine du Brévent** (☎ 04 50 53 13 18; 29 rte Henriette d'Angeville; Chamonix-Brévent adult/4-15yr/family return €22/17.40/66, Chamonix-Planpraz adult/4-15yr return €12/9.60; ⌚ 8am-5.45pm Jun-Aug, 8.45am-4.45pm mid-Dec–Apr), from the end of rue de la Mollard.

MER DE GLACE

The **Mer de Glace** (Sea of Ice) is the second-largest glacier in the Alps, 14km long, 1800m wide and up to 400m deep. A quaint red mountain train links **Gare du Montenvers** (☎ 04 50 53 12 54; 35 place de la Mer de Glace; adult/4-15yr/family €21/16.80/63; ⌚ 9am-4.30pm mid-Dec–Apr, 8am-6.30pm Jul & Aug, hr vary rest of year) in Chamonix with Montenvers (1913m), from where a cable car transports tourists in summer down to the glacier and the **Grotte de la Mer de Glace** (⌚ late Dec–Apr & mid-Jun–Sep), an ice cave that has been carved every spring since 1946.

Activities

For activities out and about on the mountain – whether that means summer hiking or winter skiing – the **Maison de la Montagne** (190 place de l'Église; ⌚ 8.30am-noon & 3-7pm), across the square from the tourist office, supplies comprehensive details on practically every imaginable pastime in the Mont Blanc area.

Sleeping

Les Deux Glaciers (☎ 04 50 53 15 84; les2glaciers.com; 80 rte des Tissières; camp sites per 2 adults & tent €14.30; ⌚ mid-Dec–mid-Nov) The only year-round camping ground, the Two Glaciers is in Les Bossons, 3km south of Chamonix.

Gîte Le Vagabond (☎ 04 50 53 15 43; www.gitevagabond.com; 365 av Ravanel-le-Rouge; dm €16.80, incl breakfast/half-board €19.40/38.60; ⌚ reception 8-10am & 4.30-10pm; 💻) This legendary bunkhouse, where cool dudes free-ride by day and eat, drink and party by night, is run and populated almost exclusively by Brits.

Auberge de Jeunesse Chamonix (☎ 04 50 53 14 52; www.fuaj.org; 127 montée Jacques Balmat; dm incl sheets & breakfast €18, half-board €27.80; ⌚ reception 8am-noon, 5-7.30pm & 8.30-10pm Dec-May & Jun-Sep) Bright, well-run hostel with impeccable two- to six-bed dorms (but no kitchen). It's 2km south of Chamonix in Les Pélerins. Take the Chamonix–Les Houches bus line and get off in Les Pélerins d'en Haut.

Hôtel Les Crêtes Blanches (☎ 04 50 53 05 62; www.cretes-blanches.com; 16 impasse du Génépy; s/d/tr/chalet summer from €50/56/78/105, winter from €62/76/96/119) This tip-top establishment in central Chamonix with crisp, modern bedrooms is excellent value for money, but it's often booked out in advance by tour operators.

Hôtel Gustavia (☎ 04 50 53 00 31; 272 av Michel Croz; s/d/tr from €50/80/111) Going strong since 1890, this charming manor-house hotel with

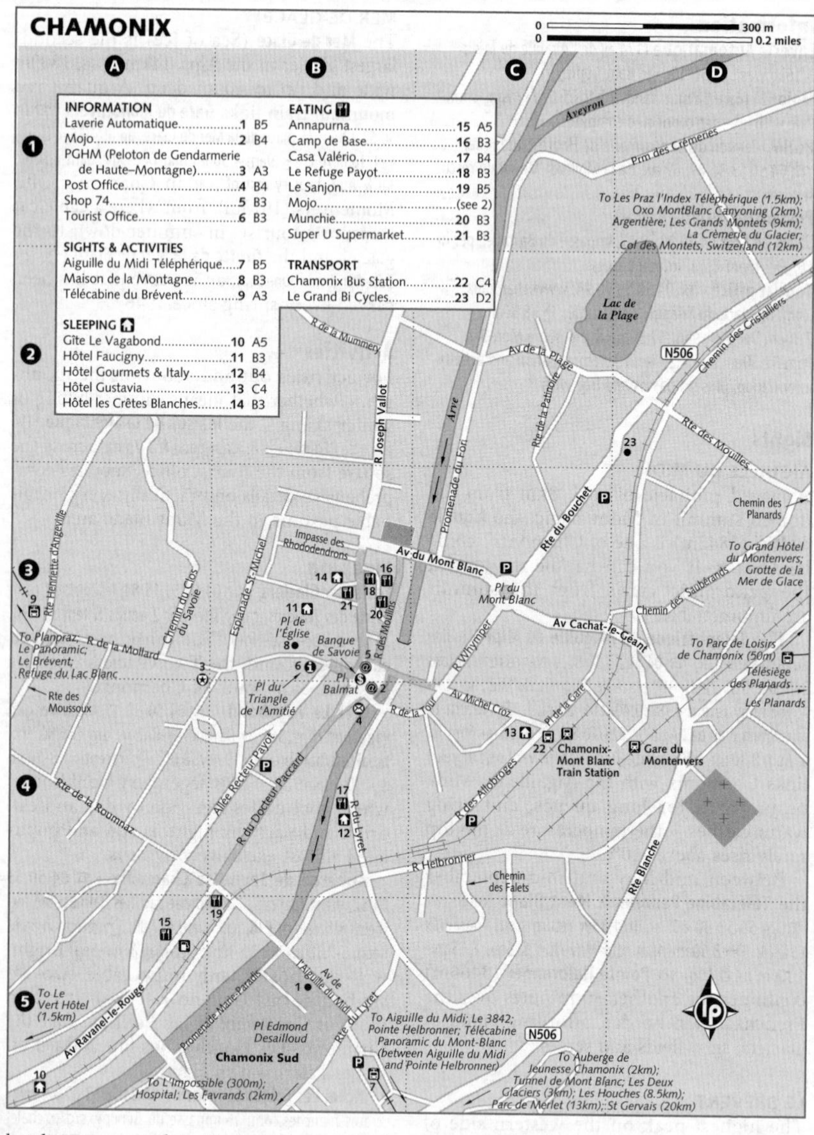

bottle green wooden window shutters and wrought-iron balconies oozes soul. Rooms feature denim-coloured duvets and wood furnishings.

Hôtel Faucigny (☎ 04 50 53 01 17; www.hotelfaucigny-chamonix.com; 118 place de l'Église; d/tr/q low season €68/82/98, high season €79/93/112; mid-May–mid-Nov & mid-Dec–mid-Apr;) This tidy hotel optimises space and comfort (made-to-measure furniture, heating mirrors etc) in a charming old building. There's a flower-decked terrace with vertigo-inducing Mont Blanc views.

Hôtel Gourmets & Italy (☎ 04 50 53 01 38; www.hotelgourmets-chamonix.com; 96 rue du Lyret; d €78-99, tr €104-150;) At Chamonix' most understated address, rooms are neutral in beige but comfortable, with great designer bathrooms, a sauna and the essential Mont Blanc outlook.

Eating

Mojo (21 place Balmat; sandwiches €5-6; 9am-8pm) The latest arrival on the sandwich scene, Mojo is smack bang on the main square, with views of Le Brévent, Mont Blanc and l'Aiguille du Midi to boot. *Bon appétit*.

Annapurna (04 50 55 81 39; 62 av Ravanel-le-Rouge; mains €10-15; lunch & dinner Wed-Sun, dinner Tue) Named after the 8000m-plus Himalayan mountain, this place takes it culinary cue from spicier climes – tandooris, biryanis and kormas are served inhouse or to take away.

Casa Valério (04 50 55 93 40; 88 rue du Lyret; mains €10-20; lunch & dinner, closes at 2am) One of Chamonix' most popular eateries, this restaurant doubles as a happening hang-out in the evenings, when young 'seasonaires' devour pasta or pizza by the bar counter.

Le Sanjon (04 50 53 56 44; 5 av Ravanel-le-Rouge; menus €12-35; lunch & dinner) The usual Alpine cheese overload on the menu, plus unusual dishes such as *potée Savoyarde* (*diot* sausage, potatoes, onions and, yes, cheese) and *moëlleux Savoyard* (cheese, ham and potatoes cooked in pine-tree bark).

Munchie (04 50 53 45 41; 87 rue des Moulins; mains €17-25; dinner Mon-Sun) Think fusion at this trendy hang-out with great pan-Asian food. Mains include sashimi, sushi, laksa, fish cakes and spare ribs.

A food market fills place du Mont Blanc on Saturday morning.

Camp de Base (04 50 18 47 76; 107 rue des Moulins; 3-8pm) English grocery shop, combined with internet cafe (per hour €5).

Le Refuge Payot (04 50 53 18 71; www.refugepayot.com; 166 rue Joseph Vallot) Local produce: cheese, smoked meats, sausages.

Super U (117 rue Joseph Vallot) Supermarket.

Getting There & Away

Next to the train station, **Chamonix bus station** (04 50 53 01 15; www.altibus.com; 6.45-10.30am & 1.25-4.45pm Mon-Fri, 6.45-11am Sat & Sun) runs buses to/from Geneva airport and bus station (one way/return €35/55, 1½ to 2 hours, three daily) and Courmayeur (one way/return €11/18, 45 minutes, two to three daily). Advanced booking only.

From Chamonix–Mont Blanc **train station** (04 50 53 12 98; place de la Gare) trains trundle to St-Gervais–Le Fayet station, 23km west of Chamonix, from where there are trains to most major French cities.

Getting Around

Local buses are provided by **Chamonix Bus** (04 50 53 05 55; www.chamonix-bus.com; 591 promenade Marie-Paradis; 7am-7pm winter, 8am-noon & 2-7pm Jun-Aug).

Le Grand Bi Cycles (04 50 53 14 16; 240 rte du Bouchet; 9am-7pm Jul & Aug, 9am-7pm Tue-Sun Sep-Jun, closed Nov) rents bikes for €25 a day.

ANNECY

pop 51,000 / elev 448m

Fresh from a 50-year clean-up, the glittering Lac d'Annecy is now one of the purest in the world, receiving only rainwater, spring water and mountain streams. Swimming in this shimmering lake surrounded by snowy mountains really is an Alpine highlight, as is strolling the geranium-lined streets of Old Annecy.

Orientation

The train and bus stations are 500m northwest of Vieil Annecy, also called the Vieille Ville (Old Town), huddled around the Thiou River (split into Canal du Thiou to the south and Canal du Vassé to the north). The town centre is between the post office and the purpose-built shopping mall, Centre Bonlieu, near Lac d'Annecy.

Information

Larache Télécom (04 50 33 08 95; 3 rue de l'Industrie; per 15min/1hr €1/3; 9am-11pm) Internet access.

Lav'Confort Express (6 rue de la Gare; 7am-9pm)

Post office (4bis rue des Glières)

Tourist office (04 50 45 00 33; www.lac-annecy.com; 1 rue Jean Jaurès, Centre Bonlieu; 9am-12.30pm & 1.45-6pm Mon-Sat mid-Sep–mid-May, 9am-6.30pm Mon-Sat mid-May–mid-Sep, 10am-1pm Sun Mar-May)

Sights & Activities

Wandering around the Vieille Ville and the lakefront is the essence of Annecy. Just east, behind the Hôtel de Ville, are the **Jardins de l'Europe**, linked to the park of **Champ de Mars** by the **Pont des Amours** (Lovers' Bridge).

With labyrinthine narrow streets and colonnaded passageways, the Old Town retains much of its 17th-century appearance. On the central island, imposing **Palais de l'Isle** (04 50 33 87 30; 3 passage de l'Île; adult/concession €3.40/1, 1st Sun of month Oct-May free; 10.30am-6pm Jun-Sep, 10am-noon

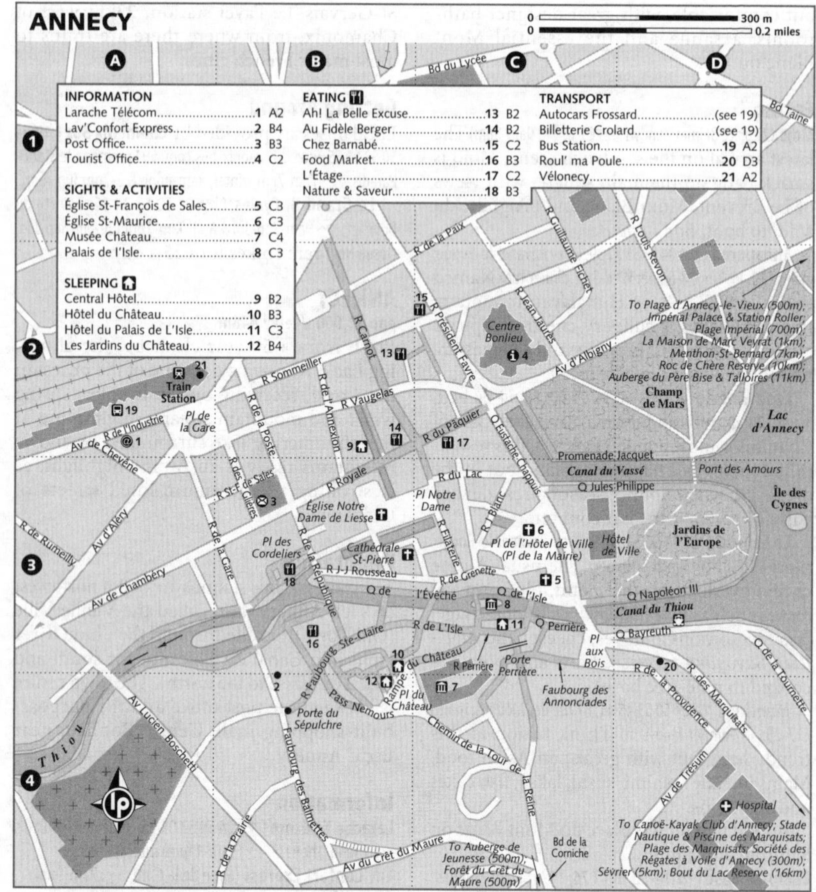

& 2-5pm Wed-Mon Oct-May) was a prison, but now hosts local-history displays.

In the 13th- to 16th-century castle above town, the eclectic **Musée Château** (☎ 04 50 33 87 30; adult/concession €4.80/2; ⏲ 10.30am-6pm Jun-Sep, 10am-noon & 2-5pm Wed-Mon Oct-May) explores traditional Savoyard art, crafts and Alpine natural history. A combined ticket covering the palace and the Musée Château costs €6.20.

Parks and grassy areas line the lakefront. Public beach **Plage d'Annecy-le-Vieux** (admission free; ⏲ Jul & Aug) is 1km east of Champ de Mars. Closer to town, privately run **Plage Impérial** (admission €3.50; ⏲ Jul & Aug) sits beneath the pre-WWI **Impérial Palace**. **Plage des Marquisats** (admission free; ⏲ Jul & Aug) is 1km south of the Vieille Ville along rue des Marquisats.

Sleeping

Auberge de Jeunesse (☎ 04 50 45 33 19; www.fuaj.org; 4 rte du Semnoz; dm incl breakfast & sheets €17.60; ⏲ reception 8am-noon & 3-10pm mid-Jan–Nov) Ten minutes from the centre, Annecy's wood-clad hostel sports tip-top facilities (bar, kitchen, wi-fi, TV room). Dorms are small but have en-suite showers (toilets are on the landing).

Central Hôtel (☎ 04 50 45 05 37; www.hotelcentralannecy.com, in French; 6bis rue Royale; d/tr €33/42, with shower €40/47, with shower & toilet €45/52) Spread across three floors in a rambling building, the rooms at this establishment are simple but cosy. Eight rooms (out of 16) have balconies overlooking the canal.

Hôtel du Château (☎ 04 50 45 27 66; www.annecy-hotel.com; 16 rampe du Château; s/d/tr/q Oct-Apr

€43/55/73/83, May-Sep €49/68/73/83) This hotel's trump card is its sun-drenched, panoramic breakfast terrace. Rooms are sweet with their pine furniture and pastel tones, but a little small.

Les Jardins du Château (☎ 04 50 45 72 28; jardinduchateau@wanadoo.fr; 1 place du Château; d €65-90, tr/q €100/130) All rooms and studios at this *chambre d'hôte* are equipped with kitchenettes and many have balconies and terraces where you can eat, sunbathe and generally chill while taking in the view.

Hôtel du Palais de L'Isle (☎ 04 50 45 86 87; www.hoteldupalaisdelisle.com; 13 rue Perrière; s/d from €67/83; 💻) Sleep in the heart of old-town action at this 18th-century house, with contemporary rooms sporting assorted views of the Palais, the castle or the Old Town's roofs.

Eating

Chez Barnabé (☎ 04 50 45 90 62; 29 rue Sommeiller; mains from €3.60; ⌚ 10am-7pm Mon-Sat) The concept of hot or cold buffet served in different-sized boxes is nothing new, but it's a winner when done well: everything here is 100% fresh and prepared on the premises daily.

Au Fidèle Berger (☎ 04 50 45 00 32; 2 rue Royale; ⌚ 9.15am-7pm Tue-Sat) This old-England style tearoom serves decadent cakes, mountains of macaroons and homemade ice creams for the sweet-toothed among you.

Ah! La Belle Excuse (☎ 04 50 51 20 05; cour du Pré Carré, 10 rue Vaugelas; mains €10-15; ⌚ lunch & dinner Mon-Sat) In a funky, red-and-green wood-clad house with an unbeatable summer deck, the Beautiful Excuse serves up grilled meats, salads and *parmentiers* (mashed potato baked with different toppings).

L'Étage (☎ 04 50 51 03 28; 13 rue du Pâquier; mains €15; ⌚ lunch & dinner) At L'Étage *le fromage* is given pride of place, even if you're not having a Savoyard speciality (think steak with cheese sauce, yum). The decor is a little passé but the cheerful staff more than make up for it.

Nature & Saveur (☎ 04 50 45 82 29; www.nature-saveur.com; place des Cordeliers; lunch €18-22, dinner €36-52; ⌚ lunch Tue-Sat, dinner Fri & Sat) The new kid on the 'alternative' block, Nature & Saveur only uses organic and wholesome ingredients from local farms, but it's no tree-hugger's hut – check out the discerning boho-chic clientele.

In the Vieille Ville, there's a **food market** (rue Faubourg Ste-Claire; ⌚ 8am-noon Sun, Tue & Fri).

Getting There & Away

From the **bus station** (Gare Routière Sud; rue de l'Industrie), **Billetterie Crolard** (☎ 04 50 45 08 12; www.voyages-crolard.com; ⌚ 7.15am-12.30pm & 1.30-7.15pm Mon-Sat, Sun in high season) runs up to five buses daily to/from Lyon St-Exupéry airport (one way/return €30/45, two hours).

Next door, **Autocars Frossard** (☎ 04 50 45 73 90; ⌚ 7.45-11am & 2-7.15pm Mon-Fri, 7.45am-1pm Sat) sells tickets for Geneva (€10.50, 1¾ hours, up to 12 daily), Thonon-les-Bains (€16.50, two hours, twice daily), Évian-les-Bains (€18.50, 2½ hours, twice daily) and Chambéry (€6, one hour).

From the **train station** (place de la Gare), there are trains to/from Aix-les-Bains (€6.80, 30 minutes), Chambéry (€8.60, 45 minutes), Lyon (€21.60, 2¼ hours) and Paris' Gare de Lyon (€69.80, four hours).

Bikes can be hired from **Vélonecy** (☎ 04 50 51 38 90; place de la Gare; ⌚ 9.30am-noon & 1.30-6.30pm Wed-Sat, 1.30-6.30pm Tue) at the train station, for adult/student €15/3 per day. **Roul' ma Poule** (☎ 04 50 27 86 83; www.annecy-location-velo.com; 4 rue des Marquisats; ⌚ 9.30am-12.30pm & 2-6pm Wed-Mon Apr-Jun, Sep & Oct, 9am-8pm Jul & Aug) also rents bikes (€10/15) and rollerblades (€9/14 per half-/full day).

GRENOBLE

pop 155,100

Wherever you turn in big-city Grenoble, you'll be treated to intoxicating Alpine views. But Grenoble isn't just a mountain base: since the 1960s the city has been a leading technology hub and a cultural centre, with some outstanding museums, a lively arts scene and 60,000 students to lap it all up.

Orientation

The old city is centred around place Grenette and place Notre Dame, both 1km east of the train and bus stations. The main university campus is a couple of kilometres east of the old centre on the southern side of the Isère River.

Information

Celsius Café (☎ 04 76 00 13 60; 15 rue Jean-Jacques Rousseau; per 30/60min €1.50/2.50; ⌚ 9am-11pm Mon-Sat & 1-8pm Sun)

Laverie Berriat (88 cours Berriat; ⌚ 7am-8pm)

Neptune Internet (☎ 04 76 63 94 18; 2 rue de la Paix; per 30/60min €2.50/3.50; ⌚ 1-7pm Mon-Sat & 2-6pm Sun) Cybercafe with qwerty keyboards.

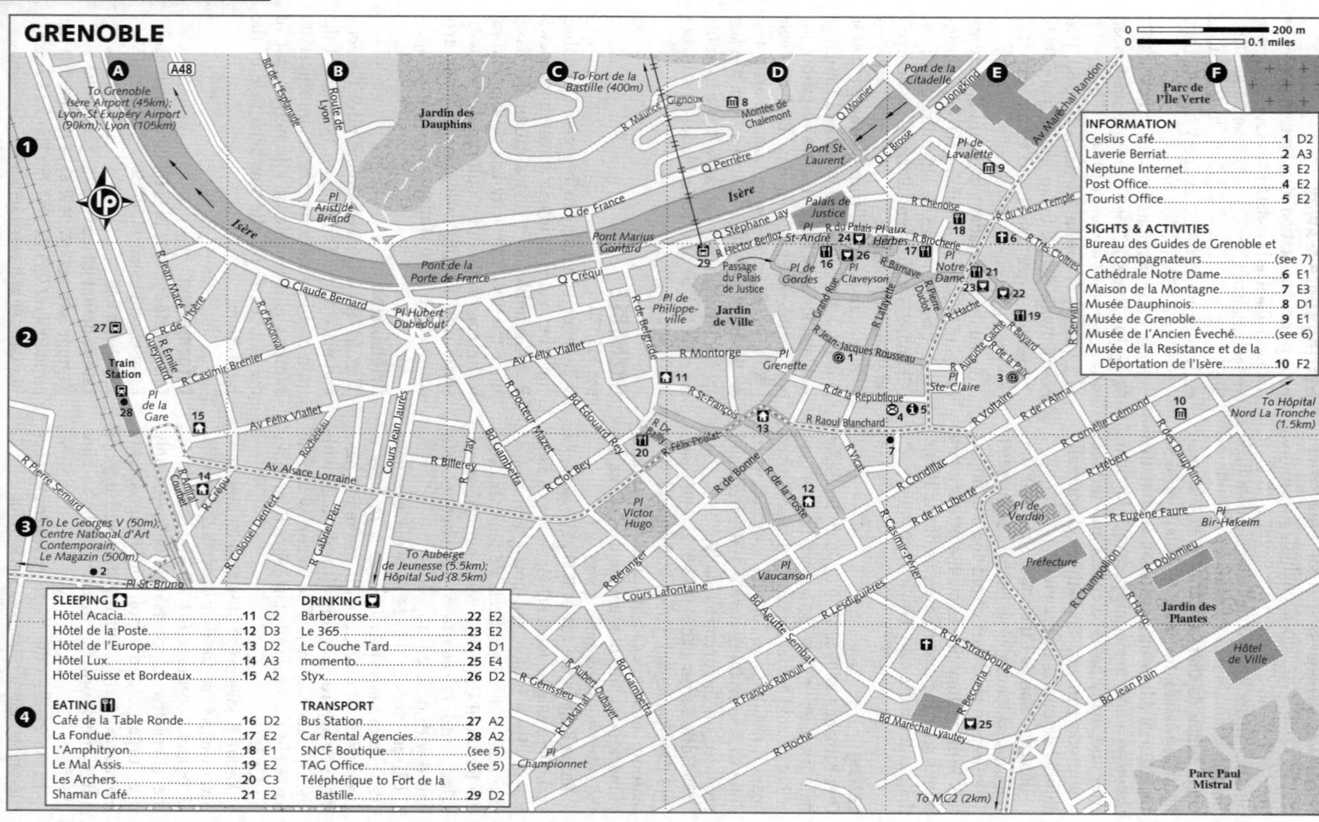
FRANCE
GRENOBLE
0 200 m
0 0.1 miles
To Grenoble Isère Airport (45km); Lyon-St Exupéry Airport (90km); Lyon (105km)
A48
To Fort de la Bastille (400m)
Jardin des Dauphins
Parc de l'Île Verte
Isère
Pont de la Citadelle
Pont St-Laurent
Pont Marius Gontard
Pont de la Porte de France
Pl Hubert Dubedout
Pl Aristide Briand
Train Station
Pl de la Gare
Palais de Justice
Passage du Palais de Justice
Jardin de Ville
Pl de Philippe-ville
Pl Grenette
Pl de Gordes
Pl Claveyson
Pl Notre Dame
Pl Ste-Claire
Pl de Lavalette
Pl Victor Hugo
Pl Vaucanson
Pl de Verdun
Préfecture
Pl Bir-Hakeim
Jardin des Plantes
Hôtel de Ville
Parc Paul Mistral
Pl Championnet
To Hôpital Nord La Tronche (1.5km)
To Le Georges V (50m); Centre National d'Art Contemporain; Le Magazin (500m)
To Auberge de Jeunesse (5.5km); Hôpital Sud (8.5km)
To MC2 (2km)
INFORMATION
Celsius Café....1 D2
Laverie Berriat....2 A3
Neptune Internet....3 E2
Post Office....4 E2
Tourist Office....5 E2
SIGHTS & ACTIVITIES
Bureau des Guides de Grenoble et Accompagnateurs....(see 7)
Cathédrale Notre Dame....6 E1
Maison de la Montagne....7 E3
Musée Dauphinois....8 D1
Musée de Grenoble....9 E1
Musée de l'Ancien Évêché....(see 6)
Musée de la Resistance et de la Déportation de l'Isère....10 F2
SLEEPING
Hôtel Acacia....11 C2
Hôtel de la Poste....12 D3
Hôtel de l'Europe....13 D2
Hôtel Lux....14 A3
Hôtel Suisse et Bordeaux....15 A2
EATING
Café de la Table Ronde....16 D2
La Fondue....17 E2
L'Amphitryon....18 E1
Le Mal Assis....19 E2
Les Archers....20 C3
Shaman Café....21 E2
DRINKING
Barberousse....22 E2
Le 365....23 E2
Le Couche Tard....24 D1
momento....25 E4
Styx....26 D2
TRANSPORT
Bus Station....27 A2
Car Rental Agencies....28 A2
SNCF Boutique....(see 5)
TAG Office....(see 5)
Téléphérique to Fort de la Bastille....29 D2

Post office (rue de la République) Next to the tourist office.

Tourist office (☎ 04 76 42 41 41; www.grenoble-isere-tourisme.com; 14 rue de la République; ⌚ 9am-6.30pm Mon-Sat, 10am-1pm Sun Oct-Apr, 10am-1pm & 2-5pm May-Sep) Sells maps and guides, arranges city tours.

Sights

Looming above the old city on the northern side of the Isère River, the grand 16th-century **Fort de la Bastille** is Grenoble's best-known landmark. The views are spectacular, with vast mountains on every side and the grey waters of the Isère River below. To get to the fort, hop aboard the riverside **Téléphérique Grenoble Bastille** (☎ 04 76 44 33 65; quai Stéphane Jay; adult/under 5yr/student one way €4.15/free/3.35, return €6.10/free/4.85; ⌚ Feb-Nov).

The sleek glass-and-steel exterior of the **Musée de Grenoble** (☎ 04 76 63 44 44; www.museedegrenoble.fr, in French; 5 place de Lavalette; adult/student €5/2, 1st Sun of month free; ⌚ 10am-6.30pm Wed-Mon) is renowned for its distinguished modern collection, including various works by Chagall, Matisse, Modigliani, Monet and Picasso, among others.

The **Musée Dauphinois** (☎ 04 57 58 89 01; www.musee-dauphinois.fr, in French; 30 rue Maurice Gignoux; admission free; ⌚ 10am-7pm Wed-Mon Jun-Sep, to 6pm Oct-May) beautifully documents the cultures, crafts and traditions of Alpine life, including a fantastic exhibition devoted to the region's skiing history.

The imposing **Cathédrale Notre Dame** and adjoining 14th-century **Bishops' Palace** – home to Grenoble's bishops until 1908 – form the **Musée de l'Ancien Évêché** (☎ 04 76 03 15 25; www.ancien-eveche-isere.com; 2 rue Très Cloîtres; admission free; ⌚ 9am-6pm Wed-Sat & Mon, 10am-7pm Sun, 1.30-6pm Tue), which traces local history.

The moving **Musée de la Résistance et de la Déportation de l'Isère** (☎ 04 76 42 38 53; www.resistance-en-isere.com, in French; 14 rue Hébert; admission free; ⌚ 9am-6pm Mon & Wed-Fri, 1.30-6pm Tue, 10am-6pm Sat & Sun Sep-Jun, 10am-7pm Mon & Wed-Sun, 1.30-7pm Tue Jul & Aug) examines the deportation of Jews and other 'undesirables' from Grenoble, and explores the role of the Vercors region in the French Resistance. Captions are in French, English and German.

Activities

The authorities on mountain activities around Grenoble reside in the **Maison de la Montagne** (☎ 04 76 44 67 03; 3 rue Raoul Blanchard; ⌚ 9.30am-12.30pm & 1-6pm Mon-Fri, 10am-1pm & 2-5pm Sat), including the **Bureau des Guides de Grenoble et Accompagnateurs** (☎ 04 76 44 67 03; www.guide-grenoble.com, in French; Maison de la Montagne).

Sleeping

Auberge de Jeunesse (☎ 04 76 09 33 52; grenoble@fuaj.org; 10 av du Grésivaudan; B&B €16.70; ⌚ reception 7.30am-11pm) This excellent hostel has everything: a bar, self-catering kitchen and sun deck, plus impeccable two- to four-bed dorms, many with en suite. The only downside is that it's located 5km south of the train station. From cours Jean Jaurès, take bus 1 to the Quinzaine stop (just outside the Casino supermarket) or tram A to La Rampe and walk 15 minutes.

Hôtel de l'Europe (☎ 04 76 46 16 94; www.hoteleurope.fr; 22 place Grenette; s with washbasin/shower €31/42, d €40-80) A good bet for central hotel accommodation, with a choice of grand spiral staircase or lift.

Hôtel de la Poste (☎ 04 76 46 67 25; 25 rue de la Poste; s/d/tr €34/41/50) Oozing old-school charm, the rooms in the rambling flats at Hôtel de la Poste are Grenoble's best-kept secret. Some have shared bathroom and toilets, and there's a communal guests' kitchen.

Hôtel Lux (☎ 04 76 46 41 89; www.hotel-lux.com; 6 rue Crépu; s €37-50, d €51-55) Despite its name, Hôtel Lux is not a luxurious affair: rooms are pretty basic and the decor neutral, but it's close to the station and has wi-fi.

Hôtel Acacia (☎ 04 76 87 29 90; 13 rue de Belgrade; s €40, d €44-62) As boxy and boring as it is, this dead-central hotel could not be closer to the action. Rooms with shared toilets (but their own shower) are cheaper.

Hôtel Suisse et Bordeaux (☎ 04 76 47 55 87; www.hotel-sb-grenoble.com; 6 place de la Gare; s/d/tr €48/57/69) They've gone overboard with the flowery bedspreads and matching curtains, but it's otherwise spacious and clean. Rear rooms are quieter, but you won't get a balcony.

Eating

L'Amphitryon (☎ 04 76 51 38 07; 9 rue Chenoise; mains €10; ⌚ dinner Mon-Sat) The decor is an odd mix of cardboard cut-out dunes, steel door, blue lights and 16th-century building, but the food's authentically oriental: the house speciality is *brik*, a thin pastry stuffed with fillings.

Café de la Table Ronde (☎ 04 76 44 51 41; 7 place St-André; dishes €10-22; ⌚ 7am-midnight Mon-Sat)

This historic 1739 cafe was Stendhal's and Rousseau's favourite haunt, and serves everything from hot goat's cheese salad to *tournedos Rossini* (€20; beef served with foie gras and Madeira wine).

Shaman Café (☎ 04 38 37 23 56; 1 place Notre Dame; menus from €12.50; ⏰ 8am-midnight) With its oriental decor and big chill music, this place offers a good-value mix of Japanese, Lebanese, Chinese and Thai.

Les Archers (☎ 04 76 46 27 76; 2 rue Docteur Bailly; mains €15; ⏰ 11-2am Tue-Sat, 11-1am Sun & Mon) Old-school French brasserie serving seafood platters, heaps of snails or a winter-warming sauerkraut.

La Fondue (☎ 04 76 15 20 72; 5 rue Brocherie; fondues per person €17; ⏰ dinner Mon, lunch & dinner Tue-Sat) La Fondue does what it says on the tin: 16 different types of fondue (with Génépi, chartreuse, kirsch, different types of cheeses etc). There's even a dessert variety (chocolate).

Le Mal Assis (☎ 04 76 54 75 93; 7 rue Bayard; mains €20; ⏰ dinner Tue-Sat) 'The Badly Seated' is an intimate place where traditional French dishes turn up as the usual tasty mains or less-conventional platters (crostini, foie gras, terrines) for a tapas-style meal.

Drinking

Like every good student city, Grenoble does a mean party.

Le 365 (☎ 04 76 51 73 18; 3 rue Bayard; ⏰ 3pm-1am or 2am Tue-Sat) Sip wines and *chocolat chartreuse* (hot chocolate with herbal liquor chartreuse) in a relaxed vibe surrounded by cluttered bottles, frames and candles.

Barberousse (☎ 04 76 57 14 53; 8 rue Hache; ⏰ 6pm-2am Tue-Sat) If you're after cheap drinks and a boogie, this is the place: shots, lairy students and loud music are regular fixtures.

momento (☎ 04 76 26 21 59; 2 rue Beccaria; ⏰ noon-1am Sun-Wed, to 2am Thu-Sat) A feast of fluoro lights, this is a bit like an American diner à la 21st century: big burgers, big cocktails (pitchers), big music.

Styx (☎ 04 76 44 09 99; 6 place Claveyson; ⏰ 1pm-2am Mon-Sat) If you're too cool for school, this is the venue for you: designer cocktails, DJs, soft red light and attitude by the shaker-load.

Le Couche Tard (☎ 04 76 44 18 79; 1 rue du Palais; ⏰ 7pm-2am Mon-Sat) The 'go to bed late' grungy pub must be the only place on earth that will encourage you to graffiti its walls, so make the best of it!

Getting There & Away

AIR

A clutch of budget airlines, including Ryanair and easyJet, fly to/from **Grenoble Isère airport** (☎ 04 76 65 48 48; www.grenoble-airport.com), 45km northwest of Grenoble. Shuttle buses run by **Transisère** (☎ 08 20 08 38 38) travel to/from the city centre (one way/return €4/8, 45 minutes, four to eight daily).

BUS

The **bus station** (☎ 04 76 87 90 31; rue Émile Gueymard) is served by several bus companies, including **VFD** (☎ 08 20 83 38 33; www.vfd.fr, in French) and **Transisère** (☎ 08 20 08 38 38; www.transisere.fr, in French). Destinations include Chambéry (€5.10, two hours), Geneva airport (€43, 2½ hours), and Lyon St-Exupéry airport (€20, one hour).

Eurolines (☎ 04 76 46 19 77; www.eurolines.fr; at the bus station; ⏰ 10am-noon & 2-7pm Tue-Sat) handles international destinations.

TRAIN

From the **train station** (rue Émile Gueymard), trains run to/from Paris' Gare de Lyon (from €74.70, 3½ hours), Chambéry (€9.90, one hour, 10 to 13 daily) and Lyon (€18, 1½ hours, five daily). Train tickets are sold in town at the **SNCF boutique** (15 rue de la République; ⏰ 9am-12.30pm & 2-6.30pm Mon-Fri, 9.30am-12.30pm & 2-6pm Sat).

Getting Around

BICYCLE

Métrovélo (☎ 08 20 22 38 38; ⏰ 7am-8pm Mon-Fri, 9am-noon & 2-7pm Sat & Sun Apr-Oct, 9am-noon Sat & 2-7pm Sun Nov-Mar), underneath the train station, rents out bikes for €3/5 per half-/full day. You'll need ID and a €50 deposit.

BUS & TRAM

Grenoble's three tram lines – A, B and C – run through the heart of town. A single-trip bus and tram ticket costs €1.30, sold at tram and bus stops or by drivers. Time-stamp tickets in the blue machines before boarding. *Carnets* of 10 tickets (€10.90) and day passes (€3.60) are sold at the **TAG office** (☎ 08 20 48 60 00; www.semitag.com; ⏰ 8.30am-6.30pm Mon-Fri, 9am-6pm Sat) inside the tourist office or next to the train station. Trams run from around 5am to 1am; buses stop between 6pm and 9pm.

BESANÇON

pop 116,100

Old town, young heart: that's Besançon, capital of the Franche-Comté region. The city boasts one of the country's largest foreign student populations and an innovative spirit, most obvious in the buzzing bars of the Battant quarter. A new TGV station outside Besançon (in Auxon, 10km north) will open in late 2011, allowing nonstop travel from the Rhine to the Rhône.

Orientation

The old city nestles in a curve of the Doubs River. The tourist office and train station sit just outside this loop. The Battant quarter straddles the northwest bank of the river around rue Battant. Grande Rue, the pedestrianised main street, slices through the old city from the river to the citadel.

Information

ID PC (28 rue de la République; per hr €3; 9.30am-noon & 2-7pm Tue-Sat) Computer shop with internet terminals.

Le Lavoir (14 rue de la Madeleine; per 5kg €3.50; 8am-8pm) Laundrette.

Post office (23 rue Proudhon; 8am-7pm Mon-Fri, 8.30am-noon Sat)

Tourist office (03 81 80 92 55; www.besancon-tourisme.com; 2 place de la 1ère Armée Française; 9.30am-7pm Tue-Sat, 10am-6pm Mon, 11am-1pm Sun) Sells city maps and guides; organises city tours (in French only).

Sights

Built by Vauban for Louis XIV between 1688 and 1711, Besançon's **citadel** (03 81 87 83 33; www.citadelle.com; rue des Fusillés de la Résistance; adult/4-14yr €7.80/4.50; 9am-7pm Jul & Aug, 9am-6pm Apr-Jun, Sep & Oct, 10am-5pm Nov-Mar) is a steep 15-minute walk from **Porte Noire** (rue de la Convention), a triumphal arch left over from the city's Roman days. Inside the citadel, the **Musée Comtois** zooms in on local traditions, the **Musée d'Histoire Naturelle** covers natural history, and the harrowing **Musée de la Résistance et de la Déportation** examines the rise of Nazism and the French Resistance movement. Less sobering are the insects, fish and animals inhabiting the **insectarium**, **aquarium**, **noctarium** and **parc zoologique**. Citadel admission covers entry to all the museums.

Thought to be France's oldest museum, the **Musée des Beaux-Arts** (03 81 87 80 49; www.musee-arts-besancon.org; 1 place de la Révolution; adult/student €5/2.50; 9.30am-noon & 2-6pm Wed-Mon) houses archaeological, medieval and Renaissance works in a very modern building.

The highlight of the 18th-century **Cathédrale St-Jean** (rue de la Convention; adult/under 18yr €3/free; 7 guided tours daily Wed-Mon Apr-Sep, Thu-Mon Oct-Mar) is an incredible astronomical clock with 30,000 moving parts, 57 faces and 62 dials; among other things, it tells the time in 16 destinations, the tides in eight French ports, and the time of sunrise and sunset.

Sleeping

Les Oiseaux (03 81 40 32 00; www.fjtlesoiseaux.fr, in French; 48 rue des Cras; dm incl breakfast €23; reception 8am-8pm) This tower-block hostel 2km east of the train station is a bit of an eyesore but the rooms themselves are clean and good value. Take bus 7 from the tourist office.

Hôtel du Nord (03 81 81 34 56; www.hotel-du-nord-besancon.com; 8 rue Moncey; d €39-61, q €61-77) Right in the centre of town, this is a good-value hotel: rooms are fairly old-fashioned but clean, there's free wi-fi, a private garage and lovely staff.

Hôtel Granvelle (03 81 81 33 92; www.hotel-granvelle.fr; 13 rue Général du Lecourbe; d €50-60, tr €62-71) Thirty clean, functional rooms in a lovely stone building at the back of a courtyard below the citadel.

our pick **Charles Quint Hôtel** (03 81 82 05 49; www.hotel-charlesquint.com; 3 rue du Chapitre; d €87-138;) Besançon's stunning boutique hotel in an 18th-century town house oozes charm, with parquet floors, period furniture, sumptuous fabrics, a heavenly garden and wood-panelled dining room.

Hôtel Castan (03 81 65 02 00; www.hotelcastan.fr; 6 sq Castan; d €110-170; closed 2 or 3 weeks Aug;) Original monumental fireplaces, canopy beds, stag heads and ornate grandfather clocks add authenticity to this lovely ivy-covered town house on a peaceful old-town square.

Eating

Au Gourmand (03 81 81 40 56; 5 rue Mégevand; mains from €7; lunch & dinner Tue-Fri, lunch Sat) With its vinyl-coated tablecloths and salt straight out of the supermarket pot, this is a no-frills but charming place. *Les parmentières* (a mound of mashed potato with various toppings) is particularly good.

Pum (03 81 81 18 47; cnr rue Jean Petit & rue Gustave Courbet; mains from €7.50; lunch & dinner, to 1am Sun-Thu, to 2am Fri & Sat) Bright-orange Pum is a great place for tight budgets. Thai staples such as stir-fries and green curries are served up at long wooden tables.

La Petite Adresse (☎ 03 81 82 35 09; 28 rue Claude Pouillet; mains €15; ⏰ lunch & dinner Mon-Sat) Enjoy some solid regional cooking in this tiny hole-in-the-wall establishment on Besançon's most happening street.

MI:AM (☎ 03 81 82 09 56; 8 rue Morand; mains €15; ⏰ 11.30am-midnight Tue-Sun) *Apéro dînatoire* (casual dinners) is what trendy MI:AM (as in YUM!) is best at, but the lunchtime *tartines* (toasted bread topped with ingredients) aren't bad either. The same set run next-door La Femme du Boulanger (☎ 03 81 82 86 93; open 8am to 7pm Monday to Saturday), paradise for cake lovers.

La Table des Halles (☎ 03 81 50 62 74; 22 rue Gustave Courbet; lunch/dinner menus €16/20; ⏰ lunch & dinner Tue-Sat) The urban loft decor is Manhattanesque – industrial rigging, starch-white walls – but the cuisine is resolutely French: Morteau sausages with Mont d'Ŏr mash or poultry in *savagnin* (a local white wine). Fabulous.

Self-caterers can shop at the **indoor market** (cnr rue Paris & rue Claude Goudimel), the **outdoor market** (place de la Révolution; ⏰ Tue, Fri & Sat morning) or the supermarket, **Monoprix** (10 Grande Rue; ⏰ 8.30am-8pm Mon-Sat).

Drinking

Nightlife centres on the Battant quarter, rue Claude Pouillet and parallel quai Vauban.

Le Gibus (☎ 03 81 81 09 99; 11 rue Claude Pouillet; ⏰ 5pm-1am) A rocking crowd gathers in the 1950s pin-up decor most evenings for live music and DJs.

Carpe Diem (☎ 03 81 83 11 18; 2 place Jean Gigoux; ⏰ 9am-1am Mon-Thu, 9am-2am Fri & Sat, 9am-8pm Sun) The archetypal local French cafe, with a crowd of regulars. Regular gigs feature, when a drink surcharge of €0.40 kicks in.

Les Passagers du Zinc (☎ 03 81 81 54 70; 5 rue Vignier; ⏰ 5pm-1am Tue-Fri, 5pm-2am Sat & Sun) Grungy bar-club with battered sofas, multicoloured lights, and a door made of an old Citroën DS, plus plenty of live bands.

Getting There & Away

There is no bus station in Besançon. Daily services to Ornans (€3.30, 45 minutes) and Pontarlier (€7.50, 1¼ hours) stop at the train station.

From Besançon Gare Viotte, 800m uphill from the centre, there are trains to/from Paris' Gare de Lyon (€63.60, 2¾ hours, three daily), Dijon (train/TGV, €13.30/17.60, 50/70 minutes, 20 daily), Lyon (€31, 2¼ hours, seven daily), Belfort (€14, 1¼ hours, 15 daily), Arbois (€8.10, 45 minutes, eight to 10 daily) and Arc-et-Senans (€6.10, 30 minutes, up to 10 daily). Buy tickets at the train station or from the **Boutique SNCF** (44 Grande Rue; ⏰ 9am-7pm Mon-Fri, 9am-6pm Sat) in town.

Getting Around

Borrow a bicycle, pram or shopping caddie from the local bus company office, **Boutique Ginko** (☎ 08 25 00 22 44; www.ginkobus.com; 4 place du 8 Septembre; ⏰ 10am-7pm Mon-Sat). The boutique sells bus tickets costing €1.15/3.50/9.80 for a single ticket/day ticket/*carnet* of 10.

AROUND BESANÇON

Envisaged by its designer, Claude-Nicolas Ledoux, as the 'ideal city', the 18th-century **Saline Royale** (Royal Saltworks; ☎ 03 81 54 45 45; www.salineroyale.com, in French; adult/6-15yr/16-25yr €7.50/3.50/5; ⏰ 9am-7pm Jul & Aug, 9am-noon & 2-6pm Apr-Jun, Sep & Oct, 10am-noon & 2-5pm Nov-Mar, closed Jan)

LOUIS PASTEUR

Almost every town in France has a street, square or garden named after Jura-born Louis Pasteur, the great 19th-century chemist who invented pasteurisation and developed the first rabies vaccine.

Pasteur was born in **Dole**, 20km west of Arc-et-Senans. His childhood home, **La Maison Natale de Pasteur** (☎ 03 84 72 20 61; www.musee-pasteur.com; 43 rue Pasteur; adult/under 12yr/student €5/free/3; ⏰ 10am-6pm Mon-Sat, 2-6pm Sun Jul & Aug, 10am-noon & 2-6pm Mon-Sat, 2-6pm Sun Apr-Jun, Sep & Oct, 10am-noon & 2-6pm Sat & Sun Nov-Mar) is now an atmospheric museum housing letters, artefacts and exhibits including his university cap and gown.

In 1827 the Pasteurs settled in **Arbois**, 35km east of Dole. His laboratory and workshops in Arbois are on display at **La Maison de Louis Pasteur** (☎ 03 84 66 11 72; 83 rue de Courcelles; adult/7-15yr €5.80/2.90; ⏰ guided tours hourly 9.45-11.45am & 2-6pm Jun-Sep, hourly 2.15-5.15pm Apr, May & 1-15 Oct).

in **Arc-et-Senans**, 30km southwest of Besançon, is a showpiece of early Industrial Age town planning. Regular trains link Besançon and Arc-et-Senans (€6.10, 30 minutes, up to 10 daily).

PARC NATUREL RÉGIONAL DU HAUT-JURA

Experience the Jura at its rawest in the Haut-Jura Regional Park, an area of 757 sq km stretching from Chapelle-des-Bois almost to the western tip of Lake Geneva. Each year in February its lakes, mountains and low-lying valleys host the Transjurassienne, the world's second-longest cross-country skiing race.

Highlights include **Les Rousses** (population 2850, elevation 1100m), the park's main sports hub, both in winter (for skiing) and summer (for walking and mountain biking), and the incredible views from the **Telesiège Val Mijoux** (chairlift; return €6; 9am-1pm & 2.15-5.30pm Fri-Sun mid-Jul–mid-Aug), which travels from the ski resort of Mijoux to Mont Rond (elevation 1533m). Even more stunning is the view from the **Col de la Faucille**, 20km south of Les Rousses.

The **Château de Voltaire** (☎ 04 50 40 53 21; allée du Château; admission free; tours 10.30am, 11.30am, 2.30pm, 3.30pm & 4.30pm Tue-Sun mid-May–mid-Sep), where the great writer lived from 1759 until his return to Paris and death in 1778, is also worth visiting. Guided tours take in the chateau, chapel and 7-hectare park.

Public transport in the park is almost non-existent, so you'll need wheels.

THE DORDOGNE & QUERCY

If it's the heart and soul of France you're searching for, then look no longer. Tucked away in the country's southwestern corner, the neighbouring regions of the Dordogne and Quercy combine history, culture and culinary sophistication in one unforgettably scenic package. The Dordogne is best known for its sturdy *bastides* (fortified towns), clifftop chateaux and spectacular prehistoric cave paintings, while the Mediterranean-tinged region of Quercy is home to endless vintage vineyards and the historic city of Cahors.

SARLAT-LA-CANÉDA

pop 10,000

A pretty tangle of honey-coloured buildings, alleyways and secret squares make up Sarlat-la-Canéda, one of the unmissable villages of the Dordogne, and an ideal (if highly touristy) launch pad for exploring the Vézère Valley.

Sarlat's **tourist office** (☎ 05 53 31 45 45; www.ot-sarlat-perigord.fr; rue Tourny; 9am-7pm Mon-Sat, 10am-noon Sun Apr-Oct, 9am-noon & 2-7pm Mon-Sat Nov-Mar) is attached to a building next to the cathedral and books accommodation for a small fee.

Part of the fun in Sarlat is getting well and truly lost in the twisting alleyways and backstreets. **Rue Jean-Jacques Rousseau** or the area around **Le Présidial** both make good starting points, but for the grandest buildings and *hôtels particuliers* you'll want to explore **rue des Consuls**.

The **Cathédrale St-Sacerdos** was once part of Sarlat's Cluniac abbey, and is a real mix of architectural styles and periods; the belfry and western facade are the oldest parts, while the nave, organ and interior chapels are later additions.

Two medieval courtyards, the **Cour des Fontaines** and the **Cour des Chanoines**, can be reached via an alleyway off rue Tourny. Nearby is the **Jardin des Enfeus**, Sarlat's first cemetery, and the rocket-shaped **Lanterne des Morts** (Lantern of the Dead), built to honour a visit by St Bernard, one of the founders of the Cistercian order, in 1147.

Sleeping & Eating

Hôtel Les Récollets (☎ 05 53 31 36 00; www.hotel-recollets-sarlat.com; 4 rue Jean-Jacques Rousseau; d €43-69) Lost in the medieval maze of the Old Town, the Récollets is a budget beauty. Nineteen topsy-turvy rooms and a charming vaulted breakfast room are rammed in around the medieval *maison*.

Hôtel La Couleuvrine (☎ 05 53 59 27 80; www.la-couleuvrine.com; 1 place de la Bouquerie; d €52-80) Gables, chimneys and red-tile rooftops adorn this rambling hotel, which originally formed part of Sarlat's city wall. It's old, odd and endearingly musty; a couple of rooms are in the hotel's turret.

Hôtel Montaigne (☎ 05 53 31 93 88; www.hotelmontaigne.fr; 2 place Pasteur; d €54-64) Popular with the coach-tour crowd, this imposing stone-front hotel offers modern rooms, all with private bathrooms and cosy decor. They're hardly exciting, but the buffet brekkie is great.

Chez Le Gaulois (☎ 05 53 59 50 64; 3 rue Tourny; mains €9-13; ⏲ lunch & dinner Tue-Sat) Stonking plates of smoked sausage, cold meats and cheese are served up Savoyard-style on wooden platters, as well as authentic *tartiflettes* (cheese, potato and bacon bake) and fondues.

Le Bistrot (☎ 05 53 28 28 40; place du Peyrou; menus €15-24; ⏲ lunch & dinner Mon-Sat) Best of the bunch on place du Peyrou. Red-check tablecloths create an intimate atmosphere, and the menu's heavy on Sarlat classics: *magret de canard* (duck breast) and *pommes sarlardaises* (potatoes cooked in duck fat).

Sarlat's chaotic **Saturday market** (place de la Liberté & rue de la République) takes over the streets around the cathedral from 8am. A smaller **fruit and vegetable market** (⏲ 8.30am-1pm) is held on Wednesday mornings on place de la Liberté.

Getting There & Away

Bus services from Sarlat are practically non-existent. The **train station** (☎ 05 53 59 00 21) is 1.3km south of the old city. Destinations include Périgueux (via Le Buisson; €13.20, 1¾ hours, three daily) and Les Eyzies (change at Le Buisson; €8.20, 50 minutes to 2½ hours depending on connections, three daily).

LES EYZIES-DE-TAYAC-SIREUIL

pop 850

The village of Les Eyzies is little more than a string of touristy shops strung along a central street, but it's worth a visit for the **Musée National de Préhistoire** (☎ 05 53 06 45 45; adult/under 18yr/18-25yr €5/free/3.50, 1st Sun of month free; ⏲ 9.30am-6.30pm Jul & Aug; 9.30am-6pm Wed-Mon Jun & Sep, 9.30am-noon & 2-5.30pm Wed-Mon Oct-May) contains the most comprehensive collection of prehistoric finds in France, including stone-age tools, jewellery and amazing stone frieze of horses and bison.

About 250m north of the museum is the Cro-Magnon shelter of **Abri Pataud** (☎ 05 53 06 92 46; www.semitour.com; adult/under 6yr/6-12yr €5.80/free/3.80; ⏲ 10am-7pm Jul-Sep, 10am-12.30pm & 2-6pm Mon-Sat Sep-Jun), with an ibex carving dating from about 19,000 BC.

For details of the train to Les Eyzies, see left.

CAHORS

pop 21,400

Sheltered in a U-shape *boucle* (curve) in the Lot River, the bustling city of Cahors has the feel of a sunbaked Mediterranean

WORTH THE TRIP: PREHISTORIC PAINTINGS

The Vézère Valley is renowned for its fantastic prehistoric **caves**, many of which contain the finest examples of cave art ever found. Most of the caves are closed in winter, and get very busy in summer. Visitor numbers are strictly limited, so you'll need to reserve well ahead.

Of the Vézère Valley's 175 known sites, the most famous ones include the **Grotte de Font de Gaume** (☎ 05 53 06 86 00; www.leseyzies.com/grottes-ornees; adult/under 18yr/18-25yr €6.50/free/4.50; ⏲ 9.30am-5.30pm mid-May–mid-Sep, 9.30am-12.30pm & 2-5.30pm mid-Sep–mid-May), 1km northeast of Les Eyzies. About 14,000 years ago, the prehistoric artists created the gallery of over 230 figures, including bison, reindeer, horses, mammoths, bears and wolves, of which 25 are on permanent display.

The **Abri du Cap Blanc** (☎ 05 53 06 86 00; adult/under 18yr €6.50/free; ⏲ 9.30am-5.30pm mid-May–mid-Sep, 9.30am-12.30 & 2-5.30pm mid-Sep–mid-May, closed Sat year-round) contains an unusual sculpture gallery of horses, bison and deer about 7km east of Les Eyzies.

Hidden in woodland 15km north of Les Eyzies, **Grotte de Rouffignac** (☎ 05 53 05 41 71; www.grottederouffignac.fr; adult/child €6.20/3.90; ⏲ tours in French 9-11.30am & 2-6pm Jul-Aug, 10-11.30am & 2-5pm Mar-Jun & Sep-Oct) is sometimes known as the 'Cave of 100 Mammoths', thanks to the large number of mammoths painted on the ceiling and walls. Access to the caves is provided by a trundling electric train.

Most famous of all are the **Lascaux Caves** (☎ 05 53 51 95 03; www.semitour.com; adult/6-12yr €8.30/5.30, joint ticket with Le Thot €11.50/7.80; ⏲ 9am-8pm Jul-Aug, 9.30am-6.30pm Sep & Apr-Jun, 10am-12.30pm & 2-6pm Oct–mid-Nov, 10am-12.30pm & 2-5.30pm mid-Nov–Mar), 2km southeast of Montignac, featuring an astonishing menagerie including oxen, deer, horses, reindeer and mammoth, as well as an amazing 5.5m bull, the largest cave drawing ever found. The original cave was closed to the public in 1963 to prevent damage to the paintings, but the most famous sections have been meticulously recreated in a second cave nearby – a massive undertaking that required some 20 artists and took 11 years.

town, a reminder that the southern region of Languedoc lies just to the south. The town's most famous landmark is the Pont du Valentré, one of France's finest medieval bridges, consisting of six arches and three tall towers.

The **tourist office** (☎ 05 65 53 20 65; officetourisme@mairie-cahors.fr; place François Mitterrand; 🕑 9am-6.30pm Mon-Sat, 10am-1pm Sun Jul & Aug, 9am-12.30pm & 1.30-6pm Mon-Sat Sep-Jun) is just off the blvd Léon Gambetta, which neatly divides the old and new parts of town.

The old **medieval quarter** is east of blvd Léon Gambetta, which cuts through the centre of the modern city. In the Middle Ages, Cahors was a prosperous commercial and financial centre, and reminders of the city's wealth are clearly visible along the narrow streets and alleyways of the old city, which is densely packed with elegant houses and merchant's mansions.

Sleeping

Auberge de Jeunesse (☎ 05 65 35 64 71; fjt46@wanadoo.fr; 20 rue Frédéric Suisse; dm €12.10-15.70; 🕑 9am-12.30pm & 2-7pm; 💻) Cahors' youth hostel is friendly and functional, with 50 beds in four- to 10-bed dorms in an old convent.

Hôtel Jean XXII (☎ 05 65 35 07 66; www.hotel-jeanxxii.com; 2 rue Edmond-Albé; s/d/tr €44/53/57; 🕑 reception 4.40-8pm) Huddled next to the Tour Jean XXII, this excellent little hotel mixes plenty of original stone, potted plants and well-worn wood with a flash of metropolitan minimalism. The rooms are plain and smart, keeping clutter to a minimum.

Hôtel de la Paix (☎ 05 65 35 03 40; www.hoteldelapaixcahors.com; 30 place St-Maurice; s €48, d €54-70) Housed in a pale-pink tenement, this friendly hotel is dingy in places, but the better rooms have balconies overlooking place St-Maurice. Downstairs the Blue Angel *salon de thé* is perfect for sticky treats.

Eating

Le Saint Urcisse (☎ 05 65 35 06 06; place St-Urcisse; mains €19.50-25.50; 🕑 lunch & dinner Tue-Sat) Homespun cooking *à la grand-mère,* served in a cosy kitchen-style dining room or a walled courtyard. It's popular for its *picadors brochettes* (kebabs), which come with duck, chicken, prawns or lamb.

Le Marché (☎ 05 65 35 27 27; place Jean-Jacques Chapon; menus €25-35; 🕑 lunch & dinner Tue-Sat) Fusion food in funky surroundings. Puce-and-cream armchairs, razor-edge wood and slate walls set the designer tone, and the menu swings from roast tarragon beef to lemon-scented sea bass.

Top place for self-catering supplies is the **Marché Couvert** (place des Halles; 🕑 8am-12.30pm & 3-7pm Tue-Sat, 9am-noon Sun). The twice-weekly open-air market takes place on place Chapon on Wednesdays and Saturdays.

Getting There & Away

Cahors' **train station** (place Jouinot Gambetta, aka place de la Gare) is on the main line (eight to 10 daily) to Paris' Gare d'Austerlitz (€63.80, five hours) via Brive-la-Gaillarde (€16.90, one hour), Limoges (€28.70, two hours), and Souillac (€12.30, 40 minutes), from where coaches go to Sarlat (€15, three hours, two daily).

THE ATLANTIC COAST & THE FRENCH BASQUE COUNTRY

Though the Côte d'Azur is the most popular beach spot in France, the many seaside resorts along the Atlantic coast are fast catching up. If you're a surf-nut or a beach bum, then the sandy bays around Biarritz will be right up your alley, while oenophiles can sample the fruits of the vine in the high temple of French winemaking, Bordeaux. Towards the Pyrenees you'll find the Basque Country, which in many ways is closer to the culture of northern Spain than to the rest of France.

NANTES

pop 280,600

You can take Nantes out of Brittany (as happened when regional boundaries were redrawn during WWII), but you can't take Brittany out of its long-time capital, Nantes ('Naoned' in Breton). Spirited and innovative, this city has a long history of reinventing itself. Founded by Celts, the city later became France's foremost port, industrial centre and shipbuilding hub, and has recently reinvented itself again as a cultural centre and youthful metropolis – one in two Nantais are aged under 40.

Orientation

On the Loire's northern bank, central Nantes' two main arteries, both served by tram lines, are the partly pedestrianised cours des 50 Otages and a broad east–west boulevard that connects the train station with quai de la Fosse. They intersect near the Gare Centrale bus/tram hub. The old city is to the east, between cours des 50 Otages and the Château des Ducs de Bretagne.

Information

Cyber City (☎ 02 40 89 57 92; 14 rue de Strasbourg; per hr €3; 11am-midnight) Internet access.
Main post office (place de Bretagne)
Tourist office – Feydeau (☎ 02 72 64 04 79; www.nantes-tourisme.com; cours Olivier de Clisson; 10am-6pm, from 10.30am Thu, closed Sun)
Tourist office – St-Pierre (2 place St-Pierre; 10am-1pm & 2-6pm, from 10.30am Thu, closed Mon)

Sights

Forget fusty furnishings – the stripped, light-filled interior of the restored **Château des Ducs de Bretagne** (☎ 02 51 17 49 00; museum/exhibitions each adult/child €5/3 or both €8/4.80, admission to grounds free; 9am-8pm mid-May–mid-Sep, 10am-7pm Wed-Mon mid-Sep–mid-May) houses multimedia-rich new exhibits detailing the city's history.

French painting forms the centrepiece of the **Musée des Beaux-Arts** (☎ 02 51 17 45 00; 10 rue Georges Clemenceau; adult/child €3.10/1.60; 10am-6pm Wed-Mon, to 8pm Thu), with works by Georges de La Tour, Chagall, Monet, Picasso and Kandinsky among others.

Overlooking the river 2km southwest of the tourist office (Feydeau branch), the **Musée Jules Verne** (☎ 02 40 69 72 52; www.julesverne.nantes.fr, in French; 3 rue de l'Hermitage; adult/student & child €3/1.50; 10am-noon & 2-6pm Mon & Wed-Sat, 2-6pm Sun) features first-edition books, manuscripts and cardboard cut-outs inspired by the work of Jules Verne, born in Nantes in 1828. Look out for statues of Captain Nemo and a boyish Jules Vernes in the adjoining park.

Île Feydeau (the quarter south of the Gare Centrale) ceased to be an island after WWII when the riverbeds dried up, while nearby **Île de Nantes** languished after Nantes' shipyards closed, but is now being regenerated as a civic hub. The quirky **Les Machines de l'Île de Nantes** (☎ 08 10 12 12 25; www.lesmachines-nantes.fr) creates amazing mechanisms such as a 12m-high mechanical elephant (40-minute rides adult/child €6/4.50); the adjoining gallery illustrates future projects such as a triple-decker carousel with Jules Verne–inspired mechanical sea creatures, due for completion in 2010. Gallery tickets admit you to the workshop where you can watch these fantastical contraptions being built.

Sleeping

Auberge de Jeunesse La Manu (☎ 02 40 29 29 20; nanteslamanu@fuaj.org; 2 place de la Manu; dm incl breakfast €17; reception closed noon-5pm, hostel closed Christmas period;) Housed in a converted factory, this well-equipped 123-bed hostel is a 15-minute walk from the centre. Take tram 1 to the Manufacture stop.

Hôtel Renova (☎ 02 40 47 57 03; www.hotel-renova.com, in French; 11 rue Beauregard; s €35-45, d €45-50, tr €70) Over six steep mosaic-tiled flights of stairs, this narrow hotel of 24 rooms with original polished floorboards is a simple one-star place with an absolutely superstar city-centre location.

Hôtel des Colonies (☎ 02 40 48 79 76; www.hoteldescolonies.fr; 5 rue du Chapeau Rouge; s €54-72.50, d €61-72.50;) Local art exhibitions, cherry-red public areas and rooms in purple, green and orange make this an attractive option. Wi-fi's free.

Hôtel Graslin (☎ 02 40 69 72 91; www.hotel-graslin.com; 1 rue Piron; r €82-94) An unlikely (but very Nantes) marriage of art deco and '70s style: velour, eggplant-and-orange wing chairs in the lounge, plus spiffy rooms featuring faux timber and edgy colour combos.

Eating

Nantes' most cosmopolitan dining is in the medieval Bouffay quarter. Breton crêperies are plentiful throughout town.

Crêperie Heb-Ken (☎ 02 40 48 79 03; 5 rue de Guérande; crêpes €4.80-17.90; lunch & dinner Mon-Sat) Dozens of varieties of crêpe (such as a delicious trout-and-leek combo, or honey, lemon and almond for dessert) are made with love at this cosy spot. A sure sign of its authenticity.

Brasserie La Cigale (☎ 02 51 84 94 94; 4 place Graslin; breakfasts €11, brunches €20, mains €12.20-24.50; 7.30am-12.30am) No visit to Nantes is complete without a cafe or an all-out feast at 1890s brasserie La Cigale, with its art deco salons and white-aproned waiters.

Le Bistrot de l'Écrivain (☎ 02 51 84 15 15; 15 rue Jean-Jacques Rousseau; menus €14.50-18.50; lunch & dinner Mon-Sat) Splashed wine bottles and checked tablecloths, Le Bistrot de l'Écrivain serves authentic Nantaise cuisine like *sandre* (pike-perch) in *beurre blanc* (white sauce).

Un Coin en Ville (☎ 02 40 20 05 97; 2 place de la Bourse; mains €15-19.50; lunch Tue-Fri, dinner Tue-Sat) Flickering tealights, soulful jazz and blues, and cooking that combines local produce with exotic styles, such as Moroccan tagines with local leeks and turnips.

Sardines are sold at street stalls throughout town between March and November. Stock up on picnic supplies at **Marché de Talensac** (rue Talensac; 7.30am-1pm Tue-Sun). Central supermarkets include **Monoprix** (2 rue du Calvaire; 9am-9pm Mon-Sat).

Getting There & Away

AIR

Aéroport International Nantes-Atlantique (☎ 02 40 84 80 00; www.nantes.aeroport.fr) is 12km southeast of town. The public bus TAN-Air links the airport with the Gare Centrale bus–tram hub and the train station's southern entrance (€6, 20 minutes) from about 5.30am until 9pm.

BUS

The southbound **bus station** (☎ 08 25 08 71 56), across from 13 allée de la Maison Rouge, is used by CTA buses serving areas of the Loire-Atlantique *département* south of the Loire River, while the **Lila** (☎ 08 25 08 71 56) bus covers the entire Loire-Atlantique *département*. Tickets cost €2/16 per single/10 rides.

Eurolines (☎ 02 51 72 02 03; allée de la Maison Rouge; 9.30am-12.30pm & 1.30-6pm Mon-Sat) has an office in town.

TRAIN

The **train station** (☎ 36 35; 27 blvd de Stalingrad) is well connected to most of the country. Destinations include Paris' Gare Montparnasse (€49.10 to €61.40, 2¼ hours, 15 to 20 daily), Bordeaux (€37, four hours, three or four daily) and La Rochelle (€21, 1¾ hours, three or four daily). For tickets and information, try the **SNCF ticket office** (La Bourse, 12 place de la Bourse; 10am-7pm Mon, 9am-7pm Tue-Sat).

Getting Around

The **TAN network** (☎ 08 10 44 44 44; www.tan.fr, in French) includes three modern tram lines that intersect at the Gare Centrale (Commerce), the main bus/tram transfer point. Buses run from 7.15am to 9pm. Night services continue until 12.30am. Combo bus/tram tickets (€1.20) are sold by bus drivers and tram-stop ticket machines. They're valid for one hour after being time-stamped. A *ticket journalier*, good for 24 hours, costs €3.30; time-stamp it only the first time you use it.

POITIERS

pop 87,000

Inland from the coast, history-steeped Poitiers rose to prominence as the former capital of Poitou, the region governed by the Counts of Poitiers in the Middle Ages. Poitiers has one of the oldest universities in the country, first established in 1432 and today a lynchpin of this lively city.

Orientation

The train station is 600m downhill (west) from the old city, which begins north of Poitiers' main square, place du Maréchal Leclerc, and stretches northeast to Église Notre Dame la Grande. Rue Carnot heads south from place du Maréchal Leclerc.

Information

Post office (21 rue des Écossais) Changes money.

Tourist office (☎ 05 49 41 21 24; www.ot-poitiers.fr; 45 place Charles de Gaulle; 10am-11pm Mon-Sat, 10am-6pm & 7-11pm Sun 21 Jun-Aug, 10am-10pm Mon-Sat, 10am-6pm & 7-10pm Sun 1-17 Sep, 10am-6pm Mon-Sat 18 Sep-20 Jun) Near Église Notre Dame.

Virtual 86 (☎ 05 49 53 63 42; 13 rue Magenta; per 15min/1hr €0.50/2; 10am-2am) Internet access.

Sights

Strolling Poitiers' streets is the best way to get a feel for the city's past. Along the footpaths, red, yellow and blue lines correspond with three **self-guided walking tours** detailed on a free map handed out by the tourist office.

Within today's Palais de Justice (law courts), at the northeastern end of rue Gambetta, the vast, partly 13th-century great hall, **Salle des Pas-Perdus** (8.45am-6pm Mon-Fri), is a reminder of the building's history as the former palace of the counts of Poitou and the dukes of Aquitaine.

Every evening from 21 June to the third weekend in September, spectacular colours are cinematically projected onto the west facade of the Romanesque **Église Notre Dame la Grande** (place Charles de Gaulle; 8.30am-7pm Mon-Sat, 2-7pm Sun). The 13th-century stained-glass window at the Gothic **Cathédrale St-Pierre** (rue de la Cathédrale; 8am-6pm) is one of the oldest in France.

WORTH THE TRIP: FUTUROSCOPE

Piercing the countryside with gleaming domes, pods and towers, the attractions at the famous and futuristic theme park **Futuroscope** (☎ 05 49 49 30 80; www.futuroscope.com; Jaunay-Clan; adult/under 16yr €33/25; ⌚ from 10am, seasonal closing times vary, closed Jan–early Feb) include a roller-coaster cinema, a virtual-reality zone where you can 'catch' various creatures in your hands, and a 3-D journey through the solar system. Allow at least five hours to see the major attractions.

Futuroscope is 10km north of Poitiers. TGV trains link the park's TGV station with cities including Paris and Bordeaux. Local **Vitalis bus** (☎ 05 49 44 66 88) bus 9 (€1.30, 30 minutes) links Futuroscope with Poitiers' train station; there are one to two buses an hour from 6.15am until 7.30pm or 9pm.

Seven statues by Camille Claudel are displayed at the **Musée Ste-Croix** (☎ 05 49 41 07 53; www.musees-poitiers.org, in French; 3 rue Jean Jaurès; adult/child €3.70/free; ⌚ 1.15-6pm Mon, 10am-noon & 1.15-6pm Tue-Fri, 10am-noon & 2-6pm Sat & Sun Jun-Sep, to 5pm Mon-Fri & afternoons Sat & Sun Oct-May).

Sleeping

Hôtel Griotte Central (☎ 05 49 01 79 79; www.centralhotel86.com, in French; 35 place du Maréchal Leclerc; d €36-53) At the southern edge of this charming pedestrian district of half-timbered houses, this two-star place is a terrific little bargain. It has snug but sunlit rooms with showers or bath-tubs.

Hôtel de l'Europe (☎ 05 49 88 12 00; www.hotel-europe-poitiers.com; 39 rue Carnot; d €52-83) Behind a dramatically recessed entrance, the main building of this elegant, very un-two-star-like hotel dates from 1710, with a sweeping staircase, oversized rooms and refined furnishings.

Le Grand Hôtel (☎ 05 49 60 90 60; www.grandhotelpoitiers.fr; 28 rue Carnot; s €67-70, d €77-85; ❄) Poitiers' premier hotel lives up to its name. Faux-art deco furnishings and fittings fill the public areas with character, and rooms are spacious and well equipped.

Eating

our pick **La Serrurerie** (☎ 05 49 41 05 14; 28 rue des Grandes Écoles; mains €12-17.50, weekend brunches €15; ⌚ 8am-2am) Showcasing local art, sculpture and retro toys, this mosaic-and-steel bistro-bar is Poitiers' communal lounge–dining room. A chalked blackboard menu lists specialities like *tournedos* (thick slices) of salmon, sensational pastas and a divine *crème brûlée*.

Other good dining bets are the atrium-style bistro **La Gazette** (☎ 05 49 61 49 21; 1 rue Gambetta; menus €11-12; ⌚ lunch & dinner Mon-Sat), and little **La Table du Jardin** (☎ 05 49 41 68 46; 42 rue du Moulin à Vent; menus €9.90, mains €13-18; ⌚ closed Sun, Mon & last 2 weeks Jun), serving exclusively seasonal market-fresh produce.

The covered market **Marché Notre Dame** (⌚ 7am-1pm Tue-Sat) is next to Église Notre Dame la Grande, and there's an open-air market from 7am to 1pm on Saturdays.

Getting There & Away

The **train station** (☎ 08 36 35 35 35; blvd du Grand Cerf) has direct links to Bordeaux (from €29.70, 1¾ hours), Nantes (€25.70, 3¼ hours) and Paris' Gare Montparnasse (from €48.20, 1½ hours, 12 daily).

BORDEAUX

pop 229,500

The new millennium was a major turning point for the city long known as La Belle Au Bois Dormant (Sleeping Beauty), when the mayor, ex-Prime Minister Alain Juppé, roused Bordeaux, pedestrianising its boulevards, restoring its neoclassical architecture, and implementing a hi-tech public transport system. His efforts paid off: in mid-2007 half of the entire city was Unesco listed, making it the largest urban World Heritage site. Bolstered by its students and some 2.5 million tourists, La Belle Bordeaux now scarcely seems to sleep at all.

Orientation

The city centre lies between the flower-filled place Gambetta and the Garonne River. From place Gambetta, place de Tourny is 500m north-east, from where the tourist office is 400m to the east. Bordeaux' train station, Gare St-Jean, is about 3km southeast of the city centre.

Information

Bordeaux Monumental (☎ 05 56 48 04 24; 28 rue des Argentiers; ⌚ 9.30am-1pm & 2-7pm Mon-Sat, 10am-1pm & 2-6pm Sun Jul & Aug, 9.30am-1pm & 2-6pm

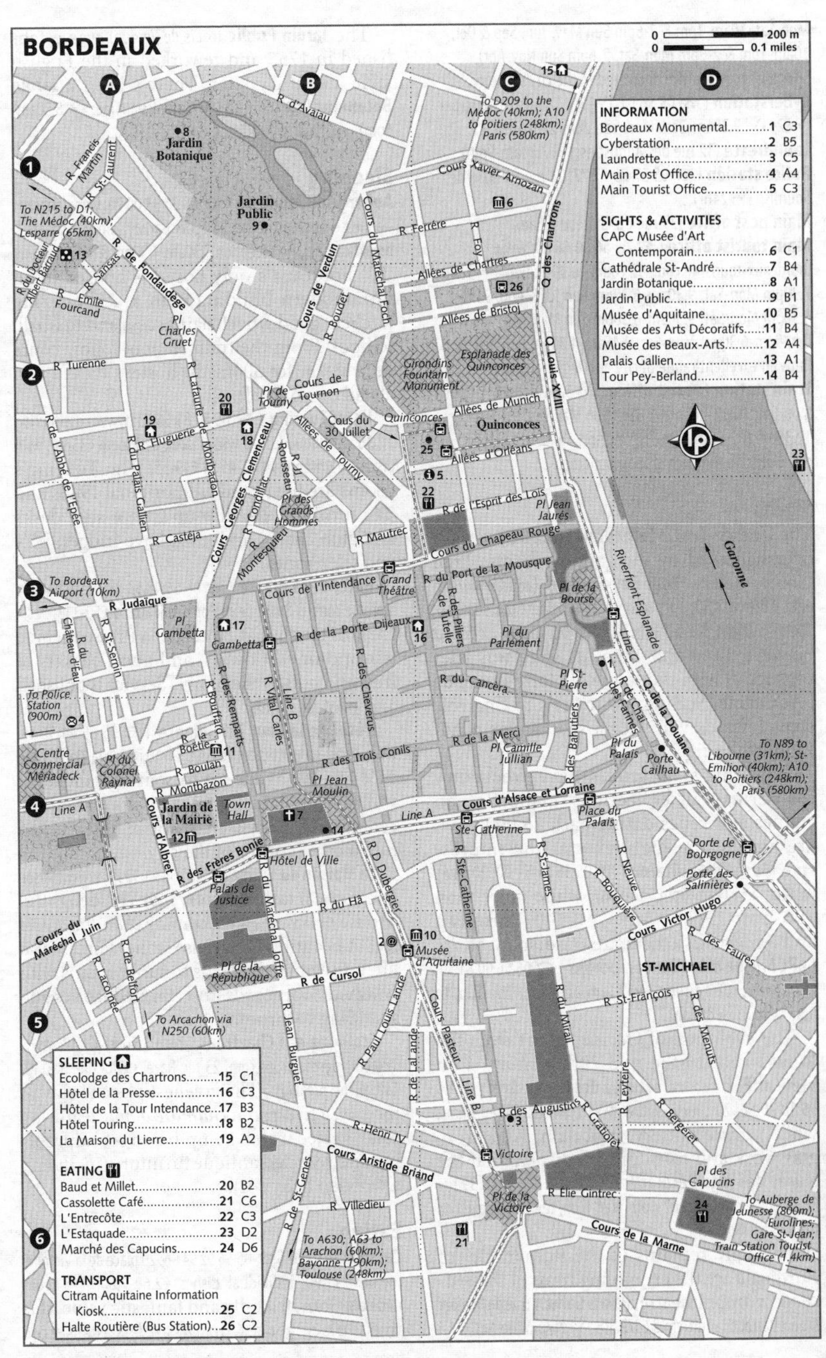
BORDEAUX
0 200 m
0 0.1 miles
INFORMATION
Bordeaux Monumental....1 C3
Cyberstation....2 B5
Laundrette....3 C5
Main Post Office....4 A4
Main Tourist Office....5 C3
SIGHTS & ACTIVITIES
CAPC Musée d'Art Contemporain....6 C1
Cathédrale St-André....7 B4
Jardin Botanique....8 A1
Jardin Public....9 B1
Musée d'Aquitaine....10 B5
Musée des Arts Décoratifs....11 B4
Musée des Beaux-Arts....12 A4
Palais Gallien....13 A1
Tour Pey-Berland....14 B4
SLEEPING
Ecolodge des Chartrons....15 C1
Hôtel de la Presse....16 C3
Hôtel de la Tour Intendance....17 B3
Hôtel Touring....18 B2
La Maison du Lierre....19 A2
EATING
Baud et Millet....20 B2
Cassolette Café....21 C6
L'Entrecôte....22 C3
L'Estaquade....23 D2
Marché des Capucins....24 D6
TRANSPORT
Citram Aquitaine Information Kiosk....25 C2
Halte Routière (Bus Station)....26 C2
To D209 to the Médoc (40km); A10 to Poitiers (248km); Paris (580km)
To N215 to D1; The Médoc (40km); Lesparre (65km)
To Bordeaux Airport (10km)
To Police Station (900m)
To N89 to Libourne (31km); St-Emilion (40km); A10 to Poitiers (248km); Paris (580km)
To Arcachon via N250 (60km)
To A630; A63 to Arachon (60km); Bayonne (190km); Toulouse (248km)
To Auberge de Jeunesse (800m); Eurolines; Gare St-Jean; Train Station Tourist Office (1.4km)
Jardin Botanique
Jardin Public
Quinconces
Esplanade des Quinconces
Girondins Fountain-Monument
Garonne
Riverfront Esplanade
Grand Théâtre
Gambetta
Pl Gambetta
Centre Commercial Mériadeck
Jardin de la Mairie
Town Hall
Hôtel de Ville
Palais de Justice
Pl de la République
Musée d'Aquitaine
Ste-Catherine
Place du Palais
Porte Cailhau
Porte de Bourgogne
Porte des Salinières
ST-MICHAEL
Victoire
Pl de la Victoire
Pl des Capucins
Cours de Verdun
Cours Georges Clemenceau
Cours du Chapeau Rouge
Cours de l'Intendance
Cours d'Alsace et Lorraine
Cours Victor Hugo
R de Cursol
Cours Pasteur
Cours Aristide Briand
Cours de la Marne
Cours d'Albret
Cours du Maréchal Juin
Q des Chartrons
Q Louis XVIII
Q de la Douane
R Judaïque
R Ste-Catherine
R du Mirail
R Elie Gintrec
R Villedieu
R Henri IV
Line A
Line B
Line C
FRANCE

Mon-Sat, 10am-1pm & 2-6pm Sun May, Jun, Sep & Oct, 10am-1pm & 2-6pm Mon-Sat, 2-6pm Sun Nov-Apr) Specialist tourist office dedicated to the city's history.

Cyberstation (☎ 05 56 01 15 15; 23 cours Pasteur; per hr €2; 9.30am-2am Mon-Sat, 2pm-2am Sun)

Laundrette (32 rue des Augustins; 7.30am-9pm)

Police station (☎ 05 57 85 77 77; 23 rue François de Sourdis; 24hr)

Main post office (37 rue du Château d'Eau)

Main tourist office (☎ 05 56 00 66 00; www.bordeaux-tourisme.com; 12 cours du 30 Juillet; 9am-7.30pm Mon-Sat, 9.30am-6.30pm Sun Jul & Aug, 9am-6.30pm Mon-Sat, 9.30am-6.30pm Sun May, Jun, Sep & Oct, 9am-6.30pm Mon-Sat, 9.45am-4.30pm Sun Nov-Apr) Runs an excellent range of city and regional tours.

Train station tourist office (9am-noon & 1-6pm Mon-Sat, 10am-noon & 1-3pm Sun May-Oct, 9.30am-12.30pm & 2-6pm Mon-Fri Nov-Apr) Small but helpful office outside the train station building.

Sights

The Unesco-listed **Cathédrale St-André** is almost overshadowed by the gargoyled, 50m-high Gothic belfry, **Tour Pey-Berland** (adult/child/student €5/free/3.50; 10am-1.15pm & 2-6pm Jun-Sep, 10am-12.30pm & 2-5.30pm Tue-Sun Oct-May). Erected between 1440 and 1466, its spire was later topped off with the statue of Notre Dame de l'Aquitaine. Scaling the tower's 232 narrow steps rewards you with a spectacular panorama of the city.

Bordeaux's museums have free entry for permanent collections. Gallo-Roman statues and relics dating back 25,000 years are among the highlights at the impressive **Musée d'Aquitaine** (☎ 05 56 01 51 00; 20 cours Pasteur; 11am-6pm Tue-Sun), while more than 700 post-1960s works by 140 European and American artists are on display at the **CAPC Musée d'Art Contemporain** (☎ 05 56 00 81 50; Entrepôt 7, rue Ferrére; 11am-6pm Tue, Thu-Sun, to 8pm Wed, closed Mon).

The evolution of Occidental art from the Renaissance to the mid-20th century is on view at Bordeaux's **Musée des Beaux-Arts** (☎ 05 56 10 20 56; 20 cours d'Albret; 11am-6pm Wed-Mon), while *faïence* pottery, porcelain, gold, iron, glasswork and furniture are displayed at the **Musée des Arts Décoratifs** (☎ 05 56 00 72 50; 39 rue Bouffard; museum 2-6pm Wed-Mon, temporary exhibits from 11am Mon-Fri).

The only remains of the Roman city of Burdigala are the crumbling ruins of the 3rd-century amphitheatre, **Palais Gallien** (rue du Docteur Albert Barraud; adult/child €3/2.50; 2-7pm Jun-Sep).

The **Jardin Public** (cours de Verdun) was established in 1755 and reworked in the English style a century later. There's been a **Jardin Botanique** (☎ 05 56 52 18 77; admission free; 8.30am-6pm) on this site since 1855.

Sleeping

Auberge de Jeunesse (☎ 05 56 33 00 70; www.auberge-jeunesse-bordeaux.com; 22 cours Barbey; dm incl sheets & breakfast €21; reception 7.30am-1.30pm & 3.30-9.30pm;) Bordeaux's only hostel is housed in an ultramodern building with a self-catering kitchen, good wheelchair access and fussball, to boot. From the train station, follow cours de la Marne for 300m; the hostel's about 250m ahead on your left.

Hôtel Touring (☎ 05 56 81 56 73; www.hoteltouring.fr; 16 rue Huguerie; s/d with shared bathroom €35/40, with private bathroom s €42-45, d €49-53) The Touring's rooms are furnished with original 1940s and '50s furniture, like flip-up school-style desks and club chairs, and most have fridges, TVs and telephones.

Hôtel de la Presse (☎ 05 56 48 53 88; www.hoteldelapresse.com; 6-8 rue de la Porte-Dijeaux; d €50-113;) Elegant touches at Hôtel de la Presse include silk and dried flowers, and guest baskets of fruit and nuts in the rooms. Service is polished and professional.

Hôtel de la Tour Intendance (☎ 05 56 44 56 56; www.hotel-tour-intendance.com; 14-16 rue de la Vieille Tour; d €58-129;) Wake up to soaring sandstone walls, stone-laid floors and wood-beamed ceilings at this stylised boutique hotel tucked into a quiet corner of the city.

La Maison du Lierre (☎ 05 56 51 92 71; www.maisondulierre.com; 57 rue Huguerie; d €78-99) The delightful 'House of Ivy' has a welcoming *chambre d'hôte* feel. A beautiful Bordelaise stone staircase (no lift, unfortunately) leads to sunlit rooms with polished floorboards, rose-printed fabrics and sparkling bathrooms.

Ecolodge des Chartrons (☎ 05 56 81 49 13; www.ecolodgedeschartrons.com; 23 rue Raze; s €90-100, d €110-140, all incl breakfast) The greenest place to stay in the city, a five-room *chambre d'hôte* featuring solar-heated water, hemp-based soundproofing and recycled antique furniture (including a wooden baby cot).

Eating

Cassolette Café (☎ 05 56 92 94 96; 20 place de la Victoire; menus €11.90, individual dishes €2.60-7.60; noon-midnight) Fun, friendly and fantastic value, this lively place serves up *cassoulets* (casserole dishes) cooked on terracotta plates, created from ingredients you tick off on a checklist.

L'Entrecôte (☎ 05 56 81 76 10; 4 cours du 30 Juillet; menus €16.50; ⏰ lunch & dinner) Opened in 1966, this unpretentious place doesn't take reservations, and it only has one menu option: succulent thin-sliced meat, heated by tealights, cooked in a special shallot sauce and accompanied by homemade *frites* (chips).

Baud et Millet (☎ 05 56 79 05 77; 19 rue Huguerie; menus €19-24; ⏰ 10am-11pm Mon-Sat) Over 250 different cheeses are offered at this cosy, mostly vegetarian place. Serious *fromage* fans should go for the all-you-can-eat cheesy buffet.

L'Estaquade (☎ 05 57 54 02 50; quai de Queyries; mains €22-26; ⏰ lunch & dinner) Set on stilts and jutting from the river's eastern bank, this restaurant is notable for its seafood (bass, cod, scampi, scallops) and magical views of Bordeaux's neoclassical architecture.

On Sunday mornings head to the quai des Chartrons' *bio* (organic) market; otherwise, stock up at the covered market, **Marché des Capucins** (place des Capucins; ⏰ 6am-1pm Tue-Sun).

Getting There & Away

Bordeaux airport (☎ 05 56 34 50 50; www.bordeaux.aeroport.fr) is in Mérignac, 10km west of the city centre, with domestic and some international services. The train station, place Gambetta and the main tourist office are connected to the airport (one way €7) by **Jet'Bus** (☎ 05 56 34 50 50), with buses at 45-minute intervals till 9.45pm or 10.45pm.

Citram Aquitaine (☎ 05 56 43 68 43; www.citram.fr, in French) runs most buses to destinations in the Gironde. **Eurolines** (☎ 05 56 92 50 42; 32 rue Charles Domercq; ⏰ 9am-12.30pm & 1.30-7pm Mon-Fri, 9am-noon & 2-6pm Sat) faces the train station.

Bordeaux is one of France's major rail-transit points. The station, Gare St-Jean, is about 3km from the city centre. Destinations include Paris' Gare Montparnasse (€66.20, three hours, at least 16 daily), Bayonne (€28.80, 1¾ hours), Nantes (€41.60, four hours), Poitiers (€33.90, 1¾ hours) and Toulouse (€33.30, 2¼ hours).

BIARRITZ

pop 30,700

As ritzy as its name suggests, this stylish coastal town, 8km west of Bayonne, took off in the mid-19th century when Napoleon III visited regularly. It glimmers with architectural treasures from the belle époque and art deco eras, but these days its big waves and beachy lifestyle are more popular with European surfers.

Orientation

Place Clemenceau, the heart of town, is just south of the main beach (La Grande Plage). Pointe St-Martin rounds off Plage Miramar, the northern continuation of La Grande Plage, bounded on its southern side by Pointe Atalaye. The train station and airport are about 3km southeast of the centre.

Information

Form@tic (☎ 05 59 22 12 79; 15 av de la Marne; per hr €4; ⏰ 9am-8pm Mon-Sat) Bright, stylish internet cafe.

Laundrettes (⏰ 7am-9pm) Wash your togs at 11 av de la Marne and 4 av Jaulerry.

Post office (rue de la Poste)

Tourist office (☎ 05 59 22 37 00; www.biarritz.fr; Sq d'Ixelles; ⏰ 9am-7pm daily Jul & Aug, 9am-6pm Mon-Sat, 10am-5pm Sun Sep-Jun) Has internet access (€3 for every 15 minutes) and publishes *Biarritz Scope et Shops*, a free what's-on guide.

Sights & Activities

Biarritz' fashionable beaches, particularly the **Grande Plage** and **Plage Miramar**, are end-to-end bodies on hot summer days. North of Pointe St-Martin, the adrenaline-pumping surfing beaches of **Anglet** (the final *t* is pronounced) continue northwards for more than 4km. Take eastbound bus 9 (line C on Sunday and public holidays) from the bottom of av Verdun (just near av Édouard VII).

Beyond long, exposed **Plage de la Côte des Basques**, some 500m south of Port Vieux, are **Plage de Marbella** and **Plage de la Milady**. Take westbound bus 9 (line C on Sunday and public holidays) from rue Gambetta where it crosses rue Broquedis.

Biarritz' history as a fishing and whaling marine is explored at the **Musée de la Mer** (☎ 05 59 22 33 34; www.museedelamer.com; Esplanade du Rocher de la Vierge; adult/child €7.80/5; ⏰ 9.30am-12.30pm & 2-6pm, closed Mon Nov-Mar) alongside underwater life collected from the Bay of Biscay (Golfe de Gascogne).

The 4km-long stretch of Anglet's beaches ranks among Europe's finest surfing venues. For gear, try **Rip Curl Surf Shop** (☎ 05 59 24 38 40; 2 av de la Reine Victoria) or the **Quiksilver Surf School** (☎ 05 59 22 03 12; www.biarritz-boardriders.com, in French).

Sleeping

Biarritz Camping (☎ 05 59 23 00 12; www.biarritz-camping.fr; 28 rue d'Harcet; camp sites €15-23; ⏲ mid-May–mid-Oct;) This camping ground, 2km southwest of the centre, has spacious, shady sites. Take bus 9 to the Biarritz Camping stop.

Auberge de Jeunesse de Biarritz (☎ 05 59 41 76 00; www.hibiarritz.org; 8 rue Chiquito de Cambo; dm incl sheets & breakfast €17.10-18.10; ⏲ reception 8.30am-11.30am & 6-9pm, to noon & 10pm Apr-Sep, closed mid-Dec–early Jan;) This popular place offers outdoor activities including surfing. Rooms for two to four hostellers have an en-suite bathroom. From the train station, follow the railway westwards for 800m.

Hôtel Maïtagaria (☎ 05 59 24 26 65; www.hotel-maitagaria.com; 34 av Carnot; s €49-54, d €57-69, tr €76-90) Spotless modern rooms with art deco furniture and immaculate bathrooms, as well as a lovely summer terrace tailor-made for lounging.

La Maison du Lierre (☎ 05 59 24 06 00; www.maisondulierre.com; 3 av du Jardin Public; r €56-139) Run by the owners of the Maison du Lierre in Bordeaux (p300), this place has 23 exquisitely decorated rooms named for local plants in the adjacent Jardin Public, and many rooms have garden views.

Hôtel Mirano (☎ 05 59 23 11 63; www.hotelmirano.fr, in French; 11 av Pasteur; r €70-110) Squiggly purple, orange and black wallpaper and oversize orange perspex light fittings are some of the rad '70s touches at this boutique retro hotel, a 10-minute stroll from the town centre.

Eating

See-and-be-seen cafes and restaurants line Biarritz' beachfront.

Le Corsaire (☎ 05 59 24 63 72; Port des Pêcheurs; mains €11-23.50; ⏲ lunch & dinner Tue-Sat) Down by the water's edge, sit out on the terrace to savour dishes like grilled cod with chorizo. The neighbouring seafood restaurants in this little harbourside setting offer similar quality and prices.

Tikia (☎ 05 59 24 46 09; 1 place Ste-Eugénie; menus €12.80-20; ⏲ lunch & dinner) The premises may be *tikia* ('small' in Basque) but the same can't be said of this rustic restaurant's giant *brochettes* (skewers) of duck, steak or seafood.

Bistrot des Halles (☎ 05 59 24 21 22; 1 rue du Centre; mains €14.50-17; ⏲ lunch & dinner) One of a cluster of decent restaurants along rue du Centre that get their produce directly from the nearby covered market, this bustling place serves excellent fish and other fresh fare from the blackboard menu.

Just downhill from Biarritz' **covered market**, **La Table de Don Quichotte** (12 av Victor Hugo) sells all sorts of Spanish hams, sausages, pickles and wines. You'll find a tempting array of cheeses, wines and pâtés at nearby **Mille et Un Fromages** (8 av Victor Hugo). At sea level, **Épicerie Fine du Port Vieux** (41bis rue Mazagran) is another excellent delicatessen.

Drinking

There are some great bars on and around rue du Port Vieux, place Clemenceau and the central food-market area.

Bar Basque (☎ 05 59 24 60 92; 1 rue du Port Vieux) This rustic-chic newcomer serves bite-size Basque tapas (€1.20 to €7) washed down with a fantastic selection of wines.

Le Surfing (☎ 05 59 24 78 72; 9 blvd Prince des Galles) After a hard day's surfing, drop in to this memorabilia-filled surf bar to compare waves and wipe-outs.

Arena Café Bar (☎ 05 59 24 88 98; Plage du Port Vieux; ⏲ 9am-2am daily Apr-Sep, 10am-2am Wed-Sun Oct-Mar) Tucked into a tiny cove, this beachfront hangout combines a style-conscious restaurant (mains €15 to €22) with a fuchsia-tinged bar with DJs on the turntables.

Getting There & Away

Biarritz–La Négresse train station is about 3km south of the town centre, and is served by buses 2 and 9 (B and C on Sundays).

From place des Basques, **ATCRB buses** (☎ 05 59 26 06 99) follow the coast to the Spanish border. There are nine services daily to St-Jean de Luz (€3, 40 minutes) with connections for Hendaye (€3, one hour). Summer beach traffic can double journey times.

Transportes Pesa (☎ in Spain 902 10 12 10; www.pesa.net) buses leave twice a day Monday to Saturday for Bilbao in Spain, calling by Biarritz, St-Jean de Luz, Irún and San Sebastián.

From the train station, **RDTL** (☎ 05 59 55 17 59; www.rdtl.fr, in French) runs services northwards into Les Landes. For beaches north of Bayonne, such as Mimizan Plage and Moliets Plage, get off at Vieux Boucau (1¼ hours, six or seven daily).

Eurolines is represented in Biarritz by **Voyages Domejean** (☎ 05 59 59 19 33; 3 place Charles de Gaulle). Buses stop in the square, opposite this travel agent's office.

LOURDES

pop 15,700 / elev 400m

Lourdes has been one of the world's most important pilgrimage sites since 1858, when 14-year-old Bernadette Soubirous (1844–79) saw the Virgin Mary in a series of 18 visions that came to her in a grotto. The town now feels dangerously close to a religious theme park, with a roll-call of over six million miracle-seeking visitors and endless souvenir shops selling statues and Virgin Mary–shaped plastic bottles (just add holy water at the shrine). Thankfully the commercialism doesn't extend to the *sanctuaires* (sanctuaries) themselves, which are mercifully souvenir-free.

The most revered site is the **Grotte de Massabielle** (Massabielle Cave), lit by flickering candles left by previous pilgrims. The 19 holy **baths** (generally 9-11am & 2.30-4pm Mon-Sat, 2-4pm Sun & holy days) are said to cure all kinds of diseases and ailments – the most recent confirmed case was that of an Italian, Anna Santaniello, who was apparently cured of chronic rheumatism in 2005.

The main 19th-century section of the **sanctuaries** is divided between the neo-Byzantine Basilique du Rosaire, the crypt and the spire-topped Basilique Supérieure (Upper Basilica). From Palm Sunday to at least mid-October, solemn torchlight processions nightly start from the Massabielle Grotto at 9pm, while at 5pm there's the Procession Eucharistique (Blessed Sacrament Procession) along the Esplanade des Processions. All four places of worship open 6am to 10pm in summer and 7am to 7pm in winter.

Lourdes is well connected by train; destinations include Bayonne (€18.90, 1¾ hours, up to four daily) and Toulouse (€22.20, 1¾ hours, six daily). There are four daily TGVs to Paris' Gare Montparnasse (€91.80, six hours).

LANGUEDOC-ROUSSILLON

Languedoc-Roussillon is three separate regions rolled into one. Bas Languedoc (Lower Languedoc) is known for bullfighting, rugby and robust red wines and is home to all the major sights, including the Roman amphitheatre at Nîmes and the turret-topped town of Carcassonne. Inland is the mountainous region of Haut Languedoc (Upper Languedoc), while Roussillon sits beside the rugged Pyrenees and shares more than just a border with nearby Catalonia. Meanwhile Languedoc's traditional centre, Toulouse, was hived off when regional boundaries were redrawn almost half a century ago, but we've chosen to include it in this section.

CARCASSONNE

pop 45,500

With its witch's hat turrets and walled city, Carcassonne looks like some fairy-tale fortress from afar – but the medieval magic's more than a little tarnished by an annual influx of over four million visitors. It can be a tourist hell in high summer, so pitch up out of season to see the town at its best (and quietest).

You can borrow an audio guide to **La Cité** (The Old City; €3 for 2hr) at the **tourist office** (☎ 04 68 10 24 30; www.carcassonne-tourisme.com; 28 rue de Verdun; 9am-7pm Jul & Aug, 9am-6pm Mon-Sat, 9am-1pm Sun Sep-Jun) or one of the summer **annexes** (La Cité Porte Narbonnaise; year-round; Ville Basse av Joffre; mid-Apr–Oct).

The old city is dramatically illuminated at night and enclosed by two **rampart walls** punctuated by 52 stone towers, Europe's largest city fortifications. Successive generations of Gauls, Romans, Visigoths, Moors, Franks and Cathars reinforced the walls, but only the lower sections are original; the rest, including the turrets, were stuck on by the 19th-century architect Viollet-le-Duc.

A drawbridge leads to the old gate of **Porte Narbonnaise** and rue Cros Mayrevieille en route to place Château and the 12th-century **Château Comtal** (adult/under 18yr/18-25yr €7.50/free/4.80; 10am-6.30pm Apr-Sep, 9.30am-5pm Oct-Mar). South of place du Château is **Basilique St-Nazaire** (9-11.45am & 1.45-5.30pm Mon-Sat, 9-10.45am & 2-6pm Sun), illuminated by delicate medieval rose windows.

Bus services are extremely patchy, but Carcassonne is on the main line to Toulouse (€13.30, 50 minutes, frequent).

NÎMES

pop 145,000

The buzzy city of Nîmes boast some of France's best-preserved classical buildings, including a famous Roman amphitheatre, although the city is most famous for its sartorial export, *serge de Nîmes* – better-known to cowboys, clubbers and couturiers as denim.

Information

Avenue PC Gamer (2 rue Nationale; per hr €2; 10.30am-11.30pm) Internet access.
Laundrette (14 rue Nationale; 7am-9pm)
Main post office (blvd de Bruxelles)
Net@Games (place de la Maison Carrée; per hr €2.50, wi-fi per hr €2; 9am-1am Mon-Sat, noon-1am Sun) Internet access.
Tourist office (04 66 58 38 00; www.ot-nimes.fr; 6 rue Auguste; 8.30am-8pm Mon-Fri, 9am-7pm Sat, 10am-6pm Sun Jul & Aug; core hr 8.30am-6.30pm Mon-Fri, 9am-6.30pm Sat, 10am-5pm Sun Sep-Jun) Rents out audio guides (one/two terminals €8/10).

Sights

A **combination ticket** (adult/child €9.80/7.50), valid for three days, covers all three of Nîmes major sights.

The magnificent **Roman Amphitheatre** (adult/under 7yr/7-17yr incl audio guide €7.70/free/5.90; 9am-7pm Jun-Aug, 9am-6pm or 6.30pm Mar-May, Sep & Oct, 9.30am-5pm Nov-Feb), the best preserved in the whole of the Roman Empire, was built around AD 100 to seat 24,000 spectators. Gladiators and exotic animals once fought each other to the death in this stately arena, and bullfights are still held here almost two millennia later. If you time it right, you might catch a couple of actors in full combat gear slugging it out in the arena.

The **Maison Carrée** (place de la Maison Carrée; adult/under 7yr/7-17yr €4.50/free/3.70; 10am-7pm or 7.30pm Apr-Sep, 10am-6.30pm Mar & Oct, 10am-1pm & 2-5pm Nov-Feb) is a rectangular Roman temple, constructed around AD 5 to honour Emperor Augustus' two adopted sons.

A 10- to 15-minute uphill walk to the top of the gardens brings you to the crumbling shell of the **Tour Magne** (adult/under 7yr/7-17yr €2.70/free/2.30; 9.30am-6.30pm or 7pm Jun-Sep, 9.30am-1pm & 2-4.30pm or 6pm Oct-Mar), raised around 15 BC and the largest of a chain of towers that once punctuated the city's 7km-long Roman ramparts.

Nîmes also has free museums exploring the city's history and archaeology, but you'll have to pay to visit the **Musée des Beaux-Arts** (rue de la Cité Foulc; adult/under 7yr/7-17yr €5.10/free/3.70) and the **Musée d'Art Contemporain** (place de la Maison Carrée; adult/under 7yr/7-17yr €5.10/free/3.70).

Festivals & Events

Nîmes becomes more Spanish than French during its two *férias* (bullfighting festivals): the five-day **Féria de Pentecôte** (Whitsuntide Festival) in June, and the three-day **Féria des Vendanges** celebrating the grape harvest on the third weekend in September.

Sleeping

Auberge de Jeunesse (04 66 68 03 20; www.hinimes.com; 257 chemin de l'Auberge de Jeunesse, la Cigale; dm/d/q €12.75/32/51; Feb-Dec) This sterling, well-equipped youth hostel with self-catering facilities has everything from dorms to cute houses for two to six in its extensive grounds, 3.5km northwest of the train station. Take bus I, direction Alès or Villeverte, and get off at the Stade stop.

Hôtel Central (04 66 67 27 75; www.hotel-central.org; 2 place du Château; s/d with shared bathroom €35/40, s/d/tr/q with private bathroom €43/48/58/68) With its creaky floorboards and bunches of wild flowers painted on each bedroom door, this friendly hotel is full of character.

Hôtel Amphithéâtre (04 66 67 28 51; http://pagesperso-orange.fr/hotel-amphitheatre; rue des Arènes; s €41-45, d €53-70; Feb-Dec;) The welcoming, family-run Amphithéâtre is just up the road from its namesake. Once a pair of 18th-century mansions, it has 15 rooms decorated in warm, woody colours, each named after a writer or painter.

Royal Hôtel (04 66 58 28 27; www.royalhotel-nimes.com, in French; 3 blvd Alphonse Daudet; s €60-65, d €75-85) This boho hotel's a treat: rooms are furnished with flair, and some overlook pedestrian place d'Assas, a work of modern art in its own right – although light sleepers might not appreciate the traffic noise.

Eating

Nîmes' gastronomy owes as much to Provence as to Languedoc. Look out for *cassoulet* (pork, sausage and white bean stew, sometimes served with duck), aïoli and *rouille* (a spicy chilli mayonnaise).

Haddock Café (04 66 67 86 57; www.haddock-café.fr, in French; 13 rue de l'Agau; daily specials €8, mains €10-14.50, menus €15-20; lunch & dinner Mon-Fri, 7pm-2am Sat) This cheerful cafe began life as a convent. Traditional food, local wines and live music at least twice a week.

Au Plaisir des Halles (04 66 36 01 02; 4 rue Littré; mains €10, menus €22-44; Tue-Sat) Near the covered market, ingredients here are all locally sourced and the lunchtime three-course *menu* is excellent value. Local winegrowers feature both on the walls and in the wine-racks.

Le Marché sur la Table (04 66 67 22 50; 10 rue Littré; mains €15-18; Tue-Sun) You *could* just pop in for a glass of wine at this up-and-coming bistro, but you'd be missing out on Éric Vidal's market-fresh food. Eat in the attractively furnished interior or quiet rear courtyard.

Le 9 (☎ 04 66 21 80 77; 9 rue de l'Étoile; lunch menus €15, mains €15-18; ⏰ Mon-Sat & lunch Sun May-Sep, dinner Fri & Sat only Oct-Apr) Tucked away behind high green doors you'll find a converted stables and a vine-clad courtyard. Everything except the lunch *menu* is à la carte.

For self-catering:

Covered market (rue Aimé Ramond; ⏰ Mon-Sat)
La Ferme (☎ 04 68 25 02 15; 26 rue Chartran) Well-stocked deli.
L'Art Gourmand (13 rue St-Louis) Divine chocolates and 33 flavours of ice cream.
Open-air market (place Carnot; ⏰ Tue, Thu & Sat)

Getting There & Away

Nîmes airport (☎ 04 66 70 49 49), 10km southeast of the city on the A54, is served by Ryanair to/from London (Luton), Liverpool and Nottingham East Midlands.

The **bus station** (☎ 04 66 38 59 43; rue Ste-Félicité) connects with the train station. International operators **Eurolines** (☎ 04 66 29 49 02) and **Line Bus** (☎ 04 66 29 50 62) both have kiosks. Regional destinations include Pont du Gard (€6.50, 30 minutes, five daily) and Alès (€8, 1¼ hours, five daily).

More than 12 TGVs daily run to/from Paris' Gare de Lyon (€68.50 to €96, three hours), while regional trains run to/from Avignon (€8.10, 30 minutes), Marseille (€17.90, 1¼ hours) and Montpellier (€8.20, 30 minutes).

PONT DU GARD

The Pont du Gard, a Unesco World Heritage site, is an exceptionally well-preserved, three-tiered Roman aqueduct. It's part of a 50km-long system of canals built about 19 BC by the Romans to bring water from near Uzès to Nîmes. The scale is huge: the 35 arches of the 275m-long upper tier, running 50m above the Gard River, contain a watercourse designed to carry 20,000 cubic metres of water per day and the largest construction blocks weigh over five tonnes.

From car parks (€5) either side of the Gard River, you can walk along the road bridge, built in 1743. The best view of the Pont du Gard is from upstream, beside the river, where you can swim on hot days.

TOULOUSE

pop 437,100

Often known as *la ville rose* (the pink city), funky Toulouse is one of the nation's liveliest and fastest-growing metropolises. Sliced through by the twin rivers of Canal du Midi and the Garonne, it's a city with both a long history and a forward-looking attitude: medieval streets and old churches fill the Old Town, while buzzy bars, grungy gig venues and over 100,000 students give the place a youthful kick.

Orientation

The heart of Toulouse is bounded by the River Garonne (west), blvd de Strasbourg, blvd Lazare Carnot (east). From place Wilson, allée Jean Jaurès leads to the bus station and Gare Matabiau, the train station.

Information

Laverie des Lois (☎ 05 61 23 71 45; 19 rue des Lois; http://laveriedeslois.spaces.live.com; per hr €4; ⏰ cybercafe 11am-9pm Tue-Sat, laundrette 8am-9pm daily) Surf the net while your smocks wash.
Post office (9 rue la Fayette)
Tourist office (☎ 05 61 11 02 22; www.toulouse-tourisme.com; Sq Charles de Gaulle; ⏰ 9am-7pm Mon-Sat, 10am-1pm & 2-6.15pm Sun Jun-Sep, 9am-6pm Mon-Fri, 9am-12.30pm & 2-6pm Sat, 10am-12.30pm & 2-5pm Sun Oct-May) Inside a 16th-century tower. Runs walking tours (two hours; adult/10 to 16 years €9/6) of historic Toulouse, metro art and night time Toulouse (adult/10 to 16 years €10/7).

Sights

Bustling **place du Capitole** is the city's main square. On the ceiling of the arcades on its western side are 29 vivid illustrations of the city's history by contemporary artist Raymond Moretti. On the square's eastern side is the 128m-long facade of the **Capitole**, Toulouse's city hall built in the 1750s.

Once an important stop on the Chemin de St-Jacques pilgrimage route, the **Basilique St-Sernin** (☎ 05 61 21 80 45; place St-Sernin; ⏰ 8.30am-6.15pm Mon-Sat, 8.30am-7.30pm Sun Jul-Sep, 8.30-11.45am & 2-5.45pm Mon-Sat, 8.30am-12.30pm & 2-7.30pm Sun Oct-Jun) is France's largest Romanesque structure and is topped by an octagonal 13th-century tower and 15th-century spire.

Inside an old Augustinian monastery, the **Musée des Augustins** (☎ 05 61 22 21 82; 21 rue de Metz; adult/under 18yr €3/free, temporary exhibitions €6/free, 1st Sun of month free; ⏰ 10am-6pm Thu-Tue, 10am-9pm Wed) houses a superb fine-art collection ranging from Roman artefacts to paintings by Rubens, Delacroix and Toulouse-Lautrec.

The **Cathédrale St-Étienne** (Cathedral of St Stephen; place St-Étienne; ⌚ 8am-7pm Mon-Sat, 9am-7pm Sun) is a hotchpotch of styles: highlights include a glorious rose window dating from 1230, and a 13th-century choir.

The city's old red-brick abattoir has been transformed into the cutting-edge **Musée d'Art Moderne et Contemporain** (☎ 05 62 48 58 00; www.lesabattoirs.org, in French; 76 allées Charles de Fitte; admission €5-10 depending on exhibition, 1st Sun of month free; ⌚ 11am-7pm Tue-Sun).

Boat trips along the Canal du Midi and Garonne River run by **Toulouse Croisières** (☎ 05 61 25 72 57; www.toulouse-croisieres.com, in French) and **Les Bateaux Toulousains** (☎ 05 61 80 22 26; www.bateaux-toulousains.com) leave from quai de la Daurade.

Sleeping

Hôtel La Chartreuse (☎ 05 61 62 93 39; www.chartreusehotel.com; 4bis blvd de Bonrepos; d/tr €37/48) *Bon repos* (good rest) is the order of the day at this good-value hotel across from the train station.

Hôtel des Arts (☎ 05 61 23 36 21; couleurs.suds@club-internet.fr; 1bis rue Cantegril; d with shared/private shower €42/54) Price is the trump card for this modest place: all rooms feature shared toilets and in-room shower cubicles.

our pick **Hôtel St-Sernin** (☎ 05 61 21 73 08; www.hotelstsernin.com; 2 rue St-Bernard; s/d/tr from €58/68/83) Exciting change is afoot at this boutique hotel: Parisian couple Julien and Aurore bought it in 2008 and are renovating floor by floor. Rooms 4, 9, 15 and 20 are to die for, and many have prime views of Basilique St-Sernin.

Hôtel Castellane (☎ 05 61 62 18 82; www.castellanehotel.com, in French; 17 rue Castellane; d/tr/q €72/84/88; ⌘) Unbeatable value, brilliantly placed and ranking sky-high in the friendliness stakes, this unpretentious two-starrer boasts family rooms and a sunlit interior patio.

Eating

Michel, Marcel, Pierre et les Autres (☎ 05 61 22 47 05; www.michelmarcelpierre.com; 35 rue de Rémusat; starters/mains/desserts €7/13/7, 2-/3-course menus €17/23; ⌚ lunch & dinner Tue-Sat) This classic bistro with a quirk is *the* place for bistro fare (mackerel fillets, pastry-baked cheese, *rillettes de canard* etc).

Les Halles Victor Hugo (place Victor Hugo; menus €10-20; ⌚ lunch Tue-Sun) Toulouse's best-value meals are on offer at the small, lunchtime-only restaurants above the busy covered market. Food is fast, delicious and totally French.

our pick **Chez Navarre** (☎ 05 62 26 43 06; 49 Grande Rue Nazareth; lunch/dinner menus €12.50/20; ⌚ lunch & dinner Tue-Fri, dinner Sat) Fed up with restaurant dining? This fabulous 16th-century *table d'hôtes* with red-brick walls, old wooden bar, beamed ceiling and shared candlelit tables is perfect. The rustic French cuisine of simple terrines, soups and one fixed meal emphasise the down-home feel.

Au Coin de la Rue (☎ 05 61 21 99 45; 2 rue Pargaminières; 2-/3-course menus €19/22, salads €14; ⌚ lunch & dinner daily) With wooden window shutters and a well-aged bottle of Armagnac planted on the bar, this contemporary spot has a handful of tables in the sun and several in the shade.

Buy fresh produce (and/or wine for €1.20 a litre!) at **Les Halles Victor Hugo** (place Victor Hugo; ⌚ 7am-1pm Tue-Sun) or **Marché des Carmes** (place des Carmes; ⌚ 7am-1pm Tue-Sun).

Imaginative breads (chestnut, nut, chorizo, onion, fig etc) make **La Panetière aux Saveurs d'Antan** (39 blvd de Strasbourg; ⌚ 7am-8.30pm Wed-Mon) a satisfying picnic stop.

Drinking

Almost every square in the Vieux Quartier has at least one bustling cafe.

Au Père Louis (☎ 05 61 21 33 45; 45 rue des Tourneurs; ⌚ 8.30am-3pm & 5-10.30pm Mon-Sat) Top of our list for irresistible old-fashioned charm, 'Father Louis' is Toulouse's oldest bar (franked 1889).

La Maison (☎ 05 61 62 87 22; 9 rue Gabriel Péri; ⌚ 5pm-2am Sun-Fri, 5pm-5am Sat) This crumbling old house is all about old-fashioned atmosphere – there's a vintage fireplace, retro chairs and sofas to lounge on.

La Tireuse (☎ 05 61 12 28 29; 24 rue Pargaminières; ⌚ 5pm-2am Mon-Sat, 6pm-2am Sun) Friendly beer bar with 20 beers *en pression* (on tap), surrounded by kebab and burger joints.

Havana Café (☎ 05 62 88 34 94; www.havana-café.fr; 2 av des Crêtes, Ramonville St-Agne; admission free-€20) Reggae, rock, blues, heavy metal and gospel make this Toulouse's best live-music venue; it's at the end of metro line B, 8km south of the city (Ramonville stop).

Le Bikini (☎ 05 62 24 09 50; www.lebikini.com; rue Hermès, Ramonville St-Agne; admission €5-20) The stuff of Toulousien legend for 25 years or so, also at the end of metro line B (Ramonville metro stop).

Getting There & Away

From **Toulouse-Blagnac airport** (☎ 08 25 38 00 00; www.toulouse.aeroport.fr), 8km northwest of the centre, there are daily flights to/from Paris (Air France and easyJet) and other European cities. The **Navette Aéroport** (airport shuttle; ☎ 05 34 60 64 00; www.navette-tisseo-aeroport.com) links the airport (one way/return €4/6.30, 20 minutes, every 20 minutes from 5am/7.25am to 8.20pm/midnight from town/airport) with the bus station, Jean Jaurès metro station or place Jeanne d'Arc.

Trains are the quickest and easiest transport from Toulouse, with regular destinations including Bayonne (€37.30, 3¾ hours), Bordeaux (€34.80, two to three hours), Carcassonne (€13.30, one hour) and Lourdes (€23.40, 1¾ hours). Buy tickets at the **SNCF boutique** (5 rue Peyras) or **Gare Matabiau** (blvd Pierre Sémard), 1km northeast of the centre.

Local buses and the two-line metro are run by **Tisséo** (☎ 05 61 41 70 70; www.tisseo.fr, in French), which has ticket kiosks located on place Jeanne d'Arc and cours Dillon. A one-way/return ticket for either costs €1.40/2.50, a 10-ticket *carnet* is €11.70 and a one-/two-day pass is €4.20/7.

PROVENCE

Provence conjures up images of rolling lavender fields, blue skies, gorgeous villages, wonderful food and superb wine. It certainly delivers on all those fronts, but it's not just worth visiting for its good looks – dig a little deeper and you'll also discover the multicultural metropolis of Marseille, the artistic haven of Aix-en-Provence and the old Roman city of Arles.

MARSEILLE

pop 826,700

There was a time when Marseille was the butt of French jokes and on the receiving end of some pretty bad press. No longer. The *cité phocéenne* has made an unprecedented comeback, undergoing a vast makeover. Marseillais will tell you that the city's rough-and-tumble edginess is part of its charm and that, for all its flaws, it is a very endearing place. They're right: Marseille grows on you with its unique history, souklike markets, millennia-old port and spectacular *corniches* (coastal roads).

Orientation

The city's main thoroughfare, blvd La Canebière, stretches eastwards from the Vieux Port (Old Port). The train station is north of La Canebière at the northern end of blvd d'Athènes. A few blocks south of La Canebière is the cours Julien, a large pedestrianised square. The ferry terminal is west of place de la Joliette, a few minutes' walk north of the Cathédrale de la Major. Addresses below include arrondissements (1er being the most central).

Information

There are banks and exchange bureaux on La Canebière near the Vieux Port.

Canebière Change (39 La Canebière, 1er; ⌚ 8am-6pm Mon-Fri, 8.30am-noon & 2-4.30pm Sat; Ⓜ Vieux Port)
Info Café (☎ 04 91 33 74 98; 1 quai de Rive Neuve, 1er; per hr adult/student €3.80/3; ⌚ 9am-9pm Mon-Sat, 2.30-7.30pm Sun; Ⓜ Vieux Port)
Laverie des Allées (15 allées Léon Gambetta, 1er; ⌚ 8am-8pm; Ⓜ 🚊 Réformés Canebière)
Main post office (1 place de l'Hôtel des Postes, 1er; Ⓜ Colbert) Offers currency exchange.
Tourist office (☎ 04 91 13 89 00; www.marseille-tourisme.com; 4 La Canebière, 1er; ⌚ 9am-7pm Mon-Sat, 10am-5pm Sun; Ⓜ Vieux Port)

Dangers & Annoyances

Marseille isn't a hotbed of crime, but petty crimes and muggings are commonplace. There's no need for paranoia but you should avoid the Belsunce area. Women *will* get unsolicited attention, ranging from wolf-whistling to sometimes aggressive chat-up routines – but keep your wits about you and you should be fine.

Sights

MUSEUMS

Built as a charity shelter for the town's poor, the stunning **Centre de la Vieille Charité** (☎ 04 91 14 58 80; 2 rue de la Charité, 2e; Ⓜ Joliette) now houses Marseille's **Musée d'Archéologie Méditerranéenne** (Museum of Mediterranean Archeology; ☎ 04 91 14 58 59) and **Musée d'Arts Africains, Océaniens & Amérindiens** (Museum of African, Oceanic & American Indian Art; ☎ 04 91 14 58 38). An all-inclusive ticket costs €5/2.50 adult/student.

A fascinating insight into Marseille's cultural heritage, the **Musée d'Histoire de Marseille** (☎ 04 91 90 42 22; ground fl, Centre Bourse shopping centre, 1er; adult/child €2/1; ⌚ noon-7pm Mon-Sat; Ⓜ Vieux Port) has some extraordinary exhibits, including the

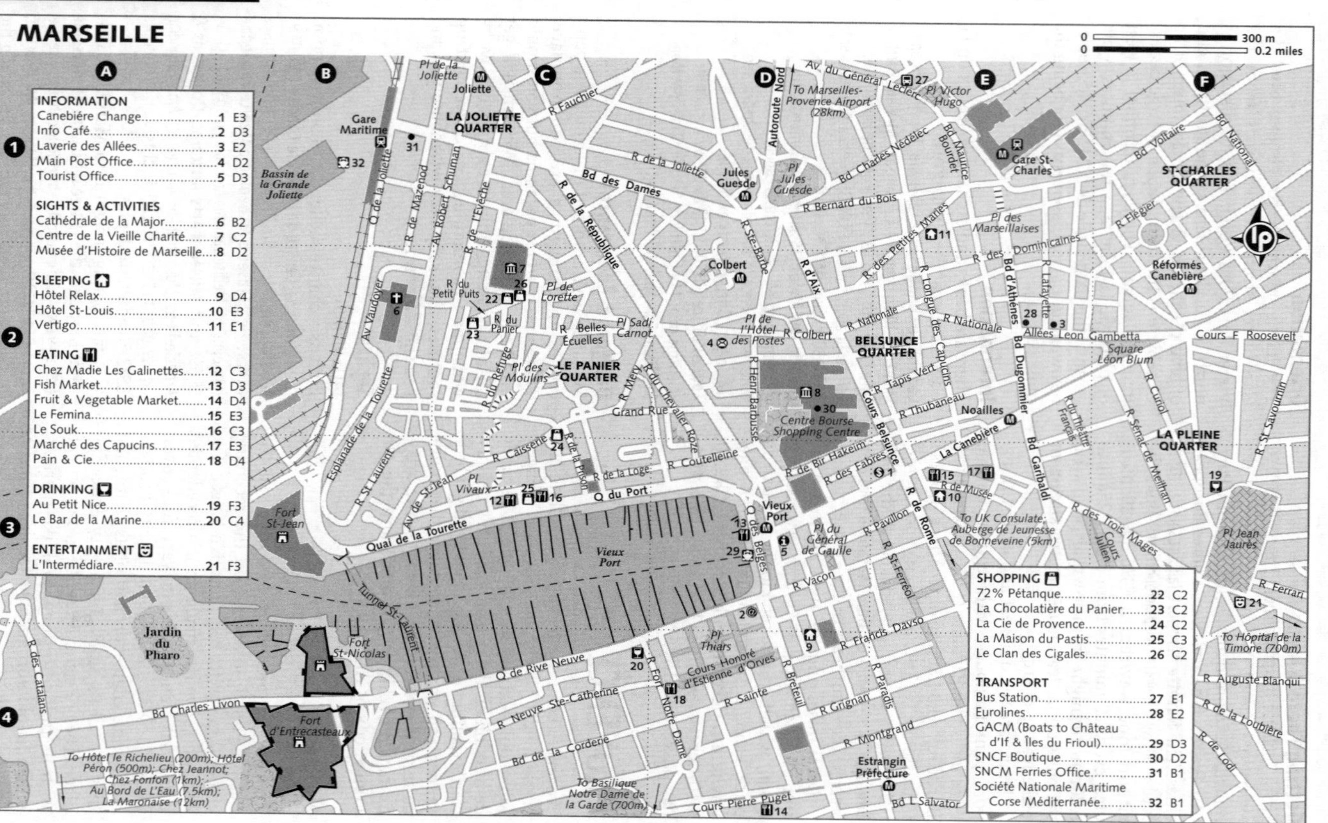
MARSEILLE
0 300 m
0 0.2 miles
INFORMATION
Canebière Change....1 E3
Info Café....2 D3
Laverie des Allées....3 E2
Main Post Office....4 D2
Tourist Office....5 D3
SIGHTS & ACTIVITIES
Cathédrale de la Major....6 B2
Centre de la Vieille Charité....7 C2
Musée d'Histoire de Marseille....8 D2
SLEEPING
Hôtel Relax....9 D4
Hôtel St-Louis....10 E3
Vertigo....11 E1
EATING
Chez Madie Les Galinettes....12 C3
Fish Market....13 D3
Fruit & Vegetable Market....14 D4
Le Femina....15 E3
Le Souk....16 C3
Marché des Capucins....17 E3
Pain & Cie....18 D4
DRINKING
Au Petit Nice....19 F3
Le Bar de la Marine....20 C4
ENTERTAINMENT
L'Intermédiare....21 F3
SHOPPING
72% Pétanque....22 C2
La Chocolatière du Panier....23 C2
La Cie de Provence....24 C2
La Maison du Pastis....25 C3
Le Clan des Cigales....26 C2
TRANSPORT
Bus Station....27 E1
Eurolines....28 E2
GACM (Boats to Château d'If & Îles du Frioul)....29 D3
SNCF Boutique....30 D2
SNCM Ferries Office....31 B1
Société Nationale Maritime Corse Méditerranée....32 B1
LA JOLIETTE QUARTER
LE PANIER QUARTER
BELSUNCE QUARTER
ST-CHARLES QUARTER
LA PLEINE QUARTER
Vieux Port
Gare Maritime
Gare St-Charles
Bassin de la Grande Joliette
Fort St-Jean
Fort St-Nicolas
Fort d'Entrecasteaux
Jardin du Pharo
Centre Bourse Shopping Centre
Tunnel St-Laurent
Quai de la Tourette
Q du Port
Q de Rive Neuve
La Canebière
Cours Belsunce
R de la République
R d'Aix
R de Rome
Bd des Dames
Bd Charles Livon
To Marseilles-Provence Airport (28km)
To UK Consulate; Auberge de Jeunesse de Bonneveine (5km)
To Hôpital de la Timone (700m)
To Basilique Notre Dame de la Garde (700m)
To Hôtel le Richelieu (200m); Hôtel Péron (500m); Chez Jeannot; Chez Fonfon (1km); Au Bord de L'Eau (7.5km); La Maronaise (12km)

remains of a merchant vessel discovered in the Vieux Port in 1974.

BASILIQUE NOTRE DAME DE LA GARDE

Be blown away by the celestial views and knock-out 19th-century architecture at the hilltop **Basilique Notre Dame de la Garde** (☎ 04 91 13 40 80; montée de la Bonne Mère; admission free; ⏲ basilica & crypt 7am-7pm, longer hr summer), the resplendent Romano-Byzantine basilica 1km south of the Vieux Port that dominates Marseille's skyline. The domed basilica was built between 1853 and 1864 and is ornamented with coloured marble, murals and mosaics restored in 2006. Bus 60 links the Vieux Port with the basilica.

CHÂTEAU D'IF

Immortalised in Alexandre Dumas' 1840s novel *Le Comte de Monte Cristo* (The Count of Monte Cristo), the 16th-century island prison of **Château d'If** (☎ 04 91 59 02 30; adult/student €5/3.50; ⏲ 9.30am-6.30pm May-Aug, 9.30am-5.30pm Tue-Sun Sep-Mar, 9.30am-5.30pm daily Apr) sits 3.5km west of the Vieux Port. Political prisoners of all persuasions were incarcerated here, along with Protestants, the Revolutionary hero Mirabeau and the Communards of 1871.

Boats run by **Frioul If Express** (☎ 04 91 46 54 65; www.frioul-if-express.com; 1 quai des Belges, 1er) leave from the Vieux Port (€10 return, 20 minutes, 15 boats daily in summer, fewer in winter).

VIEUX PORT

Ships have docked for more than 26 centuries at Marseille's colourful Vieux Port. Although the main commercial docks were transferred to the Joliette area on the coast north of here in the 1840s, it still overflows with fishing craft, yachts and local ferries.

Guarding the harbour are **Fort St-Nicolas** on the southern side and, across the water, **Fort St-Jean**, founded in the 13th century by the Knights Hospitaller of St John of Jerusalem. Standing guard between the old and the 'new' port, is the striking Byzantine-style **Cathédrale de la Major**. Its 'stripy' facade is made of Cassis stone (local white stone) and green marble from Florence.

Sleeping

Auberge de Jeunesse de Bonneveine (☎ 04 91 17 63 30; www.fuaj.org; impasse du Docteur Bonfils, 8e; dm €17.10, d incl sheets & breakfast €40.60; ⏲ Feb-Dec; 💻) The building looks like a primary school, the rooms are spartan and it's a fair way out of town, but beach activities including kayaking, hiking and kitesurfing make up for that. Bus 44 (stop Bonnefon) is just 200m away.

ourpick Vertigo (☎ 04 91 91 07 11; www.hotelvertigo.fr; 42 rue des Petites Maries, 1er; dm €23.90, d €55-65; Ⓜ Gare St-Charles SNCF; 💻) This new boutique hostel swaps dodgy bunk beds and hospital-like decor for vintage posters, a chrome kitchen and groovy communal spaces. Obviously, there's no curfew. Check out the *cabanons* (fishing cabins) doubles.

Hôtel Relax (☎ 04 91 33 15 87; http://relaxhotel.free.fr, in French; 4 rue Corneille, 1er; s €40, d €55-60; Ⓜ Vieux Port; ❄) In a dress-circle location overlooking Marseille's art deco Opera House, this 20-room hotel is run by a lovely family. Noise insulation isn't great, but it's a bargain for the location.

Hôtel le Richelieu (☎ 04 91 31 01 92; www.lerichelieu-marseille.com; 52 corniche Président John F Kennedy, 7e; d €46-110) This beach-house-type hotel has gone a little over the top on the colour schemes, but the balconies, sea views and idyllic breakfast terrace are still present and correct.

Hôtel Péron (☎ 04 91 31 01 41; www.hotel-peron.com; 119 corniche Président John F Kennedy, 7e; d €60-85; 💻) This unusual 1920s period piece has touches including original art deco bathrooms and geometric parquet floors. Balconies have sea views, although you'll have to put up with road noise.

Hôtel St-Louis (☎ 04 91 54 02 74; www.hotel-st-louis.com; 2 rue des Récollettes, 1er; d €65-90; 🚊 Canebière Garibaldi, Ⓜ Noailles; ❄ 💻) Behind the scarlet 1800s facade and pale-green shutters, this gorgeous boutique place reveals character-filled rooms – round windows, high or sloping ceilings, four-poster beds, expensive mattresses and discreet vintage furniture.

Eating

The Vieux Port overflows with restaurants. Cours Julien and its surrounding streets are jammed with French, Indian, Antillean, Pakistani, Thai, Armenian, Lebanese, Tunisian and Italian restaurants.

Le Femina (☎ 04 91 54 03 56; 1 rue de Musée, 1er; menus €15; ⏲ closed Sun & Mon; 🚊 Canebière Garibaldi, Ⓜ Noailles) Heading east from the Vieux Port towards cours Julien, Le Femina is a great – and affordable – Algerian place for succulent couscous (you should definitely try the barley semolina).

ourpick Chez Madie Les Galinettes (☎ 04 91 90 40 87; 138 quai du Port, 2e; menus €15-27, mains €25-50;

lunch & dinner Mon-Sat, closed Sat lunch summer) They're so friendly at Madie's that you'll leave feeling as though you've just had dinner with friends. The portside terrace is perfect for those long summer evenings, and the menu's stocked with fish and a fantastic bouillabaisse that you'll need to order in advance.

Pain & Cie (04 91 33 55 00; 18 place aux Huiles, 1er; brunches €19; Tue-Sat 8am-10.30pm, 8am-6pm Sun & Mon; M Vieux Port) Trendy locals brunch here at the weekend or come for a quick *tartine* at lunchtime, or cake and coffee in the afternoon.

Chez Jeannot (04 91 52 11 28; 129 rue du Vallon des Auffes; mains €15-22; lunch & dinner Tue-Sat, lunch Sun, closed Mon) An institution among Marseillais, the rooftop terrace is booked out days in advance. The atmosphere is jovial and uncomplicated, just like the thin-crust pizzas, *grillades* (grilled meats) and seafood on your plate.

Le Souk (04 91 91 29 29; 100 quai du Port, 2e; menus €20-30; lunch & dinner Tue-Sat, lunch Sun; M Vieux Port) Thanks to Marseille's heritage, you'll eat some of the best North African food this side of the Med, and Le Souk does the town's top *tajines* (slow-cooked meat and vegetable stews).

Chez Fonfon (04 91 52 14 38; 140 rue du Vallon des Auffes, 7e; mains around €40; lunch & dinner Tue-Sat, dinner Mon) Overlooking the enchanting little harbour Vallon des Auffes, Chez Fonfon is famed for its bouillabaisse. The place is quite formal, although the wonderful views brighten things up. Book ahead.

The small but enthralling **fish market** (quai des Belges; 8am-1pm; M Vieux Port) is a daily fixture at the Vieux Port docks. Cours Julien hosts a Wednesday-morning organic fruit and vegetable market.

Stock up on fruit and vegetables at **Marché des Capucins** (place des Capucins, 1er; 8am-7pm Mon-Sat; Canebière Garibaldi, M Noailles), one block south of La Canebière; and at the **fruit and vegetable market** (cours Pierre Puget, 6e; 8am-1pm Mon-Fri; M Estrangin Préfecture).

There are a couple of supermarkets in the Centre Bourse shopping centre.

Drinking & Entertainment

Options for a coffee or something stronger abound on and around the Vieux Port.

Au Petit Nice (04 91 48 43 04; 28 place Jean Jaurès, 6e; 6.30am-2am; M Notre Dame du Mont-Cours Julien) A living illustration of what cheap and cheerful means: €2 a drink, whatever it is – how could you not be happy?

Le Bar de la Marine (04 91 54 95 42; 15 quai de Rive Neuve, 7e; 7am-1am; M Vieux Port) Marcel Pagnol filmed the card party scenes in *Marius* at this Marseille institution.

L'Intermédiaire (04 91 47 01 25; 63 place Jean Jaurès, 6e; 7pm-2am Mon-Sat; M Notre Dame du Mont-Cours Julien) This grungy place with its graffitied walls is one of the best venues in town for live music, bands and DJs.

La Maronaise (04 91 72 79 39; rte de la Maronaise, 8e; admission €20; 9am-5am Wed-Sat early May-early Sep) At this uberhip hang-out at Les Goudes on Cap Croisette, slide into a sun lounge and enjoy the private little sand beach before dancing under the stars till dawn. Take bus 19.

Getting There & Away

AIR

Aéroport Marseille-Provence (04 42 14 14 14; www.marseille.aeroport.fr), also known as Aéroport Marseille-Marignane, is 25km northwest of town. It has numerous budget flights to various European destinations. **Navette shuttle buses** (Marseille 04 91 50 59 34; airport 04 42 14 31 27; €8; 25min) run to Marseille's train station every 20 minutes between 5.30am and 10.50pm.

WORTH THE TRIP: MARSEILLE'S BASKET

North of the Vieux Port, Marseille's old city, Le Panier quarter (2e), translates as 'the basket', and was the site of the Greek *agora* (marketplace) – it's still the best place in town to shop.

Sniff scented soaps at **La Cie de Provence** (04 91 56 20 94; 1 rue Caisserie). Olive soaps, olive oils and preserves fill **72% Pétanque** (04 91 91 14 57; 10 rue du Petit Puits). For sustenance, **Le Clan des Cigales** (06 63 78 07 83; 8 rue du Petit Puits) serves homemade aïoli and savoury tarts, while hand-made chocolates such as fig and *calisson* (marzipan) stock the shelves of **La Chocolatière du Panier** (04 91 91 67 66; 49 rue du Petit Puits). At **La Maison du Pastis** (04 91 90 86 77; 108 quai du Port), you can sample more than 90 varieties of the local tipple, pastis (an aniseed-flavoured *apéritif*).

BOAT

Marseille's **Gare Maritime** (passenger ferry terminal; ☎ 04 91 39 40 00; www.marseille-port.fr; M Joliette) is 250m south of place de la Joliette (1er). The **Société Nationale Maritime Corse-Méditerranée** (SNCM; ☎ 08 25 88 80 88; www.sncm.fr; 61 blvd des Dames, 2e; 8am-6pm Mon-Fri, 8.30am-noon & 2-5.30pm Sat; M Joliette) links Marseille with Corsica Sardinia and Tunisia.

BUS

The **bus station** (☎ 08 91 02 40 25; 3 rue Honnorat, 3e; M Gare St-Charles SNCF) is at the back of the train station. Tickets can be purchased from the information desk inside the train station or from the driver. Buses travel to Aix-en-Provence (€4.60, 35 minutes, every five to 10 minutes), Avignon (€18.50, two hours, one daily), Cannes (€25, two hours, up to three daily), Nice (€26.50, three hours, up to three daily) and other destinations.

Eurolines (☎ 08 92 89 90 91; www.eurolines.com; 3 allées Léon Gambetta; 10am-6pm Mon-Fri, 10am-2pm Sat) has international coach services.

TRAIN

Marseille's train station, **Gare St-Charles**, is served by both metro lines. There's an **information and ticket reservation office** (9am-8pm Mon-Sat, 5.15am-10pm for ticket purchases), plus a **left-luggage office** (from €3.50; 7.30am-10pm) next to platform A. In town, tickets can be bought at the SNCF Boutique inside the Centre Bourse shopping centre.

Useful destinations include Paris' Gare de Lyon (€80.20, three hours, 21 daily), Nice (€27.80, 2½ hours, 21 daily), Avignon (€23.10, 35 minutes, 27 daily) and Lyon (€57.60, 1¾ hours, 16 daily).

Getting Around

Marseille has two metro lines (Métro 1 and Métro 2), two tram lines (yellow and green) and an extensive bus network. The metro runs between 5am and 10.30pm Monday to Thursday and until 12.30am Friday to Sunday; the tram runs between 5am and 1am. Bus services stop around 9.30pm, when night buses take over until 12.30am.

Most leave from **Espace Infos RTM** (☎ 04 91 91 92 10; 6 rue des Fabres, 1er; 8.30am-6pm Mon-Fri, 9am-12.30pm & 2-5.30pm Sat; M Vieux Port), where you can obtain information and tickets. Bus, metro or tram tickets (€1.70) are valid for one hour after being time-stamped. A one-/three-day pass costs €4.50/10.

AIX-EN-PROVENCE

pop 141,200

Aix-en-Provence is to Provence what the Left Bank is to Paris: a pocket of Bohemian chic with an edgy student crowd. It's hard to believe that 'Aix' (pronounced ex) is just 25km from chaotic, exotic Marseille. The city has been a cultural centre since the Middle Ages (two of the town's most famous sons are painter Paul Cézanne and novelist Émile Zola) but for all its polish, it's still a laid-back Provençal town at heart.

Information

Netgames (☎ 04 42 26 60 41; 52 rue Aumône Vieille; per hr €3; 10am-midnight) Central and state-of-the-art.
Post office (place de l'Hôtel de Ville)
Tourist office (☎ 04 42 16 11 61; www.aixenprovencetourism.com; 2 place du Général de Gaulle; 8.30am-7pm Mon-Sat, 10am-1pm & 2-6pm Sun) Longer hours in summer; very proactive and helpful.

Sights

Art, culture, and architecture abound in Aix, especially thanks to local lad Paul Cézanne (1839–1906). To see where he ate, drank, studied and painted, you can follow the **Circuit de Cézanne**, marked by footpath-embedded bronze plaques inscribed with the letter C. An informative English-language guide to the plaques, *Cézanne's Footsteps*, is available free from the tourist office.

The trail takes in Cézanne's last studio, **Atelier Paul Cézanne** (☎ 04 42 21 06 53; www.atelier-cezanne.com; 9 av Paul Cézanne; adult/student €5.50/2; 10am-noon & 2-5pm Oct-Mar, to 6pm Apr-Jun & Sep, 10am-6pm Jul & Aug), 1.5km north of the tourist office, as well as the **Bastide du Jas de Bouffan**, the family home where Cézanne started painting, and the **Bibémus quarries**, where he did most of his Montagne Ste-Victoire paintings. Head to the tourist office for bookings (required) and information on these sites.

Cézanne also features at the **Musée Granet** (☎ 04 42 52 88 32; place St-Jean de Malte; 11am-7pm Wed-Mon Jun-Sep, noon-6pm Wed-Mon Oct-May), which houses nine of the artist's canvases alongside works by Picasso, Léger, Matisse, Tal Coat and Giacometti.

A potpourri of architectural styles, the **Cathédrale St-Sauveur** (rue Laroque; 8am-noon &

2-6pm) was begun in the 12th century and successively enlarged over the next few hundred years: it's worth a visit for the memorable Gregorian chants, usually sung at 4.30pm Sunday.

Sleeping

Auberge de Jeunesse du Jas de Bouffan (☎ 04 42 20 15 99; www.fuaj.org; 3 av Marcel Pagnol; dm incl breakfast & sheets €17.50-29.50; reception 7am-1pm & 5pm-midnight, closed mid-Dec–Jan) Shiny new with a bar, tennis courts, bike shed and massive summer BBQs, this HI hostel is 2km west of the centre; shame about the motorway. Take bus 4 from La Rotonde to the Vasarely stop.

Camping Arc-en-Ciel (☎ 04 42 26 14 28; rte de Nice; camp sites for 2 people plus car €18.50; Apr-Sep;) Tranquil wooded hills and a busy motorway frame this four-star camping ground. It's 2km southeast of town; take bus 3 to Les Trois Sautets stop.

Hôtel La Caravelle (☎ 04 42 21 53 05; www.lacaravelle-hotel.com; 29 blvd du Roi René; s €45, d €65-70) Central and friendly, the 30 rooms here range from air-conditioned doubles to singles with adjoining toilets. Wi-fi's free and wheelchair access is good.

Hôtel des Quatre Dauphins (☎ 04 42 38 16 39; www.lesquatredauphins.fr; 54 rue Roux Alphéran; s €55-65, d €65-100;) Close to cours Mirabeau, this sweet 13-room hotel is a symphony of Wedgwood-blue, pale-pink and beige. The tall terracotta-tiled staircase leads to four charming attic rooms with sloped beamed ceilings.

Eating & Drinking

Charlotte (☎ 04 42 26 77 56; 32 rue des Bernardines; 2-/3-course menus €14/17.50; lunch & dinner Tue-Sat) Townspeople congregate like a big extended family for home-cooked terrines, soups and savoury tarts. In summer, feasting takes place outdoors in the garden.

Le Zinc d'Hugo (☎ 04 42 27 69 69; 22 rue Lieutaud; mains €14-18; lunch & dinner Tue-Sat) Stone walls, wooden tables and a blackboard menu make for a lovely rustic bistro, so it unsurprisingly gets rammed on market days.

Le Petit Verdot (☎ 04 42 27 30 12; 7 rue Entrecasteaux; menus €17; dinner Mon-Sat) At this establishment the wine choice comes first; staff will help you make your selection from the 100-strong list, and then find a fitting dish to accompany it. It's full-on French – think duck breast, lamb shanks, even pig trotters!

The daily **produce market** (place Richelme) sells olives, goat's cheese, garlic, lavender, honey, peaches, melons and other sun-kissed products. Another **food market** (place des Prêcheurs) takes place on Tuesday, Thursday and Saturday mornings. Groceries are available at **Monoprix** (cours Mirabeau; 8.30am-9pm Mon-Sat) and **Petit Casino** (rue d'Italie; 9am-7pm Mon-Sat).

Aix' sweetest treat is the marzipanlike local speciality, *calisson d'Aix,* a small, diamond-shaped, chewy delicacy made with ground almonds and fruit syrup. Traditional *calissonniers* still make the sweets, including **Roy René** (☎ 04 42 26 67 86; www.calisson.com; 10 rue Clémenceau).

Getting There & Away

Aix' **bus station** (☎ 08 91 02 40 25; av de l'Europe) is 10 minutes southwest from La Rotonde. Routes include Marseille (€4.60, 30 to 50 minutes, every 10 minutes, every 20 minutes on Sunday), Arles (€10.40, 1½ hours, six daily Monday to Saturday) and Avignon (€14, 1¼ hours, six daily Monday to Saturday).

The only useful train from Aix' city-centre **train station** (7am-7pm) goes to Marseille (€6.50, 50 minutes). For other routes, you'll have to travel to the **TGV station**, 8km from the city centre.

Half-hourly shuttle buses run from the bus station to the TGV station (€3.70) and Aéroport Marseille-Provence (€7.90) from 4.40am to 10.30pm.

AVIGNON

pop 90,800

Hooped by 4.3km of superbly preserved stone ramparts, this graceful city is the belle of Provence's ball. Famed for its annual performing arts festival and its fabled bridge, the Pont St-Bénezet (aka the Pont d'Avignon), Avignon is an ideal spot from which to step out into the surrounding region. Wrapping around the city, Avignon's defensive ramparts were built between 1359 and 1370, and are punctuated by a series of sturdy *portes* (gates).

Information

Chez W@m (☎ 04 90 86 19 03; 34 rue Bonneterie; per hr €3; 10am-8pm Mon-Thu & 10am-10pm Fri & Sat)

Lavmatic (9 rue du Chapeau Rouge; 7am-8.30pm) A 21st-century laundrette with wi-fi.

Main post office (cours Président Kennedy) Offers currency exchange.

Tourist office (☎ 04 32 74 32 74; www.avignon-tourisme.com; 41 cours Jean Jaurès; 9am-5pm

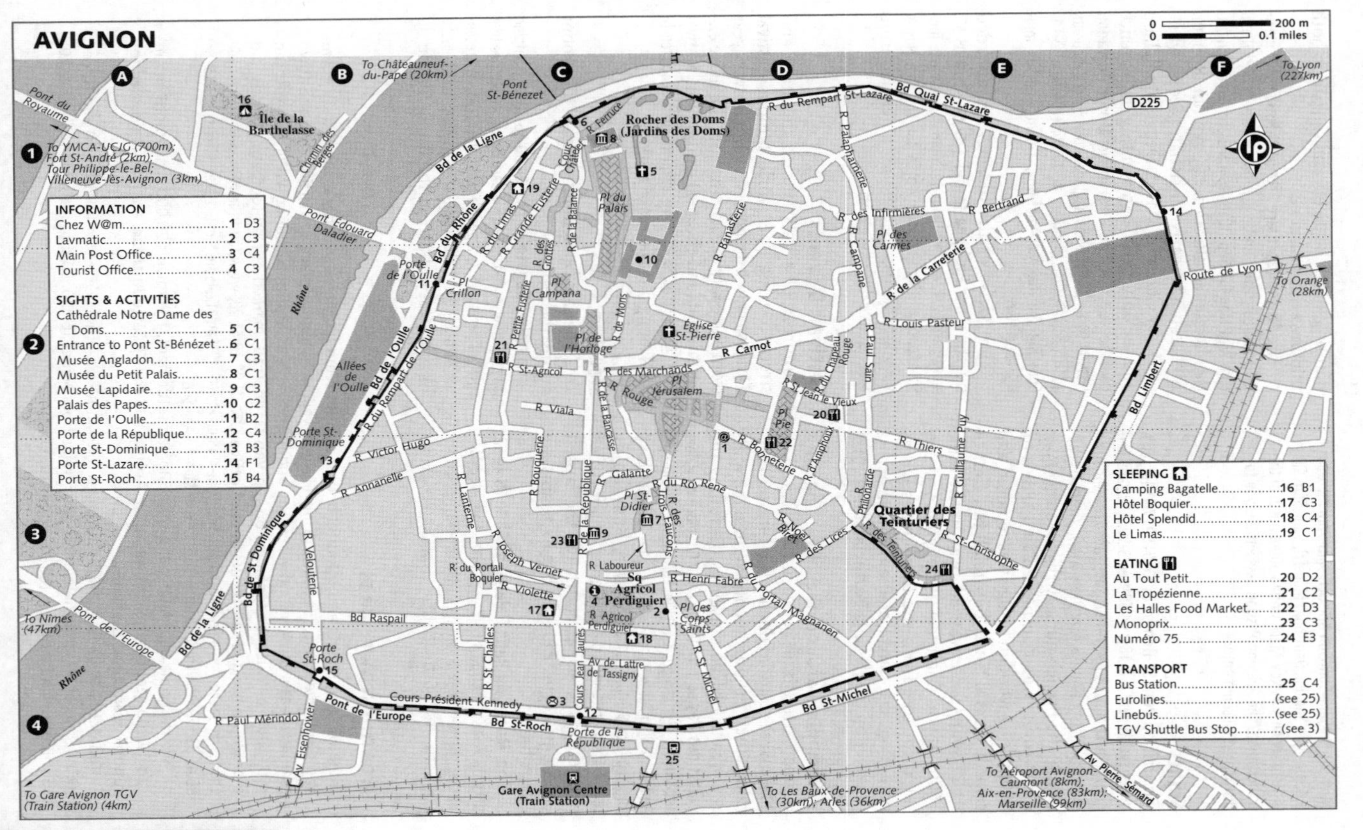
AVIGNON
INFORMATION
Chez W@m....1 D3
Lavmatic....2 C3
Main Post Office....3 C4
Tourist Office....4 C3
SIGHTS & ACTIVITIES
Cathédrale Notre Dame des Doms....5 C1
Entrance to Pont St-Bénézet....6 C1
Musée Angladon....7 C3
Musée du Petit Palais....8 C1
Musée Lapidaire....9 C3
Palais des Papes....10 C2
Porte de l'Oulle....11 B2
Porte de la République....12 C4
Porte St-Dominique....13 B3
Porte St-Lazare....14 F1
Porte St-Roch....15 B4
SLEEPING
Camping Bagatelle....16 B1
Hôtel Boquier....17 C3
Hôtel Splendid....18 C4
Le Limas....19 C1
EATING
Au Tout Petit....20 D2
La Tropézienne....21 C2
Les Halles Food Market....22 D3
Monoprix....23 C3
Numéro 75....24 E3
TRANSPORT
Bus Station....25 C4
Eurolines....(see 25)
Linebús....(see 25)
TGV Shuttle Bus Stop....(see 3)
0 200 m
0 0.1 miles
To Châteauneuf-du-Pape (20km)
To Lyon (227km)
To YMCA-UCJG (700m); Fort St-André (2km); Tour Philippe-le-Bel; Villeneuve-lès-Avignon (3km)
To Orange (28km)
To Nîmes (47km)
To Gare Avignon TGV (Train Station) (4km)
To Les Baux-de-Provence (30km); Arles (36km)
To Aéroport Avignon-Caumont (8km); Aix-en-Provence (83km); Marseille (99km)
Gare Avignon Centre (Train Station)
Rocher des Doms (Jardins des Doms)
Île de la Barthelasse
Quartier des Teinturiers
Sq Agricol Perdiguier
Pont St-Bénezet
Pont du Royaume
Pont Édouard Daladier
Pont de l'Europe
Rhône
D225
Bd Quai St-Lazare
Bd de la Ligne
Bd du Rhône
Bd de l'Oulle
Bd de St Dominique
Bd St-Roch
Bd St-Michel
Bd Limbert
Bd Raspail
Route de Lyon
Cours Président Kennedy
Cours Jean Jaurès
R Carnot
R de la Carreterie
R de la République
R Joseph Vernet
R du Rempart St-Lazare
R du Rempart de l'Oulle
Av Pierre Sémard
Av Eisenhower
Porte de l'Oulle
Porte St-Dominique
Porte St-Roch
Porte de la République
Allées de l'Oulle
Pl du Palais
Pl de l'Horloge
Pl Pie
Pl Jérusalem
Pl Crillon
Pl des Carmes
Pl des Corps Saints
Pl St-Didier
Église St-Pierre

Mon-Sat, 9.45am-5pm Sun Apr-Oct, 9am-7pm Mon-Sat, 9.45am-5pm Sun Jul, 9am-6pm Mon-Fri, 9am-5pm Sat & 10am-noon Sun Nov-Mar) Around 300m north of the train station. The Avignon Passion pass entitles you to discounted museum entry.

Sights

The fabled **Pont St-Bénezet** (☎ 04 90 27 51 16; adult/under 8yr/student & 8-18yr €4.50/free/3.50; 🕑 9am-9pm Aug, 9am-8pm Jul & early–mid-Sep, 9am-7pm Apr-Jun & mid-Sep–Oct, 9.30am-5.45pm Nov-Mar), immortalised in the French nursery rhyme *Sur le Pont d'Avignon*, was completed in 1185. The 900m-long wooden bridge was repaired and rebuilt several times before all but four of its 22 spans were washed away in the mid-1600s. If you don't feel like paying, you can see it for free from the Rocher des Doms park, Pont Édouard Daladier or from across the river on the Île de la Barthelasse's chemin des Berges.

Wrapping around the city, Avignon's ramparts were built between 1359 and 1370. They were restored during the 19th century, minus their original moats. Within the walls is a wealth of fine museums, including the **Palais des Papes** (☎ 04 90 27 50 00; place du Palais; adult/under 12yr/student & 12-18yr €6/free/3; 🕑 9am-9pm Aug, 9am-8pm Jul & early–mid-Sep, 9am-7pm Apr-Jun & mid-Sep–Oct, 9.30am-5.45pm Nov-Mar). Built during the 14th century and intended as a fortified palace for the papal court, it's the largest Gothic palace in Europe, but its rooms are rather bare.

The **Musée du Petit Palais** (☎ 04 90 86 44 58; place du Palais; adult/pass €6/3; 🕑 10am-6pm Wed-Mon Jun-Sep, 10am-1pm & 2-6pm Wed-Mon Oct-May) focuses on 13th- to 16th-century Italian religious paintings, with Botticelli and Carpaccio both making an appearance.

The **Musée Lapidaire** (☎ 04 90 86 33 84; 27 rue de la République; adult/under 12yr/pass €2/free/1; 🕑 10am-6pm Wed-Mon Jun-Sep, 10am-1pm & 2-6pm Wed-Mon Oct-May) houses a collection of Egyptian, Roman, Etruscan and early Christian pieces, while works by Cézanne. Manet, Degas, Modigliani and the only Van Gogh painting in Provence can be seen at the charming **Musée Angladon** (☎ 04 90 82 29 03; www.angladon.com; 5 rue Laboureur; adult/under 7yr/pass, student &, 7-18yr €6/free/4; 🕑 1-6pm Tue-Sun mid-Mar–mid-Nov, 1-6pm Wed-Sun mid-Nov–mid-Mar).

Fine views of the old city are afforded by the **Tour Philippe-le-Bel** (☎ 04 32 70 08 57; adult/pass €2/1.50; 🕑 10am-12.30pm & 2-6.30pm Tue-Sun Apr-Sep, 10am-noon & 2-5pm Tue-Sun Oct, Nov & Mar), 3km across the Rhône in neighbouring Villeneuve-lès-Avignon.

Festivals & Events

Hundreds of artists take to the stage and streets during the world-famous **Festival d'Avignon** (www.festival-avignon.com), held every year from early July to early August. The more experimental (and cheaper) fringe event, **Festival Off** (☎ 04 90 85 13 08; www.avignonleoff.com, in French) runs alongside the main festival.

Sleeping

You'll need to book months ahead for a room during the festival.

Camping Bagatelle (☎ 04 90 86 30 39; camping.bagatelle@wanadoo.fr; Île de la Barthelasse; camp sites tent only per person €5-7, 2 people plus car €12-20; 🕑 reception 8am-9pm) Multilingual, shaded and only 20 minutes' walk from the centre on Île de

WORTH THE TRIP: ARLES

If the winding streets and colourful houses of Arles seem familiar, it's hardly surprising – Vincent van Gogh lived here for much of his life in a yellow house on place Lamartine, and the town regularly featured in his canvases. His original house was destroyed during WWII, but you can still follow in Vincent's footsteps on the **Van Gogh Trail**, marked out by footpath plaques and a brochure handed out by the **tourist office** (☎ 04 90 18 41 20; www.tourisme.ville-arles.fr; esplanade Charles de Gaulle; 🕑 9am-6.45pm Apr-Sep, 9am-4.45pm Mon-Sat, 10am-12.45pm Sun Oct-Mar; train station ☎ 04 90 43 33 57; 🕑 9am-1.30pm & 2.30-4.45pm Mon-Fri Apr-Sep).

Two millennia ago, Arles was a major Roman settlement. The town's 20,000-seat amphitheatre and 12,000-seat theatre, known as the **Arénes** and the **Théâtre Antique**, are nowadays used for cultural events and bullfights.

Telleschi (☎ 04 42 28 40 22) runs buses to/from Aix-en-Provence (€10.40, 1½ hours) and Nîmes (€6.60, one hour), and there are regular trains from Nîmes (€7.20, 30 minutes), Marseille (€12.70, 55 minutes) and Avignon (€6.30, 20 minutes).

la Barthelasse, this camping ground offers discounts for carless campers.

YMCA-UCJG (☎ 04 90 25 46 20; www.ymca-avignon.com; 7bis chemin de la Justice; d/tr/q with shared bathroom €30/36/48, with private bathroom d €45/54/54; reception 8.30am-6pm, closed Dec–early Jan;) If you're after your own space on a shoestring, head to this spotless hostel just outside Villeneuve-lès-Avignon. There's a massive swimming pool and terrace with panoramic views of the city. Take bus 10 to the Monteau stop or take the 30-minute stroll across the bridge.

Hôtel Splendid (☎ 04 90 86 14 46; www.avignon-hotel-splendid.com; 17 rue Agricol Perdiguier; s €32-46, d €48-70, apt €70-90) This ecoconscious, cyclist-friendly place has charming rooms and self-contained studios, half overlooking the pretty neighbouring park.

Hôtel Boquier (☎ 04 90 82 34 43; www.hotel-boquier.com, in French; 6 rue du Portail Boquier; d €45-66;) Run by new owners, this great little hotel is bright, airy, spacious and central and the themed rooms are particularly attractive (try for Morocco or Lavender).

our pick **Le Limas** (☎ 04 90 14 67 19; www.le-limas-avignon.com; 51 rue du Limas; d incl breakfast €100-160, tr incl breakfast €150-180;) Behind its discreet lavender door, this chic B&B is like something out of *Vogue Living*. A state-of-the-art kitchen and minimalist white decor jostle for space with antique fireplaces and an 18th-century spiral staircase, and breakfast is served on a sun-drenched summer terrace. Lovely.

Eating

Numéro 75 (☎ 04 90 27 16 00; 75 rue Guillaume Puy; mains from €10; lunch & dinner Mon-Sat) Lodged inside the house of absinthe inventor Jules Pernod, the food at Numéro 75 screams Mediterranean cuisine: superfresh, packed with flavours, and ever so cheap.

Au Tout Petit (☎ 04 90 82 38 86; 4 rue d'Amphoux; lunch menus €10, dinner menus €18-24; lunch & dinner Mon-Sat, closed Wed night) The menu of 'The Teeny Tiny' is a foodies' treat – asparagus ravioli, salmon lasagne, apricot *tarte Tatin* with rosemary-and-madeleine ice cream. Food poetry.

Over 40 outlets fill **Les Halles' food market** (place Pie; 7am-1pm Tue-Sun), or pick up groceries at **Monoprix** (24 rue de la République; 8am-9pm Mon-Sat) and St-Tropez's famous cream-and-cake concoction, *tarte Tropézienne* at **La Tropézienne** (☎ 04 90 86 24 72; 22 rue St-Agricol; 8.30am-7.30pm Mon-Sat).

Getting There & Away

The **bus station** (☎ 04 90 82 07 35; blvd St-Roch; information window 8am-7pm Mon-Fri, 8am-1pm Sat) is near the train station. Services include Aix-en-Provence (€14, one hour), Arles (€7.10, 1½ hours), Marseille (€18.50, two hours) and Nîmes (€8.10, 1¼ hours).

Long-haul bus companies **Linebús** (☎ 04 90 85 30 48) and **Eurolines** (☎ 04 90 85 27 60; www.eurolines.com) have offices at the far end of the bus platforms.

Avignon has two train stations: **Gare Avignon Centre** (42 blvd St-Roch) has local trains to/from Arles (€6.30, 20 minutes) and Nîmes (€8.10, 30 minutes), while **Gare Avignon TGV**, 4km southwest of town, has TGV connections to/from Marseille (€23.10, 35 minutes) and Nice (€51.80, three hours). *Navette* (shuttle) buses (€1.10, 10 to 13 minutes, half-hourly between 6.15am and 11.30pm) link Gare Avignon TGV with the stop in front of the post office on cours Président Kennedy.

In July and August there's a Saturday **Eurostar** (www.eurostar.com) service from London (from €125 return, six hours) to Avignon Centre.

There is a **left luggage** (per bag from €4; 7am-7pm winter, 7am-10pm summer) facility inside the station.

CÔTE D'AZUR & MONACO

With its glistening seas, idyllic beaches and lush hills, the Côte d'Azur (Azure Coast) – otherwise known as the French Riviera – has long been a symbol of exclusivity, extravagance and excess, and it's still a favourite getaway for the European jet set, especially around the chichi resorts of St-Tropez, glamorous Cannes and super-rich, sovereign Monaco. But it's not just a high-roller's playground – every year millions of visitors descend on the southern French coast to bronze their bodies, smell the lavender and soak up the Mediterranean vibe.

NICE

pop 346,900

Nice is the Côte d'Azur's most complex and cosmopolitan city. It's a heady mix of old and new, ethnic and domestic, sunshine and smog: strollers, skaters, beach-bums, and businesspeople jostle for position along the beachfront, while tower blocks and tiny cottages stand side by side along the city's traffic-thronged streets. It's noisy, it's smelly and it's insanely touristy throughout the summer, but somehow Nice still manages to be irresistible, with a charming old city and a clutch of fantastic museums to explore.

Orientation

The modern city centre – the area north and west of place Masséna – includes the pedestrianised shopping streets rue de France and rue Masséna. The bus station is located three blocks east of place Masséna. Av Jean Médecin runs south from the train station to place Masséna.

Promenade des Anglais follows the curved beachfront from the city centre to the airport, 6km west. Vieux Nice (Old Nice) is delineated by blvd Jean Jaurès, quai des États-Unis and, east, the hill known as Colline du Château, near the port. The wealthy residential neighbourhood of Cimiez, home to outstanding museums, is north of the city centre.

Information

Barclays Bank (2 rue Alphonse Karr) Currency exchange.
Cyberpoint (☎ 04 93 92 70 63; 10 av Félix Faure; per hr €4; 🕑 10am-9pm Mon-Sat, later summer, 3-9pm Sun) One of endless cybercafes in Nice.
Laverie Mono (8 rue Belgique; 🕑 7am-9pm) Laundrette.
Lavomatique rue Pertinax (22 rue Pertinax; 🕑 7am-8pm); rue du Pont Vieux (11 rue du Pont Vieux; 🕑 7am-8pm) More laundrettes surround the station.
Main post office (23 av Thiers)
Main tourist office (☎ 08 92 70 74 07; 5 promenade des Anglais; 🕑 8am-8pm Mon-Sat, 9am-7pm Sun Jun-Sep, 9am-6pm Mon-Sat Oct-May) Right by the beach.
Train station tourist office (☎ 08 92 35 35 35; av Thiers; 🕑 8am-8pm Mon-Sat, 9am-7pm Sun Jun-Sep, 8am-7pm Mon-Sat, 10am-5pm Sun Oct-May)

Sights

VIEUX NICE

Go off-map in the Old Town's tangle of tiny 18th-century pedestrian passages and alleyways, where you'll find several historic churches including the baroque **Cathédrale Ste-Réparate** (place Rossetti) and the mid-18th-century **Chapelle de la Miséricorde**, next to place Pierre Gautier.

At the eastern end of quai des États-Unis, steep steps and a **cliffside lift** (per person €1; 🕑 9am-8pm Jun-Aug, 9am-7pm Apr, May & Sep, 10am-6pm Oct-Mar) climb to the **Parc du Château**, a beautiful hilltop park with great views over the old city and the beachfront. The chateau itself was razed by Louis XIV in 1706 and never rebuilt.

MUSEUMS

The excellent **Mamac** (☎ 04 97 13 42 01; www.mamac-nice.org; Promenade des Arts; admission free; 🕑 10am-6pm Tue-Sun) is worth a visit for its stunning architecture alone, but it also houses some fantastic avant-garde art from the 1960s to the present, including iconic pop art from Roy Lichtenstein, and Andy Warhol's 1965 *Campbell's Soup Can*.

The small **Musée National Message Biblique Marc Chagall** (☎ 04 93 53 87 20; www.musee-chagall.fr, in French; 4 av Dr Ménard; permanent collection adult/student €6.50/4.50, temporary exhibitions additional €1.20; 🕑 10am-5pm Wed-Mon Oct-Jun, to 6pm Jul-Sep) houses the largest public collection of the Russian-born artist's seminal *Old Testament* paintings.

Heading northeast from the Chagall museum (about 2.5km from the city centre) brings you to the **Musée Matisse** (☎ 04 93 81 08 08; www.musee-matisse-nice.org; 164 av des Arènes de Cimiez; admission free; 🕑 10am-6pm Wed-Mon), which contains a fantastic collection of exhibits and paintings spanning Matisse's entire career, including his famous paper cut-outs *Blue Nude IV* and mixed-media *Woman with Amphora*.

RUSSIAN ORTHODOX CATHEDRAL OF ST-NICOLAS

Crowned by six multicoloured onion domes, the **Cathédrale Orthodoxe Russe St-Nicolas** (Russian Orthodox Cathedral of St-Nicolas; ☎ 04 93 96 88 02; av Nicolas II; admission €3; 🕑 9am-noon & 2.30-5pm Mon-Sat, 2.30-5pm Sun) was built between 1902 and 1912 in early-17th-century style, and is the largest cathedral outside Russia. Shorts, miniskirts and sleeveless shirts are forbidden.

BEACHES

You'll need at least a beach mat to cushion your tush from Nice's pebbly **beaches**. Free sections of beach alternate with 15 sun lounge–lined **plages concédées** (private beaches; 🕑 late Apr or early May-15 Sep), for which you have to pay by renting a chair (around €15 a day) or mattress (around €10).There are outdoor showers on every beach, and indoor toilets and showers opposite 50 promenade des Anglais.

Tours

Trans Côte d'Azur (☎ 04 92 00 42 30; www.trans-cote-azur.com; quai Lunel; 🕑 Apr-Oct) runs scenic one-hour coastal cruises (adult/child under 10 years

€14/8.50) as well as day trips to the offshore islands of Îles de Lérins (adult/child €32/23), as well as St-Tropez (adult/child €52/39) and Monaco (adult/child €29/21).

Festivals & Events

Carnaval de Nice (www.nicecarnaval.com) Two-week carnival with flower floats and fireworks.

Nice Jazz Festival (www.nicejazzfestival.fr) In July, Nice swings to the week-long jazz festival at the Arènes de Cimiez, amid the Roman ruins.

Sleeping

Nice has a suite of places to sleep, from stellar independent backpacker hostels to international art-filled icons, but you'll obviously pay a premium for a beachfront location. Prices also rocket upwards in the summer season.

our pick **Villa Saint-Exupéry** (☎ 04 93 84 42 83; www.vsaint.com; 22 av Gravier; dm €18-25, s €35, d €55-80, all incl breakfast; 🖳) Why can't all hostels be like this? Set in a lovely converted monastery in the north of the city, this backpacker's palace features a 24-hour common room in a converted chapel, state-of-the-art-kitchens, barbecue terraces and lovely dorms; they'll even pick you up from the nearby Comte de Falicon tram stop or St Maurice stop for bus 23 (from the airport).

Auberge de Jeunesse – Les Camélias (☎ 04 93 62 15 54; www.fuaj.org, in French; 3 rue Spitalieri; dm incl breakfast & sheets €20.70; 🖳) This squeaky-clean 136-bed hostel is a signature Fédération Unie des Auberges de Jeunesse (FUAJ) establishment: bright and spacious, with bar, self-catering kitchen and laundry. No curfew, but you'll be kicked out from 11am to 3pm.

our pick **Hôtel Wilson** (☎ 04 93 85 47 79; www.hotel-wilson-nice.com; 39 rue de l'Hôtel des Postes; s €29-50, d €34-65) Many years of travelling and an experimental nature have turned Jean-Marie's rambling flat into a compelling place to stay. The 16 rooms have carefully crafted decor, there's a dining room filled with photos, African statues and a pair of resident tortoises. There's no lift, and the cheapest rooms don't have en suite, but who cares? This place is practically perfect.

Villa la Tour (☎ 04 93 80 08 15; www.villa-la-tour.com; 4 rue de la Tour; s €45-129, d €48-139; ❄) Small but perfectly formed, the Villa la Tour offers romantic Provençal rooms, a stellar Old Nice location, and a flower-decked terrace with views of Nice's rooftops.

Hôtel Paradis (☎ 04 93 87 71 23; www.paradishotel.com; 1 rue Paradis; d €55-110) This sun-filled, spotless hotel is a stone's throw from the promenade. Top-floor and courtyard rooms have air-con and all rooms are equipped with fridges; three have balconies.

Nice Garden Hôtel (☎ 04 93 87 35 63; www.nicegardenhotel.com; 11 rue du Congrès; d €60-98; ❄) Behind heavy iron gates hides this little gem of a hotel: nine beautifully appointed rooms overlooking an exquisite garden with a glorious orange tree. Amazingly, it's just two blocks from the promenade.

Hôtel Armenonville (☎ 04 93 96 86 00; www.hotel-armenonville.com; 20 av des Fleurs; d €62-98, tr €79-112; 🖳) Tucked down an alleyway and shielded by its large garden, this grand early-20th-century mansion has sober rooms, three of them (Nos 12, 13 and 14) with a huge terrace overlooking the garden. There is a free car park and wi-fi.

Hôtel Windsor (☎ 04 93 88 59 35; www.hotelwindsornice.com; 11 rue Dalpozzo; d €90-175; ❄ 🖳 🏊) Wherever you look at this boutique hotel, you'll be treated to real wit and imagination – from the graffiti mural by the pool, the weird and wonderful artist-designed rooms, or the luxurious garden with its exotic plants.

Eating

Niçois nibbles include *socca* (a thin layer of chickpea flour and olive oil batter), *salade niçoise*, and *farcis* (stuffed vegetables). Restaurants in Vieux Nice are a mixed bag, so choose carefully.

Chez René Socca (☎ 04 93 92 05 73; 2 rue Miralhéti; dishes from €2; 🕑 9am-9pm Tue-Sun, to 10.30pm Jul & Aug, closed Nov) Forget about presentation; here, it's all about taste. Grab a portion of *socca* or a plate of *petits farçis* and head across the street for a *grand pointu* (glass) of red, white or rosé.

Nissa Socca (☎ 04 93 80 18 35; 7 rue Ste-Réparate; mains from €8; 🕑 lunch & dinner Tue-Sat) This inexpensive Old Town joint is a good bet for *niçoise* cuisine, including *socca* and *pissaladière* (a thick crust topped with onions, garlic, anchovies and olives).

La Table Alziari (☎ 04 93 80 34 03, 4 rue François Zanin; mains €8-14, 🕑 noon-2pm & 7.30-10pm Tue-Sat) Run by the grandson of the Alziari olive oil family, this citrus-coloured restaurant does local specialities such as *morue à la niçoise* (cod served with potatoes, olives and a tomato sauce), *daube* (stew) or grilled goat's cheese.

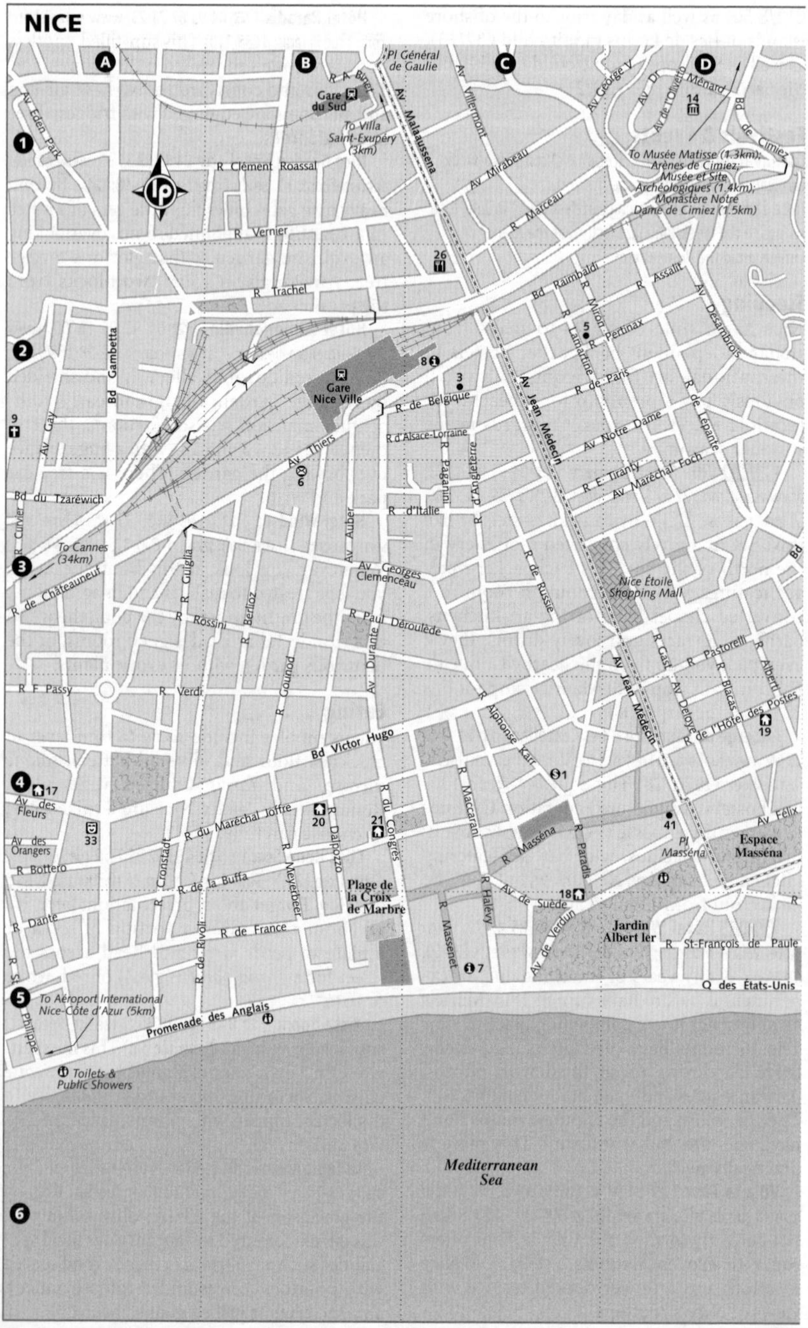

NICE

A
B
C
D
1
2
3
4
5
6

Pl Général de Gaulie
R A Binet
Gare du Sud
To Villa Saint-Exupéry (3km)
Av Malausséna
Av Villermont
Av George V
Av Dr Ménard
Av de l'Olivetto
14
Bd de Cimiez
To Musée Matisse (1.3km); Arènes de Cimiez; Musée et Site Archéologiques (1.4km); Monastère Notre Dame de Cimiez (1.5km)
Av Edem Park
R Clément Roassal
Av Mirabeau
R Marceau
R Vernier
26
R Trachel
Bd Raimbaldi
R Miron
R Assalit
Av Desambrois
R Lamartine
5
R Pertinax
8
3
Gare Nice Ville
Bd Gambetta
9
Av Gay
R de Belgique
R de Paris
Av Jean Médecin
R de Lépante
R d'Alsace-Lorraine
Av Notre Dame
R Paganini
R d'Angleterre
R E Tiranty
Av Maréchal Foch
Av Thiers
6
Bd du Tzaréwich
R d'Italie
R Curvier
To Cannes (34km)
Av Auber
R de Russie
Nice Étoile Shopping Mall
Bd
R de Châteauneuf
R Guiglia
Av Georges Clemenceau
R Berlioz
R Rossini
R Paul Déroulède
R Gounod
Av Durante
R Gioffredo
R Cast
R Pastorelli
R Alberti
R F Passy
R Verdi
Av Deloye
R Blacas
R Alphonse Karr
R de l'Hôtel des Postes
19
Bd Victor Hugo
1
R Maccarani
4
17
Av des Fleurs
Av des Orangers
33
R du Maréchal Joffre
20
R Dalpozzo
21
R du Congrès
41
Av Félix
Pl Masséna
Espace Masséna
R Masséna
R Paradis
R Bottero
R Cronstadt
R Meyerbeer
R de la Buffa
Plage de la Croix de Marbre
R Halévy
18
Av de Suède
R Dante
R de France
R Massenet
Av de Verdun
Jardin Albert Ier
R St-François de Paule
R de Rivoli
7
R St Philippe
Q des États-Unis
To Aéroport International Nice-Côte d'Azur (5km)
Promenade des Anglais
Toilets & Public Showers

Mediterranean Sea

FRANCE

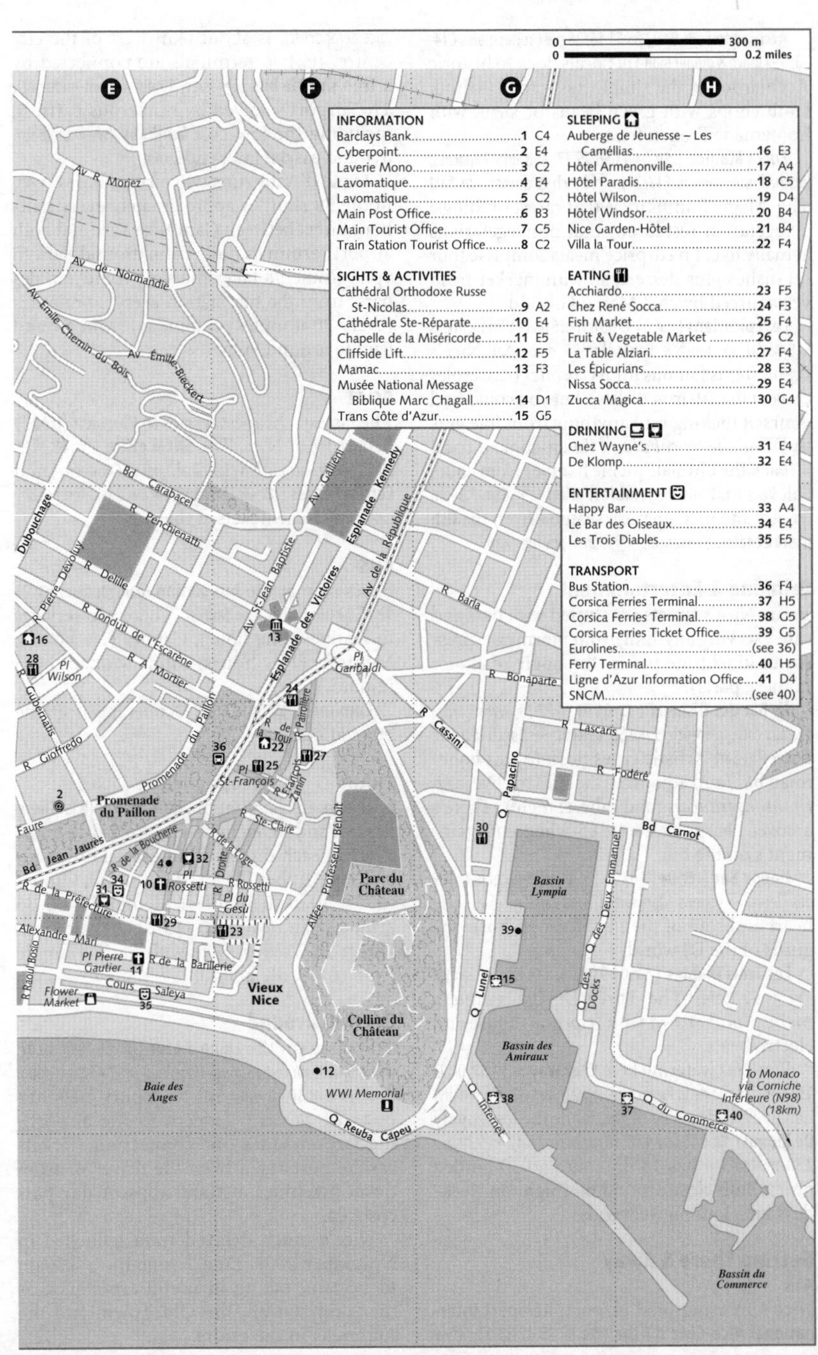
0 300 m
0 0.2 miles
E
F
G
H
INFORMATION
Barclays Bank....1 C4
Cyberpoint....2 E4
Laverie Mono....3 C2
Lavomatique....4 E4
Lavomatique....5 C2
Main Post Office....6 B3
Main Tourist Office....7 C5
Train Station Tourist Office....8 C2
SIGHTS & ACTIVITIES
Cathédral Orthodoxe Russe St-Nicolas....9 A2
Cathédrale Ste-Réparate....10 E4
Chapelle de la Miséricorde....11 E5
Cliffside Lift....12 F5
Mamac....13 F3
Musée National Message Biblique Marc Chagall....14 D1
Trans Côte d'Azur....15 G5
SLEEPING
Auberge de Jeunesse – Les Camélias....16 E3
Hôtel Armenonville....17 A4
Hôtel Paradis....18 C5
Hôtel Wilson....19 D4
Hôtel Windsor....20 B4
Nice Garden-Hôtel....21 B4
Villa la Tour....22 F4
EATING
Acchiardo....23 F5
Chez René Socca....24 F3
Fish Market....25 F4
Fruit & Vegetable Market....26 C2
La Table Alziari....27 F4
Les Épicurians....28 E3
Nissa Socca....29 E4
Zucca Magica....30 G4
DRINKING
Chez Wayne's....31 E4
De Klomp....32 E4
ENTERTAINMENT
Happy Bar....33 A4
Le Bar des Oiseaux....34 E4
Les Trois Diables....35 E5
TRANSPORT
Bus Station....36 F4
Corsica Ferries Terminal....37 H5
Corsica Ferries Terminal....38 G5
Corsica Ferries Ticket Office....39 G5
Eurolines....(see 36)
Ferry Terminal....40 H5
Ligne d'Azur Information Office....41 D4
SNCM....(see 40)
Av R Moriez
Av de Normandie
Av Emile Chemin du Bois
Av Émile Bieckert
Bd Carabacel
R Penchienatti
Dubouchage
R Pierre Dévoluy
R Delille
R Tonduti de l'Escarène
R A Mortier
Pl Wilson
R Gubernatis
R Gioffredo
Promenade du Paillon
Av St-Jean Baptiste
Esplanade des Victoires
Av Gallieni
Esplanade Kennedy
Av de la République
R Barla
Pl Garibaldi
R Bonaparte
R Cassini
R Lascaris
R Fodéré
Q Papacino
Bd Carnot
R de la Tour
R Pairolière
Pl St-François
R François Zanin
R Ste-Claire
Faure
Bd Jean Jaurès
R de la Boucherie
R de la Loge
R Droite
Pl Rossetti
R Rossetti
Pl du Gesù
R de la Préfecture
Alexandre Mari
R Raoul Bosio
Pl Pierre Gautier
R de la Barillerie
Cours Saleya
Flower Market
Vieux Nice
Allée Professeur Benoît
Parc du Château
Colline du Château
WWI Memorial
Q Rauba Capeu
Baie des Anges
Bassin Lympia
Q des Deux Emmanuel
Q des Docks
Q Lunel
Bassin des Amiraux
Q Infernet
Q du Commerce
To Monaco via Corniche Inférieure (N98) (18km)
Bassin du Commerce
FRANCE

Acchiardo (☎ 04 93 85 51 16; 38 rue Droite; mains €14-20; ⌚ lunch & dinner Mon-Fri) Locals flock to historic Acchiardo for the simple, tasty food – think lamb chops with green beans or steak with homemade French fries.

Zucca Magica (☎ 04 93 56 25 27; 4bis quai Papacino; lunch/dinner menus €17/27; ⌚ lunch & dinner Tue-Sat) The 'Magic Pumpkin' is that rarest of things: a vegetarian restaurant that nonvegetarians actually like. Fixed-price meals comprise four set dishes plus dessert, all with market-fresh veg sourced by chef Marco Folicaldi.

Les Épicuriens (☎ 04 93 80 85 00; 6 place Wilson; mains €18-45.50; ⌚ lunch & dinner Mon-Fri, dinner Sat) Nice's rising star is famous for its *cocottes* (casseroles cooked in cast-iron dishes), but you could find yourself tucking into anything from foie gras to *brandade de cabillaud* (oven-cooked cod).

Pack the ultimate picnic hamper from cours Saleya's **fruit and vegetable market** (⌚ 6am-1.30pm Tue-Sun) and pick up fresh seafood from the **fish market** (place St-François; ⌚ 6am-1pm Tue-Sun).

Drinking & Entertainment

Vieux Nice's streets are stuffed with bars and cafes, serving anything from morning espressos to lunchtime pastis (the tipple of choice in these parts).

Le Bar des Oiseaux (☎ 04 93 80 27 33; www.bardesoiseaux.com, in French; 5 rue St- Vincent; ⌚ lunch Mon-Fri, dinner Thu-Sat) Artistic types flock to this bohemian bar (and adjoining theatre) for live jazz, *chansons française* and cabaret nights. There's a cover charge of about €5 when entertainment's on the bill.

Happy Bar (☎ 04 97 07 26 26; www.hi-hotel.net; 3 av des Fleurs; ⌚ opens 10pm with DJs, to 2am Fri & Sat) The heart and soul of the hip Hôtel Hi hosts the gurus of the DJ world.

Les Trois Diables (☎ 04 93 62 47 00; 2 cours Saleya; ⌚ 5pm-2.15am) 'The Three Devils' tempts a mainly local crowd with trip-hop, house and electro beats.

Raucous watering hole **Chez Wayne's** (☎ 04 93 13 46 99; 15 rue de la Préfecture; ⌚ 2.30pm-12.30am daily) has live bands every night, while the less rowdy **De Klomp** (☎ 04 93 92 42 85; 8 rue Mascoïnat; ⌚ 5.30pm-2.30am Mon-Sat) has 18 draught and 50 bottled beers. Both close around midnight on weekdays and 3am on weekends.

Getting There & Away

AIR

Nice's international airport, **Aéroport International Nice-Côte d'Azur** (☎ 08 20 42 33 33; www.nice.aeroport.fr), is about 6km west of the city centre. Its two terminals are connected by a free **shuttle bus** (⌚ every 10min 4.30am-midnight). The airport's served by numerous carriers, including the low-cost **bmibaby** (www.bmibaby.com) and **easyJet** (www.easyjet.com).

Ligne d'Azur runs two airport buses (€4). Route 99 shuttles approximately every half-hour direct between Gare Nice Ville and both airport terminals daily from around 8am to 9pm. Route 98 takes the slow route and departs from the bus station every 20 minutes (every 30 minutes on Sunday) from around 6am to around 9pm.

BOAT

The fastest, cheapest ferries to Corsica (p327) depart from Nice. The **SNCM office** (☎ 08 25 88 80 88; www.sncm.fr; ferry terminal, quai du Commerce) and **Corsica Ferries** (☎ 08 25 09 50 95; www.corsicaferries.com; quai Lunel) issue tickets at the port.

BUS

Buses stop at the **bus station** (gare routière; ☎ 08 92 70 12 06; 5 blvd Jean Jaurès). There are services to Antibes (one hour), Cannes (1½ hours), Menton (1½ hours) and Monaco (45 minutes).

Eurolines (☎ 04 93 80 08 70) operates from the bus station.

TRAIN

Nice's main train station, **Gare Nice Ville** (av Thiers) has fast and frequent services (up to 40 trains a day in each direction) to coastal towns including Antibes (€3.80, 30 minutes), Cannes (€5.70, 30 to 40 minutes), Menton (€4.30, 35 minutes) and Monaco (€3.20, 20 minutes). Direct TGVs link Nice with Paris' Gare de Lyon (€110, 5½ hours).

Getting Around

Travelling on the **Ligne d'Azur** (☎ 08 10 06 10 07; www.lignedazur.com; 3 place Masséna; ⌚ 7.45am-6.30pm Mon-Fri & 8.30am-6pm Sat) transport network costs €1 per trip (except to the airport); the fare includes one connection. Tickets can be purchased from the driver or from ticket machines at tram stops. A day pass costs €4.

Nice's much delayed tram launched in November 2007. Line 1 runs from 4.30am to 1.30am, taking in useful areas such as the train station, the Old Town, and the Acropolis in the centre.

CANNES

pop 70,400

Everyone's heard of Cannes and its celebrity film festival, which runs for around 11 days every May and attracts big-name stars to the red carpets and flashy hotels of the blvd de la Croisette. But outside the festival season, Cannes retains a genuine small-town feel, with pleasant local shops, sparkling beaches, buzzy markets, as well as the idyllic Îles de Lérins just offshore.

The **tourist office** (☎ 04 92 99 84 22; www.cannes.travel; blvd de la Croisette; 🕑 9am-8pm Jul & Aug, 9am-7pm Mon-Sat Sep-Jun) is on the ground floor of the Palais des Festivals.

Sights & Activities

The central, sandy **beaches** along blvd de la Croisette are sectioned off for hotel patrons, where sun-worshippers pay prohibitive sums for their tans. A microscopic strip of sand near the Palais des Festivals is free, but you'll find better free sand on **Plages du Midi** and **Plages de la Bocca**, west from the Vieux Port along blvd Jean Hibert and blvd du Midi.

The **Musée de la Castre** (☎ 04 93 38 55 26; place de la Castre, Le Suquet; adult/student & under 18yr/concession €3.20/free/2; 🕑 10am-7pm Jul & Aug, 10am-1pm & 2-6pm Tue-Sun Apr-Jun & Sep, 10am-1pm & 2-5pm Tue-Sun Oct-Mar) is memorable for its ethnographic exhibits and stunning castle location at the top of Cannes' Old Town.

Although just 20 minutes away by boat, the tranquil **Îles de Lérins** feels far from the madding crowd. The closest island is **Île Ste-Marguerite**, where the mysterious Man in the Iron Mask was incarcerated during the late 17th century; it's now better known for its bone-white beaches, eucalyptus groves and small marine museum. Smaller still is **Île St-Honorat**, a monastery since the 5th century: you can visit small chapels scattered across the island and stroll among the monks' vineyards and forests.

Boats for the islands travel from quai des Îles on the western side of the harbour. **Riviera Lines** (☎ 04 92 98 71 31; ww.riviera-lines.com) runs ferries to Île Ste-Marguerite (adult/child €11/5.50 return), while **Compagnie Planaria** (☎ 04 92 98 71 38; www.cannes-ilesdelerins.com) operates boats to Île St-Honorat (adult/child €11/5.50 return).

Sleeping

Hotel prices in Cannes fluctuate wildly according to the season, and soar during the film festival, when you'll need to book months in advance.

Parc Bellevue (☎ 04 93 47 28 97; www.parcbellevue.com; 67 av Maurice Chevalier, Cannes-la-Bocca; powered camp sites per 2 adults, tent & car €26; 🕑 Apr-Sep;) About 5.5km west of the city, this is the closest camping ground to Cannes, with a huge pool and facilities galore. Bus 9 from the bus station stops 400m away.

Hôtel Albe (☎ 04 97 06 21 21; www.albe-hotel.fr; 31 rue Bivouac Napoléon; s/d from €35/45;) The rooms are nothing to write home about, but this hotel is right in the heart of the action: the street is about to become pedestrianised, which should guarantee a good night's sleep.

Le Chanteclair (☎/fax 04 93 39 68 88; 12 rue Forville; d from €48; 🕑 closed mid-Nov–mid-Jan) Right in the heart of Le Suquet and moments from the Forville Provençal market, this sweet 15-room place has an enchanting courtyard garden.

Hôtel des Orangers (☎ 04 93 39 99 92; www.hotel-orangers.com; 1 rue des Orangers; s/d from €74/81;) Perched at the edge of the Old Town, the water views from the bright west-facing rooms on the 2nd and 3rd floors are an unexpected treat, and the restaurants of rue du Suquet (five minutes) are steps away.

Hôtel Splendid (☎ 04 97 06 22 22; www.splendid-hotel-cannes.com; 4-6 rue Félix Faure; s/d from €115/128;) This elaborate 1871 building has everything it takes to rival Cannes' posher palaces: beautifully decorated rooms, fabulous

THE SCENT OF THE CÔTE D'AZUR

Around 11km west of Nice and surrounded by fields of lavender, jasmine, mimosa and orange blossom, **Grasse** is one of France's leading perfume producers. There are more than 30 **perfumeries** selling everything from scented soap to top-quality perfumes – the highly trained noses of local perfume-makers are said to be able to identify 3000 scents with a single whiff.

Fragonard (☎ 04 93 36 44 65; 20 blvd Fragonard; 🕑 9am-6pm Feb-Oct, 9am-12.30pm & 2-6pm Nov-Jan) is the easiest perfumery to reach, and the tourist office provides information on other establishments and field trips to local flower-growers, including **Domaine de Manon** (☎ 04 93 60 12 76; www.domaine-manon.com; admission €6).

FRANCE

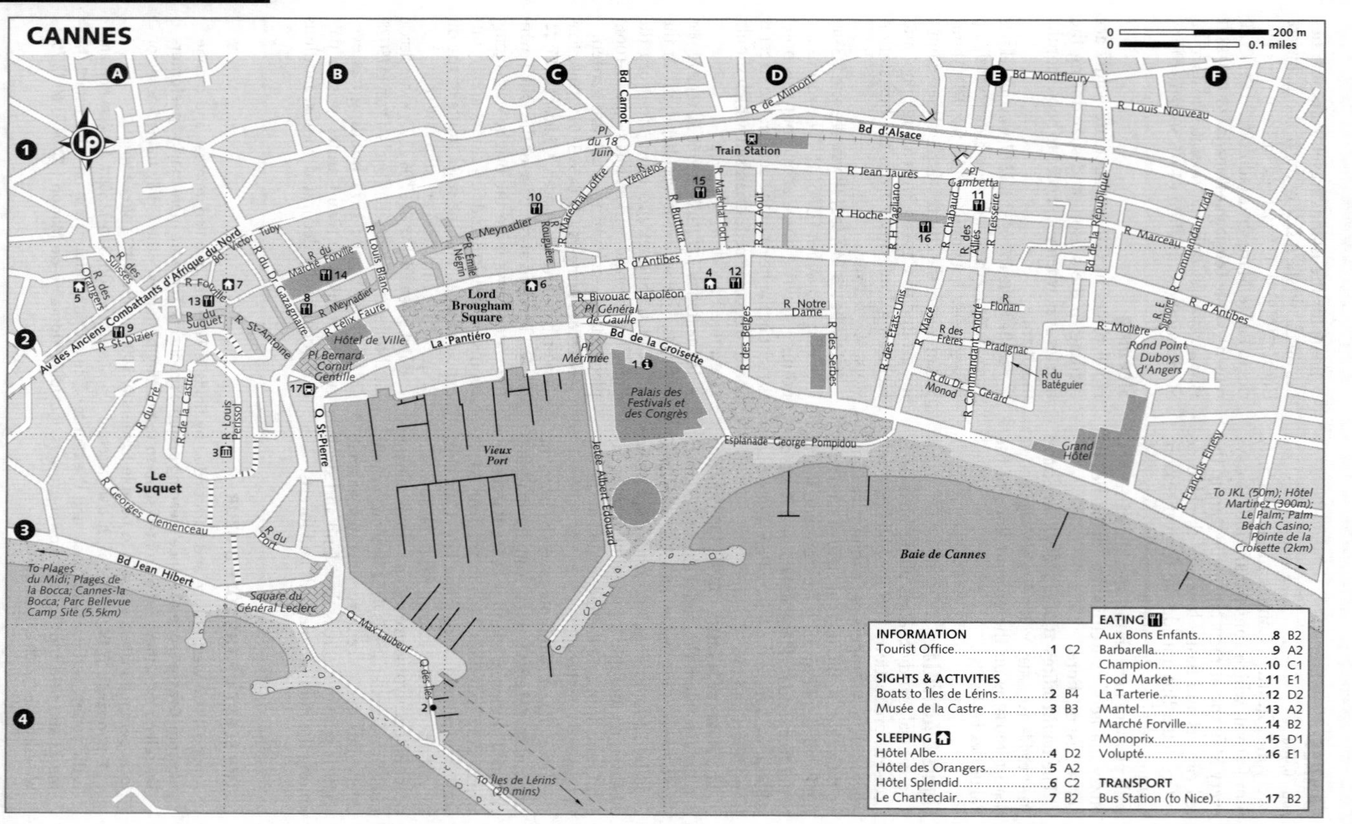
CANNES
0 200 m
0 0.1 miles
INFORMATION
Tourist Office 1 C2
SIGHTS & ACTIVITIES
Boats to Îles de Lérins 2 B4
Musée de la Castre 3 B3
SLEEPING
Hôtel Albe 4 D2
Hôtel des Orangers 5 A2
Hôtel Splendid 6 C2
Le Chanteclair 7 B2
EATING
Aux Bons Enfants 8 B2
Barbarella 9 A2
Champion 10 C1
Food Market 11 E1
La Tarterie 12 D2
Mantel 13 A2
Marché Forville 14 B2
Monoprix 15 D1
Volupté 16 E1
TRANSPORT
Bus Station (to Nice) 17 B2
Baie de Cannes
Vieux Port
Le Suquet
Lord Brougham Square
Palais des Festivals et des Congrès
Hôtel de Ville
Train Station
Grand Hôtel
Bd d'Alsace
Bd Carnot
Bd de la Croisette
Bd Jean Hibert
Bd Montfleury
Bd de la République
R d'Antibes
R Jean Jaurès
R Hoche
La Pantiéro
Q St-Pierre
Q Max Laubeuf
Q des Îles
Jetée Albert Édouard
Esplanade George Pompidou
Square du Général Leclerc
Rond Point Duboys d'Angers
Av des Anciens Combattants d'Afrique du Nord
R Georges Clemenceau
To JKL (50m); Hôtel Martinez (300m); Le Palm; Palm Beach Casino; Pointe de la Croisette (2km)
To Plages du Midi; Plages de la Bocca; Cannes-la Bocca; Parc Bellevue Camp Site (5.5km)
To Îles de Lérins (20 mins)

location, stunning views, as well as 15 rooms with self-catering kitchenettes.

Eating

Generally, you'll find the less expensive restaurants on and around rue du Marché Forville, northeast of Vieux Port. Hipper, pricier establishments line the buzzing rues St-Antoine and du Suquet.

Volupté (☎ 04 93 39 60 32; 32 rue Hoche; snacks €4.50, mains €13-15; 9am-8pm Mon-Sat) With its 140 types of tea, all neatly stocked in red and white tins, this elegant tearoom draws a happening crowd of young and beautiful things.

La Tarterie (☎ 04 93 39 67 43; 33 rue Bivouac Napoléon; dishes €6-13; 8.30am-6pm Mon-Sat) A bakery with a difference, offering megasalads and fancy tarts at a fast-food price. We like it.

Aux Bons Enfants (80 rue Meynadier; menus €23; lunch & dinner Tue-Sat) This familial little place doesn't have a phone, but it doesn't seem to matter – it's always full. The lucky ones who get a table (get there early or late) can feast on top-notch regional dishes.

Barbarella (☎ 04 92 99 17 33; 16 rue St-Dizier; mains €25-35; 7-11.30pm Tue-Sun) You've seen the film, now go to the err…restaurant. It's as kitsch as the movie (trompe l'œil–painted building, see-through chairs, psychedelic lighting, groovy atmosphere) and its fusion food is fine.

our pick **Mantel** (☎ 04 93 39 13 10; 22 rue St-Antoine; lunch menus €25, dinner menus €36-58; lunch & dinner, closed Wed & lunch Tue & Thu) The Italian maître d' will make you feel like a million dollars and you'll melt for Noël Mantel's divine cuisine and great-value prices. Best of all, you get not one but two desserts with your menu (oh, the pannacotta…).

The **Marché Forville** (rue du Marché Forville; Tue-Sun mornings) is where many of the city's restaurants shop and where you should get your picnic supplies. The **food market** (place Gambetta; morning) is another good address for fruit and veg.

Large supermarkets:

Champion (6 rue Meynadier; 8.30am-7.30pm Mon-Sat)
Monoprix (9 rue Maréchal Foch; 8.30am-8pm Mon-Sat)

Getting There & Away

Regular buses go to Nice (bus 200, €1, 1½ hours) and Nice airport (bus 210, €14.20, 50 minutes, half-hourly from 8am to 6pm). Trains serve Nice (€5.70, 30 to 40 minutes), Grasse (€3.60, 25 minutes) and Marseille (€24.80, two hours).

ST-TROPEZ

pop 5640

In the soft autumn or winter light, it's hard to believe that the pretty terracotta fishing village of St-Tropez is yet another stop on the Riviera celebrity circuit. It seems far removed from its glitzy siblings further up the coast, but come spring or summer, it's a different world: the town's population increases tenfold, prices triple, and celebrities (including Gallic crooner Johnny Hallyday) monopolise town.

Orientation & Information

The beaches where A-listers sunbathe, in the Baie de Pampelonne, lie 4km southeast of town. The village itself is on the southern side of the Baie de St-Tropez. The Old Town sits snugly between quai Jean Jaurès (the main quay of the luxury yacht-packed Vieux Port), place des Lices and a lofty 16th-century citadel overlooking the town from the northeastern edge.

The **tourist office** (☎ 04 94 97 45 21; www.ot-saint-tropez.com; quai Jean Jaurès; 9.30am-8pm Jul & Aug, 9.30am-12.30pm & 2-7pm Apr-Jun & Sep–mid-Oct, 9.30am-12.30pm & 2-6pm mid-Oct–Mar) organises 1½-hour **guided walking tours** (tours €6; 10am Wed Apr-Oct) in French; call to see if an English-speaking guide is available.

Sights & Activities

A quick wander around the historical quarter will dispel any notion that St-Tropez is all glitz, no substance. The **Musée de l'Annonciade** (☎ 04 94 17 84 10; place Grammont, Vieux Port; adult/student €5/3, exhibitions €6/4; 10am-noon & 3-7pm Wed-Mon Jun-Sep, 10am-noon & 2-6pm Wed-Mon Oct & Dec-May) displays paintings by Matisse, Bonnard, Dufy and especially Signac, who set up his home and studio in St-Tropez.

The panoramas of St-Tropez' bay from the elevated 17th-century **Citadelle de St-Tropez** (☎ 04 94 97 59 43; admission €2.50; 10am-6.30pm Apr-Sep, 10am-12.30pm & 1.30-5.30pm Oct-Mar) are definitely worth the climb.

But as is so often the case along the Côte d'Azur, it's the beaches that take centre stage in St-Tropez. The glistening **Plage de Tahiti**, 4km southeast of town, morphs into the 5km-long **Plage de Pampelonne**, which in summer incorporates a sequence of exclusive restaurant/clubs. To get here, head out of town along av de la Résistance to rte de la Belle Isnarde and then rte de Tahiti, or catch the bus to Ramatuelle, which stops at various points along a road 1km inland from the beach.

Sleeping & Eating

St-Tropez is no shoestring destination, but there are plenty of multistar camping grounds to the southeast along Plage de Pampelonne.

Hôtel La Méditerranée (☎ 04 94 97 00 44; www.hotelmediterranee.org; 21 blvd Louis Blanc; d low season €50-100, high season €85-250; ❄) It's hard to believe such authentic places still exist in St-Tropez. Sixteen rooms with a simple but romantic decor, with a bar-restaurant (mains €15) overlooking a gorgeous summery garden.

Hôtel Sube (☎ 04 94 97 30 04; www.hotel-sube.com; 15 quai Suffren; d low season €115-190, high season €140-290; ❄) This marine-style hotel has the most coveted location in town, right on the waterfront. Portside rooms and their fabulous views provide the perfect excuse to stare unashamedly at the yachts moored below.

Ô Vents d'Anges (☎ 04 94 43 31 33; 7 quai de l'Epi; mains €12-25; 🕒 lunch & dinner) Right by the port, in one of the town's party corners, this cheap and cheerful place serves up grilled fish and meat.

La Table du Marché (☎ 04 94 97 85 20; 38 rue Georges Clémenceau; mains €24-36; 🕒 lunch & dinner) Chef Christophe Leroy's St-Tropez pad is a must, be it for scrumptious tea-time *pâtisseries* (pastries and cakes) or heavenly cuisine come dinner-time.

The **place des Lices market** (🕒 mornings Tue & Sat) is a highlight of local life, with colourful stalls groaning under the weight of plump fruit and veg, mounds of olives, local cheeses, chestnut purée and fragrant herbs. The **fish market** (🕒 Tue-Sun, daily summer) on place aux Herbes is joined by a fruit and vegetable market in summer.

For groceries, try **Monoprix** (9 av du Général Leclerc; 🕒 8am-8pm Mon-Sat).

Getting There & Away

St-Tropez' **bus station** (av Général de Gaulle) is on the southwestern edge of town on the main road. There's an **information office** (☎ 04 94 54 62 36; 🕒 8.30am-noon & 2-4.30pm Mon-Fri, 8.30am-noon Sat) at the station. **Sodetrav** (☎ 08 25 00 06 50) runs eight buses daily (15 in summer) from St-Raphaël Valescure train station to St-Tropez bus station (€10.30, 1¼ hours), via Fréjus.

Trans Côte d'Azur (p316) runs day trips from Nice and Cannes between Easter and September.

MONACO

☎ 377 / pop 32,000

Your first glimpse of this pocket-sized principality will probably make your heart sink: after all the gorgeous medieval hilltop villages, glittering beaches and secluded peninsulas of the surrounding area, Monaco's concrete high-rises and astronomic prices might come as a shock.

But Monaco has a surprising amount to offer, much more, in fact, than the customary spin at its casino's roulette table. In its 1.95 sq km, the world's second-smallest state (a smidgen bigger than the Vatican) has managed to squeeze in not only a thriving performing art and sport scene, but also a world-famous circus festival, a world-class aquarium, a beautiful Old Town, stunning gardens, interesting architecture throughout and a royal family on a par with British royals for best gossip fodder.

Monaco is a sovereign state but there is no border control. It has its own flag (red and white), national holiday (19 November), postal system and telephone code (☎ 377), but the official language is French and the country uses the euro even though it is not part of the European Union. Today there are just 7800 Monégasque citizens of a total population of 32,000, all of whom live a tax-free life of cradle-to-grave security.

Orientation

Monaco consists of six areas: Monaco Ville (the old city), with its narrow, medieval streets leading to the Palais du Prince (Prince's Palace); the capital, Monte Carlo, north of the port; La Condamine, the flat area immediately southwest of the port; Fontvieille, the industrial area southwest of Monaco Ville; Moneghetti, the hillside suburb west of La Condamine; and Larvotto, the beach area north of Monte Carlo, from where the French town of Beausoleil is just three streets uphill.

Information

Calls between Monaco and France are international calls. Dial ☎ 00 followed by Monaco's country code (☎ 377) when calling Monaco from abroad. To phone France from Monaco, dial 00 and France's country code (☎ 33).

Monaco-imprinted euros are highly prized by coin collectors.

Change Bureau (Jardins du Casino; 🕒 9am-7.30pm)

Laverie (1 Escalier de la Riviera, Beausoleil; 🕒 7am-7pm)

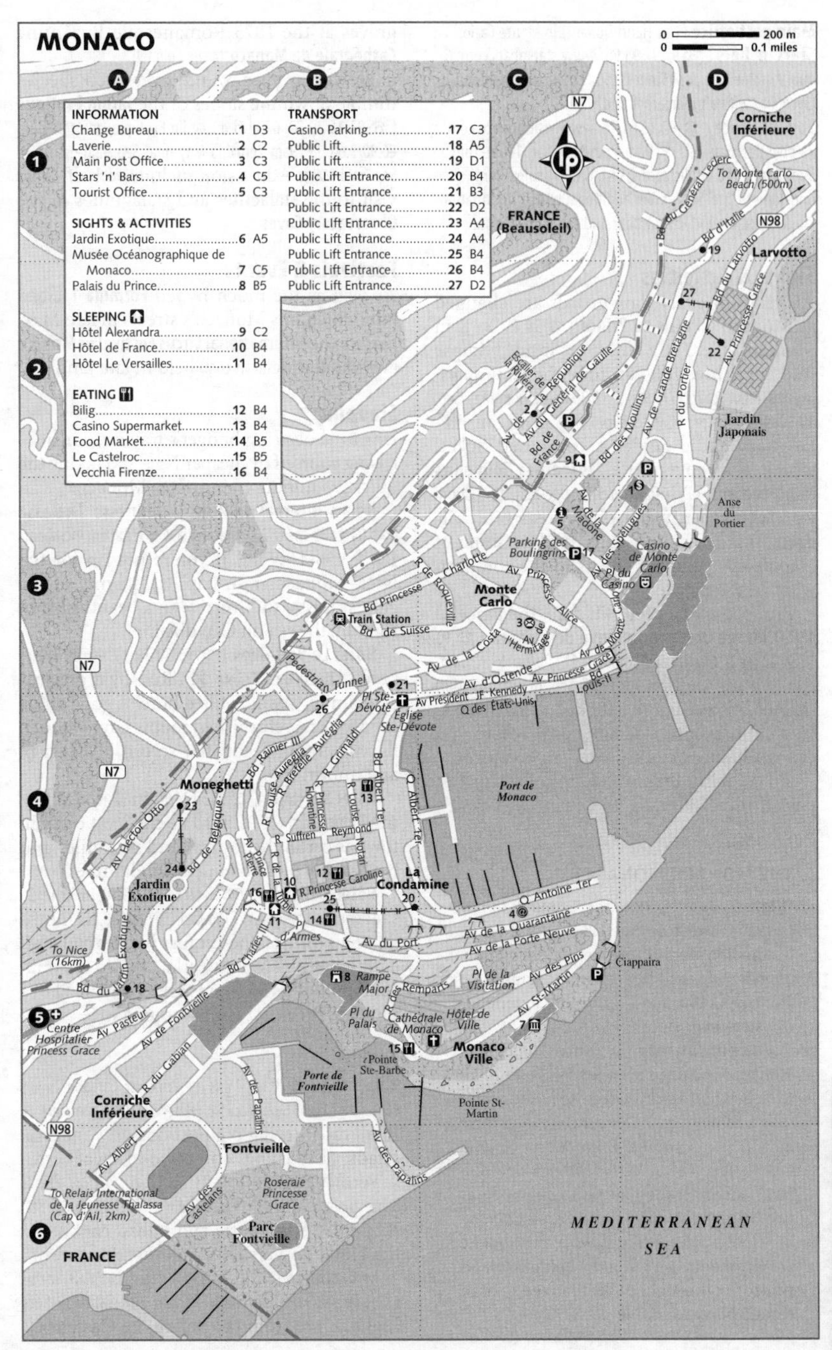
MONACO
0 200 m
0 0.1 miles
A
B
C
D
1
2
3
4
5
6
INFORMATION
Change Bureau 1 D3
Laverie 2 C2
Main Post Office 3 C3
Stars 'n' Bars 4 C5
Tourist Office 5 C3
SIGHTS & ACTIVITIES
Jardin Exotique 6 A5
Musée Océanographique de Monaco 7 C5
Palais du Prince 8 B5
SLEEPING
Hôtel Alexandra 9 C2
Hôtel de France 10 B4
Hôtel Le Versailles 11 B4
EATING
Bilig 12 B4
Casino Supermarket 13 B4
Food Market 14 B5
Le Castelroc 15 B5
Vecchia Firenze 16 B4
TRANSPORT
Casino Parking 17 C3
Public Lift 18 A5
Public Lift 19 D1
Public Lift Entrance 20 B4
Public Lift Entrance 21 B3
Public Lift Entrance 22 D2
Public Lift Entrance 23 A4
Public Lift Entrance 24 A4
Public Lift Entrance 25 B4
Public Lift Entrance 26 B4
Public Lift Entrance 27 D2
N7
Corniche Inférieure
To Monte Carlo Beach (500m)
FRANCE (Beausoleil)
Bd du Général Leclerc
Bd d'Italie
N98
Larvotto
Bd du Larvotto
Av Princesse Grace
Escalier de la Riviera
Av de la République
Av du Général de Gaulle
Bd de France
Bd des Moulins
Av de Grande Bretagne
R du Portier
Jardin Japonais
Anse du Portier
Av de la Madone
Av des Spélugues
Parking des Boulingrins
Casino de Monte Carlo
Pl du Casino
Av de Monte Carlo
Monte Carlo
Av Princesse Alice
R de Roqueville
Bd Princesse Charlotte
Train Station
Bd de Suisse
Av de l'Hermitage
Av de la Costa
Av d'Ostende
Av Princesse Grace
Bd Louis-II
Pedestrian Tunnel
Pl Ste-Dévote
Av Président JF Kennedy
Q des États-Unis
Église Ste-Dévote
Bd Rainier III
R Louise Aureglia
R Bretelle Aureglia
R Grimaldi
Bd Albert 1er
Q Albert 1er
Port de Monaco
Moneghetti
R Princesse Florentine
R Louise
R Suffren Reymond
R Notari
Av Hector Otto
Bd de Belgique
Jardin Exotique
Av Prince Pierre
R de la Turbie
R Princesse Caroline
La Condamine
Q Antoine 1er
Pl d'Armes
Av du Port
Av de la Quarantaine
Av de la Porte Neuve
Ciappaira
To Nice (16km)
Av du Jardin Exotique
Bd du Jardin Exotique
Bd Charles III
Rampe Major
R des Remparts
Pl de la Visitation
Av des Pins
Av St-Martin
Centre Hospitalier Princess Grace
Av Pasteur
Av de Fontvieille
Pl du Palais
Cathédrale de Monaco
Hôtel de Ville
Monaco Ville
R du Gabian
Pointe Ste-Barbe
Porte de Fontvieille
Av des Papalins
Pointe St-Martin
Corniche Inférieure
N98
Fontvieille
Av Albert II
To Relais International de la Jeunesse Thalassa (Cap d'Ail, 2km)
Av des Castelans
Roseraie Princesse Grace
Parc Fontvieille
FRANCE
MEDITERRANEAN SEA

FRANCE

Main post office (1 av Henri Dunant) In Monte Carlo.

Stars 'n' Bars (☎ 97 97 95 95; www.starsnbars.com; 6 quai Antoine 1er; per 15min €2.50; 11am-midnight) Lively bar with a cybercorner and wi-fi.

Tourist office (☎ 92 16 61 16; www.visitmonaco.com; 2a blvd des Moulins; 9am-7pm Mon-Sat, 10am-1pm Sun) Across the public gardens from the casino. From mid-June to late-September additional tourist information kiosks open around the harbour and the train station.

Sights & Activities

At 11.55am every day, guards are changed at Monaco's **Palais du Prince** (☎ 93 25 18 31) in Monaco Ville. For a half-hour inside glimpse into royal life, you can tour the **state apartments** (adult/child €7/3.50; 9.30am-6.30pm May-Sep, 10.30am-6pm Apr, 10am-5.30pm Oct) with an 11-language audio guide. A combined ticket, which also covers the **Musée des Souvenirs Napoléoniens** (10.30am-5pm Dec-Mar, to 5.30pm Oct & Apr, 9.30am-6.30pm May-Sep), costs €9 (children €4.50). The museum displays some of Napoleon's personal effects in the southern wing of the palace.

Propped on a sheer cliff-face, the graceful 1910 **Musée Océanographique de Monaco** (☎ 93 15 36 00; av St-Martin; adult/student €12.50/6; 9.30am-7pm Jul & Aug, to 6.30pm Apr-Jun & Sep, to 6pm Oct-Mar) houses an aquarium stocked with sharks, tropical fish, and a tactile basin where you can get hands-on with local sea creatures.

An adoring crowd continually shuffles past Prince Rainier's and Princess Grace's graves at the 1875 Romanesque-Byzantine **Cathédrale de Monaco** (4 rue Colonel).

Flowering year-round, over 1000 species tumble down the slopes of the **Jardin Exotique** (☎ 93 15 29 80; 62 blvd du Jardin Exotique; adult/student €6.90/3.60; 9am-7pm mid-May–mid-Sep, 9am-6pm mid-Sep–mid-May). Admission includes a half-hour visit to the stalactites and stalagmites in the **Observatory Caves**.

THE MONACO MONARCHY

Originally from Genoa, the Grimaldi family has ruled Monaco since 1297, except for its occupation during the French Revolution. Its independence was again recognised by France in 1860, and it's been an independent state ever since.

Since the marriage of Prince Rainier III of Monaco (who ruled between 1949 and 2005) to Hollywood actress Grace Kelly, Monaco's ruling family has been a nonstop feature in gossip magazines. Even Albert II, who has been prince since his father's death in 2005, hasn't escaped media scrutiny: he has two illegitimate children but no legitimate heirs, although his charity work and athletic achievements (he's a judo black-belt and played for the Monaco football team) have earned him favourable press.

Festivals & Events

As well as the much-hyped **Formula 1 Grand Prix**, which hits Monaco's streets in late May, there's the **International Circus Festival of Monaco** (www.montecarlofestivals.com) held in late January.

Sleeping

If your shoestring budget's fraying, consider basing yourself in cheaper Nice and taking the quick 20-minute train trip to Monaco.

Relais International de la Jeunesse Thalassa (☎ 04 93 78 18 58; 2 av Gramaglia, Cap d'Ail; dm incl sheets €17; closed Nov-Mar) If you're not up for the Nice–Monaco train trip, try staying at the closest hostel to Monaco, in a beautiful spot right by the sea on Cap d'Ail.

Hôtel Le Versailles (☎ 93 50 79 34; 4-6 av Prince Pierre; s €70-90, d €100-160;) Run by a gregarious family, this sun-filled hotel is good value for Monaco: refurbished rooms have wooden floors, simple decor, flat-screen TVs, wi-fi, and minifridges.

Hôtel de France (☎ 93 30 24 64; fax 92 16 13 34; 6 rue de la Turbie; s/d/tr €80/90/108) The cheapest place in town is certainly no-frills and no-smiles, but it's handily plonked in La Condamine.

Hôtel Alexandra (☎ 93 50 63 13; fax 92 16 06 48; 35 blvd Princesse Charlotte; s €100-125, d €120-160, tr €170-190;) This turn-of-the-century hotel is conveniently located in Monte Carlo, close to the train stations, but its 56 rooms are in dire need of a revamp. Breakfast is a whopping €15.

Eating

Bilig (☎ 97 98 20 43; 11bis rue Princesse Caroline; mains €6-12; 11am-6pm Mon-Sat winter, to 10pm summer) A small cafe serving big portions of wonderful salads, tasty crêpes and the odd meat dish.

Vecchia Firenze (☎ 93 30 27 70; 4-6 av Prince Pierre; mains €12-27; lunch & dinner Tue-Fri, dinner Sat) Authentic pizza, pasta and Italian cooking at the Hôtel Le Versailles' inhouse restaurant.

Le Castelroc (☎ 93 30 36 68; place du Palais; mains €22-27; 9am-3pm daily, dinner Tue-Sat May-Sep) Right across from the Palace, Le Castelroc's

> **FEELING LUCKY?**
>
> Monte Carlo's monumental 1910 **Casino de Monte Carlo** (☎ 98 06 21 21; www.casinomontecarlo.com; place du Casino; 🕑 European Rooms from noon Sat & Sun, from 2pm Mon-Fri) is the perfect place to live out those Bond fantasies, but it sure ain't cheap: admission is €10 for the European Rooms, with poker/slot machines, French roulette and *trente et quarante* (a card game), and €20 for the Private Rooms, which offer baccarat, blackjack, craps and American roulette. And that's before you've even bought a chip.
>
> There's a strict jacket-and-tie dress code after 10pm, and a minimum age of 18; bring photo ID.

alfresco terrace is the perfect place to try genuine Monégasque specialities like *barbajuan* (a beignet filled with spinach and cheese) and *cundyun* (Monaco's version of *salade niçoise*).

Pit stops for self-catering include a **food market** (place d'Armes; 🕑 7am-2pm) and a **Casino Supermarket** (blvd Albert 1er), both in La Condamine.

Getting There & Away

Monaco's **train station** (av Prince Pierre) has frequent trains to Nice (€3.20, 20 minutes), and east to Menton (€1.80, 10 minutes), and the Italian town of Ventimiglia (€3.20, 20 minutes).

CORSICA

The rugged island of Corsica (Corse in French) is officially a part of France, but remains fiercely proud of its own culture, history and language. It's one of the Meditteranean's most dramatic islands, with a bevy of beautiful beaches, glitzy ports, and a mountainous, maquis-covered interior to explore, as well as a wild, independent spirit all of its own.

The island has long had a love–hate relationship with the mother mainland – you'll see plenty of anti-French slogans and 'Corsicanised' road signs – but that doesn't seem to deter the millions of French tourists who descend on the island every summer. Prices skyrocket and accommodation is at a premium during the peak season between July and August, so you're much better off saving your visit for spring and autumn.

BASTIA

pop 37,800

While ramshackle Bastia might not measure up to the sexy style of Ajaccio or the architectural appeal of Bonifacio, in many ways it's a more authentic snapshot of modern-day Corsica, a lived-in, well-loved city that's resisted the urge to polish up its image just to please the tourists. Narrow alleyways climb from the old harbour to the 16th-century citadel, currently undergoing one of the largest (and costliest) renovation projects in the island's history.

Information

Oxy Cyber Café (☎ 06 84 76 11 65; 1 rue Salvatore Viale; per hr €3.10; 🕑 10am-2am Mon-Sat, 1pm-2am Sun)

Post office (av Maréchal Sébastiani; 🕑 8am-7pm Mon-Fri, 8am-noon Sat)

Tourist office (☎ 04 95 54 20 40; www.bastia-tourisme.com; place St-Nicolas; 🕑 8am-8pm Mon-Sat, 9am-noon & 4-7pm Sun Jul & Aug, 8.30am-noon & 2-6pm Mon-Sat, 9.30am-1pm Sun Apr-Jun, Sep & Oct, 8.30am-noon & 2-6pm Mon-Fri, 8.30am-noon Sun Nov-Mar) Multilingual tourist office on place St-Nicolas.

Sights & Activities

Even by Corsican standards, Bastia is a pocket-sized city. The 19th-century square of **place St-Nicholas** sprawls along the seafront between the ferry port and the harbour. Named after the patron saint of sailors – a nod to Corsica's seagoing heritage – the square is lined with plane trees and busy cafes, as well as a **statue of Napoleon Bonaparte**, Corsica's most famous son.

A network of narrow lanes leads south towards the old port and the neighbourhood of **Terra Vecchia**, a muddle of crumbling apartments and balconied blocks. Further south is the Vieux Port (Old Port), ringed by pastel-coloured tenements and buzzy brasseries, as well as the twin-towered **Église St-Jean Baptiste**. The best views of the harbour are from the **Jetée du Dragon** (Dragon Jetty) or from the hillside park of **Jardin Romieu** (Romieu Garden), reached via a twisting staircase from the waterfront. Behind the garden looms Bastia's sunbaked **citadel**, built from the 15th to 17th centuries as a stronghold for the city's Genoese masters.

Sleeping

Hôtel Univers (☎ 04 95 31 03 38; www.hotelunivers.org, in French; 3 av Maréchal Sébastiani; s €45-60, d €50-70;) Near place St-Nicolas, the Univers makes a decent base, but don't expect any frills. A scruffy staircase leads to whitewashed rooms with blue-and-yellow bedspreads and laminate floors; double-glazing shuts out (most) street noise.

Hôtel Posta Vecchia (☎ 04 95 32 32 38; www.hotel-postavecchia.com; quai des Martyrs de la Libération; d €55-92, f €65-100;) If it's sea views you're after, make a beeline for the Posta Vecchia – the only place in town where you can watch bobbing boats and Mediterranean waves from your bed (worth the €10 surcharge).

Hôtel Central (☎ 04 95 31 71 12; www.centralhotel.fr; 3 rue Miot; s €55-75, d €65-95, apt €85-105;) The pick of Bastia's town-centre hotels. Rooms feature timber floors and nautical pictures; a €10 supplement buys a titchy garden balcony. Apartments with self-contained kitchenettes are available.

Eating

Cafes and restaurants line place St-Nicolas and the old port.

our pick A Casarella (☎ 04 95 32 02 32; rue du Dragon; mains €9-28; lunch Mon-Fri, dinner Mon-Sat) In the citadel, this well-hidden restaurant boasts the loveliest port-view patio in Bastia. Tuck into traditional Corsican cuisine – tuna with caramelised figs, or sardines stuffed with *brocciu* (ewe or goat's milk cheese).

Le Bouchon (☎ 04 95 58 14 22; 4bis rue St-Jean; mains €15-21, no credit cards; closed Sun) Dinky, down-to-earth bistro from the Lyonnaise school, with a blackboard of specials running the gamut from Corsican sausages to pork steaks. A terrace spills onto the old port.

U Tianu (☎ 04 95 31 36 67; 4 rue Rigo; menus €19; dinner Mon-Sat, closed Aug) Tiny restaurant with the air of a traditional Corsican kitchen. Hunting rifles and country knick-knacks cover the walls, and you'll tuck into five-course platters of Corsican food including cheese, aperitif and coffee. Climb the stairs from the alley just behind the old port.

Cheese, fish, fruit, veg and Corsican charcuterie fills the morning **food market** (place de l'Hôtel de Ville; Tue-Sun), or you can pick up supplies at Spar supermarkets on rue César Campinchi and blvd Paoli.

Getting There & Away

AIR

Aéroport Bastia-Poretta (☎ 04 95 54 54 54; www.bastia.aeroport.fr) is 24km south of the city. Buses (€8.50, eight daily) depart from outside the Préfecture building. The first bus from town is around 6am and the last bus from the airport is around 9pm; schedules are posted at the bus stop.

BOAT

Bastia's two ferry terminals are connected by a free shuttle bus. All the ferry companies have information offices in the southern terminal, which usually open for same-day ticket sales a couple of hours before each sailing.

Corsica Ferries (☎ 04 95 32 95 95; www.corsicaferries.com; 15bis rue Chanoine Leschi; 8.30am-noon & 2-6pm Mon-Fri, 9am-noon Sat) Opposite the northern terminal.

Moby Lines (☎ 04 95 34 84 94; www.mobylines.it; 4 rue du Commandant Luce de Casabianca; 8am-noon & 2-6pm Mon-Fri, 8am-noon Sat)

SNCM (☎ 04 95 54 66 81; www.sncm.com; 8-11.45am & 2-5.45pm Mon-Fri, 8am-noon Sat)

BUS

There are three bus stops in Bastia: outside the tourist office, at the train station, and at the 'bus station' north of Sq St-Victor.

Beaux Voyages (☎ 04 95 65 11 35) Travels to Île Rousse (€10, 90 minutes) and Calvi (€16, two hours) daily except Sunday. Buses leave from the train station.

Eurocorse (☎ 04 95 31 73 76) Travels to Ajaccio (€22, three hours) via Corte (€11, two hours) twice daily except on Sundays from Bastia's 'bus station'.

TRAIN

The **train station** (☎ 04 95 32 80 61; av Maréchal Sébastiani; 6am-8.30pm Mon-Sat, 8.30am-8.30pm Sun) is on Sq Maréchal Leclerc. Main destinations include Ajaccio (€23.90, four daily) via Corte (€11.20), and Calvi (€18.10. three hours, three or four daily) via Île Rousse (€15).

CALVI

pop 5600

Basking between the fiery orange bastions of its 15th-century citadel and the glittering waters of a moon-shaped bay, Calvi feels closer to the chichi sophistication of a Côte d'Azur resort than a historic Corsican port – and has sky-high prices to match. Palatial yachts dock along its harbourside, while above the quay the watchtowers of the town's Genoese stronghold stand guard.

The **main tourist office** (☎ 04 95 65 16 67; www.balagne-corsica.com; Port de Plaisance; ⏰ 9am-noon & 3-6.30pm Jul & Aug, 9am-noon & 2-6pm Mon-Sat May, Jun, Sep & Oct, 9am-noon & 2-6pm Mon-Fri Nov-Apr) is opposite the marina.

Calvi's 15th-century **citadel** – also known as the Haute Ville (Upper City) – sits on a rocky promontory above the Basse Ville (Lower Town). The **Palais des Gouverneurs** (place d'Armes), once the seat of power for the Genoese administration, now serves as a base for the French Foreign Legion. Uphill from Caserne Sampiero is the 13th-century **Église St-Jean Baptiste**, rebuilt in 1570.

Sunworshippers don't have far to stroll – Calvi's stellar 4km beach begins at the marina and runs east around the Golfe de Calvi. You can rent out kayaks and windsurfers from the **Calvi Nautique Club** (☎ 04 95 65 10 65; www.calvinc.org; Base Nautique, Port de Plaisance; ⏰ May-Oct).

Sleeping

Most of Calvi's hotels are closed in winter.

Camping La Pinède (☎ 04 95 65 17 80; www.camping-calvi.com; rte de la Pinède; camp sites adult €6.50-9, tent €2.50-3.50, car €2.50-3.50; ⏰ mid-May–mid-Oct; 🏊) Handy for Calvi town and the beach, this shady spot has sites sheltered under tall pines.

Hôtel Le Belvedere (☎ 04 95 65 01 25; www.calvi-location.fr; place Christophe Colomb; d €47-117, tr €72-132; ❄) With top-notch views of the citadel, this hotel has wooden floors and Mediterranean accents throughout, plus a panoramic breakfast room overlooking the bay.

Hôtel Le Magnolia (☎ 04 95 65 19 16; www.hotel-le-magnolia.com; rue Alsace Lorraine; r €60-140) An old-fashioned oasis from the harbourside fizz, set behind a courtyard. Rooms are plain and small – definitely fork out for the sea-view rooms.

Eating

Calvi's quayside is chock-a-block with restaurants, but many focus more on the ocean ambience than the quality of the food.

U Callelu (☎ 04 95 65 22 18; quai Landry; menus €23, mains €12-28) This home-spun eatery is run with passion by a born-and-bred islander, and the menu's 100% local – meat from the market, wine from the vineyards, fish straight off the quay.

Île de Beauté (☎ 04 95 65 00 46; quai Landry; mains €15-35; ⏰ lunch & dinner mid-Mar–Dec) As chic as any Côte d'Azur bistro, this seafood palace serves Calvi's finest *fruits de mer*, including authentic bouillabaisse.

U Minellu (☎ 04 95 65 05 52; Traverse à l'Église; menus from €17; ⏰ lunch & dinner, closed Sun winter) Duck under the awning and prepare for hearty portions of Corsican wild boar stew, *brocciu* cannelloni and chestnut cake.

Piping-hot paninis are sold at the *sandwicherie* **Best Of** (1 rue Clemenceau; sandwiches €4-7; ⏰ 11.30am-10pm). You can pick up fresh fruit and veg from the **Alimentation du Golfe** (rue Clemenceau; ⏰ Apr-Oct) across the street or the **covered market** (marché couvert; ⏰ 8am-noon Mon-Sat) near Église Ste-Marie Majeure.

For souvenirs and Corsican goodies, seek out **Annie Traiteur** (rue Clemenceau; ⏰ Apr-Oct).

Getting There & Away

AIR

Seven kilometres southeast of town is **Aéroport Calvi Ste-Catherine** (☎ 04 95 65 88 88; www.calvi.aeroport.fr), with regular Air France (CCM) flights to Nice, Marseille and Paris Orly, plus seasonal flights. There's no airport bus: taxis with **Radio Taxis Calvis** (☎ 04 95 65 30 36) or **Association Abeille Taxis** (☎ 04 95 65 03 10) cost about €25.

BOAT

Calvi's ferry terminal is at the northeastern end of quai Landry. Regular ferries to Nice are offered by both SNCM and Corsica Ferries.

BUSES

Les Beaux Voyages (☎ 04 95 65 15 02; place de la Porteuse d'Eau) runs daily buses to Bastia (€16, two hours) via Algajola and Île Rousse (€4, 15 minutes).

WORTH THE TRIP: RÉSERVE NATURELLE DE SCANDOLA

Situated between Ajaccio and the coastal town of Porto, the Réserve Naturelle de Scandola is Corsica's only Unesco-protected marine reserve. It's a paradise for divers and snorkellers, and lots of operators run boat trips (€35 to €45) there from Porto's quayside, from April to October.

Nave Va (☎ 04 95 26 15 16; www.naveva.com)
Pass'Partout (☎ 06 75 99 13 15; www.lepasspartout.com)
Porto Linea (☎ 04 95 21 52 22; www.portolinea.com)
Via Mare (☎ 06 07 28 72 72)

TRAIN

Calvi's **train station** (☎ 04 95 65 00 61; ⏲ to 7.30pm) connects with Ajaccio (€27.80, five hours, two daily) via Corte (€15.10, four hours two daily) and Bastia (€18.10, three hours).

From April to October, the CFC's **Tramway de la Balagne** clatters to the glittering beaches between Calvi and Île Rousse (45 minutes). The line has three sectors – you need one ticket for each sector. *Carnets* (books) of six tickets (€8) are sold at stations.

LES CALANQUES

One of Corsica's most stunning natural sights is about 85km south of Calvi: **Les Calanques de Piana** (E Calanche in Corsican), a spectacular landscape of red granite cliffs and spiky outcrops, carved into bizarre shapes by the forces of wind, water and weather. Less-rocky areas support pine and chestnut forests, whose green foliage contrasts dramatically with the technicoloured granite.

AJACCIO

pop 52,900

The spectre of Corsica's great (little) general looms over the elegant port city of Ajaccio (pronounced a-zhaks-jo). Napoleon Bonaparte was born here in 1769, and the city is dotted with relics relating to the diminutive dictator. Often dubbed La Cité Imperiale in recognition of its historic importance, Ajaccio is the capital of the Corse-du-Sud *département* and is the island's main metropolis.

Orientation

Ajaccio's main street, cours Napoléon, stretches from place de Gaulle northwards to the train station and beyond. The old city is south of place Foch. The port is on the eastern side of town, from where a promenade leads west along plage St-François.

Information

CyberEspace (rue Dr Versini; per 30min/1hr €2/3; ⏲ 10am-12.30am Mon-Sat) Internet access.

Main post office (13 cours Napoléon)

Tourist office (☎ 04 95 51 53 03; www.ajaccio-tourisme.com; 3 blvd du Roi Jérôme; ⏲ 9am-6pm Mon-Sat, 9am-1pm Sun Jun-Sep, 8.30am-11.30am & 1.30-4pm Mon-Fri Oct-May) Free internet kiosk.

Sights

The Napoleonic saga begins at the **Musée National de la Maison Bonaparte** (☎ 04 95 21 43 89; rue St-Charles; adult/concession €5/3.50; ⏲ 9am-11.30am & 2-5.30pm Tue-Sun, 2-5.50pm Mon Apr-Sep, 10-11.30am & 2-4.15pm Tue-Sun, 2-4.15pm Mon Oct-Mar), the grand building in the old city where Napoleon was born and spent the first nine years of his childhood.

Established by Napoleon's uncle, the **Musée Fesch** (rue du Cardinal Fesch), one of the island's flagship museums, is currently closed for major renovations until late 2009.

Two companies run boat trips around the Golfe d'Ajaccio and the Îles Sanguinaires (€25), and excursions to the Scandola Nature Reserve (adult/four to 10 year-olds €50/35). **Découvertes Naturelles** (☎ 06 24 69 48 80; www.promenades-en-mer.org; ⏲ May-Sep) also offers a sunset cruise to the Îles Sanguinaires (€25), returning around 10pm, while **Nave Va** (☎ 04 95 51 31 31; www.naveva.com; ⏲ May-Sep) offers a cultural tour (adult/four to 10 year-olds €28/20) and a voyage down to Bonifacio (€57/40).

Sleeping

Ajaccio's hotels are pricey, especially in the high season.

Hôtel Le Dauphin (☎ 04 95 21 12 94; www.ledauphinhotel.com; 11 blvd Sampiero; s €52-59, d €60-79, tr €79-96; ❄) Ajaccio's idea of a budget hotel, with cheap(ish), functional rooms, some with port-view balconies overlooking the hectic road and ground-floor cafe-bar.

our pick **Hôtel Kallisté** (☎ 04 95 51 34 45; www.hotel-kalliste-ajaccio.com, in French; 51 cours Napoléon; s €56-69, d €64-79, tr €79-99; ❄ 💻) Exposed brick, neutral tones, terracotta tiles and a glass lift conjure a neo-boutique feel at the Kallisté, and the facilities are fab – wi-fi, satellite TV, and a stonking buffet brekkie.

Hôtel Marengo (☎ 04 95 21 43 66; www.hotel-marengo.com; 2 rue Marengo; d €61-79, tr €75-95; ❄) For something more personal, try this jolly, hospitably run little bolthole. Expect pastel rooms (all with balconies) and a quiet courtyard, all a stroll from the beach.

Eating

U Pampasgiolu (☎ 06 09 39 26 92; 15 rue de la Porta; mains €14-24, platters €26-27; ⏲ dinner) The arch-vaulted dining room of this Ajaccio institution is always packed, thanks to the first-rate Corsican food. If you're a novice, the *planches* (platters) offer bite-sized dishes of local staples.

L'Altru Versu (☎ 04 95 50 05 22; 16 rue J Baptiste Marcaggi; mains €22-28; ⏲ lunch Tue-Sat, dinner Tue-Sun) One of the top tables for Corsican cuisine: dishes at 'The Other Side' include prawn and

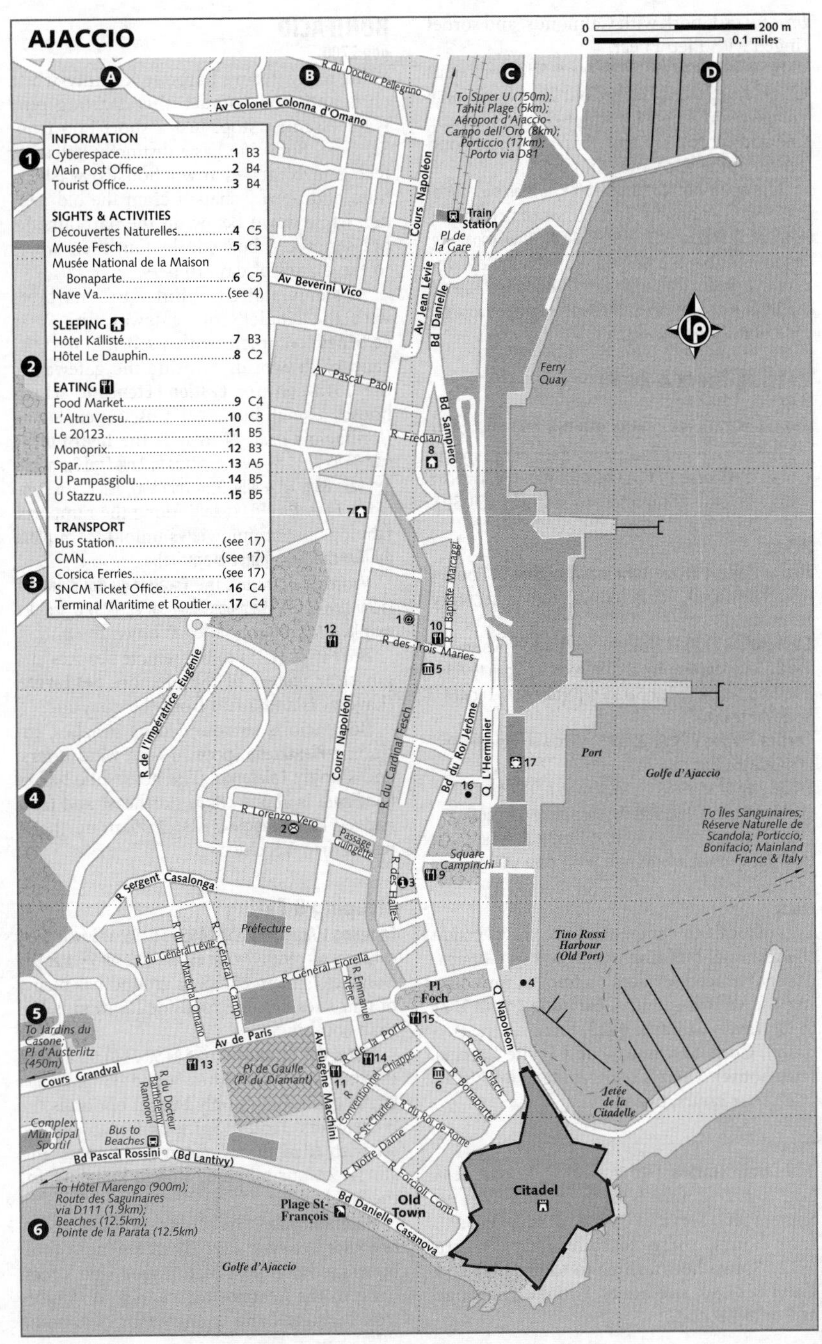
AJACCIO
0 200 m
0 0.1 miles
INFORMATION
Cyberespace 1 B3
Main Post Office 2 B4
Tourist Office 3 B4
SIGHTS & ACTIVITIES
Découvertes Naturelles 4 C5
Musée Fesch 5 C3
Musée National de la Maison Bonaparte 6 C5
Nave Va (see 4)
SLEEPING
Hôtel Kallisté 7 B3
Hôtel Le Dauphin 8 C2
EATING
Food Market 9 C4
L'Altru Versu 10 C3
Le 20123 11 B5
Monoprix 12 B3
Spar 13 A5
U Pampasgiolu 14 B5
U Stazzu 15 B5
TRANSPORT
Bus Station (see 17)
CMN (see 17)
Corsica Ferries (see 17)
SNCM Ticket Office 16 C4
Terminal Maritime et Routier 17 C4
R du Docteur Pellegrino
Av Colonel Colonna d'Omano
To Super U (750m); Tahiti Plage (5km); Aéroport d'Ajaccio-Campo dell'Oro (8km); Porticcio (17km); Porto via D81
Train Station
Pl de la Gare
Cours Napoléon
Av Beverini Vico
Av Jean Lévie
Bd Danielle
Av Pascal Paoli
Ferry Quay
R Frediani
Bd Sampiero
R J Baptiste Marcaggi
R des Trois Maries
R de l'Impératrice Eugénie
Cours Napoléon
R du Cardinal Fesch
Bd du Roi Jérôme
Q L'Herminier
Port
Golfe d'Ajaccio
To Îles Sanguinaires; Réserve Naturelle de Scandola; Porticcio; Bonifacio; Mainland France & Italy
R Lorenzo Vero
Passage Guingette
Square Campinchi
R des Halles
R Sergent Casalonga
Préfecture
R du Général Lévie
R du Maréchal Ornano
R Général Campi
R Général Fiorella
R Emmanuel Arène
Pl Foch
Tino Rossi Harbour (Old Port)
Q Napoléon
To Jardins du Casone; Pl d'Austerlitz (450m)
Av de Paris
Cours Grandval
R du Docteur Barthelemy Ramoroni
Pl de Gaulle (Pl du Diamant)
Av Eugène Macchini
R de la Porta
R Conventionnel Chiappe
R St-Charles
R du Roi de Rome
R Bonaparte
R des Glacis
Jetée de la Citadelle
Complex Municipal Sportif
Bus to Beaches
Bd Pascal Rossini (Bd Lantivy)
R Notre Dame
R Forcioli Conti
Citadel
To Hôtel Marengo (900m); Route des Saguinaires via D111 (1.9km); Beaches (12.5km); Pointe de la Parata (12.5km)
Plage St-François
Old Town
Bd Danielle Casanova
Golfe d'Ajaccio
FRANCE

brocciu tart, pork with Calmonds, and sorbet tinged with Pietra beer.

Le 20123 (☎ 04 95 21 50 05; 2 rue du Roi de Rome; menus €32; ⏰ dinner Tue-Sun) Decked out like a traditional village (complete with water pump, washing line and central square), this is another good bet for authentic Corsican fare.

The open-air **food market** (⏰ to noon, closed Mon) is on Sq Campinchi, and Corsican produce is sold at **U Stazzu** (☎ 04 95 51 10 80; 1 rue Bonaparte; ⏰ 9am-12.30pm & 2.30-7pm). Supermarkets include a **Spar** (cours Grandval; ⏰ 8.30am-12.30pm & 3-7.30pm Mon-Sat) and **Monoprix** (cours Napoléon; ⏰ 8.30am-7.15pm Mon-Sat).

Getting There & Away

AIR

Aéroport d'Ajaccio-Campo dell'Oro (☎ 04 95 23 56 56) is 8km east of the city centre. Transports Corse d'Ajaccio (TCA) bus 8 links the airport with Ajaccio's train and bus stations (€4.50).

BOAT

Boats depart from **Terminal Maritime et Routier** (quai l'Herminier), the combined bus/ferry terminal.

CMN (☎ 08 10 20 13 20; www.cmn.fr; blvd Sampiero; ⏰ 8.15am-6pm Mon-Fri, 8.15am-noon Sat, open to 7pm Mon-Fri & from 4.30-7pm Sat on departure days) Located inside the terminal.

Corsica Ferries (☎ 08 25 09 50 95; www.corsicaferries.fr) Inside the terminal.

SNCM (☎ 04 95 29 66 99; www.sncm.fr; ⏰ 8am-8pm Tue-Fri, 8am-1pm Sat) The main office is on quai L'Herminier, and there's a ticket and information kiosk inside the terminal, which opens before most sailings.

BUS

Lots of local bus companies have kiosks inside the terminal building. As always in Corsica, expect reduced services on Sunday and during the winter months. **Eurocorse** (☎ 04 95 21 06 30) travels to Bastia (€22, three hours, two daily), Corte (1¾ hours) and Ponte Lecchia (two hours). There's also a route to Bonifacio (€22, four hours, two daily).

TRAIN

The **train station** (☎ 04 95 23 11 03; place de la Gare) is staffed until 6.30pm (to 8pm May to September). Services include Bastia (€23.90, four hours, three to four daily), Corte (€12.70, two hours, three to four daily) and Calvi (€27.80, five hours, two daily; change at Ponte Leccia).

BONIFACIO

pop 2700

With its glittering harbour, creamy-white cliffs and stout citadel, this dazzling port is an essential stop. Just a short hop from Sardinia, Bonifacio has a distinctly Italianate feel: sun-bleached town houses, washing lines and murky chapels cram the old citadel, while down below on the harbourside, brasseries and boat-kiosks tout their wares to the droves of day trippers.

A steep staircase links the harbour with the citadel's old gateway, the **Porte de Gênes**, complete with its original 16th-century drawbridge. Inside the gateway is the 13th-century **Bastion l'Étendard**, which houses a small historical museum exploring Bonifacio's past. Nearby is the **tourist office** (☎ 04 95 73 11 88; www.bonifacio.fr; 2 rue Fred Scamaroni; ⏰ 9am-8pm Jul & Aug, 9am-7pm May, Jun & Sep, 9am-noon & 2-6pm Mon-Fri Oct-Apr). Along the ramparts, fabulous panoramic views unfold from **place du Marché** and **place Manichella**.

From the citadel, the **Escalier du Roi d'Aragon** (admission €2; ⏰ 9am-6pm Mon-Sat Apr-May & Sep-Oct, daily Jul & Aug) staircase leads down the cliff.

Boat trips (€25) to the remote beaches and gin-clear waters of the offshore **Îles Lavezzi** (Lavezzi Islands) run from the quayside.

Bonifacio is surrounded by beaches, including **Piantarella** (popular with windsurfers) and shingly **Calalonga**. The horseshoe bay of **Rondinara** is about 18km northeast and tree-fringed **Palombaggia** is about 30km northeast near Porto-Vecchio.

Sleeping & Eating

Camping L'Araguina (☎ 04 95 73 02 96; av Sylvère Bohn; camp sites per person/tent/car €5.85/2.40/2.40; ⏰ Mar-Oct) Bonifacio's main camping ground has plenty of tent sites, but the roadside location is less than soothing.

Hôtel des Étrangers (☎ 04 95 73 01 09; hoteldesetrangers.ifrance.com; av Sylvère Bohn; d €35-70; ⏰ Apr-Oct; ❄) Bonifacio's only budget option is the 'Foreigners' Hotel'. Spick-and-span rooms, all with tiled floors, clean bathrooms and simple colour schemes almost make up for the road racket.

Hôtel Colomba (☎ 04 95 73 73 44; www.hotel-bonifacio.fr; rue Simon Varsi; d €78-155; ❄) A not-quite-boutique hotel in a picturesque side street, bang in the heart of the citadel. Wrought-iron bedsteads and country fabrics in some rooms, carved bedheads and chequerboard tiles in others.

Kissing Pigs (☎ 04 95 73 56 09; quai Banda del Ferro; mains €8-15; ⏲ lunch & dinner daily) Diners pack into this cosy wine bar among swinging sausages for platters of Corsican meats and cheeses.

our pick **Cantina Doria** (☎ 04 95 73 50 49; 27 rue Doria; mains €10-14; ⏲ Apr-Oct) *The* place in Bonifacio for Corsican country food, served at wooden benches amid copper pots, rustic tools and dented signs. There's a sister place on the quay, Cantina Grill (☎ 04 95 70 49 86).

L'Archivolto (☎ 04 95 73 17 58; rue de l'Archivolto; mains €10-16; ⏲ dinner Mon-Sat mid-Mar–Oct) Part jumble sale, part antique shop and part fine-dining restaurant, this wonderful place sells Corsican fare among bric-a-brac, dangling guitars and mix-and-match furniture.

Getting There & Away

AIR

Bonifacio's airport, **Aéroport de Figari** (☎ 04 95 71 10 10), is 21km north of town. A shuttle bus runs from the town centre in July and August (€9, 30 to 40 minutes) five times daily.

BOAT

Saremar (☎ 04 95 73 00 96; www.saremar.it, in Italian) and **Moby Lines** (☎ 04 95 73 00 29; www.mobylines.it) offer services between Bonifacio and Santa Teresa (on the neighbouring island of Sardinia) in summer.

BUS

From Monday to Saturday, **Eurocorse** (☎ 04 95 21 06 30) has a twice-daily service to Porto-Vecchio (€7.50, 30 minutes), with onward connections to Ajaccio (€22, four hours).

FRANCE DIRECTORY

ACCOMMODATION

Accommodation is listed in this chapter by price: budget doubles cost up to €60 (€70 in Paris); 'midrange' hotels charge €61 to €140 (up to €160 in Paris); and top-end rooms cost anything upwards of €141 (€161 in the capital). You can sometimes cut costs by opting for cheaper rooms with shared bathrooms and/or a hall toilet. Unless otherwise noted, prices quoted in this chapter are for single/double rooms with en suite bathroom. We've also tried to quote for prices in high season, but many places add an extra premium in July and August, when the French typically take their annual holiday. Prices also take a hike upwards over Christmas and Easter (especially during the school holidays).

You should be able to sleep easy as smoking has been banned in all public spaces, including hotels.

B&Bs

Some of France's most charming (and best value) accommodation can be found in *chambres d'hôtes* (bed and breakfasts). Local tourist offices always have a list of local establishments, or you can contact the **Fédération Nationale des Gîtes de France** (Map pp212-13; ☎ 01 49 70 75 75; www.gites-de-france.fr; 59 rue St-Lazare, 9e, Paris; Ⓜ Trinité). Other useful websites:

Bienvenue à la Ferme (Map pp212-13; ☎ 01 53 57 11 44; www.bienvenue-a-la-ferme.com; 9 av George V, 8e, Paris; Ⓜ Alma-Marceau, George V) Specialist for farm-stays.

Fleurs de Soleil (http://fleursdesoleil.fr, in French)

Samedi Midi Éditions (www.samedimidi.com)

Camping & Caravan Parks

Camping is popular in France, although many camping grounds close from October to April. Hostels sometimes let travellers pitch tents in their grounds. Gîtes de France and Bienvenue à la Ferme coordinate camping on farms. Camping in nondesignated spots, or *camping sauvage*, is usually illegal.

Hostels & Foyers

A dorm bed in an *auberge de jeunesse* (youth hostel) costs about €25 in Paris, and anything from €10.30 to €28 in the provinces; breakfast is often included. Sheets are provided but sleeping bags are no longer permitted to prevent bedbugs. Facilities vary, although most places have self-catering kitchens. All hostels are now nonsmoking.

You'll need an annual Hostelling International card (€11/16 for under/over 26s) or a nightly Welcome Stamp (€1.80 to €2.90) to stay at hostels run by the two hostelling associations:

Fédération Unie des Auberges de Jeunesse (FUAJ; Map pp212-13; ☎ 01 44 89 87 27; www.fuaj.org; 27 rue Pajol, 18e, Paris; Ⓜ Marx Dormoy)

> **TOP TIP**
>
> In France, computer keyboards are laid out differently, which can make typing difficult. To change the keyboard language, hold down Alt and the Maj (majuscule) button – and hey presto, you can type away to your heart's content.

Ligue Française pour les Auberges de la Jeunesse (LFAJ; Map pp212-13; ☎ 01 44 16 78 78; www.auberges-de-jeunesse.com; 7 rue Vergniaud, 13e, Paris; Ⓜ Glacière)

Hotels

French hotels vary greatly in quality, ranging from low-budget no-star places to full-blown pleasure palaces, but there are a few general guidelines shared by most establishments.

French hotels almost never include breakfast in their advertised nightly rates. Unless specified otherwise, prices quoted in this guide don't include breakfast, which costs around €6.50/8/18 in a budget/midrange/top-end hotel. When you book, hotels usually ask for a credit-card number; some require a deposit.

A double room generally has one double bed (or two combined singles); a room with twin beds *(deux lits)* is usually more expensive, as is a room with a bathtub instead of a shower.

We've tried to steer clear of chain hotels, but some of the chains you'll encounter:

Citôtel (www.citotel.com)
Contact Hôtel (www.contact-hotel.com)
Inter-Hotel (www.inter-hotel.fr)
Logis de France (☎ 01 45 84 83 84; www.logis-de-france.fr)

ACTIVITIES

From the peaks, rivers and canyons of the Alps to the shining coastline, France offers a cornucopia of outdoor adventures.

Cycling

The French take cycling very seriously – the country practically grinds to a halt during the annual Tour de France. Mountain-biking (known in France as VTT, or *vélo tout-terrain)* is gaining popularity around the Alps and Pyrenees, but road-cycling still rules the roost. A *piste cyclable* is a cycling path – you'll find plenty of routes in the Dordogne and the Loire Valley.

Association Française de Développement des Véloroutes et Voies Vertes (www.af3v.org) Has a database of 250 signposted *véloroutes* (bike paths) and *voies vertes* (greenways).
Fédération Française de Cyclotourisme (www.ffct.org, in French) Promotes bicycle touring and mountain biking.

Extreme Sports

Be it canyoning, diving, ice-driving or kitesurfing, France sets the pulse racing. Adventures in *alpinisme* (mountaineering), *escalade* (rock climbing) and *escalade de glace* (ice climbing) can be arranged through the **Club Alpin Français** (www.ffcam.fr, in French).

Deltaplane (hang-gliding) and *parapente* (paragliding) are all the rage in the Pyrenees, Brittany and Languedoc-Roussillon; contact the Nice-based **Fédération Française de Vol Libre** (☎ 04 97 03 82 82; http://federation.ffvl.fr, in French). The **Fédération Française de Vol à Voile** (FFVV; ☎ 01 45 44 04 78; www.ffvv.org, in French; 29 rue de Sèvres, 6e, Paris) provides details of gliding clubs.

Hiking

The French countryside is criss-crossed by a staggering 120,000km of *sentiers balisés* (marked walking paths), including the *sentiers de grande randonnée* (GR) trails, long-distance footpaths marked by red-and-white-striped track indicators.

The **Fédération Française de la Randonnée Pédestre** (FFRP; French Ramblers' Association; www.ffrp.asso.fr, in French) has an **information centre** (Map pp212-13; ☎ 01 44 89 93 93; 64 rue du Dessous des Berges, 13e, Paris; Ⓜ Bibliothèque François Mitterrand) in Paris.

Skiing & Snowboarding

France has over 400 ski resorts, which are located in the Alps, the Jura, the Pyrenees, the Vosges and Massif Central – and even the mountains of Corsica. The season generally lasts from mid-December to late March or April, but the slopes get very crowded during the February/March school holidays. Package deals including lift passes and accommodation are available for all main resorts.

Paris-based **Ski France** (www.skifrance.fr) has information and an annual brochure covering more than 90 ski resorts. **CAF** (www.ffcam.fr, in French) can also provide information on mountain activities.

Water Sports

France has fine beaches along all its coasts – the English Channel, the Atlantic and the Mediterranean. The beautifully sandy beaches along the Atlantic coast are less crowded than their counterparts on the Côte d'Azur and Corsica, while Brittany, Normandy and the Channel coast are also popular, albeit cooler, beach destinations.

The best surfing in France is on the Atlantic coast around Biarritz (p301). White-water rafting, canoeing and kayaking are practised on many French rivers, especially in the Massif Central and the Alps.

BUSINESS HOURS

French business hours are regulated by a maze of government regulations, including the 35-hours-a-week work limit. Shop hours are usually 9am or 9.30am to 7pm or 8pm, often with a midday break from noon or 1pm to 2pm or 3pm. The midday break is uncommon in Paris but gets longer the further south you go. French law requires that most businesses close on Sunday; exceptions include grocery stores, *boulangeries* (bakeries), cake shops, and businesses catering exclusively to the tourist trade. In some places many shops also close on Monday.

Most (but not all) national museums are closed on Tuesday, while most local museums are closed on Monday. Many close at lunchtime.

Banks are usually open from 8am or 9am to some time between 11.30am or 1pm and then from 1.30pm or 2pm to 4.30pm or 5pm, Monday to Friday or Tuesday to Saturday.

See p210 for details of opening hours of restaurants, cafes and bars.

EMBASSIES & CONSULATES

All foreign embassies are in Paris. Many countries – including the United States, Canada and a number of European countries – also have consulates in other major cities.

Australia Paris (Map pp212-13; ☎ 01 40 59 33 00; www.france.embassy.gov.au; 4 rue Jean Rey, 15e; Ⓜ Bir Hakeim)

Belgium Paris (Map pp212-13; ☎ 01 44 09 39 39; www.diplomatie.be/paris; 9 rue de Tilsitt, 17e; Ⓜ Charles de Gaulle-Étoile)

Canada Paris (Map pp212-13; ☎ 01 44 43 29 00; www.amb-canada.fr; 35 av Montaigne, 8e; Ⓜ Franklin D Roosevelt); Nice consulate (☎ 04 93 92 93 22; 10 rue Lamartine, Nice)

Germany Paris Embassy & Consulate (Map pp212-13; ☎ 01 53 83 45 00; www.paris.diplo.de, in French & German; 13 av Franklin D Roosevelt, 8e; Ⓜ Franklin D Roosevelt)

Ireland Paris (Map pp212-13; ☎ 01 44 17 67 00; www.embassyofirelandparis.com; 12 av Foch, 16e; Ⓜ Argentine)

Italy Paris Embassy (Map pp212-13; ☎ 01 49 54 03 00; www.amb-italie.fr; 51 rue de Varenne, 7e; Ⓜ Rue du Bac); Paris Consulate (Map pp212-13; ☎ 01 44 30 47 00; 5 blvd Émile Augier, 16e; Ⓜ La Muette)

Japan Paris (Map pp212-13; ☎ 01 48 88 62 00; www.amb-japon.fr; 7 av Hoche, 8e; Ⓜ Courcelles)

Netherlands Paris (Map pp212-13; ☎ 01 40 62 33 00; www.amb-pays-bas.fr; 7 rue Eblé, 7e; Ⓜ St-François Xavier)

New Zealand Paris (Map pp212-13; ☎ 01 45 01 43 43; www.nzembassy.com; 7ter rue Léonard de Vinci, 16e; Ⓜ Victor Hugo)

Spain Paris (Map pp212-13; ☎ 01 44 43 18 00; www.amb-espagne.fr; 22 av Marceau, 8e; Ⓜ Alma-Marceau)

Switzerland Paris Embassy (Map pp212-13; ☎ 01 49 55 67 00; www.amb-suisse.fr; 142 rue de Grenelle, 7e; Ⓜ Varenne)

UK Paris Embassy (Map pp212-13; ☎ 01 44 51 31 00; www.amb-grandebretagne.fr; 35 rue du Faubourg St-Honoré, 8e; Ⓜ Concorde); Paris Consulate (Map pp212-13; ☎ 01 44 51 31 00; 18bis rue d'Anjou, 8e; Ⓜ Madeleine); Marseille Consulate (off Map p308; ☎ 04 91 54 92 00; place Varian Fry, 6e)

USA Paris Embassy (Map pp212-13; ☎ 01 43 12 22 22; http://france.usembassy.gov; 2 av Gabriel, 8e; Ⓜ Concorde); Paris Consulate (Map pp212-13; ☎ 01 43 12 26 71; 4 av Gabriel, 8e; 🕘 9am-noon Mon-Fri except US & French holidays; Ⓜ Concorde)

FESTIVALS & EVENTS

Most French cities, towns and villages have at least one major arts festival each year.

February

Carnaval de Nice (p326; www.nicecarnaval.com) Merrymaking in Nice during France's largest street carnival (last half of February).

May & June

May Day Across France, workers' day is celebrated with parades and protests. People give each other *muguets* (lilies of the valley) for good luck. No one works – except waiters and *muguet* sellers (1 May).

Fête de la Musique (www.fetedelamusique.culture.fr, in French) Bands and buskers take to the streets for this nationwide celebration of music (21 June).

July

Festival d'Aix-en-Provence (p311; www.festival-aix.com) Attracts some of the world's best classical music, opera, ballet and buskers (late June to mid-July).
Bastille Day Fireworks, balls, processions – including a military parade down Paris' Champs-Élysées for France's National Day (14 July).
Festival d'Avignon (p314; www.festival-avignon.com) Avignon has an official and fringe festival (mid-July).
Nice Jazz Festival (p317; www.nicejazzfest.fr) Jazz cats among the Roman ruins of Nice (mid-July).

August & September

Braderie de Lille (p242) Three days of mussel-munching as this colossal flea market engulfs the city with antiques, handicrafts and bric-a-brac (first weekend in September).

December

Christmas Markets in Alsace (p260) Last weekend in November through Christmas or New Year.
Fête des Lumières (www.lumieres.lyon.fr) France's biggest and best light show transforms Lyon (8 December).

GAY & LESBIAN TRAVELLERS

France is one of Europe's most liberal countries when it comes to homosexuality. Paris has been a thriving gay and lesbian centre since the late 1970s. Bordeaux, Lille, Lyon, Montpellier, Toulouse and many other towns also have significant active communities. Attitudes towards homosexuality tend to be more conservative in the countryside and villages. Gay Pride marches are held in French cities in July. For online info:

France Queer Resources Directory (www.france.qrd.org, in French)
French Government Tourist Office (http://us.franceguide.com/Special-Interests/Gay-friendly)
Gayscape (www.gayscape.com) Hundreds of links to gay- and lesbian-related sites.

HOLIDAYS

The following *jours fériés* (public holidays) are observed in France:

New Year's Day (Jour de l'An) 1 January
Easter Sunday & Monday (Pâques & lundi de Pâques) Late March/April
May Day (Fête du Travail) 1 May – traditional parades
Victoire 1945 8 May – commemorates the Allied victory in Europe that ended WWII
Ascension Thursday (Ascension) May – celebrated on the 40th day after Easter
Pentecost/Whit Sunday & Whit Monday (Pentecôte & lundi de Pentecôte) Mid-May to mid-June – celebrated on the seventh Sunday after Easter
Bastille Day/National Day (Fête Nationale) 14 July – *the* national holiday
Assumption Day (Assomption) 15 August
All Saints' Day (Toussaint) 1 November
Remembrance Day (L'onze Novembre) 11 November – marks the WWI armistice
Christmas (Noël) 25 December

LEGAL MATTERS

French police have wide powers of stop-and-search and can demand proof of identity at any time. Foreigners must be able to prove their legal status in France (eg passport, visa, residency permit). If the police stop you, be polite and don't argue. Don't leave baggage unattended at airports or train stations.

MONEY

The official currency of France is the euro.

Bureaux de change are available in most major cities, and most large post offices offer currency exchange and cash travellers cheques. Commercial banks charge a stiff fee for changing money – generally it's cheaper to use the *distributeurs automatiques de billets* (DAB, otherwise known as ATMs). Most ATMs are linked to the Cirrus, Plus and Maestro networks – check with your bank back home for overseas fees.

Visa and MasterCard (Access or Eurocard) are widely accepted at shops, restaurants and hotels; you'll need to know your *code* (PIN number).

For lost cards, call:

Amex (☎ 01 47 77 72 00)
Diners Club (☎ 08 10 31 41 59)
MasterCard, Eurocard & Access (Eurocard France; ☎ 08 00 90 13 87, 01 45 67 84 84)
Visa (Carte Bleue; ☎ 08 00 90 20 33)

POST

French post offices are flagged with a yellow or brown sign reading 'La Poste'. Since La Poste also has banking, finance and bill-paying functions, queues can be long but automatic machines dispense postage stamps.

Domestic letters weighing up to 20g cost €0.55. For international post, a letter/package under 20g/2kg costs €0.65/12.30 to Zone 1 (EU and Switzerland) and €0.85/14 to Zone 2 (the rest of the world). All mail to France *must* include the five-digit *code postal* (postcode/ZIP code), which begins with the two-digit number of the *département*.

EMERGENCY NUMBERS

- Ambulance ☎ 15
- Fire ☎ 18
- Police ☎ 17

TELEPHONE

Area codes are an integral part of phone numbers in France and are included in the phone numbers listed this chapter.

International Dialling

To call someone outside France, dial the international access code (☎ 00), the country code, the area code (without the initial zero if there is one) and the local number.

Numbers beginning ☎ 08 00 or ☎ 08 05 are free but other ☎ 08 numbers are not.

For France Telecom's *service des renseignements* (directory inquiries) dial ☎ 11 87 12 (€1.18 per call from a fixed-line phone). Not all operators speak English. For help in English with France Telecom's services, see www.francetelecom.com or call ☎ 08 00 36 47 75.

Mobile Phones

French mobile phone numbers begin ☎ 06. Dialling from a fixed-line phone or another mobile can be very expensive.

France uses GSM 900/1800, which is compatible with the rest of Europe and Australia but not with Japanese or North American systems. Using a mobile phone outside your home country can be hideously expensive, so it will almost certainly be cheaper to buy your own French SIM card (€20 to €30), rechargeable at most *tabacs* and newsagents.

SIMs are available from all three of France's mobile companies, **Bouygues** (☎ 08 10 63 01 00; www.bouyguestelecom.fr), France Telecom's **Orange** (www.orange.fr, in French) and **SFR** (☎ 08 11 70 70 73; www.sfr.com).

Public Phones & Telephone Cards

Most public phones operate using a credit card or two kinds of *télécartes* (phonecards): *cartes à puce* (cards with a magnetic chip) and *cartes à code* (which use a free access number and a scratch-off code). Both types are sold at *tabacs*, newsagents and post offices in various denominations; phonecards with codes offer *much* better international rates than their chip equivalents.

VISAS

For visa requirements, see the **French Foreign Affairs Ministry site** (www.diplomatie.gouv.fr) and select 'Going to France'.

EU nationals and citizens of Iceland, Norway and Switzerland need only a passport or a national identity card in order to enter France. Citizens of Australia, Canada, Israel, Hong Kong, Japan, Malaysia, New Zealand, Singapore, the USA and many Latin American countries do not need visas to visit France as tourists for up to 90 days. Other countries will require a visa: application should be made to the consulate of the country you are entering first. You'll need to supply evidence of insurance and sufficient funds to support your stay.

TRANSPORT IN FRANCE

GETTING THERE & AWAY

Air

AIRPORTS

France's two major international airports, both outside Paris, are **Roissy Charles de Gaulle** (CDG; ☎ 01 48 62 22 80; www.aeroportsdeparis.fr) and **Orly** (ORY; ☎ 01 49 75 15 15; www.aeroportsdeparis.fr). Other major French airports:

Bordeaux (BOD; ☎ 05 56 34 50 50; www.bordeaux.aeroport.fr)
Lille (LIL; ☎ 03 20 49 67 47, 08 91 67 32 10; www.lille.aeroport.fr)
Lyon (LYS; ☎ 08 26 80 08 26; www.lyon.aeroport.fr)
Marseille (MRS; ☎ 04 42 14 14 14; www.mrsairport.com)
Nantes (NTE; ☎ 02 40 84 80 00; www.nantes.aeroport.fr)
Nice (NCE; ☎ 08 20 42 33 33; www.nice.aeroport.fr)
Strasbourg (SXB; ☎ 03 88 64 67 67; www.strasbourg.aeroport.fr)
Toulouse (TLS; ☎ 08 25 38 00 00; www.toulouse.aeroport.fr)

AIRLINES

Major airlines that fly into and out of France:

Air Canada (AC; ☎ 08 25 88 29 00; www.aircanada.ca)
Air France (AF; ☎ 36 54; www.airfrance.com) France's flag carrier, now joined with KLM.
Alitalia (AZ; ☎ 08 20 31 53 15; www.alitalia.com)
American Airlines (AA; ☎ 01 55 17 43 41; www.americanairlines.com)

BMI (BD; ☎ in UK 0870-6070 555 or 01332-64 8181; www.flybmi.com)
British Airways (BA; ☎ 08 25 82 54 00; www.britishairways.com)
Continental (CO; ☎ 01 71 23 03 35; www.continental.com)
Delta Airlines (DL; ☎ 08 11 64 00 05; www.delta.com)
KLM (KL; ☎ 32 72; www.klm.com)
Lufthansa (LH; ☎ 08 26 10 33 34; www.lufthansa.com)
Qantas Airways (QF; ☎ 08 11 98 00 02; www.qantas.com)
Singapore Airlines (SQ; ☎ 08 21 23 03 80; www.singaporeair.com)
Thai Airways International (TG; ☎ 01 55 68 80 70; www.thaiair.com)
United (UA; ☎ 08 10 72 72 72; www.united.fr)

Budget carriers:
Air Berlin (AB; www.airberlin.com) Links EuroAirport (Mulhouse) and Nice with destinations around Western Europe.
Air Transat (TS; www.airtransat.com) Flights from Canada.
bmibaby (BD; www.bmibaby.com)
easyJet (U2; www.easyjet.com) UK budget carrier.
Flybe (BE; www.flybe.com) Links a dozen French cities with the UK.
Flyglobespan (Y2; www.flyglobespan.com) Scottish budget carrier.
germanwings (4U; www.germanwings.com) German budget carrier.
Jet2.com (LS; www.jet2.com) Links French cities with the UK.
Myair (MYW; www.myair.com) Flights to Italy.
Ryanair (FR; www.ryanair.com) Services from Ireland and the UK; flies to many small, touristy places in France, such as Carcassonne.
Transavia.com (HV; www.transavia.com) Budget subsidiary of Air France–KLM.
TUIfly (X3; www.tuifly.com) German budget carrier.

Land

BUS

Europe's international buses are slower and less comfortable than trains but are considerably cheaper, especially if you are under 26 or over 60.

Eurolines (☎ 08 92 89 90 91; www.eurolines.eu), a network of European and Russian long-haul coach-operators, provides bus services to various destinations throughout France. Return fares are about 20% cheaper than two one-way fares. In summer reservations are recommended at least two working days in advance.

Buses run by London-based **Busabout** (☎ in UK 0207-950 1661; www.busabout.com; 1/2/3 loops US$639/1069/1319) link 29 Continental European cities from early May to October. In France, stops are in Bordeaux, Tours, Paris, Avignon and Nice.

CAR & MOTORCYCLE

Arriving in France by car is easy. At some border points you may need a passport or EU national identity card (your driver's licence will not be sufficient ID).

From the UK, the Channel Tunnel runs high-speed **Eurotunnel trains** (☎ in UK 08705-35 35 35, in France 08 10 63 03 04; www.eurotunnel.com) from Folkestone to Coquelles, 5km southwest of Calais. Shuttles run 24 hours a day, and the earlier you book the cheaper the fare. Depending on the date and time of travel, one-way car fares range from UK£49 to UK£145 (€69 to €217).

TRAIN

Rail services link France with virtually every country in Europe. Tickets and information are available from **Rail Europe** (www.raileurope.com). In France ticketing is handled by **SNCF** (☎ in France 36 35, from abroad 08 92 35 35 35; www.sncf.com). See p341 for more on ticketing.

For details on Europe's rail network, see www.railpassenger.info. Certain services between France and its continental neighbours are marketed under separate brand names: **Alleo** heads to Germany; **Artésia** (www.artesia.eu) serves Italian cities such as Milan, Venice, Florence and Rome; **Elipsos** (www.elipsos.com) has luxurious 'train-hotel' services to Spain; and **TGV Lyria** (www.tgv-lyria.fr) takes passengers to Switzerland. **Thalys** (www.thalys.com) links Paris' Gare du Nord with destinations including Brussels-Midi (from €82, 82 minutes, up to 25 per day), Amsterdam CS (from €105, 4¼ hours, seven per day) and Cologne's Hauptbahnhof (€91, 3¾ hours, six per day).

The civilised **Eurostar** (☎ in UK 08705-186-186, in France 08 92 35 35 39; www.eurostar.com) whisks you between London St Pancras and Paris Gare du Nord in just 2¼ hours, with onward connections to Calais, Lille and Disneyland Resort Paris. As always, booking early secures the best fares: a standard 2nd-class one-way/return ticket from London to Paris costs a whopping UK£154.50/309 (€232.50/435), but superdiscount returns go for as little as UK£59.

For details on Europe-wide rail passes, see p969.

Sea

Regular ferries travel to France from Italy, the UK, Channel Islands and Ireland.

FROM IRELAND

Irish Ferries has overnight services from Rosslare to either Cherbourg (17½ hours) or Roscoff (17½ hours; mid-May to mid-September only) every other day (three times a week from October to May, except late December and January).

From about March to early November, **Brittany Ferries** runs a car ferry from Cork (Ringaskiddy) to Roscoff (14 hours).

FROM ITALY

Every two or three days during the warm half of the year, **SNCM** runs an overnight car ferry from Marseille to Porto Torres on the Italian island of Sardinia (Sardaigne). The crossing takes 14½ to 17½ hours. Several ferry companies ply the waters between Corsica and Italy.

FROM UK

As with budget airlines, ferry travel costs to the UK vary hugely depending on when you travel: booking early, avoiding peak times and avoiding July and August will cut costs. To get the best fare, check out the comparison service offered by **Ferry Savers** (☎ in UK 0844-576 8835; www.ferrysavers.com). Booking by phone incurs a UK£25 fee.

Brittany

Condor Ferries runs car ferries from Poole to St-Malo (from 4½ hours) from late May to September; and from Weymouth to St-Malo (5¼ hours) daily from late March to October and at least once a week in winter.

Brittany Ferries links Plymouth with Roscoff (6½ hours by day, nine hours overnight, one to three daily from mid-March to early November, almost daily in winter); and Portsmouth with St-Malo (8¾ hours by day, 10¾ hours overnight, one daily from March to October, almost daily in winter).

Normandy

Transmanche Ferries (☎ in Britain 0800-917-1201, in France ☎ 0800-650-100; www.transmancheferries.com) operates car ferries from Newhaven to Dieppe (up to three daily, four hours).

Condor Ferries links Portsmouth with Cherbourg (5½ hours) each Sunday from late May to early September.

Brittany Ferries links Cherbourg with both Poole (high-speed ferry 2¼ hours, regular ferry 4½ to 6½ hours, two or three daily) and Portsmouth (three hours, one or two sailings daily). The company also has car-ferry services from Portsmouth to Ouistreham (5¾ to seven hours, two to four daily), 14km northeast of Caen; high-speed ferries (3¾ hours) ply this route from mid-March to late October.

Northern France

The extremely popular Dover–Calais crossing is handled by **SeaFrance** (80 to 90 minutes, 15 daily) and **P&O Ferries** (75 to 90 minutes, 35 daily). Foot passengers are not allowed on night sailings (ie sailings departing after sometime between 7pm and 9.30pm and before 7am or 8am).

Car ferries run by **Norfolk Line** link Loon Plage, located about 25km west of Dunkirk (Dunkerque), with Dover (1¾ hours).

Ultramodern, ultrafast car catamarans run by **Speed Ferries** link Dover with Boulogne-sur-Mer (50 minutes, three to five daily).

GETTING AROUND

Air

Air France (☎ 36 54; www.airfrance.com) and its subsidiaries **Brit Air** (www.britair.fr) and **Régional** (☎ 36 54; www.regional.com) control the lion's share of France's domestic airline industry, although budget airlines including **easyJet** (www.easyjet.com), **Airlinair** (www.airlinair.com) and **Twin Jet** (www.twinjet.net) are steadily making inroads. Thanks to France's generous state subsidy for the domestic rail network, short-haul air travel within France is rare. You'll find it far easier, much faster (and generally much, much cheaper) to travel everywhere by train instead of taking a plane.

Students, people aged 12 to 24 and over 60s receive hefty discounts. Special last-minute offers appear on the Air France website every Wednesday.

Bus

You're nearly always better off travelling by train in France if possible, as the SNCF domestic railway system is heavily subsidised by the government and is much more reliable than local bus companies. Nevertheless, buses are widely used for short-distance travel within *départements*, especially in rural areas with relatively few train lines (eg Brittany and Normandy).

Car & Motorcycle

A car gives you exceptional freedom and allows you to visit more-remote parts of France. Unfortunately it can be expensive and, in cities, parking and traffic are frequently a major headache. Motorcyclists will find France great for touring, with winding roads of good quality and lots of stunning scenery. For assistance, try **Automobile Club de France** (☎ 0821 74 11 11; www.automobileclub.org, in French).

BRING YOUR OWN VEHICLE

All foreign motor vehicles entering France must display a sticker or licence plate identifying its country of registration. If you're bringing a right-hand-drive vehicle remember to fix deflectors on your headlights to avoid dazzling oncoming traffic.

DRIVING LICENCE & DOCUMENTS

All drivers must carry a national ID card or passport; a valid driving licence (*permis de conduire;* most foreign licences can be used in France for up to a year); car-ownership papers, known as a *carte grise* (grey card); and proof of third party (liability) insurance.

FUEL & TOLLS

Essence (petrol), also known as *carburant* (fuel), costs around €1.40/L for 95 unleaded (Sans Plomb 95 or SP95, usually available from a green pump) and €1.30 for diesel (*diesel, gazole* or *gasoil,* usually available from a yellow pump). Filling up *(faire le plein)* is most expensive along autoroutes.

Many French motorways (autoroutes) are fitted with toll *(péage)* stations that charge a fee based on the distance you've travelled; remember to factor in these costs when driving.

HIRE

To hire a car you'll usually need to be over 21 and in possession of a valid driving licence and a credit card. Major rental companies include:

ADA (☎ 08 25 16 91 69; www.ada.fr, in French)
Avis (☎ 08 20 05 05 05; www.avis.com)
Budget (☎ 08 25 00 35 64; www.budget.com or www.budget.fr, in French)
Easycar (☎ in UK 0906-333 333 3; www.easycar.com)
Europcar (☎ 08 25 35 83 58; www.europcar.com)
Hertz (☎ 01 39 38 38 38; www.hertz.com)
National-Citer (www.nationalcar.com or www.citer.fr)
Renault Rent (☎ 08 10 40 50 60; www.renault-rent.com, in French) Renault's new car-rental arm.
Sixt (☎ 08 20 00 74 98; www.sixt.fr, in French)

Cheap deals can often be found with **Auto Europe** (☎ in USA 1-888-223-5555; www.autoeurope.com) in the US and **Holiday Autos** (☎ in UK 0871-472 5229; www.holidayautos.co.uk).

Auto transmissions are *very* rare in France; you'll need to order one well in advance.

INSURANCE

Unlimited third party liability insurance is mandatory in France. Third party liability insurance is provided by car-rental companies, but collision-damage waivers (CDW) vary between companies. When comparing rates check the *franchise* (excess), which is usually €350 for a small car. Your credit card may cover CDW if you use it to pay for the car rental.

ROAD RULES

Cars drive on the right in France. All passengers must wear seat belts, and children who weigh less than 18kg must travel in backward-facing child seats. The speed limits on French roads are as follows:

- 50km/h in built-up areas
- 90km/h (80km/h if it's raining) on N and D highways
- 110km/h (100km/h if it's raining) on dual carriageways
- 130km/h (110km/h if it's raining) on autoroutes.

Under the *priorité à droite* (priority to the right) rule, any car entering an intersection from a road on your right has the right-of-way, unless the intersection is marked *'vous n'avez pas la priorité'* (you do not have right of way) or *'cédez le passage'* (give way).

It is illegal to drive with a blood-alcohol concentration over 0.05% – the equivalent of two glasses of wine for a 75kg adult. Mobile phones may only be used when accompanied by a hands-free kit or speakerphone.

Riders of any type of two-wheeled vehicle with a motor (except motor-assisted bicycles) must wear a helmet.

TOP TIP

Don't forget on many trains, trams and buses in France, you must time-stamp your ticket in a *composteur*. If you forget, find a conductor so they can punch it for you to avoid being fined.

Since July 2008, all French vehicles must carry a reflective safety jacket and a reflective triangle; the fine for not carrying one/both is €90/135.

Train

France's superb rail network is operated by the state-owned SNCF (www.sncf.com). Many towns not on the SNCF train network are served by SNCF buses.

The flagship trains on French railways are the superfast TGVs, which reach speeds in excess of 200mph and can whisk you from Paris to the Côte d'Azur in as little as three hours.

Many non-high-speed lines are also served by TGV trains; otherwise you'll find yourself aboard a non-TGV train, referred to as a *corail* or TER *(train express régional)*.

The main TGV lines and key stations served are as follows:

TGV Nord, Thalys & Eurostar Paris' Gare du Nord to Arras, Lille, Calais, Brussels, Amsterdam, Cologne and London St Pancras.

TGV Est Européen New line connecting Paris' Gare de l'Est with Reims, Nancy, Metz, Strasbourg, Zürich and Germany, including Frankfurt, Stuttgart and Luxembourg. At the time of writing, the high-speed section of the line only stretched as far east as Lorraine; plans to extend the superfast line all the way to Strasbourg are scheduled for completion in 2012.

TGV Sud-Est & TGV Midi-Méditerranée Paris' Gare de Lyon with the southeast, including Dijon, Lyon, Geneva, the Alps, Avignon, Marseille, Nice and Montpellier.

TGV Atlantique Sud-Ouest & TGV Atlantique Ouest Paris' Gare Montparnasse to western and southwestern France, including Brittany (Rennes, Brest, Quimper), Nantes, Tours, Poitiers, La Rochelle, Bordeaux, Biarritz and Toulouse.

COSTS

Full-fare tickets can be quite expensive, and are always pricier during peak periods, eg workday rush hours, on Friday evening and at the beginning and end of holiday periods. Special deals are published online every Tuesday at www.sncf.com, and the new website www.idtgv.com sells tickets for as little as €19 for TGV travel on 20 routes to/from Paris.

Reductions of between 25% and 60% are available with several discount cards:

Carte 12-25 (www.12-25-sncf.com; €49) For travellers aged 12 to 25.

Carte Enfant Plus (www.enfantplus-sncf.com, in French; €65) For one to four adults travelling with a child aged four to 11.

Carte Sénior (www.senior-sncf.com, in French; €55) For over 60s.

Carte Escapades (www.escapades-sncf.com, in French; €85) For people aged 26 to 59. Gets you discounts on return journeys of at least 200km that include a Saturday night away or only involve travel on a Saturday or Sunday.

TICKETS

Buying online at the various SNCF websites can reward with you some great reductions on fares, but be warned – these are generally intended for domestic travellers, and if you're buying abroad it pays to be aware of a few pitfalls. Many tickets can't be posted outside France, and if you buy with a non-French credit card, you might not be able to use it in the automated ticket collection machines at many French stations. Buying from a ticket office may not secure you the cheapest fare, but at least you'll be sure of being able to pick up your ticket…

TRAIN PASSES

The **InterRail One Country Pass** (www.interrailnet.com) valid in France entitles nonresidents to unlimited travel on SNCF trains for three to eight days over a month. For three/four/six/eight days, the cost is €189/209/269/299 for adults and €125/139/175/194 for young people aged 12 to 25.

Greece Ελλάδα

There is something mystical and magical about Greece that makes it one of the most popular destinations on the planet. The alluring combination of history and hedonism attracts all sorts. Within easy reach of magnificent archaeological sites are breathtaking beaches and relaxed tavernas serving everything from octopus to ouzo. It's a combination that makes for guilt-free travel – throw in welcoming locals with an enticing culture and captivating music, and it's easy to see why most visitors head home vowing to come back.

Adrenalin-focussed travellers can mountain climb, hike, windsurf, dive and even hit the ski slopes. Party types can enjoy pulsating nightlife in Greece's vibrant modern cities and on islands such as Mykonos, Ios and Santorini. Wanderers can just island-hop to their heart's content. No matter what you are there for, however, you cannot go far without stumbling across a broken column, a crumbling bastion or a tiny Byzantine church, each neglected and forgotten but retaining an aura of its former glory.

Perhaps, though, the true allure of Greece is due to less tangible attributes – the dazzling clarity of the light and the Aegean waters, the floral aromas that permeate the air, the spirit of the place – for there is hardly a grove, mountain or stream that is not sacred to a deity, and the ghosts of the past still linger everywhere.

Among the myriad attractions, travellers to Greece inevitably end up with a favourite site they long to return to – get out there and find yours.

FAST FACTS

- **Area** 131,944 sq km
- **Capital** Athens
- **Currency** euro (€); US$1 = €0.73; UK£1 = €1.06; A$1 = €0.50; ¥100 = €0.76; NZ$1 = €0.41
- **Famous for** ancient ruins, beautiful beaches
- **Official language** Greek
- **Phrases** *yasas* (hello); *andio* (goodbye); *parakalo* (please); *efharisto* (thank you); *ne* (yes); *ohi* (no)
- **Population** 11.1 million
- **Telephone codes** country code ☎ 30; international access code ☎ 00; reverse-charge code ☎ 161
- **Visas** not needed for most visitors for stays of up to three months; see p422

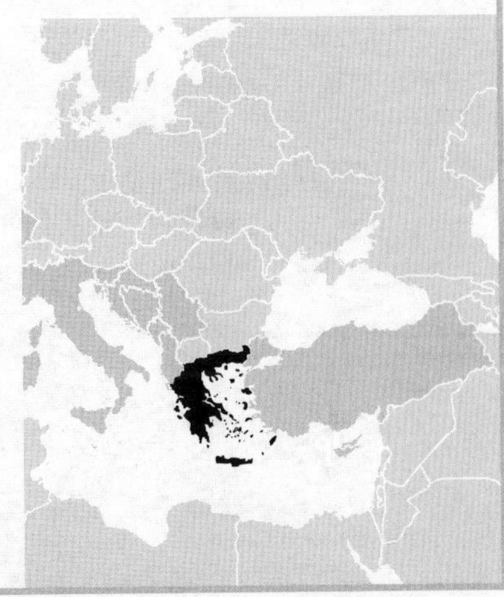

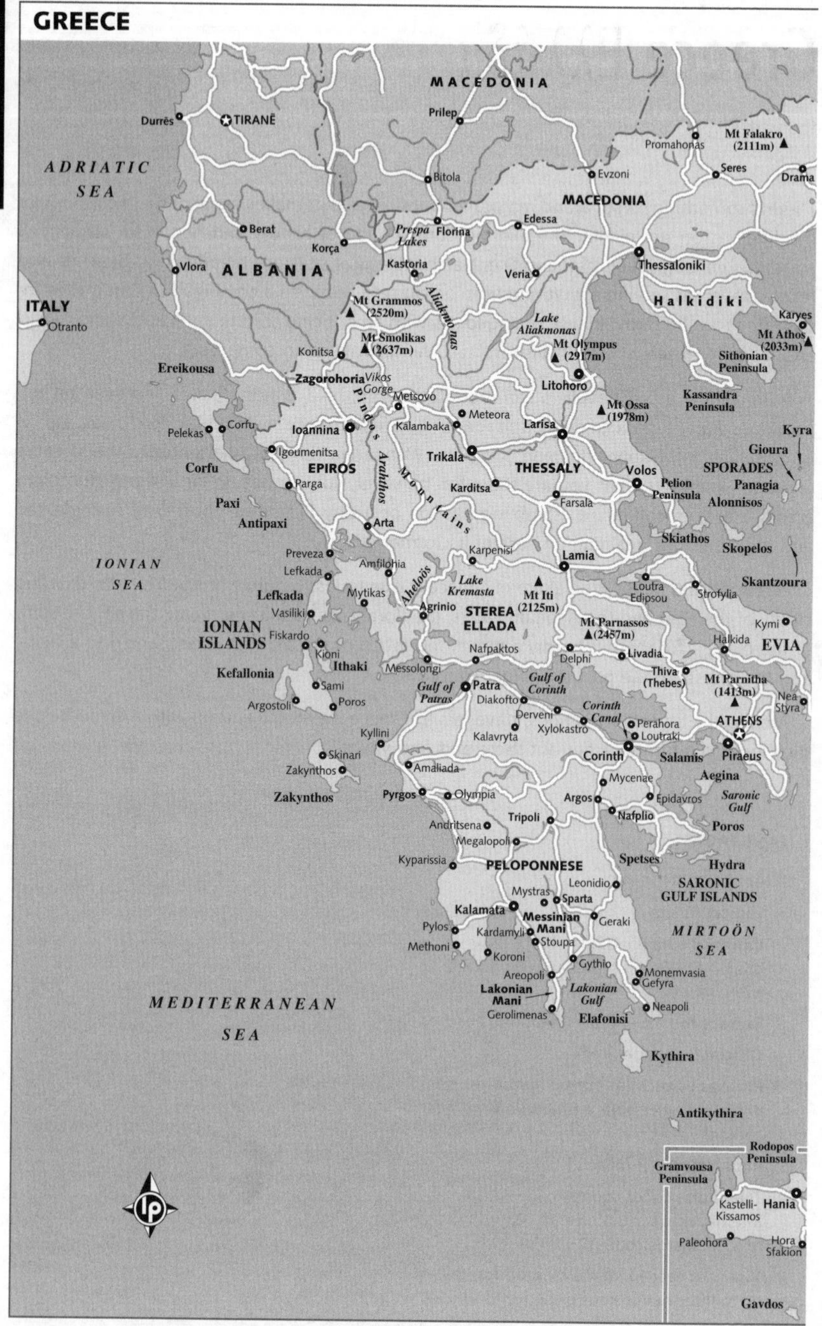
GREECE
MACEDONIA
Prilep
Durrës
TIRANË
Promahonas
Mt Falakro (2111m)
ADRIATIC SEA
Bitola
Evzoni
Seres
Drama
MACEDONIA
Edessa
Berat
Prespa Lakes
Florina
Korça
Thessaloniki
Vlora
ALBANIA
Kastoria
Veria
ITALY
Otranto
Mt Grammos (2520m)
Aliakmonas
Halkidiki
Karyes
Lake Aliakmonas
Mt Athos (2033m)
Mt Smolikas (2637m)
Mt Olympus (2917m)
Konitsa
Sithonian Peninsula
Ereikousa
Zagorohoria
Vikos Gorge
Litohoro
Kassandra Peninsula
Pindos Mountains
Metsovo
Mt Ossa (1978m)
Meteora
Pelekas
Corfu
Ioannina
Kalambaka
Larisa
Kyra
Igoumenitsa
Trikala
Gioura
Corfu
EPIROS
THESSALY
Volos
SPORADES
Arahthos
Pelion Peninsula
Panagia
Parga
Karditsa
Farsala
Alonnisos
Paxi
Antipaxi
Arta
Skiathos
Skopelos
Preveza
Karpenisi
Lamia
IONIAN SEA
Lefkada
Amfilohia
Skantzoura
Acheloös
Lake Kremasta
Mt Iti (2125m)
Loutra Edipsou
Strofylia
Lefkada
Mytikas
Vasiliki
Agrinio
STEREA ELLADA
Kymi
IONIAN ISLANDS
Mt Parnassos (2457m)
Fiskardo
Halkida
EVIA
Kioni
Nafpaktos
Delphi
Livadia
Kefallonia
Ithaki
Messolongi
Thiva (Thebes)
Mt Parnitha (1413m)
Sami
Gulf of Patras
Patra
Gulf of Corinth
Nea Styra
Argostoli
Poros
Diakofto
Corinth Canal
Derveni
Xylokastro
Perahora
ATHENS
Kyllini
Kalavryta
Loutraki
Skinari
Corinth
Salamis
Piraeus
Zakynthos
Amaliada
Mycenae
Aegina
Pyrgos
Olympia
Argos
Epidavros
Saronic Gulf
Zakynthos
Nafplio
Tripoli
Poros
Andritsena
Megalopoli
Spetses
Hydra
Kyparissia
PELOPONNESE
SARONIC GULF ISLANDS
Leonidio
Mystras
Sparta
Kalamata
Messinian Mani
Geraki
MIRTOÖN SEA
Pylos
Kardamyli
Stoupa
Methoni
Koroni
Gythio
Areopoli
Monemvasia
Gefyra
Lakonian Mani
Lakonian Gulf
MEDITERRANEAN SEA
Gerolimenas
Neapoli
Elafonisi
Kythira
Antikythira
Rodopos Peninsula
Gramvousa Peninsula
Kastelli-Kissamos
Hania
Paleohora
Hora Sfakion
Gavdos

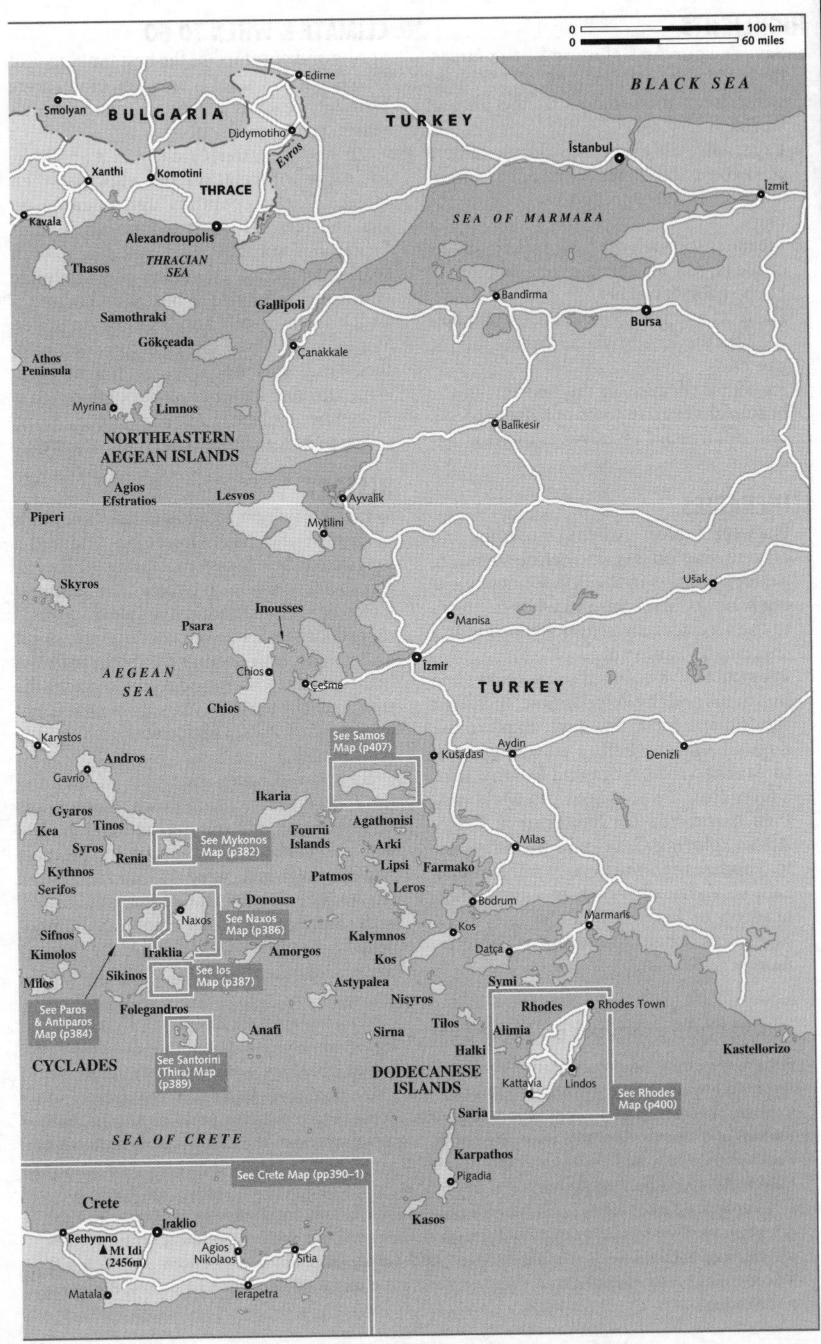
0 100 km
0 60 miles
BLACK SEA
Edirne
Smolyan
BULGARIA
TURKEY
Didymotiho
Evros
İstanbul
Xanthi
Komotini
THRACE
İzmit
Kavala
SEA OF MARMARA
Alexandroupolis
Thasos
THRACIAN SEA
Bandirma
Samothraki
Gallipoli
Bursa
Gökçeada
Athos Peninsula
Çanakkale
Myrina
Limnos
Balikesir
NORTHEASTERN AEGEAN ISLANDS
Agios Efstratios
Lesvos
Ayvalik
Piperi
Mytilini
Skyros
Uşak
Inousses
Manisa
Psara
İzmir
AEGEAN SEA
Chios
Çeşme
TURKEY
Chios
Karystos
See Samos Map (p407)
Aydin
Kuşadasi
Denizli
Andros
Gavrio
Ikaria
Gyaros
Agathonisi
Kea
Tinos
Fourni Islands
See Mykonos Map (p382)
Milas
Syros
Arki
Renia
Lipsi
Farmako
Kythnos
Patmos
Serifos
Leros
Donousa
Bodrum
Naxos
See Naxos Map (p386)
Marmaris
Sifnos
Kalymnos
Kos
Kimolos
Iraklia
Amorgos
Datça
Kos
Sikinos
See Ios Map (p387)
Milos
Astypalea
Symi
See Paros & Antiparos Map (p384)
Folegandros
Nisyros
Rhodes
Rhodes Town
Tilos
Anafi
Sirna
Alimia
See Santorini (Thira) Map (p389)
Halki
Kastellorizo
CYCLADES
DODECANESE ISLANDS
Kattavia
Lindos
See Rhodes Map (p400)
Saria
SEA OF CRETE
Karpathos
See Crete Map (pp390–1)
Pigadia
Crete
Kasos
Iraklio
Rethymno
▲Mt Idi (2456m)
Agios Nikolaos
Sitia
Matala
Ierapetra

HIGHLIGHTS

- Savour your first glimpse of the **Acropolis** (p353) in Athens, one of the most spectacular monuments of the ancient world.
- Experience the dramatic volcanic caldera of incomparable **Santorini** (p388), arguably the most stunning Greek dot on the map.
- Meander through the atmospheric streets of the largest inhabited medieval town in Europe, **Rhodes** (p399).
- Dash off a quick 100m at ancient **Olympia** (p372), the evocative birthplace of the games.
- Sip sunset drinks on the seafront in the beautiful Venetian town of **Nafplio** (p368), one of Greece's most romantic destinations.

ITINERARIES

- **One week** Explore Athens' museums and ancient sites on day one before spending a couple of days in the Peloponnese visiting Nafplio, Mycenae and Olympia; ferry to the Cyclades and enjoy Mykonos and spectacular Santorini.
- **One month** Give yourself some more time in Athens and the Peloponnese, then visit the Ionians for a few days. Explore the Zagoria villages before travelling back to Athens via Meteora and Delphi. Take a ferry from Piraeus south to Mykonos, then island-hop via Santorini to Crete. After exploring Crete, take the ferry east to Rhodes, then north to Symi, Kos and Samos. Carry on north to Chios, then head on to Lesvos. Take the ferry back to Piraeus when you're out of time or money.

CLIMATE & WHEN TO GO

Spring and autumn are the best times to visit Greece – the weather is fine, temperatures are pleasant, beaches are uncrowded and low-season prices are in effect.

Orthodox Easter (usually in April/May; for more information see p420) is when Greece starts repainting and opening up the shutters. From late June until mid-September summer is in full swing, with soaring temperatures, ancient sites swarming with tourists, crowded beaches, accommodation booked solid and high-season prices. Winter is quiet and can be surprisingly cold; the islands and much of their tourist infrastructure are in hibernation between late November and early April.

See p944 for climate charts for Athens.

HISTORY

With its strategic position at the crossroads of Europe and Asia, Greece has endured a long and turbulent history. During the Bronze Age (3000–1200 BC in Greece), the advanced Cycladic, Minoan and Mycenaean civilisations flourished. The Mycenaeans were swept aside in the 12th century BC by the warrior-like Dorians, who introduced Greece to the Iron Age. The next 400 years are often referred to as the dark ages, a period about which little is known.

By 800 BC, when Homer's *Odyssey* and *Iliad* were first written down, Greece was undergoing a cultural and military revival with the evolution of the city-states, the most powerful of which were Athens and Sparta. Greater Greece, Magna Graecia, was created, with southern Italy as an important component. The unified Greeks repelled the Persians twice, at Marathon (490 BC) and Salamis (480

CONNECTIONS: MOVING ON FROM GREECE

For those visiting Greece as part of a trip around Europe, there are various exciting options for reaching onward destinations overland or by sea.

There are regular ferry connections between Greece and the Italian ports of Ancona, Bari, Brindisi and Venice. Similarly, there are ferries operating between the Greek islands of Rhodes, Kos, Samos, Chios and Lesvos and the Aegean coast of Turkey (p423). Island-hopping doesn't have to take you back to Athens.

Overland, it's possible to reach Albania, Bulgaria, Macedonia and Turkey from Greece. If you've got your own wheels, you can drive through border crossings with these four countries. There are bus connections with Albania, Bulgaria and Turkey, and train connections with Bulgaria, Macedonia and Turkey (p423). In summer there are direct train services to Moscow, Bratislava and Prague.

BC). Victory over Persia was followed by unparalleled growth and prosperity known as the classical (or Golden) age.

The Golden Age

During this period, Pericles commissioned the Parthenon, Sophocles wrote *Oedipus the King* and Socrates taught young Athenians to think. The Golden Age ended with the Peloponnesian War (431–404 BC), when the militaristic Spartans defeated the Athenians. They failed to notice the expansion of Macedonia under King Philip II, who easily conquered the war-weary city-states.

Philip's ambitions were surpassed by those of his son, Alexander the Great, who marched triumphantly into Asia Minor, Egypt, Persia and what are now parts of Afghanistan and India. In 323 BC he met an untimely death at the age of 33, and his generals divided his empire between themselves.

Roman Rule & the Byzantine Empire

Roman incursions into Greece began in 205 BC. By 146 BC Greece and Macedonia had become Roman provinces. After the subdivision of the Roman Empire into eastern and western empires in AD 395, Greece became part of the Eastern (Byzantine) Empire, based at Constantinople.

In the centuries that followed, Venetians, Franks, Normans, Slavs, Persians, Arabs and, finally, Turks took turns chipping away at the Byzantine Empire.

The Ottoman Empire & Independence

After the end of the Byzantine Empire in 1453, when Constantinople fell to the Turks, most of Greece became part of the Ottoman Empire. Crete was not captured until 1670, leaving Corfu as the only island not occupied by the Turks. By the 19th century the Ottoman Empire was in decline. The Greeks, seeing nationalism sweep through Europe, fought the War of Independence (1821–22). Greek independence was proclaimed on 13 January 1822, only for arguments among the leaders who had been united against the Turks to escalate into civil war. The Turks, with the help of the Egyptians, tried to retake Greece, but the great powers – Britain, France and Russia – intervened in 1827, and Ioannis Kapodistrias was elected the first Greek president.

Kapodistrias was assassinated in 1831 and the European powers stepped in once again, declaring that Greece should become a monarchy. In January 1833 Otho of Bavaria was installed as king. His ambition, called the Great Idea, was to unite all the lands of the Greek people to the Greek motherland. In 1862 he was peacefully ousted and the Greeks chose George I, a Danish prince, as king.

During WWI Prime Minister Venizelos allied Greece with France and Britain. King Constantine (George's son), who was married to the kaiser's sister Sophia, disputed this and left the country.

HOW MUCH?

- **Local telephone call** €0.30 per minute
- **Minimum taxi fare** €4
- **Greek coffee** €1.50
- **Bottle of retsina** €5 to €10
- **International Herald Tribune newspaper** €2.50

LONELY PLANET INDEX

- **1L petrol** €0.88
- **1L bottled water** €1
- **Bottle of beer** €2.50
- **Souvenir T-shirt** €15
- **Gyros** €2

Smyrna & WWII

After the war Venizelos resurrected the Great Idea. Underestimating the new-found power of Turkey under the leadership of Atatürk, he sent forces to occupy Smyrna (the present-day Turkish port of İzmir), with its large Greek population. The army was heavily defeated and this led to a brutal population exchange between the two countries in 1923.

In 1930 George II, Constantine's son, was reinstated as king and appointed the dictator General Metaxas as prime minister. Metaxas' grandiose ambition was to combine aspects of Greece's ancient and Byzantine past to create a Third Greek Civilisation. However, his chief claim to fame is his celebrated *ohi* (no) to Mussolini's request to allow Italian troops into Greece in 1940.

Greece fell to Germany in 1941 and resistance movements, polarised into royalist and communist factions, staged a bloody civil war lasting until 1949. The civil war was the trigger for a mass exodus that saw almost one million Greeks head off to places such as Australia, Canada and the USA. Entire villages were abandoned as people gambled on a new start in cities such as Melbourne, Toronto, Chicago and New York.

The Colonels' Coup

Continuing political instability led to the colonels' coup d'état in 1967. King Constantine (son of King Paul, who succeeded George II) staged an unsuccessful counter-coup and fled the country. The colonels' junta distinguished itself with its appalling brutality, repression and political incompetence. In 1974 they attempted to assassinate Cyprus' leader, Archbishop Makarios, and when he escaped the junta replaced him with the extremist Nikos Samson, prompting Turkey to occupy North Cyprus. The continued Turkish occupation of Cyprus remains one of the most contentious issues in Greek politics. The junta had little choice but to hand back power to the people. In November 1974 a plebiscite voted against restoration of the monarchy. Greece became a republic with the right-wing New Democracy (ND) party taking power.

The Socialist 1980s

In 1981 Greece entered the European Community (now the EU). Andreas Papandreou's Panhellenic Socialist Movement (Pasok) won the next election, giving Greece its first socialist government. Pasok promised the removal of US air bases and withdrawal from NATO, but delivered only rising unemployment and spiralling debt.

Scandal during 1989 involving the Bank of Crete led to an unprecedented conservative and communist coalition taking power. Papandreou and four ministers were ordered to stand trial, and the coalition ordered fresh elections in October 1990.

The 1990s

The elections brought the ND party back to power with a slight majority. Tough economic reforms introduced by Prime Minister Konstantinos Mitsotakis soon made his government unpopular and corruption allegations forced Mitsotakis to call an election in October 1993.

Greeks again turned to Pasok and the ailing Papandreou, who was eventually cleared of all charges. He had little option but to continue with the austerity program begun by Mitsotakis, quickly making his government equally unpopular.

Papandreou stood down in January 1996 due to ill health and the party abandoned its leftist policies, electing economist and lawyer Costas Simitis as leader. Simitis romped to a comfortable majority at a snap poll called in October 1996.

The New Millennium

Simitis' government focused strongly on further integration with Europe and in January 2001, admission to the euro club was approved; Greece duly adopted the currency in 2002 and prices have been on the rise ever since.

Simitis was rewarded with a further four-year mandate in April 2000, but after suffering a serious popularity slump he announced an election as well as his retirement. Greece tilted to the right and in March 2004 elected the ND party led by Costas Karamanlis. This new broom was fortuitous, as the Olympic preparations were running late and suffering budget problems. While the Olympics were successful, Greece is still counting the cost.

During the long hot summer of 2007, forest fires threatened Athens and caused untold damage in the western Peloponnese, Epiros and Evia. Later the same year, Karamanlis' government was returned to power for a second term.

Greece's foreign policy is dominated by a perceptibly warming, yet still sensitive relationship with Turkey – with Greece continuing to support Turkey's bid to join the EU.

PEOPLE

Greece's population has exceeded 11.1 million, with around one-third of the people living in the Greater Athens area and more than two-thirds living in cities – confirming that Greece is now a primarily urban society. Less than 15% live on the islands, the most populous being Crete, Evia and Corfu. Greece has an ageing population and declining birth rate, with big families a thing of the past. Population growth over the last couple of decades is due to a flood of migrants, both legal and illegal. Previously, Greece had been a nation of emigrants and there are an estimated five million people of Greek descent living around the world.

RELIGION

About 95% of the Greek population belongs to the Greek Orthodox Church. The remainder are split between the Roman Catholic, Protestant, Evangelist, Jewish and Muslim faiths. While older Greeks and those in rural areas tend to be deeply religious, most young people are decidedly more secular.

The Greek year is centred on the saint's days and festivals of the church calendar. Namedays (celebrating your namesake saint) are celebrated more than birthdays. Most people are named after a saint, as are boats, suburbs and train stations.

Orthodox Easter is usually at a different time than Easter celebrated by the Western churches, though generally in April/May.

ARTS

The arts have been integral to Greek life since ancient times, with architecture having had the most profound influence. Greek temples, seen throughout history as symbolic of democracy, were the inspiration for architectural movements such as the Italian Renaissance. Today masses of cheap concrete apartment blocks built in the 20th century in Greece's major cities belie this architectural legacy.

Thankfully, the great works of Greek literature are not as easily besmirched. The first and greatest Ancient Greek writer was Homer, author of *Iliad* and *Odyssey*, telling the story of the Trojan War and the subsequent wanderings of Odysseus.

Pindar (c 518–438 BC) is regarded as the pre-eminent lyric poet of ancient Greece and was commissioned to recite his odes at the Olympic Games. The great writers of love poetry were Sappho (6th century BC) and Alcaeus (5th century BC), both of whom lived on Lesvos. Sappho's poetic descriptions of her affections for women gave rise to the term 'lesbian'.

The Alexandrian, Constantine Cavafy (1863–1933) revolutionised Greek poetry by introducing a personal, conversational style. Later, poet George Seferis (1900–71) won the Nobel Prize for literature in 1963, as did Odysseus Elytis (1911–96) in 1979. Nikos Kazantzakis, author of *Zorba the Greek* and numerous novels, plays and poems, is the most famous of 20th-century Greek novelists.

Greece's most famous painter was a young Cretan called Domenikos Theotokopoulos, who moved to Spain in 1577 and became known as the great El Greco. Famous painters of the 20th century include Konstantinos, Partenis and, later, George Bouzianis, whose work can be viewed at the National Art Gallery in Athens.

Music has been a facet of Greek life since ancient times. When visiting Greece today, your trip will inevitably be accompanied by the plucked-string sound of the ubiquitous bouzouki. The bouzouki is one of the main instruments of *rembetika* music – which is in many ways the Greek equivalent of the American blues and has its roots in the sufferings of the refugees from Asia Minor in the 1920s.

Dance is also an integral part of Greek life. Whether at a wedding, nightclub or village celebration, traditional dance is widely practised.

Drama continues to feature in domestic arts, particularly in Athens and Thessaloniki. In summer Greek dramas are staged in the ancient theatres where they were originally performed.

Greek film has for many years been associated with the work of film-maker Theo Angelopoulos, who won Cannes' Palme d'Or in 1998 with *An Eternity and One Day*. Since the late '90s, Greek cinema has witnessed a minor renaissance, with films such as *Safe Sex* (2000) luring Greek movie-goers back to the cinema.

Greek TV is dominated by chat shows, sport and foreign movies, only to be interrupted by localised versions of the latest American 'reality TV' hit.

ENVIRONMENT

The Land

Greece sits at the southern tip of the Balkan Peninsula. Of its 1400 islands, only 169 are inhabited. The land mass is 131,944 sq km and Greek territorial waters cover a further 400,000 sq km. Nowhere in Greece is much more than 100km from the sea.

Around 80% of the land is mountainous, with less than a quarter of the country suitable for agriculture.

Greece sits in one of the most seismically active regions in the world – the eastern Mediterranean lies at the meeting point of three continental plates: the Eurasian, African and Arabian. Consequently, Greece has had more than 20,000 earthquakes in the last 40 years, most of them very minor.

Wildlife

The variety of flora in Greece is unrivalled in Europe, with a dazzling array of spectacular wildflowers best seen in the mountains of Crete and the southern Peloponnese.

You won't encounter many animals in the wild, mainly due to hunting. Wild boar, still found in the north, is a favourite target. Squirrels, rabbits, hares, foxes and weasels are all fairly common on the mainland. Reptiles are well represented by snakes, including several poisonous viper species.

Lake Mikri Prespa in Macedonia has the richest colony of fish-eating birds in Europe, while the Dadia Forest Reserve in Thrace counts such majestic birds as the golden eagle and the giant black vulture among its residents.

The brown bear, Europe's largest land mammal, still survives in very small numbers in the mountains of northern Greece, as does the grey wolf.

Europe's rarest mammal, the monk seal, once very common in the Mediterranean Sea, is now on the brink of extinction in Europe. There are about 400 left in Europe, half of which live in Greece. About 40 frequent the Ionian Sea and the rest are found in the Aegean.

The waters around Zakynthos are home to Europe's last large sea turtle colony, that of the loggerhead turtle *(Careta careta)*. The **Sea Turtle Protection Society of Greece** (☎/fax 21052 31342; www.archelon.gr) runs monitoring programs and is always on the look-out for volunteers.

National Parks

While facilities in Greek national parks aren't on par with many other countries, all have refuges and some have marked hiking trails. The most visited parks are Mt Parnitha, north of Athens, and the Samaria Gorge on Crete. The others are Vikos-Aoös and Prespa National Parks in Epiros; Mt Olympus on the border of Thessaly and Macedonia; and Parnassos and Iti National Parks in central Greece. There is also a national marine park off the coast of Alonnisos, and another around the Bay of Laganas area off Zakynthos.

Environmental Issues

Greece is belatedly becoming environmentally conscious but, regrettably, it's too late for some regions. Deforestation and soil erosion are problems that go back thousands of years, with olive cultivation and goats being the main culprits. Forest fires are also a major problem, with an estimated 250 sq km destroyed every year. In 2007 there were particularly devastating fires, many of which are thought to have been lit deliberately. Epiros and Macedonia in northern Greece are the only places where extensive forests remain.

General environmental awareness remains at a depressingly low level, especially where litter is concerned. The problem is particularly bad in rural areas, where roadsides are strewn with aluminium cans and plastic packaging hurled from passing cars. It is somewhat surprising that the waters of the Aegean are as clear as they are considering how many cigarette butts are tossed off ferries.

FOOD & DRINK

Staples & Specialities

SNACKS

Greece has a great range of fast-food options. Foremost among them are gyros and souvlaki. The gyros is a giant skewer laden with seasoned meat that grills slowly as it rotates, the meat being steadily trimmed from the outside. Souvlaki are small cubes of meat cooked on a skewer. Both are served wrapped in pitta bread with salad and lashings of tzatziki (a yogurt, cucumber and garlic dip). Other snacks are pretzel rings, spanakopitta (spinach and cheese pie) and *tyropitta* (cheese pie).

STARTERS

Greece is famous for its appetisers, known as *mezedes* (literally, 'tastes'; meze for short). Standards include tzatziki, *melitzanosalata* (aubergine dip), taramasalata (fish-roe dip), dolmadhes (stuffed vine leaves), *fasolia* (beans) and *oktapodi* (octopus). A selection of three or four starters represents a good meal and makes an excellent vegetarian option.

MAIN DISHES

You'll find moussaka (layers of aubergine and mince, topped with béchamel sauce and baked) on every menu, alongside a number of other taverna staples. They include *moschari* (oven-baked veal and potatoes), *keftedes* (meatballs), *stifado* (meat stew), *pastitsio* (baked dish of macaroni with minced meat and béchamel sauce) and *yemista* (either tomatoes or green peppers stuffed with minced meat and rice).

Kalamaria (fried squid) is the most popular (and cheapest) seafood, while *barbouni* (red mullet) and *sifias* (swordfish) tend to be more expensive than meat dishes.

Fortunately for vegetarians, salad is a mainstay of the Greek diet. The most popular is *horiatiki salata,* normally listed on English-language menus as Greek salad. It's a delicious mixed salad comprising cucumbers, peppers, onions, olives, tomatoes and feta cheese. For the full scoop on Greece's legendary feta cheese, check out www.feta.gr.

DESSERTS

Most Greek desserts are Turkish in origin and are variations on pastry soaked in honey, such as baklava (thin layers of pastry filled with honey and nuts). Delicious Greek yogurt also makes a great dessert, especially with honey.

DRINKS

Bottled mineral water is cheap and available everywhere, as are soft drinks and packaged juices.

Mythos, in its distinctive green bottle, and Alfa, are popular Greek beers. Locally brewed Amstel and Heineken are commonly available.

Greece is traditionally a wine-drinking society. An increasingly good range of wines made from traditional grape varieties is available. Wine enthusiasts should take a look at www.allaboutgreekwine.com. Retsina, wine flavoured with pine-tree resin, is a tasty alternative – though an acquired taste for some. Most tavernas will offer locally made house wines by the carafe.

Aniseed-flavoured ouzo embodies a way of socialising in Greece. It is best mixed with water and ice (turning a cloudy white) and enjoyed with conversation. Metaxa, Greece's dominant brandy, is sweet, while if you are offered some raki, make sure to take a small sip first!

'Greek' coffee should be tried at least once. Don't drink the mudlike grounds at the bottom!

Where to Eat & Drink

The most common variety of restaurant in Greece is the taverna, traditionally an extension of the Greek home table. *Estiatorio* is Greek for restaurant and often has the same dishes as a taverna but with higher prices. A *psistaria* specialises in charcoal-grilled dishes while a *psarotaverna* specialises in fish. *Ouzeria* (ouzo bars) often have such a range of *mezedes* that they can be regarded as eateries.

Kafeneia are the smoke-filled cafes where men gather to drink 'Greek' coffee, play backgammon and cards, and engage in heated political discussion. Every Greek town you'll visit now has at least one cafe-bar where Greece's youth while away hours over a frappé (frothy ice coffee).

Buying and preparing your own food is easy in Greece – every town of consequence has a supermarket, as well as fruit and vegetable shops.

To have a go at producing your own Greek culinary masterpieces, check out www.gourmed.gr. You'll also find information on the healthy Greek diet at www.mediterranean-diet.gr, while www.oliveoil.gr can tell you all about one of Greece's best-known products.

Greece is a nation of heavy smokers. Very few places to eat or drink have a nonsmoking area, let alone a nonsmoking policy.

For more on opening hours, see p419.

ATHENS ΑΘΗΝΑ

pop 3.7 million

Stroll around a corner in Athens and come face to face with breathtaking archaeological treasures, evocations of classical mythology and reminders of the city's enormous historical influence on Western civilisation. With the makeover that accompanied the 2004 Olympics, Athens also presented its cosmopolitan, chic side on the world stage. Though the city still suffers from traffic congestion, pollution and urban sprawl, take the time to look beneath her skin and you will discover a complex metropolis full of vibrant subcultures. Couture-clad fashionistas ply the streets alongside leather-bedecked punks. Elegant Michelin-star restaurants abut traditional family tavernas, funky new cafes sit beside neighbourhood *ouzeria,* and *rembetika* is performed at one bar while a DJ spins trance at a club across the street.

HISTORY

The early history of Athens, named after the goddess of wisdom, Athena, is inextricably interwoven with mythology, making it impossible to disentangle fact from fiction. What is known is that the hilltop site of the Acropolis,

ATHENS IN TWO DAYS

Walk the deserted morning streets of the charming Plaka district to reach the **Acropolis** (opposite) and **Agora** (p356) before the crowds. Dig in to *mezedes* at **Tzitzikas** and **Mermingas** (p360), before spending the afternoon at the **National Archaeological Museum** (p357). Enjoy Parthenon views and haute cuisine over dinner at **Varoulko** (p360) or sup on gyros at **Savas** (p360).

On the second day, visit the wonderful **Benaki Museum** (p357) or **Museum of Cycladic Art** (p357), then rest up for a night out eating (**Sardelles, p361**), drinking (wander Psyrri or try **Hoxton**, p361) and dancing (hit **Envy**, p362).

with two abundant springs, drew some of Greece's earliest Neolithic settlers. When a peaceful agricultural existence gave way to war-orientated city-states, the Acropolis provided an ideal defensive position.

Athens' golden age, the pinnacle of the classical era, came after the Persian Empire was repulsed at the battles of Salamis and Plataea (480–479 BC). The city has passed through many hands and cast off myriad invaders from Sparta to Philip II of Macedon, the Roman and Byzantine Empires, and, most recently, the Ottoman Empire. In 1834 Athens superseded Nafplio as the capital of independent Greece.

ORIENTATION

Athens is a sprawling city but most sights are within a manageable distance. Syntagmatos Sq, or Syntagma (*syn*-tag-ma), is the city's heart. Surrounded by luxury hotels, banks and travel offices, it's dominated by the Greek parliament building. Omonia Sq (Plateia Omonias) lies to the north of Syntagma; Gazi, Psyrri and Monastiraki Sq (Plateia Monastirakiou) are to its west; the Plaka district borders it to the south; and Kolonaki is at its east.

The city's major landmarks, the Acropolis and Lykavittos Hill, serve as good reference points as they're visible from most places.

All of Athens' major central streets meet in Omonia Sq. Panepistimiou (El Venizelou) and Stadiou run parallel southeast to Syntagma, while Athinas heads south to the market district of Monastiraki and the nightlife area of Psyrri.

Monastiraki is linked to Syntagma by the pedestrianised shopping streets Ermou and Mitropoleos, which skirts the northern edge of Plaka. Plaka, a charming old neighbourhood of labyrinthine streets (now inundated with souvenir shops and tavernas) nestles on the northeastern slope of the Acropolis with most ancient sites nearby.

INFORMATION

Bookshops

Bigger *periptera* (kiosks) stock a range of English-language magazines and international newspapers.

Compendium Books (Map p358; ☎ 210 322 1248; Nikis 28, Plaka; Ⓜ Syntagma) Specialises in English-language books and offers an excellent selection of Greek history and literature.

Eleftheroudakis Books Plaka (Map p358; ☎ 210 322 9388; Nikis 20; Ⓜ Syntagma); Syntagma (Map p358; ☎ 210 325 8440; Panepistimiou 17; Ⓜ Syntagma)

Public (Map p358; ☎ 210 324 6210; Syntagma Sq; Ⓜ Syntagma) English-language books on 3rd floor.

Emergency

Athens Central Police Station (Map pp354-5; ☎ 210 770 5711 17; Leoforos Alexandras 173, Ambelokipi; Ⓜ Ambelokipi) With a branch at Syntagma Sq (☎ 210 725 7000).

Fire brigade (☎ 199)

First-aid service (☎ 166)

Police emergency (☎ 100)

Tourist police (☎ 171; 🕒 24hr) General tourist info and emergency help.

Internet Access

There are free wireless hot spots at Syntagma Sq, Gazi and the port of Piraeus, as well as in Starbucks cafes and some McDonald's outlets. Internet cafes charge €2 to €4 per hour.

Bits & Bytes Internet Café (Map p358; Kapnikareas 19, Monastiraki; per hr €3; 🕒 24hr; Ⓜ Monastiraki)

Internet Cyberzone (Map pp354-5; ☎ 210 520 3939; Satovriandou 7, Omonia; per hr €2; 🕒 24hr; Ⓜ Omonia) Prices drop after midnight.

Laundry

Plaka Laundrette (Map p358; ☎ 210 321 3102; Angelou Geronta 10, Plaka; Syntagma; 5kg wash & dry €9; 🕒 8am-7pm Mon-Sat, to 1pm Sun; Ⓜ Monastiraki)

Left Luggage

Most hotels store luggage free for guests but this may mean leaving your bags unsecured in a hallway, so check ahead if you need to leave luggage long-term. Facilities are available at the airport and train station.

Medical Services

Ambulance/First-Aid Advice (☎ 166)
Duty Doctors & Hospitals (☎ 1434, in Greek) Published in *Kathimerini*.
Pharmacies (☎ 1434, in Greek) Check pharmacy windows for notice of nearest duty pharmacy.
SOS Doctors (☎ 1016, 210 821 1888; 24hr) Pay service with English-speaking doctors.

Money

Most banks have branches located around Syntagma Sq.
Eurochange Omonia (Map pp354-5; ☎ 210 552 0314; Omonia Sq; 9am-9pm; M Omonia); Syntagma (Map p358; ☎ 210 331 2462; Karageorgi Servias 2; 8am-9pm; M Syntagma)

Post

Athens Central Post Office (Map pp354-5; Eolou 100, Omonia; 7.30am-8pm Mon-Fri, to 2pm Sat; M Omonia) All poste restante is sent here unless specified otherwise.
Parcel Post Office (Map p358; Stadiou 4, Syntagma; 7.30am-2pm Mon-Fri; M Syntagma) Parcels over 2kg going abroad must be taken here, unwrapped for inspection.
Syntagma Post Office (Map p358; ☎ 210 331 9500; cnr Mitropoleos & Syntagma Sq; 7.30am-8pm Mon-Fri, to 2pm Sat, 9am-1.30pm Sun; M Syntagma) If staying in Plaka, get poste restante sent here.

Telephone

Public phones are everywhere and take phonecards, readily available from kiosks, as are prepaid SIM cards for mobiles.

Toilets

Public toilets are thin on the ground. Try fast-food outlets, bars, cafes and hotels.

Tourist Information

Greek National Tourist Organisation/EOT Syntagma (Map p358; ☎ 210 331 0392; Amalias 26; 9am-7pm Mon-Fri, 10am-6pm Sat & Sun; M Syntagma); airport (☎ 210 353 0445; arrivals hall; 9am-7pm Mon-Fri, 10am-4pm Sat & Sun); head office (Map pp354-5; ☎ 210 870 7000; www.gnto.gr; Tsoha 7; 9am-2pm Mon-Fri; M Ambelokipi)

DANGERS & ANNOYANCES

Like any big city, Athens has its hot spots. Omonia is home to pickpockets, prostitutes and drug dealers. Women should avoid walking alone here at night. Also watch for pickpockets on the metro and at the Sunday market.

When taking taxis, establish whether the driver's going to use the meter or negotiate a price in advance. Ignore drivers' stories that the hotel you've directed them to is closed or full – they're angling for a commission from another hotel that you'll end up paying for.

Bar scams are commonplace, particularly in Plaka and Syntagma. They go something like this: friendly Greek approaches solo male traveller, discovers traveller is new to Athens, and reveals that he, too, is from out of town. However, friendly Greek knows a great bar where they order drinks and equally friendly owner offers another drink. Women appear, more drinks are served and the crunch comes at the end of the night when traveller is hit with an exorbitant bill.

On the lighter side, many Athenian footpaths are marble, which get slippery when wet – ridged rubber soles work best.

SIGHTS

Acropolis

Arguably the most important ancient monument in the Western world, the **Acropolis** (Map p358; ☎ 210 321 0219; sites & museum adult/concession €12/6; 8am-7pm Apr-Oct, to 5.30pm Nov-Mar; M Akropoli) attracts multitudes of tourists, so visit in one early morning or late afternoon.

The site was inhabited in Neolithic times and the first temples were built during the Mycenaean era in homage to the goddess Athena. People lived on the Acropolis until the late 6th century BC, but in 510 BC the Delphic oracle declared that the Acropolis should be the province of the gods. When all of the buildings were reduced to ashes by the Persians on the eve of the Battle of Salamis (480 BC), Pericles set about rebuilding a city purely of temples.

CHEAPER BY THE HALF-DOZEN

The €12 admission charge at the Acropolis includes entry to the other significant ancient sites: Ancient Agora, Roman Agora, Keramikos, Temple of Olympian Zeus and the Theatre of Dionysos. The ticket is valid for four days.

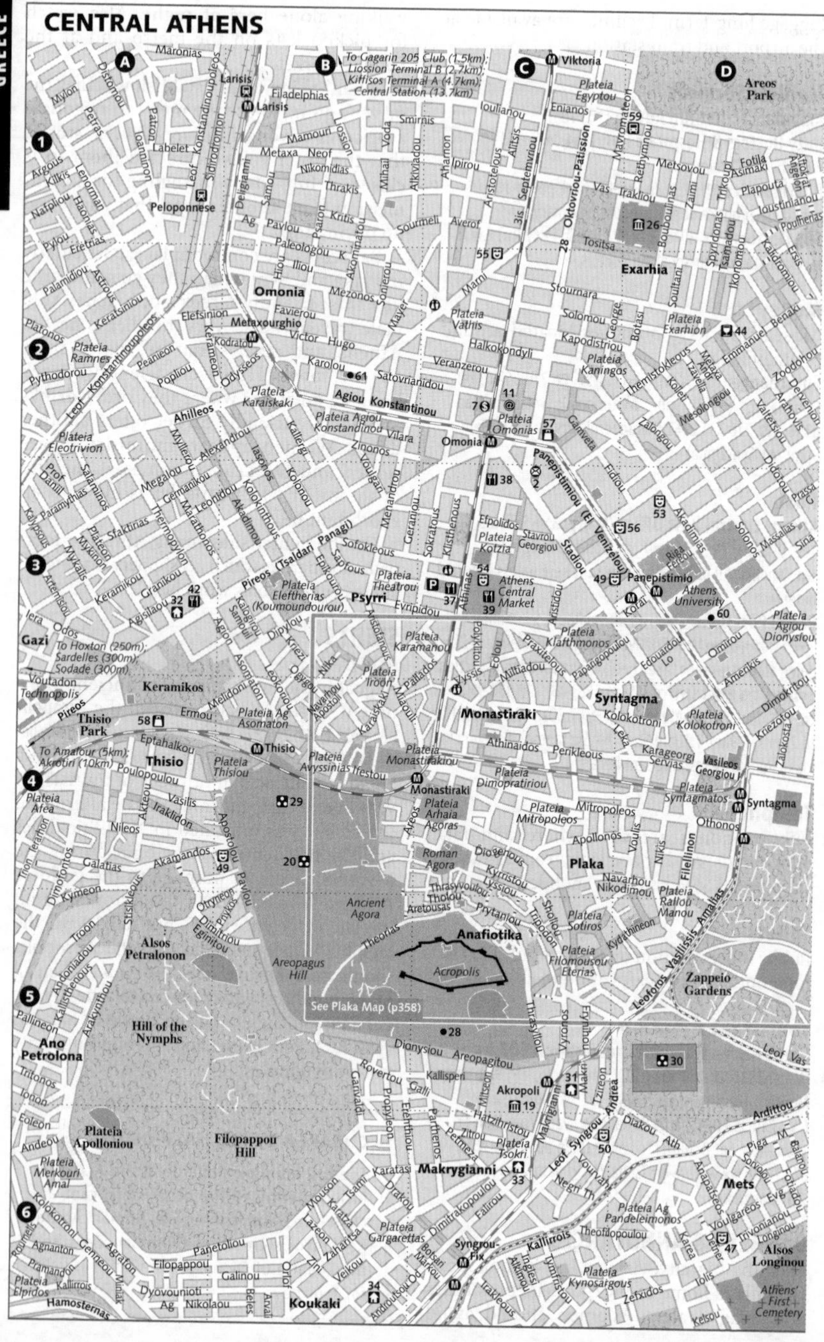
CENTRAL ATHENS
A
B
C
D
1
2
3
4
5
6
To Gagarin 205 Club (1.5km); Liossion Terminal B (2.7km); Kifisos Terminal A (4.7km); Central Station (13.7km)
Viktoria
Areos Park
Maronias
Distomou
Mylon
Petras
Larisis
Filadelphias
Plateia Egyptou
Enianos
Ioulianou
Mavromateon
59
Patron
Ioannou
Konstantinoupoleos
Sidirodromon
Leof
Labelet
Mamouri
Metaxa
Neof
Smirnis
Nikomidias
Thrakis
Liossion
Voda
Mihail
Alkiviadou
Aharnon
Ipirou
Aristotelous
Alitsis
3is Septemvriou
Oktovriou-Patission
28
Rethymnou
Metsovou
Fotila
Asimaki
Argous
Kilkis
Lenorman
Napliou
Haonias
Peloponnese
Deligianni
Samou
Ag
Pavlou
Kritis
Psaron
Sourmeli
Averof
Vas
Irakliou
Bouboulinas
Zaimi
Trikoupi
Plapouta
Ioustinianou
Poulherias
26
Tositsa
Exarhia
Spyridonos
Tsamadou
Ikonomou
Kalidromiou
Ersis
Pylou
Eretrias
Paleologou
K
Iliou
Hiou
Akominatou
Sonierou
55
Palamidiou
Astrous
Omonia
Mezonos
Mayer
Marni
Stournara
Keratsiniou
Elefsiniou
Metaxourghio
Favierou
Plateia Vathis
Solomou
Soultani
Botasi
George
Plateia Exarhion
44
Platonos
Plateia Ramnes
Kodratou
Victor Hugo
Halkokondyli
Kapodistriou
Emmanuel Benaki
Pythodorou
Leof Konstantinoupoleos
Peanieon
Odysseos
Karolou
Veranzerou
Plateia Kaningos
Themistokleous
Metaxa
Andr
Tzavela
Zoodohou
Popliou
61
Satovrianidou
11
Kolleti
Mesolongiou
Derveniou
Arahovis
Valtetsiou
Plateia Karaiskaki
Agiou Konstantinou
7
Plateia Omonias
57
Ahilleos
Plateia Agiou Konstandinou
Vilara
Omonia
Gamveta
Zalongou
Plateia Eleotrivion
Keramikou
Mylerou
Alexandrou
Zinonos
Panepistimiou (El Venizelou)
Fidiou
Didotou
Prof Daniil
Salaminos
Paramythias
Germanikou
Megalou
Leonidou
Marathonos
Thermopylon
Akadimou
Kolokinthous
Iasonos
Kolonou
Kallergi
Voulgari
Menandrou
38
2
53
Prassa
Kalypsous
Mykonou
Mykalis
Plateon
Sfaktirias
Sofokleous
Geraniou
Sokratous
Klisthenous
Efpolidos
Plateia Kotzia
Stavrou Georgiou
Stadiou
56
Akadimias
Solonos
Massalias
Sina
Riga Fereou
Pireos (Tsaldari Panagi)
Sapfous
Epikourou
Plateia Theatrou
54
Athens Central Market
Artemisiou
Granikou
Keramikou
42
32
Agisilaou
Kalogirou Samouil
Plateia Eleftherias (Koumoundourou)
Psyrri
P
37
Athinas
39
49
Panepistimio
Athens University
Kolokotroni
Aristidou
Evripidou
60
Plateia Agiou Dionysiou
Iera Odos
Gazi
To Hoxton (250m); Sardelles (300m); Sodade (300m)
Agion
Asomaton
Dipylou
Kriezi
Ogygou
Nika
Plateia Karamanou
Aristofanous
Polykleitou
Eolou
Plateia Klafthmonos
Praxitelous
Papangopoulou
Edouardou Lo
Omirou
Voutadon
Technopolis
Keramikos
Melidoni
Leokoriou
Plateia Iroon
Navarhou Apostoli
Karaiskaki
Pallados
Miaouli
Lyssis
Miltiadou
Monastiraki
Syntagma
Amerikis
Dimokritou
Pireos
Thisio Park
58
Ermou
Plateia Ag Asomaton
Kolokotroni
Plateia Kolokotroni
Leka
Kriezotou
Eptahalkou
Thisio
Athinaidos
Perikleous
Karageorgi Servias
Vasileos Georgiou I
Zalokosta
To Amalour (5km); Akrotiri (10km)
Thisio
Plateia Thisiou
Poulopoulou
Plateia Avyssinias
Ifestou
Plateia Monastirakiou
Plateia Dimopratiriou
Monastiraki
Plateia Syntagmatos
Syntagma
Plateia Afea
Vasilis
Iraklidon
Akteou
29
Plateia Arhaia Agoras
Areos
Plateia Mitropoleos
Mitropoleos
Othonos
Nileos
Apollonos
Voulis
Nikis
Filellinon
Teraton
Galatias
Akamandos
49
Apostolou Pavlou
20
Roman Agora
Diogenous
Kyrristou
Lyssiou
Plaka
Navarhou Nikodimou
Dimofontos
Kymeon
Thrasyvoulou
Tholou
Aretousas
Prytaniou
Plateia Rallou Manou
Otryneon
Dimitriou Eginitou
Ancient Agora
Shoileiou
Tripodon
Plateia Sotiros
Troon
Stisikleous
Alsos Petralonon
Theorias
Anafiotika
Kydathineon
Apostolou
Kallisthenous
Areopagus Hill
Acropolis
Plateia Filomousou Eterias
Leoforos Vasilissis Amalias
Zappeio Gardens
Arakynthou
See Plaka Map (p358)
Pallineon
Hill of the Nymphs
Ano Petrolona
28
Vyronos
Erynhou
Thrasyllou
30
Dionysiou Areopagitou
Leof Vas
Tritonos
Ionon
Rovertou Galli
Kallisperi
Akropoli
31
Makri
Tzireon
Andrea
Ardittou
Garivaldi
Propyleon
Erehthiou
Mitseon
19
Eoleon
Andeou
Plateia Apolloniou
Filopappou Hill
Parthenos
Hatzihristou
Zitrou
Petmeza
Plateia Tsokri
Makrygianni
Leof Syngrou
Diakou
Ath
Piga
Sorvolou
Fotiadou
Plateia Merkouri Amal
Karatasi
Makrygianni
33
50
Vourvahi
Negri Th
Anapafseos
Mets
Evg
Kolokotroni
Mouson
Tsami Karatza
Drakou
Dimitrakopoulou
Falirou
Plateia Ag Pandeleimonos
Voulgareos
Trivonianou
Longinou
Rouvelis
Agnanton
Genneou
Agrafon
Lazeon
Zahartsa
Plateia Gargarettas
Theofilopoulou
Karea
Deimer
47
Alsos Longinou
Pramandon
Panetoliou
Zini
Veikou
Botsari
Markou
Syngrou-Fix
Kallirrois
Inglesi
Alkimou
Tymfristou
Plateia Elpidos
Kallirrois
Filopappou
Galinou
Orloff
Plateia Kynosargous
Zefxidos
Iolis
Athens' First Cemetery
Dyovounioti
Ag
Nikolaou
Beles
Arvali
Koukaki
34
Androutsou Od
Irakleous
Kelsou
Hamosternas
Minlak

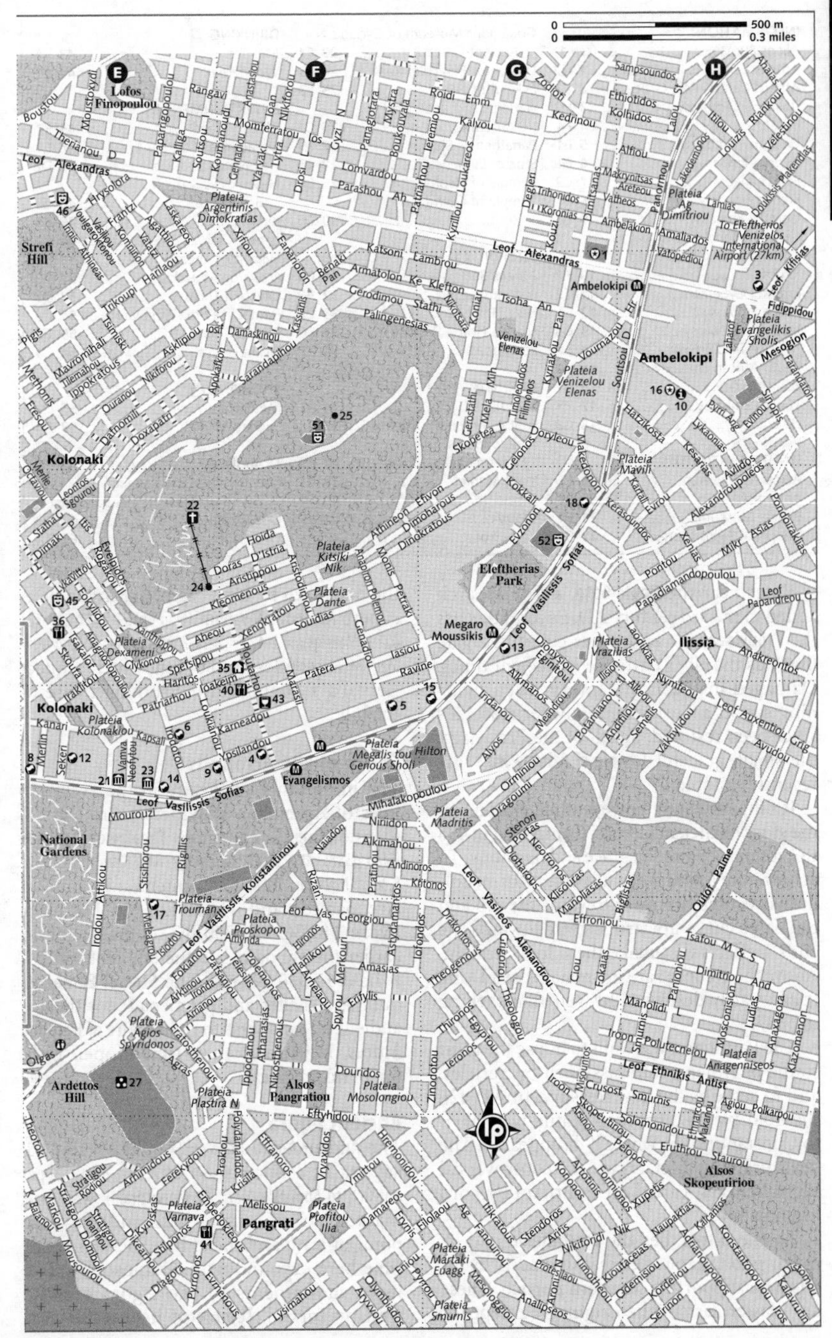
0 500 m
0 0.3 miles
Lofos Finopoulou
Strefi Hill
Kolonaki
Ambelokipi
Eleftherias Park
Megaro Moussikis
Evangelismos
Ilissia
National Gardens
Ardettos Hill
Alsos Pangratiou
Pangrati
Alsos Skopeutiriou
Plateia Argentinis Dimokratias
Plateia Kitsiki Nik
Plateia Dante
Plateia Dexameni
Plateia Kolonakiou
Plateia Megalis tou Genous Sholi
Plateia Madritis
Plateia Vrazilias
Plateia Mavili
Plateia Venizelou Elenas
Plateia Evangelikis Sholis
Plateia Ag Dimitriou
Plateia Trouman
Plateia Proskopon
Plateia Agios Spyridonos
Plateia Plastira
Plateia Mosolongiou
Plateia Varnava
Plateia Profitou Ilia
Plateia Martaki Euagg.
Plateia Smurnis
Plateia Anagenniseos
Leof Alexandras
Leof Vasilissis Sofias
Leof Vasilissis Konstantinou
Leof Vasileos Alexandrou
Leof Kifisias
Leof Ethnikis Antist
Leof Vas Georgiou
Mesogion
Oulof Palme
Hilton
To Eleftherios Venizelos International Airport (27km)

INFORMATION
Aliens Bureau (see 1)
Athens Central Police Station 1 G2
Athens Central Post Office 2 C3
Australian Embassy 3 H2
British Embassy 4 F4
Canadian Embassy 5 F4
Cypriot Embassy 6 E4
Eurochange 7 C2
French Embassy 8 E4
German Embassy 9 E4
Greek National Tourist Organisation/EOT Head Office 10 H2
Internet Cyberzone 11 C2
Italian Embassy 12 E4
Japanese Embassy 13 G3
New Zealand Embassy 14 E4
South African Embassy 15 G4
Tourist Police 16 H2
Turkish Embassy 17 E5
US Embassy 18 G3

SIGHTS & ACTIVITIES
Acropolis Museum 19 C5
Ancient Agora 20 B4
Benaki Museum 21 E4
Chapel of Agios Giorgios 22 E3
Goulandris Museum of Cycladic & Ancient Greek Art 23 E4
Lykavittos Funicular Railway 24 E3
Lykavittos Hill 25 F2
National Archaeological Museum 26 D1
Panathenaic Stadium 27 E5
Stoa of Eumenes 28 C5
Temple of Hephaestus 29 B4
Temple of Olympian Zeus 30 D5

SLEEPING
Athens Backpackers 31 C5
Eridanus 32 A3
Hera Hotel 33 C6
Marble House Pension 34 B6
Periscope 35 F3

EATING
Entryfish 36 E3
Fruit & Vegetable Market 37 C3
Marinopoulos Supermarket 38 C3
Meat Market 39 C3
Oikeio 40 F4
Spondi 41 E6
Varoulko 42 A3

DRINKING
Mai-Tai 43 F4
Wonderbar 44 D2

ENTERTAINMENT
Alekos' Island 45 E3
Decadence 46 E1
Half Note Jazz Club 47 D6
Hellenic Festival Box Office 48 C3
Kirkis 49 B4
Lamda Club 50 C6
Lykavittos Theatre 51 F2
Megaron Mousikis 52 G3
Olympia Theatre 53 D3
Rembetika Stoa Athanaton 54 C3
Rodon Club 55 C2
Ticket House 56 C3

SHOPPING
Metropolis Music 57 C2
Sunday Market 58 A4

TRANSPORT
Mavromateon Bus Terminal (Southern Attica) 59 D1
OSE Office 60 D3
OSE Office 61 B2

Enter near the **Beule Gate**, a Roman arch added in the 3rd century AD. Beyond this lies the **Propylaea**, the enormous columned gate that was the city's entrance in ancient times. Damaged in the 17th century when lightning set off a Turkish gunpowder store, it's since been restored. South of the Propylaea, the small, graceful **Temple of Athena Nike** was recently restored.

It's the **Parthenon**, however, that epitomises the glory of ancient Greece. Completed in 438 BC, it's unsurpassed in grace and harmony. To achieve the appearance of perfect form, columns become narrower towards the top and the bases curve upward slightly towards the ends – effects that make them look straight. Above the columns are the remains of a Doric frieze, partly destroyed by Venetian shelling in 1687.

The Parthenon was built to house the great statue of Athena commissioned by Pericles, and to serve as the new treasury. In AD 426 the gold-plated 12m-high statue was taken to Constantinople, where it disappeared. The best surviving artefacts are the controversial Elgin Marbles, carted off to Britain by Lord Elgin in 1801.

To the north, lies the **Erechtheion** and its much-photographed Caryatids, the six maidens who support its southern portico. These are plaster casts – the originals (except for the one taken by Lord Elgin) are in the new, superb **Acropolis Museum** (Map pp354-5; 210 321 0219; Makrigianni 2-4; 8am-7pm Apr-Oct, to 5pm Nov-Mar; M Akropoli) designed by renowned architect Bernard Tschumi, on the southern base of the hill.

South of the Acropolis

The importance of theatre in the everyday lives of Athenians is evident from the dimensions of the enormous **Theatre of Dionysos** (Map p358; 210 322 4625; 8am-7pm Apr-Oct, to 5.30pm Nov-Mar; M Akropoli); enter via Dionysiou Areopagitou and Thrasillou Sts. Built between 340 BC and 330 BC on the site of an earlier theatre dating to the 6th century BC, it held 17,000 people. The **Stoa of Eumenes**, built as a shelter and promenade for theatre audiences, runs west to the **Theatre of Herodes Atticus**, built in Roman times (open only for performances).

Ancient Agora

The **Ancient Agora** (Map pp354-5; 210 321 0185; Adrianou 24; adult/concession €4/2; 8am-6.30pm Apr-Oct, to 5pm Nov-Mar; M Monastiraki) was the marketplace of early Athens and the focal point of civic and social life. Socrates spent time here expounding his philosophy. The main monuments of the Agora are the well-preserved **Temple of Hephaestus** (Map pp354-5), the 11th-century **Church of the Holy Apostles** (Map p358) and the reconstructed **Stoa of Attalos** (Map p358), which houses the site's excellent museum.

Roman Agora

The Romans built their **agora** (Map p358; ☎ 210 324 5220; cnr Pelopida Eolou & Markou Aureliou; adult/concession €2/1; 🕒 8am-7pm Apr-Oct, to 5pm Nov-Mar; Ⓜ Monastiraki) just east of the ancient Athenian Agora. The wonderful **Tower of the Winds** was built in the 1st century BC by a Syrian astronomer, Andronicus. Each side represents a point of the compass and has a relief carving depicting the associated wind.

Temple of Olympian Zeus & Panathenaic Stadium

Begun in the 6th century BC, Greece's largest **temple** (Map pp354-5; ☎ 210 922 6330; adult/concession €2/1; 🕒 8am-7pm Apr-Oct, to 5pm Nov-Mar; Ⓜ Akropoli), behind **Hadrian's Arch**, took more than 700 years to build, with Emperor Hadrian overseeing its completion in AD 131. It's impressive for the sheer size of its Corinthian columns – 17m high with a base diameter of 1.7m. East of the temple, the **Panathenaic Stadium** (Map pp354-5), built in the 4th century BC as a venue for the Panathenaic athletic contests, hosted the first modern Olympic Games in 1896.

National Archaeological Museum

One of the world's great museums, the **National Archaeological Museum** (Map pp354-5; ☎ 210 821 7717; www.culture.gr; Patission 44; adult/concession €7/3; 🕒 1-7.30pm Mon, 8am-7.30pm Tue-Sun Apr-Oct, 1-7.30pm Mon, 8.30am-3pm Tue-Sun Nov-Mar; Ⓜ Viktoria) contains significant finds from major archaeological sites throughout Greece. The vast collections include exquisite gold artefacts from Mycenae, spectacular Minoan frescoes from Santorini and intricate Cycladic figurines.

FREE THRILLS

A simple wander through the streets brings eye candy galore or take in:

- **National Gardens** (right)
- **Changing of the Guard** (p358)
- **Monastiraki Flea Market** (p363)
- **Sunday Market** (p363)
- **Lykavittos Hill** (right)

Benaki Museum

This superb **museum** (Map pp354-5; ☎ 210 367 1000; www.benaki.gr; cnr Leof Vasilissis Sofias & Koumbari 1, Kolonaki; adult/concession €6/3; 🕒 9am-5pm Mon, Wed, Fri & Sat, to midnight Thu, to 3pm Sun; Ⓜ Syntagma) houses the extravagant collection of Antoine Benaki, the son of an Alexandrian cotton magnate. The splendid displays include ancient sculpture, Persian, Byzantine and Coptic objects, Chinese ceramics, icons, El Greco paintings and fabulous traditional costumes. The museum also runs annexes around the city containing Islamic art, archives and rotating exhibitions.

Goulandris Museum of Cycladic & Ancient Greek Art

This wonderful private **museum** (Map pp354-5; ☎ 210 722 8321; www.cycladic-m.gr; Neofytou Douka 4, Kolonaki; adult/concession €5/2.50; 🕒 10am-4pm Mon & Wed-Fri, to 3pm Sat; Ⓜ Evangelismos) was custom-built to display its extraordinary collection of Cycladic art, with an emphasis on the early Bronze Age. It's easy to see how the graceful marble statues influenced the art of Modigliani and Picasso.

Lykavittos Hill

Pine-covered **Lykavittos** (Hill of Wolves; Map pp354-5; Ⓜ Evangelismos) is the highest of the eight hills that are dotted around Athens. You can climb to the summit for stunning views of the city, the Attic basin and the islands of Salamis and Aegina (pollution permitting of course). The little **Chapel of Agios Giorgios** is floodlit at night and looks like a vision from a fairy tale from the streets below. The open-air **Lykavittos Theatre** is used for concerts in summer.

The main path to the summit starts at the top of Loukianou, or you can take the **funicular railway** (Map pp354-5; admission €5.50; 🕒 9.15am-11.45pm) from the top of Ploutarhou.

National Gardens

A delightful, shady refuge during summer, the **National Gardens** (Map p358; entrances on Leoforos Vasilissis Sofias & Leoforos Vasilissis Amalias, Syntagma; 🕒 7am-dusk; Ⓜ Syntagma) contain a large children's **playground**, a duck pond and a relaxing cafe.

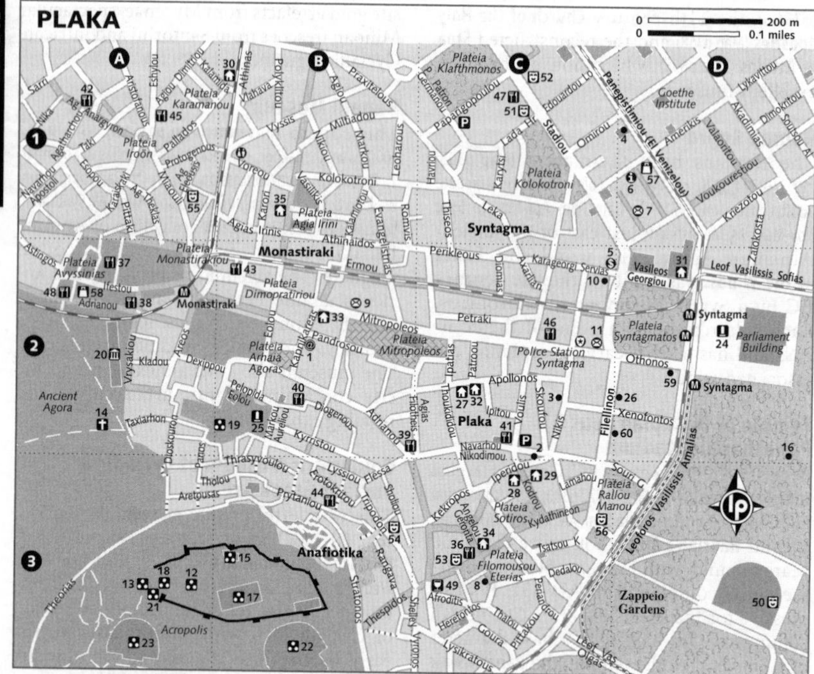

Changing of the Guard

The traditionally costumed *evzones* (guards) guarding the **Tomb of the Unknown Soldier** (Map p358), in front of the parliament building on Syntagma Sq, change every hour on the hour. On Sunday at 11am, a whole platoon marches down Vasilissis Sofias to the tomb, accompanied by a band.

TOURS

Trekking Hellas (Map p358; ☎ 210 331 0323; www.outdoorsgreece.com; Filellinon 7, Plaka; Ⓜ Syntagma) runs activities ranging from Athens walking tours (€40) to bungee jumping in the Corinth Canal (€60).

FESTIVALS & EVENTS

The annual **Hellenic Festival** (www.greekfestival.gr; ☎ 210 928 2900), the city's most important cultural event, runs from mid-June to August. International music, dance and theatre go on at venues across the city and in the ancient theatre in Epidavros (see p369). Check the program and book tickets online, by phone (☎ bookings 210 327 2000), or at the **festival box office** (Map pp354-5; Panepistimiou 39; Ⓜ Omonia).

SLEEPING

Athenians go out late and like to party, so most of these sleeping options are close to the action but quiet. Popular Plaka is close to the sights. Book well ahead for July and August. Most hotels give good discounts in the low season, for longer stays and on the internet.

Monastiraki & Syntagma

Tempi Hotel (Map p358; ☎ 210 321 3175; www.tempihotel.gr; Eolou 29, Monastiraki;, s/d with shared bathroom €43/57, d/tr with private bathroom €64/78; Ⓜ Monastiraki) No-frills rooms may be tiny, but some have balconies overlooking Plateia Agia Irini. A communal kitchen and nearby markets make it ideal for self-caterers.

Hotel Cecil (Map p358; ☎ 210 321 7079; www.cecil.gr; Athinas 39, Monastiraki, s/d incl breakfast €70/99; Ⓜ Monastiraki; ❄) Aromatic spices waft into the lobby from nearby Asian markets, but double-pane windows keep the high-ceilinged rooms in this old classical building cosy and quiet. Close to the Psyrri nightlife and sights.

Plaka Hotel (Map p358; ☎ 210 322 2096; www.plakahotel.gr; Kapnikareas 7 & Mitropoleos, Monastiraki; s/d/tr €120/145/165; Ⓜ Monastiraki; ❄ 💻) Folks come

INFORMATION	
Bits & Bytes Internet Café	1 B2
Compendium Books	2 C2
Eleftheroudakis Books	3 C2
Eleftheroudakis Books	4 D1
Eurochange	5 C2
Greek National Tourist Organisation/EOT	6 D1
Parcel Post Office	7 D1
Plaka Laundrette	8 C3
Post Office	9 B2
Public	10 C2
Syntagma Post Office	11 C2
SIGHTS & ACTIVITIES	
Acropolis	12 A3
Beule Gate	13 A3
Church of the Holy Apostles	14 A2
Erechtheion	15 B3
National Gardens	16 D2
Parthenon	17 B3
Propylaea	18 A3
Roman Agora	19 B2
Stoa of Attalos	20 A2
Temple of Athena Nike	21 A3
Theatre of Dionysos	22 B3
Theatre of Herodes Atticus	23 A3
Tomb of the Unknown Soldier (Changing of the Guard)	24 D2
Tower of the Winds	25 B2
Trekking Hellas	26 D2
SLEEPING	
Central Athens Hotel	27 C2
Hotel Acropolis House	28 C3
Hotel Adonis	29 C3
Hotel Cecil	30 B1
Hotel Grande Bretagne	31 D2
Hotel Hermes	32 C2
Plaka Hotel	33 B2
Student & Travellers' Inn	34 C3
Tempi Hotel	35 B1
EATING	
Byzantino	36 C3
Café Avyssinia	37 A2
Dioskouri	38 A2
Eat	39 B2
O Platanos	40 B2
Paradosiako	41 C2
Pica Pica	42 A1
Savas	43 B2
Taverna tou Psara	44 B3
Taverna tou Psiri	45 A1
Tzitzikas & Mermingas	46 C2
Vasilopoulou	47 C1
Viasos	48 A2
DRINKING	
Brettos	49 C3
ENTERTAINMENT	
Aigli	50 D3
Apollon	51 C1
Astor	52 C1
Cine Paris	53 C3
Dora Stratou Dance Company	54 B3
Envy	55 A1
Lava Bore	56 C3
SHOPPING	
Attica Department Store	57 D1
Monastiraki Flea Market	58 A2
TRANSPORT	
Aegean Airlines	59 D2
Olympic Airlines	60 D2

here not for the tidy, bland rooms but for the excellent Acropolis views from the rooftop garden and top-floor digs. Spacious elevator.

Hotel Grande Bretagne (Map p358; ☎ 210 333 0000; www.grandebretagne.gr; Vasileos Georgiou 1, Syntagma; r/ste from €345/480; M Syntagma;) Dripping with elegance and old-world charm, *the* place to stay in Athens has always has been the deluxe Hotel Grande Bretagne. Built in 1862 to accommodate visiting heads of state, it ranks among the great hotels of the world. From the decadent, chandeliered lobby, to the exquisite guest rooms, divine spa and rooftop restaurant, this place is built for pampering.

Plaka, Koukaki & Makrigianni

Athens Backpackers (Map pp354-5; ☎ 210 922 4044; www.backpackers.gr; Makri 12, Makrigianni; dm €25, 2-/4-person studio with kitchen €80/120; M Akropoli;) This excellent, popular hostel boasts a rooftop party bar with Acropolis views, cafe, kitchen, daily movies, and the friendly Aussie management hosts (free!) barbecues. Breakfast and nonalcoholic drinks are included, and long-term storage, laundry, airport pick-up and tours are available. There's a three-day minimum stay.

Student & Travellers' Inn (Map p358; ☎ 210 324 4808; www.studenttravellersinn.com; Kydathineon 16, Plaka; dm €26, 4-person dm/d with shared bathroom €26/68, 4-person dm/d with private bathroom €28/73; M Akropoli;) Travellers like to chill in the courtyard of this well-situated hostel. Rooms may be spartan and housekeeping a bit lean, but extras (laundry, left luggage, travel service and tours) make up for this.

Marble House Pension (Map pp354-5; ☎ 210 922 8294; www.marblehouse.gr; Zini 35, Koukaki; d/tr with shared bathroom €46/52; s/d/tr with private bathroom €46/52/59; M Syngrou-Fix;) This long-standing Athens favourite lies on a quiet cul-de-sac 10 minutes' walk from Plaka. Step through the garden pergola to quiet, spotless rooms with fridges, ceiling fans and safety boxes. For air-con add €9.

Hotel Acropolis House (Map p358; ☎ 210 322 2344; hotel@acropolishouse.gr; Kodrou 6-8, Plaka; d with shared bathroom €65, s/d/tr with private bathroom & incl breakfast from €50/78/113; M Syntagma;) This well-situated hotel in a 19th-century house feels more pension than hotel, with a comfy sitting room and hospitable management. Guests chat amicably over breakfast.

Hotel Adonis (Map p358; ☎ 210 324 9737; www.hotel-adonis.gr; Kodrou 3, Plaka; s/d/tr incl breakfast from €66/92/120; M Syntagma;) Stroll up the peaceful, pedestrianised street to this immaculate wee hotel. Guests return for the friendly welcome, great location and super Acropolis views from the roof garden.

our pick **Central Athens Hotel** (Map p358; ☎ 210 323 4357; www.centralhotel.gr; Apollonos 21, Plaka; s/d incl breakfast from €99/121; M Syntagma;) Pass through the sleek, modern lobby and by the attentive staff to spacious white rooms hung with original art and decked out with all the mod cons.

SPLURGE

Competition is fierce for the honorary title of Athens' best restaurant. The two front-runners at the time of writing are:

Varoulko (Map pp354-5; ☎ 210 522 8400; www.varoulko.gr; Pireos 80, Gazi; mains €22-30; closed Sun; M Keramikos) For a magical Greek dining experience, you can't beat the winning combination of Acropolis views and delicious seafood by celebrated Greek chef Lefteris Lazarou. This Michelin-starred seafood restaurant remains popular with Athenian celebrities and food tourists who sup on sublime crayfish dolmas wrapped in sorrel leaves, squid-ink soup and smoked swordfish, all served up on simple minimalist white linen in an airy glass-fronted dining room.

Spondi (Map pp354-5; ☎ 210 756 4021; www.spondi.gr; Pyrronos 5, Pangrati; mains €36-50; 8pm-midnight) Dining in this superb restaurant's gorgeous vaulted cellar or in its bougainvillea-draped courtyard in summer is quite an understatedly elegant affair. Chef Arnaud Bignon has won two Michelin stars creating extravagant seasonal menus using local ingredients. The world-class haute cuisine stays true to French technique but embodies vibrant Greek flavours.

Some balconies have Acropolis views as does the rooftop where you can sunbake and relax in the Jacuzzi.

Hotel Hermes (Map p358; ☎ 210 323 5514; www.hermeshotel.gr; Apollonos 19, Plaka; s/d/tr incl breakfast €120/145/165; M Syntagma;) Next to the Central, with similar amenities, but not quite as swishy.

Hera Hotel (Map pp354-5; ☎ 210 923 6682; www.herahotel.gr; Falirou 9, Makrigianni; s/d incl breakfast €135/155; M Akropoli;) The interior of this exquisite boutique hotel matches its lovely neoclassical facade. The rooftop garden, restaurant and bar boast spectacular views and it is a short walk to the Acropolis and Plaka.

Gazi

Eridanus (Map pp354-5; ☎ 210 520 5360; www.eridanus.gr; Pireos 78, Gazi; d incl breakfast from €185; M Keramikos;) After a late night partying in Gazi or nearby Psyrri, soak in your marble bathtub and lounge around in the fluffy white robe. Helpful staff cater to your every whim, and the rooftop garden has Acropolis views.

Kolonaki

Periscope (Map pp354-5; ☎ 210 729 7200; www.periscope.gr; Haritos 22, Kolonaki; r from €160; M Evangelismos;) A hip hotel with a cool, edgy look (and Mini Cooper seats for chairs in the ground floor cafe-bar), this place has comfortable minimalist rooms with all the mod cons and a quiet location in chic Kolonaki.

EATING

In addition to the mainstay tavernas, Athens has developed a flock of bistros, swank eateries, and high-end *mezedes* bars. Many popular top restaurants lie outside the heavily touristed neighbourhoods but are worth the walk or cab ride. Wear your most stylish togs at night, as Athenians dress up to eat out.

Monastiraki & Syntagma

Savas (Map p358; Mitropoleos 86-88, Monastiraki; gyros €2; M Monastiraki) This joint serves enormous grilled-meat plates (€8.50) and the tastiest gyros (pork, beef or chicken) in Athens. Take away or sit down in what becomes one of the city's busiest eat streets late at night.

Tzitzikas & Mermingas (Map p358; ☎ 210 324 7607; Mitropoleos 12-14, Syntagma; mezedes €6-8; M Syntagma) Greek merchandise lines the walls of this cheery, modern *mezedhopoleio.* The great range of delicious and creative *mezedes* draws a bustling local crowd.

Café Avyssinia (Map p358; ☎ 210 321 7407; Kynetou 7, Monastiraki; mains €8.50-14.50; M Monastiraki) Hidden away on the edge of grungy Plateia Avyssinias in the middle of the Flea Market, this *mezedhopoleio* gets top marks for atmosphere and the food is not far behind. Often has live music on weekends.

Also recommended in Monastiraki: **Viasos** (Map p358; Adrianou 19) and **Dioskouri** (Map p358; Adrianou 37). Young local crowds chat over juicy gyros (€2) and generous *mezedes* (€7 to €12) on one of Athens' most atmospheric pedestrian streets.

Plaka

Byzantino (Map p358; ☎ 210 322 7368; Kydathineon 18; mains €6-16; M Syntagma) If you must eat in the heart of Plaka, this is one of the better choices for hearty traditional cuisine and veg options in a pleasant shady spot that's great for people-watching.

O Platanos (Map p358; ☎ 210 322 0666; Diogenous 4; mains €7-9; Ⓜ Monastiraki) Laid-back O Platanos (Plane Tree) serves tasty, home-cooked-style Greek cuisine. The lamb dishes are delicious and we love the leafy courtyard.

Paradosiako (Map p358; ☎ 210 321 4121; Voulis 44a; mains €7-14; Ⓜ Syntagma) For great traditional fare you can't beat this inconspicuous, no-frills taverna on the periphery of Plaka. Choose from daily specials like delicious shrimp *saganaki*.

Eat (Map p358; ☎ 210 324 9129; Adrianou 91; mains €8-17; Ⓜ Syntagma) A sleek alternative to the endless traditional tavernas, Eat serves interesting salads and pastas and modern interpretations of Greek classics like shrimp dolmas with sun-dried tomatoes (€9).

Taverna tou Psarra (Map p358; ☎ 210 321 8734; Eretheos 16; mains €8-23; Ⓜ Monastiraki) On a path leading up towards the Acropolis, this gem of a taverna is one of Plaka's best, serving scrumptious *mezedes* and excellent fish and meat classics on a tree-lined terrace.

Psyrri & Gazi

Pica Pica (Map p358; ☎ 210 325 1663; Ag Anargyron 8, Psyrri; mains €4-11; Ⓜ Monastiraki) Head to this hip, beautiful hang-out for tasty, authentic Spanish tapas, including *gambas* (prawns), *pulpo* (octopus) and the like. Sip sangria and listen to the funky, ambient music as the party crowds swirl through Psyrri.

Taverna tou Psiri (Map p358; ☎ 210 321 4923; Eshylou 12, Psyrri; mains €6-11; Ⓜ Monastiraki) This atmospheric taverna is popular with locals who come for the daily specials menu. It's tucked away off Plateia Iroon; look for the apt mural of a drunk leaning against a lamppost.

Sardelles (off Map pp354-5; ☎ 210 347 8050; Persefonis 15, Gazi; fish mains €9.50-15; Ⓜ Keramikos) As the name (sardines) suggests and the novel fishmonger paper tablecloths confirm, this modern fish taverna specialises in seafood *mezedes*. It's a friendly place with tables outside, opposite the illuminated gasworks.

Kolonaki & Nea Smyrni

Oikeio (Map pp354-5; ☎ 210 725 9216; Ploutarhou 15, Kolonaki; Ⓜ Evangelismos; mains €8-11) With excellent home-style cooking, this modern taverna lives up to its name (homey). The intimate bistro atmosphere spills out to tables on the pavement for glitterati-watching without the normal high Kolonaki bill. Reservations recommended.

our pick **Entryfish** (Map pp354-5; ☎ 210 361 7666; Skoufa 52, Kolonaki; mezedes €11-20; Ⓜ Syntagma) Brush shoulders with CEOs at this packed, new, swank seafood salon. Funky newsprint and art glass line the walls, and the *mezedes* all have exquisitely delicate flavours. Reservations recommended.

Amalour (off Map pp354-5; ☎ 210 933 7710; N Plastira Nikolau 45 cnr Filadelfeias St, Nea Smyrni; mains €11-24) In a beautiful restored mansion in a residential neighbourhood, the warmly modern upstairs dining area serves up delicious Mediterranean cuisine. Crowds migrate downstairs to the rococo bar for drinks afterward.

Self-Catering

You'll find the best selection of fresh produce at the **fruit and vegetable market** (Map pp354–5) on Athinas, opposite the **meat market** (Map pp354–5). Decent supermarkets in central Athens include **Marinopoulos** (Map pp354-5; Athinas 60, Omonia) and **Vasilopoulou** (Map p358; Stadiou 19, Syntagma). They are closed Sunday.

DRINKING

Athenians know how to party. Everyone has their favourite *steki* (hang-out), but expect people to show up after midnight. To be around locals, head to Psyrri (around Agatharchou St), Gazi (around Voutadon St and the Keramikos metro station) and Kolonaki (around Ploutarhou and Haritos Sts or Skoufa and Omirou Sts) and explore! In summer most of the action heads to Piraeus, Glyfada and the islands.

Bars & Pubs

our pick **Hoxton** (off Map pp354-5; ☎ 210 341 3395; Voutadon 42, Gazi; Ⓜ Keramikos) Kick back on overstuffed leather couches under modern art in this industrial space that fills up late with bohemians, ruggers and the occasional pop star.

Mai-Tai (Map pp354-5; Ploutarhou 18, Kolonaki; Ⓜ Evangelismos) Jam-packed with well-healed young Athenians, this is just one in a group of happening spots in the middle of Kolonaki.

Brettos (Map p358; ☎ 210 323 2110; Kydathineon 41, Plaka; Ⓜ Syntagma) This distillery, bottle shop and bar is back-lit by an eye-catching collection of coloured bottles.

Wonderbar (Map pp354-5; ☎ 210 381 8577; Themistokleous 80, Exarhia; Ⓜ Omonia) Relaxed by day, packed by night, this lounge bar attracts hip young Athenians who come for some of Athens' best DJs.

Cafes

Athens' cafes have some of the highest prices for coffee in Europe, yet if you do what the locals do and sit on a frappé for hours, you can laze the day away. Kolonaki has a mind-boggling array of cafes off Plateia Kolonakiou, on Skoufa and Tsakalof Sts.

ENTERTAINMENT

The *Kathimerini* supplement inside the *International Herald Tribune* contains daily event listings and a cinema guide.

Nightclubs

Athenians go clubbing after midnight and dress up. Head to beachfront venues in summer.

Envy (Map p358; ☎ 210 331 7801; Agias Eleousis & Kakourgodikiou, Psyrri; admission varies; ⏲ Wed-Sat) The name changes at this popular club that plays the latest dance music in Psyrri during winter and moves to ever-changing beachside spots in summer.

Decadence (Map pp354-5; ☎ 210 882 3544; cnr Pouliherias & Voulgaroktonou 69, Lofos Strefi; admission €6-8) For indie and alternative music lovers, a quieter bar scene occupies the lower floor and a club the upper.

Lava Bore (Map p358; ☎ 210 324 5335; Filellinon 25, Plaka; admission varies) A popular place for tourists, it stays open year-round.

Akrotiri (off Map pp354-5; ☎ 210 985 9147; Vasileos Georgiou B 5, Agios Kosmas; admission €10; ⏲ 10pm-5am) This massive beach club has a capacity for 3000, bars and lounges over different levels, and hosts great party nights with top DJs.

Live Music

In summer, concerts are often held in plazas and parks; some clubs shut down.

POP, ROCK & JAZZ

Get tickets for concerts at **Ticket House** (Map pp354-5; ☎ 210 360 8366; Panepistimiou 42). Popular venues:

our pick Half Note Jazz Club (Map pp354-5; ☎ 210 921 3310; Trivonianou 17, Mets) Jazz buffs won't be disappointed – this dark, smoky club is the main venue for serious jazz.

Gagarin 205 Club (off Map pp354-5; ☎ 210 854 7601; Liossion 205) The city's coolest space attracts the most interesting international and local acts.

Rodon Club (Map pp354-5; ☎ 210 524 7427; Marni 24, Omonia) You'll either love or hate this grungy club – the city's main venue for rock and metal – but die-hard fans swear by it.

REMBETIKA

Traditional *rembetika* is hard to catch during the summer months when most of the authentic venues close, but you can see a popularised version at some tavernas in Psyrri.

Rembetika Stoa Athanaton (Map pp354-5; ☎ 210 321 4362; Sofokleous 19; ⏲ 3.30-6pm & midnight-late Mon-Sat Oct-May) Located above the meat market, this is still *the* place to listen to *rembetika*.

Classical Music, Opera & Dance

In summer the excellent Hellenic Festival (p358) swings into action.

Dora Stratou Dance Company (Map p358; ☎ 210 921 4650; www.grdance.org; Filopappou Hill; tickets €15; ⏲ 9.30pm Tue-Sat, 8.15pm Sun May-Sep) Traditional folk-dancing shows feature more than 75 musicians and dancers in an open-air amphitheatre.

Megaron Mousikis (Athens Concert Hall; Map pp354-5; ☎ 210 728 2333; www.megaron.gr; cnr Leof Vasilissis Sofias & Kokkali) This superb concert venue hosts winter performances by local and international artists.

Olympia Theatre (Map pp354-5; ☎ 210 361 2461; www.nationalopera.gr; Akadimias 59, Exarhia) The Greek National Opera season of classical opera, ballet and orchestral concerts runs from November to June.

Cinemas

Most cinemas show recent releases in English and cost around €8. Two of the major movie houses in central Athens are **Apollon** (Map p358; ☎ 210 323 6811; Stadiou 19) and **Astor** (Map p358; ☎ 210 323 1297; Stadiou 28).

In summer take your movie going outdoors. The most historic open-air cinema is the refurbished **Aigli** (Map p358; ☎ 210 336 9369) in the verdant Zappeio Gardens, or try to nab a seat with Acropolis views (seats on the right) on the rooftop of Plaka's **Cine Paris** (Map p358; ☎ 210 322 0721; Kydathineon 22).

Gay & Lesbian Venues

The greatest number of gay bars cluster in Makrigianni, south of the Temple of Olympian Zeus, Exarhia, Psyrri and Gazi. Check out www.gay.gr or a copy of the *Greek Gay Guide* booklet at *periptera* (street kiosks).

Lamda Club (Map pp354-5; ☎ 210 942 4202; Lembesi 15, Makrigianni) Athens' best gay dance club gets crowded late.

Sodade (Map pp354-5; ☎ 210 346 8657; Triptolemou 10, Gazi) Attracts a younger crowd.

Alekos' Island (Map pp354-5; Sarri 41, Psyrri) This long-standing gay bar is popular with a mellow older crowd.

Kirkis (Map pp354-5; ☎ 210 346 6960; Apostolou Pavlou 31, Thisio) Head to this hip gay and lesbian hangout to find out what's hot in Athens when you're visiting.

SHOPPING

Athens is the place to shop for cool jewellery, chic clothes and shoes, as well as souvenirs such as backgammon sets, hand-woven textiles, olive oil skin products, worry beads and colourful ceramics. You'll find boutiques on Ermou; designer brands and cool shops in Kolonaki; and souvenirs, folk art and leather in Plaka and Monastiraki.

Attica department store (Map p358; ☎ 211 180 2600; Panepistimiou 9) This store is home to several floors of funky fashion sourced from around the globe, including Greek designers, along with accessories, cosmetics and travel goods.

Metropolis Music (Map pp354-5; ☎ 210 383 0804; Panepistimiou 64, Omonia) This store is a music haven; it's well-stocked with Greek and international CDs.

The enthralling **Monastiraki flea market** (Map p358) starts at Plateia Monastirakiou. On weekends, visit the jam-packed **Sunday market** (Map pp354-5; 🕑 7am-2pm) at the end of Ermou, towards Gazi.

GETTING THERE & AWAY

Air

Athens is serviced by **Eleftherios Venizelos International airport** (ATH; ☎ 210 353 0000; www.aia.gr) at Spata, 27km east of Athens. Facilities are excellent, with a 24-hour information desk, a good selection of reasonably priced cafes and decent duty-free shopping. For phone numbers for international airlines in Athens, see p422.

The majority of domestic flights are handled by Greece's much-maligned national carrier, **Olympic Airlines** (OA; Map p358; ☎ 210 926 4444; www.olympicairlines.com; Filellinon 15, Syntagma). Crete-based **Aegean Airlines** (A3; Map p358; ☎ 210 626 1000; www.aegeanair.com; Othonos 10, Syntagma) offers flights to many of the same destinations. Several European budget carriers, such as **easyJet** (☎ 210 353 0300), **Blue 1** (☎ 210 353 0373), **SkyEurope** (☎ +421 233 017 301) and **clickair** (☎ 210 353 7600) serve Athens.

Bus

Athens has two main intercity **KTEL** (www.ktel.org) bus stations, one 5km, and one 7km to the north of Omonia. Timetables are available at EOT offices (see p353).

Kifissos Terminal A (off Map pp354-5; ☎ 210 512 4910; Kifissou 100) has buses running to the Peloponnese, Igoumenitsa, Ionian Islands, Florina, Ioannina, Kastoria, Edessa and Thessaloniki, among other destinations. Taxis from Syntagma cost about €6.

Liossion Terminal B (off Map pp354-5; ☎ 210 831 7153; Liossion 260) has departures to Trikala (for Meteora), Delphi, Larissa, Thiva, Volos and other destinations. To get here take bus 024 from outside the main gate of the National Gardens on Amalias. Get off the bus at Liossion 260, turn right onto Gousiou and you'll see the terminal.

Buses for destinations in southern Attica leave from the **Mavromateon terminal** (Map pp354-5; ☎ 210 880 8000; Alexandras & 28 Oktovriou-Patision, Pedion Areos), about 250m north of the National Archaeological Museum.

Car & Motorcycle

Syngrou Rd, south of the Temple of Olympian Zeus, is packed solid with car-hire firms. National Rd 1 is the main route north from Athens, starting at Nea Kifissia: take Vasilissis Sofias from Syntagma and follow the signs. National Rd 8, which begins beyond Dafni, is the road to take for the Peloponnese: take Agiou Konstantinou from Omonia.

Ferry

See p424 for information on ferries travelling to and from the islands.

Train

Intercity trains to central and northern Greece depart from the central **Larisis train station** (Map pp354–5), about 1km northwest of Omonia Sq (metro Line 2).

For information or bookings, call or visit an **OSE office** (Omonia Map pp354-5; ☎ 210 524 0647; Karolou 1; 🕑 8am-3pm Mon-Fri; Syntagma Map pp354-5; ☎ 210 362 4402; Sina 6; 🕑 8am-3.30pm Mon-Fri, 8am-3pm Sat).

For the Peloponnese, take the suburban rail (www.isap.gr) to Kiato and change for other OSE services there, or check for available lines at the Larisis station. A new rail hub is going to be located about 20km north of the city.

For international trains, see p423.

GETTING AROUND

The metro system makes getting around central Athens and to Piraeus easy, but Athens' road traffic is still horrendous. A 24-hour travel pass (€3) is valid for all forms of public transport, and at the time of writing a new integrated ticket (€0.80) good for 1½ hours was due to be introduced.

To/From the Airport

The 24-hour airport information desks are loaded with transport information.

BUS

Bus X93 operates between the airport and the Terminal A (Kifissos) Bus Station (35 minutes, every 30 minutes).

Bus X94 operates between the airport and metro Line 3 at Ethniki Amyna (25 minutes, every 10 minutes, 7.30am to 11.30pm).

Bus X95 operates between the airport and Syntagma Sq (60 to 90 minutes, every 30 minutes, 24 hours). The Syntagma stop is on Othonos St.

Bus X96 operates between the airport and Plateia Karaiskaki in Piraeus (60 to 90 minutes, every 20 minutes, 24 hours).

Tickets for all these services cost €3.20.

METRO

Line 3 of the metro links the airport to the city centre in around 30 minutes; it operates from Monastiraki from 5.50am to 10.50pm, and from the airport from 6.30am to 11.30pm. Tickets cost €6 and are valid for all forms of public transport for 90 minutes. At the time of research there was construction underway on this metro line and service terminated at the Ethniki Amyna station, before reaching the airport.

TAXI

Taxi fares vary according to the time of day and level of traffic, but you should expect to pay from €25 to €30 to get from the airport to the city centre, and €30 from the airport to Piraeus, depending on traffic conditions. Both trips can take up to an hour.

Public Transport

BUS & TROLLEYBUS

Blue-and-white suburban buses and yellow trolleybuses operate every 15 minutes from 5am to midnight. Route numbers and destinations are listed on the free EOT map. Get timetables at EOT tourist offices or the **Athens Urban Transport Organisation** (OASA; ☎ 210 883 6076; www.oasa.gr).

Special buses to Piraeus operate 24 hours, running every 20 minutes from 6am to midnight, and then hourly until 6am. Bus 040 leaves from the corner of Syntagma and Filellinon, and bus 049 leaves from the Omonia end of Athinas.

Tickets for all services cost €0.50 and must be purchased before boarding from a ticket booth or a *periptera*. The same tickets can be used on either buses or trolleybuses and must be validated as you board.

METRO

The metro operates from 5am to midnight. Trains run every three minutes during peak periods and every 10 minutes at other times. For metro timetables visit www.ametro.gr. Travel within one section costs €0.70 and a journey covering two or more sections costs €0.80. Tickets must be validated before travelling.

Taxi

Athenian taxis are yellow and hard to hail. The flag fall is €1 with an additional surcharge of €1 from ports and train and bus stations, and a €3.20 surcharge from the airport. After that, the day rate (tariff 1 on the meter) is €0.30 per kilometre. The rate doubles between midnight and 5am (tariff 2 on the meter). Baggage is charged at the rate of €0.30 per item over 10kg. The minimum fare is €3. Booking a radio taxi costs €2.50 extra.

Train

A fast **suburban rail** (☎ 1110; www.proastiakos.gr; 🕐 24hr) connects Athens with the airport, Piraeus, the outer regions and the Peloponnese. It connects to the metro at Larisis and Doukissis Plakentias stations and spans from the airport to Kiato (1¾ hours, €10).

AROUND ATHENS

PIRAEUS ΠΕΙΡΑΙΑΣ

pop 175,700

The highlights of Greece's main port and ferry hub, Piraeus, are the otherworldly rows of ferries, ships and hydrofoils filling its seemingly endless quays. It takes around 25 minutes to get here from the centre of Athens by metro (avoid taking a bus or taxi – the streets are even more clogged than they are in Athens), so there's no reason to stay in shabby Piraeus. However, a trip to tranquil Mikrolimano (Small Harbour), with its cafes and fish restaurants, reveals a gentler Piraeus.

Orientation & Information

Piraeus consists of a peninsula surrounded by harbours. The largest of its three harbours is the Megas Limin (Great Harbour) on the western side, from where all the ferries leave, along with hydrofoils and catamarans to the Saronic Gulf and the Cyclades. Zea Marina (Limin Zeas) and Mikrolimano, on the eastern side of the peninsula, are for private yachts. Check email at **Internet Center** (Akti Poseidonos 24; per hr €3.50; 10am-11pm) on the main road, across from the main harbour.

Eating

If you're killing time in Piraeus, take Trolleybus 20 to Mikrolimano for a good harbourfront seafood feed. One among many cafes

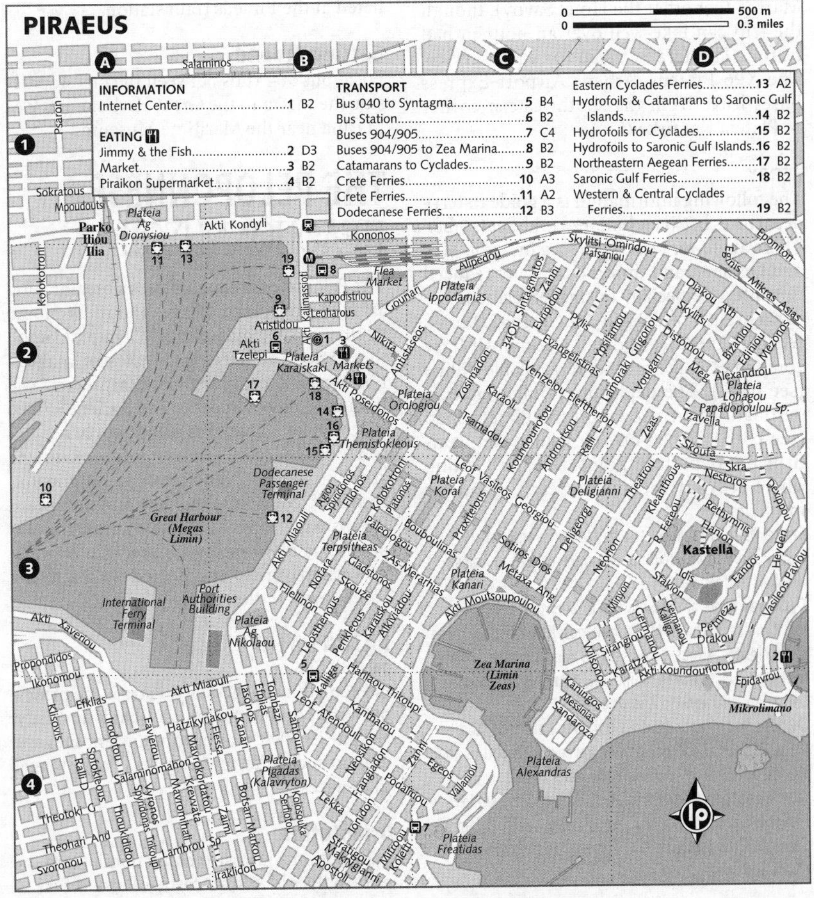

and restaurants, **Jimmy & the Fish** (☎ 210 412 4417; Koumoundourou 46; mains €16; ⏰ 1pm-1am) serves up excellent seafood in stylish surrounds.

Stock up on supplies before a ferry trip at the general **market** (⏰ 6am-4pm Mon-Fri) on Dimosthenous or **Piraikon Supermarket** (☎ 210 417 5764; Ippokratous 1; ⏰ 8am-8pm Mon-Fri, to 4pm Sat).

Getting There & Away

BUS

Two 24-hour bus services operate between central Athens and Piraeus. Bus 049 runs from Omonia to the bus station at the Great Harbour, and bus 040 runs from Syntagma to the Great Harbour bus station and the tip of the Piraeus peninsula. Bus 040 is the service to catch from Athens for Zea Marina (get off at the Hotel Savoy), though the trip can take well over an hour in bad traffic. The fare is €0.50 for each service. The X96 Piraeus–Athens Airport Express buses leave from the southwestern corner of Plateia Karaïskaki.

FERRY

The following information is a guide to ferry departures between June and mid-September. There are fewer ferries running in April, May and October, and they are radically reduced in winter – especially to smaller islands. The main branch of EOT in Athens (p353) has a reliable schedule, updated weekly. All ferry companies make timetables available online (see p424). The departure points for ferry destinations are shown on the Piraeus map (see p365). When buying your ticket, confirm the departure point. See the Getting There & Away sections for each island for more details.

Crete There are two boats a day to Hania and Iraklio, a daily service to Rethymno, and three a week to Agios Nikolaos and Sitia.

Cyclades There are daily ferries to Amorgos, Folegandros, Ios, Kimolos, Kythnos, Milos, Mykonos, Naxos, Paros, Santorini, Serifos, Sifnos, Sikinos, Syros and Tinos; two or three ferries a week to Iraklia, Shinoussa, Koufonisi, Donoussa and Anafi; and none to Andros or Kea.

Dodecanese There are daily ferries to Kalymnos, Kos, Leros, Patmos and Rhodes; three a week to Karpathos and Kassos; and weekly services to the other islands.

Northeastern Aegean Islands Daily ferries to Chios, Lesvos (Mytilini), Ikaria and Samos; twice weekly to Limnos.

Saronic Gulf Islands Daily ferries head to Aegina, Poros, Hydra and Spetses year-round.

HYDROFOIL & CATAMARAN

Hellenic Seaways (www.hellenicseaways.gr) operates high-speed hydrofoils and catamarans to the Cyclades from early April to the end of October, and year-round services to the Saronic Gulf Islands.

METRO

The fastest and most convenient link between the Great Harbour and Athens is the metro (€0.80, 25 minutes). The station is close to the ferries, at the northern end of Akti Kalimassioti. Trains run every 10 minutes from 5am to midnight.

TRAIN

At the time of research, all services to the Peloponnese from Athens started and terminated at the Piraeus train station.

Getting Around

Local bus 904 runs between the bus stop beside the metro to the Great Harbour and Zea Marina near the Maritime Museum.

THE PELOPONNESE ΠΕΛΟΠΟΝΝΗΣΟΣ

The Peloponnese encompasses a breathtaking array of landscapes, villages and ruins. Home to Olympia, birthplace of the Olympic Games; the ancient archaeological sites of magical Epidavros, Mycenae and Corinth; the fairy-tale Byzantine city of Mystras; and ancient Sparta, much Greek history has played out here.

Two of Greece's most gorgeous towns grace its shores – Venetian-style Nafplio and romantic Monemvasia. The isolated Mani Peninsula, known for its wild landscape and people, is blanketed with spectacular wildflowers in spring and dotted with striking stone tower settlements.

PATRA ΠΑΤΡΑ

pop 185,700

Greece's third-largest city, Patra is the principal ferry port for the Ionian Islands and Italy. Despite its 3000-year history, ancient sites and vibrant social life, few travellers linger longer than necessary.

Orientation

Laid out on a grid stretching uphill from the port to the old *kastro* (castle), Patra is easy to negotiate. The tourist office, ports, train and bus stations, and other services for travellers, are all along the waterfront on Othonos Amalias, in the centre of town, and within easy walking distance of each other.

Information

Cyberia (☎ 26012 79790; Gerokostopoulou 5; per hr €2.40; 🕑 24hr) Near corner of Andreou.
Main post office (☎ 26106 20644; cnr Zaimi 23 & Mezonos; 🕑 7.30am-8pm Mon-Fri, 7.30am-2pm Sat, 9am-1.30pm Sun)
Tourist office (☎ 26104 61741; www.infocenterpatras.gr; Othonos Amalias 6; 🕑 8am-10pm) The friendly multilingual staff easily run the best tourist office in Greece, with plentiful information on transport and free stuff to do in town, free bicycles and internet access. Kiosk in central Plateia Trion Symahon (🕑 9am-4pm).
Tourist police (☎ 26104 55833; Gounari 52; 🕑 7am-9pm)

Sights

The Byzantine **kastro** (🕑 8.30am-3pm Tue-Sun), built by the Emperor Justinian, has excellent views to the Ionian Islands. Patra's **museum** (☎ 26102 76207; Mezonos 42; 🕑 8.30am-3pm Tue-Sun) has a small archaeological collection from the Mycenaean, Hellenic and Roman eras. The impressive **Roman Odeon** (cnr Germanou & Sotiriadou; 🕑 8.30am-3pm Tue-Sun) is a magical spot to see a performance.

Sleeping

Pension Nicos (☎ 26106 23757; cnr Patreos 3 & Agiou Andreou 121; s/d with shared bathroom €23/33, s/d/tr with private bathroom €28/38/45) Marble stairs lead to spotlessly clean rooms smack in the city centre.

Primarolia Art Hotel (☎ 2610 624 900; www.arthotel.gr; Othonos Amalias 33; s/d incl breakfast €135/150; ❄ 🖳) This stylish place oozes individuality, with sleeping spaces ranging from the bold, contemporary and minimalist to the florid, romantic and baroque.

Eating & Drinking

Scores of stylish cafes and fast-food eateries lie between Kolokotroni and Ermou, while drinking hot spots cluster on Agios Nikolaos and Radinou (off Riga Fereou). Pedestrianised Trion Navarhon is lined with tavernas.

Mythos (☎ 26103 29984; cnr Trion Navarhon 181 & Riga; mains €6-9; 🕑 7pm-late) Friendly waiters serve excellent home-cooked Greek classics in a chandelier-strewn town house.

Kitchen of Kornelia (☎ 26102 72987; Plateia Kapodistrio 4; mains €8-14; 🕑 1.30pm-midnight Tue-Sat, to 5pm Sun) Dig in to Turkish braised beef with aubergine puree (€14) and other delicate specialities in this cool bistro tucked in the corner of a quiet square.

Provision for your journey at **Dia Discount Supermarket** (Agiou Andreou 29; 🕑 closed Sun).

Getting There & Away

From **Patra train station** (☎ 26106 39108; Othonos Amalias 27) there are seven trains a day to Athens via Corinth, terminating at Piraeus or the airport. Four are InterCity express trains (€12, 3½ hours), while three are slow trains (€8.80, four to seven hours). Between four and eight trains run south daily to Pyrgos (for Olympia, €6, two hours) and Kalamata (€9.70, five hours).

The **KTEL Achaia bus station** (☎ 26106 23886; cnr Zaimi 2 & Othonos Amalias) has regular services to Athens (€16.20, three hours, half-hourly) via Corinth, and serves Ioannina (€19.70, 4½ hours, two daily), Thessaloniki (€37.80, 10 hours, four daily), Pyrgos (for Olympia, €8.40, two hours, nine to 10 daily) and Kalamata (€19.30, four hours, two daily). Buses to the Ionian Islands, via the port of Kyllini, leave from the **KTEL Lefkada & Zakynthos bus station** (☎ 26102 20993/22224; Othonos Amalias 47) or nearby **KTEL Kefallonia bus station** (☎ 26102 74938; Othonos Amalias 58).

Ionian Ferries (☎ 2103 249 997) depart for Zakynthos (€10, 1½ hours, four to five daily). **Strintzis** (☎ 2610 240 000) and Ionian Ferries head to Kefallonia (€14.50, 2½ hours, nine daily). Strintzis also goes to Ithaki (€14.50, 3½ hours, two daily), and **Minoan Lines** (☎ 2610 426 000) and **ANEK Lines** (☎ 2610 226 053) sail to Corfu (€33, seven hours, two daily). For services to Italy see p423. The tourist office (left) provides timetables. Ticket agencies line the waterfront.

DIAKOFTO–KALAVRYTA RAILWAY
ΔΙΑΚΟΦΤΟ – ΚΑΛΑΒΡΥΤΑ

This spectacular rack-and-pinion line crawls up the deep gorge of the Vouraikos River from the small coastal town of Diakofto to the mountain resort of Kalavryta, 22km away. It's a thrilling one-hour journey, with dramatic scenery best viewed from 1st class (€5), where you face forward, rather than 2nd (€4). There are five trains a day in each direction. Diakofto is one hour east of Patra on the main train line to Athens. It can be tough to get a ticket, so buy in advance from any train station in Greece. At the time of research, the line was closed for upgrades.

CORINTH ΚΟΡΙΝΘΟΣ

pop 29,800

Drab, modern Corinth (*ko*-rin-thoss), 6km west of the Corinth Canal, is an uninspiring town; it's better to stay in the village near ancient Corinth if visiting the ruins.

At Lecheon, about 4km west of Corinth, **Blue Dolphin Camping** (☎ 27410 25766; www.camping-blue-dolphin.gr; camp sites per tent/adult €6/6.50;) just after the ancient Corinth turn-off, has a beach and decent facilities and offers tours. Buses from Corinth to Lecheon stop here.

The basic **Hotel Apollon** (☎ 27410 22587; www.hotelapollongr.com; Damaskinou 2; s/d €50/60;), handily situated near the bus station and offering good discounts, is the best accommodation option in town.

Buses to Athens (€6, 1½ hours, half-hourly) and Lecheon and ancient Corinth (€0.90, 20 minutes, hourly) leave from the **KTEL Korinthos bus station** (☎ 27410 75425; Dimocratias 4), while buses to Nafplio leave from **Argolis bus station** (cnr Ethnikis Antistaseos & Aratou). All buses to other regions in the Peloponnese can be caught from the new KTEL bus station on the Peloponnese side of the Corinth Canal. To get there from Corinth, catch one of the frequent local buses to Loutraki.

It's more convenient to take the train to Patra and Athens (14 daily, four of which are InterCity services). A handy new train service (the *proastiako*) runs between Corinth and Athens airport (€8, one hour, eight daily).

Trains also head to Kalamata (€9, 4½ hours, three daily) via Argos (for Nafplio, €4, one hour, five daily).

ANCIENT CORINTH & ACROCORINTH ΑΡΧΑΙΑ ΚΟΡΙΝΘΟΣ & ΑΚΡΟΚΟΡΙΝΘΟΣ

Seven kilometres southwest of Corinth's modern town, the ruins of **ancient Corinth** (☎ 27410 31207; site & museum €6; 8am-7.30pm Apr-Oct, to 3pm Nov-Apr) lie at the edge of the village of early Corinth in the midst of fields sweeping to the sea. It was one of ancient Greece's wealthiest cities, but earthquakes and invasions have left little standing. The only Greek monument remaining is the imposing **Temple of Apollo**; the others are Roman. **Acrocorinth**, the ruins of a citadel built on a massive outcrop of limestone, looms majestically over the site.

The great-value digs at **Tasos Taverna & Rooms** (☎ 27410 31225; fax 27410 31183; centre of town, 200m from museum; s/d/q €30/40/50;) are spotlessly clean and above an excellent eatery serving home-style Greek classics. Take in the views while chatting with the gregarious owner. Breakfast costs €6.

NAFPLIO ΝΑΥΠΛΙΟ

pop 14,500

Elegant Venetian houses and neoclassical mansions dripping with crimson bougainvillea cascade down Nafplio's hillside to the azure sea. Vibrant cafes, shops and restaurants fill winding pedestrian streets. Crenulated Palamidi Fortress perches above it all. What's not to love?

Information

Echorama (☎ 27520 26050; Vas Alexandrou 9; per hr €3; 10am-10pm) A CD shop with internet terminals in the heart of the Old Town, near the corner of Siokou.

Kasteli Travel & Tourist Agency (☎ 27520 29395; 38 Vas Konstantinou; 9am-2pm year-round & 6-8pm Jun-Sep) At Syngrou, the friendly English-speaking staff here book rooms, rent cars and sell transport tickets.

Municipal tourist office (☎ 27520 24444; 25 Martiou; 9am-1pm & 4-8pm) Generally unhelpful. A kiosk in Fillenon Sq offers free headsets for walking tours (10am to 1pm and 6pm to 8pm).

Odyssey Bookshop (☎ 27520 23430; Plateia Syntagmatos) Excellent range of international papers, magazines and novels.

Tourist police (☎ 27520 28131; Kountouridou 16)

Sights

Enjoy spectacular views of the town and surrounding coast from the magnificent hilltop **Palamidi Fortress** (☎ 27520 28036; admission €4; 8.30am-6.45pm Jun-Aug, to 2.45pm Sep-May), built by the Venetians between 1711 and 1714. The **Vasilios Papantoniou Museum** (☎ 27520 28379; 1 Vas Alexandrou St; adult/concession €4/2; 9am-2.30pm & 5.30-10.30pm) is one of Greece's best small museums, with its displays of vibrant regional costumes and rotating exhibits. The **Alexandros Soutzos Museum** (Sidiras Merarhias 23; adult/concession €3/1.50, admission free Mon; 10am-3pm & 5-8pm Wed-Mon, 10am-2pm Sun) showcases the 1821 Greek War of Independence in a stunningly restored neoclassical building.

GREECE

Sleeping

Per capita, Nafplio has some of the most exquisite hotels in Greece. The Old Town is *the* place to stay, with plenty of pensions, but limited budget options. Midweek prices are lower than weekend rates (Friday to Sunday) when town fills up – book ahead. While cheaper rooms can be found on the road to Argos and Tolo, you'll have transport costs into town.

Pension Dimitris Bekas (☎ 27520 24594; Efthimiopoulou 26; s/d/tr €28/28/39) The only good, central budget option. Clean, homey rooms have a top-value location on the slopes of the Akronafplia, and the owner has a killer baseball-cap collection.

Kapodistrias (☎ 27520 29366; www.hotelkapodistrias.gr; Kokinou 20; s/d incl breakfast €50/75;) Beautiful rooms, many with elegant canopy beds, come with sea or old-town views.

Hotel Byron (☎ 27520 22351; www.byronhotel.gr; Platonos 2; d €60-80;) Tucked into two fine Venetian buildings, iron bedsteads, rich carpets and period furniture fill immaculate rooms.

Pension Marianna (☎ 27520 24256; www.pensionmarianna.gr; Potamianou 9; s/tr incl breakfast €60/100, d incl breakfast €70-85;) Welcoming owners epitomise Greek *filoxenia* (hospitality) and serve delicious organic breakfasts. Up a steep set of stairs, and tucked under the fortress walls, a dizzying array of rooms intermix with sea-view terraces.

our pick **Amfitriti Pension** (☎ 27520 96250; www.amfitriti-pension-nafplio.com; Kapodistriou 24; s/d/tr incl breakfast €70/85/120) Quaint antiques fill these intimate rooms in an Old Town house. Enjoy stellar views at its nearby sister hotel, Amfitriti Belvedere (double €85 to €110), which is chock full of brightly coloured tapestries and emits a feeling of cheery serenity.

Hotel Grande Bretagne (☎ 27520 96200; www.grandebretagne.com.gr; Filellinon Sq; s/d incl breakfast €120/170) In the heart of Nafplio's cafe action and overlooking the sea, this splendidly restored hotel with high ceilings, antiques and chandeliers radiates plush opulence.

Eating

Nafplio's Old Town streets are loaded with restaurants; the tavernas on Staïkopoulou and those overlooking the port on Bouboulinas get jam-packed on weekends.

Antica Gelateria di Roma (☎ 27520 23520; cnr Farmakopoulou 6 & Komninou) The best (yes, best) traditional gelati outside Italy.

To Kenitrikon (☎ 27520 29933; Plateia Syntagmatos; mains €4-10) Relax under the shady trees on this pretty square and enjoy the extensive breakfasts.

Taverna Aeolos (☎ 27520 26828; V Olgas 30; mains €5-13) This boisterous taverna lined with copper pans gets packed with locals sharing generous mixed-grill plates (€8.50). It has great live music during summer.

Taverna O Vassilis (☎ 27520 25334; Staïkopoulou 20-24; mains €6-14) Delicious smells of home-style classic Greek dishes waft from the busiest taverna on this atmospheric eating strip.

Shopping

Nafplio shopping is a delight, with jewellery workshops, boutiques and wonderful regional products, such as honey, wine and handicrafts.

Metallagi (☎ 27520 21267; Sofroni 3) Here, young jeweller Maria Koitsoidaki handcrafts elegant nature-inspired jewellery from silver and fine metals, gems and stones.

Art Shop (☎ 27520 29546; Ypsilantou 14) This airy boutique carries a range of carefully selected original art, ceramics, clothes, and kids' painting supplies and games.

Getting There & Away

The **KTEL Argolis bus station** (☎ 27520 27323; Syngrou 8) has hourly buses to Athens (€11.30, 2½ hours) via Corinth. Buses go to Argos (for Peloponnese connections), Mycenae and Epidavros; these cost about €2.50 and take 30 to 45 minutes.

EPIDAVROS ΕΠΙΔΑΥΡΟΣ

Spectacular World Heritage–listed **Epidavros** (☎ 27530 22006; admission €6; 8am-7pm Apr-Sep, to 5pm Oct-Mar) was the sanctuary of Asclepius, god of medicine. Amid pine-covered hills, the magnificent **theatre** is still a venue during the Hellenic Festival (see p358), but don't miss the peaceful **Sanctuary of Asclepius**, an ancient spa and healing centre.

For an early-morning visit to the site, stay at the **Hotel Avaton** (☎ 27530 22178; s/d €45/69;), just 1km away, at the junction of the road to Kranidi, or go as a day trip from Nafplio (€2.15, 45 minutes, four daily).

MYCENAE ΜΥΚΗΝΕΣ

Although settled as early as the 6th millennium BC, **Ancient Mycenae** (☎ 27510 76585; admission €8; 8.30am-7pm Jun-Oct, to 3pm Nov-May) was at its most powerful from 1600 to 1200 BC. Mycenae's entrance, the **Lion Gate**, is Europe's oldest monumental sculpture. Homer accurately described Mycenae as being 'rich in gold': excavations of **Grave Circle A** by Heinrich Schliemann in the 1870s uncovered magnificent gold treasures, such as the Mask of Agamemnon, now on display at the National Archaeological Museum (p357).

Most people visit on day trips from Nafplio, but the bare **Belle Helene Hotel** (☎ 27510 76225; Christou Tsounta; s/d incl breakfast €35/50) on the main street, is where Schliemann lived during the excavations.

Three buses go daily to Mycenae from Argos (€1.50, 30 minutes) and Nafplio (€2.15, one hour).

SPARTA ΣΠΑΡΤΗ

pop 19,600

Cheerful, unpretentious modern Sparta (*spartee*) is at odds with its ancient Spartan image of discipline and deprivation. Although there's little to see, the town makes a convenient base from which to visit Mystras.

Sparta's street grid system sees Palaeologou running north–south through the town, and Lykourgou running east–west. Get online at **Cosmos Video** (☎ 27310 21500; Palaeologou 34; per hr €2; 8.30am-11pm), above a DVD/games store. The **tourist police** (☎ 27310 20492; Theodoritou 20) can provide information. The **post office** (Archidamou 10; 7.30am-2pm Mon-Fri) is at Archidamou.

Camping Paleologou Mystras (☎ 27310 22724; camp sites per tent/adult €3.50/6.50;), 2km west of Sparta on the road to Mystras, has basic facilities, but a gorgeous setting. Buses to Mystras will drop you there.

In a cheery yellow building, **Hotel Cecil** (☎ 27310 24980; fax 27310 81318; Palaeologou 125; s/d €35/45;) has austere rooms with balconies overlooking the quiet end of the strip.

Modern **Hotel Lakonia** (☎ 27310 28951; www.lakoniahotel.gr; Palaeologou 89; s/d incl breakfast €45/70;) maintains comfy, welcoming rooms with spotless bathrooms.

The sweet smell of spices inundates **Restaurant Elysse** (☎ 27310 29896; Palaeologou 113; mains €4.50-12), which is run by a friendly Greek-Canadian family. Locals chill out next door at **Café Ouzeri** (☎ 27310 081565; mains €2-6).

Sparta's **KTEL Lakonias bus station** (☎ 27310 26441; cnr Lykourgou & Thivronos), on the east edge of town, services Athens via Corinth (€16.80, 3½ hours, nine daily), Gythio (€4, one hour, five daily), Monemvasia (€8.70, two hours, three daily), Mystras (€1.20, 30 minutes, 14 daily) and other destinations.

MYSTRAS ΜΥΣΤΡΑΣ

Magical **Mystras** (☎ 27310 83377; adult/concession €6/3; 8am-7.30pm Apr-Oct, to 3.30pm Nov-Mar) was once the effective capital of the Byzantine Empire. Ruins of palaces, monasteries and churches, most of them dating from between 1271 and 1460, nestle at the base of the Taÿgetos Mountains, and are surrounded by verdant olive and orange groves.

Allow half a day to explore the site. While only 7km from Sparta, staying in the village nearby allows you to get there early before it heats up. Enjoy exquisite views and a beautiful swimming pool at **Hotel Byzantion** (☎ 27310 83309; www.byzantionhotel.gr; s/d €40/65;), near the main square. Have a decadent escape at **Hotel Pyrgos Mystra** (☎ 27310 20870; www.pyrgosmystra.com; Manousaki 3; s/d €150/220;), with its lovingly appointed rooms in a restored mansion.

GEFYRA & MONEMVASIA ΓΕΦΥΡΑ & ΜΟΝΕΜΒΑΣΙΑ

pop 1320

Slip out along a narrow causeway, up around the edge of a towering rock rising dramatically from the sea and arrive at the exquisite walled village of Monemvasia. Enter the *kastro* (castle), which was separated from mainland Gefyra by an earthquake in AD 375, through a narrow tunnel on foot, and emerge into a stunning (carless) warren of cobblestone streets and stone houses. Beat the throngs of day trippers by staying over.

Signposted steps lead up to the ruins of a **fortress** built by the Venetians in the 16th century, and the Byzantine **Church of Agia Sophia**, perched precariously on the edge of the cliff. Views are spectacular, and wildflowers shoulder-high in spring.

Sleeping & Eating

Staying in a hotel in the *kastro* could be one of the most romantic things you ever do (ask for discounts in the low season), but if you're on a tight budget stay in Gefyra.

Hotel Aktaion (☎ 27320 61234; fax 27320 63026; s/d €30/40) This clean, sunny hotel, on the Gefyra end of the causeway, has balconies and views of the sea and 'the rock'.

Hotel Malvasia (☎ 27320 61113; d from €80, apt €160;) A variety of cosy, traditionally decorated rooms and apartments (most with sea views) are scattered around the Old Town.

Taverna O Botsalo (☎ 27320 61491; Port, Gefyra; mains €4-9) Spot the cluster of checked tablecloths just down the wharf a bit, and you'll come to this tiny bistro serving savoury meals.

Matoula (☎ 27320 61660; main street, Monemvasia; mains €9-14) The pick of the places in the Old Town. Enjoy a selection of local delights on its terrace, beneath vine-covered trellises overlooking the sea.

Getting There & Away

Buses stop in Gefyra at the friendly **Malvasia Travel** (☎ 27320 61752) where you can buy tickets. Four daily buses travel to Athens (€25.40, 5½ hours) via Corinth and Sparta (€8.70).

GYTHIO ΓΥΘΕΙΟ

pop 4490

Gythio (*yee*-thih-o) was once the port of ancient Sparta. Now it's an earthy fishing town on the Lakonian Gulf and gateway to the rugged, much more beautiful Mani Peninsula.

Peaceful **Marathonisi islet**, linked to the mainland by a causeway, is said to be ancient Cranae, where Paris (prince of Troy) and Helen (the wife of Menelaus of Sparta) consummated the love affair that sparked the Trojan War. You'll find the tiny **Museum of Mani History** (☎ 27330 24484; admission €1.50; 8am-2.30pm) here in an 18th-century tower.

Sleeping & Eating

Camping Meltemi (☎ 27330 22833; www.campingmeltemi.gr; camp sites per tent/adult €5/5.50;) Birds chirp in these idyllic silver olive groves, 3km south of Gythio. It has its own beach, swimming pool and summer beauty contests! The Areopoli bus stops here.

Xenia Karlaftis Rooms to Rent (☎ 27330 22719; opposite Marathonisi islet; s/d/tr €25/35/45) Friendly owner Voula keeps clean rooms and offers kitchen access. Several nearby places are of similar quality if you can't get in here.

Hotel Aktaion (☎ 27330 23500; Vassilis Pavlou 39; s/d €60/80;) This elegant neoclassical building has a bit of an old resort feel with nondescript but clean rooms and balconies with sea views.

The waterfront areas on the harbour and port are packed with fish tavernas and cafes.

I Gonia (☎ 27330 24024; Vassilis Pavlou; mains €6-15) Watch all the action while supping on delectable taverna standards. It's on the corner, opposite the port.

Isalos (☎ 27330 24024; Vassilis Pavlou; mains €9-17) This taverna, close to Hotel Aktaion, has won awards for its creative flair with seafood and pasta.

Getting There & Away

The **KTEL Lakonias bus station** (☎ 27330 22228; cnr Vasileos Georgios & Evrikleos), on the square near Hotel Aktion, has buses to Athens (€30.50, 4½ hours, six daily), Sparta (€3.70, one hour, four daily), Areopoli (€2.30, 30 minutes, four daily) and the Diros Caves (€3.20, one hour, one daily). **ANEN Lines** (www.anen.gr) runs five ferries weekly to Kissamos, Crete (€22, seven hours), via Kythira (€10, 2½ hours) in summer. The schedule changes so check with **Rozakis Travel** (☎ 27330 22207) on the waterfront.

THE MANI Η ΜΑΝΗ

The exquisite Mani completely lives up to its reputation for rugged beauty, abundant wildflowers in spring, and dramatic juxtapositions of sea and the Taÿgetos Mountains (threaded with wonderful walking trails). The Mani occupies the central peninsula of the southern Peloponnese and is divided into two regions: the arid Lakonian (inner) Mani in the south and the verdant Messinian (outer) Mani in the northwest near Kalamata. Explore the winding roads by car.

Lakonian Mani

For centuries the Maniots were a law unto themselves, renowned for their fierce independence and their spectacularly murderous internal feuds. To this day, bizarre tower settlements built as refuges during clan wars dot the rocky slopes of Lakonian Mani.

Areopoli, some 30km southwest of Gythio, is a warren of cobblestone and ancient towers. **Tsimova Rooms** (☎ 27330 51301; Kapetan Matepan; s/d €55/60) is in a renovated tower tucked behind the Church of Taxiarhes. Enter a dreamlike courtyard to reach the excellent **Pyrgos Kapetanakas** (☎ 27330 51233; access off Kapetan Matepan; s/d/tr €40/50/75;), in a splendid tower house built by the powerful Kapetanakas family at the end of the 18th century.

Step behind the counter to choose from the scrumptious specials at **Nicola's Corner Taverna** (☎ 27330 51366; Plateia Athanaton; mains €4-9), on the central square.

The **bus station** (☎ 27330 51229; Plateia Athanaton) services Gythio (€2.30, 30 minutes, four daily), Itilo (for the Messinian Mani, €2, 20 minutes, three daily) and the Diros Caves (€2, 15 minutes, one daily).

Eleven kilometres south, the extensive, though touristy **Diros Caves** (☎ 27330 52222; adult/concession €12/7; 8.30am-5.30pm Jun-Sep, to 3pm Oct-May), contain a subterranean river.

Gerolimenas, a tranquil fishing village on a sheltered bay 20km further south, is home to the exceedingly popular boutique **Kyrimai Hotel** (☎ 27330 54288; www.kyrimai.gr; d from €85;). Groovy music and mood lighting fill this exquisitely renovated castle with a seaside swimming pool and top-notch restaurant.

Messinian Mani

Stone hamlets dot aquamarine swimming coves. Silver olive groves climb the foothills to the snowcapped Taÿgetos Mountains. Explore the splendid meandering roads and hiking trails from Itilo to Kalamata.

The people of the enchanting seaside village of **Kardamyli**, 37km south of Kalamata, know how good they've got it. Sir Patrick Leigh Fermor famously wrote about his rambles here in *Mani: Travels in the Southern Peloponnese*. Trekkers come for the magnificent **Vyros Gorge**. Walks are well organised and colour-coded.

Kardamyli has a good choice of small hotels and *domatia* (rooms usually in private homes) to suit all budgets: all are well signposted and easy to find, but book ahead for summer.

Olympia Koumounakou Rooms (☎ 27210 73623; r €30) is basic but clean and popular with backpackers who like the communal kitchen and courtyard.

Run by the former housekeeper to Patrick Leigh Fermor, **Lela's Rooms** (☎ 27210 73541; fax 27210 64130; s/d/f €55/65/70;) has basic charming rooms on the sea, while the adjoining Lela's Taverna serves up tasty home-style Greek cuisine (mains €10) under pergolas on water's edge.

Notos Hotel (☎ 27210 73730; www.notoshotel.gr; studios €105, apt €125-150;) is really a boutique hamlet of individual stone houses, perched on a hill overlooking the village, the mountains, and the sea! Each elegantly decorated wee house has a fully equipped kitchen, a veranda and a view.

Kardamyli is on the main bus route from Itilo to Kalamata (€2.50, one hour) and two to three buses stop daily at the central square. The hotels mentioned earlier will help with tickets and flagging the busses down.

OLYMPIA ΟΛΥΜΠΙΑ

pop 1000

Tucked along the Klados River, in fertile delta country, the modern town of Olympia supports the extensive ruins of the same name. The first Olympics were staged here in 776 BC, and every four years thereafter until AD 394 when Emperor Theodosius I banned them. During the competition the city-states were bound by a sacred truce to stop fighting and take part in athletic events and cultural exhibitions.

The folks at the **Olympia Municipal Tourist Office** (☎ 26240 23100; Praxitelous Kondyli) don't speak much English but have transport schedules. Check email at the excellent wireless **Ep@th Ion C@fé** (☎ 26240 23894; Stefanopoulou 2; per 30min €2; 10am-late).

Ancient Olympia (☎ 26240 22517; adult/concession €6/3, site & museum €9/5; 8am-7pm May-Oct, to 5pm Nov-Apr) is dominated by the immense ruined **Temple of Zeus**, to whom the games were dedicated. Don't miss the statue of **Hermes of Praxiteles**, a classical sculpture masterpiece, at the exceptional **museum** (adult/concession €6/3; 10.30am-7pm Mon, 8am-7pm Tue-Sun May-Oct, to 5pm Nov-Apr).

Pitch your tent in the leafy grove at **Camping Diana** (☎ 26240 22314; fax 26240 22425; camp sites per tent/adult €6/8;), 250m west of town.

Sparkling clean **Pension Posidon** (☎ 26240 22567; www.pensionposidon.gr; Stefanopoulou 9; s/d/tr €35/45/60;) and quiet, spacious **Hotel Pelops** (☎/fax 26240 22543; www.hotelpelops.gr; Varela 2; s/d/tr incl breakfast €45/65/82;) offer the best value in the centre. Family-run **Best Western Europa** (☎ 26240 22650/23850; www.hoteleuropa.gr; Drouva 1; s/d €90/130;) perches on a hill above town and has gorgeous sweeping vistas from rooms' balconies and the wonderful swimming pool.

Tucked beneath the trees, **Taverna Gefsis Melathron** (☎ 26240 22916; George Douma 3; mains €5-8) is by far the best place to eat delicious traditional cuisine, including scrumptious vegetarian options, such as fried baby zucchini balls. Mum is chef, daughter handles the floor and dad provides the organic wines.

Catch buses at the stop on the north end of town. All northbound buses go via Pyrgos (€1.70, 30 minutes) where you connect to buses for Athens, Corinth and Patra.

Two buses go east from Olympia to Tripoli (€10, 2½ hours). Trains run daily to Pyrgos (€0.70, 30 minutes) where you can switch for Athens, Corinth and Patra.

CENTRAL GREECE ΚΕΝΤΡΙΚΗ ΕΛΛΑΔΑ

This dramatic landscape of deep gorges, rugged mountains and fertile valleys is home to the magical stone pinnacle-topping monasteries of Meteora and the iconic ruins of ancient Delphi, where Alexander the Great sought advice from the Delphic Oracle.

DELPHI ΔΕΛΦΟΙ

pop 2800

Modern Delphi and its adjoining ruins hang stunningly on the slopes of Mt Parnassos overlooking the shimmering Gulf of Corinth.

The bus station, post office, OTE, banks and **EOT** (☎ 22650 82900; Vasileon Pavlou 44; 7.30am-2.30pm Mon-Fri) are all on modern Delphi's main street, Vasileon Pavlou.

The ancient Greeks regarded Delphi as the centre of the world. According to mythology, Zeus released two eagles at opposite ends of the world and they met here. By the 6th century BC, **ancient Delphi** (☎ 22650 82312; site or museum €6 year-round, combined adult/concession €9/5 year-round, free Sun Nov-Mar; site 7.30am-7.30pm Apr-Oct, 8am-5pm Nov-Mar; museum 7.30am-7.30pm daily Apr-Oct, 8.30am-6.45pm Mon-Fri, 8.30am-3pm Sat, Sun & public holidays Nov-Mar) had become the Sanctuary of Apollo. Thousands of pilgrims flocked here to consult the middle-aged female oracle, who sat at the mouth of a fume-emitting chasm. After sacrificing a sheep or goat, pilgrims would ask a question, and a priest would translate the oracle's response into verse. Wars, voyages and business transactions were undertaken on the strength of these prophecies. From the entrance, take the **Sacred Way** up to the **Temple of Apollo**, where the oracle sat. From here the path continues to the **theatre** and **stadium**.

Opposite the main site and down the hill some 100m, don't miss the **Sanctuary of Athena** and the much-photographed **Tholos** – a 4th-century-BC columned rotunda of Pentelic marble.

Apollon Camping (☎ 22650 82762; apollon4@otenet.gr; camp sites per tent/adult €3.50/5;)), 2km west of town, has good facilities, including a restaurant, minimarket and barbecue.

In the town centre, the welcoming **Hotel Hermes** (☎ 22650 82318; Vasileon Pavlou-Friderikis 27; s/d incl breakfast €55/70;) has spacious rooms sporting balconies with stunning valley views.

Locals pack **Taverna Gargadouas** (☎ 22650 82488; Vasileon Pavlou & Friderikis; mains €4-7) for grilled meats and slow-roasted lamb (*provatina*; €6.50).

Six buses a day go from the **bus station** (☎ 22660 82317) on the main road to Athens (€13, three hours). Take a bus to Lamia (€7.80, two hours, two to three per day) or Trikala (€13.80, 4½ hours, two per day) to transfer for Meteora.

METEORA ΜΕΤΕΩΡΑ

Meteora (meh-*teh*-o-rah) should be a certified Wonder of the World with its magnificent late-14th-century monasteries perched dramatically atop enormous rocky pinnacles. Try not to miss it. Meteora's stunning rocks are also a climbing mecca.

While there were once monasteries on all 24 pinnacles, only six are still occupied: **Megalou Meteorou** (Grand Meteoron; 9am-5pm Wed-Mon), **Varlaam** (9am-2pm & 3.20-5pm Fri-Wed), **Agiou Stefanou** (9am-2pm & 3.30-6pm Tue-Sun), **Agias Triados** (Holy Trinity; 9am-12.30pm & 3-5pm Fri-Wed), **Agiou Nikolaou Anapafsa** (9am-3.30pm Sat-Thu) and **Agias Varvaras Rousanou** (9am-6pm). Admission is €2 for each monastery and strict dress codes apply (no bare shoulders or knees and women must wear skirts; borrow a long skirt at the door if you don't have one). Walk the footpaths between monasteries or drive the back road.

The tranquil village of **Kastraki**, 2km from Kalambaka, is the best base for visiting Meteora.

Sleeping & Eating

Vrachos Camping (☎ 24320 22293; camping-kastraki@kmp.forthnet.gr; camp sites per tent/adult €5/5;) This camping ground has great views, a good taverna, a barbecue and a pool, and is a short stroll from Kastraki.

our pick **Doupiani House** (☎ 24320 75326; doupiani-house@kmp.forthnet.gr; s/d/tr €30/45/55), Around 500m from the town square, gregarious hosts Thanassis and Toula Nakis offer this comfy home from which to explore or simply sit and enjoy the panoramic views. Ask for a room with a balcony, and reconfirm your booking.

Taverna Gardenia (Kastrakiou St; mains €3-8) You'll find the freshest Greek food served with aplomb here; the splendid views of Meteora and fragrant scent of gardenias are a bonus. The owners also have good-value and spacious rooms (some with views) at Plakjas (☎ 24320 22504; single/double/triple €30/40/50), behind the restaurant.

Getting There & Away

Local buses shuttle between Kalambaka and Kastraki (€1.90), two of which go to Moni Megalou Meteoron. Hourly buses from Kalambaka go to the transport hub of Trikala (€1.90, 30 minutes), from where there are buses to Ioannina (€10.50, three hours, two daily) and Athens (€23, 5½ hours, seven daily). From Kalambaka, there are also express trains to Athens (€20, five hours, two daily) and Thessaloniki (€17, four hours, two daily) via Paliofarsalos.

NORTHERN GREECE ΒΟΡΕΙΑ ΕΛΛΑΔΑ

Northern Greece is stunning, graced as it is with magnificent mountains, thick forests, tranquil lakes and archaeological sites. Most of all, it's easy to get off the beaten track and experience aspects of Greece noticeably different to other mainland areas and the islands.

THESSALONIKI ΘΕΣΣΑΛΟΝΙΚΗ

pop 800,800

Dodge cherry sellers in the street, smell spices in the air and enjoy waterfront breezes in Thessaloniki (thess-ah-lo-*nee*-kih), also known as Salonica (Saloniki). The second city of Byzantium and of modern Greece boasts countless Byzantine churches, a smattering of Roman ruins, engaging museums, shopping to rival Athens, fine restaurants and a lively cafe scene and nightlife.

Orientation

Laid out on a grid system, the main thoroughfares of Tsimiski, Egnatia and Agiou Dimitriou run parallel to Leof Nikis, on the waterfront. Plateias Eleftherias and Aristotelous, both off Leof Nikis, are the main squares.

Information

Bianca Laundrette (Panagias Dexias 3; per 6kg load €7; 🕑 8am-8.30pm Tue, Thu & Fri, to 3pm Mon, Wed & Sat)
E-global Internet (Vas Irakliou 40; per hr €2.50; 🕑 24hr)
First-aid centre (☎ 23105 30530; Navarhou Koundourioti 10) Near the port.
Main post office (Aristotelous 26; 🕑 7.30am-8pm Mon-Fri, 7.30am-2.15pm Sat, 9am-1.30pm Sun)
Tourist information office (☎ 23102 21100; the-info_office@gnto.gr; Tsimiski 136; 🕑 8am-2.45pm Mon-Fri, to 2pm Sat)
Tourist police (☎ 23105 54871; 5th fl, Dodekanisou 4; 🕑 7.30am-11pm)

Sights

Check out the seafront **White Tower** (☎ 2310 267 832; Lefkos Pyrgos; adult €2; 🕑 8am-7pm Tue-Sun, 12.30-7pm Mon) and wander the churches and *hamams* (Turkish baths) before stopping in at the award-winning **Museum of Byzantine Culture** (☎ 23108 68570; Leoforos Stratou 2; admission €4; 🕑 1-7.30pm Mon, 8am-3pm Tue-Fri), one of Greece's best, with splendid sculptures, mosaics, icons and other intriguing artefacts beautifully displayed. The exquisite finds at the **Archaeological Museum** (☎ 23108 30538; Manoli Andronikou 6; admission €4; 🕑 8.30am-3pm) include Macedonian gold from Alexander the Great's time. The compelling **Thessaloniki Centre of Contemporary Art** (☎ 23105 46683; admission free; 🕑 11am-7pm) and small **Museum of Photography** (☎ 23105 66716; admission free; 🕑 11am-7pm Mon-Fri, to 9pm Sat & Sun) beside the port, are worth an hour of your time.

Sleeping

Steep discounts abound during summer.

Acropol Hotel (☎ 23105 36170; Tandalidou 4; s/d with shared bathroom €20/25) A bit worse for wear, it's still the best budget option.

Hotel Pella (☎ 23105 24221; pellahot@otenet.gr; Ionos Dragoumi 63; s/d €36/52; ❄) Tidy, quiet and family-run with spotless rooms.

Hotel Tourist (☎ 23102 70501; www.touristhotel.gr; Mitropoleos 21; s/d incl breakfast €55/70; ❄ 💻) Spacious rooms in a charming, central, neoclassical building are maintained by friendly staff.

City Hotel (☎ 23102 69421; www.cityhotel.gr; Komninon 11; s/d incl breakfast €115/135; ❄ 💻) Ask for a light-filled front room in this excellently located sleek, stylish hotel.

Electra Palace Hotel (☎ 23102 94011; www.electrahotels.gr; Plateia Aristotelous 9; d €135-220; ❄ 💻 🏊)

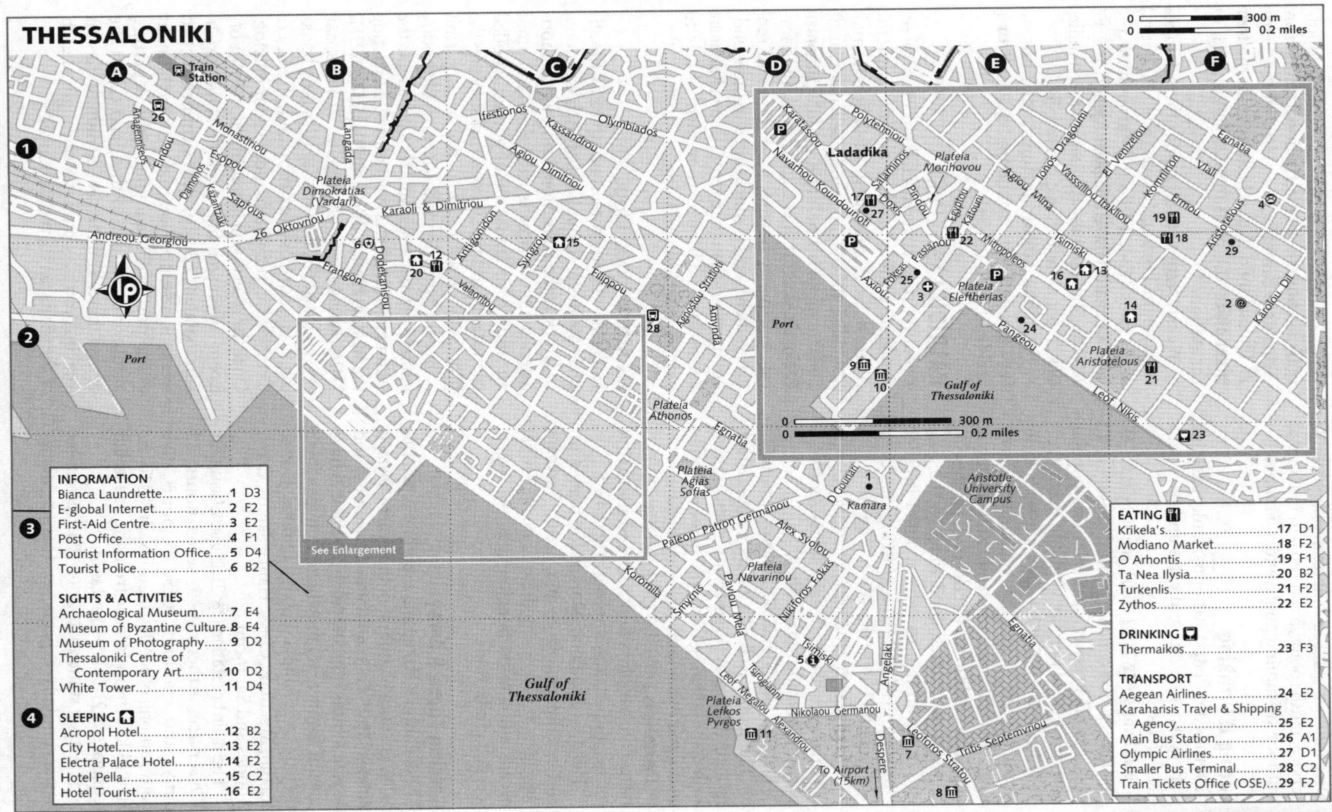
THESSALONIKI
0 300 m
0 0.2 miles
Train Station
Port
Gulf of Thessaloniki
See Enlargement
Ladadika
Plateia Dimokratias (Vardari)
Plateia Athonos
Plateia Agias Sofias
Plateia Navarinou
Plateia Lefkos Pyrgos
Plateia Morihovou
Plateia Eleftherias
Plateia Aristotelous
Aristotle University Campus
To Airport (15km)
INFORMATION
Bianca Laundrette....1 D3
E-global Internet....2 F2
First-Aid Centre....3 E2
Post Office....4 F1
Tourist Information Office....5 D4
Tourist Police....6 B2
SIGHTS & ACTIVITIES
Archaeological Museum....7 E4
Museum of Byzantine Culture....8 E4
Museum of Photography....9 D2
Thessaloniki Centre of Contemporary Art....10 D2
White Tower....11 D4
SLEEPING
Acropol Hotel....12 B2
City Hotel....13 E2
Electra Palace Hotel....14 F2
Hotel Pella....15 C2
Hotel Tourist....16 E2
EATING
Krikela's....17 D1
Modiano Market....18 F2
O Arhontis....19 F1
Ta Nea Ilysia....20 B2
Turkenlis....21 F2
Zythos....22 E2
DRINKING
Thermaikos....23 F3
TRANSPORT
Aegean Airlines....24 E2
Karaharisis Travel & Shipping Agency....25 E2
Main Bus Station....26 A1
Olympic Airlines....27 D1
Smaller Bus Terminal....28 C2
Train Tickets Office (OSE)....29 F2

Dive into five-star seafront luxury: impeccable service, plush rooms, a rooftop bar, indoor and outdoor swimming pools, and a *hamam*.

Eating & Drinking

Tavernas dot Plateia Athonos, funky bars line Plateia Aristotelous and cafes and bars pack Leof Nikis.

O Arhontis (☎ 23102 80202; Ermou 26; mains €5; 🕑 11am-5pm) Eat delicious grilled sausages and potatoes off butcher's paper at this popular working-class eatery in Modiano market.

Zythos (☎ 23105 40284; Katouni 5; mains €5-10) Popular with locals, this excellent taverna with two locations and friendly staff serves up delicious traditional Greek food, interesting regional specialities, good wines by the glass and beers on tap. Its second outlet is called Dore Zythos (☎ 2310 279 010), located at Tsirogianni 7, near the White Tower.

Ta Nea Ilysia (☎ 23105 36996; Leontos Sofou 17; mains €6) This no-nonsense taverna serves enormous portions of traditional dishes.

Krikela's (☎ 23105 01600; Salaminos 6; mains €12-30) The iconic Krikela's offers a superlative, refined dining experience for gastronomes, with dishes ranging from wild game to Cretan snails and other local Greek specialities.

Thermaikos (☎ 23102 39842; Leof Nikis 21) This retro-cool bar plays funk, jazz and alternative music, and attracts a young arty crowd.

Head to Modiano Market for fresh fruit and vegetables, olives and bread. **Turkenlis** (Aristotelous 4) is renowned for *tzoureki* (sweet bread) and a mind-boggling array of sweet-scented confections.

Getting There & Away

Thessaloniki's **Makedonia airport** (SKG; ☎ 23104 73700) is 16km southeast of the centre. **Olympic Airlines** (☎ 23103 68666; Navarhou Koundourioti 3) and **Aegean Airlines** (☎ 23102 80050; El Venizelou 2) have several flights a day to Athens. Between them they fly to Ioannina, Lesvos, Limnos, Corfu, Iraklio, Mykonos, Chios, Hania, Samos, Crete, Rhodes and Santorini.

The **main bus station** (☎ 23105 95408; Monastiriou 319) services Athens (€35, seven hours, 12 daily) and Ioannina (€25, six hours, five daily) among other destinations. Buses to the Halkidiki Peninsula leave from the **smaller bus terminal** (☎ 23103 16555; Karakasi 68).

The **train station** (☎ 23105 17517; Monastiriou) has seven daily express services to Athens (€36, 5½ hours) and two to Alexandroupolis (€10, six hours). All international trains from Athens (to Belgrade, Sofia, İstanbul etc) stop at Thessaloniki. Get schedules from the **train ticket office** (OSE; ☎ 23105 98120; Aristotelous 18) or the station.

Weekly ferries go to, among others, Limnos (€22, eight hours), Lesvos (€34, 14 hours) and Chios (€34, 19 hours) throughout the year. **Karaharisis Travel & Shipping Agency** (☎ 23105 24544; fax 23105 32289; Navarhou Koundourioti 8) handles tickets for all ferries and hydrofoils.

From the airport to town, take bus 78 (€0.50, one hour, from 5am to 10pm) or a taxi (€20, 20 minutes).

HALKIDIKI ΧΑΛΚΙΔΙΚΗ

Beautiful pine-covered Halkidiki is a three-pronged peninsula that extends into the Aegean Sea, southeast of Thessaloniki. Splendid, if built-up, sandy beaches rim its 500km of coastline. The middle **Sithonian Peninsula** is most spectacular, with pine forests and pretty beaches (and rooms to rent everywhere) and is more suited to independent travellers than the overdeveloped **Kassandra Peninsula**. You'll need your own wheels to explore Halkidiki properly.

Mt Athos Αγιος Ορος

Halkidiki's third prong is occupied by the all-male Monastic Republic of Mt Athos (known in Greek as the Holy Mountain), where monasteries full of priceless treasures stand amid an impressive landscape of gorges, wooded mountains and precipitous rocks. While the process for obtaining a four-day visitor permit is becoming easier, only 10 non-Orthodox adult males may enter Mt Athos per day, so the summer waiting list is long. Start by contacting the **Mt Athos Pilgrims' Office** (☎ 23102 52578; fax 23102 22424; pilgrimsbureau@c-lab.gr; Egnatia 109, Thessaloniki; 🕑 9am-2pm Mon-Fri, 10am-noon Sat) to make a booking. Fax your passport copy and, if you are Orthodox, certified evidence of your religion. Once the reservation is confirmed, visit the office to collect your final permit (*diamonitirion*, adult/student €30/10). If it's confirmed two weeks in advance, you may proceed straight to the port of Ouranoupolis (the departure point for boats to Mt Athos) and collect the permit there. You can visit 20 monasteries on foot, but you may only stay one night at each of the monasteries you've booked.

ALEXANDROUPOLIS ΑΛΕΞΑΝΔΡΟΥΠΟΛΗ

pop 49,200

Alexandroupolis and nearby Komotini (ko-mo-tih-*nee*) enjoy lively student atmospheres that make for a satisfying stopover on the way to Turkey or Samothraki.

Hotel Mitropolis (☎ 25510 26443; Athanasiou Dhiakou 11; s/d €35/40) is the best budget option, with spotlessly cleans rooms with TV and fridge. Fourth-floor rooms have enormous terraces.

Traditional blue-and-white decor and fresh flowers bedeck **To Nisiotiko** (☎ 25510 20990; Zarifi 1; mains €5-12). Specialising in seafood, it serves up some of the tastiest in Greece – try a plate of grilled octopus (€8) and a bottle of Drama chardonnay and you'll be in heaven.

Locals seem to do more drinking than eating. A young crowd frequents the scores of cafe-bars on Leof Dimokratias between Ionos Dragoumi and Mitropolitou Kaviri. University students fill bars on Nikiforou Foka, while the older folk like the waterfront places.

Head to **Vatitsis Shipping Agency** (☎ 25510 26721; a_vati@otenet.gr; Kyprou 5) for local ferries and tickets to Samothraki and Limnos. **Sever Travel** (☎ 25510 22555; sever1@otenet.gr; Megalou Alexandrou 24) handles long-distance and international ferries, and airlines (several flights a day to Athens). To Thessaloniki, there are trains (€10, seven hours, six daily) and buses (€25, six hours, six daily). To İstanbul (Turkey) there's a daily train (€36, seven hours) and a daily OSE bus (€15, six hours), while to Svilengrad (Bulgaria) there's a daily train (€5, four hours).

MT OLYMPUS ΟΛΥΜΠΟΣ ΟΡΟΣ

Greece's highest mountain, Mt Olympus, was the ancient home of the gods. The highest of its eight peaks is Mytikas (2917m), popular with trekkers, who use Litohoro (5km inland from the Athens–Thessaloniki highway) as their base. The main route to the top takes two days, with a stay overnight at one of the refuges (open May to October). Good protective clothing is essential, even in summer. If you trek outside the official season, you do so at your own risk. The **EOS office** (☎ 23520 84544; Plateia Kentriki; 🕑 9.30am-12.30pm & 6-8pm Mon-Sat, Jun-Sep) has information on treks.

Olympos Beach Camping (☎ 23520 22111/2; www.olympos-beach.gr; Plaka Litohoro; camp sites per adult/tent €6/7; 🕑 Apr-Oct) has decent bungalows, a good taverna, a funky waterfront lounge bar and a pleasant beach.

The romantic guest house **Xenonas Papanikolaou** (☎ 23520 81236; xenpap@otenet.gr; Nikolaou Episkopou Kitrous 1; s/d €40/45) sits in a flowery garden up in the backstreets, a world away from the tourist crowds. Tasteful rooms are enhanced by lovely views of traditional terracotta rooftops.

One of Greece's best country restaurants, **Gastrodromio El Olympio** (☎ 23520 21300; Plateia Kentriki; mains €7-11) serves up specialities like *soutzoukakia* (minced meat with cumin and mint) and delicious wild mushrooms with an impressive regional wine list and gorgeous Olympus views.

From the **bus stop** (☎ 23520 81271) 10 buses daily go to Thessaloniki (€8, 1½ hours) via Katerini, and three to Athens (€25, 5½ hours). Litohoro's train station, 9km away, gets 10 daily trains on the Athens–Volos–Thessaloniki train line.

IOANNINA ΙΩΑΝΝΙΝΑ

pop 61,700

Charming Ioannina (ih-o-*ah*-nih-nah) on the western shore of Lake Pamvotis at the foot of the Pindos Mountains, was a major intellectual centre during Ottoman rule. Today it's a thriving university town with a lively waterfront cafe scene.

The main streets meet in the town centre, around Plateia Dimokratias. Access the internet at **Web** (☎ 26510 26813; Pyrsinella 21; per hr €2.50; 🕑 24hr) and regional tourist information at **EOT** (☎ 26510 41142; Dodonis 39; 🕑 7.30am-2.30pm).

Sights

The narrow stone streets of the **Old Town** sit on a small peninsula jutting into the lake. Within its impressive fortifications, the **kale**, an inner citadel with lovely grounds and lake views, is home to the splendid **Fetiye Cami** (Victory Mosque), built in 1611 and the gem-like **Byzantine Museum** (☎ 26510 25989; admission €3; 🕑 8am-5pm). The serene **nisi** (island) shelters four monasteries among its trees. Ferries (€1.80, half-hourly summer, hourly winter) to the island leave from near the waterfront cafes and Plateia Mavili.

Sleeping & Eating

Limnopoula Camping (☎ 26510 20541; Kanari 10; camp sites per tent/adult €4/8; ⏲ May-Oct) Pitch a tent at this tree-lined camping ground, splendidly set on the edge of the lake 2km northwest of town.

Hotel Kastro (☎ 26510 22866; Andronikou Paleologou 57; s/d incl breakfast €50/80; ❄) Ask for a high-ceilinged upstairs room at this quaint hotel, across from the kale.

Filyra (☎ 26510 83560; alley off Andronikou Paleologou 18; r €65; ❄) In the Old Town, popular Filyra has rooms with kitchens and fills up fast.

Taberna To Manteio (☎ 26510 25452; Plateia Georgiou 15; mains €7-8) Join local families along the flower-filled kale wall at this place for deliciously simple *mezedes,* salads and grills.

Scores of cafes and restaurants, like **Limni** (☎ 26510 78988; Papagou 26; mains €7-15) with its hearty portions, or the elegant **Agnanti** (☎ 26510 22010; Pamvotidhas 2; mains €8-20), line the waterfront. Sit with a cold beer on a sunny day in the kale at its exquisitely situated cafe (mains cost from €3 to €7).

Getting There & Away

Aegean Airlines (☎ 26510 64444) and **Olympic Airlines** (☎ 26510 26518) fly twice a day to Athens. Slow buses ply the 2km road into town.

The **main bus station** (☎ 26510 26211; Zossimadon), 300m north of Plateia Dimokratias, services Athens (€35, 7½ hours, nine daily), Igoumenitsa (€8, 2½ hours, eight daily), Thessaloniki (€28, seven hours, six daily) and Trikala (€12.30, 3½ hours, two daily).

ZAGOROHORIA & VIKOS GORGE ΤΑ ΖΑΓΟΡΟΧΩΡΙΑ & ΧΑΡΑΔΡΑ ΤΟΥ ΒΙΚΟΥ

Do not miss the spectacular Zagori region, with its deep gorges, raging rivers, dense forests and snowcapped mountains. Some 46 charming villages, famous for their grey-slate architecture, and known collectively as the Zagorohoria, are sprinkled across a large expanse of the Pindos Mountains north of Ioannina. Formerly connected by stone paths and arching footbridges, paved roads now wind between these beautifully restored gems. Book ahead during high season (Christmas, Greek Easter and August).

Tiny, carless **Dilofo** makes a peaceful sojourn, especially if you lodge at excellent **Gaia** (☎ 26530 22570; www.gaia-dilofo.gr; s/d from €70/100) and tuck into a delicious meal (mains €6 to €8) at **Taverna Lidthos**, overlooking the village.

Delightful **Monodendri**, known for its special pitta bread, is a popular departure point for treks through dramatic **Vikos Gorge**, with its sheer limestone walls. Get cosy at quaint **Archontiko Zarkada** (☎ 26530 71305; www.monodendri.com; s/d incl breakfast €35/45), one of Greece's best-value small hotels.

It's a strenuous 7½-hour walk along well-marked paths from here to the remote (but popular) twin villages of **Megalo Papingo** and **Mikro Papingo**. Get information on the walks from Ioannina's EOT office (p377). Visit the **WWF's Information Centre** (Mikro Papingo; ⏲ 10.30am-6pm Fri-Wed) to learn about the area.

Exquisite inns with attached tavernas abound, and are a steal in low season. Prices here are for high season. In Megalo Papingo, simple **Lakis** (☎ 26530 41087; fax 26530 41120; d €50) is a *domatia,* taverna and store. Stylish **Tsoumani** (☎ 26530 41893; www.tsoumanisnikos.gr; d from €90) also serves some of the best food around. Two friendly brothers run charming **Xenonas tou Kouli** (☎ 26530 41115; d €90).

Mikro Papingo's sweetly rustic **Xenonas Dias** (☎ 26530 41257; s/d €60/80) now has competition from the fabulous, sumptuously minimalist **1700** (☎ 26530 41179; www.mikropapigo.gr; d €65-150) and the elegantly appointed **Antalki** (☎ 26530 41441; www.antalki.gr; d €60-130).

Infrequent buses run from Monodendri (€3.10, one hour, twice weekly) and the Papingos (€5, two hours, three weekly) to Ioannina.

IGOUMENITSA ΗΓΟΥΜΕΝΙΤΣΑ

pop 9110

Though tucked beneath verdant hills and lying on the sea, this characterless west-coast port is little more than a ferry hub – keep moving.

If you must stay the night, look for *domatia* signs or have a '70s flashback at **Hotel Oscar** (☎ 26650 23338; Ag Apostolon 149; s/d €30/40), across from the Corfu ticket booths.

Tasty **Taverna Emily Akti** (☎ 26650 23763; Podou 13; mains €6-8) manages to eke out some character under a pergola near the Corfu ferry quay.

The **bus station** (☎ 26650 22309; Kyprou 29) services Ioannina (€8.20, 2½ hours, eight daily) and Athens (€33, eight hours, five daily).

Several companies operate ferries to Corfu (person/car €7/33, 1½ hours, hourly) between 5am and 10pm, and hydrofoils in summer.

International services go to the Italian ports of Ancona, Bari, Brindisi, Trieste and Venice. Ticket agencies line the port.

SARONIC GULF ISLANDS ΝΗΣΙΑ ΤΟΥ ΣΑΡΩΝΙΚΟΥ

Scattered about the Saronic Gulf, these islands offer authentic and rewarding Greek-island experiences within easy reach of Athens. The Saronics are named after the mythical King Saron of Argos, a keen hunter who drowned while chasing a deer that had swum into the gulf to escape.

AEGINA ΑΙΓΙΝΑ

pop 10,500

Once a major player in the Hellenic world, thanks to its strategic position at the mouth of the gulf, Aegina (*eh*-yee-nah) now enjoys its position as Greece's premier producer of pistachios. Pick up a bag before you leave!

Bustling **Aegina Town**, on the west coast, is the island's capital and main port. There is no official tourist office, but there are plenty of booking agencies along the waterfront that will be keen to help you out. Further information can be gleaned at www.aeginagreece.com. **Surf and Play** (☎ 22970 29096; Afeas 42; per 30min €2; 9am-late) provides internet access.

The impressive **Temple of Aphaia** (☎ 22970 32398; adult/under 18/concession €4/free/2; 8am-6.30pm) is a well-preserved Doric temple 12km east of Aegina Town. It's said to have served as a model for the construction of the Parthenon. Standing on a pine-clad hill with imposing views out over the gulf, it is well worth a visit. Buses from Aegina Town to the small resort of Agia Marina can drop you at the site.

In Aegina Town, at the northern end of the waterfront, **Hotel Plaza** (☎ 22970 25600; s/d/tr €35/40/60) is a popular budget choice with enthusiastic owners. **Hotel Brown** (☎ 22970 22271; www.hotelbrown.gr; s/d/tr €60/75/100;) with its comfortable rooms and generous buffet breakfast is another excellent option at the south end of the harbour. Book ahead, especially at weekends.

A flotilla of ferries (€8.20, 70 minutes) and hydrofoils (€13, 35 minutes) plies the waters between Aegina and Piraeus with great regularity. There is a good public bus service on the island.

HELLENIC WILDLIFE REHABILITATION CENTRE

While some Greeks may not appear too environmentally minded, others are making a sterling effort to face the country's ecological problems head on. The **Hellenic Wildlife Rehabilitation Centre** (☎ 22970 31338; www.ekpaz.gr; 10am-7pm) is one such place on the Saronic Gulf island of Aegina. The centre tackles the damage caused to wild birds and animals due to hunting and pollution, and runs projects such as the release of raptors into the wilds of Crete and Northern Greece. You can visit the centre for free, though donations are appreciated. Better yet, the centre welcomes volunteers and accommodation is supplied.

POROS ΠΟΡΟΣ

pop 4500

Only a few hundred metres from the village of Galatas on the shores of the mountainous Peloponnese, Poros has a friendly feel and is worth the effort. Poros Town, on the island's southern coast, is a haven for yachties, and with boats from all over tied up along the waterfront, there is a happy mood in the air.

There is no tourist office, but also no shortage of businesses hoping to sell you your onward ticket. Hit www.poros.com.gr for extensive information. Internet is available at the waterfront **bookshop** (per 15min €3) and various cafes.

Call Tryfon at **Villa Tryfon** (☎ 22980 22215; villatryfon@poros.com.gr; s/d 40/55;) for a friendly reception at his good-value rooms with views over the waterfront. Nearby in St George's Sq, delve into tasty local cuisine at **Platanos** (☎ 22980 25409; mains €5-12),under the spectacular old plane tree.

There are four ferry (€11.60, 2½ hours) and eight hydrofoil (€19.30, one hour) services daily between Poros and Piraeus. The ferries go via Aegina (€8, 1¼ hours), while the hydrofoils go direct. Many of the outbound boats head on to Hydra and Spetses.

HYDRA ΥΔΡΑ

pop 2900

The showcase of the Saronics, Hydra (*ee*-drah) is considered the most stylish destination of the group. Hydra Town, on the northern coast, has a picturesque horseshoe-shaped harbour with gracious white and pastel stone mansions stacked up the rocky hillsides that surround it. The island is known as a retreat for artists, writers and celebrities, and wears its celebrity with panache.

A major attraction is Hydra's tranquillity. Forget noisy motorbikes keeping you awake half the night! There are no motorised vehicles – apart from sanitation and construction vehicles – and the main forms of transport are by foot and donkey.

Hydra Town is on the island's north coast. There is no tourist office, but check out www.hydradirect.com for detailed information. **Satis Tours** (☎ 22980 52184) on the waterfront is helpful, while just around the corner on Tombazi, **Flamingo Internet Café** (☎ 22980 53485; per 15min €3; ⏰ 8.30am-10pm) has internet access.

Pension Erofili (☎ 22980 54049; www.pensionerofili.gr; Tombazi; s/d/tr €45/55/65; ❄), tucked away in the inner town, has clean, comfortable rooms and an attractive courtyard. **Hotel Miranda** (☎ 22980 52230; www.mirandahotel.gr; Miaouli; s/d/tr incl breakfast €85/118/170; ❄) is worth a splurge. Originally built in 1810 as the mansion of a wealthy Hydriot sea captain, this stylish place retains much of its historical character.

Catamaran and hydrofoil (€28, 1½ hours) services connect Hydra with Piraeus four times daily in winter and up to eight times daily or more in summer via Poros (€9.50, 30 minutes).

SPETSES ΣΠΕΤΣΕΣ

pop 4000

Spetses is an attractive island that is packed with visitors in summer. Known in antiquity as Pityoussa (meaning 'pine-covered'), the original pine forests disappeared long ago. The island's present attractiveness is largely thanks to Spetses-born philanthropist Sotirios Anargyrios, who made a fortune in the US after emigrating in 1848. Anargyrios returned in 1914, bought two-thirds of the then-barren island, planted Aleppo pines, financed the island's road system, and commissioned many of the town's grandest buildings.

Spetses Town, the main port, sprawls along half the northeast coast of the island. There is no tourist office, but **Mimoza Travel** (☎ 22980 75170) on the waterfront can help with accommodation and other services. Take a look at www.spetsesdirect.com for more information. **1800 Net Café** (☎ 22980 29498; per 30min €2.50; ⏰ 9am-midnight) provides internet access.

Opposite the small town beach to the east of the ferry quay, **Villa Marina** (☎ 22980 72646; s/d €40/56; ❄) is a welcoming place with tidy rooms containing a fridge. Ask for a sea view.

A daily ferry connects Spetses to Piraeus (€15.30, four hours) via Hydra (€6.50, one hour) and Aegina (€12.10, three hours). There are at least six hydrofoils daily to Piraeus (€37, 2½ hours). There are also boats to Kosta, Ermioni and Porto Heli on the Peloponnese mainland.

CYCLADES ΚΥΚΛΑΔΕΣ

The Cyclades (kih-*klah*-dez) are Greek Islands to dream about. Named after the rough *kyklos* (circle) they form around the island of Delos, they are rugged outcrops of rock in the azure Aegean, speckled with white cubist buildings and blue-domed Byzantine churches. Throw in sun-blasted golden beaches, a dash of hedonism and a fascinating culture, and it's easy to see why many find the Cyclades irresistible.

Some of the islands, such as Mykonos, Ios and Santorini, have seized tourism with great enthusiasm. Prepare to battle the crowds if you turn up at the height of summer. Others are little more than clumps of rock, with a village, secluded coves and a few curious tourists. Ferry services rarely run in winter, while from July to September the Cyclades are vulnerable to the *meltemi*, a fierce northeasterly wind that can cull ferry schedules.

History

Said to have been inhabited since at least 7000 BC, the Cyclades enjoyed a flourishing Bronze Age civilisation (3000–1100 BC), more or less concurrent with the Minoan civilisation. From the 4th century AD, the islands, like the rest of Greece, suffered a series of invasions and occupations. The Turks turned up in 1537 but neglected the Cyclades to the extent that they became backwaters prone to raids by pirates – hence the labyrinthine character of their towns, which was meant to confuse attackers. On some islands the whole population moved into the mountainous interior to escape the pirates, while on others they braved it out on the coast. Consequently, the *hora* (main town) is on the coast on some islands, while on others it is inland.

The Cyclades became part of independent Greece in 1827. During WWII they were occupied by the Italians. Before the revival of the islands' fortunes by the tourist boom that began in the 1970s, many islanders lived in poverty and many more headed for the mainland or emigrated to America or Australia in search of work.

MYKONOS ΜΥΚΟΝΟΣ

pop 9700

Sophisticated Mykonos glitters happily under the Aegean sun, shamelessly surviving on tourism. The island has something for everyone with marvellous beaches, romantic sunsets, chic boutiques, excellent restaurants and bars, and its long-held reputation as a mecca for gay travellers. The maze of white-walled streets in Mykonos Town was designed to confuse pirates, and it certainly manages to captivate and confuse the crowds that consume the island's capital in summer.

Orientation & Information

Mykonos Town has two ferry quays. The old quay, where the smaller ferries and catamarans dock, is 400m north of the town waterfront. The new quay, where the bigger boats dock, is 2.5km north of town. Buses meet arriving ferries. When leaving Mykonos, double-check which quay your boat leaves from.

The **Tourist Information Office** (☎ 22890 25250; www.mykonos.gr; 9am-9pm Jul & Aug, 10am-5pm Easter-Jun, Sep & Oct) is at the western end of the waterfront. This is a new venture for Mykonos and time will tell if it survives. **Island Mykonos Travel** (☎ 22890 22232; www.discovergreece.org), on Taxi Sq, where the port road meets the town, is helpful for travel information. At the old port, the same building houses the **Hoteliers Association of Mykonos** (☎ 22890 24540; www.mha.gr; 8am-4pm) and the **Association of Rooms, Studios & Apartments** (☎ 22890 24860; www.mykonosfamilyhotels.com; 9am-4pm). Both can book accommodation.

Angelo's Internet Café (☎ 22890 24106; Xenias; per hr €4.50) is on the road between the southern bus station and the windmills.

Sights & Activities

A stroll around **Mykonos Town**, shuffling through snaking streets with blinding white walls and balconies of flowers is a must for any visitor. Don't forget your sunglasses! **Little Venice**, where the sea laps up to the edge of the restaurants and bars, and Mykonos' famous hilltop row of **windmills** should be included in the spots-to-see list. You're bound to run into one of Mykonos' famous resident pelicans on your walk.

The island's most popular beaches are on the southern coast. **Platys Gialos** has wall-to-wall sun lounges, while nudity is not uncommon at **Paradise Beach**, **Super Paradise**, **Agrari** and gay-friendly **Elia**.

Sleeping

Mykonos has two camping areas, both on the south coast. Minibuses from both meet the ferries and buses go regularly into town. Rooms in town fill up quickly in the high season.

Paradise Beach Camping (☎ 22890 22852; www.paradisemykonos.com; camp sites per tent/person €5/9;) There are lots of options here, including camping, beach cabins and apartments, as well as bars, a swimming pool, games etc. It is skin-to-skin mayhem in summer with a real party atmosphere.

Mykonos Camping (☎ 22890 24578; www.mycamp.gr; camp sites per tent/person €5/10) This place, right on Paraga Beach, also has plenty of options, ranging from tents to dorm rooms to apartments. There's a minimarket, self-service restaurant and bar.

Hotel Apollon (☎ 22890 22223; fax 22890 24237; Paralia, Mykonos Town; s/d with shared bathroom €50/65) Prepare for some old-world Mykonian charm in the middle of the main waterfront. Rooms are traditional and well kept, and the owner is friendly.

Hotel Philippi (☎ 22890 22294; chriko@otenet.gr; 25 Kalogera, Mykonos Town; s €60-90, d €75-120;) In the heart of the *hora*, Philippi has spacious, bright, clean rooms that open onto a railed veranda overlooking a lush garden. An extremely pleasant place to stay.

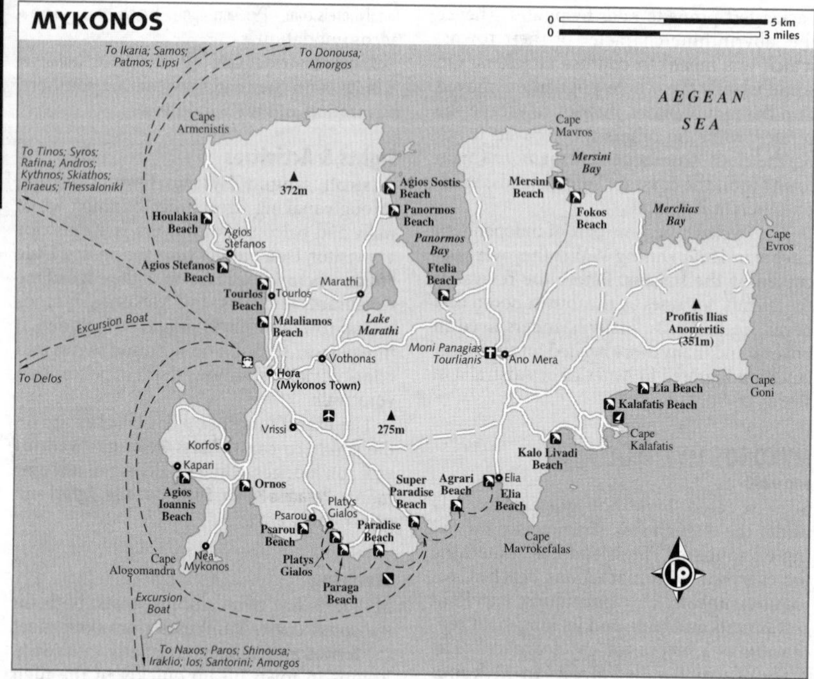

Hotel Lefteris (☎ 22890 27117; www.lefterishotel.gr; 9 Apollonas, Mykonos Town; s/d €90/115, studios €180-230;) Tucked away just up from Taxi Sq, Lefteris has bright and comfy rooms, and a relaxing sun terrace with superb views over town. A good international meeting place.

Eating & Drinking

There is no shortage of places to eat and drink in Mykonos Town. If you're on a budget, steer clear of the waterfront and head into the back of the maze that is Mykonos Town, where there are plenty of cheap eats.

Madupas (☎ 22890 22224; Paralia; mains €5-12) On the waterfront, Madupas serves a mean Mykonian sausage and is a great spot to chill out with a Mythos and watch the parade of passers-by.

Paraportiani (☎ 22890 23531; mains from €7) Just above the western end of the waterfront, Paraportiani does superb seafood and benefits from having the town's top tout, one of Mykonos' resident pelicans.

Fato a Mano (☎ 22890 26256; Meletopoulou Sq; mains €8-15) In the back of the maze, Fato a Mano is worth taking the effort to find, serving up tasty Mediterranean and traditional Greek dishes.

Katerina's Bar (☎ 22890 23084; Agion Anargion) In Little Venice, this place has dreamy views from its balcony and water lapping below your feet.

Cavo Paradiso (☎ 22890 27205; www.cavoparadiso.gr) For those who want to go the whole hog, this club 300m above Paradise Beach picks up around 2am and boasts a pool the shape of Mykonos. A bus transports clubbers from town in summer.

Long feted as a gay travel destination, Mykonos has plenty of gay-centric clubs and hang-outs. In Little Venice, **Kastro** (☎ 22890 23072; Agion Anargion) is the spot to start the night with cocktails as the sun sets. **Pierro's** (☎ 22890 22177), just near Taxi Sq, is a popular dance club for rounding off the night.

Getting There & Around

There are daily flights connecting Mykonos airport (JMK) to Athens (€65). **Olympic Airlines** (OA; ☎ 22890 22327) is by the southern bus station, or call **Aegean Airlines** (A3; ☎ 22890 28720; airport). **Sky Express** (SEH; ☎ 28102 23500; www.skyexpress.gr) flies to Iraklio (Crete), Santorini and Rhodes with varying regularity.

Daily ferries arrive from Piraeus (€25, six hours). From Mykonos, there are daily ferries and hydrofoils to most major Cycladic islands, daily services to Crete, and less-frequent services to the northeastern Aegean Islands and the Dodecanese. Head to Island Mykonos Travel (p381) for details and tickets.

The northern bus station is near the old port. It serves Agios Stefanos, Elia, Kalafatis and Ano Mera. The southern bus station, a 300m walk up from the windmills, serves Agios Ioannis, Psarou, Platys Gialos and Paradise Beach. In summer, caiques (small fishing boats) from Mykonos Town and Platys Gialos putter to Paradise, Super Paradise, Agrari and Elia Beaches.

PAROS ΠΑΡΟΣ

pop 13,000

Paros is a friendly, attractive laid-back island with an enticing main town, good swimming beaches and terraced hills that build up to Mt Profitis Ilias (770m). It has long been prosperous, thanks to an abundance of pure white marble from which the *Venus de Milo* and Napoleon's tomb were sculpted.

Orientation & Information

Paros' main town and port is Parikia, on the west coast. Opposite the ferry terminal, on the far side of Windmill roundabout, is Plateia Mavrogenous, the main square. Agora, also known as Market St, the main commercial thoroughfare, runs southwest from the far end of the square.

There is no tourist office, but travel agencies such as **Santorineos Travel** (☎ 22840 24245; bookings@santorineos-travel.gr), on the waterfront near Windmill roundabout, oblige with information. Check also www.parosweb.com. From the ferry quay it's easy to spot Mike's Rooms. Further down that street and around the corner is **Planet Internet Café** (☎ 22840 25060; per 30min €1.50; 🕑 10am-2am).

Sights & Activities

Panagia Ekatontapyliani (☎ 22840 21243; 🕑 7.30am-9.30pm), known for its beautiful ornate interior, is one of the most impressive churches in the Cyclades, dating from AD 326. Within the church compound, the **Byzantine Museum** (admission €1.50; 🕑 9.30am-2pm & 6-9pm) has an interesting collection of icons and other artefacts.

A great option on Paros is to rent a scooter or car at one of the many outlets in Parikia and cruise around the island. There are sealed roads the whole way, and the opportunity to explore villages such as **Naoussa**, **Marpissa** and **Aliki**, and swim at beaches such as **Logaras**, **Punda** and **Golden Beach**. Naoussa is a cute little fishing village on the northeastern coast that is all geared up to welcome tourists.

WORTH THE TRIP: DELOS ΔΗΛΟΣ

Southwest of Mykonos, the island of **Delos** (☎ 22890 22259; sites & museum €5; 🕑 9am-3pm Tue-Sun) is the Cyclades' archaeological jewel. The opportunity to clamber among the ruins shouldn't be missed.

According to mythology, Delos was the birthplace of Apollo – the god of light, poetry, music, healing and prophecy. The island flourished as an important religious and commercial centre from the 3rd millennium BC, reaching its apex of power in the 5th century BC.

Ruins include the **Sanctuary of Apollo**, containing temples dedicated to him, and the **Terrace of the Lions**. These proud beasts were carved in the early 6th century BC using marble from Naxos to guard the sacred area. The original lions are in the island's museum, with replicas on the original site. The **Sacred Lake** (dry since 1926) is where Leto supposedly gave birth to Apollo, while the **Theatre Quarter** is where private houses were built around the **Theatre of Delos**.

The climb up **Mt Kynthos** (113m), the island's highest point, is a highlight. The view of Delos and the surrounding islands is spectacular, and it's easy to see how the Cyclades got their name.

Take a sunhat, sunscreen, sturdy footwear, food and drinks. The island's cafeteria goes from operating one year to be closed the next, so don't bank on it being open when you turn up. Overnighting on Delos is forbidden.

Numerous boat companies offer trips from Mykonos to Delos (€12.50 return, 30 minutes) between 9am and 12.50pm. The return boats leave Delos between noon and 3pm. There is also a €5 per person entry fee on arrival at Delos.

Boats also operate to Delos from Naxos (€40) and Paros (€40).

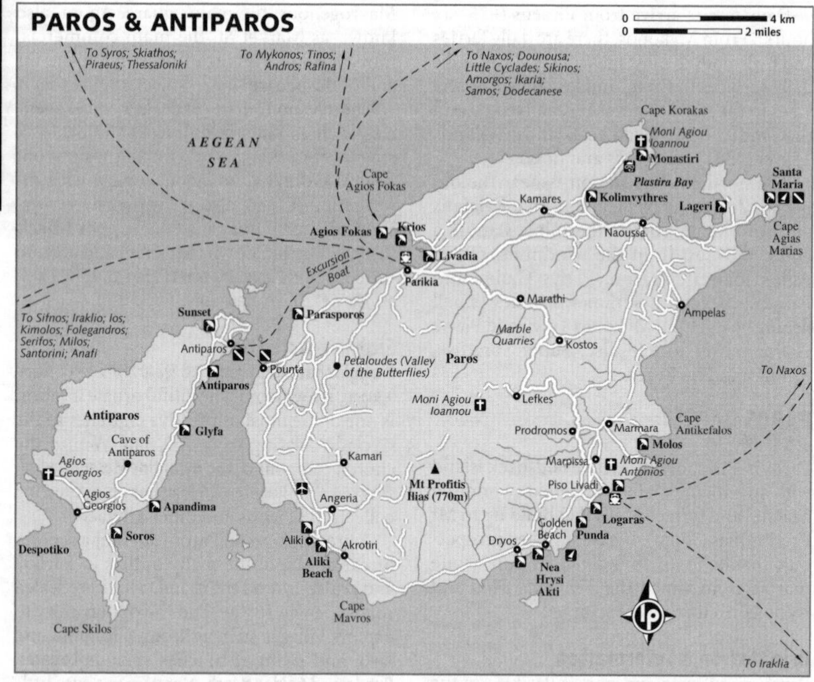

Less than 2km from Paros, the small island of **Antiparos** has fantastic beaches, which have made it wildly popular. Another attraction is its **Cave of Antiparos** (admission €3.50; 10.15am-3.45pm Jun-Sep), considered to be one of Europe's best.

Sleeping

The **Rooms Association** (22840 22722; 9am-1am) has a helpful kiosk on the quay. There's loads of camping around Paros, with charges of around €6 per person and €4 per tent.

Rooms Mike (22840 22856; www.roomsmike.com; s/d/tr €30/40/50) A popular and friendly place, Mike's offers good location and local advice. There are options of rooms with shared facilities through to fully self-contained units with kitchens. Mike's sign is easy to spot from the quay, away to the left.

Rooms Rena (22840 22220; www.cycladesnet.gr/rena; Epitropakis; s/d/tr €30/40/50;) The quiet and well-kept rooms here are excellent value. Turn left from the pier then right at the ancient cemetery and follow the signs.

our pick Pension Sofia (22840 22085; www.sofiapension-paros.com; s/d/tr €60/70/80;) If you've got a few extra euros and don't mind the stroll to town, this place, with its beautifully tended garden and immaculate rooms, is a great option that won't be regretted.

Eating & Drinking

Happy Green Cows (22840 24691; mains from €5; 7pm-midnight) Just off the back of the main square, this place is popular with vegetarians. The menu and meal names are both creative, and the bar stays open after the kitchen closes.

Porphyra (22840 22693; mains from €5) A family-run place, Porphyra serves excellent fresh seafood next to the ancient cemetery. It's 200m east of the ferry quay.

Levantis (22840 23613; mains €9-15) This popular long-established place in the Kastro area features a relaxing courtyard setting and imaginative cuisine.

Pebbles Bar (22840 22283) Perched above the waterfront west of the quay, Pebbles has stunning views, and plays classical music by day and jazz in the evenings.

Getting There & Around

Paros' airport (PAS) has daily flight connections with Athens (€60); contact **Olympic Airlines** (OA; ☎ 22840 21257; Plateia Mavrogenous, Parikia) for details.

Parikia is a major ferry hub with daily connections to Piraeus (€30, five hours) and frequent ferries and catamarans to Naxos, Ios, Santorini, Mykonos and Crete. The fast boats generally take half the time but are more expensive, eg a fast boat to Piraeus costs €45. The Dodecanese and the northeastern Aegean Islands are also well serviced from here. Head to Santorineos Travel (p383) for tickets.

From Parikia there are frequent bus services to the entire island. In summer there are excursion boats to Antiparos from Parikia port, or you can catch a bus to Pounta and ferry across.

NAXOS ΝΑΞΟΣ

pop 18,200

The biggest and greenest of the Cyclades group, Naxos could probably survive without tourism – unlike many of its neighbouring islands. Deeply fertile, Naxos produces olives, grapes, figs, citrus, corn and potatoes. The island is well worth taking the time to explore with its fascinating main town, excellent beaches and striking interior.

Orientation & Information

Naxos Town, on the west coast, is the island's capital and port. The ferry quay is at the northern end of the waterfront, with the bus terminal out front. The island website is www.naxos-greece.net.

Naxos Tourist Information Centre (NTIC; ☎ 22850 25201; www.naxostownhotels.com; 8am-midnight), a privately owned organisation just opposite the port, offers help with accommodation, tours, luggage storage and laundry. Next door, **Zas Travel** (☎ 22850 23330; 8am-midnight) sells ferry tickets and offers internet access for €4 an hour.

Sights & Activities

Behind the waterfront in Naxos Town, narrow alleyways scramble up to the spectacular hilltop 13th-century **kastro**, where the Venetian Catholics lived. The *kastro* looks out over the town, and has a well-stocked **archaeological museum** (☎ 22850 22725; admission €3; 8.30am-3pm Tue-Sun).

The beach of **Agios Georgios** is a 10-minute walk south from the main waterfront. Beyond it, wonderful sandy beaches stretch as far south as **Pyrgaki Beach**. **Agia Anna Beach**, 6km from town, and **Plaka Beach** are lined with accommodation and packed in summer.

A hire car or scooter will help reveal Naxos' dramatic landscape. The **Tragaea region** has tranquil villages, churches atop rocky crags and huge olive groves. **Filoti**, the largest inland settlement, perches on the slopes of **Mt Zeus** (1004m), the highest peak in the Cyclades.

In **Apollonas** there's the mysterious 10.5m **kouros** (naked male statue), constructed c 7th century, lying abandoned and unfinished in an ancient marble quarry.

Sleeping

Camping Maragas (☎ 22850 42552; www.maragascamping.gr/naxos-camping.htm; camp sites €9, d/studio €45/70) On Agia Anna Beach to the south of town, this place has all sorts of options, including camping, rooms and studios, and there is a restaurant and minimarket on site.

Hotel Grotta (☎ 22850 22215; www.hotelgrotta.gr; s/d incl breakfast €70/85;) Overlooking Grotta Beach at the northern end of town, this modern hotel has comfortable and immaculate rooms, a jacuzzi and minipool, and offers great sea views. Service is friendly and internet use, including wi-fi, is free.

our pick **Pension Sofi** (☎ 22850 23077; www.pensionsofi.gr; r €30-75;) and **Studios Panos** (☎ 22850 26078; www.studiospanos.com; Agios Georgios Beach; r €30-60;) are both run by members of the friendly Koufopoulos family. Sofi's in town, while Panos is a 10-minute walk away near Agios Georgios Beach. Guests are met with a glass of family-made wine or ouzo and rooms are immaculate with bathroom and kitchen. Highly recommended; rates at both places halve out of the high season. Call ahead for a pick-up at the port. Sofi is open year-round; Panos opens from April to October.

Eating & Drinking

Naxos Town's waterfront is lined with eating and drinking establishments.

Meze 2 (☎ 22850 26401; Paralia; mains €2.50-9) An excellent old-style *mezedopoleio-ouzeri* (restaurant specialising in appetisers and ouzo) on the waterfront, this place is popular with locals and serves up superb seafood dishes. Even the local fishermen eat here.

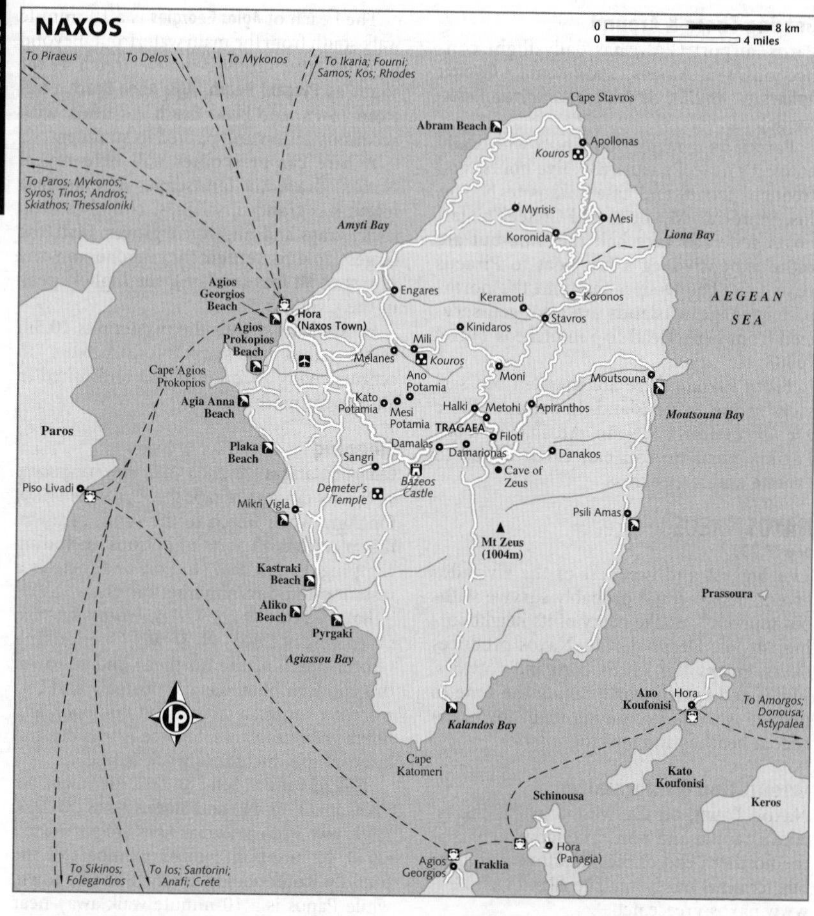

To Smyrneiko (☎ 22850 24443; mains from €5) Another top pick among many restaurants along the waterfront, this place also does seafood well.

our pick Picasso Mexican Bistro (☎ 22850 25408; mains from €5) This is a stylish and popular place that does sensational Tex-Mex 20m off Court Sq, a few minutes' walk south of the main waterfront. Receives rave reviews.

Lemon (☎ 22850 24734; Protopapadaki) A cool cocktail bar and cafe right in the middle of the waterfront. Relax with a drink and watch the world go by.

Ocean (☎ 22850 26766; admission €10; from 11.30pm) At the southern end of the waterfront, this place goes wild after midnight, featuring guest DJs and some modern Greek music.

Getting There & Around

Naxos airport (JNX) has daily flight connections with Athens (€60), and Olympic Airlines is represented by **Naxos Travel** (☎ 22850 22095). There are daily ferries (€30, five hours) and catamarans (€45, 3¾ hours) from Naxos to Piraeus, and good ferry and hydrofoil connections to most Cycladic islands and Crete. There are also ferries to Thessaloniki (€48, 15 hours, weekly) and Rhodes (€32, 14 hours, twice weekly). Zas Travel (p385) can provide ferry details and sells tickets.

Buses travel to most villages regularly from the bus terminal in front of the port. Car and motorcycle rentals are available off Court Sq.

IOS ΙΟΣ

pop 1850

Ios has long held a reputation as 'Party Island'. There are wall-to-wall bars and nightclubs in 'the village' (Hora) that thump all night, and fantastic fun facilities at Milopotas Beach that entertain all day. You won't leave disappointed if you're there to party.

But there's more to Ios than just hedonistic activities. British poet and novelist Lawrence Durrell thought highly of Ios as a place of poetry and beauty, and there is an enduring claim that Homer was buried on Ios, with his alleged tomb in the north of the island.

Orientation & Information

Ios' three population centres are close together on the west coast. Ormos is the port, where ferries arrive. Two kilometres inland is 'the village', Hora, while 2km down from Hora to the southeast is Milopotas Beach. The young tend to stay in 'the village' or Milopotas, and the others at Ormos.

There is no tourist office, but **Acteon Travel** (☎ 22860 91343; www.acteon.gr) has offices in Ormos, the village and Milopotas and is helpful. **Double Click Internet** (☎ 22860 92155; Hora; per hr €4) is one of dozens of places providing internet access. Check out www.iosgr eece.com.

Sights & Activities

The village has an intrinsic charm with its labyrinth of white-walled streets, and it's very easy to get lost, even if you haven't had one too many.

Apart from the nightlife, it's the beaches that lure travellers to Ios. While **Gialos Beach** near the port is crowded, **Koubara Beach**, a 1.3km walk west of Gialos, is less so and is the nudist beach.

Milopotas has everything a resort beach could ask for and parties hard. **Meltemi Water Sports** (☎ 22860 91680; www.meltemiwatersports.com) at the beach's far end has rental windsurfers, sailboats and canoes.

Isolated **Manganari** on the south coast is known as Ios' most beautiful beach and is reached by bus or excursion boat in summer.

More and more roads are being sealed on Ios, and a rental car or scooter is becoming a good option for exploring the island. Homer's Tomb is 12km north of Hora.

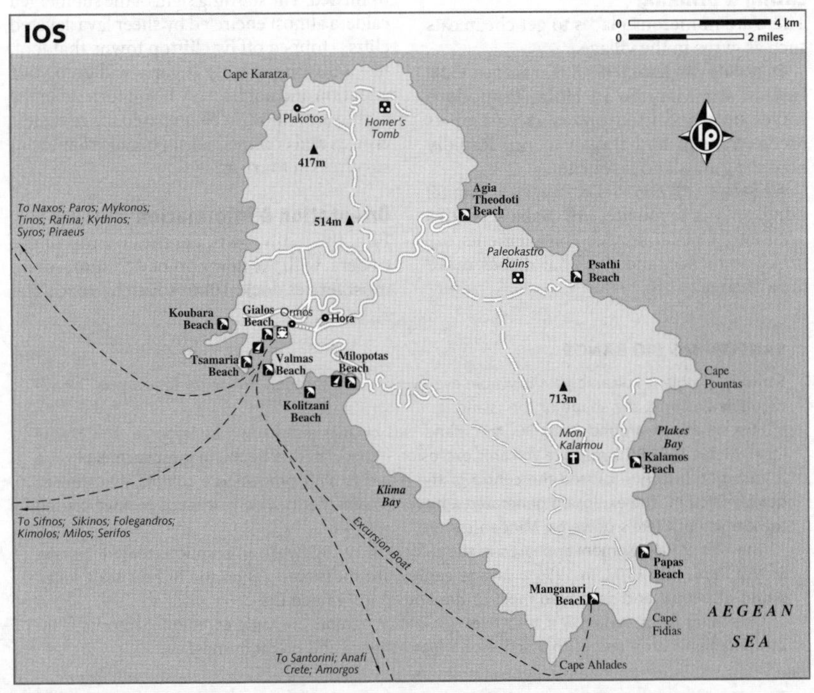

Sleeping

Far Out Camping & Beach Club (☎ 22860 91468; www.faroutclub.com; Milopotas; camp sites per person €12, bungalows €12-20, studios €90;) Right on Milopotas Beach, this place has tons of options. Facilities include camping, bungalows and hotel rooms, and its pools are open to the public. Details are on the website.

Francesco's (☎ 22860 91223; www.francescos.net; Hora; dm/s/d €15/35/45;) A lively meeting place in the village with superlative views from its terrace bar, Francesco's is convenient for party-going and rates halve out of the high season. The party spirit rules here, especially in the new 'giant Jacuzzi'.

Hotel Nissos Ios (☎ 22860 91610; www.nissosios-hotel.com; Milopotas; s/d/tr €50/70/85;) This cheerful place is on Milopotas Beach. Rooms feature huge colourful wall murals, and the excellent Bamboo Restaurant & Pizzeria on site.

Hotel Poseidon (☎ 22860 91091; www.poseidonhotelios.gr; Ormos; s/d/tr €70/80/100;) Near the ferry quay in Ormos, the Poseidon offers superb views, spacious rooms and a refreshing pool for a quieter stay on Ios.

Eating & Drinking

There are numerous places to get cheap eats such as gyros in the village.

Pomodoro (☎ 22860 91387; Hora; mains from €5.50) Just off the Main Sq in Hora, Pomodoro serves up wood-fired pizzas as part of its Mediterranean and Italian menu. Rapidly becoming an island favourite.

Ali Baba's (☎ 22860 91558; Hora; mains from €6) Long an Ios favourite, Ali Baba's parties until late. Upbeat service complements the funky ambience, and the Thai dishes make for a change.

our pick **Pithari** (☎ 22860 92440; Hora; mains from €8) Behind the cathedral at the entrance to Hora, Pithari offers an excellent array of tasty dishes. The seafood spaghetti is especially good.

At night, the compact little village erupts with bars. Its tiny central square gets so packed that by midnight you won't be able to fall over even if you want to. Perennial favourites include **Red Bull** (☎ 22860 91019), **Slammers** (☎ 22860 92119) and **Blue Note** (☎ 22860 92271).

Getting There & Around

Ios has daily ferry connections with Piraeus (€25, seven hours) and there are frequent hydrofoils and ferries to the major Cycladic islands and Crete. There are buses every 15 minutes between the port, the village and Milopotas Beach until early morning, and two to three a day to Manganari Beach (€8, 45 minutes). Head to Acteon Travel (p387) for details and tickets.

SANTORINI (THIRA) ΣΑΝΤΟΡΙΝΗ (ΘΗΡΑ)

pop 13,500

Stunning Santorini is unique and should not be missed. The startling sight of the submerged caldera almost encircled by sheer lava-layered cliffs – topped off by clifftop towns that look like a dusting of icing sugar – will grab your attention and not let it go. If you turn up in the high season though, be prepared for relentless crowds and commercialism because Santorini survives on tourism.

Orientation & Information

Fira, the main town, perches on top of the caldera, with the new port of Athinios, where most ferries dock, 10km south by road. The

SANTORINI'S BIG BANGS

Santorini's violent volcanic past is visible everywhere, and through the centuries eruptions have regularly changed the shape of the island.

First inhabited around 3000 BC, the island was circular and known as Strongili (the Round One). About 1650 BC a massive volcanic explosion – speculated to be the biggest such explosion in recorded history – caused the centre of the island to sink, producing a caldera that the sea quickly filled in. The explosion generated a huge tsunami that is widely believed to have caused the demise of Crete's powerful Minoan culture.

The islet of Palia Kameni appeared in the caldera in 197 BC, while an eruption created the islet of Nea Kameni in 1707. In 1956 a savage earthquake measuring 7.8 on the Richter scale killed scores of people and destroyed most of the houses in Fira and Oia.

One thing is for certain – it isn't over yet. Minor tremors are fairly common. Santorini is incomparable when it comes to a sense of impermanence and precariousness.

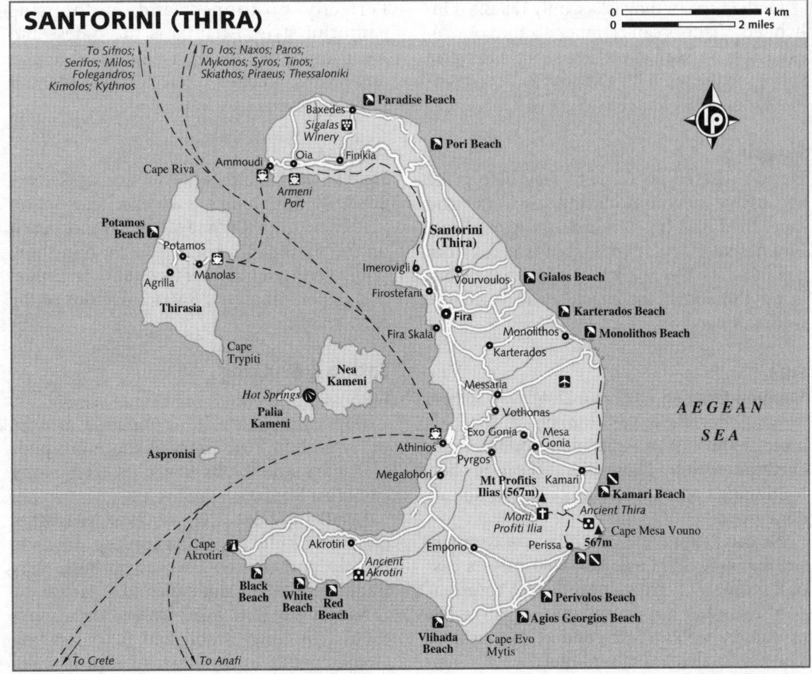

old port of Fira Skala, used by cruise ships and excursion boats, is directly below Fira and accessed by cable car (adult/child €4/2 one way), donkey (€4, up only) or by foot (588 steps).

The bus station and taxi station are just south of Fira's main square, Plateia Theotokopoulou.

Dakoutros Travel (☎ 22860 22958; www.dakoutrostravel.gr; 🕙 8.30am-10pm), opposite the taxi station, is extremely helpful, and there is a batch of other agencies around the square. Check out www.santorini.net for more info. Internet access is available at **PC World** (☎ 22860 25551; Central Sq; per 30min €2.10). The post office is one block south of the taxi station.

Sights & Activities

FIRA

The stunning caldera views from Fira are unparalleled.

The exceptional **Museum of Prehistoric Thira** (☎ 22860 23217; admission €3; 🕙 8.30am-3pm Tue-Sun), which has wonderful displays of artefacts predominantly from ancient Akrotiri, is two blocks south of the main square. **Megaron Gyzi Museum** (☎ 22860 22244; admission €3.50; 🕙 10.30am-1pm & 5-8pm Mon-Sat, 10.30am-4.30pm Sun), behind the Catholic cathedral, houses local memorabilia, including photographs of Fira before and after the 1956 earthquake.

AROUND THE ISLAND

Santorini's black-sand **beaches** of **Perissa** and **Kamari** sizzle – beach mats are essential. It's a strange feeling to walk over black sand then out onto smooth lava when going for a dip.

Excavations in 1967 uncovered the remarkably well-preserved Minoan settlement of **Akrotiri** at the south of the island with its remains of two- and three-storey buildings. A section of the roof collapsed in 2005 killing one visitor, and at the time of research, the site's future as a visitor attraction was up in the air.

On the north of the island, the flawless village of **Oia** (ee-ah), famed for its postcard sunsets, is less hectic than Fira and a must-visit. Its caldera-facing tavernas are superb spots for brunch. There's a path from Fira to Oia along the top of the caldera that takes three to four hours to walk.

Of the surrounding islets, only **Thirasia** is inhabited. Visitors can clamber around on volcanic lava on **Nea Kameni** then swim into warm springs in the sea at **Palia Kameni**; there are various excursions available to get you there.

Sleeping

Decide where you want to stay before the aggressive accommodation owners who meet the boats try to decide things for you. Fira has spectacular views, but is miles from the beaches. Perissa has a great beach but is on the southeast coast, away from the caldera views.

FIRA

Santorini Camping (☎ 22860 22944; www.santorinicamping.gr; Fira; camp sites per person €9;) This place, 500m east of Fira's main square, is the cheapest option. There is a restaurant, bar, minimarket and swimming pool, but no caldera views.

Pension Petros (☎ 22860 22573; www.astirthira.gr/petros; r €30-60;) three hundred metres east of the square, Petro's offers decent rooms at good rates, free airport and port transfers, but no caldera views. It's a good budget option. The family also has other hotels.

Hotel Keti (☎ 22860 22324; www.hotelketi.gr; Agiou Mina; d/tr €80/105;) Overlooking the caldera, with views to die for, Hotel Keti has traditional rooms carved into the cliffs. Half of the rooms have jacuzzis.

our pick Hotel Atlantis (☎ 22860 22232; www.atlantishotel.gr; s/d incl breakfast €200/284;) Perfectly positioned and epitomising Santorini style, Atlantis is the oldest and most impressive place in Fira. With bright, airy rooms, relaxing terraces and lounges, it is a superb place to stay.

PERISSA

Stelio's Place (☎ 22860 81860; www.steliosplace.com; r €30-80;) Stelio's is an excellent option just back from Perissa's black-sand beach on the southeast coast. There's a refreshing pool, very friendly service, and free port and airport transfers. Rates halve out of the high season.

Eating & Drinking

FIRA

Cheap eateries are in abundance around the square in Fira. Most of the more popular bars and clubs are clustered along Erythrou Stavrou.

Fanari (☎ 22860 25107; www.fanari-restaurant.gr; mains from €5) On the street leading down to the old port, Fanari's serves up both tasty traditional dishes and superlative views.

Nikolas (☎ 22860 24550; Erythrou Stavrou; mains €5-10) This long-established place serving Greek cuisine in the heart of Fira receives rave reviews from diners. From the main square, head straight up the pedestrian mall (Danezi) and take the first right.

Kira Thira (☎ 22860 22770) Opposite Nikolas restaurant, Kira Thira is Fira's oldest bar and plays smooth jazz, ethnic sounds and occasional live music.

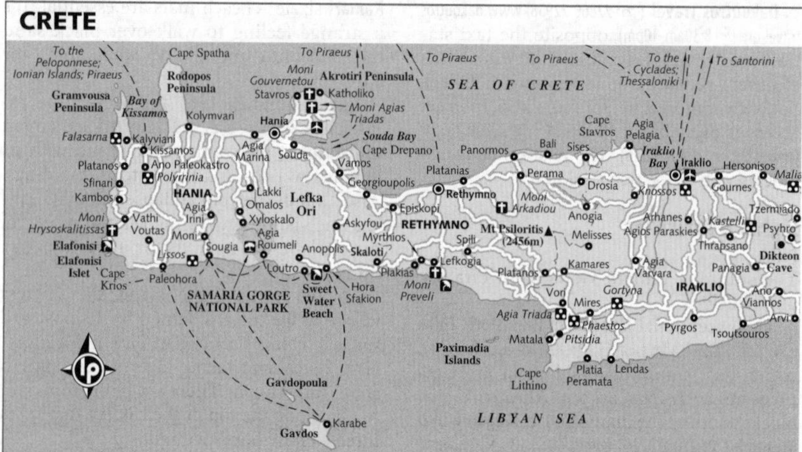

PERISSA

Great eating and drinking options line the waterfront in Perissa.

Taverna Lava (☎ 22860 81776; mains €3-8) On Perissa's waterfront, this islandwide favourite has a mouth-watering menu. You can visit the kitchen and pick what looks good.

Full Moon Bar (☎ 22860 81177; 🕒 9pm-late) On the main street in Perissa, this lively nightspot goes off until the wee hours.

Getting There & Around

Santorini airport (JTR) has daily flight connections with Athens (€60). Call **Olympic Airlines** (OA; ☎ 22860 22493) or **Aegean Airlines** (A3; ☎ 22860 28500) for details. **Sky Express** (SEH; ☎ 28102 23500; www.skyexpress.gr) has connections with Crete, Mykonos and Rhodes with varying regularity.

There are daily ferries (€28, nine hours) and fast boats (€45, 5¼ hours) to Piraeus; daily connections in summer to Mykonos, Ios, Naxos, Paros and Iraklio; and ferries to the smaller islands in the Cyclades. Large ferries use Athinios port, where they are met by buses (€1.20) and taxis. Get your tickets from Dakoutros Travel (p389).

Buses go frequently to Oia, Kamari, Perissa and Akrotiri from Fira. Port buses usually leave Fira, Kamari and Perissa one to 1½ hours before ferry departures. A rental car or scooter is a great option on Santorini.

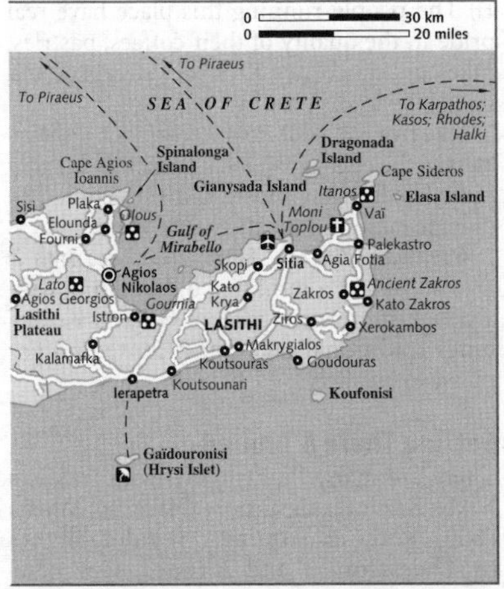

CRETE ΚΡΗΤΗ

pop 540,000

Crete is Greece's largest and most southerly island and its size and distance from the rest of Greece gives it the feel of a different country. With its dramatic landscape and unique cultural identity, Crete is a delight to explore.

The island is split by a spectacular chain of mountains running east to west. Major towns are on the more hospitable northern coast, while most of the southern coast is too precipitous to support large settlements. The rugged mountainous interior, dotted with caves and sliced by dramatic gorges, offers rigorous hiking and climbing.

While Crete's proud, friendly and hospitable people have enthusiastically embraced tourism, they continue to fiercely protect their traditions and culture – and it is the people that remain a major part of the island's appeal.

For more detailed information, snap up a copy of Lonely Planet's *Crete*. Good websites on Crete include www.interkriti.org, www.infocrete.com and www.explorecrete.com.

History

Crete was the birthplace of Minoan culture, Europe's first advanced civilisation, which flourished between 2800 and 1450 BC. Very little is known of Minoan civilisation, which came to an abrupt end, possibly destroyed by Santorini's volcanic eruption in around 1650 BC. Later, Crete passed from the warlike Dorians to the Romans, and then to the Genoese, who in turn sold it to the Venetians. Under the Venetians, Crete became a refuge for artists, writers and philosophers who fled after it fell to the Turks. Their influence inspired the young Cretan painter Domenikos Theotokopoulos, who moved to Spain and there won immortality as the great El Greco.

The Turks conquered Crete in 1670. In 1898 Crete became a British protectorate after a series of insurrections and was united with independent Greece in 1913. There was fierce fighting during WWII when a German airborne invasion defeated Allied forces in the 10-day Battle of Crete. A fierce resistance movement drew heavy German reprisals, including the slaughter of whole villages.

IRAKLIO ΗΡΑΚΛΕΙΟ

pop 131,000

Iraklio (ee-*rah*-klee-oh; often spelt Heraklion), Crete's capital, is a bustling modern city and the fifth-largest in Greece. It has a lively city centre, an excellent archaeological museum and is close to Knossos, Crete's major visitor attraction.

Orientation & Information

Iraklio's harbours face north into the Sea of Crete. The old harbour is instantly recognisable as it is protected by the old Venetian fortress. The new harbour is 400m east. Plateia Venizelou, known for its Lion Fountain, is the heart of the city, 400m south of the old harbour up 25 Avgoustou.

The **tourist office** (☎ 28102 46299; Xanthoudidou 1; 🕑 8.30am-8.30pm Apr-Oct, to 3pm Nov-Mar) is opposite the archaeological museum. There is good information at www.heraklion-city.gr. **KTEL** (www.ktel.org), which runs the buses on Crete, has useful tourist information inside Bus Station A.

Skoutelis Travel (☎ 28102 80808; www.skoutelis.gr; 25 Avgoustou 20), between Plateia Venizelou and the old harbour, handles airline and ferry bookings, and rents cars. **Gallery Games** (☎ 28102 82804; Korai 14; per hr €1.50; 🕑 24hr) and a host of other places have high-speed internet access.

Sights

Iraklio's **archaeological museum** (☎ 28102 79000; Xanthoudidou 2; adult/student €6/3; 🕑 12.30-7pm Mon, 8am-7pm Tue-Sun) has an outstanding Minoan collection, second only to the national museum in Athens.

Protecting the old harbour is the impressive **Koules Venetian Fortress** (☎ 28102 46211; adult/student €2/1; 🕑 9am-6pm Tue-Sun), also known as Rocca al Mare, which, like the city walls, was built by the Venetians in the 16th century.

The **Battle of Crete Museum** (☎ 28103 46554; cnr Doukos Beaufort & Hatzidaki; admission free; 🕑 8am-3pm) chronicles the historic WWII battle with photographs, letters, uniforms and weapons.

Sleeping

Rent Rooms Hellas (☎ 28102 88851; Handakos 24; dm/d/tr with shared bathroom €11/30/42) A popular budget choice, this place has a lively atmosphere, packed dorms, a rooftop bar and a bargain breakfast (from €2.50).

Hotel Mirabello (☎ 28102 85052; www.mirabello-hotel.gr; Theotokopoulou 20; s/d €35/44; 💻 ❄) A pleasant, relaxed budget hotel on a quiet street in the centre of town, this place is run by an ex-sea captain who has travelled the world. A good-value option. Check out the excellent website.

Hotel Kronos (☎ 28102 82240; www.kronoshotel.gr; Sofokli Venizelou 2; s/d €49/65; ❄ 💻) Down by the old harbour, this well-maintained older hotel has large, airy rooms that come with phone and TV. Ask for a room with a sea view.

our pick **Lato Boutique Hotel** (☎ 28102 28103; www.lato.gr; Epimenidou 15; s/d €100/127; ❄ 💻) A top place to stay is this stylish boutique hotel overlooking the waterfront. Ask for a room with harbour views. The contemporary interior design extends to the bar, breakfast restaurant and Brilliant (☎ 28103 34959), the superb fine-dining restaurant on the ground floor.

Eating & Drinking

There's a congregation of cheap eateries in the Plateia Venizelou and El Greco Park area, as well as a bustling, colourful market all the way along 1866.

Giakoumis Taverna (☎ 28102 80277; Theodosaki 5-8; mains €2.50-8; 🕑 closed Sun) With its full menu of Cretan specialities, Giakoumis is the best of a bunch of cheap tavernas in the market area. Take the first left heading inland up 1866.

Ippokambos Ouzeri (☎ 28102 80240; Mitsotaki 2; mains €3.50-8) On the waterfront, this place serves up a popular, well-priced menu. Enjoy eating at a pavement table or on the promenade across the road.

Samaria Delizioso (☎ 28102 86203; Kantanoleon 11) The people running this place have real pride in the quality of their coffees, pastries, cakes and chocolates. Kick back streetside and watch the locals pass by.

Take Five (☎ 28102 26564; Akroleondos 7; 🕑 10am-late) On the edge of El Greco Park, this friendly place has low-key music and ambience. The outside tables fill up after sundown.

Guernica (☎ 28102 82988; Apokoronou Kritis 2; 🕑 10am-late) In a rambling old building with a delightful terrace garden, Guernica combines traditional decor and contemporary music exquisitely.

Getting There & Around

There are many flights daily from Iraklio's Nikos Kazantzakis airport (HER) to Athens (€60) and, in summer, regular flights to Thessaloniki and Rhodes. Get your

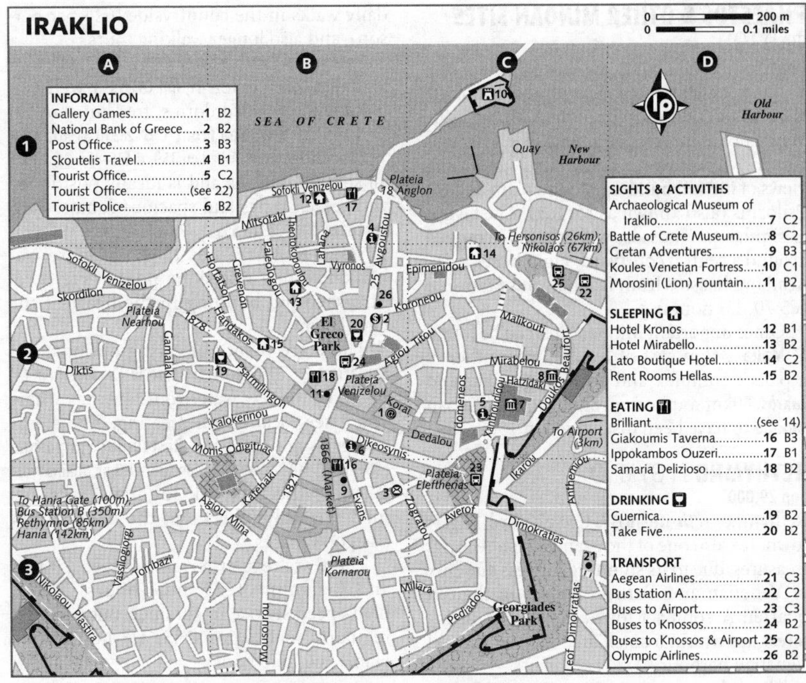

tickets from **Olympic Airlines** (OA; ☎ 28102 44824; 25 Avgoustou 27) or **Aegean Airlines** (A3; ☎ 28103 44324; Leof Dimokratias 11). **Sky Express** (SEH; ☎ 28102 23500; www.skyexpress.gr), based in Iraklio, generally flies routes that Olympic and Aegean don't. Check its website for up-to-date options.

Daily ferries service Piraeus (€30, seven hours), and most days boats go to Santorini and continue on to other Cycladic islands. Head to Skoutelis Travel (opposite) for schedules and tickets.

Iraklio has two bus stations. Bus Station A is just inland from the new harbour and serves eastern Crete (Agios Nikolaos, Ierapetra, Sitia, Malia and the Lasithi Plateau). The Hania and Rethymno terminal is opposite Bus Station A.

Bus Station B, 50m beyond the Hania Gate, serves the southern route (Phaestos, Matala and Anogia). Check out www.ktel .org for long-distance bus information.

Bus 1 travels between the airport and city centre (€1.20) every 15 minutes from 6am to 1am. It stops at Plateia Eleftherias, across the road from the archaeological museum.

KNOSSOS ΚΝΩΣΣΟΣ

Five kilometres south of Iraklio, **Knossos** (☎ 28102 31940; admission €6; 🕒 8am-7pm Jun-Oct, to 5pm Nov-May) was the capital of Minoan Crete, and is now the island's major tourist attraction.

Knossos (k-nos-*os*) is the most famous of Crete's Minoan sites and is the inspiration for the myth of the Minotaur. According to legend, King Minos of Knossos was given a magnificent white bull to sacrifice to the god Poseidon, but decided to keep it. This enraged Poseidon, who punished the king by causing his wife Pasiphae to fall in love with the animal. The result of this odd union was the Minotaur – half-man and half-bull – who lived in a labyrinth beneath the king's palace, munching on youths and maidens.

In 1900 Arthur Evans uncovered the ruins of Knossos. Although archaeologists tend to disparage Evans' reconstruction, the buildings – incorporating an immense palace, courtyards, private apartments, baths, lively frescoes and more – give a fine idea of what a Minoan palace might have looked like.

Buses to Knossos (€1.15, three per hour) leave from Bus Station A.

PHAESTOS & OTHER MINOAN SITES ΦΑΙΣΤΟΣ

Phaestos (☎ 29820 42315; admission €4; 🕑 8am-7pm May-Oct, to 5pm Nov-Apr), 63km southwest of Iraklio, is Crete's second-most important Minoan site. While not as impressive as Knossos, Phaestos (fes-*tos*) is still worth a visit for its stunning views of the surrounding Mesara plain and Mt Psiloritis (also known as Mt Ida). The layout is similar to Knossos, with rooms arranged around a central courtyard. Eight buses a day head to Phaestos from Iraklio's Bus Station B (€5.70, 1½ hours).

Other important Minoan sites can be found at **Malia**, 34km east of Iraklio, where there's a palace complex and adjoining town, and **Zakros**, 40km southeast of Sitia, the last Minoan palace to have been discovered in 1962.

RETHYMNO ΡΕΘΥΜΝΟ

pop 29,000

Rethymno (*reth*-im-no) is Crete's third-largest town. It's also one of the island's architectural treasures, due to its stunning fortress and mix of Venetian and Turkish houses in the old quarter. A compact town, most spots of interest are within a small area around the old Venetian harbour.

The old quarter is on a peninsula that juts out into the Sea of Crete; the fortress sits at the head of the peninsula, while the Venetian harbour, ferry quay and beach are on its eastern side. El Venizelou is the main strip along the waterfront and beach. Running parallel behind it is Arkadiou, the main commercial street.

The **municipal tourist office** (☎ 28310 29148; www.rethymno.gr; Eleftheriou Venizelou; 🕑 9am-8.30pm; Mar-Nov), on the beach side of El Venizelou, is convenient and helpful. **Ellotia Tours** (☎ 28310 24533; www.rethymnoatcrete.com; Arkadiou 155) will answer all transport, accommodation and tour inquiries. **Galero Café** (☎ 28310 54345; per hr €3), beside the Rimondi fountain with its spouting lion heads, has internet access.

Rethymno's 16th-century **Venetian fortress** (fortezza; ☎ 28310 28101; Paleokastro Hill; admission €3; 🕑 8am-8pm) is the site of the city's ancient acropolis and affords great views across the town and mountains. The main gate is on the eastern side of the fortress, opposite the interesting **archaeological museum** (☎ 28310 54668; admission €3; 🕑 8.30am-3pm Tue-Sun), which was once a prison.

Happy Walker (☎ 28310 52920; www.happywalker.com; Tombazi 56) runs an excellent program of daily walks in the countryside (€25 per person), and also longer walking tours.

Rethymno Youth Hostel (☎ 28310 22848; www.yhrethymno.com; Tombazi 41; dm €9) is a well-run place with crowded dorms, free hot showers and no curfew. **Sea Front** (☎ 28310 51981; www.rethymnoatcrete.com; Arkadiou 159; d €35-45; ❄) has all sorts of options and is ideally positioned with beach views and spacious rooms. **Hotel Fortezza** (☎ 28310 55551; www.fortezza.gr; Melissinou 16; s/d incl breakfast €57/69; ❄ 🏊) is more upmarket; with a refreshing pool, it's in a refurbished old building in the heart of the Old Town.

There are plenty of eating options, but **Samaria** (☎ 28310 24681; El Venizelou 39; mains from €4) is one of the few waterfront tavernas where you'll see local families eating. The soups and grills are excellent. **Restaurant Symposium** (☎ 28310 50538; www.symposium-kriti.gr; mains from €5), near the Rimondi fountain, takes its food seriously (check out the website) but has good prices.

There are regular ferries between Piraeus and Rethymno (€29, nine hours), and a high-speed service in summer. Buses depart regularly to Iraklio (€6.5, 1½ hours) and Hania (€6, one hour).

HANIA ΧΑΝΙΑ

pop 53,500

Crete's most romantic, evocative and alluring town, Hania (hahn-*yah*; often spelt Chania) is the former capital and the island's second-largest city. There is a rich mosaic of Venetian and Ottoman architecture, particularly in the area of the old harbour, which lures tourists in droves. Modern Hania retains the exoticism of a city caught between East and West. Hania is an excellent base for exploring nearby idyllic beaches and a spectacular mountainous interior.

Orientation & Information

Hania's bus station is on Kydonias, two blocks southwest of Plateia 1866, one of the city's main squares. From Plateia 1866, the old harbour is a short walk down Halidon.

The **tourist information office** (☎ 28210 36155; Kydonias 29; 🕑 8am-2.30pm), under the Town Hall, is helpful and provides practical information and maps. The city's website at www.chania.gr is worth a look for more information and upcoming events. **Tellus Travel** (☎ 28210 91500; www.tellustravel.gr; Halidon 108; 🕑 8am-11pm) can help with schedules and ticketing, and also rents out cars. **Triple W Internet Café** (☎ 28210 93478; Validinon & Halidon; per 30min €1; 🕐 24hr) provides internet access.

Sights & Activities

A stroll around the **old harbour** is a must for any visitor to Hania. It is worth the 1.5km walk around the sea wall to get to the Venetian **lighthouse** at the entrance to the harbour.

The **archaeological museum** (☎ 28210 90334; Halidon 30; admission €2; 🕐 8.30am-3pm Tue-Sun) is in a 16th-century Venetian Church that the Turks made into a mosque. The building became a movie theatre in 1913 and then was a munitions depot for the Germans during WWII.

Hania's covered **food market**, in a massive cross-shaped building, is definitely worth an inspection.

Sleeping

Camping Hania (☎ 28210 31138; camp sites per tent/person €4/5) Take the Kalamaki Beach bus from the east corner of Plateia 1866 (every 15 minutes) to get to this camping ground, which is 3km west of town on the beach. There is a restaurant, bar and minimarket.

Pension Lena (☎ 28210 86860; www.lenachania.gr; Ritsou 5; s/d €35/55; ❄) For some real character in where you stay, Lena's pension in an old Turkish building near the mouth of the old harbour is the place to go. Help yourself to one of the appealing rooms if Lena isn't there –

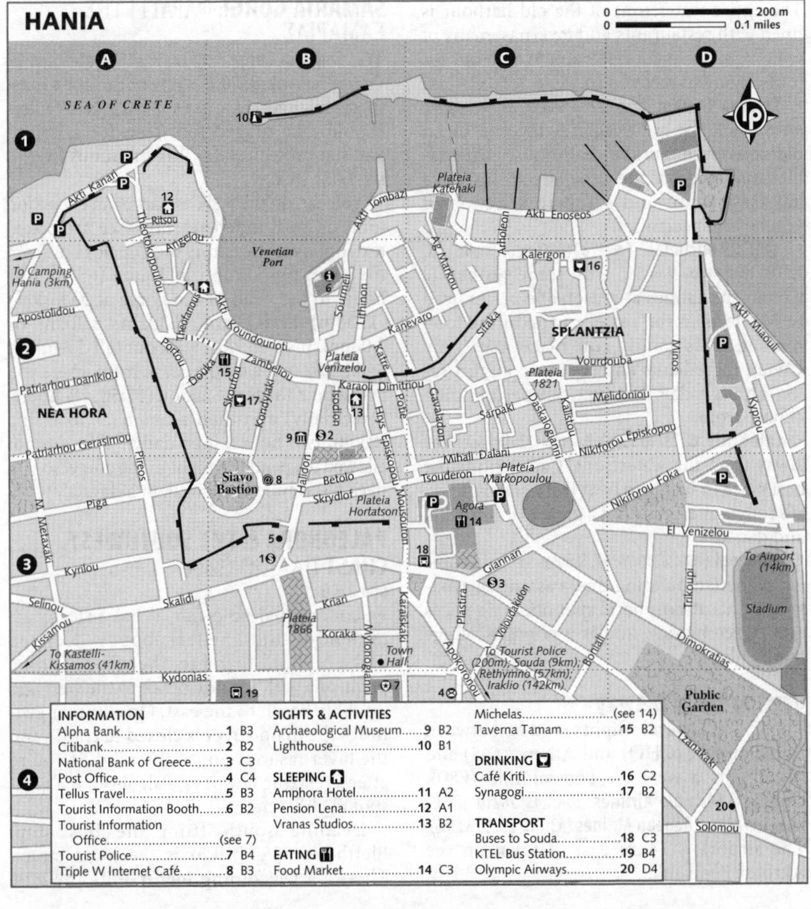

pick from the available ones on the list on the blackboard.

Vranas Studios (☎ 28210 58618; www.vranas.gr; Agion Deka 10; studio €40/70;) At the back of the cathedral, this place has immaculately maintained studios with kitchenettes. It also runs the internet cafe downstairs.

our pick Amphora Hotel (☎ 28210 93224; www.amphora.gr; Parodos Theotokopoulou 20; s/d €75/90;) Most easily found from the waterfront, this is Hania's most historically evocative hotel. Amphora is in an impressively restored Venetian mansion with elegantly decorated rooms around a courtyard. The hotel also runs the waterfront restaurant, which ranks as the best along that golden mile.

Eating & Drinking

The entire waterfront of the old harbour is lined with restaurants and tavernas, many of which qualify as tourist traps. Watch out for touts trying to reel you in.

Taverna Tamam (☎ 28210 58639; Zambeliou 49; mains €4-6.50; 1pm-12.30am) A taverna in an old converted Turkish bathhouse, with tables that spill out onto the street, this place has tasty soups and a superb selection of vegetarian specialities.

our pick Michelas (☎ 28210 90026; mains €5-7; 10am-4pm Mon-Sat) For some authentic Cretan specialities at reasonable prices head to Michelas in the eastern wing of the food market. This family-run place uses only Cretan ingredients and cooks up a great selection each day that you can peruse, then choose from.

Café Kriti (☎ 28210 58661; Kalergon 22; 8pm-late) Away from the waterfront, Café Kriti is the best place in Hania to hear live Cretan music. It's rough-and-ready but a great place to drink and dance.

Synagogi (☎ 28210 96797; Skoufou 15) In a roofless Venetian building that was once a synagogue, this atmospheric spot offers up juices and coffee by day, and is a popular lounge bar by night.

Getting There & Away

There are several flights a day between Hania airport (CHQ) and Athens (€65) and five flights a week to Thessaloniki (€80). Contact **Olympic Airlines** (OA; ☎ 28210 58005; Tzanakaki 88) or **Aegean Airlines** (A3; ☎ 28210 63366). The airport is 14km east of town on the Akrotiri Peninsula.

Daily ferries sail between Piraeus (€30, nine hours) and the port of Souda, 9km southeast of Hania. Get your tickets at Tellus Travel (p394).

Frequent buses run along Crete's northern coast to Iraklio (€11, 2¾ hours, 21 daily), Rethymno (€6, one hour, 21 daily) and Kastelli-Kissamos (€4, one hour, 14 daily); buses run less frequently to Paleohora (€6.50, one hour 50 minutes, four daily), Omalos (€5.90, one hour, four daily) and Hora Sfakion (€6.50, 1¼ hours, three daily) from the main bus station on Kydonias.

Buses for Souda's port (€1.15) leave from outside the food market. Buses for the beaches west of Hania leave from the eastern side of Plateia 1866.

SAMARIA GORGE ΦΑΡΑΓΓΙ ΤΗΣ ΣΑΜΑΡΙΑΣ

The **Samaria Gorge** (☎ 28250 67179; admission €5; 6am-3pm May–mid-Oct) is one of Europe's most spectacular gorges and a superb hike. Walkers should take rugged footwear, food, drinks and sun protection for this strenuous five- to six-hour trek.

You can do the walk as part of an excursion tour, or do it independently (see the boxed text, opposite) by taking the Omalos bus from the main bus station in Hania (€5.90, one hour) to the head of the gorge at Xyloskalo (1230m) at 6.15am, 7.30am, 8.30am or 2.00pm. It's a 16.7km walk out (all downhill) to Agia Roumeli on the coast, from where you take a boat to Hora Sfakion (€7.50, 1¼ hours, three daily) and then a bus back to Hania (€5.40, two hours, four daily). You are not allowed to spend the night in the gorge, so you need to complete the walk in a day.

PALEOHORA & THE SOUTHWEST COAST ΠΑΛΑΙΟΧΩΡΑ

pop 2200

Paleohora (pal-ee-o-*hor*-a) has a sleepy at-the-end-of-the-line feel about it. Isolated and a bit hard to get to, the village is on a peninsula with a sandy beach to the west and a pebbly beach to the east. On summer evenings the main street is closed to traffic and the tavernas move onto the road. If you're after a relaxing few days, Paleohora is a great spot to chill out.

Heading south from the bus stop, Eleftheriou Venizelou is the main street. There's a welcoming **tourist office** (☎ 28230

BEAT THE CROWDS AT SAMARIA

The Samaria Gorge walk is extremely popular and can get quite crowded, especially in summer. Most walkers have given the gorge a day and are on a rushed trip from Hania and other northern-coast cities.

If you've got a bit of time on your hands, and decide to do things on your own, there are a couple of excellent options.

One is to take the 2pm bus from Hania and spend the night in the Cretan mountains at 1200m above sea level in **Omalos** (population 30) at the very pleasant **Neos Omalos Hotel** (☎ 28210 67269; www.neos-omalos.gr; s/d €20/30). The hotel's restaurant serves excellent Cretan cuisine, local wine by the litre (€6), and they will shuttle you to the start of the gorge track the next morning.

Another option is to leave from Hania in the morning, but let the sprinters go and take your time hiking through this stupendous gorge. When you hit the coast at **Agia Roumeli** (population 125), down a cool beer, take a dip in the refreshing Libyan Sea, savour the tasty Cretan specials at **Faragi Restaurant & Rooms** (☎ 28250 91225; s/d/tr €20/30/35;) and stay the night in the tidy rooms above the restaurant. The next day you can take a ferry either west to Sougia or Paleohora, or east to Loutro or Hora Sfakion.

41507; 10am-1pm & 6-9pm Wed-Mon May-Oct) on the pebble beach road near the harbour and ferry quay. The opening hours listed are indicative only! Back on the main street, **Notos Rentals/Tsiskakis Travel** (☎ 28230 42110; notosgr@yahoo.gr; 8am-10pm) handles almost everything, including tickets, rental cars/scooters, laundry and internet access (€2 per hour). There's more information at www.west-crete.info/paleohora.htm.

The ruins of the 13th-century **Venetian castle** are worth clambering over, although there's not much left after the fortress was destroyed by the Turks, the pirate Barbarossa in the 16th-century and then the Germans during WWII.

Camping Paleohora (☎ 28230 41120; camp sites per tent/person €3/5) is 1.5km northeast of town, near the pebble beach. There's a taverna but no minimarket here. **Homestay Anonymous** (☎ 28230 41509; www.anonymoushomestay.com; s/d/tr with shared bathroom €22/25/28) is a great option with its warm service and communal kitchen. Manolis, the owner, is an excellent source of local information. Across the road from the sandy beach, the refurbished **Poseidon Hotel** (☎ 28230 41374; www.interkriti.net/hotel/paleohora/poseidon; s/d/apt €35/40/50;) has a mix of tidy double rooms, studios and apartments. There is also a good cafe on site.

There are plenty of eating options on the main street. Vegetarians rave about **Third Eye** (☎ 28230 41234; mains from €5), just inland from the sandy beach. Specialities include a tempting range of Greek-Asian fusion dishes.

Further east along Crete's southwest coast are **Sougia**, **Agia Roumeli** (at the mouth of the Samaria Gorge; see the boxed text, above), **Loutro** (see the boxed text, p398) and **Hora Sfakion**. No road links the coastal resorts, but a daily boat from Paleohora to Sougia (€7.50, one hour), Agia Roumeli (€11, 1½ hours), Loutro (€13, 2½ hours) and Hora Sfakion (€14, three hours) connects the villages in summer. The ferry leaves Paleohora at 9.45am and returns from Hora Sfakion at 1pm. It's also possible to walk right along this southern coast.

There are at least five buses daily between Hania and Paleohora (€6.50, two hours). A bus for Samaria Gorge hikers (see opposite) leaves for Omalos (€5.50, two hours) each morning at 6.15am.

LASITHI PLATEAU ΟΡΟΠΕΔΙΟ ΛΑΣΙΘΙΟΥ

The impressive mountain-fringed Lasithi Plateau in eastern Crete is laid out like an immense patchwork quilt. At 900m above sea level, it is a vast flat expanse of orchards and fields, which was once dotted with thousands of stone windmills with white canvas sails. There are still plenty of windmills, but most are now of the rusted metal variety and don't work.

There are 20 villages around the periphery of the plain, the largest being **Tzermiado** (population 750), **Agios Georgios** (population 550) and **Psyhro** (population 210).

The **Dikteon Cave** (☎ 28440 31316; admission €4; 8am-6pm) is where, according to mythology,

WORTH THE TRIP: LOUTRO

The tiny village of **Loutro** (population 90) is a particularly picturesque spot, curled around the only natural harbour on the southern coast of Crete. It's a great place for a break. With no vehicle access, the only way in is by boat or on foot. Ferries drop in daily from Hora Sfakion to the east, and from Paleohora, Sougia and Agia Roumeli to the west.

Hotel Porto Loutro (☎ 28250 91433; www.hotelportoloutro.com; s/d/tr incl breakfast €45/55/65; ❄) has tasteful rooms with balconies overlooking the harbour. The village beach, excellent walks, rental kayaks, and boat transfers to Sweetwater Beach will help to fill in a peaceful few days. Take a book and chill out.

Rhea hid the newborn Zeus from Cronos, his offspring-gobbling father. The cave is 1km from the village of Psyhro, where the **Zeus Hotel** (☎ 28440 31284; s/d €25/30) is convenient. On the main street, **Stavros** (☎ 28440 31453; mains €5-8) serves tasty home-style Cretan dishes with produce mostly from the family farm.

There are daily buses to the area from Iraklio (€5, two hours) and Agios Nikolaos (€3.50, 2½ hours), though having your own wheels would make life a lot easier.

AGIOS NIKOLAOS ΑΓΙΟΣ ΝΙΚΟΛΑΟΣ

pop 11,000

Agios Nikolaos (*ah*-yee-os nih-*ko*-laos) is an attractive former fishing village on Crete's northeast coast. The de facto town centre is around the picturesque **Voulismeni Lake**, which is ringed with cafes and tavernas, and is linked to the sea by a short canal. The ferry port is 150m past the canal.

The very helpful **municipal tourist office** (☎ 28410 22357; www.agiosnikolaos.gr; 🕑 8am-9.30pm Apr-Nov) is on the north side of the bridge over the canal and does a good job of finding sleeping options. **Polyhoros Internet Café** (☎ 28410 24876; 28 Oktovriou 13; per hr €4; 🕑 9am-2am) is just up from the canal.

The two nice little beaches in town, **Kytroplatia Beach** and **Ammos Beach**, get a bit crowded in summer. **Almyros Beach**, about 1km south, gets less so. Agios Nikolaos acts as a base for excursion tours to **Spinalonga Island**. The island's massive fortress was built by the Venetians in 1579 but taken by the Turks in 1715. It later became a leper colony. Nowadays it's a fascinating place to explore. Tours cost around €20.

Pergola Hotel (☎ 28410 28152; Sarolidi 20; s/d €20/40; ❄) is a friendly family-run place out near the ferry port, with clean rooms, balconies and sea views. **Du Lac Hotel** (☎ 28410 22711; www.dulachotel.gr; Oktovriou 17; s/d €40/60) is a refurbished hotel in a great location with views out over the lake.

Finding a place to eat will not be a problem. **Taverna Itanos** (☎ 28410 25340; Kyprou 1; mains €4-10), tucked away on a backstreet off the main square, is superb, has reasonable prices and offers the opportunity to wander into the kitchen and see what looks good. **Migomis** (☎ 28410 24353; N Plastira 20; mains from €10-15) overlooks the lake from high on the south side, providing superb ambience and views.

Ferries depart for Rhodes (€30, 11 hours) via Sitia, Kasos, Karpathos and Halki three times a week. There are also three weekly ferries to Piraeus (€34, 12 hours). Buses to Iraklio run every 30 minutes (€6.20, 1½ hours) and to Sitia (€5.90, 1½ hours, six times daily).

SITIA ΣΗΤΕΙΑ

pop 8750

Sitia (si-*tee*-a) is a laid-back little town in the northeastern corner of Crete that has escaped much of the tourism frenzy along the north coast. It is on an attractive bay flanked by mountains, and is an easy place to unwind.

The helpful **tourist office** (☎ 28430 28300; Karamanli; 🕑 9.30am-2.30pm & 5-8.30pm), on the waterfront, has town maps. The main square, Plateia Iroon Plytehniou, is in the corner of the bay, recognisable by its palm trees and statue of a dying soldier. The ferry port is about 500m to the northeast. Internet access is available at Itanos Hotel (opposite).

Porto Belis Travel (☎ 28430 22370; www.portobelis-crete.gr; Karamanli Aven 34; 🕑 9am-8.30pm), on the waterfront just before the start of the town beach, is a one-stop shop, handling ticketing, rental cars and scooters, and accommodation bookings in town. It also runs **Porto Belis House** (☎ 28430 22370; d/q €34/57; ❄) above the travel agency. These rooms are immaculate, have kitchens and look straight out onto the beach. Check out the website.

Hotel Arhontiko (☎ 28430 28172; Kondylaki 16; d/studio €30/33), two blocks uphill from the port, has spotless rooms with shared bathrooms in a beautifully maintained neoclassical building. **Itanos Hotel** (☎ 28430 22900; www.itanoshotel.com; Karamanli 4; s/d incl breakfast €42/56;) is an upmarket establishment next to the square with its own excellent **Itanos Taverna** (mains €3-12) on the waterfront outside the front door.

The waterfront is lined with tavernas. Popular with locals is **Gato Negro** (☎ 28430 25873; mains €6-12), serving Cretan specialities using produce from the owner's farm. It's the closest taverna to the ferry quay. **Balcony** (☎ 28430 25084; Foundalidou 19; mains €10-18), a couple of streets back from the waterfront, is the finest dining in Sitia in a charmingly decorated neoclassical building.

Sitia airport (JSH) has four flights a week to Athens (€66) with **Olympic Airlines** (OA; ☎ 28430 22270; 4 Septemvriou 3). There are three ferries per week via Kasos, Karpathos and Halki to Rhodes (€27, 14 hours). Porto Belis Travel (opposite) has details and sells tickets. There are five buses daily to Iraklio (€13.10, 3½ hours) via Agios Nikolaos (€6.90, 1½ hours).

DODECANESE ΔΩΔΕΚΑΝΗΣΑ

Strung out along the coast of western Turkey, the 12 main islands of the Dodecanese (*dodeca* means twelve) have suffered a turbulent past of invasions and occupations that has endowed them with a fascinating diversity.

In 1291 the Knights of St John, having fled Jerusalem, came to Rhodes and established themselves as masters of the Dodecanese. In 1522 Süleyman I staged a massive attack and took Rhodes Town, claiming the islands for the Ottoman Empire. In 1912 it was the Italians who ousted the Turks, and in 1944 the Germans took over. The following year Rhodes was liberated by British and Greek commandos. In 1947 the Dodecanese became part of Greece. These days, tourists rule.

The islands themselves range from the verdant and mountainous to the rocky and dry. While Rhodes and Kos host highly developed tourism, the more remote islands await those in search of traditional island life.

RHODES ΡΟΔΟΣ

pop 98,000

Rhodes (Rodos in Greek) is the largest island in the Dodecanese. According to mythology, the sun god Helios chose Rhodes as his bride and bestowed light, warmth and vegetation upon her. The blessing seems to have paid off, for Rhodes produces more flowers and sunny days than most Greek Islands. Throw in an east coast of virtually uninterrupted sandy beaches and it's easy to understand why sun-starved northern Europeans flock here.

GETTING THERE & AWAY

There are plenty of flights daily between Rhodes airport (RHO) and Athens (€77), two daily to Karpathos (€28) and one daily to Iraklio (€65). Call **Olympic Airlines** (OA; ☎ 22410 24571; Ierou Lohou 9) or **Aegean Airlines** (A3; ☎ 22410 98345; Diagoras airport). In summer there are regular flights to Kastellorizo. **Sky Express** (SEH; ☎ 28102 23500; www.skyexpress.gr) has options to Iraklio and Santorini.

Rhodes is the main port of the Dodecanese and there is a complex array of departures. There are daily ferries from Rhodes to Piraeus (€40, 15 to 18 hours). Most sail via the Dodecanese north of Rhodes, but at least three times a week there is a service via Karpathos, Crete and the Cyclades.

Excursion boats (€22 return) and hydrofoils (€13 one way) travel daily to Symi. Ferries (€8 one way) travel less often. Similar services also run to Kos, Kalymnos, Nisyros, Tilos, Patmos and Leros.

There are boats between Rhodes and Marmaris in Turkey (one way/return €50/70, 1¼ hours). Check www.marmarisinfo.com for up-to-date details.

For details on all your options, contact Triton Holidays (p400).

Rhodes Town

pop 56,000

Rhodes' capital is Rhodes Town, on the northern tip of the island. Its World Heritage–listed Old Town, the largest inhabited medieval town in Europe, is enclosed within massive walls and is a joy to explore. To the north is New Town, the commercial centre.

The main port, Commercial Harbour, is east of the Old Town, and north of here is Mandraki Harbour, the supposed site of the Colossus of Rhodes, a 32m-high bronze statue of Apollo built over 12 years (294–282 BC).

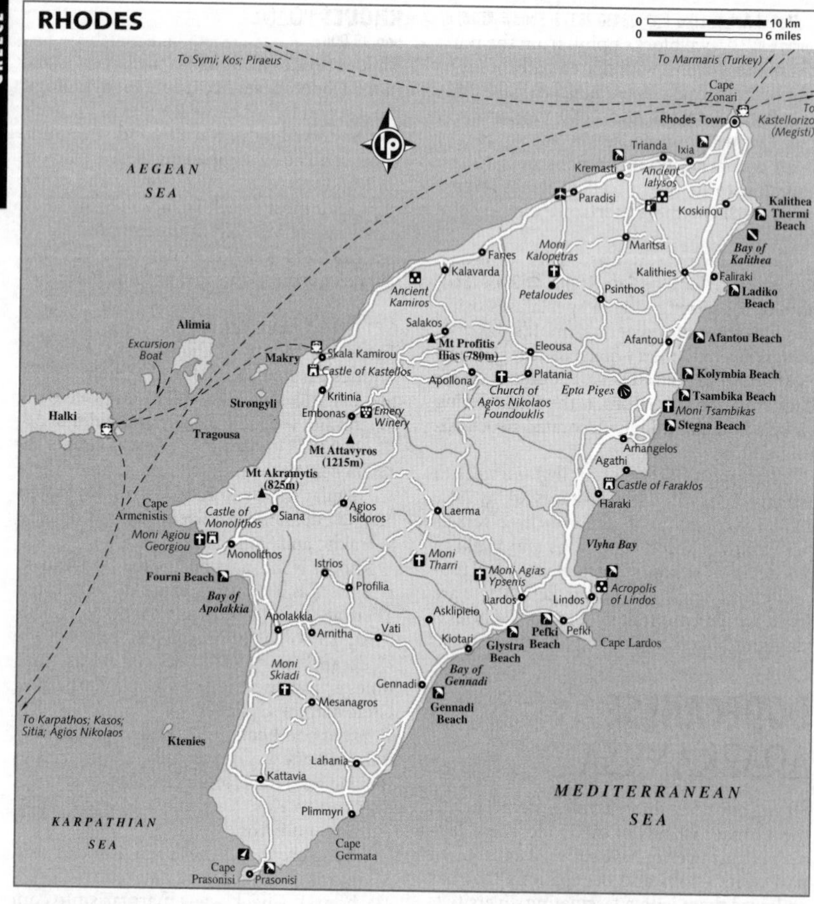

The statue stood for a mere 65 years before being toppled by an earthquake.

INFORMATION

For information about the island, visit www .ro dos.gr.

Mango Café Bar (☎ 22410 24877; www.mango.gr; Plateia Dorieos 3, Old Town; per hr €5; 9.30am-midnight) Provides internet access and everything else.

Tourist information office (EOT; ☎ 22410 35226; cnr Makariou & Papagou; 8am-2.45pm Mon-Fri) Has brochures, maps and *Rodos News*, a free English-language newspaper.

Triton Holidays (☎ 22410 21690; www.tritondmc .gr; Plastira 9, Mandraki) In the New Town, this place is exceptionally helpful, handling accommodation bookings, ticketing and rental cars.

SIGHTS & ACTIVITIES

The Old Town is reputedly the world's finest surviving example of medieval fortification, with 12m-thick walls. The Knights of St John lived in the Knights' Quarter in the northern end of the Old Town.

The cobbled **Odos Ippoton** (Ave of the Knights) is lined with magnificent medieval buildings, the most imposing of which is the **Palace of the Grand Masters** (☎ 22410 23359; admission €6; 8.30am-7.30pm Tue-Sun), which was restored, but never used, as a holiday home for Mussolini.

The 15th-century Knight's Hospital now houses the **archaeological museum** (☎ 22410 27657; Plateia Mousiou; admission €3; 8am-4pm Tue-Sun). The splendid building was restored by the

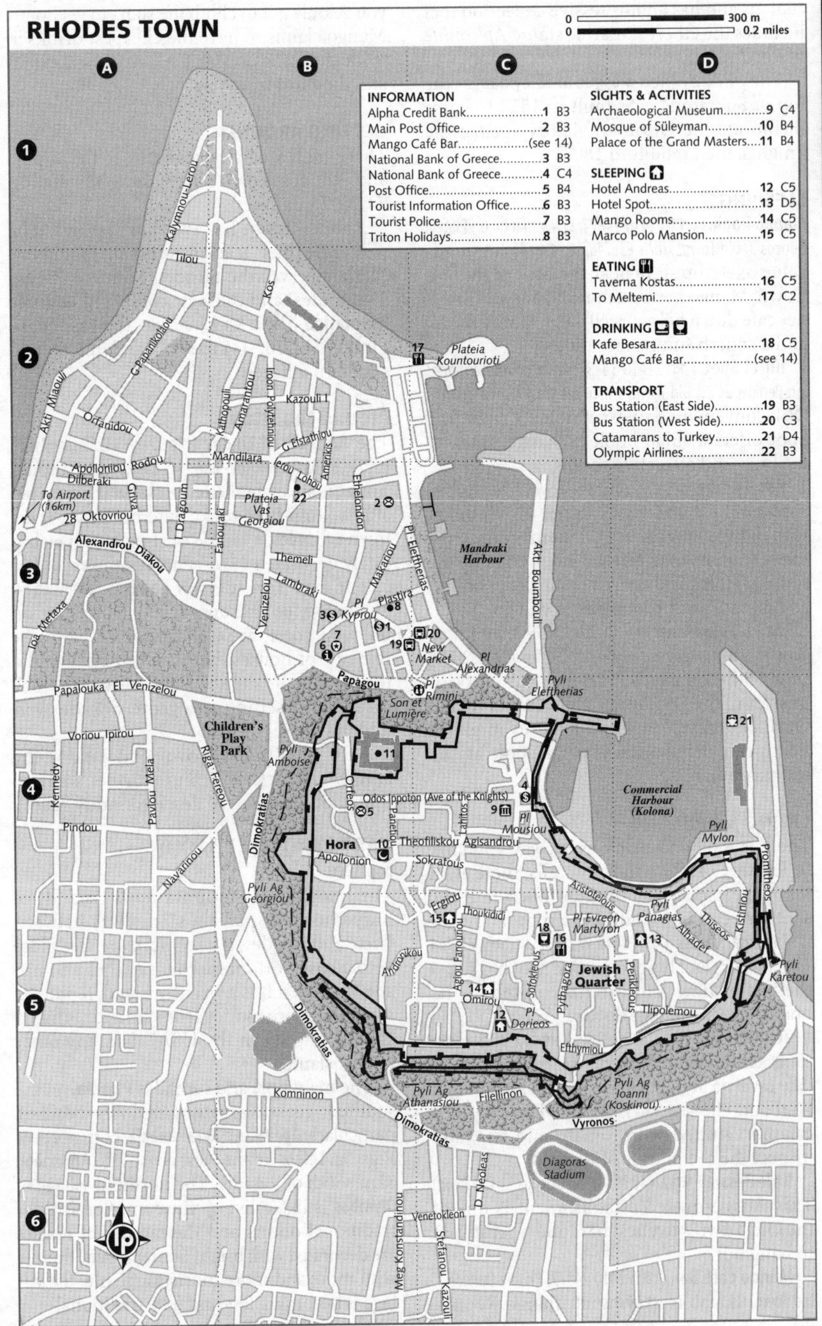
RHODES TOWN
0 300 m
0 0.2 miles
INFORMATION
Alpha Credit Bank 1 B3
Main Post Office 2 B3
Mango Café Bar (see 14)
National Bank of Greece 3 B3
National Bank of Greece 4 C4
Post Office 5 B4
Tourist Information Office 6 B3
Tourist Police 7 B3
Triton Holidays 8 B3
SIGHTS & ACTIVITIES
Archaeological Museum 9 C4
Mosque of Süleyman 10 B4
Palace of the Grand Masters 11 B4
SLEEPING
Hotel Andreas 12 C5
Hotel Spot 13 D5
Mango Rooms 14 C5
Marco Polo Mansion 15 C5
EATING
Taverna Kostas 16 C5
To Meltemi 17 C2
DRINKING
Kafe Besara 18 C5
Mango Café Bar (see 14)
TRANSPORT
Bus Station (East Side) 19 B3
Bus Station (West Side) 20 C3
Catamarans to Turkey 21 D4
Olympic Airlines 22 B3
Plateia Kountourioti
Mandraki Harbour
Commercial Harbour (Kolona)
To Airport (16km)
Plateia Vas Georgiou
New Market
Pl Alexandrias
Pyli Eleftherias
Pl Rimini
Son et Lumière
Children's Play Park
Pyli Amboise
Odos Ippoton (Ave of the Knights)
Pl Mousiou
Hora
Apollonion
Pyli Ag Georgiou
Pyli Mylon
Pl Evreon Martyron
Pyli Panagias
Pyli Karetou
Jewish Quarter
Pl Dorieos
Pyli Ag Athanasiou
Pyli Ag Ioanni (Koskinou)
Diagoras Stadium
Kalymnou-Lerou
Tilou
Kos
G Papanikolaou
Akti Miaouli
Orfanidou
Kazouli I
G Efstathiou
Mandilara
Ierou Lohou
Amerikis
Apolloniou Rodou
Dilberaki
Griva
28 Oktovriou
Alexandrou Diakou
Dragoumi
Fanouraki
Kathopouli
Amarantou
Iroon Polytehniou
Ethelondon
Makariou
Pl Eleftherias
Akti Boumbouli
Themeli
Lambraki
Plastira
Pl Kyprou
Ioa Metaxa
S Venizelou
Papagou
Papalouka El Venizelou
Voriou Ipirou
Kennedy
Pindou
Pavlou Mela
Riga Fereou
Navarinou
Dimokratias
Orfeos
Panetiou
Lahitos
Theofiliskou
Agisandrou
Sokratous
Ergiou
Thoukididi
Aristotelous
Thiseos
Alhadef
Kistiniou
Promitheos
Andronikou
Agiou Fanouriou
Sofokleous
Pythagora
Perikleous
Omirou
Tlipolemou
Efthymiou
Filellinon
Komninon
Vyronos
Meg Konstandinou
Venetokleon
D. Neoleas
Stefanou Kazouli
A
B
C
D
1
2
3
4
5
6

Italians and has an impressive collection that includes the ethereal marble statue *Aphrodite of Rhodes*.

The pink-domed **Mosque of Süleyman**, at the top of Sokratous, was built in 1522 to commemorate the Ottoman victory against the knights, then rebuilt in 1808.

SLEEPING

Mango Rooms (☎ 22410 24877; www.mango.gr; Plateia Dorieos 3, Old Town; s/d/tr €36/46/56;) A good-value one-stop shop near the back of the Old Town, Mango has a restaurant, bar and internet cafe down below, well-kept rooms above, and a superb sun terrace on top.

Hotel Spot (☎ 22410 34737; www.spothotelrhodes.gr; Perikleous 21, Old Town; s/d/tr incl breakfast €45/60/80;) Convenient and exceptionally clean, the Spot offers a small book exchange, internet facilities and attractive rooms.

Hotel Andreas (☎ 22410 34156; www.hotelandreas.com; Omirou 28d, Old Town; s/d €50/75;) Tasteful, with individually decorated rooms and terrific views from its roof-terrace, rates differ by the room at Hotel Andreas. Check it all out online, and choose your room before you go.

Marco Polo Mansion (☎ 22410 25562; www.marcopolomansion.gr; Agiou Fanouriou 40, Old Town; d €90-170) In a 15th-century building in the Turkish quarter of the Old Town, this place is rich in Ottoman-era colours and features in glossy European magazines. Take a look at the rooms online.

EATING & DRINKING

There is food and drink every way you look in Rhodes. Outside the city walls, there are a lot of cheap places in the New Market, at the southern end of Mandraki Harbour.

Taverna Kostas (☎ 22410 26217; Pythagora 62, Old Town; mains €5-10) This good-value spot has stood the test of time and can't be beaten for its quality grills and fish dishes.

To Meltemi (☎ 22410 30480; Kountourioti 8; mains €5-12) Gaze out on Turkey from this beach-side taverna at the northern end of Mandraki Harbour. The seafood is superb. Try the grilled calamari stuffed with tomato and feta, and inspect the old photos of Rhodes.

Kafe Besara (☎ 22410 30363; Sofokleous 11, Old Town) This Aussie-owned establishment is one of the Old Town's liveliest bars and a great spot to hang out.

Mango Café Bar (☎ 22410 24877; Plateia Dorieos 3, Old Town) If you're staying at Mango Rooms, you've only got to climb the stairs to get home. Mango claims to have the cheapest drinks in town and is the preferred haunt of local expats and die-hard travellers.

GETTING AROUND

There are frequent buses between the airport and Rhodes Town's west-side bus station (€1.90, 25 minutes).

Rhodes Town has two bus stations. The west-side bus station, next to the New Market, serves the airport, Kamiros (€4.60, 55 minutes) and the west coast. The **east-side bus station** (Plateia Rimini) serves the east coast, Lindos (€4.70, 1½ hours) and the inland southern villages.

Around the Island

The **Acropolis of Lindos** (☎ 22440 31258; admission €6; 8.30am-6pm Tue-Sun), 47km from Rhodes Town, is an ancient city spectacularly perched atop a 116m-high rocky outcrop. Below is the town of **Lindos**, a tangle of streets with elaborately decorated 17th-century houses.

The extensive ruins of **Kamiros** (admission €4; 8am-5pm Tue-Sun), an ancient Doric city on the west coast, are well preserved, with the remains of houses, baths, a cemetery and a temple, but the site should be visited as much for its lovely setting on a gentle hillside overlooking the sea.

Between Rhodes Town and Lindos the **beaches** are packed. Venture further south to find good stretches of deserted sandy beach.

KARPATHOS ΚΑΡΠΑΘΟΣ

pop 6000

The elongated, mountainous island of Karpathos (*kar*-pah-thos), midway between Crete and Rhodes, is a scenic, hype-free place with a cosy port, numerous beaches and unspoilt villages. It is a wealthy island, reputedly receiving more money from emigrants living abroad (mostly in the USA) than any other Greek island.

The main port and capital is **Pigadia**, on the southeast coast. Karpathos has lovely beaches, particularly **Apella** and **Kyra Panagia**, both north of Pigadia, **Lefkos** on the west coast, and **Ammoöpi**, 8km south of Pigadia. The northern village of **Olymbos** is like a living museum. Locals wear traditional outfits and the facades of houses are decorated with bright plaster reliefs, though with more and more tourists arriving, the village is becoming less and less 'traditional'.

In Pigadia, a booth on the harbour serves as **municipal tourist office** (☎ 22450 23835; ⏲ Jul & Aug). For more information on the island, check out www.inkarpathos.com. **Possi Travel** (☎ 22450 22148; possitvl@hotmail.com) on the waterfront can suggest local tours and handles air and ferry tickets. **Pot Pourri** (☎ 22450 29073; Apodimon Karpathion; per hr €3; ⏲ 7am-1am), on the western side of the harbour, offers internet access.

Elias Rooms (☎ 22450 22446; www.eliasrooms.com; s/d €20/25) is an excellent accommodation option. Owner Elias is a mine of information and his rooms have great views while being in a quiet part of town.

Hotel Titania (☎ 22450 22144; www.titaniakarpathos.gr; s/d €40/55; ❄) is in the centre of Pigadia and has spacious rooms with fridge, phone and TV.

Try the Karpathian goat *stifado* at **To Helliniko** (☎ 22450 23932; mains €5-11) on the waterfront. Head for **I Anna** (☎ 22450 22820; mains from €5) near the quay for Pigadia's freshest fish. The Karpathian sardines in oil is a good choice.

In summer, Karpathos airport (AOK), 13km southwest of town, has daily flights to Rhodes (€28) and Athens (€80). The **Olympic Airlines** (OA; ☎ 22450 22150) office is on the central square in Pigadia. There are three ferries a week to Rhodes (€18.50, four hours) and four to Piraeus (€33, 19 hours) via Crete and the Cyclades. The ferries between Rhodes and Crete stop at Pigadia and the small northern port of Diafani on Karpathos. In summer there are daily excursion boats from Pigadia to Apella and Kyra Panagia beaches.

There are also excursions from Pigadia to Diafani that include a bus trip to Olymbos. Local buses drop you at Lefkos and Ammoöpi beaches.

SYMI ΣΥΜΗ

pop 2600

Simply superb, Symi is an inviting island to the north of Rhodes. The port town of Gialos is a Greek treasure, with pastel-coloured mansions heaped up the hills surrounding the protective little harbour. Symi is swamped by day trippers from Rhodes, and it's worth staying over to enjoy the island in cruise control. The town is divided into Gialos, the port, and the tranquil *horio* (village) above it, accessible by taxi, bus or 360 steps from the harbour.

There is no tourist office. The best source of information is the free, widely available monthly English-language *Symi Visitor* (www.symivisitor.com), which includes maps of the town. **Kalodoukas Holidays** (☎ 22460 71077; www.kalodoukas.gr) handles accommodation bookings, ticketing and has a book of walking trails on the island. For internet access head to **Roloï Bar** (☎ 22460 71595; per hr €4; ⏲ 9am-3am), a block back from the waterfront.

The **Monastery of Panormitis** (⏲ dawn-sunset; admission free) is a hugely popular complex at the southern end of the island. Its **museum** (admission €1.50) is impressive, but try to avoid the hordes of day trippers who arrive about 10.30am on excursion boats from Rhodes.

Budget accommodation is scarce. **Rooms Katerina** (☎ 22460 71813, 69451 30112; d €30; ❄) is excellent, but get in quick as there are only three rooms. There is a communal kitchen with breathtaking views down over the port, and helpful Katerina is happy to answer all your questions.

Pension Catherinettes (☎ 22460 71671; marina-epe@rho.forthnet.gr; d €58; ❄ 💻) has airy rooms on the north side of the harbour. It's where the treaty surrendering the Dodecanese to the Allies was signed in 1945. On the waterfront next to the clock tower, **Hotel Nireus** (☎ 22460 72400; www.nireus-hotel.gr; s/d incl breakfast €50/80; ❄ 💻) is bright, friendly and has free wi-fi access.

Taverna Neraida (☎ 22460 71841; mains from €5), back from the waterfront by the square, serves solid Greek dishes and features intriguing old photos of Symi on its walls. **Vapori Bar** (☎ 22460 72082) is open all day. Drop by to use the internet (per hour €4) or read the free newspapers by day, or for drinks and cruising at night.

There are frequent ferries and hydrofoils between Rhodes and Kos that stop at Symi, as well as daily excursion boats from Rhodes. Small taxi boats visit inaccessible east-coast beaches daily in summer, including spectacular Agios Georgious, backed by a 150m sheer cliff.

KOS ΚΩΣ

pop 17,900

Captivating Kos, only 5km from the Turkish peninsula of Bodrum, has its own legion of fans. Popular with history buffs as the birthplace of Hippocrates (460–377 BC), the father of medicine, Kos also attracts an entirely different crowd – sun-worshipping beach lovers from northern Europe who flock in on charter flights during summer. Tourism rules the roost, and whether you are there to explore the Castle of the Knights or to party till you drop, Kos should keep you happy for at least a few days.

Orientation & Information

Kos Town is based around a circular harbour, protected by the imposing Castle of the Knights, at the eastern end of the island. The ferry quay is north of the castle. Akti Koundourioti is the main drag around the harbourfront.

The **municipal tourist office** (☎ 22420 24460; www.kosinfo.gr; Vasileos Georgiou 1; 🕒 8am-2.30pm & 3-10pm Mon-Fri, 9am-2pm Sat) is on the waterfront directly south of the port and provides maps and accommodation information. **Exas Travel** (☎ 22420 28545; www.exas.gr), near the archaeological museum in the heart of town to the southwest of the harbour, handles schedules, ticketing and excursions.

Café Del Mare (☎ 22420 24244; www.cybercafe.gr; Megalou Alexandrou 4; per 30min €2; 🕒 9am-1am) is a well-equipped internet cafe near the harbour.

Sights & Activities

The focus of the **archaeological museum** (☎ 22420 28326; Plateia Eleftherias; adult/student €3/2; 🕒 8am-2.30pm Tue-Sun) is sculpture from excavations around the island.

The **ancient agora**, with the ruins of the **Shrine of Aphrodite** and **Temple of Hercules**, is just off Plateia Eleftherias. North of the agora is the **Hippocrates Plane Tree**, under which the man himself is said to have taught his pupils.

The **Castle of the Knights** (☎ 22420 27927; admission €4; 🕒 8am-2.30pm Tue-Sun), built in the 14th century, protected the knights from the encroaching Ottomans, and was originally separated from town by a moat. That moat is now Finikon, a major street. Entrance to the castle is over the stone bridge behind the Hippocrates Tree.

On a pine-clad hill, 4km southwest of Kos Town, stand the extensive ruins of the renowned healing centre of **Asklipieion** (☎ 22420 28763; adult/student €4/3; 🕒 8.30am-6pm Tue-Sun), where Hippocrates practised medicine. Groups of doctors come from all over the world to visit.

If the history is all too much, wander around and relax at the town **beach** past the northern end of the harbour.

Therma Loutra, 12km southeast of town, has hot mineral springs that warm the sea.

Sleeping

Pension Alexis (☎ 22420 28798; fax 22420 25797; Irodotou 9; s/d €25/30; ❄) This highly recommended place has long been a budget favourite with travellers. It has large rooms with shared facilities, and a relaxing verandah and garden. It's back behind Dolphin Sq.

Hotel Camelia (☎ 22420 28983; www.camelia-hotel.com; Artemisias; s/d €30/50; 💻) On a quiet tree-lined street south of town, this place has simple, comfortable rooms and a satellite TV lounge.

our pick **Hotel Afendoulis** (☎ 22420 25321; www.afendoulishotel.com; Evripilou 1; s/d €35/50; ❄ 💻) In a pleasant, quiet area about 500m south of the ferry quay, this well-kept hotel won't disappoint. Run by the charismatic English-speaking Alexis, this is a great place to relax and enjoy Kos.

Eating & Drinking

Restaurants line the central waterfront, but you might want to hit the backstreets for value. There are a dozen discos and clubs around the streets of Diakon and Nafklirou, just north of the agora.

Barbas (☎ 22400 27856; Evripilou 6; mains €3-5) Opposite Hotel Afendoulis, Barbas specialises in grills and has a mouth-watering chicken souvlaki. Sit at the streetside tables and watch the locals pass by.

Olympiada (☎ 22420 23031; Kleopatras 2; mains €3.50-4) Back in the ruins area, behind the Olympic Airlines office, Olympiada serves up reliable, unpretentious Greek dishes.

Angelica's Beach Taverna (☎ 22420 24825; Antimachou 2) Right on the beach to the north of the harbour, Angelica, or Mama as she is better known, serves up succulent Greek dishes you can tuck into while still in your bathing suit.

Kalua (☎ 22420 24938; Akti Zouroudi 3) Just along the beach from Angelica's Kalua is a popular outdoor venue with a swimming pool.

Getting There & Around

There are daily flights to Athens (€75) from Kos' **Ippokratis airport** (KGS) with **Olympic Airlines** (OA; ☎ 22420 28330). The airline runs buses (€4) to the airport, which is 28km southwest of Kos Town. **Sky Express** (SEH; ☎ 28102 23500; www.skyexpress.gr) operates flights to Iraklio and Thessaloniki.

There are frequent ferries from Rhodes to Kos that continue on to Piraeus (€40, 12 to

15 hours) via Kalymnos, Leros and Patmos. Daily fast-boat connections head north to Patmos and Samos, and south to Symi and Rhodes.

In summer ferries depart daily for Bodrum in Turkey (€25 return, one hour). Get details and tickets at Exas Travel, near the archaeological museum (opposite).

There is a good public bus system on Kos, with the bus station on Kleopatras, near the ruins at the back of town.

Next to the tourist office is a blue mini-train for Asklipion (€5 return, hourly) and a green mini-train that does city tours (€4, 20 minutes).

PATMOS ΠΑΤΜΟΣ

pop 3050

Patmos has a sense of 'spirit of place', and with its great beaches and relaxed atmosphere, is a superb place to unwind. For the religiously motivated it is a place not to be missed. Orthodox and Western Christians have long made pilgrimages to Patmos, for it was here that John the Divine ensconced himself in a cave and wrote the Book of Revelation.

Orientation & Information

The main town and port of Skala is about halfway down the east coast of Patmos, with a protected harbour. Towering above Skala to the south is the *hora*, crowned by the immense Monastery of St John the Theologian.

The **tourist office** (☎ 22470 31666; 🕑 8am-6pm Mon-Fri Jun-Sep), post office and police station are in the white building opposite the port in Skala. For further information on the island, visit www.patmosweb.gr or www.patmos-island.com. **Apollon Travel** (☎ 22470 31324; apollontravel@stratas.gr), on the waterfront, handles schedules and ticketing. **Blue Bay Internet Café** (☎ 22470 31165; per hr €4; 🕑 9am-2pm & 5-8pm) is 200m south from the port in the Blue Bay Hotel.

Sights & Activities

The **Cave of the Apocalypse** (☎ 22470 31234; admission free, treasury €6; 🕑 8am-1.30pm daily & 4-6pm Tue, Thu & Sun), where St John wrote his divinely inspired Book of Revelation, is halfway between the port and *hora*. Take a bus from the port or hike up the **Byzantine path**, which starts from a signposted spot on the Skala–*hora* road.

The **Monastery of St John the Theologian** (☎ 22470 31398; admission free; 🕑 8am-1.30pm daily & 4-6pm Tue, Thu & Sun) looks more like a castle than a monastery and tops Patmos like a crown. It exhibits all kinds of monastic treasures.

Patmos' coastline provides secluded coves, mostly with pebble beaches. The best is **Psili Ammos**, in the south, reached by excursion boat from Skala port. **Lambi Beach**, on the north coast, is a pebble-beach lover's dream come true.

Sleeping & Eating

Katina's Rooms (☎ 22470 31327, 69734 17241; s/d €35/50) The smiling Katina meets most boats and is happy to provide a ride to her four immaculately clean rooms at the northern end of the harbour. Enthusiastic and helpful, she has contacts with other tidy rooms in her neighbourhood if hers are full.

Yvonni Studios (☎ 22470 33066; www.12net.gr/yvonni; s/d €35/50) On the western side of Skala, these exceptionally clean and pleasant studios are fully self-contained and big on privacy. Call ahead for a booking or drop into Yvonni's gift shop in Skala and ask for Theo.

our pick Blue Bay Hotel (☎ 22470 31165; www.bluebaypatmos.gr; s/d/tr €72/100/130; ✽ 💻) At the quieter southern end of Skala, this waterfront hotel has superb rooms, internet access, and breakfast included in its rates (which tumble out of the high season).

Hiliomodi Ouzeri (☎ 22470 34080; mains from €3) A favourite with locals, Hiliomodi is known for its excellent and reasonably priced seafood dishes. It's 100m up the road to the *hora* on the left.

Girovolies tou Magou (☎ 22470 33226; mains from €3) Meat lovers will croon over this place 100m south of the port. There are tables on the beach, and the speciality of the house is rotisseried and skewered meats. Bring your appetite.

Getting There & Away

Patmos is well connected, with ferries to Piraeus (€35, eight hours, two weekly) and south to Rhodes (€32, 7½ hours, two weekly). In summer daily Flying Dolphin hydrofoils head south to Kos and Rhodes, and north to Samos. Apollon Travel (left) has details and tickets.

NORTHEASTERN AEGEAN ISLANDS ΤΑ ΝΗΣΙΑ ΤΟΥ ΒΟΡΕΙΟ ΑΝΑΤΟΛΙΚΟ ΑΙΓΑΙΟΥ

One of Greece's best-kept secrets, these far-flung islands are strewn across the northeastern corner of the Aegean, closer to Turkey than mainland Greece. They harbour unspoilt scenery, welcoming locals, fascinating independent cultures, and remain relatively calm even when other Greek islands are sagging with tourists at the height of summer.

SAMOS ΣΑΜΟΣ

pop 32,800

A lush mountainous island only 3km from Turkey, Samos has a glorious history as the legendary birthplace of Hera, wife and sister of god-of-all-gods Zeus. Samos was an important centre of Hellenic culture, and the mathematician Pythagoras and storyteller Aesop are among its sons. The island has beaches that bake in summer, and a hinterland that is superb for hiking. Spring brings with it pink flamingos, wildflowers, and orchids that the island grows for export, while summer brings throngs of package tourists.

Samos has two main ports: Vathy (Samos Town) in the northeast and Pythagorio on the southeast coast. Those coming from the south generally arrive in Pythagorio. Big ferries use Vathy. Once you're on Samos and have onward tickets, double-check where your boat is leaving from. Buses between the two take 25 minutes.

GETTING THERE & AROUND

There are daily flights to Athens (€75) from **Samos airport** (SMI), 4km west of Pythagorio, and five weekly to Thessaloniki (€95) with **Olympic Airlines** (OA; ☎ 22730 27237; cnr Kanari & Smyrnis, Vathy). **Sky Express** (SEH; ☎ 28102 23500; www.skyexpress.gr) has flights to Iraklio, Crete.

A maritime hub, Samos offers daily ferries to Piraeus (€35, 13 hours), plus ferries heading north to Chios, west to the Cyclades and south to the Dodecanese. Daily hydrofoils ski south to Patmos (€20, one hour), carrying on to Leros, Kalymnos and Kos (€34, 3½ hours).

There are daily ferries to Kuşadası (for Ephesus) in Turkey (€37/47 one way/return plus €10 port taxes). Day excursions are also available from April to October. Check with **ITSA Travel** (☎ 22730 23605; www.itsatravel.com) in Vathy for up-to-date details.

You can get to most of the island's villages and beaches by bus. Rental cars and scooters are readily available around the island.

Pythagorio Πυθαγόρειο

pop 1300

Pretty Pythagorio, where you'll disembark if you've come from Patmos, is a small enticing town with a yacht-lined harbour and a holiday atmosphere.

The cordial **municipal tourist office** (☎ 22730 61389; deap5@otenet.gr; 8am-9.30pm) is two blocks from the waterfront on the main street, Lykourgou Logotheti. The bus stop is two blocks further inland on the same street, next to the post office. On the waterfront near the quay, **Pythagoras Internet Café** (☎ 22730 62722; per hr €2.50; 9am-2am) provides internet access.

The excellent **statue of Pythagoras** and his triangle, on the waterfront opposite the ferry quay, should have you recalling his theorem from your high school maths days. If not, buy a T-shirt emblazoned with it to remind you.

The 1034m-long **Evpalinos Tunnel** (☎ 22730 61400; adult/student €4/2; 8.45am-2.45pm Tue-Sun), built in the 6th century BC, was dug by political prisoners and used as an aqueduct to

'THE JUST CUP OF PYTHAGORAS'

The great Samian mathematician Pythagoras did more than just play with triangles. He also came up with an ingenious invention that ensures that drinkers can't overdo it. His *dikiakoupa tou Pythagora* – 'The Just Cup of Pythagoras' – is a multiholed drinking vessel that holds its contents perfectly well until filled past the engraved line. If overfilled, it mysteriously drains from the bottom and the overly enthusiastic drinker is punished for gluttony.

These days, faithful reproductions of the *dikiakoupa tou Pythagora* are available in gift shops on Samos – a reminder of the Apollan Mean (the ancient Greek maxim of Apollo): 'Everything in moderation'.

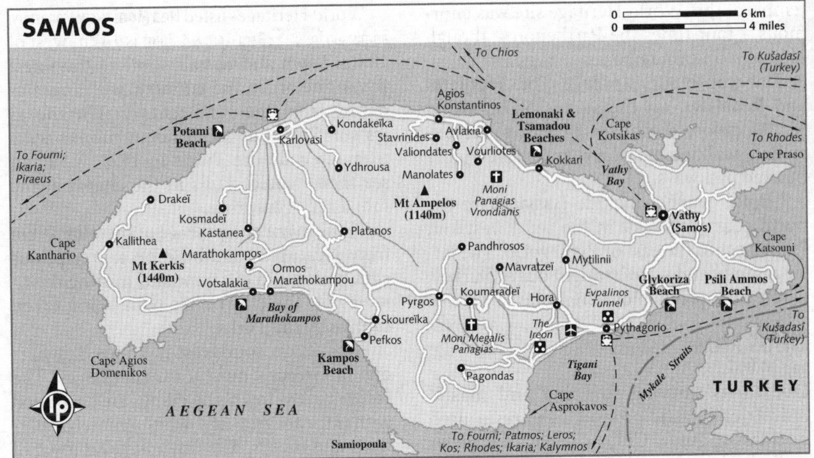

bring water from the springs of Mt Ampelos (1140m). In the Middle Ages, locals used the tunnel as a hideout during pirate raids. Part of it can still be explored. It's a 20-minute walk north of town.

Hotel Labito (☎ 22730 61086; www.labito.gr; s/d incl breakfast €45/55), a block back from the waterfront, is a friendly hotel with cosy rooms, most with a balcony. On the waterfront, **Polyxeni Hotel** (☎ 22730 61590; www.polyxeni.com; d €65;) is a homely place with nicely furnished, clean and comfortable rooms; it's a good option, especially the rooms with a harbour view.

Poseidon Restaurant (☎ 22730 62530; mains from €5), on the small town beach, past the jetty with the Pythagoras statue on it, offers superb seafood. **Iliad Bar** (☎ 22730 62207; cocktails from €5), on the waterfront, serves wicked cocktails till the wee hours and is run by an expat Kiwi.

Vathy (Samos) Βαθύ Σάμος

pop 2030

Busy Vathy, 25 minutes north of Pythagorio by bus, is an attractive working port town. Most of the action is along Themistokleous Sofouli, the main street that runs along the waterfront. The main square, Plateia Pythagorou, in the middle of the waterfront, is recognisable by its four palm trees and statue of a lion.

The rarely open and hard-to-find **tourist office** (☎ 22730 28582; Jun-Sep) is in a side street one block north of the main square. **ITSA Travel** (☎ 22730 23605; www.itsatravel.com), opposite the quay, is helpful with travel inquiries, excursions, accommodation and luggage storage. To get to Vathy's bus station, follow the waterfront south and turn left onto Lekati, 250m south of Plateia Pythagorou (just before the police station). Pythagoras Hotel (below) offers internet access for €2.50 per hour.

The **archaeological museum** (☎ 22730 27469; adult/student €3/2; 8.30am-3pm Tue-Sun), by the municipal gardens, is first rate. The highlight is a 5.5m *kouros* statue.

Pythagoras Hotel (☎ 22730 28601; www.pythagorashotel.com; Kallistratou 12; s/d €20/35;) is a friendly, great-value place with a convivial atmosphere re run by English-speaking Stelio. There is a restaurant serving tasty home-cooked meals, a bar, satellite TV and internet access (wi-fi, too) on site. Facing inland, the hotel is 400m to the left of the quay. Call ahead for free pick-up on arrival.

Ino Village Hotel (☎ 22730 23241; www.inovillagehotel.com; Kalami; s/d/tr incl breakfast €59/74/100;) is an impressive, elegant place in the hills north of the ferry quay. Its Elea Restaurant on the terrace serves up both invigorated Greek cuisine and views over town and the harbour.

Garden Taverna (☎ 22730 24033; Manolis Kalomiris; mains €4-9) serves good Greek food in a lovely garden setting; it's up to the left behind the main square.

Around Samos

Ireon (☎ 22730 95277; adult/student €4/3; 8.30am-3pm Tue-Sun), the legendary birthplace of the goddess Hera, is 8km west of Pythagorio. The temple at this World Heritage site was enormous – four times the Parthenon – though only one column remains.

The captivating villages of **Vourliotes** and **Manolates**, on the slopes of imposing Mt Ampelos, northwest of Vathy, are excellent walking territory and have many marked pathways.

Choice beaches include **Tsamadou** on the north coast, **Votsalakia** in the southwest and **Psili Ammos** to the east of Pythagorio. The latter is sandy and stares straight out at Turkey, barely a couple of kilometres away.

CHIOS ΧΙΟΣ

pop 54,000

Due to its thriving shipping and mastic industries (mastic produces the resin used in chewing gum), Chios (*hee*-os) has never really bothered much with tourism. If you are an off-the-beaten-track type of Greek Island traveller, you'll find Chios all the more appealing.

One great attraction lies in exploring the island's inland villages, including the *mastihohoria* (mastic villages) that were spared during an 1822 Turkish massacre because of the sultan's fondness for chewing gum.

Orientation & Information

Chios Town, on the island's eastern coast, is a working port and home to half the island's inhabitants. A main street runs in a semicircle around the port, with most ferries docking at its northern end. The *kastro* (old Turkish quarter) is to the north of the ferry quay, and Plateia Vounakiou, the main square, is just south and inland from the quay.

The **municipal tourist office** (☎ 22710 44389; infochio@otenet.gr; Kanari 18; 🕑 7am-10pm Apr-Oct, to 4pm Nov-Mar) is on the street that runs inland to the main square. It provides information on accommodation, schedules and rentals.

Agean Travel (☎ 22710 41277; aegeantr@otenet.gr; Leoforos Egeou 114), at the southern end of the harbour, handles ticketing, while **InSpot Internet Café** (☎ 22710 43438; Leoforos Egeou 86; per hr €2.40) has internet access on the waterfront closer to the ferry quay.

Sights & Activities

In Chios Town, **Philip Argenti Museum** (☎ 22710 23463; Korais; admission €1.50; 🕑 8am-2pm Mon-Thu, 8am-2pm & 5-7.30pm Fri, 8am-12.30pm Sat) contains the treasures of the wealthy Argenti family.

World Heritage–listed **Nea Moni** (New Monastery; admission free; 🕑 8am-1pm & 4-8pm) is 14km west of Chios Town and reveals some of the finest Byzantine art in the country, with mosaics dating from the 11th century. The mosaics survived, but the resident monks were massacred by the Turks in 1822. You can see their dented skulls in the chapel at the monastery's entrance.

Those in the ghost village of **Anavatos**, 10km from Nea Moni and built on a precipitous cliff, preferred a different fate, hurling themselves off the cliff rather than being taken captive by the Turks.

Pyrgi, 24km southwest of Chios Town, is one of Greece's most unusual villages. The facades of the town's dwellings are decorated with intricate grey-and-white geometric patterns and motifs. The tiny medieval town of **Mesta**, 10km from Pyrgi and nestled within fortified walls, features cobbled streets, overhead arches and a labyrinth of streets designed to confuse pirates.

Sleeping & Eating

Chios Rooms (☎ 22710 20198; www.chiosrooms.gr; Leoforos Egeou 110; s/d/tr €25/35/45) A top location to stay, this place is upstairs in a restored neoclassical house on the waterfront at the southern end of the harbour. It has bright, airy rooms, some with en suite bathrooms, and is being restored lovingly by its Kiwi owner, who is a mine of information on Chios.

Hotel Kyma (☎ 22710 44500; kyma@chi.forthnet.gr; Evgenias Handris 1; s/d/tr incl breakfast €71/90/111; ❄) Around the corner from Chios Rooms, this place occupies a charismatic century-old mansion and is run by the enthusiastic multilingual Theodoris. Ask for a room overlooking the sea.

our pick **Hotzas Taverna** (☎ 22710 42787; Kondyli 3; mains from €5) Up the back of town and away from the waterfront, Hotzas is known by locals to provide the best Greek fare on the island. It's worth the effort to find it. Get a local to mark it on a map and enjoy the walk.

Taverna Petrino (☎ 22710 29797; Leoforos Egeou 80; mains from €5) Features friendly service, attractive decor, a handwritten menu and delicious local delicacies on the waterfront.

Getting There & Around

There are daily flights from Chios airport (JKH) to Athens (€60) and five per week to Thessaloniki (€60) with **Olympic Airlines** (OA;

(☎ 22710 20359). The airport is 4km south of Chios Town.

Ferries sail daily to Piraeus (€32.50, six hours) and Lesvos (€19.50, two hours 15 minutes), and weekly to Thessaloniki (€40, 18 hours). There are four ferries a week to Samos (€15, four hours) from where there are connections south.

Boats to Turkey run all year from Chios, with daily sailings from July to September to Çeşme (one way/return €22/25). For details, check out **Miniotis Lines** (☎ 22710 24670; www.miniotis.gr; Neorion 24).

Chios Town has two bus stations. Blue buses go regularly to local villages and Karfas Beach, and leave from the local bus station at the main square. Buses to Pyrgi (€2.70) and Mesta (€3.10) and other distant points leave from the long-distance bus station on the waterfront near the ferry quay.

LESVOS (MYTILINI) ΛΕΣΒΟΣ (ΜΥΤΙΛΗΝΗ)

pop 93,500

Lesvos, or Mytilini as it is often called, tends to do things in a big way. The third-largest of the Greek Islands after Crete and Evia, Lesvos produces half the world's ouzo and is home to over 11 million olive trees. Mountainous yet fertile, the island presents excellent hiking and birdwatching opportunities, but remains relatively untouched in terms of tourism development.

Lesvos has always been a centre of philosophy and artistic achievement, and to this day is a spawning ground for innovative ideas in the arts and politics. An excellent source of information on the island is www.greeknet.com.

The two main towns on the island are the capital of Mytilini on the southeast coast, and attractive Mithymna on the north coast.

GETTING THERE & AWAY

Written up on flight schedules as Mytilene, Lesvos' Odysseas airport (MJT) has daily connections with Athens (€78) and Thessaloniki (€88), and two a week to Chios (€28) with **Olympic Airlines** (OA; ☎ 22510 28659) and **Aegean Airlines** (A3; ☎ 22510 61120). **Sky Express** (SEH; ☎ 28102 23500; www.skyexpress.gr) operates to Iraklio, Crete and Thessaloniki.

In summer there are daily boats to Piraeus (€30, 12 hours) via Chios, and one boat a week to Thessaloniki (€35, 13 hours). There are four ferries a week to Ayvalik in Turkey (one way/return €30/45). Stop by Zoumboulis Tours (below) for ticketing and schedules.

Mytilini Μυτιλήνη

pop 27,300

The capital and main port, Mytilini, is built between two harbours (north and south) with an imposing fortress on the promontory to the east. All ferries dock at the southern harbour, and most of the town's action is around this waterfront. With a large university campus, Mytilini is a lively place year-round.

The **tourist office** (☎ 22510 42511; 6 Aristarhou; 9am-1pm Mon-Fri), 50m up Aristarhou inland from the quay, offers brochures and maps, but its opening hours are limited. The **tourist police** (☎ 22510 22776) are at the entrance to the quay and are helpful if you're outside tourist-office hours. **Zoumboulis Tours** (☎ 22510 37755; Kountourioti 69), on the waterfront, handles flights, boat schedules, ticketing and excursions to Turkey. At the southern end of the harbour, **InSpot** (☎ 22510 45760; Hristougennon 12; per hr €2.40) has impressive internet access.

SIGHTS & ACTIVITIES

Mytilini's excellent neoclassical **archaeological museum** (☎ 22510 22087; 8 Noemvriou; adult/child €3/2; 8am-7.30pm) has a fascinating collection from Neolithic to Roman times.

A superb place for a stroll or a picnic is the pine forest surrounding Mytilini's impressive **fortress** (adult/student €2/1; 8am-2.30pm Tue-Sun), which was built in early Byzantine times and enlarged by the Turks.

Theophilos Museum (☎ 22510 41644; admission €2; 9am-2.30pm & 6-8pm Tue-Sun), 4km south of Mytilini in Varia village, is a shrine to the prolific folk painter Theophilos. Next door is the **Teriade Museum** (☎ 22510 23372; admission €2; 9am-5pm Tue-Sun) with an astonishing collection of paintings by world-renowned artists.

SLEEPING

Pension Thalia (☎ 22510 24640; Kinikiou 1; s/d €25/30) This pension has clean, bright rooms in a large house. It is about a five-minute walk north of the main square, up Ermou, the road that links the south and north harbours. Follow the signs from the corner of Ermou and Adramytiou.

Hotel Sappho (☎ 22510 22888; Kountourioti 31; s/d/tr €35/55/66) On the waterfront, rooms here are simple but clean. It's easy to find, and has the attraction of a 24-hour reception as ferries into Mytilini tend to arrive at nasty hours.

SAPPHO, LESBIANS & LESVOS

Sappho, one of Greece's great ancient poets, was born on Lesvos during the 7th century BC. Most of her work was devoted to love and desire, and the objects of her affection were often female. Because of this, Sappho's name and birthplace have come to be associated with female homosexuality.

These days, Lesvos is visited by many lesbians paying homage to Sappho. The whole island is very gay-friendly, in particular the southwestern beach resort of Skala Eresou, which is built over ancient Eresos where Sappho was born. The village is well set up to cater to lesbian needs and has a 'Women Together' festival held annually in September. Check out www.sapphotravel.com for details.

There is an excellent statue of Sappho in the main square on the waterfront in Mytilini.

Porto Lesvos 1 Hotel (☎ 22510 41771; www.portolesvos.gr; Komninaki 21; s/d €60/90; ⚹ ▣) This hotel has good rooms and service – right down to robes and slippers – in a restored building one block back from the waterfront.

EATING & DRINKING

our pick Diavlos (☎ 22510 22020; Ladadika 30; mains from €4) Head straight to Diavlos for the best in both local cuisine and art; paintings by local artists line the walls and can be purchased should you get the urge.

Kalderimi (☎ 22510 46577; Thasou 3; mains from €6) Popular with locals, Kalderimi has an excellent ambience with tables in a vine-covered pedestrian street just back from the Sappho statue on the main harbour.

Ocean Eleven Bar (☎ 22510 27030; Kountourioti 17) In the corner on the waterfront, this is a superb spot to relax with a drink and partake in some Mytilini people-watching.

GETTING AROUND

Mytilini has two bus stations. For local buses, head along the waterfront to the main square. For long-distance buses, walk 600m from the ferry along the waterfront to El Venizelou and turn right until you reach Agia Irinis park, which is next to the station. There are regular services in summer to Mithymna, Petra, Agiasos, Skala Eresou, Mantamados and Agia Paraskevi.

Mithymna Μήθυμνα

pop 1500

The gracious, preserved town of Mithymna (known by locals as Molyvos) is 62km north of Mytilini. Cobbled streets canopied by flowering vines wind up the hill below the impressive castle. The town is full of cosy tavernas and genteel stone cottages.

From the bus stop, walk straight ahead towards the town for 100m to the helpful **municipal tourist office** (☎ 22530 71347; www.mithymna.gr; 🕑 8am-9pm Mon-Fri, 9am-7pm Sat & Sun), which has good maps. Some 50m further on, the cobbled main thoroughfare of 17 Noemvriou heads up to the right. Going straight at this point will take you to the colourful fishing port. There are three internet cafes along the port road.

The noble **Genoese castle** (☎ 22530 71803; admission €2; 🕑 8am-7pm Tue-Sun) perches above the town like a crown and affords tremendous views out to Turkey. Pebbly **Mithymna Beach** sits below the town and is good for swimming. Don't forget to stroll down to the harbour.

Eftalou hot springs (☎ 22530 71245; public/private bath per person €3.50/5; 🕑 public bath 10am-2pm & 4-8pm, private bath 9am-6pm), 4km from town on the beach, is a superb bathhouse complex with a whitewashed dome and steaming, pebbled pool. There are also private baths where you don't need a bathing suit.

Nassos Guest House (☎ 22530 71432; www.nassosguesthouse.com; Arionis; d & tr €20-35) is an airy, friendly place with shared facilities and a communal kitchen, in an old Turkish house oozing with character. With rapturous views, it's highly recommended. It's easy to spot as it's the only blue house below the castle.

Betty's Restaurant (☎ 22530 71421; Agora; mains from €5) has superb home-style Greek food, views and atmosphere in a building that was once a notorious bordello. Betty also has a couple of cottages (☎ 22530 71022; www.bettyscottages.molivos.net) with kitchens in her garden that sleep up to four for €50.

Buses to Mithymna (€5) take 1¾ hours from Mytilini, though a rental car is a good option.

Around the Island

Southern Lesvos is dominated by **Mt Olympus** (968m) and the very pretty village of **Agiasos**, which has good artisan workshops making everything from handcrafted furniture to pottery.

Western Lesvos is known for its petrified forest, with petrified wood at least 500,000 years old, and for the gay-friendly town of Skala Eresou, the birthplace of Sappho (see opposite).

SPORADES ΣΠΟΡΑΔΕΣ

Scattered to the southeast of the Pelion Peninsula, to which they were joined in prehistoric times, the 11 islands that make up the Sporades group have mountainous terrain, dense vegetation and are surrounded by scintillatingly clear seas.

The main ports for the Sporades are Volos and Agios Konstantinos on the mainland.

SKIATHOS ΣΚΙΑΘΟΣ

pop 6150

Lush and green, Skiathos has a beach-resort feel about it. Charter flights bring loads of package tourists, but the island still oozes enjoyment. Skiathos Town and some excellent beaches are on the hospitable south coast, while the north coast is precipitous and less accessible. Skiathos Town was recently used as a shooting location in the filming of *Mamma Mia*.

Orientation & Information

Skiathos Town's main thoroughfare is Papadiamanti, running inland opposite the quay. There's a **tourist information booth** (☎ 24270 23172) at the port, but it opens irregularly. The helpful **tourist police** (☎ 24270 23172; 🕑 8am-9pm), about halfway along Papadiamanti next to the high school, can provide information and maps.

Heliotropio Travel (☎ 24270 22430; helio@skiathos.gr), opposite the ferry quay, handles ticketing and rents cars and scooters. **Enter Internet** (☎ 69984 24460; per hr €3; 🕑 9am-1am) is one block back from the port with heaps of signage.

Sights

Skiathos has superb beaches, particularly on the south coast. **Koukounaries** is popular with families. A stroll over the headland, **Big Banana Beach** is stunning, but if you want an all-over tan, head a tad further to **Little Banana Beach**, where bathing suits are a rarity.

At the Old Port in Skiathos Town, there are all sorts of offerings in terms of boat excursions – trips to nearby beaches (€10), trips around Skiathos Island (€25) and full-day trips that take in Skopelos, Alonnisos and the Marine Park (€35).

Sleeping

The **Rooms to Let** (☎ 24270 22990) bookings kiosk on the waterfront opens when ferries and hydrofoils arrive. There are not a lot of budget options on Skiathos.

Camping Koukounaries (☎ 24270 49250; camp sites per tent/person €4/8) This place, 30 minutes away from town by bus at beautiful Koukounaries Beach, has good facilities, a minimarket and a taverna.

Pension Pandora (☎ 24270 24357, 69441 37377; www.skiathos.gr/html/advert/pans_pandora; r €30-70; ❄) Run by the effervescent Georgina, this family-run place is 10 minutes' walk north of the quay. The spotless rooms have TV, kitchens and balconies. Georgina also has two exceptional apartments just off Papadiamanti.

Villa Orsa (☎ 24270 22430; s/d incl breakfast €70/80; ❄) Perched above the old harbour, this mansion features traditionally styled rooms and a garden terrace overlooking the sea.

Eating & Drinking

Skiathos Town is brimming with eateries.

Psaradika Ouzeri (☎ 24270 23412; mains €4-10) By the fish market at the far end of the old port, Psaradika is the seafood winner, specialising in fresh fish at decent prices.

Piccolo (☎ 24270 22780; mains from €7) Heading up from the Old Port, in the tiny square behind the church, Piccolo does exquisite pizzas and pastas in a lovely setting. Try the Greek pizza (€8).

our pick 1901 (☎ 69485 26701; mains from €7) A tad further back from Piccolo, 1901 is a superb fine-dining restaurant with a glowing reputation. Relax at the streetside tables and enjoy food produced with pride.

Kentavros (☎ 24270 22980) Just off Plateia Papadiamanti, Kentavros is popular with locals and expats alike for its mellow ambience and mixture of rock, jazz and blues.

Getting There & Around

In summer there is a daily flight from Athens to Skiathos (€55). There is an **Olympic Airlines office** (OA; ☎ 24270 22200) at Skiathos airport (JSI).

There are frequent daily hydrofoils to/from the mainland ports of Volos (€25, 1¼ hours) and Agios Konstantinos (€28, 1½ hours), as well as cheaper ferries. The hydrofoils head to and from Skopelos (€12.50, 35 minutes) and Alonnisos (€14.70, one hour). In summer there is a daily hydrofoil to Thessaloniki (€35.30, 3½ hours).

Crowded buses ply the south-coast road between Skiathos Town and Koukounaries every 30 minutes between 7.30am and 11pm year-round, stopping at all the beaches along the way. The bus stop is at the eastern end of the harbour.

SKOPELOS ΣΚΟΠΕΛΟΣ

pop 4700

A mountainous island, Skopelos is covered in pine forests, vineyards, olive groves and fruit orchards. While the northwest coast is exposed with high cliffs, the southeast is sheltered and harbours pleasant pebbled beaches. The island's main port and capital of Skopelos Town, on the east coast, skirts a semicircular bay and clambers in tiers up a hillside, culminating in a ruined fortress.

Recent claims to fame for Skopelos are the legendary Skopelos pie, which can be bought all over Greece, and its use as a location for the filming of *Mamma Mia*. The crew took over Skopelos Town's accommodation for a month and filmed at Agnontas and Kastani beaches on the western coast.

In Skopelos Town, there is no tourist office, but **Thalpos Holidays** (☎ 24240 29036; www.holidayislands.com), on the waterfront between the ferry quay and the excursion-boat quay, is handy for accommodation and tours. Head 50m up the road opposite the port entrance to find Souvlaki Sq. Along Doulidi, the street heading left off the square, is the **Skopelos Internet Café** (☎ 24240 23093; per hr €3; 9am-midnight), post office and a stack of popular nightspots. The bus station is next to the port. Excursion boats along the waterfront offer trips into the Marine Park.

ECOTOURISM ON THE RISE

In a country not noted for its ecological long-sightedness, locals (especially the fishermen) initially struggled with the idea of the National Marine Park of Alonnisos when it was established in 1992 to protect the highly endangered Mediterranean monk seal and to promote the recovery of fish stocks.

These days though, the people of the Sporades have caught on to the advantages of having such a park on their doorstep. Ecotourism is on the rise, with daily excursions on licensed boats into the park from Skiathos, Skopelos and Alonnisos. Though your odds of seeing the shy monk seal aren't great – it's on the list of the 20 most endangered species worldwide – the chances of cruising among pods of dolphins (striped, bottlenose and common) are high.

Pension Sotos (☎ 24240 22549; www.skopelos.net/sotos; s/d €20-55;), in the middle of the waterfront, has big rooms in an enchanting old Skopelete building. There's also a communal kitchen, terrace and courtyard. Check out individual rooms and its different prices online before you go. **Hotel Regina** (☎ 24240 22138; www.skopelosweb.gr/regina; s/d incl breakfast €40/55;) has bright and cheery rooms with balconies. The hotel's rooftop signage is easily spotted from the waterfront.

Head to Souvlaki Sq, 100m up from the dock, for cheap eats such as gyros and souvlaki. The top spot in town to chill out is under the huge plane tree at **Platanos Jazz Bar** (☎ 24240 23661) on the waterfront. It's open all day, plays wicked jazz and blues until the late hours, and is the ideal place to recover from, or prepare for, a hangover. Next door is **Taverna Ta Kimata O Angelos** (☎ 24240 22381; mains from €4), a traditional taverna that is the oldest one on the island.

Flying Dolphin hydrofoils dash several times a day to Skiathos (€12.50, 45 minutes), Alonnisos (€7.70, 20 minutes), Volos (€26.30, 2¼ hours) and Agios Konstantinos (€27.40, 2½ hours). Most hydrofoils also call in at Loutraki, the port below Glossa on the northwest coast of the island. There is also a daily ferry along the same route that costs less but takes longer. There are frequent buses from Skopelos Town to Glossa (€3.90, one hour) stopping at all beaches along the way.

ALONNISOS ΑΛΟΝΝΗΣΟΣ

pop 2700

Green, serene, attractive Alonnisos is at the end of the line and is thereby the least visited of the Sporades' main islands. The west coast is mostly precipitous cliffs, but the east coast is speckled with pebble-and-sand beaches.

The port village of Patitiri was slapped together in 1965 after an earthquake destroyed the hilltop capital of Alonnisos Town. There are two main thoroughfares; facing inland from the ferry quay, Pelasgon is to the left and Ikion Dolopon is to the far right.

There is no tourist office or tourist police, but the post office, police and **Play Internet** (☎ 24240 66119; per hr €3; 🕑 9am-2pm & 6-9pm) are on Ikion Dolopon. On the waterfront itself, **Alonnisos Travel** (☎ 24240 66000; www.alonnisostravel.gr) handles boat scheduling and ticketing. **Ikos Travel** (☎ 24240 65320; www.ikostravel.com) runs a popular round-the-island excursion. The bus stop is on the corner of Ikion Dolopon and the waterfront.

The tiny *hora,* **Old Alonnisos**, is a few kilometres inland. Its streets sprout a profusion of plant life, alluring villas of eclectic design and dramatic vistas.

Alonnisos is ideal for walking. Waterfront travel agencies offer guided tours or there's an excellent trail guide called *Alonnisos on Foot: A Walking & Swimming Guide* by Bente Keller and Elias Tsoukanas, which is available at newsstands for €9.

The **Rooms to Let service** (☎ 24240 66188; fax 24240 65577; 🕑 10am-2pm & 6-10pm), opposite the quay, books accommodation all over the island. **Camping Rocks** (☎ 24240 65410; camp sites per person €6) is a shady, basic camping ground. It is a steep hike about 1.5km from the port; go up Pelasgon and take the first road on your left. **Pension Pleiades** (☎ 24240 65235; www.pleiadeshotel.gr; s/d/tr €25/35/50; ❄ 💻) looks out over the harbour and is visible from the quay. The rooms are immaculate, balconied, bright and cheerful. There's also a good restaurant. **Liadromia Hotel** (☎ 24240 65521; www.liadromia.gr; d/tr/ste €50/70/85; ❄ 💻) is an excellent-value place with tons of character overlooking Patitiri's harbour. Follow the stairway opposite the National Bank.

Anais (☎ 24240 65243; mains from €5) is a traditional island eatery opposite the hydrofoil quay. **Café Flisvos** (☎ 24240 65307; mains from €5) offers excellent oven-ready dishes at decent prices.

There are ferries with varying regularity connecting Alonnisos to Volos and Agios Konstantinos via Skopelos and Skiathos. Flying Dolphin hydrofoils provide the most regular schedules between the islands. They travel several times a day to Skopelos Town (€7.70, 20 minutes), Skiathos (€14.70, 1½ hours), Volos (€32.50, three hours) and Agios Konstantinos (€36.50, three hours).

The local bus (€1.20) runs to the *hora* every hour.

IONIAN ISLANDS ΤΑ ΕΠΤΑΝΗΣΑ

The idyllic cypress- and fir-covered Ionian Islands stretch down the western coast of Greece from Corfu in the north to Kythira, off the southern tip of the Peloponnese. Mountainous, with dramatic cliff-backed beaches, soft light and turquoise water, they're more Italian in feel, offering a contrasting experience to other Greek islands. Invest in a hire car to get to small villages tucked along quiet back roads. Prices drop in low season.

CORFU ΚΕΡΚΥΡΑ

pop 114,000

Many consider Corfu to be Greece's most beautiful island – the unfortunate consequence of which is that it's often overrun with crowds.

GETTING THERE & AWAY

Ioannis Kapodistrias airport (CFU; ☎ 26610 30180) is 3km from Corfu Town. **Olympic Airlines** (☎ 26610 22962) and **Aegean Airlines** (☎ 26610 27100) fly daily to Athens. Olympic flies a few times a week to other Ionian islands and Thessaloniki. Hourly ferries go to Igoumenitsa (€7, 1½ hours). In summer daily ferries and hydrofoils go to Paxi, and international ferries (see p423 for more details) stop in Patra (€33, six hours). Daily buses to Athens (€44, 8½ hours) and Thessaloniki (€42, eight hours) leave from the Avrami terminal.

Corfu Town

pop 39,500

Built on a promontory and wedged between two fortresses, Corfu's Old Town is a tangle of narrow walking streets through gorgeous Venetian buildings. Explore the

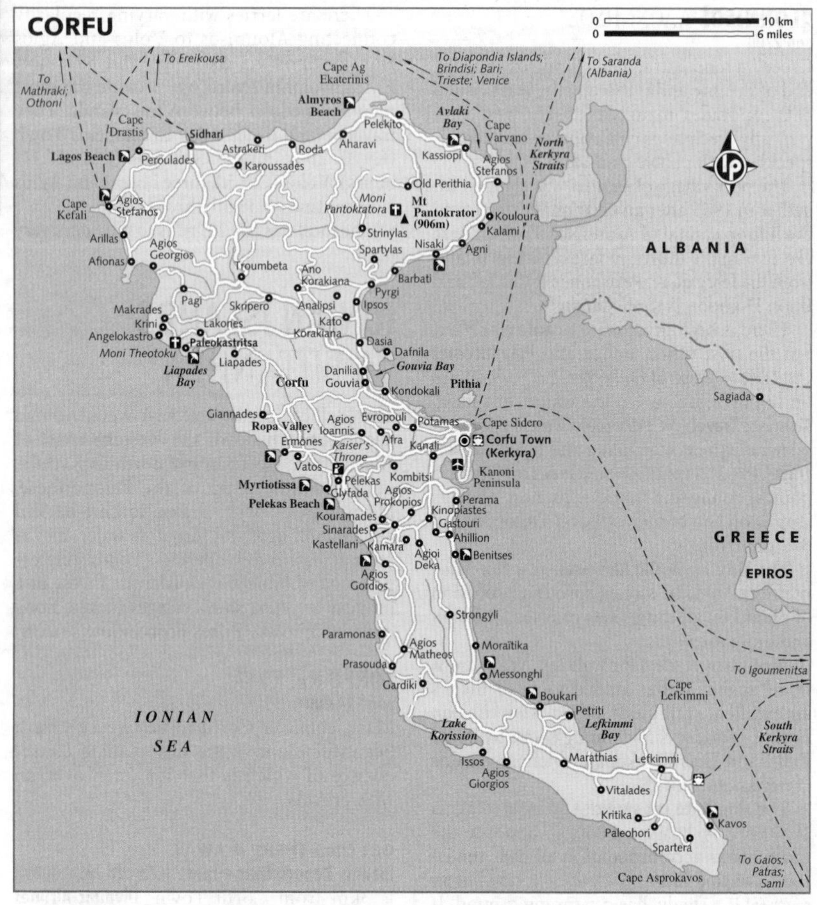

winding alleys and surprising plazas in the early morning or late afternoon to avoid the hordes of day trippers searching for souvenirs.

The Palaio Frourio (Old Fortress) stands on an eastern promontory, separated from the town by seafront gardens known as the Spianada. The Neo Frourio (New Fortress) lies to the northwest. Ferries dock at the new port, just west of the Neo Frourio. The **long-distance bus station** (☎ 26610 28900; Avrami) lies inland from the port. The **tourist police** (☎ 26610 30265; 3rd fl, Samartzi 4) provide helpful info. Check email at **Netoikos** (Kaloheretou 14; per hr €3), behind the Church of Agios Spyridon.

SIGHTS

The **Archaeological Museum** (☎ 26610 30680; Vraïla 5; admission €3; 🕒 8.30am-3pm Tue-Sun) houses a collection of finds from Mycenaean to classical times. The richly decorated **Church of Agios Spiridon** (Agios Spiridonos) displays the remains of St Spiridon, paraded through town four times a year.

SLEEPING & EATING

Accommodation prices fluctuate wildly depending on season; book ahead.

If you're after a bite, cafes and bars line the arcaded Liston.

Hotel Astron (☎ 26610 39505; hotel_astron@hol.gr; Donzelot 15, Old Port; s €45-55, d €55-65) Recently renovated and with some sea views, light-filled rooms are managed by friendly staff.

Hotel Konstantinoupolis (☎ 26610 48716; www.konstantinoupolis.com.gr; K Zavitsianou 1, Old Port; s €70-100, d €88-118; ❄ 💻) Old-world and a bit rumpled; book a front room overlooking the lovely harbour.

our pick **Bella Venezia** (☎ 26610 46500; www.bellaveneziahotel.com; N Zambeli 4; s/d incl breakfast from €85/105; ❄ 💻) Impeccable and understated, contemporary rooms are decked out in cream linens and marbles.

To Tsipouzadiko (☎ 26610 82240; mains €5-8; 🕑 dinner) Old 45 *rembetika* records line the walls, and the gregarious owner serves up generous portions of fresh (cheap) Greek food. It's on the lane behind the courthouse and Hotel Konstantinoupolis in Old Port.

To Dimarchio (☎ 26610 39031; Plateia Dimarchio; mains €8-25) Relax in a luxuriant rose garden on a charming square. Attentive staff serve elegant, inventive Italian and Greek dishes, prepared with the freshest ingredients.

La Cucina (☎ 26610 45029; Guilford 17; mains €10-15) Every detail is cared for at this intimate bistro, from the hand-rolled tortellonis to the inventive pizzas and muraled walls.

GETTING AROUND

Buses for villages close to Corfu Town leave from Plateia San Rocco. Services to other destinations leave from Avrami terminal. A taxi from the airport to the Old Town costs around €15.

Around the Island

Book dives at **Corfu Divers** (☎ 26630 81038; www.corfu-divers.com) in **Kassiopi**.

To gain an aerial view of the gorgeous cypress-backed bays around **Paleokastritsa**, the west coast's main resort, go to the quiet village of **Lakones**. Further south, good beaches surround tiny **Agios Gordios**. Backpackers head to low-key **Sunrock** (☎ 26610 94637; Pelekas Beach; dm/r per person €18/24; 💻 🍽) for its full-board hostel and genial atmosphere.

LEFKADA ΛΕΥΚΑΔΑ

pop 22,500

Joined to the mainland by a narrow isthmus, fertile Lefkada with its mountainous interior pine forests also boasts truly splendid beaches and one of the hottest windsurfing spots in Europe.

IN CASE OF A WATER LANDING

Ferry schedules and routes around the Ionian Islands and the mainland fluctuate wildly depending on season. Circumvent the issue by catching one of the sleek, efficient **AirSea Lines** (☎ 80111 800600; www.airsealines.com) pontooned sea planes that hopscotch the islands.

GETTING THERE & AROUND

Olympic Airlines flies to **Preveza-Aktio airport** (PVK), 20km to the north. **Four Island Ferries** operates daily ferries between Nydri, Frikes (Ithaki), Fiskardo (Keffalonia) and Vasiliki. Most trips take about 60 minutes and tickets cost €7 per person and €30 per car. Get times and tickets from **Borsalino Travel** (☎ 26450 92528; Nydri) or **Samba Tours** (☎ 26450 31520; Vasiliki). Rent cars in Lefkada Town, Nydri or Vasiliki.

Lefkada Town

Most travellers' first port of call, Lefkada Town remains laid-back except for when it is overrun in August. The town's unique earthquake-resistant corrugated-steel architecture somehow blends with its attractive marina, waterfront cafes and vibrant pedestrian thoroughfares.

Restaurants and cafes line the main street, Dorpfeld, central Lefkas Sq and the waterfront.

The best rooms at **Hotel Santa Maura** (☎ 26450 21308; Dorpfeld; s/d incl breakfast €55/75; ❄) are on the top floor. Think tropical Bahamas with sky-blue and shell-pink interiors and breezy balconies.

Pension Pirofani (☎ 26450 25844; Dorpfeld; d €95) has been renovated recently and sleek rooms have balconies for prime people-watching.

Gustoso (☎ 26450 24603; Agelou Sikelianou, western seafront; mains €6-20) is an attractive Italian pizzeria serving delicious salads and the best wood-fired-oven pizzas outside of Napoli.

Around the Island

With its lovely bay, **Nydri** is somewhat blighted by tacky souvenir shops and touristy tavernas. Escape instead to exquisite **Nhion** (☎ 26450 41624; Kiafa village; www.neion.gr; d €65), a pristine mountain retreat with stellar views and restored stone buildings.

Lefkada's true gifts are its west coast beaches. Cliffs drop to broad sweeps of white sand and turquoise waters. Explore! Tiny, laid-back **Agios Nikitas** village draws travellers, but gets very crowded in summer.

Southernmost eucalyptus-scented **Vasiliki** is popular with windsurfers. Organise lessons through **Club Vass** (☎ 26450 31588; www.clubvass.com) or guided treks, kayaking and other activities through **Trekking Hellas** (☎ 26450 31130; www.trekking.gr). Overlooking the port, **Pension Holidays** (☎ 26450 31426; d €55;) has great-value rooms with kitchens.

ITHAKI ΙΘΑΚΗ

pop 3700

Odysseus' long-lost home in Homer's *Odyssey*, Ithaki, or ancient Ithaca, remains a verdant pristine island blessed with cypress-covered hills and beautiful turquoise coves.

GETTING THERE & AROUND

Four Island Ferries operates seasonal ferries between Frikes, Fiskardo (Keffalonia), and Nydri and Vasiliki (Lefkada). Buy tickets at the Frikes dock just before departure. Most trips take an average of 90 minutes and cost €7 per person and €33 per car. Check routes and schedules at **Delas Tours** (☎ 26740 32104; www.ithaca.com.gr; Vathy).

Kioni

Tucked in a tiny, tranquil bay, this is a wonderful place to chill for a few days. Check email at comfy **Cafe Spavento** (per hr €4) near the waterfront.

Individuals rent rooms; some lie on the southern edge of the port (☎ 26740 31014; room with shared/private bathroom €30/40) and have kitchens and sea views. **Captain's Apartments** (☎ 26740 31481; www.captains-apartments.gr; studio/apt €65/90;) is owned by an affable former merchant navy captain. His shipshape, spacious apartments come with kitchens, satellite TV and balconies overlooking the valley and village.

Several tavernas line up like yachts along the harbour. Try **Mythos** (mains €6-8) for excellent *pastichios* and Greek staples.

Around the Island

The dusty, relaxed port of **Frikes**, where the ferries dock, is a funkier alternative to Kioni and has rooms to rent.

Vathy, Ithaki's small, bustling capital, is the spot for hiring cars and getting cash – no banks in Kioni. Elegant mansions rise from around its bay and **Hotel Perantzada** (☎ 26740 33496; www.arthotel.gr/perantzada/; Odissea Androutsou; d €176-365;) occupies two with sensational individually decorated rooms.

KEFALLONIA ΚΕΦΑΛΛΟΝΙΑ

pop 45,000

Tranquil cypress- and fir-covered Kefallonia has fortunately not succumbed to package tourism to the extent some of the other Ionian islands have, despite being thrust under the spotlight following its starring role in *Captain Corelli's Mandolin*. The largest Ionian island is breathtakingly beautiful in parts and remains low-key outside the resort areas.

GETTING THERE & AROUND

Daily flights go to Athens from **Keffalonia airport** (EFL; ☎ 26710 41511), 9km south of Argostoli. Four Island Ferries operates seasonal routes between Fiskardo, Frikes (Ithaki), and Nydri and Vasiliki (Lefkada). In Fiskardo, get tickets from **Nautilus Travel** (☎ 26740 41440; fax 26740 41470) or the dock before departure. Most trips average 90 minutes and cost €7 per person and €30 per car. In high season, ferries go from Pesada to Agios Nikolaos (Zakynthos). Daily ferries operate from Sami to Patra (€15, 2½ hours) and Pisaetos and Vathy (Ithaki), and from Argostoli and Poros to Kyllini (the Peloponnese).

A car is best for exploring Kefallonia. **Pama Travel** (☎ 26740 41033; www.pamatravel.com; Fiskardo) rents cars and boats, books accommodation and has internet access.

Fiskardo

Pretty Fiskardo, with its pastel-coloured Venetian buildings set around a picturesque bay, was the only Kefallonian village not to be destroyed by the 1953 earthquake. Despite its popularity with European yachties and upmarket package tourists, it's still peaceful enough to appeal to independent travellers, and is a sublime spot to hang for a few days. Take lovely walks to sheltered coves for swimming.

SLEEPING

Regina's Rooms (☎ 26740 41125; d €50-70) On the car park overlooking the village, this budget bargain is ideal for self-caterers. All of its colourful, breezy rooms have TV, fridge and balconies, some with gorgeous bay views or kitchenettes.

Archontiko (☎ 26740 41342; r from €80;) Overlooking the harbour, people-watch from the balconies of these luxurious rooms in a restored stone mansion.

Faros Suites (☎ 26740 41355; www.myrtoscorp.com; ste incl breakfast from €115;) Hospitable South African-Greek owners make you feel at home at this supercomfortable boutique hotel in the next baylet over from the village. Spacious suites are more like apartments with fully equipped kitchens, some with sea views.

EATING

Fiskardo has no shortage of excellent waterside restaurants.

Tassia (☎ 26740 41205; mains €8-18) Unassuming but famous Tassia is run by a charming family with an impeccable culinary pedigree. They serve up excellent seafood and Greek dishes.

Café Tselenti (☎ 26740 41344; mains €8-20) This cafe is tucked back a bit in a romantic plaza. Enjoy elegant Italian classics served by friendly waiters.

Vasso's (☎ 26740 41276; mains €10-40) Whether it's fresh grilled fish or pasta with crayfish, Vasso's is *the* place to head for exceptional seafood.

Around the Island

Straddling a slender isthmus on the northwest coast, the petite pastel-coloured village of **Assos** watches over the ruins of a Venetian fortress perched upon a pine-covered peninsula. Popular with upmarket package tourists, there are several tavernas on the waterfront, but little else to interest independent travellers. Splendid **Myrtos Beach**, 13km south of Assos, is spellbinding from both above, where the postcard views from the precarious roadway are breathtaking, and below, where you'll think you've discovered the perfect beach.

ZAKYNTHOS ΖΑΚΥΝΘΟΣ

pop 38,600

The beautiful island of Zakynthos, or Zante, has stunning coves, dramatic cliffs and laid-back beaches, but unfortunately is swamped by package tourist groups, so only a few special spots warrant your time.

GETTING THERE & AROUND

Zakynthos' **airport** (ZTH; ☎ 26950 28322) is 6km from Zakynthos Town. **Olympic Airlines** (☎ 26950 28322) has daily flights to Athens and other Ionian Islands. Seasonal ferries go between Zakynthos Town and Kyllini in the Peloponnese (per person/car €6.50/31.50, 1¼ hours) and from Agios Nikolaos to Pesada in southern Kefallonia (€6, 1½ hours). In high season two daily buses go from Pesada to Argostoli (Kefallonia), and just two per week to Agios Nikolaos, which makes crossing without your own transport difficult. Alternatively, cross to Kyllini and catch another ferry to Kefallonia. As bus services are poor, explore the island by car. Try **Europcar** (☎ 26950 41541; Plateia Agiou Louka, Zakynthos Town).

Zakynthos Town

The island's attractive Venetian capital and port was painstakingly reconstructed after the 1953 earthquake. Its elegant arcades and lively cafe scene make it the best base from which to explore the island.

Along the waterfront, Lombardou and its surrounding streets are home to touristy tavernas and travel agencies. Plateia Agiou Markou is the bustling main square, off which runs Alexandrou Roma, the main pedestrian shopping street. Look out for traditional sweet stores selling *mandolato,* the local soft nougat.

The **Byzantine Museum** (☎ 26950 42714; Plateia Solomou; admission €3; 8.30am-3pm Tue-Sun) houses fabulous ecclesiastical art rescued from churches razed in the earthquake.

Hotel Strada Marina (☎ 26950 42761; www.stradamarina.gr; Lombardou 14; s/d €75/120;) may have uninspiring rooms and a rooftop swimming pool that's only filled in summer, but it's well situated, and portside rooms have balconies with sea views.

Avoid eating on the touristy Plateia Agiou Markou and do what the locals do – hit Alexandrou Roma for cheap eats.

Owned by two guys called Dionysus, **2D** (☎ 26950 27008; Alexandrou Roma 32; gyros from €2.50) does the most delicious gyros and juicy roast chickens in town.

Take a short stroll north of the centre along the waterfront for a memorable night at **Arekia** (☎ 26950 26346; Krioneriou 92; mains €3-10). Munch Greek specialities to the melodies of live *kantades* (serenades) and *arekia* (folk songs).

Around the Island

Most people head to Zakynthos for the famous **Shipwreck Beach** in the northwest. While Zakynthos is best explored by car, for a sea-level look take a boat from Cape Skinari near Agios Nikolaos, Porto Vromi or Alykes.

Continue south and try to arrive early at gorgeous **Limnionas** for swimming in crystal-clear turquoise coves, as there's barely any space to sunbathe on the rocks. The only eatery at the cove, **Taverna Porto Limnionas** (mains €3-15) serves up delicious Greek classics (try the excellent *mezedes* plate) in a sublime setting overlooking the sea.

Cape Keri near the island's southernmost point has spectacular views of sheer cliffs and splendid beaches. **Keri Beach** is overrated. The **Bay of Laganas** has been declared a national marine park by the Greek government in order to protect the endangered loggerhead turtles that come ashore to lay their eggs in August – the peak of the tourist invasion. It's best not to risk one more beach umbrella piercing an unborn baby turtle's shell, – soak up some sun elsewhere.

GREECE DIRECTORY

ACCOMMODATION

Greece has a wide range of accommodation options from excellent camping grounds to flashy designer hotels and everything in between. Prices quoted in this book are for the high season (usually July and August) and include a private bathroom, unless otherwise stated. In general, budget rooms cost up to €60, midrange from €60 to €150, while top-end rooms start from there. Prices can be up to 50% cheaper between October and May, but note that some places virtually board up during winter. Greek accommodation is subject to strict price controls, and by law a notice must be displayed in every room stating the category of the room and the seasonal price. If you think there's something amiss, contact the tourist police.

Greece has around 340 camping grounds, many of them in wonderfully scenic locations. They're generally open from April to October. The **Panhellenic Camping Association** (www.panhellenic-camping-union.gr) has detailed information. Standard facilities include hot showers, kitchens, restaurants and minimarkets – and often a swimming pool. Prices vary according to facilities, but reckon on €8 per adult, €5 for children aged four to 12, €5 for a small tent and €8 for a large one.

Greece has more than 50 mountain refuges, which are listed in the booklet *Greece Mountain Refuges & Ski Centres,* available free of charge at EOT and EOS (Ellinikos Orivatikos Syndesmos, the Greek Alpine Club) offices.

You'll find youth hostels in most major towns and on some islands. Most hostels throughout Greece are affiliated with the **Greek Youth Hostel Organisation** (☎ 21075 19530; y-hostels@otenet.gr). Most charge around €12 for a dorm bed, and you don't have to be a member to stay.

Domatia are the Greek equivalent of a bed and breakfast – minus the breakfast. They are often purpose-built additions to a family house, but can be great value if you are on a budget. Expect to pay about €25 to €35 for a single and €40 to €50 for a double. Don't worry about finding them – owners will find you as they greet ferries and buses shouting 'room!'.

Hotels in Greece are classified as deluxe, or A, B, C, D or E class. The ratings seldom seem to have much bearing on the price, which is determined more by season and location. Some places are classified as pensions and are rated differently. Both hotels and pensions are allowed to levy a 10% surcharge for stays of less than three nights, but they seldom do.

You'll be hard pressed to find accommodation with nonsmoking areas, let alone an overall nonsmoking policy.

ACTIVITIES

Diving & Snorkelling

Snorkelling can be enjoyed just about anywhere along Greece's magnificent coastlines. Corfu, Mykonos and Santorini are just some of the good areas to snorkel. Diving, however, must take place under the supervision of a diving school to protect the antiquities still in the deep.

Hiking

Greece is a hiker's paradise. Outside the main popular routes, however, the trails are generally overgrown and poorly marked. Several companies run organised hikes; **Trekking Hellas** (Map p358; ☎ 21033 10323; www.outdoorsgreece.com; Filellinon 7, Athens) has options throughout Greece. **Cretan Adventures** (Map p393; ☎ 28103 32772; www.cretanadventures.gr; Evans 10, Iraklio) specialises in activities on Crete.

Skiing

Greece offers inexpensive European skiing with more than a dozen resorts dotted around the mainland, mainly in the north. It's no Switzerland, however, and the resorts are basic, catering mainly to Greek skiers. The main areas are Mt Parnassos (195km northwest of Athens) and Mt Vermio (110km west of Thessaloniki). A good season starts in early January and goes through to April. Take a look at www.snowreport.gr for snow reports and web cams.

Windsurfing & Kitesurfing

Greece is a fantastic windsurfing destination. You'll find that sailboards are widely available for hire, and are usually priced from €12 to €15 per hour. The top spots for windsurfing are Hrysi Akti on Paros, and Vasiliki on Lefkada, which is a popular place to learn. Kitesurfers should contact the **Greek Wakeboard & Kitesurf Association** (www.gwa.gr).

Yachting

Set aside your prejudices about those who wear deck shoes and knot their cardigans around their neck: yachting is a brilliant way to see the Greek Islands. All you need is a couple of certified sailors in your group and you can hire a 28ft bare boat (no crew) that sleeps six for around €1000 per week, although hiring a skipper will nearly double that price. The **Hellenic Yachting Server** (www.yachting.gr) is packed with information.

BUSINESS HOURS

Banks in Greece are open from 8am to 2pm Monday to Thursday, and to 1.30pm Friday. Some banks in the larger cities and towns are also open from 3.30pm to 6.30pm and on Saturday (8am to 1.30pm). Post offices are open from 7.30am to 2pm Monday to Friday; in major cities they're open until 8pm and also open from 7.30am to 2pm on Saturday.

In summer, shops are generally open from 8am to 1.30pm and 5.30pm to 8.30pm on Tuesday, Thursday and Friday, and 8am to 2.30pm on Monday, Wednesday and Saturday. Shops generally open 30 minutes later during winter. *Periptera* will often be your saviour: open from early morning to late at night, they sell everything from beer to bus tickets.

Restaurants in tourist areas generally open at 11am and stay open through to midnight; normal restaurant hours are 11am to 2pm and from 7pm to midnight or 1am. Cafes tend to open between 9am and 10am and stay open until midnight. Bars open around 8pm and close late, and while discos might open at 10pm, you'll drink alone until midnight. Nightclubs generally close around 4am, but many go through to dawn during summer.

CHILDREN

Greece is an easy destination to travel through with children. Hotels and restaurants (plenty of kids' menus) are used to having children around and the Greeks, being so family-oriented, are very welcoming. However, the summer heat can be challenging, and running around poorly maintained tourist sites (such as ruins), requires a watchful eye – as does crossing any road in Greece!

CUSTOMS

You may bring the following into Greece duty-free: 200 cigarettes or 50 cigars; 1L of spirits or 2L of wine; 50ml of perfume; and 250ml of eau de cologne.

DANGERS & ANNOYANCES

Greece has the lowest crime rate in Europe, however, you might doubt that statistic if you head down the wrong street in Omonia, Athens.

For more on information on dealing with dangers and annoyances, see the Regional Directory, p353.

EMBASSIES & CONSULATES

All foreign embassies in Greece are in Athens and its suburbs.

Australia (Map pp354-5; ☎ 210 870 4000; Leoforos Alexandras & Kifisias, Ambelokipi, GR-115 23)
Bulgaria (☎ 210 674 8105; Stratigou Kalari 33a, Psyhiko, Athens GR-154 52)
Canada (Map pp354-5; ☎ 210 727 3400; Genadiou 4, GR-115 21)
Cyprus (Map pp354-5; ☎ 210 723 7883; Irodotou 16, GR-106 75)
France (Map pp354-5; ☎ 210 361 1663; Leof Vasilissis Sofias 7, GR-106 71)
Germany (Map pp354-5; ☎ 210 728 5111; cnr Dimitriou 3 & Karaoli, Kolonaki GR-106 75)
Ireland (Map pp354–5; 210 723 2771; Vasileos Konstandinou 7; Athens GR-106 74)
Italy (Map pp354-5; ☎ 210 361 7260; Sekeri 2, GR-106 74)
Japan (Map pp354-5; ☎ 210 775 8101; Athens Tower, Leoforos Messogion 2-4, GR-115 27)

Netherlands (Map pp354–5; 210 725 4900; Vasileos Konstandinou 5-7; Athens GR-106-74)
New Zealand (Map pp354-5; ☎ 210 687 4701; Kifissias 268, Halandri)
South Africa (Map pp354-5; ☎ 210 680 6645; Kifissias 60, Maroussi, GR-151 25)
Turkey (Map pp354-5; ☎ 210 724 5915; Vasilissis Georgiou 8, GR-106 74)
UK (Map pp354-5; ☎ 210 723 6211; Ploutarhou 1, GR-106 75)
USA (Map pp354-5; ☎ 210 721 2951; Leoforos Vasilissis Sofias 91, GR-115 21)

FESTIVALS & EVENTS

In Greece, the number of celebrations means it is probably easier to list the dates when festivals and events are *not* on! Some festivals are religious, some cultural, and others are seemingly just an excuse to party. It is worth timing at least part of your trip to coincide with one festival or event, as you will be warmly invited to join in the revelry. The following list is by no means exhaustive, and further details can be found at www.cultureguide.gr and www.whatsonwhen.com.

January

Epiphany (Blessing of the Waters) Christ's baptism is celebrated on the 6th when seas, lakes and rivers are blessed. The largest ceremony occurs at Piraeus.

February

Carnival Season The three-week period before the beginning of Lent is celebrated all over Greece with fancy dress, feasting and traditional dance.

March

Independence Day On 25 March, parades and dancing mark the anniversary of the hoisting of the Greek flag that started the War of Independence.

April

Easter The most important festival of the Greek Orthodox religion occurs March/April. The emphasis is on the Resurrection rather than the Crucifixion so it's a celebratory event. The most significant part of the event is midnight on Easter Saturday when candles are lit (symbolising the Resurrection) and a fireworks and candlelit procession hits the streets. Orthodox Easter is usually at a different time than Easter celebrated by the Western churches.

May

May Day The celebrations on 1 May see a mass exodus from towns to the countryside to picnic and gather wildflowers, with which to make wreaths for adorning homes.

June

Hellenic Festival (www.greekfestival.gr) The most important of summer festivals, events are staged throughout Greece; however, the Theatre of Herodes Atticus in Athens and the Theatre of Epidavros, near Nafplio, are venues for traditional events.

July

Feast of Agia Marina (St Marina) This feast day is celebrated on 17 July in many parts of Greece, and is a particularly important event on the Dodecanese island of Kasos.

August

Feast of the Assumption Greeks celebrate this day (15 August) with family reunions and many expats head back to their home town for the festivities.
Samothraki World Music Festival The northeastern Aegean island of Samothraki plays host to Greece's biggest rave party for a week starting at the end of August.

September

Genesis tis Panagias The birthday of the Virgin Mary is celebrated on 8 September with religious services and feasting.

October

Feast of Agios Dimitrios This feast day, on 26 October, is celebrated in Thessaloniki with much revelry.
Ohi (No) Day Metaxas' refusal to allow Mussolini's troops free passage through Greece in WWII is commemorated on 28 October with parades, folk dancing and feasting.

December

Christmas Day Although not as important as Easter, Christmas Day is still celebrated with religious services and feasting. Nowadays, much 'Western' influence is apparent, including Christmas trees, decorations and presents.

GAY & LESBIAN TRAVELLERS

In a country where the church plays a significant role in shaping society's views on issues such as sexuality, it's not surprising that homosexuality is generally frowned upon. While there is no legislation against homosexual activity, it is wise to be discreet and to avoid open displays of togetherness. Greece is a popular destination for gay travellers. Athens has a busy gay scene that packs up and heads to the islands for summer. Mykonos has long been famous for its bars, beaches and hedonism, and a visit to Eresos on Lesvos has become something of a pilgrimage for lesbians.

HOLIDAYS

New Year's Day 1 January
Epiphany 6 January
First Sunday in Lent February
Greek Independence Day 25 March
Good Friday/Easter Sunday March/April
May Day (Protomagia) 1 May
Feast of the Assumption 15 August
Ohi Day 28 October
Christmas Day 25 December
St Stephen's Day 26 December

INTERNET ACCESS

Greece has embraced the internet big time. Charges differ wildly (as does the speed of access) – from €1.50 per hour in big cities to up to €6 per hour on some of the islands. Some midrange and most top-end hotels offer some form of internet connection. Laptop-wielding visitors will often be able to connect to wi-fi at hotels and most internet cafes.

INTERNET RESOURCES

Culture Guide (www.cultureguide.gr) Plenty of information about contemporary culture and the arts.
Greek National Tourist Organisation (www.gnto.gr) Concise tourist information.
Greek Travel Pages (www.gtp.gr) Useful directory for travel businesses.
Lonely Planet (www.lonelyplanet.com) Has postcards from other travellers and the Thorn Tree bulletin board, where you can pose those tricky questions or help answer other travellers' questions on your return.
Ministry of Culture (www.culture.gr) Information on ancient sites, art galleries and museums.

LANGUAGE

Greeks are naturally delighted if you can speak a little of their language, but you don't need Greek to get around the major tourism sites. Many Greeks have lived abroad, usually in Australia or the USA, and English is widely spoken, but venturing to remote villages can prove more of a challenge.

MONEY

Banks, post offices and currency exchange offices are all over the place and will exchange all major currencies. ATMs are everywhere except the smallest villages.

Greece is still a cheap destination by northern European standards, but it's no longer dirt cheap. A daily budget of €40 would entail staying in youth hostels or camping, staying away from bars, and only occasionally eating in restaurants or taking ferries. Allow at least €80 per day if you want your own room and plan to eat out regularly and see the sights. If you really want a holiday (comfortable rooms and restaurants all the way) you'll need closer to €120 per day.

Your money will go a lot further if you travel in the quieter months, as accommodation is generally much cheaper outside the high season when there are more opportunities to negotiate better deals.

Greece adopted the euro in 2002. Value-added tax (VAT) varies from 15% to 18%. A tax-rebate scheme applies at a restricted number of shops and stores; look for a Tax Free sign. You must fill in a form at the shop and then present it with the receipt at the airport on departure. A cheque will (hopefully) be sent to your home address.

In restaurants the service charge is included on the bill, but it is the custom to leave a small tip – just round up the bill. Accommodation is nearly always negotiable outside peak season, especially for longer stays. While souvenir shops will generally bargain, prices in other shops are normally clearly marked and non-negotiable.

POST

Tahydromia (post offices) are easily identified by the yellow sign outside. Regular post boxes are yellow; red post boxes are for express mail. The postal rate for postcards and airmail letters within the EU is €0.60, to other destinations it's €0.65.

Mail can be sent poste restante to any main post office and is held for up to one month. Your surname should be underlined and you will need to show your passport when you collect your mail.

SOLO TRAVELLERS

Greece is a great destination for solo travellers, particularly during summer when the islands are full of travellers meeting and making friends. Hostels, as well as other backpacker-friendly accommodation, are excellent places to meet other travellers. Solo women are quite safe – which is not to say that problems don't occur, but violent offences are rare.

TELEPHONE

The Greek telephone service is maintained by Organismos Tilepikoinonion Ellados, always referred to by its acronym OTE (o-*teh*). Public

EMERGENCY NUMBERS

- Ambulance ☎ 166
- Fire ☎ 199
- Police ☎ 100
- Roadside Assistance (ELPA) ☎ 104
- Tourist Police ☎ 171

phones are easy to use and pressing the 'i' button brings up the operating instructions in English. Public phones are everywhere and all use phonecards.

For directory inquiries within Greece, call ☎ 131 or ☎ 132; for international directory inquiries, it's ☎ 161 or ☎ 162.

Mobile Phones

Mobile phones have become the must-have accessory in Greece. If you have a compatible GSM phone from a country with a global roaming agreement with Greece, you will be able to use your phone there. Make sure you have global roaming activated before you leave your country of residence. There are several mobile service providers in Greece; **CosmOTE** (www.cosmote.gr) has the best coverage. You can purchase a Greek SIM card for around €20 and cards are available everywhere to recharge the SIM card.

Phone Codes

Telephone codes are part of the 10-digit number within Greece. The landline prefix is 2 and for mobiles it's 6.

Phonecards

All public phones use OTE phonecards, sold at OTE offices and *periptera* (kiosks). These cards are sold in €3, €5 and €10 versions, and a local call costs €0.30 for three minutes. There are also excellent discount-card schemes available that offer much better value for money.

TOURIST INFORMATION

Tourist information is handled by the Greek National Tourist Organisation (GNTO), known as EOT in Greece. There is either an EOT office or a local tourist office in almost every town of consequence and on many of the islands. Popular destinations have tourist police who can also provide information.

TRAVELLERS WITH DISABILITIES

If mobility is a problem, the hard fact is that most hotels, museums and ancient sites are not wheelchair accessible. While facilities in Athens are steadily improving – such as at the Acropolis (p353), which now has a wheelchair lift – elsewhere the uneven terrain is an issue even for able-bodied people.

Useful information on travelling with disabilities is available on the internet at www.sath.org and www.access-able.com.

VISAS

Visitors from most countries don't need a visa for Greece. The list of countries whose nationals can stay in Greece for up to three months include Australia, Canada, all EU countries, Iceland, Israel, Japan, New Zealand and the USA. For longer stays, apply at a consulate abroad or at least 20 days in advance to the **Aliens Bureau** (Map pp354-5; ☎ 210 770 5711; Leoforos Alexandras 173, Athens; 🕒 8am-1pm Mon-Fri) at the Athens Central Police Station. Elsewhere in Greece, apply to the local authority.

TRANSPORT IN GREECE

GETTING THERE & AWAY

Air

There are 16 international airports in Greece, but most of them handle only summer charter flights to the islands. **Eleftherios Venizelos airport** (ATH; ☎ 21035 30000; www.aia.gr), near Athens, handles the vast majority of international flights and has regular scheduled flights to all the European capitals.

Thessaloniki is well served by **Macedonia airport** (SKG; ☎ 23104 73700). There are also scheduled international flights to/from Iraklio's **Nikos Kazantzakis airport** (HER; ☎ 28102 28401) and Rhodes' **Diagoras airport** (RHO; ☎ 22410 83222). Other international airports are located at Mykonos, Santorini (Thira), Hania (Crete), Iraklio (Crete), Kos, Karpathos, Samos, Skiathos, Hrysoupoli (for Kavala), Aktion (for Lefkada), Kefallonia and Zakynthos. These airports are used for charter flights, mainly from Germany, the UK and Scandanavia.

National carrier **Olympic Airlines** (OA; ☎ 80111 44444; www.olympicairlines.com) and **Aegean Airlines** (A3; ☎ 80111 20000; www.aegeanair.com) are Greek companies operating a growing number of international routes. Other airlines with services to Greece:

Air Berlin (AB; ☎ 210 353 5264; www.airberlin.com)
Air France (AF; ☎ 210 353 0380; www.airfrance.com)
Alitalia (AZ; ☎ 210 353 4284; www.alitalia.it)
American Airlines (AA; ☎ 210 331 1045; www.aa.com)
British Airways (BA; ☎ 210 890 6666; www.britishairways.com)
Brussels Airlines (SN; brusselsairlines.com)
Cyprus Airways (CY; ☎ 210 372 2722; www.cyprusair.com.cy)
Delta Airlines (DL; ☎ 210 331 1660; www.delta.com)
easyJet (U2; ☎ 210 967 0000; www.easyjet.com)
Emirates Airlines (EK; ☎ 210 933 3400; www.emirates.com)
Flyglobespan (Y2; www.flyglobespan.com)
germanwings (4U; germanwings.com)
Iberia (IB; ☎ 210 323 4523; www.iberia.com)
Jet2.com (LS; www.jet2.com)
KLM (KL; ☎ 210 353 1295; www.klm.com)
Lufthansa (LH; ☎ 210 617 5200; www.lufthansa.com)
SAS (SK; ☎ 210 361 3910; www.flysas.com)
Singapore Airlines (SQ; ☎ 210 372 8000, 21035 31259; www.singaporeair.com)
Thai Airways (TG; ☎ 210 353 1237; www.thaiairways.com)
Transavia (HV; www.transavia.com)
TUIfly (X3; www.TUIfly.com)
Turkish Airlines (TK; ☎ 210 322 1035; www.turkishairlines.com)
Wizz Air (W6; www.wi zzair.com)

Land

BORDER CROSSINGS

From Albania

There are four crossing points between Greece and Albania. Kakavia, 60km northwest of Ioannina, is the main one. Others are Sagiada (near Igoumenitsa), Mertziani (near Konitsa) and Krystallopigi (near Kotas).

From Bulgaria

There are two Bulgarian border crossings: one at Promahonas (109km northeast of Thessaloniki) and the other at Ormenio (in northeastern Thrace).

From Macedonia

There are three border crossings here: Evzoni (68km north of Thessaloniki); Niki; and Doïrani.

From Turkey

The crossing points for Turkey are at Kipi, 43km east of Alexandroupolis, and, less conveniently, at Kastanies, 139km northeast of Alexandroupolis.

BUS

The Hellenic Railways Organisation (OSE) operates an overnight bus between Athens (500m west of the Larisis train station) and Tirana, Albania (€35.20, 16 hours, daily) via Ioannina and Gjirokastra. To Bulgaria, the OSE operates an Athens–Sofia bus (€45.50, 15 hours, daily except Monday), as well as a Thessaloniki–Sofia service (€19, 7½ hours, four daily). To Turkey, the OSE operates from Athens to İstanbul (€67.50, 22 hours, daily except Wednesday). This stops at Thessaloniki (€44) and Alexandroupolis (€15).

CAR & MOTORCYCLE

You can drive or ride through the border crossings listed (left) with your own transport, but if you are in a hire car, make sure that your insurance can cover this, and find out whether the car-hire company has roadside assistance coverage in these countries.

TRAIN

There is a daily train between Sofia and Athens (€32, 18 hours) via Thessaloniki. Daily trains operate between İstanbul and Thessaloniki (€48, around 12 hours), and to Macedonia there are two trains daily from Thessaloniki to Skopje (€14, five hours).

Sea

You'll find all the latest information about ferry routes, schedules and services online at www.ferries.gr. This site will also provide links to individual ferry company websites.

The following ferry services are for the high season (July and August), and prices are for one-way deck class. Prices are about 30% less in the low season.

ALBANIA

Corfu-based **Petrakis Lines** (☎ 26610 38690; www.ionian-cruises.com) has daily hydrofoils to the Albanian port of Saranda (€15, 25 minutes).

CYPRUS & ISRAEL

Passenger services from Greece to Cyprus and Israel have been suspended indefinitely.

ITALY

There are ferries between the Italian ports of Ancona, Bari, Brindisi and Venice and Patra, Igoumenitsa, Corfu and Kefallonia. If you want to take a vehicle across, it's a good idea to make a reservation beforehand.

Ancona

Blue Star Ferries and Superfast Ferries run two boats daily to Patra (€60 to €70, 19 hours or 21 hours via Igoumenitsa). Tickets are available through **Morandi & Co** (☎ 071-20 20 33; Via XXIX Settembre 2/0). Superfast accepts Eurail passes. **ANEK Lines** (☎ 071-207 23 46; Via XXIX Settembre 2/0) does the trip daily (€70) in 19½ hours via Igoumenitsa.

Bari

Superfast Ferries (☎ 080 52 11 416; Corso de Tullio 6) has daily sailings to Patra via Igoumenitsa. **Ventouris Ferries** (☎ 080 521 7609) has daily boats to Corfu (10 hours) and Igoumenitsa (11½ hours) for €53.

Brindisi

The trip from Brindisi operates only between April and early October. **Hellenic Mediterranean Lines** (☎ 0831-548001; Costa Morena) offers services to Patra (€50), calling at Igoumenitsa, Corfu, Kefallonia, Paxi and Zakynthos on the way. **Agoudimos Lines** (☎ 0831-550180; Via Provinciale per Lecce 29) and **Fragline** (☎ 0831-54 85 40; Via Spalato 31) sail only to Igoumenitsa.

Venice

Minoan Lines (☎ 041-24 07 177; Stazione Marittima 123) has boats to Patra (€75, 29 hours) calling at Corfu and Igoumenitsa. **Blue Star Ferries** (☎ 041-277 0559; Stazione Marittima 123) sails the route four times weekly for €64.

TURKEY

Five regular ferry services operate between Turkey's Aegean coast and the Greek Islands. For more information about these services, see Rhodes (p399), Chios (p408), Kos (p404), Lesvos (p409) and Samos (p406).

GETTING AROUND

Greece is a relatively straightforward destination to travel around thanks to its comprehensive transport system. On the mainland, buses travel to just about every town on the map and trains offer a good alternative where available. Island-hopping is what most people think of when travelling within Greece and there are myriad ferries that criss-cross the Adriatic and Aegean Seas. There is also an extensive and well-priced domestic air network. Note that timetables are seasonal and change in at least some way every year.

Air

Domestic air travel is becoming very price competitive, and it's sometimes cheaper to fly than take the ferry, especially if you book ahead online.

Greece's national carrier, **Olympic Airlines** (OA; ☎ 801 114 4444; www.olympicairlines.com) has the most extensive network. Private company **Aegean Airlines** (A3; ☎ 80111 20000; www.aegeanair.com) is their big competition, offering newer aircraft and similar prices on popular routes.

A recent addition to the skies over Greece is **Sky Express** (SHE; ☎ 28102 23500; www.skyexpress.gr), based in Iraklio, Crete, which mainly flies routes that the big two don't. Its schedule is growing (and changing!) by the year, so check the website for up-to-date details.

Bicycle

Given Greece's hilly terrain, stifling summer heat and many drivers' total disregard of road rules, cycling is not a popular form of transport. You can hire bicycles at most tourist centres, but these are generally for pedalling around town rather than for serious riding. Prices generally range from €10 to €12 per day. If you wish to do a cycling tour of Greece, bicycles are carried for free on ferries.

Boat

Island-hopping by boat in the Greek Islands is great fun. Keep in mind though that domestic sea travel options are constantly changing. Operations are highly seasonal and changes to schedules can take place at the last minute. Be prepared to be flexible. Boats seldom arrive early, but often arrive late! And some don't come at all. Think of it as part of the fun.

Check out www.ferries.gr for schedules, costs and links to individual boat company websites.

FERRY

Every island has a ferry service of some sort, although in winter these are pared back. Services pick up from April, and during July and August Greece's seas are a mass of wake and wash. The ferries come in all shapes and sizes, from the state-of-the-art 'superferries' that run on the major routes to the ageing open ferries that operate local services to outlying islands.

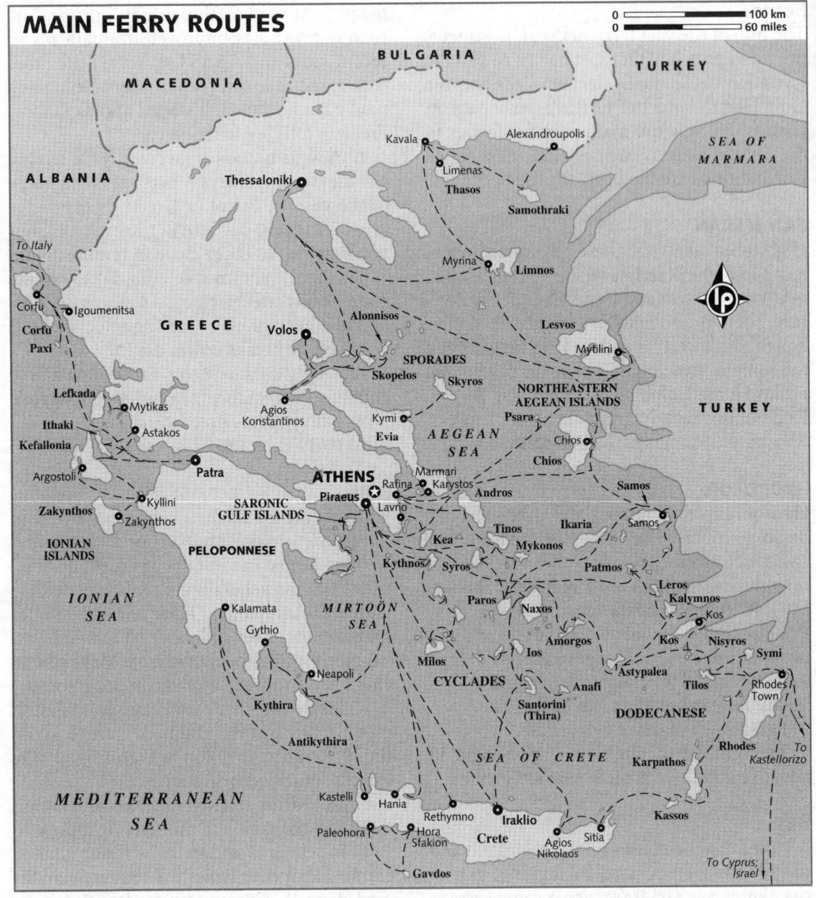

The newer high-speed ferries are slashing travel times on some of the longer routes, but generally cost much more.

Classes

'Classes' on ferries are largely a thing of the past. Basically, you have the option of 'deck class', which is the cheapest ticket and is the class that most travellers use, or 'cabin class' with air-con cabins and a decent lounge and restaurant. It doesn't make much difference on short trips, but on overnight trips you might want to go for one of the cabin options.

Children under four travel free, those between four and 10 years pay half-fare. Children over 10 pay full fare. When buying tickets you will automatically be given deck class.

Costs

It's worth noting that boat fares seem to be going up at an alarming pace while air fares seem to be coming down with increased competition. Check out your options.

The small differences in boat prices you may find between ticket agencies are the result of some agencies sacrificing part of their designated commission to qualify as a discount service. The discount offered seldom amounts to much. Generally, tickets can be bought at the last minute at the dock, but in the high season, some boats may be full – plan ahead.

Routes

The hub of the vast ferry network is Piraeus, the main port of Athens. It has ferries to the Cyclades, Crete, the Dodecanese, the Saronic Gulf Islands and the northeastern Aegean Islands. Patra is the main port for ferries to the Ionian Islands, while Volos and Agios Konstantinos are the ports for the Sporades.

CATAMARAN

High-speed catamarans have become an important part of the island travel scene. They are just as fast as hydrofoils and are much more comfortable. They are also much less prone to cancellation in rough weather and the fares are generally the same as hydrofoils. The main players are Hellas Flying Dolphins and Blue Star Ferries. Dodekanisos Seaways runs catamarans between Rhodes and Patmos in the Dodecanese.

HYDROFOIL

Hydrofoils offer a faster alternative to ferries on some routes. They take half the time, but cost twice as much. Most routes will operate only during the high season. **Hellenic Seaways** (☎ 21041 99000; www.hellenicseaways.gr) travels from Piraeus to the Saronic Gulf Islands and the ports of the eastern Peloponnese, as well as to the Sporades from Agios Konstantinos and Volos. **Aegean Hydrofoils** (☎ 22410 24000), based in Rhodes, serves the Dodecanese.

Tickets for hydrofoils must be bought in advance and there is often seat allocation.

Bus

All long-distance buses on the mainland and the islands are operated by regional collectives known as **KTEL** (Koino Tamio Eispraxeon Leoforion; www.ktel.org). Fares are fixed by the government and service routes can be found on the company's website.

Greece's buses are comfortable, they generally run on time, and there are frequent services on all the major routes. Buses are reasonably priced – eg Athens–Thessaloniki (€31, 7½ hours) and Athens–Patra (€14, three hours). Tickets should be bought at least an hour in advance to ensure a seat. Buses don't have toilets and refreshments, but stop for a break every couple of hours.

Car & Motorcycle

A great way to explore areas in Greece that are off the beaten track is by car. However, it's worth bearing in mind that Greece has the highest road-fatality rate in Europe. The road network has improved dramatically in recent years and places that were little more than a one-lane dirt track masquerading as a road have now been widened and asphalted. Freeway tolls are fairly hefty.

Almost all islands are served by car ferries, but they are expensive. Costs vary by the size of the vehicle. Petrol in Greece is expensive at around €1.50 per litre in the big cities, but you'll pay up to €0.20 more in remote areas.

The Greek automobile club, **ELPA** (www.elpa.gr), generally offers reciprocal services to members of other national motoring associations. If your vehicle breaks down, dial ☎ 104.

EU-registered vehicles are allowed free entry into Greece for six months without road taxes being due. A green card (international third party insurance) is all that's required.

HIRE

Hire cars are available just about anywhere in Greece. The major multinational companies are represented in most major tourist destinations. You can generally get a much better rate with local companies. Their advertised rates are generally lower and they're often willing to bargain, especially out of season. Make sure to check the insurance waivers on these companies closely and check how they can assist in case of a breakdown. Also make sure to advise the hire company if you're planning to take the car somewhere on a ferry.

High-season weekly rates start at about €280 for the smallest models, dropping to €200 in winter – and that's without tax and extras. Major companies will request a credit-card deposit. The minimum driving age in Greece is 18, but most car-hire firms require a driver of 21 or over.

Mopeds and motorcycles are available for hire everywhere; however, regulations stipulate that you need a valid motorcycle licence stating proficiency for the size of motorcycle you wish to rent – from 50cc upwards.

Motorcycles are a cheap way to travel around Greece. Mopeds and 50cc motorcycles range from €10 to €20 per day or from €25 per day for a 250cc motorcycle. Outside the high season, rates drop considerably. Ensure the bike is in good working order and the brakes work well.

If you plan to hire a motorcycle or moped, check that your travel insurance covers you for injury resulting from motorcycle accidents.

ROAD RULES

While it sometimes appears that there aren't any road rules in Greece, you are apparently supposed to drive on the right and overtake on the left. No casual observer would ever guess that it is compulsory to wear seat belts in the front seats of vehicles, and in the back if they are fitted.

The speed limit for cars is 120km/h on toll roads, 90km/h outside built-up areas and 50km/h in built-up areas. For motorcycles up to 100cc, the speed limit outside built-up areas is 70km/h and for larger motorbikes, 90km/h. Drivers exceeding the speed limit by 20/40% receive a fine of €60/160; however, most tourists escape with a warning.

Drink-driving laws are strict; a blood alcohol content of 0.05% incurs a fine of around €150 and over 0.08% is a criminal offence.

Public Transport

BUS

Most Greek towns are small enough to get around on foot. All major towns have local bus systems, but the only places that you're likely to need them are Athens, Kalamata and Thessaloniki.

METRO

Athens is the only city large enough to warrant a metro system. See p364 for details.

TAXI

Taxis are widely available in Greece and they are reasonably priced. Yellow city cabs are metered. Flag fall is €0.75, followed by €0.28 per kilometre in towns and €0.53 per kilometre outside towns. The rate doubles from midnight to 5am. Additional charges are €3 from airports; €0.80 from ports, bus stations and train stations; and €0.30 per luggage item over 10kg.

Taxi drivers in Athens are gifted in their ability to make a little extra with every fare. If you have a complaint, note the cab number and contact the tourist police. In rural areas taxis don't have meters, so make sure you agree on a price before you get in – drivers are generally honest, friendly and helpful.

Train

Trains are operated by the **Greek Railways Organisation** (OSE; www.ose.gr) Greece has only two main lines: Athens north to Thessaloniki and Alexandroupolis, and Athens to the Peloponnese. In addition there are a number of branch lines, such as the Pyrgos–Olympia line and the spectacular Diakofto–Kalavryta mountain railway.

Inter-Rail and Eurail passes are valid in Greece, but you still need to make a reservation. In summer make reservations at least two days in advance.

MEDITERRANEAN TREASURES

Stretching 4500km from the Portuguese coast to eastern Turkey, Mediterranean Europe encompasses a huge variety of peoples, places and beliefs. The region defies easy categorisation but there are some things that all Med folk share – a handsome and ancient landscape, a love of beauty and an unabashed ability to enjoy life. Here we celebrate the very best the region has to offer.

Timeless Landscapes

The Mediterranean of the mind's eye is an area of silky beaches, azure seas and ancient olive groves. But this tells only part of the story. Encompassing everything from Saharan sand dunes to fjords and ancient volcanoes, the Med's landscape is as diverse as it is thrilling.

❶ Santorini

Stunning volcanic scenery goes hand in hand with a thumping nightlife on the Greek island of Santorini (p388). The result of a volcanic eruption 3600 years ago, it's a classic island beauty with sheer lava-clad cliffs, black beaches and whitewashed villages.

❷ Turkish Caves

Deep in the heart of the country, Turkey's number one natural attraction is a bizarre, lunar-landscape of cave homes, fairy chimneys and honeycomb cliffs. The Unesco-listed village of Göreme (p915) makes a good base.

❸ Colourful Provence

Captured on canvas by Van Gogh and Cézanne, Provence (p307) is a picture of bold primary colours and bucolic landscapes. For a blast of urban grit, head to Marseille (p307), the region's tough and compelling capital.

❹ Saharan Sand Dunes

Saddle up and head into the Erg Chebbi (p652), a magical chain of vast, shifting sand dunes in the Moroccan Sahara. The golden colours and otherworldly sense of space make for an unforgettable desert experience.

❺ Bay of Kotor

Imagine the Norwegian fjords with beaches, a laid-back Mediterranean vibe and Venetian-style architecture and you've got the Bay of Kotor (p581). Montenegro's top beauty spot is a wonderful place to slow down into the southern pace of life.

❻ Sardinia's Coast

More than 250km off the Italian mainland, the Sardinian coastline is spectacular and surprisingly unspoiled. A highlight is the imperious Gulf of Orosei (p541), a stunning stretch of tree-flecked cliffs, brooding peaks and hidden coves.

Gourmet Treats

There's no finer place to indulge your appetite than the Mediterranean. Since the Epicureans raised the pursuit of pleasure to a philosophy, food and its enjoyment have had a special place in the region's heart.

❸ Turkish Delight

A Turkish staple (p860), the *kebap* (kebab) comes in various forms, from the classic *döner kebap* to the more sophisticated İskender *kebap,* a bed of bread covered with sliced lamb, tomato purée and yoghurt. The other kind of Turkish delight – sweet *lokum* – is pretty good, too.

❶ Port Wine in Portugal

Get to grips with Portugal's national drink (p693) in the riverside city of Porto (p689). Much of the country's port is produced in the nearby Douro Valley.

❷ French Wine

Champagne, Bordeaux, Burgundy – French wines have been setting the standards for centuries. Treat yourself to a tipple on a tour of Burgundy's Côte d'Or vineyards (p276).

❹ Pizza, Pasta & Gelato

Italy is a foodie paradise. Every town has its own recipes and culinary traditions that are jealously guarded. Pizza rules in Naples (p514), pasta is a national treasure and gelato is a dream.

❺ Spanish Thrills

Snack on tapas as you bar-hop around Madrid (p759), Spain's vibrant and energetic capital. Valencia (p807) is the place for paella, a steaming saffron-infused dish of rice, seafood, chicken and the odd vegetable.

1

Artistic Visions

Guardian to much of the Western world's greatest art and architecture, Mediterranean Europe offers everything from classical ruins to contemporary icons, Renaissance treasures and Islamic masterpieces.

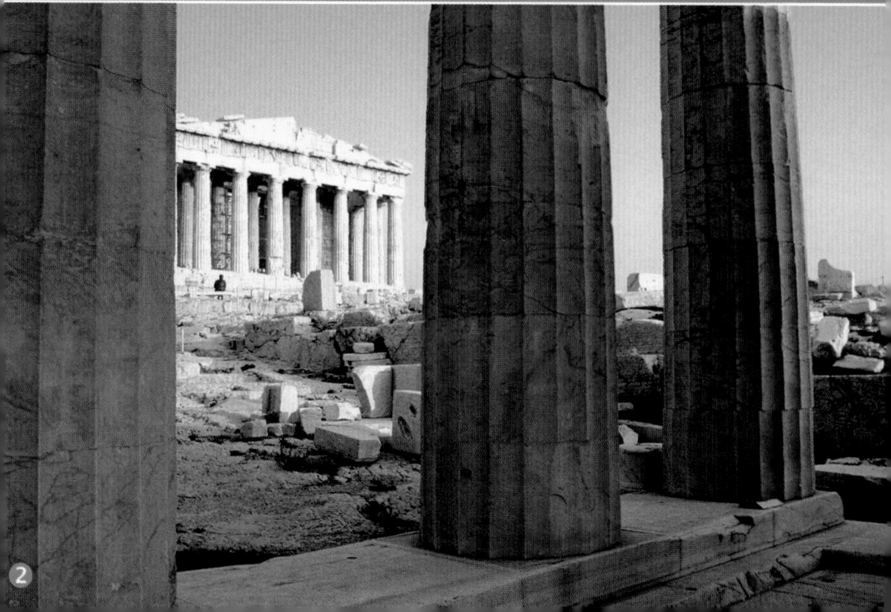

2

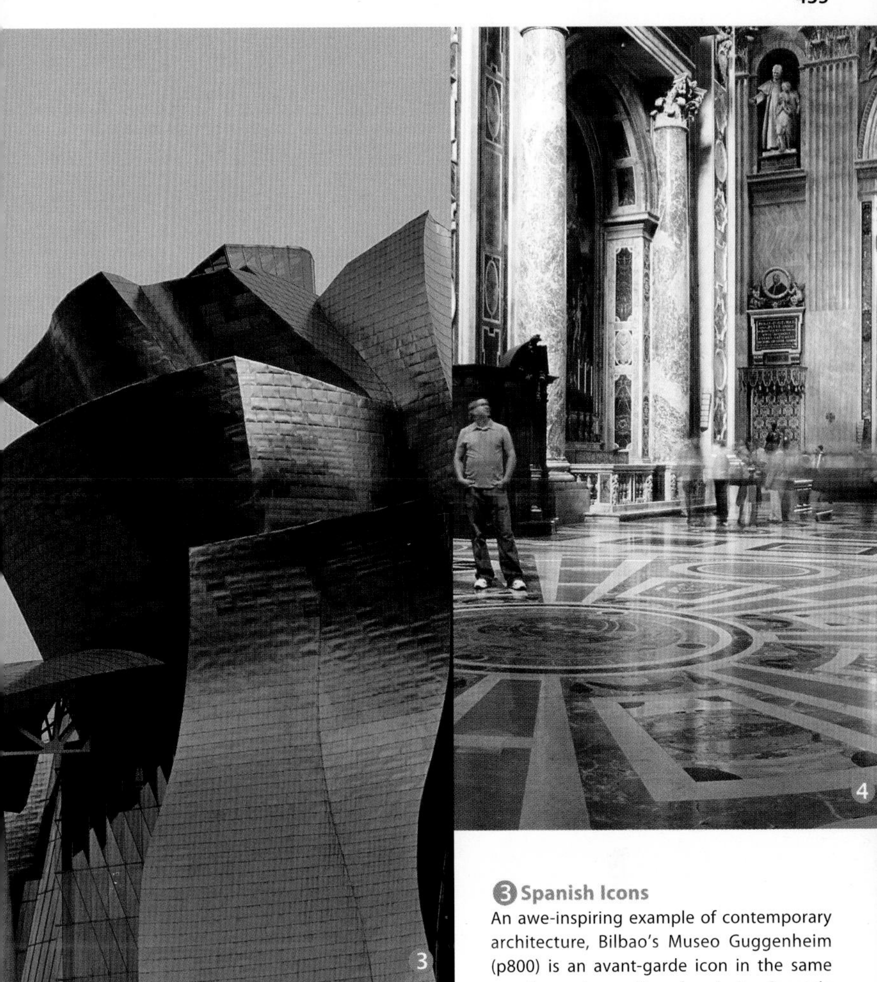

❶ The Louvre
One of the world's most famous museums, the Musée du Louvre (p222) houses an estimated 35,000 works of art. The one that no one wants to miss is Leonardo da Vinci's *Mona Lisa*.

❷ Classical Architecture
Classical architecture has had a profound influence on Western building styles. The great Renaissance architects found inspiration in the harmonious design of classical temples, such as the Parthenon (p356) in Athens and the Pantheon (p452) in Rome.

❸ Spanish Icons
An awe-inspiring example of contemporary architecture, Bilbao's Museo Guggenheim (p800) is an avant-garde icon in the same creative vein as Barcelona's La Sagrada Família (p784).

❹ Vatican City
The majesty of St Peter's Basilica (p449), the glory of the Sistine Chapel (p450) – the world's smallest state is a masterpiece in its own right.

❺ Aya Sofya
For more than 1000 years, the monumental Aya Sofya (p865) was the largest and most impressive church in Christendom. It later became a mosque and then a museum.

A Sporting Life

With its warm seas, mountainous hinterland and favourable climate, the Mediterranean is a paradise for sports lovers. Whether it's chic ski resorts you're after or roaring surf, you'll find many opportunities to flex your muscles.

① Mountain Fun

Skiers, snowboarders and climbers throng to the Alpine resorts, while to the south there's great skiing to be found in Bosnia and Hercegovina (p108) and Montenegro (p596). In the summer, the snowless slopes offer wonderful hiking and cycling.

② Diving

Warm crystalline waters, underwater grottoes, submerged wrecks and a rich flora and fauna make for fabulous diving. Hot spots include the Maltese island of Gozo (p567), Montenegro (p597) and Croatia (p170).

③ Surf's Up

Surfers head to the western edge of the continent for the thundering surf that crashes in from the Atlantic. The wind-whipped waters off the Algarve (p679) and southern Spain are favourite destinations. Tarifa (p839), near Gibraltar, is king of the windsurfing scene.

Italy

The world's love affair with Italy continues. The *bel paese* (beautiful country) might no longer be a blushing bride but this most beguiling of countries still has the power to thrill, to throw up surprises and excite emotion.

Ever since tourism began Italy has attracted attention. English gentlemen stopped off on the 18th-century Grand Tour and fragile artists sought inspiration in the southern sun. Later, classical scholars trawled ancient ruins and Hollywood stars lived *la dolce vita* (the sweet life). These days, Italy is one of Europe's top tourist destinations and a favourite with holiday-home buyers. The market might have been done to death in Tuscany but the agencies will happily point you towards Puglia, currently Italy's hottest destination.

Italy's enduring appeal is easy to explain. Rome's martial monuments, Florence's Renaissance glories and the drama of the Amalfi Coast are all well known. Less famous is the red-blooded hedonism of Italy's foodie capital, Bologna, and the edgy atmosphere of Naples' high-voltage historic centre. Much of southern Italy is mountainous and remote, its forbidding landscape largely overlooked by foreign visitors.

Alongside Italy's art treasures, you'll find plenty to keep you busy in the countryside. You can ski in the Alps, hike the Dolomites or dive off Sardinia's golden coast. Adrenalin junkies can catch fireworks on Sicily's volatile volcanoes.

But as much as all of this, a trip to Italy is about lapping up the lifestyle. It's about idling over a coffee at a streetside cafe or lingering over a long lunch in the hot Mediterranean sun.

FAST FACTS

- **Area** 301, 230 sq km
- **Capital** Rome
- **Currency** euro (€); US$1 = €0.73; UK£1 = €1.06; A$1 = €0.50; ¥100 = €0.76; NZ$1 = €0.41
- **Famous for** long lunches, ancient ruins, Renaissance art, Tuscany, crazy driving
- **Official language** Italian
- **Phrases** *buon giorno* (hello); *arrivederci* (goodbye); *per favore* (please); *grazie* (thanks); *mi scusi* (excuse me)
- **Population** 59.1 million
- **Telephone codes** country code ☎ 39; international access code ☎ 00; reverse-charge code ☎ 170
- **Visas** not needed by EU citizens or nationals of Australia, Canada, Israel, Japan, New Zealand, Switzerland and the USA for stays of up to 90 days; see p548

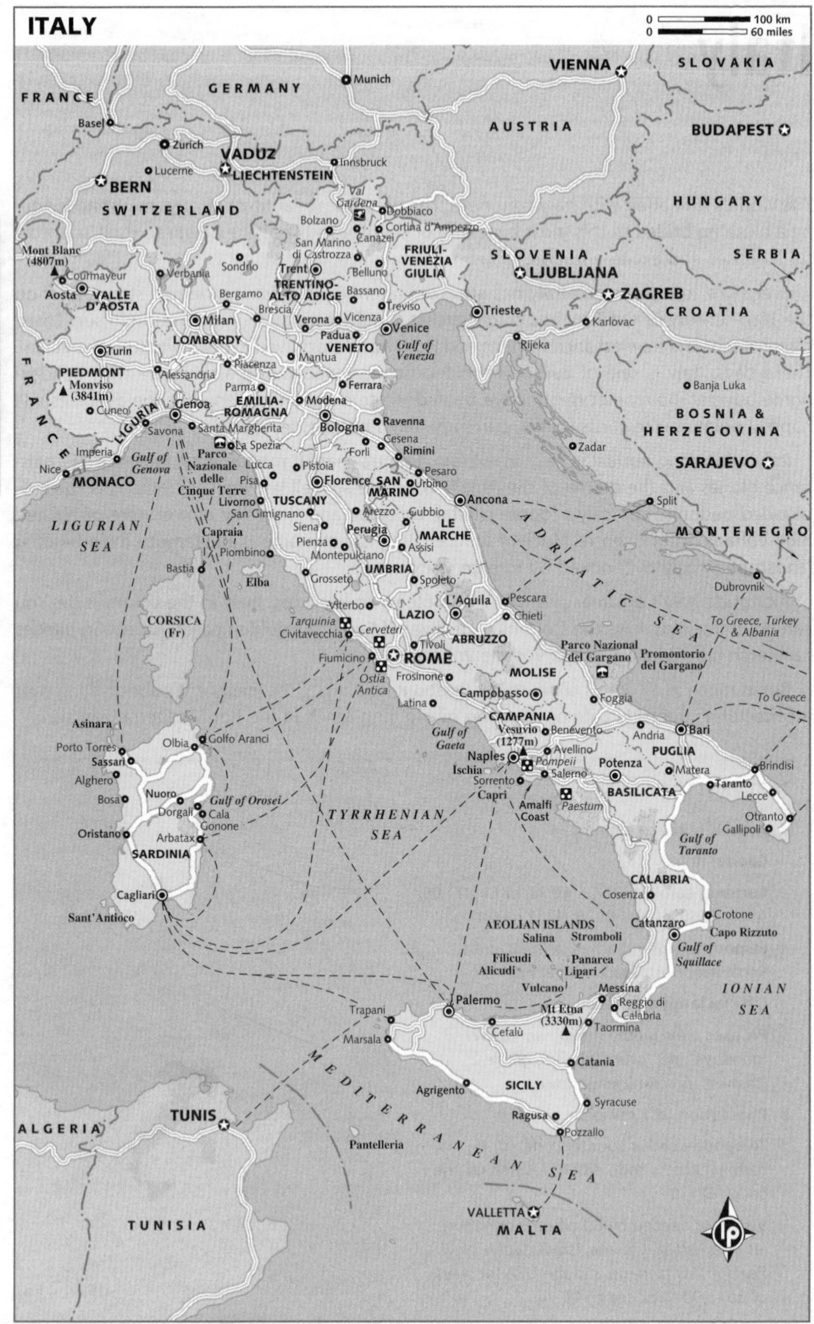
ITALY
0 100 km
0 60 miles
GERMANY
FRANCE
Munich
VIENNA
SLOVAKIA
AUSTRIA
BUDAPEST
Basel
Zurich
VADUZ
Innsbruck
Lucerne
LIECHTENSTEIN
BERN
SWITZERLAND
Val Gardena
Dobbiaco
HUNGARY
Bolzano
Cortina d'Ampezzo
Canazei
San Marino di Castrozza
FRIULI-VENEZIA GIULIA
SLOVENIA
SERBIA
Mont Blanc (4807m)
Sondrio
Trent
Belluno
LJUBLJANA
Courmayeur
Verbania
TRENTINO-ALTO ADIGE
Aosta
VALLE D'AOSTA
Bergamo
Bassano
ZAGREB
Brescia
Treviso
Trieste
CROATIA
Milan
Verona
Vicenza
Karlovac
Padua
Venice
LOMBARDY
VENETO
Gulf of Venezia
Rijeka
Turin
Mantua
Piacenza
PIEDMONT
Alessandria
FRANCE
Monviso (3841m)
Parma
Ferrara
Banja Luka
Modena
EMILIA-ROMAGNA
Cuneo
Genoa
Bologna
Ravenna
BOSNIA & HERZEGOVINA
LIGURIA
Savona
Santa Margherita
Cesena
Imperia
La Spezia
Forlì
Rimini
Zadar
Gulf of Genova
Parco Nazionale delle Cinque Terre
Lucca
Pistoia
Pesaro
Nice
MONACO
Pisa
Florence
SAN MARINO
Urbino
SARAJEVO
Livorno
TUSCANY
Ancona
Split
San Gimignano
Arezzo
Gubbio
LIGURIAN SEA
Siena
Perugia
LE MARCHE
MONTENEGRO
Capraia
Pienza
Assisi
Montepulciano
Piombino
Bastia
UMBRIA
Elba
Grosseto
Spoleto
Dubrovnik
ADRIATIC SEA
Viterbo
L'Aquila
Pescara
CORSICA (Fr)
LAZIO
Chieti
Tarquinia
Cerveteri
To Greece, Turkey & Albania
Civitavecchia
Tivoli
ABRUZZO
Parco Nazionale del Gargano
Promontorio del Gargano
Fiumicino
ROME
MOLISE
Ostia Antica
Frosinone
Campobasso
Foggia
To Greece
Latina
CAMPANIA
Asinara
Vesuvio (1277m)
Benevento
Bari
Gulf of Gaeta
Andria
Olbia
Golfo Aranci
Porto Torres
Naples
Avellino
PUGLIA
Sassari
Ischia
Pompeii
Potenza
Matera
Brindisi
Alghero
Salerno
Sorrento
Taranto
Nuoro
Capri
BASILICATA
Bosa
Gulf of Orosei
Lecce
Dorgali
Cala Gonone
Amalfi Coast
Paestum
Otranto
TYRRHENIAN SEA
Oristano
Arbatax
Gallipoli
SARDINIA
Gulf of Taranto
CALABRIA
Cagliari
Cosenza
Sant'Antioco
Crotone
AEOLIAN ISLANDS
Catanzaro
Salina
Stromboli
Capo Rizzuto
Filicudi
Panarea
Gulf of Squillace
Alicudi
Lipari
Vulcano
Messina
IONIAN SEA
Palermo
Reggio di Calabria
Trapani
Mt Etna (3330m)
Cefalù
Taormina
Marsala
Catania
SICILY
Agrigento
MEDITERRANEAN SEA
Syracuse
TUNIS
Ragusa
ALGERIA
Pozzallo
Pantelleria
VALLETTA
MALTA
TUNISIA

HIGHLIGHTS

- Lap up the *dolce vita* in **Rome** (p443), city of emperors, popes, lovers and artists.
- Check out vibrant **Turin** (p472) a forward-looking city waiting to surprise you. So much more than Fiat and factories!
- Soak up the incomparable Byzantine beauty of **Venice** (p481), Italy's canal city.
- Blow your mind on madcap baroque architecture in **Lecce** (p528), the elegant Florence of the South.
- Explore Sardinia's stunning coastline from **Cala Gonone** (p541) on the spectacular Gulf of Orosei.

ITINERARIES

- **One week** After a couple of days exploring Venice, head south to Florence. Two days is not long there but it'll whet your appetite for the treasures that await in Rome, your final destination.
- **Two weeks** In the second week, continue south for some sea and southern passion. Spend a day dodging traffic in Naples, a day investigating Pompeii and a day or two admiring the Amalfi Coast. Then backtrack to Naples for a ferry to Palermo and the gastronomic delights of Sicily. Or maybe Cagliari and Sardinia's magical beaches. You choose.

CLIMATE & WHEN TO GO

You can usually rely on sun between May and September with the hottest temperatures arriving in July and August. Italian winters are mild compared to northern climes but snow is an annual fixture in mountainous areas. November is Italy's wettest month.

The best times to visit are spring (April to June) and early autumn (September and October) – the weather's generally good and the crowds are bearable. Beaches are at their busiest in August when prices skyrocket on the coast. Winter is a peaceful and cost-effective time to visit the cities.

See p944 for climate charts.

HISTORY

Of the many Italic tribes that emerged from the Stone Age, the Etruscans left the most enduring mark. By the 7th century BC they were the dominant force in central Italy, rivalled only by the Greeks on the south coast. Greek traders had been settling in Italy since the 8th century BC, founding a number of independent city-states, collectively known as Magna Graecia. Both groups thrived until the 3rd century BC when Rome's rampaging legionnaires came crashing in.

Rise & Fall of Rome

Rome's origins are mired in myth but it's generally accepted that Romulus was the first of Rome's seven kings and that the Etruscan Tarquinius Superbus was the last. He was ousted in 509 BC and the Roman Republic was founded.

The fledgling republic got off to a shaky start but it soon colonised much of the Mediterranean and, under Julius Caesar, Gaul. Caesar, the last of the Republic's consuls, was assassinated in 44 BC, sparking a power struggle between his great-nephew Octavian and Mark Antony. Octavian prevailed and in 27 BC became Augustus, Rome's first emperor.

The Roman Empire reached its zenith in the 2nd century AD, but by the 3rd century economic decline and the spread of Christianity were fuelling discontent. Diocletian tried to stop the rot by splitting the empire into eastern and western halves, but when his successor, Constantine (the first Christian emperor), moved his court to Constantinople, Rome's days were numbered. Sacked by the Goths in 410 and plundered by the Vandals in 455, the Western Empire finally fell in 476.

From the Renaissance to the Risorgimento

Medieval Italy was a patchwork of rival city-states ruled by powerful families – the Sforza

CONNECTIONS: MOVING ON FROM ITALY

Milan and Venice are northern Italy's two main transport hubs. From Milan, trains run to cities across Western Europe, including Barcelona, Paris, Amsterdam, Zürich, Munich and Vienna. Venice is better placed for Eastern Europe, with rail connections to Prague, Ljubljana, Zagreb, Belgrade, Budapest and Bucharest. You can also pick up ferries in Venice for Corfu, Igoumenitsa and Patra (p490). Down the east coast, there are ferries from Bari to various Greek ports, as well as to Durrës, Bar and Dubrovnik (p550). At the other end of the country, Genoa has ferries to Barcelona and Tunis (p550).

in Milan, the Este in Ferrara and the Medici in Florence. Enthusiastic patrons of the arts, it was the Medici, along with the Roman popes, who financed much of the 15th- and 16th-century Renaissance.

By the end of the 16th century most of Italy was in foreign hands – the Spanish in the south and the Austrians in the north. Three centuries later, Napoleon's brief Italian interlude gave rise to the Risorgimento (unification movement). With Count Cavour providing the political vision and Garibaldi the military muscle, the movement culminated in the 1861 unification of Italy under King Vittorio Emanuele. In 1870 Rome was wrested from the papacy and became Italy's capital.

Fascism, WWII & the Italian Republic

Following a meteoric rise to power, Benito Mussolini became Italy's leader in 1925, six years after he'd founded his Fascist Party. Invoking Rome's imperial past, he embarked on a disastrous invasion of Abyssinia (modern-day Ethiopia) and, in 1940, entered WWII on Germany's side. Three years later the Allies invaded Sicily and his nation rebelled: King Vittorio Emanuele III had Mussolini arrested and Italy surrendered soon after. Mussolini was killed by Italian partisans in April 1945.

In the aftermath of the war Italy voted to abolish the monarchy and, in 1946, declared itself a constitutional republic.

A founding member of the European Economic Community, Italy enjoyed a largely successful postwar period. Consistent economic growth survived a period of domestic terrorism in the 1970s and continued well into the 1980s.

HOW MUCH?

- **Cappuccino and cornetto** €2
- **Museum admission** €6 to €14
- **City bus ticket** €1
- **Gelato** €1.50 to €3
- **Gondola ride** €80

LONELY PLANET INDEX

- **1L petrol** €1.17
- **1L bottled water** €1.50
- **Peroni beer** €1.50 to €6
- **Souvenir T-shirt** €10 to €15
- **Slice of pizza** €1.50 to €4

The Berlusconi Era

The 1990s heralded a period of crisis. In 1992 a minor bribery investigation ballooned into a nationwide corruption scandal known as *Tangentopoli* ('kickback city'). Top business figures were imprisoned and the main political parties were reduced to tatters, creating a power vacuum into which billionaire media-mogul Silvio Berlusconi deftly stepped. After a short period as prime minister in 1994, he won the elections again in 2001 and went on to become Italy's longest serving postwar PM. But his tenure was rarely free of controversy as opponents railed against his hold over Italian TV and support for American intervention in Iraq. The party came to an end in 2006, when, after an acrimonious election campaign, Romano Prodi's centre-left coalition claimed the narrowest of electoral victories.

The Prodi interlude was short-lived, though, and in April 2008, *Il Cavaliere* (The Knight, as Berlusconi is known) once again returned to the top job, this time beating Walter Veltroni, the former mayor of Rome.

Natural Disaster

As one of the world's most earthquake-prone countries, Italy has a long history of natural disaster. The country's deadliest ever earthquake struck in 1908, razing the Sicilian town of Messina to the ground and claiming up to 200,000 lives. The latest devastating quake struck the central region of Abruzzo on 6 April 2009, killing some 294 people and leaving up to 17,000 homeless. The epicentre was near regional capital L'Aquila, but shock waves were felt as far away as Rome, 90km to the southwest. Much of L'Aquila's medieval centre was destroyed and an estimated 500 historic churches were damaged, including the 13th-century Basilica di Santa Maria di Collemaggio, Abruzzo's most famous sight.

PEOPLE

They're not quite extinct, but Italian children are in increasingly short supply. Italy's birth rate is one of the lowest in the Western world and with one-fifth of the 59.1 million population over 65, there are more grandparents than grandchildren. In fact, were it not for immigration, Italy's population would be diminishing.

ORGANISED CRIME PAYS

A publishing phenomenon, Roberto Saviano's book *Gomorrah* brought the cold, hard facts of the Camorra to the world's attention. According to the author, the 6700 members of the Neapolitan mafia are active in businesses ranging from construction and illegal waste disposal to drugs, arms dealing and illicit clothes manufacture. In one of the book's more startling revelations, Saviano claims that the suit Angelina Jolie wore to the 2001 Oscars' ceremony was actually made by a Camorra tailor in an underground sweatshop.

The Camorra is one of four criminal organisations collectively known as the mafia. The others are Sicily's Cosa Nostra, the 'Ndrangheta in Calabria, and Puglia's Sacra Corona Unita, the youngest and smallest of the four. Together their annual income is put at about €90 billion, equivalent to 7% of Italy's GDP.

The groups are deeply entrenched in their territories but their reach extends beyond regional borders. The 'Ndrangheta is said to control distribution of South American cocaine in Europe, and Camorra companies run much of Italy's illegal waste-disposal business. Up to 43% of Italy's rubbish and toxic waste ends up in Campania, according to Saviano, where it's either burned or dumped.

Against this bleak reality, breakthroughs are hard fought. The latest came in June 2008 with the culmination of the Spartacus trial. After 10 years and 500 witnesses, judges handed down life sentences to 16 members of the Casalesi clan, one of the Camorra's most aggressive families based in the province of Caserta.

Italy's foreign population has grown from just over 350,000 in 1991 to 2.9 million in 2007.

Traditionally, Italians are very conscious of their regional identity and very family orientated. Times are changing, but it's still common for Italian children to remain at home until they marry.

RELIGION

Italians have an ambiguous relationship with religion. More than 80% of the country professes to be Catholic but only about a third regularly attend church. Similarly, the Vatican is a powerful voice in national debate, yet it can't find enough priests for its parish churches. Still, first Communions, church weddings and regular feast days remain an integral part of life.

There are no official figures but it's estimated that there are about 1.3 million Muslims in Italy, making Islam Italy's second religion. There are also about 400,000 evangelical Protestants, 350,000 Jehovah's Witnesses and smaller numbers of Jews and Buddhists.

ARTS

Literature

Italian literature runs the gamut from Virgil's *Aeneid,* to the chilling war stories of Primo Levi and the fantastical tales of Italo Calvino.

Dante, whose *Divina commedia* (Divine Comedy) dates to the early 1300s, was one of three 14th-century greats alongside Petrarch and Giovanni Boccaccio, considered the first Italian novelist.

In ensuing centuries, Machiavelli taught how to manipulate power in *Il principe* (The Prince) and Alessandro Manzoni wrote of star-crossed lovers in *I promessi sposi* (The Betrothed).

Italy's southern regions provide rich literary pickings. Giuseppe Tomasi di Lampedusa depicts Sicily's wary mentality in *Il gattopardo* (The Leopard), a theme that Leonardo Sciascia later returns to in *Il giorno della civetta* (The Day of the Owl). Carlo Levi denounces southern poverty in *Cristo si é fermato a Eboli* (Christ Stopped at Eboli), an account of his internal exile under the Fascists. More recently, Andrea Camilleri's Sicilian-based Montalbano detective stories have enjoyed great success.

Cinema

The influence of Italian cinema goes well beyond its success at the box office. In creating the spaghetti western Sergio Leone inspired generations of film-makers, as did horror master Dario Argento and art-house genius Michelangelo Antonioni.

The heyday of Italian cinema was the post-WWII period, when the neo-realists Roberto Rossellini, Vittorio de Sica and Luchino Visconti turned their cameras onto the war-weary Italians. Classics of the genre include *Ladri di biciclette* (Bicycle Thieves; 1948) and *Roma città aperta* (Rome Open City; 1945).

Taking a decidedly different turn, Federico Fellini created his own highly visual style and won an international audience with films such as *La dolce vita* (The Sweet Life; 1959).

Of Italy's contemporary directors, Roberto Benigni won an Oscar for *La vita è bella* (Life is Beautiful; 1997) and Nanni Moretti (1953–) won Canne's Palme D'Or for *La stanza del figlio* (The Son's Room, 2001). Fast forward to 2008 when two of Italy's most talked-about films jostled for the honours at Cannes. Paolo Sorrentino's *Il divo*, a portrait of Giulio Andreotti, Italy's controversial seven-time PM, took the Jury Prize, and *Gomorra*, directed by Matteo Garrone and based on Roberto Saviano's bestselling exposè of the Neapolitan Camorra, walked off with the Festival Grand Prix.

Music

Emotional and highly theatrical, opera has always appealed to Italians. Performances of Verdi and Puccini are regularly staged at legendary theatres such as Milan's Teatro alla La Scala (p477) and Naples' Teatro San Carlo (p520).

On the classical front, Antonio Vivaldi (1675–1741) created the concerto in its present form and wrote *Le quattro stagione* (The Four Seasons). In more recent times, Neapolitan dub and techno outfit Almamegretta have achieved international success.

Architecture & Visual Arts

Everywhere you go in Italy you're faced with reminders of the country's convoluted history. The Greek temples at Agrigento (p537) tell of glories long past, while the skeletal ruins of Pompeii (p521) offer insights into the day-to-day life of ancient Romans. Byzantine mosaics in Ravenna (p495), Venice (p481) and Palermo (p530) reveal eastern influences.

Sweeping through 15th and 16th century Europe, the Renaissance left an indelible mark, particularly in Florence and Rome. Filippo Brunelleschi defied the architectural laws of the day to create the dome on Florence's Duomo (p500) and Michelangelo Buonarrotti swept aside all convention to decorate the Sistine Chapel (p449). Contemporaries Leonardo da Vinci and Raphael further brightened the scene.

Controversial and highly influential, Michelangelo Merisi da Caravaggio dominated the late 16th century with his revolutionary use of light and penchant for warts-and-all portraits. There was little warts-and-all about the 17th-century baroque style, visible in many of Italy's great churches. Witness the Roman works of Gian Lorenzo Bernini and Francesco Borromini, and Lecce's flamboyant *centro storico* (p528).

Signalling a return to sober classical lines, neoclassicism majored in the late 18th and early 19th centuries. Its most famous Italian exponent was Canova who carved a name for himself with his smooth sensual style. Rome's Spanish Steps (p453) and Trevi Fountain (p453) both date to this period.

In sharp contrast to backward-looking neoclassicism, Italian futurism provided a rallying cry for modernism with Giacomo Balla proving hugely influential. Caught up in the modernist spirit, the 1920s *razionalisti* (rationalists) provided the architectural vision behind the EUR district in Rome.

Continuing in this modernist tradition are Italy's two superstar architects: Renzo Piano, the visionary behind Rome's Auditorium (p464), and Rome-born Massimiliano Fuksas.

ENVIRONMENT

Bound on three sides by four seas (the Adriatic, Ligurian, Tyrrhenian and Ionian), Italy has more than 8000km of coastline. Inland, about 75% of the peninsula is mountainous – the Alps curve around the northern border and the Apennines extend down the boot.

The peninsula and its surrounding seas harbour a rich fauna. You're unlikely to spot them but there are bears, wolves and wildcats in the national parks of central Italy, as well as over 150 types of bird. Swordfish, tuna and dolphins are common along the coastline and although white sharks are known to exist, attacks are rare.

Italy has 21 national parks, covering about 5% of the country, and more than 400 nature reserves, natural parks and wetlands. It also boasts over 40 Unesco World Heritage sites, more than any other country.

But Italy is not without its environmental problems. The two most obvious are air pollution and waste disposal. Heavy industry and high levels of car ownership have combined to produce dense smog, particularly in the industrialised north. Inadequate waste disposal has also led to pollution, as illegal, sometimes toxic, refuse is pumped out to sea or buried in illegal dumps by organised-crime outfits.

Other problems include unfettered coastal development, erosion and forest fires.

As a visitor, there's not a huge amount you can do to affect these things, but you can try to tread lighter. Practical tips include staying in locally run accommodation, refilling plastic water bottles at drinking fountains, turning off the air-con when you leave your hotel room, and using trains, buses and ferries as opposed to flying. Italian food organisation Slow Food promotes traditional food products so any trattoria or restaurant bearing a Slow Food sticker promises good things.

FOOD & DRINK

Despite the ubiquity of pasta and pizza, Italian cuisine is highly regional. Local specialities abound and regional traditions are proudly maintained, so expect pesto in Genoa, pizza in Naples, and *ragù* (bolognese sauce) in Bologna. It's the same with wine – Piedmont produces Italy's great reds, Barolo, Barbaresco and Dolcetto, while Tuscany's famous for its Chianti, Brunello and white Vernaccia.

Vegetarians will find delicious fruit and veg in the hundreds of daily markets, and although few restaurants cater specifically to vegetarians most serve vegetable-based antipasti (starters), pastas, *contorni* (side dishes) and salads.

Where to Eat & Drink

The most basic sit-down eatery is a *tavola calda* (literally 'hot table'), which offers canteen-style food. Pizzerias, the best of which have a *forno a legna* (wood-fired oven), serve the obvious but often a full menu as well. For takeaway, a *rosticceria* sells cooked meats and *pizza al taglio* (pizza by the slice).

For wine make for an *enoteca*, a wine bar, many of which also serve light snacks and a few hot dishes. Alternatively, most bars and cafes serve *tramezzini* (sandwiches) and panini (bread rolls). A cheaper option is to go to an *alimentari* (delicatessen) and ask them to make a panino with the filling of your choice. At a *pasticceria* you can buy pastries, cakes and biscuits. *Forni* (bakeries) are another good choice for a cheap snack.

For a full meal you'll want a trattoria or a *ristorante*. Traditionally, trattorias were family-run places that served a basic menu of local dishes at affordable prices and thankfully, a few still are. *Ristoranti* offer more choice and smarter service.

Restaurants, all of which are nonsmoking, usually open for lunch from noon to 3pm and for dinner from 7.30pm, earlier in tourist areas. For more on opening hours, see the Italy Directory, p545.

On the bill expect to be charged for *pane e coperto* (bread and a cover charge). This is standard and is added even if you don't ask for or eat the bread. Typically it ranges from €1 to €4. *Servizio* (service charge) of 10% to 15% might or might not be included; if it's not, tourists are expected to round up the bill or leave 10%.

Habits & Customs

A full Italian meal consists of an antipasto, a *primo* (first course), *secondo* (second/main course) with an *insalata* (salad) or *contorno* (vegetable side dish), and *dolci* (dessert). When eating out it's perfectly acceptable to order, say, a *primo* followed by an *insalata* or *contorno*.

Italians don't tend to eat a sit-down *colazione* (breakfast), preferring instead a cappuccino and *cornetto* (croissant) at a bar. *Pranzo* (lunch) was traditionally the main meal of the day, although many people now have a light lunch and bigger *cena* (dinner). Italians are late diners, often not eating until after 9pm.

ROME

pop 2.7 million

An epic, monumental metropolis, Rome has been in the spotlight for close to 3000 years. As the showcase seat of the Roman Empire, it was the all-powerful Caput Mundi (Capital of the World). Later, as the Renaissance capital of the Catholic world, its name sent shivers of holy terror through believers and infidels alike. Some 500 years on and its name still exerts a powerful hold. Fortunately, its reality is every bit as enticing as its reputation. With its architectural and artistic treasures, its romantic corners and noisy, colourful markets, Rome is a city that knows how to impress.

They say a lifetime's not enough for Rome *(Roma, non basta una vita)*. And while it's true that few cities can match its cultural legacy, you don't need to be an expert to enjoy it. In fact, all you've got to do is walk its animated streets. Even without trying you'll be swept up in the emotion of a city that has been inspiring artists and lovers since time immemorial.

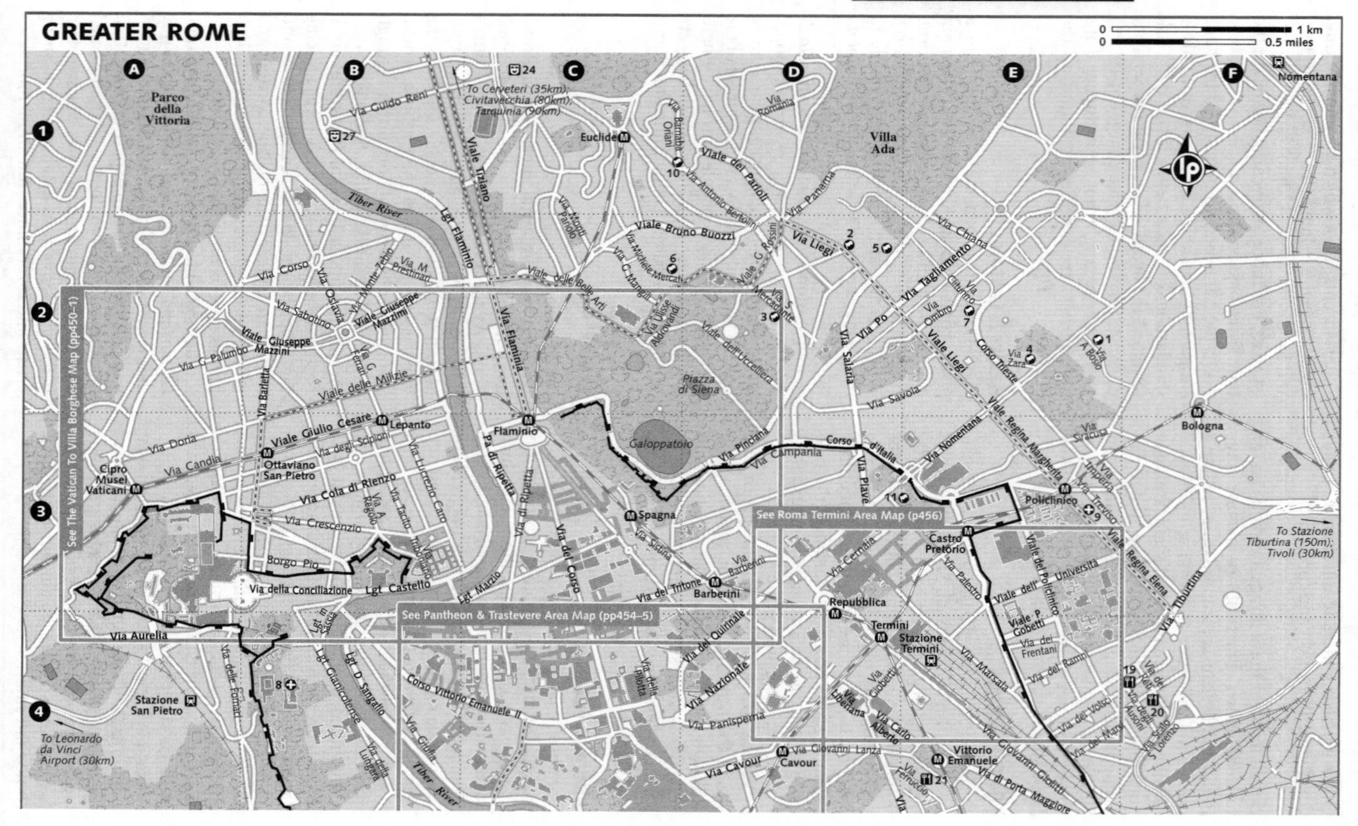
GREATER ROME
0 1 km
0 0.5 miles
Parco della Vittoria
Villa Ada
Nomentana
Euclide
Bologna
Policlinico
Castro Pretorio
Stazione Termini
Termini
Repubblica
Vittorio Emanuele
Cavour
Barberini
Spagna
Flaminio
Lepanto
Ottaviano San Pietro
Cipro Musei Vaticani
Stazione San Pietro
Galoppatoio
Piazza di Siena
Tiber River
Via Guido Reni
Viale Tiziano
Lgt Flaminio
Via Flaminia
Viale dei Parioli
Viale Bruno Buozzi
Via Liegi
Viale Liegi
Via Po
Via Tagliamento
Via Salaria
Corso Trieste
Viale Regina Margherita
Via Nomentana
Viale Regina Elena
Via Tiburtina
Corso d'Italia
Via Campania
Via Pinciana
Via Piave
Via del Corso
Via di Ripetta
Viale Giulio Cesare
Via Cola di Rienzo
Via Crescenzio
Borgo Pio
Via della Conciliazione
Lgt Castello
Via Aurelia
Via delle Fornaci
Corso Vittorio Emanuele II
Via Nazionale
Via Cavour
Via Giovanni Giolitti
Via Marsala
Via di Porta Maggiore
To Cerveteri (35km); Civitavecchia (80km); Tarquinia (90km)
To Stazione Tiburtina (150m); Tivoli (30km)
To Leonardo da Vinci Airport (30km)
See The Vatican To Villa Borghese Map (pp450–1)
See Pantheon & Trastevere Area Map (pp454–5)
See Roma Termini Area Map (p456)

INFORMATION
Australian Embassy 1 E2
Austrian Consulate 2 D2
Austrian Embassy 3 D2
Canadian Consulate 4 E2
Canadian Embassy 5 D2
Dutch Embassy 6 C2
New Zealand Embassy 7 E2
Ospedale Bambino Gesù 8 B4
Ospedale G Eastman 9 E3
Swiss Embassy 10 C1
UK Embassy 11 E3
SIGHTS & ACTIVITIES
Appia Antica Regional Park Information Point 12 D7
Basilica di San Clemente 13 D5
Basilica di San Giovanni in Laterano 14 E5
Catacombs of San Callisto 15 E8
Catacombs of San Sebastiano 16 E8
Terme di Caracalla 17 D6
EATING
Pizzeria Remo 18 C5
Pommidoro 19 F4
Tram Tram 20 F4
Vecchia Roma 21 E4
Volpetti Più 22 C6
ENTERTAINMENT
AKAB 23 C6
Auditorium Parco della Musica 24 C1
Big Mama 25 B5
Goa 26 C7
Teatro Olimpico 27 B1
Villaggio Globale 28 B6
SHOPPING
Porta Portese Flea Market 29 C5
Via Sannio Market 30 E5
5
6
7
8
Villa Doria Pamphilj
Via Aurelia Antica
Via del Vascello
Gianicolo (Janiculum)
Via G Medici
Via Calandrelli
Via G Rossetti
Via dell' Francesco Ongaro
Viale di Trastevere
Via Portuense
Stazione Trastevere
Via A Bellani
Via A Pacinotti
Via Enrico Fermi
Tiber River
To Ostia Antica (25km); Camping Internazionale Castelfusano (28km)
Clivio Portuense
Porta di Ripa Grande
Isola Tiberina
Lgt dei Pierleoni
Lgt Ripa
Via Marmorata
Piazza Santa Maria Liberatrice
Via A Volta
Cimitero Acattolico
Via del Gazometro
Via del Commercio
Stazione Roma-Ostia
Piramide
Via Ostiense
Garbatella
San Paolo
Orti Farnesiani
Via dei Cerchi
Via del Circo Massimo
Circo Massimo
Colosseo
Piazza del Colosseo
Via di San Gregorio
Parco di Porta Capena
Viale Guido
Viale Giotto
Viale Marco Polo
Via Tata Giovanni
Stazione Roma-Ostiense
Viale delle Terme di Caracalla
Via Druso
Via della Navicella
Via Labicana
Merulana
Viale Manzoni
Manzoni
Via Emanuele Filiberto
Via dell'Amba Aradam
Via Ipponio
Via Licia
Via Pannonia
Viale Metronio
Via Gallia
Via Luni
Via Vetulonia
Via Cilicia
Via Ardeatina
Via delle Sette Chiese
Via Appia Antica
Via Cristoforo Colombo
San Giovanni
Viale Carlo Felice
Via La Spezia
Via Taranto
Via Aosta
Re di Roma
Via Tabarini
Via Imera
Ponte Lungo
Furio Camillo
Via Latina
Colli Albani
To Ciampino Airport (15km)
Via Cecilia Metella
ITALY

HISTORY

According to the legend of Romulus and Remus, Rome was founded in 753 BC. Historians debate this, but they do acknowledge that Romulus was the first king of Rome and that the city was an amalgamation of Etruscan, Latin and Sabine settlements on the Palatine, Esquiline and Quirinal Hills. Archaeological discoveries have confirmed the existence of a settlement on the Palatine in that period.

In 509 BC the Roman Republic was founded. Civil war put an end to the republic following the murder of Julius Caesar in 44 BC and a bitter civil war between Octavian and Mark Antony. Octavian emerged victorious and was made the first Roman emperor with the title Augustus.

By AD 100 Rome had a population of 1.5 million and was the Caput Mundi (Capital of the World). But by the 5th century decline had set in and in 476 Romulus Augustulus, the last emperor of the Western Roman Empire, was deposed.

By this time Rome's Christian roots had taken firm hold. Christianity had been spreading since the 1st century AD, and under Constantine it received official recognition. Pope Gregory I (590–604) did much to strengthen the Church's grip over the city, laying the foundations for its later role as capital of the Catholic Church.

Under the Renaissance popes of the 15th and 16th centuries, Rome was given an extensive facelift. But trouble was never far away and in 1527 the city was sacked by Spanish forces under Charles V.

Once again Rome needed rebuilding and it was to the 17th-century baroque masters Bernini and Borromini that the city turned. With their exuberant churches, fountains and *palazzi*, these two bitter rivals changed the face of the city. The building boom following the unification of Italy and the declaration of Rome as its capital also profoundly influenced the look of the city, as did Mussolini and hasty post-WWII expansion.

ORIENTATION

Rome is a sprawling city but most sights are concentrated in the area between Stazione Termini and the Vatican on the other side of the Tiber River. Halfway between the two, the Pantheon and Piazza Navona lie at the heart of the *centro storico* (historic centre).

ROME IN TWO DAYS

Get to grips with ancient Rome at the Colosseum (opposite), the Roman Forum and Palatine Hill (p448). In the afternoon, check out the Capitoline Hill (p451) before an evening in Trastevere (p461).

On day two, hit the Vatican. Marvel at St Peter's Basilica (p449) and the vast Vatican Museums (p449). Lunch at Dino e Tony (p461) and then spend the afternoon in the *centro storico*.

To the southeast, the Colosseum is an obvious landmark. Distances are not great and walking is the best way to get around.

Roma Termini, known as Stazione Termini, is the city's main transport hub. International, intercity and local trains stop here and city buses depart from the square outside, Piazza dei Cinquecento.

Rome's two airports are well connected with the city centre. From outside Termini, buses depart for Ciampino airport, while trains run regularly to/from Leonardo da Vinci airport. For further details see p466.

INFORMATION

Bookshops

Feltrinelli International (Map p456; Via VE Orlando 84; 9am-8pm Mon-Sat, 10.30am-1.30pm & 4-7.30pm Sun) Has an extensive selection of maps and books in English and other languages.

Discount Cards

Roma Pass (3 days €20) Provides free admission to two museums or sites, as well as reduced entry to extra sites, unlimited city transport and reduced entry to other exhibitions and events; see p449.

Emergency

Police station (Questura; Map pp454-5; 06 468 61; Via San Vitale 15)

Internet Access

Internet cafes are plentiful and most hostels and many hotels offer access.

Splashnet (Map p456; Via Varese 33; per hr €1.50; 8.30am-11pm) Also a laundry – €6 per 7kg wash and dry and left luggage – €2 per bag per day.

Telephone Center International (Map p456; Via Volturno 52; per hr €2; 7am-midnight) Also good rates on international calls.

Internet Resources

Pierreci (www.pierreci.it) Has the latest on museums, monuments and exhibitions. Book tickets online here.
Roma Turismo (www.romaturismo.it) Rome Tourist Board's website lists useful numbers, all official accommodation, sites, transport and much more.
Vatican (www.vatican.va) The Holy See's official website with practical information on Vatican sites.

Left Luggage

Stazione Termini (Map p456; 1st 5hr €3.80, 6-12hr per hr €0.60, 13hr & over per hr €0.20; 6am-midnight) On the lower-ground floor under platform 24.

Medical Services

For emergency treatment, go straight to the *pronto soccorso* (casualty) section of an *ospedale* (hospital). Pharmacists will serve prescriptions and can provide basic medical advice.
24-hour Pharmacy (Map p456; 06 488 00 19; Piazza dei Cinquecento 49/50/51)
Ospedale Bambino Gesù (Map pp444-5; 06 685 92 351; Piazza di Sant'Onofrio 4) For paediatric assistance.
Ospedale G Eastman (Map pp444-5; 06 84 48 31; Viale Regina Elena 287b) A dental hospital.
Ospedale Santo Spirito (Map pp450-1; 06 683 51; Lungotevere in Sassia 1) Near the Vatican; multilingual staff.

Money

ATM's are liberally scattered around the city.
American Express (Map pp450-1; 06 676 41; Piazza di Spagna 38; 9am-5.30pm Mon-Fri, 9am-12.30pm Sat) Offers exchange facilities and travel services.

Post

Main post office (Map pp450-1; 06 697 37 213; Piazza di San Silvestro 19)
Vatican post office (Map pp450-1; 06 698 83 406; St Peter's Square)

Tourist Information

Centro Servizi Pellegrini e Turisti (Map pp450-1; 06 698 81 662; St Peter's Square; 8.30am-4.15pm Mon-Sat) The Vatican's official tourist office.
Enjoy Rome (Map p456; 06 445 68 90; www.enjoyrome.com; Via Marghera 8a; 8.30am-7pm Mon-Fri, to 2pm Sat) A private tourist office that arranges walking tours and has a free hotel-reservation service.
Rome Tourist Board (Map p456; 06 48 89 91; Via Parigi 5; 9am-7pm Mon-Sat) Can provide maps and plenty of printed material.

The Comune di Roma runs a **multilingual tourist infoline** (820 59 127; 9am-7pm) and information points across the city:
Castel Sant'Angelo (Map pp450-1; 06 688 09 707; Piazza Pia; 9.30am-7pm)
Fiumicino airport (Terminal C, International Arrivals; 9am-7pm)
Imperial Forums Visitor Centre (Map pp454-5; 06 699 24 307; Via dei Fori Imperiali; 9.30am-6.30pm)
Piazza Cinque Lune (Map pp454-5; 06 688 09 240; 9.30am-7pm) Near Piazza Navona.
Piazza Sonnino (Map pp454-5; 06 583 33 457; 9.30am-7pm) In Trastevere.
Santa Maria Maggiore (Map p456; 06 474 09 55; Via dell'Olmata; 9.30am-7pm) Near the basilica.
Stazione Termini (Map p456; 06 478 25 194; 8am-9pm) In the hall parallel to platform 24.
Via Marco Minghetti (Map pp454-5; 06 678 29 88; 9.30am-7pm) Near the Trevi Fountain.
Via Nazionale (Map pp454-5; 06 478 24 525; 9.30am-7pm)

SIGHTS & ACTIVITIES

With more sights than many small nations, Rome can be a daunting prospect. The trick is to relax and not try to see everything. Half the fun of Rome is just hanging out, enjoying the atmosphere.

Colosseum

Rome's iconic monument is a thrilling site. The 50,000 seater **Colosseum** (Map pp454-5; 06 399 67 700; admission incl Palatine Hill €11; 9am-1hr before sunset; M Colosseo) was ancient Rome's most feared arena and is today one of Italy's top tourist attractions. Queues are inevitable but you can usually avoid them by buying your ticket at the nearby Palatine Hill. Alternatively, join a walking tour (€9 on top of ticket price) and use the shorter ticket line.

Originally known as the Flavian Amphitheatre, the Colosseum was started by Emperor Vespasian in AD 72 and fin-

BE ON YOUR GUARD

Outside the Colosseum, you'll almost certainly be hailed by centurions offering to pose for a photo. They are not doing this for love and will expect payment. There's no set rate but €5 is a perfectly acceptable sum – and that's €5 period, not €5 per person. To avoid ugly scenes always agree on a price beforehand.

ished by his son Titus in AD 80. It was clad in travertine and covered by a huge canvas awning that was held aloft by 240 masts. Inside, tiered seating encircled the sand-covered arena, itself built over underground chambers where animals were caged. Games involved gladiators fighting wild animals or each other. Contrary to Hollywood folklore, bouts between gladiators rarely ended in death as the games' sponsor was required to pay the owner of a killed gladiator 100 times the gladiator's value.

To the west of the Colosseum, the **Arco di Costantino** was built to celebrate Constantine's victory over rival Maxentius at the battle of Milvian Bridge in AD 312.

Roman Forum & Palatine Hill

Now a collection of fascinating, if rather confusing, ruins, the **Roman Forum** (Map pp454-5; ☎ 06 399 67 700; admission free; ⏰ 9am-1hr before sunset Mon-Sat; Ⓜ Colosseo) was once the showpiece centre of the Roman Republic. Originally an Etruscan burial ground, it was first developed in the 7th century BC, expanding to become the social, political and commercial core of the Roman world. Its importance declined after the fall of the Roman Empire, until eventually the site was used as pasture land and plundered for marble. The area was systematically excavated in the 18th and 19th centuries and excavations continue.

As you enter at Largo Romolo e Remo, ahead to your left is the **Tempio di Antonino e Faustina**, built by the senate in AD 141 and transformed into a church in the 8th century. To your right, the **Basilica Aemilia**, built in 179 BC, was 100m long with a two-storey porticoed facade lined with shops. At the end of the short path **Via Sacra** traverses the Forum from northwest to southeast. Opposite the basilica stands the **Tempio di Giulio Cesare**, erected by Augustus in 29 BC on the site where Caesar's body had been burned.

Head right up Via Sacra and you reach the **Curia**, once the meeting place of the Roman senate and later converted into a church. In front of the Curia is the **Lapis Niger**, a large piece of black marble that purportedly covered Romulus' grave.

At the end of Via Sacra, the **Arco di Settimio Severo** was erected in AD 203 to honour Emperor Septimus Severus and his two sons and celebrate victory over the Parthians. It is considered one of Italy's major triumphal arches. Nearby, the **Millarium Aureum** marked the centre of ancient Rome, from which distances to the city were measured.

Southwest of the arch, eight granite columns are all that remain of the **Tempio di Saturno**, one of ancient Rome's most important temples. Inaugurated in 497 BC, it was later used as the state treasury.

To the southeast, you'll see the Piazza del Foro, the Forum's main market and meeting place, marked by the 7th-century **Colonna di Foca** (Column of Phocus). To your right are the foundations of the **Basilica Giulia**, a law court built by Julius Caesar in 55 BC. At the end of the basilica is the **Tempio di Castore e Polluce**, built in 489 BC in honour of the Heavenly Twins, Castor and Pollux. It is easily recognisable by its three remaining columns. Southeast of the temple, and closed to the public, is the **Chiesa di Santa Maria Antiqua**, the oldest Christian church in the Forum.

Back towards Via Sacra, the **Casa delle Vestali** was home of the virgins whose job it was to keep the sacred flame alight in the adjoining **Tempio di Vesta**. The vestal virgins were selected at the age of 10 for their beauty and virtue. They were required to stay chaste and committed to keeping the flame for 30 years.

Continuing up Via Sacra, you come to the vast **Basilica di Costantino**, also known as the Basilica di Massenzio, whose impressive design inspired Renaissance architects. The **Arco di Tito**, at the Colosseum end of the Forum, was built in AD 81 in honour of the victories of the emperors Titus and Vespasian against Jerusalem.

From here, climb the **Palatine** (Map pp454-5; ☎ 06 399 67 700; entrances Via San Gregorio 30 or Piazza

FREE THRILLS

Surprisingly, some of Rome's most famous sights are free. Try the following:

- **Roman Forum** (left)
- **Trevi Fountain** (p453)
- **Spanish Steps** (p453)
- **Pantheon** (p452)
- **Bocca della Verità** (p457)
- **All churches**, including St Peter's Basilica (opposite)
- **Vatican Museums** (opposite) on the last Sunday of the month.

Santa Maria Nova 53; admission incl Colosseum €11; 9am-1hr before sunset; M Colosseo), where Romulus is said to have founded the city in 753 BC. Archaeological evidence shows that the earliest settlements in the area were in fact on the Palatine and date back to the 8th century BC. The Palatine was ancient Rome's poshest neighbourhood and the emperor Augustus lived here all his life. After Rome's fall, it fell into disrepair and in the Middle Ages churches and castles were built over the ruins. During the Renaissance, members of wealthy families established gardens on the hill.

Most of the Palatine is covered by the ruins of Emperor Domitian's vast complex, which served as the main imperial palace for 300 years. Divided into the **Domus Flavia** (imperial palace), **Domus Augustana** (the emperor's private residence) and a **stadio** (stadium), it was built by the architect Rabirius in the 1st century AD.

Among the best-preserved buildings on the Palatine is the **Casa di Livia**. Home to Augustus' wife Livia, it was decorated with frescoes of mythological scenes, landscapes, fruits and flowers. Also of note is the **Tempio della Magna Mater**, built in 204 BC.

Vatican City

The world's smallest sovereign state, the Vatican is the jealous guardian of one of the world's greatest artistic and architectural patrimonies.

Covering just 0.44 sq km, the Vatican is all that's left of the Papal States. For more than 1000 years, the Papal States encompassed Rome and much of central Italy, but after Italian unification in 1861 the pope was forced to give up his territorial possessions. Relations between Italy and the landless papacy remained strained until 1929 when Mussolini and Pius XI signed the Lateran Treaty and formerly established the Vatican State.

As an independent state, the Vatican has its own postal service, currency, newspaper, radio station and army of Swiss Guards.

ST PETER'S BASILICA

In a city of churches, none can hold a candle to **St Peter's Basilica** (Map pp450-1; ☎ 06 698 85 518; Piazza San Pietro; admission free; 7am-7pm Apr-Sep, to 6.30pm Oct-Mar; M Ottaviano-San Pietro), Italy's biggest, richest, and most spectacular church. Built over the spot where St Peter was buried, the first basilica was consecrated by Constantine in the 4th century. Later, in 1503, Bramante designed a new basilica, which took more than 150 years to complete. Michelangelo took over the project in 1547, designing the grand dome, which soars 120m above the altar. The cavernous 187m-long interior contains numerous treasures, including two of Italy's most celebrated masterpieces: Michelangelo's *Pietà*, the only work to carry his signature; and Bernini's 29m-high baldachin over the high altar.

PAPAL AUDIENCES

At 11am on Wednesday, the pope addresses his flock at the Vatican (in July and August in Castel Gandolfo near Rome). For free tickets, contact the **Prefettura della Casa Pontificia** (Map pp450-1; ☎ 06 698 84 857; fax 06 698 85 863; 9am-1pm), through the bronze doors under the colonnade to the right of St Peter's.

When he is in Rome, the Pope blesses the crowd in St Peter's Square on Sunday at noon. No tickets are required.

Entrance to the **dome** (8am-6pm Apr-Sep, 8am-5pm Oct-Mar) is to the right as you climb the stairs to the basilica's atrium. Make the climb on foot (€5) or by lift (€7).

Dress rules and security are stringently enforced at the basilica – no shorts, miniskirts or sleeveless tops, and be prepared to have your bags searched.

ST PETER'S SQUARE

The Vatican's central piazza, **St Peter's Square** (Piazza San Pietro; Map pp450-1; M Ottaviano-San Pietro) was laid out between 1656 and 1667. Seen from above it resembles a giant keyhole: two semicircular colonnades, each consisting of four rows of Doric columns, bound by a giant ellipse that straightens out to funnel believers into the basilica. The effect was deliberate – designer Gian Lorenzo Bernini described the colonnade as representing 'the motherly arms of the church'.

In the centre, the 25m obelisk was brought to Rome by Caligula from Heliopolis in Egypt and later used by Nero as a turning post for the chariot races in his circus.

VATICAN MUSEUMS

Boasting one of the world's great art collections, the **Vatican Museums** (Map pp450-1; adult/

ITALY

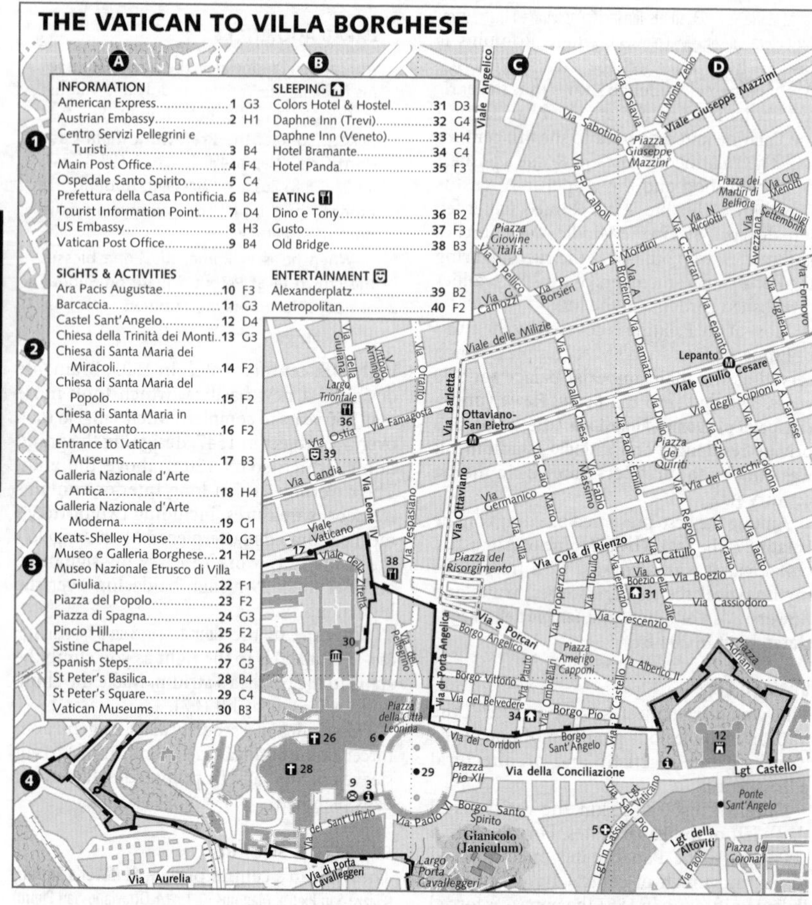

concession €14/8, last Sun of month free; 8.30am-4pm Mon-Sat, 8.30am-12.30pm last Sun of month; Ⓜ Ottaviano-San Pietro) are housed in the *Palazzo Apostolico Vaticano*. Every inch of this vast 5.5-hectare complex is crammed with art, and you'll need several hours just for the highlights. There are four colour-coded itineraries that take anything from 45 minutes to five hours. Each finishes at the Sistine Chapel, so if you want you can walk straight there, although bear in mind that you can't backtrack once you're there. Audioguides are available for €6.

Home to some spectacular classical statuary, the **Museo Pio-Clementino** is to the left of the entrance complex. Highlights include the *Apollo belvedere* and the 1st-century *Laocoön*, both in the Cortile Ottagono. Further on, the 175m-long **Galleria delle Carte Geografiche** (Map Gallery) is hung with 40 huge topographical maps. Beyond that are the magnificent **Stanze di Raffaello** (Raphael Rooms) which were once Pope Julius II's private apartments and are decorated with frescoes by Raphael. Of the paintings, *La scuola d'Atene* (The School of Athens) in the **Stanza della Segnatura** is considered one of Raphael's great masterpieces.

The place in the Vatican Museums that not a single one of the four million annual visitors wants to miss is the **Sistine Chapel** (Cappella Sistina; Map pp450–1). The chapel was originally built in 1484 for Pope Sixtus IV, after whom it is named, but it was Julius II who commissioned Michelangelo to decorate it in 1508. Over the next four years,

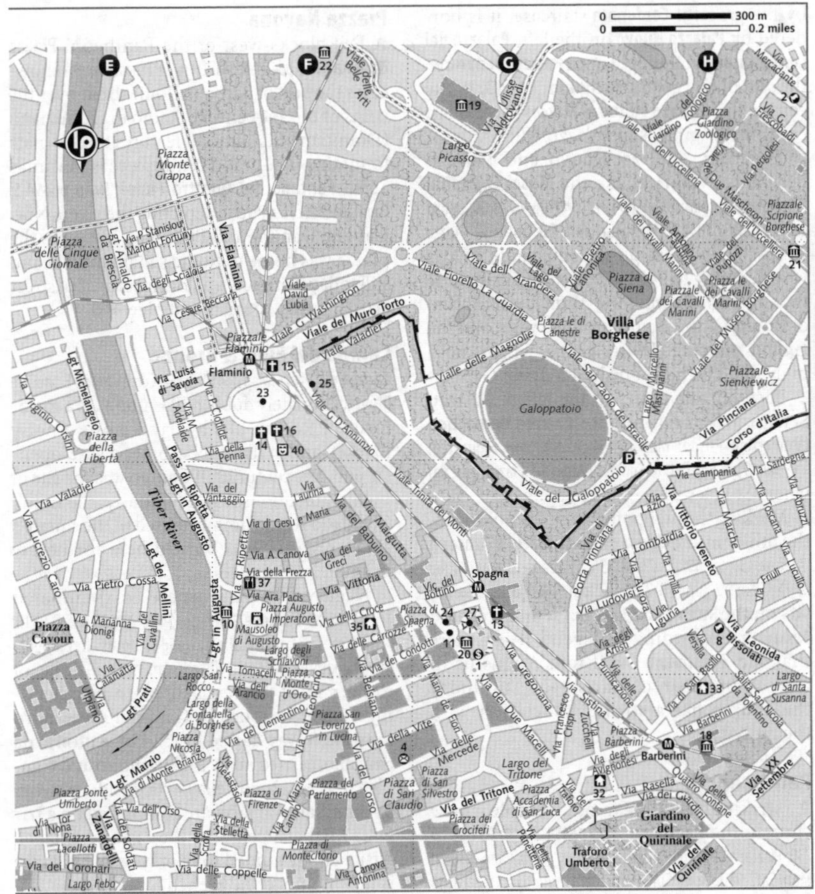

the artist painted the remarkable *Genesis* (Creation; 1508–12) on the barrel-vaulted ceiling. Twenty-two years later he returned at the behest of Pope Clement VII to paint the *Giudizio universale* (Last Judgement; 1534–41) on the end wall.

The other walls of the chapel were painted by artists including Botticelli, Ghirlandaio, Pinturicchio and Signorelli.

Castel Sant'Angelo

An instantly recognisable landmark, the chunky, round-keeped **Castel Sant'Angelo** (Map pp450-1; ☎ 06 681 91 11; Lungotevere Castello 50; admission €7; 🕑 9am-7.30pm Tue-Sun; 🚌 Piazza Pia) was commissioned by Emperor Hadrian in 123 BC as a mausoleum for himself and his family. In the 6th century, it was converted into a papal fortress, and it's now a museum with an assorted collection of sculptures, paintings, weapons and furniture. The terrace offers fine views over Rome.

Piazza del Campidoglio & Musei Capitolini

The lowest of Rome's seven hills, the Capitoline (Campidoglio) was considered the heart of the Roman Republic. At its summit were ancient Rome's two most important temples: one dedicated to Juno Moneta and another to Jupiter Capitolinus, where Brutus is said to have hidden after assassinating Caesar.

The centrepiece is the Michelangelo-designed Piazza del Campidoglio. Accessible by the graceful **Cordonata** staircase, it is bordered by **Palazzo Nuovo** on the left, **Palazzo dei Conservatori** on the right, and **Palazzo Senatorio**, the seat of city government since 1143. In the centre, the bronze **statue of Marcus Aurelius** is a copy; the original is in Palazzo Nuovo.

Together, Palazzo Nuovo and Palazzo dei Conservatori house the **Musei Capitolini** (Capitoline Museums; Map pp454-5; ☎ 06 96 74 00; adult/concession €6.50/4.50; 🕑 9am-8pm Tue-Sun; 🚌 Piazza Venezia), the oldest public museums in the world, dating to 1471. Showstoppers include the *Lupa capitolina* (She-Wolf), a sculpture of Romulus and Remus under a wolf, and the *Galata morente* (Dying Gaul), which movingly depicts the anguish of a dying Gaul.

Back outside, stairs to the left of Palazzo Senatorio lead down to the **Carcere Mamertino** (Mamertine Prison; Map pp454-5; donation requested; 🕑 9am-7pm Apr-Oct, to 5pm Nov-Mar; 🚌 Piazza Venezia) where St Peter was once imprisoned.

Marking the highpoint of the Campidoglio, the 6th-century **Chiesa di Santa Maria d'Aracoeli** (Map pp454-5; ☎ 06 679 81 55; Piazza del Campidoglio 4; 🕑 9am-12.30pm & 2.30-5.30pm; 🚌 Piazza Venezia) sits on the site of the Roman temple to Juno Moneta. According to legend it was here that the Tiburtine Sybil told Augustus of the coming birth of Christ, and still today the church has a strong association with the nativity.

Pantheon

A striking 2000-year-old temple, now church, the **Pantheon** (Map pp454-5; ☎ 06 683 00 230; Piazza della Rotonda; admission free; 🕑 8.30am-7.30pm Mon-Sat, 9am-6pm Sun, 9am-1pm holidays; 🚌 Largo di Torre Argentina) is the best preserved of ancient Rome's great monuments. In its current form it dates to around AD 120 when the Emperor Hadrian built over Marcus Agrippa's original 27 BC temple (Agrippa's name remains inscribed on the pediment). The dome, considered the Romans' most important architectural achievement, is the largest masonry vault ever built, a structure so sophisticated that had it been built with modern concrete it would long ago have collapsed under its own weight. Light enters through an oculus, which also acts as a compression ring, absorbing and redistributing the dome's vast structural forces. Inside, you'll find the tomb of Raphael, alongside those of kings Vittorio Emanuele II and Umberto I.

Piazza Navona

A few blocks west of the Pantheon, **Piazza Navona** (Map pp454-5; 🚌 Corso del Rinascimento) showcases the best of baroque Rome. Built over the ruins of the 1st-century Stadio di Domiziano (Domitian's Stadium), it features three ornate fountains. The grand centrepiece is Bernini's 1651 **Fontana dei Quattro Fiumi** (Map pp454-5; Fountain of the Four Rivers), depicting the rivers Nile, Ganges, Danube and Plate. For 300 years the piazza was home to Rome's main market and still today it attracts a colourful crowd of street artists, locals, tourists and pigeons.

Campo de' Fiori & Around

Campo de' Fiori (Map pp454-5; 🚌 Corso Vittorio Emanuele II), affectionately dubbed 'Il Campo', is a major focus of Roman life: by day it hosts a noisy market, and at night it becomes a vast, open-air pub. For centuries, Il Campo was the site of public executions. Most famously, the monk Giordano Bruno, immortalised in the square's sinister statue, was burned here for heresy in 1600.

Nearby, Piazza Farnese is dominated by **Palazzo Farnese** (Map pp454-5; ☎ 06 688 92 818; visitefarnese@france-italia.it; guided tours free, booking obligatory; 🚌 Corso Vittorio Emanuele II), one of Rome's most impressive Renaissance buildings. Commissioned by Cardinal Alessandro Farnese, it was started in 1514 by Antonio da Sangallo, carried on by Michelangelo and completed by Giacomo della Porta. Inside, frescoes by Annibale Carracci are considered on a par with Michelangelo's in the Sisitine Chapel. Visits are by guided tour only as the *palazzo* is now home to the French Embassy.

The twin fountains in the piazza are enormous granite baths taken from the **Terme di Caracalla** (Baths of Caracalla; see p457).

Villa Borghese

Once the estate of Cardinal Scipione Borghese, **Villa Borghese** (Map pp450-1; 🚌 Porta Pinciana) is a good spot for a picnic and a breath of fresh air. Bike hire is available at various points, typically costing about €4 per hour. There are also several museums, including the **Museo e Galleria Borghese** (Map pp450-1; ☎ 06 3 28 10; www.galleriaborghese.it; Piazzale del Museo Borghese; adult/concession €8.50/5.50, plus obligatory booking fee €2; 🕑 8.30am-7.30pm Tue-Sun; 🚌 Via Pinciana), Rome's finest art gallery. With works by Caravaggio, Bernini, Botticelli and Raphael, there are too many highlights to list here, but try not to miss Bernini's *Ratto di*

> **MUSEUM DISCOUNTS**
>
> If you're planning to blitz the sights, consider the **Roma Pass**. Valid for three days, it costs €20 and provides free admission to two museums or sites, as well as unlimited city transport, and reduced entry to other sites, exhibitions and events. It's available at all participating sites and tourist information points.
>
> Note that EU citizens aged between 18 and 25, and students from countries with reciprocal arrangements, generally qualify for a discount (usually half price) at galleries and museums. Under 18s and over 65s often get in free. In all cases you'll need proof of your age, ideally a passport or ID card.

Proserpina (Rape of Persephone) and *Apollo e Dafne*, and the six Caravaggio's in room VII.

In the north of the park is the **Galleria Nazionale d'Arte Moderna** (Map pp450-1; ☎ 06 32 29 81; Viale delle Belle Arti 131; admission €6.50; 🕑 8.30am-7.30pm Tue-Sun; 🚌 Viale delle Belle Arti), a belle époque palace housing 19th- and 20th-century paintings. Nearby, the **Museo Nazionale Etrusco di Villa Giulia** (Map pp450-1; ☎ 06 320 05 62; Piazzale di Villa Giulia; admission €4; 🕑 8.30am-7.30pm Tue-Sun; 🚌 Viale delle Belle Arti) displays Italy's finest collection of Etruscan treasures.

Trevi Fountain

Immortalised by Anita Ekberg's sensual dip in Fellini's *La dolce vita*, the **Fontana di Trevi** (Map pp454-5; Piazza di Trevi; Ⓜ Barberini) was designed by Nicola Salvi in 1732 and depicts Neptune's chariot being led by Tritons, with sea horses representing the moods of the sea. The water comes from the *aqua virgo*, a 1st-century BC underground aqueduct, and the name 'Trevi' refers to the *tre vie* (three roads) that converge at the fountain. The custom is to throw a coin over your shoulder into the fountain, thus ensuring your return to Rome. On an average day about €3000 is chucked away.

Piazza di Spagna & Spanish Steps

A hang-out for flirting adolescents and footsore tourists, **Piazza di Spagna** (Map pp450–1) and the **Spanish Steps** (Scalinata della Trinità dei Monti) have been a magnet for foreigners since the 18th century. Built with a legacy from the French in 1725, but named after the Spanish embassy to the Holy See, the steps were constructed to link the piazza with the well-heeled folks living above it. Looming over the Steps is the **Chiesa della Trinità dei Monti** (Map pp450-1; ☎ 06 679 41 79; Piazza Trinità dei Monti; 🕑 10am-noon & 4-6pm; Ⓜ Spagna).

To the right as you face the steps is the **Keats-Shelley House** (Map pp450-1; ☎ 06 678 42 35; Piazza di Spagna 8; 🕑 9am-1pm & 3-6pm Mon-Fri, 11am-2pm & 3-6pm Sat; Ⓜ Spagna), where Keats spent the last three months of his life in 1821. At the foot of the steps, the fountain of a sinking boat, the **Barcaccia** (1627), is believed to be by Pietro Bernini, father of the more famous Gian Lorenzo. Opposite, **Via dei Condotti** is Rome's top shopping strip.

Piazza del Popolo & Around

One of Rome's landmark squares, **Piazza del Popolo** (Map pp450-1; Ⓜ Flaminio) was laid out in 1538 at the point of convergence of three roads – Via di Ripetta, Via del Corso and Via del Babuino – which form a trident at what was once Rome's northern entrance. Today, this part of central Rome is known as Il Tridente. Guarding the southern approach to the piazza are the twin 17th-century churches of **Santa Maria dei Miracoli** and **Santa Maria in Montesanto.** On the other side of the square, the **Chiesa di Santa Maria del Popolo** (Piazza del Popolo 12; 🕑 7am-noon & 4-7pm Mon-Sat, 8am-1.30pm & 4.30-7.30pm Sun; Ⓜ Flaminio) houses two magnificent Caravaggio's: the *Conversione di San Paolo* (Conversion of St Paul) and the *Crocifissione di San Pietro* (Crucifixion of St Peter). Rising above the piazza is the **Pincio Hill**, which affords great views of the city.

South of the piazza on Via di Ripetta, the **Ara Pacis Augustae** (Altar of Peace; Map pp450-1; ☎ 06 671 03 887; admission €6.50; 🕑 9am-7pm Tue-Sun; Ⓜ Flaminio) is a monument to the peace that Augustus established both at home and abroad. Housed in Richard Meier's controversial white pavilion, it is considered one of the most important works of ancient Roman sculpture.

Museo Nazionale Romano

Spread over five sites, the **Museo Nazionale Romano** (National Roman Museum) houses one of the world's most important collection of classical art and statuary. A combined ticket including each of the sites costs €7 and is valid for three days.

Lovers of ancient sculpture should make a beeline for **Palazzo Altemps** (Map pp454-5; ☎ 06 683 37 59; Piazza Sant'Apollinare 44; 🕑 9am-7.45pm Tue-Sun;

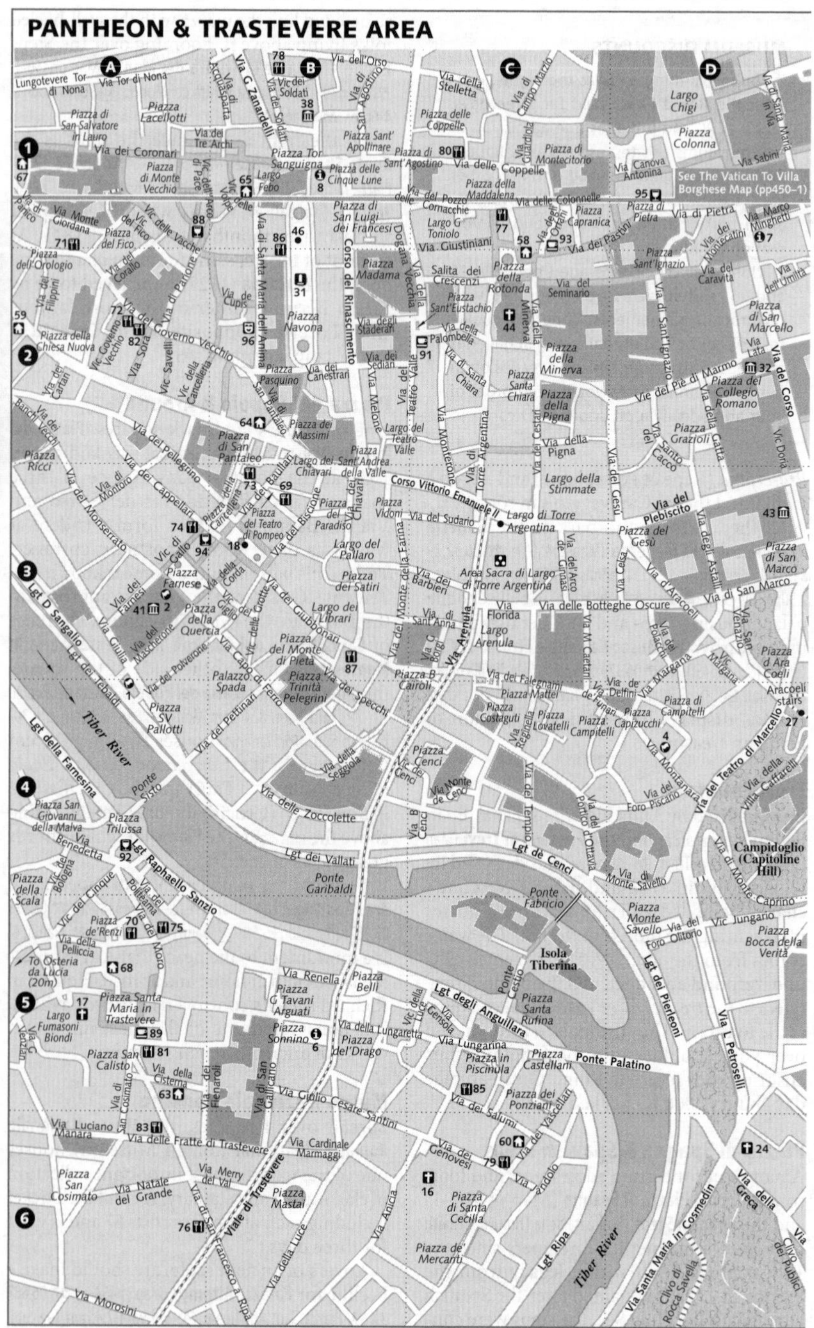
PANTHEON & TRASTEVERE AREA
A
B
C
D
1
2
3
4
5
6
Lungotevere Tor di Nona
Via Tor di Nona
Via di Acquasparta
Via G Zanardelli
Vic dei Soldati
Via dei Soldati
Via dell'Orso
Via di San Agostino
Via della Stelletta
Via di Campo Marzio
Largo Chigi
Via di Santa Maria in Via
Piazza Colonna
Via Sabini
Piazza di San Salvatore in Lauro
Piazza Lancellotti
Via dei Tre Archi
Piazza delle Coppelle
Piazza Sant' Apollinare
Via della Guardiola
Piazza di Montecitorio
Via dei Coronari
Piazza di Monte Vecchio
Vic del Pace
Vic dell'Arco della Pace
Via delle Volpe
Piazza Tor Sanguigna
Largo Febo
Piazza delle Cinque Lune
Piazza di Sant'Agostino
Via delle Coppelle
Piazza della Maddalena
Via Canova
Antonina
See The Vatican To Villa Borghese Map (pp450–1)
Via di Panico
Via Monte Giordana
Vic del Fico
Piazza del Fico
Vic delle Vacche
Via del Pozzo delle Cornacchie
Via delle Colonnelle
Piazza di Pietra
Via di Pietra
Via Marco Minghetti
Piazza dell'Orologio
Via del Corallo
Via di Santa Maria dell'Anima
Piazza di San Luigi dei Francesi
Largo G Toniolo
Via Giustiniani
Piazza Capranica
Via degli Orfani
Via dei Pastini
Via dei Montecatini
Piazza Sant'Ignazio
Via del Caravita
Via dell'Umiltà
Via dei Filippini
Via de' Cupis
Piazza Madama
Dogana Vecchia
Salita dei Crescenzi
Piazza della Rotonda
Via del Seminario
Piazza Sant'Eustachio
Via della Palombella
Piazza di San Marcello
Via del Governo Vecchio
Vic Savelli
Vic Governo Vecchio
Via Sora
Piazza della Chiesa Nuova
Piazza Navona
Corso del Rinascimento
Via degli Staderari
Via dei Sediari
Via della Minerva
Piazza della Minerva
Via di Sant'Ignazio
Via Lata
Via del Corso
Via dei Cartari
Vic della Cancelleria
Piazza Pasquino
Via dei Canestrari
Via del Teatro Valle
Via di Santa Chiara
Piazza Santa Chiara
Piazza della Pigna
Vie del Piè di Marmo
Piazza del Collegio Romano
Via dei Banchi Vecchi
Via di San Pantaleo
Piazza dei Massimi
Via Melone
Largo del Teatro Valle
Via Monterone
Via di Torre Argentina
Via dei Cestari
Via della Pigna
Via della Gatta
Piazza Grazioli
Via del Santo Cacco
Vic Doria
Piazza Ricci
Via del Pellegrino
Piazza di San Pantaleo
Largo dei Sant'Andrea Chiavari della Valle
Largo della Stimmate
Via del Gesù
Via di Montoro
Via dei Cappellari
Via della Cancelleria
Via dei Baullari
Via del Biscione
Via dei Chiavari
Corso Vittorio Emanuele II
Piazza del Teatro di Pompeo
Piazza del Paradiso
Piazza Vidoni
Via del Sudario
Largo di Torre Argentina
Via del Plebiscito
Via degli Astalli
Piazza del Gesù
Via del Monserrato
Vic di Gallo
Largo del Pallaro
Via dell'Arco de' Ginnasi
Piazza di San Marco
Piazza Farnese
Via della Corda
Via dei Farnesi
Piazza dei Satiri
Via dei Barbieri
Area Sacra di Largo di Torre Argentina
Via Celsa
Via d'Aracoeli
Via di San Marco
Lgt D Sangallo
Via Giulia
Via del Mascherone
Vic del Gallo
Piazza della Quercia
Vic delle Grotte
Via dei Giubbonari
Largo dei Librari
Via di Sant'Anna
Via Florida
Via delle Botteghe Oscure
Via di San Venanzio
Largo Arenula
Via C Borgi
Via Arenula
Via M Caetani
Via dei Polacchi
Via del Polverone
Via Capo di Ferro
Piazza del Monte di Pietà
Via del Monte della Farina
Piazza d'Ara Coeli
Lgt dei Tebaldi
Palazzo Spada
Piazza Trinità Pelegrini
Via dei Specchi
Piazza B Cairoli
Via dei Falegnami
Piazza Mattei
Via dei Delfini
Via Margana
Vic Margana
Aracoeli stairs
Tiber River
Piazza SV Pallotti
Via del Pettinari
Piazza Costaguti
Via de' Funari
Piazza Lovatelli
Piazza Campitelli
Piazza Capizucchi
Piazza di Campitelli
Via della Reginella
Lgt della Farnesina
Via della Seggiola
Piazza Cenci
Vic dei Cenci
Via Monte de Cenci
Via Montanara
Via del Teatro di Marcello
Via della Villa Caffarelli
Ponte Sisto
Via delle Zoccolette
Via del Tempio
Via del Portico d'Ottavia
Via del Foro Piscario
Piazza San Giovanni della Malva
Piazza Trilussa
Via Benedetta
Via B Cenci
Lgt dei Vallati
Lgt de Cenci
Campidoglio (Capitoline Hill)
Lgt Raphaello Sanzio
Vic del Bologna
Piazza della Scala
Vic del Cinque
Via del Politeama
Ponte Garibaldi
Via di Monte Savello
Via di Monte Caprino
Ponte Fabricio
Piazza de' Renzi
Via del Moro
Piazza Monte Savello
Via del Foro Olitorio
Vic Jungario
Via della Pelliccia
To Osteria da Lucia (20m)
Isola Tiberina
Piazza Bocca della Verità
Via Renella
Piazza Belli
Piazza G Tavani Arguati
Lgt degli Anguillara
Ponte Cestio
Lgt dei Pierleoni
Largo Fumasoni Biondi
Piazza Santa Maria in Trastevere
Vic della Luce
Via della Gensola
Piazza Santa Rufina
Via G Venezian
Piazza Sonnino
Via della Lungaretta
Via Lungarina
Piazza del Drago
Via L Petroselli
Piazza San Calisto
Via della Cisterna
Via dei Fienaroli
Via di San Gallicano
Piazza in Piscinula
Piazza Castellani
Ponte Palatino
Via di San Cosimato
Via Giulio Cesare Santini
Piazza dei Ponziani
Via dei Salumi
Via dei Vascellari
Via Luciano Manara
Via delle Fratte di Trastevere
Via Cardinale Marmaggi
Via dei Genovesi
Via Anicia
Via Jandolo
Piazza San Cosimato
Via Natale del Grande
Via Merry del Val
Viale di Trastevere
Piazza Mastai
Piazza di Santa Cecilia
Via della Greca
Via di San Francesco a Ripa
Via della Luce
Piazza de' Mercanti
Lgt Ripa
Via Santa Maria in Cosmedin
Clivo di Rocca Savella
Clivo dei Publici
Via Morosini
1
2
4
6
7
8
16
17
18
24
27
31
32
38
41
43
44
46
58
59
60
63
64
65
67
68
69
70
71
72
73
74
75
76
77
78
79
80
81
82
83
85
86
87
88
89
91
92
93
94
95
96

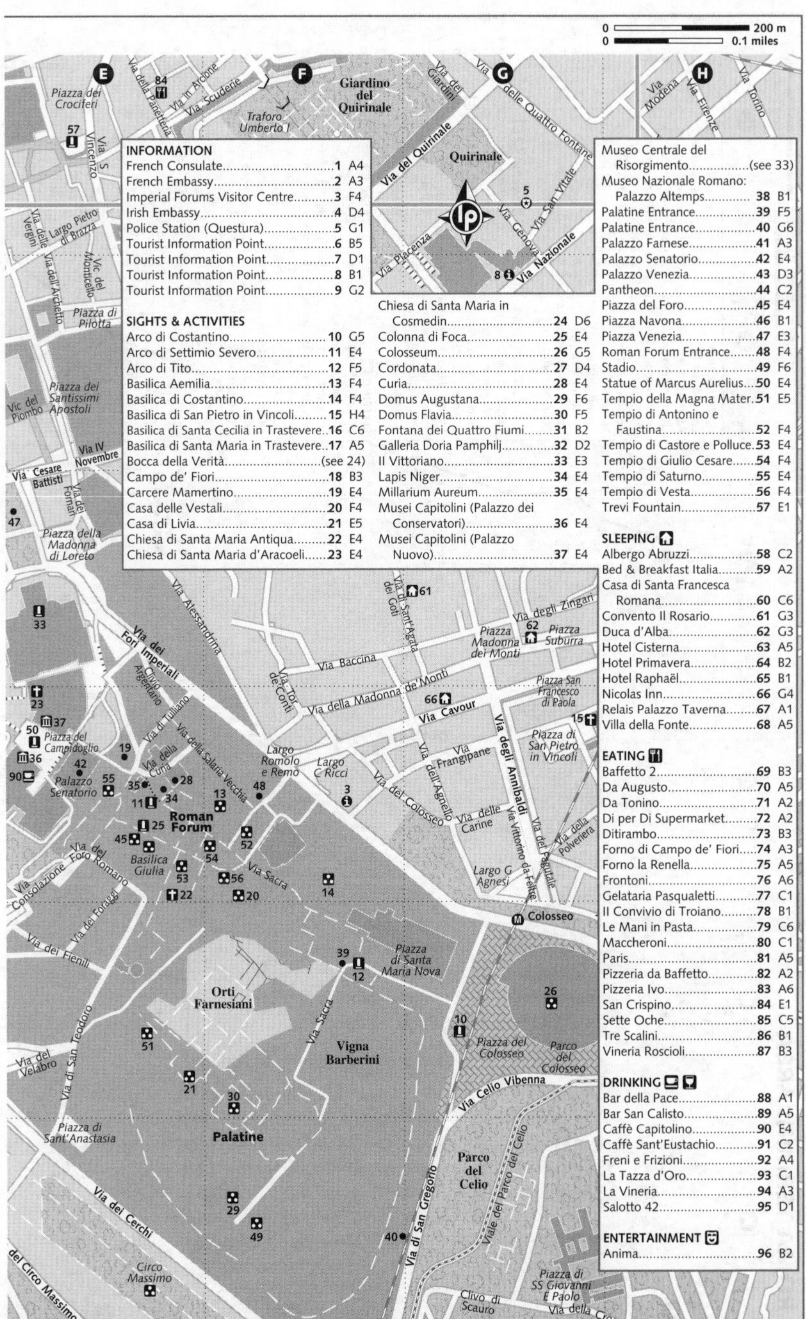
0 200 m
0 0.1 miles
E
F
G
H
INFORMATION
French Consulate....1 A4
French Embassy....2 A3
Imperial Forums Visitor Centre....3 F4
Irish Embassy....4 D4
Police Station (Questura)....5 G1
Tourist Information Point....6 B5
Tourist Information Point....7 D1
Tourist Information Point....8 B1
Tourist Information Point....9 G2
SIGHTS & ACTIVITIES
Arco di Costantino....10 G5
Arco di Settimio Severo....11 E4
Arco di Tito....12 F5
Basilica Aemilia....13 F4
Basilica di Costantino....14 F4
Basilica di San Pietro in Vincoli....15 H4
Basilica di Santa Cecilia in Trastevere..16 C6
Basilica di Santa Maria in Trastevere..17 A5
Bocca della Verità....(see 24)
Campo de' Fiori....18 B3
Carcere Mamertino....19 E4
Casa delle Vestali....20 F4
Casa di Livia....21 E5
Chiesa di Santa Maria Antiqua....22 E4
Chiesa di Santa Maria d'Aracoeli....23 E4
Chiesa di Santa Maria in Cosmedin....24 D6
Colonna di Foca....25 E4
Colosseum....26 G5
Cordonata....27 D4
Curia....28 E4
Domus Augustana....29 F6
Domus Flavia....30 F5
Fontana dei Quattro Fiumi....31 B2
Galleria Doria Pamphilj....32 D2
Il Vittoriano....33 E3
Lapis Niger....34 E4
Millarium Aureum....35 E4
Musei Capitolini (Palazzo dei Conservatori)....36 E4
Musei Capitolini (Palazzo Nuovo)....37 E4
Museo Centrale del Risorgimento....(see 33)
Museo Nazionale Romano: Palazzo Altemps....38 B1
Palatine Entrance....39 F5
Palatine Entrance....40 G6
Palazzo Farnese....41 A3
Palazzo Senatorio....42 E4
Palazzo Venezia....43 D3
Pantheon....44 C2
Piazza del Foro....45 E4
Piazza Navona....46 B1
Piazza Venezia....47 E3
Roman Forum Entrance....48 F4
Stadio....49 F6
Statue of Marcus Aurelius....50 E4
Tempio della Magna Mater....51 E5
Tempio di Antonino e Faustina....52 F4
Tempio di Castore e Polluce....53 E4
Tempio di Giulio Cesare....54 F4
Tempio di Saturno....55 E4
Tempio di Vesta....56 F4
Trevi Fountain....57 E1
SLEEPING
Albergo Abruzzi....58 C2
Bed & Breakfast Italia....59 A2
Casa di Santa Francesca Romana....60 C6
Convento Il Rosario....61 G3
Duca d'Alba....62 G3
Hotel Cisterna....63 A5
Hotel Primavera....64 B2
Hotel Raphaël....65 B1
Nicolas Inn....66 G4
Relais Palazzo Taverna....67 A1
Villa della Fonte....68 A5
EATING
Baffetto 2....69 B3
Da Augusto....70 A5
Da Tonino....71 A2
Di per Di Supermarket....72 A2
Ditirambo....73 B3
Forno di Campo de' Fiori....74 A3
Forno la Renella....75 A5
Frontoni....76 A6
Gelataria Pasqualetti....77 C1
Il Convivio di Troiano....78 B1
Le Mani in Pasta....79 C6
Maccheroni....80 C1
Paris....81 A5
Pizzeria da Baffetto....82 A2
Pizzeria Ivo....83 A6
San Crispino....84 E1
Sette Oche....85 C5
Tre Scalini....86 B1
Vineria Roscioli....87 B3
DRINKING
Bar della Pace....88 A1
Bar San Calisto....89 A5
Caffè Capitolino....90 E4
Caffè Sant'Eustachio....91 C2
Freni e Frizioni....92 A4
La Tazza d'Oro....93 C1
La Vineria....94 A3
Salotto 42....95 D1
ENTERTAINMENT
Anima....96 B2
Piazza dei Crociferi
Giardino del Quirinale
Traforo Umberto I
Quirinale
Via del Quirinale
Via delle Quattro Fontane
Via Nazionale
Via Piacenza
Via Genova
Via San Vitale
Via Torino
Via Firenze
Via Modena
Via dei Giardini
Via della Panetteria
Via in Arcione
Via Scuderie
Via S Vincenzo
Largo Pietro di Brazzà
Via dell'Archetto
Vic del Monticello
Piazza di Pilotta
Piazza dei Santissimi Apostoli
Vic del Piombo
Via IV Novembre
Via Cesare Battisti
Via dei Fornari
Piazza della Madonna di Loreto
Via Alessandrina
Via dei Fori Imperiali
Clivo Argentario
Via di Tulliano
Via della Salaria Vecchia
Via della Curia
Piazza del Campidoglio
Palazzo Senatorio
Roman Forum
Basilica Giulia
Via del Foro Romano
Via Consolazione
Via dei Foraggi
Via dei Fienili
Via Sacra
Largo Romolo e Remo
Largo C Ricci
Via del Colosseo
Via Baccina
Via Tor de' Conti
Via della Madonna de' Monti
Via Cavour
Via di Sant'Agata dei Goti
Via degli Zingari
Piazza Madonna dei Monti
Piazza Suburra
Piazza San Francesco di Paola
Via degli Annibaldi
Piazza di San Pietro in Vincoli
Via Frangipane
Via dell'Agnello
Via delle Carine
Via Vittorino da Feltre
Via del Fagutale
Via della Polveriera
Largo G Agnesi
Colosseo
Piazza di Santa Maria Nova
Orti Farnesiani
Vigna Barberini
Piazza del Colosseo
Parco del Colosseo
Via Celio Vibenna
Via del Velabro
Via di San Teodoro
Palatine
Piazza di Sant'Anastasia
Via dei Cerchi
Via del Circo Massimo
Circo Massimo
Via di San Gregorio
Parco del Celio
Viale del Parco del Celio
Piazza di SS Giovanni E Paolo
Clivo di Scauro
Via della Croce

ITALY

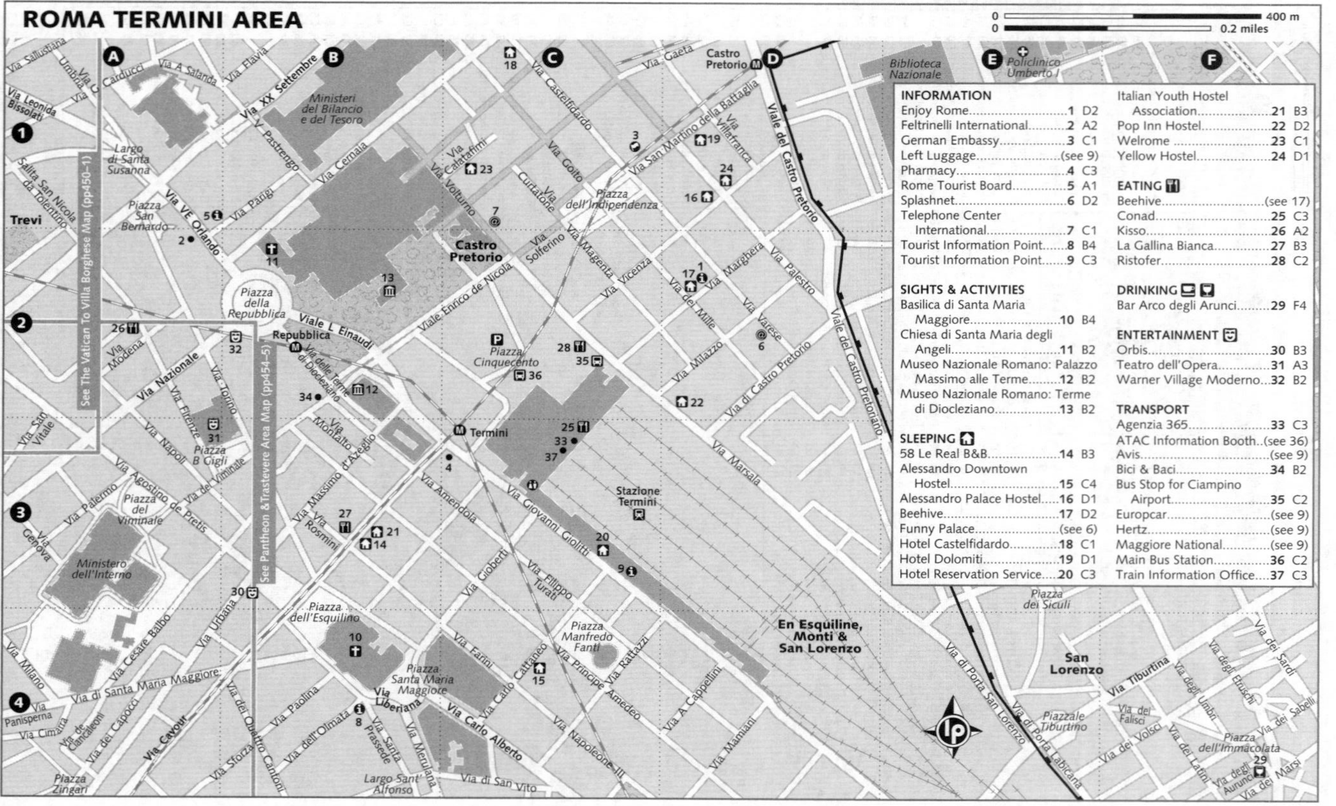
ITALY
ROMA TERMINI AREA
0 400 m
0 0.2 miles
INFORMATION
Enjoy Rome....1 D2
Feltrinelli International....2 A2
German Embassy....3 C1
Left Luggage....(see 9)
Pharmacy....4 C3
Rome Tourist Board....5 A1
Splashnet....6 D2
Telephone Center International....7 C1
Tourist Information Point....8 B4
Tourist Information Point....9 C3
SIGHTS & ACTIVITIES
Basilica di Santa Maria Maggiore....10 B4
Chiesa di Santa Maria degli Angeli....11 B2
Museo Nazionale Romano: Palazzo Massimo alle Terme....12 B2
Museo Nazionale Romano: Terme di Diocleziano....13 B2
SLEEPING
58 Le Real B&B....14 B3
Alessandro Downtown Hostel....15 C4
Alessandro Palace Hostel....16 D1
Beehive....17 D2
Funny Palace....(see 6)
Hotel Castelfidardo....18 C1
Hotel Dolomiti....19 D1
Hotel Reservation Service....20 C3
Italian Youth Hostel Association....21 B3
Pop Inn Hostel....22 D2
Welrome....23 C1
Yellow Hostel....24 D1
EATING
Beehive....(see 17)
Conad....25 C3
Kisso....26 A2
La Gallina Bianca....27 B3
Ristofer....28 C2
DRINKING
Bar Arco degli Arunci....29 F4
ENTERTAINMENT
Orbis....30 B3
Teatro dell'Opera....31 A3
Warner Village Moderno....32 B2
TRANSPORT
Agenzia 365....33 C3
ATAC Information Booth....(see 36)
Avis....(see 9)
Bici & Baci....34 B2
Bus Stop for Ciampino Airport....35 C2
Europcar....(see 9)
Hertz....(see 9)
Maggiore National....(see 9)
Main Bus Station....36 C2
Train Information Office....37 C3
See The Vatican To Villa Borghese Map (pp450–1)
See Pantheon & Trastevere Area Map (pp454–5)
En Esquiline, Monti & San Lorenzo

(Corso del Rinascimento) near Piazza Navona. This lovely 15th-century *palazzo* holds the best of the museum's classical sculpture, with many pieces from the Ludovisi collection.

Up near Termini, **Palazzo Massimo alle Terme** (Map p456; 06 399 67 700; Largo di Villa Peretti 1; 9am-7.45pm Tue-Sun; Termini) features yet more sculpture, although the highlights are the amazing frescoes and wall paintings on the 2nd floor. Nearby, the **Terme di Diocleziano** (Baths of Diocletian; Map p456; 06 488 05 30; Via Enrico de Nicola 79; 9am-7.45pm Tue-Sun; Termini) are a sight in themselves. Built at the turn of the 3rd century, they were Rome's largest baths complex, covering 13 hectares and capable of accommodating 3000 people. Nowadays, they are home to a large selection of archaeological artefacts, sarcophagi and terracotta objects.

Trastevere

Trastevere is one of central Rome's most vivacious neighbourhoods, a tightly packed district of ochre *palazzi*, ivy-clad facades and photogenic lanes. Taking its name from the Latin *trans Tiberium*, meaning over the Tiber, it was originally a working-class district but it has since been gentrified and today it's a trendy hang-out full of bars, trattorias and restaurants.

Trastevere's focal point is Piazza Santa Maria in Trastevere. Here, nestled in a quiet corner, is the **Basilica di Santa Maria in Trastevere** (Map pp454-5; 06 581 48 02; Piazza Santa Maria in Trastevere; 7.30am-12.30pm & 3.30-7.30pm; Viale di Trastevere), believed to be the oldest Roman church dedicated to the Virgin Mary. The original church dates to the 4th century, but a 12th-century makeover saw the addition of a Romanesque bell tower and frescoed facade. Inside it's the glittering 12th-century mosaics that are the main drawcard.

Over on the eastern side of Trastevere, the **Basilica di Santa Cecilia in Trastevere** (Map pp454-5; 06 589 92 89; Piazza di Santa Cecilia; basilica/fresco free/€2; basilica 9am-12.30pm & 4-6.30pm, fresco 10.15am-noon Mon-Sat, 11.15am-12.15pm Sun; Viale di Trastevere) harbours fragments of a spectacular 13th-century fresco, Pietro Cavallini's *The Last Judgement*.

Appia Antica & the Catacombs

Known to the ancient Romans as the *regina viarum* (queen of roads), Via Appia Antica (Appian Way) was named after Appius Claudius Caecus, who laid the first 90km section in 312 BC. It was extended in 190 BC to reach Brindisi some 540km away on the Adriatic coast. It was on Via Appia Antica that Spartacus and 6000 of his slave rebels were crucified in 71 BC and it's here that you'll find Rome's most celebrated catacombs.

The easiest way to get to the road is to take Metro Line A to Colli Albani, then bus 660. It's traffic-free on Sunday if you want to walk or cycle it. For information on bike hire or to join a guided tour, head to the **Appia Antica Regional Park Information Point** (Map pp444-5; 06 513 53 16; www.parcoappiaantica.org; Via Appia Antica 58-60; 9.30am-5.30pm summer, to 4.30pm winter; Via Appia Antica).

Rome's extensive network of catacombs was built as communal burial grounds. A Roman law banned burials within the city walls, and persecution left the early Christians little choice but to dig. On Via Appia Antica, you can visit the **Catacombs of San Callisto** (Map pp444-5; 06 446 56 10; Via Appia Antica 110; adult/concession €5/3; 9am-noon & 2-5pm Thu-Tue, until 5.30pm Jun-Sep, closed Feb; Via Appia Antica), Rome's largest, most famous and busiest catacombs, and, a short walk away, the **Catacombs of San Sebastiano** (Map pp444-5; 06 785 03 50; Via Appia Antica 136; adult/concession €5/3; 9am-noon & 2-5pm Mon-Sat, until 5.30pm Jun-Sep, closed mid-Nov–mid-Dec; Via Appia Antica).

Terme di Caracalla

The vast ruins of the **Terme di Caracalla** (Baths of Caracalla; Map pp444-5; 06 39 96 77 00; Via delle Terme di Caracalla 52; admission €6; 9am-1hr before sunset Tue-Sun, to 2pm Mon; Circo Massimo) are an awe-inspiring sight. Begun by Caracalla and inaugurated in AD 217, the 10-hectare leisure complex could hold up to 1600 people and included richly decorated pools, gymnasiums, libraries, shops and gardens. The baths were used until 537 and the ruins are now used to stage summer opera.

Churches & Cathedrals

One of Rome's four patriarchal basilicas, the **Basilica di Santa Maria Maggiore** (Map p456; 06 48 31 95; Piazza Santa Maria Maggiore; 7am-7pm, to 6pm winter; Piazza Santa Maria Maggiore) was built by Pope Liberius in AD 352 after the Virgin Mary instructed him to construct a church on the spot where the next snow fell. An architectural hybrid, it has a 14th-century Romanesque belfry; an 18th-century baroque facade, a largely baroque interior and some stunning 5th-century mosaics on the triumphal arch and nave.

Similarly impressive is the great white **Basilica di San Giovanni in Laterano** (Map pp444-5; ☎ 06 698 86 433; Piazza di San Giovanni in Laterano 4; 7am-7pm, to 6pm winter; M San Giovanni). Consecrated in 324 AD, this was the first Christian basilica to be built in Rome and, until the late 14th century, was the pope's principal residence. Nowadays, it's Rome's official cathedral and the pope's seat as Bishop of Rome. It has been rebuilt various times over the centuries, most notably in the late 18th century when the monumental facade was added.

Just off Via Cavour, the **Basilica di San Pietro in Vincoli** (Map pp454-5; Piazza di San Pietro in Vincoli; 8am-12.30pm & 3-7pm; M Cavour) displays Michelangelo's magnificent *Moses*, as well as the chains worn by St Peter before his crucifixion; hence the church's name (St Peter in Chains).

The **Basilica di San Clemente** (Map pp444-5; ☎ 06 774 00 21; Via di San Giovanni in Laterano; 9am-12.30pm & 3.30-6.30pm; M Colosseo), east of the Colosseum, is a multilayered affair. The 12th-century church at street level was built over a 4th-century church that was, in turn, built over a 1st-century Roman house with a temple dedicated to the pagan god Mithras.

Considered one of the finest medieval churches in Rome, the **Chiesa di Santa Maria in Cosmedin** (Map pp454-5; ☎ 06 678 14 19; Piazza della Bocca della Verità 18; 9am-1pm & 2.30-6pm; Via dei Cerchi) is most famous for the **Bocca della Verità** (Mouth of Truth) in its portico. Legend has it that if you put your right hand into the stone mouth and tell a lie, it will bite your hand off.

Facing onto Piazza della Repubblica, the hulking **Chiesa di Santa Maria degli Angeli** (Map p456; Piazza della Repubblica; 7am-6.30pm Mon-Sat, to 7.30pm Sun; M Repubblica) occupies what was once the central hall of Diocletian's enormous baths complex (see p453). Its most interesting feature is the double meridian in the transept.

Piazza Venezia & Around

Piazza Venezia is dominated by the mountain of white marble that is **Il Vittoriano** (Map pp454-5; Piazza Venezia), aka the Altare della Patria. Begun in 1885 to commemorate Italian unification and honour Victor Emmanuel II, it incorporates the **tomb of the Unknown Soldier**, as well as the **Museo Centrale del Risorgimento** (☎ 06 679 35 98; Via San Pietro in Carcere; admission free; 9.30am-6pm), documenting Italian unification. Over the square, the 15th-century **Palazzo Venezia** (Map pp454-5; ☎ 06 699 94 318; Via del Plebiscito 118; admission €4; 8.30am-7.30pm Tue-Sun) was the first of Rome's great Renaissance *palazzi*. Mussolini had his office here and there's now a museum of medieval and Renaissance art.

Just off Via del Corso, the **Galleria Doria Pamphilj** (Map pp454-5; ☎ 06 679 73 23; www.doriapamphilj.it; entrance at Piazza del Collegio Romano 2; admission €8; 10am-5pm Fri-Wed; Piazza Venezia) boasts one of Rome's finest private art collections, with works by Raphael, Tintoretto, Brueghel and Titian.

Galleria Nazionale d'Arte Antica

A must for anyone into Renaissance and baroque art, the **Galleria Nazionale d'Arte Antica** (Map pp450-1; ☎ 06 481 45 91; www.galleriaborghese.it; Via Quattro Fontane 13; admission €5; 8.30am-7pm Tue-Sun; M Barberini) is housed in the spectacular Palazzo Barberini, itself a notable work of art. Inside, you'll find works by Raphael, Caravaggio, Guido Reni, Bernini, Filippo Lippi and Holbein, as well as Pietro da Cortona's breathtaking *Trionfo della Divina Provvidenza* (Triumph of Divine Providence) in the main salon.

FESTIVALS & EVENTS

Rome's year-round festival calendar ranges from the religious to the ribald with traditional religious/historical celebrations, performing arts festivals and an international film festival. Summer and autumn are the best times to catch an event.

March–May

Easter On Good Friday the pope leads a candlelit procession around the Colosseum. At noon on Easter Sunday he blesses the crowds in St Peter's Square.

Settimana della Cultura Public museums and galleries open free of charge during culture week, held between March and May.

Natale Di Roma (21 April) Rome celebrates its birthday with music and fireworks.

Primo Maggio (May 1) Rome's biggest open-air rock concert attracts huge crowds to Piazza di San Giovanni.

June–August

Estate Romana Between June and September, Rome's big cultural festival hosts events ranging from book fairs to raves and gay parties.

Festa dei Santi Pietro e Paolo (June 29) Romans celebrate patron saints Peter and Paul around St Peter's Basilica and Via Ostiense.

Festa di Noantri Trastevere's annual party takes over the neighbourhood for the last two weeks of July.
Festa della Madonna della Neve (August 5) A miraculous 4th-century snowfall is celebrated at the Basilica di Santa Maria Maggiore.

September–November

Romaeuropa Rome's premier music and dance festival runs from late September to November.
Festival International del Film di Roma Rome's film festival rolls out the red carpet for Hollywood big guns in October (from 15 to 23 October in 2009).

SLEEPING

There's no point beating around the bush, Rome is expensive. If you can afford it, the best place to stay is in the *centro storico*, but if you're on a tight budget you'll probably end up in the Termini area, where many hostels and cheap *pensioni* (guest houses) are located. Always try to book ahead, even if it's just for the first night. **Rome Tourist Board** (www.romaturismo.it) has a full accommodation listing. For B&Bs or longer-term accommodation, try www.cross-pollinate.com.

If you arrive without a booking, there's a hotel **reservation service** (Map p456; ☎ 06 699 10 00; booking fee €3; 7am-10pm) next to the tourist office at Stazione Termini. The head office of the **Italian Youth Hostel Association** (Map p456; ☎ 06 487 11 52; www.ostellionline.org; Via Cavour 44) has information about youth hostels throughout the country.

Budget

Camping Internazionale Castelfusano (off Map pp444-5; ☎ 06 562 33 04; www.romacampingcastelfusano.it; sites per person/tent/car €9.50/4/5, 2-person bungalows €32-48;) Immersed in seafront shrubbery near Ostia, this is a well-equipped camping ground with tent pitches, bungalows, a mini-market and kids playground. Take bus 061 from Via Cristoforo Colombo near Fermi metro station.

Pop Inn Hostel (Map p456; ☎ 06 495 98 87; www.popinnhostel.com; Via Marsala 80; dm €16-31, s €40-105, d €42-120) A backpacker favourite, the Pop Inn is relaxed, lively and no-frills. Of the various sleeping options the six-bed mixed dorms are the best value. Extras are thin on the ground but you get 15 minutes free at a nearby internet point and discounts at a local laundry. Rooms with shared bathrooms are available at the cheaper rates listed.

Alessandro Palace Hostel (Map p456; ☎ 06 44 61 958; www.hostelsalessandro.com; Via Vicenza 42; dm €18-24, d €66-120, tr €58-144;) One of the slicker Termini hostels, this buzzing spot offers spick-and-span hotel-style rooms, as well as four- to six-person dorms. It's run by a friendly international crew and its brick-vaulted bar is a great place to catch up with fellow travellers. On the other side of Termini, Alessandro Downtown Hostel (Map p456) offers more of the same.

Yellow Hostel (Map p456; ☎ 06 493 82 682; www.the-yellow.com; Via Palestro 44; dm €18-38;) No place for shrinking violets, the Yellow is a hardcore hostel for a young, fit crowd. Dorms are mixed and, while clean and reasonably sized, they can be noisy. There's no common room but most people hang out in the bar or games room. Extras include free internet, wi-fi and left luggage.

Beehive (Map p456; ☎ 06 447 04 553; www.the-beehive.com; Via Marghera 8; dm €20-25, d €70-80;) A brilliant boutique hostel run by an environmentally conscious American couple, the Beehive boasts quiet rooms, a vegetarian cafe and a small walled garden. Environmental touches include homemade soap and recycling bins.

Colors Hotel & Hostel (Map pp450-1; ☎ 06 687 40 30; www.colorshotel.com; Via Boezio 31; dm €20-27, d €65-130, tr €75-145;) A laid-back hostel-cum-hotel near the Vatican, Colors has spotless, multicoloured dorms, snazzy private rooms and superhelpful staff. Hostel-stayers can cook in the fully equipped kitchen and dine alfresco on the tiny terrace. Rooms with shared bathrooms are available at the cheaper rates listed.

Funny Palace (Map p456; ☎ 06 447 03 523; www.funnyhostel.com; Via Varese 33; dm €20-30, d €79-89;) To find this popular hostel head for the Splashnet laundry, which doubles as the reception and internet point. Upstairs, the mixed dorms are big, sleeping up to 14 people, but are clean and well maintained. No credit cards.

Welrome (Map p456; ☎ 06 478 24 343; www.welrome.it; Via Calatafimi 15-19; s €50-100, d €50-110) This is a lovely, low-key hotel. Owner Mary takes great pride in looking after her guests, and her seven rooms provide welcome respite from Rome's relentless streets. Breakfast costs extra.

Convento Il Rosario (Map pp454-5; ☎ 06 679 23 46; irodopre@tin.it; Via di Sant'Agata dei Goti 10; s/d €55/98) In the cobbled Monti area, this is a quiet, convent-run guest house. It's fairly basic but

ITALY

the location is good, the rates are excellent and the rooms are perfectly comfortable. Note the 11pm curfew and cash-only payment.

Hotel Panda (Map pp450-1; ☎ 06 678 01 79; www.hotelpanda.it; Via della Croce 35; s €63-75, d €98-108, tr €130-140, q €170-180;) A budget bolthole near the Spanish Steps, the Panda is deservedly popular. Its superb position, attractive high-ceilinged rooms and honest rates ensure a year-round stream of travellers. Air-con costs €6 and wi-fi is available. No breakfast.

Also recommended is **Hotel Castelfidardo** (Map p456; ☎ 06 446 46 38; www.hotelcastelfidardo.com; Via Castelfidardo 31; s €40-70, d €60-100), a family-run one-star not far from Stazione Termini.

ITALY

Midrange

Hotel Dolomiti (Map p456; ☎ 06 495 72 56; www.hotel-dolomiti.it; Via San Martino della Battaglia 11; s €60-100, d €80-150, tr €110-180, q €135-225;) A warm, family-run hotel, the Dolomiti is a reliable choice, offering comfortable, airy rooms, attractive bathrooms and value-for-money rates.

58 Le Real B&B (Map p456; ☎ 06 482 35 66; www.58viacavour.it; Via Cavour 58; r €70-150;) This swish 12-room B&B is on the 4th floor of a towering 19th-century townhouse. Room decor is a stylish mix of leather armchairs, plasma TVs, Murano chandeliers, polished-wood bedsteads and parquet floors. Topping everything is a panoramic roof terrace.

Casa di Santa Francesca Romana (Map pp454-5; ☎ 06 581 21 25; www.sfromana.it; Via dei Vascellari 61; s/d/tr/q €80/115/150/175;) This Catholic-run inn is housed in a 15th-century *palazzo* in Trastevere. Rooms are fairly bland but the downstairs public rooms exude character and the cloistered garden is a delight with its perfumed orange trees.

Relais Palazzo Taverna (Map pp454-5; ☎ 06 203 98 064; www.relaispalzzotaverna.com; Via dei Gabrielli 92; s €80-150, d €100-210, tr €120-240;) Boutique style at less than designer prices is the drawcard here. That, and a perfect location in a quiet *centro storico* cul-de-sac. Each of the 11 individually decorated rooms sports a contemporary look with hand-printed wallpaper and funky, floral motifs.

Hotel Cisterna (Map pp454-5; ☎ 06 58 17 212; www.cisternahotel.it; Via della Cisterna 7-9; s/d €90/140;) Offering a prime location near Trastevere's Piazza Santa Maria in Trastevere, the Cisterna has bright modest rooms with creamy yellow walls and unobtrusive furniture. Service is courteous and there's a small internal courtyard.

Nicolas Inn (Map pp454-5; ☎ 06 976 18 483; www.nicolasinn.com; Via Cavour 295; d €100-180;) This bright B&B is at the bottom of Via Cavour, a stone's throw from the Forums. It has four big guest rooms, each with homely furnishings, colourful pictures and large, en suite bathrooms. Breakfast is available in a nearby bar any time between 5am and 11am.

Villa della Fonte (Map pp454-5; ☎ 06 580 37 97; www.villafonte.com; Via della Fonte dell'Olio 8; s €110-120, d €150-180;) Near Piazza Santa Maria in Trastevere, this charming little hotel is a gem. The five rooms are simple but tasteful with white walls, earth-coloured floors and modern en suite bathrooms. Outside, a picturesque garden terrace is a good place for a sundowner.

our pick **Daphne Inn** (Map pp450-1; ☎ 06 874 50 086; www.daphne-rome.com; Via di San Basilio 55 & Via degli Avignonesi 20; s €110-160, d €90-200, ste €320-550;) Daphne is a star. Spread over two sites near Piazza Barberini, it offers value for money, exceptional service and fashionably attired rooms. The look is modern with cooling earth tones, leather chairs and linear, unfussy furniture. Particularly eye-catching are the stunning suites at the Daphne Trevi. Extras include irons and boards, tea and coffee-making sets.

Also recommended is **Hotel Primavera** (Map pp454-5; ☎ 06 688 03 109; www.hotelprimavera-roma.eu; Piazza di San Pantaleo 3; s €70-100, d €90-130;), a modest, fairly priced *pensione* overlooking Corso Vittorio Emanuele II.

Top End

Duca d'Alba (Map pp454-5; ☎ 06 48 44 71; www.hotelducadalba.it; Via Leonina 14; s €70-210, d €80-260, tr €100-290;) Small but refined, the Duca d'Alba is on an atmospheric street near Cavour metro station. No two rooms are exactly alike but the best are decked out with leather bedsteads, blond parquet and contemporary art. At the time of writing there were plans to introduce a fitness area, wine bar and internet point.

Hotel Bramante (Map pp450-1; ☎ 06 688 06 426; www.hotelbramante.com; Via delle Palline 24; s €100-160, d €150-240;) Housed in a Renaissance *palazzo* by the Vatican City wall, this charmer is a model of effortless elegance. Antique furniture, wood-beamed ceilings, marble bathrooms and fresh flowers combine to create an inviting small-inn feel.

Albergo Abruzzi (Map pp454-5; ☎ 06 679 20 21; www.hotelabruzzi.it; Piazza della Rotonda 69; s €140-170, d €195-220; ❄) More than the rooms, what you're paying for here, and paying a lot for, is the location – bang opposite the Pantheon. That said, the 80 rooms are perfectly attractive with parquet and cherry-wood furnishings. They are small, though, and noise from the piazza can be a nuisance.

Hotel Raphaël (Map pp454-5; ☎ 06 68 28 31; www.raphaelhotel.com; Largo Febo 2; s €200-280, d €250-350; ❄ 💻) An ivy-clad landmark just off Piazza Navona, the Raphaël is a Roman institution. With its gallery lobby – look out for the Picasso ceramics and Miro lithographs – and sleek Richard Meier–designed rooms, this place knows how to lay out the red carpet. Breakfast is not included.

EATING

Like all Italians, Romans love eating out. The best places to eat are in the *centro storico* and Trastevere, but there are also excellent choices in San Lorenzo and Testaccio. The Termini area is best avoided although you'll find some decent takeaways, particularly around Piazza Vittorio Emanuele II.

Roman specialities include *trippa alla Romana* (tripe with potatoes, tomato and pecorino cheese), *fiori di zucca* (fried courgette flowers) and *carciofi alla romana* (artichokes with garlic, mint and parsley). Of the pastas, *cacio e pepe* (with pecorino cheese, black pepper and olive oil) and *all'amatriciana* (with tomato, pancetta and chilli) are Roman favourites.

City Centre & Jewish Ghetto

Gusto (Map pp450-1; ☎ 06 322 62 73; Piazza Augusto Imperatore 9; pizzas €8) This big, '90s-style warehouse operation is a lunchtime favourite with local office workers, serving everything from thick-crust pizza to cheese platters, salads and overpriced fusion food. At lunch the €9 salad buffet is a good bet.

Pizzeria da Baffetto (Map pp454-5; ☎ 06 686 16 17; Via del Governo Vecchio 114; pizzas €8; 🕑 6.30pm-1am) For the full-on, Roman pizza experience get down to this local institution. Meals here are raucous, chaotic and fast, but the thin-crust pizza's good and the vibe is fun. To partake, join the queue and wait to be squeezed in wherever there's room. There's now a Baffetto 2 (☎ 06 682 10 807) on Piazza del Teatro di Pompeo 18 (Map pp454–5) near Campo de' Fiori (note that it's closed Tuesdays).

Da Tonino (Map pp454-5; ☎ 06 687 70 02; Via del Governo Vecchio 18; meals €18; 🕑 Mon-Sat) This low-key neighbourhood trattoria sits among the bohemian boutiques and trendy bars on fashionable Via del Governo Vecchio. It's old-school so don't expect frills, just filling Roman cooking served fast and served cheap.

Maccheroni (Map pp454-5; ☎ 06 683 07 895; Piazza delle Coppelle 44; meals €35) Popular with locals and tourists alike, this is the archetypal *centro storico* trattoria. It's boisterous, busy and fancy-free with a classic Roman menu and an attractive setting near the Pantheon. Reliable staples include *cacio e pepe*, *amatriciana* and *trippa*.

Ditirambo (Map pp454-5; ☎ 06 687 16 26; Piazza della Cancelleria 72; meals €40; 🕑 closed Sun lunch) Beautifully located near Campo dei' Fiori, this hugely popular trattoria has made a name for itself with innovative, organic cooking. Vegetarians are catered for, as are seafood fans with dishes such as sea bass with wholemeal pasta, artichoke and mint.

Vineria Roscioli (Map pp454-5; ☎ 06 687 52 87; Via dei Giubbonari 21; meals €55; 🕑 Mon-Sat) Worth a look even if you're not going to eat here, this is a foodie paradise. Under the brick arches, you'll find a mouth-watering array of olive oils, conserves, cheeses and hams, while out back the small restaurant serves classic Italian dishes. Wine buffs can peruse the 1100-strong wine list. Glasses of wine are available from €4.50.

Il Convivio de Troiani (Map pp454-5; ☎ 06 68 69 432; www.ilconviviotroiani.com; Vicolo dei Soldati 31; meals €100; 🕑 Mon-Sat) One for a special occasion, this swish restaurant is one of the best in Rome. Menus are seasonal but always luxurious, so you could find yourself sitting down to roasted quails with semolina dumplings, spicy mango and foie gras sauce. The wine list runs to more than 2000 labels and service is impeccable.

Trastevere, Testaccio & The Vatican

Pizzeria Remo (Map pp444-5; ☎ 06 574 62 70; Piazza Santa Maria Liberatice 44; pizzas €6) One of Rome's most popular pizzerias, this rowdy Testaccio spot is a favourite with young Saturday-nighters. Queues are the norm but the large, thin-crust pizzas and delicious *bruschette* (toasted bread drizzled with olive oil and selected toppings) make the chaos bearable.

Pizzeria Ivo (Map pp454-5; ☎ 06 581 70 82; Via di San Francesco a Ripa 158; pizzas €6; Wed-Mon) A perennially popular Trastevere pizzeria, Ivo fits the stereotype. With the TV on in the corner and waiters skilfully manoeuvring plates over the noisy hordes, diners chow down on classic thin-crust pizzas. If you don't fancy pizza, there's a range of grilled meats and *scamorza* (smoked cheese).

Volpetti Più (Map pp444-5; ☎ 06 574 43 06; Via A Volta 8; meals €10-15) A sumptuous *tavola calda*, this is one of the few places in town where you can sit down and eat well for less than €15. Choose from pizza, pasta, soup, meat, vegetables and fried nibbles.

Da Augusto (Map pp454-5; ☎ 06 580 37 98; Piazza de' Renzi 15; meals €23; lunch & dinner Mon-Fri, lunch Sat Sep-Jul) You don't get any frills here, just old-fashioned Mamma-style cooking served by a team of jaded waiters. The menu is rigorously Roman, so expect dishes like *rigatoni all' amatriciana* followed by *involtini in sugo* (meat rolls in tomato sauce).

our pick **Dino e Tony** (Map pp450-1; ☎ 06 397 33 284; Via Leone IV 60; meals €25; Mon-Sat) Something of a rarity, Dino e Tony is an authentic trattoria in the Vatican area. Famous for its *amatriciana*, it serves a monumental antipasto that might well see you through to dessert. If you've got room, finish up with a *granita di caffé*, a crushed ice coffee served with a full inch of whipped cream.

Sette Oche (Map pp454-5; ☎ 06 58 09 753; Via dei Salumi 36; lunch & drink €6.50-7.50, meals €25; Tue-Sun) Duck down into the cool, whitewashed interior for a relaxed glass of wine, tasty food and occasional live music. Particularly good is the house antipasto (€10.50), a grand platter of cheeses and cold cuts.

Osteria da Lucia (off Map pp454-5; ☎ 06 580 36 01; Via del Mattinato 2; meals €28; Tue-Sun) In an atmospheric corner of Trastevere, da Lucia is a terrific neighbourhood trattoria. It's a good place to get your teeth into some authentic *trippa alla romano*.

Le Mani in Pasta (Map pp454-5; ☎ 06 58 16 017; Via dei Genovesi 37; meals €32; Tue-Sun) This tasty Trastevere *osteria* specialises in pasta and grilled mains. Try *fettucine con ricotta e pancetta* (ribbon pasta with ricotta cheese and bacon) followed by grilled scampi.

Paris (Map pp454-5; ☎ 06 581 53 78; Piazza San Calisto 7; meals €50; lunch & dinner Tue-Sat, lunch Sun) Outside of the Jewish Ghetto, this elegant, old-fashioned restaurant is the best place for traditional Roman-Jewish cooking. Specialities include *carciofi alle giudia* (deep-fried artichoke) and *fritto misto con baccalà* (fried vegetables with salted cod).

Termini & San Lorenzo

Ristofer (Map p456; Via Marsala 13; meals €7.50) Huge helpings for hungry workers. Rome's railway workers' canteen serves the cheapest full meals in Rome and although the food is hardly cordon bleu, it does the job. Ideal for travellers wanting a fill-up before a long train journey.

Kisso (Map p456; ☎ 06 478 24 677; Via Firenze 30; meals €12-35; Mon-Sat) An affordable and popular Japanese restaurant just off Via Nazionale. Sushi and sashimi dishes range from €13.50 to €48, making the €12 lunchtime menu seem even better value. Sit yourself on a stool and pick three dishes off the conveyor belt to go with soup, tofu and salad.

Beehive (Map p456; ☎ 06 447 04 553; Via Marghera 8; meals €20) In the hostel of the same name (see p459), this small organic cafe serves delicious vegetarian food. The menu changes daily but staples include homemade pasta, quiches, vegie burgers and couscous. You can also order packed lunches, and on Sunday brunch is served between 7am and 1pm.

Vecchia Roma (Map pp444-5; ☎ 06 446 71 43; Via Ferruccio 12; meals €20; Mon-Sat) Good, filling food at reasonable prices is what you get at this brick-vaulted trattoria near Piazza Vittorio Emanuele. The buffet antipasto sets you off well, whetting the appetite for classic pastas such as spaghetti *cacio e pepe* and traditional main courses.

La Gallina Bianca (Map p456; ☎ 06 474 37 77; Via Rosmini 9; meals €30, pizzas from €6) On a small street off Via Cavour, this choice restaurant offers a welcome respite from the tourist rip-off joints near Termini. It specialises in grilled vegetables and meats, although its supersized salads (€9.50) make for a lovely lunch. Pizza is also available.

Pommidoro (Map pp444-5; ☎ 06 445 26 92; Piazza dei Sanniti 44; meals €35; Mon-Sat) A much-loved San Lorenzo institution, Pommidoro continues to do what it has always done – serve traditional food to crowds of appreciative diners. Celebs often drop by, including in recent times Nicole Kidman and Fabio Capello, but it's an unpretentious place with a laid-back vibe and excellent food.

Tram Tram (Map pp444-5; ☎ 064 470 25 85; Via dei Reti 44; meals €50; Tue-Sun) Taking its name from the

ICE CREAM, YOU SCREAM, WE ALL SCREAM FOR ICE CREAM

To get the best out of Rome's *gelaterie* (ice-cream parlours) look for the words 'produzione proprio', meaning 'own production'. Here is a choice of the city's finest:

- **San Crispino** (Map pp454-5; Via della Panetteria 42) Near the Trevi Fountain, this place sells the best gelato in Rome. Flavours are natural and seasonal – think *crema* with honey – and served in tubs only.
- **Old Bridge** (Map pp450-1; Via Bastioni di Michelangelo 5) The huge helpings sold at this hole in the wall work wonders after the Vatican Museums.
- **Tre Scalini** (Map pp454-5; Piazza Navona 30) This Piazza Navona spot is famous for its *tartufo nero*, a €10 ball of chocolate ice cream filled with chunks of choc and served with cream.
- **Gelateria Pasqualetti** (Map pp454-5; Piazza della Maddalena 3a) Serves superb cream-based and fruit ice creams just around the corner from the Pantheon.

trams that rattle past outside, this is a trendy San Lorenzo eatery. Seafood from southern Italy is the house speciality – if it's on, try the *riso, cozze e patate* (rice, mussels and potato) – and the excellent wine list highlights small producers.

Quick Eats & Self-Catering

Self-caterers can stock up at Rome's produce markets that generally operate from 7am to 1.30pm. They include Campo de' Fiori; the Nuovo Mercato Esquilino, near Piazza Vittorio Emanuele; Piazza San Cosimato in Trastevere; and Piazza Testaccio.

Frontoni (Map pp454-5; Viale di Trastevere 52-56) Get a panino made up at the downstairs deli or head upstairs for a sit-down bowl of pasta for about €7.

Forno la Renella (Map pp454-5; Via del Moro 15-16) Follow your nose to this historic Trastevere bakery and choose from the daily batch of delicious wood-fired pizza, bread, and biscuits.

Forno di Campo de' Fiori (Map pp454-5; Campo de' Fiori 22) Aficionados claim you should order pizza *bianca* (white pizza) here, although the panini and pizza *rossa* (with tomato) is just as good.

Supermarkets are thin on the ground in the centre, but you'll find a **Conad** (Map p456; 6am-midnight) at Termini station, and a **Di per Di** (Map pp454-5; Via del Governo Vecchio 119; 8am-9pm) near Piazza Navona.

DRINKING

Drinking in Rome is all about looking the part and enjoying the atmosphere. Hardcore boozing does take place, mainly on Campo dei' Fiori, but Rome is not really a heavy drinking town. There are an inordinate number of bars and cafes across the city, as well as a growing number of pubs.

Much of the action is in the *centro storico*, on Campo de' Fiori and around Piazza Navona. Over the river, Trastevere is another popular spot with dozens of bars and pubs. To the east of Termini, San Lorenzo is a favourite of students and bohemian uptowners.

Cafes

our pick **Caffè Sant'Eustachio** (Map pp454-5; Piazza Sant'Eustachio 82) Aficionados claim that this unassuming cafe serves the best coffee in Rome. And, after extensive research, we agree. Served sugared and with a layer of froth, the espresso is unique, a smooth, creamy blend with a reassuringly strong caffeine kick.

La Tazza d'Oro (Map pp454-5; Via degli Orfani 84-86) Not only does this busy, stand-up bar serve a superb espresso, but it also does a mean *granita di caffè*, a crushed-ice coffee concoction, served with a big dollop of cream.

Caffè Capitolino (Map pp454-5; Musei Capitolini, Piazza del Campidoglio) Hidden behind the Musei Capitolini, this stylish cafe commands memorable views. It's a good place for a museum timeout, although you don't need a ticket to drink here – it's accessible via an entrance behind Piazza dei Conservatori.

Bars & Pubs

Bar San Calisto (Map pp454-5; Piazza San Calisto; Mon-Sat) Drug dealers, drunks, bohemian diners, foreign students – they all flock to this Trastevere landmark for the cheap prices and laid-back atmosphere. It's famous for its chocolate, drunk hot or eaten as ice cream.

La Vineria (Map pp454-5; Campo de'Fiori 15) A good spot to watch the nightly Campo de' Fiori circus, this is the hippest of the square-side bars. It has a small, bottle-lined interior and several outside tables.

Bar della Pace (Map pp454-5; Via della Pace 3-7) Style hounds looking for the archetypal *dolce vita* bar should stop here. With its art nouveau interior, ivy-clad facade and well-dressed customers, it's the very epitome of Italian style.

Bar Arco degli Aurunci (Map p456; Via degli Aurunci 42) On a car-free piazza in San Lorenzo, this attractive modern bar is a cool spot for a drink or light meal. Come between 7pm and 9pm and you can combine the two by ordering an *aperitivo* (€7, including buffet).

Salotto 42 (Map pp454-5; Piazza di Pietra; 4pm-2am Tue-Sat, to midnight Sun) A laid-back living-room bar on a picturesque *centro storico* piazza. Salotto 42 is hip yet unpretentious with soft sofas, coffee-table books and an excellent *aperitivo* spread.

Freni e Frizioni (Map pp454-5; Piazza Trilussa) In a bohemian corner of Trastevere, this is one of the in-spots for *aperitivo*. It's housed in a former garage (hence the name – 'brakes and clutches') and attracts a young, fashionable crowd.

ENTERTAINMENT

In the past few years there's been a marked increase in the quality, and quantity, of concerts in Rome. That said, the music scene remains conservative and nightclubbers will find little to compare with the club scene in Berlin, say, or London. Lovers of jazz and classical music are better served with a year-round calendar of concerts and festivals, many of which are staged in beautiful outdoor settings.

The best listings guide is *Roma C'è* (www.romace.it, in Italian), with an English-language section, published on Wednesday (€1.50). Another useful guide is *Trova Roma*, a free insert with *La Repubblica* newspaper every Thursday. Both are available at newsstands.

Two good ticket agencies are **Orbis** (Map p456; ☎ 06 48 27 403; Piazza dell'Esquilino 37; 9.30am-1pm & 4-7.30pm Mon-Fri, 9.30am-1pm Sat) and the online agency **Hello** (☎ 800 90 70 80; www.helloticket.it, in Italian).

Classical Music & Opera

Rome's premier concert complex is the **Auditorium Parco della Musica** (Map pp444-5; ☎ 06 802 41 281; www.auditorium.com; Viale Pietro de Coubertin 34). With its three concert halls and 3000-seater open-air arena, it stages everything from Beethoven to Bjork.

The auditorium is also home to Rome's top classical-music organisation, the **Accademia di Santa Cecilia** (☎ box office 06 808 20 58; www.santacecilia.it), which organises a world-class symphony season and short festivals dedicated to single composers. The **Accademia Filarmonica Romana** (☎ 06 320 17 52; www.filarmonicaromana.org) concentrates on classical and chamber music, although it also stages opera, ballet and multimedia events at the **Teatro Olimpico** (Map pp444-5; ☎ 06 326 59 91; www.teatroolimpico.it; Piazza Gentile da Fabriano 17).

Rome's opera season runs from December to June. The main venue is the **Teatro dell'Opera** (Map p456; ☎ 06 481 601; www.operaroma.it; Piazza Beniamino Gigli 7), which also houses the city's ballet company. Ticket prices tend to be steep. In summer, opera is performed outdoors at the spectacular Terme di Caracalla (see p457).

Nightclubs & Live Music

Rome's nightclub scene is centred on Testaccio and the up-and-coming Ostiense area, although you'll also find places in Trastevere and the *centro storico*. You'll need to dress the part to get into the big clubs, which rarely get going much before midnight. Admission is often free but drinks are expensive, typically €10 to €15.

AKAB (Map pp444-5; Via Monte Testaccio 68-69) One of the most popular clubs on the Testaccio clubbing strip, AKAB serves a steady supply of house, R&B and techno. Sweat to the tunes in the underground cellar or chill in the Zen garden.

Alexanderplatz (Map pp450-1; ☎ 06 397 42 171; www.alexanderplatz.it; Via Ostia 9) Rome's top jazz joint attracts international performers and a passionate, knowledgeable crowd. In July and August the club ups sticks and transfers to the grounds of Villa Celimontana.

Anima (Map pp454-5; Via di Santa Maria dell' Anima 57) A young crowd of Romans and tourists squeeze into this cool *centro storico* bar to get close over a cocktail and high-octane hip hop. Come early for a drink or drop by late to dance.

Big Mama (Map pp444-5; ☎ 06 581 24 51; www.bigmama.it; Via San Francesco a Ripa 18) This Trastevere basement is Rome's self-styled home of blues. It plays host to the world's top blues musicians and stages soul, jazz and funk.

Goa (Map pp444-5; Via Libetta 13) Top DJs whip the dressed-up crowd into a house-induced frenzy at Rome's top mega-club. Last Sunday of the month is lesbian night with 'Venus Rising'.

Villaggio Globale (Map pp444-5; Lungotevere Testaccio) This alternative venue is housed in Rome's ex-slaughterhouse. The scene is cheap beer, spliff and dreadlocks, and the gigs, including a recent set by the Prodigy, are great.

Cinema

Several cinemas show films in English, including the **Warner Village Moderno** (Map p456; ☎ 892 11 11; Piazza della Repubblica 45/46), showing Hollywood blockbusters and Italian films, and the **Metropolitan** (Map pp450-1; ☎ 06 320 09 33; Via del Corso 7), a four-screen multiplex near Piazza del Popolo. Expect to pay €7 to €7.50, with discounts on Wednesday.

SHOPPING

Shopping is fun in Rome. With everything from designer flagship stores to antique emporiums, flea markets and bohemian boutiques, there's something for all tastes.

For the big-gun designer names head for Via dei Condotti and the area between Piazza di Spagna and Via del Corso. Moving down a euro or two, Via Nazionale, Via del Corso, Via dei Giubbonari and Via Cola di Rienzo are good for midrange clothing stores. For something more left field, try the small fashion boutiques and vintage clothes shops on Via del Governo Vecchio. Trastevere also has some interesting offbeat shops.

The best places for art and antiques are Via dei Coronari and Via Margutta, where the shops resemble galleries and the prices exhibit no mercy. A cheaper option is to try one of the city's markets. The most famous, **Porta Portese** (Map pp444-5; 🕑 7am-1pm Sun) is held every Sunday morning near Trastevere and sells everything from antiques to clothes, bikes, bags and furniture. Near Porta San Giovanni, the **Via Sannio market** (Map pp444-5; Via Sannio; 🕑 morning Mon-Sat) sells new and secondhand shoes and clothes.

GETTING THERE & AWAY

Air

Rome's main international airport **Leonardo da Vinci** (FCO; ☎ 06 6 59 51; www.adr.it), better known as Fiumicino, is on the coast 30km west of the city. The much smaller **Ciampino airport** (CIA; ☎ 06 6 59 51; www.adr.it), 15km southeast of the city centre, is the hub for low-cost carriers including **Ryanair** (www.ryanair.com) and **easyJet** (www.easy jet.com).

Boat

Rome's main port is at Civitavecchia, about 80km north of Rome. The main ferry companies:

Corsica Sardinia Ferries (☎ 199 400 500; www.sardiniaferries.com) For Golfo Aranci, Sardinia.
Grimaldi Lines (☎ 091 58 74 04; www.grimaldi.it) For Barcelona, Toulon and Tunis.
SNAV (☎ 081 428 55 55; www.snav.it) For Palermo and Olbia.
Tirrenia ☎ 892 123; www.tirrenia.it) For Sardinia – Arbatax, Cagliari and Olbia.

Bookings can be made at the Termini-based **Agenzia 365** (Map p456; 🕑 8am-8pm), at travel agents or online at www.traghettionline.net. You can also buy directly at the port.

Half-hourly trains depart from Roma Termini to Civitavecchia (€4.50 to €8.50, one hour). On arrival, it's about a 15-minute walk to the port (to your right) as you exit the station.

See p550 for more information on ferry companies and routes.

Bus

Long-distance national and international buses use the bus terminus on Piazzale Tiburtina, in front of Stazione Tiburtina. Take metro line B from Termini to Tiburtina.

You can get tickets from the offices next to the bus terminus or at travel agencies. National companies include the following:

ARPA (☎ 199 166 952; www.arpaonline.it) For L'Aquila and Abruzzo.
Cotral (www.cotralspa.it, in Italian) For the Lazio region.
Interbus (☎ 0935 56 51 11; www.interbus.it, in Italian) For destinations in Sicily, including Messina, Catania and Palermo.
Marozzi (☎ 080 579 01 11; www.marozzivt.it, in Italian) To/from Sorrento, Bari, Matera and Lecce.
SAIS (☎ 091 616 60 28; www.saisautolinee.it, in Italian) For Sicily.
SENA (☎ 0577 20 82 82; www.senabus.it) To/from Siena, Milan and Bologna.
Sulga (☎ 800 099 661; www.sulga.it) For Perugia, Assisi and Ravenna.

Car & Motorcycle

It's no holiday driving into central Rome. You'll have to deal with traffic restrictions, one-way systems, an almost total lack of street parking and a few hundred thousand lunatics vying for your road space.

Rome is circled by the Grande Raccordo Anulare (GRA) to which all *autostrade* (motorways) connect, including the main A1 north–south artery (the Autostrada del Sole), and the A12, which connects Rome to Civitavecchia and Fiumicino airport.

From Rome, these are the most important roads:

SS1 (Via Aurelia) Heads northeast from the Vatican, following the coast to Pisa and Genoa.
SS2 (Via Cassia) Connects with Viterbo, Siena and Florence.
SS3 (Via Flaminia) Parallel to Via Cassia before forking northeast to Le Marche.
SS4 (Via Salaria) For Rieti and Le Marche.
SS5 (Via Tiburtina) Links Rome with Tivoli and Pescara.
SS7 (Via Appia Nuova) Heads south, via Ciampino airport, to Brindisi.
SS8 (Via del Mare/Via Ostiense) Via del Mare heads southwest to Ostia; it becomes Via Ostiense inside the GRA.

Car-hire offices at Stazione Termini include **Avis** (☎ 06 481 43 73; www.avis.com), **Europcar** (☎ 06 488 28 54; www.europcar.com), **Hertz** (☎ 06 474 03 89; www.hertz.com) and **Maggiore National** (☎ 06 488 00 49; www.maggiore.com). All have offices at both airports as well.

Near Termini, **Bici & Baci** (Map p456; ☎ 06 482 84 43; www.bicibaci.com; Via del Viminale 5; 8am-7pm) rents out scooters from €19 per day and motorbikes from €95.

Train

Almost all trains arrive at and depart from Stazione Termini. There are regular connections to other European countries, all major Italian cities, and many smaller towns. On the main concourse, the **train information office** (Map p456; 7am-9.45pm) is helpful (English is spoken) but often very busy. To avoid the queues, you can get information online at www.trenitalia.com or, if you speak Italian, by calling ☎ 89 20 21.

Rome's second train station is Stazione Tiburtina, a short ride away on metro line B.

GETTING AROUND

To/From the Airport

FIUMICINO

The efficient *Leonardo Express* train service leaves from platform 24 at Stazione Termini and travels direct to the airport every 30 minutes from 5.52am until 10.52pm. It costs €11 and takes about 30 minutes. From Fiumicino, trains start at 6.35am and run half-hourly until 11.35pm.

If you want to get to Termini from the airport, don't take the train marked Orte or Fara Sabina. These slower trains stop at Trastevere, Ostiense and Tiburtina stations but not Termini. They cost €5.50 and run every 15 minutes (hourly on Sunday and public holidays) from 5.57am to 11.27pm, and from Tiburtina between 5.06am and 10.36pm.

During the night, **Cotral** (www.cotralspa.it, in Italian) runs a bus from Stazione Tiburtina via Stazione Termini to Fiumicino. It departs Tiburtina at 12.30am, 1.15am, 2.30am and 3.45am, returning at 1.15am, 2.15am, 3.30am and 5am. Tickets, available on the bus, cost €4.50 to the airport and €7 from the airport.

The set taxi fare to/from the city centre is €40, which is valid for up to four passengers with luggage.

CIAMPINO

Terravision (☎ 06 454 41 345; www.terravision.eu) buses depart from Via Marsala outside Stazione Termini two hours before each scheduled flight and from Ciampino soon after flight arrivals. Get tickets (€8) online, on board, from Agenzia 365 at Stazione Termini or at Ciampino airport.

Alternatively, **SIT** (☎ 06 591 68 26; www.sitbusshuttle.com) covers the same route, with regular departures from Termini between 4.30am and 9.15pm, and from Ciampino between 8.30am and midnight. Buy tickets (€6) on board.

Cotral runs two night services: from Termini at 4.45am and 4.50am, and from Ciampino at 11.50pm and 12.15am. Tickets (€5) are available on the bus.

Regular Cotral buses connect with Anagnina metro station (€1.20, about 15 minutes) where you can get the metro direct to Stazione Termini. Another option is to get a local orange bus to Ciampino train station (€1) from where regular trains connect with Termini.

By taxi the set rate to/from Ciampino is €30.

Car & Motorcycle

Driving in Rome is exhilarating, terrifying, fun and often pointless, given the perpetual gridlock. Riding a scooter is hairier but gives you greater freedom and makes parking easier.

Most of the historic centre is closed to normal traffic. You're not allowed to drive in the centre from 6.30am to 6pm Monday to Friday and from 2pm to 6pm Saturday unless you're a resident or have special permission.

Parking is no fun. Blue lines denote pay-and-display spaces with tickets available from meters (coins only) and *tabacchi* (tobacconists). Costs vary but in the centre expect to pay at least €1 per hour between 8am and 8pm. If your car gets towed away, check with the **traffic police** (☎ 06 6 76 91). It will cost at least €100 to get it back, plus a hefty fine.

The most convenient car park is at Villa Borghese; entry is from Piazzale Brasile at the top of Via Vittorio Veneto. There are also supervised car parks at Stazione Termini; at Piazzale dei Partigiani, just outside Stazione Roma-Ostiense; and at Stazione Tiburtina.

See p465 for information about car and scooter rental.

Public Transport

Rome has an integrated public transport system, so the same ticket is valid for all modes of transport: bus, tram, metro and suburban railway. You can buy tickets at *tabacchi*, newsstands and from vending machines at main bus stops and metro stations. Single tickets cost €1 for 75 minutes, during which time you can use as many buses or trams as you like but only go once on the metro. Daily tickets cost €4 and give you unlimited trips; a three-day ticket costs €11; and a weekly ticket €16. Tickets must be purchased before you get on the bus/train and validated in the yellow machine, or at the entrance gates for the metro. Ticketless riders risk an on-the-spot €50 fine.

Rome's buses and trams are run by **ATAC** (☎ 06 57 003; www.atac.roma.it). The **main bus station** (Map p456; Piazza dei Cinquecento) is in front of Stazione Termini, where there's an **information booth** (🕑 7.30am-8pm). Largo di Torre Argentina, Piazza Venezia and Piazza San Silvestro are also important hubs. Buses generally run from about 5.30am until midnight, with limited services throughout the night.

The Metropolitana has two lines, A and B, which both pass through Termini. Take line A for the Trevi Fountain (Barberini), Spanish Steps (Spagna), and Vatican (Ottaviano-San Pietro); and line B for the Colosseum (Colosseo) and Circus Maximus (Circo Massimo). Trains run on line B between 5.30am and 11.30pm (1.30am on Friday and Saturday) and to 10pm on line A. From 10pm until 11.30pm (1.30am on Friday and Saturday) two temporary bus lines follow metro line A: MA1 from Battistini to Arco di Travertino, and MA2 from Viale G Washington (off Piazzale Flaminio) to Anagnina.

Taxi

Rome's taxi drivers are no better or worse than in any other city. Some will try to fleece you, others won't. To minimise the risk make sure your taxi is licensed and metered, and always go with the metered fare, never an arranged price (the set fares to and from the airports are exceptions to this rule). Official rates are posted in taxis.

You can't hail a taxi, but there are major taxi ranks at the airports, Stazione Termini and Largo di Torre Argentina. To phone, try the following:

Cosmos (☎ 06 8 81 77)
La Capitale (☎ 06 49 94)
Pronto Taxi (☎ 06 66 45)
Radio Taxi (☎ 06 35 70)
Samarcanda (☎ 06 55 51)
Tevere (☎ 06 41 57)

AROUND ROME

OSTIA ANTICA

An easy day trip from Rome, Ostia Antica is well worth a visit. Ostia was ancient Rome's port, and the clearly discernible ruins of restaurants, laundries, shops, houses and public meeting places give a good impression of what life must once have been like in the 100,000-strong town. It was founded in the 4th century BC and thrived until the 5th century AD, when barbarian invasions and an outbreak of malaria led to its eventual abandonment, and its slow burial in river silt, thanks to which it has survived so well.

The **ruins** (☎ 06 563 58 099; adult/concession €6.50/3.25; 🕑 8.30am-6pm Apr-Sep, to 5pm Mar & Oct, to 4pm Nov-Feb) are spread out and you'll need a few hours to do them justice. Highlights include the **Terme di Nettuno** (Baths of Neptune) and adjacent **amphitheatre**, built by Agrippa and later enlarged to hold 3000 people. Behind it, the **Piazzale delle Corporazioni** (Forum of the Corporations) housed Ostia's merchant guilds and is decorated with well-preserved mosaics.

To get to Ostia Antica from Rome take metro line B to Piramide, then the Ostia Lido train (25 minutes, half-hourly). The journey is covered by standard public transport tickets (see p467). By car, take Via del Mare or Via Ostiense.

TIVOLI

pop 51,850

An ancient resort town and playground for the Renaissance rich, hilltop Tivoli is home to two Unesco-listed sites: Villa Adriana and Villa d'Este. The former is Emperor Hadrian's vast villa complex; the latter a Renaissance villa famous for its garden fountains. Both warrant the easy 30km journey from Rome.

Information is available at the **tourist information kiosk** (☎ 0774 31 35 36; Piazzale delle Nazioni Unite; 🕑 10am-2pm & 3-6pm Tue-Sun, morning only Aug) near the bus stop at the top of the hill.

Sights

Five kilometres from Tivoli proper, Hadrian's sprawling summer residence, **Villa Adriana** (☎ 0774 38 27 33; with/without exhibition €10/6.50; 🕑 9am-6pm summer, to 3.30pm winter), dates to the 2nd century AD. One of the largest and most sumptuous villas in the Roman Empire, it was subsequently plundered for building materials, although enough remains to convey its magnificence.

The Renaissance **Villa d'Este** (☎ 0774 33 34 04; Piazza Trento; with/without exhibition €9/6.50; 🕑 8.30am-6.45pm Tue-Sun summer, to 4pm winter) was built in the 16th century for Cardinal Ippolito d'Este. More than the villa itself, it's the elaborate gardens and their spectacular fountains that are the main attraction.

A short walk from the villa, the **Parco Villa Gregoriana** (☎ 06 399 67 701; adult/child €4/2.50; 🕑 10am-6.30pm Tue-Sun summer, to 2.30pm winter) descends down a steep gorge, over which water crashes to the bottom 100m below.

Getting There & Away

Tivoli is 30km east of Rome and accessible by Cotral bus (€2, one hour, every 20 minutes) from outside Ponte Mammolo station on metro line B. The fastest route by car is on the Rome–L'Aquila *autostrada* (A24).

To get to Villa Adriana from Tivoli town centre, take CAT bus 4X (€1, 10 minutes, hourly) from Largo Garibaldi.

TARQUINIA

pop 16,200

Some 90km northwest of Rome, Tarquinia is the most famous of Lazio's Etruscan centres. The highlight is the magnificent Unesco-listed necropolis, but the fascinating Etruscan museum is the best outside of Rome, and the atmospheric medieval quarter is a lovely place for a stroll. Founded in the 12th century BC, Tarquinia grew to rival Athens, and its kings were among the first rulers of the nascent city of Rome. It reached its prime in the 4th century BC, before a century of struggle ended with surrender to Rome in 204 BC.

The **tourist information office** (☎ 0766 84 92 82; Piazza Cavour 1; 🕑 8am-2pm Mon-Sat) is just inside the town's medieval gate (Barriera San Giusto).

Sights

Beautifully housed in the 15th-century Palazzo Vitelleschi, the **Museo Nazionale Tarquiniense** (☎ 0766 85 60 36; Piazza Cavour; admission €6, incl necropolis €8; 🕑 8.30am-7.30pm Tue-Sun) is a treasure trove of Etruscan artefacts. Highlights include a beautiful terracotta frieze of winged horses (the Cavalli Alati); a room full of painted friezes; displays of sarcophagi, jewellery and amphorae; and some plates embellished with illustrations of acrobatic sex. The Etruscans were famous for their sexual dexterity and the words 'Etruscan' and 'prostitute' were apparently often used interchangeably.

The 7th-century-BC **necropolis** (☎ 0766 85 63 08; Via Ripagretta; admission €6, incl museum €8.50; 🕑 8.30am-6.30pm Tue-Sun summer, to 2pm winter) is 2km outside of the town centre. Almost 6000 tombs have been excavated since the first digs in 1489, of which 60 are painted, including the Tomba della Caccia e della Pesca, Tomba delle Leonesse, and Tomba della Fustigazione. To get to the necropolis take bus D (€0.60, seven daily) from outside the tourist office.

Sleeping & Eating

Tarquinia is a long day trip from Rome. If you want to overnight, the tourist office can provide details of local B&Bs, the best bet for the historic centre. If you're after a bite to eat, the **Trattoria Arcadia** (☎ 0766 85 55 01; Via Mazzini 6; meals €30) serves excellent seafood and delicious grilled meat.

Getting There & Away

The easiest way to get to Tarquinia is by train – take the Pisa train from Termini (€6.20, 1¼ hours, seven daily). At Tarquinia station take bus BC (€0.60, every 30 to 50 minutes) to the town centre.

By car, take the *autostrada* for Civitavecchia and then Via Aurelia (SS1).

CERVETERI

pop 33,400

With its hilltop *centro storico* and haunting Etruscan tombs, Cerveteri makes a rewarding day trip from Rome. Cerveteri was one of the most important commercial centres in the Mediterranean from the 7th to the 5th century BC. But as Roman power grew so Cerveteri's fortunes faded, and in 358 BC the city was annexed by Rome.

The superhelpful **tourist office** (☎ 06 995 51 971; Piazza Risorgimento 19; 9.30am-12.30pm & 5-7.30pm Tue-Sat) can provide information on local sites, accommodation and transport.

Cerveteri's Etruscan tombs are concentrated in the Unesco-listed **Necropoli di Banditaccia** (☎ 06 994 00 01; Piazzale Moretti; admission €6, incl museum €8; 8.30am-6.30pm Tue-Sun summer, 8.30am-3.30pm Tue-Sun winter). The tombs are built into *tumoli* (mounds of earth with carved stone bases), laid out in the form of a town. The best preserved is the 6th-century-BC **Tomba dei Rilievi**, adorned with painted reliefs depicting household items and cooking implements. To get to the necropolis take bus G from the town centre.

In town you can get decent pizza at **Trattoria Pizzeria Roma** (☎ 06 994 0040; Via Roma 22; pizzas €7; closed Mon). For something more upmarket book a table at the **Antica Locanda Le Ginestre** (☎ 06 994 06 72; Piazza Santa Maria 5; meals €50; closed Mon), one of Lazio's top restaurants.

Cerveteri is accessible from Rome by Cotral bus (€2.50, 1¼ hours, every 45 minutes) from outside Cornelia station on metro line A.

NORTHERN ITALY

Italy's well-heeled north is a fascinating area of historical wealth and natural diversity. Bordered by the northern Alps and boasting some of the country's most spectacular coastline, it also encompasses Italy's largest lowland area, the decidedly nonpicturesque Po Valley plain. Of the cities it's Venice that hogs the limelight, but in their own way Turin, Genoa and Bologna offer plenty to the open-minded traveller. Verona is justifiably considered one of Italy's most beautiful cities, while the medieval centres of Padua, Ferrara and Ravenna all reward the visitor.

GENOA

pop 615,700

Genoa (Genova) is a city of aristocratic *palazzi* (mansions, palaces) and malodorous alleyways, of Gothic architecture and industrial sprawl. You need only walk the labyrinthine, sometimes seedy, streets of the *centro storico* to feel its raw energy. Birthplace of Christopher Columbus (1451–1506) and home to Europe's largest aquarium, it was once a powerful maritime republic known as La Superba; nowadays it's a fascinating port city that's worth a stopover, particularly as it's the gateway to the magnificent Cinque Terre National Park.

Orientation & Information

Central Genoa is concentrated between the two main train stations: Stazione Brignole and Stazione Principe. The central shopping strip, Via XX Settembre, starts a short walk southwest of Stazione Brignole and leads up to Piazza de Ferrari. From adjacent Piazza Giacomo Matteotti, Via San Lorenzo leads to the waterfront and historic centre.

For information, head to the **tourist office** (☎ 010 868 74 52; www.apt.genova.it; Piazza Giacomo Matteotti; 9.30am-7.45pm). For information about the port, go to its **information booth** (10am-7pm). Check your email at **Nondove Internet Point** (Corso Buenos Aires 2; per hr €5; 9.30am-7.30pm) near Brignole train station.

Sights

Genoa's central square, Piazza de Ferrari, is a good place to start exploring the city. Grandiose and impressive, it's flanked by imposing *palazzi* – **Palazzo della Borsa** (closed to the public), the city's historic opera house, **Teatro Carlo Felice**, and the huge **Palazzo Ducale** (☎ 010 557 40 04; www.palazzoducale.genova.it, in Italian; entrance Piazza Giacomo Matteotti 9; admission varies according to exhibition; 9am-6.30pm Tue-Sun).

A short walk west, the 12th-century **Cattedrale di San Lorenzo** (Piazza San Lorenzo; 8-11.45am & 3-6.45pm) is most notable for its stunning Italian Gothic facade.

Genoa's **Porto Antico** (Old Port; ☎ information 010 248 57 10; www.portoantico.it) was given a makeover before the city's stint as European City of Culture in 2004. The main point of interest is the **Acquario di Genova** (☎ 010 234 56 78;

www.acquariodigenova.it; Ponte Spinola; adult/child €16/10; 9am-7.30pm Mon-Fri, 8.45am-8.30pm Sat & Sun Mar-Jun, Sep & Oct, 8.30am-10pm Jul & Aug, 9.30am-7.30pm Mon-Fri, 9.30am-8.30pm Sat & Sun Jan, Feb, Nov & Dec), Europe's largest aquarium. Designed by architect Renzo Piano, it houses 5000 animals in six million litres of water.

Genoa's main museums are in a series of *palazzi* on Via Garibaldi. The three most important, known collectively as the **Musei di Strada Nuova** (010 247 63 51; adult/child €8/6; 9am-7pm Tue-Fri, from 10am Sat & Sun), are housed in **Palazzo Bianco** (www.museopalazzobianco.it; Via Garibaldi 11), **Palazzo Rosso** (www.museopalazzorosso.it; Via Garibaldi 18) and **Palazzo Doria-Tursi** (www.museopalazzotursi.it; Via Garibaldi 9). The first two feature works by Flemish, Dutch, Spanish and Italian old masters, while the third displays the personal effects of Niccolò Paganini, Genoa's legendary violinist. Tickets, valid for all three museums, are available from the bookshop in Palazzo Doria-Tursi.

Sleeping

Ostello di Genova (010 242 24 57; www.ostellogenova.it; Via Costanzi 120; per person dm/s/d €16.50/25/23; closed Jan) Genoa's HI hostel is a functional, modern affair that makes little lasting impression, apart from its panoramic city views. There's a mid-afternoon lock-out. Take bus 40 or 640 from Stazione Brignole; or bus 35 and then bus 40 or 640 from Stazione Principe.

Albergo Carola (010 839 13 40; www.pensionecarola.it; 3rd fl, Via Gropallo 4; s with shared bathroom €28-35, d €46-70) Conveniently close to Stazione Brignole, this is a classic old-school *pensione*. Rooms and shared bathrooms are simple, small and spotless. The price doesn't include breakfast. Rooms with shared bathrooms are available at cheaper rates.

Hotel Bel Soggiorno (010 54 28 80; www.belsoggiornohotel.com; 2nd fl, Via XX Settembre 19; s €60-85, d €70-107;) An endearing mix of the modern and the antique, the Bel Soggiorno offers comfortable rooms with modern amenities such as satellite TV. It's in an excellent location and has a friendly owner.

Locanda di Palazzo Cicala (010 251 88 24; www.palazzocicala.it; Piazza San Lorenzo 16; s €133-391, d €175-391;) Hidden in a 16th-century *palazzo* opposite the cathedral, this hip hotel has huge high-ceilinged rooms with their own computer terminals. The common areas sport designer furniture and the staff are extremely helpful.

Eating

Ligurian specialities include pesto (a sauce of basil, garlic, pine nuts and Parmesan) served with *trofie* (pasta curls). Other regional dishes include *pansoti* (ravioli in ground walnut sauce) and focaccia (flat bread made with olive oil). Look out for *tripperie* (stalls selling tripe cooked in huge copper pots) and *friggitore* (stalls selling fritters made with chickpea flour or baccalà). Many of the city's cafes and restaurants are closed on Sunday.

Panarello (010 56 10 37; Via Galata 67r) Come to this branch of the popular local chain to sample *pandolce Genovese*, a delicious cake made with raisins, candied fruit and pine nuts. It's bar service only.

Ristorante Pizzeria Piedigrotta (010 58 05 53; Piazza Savonarola 27; pizzas €5-7.50) If you like your pizzas huge, cheap and tasty, you'll love Piedigrotta. Enormously popular with locals, it has a welcoming interior and friendly staff. To find it, walk down Via XX Settembre and continue on its extension Corso Buenos Aires until you see Piazza Savonarola on your right.

Antica Cantina i Tre Merli (010 247 40 95; Vico dietro il Coro Maddalena 26r; meals €35; closed Sat lunch & Sun) An atmospheric option just off Via Garibaldi, 'The Three Crows' serves Ligurian cuisine with an emphasis on fish. There are a number of regional specialities on offer – try the delicious *focaccia di Recco col formaggio* (focaccia stuffed with cheese from Recco on the Riviera di Levante).

Ristorante Da Rina (010 246 64 75; Mura delle Grazie 3r; meals €40; closed Mon & Aug) If you're keen to sample local seafood, this famous place overlooking the port will fit the bill. It opened in 1946 and has been a favourite with locals ever since.

Drinking & Entertainment

Action centres on the *centro storico*, with a number of good bars clustered around Piazza delle Erbe.

Il Clan (010 254 10 98; www.ilclan.biz; Salita Pallavinci 16r, off Via XXX Aprile; 6.30pm-2am Tue-Sun) The city's most stylish bar-nightclub is conveniently located just off Piazza de Ferrari. Enjoy an *aperitivo* or rock up later, when fashion parades or photography exhibitions are regular occurrences.

Mentelocale Café (010 595 96 48; Piazza Giacomo Matteotti 9; 8am-10pm Mon-Thu, to 1am Fri, 10am-1am Sat & Sun) This swish cafe is by the entrance to the Palazzo Ducale. Sit on the Dalì-inspired red sofas and sip on something cool as you eye up fellow drinkers.

Storico Lounge Café (☎ 010 247 45 48; Piazza de Ferrari 34/36r; 6am-3am) The *aperitivo* buffet here is a favourite with the city's fashionable young things, who love congregating at the pavement tables overlooking the Teatro Carlo Felice.

Getting There & Around

AIR

Genoa's **Cristoforo Colombo airport** (GOA; ☎ 010 60 151; www.airport.genova.it; Sestri Ponente) is 6km west of the city.

The **Volabus** (☎ 010 558 24 14; 6.05am-11.20pm) shuttle travels between the airport and Stazione Principe (€4, 20 minutes, hourly). A taxi costs approximately €24.

BUS

The main bus terminal is on Piazza della Vittoria, south of Stazione Brignole. Book tickets at **Geotravels** (☎ 010 587181; Piazza della Vittoria 57; 9am-12.30pm & 3-7pm Mon-Fri, 9am-12.30pm Sat).

Tickets on local AMT buses cost €1.20 and are valid for 90 minutes. Bus 33 runs between Stazione Principe and Stazione Brignole, stopping at Piazza Ferrari en route.

FERRIES

Ferries sail from the **ferry terminal** (☎ 166 152 39 393; www.porto.genova.it; Via Milano 51), west of the city centre. Ferry companies:

Grandi Navi Veloci (☎ 800 46 65 10; www2.gnv.it) To/from Sardinia (Porto Torres €29 to €139, 11 hours; Olbia €29 to €45, nine to 10 hours), Sicily (Palermo €133, 20 hours), Barcelona (€137 to €156, 18 hours), Tangier (€295, 46 hours) and Tunis (€74, 24 hours).

Moby Lines (☎ 010 254 15 13; www.mobylines.it) To/from Corsica (Bastia €5 to €12, five hours) and Sardinia (Porto Torres €16 to €139, 10 hours; Olbia €18 to €139, 9½ hours).

Tirrenia (☎ 800 82 40 79; www.tirrenia.it) To/from Sardinia (Porto Torres €35 to €124, 10 hours; Olbia €52 to €144, 9¾ hours; Arbatax €53 to €179, 14½ hours).

TRAIN

There are direct trains to Milan (€15.50, 1½ hours, up to 25 daily), Pisa (€15, two hours, half-hourly), Rome (€36.30, 5½ hours, eight daily) and Turin (€15, 1¾ hours, up to 20 daily). Regional trains to La Spezia service the Cinque Terre (€5.30, two hours 20 minutes, half-hourly).

It generally makes little difference whether you leave from Brignole or Principe.

CINQUE TERRE

Liguria's eastern Riviera boasts some of Italy's most dramatic coastline, the highlight of which is the Parco Nazionale delle Cinque Terre (Cinque Terre National Park), just north of La Spezia. Summer gets very crowded, so try to visit in spring or autumn. You can either visit on a day trip from Genoa, or stay overnight in one of the five villages.

Online information about the park is available at www.parconazionale5terre.it. The park's main **information office** (☎ 0187 92 06 33; 8.30am-7.30pm Mon-Fri, 8.30am-9.30pm Sat & Sun) is to the right as you exit the train station at Riomaggiore and there are other offices in the train stations at Manarola, Corniglia, Vernazza, Monterosso and La Spezia (most open from 7am to 8pm). **Internet access** (per 10min €0.80) is available at the Riomaggiore office.

Sights & Activities

Named after its five tiny villages (Riomaggiore, Manarola, Corniglia, Vernazza and Monterosso), the Unesco-listed **Parco Nazionale delle Cinque Terre** encompasses some of Italy's most picturesque and environmentally sensitive coastline. The villages are linked by the 12km **Blue Trail** (Sentiero Azzurro), a magnificent, mildly challenging 9km (five hour) trail. To walk it, you'll need to buy a **Cinque Terre Card** (adult/under 4yr/4-12yr 1 day €5/free/2.50, 2 days €8/free/4), available in all of the park offices. If you prefer, you can buy a **Cinque Terre Treno Card** (adult/under 4yr/4-12yr 1 day €8.50/free/4.30, 2 days €14.70/free/7.40), which includes the walk plus unlimited train travel between Levanto and La Spezia, including all five villages.

The walk is in four stages, the easiest of which are the first stage from Riomaggiore to Manarola (Via d'Amore, 20 minutes) and the second from Manarola to Corniglia (40 minutes). For the final two stages, you'll need to be fit and wearing proper walking shoes. The stretch from Corniglia to Vernazza takes approximately 1½ hours and from Vernazza to Monterosso it's two hours. Make sure you bring a hat, water and sunscreen if you're walking in hot weather.

The Blue Trail is just one of a network of footpaths and cycle trails that crisscross the park; details are available from the park offices (see above). If water sports are more your thing, you can hire snorkelling gear (€10 per day) and kayaks (€7 per hour) at the **Diving Center 5 Terre** (☎ 0187 92 00 11; www.5terrediving.com; Via San Giacomo) in Riomaggiore. It also offers a snorkelling boat tour for €14.

Sleeping & Eating

Ostello 5 Terre (☎ 0187 92 02 15; www.cinqueterre.net/ostello; Via B Riccobaldi 21, Manarola; dm €20-23, d €55-65; closed Nov-Feb;) There are no age limits or hostel memberships required at this popular private eco-hostel. Beds are in clean and bright six-person single-sex dorms with shared bathroom, or in twins or quads with private bathrooms. Extras include a restaurant offering well-priced set meals, and laundry facilities. Book ahead.

Hotel Ca' d'Andrean (☎ 0187 92 00 40; www.cadandrean.it; Via Doscovolo 101, Manarola; s €55-70, d €70-96;) A excellent small hotel in the upper part of Manarola village, Ca' d'Andrea has modern rooms with satellite TV and private bathrooms; some even have private terraces. Breakfast, which is served in a garden filled with lemon trees, costs an extra €6.

L'Eremo Sul Mare (☎ 339 26 85 617; www.eremosulmare.com; Sentiero Azzurro, Vernazza; r €80-110;) This attractive B&B (its name means Hermitage by the Sea) has only three rooms, all of which come with private bathrooms. There's a panoramic terrace, a kitchen for guests' use and two large living rooms with fireplaces. Cash only.

Focacceria Enoteca Antonia (☎ 0187 82 90 39; Via Fegina 124, Monterosso; focaccia per slice around €2.50; 9am-8pm Fri-Wed Mar-Oct) A great place to pick up picnic provisions of focaccia and the local *vino*.

Marina Piccola (☎ 0187 92 01 03; www.hotelmarinapiccola.com; Via Birolli 120, Manarola; meals €27) In pretty Manarola, this welcoming place has an outdoor terrace with a lovely water view. Specialities include *zuppa di pesce* (fish soup) and *antipasti di mare* (seafood antipasti). It also offers small but comfortable air-conditioned rooms (single/double €87/105).

Trattoria La Lanterna (☎ 0187 92 05 89; Via San Giacomo 46, Riomaggiore; meals €34; 24hr) Overlooking the marina in Riomaggiore, La Lanterna has a few tables on the terrace and a breezy dining room with windows overlooking the water. The menu is dominated by fresh and tasty fish dishes.

Getting There & Away

Regional train services from Genoa to Riomaggiore stop at each of the Cinque Terre villages (€4.40, two to 2½ hours). These services run every one to two hours between 4.53am and 10.20pm; the last train back to Genoa is at 11.19pm.

Trains run between La Spezia and Levanto every 30 to 60 minutes between 4.30am and 11.10pm, stopping at all of the villages en route.

Consorzio Marittimo Turistico 5 Terre (☎ 0187 81 84 40) runs ferries between four of the villages (not Corniglia) every day in summer (adult/child €12.50/6.50 return, €8/4 one way). These leave Monterosso every hour from 10.30am until 5.50pm (there's an extra service at 9.30am on weekends). The last return ferry from Riomaggiore is at 5.45pm.

In summer, **Golfo Paradiso** (☎ 0185 77 20 91; www.golfoparadiso.it) runs ferries between Genoa's Porto Antico and Vernazza. These operate on Tuesdays in July and on Tuesdays and Thursdays in August and allow a stop of four hours in Vernazza. Departure is at 8.40am and the cost is €20 one way, €29 return. Schedules can change – check at the information booth at the Porto Antico in Genoa.

TURIN

pop 900,600

First-time visitors are often surprised by Turin (Torino). Expecting a bleak, industrial sprawl dominated by Fiat factories, they are instead confronted with a dynamic and attractive city full of royal *palazzi*, historic cafes, baroque piazzas and world-class museums. Surprise almost inevitably turns to fascination when they learn of the city's occult aspect. Situated on the 45th parallel, it is said to be one of the three apexes of the white-magic triangle with Lyon and Prague, and also the black-magic counterpart of London and San Francisco.

Orientation & Information

At the time of research Stazione Porta Nuova was the main point of arrival, but most trains will be using the revamped Stazione Porta Susa in the future. From Porta Nuova cross Piazza Carlo Felice and follow Via Roma to reach Turin's two focal piazzas: San Carlo and Castello.

Maps, free walking-tour brochures and city information are available from the incredibly helpful **'Torino & You' Tourist Booths** (9am-

7pm) on Via Giuseppe Verdi near the Mole Antonelliana and on Piazza San Carlo.

Internet access is available at **1PC4You** (Via Giuseppe Verdi 20g; per hr €4; 9am-9pm Mon-Fri, 10am-8pm Sat, 2-8pm Sun).

Sights

Serious sightseers should consider the **Torino & Piedmont Card** (48hr card adult/child €18/10), available at tourist information booths around the city, at the airport and at the main train station. This is valid for public transport (not the metro) and gives discounts or entry to 140 museums, monuments and castles. One child aged under 12 is covered by each adult's Torino Card.

Turin's grandest square is **Piazza Castello**, bordered by porticoed promenades and regal palaces. Dominating the piazza, **Palazzo Madama** (www.palazzomadamatorino.it) is home to the **Museo Civico d'Arte Antica** (011 442 99 12; Piazza Castello; adult/child/concession/€7.50/free/6; 10am-6pm Tue-Fri & Sun, to 8pm Sat), with a small collection of Gothic and early Renaissance paintings and an impressive exhibit of porcelain and maiolica. To the north, statues of Castor and Pollux guard the entrance to the enormous **Palazzo Reale** (Royal Palace; 011 436 14 55; Piazza Castello; adult/child/concession €6.50/free/3.25; 8.30am-7.30pm Tue-Sun), built for Carlo Emanuele II in the mid-17th century. The palace's **Giardino Reale** (Royal Garden; admission free; 9am-1hr before sunset) was designed in 1697 by Louis le Nôtre, noted for his work at Versailles.

A short walk away, elegant **Piazza San Carlo**, known as Turin's drawing room, is famous for its cafes and twin baroque churches **San Carlo** and **Santa Cristina**.

Turin's main cathedral, the **Cattedrale di San Giovanni Battista** (011 436 15 40; Piazza San Giovanni; 7am-noon & 3-7pm Mon-Sat, from 8am Sun), houses the *Sindone* (Turin Shroud), a copy of which is on permanent display in front of the altar (the real thing is kept in a vacuum-sealed box and rarely revealed). Believers claim the linen cloth was used to wrap the crucified Christ.

The **Museo Egizio** (Egyptian Museum; 011 440 69 03; www.museoegizio.it; Via Accademia delle Scienze 6; adult/child/concession €7/free/3.50; 8.30am-7.30pm Tue-Sun) houses an engrossing collection of ancient Egyptian art that is considered the world's most important outside of Cairo and London.

Towering 167m over the city centre, the **Mole Antonelliana** (Via Montebello 20) houses the **Museo Nazionale del Cinema** (011 813 85 60; www.museocinema.it; adult/child €6.50/2; 9am-8pm Tue-Fri & Sun, to 11pm Sat) and its comprehensive collection of cinematic memorabilia. Modern, interactive and enormously enjoyable, the museum will delight adults and children alike. Don't miss the glass **panoramic lift** (adult/child €4.50/3.20), which whisks you up 85m in 59 seconds. Joint tickets for the museum and lift cost €8/4.50.

There are a number of top-notch private galleries and contemporary art museums in Turin, including the Renzo Piano–designed **Pinacoteca Giovanni e Marella Agnelli** (011 006 27 13; www.pinacoteca-agnelli.it; Via Nizza 262; adult/child for temporary & permanent exhibitions €7/6, for permanent exhibitions only €4/2.50; 10am-7pm Tue-Sun) and the **Castello di Rivoli Museo d'Arte Contemporanea** (011 956 52 20; www.castellodirivoli.org; Piazza Mafalda di Savoia; adult/child €6.50/free; 10am-5pm Tue-Thu, 10am-9pm Fri-Sun). Check www.turismotorino.org for others.

Sleeping

Ostello Torino (011 660 29 39; www.ostellotorino.it; Via Alby 1; dm/s with shared bathroom €15/21, tw with private bathroom €40; closed mid-Dec–mid-Jan;) Turin's HI hostel is quiet, comfortable and clean with three- or eight-person dorms and a variety of room types. Wi-fi and a laundry service are further pluses. Catch bus 52 from Porta Nuova (64 on Sunday), otherwise it's a steep 2km walk.

L'Orso Poeta (011 517 89 96;; Corso Vittorio Emanuele II 10; s/d from €70/110;) Everyone will feel welcome at this B&B in an historic apartment building by the river opposite Parco Valentino. Its two small rooms have bathrooms and lots of character.

our pick **Alpi Resort Hotel** (011 812 96 77; www.hotelalpiresort.it; Via A. Bonafous 5; s/d from €80/90;) This excellent midrange option is just off Piazza Vittorio Veneto. Impeccably clean and well-equipped rooms are quiet and comfortable; some even have jacuzzis. The breakfast spread is both lavish and delicious.

Art Hotel Boston (011 50 03 59; www.hotelbostontorino.it; Via Massena 70; s €110-150, d €150-190;) The Boston's austere facade gives no clues as to its colourful, modern interior. Individually decorated rooms have all the mod cons and public spaces are filled with works by Andy Warhol, Mario Mertz and Roy Lichtenstein, among others.

ITALY

CRAZY ABOUT COFFEE

As well as being the base of international coffee brand Lavazza, Turin is home to an impressive array of historic cafes. Don't leave town without propping up the bar and downing an excellent espresso in the following:

- **Baratti & Milano** (☎ 011 440 7138; Piazza Castello 29; ⏲ closed Wed) Serving coffee and confectionary since 1873.
- **Caffè San Carlo** (☎ 011 53 25 86; Piazza San Carlo 156) Dates from 1828.
- **Caffè Torino** (☎ 011 54 51 18; Piazza San Carlo 204) A relative newcomer, this art nouveau gem opened in 1903.
- **Neuv Caval'd Brônz** (☎ 011 545354; Piazza San Carlo 155) Also has an atmospheric branch in Palazzo Reale (open from 8.30am to 7pm Tuesday to Sunday).
- **San Tommaso 10** (☎ 011 53 42 01; Via San Tommaso 10; ⏲ 8am-7pm Mon-Sat) This is where Lavazzo started. Now modernised, it serves an unorthodox array of flavoured coffees as well as the classic versions.

Eating & Drinking

Da Ciro (☎ 011 531 925; Corso Vinzaglio 17; pizzas €5-8; ⏲ closed Sat lunch & Sun) The thin-crust pizzas that emerge from the wood-fired oven here are quite delicious. Decor is unpretentious and service is jovial – great stuff.

Otto Etre Quarti (8¼; ☎ 011 517 63 67; www.ottoetrequarti.it; Piazza Solferino 8C; lunch €15, dinner €30) Do as the locals do: claim a table in one of 8¼'s high-ceilinged dining rooms or on the front terrace and order from its simple yet scrumptious menu. The young waiters are enthusiastic, the ambience is casual yet chic and the prices are right – particularly at lunchtime.

Turin is rightly famous for its coffee (see the boxed text, above), but it also has a reputation for magnificent gelato. Sample it at **Grom** (branches at Via Accademia delle Scienze 4, Via Garibaldi 11 & Piazza Paleocapa 1d); **Caffé Pepino** (Piazza Carignano 8; ⏲ closed Mon); and **Fiorio** (Via Po 8).

Early evening is the time to make for one of the city's cafes and enjoy an *aperitivo* accompanied by a sumptuous buffet of *antipasti* (included in the price). The most happening *aperitivo* precinct in the city is on and around Piazza Emanuele Filiberto: try **Arancia di Mezzanotte** (☎ 011 439 04 23; Piazza Emanuele Filiberto 11; ⏲ 5pm-4am Tue-Sun), **Pastis** (☎ 011 521 10 85; Piazza Emanuele Filiberto 9; ⏲ 9am-3.30pm & 6pm-2am) or **I Tre Galli** (☎ 011 521 60 27; Via Sant'Agostino 25; ⏲ noon-midnight). The *aperitivo* drinks cost around €8 at all of these.

Getting There & Around

In Caselle, 16km northwest of the city centre, **Turin airport** (TRN; ☎ 011 567 63 61; www.turin-airport.com) operates flights to/from European and national destinations. **Sadem** (☎ 011 300 01 66; www.sadem.it, in Italian) runs an airport shuttle (€5.50, 40 minutes, every 45 minutes) between the airport and Porta Nuova/Porta Suza train stations. It operates between 5.15am and 11.15pm; tickets are €0.50 more expensive if purchased on the bus. A taxi costs approximately €30.

There's also a train to the airport. It leaves from Stazione Dora between 8am and 5pm Monday to Friday only and takes 30 minutes. Cost is €3.30 (free with the Torino Card).

Trains connect Turin with Milan (€13.50, two hours, up to 30 daily), Venice (€35.25, five hours, five daily), Florence (€32, five hours, three daily), Genoa (€15, two hours, up to 20 daily), and Rome (€76, seven hours, seven daily).

MILAN

pop 1.3 million

You may love it, you may hate it, but one thing's for sure – you won't remain indifferent to Milan (Milano). Italy's financial and fashion capital is expensive, noisy, dirty and strictly for city lovers – all of whom end up dazzled by its vibrant cultural scene, sensational shopping and wicked nightlife.

Originally founded by Celtic tribes in the 7th century BC, Milan was conquered by the Romans in 222 BC and developed into a major trading and transport centre. From the 13th century it flourished under the rule of two powerful families, the Visconti and the Sforza.

Orientation

From Stazione Centrale, take the yellow MM3 underground (Metropolitana Milanese) train line to Piazza del Duomo. The city's main attractions are concentrated in the area between the piazza and Castello Sforzesco.

Information

Main post office (Via Cordusio 4)
Mondadori (Piazza del Duomo; per hr €3; 7am-11pm) Internet access is available on the 2nd floor of this bookshop.
Pharmacy (02 669 07 35; Stazione Centrale; 24hr)
Police station (Questura; 02 622 61; Via Fatebenefratelli 11)
Tourist offices Piazza del Duomo (02 774 04 343; www.milanoinfotourist.com; Piazza Duomo 19a; 8.45am-1pm & 2-6pm Mon-Sat, 9am-1pm & 2-5pm Sun); Stazione Centrale (02 774 04 318; 9am-6pm Mon-Sat, 9am-1pm & 2-5pm Sun) Pick up the free guides *Hello Milano* and *Milanomese.*

Sights

With a capacity of 40,000 people, Milan's landmark **Duomo** (Piazza del Duomo; admission free; 7am-7pm) is the world's largest Gothic cathedral. Commissioned in 1386 to a florid French-Gothic design and finished nearly 600 years later, it's a fairy-tale ensemble of 3400 statues, 135 spires and 155 gargoyles. Climb up to the **roof** (stairs/elevator €5/7; 9am-5.20pm, to 8.30pm high summer) for memorable views of the city.

Nearby, on the northern flank of Piazza del Duomo, the elegant iron and glass **Galleria Vittorio Emanuele II** shopping arcade leads towards the famous **Teatro alla Scala** (02 720 03 744; www.teatroallascala.org; Piazza delle Scala; admission €5; 9am-12.30pm & 1.30-5.30pm when no performances are scheduled).

To the west, the dramatic 15th-century **Castello Sforzesco** (02 884 63 700; www.milanocastello.it; Piazza Castello 3; admission free; 9am-5.30pm Tue-Sun) was the Renaissance residence of the Sforza dynasty. It now shelters the **Musei del Castello** (02 884 63 703; adult/concession €3/1.50; 9am-5.30pm), a group of museums dedicated to art, sculpture, furniture, archaeology and music. Entry is free on Friday between 2pm and 5.30pm and from Tuesday to Sunday between 4.30pm and 5.30pm.

Art addicts shouldn't miss the **Pinacoteca di Brera** (02 894 21 146; www.brera.beniculturali.it; Via Brera 28; adult/concession €5/2.50; 8.30am-7.15pm Tue-Sun), whose heavyweight collection includes Andrea Mantegna's masterpiece, the *Dead Christ*, and Raphael's *Betrothal of the Virgin*.

Milan's most famous tourist attraction – Leonardo da Vinci's mural of *The Last Supper* – is in the **Cenacolo Vinciano** (02 894 21 146; www.cenacolovinciano.org; Piazza Santa Maria delle Grazie 2; booking compulsory, adult/child €6.50/free plus booking fee of €1.50; 8.15am-6.45pm Tue-Sun), just west of the city centre. Although we have been lucky in the past and scored a ticket on the day (go at lunch-time), it's much safer to book ahead.

Tours

Autostradale (02 339 10 794; www.autostradale.it) runs three-hour bus tours that take in the Duomo, Galleria Vittorio Emanuele II, La Scala, Castello Sforzesco and the Cenacolo Vinciano. If you haven't booked ahead for your *Last Supper* ticket, this may be the only opportunity you'll have to see it, as the €55 ticket (€45 for children) for this tour includes entry to see the famous mural. Tickets are available from the tourist office at Piazza Duomo. The multilingual tours depart from outside the office at 9.30am every morning except Monday.

Sleeping

Prepare yourself for a budget blow-out when booking a hotel here – everything is ridiculously expensive, particularly when trade fairs are on (which is often). Booking is essential at all times of the year.

Hotel De Albertis (02 738 34 09; www.hoteldealbertis.it; Via De Albertis 7; s €50-100, d €50-160;) This small, family-run two-star choice is in a leafy residential street that's a 20-minute walk from the Duomo (or catch tram 27). Rooms are clean, cheerful and attractive. Breakfast is served in the welcoming breakfast room or pretty garden.

Hotel Nuovo (02 864 64 444; www.hotelnuovomilano.com; Piazza Beccaria 6; r €60-150) In a city where 'cheap' is an ugly word, the Nuovo is a bastion of budget accommodation. Rooms are basic but clean, and the location, just off Corso Vittorio Emanuele II, is a winner. Rates don't include breakfast.

Ariston Hotel (02 720 00 556; www.aristonhotel.com; Largo Carrobbio 2; s €100-220, d €140-320;) Claiming to be Milan's first 'ecological hotel' (hmm), the Ariston offers comfortable but characterless rooms with jacuzzis and

ITALY

CENTRAL MILAN
0 400 m
0 0.2 miles
INFORMATION
24-Hour Pharmacy....1 D1
Central Tourist Office....2 B4
Main Post Office....3 B4
Mondadori....4 C4
Police Station....5 C3
Tourist Office....6 D1
SIGHTS & ACTIVITIES
Castello Sforzesco....7 A3
Duomo....8 C4
Galleria Vittorio Emanuele II....9 C4
Museo Teatrale alla Scala....(see 24)
Museo d'Arte Antica....(see 7)
Museo degli Strumenti Musicali....(see 7)
Museo della Preistoria....(see 7)
Pinacoteca di Brera....10 B3
Teatro alla Scala....(see 10)
The Last Supper....11 A4
SLEEPING
Alle Meravigale....12 B4
Ariston Hotel....13 B5
Hotel Nuovo....14 C4
EATING
Di per Di Supermarket....15 D2
Il Brellin....16 A6
Peck Delicatessan....17 B4
Peck Italian Bar....18 B4
Premiata Pizzeria....19 A6
Rinomata....20 A6
DRINKING
Zucca in Galleria....21 C4
ENTERTAINMENT
Blue Note....22 B1
Box Office....(see 9)
MITO (Milano & Torino) Settembre Musica Festival Box Office....23 C4
Teatro alla Scala....24 C4
TRANSPORT
Bus Station....25 B1
Bus Stop for Starfly Buses to Linate Airport....26 C4
Left Luggage....27 D1
Left Luggage....28 A4
Malpensa Shuttle, Malpensa Express Bus & Autostradale Shuttle Buses....29 A4
Cimitero Monumentale
Piazza Fidia
Piazzale Lagosta
Sondrio
Stazione Centrale
Isola
Piazzale Archinto
Stazione Porta Garibaldi
Gioia
Centrale FS
Piazza Duca d'Aosta
Piazza Luigi di Savoia
Garibaldi
Piazza Sigmund Freud
Piazzale XXV Aprile
Viale F Crispi
Bastioni di Porta Nuova
Repubblica
Largo La Foppa
Moscova
To Malpensa Airport (50km)
Piazza Sempione
Parco Sempione
Turati
Giardini Pubblici
Bastioni di Porta Venezia
Porta Venezia
Brera
Lanza
Piazza Cavour
Palestro
Stazione Nord (Stazione Cadorna)
Piazza Croce Rossa
Monte Napoleone
Cairoli
Cadorna Triennale
Piazza della Scala
Piazza del Tricolore
San Babila
Cordusio
Piazza del Liberty
Duomo
Piazza del Duomo
To Hotel De Albertis (1.5km); Linate Airport (5.5km); Orio al Serio Airport (50km)
Piazza Pia XI
Piazza S Maria Beltrade
Piazza Beccaria
Sant' Ambrogio
Basilica di Sant'Ambrogio
Corso di Porta Vittoria
Piazza Cinque Giornate
Missori
Piazza Velasca
Giardino della Guastalla
Porta Romana
Sant' Agostino
Piazza Vetra
Piazza San Nazaro in Brolo
Ospedale Maggiore Policlinico
To Stadio Giuseppe Meazza (6km)
Crocetta
Parco delle Basiliche
Piazza Sant' Eustorgio
Porta Genova
Darsena
Piazza XXIV Maggio
Viale Gian Galeazzo
Corso di Porta Romana
Corso Venezia
Corso Magenta
Corso Genova
Corso Italia
Corso San Gottardo
Corso di Porta Ticinese
Alzaia Naviglio Grande
Viale Gabriele d'Annunzio

flat-screen TVs. It's in a great location and has excellent low-season deals.

Alle Meraviglie (☎ 02 805 10 23; www.allemeraviglie.it; Via San Tomaso 8; r from €182; ❄ 💻) Boutique with a capital B, this stylish place has only six rooms, all of which balance simplicity and style to great effect. Rooms are individually decorated and feature gorgeous linen and fabrics. Breakfast costs €15.

Eating

Premiata Pizzeria (☎ 02 894 00 648; Via Alzaia Naviglio Grande 2; pizzas €5-10) Right on the canal in trendy Navigli, perennially busy Premiata serves up huge thick-crust pizzas that are perfect fodder after a few hours spent in surrounding bars.

our pick **Peck Italian Bar** (☎ 02 869 30 17; Via Cesare Cantù 3; meals €40; 🕑 11.30am-8pm) This place truly encapsulates Milan – chic and sleek surrounds, top-quality produce and a glamorous clientele. The delicious Milanese menu features classics such as *cotolleto* (breaded veal cutlet) and risotto.

Il Brellin (☎ 02 581 01 351; Via Alzaia Naviglio Grande 14; meals €46; 🕑 closed Sun) Set around a laundry dating from the 1700s, atmosphere-laden Il Brellin is a great place to linger over dinner. The three-course traditional Milanese tasting menu (€46) is a great idea, and the passing parade makes for an entertaining evening. Its bar is a great place for an *aperitivo* (open 7pm to 9.30pm).

After dinner at either Premiata Pizzeria or Il Brellin, think about sampling the gelato at **Rinomata** (☎ 02 58113877; Ripa di Porta Ticinese). Its fabulous interior features old-fashioned fridges and glass-fronted cabinets filled with cones – and the gelato is good, too!

Self-caterers can shop at the two supermarkets at Stazione Centrale (one on the upper level and one on the western side), at nearby **Di per Di** (Via Felice Casati 30; 🕑 8.30am-8pm Mon-Sat) or at the expensive but utterly irresistible **Peck Delicatessen** (☎ 02 802 31 61; Via Spadari 9; 🕑 3.30-7.30pm Mon, 9.15am-7.30pm Tue-Fri, 8.45am-7.30pm Sat).

Drinking

Milan's bar scene is famous throughout Italy, and it moves around the city's neighbourhoods. Brera and Navigli are always popular, and when this book went to print the scenes around Stazione Garibaldi (Corso Garibaldi and Corso Como), Piazzale Lagosta and Isola were hot, hot, hot.

For coffee, bypass the pricey table service and prop up the bar at **Zucca in Galleria** (Caffè Miani; ☎ 02 864 64 435; Galleria Vittorio Emanuele II 21), the city's most famous cafe (it dates from 1867).

Entertainment

The opera season at **Teatro alla Scala** (☎ 02 720 03 744; www.teatroallascala.org; Piazza della Scala; tickets €10-110) runs from November to July. Tickets are available online or from the **box office** (Galleria del Sagrato, Piazza del Duomo; 🕑 noon-6pm) beneath Piazza del Duomo.

Tickets for the **MITO (Milano & Torino) Settembre Musica festival** (www.mitosettembremusica.it) are sold from late August to late September at the **box office** (☎ 02 365 08 343; Galleria Vittorio Emanuele II 12; 🕑 10.30am-6.30pm).

Milan's jazz aficionados gravitate towards **Blue Note** (☎ 02 690 16 888; www.bluenotemilano.com; Via Borsieri 37, Isola; admission from €20; 🕑 2-7pm Mon, 2pm-midnight Tue-Sat, 7-11pm Sun). It's affiliated with the New York club of the same name, so big names often appear.

A mecca for football fans, the **Stadio Giuseppe Meazza** (San Siro; ☎ 02 404 24 32; Via Piccolomini 5; Ⓜ Lotto) is home to AC Milan and Internazionale. Match tickets (from €15) are available from branches of Cariplo bank (AC Milan) and Banca Popolare di Milano (Inter). To get to the stadium on match days, take tram 16 from Orefici or the free shuttle bus from the Lotto (MM1) metro station.

Shopping

For designer clobber head to the so-called Golden Quad, the area around Via della Spiga, Via Sant'Andrea, Via Monte Napoleone and Via Alessandro Manzoni. Street markets are held around the canals, notably on Viale Papiniano on Tuesday and Saturday mornings.

Getting There & Away

AIR

Most international flights fly into **Malpensa airport** (MXP; 🕑 02 748 52 200; www.sea-aeroportimilano.it), about 50km northwest of Milan. Domestic and some European flights use **Linate airport** (LIN; 🕑 02 748 52 200 www.sea-aeroportimilano.it), about 7km east of the city; and low-cost airlines are increasingly using **Orio al Serio airport** (BGY; 🕑 035 32 63 23; www.sacbo.it), near Bergamo.

WORTH THE TRIP: MANTUA

Placid Mantua (Mantova in Italian) is a popular day trip from both Milan and Verona. Best known as the place where Shakespeare exiled Romeo, it was for centuries (1328 to 1707) the stronghold of the Gonzaga family, one of Italy's most powerful Renaissance dynasties.

The **tourist office** (☎ 0376 43 24 32; www.turismo.mantova.it; 9.30am-6.30pm) is on Piazza Andrea Mantegna 6, close to the city's major attraction, the enormous **Palazzo Ducale** (☎ 0376 22 48 32; Piazza Sordello; adult/child/EU student 18-25yr /€6.50/free/3.25; 8.45am-7.15pm Tue-Sun). The highlight of this former seat of the Gonzaga family is its **Camera degli Sposi** (Bridal Chamber), home to extraordinary 15th-century frescoes by Andrea Mantegna. To visit the *Camera* between 15 March and 15 June or between 1 September and 15 October you need to book ahead of time (☎ 041 241 18 97).

For lunch, sit beneath 15th-century frescoes in the vaulted dining room of **Ristorante Masseria** (☎ 0376 36 53 03; Piazza Broletto 7; pizza €5-7.50, meals €26; closed Thu) to enjoy local specialities such as *tortelli di zucca* (ring-shaped pasta stuffed with pumpkin). Or perhaps have a peek at the frescoes but opt to enjoy your meal outside in the attractive 13th-century piazza.

The best way to get here is by regional train from Milan (€8.55, 2¼ hours, eight daily) or Verona (€2.55, 45 minutes, 16 daily).

TRAIN

Regular trains depart Stazione Centrale for Venice (€22, three hours, hourly), Florence (€26, 3½ hours, hourly), Rome (€45, six hours, hourly) and other Italian and European cities. Most regional trains stop at Stazione Nord in Piazzale Cadorna. Fast Eurostar Alta Velocità (ES AV) trains began operating in December 2008, cutting travel times considerably: Florence (€39.90, two hours and nine minutes, hourly), Rome (€67.50, 3½ to four hours, hourly) and Bologna (€33.30, one hour and five minutes, hourly). ES AV trains also depart from Centrale.

Getting Around

TO/FROM THE AIRPORT

Malpensa Shuttle (☎ 02 585 98 31 85; www.malpensashuttle.it) coaches run to/from Piazza Luigi di Savoia next to Stazione Centrale every 20 minutes between 4.15am and 11.15pm. Tickets for the 50-minute journey cost €7/3.50 per adult/child one way (€12/5 return). **Malpensa Bus Express** (☎ 02 339 10 794) buses depart half-hourly from the same piazza between 4.15am and 11.15pm; tickets cost €7.50 one way and the trip takes 50 minutes.

By train, take the **Malpensa Express** (☎ 02 851 14 382; www.malpensaexpress.it) from Cadorna underground station – there are hourly or half-hourly departures between 5.57am and 8.57pm (buses take over from 10.27pm to 5am). The 50-minute journey costs €11.

For Linate, **Starfly** (☎ 02 585 87 237) buses depart from Piazza Luigi di Savoia half-hourly between 5.40am and 9.30pm; tickets cost €4.50, journey time is 30 minutes. Alternatively, use local bus 73 from Piazza San Babila (€1, 20 minutes).

Autostradale (☎ 035 31 84 72; www.autostradale.it) run half-hourly buses from Piazza Luigi di Savoia to Orio al Serio between 4am and 11.30pm; the journey lasts one hour and tickets cost €8.90.

BUS & METRO

Milan's excellent public transport system is run by **ATM** (www.atm-mi.it). Tickets (€1), are valid for one underground ride or up to 75 minutes travel on city buses and trams. You can buy them at metro stations, *tabacchi* and newsstands.

VERONA

pop 260,800

Wander Verona's atmospheric streets and you'll understand why Shakespeare set *Romeo and Juliet* here – this is one of Italy's most beautiful and romantic cities. Known as *piccola Roma* (little Rome) for its importance in imperial days, its heyday came in the 13th and 14th centuries under the Della Scala (aka Scaligeri) family, a period noted for the savage family feuding on which Shakespeare based his tragedy.

Information is available at the three **tourist offices** (www.tourism.verona.it; airport ☎ 045 861 91 63; 9am-5pm Mon & Tue, 9am-6pm Wed-Sat, 10am-4pm Sun;

city centre (☎ 045 806 86 80; Piazza Brà; ⏲ 9am-7pm Mon-Sat, to 4pm Sun; train station ☎ 045 800 08 61; ⏲ 8am-7pm Mon-Sat, to 3pm Sun). Internet access is available at **Internet Etc** (Via Quattro Spade 3b; per hr €5.50; ⏲ 2.30pm-7.45pm Mon, 9.30am-7.45pm Tue-Fri, 10.30am-7.45pm Sat, 3.30-7.45pm Sun).

Sights & Activities

The **Verona Card** (1/3 days €8/12) covers city transport and the main monuments. It's available from tourist offices and most sights.

In the corner of Piazza Brà, the 1st-century pink-and-white **amphitheatre** (☎ 045 800 03 60; www.arena.it; Piazza Brà; adult/child/concession €6/1/4.50; ⏲ 8.30am-7.15pm Tue-Sun, 1.30-7.15pm Mon Oct-Jun, 8am-3.30pm Jul-Sep), known as the Arena, is the third-largest Roman amphitheatre in existence, with a capacity of 20,000. These days it's most famous as Verona's summer opera house (see p480).

From the Arena, walk along Via Mazzini, Verona's premier shopping strip, to Via Cappello and the **Casa di Giulietta** (☎ 045 803 43 03; Via Cappello 23; courtyard free, museum adult/child/concession €6/1/4.40; ⏲ 8.30am-7.30pm Tue-Sun, 1.30-7.30pm Mon), a clever tourist attraction created by local authorities a few decades ago and marketed as Juliet's house. Its pretty balcony is a much-loved happy-snap spot, and romantic superstition suggests that rubbing the right breast of Juliet's statue (in the courtyard below the balcony) will bring you a new lover. Further along the street is **Porta Leoni**, one of the city's Roman gates; the other, **Porta Borsari**, is north of the Arena.

Set over the city's Roman forum, **Piazza delle Erbe** is lined with sumptuous palaces and filled with touristy market stalls. Through the **Arco della Costa**, the quieter **Piazza dei Signori** is flanked by the **Loggia del Consiglio**, the medieval town hall regarded as Verona's finest Renaissance structure, and **Palazzo degli Scaligeri**, the former residence of the Della Scala family.

The Romanesque **Basilica di San Zeno Maggiore** (Piazza San Zeno; ⏲ 8.30am-6pm Mon-Sat, 1-5pm Sun Mar-Oct, 10am-4pm Tue-Sat, 1-5pm Sun Nov-Feb) honours the city's patron saint. Look out for the rose window and Mantagna's *Maestà della Vergine* (The Majesty of the Virgin), above the high alter.

The tourist office at the train station offers **free bike hire**. There are 10 bikes available (first come, first served); leave ID as security.

Sleeping

High-season prices apply during the opera season and it is absolutely essential to book ahead during this period.

Ostello Villa Francescatti (☎ 045 59 03 60; www.villafrancescatti.com, in Italian; Salita Fontana del Ferro 15; dm incl breakfast €17.50-19, d €36) This beautiful hostel is housed in a 16th-century villa set in extensive grounds. To save yourself a steep uphill walk, take bus 73 from the train station (90 on Sunday). There's a strict 11.30pm curfew.

Hotel Torcolo (☎ 045 800 75 12; www.hoteltorcolo.it; Vicolo Listone 3; s €50-103, d €70-150; ❄) Not 50m from Piazza Brà, the homely Torcolo is ideally located. Its comfortable mid-sized rooms have double-glazing and satellite TV. If weather permits, breakfast (included in high-season prices only) is served in the small piazza in front of the hotel.

Hotel Aurora (☎ 045 59 47 17; www.hotelaurora.biz; Piazza delle Erbe; s €58-125, d €100-145; ❄) A top of the range two-star, the Aurora has friendly staff and clean and comfortable rooms with an understated decor. The lavish breakfast can be enjoyed on a lovely terrace overlooking Piazza delle Erbe. Single rooms with a shared bathroom are available for cheaper rates.

L'Ospite (☎ 045 803 69 94; www.lospite.com; Via XX Settembre 3; apt for 3 €110-160, apt for 4 €125-180; ❄) Over the river from the *centro storico*, L'Ospite has six self-contained flats for up to four people. Simple and bright with wood-beamed ceilings and fully equipped kitchens, they come with wi-fi and are ideal for families.

Eating

Boiled meats are a Veronese speciality, as is crisp Soave white wine.

Hosteria All'Orso (☎ 045 597214; Via Sottoriva 3/c; meals €30; ⏲ closed Sun & Mon lunch) This is a charming spot in Verona's trendy riverside district. Grab a table under the timber-beamed porticoes or in the rustic-chic interior and order from the menu of tempting north-Italian staples.

Al Pompiere (☎ 045 59 42 91; Vicolo Regina d'Ungheria 5; meals €45; ⏲ closed Sun & Mon lunch) There's no secret to the success of this much-loved trattoria – top-notch seasonally inspired food and welcoming surroundings. It's a must for cheese fans, with some 120 on the menu.

our pick **Antica Bottega del Vino** (☎ 045 80 04 535; Via Scudo di Francia 3; meals €50; ⏲ closed Tue) Established in 1890, this wine bar–restaurant is one of the essential stops while you're in town. You can enjoy a glass of wine (€1 to €11) from a mind-boggling array of choices while standing at the bar, or book a table for a meal. The food is rustic and delicious – freshly made *bigoli all'anatra* (pasta with a duck *ragù*), soupy *risotto all'Amarone* (rice cooked with Amarone wine) and a variety of perfectly cooked meat dishes. The surrounds couldn't be more atmospheric.

Entertainment

The opera season at the Roman **Arena** (☎ 045 800 51 51; www.arena.it; tickets €22.50-198) runs from late June to the end of August – if you attend a performance make sure you take your own food and drinks (stuff sold in the Arena is outrageously overpriced) and perhaps something to sit on, as the stone seating can be very uncomfortable. There's also a winter season of classical and modern music, ballet and opera at the 18th-century **Teatro Filarmonico** (☎ 045 800 51 51; www.arena.it; Via dei Mutilati 4).

Nightlife is centred on the bars and trattorias of Via Sottoriva.

Getting There & Around

Valerio Catullo airport (☎ 045 809 56 66; www.aeroportidelgarda.it) is 12km outside the city and accessible by bus from the train station (€4.50, 20 minutes, every 20 minutes between 5.40am and 11.10pm). Ryanair flies to **Brescia airport** (VBS; ☎ 030 965 65 99), from where **CGA** (www.cgabrescia.it) shuttle buses (€11, one hour, one daily) connect to Verona's main train station.

From the main bus terminal in front of the train station, buses 72 and 73 leave Stand F going to Piazza Erbe. Buses 11, 12 and 13 leave Stand A going to the Arena. Tickets cost €1.20 on the bus, €1 at the station's *tabacchi*. A taxi from the train station to the centre costs around €8.

Verona is directly linked by rail to Milan (€12.50, two hours, half-hourly), Venice (€13.50, 1½ hours, half-hourly), Bologna (€15, 1¾ hours, hourly) and Rome (Eurostar €48.50, six hours, hourly).

PADUA

pop 210,400

A lively university city, Padua (Padova) is a fun place to hang out. But what really makes a visit worthwhile are the stunning Giotto frescoes in the Cappella degli Scrovegni.

From the train station, follow Corso del Popolo and its continuation Corso Garibaldi until you see a park on your left – the *cappella* is here. Continue on Corso Garibaldi and its extension Via VII Febbraio, to reach the *centro storico*.

Information is available at the three **tourist offices** (www.turismopadova.it; Galleria Pedrocchi ☎ 049 876 79 27; 🕑 9am-1.30pm & 3-7pm Mon-Sat; Piazza Del Santo ☎ 049 875 30 87; 🕑 9am-1.30pm & 3-6pm Mon-Sat, 10am-1pm & 3-6pm Sun Apr-Oct only; train station ☎ 049 875 20 77; 🕑 9am-7pm Mon-Sat, 9am-12.30pm Sun).

Sights

The **PadovaCard** (☎ 049 876 79 27; www.padovacard.it; 2/3 days for 1 adult & 1 child under 14yr €15/20), available from tourist offices and participating sights, provides free public transport, parking and entry to many sights, including the Cappella degli Scrovegni (plus €1 booking fee).

Many people visit Padua just to see Giotto's extraordinary frescoes in the **Cappella degli Scrovegni** (☎ 049 201 00 20; www.cappelladegliscrovegni.it; Piazza Eremitani 8; tickets incl entry into the adjoining Musei Civici agli Eremitani adult/child/student €12/5/8; 🕑 9am-7pm). The 38 colourful panels (c 1304–1306) depicting Christ's life cover the chapel from floor to ceiling. It's best to book tickets at least 24 hours in advance, though it's sometimes possible to buy tickets on the spot. Visits are limited to 15 minutes.

From 1 March to 6 January, the Cappella (but not the Musei Civici agli Eremitani) is open until 10pm. Tickets for these evening openings cost adult/student and child €8/6 – it's also possible to buy a 'double turn' ticket (€12) at these times, which gives you 30 minutes rather than 15.

On the other side of the *centro storico* is the **Basilica di Sant'Antonio** (Basilica del Santo; ☎ 049 824 28 11; Piazza del Santo; admission free; 🕑 6.30am-7.45pm). Home to the surprisingly gaudy **tomb** of St Anthony, Padua's patron saint, it's one of Italy's major pilgrimage sights.

In the square outside the basilica, the bronze equestrian statue, the *Gattamelata* (Honeyed Cat), is by the Renaissance sculptor Donatello.

Sleeping

Ostello della Città di Padova (☎ 049 875 22 19; www.ostellopadova.it; Via Aleardo Aleardi 30; dm incl breakfast from €16.50) Functional and friendly, Padua's HI hostel has beds in large single-sex dorms and four- or six-person family rooms. Take the tram (€1) from the train station to Via Cavalletto, turn right into Via Marin and then left at the Torresino church.

Albergo Verdi (☎ 049 836 41 63; www.albergoverdipadova.it; Via Dondi dall'Orologio 7; s €40-100, d €40-150; ❄) This stylish modern choice offers quiet rooms with bright colour schemes and mod cons such as satellite TV. An excellent location just off Piazza del Capitaniato completes a well-priced and welcoming package.

Hotel Sant'Antonio (☎ 049 875 13 93; www.hotelsantantonio.it; Via San Fermo 118; s €39-67, d €84-94; ❄) On the edge of the historic centre, the three-star Sant'Antonio is a safe, if rather staid, option. Breakfast costs an extra €7.50 and single rooms with a shared bathroom are available for cheaper rates.

Eating & Drinking

L'Anfora (☎ 049 65 66 29; www.osterianfora.it; Via dei Sconcin 13; meals €27; ⏰ closed Sun) A typical old-school *osteria* with bare wooden tables and racked wine bottles, L'Anfora serves hearty meals such as *pasta e fagioli* (pasta and beans) or *fegato alla veneziana con polenta* (liver and onions served with polenta). There's sometimes live jazz to accompany your meal – check the website for details.

Trattoria San Pietro (☎ 049 876 0303; Via San Pietro 95; meals €32; ⏰ closed Jul, Sun Jun, Aug & Sep) The unassuming facade here gives no clue as to the excellence of the restaurant within. Dishes from the Veneto join specialities from Lombardy on the menu.

There are a number of stylish contemporary *enoteche* in the centre of town, including **Godenda** (☎ 049 877 41 92; Via Squarcione Francesco 4; ⏰ closed Sun) and **K Foccaccia e Champagne** (☎ 049 876 16 51; Piazzetta Garzena 6, off Via VIII Febbraio; ⏰ closed Mon). The charming **Enoteca Angelo Rasi** (☎ 049 871 97 97; Riviera Paleocapa 7; ⏰ from 6pm Tue-Sun) is on a canal to the southwest of the centre – it's also a great place for dinner (meals €50).

The most atmospheric spot for coffee is historic **Caffè Pedrocchi** (☎ 049 878 12 31; Via VIII Febbraio 15), where Stendhal once held court.

Getting There & Away

SITA buses (☎ 049 820 68 44; www.sitabus.it, in Italian) arrive from Venice (€3.55, 45 minutes, hourly) at Piazzale Boschetti, next to the Cappella Scrovegni.

There are regional trains to/from Venice (€2.90, 45 minutes, every 20 minutes) and direct services to Verona (€8.50, 50 minutes, every 20 minutes) and Bologna (€13, 1½ hours, every 45 minutes).

VENICE

pop 269,000

Venice (Venezia) is a hauntingly beautiful city. At every turn you're assailed by unforgettable images – tiny bridges crossing limpid canals, delivery barges jostling chintzy gondolas, tourists posing under flocks of pigeons. But to reduce Venice to a set of pictures is as impossible as describing it in sound bites. To discover its romantic and melancholic nature you really need to walk its hidden back lanes. Parts of the Cannaregio, Dorsoduro and Castello *sestieri* (districts) rarely see many tourists, and you can lose yourself for hours in the streets between the Accademia and the train station. Stroll late at night to feel an eerie atmosphere, redolent of dark passions and dangerous secrets.

The reality of modern Venice is, however, a city besieged by rising tides and up to 20 million visitors a year. This and the sky-high property prices mean that most Venetians live over the lagoon in Mestre.

History

Venice's origins date to the 5th and 6th centuries when barbarian invasions forced the Veneto's inhabitants to seek refuge on the lagoon's islands. First ruled by the Byzantines from Ravenna, it wasn't until AD 726 that the Venetians elected their first *doge* (duke).

Over successive centuries, the Venetian Republic grew into a great merchant power, dominating half the Mediterranean, the Adriatic and the trade routes to the Levant – it was from Venice that Marco Polo set out for China in 1271. Decline began in the 16th century and in 1797 the city authorities opened the gates to Napoleon who, in turn, handed the city over to the Austrians. In 1866, Venice was incorporated into the Kingdom of Italy.

Orientation

Everybody gets lost in Venice (Venezia). With 117 islands, 150-odd canals and 400 bridges (only three of which – the Rialto, the Accademia and, at the train station, the Scalzi – cross the Grand Canal) it's impossible not to.

It gets worse: Venetian addresses are almost meaningless to all but local posties. Instead of a street and civic number, local addresses often consist of no more than the *sestiere* (Venice is divided into six districts: Cannaregio, Castello, San Marco, Dorsoduro, San Polo and Santa Croce) followed by a long number. Some, however, do have street names and where

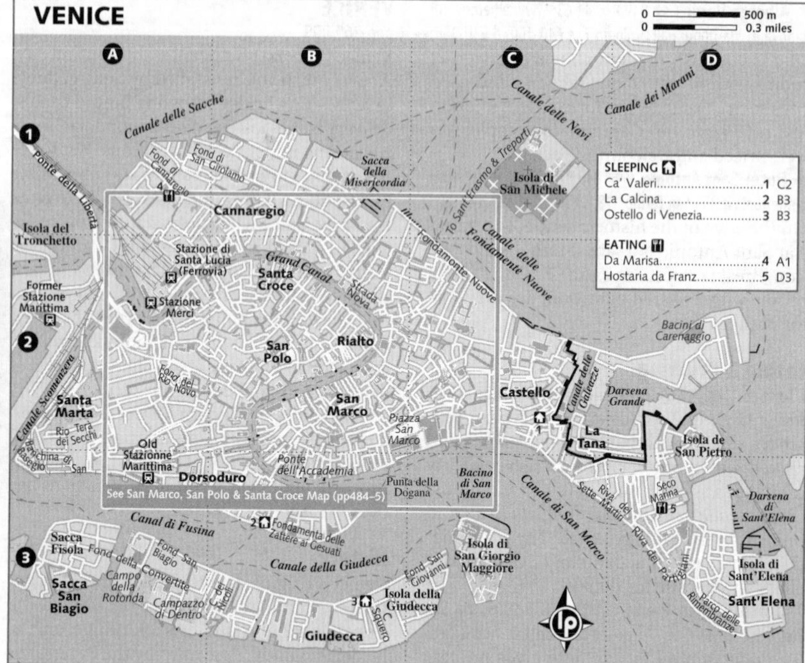

possible we've provided them. You'll still need to know that a street can be a *calle*, *ruga* or *salizada*; beside a canal it's a *fondamenta*. A canal is a *rio*, a filled canal-turned-street a *rio terrà*, and a square a *campo* (Piazza San Marco is Venice's only piazza).

The most helpful points of reference are Santa Lucia train station and Piazzale Roma in the northwest and Piazza San Marco (St Mark's Square) in the south. The signposted path from the train station *(ferrovia)* to Piazza San Marco (the nearest Venice has to a main drag) is a good 40 to 50 minute walk.

Information

EMERGENCY

Police station (Questura; Map pp484-5; ☎ 041 274 70 70; Fondamenta di San Lorenzo, Castello 5053)

INTERNET ACCESS

There are lots of internet cafes in Venice, none cheap.

botteg@ internet (Map pp484-5; Calle delle Botteghe, San Marco 2970; per 15min €3; 🕑 7am-midnight) Also an art gallery and secondhand English bookshop.

Libreria Mondadori (Map pp484-5; Salizada San Moisè 1345, San Marco; per 10min €1; 🕑 10am-8pm Mon-Sat, 11am-7.30pm Sun) The cheapest in town, but only a few terminals available.

Planet Internet (Map pp484-5; Rio Terà San Leonardo, Cannaregio 1520; per 15min €3; 🕑 9am-midnight)

LAUNDRY

Speedy Wash (Map pp484-5; Rio Terà San Leonardo, Cannaregio 1520; 8kg wash/dry €6/3; 🕑 8am-11pm) Next to Planet Internet.

MEDICAL SERVICES

Twenty-four-hour pharmacies are listed in *Un Ospite a Venezia* (A Guest in Venice), a free guide available in many hotels.

Ospedale Civile (Hospital; Map pp484-5; ☎ 041 529 41 11; Campo SS Giovanni e Paolo 6777)

POST

Post office (Map pp484-5; Salizada del Fontego dei Tedeschi; 🕑 9am-6.30pm Mon-Fri). There's also a branch just off Piazza San Marco (limited hours only).

TOURIST INFORMATION

Pick up the free *Shows & Events* guide at tourist offices. It contains comprehensive city listings and a useful public transport map on the inside back cover. The tourist offices also sell a useful map of the city (€2.50).

Azienda di Promozione Turistica (Venice Tourist Board; ☎ central information line 041 529 87 11; www.turismovenezia.it) Lido (Gran Viale Santa Maria Elisabetta 6a; 9am-noon & 3-6pm Jun-Sep); Marco Polo airport (Arrivals Hall; 9am-9pm); Piazza San Marco (Map pp484-5; Piazza San Marco 71f; 9am-3.30pm); Piazzale Roma (Map pp484-5; 9.30am-4.30pm Jun-Sep); train station (Map pp484-5; 8am-6.30pm).

Sights

A good way to whet your sightseeing appetite is to take *vaporetto* (small passenger ferry) No 1 along the **Grand Canal**, which is lined with rococo, Gothic, Moorish and Renaissance palaces. Alight at Piazza San Marco, Venice's most famous sight.

PIAZZA SAN MARCO

Piazza San Marco beautifully encapsulates the splendour of Venice's past and its tourist-fuelled present. Flanked by the arcaded **Procuratie Vecchie** and **Procuratie Nuove**, it's filled for much of the day with tourists, pigeons, balloon-vendors and policemen. While you're taking it all in, you might see the bronze *mori* (Moors) strike the bell of the 15th-century **Torre dell'Orologio** (clock tower).

But it's to the remarkable **Basilica di San Marco** (St Mark's Basilica; Map pp484-5; ☎ 041 522 52 05; Piazza San Marco; admission free; 9.45am-5pm Mon-Sat, 2-4pm Sun Apr-Sep, 9.45am-4.45pm Mon-Sat, 2-4.30pm Sun Oct-Mar) that all eyes are drawn. Sporting spangled spires, Byzantine domes, luminous mosaics and lavish marble work, it was originally built to house the remains of St Mark. According to legend, the Evangelist's body was stolen from Alexandria in Egypt and smuggled to Venice in a barrel of pork. He's since been buried several times, his body now resting under the high altar. The original chapel was destroyed by fire in AD 932 and a new basilica was consecrated in its place in 1094. For the next 500 years it was a work in progress as successive *doges* added mosaics and embellishments looted from the East. The bronze horses above the entrance are replicas of statues 'liberated' from Constantinople in the Fourth Crusade (1204). Behind the main altar is the **Pala d'Oro** (admission €2; 9.45am-5pm Mon-Sat, 2-4.30pm Sun Apr-Sep, to 4pm Oct-Apr), a stunning gold altarpiece decorated with priceless jewels.

The basilica's 99m freestanding **campanile** (bell tower; adult/child €8/4; 9am-7pm Apr-Jun, Sep & Oct, to 9pm Jul & Aug, 9.30am-4.15pm Nov-Mar) dates from the 10th century, although it suddenly collapsed on 14 July 1902 and had to be rebuilt. A lift takes you to the top.

PALAZZO DUCALE

The official residence of the *doges* from the 9th century and the seat of the Republic's government, **Palazzo Ducale** (Doge's Palace; Map pp484-5; ☎ 041 271 59 11; Piazzetta di San Marco; admission with Museum Pass or San Marco Plus Ticket; 9am-7pm Apr-Oct, to 5pm Nov-Mar) also housed Venice's prisons. On the 2nd floor, the massive **Sala del Maggiore Consiglio** is dominated by Tintoretto's *Paradiso* (Paradise), one of the world's largest oil paintings, which measures 22m by 7m.

The **Ponte dei Sospiri** (Bridge of Sighs) connects the palace to an additional wing of the city dungeons. It's named after the sighs that prisoners – including Giacomo Casanova – emitted en route from court to cell.

GALLERIA DELL'ACCADEMIA

One of Venice's top galleries, the **Galleria dell'Accademia** (Map pp484-5; ☎ 041 522 22 47; Dorsoduro 1050; adult/child/concession €6.50/free/3.50; 8.15am-2pm Mon, to 7.15pm Tue-Sun) traces the development of Venetian art from the 14th to the 18th century. You'll find works by Bellini, Titian, Carpaccio, Tintoretto, Giorgione and Veronese.

COLLEZIONE PEGGY GUGGENHEIM

For something more contemporary, visit the **Collezione Peggy Guggenheim** (Map pp484-5; ☎ 041 240 54 11; www.guggenheim-venice.it; Palazzo Venier dei Leoni, Dorsoduro 701; adult/child/student/senior €10/free/5/8; 10am-6pm Wed-Mon). Housed in the American heiress's former home, the spellbinding collection runs the gamut of modern art with works by, among others, Bacon, Pollock, Picasso and Dalí. In the sculpture garden you'll find the graves of Peggy and her dogs.

PALAZZO GRASSI

In 2005 French businessman and art collector François Pinault purchased one of the Grand Canal's most impressive buildings, the 18th-century **Palazzo Grassi** (Map pp484-5; ☎ 041 523 16 80; www.palazzograssi.it; Campo San Samuele 3231; adult/student & child €10/6; 10am-7pm Wed-Mon), and commissioned Japanese architect Tadeo Ando to renovate the building. Since opening

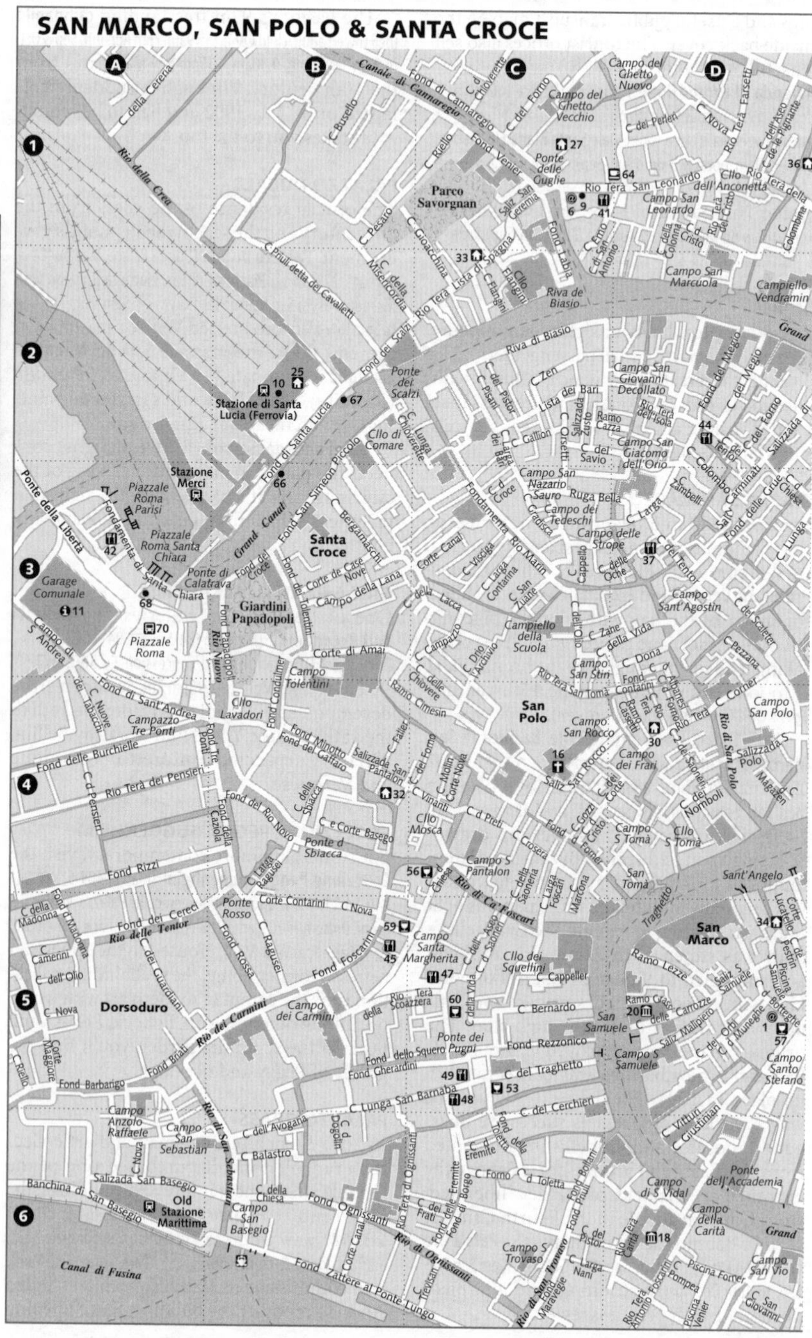
SAN MARCO, SAN POLO & SANTA CROCE
A
B
C
D
1
2
3
4
5
6
Canale di Cannaregio
Rio della Crea
C della Cerena
Fond di Cannaregio
Campo del Ghetto Nuovo
Campo del Ghetto Vecchio
C del Forno
C d Chiovere
C del Perleri
C Nova
Rio Terà Farsetti
27
Ponte delle Guglie
Fond Venier
C Riello
C Busello
Parco Savorgnan
64
36
Rio Terà San Leonardo
Cllo dell'Anconetta
Campo San Leonardo
6
9
41
C Pesaro
C Gioacchina
C della Misericordia
C Priuli detta dei Cavallotti
33
Rio Terà Lista di Spagna
Cllo Flangini
Fond Labia
Riva de Biasio
Campo San Marcuola
Campiello Vendramin
Grand
Riva di Biasio
Fond dei Scalzi
Ponte dei Scalzi
25
10
Stazione di Santa Lucia (Ferrovia)
67
Fond di Santa Lucia
C Zen
Lista dei Bari
Campo San Giovanni Decollato
Rio Terà dell'Isola
Ramo Cazza
Campo San Giacomo dell'Orio
44
Fond del Megio
C del Megio
C del Forno
C Lunga Chioverette
Cllo di Comare
C Gallion
C Orsetti
C del Savio
Stazione Merci
66
Fond San Simeon Piccolo
Piazzale Roma Parisi
Ponte della Libertà
42
Piazzale Roma Santa Chiara
Grand Canal
Fondamenta di Santa Chiara
Campo San Nazario Sauro
Ruga Bella
Campo dei Tedeschi
C Larga
C Zambelli
C Colombo
Campo delle Strope
37
C del Tentor
C Bergamaschi
Santa Croce
Corte Canal
Fondamenta Rio Marin
3
Garage Comunale
11
Ponte di Calatrava
Fond dei Croce
C Corte de Case Nove
Campo della Lana
Fond dei Tolentini
68
Giardini Papadopoli
C della Lacca
Campo Sant'Agostin
70
Piazzale Roma
Campo di S Andrea
Fond Papadopoli
Rio Nuovo
Campiello della Scuola
C della Vida
C Zane
Corte di Amai
Campo Tolentini
Campo San Stin
Rio Terà San Tomà
C Dona
Fond Contarini
C Pezzana
C Corner
Campo San Polo
Fond di Sant'Andrea
C Nuove dei Tabacchi
Campazzo Tre Ponti
Cllo Lavadori
Fond Condulmer
Ramo Cimesin
San Polo
Campo San Rocco
30
Rio di San Polo
Salizzada S Polo
Fond delle Burchielle
Fond Tre Ponti
Fond Minotto
Fond del Gaffaro
Salizzada San Pantalon
C del Forno
Corte Nova
16
Salizz San Rocco
Campo dei Frari
C dei Nomboli
Rio Terà dei Pensieri
C d Pensieri
Fond del Rio Novo
Fond della Caziola
C della Sbiacca
32
C Vinanti
Cllo Mosca
C d Preti
C Crosera
Campo S Tomà
Cllo S Tomà
C e Corte Basego
Ponte d Sbiacca
Fond Rizzi
C Larga Ragusei
56
Rio di Ca' Foscari
Campo S Pantalon
San Tomà
Sant'Angelo
Traghetto
Corte Contarini
C Nova
Ponte Rosso
Fond dei Cereri
Rio delle Tentor
C della Madonna
Fond d Madonna
C Camerini
C dei Guardiani
Fond Rossa
C Ragusei
59
45
Campo Santa Margherita
Fond Foscarini
Cllo dei Squellini
C Cappeller
San Marco
34
Ramo Lezze
C dell'Olio
47
Rio Terà della Scoazzera
60
Dorsoduro
Campo dei Carmini
Rio dei Carmini
C Bernardo
Ramo Grassi
20
San Samuele
1
57
C Nova
Corte Maggiore
C Riello
Ponte dei Pugni
Fond Rezzonico
Campo S Samuele
Campo Santo Stefano
Fond Briati
Fond dello Squero
Fond Gherardini
C del Traghetto
49
Fond Barbarigo
48
53
C Lunga San Barnaba
C del Cerchieri
Campo Anzolo Raffaele
Campo San Sebastian
C Nova
C dell'Avogaria
C d Dogolin
C Balastro
Rio di San Sebastian
C Vitturi
C Giustinian
Ponte dell'Accademia
Salizada San Basegio
Banchina di San Basegio
Old Stazione Marittima
C della Chiesa
Campo San Basegio
Fond Ognissanti
Rio Terà di Ognissanti
C dei Frati
Fond delle Eremite
Fond di Borgo
C d Eremite
C Forno
C d Toletta
Fond Bollani
Campo di S Vidal
Campo della Carità
Grand
18
Canal di Fusina
Rio di Ognissanti
Campo S Trovaso
C del Pistor
C Larga Nani
Rio Terà Carità
Rio di San Trovaso
Piscina Forner
C Pompea
Campo San Vio
Fond Zattere al Ponte Lungo
C Trevisan
Fond Maravegie
Rio Terà Antonio Foscarini
Piscina Venier
C San Giovanni

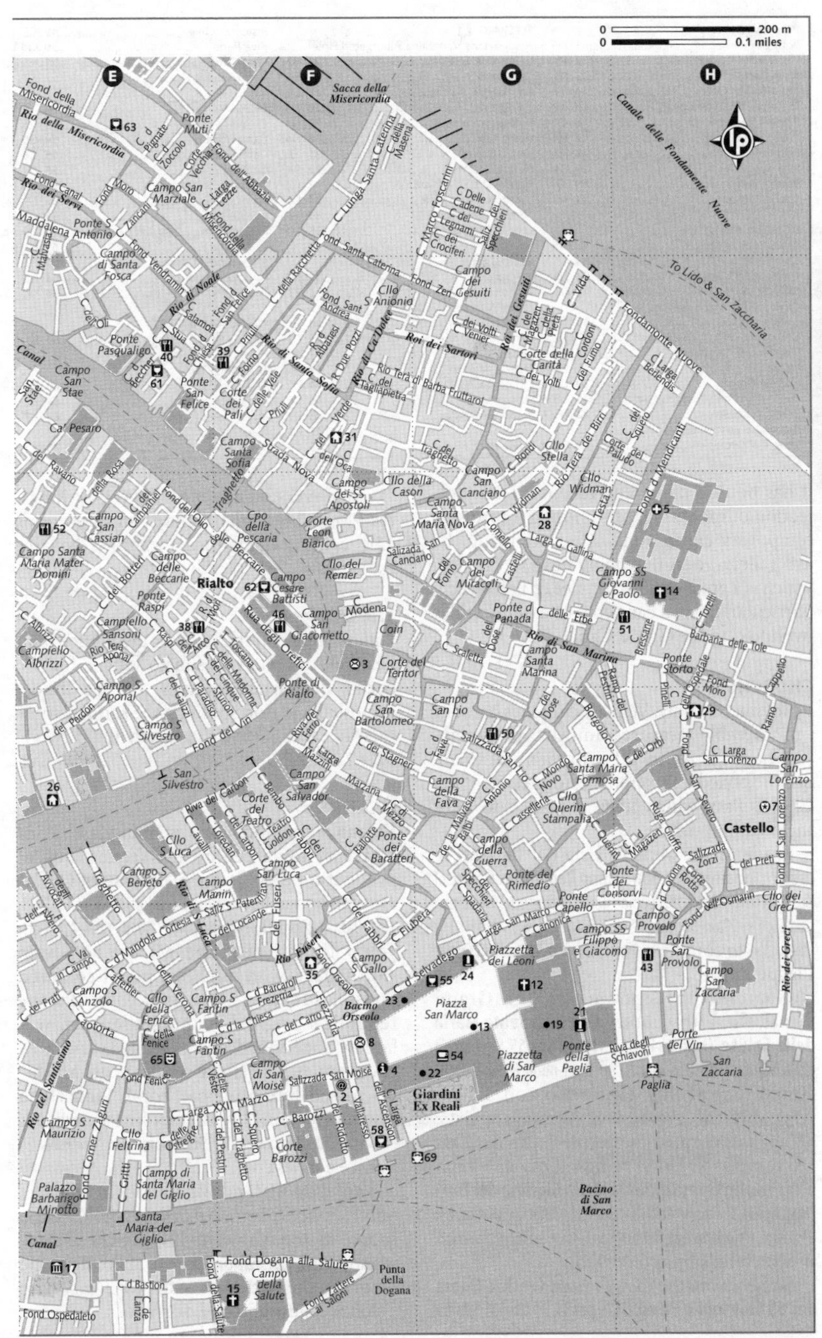
0 200 m
0 0.1 miles
E
F
G
H
Sacca della Misericordia
Canale delle Fondamente Nuove
To Lido & San Zaccaria
Fondamonte Nuove
Fond della Misericordia
Rio della Misericordia
Rio dei Servi
Maddalena
Ponte S Antonio
Campo di Santa Fosca
Fond Vendramin
Rio di Noale
Ponte Muti
Campo San Marziale
Fond dell'Abbazia
Fond della Misericordia
C Lunga Santa Caterina
Fond Santa Caterina
Fond Zen
Campo dei Gesuiti
Rio dei Gesuiti
Rio di Santa Sofia
Rio di Ca' Dolce
Roi dei Sartori
Rio Terà di Barba Fruttarol
Corte della Carità
Ponte Pasqualigo
Ponte San Felice
Corte dei Pali
Campo San Stae
Canal
Ca' Pesaro
Campo Santa Sofia
Strada Nova
Campo dei SS Apostoli
Cllo della Cason
Campo San Canciano
Campo Santa Maria Nova
Cllo Stella
Rio Terà dei Birri
Cllo Widman
Fond d Mendicanti
Campo San Cassian
Campo Santa Maria Mater Domini
Cpo della Pescaria
Corte Leon Bianco
Cllo del Remer
Campo delle Beccarie
Rialto
Campo Cesare Battisti
Campo San Giacometto
Rua degli Orefici
Ponte di Rialto
Campo dei Miracoli
Ponte d Panada
Rio di San Marina
Campo Santa Marina
Campo SS Giovanni e Paolo
Barbaria delle Tole
Ponte Storto
Campiello Sansoni
Campiello Albrizzi
Campo S Aponal
Campo S Silvestro
Fond del Vin
San Silvestro
Corte del Tentor
Campo San Bartolomeo
Campo San Lio
Salizzada San Lio
Campo Santa Maria Formosa
C Larga San Lorenzo
Campo San Lorenzo
Castello
Campo San Salvador
Marzaria
Riva del Carbon
Corte del Teatro
Cllo S Luca
Campo della Fava
Cllo Querini Stampalia
Ponte dei Baratteri
Campo della Guerra
Ponte del Rimedio
Ponte dei Consorvi
Salizzada Zorzi
Cllo dei Greci
Campo S Beneto
Campo Manin
Rio di S Luca
Campo San Luca
Rio Fuseri
Campo S Gallo
C Larga San Marco
Piazzetta dei Leoni
Campo SS Filippo e Giacomo
Campo S Provolo
Ponte San Provolo
Campo San Zaccaria
Rio dei Greci
Campo S Anzolo
Cllo della Fenice
Campo S Fantin
Bacino Orseolo
Piazza San Marco
Piazzetta di San Marco
Ponte della Paglia
Riva degli Schiavoni
Porte del Vin
San Zaccaria
Paglia
Rio del Santissimo
Campo di San Moisè
Salizzada San Moisè
Giardini Ex Reali
C Larga XXII Marzo
Campo S Maurizio
Cllo Feltrina
Corte Barozzi
Campo di Santa Maria del Giglio
Palazzo Barbarigo Minotto
Santa Maria del Giglio
Bacino di San Marco
Fond Dogana alla Salute
Campo della Salute
Punta della Dogana
Fond Zattere al Saloni
C d Bastion
Fond Ospedaleto
2
3
4
5
7
8
12
13
14
15
17
19
21
22
23
24
26
28
29
31
35
38
39
40
43
46
50
51
52
54
55
58
61
62
63
65
69

INFORMATION		
botteg@internet	1	D5
Libreria Mondadori	2	F5
Main Post Office	3	F3
Main Tourist Office	4	F5
Ospedale Civile (Hospital)	5	H3
Planet Internet	6	C1
Police Station	7	H4
Post Office	8	F5
Speedy Wash	9	C1
Tourist Office	10	B2
Tourist Office	11	A3
SIGHTS & ACTIVITIES		
Basilica di San Marco	12	G5
Campanile	13	G5
Chiesa dei SS Giovanni e Paolo	14	H3
Chiesa di Santa Maria della Salute	15	F6
Chiesa Santa Maria Gloriosa dei Frari	16	C4
Collezione Peggy Guggenheim	17	E6
Gallerie dell'Accademia	18	D6
Palazzo Ducale	19	G5
Palazzo Grassi	20	D5
Ponte dei Sospiri (Bridge of Sighs)	21	G5
Procuratie Nuove	22	G5
Procuratie Vecchie	23	F5
Torre dell'Orologio	24	G5
SLEEPING		
Associazione Veneziana Albergatori Hotel Booking Service	25	B2
Ca' Angeli	26	E4
Ca' Pozzo	27	C1
Ca' Riccio	28	G3
Foresteria Valdese	29	H4
Hotel Alex	30	D4
Hotel Bernardi	31	F2
Hotel Dalla Mora	32	B4
Hotel Minerva & Nettuno	33	C2
Locanda Antico Fiore	34	D5
Locanda Orseola	35	F5
Ostello Santa Fosca	36	D1
EATING		
Ae Oche	37	D3
All'Arco	38	E3
Antica Adelaide	39	F2
Billa	40	E2
Cannaregio Fish & Produce Market	41	C1
Coop	42	A3
Osteria da Baco	43	H5
Osteria La Zucca	44	D2
Pizza al Volo	45	B5
Produce Market	46	F3
Punto Sma	47	C5
Ristorante La Bitta	48	C5
Ristoteca Oniga	49	C5
Riva Reno	50	G4
Rosa Salva	51	H3
Vecio Fritolin	52	E3
DRINKING		
Caffè Bar Ai Artisi	53	C5
Caffè Florian	54	G5
Caffè Quadri	55	G5
Chet Bar	56	C4
Gelateria Paolin	57	D5
Harry's Bar	58	F6
Il Caffè	59	C5
Imagina Café	60	C5
La Cantina	61	E2
Muro Vino e Cucina	62	F3
Paradiso Perduto	63	E1
Torrefazione Costarica	64	D1
ENTERTAINMENT		
Gran Teatro La Fenice	65	E5
TRANSPORT		
ACTV Booth	66	B3
ACTV Booth	67	B2
ACTV Ticket Point	68	A3
Alilaguna Fast Ferry to Airport	69	G6
Bus Station	70	A3

it has housed his extensive and eclectic collection of modern art and hosted impressive temporary exhibitions. After admiring the art, gallery-goers inevitably head to the cafe, which is a great spot for a coffee or light lunch, particularly if you can score one of the tables overlooking the Grand Canal.

CHURCHES

As in much of Italy, Venice's churches harbour innumerable treasures; unusually, though, you have to pay to get into many of them. See the boxed text, opposite, for details of the Chorus Pass, which gives admission to 16 of the most important.

Scene of the annual Festa del Redentore (see opposite), the **Santissimo Redentore** (Church of the Redeemer; Map p482; Campo del SS Redentore 194; admission €3; 10am-5pm Mon-Sat, 1-6pm Sun) was built by Palladio to commemorate the end of the Great Plague in 1577.

Guarding the entrance to the Grand Canal, the 17th-century **Chiesa di Santa Maria della Salute** (Map pp484-5; 041 522 55 58; Campo della Salute 1/b; sacristy €2; 9am-noon & 3.30-6pm) contains works by Tintoretto and Titian. Arguably the greatest of Venice's artists, Titian's celebrated masterpiece the *Assunta* (Assumption; 1518) hangs above the high altar in the **Chiesa di Santa Maria Gloriosa dei Frari** (Map pp484-5; Campo dei Frari, San Polo 3004; admission €3; 9am-6pm Mon-Sat, 1-6pm Sun), the same church in which he's buried.

Some way to the east, the vast Gothic **Chiesa dei SS Giovanni e Paolo** (Map pp484-5; 041 523 59 13; Campo SS Giovanni e Paolo; admission €3; 9.30am-7pm Mon-Sat, 1-6pm Sun) is famous for its glorious 15th-century stained-glass window, the largest in Venice.

THE LIDO

Unless you're on the Lido for the Venice Film Festival, the main reason to visit is for the beach. Be warned, though, that it's almost impossible to find space on the sand in summer. It's accessible by *vaporetti* 1, 2, LN, 51, 52, 61 and 62.

ISLANDS

Murano is the home of Venetian glass. Tour a factory for a behind-the-scenes look at production or visit the **Glass Museum** (041 73 95 86; Fondamenta Giustinian 8; adult/student €5.50/3; 10am-4.30pm Thu-Tue Nov-Mar, 10am-6pm Apr-Oct); you'll find it near the Museo *vaporetto* stop. **Burano**, with its cheery pastel-coloured houses, is renowned for its lace. **Torcello**, the republic's original island settlement, was largely abandoned due to malaria and now counts no more than 80 residents. Its not-to-be-missed Byzantine cathedral, **Santa Maria Assunta** (041 270 24 64; Piazza Torcello; adult/child €4/3; 10.30am-6pm Mar-Oct, 10am-5pm Nov-Feb), is Venice's oldest.

Vaporetto 41 (and *vaporetto* 5 in summer only) services Murano from the San Zaccaria *vaporetto* stop. *Vaporetto* LN services all three islands from the *vaporetto* stop at Fondamente Nuove in the northeast of the city. *Vaporetto* T connects Burano and Torcello.

Activities

Be prepared to pay through the nose for that most quintessential of Venetian experiences, a **gondola ride**. Official rates per gondola (maximum six people) start at €80 (€100 at night) for a short trip including the Rialto but not the Grand Canal, and €120 (€150 at night) for a 50-minute trip including the Grand Canal. Haggling may or may not get you a reduction.

If you're a solo traveller in Venice, the cheapest way for you to enjoy a gondola ride is to book in for the 2½-hour 'Ice-cream & Gondola' tour (€40) offered by **Turismo Ricettivo Veneziano** (www.turive.it). This includes a guided walking tour (taken in English), a gelato and a 40-minute gondola ride. It leaves from the San Marco Tourist Office every day at 3pm. The same company offers a two-hour 'Walking Venice' tour (€35, or €22 if you have a Museum Pass) leaving from the office every day at 9.15am. Both tours run between 1 April and 31 October only.

Festivals & Events

Carnevale The major event of the year, when some Venetians and loads of tourists don Venetian-made masks and costumes for a weeklong party in the lead-up to Ash Wednesday. It's been going since 1268.

Palio delle Quattro Repubbliche Marinare Venice, Amalfi, Genoa and Pisa take turns to host this historic regatta. It's in Venice in early June 2011.

Festa del Redentore Held on the third weekend in July; celebrations climax with a spectacular fireworks display.

Regata Storica Costumed parades precede gondola races on the Grand Canal; held on the first Sunday in September.

Venice Architecture Biennale This major architecture shindig is held every even-numbered year from September to November.

Venice Biennale This major exhibition of international visual arts is held every odd-numbered year from June to November.

Venice International Film Festival (Mostra del Cinema di Venezia) Italy's top film fest is held in late August and September at the Lido's Palazzo del Cinema.

Sleeping

Venice is Italy's most expensive city. It's always advisable to book ahead, especially at weekends, in May and September, and during Carnevale and other holidays. At the train station, the **Associazione Veneziana Albergatori** (Map p482; ☎ 800 843 006; 🕑 8am-10pm Easter-Oct, to 9pm Nov-Easter) will book you a room for a small fee.

BUDGET

Ostello Santa Fosca (Map pp484-5; ☎ 041 71 57 75; www.santafosca.it; Cannaregio 2372; dm/d with shared bathroom €20/50) Here, you can sunbathe in an enclosed garden near the Rialto before retiring to your dormitory for the night. There's a kitchen for guests to use (summer only). With a Rolling Venice Card rates are €2 cheaper. Breakfast isn't included in the price.

Ostello di Venezia (Map p482; ☎ 041 523 82 11; www.ostellovenezia.it; Fondamenta delle Zitelle 86; dm €21) Venice's cheap but charmless HI hostel is over the water from Piazza San Marco on the island of Giudecca. Take *vaporetto* 41, 42 or 82 from the train station, alighting at Zitelle. There's an 11.30pm curfew.

ITALY

ADMISSION DISCOUNTS

The **Rolling Venice Card** (€4) is for visitors aged 14 to 29 years; it offers discounts on food, accommodation, shopping, transport and museums. You can get it at tourist offices, and at HelloVenezia offices. You'll need ID.

The **Venice Card** (www.venicecard.it; under 30yr 3/7 days €53.50/76, 30yr & over €62/85) entitles holders to free entry at all of Venice's civic museums (including Palazzo Ducale and the Murano Glass Museum), free entry to the 16 Chorus churches, unlimited use of ACTV public transport, discounted car parking and use of public toilets. It doesn't always represent a saving, so check before buying. It's cheaper if you buy it online; otherwise, it's sold at tourist and HelloVenezia offices.

To visit the museums on Piazza San Marco you'll need to buy either a **Museum Pass** (☎ 041 240 52 11; www.museicivicivenezianі.it; adult/under 5yr/6-14yr/EU citizen €18/free/12/12), which gives entry to the museums on Piazza San Marco and six other civic museums; or a **San Marco Plus Ticket** (€13/free/7.50), which gives entry to the San Marco Museums and your choice of one other civic museum. Both are available at participating museums.

The **Chorus Pass** (☎ 041 275 04 62; www.chorusvenezia.org; adult/student under 29yr/family €9/6/18) covers admission to 16 of Venice's major churches. Otherwise entry to each church is €3.

Foresteria Valdese (Map pp484-5; ☎ 041 528 67 97; www.foresteriavenezia.it; Centro Culturale P Cavagnis, Castello 5170; dm €24-26, d €82-86; 💻) Run by the Waldensian and Methodist Church and housed in a rambling old mansion, this well-run hostel is deservedly popular. Follow Calle Lunga Santa Maria Formosa from Campo Santa Maria Formosa. Only groups can book ahead; for everyone else it's first come, first served.

Hotel Bernardi (Map pp484-5; ☎ 041 522 72 57; www.hotelbernardi.com; SS Apostoli Calle dell'Oca, Cannaregio 4366; s €55, d with shared bathroom €55-70, d with private bathroom €80-110; ❄) Comfortable rooms, hospitable owners and keen prices mean that this top choice is always heavily booked.

Hotel Alex (Map pp484-5; ☎ 041 523 13 41; www.hotelalexinvenice.com; Rio Terá, San Polo 2606; s €35-50, d €40-108) The welcoming Alex is in a quiet spot near Campo dei Frari. Spread over three floors (no lift), most of the rooms are a decent size and all are decorated with simple efficiency. There are rooms with shared bathrooms available for cheaper rates.

Hotel Minerva & Nettuno (Map pp484-5; ☎ 041 71 59 68; www.minervaenettuno.it; Lista di Spagna, Cannaregio 230; s/d with shared bathroom €45/70, with private bathroom €65/110; ❄) Stay at this place near the train station and do your bit for the environment. All the mod cons in the antique-laden rooms are fired by electricity produced from renewable sources.

Hotel Dalla Mora (Map pp484-5; ☎ 041 71 07 03; www.hoteldallamora.it; Salizada San Pantalon, Santa Croce 42a; d with shared bathroom €80-83, s/d with private bathroom €70/100) This family-run one-star choice has small but clean and airy rooms in two buildings, some of which overlook a canal. There's a pleasant terrace, too.

MIDRANGE & TOP END

La Calcina (Map p482; ☎ 041 520 64 66; www.lacalcina.com; Fondamenta Zattere ai Gesuati, Dorsoduro 780; s €65-110, d €99-225; ❄ 💻) A charming place with 29 rooms and a small garden, La Calcina offers immaculate and elegant rooms with parquet floors and timber furnishings. In summer, breakfast is served on a terrace overlooking the Guidecca Canal. Cheaper rates are available for single rooms with a shared bathroom.

Ca' Valeri (Map p482; ☎ 041 241 15 30; www.locandacavaleri.com; Ramo Corazzieri, Castello 3845; r €69-169, ste €79-179; ❄) The drawcard here is an extremely quiet location and beautifully decorated rooms with excellent bathrooms. And there's only one way to describe the low-season prices – a total steal.

Locanda Antico Fiore (Map pp484-5; ☎ 041 71 51 80; www.anticofiore.com; Corte Lucatello, San Marco 3486; r €70-145; ❄ 💻) Warm colours and an overload of chintz are the decorative hallmarks of this comfortable hotel, which is located in an 18th-century *palazzo* just off the Grand Canal.

Ca'Riccio (Map pp484-5; ☎ 041 52 82 334; www.cariccio.com; Campo dei Miracoli, Cannaregio 5394a; s €77-99, d €99-154; ❄) Located behind the magnificent Chiesa dei Miracoli, this 14th-century residence offers beautifully restored rooms overlooking a pretty courtyard.

our pick **Ca' Angeli** (Map pp484-5; ☎ 041 523 24 80; www.caangeli.it; Calle del Tragheto della Madoneta, San Polo 1434; s €80-150, d €105-215, ste €195-315; ❄) A fabulous choice overlooking the Grand Canal, Ca' Angeli is notable for its extremely comfortable rooms, helpful staff and truly magnificent breakfast spread. If you can possibly afford it, opt for a suite with a Grand Canal view.

Ca' Pozzo (Map pp484-5; ☎ 041 524 05 04; www.capozzovenice.com; Sotoportego Ca'Pozzo, Cannaregio 1279; s €90-175, d €120-205; ❄ 💻) Its motto is 'accommodation and art', and this very stylish boutique hotel in the Ghetto melds the two perfectly. Rooms are decorated with a minimalist aesthetic but have all the mod cons you'll need; some have a private terrace or courtyard. The rates are extremely reasonable for what's on offer.

Locanda Orseola (Map pp484-5; ☎ 041 520 48 27; www.locandaorseolo.com; Corte Zorzi, San Marco 1083; s €90-190, d €120-300; ❄) You can watch the gondolas skimming over the Orseolo canal from the breakfast room of this impressive hotel. The richly decorated rooms are comfortable and have buckets of charm.

Eating

Venetian specialities include *risi e bisi* (pea soup thickened with rice) and *sarde di saor* (fried sardines marinated in vinegar and onions).

RESTAURANTS

Ae Oche (Map pp484-5; ☎ 041 524 11 61; Calle del Tentor, Santa Croce 1552a/b; pizza €7-10) Students adore the Tex-Mex decor and huge pizza list at this bustling place. It's on the main path between the *ferrovia* and San Marco.

Antica Adelaide (Map pp484-5; ☎ 041 523 26 29; Calle Priuli, Cannaregio 3728; meals €30) The ancient Adelaide was (under different names) in the food business as far back as the 18th century. You can pop in for a drink and *cicheti* (bar snacks) or tuck into a hearty bowl of pasta or full meal.

Osteria La Zucca (Map pp484-5; ☎ 041 524 15 70; Calle del Tentor, Santa Croce 1762; meals €32; ⏰ closed Sun) A wonderful, unpretentious little restaurant in an out-of-the-way spot, 'The Pumpkin' serves a range of innovative Mediterranean dishes prepared with fresh, seasonal ingredients.

Da Marisa (Map p482; ☎ 041 72 02 11; Fondamenta di San Giobbe 652b, Cannaregio; set menu incl wine & coffee €35-40; ⏰ lunch daily, dinner Tue & Thu-Sat) You can watch the sun setting over the lagoon from the canalside tables here. Locals tie up their boats and sit down to enjoy generous servings of truly excellent local food – they almost always outnumber tourists. Devotees overlook the fact that service can be brusque, meal times are set (noon and 8pm), credit cards aren't accepted and there's no opportunity to vary the daily menu, which is mostly meat but sometimes seafood.

Ristorante La Bitta (Map pp484-5; ☎ 041 523 05 31; Calle Lunga San Barnaba, Dorsoduro 2753a; meals €40; ⏰ closed Sun) The bottle-lined dining room and attractive internal courtyard are a lovely setting in which to enjoy your choice from a small, meat-dominated menu that changes with the season. No credit cards.

Ristoteca Oniga (Map pp484-5; ☎ 041 522 44 10; Campo San Barnaba, Dorsoduro 2852; meals €46; ⏰ closed Tue) We agonised over whether to recommend this stylish restaurant – its food and ambience are top-class, but its service is possibly the worst we encountered in Venice (and that's saying a lot). In the end, we decided that the superb homemade pasta dishes and piazza setting came up trumps.

Vecio Fritolin (Map pp484-5; ☎ 041 522 28 81; Calle della Regina, Santa Croce 2262; meals €50; ⏰ dinner Tue, lunch & dinner Wed-Mon) Traditionally, a *fritolin* was an eatery where diners sat at a common table and tucked into fried seafood and polenta. This is the modern equivalent, only the food is sophisticated, the menu is varied and the decor is stylish rather than rustic. The owners also run a chic cafe in the Palazzo Grassi – if you see an exhibition here make sure you pop in for a well-priced light lunch.

our pick **Hostaria da Franz** (Map p482; ☎ 041 522 70 24; Calle del Pestrin, Castello 3886; meals €70-90) Expensive? Yes. Elegant? Excessively. Delicious? You said it! This is one of the best seafood restaurants in the city, and it's also world-renowned for its creamy tiramisu. On a quiet canal away from any tourist action, it's where the arty-glitterati love to eat when they come for the Biennale.

QUICK EATS

All'Arco (Map pp484-5; ☎ 041 520 56 66; Calle dell'Arco, San Polo 436; chiceti €1.50-4, panini €4; ⏰ 7.30am-9pm Mon-Sat) Popular with locals, this tiny *osteria* serves wonderful, fresh panini, a range of *cicheti* and wine by the glass.

Osteria da Baco (Map pp484-5; ☎ 041 522 28 87; Calle delle Rasse, Castello 6672) A friendly local bar where gondoliers like to relax between trips, Osteria da Baco offers a range of tasty *tremezzini* (sandwiches, €1.30) that can be washed down with a beer (€3) or glass of *fragolino* (fragrant strawberry wine, €2).

Pizza al Volo (Map pp484-5; ☎ 041 522 54 30; Campo Santa Margherita, Dorsoduro 2944; pizza slice from €2.50) In need of a pizza pit stop? Here's your opportunity. You'll be in the company of a steady stream of interns from the Guggenheim.

Riva Reno (Map pp484-5; ☎ 041 2411821; Salizada S Lio, Castello 5662) This sleek branch of the excellent national gelato chain is conveniently located between the Rialto and Piazza San Marco.

Rosa Salva (Map pp484-5; ☎ 041 522 79 49; Campo SS Giovanni e Paolo, Castello 6779; ⏰ closed Wed) Stop by this historic cafe for sensational *fritalle* (fried pastry puffs filled with zabaglione or cream).

SELF-CATERING

For fruit and veg, as well as deli items, head for the markets near the Rialto bridge, or on the Rio Terà San Leonardo. There are also supermarkets: **Punto Sma** (Map pp484-5; Campo Santa Margherita), **Billa** (Map pp484-5; Strada Nova, Cannaregio 3660) and **Coop** (Map pp484-5; Fondamenta di Santa Chiara, Piazzale Roma 506a).

Drinking

BARS

Caffè Bar Ai Artisti (Map pp484-5; ☎ 041 523 89 44; Fondamenta della Toletta, Dorsoduro 1169a) On Campo S Barnaba, this welcoming place is good for coffee during the day, but even better for a drink or two at night.

Chet Bar (Map pp484-5; ☎ 041 523 87 27; Campo Santa Margherita, Dorsoduro 3684) Late at night, patrons at this laid-back drinking den spill out of the bar and sit on the steps of the nearby bridge. It's one of the most popular venues on buzzing Campo Santa Margherita.

ITALY

Harry's Bar (Map pp484-5; ☎ 041 528 57 77; Calle Vallaresso, San Marco 1323) To drink a Bellini (white-peach pulp and *prosecco* – Venetian sparkling white) at the bar that invented them is an expensive experience to tick off the list rather than a holiday highlight. Nevertheless, this bar to the stars is always full.

Il Caffè (Map pp484-5; ☎ 041 528 79 98; Campo Santa Margherita, Dorsoduro 2963) Popular with foreign and Italian students, this is one of Venice's historic drinking spots. Known to locals as Café Rosso because of its red frontage, it's got outdoor seating and great *sprizze* (a type of apéritif).

Imagina Café (Map pp484-5; ☎ 041 241 06 25; Rio Terà Canal, Dorsoduro 3126) A constantly changing exhibition program means that patrons can enjoy art with their *aperitivo* at this hip modern bar.

La Cantina (Map pp484-5; ☎ 041 52 28 258; Campo San Felice 3689, Cannaregio; 🕒 closed Mon, 2 weeks Jul & Aug, 2 weeks Jan) Sit at one of the outdoor tables at this *enoteca* and watch the passing traffic promenade up and down the Strada Nuova. A good choice of wines by the glass and classy *chicheti* make it deservedly popular.

Paradiso Perduto (Map pp484-5; ☎ 041 72 05 81; Fondamenta della Misericordia, Cannaregio 2540; 🕒 closed Mon) Queer-friendly and flamboyant, this restaurant-cum-club heats up late, but when the DJs pump up the decibels it jives. There's live music most weekends.

Muro Vino e Cucina (Map pp484-5; ☎ 041 523 47 40; Campo Cesare Battisti, San Polo 222; 🕒 closed Sun) The centre of a happening nightlife scene in the market squares of the Rialto, Muro joins a number of bars in attracting huge gaggles of young locals, who spill out into the square with their drinks. It also serves excellent, if pricey, food.

CAFES

Caffè Florian (Map pp484-5; ☎ 041 520 56 41; Piazza San Marco 56/59) If you think it's worth paying up to four times the usual price for a coffee, emulate Byron, Goethe and Rousseau and pull up a seat at Piazza San Marco's most famous cafe. Here you can watch life on the square as you're serenaded by the in-house musicians.

Caffè Quadri (Map pp484-5; ☎ 041 528 92 99; Piazza San Marco 120; coffee €7-10) On the opposite side of the square, Caffè Quadri offers more of the same.

Gelateria Paolin (Map pp484-5; ☎ 041 522 55 76; Campo Santo Stefano, San Marco 2962) A lovely sunny spot for a morning coffee, and an essential gelato stop (eat in or take out) in the afternoon or evening.

Torrefazione Costarica (Map pp484-5; ☎ 041 71 63 71; Rio Terá San Leonardo, Cannaregio 1337) Connoisseurs come here for Venice's best coffee. Espressos are smooth yet charged with flavour, and cappuccinos are exactly as they should be, warm and creamy.

Entertainment

Tickets for the majority of events in Venice are available from **HelloVenezia ticket outlets** (www.hellovenezia.it), run by the ACTV transport network. You'll find them in front of the train station and at Piazzale Roma.

Gran Teatro La Fenice (Map pp484-5; ☎ for guided tours 041 24 24; www.teatrolafenice.it; Campo San Fantin, San Marco 1977; tickets from €15) One of Italy's most important opera houses, the fully restored Fenice is back to its sumptuous best after being destroyed by fire in 1996.

Shopping

Classic Venetian gift options include Murano glass, lace from Burano, Carnevale masks and *carta marmorizzata* (marbled paper). There are any number of shops selling these items, but if you want the best deal go to the source. Be warned that genuine Burano lace is expensive; much of the cheaper stuff sold round town is imported from the Far East.

The main shopping area is between San Marco and the Rialto, although if you're after designer clobber you should head to the area west of Piazza San Marco.

Getting There & Away

AIR

Most European and domestic flights land at **Marco Polo airport** (VCE; ☎ 041 260 92 60; www.veniceairport.it), 12km outside Venice. Ryanair flies to **Treviso airport** (TSF; ☎ 0422 31 51 11; www.trevisoairport.it), about 30km from Venice.

BOAT

Minoan Lines (☎ 041 240 71 01; www.minoan.gr) runs ferries to Corfu (€69 to €91, 23½ hours), Igoumenitsa (€69 to €91, 22 hours) and Patra (€69 to €182, 36 hours) daily in summer and four times per week in winter.

BUS

ACTV (☎ 041 24 24; www.actv.it) buses service surrounding areas, including Mestre, Padua and Treviso. Tickets and information are available at the bus station (Map pp484–5) in Piazzale Roma.

TRAIN

Venice's Stazione di Santa Lucia is directly linked by regional trains to Padua (€2.90, 45 minutes, every 20 minutes), Verona (€13.50, 1½ hours, half-hourly) and Ferrara (€6.15, two hours, half-hourly). It is easily accessible from Bologna, Milan, Rome and Florence. You can also reach points in France, Germany, Austria, Switzerland, Slovenia and Croatia from here.

Getting Around

TO/FROM THE AIRPORT

To get to Marco Polo there are various options: **Alilaguna** (Map pp484-5; www.alilaguna.com) operates a fast ferry service from the San Marco ferry stop (€12, 70 minutes, approximately every hour); alternatively, from Piazzale Roma take either an **ATVO** (☎ 041 520 55 30; www.atvo.it, in Italian) bus (€3, 20 minutes, every half-hour) or ACTV bus 5d (€2, 25 minutes, every half-hour).

For Treviso airport, take the ATVO Ryanairbus (€5, 70 minutes, 16 daily) from Piazzale Roma two hours and 10 minutes before your flight departure. The last service is at 7.40pm.

BOAT

The city's main mode of public transport is the *vaporetto*. The most useful routes:

1 From Piazzale Roma to the train station and down the Grand Canal to San Marco and the Lido.

2 From S Zaccaria (near San Marco) to the Lido via Giudecca, Piazzale Roma, the train station and the Rialto.

3 From Piazzale Roma to San Marco via the Rialto and Accademia.

17 Car ferry between Tronchetto and the Lido.

LN From Fondamenta Nuove to Murano, Burano and Torcello.

T Runs between Burano and Torcello.

Tickets, available from ACTV booths at the major *vaporetti* stops, are expensive: €6.50 for a single trip; €14 for 12 hours; €16 for 24 hours; €21 for 36 hours; €26 for 48 hours and €31 for 72 hours (€18 if you have a Rolling Venice card).

The poor man's gondola, *traghetti* (€0.50 per crossing) are used by Venetians to cross the Grand Canal where there's no nearby bridge.

CAR & MOTORCYCLE

Vehicles must be parked on Tronchetto or at Piazzale Roma (cars are allowed on the Lido – take car ferry 17 from Tronchetto). The car parks are not cheap – €24 every 24 hours – so you're better off leaving your car in Mestre and getting a train over to Venice.

FERRARA

pop 133,300

Ferrara retains much of the austere splendour of its Renaissance heyday, when it was the seat of the powerful Este family (1260–1598). Overshadowed by the menacing Castello Estense, the compact medieval centre is atmospheric and lively.

Information is available from the main **tourist office** (☎ 0532 29 93 03; www.ferrarainfo.com; 9am-1pm & 2-6pm Mon-Sat, 9.30am-1pm & 2-5.30pm Sun) inside Castello Estense. For internet, try **Sun Rise Internet Point** (Via Garibaldi 37/13-15; per hr €4; 9am-9.30pm).

Sights

If you're planning to visit the major monuments, buy a **Museum Card** (adult/child 11-17yr €14/10), which gives free entry to all municipal museums. They're available from both the Cathedral Museum and Palazzo Schifanoia.

Easily explored on foot, Ferrara's *centro storico* lies to the south of **Castello Estense** (☎ 0532 29 92 33; www.castelloestense.it; Viale Cavour; adult/child €7/6, Lion's Tower extra €1; 9.30am-5.30pm, closed Mon Jun-Feb). Complete with moat and drawbridges, the castle was begun by Nicolò II d'Este in 1385 and became the Este family's residence. Highlights include the **Sala dei Giganti** (Giant's Room) and **Salone dei Giochi** (Games Salon) with frescoes by Camillo and Sebastiano Filippi.

Nearby, the pink-and-white 12th-century **Duomo** (☎ 0532 20 74 49; Piazza Cattedrale; 7.30am-noon & 3-6.30pm Mon-Sat, 7.30am-12.30pm & 3.30-7.30pm Sun) is most notable for its superb three-tiered marble facade with a Gothic depiction of the Last Judgement.

Fresco fans won't want to miss **Palazzo Schifanoia** (☎ 0532 24 49 49; Via Scandiana 23; adult/child €5/free; 9am-6pm Tue-Sun), one of Ferrara's earliest Renaissance buildings and another of the Este palaces. In the **Sala dei Mesi** (Room of the Months), the 15th-century frescoes are considered among the best examples of their type in Italy. Sadly, though, they're not in great nick.

Sleeping

You won't need to overnight to see Ferrara's sights, but it's a cheap alternative to Bologna, and a viable base for Venice.

Pensione Artisti (☎ 0532 76 10 38; Via Vittoria 66; s/d with shared bathroom €28/48, d with private bathroom €60) Put simply, this is the best budget option in town. Its scrubbed white rooms sparkle, the location is excellent, there are kitchen facilities for guests, and the owners are superfriendly.

Hotel de Prati (☎ 0532 24 19 05; www.hoteldeprati.com; Via Padiglioni 5; s €49-85, d €75-120; ☒) The large, individually decorated and extremely comfortable rooms here sport features such as satellite TV and wi-fi. Downstairs, the yellow and orange walls stage contemporary art exhibitions. Great location.

Eating & Drinking

Trattoria Il Mandolino (☎ 0532 76 00 80; Via Carlo Mayr 83; meals €25; ⏲ lunch & dinner Wed-Sun, lunch Mon) Taking its name from the mandolin on the wall, this charmingly cluttered trattoria is a memorable place to dine on Ferrarese food. Menu staples include the house speciality, *salama da sugo con purè* (salty braised salami on a bed of mashed potato).

Messisbugo (☎ 0532 76 40 60; Via Carlo Mayr 79; ⏲ 7pm-2am Tue-Sun) Despite a name that suggests Tex-Mex tack, Messisbugo is actually a cool, brick-vaulted bar favoured by bohemians and students, with friendly staff, great wines and a laid-back vibe.

Getting There & Around

Ferrara is easy to reach by train. There are regional trains to Bologna (€3.10, 35 minutes, every 30 to 60 minutes), Venice (€6.15, two hours, half-hourly) and nearby Ravenna (€4.50, 75 minutes, 10 daily).

From the station take bus 1 or 9 for the historic centre.

BOLOGNA

pop 374,000

Boasting a boisterous bonhomie rare in Italy's reserved north, Bologna is worth a few days of anyone's itinerary, not so much for its specific attractions, but for the sheer fun of strolling its animated, arcaded streets. A university town since 1088 (Europe's oldest), it's riddled with bars, cafes and trattorias.

Bologna is also famous as one of the country's foremost foodie destinations. Besides the eponymous bolognese sauce (*ragù*), classic pasta dishes such as tortellini and lasagne were invented here, as was mortadella (aka baloney or Bologna sausage). Treats such as these are enjoyed in welcoming trattorias throughout the city, washed down with fizzy Lambrusco red wine. After dinner, locals love to wander through the city's arcades to their favourite bar or nightclub and party the night away – this is not a town that goes to sleep early.

Information

Iperbole (☎ 051 219 31 84; URP, Piazza Maggiore 6; ⏲ 9.30am-6.30pm Mon-Fri, 9.30am-1.30pm & 3.30-6.30pm Sat) Free internet access is offered at the commune-funded URP library.
Lava e Asciuga (Via Irnerio 35b; wash load €3, dry €1.30; ⏲ 7am-midnight) Conveniently located self-service laundrette.
Liong@te Internet Point (www.liongate.it; 1st fl, Via Rizzoli 9; per hr €2; ⏲ 10am-midnight)
Ospedale Maggiore (Hospital; ☎ 051 647 81 11)
Police station (Questura; ☎ 051 640 11 11; Piazza Galileo 7)
Post office (Piazza Minghetti 1)
Tourist information (☎ 051 23 96 60; www.bolognaturismo.info) airport (⏲ 8am-8pm); Piazza Maggiore 1 (⏲ 9.30am-7.30pm); train station (⏲ 9am-7pm Mon-Sat, 9am-3pm Sun) Ask for a copy of the free *bé* 'what's on' booklet.

Sights & Activities

Bologna's porticoed *centro storico* is a vibrant and atmospheric place to wander. The place to start is pedestrianised **Piazza Maggiore** and adjoining **Piazza del Nettuno**. Here you'll find the **Fontana del Nettuno** (Neptune's Fountain), sculpted by Giambologna in 1566 and featuring an impressively muscled Neptune. On the western flank of Piazza Maggiore is the **Palazzo Comunale** (Town Hall; ☎ 051 20 31 11; admission free), home to the **Collezioni Comunali d'Arte** (Civic Art Collection; admission free; ⏲ 9am-3pm Tue-Fri, 10am-6.30pm Sat & Sun) and a museum dedicated to the work of artist **Giorgio Morandi** (admission free; ⏲ 9am-3pm Tue-Fri, 10am-6.30pm Sat & Sun).

To the south, the Gothic **Basilica di San Petronio** (☎ 051 22 54 22; Piazza Maggiore; ⏲ 7.45am-12.30pm & 3-6pm) is dedicated to the city's patron saint, Petronius. Its partially complete facade doesn't diminish its status as the world's fifth-largest basilica. Inside, don't miss Giovanni da Modena's bizarre *l'Inferno* fresco in the fourth chapel on the left.

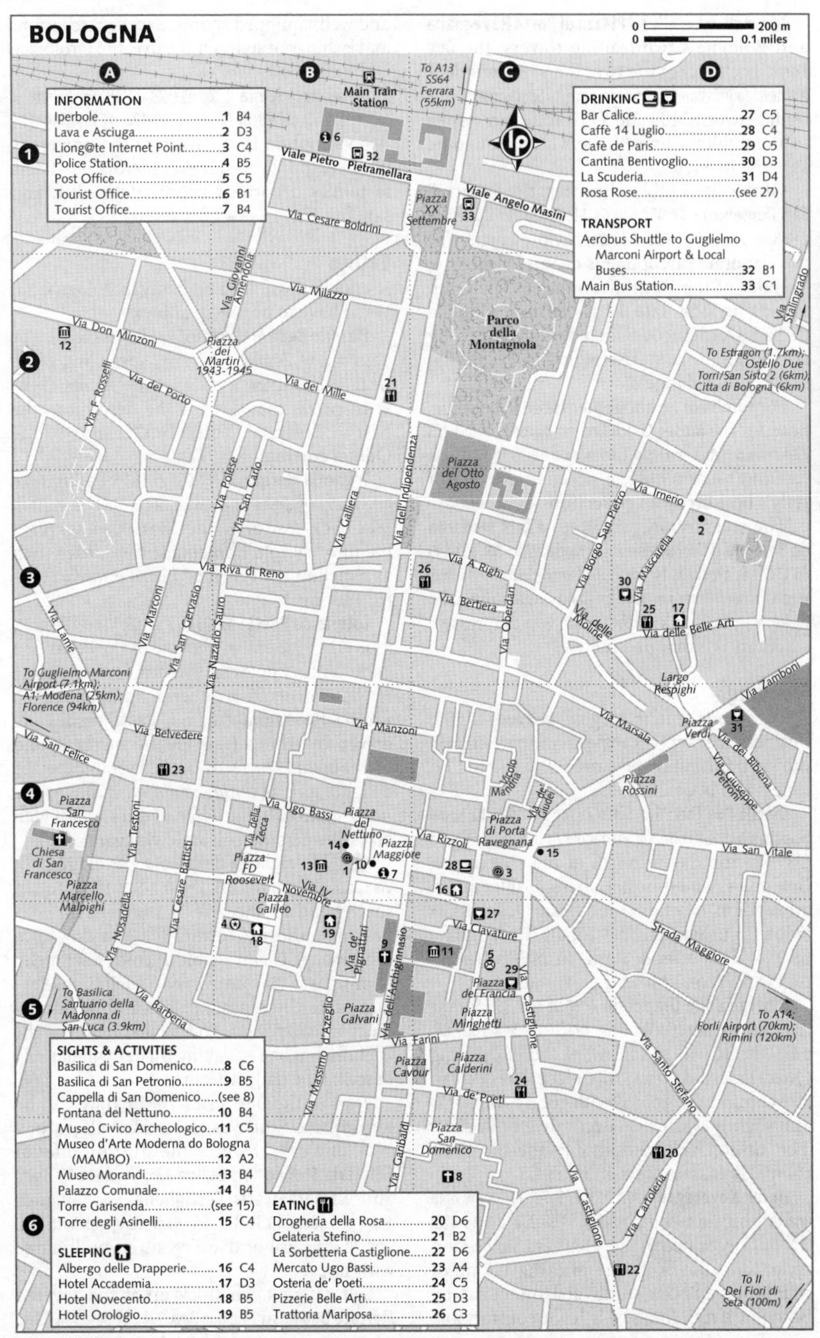
BOLOGNA
0 200 m
0 0.1 miles
INFORMATION
Iperbole 1 B4
Lava e Asciuga 2 D3
Liong@te Internet Point 3 C4
Police Station 4 B5
Post Office 5 C5
Tourist Office 6 B1
Tourist Office 7 B4
DRINKING
Bar Calice 27 C5
Caffè 14 Luglio 28 C4
Cafè de Paris 29 C5
Cantina Bentivoglio 30 D3
La Scuderia 31 D4
Rosa Rose (see 27)
TRANSPORT
Aerobus Shuttle to Guglielmo Marconi Airport & Local Buses 32 B1
Main Bus Station 33 C1
SIGHTS & ACTIVITIES
Basilica di San Domenico 8 C6
Basilica di San Petronio 9 B5
Cappella di San Domenico (see 8)
Fontana del Nettuno 10 B4
Museo Civico Archeologico 11 C5
Museo d'Arte Moderna do Bologna (MAMBO) 12 A2
Museo Morandi 13 B4
Palazzo Comunale 14 B4
Torre Garisenda (see 15)
Torre degli Asinelli 15 C4
SLEEPING
Albergo delle Drapperie 16 C4
Hotel Accademia 17 D3
Hotel Novecento 18 B5
Hotel Orologio 19 B5
EATING
Drogheria della Rosa 20 D6
Gelateria Stefino 21 B2
La Sorbetteria Castiglione 22 D6
Mercato Ugo Bassi 23 A4
Osteria de' Poeti 24 C5
Pizzerie Belle Arti 25 D3
Trattoria Mariposa 26 C3
Main Train Station
To A13 SS64 Ferrara (55km)
Viale Pietro Pietramellara
Viale Angelo Masini
Piazza XX Settembre
Via Cesare Boldrini
Via Giovanni Amendola
Via Milazzo
Parco della Montagnola
Via Don Minzoni
Piazza dei Martiri 1943-1945
Via del Porto
Via dei Mille
Via F Rosselli
Via Stalingrado
To Estragon (1.7km); Ostello Due Torri/San Sisto 2 (6km); Citta di Bologna (6km)
Piazza del Otto Agosto
Via Polese
Via San Carlo
Via Galliera
Via dell'Indipendenza
Via Irnerio
Via Borgo San Pietro
Via Mascarella
Via Riva di Reno
Via A Righi
Via Bertiera
Via Oberdan
Via delle Moline
Via delle Belle Arti
Via Lame
Via Marconi
Via San Gervasio
Via Nazario Sauro
To Guglielmo Marconi Airport (7.1km); A1; Modena (25km); Florence (94km)
Largo Respighi
Via Zamboni
Via Marsala
Piazza Verdi
Via dei Bibiena
Via Giuseppe Petroni
Via Belvedere
Via San Felice
Via Manzoni
Vicolo Mandria
Via de' Giudei
Piazza Rossini
Piazza San Francesco
Chiesa di San Francesco
Via Testoni
Via della Zecca
Via Ugo Bassi
Piazza del Nettuno
Piazza Maggiore
Via Rizzoli
Piazza di Porta Ravegnana
Via San Vitale
Piazza FD Roosevelt
Via IV Novembre
Piazza Galileo
Piazza Marcello Malpighi
Via Nosadella
Via Cesare Battisti
Via de' Pignattari
Via dell'Archiginnasio
Via Clavature
Strada Maggiore
Piazza del Francia
Via Castiglione
To Basilica Santuario della Madonna di San Luca (3.9km)
Via Barberia
Piazza Galvani
Via Massimo d'Azeglio
Piazza Minghetti
To A14; Forli Airport (70km); Rimini (120km)
Via Farini
Piazza Cavour
Piazza Calderini
Via Santo Stefano
Via de' Poeti
Piazza San Domenico
Via Garibaldi
Via Cartoleria
To Il Dei Fiori di Seta (100m)
ITALY

It's a short walk to **Piazza di Porta Ravegnana** and Bologna's two leaning towers, the **Due Torri**. The taller of the two, the 97m **Torre degli Asinelli** (admission €3; 9am-6pm, to 5pm winter), was built between 1109 and 1119 and is now open to the public. Climb the 498 steps for some superb city views.

Of the city's other churches, the **Basilica di San Domenico** (051 640 04 11; Piazza San Domenico; 8am-12.30pm & 3.30-6.30pm) is noteworthy for the elaborate sarcophagus of San Domenico, founder of the Dominican order. The tomb stands in the late-12th-century Capella di San Domenico, which was designed by Nicolò Pisano and later added to by, among others, Michelangelo.

For tombs of an altogether more sober style, head for the **Museo Civico Archeologico** (051 275 72 11; Via dell'Archiginnasio 2; admission free; 9am-3pm Tue-Fri, 10am-6.30pm Sat & Sun), which houses one of Italy's best Etruscan collections.

The recently opened **Museo d'Arte Moderna do Bologna** (MAMBO, Museum of Modern Art; 051 649 66 11; Via Don Minzoni 14; admission free; 10am-6pm Tue, Wed & Fri-Sun 10am-6pm, to 10pm Thu) is in a converted bakery in Bologna's new – and very impressive – arts and culture precinct.

Sleeping

Accommodation is largely geared to the business market. It's expensive (particularly during trade fairs) and can be difficult to find unless you book ahead.

Ostello Due Torri/San Sisto 2 (051 50 18 10; hostelbologna@hotmail.com; Via Viadagola 5; dm €16, s €25, d €38;) Some 6km north of the city centre, Bologna's two HI hostels, barely 100m apart, are modern, functional and cheap. Take bus 93 (Monday to Saturday day time), 301 (Sunday) or 21b (daily after 8.30pm) from Via Irnerio or Via Marconi. Mind the 11pm curfew.

Albergo delle Drapperie (051 22 39 55; www.albergodrapperie.com; Via delle Drapperie 5; s €60-105, d €75-140;) In the heart of the happening Quadrilatero district, this place offers clean and comfortable rooms with good bathrooms and slightly whimsical decorative flourishes. The air-con can be dodgy in the top-floor rooms. Breakfast costs an extra €5.

Hotel Novecento (051 745 73 11; www.bolognarthotels.it; 3rd fl, Piazza Galileo 4; s €90-230, d €140-328;) Decorated in the Viennese Succession style, this chic boutique offering is one of four hotels and one studio apartment run by Bologna Arts Hotels. All have comfortable and well-equipped rooms, excellent locations and lashings of style. Of the five, the Orologico is the cheapest.

Hotel Accademia (051 23 23 18; www.hotelaccademia.it; Via delle Belle Arti 6; s €100-128, d €155-180;) A good option in the thick of the university quarter, the three-star Accademia has fresh, tastefully decorated rooms with wi-fi and satellite TV.

Eating

It's not impossible to eat badly in Bologna, but you'd have to be pretty unlucky.

Pizzerie Belle Arti (051 22 55 81; Via Belle Arti 14; pizzas from €4.50, meals €25) This sprawling place near the university serves delicious thin-crust pizzas that deserve the descriptor 'the best in Bologna'. You'll find it next to the Odeon cinema.

Trattoria Mariposa (051 22 56 56; Via Bertiera 12; meals €20; closed Sun & Mon, dinner Thu) A genial, laid-back trattoria, the Mariposa serves a menu of simple homemade favourites such as tortellini with *ragù* or *burro e salvia* (butter and sage).

Osteria de'Poeti (051 23 61 66; Via de' Poeti 1b; meals €32; closed Mon, lunch Sun) In the cellar of a 14th-century *palazzo*, this atmospheric place is a bastion of old-style service and top-notch Emilia-Romagna cuisine. Pasta dishes are driven by what's fresh in the markets, and mains include perfectly cooked yet unexpected delights such as *ventaglio d'anatra con prugne nere e aceto balsamico* (fan of duck breast with black prunes and balsamic vinegar sauce).

our pick **Drogheria della Rosa** (051 22 25 29; Via Cartoleria 10; meals €45; Mon-Sat) Its wooden shelves and apothecaries' jars and bottles signal this trattoria's former life as a *drogheria* (pharmacy). Claim a table to enjoy a set menu of antipasto (including mortadella), a selection of excellent pasta dishes and wonderful meat or fish *secondi*. There's no menu, but the friendly English-speaking owner will happily describe the daily offerings.

Two of the best *gelaterie* in Italy can be found here (and yes, we realise that's one heck of a call). Sample the stuff on offer at **Gelateria Stefino** (Via Galleria 49b; noon-12.30am) and **La Sorbetteria Castiglione** (Via Castiglione 44; 8.30am-10.30 Tue-Fri, 9am-midnight Sat& Sat, 9am-10.30pm Sun) and we're sure you'll agree with us.

Self-caterers can stock up at the covered **Mercato Ugo Bassi** (Via Ugo Bassi 27; closed Sun).

Drinking

There are so many bars in Bologna that it seems silly to single out only a few. Popular drinking strips include the Quadrilatero, east of Piazza Maggiore, where you'll find uber-fashionable **Café de Paris** (☎ 051 23 49 80; www.cafedeparisbologna.org; Piazza del Francia 1c; 8am-1am Mon-Thu, 8am-late Fri & Sat), **Rosa Rose** (☎ 051 22 50 71; Via Clavature 18b) and **Bar Calice** (☎ 051 26 45 06; Via Clavature 13a). Other popular bars are scattered around Piazza Verdi; jazz-focussed **Cantina Bentivoglio** (☎ 051 26 54 16; www.cantinabentivoglio.it; Via Mascarella 4b; 8pm-2am Sep-May, closed Sun Jun-Aug) and bohemian **La Scuderia** (☎ 051 656 96 19; www.lascuderia.bo.it; Piazza Verdi 2; 8am-2am Mon-Sat) are both here. Most of these places also serve good food.

For coffee, make your way to **Caffè 14 Luglio** (Via Orefici 6; 7am-8.30pm Mon-Sat). The flagship store of a generations-old coffee company, it sells freshly roasted beans and serves fantastic coffee in its small modern cafe.

Getting There & Around

European and domestic flights arrive at Bologna's **Guglielmo Marconi airport** (BLQ; ☎ 051 647 96 15; www.bologna-airport.it), 6km northwest of the city. An Aerobus shuttle (€5, 30 minutes, three times hourly) departs from the main train station; buy your ticket at the ACTV office behind the taxi rank. Ryanair flies to **Forlì** (FRL; ☎ 0543 47 49 21; www.forli-airport.it), 70km southeast of Bologna. **Ebus** (☎ 199 11 55 77) buses run between Forlí and the main train station to coincide with flights. The trip takes 1½ hours and costs €10.

Bologna is a major rail hub. From the **main train station** (Piazza delle Medaglie d'Oro), trains run to Venice (€15.10, two hours, half-hourly), and to the following on the fast Eurostar Alta Velocità (ES AV) trains: Florence (€16.20, one hour, hourly), Rome (€45.60, 2¾ hours, hourly) and Milan (€33, one hour, hourly).

National and international coaches depart from the main **bus station** (Piazza XX Settembre).

Traffic is restricted in Bologna's centre. To get to the centre from the train station take bus 25 or 30 (€1).

RAVENNA

pop 152,000

Most people visit Ravenna to see its remarkable Unesco-protected mosaics. Relics of the city's golden age as capital of the Western Roman and Byzantine Empires, they are described by Dante in his *Divine Comedy*, much of which was written here. Easily accessible from Bologna, this refined and polished town is worth a day trip at the very least. Its national profile is raised each year during June and July when the **Ravenna Festival** (www.ravennafestival.org) is held. Performances are in venues including the Basilica di San Vitale, and the involvement of Italy's top conductor, Riccardo Muti, means the classical component is always strong.

The city's **main tourist office** (☎ 0544 354 04; www.turismo.ravenna.it; Via Salara 8/12; 8.30am-7pm Mon-Sat, 10am-6pm Sun summer, 8.30am-6pm Mon-Sat, 10am-4pm Sun winter) is in the *centro storico*. There's another office in **Classe** (Via Romea Sud 266; 9.30am-12.30pm & 2.30-5.30pm).

Sights

Ravenna's five main **monuments** (www.ravennamosaici.it; adult/under 10yr/concession €8.50/free/7.50) are covered by a single ticket. Available at any one of the five monuments and valid for seven days, it gives entry to the Basilica di San Vitale, the Mausoleo di Galla Placida, the Basilica di Sant'Appollinare Nuovo, the Museo Arcivescovile and Battistero Neoniano. In summer there's an extra €2 booking fee for the Mausoleo di Galla Placida.

On the northern edge of the *centro storico*, the sombre exterior of the 6th-century **Basilica di San Vitale** (☎ 0544 21 51 93; Via Fiandrini; 9am-7pm Apr-Sep, 9am-5.30pm Mar & Oct, 9.30am-5pm Nov-Feb) hides a dazzling interior with mosaics depicting Old Testament scenes. Nearby, the **Mausoleo di Galla Placidia** (☎ 0544 21 51 93; Via Fiandrini; 9am-7pm Apr-Sep, 9am-5.30pm Mar & Oct, 9.30am-5pm Nov-Feb) contains the city's oldest mosaics. Adjoining Ravenna's unremarkable cathedral, the **Museo Arcivescovile** (☎ 0544 21 52 91; Piazza Arcivescovado; 9am-7pm Apr-Sep, 9.30am-5.30pm Mar & Oct, 10am-5pm Nov-Feb) boasts an exquisite 6th-century ivory throne, while next door in the **Battistero Neoniano** (Via Battistero; 9am-7pm Apr-Sep, 9.30am-5.30pm Mar & Oct, 10am-5pm Nov-Feb), the baptism of Christ and the apostles is represented in the domed roof mosaics. To the east the **Basilica di Sant'Apollinare Nuovo** (☎ 0544 21 95 18; Via di Roma; 9am-7pm Apr-Sep, 9.30am-5.30pm Mar & Oct, 10am-5pm Nov-Feb) boasts, among other things, a superb mosaic depicting a procession of martyrs headed towards Christ and his apostles. It was being restored at the time of research.

Five kilometres southeast of the city, the apse mosaic of the **Basilica di Sant'Apollinare in Classe** (☎ 0544 47 35 69; Via Romea Sud, Classe; adult/child/

concession €3/free/1.50; ⌚ 8.30am-7.30pm) is a must-see. Take bus 4 or 44 (€1) from Piazza Caduti per la Libertà. These run half-hourly.

Dante spent the last 19 years of his life in Ravenna after Florence expelled him in 1302. As a perpetual act of penance, Florence supplies the oil for the lamp that burns in his **tomb** (Via Dante Alighieri 9; admission free; ⌚ 9am-7pm).

Sleeping & Eating

Ostello Dante (☎ 0544 42 11 64; www.hostelravenna.com; Via Nicolodi 12; dm/s/d €14/22/40; 💻) Ravenna's vibrant HI youth hostel is in a modern building 1km east of the train station. There's wi-fi in the lobby. Take bus 1.

Hotel Diana (☎ 0544 391 64; www.hoteldiana.ra.it; via Girolamo Rossi, 47; s €42-61, d €63-86; ❄) A modern three-star hotel occupying an 18th-century townhouse, Hotel Diana offers 33 extremely comfortable rooms and a lavish buffet breakfast.

Cá de Vén (☎ 0544 301 63; Via Corrado Ricci 24; 1st/2nd courses €8/13; ⌚ closed Mon) The food's nothing special at this cavernous, high-ceilinged *enoteca*-cum-restaurant, but locals and tourists alike enjoy popping in for a glass of wine and *piadina* (flat-bread sandwich). It's the most famous eatery in town.

Locanda del Melarancio (☎ 0544 215 258; Via Mentana 33; ⌚ closed Wed) Choose between the downstairs *osteria* (mains €12) or the elegant upstairs *ristorante* (mains €20) at this popular eatery. The delicious menu is seasonally driven and dishes are perfectly executed. At night the *osteria* morphs into a pub.

Getting There & Around

Regional trains connect the city with Bologna (€5, 1½ hours, 13 daily) and Ferrara (€4.50, 1¼ hours, 11 daily).

In town, cycling is popular. The tourist office in town has 20 bikes that it makes available to visitors aged 18 or over at no charge.

THE DOLOMITES

Stretching across Trentino-Alto Adige and into the Veneto, the stabbing sawtooth peaks of the Dolomites provide some of Italy's most thrilling scenery. With their jagged silhouettes and colourful tints (blue-grey turning to red, then purple as the sun sets), they are popular all year – in winter for the skiing, in summer for the superb hiking.

Resorts range from exclusive Cortina d'Ampezzo (see opposite) to family-oriented resorts in the Val Gardena (opposite). Ski passes cover either single resorts or a combination of slopes; the most comprehensive is the **Superski Dolomiti pass** (www.dolomitisuperski.com; high season 3/6 days €125/220), which accesses 464 lifts and 1220km of runs in 12 valleys.

Hiking opportunities run the gamut from kid-friendly strolls to hard-core mountain treks. Trails are well marked with numbers on red-and-white bands on trees and rocks, or by numbers inside coloured triangles for the four *Alte Vie* (High Routes). Recommended areas include the Alpe di Siusi, a vast plateau above the Val Gardena; the area around Cortina; and Pale di San Martino, accessible from San Martino di Castrozza.

For more information on skiing and cycling, see the Activities section in the Italy Directory, p545.

Information

Information on Trentino-Alto Adige can be obtained in Trent at the **tourist office** (☎ 0461 98 38 80; www.apt.trento.it; Via Manci 2; ⌚ 9am-7pm). Bolzano's **tourist office** (☎ 0471 30 70 00; www.bolzano-bozen.it; Piazza Walther 8; ⌚ 9am-6.30pm Mon-Fri, to 12.30pm Sat) can also help.

For activities and accommodation in the Veneto, ask at the tourist office in Cortina – see opposite.

The best online resource option is www.dolomiti.org, which has a great deal of useful information.

Getting There & Around

In Trentino-Alto Adige, **Bolzano airport** (BZO; ☎ 0471 25 52 55; www.abd-airport.it) is served by ski charter flights from the UK in winter and daily year-round flights from Rome and Milan.

> **WARNING**
>
> Even in summer the weather is extremely changeable in the Alps; though it may be sweltering when you set off, be prepared for very cold, wet weather on even the shortest walks. Essentials include good-quality, worn-in walking boots, a waterproof jacket, warm hat and gloves, light food, plenty of water and a decent map. The best maps are the Tabacco 1:25,000 series, widely available throughout the area.

Otherwise the nearest airports are in Verona (see p480) or Bergamo (see p477).

On terra firma, the area's excellent bus network is run by **Trentino Trasporti** (☎ 0461 82 10 00; www.ttspa.it, in Italian) in Trent; **SAD** (☎ 800 84 60 47; www.sii.bz.it) in Alto Adige; and **Dolomiti Bus** (www.dolomitibus.it, in Italian) in the Veneto. During winter, most resorts offer 'ski bus' services.

The main towns and the many ski resorts can be reached directly from cities such as Rome, Florence, Venice, Bologna, Milan and Genoa. Information is available from tourist offices and regional bus stations.

CORTINA D'AMPEZZO

Surrounded by some of the Dolomites' most dramatic scenery, Cortina is one of Italy's most famous, fashionable and expensive ski resorts. Predictably it boasts first-class facilities (skiing, skating, sledding, climbing) and superb hiking; less obviously, it has some reasonably priced accommodation. Ask at the **tourist office** (☎ 0436 32 31; www.infodolomiti.it; Piazzetta San Francesco 8; 🕑 9am-12.30pm & 3.30-6.30pm) for listings.

SAD buses connect Cortina with Dobbiaco (€1, 45 minutes, three times daily), where you can change for Bolzano. ATVO runs a service to/from Venice (€11, 3½ hours) on weekends from September to May and daily from mid-June to the end of August.

CANAZEI

One of the best-known resorts in the Val di Fassa, Canazei is a great spot for serious skiers. It has 120km of downhill and cross-country runs and is linked to the challenging Sella Ronda ski network. There's even summer skiing on the Marmolada glacier, whose stunning 3342m-summit marks the highest point in the Dolomites.

Spend a cheap night at the Marmolada **camping ground** (☎ 0462 60 16 60, fax 0462 60 17 22; Strèda de Parèda 60; per person/tent €9.50/9.50; 🕑 year-round), or contact the **tourist office** (☎ 0462 60 96 00; www.fassa.com; Piazza Marconi 5; 🕑 8.30am-12.15pm & 3-7pm Mon-Sat, 10am-12.30pm Sun) for accommodation lists. The resort is accessible by **Trentino Trasporti bus** (www.ttspa.it, in Italian) from Trent (€5.50, 2½ hours, three daily).

VAL GARDENA

Branching northeast off the Val di Fassa, the Val Gardena is a popular skiing area with great facilities and accessible prices. In summer, hikers head to the Sella Group and the Alpe di Siusi for rugged, high-altitude walks and to the Vallunga for more accessible family strolls.

The valley's main towns are Ortisei, Santa Cristina and Selva, all offering plenty of accommodation and easy access to runs. Further information is available online at www.gardena.org, or from the towns' tourist offices:

Ortisei (☎ 0471 77 76 00; Via Rezia 1; 🕑 8.30am-12.30pm & 2.30-6.30pm Mon-Sat, 10am-noon & 5-6.30pm Sun)

Santa Cristina (☎ 0471 77 78 00; Via Chemun 9; 🕑 8am-noon & 2.30-6.30pm Mon-Sat, 9.30am-noon Sun)

Selva (☎ 0471 77 79 00; Via Mëisules 213; 🕑 8am-noon & 3-6.30pm Mon-Sat, 9am-noon & 5-6.30pm Sun)

The Val Gardena is accessible from Bolzano by SAD bus and from Canazei in summer.

SAN MARTINO DI CASTROZZA

At the foot of the imposing Pale di San Martino range, San Martino di Castrozza acts as a gateway to the Parco Naturale Paneveggio - Pale di San Martino. The **tourist office** (☎ 0439 76 88 67; www.sanmartino.com; Via Passo Rolle 165; 🕑 9am-noon & 3-7pm Mon-Sat, 9.30am-12.30pm Sun) can provide skiing information and help with accommodation.

Trentino Trasporti buses run to/from Trent (€5.80, 2½ hours, four daily).

TUSCANY

Tuscany is one of those places that well and truly lives up to its press. Its fabled rolling landscape has long been considered the embodiment of rural chic, a favourite of holidaying PMs and retired advertising executives, while its cities are home to a significant portfolio of the world's medieval and Renaissance art. Some people never venture beyond the region's crowded capital, but with some of Italy's most charming towns an easy trip away, to do so would be a waste, particularly as there are so many chances to sample the region's famous food and wine along the way.

FLORENCE

pop 366,000

Poets of the 18th and 19th centuries swooned at the beauty of Florence (Firenze), and once here you'll appreciate why. An essential stop on everyone's Italian itinerary, this Renaissance treasure trove is busy year-round. Fortunately, the huge crowds fail to diminish the city's lustre. A list of its famous sons

TOP FIVE TUSCAN TREASURES

- Ogle **David** (p502), Michelangelo's perfect man, in the Galleria dell'Accademia, Florence.
- Fall in love with Botticelli's **Spring** and **Venus** (p500) in the Galleria degli Uffizi, Florence.
- See that it's no misnomer: the **Leaning Tower of Pisa** (p506) really is a long way from vertical.
- Admire Siena's symbol of civic pride, Ambrogio Lorenzetti's **Allegory of Good & Bad Government** (p507) mural in the city's Museo Civico.
- Picnic and pedal atop Lucca's monumental Renaissance **city walls** (p510).

reads like a Renaissance who's who – under 'M' alone you'll find Medici, Machiavelli and Michelangelo – and its celebrated cityscape lingers in the memory long after you've said your farewells.

History

Many hold that Florentia was founded by Julius Caesar around 59 BC, but archaeological evidence suggests an earlier village, possibly founded by the Etruscans around 200 BC. A rich merchant city by the 12th century, its golden age arrived in the 15th century. Under the Medici prince Lorenzo il Magnifico (1469–92), the city's cultural, artistic and political fecundity culminated in the Renaissance.

The Medici were succeeded in the 18th century by the French House of Lorraine, which ruled until 1860, when the city was incorporated into the kingdom of Italy. From 1865 to 1870, Florence was, in fact, capital of the fledgling kingdom.

During WWII, parts of the city were destroyed by bombing, including all of its bridges except for Ponte Vecchio. In 1966 a devastating flood destroyed or severely damaged many important works of art. More recently, in 1993, the Mafia exploded a massive car bomb, killing five people and destroying part of the Uffizi Gallery.

Orientation

From the main train station, Santa Maria Novella, it's a 550m walk along Via de' Panzani and Via de' Cerretani to the Duomo. From Piazza di San Giovanni, next to the Duomo, Via Roma leads down to Piazza della Repubblica and continues as Via Calimala and Via Por Santa Maria to the Ponte Vecchio.

Information

BOOKSHOPS

Feltrinelli International (Map p501; ☎ 055 21 95 24; Via Cavour 12r; 🕑 9am-7.30pm Mon-Sat) Great selection of fiction and nonfiction in English.

Paperback Exchange (Map p501; ☎ 055 29 34 60; Via delle Oche 4r; 🕑 9am-7.30pm Mon-Fri, 10.30am-7.30pm Sat) New and secondhand books in English.

EMERGENCY

Police station (Questura; Map p499; ☎ 055 497 71; Via Zara 2)

INTERNET ACCESS

Cyber Link (Map p501; Via del Giglio 29r; per hr €4, students €3; 🕑 9.30am-12.30am) Also offers a left luggage service (€5 per 24 hour).

Internet Train (per hr €4.30, students €3.20); Via Porta Rossa 38 (Map p501; 🕑 9.30am-midnight Mon-Sat, 10am-midnight Sun); Borgo San Jacopo 30r (Map p501; ☎ 055 265 79 35) There are also branches at Via dell'Oriuolo 40r (Map p501), Via Guelfa 24a (Map p499) and beneath Stazione Santa Maria Novella (Map p499). Hours vary.

LAUNDRY

Wash & Dry Lavarapido (☎ 800 23 11 72; 8kg wash or dry €3.50; 🕑 8am-10pm) There are branches at Borgo San Frediano 39r (Map p499), Via dei Servi 105r (Map p499), Via del Sole 29r (Map p501), Via della Scala 52-54r (Map p499), Via Dell'Agnolo 21r (Map p499), Via de' Serragli 87r (Map p499) and Via Nazionale 129r (Map p499).

MEDICAL SERVICES

Farmacia Comunale (Map p499; ☎ 055 28 94 35; Stazione di Santa Maria Novella; 🕑 24hr) Inside the train station.

Misericordia di Firenze (Map p501; ☎ 055 21 22 22; Vicolo degli Adimari 1, Piazza del Duomo; 🕑 2-6pm Mon-Fri Mar-Oct) Fee-paying medical service.

Tourist Medical Service (Map p499; ☎ 055 47 54 11; Via Lorenzo il Magnifico 59; 🕑 24hr)

POST

Post office (Map p501; Via Pellicceria 3)

TELEPHONE

Telecom office (Map p499; Via Cavour 21r; 🕑 7am-11pm) Public payphones.

FLORENCE
0 500 m
0 0.2 miles
A
B
C
D
1
2
3
4
5
6
INFORMATION
Farmacia Comunale.............1 A3
Internet Train.....................2 B3
Police Station.....................3 C2
Telecom Office....................4 C4
Tourist Medical Service........5 C2
Tourist Office.....................6 B4
Tourist Office.....................7 B4
Wash & Dry Lavarapido......8 C3
Wash & Dry Lavarapido......9 B3
Wash & Dry Lavarapido....10 A5
Wash & Dry Lavarapido....11 D5
Wash & Dry Lavarapido....12 A5
Wash & Dry Lavarapido....13 A4
SIGHTS & ACTIVITIES
Florence by Bike................14 C3
Galleria dell'Accademia......15 C3
Piazzale Michelangelo...........16 D6
Porta Romana.......................17 A6
SLEEPING
Campeggio Michelangelo......18 D6
Hotel Morandi alla Crocetta...19 C3
Johlea & Johanna..................20 C3
Ostello Archi Rossi...............21 B3
Ostello Santa Monaca...........22 A5
EATING
Borgo Antico........................23 A5
Standa.................................24 C4
Trattoria Casalinga...............25 B5
Trattoria Cibrèo....................26 D4
Trattoria Mario.....................27 B3
DRINKING
Negroni.............................28 C5
TRANSPORT
ATAF Bus Stop...................29 B3
Avis....................................30 A4
Hertz..................................31 A4
SITA Bus Station.................32 A4
To Ostello Villa Camerata (3.5km)
Via Faentina
Via I Settembrini
Piazza delle Cure
Viale dei Mille
Via G Berchet
Giardino dell's Orticltura
Via Vittorio Emanuele II
Via Bolognese
Ponte Rosso
Viale G Milton
Viale Don G Minzoni
Via Lorenzo il Magnifico
Piazza della Libertà
Via Fra' Bartolommeo
Via Masaccio
Via S Botticelli
Via L Giordano
Via Fra Buonvicini
To Villa Medicea di Careggi (3km); Villa Medicea La Petraia (4.5km); Villa di Medicea Castello (6km)
Via A Poliziano
Via dello Statuto
To Aeroport di Firenze (Florence Airport; 5km); Provincia di Firenze Tourist Office (5km); Uffico Depositeria Comunlae (5km); Tenax (5km)
Fortezza da Basso
Palazzo delle Esposizioni
Viale Spartaco Lavagnini
Via delle Mantellate
Via Duca d'Aosta
Via Bonifacio Lupi
Piazza Savonarola
Viale Filippo Strozzi
Via Cittadella
Piazza della Indipendenza
Via Santa Caterina d'Alessandria
Via delle Ruote
Via Zara
Via San Gallo
Via Gustavo Modena
Via Venezia
Viale Giacomo Matteotti
Via dei della Robbia
Via M Ficino
Via degli Artisti
Via Pier Capponi
Viale Fratelli Rosselli
Via della Fortezza
Via Santa Reparata
Via San Zanobi
Via Giorgio la Pira
Giardino dei Semplici
Giardino della Gherardesca
Piazzale Donatello
Via Jacopo da Diacceto
Via Luigi Alamanni
Via Valfonda
Via Fiume
Via Faenza
Via Nazionale
Via Guelfa
Piazza San Marco
Via Cesare Battisti
Via Gino Capponi
Via Giuseppe Giusti
Stazione di Santa Maria Novella
Via Rosina
Via Taddea
Mercato Centrale
Via de' Ginori
Via Cavour
Piazza della SS Annunziata
Via Laura
Via P Giordani
Via Bernardo Rucellai
Via degli Orti Oricellari
Piazza della Stazione
Via Sant'Antonino
Borgo la Noce
Via degli Alfani
Via della Pergola
Via della Colonna
Piazza Massimo d'Azeglio
Via Giosuè Carducci
Via della Mattonaia
To Teatro Communale (100m)
Via Palazzuolo
Via della Scala
Via Panzani
Via de' Cerretani
Piazza del Duomo
Via Bufalini
Santa Croce
Borgo Pinti
Via Fiesolana
Via dei Pilastri
Borgo Ognissanti
Via Montebello
Lungarno Amerigo Vespucci
Ponte Amerigo Vespucci
Piazza degli Antinori
Via de' Tornabuoni
Piazza della Repubblica
Via de' Calzaiuoli
Via dell'Oriuolo
Via di Mezzo
Piazza Sant' Ambrogio
Borgo degli Albizi
Via Pietrapiana
Borgo la Croce
Piazza Lorenzo Ghiberti
Via F Paolieri
To UNA Vittoria Hotel (500m); Pisa International Airport Galileo Galilei (44km)
Ponte alla Carraia
Lungarno Corsini
Borgo Allegri
Via dell'Agnolo
Piazza de Nerli
Borgo San Frediano
Lungarno Guicciardini
Ponte Santa Trinità
Via dei Macci
Via delle Conce
Via di San Giuseppe
Via delle Casine
Via Pietro Thouar
Viale della Giovine Italia
Piazza Piattellina
Via Santa Monaca
Via dell'Ardiglione
Via Maffia
Via de' Michelozzi
Ponte Vecchio
Lungarno Generale Diaz
Piazza dei Cavalleggeri
Via dei Molcontenti
San Frediano
Santo Spirito
Via Tripoli
Piazza Piave
Via Maggio
Via Mazzetta
Via de' Guicciardini
Piazza de' Pitti
Costa di San Giorgio
Via de' Bardi
Ponte alle Grazie
Lungarno delle Grazie
Lungarno della Zecca Vecchia
Lungarno G Pecori Giraldi
Arno
Giardino Torrigiani
Via della Chiesa
Via del Campuccio
Piazza San Felice
Vicolo della Cava
Lungarno Serristori
V dei Renai
Lungarno Benvenuto Cellini
Giardino di Bardini (Bardini Gardens)
Via San Niccolò
Piazza Giuseppe Poggi
Via della Fornace
Via de' Serragli
Via Romana
See Around The Duomo Map (p501)
Viale Francesco Petrarca
Fontana del Forcone
Via della Meridiana
Via di San Leonardo
Viale Michelangelo
Giardino di Boboli (Boboli Gardens)
Piazza della Calza
Viale dei Cipressi
Isolotto
Via del Bellosguardo
Via dei Belvedere
San Niccolò
Monte Alle Croci
To Certosa di Firenze (3km)

ITALY

TOURIST INFORMATION

Tourist offices (www.firenzeturismo.it) main office (Map p499; ☎ 055 29 08 32; Via Cavour 1r; 8.30am-6.30pm Mon-Sat, to 1.30pm Sun); airport (☎ 055 31 58 74; 8.30am-8.30pm); Borgo Santa Croce 29r (Map p501; ☎ 055 234 04 44; 9am-7pm Mon-Sat, to 2pm Sun Mar–mid-Nov, 9am-5pm Mon-Sat, to 2pm Sun mid-Nov–Feb); Piazza della Stazione 4 (Map p499; ☎ 055 21 22 45; www.commune.fi.it; 8.30am-7pm Mon-Sat, to 2pm Sun)

Sights & Activities

Sightseeing in Florence inevitably means time spent in queues. You'll never avoid them altogether, but by pre-booking museum tickets you'll save time. For €4 extra per museum you can book tickets for the Uffizi, Palazzo Pitti, Galleria dell'Accademia and Cappelle Medicee through **Firenze Musei** (☎ 055 29 48 83; www.firenzemusei.it; booking service 8.30am-7pm Tue-Sun). Buy or collect your tickets from the information desks at the Uffizi or Palazzo Pitti.

PIAZZA DEL DUOMO & AROUND

Pictures don't do justice to the exterior of Florence's Gothic **Duomo** (Map p501; ☎ 055 230 28 85; 10am-5pm Mon-Wed & Fri, 10am-3.30pm Thu, 10am-4.45pm Sat, 10am-3.30pm 1st Sat of every month, 1.30-4.45pm Sun). While they reproduce the startling colours of the tiered red, green and white marble facade and the beautiful symmetry of the dome, they fail to give any sense of its size. One of the world's largest cathedrals – officially known as the Cattedrale di Santa Maria del Fiore – it was begun in 1294 by Sienese architect Arnolfo di Cambio and consecrated in 1436. Its most famous feature, the enormous octagonal **cupola** (dome; admission €6; 8.30am-6.20pm Mon-Fri, to 5pm Sat) was built by Brunelleschi after his design won a public competition in 1420. The interior is decorated with frescoes by Vasari and Zuccari, and the stained-glass windows are by Donatello, Paolo Uccello and Lorenzo Ghiberti. The facade is a 19th-century replacement of the unfinished original, pulled down in the 16th century.

Beside the cathedral, the 82m **campanile** (Map p501; admission €6; 8.30am-6.50pm Nov-May, to 10.20pm Jun-Oct) was begun by Giotto in 1334 and completed after his death by Andrea Pisano and Francesco Talenti. The views from the top make the 414-step climb worthwhile.

To the west, the Romanesque **battistero** (baptistery; Map p501; Piazza di San Giovanni; admission €3; 12.15-6.30pm Mon-Sat, 8.30am-1.30pm 1st Sat of every month, 8.30am-1.30pm Sun) is one of the oldest buildings in Florence and it was here that Dante was baptised. Built on the site of a Roman temple between the 5th and 11th centuries, it's famous for its gilded-bronze doors, particularly Lorenzo Ghiberti's *Gate of Paradise*. Andrea Pisano's south door (1336) is the oldest.

GALLERIA DEGLI UFFIZI (UFFIZI GALLERY)

Home to the world's greatest collection of Italian Renaissance art, the **Galleria degli Uffizi** (Map p501; ☎ 055 238 86 51; www.uffizi.firenze.it; Piazza degli Uffizi 6; admission €10; 8.15am-6.35pm Tue-Sun) attracts some 1.5 million visitors annually. They won't all be there when you visit, but unless you've booked a ticket (see Firenze Musei, left), expect to queue.

The gallery houses the Medici family collection, bequeathed to the city in 1743 on the condition that it never leave the city. Highlights include *La nascita di Venere* (Birth of Venus) and *Allegoria della primavera* (Allegory of Spring) in the Botticelli Rooms (10 to 14); Leonardo da Vinci's *Annunciazione* (Annunciation; room 15); Michelangelo's *Tondo doni* (Holy Family; Room 25); and Titian's *Venere d'Urbino* (Venus of Urbino; Room 28). Elsewhere you'll find works by Giotto and Cimabue, Filippo Lippi, Fra Angelico and Paolo Uccello, Raphael, Andrea del Sarto, Tintoretto and Caravaggio.

PIAZZA DELLA SIGNORIA

Traditional hub of Florence's political life, Piazza della Signoria is dominated by **Palazzo Vecchio** (Map p501; ☎ 055 276 82 24; adult/child/concession €6/2/4.50; 9am-7pm Fri-Wed, to 2pm Thu), the historical seat of the Florentine government. Characterised by the 94m **Torre d'Arnolfo**, it was designed by Arnolfo di Cambio and built between 1298 and 1340. Visit the Michelozzo courtyard and the lavish upstairs apartments.

To the south, the famous **Loggia della Signoria** (Map p501) is a 14th-century sculpture showcase. The statue of *David* is a copy of Michelangelo's original, which stood here until 1873 but is now in the Galleria dell'Accademia (p502).

PONTE VECCHIO

Lined with jewellery shops, the 14th-century **Ponte Vecchio** (Map p501) was originally flanked by butchers' shops. But when the Medici built a corridor through the bridge to link Palazzo Pitti with Palazzo Vecchio, they

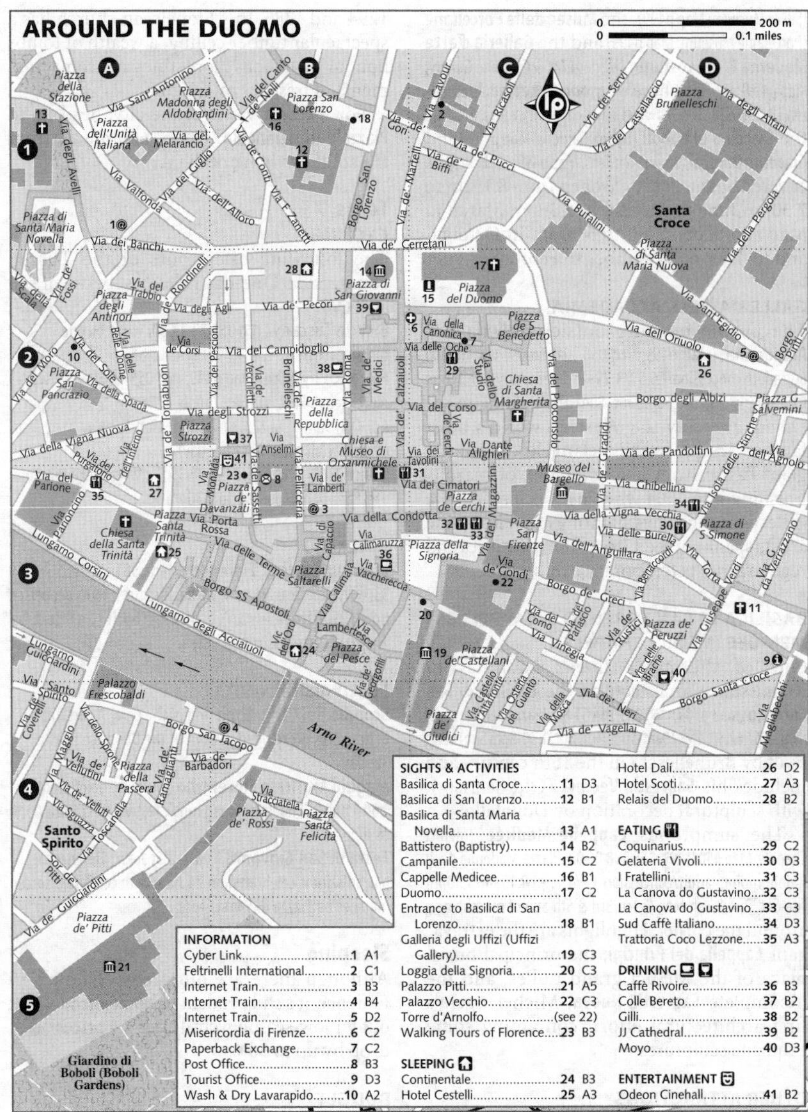

ordered that the smelly butchers be replaced with goldsmiths.

PALAZZO PITTI

Built for the Pitti family, great rivals of the Medici, the vast 15th-century **Palazzo Pitti** (Map p499; ☎ 055 238 86 14; Piazza de' Pitti) was bought by the Medici in 1549 and became their family residence. Today it houses four museums, of which the **Galleria Palatina** (Palatine Gallery; Map p499; ☎ 055 238 86 14; adult/concession €12/6, ticket valid 3 days; 🕓 8.15am-6.50pm Tue-Sun) is the most important. Works by Raphael, Filippo Lippi, Titian and Rubens adorn lavishly decorated rooms, culminating in the royal apartments. Three other museums – the **Museo degli Argenti**

(Silver Museum; Map p499), the **Museo delle Porcellane** (Porcelaine Museum; Map p499) and the **Galleria d'arte Moderna & del Costume** (Modern Art & Costume Gallery; Map p499) are also here. A **group ticket** (adult/EU citizen 18-25yr €10/5) gets you in to all three, as well as the **Giardino di Boboli** (Boboli Gardens; Map p499) and **Giardino Bardini** (Bardini Gardens; Map p499). All sights covered by the ticket are open from 8.15am to 7.30pm June to August, to 6.30pm March to May and September, to 5.30pm in October, and to 4.30pm November to February.

GALLERIA DELL'ACCADEMIA

The people queuing outside **Galleria dell' Accademia** (Map p499; ☎ 055 238 86 09; Via Ricasoli 60; adult/concession €6.50/3.25, incl temprary exhibition €10/5; 8.15am-6.50pm Tue-Sun) are waiting to see *David,* arguably the Western world's most famous sculpture. Michelangelo carved the giant figure from a single block of marble, finishing it in 1504 when he was just 29. The gallery also displays paintings by Florentine artists spanning the 13th to 16th centuries and regularly hosts temporary exhibitions.

BASILICA DI SAN LORENZO & CAPPELLE MEDICEE (MEDICI CHAPELS)

One of the city's finest examples of Renaissance architecture, the **Basilica di San Lorenzo** (Map p501; ☎ 055 264 51 84; Piazza San Lorenzo; admission €2.50; 10am-5pm Mon-Sat, 1.30-5pm Sun) was built by Brunelleschi in the 15th century and includes his **Sagrestia Vecchia** (Old Sacristy), with sculptural decoration by Donatello.

The sumptuous **Cappelle Medicee** (Medici Chapels; Map p501; ☎ 055 238 86 02; Piazza Madonna degli Aldobrandini; adult/concession €6/4; 8.15am-5.50pm Tue-Sat, 2nd & 4th Mon & 1st, 3rd & 5th Sun of month) are around the corner. Highlights are the extravagant **Cappella dei Principi**, the principal burial place of the Medici grand dukes, and the incomplete **Sagrestia Nuova**, Michelangelo's first architectural effort, containing some exquisite sculptures.

OTHER ATTRACTIONS

The French writer Stendhal was so dazzled by the **Basilica di Santa Croce** (Map p501; ☎ 055 246 61 05; adult/under 10yr/11-17yr €5/free/3; 9.30am-5.30pm Mon-Sat, 1-5.30pm Sun) that he was barely able to walk for faintness. He is apparently not the only one to have felt so overwhelmed by the beauty of Florence; Florentine doctors are said to treat a dozen cases of 'Stendhalismo' each year. Designed by Arnolfo di Cambio between 1294 and 1385, this Franciscan church has a spectacular timber ceiling, a wealth of tombs honouring famous Florentines and some fragments of frescoes by Giotto.

For the best views of the city, head up to **Piazzale Michelangelo**, a steep 600m walk from the southern bank of the Arno.

Tours

CYCLING

The following offer tours of the Tuscan countryside. One-day rides cost between €60 and €90.

Bicycle Tuscany (☎ 055 22 25 80; www.bicycletuscany.com)

Florence by Bike (Map p499; ☎ 055 48 89 92; www.florencebybike.it; Via San Zanobi 120r; 9am-7.30pm Apr-Oct, 9am-1pm & 3.30-7.30pm Mon-Sat Nov-Mar) Also offers city bike hire (€14 per day).

I Bike Italy (☎ 055 347 638 39 76; www.ibikeitaly.com; 8am-6pm Mon-Sat, to 1.30pm Sun)

WALKING

Walking Tours of Florence (Map p501; ☎ 055 264 50 33; www.italy.artviva.com; Via de' Sassetti 1; tours per person from €25) offers a range of city tours, all led by English-speaking guides.

Festivals & Events

Scoppio del Carro (Explosion of the Cart) A cart full of fireworks is exploded in front of the Duomo on Easter Sunday.

Maggio Musicale Fiorentino (www.maggiofiorentino.com) Italy's longest-running music festival held from April to June.

Festa di San Giovanni (Feast of St John) Florence's patron saint is celebrated on 24 June with costumed soccer matches on Piazza di Santa Croce.

Sleeping

Although there are hundreds of hotels in Florence, it's still prudent to book ahead. Look out for low-season website deals – prices often drop by up to 50%.

BUDGET

Campeggio Michelangelo (Map p499 ☎ 055 681 19 77; Viale Michelangelo 80; www.ecvacanze.it; per person €9-10.30, per tent/car €5.50/5.50) Just off Piazzale Michelangelo, this large and well-equipped camping ground is the nearest to the city centre. Take bus 12 from the train station to Piazzale Michelangelo.

Ostello Santa Monaca (Map p499; ☎ 055 26 83 38; www.ostello,it; Via Santa Monaca 6; dm €16-20;)

Occupying a 15th-century convent, this large and popular hostel offers single-sex dorms with four, five, six, eight and 10 beds (lockout applies between 10am and 2pm). There's a kitchen for guests' use, a laundrette, free wi-fi and a couple of computers. The 2am curfew is enforced and breakfast isn't included in the price.

Ostello Villa Camerata (off Map p499; ☎ 055 60 14 51; www.ostellofirenze.it; Viale Augusto Righi 2-4; dm €17.50-20; 💻) Housed in a beautiful 17th-century villa 5km northeast of the train station, Florence's HI hostel has 322 beds in various room combinations. Take bus 17A or 17B from the train station. Reservations are essential in summer.

Ostello Archi Rossi (Map p499; ☎ 055 29 08 04; ostelloarchirossi@hotmail.com; Via Faenza 94r; dm €20-26; 💻) A faux-frescoed private hostel, the Archi is a busy, boisterous backpacker pad. Near the train station, it's equipped with washing machines and microwaves, and offers free internet access and walking tours.

Hotel Dali (Map p501; ☎ 055 234 07 06; www.hoteldali.com; Via dell'Oriuolo 17; s €34-40, d €56-80) Escape the crowds at this excellent budget hotel. Owners Marco and Samanta go out of their way to ensure a pleasant stay, while the spotless, sunny rooms provide a homely retreat from the ever-present masses down the road at the Duomo. Cheaper rates are available for rooms with a shared bathroom.

MIDRANGE & TOP END

Hotel Scoti (Map p501; ☎ 055 29 21 28; www.hotelscoti.com; Via de' Tornabuoni 7; s €45-75, d €75-125) On Florence's smartest shopping strip, the friendly Scoti is a gem. Housed in a 16th-century *palazzo*, it has an amazing frescoed living room and comfortable, characterful rooms.

our pick Relais del Duomo (Map p501; ☎ 055 21 01 47; www.relaisdelduomo.it, in Italian; Piazza dell'Olio 2; s €50-80, d €60-120; ❄ 💻) Florentine B&Bs don't come much better than this one. Located in the shadow of the Duomo, it has four light and airy rooms with attractive furnishings and lovely little bathrooms. Privacy levels are high and management is extremely helpful.

Johlea & Johanna (Map p499; ☎ 055 463 32 92; www.johanna.it; Via San Gallo 80; s €70-120, d €85-175; ❄) This highly regarded B&B has more than a dozen tasteful, individually decorated rooms housed in five historic residences. There are also two charming suite apartments (€160 to €280).

Hotel Cestelli (Map p501; ☎ 055 21 42 13; www.hotelcestelli.com; Borgo SS Apostoli 25; s with shared bathroom €60-80, d with private bathroom €100-115; ❄) The Cestelli gets rave reviews in innumerable guidebooks for good reason. Run by Florentine photographer Alessio and his Japanese partner Asumi, it offers attractively decorated rooms and as much friendly and informed advice about Florence as you could possibly need.

Hotel Morandi alla Crocetta (Map p499; ☎ 055 234 47 47; www.hotelmorandi.it; Via Laura 50; s €110-140, d €177-220; ❄) This medieval convent-turned-hotel, away from the madding crowds, is a stunner. Rooms are charmingly decorated (try for the frescoed No 29) and extremely well equipped, with added features such as wi-fi. Breakfast costs €12.

UNA Vittoria Hotel (off Map p499; ☎ 055 227 71; www.unahotels.it; Via Pisana 59; r €114-243; ❄ 💻) When we saw the extremely reasonable web rates (cited) for rooms at this sleek hotel in the San Frediano district we couldn't believe our eyes. Rooms have loads of facilities (plasma TV, wi-fi, pillow menu etc) and are decorated in a hip, uncompromisingly modern style that's provides a refreshing change from the Renaissance furbelows at many Florentine hotels.

Continentale (Map p501; ☎ 055 2 72 62; www.lungarnohotels.com; Viccolo dell'Oro 6r; s €180-220, d €180-450; ❄ 💻) If you thought Ferragamo was only known for its shoes and bags, think again. This hip hotel was designed by Michele Bönan for the Florentine fashion house, and it's where trend-setters gravitate when they come to town. The high-tech rooms, spectacular lounge bar and great location overlooking the Arno are the knockout features.

Eating

Classic Tuscan dishes include *ribollita*, a heavy vegetable soup, *cannellini* (white beans) and *bistecca alla Fiorentina* (Florentine steak served rare). Chianti is the local tipple.

RESTAURANTS

Borgo Antico (Map p499; ☎ 055 21 04 37; Piazza Santo Spirito 6r; pizzas €7-10, meals €25) On a vibrant piazza, this trendy eatery is great for whiling away a summer evening over a pizza and glass of something cool. Select from the menu of leafy salads, wood-fired pizzas and Tuscan specialities.

ITALY

Sud Caffé Italiano (Map p501; ☎ 055 28 93 68; Via della Vigna Vecchia; pizza €9.50, pasta €8-10.50; closed Sun & Mon) An ode to southern-Italian-style casual chic, this place is perfect for a simple meal of pasta or pizza washed down by your choice from an impressive list of wines by the glass.

Trattoria Casalinga (Map p499; ☎ 055 21 86 24; Via de'Michelozzi 9r; meals €15; closed Sun) If you're after a filling meal at rock-bottom prices, look no further. Family-run and refreshingly unpretentious, it's always full of locals.

Trattoria Mario (Map p499; Via Rosina 2r; meals €18; lunch Mon-Sat, closed 3 weeks Aug) Lunch at Mario's is fun, filling and frenetic. A noisy, cheerful place full of market workers and tourists, it serves hearty pastas and meaty main courses at keen prices.

our pick **La Canova do Gustavino** (Map p501; ☎ 055 239 98 06; Via della Condotta 29r; meals €20) There aren't too many opportunities to enjoy a delicious cheap meal in stylish surrounds here in Florence, which is why this friendly *enoteca* is such a find. Crunchy bruschetta, hearty soups and excellent pasta dishes are constant features on a small menu. There's also a great wine list. The adjoining restaurant (meal €42; open for dinner Monday to Friday, lunch and dinner Saturday and Sunday) offers a more sophisticated menu.

Trattoria Coco Lezzone (Map p501; ☎ 055 28 71 78; Vai Parioncino 26r; meals €25; closed Sun) The name means 'the slovenly chef', but there's nothing slovenly about this Florentine institution. Classic Tuscan fare such as *ribollita, arista di maiale* (roasted pork loin) and *papa al pomodoro* (tomato and bread soup) take centre stage. No credit cards and no coffee.

Trattoria Cibrèo (Map p499; Viadei Macci 122r; meals €26; closed Mon & Aug) The small dining room here is run with charm and efficiency by a maitre d' who will happily explain the menu and suggest a matching wine. *Secondi* comprise a small main dish matched with a side of seasonal vegetables; everything is utterly delicious and exceptionally well priced considering its quality. No reservations and no credit cards.

Coquinarius (Map p501; ☎ 055 230 21 53; Via della Oche 15r; meals €30; closed Sun dinner) Close to Piazza Signoria, this modern *enoteca* is a perfect spot for lunch or a light dinner. The pasta dishes are uniformly good, and there's almost always a few unusual and delicious salads on the menu.

QUICK EATS & SELF-CATERING

Gelateria Vivoli (Map p501; ☎ 055 29 23 34; Via dell'Isola delle Stinche 7; closed Mon & mid-Aug) Ice-cream aficionados rate the gelati here the city's best – we'd go as far as to say that it's up there with the best in the country. No cones, just a fabulous array of fresh flavours served in cups.

I Fratellini (Map p501; ☎ 055 239 60 96; Via dei Cimatori 38r; panini €2-3; 8am-8pm, closed Sat & Sun Jul & Aug, 2 weeks Mar & Aug) Although no more than a hole-in-the-wall panino bar, I Fratellini is a city institution. Locals flock to its tiny counter for fresh-filled panini ready in the twinkle of an eye, chased down with a glass of vino.

Fresh produce is available at the central **food market** (Map p501; Piazza San Lorenzo; 7am-2pm Mon-Sat). Alternatively, there's a **supermarket** (Map p499; Stazione di Santa Maria Novella) at the train station, and a **Standa** (Map p499; Via Pietrapiana 94) east of Piazza del Duomo.

Drinking

our pick **Caffè Rivoire** (Map p501; ☎ 055 21 44 12; Piazza della Signoria; closed Mon & 2nd half Jan) Famous for its chocolate (try a cup of the hot stuff), Rivoire's terrace has the best view in the city. Settle in for a long *aperitivo* or coffee break – it's worth the high prices.

Colle Bereto (Map p499; ☎ 055 28 31 56; Piazza Strozzi 5r) Slip into something Dolce & Gabbana and join the fashionistas at this glam bar. It's known for excellent cocktails and a lavish *aperitivo* spread.

Gilli (Map p501; ☎ 055 21 38 96; Piazza della Repubblica 39r; closed Mon & Tue) The city's grandest cafe, Gilli has been serving excellent coffee and delicious cakes since 1733. Claiming a table on the piazza is *molto* expensive – we prefer standing at the spacious art nouveau bar.

JJ Cathedral (☎ 055 265 68 92; Piazza di San Giovanni 4r) JJ's is a magnet for foreign students on holiday, who come here to swill beer and admire the views of the Duomo. Try to snaffle the upstairs balcony table.

Moyo (Map p501; ☎ 055 247 97 38; Via de' Benci 23r) A mixed crowd of young locals and foreign students drink at this funky modern bar. It's good for coffee and free wi-fi during the day, drinks and upbeat music at night.

Negroni (Map p499; ☎ 055 24 36 47; Via dei Renai 17r) The famous Florentine cocktail gives its name to this popular bar in the trendy

San Nicolò district. It's known for its art exhibitions, excellent *aperitivo* spread and cheap lunch buffet. A great spot to come to after admiring the sunset from Piazzale Michelangelo.

Entertainment

Florence's definitive monthly listings guide *Firenze Spettacolo* is sold at newsstands (€1.80).

Concerts, opera and dance are performed year-round at the **Teatro Comunale** (off Map p499; ☎ 800 11 22 11; Corso Italia 16), which is also the venue for events organised by the Maggio Musicale Fiorentino (see Festivals & Events, p502).

English-language films are screened at the **Odeon Cinehall** (Map p501; ☎ 055 21 40 68; www.cinehall.it, in Italian; Via dei Sassetti 1; tickets €7.50).

Shopping

Shopping is concentrated between the Duomo and the Arno, with boutiques along Via Roma, Via de' Calzaiuoli and Via Por Santa Maria. For the big fashion guns, head to Via de' Tornabuoni and Via della Vigna Nuova.

Just north of the Duomo, the **Mercato de San Lorenzo** (Map p501; Piazza San Lorenzo; Tue-Sun) is the place for leather goods, clothing and jewellery, although quality and prices vary.

Getting There & Away

AIR

The main airport serving Florence is Pisa's **Galileo Galilei airport** (PSA; ☎ 050 84 93 00; www.pisa-airport.com). There's also a small city airport 5km north of Florence, **Aeroporto di Firenze** (Aeroporto Vespucci; FLR; ☎ 055 306 13 00; www.aeroporto.firenze.it).

BUS

The **SITA bus station** (Map p499; ☎ 800 37 37 60; www.sita-on-line-it, in Italian; Via Santa Caterina da Siena 17) is just south of the train station. Buses leave for Siena (€6.80, 1½ hours, every 30 to 60 minutes) and San Gimignano (€6, 1¼ hours, 14 daily).

CAR & MOTORCYCLE

Florence is connected by the A1 *autostrada* to Bologna and Milan in the north and Rome and Naples to the south. The A11 links Florence with Pisa and the coast, and a *superstrada* (expressway) joins the city to Siena.

TRAIN

Florence is well connected by train. There are regular services to/from Pisa (Regional €5.60, 1¼ hours, every 10 to 30 minutes), Rome (Eurostar AV, €36.50, 70 minutes, hourly), Bologna (Eurostar AV, €16.20, one hour, hourly), Venice (Eurostar €32.30, 2¾ hours, 10 daily) and Milan (Eurostar AV, €16.20, one hour, hourly). Check times at the **train information office** (Map p499; ☎ 7am-9pm) in the station's main foyer.

Getting Around

TO/FROM THE AIRPORT

Terravision (☎ 06 321 20 011; www.terravision.it) runs a bus service between the train station and Galileo Galilei airport (adult/child five to 12 €8/4, 70 minutes, 12 daily). Otherwise there are regular trains (€5.10, 1½ hours, hourly between 6.37am and 8.37pm).

Volainbus (☎ 800 42 45 00; www.ataf.net) runs a shuttlebus (€4.50, 25 minutes, half-hourly from 5.30am to 11pm) connecting Florence airport with the SITA bus station.

BICYCLE

Alinari (Map p499; ☎ 055 28 05 00; www.alinarirental.com; Via San Zanobi 38r; 9.30am-1pm & 2.45-6pm Mon-Sat, 10am-1pm Sun) rents out bikes for €7/12/24 per five hours/day/weekend and scooters for €35/55/125.

BUS

ATAF (Map p499; ☎ 800 42 45 00; www.ataf.net) buses service the city centre and Fiesole, a small town in the hills 8km northeast of Florence. The most useful terminal is just outside the train station's eastern exit. Take bus 7 for Fiesole, and 12 or 13 for Piazzale Michelangelo. Tickets (70 minute/24 hour €1.20/5) are sold at *tabacchi* and newsstands – you can also buy a 70-minute ticket on board the bus (€2).

CAR & MOTORCYCLE

Much of the city centre is restricted to traffic so the best advice is to leave your car in a car park and use public transport. Details of car parks are available from **Firenze Parcheggi** (☎ 055 500 19 94; www.firenzeparcheggi.it, in Italian). If your car is towed away, call ☎ 055 78 38 82.

To rent, try **Hertz** (Map p499; ☎ 199 11 22 11; Via M Finiguerra 33r) or **Avis** (Map p499; ☎ 199 10 01 33; Borgo Ognissanti 128r).

PISA

pop 88,000

One of Italy's most recognisable monuments, the Leaning Tower of Pisa (Torre Pendente) is a genuinely astonishing sight. Veering upwards at an alarming angle, it stands in permanent defiance of the laws of gravity. Tower aside, Pisa is an unassuming university town that while pleasant enough, won't claim your attention for long.

Pisa's golden age came in the 12th and 13th centuries when it was a maritime power rivalling Genoa and Venice. It was eventually defeated by the Genoese in 1284 and, in 1406, fell to Florence. Under the Medici, the arts and sciences flourished and Galileo Galilei (1564–1642) taught at the university.

Orientation & Information

From Piazza Vittorio Emanuele II, just north of the train station, the Leaning Tower is a straightforward 1.5km walk – follow Corso Italia to the Arno, cross the river and continue down Borgo Stretto. At the end of Via G Carducci, bear left down Via Cardinale Pietro Maffi. You could also take bus 3 or shuttle A from the train station.

For city information, check www.pisaturismo.it or ask at one of the three **tourist offices** (airport ☎ 050 50 37 00; ⏰ noon-10pm; city centre ☎ 050 4 22 91; Piazza Vittorio Emanuele II 16; ⏰ 9am-7pm Mon-Fri, to 1.30pm Sat; Leaning Tower ☎ 050 56 04 64; Piazza del Duomo 1; ⏰ 10am-7pm).

Go online at **Internet Planet** (☎ 050 83 07 02; Piazza Cavallotti 3-4; per hr €3.50; ⏰ 9am-midnight Mon-Fri, 10am-10pm Sat & Sun).

Sights

The entry times listed here are those in force at the time of research, but they change frequently – call ☎ 050 387 22 10 or log onto www.opapisa.it for confirmation.

Pisans claim that the **Campo dei Miracoli** (Field of Miracles) is among the most beautiful squares in the world. Certainly, the immaculate walled lawns provide a gorgeous setting for the cathedral, baptistry and tower; on the other hand, few places boast so many tat-waving hawkers. You can purchase group tickets for the sights (not including the Leaning Tower); these cost €6 for the cathedral and baptistery and €10 for the cathedral, baptistery and cemetery.

Forming the centrepiece of the Campo's Romanesque trio, the candy-striped **cathedral** (☎ 050 56 09 21; admission €2; ⏰ 10am-1pm & 2-5pm Nov-Feb, 10am-10pm Apr-Sep, to 7pm Oct, to 6pm Mar), begun in 1063, has a graceful tiered facade and cavernous interior. The transept's bronze doors are by Bonanno Pisano, but the 16th-century entrance doors are by Giambologna.

To the west, the cupcake-like **battistero** (baptistery; admission €5; ⏰ 10am-5pm Nov-Feb, 9am-6pm Mar, 8am-8pm Apr-Sep, 9am-7pm Oct) was started in 1153 and completed by Nicola and Giovanni Pisano in 1260. Inside, note Nicola Pisano's beautiful pulpit.

But it's to the *campanile*, better known as the **Leaning Tower** (Torre Pendente; www.opapisa.it; admission €15 plus booking fee €2; ⏰ 10am-7pm Nov-Feb, 9am-6pm Mar, 8.30am-8.30pm Apr-Sep, 9am-7pm Oct), that all eyes are drawn. Bonanno Pisano began building in 1173, but almost immediately his plans came a cropper in a layer of shifting soil. Only three of the tower's seven tiers were completed before it started tilting – continuing at a rate of about 1mm per year. By 1990 the lean had reached 5.5 degrees – a tenth of a degree beyond the critical point established by computer models. Stability was finally ensured in 1998 when a combination of biased weighting and soil drilling forced the tower into a safer position. Today it's almost 4.1m off the perpendicular.

Visits are limited to groups of 30; entry times are staggered and queuing is predictably inevitable. It is wise to book ahead.

Flanking the Campo, the beautiful **Camposanto cemetery** (admission €5; ⏰ 10am-5pm) is said to contain soil shipped from Calvary during the crusades – soil that's reputed to reduce cadavers to skeletons within days.

Sleeping

There are no budget options in Pisa worth recommending.

Hotel di Stefano (☎ 050 55 35 59; www.hoteldistefano.pisa.it; Via Sant'Apollonia 35-37; s €45-140, d €65-170; ❄) There are three reasons to stay at this friendly three-star: its location in a quiet backstreet in the medieval quarter; its smart, simple rooms; and its terrace with views of the tower's top half. Deluxe rooms in the recently renovated Casa Torre (c 1045) feature wooden-beamed ceilings and exposed stone walls. There are cheaper rates on offer for rooms with a shared bathroom.

Hotel Francesco (☎ 050 55 54 53; www.hotelfrancesco.com; Via Santa Maria 129; r €70-150; ❄ 💻) The best of the hotels lining busy Via Santa Maria (just off Campo dei Miracoli), the small family-run Francesco offers a warm welcome and bright, mod-conned rooms. It also hires out bikes (€10 per day).

Eating

Trattoria della Faggiola (☎ 050 55 61 79; Via della Faggiola 1; meals €20; ⏰ lunch Mon-Thu, lunch & dinner Fri & Sat) This much-loved local eatery offers a limited menu of seasonal specialities. The food is simple but well cooked.

Antica Trattoria il Campano (☎ 050 58 05 85; Via Cavalca 19; meals €30; ⏰ lunch & dinner Fri-Tue, dinner Thu) This atmospheric trattoria serves adventurous regional fare in a medieval setting. It has the dubious distinction of being one of the Hairy Bikers' top 10 world eateries.

Getting There & Away

The city's **Galileo Galilei airport** (PSA; ☎ 050 50 07 07; www.pisa-airport.com) is linked to the centre by train (€1.10, five minutes, 15 daily), or by bus 1 (€0.95, 10 minutes, every 10 minutes).

VAI (☎ 050 462 88; www.lazzi.it, in Italian) buses depart from the airport to Florence (€7.80, two hours, hourly) via Lucca. **Train SpA** (www.trainspa.it) buses go to Siena (€14, two daily).

Regular trains run to Florence (Regional €5.60, 1¼ hours, every 10 to 30 minutes), Rome (Regional €17.15, four hours, five daily) and Genoa (€15, two hours, half-hourly).

SIENA

pop 53,900

Famous for its annual horse race (Il Palio), Siena is one of Italy's most enchanting medieval towns. Its walled centre, a beautifully preserved warren of dark lanes punctuated by Gothic *palazzi*, piazzas and eye-catching churches, is a lovely place to get lost. The action centres on Piazza del Campo (known as Il Campo), the sloping square that serves as a communal sunbed to scores of day trippers.

According to legend, Siena was founded by the sons of Remus. In the Middle Ages its dramatic rise caused political and cultural friction with Florence. Painters of the Sienese School (most notably in the 13th to 15th centuries) produced significant works of art, and the city was home to Saints Catherine and Benedict.

Orientation

From the train station take bus 8, 9 or 10 (€0.95) to Piazza Gramsci, from where Piazza del Campo is a short, signposted walk away. From the bus station it's a 10-minute walk up Via La Lizza and Via delle Terme. The centre's main streets – the Banchi di Sopra, Via di Città and Banchi di Sotto – curve around Il Campo.

Visitors' cars aren't permitted in the centre.

Information

Book Shop (☎ 0577 22 65 94; Via San Pietro 10) Good selection of English-language books.
Internet Train (Via di Città 121 & Via di Pantaneto 57; per hr €4; ⏰ 10am-10pm)
Left Luggage At the bus station (per day €5.50).
Police station (Questura; ☎ 0577 20 11 11; Via del Castoro 23)
Post office (Piazza Matteotti 1)
Tourist office (☎ 0577 28 05 51; www.terresiena.it; Piazza del Campo 56; ⏰ 9am-7pm)

Sights

Ever since the 14th century, the slanting, shell-shaped **Piazza del Campo** has been the city's civic centre. Forming the base of the piazza, the **Palazzo Pubblico** (Palazzo Comunale) is a magnificent example of Sienese Gothic architecture. Inside, the **Museo Civico** (☎ 0577 29 26 14; adult/child/concession €7.50/free/04.50; ⏰ 10am-7pm mid-Mar–Oct, to 6pm Nov–mid-Mar) houses some extraordinary frescoes, including Simone Martini's famous *Maestà* (Virgin Mary in Majesty) and Ambroglio Lorenzetti's *Allegories of Good and Bad Government*. Soaring above the *palazzo* is the 102m **Torre del Mangia** (admission €7; ⏰ 10am-7pm mid-Mar–end Oct, to 4pm Nov–mid-Mar), which dates from 1297. A combined ticket to the two costs €12 and is only available at the Torre del Mangia ticket office.

The spectacular **Duomo** (☎ 0577 473 21; admission €3; ⏰ 10.30am-8pm Mon-Sat, 1.30-6pm Sun mid-Mar–Sep, 10.30am-7.30pm Mon-Sat, 1.30-6pm Sun Oct, 10.30am-6.30pm Mon-Sat, 1.30-5.30pm Sun Nov–mid-Mar) is another Gothic masterpiece. Begun in 1196 it was completed in 1215, although work continued well into the 13th century. Subsequent expansion plans were stymied by the plague of 1348. The striking facade of green, red and white marble was designed by Giovanni Pisano, who also helped his dad, Nicola, craft the cathedral's intricate pulpit. Inside, it's the 14th-century **inlaid-marble floor** (viewing €6; ⏰ 10.30am-7.30pm mid-Aug–Oct), decorated with 56 biblical panels, that's the highlight. Other noteworthy features include Donatello's bronze of St John the Baptist and statues of St Jerome and Mary Magdalene by Bernini.

Behind the cathedral and down a flight of stairs, the **battistero** (baptistery; Piazza San Giovanni; admission €3; 9.30am-8pm Mar-Sep, to 7.30pm Oct, 10am-5pm Nov-Feb) has a Gothic facade and a rich interior of 15th-century frescoes.

On the western edge of the walled city, the **Chiesa di San Domenico** (Piazza San Domenico 1; admission free; 7.30am-1pm & 3-6.30pm) is the last resting place of St Catherine's head and thumb.

Festivals & Events

Siena's great annual event is the **Palio** (2 Jul & 16 August), a pageant culminating in a bareback horse race round Il Campo. The city is divided into 17 *contrade* (districts), of which 10 are chosen annually to compete for the *palio* (silk banner). The only rule in the three-lap race is that jockeys can't tug the reins of other horses.

Sleeping

It's always advisable to book in advance, but for August and the Palio, it's essential.

Ostello Guidoriccio (0577 522 12; siena@ostellionline.org; Via Fiorentina 89; per person €14.45;) An inconvenient 20-minute bus ride from the town centre, Siena's HI hostel has 46 neat but dark two-bed rooms and one single-sex eight-bed dorm. Take bus 10 or 15 from Piazza Gramsci, or 77 from the train station and tell the driver you're after the *ostello* (hostel).

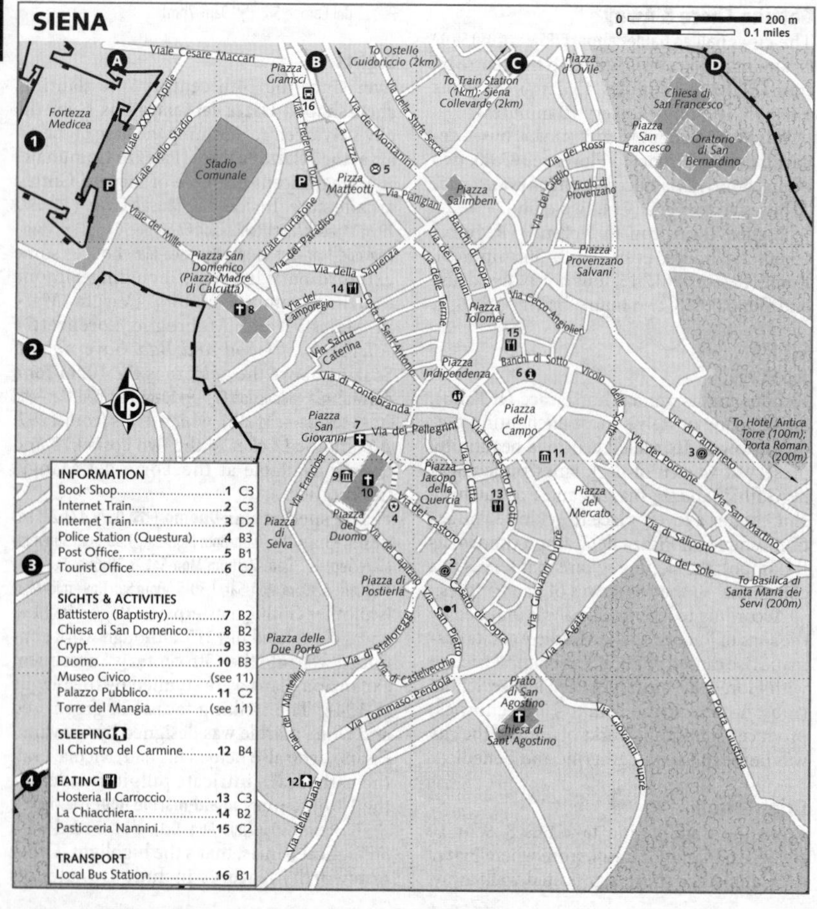

WORTH THE TRIP: SAN GIMIGNANO

Dubbed the medieval Manhattan, San Gimignano is a tiny hilltop town deep in the Tuscan countryside. A mecca for day-trippers from Florence and Siena, it owes its nickname to the 11th-century towers that soar above its pristine *centro storico*. Originally 72 were built as monuments to the town's wealth but only 14 remain. To avoid the worst of the crowds try to visit midweek, preferably in deep winter.

The **tourist office** (☎ 0577 94 00 08; www.sangimignano.com; Piazza del Duomo 1; 🕒 9am-1pm & 3-7pm Mar-Oct, 9am-1pm & 2-6pm Nov-Feb) is a short walk from Piazza dei Martiri di Montemaggio, the nearest San Gimignano has to a bus terminal. On the southern edge of Piazza del Duomo, the **Palazzo Comunale** (☎ 0577 99 03 12; Piazza del Duomo; adult/child €5/4; h9.30am-7pm Mar-Oct, 10am-5.30pm Nov-Feb) houses San Gimignano's art gallery (the **Pinacoteca**) and tallest tower, the **Torre Grossa**. Climb to the top for some unforgettable views.

Nearby, the Romanesque **basilica** (☎ 0577 94 00 08; Piazza del Duomo; adult/child €3.50/1.50; h9.30am-7.10pm Mon-Fri, to 5.10pm Sat & Sun Apr-Oct, 9.30am-4.40pm Mon-Sat, 12.30-4.40pm Sun Feb, Mar & Nov-Jan), known also as the Collegiata, boasts frescoes by Ghirlandaio.

Sample the local wine, vernaccia, at **Enoteca Gustavo** (☎ 0577 94 00 57; Via San Matteo 29; snacks from €3), an atmospheric brick-vaulted *enoteca* serving a range of delicious bruschette, panini and wine by the glass.

Regular buses link San Gimignano with Florence (€6, 1¼ hours, 14 daily) and Siena (€5.30, 1¼ hours, hourly). Most require a change at Poggibonsi.

Hotel Antica Torre (☎ 0577 22 22 55; www.anticatorresiena.it; Via di Fiera Vecchia 7; s €65-90, d €90-120; ❄) Three-star facilities meet two-star prices at this excellent choice. Eight pretty rooms with Tuscan-style decor are on offer in a restored 16th-century tower; the two at the top offer spectacular views over the surrounding countryside (no lift).

Il Chiostro del Carmine (☎ 0577 22 34 76; www.chiostrodelcarmine.com; Via della Diana 4; r €129-189; ❄ 💻) Sleeping in a 14th-century Carmelite Monastery is good postcard-writing fodder, but this choice just inside the Porta San Marco offers more than just atmosphere. Rooms are large, quietly stylish and extremely comfortable.

Eating & Drinking

Pasticceria Nannini (☎ 0577 23 60 09; 24 Via Banchi di Sopra) For the finest *cenci* (fried sweet pastry), *panforte* (dense fruit and nut cake) and *ricciarelli* (almond biscuits) in town, enjoyed with a cup of excellent coffee, you need go no further than this Sienese institution.

La Chiacchiera (☎ 0577 28 06 31; Costa di Sant'Antonio 4; pasta €7, meals €18) With its rustic wooden tables and stone walls, this is an atmospheric spot. The food is seasonal, earthy and filling. In summer, there's outdoor seating on a quiet pedestrian street.

Hosteria Il Carroccio (☎ 0577 411 65; Via del Casato di Sotto 32; meals €30; 🕒 closed dinner Tue & Wed winter) Recommended by the prestigious Slow Food movement (always a good sign), Il Carroccio specialises in traditional Sienese cooking. Staples include *pici* (thick spaghetti) and succulent *bistecca di chianina alla brace* (grilled steak).

Getting There & Away

Siena is not on a main train line so it's easier to take a bus. From the bus station on Piazza Gramsci, **Train SpA** (www.trainspa.it) and SITA buses run to/from Florence (€6.80, 1½ hours, every 30 to 60 minutes), Pisa airport (€14, two daily) and San Gimignano (€5.30, 1¼ hours, hourly), either direct or via Poggibonsi.

Sena (☎ 0577 28 32 03; www.sena.it) operates services to/from Rome (€18.50, three hours, 10 daily).

Both Train SpA and Sena have ticket offices underneath the piazza.

LUCCA

pop 82,300

Lucca is a love-at-first-sight type of place. Hidden behind monumental Renaissance walls, its historic centre is chock-full of handsome churches, excellent restaurants and tempting *pasticcerie*. Founded by the Etruscans, it became a city state in the 12th century and stayed that way for 600 years. Most of its streets and monuments date from this period.

Orientation

From the train station walk across Piazza Ricasoli, cross Viale Regina Margherita and then follow the path across the grass and through the wall to reach the historic centre. The bus station is near Piazzale Giuseppe Verdi, near Porta Vittorio Emanuele Santa Anna.

Information

Ali's Call Center & Internet (Via Gemma Galgani 9b; internet per hr €3; 9am-11pm)

Left Luggage At the Piazzale Verdi Tourist Office (per hour €1.50).

Post office (Via Vallisneri 2)

Tourist offices (☎ 0583 355 51 00; www.turislucca.com) Piazza Ducale (10am-1pm & 2-6pm Mon-Sat); Piazza Santa Maria (9am-8pm); Piazza Verdi (9am-7pm) Makes accommodation recommendations and bookings, and offers advice and maps. The Piazza Santa Maria office also offers internet access (per hour €3.50).

Sights & Activities

Lucca's 12m-high **city walls** were built around the old city in the 16th and 17th centuries and were once defended by 126 cannons. In the 19th century they were crowned with a wide, tree-lined footpath that is now the centre of local Lucchese life. To join the locals in walking, jogging, rollerblading or cycling the 4km-long footpath, access it via Piazzale Verdi or Piazza Santa Maria; bike hire is available at the tourist office at Piazzale Verdi (per hour €2.50) or at one of two bike-rental shops (bikes per hour €2.50, tandems €5.50) at Piazza Santa Maria.

The predominantly Romanesque **Cattedrale di San Martino** (☎ 0583 95 70 68; www.museocattedralelucca.it, in Italian; Piazza San Martino; 9.30am-5.45pm Mon-Fri, to 6.45pm Sat, 9am-10.45am & noon-6pm Sun Mar-Oct, 9.30am-4.45pm Mon-Fri, to 6.45pm Sat, 11.20am-11.50am & 1-4.45pm Sun Nov-Feb) dates to the 11th century. Its exquisite facade was designed to accommodate the pre-existing *campanile*, and the reliefs over the left doorway of the portico are believed to be by Nicola Pisano. Inside, there's a magnificent *Last Supper* by Tintoretto.

Festivals & Events

Opera buffs from around the world come here to pay their respects to the memory of the great Giacomo Puccini (1858–1924). Born in Lucca, Puccini worked as an organist and choirmaster here before studying composition in Milan. He returned to Lucca in 1891, moving to nearby Torre del Lago. In July each year, the **Puccini Festival** (☎ 0584 35 93 22; www.puccinifestival.it; Lucca ticket office Piazza Anfiteatro) is held in a purpose-built outdoor theatre in Torre del Lago. During the festival, **TAU Touring** (☎ 393 904 15 45) runs bus transfers between Lucca's Porta San Pietro and Torre del Lago for €20 return.

Sleeping & Eating

Ostello San Frediano (☎ 0583 46 99 57; www.ostellolucca.it; Via della Cavellerizza12; dm €18-19.50, d €50;) Comfort and service levels are high at this HI-affiliated hostel. There are 141 rooms, a bar and a restaurant. Breakfast costs €3.

San Frediano Guesthouse (☎ 0583 46 96 30; www.sanfrediano.com; Via degli Angeli 19; s €38-90, d €48-110;) Repeat visitors are often spotted at this well-located B&B, lured back by its small but well-maintained rooms and reasonable prices. The cheaper rates available are for rooms with a shared bathroom.

La Corte degli Angeli (☎ 0583 46 92 04; www.allacortedegliangeli.com; Via degli Angeli 23; s €80-140, d €119-180;) The room decor in this 15th-century townhouse might be a bit decorative for some, but high comfort levels and mod cons such as wi-fi and iPod docking stands end up winning everyone over.

Giurlani (☎ 0583 46 76 36; Via Fillungo 239) The best way to enjoy a Lucchese lunch is to picnic on the wall, particularly if you buy delectable provisions from this artisan produce shop.

Trattoria da Leo (☎ 0583 49 22 36; Via Tegrimi 1; meals €20; closed Sun) A terrific trattoria that is greatly beloved of locals, da Leo serves delicious and extraordinarily well-priced meals. Choose from the colourful antipasto buffet (€8 per plate) or order a pasta, risotto or *secondo* from a large list.

our pick **La Buca di San Antonio** (☎ 0583 55 881; Via della Cervia 3; closed Mon, dinner Sun & 2 weeks Jan) Ask locals to recommend the best restaurant in town, and most will nominate this romantic eatery, which first opened its doors in 1782. The menu features traditional Lucchese dishes, perfectly cooked.

Getting There & Away

From the bus station near Piazzale Giuseppe Verdi, VAI buses run to/from Florence (€5, 80 minutes, hourly), Pisa airport (€2.80, 30 minutes, hourly Monday to Saturday and every two hours Sunday) and Pisa (€2.80, 30 minutes, half-hourly).

Lucca is on the Florence–Pisa–Viareggio train line. Regional trains run to/from Florence (€5, 1½ hours, hourly) and Pisa (€2.40, 30 minutes, half-hourly).

UMBRIA & LE MARCHE

Dubbed the 'green heart of Italy', the predominantly rural region of Umbria harbours some of Italy's best-preserved historic *borghi* (villages) and many important artistic, religious and architectural treasures. The regional capital Perugia provides a convenient base, with Assisi an easy day trip away.

To the east, mountainous Le Marche offers more of the same, its appeal encapsulated in the medieval, fairy-tale centre of Urbino.

PERUGIA

pop 162,000

With its hilltop medieval centre and international student population, Perugia is Umbria's largest and most cosmopolitan city. There's not a lot to see here, but the presence of the University for Foreigners ensures a buzz that's not always apparent in the region's sleepy hinterland. In July, music fans inundate the city for the prestigious **Umbria Jazz festival** (www.umbriajazz.com, in Italian).

Perugia has a bloody and lively past. In the Middle Ages, the Baglioni and Oddi families fought for control of the city, while later, as a papal satellite, the city fought with its neighbours. All the while art and culture thrived: painter Perugino and Raphael, his student, both worked here.

Orientation & Information

The historic centre is on top of the hill, the train station is at the bottom and the regional bus station, Piazza dei Partigiani, is halfway between the two. From Piazza Partigiani there are *scale mobili* (elevators) going up to Piazza Italia, where local buses terminate. From Piazza Italia, pedestrianised Corso Vannucci runs up to Piazza IV Novembre, the city's focal point. City maps are available at the **tourist office** (☎ 075 573 64 58; www.perugia.umbria2000.it; Piazza Matteotti 18; 8.30am-6.30pm) opposite the **post office** (☎ 075 573 69 77; Piazza Matteotti).

To check your email try **Tempo Reale** (Via del Forno 17; per hr €1.50; 10am-11.30pm) in the historic centre.

Sights

Flanking Piazza IV Novembre, the austere 14th-century **Duomo** (☎ 075 572 38 32; Piazza IV Novembre; 7am-12.30pm & 4-6.45pm Mon-Sat, 8am-12.45pm & 4-6.45pm Sun) has an unfinished two-tone facade and, inside, an altarpiece by Signorelli and sculptures by Duccio.

In the centre of the piazza, the stolid **Fontana Maggiore** was designed by Fra Bevignate and carved by Nicola and Giovanni Pisano between 1275 and 1278.

The 13th-century **Palazzo dei Priori** houses Perugia's best museums, including the **Galleria Nazionale dell'Umbria** (☎ 800 961 993; www.gallerianazionaleumbria.it; Corso Vannucci 19; adult/under 18yr/concession €6.50/free/3.25; 8.30am-7.30pm Tue-Sun), whose collection contains works by local heroes Perugino and Pinturicchio. Close to the *palazzo*, the impressive **Nobile Collegio del Cambio** (Exchange Hall; ☎ 075 572 85 99; Corso Vannucci 25; adult/concession €4.50/2.60; 9am-12.30pm & 2.30-5.30pm Mon-Sat, 9am-1pm Sun) is home to impressive frescoes by Perugino.

Courses

The **Università per Stranieri** (University for Foreigners; ☎ 075 574 61; www.unistrapg.it; Piazza Fortebraccio 4) runs hundreds of courses in language, art, history, music and architecture.

Sleeping

Centro Internazionale per la Gioventù (☎ 075 572 28 80; www.ostello.perugia.it; Via Bontempi 13; dm €15; closed mid-Dec–mid-Jan;) This is a private hostel with decent four- to six-bed dorms, a frescoed TV room, a kitchen for guests' use and great views from the terrace. The lockout (10am to 4pm) and 1am curfew are strictly enforced. The price doesn't include breakfast and sheets cost €2.

Bed & Breakfast Spagnoli (☎ 075 573 51 27; www.perugiaonline.com/bbspagnoli; Via Cesare Caporali 17; s with shared bathroom €30-40, d with shared bathroom €45-60) The motto here is *semplice* (simple) and the three spacious rooms in this family home near Piazza Italia offer great value.

Primavera Mini Hotel (☎ 075 572 16 57; www.primaveraminihotel.com; Via Vincioli 8; s €42-65, d €65-75;) On the top floor of a 16th-century *palazzo* (think memorable views) this intimate two-star has spruce modern rooms

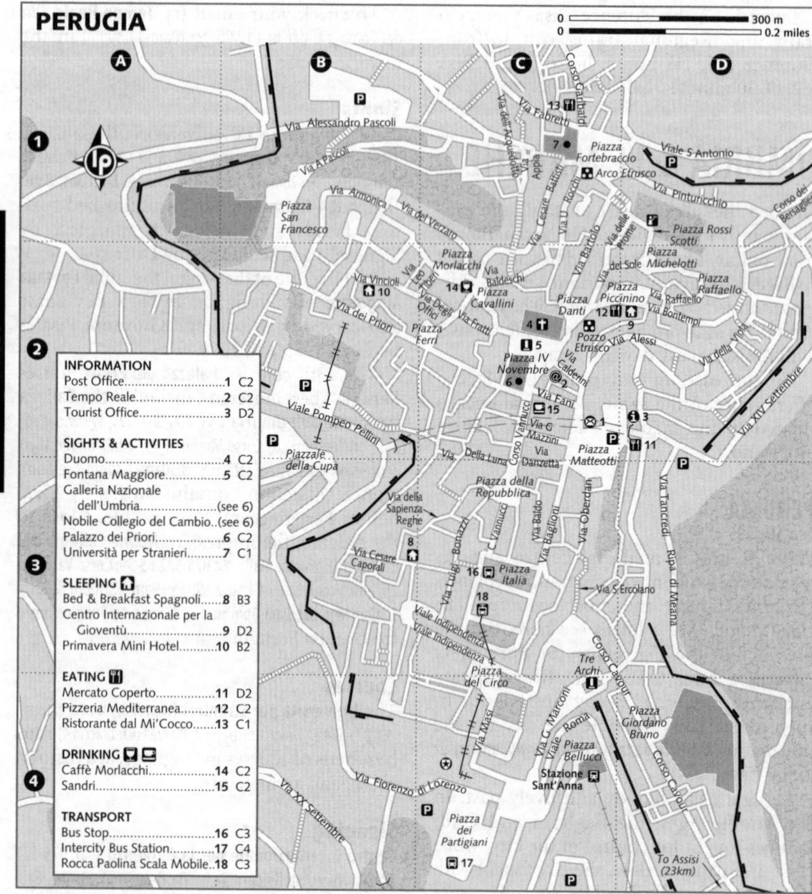

decorated with understated style. Not all rooms have air-con, and breakfast costs an extra €3 to €6. It's deservedly popular, so book well ahead.

Eating & Drinking

Pizzeria Mediterranea (☎ 075 572 13 22; Piazza Piccinino 11/12; pizzas €3.70-12; closed Tue) The wood-fired oven in the middle of the dining room is put to excellent use at this busy pizzeria. You can opt for a simple topping or lash out and order delectable *mozzarella di bufala* (fresh buffalo-milk mozzarella) to go on top for a small surcharge.

Ristorante dal Mi'Cocco (☎ 075 573 25 11; Corso Giuseppe Garibaldi 12; set menu €13; closed Mon) Loads of fun and long communal tables are on offer at this ebullient eatery. The three-course meals are dished up at set times – lunch 1pm, dinner 8.15pm – and change daily. It's wildly popular, so book ahead.

our pick Sandri (☎ 075 44 9 41; Corso Vannucci 32; closed Mon) Sandri has been serving exquisite cakes and the best coffee in town since 1860. Sit at tables on the corso or stand at the stunning bar and eye off the decadent cakes, pastries and chocolates on offer.

Caffè Morlacchi (☎ 075 572 17 60; Piazza Morlacchi 6/8; closed Sun) The local literati adore this effortlessly hip cafe. It has a laid-back vibe during the day, but revs up at night.

Mercato Coperto (Covered markets; Piazza Matteotti; 7am-1.30pm Mon-Fri, 7am-1.30pm & 4.30-7.30pm Sat) Stock up on fruit, bread, cheese and meat.

Getting There & Away

From the intercity bus station on Piazza dei Partigiani, **Sulga** (☎ 800 09 96 61; www.sulga.it, in Italian) buses depart for Florence (€10.50, two hours, one daily) and Rome (€21, three hours, two daily), continuing onto Fiumicino airport (€21, four hours). **Sena** (☎ 800 93 09 60; www.sena.it, in Italian) serves Siena (€12, 1½ hours, three daily), while **APM** (☎ 800 51 21 41; www.apmperugia.it, in Italian) buses head up to Assisi (€3.10, one hour, 13 daily).

Regional trains connect with Rome (€10.50, 2¾ hours, 20 daily), Florence (€8.75, 2¼ hours, 14 daily) and Assisi (€2.05, 20 minutes, hourly).

Getting Around

From the train station, take bus G, R, TD or 24 (€1) to get to Piazza Italia. Bus C leaves from outside the UPIM building opposite the station and goes to Piazza Cavallini, near the Duomo. From the intercity bus station on Piazza dei Partigiani, take the free *scala mobila*.

The centre is mostly closed to traffic so park in one of the supervised car parks near the bus station.

ASSISI

pop 26,800

Seen from afar, the only clue to Assisi's importance is the imposing form of the Basilica di San Francesco jutting over the hillside. Thanks to St Francis, born here in 1182, this quaint medieval town is a major destination for millions of pilgrims.

The **tourist office** (☎ 075 81 25 34; info@iat.assisi.pg.it; Piazza del Comune 22; 8am-2pm & 3-6pm Mon-Sat, 10am-1pm Sun) can provide practical information.

Sights

Dress rules are applied rigidly at the main religious sights, so no shorts, miniskirts, low-cut dresses or tops. To book guided tours (in English) of the Basilica di San Francesco, email its **information office** (☎ 075 81 90 84; AssisiSanFrancesco@libero.it; Piazza San Francesco; 9am-noon & 2-5.30pm Mon-Sat).

The **Basilica di San Francesco** (www.sanfrancescoassisi.org; Piazza di San Francesco) comprises two churches. The **upper church** (8.30am-6.45pm Easter-Nov, to 5.45pm daily Nov-Easter) was damaged during a severe earthquake in 1997, but has since been restored to its former state. Built between 1230 and 1253 in the Italian Gothic style, it features superb frescoes by Giotto and works by Cimabue and Pietro Cavallini.

Downstairs in the dimly lit **lower church** (6am-6.45pm Easter-Nov, to 5.45pm Nov-Easter), constructed between 1228 and 1230, you'll find a series of colourful frescoes by Simone Martini, Cimabue and Pietro Lorenzetti. The crypt where St Francis is buried is below the church.

The 13th-century **Basilica di Santa Chiara** (☎ 075 81 22 82; Piazza Santa Chiara; 6.30am-noon & 2-7pm Apr-Oct, to 6pm Nov-Mar) contains the remains of St Clare, friend of St Francis and founder of the Order of Poor Clares.

ITALY

Sleeping & Eating

You'll need to book ahead during peak times: Easter, August and September, and the Feast of St Francis (3 and 4 October).

Ostello della Pace (☎ 075 81 67 67; www.assisihostel.com; Via Valecchie 177; dm €16-18;) In a pretty and quiet location between the train station and the Old Town, this family-run HI hostel offers a bar, restaurant, laundry room and bikes for hire.

Camere Santa Chiara (☎ 075 81 34 67; camere.santachiara@yahoo.it; Vicolo Sant'Antonio 1; s/d €50/60) This place has atmosphere and services in spades. There are only six rooms, but all are well-equipped and one even has a private terrace.

Osteria Piazzetta dell'Erba (☎ 075 81 53 52; Via S. Gabriele dell'Addolorata; pastas €9-12, salads €6-8, meals €30) After admiring the churches, why not claim a table under the plane trees and enjoy a light lunch? This *osteria* close to Piazza del Commune serves modern Italian dishes that are as good to eat as they are to look at. Salads, pasta and antipasti platters are the best bets.

Trattoria Pallotta (☎ 075 81 26 49; Vicolo della Volta Pinta 2; meals €25; closed Tue) Duck under the frescoed Volta Pinta (Painted Vault) off Piazza del Comune to this brick-vaulted, wood-beamed trattoria. The menu is unapologetically local, featuring homemade *strangozzi* (like tagliatelle), roast pigeon and rabbit stew.

Getting There & Away

It is better to travel to Assisi by bus rather than train, as the train station is 4km from Assisi proper in Santa Maria degli Angeli. Buses arrive at and depart from Piazza Matteotti in the *centro storico*.

APM buses connect Assisi with Perugia (€3.10, one hour, 13 daily). Sulga operates buses to Rome (€17.50, three hours, two daily) and Florence (€12, 2½ hours, one daily).

If you arrive by train, a bus (Linea C, €1, half-hourly) runs between Piazza Matteotti and the station. Regional trains run to Perugia (€2.05, 20 minutes, hourly).

URBINO

pop 15,400

If you visit only one town in Le Marche, make it Urbino. It's difficult to get to, but as you wander its steep, Unesco-protected streets you'll appreciate the effort. Birthplace of Raphael and Bramante and a university town since 1564, it continues to be a bustling centre of culture and learning. In July, it hosts the internationally famous **Urbino Musica Antica** (Urbino Festival of Ancient Music; www.fima-online.org, in Italian).

To get to the centre from the bus terminal on Borgo Mercatale, head up Via Mazzini or take the *ascensore* (lift) up to Via Garibaldi (€0.50).

Information and accommodation listings are available at the town's two **tourist offices** (☎ 0722 26 13; iat.urbino@regione.marche.it; centre Via Puccinoti 35; 9am-1pm Mon, 9am-1pm & 3-6pm Tue-Sat, 9am-1pm Sun summer, closed Sun & Sat afternoon winter; bus terminus 9am-6pm Mon-Sat, 9am-1pm Sun). For internet, head to **Netgate** (Via G Mazzini 17; per hr €4; 9am-10pm Mon-Sat).

Urbino's centrepiece is the Renaissance **Palazzo Ducale** (☎ 0722 32 26 25; Piazza Duca Federico; adult/concession €8/4; 8.30am-7.15pm Tue-Sun, to 2pm Mon), completed in 1482. Inside, the **Galleria Nazionale delle Marche** features works by Raphael, Paolo Uccello, della Francesca and Verrocchio.

Right in the heart of the walled town, **Albergo Italia** (☎ 0722 27 01; www.albergo-italia-urbino.it; Corso Garibaldi 32; s €47-70, d €70-120;) has a bland modern interior offset by helpful staff, a pleasant garden terrace and comfortable rooms.

The owner-chef of **La Trattoria del Leone** (☎ 0722 32 98 94; Via Cesare Battisti; meals €16-20; dinner daily, lunch Sat & Sun) is understandably proud of the Marchigiani food he serves at this unassuming trattoria on the main square. There are well-priced set meals or you can order à la carte.

Locals celebrating major milestones always choose one place as the venue: the classically elegant **Vecchia Urbino** (☎ 0722 44 47; Via dei Vasari 3; meals €35; closed Tue). In a 16th-century *palazzo,* it serves exceptionally well-executed local specialities in evocative surrounds.

Trains don't run to Urbino. **Autolinee Ruocco** (☎ 800 90 15 91, 0975 790 33) runs a daily bus to Perugia (€13, 1¾ hours), for which it is essential to book a seat in advance. **Autolinee Bucci** (☎ 0721 324 01; www.autolineebucci.com) runs two buses per day to Rome (€20.80, 4½ hours). **Soget** (☎ 0721 54 96 20) buses link with Pesaro (€2.75 to €3, 75 minutes, 15 daily), where you can pick up a train for Bologna (€15, 90 minutes, hourly).

SOUTHERN ITALY

A sun-bleached land of spectacular coastlines, silent, windswept hills and proud towns, southern Italy is an altogether more raw prospect than the manicured north. Its stunning scenery, graphic ruins and fabulous beaches often go hand in hand with urban sprawl and scruffy coastal development, sometimes in the space of a few kilometres.

Yet for all its troubles, *il mezzogiorno* (the midday sun, as southern Italy is known) has much to offer. Centuries of foreign dominion have led to a fruitful fusion of architectural, artistic and culinary styles. Nature has done her bit too, dealing the area a dramatic topography that for centuries caused isolation and tribulation. It was only with the onset of 20th-century tourism that the Amalfi Coast, Matera and Sardinia began to escape grinding poverty.

Of Italy's southern regions, Puglia is currently attracting the most attention with its enviable cuisine, cracking coastline and beautiful, historic towns.

NAPLES

pop 975,200

A raucous hell-broth of a city, Naples (Napoli) is loud, anarchic, dirty and edgy. Its manic streets and in-your-face energy leave you disorientated, bewildered and hungry for more. Founded by Greek colonists, it became a thriving Roman city and was later the Bourbon capital of the Kingdom of the Two Sicilies. In the 18th-century it was one of Europe's great cities, something you'll readily believe as you marvel at its imperious palaces. Many of Naples finest *palazzi* now house museums and art galleries, the best of which is the Museo Archeologico Nazionale, one of Italy's premier museums and reason enough for a city stopover.

Orientation

Naples lazes along the waterfront and is divided into *quartieri* (districts). A convenient point of reference is Stazione Centrale, which forms the eastern flank of Piazza Garibaldi, Naples' ugly transport hub. From Piazza Garibaldi, Corso Umberto I skirts the *centro storico*, which is centred on two parallel roads: Via San Biagio dei Librai and its continuation Via Benedetto Croce (together known as Spaccanapoli); and Via dei Tribunali. West of the *centro storico*, Via Toledo, Naples' main shopping strip, leads down to Piazza del Plebiscito. South of here lies the seafront Santa Lucia district; to the west is Chiaia, a rich, fashionable area. Above it all, Vomero is a natural balcony with grand views.

Information

DISCOUNT CARDS

Campania ArteCard (☎ 800 600 601; www.campaniaartecard.it; 3 days Naples/3 days Campania/7 days Campania €13/25/28) Free or discounted admission to dozens of museums, plus free public transport. Available at train stations, newsagents, participating museums, the internet or through the call centre.

EMERGENCY

Police station (Questura; ☎ 081 794 11 11; Via Medina 75)

INTERNET ACCESS

Navig@ndo (Via Santa Anna di Lombardi 28; per hr €2; 🕒 9am-8.30pm Mon-Fri, 9.30am-2pm Sat)

LEFT LUGGAGE

Stazione Centrale (1st 5hr €3.80, 6-12hr per hr €0.60, 13hr & over per hr €0.20; 🕒 7am-11pm)

MEDICAL SERVICES

Ospedale Loreto-Mare (Hospital; ☎ 081 20 10 33; Via Amerigo Vespucci 26) On the waterfront, near the train station.

Pharmacy (☎ 081 26 88 81; Stazione Centrale; 🕒 7am-9.30pm) At the main train station.

POST

Main post office (☎ 081 790 47 54; Piazza Matteotti)

TOURIST INFORMATION

Pick up a copy of *Qui Napoli*, a useful bilingual monthly publication with details of sights, transport, accommodation, and major events.

There are several tourist offices:

Piazza del Gesù Nuovo 7 (☎ 081 552 33 28; www.inaples.it; 🕒 9.30am-1.30pm & 2.30-6pm Mon-Sat, 9am-1.30pm Sun)

Stazione Centrale (☎ 081 20 66 66; 🕒 9am-7pm daily) On the main concourse.

Via San Carlo 9 (☎ 081 40 23 94; 🕒 9.30am-1.30pm & 2.30-6pm Mon-Sat, 9am-1.30pm Sun) Opposite Teatro San Carlo.

Dangers & Annoyances

Despite Naples' notoriety as a mafia hotspot, the city is pretty safe. That said, travellers should be careful about walking alone late at night near Stazione Centrale and Piazza Dante.

Petty crime is also widespread. Be especially vigilant for pickpockets and moped bandits, many of whom target out-of-towners with expensive watches.

Car and motorcycle theft is also rife, so think twice before bringing a vehicle into town and never leave anything visible in a parked car.

And never ever buy electronic gear on Piazza Garibaldi – you'll almost certainly be ripped off.

Sights

CENTRO STORICO & AROUND

If you visit only one museum in southern Italy, make it the **Museo Archeologico Nazionale** (☎ 081 442 21 49; Piazza Museo Nazionale 19; adult/concession €6.50/3.25; 🕒 9am-7.30pm Wed-Mon), home to one of the world's most important collections of Graeco-Roman antiquities. Many of the exhibits once belonged to the Farnese family, including the colossal *Toro Farnese* (Farnese Bull) and gigantic *Ercole* (Hercules). On the mezzanine floor, *La battaglia di Alessandro contro Dario* (The Battle of Alexander against Darius) is one of many awe-inspiring mosaics from Pompeii. On the same floor, the **Gabinetto Segreto** (Secret Room) features some saucy sculpture and a series of impressive phalluses.

A short walk south of the museum, Piazza del Gesù Nuovo, is flanked by the 16th-century ashlar facade of the **Chiesa del Gesù Nuovo** (☎ 081 557 81 11; 🕒 7am-12.30pm & 4-7.30pm) and the **Basilica di Santa Chiara** (☎ 081 552 62 09; Via Santa Chiara 49; 🕒 7.30am-1pm & 4-8pm Mon-Sat). This hulking Gothic complex was restored

to its original 14th-century look after being severely damaged by WWII bombing. The main attraction is the tiled **Chiostro delle Clarisse** (Nuns' Cloisters; admission €5; 9.30am-5.30pm Mon-Sat, 9.30am-1pm Sun), adjacent to the main basilica.

Just off Via Benedetto Croce, the **Cappella di San Severo** (081 551 84 70; Via de Sanctis 19; admission €6; 10am-5.40pm Mon & Wed-Sat, 10am-1.10pm Sun) reveals a sumptuous baroque interior and the remarkable *Cristo velato* (Veiled Christ), Giuseppe Sanmartino's incredible depiction of Jesus covered by a veil.

Naples' spiritual heart is the **Duomo** (081 44 90 97; Via Duomo; 8am-12.30pm & 4.30-7pm Mon-Sat, 8.30am-1.30pm & 5-7.30pm Sun). Built by the Angevins at the end of the 13th century,

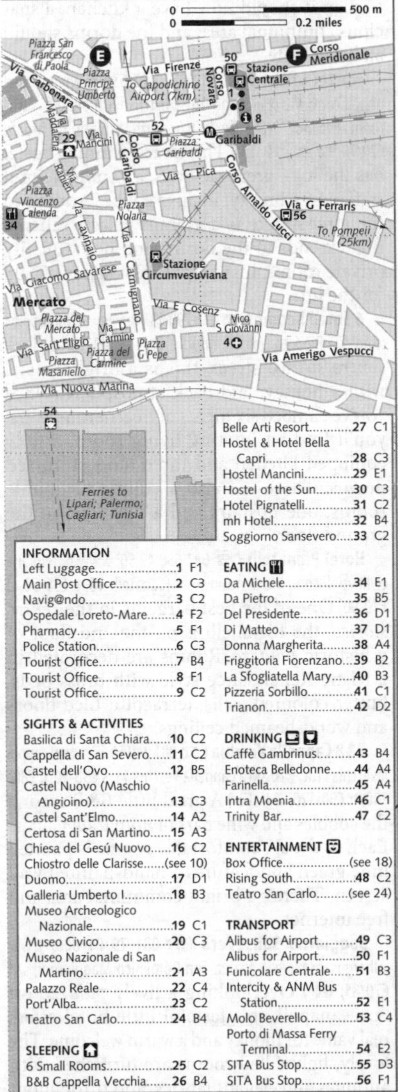

it has a 19th-century neo-Gothic facade and a largely baroque interior. Inside, the holy of holies is the 17th-century **Cappella di San Gennaro**, containing the head of St Januarius (the city's patron saint) and two vials of his congealed blood. The saint is said to have saved the city from disasters on various occasions.

At the western end of Via dei Tribunali, **Port' Alba** was one of the city's 17th-century gates.

CHIAIA & SANTA LUCIA

At the bottom of Via Toledo, beyond the glass atrium of the **Galleria Umberto 1** shopping arcade, Piazza Trieste e Trento leads onto **Piazza del Plebiscito**, Naples' most impressive piazza. Forming one side of the square, the rusty-red **Palazzo Reale** (☎ 081 794 40 21; Piazza del Plebiscito I; admission €4; 9am-8pm Thu-Tue) was the official residence of the Bourbon and Savoy kings and now houses a rich collection of baroque and neoclassical furnishings, statues and paintings.

Next door, the **Teatro San Carlo** (☎ 081 553 45 65; Via San Carlo 98; tours €5; 9am-5.30pm Thu-Mon) opera house is famed for its perfect acoustics and passionate audiences. Visit its lavish interior or go for a show (see p520).

Overlooking the seafront, **Castel Nuovo** is one of Naples' landmark sites, a hulking 13th-century castle known to locals as the Maschio Angioino (Angevin Keep). Inside, the **Museo Civico** (☎ 081 795 20 03; adult/concession €5/4; 9am-7pm Mon-Sat, to 2pm Sun) displays some interesting 14th- and 15th-century frescoes and sculptures.

A second castle, the improbably named **Castel dell'Ovo** (Castle of the Egg; ☎ 081 24 00 055; Borgo Marinaro; admission free; 8am-6pm Mon-Sat, to 2pm Sun) marks the eastern end of the *lungomare* (seafront). Standing on the Borgo Marinaro, a small fishing village now given over to restaurants and bars, it was originally a Norman castle and then an Angevin fortress.

VOMERO

The highpoint (quite literally) of Neapolitan baroque, the stunning **Certosa di San Martino** is one of Naples' must-see sights. Originally a 14th-century Carthusian monastery, it was given a 17th-century facelift by baroque maestro Cosimo Fanzago, and now houses the **Museo Nazionale di San Martino** (☎ 081 558 64 08; Piazzale San Martino 5; admission €6; 8.30am-7.30pm Thu-Tue). Highlights include the main church, the Chiostro Grande (Great Cloister) and the Sezione Presepiale, dedicated to rare 18th- and 19th-century *presepi* (nativity scenes). There's also a collection of Bourbon carriages and a monastic spicery.

Commanding spectacular views across the city, **Castel Sant' Elmo** (☎ 081 578 40 30; Via Tito Angelini

20; admission €3; 9am-6.30pm Tue-Thu) dates to 1329 and hosts art exhibits.

The easiest way up to Vomero is to take the Funicolare Centrale from Via Toledo.

CAPODIMONTE

A bus ride from the city centre, Capodimonte is worth a day of anyone's time. The colossal 18th-century Palazzo Reale di Capodimonte houses one of southern Italy's top fine-art museums, and the 130-hectare park is a top picnic spot.

The **Museo di Capodimonte** (081 749 91 11; Parco di Capodimonte; adult/child €7.50/3.75; 8.30am-7.30pm Thu-Tue) is spread over three floors and 160 rooms. You'll never see everything but a morning should be enough for an abridged tour. With works by Bellini, Botticelli, Titian and Andy Warhol, there's no shortage of talking points, but the piece that many come to see is Caravaggio's striking *Flagellazione* (Flagellation).

Take bus R4 to reach Capodimonte.

Festivals & Events

The **Festa di San Gennaro** honours the city's patron saint and is held three times a year (first Sunday in May, 19 September and 16 December). Thousands pack into the Duomo to witness the saint's blood liquefy, a miracle said to save the city from potential disasters.

Sleeping

Accommodation is plentiful and you should have no problem finding somewhere to stay. Most of the budget accommodation is in the ugly area around Stazione Centrale and down near the port. The *centro storico* has some good places, most hidden in centuries-old *palazzi*.

Hostel & Hotel Bella Capri (081 552 92 65; www.bellacapri.it; Via Melisurgo 4; dm €16-21, s €55-70, d €60-80, tr €80-100, q €90-110;) A hybrid hotel-cum-hostel, this is an excellent portside choice. The hotel rooms are smallish but comfy with air-con and unfussy decor, and some even have balconies overlooking Vesuvius. On the 7th floor, the hostel is colourful and welcoming. Cheaper rooms with shared bathrooms are also available.

Hostel Mancini (081 553 67 31; www.hostelpensionemancini.com; Via Mancini 33; dm €18, s €45-55, d €50-65, tr €80-90, q €80-90) One of the better options in the Stazione Centrale area, this no-frills hostel/*pensione* was about to be given a facelift when we passed. If everything went according to plan it should now have a kitchen, a spacious communal area, and the dorms should all be en suite.

Hostel of the Sun (081 420 63 93; www.hostelnapoli.com; Via Melisurgo 15; s/d/tr/q with shared bathroom €45/56/70/80, dm/d/tr/q with private bathroom €20/70/90/100;) This award-winning hostel has the lot – great facilities, a young, helpful staff, and a breezy, inclusive vibe. Adding to the atmosphere is a vibrant colour scheme that extends to the dorms and hotel-quality private rooms. Just make sure you have €0.05 for the lift.

6 Small Rooms (081 790 13 78; www.6smallrooms.com; Via Diodato Lioy 18; dm/d €22/45;) In a dark *centro storico* street, this is a bright hostel with a homey, laid-back atmosphere. Once you've climbed six flights of treacherous stairs, you'll find an inviting living room, a fully equipped kitchen and three modest, mixed dorms. There are also a couple of double rooms, one upstairs and a tiny one on the ground floor.

Hotel Pignatelli (081 658 49 50; www.hotelpignatellinapoli.com; Via San Giovanni Pignatelli 16; s €35-50, d €70-90) One of the best bargains in the *centro storico*, the Pignatelli is on the 2nd floor of a historic *palazzo*. Rooms are decorated in a rustic Renaissance style with brass beds, butter-coloured walls, terracotta-tiled floors and wood-beamed ceilings.

B&B Cappella Vecchia (081 240 51 17; www.cappellavecchia11.it; Vico SM a Cappella Vecchia 11; s €50-70, d €80-100, tr €90-120;) A great little B&B among the cobbles and wine bars of upmarket Chiaia. Each of the six comfortable rooms is painted lime green and features a hand-painted wall screen. There's a bright communal area and free internet.

Soggiorno Sansevero (081 79 01 000; www.albergosansevero.it; Piazza San Domenico Maggiore 9; s/d €70/85;) Overlooking a lively *palazzo* on Spaccanapoli, this tasteful little hotel offers real value for money and a warm welcome. The lovely, light-filled rooms are furnished with antiques and elegant fabrics, and throughout there's a quiet, homey atmosphere.

Belle Arti Resort (081 557 10 62; www.belleartiresort.com; Via Santa Maria di Costantinopoli 27; r from €80;) Behind an impenetrable wall near Piazza Bellini, this is an exquisite boutique hideaway. The seven rooms are a picture of sensitive design, combining frescoed ceilings and original stucco with sharp modern furniture, sexy lighting and marble bathrooms.

mh Hotel (☎ 081 195 71 576; www.mhhotel.it; Via Chiaia 245; s €99-150, d €105-230;) Claiming to be the first 'design' hotel in Naples, the mh sports a linear, Prada-inspired look. Blacks, greys and whites form the backdrop to the sleek, modern rooms equipped with mod cons and gleaming bathrooms.

Eating

Neapolitans are justifiably proud of their food. Pizza was created here, the city's famous for it, and nowhere will you eat it better. There are any number of toppings but locals favour *margherita* (tomato, mozzarella and basil) or *marinara* (tomato, garlic, oregano and olive oil), cooked in a wood-fired oven. Pizzerias serving the 'real thing' have a sign on their door – *la vera pizza napoletana* (the real Neapolitan pizza).

Neapolitan street food is good. *Misto di frittura* – deep-fried vegetables – are available at takeaways called *friggatorie* all over town. For something sweet try a *sfogliatella* (a flaky pastry filled with sweet cinnamon ricotta).

PIZZA

Trianon (☎ 081 553 94 26; Via Colletta 46; pizzas €4) A city institution, this marble-clad pizzeria has been on the dough since 1923. Queues wait to tuck into the usual range of pizzas prepared with practised flair by the hardworking *pizzaioli* (pizza makers).

Da Michele (☎ 081 553 92 04; Via Cesare Sersale 1/3; pizzas €4; Mon-Sat) The godfather of Neapolitan pizzerias, this place takes the no-frills ethos to its extremes. It's dingy, old-fashioned and serves only two types of pizza – *margherita* and *marinara*. But, boy are they good!

Di Matteo (☎ 081 45 52 62; Via dei Tribunali 94; pizzas €5; 9am-midnight Mon-Sat) Not much more than a hole-in-the-wall, this is one of three top pizzerias on Via dei Tribunali. Locals flock here on weekend nights to stock up on fried snacks from the street-front counter or wolf down pizza in the broiling interior.

our pick **Del Presidente** (☎ 081 21 09 03; Via dei Tribunali 120/121; pizzas €5) This is where British uber-chef Heston Blumenthal came when researching pizza for his TV series *In Search of Perfection*. He thought the *margherita* was pretty damn good, as did this author, who valiantly braved the crowds and scary service to put Heston's verdict to the test.

Pizzeria Sorbillo (☎ 081 44 66 43; Via dei Tribunali 32; pizzas €5; Mon-Sat) The smartest of the Via dei Tribunali pizzerias, the Sorbillo is hugely popular. So much so that eating here is much like sitting down to a meal in rush hour. But the locals know their pizza and they wouldn't come if it wasn't top notch.

NOT PIZZA

Friggitoria Fiorenzano (☎ 081 551 27 88; Piazza Montesanto; snacks from €1; Mon-Sat) Choose from piles of crunchy deep-fried aubergines and artichokes, croquets filled with prosciutto and mozzarella, and a whole lot more.

La Sfogliatella Mary (☎ 081 40 22 18; Via Toledo 66; Tue-Sun) The place to grab a quick, on-the-go *sfogliatella*. Warm from the oven, they're the best €1.20 you'll ever spend.

Da Pietro (☎ 081 807 10 82; Borgo Marinaro 29-30; meals €23; Tue-Sun) On trendy Borgo Marinaro, this modest harbour-side restaurant serves wonderful seafood. The menu, chalked up daily, depends on the day's catch but expect bowls of local mussels, grilled fish and simple house wine.

Donna Margherita (☎ 081 40 01 29; Vico II Alabardieri 4-6; meals €25) For huge helpings of uncomplicated, tasty food this trattoria-cum-pizzeria hits the spot. The rich antipasti buffet makes for a good start and the vast pastas ensure you won't be running anywhere in a hurry.

Drinking

Caffè Gambrinus (☎ 081 41 75 82; Via Chiaia 12) Naples' most venerable cafe features a showy art nouveau interior and a cast of self-conscious drinkers served by smart, waistcoated waiters.

Farinella (☎ 081 423 84 55; Via Alabadieri 10) Join the Chiaia style-cats for an *aperitivo* at this snazzy NY-style restaurant lounge bar. Chic atmosphere with prices to match.

Enoteca Belledonne (☎ 081 40 31 62; Vico Belledonne a Chiaia 18) Exposed brick walls, ambient lighting and bottle-lined shelves set the scene at this much-loved Chiaia wine bar.

Intra Moenia (☎ 081 29 07 20; Piazza Bellini 70) Attracting a bohemian crowd, this arty cafe-cum-bookshop is beautifully located on Piazza Bellini. It's a great place to while away a long summer evening with friends and something cool.

Trinity Bar (☎ 081 551 45 69; Calata Trinita Maggiore 5) The most popular of the bars around Piazza del Gesù Nuovo. Grab a beer and kick back with the students.

Entertainment

For cultural listings pick up the monthly *Qui Napoli* at tourist offices. You can buy tickets for most sporting and cultural events at **Box Office** (☎ 081 551 91 88; www.boxofficenapoli.it; Galleria Umberto I 15-16).

During May free concerts and cultural events are often held at weekends. Ask at the tourist offices for details.

Opera fans will enjoy an evening at **Teatro San Carlo** (☎ box office 081 797 23 31; www.teatrosancarlo.it; Via San Carlo 98; tickets from €25), one of Italy's top opera houses, which has a year-round program of opera and ballet. For something more contemporary, **Rising South** (Via San Sebastiano 19) is a popular *centro storico* nightclub.

Getting There & Away

AIR

Capodichino airport (NAP; ☎ 848 88 87 77; www.gesac.it), 7km northeast of the city centre, is southern Italy's main airport. Flights operate to most Italian cities and up to 30 European destinations, as well as New York. Some 27 airlines serve the airport, including Alitalia, Air One, easyJet, Meridiana, BA, BMI and Air France.

BOAT

A fleet of *traghetti* (ferries), *aliscafi* (hydrofoils) and *navi veloci* (fast ships) connect Naples with Sorrento, the bay islands, the Amalfi Coast, Salerno, Sicily and Sardinia. Hydrofoils leave from Molo Beverello and Megellina; ferries depart from the Porta di Massa ferry terminal.

Tickets for shorter journeys can be bought at Molo Beverello or Mergellina. For longer journeys try ferry company offices at Porto di Massa or a travel agent. You can also buy online.

Qui Napoli lists timetables for Bay of Naples services. Note, however, that ferry services are pared back in winter and adverse sea conditions may affect sailing schedules.

The major companies out of Naples:

Alilauro (☎ 081 761 10 04; www.alilauro.it) To/from Sorrento (hydrofoil €11.50, 35 minutes), Ischia (hydrofoil €17, 45 minutes).

Caremar (☎ 081 551 38 82; www.caremar.it) To/from Capri (ferry €5.60, 1¼ hours), Ischia (hydrofoil €14, 55 minutes), Procida (hydrofoil €9.25, 45 minutes).

Metro del Mare (☎ 199 600 700; www.metrodelmare.com) To/from Amalfi (ferry €15, 1½ hours), Positano (ferry €14, 55 minutes), Sorrento (ferry €6.50, 45 minutes).

NLG (☎ 081 552 07 63; www.navlib.it) To/from Capri (hydrofoil €17, 30 minutes).

Siremar (☎ 081 89 21 23; www.siremar.it) To/from Lipari (ferry €12.60, 10½ hours).

SNAV (☎ 081 428 55 55; www.snav.it) To/from Capri (hydrofoil €20, 45 minutes), Palermo (ferry €46, 10½ hours).

Tirrenia (☎ 081 89 21 23; www.tirrenia.com) To/from Palermo (ferry €48, 10¼ hours), Cagliari (€45, 16¼ hours).

Note that these prices are for high season and may fluctuate depending on fuel surcharges.

BUS

Most buses leave from Piazza Garibaldi. **SITA** (☎ 199 73 07 49; www.sitabus.it, in Italian) runs buses to Pompeii (€2.40, 40 minutes, hourly), Sorrento (€3.30, one hour 20 minutes, three daily), Positano (€3.30, two hours, three daily), Amalfi (€3.30, two hours, eight daily) and Bari (€19.50, three hours, one daily). Buy tickets and catch buses from the terminus near Porto di Massa or from Via G Ferraris, near Stazione Centrale.

Miccolis (☎ 081 200 380) serves Lecce (€28, 5½ hours) and Brindisi (€25.60, five hours).

CAR & MOTORCYCLE

If you value your sanity, skip driving in Naples. If you want to tempt fate, the city is easily accessible from Rome on the A1 *autostrada*. The Naples–Pompeii–Salerno motorway (A3) connects with the coastal road to Sorrento and the Amalfi Coast.

TRAIN

Naples is southern Italy's main rail hub. Most trains stop at Stazione Centrale or, underneath the main station, Stazione Garibaldi. There are up to 30 trains daily to Rome (€19.50 to €27.60, two hours) and some 20 to Salerno (€6.50, 35 minutes).

The **Circumvesuviana** (☎ 800 05 39 39; www.vesuviana.it), accessible from Stazione Centrale, operates trains to Sorrento (€3.30, one hour 10 minutes) via Ercolano (€1.80, 20 minutes), Pompeii (€2.40, 40 minutes) and other towns along the coast. There are about 40 trains daily running between 5am and 10.40pm, with reduced services on Sunday.

The Ferrovia Cumana and the **Circumflegrea** (☎ 800 00 16 16; www.sepsa.it), based at Stazione Cumana di Montesanto, operate services to Pozzuoli (€1.10, every 25 minutes) and Cuma (€1.10, six daily).

WORTH THE TRIP: PALAZZO REALE

Dubbed the Italian Versailles, Caserta's monumental **Palazzo Reale** (☎ 0823 44 80 84; Corso Pietro Giannone 1; adult/concession €6/3; ⌚ 8.30am-7pm Wed-Mon) is one of the greatest achievements of Italian baroque architecture. The Reggia di Caserta, as it's better known, was designed and built by Neapolitan Luigi Vanvitelli to triumphant effect. With its 1200 rooms, 1790 windows, 34 staircases and a 250m-long facade, it was reputedly the largest building in 18th-century Europe. Outside, the gardens are equally grandiose.

Caserta is easily reached by bus or train from Naples.

Getting Around

TO/FROM THE AIRPORT

By public transport you can either take the regular **ANM** (☎ 800 639 525; www.anm.it) bus 3S (€1.10, 30 minutes, half-hourly) from Piazza Garibaldi, or the Alibus airport shuttle (€3.10, 20 minutes, half-hourly) from Piazza del Municipio or Stazione Centrale.

Taxi fares are set at €19 to/from a seafront hotel, €16 to/from Piazza Municipio, and €12.50 to/from Stazione Centrale.

PUBLIC TRANSPORT

You can travel Naples by bus, metro and funicular. Journeys are covered by the Unico Napoli ticket, which comes in various forms: the standard ticket, valid for 90 minutes, costs €1.10; a daily pass is €3.10; and a weekend daily ticket is €2.60. Note that these tickets are not valid to Pompeii or Ercolano on the Circumvesuviana line. Campania ArteCards (p515) are also valid on all forms of public transport.

There's no central bus station but most buses pass through Piazza Garibaldi. A useful one is bus R2, which runs along Corso Umberto I to Piazza del Municipio and Piazza Trieste e Trento.

POMPEII

An ancient town frozen in its 2000-year-old death throes, Pompeii was a thriving commercial town until Mt Vesuvius erupted on 24 August AD 79, burying it under a layer of *lapilli* (burning fragments of pumice stone) and killing some 2000 people. The skeletal, Unesco-listed **ruins** (☎ 081 857 53 47; www.pompeiisites.org; adult/concession €11/5.50, audio guides €6.50; ⌚ 8.30am-7.30pm Apr-Oct, 8.30am-5pm Nov-Mar, last entry 1½ hr before closing) provide a remarkable model of a working Roman city, complete with temples, a forum, an amphitheatre, apartments, a shopping district, and a brothel. Dotted around the 44-hectare site are a number of creepy body casts, made in the late 19th century by pouring plaster into the hollows left by disintegrated bodies. They are so lifelike you can still see clothing folds, hair, even the expressions of terror on their faces.

There is a **tourist office** (☎ 081 536 32 93; pompeiturismo@email.it; Piazza Porta Marina Inferiore 12; ⌚ 9am-3.30pm Mon-Sat) just outside the excavations at Porta Marina.

The easiest way to get to Pompeii is by the Ferrovia Circumvesuviana from Naples (€2.40, 35 minutes, half-hourly) or Sorrento (€1.90, 30 minutes, half-hourly). Get off at Pompeii Scavi-Villa dei Misteri; the Porta Marina entrance is nearby.

CAPRI

pop 7260

The most visited of Naples' Bay islands, Capri is far more interesting than a quick day trip would suggest. Get beyond the glamorous veneer of chichi piazzas and designer boutiques and you'll discover an island of rugged seascapes, desolate Roman ruins and a surprisingly unspoiled rural inland.

Capri's fame dates to Roman times, when Emperor Augustus made it his private playground and Tiberius retired there in AD 27. Its modern incarnation as a tourist destination dates to the early 20th century when it was invaded by an army of European artists, writers and Russian revolutionaries, drawn as much by the beauty of the local boys as the thrilling landscape.

The island is easily reached from Naples and Sorrento. Hydrofoils and ferries dock at Marina Grande, from where it's a short funicular ride up to Capri, the main town. A further bus ride takes you up to Anacapri.

Information is available online at www.capri.it, www.capritourism.it, or from one of the three **tourist offices** (Anacapri ☎ 081 837 15 24; Via G Orlandi 59; ⌚ 9am-3pm Mon-Sat; Capri Town ☎ 081 837 06 86; Piazza Umberto I; ⌚ 8.30am-8.30pm Mon-Sat, 9am-3pm Sun summer, 9am-1pm & 3.30-6.45pm Mon-Sat winter; Marina Grande ☎ 081 837 06 34; ⌚ 9am-1pm & 3.30-6.45pm Mon-Sat).

Sights & Activities

Capri's single most famous attraction is the **Grotta Azzurra** (Blue Grotto; admission €4; 9am-1hr before sunset), a stunning sea cave illuminated by an other-worldly blue light. Try to visit early or late in the day to avoid the hordes. Boats leave from Marina Grande and the all-in round trip costs €21; allow a good hour.

Once you've explored Capri Town's dinky whitewashed streets, head over to the **Giardini di Augusto** (Gardens of Augustus) for some breathtaking views. From here the magnificent **Via Krupp** zigzags vertiginously down to Marina Piccola.

East of Capri Town, an hour-long walk along Via Tiberio, is **Villa Jovis** (admission €2; 9am-1hr before sunset), the largest and most sumptuous of the island's 12 Roman villas and Tiberius' main Capri residence. A short walk away, down Via Tiberio and Via Matermània, is the **Arco Naturale**, a huge rock arch formed by the pounding sea.

Up in Anacapri, **Villa San Michele** (081 837 14 01; Via Axel Munthe; admission €5; 9am-6pm May-Sep, to 5pm Oct & Apr, to 3.30pm Nov-Feb, to 4.30pm Mar) boasts some Roman antiquities and beautiful, panoramic gardens. For the best views on the island, take the **seggiovia** (chair lift; one way/return €6/8; 9.30am-5pm Mar-Oct, 10.30am-3pm Nov-Feb) up from Piazza Vittoria to the summit of **Mt Solaro** (589m), Capri's highest point.

Sleeping

Capri has plenty of top-end hotels but few genuinely budget options. Always book ahead as hotel space is at a premium during summer and many places close in winter.

Hotel La Tosca (081 837 09 89; www.latoscahotel.com; Via Dalmazio Birago 5; s €60-90, d €80-140; Apr-Oct;) La Tosca is one of the island's top budget hotels. With 11 sparkling white rooms, a central location, and a genial manager, it presses all the right buttons.

Hotel Bussola (081 838 20 10; www.bussolahermes.com; Trav La Vigna 14; d €70-140, tr €90-165, q €130-200;) A hospitable outpost on a quiet Anacapri lane, the year-round Bussola offers a warm welcome and sunny rooms with flat-screen TVs, white walls and blue marble floors. Depending on availability, they also set aside one or two rooms for students (€35 to €40 per person).

Hotel La Minerva (081 837 70 67; www.laminervacapri.com; Via Occhio Marino 8; d €150-390; Mar-Nov;) This romantic four-star is a model of Capri style. Sunlight streams into the tastefully decorated white rooms, washing the maiolica-tiled floors and soft furnishings in a sharp, crystal light. Outside, you can sunbathe on your private terrace or by the swimming pool.

Eating & Drinking

Island specialities include *insalata caprese*, a salad of fresh tomato, basil and mozzarella, and *ravioli caprese*, ravioli stuffed with ricotta and herbs.

Pulalli Wine Bar (081 837 4108; Piazza Umberto I; closed Tue & winter) A ritzy spot for a glass of local *limoncello* (lemon liqueur), Pulalli is perched in the clock tower overlooking 'la Piazzetta', Capri Town's main square. For a grandstand view of the action, snaffle a table on the small terrace. Light lunches and dinner are also served.

Trattoria Il Solitario (081 837 13 82; Via G Orlandi 96; pizzas from €5, meals €20; Apr-Oct) Just off Anacapri's main strip, this is a good, honest trattoria serving tasty local food. There are no surprises on the menu but you won't be disappointed with the large helpings and below-average prices. Book ahead on summer weekends.

La Pergola (081 837 74 12; Via Traversa Lo Palazzo 2; meals €32; Thu-Tue Nov-Sep) La Pergola offers a textbook rendition of the ideal Capri meal – delicious food on a vine-covered terrace overlooking the sea. The menu is inspired by the island's ingredients so expect plenty of seafood and a number of tempting lemon dishes.

Il Cucciolo (081 83 71 917; Trav Veterino 8; meals €50; Mar-Oct) Deep in the Anacapri countryside, Il Cucciolo sets the scene for a memorable meal. The romantic sunset views and wonderful, fresh seafood are not something you'll forget in a hurry. Booking is strongly advised, if nothing else to arrange a free pick-up from Anacapri.

In Capri Town, **Deco supermarket** (Via Roma; 8am-8pm Mon-Sat, 9am-1pm Sun) is a good place to load up with picnic provisions.

Getting There & Around

There are year-round hydrofoils and ferries to Capri from Naples and Sorrento. Timetables and fare details are available online at www.capritourism.com/en/timetable-and-prices. In Naples, sailing times are published in *Qui Napoli*; in Sorrento you can get timetables from the tourist office (see below).

From Naples, ferries depart from Porto di Massa and hydrofoils from Molo Beverello and Mergellina. Tickets cost €17 (hydrofoil), €14.90 (fast ferry) and €9.60 (ferry) – see p520 for further details.

From Sorrento, there are more than 25 sailings a day (less in winter). You'll pay €14.50 for the 20-minute hydrofoil crossing, €9.80 for the 25-minute fast ferry trip.

In summer, hydrofoils connect Capri with Positano (€15.50) and Amalfi (€16).

On the island, buses run from Capri Town to/from Marina Grande, Anacapri and Marina Piccola; also from Marina Grande to Anacapri. Single tickets cost €1.40 on all routes as does the funicular that links Marina Grande with Capri Town.

Contact **Rent a Scooter** (☎ 081 837 58 63; Via Roma 70; per hr €12) if you want to…well, you know.

SORRENTO

pop 16,600

Overlooking the Bay of Naples and Mt Vesuvius, Sorrento is southern Italy's main package holiday resort. Despite this, and despite the lack of a decent beach, it's an appealing place whose laid-back charm defies all attempts to swamp it in souvenir tat. There are few must-see sights but the *centro storico* is lively and the town makes a good jumping off point for the Amalfi Coast, Pompeii and Capri.

Orientation

The centre of town is Piazza Tasso, 300m northwest of the Circumvesuviana train and bus station along Corso Italia. From Marina Piccola, where ferries and hydrofoils dock, walk south along Via Marina Piccola then climb the steps to reach the piazza.

Information

Internet Train (Via degli Aranci 49; per hr €3.70; 9.30am-1.30pm & 3-8pm Mon-Sat, 9.30am-1.30pm Sun)

Lavanderia (Via degli Aranci 188; 8kg wash & dry €8; 7am-11pm) Self-service laundrette.

Ospedale Civile (Hospital; ☎ 081 533 11 11; Corso Italia 1)

Police station (Questura; ☎ 081 807 53 11; Vico III Rota) Report thefts here.

Post office (Corso Italia 210)

Tourist information office (☎ /fax 081 807 40 33; www.sorrentotourism.com; Via Luigi de Maio 35; 9am-6.30pm Mon-Sat summer, closes 4pm winter)

Sights & Activities

You'll probably spend most of your time in the *centro storico*, a tight-knit area of narrow streets lined with loud souvenir stores, cafes, churches and restaurants. To the north, the **Villa Comunale park** (8am-midnight summer, 8am-8pm winter) commands grand views over the sea to Mt Vesuvius.

Of the museums, the most interesting is the **Museo Bottega della Tarsia Lignea** (☎ 081 877 19 42; Via San Nicolà 28; admission €8; 10am-1pm & 3pm-6pm Mon-Sat) which showcases the *intarsio* (marquetry) furniture for which Sorrento is famous.

In town the two main swimming spots are **Marina Piccola** and **Marina Grande**, although neither is especially appealing. Nicer by far is **Bagni Regina Giovanna**, a rocky beach set among the ruins of a Roman villa, 2km west of town. To get there take the SITA bus for Massalubrense.

Sleeping

Nube d'Argento (☎ 081 878 13 44; www.nubedargento.com; Via del Capo 21; per person/tent/car €11/10/5; 2-person bungalows €50-85; Mar-Dec) This is a popular camping ground located 1km west of the town centre. Pitches and wooden chalet-style bungalows are set out beneath a panoply of olive trees, and the facilities, including an open-air swimming pool and a pizzeria, are excellent.

our pick **Ulisse Deluxe Hostel** (☎ 081 877 47 53; www.ulissedeluxe.com; Via del Mare 22; dm €25, d/tr/q €70/105/140) Masquerading as a three-star hotel, this recently opened hostel is quite something. With its vast reception hall, smart modern rooms, its en suite dorms and an air of quiet efficiency, it's a cut above most town-centre hotels, let alone hostels. There's access for travellers with disabilities, an internet point, and guests get discounts at the adjacent health club.

Hotel Linda (☎ 081 878 29 16; Via degli Aranci 125; s €30-38, d €50-70) A 10-minute walk from the train station, this is a classic, family-run *pensione*. It's a homey outfit with comfortable modern rooms on the 2nd floor of an unappealing block of flats. Cheaper rates are on offer for rooms with a shared bathroom. No breakfast.

La Magnolia (☎ 081 877 35 60; www.magnoliasorrento.it; Viale Caruso 14; s €50-90, d €70-120, tr €90-140) A terrific retreat just yards from Piazza Tasso. Housed in a converted villa, elegant

ITALY

rooms come with parquet, inlaid Sorrentine wood furniture and smart green bathrooms. Outside, there's a walled citrus garden where you can breakfast (for €6) in summer. Wi-fi is available.

Eating & Drinking

La Fenice (☎ 081 878 16 52; Via degli Aranci 11; pizzas €5, meals €30; ⏰ Tue-Sun) This bustling restaurant is good place to try *gnocchi alla sorrentina*, (potato gnocchi baked in tomato sauce with mozzarella), a traditional Sorrento speciality. If that doesn't appeal, there's fresh seafood or a comprehensive choice of pizzas and classic meat dishes.

Pizzeria Da Franco (☎ 081 877 20 66; Corso Italia 265; pizzas €6; ⏰ 8am-2am) Don't expect frills at this laid-back pizzeria, just queues and the best pizza in town. Grab a spot at one of the rustic wooden tables and tuck into magnificently baked pizza, served on a metal tray with plastic cutlery.

Café Latino (☎ 081 878 37 18; Vico I Fuoro 4/a; meals €30) Wow your partner with a cocktail at this romantic cafe. Tables are laid out in a tropical-looking garden full of lush orange and lemon trees. If you can't drag yourselves away, you can also eat here.

Sisa Supermercato (☎ 081 807 44 65; Via degli Aranci 157) A supermarket on the eastern edge of town.

Getting There & Away

Circumvesuviana trains run half-hourly between Sorrento and Naples (€3.30, 1¼ hours) via Pompeii and Ercolano (€1.90 to each). Regular SITA buses leave from the train station for the Amalfi Coast, stopping in Positano (€3, 50 minutes) and then Amalfi (€6, 1½ hours).

Sorrento is the main jumping-off point for Capri and ferries/hydrofoils run year-round from Marina Piccola. Get timetables from the tourist office. Tickets cost €14.50 (hydrofoil) or €9.80 (fast ferry).

Jolly Service and Rent (☎ 081 877 34 50; www.sorrentorent.com; Via degli Aranci) rents out cars/scooters from €50/25 per day.

AMALFI COAST

Stretching 50km along the southern side of the Sorrentine Peninsula, the Amalfi Coast (Costiera Amalfitana) is a postcard vision of Mediterranean beauty. Against a shimmering blue backdrop, whitewashed villages and terraced lemon groves cling to vertiginous cliffs backed by the craggy Lattari mountains. This Unesco-protected area is one of Italy's top tourist destinations, attracting hundreds of thousands of visitors each year, 70% of them between June and September.

GETTING THERE & AWAY

There are two main entry points to the Amalfi Coast: Sorrento and Salerno. Regular SITA buses run from Sorrento to Positano (€3, 50 minutes) and Amalfi (€6, 1½ hours) and from Salerno to Amalfi (€3, 1¼ hours).

Between April and September, **Metrò del Mare** (☎ 199 600 700; www.metrodelmare.com) runs boats from Naples to Sorrento (€6.50, 45 minutes), Positano (€14, 55 minutes) and Amalfi (€15, 1½ hours).

By car, pick up the SS163 coastal road at Vietri sul Mare.

WALK WITH THE GODS

Rising steeply from the coast, the densely wooded Lattari mountains provide some stunning walking opportunities. An extraordinary network of paths traverses the precipitous peaks, climbing to remote farmhouses through wild and beautiful valleys.

Probably the best-known route, the 9.3km *Sentiero degli Dei* (Path of the Gods; 5½ to six hours) follows the steep, often rocky paths linking Bomerano (near Agerola) to Nocelle, a village above Positano. It's a spectacular walk passing through some of the area's least developed countryside and offering breathtaking views. The route is marked by red and white stripes daubed on rocks and trees, although many of these have become worn and might be difficult to make out.

To the west, the tip of the Sorrentine Peninsula is another hiking hot spot. Some 110km of paths criss-cross the area, linking the spectacular coastline with the rural hinterland. Tourist offices can supply basic walking maps but if you're intent on trying one of the more demanding routes, you'll need a detailed map. Route details are also available in Lonely Planet's *Walking in Italy* guide.

Positano

pop 3930

The best way to approach Positano, the coast's most expensive and glamorous town, is by boat. As you come into dock, feast your eyes on the unforgettable view of colourful, steeply stacked houses packed onto near-vertical green slopes. In town, the main activities are hanging out on the small beach and browsing the flamboyant shop displays.

The **tourist office** (☎ 089 87 50 67; Via del Saracino 4; 9am-1.30pm & 3.30-8pm Mon-Sat) can provide information on walking in the surrounding hills.

SLEEPING & EATING

Hostel Brikette (☎ 089 87 58 57; www.brikette.com; Via Marconi 358; dm €22-27, d with shared bathroom €65-70, with private bathroom €90-110; Easter-Oct;) Near the bus stop on the coastal road, this is one of the very few hostels on the Amalfi Coast. It's decidedly no-frills with beds in six-to-20 person dorms and modest private rooms, but there's a terrace for drinks and the views are stunning.

Villa Maria Antonietta (☎ 089 87 50 71; Via C Colombo 41; r €80-100) Value for money is not something you can count on in Positano, but you'll get it here. All seven of the sunny, white-walled rooms look over a flower-filled terrace and, beyond that, the sea.

Villa Rosa (☎ 089 81 19 55; www.villarosapositano.it; Via C Colombo 127; d €160-240; Mar-Oct) This stylish little hotel has impeccable rooms decorated in classic coastal style, with white walls and cool, tiled floors. Some have private balconies but if yours doesn't, just head along to the picturesque terrace.

Da Costantino (☎ 089 87 57 38; Via Montepertuso; pizzas from €6, meals €25; Thu-Tue) About 300m above Hostel Brikette, this is one of the few authentic trattorias in town. Expect honest, down-to-earth Italian grub, pizza, char-grilled steaks, and fabulous views.

Ristorante Bruno (☎ 089 87 53 92; Via Cristoforo Colombo 157; meals €30; Feb-Oct) An unassuming restaurant on the road up to the SITA bus stop, Bruno serves superb seafood. Of the pastas, the homemade *scialatiella* (ribbon) is delicious, especially when served *con frutti di mare* (with mussels, prawns, clams, scampi and sweet cherry tomatoes).

Also recommended is **Hotel Continetale & La Tranquilita** (☎ 089 87 40 84; www.continental.praiano.it; Via Roma 21, Praiano; 2-person tent €40, s €45-65, d €70-90; Apr-Oct), between Positano and Amalfi. It has private rooms and tent pitches.

Amalfi

pop 5430

An attractive tangle of souvenir shops, dark alleyways and busy piazzas, Amalfi is the coast's main hub. Large-scale tourism has enriched the town, but it maintains a laid-back, small-town vibe, especially outside of the busy summer months.

Looming over the central piazza is the town's landmark **Duomo** (☎ 089 87 10 59; Piazza del Duomo; admission 10am-5pm €2.50, 7.30am-10am & 5pm-7.30pm free; 7.30am-7.30pm), one of the few relics of Amalfi's past as an 11th-century maritime superpower. Between 10am and 5pm, entry is through the adjacent Chiostro del Paradiso.

Four kilometres west of town, the **Grotta dello Smeraldo** (admission €5; 9am-4pm) is a haunting sea cave. Boat trips from Amalfi cost €10 return.

Get details of these and other activities from the **tourist office** (☎ 089 87 11 07; www.amalfi-touristoffice.it; Corso delle Repubbliche Marinare; 9am-1pm & 4-7pm Mon-Fri, 9am-noon Sat).

SLEEPING & EATING

A'Scalinatella Hostel (☎ 089 87 14 92; www.hostelscalinatella.com; Piazza Umberto I 5, Atrani; d/q with shared bathroom €60/100, dm/d/q with private bathroom €21/83/120;) In Atrani, this popular budget operation has 10-bed dorms, rooms and apartments scattered across the village. Extras don't run to frills but there's internet, a washing machine (€7 per load) and kitchen.

Hotel Lidomare (☎ 089 87 13 32; www.lidomare.it; Largo Duchi Piccolomini 9; s €50-65, d €70-135;) Housed in a 14th-century building on a petite piazza, the Lidomare is a lovely, family-run hotel. The spacious rooms are full of character with maiolica tiles and fine old antiques. Some also have jacuzzis and sea views.

Residence del Duca (☎ 089 87 36 365; www.residencedelduca.it; Via Mastalo II Duca 3; s €60-70, d €80-160;) Make it up the tricky staircase to the 3rd floor of this 10th-century *palazzo* and you'll be rewarded with a warm welcome and a smart room. Wood-beamed ceilings, chandeliers and antiques feature heavily.

our pick **Pizzeria Donna Stella** (☎ 338 358 84 83; Salita Rascica 2; pizzas from €5, mains €8; Tue-Sun) It's well worth searching out this delightful back-alley pizzeria. Not only does it serve superb pizza but it also boasts one of Amalfi's

ITALY

WORTH THE TRIP: RAVELLO

The refined, polished town of Ravello commands some of the finest views on the Amalfi Coast. A hairy 7km climb from Amalfi, it has been home to an impressive array of bohemians including Wagner, DH Lawrence, Virginia Woolf and Gore Vidal, whose former home can be seen on the bus ride up from Amalfi. The main attractions are the beautiful gardens at **Villa Cimbrone** and **Villa Ruffolo**. The **tourist office** (☎ 089 85 70 96; www.ravellotime.it; Via Roma 18bis; 🕑 9am-8pm) can provide details on these and Ravello's famous summer festival.

Regular SITA buses run from Amalfi to Ravello.

loveliest settings – a delightful summer garden enclosed by jasmine-clad walls. Alongside the pizza, there's also a selection of mains and baguettes.

Trattoria San Giuseppe (☎ 089 87 26 40; Salita Ruggiero II 4; pizzas €6, meals €30; 🕑 Fri-Wed) A long-standing favourite, this bustling trattoria-pizzeria is touristy but the food is good. The menu is typical of the coast, so expect plenty of seafood, thick-crust Neapolitan pizza and calorie-heavy desserts.

Self-caterers can stock up with provisions at the central **Supermercato Deco** (Salita dei Curiali; 🕑 8am-1.30pm & 5-8.30pm Mon-Sat).

MATERA

pop 57,400

Set atop two rocky gorges, Matera is one of Italy's most remarkable towns. Dotting the ravines are the famous *sassi* (cave dwellings), where up to half the town's population lived until the late 1950s. Ironically, the *sassi* are now Matera's fortune, attracting visitors from all over the world, and inspiring Mel Gibson to film *The Passion of the Christ* here.

The **tourist office** (☎ 0835 33 18 17; www.aptbasilicata.it; Via Spine Bianche 22; 🕑 8.30am-1pm & 4-7.30pm Mon-Sat, 8.30am-1pm Sun) can provide *sassi* maps and information on the surrounding area.

Sights & Activities

Within Matera there are two *sassi* areas, **Barisano** and **Caveoso**. With a map you can explore them on your own, but you'll get much more out of them with a guide. Both **Sassi Tourism** (☎ 0835 31 94 58; www.sassitourism.it; Via Bruno Buozzi 141) and **Ferula Viaggi** (☎ 0835 33 65 72; www.ferulaviaggi.it; Via Cappelluti 34) run tours. Prices start at about €10 per person (excluding admission prices) for a three-hour tour.

Inhabited since the Paleolithic age, the *sassi* were brought to public attention with the publication of Carlo Levi's book *Cristo si é fermato a Eboli* (Christ Stopped at Eboli, 1954). His description of children begging for quinine to stave off endemic malaria, shamed the authorities into action and about 15,000 people were forcibly relocated in the late 1950s. In 1993 the *sassi* were declared a Unesco World Heritage site. Today the area is a fashionable spot for a second home.

The older of the two *sassi*, Sasso Caveoso is the more evocative. Highlights include the churches of **Santa Maria d'Idris** and **Santa Lucia alle Malve** (🕑 both 9am-1pm & 3-7pm summer, 9.30am-1.30pm & 2.30-4.30pm winter) with their well-preserved 13th-century Byzantine frescoes. Both are part of the *circuito urbano delle chiese rupestri*, a group of five churches in the *sassi* area. Tickets to individual churches cost €2.50; admission to all five is €6.

The **Casa-Grotta di Vico Solitario** (☎ 0835 31 01 18; off Via Bruno Buozzi; admission €1.50; 🕑 9.30am-8.30pm summer, to 5.30pm winter) has been set up to show family life 40 years ago, when a family of 10 might have shared a cave with a donkey and several pigs, but with no running water or electricity.

The countryside outside of Matera, the **Murgia Plateau**, is littered with dozens of Palaeolithic caves and monastic developments. It's best explored with a guide.

Sleeping

The following are all in the *sassi* areas.

Le Monacelle (☎ 0835 34 40 97; www.lemonacelle.it; Via Riscatto 9/10; dm/s/d/tr/q €16/55/86/105/135; 💻) A former monastery, this hostel-cum-hotel is excellent value. Rooms are housed in the former cells and retain an air of elegant austerity, while the terrace offers unforgettable *sassi* views. Wi-fi is available.

Sassi Hotel (☎ 0835 33 10 09; www.hotelsassi.it; Via san Giovanni Vecchio 89; s/d/ste €65/95/120; ✖) Bunk down in a refurbished tufa cave at Matera's first *sassi* hotel. In the Barisano, it has a range of rooms in a rambling 18th-century *palazzo*. No two are identical, but the best are bright and spacious with tasteful, modern furniture, terraces and panoramic views.

Sant' Angelo (☎ 0835 31 40 10; www.hotelsantangelosassi.it; Piazza San Pietro Caveoso; s/d €90/120; ❄ 💻) This romantic four-star sets the standard for modern cave dwelling. Each of its 16 stylish rooms was once a *sassi* home, and you can still see nicks in the wall used to store cooking implements. Today, there are mod cons and antique furniture.

Eating & Drinking

Ginger Caffè (☎ 0835 33 53 07; Via Lucana 54) Get down to this neighbourhood cafe for an early evening *aperitivo* – buy a €6 (€4 if nonalcoholic) drink and dig into a full meal's worth of savoury snacks.

Il Terrazzino (☎ 0835 33 25 03; Vico San Giuseppe 7; meals €18; 🕑 Tue-Sun) Just off Piazza Vittorio Veneto, this teeming trattoria does a roaring trade in filling, no-nonsense pastas and simple meat dishes. Get into the swing of things with a rustic antipasto of olives, salami and cheese.

19a Buca Winery? (☎ 0835 33 35 92; Via Lombardi 3; meals €35; 🕑 11am-midnight Tue-Sun) A modish lounge bar–restaurant in an ancient water cistern 13m below Piazza Vittorio Veneto. It's a showy place with chic glass and metal decor, a virtual golf course, and a creative, contemporary menu.

Getting There & Away

The best way to reach Matera is by bus. From Rome's Stazione Tiburtina, **Marozzi** (☎ 06 225 21 47; www.marozzivt.it, in Italian) runs three daily buses (€33, 6½ hours). Matera's bus terminus is north of Piazza Matteotti near the train station.

By train, the **Ferrovie Appulo Lucano** (☎ 0835 572 52 29; www.fal-srl.it) runs regular services to Bari (€4, 1¼ hours, 14 daily).

BARI

pop 325,100

Puglia's capital is no longer the grim, crime-ridden port of yesteryear. Recent efforts to clean up the city centre have gone a long way to restoring its reputation, and while it's no model of urban decorum, it's not without charm. Its large university population ensures a buzzing social scene and there are a number of architectural gems worth more than a passing glance en route to the ferry terminal.

Orientation & Information

Orient yourself from Piazza Aldo Moro in front of the main train station. From the square, it's about 1km northwards to Bari Vecchia, the Old Town where all the major sights are located. The New Town, laid out in grid pattern, is separated from the historic centre by Corso Vittorio Emanuele II, which heads northwest out of town towards the ferry terminal.

The best bet for information is the **tourist information point** (☎ 080 990 93 41; www.infopointbari.com; Piazza Aldo Moro; 🕑 9am-7pm Mon-Sat, 9am-1pm Sun) in front of the train station.

Sights & Activities

Bari's single most important sight is the **Basilica di San Nicola** (☎ 080 573 71 11; Piazza San Nicola; 🕑 7am-1pm & 6-8pm Mon-Fri), the first great Norman church in the south and a wonderful example of Puglia's distinct Romanesque style. It was originally built to house the bones of St Nicholas (aka Father Christmas) that were stolen from Myra (in modern-day Turkey) by Baresi fishermen in 1087. His remains still lie in the crypt, ensuring a regular flow of Catholic and Greek Orthodox pilgrims.

From the basilica, it's a short walk to the **Cattedrale San Sabino** (Piazza dell'Odegitria; 🕑 8am-12.30pm & 4-7.30pm), Bari's main seat of worship. Built in the 11th century, but destroyed and rebuilt a century later, it displays a simple Romanesque style with a wide nave and a 35m-high cupola.

On the edge of the Old Town, the brooding, boxlike **Castello Svevo** (Swabian Castle; ☎ 080 528 61 11; Piazza Frederico II di Svevia; admission €2; 🕑 8.30am-2.30pm Mon, Tue, Thu & Fri, to 7pm Sat & Sun) hosts regular art exhibitions.

Sleeping & Eating

Hotel Pensione Giulia (☎ 080 521 66 30; www.hotelpensionegiulia.it; Via Crisanzio 12; s €50-60, d €65-75; ❄) One of several hotels in the same *palazzo*, the Giulia is as budget as it gets in Bari. An old-fashioned, family-run *pensione*, it has basic, plainly furnished rooms and a homey feel.

Hotel Costa (☎ 080 521 00 06; www.hotelcostabari.com; s/d €62/88) A floor up from the Giulia, the Costa is marginally more upmarket. It's not flash but rooms are a decent size, the owner's a cordial guy, and the location near the train station is convenient. Breakfast is extra.

Al Pescatore (☎ 080 523 70 39; Piazza Federico di Svevia II; meals €28) Sit down to great seafood in the

ITALY

GATEWAY TO GREECE

About 115km south of Bari, **Brindisi** has been a gateway to Greece since Roman times. These days various companies operate out of the port, sailing to Corfu, Igoumenitsa, Patra, Kefallonia and Paxos. You can check routes and book tickets at www.traghettigrecia.com.

Brindisi is easily accessible by bus and train from Bari, Lecce, Naples and Rome.

shadow of the castle. With fish fresh from the morning catch, the cooks keep it simple and you'd do well to follow suit. Try the grilled squid and you'll get the idea.

Getting There & Away

Bari is served by **Palese airport** (BRI; ☎ 080 580 02 00; www.seap-puglia.it), 8km northwest of town. An hourly shuttle bus (€4.15, 30 minutes) connects the airport with the main train station. Alternatively, take local bus 16 (€0.90).

Ferries run from Bari to Greece (Corfu–Igoumenitsa–Patra), Albania (Durazzo), Croatia (Dubrovnik) and Montenegro (Bar). Ferry companies have offices at the port, accessible by bus 20 (€0.90) from the train station. You can also get tickets at **Morfimare Travel Agency** (☎ 080 578 98 11; Corso Antonio de Tullio 36-40) opposite the port.

For information on the main companies and the routes they serve see p550.

Bari is on the main east coast train line and there are regular services to/from Rome (€36, up to 6½ hours), Brindisi (€6.80, one hour 20 minutes) and Lecce (€15, two hours), as well as many smaller towns in Puglia.

LECCE

pop 93, 600

Lecce's bombastic displays of jaw-dropping baroque architecture are one of southern Italy's highlights. Opulent to the point of excess, the local *barocco leccese* (Lecce baroque) style has earned this urbane city a reputation as the 'Florence of the South'. A lively university town with a vibrant bar scene and a graceful historic centre, Lecce is well worth a stopover.

There's a **tourist office** (☎ 0832 24 80 92; Corso Vittorio Emanuele 24; ⏲ 9am-1pm & 4-8pm Mon-Sat summer, to 7pm winter) in the historic centre, and another private one run by the **Cooperative Theutra** (☎ 0832 24 65 17; www.abitalecce.it; Castello Carlo V; ⏲ 9am-9pm summer, 9.30am-1.30pm, 4-8pm winter) at the castle.

Sights

The most celebrated example of Lecce's baroque architecture is the eye-popping **Basilica di Santa Croce** (☎ 0832 24 19 57; Via Umberto I; ⏲ 9.30am-noon & 5-8pm). It took a team of 16th- and 17th-century craftsmen more than a 100 years to create the swirling facade that you see today. A short walk away, **Piazza del Duomo** is a further orgy of architectural extravagance. The 12th-century **cathedral** (☎ 0832 30 85 57; admission free; ⏲ 7am-noon & 5-7.30pm) was completely restored by baroque master Giuseppe Zimbalo, who also fashioned the 68m-high **bell tower**. Facing the cathedral is the 15th-century **Palazzo Vescovile** (Bishop's Palace) and the 17th-century **Seminario**.

Lecce's social and commercial hub, **Piazza Sant'Oronzo** is built round the remains of a 2nd-century **Roman amphitheatre**. Originally this was the largest in Puglia, with a capacity for 15,000 people, but only the lower half of the grandstand survives.

Sleeping

Centro Storico (☎ 0832 24 27 27; www.bedandbreakfast.lecce.it; Via Vignes 2/b; s/d €40/57, ste €70-100; ❄) A modest B&B in a historic *palazzo*. The 2nd-floor rooms are bright and airy, decked out with parquet, wrought-iron beds and plain furniture. Upstairs, there's a sun terrace where evening wine tastings are held. Free wi-fi.

Sweet Place (☎ 338 87 10 295; sweet.place@fisicaonline.net; Via Ferrante d'Aragone 17b; s €40-90, d €60-90) With its 16th-century vaulted ceilings and dishy rooms, this historic centre B&B is attractive and welcoming. Decorated with a sure hand it features light, modern furniture set against exposed stone walls and pastel colours. Use of a kitchen is a further plus.

B&B Centro Storico Prestige (☎ 0832 24 33 53; www.bbprestige-lecce.it; Via S Maria del Paradiso 4; s €50-60, d €70-90; 💻) A cheerful home away from home, this is a cracking little B&B. The irrepressible Renata ushers guests into her lovingly tended 2nd-floor flat where sunlight floods into understated white guest rooms. Upstairs, there's a pretty communal terrace.

Also recommended is **Azzurretta B&B** (☎ 0832 24 22 11; www.bblecce.it; Via Vignes 2/b; s €38, d €55-70; ❄), a straightforward B&B run by the same family as the Centro Storico.

Eating and Drinking

Torre di Merlino (☎ 0832 24 18 74; Vico del Tufo; pizzas €4, meals €40; ⏰ closed Mon, dinner Sun) Lap up the *centro storico* atmosphere at this smooth, contemporary restaurant. With tables on a pretty piazza or in a barrel-vaulted interior, it offers a comprehensive menu of pizzas, pastas, mains and salads.

Trattoria Le Zie (☎ 0832 24 51 78; Via Colonello Costadura 19; meals €25; ⏰ closed Mon, dinner Sun) Also known as 'Cucina Casareccia' ('home-style cooking'), this family-run trattoria serves exactly what you hope it will – filling, *nonna*-style cooking. The emphasis is on local Salentine cooking so you'll sit down to vegetables, homemade pasta and strong, palate-kicking cheese.

Alle due Corti (☎ 0832 24 22 23; www.alleduecorti.com; Corte dei Giugni 1; meals €25) This popular restaurant is a fine place to get to grips with Salento's gastronomic heritage. Opt for *ricchietelle cule rape* (orecchiette pasta with turnip tops) followed by *pezzetti te cavallu* (horse meat in tomato sauce) for a real taste of tradition.

Of the many bars in the centre, the **Caffè Letterario** (☎ 0832 24 23 51; www.caffeletterario.org, in Italian; Via Paladini 48) is a happening spot.

Getting There & Away

Lecce is the end of the main southeastern train line and there are direct trains to Brindisi (€5.30, 35 minutes), Bari (€15, two hours), and Rome (€51.30, six hours), as well as to points throughout Puglia.

By car, take the SS16 to Bari via Monopoli and Brindisi. For Taranto take the SS7.

SICILY

The Mediterranean's largest island, Sicily is a hotbed of southern excess. Everything about the place is extreme, from the beauty of its rugged landscape to the flavours of its hybrid cuisine and the scorching power of its relentless sun.

Over the centuries, Sicily has seen off a catalogue of foreign invaders, ranging from the Phoenicians and ancient Greeks to the Spanish Bourbons and WWII Allies. All have contributed to the island's cultural landscape, leaving in turn Greek temples, Arab domes, Byzantine mosaics, Norman castles, Angevin churches and baroque facades.

This cultural complexity is complemented by Sicily's volcanic geography. Dominating the east coast, Mt Etna (3320m) is Sicily's most famous volcano, although not its most active; Stromboli usually claims that accolade. All round the island aquamarine seas lap at the craggy coastline, while inland, hilltop towns pepper the timeless countryside.

Most ferries arrive at Palermo, the island's capital and main transport hub.

Getting There & Away

AIR

Flights from Italy's mainland cities and a number of European destinations land at Sicily's two main airports: **Palermo** (PMO; www.gesap.it; ☎ 091 702 01 11) and **Catania** (CTA; ☎ 095 723 91 11; www.aeroporo.catania.it). Carriers to Sicily:

Alitalia (☎ 06 22 22; www.alitalia.it)
Air One (AP; ☎ 199 207 080; www.flyairone.it)
easyJet (U2; ☎ 899 234 589; www.easyjet.com)
Meridiana (IG; ☎ 89 29 28; www.meridiana.it)
Ryanair (FR; ☎ 899 678 910; www.ryanair.com)

BOAT

Regular car and passenger ferries cross to Sicily (Messina) from Villa San Giovanni in Calabria. The island is also accessible by ferry from Genoa, Livorno, Naples and Cagliari, as well as Malta and Tunisia. The main companies:

Grandi Navi Veloci (☎ 091 587 801; www.gnv.it) Palermo to/from Genoa and Tunis.
Grimaldi Lines (☎ 091 611 36 91; www.grimaldi-ferries.com) Palermo to/from Salerno and Tunis.
SNAV (☎ 091 631 79 00; www.snav.com) Palermo to/from Naples and Civitavecchia.
Tirrenia (☎ 892 123; www.tirrenia.it) Palermo to/from Naples and Cagliari.

Timetables are seasonal, so check with a travel agent or online at www.traghettionline.net. Book well in advance during summer, particularly if you have a car.

For information on ferries going directly to the Aeolian Islands, see p535.

BUS

Bus services between Rome and Sicily are operated by **SAIS** (☎ 091 616 60 28; www.saisautolinee.it, in Italian) and **Interbus** (☎ 0935 56 51 11; www.interbus.it, in Italian), departing from Rome's Piazza Tiburtina. There are daily buses to Messina (€41, nine hours), Catania (€46, 11 hours), Palermo (€44, 12¾ hours) and Syracuse (€47, 12 hours).

ITALY

TRAIN

Direct trains run from Milan, Florence, Rome, Naples and Reggio di Calabria to Palermo and Catania. For further information contact **Trenitalia** (☎ 89 20 21; www.trenitalia.com).

Getting Around

Generally the best way to get around Sicily is by bus. Services are pretty good and most towns are covered. Trains tend to be cheaper on the major routes, but once you're off the coast, they can be painfully slow.

Roads are generally good and *autostrade* connect major cities.

PALERMO

pop 666,600

Although it still bears the bruises of its WWII battering, Palermo is nevertheless a compelling, and chaotic, city. It takes a little work, but once you've acclimatised to the congested streets you'll be rewarded with some of southern Italy's most exotic buildings. In among chaotic street markets and bombed-out *palazzi*, you'll find palaces, castles and churches, as well as fabulous restaurants and tempting cafes.

Orientation

Palermo's centre is large but it's quite manageable to get around on foot. The main street is Via Maqueda, which runs parallel to Via Roma, the busy road running north from the train station. Corso Vittorio Emanuele crosses Via Maqueda at a junction known as the Quattro Canti (Four Corners). You'll find that most sights and hotels are within easy walking distance of this intersection.

Information

Aboriginal Café (Via Spinuzza 51; per hr €3.50; ⏰ 6pm-3am) Popular Australian-style pub with internet access.

Citysightseeing Palermo (☎ 091 58 94 29; www.palermo.city-sightseeing.it; adult/child €20/10) Hop-on, hop-off bus tours. Departures in front of Teatro Politeamo Garibaldi.

Left Luggage (1st 5hr €3.80, 6-12hr per hr €0.60, 13hr & more per hr €0.20; ⏰ 7am-11pm) At the train station.

Lo Cascio Pharmacy (☎ 091 616 21 17; Via Roma 1) All-night chemist.

Ospedale Civico (Hospital; ☎ 091 666 11 11; Via Carmelo Lazzaro)

Police station (Questura; ☎ 091 21 01 11; Piazza della Vittoria)

Post office (Palazzo della Poste; Via Roma 322)

Tourist offices (www.palermotourism.com); airport (☎ 091 59 16 98; ⏰ 8.30am-7.30pm Mon-Sat); Piazza Castelnuovo 34 (☎ 091 60 58 351; ⏰ 8.30am-2pm & 2.30-6pm Mon-Fri); Stazione Centrale (☎ 091 616 99 69; Piazza Giulio Cesare) Pick up *Agenda Turismo*, which has loads of practical info. The Stazione Centrale branch was closed at the time of research, but was due to reopen.

Sights

A good starting point is the **Quattro Canti**, a road junction where Palermo's four central districts converge. Locals call the intersection *Il teatro del sole* (Theatre of the Sun) as each of the baroque facades that surround it is lit up during the course of the day. Nearby, Piazza Pretoria is dominated by the ostentatious **Fontana Pretoria**, whose nude nymphs caused outrage when it was bought from Florence in 1573. Overlooking the fountain, **Palazzo Pretorio** is Palermo's town hall and the **Chiesa di Santa Caterina** (entrance Piazza Bellini; admission €2; ⏰ 9.30am-1pm & 3-7pm Mon-Sat, 9.30am-1pm Sun) is a fine baroque church.

Around the corner in Piazza Bellini, **La Martorana** (Chiesa di Santa Maria dell'Ammiraglio; ☎ 091 616 1692; admission free; ⏰ 8.30am-1pm & 3.30-7pm Mon-Sat, 8.30am-1pm Sun) is Palermo's most famous medieval church, and a popular wedding venue. Its best known for the 12th-century bell tower and stunning Byzantine mosaics. Next door, the red-domed **Chiesa di San Cataldo** (admission €1; ⏰ 9am-2pm & 3.30-7pm Mon-Sat, 9am-2pm Sun) is of interest more for the Arab-Norman exterior than its surprisingly bare interior.

A short walk north up Corso Vittorio Emanuele II brings you to Palermo's extraordinary **cathedral** (☎ 091 33 43 73; Corso Vittorio Emanuele; admission free; ⏰ 9.30am-5.30pm Mon-Sat, 8am-1.30pm & 4.30-6pm Sun), a visual riot of arches, cupolas, and crenellations. Modified many times over the centuries, it's a stunning example of Sicily's unique Arab-Norman architectural style. Barely less dramatic is **Palazzo Reale** (Palazzo dei Normanni; ☎ 091 626 28 33; Piazza Indipendenza; admission incl Cappella Palatina €6; ⏰ 8.30am-noon & 2-5pm Thu-Sat, Mon & Tue, 8.30am-12.30pm Sun), the theatrical seat of the Sicilian parliament. Guided tours lead you to the **Sala di Ruggero II**, the mosaic-decorated bedroom of King Roger II. Downstairs, is Palermo's premier tourist attraction, the 12th-century **Cappella Palatina** (Palatine Chapel; ☎ 091 626 28 33; admission €6; ⏰ 8.30am-noon & 2-5pm Mon-Sat, 8.30am-12.30pm Sun), a jaw-dropping jewel of Arab-Norman architecture lavishly decorated with exquisite mosaics.

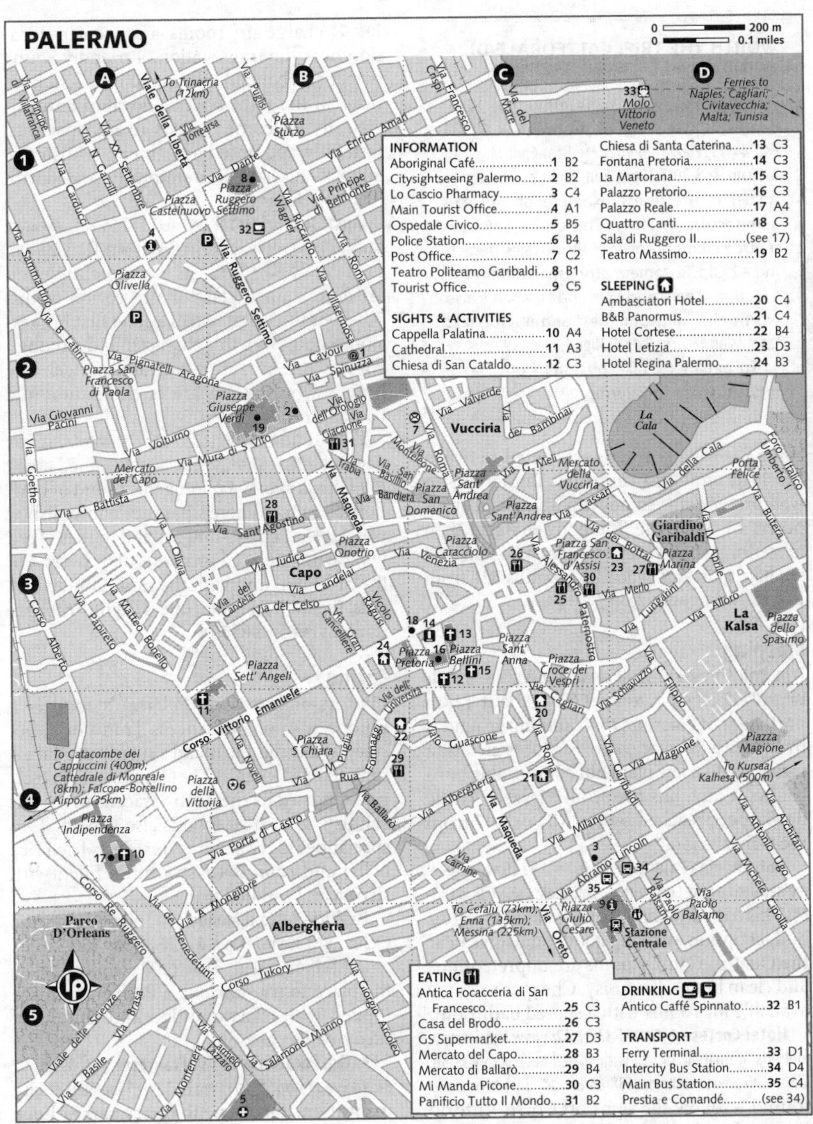

ITALY

Palermo's musical heart beats at the neoclassical opera house **Teatro Massimo** (☎ 091 609 08 31; Piazza Giuseppe Verdi; www.teatromassimo.it, in Italian; guided tours adult/concession €5/3; 🕑 10am-2.30pm Tue-Sun). Supposedly the third-largest 19th-century opera house in Europe after Paris and Vienna, it took over 20 years to build and, in 1897, opened to celebrate the unification of Italy. The theatre has since become a symbol of the triumph and tragedy of Palermo itself. Appropriately enough, the closing scene of *The Godfather III* was filmed here.

Southwest of the city centre, the macabre **Catacombe dei Cappuccini** (Capuchin Catacombs; ☎ 091 21 21 17; Piazza Cappuccini 1; admission €1.50; 🕑 9am-noon & 3-5.30pm) hold the mummified bodies of

WORTH THE TRIP: CATTEDRALE DI MONREALE

Just 8km southwest of Palermo, the 12th-century **Cattedrale di Monreale** (☎ 091 640 44 13; Piazza Duomo; 🕑 8am-6pm Mon-Sat, 8-10am & 3.30-5.30pm Sun summer, shorter hr winter) is the finest example of Norman architecture in Sicily. The entire 6400-sq-metre ceiling is covered in mosaics depicting 42 Old Testament stories, including the Creation, Adam and Eve, and Noah. It's also worth checking out the tranquil **cloisters** (admission €6; 🕑 9am-6.30pm).

To get there, take bus 389 from Piazza Indipendenza in Palermo.

some 8000 Palermitans who died between the 17th and 19th centuries. Bodies are so well preserved – some with arsenic or lime, others by 'straining' the body dry and then preserving it in vinegar – that you can still see hair, skin and eyeballs. Take bus 327 from Piazza Indipendenza.

Sleeping

Trinacria (☎ 091 53 05 90; www.campingtrinacria.it; Via Barcarello 25; per person/tent/car €7/7/4) About 12km northwest of Palermo, this camping ground is by the sea at Sferracavallo. Facilities include a pizzeria and a few plain but comfortable bungalows. Catch bus 616 from Piazzale Alcide de Gasperi, reached by bus 101 or 107 from the train station.

Hotel Regina Palermo (☎ 091 611 42 16; www.hotelreginapalermo.com; Corso Vittorio Emanuele 316; s €28, d €40-64) This friendly, family-run *pensione* is a great budget option, offering good-value digs near the Quattro Canti. Rooms are unpretentious and clean but can be noisy. Cheaper rates are available for rooms with a shared bathroom.

Hotel Cortese (☎ 091 33 17 22; www.hotelcortese.net; Via Scarparelli 16; s/d with shared bathroom €33/56, s/d/tr with private bathroom €38/66/80; ❄ 💻) Not easy to find – follow the signs off Corso Vittorio Emanuele – this welcoming haven is a stone's throw from the chaotic Ballaró markets. Space is tight in these parts and guest rooms are not the largest, but they are smart and ably decorated with period furniture and the odd framed print. There's a small terrace and a large buffet breakfast (€4).

our pick B&B Panormus (☎ 091 617 58 26; www.bbpanormus.com; Via Roma 72; s €35-45, d €70-80, tr €90-100; ❄) Large airy rooms, a convenient location near the train station, a friendly young owner and bargain rates – this excellent B&B ticks all the right boxes. Giovanni enthusiastically welcomes guests to his spacious, tastefully appointed apartment, whose five guest rooms have been simply decorated with low-key elegance.

Ambasciatori Hotel (☎ 091 610 66 881; www.ambasciatorihotelpalermo.com; 5th fl, Via Roma 111; s €55-105, d €78-155; ❄ 💻) With its warm lighting and art deco stained glass, the reception of this 5th-floor three-star makes a good first impression. Rooms lack this character and although comfortable are rather corporate in feel. The hotel's winning feature is the panoramic rooftop terrace.

Hotel Letizia (☎ 091 58 91 10; www.hotelletizia.com; Via dei Bottai 30; s €85, d €115-150; 💻) A refined hotel, the Letizia sports a photogenic brand of boudoir elegance. There's parquet and polished wood, velvet chaise-longues and bottles of red wine artfully placed on chests of drawers. On the 3rd floor, and with the same contact details, the B&B Ai Bottai offers slightly cheaper doubles (€85 to €135).

Eating

Like its architecture, Palermo's food is a unique mix of influences. Traditional yet spicy, it marries the island's superb produce – praised by Homer in *The Odyssey* – with recipes imported by the Arab Saracens in the 9th century. The street food is also superb. Two specialities to try are *arancini* (deep-fried rice balls) and *cannoli* (pastry tubes filled with ricotta and candied fruit).

Panificio Tutto Il Mondo (Via Trabia 49; snacks from €1.20; 🕑 8.30am-2.30pm & 4.30-8.30pm Mon-Sat) A small bakery near Teatro Massimo, this is the place to try *sfincioni*, a Palermitan pizza topped with tomato, onion and chunks of *caciocavallo* cheese.

Antica Focacceria di San Francesco (☎ 091 32 02 64; Via Paternostro 58; set menu €6-12; 🕑 Tue-Sun) A city institution, this frenetic eatery serves huge portions of filling Palermitan classics. Ignore the restaurant and eat in the canteen where you can choose from various set menus of pastas, fried snacks and not-to-be missed *cannoli*. Speciality of the house is *panino con la milza*, a traditional sandwich of veal innards and ricotta cheese.

Casa del Brodo (☎ 091 3 21 55; Corso Vittorio Emanuele 175; set menu €16-18, meals €27; 🕑 Mon-Sat) This historic trattoria knows what its diners want and delivers every time. And what they want is good-value Sicilian food served in a pleasantly relaxed atmosphere. Alongside an impressive antipasto spread, the menu features a number of interesting boiled-meat dishes and some fine fruity desserts.

Mi Manda Picone (☎ 091 616 06 60; Via A Paternostro 59; meals €40) Housed in a brick-clad 13th-century *palazzo,* this urbane wine bar–cum-restaurant offers contemporary Sicilian food, delicious chocolate cake, and a 450-strong wine list. Staff are knowledgeable and can help with wine selection.

For an adrenalin-charged food experience, dive into one of Palermo's legendary markets: **Capo** (Mon-Sat) on Via Sant'Agostino, or **Il Ballaró** (daily) in the Albergheria quarter, off Via Maqueda. Easier, but less fun, is the **GS supermarket** (Via Salità Partanna 1) off Piazza Marinara.

Drinking

Kursaal Kalhesa (☎ 091 616 21 11; Foro Italico Umberto I 21; noon-1.30am Tue-Sun) Recline on a silk cushion with a splash of wine at this smooth but unpretentious brick-vaulted wine bar. In winter toast yourself by the fire; in summer sip cocktails in the lush garden. There's internet access and regular live music, often jazz.

Antico Caffé Spinnato (☎ 091 58 32 31; Via Principe di Belmonte 107-15) Join Palermo's snappily dressed shoppers for an early-evening drink at this historic cafe. You can sit outside with the pianist or retire to the polished interior for every imaginable Sicilian drink, ice cream and cake. Snacks can be had for around €6.

Getting There & Away

National and international flights serve **Falcone-Borsellino airport** (PMO; ☎ 091 702 01 11; www.gesap.it), 35km west of Palermo. See p529 for a list of airlines.

The ferry terminal is northeast of the historic centre, off Via Francesco Crispi. Ferries for Cagliari (€51, 14½ hours) and Naples (€48, 10¼ hours) leave from Molo Vittorio Veneto; for Genoa (€96, 20 hours) from Molo S. Lucia. See p529 for further information.

The main intercity bus station is near Via Paolo Balsamo, east of the train station. Sicily's buses are privatised and different routes are serviced by various companies, all of whom have their own ticket offices. Main companies:

Cuffaro (☎ 091 616 15 10; www.cuffaro.info) To/from Agrigento (€7.70, two hours, nine daily).
Interbus (☎ 0935 56 51 11; www.interbus.it, in Italian) To/from Syracuse (€14, 3¼ hours, five daily).
SAIS Autolinee (☎ 091 616 60 28; www.saisautolinee.it, in Italian) To/from Catania (€13.20, 2¾ hours, 14 daily) and Messina (€14.10, 2¾ hours, six daily).

Agenda Turismo, available from the tourist office, lists destinations and the companies that serve them.

Regular trains leave from the Stazione Centrale for Messina (€18, 3½ hours, half-hourly) via Milazzo (€9.65), the jumping-off point for the Aeolian Islands. There are also slow services to Catania, Syracuse and Agrigento, as well as to nearby towns such as Cefalù. Long-distance trains go to Reggio di Calabria (€30, six hours, four daily), Naples (€47.50, nine to 10 hours, four daily) and Rome (€58, 11 to 12 hours, seven daily).

Getting Around

A half-hourly bus service run by **Prestia e Comandé** (☎ 091 58 63 51) connects the airport with the train station. Tickets for the 50-minute journey cost €5.30 and are available on the bus. There's also the hourly Trinacria Express train service (€4.50, 45 minutes) from Stazione Centrale. A taxi to the airport will cost at least €50.

Walking is the best way to get around Palermo's centre but if you want to take a bus, most stop outside or near the train station. Tickets cost €1.10 and are valid for two hours. There are two small lines – Gialla and Rossa – that operate in the historic centre.

All the major car-hire companies are represented at the airport.

AEOLIAN ISLANDS

Rising out of the cobalt-blue seas off Sicily's northeastern coast, the Unesco-protected Aeolian Islands (Isole Eolie) have been seducing visitors since Odysseus' time. With their wild, windswept mountains, hissing volcanoes and rich waters, they form a beautiful outdoor playground, ideal for divers, sun seekers and adrenalin junkies.

Part of a huge volcanic ridge, the seven islands (Lipari, Salina, Vulcano, Stromboli, Alicudi, Filicudi and Panarea) represent the very pinnacle of a 3000m-high outcrop that was formed one million years ago. Lipari is the biggest and busiest of the seven, and the main transport hub. From there you can pick up connections to all the other islands, including Vulcano, famous for its therapeutic mud, and Stromboli, whose permanently active volcano supplies spectacular fire shows.

The islands' only **tourist office** (☎ 090 988 00 95; www.aasteolie.191.it, in Italian; Corso Vittorio Emanuele 202; 8.30am-1.30pm & 4.30-7.30pm Mon-Fri) is on Lipari.

Sights & Activities

On **Lipari** you can explore the volcanic history of the islands at the **Museo Archeologico Eoliano** (☎ 090 988 01 74; admission €6; 9am-1pm & 3-7pm Mon-Sat) in the Spanish Aragon-built **citadel**. For sunbathing, head to Canneto and the Spiaggia Bianca or to Porticello for Spiaggia Papesca. Snorkelling and diving are popular – contact **Diving Center La Gorgonia** (☎ 090 981 26 16; www.lagorgoniadiving.it; Salita San Giuseppe; dives from €31) for equipment and guided dives. For tours of the islands, **Da Massimo** (☎ 338 369 44 04; www.damassimo.it; Via Maurolico 2) offers various packages, ranging from a €15 tour of Lipari and Vulcano to a €80 summit climb of Stromboli.

From Lipari, it's a short boat ride to **Vulcano**, a malodorous and largely unspoilt island. Most people come here to make the hour-long trek up the **Fossa di Vulcano**, the island's active volcano (€3 for crater entrance), or to wallow in the **Laghetto di Fanghi** mud baths (€2.50).

Famous for its spectacular fireworks, **Stromboli's volcano** is the most active in the region, last exploding in February 2007. To make the tough six- to seven-hour ascent to the 920m summit you are legally required to hire a guide. At the top you're rewarded with incredible views of the Sciara del Fuoco (Trail of Fire) and constantly exploding crater. **Magmatrek** (☎ 090 986 57 68; www.magmatrek.it) organises afternoon climbs for €25 per person (minimum 10 people).

Sleeping & Eating

Most accommodation is on Lipari. Always try to book ahead as summer is busy and many places close over winter. Prices fall considerably outside of high season.

LIPARI

Don't dismiss outright offers by touts at the port as they're often genuine.

Baia Unci (☎ 090 981 19 09; www.baiaunci.it; Marina Garibaldi 2; sites per person/tent €10/12, 4-person bungalow €52-100) The island's shady camping ground is on the sea at Canneto, 2km out of Lipari town. On-site facilities include a restaurant, bar and diving centre.

Diana Brown (☎ 090 981 25 84; www.dianabrown.it; Vico Himera 3; s €30-80, d €40-100; year-round;) Down a tiny back lane, Diana has comfortable rooms decorated in cheerful summery style. Kettles and fridges are provided and the darker downstairs rooms have a small kitchenette. Breakfast (€5) is served on the solarium.

La Piazzetta (☎ 090 981 25 22; off Corso Vittorio Emanuele; pizzas €5) This pizzeria is a long-standing favourite with a good location behind Pasticceria Subba and a lively atmosphere.

our pick Osteria Mediterranea (☎ 090 981 25 11; Corso Vittorio Emanuele; meals €20) Offering excellent value for money, prompt, friendly service, and delicious food, this is an excellent choice. Large juicy olives arrive with the wine, whetting your appetite for wonderful seafood dishes, such as grilled catch of the day with almonds and sun-dried tomatoes.

The main drag, Corso Vittorio Emanuele, is lined with eateries, takeaways and bars. Next to the tourist office there's a **Sisa supermarket** (Corso Vittorio Emanuele 230; 8am-9pm Mon-Sat) and, further down, at No 150, a takeaway where you can pick up a snack and beer for €2.50.

STROMBOLI

La Locanda del Barbablù (☎ 090 98 61 18; www.barbablu.it; Via Vittorio Emanuele 17-19; meals €40; Mar-Oct) One of Stromboli's top restaurants, this place also has six delightfully eccentric rooms (doubles €120 to €210) decorated with period furniture, silk coverlets and antique tiles.

VULCANO

Camping Togo Togo (☎ 090 985 21 28; www.campingvulcano.it; Porto Ponente; sites per person & tent €12; Apr-Sep) Campers can down tents at this tranquil camping ground near Spiaggia Sabbia Nera.

Hotel Torre (☎ 090 985 23 42; www.hoteltorrevulcano.it; Via Favaloro 1; d €40-80;) Another budget option is Hotel Torre with large, functional rooms near the port.

ALICUDI & FILICUDI

Hotel La Canna (☎ 090 988 99 56; www.lacannahotel.it; Via Rosa 43; half-board per person €60-102, d €70-140;) Filicudi is a wild and beautiful island and this is the best of its limited accommodation, with sunny, wood-beamed rooms and a fine restaurant. Half-board is compulsory between June and September.

Ericusa (☎ 090 988 99 02; www.alicudihotel.it; Via Regina Elena; r per person incl half-board €70-90; ⌚ Jun-Sep) Alicudi is even more remote, and the island's only hotel is the pleasant Ericusa on the seafront.

Getting There & Away

The main departure point for the islands is Milazzo. If arriving in Milazzo by train, you'll need to catch a bus (€1) or taxi (€10) to the port, 4km from the station. At the port you'll find ticket offices lined up on Corso dei Mille.

Ustica Lines (☎ 0923 87 38 13; www.usticalines.it) and **Siremar** (☎ 892 123; www.siremar.it) run hydrofoils to Vulcano (€15, 40 minutes) and on to Lipari (€15.80, 55 minutes). Between June and September departures are almost hourly from 7am to 8pm. There are also direct hydrofoils to Stromboli (€20.95, 2¾ hours, six daily). Siremar also runs ferries to the same destinations. These take up to twice the time and cost about €4 less.

Connecting with the mainland, Siremar has twice-weekly ferries between Milazzo and Naples (€56.70, 17 hours) calling at each of the islands, and **SNAV** (☎ 081 428 55 55; www.snav.it) has daily sailings from Naples to Lipari (€106.50, six hours).

Getting Around

Lipari is the main transport hub with regular services to Vulcano (€5.80), Stromboli (€17.80), Filicudi (€15.80), Alicudi (€18.85) and the other islands. You can get full timetable information and buy tickets at Lipari's port.

TAORMINA

pop 11,100

Spectacularly perched on a cliff-top terrace, Taormina is Sicily's glitziest resort, a sophisticated town with a pristine medieval core and grandstand coastal views. In its current guise, it was made famous by Goethe and DH Lawrence, both former residents, but in the 9th century it was Sicily's Byzantine capital.

The **tourist office** (☎ 0942 2 32 43; www.gate2taormina.com; Piazza Santa Caterina; ⌚ 8.30am-2pm & 4-7pm Mon-Thu & 8.30am-2pm Fri) can provide plenty of local information and help with booking accommodation. Head to **Net Point** (Via Jallia Bassia 34; per 20min €2; ⌚ 9am-9pm) for internet access.

Sights & Activities

The principal pastime in Taormina is wandering the pretty hilltop streets, browsing the shops and eyeing-up fellow holidaymakers. Take time to visit the stunning **Teatro Greco** (☎ 0942 2 32 20; Via Teatro Greco; adult/concession €6/3; ⌚ 9am-7pm summer, to 4.30pm winter). Built in the 3rd century BC and remodelled 400 years later by the Romans, this perfect horseshoe theatre now hosts summer concerts.

For some great views, head to the immaculate **Villa Comunale** (Via Bagnoli Croce; ⌚ 9am-midnight summer, to 10pm winter), a colourful garden bursting with Mediterranean flora. On Corso Umberto I, the pedestrianised main drag, people congregate around the ornate baroque fountain and Piazza del Duomo. On the eastern side of the piazza is the Norman-Gothic **Duomo** (⌚ 10am-noon & 5-7.30pm).

For a swim you'll need to take the **cable car** (return €3.50; ⌚ 8am-8.15pm) down to Taormina's beach, **Lido Mazzarò**, and the tiny **Isola Bella** set in its own picturesque cove.

Saistours (☎ 0942 62 06 71; Corso Umberto 222) organises excursions to several destinations including Mt Etna (from €21), Agrigento (€41) and Syracuse (€33).

Sleeping & Eating

Taormina's Odyssey (☎ 0942 2 45 33; www.taorminaodyssey.com; Trav A – Via G Martino 2; dm €17-20, d €45-60) Taormina's sole hostel is a friendly, year-round affair about 10 minutes' walk from the centre (follow signs for Hotel Andromaco). Space is tight but there's still a well-stocked kitchen and convivial common room.

Isoco Guest House (☎ 094 22 36 79; www.isoco.it; Via Salita Branco 2; s €65-120, d €85-120; ❄) A gay-friendly guest house with five individually decorated rooms, each named after an artist. There's the modern black and white Herb Ritts room, the pink Botticelli room and a Keith Haring room, littered with the artist's trademark graffiti figurines.

Hotel Villa Belvedere (☎ 0942 2 37 91; www.villabelvedere.it; Via Bagnoli Croci 79; s €70-134, d €118-212; ⌚ Mar-Nov, Christmas; ❄ 🏊) This historic hotel oozes class. The quiet rooms are simple yet refined, with cream linens and terracotta floors, and the luxuriant garden commands majestic sea views. Parking costs €7.80.

Vecchia Taormina (☎ 0942 62 55 89; Vico Ebrei 3; pizzas €6.50, meals €25) At the end of a tiny alley off Piazza del Duomo, this unpretentious trattoria serves no-nonsense local food,

ITALY

including a classic *caponata* (sweet and sour aubergine and tomato ratatouille). If you don't fancy pasta, the wood-fired pizzas are an excellent alternative.

Granduca (☎ 0942 2 49 83; Corso Umberto 172; pizza €7.50, meals €45) Famous for its spectacular terrace, Granduca offers lovely wood-charred pizza and a wide-ranging international menu. Dress the part and book ahead.

Ristorante Luraleo (☎ 0942 62 01 64; Via Bagnoli Croce 27/31, meals €25) Hanging copper pots, tacky stained glass and a vine-draped terrace set the stage for some pretty spot-on food. Think risotto with salmon and pistachio nuts followed by grilled calamari.

Getting There & Away

Taormina is best reached by bus. From the bus terminus on Via Pirandello, Interbus serves Messina (€3.50, 1¾ hours, hourly) and **Etna Trasporti** (☎ 095 53 27 16; www.etnatrasporti.it) connects with Catania (€4.40, 1½ hours, hourly).

There are regular trains to/from Messina (€5.50, 45 minutes, hourly) and Catania (€5.50, 40 minutes, hourly), but on arrival you'll have to get the Etna bus up to the town centre.

MT ETNA

The dark silhouette of Mt Etna (3330m) broods ominously over the east coast, more or less halfway between Taormina and Catania. One of Europe's highest and most volatile volcanoes, it erupts frequently, most recently in May 2008, spewing out lava and ash from four summit craters and fissures on the mountain's slopes.

By public transport the best way to get to the mountain is to take the daily AST bus from Catania. This departs from in front of the main train station at 8.30am (returning at 4.30pm, €5.15 return) and drops you at the Rifugio Sapienza (1923m) where you can pick up the **Funivia dell'Etna** (cable car, bus & guide €49; 9am-5pm summer, to 3.30pm winter) to 2500m. From here buses courier you up to the official crater zone (2920m). If you want to walk, allow up to four hours for the round trip.

Gruppo Guide Alpine Etna Sud (☎ 095 791 47 55; www.etnaguide.com) is one of hundreds of outfits offering guided tours, typically involving 4WD transport and a guided trek. Reckon on at least €60 for a summit excursion.

Armchair excursionists can enjoy Etna views by hopping on a **Ferrovia Circumetnea** (☎ 095 54 12 50; www.circumetnea.it; €6.50) train. These circle Mt Etna from Catania to Riposto in a 3½-hour trip.

Further Etna information is available from the **tourist office** (☎ 0975 730 62 55; 8am-8pm) at Catania train station.

If you want to overnight in Catania, the **Agora Hostel** (☎ 095 723 30 10; www.agorahostel.com; Piazza Curro 6; dm €21, s €30-35, d €50-55;) is a well-equipped and sociable spot with its own pub and restaurant.

SYRACUSE

pop 123,400

With its gorgeous *centro storico* and gritty ruins, Syracuse (Siracusa) is a baroque beauty with an ancient past. One of Sicily's most visited cities, it was founded in 734 BC by Corinthian settlers and became the dominant Greek city state on the Mediterranean, battling Carthaginians and Etruscans before falling to the Romans in 212 BC.

Orientation & Information

If arriving by bus, or train, you'll be dropped off at the western end of the city centre. From the train station, it's a 20-minute walk to Ortygia, the historic centre, where you'll find the best restaurants and hotels – take Via Francesco Crispi to Piazzale Marconi and then follow Corso Umberto I down to the bridge. Alternatively, jump on one of the regular shuttle buses that connect Ortygia with the station.

The **tourist office** (☎ 0931 46 42 55; Via Maestranza 33; 8.30am-1.45pm & 2.30-3.30pm Mon-Fri) is in Ortygia.

Sights

ORTYGIA

Connected to the town by bridge, the island of Ortygia is an atmospheric warren of elaborate baroque *palazzi*, lively piazzas and busy trattorias. Just off Via Roma, the 7th-century **cathedral** (Piazza del Duomo; 9am-7pm) was built over a pre-existing 5th-century-BC Greek temple, incorporating most of the original columns in its three-aisled structure. Its sumptuous baroque facade was added in the 18th century. South of Piazza del Duomo, is the **Fontana Aretusa**, where fresh water has been bubbling up since ancient times when it was the city's main water supply.

PARCO ARCHEOLOGICO DELLA NEAPOLIS

Syracuse's main attraction is the extensive **Parco Archeologico della Neapolis** (☎ 0931 6 50 68; Viale Paradiso; adult/concession €8/4; 🕑 8am-7pm summer, to 4pm winter), home to the city's ancient ruins. Hewn out of solid rock, the 5th-century-BC **Greek theatre** is where Aeschylus premiered many of his tragedies. Nearby, the **Orecchio di Dionisio** is an ear-shaped grotto whose perfect acoustics allowed Syracuse's tyrant Dionysius to eavesdrop on his prisoners. On the other side of Via Paradiso, the impressive 2nd-century **Roman amphitheatre** was used for gladiatorial games.

To get to the park take bus 1 or 4 to Corso Gelone. On foot, it's about 20 minutes from the train station.

About 500m east of the archaeological zone, the impressive **Museo Archeologico Paolo Orsi** (☎ 0931 46 40 22; Viale Teocrito 66/a; adult/concession €8/4; 🕑 9am-6pm Tue-Sat, 9am-1pm Sun) houses Sicily's most extensive archaeological collection.

Sleeping & Eating

Lol Hostel (☎ 0931 46 50 88; www.lolhostel.com; Via Francesco Crispi 94; dm/d €20/58; 💻) A terrific modern hostel near the train station. Accommodation is in mixed and girl-only dorms, and sunny, cheerfully furnished private rooms. At the time of research, refurbishment was underway to add a downstairs pub. Should be good.

Hotel Ortigia Acropoli (☎ 0931 44 93 04; www.siracusa-hotels.it; Via Roma 15; s/d/tr/q €55/75/100/120; ❄) Offering value for money and big, comfortable rooms, this Ortygia option is a good bet. From the brick-vaulted reception, an old stone staircase leads to guest rooms, which come with parquet or terracotta floors and smart furniture. Guests also have use of a kitchen.

Casa Mia (☎ 0931 46 33 49; www.bbcasamia.it; Corso Umberto 112; d €60-75; ❄ 💻) On the principal mainland strip, this is a small, homey hotel. Its characterful, old-fashioned rooms are furnished with family heirlooms and imperious beds. The owners are planning to add 10 new rooms and revamp the existing ones so the look may change.

our pick **Hotel Gutkowski** (☎ 0931 46 58 61; www.guthotel.it; Lungomare Vittorini 26; s/d €80/110; ❄ 💻) Spread over two fishermen's houses on the Ortygia seafront, this small design-hotel is a gem. Rooms and public spaces have been decorated with a masterfully light touch, allowing sunlight to illuminate the soft pastel tones and simple, modern decor. There's a small terrace overlooking the sea, service is cheerful and efficient, and breakfast is mostly organic.

Castello Fiorentino (☎ 0931 21 097; Via del Crocifisso 6, trav Via Roma; pizza €5, meals €15) This place has all the hallmarks of a classic Italian pizzeria. The pizza is excellent, the atmosphere is raucous, and the pace is quick. Expect all the usual toppings plus a few novelties involving smoked salmon and caviar.

Sicilia in Tavola (☎ 392 461 08 89; Via Cavour 28; meals €22; 🕑 Tue-Sun) Come here for delicious homemade pasta and fresh-off-the-boat seafood. Try the prawn ravioli served with tomato, mint and parsley, followed by *polpette in mucca* (fried fish cakes). It's a small, cluttered place, so book ahead.

Don Camillo (☎ 0931 6 71 33; Via Maestranza 96; meals €40; 🕑 Mon-Sat) A treat for bon viveurs, this is one of Syracuse's top restaurants. The ex-convent setting and jacketed waiters lend it a formal atmosphere but the food is top notch. Select from a fabulous antipasto spread and extensive menu.

Getting There & Away

In general, buses are quicker and more convenient than trains. Buses use the terminus in front of the train station. Both **Interbus** (☎ 091 617 54 11; www.interbus.it, in Italian) and **AST** (☎ 0931 46 48 20; www.aziendasicilianatrasporti.it) run to/from Catania (€4.70, 1½ hours, hourly) and Palermo (€14, 3¼ hours, 10 daily).

Trains service Taormina (€11.60, one hour, nine daily), Catania (€7.50, 1¼ hours, 11 daily) and Messina (€14.50, three hours, nine daily).

AGRIGENTO

pop 59,100

Agrigento enjoys fame and notoriety in equal measure. Fame for its awe-inspiring Greek temples; notoriety for the rampant *abusivismo* (illegal building) that has overrun the medieval hilltop town with high-rise tower blocks. Agrigento was founded around 581 BC by Greek settlers and became an important trading centre under the Romans and Byzantines.

Intercity buses arrive on Piazzale Rosselli where you can catch local bus 1, 2 or 3 to the Valley of the Temples. Up in the main town, the **tourist office** (☎ 800 31 55 55; Piazzale Aldo Moro; 🕑 8am-2pm & 3-7pm Mon-Fri, 8am-1pm Sat) can provide limited information on the archaeological park.

Sights

One of the most compelling archaeological sites in southern Europe, the **Valley of the Temples** is a Unesco-listed complex of temples and walls from the ancient city of Akragas, founded here in 581 BC. You'll need a full day to do justice to the **archaeological park** (☎ 0922 49 72 26; adult/concession €8/4, incl museum €10/5; 8.30am-7pm), which is divided into eastern and western zones. The most spectacular temples are in the eastern zone. First up is the oldest, the **Tempio di Ercole**, built at the end of the 6th century BC and equivalent in size to the Parthenon. Continuing east, the intact **Tempio della Concordia** was transformed into a Christian church in the 6th century and the **Tempio di Giunone** boasts an impressive sacrificial altar.

Over the road in the western zone, the remains of the 5th-century-BC **Tempio di Giove** suggest just how big the original must have been. In fact, it covered an area of 112m by 56m with 20m-high columns interspersed with *telamoni* (giant male statues), one of which now stands in the Museo Archeologico (see below). Further on, the **Tempio di Castore e Polluce** was partly reconstructed in the 19th century.

North of the temples, on the road up to Agrigento, the **Museo Archeologico** (☎ 0922 40 15 65; adult/concession incl archaeological park €10/5; 9.30am-7pm Tue-Sat, to 1pm Sun & Mon) has a huge collection of well-labelled artefacts.

Sleeping & Eating

Campeggio Internazionale San Leone (☎ 0922 41 11 15; www.campingvalledeitempli.com; Viale Emporium 192, San Leone; per person/tent/car €7/7/3;) This well-equipped camping ground is on the sea in the small town of San Leone. With a swimming pool, pizzeria, internet point, and bus shuttle to the temples and nearby beaches, it's got pretty much all you need. Take bus 2 from Agrigento train station.

B&B Foderà (☎ 0922 40 30 79; www.fodera.it; Via Foderà 11; d €50-80, tr/q €100/120;) Hidden away on a medieval side street, this is a classic family B&B. There are few luxuries but the five old-fashioned rooms are spacious and full of character with wood-beamed ceilings and cool, tiled floors.

B&B Atenea 191 (☎ 0922 59 55 94; www.atenea191.com; Via Atenea 191; s/d/tr/q €50/80/120/160) A labour of love for the artist owner, the seven rooms at this welcoming B&B are decorated with original paintings and exuberant floral stencils. Two rooms are topped by 18th-century frescoes and five have views down to the sea. Breakfast is served on the rooftop patio.

Café Girasole (Via Atenea 68-70; panino €2.50) A great little wine bar popular with lunching locals. You can prop up the bar or sit on the small terrace, shrouded in a mist of cooling water spray. Decent panini and good espresso.

Trattoria Pizzeria Manhattan (☎ 0922 2 09 11; Salita M. Angeli 9; set menu €15-18; Mon-Sat) Good for straightforward Sicilian cooking, this modest trattoria is halfway up a staircase off Via Ateneo, Agrigento's main street. Help yourself at the buffet antipasto and fill up on spaghetti *alla siciliana* (with tomato, aubergine, basil and salty ricotta).

Getting There & Away

For most destinations, the bus is the easiest way to get to and from Agrigento. **Cuffaro** (☎ 091 616 15 10; www.cuffaro.info) runs buses to Palermo (€7.70, two hours, nine daily) and **SAIS** (☎ 091 616 60 28; www.saisautolinee.it, in Italian) serves Catania (€11.60, three hours, 14 daily).

SARDINIA

To most people Sardinia means exclusive beach resorts and sky-high prices. And while it's true that the 55km-long *Costa Meralda* (Emerald Coast) is one of the priciest destinations on the Med, it is hardly representative of the whole island. Sardinia's coast stretches for 1850km, and much of it is still undeveloped. Visit out of high summer and you'll have the pick of the island's long sandy-white beaches. You'll also find that prices compare favourably with mainland Italy.

But there's more to Sardinia than transparent seas and tropical-looking beaches. The largely barren interior is a spellbinding mix of impenetrable granite gorges, forbidding peaks, and silent cork forests. Adding a sense of mystery are the 7000 *nuraghi* (circular stone towers), which pepper the landscape, all that's left of Sardinia's mysterious prehistoric past.

You can get round Sardinia on public transport but you'll discover much more with your own wheels.

Getting There & Away

AIR

Flights from Italian and European cities serve Sardinia's three main airports: **Elmas** (CAG; ☎ 070 211 211; www.sogaer.it) in Cagliari; Alghero's **Fertilia**

(AHO; ☎ 079 93 52 82; www.algheroairport.it); and the **Aeroporto Olbia Costa Smeralda** (OLB; ☎ 0789 56 34 44; www.geasar.it) in Olbia.

BOAT

Car and passenger ferries sail year-round from various Italian ports, including Civitavecchia, Genoa, Livorno, Naples and Palermo. Various companies ply these routes and services are at their most frequent between June and September. There are also several summer-only routes from Fiumicino. The following is a brief rundown of the major routes and the companies that operate them:

Civitavecchia To/from Olbia (Moby Lines, Sardinia Ferries, Tirrenia); Cagliari (Tirrenia); Golfo Aranci (Sardinia Ferries).
Genoa To/from Porto Torres (Grandi Navi Veloci, Tirrenia); Olbia (Moby Lines, Tirrenia); Arbatax (Tirrenia).
Livorno To/from Olbia (Moby Lines); Golfo Aranci (Sardinia Ferries).
Naples To/from Cagliari (Tirrenia).
Palermo To/from Cagliari (Tirrenia).

For further details see listings in individual town entries. Online, you can get up-to-date information and book tickets at www.traghetti online.net.

Getting Around

Getting round Sardinia without your own wheels can be time-consuming, although it's not impossible. In most cases buses are preferable to trains, which are nearly always slower and often involve lengthy changes. Bus services are generally cheap and efficient. The two main companies **ARST** (☎ 800 865 042; www.arst.sardegna.it, in Italian) and **FMS** (☎ 800 044 553; www.ferroviemeridionalisarde.it) cover destinations across the island. **FdS** (Ferrovie della Sardegna; ☎ 800 460 220; www.ferroviesardegna.it, in Italian) also operates bus and train services, including the **Trenino Verde** (☎ 800 460 220; www.treninoverde.com), a tiny tourist train that trundles through Sardinia's most inaccessible countryside.

CAGLIARI

pop 159,400

Sardinia's capital and largest city is a far cry from the chichi coastal resorts that most people associate with the island. A busy working port, it has not been prettified for the benefit of tourists and is all the more interesting for it. With its landmark citadel, great restaurants and popular, sandy beach, Cagliari is very much its own city.

Orientation

The main bus and train stations and port are near Piazza Matteotti, where you'll find the city tourist office. The busy seafront road Via Roma connects with the grand boulevard Largo Carlo Felice, which heads north to Piazza Yenne, the centre's focal square. Rising above everything is the historic Castello (castle) district. Much of the budget accommodation and many good-value trattorias are in the Marina neighbourhood just inland of Via Roma.

Information

Lamarù (Via Napoli 43; per hr €3; 9am-8pm Mon-Sat) Internet cafe.
Ospedale Brotzu (Hospital; ☎ 070 53 91; Via Peretti)
Police station (Questura; ☎ 070 6 02 71; Via Amat Luigi 9)
Post office (Piazza del Carmine 27)
Tourist office (☎ 070 66 92 55; Piazza Matteotti; 8.30am-1.30pm & 2-8pm)

Sights & Activities

The most interesting part of town is the Castello district, the medieval citadel that towers over the city. Here you can climb the **Torre di San Pancrazio** (Piazza Indipendenza; admission €4; 9am-1pm & 3.30-7pm Tue-Sun), one of only two 14th-century towers still standing. Nearby, in what was once Cagliari's arsenal, is the city's main museum complex, the **Citadella dei Musei**. Of its four museums, the most impressive is the **Museo Archeologico Nazionale** (☎ 070 68 40 00; Piazza dell'Arsenale; admission €4; 9am-8pm Tue-Sun), which has a fabulous collection of *nuraghi* bronzes. These provide one of the few clues to the island's mysterious native culture.

At the other end of Castello, past the 13th-century **Cattedrale di Santa Maria** (Piazza Palazzo 4; 8.30am-12.30pm & 5.30-8pm) and its imposing Romanesque pulpits, is the monumental **Bastione San Remy** (Piazza Costituzione). This was formerly a strong point in the defensive walls and commands huge views over the city and distant lagoons.

To the west of the centre, the 2nd-century **Anfiteatro Romano** (Roman Amphitheatre; Vile Fra Ignazio; admission €4.30; 9.30am-1.30pm Tue-Sat, 9.30am-1.30pm & 3.30-5.30pm Sun) is the most important Roman monument in Sardinia. During summer, concerts are staged here.

A short bus ride from the centre, Cagliari's vibrant beach, **Spiaggia di Poetto**, boasts inviting blue waters and a happening summer bar scene.

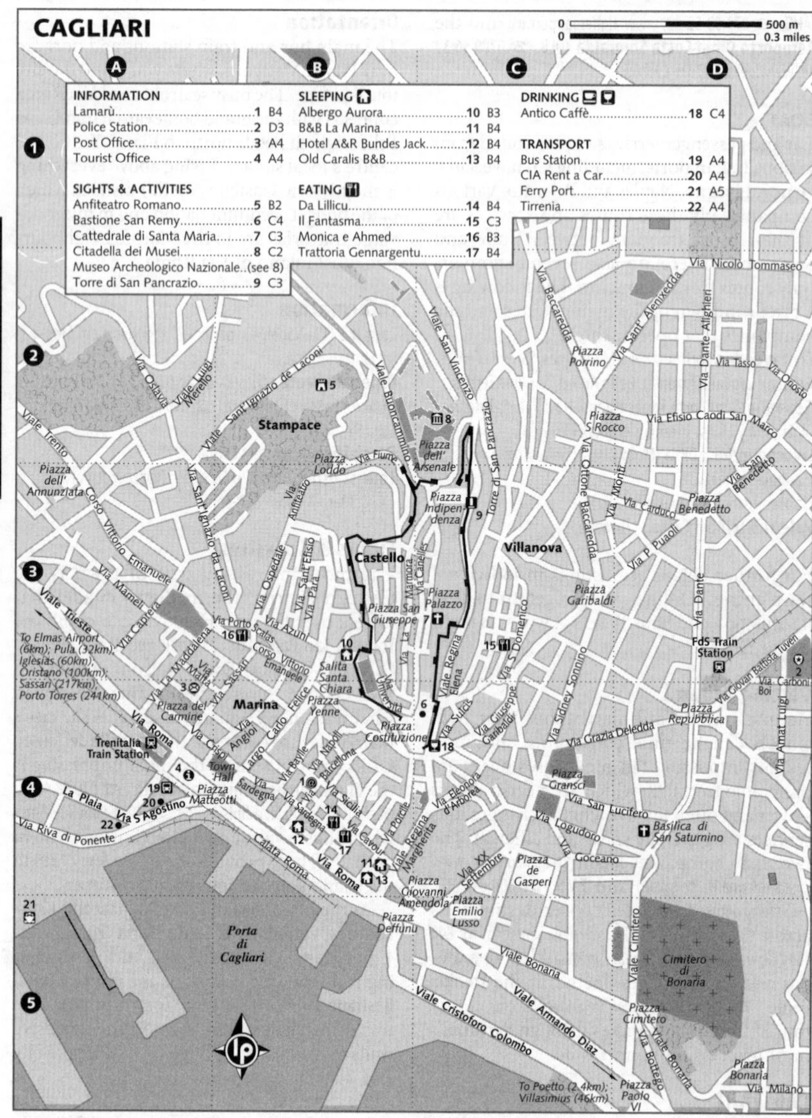

Festivals & Events

Cagliari's annual bonanza, the **Festa di Sant'Efisio**, involves four days of costumed processions from 1 May.

Sleeping

B&B La Marina (☎ 070 67 00 65; www.la-marina.it; Via Porcile 23; s €40, d €70-75; ❄) A good-value B&B in the atmospheric Marina district. The elderly couple who run the place keep a tight ship and the four white, wood-beamed rooms are pristine. There are a couple of communal breakfast rooms with fridges for guest use.

Old Caralis B&B (☎ 349 29 12 853; www.oldcaralis.it; Via Porcile 11; s €40-70, d €60-90; ❄ 💻) This cosy B&B is within walking distance of the port and train station. Housed in a 19th-century *palazzo*, the two guest rooms are not the biggest but they're tastefully decorated with wooden furniture and comfortable beds.

Hotel A&R Bundes Jack (☎/fax 070 66 79 70; www.hotelbjvittoria.it; Via Roma 75; s €48-58, d €76-88; ☒) The best budget hotel on the seafront, this is an old-fashioned family-run *pensione*. Run by a garrulous old boy, it has spacious, high-ceilinged rooms decorated with robust family furniture and sparkling chandeliers. Breakfast is not included.

T Hotel (☎ 070 474 00; www.thotel.it; Via dei Giudicati; r €99-410; ☒) Adding a dose of contemporary design to Cagliari's cityscape, the T is housed in a modernistic steel and glass tower. Inside, the vast, airport-style lobby features a sunken bar and gurgling fountain and rooms reveal a linear, modish look. Breakfast is not included in rates.

Also recommended is **Albergo Aurora** (☎ 070 65 86 25; www.hotelcagliariaurora.it; Salita Santa Chiara 19; s €32-46, d €48-68; ☒), a welcoming budget hotel just off buzzing Piazza Yenne. There are cheaper rates for rooms with a shared bathroom.

Eating & Drinking

Il Fantasma (☎ 070 65 67 49; Via San Domenico 94; pizzas €6.50; ⏰ Mon-Sat) It's quite a trek to this local favourite, but well worth it to chow down on Cagliari's best pizza. If you haven't booked you'll need to arrive early to get a table in the cheerful, brick-lined interior.

Trattoria Gennargentu (☎ 070 67 20 21; Via Sardegna 60; meals €20) It doesn't look much from outside but this no-frills Marina trattoria serves excellent food. There's a full menu of pastas and meaty mains but the seafood is particularly good. Try the *tonno alla carlofortina*, tuna chunks served cold in a sweet tomato and onion sauce.

our pick **Monica e Ahmed** (☎ 070 640 20 45; Corso Vittorio Emanuele 119; meals €25; ⏰ closed dinner Sun) A top spot for delicious seafood at affordable prices. Monica welcomes you with a smile and then plies you with a tempting array of fishy delights. Start with a lavish antipasto of fresh cuttlefish, *ricci* (sea urchins), mussels, and lobster in vinaigrette, and follow with spaghetti *ai frutti di mare* (with mussels, clams and breadcrumbs). If you've got room left, the grilled scampi looked mighty good.

Da Lillicu (☎ 070 65 29 70; Via Sardegna 78; meals €28) One of Cagliari's most famous eateries, this historic trattoria has an excellent local reputation and is nearly always packed. The menu features a number of Sardinian specialities, including *burrida* (catfish marinated in white-wine vinegar and served with nuts).

Also worth a mention is **Antico Caffè** (☎ 070 65 82 96; Piazza Costituzione), an elegant cafe where you can get a pasta lunch for around €10.

Getting There & Away

Cagliari's **Elmas airport** (CAG; ☎ 070 211 211; www.sogaer.it) is 6km northwest of the city. The airport is served by a number of airlines, including easyJet, Ryanair, and several buget carriers, with routes to/from mainland Italian cities and destinations across Europe. In summer, there are additional charter flights. Half-hourly ARST buses connect the airport with the bus station on Piazza Matteotti; the 10-minute journey costs €2.

Cagliari's ferry port is just off Via Roma. **Tirrenia** (☎ 892 123; www.tirrenia.it; Via dei Ponente 1; ⏰ 8.30am-12.20pm & 3.30-6.50pm Mon-Sat) is the main ferry operator, with year-round services to Civitavecchia (€48, 16½ hours), Naples (€45, 16¼ hours) and Palermo (€51, 14½ hours). Book tickets at the port or at travel agencies.

From the bus station, ARST runs buses to/from Oristano (€6.50, 1½ hours, four daily) and Nuoro (€14.50, 3½ hours, four daily), as well as destinations on the Costa del Sud and Costa Rei. Get tickets from the McDonalds on the square. FdS buses link with Sassari (€17, 3¼ hours, three daily) and **Turmo Travel** (☎ 0789 214 87; www.gruppoturmotravel.com) runs a daily bus to Olbia (€18, 4¼ hours).

Down by the port, you can rent cars, bikes and scooters from **CIA Rent a Car** (☎ 070 65 65 03; www.ciarent.it; Via Molo Sant'Agostino 13; car per day from €39).

Trenitalia trains run from the station on Piazza Matteotti to Oristano (€5.15, up to two hours, hourly) and Sassari (€13.65, 4¼ hours, five daily).

CALA GONONE

A popular resort with a small beach and decent accommodation, Cala Gonone makes an excellent base for exploring the spectacular Gulf of Orosei. The coastline, one of Italy's most imperious, is peppered with beaches and sea caves, many of which are only accessible by boat or on foot. Inland, the rugged, difficult terrain is ideal for hikers and climbers.

The helpful **tourist office** (☎ 0784 936 96; www.calagonone.com; Viale Bue Marino 1/a; ⏰ 9am-1pm &

3-7pm) has maps, accommodation lists and contact details for local guides. **Coop Ghivine** (☎ 349 442 55 52; www.ghivine.com; Via Montebello 5) in nearby Dorgali is one of several cooperatives that organise excursions and guided treks, starting at about €35 per person.

Sights & Activities

Beach-lovers will be spoilt for choice along Cala Gonone's coast. **Spiaggia Centrale**, the small beach in town, is good for a quick dip but the best beaches are round the coast. **Cala Fuili**, about 3.5km south of town, is a small, rocky inlet backed by a deep green valley. From here you can hike over the cliff tops to the stunning **Cala Luna**, about two hours (4km) away on foot. Alternatively, jump on a boat at Cala Gonone's tiny port and cruise the coast. The **Nuovo Consorzio Trasporti Marittimi Calagonone** (☎ 0784 9 33 05; www.calagononecrociere.it) is one of many outfits operating tours to Cala Luna (€12) and the dazzling **Grotta del Bue Marino** (€16.50, including Cala Luna €23). A series of stalactite- and stalagmite-filled caves, the Grotta (admission €8) is the last island refuge of the monk seal, although none have been seen for some time.

There's a whole range of activities for those who have time or money or both: diving, snorkelling, rock climbing, mountain biking and hiking are the most popular. The tourist office can supply details. To hire your own boat reckon on at least €80 per day for two people (petrol extra).

Sleeping & Eating

Camping Cala Gonone (☎ 0784 9 31 65; www.campingcalagonone.it; per person incl car & tent €15-19, 2-bed bungalow €48-103; Apr-Oct) By the entrance to town on the main road from Dorgali, this shady camping ground has excellent facilities including a tennis court, bar, barbecue area, pizzeria and swimming pool. Book ahead for August.

Pop Hotel (☎ 0784 9 31 85; www.hotelpop.com; per person €27-53) This is a cheerful year-round hotel is yards from the port. Rooms are spacious and sunny and the roadside restaurant is a good place to eat. There's a huge menu including a number of interesting fusion dishes. Set menus range from €16 to €28, otherwise you're looking at around €30 for a meal.

our pick **Agriturismo Nuraghe Mannu** (☎ 0784 9 32 64; www.agriturismonuraghemannu.com; off the SP 26 Dorgali–Cala Gonone Rd; d €48-80, half-board per person €40-48) Immersed in greenery and with blissful sea views, this is the real McCoy, an authentic working farm with four simple rooms and a restaurant open to all. The fixed €23 menu is a feast of home-produced cheese, salami, pork, lamb and wine. Bookings are essential. There are also five tent pitches available for €8 to €10 per person.

Hotel Costa Dorada (☎ 0784 9 33 32; www.hotelcostadorada.it; Lungomare Palmasera 45; per person €53-93; Apr-Oct) The best looking hotel in town, the flower-clad Costa Dorada offers luxurious sea views and tasteful rooms decorated with local handicrafts. It's at the southern end of the *lungomare*, just over the road from the beach.

SPLURGE

Overlooked by giant granite peaks about 20km inland from Cala Gonone, the **Hotel Su Gologone** (☎ 0784 28 75 12; www.sugologone.it; s €115-180, d €140-240, ste €340-440) is a fabulous hacienda-style rural retreat. Cobbled paths lead to a series of whitewashed cottages whose rooms are decorated with olive-wood beams, embroidered pillows, antique headboards and local handicrafts. There's a pool, a leisure centre, a huge wine cellar and plenty of walking in the surrounding countryside. The restaurant, one of Sardinia's best, specialises in traditional Sardinian cooking, including a delicious *porceddu*, spit-roasted suckling pig.

Getting There & Away

There are seven ARST buses a day from Nuoro through Dorgali to Cala Gonone (€3, 70 minutes). If travelling by car, you'll need a good road map, such as Sardegna published by the Touring Club Italiano.

ALGHERO

pop 50,600

A favourite of holidaying Brits, Alghero is the main resort on Sardinia's northwest coast. Surprisingly, though, it's not entirely given over to tourism and it is still an important fishing port. Interest is centred on the medieval *centro storico* with its robust stone ramparts and tight-knit lanes.

Alghero was founded in the 11th century by the Genovese and later became an important outpost of the Aragonese Catalans.

Still today the local dialect is a form of Catalan, and the town retains something of a Spanish atmosphere.

Orientation & Information

Alghero's historic centre is on a small promontory jutting into the sea, with the new town radiating out behind and north along the coast.

On the eastern fringe of the *centro storico*, the superhelpful **tourist office** (☎ 079 97 90 54; www.comune.alghero.ss.it, in Italian; Piazza Porta Terra 9; ⌚ 8am-8pm Mon-Sat, 10am-1pm Sun) can answer every imaginable question.

Sights & Activities

The *centro storico* is a charming mesh of narrow cobbled alleys hemmed in by Spanish Gothic *palazzi*. Of the various churches, the most interesting is the **Chiesa di San Francesco** (Via Carlo Alberto; ⌚ 7.30am-noon & 5-8.30pm), with its mix of Romanesque and Gothic styles. The cathedral's landmark **campanile** (bell tower; admission €2; ⌚ 7pm-9.30pm Tue, Thu & Sat Jul & Aug, 5-8pm Sep, by appointment rest of yr) is a fine example of Gothic-Catalan architecture.

From the port you can take a boat trip along the impressive northern coast to **Capo Caccia** and the grandiose **Grotte di Nettuno** (☎ 079 94 65 40; adult/concession €10/5; ⌚ 9am-7pm Apr-Sep, to 5pm Oct, to 4pm Jan-Mar, Nov & Dec) complex. The cheapest boat is the **Navisarda ferry** (☎ 079 95 06 03; adult/child return €14/7), which departs hourly between 9am and 5pm from June to September, and four times daily the rest of the year. Allow 2½ hours for the round-trip. Cheaper still, you can get a bus to the caves from Via Catalogna (€3.50 return, 50 minutes, three times daily summer, once winter).

Ten kilometres west of Alghero on the road to Porto Conte, the **Nuraghe di Palmavera** (☎ 079 95 32 00; admission €3; ⌚ 9am-7pm summer, shorter hr winter) is a 3500-year-old *nuraghe* village, well worth a visit.

Sleeping & Eating

There's plenty of accommodation in Alghero but you'll need to book between June and September.

Camping La Mariposa (☎ 079 95 03 60; www.lamariposa.it; Via Lido 22; sites per person/tent/car €11/13/4, 4-person bungalows €47-78; 💻; ⌚ Apr-Oct) About 2km north of the centre, this camping ground is on the beach amid pine and eucalyptus trees. This, and the excellent facilities, make it a popular choice.

Hotel San Francesco (☎ 079 98 03 30; www.sanfrancescohotel.com; Via Ambrogio Machin 2; s €45-70, d €70-105; ❄) You'll need to book early to get a room at Alghero's only *centro storico* hotel. Housed in an ex-convent, the rooms are straightforward but comfortable with white walls, pine furniture and brown tiled floors.

Angedras Hotel (☎ 079 973 50 34; www.angedras.it; Via Frank 2; s €53-68, d €75-110; ❄ 💻) A model of whitewashed Mediterranean style, the Angedas has cool, airy rooms with big French doors opening on to sunny patios. It also runs a seafront restaurant (☎ 079 973 50 78; Bastioni Marco Polo 41; meals €35) on the city ramparts.

Caffè Costantino (Piazza Civica 30; ⌚ Thu-Tue) Alghero's ritziest cafe spills onto the main square in the *centro storico*. Come here for coffee, cakes and ice cream. There's also a full food menu but prices are inflated.

Il Ghiotto (☎ 079 97 48 20; Piazza Civica 23; meals €10-15; ⌚ Tue-Sun) One of the few places in Alghero where you can sit down and fill up for as little as €10. It looks like a typical foodie souvenir shop but has a fantastic canteen, serving a daily spread of panini, pastas, salads and mains.

Osteria Machiavello (☎ 079 98 06 28; Bastioni Marco Polo 57; meals €35, set menus €16-18; ⌚ Wed-Mon) With tables on the city walls, this is a panoramic spot for a memorable dinner. The menu covers most tastes with grilled meats, including horse, and a number of classic fish dishes. Try the *zuppa di cozze e vongole* (mussel and clam soup).

Trattoria Maristella (☎ 079 97 81 72; Via Fratelli Kennedy 9; meals €27) Visitors and locals flock to this bustling little trattoria for reliable seafood – the *insalata di mare* (seafood salad) is excellent – and Sardinian specialities such as *culurgiones* (ravioli stuffed with potato, pecorino cheese and mint). And all at very honest prices.

Getting There & Away

Alghero's airport **Fertilia** (AHO; ☎ 079 93 52 82; www.algheroairport.it) is served by a number of low-cost carriers, including Ryanair and Air One, with connections to mainland Italy and destinations across Europe.

Up to 10 daily FdS buses (€0.70, 20 minutes) connect the airport with Piazza Mercede in the town centre. **Logudoro Tours**

WORTH THE TRIP: BOSA

As much for the getting there as the town itself, a trip to **Bosa** is well worth your time. The 46km road from Alghero is one of Sardinia's great coastal rides with unforgettable vistas at every turn. Bosa doesn't disappoint either, with its picturesque Old Town rising up from the Temo River.

For the journey, you can rent cars, motorcycles and bikes from **Cicloexpress** (☎ 079 98 69 50; www.cicloexpress.com; Via Garibaldi, Alghero) from €65/55/8 per day.

(☎ 079 28 17 28) runs two daily buses from the airport to Cagliari (€20, 3½ hours) and vice versa. For Sassari, there are up to 15 daily buses (€3, one hour) from Via Catalogna, or you can catch a train (€2.20, 35 minutes, 10 daily) from the station about 1km southeast of the historic centre.

ITALY DIRECTORY

ACCOMMODATION

In this chapter accommodation is divided into budget (under €110 for a high-season double), midrange (€110 to €200) and top end (€200 and up). The prices quoted are the minimum/maximum for rooms with a private bathroom, and unless otherwise stated include breakfast.

The bulk of Italy's accommodation is made up of *alberghi* (hotels) and *pensioni* – often housed in converted apartments. You'll also find youth hostels and camping grounds scattered across the country, alongside an ever-increasing number of B&Bs and *agriturismi* (farm stays). Other options include mountain *rifugi* (alpine refuges), monasteries, and villa/apartment rentals.

Rates fluctuate enormously depending on where you go (the south is generally cheaper than the north) and when. Expect to pay high-season rates at Easter, in summer (mid-June to August), and over the Christmas to New Year period. Peak season in the ski resorts runs from December to March. Note that many city-centre hotels offer discounts in August to lure guests away from the crowded coasts. Conversely, many hotels in coastal resorts shut up shop for winter, typically from November to March.

As a rough guide, reckon on at least €55 for a double room in a budget hotel.

Under Italian law, smoking is banned in all public areas in hotels, ie in receptions, lobbies, bars, dining rooms etc. Some hotels also ban it in guest rooms, although they are not legally obliged to do so. In practice, most midrange to top-end hotels have nonsmoking rooms available.

B&Bs

Bed and breakfasts (B&Bs) are also popular. The best B&Bs invariably offer great value, providing comfort way beyond what you'd get for the same price at a hotel. Prices are typically between €70 and €150 for a room. Contact **Bed & Breakfast Italia** (Map pp454-5; ☎ 06 688 01 513; www.bbitalia.it; Corso Vittorio Emanuele II 282, Rome) for further information. **Cross-pollinate** (www.cross-pollinate.com) is an online booking service with apartments, B&Bs and guest houses in Rome, Florence and Venice.

Camping

Campers are well-catered for in Italy. Lists of camping grounds are available from local tourist offices or online at www.campeggi.com, www.camping.it and www.touringclub.it. In high season expect to pay up to €12 per person and a further €15 for a tent pitch. Independent camping is not permitted in many places.

Farm-stays

To stay in the countryside, an *agriturismo* (farm stay) is often a good option, although you will usually need your own wheels. Accommodation varies from spartan billets on working farms to palatial suites at luxurious rural retreats. For information and lists check out www.agriturist.it or www.agriturismo.com.

Hostels

Italian *ostelli per la gioventù* (youth hostels) are run by the **Italian Youth Hostel Association** (Associazione Italiana Alberghi per la Gioventù; Map p456; ☎ 06 487 11 52; www.ostellionline.org; Via Cavour 44, Rome), affiliated with **Hostelling International** (HI; www.hihostels.com). A valid HI card is required, which you can get in your home country or at many hostels. Dorm rates are typically between €15 and €30, with breakfast usually included. Many places also offer dinner for around €10.

Refuges

Italy boasts an extensive network of mountain *rifugi* (refuges). Open from July to September, they offer basic dorm-style accommodation, although some larger ones have double rooms. Reckon on €17 to €26 per person per night with breakfast usually included. The best source of information is the **Club Alpino Italiano** (CAI; www.cai.it, in Italian), which owns and runs many of the refuges.

Religious accommodation is a reliable money-saver – typically about €85 for a double room. The **Chiesa di Santa Susanna** (www.santasusanna.org) has a list of convents and monasteries throughout the country. You can also try www.monasterystays.com, a specialist online booking service.

Rental Accommodation

Finding rental accommodation in the major cities can be difficult. A studio flat will typically cost from €1000 per month, with a month's rent payable in advance as a deposit. The easiest way to rent an apartment or a holiday villa is through one of the hundreds of specialist agencies. Some options:

Cottages to Castles (www.cottagesandcasteles.com.au) Oz-based specialist in villa-style accommodation.

Cuendet (www.cuendet.com) Specialises in villa rentals in Tuscany.

Guest in Italy (www.guestinitaly.com) Has apartments and B&Bs on its books in Rome, Florence and Venice.

Long Travel (www.long-travel.co.uk) Has properties in the south of Italy, Sardinia and Sicily.

ACTIVITIES

Cycling

Italy offers everything from teeth-rattling mountain biking to gentle valley rides. Tourist offices across the country can provide details on trails and guided rides. Tuscany and Umbria are favourite spots, particularly around Florence (p497) and Siena (p507). Further north, the Dolomites (p496) and northern lakes are popular with mountain-bikers, as is Sardinia's rugged interior.

The best time for cycling is spring, when it's not too hot and the countryside is looking its best. Lonely Planet's *Cycling in Italy* offers practical tips and several detailed itineraries.

Diving

Transparent topaz waters and a spiky, volcanic geology make for spectacular diving. There are hundreds of schools offering courses and guided dives for all levels. Dive hot spots include Lipari, one of Sicily's Aeolian Islands (p533), and the Golfo di Orosei (p541) on Sardinia's eastern coast, where you can investigate caves rich in flora and fauna.

Hiking & Walking

Thousands of kilometres of *sentieri* (marked trails) criss-cross Italy, ranging from hard-core mountain treks to gentle lakeside ambles. In the high season (the end of June to September), the Dolomites (p496) are a favourite destination. Other popular areas include the Cinque Terre (p471), Amalfi Coast (p524) and Mt Etna in Sicily (p536).

Useful websites include www.cai.it, in Italian, and www.parks.it. Lonely Planet's *Walking in Italy* has descriptions of more than 50 walks.

Skiing

Most of the country's top ski resorts are in the Alps, although there are excellent facilities throughout the Apennines. Skiing isn't cheap, and high-season (December to March) costs will hit your pocket hard. The best way to save money is to buy a *settimana bianca* (literally 'white week') package deal, covering seven days' accommodation, food and ski passes.

See The Dolomites section, p496, for further details.

BOOKS

To get in the mood for Italy, dip into these:

- *Gomorrah* (Roberto Saviano) Saviano is under police protection after this gripping exposé of the Neapolitan mafia.
- *La Bella Figura* (Beppe Severgnini) An acclaimed Italian journalist attempts to explain his nation's foibles.
- *The Leopard* (Giuseppe Tomasi di Lampedusa) Fifty years after it was first published, this is still the best book about Sicily.
- *The Dark Heart of Italy* (Tobias Jones) A no-holds barred study of Berlusconi and his way with power.
- *Italy* (Lonely Planet) More-detailed information on where to go and how.

BUSINESS HOURS

For the purposes of this chapter, opening hours have only been provided in the Information, Eating, Drinking, Entertainment and Shopping sections when they differ from the following standards:

Banks (8.30am-1.30pm & 2.45-4.30pm Mon-Fri)
Bars & Cafes (7.30am-8pm) Many open earlier and some stay open until the small hours. Pubs often open from noon to 2am.
Discos & Clubs (10pm-4am) The action rarely starts much before midnight.
Pharmacies (9am-1pm & 4-7.30pm Mon-Fri, to 1pm Sat) Outside of these hours, pharmacies open on a rotation basis. All are required to post a list of places open in the vicinity.
Post offices major offices (8.30am-6.50pm Mon-Fri, to 1.15pm Sat); branch offices (8.30am-1.50pm Mon-Fri, to 11.50am Sat)
Restaurants (noon-3pm & 7.30-11pm, later in summer) Most restaurants close one day a week.
Shops (9am-1pm & 3.30-7.30pm, or 4-8pm Mon-Sat) In larger cities many chain stores and supermarkets open from 9am to 7.30pm Monday to Saturday; some also open Sunday mornings, typically from 9am to1pm. Food shops are generally closed on Thursday afternoon; some other shops are closed on Monday morning.

Many museums, galleries and archaeological sites operate summer and winter opening hours. Typically, winter hours will apply between November and late March or early April.

DANGERS & ANNOYANCES

The greatest risk visitors face in Italy is from pickpockets and bag snatchers. Pickpockets follow the tourists so be on your guard in popular centres such as Rome, Florence and Venice. Be especially vigilant on public transport. Watch out for gangs of dishevelled-looking kids, and for moped thieves.

Another insidious form of theft is short-changing. This takes various forms but typically goes as follows: you pay for a €3 panino with a €20 note. The cashier then distractedly gives you a €2 coin and a €5 note before turning away. The trick here is to wait and chances are that the €10 note you're waiting for will appear without a word being said.

Road rules are obeyed with discretion, so don't take it for granted that cars will stop at red lights. To cross the road, step confidently into the traffic and walk calmly across. Tread carefully though – there's a lot of dog crap about.

For more information on dealing with dangers and annoyances, see p945.

> **NO SMOKING**
>
> In Italy smoking is banned in all public places. Exactly what constitutes a public place is open to interpretation but restaurants, pubs and bars are all nonsmoking. Most hotels forbid it but you might find some that turn a blind eye to a quick puff in your room or let you light up on a balcony.

EMBASSIES & CONSULATES

Embassies & Consulates in Italy

The following contact details refer to the embassies and consulates in Rome.

Australia (Map pp444-5; ☎ 06 85 27 21, emergencies 800 87 77 90; www.italy.embassy.gov.au; Via Antonio Bosio 5; ⏲ 8.30am-5pm Mon-Fri)
Austria Embassy (Map pp450-1; ☎ 06 844 01 41; www.bmeia.gv.at/it/ambasciata/roma; Via Pergolesi 3); Consulate (Map pp444-5; ☎ 06 855 28 80; Viale Liegi 32; ⏲ 9am-noon Mon-Fri)
Canada Embassy (Map pp444-5; ☎ 06 85 44 41; www.international.gc.ca/canada-europa/italy; Via Salaria 243) Consulate (Map pp444-5; ☎ 06 85 44 41; Via Zara 30; ⏲ 8.30am-noon, 2-4pm Mon-Fri)
France Embassy (Map pp454-5; ☎ 06 68 60 11; www.ambafrance-it.org; Piazza Farnese 67) Consulate (Map pp454-5; ☎ 06 68 60 11; Via Giulia 251; ⏲ 9am-12.30pm Mon-Fri)
Germany (Map p456; ☎ 06 49 21 31; www.rom.diplo.de; Via San Martino della Battaglia 4; ⏲ 8.30-11.30am Mon-Fri)
Ireland (Map pp454-5; ☎ 06 697 91 21; www.ambasciata-irlanda.it; Piazza Campitelli 3; ⏲ 10am-12.30pm, 3-4.30pm Mon-Fri)
Netherlands (Map pp444-5; ☎ 06 322 86 001; www.olanda.it; Via Michele Mercati 8; ⏲ 9am-noon Mon, Tue, Thu & Fri)
New Zealand (Map pp444-5; ☎ 06 853 75 01; www.nzembassy.com; Via Clitunno 44; ⏲ 8.30am-12.45pm & 1.45-5pm Mon-Fri)
Switzerland (off Map pp444-5; ☎ 06 80 95 71; www.eda.admin.ch/roma; Via Barnarba Oriani 61; ⏲ 9am-noon Mon-Fri)
UK (Map pp444-5; ☎ 06 422 00 001; www.britishembassy.gov.uk/italy; Via XX Settembre 80a; ⏲ 9am-5pm Mon-Fri)
USA (Map pp450-1; ☎ 06 4 67 41; www.usis.it; Via Vittorio Veneto 119a; ⏲ 8.30am-12.30pm Mon-Fri)

FESTIVALS & EVENTS

The following are some of Italy's most famous celebrations:

February, March & April

Carnevale In the period before Ash Wednesday, many towns stage carnival celebrations. The best known is in Venice (see p487).

Settimana Santa Italy celebrates Holy Week with processions and passion plays. On Easter Sunday, the pope gives a traditional blessing in St Peter's Square, Rome.

Scoppio del Carro A cart full of fireworks is exploded in Florence's Piazza del Duomo on Easter Saturday (see p502).

May–September

Festa di Sant'Efisio An effigy of Sardinia's patron saint is paraded around Cagliari on a bullock-drawn carriage amid a colourful procession (see p540).

Palio delle Quattro Antiche Repubbliche Marinare (Regatta of the Four Ancient Maritime Republics) Boat races between the four historical maritime republics – Pisa, Venice, Amalfi and Genoa. The event rotates between the towns and is usually held in June.

Il Palio On 2 July and 16 August, Siena stages its extraordinary bareback horse race.

Venice International Film Festival (Mostra del Cinema di Venezia) The international film glitterati disembark at Venice Lido for the annual film fest (see p487).

December

Natale In the weeks preceding Christmas, many churches set up elaborate cribs or nativity scenes known as *presepi* – Naples is famous for these.

HOLIDAYS

Most Italians take their annual holiday in August. This means that many businesses and shops close down for at least a part of the month, usually around *Ferragosto* (15 August). Easter is another busy holiday.

Public holidays include the following:

New Year's Day (Capodanno) 1 January
Epiphany (Epifania) 6 January
Easter Monday (Pasquetta) March/April
Liberation Day (Giorno delle Liberazione) 25 April
Labour Day (Festa del Lavoro) 1 May
Republic Day (Festa della Repubblica) 2 June
Feast of the Assumption (Ferragosto) 15 August
All Saint's Day (Ognisanti) 1 November
Feast of the Immaculate Conception (Immacolata Concezione) 8 December
Christmas Day (Natale) 25 December
Boxing Day (Festa di Santo Stefano) 26 December

Individual towns also have holidays to celebrate their patron saints:

St Mark (Venice) 25 April
St John the Baptist (Florence, Genoa and Turin) 24 June
Saints Peter and Paul (Rome) 29 June
St Rosalia (Palermo) 15 July
St Janarius (Naples) First Sunday in May, 19 September and 16 December
St Ambrose (Milan) 7 December

INTERNET RESOURCES

Beppe Grillo (www.beppegrillo.it) A comedian and anti-political rabble-rouser, Beppe Grillo is Italy's most famous blogger.

Delicious Italy (www.deliciousitaly.com) Whet your appetite on this foodie website.

Italia Mia (www.italiamia.com) Has links to hundreds of Italy-related sites, as well as news headlines.

Italian Government Tourist Board (www.enit.it) Particularly good for festivals and events.

Lonely Planet (www.lonelyplanet.com) Read up about Italy and exchange tips with folk who've been there.

Trenitalia (www.trenitalia.it) Plan your train trips.

MONEY

Italy's currency is the euro. The best way to carry your money is to bring a mix of ATM card, credit card, cash and one or two travellers cheques as backup. ATMs (known in Italy as *bancomat*) are widespread and will accept cards displaying the appropriate sign. Visa and MasterCard are widely recognised, as are Cirrus and Maestro; American Express is less common. If you don't have a PIN, some, but not all, banks will advance cash over the counter.

If your credit card is lost, stolen or swallowed by an ATM, telephone toll free to block it:

Amex (☎ 800 914 912)
MasterCard (☎ 800 870 866)
Visa (☎ 800 81 90 14)

Visa, Travelex and Amex are the most widely accepted travellers cheques, although changing even these in smaller cities can be difficult. You'll find exchange offices at major airports and train stations. For lost or stolen cheques call:

Amex (☎ 800 914 912)
MasterCard (☎ 800 870 866)
Travelex (☎ 800 87 20 50)
Visa (☎ 800 874 155)

You're not expected to tip on top of restaurant service charges, but if you think the service warrants it feel free to round up the bill or leave a little extra – 10% is fine. In bars, Italians often leave small change (€0.10 or €0.20).

POST

Italy's postal system, **Poste** (☎ 803 160; www.poste.it, in Italian), is not the world's most efficient but it has improved in recent years. The standard service is *posta prioritaria*, which costs €0.60 for a normal letter. Registered mail is known as *posta raccomandata*, insured mail as *posta assicurato*.

Francobolli (stamps) are available at post offices and *tabacchi* (tobacconists) – look for the official sign, a big white 'T' against a black background. Tobacconists keep regular shop hours – see p545.

TELEPHONE

Local and long-distance calls can easily be made from public phones by using a phonecard. Rates, particularly for long-distance calls, are pretty high, though. Peak rates apply from 8am to 6.30pm Monday to Friday and until 1pm on Saturday. You can usually save a bit by calling from a cut-price call centre, which you you'll find in all of the main cities. Alternatively, some internet cafes have Skype.

To make a reverse-charge (collect) international call, dial ☎ 170. All operators speak English.

To call Italy from abroad, dial ☎ 0039 and then the area code, including the first zero.

Mobile Phones

Italy uses the GSM 900/1800 network which is compatible with the rest of Europe and Australia, but not with the North American GSM 1900 or the Japanese system (although some GSM 1900/900 phones do work here).

If you have a GSM dual- or tri-band cellular phone that you can unlock (check with your service provider), you need only buy a *prepagato* (prepaid) SIM card to use it in Italy. Companies offering SIM cards include **TIM** (Telecom Italia Mobile; www.tim.it), **Wind** (www.wind.it) and **Vodafone** (www.vodafone.it). You'll need ID to open an account.

Phone Codes

The country code for Italy is 39. Mobile phone numbers begin with a three-digit prefix such as 330 or 339; toll-free (free-phone) numbers are known as *numeri verdi* and usually start with 800; national call rate numbers start with 848 or 199.

Area codes are an integral part of all Italian phone numbers, meaning that you must always use them, even when calling locally.

EMERGENCY NUMBERS

- Ambulance ☎ 118
- Fire ☎ 115
- Police ☎ 113

Phonecards

To phone from a public payphone you'll need a *scheda telefonica* (telephone card), although you'll still find some that accept credit cards and coins. You can buy phonecards (€5, €10, €20) at post offices, *tabacchi* and newsstands.

TRAVELLERS WITH DISABILITIES

Italy is not an easy country for disabled travellers. Cobbled streets, blocked pavements and tiny lifts all make life difficult. Rome-based **Consorzio Cooperative Integrate** (COIN; ☎ 06 232 69 231; www.coinsociale.it) is the best point of reference for disabled travellers. You can also check out www.romapertutti.it and www.milanopertutti.it for information on Rome and Milan.

For those travelling by train, **Trenitalia** (www.trenitalia.com) runs a telephone info line (☎ 199 30 30 60) with details of assistance available at stations.

VISAS

EU citizens do not need a visa to enter Italy. Nationals of some other countries, including Australia, Canada, Israel, Japan, New Zealand, Switzerland and the USA do not need a visa for stays of up to 90 days.

The standard tourist visa for a Schengen country is valid for 90 days, for further details see p955.

Technically, all foreign visitors to Italy are supposed to register with the local police within eight days of arrival. However, if you're staying in a hotel you don't need to bother as the hotel does this for you.

Permesso di Soggiorno

A *permesso di soggiorno* (permit to stay) is required by all non-EU nationals who stay in Italy longer than three months. In theory, you should apply for one within eight days of arriving in Italy. EU citizens do not require a *permesso di soggiorno*.

To get one you'll need an application form; a valid passport, containing a stamp with your date of entry into Italy (ask for this as it's not automatic); a photocopy of your passport; a study visa if necessary; four passport-style photographs; proof of your ability to support yourself financially (ideally a letter from an employer or school/university); and a €14.62 official stamp. Kits containing application forms are available from main post offices.

Non-EU citizens who want to study in Italy must obtain a study visa from their nearest Italian embassy or consulate.

TRANSPORT IN ITALY

GETTING THERE & AWAY

Air

You shouldn't have many problems finding a reasonably priced flight to Italy. High season is June to September, Christmas and Easter. Shoulder season runs from mid-September to the end of October and again in April. Low season is generally November to March. For further information on buying tickets see p958.

Italy's main intercontinental gateway is Rome's **Leonardo da Vinci airport** (FCO; www.adr.it), better known as Fiumicino airport, but flights also serve Milan's **Malpensa** (MXP; www.sea-aeroportomilano.it). Low-cost carriers generally fly into Italy's regional airports, including **Ciampino** (CIA; www.adr.it) in Rome, Pisa's **Galileo Galilei** (☎ 050 50 07 07; www.pisa-airport.com) and **Marco Polo** (VCE; www.veniceairport.it) in Venice. Other important provincial airports include Bologna's **Guglielmo Marconi** (BLQ; ☎ 051 647 96 15; www.bologna-airport.it); **Elmas** (CAG; ☎ 070 211 211; www.sogaer.it) in Cagliari, Sardinia; **Capodichino** (NAP; ☎ 848 88 87 77; www.gesac.it) in Naples; and the Sicilian airport of **Palermo** (PMO; www.gesap.it; ☎ 091 702 01 11)

Alitalia, Italy's national carrier, was saved from bankruptcy in late 2008 by a consortium of private investors who bought the company from the Italian government. It has since merged with Air One, but both Alitalia and Air One continue to operate. International airlines flying to/from Italy include the following:

Air Berlin (AB; ☎ 199 400 737; www.airberlin.com)
Air Canada (AC; ☎ 03 607 21 11; www.aircanada.ca)
Air Dolomiti (EN; ☎ 045 288 61 40; www.airdolomiti.it)
Air France (AF; ☎ 848 88 44 66; www.airfrance.com)
Air New Zealand (NZ; ☎ 02 434 58 390; www.airnz.co.nz)
Air One (AP; ☎ 199 207 080; www.flyairone.it)
Alitalia (AZ; ☎ 06 22 22; www.alitalia.it)
American Airlines (AA; ☎ 06 660 53 169; www.aa.com)
British Airways (BA; ☎ 199 712 266; www.britishairways.com)
Delta Air Lines (DL; ☎ 848 78 03 76; www.delta.com)
easyJet (U2; ☎ 899 234 589; www.easyjet.com)
Jet2 (LS; ☎ 199 404 023; www.jet2.com)
KLM (KL; ☎ 199 414 199; www.klm.com)
Lufthansa (LH; ☎ 199 400 044; www.lufthansa.com)
Meridiana (IG; ☎ 89 29 28; www.meridiana.it)
Qantas (QF; ☎ 848 350 010; www.qantas.com)
Ryanair (FR; ☎ 899 678 910; www.ryanair.com)
SAS (SK; ☎ 199 404 004; www.flysas.com)
Singapore Airlines (SQ; ☎ 06 478 55 360; www.singaporeair.com)
Thai Airways International (TG; ☎ 06 47 81 31; www.thaiair.com)
TUIfly (X3; ☎ 199 192 692; www.tuifly.com)
Vueling (VY; ☎ 800 78 77 88; www.vueling.com)

Land

BUS

A consortium of 32 European coach companies, **Eurolines** (☎ 055 35 70 59; www.eurolines.com) operates across Europe with offices in all major European cities. Italy-bound buses head to Ancona, Florence, Rome, Siena and Venice. Its multilanguage website gives details of prices, passes and travel agencies where you can book tickets.

CAR & MOTORCYCLE

Traversing the Alps into Italy, the main, year-round routes are the Mont Blanc tunnel from France; the Grand St Bernard tunnel and the new Lötschberg Base tunnel from Switzerland; and the Brenner Pass from Austria. All three connect with major *autostrade* (motorways).

If driving from the UK, you can cross to France by ferry or via the Channel Tunnel, operated by **Eurotunnel** (www.eurotunnel.com). Fares vary according to time and season, but single fares start at £49.

When driving into Italy always carry proof of ownership of a private vehicle. You'll also need third-party motor insurance. For more on driving in Italy see p551.

TRAIN

International trains connect with various cities, including the following:

Milan To/from Barcelona, Nice, Paris, Amsterdam, Zürich, Munich, Frankfurt and Vienna.
Rome To/from Paris, Munich and Vienna.

Venice To/from Paris, Zürich, Munich, Vienna, Prague, Ljubljana, Zagreb, Belgrade, Budapest and Bucharest.

There are also international trains from Genoa, Turin, Verona, Bologna, Florence and Naples. Details are available online at www.trenitalia.com.

Cisalpino (www.cisalpino.com) operates daily fast trains from Milan and Venice to Switzerland.

In the UK, the **Rail Europe Travel Centre** (☎ 0870 848 848; www.raileurope.co.uk) can provide fare information on journeys to/from Italy, most of which require a change at Paris.

For details of Eurail and Inter-Rail passes, both valid in Italy, see p969.

ITALY

Sea

Dozens of ferry companies connect Italy with other Mediterranean countries. For details of routes, companies and online booking log onto **Traghettionline** (www.traghettionline.net).

Unless otherwise stated, quoted prices are for a one-way *poltrona* (reclinable seat) in high season. Holders of Eurail and Inter-Rail passes should check with the ferry company if they are entitled to a discount or free passage. Timetables vary from season to season so always check ahead.

Major ferry companies:

Agoudimos (☎ 0831 52 90 91; www.agoudimos-lines.com) Bari to Igoumenitsa (€70, 10 to 12 hours), Patra (€70, 16½ hours) and Kefallonia (€70, 15½ hours); Brindisi to Corfu (€75, 6½ hours).

Endeavor Lines/Hellenic Mediterranean Lines (☎ 0831 52 85 31; www.hml.it) Brindisi to Igoumenitsa (€66, eight hours), Patra (€70, 14 hours), Corfu (€66, 11½ hours) and Kefallonia (€80, 12½ hours).

Grandi Navi Veloci (☎ 010 209 45 91; www.gnv.it) Genoa to Barcelona (€99, 18 hours) and Tunis (€151, 24 hours).

Jadrolinija (☎ Croatia +385 51 666 111; www.jadrolinija.hr) Ancona to Split (€63.50, 11 hours); Bari to Dubrovnik (€63.50, 7½ hours).

Marmara Lines (☎ 071 207 61 65; www.marmaralines.com) Ancona to Cesme in Turkey (€150, 55½ hours).

Minoan Lines (☎ 041 504 12 01; www.minoanlines.it) Ancona to Igoumenitsa (€103, 16 hours) and Patra (€103, 22 hours); Venice to Corfu (€106, 22 hours), Igoumenitsa (€106, 23½ hours) and Patra (€106, 29½ hours).

Montenegro (☎ 080 578 98 27; www.morfimare.it) Bari to Bar in Montenegro (€67, nine hours).

SNAV (☎ 081 428 55 55; www.snav.it) Ancona to Split (€90, 4½ hours); Brindisi to Corfu (€80, 5½ hours).

Superfast Ferries (☎ 899 92 92 06; www.superfast.com) Ancona to Igoumenitsa (€108, 15 hours) and Patra (€108, 21 hours); Bari to to Igoumenitsa (€85, 9½ hours) and Patra (€85, 15½ hours).

Tirrenia (☎ 892 123; www.tirrenia.it) Genoa to Tunis (€140.50, 24 hours); Bari to Durrës (€64.70, nine hours).

GETTING AROUND

You can get pretty much anywhere in Italy by train, bus or ferry – services are generally efficient and cheap. Domestic airlines connect major cities, but flights are still relatively expensive. Your own car gives you more freedom but comes at a cost – expensive petrol, motorway tolls and lack of parking are just some of the headaches you'll have to face.

Air

Italy's major domestic airlines are **Air One** (☎ 199 207 080; www.flyairone.it); **Alitalia** (☎ 06 22 22; www.alitalia.it) and **Meridiana** (☎ 89 29 28; www.meridiana.it). **Ryanair** (☎ 899 678 910; www.ryanair.com) also flies a number of domestic routes.

The main airports are in Rome, Pisa, Milan, Bologna, Genoa, Turin, Naples, Venice, Catania, Palermo and Cagliari.

Bicycle

Cycling is a popular pastime in Italy, particularly in the north. Tourist offices can provide details of designated bike trails and bike hire (rental costs are about €10 per day).

There are no particular road rules for cyclists, although you'd do well to bring a helmet, lights and a small tool kit.

Bikes can be taken on any train carrying the bike logo, but you'll need to pay a bike supplement (€3.50 on regional trains, €5 on Intercity and Eurostar services, €10 on international trains), valid for 24 hours. Bikes generally travel free on ferries.

Boat

Navi (large ferries) service Sicily and Sardinia; *traghetti* (smaller ferries) and *aliscafi* (hydrofoils) cover the smaller islands, including Elba, the Aeolian Islands, Capri, Ischia and Procida. The main embarkation points for Sardinia are Genoa, Livorno, Civitavecchia and Naples; for Sicily, it's Naples and Villa San Giovanni in Calabria. Most long-distance ferries travel overnight.

The major domestic ferry companies:

Grandi Navi Veloci (☎ 010 209 45 91; www.gnv.it)

Moby (☎ 199 30 30 40; www.mobylines.it)

Sardinia Ferries (☎ 199 400 500)

SNAV (☎ 081 428 55 55; www.snav.it)
Tirrenia (☎ 892 123; www.tirrenia.it)

For details of routes, refer to individual town entries.

Bus

Italy boasts an extensive and largely reliable bus network. Buses are not necessarily cheaper than trains, but in mountainous areas such as Umbria, Sicily and Sardinia they are often the only choice. In larger cities, companies have ticket offices or operate through agencies but in most villages and small towns tickets are sold in bars or on the bus. Reservations are usually only necessary for high-season long-haul trips.

Car & Motorcycle

Roads are generally good throughout the country and there's an excellent system of *autostrade* (motorways). There's a toll to use most *autostrade*, payable in cash or by credit card at exit barriers. Motorways are indicated by an A with a number (eg A1) on a green background; *strade statali* (main roads) are shown by an S or SS and number (eg SS7) against a blue background.

Italy's motoring organisation **Automobile Club d'Italia** (ACI; www.aci.it) is an excellent source of information and provides 24-hour roadside assistance (☎ 803 116).

As everywhere else in Europe, petrol prices have gone through the roof in Italy. At the time of writing, a litre of *benzina senza piombo* (unleaded petrol) was selling for €1.17, *gasolio* (diesel) for a cent or two less.

DRIVING LICENCE

All EU driving licences are recognised in Italy. Holders of non-EU licences must get an International Driving Permit (IDP) to accompany their national licence.

HIRE

To hire a car in Italy you'll need a valid driving licence (plus IDP if required, see above). Age restrictions vary from agency to agency but generally you'll need to be 21 or over. Also, if you're under 25 you'll probably have to pay a young-driver's supplement on top of the usual rates.

Make sure you understand what is included in the price (unlimited kilometres, tax, insurance, collision damage waiver etc) and what your liabilities are. For the best rental rates, book your car before leaving home.

The most competitive multinational car-rental agencies:

Avis (☎ 06 452 10 83 91; www.avis.com)
Budget (☎ 283 438; http://ie.budgetinternational.com)
Europcar (☎ 199 30 70 30; www.europcar.com)
Hertz (☎ 199 11 22 11; www.hertz.com)
Italy by Car (☎ 091 639 31 20; www.italybycar.it)
Maggiore (☎ 199 151 120; www.maggiore.com)

You'll have no trouble hiring a scooter or motorcycle (provided you're over 18); there are rental agencies in all Italian cities. Rates start at about €20 a day for a 50cc scooter.

INSURANCE

If you're driving your own car, you'll need an international insurance certificate, known as a *Carta Verde* (Green Card), available from your insurance company.

ROAD RULES

In Italy drive on the right, overtake on the left and give way to cars coming from the right. It's obligatory to wear seat belts, to drive with your headlights on outside built-up areas, and to carry a warning triangle and fluorescent waistcoat in case of breakdown. Wearing a helmet is compulsory on all two-wheeled vehicles. The blood alcohol limit is 0.05%.

Speed limits, unless otherwise indicated, are 130km/h (in rain 110km/h) on *autostrade*; 110km/h (in rain 90km/h) on all main, non-urban roads; 90km/h on secondary, non-urban roads; and 50km/h in built-up areas. Speeding fines range from €36 to €1485.

Most major Italian cities, including Rome, Bologna, Florence, Milan and Turin, operate restricted traffic zones. You can enter these zones on a *motorino* (moped/scooter) or in a car with foreign registration but not in private or rental cars.

Train

Trenitalia (☎ 89 20 21; www.trenitalia.com) runs most train services in Italy. There are several types of train: local *regionale* or *interregionale* trains; faster InterCity (IC) services; Eurostar (ES) trains; and since December 2008, Eurostar Alta Velocità trains (ES AV). These high-speed services operate on the main line from Milan, via Bologna and Florence, to Rome and Naples. They have cut journey times considerably but are considerably more expensive than

InterCity trains. On train timetables high-speed trains are marked with the following symbols: ES AV (Eurostar Alta Velocità); ES AV Fast (the nonstop Rome–Milan trains) and ES Fast.

COSTS

Ticket prices depend on the type of train and class (1st class costs almost double 2nd class). Regional trains are cheaper than InterCity and Eurostar services, both of which require a supplement determined by the distance you travel. Eurostar ticket prices include a compulsory reservation fee. Generally, it's cheaper to buy all local train tickets in Italy – check for yourself on the Trenitalia website.

Unless otherwise stated, train prices quoted in this chapter are for an InterCity, one-way 2nd-class ticket.

Tickets must be validated – in the yellow machines at the entrance to platforms – before boarding trains.

Children under four years travel free, while kids between four and 12 years are entitled to discounts of between 30 and 50%.

For detailed information on using trains in Italy see www.seat61.com/Italy-trains.htm.

TRAIN PASSES

Available at all major train stations, the *Carta Verde* is available to anyone between 12 and 26. It costs €40 and is valid for a year, entitling holders to discounts of 10% on national trains and up to 25% on international trains. The *Carta d'Argento* (€30) is a similar pass for the over-60s, offering 15% reductions on national routes and 25% on international journeys.

Malta

Despite being made up of three small islands on the very southern edge of Europe, Malta veritably groans under the weight of its rich and tumultuous history, dramatic and unusual geography and fascinating cultural influences. As a melting pot of pan-Mediterranean culture, Malta merits far deeper exploration than is often given to it by the package crowds whose first priority is usually hitting the beach. Nothing wrong with that of course (and Malta boasts some of the loveliest stretches of sand in Europe), but don't get caught out thinking that sun and sand are all that the magical Maltese islands have to offer.

From its historic North African and Arabic influences (listen carefully to the local language) to the Sicilian-inspired cuisine on its menus and the oddly 1950s British feel to much of the place, Malta will almost certainly surprise you. And while there has certainly been an eclectic mix of influences and a roll call of rulers over the centuries, be in no doubt, Malta is not just a notional outpost of Italy or a relic of colonial Britain; this diminutive island nation has a quirky character all of its own.

Make sure you give plenty of time to historic Valletta with its grand churches and uniform honey-coloured limestone buildings, and the fascinating Three Cities and nearby Sliema for its restaurants and bars. The old capital Mdina is another must-see, with its exquisite walled city and delightful cathedral. Don't forget little Gozo either, the highlight of many a trip, where the pace of life is that much slower and development has been far more measured than on the 'mainland'.

FAST FACTS

- **Area** 316 sq km
- **Capital** Valletta
- **Currency** euro (€); US$1=€0.73; UK£1=€1.13; A$1=€0.56; ¥100=€0.76; NZ$1=€0.44
- **Famous for** prehistoric temples, the Knights of St John, WWII heroism, falcons of the local persuasion
- **Official languages** Maltese, English
- **Population** 410,000
- **Phrases** *merħba* (hello); *saħħa* (goodbye)
- **Telephone codes** country code ☎ 356; international access code ☎ 00
- **Visas** not required for visits up to three months by citizens of the EU, US, Canada, Australia and New Zealand

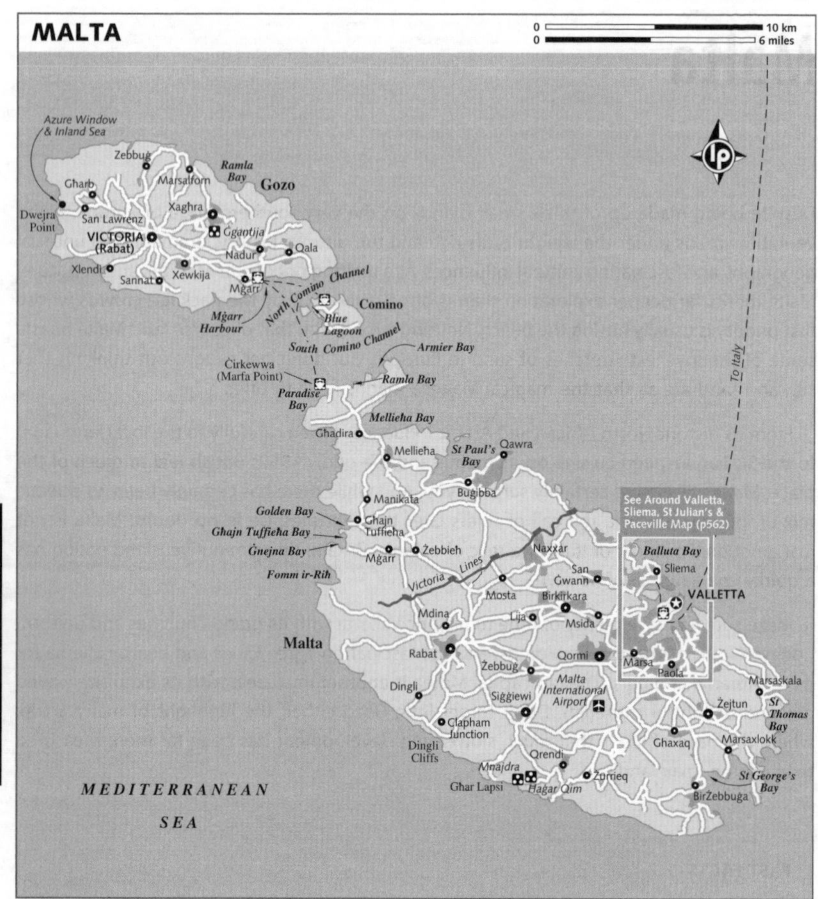

HIGHLIGHTS

- Absorb centuries of dramatic history, enjoy great food and savour the honeycomb-coloured stone architecture of delightful **Valletta** (p557).
- Soak up some sun at the beach – choose between **Golden Bay** (p566) and Gozo's **Ramla Bay** (p568), or snorkelling at Comino's **Blue Lagoon** (p569).
- Toast a town's patron saint at a **festa** (p571), amid an infectious mix of local music, food and fireworks.
- Step back in time in the silent streets of the graceful old capital, **Mdina** (p565).
- Bask in the charms of green, peaceful **Gozo** (p567), and perhaps even **dive** (p570) in its crystalline waters.

ITINERARIES

- **Three days** Start things off in Valletta to get an overview of the country – wander the streets and soak up some of the history. On your second day, head to the Hypogeum (you'll need to have booked in advance) before enjoying a meal of seafood in Marsaxlokk and the nightlife in Paceville. On the third day visit Mdina and Rabat, then escape to a beach in the northwest.
- **One week** As above, then on day four head for gorgeous Gozo. From here you can take a day trip to Comino, discover your own beaches and eat glorious food in Malta's least-discovered corner.

CLIMATE & WHEN TO GO

Malta is a year-round destination. Peak season is June to September, but it's best to avoid July and August, when it can get unbearably hot (35°C) and Malta is overrun with tourists. The ideal time to visit is in spring (April to June) and autumn (September and October). From October to May most hotels offer discounted rates (up to 50% below high-season prices). Winter weather is mild, but the Christmas and New Year period is busy, with room prices rising to peak-season rates. See p944 for climate charts.

HISTORY

Malta has a fascinating history and is crowded with physical and cultural reminders of its past. The mysterious megalithic temples built between 3600 BC and 2500 BC are the oldest surviving freestanding structures in the world, predating Egypt's Pyramids of Giza by more than 500 years. The best places to view them are on the south coast (p566) and at Xagħra (p568) on Gozo.

From around 800 BC to 218 BC, Malta was colonised by the Phoenicians and Carthaginians, and then became part of the Roman Empire. In AD 60, St Paul was shipwrecked on the island, where (according to folklore) he converted the islanders to Christianity.

Arabs from North Africa arrived in AD 870 and tolerated the local Christians. The Arabs were expelled in 1090 by the Norman king, Roger of Sicily. For the next 400 years, Malta's history was linked to Sicily, and its rulers were a succession of Normans, Angevins (French), Aragónese and Castilians (Spanish).

In 1530 the islands were given to the Knights of the Order of St John of Jerusalem by Charles V, Emperor of Spain; the local inhabitants were given no say in the matter. As soon as they arrived in Malta, the Knights began to fortify the harbour and to skirmish with Ottoman forces. In May 1565, a huge Ottoman fleet carrying more than 30,000 men laid siege to the island, but 700 knights and 8000 Maltese managed to hold them off. The Great Siege lasted for more than three months, with continuous and unbelievably ferocious fighting. After enormous bloodshed on both sides, help finally arrived from Sicily and the Turks withdrew.

The Knights were hailed as the saviours of Europe. Money and honours were heaped upon them by grateful monarchs, and the construction of the new city of Valletta and its enormous fortifications began. With fame and power came corruption, and the Knights sank into ostentatious ways, largely supported by piracy. In 1798 Napoleon arrived, seeking to counter the British influence in the Mediterranean, and the Knights, who were mostly French, surrendered to him without a fight.

The Maltese defeated the French in 1800 with British assistance, and in 1814 Malta officially became part of the British Empire. The British developed Malta into a major naval base, making it an inviting target for the Axis during WWII. Considered a linchpin in the battle for the Mediterranean, Malta was subjected to a German and Italian naval and aerial blockade between 1940 and 1943. In 1942 it suffered five months of day-and-night

HOW MUCH?

- **Room in guest house** €20 to €30 per person
- **Bus trip** €0.47-1.16
- **Cup of coffee** €1.50
- **Day hire of sun lounge** €3.50
- **One hour internet access** €2

LONELY PLANET INDEX

- **1L of petrol** €0.97
- **1L of bottled water** €1.25
- **Beer (Cisk)** €2
- **Souvenir T-shirt** €10
- **Street snack (pastizzi)** €0.25 to €0.40

CONNECTIONS: MOVING ON FROM MALTA

Malta is well connected to both Sicily and mainland Italy by sea (p572) and can be reached by an occasional ferry from Tunisia, too. Catamarans to Pozzallo and Catania in Sicily are the fastest and most frequent connection, while other services link Malta to Palermo, Genoa and Civitavecchia. The ferries from Tunis only operate *to* Malta; they then return to Genoa, making onward travel to Tunisia by sea impossible.

bombing raids, which left 40,000 homes destroyed and the population on the brink of starvation.

In 1947 the devastated island was given a measure of self-government. The country gained independence in 1964, and became a republic in 1974. In recent decades, the Maltese have achieved considerable prosperity, thanks largely to tourism. Every summer the Maltese population triples due to an influx of tourists, and development continues unabated, much to the detriment of the environment.

Malta became a member of the EU in May 2004, and adopted the euro as its national currency in 2008.

PEOPLE

Malta's population is around 410,000, with most people living in the satellite towns around Valletta, Sliema and the Grand Harbour. Approximately 31,000 live on Gozo, while Comino has a mere handful of farmers. More than 95% of the total population is Maltese-born.

Malta has long been an entry point for illegal immigration into Europe from Africa, but numbers have skyrocketed in recent years. This remains a divisive local issue and attitudes are very mixed within the country about how best to deal with the situation.

RELIGION

Despite an easy blend of Mediterranean and British culture throughout the islands, there's still a strong feeling of tradition. The Maltese are fairly conservative in outlook, with strong family values. Around 98% of the population is Roman Catholic, and the Church wields considerable influence – most noticeable on Sundays when many shops and businesses are closed. Abortion and divorce are illegal.

ARTS

Lacemaking is thought to have been introduced to Malta during the 16th century when the Knights arrived. There are plenty of stalls and shops selling traditional tablecloths and such things in more touristy areas. You should also keep an eye out for beautiful, intricate silver filigree – the art is thought to have come to Malta from Sicily in the 17th century. The Maltese glass-blowing industry has enjoyed increasing success and many pieces are now exported.

ENVIRONMENT

Environmental Issues

Malta's small surface area has been subjected to pressures of population, land use and development, a lack of protection for natural areas and, more recently, a significant increase in pollution. There is also a severe shortage of fresh water. Hunting and trapping of birds remains a (controversial) part of the Maltese way of life.

The Land

The Maltese archipelago consists of three inhabited islands: Malta (246 sq km), Gozo (67 sq km) and Comino (2.7 sq km). It lies in the middle of the Mediterranean, 93km south of Sicily, 288km east of Tunisia and 340km north of Libya.

The densely populated islands are formed of soft limestone, the golden building material used here in construction. There are some low ridges and outcrops, but no major hills. There are few trees and little greenery to soften the sun-bleached landscape; in turn, the sparse vegetation supports little in the way of wildlife. There is almost no surface water and no permanent creeks or rivers. The water table is the main source of fresh water, but it is supplemented by several desalination plants.

FOOD & DRINK

Like the Maltese language, local cuisine has been influenced by the many foreign cultures that have ruled the country. The food is rustic and meals are based on seasonal produce and the fisherman's catch.

Malta is not known as a gourmet destination, but the food is generally good and cheap, and at the top end can be excellent. Most restaurants offer inexpensive pizzas and pastas, and there are usually vegetarian options. The national dish is *fenek* (rabbit), and it can be fried in olive oil, roasted, stewed, served with spaghetti or baked in a pie. Be sure to try the locally caught fish and seafood.

Look out for *pastizzi*, a favourite local snack. These small parcels of flaky pastry are filled with ricotta cheese or mushy peas; you'll pay around €0.25 for one, so they're great for quick, budget snacks. A dish you're sure to encounter is *braġioli*, 'beef olives' prepared by wrapping a thin slice of beef around a stuffing of breadcrumbs, chopped bacon, egg and parsley, then braised in a red-wine sauce.

Local beers are good, particularly Cisk (pronounced 'chisk'), and the range of locally produced wine is surprisingly accomplished.

Most eateries are open from noon to 3pm and 7pm to 11pm Monday to Saturday; most are closed on Sundays. Outside of Valletta and its suburbs, however, be sure to get to a restaurant by 9.30pm at the latest as kitchens can close early.

Smoking is banned in all enclosed spaces, but is still allowed in closed-off, separately ventilated areas.

MALTA

VALLETTA

pop 6300

The Maltese capital is an absolute stunner. Whereas careless modern development has blighted much of the rest of Malta's coast, Valletta has retained its architectural unity and ancient charm. Built on a hilly peninsula jutting into the Mediterranean and thick with massive fortifications, Italianate churches and the city's trademark golden limestone buildings, Valletta makes a great base from which to explore the rest of the country and merits a couple of days' exploration in its own right. Commercial activity bustles around Triq ir-Repubblika and Triq il-Merkanti, but the quiet, narrow backstreets are where you'll get a feel for everyday life. The city overlooks the impressive Grand Harbour to the southeast and Marsamxett Harbour to the northwest.

Orientation

Valletta is a compact town barely 1km long and 600m wide, with a grid of narrow streets within the medieval fortifications. The main street, Triq ir-Repubblika (Republic St), runs northeast from City Gate (adjacent to City Gate bus terminus) to Fort St Elmo.

Information

Bank of Valletta (cnr Triq ir-Repubblika & Triq San Ġwann) Foreign-exchange machine and ATMs.

HSBC Bank (20 Triq ir-Repubblika) Foreign exchange and ATMs.

Police station (☎ 2122 5495; Triq Nofs in-Nhar)

Post office (Pjazza Kastilja; 🕑 8.15am-3.45pm Mon-Fri, to 12.30pm Sat)

Mater Dei (☎ 158; Tal-Qroqq, Birkirkara) This brand-new public hospital is located near the University of Malta.

Tourist office Valletta (☎ 2123 7747; Misraħ il-Ħelsien; 🕑 9am-7pm Mon-Sat, to 1pm Sun, closed public holidays); Malta International Airport (☎ 2369 6073; 🕑 10am-9pm) The branch in town is in the City Arcade on the right as you enter through City Gate

Ziffa (☎ 2122 4307; 194 Triq id-Dejqa; per hr €5; 🕑 9am-11pm Mon-Sat, 10am-4pm Sun) Internet access, wi-fi and good rates for international phone calls.

Sights & Activities

Valletta is an easy city to walk, and the views are spectacular. Be sure to stop at the **Upper Barrakka Gardens** in the southwest to take in the view that puts the grand in Grand Harbour. The **Lower Barrakka Gardens** further down the harbour also offer spectacular views.

St John's Co-Cathedral (☎ 2122 0526; Triq ir-Repubblika; admission incl Cathedral Museum adult/child/student €5.82/free/1.50; 🕑 9.30am-4.30pm Mon-Fri, to 12.30pm Sat, closed Sun, public holidays & during services), built in the 1570s, dominates the centre of town with its sombre exterior. Its baroque interior is breathtaking, though, and the floor is covered with colourful marble tombstones marking the resting place of knights and dignitaries. Side chapels built and maintained by different orders of the Knights of St John are all fascinating and well explained by the free audio tour. This is a so-called 'co-cathedral', as St Paul's

VALLETTA IN TWO DAYS

Get the day started with coffee and *pastizzi* (small pastries filled with ricotta cheese or mushy peas) at **Caffé Cordina** (p560), then gain some insight into the country by taking in the **Malta Experience** (p559). Spend a few hours wandering Valletta's historic streets, stopping to take in the views, especially from the **Upper Barrakka Gardens** (above) over Grand Harbour, from where there's a canon fired daily at noon. That evening, take in a show at **Manoel Theatre** (p559) or **St James' Cavalier Centre for Creativity** (p559). On day two, spend the morning marvelling at **St John's Co-Cathedral** (above), the **Grand Master's Palace** (p558) and the **National Museum of Archaeology** (p559), before taking a tour of the **Hypogeum** (p563). Finish with dinner at **Rubino** (p560).

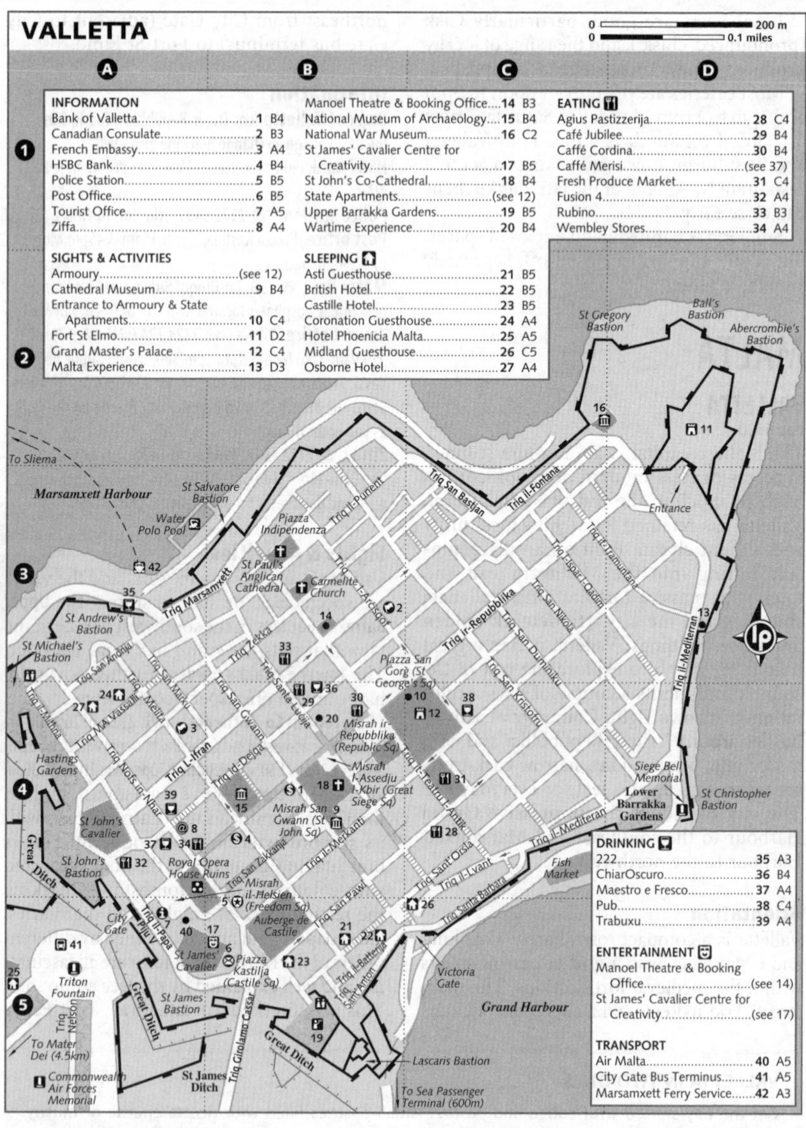

Cathedral (p565) in Mdina has historically been the seat of Malta's archbishop, but St John's was raised to equal level by a 1816 papal decree. Inside the cathedral is the entry to the **Cathedral Museum**, which houses two magnificent works by Caravaggio.

The 16th-century **Grand Master's Palace** (Pjazza San Ġorġ) is now the seat of the Maltese parliament. From the entrance on Triq il-Merkanti, it's possible to visit the **armoury** (☎ 2124 9349; adult/child/student €4.66/1.16/2.33; 🕓 10am-4pm Fri-Wed) and **State Apartments** (☎ 2124 9349; adult/child/student €4.66/2.33/1.16; 🕓 10am-4pm Fri-Wed). The corridors are lined with paintings by the Grand Masters, and there's an exquisite fresco depicting the Great Siege of 1565.

At the **National Museum of Archaeology** (☎ 2122 1623; Triq ir-Repubblika; adult/child/student €2.33/0.58/1.16; 9am-7pm) you can admire beautiful objects that have been found at Malta's prehistoric sites – check out the female figurines found at Ħaġar Qim, the so-called 'fat ladies'. Best of all is the *Sleeping Lady*, found at the Hypogeum (p563) and dating from around 3000 BC. There are free guided tours in English at 10am and 3pm daily

At the furthest point of Valletta is **Fort St Elmo**, built in 1552 by the Knights of the Order of St John. Its strategic location and design were vital to the island's defence. Today the fort is only open to the public for historical re-enactments, such as **In Guardia** (☎ 2369 6073; adult/child €4.66/1.16; late Sep-early Jul), a colourful military pageant in 16th-century costume held two to three times a month. Next to Fort St Elmo, the **National War Museum**, that commemorates Malta's heroic involvement in WWII, is currently undergoing a full refit.

The beautiful **Manoel Theatre** (☎ 2124 6389; www.teatrumanoel.com.mt; 115 Triq it-Teatru l-Antik; theatre tours €4; Mon-Sat), built in 1731, is one of the oldest theatres in Europe and functions as Malta's national theatre. There's a varied program of events from October to May (drama, concerts, opera and ballet), or you can take a guided tour (at least four daily) to see the restored baroque auditorium.

The St James' Cavalier has undergone transformation from a 16th-century fortification into the **St James' Cavalier Centre for Creativity** (☎ 2122 3200; www.sjcav.org; Triq Nofs in-Nhar), a bright, modern arts centre housing exhibition spaces, a theatre and a cinema. It's worth stopping to check out the interior and to grab a program of what's on.

Multimedia audiovisual experiences have sprung up all over Valletta, but some are better than others. The **Malta Experience** (☎ 2124 3776; www.themaltaexperience.com; Triq il-Mediterran; adult/under 14yr/student €9.50/4.50/6.50; screenings 11am, noon, 2pm, 3pm, 4pm Mon-Fri, 11am, noon, 1pm Sat & Sun) provides a good introduction to the country's history and culture in a number of languages; screenings are on the hour. The **Wartime Experience** (☎ 2122 2225; Embassy Cinema, Triq Santa Luċija; adult/child €5.50/3.50; 10am-1pm) is a poignant 45-minute film presentation depicting Malta's struggle against the odds during WWII; screenings are on the hour.

THE KNIGHTS OF WHO?

You'll encounter references to the Knights of the Order of St John all over Malta, so some background information is worth having. The Order of St John was founded during the Christian crusades of the 11th and 12th centuries to protect Christian pilgrims travelling to and from the Holy Land, and to care for the sick. The Knights were drawn from the younger male members of Europe's aristocratic families (those who were not the principal heirs). It was a religious order, with the Knights taking vows of celibacy, poverty and obedience, and handing over their patrimonies. The Order became extremely prestigious, wealthy and powerful as a military and maritime force, and as a charitable organisation that founded and operated several hospitals.

Sleeping

Valletta's hotel scene is not deeply exciting, and there's relatively little choice of places in the capital itself. One alternative is to rent an apartment, which can be done through **Valletta Studio Flats** (☎ 2123 6476; www.valletta-studioflats.org).

Coronation Guesthouse (☎ 2123 7652; 10E Triq M A Vasalli; B&B per person with shared bathroom €15) This friendly, family-run place comes complete with wonderfully old royal family paraphernalia. Of the 12 simple rooms, four have balconies with great Valletta views. All bathrooms are shared, save in the self-contained two-person flat, which can be booked out for €40 per night.

our pick Asti Guesthouse (☎ 2123 9506; http://mol.net.mt/asti; 18 Triq Sant'Orsla; B&B per person with shared bathroom €17) You'll get a taste of old-school Valletta charm here in a 350-year-old building converted into a guest house that offers the best-value accommodation in town. Asti has a charming host (though don't cross her!), simple, spacious rooms (each with hand basin), and spotless shared bathrooms. The bargain prices give little indication of the guest house's simple elegance – breakfast is served in a vaulted dining room under a chandelier.

Midland Guesthouse (☎ 2123 6024; 255 Triq Sant'Orsla; B&B per person with shared bathroom €20) Run by some rather stern Maltese matriarchs, this well-located place is spread over several floors of a large town house. The rooms are neat and pleasant – it's rather like staying at your grandmother's.

British Hotel (☎ 2122 4730; www.britishhotel.com; 40 Triq il-Batterija; s/d incl breakfast €40/60;) This 1970s time warp is a bit of a sleeper hit – rooms may be underwhelming and characterless, but the views, whether from rooms at the front of the building or from the bar, are utterly breathtaking. Skip the breakfast though.

Osborne Hotel (☎ 2123 2127/8; www.osbornehotel.com; 50 Triq Nofs in-Nhar; s/d €42/61;) The 59-room Osborne, once a hostel to the Knights of St John, has breathed some much-needed life into the Valletta hotel scene. The lobby is a gorgeous and classy affair stuffed full of antiques. Rooms are thoroughly modern and comfortable, but some on the lower floors suffer from being rather dark. There's free wi-fi in the lobby and a plunge pool (and great views) from the roof.

Castille Hotel (☎ 2124 3677/8; www.hotelcastillemalta.com; Pjazza Kastilja; s/d incl breakfast €50/100;) Enjoying a grand position in an old palazzo and with a lobby that feels far grander than you'd expect for a three-star hotel, the Castille is a great choice. Rooms have more character here than in most local hotels, and the three with balconies are very sought-after!

Hotel Phoenicia Malta (☎ 2122 5241; www.phoeniciamalta.com; The Mall, Floriana; r from €300;) This grand dame is actually just outside Valletta's city walls, but it's a short stroll from the town so can be considered a Valletta hotel. It certainly makes the most of its extra space – the walk from the hotel to the pool through the gorgeous gardens takes a good five minutes! The rooms, while comfortable, lack style, but the gorgeous bathrooms and marble floors throughout compensate somewhat. If you want to stay in a classic five star hotel, this is the place for you.

Eating

Agius Pastizzerija (273 Triq San Pawl; pastries from €0.20; 7.30am-5.30pm Mon-Sat) Search out this hole-in-the-wall place for traditional snacks, including *pastizzi* and other carb-loaded treats, at rock-bottom prices.

Caffé Merisi (☎ 2123 8027; 11 Triq Nofs in-Nhar; mains €3-8; 8am-8pm Mon-Tue, to 11pm Wed-Sun) Named after Caravaggio's real surname, this local stalwart has trendy touches, friendly staff and free wi-fi. Good coffee, full breakfasts and a range of light meals are all served here.

Café Jubilee (☎ 2125 2332; 125 Triq Santa Lučija; mains €4-8; 8am-1am) A feel-good place you can drop into anytime: for a breakfast of coffee and *pastizzi*, a lunchtime baguette, or a simple dinner of salad, pasta or risotto. Jubilee is a continental-style bistro, with low lighting, cosy nooks and poster-plastered walls. It is also one of the few places where you can eat and drink late in Valletta.

Caffé Cordina (☎ 2123 4385; 244 Triq ir-Repubblika; mains €4-10; breakfast & lunch) The prime location of this local institution makes it a great place for a coffee and cake while you watch the world go by, but do make sure you go inside and see the exquisitely painted vaulted ceiling. The food is passable but nothing special.

our pick **Rubino** (☎ 2122 4656; 53 Triq L-Ifran; mains €10-15; noon-2.30pm Mon-Fri, 7.45-10.30pm Tue & Thu-Sat) Hands down our favourite Valletta restaurant, charming, rustic Rubino is a great spot for lunch or dinner. The menu is verbal, changing daily, with modern takes on traditional Maltese cooking; the mixed starter selection (€8.95) is sublime.

Fusion 4 (☎ 2122 5255; cnr Triq Il-Papa Piju V & Triq San Ġwann Kavalier; mains €12-20; noon-3pm Mon-Fri, 7-11pm Tue-Sat) You need to look hard to find this sleek subterranean eatery, but it's well worth the effort. Its main room is under a vaulted ceiling and there's an innovative menu featuring dishes such as nori-wrapped salmon or pork fillet on a bed of red apples.

Fumia (☎ 2131 7053; Manoel Theatre, Triq it-Teatru l-Antik; mains €18-24) There are two eateries here: the charming Fumia Café in the Manoel Theatre's luminous courtyard, where light meals are served up all day and the highly stylish Fumia Restaurant in the basement, a refined, dark space housed in a vault and specialising in fish and seafood.

Wembley Stores (305 Triq ir-Repubblika; 7.15am-7pm Mon-Sat) stocks a selection of groceries and there's a **fresh produce market** (Triq il-Merkanti; 7am-1pm Mon-Sat) behind the Grand Master's Palace, where you can buy fruit and vegetables, fish, meat etc.

Drinking

Valletta is no party town – for real nightlife head to Paceville (p563). But for a pleasant and sophisticated evening look no further.

Trabuxu (☎ 2122 3036; 1 Triq id-Dejqa) Things don't come much simpler or much better than this cellar wine bar. Friendly staff are keen to introduce you to Malta's more accomplished wines, which are complemented by a menu of tasty local tapas, cheese and daily specials. Perfect.

Maestro e Fresco (☎ 2122 0357; 8/9 Triq Nofs in-Nhar) Another real charmer, this trendy space stuffed with white leather sofas and dark-wood floors is popular with a young after-work crowd.

222 (☎ 2733 3222; 222 Great Siege Rd) Holy design attack! This supercool lounge-bar could have been an abomination, built as it is into Valletta's defensive walls, but it's anything but. This cold blue tunnel of minimalism proves that not all Malta's choicest hangouts are across the bay in Sliena.

ChiarOscuro (☎ 2784 1056; 44 Triq id-Dejqa) A bistro, wine bar and nightclub offering edibles and DJ entertainment. Cover charge for the club varies.

Film buffs should raise a glass in memory of the late Oliver Reed who in 1999 slumped over and died, mid-drink at a Valletta bar simply named **Pub** (☎ 2123 7525; 136 Triq l-Arċisqof; 🕑 11.30am-11pm).

Entertainment

St James' Cavalier Centre for Creativity (☎ 2122 3200; www.sjcav.org; Triq Nofs in-Nhar) Modern arts centre housing exhibition spaces, a theatre for live performances and an art-house cinema. Pick up a program inside for the lowdown on what's showing.

Theatre lovers should check out what's on at the **Manoel Theatre** (p559), Valletta's most famous stage.

Getting There & Away

The City Gate bus terminus has services to all parts of the island (see p573). Bus 8 runs between the City Gate bus terminus and Malta's airport (€0.47) approximately every half-hour. On the return trip, the bus leaves from outside the departures hall. To do the airport–Valletta trip by taxi, arrange and pay at the designated booth in the arrivals hall.

The **Marsamxetto ferry service** (☎ 2346 3862) crosses frequently between Valletta and Sliema (€0.93, five minutes); boats operate from 8am to 6pm. Boats depart and arrive at the end of Triq San Marku. Ferries from Italy (p572) dock southwest of Valletta at the Sea Passenger Terminal, near Pinto Wharf; from here the set taxi fare is €10 to Valletta.

DIY CAPITAL BUS TOUR

Fancy a cheap, quick, DIY bus tour of the capital? Bus 98 is a circular route departing City Gate on the hour from 7am to 6pm. It does a clockwise loop around the bastions of Valletta and through Floriana, so you can take in harbour views, Fort St Elmo and the start of the new Valletta Waterfront area (encompassing Pinto Wharf). You'll see the periphery of the capital from the bus, but you'll need to 'fill in the gaps' on foot. A complete circuit takes around 15 to 20 minutes; the fare is all of €0.35.

AROUND VALLETTA

The Three Cities

You'll be awed by views of the **Three Cities** from Valletta's southern side, but make the effort to visit as well, as these ancient settlements are fast becoming Valletta's most interesting and vibrant neighbours, a world away from the commercialism of Sliema. The Three Cities are Vittoriosa, Senglea and Cospicua, and all three are crowded around Valletta's dockyards. Of the three, Vittoriosa has by far the most to offer visitors, so make this your priority.

Start with the excellent **Maritime Museum** (☎ 2166 0052; Vittoriosa Waterfront; adult/child €4.66/2.33; 🕑 9am-5pm) where Malta's naval history is gone over in great detail, from the Romans to the British; there is a free tour at 11am. From here wander down the newly renovated marina to **Fort St Angelo**, which takes up the end of the peninsula. It housed the Grand Master of the Knights of St John until 1571, and later served as headquarters of la Valette during the Great Siege. Sadly the fortress is not presently open to the public. Wandering back through Vittoriosa's backstreets, don't miss the fascinating **Inquisitor's Palace** (☎ 2182 7006; Triq il-Mina l-Kbira; adult/child €4.66/2.33; 🕑 9am-5pm), where the inquisition went about its brutal tortures (largely glossed over by the exhibits!) and home now to the **National Museum of Ethnography**. Note that a combined ticket for both the Maritime Museum and the Inquisitor's Palace costs €6.99.

There are also a selection of good eateries now open on the waterfront – try **Two and a Half Lemon** (☎ 2180 9909; Vault 5, Old Treasury Bldg, Vittoriosa Marina; mains €8-25; 🕑 lunch & dinner Mon-Sun), whose attractive waterside venue serves up unlikely culinary adventures such as rock-grilled

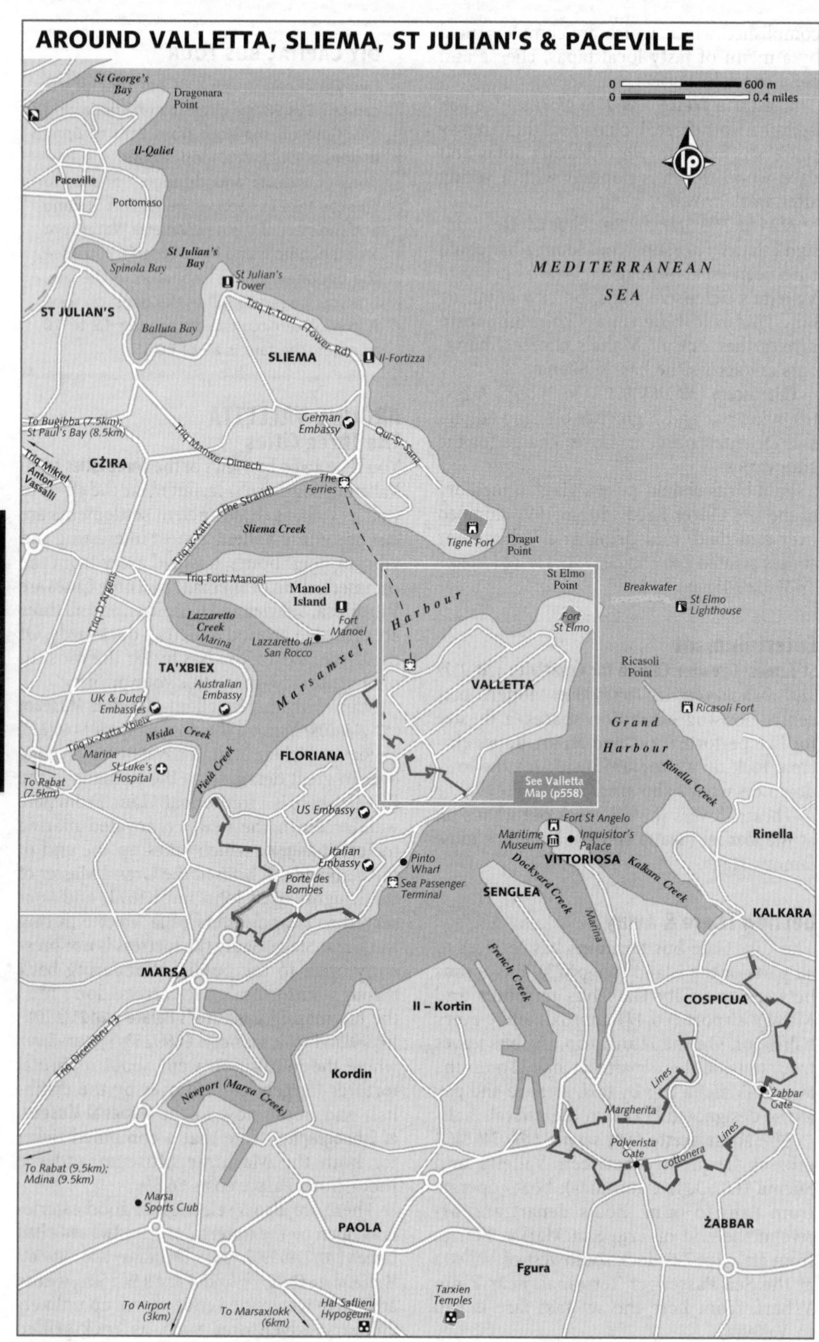
AROUND VALLETTA, SLIEMA, ST JULIAN'S & PACEVILLE
600 m
0.4 miles
St George's Bay
Dragonara Point
Il-Qaliet
Paceville
Portomaso
St Julian's Bay
Spinola Bay
St Julian's Tower
ST JULIAN'S
Balluta Bay
Triq it-Torri (Tower Rd)
SLIEMA
Il-Fortizza
MEDITERRANEAN SEA
To Bugibba (7.5km); St Paul's Bay (8.5km)
German Embassy
Qui-Si-Sana
Triq Manwel Dimech
GŻIRA
Triq Mikiel Anton Vassalli
The Ferries
Triq ix-Xatt (The Strand)
Sliema Creek
Tigné Fort
Dragut Point
Triq Forti Manoel
Triq D'Argens
Manoel Island
Fort Manoel
Lazzaretto Creek Marina
Lazzaretto di San Rocco
Marsamxett Harbour
St Elmo Point
Fort St Elmo
Breakwater
St Elmo Lighthouse
TA'XBIEX
Australian Embassy
UK & Dutch Embassies
VALLETTA
Ricasoli Point
Ricasoli Fort
Grand Harbour
Triq ix-Xatt ta Xbiex
Msida Creek
Marina
St Luke's Hospital
Pieta Creek
FLORIANA
See Valletta Map (p558)
Rinella Creek
To Rabat (7.5km)
US Embassy
Fort St Angelo
Maritime Museum
Inquisitor's Palace
Rinella
VITTORIOSA
Italian Embassy
Pinto Wharf
Sea Passenger Terminal
Porte des Bombes
SENGLEA
Dockyard Creek
Kalkara Creek
Marina
KALKARA
French Creek
MARSA
Il – Kortin
COSPICUA
Triq Dicembru 13
Kordin
Lines
Żabbar Gate
Margherita
Newport (Marsa Creek)
Polverista Gate
Cottonera
Lines
To Rabat (9.5km); Mdina (9.5km)
Marsa Sports Club
PAOLA
ŻABBAR
Fgura
Tarxien Temples
To Airport (3km)
To Marsaxlokk (6km)
Hal Saflieni Hypogeum

MALTA

kangaroo fillet with porcini dip. For something with a little bit more local flavour, head to Vittoriosa's main square, the delightful Misrah ir-Rebħa, where small and friendly local cafes serve up salads, sandwiches and fresh fish.

From Vittorisoa's waterfront there are water taxis that will take you across to Valletta for €4, or do a cruise of the harbour for €8 per person. Buses 1, 2, 4 and 6 from Valletta will take you to the bus stop on Triq 79 beneath the Poste d'Aragon (bus 2 continues to Misrah ir-Rebħa). One of these routes leaves Valletta every 15 to 20 minutes; the fare is €0.47.

Paola

The town of Paola, about 4km south of Valletta, is home to the magnificent **Hal Saflieni Hypogeum** (☎ 2180 5018/9; Triq iċ-Ċimiterju; adult/child €9.32/4.66; ⌚ tours hourly 9am-4pm), usually referred to simply as the Hypogeum. It's a complex of underground burial chambers thought to date from 3600 BC to 3000 BC. Excellent 50-minute tours of the complex are available, but the number of visitors has been restricted in order to preserve this fragile Unesco World Heritage site. Prebooking is therefore *essential* (usually a couple of weeks before you wish to visit); tickets are available in person from the Hypogeum and the National Museum of Archaeology in Valletta (p559), or online at www.heritagemalta.org. Note that kids under six are not permitted. If you have not booked ahead, fear not – every day 10 tickets go on sale at the National Museum of Archaeology for the noon tour the following day. These are sold on a first come, first served basis from 9am, and cost €20 each.

Half a dozen buses leaving from the Valetta bus station pass through Paola, including bus 1, 2, 3, 4, 6, 18, 19 and 27. Get off at the main square (Pjazza Paola); the Hypogeum is a five-minute signposted walk south.

SLIEMA, ST JULIAN'S & PACEVILLE

Valletta, while nominally Malta's capital, is something of a museum piece, with a small residential population. The nearby towns of Sliema, St Julian's and Paceville are where all the action is – and this is where Malta's younger population flocks to promenade, eat, drink, shop and play. As well as being a local playground for the cashed-up, it's where many tourists base themselves, among the growing number of high-rise hotels, apartment blocks, shops, restaurants, bars and nightclubs.

Information

MelitaNet (Triq Ball, Paceville; per hr €2; ⌚ 24hr) Large internet cafe inside Tropicana Hotel. Also offers good-value rates for international calls.

Post office Paceville (cnr Triq San Ġorġ & Triq Elija Zammit); Sliema (118 Triq Manwel Dimech)

White House (cnr Paceville Ave & Triq Schreiber, Paceville; per 75 min €2; ⌚ 7am-11pm) Fast internet access with lots of terminals.

Sights & Activities

There's not a lot to see in Sliema itself, but there are good views of Valletta from **Triq ix-Xatt** (the Strand), especially at dusk as the floodlights are switched on. Triq ix-Xatt and Triq it-Torri (Tower Rd) make for a pleasant waterfront stroll, with plenty of bars and cafes in which to quench a thirst. **Beaches** in the area are mostly shelves of bare rock, and clambering in and out of the sea can be a bit awkward. There are better facilities at the many private **lidos** along the coast, offering swimming pools, sun lounges, bars and water sports; admission costs around €5 to €7 per day.

Captain Morgan Cruises (☎ 2346 3333; www.captainmorgan.com.mt) operates from the waterfront area of Sliema known as The Ferries. The Captain has a boat trip for every traveller's taste and pocket – there's a popular tour of Grand Harbour (€15.75), or an all-day cruise around Malta and Comino (€39). Other options include day trips to the Blue Lagoon (p569), a sunset cruise, a sailing cruise on a catamaran or an 'underwater safari' in a glass-bottom boat. There are also popular 4WD jeep safaris (€54/60.50 to explore Malta/Gozo). Tickets can be purchased at any of the travel agencies on the waterfront.

Sleeping

NSTS Hibernia Residence & Hostel (☎ 2133 3859, 2133 5450; www.nsts.org; Triq Mons G Depiro, Sliema; dm €8, s/d €49/50; 💻) Malta's only hostel is perfect for those who are after quality budget accommodation. As well as the roll-call of facilities (laundry, kitchens, breakfast room/cafeteria, TV lounge, internet cafe and rooftop sun terrace), there are single-sex dorms, or twin studios with private bathroom and kitchenette. From Valletta, take bus 62, 64 or 67 to Balluta Bay and walk 300m up Triq Manwel Dimech; Triq Mons G Depiro is on the left. The hotel

MALTA

rents bikes for €13 per day. Low-season prices can be as low as €27/28 per single/double.

Hotel Valentina (☎ 2138 2232; www.hotelvalentina.com; Triq Schreiber; d incl breakfast €46-106;) Prices at split-personality Valentina are shockingly reasonable and the location is fab. There's a modern, progressive feel, but the rooms veer from handsome and rustic to those that are sleekly pared down and enlivened by splashes of colour. Rooms aren't huge, but then neither are the prices, and facilities include air-con and satellite TV. A bargain.

Hotel Juliani (☎ 2138 8000; www.hoteljuliani.com; 12 Triq San Ġorġ, Spinola Bay; r from €155;) Juliani scores points for introducing Malta to the boutique hotel concept. That it's superbly located in Spinola Bay, houses top-notch eateries and is heavily design driven means its overall satisfaction scoresheet is high. There's no beating the views from the gorgeous rooftop pool and terrace, all gleaming white tiles and glass.

Hilton Malta (☎ 2138 3383; www.malta.hilton.com; Portomaso, St Julian's; r from €175;) This luxury property sprawls around the side of the Portomaso Marina like a self-enclosed city. It's a great choice for combining the urban pursuits of St Julian's with the possibility of relaxing by the pool in a grand environment.

MALTA

Eating

While there are plenty of places cranking out so-so meals, you shouldn't need to look hard to find some gems. Fertile hunting grounds include Spinola Bay and the sleek Portomaso complex.

Gigi's Concept Café (☎ 2135 9865; 23 Triq San Ġorġ, Spinola Bay; mains €3-9) Gigi's concept is not that revolutionary, but it is mighty appealing: cafe by day, wine bar by night, then throw in some funky artwork, interesting decor and windows that open onto the street.

Avenue (☎ 2135 1753; Triq Gort, Paceville; mains €5-9; lunch Mon-Sat, dinner daily) Multicoloured and multiroomed, the Avenue is a quiet escape from Paceville's traffic with a huge pizza and pasta menu, Murano glass and Venetian masks as decor and tons of outdoor tables. With prices this decent it's no surprise that it's enormously popular.

Paparazzi (☎ 2137 4966; 159 Triq San Ġorġ, Spinola Bay; mains €8-12; 10am-midnight) The sunny terrace here is a prime people-watching spot, with a fine view of Spinola Bay. Fight your way through the huge portions on the cheeky, crowd-pleasing menu. Child- and veggie-friendly.

Hugo's Lounge (☎ 2138 2264; Triq San Ġorġ, Paceville; mains €10-15) This very cool, dark cocktail lounge and restaurant serves up well-executed Asian food ranging from sushi, Thai soups and curries to noodles and stir-fries. It's also a great spot for preclubbing cocktails in the alfresco area on Triq San Ġorġ, Paceville's party street.

our pick **Oliver's** (☎ 2138 0023; 19/21 Paceville Ave, Paceville; mains €14-21; 7-11pm Tue-Sun) This newcomer to Paceville's dining scene is a real boon. The classy, dark red interior and discreet service immediately set it apart from the crowd, though the real draw is the excellent food. Try the braised rabbit on tomato fondue, the sea bass with almond and pesto gnocchi or the red king prawns, egg noodles and leaks. Mmmmm.

Zeri's (☎ 2135 9559; Portomaso Marina, St Julian's; mains €18-20) In the otherwise rather sterile surrounds of the hyperchic Portomaso Marina, this new restaurant shines. It's not cheap, but the food is excellent: a wide-ranging, imaginative list of Italian dishes with a strong emphasis on fish and seafood.

Paranga (☎ 2376 5061; St George's Bay, St Julian's; mains €20) On a wooden deck built over the water's edge, this stylish spot overlooks the beach on St George's Bay. A great place to come for evening cocktails, it also has a large selection of seafood and pasta dishes.

Self-caterers should head to **Arkadia Foodstore** (Triq il-Knisja, Paceville; 8am-8pm Mon-Sat) or **Tower Foods Supermarket** (46 Triq il-Kbira, Sliema; 8am-7.30pm Mon-Sat).

Drinking & Entertainment

This area has a bar for everyone. The St Julian's and Sliema waterfronts have everything from chichi wine bars to traditional British pubs. Paceville is the place for partying, with wall-to-wall bars and clubs, especially around the northern end of Triq San Ġorġ. Paceville is jam-packed at the weekends year-round (nightly in summer), and all bars and clubs stay open until late – it's an in-your-face scene and won't appeal to many. Paranga, Gigi's and Hugo's Lounge (see above) are classier drinking venues without the noisy nightclub atmosphere. Listed are some of the more raucous destinations. Cover charges vary but we've noted those that have free admission.

BJ's (☎ 2137 7642; Triq Ball, Paceville) An offbeat club featuring live music nightly (primarily jazz) and drawing a more mature crowd than most of its neighbours.

Fuego (☎ 2138 6746; www.fuego.com.mt; Triq Santu Wistin, Paceville; admission free) Get hot and sweaty dancing up a storm at this popular salsa bar – head first to its free salsa-dancing classes (Mondays to Wednesdays from 8.30pm).

Havana Bar (☎ 2137 4500; www.havanamalta.com; Triq San Ġorġ, Paceville; admission free) Three dance floors, six bars and an eclectic range of music from retro '70s and '80s to soul and hip hop – this place has something for everyone.

Axis (☎ 2138 2767; www.axis.com.mt; Triq San Ġorġ, Paceville) Malta's biggest and best nightclub (and one that's managed to stand the test of time) houses three separate clubs (commercial house music is usually served up) and seven bars providing party space for more than 3000 punters. There's usually an entrance fee.

The friendly **Adam's Bar** (☎ 2138 4083; www.adamsmalta.com; Ross St, St Julian's) is Malta's much loved gay bar. It's off Triq San Ġorġ. Nearby is **Klozet** (☎ 7932 4333; www.klozetclub.com; Ball St, St Julian's), the island's only gay club.

Getting There & Away

Buses 62, 64 and 67 run regularly between Valletta and Sliema, St Julian's and Paceville (€0.47). The **Marsamxetto ferry service** (☎ 2346 3862) crosses frequently between Sliema and Valletta (€0.93, five minutes); boats operate from 8am to 6pm. Arrival and departure points are at the Strand in Sliema and at the end of Triq San Marku in Valletta.

MDINA & RABAT

Elegant, aristocratic Mdina, once the capital of Malta, is perched on a rocky outcrop in the southwest of Malta. It has been a fortified city for more than 3000 years and was the island's political centre before the Knights arrived and chose to settle around Grand Harbour. You can spend hours wandering around the quiet, narrow streets, and admiring the exquisite architectural detail. Despite the small honey pots of tourist bustle that have inevitably developed, the city has retained its historical charm. It's at its best of an evening, when the tour buses have gone and you can see just how the town got the nickname 'Silent City'.

The name Mdina comes from the Arabic for 'walled city'. Rabat (population 11,400) is the sprawling town settlement outside the walls to Mdina's south. It's not particularly picturesque, but it's full of religious sights including St Paul's Church and two sets of catacombs.

Sights

Mdina's main square is dominated by **St Paul's Cathedral** (Pjazza San Pawl; adult/student €2.50/1.75; 🕑 9.30-4.45pm Mon-Sat, 3-4.45pm Sun). It's not as impressive as St John's (p557) in Valletta, but it's still worth visiting to see the marble tombstones covering the floor and the huge fresco of St Paul's Shipwreck. The **Cathedral Museum** (☎ 2145 4697; Pjazza San Pawl; adult/student €2.50/1.75; 🕑 9.30am-4.30pm Mon-Fri, to 3.30pm Sat), opposite, is housed in a baroque 18th-century palace originally used as a seminary. It contains collections of coins, silver, vestments, manuscripts and religious paintings. Note that one ticket covers entry to both the cathedral and museum.

Also worth a visit within the town walls is the **Palazzo Falson** (☎ 2145 4516; Triq Villegaignon; adult/student €10/5; 🕑 10am-5pm Tue-Sun), a 13th-century gem and the second-oldest building in the walled city. The entire house is stuffed full of objets d'art, weapons, furniture and paintings.

Outside Mdina's Greek's Gate, **Domus Romana** (☎ 2145 4125; Wesgħa tal-Mużew; adult/child €5.82/2.91; 🕑 9am-5pm Mon-Sat) is a museum incorporating the excavated remains of a large Roman town house dating from the 1st century BC and featuring impressive mosaics.

From Domus Romana, head into Rabat by walking south along Triq San Pawl. Stop in to see **St Paul's Church** and **St Paul's Grotto** (Misraħ il Parroċċa; admission free, donations accepted; 🕑 10.30am-5pm Mon-Sat), a cave where St Paul is said to have preached during his stay on the island. Further south you'll come across **St Paul's Catacombs** (☎ 2145 4562; Triq Sant'Agata; adult/student & child €4.66/2.33; 🕑 9am-5pm), a series of rock-cut tombs thought to date back to the 3rd century. Entry includes an audioguide. More interesting are the nearby **St Agatha's Crypt & Catacombs** (☎ 2145 4503; Triq Sant'Agata; adult/child €2.50/0.50; 🕑 9am-6pm Mon-Fri, to 4pm Sat), an underground complex of burial chambers boasting some amazing Byzantine frescos. Wait by the entrance to the museum for the next guided tour.

Sleeping & Eating

our pick **Point de Vue Guesthouse & Restaurants** (☎ 2145 4117; www.pointdevuemalta.com; 5 Saqqajja, Rabat; B&B per person €35; 💻) This century-old

MALTA

12-room guest house is rightly popular thanks to a combination of affordable rates and its position just metres from Mdina's town walls. Downstairs from the large, spotless rooms (Room 4 is our favourite; it has great island views) are a cafe and restaurant with some unexpected African accents (management is South African–Maltese).

Fontanella Tea Gardens (☎ 2145 0204; Triq is-Sur, Mdina; mains €3-7; ⌚ 10am-6pm winter, to 11pm summer) This place does a roaring lunchtime trade, due largely to its great terrace views. With a dazzling array of cakes (€2.20 each) to accompany the sandwiches and pizza on the menu, it's a shame about the ordinary service.

Il Gattopardo (☎ 2145 1213; 20 Triq Villegaignon, Mdina; mains €8-10; ⌚ lunch & dinner Thu-Sat, lunch Mon-Wed Jun-Aug, lunch Mon-Sat Sep-May) The name (meaning 'The Leopard') may be Italian, but this art bistro set in a lovely old house with a shady courtyard serves up a Greek-inspired menu.

Bacchus (☎ 2145 4981; 1 Triq Iguanez, Mdina; mains €10-18) This rather hidden away restaurant is one of Mdina's very finest and makes for a great place to sample some imaginative Maltese-Italian cooking. The venue is gorgeous, set in a vault beneath the De Redin Bastion, and the service is very good.

MALTA

Getting There & Away

From Valletta, take bus 80 or 81 to reach Rabat (€0.54); from Sliema and St Julian's bus 65 (€1.16); from Buġibba bus 86 (€1.16). The bus terminus in Rabat is on Is-Saqqajja, 150m south of Mdina's Main Gate.

SOUTHWEST COAST

The views are fantastic from the top of **Dingli Cliffs**, south of Rabat. While you're here, stop by **Bobbyland Restaurant** (☎ 2145 2895; mains €9-17; ⌚ 6.30-11pm Tue-Sat, 10.30am-4pm Sun), a favourite weekend venue for locals. It's regularly crowded with diners munching contentedly on house specialities such as rabbit and lamb.

To the southeast, you'll find the village of **Qrendi** and the nearby prehistoric temples of **Ħaġar Qim & Mnajdra** (☎ 2142 4231; adult/child one temple €4.66/2.33, both temples €6.99/3.50; ⌚ 9am-5pm). Built between 3600 BC and 3000 BC, these are perhaps the best preserved and most evocative of Malta's prehistoric sites. At the time of writing a new EU-funded visitor centre was being built to better put these extraordinary ruins in context. Buses 38 and 138 run from Valletta to the temples (€1.16).

For a quick dip, call in to **Għar Lapsi**, a cove in the low cliffs that's a popular spot with locals for bathing and picnicking. If swimming has given you an appetite, there are two restaurants above the cove. No buses run to Għar Lapsi, so you'll need a car.

SOUTHEAST COAST

Marsaxlokk is a sprawling fishing village that's spread along the side of a photogenic harbour littered with colourful fishing boats. It's renowned for its seafood restaurants and can be a magnet for long-lunching locals and tourist busloads. When the buses are absent though, it's a charming place.

Duncan Guesthouse (☎ 2165 7212; http://duncanmalta.com; 33 Xatt is-Sajjieda; d from €42; 💻) is a family-run place offering decent-value rooms, each with bathroom and kitchenette. Minimum stay is four days, though, which will put many people off.

Of the numerous waterfront eateries here, locals trust **Ir-Rizzu** (☎ 2165 1569; Xatt is-Sajjieda; mains €10-20) for their fresh fish feasts, as well as nearby **Ix-Xlukkajr** (☎ 2165 2109; Xatt is-Sajjieda; mains €10-20) where rabbit, as well as fresh fish, is a speciality. For something totally different, try newly opened swanky **Southport** (☎ 2701 2600; www.southportmalta.com; Xatt is-Sajjieda), which contains no fewer than four restaurants, all catering to the smart set. The views from the upstairs terrace are gorgeous, and the whole place is great for a special occasion.

There are a few good swimming places on the eastern side of the nearby Delimara Peninsula, including the tricky-to-find **Peter's Pool**.

Bus 27 runs frequently from Valletta to Marsaxlokk (€0.47); bus 627 runs from Buġibba via Sliema to Marsaxlokk (€1.16).

NORTH COAST

The overdeveloped sprawl of **Buġibba** and **Qawra** in the northeast is the heartland of Malta's cheap-and-cheerful package-holiday trade, and it's absolutely mobbed in summer. It's crammed full of hotels, bars and restaurants – fine if you want a week or so of hedonism, but rather lacking in local charm. Buses 49 and 58 run frequently between Valletta and Buġibba (€0.47).

The north is also home to a handful of excellent beaches. Beach bums should make a beeline for **Mellieħa Bay** (also known as Għadira Bay), or **Golden Bay** if you like your facilities and water sports laid on thick. If you're after something more low-key, try **Għajn Tuffieħa Bay** or **Ġnejna Bay**.

For Mellieħa Bay, take bus 44 or 45 from Valletta (€0.58), bus 645 from Sliema/St Julian's (€1.16) and bus 48 from Buġibba (€1.16); for Golden Bay you'll need bus 47 from Valletta (€0.54), and bus 652 from Sliema/St Julian's and Buġibba (€1.16).

GOZO

Malta's little sister island has a charm all of its own. More relaxed, less populated and home to some stunning scenery, this tiny place should not be missed on any trip to Malta. Do yourself a favour and spend a few days here, as visiting on a day trip can't really do it justice.

Gozo is a favourite place for scuba diving (p570) and there are several dive operators around the island. You can also take a cruise from resorts such as Marsalforn and Xlendi; this is the best way to enjoy the breathtaking coastline, including the Azure Window and Inland Sea at Dwejra on the west coast.

VICTORIA (RABAT)

pop 16,600

Victoria, also known as Rabat, is the chief town on Gozo and sits in the centre of the island, 6km from the ferry terminal at Mġarr. Victoria's main attraction is the compact and photogenic Citadel, with its cathedral and museums. The town around it is where you'll find most shops and services on the island, and though pleasant enough, it's not usually a place visitors spend much time in.

Information

Aurora Opera House (Triq ir-Reppublika; per hr €2) Has computers for internet access in its foyer; purchase vouchers from the bar.

APS Bank (Triq ir-Repubblika)

Bank of Valletta (Triq ir-Repubblika)

Police station (☎ 2156 2040; Triq ir-Repubblika)

Post office (127 Triq ir-Repubblika; 🕑 8.15am-4.30pm Mon-Fri, to 12.30pm Sat)

Tourist office (☎ 2156 1419; Tigrija Palazz, cnr Triq ir-Repubblika & Triq Putirjal; 🕑 9am-5.30pm Mon-Sat, to 1pm Sun & public holidays) Inside a shopping arcade, near the bus station.

> **TOP 10 SWIMMING SPOTS**
>
> There are some great swimming spots scattered around Malta and Gozo, but don't expect to have them all to yourself in high season. The first six in this list are sandy beaches; the remainder offer rocky ledges for sunbathing. Take a snorkel along.
>
> - **Għajn Tuffieħa Bay** (left), North Coast
> - **Golden Bay** (opposite), North Coast
> - **Ramla Bay** (p568), Gozo
> - **Mellieħa Bay** (opposite), North Coast
> - **Ġnejna Bay** (left), North Coast
> - **Xlendi Bay** (p569), Gozo
> - **Għar Lapsi** (opposite), Southwest Coast
> - **Peter's Pool** (opposite), Southeast Coast
> - **Blue Lagoon** (p569), Comino

Sights

Pjazza Indipendenza, the main square of Victoria, is a hive of activity, with open-air cafes, treasure-trove craft shops and traders peddling fresh produce.

Victoria is built on a hill, crowned by the **Citadel** (also known as Il-Kastell, or Citadella), a miniature version of Malta's Mdina (p565). A stroll around the Citadel offers panoramic views of the island. The **Cathedral of the Assumption** (Misraħ il-Katidral; adult/child €3/free; 🕑 9am-5pm Mon-Sat) was built between 1697 and 1711. Its elegant design is marred only by the fact that funds ran out before completion and the structure remained flat-topped. This can't be detected from inside due to an elaborate trompe l'œil painted on the ceiling. Entry includes an audioguide (deposit required), and admission to the nearby cathedral museum, which displays church gold and religious art.

The handful of small **museums** inside the Citadel display reasonable collections, but if you're pushed for time, don't feel as though you've missed out – the museums in Valletta are better.

Eating

Make time to stop at the charming **Ta'Rikardu** (☎ 2155 5953; 4 Triq il-Fossos; 🕑 10am-6pm), where you can pick up souvenirs as well as local produce bursting with flavour. Enjoy a platter (€8.75 for two people) that includes cheese, bread,

MALTA

tomatoes, capers and olives, and wash it down with a glass of Gozitan wine – delicious.

Getting There & Away

See p573 for details of ferry services between Malta and Gozo. Bus 25 runs between Victoria and the ferry, timed with the ferry arrival and departure times.

Gozo's bus terminus is on Triq Putirjal, south off Triq ir-Repubblika and about 10 minutes' walk from the Citadel. All the island's bus routes are circular, starting and finishing at Victoria; the flat fare is €0.47.

MARSALFORN

Marsalforn is built around a cove and, with its good facilities, is the favoured choice for tourists in the summer months – it's particularly popular with divers. As with many towns in Malta, Marsalforn is a bit overdeveloped, but it still retains lots of friendly charm. At the head of the bay is a tiny scrap of sand; better swimming and sunbathing can be found on the rocks out to the west. Hike eastward over the hill to Ramla Bay in about 45 minutes.

our pick **Maria Giovanna Hostel** (☎ 2155 3630; www.tamariagozo.com/hostel.htm; 41 Triq ir-Rabat; s incl breakfast €20-40, d incl breakfast €40-60; 💻) is the pick of budget accommodation on Gozo. This small, extremely welcoming guest house just back from the waterfront retains a loyal clientele who come back again and again. There are now 15 rooms following recent renovations, each charmingly decorated and with beautiful new bathrooms. All rooms have balconies, with one exception, and guests are free to use the kitchen.

The incongruously large 100-room **Hotel Calypso** (☎ 2156 2000; www.hotelcalypsogozo.com; Triq il-Port; d €60-95; ❄ 💻 🏊) actually has quite a bit of style, though it's far from a Maltese experience. Rooms are modern, sleek and comfortable; avoid those on the second floor, as they don't have balconies.

The best eating option in town is **Il-Kartell** (☎ 2155 1965; Triq il-Port; mains €12), an upmarket waterfront fish restaurant with lots of interesting dishes including braised rabbit in red wine and a superb *aljotta* (fish soup). Another popular place that comes highly recommended by locals is **L'Aragosta** (☎ 2155 4104; Triq il-Port; mains €12), a small and unremarkable looking place on the seafront that does great fresh fish.

MALTA

SPLURGE

Ta'Frenc Restaurant (☎ 2155 3888; www.tafrencrestaurant.com; Triq ir-Rabat; mains €12-25; 🕒 closed Tue) For a memorable meal, this wonderful place about 1.5km south of Marsalforn en route to Victoria is widely considered to be Malta's top restaurant. Housed in a fabulous old farmhouse, the food served here is classic international but with a heavy focus on local ingredients and dishes. Don't miss the excellent rabbit ravioli. Bookings advised.

Marsalforn is a 4km walk from Victoria, or you can catch bus 21 (€0.47).

XAGHRA

The early-19th-century **Church of Our Lady of Victory** looks down on the village square of Xagħra, where old men sit and chat in the shade of the oleanders. Close by are the megalithic temples of **Ġgantija** (☎ 2155 3194; access from Triq L-Imqades; adult/student €3.49/1.75; 🕒 9am-5pm), which has a splendid view over most of southern Gozo and beyond. As the name implies (*ġgantija* means 'giantess'), locals traditionally believed that they had been constructed by giants. These are the largest of the megalithic temples found in the Maltese islands – the walls stand more than 6m high, and together the two temples are 40m wide – and they are believed to be the oldest freestanding structures in the world, built in three stages between 3600 and 3000 BC.

It's not far from here to one of Gozo's best beaches, **Ramla Bay**, which has a beautiful red-sand stretch perfect for sunbathing. Follow the signposts from town (bus 42 runs from Victoria to Ramla from July to September).

Xagħra Lodge (☎ 2156 2362; www.xaghralodge.com; Triq Dun Ġorġ Preċa; s/d incl breakfast €47/65; ❄ 🏊) is a friendly guest house with decent facilities, including air-con, bathroom, balcony and cable TV in all rooms, plus a swimming pool and an adjacent bar, and a vegetarian-friendly Chinese restaurant. It's a five-minute walk east of the town square. **Oleander** (☎ 2155 7230; Pjazza Vittorija; mains €10-16; 🕒 Tue-Sun) is a good place to try authentic Maltese cuisine – regulars rave about the rabbit dishes at this fixture on the pretty village square. The menu has an array of local favourites, including pastas, *bragioli*, fresh fish and fried rabbit in homemade red-wine sauce.

Buses 64 and 65 run between Victoria and Xagħra (€0.47).

XLENDI

Xlendi is a former fishing village situated on a deep, rocky inlet on the southwest coast. Development has turned the place into a popular resort town. Sure, it's busier now – but the bay is still beautiful. **San Antonio Guesthouse** (☎ 2156 3555; www.clubgozo.com.mt; Triq it-Torri; B&B per person €29-45;) has marvellously affordable rates that get you one of 13 rooms – surprisingly (given the price) air-con, cable TV, big private bathrooms and balconies/terraces are standard, and there's a very decent pool.

The pick of the bunch though is **St Patrick's Hotel** (☎ 2156 2951; www.vjborg.com/stpatricks; Xlendi Waterfront; B&B per person interior room/seaview €36/60;), which is located right in the centre of the town and has 65 attractive rooms. Sea views come at a premium, but are worth the price hike. For eating, try **Stone Crab** (☎ 2155 6400; Triq ix-Xatt; meals €4-15; lunch year-round, dinner Jun-Oct), a cheerful place right on the waterfront that serves up lots of seafood, local dishes and popular pizzas.

Bus 87 runs between Victoria and Xlendi (€0.47).

SAN LAWRENZ

This charming village is famous as the home of writer Nicholas Monsarrat (1910–79), whose novel *The Kappillan of Malta* is considered a classic of Maltese modern literature. The village today is home to the **Ta'Dbiegi Crafts Village** (10am-4pm), where artisans sell handicrafts, lace, glass and pottery. Beyond the crafts village is the **Kempinski Hotel San Lawrenz** (☎ 2211 0000; www.kempinski-gozo.com; Triq ir-Rokon; d from €128;), the island's very best. The sprawling complex has large, attractive rooms arranged around two large pools and looking out towards the fields around the village. The food and service are absolutely top-notch, although the hotel itself can feel somewhat sterile. For more of a local vibe, the village itself does not disappoint. You can enjoy a fantastic meal at charming **Tatitas Restaurant** (☎ 2156 6482; San Lawrenz Sq; mains €10-20; lunch & dinner March-Jul, Sep & Oct, dinner Aug), where you can dine alfresco in the square or enjoy the cosy interior. It has a great menu of modern takes on Maltese and Mediterranean classic cookery.

DWEJRA

From San Lawrenz it's a 1.5km walk or a short drive (buses are infrequent) to Dwejra, home of Gozo's most famous natural wonder, the Azure Window. Here geology and the sea have conspired to produce some of Gozo's most spectacular coastal scenery.

At this dramatic site two vast underground caverns in the limestone have collapsed to create two circular depressions now occupied by **Dwejra Bay** and the **Inland Sea**. The Inland Sea is a cliff-bound lagoon connected to the open sea by a tunnel that runs for 100m through the headland of Dwejra Point. The tunnel is big enough for small boats to sail through in calm weather and the Inland Sea has been used as a fisherman's haven for centuries. Today the fishermen supplement their income by taking tourists on boat trips (per person €3.50) through the cave.

A few minute's walk from the Inland Sea is the huge natural arch in the sea cliffs, known as the **Azure Window**. In the rocks in front of it is another geological freak called the **Blue Hole** – a vertical chimney in the limestone about 10m in diameter and 25m deep that connects with the open sea through an underwater arch about 8m down. Understandably, it's a very popular dive site, though the snorkelling is also excellent. Between the Inland Sea and the Azure Window is the little **Chapel of St Anne**, built in 1963 on the site of a much older church.

COMINO

The tiny island of Comino, smack bang between Malta and Gozo, was once reportedly the hideout of pirates and smugglers, but now hosts boatloads of sun-seeking, day-tripping invaders instead. The island's just 2.5km by 1.5km and has a permanent population of four, but the presence of a large hotel and an endless stream of summer visitors sadly will dampen your desert-island fantasies. The trick is to stay the night here.

The island's biggest attraction is the photogenic **Blue Lagoon**, a sheltered cove between the west end of the island and the uninhabited islet of Cominotto, with a white-sand sea bed and clear turquoise waters. The bay is usually inundated with people enjoying top-notch swimming and snorkelling. Take care in the shadeless summer heat; most sunbathing is done on the rocky ledges surrounding the cove. There are public toilets, deckchairs for hire, and kiosks selling drinks and snacks.

Comino Hotel (☎ 2152 9821; www.cominohotel.com; half-board per person €30-70; Apr-Oct;) is the only accommodation on the island. It offers bright, simply furnished rooms, a restaurant, cafe and bar, private beach, swimming pools and tennis courts. It also has bike rentals, dive instruction and assorted water sports.

The hotel runs its own ferry service, with crossings from Ċirkewwa in Malta and Mġarr in Gozo; nonguests can use the service, too (€8.15 return). Independent water taxis also operate regularly to the island from these two ports – from Mġarr is usually €7 return; from Ċirkewwa is €10 return. Day trips operate to the Blue Lagoon from tourist areas such as Sliema and Buġibba in Malta, and Xlendi and Marsalforn in Gozo.

MALTA

MALTA DIRECTORY

ACCOMMODATION

Accommodation is plentiful and the **Malta Tourism Authority** (www.visitmalta.com) can provide listings.

There is a handful of hostels and an array of family-run guest houses that usually represent great value for money. Hotels in Malta range from crumbling, characterful old town houses to modern palaces of five-star luxury. Rates are significantly reduced during off-peak periods. The high season is generally June to September, as well as the Christmas to New Year period.

Prices are quoted at high-season rates and include private bathroom unless otherwise stated.

Smoking is banned in all enclosed spaces, but is still allowed in closed-off, separately ventilated areas.

ACTIVITIES

The website of the **Malta Tourism Authority** (www.visitmalta.com) showcases activities available in Malta, and who can help you pursue them. Click the 'What to see & do' pages.

Diving conditions here are excellent: visibility often exceeds 30m and there's a variety of marine life. The Mediterranean's warm temperatures mean that diving is possible year-round. Favourite dive spots include Ċirkewwa on Malta, Dwejra on Gozo and various spots around Comino.

There are more than 40 diving schools to choose from. The majority are members of the **Professional Diving Schools Association** (PDSA; www.pdsa.org.mt). See also www.visitmalta.com/diving-malta for comprehensive details of dive sites, regulations and operators.

Most schools offer a half-day 'taster course' or beginner's dive costing around €35. A course that will give you an entry-level diving qualification (eg PADI Open Water Diver) should take three to five days and cost around €350. Experienced divers can hire equipment and arrange accompanied or unaccompanied dives with most operators.

Potential divers will need to answer a medical questionnaire and may be required to undergo a medical examination (dive centres will help arrange this). If you plan to dive, make sure your travel insurance covers this activity.

BUSINESS HOURS

The standard opening hours for banks are 8.30am to 12.30pm Monday to Friday and 8.30am to 11.30am Saturdays. There are slightly longer hours from June to September. Government museums open 9am to 5pm daily (last entry at 4.30pm) and are closed on major public holidays. Eateries open from noon to 3pm and 7pm to 11pm, while shops open from 9am to 1pm and 4pm to 7pm Monday to Saturday; they are closed Sundays and public holidays. Some shops stay open all day in summer, especially in tourist areas. Note that on Sundays the large majority of restaurants, cafes and shops are closed.

ELECTRICITY

Malta's electricity supply is 240V/50Hz and plugs have three flat pins as in the UK. Adaptors for Continental European appliances (plugs with two round pins) are widely available.

EMBASSIES & CONSULATES

Full lists of Maltese embassies abroad and foreign embassies in Malta can be found at www.foreign.gov.mt. Countries with representation in Malta:

Australia (Map p562; ☎ 2133 8201; Villa Fiorentina, Rampa Ta'Xbiex, Ta'Xbiex)
Canada (Map p558; ☎ 2552 3233; 103 Triq l-Arċisqof, Valletta)
France (Map p558; ☎ 2248 0600; www.ambafrance-mt.org; 130 Triq Melita, Valletta)
Germany (Map p562; ☎ 2133 6520; www.valletta.diplo.de; Il-Piazzetta, Entrance B, 1st fl, Triq it-Torri, Sliema)
Italy (Map p562; ☎ 2123 3157/8/9; www.amblavalletta.esteri.it; 5 Triq Vilhena, Floriana)
Netherlands (Map p562; ☎ 2131 3980; www.mfa.nl/val; Whitehall Mansions, Xatt Ta'Xbiex, Ta'Xbiex)
UK (Map p562; ☎ 2323 0000; www.ukinmalta.fco.gov.uk; Whitehall Mansions, Xatt Ta'Xbiex, Ta'Xbiex)
USA (Map p562; ☎ 2561 4000; http://valletta.usembassy.gov; 3rd fl, Development House, Triq Sant'Anna, Floriana)

FESTIVALS & EVENTS

Each village has a *festa* (feast day) honouring its patron saint, and you can't avoid getting caught up in the celebrations. Religious enthusiasm starts in the days leading up to and during the *festa* as families flock to the churches to give thanks. The streets are illuminated and the festivities culminate in a huge procession, complete with fireworks, marching brass bands and a life-sized statue of the patron saint. *Festa* season runs from May to September. But a *festa* isn't the only excuse to throw a party in Malta, and the website www.maltafestivals.com lists what's on, where and when (including links to *festa* dates and locations).

HOLIDAYS

New Year's Day 1 January
St Paul's Shipwreck 10 February
St Joseph's Day 19 March
Freedom Day 31 March
Good Friday March/April
Labour Day 1 May
Commemoration of 1919 Independence Riots 7 June
Feast of Sts Peter and Paul (L-Imnarja Festival) 29 June
Feast of the Assumption 15 August
Victory Day 8 September
Independence Day 21 September
Feast of the Immaculate Conception 8 December
Republic Day 13 December
Christmas Day 25 December

INTERNET ACCESS

Malta has numerous internet cafes and many hotels have a computer available for guests' use. More and more access is via wi-fi, usually free in well-run hotels, but sometimes still charged. Many computers belong to the **MelitaNet** (www.internetcafe.com.mt) or **Yellow Blue** (www.yellowblue.net) networks – if you purchase a voucher for one network, you receive a password allowing the voucher to be used at any of their computers throughout Malta. The websites for each network list computer locations.

INTERNET RESOURCES

About Malta (www.aboutmalta.com) Directory of Malta sites.
Gozo (www.gozo.com) Gozo-specific travel information.
Malta Tourism Authority (www.visitmalta.com) Huge official site.
Maltese Islands (www.malteseislands.com) Extensive travel information.
Search Malta (www.searchmalta.com) Directory of links to Malta-related websites.
StarWeb Malta (www.starwebmalta.com) Malta's 'first on-line concierge' with great listings.

MONEY

Malta adopted the euro in January 2008. To avoid stealth price hikes, the cost of all goods is legally required to be listed in Maltese lira as well as euros, hence the often bizarre prices for museum tickets, public transport and other state-run services.

Banks usually offer better rates of exchange than hotels. There's a 24-hour exchange bureau and ATMs at the airport, and a bank and ATMs at Pinto Wharf. ATMs can be found in almost all towns.

It's a good idea to round up a taxi fare or restaurant bill in order to leave a small tip. Shops have fixed prices; hotels and car-hire agencies offer reduced rates in the low and shoulder seasons (October to May).

TELEPHONE

Public telephones (mostly card-operated) are widely available; buy phonecards at kiosks, post offices and souvenir shops. International calls are discounted after 6pm weekdays and all day Saturday and Sunday. For local telephone inquiries, call ☎ 1182; for overseas inquiries, call ☎ 1152.

The international direct dialling code is ☎ 00. To call Malta from abroad, dial the international access code, ☎ 356 (the country code for Malta) and the eight-digit number (there are no area codes in Malta).

EMERGENCY NUMBERS

- Ambulance ☎ 112
- Fire ☎ 112
- Police ☎ 112

Most of the population have mobile phones; these numbers begin with either 79 or 99.

TOURIST INFORMATION

There are local tourist offices at Valletta (p557), Malta international airport and Victoria (p567) on Gozo.

VISAS

Visas are not needed for visits of up to three months by nationals of most Commonwealth countries (excluding South Africa, India and Pakistan), most European countries (excluding Russia), the USA and Japan. Full details of visa requirements (and visa application forms) are on the website of Malta's **Ministry of Foreign Affairs** (www.foreign.gov.mt).

TRANSPORT IN MALTA

GETTING THERE & AWAY

Air

Malta is well connected to Europe and North Africa. All flights arrive at and depart from **Malta international airport** (MLA; ☎ 2124 9600; www.maltairport.com) at Luqa, 8km south of Valletta. The modern airport has good facilities, including ATMs and currency exchange, a tourist office and a cheap bus service to/from Valletta.

The Maltese national airline is **Air Malta** (KM; Map p558; ☎ 2166 2211; www.airmalta.com; Misraħ-il-Ħelsien), with a good safety record. Other airlines flying to and from Malta include:

Aeroflot (SU; www.aeroflot.com)
Air Berlin (AB; www.germanwings.com)
Alitalia (AZ; ☎ 2123 7115; www.alitalia.com)
British Airways (BA; ☎ 2124 2233; www.ba.com)
easyJet (U2; www.easyjet.com)
Egyptair (MS; ☎ 2132 2256; www.egyptair.com.eg)
Emirates (EK; ☎ 2557 7255; www.emirates.com)
germanwings (4U; www.germanwings.com)
JAT Airways (JU; ☎ 2133 2814; www.jat.com)
KLM (KL; ☎ 2133 1010; www.klm.com)
Libyan Arab Airlines (LAA; ☎ 2122 2735)
Lufthansa (LH; ☎ 2125 2020; www.lufthansa.com)
Ryanair (FR; www.ryanair.com)
Swiss International Air Lines (LX; ☎ 2180 2777; www.swiss.com)

Sea

Malta has regular sea links with Sicily (Pozzallo and Catania), southern Italy (Reggio di Calabria and Salerno) and northern Italy (Genoa). You can also sail from Tunis to Malta (but, strangely, not from Malta direct to Tunis). Ferries dock at the Sea Passenger Terminal beside Pinto Wharf in Floriana, southwest of Valletta.

Virtu Ferries (www.virtuferries.com; ☎ Malta 2206 9022, Catania 095-535 711, Pozzallo 0932-954 062) offers the shortest, fastest Malta–Sicily crossing with its catamaran service to/from Pozzallo and Catania. The Pozzallo–Malta crossing takes only 90 minutes and operates year-round. High-season passenger fares one way/return cost €67/107.

Grimaldi Ferries (☎ 2122 6873; www.grimaldi-ferries.com) operates a weekly service year-round from Catania in Sicily as well as two other services from Genoa and Civitavecchia.

Grandi Navi Veloci (GNV; ☎ 2569 1600; www.gnv.it) operates a weekly Palermo–Malta service. GNV also offers a connection from Genoa to Malta via Tunis, which makes it possible to travel to Malta from Tunisia, but not vice versa. Check the website for details as departures are sporadic.

At the time of research, public transport links with the ferry terminal in Floriana were poor. With luggage, you'll probably need to catch a taxi to your destination – set fees are established (to Valletta costs €10, to Sliema/St Julian's costs €16.30).

Tours

There are loads of companies offering tours around the islands, by boat/bus/4WD or a combination of the three. Half-day tours cost from €25 but prices vary, so shop around. If you're pushed for time tours can be a good way to see the highlights, but itineraries can often be rushed, with little free time. Day trips to Gozo and Comino are also common.

Captain Morgan Cruises (☎ 2346 3333; www.captainmorgan.com.mt) runs a range of sailing trips, cruises and jeep safaris, primarily out of Sliema. See p563 for information on harbour tours.

GETTING AROUND

Boat

Gozo Channel Company (www.gozochannel.com; ☎ Ċirkewwa 2158 0435, Mġarr 2156 1622) runs regular car ferry services between Ċirkewwa (Malta) and Mġarr (Gozo), with crossings every 45 to 75 minutes from 6am to around 10pm (and every two hours throughout the night). The journey takes 25 minutes, and the return fare for an adult/child is €4.65/1.15; transporting a car (including driver) is €15.70. Bus 45 runs regularly from Valletta to Ċirkewwa to connect with the ferry to Gozo. Bus 25 runs between Victoria and Mġarr on Gozo.

There's also a ferry service between Valletta and Sliema (p563).

Bus

Malta and Gozo are served by a network of buses run by the **Malta Public Transport Association** (ATP; ☎ 2125 0007/8; www.atp.com.mt). Most of Malta's services originate from the chaotic City Gate terminus, just outside Valletta's city gates. The buses are bright yellow and many are relics of the 1950s – supremely stylish kings of the road that are a perennial favourite for postcard vendors. More modern (and less environmentally damaging) vehicles are slowly being introduced, much to many people's consternation.

Fares are inexpensive, but make sure you have small change for your ticket, which you purchase from the driver when boarding. Fares from Valletta cost €0.47 to €0.58; direct services between tourist areas that bypass Valletta (eg Sliema–Rabat/Mdina, Buġibba–Golden Bay) cost €1.16.

Services are regular and the more popular routes run until 11pm (with night buses operating to/from Paceville until 3am on weekends). Most services between any two points take between 30 minutes and an hour – Malta's not big enough for bus journeys longer than that, although traffic congestion has an impact. Ask at the tourist office or bus terminus for a free timetable.

On Gozo, the bus terminus is in Victoria, just south of Triq ir-Repubblika. All services (grey buses) depart from here and cost €0.47.

Car & Motorcycle

Considering the low rental rates it may make economic sense to hire a car, but beware that the Maltese have a driving style that can be politely described as 'after the Italian style'. Road rules are often ignored, roads are confusingly signposted and parking can be difficult. Distance isn't a problem, however, since Malta is so small and Gozo's half the size again. Outside urban areas, driving is a breeze, and your biggest problem will be potholed roads and getting lost due to lack of signposts.

All the major international car-hire companies are at the airport; there are also dozens of local agencies. Shop around – rates depend on season, length of rental period and the size and make of car. Daily rates for the smallest vehicles start from around €20 (for rental of seven days or longer). The age limit for rental drivers is generally 21 to 70, but drivers between 21 and 25 may be asked to pay a supplement.

The Maltese drive on the left. Speed limits are 80km/h on highways and 50km/h in urban areas, but they are rarely observed. The wearing of seat belts is compulsory for the driver and front-seat passenger. The maximum blood-alcohol concentration (BAC) level allowed in drivers is 0.08%.

Road conditions are invariably poor with lots of potholes and inadequate markings. There are no right-of-way rules at roundabouts and at intersections priority is given to whoever gets there first. Any accidents must be reported to the nearest police station (and to the rental company) – don't move your vehicle until the police have arrived.

Seaplane

Malta's only internal air service is the regular seaplane link between Valletta's waterfront and Gozo's Imgarr Harbour run by **Harbour Air** (☎ 2122 8302; www.harbourairmalta.com; adult one-way/return €42/83, child one-way/return €31/61). The flights run three times daily (early March to late November) in each direction, taking 20 minutes each way.

Taxi

Official Maltese taxis are white (with a taxi sign on top) and fitted with meters. Fares are generally expensive. If you arrive at the airport or port, there are kiosks where you pay the set tariffs upfront. Black taxis (no sign) are privately owned and usually offer cheaper rates than official taxis. To order a taxi by phone, ask at your hotel's reception or try **Wembley Motors** (☎ 2137 4141) for 24-hour service.

Montenegro
Црна Гора

Imagine a place with sapphire beaches as spectacular as Croatia's, rugged peaks as dramatic as Switzerland's, canyons nearly as deep as Colorado's, *palazzi* as elegant as Venice's and towns as old as Greece's and then wrap it up in a Mediterranean climate and squish it into an area two-thirds the size of Wales and you start to get a picture of Montenegro.

Going it alone is a brave move for a nation of this size – its entire population of 678,000 would barely fill a medium-sized city – but toughing it out is something these gutsy people have had plenty of experience in. Their national identity is built around resisting the Ottoman Empire for hundreds of years in a mountainous enclave much smaller than the current borders.

Given its natural assets, tourism is vitally important to Montenegro's future. In that respect it's done spectacularly well filling its tiny coast with Eastern European sunseekers for two months of each year, while serving up the rest of the country as bite-sized day trips. The upshot for intrepid travellers is that you can easily sidestep the hordes in the rugged mountains of Durmitor, the primeval forest of Biogradska Gora National Park or in the many towns and villages where ordinary Montenegrins go about their daily lives. This is, after all, a country where wolves and bears still lurk in forgotten corners.

Montenegro, Crna Gora, Black Mountain: the name itself conjures up romance and drama. There are plenty of both on offer as you explore this perfumed land, bathed in the scent of wild herbs, conifers and Mediterranean blossoms. Yes, it really is as magical as it sounds.

FAST FACTS

- **Area** 13,812 sq km
- **Capital** Podgorica
- **Currency** euro (€); US$1 = €0.73; UK£1 = €1.06; A$1 = €0.50; ¥100 = €0.76; NZ$1 = €0.41
- **Famous for** being really beautiful
- **Key phrases** *zdravo* (hello); *doviđenja* (goodbye); *hvala* (thanks)
- **Official language** Montenegrin
- **Population** 678,000
- **Telephone codes** ☎ 382; international access code ☎ 00
- **Visas** not required by Australian, British, Canadian, New Zealand, US or most EU citizens; see p599

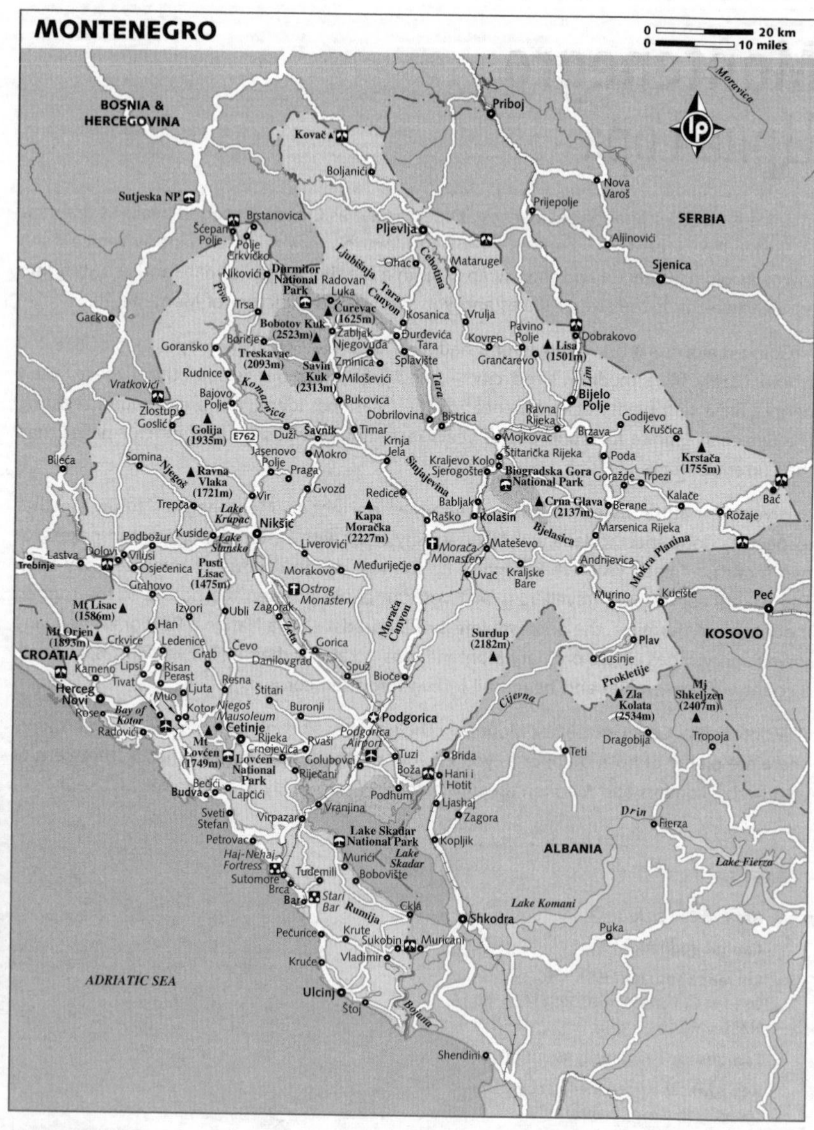

HIGHLIGHTS

- Marvel at the majesty of the **Bay of Kotor** (p581) and explore the historic towns hemmed in by the region's limestone cliffs.
- Drive the vertiginous route from Kotor to the Njegoš Mausoleum at the top of **Lovćen National Park** (p590).
- Enjoy the iconic island views while lazing on the uncrowded sands of **Sveti Stefan** (p587).
- Seek the spiritual at peaceful **Ostrog Monastery** (p595).
- Float through paradise, rafting between the kilometre-plus-high walls of the **Tara River** (p596).

HOW MUCH?

- **Bottle of Vranac (local red wine) from market** €2.50
- **Internet access** per hour €1
- **Cup of coffee** €1
- **Short taxi ride** €5
- **Postcard** €0.50

LONELY PLANET INDEX

- **1L petrol** €0.99
- **1L bottled water** €1
- **500mL beer** €1.50
- **Souvenir T-shirt** €12
- **Street snack (burek)** €1

ITINERARIES

- **One week** Base yourself in the Bay of Kotor for two nights. Drive through Lovćen to Cetinje, then the next day continue to Šćepan Polje via Ostrog Monastery. Go rafting the following morning and spend the night in Podgorica. Head to Virpazar for a boat tour of Lake Skadar and then take the scenic lakeside road to Ulcinj. Finish in Sveti Stefan.
- **Two weeks** Follow the itinerary above, but allow extra time in Kotor, Lake Skadar and Sveti Stefan. From Šćepan Polje head instead to Žabljak and then Biogradska Gora National Park before continuing to Podgorica.

CLIMATE & WHEN TO GO

Like most of the Mediterranean, the coast enjoys balmy summers and mild winters. The warmest months are July and August, when the temperature ranges from 19°C to 29°C (average lowest to average highest), while the coldest is January (4°C to 12°C).

You're best to avoid the height of the tourist season in July and August and aim instead for May, June, September and October. You'll still get plenty of sunshine and an average water temperature over 20°C. The ski season is roughly from December to March.

HISTORY

Before the Slavs

Historians record the Illyrians inhabiting the region by 1000 BC, establishing a loose federation of tribes across much of the Balkans. By around 400 BC the Greeks had established some coastal colonies and by AD 10 the Romans had absorbed the entire region into their empire. In 395 the Roman Empire was split into two halves, the Western half retaining Rome as capital, the Eastern half, which eventually became the Byzantine Empire, centred on Constantinople. Modern Montenegro lay on the fault line between the two entities.

In the early 7th century, the Slavs arrived from north of the Danube. Two main Slavic groups settled in the Balkans: the Croats along the Adriatic coast and the Serbs in the interior. With time most Serbs accepted the Orthodox faith, while the Croats accepted Catholicism.

First Kingdoms

In the 9th century the first Serb kingdom, Raška, arose near Novi Pazar (in modern Serbia) followed shortly by another Serb state, Duklja, which sprang up on the site of the Roman town of Doclea (present-day Podgorica). Initially allied with Byzantium, Duklja eventually shook off Byzantine influence and began to expand. Over time Duklja came to be known as Zeta, but from 1160 Raška again became the dominant Serb entity. At its greatest extent it reached from

MONTENEGRO

CONNECTIONS: MOVING ON FROM MONTENEGRO

Many travellers make the most of the proximity of Dubrovnik's Čilipi airport to Herceg Novi to tie in a visit to Croatia with a Montenegrin sojourn. At the other end of the coast, Ulcinj is the perfect primer for exploring Albania and is connected by bus to Shkodra. Likewise, Rožaje both captures elements of Kosovar culture and is well connected to Peć. A train line and frequent bus connections make a trip to Montenegro's closest cousins in Serbia a breeze. Montenegro shares a longer border with Bosnia and Hercegovina (BiH) than any of its neighbours. There are plenty of crossings for drivers, as well as regular bus services from towns.

Towns with onward international transport include Herceg Novi (p582), Kotor (p585), Bar (p589), Ulcinj (p590), and Podgorica (p594).

the Adriatic to the Aegean and north to the Danube.

Expansion was halted in 1389 at the battle of Kosovo Polje, where the Serbs were defeated by the Ottoman Turks. Thereafter the Turks swallowed up the Balkans and the Serb nobility fled to Zeta, on Lake Skadar. When they were forced out of Zeta by the Ottomans in 1480 they established a stronghold and built a monastery at Cetinje on the foothills of Mt Lovćen.

Montenegro & the Ottomans

This mountainous area became the last redoubt of Serbian Orthodox culture when all else fell to the Ottomans. It was during this time that the Venetians, who ruled Kotor, Budva and much of the Adriatic Coast, began calling Mt Lovćen the Monte Negro (Black Mountain) which lends its name to the modern state. Over time the Montenegrins established a reputation as fierce and fearsome warriors. The Ottomans opted for pragmatism, and largely left them to their own devices.

With the struggle against the Ottomans, the previously highly independent tribes began to work collaboratively by the 1600s. This further developed a sense of shared Montenegrin identity and the *vladika*, previously a metropolitan position within the Orthodox Church, began mediating between tribal chiefs. As such, the *vladika* assumed a political role, and *vladika* became a hereditary title: the prince-bishop.

While Serbia remained under Ottoman control, in the late 18th century the Montenegrins under *vladika* Petar I Petrović began to expand their territory, doubling it within the space of a little over 50 years.

A rebellion against Ottoman control broke out in Bosnia and Hercegovina (BiH) in 1875. Montenegrins joined the insurgency and made significant territorial gains as a result. At the Congress of Berlin in 1878 Montenegro and Bosnia officially achieved independence.

In the early years of the 20th century there were increasing calls for union with Serbia and rising political opposition to the ruling Petrović dynasty. The Serbian king Petar Karadjordjević attempted to overthrow King Nikola Petrović and Montenegrin-Serbian relations reached their historical low point.

The Balkans Wars of 1912–3 saw the Montenegrins joining the Serbs, Greeks and Bulgarians and succeeded in throwing the Ottomans out of southeastern Europe. Now that Serbia and Montenegro were both independent and finally shared a border, the idea of a Serbian-Montenegrin union gained more currency. King Nikola pragmatically supported the idea on the stipulation that both the Serbian and Montenegrin royal houses be retained.

The Two Yugoslavias

Before the union could be realised WWI intervened. The Serbs quickly entered the war and the Montenegrins followed in their footsteps. Austria-Hungary invaded Serbia shortly afterwards and swiftly captured Cetinje, sending King Nikola into exile in France. In 1918 the Serbian army reclaimed Montenegro, and the French, keen to implement the Serbian-Montenegrin union, refused to allow Nikola to leave France. The following year Montenegro was incorporated in the Kingdom of the Serbs, Croats and Slovenes, the First Yugoslavia.

Throughout the 1920s some Montenegrins put up spirited resistance to the union with Serbia. This resentment was increased by the abolition of the Montenegrin church, which was absorbed by the Serbian Orthodox Patriarchate.

During WWII the Italians occupied the Balkans. Tito's Partisans and the Serbian Chetniks engaged the Italians, sometimes lapsing into fighting each other. Ultimately, the Partisans put up the best fight and with the diplomatic and military support of the Allies, the Partisans entered Belgrade in October 1944 and Tito was made prime minister. Once the Communist federation of Yugoslavia was established, Tito decreed that Montenegro have full republic status and the border of the modern Montenegrin state was set. Of all the Yugoslav states, Montenegro had the highest per-capita membership of the Communist party and it was highly represented in the armed forces.

The Union & Independence

In the decades following Tito's death in 1980, Slobodan Milošević used the issue of Kosovo to whip up a nationalist storm in Serbia and ride to power on a wave of nationalism. The Montenegrins largely supported their Orthodox co-religionists. In 1991 Montenegrin paramilitary groups were responsible for the shelling of Dubrovnik and parts of the Dalmatian littoral. In 1992, by which point Slovenia, Croatia and BiH had opted for independence, the Montenegrins voted overwhelmingly in support of a plebiscite to remain in Yugoslavia with Serbia.

In 1997 Montenegrin leader Milo Djukanović broke with an increasingly isolated Milošević and immediately became the darling of the West. As the Serbian regime became an international pariah, the Montenegrins increasingly wanted to re-establish their distinct identity.

In 2000 Milošević lost the election in Serbia. Meanwhile Vojislav Koštunica came to power in Montenegro. With Milošević now toppled, Koštunica was pressured to vote for a Union of Serbia and Montenegro. In theory this union was based on equality between the two republics, however in practice Serbia was such a dominant partner that the union proved unfeasible from the outset. In May 2006 the Montenegrins voted for independence. Since then the divorce of Serbia and Montenegro has proceeded relatively smoothly. Montenegro has rapidly opened up to the West, in particular welcoming many holidaymakers, and has instituted economic, legal and environmental reforms with a view to becoming a member of the EU.

PEOPLE

In the last census (2003) 43% of the population identified as Montenegrin, 32% as Serb, 8% as Bosniak (with a further 4% identifying as Muslim), 5% as Albanian, 1% as Croat and 0.4% as Roma. Montenegrins are the majority along most of the coast and the centre of the country, while Albanians dominate in the southeast (around Ulcinj), Bosniaks in the far east (Rožaje and Plav), and Serbs in the north and Herceg Novi.

To get an idea of the population shifts caused by the recent wars you need only look at the changes since the 1981 census, when Montenegrins made up 69% of the population and Serbs only 3%.

RELIGION

Religion and ethnicity broadly go together in these parts. Over 74% of the population is Orthodox (mainly Montenegrins and Serbs), 18% Muslim (mainly Bosniaks and Albanians) and 4% Roman Catholic (mainly Albanians and Croats).

In 1993 the Montenegrin Orthodox Church (MOC) was formed, claiming to revive the autocephalous church of Montenegro's bishop-princes that was dissolved in 1920 following the formation of the Kingdom of Serbs, Croats and Slovenes in 1918. The Serbian Orthodox Church (SOC) doesn't recognise the MOC and still control most of the country's churches and monasteries.

ARTS

Montenegro's visual arts can be divided into two broad strands: religious iconography and Yugoslav-era painting and sculpture. The nation's churches are full of wonderful frescos and painted iconostases (the screen that separates the congregation from the sanctuary in Orthodox churches). Of the modern painters, an early great was Petar Lubarda (1907–1974), whose stylised oil paintings included themes from Montenegrin history.

Towering over Montenegrin literature is Petar II Petrović Njegoš (1813–51); towering so much, in fact, that his mausoleum overlooks the country from the top of the black mountain itself. This poet–prince-bishop, produced the country's most enduring work of literature *Gorski vijenac (The Mountain Wreath)*, a verse play romanticising the brutal struggle with the Ottomans.

Archbishop Jovan of Duklja was producing religious chants in the 10th century, making him the earliest known composer in the region. Traditional instruments include the flute and the one-stringed *gusle*, which is used to accompany epic poetry.

The unusual *oro* is a circle dance accompanied by the singing of the participants as they tease each other and take turns to enter the circle and perform a stylised eagle dance. For a dramatic conclusion, the strapping lads form a two-storey circle, standing on each other's shoulders.

ENVIRONMENT

The Land

Montenegro is comprised of a thin strip of Adriatic coast, a fertile plain around Podgorica and a whole lot of mountains. The highest peak is Kolac (2534m) in the Prokletije range near the Albanian border. Most of the mountains are limestone and karstic in nature and they shelter large swathes of forest and glacial lakes. Rivers such as the Tara, Piva and Morača have cut deep canyons through them.

The oddly shaped Bay of Kotor is technically a drowned river canyon although it's popularly described as a fjord. Lake Skadar, the largest in the Balkans, spans Montenegro and Albania in the southeast.

Wildlife

Among the mammals that live in Montenegro are otters, badgers, roe deer, chamois, foxes, weasels, moles, groundhogs and hares. Bears, wolves, lynxes and jackals are a much rarer sight. Tortoises, lizards and snakes are easier to find and you might spot golden and imperial eagles, white-headed vultures and peregrine falcons above the peaks. The rare Dalmatian pelican nests around Lake Skadar, along with pygmy cormorants, yellow heron and whiskered tern.

National Parks

Sometime during the lifetime of this book it's possible that Montenegro will declare a section of the Prokletije Mountains bordering Albania its fifth national park, joining Lovćen, Durmitor, Biogradska Gora and Lake Skadar. The current parks cover an area of 90,870 hectares.

Environmental Issues

For a new country, especially one recovering from a recent war, Montenegro has made some key moves to safeguard the environment, not the least declaring itself an 'ecological state' in its constitution. Yet in the rush to get bums on beaches, the preservation of the nation's greatest selling point sometimes plays second fiddle to development.

Water shortages continue to affect the coast and in 2008 high salinity levels rendered Tivat's supply undrinkable. A new desalination plant has been constructed near Budva but these operations are notoriously energy intensive.

The country currently imports 40% of its electricity and ideas mooted for increasing supply have included new hydro projects, requiring the flooding of river canyons, or potentially nuclear energy.

There's little awareness of litter as a problem. It's not just the ubiquitous practice of throwing rubbish out of car windows; we've seen waitresses clear tables by throwing refuge straight into a river and we've heard reports of train employees doing the same. Along the coast, fly-tipping of rubble from building sites is a problem. On an encouraging note, recycling is being trialled in Herceg Novi.

FOOD & DRINK

Loosen your belt, you're in for a treat. Eating in Montenegro is generally an extremely pleasurable experience. By default, most of the food is local, fresh and organic, and hence very seasonal. The only downside is a lack of variety. By the time you've been here a week, menu déjà vu is likely to have set in.

The food on the coast is virtually indistinguishable from Dalmatian cuisine: lots of grilled seafood, garlic, olive oil and Italian dishes. Inland it's much more meaty and Serbian-influenced.

Staples & Specialities

The village of Njeguši in the Montenegrin heartland is famous for its *pršut* (dried ham) and cheese. Anything with Njeguški in its name is going to be a true Montenegrin dish and stuffed with these goodies.

In the mountains, meat roasted *ispod sača* (under a metal lid covered with hot coals) comes out deliciously tender. Lamb is also slowly cooked in milk. You might eat it with *kačamak*, a cheesy, creamy cornmeal or buckwheat dish – heavy going but comforting on those long winter nights.

On the coast, be sure to try the fish soup, grilled squid (served plain or stuffed with *pršut* and cheese) and black risotto (made from squid ink). Whole fish are often presented to the table for you to choose from and are sold by the kilogram.

Montenegro's domestic wine is eminently drinkable and usually the cheapest thing on the menu. Vranac and Krstač are the indigenous red and white grapes, respectively. Nikšićko Pivo (try saying that after a few) is the local beer and a good thirst-quencher. Many people distil their own *rakija* (brandy), made out of just about anything (grapes, pears, apples etc). They all come out tasting like rocket fuel, although the plum variety *(šljivovica)* is the most lethal.

The coffee is universally excellent. In private houses it's generally served Turkish-style, 'black as hell, strong as death and sweet as love'.

Where to Eat & Drink

Fast-food outlets and bakeries *(pekara)*, serving *burek* (meat- or spinach-filled pastries),

MONTENEGRO

pizza slices and *palačinke* (pancakes), are easy to find. Anywhere that attracts tourists will have a selection of restaurants and *konoba* (small family-run affairs). There is generally no distinction between a cafe and bar. Restaurants open at around 8am and close around midnight, while cafe-bars may stay open until 2am or 3am.

Nonsmoking sections are a rumour from distant lands that have yet to trouble the citizens of Montenegro.

Vegetarians & Vegans

Eating in Montenegro can be a trial for vegetarians and almost impossible for vegans. Pasta, pizza and salad are the best options.

Habits & Customs

Lunch has traditionally been the main family meal but with Western working hours catching on, this is changing. Bread is served free of charge with most meals.

BAY OF KOTOR

Coming from Croatia, the Bay of Kotor (Boka Kotorska) starts simply enough, but as you progress through fold upon fold of the bay and the surrounding mountains get steeper and steeper, the beauty meter gets close to bursting. It's often described as Southern Europe's most spectacular fjord and even though the label's not technically correct, the sentiment certainly is.

HERCEG NOVI ХЕРЦЕГ НОВИ

☎ 031 / pop 12,700

It's easy to drive straight through Herceg Novi without noticing anything worth stopping for, especially if you've just come from Croatia with visions of Dubrovnik still dazzling your brain. However, just below the uninspiring roadside frontage hides an appealing Old Town with ancient walls, sunny squares and a lively atmosphere. The water's cleaner here near the mouth of the bay, so the pebbly beaches and concrete swimming terraces are popular.

> **BAY OF KOTOR IN TWO DAYS**
>
> Drive around the Bay, stopping where the mood takes you. Start with breakfast in **Herceg Novi** (above), check out the mosaics in **Risan** (p583) and allow plenty of time to visit **Perast** (p583) and its islands. Stop for the night near **Kotor** (p583) and spend the next day exploring the **Stari Grad** (p583).

Information

There's a cluster of banks with ATMs around Trg Nikola Đurkovića, while the main street Njegoševa has the post office and an internet cafe. The **tourist office** (☎ 350 820; www.hercegnovi.travel; Jova Dabovica 12; 🕑 8am-3pm Mon-Fri) is on the 1st floor above a house.

Sights

The big fort visible from the main road is the **Kanli-Kula** (Bloody Tower; admission €1; 🕑 8am-midnight), a notorious prison during Turkish rule (roughly 1482–1687). You can walk around its sturdy walls and enjoy views over the town. The bastion at the town's seaward edge, **Fortemare**, was rebuilt by the Venetians during their 110-year stint as overlords.

The elegant crenulated **clocktower**, built in 1667, was once the main city gate. Just inside the walls is Trg Herceg Stjepana (commonly called Belavista Sq), a gleaming white piazza that's perfect for relaxing, drinking and chatting in the shade. At its centre is the Orthodox **Archangel Michael's Church** (built 1883–1905), its lovely proportions capped by a dome and flanked by palm trees. Its Catholic counterpart, **St Jerome's** (1856), is further down the hill, dominating Trg Mića Pavlovića.

From its hillside location in the town's eastern fringes, **Savina Monastery** (☎ 345 300; Manastirska 21; 🕑 6am-8pm) enjoys wonderful coastal views. This peaceful complex is dominated by the elegant 18th-century Church of the Dormition, carved from pinkish stone. Inside there's a beautiful gilded iconostasis but you'll need to be demurely dressed to enter (no shorts, singlets or bikinis). The smaller church beside it has the same name but is considerably older (possibly from the 14th century) and has the remains of frescos. The monastery is well signposted from the highway.

Apart from the building itself (a fab bougainvillea-shrouded baroque palace with absolute sea views), the highlight of the **Regional Museum** (☎ 322 485; www.rastko.org.yu/rastko-bo/muzej; Mirka Komnenovića 9; admission €1.50; 🕑 9am-6pm Mon-Sat winter, 9am-8pm Tue-Sun summer) is its impressive icon gallery.

High above the town, on the other side of the main road, is the **Španjola fortress**, which was started and finished by the Turks but named after the Spanish (yep, in 1538 they had a brief stint here as well). If the graffiti and empty bottles are anything to go by, it's now regularly invaded by local teenagers.

Activities

Herceg Novi is shaping up as the best base for arranging active pursuits, largely due to a network of expats running professional, customer-focused, environmentally-aware businesses. A good place to start is **Black Mountain** (☎ 321 968; www.montenegroholiday.com; Šetalište Pet Danica 41), an agency that can arrange pretty much anything, including diving, rafting, hiking and paragliding. They offer mountain bike tours (about €20 per person), rent out bikes (€15 per day) and have a second office at the bus station.

Another excellent outfit run by British expats, **Kayak Montenegro** (☎ 067-887 436; www.kayakmontenegro.com; Šetalište Pet Danica bb; hire 1-/4-/8-hr €5/15/25) rents kayaks and offers paddling tours across the bay (€45, including equipment), as well as day trips to explore Lake Skadar from Rijeka Crnojevića (price on application). In October they work with Black Mountain to stage the **Adventure Race Montenegro** (p598).

From May to September **Diving Center Marina** (☎ 069-637 915; www.dcmarina.com) organises dives to about 20 sites in the vicinity of the bay and Budva, including various wrecks and caves. A two-dive trip costs €55 including tanks, weights and the boat trip.

Yachting Club 32 (☎ 069-333 011; Šetalište Pet Danica) offers parasailing (single/double €40/60 per 10 minutes) and hires jet skis (€50 per 20 minutes), paddleboats (per hour €8) and mountain bikes (hour/three hours/day €3/6/15).

Sleeping

In summer there are often people around the bus station touting private accommodation. Black Mountain (above) can fix you up with rooms starting from around €15 per person, although most of their apartments are at a higher level.

Hotel Perla (☎ 345 700; www.perla.cg.yu; Šetalište Pet Danica 98; s €61-104, d €76-130, tr €111-189, apt €140-210; ❄) It's a fair stroll from the centre but if it's beach you're after, Perla's possie is perfect. The helpful staff speak excellent English and the front rooms of this medium-sized modern block have private terraces and sea views.

our pick **Hotel Aurora** (☎ 321 620; www.auroramontenegro.com; Šetalište Pet Danica 42; tw €70-100, d €80-100, tr €105-120; ❄) You'd never suspect that this handsome stone building was once the railway station, especially given its prime waterfront location at the foot of the Old Town. Oscar-nominated filmmaker Emir Kusturica was behind its loving transformation into a chic and comfortable eight-room boutique hotel, hence the three tiny cinemas of the Aurora Artplex (admission €3) on the ground floor.

Eating & Drinking

If you want to take on the local women in a tussle for the best fresh fruit and vegetables, get to the **market** (Trg Nikole Đurkovića) by around 8am.

Konoba Hercegovina (☎ 322 800; Trg Nikole Đurkovića; mains €2-6) A firm favourite with the locals, this all-year-long eatery serves everything from burgers and *ćevapčići* to traditional meat and fish grills and more-exotic dishes like Hungarian goulash.

our pick **Portofino** (Trg Herceg Stjepana; breakfast €2.50-5, mains €6-16) Its blissful location in Herceg Novi's prettiest square makes it tempting to linger here all day, which is exactly what the town's expat community seems to do. The Italianate menu features creamy pastas and juicy steaks.

Konoba Feral (Šetalište Pet Danica 47; mains €7.50-15) Feral is a local word for a ship's lantern, so it's seafood (not wild cat) that takes pride of place on the menu. The grilled squid is amazing and comes with a massive serving of seasonal vegetables and salads.

Getting There & Around

BUS

At the time of research the **bus station** (☎ 321 225; Jadranska Put; 🕑 6am-9pm) was on the main highway above the centre, but there were plans to move international services to the western approach to town. Hopefully through-services will continue to stop at the old station. There are frequent buses to Kotor (€3.50, one hour), Budva (€5, 1¾ hours) and Podgorica (€9, three hours).

From Herceg Novi there are buses to Dubrovnik (€8, two hours, two daily), Sarajevo (€22, seven hours, four daily) and Belgrade (€30, 13 hours, nine daily).

CAR

A tortuous, often grid-locked, one-way system runs through the town, so you're best to park on the highway. If you're driving to Tivat or Budva it's usually quicker to take the **ferry** (car/motorcycle/passenger €4/1.50/free; 24hr) from Kamenari (15km northeast of Herceg Novi) to Lepetane (north of Tivat). Queues can be horrendously long in summer.

Budget (☎ 321 100; www.budget.com; Njegoševa 90) Rents cars from €68 for one day. If you need a taxi, call **Taxi More** (☎ 9730).

BOAT

Taxi boats ply the coast during summer, charging about €10 for a trip to the beaches on the Luštica Peninsula.

PERAST ПЕРАСТ

Looking like a chunk of Venice has floated down the Adriatic and anchored itself onto the bay, Perast's streets hum with melancholy memories of the days when it was rich and powerful. This tiny town boasts 16 churches and 17 formerly grand *palazzi*, one of which has been converted into **Perast Museum** (☎ 373 519; admission €2.50; 9am-6pm Mon-Sat, to 2pm Sun) and showcases the town's proud seafaring history.

The 55m belltower belongs to **St Nicholas' Church**, which also has a **museum** (admission €1; 10am-6pm) containing bits of saints and beautifully embroidered vestments.

Just offshore are two peculiarly picturesque islands. The smaller **Sv Đorđe** (St George's Island) rises from a natural reef and houses a Benedictine monastery shaded by cypresses. Its big sister, **Gospa od Škrpjela** (Our-Lady-of-the-Rock Island), was artificially created in the 15th century and every year on 22 July the locals row over with stones to continue the task. Its magnificent church was erected in 1630. Boats regularly ply to the islands for around €3.

Perast makes an atmospheric and peaceful base from which to explore the bay. Several houses rent rooms or you can try the **Hotel Conte** (☎ 032-373 687; www.hotel-conte.com; apt €90-250;), a series of delux studio to two-bedroom sea-view apartments in historic buildings scattered around St Nicholas' Church. It has wi-fi and its wonderful restaurant, **Conte Nautilus** (mains €6.50-14), serves fresh fish with lashings of romance on its waterside terrace.

Not far from Perast, **Risan** is the oldest town on the bay, dating to at least the 3rd century BC. Signposts point to some superb **Roman mosaics** (admission €2; 8am-8pm 15 May-15 Oct), discovered in 1930.

KOTOR КОТОР

☎ 032 / pop 13,500

Those prone to operatic outbursts may find themselves launching into Wagner at their first glimpse of this dramatically beautiful town. Its sturdy walls – started in the 9th century and tweaked until the 18th – arch steeply up the slopes behind it. From a distance they're barely discernable from the mountain's grey hide but at night they're spectacularly lit, reflecting in the water to give the town a golden halo. Within those walls lie labyrinthine marbled lanes, where churches, shops, bars and restaurants surprise you on hidden piazzas.

Orientation

Kotor's funnel-shaped Stari Grad (Old Town) sits between the bay and the lower slopes of Mt Lovćen. Newer suburbs surround the town, linking up to the old settlements of Dobrota to the north, Muo to the west and, beyond this, Prčanj. The main road to Tivat and Budva turns off the waterfront road at a baffling uncontrolled intersection south of the Stari Grad and heads through a long tunnel.

Information

You'll find a choice of banks with ATMs, an internet cafe called **Forza** (☎ 304 352; Trg od Oružja; 7am-midnight), and the post office on the main square, Trg od Oružja. There's a **tourist information booth** (☎ 325 950; www.kotor.travel; outside Vrata od Mora; 8am-8pm) just outside the main gate

Sights

The best thing to do in Kotor is to get lost and found again in the maze of streets. You'll

FREE THRILLS

Many of Montenegro's most memorable experiences can be had for free:

- Wander the marbled lanes of **Kotor's Stari Grad** (above).
- Take the **back road** (p585) from Kotor to Lovćen.
- Enjoy the iconic view of **Sveti Stefan** (p587) from the highway.
- Call into either of the Centre for Contemporary Art's two **Podgorica galleries** (p593).
- Visit **Ostrog Monastery** (p595).

soon know every corner, as the town is quite small, but there's plenty of old churches to pop into and many coffees to be drunk in the shady squares.

Stepping through the main entrance, **Vrata od Mora** (Sea Gate, 1555), onto Trg od Oružja (Square of Arms) you'll see the strange stone pyramid in front of the **clock tower** (1602) that was once used as a pillory to shame wayward citizens.

Kotor has a proud history as a naval power and the **Maritime Museum** (☎ 069-045 447; Trg Bokeljske Mornarice, Stari Grad; admission €4 incl audioguide; 🕒 8am-11pm Jul-Aug, 8am-7pm Mon-Sat & 9am-1pm Sun Apr-Jun & Sep, 8am-2pm Mon-Sat & 9am-1pm Sun Oct-Mar) celebrates it with three storeys of displays housed in a wonderful early 18th-century palace.

The town's most impressive building is the Catholic **St Tryphon Cathedral** (Trg Sv Tripuna, Stari Grad; admission €1.50; 🕒 8.30am-7pm), originally built in the 12th century but reconstructed after several earthquakes. The Cathedral's gently hued interior is a masterpiece of Romanesque-Gothic architecture, with slender Corinthian columns alternating with pillars of pink stone, thrusting upwards to support a series of vaulted roofs. Its gilded silver-relief altar screen is considered Kotor's most valuable treasure.

The energetic can make the 1200m ascent via 1350 steps up the **fortifications** (admission €2, charged May to Sep) for unforgettable views and a huge sense of achievement. There are entry points near the North Gate and Trg od Salata.

Sleeping

Although the Stari Grad is a charming place to stay, you'd better pack earplugs. In summer the bars blast music onto the streets until 1am every night and rubbish collectors clank around at 6am. Some of the best options are just out of Kotor in quieter Dobrota, Muo and Prčanj.

Enquire about private accommodation at the city's information booth (p583). **Meridian Travel Agency** (☎ 323 448; www.tameridian.cg.yu; 🕒 9am-3pm & 6-9pm Mon- Sat), near Trg od Oružja, in the lane behind the clock tower, has rooms on their books at around €15 to €30 per person and can also book hotels.

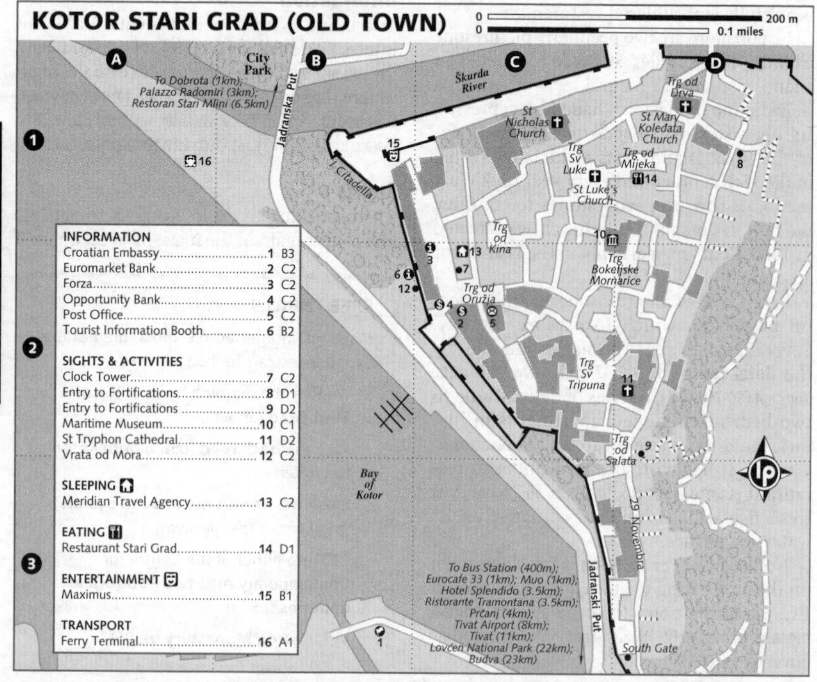

DETOUR: BACK ROAD TO MT LOVĆEN

Looming above Kotor is **Mt Lovćen**. The journey to this ancient core of the country is one of the world's great drives. Take the road heading towards the Tivat tunnel and turn right just past the graveyard (there's no sign). After 5km, follow the sign to Cetinje on your left opposite the fort. From here there's 17km of good but narrow road snaking up 25 hairpin turns, each one revealing a vista more spectacular than the last. Take your time and keep your wits about you; you'll need to pull over and be prepared to reverse if you meet oncoming traffic. From the top the views stretch over the entire bay to the Adriatic. At the entrance to Lovćen National Park you can continue straight ahead for the shortest route to Cetinje or turn right and continue on the scenic route through the park.

Eurocafe 33 (☎ 069-047 712; lemaja1@cg.yu; Muo 33; r €20-25 per person;) On the Muo waterfront, this traditional stone building with a small private beach enjoys possibly the best views of Kotor. The top two floors have a scattering of differently configured rooms, some of which share bathrooms. The owner's an ex-footballer turned assistant coach for the national side and speaks excellent English. If there are a few of you enquire about booking a floor.

our pick **Palazzo Radomiri** (☎ 333 172; www.palazzoradomiri.com; Dobrota; s €60-160, d €100-200, ste €60-280;) Exquisitely beautiful, this honey-coloured early 18th-century *palazzo* has been transformed into a first-rate boutique hotel. Some rooms are bigger and grander than others (hence the variation in prices), but all 10 have sea views and luxurious furnishings. Guests can avail themselves of a small workout area, sauna, pool, private jetty, bar and restaurant; half-board is included in the summer prices and wi-fi is available.

Hotel Splendido (☎ 301 700; www.splendido-hotel.com; Prčanj; s €65-116, d €93-166, apt €119-199;) Negotiating the 4km drive along the narrow waterfront road from Kotor can be stressful, but aside from that Splendido is magnifico. Completely gutted and fitted with comfortable modern rooms, this large stone *palazzo* still surveys the bay as solidly as it's ever done, although there's now a blissful terrace and swimming pool separating it from the water's edge. Wi-fi is available.

Eating & Drinking

There are tons of small bakeries and takeaway joints on the streets of Kotor.

This town is full of cafe-bars that spill into the squares and are abuzz with conversation during the day. All chitchat stops abruptly in the evening, when speakers are dragged out onto the ancient lanes and the techno cranked up to near ear-bleeding volumes.

our pick **Ristorante Tramontana** (☎ 301 700; Prčanj; mains €4-16) It's hard to top the romantic setting of this Italian restaurant on the terrace of the Hotel Splendido. The food is equally memorable, from sublime pasta to perfectly tender grilled squid.

Restaurant Stari Grad (☎ 322 025; Trg od Mlijeka; mains €8-18) Head straight through to the stone-walled courtyard, grab a seat under the vines and prepare to get absolutely stuffed full of fabulous food – the serves are huge. Either point out the fish that takes your fancy or order from the traditional à la carte menu.

Restoran Stari Mlini (☎ 333 555; Jadranska Put, Ljuta; meals €11-21) It's well worth making the 7km trip to Ljuta for this magical restaurant set in and around an old mill by the edge of the bay. If you've got time to spare and don't mind picking out bones, order the Dalmatian fish stew with polenta for two. The steaks are also excellent, as are the bread, wine and service.

Entertainment

Maximus (☎ 334 342; admission €2-5; 11pm-5am Thu-Sat, nightly summer) Montenegro's most pumping club comes into its own in summer, hosting big name international DJs and local starlets.

Getting There & Away

The **bus station** (☎ 325 809, 6am-9pm) is to the south of town, just off the road leading to the Tivat tunnel. Buses to Herceg Novi (€3.50, one hour), Budva (€3, 40 minutes) and Podgorica (€7, two hours) are at least hourly.

A taxi to Tivat airport costs around €8.

Azzurra Lines (www.azzurraline.com) ferries connect Kotor and Bar with Bari, Italy (€65, nine hours, weekly in summer).

TIVAT ТИВАТ

☎ 032 / pop 9,450

Big things are planned for this town, which is not a bad thing, as Tivat doesn't have a lot to lose from development. At present it's the airport that's the drawcard, although there are a lot of sweet villages and beaches to explore on the coast between here and Kotor and on the Luštica Peninsula. The helpful **tourist office** (☎ 671 324; www.tivat.travel; Palih Boraca 8; 8am-3pm Mon-Sat, to 2pm Sun) can point you in the direction of some terrific walks.

If you've got an early flight, the **Hotel Villa Royal** (☎ 675 310; www.hotelvillaroyal.cg.yu; Kalimanj bb; s €42-65, d €68-102, apt €102-141;) is a bright modern block with clean rooms and friendly staff.

From the **bus station** (Palih Boraca bb) there are frequent buses to Budva (€2) via the airport (€0.50), as well as services to Kotor (€1, six daily) and Herceg Novi (€3, seven daily).

Tivat Airport is 3km south of town and 8km through the tunnel from Kotor. Airport minibuses leave when full and head to Budva (€3.50) and Herceg Novi (€8).

ADRIATIC COAST

Much of Montenegro's determination to reinvent itself as a tourist mecca has focused on this gorgeous stretch of beaches. In July and August it seems that the entire Serbian world and a fair chunk of its Orthodox brethren can be found crammed onto this less-than-100km-long stretch of coast. Avoid these months and you'll find a charismatic set of small towns and fishing villages to explore, set against clear Adriatic waters and Montenegro's mountainous backdrop.

BUDVA БУДВА

☎ 033 / pop 10,100

The poster child of Montenegrin tourism, Budva – with its atmospheric Old Town and numerous beaches – certainly has a lot to offer. Yet the child has quickly moved into a difficult adolescence, fuelled by rampant development that has leeched much of the charm from the place. In the height of the season the sands are blanketed with package holidaymakers from Russia and the Ukraine, while by night you'll run the gauntlet of glorified strippers attempting to cajole you into the beachside bars.

It's the buzziest place on the coast so if you're in the mood to party, bodacious Budva will be your best buddy.

Orientation & Information

Apart from the Old Town, hardly any streets have names and even fewer have signs. The main beachside promenade is pedestrianised Slovenska Obala, which in summer is lined with fast-food outlets, beach bars, travel agencies hawking tours, internet cafes and a fun park. The post office and a cluster of banks are on and around ulica Mediteranska. The **tourist office** (☎ 452 750; Njegoševa bb, Stari Grad; 9am-9pm May-Oct) has brochures on sights and accommodation.

Sights & Activities

Budva's best feature and star attraction is the Stari Grad – a mini Dubrovnik with marbled streets and Venetian walls rising from the clear waters below. Much of it was ruined in two earthquakes in 1979 but it has since been completely rebuilt and now houses more shops, bars and restaurants than residences. At its seaward end, the **Citadel** (admission €2; 8am-midnight May-Nov) offers striking views, a small museum and a library full of rare tomes and maps. In the square in front of the citadel are a cluster of interesting churches. Nearby is the **entry to the town walls** (admission €1; 9am-5pm Mon-Sat).

The **Archaeological Museum** (☎ 453 308; Petra I Petrovića 11, Stari Grad; adult/child €2/1; 9am-10pm) shows off the town's ancient and complicated history – dating back to at least 500 BC – over three floors of exhibits. Also in the Old Town is the **Museum of Modern Art** (☎ 451 343; Cara Dušana 19; admission free; 8am-2pm & 5-8pm), an attractive gallery staging temporary exhibitions.

The **Montenegro Adventure Centre** (☎ 067-580 664; www.montenegrofly.com; Lapčići) offers plenty of action from its perch high above Budva. Rafting, hiking, mountain biking, diving and accommodation can all be arranged, as well as paragliding from launch sites around the country. An unforgettable tandem flight landing 750m below at Bečići beach costs €65.

Sleeping & Eating

The tourist office (above) produces an excellent hotel directory and private accommodation booklet.

Hotel Kangaroo (☎ 458 653; www.kangaroo.cg.yu; Velji Vinogradi bb; s €29-69, d €39-69, tr €59-104;)

Bounce into a large clean room with a desk, terrace and excellent bathroom at this mid-sized hotel that's a hop, skip and jump from the beach and has wi-fi. The owners once lived in Perth, hence the name and the large mural of Captain Cook's *Endeavour* in the popular restaurant below.

Hotel Astoria (☎ 451 110; www.hotelastoria.cg.yu; Njegoševa 4; s €130-190, d €170-230, ste €180-380;) Water shimmers down the corridor wall as you enter this chic boutique hotel hidden in the Old Town's fortifications. The rooms are on the small side but they're beautifully furnished; the seaview suite is spectacular. The wonderful guest-only roof terrace is Budva's most magnificent dining area.

Knez Konoba (Mitrov Ljubiše bb; mains €9-15) Hidden within Stari Grad's tiny lanes this atmospheric eatery only sports two outdoor tables and a handful inside. Try the black risotto – it's more expensive than most (€10) but they present it beautifully, with slices of lemon and orange, along with tomato, cucumber and olives.

Getting There & Away

The **bus station** (☎ 456 000; Ivana Milutinovića bb) has regular services to Herceg Novi (€5, 1¾ hours), Kotor (€3, 40 minutes) and Cetinje (€3, 40 minutes). **Meridian Rentacar** (☎ 454 105; www.meridian-rentacar.com; Mediteranski Sportski Centar) is opposite the bus station.

You can flag down the Olimpia Express (€1.50) from the bus stops on Jadranska Put to head to Bečići (five minutes) or Sveti Stefan (20 minutes). They depart every 30 minutes in summer and hourly in winter.

SVETI STEFAN СВЕТИ СТЕФАН

☎ 033

Impossibly picturesque Sveti Stefan, 5km south of Budva, provides the biggest 'wow' moment on the entire coast. From the 15th century to the 1950s this tiny island – connected to the shore by a narrow isthmus and crammed full of terracotta-roofed dwellings – housed a simple fishing community. That was until someone had the idea to nationalise it and turn it into a luxury hotel. Until the wars of the 1990s it was a big hit with both Hollywood and European royalty.

Over the last few years tradesmen have replaced screen goddesses on its exclusive streets, but the resort will reopen during the lifetime of this book. When it does, it's likely that a day rate will once again be charged for mere mortals to wander around. In the meantime, make the most of the lovely beaches facing the island while they're comparatively uncrowded.

Sveti Stefan is also the name of the new township that's sprung up onshore. From its slopes you get to look down at that iconic view all day – which some might suggest is even better than staying in the surreal enclave below.

From the beach there's a very pleasant walk north to the cute village of **Pržno** where there are some excellent restaurants and another attractive beach.

Sleeping & Eating

Levantin Travel Agency (☎ 468 206; www.geocities.com/levantin88/levantin; Vukice Mitrović 3) Not only does the charming, helpful owner bear a striking likeness to Michael Palin in the *Life of Brian*, he can sort you out with private accommodation, apartments and other travel arrangements.

our pick **Vila Drago** (☎ 468 477; www.viladrago.com; Slobode 32; d €34-68, tr €58-100, apt €103-170;) The only problem with this place is that you may never want to leave your terrace, as the views are so sublime. The supercomfy pillows and fully stocked bathrooms are a nice touch, especially at this price. Watch the sunset over the island from the grapevine-covered terrace restaurant (mains €4 to €11) and enjoy specialities from the local Paštrovići clan, like roast suckling pig (€15 per kilogram).

Getting There & Away

Olimpia Express buses head to and from Budva (€1.50, 20 minutes) every 30 minutes in summer and hourly in winter, stopping on Ulica Slobode near the Vila Drago.

PETROVAC ПЕТРОВАЦ

☎ 033

The Romans had the right idea, building their summer villas on this lovely bay. The pretty beachside promenade is perfumed with the scent of lush Mediterranean plants and a picturesque 16th-century **Venetian fortress** guards a tiny stone harbour. This is one of the best places on the coast for families: the accommodation is reasonably priced, the water's clear and kids roam the esplanade at night with impunity.

In July and August you'll be lucky to find an inch of space on the town beach but wander south and there's cypress and oleander-lined

TAKING THE BAR EXAM

One of the legacies of the former Yugoslavia's communist years is a rigorous education system. We asked English teacher Daniela Đuranović to teach us a thing or two about her home town and country.

Where's a good place to begin? First swim in the sea. Bar's most beautiful beaches are a little out of town. For me, Montenegro's best beach is Pržno, near Sveti Stefan.

What else shouldn't be missed? You must visit the mountains. They're beautiful in summer but I like them at winter covered in snow. I don't ski, though. I just drink coffee and tea and enjoy the nature.

You seem to have a good life here. I see TV programs about Provence (France), talking about the nature, the cheese, the produce. I can eat that food every day. In summer I have everything I need right here.

Lučice Beach and beyond it the 2.5km-long sweep of **Bulgarica Beach**.

Sleeping & Eating

Mornar Travel Agency (☎ 033-461 410; www.mornar-travel.com; 8am-8pm summer, to 2pm winter) An excellent local agency offering private accommodation from €23 per person.

Hotel W Grand (☎ 033-461 703; www.wgrandpetrovac.com; s €41-71, d €54-94, tr €81-141; P) The colour scheme simulates the effect of waking up inside an egg-yolk but this modern mid-sized hotel has roomy rooms with comfy beds and puts on a brilliant breakfast buffet on its view-hungry terrace. Wi-fi is available too.

Konoba Bonaca (☎ 069-084 735; mains €8-15) Set back slightly from the main beach drag, this traditional restaurant focuses mainly on seafood but the local cheeses and olives are also excellent. Grab a table under the grapevines on the terrace and gaze out to sea.

Getting There & Away

Petrovac's **bus station** (☎ 068-838 184) is near the top of town. Regular services head to Budva and Bar (both €2, 30 minutes).

BAR БАР

☎ 030 / pop 13,800

Dominated by Montenegro's main port and a large industrial area, Bar is unlikely to be anyone's highlight, but it is a handy transport hub welcoming trains from Belgrade and ferries from Italy. More interesting are the ruins of Stari Bar (Old Bar) in the mountains behind.

Orientation & Information

Bar's centre is immediately east of the marina and ferry terminal. Beaches stretch north from here, while the port and industrial area are to the south. There are several banks with ATMs around ulica Maršala Tita and ulica Vladimira Rolovića.

Accident & Emergency Clinic (☎ 124; Jovana Tomeševića 42)

Post office (☎ 301 300; Jovana Tomeševića bb)

Tourist information centre (☎ 311 633; Obala 13 Jula bb; 7am-9pm Jul & Aug, to 2pm Mon-Fri Sep-Jun) Helpful staff with good English; stocks useful brochures listing sights and private accommodation.

Sights

Presenting an elegant facade to the water, **King Nikola's Palace** (☎ 314 079; Šetalište Kralje Nikole; admission €1; 8am-3pm) has been converted into a museum housing a collection of antiquities, folk costumes and royal furniture. Its shady gardens contain plants cultivated from seeds and cuttings collected from around the world by Montenegro's sailors.

Impressive **Stari Bar** (adult/child €1/0.50; 8am-8pm), Bar's original settlement, stands on a bluff 4km northeast off the Ulcinj road. A steep cobbled hill takes you past a cluster of old houses and shops to the fortified entrance where a short dark passage pops you out into a large expanse of vine-clad ruins and abandoned streets overgrown with grass and wild flowers. A small **museum** just inside the entrance explains the site and its history. The Illyrians founded the city in around 800 BC. It passed in and out of Slavic and Byzantine rule until the Venetians took it in 1443 and held it until it was taken by the Ottomans in 1571. Nearly all the 240 buildings now lie in ruins, a result of Montenegrin shelling, when the town was captured in 1878.

Buses marked Stari Bar depart from the centre of new Bar every hour (€1).

Sleeping & Eating

Hotel Princess (☎ 300 100; www.hotelprincess-montenegro.com; Jovana Tomaševića 59; s €80-140, d €100-200, apt €150-450;) It's pricey and generic but this resort-style hotel is the only decent option in town. Make the most of your money at the private beach, swimming pool and spa centre. Wi-fi available.

Konoba Spilja (☎ 340 353; Stari Bar bb; mains €3-15) So rustic you wouldn't be surprised if a goat wandered through, this is a terrific spot for a traditional meal after exploring Stari Bar.

Getting There & Away

The **bus station** (☎ 346 141) and adjacent **train station** (☎ 301 622; www.zeljeznica.cg.yu) are 1km southeast of the centre. Destinations include Podgorica (€5, seven daily) and Ulcinj (€2.50, six daily). Trains to Podgorica (€3, one hour, 14 daily) also stop at Virpazar (€2).

Montenegro Line (www.montenegrolines.net) ferries to Bari (€60, nine hours, three weekly) and Ancona (€71, 11 hours, twice weekly in summer) in Italy, and **Azzurra Lines** (www.azzurraline.com) ferries to Bari (€65, nine hours, weekly in summer) leave from the **ferry terminal** (Obala 13 Jula bb) near the centre. You can book your Montenegro Lines ferry tickets here and there's a post office and ATM. Azzura Line can be booked at **Mercur** (☎ 313 617; Vladimir Rolovića bb).

ULCINJ УЛЦИЊ

☎ 030 / 10,850

If you want a feel for Albania without actually crossing the border, buzzy Ulcinj's the place to go. The population is 72% Albanian and in summer it swells with Kosovar holidaymakers for the simple reason that it's a hell of a lot nicer than any of the Albanian seaside towns. The elegant minarets of numerous mosques give Ulcinj a distinctly Eastern feel, as does the music echoing out of the kebab stands.

For centuries Ulcinj had a reputation as a pirate's lair. By the end of the 16th century as many as 400 pirates, mainly from Malta, Tunisia and Algeria, made Ulcinj their main port of call – wreaking havoc on passing vessels and then returning to party up large on Mala Plaža. Ulcinj became the centre of a thriving slave trade, with people – mainly from North Africa – paraded for sale on the town's main square.

You'll find banks, internet cafes, supermarkets, pharmacies and the post office on Rr Hazif Ali Ulqinaku.

Sights & Activities

The ancient Stari Grad overlooking Mali Plaža is still largely residential and somewhat dilapidated – a legacy of the 1979 earthquake. A steep slope leads to the **Upper Gate**, where there's a small **museum** (☎ 421 419; admission €1; 6am-noon & 5-9pm) containing Roman and Ottoman artefacts just inside the walls.

Mala Plaža may be a fine grin of a cove but it's hard to see the beach under all that suntanned flesh in July and August. You're better to stroll south, where a succession of rocky bays offer a little more room to breathe. **Ladies' Beach** (admission €1.50) has a strict women-only policy, while a section of the beach in front of the Hotel Albatross is clothing-optional.

The appropriately named **Velika Plaža** (Big Beach) starts 4km southeast of the town and stretches for 12 sandy kilometres. Sections of it sprout deckchairs but there's still plenty of space to lose yourself. To be frank, this large flat expanse isn't as picturesque as it sounds and the water is painfully shallow – great for kids but you'll need to walk a fair way for a decent swim.

On your way to Velika Plaža you'll pass the murky **Milena canal**, where local fishermen use nets suspended from long willow rods attached to wooden stilt houses. The effect is remarkably redolent of South East Asia. There are more of these contraptions on the banks of the **Bojana River** at the other end of Veliki Plaža.

Divers wanting to explore various wrecks and the remains of a submerged town should contact the **D'olcinium Diving Club** (☎ 067-319 100; www.uldiving.com; introductory dive €30, 2 dives incl equipment €40). They also hire snorkelling (€3) and diving (€15) gear.

Sleeping

Real Estate Travel Agency (☎ 421 609; www.realestate-travel.com; Hazif Ali Ulqinaku bb; 8am-9pm) This strangely named agency has obliging English-speaking staff who can help you find private rooms (from €10 per person), apartments or hotel rooms. They also rent cars, run tours and sell maps of Ulcinj.

Hotel Dolcino (☎ 422 288; www.hoteldolcino.com; Hazif Ali Ulqinaku bb; s/d/q/ste €40/50/60/70;) You can't quibble over the exceptionally reasonable prices of this modern business-orientated minihotel in the centre of town. The quieter rooms at the back have spacious terraces, although the small front balconies are great for watching the passing parade.

Dvori Balšića & Palata Venecija (☎ 421 457; www.realestate-travel.com; Stari Grad; s/d/q/apt €75/100/140/190; ⊠) If you've ever fancied being king of the castle, these grand stone *palazzi* in the Old Town should satisfy the urge. The sizeable rooms all have kitchenettes, romantic sea views, wi-fi and stucco and dark wooden interiors.

Eating & Drinking

Restaurant Pizzeria Bazar (☎ 421 639; Hazif Ali Ulqinaku bb; mains €4-10) An upstairs restaurant that's a great idling place when the streets below are heaving with tourists. People-watch in comfort as you enjoy a plate of *Lignje na žaru* (grilled squid), the restaurant's speciality.

Riblja Čorba (☎ 401 720; Bojana River; mains €6-10) Not actually in Ulcinj but well worth the 14km drive, this memorable fish restaurant is one of several that jut out over the Bojana River just before the bridge to Ada Bojana. The name means fish soup and their broth is indeed sublime: thick with rice and served in a metal pot that will fill your bowl twice over.

Getting There & Away

The **bus station** (☎ 413 225) is on the north-eastern edge of town just off Bul Vëllazërit Frashëri. Services head to Bar (€2.50, 30 minutes, six daily), Podgorica (€7, one hour, daily), Shkodra (Albania; €4.50, 90 minutes, daily) and Pristina (Kosovo; €22.50, eight hours, three daily).

Minibuses head to Shkodra at 9am and 3pm (or when they're full) from the carpark beside Ulcinj's market (about €5).

CENTRAL MONTENEGRO

The heart of Montenegro – physically, spiritually and politically – is easily accessed as a day trip from the coast but it's well deserving of a longer exploration. Two wonderful national parks separate it from the coast and behind them lie the two capitals, the ancient current one and the newer former one.

LOVĆEN NATIONAL PARK ЛОВЋЕН

Directly behind Kotor is **Mt Lovćen** (1749m), the black mountain that gave *Crna Gora* (Montenegro) its name (*crna/negro* means 'black', *gora/monte* means 'mountain' in Montenegrin and Italian respectively). This locale occupies a special place in their hearts of all Montenegrins. For most of its history it represented the entire nation – a rocky island of Slavic resistance in an Ottoman sea. The old capital of Cetinje nestles in its foothills.

The national park's 6220 hectares are home to 85 species of butterfly, 200 species of birds and mammals, including brown bears and wolves. It's criss-crossed with well-marked hiking paths.

The **National Park Office** (☎ 033-761 128; www.nparkovi.cg.yu; Ivanova Korita bb; ⏲ 9am-5pm Apr-Oct, less in winter) is near its centre and offers accommodation in four-bedded bungalows (€40). If you're planning some serious walking, buy a copy of the *Lovćen Mountain Touristic Map* (scale 1:25,000), available from the office and park entries.

Lovćen's star attraction is the magnificent **Njegoš Mausoleum** (admission €3) at the top of its second-highest peak, Jezerski Vrh (1657m). Take the 461 steps up to the entry, where two granite giantesses guard the tomb. Inside, under a golden mosaic canopy, a 28-ton Vladika Petar II Petrović Njegoš rests in the wings of an eagle, carved from a single block of black granite. The actual tomb lies below and a path at the rear leads to a dramatic circular viewing platform. A photographer stationed near the entrance has a stash of folk costumes for a quirky souvenir photo (€5).

If you're driving, the park can be approached from either Kotor or Cetinje (entry fee €2). The back route between the two shouldn't be missed (see p585).

CETINJE ЦЕТИЊЕ

☎ 041 / pop 15,150

Rising from a green vale surrounded by rough, grey mountains, Cetinje is an odd mix of former capital and overgrown village, where single-storey cottages and stately mansions share the same street. Pretty Njegoševa is a partly pedestrianised thoroughfare lined with interesting buildings, including the **Presidential Palace** and various former embassies marked with plaques. Everything of significance is in the immediate vicinity. There's not much English spoken at the **tourist information centre** (☎ 078-108 788; Novice Cerovića bb; ⏲ 8am-8pm Mon-Sat, 9am-5pm Sun) but you can buy souvenirs and Cetinje guidebooks (€10).

Sights

MUSEUMS

The **National Museum of Montenegro** (Narodni muzej Crne Gore; all museums adult/child €8/4; ⏲ 9am-5pm, last admission 4.30pm) is actually a collection of five museums housed in a clump of important buildings. A joint ticket will get you into all of them or you can buy individual tickets.

Two are housed in the former parliament (1910), Cetinje's most imposing building. The fascinating **History Museum** (Istorijski muzej; ☎ 230 310; Novice Cerovića 7; adult/child €3/1.50) is very well laid out, following a timeline from the Stone Age to 1955. There are few English signs but the enthusiastic staff will walk you around and give you an overview, before leaving you to your own devices.

Upstairs is the equally excellent **Art Museum** (Umjetnički muzej; adult/child €3/1.50). There's a small collection of icons, the most important being the precious 9th-century *Our Lady of Philermos,* which was traditionally believed to be painted by St Luke himself. Elsewhere in the gallery all of Montenegro's great artists are represented, with the most famous having their own separate spaces. Expect a museum staff member to be hovering as you wander around.

While the hovering at the Art Museum is annoying, the **King Nikola Museum** (Muzej kralja Nikole; ☎ 230 555; Trg Kralja Nikole; adult/child €5/2.50) can be downright infuriating. Entry is only by guided tour, which the staff will only give to a group, even if you've pre-paid a ticket and they've got nothing else to do. Still, this 1871 palace of Nikola I, last soverign of Montenegro, is worth the hassle.

Opposite the National Museum, the castle-like **Njegoš Museum** (Njegošev Muzej; ☎ 231 050; Trg Kralja Nikole; adult/child €3/1.50) was the residence of Montenegro's favourite son, prince-bishop–poet Petar II Petrović Njegoš. The hall was built and financed by the Russians in 1838 and housed the nation's first billiard table, hence the museum's alternative name, Biljarda. The bottom floor is devoted to military costumes, photos of soldiers with outlandish moustaches and exquisitely decorated weapons. Njegoš's personal effects are displayed upstairs.

When you leave the museum turn right and follow the walls to the glass pavilion housing a fascinating large scale **relief map** (adult/child €1/0.50) of Montenegro created by the Austrians in 1917.

Occupying the former Serbian Embassy, the **Ethnographic Museum** (Etnografski muzej; Trg Kralja Nikole; adult/child €2/1) is the least interesting of the five but if you've bought a joint ticket you may as well check it out. The collection of costumes and tools is well presented and has English notations.

CETINJE MONASTERY

It's a case of three times lucky for **Cetinje Monastery** (☎ 231 021; 🕒 8am-6pm), having been repeatedly destroyed during Ottoman attacks and rebuilt after. This sturdy incarnation dates from 1785, with its only exterior ornamentation being the capitals of columns recycled from the original building, founded in 1484.

The chapel to the right of the courtyard holds the monastery's proudest possessions: a shard of the 'true cross' and the mummified right hand of St John the Baptist. The hand's had a fascinating history, having escaped wars and revolutions and passing through the hands of Byzantine emperors, Ottoman sultans, the Knights Hospitalier, Russian tsars and Serbian kings. It's now housed in a bejewelled golden casket by the chapel's window, draped in heavy fabric. The casket's only occasionally opened for veneration, so if you miss out you can console yourself that it's not a very pleasant sight.

The monastery **treasury** (admission €2; 🕒 8am-4pm) is only open to groups, but if you are persuasive enough and prepared to wait around, you may be able to get in. It holds a wealth of fascinating objects that form a blur as you're shunted around the rooms by one of the monks. These include jewel-encrusted vestments, ancient handwritten texts, icons, royal crowns and a copy of the 1494 *Oktoih* (Book of the Eight Voices), the first book printed in Serbian.

If your legs, shoulders or cleavage are on display you'll either be denied entry or given a smock to wear.

Sleeping & Eating

Accommodation in Cetinje is limited and there are only a few proper restaurants.

Hotel Grand (☎ 242 400; hotelgrand@cg.yu; Njegoševa 1; s €45-60, d €64-80, apt €120) 'Fading grandeur' would be a more apt description than 'Grand', but aside from a few pigeons roosting in the walls, Cetinje's only hotel is a pleasant place to stay. The comfy beds, new linen and spongy carpet strips certainly help.

Vinoteka (☎ 068-555 771; Njegoševa 103; mains €2.20-5) The wood-beamed porch looking onto the garden is such a nice spot that the excellent and reasonably priced pizza and pasta feels like a bonus – the decent wine list even more so.

Getting There & Away

Cetinje's on the main highway between Budva and Podgorica and can also be reached by a glorious back road from Kotor via Lovćen National Park; see p585. The **bus station** (Trg Golootočkih Žeta) is only two blocks from the main street but it doesn't have a timetable, ticket counter or even a phone. Buses leave every 30 minutes for Podgorica (€3) and hourly for Budva (€3).

LAKE SKADAR NATIONAL PARK СКАДАРСКО ЈЕЗЕРО

The Balkans' largest lake, dolphin-shaped Lake Skadar has its tail and two-thirds of its body in Montenegro and its nose in Albania. Covering between 370 and 550 sq km (depending on the time of year), it's one of the most important reserves for wetland birds in the whole of Europe. The endangered Dalmatian pelican nests here, along with 256 other species, while 48 known species of fish lurk beneath its smooth surface. On the Montenegrin side, an area of 400 sq km has been protected by a national park since 1983. It's a blissfully pretty area, encompassing steep mountains, hidden villages, historic churches, clear waters and floating meadows of waterlilies.

The **National Park Visitors' Centre** (☎ 020-879 100; www.skadarlake.org; Vranjina bb; admission €2; 🕑 8am-4pm) is on the opposite side of the causeway heading to Podgorica from Virpazar. This modern facility has excellent displays about all the national parks, not just Lake Skadar, and sells park entry tickets (per day €4) and fishing permits (per day €5).

In the busy months, various tour operators set up kiosks in the vicinity. **Kings Travel** (☎ 020-202 800) hires rowboats (per hour/day €25/100) and speed boats with drivers (per hour/day €60/300).

Just along the causeway are the remains of the 19th-century fortress **Lesendro**. The busy highway and railway tracks prevent land access to the site.

Rijeka Crnojevića Ријека Црнојевића

The northwestern end of the lake thins into the serpentine loops of the Rijeka Crnojevića (Crnojević River) and terminates near the pretty village of the same name. It's a charming, tucked-away kind of place, accessed by side roads that lead off the Cetinje–Podgorica highway. Occupying four wooden huts that jut out over the river on stilts is a **National Park Visitors' Centre** (admission €1; 🕑 8am-4pm), which houses a historical display.

You wouldn't expect it but this sleepy place is home to one of Montenegro's best restaurants. **Stari Most** (☎ 033-239 505; fish per kg €25-45, 5-course set menu €40-50) is well located on the marble riverside promenade, looking towards the photogenic arched stone bridge (1854) from which it derives its name. Fish, particularly eel, is the speciality here and the fish soup alone is enough to justify a drive from Podgorica.

Virpazar Вирпазар

This sweet little town serves as the main gateway to the national park. It's centred on a pretty town square and a river blanketed with waterlilies. Most of the boat tours of the lake depart from here, so the tranquillity is briefly shattered at around 10.30am, when the tour buses from the coast pull in. There's a **National Park kiosk** by the marina that sells entry tickets and fishing permits but doesn't offer much information.

The **Pelikan Hotel** (☎ 020-711 107; pelikanzec@cg.yu; r €52-75; ❄) is a well-run one-stop shop offering accommodation, an excellent traditional restaurant (main €5 to €12) and 2½-hour boat tours that explore the lake's northern reaches (€30). The rooms are clean and have nice views over the square, although some of them are tiny.

Virpazar doesn't have a bus station but buses on the Bar–Podgorica route stop here. The decrepit **train station** (☎ 020-441 435) is off the main road, 800m south of town. There are regular services to Bar (€2) and Podgorica (€2.50).

Murići Мурићи

The southern edge of the lake is the most dramatic, with the Rumija Mountains rising precipitously from the water. From Virpazar there's a wonderful drive following the contours of the lake through the mountains towards the border before crossing the range and turning back towards Ulcinj. About halfway, a steep road descends to the village of **Murići**. This is one of the lake's best swimming spots. Local boatmen offer trips to the monasteries on the nearby islands for around €10 per hour.

The **Murići Vacation Resort** (☎ 069-688 288; www.nacionalnipark-izletistemurici.com; per person €35) has simple log cabins nestled within an olive grove. A decent ablutions block is shared and the price includes three meals in the shady outdoor

MONTENEGRO

restaurant (mains €5-9). They also organise **lake tours** (€16) that visit the islands and Virpazar.

PODGORICA ПОДГОРИЦА

☎ 020 / pop 136,480

Podgorica's never going to be Europe's most happening capital but if you can get past the sweltering summer temperatures and concrete apartment blocks you'll find a pleasant little city with lots of green space and some decent galleries, restaurants and bars.

The city sits at the confluence of two rivers. West of the broad Morača is what passes for the business district. The smaller Ribnica River divides the eastern side in two. To the south is Stara Varoš, the heart of the former Ottoman town. North of the Ribnica is Nova Varoš, an attractive, mainly low-rise precinct of late 19th-/early 20th-century buildings housing a lively mixture of shops and bars. At its centre is the attractive main square, Trg Republika.

Information

You'll find plenty of ATMs scattered around the inner city.

Accident & Emergency clinic (Hitna Pomoć; ☎ 124; Vaka Djurovića bb)

Montenegro Adventures (☎ 202 380; www.montenegro-adventures.com; Moskovska 63-4) The commercial wing of the nonprofit Centre for Sustainable Tourism Initiatives (www.cstimontenegro.org), with whom they share an office. They organise tours, accommodation and the like.

Tourist Organisation Podgorica (TOP; ☎ 667 535; www.podgorica.travel; Slobode 47)

www.club (Bokaška 4; per hr €1.50; 🕓 8am-2am) Decent cafe-bar with internet terminals.

Sights

Despite Cetinje nabbing most of the national endowment, the new capital is well served by the **Podgorica Museum & Gallery** (☎ 242 543; Marka Miljanova 4; adult/child €5/1; 🕓 9am-8pm). There's an interesting section on the city's history, including antiquities surviving from its Roman incarnation, Doclea. The gallery features local big hitters such as Dado Đurić and Petar Lubarda, whose large canvas *Titograd* (1956) takes pride of place in the foyer.

The Centre for Contemporary Art operates two galleries in Podgorica. The bottom two floors of the once-royal palace **Dvorac Petrovića** (☎ 243 513; Kruševac bb; admission free; 🕓 8am-2pm & 4-9pm Mon-Fri & 10am-4pm Sat summer, 8am-8pm Mon-Fri & 8am-2pm Sat winter) are given over to high-profile exhibitions, while the top floor has an oddball collection of miscellanea. Temporary exhibitions are also staged in the small **Galerija Centar** (☎ 665 409; Njegoševa 2; admission free; 🕓 9am-2pm & 5-9pm Mon-Fri, 10am-2pm Sat).

An indicator of the healthy state of Orthodoxy in Montenegro is the immense **Hram Hristovog Vaskrsenja** (Temple of Christ's Resurrection; Bul Džordža Vašingtona). It's still incomplete after 15 years' construction, but its large dome, white stone towers and gold crosses are a striking addition to Podgorica's skyline.

Sleeping

Most visitors to Podgorica are here for business, either commerce or government-related. Hotels set their prices accordingly and private accommodation isn't really an option.

Hotel Evropa (☎ 623 444; www.hotelevropa.cg.yu; Orahovačka 16; s €55-70, d/tr €90/120; ❄ 💻) It's hardly a salubrious location, but Evropa is handy to the train and bus station and offers clean rooms with comfortable beds, writing desks and decent showers. Despite its diminutive size there's a sauna, fitness room, wi-fi and ample parking.

Hotel Eminent (☎ 664 646; eminent@cg.yu; Njegoševa 25; s/d/tr €80/130/160, apt €90-140; ❄) Given its location and excellent facilities, the Eminent seems to be set up for business people keen on an after-work tipple. The front rooms can be noisy but the funky mezzanine apartments open on to a covered veranda at the back. Wi-fi is available.

Eating & Drinking

Head to the **little market** (Moskovska bb) or the **big market** (Bratstva Jedinstva bb) for fresh fruit and vegetables.

Laterna (☎ 232 331; Marka Miljanova 41; mains €4-13; 🕓 9am-midnight Mon-Sat) Farm implements hang from the rough stone walls, creating a surprisingly rustic ambience in the centre of the city. A selection of meat and fish grills is offered but it's hard to go past the crispy-based pizza – it's quite possibly Montenegro's best.

Leonardo (☎ 242 902; Svetozara Markovića bb; mains €4-13) Leonardo's unlikely position at the centre of a residential block makes it a little tricky to find but the effort's well rewarded by accomplished Italian cuisine. The pasta dishes are delicious and reasonably priced, given the upmarket ambience, while the €4 pizzas should leave even those on a budget with a Mona Lisa smile.

Buda Bar (☎ 067-344 944; Stanka Dragojevića 26; 🕓 8am-2am) A golden Buddha smiles serenely

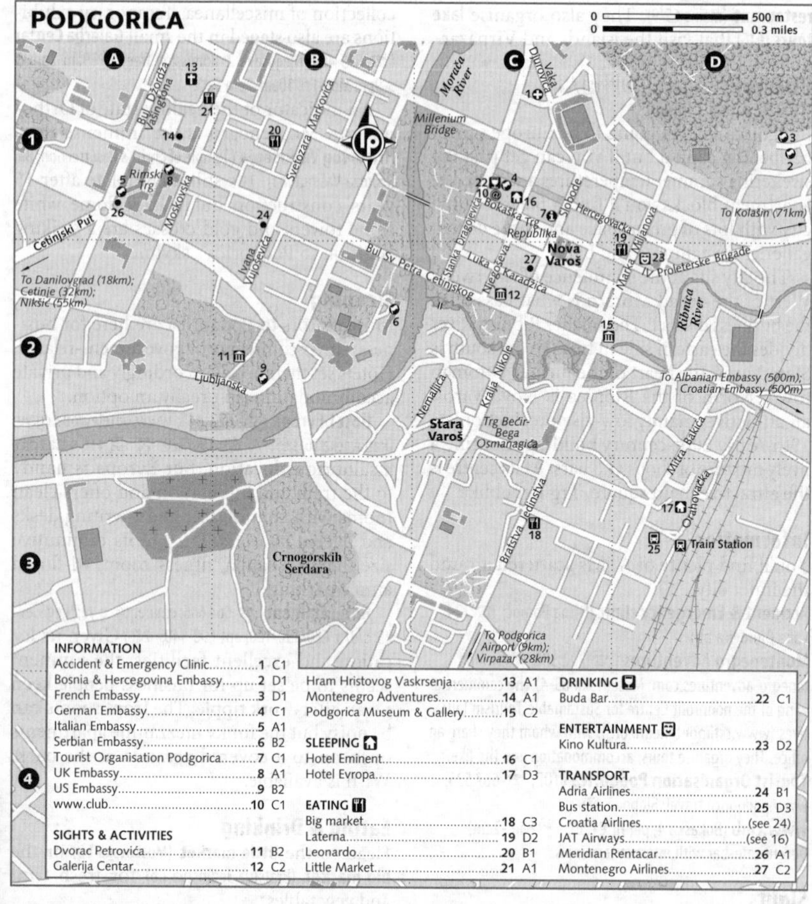

as you meditate over your morning coffee or search for the eternal truth at the bottom of a cocktail glass. This is one slick watering hole; the tent-like semi-enclosed terrace is the place to be on balmy summer nights.

Entertainment

Kino Kultura (IV Proleterske Brigade 1; admission €2.50) The screenings aren't as regular as you might expect for the city's only cinema but you might luck upon an English-language movie with Montenegrin subtitles.

Getting There & Away

BUS

Podgorica's **bus station** (☎ 620 430; Trg Golootočkih Žrtava; 🕑 5am-10pm) has a left-luggage service, ATM and services to all major towns, including Herceg Novi (€9, three hours), Kotor (€7, two hours) and Ulcinj (€7, one hour).

TRAIN

Don't expect any English or a lot of help from the information desk at the **train station** (☎ 441 211; www.zeljeznica.cg.yu; Trg Golootočkih Žrtava 13; 🕑 5am-11pm). Thankfully, timetables are posted. Destinations include Bar (€3, one hour, 14 daily), Virpazar (€2.50, 40 minutes, 14 daily), Kolašin (€4.50, 1½ hours, three daily) and Belgrade (€22, 7½ hours, four daily).

CAR

The major rental car agencies all have counters at Podgorica airport. Excellent local agency

Meridian Rentacar (☎ 234 944, 069-316 666; www.meridian-rentacar.com; Bul Džordža Vašingtona 85) also has a city office.

Getting Around

It's not difficult to get around town on foot but if you fancy trying a local bus they cost €0.60 for a short journey. **Podgorica Airport** (☎ 020-872 016) is 9km south of the city. Montenegro Airlines runs a shuttle bus (€3) between the airport and Trg Republika, timed around their flights. Airport taxis have a standard €15 fare to the centre but ordinary taxis should only charge about €8.

OSTROG MONASTERY МАНАСТИР ОСТРОГ

Resting in a cliff-face 900m above the Zeta valley, the gleaming white **Ostrog Monastery** is the most important site in Montenegro for Orthodox Christians. Even with its masses of pilgrims, tourists and trashy souvenir stands, it's a strangely affecting place.

Leaving the main Podgorica–Nikšić highway 19km past Danilovgrad, a narrow road twists uphill for 7km before it reaches the **Lower Monastery** (1824). In summer you'll be greeted with sweet fragrances emanating from the mountain foliage. The church has vivid frescos and behind it is a natural spring, where you can fill your bottles with deliciously fresh water and potentially benefit from an internal blessing as you sup it. From here the faithful, many of them barefoot, plod up another two steep kilometres to the main shrine. Nonpilgrims and the pure of heart may drive to the upper carpark.

The **Upper Monastery** (the really impressive one) is dubbed 'Sv Vasilije's miracle', because no-one seems to understand how it was built. Constructed in 1665 within two large caves, it gives the impression that it has grown out of the very rock. Sv Vasilije (St Basil), a bishop from Hercegovina, brought his monks here after the Ottomans destroyed Tvrdos Monastery near Trebinje. Pilgrims queue to go into the atmospheric shrine where the Saint's fabric-wrapped bones are kept. To enter you'll need to be wearing a long skirt or trousers (jeans are fine) and cover your shoulders.

One of the only nonsmoking establishments in the country, the **guest house** (☎ 067-405 258; dm €4) near the Lower Monastery offers tidy single-sex dorm rooms, while in summer many pilgrims lay sleeping mats in front of the Upper Monastery.

There's no public transport but numerous tour buses head here from all of the tourist hot spots. Expect to pay about €15 to €20 for a daytrip from the coast.

NORTHERN MOUNTAINS

This really is the full Monte: soaring peaks, hidden monasteries, secluded villages, steep river canyons and a whole heap of 'wild beauty', to quote the tourist slogan. It's well worth hiring a car for a couple of days to get off the beaten track – some of the roads are truly spectacular.

DURMITOR NATIONAL PARK ДУРМИТОР

☎ 052 / pop 4900

Magnificent scenery ratchets up to the stupendous in this national park, where ice and water have carved a dramatic landscape from the limestone. Some 18 glacial lakes known as *gorske oči* (mountain eyes) dot the Durmitor range, with the largest, **Black Lake** (Crno Jezero), a pleasant 3km walk from Žabljak. The rounded mass of **Međed** (The Bear, 2287m) rears up behind the lake flanked by others of the park's 48 peaks over 2000m, including the highest, **Bobotov Kuk** (2523m). In winter (December to March) Durmitor is Montenegro's main ski resort; in summer it's a popular place for hiking, rafting and other active pursuits.

The park is home to enough critters to cast a Disney movie, including 163 species of bird, about 50 types of mammals and purportedly the greatest variety of butterflies in Europe.

Žabljak, at the eastern edge of the range, is the park's principal gateway and the only town within its boundaries. It's not very big and nor is it attractive, but it has a supermarket, post office, bank, hotels and restaurants, all gathered around the parking lot that masquerades as the main square.

Information

Durmitor National Park Visitor Centre (☎ 360 228; www.nparkovi.cg.yu; 🕑 7am-2pm autumn & spring, 8am-6pm winter & summer) On the road to the Black Lake, this centre includes a wonderful micromuseum focusing on the park's flora and fauna. The knowledgable English-speaking staff sells local craft, fishing permits (river/lake €15/10), maps (€8) and hiking guidebooks.

Summit Travel Agency (☎ 361 502; anna.grbovic@cg.yu; Njegoševa bb, Žabljak) Owner Anna Grbović speaks good English and can arrange jeep tours (€100 for up to three people), rafting trips and mountain bike hire (per hour/day €2/10).

Activities

RAFTING

Slicing through the mountains at the northern edge of the national park like they were made from the local soft cheese, the **Tara River** forms a canyon that at its peak is 1300m deep. By way of comparison, Colorado's Grand Canyon is only 200m deeper.

Rafting along the river is one of the country's most popular tourist activities, with various operators running trips daily between May and October. The river has a few rapids but don't expect an adrenaline-fuelled white-water experience. You'll get the most excitement in May, when the last of the melting snow still revs up the flow.

The 82km section that is raftable starts from Splavište, south of the impressive 150m high Tara Bridge, and ends at Šćepan Polje on the Bosnian border. The classic two-day trip heads through the deepest part of the canyon on the first day, stopping overnight at Radovan Luka. Most of the day-tours from the coast traverse only the last 18km – this is outside the national park and hence avoids hefty fees. You'll miss out on the canyon's depths but it's still a beautiful stretch, including most of the rapids. The buses follow a spectacular road along the Piva River, giving you a double dose of canyon action.

If you've got your own wheels you can save a few bucks and avoid a lengthy coach tour by heading directly to Šćepan Polje. **Tara Tour** (☎ 069-086 106; www.tara-tour.com) offers an excellent half-day trip (with/without breakfast and lunch €40/30) and has a cute set of wooden chalets with squat toilets and showers in a separate block; accommodation, three meals and a half-day's rafting costs €55. Another good operator is **Kamp Grab** (☎ 083-200 598; www.tara-grab.com), with lodgings blissfully located 18km upstream at Brstanovica.

Summit Travel Agency (above) offers a range of tours from Žabljak starting from Splavište (half-/one-/two-day tour €50/110/200).

HIKING

Durmitor is one of the best-marked mountain ranges in Europe. Some suggest it's a little too well labelled, encouraging novices to wander around seriously high altitude paths that are prone to fog and summer thunderstorms. Check the weather forecast before you set out, stick to the tracks and prepare for sudden drops in temperature. You'll be charged €2 per day to enter the park and paths can be as easy as a 4km stroll around the Black Lake.

SKIING

On the slopes of **Savin Kuk** (2313m), 5km from Žabljak, you'll find the main ski centre. Its 3.5km run starts from a height of 2010m and is best suited to advanced skiers. On the outskirts of town near the bus station, **Javorovača** is a gentle 300m slope that's good for kids and beginners. The third centre at **Mali Štuoc** (1953m) should have reopened by the time you read this; it has terrific views over the Black Lake, Međed and Savin Kuk, and slopes to suit all levels of experience.

One of the big attractions for skiing here is the cost: day passes are around €15, weekly passes €70 and ski lessons between €10 and €20. You can rent ski and snowboard gear from **Sport Trade** (☎ 069-538 831; Vuka Karadžića 7, Žabljak) for €10 per day.

Sleeping & Eating

Summit Travel Agency (left) can help you source private accommodation, starting from around €10 per person. Most of the giant Yugoslav-era hotels were either closed for renovation when we visited or deserved to be.

Autokamp Mlinski Potok Mina (☎ 069-497 625; camp sites per person €3, bed €10) With a fabulously hospitable host (there's no escaping the *rakija* shots), this camping ground above the National Park Visitors Centre is an excellent option. The owner's house can sleep 12 guests in comfortable wood-panelled rooms and he has another house sleeping 11 by the Black Lake.

MB Hotel (☎ 361 601; www.mb-hotel.com; Tripka Đakovića bb, Žabljak; s/d/villa €30/57/100) In a quiet backstreet halfway between the town centre and the bus station, this little hotel offers modern rooms, English-speaking staff and an attractive restaurant and bar. The restaurant even has a nonsmoking section – something even less likely to be seen in these parts than wolves. Wi-fi available.

Eko-Oaza Suza Evrope (☎ 067-511 755; eko-oaza@cg.yu; Dobrilovina; cottage €50) Situated 25km west of Mojkovac at the beginning of the arm of the park that stretches along the Tara River, this 'eco oasis' consists of four comfortable wooden cottages, each sleeping five people. From here you can hike up the mountain and stay overnight in a hut near the glacial Lake Zaboj (1477m).

National Eco Restaurant (☎ 361 337; Božidara Žugića 8, Žabljak; mains €3-10) A great place to try traditional mountain food, such as lamb or veal roasted 'under the pan' (€24 per kilogram). It's all locally sourced and hence organic, without trying very hard.

Getting There & Away

The most reliable road to Žabljak follows the Tara River west from Mojkovac. In summer this 70km route takes about 90 minutes. If you're coming from Podgorica the quickest route is through Nikšić and Šavnik, but the road can be treacherous in winter. The main highway north from Nikšić follows the dramatic Piva Canyon to Šćepan Polje.

There's a petrol station near the **bus station** (☎ 361 318) at the southern end of Žabljak on the Nikšić road. Buses head to Belgrade (€25, nine hours, two daily) and Podgorica (€9.50, 3½ hours, three daily).

BIOGRADSKA GORA NATIONAL PARK БИОГРАДСКА ГОРА

Nestled in the heart of the Bjelasica Mountain Range, this pretty national park has as its heart 1600 hectares of virgin woodland – one of Europe's last three remaining primeval forests. The main entrance to the park is between Kolašin and Mojkovac on the Podgorica–Belgrade route. After paying a €2 entry fee you can drive the further 4km to the lake.

You can hire rowboats (per hour €5) and buy fishing permits (per day €20) from the **park office** (☎ 020-865 625; www.nparkovi.cg.yu) by the carpark. If you're planning to tackle the excellent hiking tracks it's worth buying a copy of the *Mountains of Bjelasica* booklet (€3).

Nearby there's a **camping ground** (small/large tent €3/5) with basic squat toilets and a cluster of 11 new windowless log cabins, each with two beds (€20). The ablutions block for the cabins is much nicer. **Restoran Biogradsko Jezero** (mains €5.50-9.20) has a wonderful terrace where you can steal glimpses of the lake through the trees as you tuck into a traditional lamb or veal dish.

The nearest bus stop is an hour's walk away at Kraljevo Kolo and the nearest train station is a 90-minute walk at Štitarička Rijeka. The next major town with decent hotels and an excellent **tourist office** (☎ 020-865 110; Trg Borca 2; 🕒 8am-4pm) is Kolašin, 15km south of the park entrance.

MONTENEGRO DIRECTORY

ACCOMMODATION

A tidal wave of development has seen hotels large and small spring up in the popular destinations. Prices are very seasonal, peaking in July and August on the coast. Where the prices vary according to the season we've listed a range from the cheapest low-season price through to the most expensive high-season rate for each room category. Budget rooms can cost up to €30 per night, and you should be able to find a midrange option for less than €90. Top-end rooms start from this mark and head into the hundreds. Unless otherwise mentioned the rooms have bathrooms and the tariff usually includes breakfast.

The cheapest option is private accommodation and apartment rentals. These can be arranged through travel agencies or, in season, you may be approached at the bus stop or see signs hanging outside of houses. Some local tourist offices publish handy guides.

Facilities at camp grounds tend to be basic, often with squat toilets and limited water. The national parks have cabin-style accommodation.

An additional tourist tax (less than €2 per night) will be added to the rate for all accommodation types.

ACTIVITIES

Hooking up with activity operators can be difficult due to language difficulties, lack of permanent offices and out-of-date websites. Luckily there are some excellent travel agencies who will do the legwork for you, including Black Mountain (p582), Montenegro Adventures (p593), and the London-based agency **So Montenegro** (☎ in the UK 20-3039 5651; www.somontegro.co.uk).

The National Tourist Office, in association with mountain clubs, has developed the resource *Wilderness Hiking & Biking* which outlines five magical routes (downloadable from www.montenegro.travel/xxl/en/brochures /index.html). At the same web address you can download the *Wilderness Biking Montenegro* pamphlet, outlining five 'top trails' and the mother of all mountain biking routes, the 14-day, 1276km Tour de Montenegro.

For diving, head to Herceg Novi (p582) and Ulcinj (p589). Kayaking is possible at Herceg Novi (p582), and Budva offers paragliding (p586). For rafting, try the Tara River (p596) and for skiing head to Durmitor (p596).

BUSINESS HOURS

Business hours in Montenegro are a relative concept. Even if hours are posted on the doors of museums or shops, don't be surprised if they're not heeded. Banks are usually open from 8am to 5pm Monday to Friday and until noon Saturday. Shops in busy areas often start at around 8am or 9am and close at a similar time in the evening. Sometimes they'll close for a few hours in the late afternoon. Restaurants open at around 8am and close around midnight, while cafe-bars may stay open until 2am or 3am.

CUSTOMS REGULATIONS

In a bid to stop tourists from neighbouring countries bringing all their holiday groceries with them, Montenegro now restricts what food can be brought into the country. For other customs information, see p945.

DANGERS & ANNOYANCES

Montenegro's towns and villages are generally safe places. Montenegro's roads, on the other hand, can be treacherous, due to some kamikaze-style local driving habits.

Chances are you'll see some snakes if you're poking around ruins during summer. Montenegro has two types of venomous viper, but they'll try their best to keep out of your way. If bitten you should head to a medical centre for the antivenom.

EMBASSIES & CONSULATES

For a full list, see www.vlada.cg.yu/eng/mini nos/. The following are all in Podgorica, unless otherwise stated:

Albania (off Map p594; ☎ 020-652 796; Zmaj Jovina 30)
Bosnia and Hercegovina (Map p594; ☎ 020-618 105; Atinska 58)
Croatia Podgorica (off Map p594; ☎ 020-269 760; Vladimira Ćetkovića 2); Kotor (☎ 032-323 127; Šušanj 248)
France (Map p594; ☎ 020-655 348; Atinska 35)
Germany (Map p594; ☎ 020-667 285; Hercegovačka 10)
Italy (Map p594; ☎ 020-234 661; Bul Džordža Vašingtona 83)
Serbia (Map p594; ☎ 020-402 500; Hotel Podgorica, Bul Svetog Petra Cetinjskog 1)
UK (Map p594; ☎ 020-205 460; Bul Svetog Petra Cetinjskog 149)
USA (Map p594; ☎ 020-225 417; Ljubljanska bb)

FESTIVALS & EVENTS

Most of the coastal towns host summer festivals and the former Venetian towns have a tradition of masked carnivals.

Active types should enter the awesome **Adventure Race Montenegro** (www.adventurerace montenegro.com; 1-/2-day entry €120/200). This two-day event in early October combines kayaking, mountain biking, trekking and orienteering with brilliant scenery, environmental awareness and fundraising for local charities.

GAY & LESBIAN TRAVELLERS

Although homosexuality was decriminalised in 1977, you won't find a single gay or lesbian venue in Montenegro. Attitudes to homosexuality remain hostile and life for gay people is extremely difficult, exacerbated by the fact that most people are expected to live at home until they're married.

Many gay men resort to online connections (try www.gayromeo.com) or take their chances at a handful of cruisy beaches.

HOLIDAYS

Public holidays in Montenegro include:

New Year's Day 1 January
Orthodox Christmas 7 January
Orthodox Easter Monday April/May
Labour Day 1 May
Independence Day 21 May
Statehood Day 13 July

MONEY

Montenegro uses the euro (€). You'll find banks with ATMs in all the main towns, most of which accept Visa, MasterCard, Maestro and Cirrus. Don't rely on restaurants, shops or smaller hotels accepting credit cards.

Tipping isn't expected although it's common to round up to the nearest euro.

POST

Every town has a post office, which locals use for paying their bills: be prepared for horren-

EMERGENCY NUMBERS

- Ambulance ☎ 124
- Fire ☎ 123
- Police ☎ 122

dous queues. Parcels should be taken unsealed for inspection. You can receive mail, addressed *poste restante,* in all towns for a small charge. International postal services are slow.

TELEPHONE

Montenegro has recently been given its own country code (☎ 382) and a new set of local codes. Partly because of the changes, many businesses advertise their mobile numbers (starting with ☎ 06) instead of land lines.

The international access prefix is ☎ 00 or + from a mobile phone. Post offices are the best places to make international calls.

Local SIM cards are a good idea if you're planning a longer stay. The main providers are T-Mobile, M:tel and Promonte; they have storefronts in most towns.

VISAS

Visas are not required for citizens of most European countries, Australia, New Zealand, Canada, UK and the USA. In most cases this allows a stay of up to 90 days.

WOMEN TRAVELLERS

Other than a cursory interest shown by men towards solo women travellers, travelling is hassle-free and easy. In Muslim areas a few women wear a headscarf but most adopt Western fashions.

TRANSPORT IN MONTENEGRO

GETTING THERE & AWAY

Air

Both **Tivat** (TIV; ☎ 032-617 337) and **Podgorica** (TGD; ☎ 020-872 016) have airports and Dubrovnik's airport (p172) is very near the border. The following airlines fly to/from Montenegro:

Adria Airlines (JP; Map p594; ☎ 020-201 201; www.adria-airways.com; Ivana Vujoševića 46, Podgorica) Flies from Ljubljana and Sarajevo to Podgorica.

Aerosvit (VV; ☎ 380-44-496 7975; www.aerosvit.com) Flies from Kiev to Tivat.

Atlant-Soyuz Airlines (3G; ☎ 7-495-436 7045; www.atlant-soyuz.ru) Flies from Moscow to Tivat.

Austrojet (AUJ; www.austrojet.at) Flies from Banja Luka to Tivat.

Croatia Airlines (OU; Map p594; ☎ 020-201 201; www.croatiaairlines.com; Ivana Vujoševića 46, Podgorica) Flies from Zagreb to Podgorica.

JAT Airways (JU; www.jat.com) Budva (☎ 033-451 641; Mediteranska 2); Podgorica (Map p5944; ☎ 020-664 750; Njegoševa 25) Flies from Belgrade and Niš (summer only) to Tivat and from Belgrade to Podgorica.

Malév Hungarian Airlines (MA; ☎ 36-1-235 3888; www.malev.hu) Flies from Budapest to Podgorica.

Montenegro Airlines (YM; www.montenegroairlines.com) Budva (☎ 033-454 900; Slovenska Obala bb); Podgorica (Map p594; ☎ 020-664 411; Slobode 23) Flies from Belgrade, Moscow and Niš (summer only) to Tivat. Also from Belgrade and Ljubljana to Podgorica.

Moskovia Airlines (3R; ☎ 033-455 967; www.ak3r.ru; Mediteranska 23, Budva) Flies from Moscow to Tivat and Podgorica.

Rossiya Airlines (FV; ☎ 7-495-995 2025; www.rossiya-airlines.ru) Flies from St Petersburg to Tivat.

S7 Airlines (S7; ☎ 033-459 706; www.s7.ru) Flies from Moscow to Tivat and Podgorica.

Ukraine International Airlines (PS; ☎ 380-44-581 5050; www.flyuia.com) Flies from Kiev to Tivat (summer only).

Ural Airlines (U6; ☎ 7-343-345 3645; www.uralairlines.ru) Flies from Yekaterinburg to Tivat (summer only).

Land

There are two main crossings between Albania and Montenegro, linking Shkodra to Ulcinj (Sukobin) and to Podgorica (Hani i Hotit).

For Bosnia, two checkpoints link Nikšić to Trebinje (Dolovi) and to Srbinje (Šćepan Polje). There's a more remote crossing halfway between the two at Vratkovići and another in the Kovač Mountains in the far north.

There's a busy checkpoint on the Adriatic highway between Herceg Novi and Dubrovnik, Croatia; expect delays.

There's only one crossing between Kosovo and Montenego, on the road between Rožaje and Peć.

If you're heading to Serbia, the busiest crossing is north of Bijelo Polje near Dobrakovo, followed by the checkpoint northeast of Rožaje and another east of Pljevlja.

BUS

There's a well-developed bus network linking Montenegro with the major cities of the region. Podgorica is the main hub but buses stop at many coastal towns as well. For details of bus travel from specific towns see p582 and p590.

CAR & MOTORCYCLE

Drivers need an International Driving Permit (IDP) and vehicles need Green Card insurance or insurance must be bought at the border.

TRAIN

Montenegro's only working passenger train line starts at Bar and heads into Serbia. For details on the train to Belgrade, see p594.

SEA

For details on ferries to Italy from Kotor and Bar, see p585 and p589.

GETTING AROUND

Bicycle

Cyclists are a rare species, even in the cities. Don't expect drivers to be considerate. Wherever possible, try to get off the main roads. The National Tourist Office has been developing a series of wilderness mountain biking trails (p597).

Bus

The local bus network is extensive and reliable. Buses are usually comfortable, air conditioned and rarely full. It's slightly cheaper to buy your ticket on the bus rather the station, but a station-bought ticket theoretically guarantees you a seat. Luggage carried below the bus is charged at €1 per piece.

Car & Motorcycle

Independent travel by car or motorcycle is an ideal way to gad about and discover the country; some of the drives are breathtakingly beautiful. Traffic police are everywhere, so stick to speed limits and carry an IDP. Allow more time than you'd expect for the distances involved, as the terrain will slow you down.

The major European car-hire companies have a presence in various centres, but **Meridian Rentacar** (☎ 454 105; www.meridian-rentacar.com), which has offices in Budva, Bar and Podgorica (Map p594), is a reliable local option; one-day hire starts from €45.

Train

Željeznica Crne Gore (☎ 441 211; www.zeljeznica.cg.yu) runs the only passenger train line, heading north from Bar. The trains are old and stiflingly hot in summer but they're priced accordingly and the route through the mountains is spectacular. Useful stops include Virpazar, Podgorica and Kolašin.

Morocco

For many travellers, Morocco might just be a short hop away by ferry or by one of the myriad budget airlines from Spain, but it's a much further distance to travel culturally. The regular certainties of Europe are suddenly swept away by the arrival in full technicolour of Africa and Islam. It's a complete sensory overload.

Tangier, that faded libertine on the coast, has traditionally been a first port of call, but the winds blow you quickly along the Atlantic coast to the cosmopolitan and movie-star famous Casablanca, and whitewashed fishing port gems of Asalih and Essaouira. Inland, the great imperial cities of Marrakesh and Fez attract visitors in droves as they have done for centuries. The winding streets of their ancient medinas have enough surprises around each corner to fill a dozen repeat trips. Away from the urban beat, you'll find Roman ruins and dramatically craggy valleys to distract you.

If you really want to escape from everything, Morocco still has a couple of trump cards. The High Atlas mountains seem custom-made for hiking boots, with endless trails between Berber villages, and North Africa's highest peak to conquer. Or if you prefer someone else to do the walking, simply saddle up your camel and ride it straight into the Sahara, to watch the sun setting over an ocean of sand.

FAST FACTS

- **Area** 446,550 sq km
- **Capital** Rabat
- **Currency** dirham (Dh); €1 = Dh11.22; UK£1 = Dh12.84; US$1 = Dh8.14; A$1 = Dh6.31; ¥100 = Dh8.6; NZ$1 = Dh4.95
- **Famous for** Humphrey Bogart and *Casablanca*, Marrakesh, tajines and couscous, trendy riad hotels
- **Official languages** Darija (Moroccan Arabic), French, Berber
- **Population** 33.7 million
- **Phrases** *ssalamu'lekum* (hello); *shukran* (thanks); *insh'allah* (God willing)
- **Telephone codes** country code ☎ 212; international access code ☎ 00
- **Visas** The vast majority of nationalities can enter Morocco for 90 days without a visa; see p955 for more details

HIGHLIGHTS

- Get lost in the alleyways of the **Fez medina**, Islam's greatest living medieval city (p631).
- Taste *1001 Nights* in the open-air spectacle of the Djemaa el-Fna square in **Marrakesh** (p641).
- Chill in the Rif Mountains in the dazzling blue town of **Chefchaouen** (p614).
- Catch the sea breeze in **Essaouira** (p627), Morocco's hippest resort.
- Watch a Sahara desert sunset over the sand dunes of **Erg Chebbi** (p652).

ITINERARIES

- **One week** From Tangier, make a beeline for Fez and Marrakesh, imperial cities in the Moroccan interior that deserve as much time as you can spare. After that, a detour to artsy Essaouira is a wonderful way to step down a gear after the onslaught of Morocco's most clamorous cities.
- **Two weeks** Follow the itinerary above, but en route south head via chilled-out Chefchaouen. Meknès is a great detour from Fez, but once into the south past Marrakesh, make time either to head into the High Atlas for hiking, or the Saharan sand at Merzouga or M'Hamid.

CLIMATE & WHEN TO GO

Morocco is at its best in spring (mid-March to May), when the country is lush and green, followed by autumn (September to November), when the heat of summer has eased. At other times, don't underestimate the extremes of summer heat and winter, particularly in the High Atlas, where snow-capped peaks persist from November to July. If you are travelling in winter, head for the south, although be prepared for bitterly cold nights. The north coast and Rif Mountains are frequently wet and cloudy in winter and early spring.

Apart from the weather, the timing of Ramadan, the traditional month of fasting and purification, is another important consideration as some restaurants and cafes close during the day and general business hours are reduced.

See the climate charts, p944, for more information.

CONNECTIONS: MOVING ON FROM MOROCCO

The cheap flight revolution has well and truly arrived in Morocco, and budget airlines link Casablanca, Marrakesh and, to a lesser extent, Fez and Tangier to the major European air hubs (p657). If you have time, a more enjoyable way of connecting to mainland Europe is by ferry, either zipping across the Straits of Gibraltar from Tangier to Algeciras (p838) or Tarifa (p839) in Spain, or from Spain's enclaves of Ceuta and Melilla (p657), to connect with the Spanish rail network.

HISTORY

The Berbers & Romans

Morocco's first-known inhabitants were Near Eastern nomads who may have been distant cousins of the ancient Egyptians. Phoenicians appear to have arrived around 800 BC. When the Romans arrived in the 4th century BC, they called the expanse of Morocco and western Algeria 'Mauretania' and the indigenous people 'Berbers', meaning 'barbarians'.

In the 1st century AD, the Romans built up Volubilis (p640) into a city of 20,000 mostly Berber people, but, fed up with the persistently unruly locals, the Roman emperor Caligula declared the end of Berber autonomy in North Africa in 40 AD. But whereas the Vandals and Byzantines failed to oust the Romans from their home turf, Berbers in the Rif and the Atlas ultimately succeeded through a campaign of near-constant harassment – a tactic that would later put the squeeze on many an unpopular Moroccan sultan.

As Rome slipped into decline, the Berbers harried and hassled any army that dared to invade to the point where the Berbers were free to do as they pleased.

The Islamic Dynasties

In the second half of the 7th century, the soldiers of the Prophet Mohammed set forth from the Arabian Peninsula and overwhelmed the peoples of North Africa. Within a century, nearly all Berber tribes had embraced Islam, although, true to form, local tribes developed their own brand of Islamic Shi'ism, which sparked rebellion against the eastern Arabs.

By 829, local elites had established an Idrissid state with its capital at Fez, dominating all of Morocco. Thus commenced a

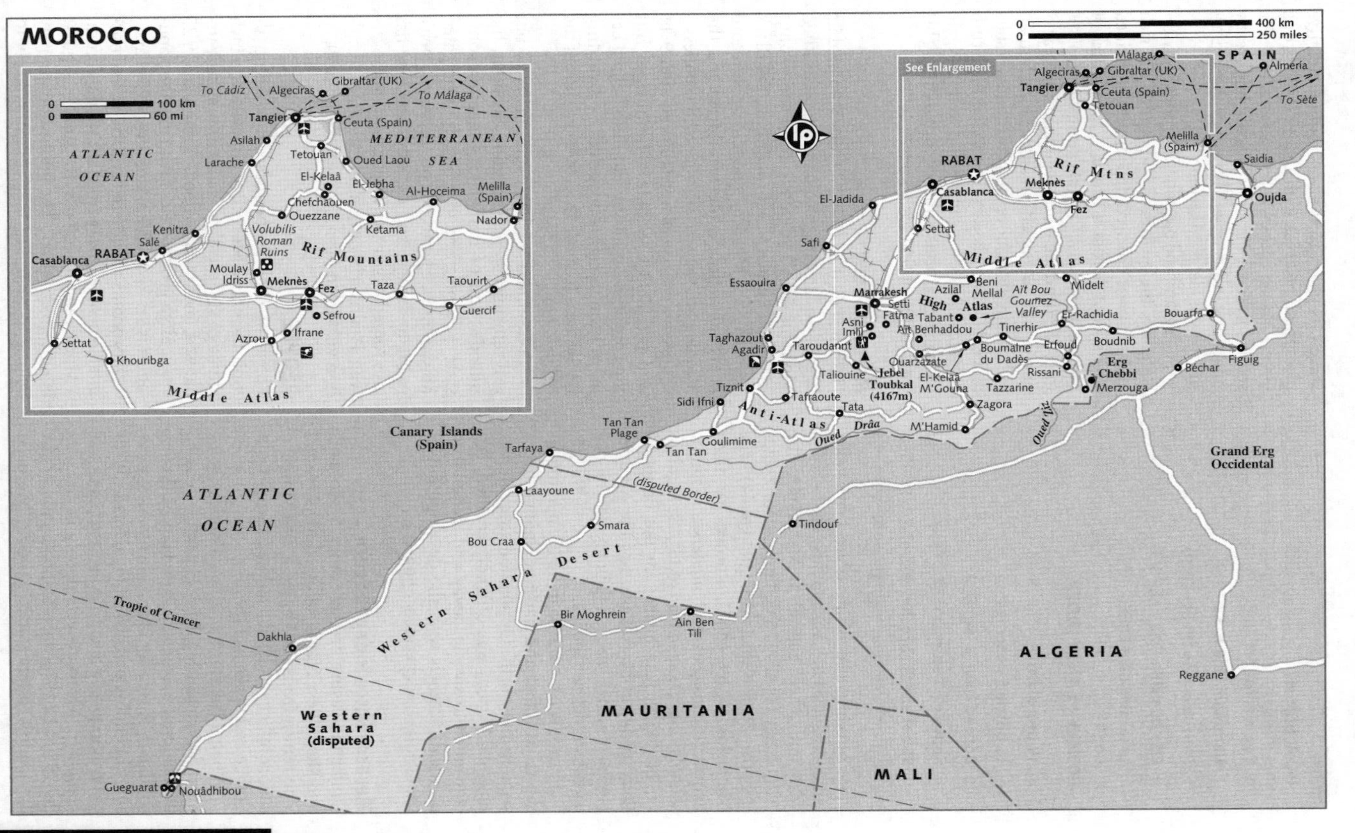
MOROCCO
0 400 km
0 250 miles
SPAIN
Almería
To Sète
Málaga
Gibraltar (UK)
Algeciras
Ceuta (Spain)
Tetouan
Tangier
Melilla (Spain)
Saïdia
Oujda
See Enlargement
RABAT
Casablanca
Settat
Rif Mtns
Meknès
Fez
Middle Atlas
Midelt
Beni Mellal
Azilal
Aït Bou Goumez Valley
High Atlas
Tabant
Er-Rachidia
Boudnib
Bouarfa
Figuig
Béchar
Erg Chebbi
Merzouga
Erfoud
Rissani
Tinerhir
Boumalne du Dadès
Aït Benhaddou
Ouarzazate
El-Kelaâ M'Gouna
Tazzarine
Zagora
M'Hamid
Oued Ziz
Marrakesh
Setti Fatma
Asni
Imlil
Jebel Toubkal (4167m)
Taliouine
Taroudannt
Tata
Oued Drâa
Tafraoute
Anti-Atlas
El-Jadida
Safi
Essaouira
Taghazout
Agadir
Tiznit
Sidi Ifni
Goulimime
Tan Tan
Tan Tan Plage
Canary Islands (Spain)
Tarfaya
Laayoune
(disputed Border)
Smara
Bou Craa
Tindouf
Western Sahara Desert
Bir Moghrein
Ain Ben Tili
Grand Erg Occidental
ALGERIA
Reggane
MAURITANIA
MALI
ATLANTIC OCEAN
Tropic of Cancer
Dakhla
Western Sahara (disputed)
Gueguarat
Nouâdhibou
0 100 km
0 60 mi
To Cádiz
Algeciras
Gibraltar (UK)
To Málaga
Tangier
Ceuta (Spain)
MEDITERRANEAN SEA
ATLANTIC OCEAN
Asilah
Larache
Tetouan
Oued Laou
El-Kelaâ
El-Jebha
Al-Hoceima
Melilla (Spain)
Chefchaouen
Ouezzane
Ketama
Nador
Kenitra
Salé
RABAT
Casablanca
Volubilis Roman Ruins
Rif Mountains
Moulay Idriss
Meknès
Fez
Taza
Taourirt
Guercif
Sefrou
Ifrane
Azrou
Settat
Khouribga
Middle Atlas

MOROCCO

HOW MUCH?

- **Pot of mint tea** Dh8
- **Hammam** Dh8 to Dh12
- **Petit-taxi ride** Dh5 to Dh10
- **City bus ride** Dh2 to Dh3
- **Local sim card** Dh30

LONELY PLANET INDEX

- **1L petrol** Dh12
- **1L bottled water** Dh6
- **Bottled beer (Flag)** Dh8
- **Souvenir T-shirt** Dh120
- **Street snack (brochette)** Dh30 to Dh40

cycle of rising and falling Islamic dynasties, which included the Almoravids (1062–1147), who built their capital at Marrakesh; the Almohads (1147–1269), famous for building the Koutoubia Mosque (p644); the Merenids (1269–1465), known for their exquisite mosques and *medersas* (Islamic schools), especially in Fez (p633); the Saadians (1524–1659), responsible for the Palais el-Badi (p644) in Marrakesh; and the Alawites (1659–present), who left their greatest monuments in Meknès (p638).

France took control in 1912, making its capital at Rabat and handing Spain a token zone in the north. Opposition from Berber mountain tribes was officially crushed, but continued to simmer away and moved into political channels with the development of the Istiqlal (independence) party.

Morocco Since Independence

Under increasing pressure from Moroccans and the Allies, France allowed Mohammed V to return from exile in 1955, and Morocco successfully negotiated its independence from France and Spain in 1956.

When Mohammed V died suddenly of heart failure in 1961, King Hassan II became the leader of the new nation. Hassan II consolidated power by crackdowns on dissent and suspending parliament for a decade. With heavy borrowing and an ever-expanding bureaucracy, Morocco was deeply in debt by the 1970s. In 1973 the phosphate industry in the Spanish Sahara started to boom. Morocco staked its claim to the area and its lucrative phosphate reserves with the 350,000-strong Green March into Western Sahara in 1975, settling the area with Moroccans while greatly unsettling indigenous Sahrawi people agitating for self-determination.

Such grand and patriotic flourishes notwithstanding, the growing gap between the rich and the poor ensured that dissent remained widespread across a broad cross-section of Moroccan society. Protests against price rises in 1981 prompted a brutal government crackdown, but sustained pressure from human rights activists achieved unprecedented results in 1991, when Hassan II founded the Truth & Reconciliation Commission to investigate human rights abuses that occurred during his own reign – a first for a king.

Morocco Today

Hassan II died in 1999 and Morocco held its breath. In his first public statement as king, Mohammed VI vowed to right the wrongs of the era known to Moroccans as 'the Black Years'. Today, Morocco's human rights record is arguably the cleanest in Africa and the Middle East, though still not exactly spotless – repressive measures were revived after 9/11 and the 2003 Casablanca bombings. But the commission has nonetheless helped cement human rights advances by awarding reparations to more than 9000 victims of the Black Years.

Mohammed VI has overseen small but real reformist steps, including elections, the introduction of Berber languages in some state schools, and the much-anticipated Mudawanna, a legal code protecting women's rights to divorce and custody. The king has also forged closer ties with Europe and overseen a tourism boom, aiming to attract 10 million visitors to Morocco by the year 2010.

PEOPLE

People of Arab-Berber descent make up almost the entire Moroccan population, which although still mostly rural, is increasingly urbanised, and young to boot – 55% are under 25 years. High growth rates mean that the population is set to double almost every 25 years.

Moroccans are inherently sociable and hospitable people. Away from the tourist scrum, a Moroccan proverb tells the story – 'A guest is a gift from Allah'. The public domain may belong to men, but they're just as likely to invite you home to meet the family. If this happens, consider yourself truly privileged but remember: remove your shoes before stepping on the carpet; keep your (ritually unclean) left hand firmly out of the communal dish; and feel free to slurp your tea and belch your appreciation loudly.

RELIGION

Morocco is a Muslim country. Muslims share their roots with Jews and Christians and respect these groups as *Ahl al-Kteb,* People of the Book. Fundamentalism is mostly discouraged but remains a presence, especially among the urban poor who have enjoyed none of the benefits of economic growth. That said, the majority of Muslims do not favour such developments and the popularity of fundamentalism is not as great as Westerners imagine.

Emigration to France, Israel and the US has reduced Morocco's once robust Jewish community to about 7000 from a high of around 300,000 in 1948.

ARTS

Architecture

Moroccan religious buildings are adorned with hand-carved detailing, gilded accents, chiselled mosaics and an array of other decorative flourishes. A mosque consists of a courtyard, an arcaded portico and a main prayer hall facing Mecca. Great examples include the 9th-century Kairaouine Mosque (p633) in Fez and the colossal Hassan II Mosque (p624) in Casablanca. While all but the latter are closed to non-Muslims, the *medersas* that bejewel major Moroccan cities are open for visits.

Although religious architecture dominates, Casablanca in particular boasts local architectural features grafted onto whitewashed European edifices in a distinctive crossroads style that might be described as Islamic geometry meets art deco.

The street facade of the Moroccan *riads* (traditional courtyard houses; also called *dars*) usually conceals an inner courtyard that allows light to penetrate during the day and cool air to settle at night. Many classy guest houses occupy beautifully renovated traditional *riads*.

Music

The most renowned Berber folk group is the Master Musicians of Jajouka, who famously inspired the Rolling Stones and collaborated with them on some truly experimental fusion. Lately the big names are women's, namely the all-female group B'net Marrakech and the bold Najat Aatabou, who sings protest songs in Berber against restrictive traditional roles.

Joyously bluesy with a rhythm you can't refuse, Gnaoua music, which began among freed slaves in Marrakesh and Essaouira, may send you into a trance – and that's just what it's meant to do. To sample the best in Gnaoua, head to Essaouira on the third weekend in June for the Gnaoua & World Music Festival.

Rai, originally from Algeria, is one of the strongest influences on Moroccan contemporary music, incorporating elements of jazz, hip hop and rap. A popular artist is Cheb Mami, famous for vocals on Sting's 'Desert Rose'.

ENVIRONMENT

Morocco's three ecological zones – coast, mountain and desert – host more than 40 different ecosystems and provide habitat for many endemic species, including the iconic and sociable Barbary macaque (also known as the Barbary ape). Unfortunately, pressure from sprawling urban areas and the encroachment of industrialisation in Morocco's wilderness means that 18 mammal (a staggering 15% of the total) and a dozen bird species are considered endangered.

Pollution, desertification, overgrazing and deforestation are the major environmental issues facing the Moroccan government. Despite plantation programs and the development of new national parks, less than 0.05% of Moroccan territory is protected, one-third of Morocco's ecosystems are disappearing, 10% of vertebrates are endangered and 25,000 hectares of forest are lost every year.

Global warming has stolen valuable snowfall from mountain regions whose rivers depend upon the melt; in the south, most rivers have been dry for at least 10 years. Population pressures also result in more intensive farming practices and deforestation, while overgrazing is picking the land clean, thereby accumulating the pressures heaped upon the land by global environmental change. Desertification is the result, rendering crops defenceless against whipping sandstorms or torrential flooding. In the end, the ravaged villages confront a crisis of food and water supply in which poor health and sanitation fester, land becomes unsuitable for farming and pristine environments are lost forever. Pollution is another problem that threatens to choke Morocco's environment. Industrial waste is routinely released into the sea, soil and waterways, thereby contaminating water supplies used for drinking and irrigation. The draining of coastal wetlands – which provide important habitats for endangered species – continues apace to address the rising demand and falling supply of water for irrigation, a problem that becomes increasingly acute with water-hungry tourist developments.

FOOD & DRINK

Influenced by Berber, Arabic and Mediterranean traditions, Moroccan cuisine features a sublime combination of spices and fresh produce.

It would be a culinary crime to skip breakfast in Morocco. Pavement cafes and kiosks put a local twist on a continental breakfast with Moroccan pancakes and doughnuts, French pastries, coffee and mint tea. Follow your nose into the *souqs* (markets), where you'll find tangy olives and local *jiben* (fresh goat's or cow's milk cheeses) to be devoured with fresh *khoobz* (Moroccan-style flat bread baked in a wood-fired oven).

Lunch is traditionally the biggest meal of the day in Morocco. The most typical Moroccan dish is tajine, a meat and vegetable stew cooked slowly in an earthenware dish. Couscous, fluffy steamed semolina served with tender meat and vegetables, is another staple. Fish dishes also make an excellent choice in coastal areas, while *harira* is a thick soup made from lamb stock, lentils, chickpeas, onions, tomatoes, fresh herbs and spices. *B'stilla*, a speciality of Fez, includes poultry (chicken or pigeon), almonds, cinnamon, saffron and sugar, encased in layer upon layer of very fine pastry.

Vegetarians shouldn't have many problems – fresh fruit and vegetables are widely available, as are lentils and chickpeas. Salads are ubiquitous in Morocco, particularly the traditional *salade marocaine* made from diced green peppers, tomatoes and red onion. Ask for your couscous or tajine *sans viande* (without meat).

For dessert, Moroccan patisseries concoct excellent French and Moroccan sweets. Local sweets include flaky pastries rich with nuts and aromatic traces of orange-flower water. Another variation is a sweet *b'stilla* with toasted almonds, cinnamon and cream.

Cafe culture is alive and well in Morocco and mint tea, the legendary 'Moroccan whisky', is made with Chinese gunpowder tea, fresh mint and copious sugar. It's not advisable to drink tap water in Morocco but fruit juices, especially freshly squeezed orange juice, are the country's greatest bargain. Beer is easy to find in the *villes nouvelles* (new towns); Flag is the most common brand.

Smoking is something of a national pastime for (male) Moroccans, although most restaurants tend to be reasonably smokefree.

For more on opening hours, see the Morocco Directory, p654.

MEDITERRANEAN COAST & THE RIF

Bounded by the red crags of the Rif Mountains and the crashing waves of the Mediterranean, northern Morocco's wildly beautiful coastline conceals attractions as diverse as the cosmopolitan hustle of Tangier, the Spanish enclaves of Ceuta and Melilla, the old colonial capital of Tetouan, and the superbly relaxing town of Chefchaouen.

TANGIER

pop 650,000

Like the dynamic strait upon which it sits, Tangier is the product of 1001 currents, including Islam, Berber tribes, colonial masters, a highly strategic location, a vibrant port, the Western counterculture and the international jet set. It has been Morocco's face to the world for longer than anyone cares to remember, and has regularly passed between Moroccan and Western control – for half the 20th century is was under the dubious control of an international council, making it a byword for licentious behaviour and dodgy dealings.

Some of the hustlers remain, notably looking out for tourists fresh off the ferry from Spain, although the ministrations of the tourist police have greatly reduced these stresses. Many travellers simply pass through, but if you take it head-on and learn to handle the hustlers, you'll find it a lively, cosmopolitan place with an energetic nightlife.

Orientation

Tangier's small medina climbs up the hill to the northeast of the city, while the *ville nouvelle* surrounds it to the west, south and southeast. The large, central square known as the Grand Socco (officially renamed Place du 9 Avril 1947) provides the link between the two. For details on getting to/from the airport, see p610.

Information

Blvds Pasteur and Mohammed V are lined with numerous banks with ATMs and *bureau de change* counters. Blvd Pasteur also has plenty of internet places.

Clinique du Croissant Rouge (Red Cross Clinic; ☎ 039 946976; 6 Rue al-Mansour Dahabi)

Délégation Régionale du Tourisme (ONMT; ☎ 039 948050; 29 Blvd Pasteur; 8.30am-4.30pm Mon-Fri) Local tourist office.

Espace Net (16 Ave Mexique; per hr Dh5; 9.30am-1am)

Main post office (Blvd Mohammed V)

Sights

The **kasbah** sits on the highest point of Tangier, behind stout walls. Coming from the medina, you enter through Bab el-Aassa, the southeastern gate, to find the **Kasbah Museum** (☎ 039 932097; admission incl Sultan's Gardens Dh10; 9am-12.30pm Wed-Mon, 3-5.30pm Wed, Thu & Sat-Mon), housed in the 17th-century palace of Dar el-Makhzen. It's now a worthwhile museum devoted to Moroccan arts. Before leaving, take a stroll around the Andalucian-style **Sultan's Gardens**.

In the southwest corner of the medina, the **Old American Legation Museum** (☎ 039 935317; www.legation.org; 8 Rue d'Amerique; admission free; 10am-1pm & 3-5pm Mon-Fri) is an intriguing relic of the international zone with a fascinating collection of memorabilia from the international writers and artists who passed through Tangier. Donations appreciated.

Housed in a former synagogue, the **Musée de la Fondation Lorin** (☎ 039 930306; lorin@wanadoo.net.ma; 44 Rue Touahine; admission free; 11am-1pm & 3.30-7.30pm Sun-Fri) has an engaging collection of photographs, posters and prints of Tangier from 1890 to 1960. Donations appreciated.

Heading uphill, you eventually emerge at **Bab Fass**, the keyhole-shaped gate that opens to the renovated plaza of **Grand Socco**. A short walk up Rue d'Angleterre brings you to one of the more charming oddities of Tangier, the Victorian-era **St Andrews Church** (services Sun 8.30am, 11am), which has the Lord's Prayer in Arabic above the nave.

Sleeping

Hotel Mamora (☎ 039 934105; 19 Rue des Postes; s Dh60-200, d Dh120-230) With a variety of rooms at different rates (some with just a sink, some with toilet or shower), this is a good bet. It's a bit institutional, like an old school, but clean, well run and strong value for the money. The rooms overlooking the green-tiled roof of the Grande Mosqué are the most picturesque, if you don't mind the muezzin's call.

Hotel El-Muniria (☎ 039 935337; 1 Rue Magellan; s/d Dh150/200) This is your best low-end option in the *ville nouvelle*, an important cut above the gloomy and often dirty competition. French windows and bright, flowery fabrics set it apart, revealing the careful touch of a hands-on family operation. Room 4 is a great hideaway, a quiet corner double with lots of light, as is Room 8, a quiet single with a harbour view. Potential noise from the bar below is the only drawback.

La Tangerina (☎ 039 947731; www.latangerina.com; Riad Sultan Kasbah, d incl breakfast Dh400-1000) This is easily the best midrange choice in Tangier. It's a perfectly renovated *riad* at the very top of the kasbah, with 10 rooms of different personalities, fairly priced and with highly attentive hosts. Bathed in light and lined with rope banisters, it feels like an elegant, Berber-carpeted steamship cresting the medina, with the roof terrace overlooking the ancient crenellated walls of the kasbah. Dinner is available on request.

Hotel Marco Polo (☎ 039 941124; www.marco-polo.ma; 2 Rue al-Antaki; s/d Dh420/560) This newly renovated hotel is the perfect choice if you aren't looking for local atmosphere. Lots of light, sparkling marble floors and pastel walls make this a bright and welcoming, though generic, space. An excellent, central location across from the beach provides easy access to both the *ville nouvelle* and the medina. During low season you pay Dh330/400 for a single/double. Breakfast costs Dh35.

El-Minzah (☎ 039 935885; www.elminzah.com; 85 Rue de la Liberté; s/d incl breakfast from Dh1700/2100;) The classiest five-star hotel in Tangier proper, and a local landmark, this beautifully maintained 1930s period piece offers three excellent restaurants, three equally good bars, a fitness centre, a spa, pleasant gardens and

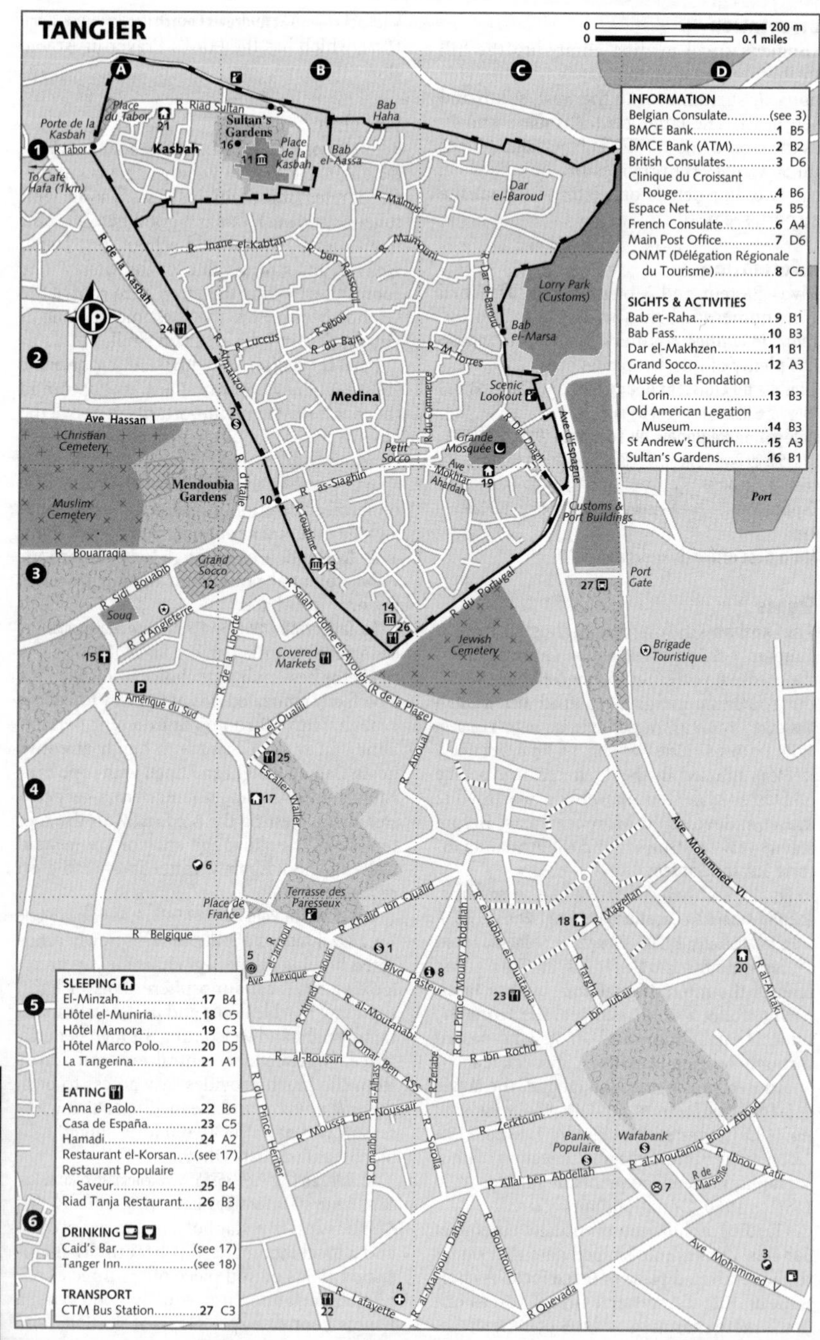
TANGIER
INFORMATION
Belgian Consulate............(see 3)
BMCE Bank.........................1 B5
BMCE Bank (ATM)............2 B2
British Consulates..............3 D6
Clinique du Croissant Rouge..........................4 B6
Espace Net.........................5 B5
French Consulate...............6 A4
Main Post Office...............7 D6
ONMT (Délégation Régionale du Tourisme)................8 C5
SIGHTS & ACTIVITIES
Bab er-Raha......................9 B1
Bab Fass..........................10 B3
Dar el-Makhzen...............11 B1
Grand Socco..................12 A3
Musée de la Fondation Lorin............................13 B3
Old American Legation Museum.........................14 B3
St Andrew's Church.........15 A3
Sultan's Gardens.............16 B1
SLEEPING
El-Minzah........................17 B4
Hôtel el-Muniria...............18 C5
Hôtel Mamora..................19 C3
Hôtel Marco Polo.............20 D5
La Tangerina....................21 A1
EATING
Anna e Paolo....................22 B6
Casa de España................23 C5
Hamadi............................24 A2
Restaurant el-Korsan.....(see 17)
Restaurant Populaire Saveur.........................25 B4
Riad Tanja Restaurant.....26 B3
DRINKING
Caid's Bar......................(see 17)
Tanger Inn......................(see 18)
TRANSPORT
CTM Bus Station.............27 C3
Kasbah
Medina
Sultan's Gardens
Place du Tabor
Place de la Kasbah
Porte de la Kasbah
To Café Hafa (1km)
Bab Haha
Bab el-Aassa
Dar el-Baroud
Lorry Park (Customs)
Bab el-Marsa
Scenic Lookout
Grande Mosquée
Petit Socco
Christian Cemetery
Muslim Cemetery
Mendoubia Gardens
Grand Socco
Souq
Covered Markets
Jewish Cemetery
Customs & Port Buildings
Port
Port Gate
Brigade Touristique
Terrasse des Paresseux
Place de France
Bank Populaire
Wafabank
Ave Hassan I
Ave d'Espagne
Ave Mohammed VI
Ave Mohammed V
R Riad Sultan
R Tabor
R de la Kasbah
R Jnane el-Kabtan
R ben Raissouli
R Malmusi
R Maimouni
R Dar el-Baroud
R Lucus
R Sebou
R du Bain
R M Torres
R Almanzor
R du Commerce
R Dar Dbagh
Ave Mokhtar Ahardan
R d'Italie
R as-Siaghin
R Touahine
R du Portugal
R Bouarraqia
R Sidi Bouabib
R d'Angleterre
R de la Liberté
R Salah Eddine el-Ayoubi (R de la Plage)
R Amérique du Sud
R el-Oualili
Escalier Waller
R Anoual
R Belgique
R Khalid ibn Oualid
R el-Jarraoui
Ave Mexique
Blvd Pasteur
R Ahmed Chaouki
R al-Moutanabi
R du Prince Moulay Abdallah
R el-Jabha el-Ouatania
R Magellan
R Targha
R ibn Jubair
R al-Antaki
R al-Boussiri
R Omar Ben ASS
R Zeriabe
R ibn Rochd
R du Prince Heritier
R al-Alhass
R Moussa ben-Noussair
R Sorolla
R Zerktouni
R Omaribn
R Allal ben Abdellah
R al-Moutamid Bnou Abbad
R Ibnou Katir
R de Marseille
R al-Mansour Dahabi
R Bouhtouri
R Lafayette
R Quevada
200 m
0.1 miles

even a babysitting service. Shaped like an enormous hollow square, with a tremendous Spanish–Moorish courtyard, it has history oozing from its walls. Portside rooms offer beautiful views. Low-season prices drop to Dh1300/1700 for a single/double.

Eating

In the medina there's a host of cheap eating possibilities around the Petit Socco and the adjacent Ave Mokhtar Ahardan, with rotisserie chicken, sandwiches and brochettes all on offer. In the *ville nouvelle,* try the streets immediately south of Place de France, which are flush with fast-food outlets, sandwich bars and fish counters.

MEDINA

Hamadi (☎ 039 934514; 2 Rue de la Kasbah; mains Dh40-70; ⏰ 9.30-3.30am & 7.30-11pm) A so-called 'palace restaurant' offering multicourse local cuisine, uniformed staff, live music (and perhaps belly dancing) at a fixed price, all of it aimed at the next tour bus. But the price is right, the decor bright and the location pleasant.

Restaurant Populaire Saveur (☎ 039 336326; 2 Escalier Waller; set menu Dh150; ⏰ 12.30-4pm & 7-10pm, Sat-Thu) This charming little seafood restaurant offers excellent, filling set menus in rustic surroundings. The owner, a self-described Popeye lookalike, serves inventive plates of fresh catch with sticky *seffa* (sweet couscous) for dessert, all of it washed down with a homemade juice cocktail made from 15 kinds of fruit (have a look at the vat in back.) Not just a meal, a whole experience.

Riad Tanja Restaurant (☎ 039 333538; www.riadtanja.com; Rue du Portugal; set menu Dh300) With a reputation for some of the best food in the city and for a romantic view of the *ville nouvelle* climbing up the opposite hill, this is a great place to splurge, particularly with that special someone. The bi-level dining area feels more like a well-designed living room, with a dozen tables, high ceilings and international decor.

VILLE NOUVELLE

Casa de España (☎ 039 947359; 11 Rue el-Jebha el-Ouatania; mains from Dh60, lunch set menu Dh60) With its attractive minimal style, this contemporary Spanish bar-restaurant is a breath of fresh air after so many mosaic interiors. Snappily dressed waiters serve up classic Spanish dishes, with some wonderful specials such as lamb with summer fruits, and there are free tapas with drinks.

Anna e Paolo (☎ 039 944617; 77 Ave Prince Heretier; mains from Dh60) This is the top Italian bistro in the city, a family-run restaurant with Venetian owners that feels like you have been invited for Sunday dinner. Expect a highly international crowd, lots of cross-table conversations about the events of the day, wholesome food and a shot of grappa on the way out the door. Watch your head on the way upstairs.

Restaurant el-Korsan (☎ 039 935885; El-Minzah, 85 Rue de la Liberté; mains around Dh130; ⏰ 8-11pm) One of Tangier's top restaurants, this chic and classy place inside the El-Minzah (p607) offers a smaller, more-intimate version of a palace restaurant theme – without the bus tours. Well-presented Moroccan classics are served to the soft playing of live musicians, and often traditional dancing. Reservations are necessary, including a day's notice for lunch. Dress well.

Drinking

Café Hafa (Ave Mohammed Tazi; ⏰ 10am-8pm) With a shady terrace overlooking the straits, Hafa is where Paul Bowles and the Rolling Stones came to smoke dope and the indolent air still lingers among the locals who hang out here to enjoy the view and a game of backgammon.

Caid's Bar (El-Minzah, 85 Rue de la Liberté; wine from Dh20; ⏰ 10am-midnight) Welcome to Rick's Café – the real-life model for the bar in *Casablanca.* Long the establishment's drinking hole of choice, this El-Minzah landmark is a classy relic of the grand days of international Tangier, and photos of the famous and infamous adorn the walls. Women are more than welcome, and the adjacent wine bar is equally good.

Entertainment

Tangier's nightlife picks up in summer. Nightclubs cluster near Place de France and line the beach. Cover charges vary and may be rolled into drink prices. **Loft** (☎ 073 280927; www.loftclub-tanger.com) is the premier nightspot, a state-of-the-art club that feels like an enormous silver cruise ship, with upper storey balconies, sparkling metal railings, billowing sail-like curtains, spot lights cutting through artificial fog – and no cover. Tangier's gay scene has long since departed for Marrakesh, but **Tanger Inn** (Hotel El-Muniria, 1 Rue Magellan; beer Dh10; ⏰ 10.30pm-1am, to 3am Fri & Sat) and some of the bars along the beach attract gay clientele, particularly late on weekends.

FRESH OFF THE BOAT?

For many people Tangier is a first: first time in Africa, first time in a Muslim country, first time in a developing country, or some combination of the above. If you've taken the ferry, drawn by the exotic scent from across the strait, here are some tips to ease your arrival (and departure) stress:

The hordes of touts that would descend in packs on unwary travellers have largely disappeared from Tangier's port, but you're still likely to be greeted by a few multilingual 'guides'. The best way to deal with this is to look blasé, claim that you already know the city and politely decline any offers of assistance. Smile and keep moving. It helps to know exactly where you're going, so you can jump quickly into a cab if necessary. A *petit taxi* (local taxi) into the centre will cost around Dh10 and a *grand taxi* (shared taxi) around Dh30 between all passengers. Remember to change money on the boat to pay the fare. Tackling anywhere unfamiliar after dark is always more traumatic, so try to arrive early in the day and, above all, with a good sense of humour.

If you're catching the ferry *from* Tangier and arrive at the port on foot, you'll be approached by touts intent on getting you into one or other of the numerous ticket offices and travel agencies along Ave d'Espagne. To minimise the hassle, you might buy your ticket in advance or take a taxi to the terminal building. In any case, be sure to pick up an exit form with your ticket. The scribes who distribute them at the port will expect a tip for their 'assistance' filling out the form. Allow a good 90 minutes before your boat sails for getting tickets and getting through passport control.

Getting There & Away

For ferry options, see p657.

BUS

The **CTM station** (☎ 039 931172) is conveniently located beside the port gate. Destinations include Casablanca (Dh120, six hours), Rabat (Dh90, 4½ hours), Marrakesh (Dh210, 10 hours), Fez (Dh100, six hours), Meknès (Dh80, five hours), Chefchaouen (Dh40, three hours) and Tetouan (Dh20, one hour). Cheaper bus companies operate from the **main bus station** (gare routière; ☎ 039 946928; Place Jamia el-Arabia), about 2km south of the city centre.

TAXI

You can hail *grands taxis* (shared taxis) to places outside Tangier from a lot next to the main bus station. The most common destinations are Tetouan (Dh25, one hour), Asilah (Dh20, 30 minutes) and, for Ceuta, Fnideq (Dh40, one hour).

TRAIN

Four trains depart daily from Tanger Ville, the swish new train station 3km southeast of the centre (Dh10 in a local *petit taxi*). One morning and one afternoon service go to Casa-Voyageurs in Casablanca (Dh118, 5½ hours); four trains via Meknès (Dh80, four hours) to Fez (Dh97, five hours), although three involve changing at Sidi Kacem. A night service goes all the way to Marrakesh (seat Dh197, couchette Dh350, 12 hours).

Getting Around

Distinguishable by their ultramarine colour with a yellow stripe down the side, *petits taxis* do standard journeys around town for Dh7 to Dh10. From **Ibn Batouta airport** (☎ 039 393720), 15km southeast of the city, take a cream-coloured *grand taxi* (Dh150).

AROUND TANGIER

Just 14km west of Tangier lies the dramatic **Cap Spartel**, the northwestern extremity of Africa's Atlantic coast. Below Cap Spartel, the lovely beach **Plage Robinson** stretches to the south. Five kilometres along here you reach the **Grottes d'Hercule** (admission Dh5), next to Le Mirage hotel. These caves are said to have been the dwelling place of the mythical Hercules when he mightily separated Europe from Africa.

CEUTA

pop 76,000

Jutting out east into the Mediterranean, this 20 sq km peninsula has been a Spanish enclave since 1640, and its relaxed, well-kept city centre with bars, cafes and Andalucian atmosphere provides a sharp contrast to the other side of the border. Nonetheless, Ceuta is still recognisably African. Between a quarter and a third of the population are of Rif

Berber origin, giving the enclave a fascinating Iberian–African mix.

Orientation & Information

Most of the hotels, restaurants and offices of interest are on the narrow spit of land linking the peninsula to the mainland. The Plaza de Africa, unmistakable for its giant cathedral, dominates the city centre. The port and ferry terminal are a short walk to the northwest. The border is 2km to the south along the Avenida Martinez Catena.

To phone Ceuta from outside Spain, dial ☎ 0034 before the nine-digit phone number. Also remember that Ceuta is on Spanish time and uses the euro.

Banks with ATMs are plentiful around the pedestrianised Paseo de Revellín, and Plaza Ruiz.

Cyber Ceuta (☎ 956 512303; Paseo Colón; per hr €2.40; 11am-2pm & 5-10pm Mon-Sat, 5-10pm Sun)

Main tourist office (☎ 956 200560; Baluarte de los Mallorquines; 8.30am-8.30pm Mon-Fri, 9am-8pm Sat & Sun) Friendly and efficient, with good maps and brochures.

Post office (59 Calle Real; 8.30am-8.30pm Mon-Fri, 9.30am-2pm Sat)

Sights

Ceuta's history is marked by the **Ruta Monumenta**, a series of excellent information boards in English and Spanish outside key buildings and monuments.

The impressively restored **royal city walls** (☎ 956 511770; Ave González Tablas; admission free incl gallery; 10am-2pm & 5-8pm) are worth a visit, and contain the striking **Museo de los Muralles Reales** art gallery tucked inside.

The most intriguing museum is the underground **Museo de la Basilica Tardorromana** (Calle Queipo de Llano; 10am-1.30pm & 5-7.30pm Mon-Sat, 10am-1.30pm Sun). It's integrated into the architectural remains of an ancient basilica discovered during street work in the 1980s and includes a bridge over open tombs, skeletons included.

Sleeping

Pensión La Bohemia (☎ 956 510615; 16 Paseo de Revellín; s/d €25/35) This well-run operation, one flight above a shopping arcade, offers a bright and spotless set of rooms arranged around a central court, with potted plants, shiny tile floors and a surfeit of pictures of Marilyn Monroe. Bathrooms are shared, with plenty of hot water and communal showers. Rooms have small TVs and fans.

Hostal Central (☎ 956 516716; www.hostalesceuta.com; Paseo del Revellín; s/d/tr €34/44/54;) This good-value, centrally located two-star hotel is the next step up from a pension, but has the same cosy charm. Bright rooms are small but spotless, and all come with bathroom and fridge. Low-season discounts can tip this place into the budget bracket.

Hostal Plaza Ruiz (☎ 956 516733; www.hostalesceuta.com; 3 Plaza Ruiz; s €34-45, d €44-60, tr €54-76;) Sister hotel to the Central, this place has a similar, welcoming style and a charming location. Rooms are airy, with nice pine furniture; the best have wrought-iron balconies overlooking the cafes of the plaza. Bathrooms and fridges are standard.

Parador Hotel La Muralla (☎ 956 514940; ceuta@parador.es; 15 Plaza de Africa; s/d from €65/90;) Ceuta's top address is this spacious four-star hotel perfectly situated on the Plaza de Africa. Rooms are comfortable, but not luxurious, with simple wooden doors and plain ceramic tiles. Balconies overlook a pleasant garden overflowing with palm trees. A bar-cafe and gym add value, but the best asset is the bargain price.

Eating

In addition to the places listed here, the Pablado Marinero (Seamen's Village) beside the yacht harbour is home to a variety of decent restaurants. The best place to look for tapas bars is in the streets behind the post office and around Millán Astray to the north of Calle Camoens.

La Marina (☎ 956 514007; 1 Alférez Bayton; mains from €12, set menu €8; Mon-Sat Mar-Jan) This smart, friendly restaurant is often crowded at lunchtime. It specialises in fish dishes, but also does a great-value three-course set menu of the chicken or fish and chips variety.

El Angulo (☎ 956 515810; 1 Muralles Reales; mains from €15; noon-4pm & 8.30-midnight Mon-Sat) Here's your chance to eat inside the royal walls. The local meats and seafood are as good as the unique atmosphere. White tablecloths and stone fortifications work surprisingly well together.

Cala Carlota (☎ 956 525061; Calle Edrisis; set menu from €7) This simple restaurant has a prime location in the Club Nautico overlooking the yacht harbour and outdoor seating in season. The three-course *menú del diá* (daily set menu) is a popular choice; the luscious fish dishes will set you back the same amount on their own.

Getting There & Away

Bus 7 runs up to the Moroccan *frontera* (border) every 10 minutes from Plaza de la Constitución (€0.60). The large *grand taxi* lot next to Moroccan border control has departures to Tetouan (Dh30, 40 minutes). For Tangier, take a *grand taxi* to Fnideq (Dh5, 10 minutes), just south of the border, and change there.

The **estación marítima** (ferry terminal; Calle Muelle Cañonero Dato) is west of the town centre and from here there are several daily high-speed ferries to Algeciras (p657).

TETOUAN

pop 320,000

Tetouan occupies a striking location at the foot of the Rif Mountains. From 1912 until 1956 it was the capital of the Spanish Protectorate in Morocco. This and the town's long relationship with Andalucía have left it with a Hispano-Moorish character that is unique in Morocco. This is physically reflected in the Spanish part of the city (whose white buildings and broad boulevards have recently been restored to their original condition) and the Unesco World Heritage–listed medina.

If you want to see the sea, the small port of Martil is a 15-minute cab ride from the Tetouan centre – well worth a day trip.

Information

There are plenty of banks with ATMs along Ave Mohammed V.

BMCE foreign exchange office (Place Moulay el-Mehdi; 10am-2pm & 4-8pm) Change cash and travellers cheques outside regular banking hours.

Délégation Régionale du Tourisme (ONMT; 039 961915; 30 Ave Mohammed V; 8.30am-12.30pm & 1.30-4.30pm Mon-Fri) Local tourist office – poor service.

Main hospital (039 972430; Martil Rd) About 2km out of town.

Post office (Place Moulay el-Mehdi; 8am-4.30pm Mon-Fri)

Remote Studios (13 Ave Mohammed V; per hr Dh9; 9am-midnight) Internet access.

Sights

The whitewashed **medina** (home to some 40 mosques, of which the **Grande Mosqué** and **Saidi Mosque** are the most impressive) opens through its main gate, Bab er-Rouah, onto Place Hassan II, Tetouan's grand main square. At the opposite end of the medina, the **Musée Marocaine** (Musée Ethnographique; admission Dh10; 9.30am-noon & 3.30-6.30pm Mon-Fri) is housed inside the bastion in the town wall.

Just outside Bab el-Okla is the **Artisanal School** (039 972721; admission Dh10; 8am-noon & 2.30-5.30pm Mon-Fri), offering a fascinating opportunity to see masters teaching apprentices traditional arts, including ornamental woodwork, carved plaster and intricate mosaics.

Sleeping

Pension Iberia (039 963679; 5 Place Moulay el-Mehdi; s/d/tr with shared bathroom Dh50/80/120) This is the best budget option, with classic high-ceilinged rooms and shuttered balconies that open out onto the Place Moulay el-Mehdi. Views of the white city washing over the hills, and the fountain in the square – better observed from here than the street – add a dash of romance. Hot showers cost an extra Dh10.

Riad Dalia (018 025049; www.riad-dalia.com; 25 Rue Ouessaa; s with shared bathroom Dh150, ste Dh400-600) The first *riad* hotel in the medina, this funky, family-run option is an eclectic adventure. The 300-year-old former Dutch consul's house has been transformed into a hotel without much renovation, so it feels like the consul may turn up at any moment. The master suite is immense and fit for royalty, but mixed pricing allows a room for every budget.

El Reducto (039 968120; www.riadtetouan.com; Zanqat Zawya 38; s/d incl breakfast Dh425/550, half-board Dh500/700) This is the premier place to stay in Tetouan if you want an upscale medina experience at a very reasonable price. The spotless, palatial rooms are truly fantastic with big bathrooms, the highest quality antique furniture and beautiful silk bedspreads. Marble staircases and elegant tiled walls complete the royal ambiance, the product of a two-year restoration completed in 2006.

Eating

Jenin (039 962246; 8 Rue al-Ouahda; 6am-9.30pm winter, to 11pm summer, closed Fri afternoons) This sparkling, modern cafe is the trendiest in town. The ten blenders full of different fruit juices are the highlight, along with the presence of courting couples and groups of young women. A world away from the smoky male cafes on the same block. Coffee costs Dh8.

Restaurant Restinga (21 Ave Mohammed V; fish dishes from Dh50; noon-9pm) The open-air courtyard

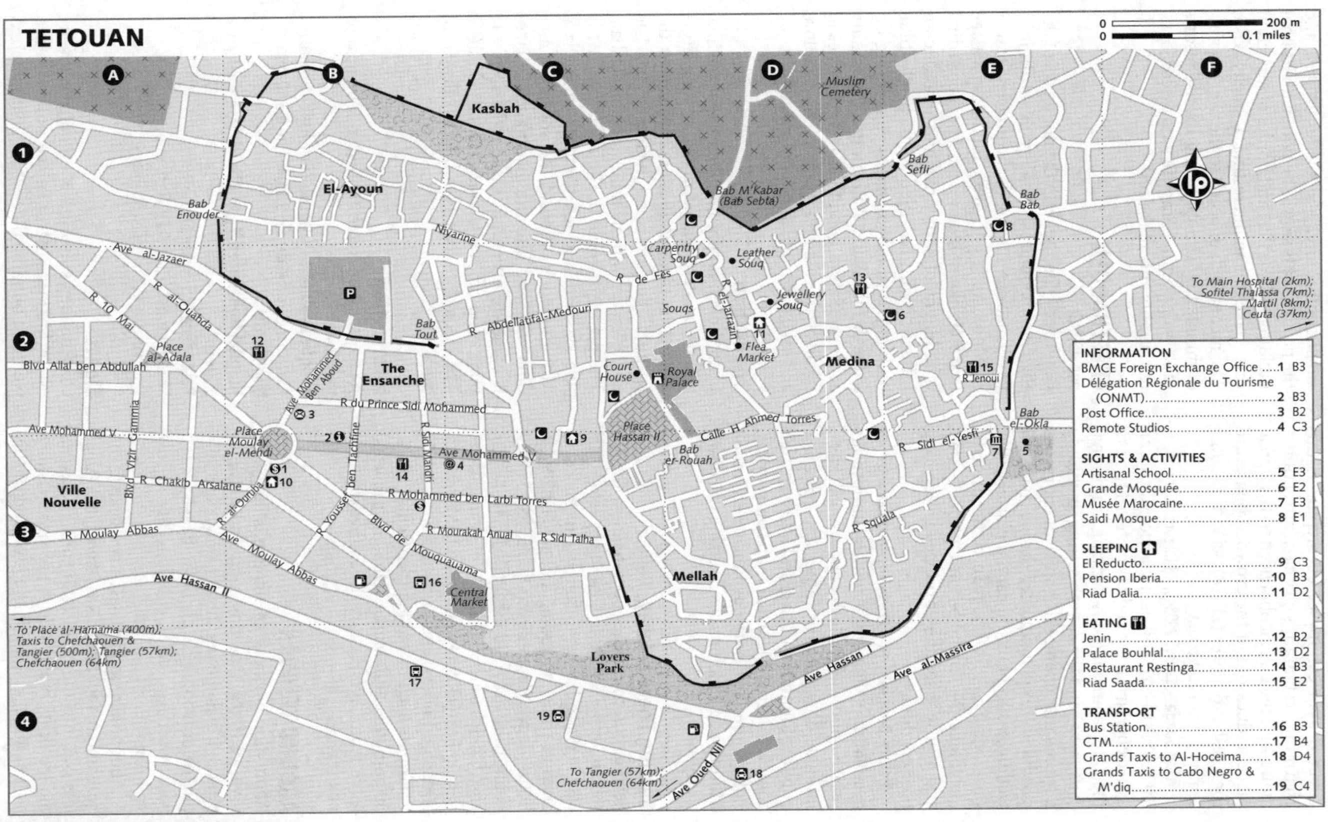
TETOUAN
0 200 m
0 0.1 miles
A
B
C
D
E
F
1
2
3
4
Kasbah
Muslim Cemetery
El-Ayoun
Bab Enouder
Niyarine
Ave al-Jazaer
R al-Ouahda
R 10 Mai
Place al-Adala
Blvd Allal ben Abdullah
Ave Mohammed Ben Aboud
The Ensanche
R du Prince Sidi Mohammed
Ave Mohammed V
Place Moulay el-Mehdi
Blvd Vizir Gammia
R Chakib Arsalane
Ville Nouvelle
R al-Ouruba
R Youssef ben Tachfine
R Sidi Mandri
R Mohammed ben Larbi Torres
Blvd de Mouquauama
R Mourakah Anual
R Sidi Talha
R Moulay Abbas
Ave Moulay Abbas
Ave Hassan II
Central Market
To Place al-Hamama (400m); Taxis to Chefchaouen & Tangier (500m); Tangier (57km); Chefchaouen (64km)
Lovers Park
To Tangier (57km); Chefchaouen (64km)
Ave Oued Nil
Ave Hassan I
Ave al-Massira
Bab Tout
R Abdellatif al-Medouri
R de Fès
Carpentry Souq
Leather Souq
Bab M'Kabar (Bab Sebta)
Souqs
R el-Jarrazin
Jewellery Souq
Flea Market
Court House
Royal Palace
Place Hassan II
Bab er-Rouah
Calle H Ahmed Torres
Medina
Mellah
R Squala
R Sidi el-Yesfi
Bab Sefli
Bab Bab
R Jenoui
Bab el-Okla
To Main Hospital (2km); Sofitel Thalassa (7km); Martil (8km); Ceuta (37km)
INFORMATION
BMCE Foreign Exchange Office 1 B3
Délégation Régionale du Tourisme (ONMT) 2 B3
Post Office 3 B2
Remote Studios 4 C3
SIGHTS & ACTIVITIES
Artisanal School 5 E3
Grande Mosquée 6 E2
Musée Marocaine 7 E3
Saidi Mosque 8 E1
SLEEPING
El Reducto 9 C3
Pension Iberia 10 B3
Riad Dalia 11 D2
EATING
Jenin 12 B2
Palace Bouhlal 13 D2
Restaurant Restinga 14 B3
Riad Saada 15 E2
TRANSPORT
Bus Station 16 B3
CTM 17 B4
Grands Taxis to Al-Hoceima 18 D4
Grands Taxis to Cabo Negro & M'diq 19 C4

covered by a canopy of eucalyptus is this charming restaurant's primary attraction – along with the rare alcohol licence. It's a great place to duck out of the crowded boulevard for a rest and a beer (Dh18), as well as some seafood from the coast.

Riad Saada (☎ 061 299846; 18 Rue Jenoui; set menu Dh100; 🕓 8am-late) This is a classic Moroccan experience, from the endless plates of food to the entertainment (belly dancing, traditional musicians) and the superb setting, including a spectacular open ceiling with an enormous pendulum lamp, two golden throne chairs for weddings and beautiful carved plaster walls. Enter via Bab el-Okla, turn right immediately, take the second left at Optique Seffar, and you will see the entrance, a very long tiled corridor.

Palace Bouhlal (☎ 039 998797; 48 Jamaa Kebir; set menu Dh100; 🕓 10am-4pm) Another sumptuous palace option with plush couches, wall rugs, intimate dining spaces (especially upstairs), gurgling fountains and a grand Moorish arch complementing the usual four-course meal. Follow the lane north around the Grande Mosqué and look for signs directing you down a tiny alley.

Getting There & Away

Several bus companies operate from the **bus station** (cnr Rue Sidi Mandri & Rue Moulay Abbas). **CTM** (☎ 039 961688) has buses running to the usual array of places, including Tangier (Dh20, 1¼ hours, daily), Casablanca (Dh125, six to seven hours, twice daily) via Rabat (Dh10, 4½ hours), and Chefchaouen (Dh25, 1½ hours, three daily), Fez (Dh93, four hours), Marrakech (Dh235, 11 hours) and many more.

Grands taxis to Fnideq (for Ceuta; Dh30, 30 minutes) and Martil (Dh5, 15 minutes) leave from Ave Hassan II, southeast of the bus station.

AROUND TETOUAN

About 8km northeast of Tetouan is the beach town of **Martil**. One-time port and home to pirates, it's altogether quieter now, especially out of season. The pleasant beach, lined with waterfront cafes, comes to life in July and August.

About 5km up the coast from Martil, the headland of **Cabo Negro** (Ras Aswad in Arabic) juts out into the Mediterranean. Tucked in the lee of its north side is the small fishing port of **M'diq**. Fishing is the lifeblood of this small community. The hassles are few and the pace of life is slow. The port, with its boat building, fishing fleet and hordes of expectant cats, makes for an interesting (if smelly) visit. The nice stretch of beach to the north is now dominated by the sprawling tourist resorts of Restinga-Smir, complete with discos, bars, restaurants and all the rest.

CHEFCHAOUEN

pop 45,000

Beautifully sited beneath the raw peaks of the Rif, Chefchaouen (also known by its diminutive 'Chaouen') is one of the prettiest towns in Morocco. It's an artsy mountain village that feels like its own world. The old medina is a delight of Moroccan and Andalucian influence with red-tiled roofs, bright blue buildings and narrow lanes converging on a delightful square. With a variety of quality accommodation, good food and no hassles to speak of, this is a great place to relax, explore and take day trips in the cool green hills.

Orientation

Chefchaouen is split into the eastern medina, and the western *ciudad nueva,* or new city – a hangover from its 1920s occupation by the Spanish. The heart of the medina is Plaza Uta el-Hammam, with its unmistakeable kasbah. The principal route of the *ciudad nueva* is Ave Hassan II, which stretches from Plaza Mohammed V, around the southern medina wall, and into the medina itself. Here it comes to an end at Place el-Majzen, the main drop-off point, which faces the kasbah. The bus station is a 1km hike southwest of the town centre.

Information

A tourist office is due to open in 2009 next to the Hotel Parador.

Banque Populaire Ciudad nueva (Ave Hassan II); Medina (Plaza Uta el-Hammam; 🕓 9.30am-1pm & 3.30-9pm Mon-Fri) ATM

Hospital Mohammed V (☎ 039 986228; Ave al-Massira al-Khadra)

Post office (Ave Hassan II)

Saadoune.net (Plaza Uta el-Hammam; per hr Dh10; 🕓 9am-2pm & 3pm-midnight) Internet access.

Sights

Chefchaouen's medina is one of the loveliest in Morocco. Most of the buildings are painted a blinding blue-white, giving them a

MOROCCO

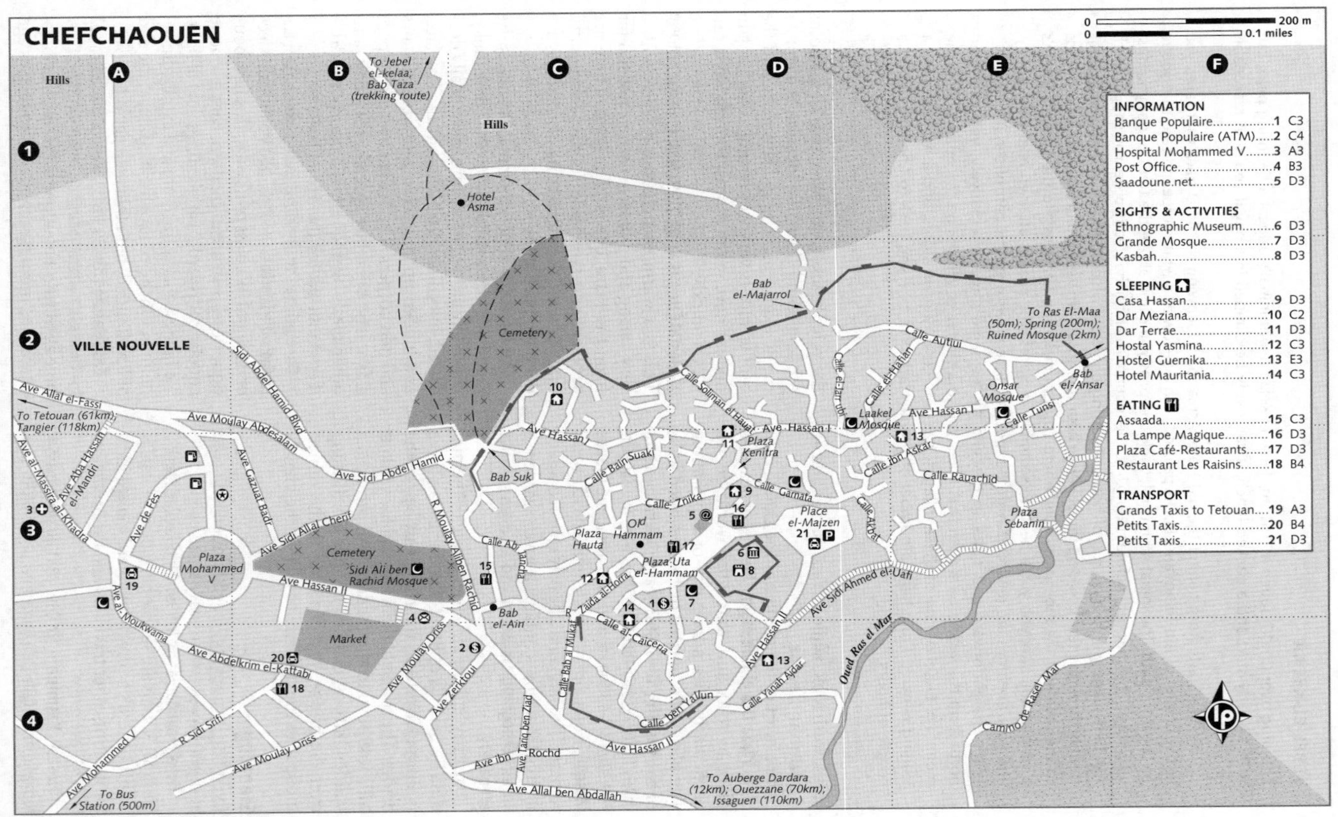
CHEFCHAOUEN
0 200 m
0 0.1 miles
INFORMATION
Banque Populaire 1 C3
Banque Populaire (ATM) 2 C4
Hospital Mohammed V 3 A3
Post Office 4 B3
Saadoune.net 5 D3
SIGHTS & ACTIVITIES
Ethnographic Museum 6 D3
Grande Mosque 7 D3
Kasbah 8 D3
SLEEPING
Casa Hassan 9 D3
Dar Meziana 10 C2
Dar Terrae 11 D3
Hostal Yasmina 12 C3
Hostel Guernika 13 E3
Hotel Mauritania 14 C3
EATING
Assaada 15 C3
La Lampe Magique 16 D3
Plaza Café-Restaurants 17 D3
Restaurant Les Raisins 18 B4
TRANSPORT
Grands Taxis to Tetouan 19 A3
Petits Taxis 20 B4
Petits Taxis 21 D3
Hills
To Jebel el-kelaa; Bab Taza (trekking route)
Hotel Asma
VILLE NOUVELLE
Cemetery
Bab el-Majarrol
To Ras El-Maa (50m); Spring (200m); Ruined Mosque (2km)
Bab el-Ansar
Onsar Mosque
Laakel Mosque
Plaza Kenitra
Bab Suk
Old Hammam
Plaza Hauta
Plaza Uta el-Hammam
Place el-Majzen
Plaza Sebanin
Bab el-Ain
Sidi Ali ben Rachid Mosque
Plaza Mohammed V
Market
Oued Ras el Mar
To Tetouan (61km); Tangier (118km)
To Bus Station (500m)
To Auberge Dardara (12km); Ouezzane (70km); Issaguen (110km)
Ave Allal el-Fassi
Ave Moulay Abdesalam
Sidi Abdel Hamid Blvd
Ave Sidi Abdel Hamid
Ave Aba Hassan el-Mandri
Ave al-Massira al-Khadra
Ave de Fès
Ave Gazuat Badr
Ave Sidi Allal Cherif
Ave Hassan II
Ave al-Moukwama
Ave Abdelkrim el-Kattabi
R Moulay Aliben Rachid
Ave Moulay Driss
Ave Zerktouni
R Sidi Srifi
Ave Mohammed V
Ave Ibn Rochd
Ave Tariq ben Ziad
Ave Allal ben Abdallah
Ave Hassan I
Calle Soliman el Haual
Calle Autiui
Calle el-Jarrubi
Calle el-Haflan
Calle Tunsi
Calle Bain Suaki
Calle Znika
Calle Garnata
Calle ibn Askar
Calle Rauachid
Calle Akbat
Calle Abi Jancha
Zaida al-Horra
Calle al-Caiceria
Calle Bab al Mukar
Calle ben Yallun
Calle Yanah Ajdar
Ave Sidi Ahmed el-Uafi
Camino de Rasel Mar

MOROCCO

JEBEL EL-KELAÂ

Looming over Chefchaouen at 1616m, Jebel el-Kelaâ might initially appear a daunting peak, but with an early start and a packed lunch, it can easily be climbed in a day if you're in reasonably good shape.

The hike starts from behind the old Hôtel Asma road, following the 4WD track that takes you to the hamlet of Aïn Tissimlane. Rocks painted with a yellow and white stripe indicate that you're on the right path. The initial hour is relatively steep, as you climb above the trees to get your first views over Chefchaouen, before cutting into the mountains along the steady piste. You should reach Aïn Tissemlane within a couple of hours of setting out, after which the path climbs and zigzags steeply through great boulders for nearly an hour to a pass. Turn west along the track, which leads to the saddle of the mountain, from where you can make the final push to the summit. There's a rough path, although you'll need to scramble in places. The peak is attained relatively quickly, and your exertions are rewarded with the most sublime views over this part of the Rif.

It's straightforward and quick to descend by the same route. Alternatively, you can head north from the saddle on a path that takes you to a cluster of villages on the other side of the mountain. El-Kelaâ, one of these villages, has 16th-century grain stores, and a mosque with a leaning minaret. From here, a number of simple tracks will take you back to Chefchaouen in a couple of hours.

clean, fresh look, while terracotta tiles add an Andalucian flavour.

The heart of the medina is the shady, cobbled **Plaza Uta el-Hammam**. This is a peaceful place to relax and watch the world go by, particularly after a long day of exploration. The plaza is dominated by the red-hued walls of the **kasbah** (☎ 039 986343; admission incl museum & gallery Dh10; ⏲ 9am-1pm & 3-6.30pm Wed, Thu, Sat-Mon, 9-11.30am & 3-4.30pm Fri) and the adjacent **Grande Mosqué**, noteworthy for its unusual octagonal minaret. The kasbah is a heavily restored walled fortress that now contains a lovely garden, a small **ethnographic museum** and an even smaller **art gallery**.

Just beyond the far eastern gate of the medina lie the falls of **Ras El-Maa**. In season there is a popular cafe on the right, just before the bridge. The sound of the water and the verdant hills just beyond the medina wall provides a sudden, strong dose of nature. Continuing over the bridge, you can walk to the ruined mosque in the distance to take in the views.

Sleeping

Even late into spring, Chefchaouen gets cold at night, so ask for an extra blanket.

Hotel Mauritania (☎ 039 986184; 15 Rue Qadi Alami; s/d Dh45/80) Rooms are simple here, but the staff is helpful, there's a comfy courtyard lounge ideal for meeting other travellers and the breakfasts (Dh20) are great.

Hostal Yasmina (☎ 039 883118; yasmina45@hotmail.com; 12 Calle Lalla Horra; r per person Dh70) For the price bracket, this place sparkles. Rooms are bright and clean, the location is a stone's throw from Plaza Uta el-Hammam, and the roof terrace is very welcoming. This bargain doesn't have many rooms, though, so it can fill up quickly.

Hostal Guernika (☎ 039 987434; 49 Onssar; r Dh200) This is a warm and charming place, with a very caring and attentive owner, not too far from the Plaza Uta el-Hammam. There are several great streetside rooms – large and bright, facing the mountains – but others are dark. All have showers.

Dar Terrae (☎ 039 987598; darterrae@hotmail.com; Ave Hassan I; s/d/tr incl breakfast Dh250/350/450) These funky, cheerfully painted rooms are individually decorated, inlcuding own bathroom and fireplace, and hidden up and down a tumble of stairs and odd corners. The Italian owners prepare a fantastic breakfast spread every day, and other meals on request. It's poorly signed – if in doubt ask for the 'Hotel Italiano'.

Dar Meziana (☎ 039 987806; www.darmeziana.com; Rue Zagdud; s/d/tr from Dh475/650/950; ❄) Beautifully decorated, and in a class of its own, this new boutique hotel is an artful creation, with a unique angular courtyard, lush plantings, lots of light, the highest quality furniture and extraordinary ceilings. On the edge of the medina, at the end of Rue Zagdud, but otherwise perfect.

Casa Hassan (☎ 039 986153; www.casahassan.com; 22 Rue Targui; s/d/tr with half-board from Dh500/650/800; ❄) A large hotel with a boutique hotel feel, this long-established upmarket choice is showing its age a bit, but still has sizable rooms with creative layouts, including beds tucked into coves and an in-house *hammam* (traditional bathhouse). The terrace provides an elegant lounge, and the cosy Restaurant Tissemlal a warm hearth.

Eating

A popular eating option in Chefchaouen is to choose one of about a dozen cafe-restaurants on the main square (Plaza Uta el-Hamman). Menus are virtually identical – continental breakfasts, soups and salads, tajines and seafood – but the food (breakfast from Dh15, mains from Dh25) is generally pretty good, and the ambience lively. Open 8am to 11pm.

Restaurant Les Raisins (☎ 067 982878; 7 Rue Sidi Sifri; tajines Dh20, set menu from Dh40; ⏰ 7am-9pm) A bit out of the way, this family-run place is a perennial favourite with locals and tourists alike, and known for its couscous royal. Late, lazy lunches are the best, with the front terrace catching the afternoon sun.

Assaada (☎ 066 317316; Bab Ain; set menu Dh40) This reliable cheapie tries hard to please. Located on both sides of the alley just prior to Bab el-Ain, it offers the usual set menu, but also great fruit shakes. It has a funky graffiti rooftop terrace that exudes an urban charm. The staircase is not for the faint-hearted.

La Lampe Magique (☎ 065 406464; Rue Targui; mains from Dh45, set menu Dh75) This magical place overlooking Plaza Uta el-Hammam serves delicious Moroccan staples in a grand setting. Three bright blue floors include a laid-back lounge, a more formal dining area and a rooftop terrace. The menu – featuring favourites such as lamb tajine with prunes and some great cooked salads – is better than average, but this place is really about atmosphere.

Shopping

Chefchaouen remains an artisan centre, especially for woven rugs and blankets in bright primary colours. Many shops have looms in situ, and although most weaving is now woollen, silk was once the material of choice: the mulberry trees in Plaza Uta el-Hammam are a legacy of those times.

The largest concentration of tourist shops is around the Uta el-Hammam and Place el-Majzen.

Getting There & Away

Many bus services from Chefchaouen originate elsewhere and are often full on arrival, so buy your ticket a day in advance if possible. **CTM** (☎ 039 987669) serves Casablanca (Dh120, eight hours), Rabat (Dh90, six hours), Tetouan (Dh20, 1½ hours), Fez (Dh70, four hours) Tangier (Dh40, three hours) and further destinations.

Grands taxis heading to Tetouan (Dh30, one hour) leave from just below Plaza Mohammed V – change for Tangier or Ceuta.

MELILLA

pop 65,000

Occupied by the Spanish since 1496, Melilla is the smaller and less affluent of the two enclaves that mark the last vestiges of Spain's African empire. With nearly half of its inhabitants being of Rif Berber origin, it has an atmosphere all of its own – neither quite Europe nor Africa. The centre of Melilla is a delight of modernist architecture and quiet gardens.

Information

To phone Melilla from Morocco, dial ☎ 0034, then the number. Note that Melilla operates on Spanish time and the unit of currency here is the euro. You'll find several banks (with ATMs) around Avenida de Juan Carlos I Rey. On the Moroccan side of the border you can change cash at the Crédit du Maroc.

Hospital Comarcal (☎ 956 670000) South side of Río de Oro.

Locutoria Dosmil (Calle Ejército España, local 14-25; per hr €2; ⏰ 9am-2pm & 4-9pm) Internet access.

Main post office (Correos y telégrafos; Calle Pablo Vallescá; ⏰ 8.30am-8.30pm Mon-Fri, 9.30am-1pm Sat)

Oficina del Turismo (☎ 952 976151; www.melillaturismo.com; 21 Calle Fortuny; ⏰ 9am-2pm & 5-8pm Mon-Fri) Main tourist office.

Sights

Up until the end of the 19th century virtually all of Melilla was contained within a single impregnable fortress of **Melilla la Vieja** (Old Melilla), perching over the Mediterranean. The main entrance is **Puerta de la Marina**, from where you ascend passing by several small museums. The first is the **Museo de Arqueología e Historia** (☎ 952 976216; Plaza Pedro de Estopiñán; admission free; ⏰ 10am-2pm & 4-8.30pm Tue-Sat, 10am-2pm Sun winter, 10am-2pm & 5-9.30pm Tue-Sat, 10am-2pm Sun summer), which has a nifty little collection of archaeological finds, signed in English. The small door across the courtyard leads into the cavelike **Aljibes de las Peñuelas** (admission free; ⏰ 10am-2pm & 5-9.30pm Tue-Sat, 10am-2pm Sun Apr-Sep,

10am-2pm & 4-8.30pm Tue-Sat, 10am-2pm Sun Oct-Mar), an other-worldly cistern. The construction across the way is the new Berber museum, due to open by 2010.

The new part of town, west of the fortress, is considered by some to be Spain's 'second modernist city', after Barcelona. The best way to appreciate this heritage is to stroll around the area to the north of Parque Hernandez, known as 'the golden triangle'. Several fine examples are on the **Plaza de España** including the art deco **Palacio de Asamblea**, the **Casino Militar** whose facade depicts a republican coat of arms; and the **Banco de España**.

Sleeping & Eating

Hostal La Rosa Blanca (☎ 952 682738; 7 Calle Gran Capitán; s/d €20/32) A very basic option, the rooms are clean but vary in quality, so make sure you look before you buy, and beware those tattered bedspreads. Rooms have sinks and shared baths.

Hostal Residencia Cazaza (☎ 956 684648; 6 Calle Primo de Rivera; s/d €26/36) While the rooms here are beat-up, this old building with its high ceilings and small balconies manages to be charming, and it has a central location in the Golden Triangle. Management is friendly.

Parador de Melilla (☎ 956 684940; Avenida Cándido Lobera; s/d €94/118;) This is a very classy choice with large, grand rooms, a warm use of wood throughout, a high level of quality furnishings, and balconies with great views to sea. The circular dining room overlooking the city is an elegant touch. The adjacent Parque Lobera is great for kids.

Parnaso (☎ 952 684184; 30 Avenida Duquesa de la Victoria; sandwiches from €2.50; 7am-1am Mon-Sat) This hopping bistro with outdoor seating on a tree-lined avenue offers inexpensive but tasty sandwiches and tapas. Popular during lunch and with the after-work crowd.

La Pérgola (Calle General Marcías; noon-midnight) A waterfront terrace, white tablecloths and cafe music make this classy spot a very pleasant place for a meal or just a late-afternoon drink. The speciality is seafood, and at €10 the fixed-price menu cannot be beaten.

Los Salazones (☎ 952 673652; Calle Conde de Alcaudete 15; mains from €12; 1.30-4.30pm & 9pm-close) Another local favourite, this meat and seafood restaurant is a block from the beach, and is the perfect place to end a day in the sun. Sit at the marble-topped barrels and enjoy the grilled fish.

Getting There & Away

To get to the border, you'll need to catch the local bus 2 (marked 'Aforos'), which runs between Plaza de España and the Beni Enzar border post (€0.60) every 30 minutes from 7.30am to 11pm. On the Moroccan side of the border, bus 19 runs hourly to Nador (Dh23, 25 minutes). Frequent *grands taxis* (Dh5, 15 minutes) to Nador are tucked away on a lot to the right of this crossroad.

There are daily ferries to Málaga and Alméria. Ferry tickets are available for purchase at the **estación marítima** (ferry terminal; ☎ 956 681633).

THE ATLANTIC COAST

Morocco's Atlantic littoral is surprisingly varied, with sweeping beaches and lagoons, and the pretty fishing ports-cum-tourist drawcards of Essaouira and Asilah. It's also the economic motor of the urban sprawl around the political and economic capitals of Rabat and Casablanca.

ASILAH

pop 30,000

A strategic port since the days of Carthage and Rome, the gorgeous whitewashed resort town of Asilah feels as much like somewhere on a Greek Island than North Africa. It's an intimate, sophisticated introduction to Morocco, with galleries lining the narrow streets. It swarms in summer with holidaying Moroccans and with foreigners trying to find property bargains. Given its increasing popularity, consider visiting out of season to appreciate the old-world charm of this lovely town at its best.

Sights

Asilah's **medina** is surrounded by the sturdy stone fortifications built by the Portuguese in the 15th century and it is these walls, flanked by palms, that have become the town's landmark. The medina and ramparts have been largely restored (overrestored some would say) in recent years and the tranquil narrow streets lined by whitewashed houses are well worth a wander. Craftspeople and artists have opened workshops along the main streets and invite passers-by in to see them work. The southwestern bastion of the ramparts is the place for views over the ocean.

Paradise Beach, Asilah's best beach, is 3km south of town and is a gorgeous, pristine spot that really does live up to its name.

Sleeping

During high season (Easter week and July to September), the town is flooded with visitors so it's advisable to book well in advance, but touts meeting the buses or trains offer basic accommodation in the medina for about Dh75.

Hôtel Sahara (☎ 039 417185; 9 Rue de Tarfaya; s/d/tr Dh98/136/204) This small, immaculately kept hotel offers simple rooms set around an open courtyard and a very Moroccan atmosphere. Patterned tiles and potted plants adorn the lovely entrance, and the compact rooms are comfortable and well maintained. The sparkling shared toilets and showers are all new and scrubbed till they gleam. Hot showers cost Dh5.

Hôtel Patio de la Luna (☎ 039 416074; 12 Place Zellaka; s/d Dh300/450) The only accommodation option in Assilah with any local character is this intimate Spanish-run place secluded behind an unassuming door on the main drag. The simple, rustic rooms have wooden furniture, woven blankets and tiled bathrooms and are set around a lovely leafy patio. It's very popular, so book ahead.

Hôtel Azayla (☎ 039 416717; e-elhaddad@menara.ma; 20 Rue ibn Rochd; s Dh300-390, d Dh380-480) Big, bright, comfy and well equipped, the rooms here are a really good deal. The bathrooms are new, the decor is tasteful with great photographs of Morocco by the owner, and the giant windows bathe the rooms in light. The place may lack local character, but the staff is very friendly, helpful and reliable. Higher prices kick in from July to September.

Eating

Asilah has a string of restaurants clustered around Bab Kasaba and along the medina walls on Ave Hassan II. There are a few other cheap options on Rue Ahmed M'dem near the banks on Place Mohammed V.

Restaurant Yali (☎ 071 043277; Ave Hassan II; mains Dh25-50) Although there's little to choose between them, this is one of the most popular of the string of restaurants along the medina walls. It serves up a good selection of fish, seafood and traditional Moroccan staples.

Restaurant de la Place (☎ 039 417326; 7 Ave Moulay Hassan ben el-Mehdi; mains Dh40-80) Friendly, less formal and more varied than its neighbours, this restaurant offers a choice of traditional Moroccan dishes as well as the ubiquitous fish and seafood. The delicious fish tajine provides the best of both worlds.

Casa García (☎ 039 417465; 51 Rue Moulay Hassan ben el-Mehdi; mains Dh55-80) Spanish-style fish dishes and fishy tapas are the speciality at this small restaurant opposite the beach. Go for succulent grilled fresh fish or octopus, eels, shrimp and barnacles, served with a glass of crisp Moroccan rosé wine on the large and breezy terrace. The paella is delicious, too.

Getting There & Away

Asilah is 46km south of Tangier and has good bus connections to most towns. The tiny bus station is on the corner of Ave Moulay Ismail and the Tangier–Rabat Rd. CTM doesn't serve Asilah, but several private bus companies offer services including to Rabat (Dh60, 3½ hours), Marrakech (Dh130, nine hours), Tangier (Dh10, one hour) and Fez (Dh60, 4½ hours). Buses to Tangier and Casablanca leave roughly every half-hour.

Three trains run daily to Rabat (Dh77, 3½ hours) and Casablanca (Dh101, 4½ hours), one to Meknès (Dh66, three hours) and Fez (Dh81, four hours) and six daily to Tangier (Dh14, 45 minutes). One overnight train goes direct to Marrakesh (Dh174, nine hours), but this train originates (and fills up) in Tangier, so buy your ticket in advance.

Grands taxis to Tangier (Dh20) depart when full from Ave Moulay Ismail, across from the mosque.

RABAT

pop 1.7 million

Rabat, Morocco's political and administrative capital since independence in 1956, hasn't established itself as a tourist destination, but the few visitors who do go find a gem of a city. The colonial architecture is stunning, the palm-lined boulevards are well kept and the atmosphere is cosmopolitan. You'll be blissfully ignored on the streets and *souqs*, so it's easy to discover the city's monuments and hidden corners at your own pace. The picturesque kasbah is also a place to explore with its narrow alleys, art galleries and magnificent ocean views.

Orientation

Ave Hassan II divides the medina from the *ville nouvelle* and follows the line of the medina

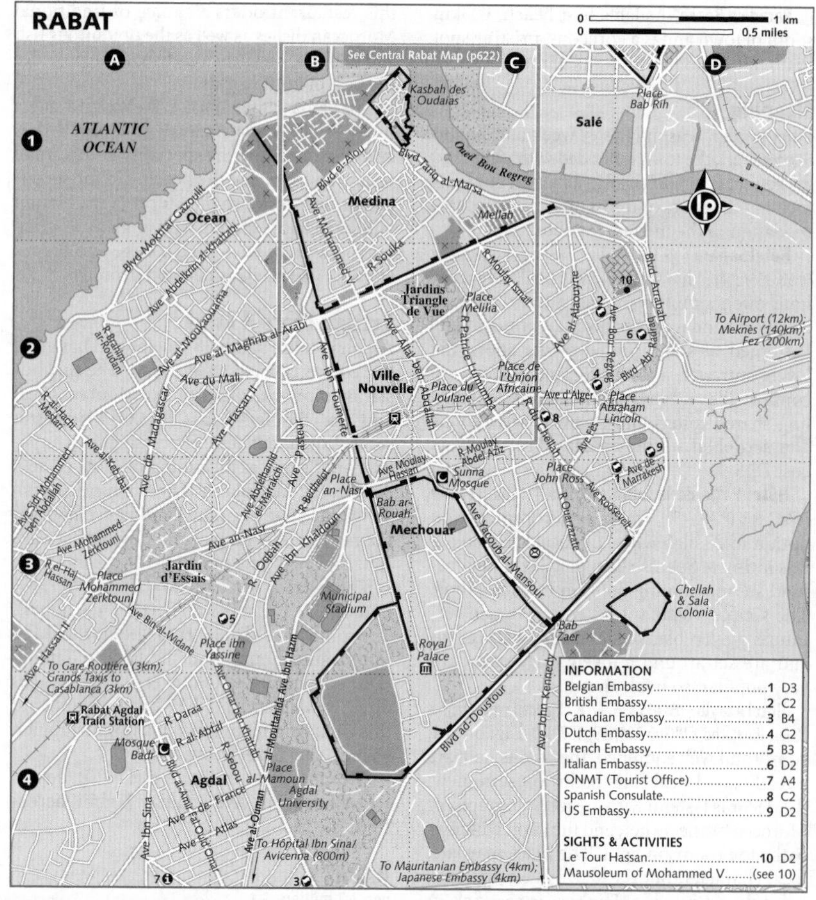

walls to the Oued Bou Regreg, the river that separates the twin cities of Rabat and Salé. The city's main thoroughfare – the wide, palm-lined Ave Mohammed V – is home to many hotels, while most embassies cluster around Place Abraham Lincoln and Ave Fès east of the centre; see p654 for addresses.

Information

Numerous banks (with ATMs) are concentrated along Ave Mohammed V.

American Bookshop (Map p622; cnr Rue Moulay Abdelhafid & Rue Boujaad)

BMCE (Map p622; Ave Mohammed V; 8am-8pm Mon-Fri) Bank with ATM.

Hôpital Ibn Sina/Avicenna (off Map p622; ☎ 037 672871/037 674450 for emergencies; Place Ibn Sina, Agdal)

Librairie Livre Service (Map p622; ☎ 037 724495; 46 Ave Allal ben Abdallah; per hr Dh7; 9am-noon & 3-8pm Mon-Sat)

Main post office (Map p622; cnr Rue Soékarno & Ave Mohammed V)

Office National Marocain du Tourisme (ONMT; Map p620; ☎ 037 674013; visitmorocco@onmt.org.ma; cnr Rue Oued el-Makhazine & Rue Zalaka, Agdal; 8.30am-noon & 3-6.30pm Mon-Fri)

Sights

Barely 400 years old, Rabat's **medina** is tiny compared to Fez or Marrakesh, although it still piques the senses with its rich mixture of spices, carpets, crafts, cheap shoes and bootlegged DVDs. The **Kasbah des Oudaias** (Map p622) sits high up on the bluff overlooking the Oued Bou Regreg and contains within its walls the oldest **mosque** (Map p622) in Rabat, built in the 12th century and restored in the 18th. The kasbah's southern corner is home to the **Andalusian Gardens** (Map p622; sunrise-sunset), laid out by the French during the colonial period. The centrepiece is the grand 17th-century palace containing the **Musée des Oudaia** (Map p622; 037 731537; admission Dh10; 9am-noon & 3-5pm Oct-Apr, to 6pm May-Sep).

Towering above the Oued Bou Regreg is Rabat's most famous landmark, **Le Tour Hassan** (Hassan Tower; Map p620). In 1195 the Almohad sultan Yacoub al-Mansour began constructing an enormous minaret, intending to make it the highest in the Muslim world, but he died before the project was completed. Abandoned at 44m, the beautifully designed and intricately carved tower still lords over the remains of the adjacent mosque.

The cool marble **Mausoleum of Mohammed V** (Map p620; admission free; sunrise-sunset), built in traditional Moroccan style, lies opposite the tower. The present king's father (the late Hassan II) and grandfather are laid to rest here, surrounded by intensely patterned *zellij* mosaics from floor to ceiling.

Abandoned, crumbling and overgrown, the combined ancient Roman city of **Sala Colonia** (Map p620) and Merenid necropolis of **Chellah** (Map p620; cnr Ave Yacoub al-Mansour & Blvd Moussa ibn Nassair; admission Dh10; 9am-5.30pm) is one of Rabat's most evocative sights. Rarely visited and overgrown with fruit trees and wildflowers, it's an atmospheric place to roam around, although making out some of the structures takes a bit of imagination. An incredible colony of storks has taken over the ruins, lording over the site from their treetop nests.

Sleeping

Hôtel Dorhmi (Map p622; 037 723898; 313 Ave Mohammed V; s/d Dh80/120) Immaculately kept, very friendly and keenly priced, this family-run hotel is the best of the medina options. The simple rooms are bright and tidy and surround a central courtyard. Hot showers cost Dh10.

Hôtel Splendid (Map p622; 037 723283; 8 Rue Ghazza; s/d with private bathroom Dh128/187, s/d with shared bathroom Dh104/159) Right in the heart of town, this hotel has spacious, bright rooms with high ceilings, big windows, cheerful colours and simple wooden furniture. Bathrooms are new and even rooms without bathrooms have a hot-water washbasin. The hotel is set around a pleasant courtyard.

Hôtel Balima (Map p622; 037 707755; Ave Mohammed V; s/d Dh450/580;) The grand dame of Rabat hotels is not as grand as it used to be but still offers newly decorated and comfortable rooms with bathrooms, all immaculately kept with great views over the city. The hotel has a decent restaurant and nightclub and a glorious shady terrace facing Ave Mohammed V, still the place to meet in Rabat.

Le Piétri Urban Hotel (Map p622; 037 707820; www.lepietri.com; 4 Rue Tobrouk; s/d/ste Dh600/650/1050;) The former Hôtel Oudayas was totally renovated and is now a good value boutique hotel in a quiet side street in a still central but more residential part of town. The 36 spacious bright rooms with wooden floors are very comfortable, well equipped, and decorated in warm colours in a stylish contemporary style. The hotel has an excellent and trendy restaurant with a small garden for elegant alfresco dining.

Riad Oudaya (Map p622; 037 702392; www.riadoudaya.com; 46 Rue Sidi Fateh; r/ste Dh1350/1650) Tucked away down an alleyway in the medina, this gorgeous guest house is a real hidden gem. The rooms around a spectacular courtyard are tastefully decorated with a wonderful blend of Moroccan style and Western comfort. Subtle lighting, open fires, balconies and the gentle gurgling of the fountain in the tiled courtyard below complete the romantic appeal. Meals here are wonderful but must to be ordered in advance.

Eating

For quick eating, go to Ave Mohammed V just inside the medina gate, where you'll find a slew of hole-in-the-wall joints dishing out tajines, brochettes, salads and chips.

Café Maure (Map p622; Kasbah des Oudaias; 9am-5.30pm) Sit back, relax and just gaze out over the estuary to Salé from this chilled open-air cafe spread over several terraces in the Andalusian Gardens. Mint tea is the thing here, accompanied by little almond biscuits delivered on silver trays. It's an easy place to pass time writing postcards and a relaxed venue for women.

Restaurant de la Libération (Map p622; 256 Ave Mohammed V; mains Dh30) Cheap, cheerful and marginally more classy than the string of other eateries along this road (it's got plastic menus and tablecloths), this basic restaurant does a steady line in traditional favourites. Friday is

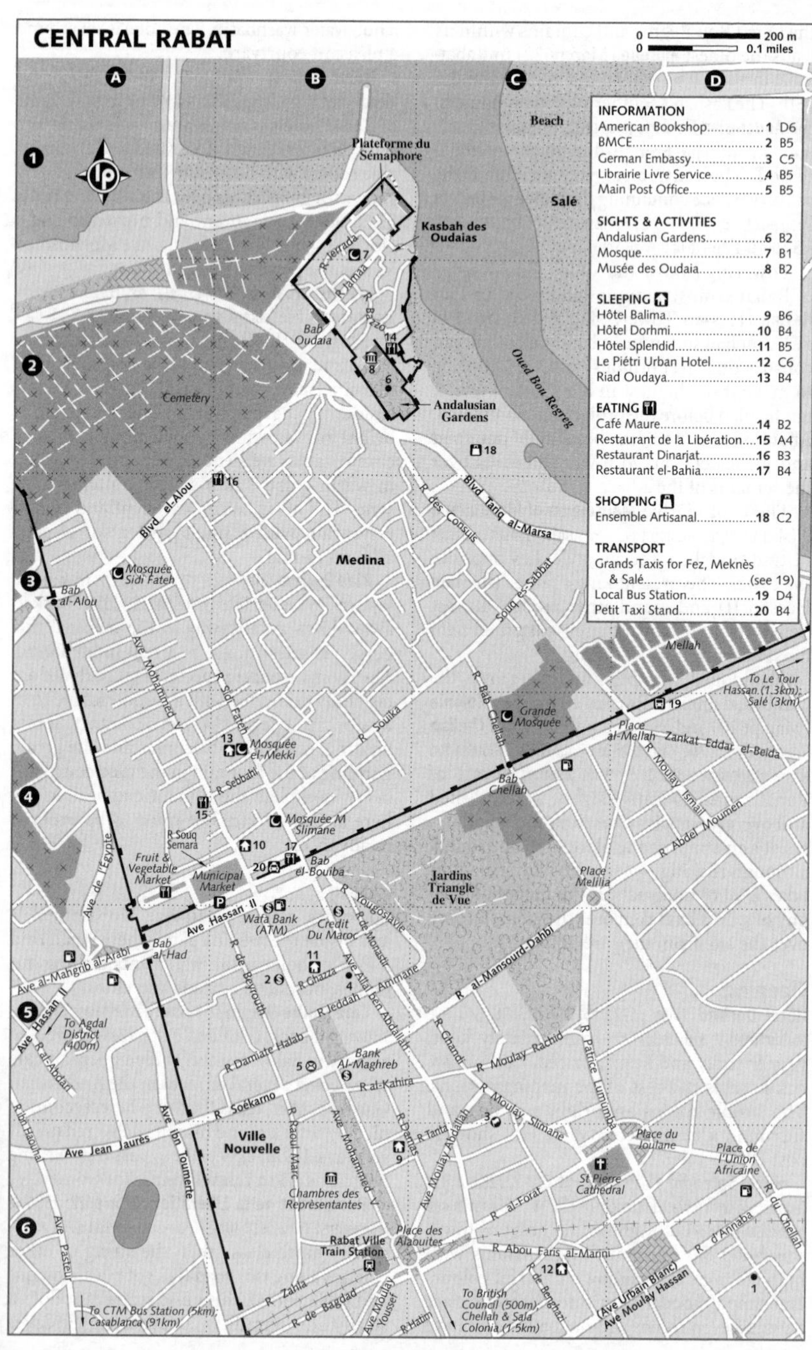
CENTRAL RABAT
0 200 m
0 0.1 miles
INFORMATION
American Bookshop 1 D6
BMCE 2 B5
German Embassy 3 C5
Librairie Livre Service 4 B5
Main Post Office 5 B5
SIGHTS & ACTIVITIES
Andalusian Gardens 6 B2
Mosque 7 B1
Musée des Oudaia 8 B2
SLEEPING
Hôtel Balima 9 B6
Hôtel Dorhmi 10 B4
Hôtel Splendid 11 B5
Le Piétri Urban Hotel 12 C6
Riad Oudaya 13 B4
EATING
Café Maure 14 B2
Restaurant de la Libération 15 A4
Restaurant Dinarjat 16 B3
Restaurant el-Bahia 17 B4
SHOPPING
Ensemble Artisanal 18 C2
TRANSPORT
Grands Taxis for Fez, Meknès & Salé (see 19)
Local Bus Station 19 D4
Petit Taxi Stand 20 B4
Beach
Plateforme du Sémaphore
Kasbah des Oudaias
Salé
Oued Bou Regreg
Bab Oudaia
Andalusian Gardens
Cemetery
Blvd el-Alou
Blvd Tariq al-Marsa
R des Consuls
Medina
Mosquée Sidi Fateh
Bab al-Alou
Souq es-Sabbat
Mellah
To Le Tour Hassan (1.3km); Salé (3km)
Ave Mohammed V
R Sidi Fateh
R Bab Chellah
Grande Mosquée
Place al-Mellah
Zankat Eddar el-Beida
R Moulay Ismail
R Souika
Mosquée el-Mekki
R Sebbahi
Bab Chellah
R Abdel Moumen
Mosquée M Slimane
R Souq Semara
Fruit & Vegetable Market
Municipal Market
Bab el-Bouiba
Jardins Triangle de Vue
Place Melilia
Ave de l'Egypte
Ave Hassan II
Wafa Bank (ATM)
Credit Du Maroc
R Yougoslavie
R de Monastir
Bab al-Had
Ave al-Mahgrib al-Arabi
R de Beyrouth
R Ghazza
Ave Allal ben Abdallah
R Ammane
R al-Mansour-Dahbi
Ave Hassan II
R al-Abdari
To Agdal District (400m)
R Jeddah
R Damiate Halab
Bank Al-Maghreb
R Ghandi
R Moulay Rachid
R Patrice Lumumba
R al-Kahira
R Soékarno
R Moulay Slimane
R Ibn Haoufal
Ave Ibn Toumerte
R Raoul Marc
Ave Mohammed V
R Damas
R Tanta
Ave Moulay Abdallah
Place du Joulane
Place de l'Union Africaine
Ave Jean Jaurès
Ville Nouvelle
St Pierre Cathedral
Chambres des Représentantes
R al-Forat
R du Chellah
Ave Pasteur
Place des Alaouites
Rabat Ville Train Station
R Abou Faris al-Marini
R d'Annaba
R de Benghazi
R Zahla
R de Bagdad
Ave Moulay Youssef
R Hatim
To British Council (500m); Chellah & Sala Colonia (1.5km)
(Ave Urbain Blanc) Ave Moulay Hassan
To CTM Bus Station (5km); Casablanca (91km)

couscous day when giant platters of the stuff are delivered to the eager masses.

Restaurant el-Bahia (Map p622; ☎ 037 734504; Ave Hassan II; mains Dh50; 6am-midnight summer, to 10.30pm winter) Built into the outside of the medina walls and a good spot for people-watching, this laid-back restaurant has the locals lapping up hearty Moroccan fare. Choose to sit on the pavement terrace, in the shaded courtyard or upstairs in the traditional salon.

Restaurant Dinarjat (Map p622; ☎ 037 724239; 6 Rue Belgnaoui; set menu Dh450) Very stylish and the most elegant of medina restaurants, Dinarjat is a favourite with well-heeled locals and visitors alike. Set in a superb 17th-century Andalucian-style house at the heart of the medina, carefully restored and decorated in a contemporary style but in keeping with tradition, the tajines, couscous and salads are prepared with the freshest ingredients. Book in advance.

Shopping

Rabat's merchants are a lot more laid-back than in Marrakesh, so you can stroll around the stalls in relative peace, but there's also less space to bargain. The *souqs* still have a good selection of handicrafts, particularly in and around the Rue des Consuls in the medina, and Blvd Tariq al-Marsa towards the kasbah. Weaving was one of the most important traditional crafts in Rabat, and on Tuesday and Thursday mornings women descend from the villages to auction their carpets to local salesmen at the carpet *souq* off Rue des Consuls. For fixed prices head for the **Ensemble Artisanal** (Map p622; ☎ 037 730507; Blvd Tariq al-Marsa; 9am-noon & 2.30-6.30pm).

Getting There & Away

Rabat Ville train station (Map p622; ☎ 037 736060) is right in the centre of town, and not to be confused with Rabat Agdal train station to the west of the city. Trains run every 30 minutes until 10.30pm to Casa-Port train station in Casablanca (Dh36, one hour), with services to Fez (Dh76, 3½ hours, eight daily) via Meknès (Dh60, 2½ hours), Tangier (Dh91, 4½ hours, seven daily) and Marrakesh (Dh112, 4½ hours, eight daily).

Rabat has two bus stations: the main **gare routière** (off Map p620; ☎ 037 795816), where most buses depart and arrive, and the less chaotic **CTM bus station** (off Map p622; ☎ 037 281488). Both are about 5km southwest of the city centre on the road to Casablanca. CTM has eight daily services to Casablanca (Dh35, 1½ hours), three to Essaouira (Dh115, three hours), seven to Fez (Dh68, 3½ hours), three to Marrakesh (Dh120, five hours), five to Tangier (Dh90, 4½ hours) and one to Tetouan (Dh88, five hours). The main *gare routière* has 13 separate ticket windows, each one clearly marked by destination. Arriving by bus from the north, you may pass through central Rabat, so it's worth asking if you can be dropped off in town.

Grands taxis leave for Casablanca (Dh35) from just outside the intercity bus station. Other *grands taxis* leave for Fez (Dh65), Meknès (Dh50) and Salé (Dh4) from a lot off Ave Hassan II behind the Hôtel Bouregreg.

Getting Around

Rabat's blue *petits taxis* are plentiful, cheap and quick. A ride around the centre of town will cost about Dh10.

AROUND RABAT

Salé

pop 400,000

A few hundred metres and half a world away, Salé is a walled city and strongly traditional backwater on the far side of the Oued Bou Regreg estuary. But change is coming, and by 2010 the Amwaj mega project will link Rabat and Salé by developing the waterfront on both sides of the river.

Salé is best seen on a half-day trip from Rabat. The main entrance to the **medina** is Bab Bou Haja, on the southwestern wall, which opens onto Place Bab Khebaz. The **Grande Mosqué** is 500m further northwest along Rue Ras ash-Shajara; it's closed to non-Muslims, but the **medersa** (admission Dh10; 9am-noon & 2.30-6pm) is open as a museum.

Shaded by trees and unchanged for centuries, the **Souq el-Ghezel** (Wool Market), makes an interesting stop. In the nearby **Souq el-Merzouk**, textiles, basketwork and jewellery are crafted and sold.

The most atmospheric way to reach Salé is to take one of the small row boats (Dh1 per person) that cross the Oued Bou Regreg from just below the *mellah* (walled Jewish quarter). Alternatively, take bus 12, 13, 14 or 16 (Dh4) and get off after passing under the railway bridge.

In the village of Oulja, 3km southeast of Salé, the **Complexe de Potiers** (potters' cooperative; sunrise-sunset) is a top spot for the souvenir hunter. A huge selection of ceramics is produced and sold here, including tajine dishes of every size and colour.

Jardins Exotiques

The gardens created by the French horticulturist Marcel François in 1951, the **Jardins Exotiques** (adult/child Dh10/5; 9am-5pm winter, to 7pm summer) reopened after several years of restoration in 2005. The gardens are tranquil on weekends. Colour-coded paths lead through overgrown Brazilian rainforest, Polynesian jungle, Japanese pleasure grounds and an Andalucian garden. This is a great place to bring children and a popular spot for courting couples. The gardens are 13km north of Rabat on the road to Kenitra. Take bus 28 from Ave Moulay Hassan in Rabat, or Bab Fès, the main gate at Salé medina.

CASABLANCA

pop 4 million

Many travellers stay in CasaCasa, as Casablanca is popularly known, just long enough to change planes or catch a train, but Morocco's economic heart offers a unique insight into the country. This sprawling, European-style city is home to racing traffic, simmering social problems, wide boulevards, parks and imposing Hispano-Moorish and art deco buildings. Their facades stand in sharp contrast to Casablanca's modernist landmark: the enormous and incredibly ornate Hassan II mosque.

Orientation

The medina – the oldest part of town – is relatively small and sits in the north of the city close to the port. To the south of the medina is Place des Nations Unies, a large traffic junction that marks the heart of the city. The CTM bus station and Casa-Port train station are in the centre of the city. Casa-Voyageurs station is 2km east of the centre and the airport is 30km southeast of town.

Information

There are banks – most with ATMS and foreign exchange offices – on almost every street corner in the centre of Casablanca.

BMCE (Hyatt Regency Hotel; Place des Nations Unis; 9am-9pm) Good for after-hours and weekend services.

Central Market post office (cnr Blvd Mohammed V & Rue Chaouia)

Crédit du Maroc (☎ 022 477255; 48 Blvd Mohammed V) Separate *bureau de change* that is very central.

Gig@net (☎ 022 484810; 140 Blvd Mohammed Zerktouni; per hr Dh10; 24hr)

LGnet (☎ 022 274613; 81 Blvd Mohammed V; per hr Dh6; 9am-midnight)

Main post office (cnr Blvd de Paris & Ave Hassan II)

Office National Marocain du Tourisme (ONMT; ☎ 022 271177; 55 Rue Omar Slaoui; 8.30am-4.30pm Mon-Fri)

Service d'Aide Médicale Urgente (SAMU; ☎ 022 252525; 24hr) Private ambulance service.

Sights

Rising above the Atlantic northwest of the medina, the **Hassan II Mosque** is the world's third-largest mosque, built to commemorate the former king's 60th birthday. The mosque rises above the ocean on a rocky outcrop reclaimed from the sea, a vast building that holds 25,000 worshippers and can accommodate a further 80,000 in the courtyards and squares around it. To see the interior of the mosque you must take a **guided tour** (☎ 022 482886; adult/child/student Dh120/30/60; 9am, 10am, 11am & 2pm Sat-Thu).

Central Casablanca is full of great art deco and Hispano-Moorish buildings. The best way to take them all in is by strolling in the area around the **Central Market** (Marché Central) and **Place Mohammed V**. The grand square is surrounded by public buildings that were later copied throughout Morocco, including the law courts, the splendid Wilaya, the Bank al-Maghrib and the main post office. After that, explore the slightly dilapidated 19th-century **medina** near the port.

Set in a beautiful villa surrounded by lush gardens, the **Jewish Museum of Casablanca** (☎ 022 994940; 81 Rue Chasseur Jules Gros, Oasis; admission Dh20, with guide Dh30; 10am-5pm Mon-Fri) is the only Jewish museum in the Islamic world.

Sleeping

Youth Hostel (☎ 022 220551; frmaj1@menara.com; 6 Place Ahmed el-Bidaoui; dm/d/tr incl breakfast Dh45/120/180; 8-10am & noon-11pm;) Clustered around a bright central lounge area, the rooms are basic but well kept and quiet, with high ceilings and a lingering smell of damp in winter. Good hot showers in the morning and a small kitchen for guest use. Sheets cost an extra Dh5.

Hôtel Galia (☎ 022 481694; 19 Rue Ibn Batouta; s/d/tr with shared bathroom Dh150/220/300, with private bathroom Dh170/250/330) Tiled floors, plastic flowers, gold tasselled curtains and matching bedspreads adorn the rooms at the Galia, a top-notch

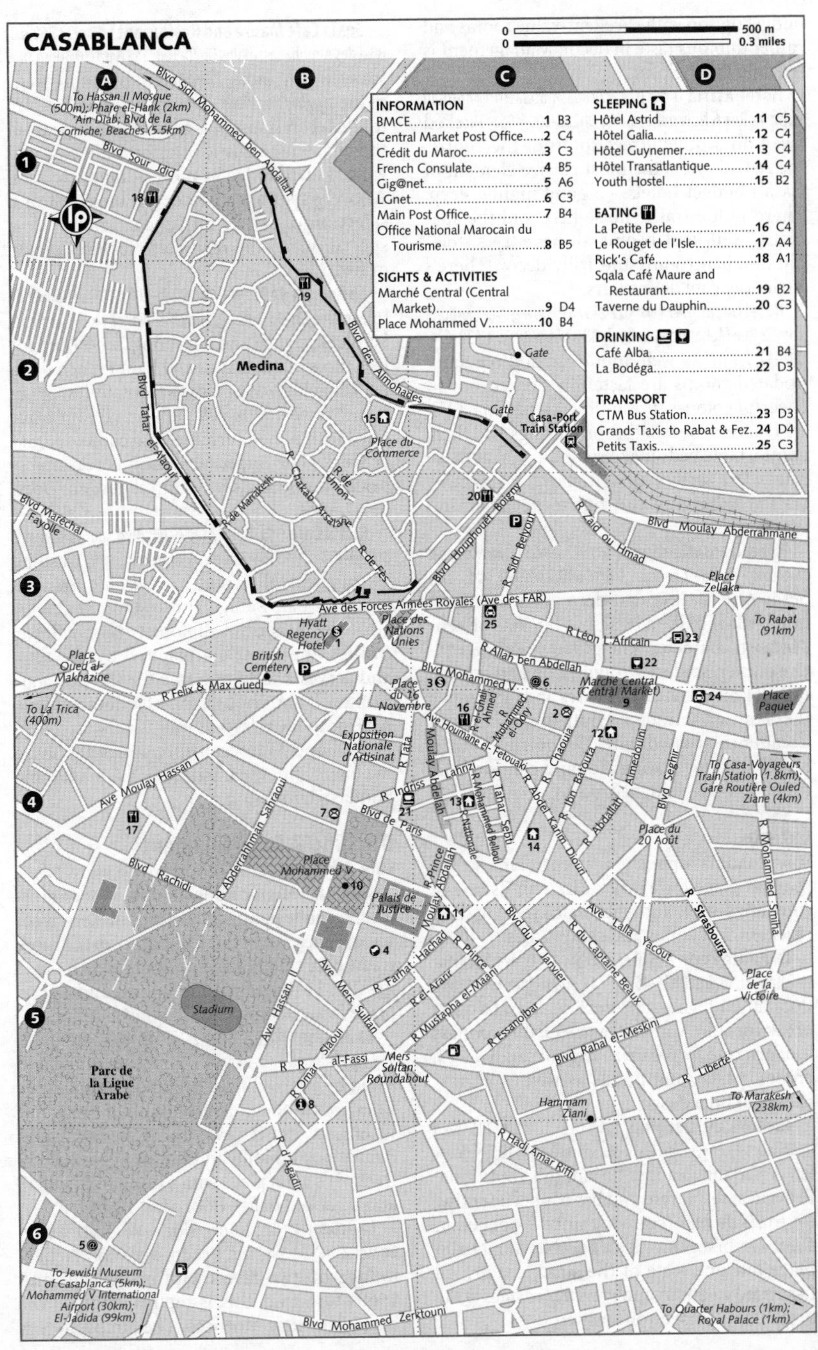
CASABLANCA
0 500 m
0 0.3 miles
A
B
C
D
1
2
3
4
5
6
INFORMATION
BMCE 1 B3
Central Market Post Office 2 C4
Crédit du Maroc 3 C3
French Consulate 4 B5
Gig@net 5 A6
LGnet 6 C3
Main Post Office 7 B4
Office National Marocain du Tourisme 8 B5
SIGHTS & ACTIVITIES
Marché Central (Central Market) 9 D4
Place Mohammed V 10 B4
SLEEPING
Hôtel Astrid 11 C5
Hôtel Galia 12 C4
Hôtel Guynemer 13 C4
Hôtel Transatlantique 14 C4
Youth Hostel 15 B2
EATING
La Petite Perle 16 C4
Le Rouget de l'Isle 17 A4
Rick's Café 18 A1
Sqala Café Maure and Restaurant 19 B2
Taverne du Dauphin 20 C3
DRINKING
Café Alba 21 B4
La Bodéga 22 D3
TRANSPORT
CTM Bus Station 23 D3
Grands Taxis to Rabat & Fez 24 D4
Petits Taxis 25 C3
To Hassan II Mosque (500m); Phare el-Hank (2km) 'Ain Diab; Blvd de la Corniche; Beaches (5.5km)
Blvd Sidi Mohammed ben Abdallah
Blvd Sour Jdid
Medina
Blvd Tahar el-Alaoui
Blvd des Almohades
Gate
Casa-Port Train Station
Place du Commerce
R Chakab Arsalane
R de Union
R de Marrakesh
R de Fès
Blvd Maréchal Fayolle
Blvd Houphouet Boigny
R Sidi Belyout
R Zaid ou Hmad
Blvd Moulay Abderrahmane
Place Zellaka
Ave des Forces Armées Royales (Ave des FAR)
Hyatt Regency Hotel
Place des Nations Unies
R Léon L'Africain
To Rabat (91km)
R Allah ben Abdellah
Place Oued al-Makhazine
British Cemetery
R Felix & Max Guedj
Blvd Mohammed V
Place du 16 Novembre
Marché Central (Central Market)
Place Paquet
To La Trica (400m)
Exposition Nationale d'Artisinat
R Tata
R el-Ghali Ahmed
R Mohammed el-Qory
Ave Houmane el-Fetouaki
R Chaouia
R Ibn Batouta
R Almedouini
Blvd Seghir
To Casa-Voyageurs Train Station (1.8km); Gare Routière Ouled Ziane (4km)
Ave Moulay Hassan I
R Indriss Lahrizi
Moulay Abdelah
R Tahar Sebti
R Abdel Karim Diouri
R Abdallah
Place du 20 Août
R Mohammed Smiha
Blvd de Paris
R Nationale
R Mohammed Belloul
R Abderrahman Sahraoui
Blvd Rachidi
Place Mohammed V
Palais de Justice
R Prince Moulay Abdallah
Blvd du 11 Janvier
Ave Lalla Yacout
R Strasbourg
R du Captaine Beaux
Place de la Victoire
R Farhat Hachad
R Prince
R el-Ararir
R Mustapha el-Maani
R Essanoubar
Ave Mers Sultan
Ave Hassan II
Stadium
R Omar Slaoui
R al-Fassi
Mers Sultan Roundabout
Blvd Rahal el-Meskini
R Liberté
Parc de la Ligue Arabe
To Marakesh (238km)
Hammam Ziani
R Hadj Amar Riffi
R d'Agadir
To Jewish Museum of Casablanca (5km); Mohammed V International Airport (30km); El-Jadida (99km)
Blvd Mohammed Zerktouni
To Quarter Habours (1km); Royal Palace (1km)

budget option with excellent-value rooms and rather dubious taste in decor. Management is friendly and helpful.

Hôtel Astrid (☎ 022 277803; hotelastrid@hotmail.com; 12 Rue 6 Novembre; s/d/tr Dh256/309/405) Tucked away on a quiet street south of the centre, the Astrid offers the most elusive element of Casa's budget hotels – a good night's sleep. There's little traffic noise here and the spacious, well-kept rooms all have TVs, telephones, bathrooms and frilly decor. There's a friendly cafe downstairs.

Hôtel Guynemer (☎ 022 275764; www.guynemerhotel.com; 2 Rue Mohammed Belloul; B&B s/d/tr Dh398/538/676;) The 29 well-appointed and regularly updated rooms are tastefully decked out in cheerful colours. Fresh flowers, plasma TVs, wi-fi access, new bathroom fittings and firm, comfortable beds make rooms a steal at these rates. The service is well above average: its staff will happily run out to get anything you need.

Hôtel Transatlantique (☎ 022 294551; www.transatcasa.com; 79 Rue Chaouia; s/d/tr 600/750/950;) Set in one of Casa's art deco gems, this 1922 hotel, shaped like a boat, has buckets of neo-Moorish character. The grand scale, decorative plaster, spidery wrought iron and eclectic mix of knick-knacks, pictures and lamps give the Transatlantique a whiff of colonial-era decadence crossed with '70s retro. It has a lovely outdoor seating area and comfortable, though fairly plain, bedrooms.

Eating

Rue Chaouia, opposite the central market, is the best place for a quick eat, with its line of rotisseries, stalls and restaurants serving roast chicken, brochettes and sandwiches.

La Petite Perle (☎ 022 272849; 17-19 Ave Houmane el-Fetouaki; mains Dh25-45; 11.30am-3pm & 6-11pm) Popular with young professionals and a quiet break for solo women travellers, this spotless modern cafe serves up a range of sandwiches, crêpes, pastas and pizzas as well as a great choice of breakfasts.

Taverne du Dauphin (☎ 022 221200; 115 Blvd Houphouet Boigny; mains Dh70-90, set menu Dh110; Mon-Sat) A Casablanca institution, this traditional Provençal restaurant and bar has been serving up *fruits de mer* (seafood) since it opened in 1958. On first glance it's a humble, family-run place but one taste of the succulent grilled fish, fried calamari and *crevettes royales* (king prawns) will leave you smitten.

Sqala Cafe Maure and Restaurant (☎ 022 260960; Blvd des Almohades; mains Dh70-160; 8am-10.30pm Tue-Sun winter, daily summer) Nestled in the ochre walls of the *sqala*, an 18th-century fortified bastion, this lovely restaurant is a tranquil escape from the city, with a rustic interior and delightful garden surrounded by flower-draped trellises. A lovely spot for a Moroccan breakfast or a selection of salads for lunch. Tajines are a speciality, but the menu also features plenty of fish.

Le Rouget de l'Isle (☎ 022 294740; 16 Rue Rouget de l'Isle; mains Dh110-130; lunch & dinner Mon-Fri, dinner Sat) Sleek, stylish and charming, renowned for its simple but delicious and light French food, Le Rouget is one of Casa's top eateries. Set in a renovated 1930s villa, it is an elegant place filled with period furniture and contemporary artwork. The impeccable food is reasonably priced and there's a beautiful garden. Book in advance.

Rick's Cafe (☎ 022 274207; 248 Blvd Sour Jdid; mains Dh130-160; noon-3.30pm & 6pm-midnight) Cashing in on the Hollywood hit *Casablanca*, this beautiful bar, lounge and restaurant run by a former American diplomat has furniture, fittings and nostalgia inspired by the film, and serves a taste of home for the nostalgic masses. Lamb chops, chilli, hamburgers and American breakfasts as well as a few excellent French and Moroccan specialities are all on the menu, plus there's an in-house pianist and Sunday jazz session.

Drinking & Entertainment

Café Alba (☎ 022 227154; 59-61 Rue Indriss Lahrizi; 8am-1am) High ceilings, swish, modern furniture, subtle lighting and a hint of elegant colonial times, mark this cafe out from the more traditional smoky joints around town. It offers hassle-free downtime for women and a great place for watching Casa's up-and-coming.

La Bodéga (☎ 022 541842; 129 Rue Allah ben Abdellah; 12.30-3pm & 7pm-midnight) Hip, happening and loved by a mixed-aged group of Casablanca's finest, La Bodéga is essentially a tapas bar where the music (everything from salsa to Arabic pop) is loud and the Rioja wine flows freely. It's a fun place with a lively atmosphere and a packed dance floor after 10pm.

La Trica (☎ 022 220706; 5 Rue el-Moutanabi, Quartier Gauthier; 12pm-1am Mon-Fri, dinner Sat) A bar-lounge on two levels with brick walls and 1960s furniture, this is the place to feel the beat of the new Morocco. The atmosphere is

BUSES FROM CASABLANCA

Destination	Cost (Dh)	Duration (hr)	Frequency
Essaouira	130	7	2 daily
Fez	100	5	10 daily
Marrakesh	80	4	9 daily
Meknès	80	4	11 daily
Rabat	30	1	hourly
Tangier	130	6	6 daily
Tetouan	130	7	3 daily

hot and trendy at night, stirred by the techno beat and a flow of beer and mojitos, but things are a lot calmer at lunchtime.

The beachfront suburb of Aïn Diab is the place for late-night drinking and dancing in Casa. Hanging out with Casablanca's beautiful people for a night on the town doesn't come cheap, though. You can expect to pay at least Dh100 to get in and as much again for drinks.

Getting There & Away

All long-distance trains, as well as trains to Mohammed V International Airport, depart from **Casa-Voyageurs train station** (☎ 022 243818), 4km east of the city centre. Catch bus 30 (Dh3.50), which runs down Blvd Mohammed V, or hop in a taxi and pay about Dh10 to get there. Destinations include Marrakesh (Dh84, three hours, nine daily), Fez (Dh103, 4½ hours, nine daily) via Meknès (Dh86, 3½ hours) and Tangier (Dh118, 5¾ hours, three daily).

The **Casa-Port train station** (☎ 022 223011) is a few hundred metres northeast of Place des Nations Unies. Although more conveniently located, trains from here run only to Rabat (Dh36, one hour).

The modern **CTM bus station** (☎ 022 541010; 23 Rue Léon L'Africain) has daily CTM departures, for details on price and frequency, see the boxed text, above.

The modern **Gare Routière Ouled Ziane** (☎ 022 444470), 4km southeast of the centre, is the bus station for non-CTM services.

Getting Around

The easiest way to get from Mohammed V International Airport to Casablanca is by train (2nd class Dh30, 35 minutes); they leave every hour from 6am to midnight from below the ground floor of the airport terminal building.

A *grand taxi* between the airport and the city centre costs Dh250.

Expect to pay Dh10 in or near the city centre for a trip in one of the red *petits taxis*.

ESSAOUIRA

pop 70,000

Perennially popular Essaouira has long been a favourite on the travellers' trail. It's laid-back and artsy with sea breezes and picture-postcard ramparts, all of which conspire to make a short visit from Marrakesh turn into a stay of several nights. Although it can appear swamped with visitors in the height of summer, when the day trippers get back on the buses there's more than enough space to sigh deeply and just soak up the atmosphere.

Information

There are several banks with ATMs around Place Moulay Hassan. There are plentiful internet cafes, most opening from 9am to 11pm and charging Dh8 to Dh10 per hour.

Cyber Les Remparts (12 Rue du Rif)
Délégation du Tourisme (☎ 024 783532; www.essaouira.com; 10 Rue du Caire; 🕒 9am-noon & 3-6.30pm Mon-Fri) Very helpful staff.
Espace Internet (8bis, Rue du Caire)
Hôpital Sidi Mohammed ben Abdallah (☎ 024 475716; Blvd de l'Hôpital) Emergencies.
Main post office (Ave el-Mouqawama)

Sights & Activities

Essaouira's walled **medina** was added to Unesco's World Heritage list in 2001, its well-preserved, late-18th-century fortified layout a prime example of European military architecture in North Africa. The mellow atmosphere, narrow, winding streets lined with colourful shops, whitewashed houses and heavy old wooden doors make it a wonderful place to stroll. The easiest place to access the ramparts is **Skala de la Ville**, the impressive sea bastion built along the cliffs. Down by the harbour, the **Skala du Port** (adult/child Dh10/3; 🕒 8.30am-noon & 2.30-6pm) offers picturesque views over the fishing port and the **Île de Mogador**.

A number of outlets rent water-sports equipment and offer instruction along Essaouira's wide, sandy beach. **Océan Vagabond** (☎ 024 783934; www.oceanvagabond.com, in French; 🕒 8am-8pm daily) rents surfboards (three days Dh500) and gives two-hour surfing lessons (Dh350). It also offers kitesurfing lessons (six hours Dh1950) and rental (three days Dh1200), and windsurfing

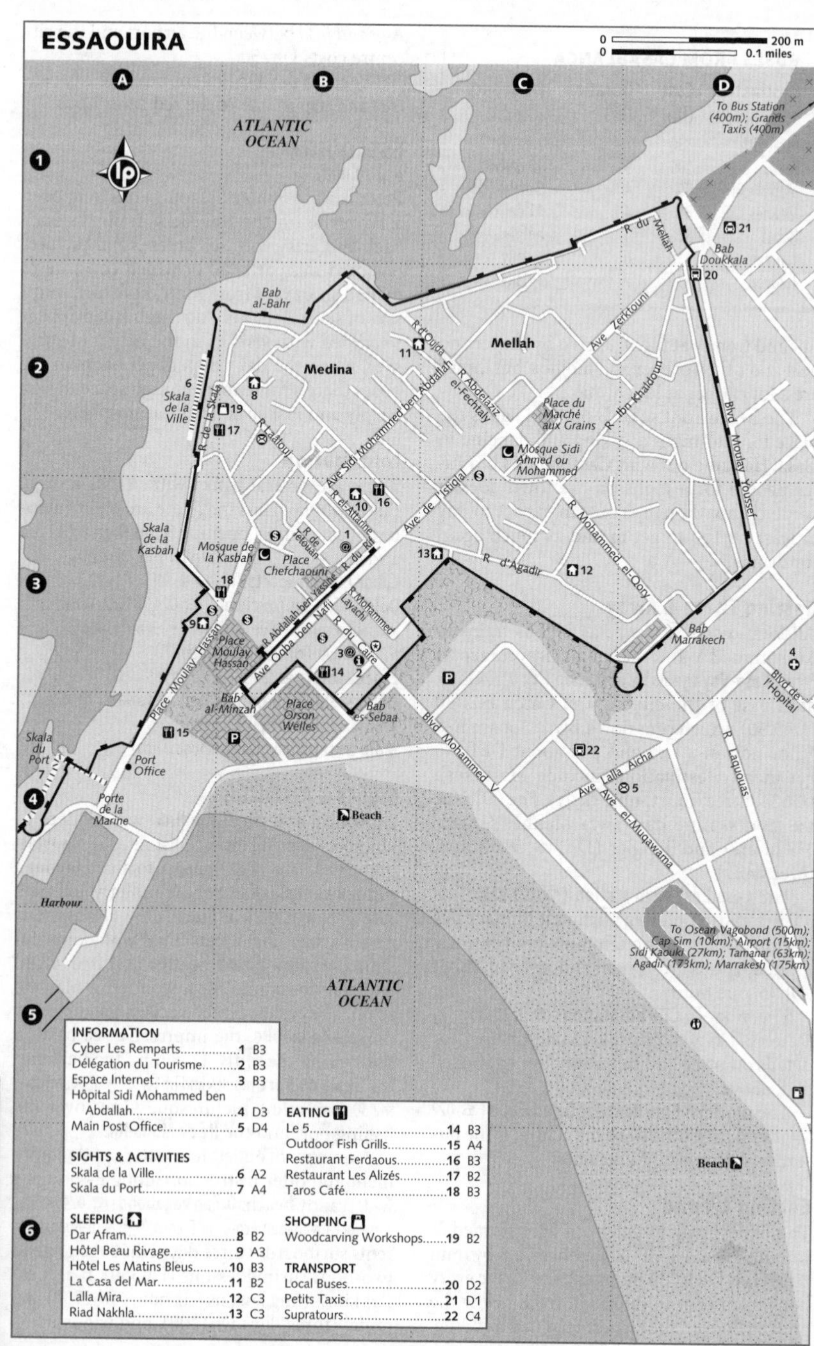
ESSAOUIRA
0 200 m
0 0.1 miles
A
B
C
D
1
2
3
4
5
6
ATLANTIC OCEAN
To Bus Station (400m); Grands Taxis (400m)
R du Mellah
Bab Doukkala
Bab al-Bahr
R d'Oujda
Mellah
Medina
Ave Zerktouni
R Ibn Khaldoun
Skala de la Ville
R de la Skala
R Laâlouj
Ave Sidi Mohammed ben Abdallah
R Abdelaziz el-Fechtaly
Place du Marché aux Grains
Mosque Sidi Ahmed ou Mohammed
Blvd Moulay Youssef
R el-Attarine
Ave de l'Istiqlal
R Mohammed el-Qory
Skala de la Kasbah
Mosque de la Kasbah
R de Tetouan
R du Rif
Place Chefchaouni
R d'Agadir
R Abdallah ben Yassine
R Mohammed Layachi
Place Moulay Hassan
Ave Oqba ben Nafii
R du Caire
Bab Marrakech
Blvd de l'Hôpital
Place Moulay Hassan
Bab al-Minzah
Place Orson Welles
Bab es-Sebaa
Blvd Mohammed V
Skala du Port
Port Office
R Laqouas
Ave Lalla Aicha
Ave el-Muqawama
Porte de la Marine
Beach
Harbour
To Ocean Vagabond (500m); Cap Sim (10km); Airport (15km); Sidi Kaouki (27km); Tamanar (63km); Agadir (173km); Marrakesh (175km)
ATLANTIC OCEAN
Beach
INFORMATION
Cyber Les Remparts....1 B3
Délégation du Tourisme....2 B3
Espace Internet....3 B3
Hôpital Sidi Mohammed ben Abdallah....4 D3
Main Post Office....5 D4
SIGHTS & ACTIVITIES
Skala de la Ville....6 A2
Skala du Port....7 A4
SLEEPING
Dar Afram....8 B2
Hôtel Beau Rivage....9 A3
Hôtel Les Matins Bleus....10 B3
La Casa del Mar....11 B2
Lalla Mira....12 C3
Riad Nakhla....13 C3
EATING
Le 5....14 B3
Outdoor Fish Grills....15 A4
Restaurant Ferdaous....16 B3
Restaurant Les Alizés....17 B2
Taros Café....18 B3
SHOPPING
Woodcarving Workshops....19 B2
TRANSPORT
Local Buses....20 D2
Petits Taxis....21 D1
Supratours....22 C4

lessons (one hour/six hours Dh500/1200) and rental (per hour Dh60). Be aware of strong Atlantic currents.

The **Gnaoua & World Music Festival** (third weekend June) is a four-day musical extravaganza with concerts on Place Moulay Hassan.

Sleeping

Dar Afram (☎ 024 785657; www.darafram.com; 10 Rue Sidi Magdoul; s Dh250, d Dh400-450) This extremely friendly guest house has simple, spotless rooms with shared bathrooms and a funky vibe. The guest house's Aussie–Moroccan owners are musicians and an impromptu session often follows the evening meals shared around a communal table. It also has a lovely tiled *hammam*. In the low season prices drop by around Dh100.

Hotel Beau Rivage (☎ 024 475925; beaurivage@menara.ma; 14 Place Moulay Hassan; s/d/tr Dh250/350/450) A long-time backpacker's favourite, this cheery hotel on the central square could hardly be better located. Rooms are clean, comfy and airy. They have bathrooms and a few face onto a rooftop terrace with views over the town that make it ideal for lazy-late morning breakfasts (Dh 20).

Riad Nakhla (☎/fax 024 474940; www.essaouiranet.com/riad-nakhla; 2 Rue Agadir; s Dh225, d Dh325, ste Dh400-500) Riad Nakhla looks like any other budget place from the outside, but inside the weary traveller is met with a friendly reception in a beautiful courtyard, with elegant stone columns and trickling fountain. The well-appointed bedrooms are simple but comfortable and immaculately kept. Breakfast on the stunning roof terrace with views over the ocean and town is another treat. All in all, it's an incredible bargain at this price.

Hôtel Les Matins Bleus (☎ 024 785363/066 308899; www.les-matins-bleus.com; 22 Rue de Drâa; s/d/ste Dh300/460/920) Hidden down a dead end, this charming hotel has bright, traditionally styled rooms surrounding a central courtyard painted in cheerful colours. The rooms all have plain white walls, lovely local fabrics and spotless bathrooms. Breakfast is served on the sheltered terrace from where you'll get good views over the medina.

Lalla Mira (☎ 024 475046; 14 Rue d'Algerie; www.lallamira.net; s/d/ste Dh436/692/920; 💻) This gorgeous little place, the town's first eco-hotel, has simple rooms with ochre *tadelakt* (polished plaster) walls, wrought-iron furniture, natural fabrics and solar-powered underfloor heating. The hotel also has a great *hammam* and a good restaurant (mains Dh90 to Dh120) serving a decent selection of vegetarian food.

La Casa del Mar (☎ 024 475091; www.lacasa-delmar.com; 35 Rue D'Oujda; inc breakfast d Dh825/990) A delightful guest house that seamlessly blends contemporary design with traditional style, creating a stunning yet simple atmosphere where you can sit back, relax and just soak up the atmosphere. Retire to your room, join the other guests for a communal Moroccan meal or Spanish paella (Dh180), arrange a home visit from a masseur or henna-artist or just watch the sunset from the seafront terrace.

Eating

Place Moulay Hassan offers plenty of sandwich stands and cafes for lazy breakfasts and lunches.

our pick **Outdoor fish grills** (Place Moulay Hassan; meals Dh40-100) These unpretentious stands at port end of Place Moulay offer one of the definitive Essaouira experiences. Just choose what you want to eat from the colourful displays of freshly caught fish and shellfish at each grill, see it weighed up to arrive at a price and wait for it to be cooked on the spot and served with a pile of bread and salad.

Restaurant Ferdaous (☎ 024 473655; 27 Rue Abdesslam Lebadi; mains Dh60-80, set menu Dh105; 🕑 closed Mon) Delightful Moroccan restaurant, and one of the few places in town that serves real, home-cooked traditional Moroccan food. The seasonal menu offers an innovative take on traditional recipes, the service is very friendly and the low tables and padded seating make it feel like the real McCoy.

Taros Café (☎ 024 476407; 2 Rue de la Skala; mains Dh70-120; 🕑 8am-11pm Mon-Sat) The roof terrace at the Taros is a wonderful place for afternoon tea or for evening cocktails lit by giant Moroccan lamps. The salons in this beautifully restored house are lined with artworks and although the restaurant is a bit hit-and-miss for food, it has live music and belly dancing most nights.

Restaurante Les Alizés (☎ 024 476819; 26 Rue de la Skala; mains Dh75-90) Above Pension Smara, this popular place run by a charming Moroccan couple in an 19th-century house has delicious Moroccan dishes, particularly the couscous with fish and the tajine of *boulettes de sardines* (sardine balls). Book well ahead as it fills up every night, both with Moroccans and visitors.

Le 5 (☎ 024 784726; 5 Rue Youssef el-Fassi; menu Dh180; 7-11pm Wed-Mon, noon-3pm Sat & Sun) Deep-purple seating, warm stone arches and giant lampshades dominate this trendy restaurant that serves well-cooked and original Mediterranean and Moroccan dishes. One of the most popular places to head for dinner.

Shopping

Essaouira is well known for its woodwork and you can visit the string of **woodcarving workshops** near the Skala de la Ville. The exquisite marquetry work on sale is made from local fragrant thuya wood, unfortunately now endangered. Essaouira also has a reputation as an artists' hub and plenty of galleries around town sell works by local painters.

Getting There & Away

The **bus station** (☎ 024 785241) is about 400m northeast of the medina, an easy walk during the day but better in a *petit taxi* (Dh10) if you're arriving/leaving late at night. **CTM** (☎ 024 784764) has several buses daily for Casablanca (Dh125, six hours), and one apiece to Marrakesh (Dh75, 2½ hours) and Agadir (Dh70, three hours). Other companies run cheaper and more frequent buses to the same destinations as well as Taroudannt (Dh70, six hours) and Rabat (Dh90, six hours).

Supratours (☎ 024 475317) operates from outside the medina and runs buses to Marrakesh train station (Dh80, 2½ hours, four daily) to connect with trains to Casablanca. You should book several days in advance for this service, particularly in summer.

AGADIR

pop 680,000

Completely destroyed by an earthquake in 1960, Agadir has rebuilt itself as Morocco's premier beach resort, with spacious streets and a new marina. Although it's best known for package tourism, Agadir has an increasing number of attractions for independent travellers and is a good place to stop, not only for some good old-fashioned R&R and for its improved restaurants, but for its gentle sights – the ruined kasbah, and its huge sandy bay, which is more sheltered than many other Atlantic beaches.

Orientation

Agadir's bus stations and most of the budget hotels are in the business centre of Nouveau Talborjt, inland, on the northeast side of the town. From here it's about a 15-minute walk down to Blvd du 20 Août, the main strip, which is lined with cafes and restaurants and big hotels.

Information

Banks with ATMs proliferate along Blvd Hassan II; those listed here also have *bureaux de change.*

Banque Populaire (Blvd Hassan II)

Délégation Régionale du Tourisme (ONMT; ☎ 028 846377; Immeuble Ignouan, Ave Mohammed V; 8.30am-noon & 2.30-6.30pm Mon-Thu, 8.30-11.30am & 3-6.30pm Fri) The best place for local and regional information.

Internet Swiss (Blvd Hassan II; per hr Dh10; 9am-11pm) The busiest and most conveniently located cybercafe.

Main post office (Ave Sidi Mohammed; 8.30am-6.30pm Mon-Fri, to noon Sat)

Wafa Bank (Blvd Hassan II)

Sights

The old **kasbah**, on a hill 7km northwest of the centre and visible from much of Agadir, is a rare survivor of the earthquake, and dates from 1541. The grassy area below the kasbah, **Ancienne Talborjt**, covers the remains of old Agadir town and constitutes a mass grave for all those who died in the 1960 earthquake. The walk up to the kasbah is long, hot and uncomfortable: get a taxi up (Dh20 to Dh25) and walk back down.

The small **Musée du Patrimoine Amazigh** (☎ 028 821632; Aït Souss, Blvd Hassan II; admission Dh20; 9.30am-5.30pm Mon-Sat) has an excellent display of Berber artefacts and is especially strong on jewellery.

Four kilometres south, on the Inezgane road, is **La Médina d'Agadir** (☎ 028 280253; www.medinapolizzi.com, in French; Aghroud Ben Sergao; adult/child Dh40/20; 8.30am-6.30pm), an idealised Berber village, built using traditional techniques and materials, with workshops for 30 independent artisans. Shuttle buses (adult/child Dh60/30) come out here from the kiosk on Blvd du 20 Août, picking up at several hotels on the way.

Sleeping

Hôtel Canaria (☎ 028 846727; Place Lahcen Tamri; s/d Dh80/100) The hotel overlooks a pleasant square, although the rooms, with pine furniture and potted plants, all face into the internal upper

MOROCCO

courtyard. Rooms without bathrooms are Dh10 cheaper. It's near the bus offices.

Hôtel Tiznine (☎ 028 843925; 3 Rue Drarga; s/d with private bathroom Dh120/150, with shared bathroom Dh100/150) One of Agadir's best budget places, with a dozen good-sized rooms around a green-and-white tiled flowering courtyard. Some rooms have en suite bathrooms, but if not the communal ones are spotless. The manager speaks good English.

Hôtel Kamal (☎ 028 842817; fax 028 843940; Ave Hassan II; s/d Dh403/462) An extremely popular and well-run downtown hotel in a modernist white block near the town hall. The Kamal manages to appeal to a wide range of clients, including package-tour groups and travelling Moroccans. The rooms have bathrooms and are bright and clean, the staff are helpful and there's a pool large enough to swim laps.

Sofitel Agadir (☎ 028 820088; www.sofitel.com; Baie des Palmiers, Ben Sergao; s/d from Dh750/900;) The Sofitel stands out from the large range of resort hotels. Built like a low-rise kasbah, it manages to seem smaller than its 240 rooms, all of which have had a recent upgrade. Luxury facilities include an excellent thalassotherapy spa, *hammam*, several swimming pools, a well-tended beach and a range of restaurants. It also boasts Agadir's most happening nightclub.

Eating

The cheap snack bars in Nouveau Talborjt and around the bus stations are open after hours. For ultrafresh, no-nonsense fish, try one of the many **fish stalls** (meals around Dh50) at the entrance to the commercial port. There are plenty of places along the beach to chill at midday or toast the sunset. Some of the places along Palm Beach stay open till 1am in summer.

Bab Marrakesh (☎ 028 826144; Rue de Massa; sandwiches Dh25-35, couscous Dh70, 2-person tajine Dh100) Near Souq al-Had, this is the real thing, far removed from the tourist traps near the beach. Highly regarded by locals, it serves authentic Moroccan food at authentic prices.

Les Blancs (☎ 028 828388; Marina; mains from Dh90) The best-located restaurant in Agadir by a long way. At the very northern end of the beach and at the entrance to the new marina development, Les Blancs is a chilled, elegant, white-tiled bar, lounge and restaurant. A Spaniard runs the kitchen serving a mix of Andalucian and Moroccan dishes. Service can be slow.

La Scala (☎ 028 846773; Rue du Oued Souss; meals incl wine Dh350) Excellent Moroccan restaurant, popular with wealthy Moroccans, Arab tourists and Westerners, which makes for a pleasantly cosmopolitan atmosphere. The food is elegant and fresh, and beautifully presented.

Getting There & Away

Although a good number of buses serve Agadir, it is quite possible you'll end up in the regional transport hub of Inezgane, 13km south – check before you buy your ticket. Plenty of *grands taxis* (Dh8) and local buses shuttle between there and Agadir.

The **bus station** is on Rue Chair al-Hamra Mohammed ben Brahim, past the Souq el-Had. **CTM** (☎ 028 825341; www.ctm.co.ma) has buses to Casablanca (Dh180, eight hours, six daily). The 10.30pm continues to Rabat (Dh195, 10 hours). There are also departures for Marrakesh (Dh80, four hours, seven daily), Essaouira (Dh60, two hours, one daily), as well as Fez and Tangier. **Supratours** (☎ 028 224010) has fast services to Marrakesh train station (Dh90, four hours, several daily) and Essaouira (Dh60, three hours).

The main *grand taxi* rank is at the south end of Rue de Fès. Destinations include Taroudannt (Dh35), Essaouira (Dh70) and Marrakesh (Dh120). A *grand taxi* to the airport costs Dh150 by day, Dh200 at night. Orange *petits taxis* run around town.

IMPERIAL CITIES & THE MIDDLE ATLAS

The rolling plains that sweep across the north along the base of the Middle Atlas are Morocco's most fertile agricultural region, dotted with olive groves and wheat fields. Several of Morocco's most important cities have also taken root here, including ancient Fez with its teeming medina, imperial Meknès and the Roman city of Volubilis, now Morocco's most interesting archaeological site.

FEZ

pop 1 million

Marrakesh might be modern Morocco's tourist capital, but 1400-year old Fez is Morocco's spiritual beating heart. Its medina (Fès el-Bali) is the largest living medieval Islamic city in the world, and the world's largest

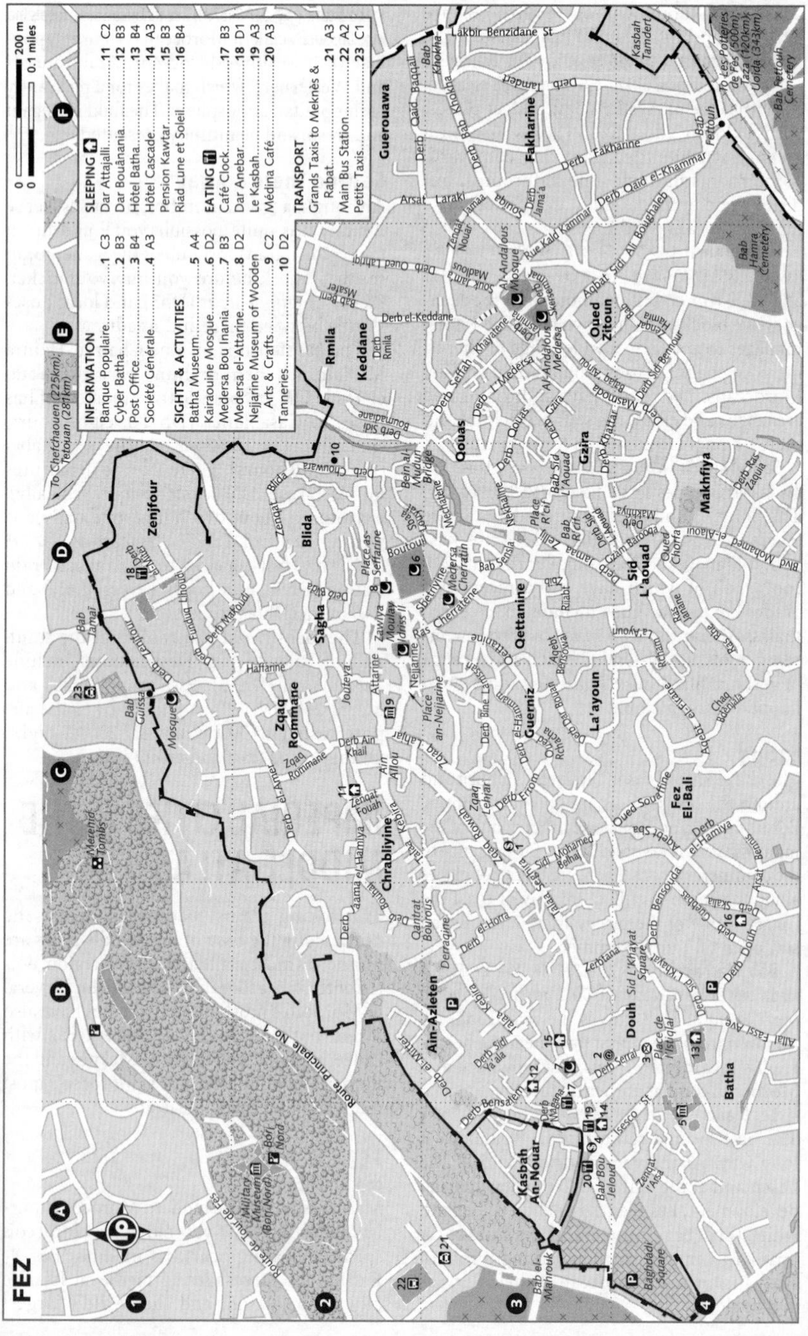

FEZ

0 — 200 m
0 — 0.1 miles

INFORMATION

Banque Populaire	1	C3
Cyber Batha	2	B3
Post Office	3	B4
Société Générale	4	A3

SIGHTS & ACTIVITIES

Batha Museum	5	A4
Kairaouine Mosque	6	D2
Medersa Bou Inania	7	B3
Medersa el-Attarine	8	D2
Nejjarine Museum of Wooden Arts & Crafts	9	C2
Tanneries	10	D2

SLEEPING

Dar Attajalli	11	C2
Dar Bouânania	12	B3
Hôtel Batha	13	B4
Hôtel Cascade	14	A3
Pension Kawtar	15	B3
Riad Lune et Soleil	16	B4

EATING

Café Clock	17	B3
Dar Anebar	18	D1
Le Kasbah	19	A3
Médina Café	20	A3

TRANSPORT

Grands Taxis to Meknès & Rabat	21	A3
Main Bus Station	22	A2
Petits Taxis	23	C1

car-free urban environment. A first visit can be overwhelming, an assault on the eyes, ears and nose through covered bazaars, winding alleys, mosques and workshops, amid people and pack animals, all of which seem to take you out of the 21st century and back to an imagined era of *1001 Arabian Nights*.

Orientation

Fez can be neatly divided into three distinct parts: Fès el-Bali (the core of the medina; the main entrance is Bab Bou Jeloud) in the east; Fès el-Jdid (containing the *mellah* and Royal Palace) in the centre; and the *ville nouvelle,* the modern administrative area constructed by the French, to the southwest. It's a 45-minute walk between the *ville nouvelle* and the medina, or a short Dh10 hop in a *petit taxi*.

Information

INTERNET ACCESS

Cyber Batha (Map p632; Derb Douh; per hr Dh10; ⌚ 9am-10pm) Has English as well as French keyboards.
Cyber Club (Map p634; Blvd Mohammed V; per hr Dh6; ⌚ 9am-10pm)

MEDIA

View from Fez (http://riadzany.blogspot.com) Essential news and views blog for keeping up-to-date with what's happening in Fez.

MEDICAL SERVICES

Hôpital Ghassani (off Map p634; ☎ 055 622777) One of the city's biggest hospitals; located east of the *ville nouvelle* in the Dhar Mehraz district.
Night Pharmacy (Map p634; ☎ 035 623493; Blvd Moulay Youssef; ⌚ 9pm-6am) Located in the north of the *ville nouvelle;* staffed by a doctor and a pharmacist.

MONEY

There are plenty of banks (with ATMs) in the *ville nouvelle* along Blvd Mohammed V. In the medina:

Banque Populaire (Map p632; Ave des Français; ⌚ 8.45am-noon & 2.45-6pm Mon-Thu, 8.45am-noon Sat) ATM and foreign exchange.
Société Générale (Map p632; Ave des Français; ⌚ 8.45am-noon & 2.45-6pm Mon-Thu, 8.45-11am Fri, 8.45am-noon Sat) ATM and foreign exchange.

POST

Main post office (Map p634; cnr Ave Hassan II & Blvd Mohammed V) Poste restante is at the far left; the parcels office is through a separate door.
Post office (Map p632; Place Batha) Located in the medina; also has an ATM.

TOURIST INFORMATION

There is no tourist information in the medina.
Tourist Information Office (Syndicat d'Initiative; Map p634; ☎ 035 623460; Place Mohammed V)

Dangers & Annoyances

Fez has long been notorious for its *faux guides* (unofficial guides) and carpet-shop hustlers. *Faux guides* tend to congregate around Bab Bou Jeloud, the main western entrance to the medina, although crackdowns by the authorities have greatly reduced their numbers and hassle. Also watch out for touts on trains arriving into Fez, hoping to steer you towards certain hotels. Walking alone late at night in the medina is also advised against, as knifepoint robberies aren't unknown.

Sights

THE MEDINA (FÈS EL-BALI)

Within the old walls of Fès el-Bali lies an incredible maze of twisting alleys, blind turns and hidden *souqs*. Navigation can be confusing and getting lost at some stage a certainty, but this is part of the medina's charm: you never know what discovery lies around the next corner.

If Fez is the spiritual capital of Morocco, the **Kairaouine Mosque** (Map p632) is its true heart. Built in 859 by refugees from Tunisia, and rebuilt in the 12th century, it can accommodate up to 20,000 people at prayer – Africa's largest mosque. Non-Muslims are forbidden to enter and will have to suffice with glimpses of its seemingly endless columns from the gates on Talaa Kebira and Place as-Seffarine.

Located 150m east of Bab Bou Jeloud, the 14th-century **Medersa Bou Inania** (Map p632; admission Dh10; ⌚ 9am-6pm, closed during prayers) is the finest of Fez's theological colleges constructed by the Merenids. The *zellij* (tiling), *muqarna* (plasterwork) and woodcarving are amazingly elaborate, and views from the roof are also impressive.

Founded by Abu Said in 1325 in the heart of the medina, the **Medersa el-Attarine** (Map p632; admission Dh10; ⌚ 9am-6pm, closed during prayers) displays the traditional patterns of Merenid artisanship. The *zellij* base, stucco work and cedar wood at the top of the walls and the ceiling are every bit as elegant as the artistry of the Medersa Bou Inania.

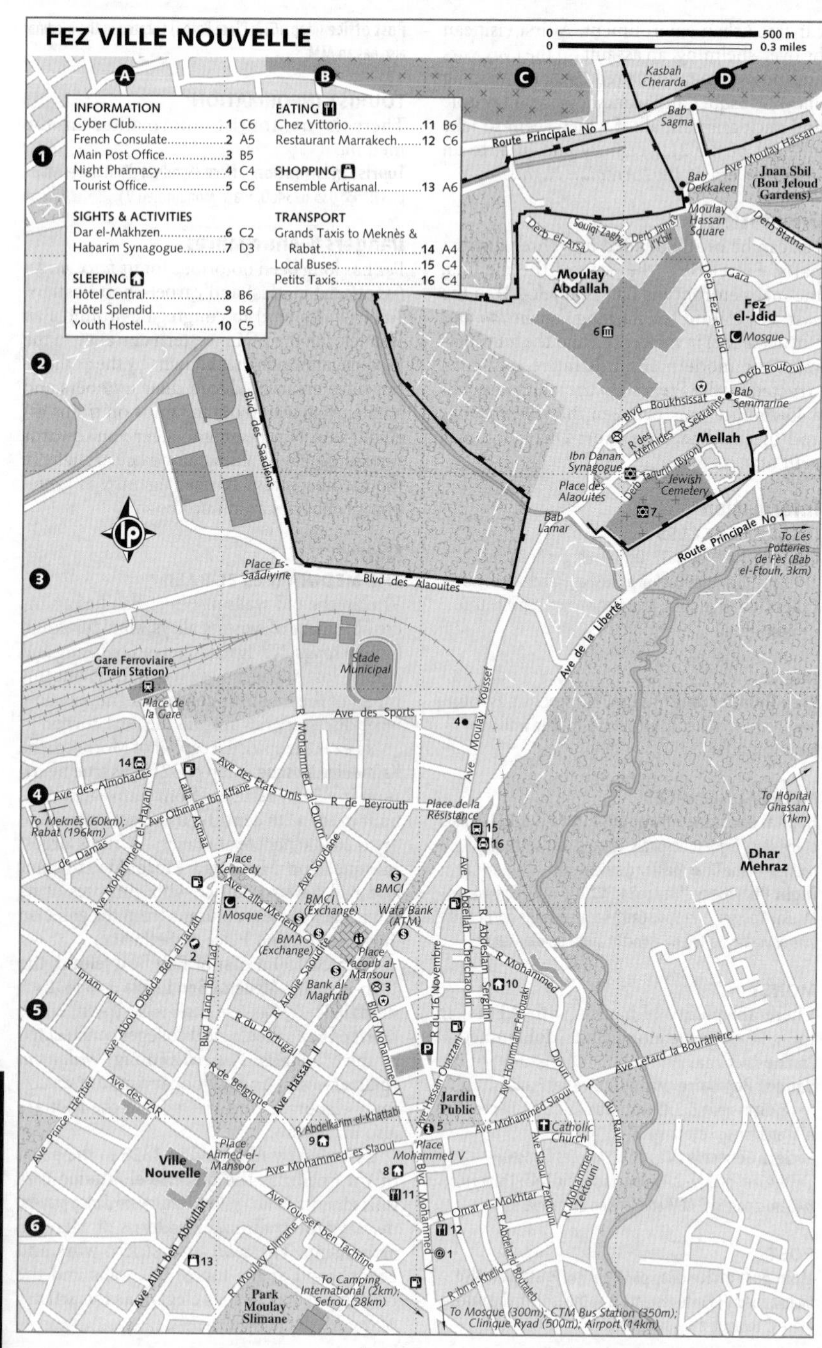
FEZ VILLE NOUVELLE
0 500 m
0 0.3 miles
INFORMATION
Cyber Club....1 C6
French Consulate....2 A5
Main Post Office....3 B5
Night Pharmacy....4 C4
Tourist Office....5 C6
SIGHTS & ACTIVITIES
Dar el-Makhzen....6 C2
Habarim Synagogue....7 D3
SLEEPING
Hôtel Central....8 B6
Hôtel Splendid....9 B6
Youth Hostel....10 C5
EATING
Chez Vittorio....11 B6
Restaurant Marrakech....12 C6
SHOPPING
Ensemble Artisanal....13 A6
TRANSPORT
Grands Taxis to Meknès & Rabat....14 A4
Local Buses....15 C4
Petits Taxis....16 C4
Kasbah Cherarda
Bab Sagma
Route Principale No 1
Ave Moulay Hassan
Jnan Sbil (Bou Jeloud Gardens)
Bab Dekkaken
Moulay Hassan Square
Derb Btatna
Derb el-Arsa
Souiqi Zagher
Derb Jama'a l'Kbir
Moulay Abdallah
Gara
Derb Fez el-Jdid
Fez el-Jdid
Mosque
Derb Bouttouil
Bab Semmarine
Blvd Boukhsissat
R Sekkakine
R des Merinides
Mellah
Ibn Danan Synagogue
Derb Taquriri (Byron)
Jewish Cemetery
Place des Alaouites
Bab Lamar
To Les Potteries de Fès (Bab el-Ftouh, 3km)
Blvd des Saadiens
Place Es-Saâdiyine
Blvd des Alaouites
Stade Municipal
Gare Ferroviaire (Train Station)
Place de la Gare
Ave des Sports
Ave de la Liberté
Ave Moulay Youssef
R Mohammed al-Quorri
Ave des Almohades
Ave des Etats Unis
R de Beyrouth
Place de la Résistance
Ave Othmane Ibn Affane
Lalla Asmaa
To Meknès (60km); Rabat (196km)
R de Damas
Ave Mohammed el-Hayani
To Hôpital Ghassani (1km)
Dhar Mehraz
Place Kennedy
Ave Lalla Meriem
Mosque
Ave Soudane
BMCI
BMCI (Exchange)
Wafa Bank (ATM)
BMAO (Exchange)
Place Yacoub al-Mansour
Bank al-Maghrib
R Arabie Saoudite
Ave Abdellah Chefchaouni
R Abdeslam Serghini
R Mohammed
R Imam Ali
Ave Abou Obeida Ben al-Jarrah
Blvd Tariq Ibn Ziad
R du Portugal
Blvd Mohammed V
R du 16 Novembre
Ave Hoummane Fetouaki
Diouri
Ave Letard la Bourallière
R de Belgique
Ave Hassan II
Ave des FAR
Ave Hassan Ouazzani
Jardin Public
R Abdelkarim el-Khattabi
Ave Mohammed Slaoui
Catholic Church
R du Ravin
Ave Prince Héritier
Place Ahmed el-Mansoor
Place Mohammed V
Ave Mohammed es Slaoui
Ville Nouvelle
Ave Slaoui Zerktouni
R Mohammed Zerktouni
Ave Youssef ben Tachfine
R Omar el-Mokhtar
R Abdelaziz Boutaleb
Ave Allal ben Abdullah
Ave Moulay Slimane
R ibn el-Khelid
To Camping International (2km); Sefrou (28km)
Park Moulay Slimane
To Mosque (300m); CTM Bus Station (350m); Clinique Ryad (500m); Airport (14km)

MOROCCO

The **Nejjarine Museum of Wooden Arts & Crafts** (Map p632; ☎ 035 740580; Place an-Nejjarine; admission Dh20; 🕑 10am-7pm) is in a wonderfully restored *funduq* (a caravanserai – for travelling merchants), with a host of fascinating exhibits. The rooftop cafe has great views over the medina. Photography forbidden.

In a wonderful 19th-century summer palace, the **Batha Museum** (Map p632; ☎ 035 634116; Rue de la Musée, Batha; admission Dh10; 🕑 8.30am-noon & 2.30-6pm Wed-Mon) houses an excellent collection of traditional Moroccan arts and crafts.

The **tanneries** (Map p632; Derb Chouwara, Blida) are one of the city's most iconic sights (and smells). Head northeast of Place as-Seffarine and take the left fork after about 50m; you'll soon pick up the unmistakeable waft of skin and dye that will guide you into the heart of the leather district. It's not possible to get in among the tanning pits themselves, but there are plenty of vantage points from the streets that line them, all occupied (with typical Fassi ingenuity) by leather shops.

Outside the medina walls, the **Merenid tombs** (Map p632) are dramatic in their advanced state of ruin. The views over Fez are spectacular and well worth the climb. Look for the black smoke in the southern part of the city, marking the potteries.

FEZ EL-JDID (NEW FEZ)

Only in a city as old as Fez could you find a district dubbed 'New' because it's only 700 years old. It's home to the Royal Palace, whose entrance at **Dar el-Makhzen** (Royal Palace; Map p632; Place des Alaouites) is a stunning example of modern restoration, but the 80 hectares of palace grounds are not open to the public.

In the 14th century, Fès el-Jdid was a refuge for Jews, thus creating a **mellah**. The *mellah's* southwest corner is home to the fascinating **Jewish Cemetery & Habarim Synagogue** (Map p634; admission free; 🕑 7am-7pm). Donations appreciated.

Sleeping

MEDINA

Pension Kawtar (Map p632; ☎ 035 740172; pension_kaw@yahoo.fr; Derb Taryana, Talaa Seghira; dm Dh60, s with shared bathroom Dh200, d with shared/private bathroom Dh300/350) Well-signed in an alley off Talaa Seghira, the Kawtar is a friendly Moroccan family-run concern, as much a home as a hostel. Amazingly, there are 10 rooms tucked into the place – those on the ground floor are a bit gloomy, but rooms get better the closer you get to the roof terrace. Great value for the price. Breakfast costs Dh25.

Hôtel Cascade (Map p632; ☎ 035 638442; 26 Rue Serrajine, Bab Bou Jeloud; dm Dh80, r Dh160) One of the grandaddies of the Morocco shoestring hotels, the Cascade still keeps drawing them in. You don't expect much for the price and you don't really get it either – it's all pretty basic – but if you're up for stretching budgets and meeting plenty of like-minded travellers then this might be the place for you. Breakfast costs Dh20.

Dar Bouânania (Map p632; ☎ 035 637282; 21 Derb be Salem, Talaa Kebira; s/d with shared bathroom Dh200-500, s/d with private bathroom Dh300/600, q Dh400) A popular choice with backpackers, this is as close as tight budgets will get to a *riad*. A traditional house with courtyard, *zellij* tiles and painted woodwork, it has several well-sized rooms on several levels, although as all face inward they can be quite dark at times. Shared bathrooms are clean, and there's a roof terrace. There's a high-season supplement of Dh100 per person. Breakfast is Dh30.

Hôtel Batha (Map p632; ☎ 035 741077; fax 035 741078; Place Batha; s/d Dh395/520; ❄ 🏊) The great location, room capacity and pool keeps the Batha perennially busy. It's a reasonably modern set-up, with fair rooms and cool, quiet areas to retreat from the hustle of the medina. It's good value, although the eccentric attitude to only providing hot water at particular (often inconvenient) hours has been a frustration for many years now.

our pick **Riad Lune et Soleil** (Map p632; ☎ 035 634523; www.riadluneetsoleil.com; 3 Derb Skalia, Batha; r Dh800-1200; ❄) Hospitality is everything at this *riad*. Each room is a cornucopia, decorated with everything from old postcards and embroidery to carvings and metalwork. There's plenty of comfort, too; several rooms have their own hot tub. You might just make it downstairs for dinner – recognised as coming from one of the best kitchens in the medina. Wi-fi is available.

Dar Attajali (Map p632; ☎ 035 637728; www.attajalli.com; Derb Qettana, Zkak Roumane; r/ste from Dh1000/1500; ❄) Dar Attajali is a magnificent testament to the art of patient and sympathetic restoration, which has maintained the building's integrity with a minimum of modern techniques and chemicals, while still managing to produce a supremely comfortable guest house. Decoration is set off with gently colour-themed Fassi fabrics – colours further reflected in the planting of the terrace roof

FESTIVALS IN FEZ

Every June the **Fez Festival of World Sacred Music** (☎ 035 740691; www.fesfestival.com) brings together music groups and artists from all corners of the globe, and has become one of the most successful world-music festivals going. Concerts are held in a variety of venues, including the Batha Museum and the square outside Bab Bou Jeloud. While the big names are a draw (Youssou N'Dour and Ravi Shankar have both played), equally fascinating are the more-intimate concerts held by Morocco's various *tariqas* (Sufi orders). Tickets can go like hot cakes and accommodation books out early – so organise as far ahead as possible if you plan on attending.

The **Festival of Sufi Culture** (www.par-chemins.org) debuted in 2007 and hosts a series of events every April including films and lectures and some spectacular concerts held in the garden of the Batha Museum with Sufi musicians from across the world.

In July the **National Festival of Berber Culture** aims to promote and protect Amazigh (Berber) culture. Its program includes musical performances as well as lectures and workshops.

Fez's biggest religious festival is also one of the country's largest. The *moussem* (saint's day) of the city's founder, Moulay Idriss, draws huge crowds. Local artisans create special tributes and there's a huge procession through the medina. Traditional music is played and followers dance and shower the musicians (and onlookers) with orange or rose water.

garden, and all designed to get you instantly relaxed (as if the organic, locally sourced breakfasts didn't get your day off to a good enough start). Wi-fi is available for guests.

VILLE NOUVELLE

Hôtel Central (Map p634; ☎ 035 622335; 50 Rue Brahim Roudani; s/d with shared bathroom Dh130/160, with private bathroom Dh150/180) A bright and airy budget option just off busy Ave Mohammed V. All rooms have external toilets; those without a shower have a sink. It's good value and popular so sometimes there are no rooms available.

Hôtel Splendid (Map p634; ☎ 035 622148; splendid@iam.net.ma; 9 Rue Abdelkarim el-Khattabi; s/d Dh318/412;) For the price, this hotel makes a valid claim for three stars. It's all modern and tidy, with good bathrooms and comfy beds, plus a pool for the heat and a bar for the evenings. There's a dining room, but breakfast isn't automatically included in the price.

Youth Hostel (Map p634; ☎ 035 624085; 18 Rue Abdeslam Serghini; dm Dh450; 8-10am, noon-3pm & 6-10pm) One of the better youth hostels in Morocco, the Fez branch is well looked after, and right in the centre of the *ville nouvelle*. Tidy rooms and facilities (including Western-style toilets) are superbly clean. If you're not a Youth Hostelling International (YHI) member, there's a Dh5 surcharge.

Eating

MEDINA

In the medina, you won't have to walk far to find someone selling food – tiny cell-like places grilling brochettes and cooking up cauldrons of soup, sandwich shops or just a guy with a push-cart selling peanut cookies. Bab Bou Jeloud has quite a cluster of options with streetside tables for people-watching.

Le Kasbah (Map p632; Rue Serrajine; mains Dh40, set menu Dh70; 8am-midnight) On several floors opposite the cheap hotels at Bab Bou Jeloud, this restaurant occupies a prime spot: the top floor looks out over the medina. The menu itself isn't overly exciting – tajines, couscous and meat from the grill, but good value (though drinks are marked up if you're not eating).

our pick **Café Clock** (Map p632; ☎ 035 637855; www.cafeclock.com; 7 Derb el-Mergana, Talaa Kebira; mains Dh55-80; 9am-10pm) In a restored town house, this funky place has a refreshing menu with offerings such as falafel, some interesting vegetarian options, a monstrously large camel burger and some delicious cakes. Better still, its 'Clock Culture' program includes sunset concerts every Sunday (cover charge around Dh20), attracting a good mix of locals, expats and curious tourists. There's wi-fi available.

Médina Café (Map p632; ☎ 035 633430; 6 Derb Mernissi, Bab Bou Jeloud; mains Dh70-100; 8am-10pm) Just outside Bab Bou Jeloud, this small restaurant is an oasis of serenity, decorated in a traditional yet restrained manner. During the day it's good for a quick bite or a fruit juice; in the evening better Moroccan fare is on offer – the lamb tajine with dried figs and apricots is a winner, while the plates of couscous are big enough for two.

Dar Anebar (Map p632; ☎ 035 635787; 25 Derb el-Miter, Zkak Roumane; mains from Dh120; 7.30pm-close) Another good *riad* for dining, you'll eat in truly fine surroundings here, in the splendid courtyard or one of the cosy salons. The menu is strictly Moroccan and of the highest standard, and you can accompany dinner with a bottle of wine.

VILLE NOUVELLE

Chez Vittorio (Map p634; ☎ 035 624730; 21 Rue Brahim Roudani; salads from Dh30, pizza or pasta from Dh56, mains from Dh80) This dependable favourite covers the rustic Italian restaurant angle well, right down to the candles and checked cloths. Food is good value, and while the initial service can be a bit creaky, your meal tends to arrive in a trice. Go for the pizzas or steak, as the pasta often disappoints. You can also enjoy a glass of wine with your meal.

Restaurant Marrakech (Map p634; ☎ 035 930876; 11 Rue Omar el-Mokhtar; mains from Dh55;) A charming restaurant that goes from strength to strength behind thick wooden doors. Red *tadelakt* walls and dark furniture plus a cushion-strewn salon at the back adds ambience, while the menu's variety refreshes the palate, with dishes such as chicken tajine with apple and olive, or lamb with aubergine and peppers. There is also a set three-course menu available.

Shopping

Fez is and always has been the artisanal capital of Morocco. The choice of crafts is wide, quality is high and prices are competitive. As usual, it's best to seek out the little shops off the main tourist routes.

Ensemble Artisanal (Map p634; Ave Allah ben Abdullah; 9am-noon & 2.30-6.30pm) Slightly out of the way in the *ville nouvelle*, the state-run Ensemble Artisanal is always a decent place to get a feel for quality and price.

Les Potteries de Fès (off Map p634; ☎ 035 669166; www.artnaji.net; Ain Nokbi; 8am-6pm) An attraction in itself, this is the home of the famous Fassi pottery. You can see the entire production process, from pot throwing to the painstaking hand painting and laying out of *zellij* – it's a joy to behold.

Getting There & Away

BUS

The main station for **CTM buses** (☎ 035 732992) is near Place Atlas in the southern *ville nouvelle*.

BUSES TO/FROM FEZ

Destination	Cost (Dh)	Duration (hr)	Frequency
Casablanca	100	5	7 daily
Chefchaouen	70	4	3 daily
Marrakesh	160	9	2 daily
Meknès	20	1.5	6 daily
Rabat	7	3.5	7 daily
Tangier	100	6	3 daily
Tetouan	93	5	2 daily

CTM runs many daily services to and from Fez; see the boxed text, above.

Non-CTM buses depart from the **main bus station** (Map p632; ☎ 035 636032) outside Bab el-Mahrouk.

TAXI

There are several *grand taxi* ranks dotted around town. Taxis for Meknès (Dh16) and Rabat (Dh59) leave from in front of the main bus station (outside Bab el-Mahrouk) and from near the train station.

TRAIN

The **train station** (Map p634; ☎ 035 930333) is in the *ville nouvelle*, a 10-minute walk northwest of Place Florence. Trains depart every two hours between 7am and 5pm for Casablanca (Dh103, 4½ hours), via Rabat (Dh76, 3½ hours) and Meknès (Dh18, one hour), plus there are two overnight trains. Eight trains travel to Marrakesh (Dh180, eight hours) and one goes to Tangier (Dh97, five hours).

Getting Around

There is a regular bus service (bus 16) between the airport and the train station (Dh3, 25 minutes), with departures every half-hour or so. *Grands taxis* from all stands charge a set fare of Dh120.

Drivers of the red *petits taxis* generally use their meters without any fuss. Expect to pay about Dh9 from the train or CTM station to Bab Bou Jeloud.

MEKNÈS

pop 690,000

Of the four imperial cities, Meknès is the most modest by far. Its proximity to Fez rather overshadows Meknès, which receives fewer visitors than it really should. Quieter and smaller than its grand neighbour, it's also more laid-back, presents less hassle yet still has all the winding narrow medina streets and grand buildings that it warrants as a one-time home of the Moroccan sultanate. Meknès is also the ideal base from which to explore the Roman ruins at Volubilis and the hilltop holy town of Moulay Idriss, two of the country's most significant historic sites.

Orientation

The valley of the (usually dry) Oued Bou Fekrane neatly divides the old medina in the west and the French-built *ville nouvelle* in the east. Ave Moulay Ismail connects them, then becomes the principal route of the *ville nouvelle,* where its name changes to Ave Hassan II.

Moulay Ismail's tomb and imperial city are south of the medina. The train and CTM bus stations are in the *ville nouvelle,* as are most offices and banks, as well as the more expensive hotels. It's a 20-minute walk from the medina to the *ville nouvelle,* but blue *petits taxis* and urban *grands taxis* shuttle between the two.

Information

There are plenty of banks with ATMs both in the *ville nouvelle* (mainly on Ave Hassan II and Ave Mohammed V) and the medina (Rue Sekkakine).

Cyber Bab Mansour (Zankat Accra; per hr Dh6; 9am-midnight) Internet access.
Délégation Régionale du Tourisme (055 524426; fax 055 516046; Place de l'Istiqlal; 8.30am-noon & 2.30-6.30pm Mon-Thu, 8-11.30am & 3-6.30pm Fri)
Hôpital Moulay Ismail (035 522805; off Ave des FAR)
Main post office (Place de l'Istiqlal) In the *ville nouvelle.*
Post office (Rue Dar Smen) In the medina.
Quick Net (28 Rue el-Emir Abdelkader; per hr Dh6; 9am-10pm)

Sights

The main sights are tied to Meknès' 17th-century heyday as imperial capital under the Alawite sultan Moulay Ismail.

The heart of the Meknès medina is **Place el-Hedim**, the large square facing Bab el-Mansour. Built by Moulay Ismail and originally used for royal announcements and public executions, it's a good place to sit and watch the world go by. A small *mellah* is to the west. To the south, Moulay Ismail's **imperial city** opens up through one of the most impressive monumental gateways in all of Morocco, **Bab el-Mansour**. Following the road around to the right, you'll come across the grand **Mausoleum of Moulay Ismail** (donations welcomed; 8.30am-noon & 2-6pm Sat-Thu), with its austere courtyards leading to a lavish tomb.

Nearly 2km southeast of the mausoleum, Moulay Ismail's immense granaries and stables, **Heri es-Souani** (admission Dh10; 9am-noon & 3-6.30pm), are an impressive sight next to the **Agdal Basin**, a stone-lined reservoir and evening promenade spot.

Overlooking Place el-Hedim is the 1882 palace that houses the **Dar Jamaï museum** (035 530863; Place el-Hedim; admission Dh10; 9am-noon & 3-6.30pm Wed-Mon). Exhibits include traditional ceramics, jewellery, rugs and some fantastic textiles and embroidery. Deeper in the medina, opposite the Grand Mosque, the **Medersa Bou Inania** (Rue Najjarine; admission Dh10; 9am-noon & 3-6pm) is typical of the exquisite interior design that distinguishes Merenid monuments.

Sleeping

Maroc Hôtel (035 530075; 7 Rue Rouamzine; s/d Dh90/180) A perennially popular shoestring option, the Maroc has kept its standards up over the many years we've been visiting. It's friendly and quiet, rooms (with sinks) are freshly painted, and the shared bathrooms are clean. The great terrace and courtyard filled with orange trees add to the ambience.

Hôtel Majestic (035 522035; 19 Ave Mohammed V; s Dh127-197, d Dh168-229) Open for business since 1937, the Majestic is one of the best art deco buildings in Meknès. There's a good mix of rooms (all have sinks), and there's plenty of character to go around from the dark-wood dado to the original deco light fittings. A quiet courtyard, roof terrace and friendly management top things off, making this a hard option to beat. Breakfast costs Dh22.

Hôtel de Nice (035 520318; nice_hotel@menara.ma; cnr Rue Accra & Rue Antserapé; s/d Dh387/482;) This hotel continues to fly the flag for quality and service. Modern, efficient and ever-so-slightly shiny, it's a surprise that room rates aren't a good Dh100 more than they actually are. Rooms are nicely decorated and well sized, and there's a decent bar and restaurant, too. Breakfast costs Dh46.

Maison d'Hôtes Riad (035 530542; www.riadmeknes.com; 79 Ksar Chaacha, Dar el-Kabir; r incl breakfast Dh650-750;) This *riad* is located amid the ruins

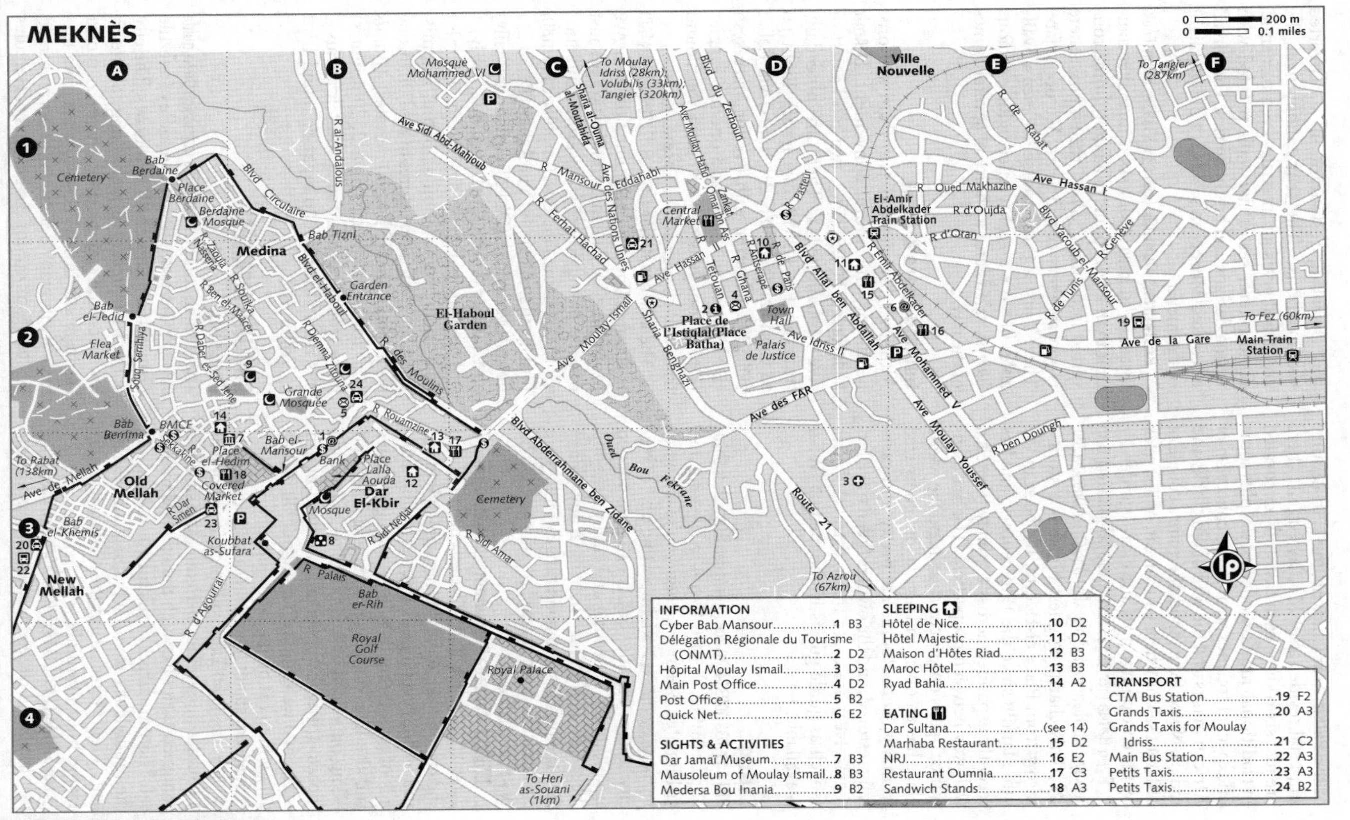
MEKNÈS
0 200 m
0 0.1 miles
Ville Nouvelle
Medina
Old Mellah
New Mellah
Dar El-Kbir
El-Haboul Garden
Royal Golf Course
Royal Palace
Cemetery
Flea Market
Covered Market
Place de l'Istiqlal(Place Batha)
Place Berdaine
Place el-Hedim
Place Lalla Aouda
Bab Berdaine
Bab el-Jedid
Bab Berrima
Bab el-Khemis
Bab el-Mansour
Bab Tizni
Bab er-Rih
Koubbat as-Sufara'
Berdaine Mosque
Grande Mosquée
Mosque Mohammed VI
Garden Entrance
Town Hall
Palais de Justice
Central Market
El-Amir Abdelkader Train Station
Main Train Station
BMCE
Bank
Mosque
Blvd Circulaire
Blvd el-Haboul
R des Moulins
Blvd Abderrahmane ben Zidane
Ave Moulay Ismail
Ave des FAR
Blvd Allal ben Abdallah
Ave Mohammed V
Ave Moulay Youssef
Ave Hassan I
Ave Hassan II
Ave des Nations Unies
Ave Moulay Hafid
Ave Idriss II
Ave de la Gare
Ave de Mellah
Ave Sidi Abd-Mahjoub
Blvd du Zerhoun
Blvd Yacoub el-Mansour
Sharia al-Ouma al-Moutahida
Sharia Benghazi
R Mansour Eddahabi
R Ferhat Hachad
R al-Andalous
R Emir Abdelkader
R de Rabat
R Oued Makhazine
R d'Oujda
R d'Oran
R Genève
R de Tunis
R ben Dough
R Pasteur
R de Paris
R Antserapé
R Ghana
R Tetouan
Zankat Omar ibn Ass
R Rouamzine
R Djemma Zitouna
R Daber es-Sed Jene
R Ben el-Maacer
R Souika
R Zaouia Nasseria
Soug Serrhiya
R Sekkakine
R Dar Smen
R d'Agourai
R Palais
R Sidi Nedjar
R Sidi Amar
Oued Bou Fekrane
Route 21
To Moulay Idriss (28km); Volubilis (33km); Tangier (320km)
To Tangier (287km)
To Fez (60km)
To Azrou (67km)
To Heri as-Souani (1km)
To Rabat (138km)
INFORMATION
Cyber Bab Mansour 1 B3
Délégation Régionale du Tourisme (ONMT) 2 D2
Hôpital Moulay Ismail 3 D3
Main Post Office 4 D2
Post Office 5 B2
Quick Net 6 E2
SIGHTS & ACTIVITIES
Dar Jamaï Museum 7 B3
Mausoleum of Moulay Ismail 8 B3
Medersa Bou Inania 9 B2
SLEEPING
Hôtel de Nice 10 D2
Hôtel Majestic 11 D2
Maison d'Hôtes Riad 12 B3
Maroc Hôtel 13 B3
Ryad Bahia 14 A2
EATING
Dar Sultana (see 14)
Marhaba Restaurant 15 D2
NRJ 16 E2
Restaurant Oumnia 17 C3
Sandwich Stands 18 A3
TRANSPORT
CTM Bus Station 19 F2
Grands Taxis 20 A3
Grands Taxis for Moulay Idriss 21 C2
Main Bus Station 22 A3
Petits Taxis 23 A3
Petits Taxis 24 B2

MOROCCO

of the Palais Ksar Chaacha, the 17th-century imperial residence of Moulay Ismail. There are just six rooms, each tastefully decorated in traditional-meets-modern style, plus some unexpected touches such as the collection of African masks and the wall of old clocks and radios. Noted for its food, there are a couple of different salons where you can eat, or just relax by the chic plunge pool and cactus garden.

Ryad Bahia (☎ 035 554541; www.ryad-bahia.com; Derb Sekkaya, Tiberbarine; r incl breakfast Dh670, ste Dh950-1200; ❄) This charming guest house is a stone's throw from Place el-Hedim. It's been in the same family since the 17th century, and has recently expanded across the alley (there's a walkway between properties). The main entrance opens onto a courtyard and the whole place has an open and airy layout compared to many *riads*. Rooms are pretty and carefully restored, and the owners (keen travellers themselves) are eager to swap travel stories as well as guide guests in the medina. Wi-fi is available.

Eating

NRJ (☎ 035 400324; 30 Rue Amir Abdelkader; salads Dh20-30, pizza Dh35-60; 🕑 24hr) If you're a young and fashionable Meknassi, then you're going to be hanging out at NRJ. Importing a bit of big-city laptop-friendly cool, it's all glass-topped tables, under-lit seating and funky tunes on the stereo. Perfect for a light meal any time of day, the paninis and good range of juices are particularly good; breakfast starts at Dh22. Wi-fi available.

our pick **Marhaba Restaurant** (23 Ave Mohammed V; tajines Dh25; 🕑 noon-10pm) The essence of cheap and cheerful, we adore this canteen-style place, and so does everyone else going by how busy it is of an evening. While you can get tajines and the like, do as everyone else does and fill up on a bowl of *harira* a plate of *makoda* (potato fritters) with bread and hard-boiled eggs – and walk out with change of Dh15. We defy you to eat better for cheaper.

Sandwich stands (Place el-Hedim; sandwiches around Dh30; 🕑 7am-10pm) Take your pick of any one of the stands lining Place el-Hedim, and sit at the canopied tables to watch the scene as well as eat. There are larger meals such as tajines, but the sandwiches are usually quick and excellent. A few places nearer the medina walls do a good line in sardines.

Dar Sultana (☎ 035 535720; Derb Sekkaya, Tiberbarine; mains from Dh70, 3-course set menu Dh150) This a small but charming restaurant in a converted medina house. The tent canopy over the courtyard gives an intimate, even romantic, atmosphere, set off by walls painted with henna designs and bright fabrics. The spread of cooked Moroccan salads is a big highlight of the menu.

Restaurant Oumnia (☎ 035 533938; 8 Ain Fouki Rouamzine; set menu Dh80) Less a formal restaurant than a few rooms of a family home converted into dining salons, the emphasis here is on warm service and hearty Moroccan fare. There's just a three-course set menu available, but it's a real winner, with delicious *harira*, salads and a choice of several tajines of the day.

Getting There & Away

Although Meknès has two train stations, head for the more convenient **El-Amir Abdelkader** (☎ 035 522763), two blocks east of Ave Mohammed V. There are nine daily trains to Fez (Dh18, one hour). Eight go to Casablanca (Dh86, 3½ hours) via Rabat (Dh59, 2¼ hours), with five for Marrakesh (Dh162, seven hours) and one for Tangier (Dh80, four hours) – or take a westbound train and change at Sidi Kacem.

The **CTM bus station** (☎ 035 522585; Ave des FAR) is about 300m east of the junction with Ave Mohammed V. The main bus station lies just outside Bab el-Khemis, west of the medina. CTM departures include: Casablanca (Dh80, four hours, six daily) via Rabat (Dh50 2½ hours), Marrakesh (Dh120, eight hours, daily) and Tangier (Dh80, five hours, three daily).

The principal *grand taxi* rank is a dirt lot next to the bus station at Bab el-Khemis. There are regular departures to Fez (Dh16, one hour) and Rabat (Dh44, 90 minutes). *Grands taxis* for Moulay Idriss (Dh12, 20 minutes) leave from opposite the Institut Français – this is also the place to organise round-trips to Volubilis.

AROUND MEKNÈS

Volubilis

The Roman ruins of **Volubilis** (admission Dh20, guide Dh140; 🕑 8am-sunset) sit in the middle of a fertile plain about 33km north of Meknès. The city is the best-preserved archaeological site in Morocco and was declared a Unesco World Heritage site in 1997. Its most amazing features are its many beautiful mosaics preserved in situ – look out for the Labours of Hercules and the erotically charged Abduction of Hylas by the Nymphs, as well as the columns of the basilica, which are often topped with storks' nests. Parking costs Dh5.

A half-day outing by *grand taxi* from Meknès will cost around Dh350, including a stop at Moulay Idriss.

Moulay Idriss

The whitewashed holy town of Moulay Idriss is named for a great-grandson of the Prophet Mohammed, the founder of Morocco's first real dynasty in the 8th century, and its most revered saint. His tomb is at the heart of the town, and is the focus of the country's largest *moussem* every August. Non-Muslims may not enter, but you can climb the twin hills the town straddles for good views. Moulay Idriss's pious reputation deters some travellers, but it's a pretty and relaxed town with a centre free of carpet shops and traffic giving you a chance to see Morocco as Moroccans experience it.

For sleeping options, try the family home–cum–guest house of **La Colombe Blanche** (☎ 035 544596; www.maisondhote-zerhoune.ma; 21 Derb Zouak Tazgha; r incl breakfast Dh300-500), or the newly opened backpacker-style **Buttons Inn** (☎ 035 544371; www.buttonsinn.com; 42 Derb Zouak Tazgha; dm/s/d/tr Dh180/250/400/600; 💻) across the street. The main square has plenty of cheap eats and cafes.

It's a 5km walk between Moulay Idriss and Volubilis, and there are regular *grands taxis* to Meknès (Dh12, 20 minutes).

CENTRAL MOROCCO & THE HIGH ATLAS

Marrakesh is the queen bee of Moroccan tourism, but look beyond it and you'll find great hiking in the dramatic High Atlas, and spectacular valleys and gorges that lead to the vast and empty sands of the Saharan dunes.

MARRAKESH

pop 2 million

Marrakesh grew rich on the camel caravans threading their way across the desert, but these days it's cheap flights from Europe bringing tourists to spend their money in the *souqs* that fatten the city's coffers. As many locals have taken the opportunity to move out of the medina into modern housing, so foreigners have arrived to transform those houses into stylish magazine-friendly guest houses.

But Marrakesh's old heart still beats strongly enough, from the time-worn ramparts that ring the city to the nightly spectacle of the Djemaa el-Fna that leaps from the pages of the *1001 Nights* on the edge of the labyrinthine medina.

Like most Moroccan cities, Marrakesh is divided into new and old sections; it's a short taxi ride or a 30-minute walk from the centre of the *ville nouvelle* to Djemaa el-Fna.

Information

EMERGENCY

Ambulance (☎ 024 443724)

Brigade Touristique (tourist police; ☎ 024 384601; Rue Sidi Mimoun; 🕒 24hr)

INTERNET ACCESS

Internet cafes ringing the Djemaa el-Fna charge Dh8 to Dh12 per hour; just follow signs reading 'c@fe'.

Cyber Café in CyberPark (Ave Mohammed V; per hr Dh10; 🕒 9.30am-8pm)

Hassan Internet (☎ 024 441989; Immeuble Tazi, 12 Rue Riad el-Moukha; per hr Dh8; 🕒 7am-1am)

MEDICAL SERVICES

Pharmacie de l'Unité (☎ 024 435982; Ave des Nations Unies, Guéliz; 🕒 8.30am-11pm)

Polyclinique du Sud (☎ 024 447999; cnr Rue de Yougoslavie & Rue Ibn Aicha, Guéliz; 🕒 24hr)

MARRAKESH IN TWO DAYS

Start the day with an orange juice on the **Djemaa el-Fna** (p644) and make your way to the **Ali ben Yousseff Medersa** (p644) and the **Musée de Marrakech** (p644), before plunging into the labyrinthine *souqs* (p646) for an afternoon of shopping. Back at the Djemaa el-Fna, take in the full spectacle before splurging on dinner at **Narwama** (p645). The next day, concentrate on the **Palais de la Bahia** (p644), the **Saadian Tombs** (p644) and views of the **Koutoubia Mosque minaret** (p644). Later in the afternoon, head for the *ville nouvelle* and relax in the tranquillity of the **Jardin Majorelle** (p644). Return to the medina for sunset drinks over the square, before finishing back at Djemaa el-Fna for an utterly memorable meal at its food stands.

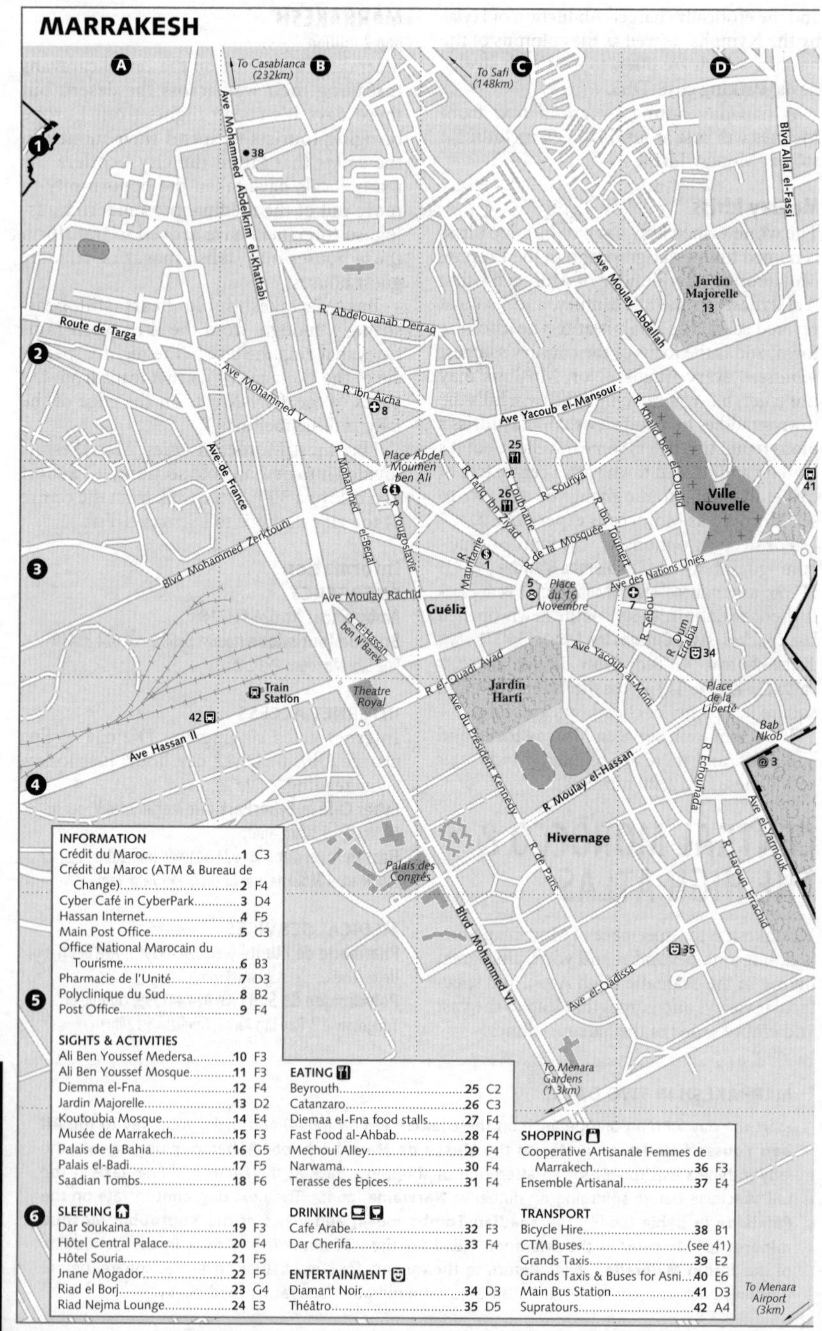
MARRAKESH
A
B
C
D
1
2
3
4
5
6
To Casablanca (232km)
To Safi (148km)
Ave Mohammed Abdelkrim el-Khattabi
38
Blvd Allal el-Fassi
Ave Moulay Abdallah
Jardin Majorelle
13
R Abdelouahab Derraq
Route de Targa
Ave Mohammed V
R ibn Aicha
8
Ave Yacoub el-Mansour
R Khalid ben el-Oualid
25
Place Abdel Moumen ben Ali
Ave de France
R Mohammed el-Beqal
6
R Yougoslavie
R Tariq ibn Ziyad
R Loubnane
26
R Souriya
Ville Nouvelle
41
Blvd Mohammed Zerktouni
R Mauritanie
1
R de la Mosquée
R ibn Toumert
Ave des Nations Unies
5
Place du 16 Novembre
7
Ave Moulay Rachid
Guéliz
R el-Hassan ben N'Barek
R Sebou
R Oum Errabia
34
Ave Yacoub al-Mrini
Train Station
R el-Quadi Ayad
Jardin Harti
Theatre Royal
Place de la Liberté
42
Ave Hassan II
Ave du President Kennedy
Bab Nkob
3
R Moulay el-Hassan
R Echouhada
Ave el-Yarmouk
Hivernage
R Haroun Errachid
Palais des Congrès
R de Paris
Blvd Mohammed VI
35
Ave el-Qadissa
To Menara Gardens (1.3km)
To Menara Airport (3km)
INFORMATION
Crédit du Maroc 1 C3
Crédit du Maroc (ATM & Bureau de Change) 2 F4
Cyber Café in CyberPark 3 D4
Hassan Internet 4 F5
Main Post Office 5 C3
Office National Marocain du Tourisme 6 B3
Pharmacie de l'Unité 7 D3
Polyclinique du Sud 8 B2
Post Office 9 F4
SIGHTS & ACTIVITIES
Ali Ben Youssef Medersa 10 F3
Ali Ben Youssef Mosque 11 F3
Djemma el-Fna 12 F4
Jardin Majorelle 13 D2
Koutoubia Mosque 14 E4
Musée de Marrakech 15 F3
Palais de la Bahia 16 G5
Palais el-Badi 17 F5
Saadian Tombs 18 F6
SLEEPING
Dar Soukaina 19 F3
Hôtel Central Palace 20 F4
Hôtel Souria 21 F5
Jnane Mogador 22 F5
Riad el Borj 23 G4
Riad Nejma Lounge 24 E3
EATING
Beyrouth 25 C2
Catanzaro 26 C3
Djemaa el-Fna food stalls 27 F4
Fast Food al-Ahbab 28 F4
Mechoui Alley 29 F4
Narwama 30 F4
Terasse des Èpices 31 F4
DRINKING
Café Arabe 32 F3
Dar Cherifa 33 F4
ENTERTAINMENT
Diamant Noir 34 D3
Théâtro 35 D5
SHOPPING
Cooperative Artisanale Femmes de Marrakech 36 F3
Ensemble Artisanal 37 E4
TRANSPORT
Bicycle Hire 38 B1
CTM Buses (see 41)
Grands Taxis 39 E2
Grands Taxis & Buses for Asni 40 E6
Main Bus Station 41 D3
Supratours 42 A4

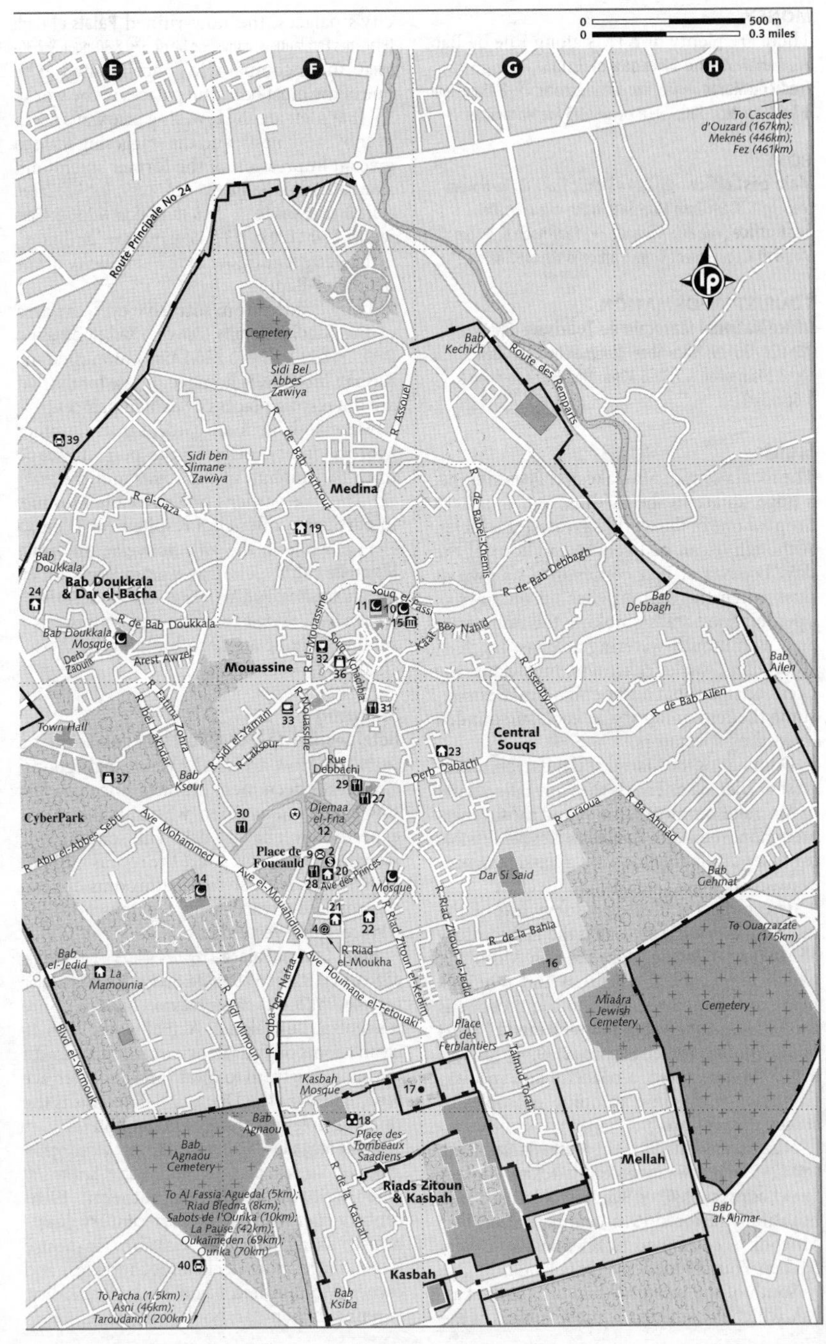
0 500 m
0 0.3 miles
E
F
G
H
To Cascades d'Ouzard (167km); Meknès (446km); Fez (461km)
Route Principale No 24
Cemetery
Sidi Bel Abbes Zawiya
Bab Kechich
Route des Remparts
R Assouel
R de Bab Tarhzout
39
Sidi ben Slimane Zawiya
Medina
R de Babel-Khemis
R el-Gaza
19
Bab Doukkala
Bab Doukkala & Dar el-Bacha
24
Souq el-Passi
R de Bab Debbagh
Bab Debbagh
R de Bab Doukkala
Bab Doukkala Mosque
Derb Zaouia
Arest Awzel
Mouassine
R el-Mouassine
Souq Kchachbia
Kaat Ben Nahid
R Issebtiyne
Bab Ailen
R de Bab Ailen
R Fatima Zohra
R Ibel Lakhdar
Town Hall
R Sidi el-Yamani
R Laksour
R Mouassine
Central Souqs
Rue Debbachi
Derb Dabachi
Bab Ksour
37
CyberPark
Djemaa el-Fna
R Graoua
R Ba Ahmad
R Abu el-Abbes Sebti
Ave Mohammed V
Place de Foucauld
Ave des Princes
Mosque
Dar Si Said
Bab Gehmat
Ave el-Mouahidine
R Riad Zitoun el-Kedim
R Riad Zitoun el-Jedid
To Ouarzazate (175km)
R Riad el-Moukha
R de la Bahia
Bab el-Jedid
La Mamounia
Ave Houmane el-Fetouaki
R Sidi Mimoun
R Oqba ben Nafaa
Place des Ferblantiers
R Talmud Torah
Miaâra Jewish Cemetery
Cemetery
Blvd el-Yarmouk
Kasbah Mosque
Place des Tombeaux Saadiens
Bab Agnaou
Bab Agnaou Cemetery
Mellah
Riads Zitoun & Kasbah
R de la Kasbah
To Al Fassia Aguedal (5km); Riad Bledna (8km); Sabots de l'Ourika (10km); La Pause (42km); Oukaïmeden (69km); Ourika (70km)
Bab al-Ahmar
Kasbah
Bab Ksiba
To Pacha (1.5km); Asni (46km); Taroudannt (200km)

MOROCCO

MONEY

There are plenty of ATMs along Rue de Bab Agnaou off the Djemaa el-Fna.

Crédit du Maroc Medina (Rue de Bab Agnaou; 8.45am-1pm & 3-6.45pm Mon-Sat); Ville Nouvelle (215 Ave Mohammed V)

POST

Main post office (024 431963; Place du 16 Novembre; 8.30am-2pm Mon-Sat) In the *ville nouvelle*.

Post office (Rue Bab Agnaou; 8am-noon & 3-6pm Mon-Fri) A convenient branch office in the medina.

TOURIST INFORMATION

Office National Marocain du Tourisme (ONMT; 024 436179; Place Abdel Moumen ben Ali, Guéliz; 8.30am-noon & 2.30-6.30pm Mon-Fri, 9am-noon & 3-6pm Sat)

Sights

The focal point of Marrakesh is **Djemaa el-Fna**, a huge square in the medina, and the backdrop for one of the world's greatest spectacles. Although it can be lively at any hour of the day, Djemaa el-Fna comes into its own at dusk when the curtain goes up on rows of open-air food stalls smoking the immediate area with mouth-watering aromas. Jugglers, storytellers, snake charmers, musicians, the occasional acrobat and benign lunatics consume the remaining space, each surrounded by jostling spectators.

Dominating the Marrakshi landscape, southwest of Djemaa el-Fna, is the 70m-tall minaret of Marrakesh's most famous and most venerated monument, the **Koutoubia Mosque**. Visible for miles in all directions, it's a classic example of Moroccan-Andalucian architecture.

The largest and oldest-surviving of the mosques inside the medina is the 12th-century **Ali ben Youssef Mosque** (closed to non-Muslims), which marks the intellectual and religious heart of the medina. Next to the mosque is the 14th-century **Ali ben Youssef Medersa** (024 441893; Place ben Youssef; admission Dh40; 9am-6pm winter, 9am-7pm summer), a peaceful and meditative place with some stunning examples of stucco decoration.

Inaugurated in 1997, the **Musée de Marrakech** (024 390911; www.museedemarrakech.ma; Place ben Youssef; admission Dh30; 9am-7pm) is housed in a beautifully restored 19th-century palace, Dar Mnebhi. A combined ticket that also covers Ali ben Youssef Medersa costs Dh60.

South of the main medina area is the **kasbah**, which is home to the most famous of the city's palaces, the now-ruined **Palais el-Badi** (Place des Ferblantiers; admission Dh10; 8.30-noon & 2.30-6pm), 'the Incomparable', once reputed to be one of the most beautiful palaces in the world. All that's left are the towering pisé walls taken over by stork nests, and the staggering scale to give an impression of the former splendour. The **Palais de la Bahia** (024 389564; Rue Riad Zitoun el-Jedid; admission Dh10; 8.30-11.45am & 2.30-5.45pm Sat-Thu, 8.30-11.30am & 3-5.45pm Fri), the 'Brilliant', is the perfect antidote to the simplicity of the nearby el-Badi.

Long hidden from intrusive eyes, the area of the **Saadian Tombs** (Rue de la Kasbah; admission Dh10; 8.30-11.45am & 2.30-5.45pm), alongside the Kasbah Mosque, is home to ornate tombs that are the resting places of Saadian princes.

Marrakesh has more gardens than any other Moroccan city, offering the perfect escape from the hubbub of the *souqs* and the traffic. The rose gardens of Koutoubia Mosque, in particular, offer cool respite near Djemaa el-Fna, while in the *ville nouvelle*, the **Jardin Majorelle** (024 301852; www.jardinmajorelle.com; cnr Ave Yacoub el-Mansour & Ave Moulay Abdullah; garden Dh30, museum Dh15; 8am-6pm summer, to 5pm winter) is a sublime mix of art deco buildings and psychedelic desert mirage.

Sleeping

Hôtel Souria (024 445970; 17 Rue de la Recette; s/d Dh130/170) 'How are you? Everything's good?' Even if it's been mere minutes since you last saw them, the women who run this place expertly never fail to ask. The sentiment is straightforward and so are the rooms – 10 no-frills rooms with shared bathrooms around a garden courtyard, with a patchwork-tiled terrace. Book yesterday.

Hôtel Central Palace (024 440235; hotelcentralpalace@hotmail.com; 59 Derb Sidi Bouloukat; d with shared bathroom Dh155, with private bathroom Dh205-305) Sure it's central, but palatial? Actually, yes. With 40 clean rooms on four floors arranged around a burbling courtyard fountain and a roof terrace lording it over the Djemaa el-Fna, this is the rare example of a stately budget hotel.

Jnane Mogador (024 426323; www.jnanemogador.com; Derb Sidi Bouloukat, 116 Riad Zitoun el-Kedim; s/d/tr/q Dh360/480/580/660;) An authentic 19th-century *riad* with all the 21st-century guesthouse fixings: prime location, in-house *hammam*, double-decker roof terraces, and owner Mohammed's laid-back hospitality. Perennially popular; book in advance.

Riad Nejma Lounge (☎ 024 382341; www.riad-nejmalounge.com; 45 Derb Sidi M'Hamed el-Haj, Bab Doukkala; d incl breakfast Dh495-795;) Lounge lizards chill on hot-pink cushions in the whitewashed courtyard and graphic splashes of colour make the wood-beamed guest rooms totally mod, though the rustic showers can be temperamental. Handy for *ville nouvelle* restaurants and shops.

our pick Dar Soukaina (☎ 061 245238; www.darsoukaina.com; 19 Derb el-Ferrane, Riad Laârouss; s Dh790, d Dh970-1400, tr Dh1150;) His'n'hers *riads:* the original is all soaring ceilings, cosy nooks and graceful archways, while the newer extension across the street is about sprawling beds, the grand patio and handsome woodwork. A 20-minute walk from the Djemaa, but worth the discovery. All prices include breakfast.

Riad el Borj (☎ 024 391223; www.riadelborj.com; 63 Derb Moulay Adbelkader; d Dh935-1540;) Once this was a grand vizier's lookout, and now you too can lord it over the neighbours in the suite with original *zellij*, double-height ceilings, and skylit tub, or the tower hideaway with the rippled ceiling and book nook. Loaf by the pool in the 'Berber annex,' or let off steam in the *hammam*. Babysitting is available.

Eating

The cheapest and most exotic place to eat in town remains the food stalls on Djemaa el-Fna, piled high with fresh meats and salads, goats' heads and steaming snails.

Fast Food Al-Ahbab (Rue de Bab Agnaou; salads Dh15-25, sandwiches Dh20-30; 7am-11pm) The awning boasting 'recommended by Lonely Planet' must be 25 years old now, and still we stand by our initial assessment of the Dh35 *shwarma* accompanied by four sauces and just-right French fries, though the avocado milkshake is best avoided.

our pick Mechoui Alley (250g lamb with bread Dh30-50; 11am-2pm daily) Just before noon, the vendors at this row of stalls start carving up steaming sides of *mechoui* (slow-roasted lamb). Point to the best-looking cut of meat, and ask for a '*nuss*' (half) or '*rubb*' (quarter) kilo. Some haggling might ensue, but it procures a baggie of falling-off-the-bone delicious lamb with fresh-baked bread, cumin and olives. It's on the east side of Souq Ablueh (Olive Souq).

Catanzaro (☎ 024 433731; 42 Rue Tariq ibn Ziyad, Guéliz; pizza or pasta Dh60-80, mains Dh80-120; noon-2.30pm & 7.30-11pm Mon-Sat;) Where are we, exactly? The thin-crust, wood-fired pizza says Italy; the wooden balcony and powerful air-con suggest the Alps; but the spicy condiments and spicier clientele are definitely midtown Marrakesh. Grilled meat dishes are juicy and generous, but the Neapolitan pizza with capers, local olives and Atlantic anchovies steals the show.

Beyrouth (☎ 024 423525; 9 Rue Loubnane; mains Dh80-150) Bright, lemony Lebanese flavours, with a mix-and-match meze that's a feast for two with tabouleh, spinach pies and felafel for Dh160. The smoky, silky *baba ghanoush* (aubergine dip) here gives Moroccan eggplant caviar serious competition for best Middle Eastern spread.

Narwama (☎ 024 442510; 30 Rue el-Koutoubia nr Djemaa el-Fna; mains Dh80-140; 8pm-1am) Opposites attract at Narwama, true to its name (fire and water) with unconventional combinations: Thai green curries and almond-and-cream *b'stilla*, a DJ spinning Brazilian/Italian/Arabic tunes, and the best Moroccan mint mojito in town – all in a 19th-century *riad* with 21st-century Zen decor. Alcohol is served.

Terrasse des Èpices (☎ 024 375904; 15 Souq Cherifia; set menu Dh100-150) Head to the roof for lunch on top of the world in a mud-brick *bhou* (booth). Check the chalkboard for the Dh100 fixed-price special: Moroccan salads followed by scrawny but scrumptious chicken-leg tajine with fries, then strawberries and mint. Reservations are handy in high season.

Drinking

The number one spot for a cheap and delicious drink is right on Djemaa el-Fna, where orange juice is freshly squeezed around the clock for just Dh4. Rooftop cafes overlook the square.

Dar Cherifa (☎ 024 426463; 8 Derb Cherfa Lakbir, near Rue Mouassine; tea/coffee Dh15-25; noon-7pm) Revive *souq*-sore eyes at this serene late-15th-century Saadian *riad*, where tea and saffron coffee are served with contemporary art and literature downstairs or terrace views upstairs.

Café Arabe (☎ 024 429728; www.cafearabe.com; 184 Rue el-Mouassine, Medina; 10am-midnight;) Gloat over *souq* purchases with cocktails on the roof at sunset or a glass of wine next to the Zen-*zellij* courtyard fountain. The food is mixed.

Entertainment

Sleeping is overrated in a city where the nightlife begins around midnight. Most of the hottest clubs are in the Hivernage district of the *ville nouvelle*. Admissions range from Dh150 to Dh350 including the first drink. Each drink thereafter costs at least Dh50. Dress to impress.

Pacha (☎ 024 388405; www.pachamarrakech.com; Complexe Pacha Marrakech, Blvd Mohammed VI, Hivernage; admission Mon-Fri before/after 10pm free/Dh150-200, Sat & Sun Dh200-300; 🕑 8pm-5am) Pacha Ibiza was the prototype for this enormous clubbing complex that's now Africa's biggest, with DJs mashing up international and Magrebi hits for huge weekend influxes of Casa hipsters and raging Rabatis. The complex includes two dazzling restaurants and a pool to lounge away afternoons in until the party starts.

Diamant Noir (☎ 024 434351; Hôtel Marrakech, cnr Ave Mohammed V & Rue Oum Errabia, Guéliz; admission from Dh100; 🕑 10pm-4am) For its rare gay-friendly clientele on weeknights and seedy charm on weekends, the gravitational pull of 'Le Dia' remains undeniable. The dark dance floor thumps with hip hop and gleams with mirrors and bronzer-enhanced skin, while professionals lurk at the shady end of the upstairs bar. Cash only.

Théâtro (☎ 024 448811; Hôtel es Saadi, Ave el-Qadissa, Hivernage; admission Dh200; 🕑 11.30pm-5am). Don't bother schmoozing the bouncer for entry to the boring VIP area because the dance floor in this converted theatre is where all of the action is: packed, sweaty, carefree, fabulous. Saturdays are white nights, with white-clad clubbers grooving 'til dawn on the signature mix of house, techno, R&B and Morocco-pop.

Shopping

Marrakesh is a shopper's paradise; its *souqs* are full of skilled artisans producing quality products in wood, leather, wool, metal, bone, brass and silver. The trick is to dive into the *souqs* and treat shopping as a game.

Ensemble Artisanal (Ave Mohammed V; 🕑 8.30am-7.30pm) To get a feeling for the quality of merchandise it is always good to start at this government-run spot in the *ville nouvelle*.

Cooperative Artisanale Femmes de Marrakesh (☎ 024 378308; 67 Souq Kchachbia; 🕑 9.30am-12.30pm & 2.30-6.30pm) This is a hidden treasure worth seeking in the *souqs*, with breezy cotton clothing and household linens made by a Marrakesh women's cooperative and a small annexe packed with varied items from nonprofits and women's cooperatives from across Morocco.

Getting There & Away

BUS

Most buses arrive and depart from the main **bus station** (☎ 024 433933; Bab Doukkala) just outside the city walls. A number of companies run buses to Fez (from Dh130, 8½ hours, at least six daily) and Meknès (from Dh120, six hours, at least three daily). **CTM** (☎ 024 434402; Window 10, Bab Doukkala bus station) operates daily buses to Fez (Dh160, 8½ hours, one daily) There are also daily services to Agadir (Dh90, four hours, nine daily), Casablanca (Dh85, four hours, three daily) and Essaouira (Dh80, 2½ hours).

Supratours (☎ 024 435525; Ave Hassan II), west of the train station, operates three daily coaches to Essaouira (Dh65, 2½ hours).

TRAIN

For the **train station** (☎ 024 447768; cnr Ave Hassan II & Blvd Mohammed VI, Guéliz), take a taxi or city bus (3, 8, 10 and 14, among others, Dh3) from the centre. There are trains to Casablanca (Dh84, three hours, nine daily), Rabat (Dh112, four hours), Fez (Dh180, eight hours, eight daily) via Meknès (Dh162, seven hours) and nightly trains to Tangier (Dh190).

Getting Around

A *petit taxi* to Marrakesh from the airport (6km) should cost no more than Dh60. Alternatively, bus 11 runs irregularly to Djemaa el-Fna. The creamy-beige *petits taxis* around town cost anywhere between Dh5 and Dh15 per journey.

HIGH ATLAS MOUNTAINS

The highest mountain range in North Africa, the High Atlas runs diagonally across Morocco, from the Atlantic coast northeast of Agadir all the way to northern Algeria, a distance of almost 1000km. In Berber it's called Idraren Draren (Mountain of Mountains) and it's not hard to see why. Flat-roofed, earthen Berber villages cling tenaciously to the valley sides, while irrigated terraced gardens and walnut groves flourish below.

Hiking

The Moroccan tourist office, Office National Marocain du Tourisme (ONMT), publishes an extremely useful booklet called *Morocco: Mountain and Desert Tourism* (2005), which has lists of *bureaux des guides* (guide offices), *gîtes d'étape* (hikers' hostels) and other useful information. Hikes of longer than a couple of days will almost certainly require a guide (Dh300 per day) and mule (Dh100) to carry kit and supplies. There are *bureaux des guides* in Imlil, Setti Fatma, Azilal, Tabant (Aït Bou Goumez Valley) and El-Kelaâ M'Gouna, where you should be able to pick up a trained, official guide. Official guides carry ID cards.

Club Alpin Français (CAF; ☎ 022 270090; 50 Blvd Moulay Abderrahman, Quartier Beauséjour, Casablanca) operates key refuges in the Toubkal area, particularly those in Imlil and Oukaïmeden and on Jebel Toubkal. The club website is a good source of hiking information and includes links to recommended guides.

JEBEL TOUBKAL HIKE

One of the most popular hiking routes in the High Atlas is the ascent of Jebel Toubkal (4167m), North Africa's highest peak. The Toubkal area is just two hours' drive south of Marrakesh and easily accessed by local transport.

You don't need mountaineering skills or a guide to reach the summit, provided you follow the standard two-day route and don't do it in winter. You will, however, need good boots, warm clothing, a sleeping bag, food and water, and you should be in good physical condition before you set out. It's not particularly steep, but it's a remorseless uphill hike all the way (an ascent of 1467m) and it can be very tiring if you haven't done any warm-up walks or spent time acclimatising.

The usual starting point is the picturesque village of **Imlil**, 17km from Asni off the Tizi n'Test road between Marrakesh and Agadir. Most hikers stay overnight in Imlil.

The first day's walk (10km; about five hours) winds steeply through the villages of Aroumd and Sidi Chamharouch to the **Toubkal Refuge** (☎ 064 071838; dm CAF members/HI members/nonmembers Dh46/69/92). The refuge sits at an altitude of 2307m and sleeps more than 80 people.

The ascent from the hut to the summit on the second day should take about four hours and the descent about two hours. It can be bitterly cold at the summit, even in summer.

There is plenty of accommodation in Imlil. Try **Hôtel el-Aïne** (☎ 024 485625; rooftop beds Dh30, r per person Dh45) or **Dar Adrar** (☎ 070 726809; http://toubkl.guide.free.fr/gite; d incl breakfast/half-board Dh220/330), at the top of the village. Imlil is also well stocked for shops with hiking supplies.

Frequent local buses (Dh15, 1½ hours) and *grands taxis* (Dh30, one hour) leave south of Bab er-Rob in Marrakesh to Asni, where you change for the final 17km to Imlil (Dh15 to Dh20, one hour).

OTHER HIKES

In summer it's quite possible to do an easy one- or two-day hike from the ski resort of **Oukaïmeden**, which also has a Club Alpin Français (CAF) refuge, southwest to Imlil or vice versa. You can get here by *grand taxi* from Marrakesh.

From **Tacheddirt** (where the CAF refuge charges Dh60 for nonmembers) there are numerous hiking options. One of these is a pleasant two-day walk northeast to the village of **Setti Fatma** (also accessible from Marrakesh) via the village of **Timichi**, where there is a welcoming *gîte*. A longer circuit could take you south to **Amsouzerte** and back towards Imlil via **Lac d'Ifni**, Toubkal, **Tazaghart** (also with a refuge and rock climbing) and **Tizi Oussem**.

TAFRAOUTE

Nestled in the enchanting **Ameln Valley** is the village of Tafraoute. Surrounded on all sides by red granite mountains, it's a pleasant and relaxed base for exploring the region. In late February and early March the villages around Tafraoute celebrate the almond harvest with all-night singing and dancing.

There are two banks in Tafraoute – **BMCE**, located behind the post office, and **Banque Populaire**, on Pl Mohammed V.

Sights & Activities

The best way to get around the beautiful villages of the Ameln Valley is by walking or cycling. Bikes can be rented from **Artisanat du Coin** (per day Dh60). You can also rent mountain bikes or book a mountain-biking trip from **Tafraoute Aventure** (☎ 061 387173) and **Au Coin des Nomades** (☎ 061 627921), who offer mountain-biking and hiking trips either up Jebel Lekst (2359m) or along the palm-filled gorges of Aït Mansour, leading towards the bald expanses of the southern Anti-Atlas.

Sleeping & Eating

Hôtel Salama (☎ 028 800026; s/d Dh199/298;) Completely renovated to higher standards, the long-established Salama mixes local materials with modern standards. The result is the best midrange hotel in town with great views from the terrace, a restaurant serving full meals and a teahouse overlooking the market square.

Hôtel Les Amandiers (☎ 028 800088; hotellesamandiers@menara.ma; s/d from Dh350/450;) Sitting like a castle on the crest of the hill overlooking the town, Les Amandiers wants to be Tafraoute's top hotel, in every sense. The kasbah-style hotel has spacious, if unglamorous rooms with bathrooms and a pool with spectacular views, as well as a bar and restaurant.

Restaurant Marrakech (☎ 063 229250; Rue Annahda; set menu Dh55) A cheap, family-run restaurant on the road up from the bus station with a small terrace and good, dependable food.

Restaurant L'Étoile d'Agadir (☎ 028 800268; Place de la Marche Verte; meals around Dh75; 8am-6pm) Locals swear by this place for its succulent tajines, all beautifully presented. This is also *the* place to ease into the day over a coffee.

Getting There & Away

Buses depart from outside the various company offices on Sharia al-Jeish al-Malaki, including to Agadir (Dh40, six hours, daily), Casablanca (Dh100, 14 hours, five daily) and Marrakesh (Dh90, seven hours, four daily).

TAROUDANNT

Hidden by magnificent red-mud walls and with the snowcapped peaks of the High Atlas beckoning beyond, Taroudannt appears a touch mysterious at first. It is, however, every inch a market town, with busy *souqs* where the produce of the rich and fertile Souss Valley is traded.

Information

There are three banks with ATMs on Place al-Alaouyine, and all have exchange facilities and accept travellers cheques. BMCE also does cash advances. The main **post office** (Rue du 20 Août) is off Ave Hassan II, to the east of the kasbah. Internet access is available at **Wafanet** (Ave Mohammed V; per hr Dh8).

Sights & Activities

The 5km of **ramparts** surrounding Taroudannt are the best preserved in Morocco, their colour changing from golden brown to the deepest red depending on the time of day. They can easily be explored on foot (1½ hours), preferably in the late afternoon.

Taroudannt is a great base for hiking in the western High Atlas region and the secluded **Tichka Plateau**, a delightful meadow of springtime flowers and hidden gorges. There are several agencies in town offering hikes, but beware as there are many stories of rip-offs and unqualified guides.

Sleeping

Naturally Morocco Guest House: Centre Culturel & Environmental (☎ 028 551628/067 297438; 422 Derb Afferdou; per person half-board Dh410) If only there were more places like this: a medina house run by locals offering a rare glimpse into Moroccan life. Dedicated to sustainable tourism and cultural contact, they can arrange ecotours on botany, birdwatching, flora and fauna. Bookings only through www.naturallymorocco.co.uk, ☎ 0044 1239 710814.

Hôtel Taroudant (☎ 028 852416; Place al-Alaouyine; s/d/tr Dh140/160/200) The Taroudant is faded, the en suite rooms, though clean, have seen better days and its bar can get rowdy. And yet its jungle-style courtyard and faintly colonial public areas have a unique atmosphere – and the bar closes early. There is a good restaurant, and the hotel can organise hikes.

Kasabat Annour (☎ 028 854576; www.kasabatannour.com; Kasbah; s/d incl breakfast Dh880/1320;) This guest house is built around a former colonel's house in the medina and has six elegant and spacious rooms around a swimming pool. Meals, *hammam* and treatments are available on request.

Eating

The best place to look for cheap eateries is around Place an-Nasr and north along Ave Bir Zaran, where you find the usual tajine, *harira* and salads. Several places around Place al-Alaouyine serve sandwiches and simple grills.

Jnane Soussia (☎ 028 854980; set menu Dh75; dinner;) Delightful restaurant, outside Bab Zorgane, with tented seating areas set around a large pool, in a garden adjacent to the ramparts. The house speciality is a mouth-watering *mechoui* (whole roast lamb), which must be ordered in advance.

Chez Nada (☎ 028 851726; Ave Moulay Rachid; set menu Dh70;) West of Bab al-Kasbah, this is a quiet modern family-run place, that is famous for its excellent and good-value tajines, including one of pigeons. There is a cafe downstairs, dining room on the first floor terrace with great views over the gardens. The food is home cooking and excellent. *B'stilla*

WORTH THE TRIP: AÏT BOU GOUMEZ VALLEY

Aït Bou Goumez Valley is often called 'the Happy Valley' and when you get there you will understand why: there is a touch of Shangri-la about this lush and unusually beautiful valley. East of Marrakesh, beyond Azilal, the Aït Bou Goumez Valley feels remote because it is. A year-round road link was opened in 2001, before which the valley was snowbound for four months a year. Even now the road is rarely busy.

The only real sight in the valley is the marabout of Sidi Moussa, though hiking in the M'Goun Massif is also possible. But the real attraction of the valley is the joy of being in so peaceful a place and seeing this landscape – the rich fertility of the valley floor and terraced hillsides – and the Berber villages, which seem to have grown out of the mud and rock on which they sit. The views over the valley from the shrine, and from the *agadir* (fortified granary) on the adjacent hill, are spectacular.

and couscous should be ordered a couple of hours ahead.

Getting There & Away

All buses leave from the main bus station outside Bab Zorgane. **CTM** (Hotel Les Arcades, Place al-Alaouyine) has the most reliable buses, with one departure per day for Casablanca (Dh150, 10 hours) via Marrakesh (Dh90, six hours).

Other companies run services through the day to both these cities plus Agadir (Dh30, 2½ hours) and Ouarzazate (Dh80, five hours).

AÏT BENHADDOU

Aït Benhaddou, 32km from Ouarzazate, is one of the most exotic and best-preserved kasbahs in the Atlas region. This is hardly surprising, given the money poured into it as a result of being used for scenes in many films, notably *Lawrence of Arabia, Jesus of Nazareth* (for which much of the village was rebuilt) and, more recently, *Gladiator*. The kasbah is now under Unesco protection. It's a very special place.

The best place to stay is **Dar Mouna** (☎ 028 843054; www.darmouna.com; s/d incl breakfast Dh480/600, s/d half-board Dh720/840, ste incl breakfast/half-board Dh780/960;), an elegant pisé guest house that threatens to steal scenes from the movie star directly across the valley. Light, high-ceilinged rooms facing the valley are the ones to get. Amenities include great food, a bar, *hammam* and bike and camel rental.

To get here from Ouarzazate, take the main road towards Marrakesh as far as the sign-posted turn-off (22km); Aït Benhaddou is another 9km down a bitumen road. *Grands taxis* run from outside Ouarzazate bus station when full (Dh20 per person) or cost Dh250 to Dh350 in total for a half-day with return.

DRÂA VALLEY

A ribbon of technicoloured *palmeraies* (palm groves), earth-red kasbahs and stunning Berber villages – the Drâa Valley is a special place. The valley eventually seeps out into the sands of the desert, and it once played a key role in controlling the ancient trans-Saharan trade routes that Marrakesh's wealth was built on.

Zagora

The iconic 'Tombouktou, 52 jours' ('Timbuktu, 52 days') signpost was recently taken down in an inexplicable government beautification scheme, but Zagora's fame as a desert outpost is indelible. The Saadians launched their expedition to conquer Timbuktu from Zagora in 1591, and the many desert caravans that passed through this oasis have added to its character.

Jebel Zagora and a *palmeraie* make a dramatic backdrop for the rather drab French colonial outpost buildings and splashy new town hall complex. But for all its recent modernisation, Zagora is still a trading post at heart, with a large market on Wednesdays and Sundays selling produce, hardware and livestock.

About 23km south of Zagora, you get your first glimpse of Saharan sand dunes, the **Tinfou Dunes**. If you've never seen a sandy desert, Tinfou is a pleasant spot to take a breather and enjoy a small taste, although the dunes at Merzouga or around M'Hamid are grander.

INFORMATION

Banks including **Banque Populaire** and **BMCE** are on Blvd Mohammed V, with ATMs and normal banking hours.

Placenet Cyber Center (95 Blvd Mohammed V; per hr Dh10) Internet access.

ACTIVITIES

Camel rides are not only still possible in Zagora, but practically obligatory. Count on around Dh350 per day if you're camping, and ask about water, bedding, toilets, and how many other people will be sharing your camp site. Decent agencies:

Caravane Dèsert et Montagne (☎ 024 846898, 066 122312; www.caravanedesertetmontagne.com; 112 Blvd Mohammed V)

Caravane Hamada Drâa (☎/fax 024 846930; www.hamadadraa.com, in French; Blvd Mohammed V)

Découverte Sud Maroc (☎ 024 846115; www.geocities.com/decousudma)

SLEEPING & EATING

Auberge Restaurant Chez Ali (☎ 024 846258; www.chezali.prophp.org; Ave de l'Atlas Zaouiate El Baraka, Zagora; garden tents per person Dh40, r per person incl breakfast/full-board Dh100/260, with terrace Dh200/360) The peacocks stalking the garden can't be bothered, but otherwise the welcome here is very enthusiastic. The skylit rooms upstairs have new pine furnishings and tiled floors though some mattresses are a tad lumpy. Meals are down-home Berber cooking. Showers cost Dh5.

Hôtel la Rose des Sables (☎ 024 847274; Ave Allal Ben Abdallah; s/d with shared bathroom Dh50/60, with private bathroom Dh60/90) Off-duty desert guides unwind in these basic, tidy rooms right off the main drag, and you might be able to coax out stories of travellers gone wild over tasty tajine meals at the sidewalk cafe (set menu Dh40 to Dh50).

Dar Raha (☎ 024 846993; http://darraha.free.fr; Amezrou; s/d incl breakfast Dh220/410, half-board Dh300/550) 'How thoughtful!' is the operative phrase here, from the heartfelt hello and half-price rates for kids to oasis-appropriate details such as local palm mats, recycled wire lamps and thick straw pisé walls eliminating the need for a pool or air-con. Enjoy home-cooked meals and chats in the kitchen like family, and check out the expo of local paintings and crafts.

Villa Zagora (☎ 024 846093; www.mavillaausahara.com; Amezrou; s berber tent/d tent with shared bathroom/d tent with private bathroom/ste tent incl breakfast Dh220/286/365/495; d with shared bathroom/d with private bathroom/ste incl breakfast half-board Dh418/506/638; ❄ 🅿) Light, breezy, and naturally charming, with staff that fuss over you like the Moroccan aunties and uncles you never knew you had. There's a talented cook in the kitchen, and a tiny pool. Forget the camels and read the day away on the verandah.

All hotels have their own restaurants and will provide set meals (Dh100 to Dh150) to nonguests by prior reservation. Moroccan fare with less flair can be had at cheap, popular restaurants along Blvd Mohammed V.

GETTING THERE & AWAY

The **CTM bus station** (☎ 024 847327) is at the southwestern end of Blvd Mohammed V, and the main bus and *grand taxi* lot is at the northern end. CTM has a daily service to Marrakesh (Dh100) and Casablanca (Dh175) via Ouazazarte. Other companies also operate buses to Boumalne du Dadès (Dh75) and Erfoud (Dh85). A bus passes through headed to M'Hamid (Dh20, two hours) in the morning; there are also minibuses (Dh25) and *grands taxis* (Dh30).

M'Hamid

Once it was a lonesome oasis, but these days M'Hamid is a wallflower no more. Today the road is flanked with hotels to accommodate travellers lured here by the golden dunes of the Sahara. This one dot on a map actually covers two towns: the M'hamid Jdid is a typical one-street administrative centre with a mosque, a few restaurants, small hotels, craft shops and a Monday market. M'Hamid Bali, the old town, is 3km away across the Oued Drâa. It has an impressive and well-preserved kasbah.

M'hamid's star attraction is **Erg Chigaga**, a mind-boggling 40km stretch of golden Saharan dunes that's the equal of Erg Chebbi near Merzouga. It's 56km away – a couple of hours by 4WD or several days by camel. A closer alternative is Erg Lehoudi, but it's in bad need of rubbish collection. **Sahara Services** (☎ 061 776766; www.saharaservices.info; 300m on right after M'Hamid entry) and **Zbar Travel** (☎ 068 517280; www.zbartravel.com) are both reliable agencies offering tours – an overnight camel trek should start at about Dh380.

If you're not sleeping with your camel in the desert, **Dar Azawad** (☎ 024 848730; www.darazawad.com; Douar Ouled Driss, M'Hamid; half-board d tent/d/ste Dh500/700/900; ❄ 🅿) is a deluxe hotel ideal for Armani-clad nomads, while **Camping Hammada du Drâa** (☎ 024 848080; per person Dh15, plus per car Dh20, Berber tents per person Dh50) offers simpler but still decent fare.

There's a daily CTM bus at 4.30pm to Zagora (Dh25, two hours), Ouarzazate (Dh70, seven hours), Marrakesh (Dh120, 11 to 13 hours) and Casablanca (Dh205, 15 hours), plus an assortment of private buses, minibuses and *grands taxis*.

DADÈS GORGE

Those art deco tourism posters you'll see all over southern Morocco showing a striking pink and white kasbah in a rocky oasis aren't exaggerating: the Dadès Gorge really is that impressive.

The main access to the gorge is from **Boumalne du Dadès**, a pleasant, laid-back place with a good Wednesday market. From there, a good sealed road wriggles past 63km of *palmeraies,* fabulous rock formations, Berber villages and some beautiful ruined kasbahs to Msemrir, before continuing as a dirt track to Imilchil in the heart of the High Atlas.

If you have plenty of time, you could easily spend several days pottering about in the gorge – watching nomads bring vast herds of goats down the cliffs to the river, fossicking for fossils and generally enjoying the natural splendour.

There are a number of places to stay; the kilometre markings of the following places refer to the distance into the gorge from Boumalne du Dadès. Nearly all hotels will let you sleep in the salon or on the terrace (even in summer you may need a sleeping bag) for around Dh25, or camp by the river for around Dh10. Most also offer half-board rates and dinner.

River views, good value and a terrace restaurant amid the chirping songbirds make **Hôtel le Vieux Chateau du Dadès** (☎ 024 831261; fax 024 830221; Km 27; half-board per person downstairs/upstairs Dh150/220) worth going the extra mile to find. The tiled rooms upstairs have better views, but the snug pisé-walled downstairs guest rooms are equally charming.

A bubbly personality overlooking the river, **Auberge des Gorges du Dadès** (☎ 024 831719; www.aubergeaitoudinar.com; Km 25.5; per person Dh15, per person incl breakfast/half-board Dh120/200) has 12 rooms with splashy Amazigh motifs and big bathrooms plus a pleasantly shaded camping area. The trek leader speaks English, French and Spanish and has more than 23 years' experience.

Romance is in the air at **Les 5 Lunes** (☎ 024 830723; Km 23, Aït Oudinar; d with shared bathroom incl breakfast/half-board Dh200/360, tr with private bathroom incl breakfast/half-board Dh300/540) a snug treehouse-style berth teetering above valley treetops, with four plain but pretty doubles and one triple and a hewn-stone bathroom. Book ahead for dinner.

Chez Pierre (☎ 024 830267; http://chezpierre.ifrance.com; Km 27; half-board per person Dh570, 2-person minimum; 🏊) is a rock-climbing hotel with eight airy rooms and one apartment shimmying right up the gorge. Decor is kept simple to focus attention on what really matters: the view over the valley from flower-filled terraces and poolside sun decks. Picnics and hikes with official guides can be arranged.

Grands taxis and minibuses run up the gorge from Boumalne du Dadès and charge Dh15 per person to the cluster of hotels in the middle of the gorge and Dh30 to Msemrir – ask to be dropped at your chosen hotel. To return, simply wait by the road and flag down a passing vehicle. Boulmane du Dadès itself has good onward connections to major destinations including Zagora (Dh65), Tinerhir (Dh25), Fez (Dh135), Casablanca (Dh150 to Dh190), Erfoud (Dh60) and Marrakesh (Dh70 to Dh90).

TODRA GORGE

Being stuck between a rock and a hard place is a fantastic experience to have in the Todra Gorge, where the massive fault dividing the High Atlas from the Jebel Sarhro is at some points just wide enough for a crystal-clear river and some hikers to squeeze through. The road from Tinerhir passes green *palmeraies* and yellowish Berber villages until, 15km along, high walls of pink and grey rock close in around the road. The approach is thrilling and urgent, as though the doors of heaven were about to close before you.

Arrivals at the Todra are best timed for the morning, when the sun briefly alights on the bottom of the gorge, providing your shining golden moment of welcome. In the afternoon it gets very dark and, in winter, bitterly cold.

There's little reason to stay in Tinerhir itself, but you'll find banks, internet cafes and onward transport there. An enormous *souq* is held about 2.5km west of the centre on Mondays.

Sights & Activities

This is prime hiking and climbing country. About a 30-minute walk beyond the main gorge is the Petite Gorge. This is the starting point of many pleasant day hikes, including one starting by the Auberge Le Festival (p652), 2km after the Petite Gorge. For a more strenuous hike, you could do a three-hour loop from north of the gorge to Tizgui, south of the gorge. Regular donkey and mule traffic keep this path well defined for most of the route. If you wanted to push on, you could walk to Tinerhir through the *palmeraies* in three or four hours.

Assettif Aventure (☎ 024 895090; www.assettif.org, in French) located 700m before the gorge, arranges hikes and horse riding (day trip Dh500) and hires out bikes (per day Dh100) and mountaineering equipment.

Sleeping & Eating

Auberge Etoile des Gorges (☎ 024 895045; fax 024 832151; s/d/tr with shared bathroom Dh50/70/100) A plucky little budget hotel in the mouth of the mighty gorge, featuring six simple rooms with orthopaedically stiff beds and solar-heated showers. Minor road noise is easily ignored on a roof deck with a close-up view of the gorge. It serves reasonable meals (three-course meals Dh60 to Dh70).

Dar Ayour (☎ 024 895271; www.darayour.com; Km 13, Gorges du Todra, Tinghir; r with shared bathroom/private bathroom Dh100/150, r incl breakfast/half-board Dh200/350) *Riads* have arrived in Todra with this warm, artsy five-storey guest house. The 2nd floor is a three-room suite that can sleep a family of seven; the 3rd storey has three guest rooms with bathrooms; and breakfast with a view is served up on the terrace.

Auberge Le Festival (☎ 061 267251; http://aubergelefestival.com; main house half-board s/d Dh300/460, tower room s/d Dh400/700, cave room d/tr Dh700/900) Get in touch with your primal instincts in a cave guest room dug right into the hillside, or do your best Romeo and Juliet impersonation on your private wrought-iron tower balcony.

Hôtel Amazir (☎ 024 895109; d/tr incl breakfast Dh400/600, half-board Dh600/800; ☒) Don't be fooled by its stern, stony exterior: inside, this place is relaxed, with pretty, unfussy rooms, a pool terrace surrounded by palms, and the lulling sound of the rushing river below. It's on a bend in the road at the southern end of the gorge, 5km before you enter, away from gorge-gawking crowds.

If you need a bed for the night in Tinerhir, the **Hôtel de l'Avenir** (☎ 024 834599; www.avenir.tineghir.net; 27 Rue Zaid Ouhmed; mattress on roof Dh30, s/d/tr 30/100/150) is a sociable spot, with cafes lining the plaza outside, bike hire and a steady stream of travellers.

Getting There & Away

Buses from Tinerhir leave from the Place Principale to Marrakesh (Dh105, five daily) via Ouarzazate (Dh45), and to Casablanca (Dh165), Erfoud (Dh30, three daily), Meknès (Dh115, six daily) and Zagora (Dh80). Anything westbound will drop you in Boumalne du Dadès (Dh15). *Grands taxis* run throughout the day to Todra Gorge (Dh8).

MERZOUGA & THE DUNES

Erg Chebbi is Morocco's only genuine Saharan erg, an impressive, drifting chain of sand dunes that can reach 160m and seems to have escaped from the much larger dune field across the nearby border in Algeria. The erg is a magical landscape that deserves much more than the sunrise or sunset glimpse many visitors give it. The dunes are a scene of constant change and fascination as sunlight transforms them from pink to gold to red. The largest dunes are near the villages of Merzouga and Hassi Labied. At night, you only have to walk a little way into the sand, away from the light, to appreciate the immense clarity of the desert sky and the brilliance of its stars.

Merzouga, some 50km south of Erfoud is a tiny village, but does have *téléboutiques*, general stores, a mechanic and, of course, a couple of carpet shops. It also has an internet place, **CyberInternet** (⏲ 9am-10pm; per hr Dh5), and is the focus of fast-expanding tourism in the area. As a result, it is acquiring a reputation for some of the worst hassle in Morocco.

Most hotels offer excursions into the dunes, which can range from Dh80 to Dh200 for a couple of hours on a sunrise or sunset camel trek. Overnight trips usually include a bed in a Berber tent, dinner and breakfast, and range from Dh300 to Dh650 per person. Outings in a 4WD are more expensive, up to Dh1200 per day for a car taking up to five passengers.

Sleeping & Eating

Purists lament the encroachment, but a string of hotels now flank the western side of Erg Chebbi from the village of Merzouga, north past the oasis village of Hassi Labied. On the upside, many of these places have spectacular dune views from rooms and terraces. Most offer half-board options, and often you can sleep on a terrace mattress or in a Berber tent for Dh30 to Dh50 per person.

HASSI LABIED

This tiny village, 5km north of Merzouga and some way off the tarmac, has a good range of accommodation.

Auberge Camping Sahara (☎ 035 577039; terrace/camping per person Dh20, s half-board Dh110, d/tr/ste half-board with private bathroom Dh140/170/250) Basic but spotless rooms and Turkish toilets in a friendly Tuareg-run place backing right onto the dunes at the southernmost end of the village. The auberge organises excursions and will even help you buy your complete Tuareg outfit in the market.

Kasbah Sable d'Or (aka Chez Isabelle & Rachid; ☎ 035 577859 http://kasbah-sable-dor.co; half-board per person with shared bathroom Dh140, with private bathroom Dh170) When the goat bleats welcome, you know you've come to the right place. There are just four rooms here, with hand-painted murals on the doors, fans instead of air-con, and tasty home-cooked dinners in the family salon. You can also camp in a Bedouin tent (Dh25), have a private overnight camel, or get up early to watch the sunrise atop a camel.

Dar el Janoub (☎ /fax 035 577852; www.dareljanoub.com; d 500-600, ste per person Dh700;) An ode to local building tradition, the architect here stuck to elemental building shapes, because when you're facing the dunes, why compete? For the price you're getting great rooms with a million-dirham view, half-board, a pool and pure poetry.

MERZOUGA

Chez Julia (☎ 035 573182; s/d/tr/q with shared bathroom Dh160/180/200/230) Pure charm in the heart of Merzouga, Chez Julia offers nine simply furnished rooms in soft, sun-washed colours with immaculate white-tiled bathrooms. The Moroccan ladies who run the place can cook up a storm of delicious Moroccan meals and Austrian dishes such as schnitzel and apfelstrudel, too.

Riad Totmaroc (☎ 070 624136; www.totmarroc.com; Merzouga; per person half-board Dh350) A modern kasbah that provides instant relief from the white-hot desert with five guest rooms in bold, eye-soothing shades of blue and green, shady patios looking right onto the dunes and an open kitchen turning out tasty meals.

Getting There & Away

Thankfully, the sealed road now continues all the way to Merzouga. Most hotels are at least a kilometre off the road at the base of the dunes, but all are accessible by car. The *pistes* (sandy tracks) can be rough and there is a possibility, albeit remote, of getting stuck in sand, so make sure you have plenty of water for emergencies and a mobile phone. Without your own transport, you'll have to rely on *grands taxis* or on the minivans that run from Merzouga to the transport junction towns of Rissani and Erfoud and back.

MOROCCO DIRECTORY

ACCOMMODATION

Auberges de jeunesses (youth hostels) operate in Casablanca, Chefchaouen, Fez, Meknès, Rabat and Tangier. Hotels vary dramatically, ranging from dingy dives to gorgeous guest houses and fancy five-stars (the latter mostly in larger cities). Cities that see many tourists also offer wonderful accommodation in the style of a *riad*.

Places to stay are listed in order of price and include a private bathroom unless otherwise stated. Prices given are for high season (June to September) and include tax; always check the price you are quoted is TTC (all taxes included).

Advance reservations are highly recommended for all places listed in this chapter, especially in summer.

You'll be hard-pressed to find nonsmoking accommodation in Morocco.

ACTIVITIES

Camel Treks & Desert Safaris

Exploring the Moroccan Sahara by camel is one of the country's signature activities and one of the most rewarding wilderness experiences, whether done on an overnight excursion or a two-week trek. The most evocative stretches of Saharan sand include the Drâa Valley (p650), especially the Tinfou Dunes and Erg Chigaga, and the dunes of Erg Chebbi (opposite) near Merzouga.

Autumn (September to October) and winter (November to early March) are the only seasons worth considering. Prices hover around Dh350 to Dh450 per person per day but vary depending on the number of people, the length of the trek and your negotiating skills.

Hammams

Visiting a *hammam* is a ritual at the centre of Moroccan society and a practical solution for those who don't have hot water at home (or in their hotel). Every town has at least one public *hammam*, and the big cities have fancy spas – both are deep-cleaning and totally relaxing. A visit to a standard *hammam* usually costs Dh10, with a massage costing an extra Dh15 or so.

Hiking

Morocco is a superb destination for mountain lovers, offering a variety of year-round hiking possibilities. It's relatively straightforward to arrange guides, porters and mules for a more independent adventure. Jebel Toubkal (4167m), the highest peak in the High Atlas (p646), attracts the lion's share of visitors, but great possibilities exist throughout the country, including in the Rif Mountains around Chefchaouen (p616). The Dadès and Todra Gorges also offer good hiking opportunities (p651). Spring and autumn are the best seasons for hiking.

Surfing & Windsurfing

With thousands of kilometres of Atlantic coastline, Morocco has some great surfing spots. The beaches in Essaouira (p627) are a highlight for windsurfers.

BUSINESS HOURS

Cafes (🕑 7am-11pm)
Post offices (🕑 8.30am-4.30pm Mon-Fri, 9am-noon Saturday)
Restaurants (🕑 noon-3pm & 7-11pm)
Shops (🕑 9am-12.30pm & 2.30-8pm Mon-Sat) Often closed longer at noon on Friday.
Tourist offices (🕑 8.30am-12.30pm & 2.30-6.30pm Mon-Thu)

DANGERS & ANNOYANCES

Morocco's era as a hippy paradise is long past. Plenty of fine *kif* (dope) is grown in the Rif Mountains, but drug busts are common and Morocco isn't a good place to investigate prison conditions.

A few years ago the *brigade touristique* was set up in the principal tourist centres to clamp down on Morocco's notorious *faux guides* and hustlers. Anyone convicted of operating as an unofficial guide faces jail time and/or a huge fine. This has reduced but not eliminated the problem of *faux guides*. You'll still find plenty of these touts hanging around the entrances to medinas and train stations (and even on trains approaching Fez and Marrakesh), and at Tangier port. Remember that their main interest is the commission gained from certain hotels or on articles sold to you in the *souqs*.

If possible, avoid walking alone at night in the medinas of the big cities. Knife-point muggings aren't unknown.

For specific information for women travellers, see p657.

EMBASSIES & CONSULATES

For details of all Moroccan embassies abroad and foreign embassies in Morocco, go to www.maecgov.ma.

All of the following are in Rabat:

Belgium (Map p620; ☎ 037 268060; info@ambabel-rabat.org.ma; 6 Ave de Marrakesh)
Canada (Map p620; ☎ 037 687400; fax 037 687430; 13 Rue Jaafar as-Sadiq, Agdal)
France (Map p620; ☎ 037 689700; www.ambafrance-ma.org; 3 Rue Sahnoun, Agdal)
Germany (Map p622; ☎ 037 709662; 7 Rue Madnine)
Ireland (☎ 022 660306; gb@copragri.co.ma; 7 Rue Madnine) In Casablanca; honorary consul only.
Italy (Map p620; ☎ 037 706598; ambaciata@iambitalia.ma; 2 Rue Idriss el-Azhar)
Japan (off Map p620; ☎ 037 631782; fax 037 750078; 39 Ave Ahmed Balafrej Souissi)
Mauritania (off Map p620; ☎ 037 656678; ambassadeur@mauritanie.org.ma; 7 Rue Thami Lamdaouar, Soussi I)
Netherlands (Map p620; ☎ 037 219600; nlgovrab@mtds.com; 40 Rue de Tunis)
Spain (Map p620; ☎ 037 633900; emb.rabat@mae.es; Rue Ain Khalouiya, Route des Zaers km 5.300, Souissi)
UK (Map p620; ☎ 037 238600; ukinmorocco.fco.gov.uk; 17 Blvd de la Tour Hassan) Provides consular support for New Zealand.
USA (Map p620; ☎ 037 762265; www.usembassy.ma; 2 Ave de Marrakesh)

FESTIVALS & EVENTS

Religious festivals are significant for Moroccans. Local *moussems* are held all over the country throughout the year and some draw big crowds.

Major festivals:

Gnaoua & World Music Festival (www.festival-gnaoua.co.ma) Held in June in Essaouira.
Festival of World Sacred Music (www.fesfestival.com) Every June in Fez.
Marrakesh Popular Arts Festival (www.maghrebarts.ma, in French) Held in July.
International Cultural Festival July/August in Asilah.
Moussem of Moulay Idriss II September/October in Fez.

GAY & LESBIAN TRAVELLERS

Homosexual acts (including kissing) are officially illegal in Morocco – in theory you can go to jail and/or be fined. In practice, although not openly admitted or shown, male homosexuality remains relatively common, and platonic affection is freely shown, more so among men than women. In most places, discretion is the key and public displays of affection should be avoided (aggression towards gay male travellers is not unheard of) – this advice applies equally to homosexual and heterosexual couples as a means of showing sensitivity to local feelings.

Some towns are certainly more gay-friendly than others, with Marrakesh winning the prize, followed by Tangier. That said, gay travellers generally follow the same itineraries as everyone else and although 'gay' bars can be found here and there, Moroccan nightlife tends to include something for everybody.

Lesbians shouldn't encounter any problems, though it's commonly believed by Moroccans that there are no lesbians in their country. Announcing that you're gay probably won't make would-be Romeos magically disappear. For Moroccan men it may simply confirm their belief that Western men don't measure up in the sexual department.

It is also worth bearing in mind that the pressures of poverty mean than many young men will consider having sex for money or gifts. Needless to say, exploitative relationships form an unpleasant but real dimension of the Moroccan gay scene.

Useful websites that give the low-down on local laws and attitudes to homosexuality include:

Behind the Mask (www.mask.org.za) Detailed information and related news stories for every African country.
Gay & Lesbian Arab Society (www.glas.org) Resources on homosexuality in the Arab world.
Global Gayz (www.globalgayz.com) A useful resource with good links on Morocco.

HOLIDAYS

All banks, post offices and most shops are shut on the main public holidays:

New Year's Day 1 January
Independence Manifesto 11 January
Labour Day 1 May
Feast of the Throne 30 July
Allegiance of Oued-Eddahab 14 August
Anniversary of the King's and People's Revolution 20 August
Young People's Day 21 August
Anniversary of the Green March 6 November
Independence Day 18 November

In addition to secular holidays there are many national and local Islamic holidays and festivals, all tied to the lunar calendar:

Eïd al-Adha Marks the end of the Islamic year. Most things shut down for four or five days.
Eïd al-Fitr Held at the end of the month-long Ramadan fast, which is observed by most Muslims. The festivities last four or five days, during which Morocco grinds to a halt. Ramadan will fall in summer during the lifetime of this guide.
Mawlid an-Nabi (Mouloud) Celebrates the birthday of the Prophet Mohammed.

INTERNET ACCESS

Internet access is widely available, efficient and cheap (Dh4 to Dh10 per hour) in internet cafes, usually with pretty impressive connection speeds. One irritant for travellers is the widespread use of French or Arabic (non-qwerty) keyboards, which will reduce most travellers to one-finger typing and fumbled searches for hidden punctuation marks.

Most top-end and many midrange hotels offer wi-fi, and it's more or less standard in most *riads* and *maisons d'hôtes*. If you're bringing your laptop, check the power supply voltage and bring a universal adaptor.

INTERNET RESOURCES

Lonelyplanet.com contains up-to-date news and destination information, and includes the Thorn Tree forum, where you can post questions.

Al-Bab (www.al-bab.com/maroc) Also called the Moroccan Gateway, Al-Bab has excellent links, especially for current affairs, news and good books about Morocco.
Maghreb Arts (www.maghrebarts.ma, in French) Up-to-the-minute coverage of theatre, film, music, festivals and media events in Morocco.
Maroc Blogs (http://maroc-blogs.com) Useful blog aggregator pulling in feeds from the entire Moroccan blogging community.
Tourism in Morocco (www.tourism-in-morocco.com/index_en.php) Morocco's official tourist information site; user-friendly, with guided tours, links and news.

MONEY

The Moroccan currency is the dirham (Dh), which is divided into 100 centimes. There is no black market, although it's forbidden to take dirhams out of the country. The Spanish enclaves of Ceuta and Melilla use the euro.

ATMs *(guichets automatiques)* are widespread and generally accept Visa, MasterCard, Electron, Cirrus, Maestro and InterBank cards.

Major credit cards are widely accepted in the main tourist centres, although their use often attracts a surcharge of around 5% from Moroccan businesses. Amex, Visa and Thomas Cook travellers cheques are also widely accepted for exchange by banks. Australian, Canadian and New Zealand dollars are not quoted in banks and are not usually accepted.

Tipping and bargaining are integral parts of Moroccan life. Practically any service can warrant a tip, and a few dirham for a service willingly rendered can make your life a lot easier. Tipping between 5% and 10% of a restaurant bill is appropriate.

POST

Post offices are distinguished by the 'PTT' sign or the 'La Poste' logo. You can sometimes buy stamps at *tabacs,* the small tobacco and newspaper kiosks you see scattered about the main city centres.

The postal system is fairly reliable, but not terribly fast. It takes about a week for letters to get to their European destinations, and two weeks or so to get to Australia and North America. Sending post from Rabat or Casablanca is quickest.

The parcel office, indicated by the sign '*colis postaux*', is generally in a separate part of the post office building. Take your parcel unwrapped for customs inspection. Some parcel offices sell boxes.

RESPONSIBLE TRAVEL

Despite extensive Westernisation, Morocco remains a largely conservative Muslim society. As a rule, a high degree of modesty is demanded of both sexes. Women are advised to keep their shoulders and upper arms covered and to opt for long skirts or trousers.

All mosques, cemeteries and religious buildings in active use are off limits to non-Muslims unless otherwise signed.

If invited into a Moroccan home, it's customary to remove your shoes before stepping onto the carpet. Food is served in common dishes and eaten with the right hand – the left hand is used for personal hygiene and should not be used to eat with or to touch any common source of food or water, or to hand over money or presents.

TELEPHONE

A few cities and towns still have public telephone offices, often next to the post office, but more common are privately run *téléboutiques,* which can be found in every town and village on almost every corner. Most public payphones are card-operated, with *télécartes* (phonecards) sold in general stores and news kiosks.

All domestic phone calls in Morocco require a nine-digit number, which includes the three-digit area code (or GSM code). When calling overseas from Morocco, dial ☎ 00, the country code and then the city code and number. Morocco's country code is ☎ 212.

Morocco has three GSM mobile phone networks – Méditel, Maroc Telecom and Wana – which cover 90% of the population. Moroccan mobile numbers start with ☎ 01, ☎ 06 or ☎ 07. A local sim card costs around Dh30 and top-up scratch cards are sold everywhere.

EMERGENCY NUMBERS

- Ambulance ☎ 15
- Fire ☎ 16
- Police ☎ 19

TOURIST INFORMATION

The national tourism body, **Office National Marocain du Tourisme** (ONMT; www.visitmorocco.com), has offices in the main cities, with the head office in Rabat. These offices are often called Délégation Régionale du Tourisme. Regional offices, called Syndicat d'Initiative are to be found in smaller towns. Although there are some notable exceptions, most tourist offices inside Morocco are of limited use, offering the standard ONMT brochures and the simplest of tourist maps, along with helpless smiles.

VISAS

Most visitors to Morocco do not require visas and are allowed to remain in the country for 90 days on entry. Exceptions to this include nationals of Israel, and most sub-Saharan African countries (including South Africa). Moroccan embassies have been known to insist that you get a visa from your country of origin. Should the standard 90-day stay be insufficient, it is possible (but difficult) to apply at the nearest police headquarters (Préfecture de Police) for an extension – the simplest thing to do is to leave (eg travel to the Spanish enclaves of Ceuta and Melilla) and come back a few days later. Your chances improve if you re-enter by a different route. The Spanish enclaves have the same visa requirements as mainland Spain.

VOLUNTEERING

There are many international and local organisations that organise voluntary work on regional development projects in Morocco. They generally pay nothing, sometimes not even lodging, and are aimed at young people looking for something different to do for a few weeks over the summer period.

A good place to start looking is the Morocco page for **Volunteer Abroad** (www.volunteerabroad.com/Morocco.cfm), which provides links to NGOs (nongovernment organisations) with Morocco-specific programs. Also worth getting hold of is Lonely Planet's *The Gap Year Book*, which lists hundreds of NGOs that organise volunteer and other work and study programs around the world – although unless you have a working knowledge of Arabic or Berber, or have specific specialist skills, many organisations will not be interested.

International or local NGOs that sometimes have Morocco placements or camps include:

Baraka Community Partnerships (www.barakacommunity.com) Near Telouet, it organises volunteers to build schools, plant trees, supply basic medical care and work on initiatives to improve local food security between partnerships.

Chantiers Sociaux Marocains (☎ 037 262400; csm@wanadoo.net.ma; Rabat) Local NGO engaged in health, education and development projects, with international volunteers aged 18 to 30.

International Cultural Youth Exchange (www.icye.org) Allows you to search for upcoming Moroccan volunteer opportunities.

Jeunesse des Chantiers Marocains (http://perso.menara.ma/youthcamps) A nonprofit group open to 18 to 30 year olds, promoting cultural exchange through three- to four-week courses in Moroccan Arabic, during which you stay with local families and take part in cultural events.

WOMEN TRAVELLERS

Women can expect a certain level of sexual harassment when travelling in Morocco. It comes in the form of nonstop greetings, leering and other unwanted attention, but it is rarely dangerous. It is best to avoid overreacting and to ignore this attention. In the case where a would-be suitor is particularly persistent, threatening to go to the police or the *brigade touristique* is amazingly effective. Women will save themselves a great deal of grief by avoiding eye contact, dressing modestly (covering knees and shoulders) and refraining from walking around alone at night.

TRANSPORT IN MOROCCO

GETTING THERE & AWAY

Air

Morocco's two main international entry points are **Mohammed V International Airport** (☎ 022 539040), 30km southeast of Casablanca and Marrakesh's **Ménara airport** (☎ 044 447865). Other international airports are in Fez, Tangier and Agadir. For comprehensive information on all Morocco's airports, check the website of **Office National des Aéroports** (www.onda.org.ma, in French).

Some budget airlines flying to Morocco:

Atlas Blue (BMM; www.atlas-blue.com)
CorsairFly (SS; www.corsairfly.com)
easyJet (EZY; www.easyjet.com)
Edelweiss Air (EDW; www.edelweissair.ch)
Jet4You (8J; www.jet4you.com)
Ryanair (FR; www.ryanair.com)
Thomsonfly (BY; www.thomsonfly.com)

Bus

The Moroccan bus company **CTM** (☎ Casablanca 022 45 80 80; www.ctm.co.ma) operates buses from Casablanca and most other main cities to France, Belgium, Spain, Germany and Italy. Another Moroccan bus service with particularly good links to Spanish networks is **Tramesa** (☎ 022 245274; http://perso.menara.ma/tramesa07, in French). **Eurolines** (www.eurolines.com) is a consortium of European coach companies that operates across Europe (including the UK) and to Morocco. It has offices in all major European cities.

Sea

Regular ferries run to Europe from several ports along Morocco's Mediterranean coast. The most trafficked is Tangier, from where there are boats to Algeciras, Spain (€31, 60 to 70 minutes, every 90 minutes); Tarifa, Spain (€40, 35 minutes, five daily); and Sete, France (€165, 36 hours, two weekly). Hourly ferries also run from Ceuta to Algeciras (€28, 35 minutes, hourly). Daily ferries go from

Al-Hoceima (summer only), Melilla and Nador to Almería and Málaga in Spain. Bringing a bicycle costs €8 to €15 extra, while a car adds €60 to €80. Children travel half-price. Tickets are available at the port of departure or from any travel agent in town.

GETTING AROUND

Air

Royal Air Maroc (RAM; ☎ 09000 0800; www.royalairmaroc.com) dominates the Moroccan airline industry, with paltry competition from one other domestic airline, **Regional Air Lines** (☎ 022 538080). Both airlines use Casablanca as their hub, with internal flights routed through Mohammed V International Airport. Student and under-26 youth discounts of 25% are available on all RAM domestic flights, but only if the ticket is bought in advance from one of its offices. For most routes, flying is an expensive and inconvenient option compared to road or rail.

Bus

A dense network of buses operates throughout Morocco, with many private companies competing for business alongside the comfortable and modern coaches of the main national carrier **CTM** (☎ in Casablanca 022 45 80 80).

The **ONCF** (www.oncf.ma, in French) train company runs buses through Supratours to widen its train network, for example running connections from Marrakesh to Essaouira. Morocco's other bus companies are all privately owned and only operate regionally. It's best to book ahead for CTM and Supratours buses, which are slightly more expensive than those of other companies.

Car & Motorcycle

Taking your own vehicle to Morocco is straightforward. In addition to a vehicle registration document and an International Driving Permit (although many foreign licences, including US and EU ones, are also acceptable), a Green Card is required from the car's insurer. Not all insurers cover Morocco.

Renting a car in Morocco isn't cheap, with prices starting at Dh3500 per week or Dh500 per day for a basic car with unlimited mileage. International hire companies are well represented, and booking in advance online secures the best deals. Most companies demand a returnable cash deposit (Dh3000 to Dh5000) unless you pay by credit card.

In Morocco you drive on the right-hand side. On a roundabout, give way to traffic entering from the right.

Taxi

Cities and bigger towns have local *petits taxis,* which are a different colour in every city. They are not permitted to go beyond the city limits, are licensed to carry up to three passengers and are usually metered. Fares increase by 50% after 8pm.

The old Mercedes vehicles you'll see belting along roads and gathered in great flocks near bus stations are *grands taxis*. They link towns to their nearest neighbours. *Grands taxis* take six extremely cramped passengers and normally only leave when full.

Train

Morocco's train network is run by **ONCF** (www.oncf.ma, in French). There are two lines that carry passengers: from Tangier in the north down to Marrakesh; and from Oujda in the northeast, also to Marrakesh, joining with the Tangier line at Sidi Kacem.

Trains are comfortable, fast and generally preferable to buses. There are different 1st- and 2nd-class fares on all these trains, but 2nd-class is more than adequate on any journey. Couchettes are available on the overnight trains between Marrakesh and Tangier. Children aged under four travel free. Those aged between four and 12 years get a reduction of 10% to 50%, depending on the service.

Two types of rail discount cards are available in Morocco. The Carte Fidelité (Dh149) is for those aged over 26 and gives you 50% reductions on eight return or 16 one-way journeys in a 12-month period. If you're under 26, the Carte Jaune (Dh99) will give you the same discounts. To apply for the card you will need one passport-sized photo as well as a photocopy of your passport.

Portugal

The once-great seafaring empire of Portugal is today a country straddling two very different worlds. Portugal is a land of old-fashioned charm, where medieval castles and picture-perfect villages lie scattered over meandering coastlines and flower-covered hillsides. Folk festivals and long-running traditions run deep, from long-time connections to the sea and vineyards that predate the Romans. Meanwhile, laid-back cities and sun-kissed beaches offer enticements of a more modern sort.

Portugal's capital, Lisbon, and its northern rival, Porto, are gems among the urban streetscapes of Europe. Both are magical places for the wanderer, with riverside views, cobblestone streets and rattling trams framed by looming cathedrals. Narrow lanes hide old book and record shops, tiny boutiques and an eclectic mix of restaurants, bars and nightclubs, giving new life to the time-worn setting.

Outside the cities, rambling vineyards and groves of cork and olives roll off into the distance towards jagged peaks in the north and gentler slopes in the south. More famous is Portugal's comely shoreline, which has long enchanted visitors. Stretching along the Atlantic are dramatic, end-of-the-world cliffs, wild dune-covered beaches, protected coves and long, sandy islands fronting calm blue seas.

Portugal's dual nature presents travellers with rewarding opportunities to see both sides of the coin, from visiting old-fashioned wine estates to gallery-hopping; from overnighting in medieval villages to people-watching at trendy beach resorts. Sometimes Portugal is a country happily in conflict with itself, and, while the scales are even, there's no better time to visit.

FAST FACTS

- **Area** 92,400 sq km
- **Capital** Lisbon
- **Currency** euro (€); US$1 = €0.73; UK£1 = €1.06; A$1 = €0.50; ¥100 = €0.76; NZ$1 = €0.41
- **Famous for** fado, football, port, *azulejos* (tiles), salted cod
- **Official language** Portuguese
- **Phrases** *bom dia* (hello); *obrigado/a* (thank you); *desculpe* (excuse me); *adeus* (goodbye); *faz favor* (please)
- **Population** 10.7 million
- **Telephone codes** country code ☎ 34; international access code ☎ 00; reverse-charge code ☎ 120
- **Visas** not needed for citizens from the EU, the USA, Australia, Canada and New Zealand; see p699

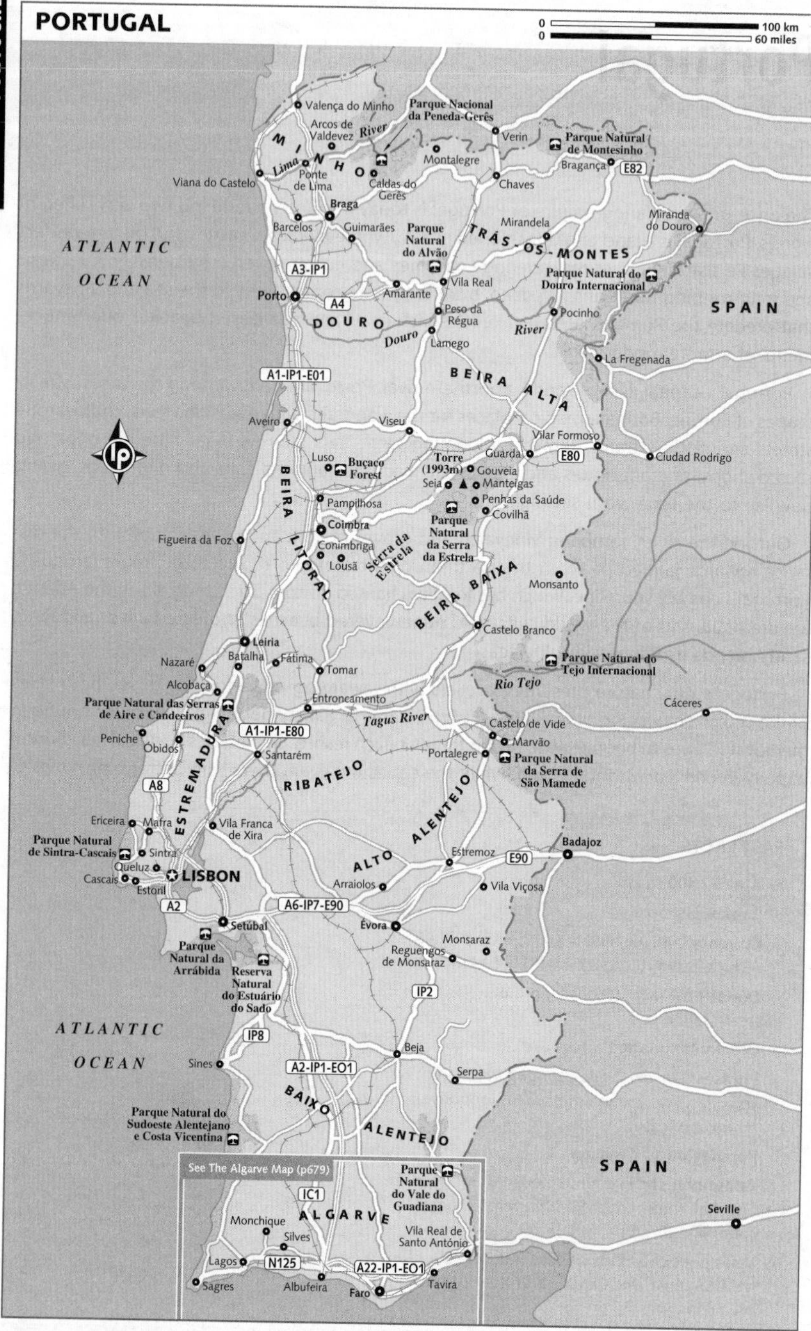
PORTUGAL
0 100 km
0 60 miles
ATLANTIC OCEAN
SPAIN
Valença do Minho
Parque Nacional da Peneda-Gerês
Arcos de Valdevez
River
Lima
MINHO
Verin
Parque Natural de Montesinho
Montalegre
Viana do Castelo
Ponte de Lima
Caldas do Gerês
Bragança
E82
Chaves
Braga
Barcelos
Guimarães
Parque Natural do Alvão
Mirandela
Miranda do Douro
TRÁS-OS-MONTES
A3-IP1
Parque Natural do Douro Internacional
Porto
A4
Amarante
Vila Real
Peso da Régua
Pocinho
DOURO
Douro
River
Lamego
La Fregenada
A1-IP1-E01
BEIRA ALTA
Aveiro
Viseu
Vilar Formoso
Guarda
E80
Ciudad Rodrigo
Luso
Buçaco Forest
Torre (1993m)
Gouveia
Seia
Manteigas
Penhas da Saúde
Pampilhosa
Covilhã
Coimbra
Parque Natural da Serra da Estrela
Figueira da Foz
Conimbriga
Lousã
Serra da Estrela
BEIRA LITORAL
BEIRA BAIXA
Monsanto
Castelo Branco
Leiria
Parque Natural do Tejo Internacional
Nazaré
Batalha
Fátima
Tomar
Alcobaça
Rio Tejo
Parque Natural das Serras de Aire e Candeeiros
Entroncamento
Cáceres
Tagus River
Castelo de Vide
A1-IP1-E80
Peniche
Óbidos
Marvão
Portalegre
Santarém
Parque Natural da Serra de São Mamede
RIBATEJO
A8
ESTREMADURA
ALENTEJO
Ericeira
Mafra
Vila Franca de Xira
Parque Natural de Sintra-Cascais
Sintra
Badajoz
Queluz
Estremoz
E90
LISBON
ALTO
Cascais
Estoril
Arraiolos
Vila Viçosa
A2
A6-IP7-E90
Setúbal
Évora
Parque Natural da Arrábida
Monsaraz
Reguengos de Monsaraz
Reserva Natural do Estuário do Sado
IP2
IP8
Beja
Sines
A2-IP1-EO1
Serpa
BAIXO ALENTEJO
Parque Natural do Sudoeste Alentejano e Costa Vicentina
See The Algarve Map (p679)
Parque Natural do Vale do Guadiana
IC1
ALGARVE
Monchique
Seville
Silves
Vila Real de Santo António
Lagos
N125
A22-IP1-EO1
Sagres
Albufeira
Faro
Tavira

HIGHLIGHTS

- Get lost in the tangle of narrow lanes in the **Alfama** (p668), a cinematic slice of old-fashioned village life in the heart of the capital.
- Take in the laid-back charms of **Tavira** (p680), before hitting some of the Algarve's prettiest beaches.
- Catch live fado in a backstreet bar in **Coimbra** (p687), a festive university town with a stunning medieval centre.
- Stroll around elegant and evocative **Sintra** (p676), studded with fairy-tale-like palaces, villas and gardens.
- Conquer the trails of the ruggedly beautiful **Parque Nacional da Peneda-Gerês** (p697).

ITINERARIES

- **One week** Devote three days to Lisbon, including a night of fado in the Alfama, bar-hopping in Bairro Alto and pastry-eating in Belém. Spend a day taking in sumptuous Sintra, before continuing on to Porto, a pretty riverside city that's well placed for sampling the great fruits of the Douro Valley – at port lodges across the river. Wind up your week in the picturesque lanes of Coimbra, Portugal's own Cambridge.
- **Two weeks** The same as for one week, plus two days in Unesco-listed Évora followed by a day in magical hilltop Monsaraz. Next, hit the road south to the Algarve (including a day each in Tavira, Lagos and Silves).

CLIMATE & WHEN TO GO

Portugal has a sunny, warm climate with mild winters. The midsummer heat can be sizzling in the Algarve, the Alentejo and in the upper Douro Valley, but tolerable elsewhere. The north is cold and wet in winter with snowfall common in the Serra da Estrela.

Avoid the Algarve's packed beach resorts in July and August. You can often save up to 50% on accommodation outside of high season (June to August).

HISTORY

Portugal has had a history of occupation and strife, stretching back to 700 BC when the Celts arrived on the Iberian Peninsula, followed by the Phoenicians, Greeks, Romans and Visigoths.

In the 8th century the Moors conquered Portugal. Arabic words filtered into the language and, today, their influence is evident in the culture, architecture and dark features of the people, particularly in the Algarve where the Moors established their capital in Silves. After the Christian conquest, Portugal's famed explorers discovered trade routes that helped create an empire extending to four continents, and made Lisbon the wealthiest city in Europe. Portugal's Gothic-style Manueline architecture dates from this time. This period of opulence was short-lived; from 1580 Spain occupied the Portuguese throne for 60 years, and their imperial momentum was lost forever.

In 1755 a massive earthquake tragically destroyed most of Lisbon, followed around 50 years later by Napoleon's thwarted invasion, which sent the king into exile in Brazil and further weakened the country. A period of civil war and political mayhem ensued, culminating in the abolition of the monarchy in 1910 and the founding of a democratic republic.

A 1926 military coup set the stage for the dictatorship of António de Oliveira Salazar until his death in 1970. Discontent with his regime and a ruinous war in Africa led to a peaceful military coup on 25 April 1974.

The subsequent granting of independence to Portugal's African colonies produced a flood of nearly a million refugees into the country. Their influence is reflected in the music and food, especially in Lisbon and Porto.

Flush with new funds, Portugal's entry into the EU in 1986 resulted in radical economic reforms and unprecedented economic growth.

CONNECTIONS: MOVING ON FROM PORTUGAL

Travelling overland from Portugal entails a trip through Spain, as it is surrounded by its former nemesis. Good places to cross the (invisible) border include Vila Real de Santo António in the Algarve, where boats ferry passengers to Ayamonte, with onward connections to Seville. There are also convenient links from Elvas (going across to Badajoz) and rail links from Valença do Minho in the north (heading up to Santiago de Compostela in Galicia). See p699 for more.

However, this opulence was short-lived and the early 1990s saw crippling corruption charges, rising inflation and a faltering economic recession.

Expo '98 gave the country a boost, and triggered vast transport and communications projects. This was further advanced by Porto's status as the European Capital of Culture in 2001, followed in 2004 by Portugal hosting the Euro 2004 football championships. Despite an initial boost to the economy, Portugal has been in an economic slump since 2000, with one of Europe's lowest growth rates and steadily rising unemployment.

Parliamentary elections in 2005 brought to power the tough-talking socialist legislator José Sócrates, who promised to revitalise the economy and tackle unemployment. He's had moderate success, while earning a few enemies by slashing pensions and privatising public services.

Sócrates, a former environment minister, set ambitious goals for Portugal in the realm of renewable energy. Under his government, enormous wind farms and solar-power plants opened, along with experimental technologies like a wave-power plant (harnessing the ocean's energy) and plans to build a nationwide network of recharging stations for electric cars by 2012.

Other big news during Sócrates' term include major improvements in the education system and a smoking ban in public indoor spaces (including restaurants) that came into effect in 2008.

HOW MUCH?

- **Short black coffee** €0.60
- **Lisbon to Porto train ticket** €20
- **Budget hotel room** €35
- **Glass of port** €2.20
- **Caldeirada (seafood stew) for two** €25

LONELY PLANET INDEX

- **1L unleaded petrol** €1.15
- **1L bottled water** €0.50
- **Beer** €1.10
- **Souvenir T-shirt** €6 to €12
- **Pastel de nata (custard tart)** €0.80

PEOPLE

Portugal's population of 10.7 million excludes the estimated three million Portuguese who are living abroad, but it includes the considerable number of African and Brazilian immigrants. Since May 2004 there has also been an influx of new immigrants from central and Eastern Europe. Foreign residents number around 200,000 and are primarily northern Europeans seeking the sunshine of the Algarve.

RELIGION

Portugal is around 85% Roman Catholic; other Christian denominations make up much of the remaining population, as well as Muslims and a small number of Jews.

ARTS

Music

The best-known form of Portuguese music is the melancholy, nostalgic songs called fado (literally 'fate') said to have originated from troubadour and African slave songs. The late Amália Rodrigues was the Edith Piaf of Portuguese fado. Today it is Mariza who has captured the public's imagination with her extraordinary voice and fresh contemporary image. Awarded 2004 Portuguese Personality of the Year, her 2005 release *Transparente* was a big worldwide seller, while her latest album *Terra* (2008) brings a more global sound to her music. Lisbon's Alfama district has plenty of fado houses (see boxed text, p674), ranging from the grandiose and tourist-conscious to small family affairs.

Architecture

Unique to Portugal is Manueline architecture, named after its patron King Manuel I (1495–1521). It symbolises the zest for discovery of that era and is hugely flamboyant, characterised by fantastic spiralling columns and elaborate carving and ornamentation.

Visual Arts

Portugal's stunning painted *azulejo* tiles coat contemporary life, covering everything from houses to churches. The art form dates from Moorish times and reached a peak in the late 19th century when the art-nouveau and art deco movements provided fantastic facades and interiors. Lisbon has its very own *azulejo* museum (p668).

THE QUEEN OF FADO

Mariza is a 35-year-old singer from Lisbon. She talked to Regis St Louis about what fado means to her.

'Fado is a really magical genre; it concerns the deepest feelings of the human being.

'The neighbourhood where I grew up in Lisbon, Mouraria, had a big role in my life and singing. I lived there since I was three years old, and it was there where I first experienced fado. I started singing at age five at my parents' tavern. It had a magical environment, coloured by the sound of the Portuguese guitar and all those beautiful voices that were my first teachers.

'I still live in Lisbon; it will always be home. If you walk around traditional neighbourhoods like the Alfama, Bairro Alto or Mouraria you will breathe fado, as it is part of Lisbon's personality. It is in my city that I learn more about fado, listening to the elders and visiting typical homes.

'Fado has the power to cross boundaries and touch anyone inside. That's when nationalities drop frontiers, and there is only emotions and the heart.'

ENVIRONMENT

The Land

Portugal is Europe's third-smallest country, stretching 563km from north to south and 220km at its widest east–west point. The country is bordered on the north and east by Spain and on the south and west by the Atlantic.

Wildlife

Portugal is home to the most endangered big cat in the world, the Iberian lynx, as well as a rare beast in the dog family, the rusty-coloured Iberian wolf. However, you are far more likely to come across deer, foxes, otters or even wild boars. Bird enthusiasts will be kept very happy with a vast range of species, including storks, eagles and, among the wetland species, flamingos, spoonbills and egrets, which can be seen in natural parks such as Ria Formosa (p680).

National Parks

Portugal has 25 natural parks, nature reserves and protected landscape areas. These areas total approximately 6500 sq km – just over 7% of Portugal's land area. There are 13 World Heritage sites in Portugal. Check them out on the web at http://whc.unesco.org.

Environmental Issues

Portugal has been slow to address its environmental problems, notably soil erosion, air and water pollution, rubbish disposal and the effects of mass tourism on fragile coastal areas. Industrial development is to blame for Portugal's most polluted seasides. That said, in 2008 around 197 Portuguese beaches claimed an international Blue Flag for cleanliness, and some areas have had clean-ups in recent years.

Brush and forest fires, brought on by years of continuing drought, are another major issue. Every year around 3% of Portugal's forest goes up in flames, worsening soil erosion and devastating farmland. Fires between 2003 and 2006 were particularly bad, burning over 9000 sq km.

Portugal's answer to its water shortages has been to erect large dams, which often bring a host of other problems. To create the Alqueva dam, Europe's largest artificial lake, over a million oak and olive trees were cut down, and some 160 rocks covered with Stone Age drawings were submerged.

On a more positive note, Portugal has set some ambitious goals in the area of renewable energy. Roughly 20% of Portugal's energy comes from renewable sources. In 2008 the world's largest solar farm opened in the Alentejo, providing energy to power 30,000 homes. Portugal also has numerous wind farms and has even launched the world's first 'wave farm' harnessing the ocean's power, just north of Porto.

FOOD & DRINK

There are a great range of offerings for diners of all budgets in Portugal. For between €2 and €7, you'll be able to eat daily specials (pork, chicken, fried fish) at casual, family-style restaurants. Midrange meals (€8 to €12) include popular Portuguese eateries serving traditional fare such as *bacalhau* (codfish) dishes, as well as vegetarian and international fare. Dining with a budget of €13 and above allows diners to sample the country's best seafood and haute cuisine.

Staples & Specialities

Portuguese cuisine is home-style cooking rather than *haute cuisine*. Seafood is the national favourite, especially *caldeirada* (seafood stew), *cataplana* (seafood and rice stew in a copper pot) *sardinhas assadas* (grilled sardines) and the omnipresent *bacalhau*, reputedly prepared in some 365 ways.

Meat dishes are a little less imaginative, though there are some standouts. Northern favourites include *cabrito assado* (roast kid), *porco preto* (black pork), *borrego* (lamb) and *posta de barosã*, an amazing beef from rare Minho cattle. Chicken is best when barbecued; *piri-piri* (chilli) sauce livens things up. When available, don't miss *leitão* (roast suckling pig), usually reserved for special occasions.

Pastelarias (pastry shops) are everywhere in Portugal and offer splendid desserts, particularly the delectable *pastel de nata* (custard tart).

Portuguese coffee has kick. A small black espresso is known as a *bica* in the south and elsewhere simply as a *café*. Half coffee, half milk is *café com leite*. Local *cerveja* (beer) includes Sagres in the south and Super Bock in the north.

Portuguese *vinho* (wine) offers excellent value in all its varieties: *tinto* (red), *branco* (white) and *vinho verde* (semisparkling young), which is usually white. Restaurants often serve drinkable *vino da casa* (house wine) for as little as €3 per 350ml jug. Port, synonymous with Portugal, is produced in the Douro Valley to the east of Porto; see the boxed text, p693 for more on the famous tipple.

Where to Eat & Drink

The line between snacks and meals is blurred. For full meals try a *tasca* (tavern), a *restaurante cervejaria* (bar-restaurant) or a *marisqueira* (seafood restaurant). Lunch time typically lasts from noon to 3pm, and evening meals from 7pm to 10.30pm.

The *prato do dia* (dish of the day) is often a bargain, as is the *ementa turistica* (tourist menu). Be wary of the *couvert* (the bread, cheese, butter, olives and other titbits at the start of a meal): they cost extra. You can send them back without causing offence. All restaurants in this chapter are open daily for lunch (noon to 3pm) and dinner (7pm to 10.30pm) unless otherwise noted.

Following the nationwide ban on smoking in public spaces passed in 2008, most restaurants are now smoke free.

Vegetarians & Vegans

The typical Portuguese menu is tough on vegetarians; *sopa de legumes* (vegetable soup), *ensalada* (salad), *omeleta* (omelette) and the requisite bread, olives and perhaps cheese are among the only reliable options. In Lisbon and Porto, international and ethnic eateries and dedicated vegetarian restaurants provide more satisfying selections, and even vegans can assemble a decent meal.

LISBON

pop 580,000

Set against a canvas of cobalt skies and the sparkling Rio Tejo, Lisbon is a city of steep hills, candy-bright houses, twisting alleys and grand plazas where locals relax in the sunshine. Add to that swirly Manueline turrets, ivory-white domes and a Moorish castle on the hillside, and you have a town that is one of Europe's under-appreciated masterpieces.

Yet Lisa, as locals nickname their city, is no superficial beauty. Step into the painting for exhilarating extremes. Retrospective and innovative, Lisbon is a twilight zone between past and future: dodgemlike trams screech through cobbled streets and Afro-Brazilian beats pulsate in the graffiti-slashed Bairro Alto; Zen-style sushi bars sidle up to one-pan family taverns; and thimble-sized haberdasheries abut eco-cool design stores. Neither time- nor trend-obsessed, Portugal's capital is refreshingly authentic.

The wanderer can spend days just scratching the surface of this fascinating city. Good places to begin include the medieval-like tangle of fado-filled streets in the Alfama, the festive nightlife centre of Bairro Alto, the baroque splendours of Belém and the elegant shops and cafes of Chiado.

ORIENTATION

Baixa is the modern city centre with its grid of streets and huge square, Praça do Comércio, to the south. To the north stands Praça Dom Pedro IV, better known as Rossio Sq, surrounded by cafes, bars and shops. Chiado and Bairro Alto districts lie

LISBON IN TWO DAYS

Take a roller-coaster ride of Lisbon on **tram 28**, hopping off to scale the vertiginous ramparts of Moorish **Castelo de São Jorge** (p668). Poke around **Alfama**'s twisting alleys, pausing for lunch in arty **Pois Café** (p672). By night, return to lantern-lit Alfama to hear first-rate fado at **Clube de Fado** (p674).

On the second day, wake up over a cinnamon-dusted *pastel de nata* (custard tart) and *bica* (espresso) at the **Antiga Confeitaria** (p673), then explore the fantastical Manueline cloisters of **Mosteiro dos Jerónimos** (p668). Head back for sundowners and twinkling skylines at **Noobai Cafe** (p674), head to dinner at **A Camponesa** (p673) and go bar-crawling in party-hearty **Bairro Alto** (p673).

above Baixa to the west. Chiado is the affluent quarter with sophisticated shops, restaurants and cafes, while the atmospheric Bairro Alto is famed for its lively nightlife.

Alfama, northeast of Baixa, is the oldest part of Lisbon with its narrow medinalike streets plunging from the castle to the river.

Belém, a peaceful suburb 6km west of Rossio, is home to the magnificent Mosteiro dos Jerónimos, and several other historical sights.

Saldanha district is situated around 2km north of Baixa; it has a couple of great museums and a metro stop, but not much else.

INFORMATION

Bookshops

Livraria Bertrand (Map pp670-1; ☎ 213 421 941; Rua Garrett 73) Bertrand has excellent selections amid 18th-century charm.

Discount Cards

Lisboa Card (24-/48-/72-hr card €15/26/32) This a cost-saving pass that covers travel on the metro, Carris buses, some trains, all trams and lifts. As well as that it gives you admission to key museums and attractions and you'll receive up to 50% discount on tours, cruises and other admission charges. Available at Ask Me Lisboa tourist offices (right).

Emergency

Police station (Map pp670-1; ☎ 217 654 242; Rua Capelo 13)

Tourist police post (Map pp670-1; ☎ 213 421 634; Palácio Foz, Praça dos Restauradores; 🕒 24hr)

Internet Access

Places listed here charge between €1.50 and €3 per hour.

@lfa.net (Map pp670-1; Rua dos Remédios 89; 🕒 9am-7.30pm)

Cyber Bica (Map pp670-1; ☎ 213 225 004; Rua Duques de Bragança; per hr €3; 🕒 noon-midnight Mon-Fri)

Web Café (Map pp670-1; ☎ 213 421 181; Rua do Diário de Notícias 126; per hr €3; 🕒 7pm-2am)

Medical Services

The rotation of emergency, night service and Sunday schedules are posted on the doors of all pharmacies.

Farmácia Estácio (Map pp670-1; ☎ 213 211 390; Rossio 62) Good central pharmacy.

Hospital Britânico (British Hospital, Hospital Inglês; Map pp666-7; ☎ 213 943 100, 213 929 360; Rua Saraiva de Carvalho 49) English-speaking staff and dental care available.

Money

Cota Câmbios (Map pp670-1; ☎ 213 220 480; Rossio 41) One of the best exchange rates in town.

Post

Main post office (Map pp670-1; Praça do Comércio; 🕒 8.30am-6.30pm Mon-Fri, 9am-noon Sat) Handles poste-restante collection.

Post office (Map pp670-1; Praça dos Restauradores; 🕒 8am-10pm Mon-Fri, 9am-6pm Sat & Sun) Opposite the Ask Me Lisboa tourist office.

Telephone

Portugal Telecom (Map pp670-1; Rossio 68; 🕒 8am-11pm) Telephone booths available and phonecards for sale.

Tourist Information

Ask Me Lisboa Belém (Map pp666-7; Largo dos Jernónimos; 🕒 10am-1pm & 2-6pm Tue-Sat); Palácio Foz (Map pp670-1; near Praça dos Restauradores; 🕒 9am-8pm); Rua Augusta (Map pp666-7; near Rua Conceição; 🕒 10am-1pm & 2-6pm); Santa Apolónia (Map pp670-1; door 47, inside train station; 🕒 8am-1pm Wed-Sat) Turismo de Lisboa runs several information kiosks; these are the most useful. Most kiosks have free maps and the bimonthly guide *Follow Me Lisboa*, and sell the Lisboa Card.

Lisboa Welcome Center (Map pp670-1; ☎ 210 312 810; www.visitlisboa.com; Praça do Comércio) Main branch of Turismo de Lisboa, providing free city maps, brochures (like *Follow Me Lisboa*) and hotel- and tour-booking services.

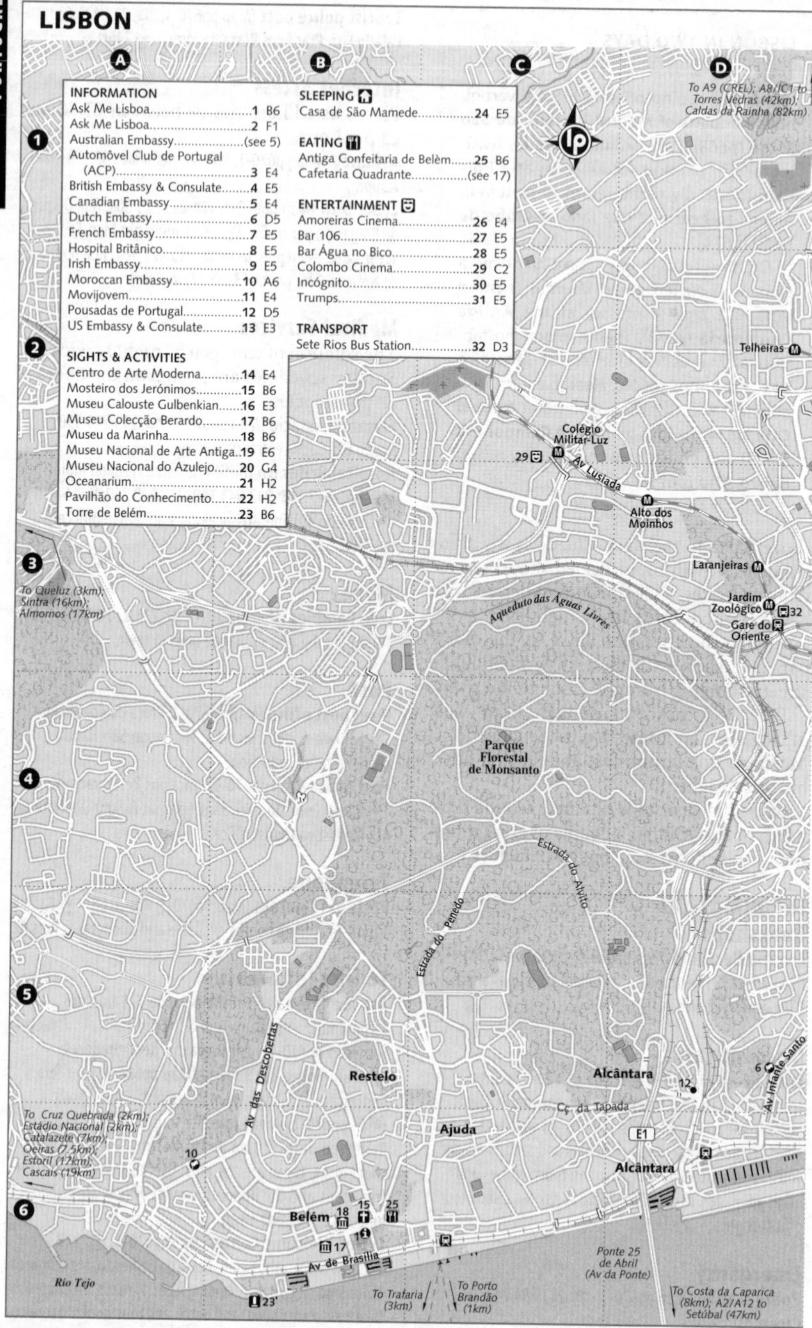
LISBON
A
B
C
D
1
2
3
4
5
6
INFORMATION
Ask Me Lisboa....1 B6
Ask Me Lisboa....2 F1
Australian Embassy....(see 5)
Automôvel Club de Portugal (ACP)....3 E4
British Embassy & Consulate....4 E5
Canadian Embassy....5 E4
Dutch Embassy....6 D5
French Embassy....7 E5
Hospital Britânico....8 E5
Irish Embassy....9 E5
Moroccan Embassy....10 A6
Movijovem....11 E4
Pousadas de Portugal....12 D5
US Embassy & Consulate....13 E3
SIGHTS & ACTIVITIES
Centro de Arte Moderna....14 E4
Mosteiro dos Jerónimos....15 B6
Museu Calouste Gulbenkian....16 E3
Museu Colecção Berardo....17 B6
Museu da Marinha....18 B6
Museu Nacional de Arte Antiga....19 E6
Museu Nacional do Azulejo....20 G4
Oceanarium....21 H2
Pavilhão do Conhecimento....22 H2
Torre de Belém....23 B6
SLEEPING
Casa de São Mamede....24 E5
EATING
Antiga Confeitaria de Belèm....25 B6
Cafetaria Quadrante....(see 17)
ENTERTAINMENT
Amoreiras Cinema....26 E4
Bar 106....27 E5
Bar Água no Bico....28 E5
Colombo Cinema....29 C2
Incógnito....30 E5
Trumps....31 E5
TRANSPORT
Sete Rios Bus Station....32 D3
To A9 (CREL); A8/IC1 to Torres Vedras (42km); Caldas da Rainha (82km)
Telheiras
Colégio Militar-Luz
Av Lusíada
Alto dos Moinhos
Laranjeiras
Jardim Zoológico
Gare do Oriente
To Queluz (3km); Sintra (16km); Almornos (17km)
Aqueduto das Águas Livres
Parque Florestal de Monsanto
Estrada do Alvito
Estrada do Penedo
Av das Descobertas
Restelo
Alcântara
Cç da Tapada
Ajuda
E1
Alcântara
Av Infante Santo
To Cruz Quebrada (2km); Estádio Nacional (2km); Catalazete (7km); Oeiras (7.5km); Estoril (17km); Cascais (19km)
Belém
Av de Brasília
Rio Tejo
To Trafaria (3km)
To Porto Brandão (1km)
Ponte 25 de Abril (Av da Ponte)
To Costa da Caparica (8km); A2/A12 to Setúbal (47km)

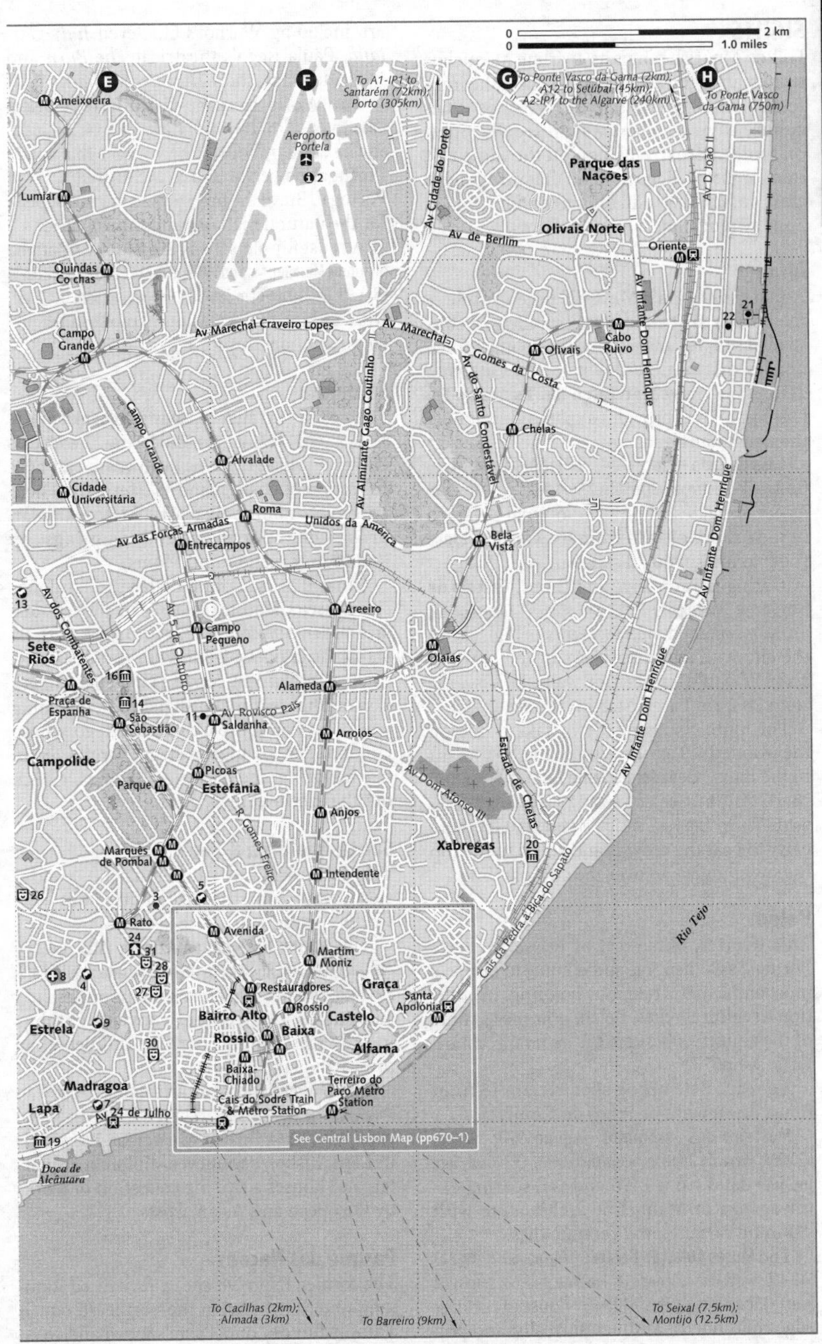

0 2 km
0 1.0 miles
E
F
G
H
To A1-IP1 to Santarém (72km); Porto (305km)
To Ponte Vasco da Gama (2km); A12 to Setúbal (45km); A2-IP1 to the Algarve (240km)
To Ponte Vasco da Gama (750m)
Ameixoeira
Aeroporto Portela
2
Parque das Nações
Av D João II
Lumiar
Av Cidade do Porto
Av de Berlim
Olivais Norte
Oriente
Quindas Co chas
Av Infante Dom Henrique
21
22
Campo Grande
Av Marechal Craveiro Lopes
Av Marechal Gomes da Costa
Cabo Ruivo
Olivais
Av Almirante Gago Coutinho
Av do Santo Condestável
Campo Grande
Chelas
Alvalade
Cidade Universitária
Roma
Unidos da América
Av das Forças Armadas
Entrecampos
Bela Vista
Av Infante Dom Henrique
13
Av dos Combatentes
Av 5 de Outubro
Areeiro
Campo Pequeno
Sete Rios
Olaias
16
Alameda
Praça de Espanha
14
São Sebastião
11
Av Rovisco Pais
Saldanha
Arroios
Estrada de Chelas
Av Infante Dom Henrique
Campolide
Picoas
Av Dom Afonso III
Parque
Estefânia
R Gomes Freire
Anjos
Marquês de Pombal
Xabregas
20
Intendente
26
3
5
Cais da Pedra à Bica do Sapato
Rato
Avenida
Rio Tejo
24
31
28
Martim Moniz
8
4
27
Restauradores
Graça
Santa Apolónia
Rossio
Bairro Alto
Castelo
Estrela
9
Rossio
Baixa
30
Alfama
Baixa-Chiado
Madragoa
Terreiro do Paço Metro Station
Cais do Sodré Train & Metro Station
Lapa
7
Av 24 de Julho
19
See Central Lisbon Map (pp670–1)
Doca de Alcântara
To Cacilhas (2km); Almada (3km)
To Barreiro (9km)
To Seixal (7.5km); Montijo (12.5km)

SIGHTS

Hilltop Moorish ramparts, twirling Manueline turrets, and a fortified Romanesque cathedral – Lisbon's heritage stash would give most cities culture envy. The best way to see the city is on foot. Alternatively, hop on the funicular, tram or metro. Keep in mind that many sights close on Mondays and offer free admission on Sunday mornings.

Alfama

Alfama is Lisbon's Moorish time capsule: a medinalike district of tangled alleys, palm-shaded squares and skinny, terracotta-roofed houses that tumble down to the glittering Tejo. The terrace at **Largo das Portas do Sol** (Map pp670–1) provides a splendid view over the neighbourhood.

Casa do Fado (Map pp670-1; ☎ 218 823 470; Largo do Chafariz de Dentro; adult/child €2.50/1.25; 🕑 10am-6pm Tue-Sun) provides vibrant audiovisual coverage of the history of fado from its working-class roots to international stardom.

Dating from Visigothic times, **Castelo de São Jorge** (Map pp670-1; ☎ 218 800 620; admission €5; 🕑 9am-9pm Mar-Oct, to 6pm Nov-Feb) sits high above the city with stunning views of the city and river. If you'd rather not walk, take scenic tram 28 from Largo Martim Moniz.

For more charming views, take a ride on the wonderful 19th-century wrought-iron lift in the Baixa, **Elevador de Santa Justa** (Map pp670-1; ☎ 213 613 054; Rua de Santa Justa & Largo do Carmo; admission €2.70; 🕑 7am-9pm, to 11pm in summer). Get there early to beat the crowds and zoom to the top for sweeping views over the city's skyline.

Belém

This quarter, 6km west of Rossio, reflects Portugal's Golden Age and is home to Lisbon's most emblematic religious building. In addition to cultural relics, Belém is home to some of the country's best *pastéis de nata* (custard tarts; see p673).

To reach Belém, hop aboard tram 15 from Praça da Figueira or Praça do Comércio.

Mosteiro dos Jerónimos (Map pp666-7; ☎ 213 620 034; Praça do Império; adult/child €6/3; 🕑 10am-5pm Tue-Sun) dates from 1496 and is a soaring extravaganza of Manueline architecture with stunning carvings and ceramic tiles.

The **Museu Colecção Berardo** (Map pp666-7; ☎ 213 612 400; www.museuberardo.pt; Praça do Império; admission free; 🕑 10am-7pm Sat-Thu, to 10pm Fri) houses a cutting-edge collection of abstract, surrealist and pop art, including Warhol's blue-eyed *Judy Garland*, Paula Rego's theatrical *The Barn* and Magritte's fantastical *The Silvery Chasm*.

The World Heritage–listed **Torre de Belém** (Map pp666-7; ☎ 213 620 034; admission €4; 🕑 10am-5pm Tue-Sun) symbolises the voyages that made Portugal powerful and is *the* tourist icon of Portugal. Brave the tiny steps to the turret peak for the natural high of panoramic views.

A must for old salts is the **Museu da Marinha** (Maritime Museum; Map pp666-7; ☎ 213 620 019; adult/child €3/1.50; 🕑 10am-6pm Tue-Sun Apr-Sep, to 5pm Oct-Mar), with all kinds of seafaring paraphernalia including model ships.

Saldanha

The celebrated **Museu Calouste Gulbenkian** (Map pp666-7; ☎ 217 823 461; Avenidae de Berna 45; adult/child €4/free; 🕑 10am-6pm Tue-Sun) showcases an epic collection of Eastern and Western art. There are Egyptian mummy masks, Mesopotamian urns, Qing porcelain and paintings by Rembrandt, Renoir and Monet.

Situated in a sculpture-dotted garden alongside Museu Calouste Gulbenkian, the **Centro de Arte Moderna** (Modern Art Centre; Map pp666-7; ☎ 217 823 474; Rua Dr Nicaulau de Bettencourt; adult/child €4/free; 🕑 10am-6pm Tue-Sun) contains a stellar collection of 20th-century Portuguese art, including works by London-based Paula Rego whose childhood in Portugal is strongly reflected in her haunting and theatrical themes. Check out the excellent restaurant.

Santa Apolónia & Lapa

The following two museums are a side-step away from the city centre, but well worth visiting.

The **Museu Nacional do Azulejo** (Map pp666-7; ☎ 218 100 340; Rua Madre de Deus 4; adult/child €4/2; 🕑 10am-6pm Wed-Sun, 2-6pm Tue) languishes in a sumptuous 17th-century convent. Exhibits include a fascinating 36m tile panel depicting pre-earthquake Lisbon.

The **Museu Nacional de Arte Antiga** (Ancient Art Museum; Map pp666-7; ☎ 213 912 800; Rua das Janelas Verdes; admission €4; 🕑 10am-6pm Wed-Sun, 2-6pm Tue) is in Lapa, Lisbon's moneyed diplomatic quarter, and houses a ripping collection of works by European and Asian artists.

Parque das Nações

The former Expo '98 site, a revitalised 2km-long waterfront area in the northeast, equals a family fun day out. There's weird and won-

FREE THRILLS

Lisbon is a superb city for euro-pinchers, as its biggest draws are outdoors: from astounding views at hilltop **miradouros** (lookouts) to urban treasure hunts in the warrenlike **Alfama**.

Many museums have free admisson on Sunday mornings. For a free cultural fix on other days, make for Belém's iconic **Museu Colecção Berardo** (opposite), **Museu do Teatro Romano** (Roman Theatre Museum; Map pp670-1; ☎ 217 513 200; Pátio do Aljube 5; 🕒 10am-1pm & 2-6pm Tue-Sun) for Roman theatre ruins and, right opposite, the fortresslike **Sé** (cathedral; Map pp670–1), built in 1150 on the site of a mosque. The **Museu Calouste Gulbenkian** (opposite) gives free musical recitals at noon on Sundays in the library foyer. Try to catch one of the free jazz concerts on Thursdays in summer at **Cafetaria Quadrante** (p673).

derful public art on display, lush gardens and casual riverfront cafes. Other highlights include the mind-blowing **Oceanarium** (Map pp666-7; ☎ 218 917 002; www.oceanario.pt; adult/child €11/5.50; 🕒 10am-7pm), Europe's second-largest, and **Pavilhão do Conhecimento** (Living Science Centre; Map pp666-7; ☎ 218 917 100; adult/child €7/3; 🕒 10am-6pm Tue-Fri, 11am-7pm Sat & Sun) with over 300 interactive exhibits for kids of all ages. Take the metro to Oriente station – an equally impressive Expo project.

Alcântara

The former wharves today house a sleek and modern strip of bars and restaurants with tables spilling onto the long promenade. It's an intriguing place for a waterfront stroll, a bite or a drink, though some find the metallic drone of traffic across the bridge a bit grating.

TOURS

Lisbon Walker (☎ 218 861 840; www.lisbonwalker.com; Rua dos Remédios 84; 3hr walk €15; 🕒 10am & 2.30pm) Well-informed, English-speaking guides lead fascinating themed walking tours through Lisbon. They depart from the northeast corner of Praça do Comércio.

Transtejo (Map pp670-1; ☎ 218 824 671; www.transtejo.pt; Terreiro do Paço ferry terminal; adult/child €20/10; 🕒 Mar-Oct) Runs cruises on the Tagus. There are great views of the city from this watery perspective.

FESTIVALS & EVENTS

The **Festa de Santo António** (Festival of Saint Anthony), from 12 June to 13 June, culminates the three-week **Festas de Lisboa**, with processions and dozens of street parties.

SLEEPING

Lisbon has seriously raised the slumber stakes recently with a new crop of design-conscious boutique hotels and upmarket backpacker digs. Book ahead during the high season (July to mid-September).

Baixa & Alfama

Lounge Hostel (Map pp670-1; ☎ 213 462 061; www.lisbonloungehostel.com; Rua de São Nicolau 41; dm/d incl breakfast €20/60; 💻) These ultrahip Baixa digs have a party vibe. Bed down in immaculate dorms and meet like-minded travellers in the funky lounge watched over by a wacky moose head.

Travellers House (Map pp670-1; ☎ 210 115 922; http://travellershouse.com; Rua Augusta 89; dm from €22; 💻) This superfriendly hostel is set in a converted 250-year-old house and offers cosy dorms, a retro lounge with beanbags, an internet corner and a communal kitchen.

Pensão Imperial (Map pp670-1; ☎ 213 420 166; Praça dos Restauradores 78; s/d €25/40) Cheery Imperial has a terrific location over the main square. The high-ceilinged rooms with rickety '70s-style furniture are nothing flash, but some have flower-draped balconies overlooking the *praça*.

Pensão Ninho das Águias (Map pp670-1; ☎ 218 854 070; Costa do Castelo 74; s/d/tr with shared bathroom €30/40/60) It isn't called 'eagle's nest' for nothing: this guest house has a Rapunzel-esque turret affording magical 360-degree views over Lisbon. Book well ahead.

Pensão São João da Praça (Map pp670-1; ☎ 218 862 591; 218862591@sapo.pt; 2nd fl, Rua de São João da Praça 97; d with shared/private bathroom €35/50) So close to the *sé* you can almost touch the gargoyles, this 19th-century guest house has a pick-and-mix of clean, sunny rooms with fridges and TVs; the best have river-facing verandahs.

Pensão Residencial Gerês (Map pp670-1; ☎ 218 810 497; www.pensaogeres.com; Calçada do Garcia 6; d with shared/private bathroom €45/55; 💻) A family-run place with some English, plus religious pics, traditional tiles and fussy comfortable rooms. Go for corner room 105 with its five-star views.

CENTRAL LISBON

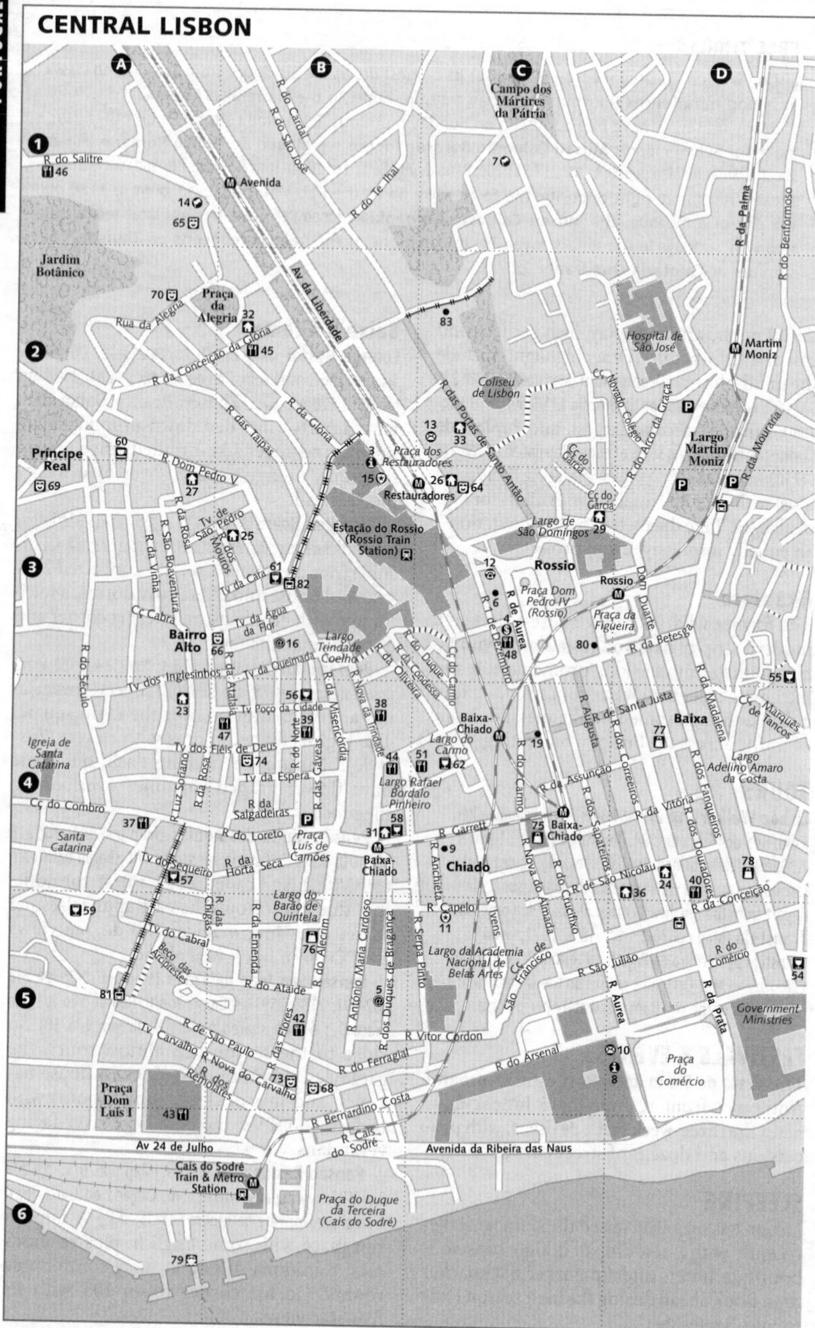

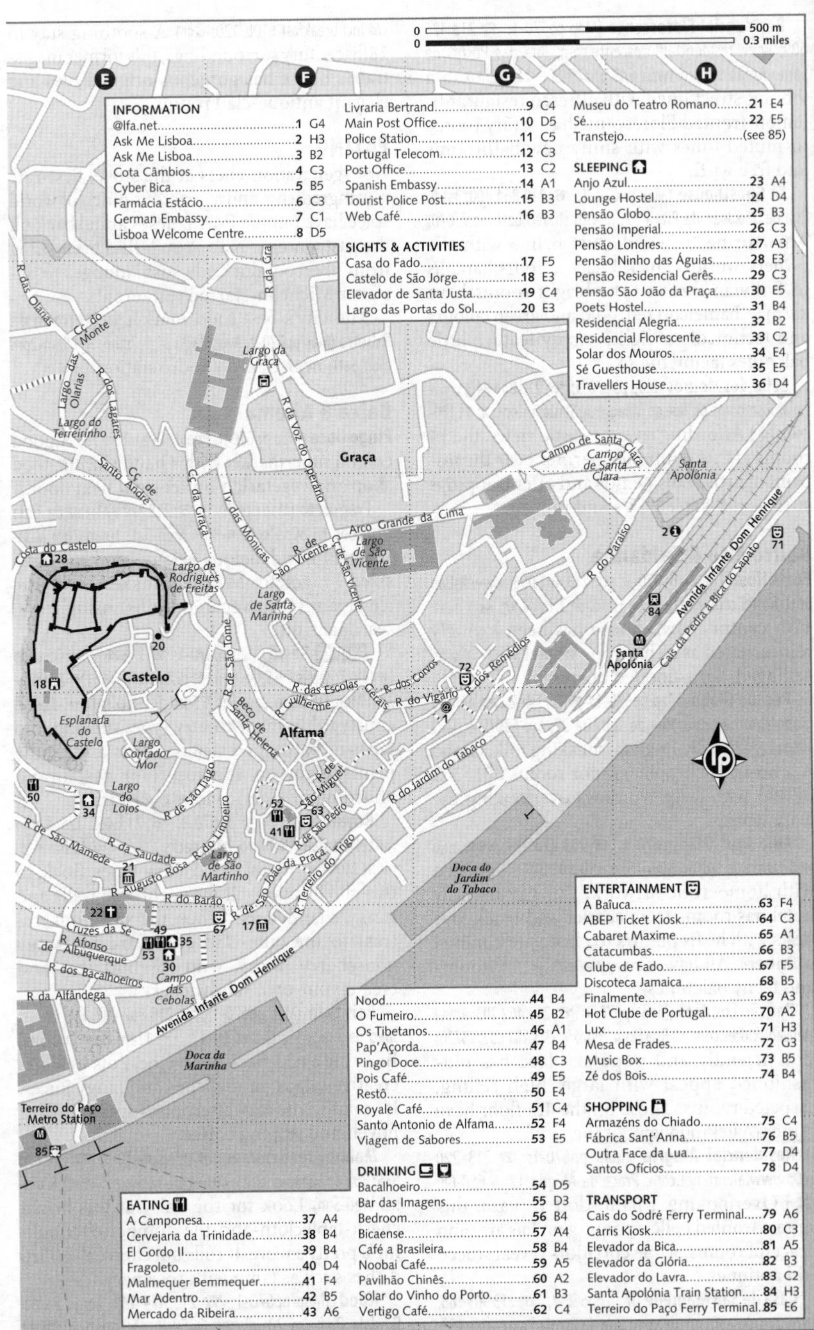
0 500 m
0 0.3 miles
E
F
G
H
INFORMATION
@lfa.net 1 G4
Ask Me Lisboa 2 H3
Ask Me Lisboa 3 B2
Cota Câmbios 4 C3
Cyber Bica 5 B5
Farmácia Estácio 6 C3
German Embassy 7 C1
Lisboa Welcome Centre 8 D5
Livraria Bertrand 9 C4
Main Post Office 10 D5
Police Station 11 C5
Portugal Telecom 12 C3
Post Office 13 C2
Spanish Embassy 14 A1
Tourist Police Post 15 B3
Web Café 16 B3
SIGHTS & ACTIVITIES
Casa do Fado 17 F5
Castelo de São Jorge 18 E3
Elevador de Santa Justa 19 C4
Largo das Portas do Sol 20 E3
Museu do Teatro Romano 21 E4
Sé 22 E5
Transtejo (see 85)
SLEEPING
Anjo Azul 23 A4
Lounge Hostel 24 D4
Pensão Globo 25 B3
Pensão Imperial 26 C3
Pensão Londres 27 A3
Pensão Ninho das Águias 28 E3
Pensão Residencial Gerês 29 C3
Pensão São João da Praça 30 E5
Poets Hostel 31 B4
Residencial Alegria 32 B2
Residencial Florescente 33 C2
Solar dos Mouros 34 E4
Sé Guesthouse 35 E5
Travellers House 36 D4
EATING
A Camponesa 37 A4
Cervejaria da Trinidade 38 B4
El Gordo II 39 B4
Fragoleto 40 D4
Malmequer Bemmequer 41 F4
Mar Adentro 42 B5
Mercado da Ribeira 43 A6
Nood 44 B4
O Fumeiro 45 B2
Os Tibetanos 46 A1
Pap'Açorda 47 B4
Pingo Doce 48 C3
Pois Café 49 E5
Restô 50 E4
Royale Café 51 C4
Santo Antonio de Alfama 52 F4
Viagem de Sabores 53 E5
DRINKING
Bacalhoeiro 54 D5
Bar das Imagens 55 D3
Bedroom 56 B4
Bicaense 57 A4
Café a Brasileira 58 B4
Noobai Café 59 A5
Pavilhão Chinês 60 A2
Solar do Vinho do Porto 61 B3
Vertigo Café 62 C4
ENTERTAINMENT
A Baîuca 63 F4
ABEP Ticket Kiosk 64 C3
Cabaret Maxime 65 A1
Catacumbas 66 B3
Clube de Fado 67 F5
Discoteca Jamaica 68 B5
Finalmente 69 A3
Hot Clube de Portugal 70 A2
Lux 71 H3
Mesa de Frades 72 G3
Music Box 73 B5
Zé dos Bois 74 B4
SHOPPING
Armazéns do Chiado 75 C4
Fábrica Sant'Anna 76 B5
Outra Face da Lua 77 D4
Santos Ofícios 78 D4
TRANSPORT
Cais do Sodré Ferry Terminal 79 A6
Carris Kiosk 80 C3
Elevador da Bica 81 A5
Elevador da Glória 82 B3
Elevador do Lavra 83 C2
Santa Apolónia Train Station 84 H3
Terreiro do Paço Ferry Terminal 85 E6
R das Olarias
Cç do Monte
Largo das Olarias
R dos Lagares
Largo do Terreirinho
Santo André
Cç de
R da Graça
Largo da Graça
R da Voz do Operário
Graça
Cç da Graça
Tv das Mónicas
Campo de Santa Clara
Campo de Santa Clara
Santa Apolónia
Arco Grande da Cima
R de São Vicente
Largo de São Vicente
Cç de São Vicente
R do Paraíso
Avenida Infante Dom Henrique
Cais da Pedra à Bica do Sapato
Costa do Castelo
Largo de Rodrigues de Freitas
Largo de Santa Marinha
R de São Tomé
Castelo
Esplanada do Castelo
R das Escolas Gerais
R dos Corvos
R do Vigário
R dos Remédios
R Guilherme
Beco de Santa Helena
Alfama
Santa Apolónia
Largo Contador Mor
Largo do Loios
R de São Tiago
R do Limoeiro
R de São Miguel
R de São Pedro
R do Jardim do Tabaco
R de São Mamede
R da Saudade
R Augusto Rosa
Largo de São Martinho
R de São João da Praça
R Terreiro do Trigo
Doca do Jardim do Tabaco
R do Barão
Cruzes da Sé
R Afonso de Albuquerque
R dos Bacalhoeiros
R da Alfândega
Campo das Cebolas
Avenida Infante Dom Henrique
Doca da Marinha
Terreiro do Paço Metro Station

Residencial Florescente (Map pp670-1; ☎ 213 426 609; www.residencialflorescente.com; Rua das Portas de Santo Antão 99; s/d/tw/tr €45/55/70/80;) On a vibrant street lined with alfresco restaurants, lemon-fronted Florescente has comfy rooms in muted tones with shiny new bathrooms and free wi-fi.

Sé Guesthouse (Map pp670-1; ☎ 218 864 400; 1st fl, Rua de São João da Praça 97; d with shared bathroom €70) This shrine to wanderlust brims with the owners' worldly knick-knacks, from pharaohs to Bolivian throws. The bright rooms have karma-chameleon red, gold and green colours and technicolour lights; many feature little balconies facing the *sé*.

Solar dos Mouros (Map pp670-1; ☎ 218 854 940; www.solardosmouros.pt; Rua do Milagre de Santo António 4; d €120-240;) Affording river or castle views, the 14 rooms at this boutique charmer bear the imprint of artist Luís Lemos and offer trappings such as flat-screen TVs and minibars.

Bairro Alto & Saldanha

Poets Hostel (Map pp670-1; ☎ 213 461 058; www.lisbonpoetshostel.com; Rua Nova da Trindade 2; dm €20;) The 17th-century town house has been lovingly reincarnated as a charming hostel with high-ceilinged, light-flooded dorms.

Pensão Globo (Map pp670-1; ☎ 213 462 279; pensaoglobo@hotmail.com; Rua do Teixeira 37; s/d €30/50;) Run by friendly English-speaking folk, Globo is a no-frills cheapie. Go for rooms 301, 302 or 303 with large windows overlooking the leafy street.

Anjo Azul (Map pp670-1; ☎ 213 478 069; www.anjoazul.com; Rua Luz Soriano 75; d €50-80;) Adorned with homoerotic artwork, this gay-friendly hotel has rooms from scarlet-and-black love nests with heart pillows to chocolate-caramel numbers. All have squeaky-clean bathrooms and teeny balconies.

Pensão Londres (Map pp670-1; ☎ 213 462 203; www.pensaolondres.com.pt; Rua Dom Pedro V 53; s/d/t €52/75/90) This friendly and popular place has old-fashioned appeal with large, high-ceiling, carpeted rooms. Those on the 4th floor have camera-clicking views of the city.

Residencial Alegria (Map pp670-1; ☎ 213 220 670; www.alegrianet.com; Praça da Alegria 12; d €58-68;) Overlooking a palm-dotted plaza, this lemon-fronted belle-époque gem has airy and peaceful rooms, while corridors reveal stucco and antiques.

Casa de São Mamede (Map pp666-7; ☎ 213 963 166; www.casadesaomamede.com; Rua da Escola Politécnica 159; s/d incl breakfast €100/120;) A soothing stay in 18th-century surroundings; this former magistrate's house has gorgeous original tiles and elegant antique-clad rooms.

EATING

New-generation chefs at the stove, first-rate raw ingredients and a generous pinch of world spice have put the Portuguese capital back on the gastronomic map. You'll find everything from ubercool dockside sushi lounges to designer Michelin-starred restaurants.

The city's best food market is **Mercado da Ribeira** (Map pp670-1; Avenida da 24 de Julho; 5am-2pm Mon-Sat), near Cais do Sodré station.

Baixa & Alfama

Pingo Doce (Map pp670-1; Rua de Dezembro 73) A good central supermarket with a handy health-food shop and vegetarian buffet right next door.

Fragoleto (Map pp670-1; ☎ 218 877 971; Rua da Prata 74; scoop €1.80; 9am-8pm Mon-Sat, 10am-7pm Mon-Sat winter) For delicious gelato, head for pint-sized Fragoleto. Manuela makes authentic ice cream (even vegan options) using fresh, seasonal fruit.

our pick **Restô** (Map pp670-1; ☎ 218 867 334; Costa do Castelo 7; tapas €4-5, restaurant dishes €10-16; 7.30pm-2am Mon-Fri, noon-2am Sat & Sun) Restô's tree-filled courtyard hums with arty types tucking into tapas or barbecued steaks. Zebra and giraffe prints glam up the top-floor restaurant, affording mesmeric views over Lisbon.

Royale Café (Map pp670-1; ☎ 213 469 125; Largo Rafael Bordalo Pinheiro 29; snacks €4-6; 10am-midnight Mon-Sat, to 8pm Sun) Media types flock to this chichi cafe – all monochrome walls and funky chandeliers. When the sun's out, retreat to the vine-clad courtyard for zingy gooseberry juices, wild-rosebud teas and create-your-own sandwiches.

Pois Café (Map pp670-1; ☎ 218 862 497; Rua de São João da Praça 93; dishes €4-12; 11am-8pm Tue-Sun) Boasting a laid-back boho vibe, Pois Café has creative salads, sandwiches and tangy juices. Its sofas invite lazy afternoons spent reading novels and sipping coffee.

Malmequer Bemmequer (Map pp670-1; ☎ 218 876 535; Rua de São Miguel 23; dishes €6-12.50; lunch & dinner Wed-Sun) Look for the daisy at this bright check-tablecloth-and-tile number overlooking a pretty square. It rolls out charcoal-grilled dishes such as lamb with rosemary.

Nood (Map pp670-1; ☎ 213 474 141; Largo Rafael Bordalo Pinheiro 20; dishes €6.50-9; noon-midnight

Sun-Thu, to 2am Fri & Sat) Young and buzzy, this Japanese newcomer is Chiado's hippest nosh spot. The scene: chilli-red walls, communal tables and flaming woks. The menu: well-prepared sushi, sashimi and noodles.

Santo Antonio de Alfama (Map pp670-1; ☎ 218 881 328; Beco de São Miguel 7; dishes €8-16; lunch & dinner Wed-Mon) Shoehorned between Alfama's candy-bright houses, this bistro wins the award for Lisbon's loveliest courtyard: all vines, twittering budgies and fluttering laundry. The menu stars its own creations such as Sophia Loren salad (pesto, rocket and salmon).

Viagem de Sabores (Map pp670-1; ☎ 218 870 189; Rua de São João da Praça 103; dishes €8.50-12.50; dinner Mon-Sat) Travel your tastebuds at this worldly haunt behind the *sé*. Amid industrial-design cool, sample tender Moroccan lamb, chocolate cannelloni and other global bites.

Avenida de Liberdade

Os Tibetanos (Map pp670-1; ☎ 213 142 038; Rua do Salitre 117; mains from €6; closed Sat & Sun;) Doubles as a Tibetan Buddhist school with Zen-style surroundings, a leafy patio and a diverse meatless menu; try the Japanese mushrooms with seaweed and tofu.

O Fumeiro (Map pp670-1; ☎ 213 474 203; Rua da Conceição da Glória 25; dishes €12-20) This cosy blue-and-white-tiled restaurant specialises in the earthy, aromatic cuisine of the mountainous Beira Alta. Suckling pig and seafood *cataplana* (stew) pair well with Portuguese wines.

Bairro Alto & Saldanha

Mar Adentro (Map pp670-1; ☎ 346 91 58; Rua do Alecrim 35; snacks €3-5; 10am-11pm Mon-Thu, 1pm-midnight Fri & Sat) Gay-friendly Mar Adentro reveals a razor-sharp industrial design with a stainless-steel arch, concrete walls and moulded plastic chairs. Lisbon creatives flock here for healthy breakfasts, yummy sandwiches such as feta, pepper and olive, and free wi-fi.

El Gordo II (Map pp670-1; ☎ 213 426 372; Travessa dos Fiéis de Deus 28; tapas €3.25-28; dinner Tue-Sun) Lit with a rosy glow from cloth lanterns, Lisbon's 'fat boy two' churns out lip-smacking tapas such as octopus in smoked paprika, pimento peppers and cod pastries. Go alfresco on the cobbled steps.

A Camponesa (Map pp670-1; ☎ 213 464 791; Rua Marechal Saldanha 23; dishes €7.50-15; lunch & dinner Mon-Fri, dinner Sat) This Santa Catarina hot spot attracts arty types with its poster-plastered walls, jazzy grooves and tables full of holiday snapshots. Savour home-grown flavours like Algarve oysters and cuttlefish with fried egg.

Cervejaria da Trindade (Map pp670-1; ☎ 213 423 506; Rua Nova da Trindade 20c; mains €8-20) This 13th-century monastery turned clattering beer hall oozes atmosphere with its vaults and *azulejos* of quaffing clerics and seasonal goddesses. Feast away on humungous steaks or lobster stew, washed down with foaming beer.

Pap'Açorda (Map pp670-1; ☎ 213 464 811; Rua da Atalaia 57; dishes €15-25) Way too sexy for Bairro Alto, Pap'Açorda lures the beauty set with its cascading chandeliers, pink-champagne walls and good-looking waitstaff. The signature dish is *açorda* (bread and shellfish stew), preferably washed down with Moët.

Belém

Antiga Confeitaria de Belém (Map pp666-7; ☎ 213 637 423; Rua de Belém 86-88) A classically tiled and elegant cafe with probably the best *pastéis de nata* on earth. Delicious!

Cafetaria Quadrante (Map pp666-7; ☎ 213 622 722; Centro Cultural de Belém; dishes €5-8; 10am-8pm Mon-Fri, to 9pm Sat & Sun) Revive over salads and soups at this light-filled cafe. Don't miss the Henry Moore sculpture on the terrace. There are free jazz concerts on Thursdays in summer.

DRINKING

All-night street parties in Bairro Alto, sunset drinks from high Alfama terraces, and sumptuous art deco cafes scattered about Chiado – Lisbon has many enticing options for imbibers.

Pavilhão Chinês (Map pp670-1; Rua Dom Pedro V 89-91) An old curiosity shop of a bar with oil paintings and model spitfires dangling from the ceiling, and cabinets brimming with glittering Venetian masks and Action Men. Play pool or bag a comfy armchair with port or beer in hand.

Bicaense (Map pp670-1; Rua da Bica de Duarte Belo 42a) Indie kids have a soft spot for this chilled Santa Catarina haunt, kitted out with retro radios, projectors and squishy beanbags. DJs spin house to the preclubbing crowd and the back room stages occasional gigs.

Café a Brasileira (Map pp670-1; ☎ 213 469 547; Rua Garrett 120; 8am-2am) A historic watering hole for Lisbon's 19th-century greats, with warm wooden innards and a busy counter serving daytime coffees and pints at night.

Bedroom (Map pp670-1; Rua do Norte 86) It's a bedroom, but these beauties aren't sleeping. Join them on the dance floor for electro and hip

PORTUGUESE SOUL

Infused by Moorish song and the ditties of homesick sailors, bluesy, bittersweet fado encapsulates the Lisbon psyche like nothing else. The melancholic, uniquely Portuguese style was born in the Alfama – still the best place in Lisbon to hear it live.

- **A Baîuca** (Map pp670-1; ☎ 218 867 284; Rua de São Miguel 20; admission minimum €25; ⌚ dinner Thu-Mon) On a good night, walking into A Baîuca is like gatecrashing a family party. It's a special place with *fado vadio*, where locals take a turn and spectators hiss if anyone dares to chat during the singing. Reserve ahead.
- **Clube de Fado** (Map pp670-1; ☎ 218 852 704; www.clube-de-fado.com; Rua de São João da Praça; admission minimum €10; ⌚ 9pm-2.30am Mon-Sat) Hosts the cream of the fado crop in vaulted, dimly lit surrounds. Big-name *fadistas* perform here alongside celebrated guitarists.
- **Mesa de Frades** (Map pp670-1; ☎ 917 029 436; www.mesadefrades.com; Rua dos Remédios 139a; admission minimum €15; ⌚ dinner Wed-Mon) A magical place to hear fado, tiny Mesa de Frades used to be a chapel. It's tiled with exquisite *azulejos* and has just a handful of tables. The show begins around 11pm.

hop, or recline on the beds in the lounge shimmering with gold wallpaper and chandeliers.

Solar do Vinho do Porto (Map pp670-1; ☎ 213 475 707; Rua São Pedro de Alcântara 45; ⌚ 11am-midnight Mon-Sat) Part of an 18th-century mansion, the low-lit, beamed cavern is ideal for nursing a glass of Portugal's finest port.

Bar das Imagens (Map pp670-1; Calçada Marquês de Tancos 1; ⌚ 11am-2am Tue-Sat, 3-11pm Sun) With a terrace affording vertigo-inducing views over the city, this cheery bar serves potent Cuba libres and other well-prepared cocktails.

Bacalhoeiro (Map pp670-1; ☎ 218 864 891; Rua dos Bacalhoeiros 125;) Nonconformist, laid-back Bacalhoeiro shelters a cosy bar and hosts everything from alternative gigs to film screenings, salsa nights and themed parties. Free wi-fi.

Noobai Café (Map pp670-1; Miradouro de Santa Catarina; ⌚ noon-midnight) Lisbon's best-kept secret is next to Miradouro de Santa Catarina, with a laid-back vibe, jazzy beats and magnificent views from the terrace.

Vertigo Café (Map pp670-1; ☎ 213 433 112; Travessa do Carmo 4; snacks €4-7; ⌚ 10am-midnight) Artists lap up the boho vibe at this glam Chiado cafe, where they can relax, read the papers and play draughts.

ENTERTAINMENT

Pick up the free monthly *Follow me Lisboa*, the *Agenda Cultural Lisboa* or quarterly *Lisboa Step By Step* from the tourist office for what's on. Check out www.visitlisboa.com (Lisbon tourist office website) and www.lisboacultural.pt (for cultural events).

Live Music

Hot Clube de Portugal (Map pp670-1; ☎ 213 467 369; www.hcp.pt; Praça da Alegria 39; ⌚ 10pm-2am Tue-Sat) This small, poster-plastered cellar has staged top-drawer jazz acts since the 1940s. Shows are at 11pm and 12.30am.

Catacumbas (Map pp670-1; Travessa da Água da Flor 43) Moodily lit and festooned with portraits of legends like Miles Davis, this den is jam-packed when it hosts live jazz on Thursday night.

Zé dos Bois (Map pp670-1; ☎ 213 430 205; www.zedosbois.org; Rua da Barroca 59) Focusing on tomorrow's performing arts and music trends, Zé dos Bois is an experimental venue with a graffitied courtyard for chilling. The boho haunt has hosted bands like Black Dice and Animal Collective.

Nightclubs

Cover charges for nightclubs vary from €5 to €20.

Music Box (Map pp670-1; Rua Nova do Carvalho 24; www.musicboxlisboa.com) Under the brick arches on Rua Nova do Carvalho lies one of Lisbon's hottest clubs. Music Box hosts loud and sweaty club nights with music shifting from electro to rock, plus ear-splitting gigs by rising bands.

Incógnito (Map pp666-7; Rua Poiais de São Bento 37) No-sign, pint-sized Incógnito offers an alternative vibe and DJs thrashing out indie rock and electro-pop. Sweat it out with a fun crowd on the tiny basement dance floor, or breathe more easily in the loft bar upstairs.

Lux (Map pp670-1; ☎ 218 820 890; www.luxfragil.com; Armazém A, Cais da Pedra a Bica do Sapato; ⏰ 11pm-6am Thu-Sat) Hollywood actor John Malkovich helped bankroll this supercool club with its peacocking beauty crowd.

Discoteca Jamaica (Map pp670-1; Rua Nova do Carvalho; ⏰ 11pm-4am) Gay and straight, black and white, young and old – everyone has a soft spot for this offbeat club. It gets going around 2am at weekends with DJs pumping out reggae, hip hop and retro.

Cabaret Maxime (Map pp670-1; www.cabaret-maxime.com; Praça da Alegria 58) Young Lisboetas flock to this former strip club for DJ nights of old-school tunes, or loud, sweaty gigs of established and upcoming local bands.

Gay & Lesbian Venues

Lisbon has a relaxed yet flourishing gay scene, with an annual Gay Pride Festival in June. Visit www.portugalgay.pt for more on the scene.

Bar 106 (Map pp666-7; www.bar106.com; Rua de São Marçal 106) Young and fun with an upbeat, preclubbing vibe and crazy events such as Sunday's message party.

Bar Água No Bico (Map pp666-7; Rua de São Marçal 170) Cheery bar with art exhibitions, shows and music from jazz to chill-out.

Finalmente (Map pp670-1; Rua da Palmeira 38) This popular club has a tiny dance floor, nightly drag shows and wall-to-wall crowds.

Trumps (Map pp666-7; www.trumps.pt; Rua da Imprensa Nacional 104b) Lisbon's hottest gay club with cruisy corners, a sizeable dance floor and events from live music to drag.

Cinemas

Lisbon has dozens of cinemas, including the multiscreen **Amoreiras Cinema** (Map pp666-7; ☎ 213 810 200; Amoreiras Shopping Center, Avenida Eng Duarte Pacheco) and **Colombo Cinema** (Map pp666-7; ☎ 217 113 222, Centro Colombo, Avenida Lusíada), both located within shopping centres.

Sport

Lisbon's football teams are Benfica, Belenenses and Sporting. Euro 2004 led to the upgrading of the 65,000-seat Estádio da Luz and the construction of a new 54,000-seat Estádio Nacional. Bullfights are staged on Thursday from May to October at **Campo Pequeno** (Map pp666-7; ☎ 217 932 442; Avenida da República; tickets €10-75). Tickets for both sports are available at **ABEP ticket kiosk** (Map pp670-1; ☎ 213 475 824; Praça dos Restauradores).

SHOPPING

Shops in Lisbon are a mix of the classic and the wild, with antiques, stuck-in-time button and tinned-fish shops, and edgy boutiques all sprinkled across the hilly landscape. Rua Garrett and nearby Largo do Chiado, across Rua da Misericórdia, are home to some of Lisbon's oldest and most upscale boutiques. Meanwhile, Bairro Alto attracts vinyl lovers and vintage fans to its cluster of late-opening boutiques.

Armazéns do Chiado (Map pp670-1; Rua do Carmo 2) This shopping complex is artfully concealed behind the restored facade of the historic main department store. The FNAC here is good for books, music and booking concert tickets.

Outra Face da Lua (Map pp670-1; ☎ 218 863 430; Rua da Assunção 22) Vintage divas make for this retro boutique in Baixa, crammed with puffball dresses, lurex skirts, 1920s hats and a trunk full of old Barbie dolls. Jazz and electronica play overhead. Revive over tea at the in-store cafe.

Fábrica Sant'Ana (Map pp670-1; Rua do Alecrim 95) and **Santos Ofícios** (Map pp670-1; Rua da Madalena 87) are touristy but have an eclectic range of Portuguese folk art.

GETTING THERE & AWAY

Air

Portugal's national airline, TAP has frequent daily flights between Lisbon and Porto, Faro and many European cities; see p699.

Bus

Lisbon's new long-distance bus terminal is **Sete Rios** (Map pp666-7; Rua das Laranjeiras), conveniently linked to both Jardim Zoológico metro station and Sete Rios train station. From here the big carriers, **Rede Expressos** (☎ 213 581 460; www.rede-expressos.pt) and **Eva/Mundial Turismo** (☎ 213 581 466; www.eva-bus.com), run frequent services to almost every major town.

The other major terminal is **Gare do Oriente** (Map pp666–7), concentrating on services to the north and to Spain. The biggest companies operating from here are **Renex** (☎ 218 956 836; www.renex.pt) and the Spanish operator **Avanza** (☎ 218 940 250; www.avanz abus.com).

Train

Santa Apolónia station (Map pp670-1; ☎ 808 208 208) is the terminus for northern and central Portugal. You can catch trains from Santa

Apolónia to Gare do Oriente train station (Map pp666–7), which has departures to the Algarve and international destinations. Cais do Sodré station (Map pp670–1) is for Belém, Cascais and Estoril. Newly reopened Rossio station (Map pp670–1) is the terminal to Sintra via Queluz.

For fares and schedules visit www.cp.pt. For more detailed information on all the above modes of transport see p699.

GETTING AROUND

To/From the airport

The AeroBus (91) runs every 20 minutes from 7.45am to 8.15pm, taking 30 to 45 minutes between the airport and Cais do Sodré; buy your ticket (€3.35) on the bus. A taxi into town is about €10, plus €1.60 for luggage.

Car & Motorcycle

On the outskirts of the city there are cheap (or free) car parks near Parque das Nações or Belém. The most central underground car park is at Praça dos Restauradores, costing around €10 to €12 per day. On Saturday afternoons and Sunday, parking is normally free in the pay-and-display areas in the centre.

Public Transport

A one-day Bilhete Carris/Metro (€3.70) gives unlimited travel on all buses, trams, metros and funiculars. Pick it up from Carris kiosks and metro stations. The Lisboa Card is good for unlimited travel on nearly all city transport (see p665).

BUS, TRAM & FUNICULAR

Buses and trams run from 6am to 1am, with a few all-night services. Pick up a transport map from tourist offices or Carris kiosks. A single ticket costs €1.35 on board or €0.81 if you buy a *bilhete único de coroa* (BUC; a one-zone city-centre ticket) beforehand. These prepaid tickets are sold at Carris kiosks – most conveniently at Praça da Figueira, at the foot of the Elevador de Santa Justa.

Don't leave the city without riding tram 28 from Largo Martim Moniz or tram 12 from Praça da Figueira through the narrow streets of the Alfama.

There are three funiculars: Elevador da Bica (Map pp670–1), Elevador da Glória (Map pp670–1) and Elevador do Lavra (Map pp670–1).

FERRY

Car, bicycle and passenger ferries leave frequently from the Cais do Sodré ferry terminal (Map pp670–1) to Cacilhas (€0.81, 10 minutes), a transfer point for some buses to Setúbal. From Terreiro do Paço terminal catamarans zip across to Montijo (€2.10, every 30 minutes) and Seixal (€1.75, every 30 minutes).

METRO

The **metro** (www.metrolisboa.pt; 1-zone single/return €1.25/1.55, 2-zone single/return €1.95/2.45; 6.30am-1am) is useful for hops across town and to the Parque das Nações. Buy a *caderneta* (10-ticket booklet; 1-/2-zone caderneta €7.40/10.35) if you'll be using the metro often.

Taxi

Lisbon's taxis are metered and best hired from taxi ranks. Beware of rip-offs from the airport. From the Rossio to Belém is around €8 and to the castle about €6. To call one, try **Rádio Táxis** (☎ 218 119 000) or **Autocoope** (☎ 217 932 756).

AROUND LISBON

SINTRA

pop 26,400

Lord Byron called this hilltop town a 'glorious Eden' and, although best appreciated at dusk when the coach tours have left, it *is* a magnificent place. Less than an hour west of Lisbon, Sintra was the traditional summer retreat of Portugal's kings. Today it's a fairy-tale setting of stunning palaces and manors surrounded by rolling green countryside.

The **tourist office** (☎ 219 231 157; www.cm-sintra.pt; Praça da República 23; 9am-7pm) has useful maps and can help with accommodation.

Sights & Activities

Although the whole town resembles a historical theme park, there are several compulsory eye-catching sights. Most are free or discounted with the Lisboa Card (see p665).

The **Palácio Nacional de Sintra** (☎ 219 106 840; Largo Rainha Dona Amélia; adult/child €5/2; 10am-5.30pm Thu-Tue) is a dizzy mix of Moorish and Gothic architecture with twin chimneys that dominate the town.

The world-class **Museu de Arte Moderna** (☎ 219 248 170; www.berardocollection.com; Avenida Heliodoro Salgado; admission €3; 10am-6pm Tue-Sun) hosts rotating exhibitions covering the entire modern-art spectrum, from kinetic and pop art to surrealism and expressionism.

An energetic, 3km greenery-flanked hike from the centre, the 8th-century ruined ramparts of **Castelo dos Mouros** (☎ 219 107 970; adult/child €5/3; ⌚ 10am-6pm mid-Sep–Apr, to 8pm May–mid-Sep) provide fine views.

Trudge on a further 20 minutes to the exuberantly kitsch **Palácio da Pena** (☎ 219 105 340; adult/child €6/4; ⌚ 10am-6.30pm Tue-Sun Apr-Oct, to 5pm Nov-May), where every room is crammed with fascinating treasures.

Monserrate Gardens (☎ 219 237 116; www.parquedesintra.pt; adult/child €5/3; ⌚ 9am-7pm Oct-May, 9am-8pm Jun-Sep) are fabulously lush botanical gardens 4km from town. A manicured lawn sweeps up to the whimsical, Moorish-inspired **palácio** (⌚ guided visits 10am-1pm & 2-6.30pm), the 19th-century romantic folly of English millionaire Sir Francis Cook. Visits are by 90-minute guided tour; reservations are essential.

En route to the gardens is **Quinta da Regaleira** ☎ 219 106 650; Rua Barbosa du Bocage; adult/child €6/3; ⌚ 10am-8pm Apr-Sep, to 6.30pm Feb, Mar & Oct, to 5.30pm Nov-Jan), a magnificent World Heritage site and, as an early-20th-century neo-Manueline extravaganza, one of Sintra's highlights.

Cabra Montêz (☎ 917 446 668; Rua D Mafalda, Belas; www.cabramontez.com) arranges all kinds of adventurous pursuits including trekking, rafting and canyoning trips.

Sleeping

Casa de Hóspedes Dona Maria da Parreirinha (☎ 219 232 490; Rua João de Deus 12-14; d €40-45) This small, homely guest house is run by a charming elderly couple. The doubles here are old-fashioned but spotless, with big windows, dark-wood furnishings and floral fabrics.

Villa Marques (☎ 219 230 027; www.vilamarques.net; Rua Sotto Mayor 1; s/d with private bathroom €50/60, with shared bathroom €35/50) Fabulous tiled pictures adorn this traditional manor house with its grand staircase, grandmotherly rooms and an outside terrace that has views of the duck pond and countryside beyond.

Lawrence's Hotel (☎ 219 105 500; www.lawrenceshotel.com; Rua Consiglieri Pedroso 38-40; s/d €130/180; ❄ 💻) Lord Byron once stayed at this 18th-century mansion turned boutique hotel. Lawrence's oozes charm in its lantern-lit, vaulted corridors, snug bar and individually designed rooms, decorated with *azulejos* and antique trunks. Lawrence's has an excellent restaurant.

Eating & Drinking

Binhoteca (☎ 219 240 849; Rua das Padarias 16; tapas €2-14) Jazzy music and exposed stone set the scene at this glam wine and tapas bar, serving Portugal's finest, from full-bodied Douros to woody Madeira whites.

Café de Paris (☎ 219 232 375; Praça da República 40; mains €6-14) Enjoy such lush grub as rocket salad with cheese, figs and nuts in this sublime 18th-century setting, complete with nymphette ceiling mural and outside terrace overlooking the main square.

Tulhas (☎ 219 232 378; Rua Gil Vicente 4; mains €9-14; ⌚ closed Wed) This converted grain warehouse is dark, tiled and quaint, with twisted chandeliers and a relaxed, cosy atmosphere. It's renowned for its *bacalhau com natas* (shredded cod with cream and potato).

Getting There & Away

The Lisbon–Sintra railway terminates in Estefânia, a 1.5km scenic walk northeast of the town's historic centre. Sintra's bus station, and another train station, are a further 1km east in the new town Portela de Sintra. Frequent shuttle buses link the historic centre with the bus station.

Train services (€1.70, 40 minutes, every 15 minutes) run between Sintra and Lisbon's Rossio station. Buses run regularly from Sintra to Cascais (€3.35, 60 minutes), Estoril (€3.35, 40 minutes) and Mafra (45 minutes).

Getting Around

It's worth buying the Scotturb *Bilhete Diário Circuito da Pena* (€4.50), a hop-on, hop-off day pass for bus 434, which runs from the train station via Sintra-Vila to Castelo dos Mouros, Palácio da Pena and back. It operates every 15 minutes from 9.15am to 7.50pm.

A taxi to Pena or Monserrate costs around €16 return.

CASCAIS

pop 33,400

Cascais is a handsome seaside resort with elegant buildings, an atmospheric Old Town and a happy abundance of bars and restaurants.

The **tourist office** (☎ 214 868 204; www.visiteestoril.com; Rua Visconde de Luz 14; 9am-7pm Mon-Sat, 10am-6pm Sun) can provide accommodation lists and bus timetables.

Sights & Activities

Cascais' three sandy bays – **Praia da Conceição**, **Praia da Rainha** and **Praia da Ribeira** – are great for a sunbake or a tingly Atlantic dip, but attract crowds in summer.

Amid the picturesque gardens of **Parque Marechal Carmona** (Avenida Rei Humberto II) is the **Museu Condes de Castro Guimarães** (☎ 214 815 304; admission €1.80; 10am-5pm Tue-Sun), a whimsical early-19th-century mansion, complete with castle turrets and Arabic cloister.

Estoril is a somewhat faded resort 2km east of Cascais with a popular sandy beach and Europe's largest **casino** (☎ 214 667 700; www.casino-estoril.pt, in Portuguese; 3pm-3am, floor show 11pm).

The sea roars into the coast at **Boca do Inferno** (Hell's Mouth), 2km west of Cascais. Spectacular **Cabo da Roca**, Europe's westernmost point, is 16km from Cascais and Sintra and is served by buses from both towns.

Wild **Guincho** beach, 3km from Cascais, is a popular surfing spot.

Sleeping & Eating

Cascais Beach Hostel (☎ 309 906 421; www.cascaisbeachostel.com; Rua da Vista Alegre 10; dm/d €20/49;) This funky newcomer is central for Cascais' beaches and nightlife. Dorms and doubles sport shiny wooden floors and citrus hues. There's a lounge, bike rental, free wi-fi and a small pool in the garden.

Residencial Solar Dom Carlos (☎ 214 828 115; www.solardomcarlos.com; Rua Latino Coelho 104; s/d €55/70;) Hidden down a sleepy alley, this 16th-century former royal residence turned guest house retains lots of original features, from chandeliers to wood beams, *azulejos* and a frescoed breakfast room.

Apeadeiro (☎ 214 832 731; Avenida Vasco da Gama 252; mains €6.50-11) With walls hung with fishing nets, this sunny restaurant is known for its superb chargrilled fish – shrimp *piri-piri* is delicious.

Getting There & Around

Trains run frequently to Cascais via Estoril (€1.70, 40 minutes) from Cais do Sodré station in Lisbon. **Transrent** (☎ 214 864 566; www.transrent.pt; Centro Commercial Cisne, Avenida Marginal) rents cars, bicycles and motorcycles.

SETÚBAL

pop 115,000

Unsurprisingly, Portugal's third-largest port is famous for its excellent seafood restaurants. Other draws are a stunning Manueline church, a castle with views and an easygoing pedestrianised centre packed with shops and cafes. Setúbal is also a fine base for exploring the aquatic wonders of the Sado estuary

Information

Instituto Português da Juventude (IPJ; ☎ 265 534 431; Largo José Afonso; 9am-5pm Mon-Fri) Has free internet access for a maximum of 30 minutes.

Regional tourist office (☎ 265 539 130; www.mun-setubal.pt, www.costa-azul.rts.pt; Travessa Frei Gaspar 10) With the oddity of a Roman fish-preserving factory under its glass floor.

Sights & Activities

Portugal's first Manueline building, the stunning **Igreja de Jesus** (Praça Miguel Bombarda; admission free; 9am-1pm & 2-5pm Tue-Sun), has maritime motifs and twisted pillars that resemble coiled ropes. The **Galeria da Pintura Quinhentista** (Rua do Balneã Rio Paula Borba; admission €1.10; 9am-noon & 2-5pm Tue-Sat), just around the corner, has a renowned collection of 16th-century paintings.

Worth the 500m schlep west uphill, the 16th-century **Castelo São Filipe** (7am-10pm) has precipitous views over town and coast. The castle was converted into a *pousada* (hotel run by the government) in the '60s. Its outdoor restaurant makes a great spot for a sundowner.

Good **beaches** west of town include Praia da Figuerinha (accessible by bus in summer). Across the estuary at Tróia is a more developed beach, plus the ruins of a Roman settlement. On the ferry trip across you may see some of the estuary's 30 or so bottle-nosed dolphins.

SAL (☎ 265 227 685; www.sal.pt, in Portuguese) organises walks from €6 per person. For jeep safaris, hiking and biking in the Serra da Arrábida, or canoe trips through the Reserva Natural do Estuário do Sado, contact **Planeta Terra** (☎ 919 471 871; www.planetaterra.pt; Praça General Luís Domingues 9). **Vertigem Azul** (☎ 265 238 000; www.vertigemazul.com; Avenida Luísa Todi 375) offers canoe and dolphin-spotting excursions. There are wine-cellar tours of **José Maria da Fonseca** (☎ 212 198 940; www.jmf.pt; Rua José Augusto Coelho 11; per person €2.50-3.50; 10am-12.30pm & 2-5pm Mon-Fri), the oldest Portuguese producer of table wine.

Sleeping

Pousada da Juventude (☎ 265 534 431; setubal@movijovem.pt; Largo José Afonso; dm/d €10/32) Adequate tidy hostel with a buzzy vibe. It has an 11pm curfew.

Residencial Bocage (☎ 265 543 080; www.residencialbocage.pt; Rua de São Cristóvão 14; s/d incl breakfast €38/50; ❄) Decorated in earthy hues with striped curtains, the recently renovated rooms here sport parquet floors, comfy beds and squeaky-clean bathrooms.

Albergaria Solaris (☎ 265 541 770; albergaria.solaris@netc.pt; Praça Marquês de Pombal 12; s/d €50/60; ❄ 💻) Overlooking a lively square, Solaris is a small and friendly option. Though rooms are plain and corporate, they're well kept.

Eating

Casa Santiago (☎ 265 221 688; Avenida Luísa Todi 92; mains €7-12; 🕐 Mon-Sat) Wafts of fish sizzling on the grill will reel you into this local favourite, where the hungry lunchtime crowds feast on huge portions of *choco frito* (fried cuttlefish).

Solar do Lago (☎ 265 238 847; Parque das Escolas 40; mains €7.50-15) This high-ceilinged restaurant exudes rustic charm with its chunky wooden tables and terracotta tiles. Tasty seafood dishes include garlicky *caldeirada* and grilled squid.

Xica Bia (☎ 265 522 559; Avenida Luisa Todi 131; mains from €9-12) Xica Bia has an elegant dinner-for-two setting with barrel-vault ceiling, exposed bricks and chandeliers. The menu includes plenty of thrills, including an exemplary *arroz de marisco* (shellfish rice).

Getting There & Away

Buses leave at least hourly from Lisbon's Praça de Espanha (€4, one hour). Ferries shuttle across the estuary to Tróia approximately every 45 minutes (€1.30, 15 minutes).

THE ALGARVE

Love it or loathe it, it's easy to see the allure of the Algarve: breathtaking cliffs, golden sands, scalloped bays and long sandy islands. Although overdevelopment has blighted parts of the coast, head inland and you'll land solidly in lovely Portuguese countryside once again. Algarve highlights include the forested slopes of Monchique, pretty riverside town of Tavira and windswept, historic Sagres. Underrated Faro is the regional capital.

FARO

pop 58,000

Faro is an attractive seaside town and makes a good place from which to explore the rest of this coastal strip. It has an attractive marina, well-maintained parks and plazas and a historic Old Town full of pedestrian lanes and outdoor cafes.

Go online at **Café Aliança** (Rua Dr Francisco Gomes; per hr €2.50; 🕐 10am-11.45pm). The central **tourist office** (☎ 289 803 604; www.cm-faro.pt; Rua da Misericórdia) has informative leaflets and maps.

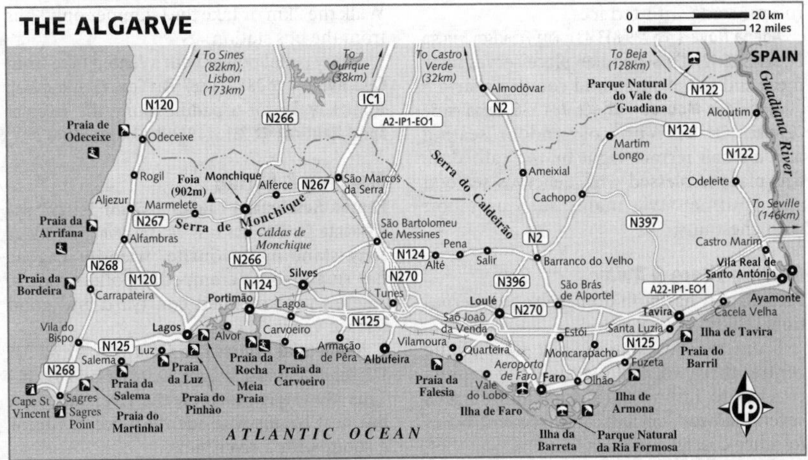

Sights & Activities

An intriguing place to wander is inside the picturesque **Cidade Velha** (Old Town), with its winding, peaceful cobbled streets and squares. The palm-clad **waterfront** around Praça de Dom Francisco Gomes has pleasant kick-back cafes. Faro's beach, **Praia de Faro** (Ilha de Faro), is 6km southwest of the city; take bus 16 from opposite the bus station. Less crowded is the unspoilt Ilha Deserta, reachable by ferry.

For visits to the **Parque Natural da Ria Formosa**, sign up for a boating or birdwatching tour with the environmentally friendly outfits of **Ria Formosa** (☎ 289 817 466; www.formosamar.pt) and **Lands** (☎ 967073846; www.lands.pt), both in the Clube Naval in Faro's marina.

Sleeping & Eating

Pousada da Juventude (☎ 289 826 521; www.pousadasjuventude.pt; Rua da Polícia de Segurança Pública 1; dm incl breakfast €13, d incl breakfast with shared/private bathroom €30/38; reception 24hr) Adjoining a small park, this hostel offers basic, clean rooms with no frills but is a good ultrabudget option.

Residencial Dandy (☎ 289 824 791; Rua Filipe Alistão 62; d with shared/private bathroom from €40/50) Plastic flowers, African masks and museum-style paraphernalia are features of this rambling place. The best rooms have antique furniture, high ceilings and wrought-iron balconies. Smaller, tile-floored rooms are in back.

Residencial Adelaide (☎ 289 802 383; www.adelaideresidencial.com; Rua Cruz dos Mestres 7; s/d incl breakfast €45/50;) This modern and pleasant guest house is good value for its clean and light rooms, some with terraces.

Adega Nova (☎ 289 813 433; Rua Francisco Barreto 24; mains €6-12) This popular place serves tasty meat and fish dishes amid country charm.

Mesa dos Mouros (☎ 966 784 536; Largo da Sé 10; mains €11-18) With cosy indoor seating and a small terrace right by the cathedral, this place is blessed with delicious seafood and gourmet-style mains such as rabbit with chestnuts.

Getting There & Away

Faro airport has both domestic and international flights (see p699).

From the bus station, just west of the centre, there are at least six daily express coaches to Lisbon (€18, four hours), plus several slower services, and frequent buses to other coastal towns.

The train station is a few minutes' walk west of the bus station. Five trains run daily to Lisbon (€20, four hours).

Getting Around

The airport is 6km from the centre. Buses 14 and 16 (€1.55) run into town until 9pm. A taxi costs about €12 from the airport to the town centre. From May to September, five ferries a day run from to/from Ilha Deserta (€5 one way).

TAVIRA

pop 12,600

Set on either side of the meandering Rio Gilão, Tavira is a charming town. The ruins of a hilltop castle, an old Roman bridge and a smattering of Gothic and Renaissance churches are among the historic attractions. The **tourist office** (☎ 281 322 511; Rua da Galeria 9) can help with accommodation and the **town hall** (Praça da Republica; 9am-9pm Mon-Fri, 10am-1pm Sat) provides free internet access.

Sights & Activities

One of the town's 30-plus churches, the 16th-century **Igreja da Misericórdia** (Rua da Galeria) is among the most striking in the Algarve. Tavira's ruined **castle** (Rua da Liberdade; admission free; 9am-5pm Mon-Fri, 10am-5pm Sat & Sun) dominates the town. Nearby, the 16th-century **Palácio da Galeria** (☎ 281 320 540; Calçada da Galeria; admission €2; 10am-noon & 4-7.30pm Tue-Sat) holds occasional exhibitions.

Ilha da Tavira is an island beach connected to the mainland by a ferry at Quatro Águas. Walk the 2km or take the (summer only) bus from the bus station.

Enjoy pedal power with a rented bike from **Casa Abilio** (☎ 281 323 467; Rua Goao Vaz C Real 23a). Rent kayaks for a paddle along the river at **Sport Nautica** (☎ 281 324 943; Rua Jacques Pessoa 26).

Sleeping & Eating

Pensão Residencial Lagôas (☎ 281 322 252; Rua Almirante Cândido dos Reis 24; s/d from €20/30) A long-standing favourite, friendly Lagôas has small (some cramped), spotless rooms. There's a plant-filled courtyard and good terrace views.

Residencial Princesa do Gilão (☎/fax 281 325 171; Rua Borda d'Água de Aguiar 10; s/d/tr €45/55/65;) This '80s-style place on the river has tight but neat rooms with identical decor. Go for a room with a river view.

Pensão Residencial Castelo (☎ 281 320 790; fax 281 320 799; Rua da Liberdade 22; s/d & apt €50/70;) Castelo offers nicely furnished rooms with spotless tile floors. Some also have balconies and castle views, and there is wheelchair access.

Restaurante Bica (☎ 281 323 843; Rua Almirante Cândido dos Reis 24; mains €6-16) Deservedly popular, Bica serves splendid food, such as fresh grilled fish, which diners enjoy with inexpensive but decent Borba wine.

Bistro 'oPorto' (☎ 968 991 401; Rua Dr José Pires Padinha 180; mains €9.50-13.50; Tue-Sat) An intimate bar and a pleasant riverside setting make for an enjoyable time at this French-owned spot. The menu is varied – think samosas to *bacalhau*.

Getting There & Away

Some 15 trains and six express buses run daily between Faro and Tavira (€3, one hour).

LAGOS

pop 25,400

In summer the pretty fishing port of Lagos has a party vibe; its picturesque cobbled streets and pretty nearby beaches pack with revellers and sunseekers. The municipal **tourist office** (☎ 282 764 111; www.lagosdigital.com, in Portuguese; Largo Marquês de Pombal) is in the centre of town. Sip coffee while emailing at cool **Café Gélibar** (Rua Lançarote de Freitas 43a; per hr €3; 9am-11pm Mon-Sat, to 8pm Sun).

Sights & Activities

The **Museu Municipal** (☎ 282 762 301; Rua General Alberto da Silveira; admission €2; 9.30am-12.30pm & 2-5pm Tue-Sun) houses an eclectic mix of archaeological and ecclesiastical treasures (and oddities). Admission includes the adjacent **Igreja de Santo António** (9.30am-12.30pm & 2-5pm Tue-Sun), one of the best baroque churches in Portugal.

The beach scene includes **Meia Praia**, a vast strip to the east; **Praia da Luz** to the west; and the smaller **Praia do Pinhão**.

Blue Ocean (☎ 964 665 667; www.blue-ocean-divers.de) organises diving, kayaking and snorkelling safaris. On the promenade, fishermen offer motorboat jaunts to nearby grottoes. **Kayak Adventures** (☎ 913 262 200) offers kayaking trips. Rent windsurfing gear from **Windsurf Point** (☎ 282 792 315, www.windsurfpoint.com).

Sleeping

Pousada da Juventude (☎ 282 761 970; www.pousadasjuventude.pt; Rua Lançarote de Freitas 50; dm €16, d with shared/private bathroom €35/43; 24hr;) One of Portugal's best, this well-run hostel is a great place to meet other travellers.

Pensâo Marazul (☎ 282 770 230; www.pensaomarazul.com; Rua 25 de Abril 13; s/d with shared bathroom €40/50;) Draws a good mix of foreign travellers to its small but cheerfully painted rooms – the best of which offer sea views.

Cidade Velha (☎ 282 762 041; www.cidadevelha.info; Rua Dr Joaquim Tello 7; s/d/tr from €45/65/75;) This friendly, welcoming guest house offers light, airy and tidy rooms with tile floors and balconies.

Eating

A Forja (☎ 282 768 588; Rua dos Ferreiros 17; mains €6.50-14; closed Sat) This buzzing place pulls in the crowds for its hearty, top-quality traditional food. Plates of the day are always reliable, as are the fish dishes.

Casinha do Petisco (☎ 282 084 285; Rua da Oliveira 51; mains €6.90-12; Mon-Sat) This tiny traditional gem comes highly recommended by locals for its seafood grills and shellfish dishes.

Meu Limão (☎ 282 767 946; Rua Silva Lopes 40; mains €8.50-12.50) This handsome tapas bar has a trendy feel, a smart crowd and a postcard view of Igreja de Santo António from the outdoor tables. There's delectable tapas on offer and heartier plates plus good wines.

Getting There & Away

Bus and train services depart frequently for other Algarve towns, and around eight times daily to Lisbon (€25, four hours).

Getting Around

A new **bus service** (one-way €1.30, 7am-8pm Mon-Sat, to 2pm Sun) provides useful connections around town, as well as to the beaches of Meia Praia and Luz. Rent bicycles and motorbikes from **Motorent** (☎ 289 769 716; www.motorent.pt; Rua Victor Costa e Silva; bike/motorcycle per day from €10/50).

MONCHIQUE

pop 6980

High above the coast, in cooler mountainous woodlands, the picturesque hamlet of Monchique makes a lovely base for exploring, with some excellent options for walking, biking or canoeing. The **tourist office** (☎ 282

911 189; Largo de São Sebastião; 9.30am-1pm & 2-5.30pm Mon-Fri) is uphill from the bus stop.

Sights & Activities

Igreja Matriz (Rua da Igreja) features a stunning Manueline portal, with its stone seemingly tied in knots. Keep climbing to reach the ruins of the 17th-century Franciscan monastery, **Nossa Senhora do Desterro**, which overlooks the town from its wooded hilltop.

Caldas de Monchique, 6km south, is a peaceful hamlet with a **spa resort** (www.monchiquetermas.com). Some 8km west is the Algarve's 'rooftop', the 902m **Fóia** peak atop the Serra de Monchique, with heady views through a forest of radio masts.

Outdoor Tours (282 969 520, 916 736 226; www.outdoor-tours.com; Mexilhoeira Grande; trips from €20) offers biking, kayaking and walking trips.

Sleeping & Eating

Residencial Miradouro Da Serra (282 912 163; Rua Combatentes do Ultramar; s/d €35/50) This 1970s hilltop place offers sweeping, breezy views and neat rooms, some with balcony.

A Charrete (282 912 142; Rua Dr Samora Gil 30-34; mains €7.50-13) Touted as the town's best eatery for its regional specialities, this place serves reliably good cuisine amid country rustic charm.

Getting There & Away

There are five to nine buses daily from Portimão (€2.80, 45 minutes) to Monchique.

SILVES

pop 10,800

The one-time capital of Moorish Algarve, Silves is a pretty town of jumbling orange rooftops scattered above the banks of the Rio Arade. Clamber around the ramparts of its fairy-tale castle for superb views. The **tourist office** (289 442 255; www.cm-silves.pt; Rua 25 de Abril) can help with accommodation. Get online at **It-Connect** (Rua Pintor Bernardo Marques; per hr €1.50).

Sleeping & Eating

Residencial Ponte Romana (282 443 275; Horta da Cruz; s/d €20/30) Floral-themed rooms beside the Roman bridge, with castle views and a cavernous bar-restaurant full of old-timers in flat caps and Portuguese families.

Quinta da Figueirinha (282 440 700; www.qdf.pt; 2-/4-/6-person apt €62/90/122;) Four kilometres outside of Silves, this 36-hectare organic farm offers simple apartments in idyllic farmlike surroundings.

Café Ingles (282 442 585; mains €7-14) Situated at the castle entrance, this English-owned funky place has vegetarian dishes, homemade soups, pasta and wood-fired pizza. In summer there's live music at weekends.

Getting There & Away

Silves train station is 2km from town; trains from Lagos (€2.10, 35 minutes) stop nine times daily (from Faro, change at Tunes), to be met by local buses. Eight buses run daily to Silves from Albufeira (€3.60, 40 minutes).

SAGRES

pop 1940

The small, elongated village of Sagres has an end-of-the-world feel with its sea-carved cliffs and empty, wind-whipped fortress high above the ocean. There is a central **tourist office** (282 624 873; Rua Comandante Matoso; Tue-Sat).

Sights & Activities

The **fort** (adult/child €3/1.50; 10am-8.30pm May-Sep, to 6.30pm Oct-Apr) offers breathtaking views over the seaside cliffs; according to legend, this is where Henry the Navigator established his navigation school and primed the early Portuguese explorers.

Visit Europe's southwestern-most point, the **Cabo de São Vicente** (Cape St Vincent), 6km to the west. A solitary lighthouse stands on this barren cape.

This coast is ideal for surfing; hire windsurfing gear at sand-dune fringed **Praia do Martinhal**. You can sign up for surfing lessons, hire bikes and arrange canoe trips with **Sagres Natura** (282 624 072; www.sagresnatura.com; Rua São Vicente).

DiversCape (965 559 073; www.diverscape.com; Porto da Baleeira) organises diving trips.

Sleeping & Eating

Casa do Cabo de Santa Maria (282 624 722; casacabosantamaria@sapo.pt; Rua Patrão António Faústino; r/apt from €50/60) These squeaky-clean rooms and apartments might not have sweeping views, but they are handsome and nicely furnished.

A Tasca (282 624 177; Porto da Baleeira; dishes €7-23) Overlooking the marina, this cosy place whips up tasty *cataplana* and other seafood dishes, best enjoyed on the sunny terrace.

Getting There & Away

Frequent buses run daily to Sagres from Lagos (€3.40, one hour), with fewer on Sunday. Three continue out to Cabo de São Vicente on weekdays.

CENTRAL PORTUGAL

The vast centre of Portugal is a rugged swath of rolling hillsides, whitewashed villages and olive groves and cork trees. Richly historic, it is scattered with prehistoric remains and medieval castles. It's also home to one of Portugal's most architecturally rich towns, Évora, as well as several spectacular walled villages. There are fine local wines and, for the more energetic, plenty of outdoor exploring in the dramatic Beiras region.

ÉVORA

pop 56,500

Évora is an enchanting place to delve into the past. Inside the 14th-century walls, Évora's narrow, winding lanes lead to a striking medieval cathedral, a Roman temple, and a picturesque town square. These old-fashioned good looks are the backdrop to a lively student town surrounded by wineries and dramatic countryside. The **tourist office** (☎ 266 777 071; www.cm-evora.pt, in Portuguese; Praça do Giraldo 73) has an excellent city map. Log on at the **Câmara Municipal** (town hall; 9am-12.30pm & 2-5pm Mon-Fri), which has free internet.

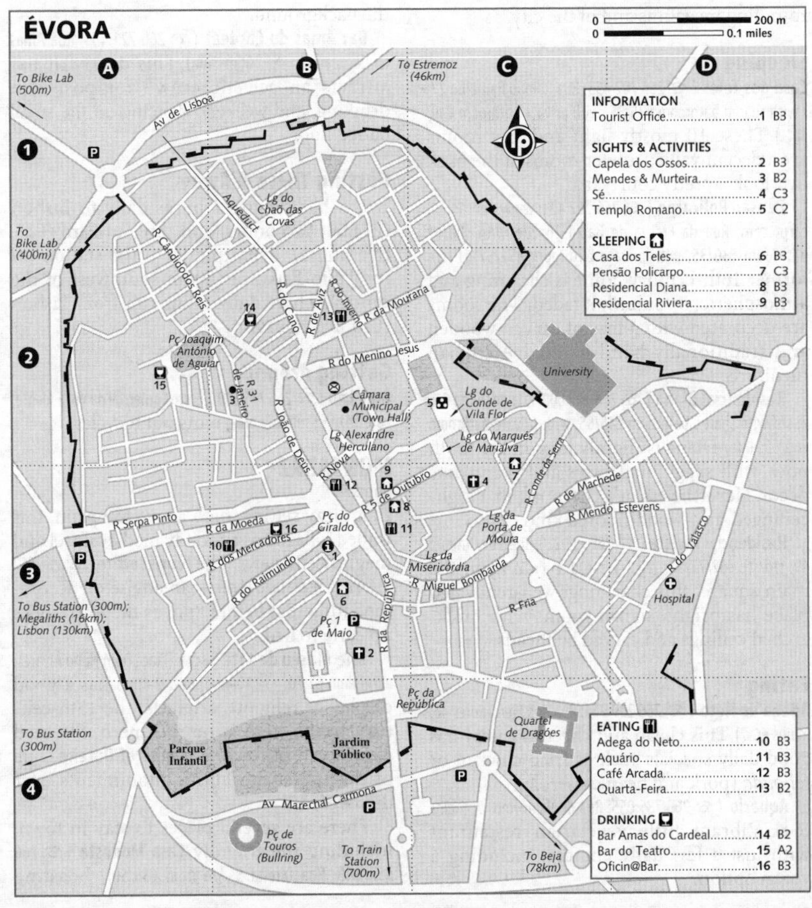

PORTUGAL

Sights & Activities

Évora's cathedral, **Sé** (Largo do Marquês de Marialva; adult/child €1/free; 9am-noon & 2-5pm), has fabulous cloisters and a museum jam-packed with ecclesiastical treasures.

The **Templo Romano** (Temple of Diana; Largo do Conde de Vila Flor) was once part of the Roman Forum; it's a heady slice of drama right in town.

Capela dos Ossos (266 744 307; Praça 1 de Maio; admission €1.50; 9am-1pm & 2.30-6pm) provides a real *Addams Family* day out. This ghoulish Chapel of Bones is constructed from the bones and skulls of several thousand people.

Tours

Mendes & Murteira (266 739 240; www.evora-mm.pt; Rua 31 de Janeiro 15a) offers half-day tours of surrounding megaliths and of the city.

Sleeping

Casa dos Teles (266 702 453; Rua Romão Ramalho 27; r with shared bathroom €25-35, with private bathroom €40;) These 10 mostly light and airy rooms are a decent value; quieter rooms at the back overlook a pretty courtyard.

Pensão Policarpo (266 702 424; www.pensaopolicarpo.com; Rua da Freiria de Baixo 16; s/d with shared bathroom €30/35, with private bathroom €52/57) This former 16th-century home is charming and atmospheric, if somewhat faded. The rooms are decorated with a mix of carved wooden and traditionally hand-painted Alentejan furniture.

Residencial Diana (266 702 008; Rua de Diogo Cão 2; s/d with shared bathroom €45/55, with private bathroom €60/65;) Diana is slightly long in the tooth now, with saggy mattresses and grannylike decor. Nevertheless, it's charming in a high-ceilinged-and-wood-floored kind of way.

Residencial Riviera (266 737 210; Rua 5 de Outubro 49; s/d/ste €62/77/92;) Just a block from the main square, this charming, well-renovated place has bright, stylish rooms with brick-arched ceilings and carved bedheads.

Eating

Adega do Neto (266 209 916; Rua dos Mercadores 46; mains €6-7) This cheap and cheerful eatery has good daily specials such as fried chicken or *feijoada* (pork and bean casserole).

Aquário (266 785 055; Rua de Valdevinos 7; mains €6-8) Vibrant little vegetarian restaurant with just a few daily choices, including a vegan option.

Café Arcada (Praça do Giraldo 10; meals €6.50-10; breakfast, lunch & dinner) An Évora institution, serving up coffee, crêpes and cakes, with outdoor tables on the plaza.

Quarta-Feira (266 707 530; Rua do Inverno 16; mains €12-20; closed Sun) Well hidden in the Moorish quarter, this jovial place serves hearty home cooking with an emphasis on game and *bacalhau.*

Drinking

Bar do Teatro (Praça Joaquim António de Aguiar; 8pm-2am) This small, inviting bar has high ceilings and old-world decor that sees a friendly mixed crowd.

Oficin@Bar (Rua da Moeda 27; 8pm-2am Mon-Sat) Attracting all ages, this is a small, relaxed bar with jazz and blues playing in the background.

Bar Amas do Cardeal (266 721 133; Rua Amas do Cardeal 4a; 10pm-3am) This darkly lit bar attracts an eclectic crowd for post-1am drinking, and weekend dancing on the small dance floor.

Getting There & Away

Évora has six to 12 buses daily to Lisbon (€11.50, two hours) and three to Faro (€15, five hours), departing from the station off Av Túlio Espanca (700m southwest of the centre). Three daily trains run from Lisbon (€10, 2½ hours).

Getting Around

Bike Lab (266 735 500; Centro Comercial da Vista Alegre, Lote 14; summer only) rents out bicycles.

MONSARAZ

pop 980

In a dizzy setting, high above the plain, this walled village has a moody medieval feel and magnificent views. The **tourist office** (266 557 136; Praça Dom Nuno Álvares) can advise on accommodation. Eat before 8pm as the town tucks up early to bed.

The **Museu de Arte Sacra** (Plaça Dom Nuno Álvares; admission €1.70; 10am-1pm & 2-6pm) has a good display of religious artefacts; the 15th-century fresco here is quite superb. Situated 3km north of town is **Menhir of Outeiro**, one of the tallest megalithic monuments ever discovered.

There are several places to stay in town, including the friendly **Casa Modesta** (266 557 388; Rua Direita 5; s/d from €35/50), boasting rooms with high ceilings and traditional hand-painted furniture.

Up to four buses per day connect Monsaraz with Reguengos de Monsaraz (€2.50, 35 minutes, Monday to Friday), with connections to Évora.

ESTREMOZ

pop 15,400

One of three marble towns in these parts, Estremoz has an attractive centre set with peaceful plazas, orange tree-lined lanes and a hilltop castle and convent. In its prime, the town was one of the most strongly fortified in Portugal with its very own palace (now a luxurious *pousada;* upmarket inn). The **tourist office** (☎ 268 339 200; www.cm-estremoz.pt, in Portuguese; Largo da República 26) is just south of Rossio.

Sights

Museu Municipal (☎ 268 339 200; Largo D Dinis; adult/child €1.50/free; 9am-12.30pm & 2-5.30pm Tue-Sun), in a beautiful 17th-century almshouse, specialises in fascinating pottery figurines, including an entire Easter parade.

Vila Viçosa, another marble town 17km from Estremoz, is home to the magnificent **Palácio Ducal** (☎ 268 980 659; Terreiro do Paça; adult/child €5/free, armoury museum €2.50; 9am-1pm & 3-5.30pm Tue-Sun), the ancestral home of the dukes of Bragança. It's rich with *azulejos*, frescoed ceilings and elaborate tapestries.

Sleeping & Eating

Residencial O Gadanha (☎ 268 339 110; www.residencialogadanha.com; Largo General Graça 56; s/d/tr €20/33/43;) This whitewashed house offers excellent value for its bright, fresh and clean rooms overlooking the square.

Café Alentejano (☎ 268 337 300; Rossio 13-15; s/d €25/40) A varied selection of ageing but characterful rooms above a handsome restaurant fronting the main square.

Adega do Isaías (☎ 268 322 318; Rua Almeida 21; mains €7.50-10) Amid wooden vats of wine, this award-winning *tasca* (tavern) grills up sizzling plates of fish, meat and Alentejan specialities.

Getting There & Away

Estremoz is linked to Évora by numerous local buses (€3.80, 1¼ hours) and two *expressos* (€7.80, 45 minutes), Monday to Saturday.

ÓBIDOS

pop 10,800

This exquisite walled village was a wedding gift from Dom Dinis to his wife Dona Isabel (beats a fondue set), and its historic centre is a delightful place to wander. Highlights include the **Igreja de Santa Maria** (Rua Direita), with fine *azulejos*, and views from the town walls. The **tourist office** (☎ 262 955 060; www.cm-obidos.pt, in Portuguese; Rua Direita) has a brochure of walks in the area and can advise on accommodation. Check your email for free at **Espaço Internet** (☎ 262 955 561; Rua Direita 107; 10am-7pm Mon-Fri, 11.30am-6.30pm Sat & Sun).

Sleeping & Eating

Óbido Sol (☎ 262 959 188; Rua Direita 40; d €40) This neatly kept Old Town house has cosy and comfortable rooms surrounding a snug living room.

Casa de São Thiago (☎ 262 959 587; www.casas-sthiago.com; Largo de São Thiago; s/d €65/80) This charming labyrinth of trim 18th-century rooms and flower-filled courtyards sits in the shadow of the castle.

Restaurante Alcaide (☎ 262 959 220; Rua Direita 60; mains €11-16) A classy place with countryside views and a menu of creative dishes like codfish with cheese, chestnuts and apple.

WORTH THE TRIP: CASTELO DE VIDE

A worthy detour north of Estremoz is the hilltop, story-book town **Castelo de Vide**, noted for its picturesque houses with Gothic doorways. Highlights are the **Judiaria** (Old Jewish Quarter), the medieval backstreets and (yet another) castle-top view. Try to spend a night here heading skywards to **Marvão**, a fabulous mountain-top walled village (population 190) 12km from Castelo de Vide. The **tourist offices** (Castelo de Vide ☎ 245 901 361; www.cm-castelo-vide.pt; Praça Dom Pedro V; Marvão ☎ 245 909 131; Largo de Santa Maria) can help with accommodation.

On weekdays, three buses run from Portalegre to Castelo de Vide (€5, 20 minutes) and two to Marvão (€4, 45 minutes). There are three buses connecting Estremoz and Portalegre (€5, one hour).

Getting There & Away

There are direct buses Monday to Friday from Lisbon (€7, 70 minutes) or via Caldas da Rainha, 10 minutes away.

NAZARÉ

pop 16,000

With a warren of narrow cobbled lanes running down to a wide cliff-backed beach, Nazaré is Estremadura's most picturesque coastal resort. The town centre is jammed with seafood restaurants, bars and local women in traditional dress hawking rooms for rent. The **tourist office** (☎ 262 561 194) is at the end of Av da República.

Sights & Activities

The **beaches** are superb, although swimmers should be aware of dangerous currents. Climb or take the funicular to the cliff-top **Sítio**, with its cluster of fishermen's cottages and great view.

Two of Portugal's big-time architectural masterpieces are close by. Follow the signs to **Alcobaça** where, right in the centre of town, is the immense **Mosteiro de Santa Maria de Alcobaça** (☎ 262 505 120; adult/child €5/2.50, church admission free; 9am-7pm, to 5pm winter) dating from 1178; don't miss the colossal former kitchen.

Batalha's massive Gothic **Mosteiro de Santa Maria de Vitória** (☎ 244 765 497; admission to cloisters & unfinished chapels adult/child €5/2.50; 9am-6pm, to 5pm winter), dating from 1388, is home to the tomb of Henry the Navigator.

Sleeping & Eating

Many townspeople rent out rooms; doubles start from €35. Check at the tourist office.

Vila Conde Fidalgo (☎ 262 552 361; http://condefidalgo.planetaclix.pt; Avenida da Independência Nacional 21a; 2-/4-person apt €45/75) This pretty little complex uphill a few blocks from the beach is built around a series of flower-filled courtyards. Rooms all have kitchenettes.

Residencial A Cubata (☎ 262 561 706; www.residencialcubata.com; Avenida da República 6; d €60) Rooms at the front of this small hotel have picturesque tiled balconies with full-on views of the coast.

Conchina da Nazaré (☎ 262 186 156; Rua de Leiria 17d; mains €5.50-10) This simple place with outdoor seating serves good-value seafood, including wood-grilled fish and delicious *açorda de marisco* (thick bread soup with seafood).

A Tasquinha (☎ 262 551 945; Rua Adrião Batalha 54; mains €6.50-10; Tue-Sun) This enormously popular family tavern serves high-quality seafood at reasonable prices. Expect queues on summer nights.

Getting There & Away

The nearest train station, 6km away at Valado, is connected to Nazaré by frequent buses. Nazaré has numerous bus connections to Lisbon (€8.60, two hours).

TOMAR

pop 17,000

A charming town straddling a river, Tomar has the notoriety of being home to the Knights Templar; check out their headquarters, the outstanding monastery **Convento de Cristo** (☎ 249 313 481; adult/child €5/2.50; 9am-6pm Jun-Sep, to 5pm Oct-May). Other rarities include a magnificent 17th-century **Aqueduto de Pegões** (aqueduct) and a medieval **synagogue** (Rua Dr Joaquim Jacinto 73; admission free; 10am-1pm & 2-6pm). The town is backed by the dense greenery of the **Mata Nacional dos Sete Montes** (Seven Hills National Forest). Tomar's **tourist office** (☎ 249 322 427; turismo.tomar@sapo.pt; Avenida Dr Cândido Madureira) can provide town and forest maps.

Sleeping & Eating

Residencial União (☎ 249 323 161; www.residencialuniao.verportugal.com; Rua Serpa Pinto 94; s/d/q €25/38/45;) Tomar's most atmospheric budget choice, this once-grand town house features large and sprucely maintained rooms with antique furniture and fixtures.

Residencial Sinagoga (☎ 249 323 083; residencial.sinagoga@clix.pt; Rua de Gil de Avô; s/d €34/49;) On a quiet residential street in the centre, this place offers tidy, if undistinguished, modern rooms.

Restaurante Tomaz (☎ 249 312 552; Rua dos Arcos 31; mains €4-7; Mon-Sat) Popular with locals, this simple, appealing place has a cosy dining room serving Portuguese favourites. There's outdoor seating on a wide, leafy street.

Bela Vista (☎ 249 312 870; Rua Fonte do Choupo 6; mains €6-10) The town's best-known restaurant, with a riverside terrace, serves dishes like roast kid.

Getting There & Away

There are at least four express buses daily to Lisbon (€8, two hours) and even more frequent trains (€8.20, two hours).

COIMBRA

pop 150,000

Coimbra is a dynamic, fashionable, yet comfortably lived-in city, with a student life centred on the magnificent 13th-century university. Aesthetically eclectic, there are elegant shopping streets, ancient stone walls and backstreet alleys with hidden *tascas* and fado bars. Coimbra was the birth and burial place of Portugal's first king, and was the country's most important city when the Moors captured Lisbon.

Information

Casa Municipal da Cultura (☎ 239 702 630; Rua Pedro Monteiro; 🕑 10am-7.30pm Mon-Fri, 2-6.30pm Sat) Free internet access near the youth hostel.

Tourist office (☎ 239 859 884; coimbraviva@cm-coimbra.pt; Praça da Porta Férrea)

Sights & Activities

Igreja de Santa Cruz (☎ 239 822 941; Praça 8 de Maio; adult/child €2.50/1.50; 🕑 9am-noon & 2-5pm) has a fabulous ornate pulpit and medieval royal tombs. Located at the bottom of the hill in the Old Town,the monastery can be reached via the elevator (one way €1.50) by the market.

Velha Universidade (Old University; ☎ 239 822 941; www.uc.pt/sri; admission €6; 🕑 10am-noon & 2-5pm) is unmissable in its grandeur. You can visit the library with its gorgeous book-lined hallways and the Manueline chapel dating back to 1517.

Capitão Dureza (☎ 239 918 148; www.capitaodureza.com, in Portuguese; Barcouça) organises rafting, canoeing, biking and hiking trips. **Basófias** (☎ 969 830 664; www.basofias.com, in Portuguese; 🕑 Tue-Sun) runs boat trips (€8, 55 minutes) on the Rio Mondego.

Festivals & Events

Coimbra's annual highlight is **Queima das Fitas**, a boozy week of fado and revelry that begins on the first Thursday in May when students celebrate the end of the academic year.

Sleeping

Pensão Residencial Larbelo (☎ 239 829 092; residencialarbelo@sapo.pt; Largo da Portagem 33; s/d €30/40; ❄) Larbelo is bang in the centre and boasts high-ceilinged rooms with wooden floors and modern furnishings. Front rooms opening onto the Largo da Portagem are especially nice.

Pensão-Restaurante Flôr de Coimbra (☎ 239 823 865; flordecoimbrahr@sapo.pt; Rua do Poço 5; s/d/tr with shared bathroom €30/35/40, with private bathroom €40/45/50) This once-grand 19th-century home with its own restaurant offers loads of character in a great location.

Pensão Residencial Antunes (☎ 239 854 720; http://residencialantunes.pt.vu; Rua Castro Matoso 8; s/d/tw €36/46/50) A few steps from the aqueduct and botanical gardens, this large old guest house in a 19th-century building offers charming, creaky doubles and wi-fi in the downstairs parlour.

Casa Pombal Guesthouse (☎ 239 835 175; www.casapombal.com, in Portuguese; Rua das Flores 18; d with shared/private bathroom €52/62) This gem near the university has pretty rooms painted in pastel colours, and rooftop views. Dutch owner Elsa's breakfast is more generous than most.

Eating & Drinking

Café Santa Cruz (☎ 239 833 617; Praça 8 de Maio; 🕑 Mon-Sat) Former chapel that has been resurrected into one of Portugal's most atmospheric cafes.

Restaurante Jardim da Manga (☎ 239 829 156; Rua Olímpio Nicolau Rui Fernanda; mains €5-7.50; 🕑 closed Sat) A student favourite, this cafeteria-style restaurant serves up tasty meat and fish dishes, with pleasant outdoor seating beside the Jardim da Manga fountain.

Zé Manel (☎ 239 823 790; Beco do Forno 12; mains €7-10; 🕑 Mon-Sat) Great food, huge servings and a zany atmosphere with walls papered with diners' comments, cartoons and poems. Vegetarian choices available.

Italia (☎ 239 838 863; Parque Dr Manuel Braga; mains €7-14) Expand your midriff at this excellent Italian restaurant on the riverfront with laden dishes of excellent pizza and pasta.

Head to the lanes west of Praça do Comércio, especially Rua das Azeiteiras, for cheap eats. Self-caterers should stop by the modern **Mercado Municipal Dom Pedro V** (Rua Olímpio Nicolau Rui Fernandes; 🕑 Mon-Sat) for fruit, vegetables and much more.

Entertainment

Coimbra-style fado is more cerebral than the Lisbon variety, and its adherents are staunchly protective.

our pick Á Capella (☎ 239 833 985; www.acapella.com.pt; Rua Corpo de Deus; admission incl 1 drink €10; 🕑 10pm-2am) Housed in a fabulous 14th-century former chapel, Á Capella regularly hosts the city's most renowned fado musicians.

DETOUR: CONIMBRIGA

Conimbriga, 16km south of Coimbra, is the site of the well-preserved ruins of a **Roman town** (9am-8pm mid-Mar–mid-Sep, 10am-6pm mid-Sep–mid-Mar), including mosaic floors, baths and fountains. There's a good **museum** (adult/child €4/free; 9am-8pm mid-Mar–mid-Sep, 10am-6pm mid-Sep–mid-Mar) here with restaurant. Frequent buses run to Condeixa, 2km from the site; direct buses (€2) depart at 9am and 9.35am (only 9.35am at weekends) from the **AVIC terminal** (Rua João de Ruão 18, Coimbra) returning at 1pm and 5pm (only 5pm at weekends).

Quebra Costas (239 836 038; Rua Quebra Costas 45) Has live jazz at weekends.

Via Latina (239 833 034; Rua Almeida Garrett 1) Fires up to a steamy dance pit late at night.

Catch live fado at **Bar Diligência** (239 827 667; Rua Nova 30; 6pm-2am) or in the open air at **Arco de Almedina** (free) nightly at 9pm in the summer.

Getting There & Away

At least a dozen buses and as many trains run daily from Lisbon (€12, 2½ hours) and Porto (€11, 1½ hours), plus frequent express buses from Faro and Évora, via Lisbon. The main long-distance train stations are Coimbra B, 2km northwest of the centre, and central Coimbra A. Most long-distance trains call at both. Other useful connections include eight daily buses to Luso/Buçaco from Coimbra A (€3, 45 minutes).

LUSO & THE BUÇACO FOREST

pop 2000

This sylvan region harbours a lush forest of century-old trees surrounded by countryside that's dappled with heather, wildflowers and leafy ferns. There's even a fairy-tale palace here, a 1907 neo-Manueline extravagance, where visitors can dine or stay overnight. Buçaco was chosen as a retreat by 16th-century monks, and it surrounds the lovely spa town of Luso.

The **tourist office** (231 939 133; Avenida Emídio Navarro 136; Mon-Sat) has maps and leaflets about the forest and trails, as well as free internet access. The **Termas** (thermal baths; 231 937 910; Avenida Emídio Navarro; admission free; May-Oct) offers a range of treatments.

Sleeping & Eating

Casa de Hóspedes Familiar (231 939 612; paulcoelho@sapo.pt; Rua Ernesto Navarro 34; d/tr €35/40) Just above town, this homey late-Victorian country house has simple cosy rooms, some with little verandahs and views.

Palace Hotel do Buçaco (231 930 101; www.almeidahotels.com; s/d from €150/180) Live a real-life fairy tale and stay at this ostentatious palace complete with gargoyles, ornamental garden and turrets. The equally elegant restaurant offers seven-course menus for around €45.

Restaurante Lourenços (231 939 474; Avenida Emídio Navarro; mains €8.50-10; closed Wed) This blandly bright modern place serves surprisingly good regional specialities.

Getting There & Away

Buses to/from Coimbra (€3, 45 minutes) run four times daily each weekday and twice daily on weekends. IR trains run four times daily from Coimbra A to Luso/Buçaco station (€1.65, 30 minutes), from where it's a solid 15-minute walk to the Luso tourist office and 30 minutes further to the Palace Hotel.

SERRA DA ESTRELA

The forested Serra da Estrela has a raw natural beauty and offers some of the country's best hiking. This is Portugal's highest mainland mountain range (1993m), and the source of its two great rivers: Mondego River and Zêzere River. The town of **Manteigas** makes a great base for hiking and exploring the area (plus skiing in winter). The **main park office** (275 980 060; pnse@icn.pt; Rua 1 de Maio 2; Manteigas; Mon-Fri) provides details of popular walks in the Parque Natural de Serra da Estrela; additional offices are at Seia, Gouveia and Guarda.

Sleeping

Casa de São Roque (275 981 125, 965 357 225; Rua de Santo António 51, Manteigas; s/d from €30/40) This beautiful, creaky old house filled with cosy lounges, antique furnishings and religious artwork is lovingly kept by its elderly owner.

Pensão Serradalto (275 981 151; Rua 1 de Maio 15, Manteigas; s/d/ste €35/45/60) In a renovated stone house, the Serradalto offers rooms with wood floors and simple antique furnishings, plus fine valley views from a sunny upstairs terrace.

Getting There & Away

Two regular weekday buses connect Manteigas with Guarda, from where there are onward services to Coimbra and Lisbon. Several buses run daily from Coimbra along the park's perimeter to Seia, Gouveia, Guarda or Covilhã.

Getting Around

No buses cross the park, although you can go around it. At least two buses link Seia, Gouveia and Guarda daily, and considerably more run between Guarda and Covilhã.

THE NORTH

Beneath the edge of Spanish Galicia, northern Portugal is a land of lush river valleys, sparkling coastline, granite peaks and virgin forests. This region is also gluttony for wine lovers: it's the home of the sprightly *vinho verde* wine and ancient vineyards along the dramatic Rio Douro. Gateway to the north is Porto, a beguiling riverside city blending both medieval and modern attractions. Smaller towns and villages also offer cultural allure, from majestic Braga, the country's religious heart, to the seaside beauty Viana do Castelo.

PORTO

pop 300,000

At the mouth of the Rio Douro, the hilly city of Porto presents a jumble of styles, eras and attitudes: narrow medieval alleyways, extravagant baroque churches, prim little squares, and wide boulevards lined with beaux-arts edifices. A lively city with chatter in the air and a tangible sense of history, Porto's old-world river-frontage district is a World Heritage site. Across the water twinkle the neon signs of Vila Nova de Gaia, the headquarters of the major port manufacturers.

Orientation

Porto centre is small enough to cover mainly by foot. The city clings to the north bank of the Douro River, spanned by five bridges across from Vila Nova de Gaia, home to the port-wine lodges. Central Porto's axis is Av dos Aliados. The picturesque Ribeira district lies along the waterfront, in the shadow of the great Ponte de Dom Luís I bridge.

Information

Branch tourist office (☎ 222 057 514; Praça Dom João I 43) Smaller but equally helpful office.

Main post office (Praça General Humberto Delgado) Located across from the main tourist office.

Main tourist office (☎ 223 393 472; www.portoturismo.pt; Rua Clube dos Fenianos 25) Next door to the tourist police office.

On web (Praça General Humberto Delgado 291; per hr €1.80; 🕒 10am-2am Mon-Sat, 3pm-2am Sun) Internet access in a basement cyber cafe with lively ambience.

Santo António Hospital (☎ 222 077 500; Largo Prof Abel Salazar) Has English-speaking staff.

Telephone office (Praça da Liberdade 62)

Sights

Head for the riverfront Ribeira district for an atmospheric stroll around, checking out the gritty local bars, sunny restaurants and river cruises.

Torre dos Clérigos (Rua dos Clérigos; admission €2; 🕒 10am-noon & 2-5pm) is atop 225 steep steps but rewards those who make it to the top with the best panorama of the city.

Dominating Porto is the **Sé** (☎ 222 059 028; Terreiro da Sé; cloisters €2; 🕒 8.45am-12.30pm & 2.30-7pm). The cathedral is worth a visit for its mixture of architectural styles and vast ornate interior.

Within the verdant gardens west of the city, the arrestingly minimalist **Museu de Arte Contemporânea** (☎ 226 156 500; www.serralves.pt; Rua Dom João de Castro 210; admission €5; 🕒 10am-7pm) features works by contemporary Portuguese artists.

Museu do Vinho do Porto (Port Wine Museum; ☎ 222 076 300; museuvinhoporto@cm-porto.pt; Rua de Monchique 45-52; admission €2; 🕒 11am-7pm Tue-Sun) traces the history of wine- and port-making with an informative short film, models and exhibits. Tastings available.

Porto's best art museum, the **Soares dos Reis National Museum** (☎ 223 393 770; Rua Dom Manuel II 44; admission €3; 🕒 10am-6pm Wed-Sun, 2-6pm Tue) exhibits Portuguese painting and sculpture masterpieces from the 19th and 20th centuries. Catch bus 78 from Praça da Liberdade.

Many of the port-wine lodges in Vila Nova de Gaia offer daily tours and tastings, including **Taylor's** (☎ 223 742 800; www.taylor.pt; Rua do Choupelo 250; admission free; 🕒 10am-6pm Mon-Fri) and **Barros** (☎ 223 746 660; www.porto-barros.pt; Rua Dona Leonor de Freitas; admission free; 🕒 10am-5.30pm Mon-Fri).

A few kilometres west of the city centre, the seaside suburb of **Foz do Douro** is a prime destination on hot summer weekends. It has

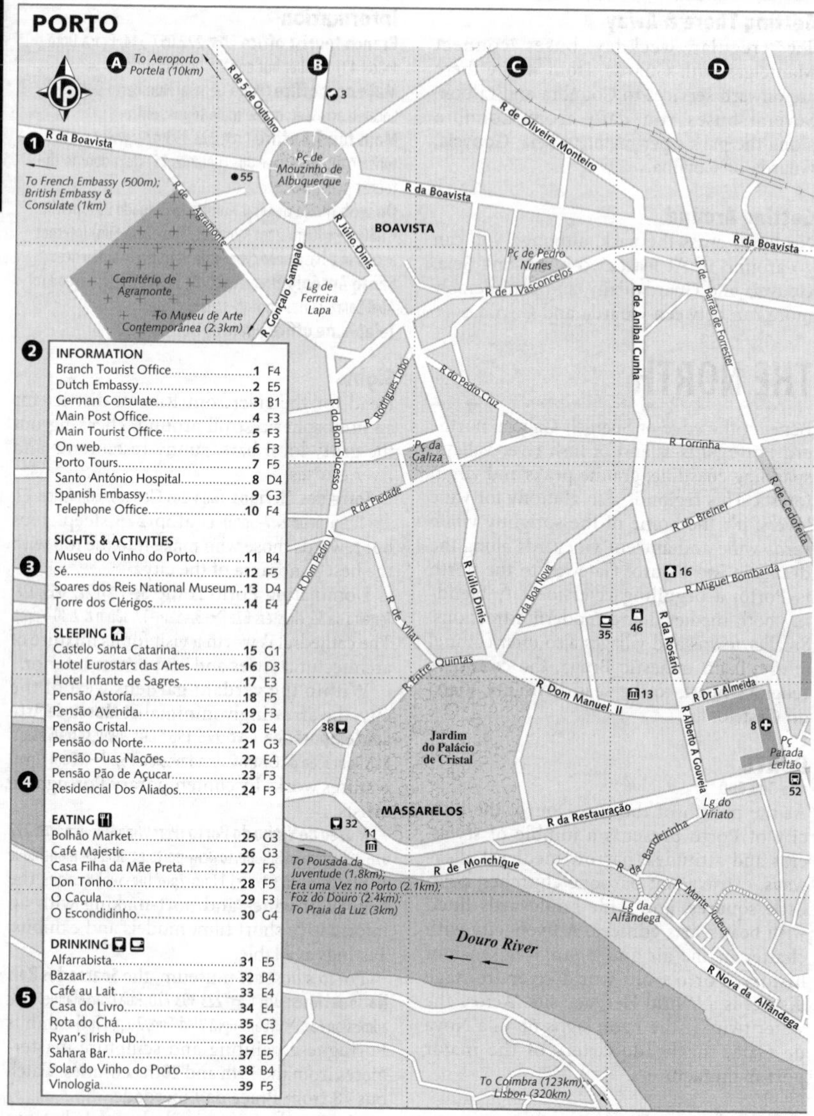

a long beach promenade and a scattering of ocean-fronting bars and restaurants.

Festivals & Events

Porto's big festivals are the international film festival, **Fantasporto,** in February and the **Festa de São João** (St John's Festival) from 20 to 24 June. The latter produces processions, live music on the city's plazas and merry-making all across town. Squeaky plastic hammers (available for sale everywhere) also come out for the unusual custom of whacking one another. Everyone is fair game - expect no mercy. Also worth catching are the **Celtic music festival** in April/May and the **rock festival** in August.

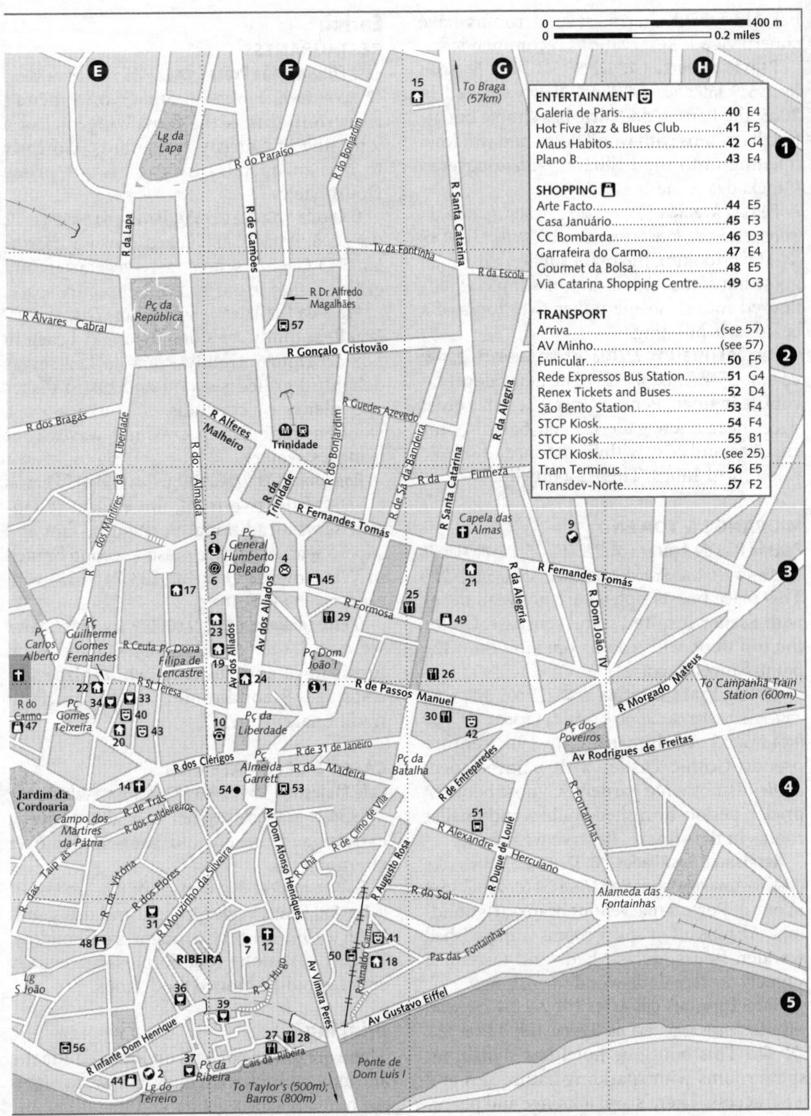

Sleeping

BUDGET

Pousada da Juventude (☎ 226 177 257; www.pousadasjuventude.pt; Rua Paulo da Gama 551; dm/d €14/38; 24hr;) This is a tastefully spruced-up hostel 4km west of the centre. Reservations are essential. To get here, take bus 500 from Aliados.

Pensão Duas Nações (☎ 222 081 616; www.duasnacoes.com.pt; Praça Guilherme Gomes Fernandes 59; s/d/tr from €14/23/36;) A backpacker favourite with walls washed in bright primary colours, and comfortable clean rooms.

Pensão Astória (☎ 222 008 175; Rua Arnaldo Gama 56; s/d from €20/30) In an austere but elegant town house above the Rio Douro, this spotless place has old-world charm; several rooms have superb views. Reservations recommended.

Pensão do Norte (☎ 222 003 503; Rua de Fernandes Tomás 579; s/d/tr from €30/40/55) Newly opened in 2008, the Pensão do Norte has simple but attractive rooms with wood floors and windows opening onto the brilliant *azulejo*-covered Capela das Almas.

Pensão Avenida (☎ 222 009 551; http://planeta.clix.pt/pensaoavenida; Avenida dos Aliados 141; s/d/tw €35/40/45;) Overlooking the main square, this small guest house has a handful of simple wood-floored rooms on the upper two floors of a beaux-arts building.

Pensão Cristal (☎ 222 002 100; Rua Galeria de Paris 48; s/d/tw/tr €35/45/50/60;) The new budget favourite in town, Pensão Cristal lies on a quiet street near a few galleries and bars. Rooms are clean and cosy with tile floors and simple wood furnishings. There's a tiny lift.

MIDRANGE & TOP END

Pensão Pão de Açucar (☎ 222 002 425; Rua do Almada 262; www.residencialpaodeacucar.com; s/d €45/60;) This place boasts upbeat art-nouveau decor with Escher-inspired spiral staircase. Go for the top floor with rooms opening onto the palm-fringed terrace.

Castelo Santa Catarina (☎ 225 095 599; www.castelosantacatarina.com.pt; Rua Santa Catarina 1347; s/d from €45/65;) A whimsical late-19th-century pseudo-Gothic castle, with palm-shaded, *azulejo*-smothered gardens. Choose between pricier, period-furnished doubles and smaller rooms in the annexe. Reserve well ahead.

Residencial Dos Aliados (☎ 222 004 853; www.residencialaliados.com; Rua Elisio de Melo 27; s/d €50/60;) Set in one of Porto's marvellous beaux-arts buildings, Aliados offers spiffy rooms with polished wooden floors, decent beds and tasteful if vaguely austere dark-wood furnishings.

Hotel Eurostars das Artes (☎ 222 071 250; www.eurostarshotels.com; Rua do Rosário 160; d from €80;) This boutique hotel has stylish but spare rooms with sparkling bathrooms and wi-fi access. There's also a lounge and peaceful terrace.

Hotel Infante de Sagres (☎ 223 398 500; www.hotelinfantesagres.pt; Praça Dona Filipa de Lencastre 62; s/d from €175/195;) An exquisite time warp with well-coiffed doormen, crystal chandeliers and ornately decorated common areas, this place feels like a royal getaway in the heart of the city.

Eating

RESTAURANTS

Casa Filha da Mãe Preta (☎ 222 055 515; Cais da Ribeira 40; mains €6-9; Mon-Sat) Smack on Ribeira's riverfront, this is the most congenial of a long line of touristy restaurants. Go early to bag an upstairs front table for prime Douro views.

O Caçula (☎ 222 055 937; Travessa do Bonjardim 20; mains €7-9; Mon-Sat) Tucked down a narrow lane, O Caçula serves tasty vegetarian and grilled dishes in a trim, contemporary space.

Praia da Luz (Avenida Brasil; mains €7-14; 9am-2am) Beautifully set along the rocky beach in Foz do Douro, trendy Praia da Luz serves delightful grilled seafood and bistro dishes and plenty of cocktails. Sit outside on a wooden deck facing crashing waves (but bring a sweater).

Don Tonho (☎ 222 004 307; Cais da Ribeira 13-15; mains €12-22) On the riverfront, this elegant restaurant serves traditional Portuguese fare and superb seafood. There's also a second branch in Vila Nova de Gaia (☎ 223 744 835) with great riverside seating.

O Escondidinho (☎ 222 001 079; Rua Passos Manuel 144; mains €13-20) Amid *azulejos,* dark-wood furnishings and starched white place settings, O Escondidinho serves excellent traditional cuisine.

CAFES & SELF-CATERING

Café Majestic (☎ 222 003 887; Rua Santa Catarina 112; 9.30am-midnight Mon-Sat) An art-nouveau extravagance where old souls linger over afternoon tea.

Bolhão market (Rua Formosa; 8am-5pm Mon-Fri, to 1pm Sat) Fruit, vegies, cheese and deli goodies in a 19th-century wrought-iron building. Further east along Rua Formosa are equally enticing old-fashioned food shops.

Drinking

There are dozens of bars on Praça da Ribeira and along the adjacent quay. On warm nights the outdoor tables get packed.

Ryan's Irish Pub (☎ 222 005 366; Rua Infante Dom Henrique 18; 6pm-2am) Expats and whisky lovers flock to this popular if predictable drinking spot.

Alfarrabista (☎ 222 012 892; Rua das Flores 46; 10am-2am Mon-Sat) The nicely designed contemporary lounge has DJs spinning world music most nights.

PORT WINE 101

With its intense flavours, silky textures and appealing sweetness, port wine is easy to love, especially when taken with its proper accompaniments: cheese, nuts and dried fruit.

It was probably Roman soldiers who first planted grapes in the Douro valley some 2000 years ago, but tradition credits the discovery of port itself to 17th-century British merchants. With their country at war with France, they turned to their old ally Portugal to meet their wine habit. According to legend, the British threw in some brandy with grape juice, both to take off the wine's bite and preserve it for shipment back to England – and port wine was the result.

Ports are wonderfully varied. The quality of the grapes, plus the ways the wine is aged and stored, determine the kind of port you get. Here's a quick primer on different varieties:

Ruby Made from average-quality grapes, and aged at least two years in vats; rich, red colours and sweet, fruity flavours.

Tawny Made from average-quality grapes, and aged for two to seven years in wooden casks; mahogany colours, drier than ruby, with nuttier flavours.

Aged tawny Selected from higher-quality grapes, then aged for many years in wood casks; subtler and silkier than regular tawny.

Late-bottled vintage (LBV) Made from very select grapes of a single year, aged for around five years in wood casks, then bottled; similar to vintage, but ready for immediate drinking once bottled, and usually smoother and lighter-bodied than vintage.

Vintage Made from the finest grape from a single year, aged in barrels two years, then aged in bottles at least 10 years and up to 100 or more; dark ruby colours, fruity yet extremely subtle and complex.

A great place to sample the goods **Solar do Vinho do Porto** (☎ 226 097 749; Rua Entre Quintas 220; ⏲ 4pm-midnight Mon-Sat), a converted 19th-century manor with hundreds of ports available – best enjoyed in the picturesque garden overlooking the Douro.

In the Ribeira, **Vinologia** (☎ 936 057 340; www.lamaisondesporto.com; Rua de São João 46; ⏲ 4-9pm Mon-Wed, to midnight Thu-Sat, 6-9pm Sun) is a cosy wine bar with over 200 different ports on offer.

Sahara Bar (☎ 969 206 037; Cais da Estiva 4; ⏲ 10pm-4am Mon-Sat) Decked out like an Arabian hideaway, this loungey place has hookahs, a festive crowd, the occasional belly dancer and sidewalk seating.

Rota do Chá (Rua Miguel Bombarda 457; tea €2) This proudly bohemian cafe has a verdant but rustic back garden and a magnificent tea selection.

Other recommended bars nearby:

Galeria de Paris (☎ 934 210 792; Rua Galeria de Paris 56; ⏲ Mon-Sat)

Casa do Livro (Rua Galeria de Paris 85; ⏲ Mon-Sat)

Café au Lait (☎ 222 025 016; Rua Galeria de Paris 44; ⏲ Mon-Sat)

Entertainment

Era uma Vez no Porto (☎ 226 164 793; www.eraumaveznoporto.com; Rua do Passeio Alegre 550; ⏲ 6-9pm & 10pm-2am Mon-Fri, 4-8pm & 10pm-2am Sat & Sun) Part tearoom, part nightclub, part experimental art gallery and part vintage-clothing shop, this riverfront town house feels as if you've entered a private party with a cash bar.

Bazaar (☎ 226 062 113; Rua de Monchique 13; ⏲ from 4pm) One of the hottest clubs in Porto, Bazaar spins high-quality house for hundreds of pretty 20- and 30-somethings.

Maus Habitos (☎ 222 087 268; 4th fl, Rua Passos Manuel 178; ⏲ 10pm-2am Wed, Thu & Sun, to 4am Fri & Sat) This bohemian multiroom space hosts art exhibits, while live bands and DJs work the back stage.

Hot Five Jazz & Blues Club (☎ 919 015 374; www.hotfive.eu; Largo Actor Dias 51; ⏲ 10pm-3am Wed-Sun) Hosts live jazz and blues as well as the acoustic, folk and all-out jam sessions.

Plano B (☎ 222 012 500; www.planobporto.com; Rua Cândido dos Reis 30; ⏲ 2.30-8pm & 10pm-2am Tue-Wed, 2.30pm-4am Thu-Sat, closed Aug) This creative space has an art gallery in front, a tall-ceilinged cafe in back, and a downstairs where DJs and live bands hold court.

Shopping

Major shopping areas are eastward around the Bolhão Market and Rua Santa Catarina.

The best central shopping mall is **Via Catarina Shopping Centre** (Rua Santa Catarina) in a tasteful building. For something a little edgier, visit **CC Bombarda** (Rua Miguel Bombarda), a gallery of stores selling urban wear, stylish home knick-knacks, Portuguese indie rock and other hipster-pleasing delights.

Port is, naturally, a popular purchase in this town. Shops with a good selection include knowledgeable **Garrafeira do Carmo** (Rua do Carmo 17), the deli **Casa Januário** (Rua do Bonjardim 352) and friendly, English-speaking **Gourmet da Bolsa** (☎ 919 088 968; Largo de São Domingos 26).

For handicrafts visit **Arte Facto** (Rua da Reboleira 37) in the Ribeira.

Getting There & Away

AIR

Porto is connected by daily flights from Lisbon and London, and almost-daily direct links from other European cities (see p699), particularly with easyJet and Ryanair.

BUS

Porto has a baffling number of private bus companies leaving from different terminals; the main tourist office can help with transport queries. In general, for Lisbon (€16.50) and the Algarve the choice is **Renex** (☎ 222 003 395; www.renex.pt; Campo Mártires de Pátria 37) or **Rede Expressos** (☎ 222 052 459; www.rede-expressos.pt; Rua Alexandre Herculano 370).

Three companies operate from or near Praceto Régulo Magauanha, off Rua Dr Alfredo Magalhães: **Transdev-Norte** (☎ 222 006 954) goes to Braga (€4.30); **AV Minho** (☎ 222 006 121) to Viana do Castelo (€6.50); and **Arriva** (☎ 222 051 383) to Guimarães (€4.50).

TRAIN

Porto is a northern Portugal rail hub with three stations. Most international trains, and all intercity links, start at Campanhã, 2km east of the centre. Inter-regional and regional services depart from Campanhã or the central **São Bento station** (☎ 225 364 141; Praça Almeida Garrett). Frequent local trains connect these two.

At São Bento station you can book tickets to any other destination.

> **ANDANTE FARES**
>
> The Andante is a euro-economising ticket covering metro, funicular, tram and some bus routes. The initial card costs €0.50, and it may then be recharged with more credit at vending machines at metro, train and bus stations. For more info, pick up a transport guide at city tourist offices.

Getting Around

TO/FROM THE AIRPORT

The metro's 'violet' line provides handy service to the airport. A one-way ride to the centre costs €1.45 and takes about 45 minutes. A daytime taxi costs €20 to €25 to/from the centre.

PUBLIC TRANSPORT

Bus

Central hubs of Porto's extensive bus system include Jardim da Cordoaria, Praça da Liberdade and São Bento station. Tickets are cheapest from STCP kiosks or news agents and tobacconists: €1.75 for a return within Porto and from €2.20 for outlying areas. Tickets bought on the bus are €1.45 for a single. There's also a €5 day pass available.

Funicular

Save your puff and hop on the funicular that shuttles up and down a steep incline from Av Gustavo Eiffel to Rua Augusto Rosa (€0.90, from 8am to 8pm).

Metro

Porto's **metro** (www.metrodoporto.pt) currently comprises four metropolitan lines that all converge at the Trinidade stop. Tickets cost €1.45 for a single ride, but you can save money by investing in an Andante card (see boxed text, left).

Tram

Porto has three antique trams that trundle around town. The most useful line 1E travels along the Douro towards the Foz district.

TAXI

To cross town, expect to pay between €5 and €7. There's a 20% surcharge at night, and an additional charge to leave city limits, which includes Vila Nova de Gaia. There are taxi ranks throughout the centre or you can call a **radio taxi** (☎ 225 076 400, 225 029 898).

ALONG THE DOURO

Portugal's best-known river flows through the country's rural heartland. In the upper reaches, port-wine grapes are grown on steep terraced hills, punctuated by remote stone villages and, in spring, splashes of dazzling white almond blossom.

The Douro River is navigable right across Portugal. Highly recommended is the train journey from Porto to Pinhão (€9.05, 2½ hours, five trains daily), the last 70km clinging to the river's edge; trains continue to Pocinho (from Porto €10.75, 3½ hours). **Porto Tours** (☎ 222 000 073; www.portotours.com; Torre Medieval, Calçada Pedro Pitões 15), situated next to Porto's cathedral, can arrange tours, including idyllic Douro cruises. Cyclists and drivers can choose river-hugging roads along either bank, and visit wineries along the way (check out www.rvp.pt for an extensive list of wineries open to visitors). You can also overnight in scenic wine lodges among the vineyards.

VIANA DO CASTELO

pop 37,500

The jewel of the Costa Verde (Green Coast), Viana do Castelo has both an appealing medieval centre and lovely beaches just outside the city. In addition to its natural beauty, Viana do Castelo whips up some excellent seafood and hosts some magnificent traditional festivals, including the spectacular **Festa de Nossa Senhora da Agonia** (see p699) in August. The **tourist office** (☎ 258 822 620; www.rtam.pt; Rua Hospital Velho) is handily located in the old centre.

Sights

The stately heart of town is Praça da República, with its delicate fountain and grandiose buildings, including the 16th-century **Misericórdia**, a striking Renaissance building, its upper storeys supported by ornate caryatids.

Atop Santa Luzia Hill, the **Templo do Sagrado Coração de Jesus** (Temple of the Sacred Heart of Jesus; ☎ 258 823 173; admission free; 8am-7pm Apr-Sep, to 5pm Oct-Mar) offers a grand panorama across the river. It's a steep 2km climb; you can also catch a ride on the newly restored funicular railway (one-way/return €2/3).

Viana's enormous arcing beach, **Praia do Cabedelo**, is one of the Minho's best, with little development to spoil its charm. It's across the river from town, best reached by ferry (adult/child €1.10/0.60, hourly 8.15am to 7pm) from the pier south of Largo 5 de Outubro.

Sleeping

Pousada da Juventude Gil Eannes (☎ 258 821 582; www.pousadasjuventude.pt; Gil Eannes; dm €8) This *hostal* is located in the bowels of a former naval hospital ship. QE2 it ain't, but the novelty factor is high.

Residencial Viana Mar (☎/fax 258 828 962; Avenida dos Combatentes da Grande Guerra 215; s/d from €30/40) This well-worn place has thin carpeting, tall ceilings and simple furnishings. Rooms in the back are gloomy; front rooms are at least bright with balconies.

Dolce Vianna (☎ 258 824 860; pizzariadolcevianna@gmail.com; Rua do Poço 44; d €40;) Set above a popular pizzeria in the town centre, the quiet rooms at Dolce Vianna are spick-and-span, with tile floors and sturdy furnishings.

Margarida da Praça (☎ 258 809 630; www.margaridadapraca.com; Largo 5 de Outubro 58; d €75;) Offers remodelled rooms in a handsome town house with a pleasant riverfront location. It sits above one of Viana's best restaurants (mains €9 to €12; open Monday to Saturday).

Eating & Drinking

The newest destination for dining or drinking is the waterfront Praça da Liberdade, with its open-air cafes and restaurants.

Scala Restaurante (☎ 258 808 060; Avenida do Atlântico 813, Praia Norte; mains €7-14) Two kilometres west of the centre overlooking the rugged Praia Norte, Scala has unrivalled views of the sea. The broad menu includes salads, crepes, seafood and Portuguese favourites.

Restaurant O Pescador (☎ 258 826 039; Largo de São Domingos 35; mains €9-13) A friendly, family-run restaurant admired by locals for its for its good seafood.

our pick **Taberna do Valentim** (☎ 258 827 505; Rua Monsignor Daniel Machado 180; mains €12-14; Mon-Sat) In the old fishermen's neighbourhood, this fantastic seafood restaurant serves grilled fish by the kilogram, and rich seafood stews – *arroz de tamboril* (monkfish rice) and *caldeirada* (fish stew).

Caffe del Rio (☎ 258 822 963; Rua da Bandeira 179-185; 1pm-2am Sun-Thu, to 4am Fri & Sat) The sleek glass-and-chrome, '60s-style bar upstairs has great river views. On weekends DJs spin house and hip hop here. It's located on the river; it's a short stroll east along the waterside promenade.

Getting There & Away

Five to 10 trains go daily to Porto (€8, two hours). There are also express buses to Porto (€6.50, 2¼ hours) and Lisbon (€17, 5½ hours).

BRAGA

pop 120,000

Portugal's third-largest city boasts an astounding array of churches, their splendid baroque facades looming above the old plazas and narrow lanes of the historic centre. Lively cafes, trim little boutiques, and some excellent restaurants add to the appeal. The **tourist office** (☎ 253 262 550; www.cm-braga.pt; Praça da República 1) can help with accommodation and maps.

Sights

In the centre of Braga is the **Sé** (Rua Dom Paio Mendes; admission free; 8.30am-6.30pm), one of Portugal's most extraordinary cathedrals, with roots dating back a thousand years. Within the cathedral you can also visit the **treasury** (€2) and **choir** (€2).

At Bom Jesus do Monte, a hilltop pilgrimage site 5km from Braga, is an extraordinary stairway, the **Escadaria do Bom Jesus**, with allegorical fountains, chapels and a superb view. City bus 2 (€1.30) runs frequently from Braga to the site, where you can climb the steps (pilgrims sometimes do this on their knees) or ascend by funicular railway (€1.20).

It's an easy day trip to **Guimarães** with its medieval town centre and a palace of the dukes of Bragança. It's also a short jaunt to **Barcelos**, a town famed for its enormous Thursday market.

Sleeping

Pousada da Juventude (☎ 253 616 163; www.pousadasjuventude.pt; Rua de Santa Margarida 6; dm/d €7/22) This bland but lively hostel is a 10-minute walk from the centre.

Albergaria da Sé (☎ 253 214 502; www.albergaria-da-se.com.pt; Rua Gonçalo Pereira 39; s/d/ste €45/55/75;) Around the corner from the cathedral, this friendly three-storey guest house has darkwood floors and airy rooms.

Hotel-Residencial Dona Sofia (☎ 253 263 160; www.hoteldonasofia.com; Largo São João do Souto 131; s/d €45/60;) On a pretty, central square, prim little Dona Sofia has spotless, carpeted rooms with very good beds.

Eating & Drinking

Livraria Café (☎ 253 267 647; Avenida Central 118; mains €4; 9am-7.30pm Mon-Sat) Tucked inside the bookshop Centésima Página, this charming cafe serves tasty quiches, salads and desserts. Outdoor tables are in the pleasantly rustic garden.

Cozinha da Sé (☎ 253 277 343; Rua Dom Frei Caetano Brandão 95; mains €7-10; Tue-Sun) A handsome Braga newcomer, Sé serves traditional, high-quality dishes (including one vegetarian selection).

Taberna do Felix (☎ 253 617 701; Praça Velha 17; mains €7-10; dinner Mon-Sat) Situated near the Arco da Porta Nova, this attractive country-style tavern prepares delightful Franco-Portuguese dishes. There are several other excellent restaurants nearby, including a vegetarian one.

Taperia Palatu (☎ 253 279 772; Rua Dom Afonso Henrique 35; mains €8-12; Mon-Sat) A Spanish/Portuguese couple serves up delectable Spanish tapas and classic Portuguese dishes on an airy courtyard.

Getting There & Away

Trains arrive twice daily from Lisbon (€22 to €30, four hours), Coimbra (€12 to €22, 2¼ hours) and Porto (€2.15, 1¼ hours), and there are daily connections north to Viana do Castelo. Daily bus services link Braga to Porto (€4.50, 1¼ hours) and Lisbon (€18, five hours). Car hire is available at **AVIC** (☎ 253 203 912; Rua Gabriel Pereira de Castro 28; Mon-Fri), with prices starting at €30 per day.

PARQUE NACIONAL DA PENEDA-GERÊS

Spread across four impressive granite massifs, this vast park encompasses boulder-strewn peaks, precipitous valleys, gorse-clad moorlands and forests of oak and pine. It also shelters more than 100 granite villages that, in many ways, have changed little since Portugal's founding in the 12th century. For nature lovers the stunning scenery is unmatched in Portugal for camping, hiking and other outdoor adventures. The park's main centre is at Vila do Gerês, a sleepy, hot-spring village.

Information

The head park office is **Adere-PG** (☎ 258 452 250; www.adere-pg.pt; Mon-Fri) in Ponte de Barca. Obtain park information and reserve cottages and other park accommodation through them. Gerês' **tourist office** (☎ 253 391 133; fax 253 391 282; closed Thu) can provide information on activities and accommodation.

Activities

HIKING

There are trails and footpaths through the park, some between villages with accommodation. Leaflets detailing these are available from the park offices.

Day hikes around Gerês are popular. An adventurous option is the old Roman road from Mata do Albergaria (10km up-valley from Gerês by taxi or hitching), past the **Vilarinho das Furnas** reservoir to Campo do Gerês. More distant destinations include **Ermida** and **Cabril**, both with simple accommodation.

CYCLING & HORSE RIDING

Mountain bikes can be hired in Campo do Gerês (15km northeast of Vila do Gerês) from **Equi Campo** (☎ 253 357 022, www.equicampo.com; per hr/day €5/17; 10am-7pm). Guides here also lead horse-riding trips, hikes and combination hiking/climbing/abseiling excursions.

WATER SPORTS

Rio Caldo, 8km south of Gerês, is the base for water sports on the Caniçada reservoir. English-run **AML** (Água Montanha e Lazer; ☎ 253 391 779, 968 021 142; www.aguamontanha.com; Lugar de Paredes, Rio Caldo) rents kayaks, pedal boats, rowing boats and small motorboats. It also organises kayaking trips along the Albufeira de Salamonde.

Sleeping & Eating

Gerês has plenty of *pensões* (guest houses), but you may find vacancies are limited; many are block-booked by spa patients in summer.

Parque Campismo de Cerdeira (☎ 253 351 005; www.parquecerdeira.com; camp sites per adult/tent/car €4.60/3.90/4.30, 2-/4-person bungalow €63/85;) In Campo de Gerês, this place has oak-shaded sites, laundry, pool, minimarket and a particularly good restaurant. The ecofriendly bungalows have French doors opening onto unrivalled mountain views. Book ahead.

Pensão Flôr de Moçambique (☎/fax 253 391 119; d from €30) The best budget option in town, this guest house offers modern rooms, most with verandahs and nice views.

Pensão Adelaide (☎ 253 390 020; www.pensaoadelaide.com.pt; d from €40;) Rooms at this attractive lemon yellow place have tiled (or wood) floors and new beds, and some have valley views.

Pensão Baltazar (☎ 253 391 131; www.pensaobaltazar.com; N308; d from €40) This friendly, family-run place just up from the tourist office has well-kept rooms, many of which look out onto a pleasant wooded park. The downstairs restaurant is excellent.

Getting There & Away

From Braga, at least five coaches daily run to Rio Caldo and Gerês, and three to Campo do Gerês (fewer at weekends). Because of the lack of transport within the park, it's good to have your own wheels. You can rent cars in Braga (opposite).

PORTUGAL DIRECTORY

ACCOMMODATION

Most tourist offices have lists of accommodation to suit a range of budgets. In this chapter the budget category for a double room is up to €45, midrange is between €46 and €80 and top end is over €80. Prices include private bathroom unless otherwise stated and are quoted for high season (June to August).

The government grades hotels with one to five stars. For a high-season double expect to pay €60 up to as much as €250. Prices drop considerably in low season.

Camping is always the cheapest option, although some camping grounds close out of season. The multilingual, annually updated *Roteiro Campista* (€5.50), sold in larger bookshops or via the www.roteiro-campista.pt website, lists Portugal's camping grounds.

Note that most accommodation options, excluding camping grounds and youth hostels, include a continental breakfast in the price.

Ecotourism & Farmstays

Private counterparts are operated under a scheme called **Turismo de Habitação** (www.turihab.pt) and a number of smaller schemes (collectively called 'Turihab'). They allow you to stay in historic, heritage or rustic properties, ranging from 17th-century manors to quaint farmhouses or self-catering cottages. Doubles run about €60 to €100.

Guest Houses

The most common types of guest house are the *residencial* and the *pensão*, which are usually simple family-owned operations. Some have cheaper rooms with shared bathrooms.

Pousadas

Pousadas are government-run former castles, monasteries or palaces, often in spectacular locations. For details contact tourist offices or **Pousadas de Portugal** (☎ 218 442 001; www.pous adas.pt).

Youth Hostels

Portugal has 36 *pousadas da juventude* (youth hostels) within the Hostelling International (HI) system. Reserve in advance by contacting **Movijovem** (Map pp666-7; ☎ 707 203 030; www.pousadasjuventude.pt; Rua Lúcio de Azevedo 27, Saldanha, Lisbon).

If you don't already have a card from your national hostel association, you can pay a €2 supplement per night (and have a one-night, six-night or year-long 'guest card').

ACTIVITIES

Off-road cycling and bike trips are growing in popularity in Portugal; good starting points are Tavira in the Algarve, Sintra and Setúbal in central Portugal and Parque Nacional da Peneda-Gerês in the north.

Despite some fine rambling country, walking is not a Portuguese passion. Some parks are establishing trails though, and some adventure-travel agencies offer walking tours.

Popular water sports include surfing, windsurfing, canoeing, white-water rafting and water skiing. For local specialists, see Lagos (p681), Sagres (p682), Tavira (p680), Coimbra (p687) and Parque Nacional da Peneda-Gerês (p697).

Modest alpine skiing is possible at Torre in the Serra da Estrela, usually from January through to March.

BUSINESS HOURS

Banks are open 8.30am to 3pm weekdays. Museums and tourist attractions are open between 10am and 5pm Tuesday to Sunday, but are often closed at lunch. Shopping hours are generally 9am to 7pm weekdays, and 9am to 1pm Saturday. Restaurants are open for lunch and dinner, unless noted. Lunch is typically served from noon to 3pm, and dinner from 7pm to 10.30pm. Tourist offices in larger towns are generally open Monday to Saturday 9am to 6pm; in smaller towns they close for lunch from between noon and 2.30pm. Portuguese post offices *(correios)* are open Monday to Friday 8.30am to 6pm. In Lisbon and Porto they are also open on Saturday mornings.

EMBASSIES & CONSULATES

Nations with embassies or consulates in Portugal include the following:

Australia (Map pp666-7; ☎ 213 101 500; https://portugal.embassy.gov.au; 2nd fl, Avenida da Liberdade 200)

Canada Lisbon (Map pp666-7; ☎ 213 164 600; http://geo.international.gc.ca/canada-europa/portugal; 3rd fl, Avenida da Liberdade 196); Faro (☎ 289 803 757; Rua Frei Lourenço de Santa Maria 1)

France Lisbon (Map pp666-7; ☎ 213 939 100; www.ambafrance-pt.org; Rua de Santos-o-Velho 5); Porto (off Map pp690-1; ☎ 226 078 220; Avenida da Boavista 1681)

Germany Lisbon (Map pp670-1; ☎ 218 810 210; www.lissabon.diplo.de; Campo dos Mártires da Pátria 38); Porto (Map pp690-1; ☎ 226 052 810; 6th fl, Avenida de França 20)

Ireland (Map pp666-7; ☎ 213 929 440; www.embassyofireland.pt; Rua da Imprensa, Estrela)

Morocco (Map pp666-7; ☎ 213 020 842; www.emb-marrocos.pt, in Portuguese; Rua Alto do Duque 21)

Netherlands Lisbon (Map pp666-7; ☎ 213 914 900; www.emb-paisesbaixos.pt; Avenida Infante Santo 43); Porto (Map pp690-1; ☎/fax 222 080 061; Rua da Reboleira 7)

New Zealand There's no New Zealand embassy in Portugal. In emergencies, New Zealand citizens can call the honorary consul (☎ 213 705 779). The nearest New Zealand embassy is in Madrid (☎ 34 915 230 226; www.nzembassy.com).

Spain Lisbon (Map pp670-1; ☎ 213 472 381; embesppt@correo.mae.es; Rua do Salitre 1, 1269-052 Lisbon); Porto (Map pp690-1; ☎ 225 363 915; cgespporto@correo.mae.es; Rua Dom João IV 341) Also in Valença do Minho and Vila Real de Santo António.

UK Lisbon (Map pp666-7; ☎ 213 924 000; www.britishembassy.gov.uk/portugal; Rua de São Bernardo 33); Porto (off Map pp690-1; ☎ 226 184 789; Travessa Barão de Forrester 86, Vila Nova de Gaia)

USA (Map pp666-7; ☎ 217 273 300; http://portugal.usembassy.gov; Avenida das Forças Armadas, LIsbon)

FESTIVALS & EVENTS

April

Holy Week Festival Easter week in Braga features colourful processions, including Ecce Homo, with barefoot penitents carrying torches.

May

Festas das Cruzes Held in Barcelos, the Festival of the Crosses is known for processions, folk music and dance, plus regional handicrafts.

June

Festa de Santo António The Festival of St Anthony fills the streets of Lisbon on 13 June.

Festa de São João Porto and Braga's big street bash is the St John's Festival, building up to 23 and 24 June.

August

Festa de Nossa Senhora da Agonia Viana do Castelo's Our Lady of Suffering Festival runs for three days, including the weekend nearest to 20 August, and is famed for its folk arts, parades and fireworks.

HOLIDAYS

New Year's Day 1 January
Carnival February/March (Shrove Tuesday)
Good Friday and the following Saturday March/April
Liberty Day 25 April (commemorating the 1975 Revolution)
Labour Day 1 May
Corpus Christi May/June (the ninth Thursday after Easter)
Portugal Day 10 June
Feast of the Assumption 15 August
Republic Day 5 October
All Saints' Day 1 November
Independence Day 1 December (celebrating independence from Spain in 1640)
Immaculate Conception 8 December
Christmas Day 25 December

MONEY

There are numerous banks with ATMs located throughout Portugal. Credit cards are accepted in many hotels, restaurants and shops.

POST

Stamps can be bought over the counter from the post office or from an automatic dispensing machine (*Correio de Portugal – Selos*).

TELEPHONE

Mobile phone numbers within Portugal have nine digits and begin with ☎ 9.

EMERGENCY NUMBERS

- Ambulance ☎ 112
- Fire ☎ 112
- Police ☎ 112

All Portuguese phone numbers consist of nine digits. These include area codes, which always need to be dialled. For general information dial ☎ 118, for international enquiries dial ☎ 179, and for reverse-charge (collect) calls dial ☎ 120.

Phonecards are the most reliable and cheapest way of making a phone call from a telephone booth. They are sold at post offices, newsagents and tobacconists in denominations of €5 and €10.

VISAS

EU nationals need only a valid passport or identity card for entry to Portugal, and can stay indefinitely. Citizens of Australia, Canada, New Zealand and the US can stay for up to 90 days in any half-year without a visa. Others, including nationals of South Africa, need a visa unless they're the spouse or child of an EU citizen.

TRANSPORT IN PORTUGAL

GETTING THERE & AWAY

Air

Portugal's main gateway is the **Aeroporto Portela** (LIS; ☎ 218 413 500) in Lisbon, approximately 8km north of the city centre. Porto's **Aeroporto Francisco Sá Carneiro** (OPO; ☎ 229 432 400) also handles international flights, as does the **Aeroporto de Faro** (FAO; ☎ 229 800 800) in the Algarve, which has the largest number of charter flights. The website for all three airports is www.ana-aeroportos.pt, in Portuguese.

TAP Portugal (TP; ☎ 707 205 700; www.flytap.com) is the main international and domestic carrier, serving dozens of destinations across Europe as well as Brazil, the USA and former Portuguese colonies in Africa.

Following is a list of the major carriers serving Portugal with the airports they use:

Lisbon, Porto or Faro. For details of carriers to/from outside Western Europe see p957.

Air France (AF; ☎ 707 202 800; www.airfrance.com) Lisbon, Porto.

British Airways (BA; ☎ 808 200 125; www.britishairways.com) Lisbon, Porto, Faro.

Bmibaby (WW; ☎ UK 44 870 126 6726; www.bmibaby.com) Lisbon, Porto, Faro.

easyJet (U2; ☎ 218 445 278; www.easyjet.com) Lisbon, Faro.

Iberia (IB; ☎ 707 200 000; www.iberia.com) Lisbon, Porto.

KLM (KL; ☎ 707 222 747; www.klm.nl) Lisbon.

Lufthansa (LH; ☎ 707 782 782; www.lufthansa.com) Lisbon, Porto, Faro.

Monarch Airlines (ZB; ☎ 800 860 270; www.flymonarch.com) Faro.

Ryanair (FR; ☎ 229 432 400; www.ryanair.com) Porto.

TAP Portugal (TP; ☎ 707 205 700; www.flytap.com) Lisbon, Porto, Faro.

Land

BUS

Eurolines (☎ UK 08705-143 219; www.eurolines.co.uk) in London departs for Portugal twice weekly with stops including Lisbon (36 hours) and Porto (34 hours). Buses depart from London's Victoria Station. The current return fare London–Lisbon is £110. From Spain, **Eurolines** (☎ Madrid 915 063 360; www.eurolines.es, in Spanish) operates several services to Portugal, including Madrid–Lisbon, Seville–Lisbon and Barcelona–Lisbon. Other bus services from Spain include an **ALSA** (☎ Madrid 902 422 242; www.alsa.es) Madrid–Lisbon service, while **Damas** (☎ Huelva 959 256 900; www.damas-sa.es) connects Seville to Faro and Lagos via Huelva, jointly with the Algarve line **EVA** (☎ Faro 289 899 700; www.eva-bus.com).

CAR & MOTORCYCLE

There is no border control in Portugal. For more information about driving in Portugal, see opposite.

TRAIN

The fastest and most convenient route to Portugal from the UK is with Eurostar from London Waterloo to Paris via the Channel Tunnel, and then onward to Lisbon via Irún (around 24 hours). Contact **Rail Europe** (☎ UK 08705-848 848; www.raileurope.co.uk; return ticket around €300). From Paris, contact **SNCF** (www.sncf.com; return ticket around €210).

The most popular train link from Spain is on the Sud Express, operated by **Renfe** (☎ Spain 902 240 202; www.renfe.es; one-way ticket from €56), which has a nightly sleeper service between Madrid and Lisbon. Badajoz–Elvas–Lisbon is slow and there is only one regional service daily, but the scenery is stunning. Coming from Galicia, in the northwest of Spain, travellers can go from Vigo to Valença do Minho (Portugal) and continue on to Porto.

GETTING AROUND

Air

TAP Portugal (TAP; ☎ 707 205 700; www.flytap.com) has daily Lisbon–Faro flights (under an hour) year-round. Overall, however, flights within Portugal are poor value; it is a lot cheaper and not terribly time consuming to travel by bus or train.

Bicycle

Mountain biking is a fine way to explore the country, although given the Portuguese penchant for overtaking on blind corners, it can be dangerous on lesser roads. Bicycle lanes are rare: veteran cyclists recommend the Parque Nacional da Peneda-Gerês (p697). A handful of towns have bike-hire outfits (around €10 a day). If you're bringing your own, pack plenty of spare tyres. Bicycles can be taken free on all regional and inter-regional trains as accompanied baggage. They can also go on a few suburban services on weekends. Most domestic bus lines won't accept bikes.

Boat

Portugal is not big on water-borne transport as a rule; however, there are river cruises along the Douro River from Porto (p695), Lisbon's river trips (p669) and commuter ferries.

Bus

Portugal's buses are generally modern and comfortable. However, there is a baffling number of privatised bus companies operating across the country. In Porto alone there are at least 18 bus companies, most based at different terminals.

Among the largest companies are **Rede Expressos** (☎ 707 223 344; www.rede-expressos.pt, in Portuguese), serving 300 destinations throughout the country. **Rodonorte** (☎ 259 340 710; www.rodonorte.pt) serves the north, while **Eva** (☎ 289 899 700; www.eva-bus.com) serves the south, including the Algarve.

Most bus-station ticket desks will give you a computer print-out of fares, and services and schedules are usually posted at major stations.

CLASSES

There are three classes of bus service: *expressos* are comfortable, fast, direct buses between major cities; *rápidas* are fast regional buses; and *carreiras* stop at every crossroad. *Expressos* are generally the best cheap way to get around (particularly for long trips, where per-kilometre costs are lowest). An under-26 card should get you a small discount, at least on the long-distance services.

COSTS

Travelling by bus in Portugal is fairly inexpensive. Refer to the Getting There & Away section of the respective city or town you are travelling to/from for more information on fares and durations.

RESERVATIONS

Advance reservations are only really necessary on the longer routes of the *expresso* service.

Car & Motorcycle

AUTOMOBILE ASSOCIATIONS

Automóvel Clube de Portugal (ACP; Map pp666-7; ☎ 808 502 502; www.acp.pt, in Portuguese; Rua Rosa Araújo 24, Lisbon) has a reciprocal arrangement with many of the better-known foreign automobile clubs, including AA and RAC. ACP provides medical, legal and breakdown assistance. The 24-hour emergency help number is ☎ 707 509 510.

FUEL & SPARE PARTS

There are plenty of self-service stations; some have garages that can replace batteries, repair punctures and do minor mechanical repairs, as well as supply some spare parts. Alternatively, they can direct you to the nearest car workshop.

HIRE

To hire a car in Portugal you must be at least 25 years old and have held your home licence for over a year (some companies allow younger drivers at higher rates). To hire a scooter of up to 50cc you must be over 18 years old and have a valid driving licence. For more powerful scooters and motorbikes you must have a valid driving licence covering these vehicles from your home country.

INSURANCE

Although most car-insurance companies within the EU will cover taking your car to Portugal, it is prudent to consider extra cover for assistance in case your car breaks down. The minimum insurance required is third party.

ROAD RULES

The various speed limits for cars and motorcycles are 50km/h within cities and public centres, 90km/h on normal roads and 120km/h on motorways (but 50km/h, 70km/h and 100km/h for motorcycles that have sidecars).

Driving is on the right side of the road. Drivers and front passengers in cars must wear seatbelts. Motorcyclists and passengers must wear helmets, and motorcycles must have headlights on day and night. Using a mobile phone while driving could result in a fine.

Drink-driving laws are strict in Portugal with a maximum legal blood-alcohol level of 0.05%.

Train

Caminhos de Ferro Portugueses (CP; ☎ 808 208 208; www.cp.pt) is the statewide train network and is generally efficient, although can be slower than long-distance buses. Most trains are *regionais* (R) or *suburbanos*, stopping at stations en route. The more costly *intercidades* (IC) trains are faster, while the most luxurious and pricey are the *alfa pendulares* (AP) trains. Both the IC and AP lines require seat reservations in advance. The most popular train routes are Lisbon–the Algarve and Lisbon–Porto.

Slovenia

It's a tiny place, about half the size of Switzerland, and counts just over two million people. But the only way to describe pint-sized Slovenia (Slovenija), an independent republic bordering Italy, Austria, Hungary, Croatia and the Adriatic Sea, is that it's 'a mouse that roars'.

Slovenia has been dubbed a lot of things since independence in 1991 – 'Europe in Miniature', 'The Sunny Side of the Alps', 'The Green Piece of Europe' – and, though they may sound like blurbs, they're all true. From beaches, snow-capped mountains, hills awash in grapevines and wide plains blanketed in sunflowers, to Gothic churches, baroque palaces and art nouveau civic buildings, Slovenia offers more diversity than countries many times its size. Its incredible mixture of climates brings warm Mediterranean breezes up to the foothills of the Alps, where it can even snow in summer. With more than half of its total area covered in forest, Slovenia truly is one of the greenest countries in the world – and in recent years it has also become Europe's activities playground.

Among Slovenia's greatest assets, though, are the Slovenes themselves – welcoming, generous, multilingual, broad-minded. As far as they are concerned, they do not live emotionally, spiritually or even geographically in 'Eastern' Europe – their home is the very heart of the continent.

FAST FACTS

- **Area** 20,273 sq km
- **Capital** Ljubljana
- **Currency** euro (€); US$1 = €0.73; UK£1 = €1.06; A$1 = €0.50; ¥100 = €0.76; NZ$1 = €0.41
- **Famous for** hiking and skiing, Lake Bled, Lipizzaner horses, *pršut* (air-dried ham)
- **Official language** Slovene
- **Phrases** *dober dan* (hello); *živijo* (hi); *prosim* (please); *hvala* (thank you); *oprostite* (excuse me); *nasvidenje* (goodbye)
- **Population** 2.018 million
- **Telephone codes** country code ☎ 386; international access code ☎ 00
- **Visas** not required for most nationalities; see p738

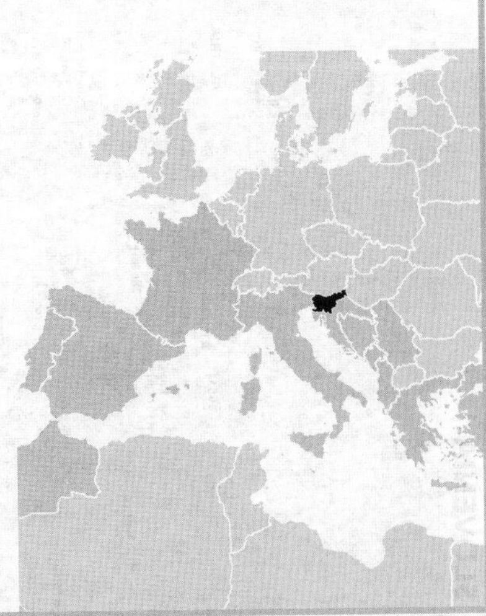

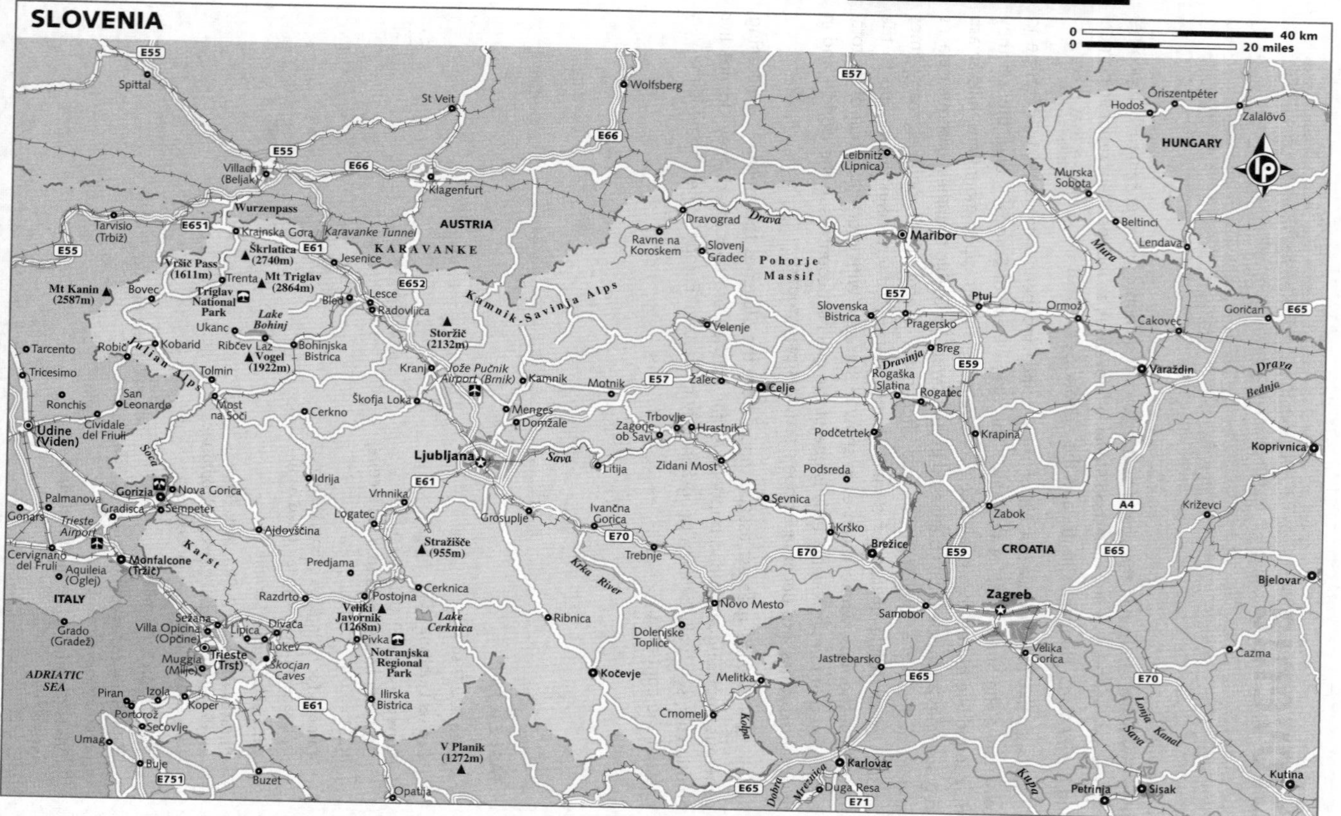
SLOVENIA
0 40 km
0 20 miles
HUNGARY
AUSTRIA
CROATIA
ITALY
ADRIATIC SEA
Zalalövő
Őriszentpéter
Hodoš
Beltinci
Lendava
Murska Sobota
Mura
Goričan
Čakovec
Varaždin
Drava
Bednja
Koprivnica
Bjelovar
Križevci
Čazma
Kutina
Lonja Kanal
Sava
Sisak
Petrinja
Kupa
Velika Gorica
Zagreb
Zabok
Krapina
Ormož
Ptuj
Maribor
Leibnitz (Lipnica)
Pragersko
Breg
Rogatec
Dravinja
Rogaška Slatina
Slovenska Bistrica
Samobor
Brežice
Podčetrtek
Podsreda
Krško
Jastrebarsko
Karlovac
Duga Resa
Mrežnica
Dobra
Pohorje Massif
Dravograd
Slovenj Gradec
Celje
Velenje
Žalec
Hrastnik
Trbovlje
Zagorje ob Savi
Zidani Most
Sevnica
Novo Mesto
Melitka
Kolpa
Črnomelj
Dolenjske Toplice
Trebnje
Wolfsberg
Ravne na Koroskem
Kamnik-Savinja Alps
Motnik
Litija
Ivančna Gorica
Krka River
Kočevje
Ribnica
Kamnik
Menges
Domžale
Grosuplje
St Veit
Klagenfurt
Karavanke
Karavanke Tunnel
Jesenice
Lesce
Radovljica
Storžič (2132m)
Jože Pučnik Airport (Brnik)
Kranj
Ljubljana
Stražišče (955m)
Cerknica
Lake Cerknica
V Planik (1272m)
Škofja Loka
Vrhnika
Logatec
Postojna
Veliki Javornik (1268m)
Pivka
Notranjska Regional Park
Ilirska Bistrica
Opatija
Villach (Beljak)
Wurzenpass
Kranjska Gora
Škrlatica (2740m)
Mt Triglav (2864m)
Bled
Bohinjska Bistrica
Lake Bohinj
Vogel (1922m)
Ribčev Laz
Ukanc
Trenta
Triglav National Park
Vršič Pass (1611m)
Cerkno
Idrija
Predjama
Ajdovščina
Razdrto
Divača
Lokev
Škocjan Caves
Lipica
Sežana
Trieste (Trst)
Villa Opicina (Općine)
Muggia (Milje)
Koper
Izola
Piran
Portorož
Sečovlje
Buje
Umag
Buzet
Spittal
Tarvisio (Trbiž)
Bovec
Kobarid
Tolmin
Most na Soči
Julian Alps
Mt Kanin (2587m)
Robič
San Leonardo
Cividale del Friuli
Soča
Nova Gorica
Šempeter
Gorizia
Gradisca
Karst
Monfalcone (Tržič)
Tarcento
Tricesimo
Ronchis
Udine (Viden)
Palmanova
Trieste Airport
Aquileia (Oglej)
Grado (Gradež)
Cervignano del Friuli
Gonars
E55
E57
E59
E61
E65
E66
E70
E71
E651
E652
E751
A4

HIGHLIGHTS

- Experience the architecture, hilltop castle, green spaces and cafe life of **Ljubljana** (p707), Slovenia's capital.
- Wax romantic at the picture-postcard setting of **Bled** (p719): the lake, the island, the hilltop castle.
- Get into the outdoors or in the bluer-than-blue Soča in the majestic mountain scenery at **Bovec** (p724), arguably the country's best outdoor activities centre.
- Explore the series of karst caves at **Škocjan** (p727) a scene straight out of Jules Verne's *A Journey to the Centre of the Earth.*
- Swoon at wonderful Venetian architecture in the romantic port of **Piran** (p730).

ITINERARIES

- **Three days** Enjoy a long weekend in Ljubljana, sampling the capital's museums and nightlife, with an excursion to Bled.
- **One week** Spend a couple of days in Ljubljana, then head north to unwind in Bohinj or romantic Bled beside idyllic mountain lakes. Depending on the season take a bus or drive over the hair-raising Vršič Pass into the valley of the vivid blue Soča River and take part in some extreme sports in Bovec or Kobarid before returning to Ljubljana.

CLIMATE & WHEN TO GO

The ski season generally lasts from December to March, though heavy snowfall can keep the Vršič Pass closed as late as May. Spring is a great time to be in the lowlands, though it can be pretty wet in May and June. At the same time, the days are getting longer and off-season rates apply. Hotel prices rise in summer, peaking in August, when rooms can be hard to come by on the coast. Warm September days are calm and ideal for hiking and climbing, while October and November can be rainy.

HISTORY

Slovenes can make a credible claim to have invented democracy. By the early 7th century their Slavic forebears had founded the Duchy of Carantania (Karantanija), based at Krn Castle (now Karnburg in Austria). Ruling dukes were elected by ennobled commoners and invested before ordinary citizens. This model was noted by the 16th-century French political theorist Jean Bodin, whose work was a key reference for Thomas Jefferson when he wrote the American Declaration of Independence in 1775–76. Carantania (later Carinthia) was fought over by Franks and Magyars from the 8th to 10th centuries, and later divided up among Austro-Germanic nobles and bishops. By 1335 Carantania and most of present-day Slovenia, with the exception of the Venetian-controlled coastal towns, were dominated by the Habsburgs.

Indeed, Austria ruled what is now Slovenia until 1918, apart from a brief interlude between 1809 and 1813 when Napoleon created six 'Illyrian Provinces' from Slovenian and Croatian regions and made Ljubljana the capital. Napoleon proved a popular conqueror as his relatively liberal regime de-Germanised the education system. Slovene was taught in schools for the first time, leading to a blossoming of national consciousness. In tribute, Ljubljana still has a French Revolution Sq (Trg Francoske Revolucije) with a column bearing a likeness of the French emperor.

Fighting during WWI was particularly savage along the Soča Valley – what would later become known as the Isonzo Front, which was occupied by Italy then dramatically retaken by German-led Austrian-Hungarian forces. The war ended with the collapse of Austria-Hungary, which handed western Slovenia to Italy as part of postwar reparations. Northern Carinthia, including the towns of Beljak and Celovec (now Villach and Klagenfurt), voted

CONNECTIONS: MOVING ON FROM SLOVENIA

As wonderful as Slovenia is, it is extremely well placed to leave. Border formalities with Slovenia's three European Union neighbours – Italy, Austria and Hungary – are almost nonexistent and all are accessible by train (p738) and (less frequently) bus (p738), as are many other European nations. Venice can also be reached by boat from Izola (p730) and Piran (p733). As a member state that forms part of the EU's external frontier, Slovenia must implement the strict Schengen border rules, so expect a somewhat closer inspection of your documents – national ID (for EU citizens) or passport and, in some cases, visa – when travelling by train or bus to/from Croatia.

HOW MUCH?

- **100km by bus/train** €9/6
- **Bicycle rental (one day)** €5 to €15
- **Bottle of ordinary/quality Slovenian wine** €4/8
- **Cup of coffee in a cafe** €1 to €2.50
- **Daily ski pass (adult/child)** €26/16

LONELY PLANET INDEX

- **1L petrol** €0.96
- **1L bottled water** €0.35 to €1
- **500mL local beer (shop/bar)** €1/3
- **Souvenir T-shirt** €10 to €15
- **Street snack (burek)** €2 to €3

to stay with Austria in a 1920 plebiscite. What remained of Slovenia joined fellow south *(jug)* Slavs in forming the Kingdom of Serbs, Croats and Slovenes, later Yugoslavia.

Nazi occupation in WWII was for the most part resisted by Slovenian partisans, though after Italy capitulated in 1943 the anti-partisan Slovenian Domobranci (Home Guards) were active in the west and, in a bid to prevent the communists from taking political control in liberated areas, threw their support behind the Germans. The war ended with Slovenia regaining Italian-held areas from Piran to Bovec, but losing Trst (Trieste) and part of divided Gorica (Gorizia).

Slovenia, with only 8% of the national population, was the economic powerhouse of Tito's Yugoslavia, producing up to 20% of the national GDP. By the 1980s the federation was becoming increasingly Serb-dominated, and Slovenes, who already felt taken for granted economically, feared losing their political autonomy. After free elections, Slovenia broke away from Yugoslavia on 25 June 1991. A 10-day war that left 66 people dead followed; rump Yugoslavia swiftly signed a truce in order to concentrate on regaining control of coastal Croatia. Slovenia was admitted to the UN in May 1992 and, together with nine other 'accession' countries, became a member of the EU in May 2004. In January 2007 Slovenia replaced the tolar with the euro as the national currency.

Slovenia shared the presidency of the EU Council with France in 2008, the same year that saw the death of President Janez Drnovšek of cancer at age 57. In the national elections of October of that year, Janez Janša's coalition government was defeated by the Social Democrats under Borut Pahor, who was able to form a coalition with three minority parties.

PEOPLE

The population of Slovenia is largely homogeneous. More than 87% are ethnic Slovenes, with the remainder being Croats, Serbians, Bosnians and Roma; there are also small enclaves of Italians and Hungarians, who have special deputies looking after their interests in parliament. Slovenes are ethnically Slavic, typically multilingual and extroverts. Just under 58% of Slovenes identify themselves as Roman Catholics.

ARTS

Slovenia's most cherished writer is the Romantic poet France Prešeren (1800–49), whose statue commands Ljubljana's central square. Prešeren's patriotic yet humanistic verse was a driving force in raising Slovene national consciousness. Fittingly, a stanza of his poem *Zdravlijca* (A Toast) comprise the lyrics of the national anthem.

Many of Ljubljana's most characteristic architectural features, including its recurring pyramid motif, were added by celebrated Slovenian architect Jože Plečnik (1872–1957), whose work fused classical architectural principles and folk-art traditions.

Slovenia has some excellent modern and contemporary artists, including Rudi Skočir, whose style reflects a taste for Viennese art nouveau. A favourite sculptor-cum-designer is Oskar Kogoj, whose work has become increasingly commercial in recent years.

Postmodernist painting and sculpture were more or less dominated from the 1980s by the multimedia group Neue Slowenische Kunst (NSK) and the artists' cooperative Irwin. It also spawned the internationally known industrial-music group Laibach, whose leader, Tomaž Hostnik, died tragically in 1983 when he hanged himself from a *kozolec*, the traditional (and iconic) hayrack found almost everywhere in Slovenia. Slovenia's vibrant music scene embraces rave, techno, jazz, punk, thrash-metal and *chanson* (torch songs from the likes of Vita Mavrič); the most popular local rock group is Siddharta, the only Slovenian band ever to appear on MTV. There's also a folk-music revival: listen for the groups Katice, Brina and Katalena, who play traditional Slovenian music with a modern twist. Terra Folk is the quintessential world music band.

Another way to hear traditional music is to attend the fun-filled Ljubljana-based 'Slovenian Evening' of folk music and dancing (audience participation mandatory) along with a four-course meal of Slovenian specialities plus wine run by an outfit called **Židana Marela** (☎ 040-363 272; www.zidanamarela.si; €33). Groups depart from the Prešeren monument at 7.15pm on Wednesday and Friday year-round and proceed to the Skriti Kot (Hidden Corner), a restaurant in the shopping mall below Trg Ajdovščina. Just follow the guide with the red umbrella.

Well-received Slovenian films in recent years include *Kruh in Mleko* (Bread & Milk, 2001), the tragic story of a dysfunctional small-town family by Jan Cvitkovič, and Damjan Kozole's *Rezerni Deli* (Spare Parts, 2003) about the trafficking of illegal immigrants through Slovenia from Croatia to Italy by a couple of embittered misfits living in the southern town of Krško, site of the nation's only nuclear power plant. Much lighter is *Petelinji Zajtrk* (Rooster's Breakfast, 2007), a romance by Marko Naberšnik set in Gornja Radgona on the Austrian border in northeast Slovenia.

ENVIRONMENT

Slovenia is amazingly green; indeed, just under 57% of its total surface area is covered in forest. It is home to almost 3200 plant species – some 70 of which are indigenous. Triglav National Park is particularly rich in native flowering plants. Among the more peculiar endemic fauna in Slovenia is a blind salamander called *Proteus anguinus* that lives deep in karst caves, can survive for years without eating and has been called a 'living fossil'.

FOOD & DRINK

It's relatively hard to find such archetypal Slovenian foods as *žlikrofi* ('ravioli' filled with cheese, bacon and chives), *brodet* (fish soup) from the coast, *ajdovi žganci z ocvirki* (buckwheat 'porridge' with savoury pork crackling/scratchings) and salad greens doused in *bučno olje* (pumpkinseed oil); generally these are dishes eaten at home. A *gostilna* or *gostišče* (inn) or *restavracija* (restaurant), which are generally open 10am or 11am to 10pm or 11pm, more frequently serves *rižota* (risotto), *klobasa* (sausage), *zrezek* (cutlet/steak), *golaž* (goulash) and *paprikaš* (piquant chicken or beef 'stew'). *Riba* (fish) is usually priced by the *dag* (100g). *Postrv* (freshwater trout) generally costs half the price of sea fish, though grilled squid *(lignji na žaru)* doused in garlic butter is usually a bargain.

Common in Slovenia are such Balkan favourites as *cevapčiči* (spicy meatballs of beef or pork), *pljeskavica* (spicy meat patties) and *ražnjiči* (shish kebabs), often served with *krompir* (potatoes).

You can snack cheaply on takeaway pizza slices or pieces of *burek* (€2 to €3), flaky pastry sometimes stuffed with meat, cheese or apple. Alternatives include *štruklji* (cottage-cheese dumplings) and *palačinke* (thin sweet pancakes).

Some restaurants have *dnevno kosilo* (set lunches), including *juha* (soup) and *solata* (salad), for as low as €5. This can be less than the price of a cheap main course, and usually one option will be vegetarian.

Tap water is safe to drink everywhere. Distinctively Slovenian wines include peppery red Teran made from Refošk grapes in the Karst region, Cviček, a dry light red – almost rosé – *vino* (wine) from eastern Slovenia and Malvazija, a straw-colour white wine from the coast that is light and dry. Slovenes are justly proud of their top vintages, but cheaper bar-standard 'open wine' (*odprto vino*) sold by the decilitre (0.1L) is often rot-gut.

Pivo (beer), whether *svetlo* (lager) or *temno* (dark), is best on *točeno* (draught).

There are dozens of kinds of *žganje* (fruit brandy) available, including *češnjevec* (made with cherries), *sadjevec* (mixed fruit), *brinjevec* (juniper), *hruška* (pears, also called *viljamovka*) and *slivovka* (plums).

Like many other countries in Europe, Slovenia bans smoking across the board in all public places, including restaurants, bars and hotels.

LJUBLJANA

☎ 01 / pop 216,200

Ljubljana is by far Slovenia's largest and most populous city. It is also the nation's political, economic and cultural capital. As such, virtually everything of national importance begins, ends or is taking place in Ljubljana.

But it can be difficult to get a grip on the place. In many ways the city whose name *almost* means 'beloved' (*ljubljena*) in Slovene

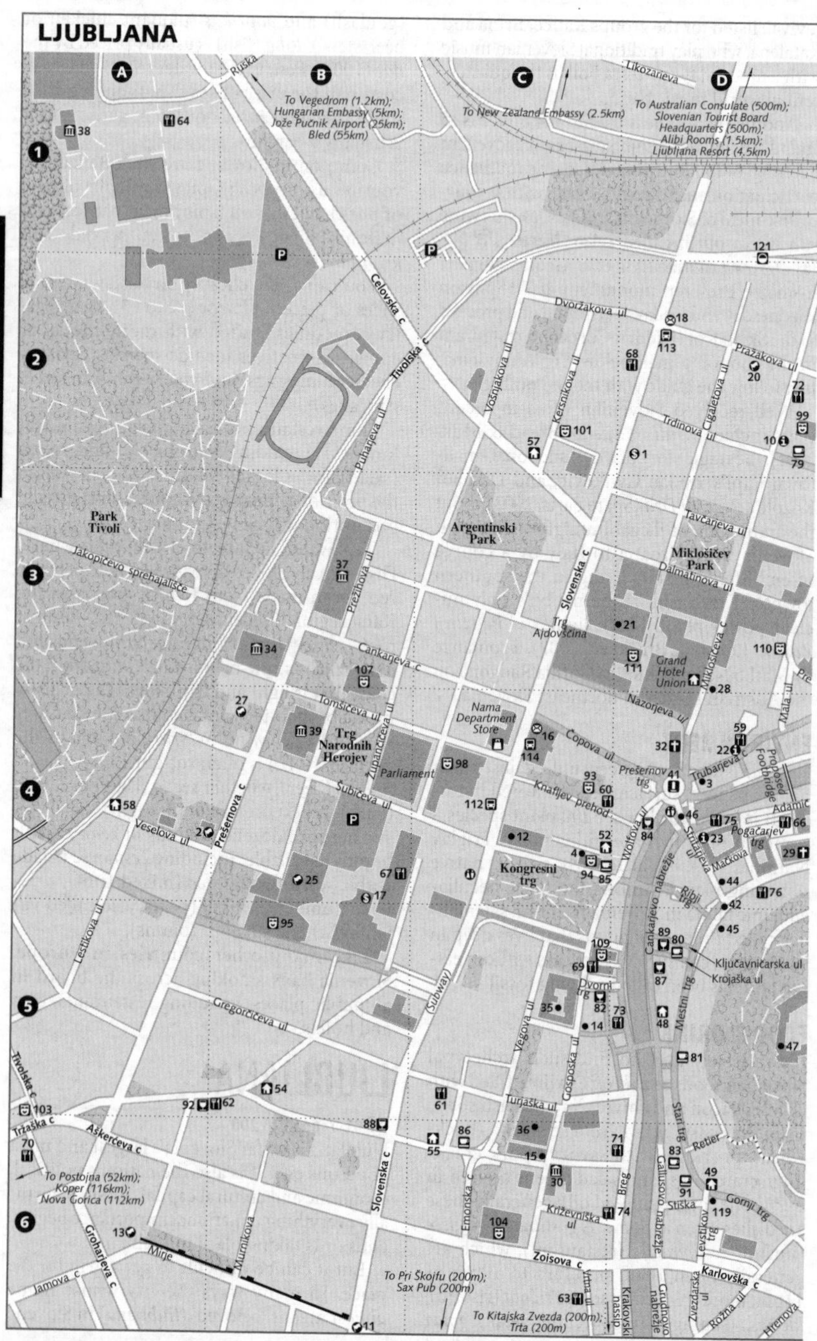
LJUBLJANA
To Vegedrom (1.2km); Hungarian Embassy (5km); Jože Pučnik Airport (25km); Bled (55km)
To New Zealand Embassy (2.5km)
To Australian Consulate (500m); Slovenian Tourist Board Headquarters (500m); Alibi Rooms (1.5km); Ljubljana Resort (4.5km)
Ruska
Likozarjeva
Celovska c
Tivolska c
Dvoržakova ul
Pražakova ul
Vošnjakova ul
Kersnikova ul
Trdinova ul
Cigaletova ul
Puharjeva ul
Park Tivoli
Argentinski Park
Tavčarjeva ul
Miklošičev Park
Dalmatinova ul
Jakopičevo sprehajališče
Prežihova ul
Slovenska c
Trg Ajdovščina
Cankarjeva c
Grand Hotel Union
Miklošičeva c
Tomšičeva ul
Nazorjeva ul
Trg Narodnih Herojev
Župančičeva ul
Nama Department Store
Čopova ul
Parliament
Prešernov trg
Trubarjeva c
Proposed Footbridge
Šubičeva ul
Knafljev prehod
Wolfova ul
Adamič
Veselova ul
Prešernova c
Pogačarjev trg
Stritarjeva ul
Kongresni trg
Mačkova
Ribji trg
Lestikova ul
Cankarjevo nabrežje
Ključavničarska ul
Krojaška ul
(Subway)
Dvorni trg
Mestni trg
Gregorčičeva ul
Vegova ul
Gosposka ul
Tivolska c
Turjaška ul
Tržaška c
Aškerčeva c
Stari trg
Retier
To Postojna (52km); Koper (116km); Nova Gorica (112km)
Emonska c
Breg
Gallusovo nabrežje
Stiška
Gornji trg
Levstikov trg
Križevniška ul
Groharjeva c
Murnikova
Mirje
Jamova c
Zoisova c
Karlovška c
To Pri Škofju (200m); Sax Pub (200m)
To Kitajska Zvezda (200m); Trta (200m)
Vrtna ul
Krakovski nasip
Grudnovo nabrežje
Zvezdarska ul
Rožna ul
Hrenova

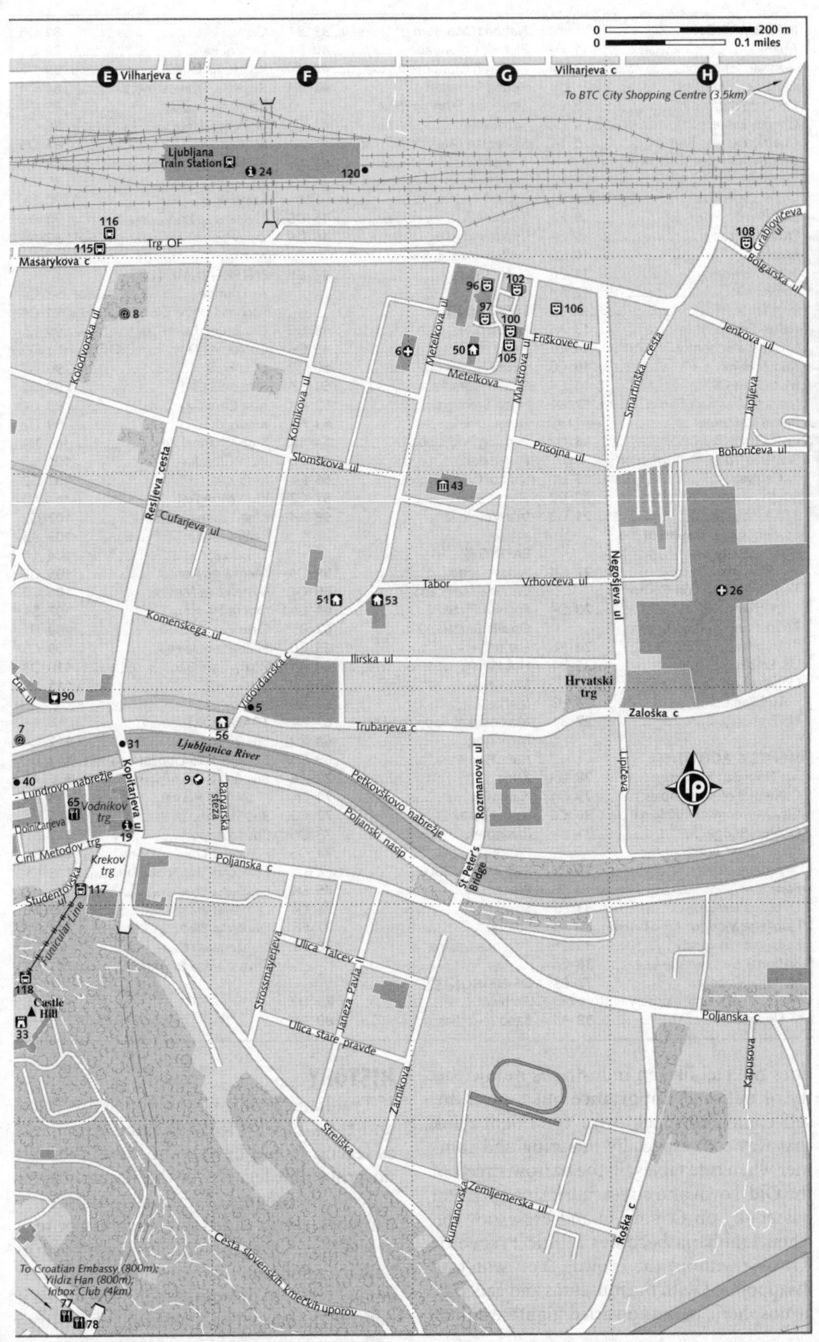
0 200 m
0 0.1 miles
E
F
G
H
Vilharjeva c
Vilharjeva c
To BTC City Shopping Centre (3.5km)
Ljubljana Train Station
24
120
116
115
Trg OF
Masarykova c
108
Grablovičeva ul
Bolgarska ul
8
Kolodvorska ul
96
102
97
100
105
106
6
50
Metelkova ul
Metelkova
Maistrova ul
Friškovec ul
Jenkova ul
Japljeva
Šmartinska cesta
Kotnikova ul
Resljeva cesta
Slomškova ul
Prisojna ul
Bohoričeva ul
43
Cufarjeva ul
Tabor
Vrhovčeva ul
26
51
53
Komenskega ul
Negošjeva ul
Ilirska ul
Vidovdanska c
Hrvatski trg
90
5
Zaloška c
56
Trubarjeva c
7
31
Ljubljanica River
40
Lundrovo nabrežje
9
Barvarska steza
Petkovškovo nabrežje
Rozmanova ul
Lipičeva
65
Vodnikov trg
Dolničarjeva
19
Kopitarjeva ul
Poljanski nasip
Ciril Metodov trg
Krekov trg
Poljanska c
St Peter's Bridge
Studentovska ul
117
Funicular Line
Ulica Talcev
Strossmayerjeva
Janeza Pavla II
118
Castle Hill
33
Ulica stare pravde
Poljanska c
Kapusova
Zarnikova
Streliška
Zemljemerska ul
Kumanovska
Roška c
Cesta slovenskih kmečkih uporov
To Croatian Embassy (800m); Yildiz Han (800m); Inbox Club (4km)
77
78
SLOVENIA

INFORMATION

Abanka 1 D2
Austrian Embassy 2 A4
Canadian Embassy (see 25)
Central Pharmacy 3 D4
Chemo Express 4 C4
Chemo Express Branch 5 F4
Community Health Centre Ljubljana 6 F2
Cyber Café Xplorer 7 E4
DrogArt 8 E2
Dutch Embassy 9 E4
Erazem 10 D2
French Embassy 11 B6
Geonavtik 12 C4
Irish Embassy (see 9)
Italian Embassy 13 A6
Knjigarna Behemot 14 C5
Kod & Kam 15 C6
Main Post Office 16 C4
Nova Ljubljanska Banka 17 B4
Portal.si Internet (see 115)
Post Office Branch 18 D2
Slovenia Tourist Information Centre 19 E4
South African Consulate 20 D2
STA Ljubljana 21 D3
Student Organisation of the University of Ljubljana 22 D4
Tourist Information Centre Ljubljana 23 D4
Tourist Information Centre Ljubljana 24 F1
UK Embassy 25 B4
University Medical Centre Ljubljana 26 H3
US Embassy 27 B4

SIGHTS & ACTIVITIES

Art Nouveau Buildings 28 D3
Cathedral of St Nicholas 29 D4
City Museum of Ljubljana 30 C6
Dragon Bridge 31 E4
Franciscan Church of the Annunciation 32 D4
Funicular (see 117)
Ljubljana Castle 33 E5
Ljubljana Modern Art Museum 34 B3
Ljubljana University 35 C5
National & University Library 36 C6
National Gallery 37 B3
Museum of Contemporary History of Slovenia 38 A1
National Museum of Slovenia 39 B4
Plečnik Colonnade 40 E4
Prešeren Monument 41 D4
Robba Fountain 42 D4
Slovenian Ethnographic Museum 43 G3
Slovenian Museum of Natural History (see 39)
Tourist Train 44 D4
Tourist Train (see 41)
Town Hall 45 D5
Triple Bridge 46 D4
Watchtower & Virtual Museum 47 D5

SLEEPING

Alibi Hostel 48 D5
Antiq Hotel 49 D6
Celica Hostel 50 G2
Dijaški Dom Tabor 51 F3
Hotel Emonec 52 C4
Hotel Park 53 F3
Penzion Pod Lipo 54 B5
Pri Mraku 55 C6
Simbol Castle Hotel 56 F4
Slamič B&B 57 C2
Vila Veselova 58 A4

EATING

Ajdovo Zrno 59 D4
Cantina Mexicana 60 C4
Foculus Pizzeria 61 C5
Gostila Rimska XXI 62 B5
Harambaša 63 C6
Hot Horse 64 A1
Market 65 E4
Market 66 D4
Maximarket Supermarket 67 B4
Mercator 68 D2
Mercator Branch 69 C5
Mirje 70 A6
Namasté 71 D6
Nobel Burek 72 D2
Paninoteka 73 D5
Pri Vitezu 74 D6
Restavracija 2000 (see 67)
Ribca 75 D4
Sokol 76 D4
Špajza 77 E6
Taverna Tatjana 78 E6

DRINKING

Ambient 79 D2
Babo Juice Bar 80 D5
Čajna Hiša 81 D5
Dvorni Bar 82 C5
Kafeterija Lan 83 D6
Kavarna Tromostovje 84 D4
Kavarna Zvezda 85 C4
Le Petit Café 86 C6
Maček 87 D5
Pr' Semaforju 88 B6
Pr' Skelet 89 D5
Salon 90 E4
Slaščičarna Pri Vodnjaku 91 D6
Žmavc 92 A5

ENTERTAINMENT

As Lounge 93 C4
Bachus Centre Club 94 C4
Cankarjev Dom 95 B5
Cankarjev Dom Ticket Office (see 67)
Gala Hala 96 G2
Jalla Jalla Club 97 G2
Jazz Club Gajo 98 C4
Kinoteka 99 D2
Klub Channel Zero (see 96)
Klub Gromka 100 G2
Klub K4 101 C2
Klub Monokel (see 102)
Klub Tiffany 102 G2
KMŠ Club 103 A5
Križanke 104 C6
Menza pri Koritu 105 G2
Metelkova Mesto 106 G2
Opera House 107 B3
Orto Bar 108 H1
Philharmonic Hall 109 C5
Roxly Café Bar 110 D3
Ultra 111 D3

TRANSPORT

Bus 27 to Inbox Club 112 C4
Bus 6 & 8 to Ljubljana Resort 113 D2
Bus 6 & 8 to Ljubljana Resort, Bus 14 to Alibi Rooms 114 C4
Bus Station 115 E1
Bus to Airport 116 E1
Funicular Lower Station 117 E4
Funicular Upper Station 118 E5
Ljubljana Bike (see 50)
Ljubljana Bike 119 D6
Ljubljana Bike 120 F1
Ljubljana Bike (see 19)
Private Vans to Airport 121 D1

does not feel like an industrious municipality of national importance but a pleasant, self-contented small town. You might think that way too, especially in spring and summer when cafe tables fill the narrow streets of the Old Town and street musicians entertain passers-by on Čopova ul and Prešernov trg. Then Ljubljana becomes a little Prague or Kraków without the crowds. You won't be disappointed with the museums and galleries, atmospheric bars and varied nightlife either.

HISTORY

If Ljubljana really was founded by Jason and the Golden Fleece–seeking Argonauts as legend would have you believe, they left no proof. But legacies of the Roman city of Emona – remnants of walls, dwellings, early churches, even a gilded statuette – can be seen everywhere. Ljubljana took its present form as Laibach under the Austrian Habsburgs, but it gained regional prominence in 1809, when it became the capital of Napoleon's short-lived

'Illyrian Provinces'. Some fine art nouveau buildings filled up the holes left by a devastating earthquake in 1895, and architect Jože Plečnik continued the remake of the city up until WWII.

ORIENTATION

Prešernov trg, on the left bank of the Ljubljanica River, is the heart of Ljubljana. Just across delightful Triple Bridge is the picturesque – if bite-sized – Old Town, which follows the north and west flanks of Castle Hill. The bus and train stations are 800m northeast of Prešernov trg up Miklošičeva c.

Ljubljana's Jože Pučnik Airport, at Brnik near Kranj, is 27km north of the city.

Maps

Excellent free maps, some of which show the city's bus network, are available from the tourist offices (see p712). The more detailed 1:20,000-scale *Mestni Načrt Ljubljana* (Ljubljana City Map; €7.70) from Kod & Kam is available at news-stands and bookshops.

INFORMATION

Bookshops

Geonavtik (☎ 252 70 27; www.geonavtik.com; Kongresni trg 1; ⌚ 8.30am-8.30pm Mon-Fri, 8.30am-4pm Sat) Stocks guides and books about Slovenia.

Knjigarna Behemot (☎ 251 13 92; www.behemot.si; Židovska steza 3; ⌚ 10am-8pm Mon-Fri, 10am-3pm Sat) Pint-size English-language bookshop for bibliophiles.

Kod & Kam (☎ 200 27 32; www.gzs-dd.si/kod&kam; Trg Francoske Revolucije 7; ⌚ 8am-8pm Mon-Fri, 8am-1pm Sat) Map specialists.

Discount Cards

The Ljubljana Card (€12.50), valid for three days (72 hours) and available from the tourist offices (p712), offers free admission to many museums, unlimited city bus travel and discounts on organised tours, accommodation and restaurants, hire cars etc.

Internet Access

Web connection is available at virtually all hostels and hotels, the Slovenia Tourist Information Centre (p712; €1 per half-hour), STA Ljubljana (p712; €1 per 20 minutes) and Student Organisation of the University of Ljubljana (p712; free). In addition:

Cyber Café Xplorer (☎ 430 19 91; Petkovškovo nabrežje 23; per 30min/hr/5hr €2.50/4/12; ⌚ 10am-10pm Mon-Fri, 2-10pm Sat & Sun) Ljubljana's best internet cafe, with 10 superfast computers, wi-fi and international phone calls at €0.10 per minute.

DrogArt (☎ 439 72 70; Kolodvorska ul 20; 1st 15min free, then per 30min/hr €1/1.80; ⌚ 10am-4pm Mon-Fri) Opposite the train station.

Portal.si Internet (☎ 234 46 00; Trg OF 4; per hr €3.80; ⌚ 7am-8.30pm) In the bus station (get code from window No 4).

Internet Resources

City of Ljubljana (www.ljubljana.si) Comprehensive information portal on every aspect of life and tourism.

Laundry

Washing machines (€5 per load) are available, even to nonguests, at the Celica Hostel (p714). Commercial laundries, including **Chemo Express** (☎ 251 44 04; Wolfova ul 12; ⌚ 7am-6pm Mon-Fri); Tabor (☎ 23107 82; Vidovdanska ul 2), charge from €4.20 per kg.

Left Luggage

Bus station (Trg OF 4; per day €2; ⌚ 5.30am-10.30pm Sun-Fri, 5am-10pm Sat) Window No 3.

Train station (Trg OF 6; per day €2-3; ⌚ 24hr) Coin lockers on platform No 1.

Medical Services

Central Pharmacy (Centralna Lekarna; ☎ 244 23 60; Prešernov trg 5; ⌚ 7.30am-8pm Mon-Fri, 8am-1pm Sat)

SLOVENIA

LJUBLJANA IN TWO DAYS

Take the funicular up to **Ljubljana Castle** (p712) to get an idea of the lay of the land. After a seafood lunch at **Ribca** (p716), explore the Old Town then cross the Ljubljanica River via St James Bridge and walk north along bust-lined Vegova ul to Kongresni trg and **Prešernov trg** (p712). Over a fortifying libation at **Kavarna Tromostovje** (p716), plan your evening: low key at **Jazz Club Gajo** (p717), chichi at **Ultra** (p717) or alternative at **Metelkova Mesto** (p717).

On your second day check out some of the city's excellent **museums and galleries** (p713), and then stroll or cycle through Park Tivoli, stopping for a oh-so-local horse burger at **Hot Horse** (p716) along the way.

Community Health Centre Ljubljana (Zdravstveni Dom Ljubljana; www.zd-lj.si; ☎ 472 37 00; Metelkova ul 9; 7.30am-7pm) For nonemergencies.

University Medical Centre Ljubljana (Univerzitetni Klinični Center Ljubljana; ☎ 522 50 50; www3.kclj.si; Zaloška c 2; 24hr) Accident and emergency service.

Money

There are ATMs at every turn, including a row of them outside the main tourist information centre (TIC) office. At both the bus and train stations you'll find **bureaux de change** (7am-8pm) changing cash for no commission but not travellers cheques.

Abanka (☎ 300 15 00; Slovenska c 50; 9am-5pm Mon-Fri)

Nova Ljubljanska Banka (☎ 476 39 00; Trg Republike 2; 8am-6pm Mon-Fri)

Post

Main post office (Slovenska c 32; 8am-7pm Mon-Fri, to 1pm Sat) Holds poste restante for 30 days and changes money.

Post office branch (Pražakova ul 3; 8am-7pm Mon-Fri, to noon Sat) Just southwest of the bus and train stations.

Tourist Information

Slovenia Tourist Information Centre (STIC; ☎ 306 45 76; www.slovenia.info; Krekov trg 10; 8am-9pm Jun-Sep, 8am-7pm Oct-May) Internet and bicycle hire also available.

Student Organisation of the University of Ljubljana (Študentska Organizacija Univerze Ljubljani; ŠOU; ☎ 433 01 76; www.sou-lj.si; Trubarjeva c 7; 9am-6pm Mon-Thu, 9am-3pm Fri) Information and free internet.

Tourist Information Centre Ljubljana Old Town (TIC; ☎ 306 12 15; www.visitljubljana.si; Kresija Bldg, Stritarjeva ul; 8am-9pm Jun-Sep, 8am-7pm Oct-May); Train station (☎ 433 94 75; Trg OF 6; 8am-10pm Jun-Sep, 10am-7pm Oct-May)

Travel Agencies

Erazem (☎ 430 55 37; www.erazem.net; basement, Miklošičeva c 26; 10am-5pm Mon-Fri Jun-Sep, noon-5pm Mon-Fri Oct-May) Staff make flight and train bookings and sell student and hostel cards.

STA Ljubljana (☎ 439 16 90; www.staljubljana.com; 1st fl, Trg Ajdovščina 1; 10am-1pm & 2-5pm Mon-Fri) Discount airfares for students; go online at their internet cafe (open 8am to midnight Monday to Saturday).

SIGHTS

Ljubljana Castle (☎ 232 99 94; www.ljubljanafestival.si; admission free; 9am-11pm May-Sep, 10am-9pm Oct-Apr) crowns a wooded hill that is the city's focal point. It's an architectural mishmash, including fortified walls dating from the early 16th century, a late-15th-century chapel and a 1970s concrete cafe. The best views are from the 19th-century **watchtower** (adult/student/child €3.50/2/2; 9am-9pm May-Sep, 10am-6pm Oct-Apr); admission includes a visit to the **Virtual Museum** below, a 23-minute, 3-D video tour of Ljubljana though the centuries. The fastest way to reach the castle is via the **funicular** (vzpenjača; adult/student/child return €3/2/2; 9am-11pm May-Sep, 10am-9pm Oct-Apr), which ascends from Krekov trg every 10 minutes, though you can also take the hourly **tourist train** (adult/child €3/2; up 9am-9pm, down 9.20am-9.20pm) from just south of the TIC on Stritarjeva ul. It takes about 15 minutes to walk to the castle from the Old Town.

Central Prešernov trg is dominated by the salmon pink, 17th-century **Franciscan Church of the Annunciation** (6.40am-noon & 3-8pm) and the **Prešeren monument** (1905), in honour of the national poet France Prešeren. Coyly observing Prešeren from a terracotta window at Wolfova ul 4 is a bust of his unrequited love (and poetic inspiration), Julija Primic. Wander north of the square along Miklošičeva c to admire the fine **art nouveau buildings**, including the landmark Grand Hotel Union at No 1, built in 1905, and the colourful former Cooperative Bank (1922) at No 8.

Leading southward from Prešernov trg is the small but perfectly formed **Triple Bridge**; prolific architect Jože Plečnik added two side bridges to the 19th-century span in 1931 to create something truly unique. The renovated baroque **Robba Fountain** stands before the Gothic **town hall** (1718) in **Mestni trg**, the 'City Square', that leads into two more: **Stari trg** (Old Sq) and **Gornji trg** (Upper Sq).

East of the Triple Bridge, the 18th-century **Cathedral of St Nicholas** (Dolničarjeva ul 1; 10am-noon & 3-6pm) is filled with pink marble, white stucco, gilt and a panoply of baroque frescoes. North and east of the cathedral is a lively open-air market (p716) selling both foodstuffs and dry goods, the magnificent riverside **Plečnik Colonnade** and the **Dragon Bridge** (Zmajski Most; 1901), a span guarded by four of the mythical creatures that are now the city's mascots.

The main building of **Ljubljana University** (Kongresni trg 12) was erected as a ducal palace in 1902. The more restrained Philharmonic Hall (p718) dates from 1898. South of the university building is the **National & University Library** (Gosposka ul 14; ⏰ 9am-6pm Mon-Fri, 9am-2pm Sat), Plečnik's masterpiece completed in 1941, with its stunning main reading room. Diagonally opposite is the excellent **City Museum of Ljubljana** (☎ 241 25 00; www.mm-lj.si; Gosposka ul 15; adult/student & child €4/2.50; ⏰ 10am-6pm Tue-Sun). The reconstructed Roman street dating back to the 1st century AD is worth a visit in itself.

Of several major galleries and museums west of Slovenska c, the best are the impressive **National Gallery** (☎ 241 54 18; www.ng-slo.si; Prešernova c 24 & Cankarjeva c 20; permanent collection free, temporary exhibits adult/student €7/3.50; ⏰ 10am-6pm Tue-Sun), which contains the nation's historical art collection and the fascinating **National Museum of Contemporary History** (☎ 300 96 10; www.muzej-nz.si; Celovška c 23; adult/student €3.35/2.50; ⏰ 10am-6pm) in Park Tivoli, with its imaginative look at 20th-century Slovenia through multimedia and artefacts. The inwardly vibrant (but outwardly drab) 1940s **Ljubljana Modern Art Museum** (☎ 241 68 00; www.mg-lj.si; Cankarjeva c 15) was undergoing extensive renovation at the time of research.

The **National Museum of Slovenia** (☎ 241 44 00; www.nms.si; Muzejska ul 1; adult/student €3/2.50, admission 1st Sun of month free; ⏰ 10am-6pm Fri-Wed, 10am-8pm Thu), in an elegant 1888 building, has rich archaeological and coin collections, including a Roman lapidarium and a Stone Age bone flute discovered near Cerkno in western Slovenia in 1995. Joint entry to the National Museum and the attached **Slovenian Museum of Natural History** (☎ 241 09 40; www2.pms-lj.si; Muzejska ul 1; adult/student €3/2.50), which keeps the same hours, costs €5/4/10 per adult/student/family.

The **Slovenian Ethnographic Museum** (☎ 300 87 00; www.etno-muzej.si; Metelkova ul 2; adult/student €4.50/2.50; ⏰ 10am-6pm Tue-Sun), housed in the 1886 Belgian Barracks on the southern edge of Metelkova, has a permanent collection on the top floor with traditional Slovenian trades and crafts – everything from beekeeping and blacksmithing to glass-painting and pottery making.

TOURS

Two-hour **walking tours** (adult/child 4-12yr €10/5; ⏰ 10am, 2pm & 5pm Apr-Oct) that are combined with a ride up to the castle on the funicular or the tourist train or a cruise on the Ljubljanica are organised by the TIC (opposite). They depart daily from the town hall on Mestni trg in season.

FESTIVALS & EVENTS

There is plenty going on in and around the capital, including **Druga Godba** (www.drugagodba.si), a festival of alternative and world music at the Križanke in late May/early June; the **Ljubljana Festival** (www.ljubljanafestival.si), the nation's premier cultural event (music, theatre and dance) held from early July to late August; and the **Ljubljana Marathon** (www.ljubljanskimaraton.si) in late October.

SLEEPING

Ljubljana is not overly endowed with accommodation choices, though it has gained several new places in the budget and midrange levels in recent years.

Budget

The TIC (opposite) has comprehensive details of **private rooms** (€20-30 per person) and **apartments** (€50-95) though only a handful are what could be called central.

Ljubljana Resort (☎ 568 39 13; www.ljubljanaresort.si/eng; Dunajska c 270; camping adult €7.50-13.50, child €5.75-10.25; ⏰ year-round; 💻 ♿) Wait till you see the facilities at this attractive 6-hectare camping ground–cum-resort 4km north of the city centre. Along with a 50-room hotel (singles €71 to €111, doubles €112 to €152) and five bungalows (€105 to €150) accommodating up to five people, there's Laguna (www.laguna.si, admission adult/child from €8/10, open June to September), a 'city beach club' (read water park) with outdoor swimming pools, fitness studio with sauna, and badminton and volleyball courts. Take bus 6 or 8 to the Ježica stop.

Dijaški Dom Tabor (☎ 234 88 40; www.d-tabor.lj.edus.si; dm/s/d €11/26/38; ⏰ late Jun–late Aug; 💻) In summer five colleges in Ljubljana open their halls of residence *(dijaški dom)* to visitors, but only this 300-bed one, a 10-minute walk southeast of the bus and train stations, is really central. Accommodation is in rooms with one to 10 beds. Enter from Kotnikova ul.

Simbol Castle Hostel (☎ 041-720 825; www.simbol.si; Petkovškovo nabrežje 47; dm/d/tr/q €16/50/54/68; 💻) A favourite new place in Ljubljana, this five-room hostel wraps around a tiny courtyard bordering the Ljubljanica, and one room has views of the castle. Rooms, with two to six beds, have their own kitchens. Internet is free.

Alibi Hostel (☎ 251 12 44; www.alibi.si; Cankarjevo nabrežje 27; dm/d €20/50; ✕ 💻) This well-situated 106-bed hostel on the Ljubljanica has brightly painted, airy dorms with four to 12 wooden bunks and five doubles. One room is air-conditioned and there's a private suite at the top for six people. Farther afield to the north in Bežigrad (bus 14 to Podmilščakova stop), Alibi Rooms (☎ 433 13 31; Kolarjeva ul 30) has eight rooms with between two and six beds (dorms €18, doubles €46) in an old villa with a lovely garden.

our pick **Celica Hostel** (☎ 230 97 00; www.hostelcelica.com; Metelkova ul 8; dm €21, s/d/tr cell €47/54/66, 4-to 5-bed room per person €27, 6-to 7-bed room per person €22; 💻) This stylishly revamped former prison (1882) in Metelkova has 20 'cells', designed by as many different architects and complete with original bars; it also has nine rooms and apartments with three to seven beds; and a packed, popular 12-bed dorm. The ground floor is home to three cafes (set lunch €5 to €7; open 7.30am to midnight) and the hostel boasts its own gallery where everyone can show their own work.

Vila Veselova (☎ 059-926 721; www.v-v.si; Veselova ul 14; dm €21, d/q €68/102; ❄ 💻) This very attractive bright yellow villa, with its own garden and 42 beds in the centre of the museum district, offers mostly hostel accommodation in five colourful rooms with four to eight beds. A double and two apartments with attached facilities and access to a kitchen make it an attractive midrange option, however. Some rooms face Park Tivoli across busy Tivolska c.

Midrange

Penzion Pod Lipo (☎ 031-809 893; www.penzion-podlipo.com; Borštnikov trg 3; d/tr/q €59/72/96; 💻) Sitting atop one of Ljubljana's oldest *gostilne* and by a 400-year-old linden tree, this 10-room inn offers excellent value in a part of the city that is filling up with bars and restaurants. Fall in love with the communal kitchen, the original hardwood floors and the east-facing terrace that catches the morning sun.

Hotel Emonec (☎ 200 15 20; www.hotel-emonec.com; Wolfova ul 12; s €59-72, d €67-77, tr/q €90/105; 💻) The decor is simple and functionally modern at this 39-room hotel and the staff is less than welcoming, but everything is spotless and you can't beat the central location.

Slamič B&B (☎ 433 82 33; www.slamic.si; Kersnikova ul 1; s €65-80, d €95-107; ❄ 💻) It's a titch away from the action but Slamič, a B&B above a famous cafe and teahouse, offers 11 bright rooms with antique(ish) furnishings and parquet floors. Choice rooms include quiet No 1 looking on to a back garden and No 9 just off an enormous terrace used by the cafe and made for smokers.

Pri Mraku (☎ 421 96 00; www.daj-dam.si; Rimska c 4; s €69-77, d €102-112, tr €121-131; ❄ 💻) Although it calls itself a *gostilna*, 'At Twilight' is really just a smallish hotel (36 rooms) in an old building with no lift and a garden. Rooms on the 1st and 4th floors have air-con.

Hotel Park (☎ 300 25 00; www.hotelpark.si; Tabor 9; s €75-80, d €104-110; 💻) A partial facelift inside and out has made this tower-block hotel an even better-value midrange choice in central Ljubljana. The 200 pleasant, well-renovated standard and comfort rooms are bright and unpretentiously well equipped. Cheaper 'hostel' rooms, some of which have shared facilities and others en-suite shower, cost €22/26 per person with shared/private bathroom in a double and €17/19 in a quad. Students with ISIC cards get a 10% discount.

Top End

Antiq Hotel (☎ 421 35 60; www.antiqhotel.si; Gornji trg 3; s €113-164, d €144-204; ❄ 💻) Ljubljana's first (and still only) boutique hotel was cobbled together from a series of townhouses on the site of a Roman workshop. It has 16 rooms and apartments, most of which are very spacious, a small wellness centre next door and multitiered back garden. The decor is kitsch with a smirk and there are fabulous little nooks and touches everywhere: glassed-in medieval courtyard; vaulted ceilings; two noncarpeted, antiallergenic floors; and bath towels trimmed with Slovenian lace. Among our favourite rooms are enormous No 8 on the 2nd floor, with swooningly romantic views of the Hercules Fountain, and No 10, an even bigger two-room suite on the top floor with a terrace and glimpses of Ljubljana Castle. The two cheapest rooms (singles/doubles €61/77), Nos 2 and 9, have their own bathrooms but they're on the corridor.

EATING

The Old Town has a fair number of appealing restaurants, but the majority of the venues here are cafes. For cheaper options, try the dull but functional snack bars around the bus and train stations, and both on and in the shopping mall below Trg Ajdovščina.

Restaurants

Harambaša (☎ 041-843 106; Vrtna ul 8; dishes €3.50-6; 🕑 10am-10pm Mon-Fri, noon-10pm Sat, noon-6pm Sun)

Here you'll find authentic Bosnian – Sarajevan to be precise – dishes like *čevapčiči* (spicy meatballs of beef or pork) and *pljeskavica* (meat patties) served at low tables in a charming modern cottage.

Kitajska Zvezda (☎ 425 88 24; Hrenova ul 19; mains €4.10-12.30; 11am-11pm) If you're looking for a fix of rice or noodles, try the 'Chinese Star' on the river just south of the Old Town. Szechuan dishes, including the *ma po doufu* (tofu with garlic and chilli), are good; they also do Cantonese and Shanghainese food.

Vegedrom (☎ 513 26 42; Vodnikova c 35; mains €5.60-12.60; 11am-10pm Mon-Fri, noon-10pm Sat) This appealing, if somewhat pricey, vegan restaurant at the northeastern edge of Park Tivoli now also dibble-dabbles (or is that nibble-nabbles?) in Indian food. The set lunch is good value at €6.90 and there's a salad bar (from €3.40).

Pri Škofju (☎ 426 45 08; Rečna ul 8; mains €7-15; 10am-midnight Mon-Fri, noon-midnight Sat & Sun) Still our off-the-beaten track favourite, this wonderful little place in tranquil Krakovo, south of the city centre, serves some of the best prepared local dishes and salads in Ljubljana, with an ever-changing menu. Weekday set lunches are good value at €5.30 to €6.90.

Sokol (☎ 439 68 55; Ciril Metodov trg 18; mains €7-20; noon-11pm) In this old vaulted house, traditional Slovenian food is served on heavy tables by costumed waiters. Along with traditional dishes like *obara* (veal stew, €7) and Krvavica sausage with cabbage and turnips (€8.50), there are the more esoteric deep-fried bull's testicles with tartare sauce and grilled stallion steak (€16).

Namasté (☎ 425 01 59; Breg 8; mains €7.50-15.50; 11am-midnight Mon-Sat, to 10pm Sun) Should you fancy a bit of Indian, head for this place on the left bank of the Ljubljanica. You won't get high street–quality curry but the thalis (from €7.50) and tandoori dishes (from €12.30) are good. The choice of vegetarian dishes is better than average and the set lunch is €8.

Cantina Mexicana (☎ 426 93 25; Knafljev prehod 3; mains €7.90-16.80; 10am-1am Sun-Tue, 10am-3am Wed-Fri, 9am-3am Sat) This stylish Mexican restaurant has an eye-catching red and blue exterior and hacienda-like decor inside. The fajitas (€7.90 to €12.90) are good.

Yildiz Han (☎ 426 57 17; Karlovška c 19; mains €8.50-15; noon-midnight Mon-Sat) If Turkish is your thing, head for authentic (trust us) 'Star House', which features belly dancing on Friday nights. Lunches are a snip at €5.

Taverna Tatjana (☎ 421 00 87; Gornji trg 38; mains €8.50-22; 3pm-midnight Mon-Sat) A wooden-beamed cottage pub with a nautical theme (think nets and seascapes), this is actually a rather exclusive fish restaurant with a lovely (and protected) back courtyard for the warmer months.

Gostilna Rimska XXI (☎ 425 20 29; Rimska c 21; mains €10-24; 12.30pm-1am Mon-Fri) This sleek new *gostilna* that changes its menu twice a day serves Mediterranean-inspired dishes till late. Set lunch is €16.

Špajza (☎ 425 30 94; Gornji trg 28; mains €14.60-22; noon-11pm Mon-Sat, to 10pm Sun) A welcome return to the Old Town is the 'Pantry', nicely decorated with its rough-hewn tables and chairs, wooden floors, frescoed ceilings and nostalgic bits and pieces. Try the 'Špajza filet' (€22), which is actually horseflesh, or a bit of *kozliček iz pečiče* (oven-roasted kid; €14.60); wines from a dozen different Slovenian producers are served. A three-course set lunch is only €10.

Pri Vitezu (☎ 426 60 58; Breg 18-20; mains €18-30; noon-11pm Mon-Sat) Located directly on the left bank of the Ljubljanica, 'At the Knight' is the place for a special meal (Mediterranean-style grills and Adriatic fish dishes), whether in the brasserie, the salon or the very cosy Knight's Room.

Ljubljana is awash in pizzerias, where pizza routinely costs €4 to €8.50. The pick of the crop includes **Foculus Pizzeria** (☎ 251 56 43; Gregorčičeva ul 3; 10am-midnight Mon-Fri, noon-midnight Sat & Sun), which boasts a vaulted ceiling painted with spring and autumn leaves; **Trta** (☎ 426 50 66; Grudnovo nabrežje 21; 11am-10.30pm Mon-Fri, noon-10.30pm Sat), on the right bank of the Ljubljanica; and **Mirje** (☎ 426 60 15; Tržaška c 5; 10am-10pm Mon-Fri, noon-5pm Sat), southwest of the city centre, which does some excellent pasta dishes, too.

Quick Eats

Nobel Burek (Miklošičeva c 30; burek €2, pizza slice €1.40; 24hr) This hole-in-the-wall serves Slovenian-style fast food round-the-clock.

Restavracija 2000 (☎ 476 69 25; Trg Republike 1; dishes €1.50-3, set lunch €6.50; 9am-7pm Mon-Fri, 9am-3pm Sat) In the basement of the Maximarket department store, this glass and chrome self-service eatery is surprisingly upbeat, and just the ticket if you want something quick while visiting the main museums.

Ajdovo Zrno (☎ 041-690 478; Trubarjeva c 7; soups & sandwiches €1.80-2, set lunch €6; 🕑 10am-7pm Mon-Fri) Vegetarian 'Buckwheat Grain' serves soups, sandwiches, fried vegetables and lots of different salads (self-service, €3 to €6). And they have terrific, freshly squeezed juices, including the unusual rose-petal juice with lemon. Enter from little Mali trg.

Paninoteka (☎ 041-529 824; Jurčičev trg 3; soups & toasted sandwiches €2.40-6; 🕑 8am-1am Mon-Sat, 9am-11pm Sun) Healthy sandwich creations on a lovely little square by the river.

Hot Horse (☎ 521 14 27; Park Tivoli; snacks & burgers €2.80-6; 🕑 9am-6am Mon, 10am-6am Tue-Sun) This place in a kiosk in the city's largest park supplies Ljubljančani with their favourite treat: horse burgers (€4). It's just down the hill from the National Museum of Contemporary History.

Ribca (☎ 425 15 44; Adamič-Lundrovo nabrežje 1; dishes €3-7.50; 🕑 8am-4pm Mon-Fri, 8am-2pm Sat) This basement seafood bar below the Plečnik Colonnade in Pogačarjev trg serves tasty fried squid, sardines and herrings to hungry market-goers. Set lunch is €7.50.

Self-Catering

Handy supermarkets include a large **Mercator** (Slovenska c 55; 🕑 7am-9pm) southwest of the train and bus stations and a smaller, more central **Mercator branch** (Kongresni trg 9; 🕑 7am-8pm Mon-Fri, 8am-3pm Sat & Sun) just up from the river.

The **Maximarket supermarket** (☎ 476 68 00; basement, Trg Republike 1; 🕑 9am-9pm Mon-Fri, 8am-5pm Sat) below the department store of the same name has the largest selection of food and wine in the city centre.

The open-air **market** (Pogačarjev trg & Vodnikov trg; 🕑 6am-6pm Mon-Fri, 6am-4pm Sat Jun-Sep, 6am-4pm Mon-Sat Oct-May), held across two squares north and east of the cathedral, sells mostly fresh fruit and vegetables.

DRINKING

Few cities of this size have central Ljubljana's concentration of inviting cafes and bars, the vast majority with outdoor seating.

Bars & Pubs

Kavarna Tromostovje (☎ 430 12 18; Prešernov trg 1; 🕑 7am-1am Apr-Oct) This cafe-bar on the southern side of Prešernov trg seems to change its name on an annual basis but remains one of the most popular places for a drink if you just want to sit outside and watch the passing parade.

Maček (☎ 425 37 91; Krojaška ul 5; 🕑 9am-1am) *The* place to be seen in Ljubljana on a sunny summer afternoon, the 'Cat' is Kavarna Tromostovje's rival on the right bank of the Ljubljanica. Happy hour is between 4pm and 7pm on weekdays.

Salon (☎ 439 87 64; Trubarjeva c 23; 🕑 9am-1am Mon-Wed, 9am-3am Thu-Sat, 3pm-1am Sun) Salon is a dazzling designer-kitsch cocktail bar featuring gold ceilings, faux leopard armchairs, heavy purple velvet drapes and excellent cocktails (€4.50 to €6.50).

Sax Pub (☎ 283 14 57; Eipprova ul 7; 🕑 noon-1am Mon, 10am-1am Tue-Sat, 4-10pm Sun) Two decades in Trnovo and decorated with colourful murals and graffiti inside and out, the Sax has live jazz at 9pm or 9.30pm on Thursdays from late August to December and February to June. Canned stuff rules at other times.

Dvorni Bar (☎ 251 12 57; Dvorni trg 2; 🕑 8am-1am Mon-Sat, 8am-midnight Sun) This wine bar is an excellent place to taste Slovenian vintages; it stocks more than 100 varieties and has wine tastings every second Wednesday of the month.

Pr' Skelet (☎ 252 77 99; Ključavničarska ul 5; 🕑 10am-3am) It might sound like a one-joke wonder, but you'll shake, rattle and roll at this skeleton-themed basement bar, where cocktails are two for one throughout the day.

Žmavc (☎ 251 03 24; Rimska c 21; 🕑 7.30am-1am Mon-Fri, 10am-1am Sat, 6pm-1am Sun) A superpopular student hang-out west of Slovenska c, with comic-strip scenes and figures running halfway up the walls.

Pr' Semaforju (☎ 040-893 664; Slovenska c 5; 🕑 7am-midnight Mon-Fri) Student (and we're talking spotty teens here) hang-out par excellence, 'At the Traffic Light' (the name is translated into a dozen languages outside) is a slightly grotty cafe-bar that rocks later in the evening.

Cafes & Teahouses

Kavarna Zvezda (☎ 421 90 90; Kongresni trg 4 & Wolfova ul 14; 🕑 7am-11pm Mon-Sat, 10am-8pm Sun) The 'Star Café' is celebrated for its shop-made cakes, especially *skutina pečena* (€2.60), an eggy cheesecake.

Le Petit Café (☎ 251 25 75; Trg Francoske Revolucije 4; 🕑 7.30am-midnight) Just opposite the Križanke, this pleasant, studenty place offers great coffee and a wide range of breakfast goodies (€2.60 to €6.50).

Ambient (☎ 430 27 56; Čufarjeva ul 5; 🕑 7am-1am Mon-Fri, 9am-1am Sat, 6pm-1am Sun) This stylish cafe-cum-bistro hidden down a narrow side street just east of Miklošičeva c caters to a diverse crowd throughout the day.

Kafeterija Lan (Gallusovo nabrežje 27; ⌚ 10am-midnight Mon-Thu, 10am-1am Fri, 11am-midnight Sat & Sun) A little greener-than-green cafe-bar on the river below Cobbler Bridge, Lan is something of a hipster gay magnet. There's a nice terrace under a spreading chestnut street.

Čajna Hiša (☎ 421 24 44; Stari trg 3; ⌚ 9am-10.30pm Mon-Fri, 9am-3pm & 6-10pm Sat) If you take your cuppa seriously, come here; the appropriately named 'Teahouse' offers a wide range of green and black teas and fruit tisanes for €1.80 to €3.40 a pot.

Babo Juice Bar (☎ 040-533 334; Krojaška ul 4; juices & smoothies €1.95-4.40; ⌚ 9am-9pm) Of the crop of juice bars that have sprouted all over Ljubljana, Babo is the best, with some excellent fruit and vegetable combinations.

Slaščičarna Pri Vodnjaku (☎ 425 07 12; Stari trg 30; ⌚ 8am-midnight) For all kinds of chocolate of the ice cream and drinking kind, the 'Confectionery by the Fountain' will surely satisfy – there are almost three-dozen flavours (€1 per scoop), as well as teas (€1.60) and fresh juices (€0.80 to €3.35).

ENTERTAINMENT

The free quarterly **Ljubljana Life** (www.ljubljanalife.com) has practical information and listings. **Ljubljana in Your Pocket** (www.inyourpocket.com; €2.90), another quarterly, will cost you, but it's a thousand times more useful. *Where to? in Ljubljana*, available from the tourist offices (p712), lists cultural and sporting events.

Nightclubs

Inbox Club (☎ 428 96 90, 428 75 01; www.inbox-club.com; Jurčkova c 224; ⌚ 9pm-dawn Thu-Sat) Ljubljana's biggest club is hidden in a shopping centre opposite the Leclerc Hypermarket (take bus 27 to NS Rudnik, the last stop) in the far southeastern suburbs

Klub K4 (☎ 438 02 61; www.klubk4.org; Kersnikova ul 4; ⌚ 8pm-2am Tue, 8pm-4am Wed & Thu, 9pm-6am Fri & Sat, 10pm-4am Sun) This evergreen venue in the basement of the Student Organisation of Ljubljana University (ŠOU) headquarters features rave-electronic music on Fridays and Saturdays, with other styles of music on weeknights, and a popular gay and lesbian night on Sundays. It closes in July and August.

Bachus Center Club (☎ 241 82 44; www.bachus-center.com; Kongresni trg 3; ⌚ 9pm-5am Mon-Sat) This place has something for everyone, including a restaurant and bar-lounge, and attracts a pretty tame, pretty mainstream crowd.

As Lounge (☎ 425 88 22; www.gostilnaas.si; Čopova 5A but enter from Knafljev prehod; ⌚ 9am-3am Wed-Sat) DJs transform this candlelit basement bar into a pumping, crowd-pulling nightclub four nights a week. The way the name sounds in Slovene might have you thinking you're going to get lucky. It just means 'ace', ace.

Ultra (☎ 070 818 979; www.ultra-club.si; Nazorjeva ul 6; ⌚ 10pm-6am Wed-Sat) Ultra is a popular dance venue with four different theme nights and a switched-on, somewhat chichi crowd.

KMŠ (☎ 425 74 80; www.klubkms.si; Tržaška ul 2; ⌚ 8am-5am Mon-Fri, 9pm-5am Sat) Located in the deep recesses of a former factory complex, the 'Maribor Student Club' is a raucous place with music and dancers all over the shop.

Metelkova Mesto (www.metelkova.org; Masarykova c 24) 'Metelkova Town', an ex-army garrison taken over by squatters after independence, is now a free-living commune – a miniature version of Copenhagen's Christiania. In this two-courtyard block, a dozen idiosyncratic venues hide behind brightly tagged doorways, coming to life generally after midnight, daily in summer and on Fridays and Saturdays the rest of the year. Entering the main 'city gate' from Masarykova c, the building to the right houses **Gala Hala** (www.galahala.com), with live bands and club nights, and **Klub Channel Zero** (www.ch0.org), with punk and hardcore. Easy to miss in the first building to the left are **Klub Tiffany** (www.ljudmila.org/siqrd/tiffany) for gay men and **Klub Monokel** (www.klubmonokel.com) for lesbians. Due south is the ever-popular **Jalla Jalla Club** (www.myspace.com/jallajallaclub), a congenial pub with concerts. Beyond the first courtyard to the southwest, **Klub Gromka** (www.metelkova.org/gromka) in the building with the conical roof has folk, live concerts, theatre and lectures. Next door is **Menza pri Koritu** (www.menzaprikoritu.org) under the strange E.T.-like figures with performances and concerts.

Live Music

Orto Bar (☎ 232 16 74; www.orto-bar.com; Graboličeva ul 1; ⌚ 8am-4am Mon-Wed, 8am-5am Thu-Sat, 6-9pm Sun) A popular bar-club for late-night drinking and dancing with occasional live music, Orto is just five minutes' walk from Metelkova.

Jazz Club Gajo (☎ 425 32 06; www.jazzclubgajo.com; Beethovnova ul 8; ⌚ 11am-2am Mon-Fri, 7pm-midnight Sat & Sun) Now in its 15th year, Gajo is the city's premier venue for live jazz and attracts both local and international talent (jam sessions 9pm Mondays).

Roxly Café Bar (☎ 430 10 21; www.roxly.si; Mala ul 5; 7am-2am Mon-Wed, to 3am Thu & Fri, 10am-3am Sat) New venue north of the Ljubljanica; there's live rock music from 10pm two or three nights a week.

Performing Arts

Philharmonic Hall (Filharmonija; ☎ 241 08 00; www.filharmonija.si; Kongresni trg 10) This century-old concert hall is home to the Slovenian Philharmonic Orchestra, founded in 1701.

Opera House (☎ 241 17 40; www.opera.si; Župančičeva ul 1) Opera and ballet are performed at the neo-Renaissance Opera House dating back to 1882.

Križanke (☎ 241 60 00, box office 241 60 26; Trg Francoske Revolucije 1-2) Hosts concerts of the Ljubljana Festival (p713) and other events both inside and out what was a sprawling monastic complex dating back to the 13th century.

Cankarjev Dom (☎ 241 71 00; www.cd-cc.si; Prešernova c 10) is Ljubljana's premier cultural centre and has two large auditoriums (the Gallus Hall has perfect acoustics) and a dozen smaller performance spaces offering a remarkable smorgasbord of performance arts. The **ticket office** (☎ 241 72 99; 11am-1pm & 3-8pm Mon-Fri, 11am-1pm Sat & 1hr before performances) is in the subway below Maximarket Supermarket.

Cinema

Kinoteka (☎ 434 25 20; www.kinoteka.si; Miklošičeva c 28) The 'Slovenian Cinematheque' screens archival art and classic films in their original languages.

GETTING THERE & AWAY

Bus

The **bus station** (☎ 234 46 00, information 090 93 42 30; www.ap-ljubljana.si; Trg OF 4; 5.30am-10.30pm Sun-Fri, 5am-10pm Sat) opposite the train station has bilingual info-phones; just pick one up and wait for the connection. Frequent buses serve Bohinj (€8.30, two hours, 86km, hourly) via Bled (€6.30, 1¼ hours, 57km). Most buses to Piran (€12, three hours, 140km, up to seven daily) go via Koper (€11.10, 2½ hours, 122km, up to 16 daily) and Postojna (€6, one hour, 53km, up to 36 daily).

International services from Ljubljana include Belgrade (€35, 7¾ hours, 536km, 10am and 10.25pm daily); Budapest (€8, six hours, 442km, 1pm Wednesday, Friday and Sunday), Frankfurt (€83, 12½ hours, 777km, 7.30pm Sunday to Friday, 9.30pm Saturday) via Munich (€48, 6¾ hours, 344km); Poreč (€17.50, 4½ hours, 162km, 1.45pm daily), Sarajevo (€38, 9½ hours, 570km, 3.15pm daily 4pm Wednesday and Sunday); Skopje (€50, 15 hours, 960km, 3pm Sunday to Friday); Split (€44, 10½ hours, 528km, 7.40pm daily) via Rijeka (€17, 2½ hours, 136km); Trieste (€11.60, 2¾ hours, 105km, 2.25pm Monday to Saturday); and Zagreb (€13.60, 2½ hours, 154km, 2.25am daily).

Train

Ljubljana's **train station** (☎ 291 33 32; www.slo-zeleznice.si; Trg OF 6; 5am-10pm) has daily services to Koper (€7.75 to €13, 2½ hours, 153km, up to five times daily). Alternatively you can take one of the more frequent Sežana-bound trains and change at Divača (€6.25 to €7.75, 1¾ hours, 104km).

Ljubljana–Vienna trains (€61.80, 6¼ hours, 385km, twice daily) via Graz (€31.40, 200km, three hours) are expensive, although Spar Schiene fares as low as €29 apply on certain trains at certain times. Otherwise save a little bit of money by going first to Maribor (from €7.70, 2½ hours, 156km, up to two dozen daily), where you can buy a Maribor–Graz ticket (€13, one hours, three daily) and then continue on domestic tickets from Graz to Vienna (€31.40, 2¾ hours, 214km). Similar savings apply via Jesenice and Villach and/or Klagenfurt.

Three trains depart daily from Ljubljana for Munich (€71.40, 6½ hours, 405km). The 11.50pm departure has sleeping carriages available.

Ljubljana–Venice trains (€25 to €47, four hours, 244km) via Sežana depart at 2.22am and 10.35am. It's cheaper to go first to Nova Gorica (€7.75, 3½ hours, 153km, five daily), cross over to Gorizia and then take an Italian train to Venice (€8.75, 2¼ hours).

For Zagreb there are seven trains daily from Ljubljana (€12.20, 2½ hours, 154km) via Zidani Most. Two trains from the capital serve Rijeka (€12.60, 2½ hours, 136km) via Postojna.

Ljubljana–Budapest trains (€57.80, 8¾ hours, 451km, twice daily) go via Ptuj and Hodoš; there are Budapest Special fares available for as low as €29 on certain trains at certain times. Belgrade (€25 to €44, 10 hours, 535km) is served by four trains a day.

GETTING AROUND

The cheapest way to Ljubljana's recently renamed **Jože Pučnik Airport** (LJU; www.lju-airport.si) at Brnik is by city bus from stop 28 (€4.10, 50 minutes, 27km) at the bus station. These run at 5.20am and hourly from 6.10am to 8.10pm Monday to Friday; on weekends there's a bus at 6.10am and then one every two hours from 9.10am to 7.10pm. A **private airport van** (☎ 041-792 865; €5) also links Trg OF near the bus station with the airport (30 minutes) up to 10 times daily between 5.20am and 10.30pm. A **taxi** (☎ 031-311 311, 041-445 406) from downtown Ljubljana will cost you about €38.

Ljubljana has an excellent network of city buses. Most operate every five to 15 minutes from 5am to 10.30pm, though some start as early as 3.15am and run till midnight. The central area is perfectly walkable, though, so buses are really only necessary if you're staying out of town. Buy metal tokens (*žetoni*; €0.80) from news-stands, or pay €1 on board.

Ljubljana Bike (per 2hr/day €1/5; 8am-7pm or 9pm Apr-Oct) has two-wheelers available from 10 locations around the city, including the train station, the STIC office (p712), Celica Hostel (p714) and opposite Antiq Hotel.

JULIAN ALPS

The Julian Alps – named in honour of Caesar himself – form Slovenia's dramatic northwest frontier with Italy. Triglav National Park, established in 1924, includes almost all of the Alps lying within Slovenia. The centrepiece of the park is, of course, Mt Triglav (2864m), Slovenia's highest mountain, but there are many other peaks here reaching above 2000m. Along with an embarrassment of fauna and flora, the area offers a wide range of adventure sports.

KRANJ

☎ 04 / pop 34,950

At the foot of the Kamnik-Savinja Alps, with the snow-capped peak of Storžič (2132m) and others looming to the north, Kranj is Slovenia's fourth-largest city. The attractive Old Town, perched on an escarpment above the confluence of the Sava and Kokra Rivers, barely measures 1km by 250m.

The frequent weekday buses between Kranj and Ljubljana airport at nearby Brnik make it possible to head straight to the Julian Alps without first going to the capital. While waiting for your onward bus to Bled (€3.60, 30 minutes, 23km), have a look at the Old Town, starting with the art nouveau **former post office** (Koroška c 2) facing Maistrov trg and its rooftop cafe, a 600m walk south from the bus station. On your way you'll pass the 87-room **Hotel Creina** (☎ 281 75 00; www.hotel-creina.si; Koroška c 5; s/d €81/102;), the only game in town and now getting a much needed refit. The **tourist office** (☎ 238 04 50; www.tourism-kranj.si; Glavni trg 2; 8am-7pm Mon-Sat, 9am-4pm Sun) can find you a private room from €25 or, in summer, a bed in a student dormitory (€15).

Most places of interest are along just three streets – pedestrianised Prešernova ul, Tavčarjeva ul and Tomišičeva ul – the first two of which lead to the **Church of St Cantianus**, with impressive frescoes and stained glass. Another 300m farther south, the Old Town dead-ends at the Serbian Orthodox **Plague Church**, built during a time of pestilence in 1470, and the 16th-century **defence tower** behind it. **Mitnica** (☎ 040-678 778; Tavčarjeva ul 35; 7am-11pm Mon-Wed, 7am-1am Thu, 7am-2am Fri & Sat, 3-11pm Sun) is a relaxing cafe-bar in the basement of a 16th-century toll house with a huge terrace backing on to the river.

From Kranj it's an easy excursion to **Škofja Loka** (population 12,275) whose main square, **Mestni trg**, contains beautifully painted houses and a **tourist office** (☎ 512 02 68; www.skofjaloka.info; Mestni trg 7). The fine **castle** (Grajska pot 13) has the **Loka Museum** (☎ 517 04 00; adult/child €3/2.10; 9am-6pm Tue-Sun Apr-Oct, 9am-5pm Sat & Sun Nov-Mar) with one of the best ethnographical collections in Slovenia. Buses for Škofja Loka (€2.30, 25 minutes, 13km) depart hourly from Kranj between 5.10am and 9.10pm.

BLED

☎ 04 / pop 5415

With an emerald-green lake, a picture-postcard church on a tiny island, a medieval castle clinging to a rocky cliff, and some of the highest peaks of the Julian Alps and the Karavanke as backdrops, Bled seems to have been designed by some god of tourism. As it is Slovenia's most popular destination, it can get pretty crowded in summer, but it's small, convenient and a delightful base from which to explore the mountains.

Information

À Propos Bar (☎ 574 40 44; Bled Shopping Centre, Ljubljanska c 4; per 15/30/60min €1.25/2.10/4.20; 8am-midnight) Internet access.

SLOVENIA

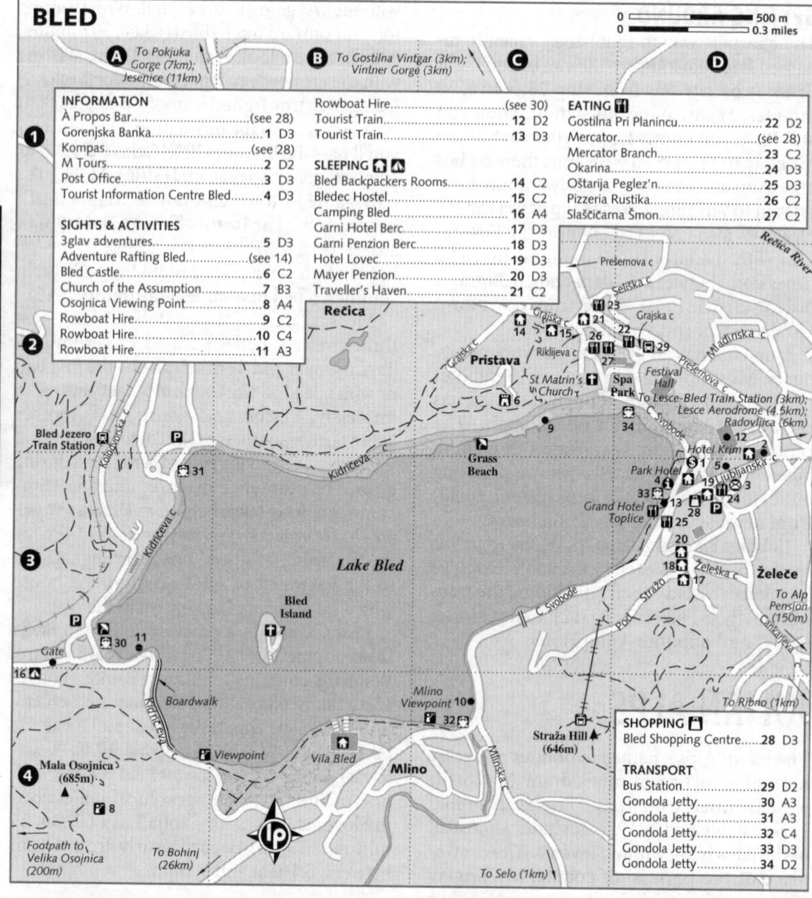

Gorenjska Banka (C Svobode 15; 9-11.30am & 2-5pm Mon-Fri, 8-11am Sat) North end of Park Hotel shop complex.

Kompas (572 75 00; www.kompas-bled.si; Bled Shopping Centre, Ljubljanska c 4; 8am-8pm Mon-Sat, 8am-noon & 4-8pm Sun Jul & Aug, 8am-7pm Mon-Sat Sep-Jun) Rents private rooms and bicycles.

M Tours (575 33 00; www.mtour.net; Ljubljanska c 7; 8am-8pm Mon-Sat, 8am-noon & 4-8pm Sun) Has private rooms.

Post office (Ljubljanska cesta 10; 8am-7pm Mon-Fri, 8am-noon Sat)

Tourist Information Centre Bled (574 11 22; www.bled.si; C Svobode 10; 8am-9pm Mon-Sat, 9am-5pm Sun Jul & Aug, 8am-7pm Mon-Sat, 11am-5pm Sun Mar-Jun & Sep-Oct, 9am-6pm Mon-Sat, noon-4pm Sun Nov, 8am-6pm Mon-Fri, 8am-1pm Sun Dec-Feb) Internet access is free for 15 minutes or pay €2.50/4 per 30/60 minutes

Sights

Sitting on its very own islet, the baroque **Church of the Assumption** (8am-dusk) is Bled's icon. Getting there by a piloted **gondola** (pletna; 041-427 155; per person €12) is the archetypal tourist experience. Gondola prices are standard from any jetty, and you'll stay on the island long enough to ring the 'lucky' bell; all in all, it's a 1½-hour trip. Ordinary row-yourself boats for three to four people cost €10 to €13 per hour.

Perched atop a 100m-high cliff, **Bled Castle** (572 9780; Grajska c 25; adult/student/child €7/6/3.50; 8am-8pm May-Oct, 8am-5pm Nov-Apr) is the perfect backdrop to a lake view. One of many access footpaths leads up from behind the Bledec Hostel. Admission includes entry to the recently revamped **museum collection**.

A short distance southeast of Bled and well served by bus (€1.80, 15 minutes, 7.5km, half-hourly), the sleepy town of **Radovljica** (population 6000) has a particularly delightful square called **Linhartov trg** in its Old Town, where there are restored and painted **manor houses**, an interesting **gallery**, the fascinating **Beekeeping Museum** (☎ 532 05 20; Linhartov trg 1; adult/student €3/2.50; ⏰ 10am-1pm & 3-6pm Tue-Sun May-Oct, 10am-noon & 3-5pm Wed, Sat & Sun Mar, Apr, Nov & Dec) and, on the edge of the square, a **tourist office** (☎ 531 53 00; www.radovljica.si; Gorenjska c 1). The square lies 400m southeast of the bus station via Gorenjska c or just 100m up narrow Kolodvorska ul from the train station to the south.

Activities

The best way to see Lake Bled is on foot; the 6km stroll around the lake shouldn't take more than a couple of hours, including the short (but steep) climb to the brilliant **Osojnica viewing point** in the southwest. If you prefer, jump aboard the **tourist train** (adult/child €3/2; ⏰ 9am-9pm May–mid-Oct, Sat & Sun Nov-Apr) for the 45-minute twirl around the lake, which departs from in front of the Sport Hall and, more centrally, from just north of the tourist office.

A popular and easy walk is to **Vintgar Gorge** (adult/student/child €4/3/2; ⏰ 8am-7pm mid-May–Oct) 4km to the northwest. The highlight is the 1600m-long wooden walkway (1893) that criss-crosses the swirling Radovna River for the first 700m or so. Thereafter the scenery becomes tamer, passing a tall railway bridge and a spray-spouting weir, and ending at the anticlimactic 13m-high **Šum Waterfall**. The easiest way to get to the gorge is via the appealing Gostilna Vintgar, an inn just three well-signed kilometres away on quiet, attractive roads from the Bledec Hostel. From early June to September, a daily bus (€3.50) leaves Bled bus station for Vintgar at 10am daily, arriving at 10.30am and returning at noon.

For something tougher, join one of the rafting or kayaking (€25 to €44) or paragliding (€85) trips on offer from **3glav adventures** (☎ 041-683 184; www.3glav-adventures.com; Ljubljanska c 1; ⏰ 9am-7pm Apr-Oct); **Adventure Rafting Bled** (☎ 574 40 41, 051-676 008; www.adventure-rafting.si; Bled Backpackers Rooms, Grajska c 21; ☎ Apr-Oct) organises rafting and canyoning. Both the tourist office (opposite) and Kompas (opposite) rent **bikes** for €3.50/6 for one-/three-hours, or €8/11 for a half-/full day.

Sleeping

Bled is now blessed with several hostels, all within spitting distance of one another. Kompas (opposite) and M Tours (opposite) in the Hotel Krim have lists of private rooms, with singles/doubles starting at €24/38.

Camping Bled (☎ 575 20 00; www.camping-bled.com; Kidričeva c 10c; adult €8.50-11.50, child €5.95-8.05; ⏰ Apr–mid-Oct) This popular 6.5-hectare site fills a small valley at the western end of the lake and boasts a popular restaurant.

Bled Backpackers Rooms (☎ 574 40 41, 051-678 008; www.bled-backpackersrooms.com; Grajska c 21; per person €17; 💻) With the attached George Best Bar open till at least midnight daily, this five-room place with 20 beds is Bled's party hostel. We love the room with the huge balcony and the storage lockers that open from the top.

Bledec Hostel (☎ 574 52 50; www.mlino.si; Grajska c 17; HI members/nonmembers dm €18/20, d €24/26; 💻) This official, somewhat old-fashioned hostel has dorms with four to seven beds and private bathrooms, a bar and an inexpensive restaurant. Laundry service (€8.50) and internet access (€2.10 per half-hour) is available.

Traveller's Haven (☎ 031-704 455, 041-396 545; www.travellers-haven.com; Riklijeva c 1; per person €19; 💻) This stunning new facility in a converted old villa (c 1909) has six rooms with between two and six beds, a great kitchen, free internet and laundry, and a chilled vibe.

Alp Penzion (☎ 576 74 50; www.alp-penzion.com; Cankarjeva c 20a; s €41, d €54-72) About 750m south of the town centre, the Alp is a bit away from the action but can be recommended for its tranquil location and lovely garden.

Garni Hotel Berc (☎ 576 56 58; www.berc-sp.si; Pod Stražo 13; s €40-45, d €65-70; 💻) This purpose-built place, reminiscent of a Swiss chalet, has 15 rooms on two floors in a quiet location above the lake. Just opposite is a second branch, Garni Penzion Berc (☎ 574 18 38; Želeška c 15; singles €35 to €40, doubles €60 to €55), with simpler rooms and cheaper rates.

Mayer Penzion (☎ 576 57 40; www.mayer-sp.si; Želeška c 7; s €45, d €70-75, apt €100; 💻) This delightful, flower-bedecked 12-room inn in a renovated 19th-century house is in the same neighbourhood as Garnic Hotel Berc. It's equally celebrated for its in-house restaurant.

Hotel Lovec (576 86 15; www.lovechotel.com; Ljubljanska c 6; s €110-151, d €128-225, ste from €245; ❄ 💻 🏊) A new favourite, the Lovec has been completely overhauled and now boasts 60 of some of the most attractive rooms in Bled. We love the rooms with blonde-wood walls, red carpet and bath with jacuzzi in front of a massive window facing the lake.

Eating

Slaščičarna Šmon (☎ 574 16 16; Grajska c 3; 🕑 7.30am-10pm) Bled's sweet of choice is *kremna rezina* (cream cake; €2.20), a layer of vanilla custard topped with whipped cream and sandwiched neatly between two layers of flaky pastry.

Gostilna Pri Planincu (☎ 574 16 13; Grajska c 8; mains €5-20.50; 🕑 10am-10pm) 'At the Mountaineers' is a homey pub-restaurant just down the hill from the hostels, with Slovenian mains like sausage and *skutini štruklji* (cheese curd pastries) and grilled Balkan specialities such as *čevapčiči* (spicy meatballs of beef or pork; €7.40) and *pljeskavica z kajmakom* (Serbian-style meat patties with mascarpone-like cream cheese; €8.40).

Ostarija Peglez'n (☎ 574 42 18; C Svobode 19A; mains €8.50-22; 🕑 11am-midnight) The best restaurant in Bled, the 'Iron Inn' is just opposite the landmark Grand Hotel Toplice, with attractively retro decor and some of the best fish dishes in town.

Okarina (☎ 574 14 58; Ljubljanska c 8; mains €9.80-24.80; 🕑 noon-midnight) This very upmarket restaurant has lots of colourful art spread over a modern dining room and serves both international favourites and decent Indian dishes like chicken *masala* and tandoori bass. There's a good choice of vegetarian dishes.

Pizzeria Rustika (☎ 576 89 00; Riklijeva c 13; pizza €5.70-9.50; 🕑 noon-midnight Tue-Sun) A marble-roll down the hill from the hostels, this place has its own wood-burning oven and seating on two levels plus an outside terrace.

You'll find a **Mercator** (Ljubljanska c 4; 🕑 7am-8pm Mon-Sat, 8am-noon Sun) at the eastern end of Bled Shopping Centre. There's a smaller **Mercator branch** (Prešernova c 48; 🕑 7am-8pm Mon-Sat, 8am-4pm Sun) close to the hostels.

Getting There & Around

Frequent buses to Bohinj (€3.60, one hour, 26km, hourly), Ljubljana (€6.30, 1¼ hours, 57km, hourly) and Kranj (€3.60, 30 minutes, 23km, half-hourly) via Radovljica (€1.80, 15 minutes, 7.5km) leave from the central bus station.

Bled has no central train station. Trains to Bohinjska Bistrica (€1.50, 20 minutes, 18km, seven daily) and Nova Gorica (€5.35, two hours, 79km, seven daily) use little Bled Jezero train station, which is 2km west of central Bled – handy for the camping ground but little else. Trains for Ljubljana (€4.10 to €7.60, 45 minutes to one hour, 51km, up to 17 daily) use Lesce-Bled train station, 4km to the east of town.

Book a taxi on ☎ 031-705 343.

BOHINJ

☎ 04 / pop 5275

Lake Bohinj, a larger and much less-developed glacial lake 26km to the southwest, is a world apart from Bled. Mt Triglav is visible from the lake and there are activities galore – from kayaking and mountain biking to hiking up Triglav via one of the southern approaches.

Bohinjska Bistrica, the area's largest village, is 6km east of the lake and only interesting for its train station. The main tourist hub on the lake is **Ribčev Laz** at the eastern end. Its miniscule commercial centre contains a supermarket, a post office (which changes money), an ATM and the **Bohinj tourist office** (☎ 574 60 10; www.bohinj-info.com; Ribčev Laz 48; 🕑 8am-8pm Mon-Sat, to 6pm Sun Jul & Aug, 8am-6pm Mon-Sat, 9am-3pm Sun Sep-Jun), which can help with accommodation and sells **fishing licences** (€25 per day for the lake, €38.50 catch and release). Central **Alpinsport** (☎ 572 34 86; www.alpinsport.si; Ribčev Laz 53; 🕑 9am or 10am-6pm or 8pm) organises a range of activities, and hires out kayaks, canoes, mountain bikes (per hour/day €4/14) and other equipment from a kiosk near the stone bridge. Next door is the delightful **Church of St John the Baptist**, which contains splendid 15th- and 16th-century frescoes, but is undergoing a protracted renovation.

The nearby village of **Stara Fužina** has an appealing little **Alpine Dairy Museum** (☎ 041-564 904; Stara Fužine 181; adult/child €2.10/1.60; 🕑 11am-7pm Tue-Sun Jul & Aug, 10am-noon & 4-6pm Tue-Sun Jan-Jun, Sep & Oct). Just opposite is a cheesemonger called **Planšar** (☎ 572 30 95; Stara Fužina 179; 🕑 1am-7pm Tue-Sun Jul & Aug, 10am-noon & 4-6pm Tue-Sun Jan-Jun, Sep & Oct), which specialises in homemade dairy products such as hard Bohinj cheese, cottage cheese and curd pie. Just 2km east is **Studor**, a village famed for its *toplarji*, the double-linked hayrack with barns or storage areas at the top, some of which date from the 18th and 19th centuries.

From June to late September, the inventively named **Tourist Boat** (☎ 041-434 986; adult/child/family one-way €8.50/6/18, return €10/7/23; 🕑 10am-6pm) departs from the pier just opposite the Alpinsport kiosk every 30 to 40 minutes

SLOVENIA

HIKING MT TRIGLAV

The Julian Alps offer some of Europe's finest hiking. In summer some 170 mountain huts (*planinska koča* or *planinski dom*) operate, none more than five hours' walk from the next. These huts get very crowded, especially on weekends, so booking ahead is wise. If the weather turns bad, however, you won't be refused refuge.

At €27 per person in a room with up to four beds or €18 in a dormitory in a Category I hut (Category II huts charge €20 and €12 respectively), the huts aren't cheap, but as they serve meals (a simple meal should cost between €4.70 and €6.20 in a Category I hut, and €3.50 and €5 in a Category II hut) you can travel light. Sturdy boots and warm clothes are indispensable, even in midsummer. Trails are generally well marked with a white-centred red circle, but you can still get lost and it's very unwise to trek alone. It's best to engage the services of a qualified (and licensed) guide, who will cost from €50/150 per two-/eight-hour period.

The tourist offices in Bled (p720), Bohinj (opposite), Kranjska Gora (p724) and Bovec (p725) all have lots of hiking information, sell maps in a variety of scales and can help book huts and guides in their regions. You might also contact the Alpine Association of Slovenia (p736) directly.

SLOVENIA

(between four and six times a day at other times), terminating a half-hour later at the Ukanc jetty at the lake's far western end. Just 300m up from the Ukanc jetty and 5km west of Ribčev Laz, a **cable car** (☎ 572 97 12 adult/child one-way €8/6, return €12/8; 🕑 8am-6pm) whisks up half-hourly to 1540m; from here, paths continue up **Mt Vogel**.

In September, the **Cows' Ball** (www.bohinj.si) at Bohinj is a zany weekend of folk dance, music, eating and drinking to mark the return of the cows from their high pastures down to the valleys.

Sleeping & Eating

Private rooms (per person €10-15) and **apartments** (d €33-44, q €48.50-70) are available through the tourist office.

Autokamp Zlatorog (☎ 572 34 82; www.aaturizem.com; Ukanc 2; per person €7-12; 🕑 May-Sep) This pine-shaded 2.5-hectare camping ground accommodating 500 guests is at the lake's western end, 4.5km from Ribčev Laz.

Hostel Pod Voglom (☎ 572 34 61; www.hostel-podvoglom.com; Ribčev Laz 60; per person with shared bathroom €19-21, with private bathroom €22-24, dm €16-18; 💻) This welcome addition to Bohinj's budget accommodation scene some 3km west of the centre has 119 beds in 46 somewhat frayed rooms in two buildings. The so-called Hostel Building has doubles, triples and dormitory accommodation with shared facilities; rooms in the Rodica Annexe, with between one and four beds, are with en suite.

Penzion Gasperin (☎ 572 36 61; www.bohinj.si/gasperin; Ribčev Laz 36A; per person €22-33; ⊠ 💻) This positively spotless chalet-style guest house with 20 rooms (nine of which are spanking new) is just 350m east of the tourist office and run by a friendly British/Slovenian couple. Some rooms (eg Nos 1, 2 and 3) have balconies.

Hotel Bellevue (☎ 572 33 31; www.hoteli-bohinj.si; Ribčev Laz 65; s €48-57, d €56-74; 💻) The shabby Bellevue has a beautiful (if somewhat isolated) and atmospheric location on a hill about 700m south of the lake. Whodunit fans take note: Agatha Christie stayed in room No 204 for three weeks in 1967. Thirty-eight of the hotel's 59 rooms are in the unattractive Savica Annexe.

Gostilna Rupa (☎ 572 34 01; Srednja Vas 87; mains €7-15; 🕑 10am-midnight Jul & Aug, 10am-midnight Tue-Sun Sep-Jun) If you're under your own steam, head for this country-style restaurants in the next village over from Studor and about 5km from Ribčev Laz. Among the excellent home-cooked dishes are *ajdova krapi*, crescent-shaped dumplings made from buckwheat and cheese, various types of local *klobasa* (sausage) and Bohinj trout.

Getting There & Around

Buses run regularly from Ukanc ('Bohinj Zlatorog' on most schedules) to Ljubljana (€8.70, two hours, 91km, hourly) via Ribčev Laz, Bohinjska Bistrica and Bled (€4.10, one hour, 34km), with six extra buses daily between Ukanc and Bohinjska Bistrica (€2.70 20 minutes, 12km). From Bohinjska Bistrica, passenger trains to Nova Gorica (€4.70, 1¼ hours, 61km, up to seven daily) make use of a century-old tunnel under the mountains that provides the only direct option for reaching the Soča Valley. In addition there are daily auto trains (*avtovlaki*) to Podbrdo (€7.50, eight minutes, 7km, five daily) and Most na Soči (€11.50, 25 minutes, 28km, three daily).

KRANJSKA GORA

☎ 04 / pop 1490

Nestling in the Sava Dolinka Valley, Kranjska Gora is Slovenia's largest and best-equipped ski resort. It's at its most perfect under a blanket of snow, but its surroundings are wonderful to explore at other times as well. There are endless possibilities for hiking and mountaineering in Triglav National Park, which is right on the town's doorstep to the south, and few travellers will be unimpressed by a trip over Vršič Pass (1611m), the gateway to the Soča Valley.

Kranjska Gora has lots of places offering ski tuition and hiring out equipment, including **ASK Kranjska Gora Ski School** (☎ 588 53 02; www.ask-kg.com; Borovška c 99A) in the same building as SKB Banka. Rent bikes from one of the **Sport Point** (☎ 588 48 83; www.sport-point.si; Borovška c 74; per hr/4hr/day €3.50/6.50/10; 9am-9pm) outlets. To watch the experts, the men's slalom and giant slalom **Vitranc Cup** (www.pokal-vitranc.com) is held in Kranjska Gora in late February and early March, and the **Ski-Jumping World Cup Championships** (www.planica.info) at nearby Planica (also in March).

Borovška c, 400m south of the bus stops, is the heart of the village, with the endearing **Liznjek House** (☎ 588 19 99; Borovška 63; adult/child €2.50/2; 10am-8pm Tue-Sat, 10am-5pm Sun May-Oct & Dec-Mar), an 18th-century museum house with a good collection of household objects and furnishings peculiar to Gorenjska province. At its western end is the **Tourist Information Centre Kranjska Gora** (☎ 580 94 40; www.kranjska-gora.si; Tičarjeva c 2; 8am-8pm Mon-Sat, 9am-6pm Sun Jun-Sep & mid-Dec–Mar, 8am-3pm Mon-Fri, 8am-4pm Sat, 9am-1pm Sun May, 8am-3pm Mon-Fri, 9am-4pm Sat Apr & Oct–mid-Dec).

Sleeping & Eating

Accommodation costs peak from December to March and in midsummer. **Private rooms** (per person €12-24) and **apartments** (d €34-50, q €68-108) can be arranged through the tourist office.

Hostel Pr' Tatko (☎ 031-479 087; Podkoren 72; www.prtatko.com; dm €13-17, q €56-76;) One of Slovenia's nicest small hostels is in Podkoren, just 3km to the northwest of Kranjska Gora. It's a four-room affair in a traditional old farmhouse, each with between four (one en suite) and eight beds. There's a decent-sized kitchen and common room. They'll teach you how to collect mushrooms in season.

Pension Borka (☎ 031-536 288; darinka2007@gmail.com; Borovška c 71; per person €20-30) Not a patch (operative word) on the Tatko but a lot more central, this very frayed property has some three-dozen rooms – mostly doubles and triples – crying out for a refit. There's a large cellar restaurant.

Hotel Kotnik (☎ 588 15 64; www.hotel-kotnik.si; Borovška c 75; s €50-59, d €60-78;) If you're not into big high-rise hotels with hundreds of rooms, choose this charming, bright yellow low-rise property. It has 15 cosy rooms, a great restaurant and pizzeria, and it couldn't be more central.

Gostilna Pri Martinu (☎ 582 03 00; Borovška c 61; mains €4-12.50; 10am-11pm) This atmospheric tavern-restaurant in an old house opposite the fire station is one of the best places in town to try local specialities, such as *telečja obara* (veal stew; €4) and *ričet* (barley stew with smoked pork ribs; €5.90).

Getting There & Away

Buses run hourly on the half-hour to Ljubljana (€8.70, two hours, 91km) via Jesenice (€3.10, 30 minutes, 23km), where you should change for Bled (€2.70, 20 minutes, 16km). There's just one direct departure to Bled (€5.20, one hour, 40km) on weekdays at 9.05am. A service to Bovec (€6.70, two hours, 46km) via Vršič Pass departs five times daily (six on Sunday) in July and August, and on Saturday and Sunday at 8.27am in June and September.

SOČA VALLEY

The Soča Valley region is defined by the 96km-long Soča River coloured a deep, almost artificial turquoise. The valley has more than its share of historical sights, most of them related to one of the costliest battles of WWI, but the majority of visitors are here for rafting, hiking, skiing and other active sports.

Bovec

☎ 05 / pop 1760

Effectively the capital of the Soča Valley, Bovec has a great deal to offer adventure-sports enthusiasts. With the Julian Alps above, the Soča River below and Triglav National Park all around, you could spend a week here hiking, kayaking, mountain biking and, in winter, skiing at Mt Kanin (2587m), Slovenia's highest ski station, without ever doing the same thing twice.

The compact village square, **Trg Golobarskih Žrtev**, has everything you'll need. There are cafes, a hotel, the helpful **Tourist Information Centre Bovec** (☎ 389 64 44; www.bovec.si; Trg Golobarskih Žrtev; 🕑 8.30am-8.30pm Jul & Aug, 9am-5pm Mon-Fri, 9am-noon & 4-6pm Sat, 9am-noon Sun Sep-Jun) and a half-dozen adrenalin-raising adventure-sports companies.

ACTIVITIES

There's no shortage of activities on offer in and around Bovec. Possibilities include **canyoning** (€43 to €45 for two hours) at Sušec, or **caving** (€35 per person with guide). Or you could try your hand at **hydrospeed** (like riding down a river on a boogie board); you'll pay €45 to €55 for a 6km to 8km ride. A guided 10km **kayaking** tour costs from €39.50 to €41.50 per person, or a one-day training course from €45 to €53.50.

From April to October, you can go **rafting** (€35/45 for a 10/20km trip). And in winter you can take a tandem paraglider flight (ie as a passenger accompanied by a qualified pilot) from atop the Kanin cable car, 2000m above the valley floor. A flight costs from €110; ask Avantura for details.

Recommended operators:

Avantura (☎ 041-718 317; www.avantura.org)
Bovec Rafting Team (☎ 388 61 28, 041-338 308; www.bovec-rafting-team.com)
Outdoor Freaks (☎ 389 64 90, 041-553 675; www.outdoorfreaks.si)
Soča Rafting (☎ 389 62 00, 041-724 472; www.socarafting.si)
Sport Mix (☎ 389 61 60, 031-871 991; www.sportmix.traftbovec.si)
Top Extreme (☎ 041-620 636; www.top.si)

SLEEPING & EATING

Alp Hotel (☎ 388 40 00; www.alp-chandler.si; Trg Golobarskih Žrtev 48; s €48-60, d €66-90; 💻 🅿) This 103-room hotel is fairly good value and as central as you are going to find in Bovec. Guests get to use the swimming pool at the nearby Hotel Kanin.

Dobra Vila (☎ 389 64 00; www.dobra-vila-bovec.com; Mala Vas 112; s €58-105, d €88-135; 💻) This positive stunner of a 12-room boutique hotel is housed in an erstwhile telephone-exchange building. It has its own small cinema, library, restaurant and wine cellar.

Martinov Hram (☎ 388 62 14; Trg Golobarskih Žrtev 27; mains €6.90-19.50; 🕑 10am-10pm Tue-Thu, to midnight Fri & Sat) Traditional restaurant in an attractive inn specialising in game, Soča trout and mushroom dishes. During the winter, pizza rears its ugly head.

Private rooms (per person €15-30) are easy to come by in Bovec through the TIC.

Camping facilities are generally better in Kobarid (p726), but **Kamp Polovnik** (☎ 388 60 69; www.kamp-polovnik.com; Ledina 8; adult €5-7, child €3.75-5.25; 🕑 Apr–mid-Oct) about 500m southeast of the town centre is much more convenient.

GETTING THERE & AWAY

Buses to Nova Gorica (€7.50, two hours, 77km, up to five a day) go via Kobarid (€3.10, half-hour, 21km). A service to Kranjska Gora (€6.70, two hours, 46km) via the spectacular Vršič Pass departs five times daily (six on Sunday) in July and August, and on Saturday and Sunday at 3.35pm in June and September.

Kobarid

☎ 05 / pop 1235

Some 21km south of Bovec, quaint Kobarid (Caporetto in Italian) lies in a broad valley on the west bank of the Soča River. Although it's surrounded by mountain peaks higher than 2200m, Kobarid somehow feels more Mediterranean than alpine. The Italian border is just 9km to the west.

The **Tourist Information Centre Kobarid** (☎ 380 04 90; www.lto-sotocje.si; Gregorčičeva ul 8; 🕑 9am-8pm Jul & Aug, 9am-12.30pm & 1.30-7pm Mon-Fri, 9am-1pm Sat Sep-Jun) is next door to the award-winning **Kobarid Museum** (☎ 389 00 00; Gregorčičeva ul 10; adult/student/child €4/3/2.50; 🕑 9am-6pm Mon-Fri, 9am-7pm Sat & Sun Apr-Sep, 10am-5pm Mon-Fri, 9am-6pm Sat & Sun Oct-Mar), devoted almost entirely to the Isonzo (Soča) Front of WWI, which formed the backdrop to Ernest Hemingway's *A Farewell to Arms*. A free pamphlet and map titled *The Kobarid Historical Trail* outlines a 5km-long route that will take you past remnant WWI troop emplacements to the impressive **Kozjak Stream Waterfalls**. More ambitious is the hike outlined in the *Pot Miru/Walk of Peace* brochure.

Kobarid is beginning to give Bovec a run for its money in extreme sports, and you'll find several outfits on or off the town's main square that can organise rafting, canyoning, canoeing and paragliding from April to October. They include the long-established

XPoint (☎ 388 53 08, 041-692 290; www.xpoint.si; Trg Svobode 6); the new and enthusiastic **Positive Sport** (☎ 040-654 475; www.positive-sport.com; Markova ul 2); and Apartma-Ra, which also organises two-hour quad-bike trips for €45.

The oldest (and, some would say, friendliest) camping ground in the valley, **Kamp Koren** (☎ 389 13 11; www.kamp-koren.si; Drežniške Ravne 33; per person €8.50-10; mid-Mar–Oct;) is a small site about 500m northeast of Kobarid on the left bank of the Soča River and just beyond the Napoleon Bridge, built in 1750.

The welcoming little **Apartma-Ra** (☎ 041-641 899; apartma-ra@siol.net; Gregorčičeva ul 6C; per person €15-25;) lies between the museum and Trg Svobode and has five rooms and apartments, some with terraces. The best place in town is the **Hotel Hvala** (☎ 389 93 00; wwww.hotelhvala.si; Trg Svobode 1; s €59-72, d €82-108;), which has 31 rooms – some recently renovated to a level unseen in provincial Slovenia – linked by a snazzy new lift, a bar, a superb Restavracija Topli Val restaurant and a Mediterranean-style cafe in the garden.

In the centre of Kobarid you'll find two of Slovenia's best restaurants, both of which specialise in fish and seafood: the incomparable **Restavracija Topli Val** (☎ 389 93 00; Trg Svobode 1; mains €9.50-25; noon-10pm) and **Restavracija Kotlar** (☎ 389 11 10; Trg Svobode 11; mains €8.50-20; noon-11pm Thu, Sun & Mon, to midnight Fri & Sat).

Buses, which arrive at and depart from in front of the Cinca Marinca bar on Trg Svobode, link Kobarid with Nova Gorica (€6, 1½ hours, 55km, up to five daily) and Ljubljana (€11.50, three hours, 130km, up to four daily) passing Most na Soči train station, which is good for Bled and Bohinj. Buses that cross over the spectacular Vršič Pass to Kranjska Gora (€7.85, three hours, 68km) depart three times a day in July and August.

Nova Gorica

☎ **05 / pop 12,585**

When the town of Gorica, capital of the former Slovenian province of Goriška, was awarded to the Italians after WWII, the new socialist government in Yugoslavia set itself to building a model town on the eastern side of the border. They called it 'New Gorica' and erected a chain-link barrier between the two towns. This rather flimsy 'Berlin Wall' was pulled down to great fanfare in 2004, leaving Piazza della Transalpina (or Trg z Mozaikom on this side) straddling the border right behind Nova Gorica's train station. There you'll now find the esoteric **Museum of the Border in Gorica 1945–2004** (☎ 333 44 00; admission free; 1-5pm Mon-Fri, 9am-7pm Sat, 10am-7pm Sun). Nova Gorica is an easy way to get to/from Italy; Italian bus 1 (€0.98) will whisk you from Via G Caprin opposite the museum to Gorizia train station.

The helpful **Tourist Information Centre Nova Gorica** (☎ 330 46 00; www.novagorica-turizem.com; Bevkov trg 4; 8am-8pm Mon-Fri, 9am-1pm Sat & Sun Jul & Aug, 8am-6pm Mon-Fri, 9am-1pm Sat Sep-Jun) is in the lobby of the Kulturni Dom (Cultural House).

One of the few inexpensive accommodation options, **Prenočišče Pertout** (☎ 330 75 50, 041-624 452; www.prenociscepertout.com; Ul 25 Maja 23; s/d/tr €24/34/51) is a five-room B&B in Rožna Dolina, south of the town centre and scarcely 100m northeast of the Italian border. The Italian restaurant **Marco Polo** (☎ 302 97 29; Kidričeva ul 13; mains €8-17; 11am-11pm Mon-Thu, 11am-midnight Fri & Sat, noon-midnight Sun), with a delightful back terrace 250m east of the tourist office, is one of the town's best places to eat, serving pizza (€4.40 to €7.80), pasta (€5.50 to €10) and more ambitious dishes.

Buses travel hourly between Nova Gorica and Ljubljana (€10.70 2½ hours, 116km) via Postojna (€6.30, one hour, 53km), and up to five times daily to Bovec (€7.50, two hours, 77km) via Kobarid (€6, 1½ hours, 55km).

Trains link Nova Gorica with Bohinjska Bistrica (€4.70, 1¼ hours, 61km, up to seven daily), a springboard for Bled, with Postojna (€5.65, two hours, 61km, six daily) via Sežana and Divača, and with Ljubljana (€7.75, 3½ hours, 153km, five daily) via Jesenice.

KARST & COAST

Slovenia's short coast (47km) is an area of both history and recreation. Three important towns full of Venetian Gothic architecture – Koper, Izola and Piran – are the main drawcards here and the southernmost resort of Portorož has some decent beaches. En route from Ljubljana or the Soča Valley, you'll cross the Karst, a huge limestone plateau and a land of olives, ruby-red Teran wine, *pršut* (air-dried ham), old stone churches and deep subterranean caves. In fact, Slovenia's two most famous caverns – Postojna and Škocjan – are here.

POSTOJNA

☎ **05 / pop 8850**

Slovenia's single most popular tourist attraction, **Postojna Cave** (☎ 700 01 00; www.postojnska-jama.si;

Jamska c 30; adult/student/child €20/16/13; tours hourly 9am-6pm Jul & Aug, to 5pm May, Jun & Sep, 10am, noon, 2pm & 4pm Apr & Oct, 10am, noon & 3pm Nov-Mar) is about 2km northwest of the town of that name. The 5.7km-long cavern is visited on a 1½-hour tour, but about 4km of it is covered by an electric train and the rest on foot. Inside, impressive stalagmites and stalactites stretch almost endlessly in all directions, as do the chattering crowds who pass them.

Close to the cave's entrance is the **Proteus Vivarium** (adult/student/child €7/6/4, with cave €24/19/14; 9.30am-5.30pm May-Sep, 10.30am-3.30pm Oct-Apr), a speliobiological research station with a video introduction to underground zoology. A 45-minute tour then leads you into a small, darkened cave to peep at some of the endemic *Proteus anguinus*, shy (and miniscule) creatures you've just learned about in the Postojna Cave.

Predjama (population 85), a village 9km northwest of Postojna, can claim the remarkable **Predjama Castle** (751 60 15; Predjama 1; www.turizem-kras.si; adult/student/child €8/7/5; 9am-7pm Jul & Aug, to 6pm May, Jun & Sep, 10am-5pm Apr & Oct, to 4pm Nov-Mar), which appears to grow out of a yawning cave. The partly furnished interior spread over four floors boasts costumed wax mannequins, one of which dangles from the dripping rock-roofed torture chamber. Beneath are stalactite-adorned **caves** (adult/student/child €7/6/4, cave & castle combination ticket €13/11/8; tours 11am, 1pm, 3pm & 5pm May-Sep), which lack Postojna's crowds but also much of its grandeur; tours last an hour.

Sleeping & Eating

Kompas Postojna (721 14 80; www.kompas-postojna.si; Titov trg 2A; r per person €18-20; 8am-7pm Mon-Fri, 9am-1pm Sat Jun-Aug, 8am-6pm Mon-Fri, 9am-1pm Sat May, Sep & Oct, 8am-5pm Mon-Fri, 9am-1pm Sat Nov-Apr) Has private rooms.

Hotel Sport (720 22 44; www.sport-hotel.si; Kolodvorska c 1; dm €20, s €55-65, d €70-90, tr 96-125, q €120-160;) A much more expensive proposition than when it opened a few short years ago, the Sport still offers reasonable value for money, with 32 spick-and-span and very comfortable rooms, including 40 hostel beds. It's just 300m north of the centre of Postojna. It rents mountain bikes (half-/full day €9/15) for exploring nearby Notranjska Regional Park.

Pizzeria Minutka (720 36 25; Ljubljanska c 14; pizza €4.90-7.10; noon-11pm) A pizzeria with a terrace, Minutka is a favourite with locals and is just south of the Hotel Sport.

Getting There & Away

Buses from Ljubljana to Koper, Piran and Nova Gorica all stop in Postojna (€6, one hour, 54km, half-hourly). The train is less useful, as the station is 1km east of town (ie almost 3km from the caves).

As close as you'll get by local bus from Postojna to Predjama (€2.30, 15 minutes, 9km, five daily Monday to Friday) and during the school year only is Bukovje, a village about 2km northeast of Predjama. A taxi from Postojna, including an hour's wait at Predjama Castle, will cost €30, which staff at Kompas Postojna can organise.

ŠKOCJAN CAVES

05

The immense system of **Škocjan Caves** (708 21 00; www.park-skocjanske-jame.si; Škocjan 2; adult/student/child €14/10/6), a Unesco World Heritage site since 1986, is far more captivating than the larger one at Postojna, and for many travellers a visit here will be a highlight of their trip to Slovenia. With relatively few stalactites, the attraction is the sheer depth of the awesome underground chasm, which you cross by a dizzying little footbridge. To see this you must join a shepherded walking tour, lasting 1½ to two hours and involving hundreds of steps and a funicular ride at the end. Tours depart hourly from 10am to 5pm from June to September, at 10am, 1pm and 3.30pm in April, May and October, and at 10am and 1pm Monday to Saturday, and 10am, 1pm and 3pm Sunday from November to March.

The nearest town with accommodation is **Divača** (population 1330), 5km to the northwest. **Gostilna Malovec** (763 12 25; Kraška 30a; per person €20) has a half-dozen basic but renovated rooms in a building beside its traditional **restaurant** (mains €5-15; 8am to 10pm). For something a bit more, well, 21st century, cross the road to **Orient Express** (763 30 10; Kraška c 67; pizza €4.60-14; 11am-11pm Sun-Fri, 11am-2am Sat), a lively pizzeria and pub.

Bus services running from Ljubljana to Koper and the coast stop at Divača (€8, 1½ hours, 82km, half-hourly), as do trains (€6.25, 1½ hours, 104km, hourly). Staff at the train station ticket office can provide you with a photocopied route map for walking to the caves and there is a copy posted outside. Alternatively, a courtesy van meets incoming trains at 10am, 11.04am, 2pm and 3.35pm and will transport those with bus or train tickets to the caves.

LIPICA

☎05 / pop 95

Lipica is where Austrian Archduke Charles, son of Ferdinand I, established a stud farm to breed horses for the Spanish Riding School in Vienna in 1580. The snow-white beauties are still born and raised at the **Lipica Stud Farm** (☎739 15 80; www.lipica.org; Lipica 5; adult/student & child from €9/4.50), which offers equestrian fans a variety of tours, as well as riding and lessons. Tour times are complex; see the website for details.

SLOVENIA

Good value is the 80-room **Hotel Klub** (☎739 15 70; s/d €32/49;) near the stud farm with a sauna and fitness centre. The nearby **Hotel Maestoso** (☎739 15 80; s/d €80/120;) has 66 more modern rooms.

A van meets incoming trains at Divača, 9km to the northeast, at 10.19am, 11.24am, 2.24pm and 3.59pm and transports ticket holders to the stud farm.

KOPER

☎05 / pop 24,630

Coastal Slovenia's largest town, Koper (Capodistria in Italian and Aegida to the Greeks) at first glance appears to be a workaday city that scarcely gives tourism a second thought. Yet its central core is delightfully medieval and far less overrun than its ritzy cousin Piran, 17km down the coast. Koper grew rich as a key port trading salt, and was the capital of Istria under the Venetian Republic during the 15th and 16th centuries. It remains Slovenia's most important port.

Orientation

The joint bus and train station is about 1.5km southeast of central Titov trg. To walk into town, just head north along Kolodvorska c in the direction of the cathedral's distinctive campanile (bell tower). Alternatively, take bus 1 or 2 to Muda Gate.

Information

Banka Koper (Kidričeva ul 14; 8.30am-noon & 3-5pm Mon-Fri, 8.30am-noon Sat)

Kompas (☎663 05 81; Pristaniška ul 17; 8am-7pm Mon-Fri, 8am-1pm Sat) Private rooms.

Palma Travel Agency (☎663 36 60; Pristaniška ul 21; 8am-7pm Mon-Fri, 9am-noon Sat) Private rooms.

Pina (☎627 80 72; Kidričeva ul 43; adult/student per hr €4.20/1.20; 4-10pm) Central internet cafe with 10 terminals.

Post office (Muzejski trg 3; 8am-7pm Mon-Fri)

Tourist Information Centre Koper (☎664 64 03; www.koper.si; Praetorian Palace, Titov trg 3; 9am-9pm Jul & Aug, 9am-5pm Mon-Fri, to 7pm Sat & Sun Sep-Jun)

Sights

You'll change centuries abruptly as you pass through **Muda Gate** (1516) leading into Prešernov trg. Continue north past the bridge-shaped **Da Ponte Fountain** (1666), and up Župančičeva ul and Čevljarska ul, the narrow commercial artery, to reach **Titov trg**. This fine central square is dominated by the 15th-century **City Tower** (adult/child €2/1.50; 9am-2pm & 4-9pm), which can be climbed, attached to the part-Gothic, part-Renaissance **Cathedral of the Assumption**. The Venetian Gothic and Renaissance **Praetorian Palace** (Titov trg 3; admission free) contains the town hall, with an old pharmacy and the tourist office on the ground floor and a ceremonial hall with exhibits on the 1st floor. Opposite, the splendid 1463 **Loggia** is now an elegant cafe (p730) and gallery. To the east of it is the circular Romanesque **Rotunda of St John the Baptist**, a baptistery dating from the second half of the 12th century.

The **Koper Regional Museum** (☎663 35 70; Kidričeva ul 19; adult/child €2.50/1.50; 9am-1pm & 6-9pm Tue-Sun Jul & Aug, 10am-6pm Tue-Fri, 9am-1pm Sat & Sun Sep-Jun), inside the Belgramoni-Tacco Palace, contains an Italianate sculpture garden. Kidričeva ul also has a few multicoloured **medieval houses** with beamed overhangs. It leads west into Carpacciov trg, the former fish market with a 15th-century **salt warehouse** and the stone **Column of St Justina** dating from 1571.

Sleeping

Both Kompas (left) and the Palma Travel Agency (left) can arrange **private rooms** (per person r €20-31) and **apartments** (2-person €32-40, 4-person €56-70), most of which are in the new town beyond the train station.

Motel Port (☎639 32 60; www.port-turizem.si; Ankaranska c 7; dm €15-17, s €29-40, d €43-48, tr €54-60;) Hidden on the 2nd floor of a shopping centre southeast of the Old Town, this place has 30 rooms, some of them en suite and air-conditioned and others dorm rooms with four to six beds. There's a breezy cafe-bar here as well.

Museum Hostel (☎626 18 70, 041-504 466; bozic.doris@siol.net; Muzejski trg 6; per person €20-25) This

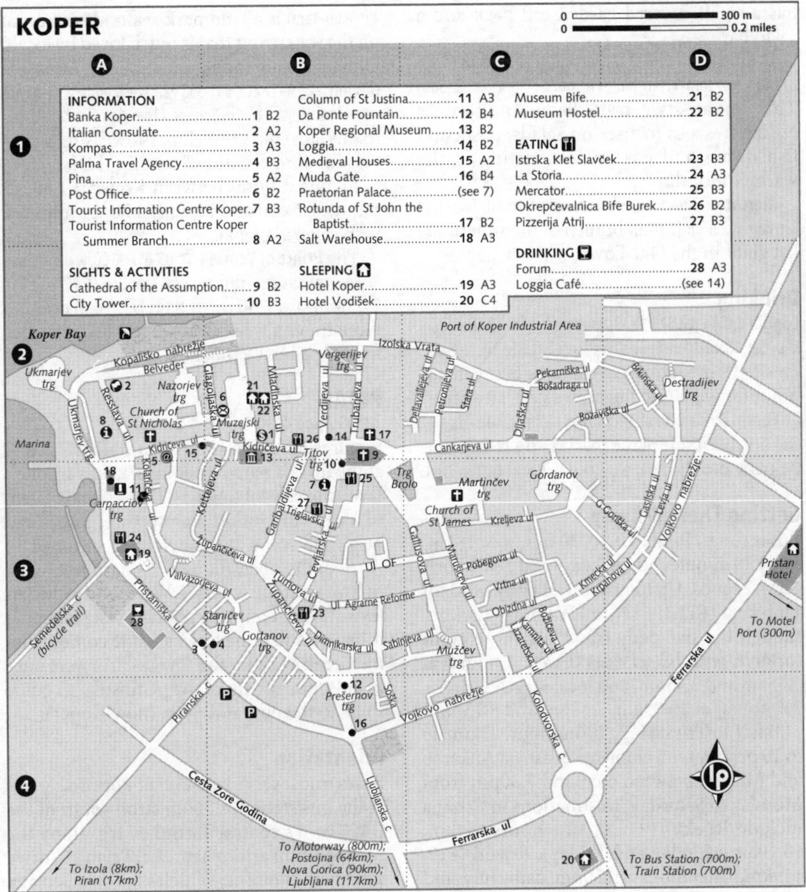

good-value place is more a series of bright apartments with modern kitchens and bathrooms than a hostel. Reception is at the little Museum Bife, a cafe-bar on Muzejski trg; the rooms are actually at Mladinska ul 7.

Hotel Vodišek (☎ 639 24 68; www.hotel-vodisek.com; Kolodvorska c 2; s €45-60, d €68-90, tr €83-110;) This hotel, with 32 small but reasonably priced rooms, is in a shopping centre halfway between the Old Town and the train and bus stations. Guests get to use the hotel's bicycles for free.

Hotel Koper (☎ 610 05 00; www.terme-catez.si; Pristaniška ul 3; s €76, d €120;) This pleasant, 65-room property on the very edge of the historic Old Town is the only central hotel in Koper.

Eating

Okrepčevalnica Bife Burek (☎ 271 347; Kidričeva ul 8; snacks €1.70-2.50; 7am-10pm) Buy good-value *burek* here and enjoy it at Titov trg for a take-away snack.

Istrska Klet Slavček (☎ 627 67 29; Župančičeva ul 39; dishes €2.50-14; 7am-10pm Mon-Fri) This 'Istrian Cellar', situated below the 18th-century Carli Palace, is one of the most colourful places for a meal in Koper's Old Town. Filling set lunches go for less than €7, and there's local Malvazija and Teran wine from the barrel.

Pizzerija Atrij (☎ 627 22 55; Triglavska ul 2; pizza €3-6.70; 9am-10pm Mon-Fri, 10am-10pm Sat) This popular pizzeria down an alleyway no wider than your average quarterback's shoulder spread has a small covered garden out back and a salad bar.

La Storia (☎ 626 20 18; Pristaniška ul 3; mains €9.90-22.50; ⌚ 11am-11pm Mon-Fri, noon-11pm Sat & Sun) This Italian-style trattoria with sky-view ceiling frescoes focuses on salads, pasta and fish dishes and has outside seating in the warmer months.

Mercator (Titov trg 2; ⌚ 7am-8pm Mon-Fri, 7am-1pm Sat, 8am-noon Sun) Small branch of the supermarket giant in the Old Town.

Drinking

Loggia Café (☎ 621 32 13; Titov trg 1; ⌚ 7.30am-10pm Mon-Sat, 10am-10pm Sun) This lovely cafe in the exquisite 15th-century Loggia is the best vantage point for watching the crowds on Titov trg.

Forum (Pristaniška ul 2; ⌚ 7am-11pm) Cafe-bar at the northern side of the market and facing a little park and the sea; a popular local hang-out.

Getting There & Away

Buses run to Piran (€3.10, 30 minutes, 18km) every 20 minutes on weekdays and half-hourly on weekends. Up to nine buses daily head for Ljubljana (€11.10, 1¾ to 2½ hours, 120km), though the five daily trains are more comfortable, with IC services (€13, 2¼ hours) at 5.55am and 2.45pm, and local services (€7.75, 2½ hours) at 10.03am, 7.12pm and 8.13pm.

Buses to Trieste (€2.80, one hour, 23km, up to 10 per day) run along the coast via Ankaran and Muggia between 6am and 7.30pm from Monday to Saturday. Destinations in Croatia include Rijeka (€11.20, two hours, 84km, 10.10am Monday and Friday), Rovinj (€12, 129km, three hours, 3.50pm daily July and August) via Poreč (€10, two hours, 88km), plus three more to Poreč only at 7.30am, 2pm and 3.55pm Monday to Friday.

IZOLA

☎ 05 / pop 11,270

Overshadowed by more genteel Piran, Izola (Isola in Italian) has a certain Venetian charm, narrow old streets, and nice waterfront bars and restaurants. Ask the helpful **Tourist Information Centre Izola** (☎ 640 10 50; www.izola.eu; Sončno nabrežje 4; ⌚ 9am-9pm Mon-Sat, 10am-5pm Sun Jun-Sep, 9am-5pm Mon-Fri, 10am-5pm Sat Oct-May) about **private rooms** (s €18-26, d €26-36) or, in July and August, check out the 174-bed **Riviera** (☎ 662 1740; branko.miklobusec@guest.arnes.si; Prekomorskih Brigad ul 7; dm €24), a student dormitory overlooking the marina. **Ribič** (☎ 641 83 13; Veliki trg 3; mains €8-18; ⌚ 8am-1am) is a landmark seafood restaurant on the waterfront that is much loved by locals. Out in Izola's industrial suburbs, **Ambasada Gavioli** (☎ 641 8212, 041-353 722; www.ambasada-gavioli.com; Industrijska c; ⌚ 8pm or 11pm-6am Fri & Sat) remains Slovenia's top club, showcasing a procession of international and local DJs.

Frequent buses between Koper (€1.80, 15 minutes, 6km) and Piran (€2.30, 20 minutes, 9.5km) go via Izola.

The **Prince of Venice** (☎ 05-617 80 00; www.kompas-online.net) catamaran serves Venice (€47 to €70, 2½ hours) at 7.30am or 8am between one and three times a week, and several times a week from April to October.

PIRAN

☎ 05 / pop 4430

Picturesque Piran (Pirano in Italian), sitting at the tip of a narrow peninsula, is everyone's favourite coastal town. Its Old Town is a gem of Venetian Gothic architecture, but it can be a mob scene at the height of summer. In April or October, though, it's hard not to fall in love with the winding Venetian Gothic alleyways and tempting seafood restaurants. It is believed that the town's name comes from the Greek word for fire *(pyr)* as fires were once lit at Punta, the tip of the peninsula, to guide ships to the port at Aegida (now Koper).

Orientation

Buses from everywhere except Portorož arrive at the bus station, a 300m stroll south of the Old Town's central Tartinijev trg, along the portside Cankarjevo nabrežje. Trying to drive a car here is insane; vehicles are stopped at a toll gate 200m south of the bus station, where the sensible choice is to use the huge Fornače car park (per hour/day €1/10) and ride the very frequent shuttle bus into town.

Information

Banka Koper (Tartinijev trg 12; ⌚ 8.30am-noon & 3-5pm Mon-Fri, 8.30am-noon Sat)

Caffe Neptun (☎ 041-724 237; www.caffeneptun.com; Dantejeva ul 4; per 15min €1; ⌚ 7am-1am Mon-Sat, 8am-10pm Sub) Modern cafe near bus station with internet access.

Maona Tourist Agency (☎ 673 45 20; www.maona.si; Cankarjevo nabrežje 7; ⌚ 9am-8pm Mon-Sat, 10am-1pm & 5-7pm Sun) Rents private rooms and bikes, organises activities and cruises.

Post office (Cankarjevo nabrežje; ⌚ 8am-7pm Mon-Fri, 8am-noon Sat)

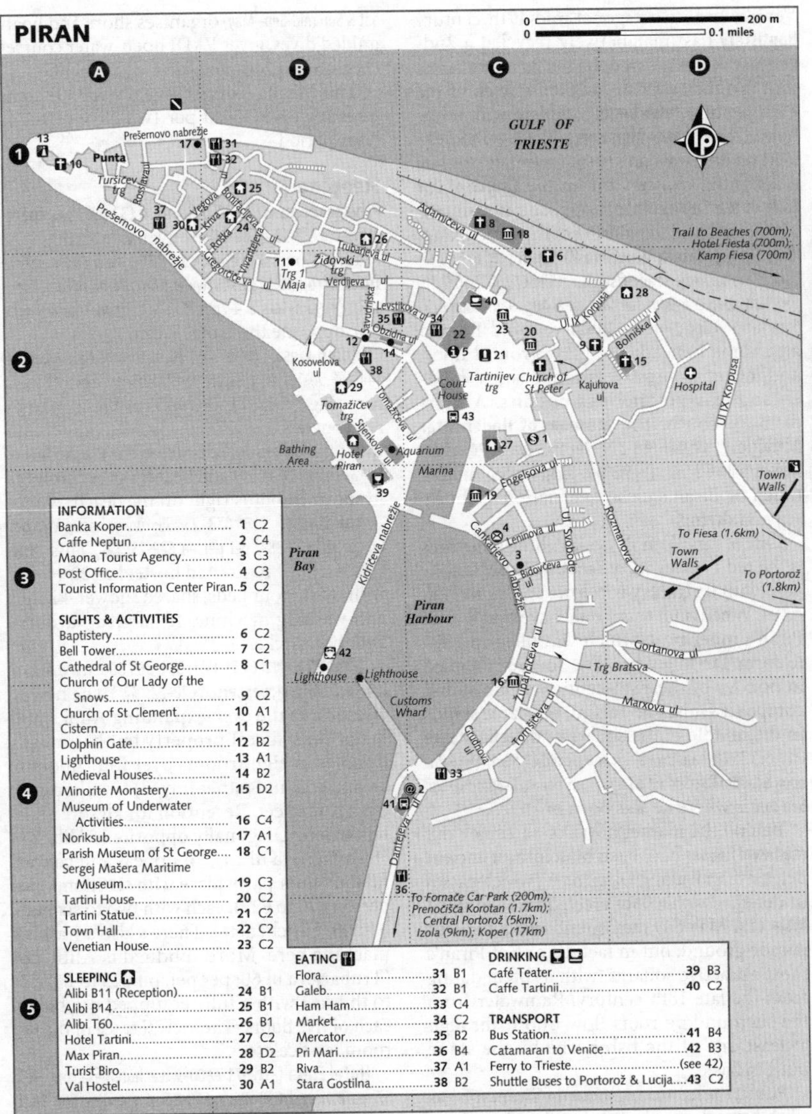

Tourist Information Center Piran (☎ 673 44 40; www.portoroz.si; Tartinijev trg 2; ⏰ 9am-7pm Jul-Sep, 9am-5pm Oct-Jun) In the impressive town hall.

Sights & Activities

Piran is watched over by the **Cathedral of St George** (Adamičeva ul 2) dating from the 16th and 17th centuries. If time weighs heavily on your hands, visit the attached **Parish Museum of St George** (☎ 673 34 40; admission €1; ⏰ 10am-1pm & 3-5pm Mon & Wed-Fri, 10am-6pm Sat & Sun), which contains church plate, paintings and a lapidary. The cathedral's free-standing **bell tower** (admission €2; ⏰ 10am-1pm & 6-9pm) dates back to 1608 and can be climbed. It was clearly modelled on the campanile at San Marco's Basilica in

Venice, and its octagonal mid-17th-century **baptistery** has imaginatively recycled a 2nd-century Roman sarcophagus as a baptismal font. To the east runs a 200m stretch of the 15th-century **town walls** complete with loop-holes. The **Minorite Monastery** (☎ 673 44 17; Bolniška ul 30) on the way down to Tartinijev trg has a delightful cloister, and in the **Church of Our Lady of the Snows** almost opposite is a superb 15th-century arch painting of the Crucifixion. The **Sergej Mašera Maritime Museum** (☎ 671 00 40; Cankarjevo nabrežje 3; adult/student/child €/3.50/2.50/2.10; ⏲ 9am-noon & 6-9pm Tue-Sun Jul & Aug, 9am-noon & 3-6pm Tue-Sun Sep-Jun) has 2000-year-old Roman amphorae beneath the glass ground floor, and lots of impressive antique ships' models and ex-voto offerings upstairs. A short distance south, the **Museum of Underwater Activities** (☎ 041-685 379; Župančičeva ul 24; adult/student/child €/3/2/2; ⏲ 9.30am-10pm Jun-Sep) makes much of Piran's close association with the sea and diving.

One of Piran's most eye-catching structures is the red 15th-century **Venetian House** (Tartinijev trg 4), with its tracery windows and stone lion relief. When built this would have overlooked Piran's inner port, which was filled in 1894 to form Tartinijev trg. The square is named in honour of the 18th-century violinist and composer Giuseppe Tartini; his **statue** stands in the middle of the square and **Tartini House** (☎ 663 35 70; Kajuhova ul 12; adult/child €1.50/1; ⏲ 9am-noon & 6-9pm Tue-Sun Jul & Aug, 11am-noon & 5-6pm Tue-Sun Sep-Jun) is where he was born in 1692.

Behind the market north of Tartinijev trg, **medieval houses** have been built into an ancient defensive wall along Obzidna ul, which passes under the **Dolphin Gate** erected in 1483. **Trg 1 Maja** (1st May Sq) may sound like a socialist parade ground, but in fact it's one of Piran's most attractive squares, with a **cistern** dating from the late 18th century. Rainwater from the surrounding roofs flow into it through at least one of the fish borne by the stone putti in back.

Punta, the historical 'snout' of Piran, still has a **lighthouse**, but today's is small and modern. Attached to it, the round, serrated tower of 18th-century **Church of St Clement** evokes the ancient beacon from which Piran got its name.

Most water-related activities take place in Portorož, but if you want to give diving a go, **Noriksub** (☎ 673 22 18, 041-746 153; www.skupinanoriksub.si; Prešernovo nabrežje 24; shore/boat dive €30/40; ⏲ 9am-noon & 1-6pm Tue-Sun Jun–mid-Sep, 10am-4pm Sat & Sun mid-Sep–May) organises shore and boat-guided dives, gives PADI open-water courses (beginners €240) and hires equipment.

The Maona Tourist Agency (p730) rents **bikes** for €6/9/15/20 per two-/five-/10-/24-hour period.

Sleeping

Private rooms (s €16-30, d €23-42, tr €32-55) and **apartments** (d €38-50, q €60-84) are available through the Maona Tourist Agency (p730) and the central **Turist Biro** (☎ 673 25 09; www.turistbiro-ag.si; Tomažičeva ul 3; ⏲ 9am-1pm & 4-7pm Mon-Sat, 10am-1pm & 4-6pm Sun), opposite the Hotel Piran.

Kamp Fiesa (☎ 674 62 30; autocamp.fiesa@siol.net; adult €8.50-10, child €3.25; ⏲ May-Sep) The closest camping ground to Piran is at Fiesa, 4km by road but less than 1km if you follow the coastal trail (*obalna pešpot*) east from the Cathedral of St George. It's tiny and becomes very crowded in summer, but is right on the beach.

Val Hostel (☎ 673 25 55; www.hostel-val.com; Gregorčičeva ul 38A; per person €22-25; 🖳) This central, partially renovated hostel has 22 rooms, with two to four beds, shared shower, kitchen and washing machine. It's a great favourite with backpackers.

Alibi B11 (☎ 673 01 41; 031-363 666; www.alibi.si; Bonifacijeva ul 11; per person €20-22; 🖳) The newest addition to the ever-expanding Alibi stable is not their nicest property but has mostly doubles in eight rooms over four floors in an ancient (and rather frayed) townhouse on a narrow street. Reception for all three hostels is here. Diagonally opposite is Alibi B14 (Bonifacijeva ul 14), an upbeat and colourful four-floor party place with six rooms (per person €20 to €22), each with two to six beds, bath and kitchenette. There's also a washing machine here. More subdued is Alibi T60 (Trubarjeva ul 60; per person €25 to €27.50) to the east with a fully equipped double on each of five floors. The view terrace of the top room is priceless.

Hotel Fiesa (☎ 671 22 00; www.hotelfiesa.com; Fiesa 57; park view d €58-78, tr €68-85, d sea view €69-98, tr €82-110) Although not in Piran itself, this 22-room pink-coloured hotel overlooking the sea near the Kamp Fiesa camping ground is one of the most atmospheric places to stay in the area.

Max Piran (☎ 673 34 36, 041-692 928; www.maxpiran.com; Ul IX Korpusa 26; s €35-40, d €60-70; 🖳) Piran's most romantic accommodation option has just six rooms – each bearing a woman's name rather than a number – in a delightful coral-coloured 18th-century townhouse. It's just down from the cathedral.

Hotel Tartini (☎ 671 10 00; www.hotel-tartini-piran.com; Tartinijev trg 15; s €56-86, d €76-112, ste €128-192;) This attractive, 45-room property faces Tartinijev trg and manages to catch a few sea views from the upper floors. The staff are especially friendly and helpful. If you've got the dosh, splash out on suite No 40a; we're suckers for eyrie-like round rooms with €1-million views.

Eating & Drinking

One of Piran's major attractions is its plethora of fish restaurants, especially along Prešernovo nabrežje, though don't expect any bargains there.

Flora (☎ 673 12 58; Prešernovo nabrežje 26; pizza €4-7.50; 10am-1am Jul & Aug, 10am-10pm Sep-Jun) The terrace of this simple pizzeria east of the Punta lighthouse has uninterrupted views of the Adriatic.

Galeb (☎ 673 32 25; Pusterla ul 5; mains €8-11; 11am-4pm & 6pm-11pm or midnight Wed-Mon) This excellent family-run restaurant with seafront seating is east of the Punta lighthouse. The food is good but takes no risks.

Pri Mari (☎ 673 47 35, 041-616 488; Dantejeva ul 17; mains €7.50-16; 10am-11pm Tue-Sun Jul & Aug, noon-10pm Tue-Sat, noon-6pm Sun Sep-Jun) This stylish Italian-owned restaurant south of the bus station serves the most inventive Mediterranean and Slovenian dishes in town. Try the fish paté and mussels in wine.

Stara Gostilna (☎ 673 31 65; Savudrijska ul 2; mains €7.50-17; 9am-11pm) This delightful bistro in the Old Town serves both meat and fish dishes, and offers some of the best and most welcoming service in town.

Riva (☎ 673 221 80; Prešernovo nabrežje; mains €8-24; 11.30am-midnight) The only seafood restaurant on Prešernovo nabrežje worth patronising is this classy place with the strip's best decor and sea views.

Café Teater (☎ 051-694 100; Stjenkova ul 1; 7am-3am Mon-Fri, 9am-3am Sat & Sun) Anyone who's anyone in Piran can be found at this cafe with a waterfront terrace and troppo furnishings.

Caffe Tartini (☎ 673 33 81; Tartinijev trg 3; 7am-3am) This cafe, housed in a classical building opposite the Venetian House, is a wonderful place for a cup of something hot and a slice of something sweet at almost any time of the day.

There's an outdoor **market** (Zelenjavni trg; 7am-2pm Mon-Sat) in the small square behind the town hall. **Mercator** (Levstikova ul 5; 7am-8pm Mon-Sat, 8am-noon Sun) has a branch in the Old Town. **Ham Ham** (Tomšičeva ul 41; 7am-midnight) is a convenience store opposite the bus station.

Getting There & Away

From the bus station, buses run every 20 to 30 minutes to Koper (€3.10, 30 minutes, 18km) via Izola, while five head for Trieste in Italy (€10, 1¾ hours, 36km) between 6.45am and 6.55pm Monday to Saturday. Between three and five daily buses go to Ljubljana (€12, 2½ to three hours, 140km) via Divača and Postojna.

From the southern end of Tartinijev trg, a shuttle bus (€1) goes every 15 minutes to Lucija via Portorož.

Venezia Lines (☎ 05-674 71 61; www.venezialines.com) catamarans sail to Venice (one way/return €46/89, 2¼ hours) at 8.30am on Wednesday from May to mid-September. A new service run by **Trieste Lines** (www.triestelines.it) links Piran and Trieste twice a day Tuesday to Sunday from late April to late September. Buy tickets (one way/return €6.80/12.60) from the TIC in Piran.

PORTOROŽ

☎ 05 / pop 2900

Portorož (Portorose in Italian), the biggest resort in Slovenia, is actually quite classy for a seaside town, even along Obala, the main drag. And with the recent reopening of the 185-room Palace, the art nouveau hotel that put Portorož on the map, it may even start to relive its glory days. Portorož's sandy beaches are relatively clean, and there are pleasant spas and wellness centres where you can take the waters or cover yourself in curative mud.

At the same time, the vast array of accommodation options makes Portorož a useful fall back if everything's full in Piran. Full listings are available at the **Tourist Information Center Portorož** (☎ 674 22 20; www.portoroz.si; Obala 16; 9am-7pm Jul & Aug, 9am-5pm Mon-Sat, 10am-2pm Sun Sep-Jun). Just off the main road between Piran and the centre of Portorož, the summer-only hostel **Prenočišča Korotan** (☎ 674 54 00; www.sd.upr.si/sdp/prenocisca; Obala 11; s €30-33, d €43-46, tr €57-60, q €€69-73; Jul & Aug;) has en-suite rooms. Be warned, though, that there is a 40/20% supplement for stays of just one/two nights. At the

SLOVENIA

other end of the scale, the 48-room **Hotel Marko** (☎ 617 40 00; www.hotel-marko.com; Obala 28; s €56-96, d €70-120), with lovely gardens just opposite Portorož Bay is delightful.

There are dozens of decent pizzerias along Obala, but the place of choice is **Pizzeria Figarola** (☎ 674 22 00; Obala 14A; pizza €6.50-10.50; 🕑 10am-10pm), with a huge terrace just up from the main pier.

Papa Chico (☎ 677 93 10; Obala 26; mains €5.80-11.30; 🕑 9am-2am Mon-Sat, 10am-2am Sun) serves 'Mexican fun food' (go figure), including fajitas (€9.40 to €11.30).

Kavarna Cacao (☎ 674 10 35; Obala 14; 🕑 8am-1am Sun-Thu, to 3am Fri & Sat) wins the award as the most stylish cafe-bar on the coast and boasts a fabulous waterfront terrace.

Every 20 minutes, a shuttle bus (€1) from Piran trundles along Obala on its way to Lucija, passing by Prenočišča Korotan.

EASTERN SLOVENIA

The rolling vine-covered hills of eastern Slovenia are attractive but much less dramatic than the Julian Alps or, indeed, the coast. If you're heading by train to Vienna via Graz in Austria it saves money to stop in lively Maribor, Slovenia's second-largest city; international tickets are very expensive per kilometre, so doing as much travelling as possible on domestic trains saves cash. While there, consider visiting postcard-perfect Ptuj just down the road.

MARIBOR

☎ 02 / pop 89,450

Slovenia's light-industrial second city really has no unmissable sights but oozes with charm thanks to its delightfully patchy Old Town. Pedestrianised central streets buzz with cafes and student life, and in late June/early July the old, riverside Lent district buzzes with the two-week **Lent International Summer Festival** (http://lent.slovenija.net) extravaganza of folklore and culture.

Maribor Castle (Grajski trg 2), on the main square's northeast corner, contains a magnificent 18th-century **rococo staircase** visible from the street and the **Maribor Regional Museum** (☎ 228 35 51; adult/student & child €3/2.50; 🕑 9am-4pm Tue-Sat, 9am-2pm Sun), one of Slovenia's richest archaeological and ethnographical collections but undergoing a protracted renovation.

Two cafe-packed blocks to the southwest, the **Cathedral** (Slomškov trg) sits in an oasis of fountain-cooled calm. Follow little Poštna ul southward into **Glavni trg** with its extravagant **town hall** (Glavni trg 14) and **plague pillar**, a lovely column of saints erected by townspeople in gratitude for having survived the plague. A block farther south down Mesarski prehod is the Drava River's north bank, where you'll find the **Stara Trta** (Vojašniška 8), the world's oldest living grapevine. It's been a source of a dark red wine called Žametna Črnina (Black Velvet) for more than four centuries.

The helpful **Tourist Information Centre Maribor** (☎ 234 66 10; www.maribor.si; Partinzanska c 6A; 🕑 9am-7pm Mon-Fri, to 6pm Sat & Sun Jul & Aug, 9am-6pm Mon-Sat, to 1pm Sun Sep-Jun) has a complete listing of places to stay. At the budget end of the spectrum, try the new **Alibi C2** (☎ 051-663 555; www.alibi.si; Cafova ul 2; dm €17-20, d per person €20-25; 💻), a superswanky hostel with seven doubles and six dorms with six beds each in a beautifully renovated 19th-century building. Just around the corner is the **Grand Hotel Ocean** (☎ 234 36 73; www.hotelocean.si; Partizanska c 39; s €70-75, d €100; ❄ 💻), a stunning 23-room boutique hotel named after the first train to pass through the city in 1846 (and, well, the most exciting thing to happen here since).

Gril Ranca (☎ 252 55 50; Dravska ul 10; dishes €3-6; 🕑 8am-11pm Mon-Sat, noon-9pm Sun) serves simple but scrumptious Balkan grills in full view of the Drava. For something more, ahem, cosmopolitan try **Toti Rotovž** (☎ 228 76 50; Glavni trg 14 & Rotovški trg 9; mains €6-18; 🕑 9am-midnight Mon-Thu, 9am-2am Fri & Sat), a peculiar place behind the town hall that serves up just about every cuisine under the sun – from Slovenian to Thai and Greek to Mexican.

Buses run to Ljubljana (€12, three hours, 127km) two to four times a day. Also served are Celje (€6.30, 1½ hours, 55km, up to 10 a day) and Ptuj (€3.60, 45 minutes, 27km, hourly). There are daily buses to Munich (€46, 7½ hours, 453km) at 6.50pm and 9.50pm, and one to Vienna (€29, 4½ hours, 258km) at 5.45pm. Of the two-dozen daily trains to/from Ljubljana (€7.75, 2½ hours, 156km), five are IC express trains costing €19.60 and taking just under two hours.

PTUJ

☎ 02 / pop 18,950

Rising gently above a wide, almost flat valley, compact Ptuj (Poetovio to the Romans) forms a symphony of red-tile roofs best viewed from across the Drava River. Its pinnacle is the well-preserved **Ptuj Castle** (Na Gradu 1), containing the fine **Regional Museum Ptuj** (☎ 787 92 30; adult/student/child €4/2.50/2.50; 9am-6pm Mon-Fri, 9am-8pm Sat & Sun Jul & Aug, 9am-6pm daily May-Jun & Sep–mid-Oct, 9am-5pm mid-Oct–Apr).

For 10 days before Mardi Gras crowds come from far and wide to spot the shaggy Kurent straw men at Slovenia's foremost traditional carnival, **Kurentovanje** (www.kurentovanje.net). A 'rite of spring', it is celebrated for 10 days up to Shrove Tuesday (February or early March; the museum has some excellent Kurentovanje-related exhibits. The **Tourist Information Centre Ptuj** (☎ 779 60 11; www.ptuj-tourism.si; Slovenski trg 3; 9am-8pm May–mid-Oct, 9am-6pm mid-Oct–Apr), facing a medieval tower in the Old Town, has reams of information and lists of places to stay. If you're looking for budget accommodation, look no further than **Hostel Eva** (☎ 771 24 41, 040-226 522; info@bikeek.si; Jadranska 22; per person €12-17), a welcoming, up-to-date hostel connected to a bike shop (per day €10) with six rooms containing two to four beds and a large, light-filled kitchen. If you'd like more comfort, continue walking west on Prešernova ul past a parade of cafes and bars to the new **Park Hotel Ptuj** (☎ 749 33 00; www.parkhotel-ptuj.si; Prešernova ul 38; s €81-98, d €108-122, ste €110-126;), a lovely new boutique hotel in an 18th-century townhouse with 15 individually designed rooms and lots of original artwork on the walls.

Eat next door at **Amadeus** (☎ 771 70 51; Prešernova ul 36; mains €6.50-20; noon-10pm Mon-Thu, noon-11pm Fri & Sat, noon-4pm Sun), a very pleasant *gostilna* above a cafe-bar serving *štruklji* (dumplings with herbs and cheese, €3.50), steak and pork dishes. More pleasant in the warmer months is **Ribič** (☎ 749 06 35; Dravska ul 9; mains €9-18; 10am-11pm Sun-Thu, to midnight Fri & Sat), the best restaurant in Ptuj, with a great riverside terrace and the ideal spot to have a fish dinner. Next to the town's open-air **market** (Novi trg; 7am-3pm) you'll find a large **Mercator** (Novi trg 3; 7.30am-7.30pm Mon-Fri, 7.30am-1pm Sat) supermarket.

Buses to Maribor (€3.60, 45 minutes, 27km) run at least hourly on weekdays but are less frequent on weekends. A half-dozen IC trains from Ljubljana (€9.20 to €13, 2½ hours, 155km) pass through Ptuj daily, two of which (10.08am and 7.03pm) are on their way to Budapest (€38.60, 4¼ hours, 313km).

SLOVENIA DIRECTORY

ACCOMMODATION

Accommodation listings throughout this guide have been ordered by price. Very roughly, budget accommodation means a double room under €50, midrange is €51 to €100 and top end is anything over €101. Accommodation is a little bit more expensive in Ljubljana. Unless otherwise indicated, rooms include en-suite toilet and bath or shower and breakfast. Smoking is banned in hotels.

Camping grounds generally charge per person, whether you're in a tent or caravan. Almost all sites close from mid-October to mid-April. Camping 'rough' is illegal in Slovenia, and this law is enforced, especially around Bled. Seek out the Slovenian Tourist Board's *Camping in Slovenia*.

Slovenia's growing stable of hostels includes Ljubljana's trendy Celica and the Alibi chain of hostels found in the capital, at Piran and now in Maribor. Throughout the country there are student dormitories (residence halls) moonlighting as hostels for visitors in July and August. Unless stated otherwise hostel rooms share bathrooms. Hostels usually cost from €15 to €22; prices are at their highest in July and August and during the Christmas break, when it can sometimes be difficult to find accommodation at any price.

Tourist information offices can help you access private rooms, apartments and tourist farms, or they can recommend private agencies that will. Such accommodation can appear misleadingly cheap if you overlook the 30% to 50% surcharge levied on stays of less than three nights. Also be aware that many such properties are in outlying villages with minimal public transport, and that the cheapest one-star category rooms with shared bathroom are actually very rare, so you'll usually pay well above the quoted minimum. Depending on the season you might save a little money by going directly to any house with a sign reading *sobe* (rooms). For more information check out the Slovenian Tourist Board's **Friendly Countryside** (www.slovenia.info/touristfarms) pamphlet listing upwards of 200 farms with accommodation.

Guest houses, known as a *penzion, gostišče,* or *prenočišča*, are often cosy and better value than full-blown hotels. Nonetheless it can be difficult to find a double room in a hotel for under €50. Beware that locally listed rates are usually quoted per person assuming double occupancy. A tourist tax – routinely €0.50 to €1 (hotel) per person per day – is usually not included.

ACTIVITIES

Extreme Sports

Several areas specialise in adrenalin-rush activities, the greatest range being available at Bovec (p725), famous for rafting, hydro-speed, kayaking and canyoning, and increasingly at Bled (p721). Bovec is also a great place for paragliding; in winter you ascend Mt Kanin via ski lift and then jump off. Gliding costs are very reasonable from Lesce near Bled. Scuba diving from Piran (p732) is also good value.

Hiking

Hiking is extremely popular, with the **Alpine Association of Slovenia** (www.pzs.si) counting some 55,000 members and Ljubljančani flocking in droves to Triglav National Park (p723) on weekends. There are more than 7000km of marked trails and paths, and in summer as many as 170 mountain huts offer comfortable trailside refuge. Several treks are outlined in Lonely Planet's more comprehensive *Slovenia.*

Skiing

Skiing is a Slovenian passion, with slopes particularly crowded over the Christmas holidays and in early February. See the Slovenian Tourist Board's **Ski Centers of Slovenia** (www.slovenia.info/skiing) for more details.

Kranjska Gora (up to 1291m; p724) has some challenging runs, and the world record for ski-jumping was set at nearby Planica, 4km to the west. Above Lake Bohinj, Vogel (up to 1800m) is particularly scenic, as is Kanin (up to 2300m) above Bovec, which can have snow as late as May. Being relatively close to Ljubljana, Krvavec (up to 1971m), northeast of Kranj, can have particularly long lift queues.

Just west of Maribor in eastern Slovenia is a popular choice and the biggest downhill skiing area in the country. Although relatively low (336m to 1347m), the Mariborsko Pohorje is easily accessible, with very varied downhill pistes and relatively short lift queues.

Other Activities

Mountain bikes are available for hire from travel agencies at Bled, Bohinj, Bovec, Kranjska Gora and Postojna.

The Soča River near Kobarid and the Sava Bohinjka near Bohinj are great for fly-fishing April to October. Licences for the latter cost €55/38 (catch/catch and release) and are sold at the tourist office and certain hotels.

Spas and wellness centres are very popular in Slovenia; see **Slovenia Spas** (www.spa-slovenia.com) website for more information. Most towns have some sort of spa complex, and hotels often offer free or bargain-rate entry to their guests.

BUSINESS HOURS

All businesses post their opening times *(delovni čas)* on the door. Many shops close Saturday afternoons. A handful of grocery stores open on Sundays, including some branches of the ubiquitous Mercator supermarket chain. Most museums close on Mondays. Banks often take lunch breaks from 12.30pm to 2pm and only a few open on Saturday mornings.

Restaurants typically open for lunch and dinner until at least 10pm, and bars until midnight, though they may have longer hours on weekends and shorter ones on Sundays.

EMBASSIES & CONSULATES

Following are among the embassies and consulates in Slovenia. Unless noted otherwise, they are all in Ljubljana.

Australia (off Map pp708-9; ☎ 01-425 42 52; Dunajska c 50; 🕒 9am-1pm Mon-Fri)

Austria (Map pp708-9; ☎ 01-479 07 00; Prešernova c 23; 🕒 8am-noon Mon-Thu, 8-11am Fri) Enter from Veselova ul.

Canada (Map pp708-9; ☎ 01-252 44 44; 12th fl, Trg Republike 3; 🕒 9am-noon Mon-Fri)

Croatia Ljubljana (Map pp708-9; ☎ 01-425 62 20; Gruberjevo nabrežje 6; 🕒 9am-1pm Mon-Fri); Maribor (☎ 02-234 66 86; Trg Svobode 3; 🕒 10am-1pm Mon-Fri)

France (Map pp708-9; ☎ 01-479 04 00; Barjanska c 1; 🕒 8.30am-12.30pm Mon-Fri)

Hungary (off Map pp708-9; ☎ 01-512 18 82; ul Konrada Babnika 5; 🕒 8am-5pm Mon-Fri)

Ireland (Map pp708-9; ☎ 01-300 89 70; Palača Kapitelj, Poljanski nasip 6; 🕒 9.30am-12.30pm & 2.30-4pm Mon-Fri)

Italy Ljubljana (Map pp708-9; ☎ 01-426 21 94; Snežniška ul 8; 🕒 9-11am Mon-Fri); Koper (Map p729; ☎ 05-627 37 49; Belvedere 2; 🕒 8.30am-noon Mon-Fri)

Netherlands (Map pp708-9; ☎ 01-420 14 61; Palača Kapitelj, Poljanski nasip 6; 🕒 9am-noon Mon-Fri)

New Zealand (off Map pp708-9; ☎ 01-580 30 55; Verovškova ul 57; 🕒 8am-3pm Mon-Fri)

South Africa (☎ 01-200 63 00; Pražakova ul 4; ⌚ 3-4pm Tue) In Kompas building.
UK (Map pp708-9; ☎ 01-200 39 10; 4th fl, Trg Republike 3; ⌚ 9am-noon Mon-Fri)
USA (Map pp708-9; ☎ 01-200 55 00; Prešernova c 31; ⌚ 9-11.30am & 1-3pm Mon-Fri)

FESTIVALS & EVENTS

Major cultural and sporting events are listed under 'Events' on the website of the **Slovenian Tourist Board** (www.slovenia.info) and in the STB's comprehensive *Calendar of Major Events in Slovenia*, issued annually.

Slovenia's biggest open-air rock concert **Rock Otočec** (www.rock-otocec.com) is a three-day event held in late June/early July at Prečna airfield, 5km northwest of Novo Mesto in southeastern Slovenia.

GAY & LESBIAN TRAVELLERS

Roza Klub (☎ 01-430 47 40; Kersnikova ul 4) in Ljubljana is made up of the gay and lesbian branches of ŠKUC (Študentski Kulturni Center or Student Cultural Centre).

GALfon (☎ 01-432 40 89; ⌚ 7-10pm Mon-Fri) is a hotline and source of general information for gays and lesbians. The websites of **Slovenian Queer Resources Directory** (www.ljudmila.org/siqrd) and **Out in Slovenia** (www.outinslovenija.com) are both extensive and partially in English.

HOLIDAYS

Slovenia celebrates 14 holidays *(prazniki)* a year. If a holiday falls on a Sunday, then the following Monday becomes the holiday.

New Year 1 and 2 January
Prešeren Day (Slovenian Culture Day) 8 February
Easter March/April
Insurrection Day 27 April
Labour Days 1 and 2 May
National Day 25 June
Assumption Day 15 August
Reformation Day 31 October
All Saints Day 1 November
Christmas Day 25 December
Independence Day 26 December

INTERNET ACCESS

Virtually every hostel and hotel now has internet access – a computer for guests' use (free or for a small fee), wi-fi, or both. Most cities and towns have at least one cyber cafe but they usually only have a handful of terminals. Be advised that Slovenian keyboards are neither qwerty nor azerty but qwertz, reversing the y and z keys, but otherwise following the Anglophone norm.

INTERNET RESOURCES

The website of the **Slovenian Tourist Board** (www.slovenia.info) is tremendously useful, as is that of **Mat'Kurja** (www.matkurja.com), a directory of Slovenian web resources. Most Slovenian towns and cities have a website accessed by typing www.town.si (or sometimes www.town-tourism.si). Especially good are **Ljubljana** (www.ljubljana.si), **Maribor** (www.maribor.si) and **Piran-Portorož** (www.portoroz.si).

MONEY

Slovenia uses the euro as its official currency. Exchanging cash is simple at banks, major post offices, travel agencies and *menjalnice* (bureaux de change), although some of the latter don't accept travellers cheques. Major credit and debit cards are accepted almost everywhere, and ATMs are ubiquitous.

POST

Local mail costs €0.27 for up to 20g, while an international airmail stamp costs €0.45. Poste restante is free; address it to and pick it up from the main post office at Slovenska c 32, 1101 Ljubljana.

TELEPHONE

Slovenia's country code is ☎ 386. Public telephones require a phonecard *(telefonska kartica* or *telekartica)*, available at post offices and some news-stands. The cheapest card (€4, 25 units) gives about 20 minutes' calling time to other European countries; the highest value is €14.60 with 300 units. Local SIM cards with €5 credit are available for €12 from **SiMobil** (www.simobil.si) and for €15 from **Mobitel** (www.mobitel.si). Mobile numbers in Slovenia are identified by the prefix ☎ 031-, 040-, 041- and 051-.

TOURIST INFORMATION

The Ljubljana-based **Slovenian Tourist Board** (off Map pp708-9; ☎ 01-589 18 40; www.slovenia.info; Dunajska

EMERGENCY NUMBERS

- Ambulance ☎ 112
- Fire ☎ 112
- Police ☎ 113
- Roadside assistance ☎ 1987

SLOVENIA

c156) has dozens of tourist information centres (TICs) in Slovenia, and overseas branches in a half-dozen European countries; see 'STB Representative Offices Abroad' on its website for details.

VISAS

Citizens of virtually all European countries, as well as Australia, Canada, Israel, Japan, New Zealand and the USA, do not require visas to visit Slovenia for stays of up to 90 days. Holders of EU and Swiss passports can enter using a national identity card.

Those who do require visas (including South Africans) can get them for up to 90 days at any Slovenian embassy or consulate – see the website of the **Ministry of Foreign Affairs** (www.mzz.gov.si) for a full listing. They cost €35 regardless of the type of visa or length of validity. You'll need confirmation of a hotel booking plus one photo, and you may have to show a return or onward ticket.

WOMEN TRAVELLERS

In the event of an emergency call the **police** (☎ 113) any time or the **SOS Helpline** (☎ 080 11 55; www.drustvo-sos.si; noon-10pm Mon-Fri, 6-10pm Sat & Sun).

TRANSPORT IN SLOVENIA

GETTING THERE & AWAY

Air

Slovenia's only international airport receiving regular scheduled flights at present – Aerodrom Maribor does limited charters only – is Ljubljana's recently renamed **Jože Pučnik Airport** (LJU; www.lju-airport.si) at Brnik, 27km north of Ljubljana. From its base here, the Slovenian flag-carrier, **Adria Airways** (JP; ☎ 080 13 00, 01-369 10 10; www.adria-airways.com), serves some 28 European destinations on regularly scheduled flights, with just as many holiday spots served by charter flights in summer. Adria can be remarkably good value and includes useful connections to İstanbul, Ohrid (Macedonia), Pristina (Kosovo) and Tirana (Albania).

Other airlines with regularly scheduled flights to and from Ljubljana:

Air France (AF; ☎ 01-244 34 47; www.airfrance.com/si) Daily flights to Paris (CDG).

Austrian Airlines (OS; ☎ 01-202 01 00; www.aua.com) Multiple daily flights to Vienna.

Brussels Airlines (SN; ☎ 04-206 16 56; www.brusselsairlines.com) Daily flights to Brussels.

ČSA Czech Airlines (OK; ☎ 04-206 17 50; www.czechairlines.com) Flights to Prague.

easyJet (EZY; ☎ 04-206 16 77; www.easyjet.com) Low-cost flights to London Stansted.

Finnair (AY; ☎ 080 13 00, 01-369 10 10; www.finnair.com) Flights to Helsinki.

JAT Airways (JU; ☎ 01-231 43 40; www.jat.com) Daily flights to Belgrade.

Malév Hungarian Airlines (MA; ☎ 04-206 16 76; www.malev.hu) Daily flights to Budapest.

Turkish Airlines (TK; ☎ 04-206 16 80; www.turkishairlines.com) Flights to İstanbul.

Land

BUS

International bus destinations from Ljubljana include Serbia, Germany, Hungary, Croatia, Bosnia and Hercegovina, Macedonia and Italy; see p718 for details. You can also catch buses to Italy and Croatia from coastal towns, including Piran (p733) and Koper (p730). Maribor (p734) also has buses to Germany and Austria.

TRAIN

It is possible to travel to Italy, Austria, Germany and Croatia by train; Ljubljana (p718) is the main hub, although you can, for example, hop on a train to Budapest at Ptuj (p735).

Train travel can be expensive. It is sometimes cheaper to travel as far as you can on domestic routes before crossing any borders. For example, you can travel on a Ljubljana–Vienna service but you will save a little bit of money by going first to Maribor; see p734 for details.

Seat reservations, compulsory on trains to and from Italy and on InterCity (IC) trains, cost €3.50, but it is usually included in the ticket price.

Sea

Piran despatches ferries to Trieste a couple of times a day and catamarans to Venice at least once a week; see p733 for details. There's also a catamaran between nearby Izola and Venice in summer months; see p730.

GETTING AROUND

Bus

It's worth booking long-distance buses ahead of time, especially when travelling on Friday afternoons. If your bag has to go in the luggage compartment below the bus, it will cost €1.50 extra. The online bus timetable, **Avtobusna Postaja Ljubljana** (www.ap-ljubljana.si), is extensive, but generally only lists buses that use Ljubljana as a hub.

Bicycle

Bicycles may be hired at some train stations, tourist offices, travel agencies and hotels.

Car

Hiring a car is recommended, and can even save you money as you can access cheaper out-of-centre hotels and farm or village homestays. Daily rates usually start at around €40/210 per day/week, including unlimited mileage, collision-damage waiver and theft protection. Unleaded petrol *(bencin)* costs €1.21 (95 octane) and €1.25 (98 octane), with diesel at €1.31. You must keep your headlights illuminated throughout the day. If you'll be doing a lot of driving consider buying Kod & Kam's 1:100,000 *Avtoatlas Slovenija* (€27).

A new law requires all cars to display a *vinjeta* (road-toll sticker) on the windscreen. They cost €35/55 for a half-/full year and are available at petrol stations, post offices and some kiosks; for a complete list consult the website www.cestnina.si. These will already be in place on a rental car but if you are driving your own vehicle, failure to display such a sticker risks a fine of €300 to €800.

Further information is available from the **Automobile Association of Slovenia** (☎ 01 530 53 00; www.amzs.si)

Hitching

Hitchhiking is fairly common and legal, except on motorways and a few major highways. Even young women hitch in Slovenia, but it's never totally safe and Lonely Planet doesn't recommend it.

Train

Slovenian Railways (Slovenske Železnice; ☎ 01-291 33 32; www.slo-zeleznice.si) has a useful online timetable that's easy to use. Buy tickets before boarding or you'll incur a €2.50 supplement. Be aware that EuroCity (EC) and InterCity (IC) trains carry a surcharge of €1.50 on top of standard quoted fares, while InterCity Slovenia ones cost €8.80/5.70 extra in 1st/2nd class.

Spain

Stretching sun-drenched and untamed to the south of the wild and majestic Pyrenees, this passionate nation works a mysterious magic. Spain is littered with hundreds of glittering beaches; flamenco *bailaors* (dancers) swirl in flounces of colour; and *toreros* (bullfighters) strut their stuff in the bullrings. Summer holidaymakers gather around great pans of steaming paella (at its tasty best in Valencia) and pitchers of sangria...

Beyond these clichéd images, a vast, unexpected panorama unfolds before you. Emerald green mountains seem to slide into the wild blue Atlantic in the north. Proud, solitary castles and medieval towns are strewn across the interior. White villages glitter in inland Andalucía. Rugged mountain ranges such as the Sierra Nevada (Europe's most southerly ski resort) are draped across the country. The Celtic music of Galicia and Asturias reminds one of the misty lands of Brittany, Scotland and Ireland.

From its Roman amphitheatres to Muslim palaces, from Gothic cathedrals and Modernista constructions, the country is a treasure chest of artistic and architectural marvels across a matchless cultural palette. More than 30 years of democracy and rapid economic development have spurred Spain's cities to bedeck themselves with sparkling new ornaments. An army of local and international architects has left a slew of daring signature buildings in Barcelona, Bilbao and Madrid, to name a few.

Up and down the country, a zest for life creates an intense, hedonistic vibe in its effervescent cities. Indeed, if there is one thing Spaniards love, it is to eat, drink and be merry, whether gobbling up tapas over fine wine in Madrid and the south, or its elaborate Basque Country equivalent, *pintxos*, over cider in the north.

FAST FACTS

- **Area** 504,782 sq km
- **Capital** Madrid
- **Currency** euro (€); US$1 = €0.73; UK£1 = €1.06; A$1 = €0.50; ¥100 = €0.76; NZ$1 = €0.41
- **Famous for** sunshine, late nights, bullfighting, *gazpacho* (cold tomato soup), *Don Quijote,* Pedro Almodóvar films
- **Official languages** Spanish (Castilian or *castellano*), Catalan, Basque, Galician *(gallego)*
- **Phrases** *hola* (hello); *gracias* (thanks); *adiós* (goodbye)
- **Population** 45 million
- **Telephone codes** country code ☎ 34; international access code ☎ 00
- **Visas** Not required for EU nationals and many others for up to 90 days; see p848

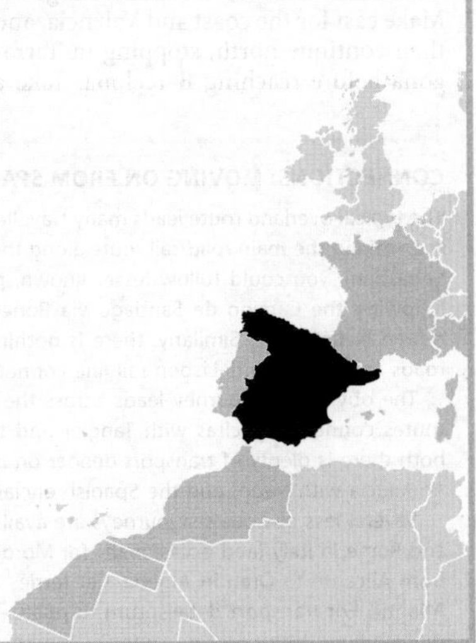

SPAIN

HIGHLIGHTS

- Visit Gaudí's singular work in progress, **La Sagrada Família** (p784), in Barcelona, an art nouveau cathedral that truly defies imagination.
- Discover the impossibly beautiful Mediterranean beaches and coves of **Menorca** (p821).
- Eat your way through **San Sebastián** (p797), a gourmand's paradise with an idyllic seaside setting.
- Join the pilgrims making their way along medieval laneways to the magnificent **Catedral del Apóstol** (p805) in Santiago de Compostela.
- Soak up the scent of orange blossom and surrender to the party atmosphere in sunny **Seville** (p823).

ITINERARIES

- **One week** Marvel at Barcelona's art nouveau–influenced Modernista architecture and seaside style before taking the train to San Sebastián, with a stop in Zaragoza on the way. Head on to Bilbao for the Guggenheim Museum and end the trip living it up on Madrid's legendary night scene.
- **One month** Fly into Seville and embark on a route exploring it and picture-perfect Ronda, Granada and Córdoba. Take the train to Madrid, from where you can check out Toledo, Ávila and Segovia. Make east for the coast and Valencia, and then continue north, stopping in Tarragona before reaching Barcelona. Take a plane or boat for the Balearic Islands, from where you can get a flight home.

CLIMATE & WHEN TO GO

Much of Spain is drenched with sunshine year-round, although the green north and snow-capped Pyrenees don't always fit the stereotype. Beach weather begins in late May and lasts until as late as early October. In the north, summer is shorter and cooler than in the south.

The Mediterranean coast is mild, but central Spain and the Pyrenees get downright cold. Rain and wind along the Atlantic coasts make winters in Galicia, Cantabria, Asturias and the Basque Country occasionally unpleasant. Winter snowfalls inland in the north, even in the plains, are not uncommon. See Climate Charts (p944) for more information.

HISTORY

Ancient History

The bridge between Africa and Europe, Spain has always been a meeting point for peoples and cultures, if not always a peaceful one. The oldest pieces of human bone in Europe have been found in Spain, in the Sierra de Atapuerca near Burgos. They are about 780,000 years old and probably come from ancestors of the later Neanderthals. Sophisticated cave paintings at Altamira (p803), near Santander, date from around 12,000 BC. North Africans settled in the peninsula from around 8000 BC and, in the millennia that followed, Celtic tribes, Phoenician merchants, Greeks and Carthaginians trickled in. The Romans ar-

CONNECTIONS: MOVING ON FROM SPAIN

The typical overland route leads many travellers from France over the Pyrenees into Spain. Rather than taking the main road/rail route along the Mediterranean coast (or between Biarritz and San Sebastián), you could follow lesser known, pretty routes over the mountains. Options include following the Camino de Santiago via Roncesvalles (Navarra) or heading down the green Val d'Aran in Catalonia. Similarly, there is nothing to stop you carrying on to Portugal. Numerous roads and the Madrid–Lisbon rail line connect the two countries.

The obvious sea journey leads across the Strait of Gibraltar to Morocco. The most common routes connect Algeciras with Tangier and the Spanish North African enclave of Ceuta. From both there is plenty of transport deeper on into Morocco. Other boats connect various ports in Andalucía with Nador and the Spanish enclave of Melilla.

Several less obvious sea journeys are available. Car ferries leave Barcelona for Genoa, Livorno and Rome in Italy (and occasionally for Morocco). For a serious change of pace, jump on a ferry from Alicante to Oran in Algeria. Car ferries also chug from Cádiz to the Canary Islands in the Atlantic. For transport details, turn to p848.

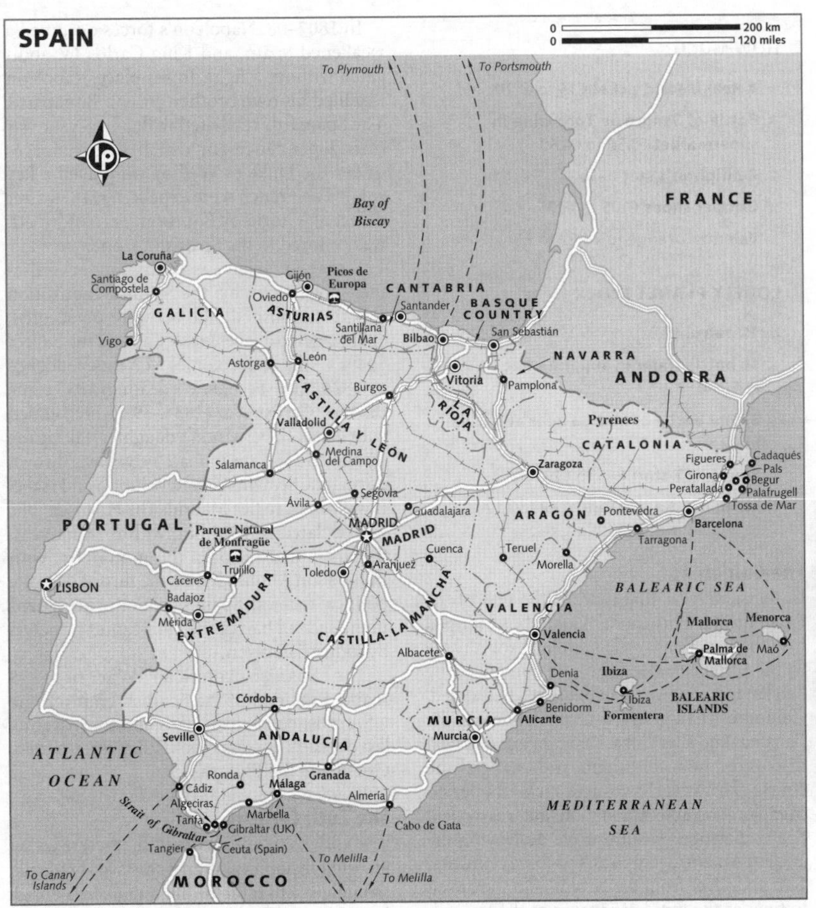

rived in the 3rd century BC but took 200 years to subdue the peninsula. By AD 410, the Christian Visigoths had established a kingdom that lasted until 711.

Muslim Spain & the Reconquista

In 711, Muslim armies invaded the peninsula, most of which they would end up occupying. Muslim dominion would last almost 800 years in parts of Spain. In Islamic Spain (known as al-Andalus), arts and sciences prospered, new crops and agricultural techniques were introduced, and palaces, mosques, schools, public baths and gardens were built.

In 1085, Alfonso VI, king of Castile, took Toledo, the first definitive victory of the Reconquista (the struggle to wrestle Spain into Christian hands). By the mid-13th century, the Christians had taken most of the peninsula, except for the emirate of Granada.

In the process, the kingdoms of Castile and Aragón emerged as Christian Spain's two main powers, and in 1469 they were united by the marriage of Isabel, princess of Castile, and Fernando, heir to Aragón's throne. Known as the Catholic Monarchs, they laid the foundations for the Spanish Golden Age, but were also responsible for one of the darkest hours in Spain's history – the Spanish Inquisition, a witch-hunt to expel or execute Jews and other non-Christians. In 1492, the last Muslim ruler of Granada surrendered to them, marking the end of the Reconquista.

HOW MUCH?

- **A Real Madrid ticket** €15 to €170
- **Bottle of Sangre de Toro wine in supermarket** €3.50 to €4.50
- **Bullfighter's suit** €2500
- **Camper shoes** €105 to €275
- **Valencia orange juice** €2 to €3

LONELY PLANET INDEX

- **1L petrol** €0.87
- **1L bottle water in supermarket** €0.30 to €0.40
- **330ml bottle of Mahou beer at bar** €2 to €2.50
- **Souvenir T-shirt** €15 to €20
- **Menú del día (set lunch)** €8 to €12

The Golden Age

In the same year that marked the end of the Reconquista, Christopher Columbus bumped into the Americas while searching for a route to the Orient (indeed, he was convinced he had landed somewhere in the East). Befuddled, Columbus (Colón in Castilian) landed in the Bahamas and later Cuba. He never guessed he'd discovered new continents and changed the course of history. His voyages sparked a period of exploration and exploitation that was to yield Spain enormous wealth, while destroying the ancient American empires. For three centuries, gold and silver from the New World were used to finance the rapid expansion of the Spanish empire but were not enough to prevent its slow decline. By the 18th century, the mighty Spanish empire was on its way out, the life sucked out of it by a series of unwise kings, a self-seeking noble class and ceaseless warfare.

The 18th & 19th Centuries

The 18th century dawned with a war over the succession to the throne when Carlos II died heirless, but all was soon put right when Felipe V, the first Bourbon king, took control and ushered in a period of stability. Peace would last until the end of the century, when Spain declared war on France and then on Britain and Portugal. The wars proved disastrous, and Spain ultimately lost several colonies and nearly all its sea power.

In 1807–08, Napoleon's forces occupied a weakened Spain, and King Carlos IV abdicated without a fight. In his place Napoleon installed his own brother, Joseph Bonaparte. The Spaniards retaliated with a five-year war of independence (in which British forces under the Duke of Wellington played a key role). The French were expelled in 1813 after defeat at Vitoria. A Bourbon, Fernando VII, was restored to the Spanish throne.

Fernando's reign was a disastrous advertisement for monarchy: the Spanish Inquisition was re-established, liberals were persecuted, Spain entered a severe recession and the bulk of Spain's American colonies won independence by 1824. After Fernando's death in 1833 came the First Carlist War (1834–39), which ended with Isabel II, Fernando's daughter, taking the throne. In 1868, the monarchy was overthrown during the Septembrina Revolution and Isabel II was forced to flee Madrid. The First Republic was declared in 1873 but, within 18 months, the army had restored the monarchy, with Isabel's son Alfonso XII on the throne. Despite political turmoil, Spain's economy prospered in the second half of the 19th century, fuelled by industrialisation.

The Spanish-American War of 1898 marked the end of the Spanish empire. The USA crushed Spanish arms and took over its last overseas possessions – Cuba, Puerto Rico, Guam and the Philippines.

The 20th Century

The early 20th century was characterised by growing instability, as anarchists and radicals struggled to overthrow the established order. In 1923, with Spain on the brink of civil war, Miguel Primo de Rivera made himself military dictator, ruling until 1930. In 1931 King Alfonso XIII fled the country and the Second Republic was declared.

Like its predecessor, the Second Republic fell victim to internal conflict. The 1936 elections split the nation in two, with the Popular Front (an uneasy alliance of leftist parties) on one side and the right-wing Nationalists (an alliance of the army, Church and the Fascist-style Falange Party) on the other.

Nationalist plotters in the army rose against the Republican government in July 1936, launching a civil war (1936–39) that would further sink the country in poverty and create bitter wounds that are still healing today. The Nationalists, led by General Francisco Franco, received military support from Nazi Germany and Fascist Italy, while the elected Republican government received support from the Soviet Union and other foreign leftists.

The war ended in 1939, with Franco the victor. Some 350,000 Spaniards died in the war, most of them on the battlefield but many others in executions, prison camps or simply from disease and starvation. After the war, thousands of Republicans were executed, jailed or forced into exile, and Franco's 36-year dictatorship began with Spain isolated internationally and crippled by recession. It wasn't until the 1950s and '60s, when the rise in tourism and a treaty with the USA combined to provide much-needed funds, that the country began to recover.

Franco died in 1975, having named Juan Carlos, the grandson of Alfonso XIII, as his successor. King Juan Carlos opted for the creation of a constitutional monarchy and a democratic government. The first elections were held in 1977 and a new constitution was drafted in 1978. Spain joined the European Community (EC) in 1986 and celebrated its return to the world stage in style in 1992, with Expo '92 in Seville and the Olympic Games in Barcelona.

Spain Today

The modern, forward-thinking Spain of today has long since thrown off the dark cloud of Franco's dictatorship. In the late 1990s, the centre-right Partido Popular (Popular Party; PP), led by José María Aznar, took control of the nation after the long-ruling Partido Socialista Obrero Español (Spanish Socialist Party; PSOE) was voted out under accusations of corruption. The PP went on to establish programs of economic decentralisation and liberalisation.

In the elections of 2004, just days after the 11 March terrorist attacks in Madrid, the PP lost the presidential election to the PSOE. Newly elected President José Luís Rodríguez Zapatero made waves immediately. Among his first actions as president was the withdrawal of Spanish troops from Iraq. He opened the way to increased devolution of powers to the regions but not without controversy. The opposition PP took special exception to Catalonia's new Estatut (autonomy statutes). Indeed, the PP maintained a divisive campaign against the government until the 2008 elections, which Zapatero also won. His efforts to reach a peace deal with the Basque terror group ETA, which ultimately failed, was one of the deepest sources of division. Under Zapatero, gay marriage was legalised and a massive amnesty legalised the presence of hundreds of thousands of illegal immigrants.

Within months of his re-election, years of economic boom came grinding to a halt amid the worldwide financial crisis unleashed by the subprime calamity in the USA. The construction industry, one of the pillars of the Spanish economy, juddered to a halt and unemployment exploded from 8.3% to 11.3% in the 12 months to October 2008. Amid the growing fears of economic recession, Zapatero pushed through a law on 'historic memory' that provoked sharp debate. Aimed at investigating the crimes and executions of the Franco years, it represented the first official attempt to deal with the country's dictatorial past.

PEOPLE

Spain has a population of approximately 45 million, descended from all the many peoples who have settled here over the millennia, among them Iberians, Celts, Romans, Jews, Visigoths, Berbers, Arabs and 20th-century immigrants from across the globe. The biggest cities are Madrid (3.13 million), Barcelona (1.59 million), Valencia (805,000) and Seville (700,000). Each region proudly preserves its own unique culture, and some – Catalonia and the Basque Country in particular – display a fiercely independent spirit.

RELIGION

Only about 20% of Spaniards are regular churchgoers, but Catholicism is deeply ingrained in the culture. As the writer Unamuno said, 'Here in Spain we are all Catholics, even the atheists'.

However, many Spaniards have a deep-seated scepticism about the Church. During the civil war, anarchists burned churches and shot clerics because they represented repression and corruption. Later, during Franco's rule, church-going was practically obligatory and those who shunned the Church were often treated as outcasts or targeted as delinquents by Franco's police.

Zapatero's introduction of gay weddings, dropping of compulsory religious education in schools and promises to ease abortion regulations all set him at odds with the conservative Spanish clerics.

Spain's most significant (and growing) religious communities after the Catholics are Protestants (around 1.4 million) and Muslims (around 1.5 million).

ARTS

Literature

One of the earliest works of Spanish literature is the *Cantar de Mío Cid* (Song of My Cid), an anonymous epic poem describing the life of El Cid, an 11th-century Christian knight buried in the Burgos cathedral. Miguel de Cervantes' novel, *Don Quijote,* is the masterpiece of the literary flowering of the 16th and 17th centuries, as well as one of the world's great works of fiction.

The next high point, in the early 20th century, grew out of the crisis of the Spanish-American War that spawned the intellectual Generation of '98. The towering figure was poet and playwright Federico García Lorca, who won international acclaim before he was murdered in the civil war for his Republican sympathies.

Popular contemporary authors include Arturo Pérez Reverte, whose *Capitán Alatriste* books are international best-sellers. Carlos Ruíz Zafon followed up his 2002 bestseller, *Shadow of the Wind,* with another, *The Angel's Game,* in 2008. Another writer with a broad following is Javier Marías. He has kept the country in thrall these past years with his 1500-page trilogy, *Tu Rostro Mañana* (Your Face Tomorrow).

Cinema

Modern Spanish cinema's best-known director is Pedro Almodóvar, whose humorous, cutting-edge films are largely set amid the Movida. His *Todo Sobre Mi Madre* (All About My Mother; 1999) and *Habla Con Ella* (Talk to Her; 2002) are both Oscar winners.

Alejandro Amenábar, the young Chilean-born director of *Abre los Ojos* (Open Your Eyes; 1997), *The Others* (2001) and the Oscar-winning *Mar Adentro* (The Sea Inside; 2004), is Almodóvar's only competition for Spain's 'best director' title. That latter film's star, Javier Bardem, won the Oscar for Best Supporting Actor in the Coen brothers' disturbing *No Country for Old Men* in 2008.

Woody Allen set his *Vicky Cristina Barcelona* (2008), a light romantic comedy, largely in Barcelona.

Architecture

Spain's earliest architectural relics are the prehistoric monuments on Menorca. Reminders of Roman times include Segovia's aqueduct (p770), the ancient theatres of Mérida (p843) and Tarragona (p793), and the ruins of Zaragoza (p796). The Muslims left behind some of the most splendid buildings in the Islamic world, including Granada's Alhambra (p830), Córdoba's awe-inspiring Mezquita (p829) and Seville's Alcázar (p823) – the latter an example of Mudéjar architecture, the name given to Islamic artistry done in Christian-held territory.

The first main Christian architectural movement was Romanesque, best seen in churches and monasteries across the north of the country. More unique still is the handful of pre-Romanesque chapels and churches, especially around Oviedo.

Later came the great Gothic cathedrals, such as those in Toledo (p774), Barcelona (p779), Burgos (p773), León (p771), Salamanca (p766) and Seville (p823) of the 13th to 16th centuries; Renaissance styles such as the plateresque work so prominent in Salamanca; and the austere work of Juan de Herrera, responsible for El Escorial (p765). Spain then followed the usual path to baroque (17th and 18th centuries) and neoclassicism (19th century), before Catalonia produced its startling Modernista movement around the turn of the 20th century, of which Antoni Gaudí's La Sagrada Família (p784) in Barcelona, is the most stunning example.

Painting

The giants of Spain's Golden Age (around 1550–1650) were Toledo-based El Greco (originally from Crete) and Diego Velázquez, considered Spain's best painter by greats including Picasso and Dalí. El Greco and Velázquez are well represented in Madrid's El Prado (p752) and were known for their insightful portraits. The genius of both the 18th and 19th centuries was Francisco Goya, whose versatility ranged from unflattering royal portraits and anguished war scenes to bullfight etchings and tapestry designs. Again, many of his works hang in El Prado.

Catalonia was the powerhouse of early-20th-century Spanish art, claiming the hugely prolific Pablo Picasso (although born in Andalucía), the colourful symbolist Joan Miró and surrealist Salvador Dalí. To get inside the latter's world, head for Figueres (p791). The Museu Picasso and Fundació Joan Miró, both in Barcelona (p779), lend deep insight into the work of these two artists.

Important artists of the late 20th century include Catalan abstract artist Antoni Tàpies and Basque sculptor Eduardo Chillida (visit his Museu Chillida Leku, p797).

Flamenco

Getting to see real, deeply emotional flamenco can be hard, as it tends to happen semispontaneously in little bars and not on big touristy stages. Andalucía is its traditional home and your best chance of catching the real thing is probably at one of the flamenco festivals in the south, usually held in summer. You'll also find quality *tablaos* (flamenco stages) in Madrid and throughout Andalucía.

ENVIRONMENT

Spain is a geographically diverse country, with landscapes ranging from the near-deserts of Almería to the emerald green countryside of Asturias and deep coastal inlets of Galicia, from the rolling sun-baked plains of Castilla-La Mancha to the rugged Pyrenees.

The country covers 84% of the Iberian Peninsula and spreads over some 505,000 sq km, about 40% of which is high *meseta* (tableland). Spain is criss-crossed by several majestic mountain chains.

The brown bear, wolf, lynx (very rare) and wild boar all survive in Spain, although only the boar exists in abundance – farmers delight in shooting and roasting the tasty pest. Spain's high mountains harbour the chamois and Spanish ibex and big birds of prey such as eagles, vultures and lammergeier. The marshy Ebro Delta and Guadalquivir estuary are important for water birds, among them the spectacular greater flamingo. Many of Spain's 5500 seed-bearing plants grow nowhere else in Europe, due to the barrier of the Pyrenees. Spring wildflowers are magnificent in many country and hill areas.

The conservation picture has improved in leaps and bounds since 1980 and Spain has 40,000 sq km of protected areas, including 14 national parks. However, overgrazing, the widespread presence of reservoirs, tourism, housing developments, agricultural and industrial effluent, fires and hunting all still threaten plant and animal life.

FOOD & DRINK

Reset your stomach's clock in Spain unless you want to eat alone or with other tourists. Most Spaniards start the day with a light *desayuno* (breakfast), perhaps coffee with a *tostada* (piece of toast) or *pastel/bollo* (pastry), although they might stop in a bar later for a mid-morning *bocadillo* (baguette).

La comida (lunch) is usually the main meal of the day, eaten between about 2pm and 4pm. The *cena* (evening meal) is usually lighter and locals won't sit down for it before 9pm (in the north and mountain areas). The further south you go, the later start times tend to be – anything from 10pm to midnight!

Staples & Specialities

Each region has its own style of cuisine and its own specialities. One of the most characteristic dishes, from the Valencia region, is paella – rice, seafood, the odd vegetable and often chicken or meat, all simmered together and traditionally coloured yellow with saffron. Another dish, of Andalucian origin, is *gazpacho,* a cold soup made from tomatoes, breadcrumbs, cucumber and green peppers. Tortillas (like omelettes) are an inexpensive stand-by snack and come in many varieties. *Jamón serrano* (cured ham) is a delicacy available in many different qualities.

Start the day with a strong coffee, either as a *cafe con leche* (half-coffee, half-milk), *cafe solo* (short black, espresso-like) or *cafe cortado* (short black with a little milk).

The most common way to order a *cerveza* (beer) is to ask for a *caña* (small draught beer). In Basque Country this is a *zurrito.* A larger beer (about 300mL) is often called a *tubo.* All these words apply to *cerveza de barril* (draught beer) – if you just ask for a *cerveza* you're likely to get bottled beer, which is a little more expensive.

Vino (wine) comes *blanco* (white), *tinto* (red) or *rosado* (rosé). Exciting wine regions include Penedès, Priorat, Ribera del Duero and Rioja. *Tinto de verano,* a kind of wine shandy, is good in summer. There are also many regional specialities, such as *jerez* (sherry) in Jerez de la Frontera and *cava* (a sparkling wine) in Catalonia. Sangria, a sweet punch made of red wine, fruit and spirits, is a summer drink and especially popular with tourists.

Agua del grifo (tap water) is usually safe to drink but it may not be very tasty in cities or near the coast. *Agua mineral con gas* (sparkling mineral water) and *agua mineral sin gas* (still mineral water) is available everywhere.

Where to Eat & Drink

Bars and cafes are open all day (see p845 for detailed hours), serving coffees, pastries, *bocadillos* and usually tapas (which generally cost from €1 to €4). In the evenings, these same bars fill with regulars looking for a quick beer or glass of house wine. You can also order *raciones,* a large-sized serving of these snacks. You can often save by ordering and eating food at the bar rather than at a table.

Self-caterers will be delighted with Spain's fresh-produce markets, located near the centre of just about every city and town. Load up on colourful veggies, fresh bread and Spanish cheeses.

Spaniards like to eat out, and restaurants (which come in different styles and with different names such as *taberna, mesón, tasca* and, oh, *restaurante*) abound even in small towns. At lunchtime, most places offer a *menú del día* – a fixed-price lunch menu and the budget traveller's best friend. For €8 to €12 you typically get three courses, bread and a drink. The *plato combinado* (combined plate) is a cousin of the *menú* and usually includes a meat dish with some vegetables.

A 2006 law obliges all establishments bigger than 100 sq metres to be smokefree; smaller places generally allow smoking. Enforcement of the nonsmoking rule is haphazard, however, so many restaurants, regardless of size, remain smoker-friendly.

After dinner, head for the bars. At many bars you can get coffee and tea, and in most cafeterias you can get beer and house wine. A bar de copas will sell beer, probably some cheap wine and an endless array of *combinados* (drinks like vodka and orange or rum and Coke) and sometimes more sophisticated cocktails.

Vegetarians & Vegans

Vegetarians may have to be creative in Spain. Although in larger cities and important student centres there's a growing awareness of vegetarianism and an array of places serving meat-free food, traditional restaurants often offer salads and egg tortillas, but little else for non-carnivores. Even salads may come laden with sausages or tuna. Pasta and pizza are readily available, as is seafood for those who eat it. Vegans will have an especially hard time away from the big cities (and not an easy time in them).

SPAIN

MADRID

pop 3.13 million

Spain's capital is a vibrant place, the hub of the country's government and commerce, and an exciting city bubbling over with creativity. Madrid has a raw, infectious energy. Explore the old streets of the centre, relax in the plazas, soak up the culture in its excellent art museums, and take at least one night to experience the city's legendary nightlife scene.

HISTORY

Madrid was little more than a muddy, mediocre village when King Felipe II declared it Spain's capital in 1561. Established as a Moorish garrison in 854, by the 16th century the population was only 12,000. That began to change when it became the permanent home of the previously roaming Spanish court.

Despite being home to generations of nobles, the city was a squalid grid of unpaved alleys and dirty buildings until the 18th century, when King Carlos III turned his attention to public works. With 175,000 inhabitants under Carlos' rule, Madrid had become Europe's fifth largest capital.

The post–civil war 1940s and '50s were trying times for the capital, with rampant poverty. When Spain's dictator, General Franco, died in 1975, the city exploded with creativity and life, giving Madrileños the party-hard reputation they still cherish.

Terrorist bombs rocked Madrid in March 2004, just before national elections, and killed 191 commuters on four trains. In 2007, two people died in a Basque terrorist bomb attack at the city's airport. With remarkable aplomb, the city quickly returned to business as usual on both occasions.

ORIENTATION

In Spain, all roads lead to Madrid's Plaza de la Puerta del Sol, kilometre zero, the physical and emotional heart of the city. Radiating out from this busy plaza are roads – Calle Mayor, Calle del Arenal, Calle de Preciados, Calle de la Montera and Calle de Alcalá – that stretch deep into the city, as well as a host of metro lines and bus routes.

South of the Puerta del Sol is the oldest part of the city, with Plaza Mayor and Los Austrias to the southwest and the busy streets of the Huertas *barrio* (district or quarter of a town or city) to the southeast. Also to the south lie La Latina and Lavapiés.

North of the plaza is a modern shopping district and, beyond that, the east–west thoroughfare Gran Vía and the gay barrio Chueca, gritty Malasaña, then Chamberí and Argüelles. East of the Puerta del Sol, across the Paseo del Prado and Paseo de los Recoletos, lie El Retiro park and chichi Salamanca. On or close to Paseo del Prado itself are the city's big three art museums.

MADRID IN TWO DAYS

Start with breakfast in the **Plaza de Santa Ana** (Map p753), then visit the **Museo del Prado** (p752). Afterwards, walk around **El Retiro** (p755), but save energy for the **Palacio Real** (p754), early evening shopping and tapas in **Chueca** (p763). At night, catch a **flamenco show** (p762).

On day two, sign up for a **tour** (p756) of historic Madrid, and then visit either the **Thyssen-Bornemisza** (p752) or the **Reina Sofía** (p754) art museums. Make time for a siesta, then hit **Viva Madrid** (p760) for drinks and dancing.

INFORMATION

Bookshops

J&J Books & Coffee (Map pp750-1; Calle del Espíritu Santo 47; 10am-10pm Mon-Thu, 10am-midnight Fri & Sat, 2-10pm Sun; M Noviciado) It claims to have 150,000 (mostly English-language) books.

La Casa del Libro (Map p753; ☎ 91 524 19 00; www.casadellibro.com; Gran Vía 29; 9.30am-9.30pm Mon-Sat, 11am-9pm Sun; M Gran Vía) This mega bookshop has tons of English- and foreign-language titles.

Petra's International Bookshop (Map p753; ☎ 91 541 72 91; Calle de Campomanes 13; 11am-9pm Mon-Sat; M Santo Domingo) A treasure trove of used books, mainly in English.

Discount Cards

Madrid Card (☎ 91 360 47 72; www.madridcard.com; 1/2/3 days €42/55/68) Great if you intend to do some intensive sightseeing and travelling on public transport. It includes free entry to more than 40 museums in and around Madrid. There's also a cheaper version (€28/32/36 for 1/2/3 days) that covers just cultural sights.

Emergency

Servicio de Atención al Turista Extranjero (Foreign Tourist Assistance Service; Map p753; ☎ 91 548 85 37, 91 548 80 08; satemadrid@munimadrid.es; Calle de Leganitos 19; 9am-10pm; M Plaza de España or Santo Domingo).

Internet Access

Madrid is full of internet cafes. Some offer student rates, while most have deals on cards for several hours' use at much-reduced rates. The Ayuntamiento's Centro de Turismo de Madrid on Plaza Mayor offers free internet for up to 15 minutes.

Bbigg (Map p753; ☎ 91 531 23 64; Calle Mayor 1; per 1/5hr €2.50/3; 9.30am-midnight; M Sol) A massive internet centre in the heart of town with separate sections for Skype, internet and games.

Left Luggage

At Madrid's Barajas airport, there are three **consignas** (left-luggage offices; 24hr). In either, you pay €3.60 for the first 24-hour period (or fraction thereof). Thereafter, it costs €4.64/4.13/3.61 per day in a big/medium/small locker. After 15 days the bag will be moved into storage (€1.85 plus a €37.08 transfer fee). Similar services operate for similar prices at Atocha and Chamartín train stations (open 7am to 11pm).

Medical Services

Anglo-American Medical Unit (Map pp750-1; ☎ 91 435 18 23; www.unidadmedica.com; Calle del Conde de Aranda 1; 9am-8pm Mon-Fri, 10am-1pm Sat for emergencies; M Retiro) For medical help in English.

Farmacia del Globo (Map p753; ☎ 91 369 20 00; Calle de Atocha 46; 24hr; M Antón Martín)

Money

Like all Spanish cities, Madrid is fairly crawling with bank branches equipped with ATMs. As a rule, exchange bureaux have longer hours but worse rates and steeper commissions.

Post

Main post office (Map pp750-1; ☎ 91 396 27 33; www.correos.es; Plaza de la Cibeles; 8.30am-9.30pm Mon-Fri, 8.30am-2pm Sat; M Banco de España) It's almost fun to wait in line (which you'll surely have to do) at the beautiful Palacio de Comunicaciones.

Tourist Information

Municipal tourist office (Centro de Turismo de Madrid; Map p753; ☎ 91 429 49 51; www.esmadrid.com; Plaza Mayor 27; 9.30am-8.30pm)

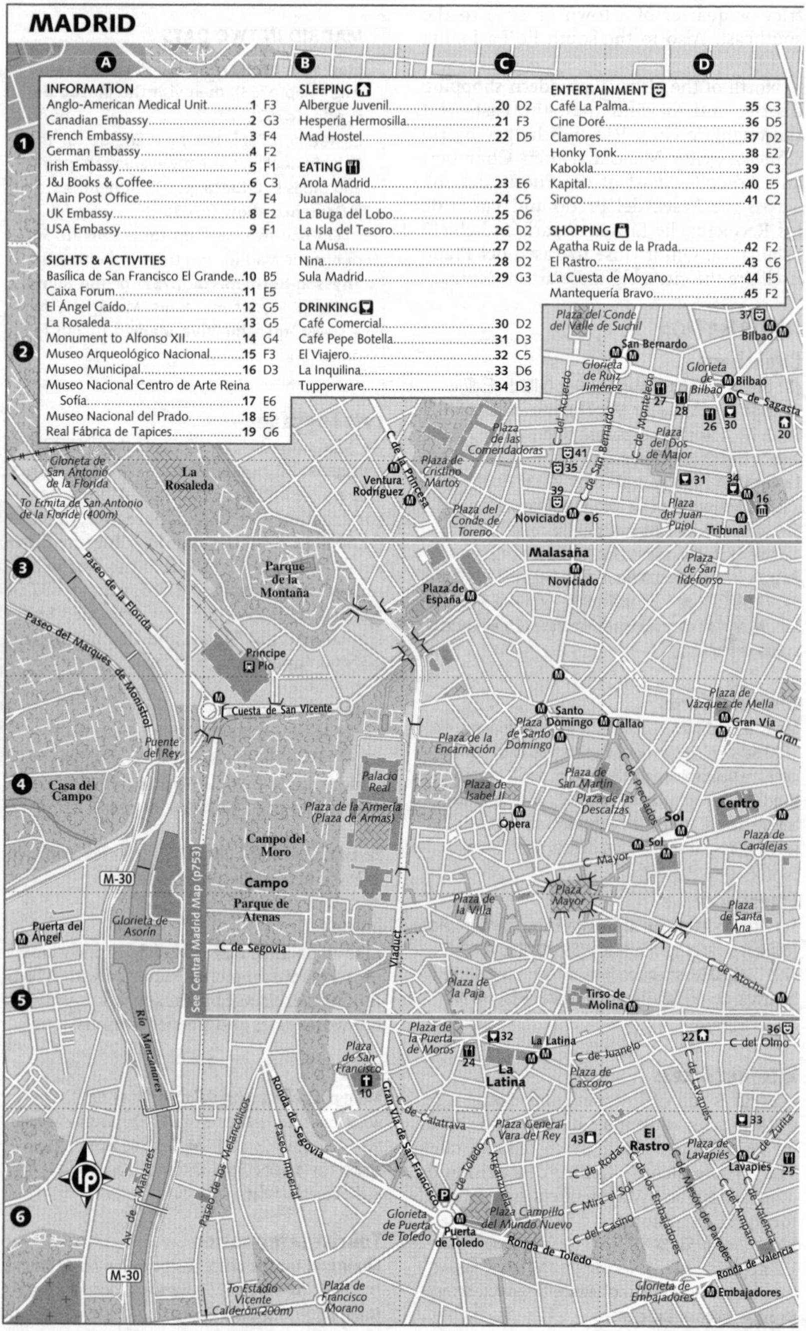
MADRID
INFORMATION
Anglo-American Medical Unit 1 F3
Canadian Embassy 2 G3
French Embassy 3 F4
German Embassy 4 F2
Irish Embassy 5 F1
J&J Books & Coffee 6 C3
Main Post Office 7 E4
UK Embassy 8 E2
USA Embassy 9 F1
SIGHTS & ACTIVITIES
Basílica de San Francisco El Grande 10 B5
Caixa Forum 11 E5
El Ángel Caído 12 G5
La Rosaleda 13 G5
Monument to Alfonso XII 14 G4
Museo Arqueológico Nacional 15 F3
Museo Municipal 16 D3
Museo Nacional Centro de Arte Reina Sofía 17 E6
Museo Nacional del Prado 18 E5
Real Fábrica de Tapices 19 G6
SLEEPING
Albergue Juvenil 20 D2
Hesperia Hermosilla 21 F3
Mad Hostel 22 D5
EATING
Arola Madrid 23 E6
Juanalaloca 24 C5
La Buga del Lobo 25 D6
La Isla del Tesoro 26 D2
La Musa 27 D2
Nina 28 D2
Sula Madrid 29 G3
DRINKING
Café Comercial 30 D2
Café Pepe Botella 31 D3
El Viajero 32 C5
La Inquilina 33 D6
Tupperware 34 D3
ENTERTAINMENT
Café La Palma 35 C3
Cine Doré 36 D5
Clamores 37 D2
Honky Tonk 38 E2
Kabokla 39 C3
Kapital 40 E5
Siroco 41 C2
SHOPPING
Agatha Ruiz de la Prada 42 F2
El Rastro 43 C6
La Cuesta de Moyano 44 F5
Mantequería Bravo 45 F2
La Rosaleda
To Ermita de San Antonio de la Florida (400m)
Glorieta de San Antonio de la Florida
Paseo de la Florida
Paseo del Marqués de Monistrol
Parque de la Montaña
Príncipe Pío
Cuesta de San Vicente
Puente del Rey
Casa del Campo
Campo del Moro
Campo
Parque de Atenas
Palacio Real
Plaza de la Armería (Plaza de Armas)
Plaza de España
Ventura Rodríguez
Plaza de Cristino Martos
Plaza del Conde de Toreno
Plaza de las Comendadoras
Malasaña
Noviciado
Plaza del Conde del Valle de Suchil
San Bernardo
Glorieta de Ruiz Jiménez
Glorieta de Bilbao
Bilbao
C de Sagasta
Plaza del Dos de Mayor
Plaza del Juan Pujol
Tribunal
Plaza de San Ildefonso
Santo Domingo
Plaza de Santo Domingo
Callao
Plaza de la Encarnación
Plaza de Vázquez de Mella
Gran Vía
Plaza de San Martín
Plaza de las Descalzas
Plaza de Isabel II
Ópera
Sol
Centro
Plaza de Canalejas
C Mayor
Plaza Mayor
Plaza de la Villa
Plaza de Santa Ana
C de Atocha
Plaza de la Paja
Tirso de Molina
M-30
Glorieta de Asorín
Puerta del Ángel
C de Segovia
Viaduct
See Central Madrid Map (p753)
Río Manzanares
Plaza de la Puerta de Moros
La Latina
C de Juanelo
Plaza de Cascorro
C del Olmo
Plaza de San Francisco
C de Calatrava
Gran Vía de San Francisco
Ronda de Segovia
Paseo Imperial
Paseo de los Melancólicos
Av de Manzanares
Plaza General Vara del Rey
El Rastro
C de Toledo
Plaza Campillo del Mundo Nuevo
Glorieta de Puerta de Toledo
Puerta de Toledo
Ronda de Toledo
C Mira el Sol
C del Casino
C de los Embajadores
C de Mesón de Paredes
Plaza de Lavapiés
Lavapiés
Ronda de Valencia
Glorieta de Embajadores
Embajadores
To Estadio Vicente Calderón (200m)
Plaza de Francisco Morano

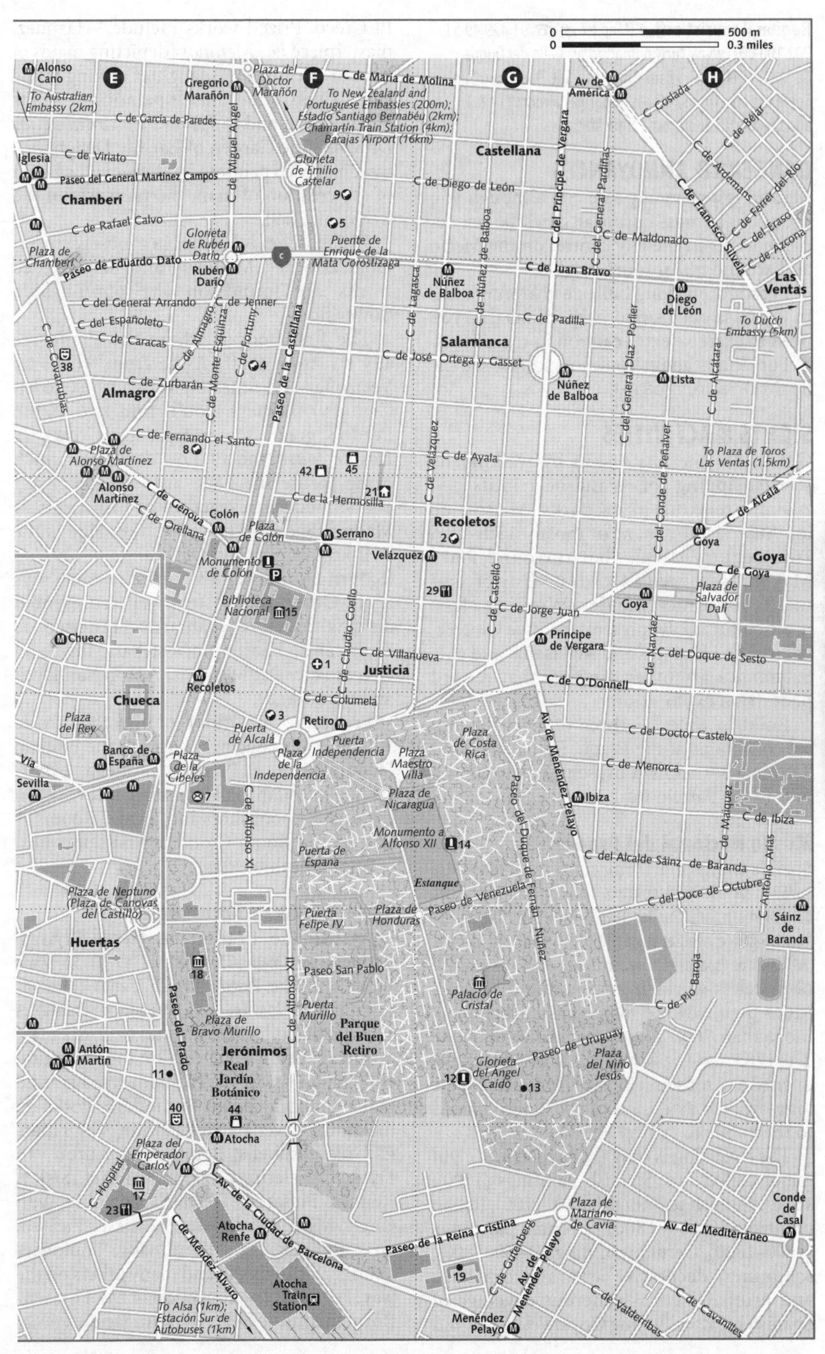
0 500 m
0 0.3 miles
E
F
G
H
Alonso Cano
To Australian Embassy (2km)
Gregorio Marañón
Plaza del Doctor Marañón
C de María de Molina
To New Zealand and Portuguese Embassies (200m); Estadio Santiago Bernabéu (2km); Chamartín Train Station (4km); Barajas Airport (16km)
Av de América
C Coslada
C de García de Paredes
Iglesia
C de Viriato
Paseo del General Martínez Campos
Glorieta de Emilio Castelar
Castellana
C de Béjar
C de Ardemans
Chamberí
C de Miguel Ángel
C de Diego de León
C del Príncipe de Vergara
C del General Pardiñas
C de Francisco Silvela
C de Ferrer del Río
C de Rafael Calvo
C del Eraso
C de Azcona
Glorieta de Rubén Darío
Puente de Enrique de la Mata Gorostizaga
C de Maldonado
Plaza de Chamberí
Paseo de Eduardo Dato
Rubén Darío
Núñez de Balboa
C de Núñez de Balboa
C de Juan Bravo
Las Ventas
C del General Arrando
C de Jenner
C de Lagasca
Diego de León
C del Españoleto
C de Padilla
To Dutch Embassy (5km)
C de Caracas
C de Almagro
C de Monte Esquinza
C de Fortuny
Salamanca
C de Covarrubias
C de José Ortega y Gasset
Paseo de la Castellana
Núñez de Balboa
Lista
C del General Díaz Porlier
C de Alcántara
C de Zurbarán
Almagro
C de Fernando el Santo
Plaza de Alonso Martínez
Alonso Martínez
C de Velázquez
C de Ayala
To Plaza de Toros Las Ventas (1.5km)
C de Génova
C de Orellana
C de la Hermosilla
C del Conde de Peñalver
C de Alcalá
Colón
Plaza de Colón
Serrano
Recoletos
Goya
Monumento de Colón
Velázquez
Goya
C de Goya
Biblioteca Nacional
C de Castelló
Goya
Plaza de Salvador Dalí
C de Jorge Juan
Chueca
C de Claudio Coello
Príncipe de Vergara
C de Narváez
C de Villanueva
C del Duque de Sesto
Justicia
Recoletos
C de O'Donnell
Chueca
C de Columela
Plaza del Rey
Retiro
C del Doctor Castelo
Puerta de Alcalá
Plaza de Costa Rica
Banco de España
Puerta Independencia
Plaza Maestro Villa
Av de Menéndez Pelayo
C de Menorca
Vía
Plaza de la Cibeles
Plaza de la Independencia
Sevilla
Plaza de Nicaragua
Ibiza
C de Alfonso XI
Paseo del Duque de Fernán Núñez
C de Ibiza
Monumento a Alfonso XII
C de Máiquez
Puerta de España
C del Alcalde Sáinz de Baranda
Estanque
Plaza de Neptuno (Plaza de Cánovas del Castillo)
C del Doce de Octubre
Paseo de Venezuela
C Antonio Arias
Puerta Felipe IV
Plaza de Honduras
Sáinz de Baranda
Huertas
Paseo San Pablo
Palacio de Cristal
C de Pío Baroja
Paseo del Prado
Puerta Murillo
C de Alfonso XII
Plaza de Bravo Murillo
Parque del Buen Retiro
Paseo de Uruguay
Antón Martín
Jerónimos
Plaza del Niño Jesús
Real Jardín Botánico
Glorieta del Ángel Caído
Atocha
Plaza del Emperador Carlos V
C Hospital
Av de la Ciudad de Barcelona
Plaza de Mariano de Cavia
Conde de Casal
Atocha Renfe
Paseo de la Reina Cristina
Av del Mediterráneo
C de Méndez Álvaro
C de Gutenberg
Av de Menéndez Pelayo
Atocha Train Station
C de Valderribas
C de Cavanilles
To Alsa (1km); Estación Sur de Autobuses (1km)
Menéndez Pelayo
SPAIN

Regional tourist office (Map p753; ☎ 91 429 49 51, 902 100 007; www.turismomadrid.es; Calle del Duque de Medinaceli 2; 8am-8pm Mon-Sat, 9am-2pm Sun) There are also tourist offices at Barajas airport (T1 & T4), and Chamartín and Atocha train stations.

DANGERS & ANNOYANCES

Madrid is a generally safe city although you should, as in most European cities, be wary of pickpockets in the city centre, on the Metro and around major tourist sights.

Prostitution along Calle de la Montera and in the Casa del Campo park means that you need to exercise extra caution in these areas.

For details about common scams, see the Spain Directory (p845).

SIGHTS & ACTIVITIES

Get under the city's skin by walking its streets, sipping coffee and beer in its plazas and relaxing in its parks. Madrid de los Austrias, the maze of mostly 15th- and 16th-century streets that surround Plaza Mayor, is the city's oldest district and makes for a nice wander. Working class, multicultural Lavapiés, alternative Chueca, bar-riddled Huertas and Malasaña, and chic Salamanca are other districts that reward pedestrian exploration.

Build in time for three of Europe's top art collections at the Prado, Reina Sofía and Thyssen-Bornemisza museums, as well as a visit to the Palacio Real.

Museo Nacional del Prado

Spain's premier art museum, the **Prado** (Map pp750-1; ☎ 91 330 28 00; http://museoprado.mcu.es; Paseo del Prado s/n; adult/under 18yr & over 65yr/student €6/free/4, Sun free, headset guide €3.50; 9am-8pm Tue-Sun; Ⓜ Banco de España) is a seemingly endless parade of priceless works from Spain and beyond. More than half the museum's collection of more than 7000 pieces is usually on show. The 1785 neo-Classical Palacio de Villanueva opened as a museum in 1819. In late 2007, the long-awaited extension of the Prado opened to the public to critical acclaim.

The collection is roughly divided into eight major collections: Spanish paintings (1100–1850), Flemish paintings (1430–1700), Italian paintings (1300–1800), French paintings (1600–1800), German paintings (1450–1800), sculptures, decorative arts, and drawings and prints. There is generous coverage of Spanish greats including Goya, Velázquez and El Greco. Prized works include Velázquez' masterpiece *Las Meninas* (depicting maids of honour attending the daughter of King Felipe IV and Velázquez himself painting portraits of the queen and king) and *El Jardín de las Delicias* (The Garden of Earthly Delights), a three-panelled painting by Hieronymus Bosch of the creation of man, the pleasures of the world, and hell.

The museum is laid out in a loosely chronological order. Medieval and Renaissance works are found on the *planta baja* (lower floor).

The first floor is where the Prado really struts its stuff. Aside from works by Velázquez and other Siglo de Oro (Golden Century) painters, you'll find two of the Prado's greatest masterpieces, Goya's *El Dos de Mayo* and *El Tres de Mayo,* which bring to life the 1808 anti-French revolt and subsequent execution of insurgents in Madrid. Showing Goya's darker side is the well-known *Saturno Devorando a Un Hijo* (Saturn Devouring his Son); the name says it all. Other old masters well represented on this floor are Spaniards Francisco de Zurbarán and Bartolomé Esteban Murillo, El Greco, Peter Paul Rubens, Anton Van Dyck and Rembrandt.

From the first floor of the Palacio de Villanueva, passageways lead to the Edificio Jerónimos, the Prado's modern extension. The main hall contains information counters, a bookshop and a cafe. Rooms A and B (and Room C on the first floor) host temporary exhibitions.

Museo Thyssen-Bornemisza

Opposite the Prado, the **Museo Thyssen-Bornemisza** (Map p753; ☎ 91 369 01 51; www.museothyssen.org; Paseo del Prado 8; adult/concession €6/4; 10am-7pm Tue-Sun; Ⓜ Banco de España) is an eclectic collection of international masterpieces. Begin your visit on the 2nd floor, where you'll start with medieval art, and make your way down to modern works on the ground level, passing paintings by Titian, El Greco, Rubens, Rembrandt, Anton van Dyck, Canaletto, Cézanne, Monet, Sisley, Renoir, Pissarro, Degas, Constable, Van Gogh, Miró, Modigliani, Matisse, Picasso, Gris, Pollock, Dalí, Kandinsky, Toulouse-Lautrec, Lichtenstein and many others on the way. Formerly the collection of the Thyssen-Bornemiszas, a German-Hungarian family

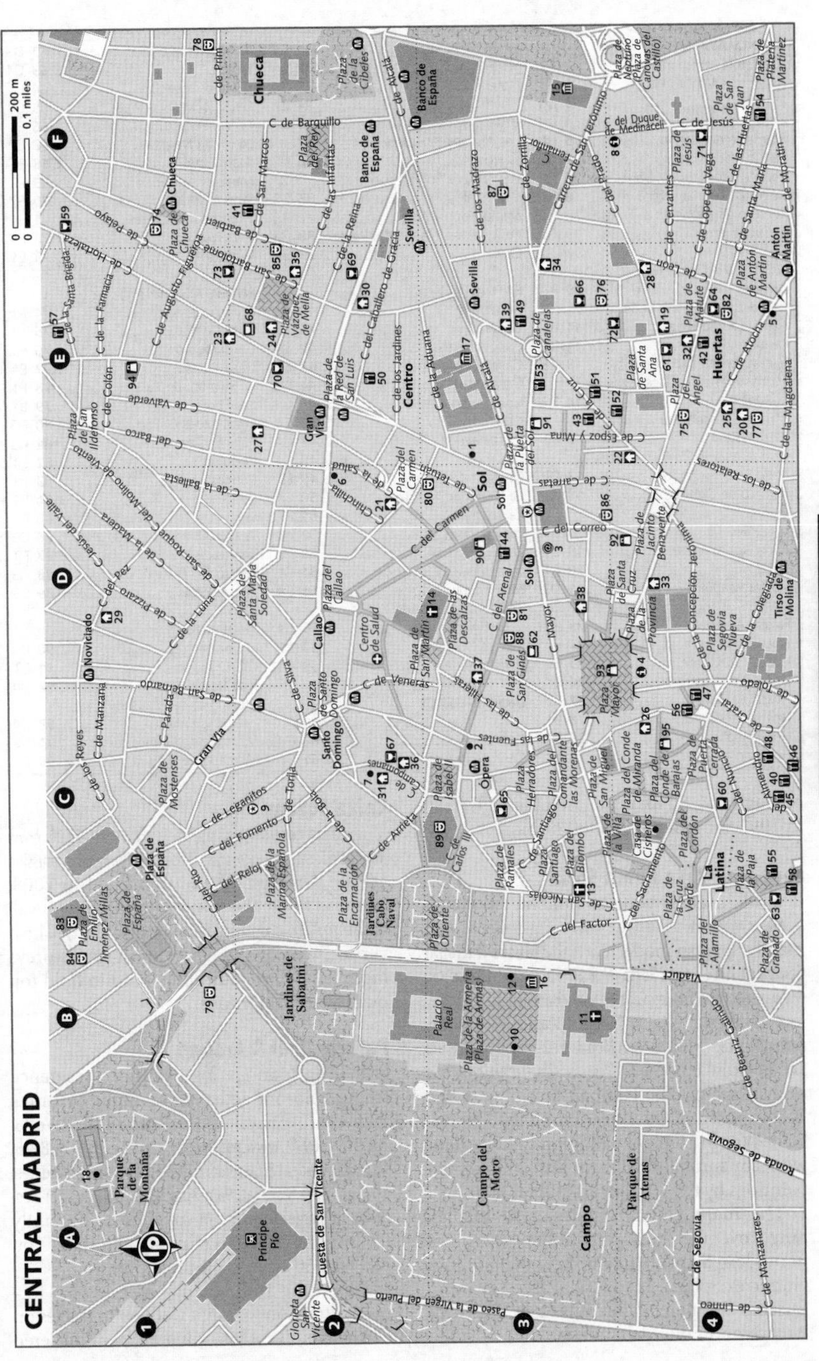
CENTRAL MADRID
0 200 m
0 0.1 miles
Parque de la Montaña
Príncipe Pío
Glorieta San Vicente
Cuesta de San Vicente
Paseo de la Virgen del Puerto
Campo del Moro
Campo
Parque de Atenas
C de Segovia
Ronda de Segovia
C de Linneo
C de Manzanares
C de Beatriz Galindo
Jardines de Sabatini
Palacio Real
Plaza de la Armería (Plaza de Armas)
Viaduct
Plaza de España
Plaza de Emilio Jiménez Millas
Jardines Cabo Naval
Plaza de Oriente
Plaza de la Encarnación
Plaza de Isabel II
Ópera
Santo Domingo
Plaza de Santo Domingo
Gran Vía
Plaza de Mostenses
Noviciado
Plaza de Santa María Soledad
Callao
Plaza del Callao
Centro de Salud
Plaza de San Martín
Plaza de las Descalzas
Plaza de San Ginés
C del Arenal
C Mayor
Plaza Mayor
Plaza de la Villa
Plaza de San Miguel
Plaza del Conde de Miranda
Plaza del Conde de Barajas
Casa de Cisneros
Plaza del Cordón
Plaza de la Cruz Verde
Plaza de Puerta Cerrada
La Latina
Plaza de la Paja
Plaza del Alamillo
Plaza de Granado
Plaza de Segovia Nueva
Tirso de Molina
Plaza de la Provincia
Plaza de Santa Cruz
Plaza de Jacinto Benavente
Sol
Plaza de la Puerta del Sol
Plaza del Carmen
C del Carmen
C de la Montera
Plaza de la Red de San Luis
Centro
Plaza de Canalejas
Plaza de Santa Ana
Plaza del Ángel
Huertas
Antón Martín
Plaza de Antón Martín
Plaza de Matute
Plaza de Jesús
Plaza de San Juan
Plaza de Platería Martínez
Plaza de Neptuno (Plaza de Cánovas del Castillo)
Carrera de San Jerónimo
C del Prado
C de Cervantes
C de Lope de Vega
C de las Huertas
C de Atocha
C de la Magdalena
C de Alcalá
Sevilla
Banco de España
Plaza de la Cibeles
Chueca
Plaza de Chueca
Plaza del Rey
Plaza de Vázquez de Mella
Plaza de San Ildefonso
C de Hortaleza
C de Fuencarral
C de Barquillo
C de Prim
C de San Bernardo
C de Toledo
Plaza de Ramales
Plaza Herradores
Plaza Comandante las Morenas
Plaza Santiago
Plaza del Biombo

INFORMATION
Academia Inhispania................1 E3
Academia Madrid Plus...............2 C3
Bbigg....................................3 D3
Centro de Turismo de Madrid....4 D4
Farmacia del Globo..................5 E4
La Casa del Libro.....................6 D2
Petra's International Bookshop....7 C2
Regional Tourist Office.............8 F4
Servicio de Atención al Turista Extranjero..........................9 C2

SIGHTS & ACTIVITIES
Armería Real..........................10 B3
Catedral de Nuestra Señora de la Almudena...................11 B3
Farmacia Real........................12 B3
Iglesia de San Nicolás.............13 C3
Monasterio de las Descalzas Reales...............................14 D3
Museo Thyssen-Bornemisza......15 F3
Palacio Real...........................16 B3
Real Academia de Bellas Artes de San Fernando.................17 E3
Templo de Debod....................18 A1

SLEEPING
Alicia Room Mate....................19 E4
Cat's Hostel............................20 E4
Hostal Acapulco.......................21 D2
Hostal Adriano.........................22 E4
Hostal América........................23 E2
Hostal Don Juan.......................24 E2
Hostal Horizonte......................25 E4
Hostal La Macarena.................26 C4
Hostal La Zona........................27 E2
Hostal Sardinero......................28 E4
Hotel Abalú.............................29 D1
Hotel de las Letras...................30 E2
Hotel Meninas.........................31 C2
Hotel Miau..............................32 E4
Hotel Plaza Mayor...................33 D4
Hotel Urban............................34 E3
Hotel Óscar.............................35 E2
Los Amigos Backpackers' Hostel..................................36 C2
Los Amigos Sol Backpackers' Hostel..................................37 D3
Mario Room Mate..................(see 36)
Petit Palace Posada del Peine....38 D3
Quo.......................................39 E3

EATING
Almendro 13...........................40 C4
Bazaar....................................41 F2
Casa Alberto...........................42 E4
Casa del Abuelo.......................43 E3
Casa Labra.............................44 D3
Casa Lucas.............................45 C4
Casa Lucio.............................46 C4
Casa Revuelta.........................47 C4
La Chata................................48 C4
La Finca de Susana..................49 E3
La Gloria de Montera...............50 E2
La Trucha...............................51 E3
Las Bravas..............................52 E4
Lhardy...................................53 E3
Maceiras.................................54 F4
Naïa Restaurante.....................55 C4
Restaurante Sobrino de Botín...............................56 C4
Ribeira Do Miño......................57 E1
Viva La Vida...........................58 C4

DRINKING
Areia.....................................59 F1
Café del Nuncio......................60 C4
Cervecería Alemana.................61 E4
Chocolatería de San Ginés........62 D3
Delic......................................63 C4
El Imperfecto..........................64 E4
Gaia Cocktail Lounge................65 C3
La Venencia............................66 E3
La Viuda Negra........................67 C2
Mamá Inés..............................68 E2
Museo Chicote........................69 E2
Stop Madrid............................70 E2
Taberna de Dolores..................71 F4
Viva Madrid............................72 E4
Why Not?...............................73 E1

ENTERTAINMENT
Café Acuarela..........................74 F1
Café Central...........................75 E4
Cardamomo............................76 E3
Casa Patas..............................77 E4
La Fulanita de Tal.....................78 F1
Las Tablas..............................79 B1
Localidades Galicia...................80 D3
Palacio Gaviria........................81 D3
Popular...................................82 E4
Princesa.................................83 B1
Renoir....................................84 B1
Sunrise...................................85 F2
Teatro Albéniz.........................86 D3
Teatro de la Zarzuela................87 F3
Teatro Joy Eslava.....................88 D3
Teatro Real.............................89 C3

SHOPPING
El Corte Inglés.........................90 D3
Gil...91 E3
José Ramírez...........................92 D4
Mercadillo de Filatelia y Numismática........................93 D4
Mercado de Fuencarral.............94 E1
Mercado de Pintura..................95 C4

of magnates, Spain purchased the collection in 1993 for a mere US$300 million.

Centro de Arte Reina Sofía

If modern art is your cup of tea, the Reina Sofía is your museum. A stunning collection of mainly Spanish modern art, the **Museo Nacional Centro de Arte Reina Sofía** (Map pp750-1; ☎ 91 774 10 00; www.museoreinasofia.es; Calle de Santa Isabel 52; adult/child & senior/student €6/free/4, 2.30-9pm Sat & 10am-2.30pm Sun free, audioguide €3; 10am-9pm Mon & Wed-Sat, 10am-2.30pm Sun; Ⓜ Atocha) is home to Picasso's *Guernica* – his protest against the German bombing of the Basque town of Guernica during the Spanish Civil War in 1937 – in addition to important works by surrealist Salvador Dalí and abstract paintings by the Catalan artist Joan Miró.

The main gallery's permanent display ranges over the 2nd and 4th floors. Key names in modern Spanish art on show include José Gutiérrez Solana, Juan Gris, Pablo Gargallo, Eusebio Sempere, Pablo Palazuelo, Eduardo Arroyo and Eduardo Chillida.

Caixa Forum

The **Caixa Forum** (Map pp750-1; ☎ 91 330 73 00; www.fundacio.lacaixa.es in Spanish; Paseo del Prado 36; admission free; 10am-10pm; Ⓜ Atocha), opened in 2008, seems to hover above the ground. On one wall is the *jardín colgante* (hanging garden), a lush vertical wall of greenery almost four storeys high. Inside are four floors used to hold top quality art exhibitions.

Palacio Real & Around

Still King Juan Carlos I's official residence (though no-one actually lives here), Madrid's 18th-century royal palace, **Palacio Real** (Map p753; ☎ 91 542 69 47; www.patrimonionacional.es; Calle de Bailén s/n; adult/student & EU senior €10/3.50, EU citizens Wed free; 9am-6pm Mon-Sat, 9am-3pm Sun & holidays Apr-Sep, closes 1hr earlier Oct-Mar; Ⓜ Ópera), is used mainly for important events of pomp and state. You can visit 50 of its 2800-plus rooms.

When the 16th-century Alcázar that formerly stood on this spot went up in flames on Christmas Eve 1734, King Felipe V ordered construction of a new palace on the same ground. The opulent Palacio Real was finished in 1755 and Carlos III moved in during 1764.

Look out for the 215 clocks of the royal clock collection and the five Stradivarius violins, used occasionally for concerts and balls. The tapestries and chandeliers throughout the palace are original.

Outside the main palace, poke your head into the **Farmacia Real** (Map p753; Royal Pharmacy), where apothecary-style jars line the shelves. Continue on to the **Armería Real** (Map p753; Royal Armoury), where you'll be impressed by the shiny (and surprisingly tiny!) royal suits of armour, most of them from the 16th and 17th centuries.

Plaza Mayor

Ringed with numerous cafes and restaurants and packed with people day and night, the 17th-century arcaded **Plaza Mayor** (Map p753) was traditionally used as a market but is now an elegant and bustling square. On Sunday morning a stamp market sets up shop.

Colourful frescoes decorate the **Real Casa de la Panaderia** (Royal Bakery), which predates the plaza and was restored after a 1790 fire. The equestrian statue of Felipe III was placed here in 1848.

Churches

The **Catedral de Nuestra Señora de la Almudena** (Map p753; ☎ 91 542 22 00; Calle de Bailén; 9am-9pm; M Ópera) is just across the plaza from the Palacio Real. Finished in 1992 after a century, the cathedral has never really won a place in the hearts of Madrileños. It's worth a quick peek but is much less captivating than the imposing 18th-century **Basílica de San Francisco El Grande** (Map pp750-1; ☎ 91 365 38 00; Plaza de San Francisco 1; admission €3; 8-11am Mon, 8am-1pm & 4-6.30pm Tue-Fri, 4-8.45pm Sat; M La Latina). Also worth a visit is the largely 15th-century **Iglesia de San Nicolás** (Map p753; ☎ 91 548 83 14; Plaza San Nicolás 6; M Ópera).

FREE THRILLS

If you plan well, there are several free attractions in Madrid. Entry to many sights, including the **Museo del Prado** (p752) and **Centro de Arte Reina Sofía** (opposite), is free on Sundays. EU citizens also enjoy free days in some sights, such as the **Palacio Real** (opposite) and **Monasterio de las Descalzas Reales** (right); Wednesday in both. Entry to the **Caixa Forum** (opposite) art gallery and **Parque del Buen Retiro** (right) is free.

Monasterio de las Descalzas Reales

Opulent inside though with a rather plain Plateresque exterior, the **Convento de las Descalzas Reales** (Convent of the Barefoot Royals; Map p753; ☎ 91 542 69 47; www.patrimonionacional.es; Plaza de las Descalzas 3; adult/child €5/2.50, EU citizens Wed free, combined ticket with Convento de la Encarnación €6/3.40; 10.30am-12.45pm & 4-5.45pm Tue-Thu & Sat, 10.30am-12.45pm Fri, 11am-1.45pm Sun; M Ópera or Sol) was founded in 1559 by Juana of Austria. Daughter of Spain's King Carlos I and Isabel of Portugal, Juana transformed one of her mother's palaces into the noblewomen's convent of choice. On the obligatory guided tour you'll see a gaudily frescoed Renaissance stairway, a number of extraordinary tapestries based on works by Rubens, and a wonderful painting entitled *The Voyage of the 11,000 Virgins*. Some 33 nuns still live here and there are 33 chapels dotted around the convent.

Parque del Buen Retiro

A stroll in the **Parque del Buen Retiro** (Map pp750-1; 7am-midnight May-Sep, 7am-10pm Oct-Apr; M Retiro), or simply El Retiro, is an integral part of Madrid life. Come on a weekend for street performers, clowns, puppet shows and the occasional theatre performance.

The pretty **estanque** (lake) is overlooked by the **Monument to Alfonso XII** (Map pp750–1). Rent a row boat at the northern end. Dotted about the park are a few interesting statues, such as the **El Ángel Caído** (Fallen Angel; Map pp750–1), unusually dedicated to the devil. Also interesting are gardens such as **La Rosaleda** (Rose Garden; Map pp750–1) and the sadly poetic **Bosque de los Ausentes** (Forest of the Missing), a tribute to the victims of the March 2004 terrorist attack, between the Puerta del Ángel Caído and Monument to Alfonso XII. The 1887 **Palacio de Cristal** (Map pp750-1; ☎ 91 574 66 14; 11am-8pm Mon-Sat, 11am-6pm Sun & holidays May-Sep, 10am-6pm Mon-Sat, 10am-4pm Sun & holidays Oct-Apr), a charming metal-and-glass structure south of the lake, hosts temporary exhibitions.

Just outside the park is the **Real Jardín Botánico** (Map pp750-1; ☎ 91 420 30 17; Plaza de Bravo Murillo 2; adult/child/concession €2/free/1; 10am-dusk), equally pleasant for strolling.

Other Sights

Brush up on the city's history and development at the **Museo Municipal** (Map pp750-1; ☎ 91 588 86 72; www.munimadrid.es/museomunicipal; Calle de Fuencarral 78; admission free; ⏰ 9.30am-8pm Tue-Fri, 10am-2pm Sat & Sun Sep-Jun, 9.30am-2.30pm Tue-Fri, 10am-2pm Sat & Sun Jul & Aug; Ⓜ Tribunal), which contains paintings and other memorabilia charting the evolution of Madrid.

The frescoed ceilings of the **Ermita de San Antonio de la Florida** (Map pp750-1; ☎ 91 542 07 22; Glorieta de San Antonio de la Florida 5; admission free; ⏰ 9.30am-8pm Tue-Fri, 10am-2pm Sat & Sun, varied hr Jul & Aug; Ⓜ Príncipe Pío) are one of Madrid's most surprising secrets. In the southern of the two small chapels you can see Goya's work in its original setting, done in 1798. The painter is buried in front of the altar.

Founded in 1721, the **Real Fábrica de Tapices** (Map pp750-1; ☎ 91 434 05 51; www.realfabricadetapices.com; Calle de Fuenterrabía 2; admission €2.50; ⏰ 10am-2pm Mon-Fri Sep-Jul; Ⓜ Menéndez Pelayo) still makes ornate tapestries and carpets by hand. Take one home for a mere €10,000 per sq metre.

Highlights of the extensive collection of the **Museo Arqueológico Nacional** (National Archaeology Museum; Map pp750-1; ☎ 91 577 79 12; http://man.mcu.es, in Spanish; Calle de Serrano 13; admission €3, free after 2.30pm Sat & Sun; ⏰ 9.30am-8pm Tue-Sat, 9.30am-3pm Sun & holidays; Ⓜ Serrano) include stunning mosaics taken from Roman villas across Spain; a gilded Mudéjar domed ceiling; and the ancient *Dama de Ibiza* and *Dama de Elche* sculptures that reveal a flourishing artistic tradition among the Iberian tribes, influenced by contact with Greek and Phoenician civilisations.

The authentically ancient **Templo de Debod** (Map p753; ☎ 91 366 74 15; www.munimadrid.es/templodebod; Paseo del Pintor Rosales; admission free; ⏰ 10am-2pm & 6-8pm Tue-Fri, 10am-2pm Sat & Sun Apr-Sep, 9.45am-1.45pm & 4.15-6.15pm Tue-Fri, 10am-2pm Sat & Sun Oct-Mar; Ⓜ Ventura Rodríguez) was transferred here stone by stone from Egypt in 1972 as a gesture of thanks to Spanish archaeologists who helped save Egyptian monuments from the rising waters of the Aswan Dam.

The somewhat fusty **Real Academia de Bellas Artes de San Fernando** (Map p753; ☎ 91 524 08 64; http://rabasf.insde.es in Spanish; Calle de Alcalá 13; adult/senior & under 18yr/student €3/free/1.50; ⏰ 9am-7pm Tue-Fri, 9am-2.30pm & 4-7pm Sat, 9am-2.30pm Sun & Mon Sep-Jun, varied hr Jul & Aug; Ⓜ Sevilla) offers a broad collection of old and modern masters, including works by Zurbarán, El Greco, Rubens, Tintoretto, Goya, Sorolla and Juan Gris.

COURSES

There's no shortage of places to learn Spanish in Madrid.

Academia Inhispania (Map p753; ☎ 91 521 22 31; www.inhispania.com; Calle de la Montera 10-12; Ⓜ Sol)

Academia Madrid Plus (Map p753; ☎ 91 548 11 16; www.madridplus.es; 6th fl, Calle del Arenal 21; Ⓜ Ópera)

TOURS

The Centro de Turismo de Madrid (p749) offers **Descubre Madrid** (Discover Madrid; ☎ 91 588 29 06; www.esmadrid.com/descubremadrid/portal.do; walking tours adult/child, student, under-25 or senior €3.30/2.70, bus tours €6.45/5.05, bicycle tours €3.30/2.70 plus €6 bike rental) – dozens of guided walking, cycling and bus itineraries.

FESTIVALS & EVENTS

Madrid's social calendar is packed with festivals and special events. Check with the tourist office (p749) or in publications such as the *Guía del Ocio* to see what's on. Major holidays and festivals include the following:

Fiesta de San Isidro Street parties, parades, bullfights and other fun events honour Madrid's patron saint on and around 15 May.

Summer Festivals Small-time but fun, the neighbourhood summer festivals, such as San Cayetano in Lavapiés, and San Lorenzo and La Paloma in La Latina, allow hot and sweaty Madrileños to drink and dance the night away in the streets.

SLEEPING

Madrid has high-quality accommodation across all price ranges and caters to every taste. During a major holiday or trade fair, prices can rise by 15% to 20%. During slower periods, you might find deep discounts. There's a good sprinkling of options around Plaza Mayor and still more in the streets running off Plaza de Santa Ana. The Malasaña and Chueca areas are chock full with places.

Los Austrias & Centro

BUDGET

Los Amigos Backpackers' Hostel (Map p753; ☎ 91 547 17 07; www.losamigoshostel.com; Calle de Campomanes 6; dm €17-19; Ⓜ Ópera; 💻) Gregarious folk will be at home here – lots of students hang at Los Amigos, staff are savvy (and speak English) and there are bright dorm-style rooms that sleep from four to 12 people (with free lockers). A similar deal is available at nearby Los Amigos Sol

Backpackers' Hostel (☎ 91 559 24 72; 4th floor, Calle de Arenal 26; dorm €16 to €19).

Cat's Hostel (Map p753; ☎ 91 369 28 07; www.catshostel.com; Calle de Cañizares 6; dm €19, d from €24; Ⓜ Antón Martín;) The fine internal courtyard here boasts lavish Andalucian tilework, a fountain, a spectacular glass ceiling and is surrounded by an open balcony. There's a supercool basement bar where occasional live flamenco cohabits with free internet connections.

Mad Hostel (Map pp750-1; ☎ 91 506 48 40; www.madhostel.com; Calle de Cabeza 24; dm €20; Ⓜ Antón Martín;) Mad Hostel is similarly buzzing to Cat's. The 1st-floor courtyard – with retractable roof – is a wonderful place to chill, while the four- to eight-bed rooms are smallish but clean. There's a small rooftop gym.

Hostal Horizonte (Map p753; ☎ 91 369 09 96; www.hostalhorizonte.com; 2nd fl, Calle de Atocha 28; s/d with shared bathroom €29/44, with private bathroom €40/55; Ⓜ Antón Martín) Billing itself as a *hostal* (high-end guest house) run by travellers for travellers, Hostal Horizonte is well run. The rooms have far more character than your average *hostal*, with high ceilings, deliberately old-world furnishings and modern bathrooms.

MIDRANGE & TOP END

Hostal Acapulco (Map p753; ☎ 91 531 19 45; www.hostalacapulco.com; Calle de la Salud 13; s/d/tr €52/62/79; Ⓜ Gran Vía;) This immaculate little *hostal* has marble floors, renovated bathrooms, double-glazed windows and comfortable beds. Street-facing rooms have balconies overlooking sunny Plaza del Carmen.

Hostal La Macarena (Map p753; ☎ 91 365 92 21; www.silserranos.com in Spanish; Cava de San Miguel 8; s/d €60/74; Ⓜ Sol;) On one of the old, cobblestone streets that runs past Plaza Mayor, this *hostal* is loaded with old-style charm. The rooms are nicely spacious and decorated in warm colours.

Hotel Plaza Mayor (Map p753; ☎ 91 360 06 06; www.h-plazamayor.com; Calle de Atocha 2; s/d from €65/85; Ⓜ Sol or Tirso de Molina;) Stylish decor, charming original elements of an 150-year-old building and helpful staff are selling points here. The rooms are attractive, some with a light colour scheme and wrought-iron furniture. The attic rooms have great views.

Mario Room Mate (Map p753; ☎ 91 548 85 48; www.room-matehoteles.com; Calle de Campomanes 4; s €90-120, d €100-140; Ⓜ Ópera;) Mario's offers sleek designer boutique chic. Rooms are spacious, with high ceilings and simple furniture, light tones contrasting smoothly with muted colours and dark surfaces.

Hotel Meninas (Map p753; ☎ 91 541 28 05; www.hotelmeninas.com; Calle de Campomanes 7; s/d from €109/129; Ⓜ Ópera;) Inside a refurbished 19th-century mansion, the Meninas combines old-world comfort with modern, minimalist style. The colour scheme is blacks, whites and greys, with dark-wood floors and splashes of fuchsia and lime-green.

Petit Palace Posada del Peine (Map p753; ☎ 91 523 81 51; www.hthotels.com; Calle de Postas 17; d €115-150; Ⓜ Sol;) Combining a splendid historic building (1610) with brilliant location, this enticing hotel also has hi-tech rooms. The bathrooms sparkle and many historical architectural features remain *in situ*. Rooms are on the small side, however.

Hotel de Las Letras (Map p753; ☎ 91 523 79 80; www.hoteldelasletras.com; Gran Vía 11; d from €165; Ⓜ Gran Vía) Hotel de las Letras started the rooftop hotel bar in Madrid. The bar's wonderful, but the whole hotel is excellent with individually styled rooms, each with literary quotes scribbled on the walls.

Sol, Huertas & Atocha

Hostal Sardinero (Map p753; ☎ 91 429 57 56; fax 91 429 41 12; Calle del Prado 16; s/d from €47/67; Ⓜ Sol or Antón Martín;) More than the cheerful rooms (high ceilings, a safe, hairdryers and renovated bathrooms), it's the friendly old couple who run Hostal Sardinero that gives it its charm.

Hostal Adriano (Map p753; ☎ 91 521 13 39; www.hostaladriano.com; 4th fl, Calle de la Cruz 26; s/d/tr €49/63/83; Ⓜ Sol) They don't come any better than this bright and cheerful *hostal* wedged in the streets that mark the boundary between Sol and Huertas. Most rooms are well sized and each has its own colour scheme.

Hotel Miau (Map p753; ☎ 91 369 71 20; www.hotelmiau.com; Calle del Príncipe 26; s/d incl breakfast €85/95; Ⓜ Sol or Antón Martín;) Close to the nightlife of Huertas, this spot boasts light tones, splashes of colour and modern art in the rooms, which are large and well-equipped. Light sleepers should bring ear plugs.

Quo (Map p753; ☎ 91 532 90 49; www.hotelesquo.com; Calle de Sevilla 4; s €90-160, d €90-195; Ⓜ Sevilla;) Quo is one of Madrid's homes of chic with black-clad staff, minimalist designer furniture, high ceilings and huge windows. Rooms have black-and-white photos of Madrid, dark-wood floors and comfy armchairs.

SPAIN

Alicia Room Mate (Map p753; ☎ 91 389 60 95; www.room-matehoteles.com; Calle del Prado 2; d €90-200; M Sol, Sevilla or Antón Martín;) With beautiful, spacious rooms, Alicia overlooks Plaza de Santa Ana. It has an ultra-modern look and the downstairs bar is oh-so-cool.

Hotel Urban (Map p753; ☎ 91 787 77 70; www.derbyhotels.com; Carrera de San Jerónimo 34; d €200-350; M Sevilla;) The towering glass edifice of Hotel Urban is the epitome of art-inspired designer cool. Dark-wood floors and dark walls are offset by plenty of light, while the bathrooms have wonderful designer fittings. The rooftop swimming pool is Madrid's best.

Malasaña & Chueca

Albergue Juvenil Map pp750-1; ☎ 91 593 96 88; www.ajmadrid.es; Calle de Mejía Lequerica 21; dm €18-24; M Bilbao or Alonso Martínez) Opened in 2007, the Albergue's rooms are spotless, no dorm houses more than six beds (each has its own bathroom) and facilities include a pool table, gymnasium, wheelchair access, free internet, laundry and TV/DVD room with a choice of movies.

Hostal Don Juan (Map p753; ☎ 91 522 31 01; Plaza de Vázquez de Mella 1; s/d/tr €38/53/71; M Gran Vía) Don John would have liked this elegant two-storey *hostal*. It's filled with art (each room has original works) and antique furniture. Rooms are simple but luminous and large.

Hostal América (Map p753; ☎ 91 522 64 48; www.hostalamerica.net; Calle de Hortaleza 19; s/d €40/55; M Gran Vía) A lovely mother-son-dog team preside over superclean, spacious and IKEA-dominated rooms. As most rooms face on to the usual interior 'patio' of the building, you should get a good night's sleep in this busy area.

Hostal La Zona (Map p753; ☎ 91 521 99 04; www.hostallazona.com; Calle de Valverde 7; s/d/tr €50/60/85;) Catering primarily to a gay clientele, the stylish Hostal La Zona has exposed brickwork, wooden pillars and a subtle colour scheme. We like a place where a sleep-in is encouraged – breakfast is from 9am to noon!

Hotel Abalú (Map p753; ☎ 91 531 47 44; www.hotelabalu.com; Calle del Pez 19; s/d from €74/105, ste €140-200; M Noviciado) Each room in this boutique special has its own design drawn from the imagination of Luis Delgado, from retro chintz to Zen, Baroque and pure white. Some of the suites have Jacuzzis and large-screen home cinemas.

our pick Hotel Óscar (Map p753; ☎ 91 701 11 73; www.room-matehoteles.com; Plaza Vázquez de Mella 12; d €90-200, ste €150-280; M Gran Vía) Hotel Óscar's designer rooms ooze style and sophistication. Some have floor-to-ceiling murals, the lighting is always funky and the colour scheme is asplash with pinks, lime greens, oranges or a more minimalist black-and-white.

Salamanca

Hesperia Hermosilla (Map pp750-1; ☎ 91 246 88 00; www.hesperia.com; Calle de la Hermosilla; s/d from €125/135; M Serrano;) If you're here to shop in Salamanca, or otherwise value quiet, exclusive streets, this stylish hotel is a terrific choice. The furnishings are vaguely minimalist, while flat-screen TVs and other creature comforts are rare luxuries in this price range.

EATING

It's possible to find just about any kind of cuisine and eatery in Madrid, from ageless traditional to trendy fusion. Madrid is a focal point of cooking from around the country and is particularly attached to seafood (despite not having a sea).

From the chaotic tapas bars of La Latina to countless neighbourhood favourites, you'll have no trouble tracking down specialities like *cochinillo asado* (roast suckling pig) or *cocido madrileño* (a hearty stew made of beans and various animals' innards).

Restaurants in Malasaña, Chueca and Huertas range from glorious old *tabernas* (taverns) to boutique eateries. For more classically classy surrounds, Salamanca and Northern Madrid are generally pricey but of the highest standard. In the central *barrios* of Los Austrias, Sol and Centro, there's a bit of everything.

Los Austrias & Centro

La Gloria de Montera (Map p753; ☎ 91 523 44 07; Calle del Caballero de Gracia 10; meals €20-25; M Gran Vía) Minimalist style, tasty Mediterranean dishes and great prices mean that you'll probably have to wait in line to eat here.

Restaurante Sobrino de Botín (Map p753; ☎ 91 366 42 17; www.botin.es; Calle de los Cuchilleros 17; meals €35-45; M La Latina or Sol) Reputedly opened in 1725, this is the oldest restaurant in Madrid. The secret of their staying power is fine *cochinillo* (€21.10) and *cordero asado* (roast lamb; €21.10) cooked in wood-fired ovens.

Sol, Huertas & Atocha

La Finca de Susana (Map p753; ☎ 91 369 35 57; Calle de Arlabán 4; meals €20-25; M Sevilla) A well-priced mix

A TAPAS TOUR

Madrid's home of tapas is La Latina, especially along Calle de la Cava Baja and the surrounding streets. **Almendro 13** (Map p753; ☎ 91 365 42 52; Calle de Almendro 13; meals €15-25; M La Latina) is regularly voted among the top tapas bars in Madrid for traditional snacks. Nearby, **Casa Lucas** (Map p753; ☎ 91 365 08 04; Calle de la Cava Baja 30; meals €20-25; lunch & dinner Thu-Tue, dinner Wed; M La Latina) and **La Chata** (Map p753; ☎ 91 366 14 58; Calle de la Cava Baja 24; meals €25-30; lunch & dinner Thu-Mon, dinner Wed; M La Latina) are popular. **Juanalaloca** (Map pp750-1; ☎ 91 364 05 25; Plaza de la Puerta de Moros 4; meals €30-35; lunch & dinner Tue-Sun, dinner only Mon; M La Latina) does a magnificent *tortilla de patatas*.

Most famous for *bacalao* (cod) is **Casa Labra** (Map p753; ☎ 91 531 00 81; Calle de Tetuán 11; meals €15-20; 11am-3.30pm & 6-11pm; M Sol), which has been around since 1860. However, many *madrileños* wouldn't eat *bacalao* anywhere but **Casa Revuelta** (Map p753; ☎ 91 366 33 32; Calle de Latoneros 3; meals €10-15; lunch & dinner Tue-Sat, lunch Sun; M La Latina).

In Huertas, **Casa del Abuelo** (Map p753; ☎ 91 521 23 19; Calle de la Victoria 12; meals €15-25; 11.30am-3.30pm & 6.30-11.30pm; M Sol) is famous for *gambas a la plancha* (grilled prawns) or *gambas al ajillo* (prawns sizzling in garlic on little ceramic plates) and a *chato* (small glass) of the heavy, sweet El Abuelo red wine. For *patatas bravas* (fried potatoes slathered with a spicy tomato sauce), **Las Bravas** (Map p753; ☎ 91 532 26 20; Callejón de Álvarez Gato 3; meals €15; 10am-11.30pm; M Sol) is the place, while **La Trucha** (Map p753; ☎ 91 532 08 82; Calle de Núñez de Arce 6; meals around €15-20; Tue-Sat; M Sol) has a counter overloaded with enticing Andalusian tapas.

of Spanish and international fare has made this an extremely popular choice with locals and tourists alike. The softly lit dining area is bathed in greenery and the sometimes innovative, sometimes traditional food draws a hip young crowd.

our pick Maceiras (Map p753; ☎ 91 429 15 84; Calle de Jesús 7; meals €20-25; lunch & diner Tue-Sun, dinner Mon; M Antón Martín) Galician tapas (think octopus, green peppers etc) never tasted so good as in this agreeably rustic bar down the bottom of the Huertas hill, especially when washed down with a crisp white Ribeiro.

Casa Alberto (Map p753; ☎ 91 429 93 56; www.casaalberto.es; Calle de las Huertas 18; meals €20-25; noon-1.30am Tue-Sat, noon-4pm Sun; M Antón Martín) Casa Alberto has been around since 1827. The secret to their staying power is vermouth on tap, excellent tapas and fine sit-down meals; *rabo de toro* (bull's tail) is a good order.

Lhardy (Map p753; ☎ 91 522 22 07; www.lhardy.com; Carrera de San Jerónimo 8; meals €50-60; lunch & dinner Mon-Sat, lunch Sun; M Sol or Sevilla) This Madrid landmark (since 1839) is an elegant treasure-trove of take-away gourmet tapas. Upstairs is the upscale preserve of house specialities such as *callos* (tripe), pheasant in grape juice and lemon soufflé.

Arola Madrid (Map pp750-1; ☎ 91 467 02 02; www.arola-madrid.com in Spanish; Calle de Argumosa 43; meals €50; 10am-9pm Mon & Wed-Sat, 10am-5pm Sun; M Atocha) Fashionable chef Sergi Arola serves up nouvelle cuisine with an emphasis on presentation and variations on a traditional Spanish base in this design den.

La Latina & Lavapiés

This area is best known for its tapas bars. See above for more.

Viva La Vida (Map p753; ☎ 91 366 33 49; www.vivalavida.vg; Costanilla de San Andrés 16; veg buffet €1.80 per 100g; 11am-midnight; M La Latina) This organic food shop has as its centrepiece an enticing vegetarian buffet with hot and cold food that's always filled with flavour. It's great at any time of the day.

La Buga del Lobo (Map pp750-1; ☎ 91 467 61 51; www.labocadellobo.com; Calle de Argumosa 11; meals €25-30; 11am-2am Wed-Mon; M Lavapiés) It's hard to get a table in this bohemian eatery filled with funky, swirling murals, contemporary art exhibitions and jazz or lounge music.

Naïa Restaurante (Map p753; ☎ 91 366 27 83; www.naiarestaurante.com in Spanish; Plaza de la Paja 3; meals €25-30; Mon-Sat; M La Latina) Naïa has a real buzz, with delightful modern Spanish cooking and a chill-out lounge downstairs. The emphasis throughout is on natural ingredients, healthy cooking and exciting tastes.

Casa Lucío (Map p753; ☎ 91 365 32 52; www.casalucio.es in Spanish; Calle de la Cava Baja 35; meals €35-45; lunch & dinner Sun-Fri, dinner Sat Sep-Jul; M La Latina) Lucio has been wowing *madrileños* with his light touch, quality ingredients and home-style local cooking for ages – think seafood, roasted meats and, a Lucio speciality, eggs in abundance.

Malasaña & Chueca

Some of the city's best (and best-priced) eateries can be found along the side streets of the trendy Chueca district.

Ribeira Do Miño (Map p753; ☎ 91 521 98 54; Calle de la Santa Brigida 1; meals €20-25; Tue-Sat; M Tribunal) The *mariscada de la casa* (€30 for two) is a platter of seafood so large that even the hungriest of visitors will leave satisfied. Leave your name with the waiter and be prepared to wait for a table.

Bazaar (Map p753; ☎ 91 523 39 05; www.restaurantbazaar.com; Calle de la Libertad 21; meals €25-30; M Chueca) Bazaar's pristine-white interior design with theatre lighting may draw a crowd that looks like it stepped out of the pages of *Hola!* Magazine, but the food is extremely well-priced and innovative. It doesn't take reservations.

La Musa (Map pp750-1; ☎ 91 448 75 58; www.lamusa.com.es; Calle de Manuela Malasaña 18; meals €25-30; M San Bernardo) The fried green tomatoes with strawberry jam and great meat dishes are fun and filled with flavour. It doesn't take reservations so sidle up to the bar, put your name on the waiting list and soak up the ambient buzz of Malasaña at its best.

La Isla del Tesoro (Map pp750-1; ☎ 91 593 14 40; Calle de Manuela Malasaña 3; meals €30; M Bilbao) The dining area is like someone's fantasy of a secret garden come to life. The jungle burger is typical in a menu that's full of surprises. Their weekday, lunchtime *menú del día* is more varied than most in Madrid, with Indonesian, Lebanese, Moroccan, French and Mexican influences.

Nina (Map pp750-1; ☎ 91 591 00 46; Calle de Manuela Malasaña 10; meals €30-35; M) The cooking is as cool as the dining area. The *foie fresco a la plancha* (grilled foie gras) is divine. Popular with a sophisticated crowd, Nina can be a hard place to get a table.

Salamanca

Sula Madrid (Map pp750-1; ☎ 91 781 61 97; www.sula.es; Calle de Jorge Juan 33; meals €70-80; Mon-Sat; M Velázquez) Sula is a gourmet food store, stylish tapas bar and clean-lined restaurant in one. Gastronomic *wunderkind* Quique Dacosta serves up a range of Mediterranean dishes.

DRINKING

Madrid lives life on the streets and plazas. Bar-hopping is a pastime enjoyed by young and old alike.

If you're after the more traditional, with tiled walls and flamenco tunes, head to the *barrio* of Huertas. For gay-friendly drinking holes, Chueca is the place. Malasaña caters to a grungy, funky crowd, while La Latina has friendly bars that guarantee atmosphere most nights of the week. In summer, the terrace bars that pop up all over the city are unbeatable.

The bulk of Madrid bars open to 2am Sunday to Thursday, and to 3am or 3.30am Friday and Saturday.

Los Austrias & Centro

Café del Nuncio (Map p753; Calle de Segovia 9; M La Latina) Lace curtains and red-wood panelling set the tone at this bustling bar. In summer, the outdoor terrace is divine.

La Viuda Negra (Map p753; Calle de Campomanes 6; M Ópera) The loungelike 'Black Widow' cocktail bar is Manhattan minimalist and draws a sophisticated crowd.

Gaia Cocktail Lounge (Map p753; www.gaiacocktail.com in Spanish; Calle de Amnistía 5; 10pm-3am Tue-Thu, 8.30pm-3.30am Fri & Sat; M Ópera) Gaia serves up delicious cocktails to a DJ soundtrack of jazz, funk, lounge and occasional house music.

Museo Chicote (Map p753; www.museo-chicote.com; Gran Vía 12; 8am-4am Mon-Sat; M Gran Vía) A timeless classic popular with socialites and film stars, the Museo Chicote has a lounge atmosphere late at night and a stream of famous faces all day.

Sol, Huertas & Atocha

Cervecería Alemana (Map p753; Plaza de Santa Ana 6; 10.30am-12.30am Sun-Thu, 10.30am-2am Fri & Sat, closed August; M Antón Martín or Sol) A classic and classy watering hole, this place is famous for its cold, frothy beers and delicious tapas. It was one of Hemingway's haunts.

Taberna de Dolores (Map p753; Plaza de Jesús 4; M Antón Martín) Here since 1908, this delightful little bar smothered in tiles has beer and wine flowing freely, along with sea salty anchovies.

our pick **La Venencia** (Map p753; Calle de Echegarary 7; M Sol) Your sherry (in several varieties) is poured straight from dusty wooden barrels and your tab is literally chalked up on the bar itself.

SPAIN

El Imperfecto (Map p753; Plaza de Matute 2; Ⓜ Antón Martín) This place has live jazz on Tuesdays (and sometimes other nights) and a drinks menu as long as a saxophone, ranging from cocktails (€6.50) and spirits to milkshakes, teas and creative coffees.

Viva Madrid (Map p753; www.barvivamadrid.com; Calle de Manuel Fernández y González 7; Ⓜ Antón Martín or Sol) A landmark smothered in beautiful coloured tiles, Viva Madrid does tapas earlier in the evening and drinks late into the night.

La Latina & Lavapiés

El Viajero (Map pp750-1; Plaza de la Cebada 11; Ⓜ La Latina) A neighbourhood favourite drawing a mixed crowd, El Viajero has a downstairs restaurant, a cosy upstairs bar and best of all, a rooftop terrace with fantastic city views.

Delic (Map p753; Costanilla de San Andrés 14; Ⓜ La Latina) Nursing a fine mojito on a warm summer's evening at Delic's outdoor tables on one of Madrid's prettiest plazas is one of life's great pleasures.

La Inquilina (Map pp750-1; Calle del Ave María 39; 🕒 7pm-2am Tue-Thu, 1-4pm & 8pm-3am Fri-Sun; Ⓜ Lavapiés) With its cool-and-casual vibe, this locals bar is run by women and there's sports art by budding local artists on the walls. Gather around the bar or take a table out the back.

Malasaña & Chueca

Areia (Map p753; www.areiachillout.com in Spanish; Calle de Hortaleza 92; Ⓜ Chueca or Alonso Martínez) The ultimate lounge bar by day, groovy DJs take over at night with deep and chill house, nu jazz, bossa and electronica.

Café Comercial (Map pp750-1; Glorieta de Bilbao 7; Ⓜ Bilbao) The faded elegance of this classic cafe appeals to intellectuals and the artsy crowd.

Café Pepe Botella (Map pp750-1; Calle de San Andrés 12; Ⓜ Bilbao or Tribunal) The cosy velvet benches and marble-topped tables give 'Joe Bottle' a retro feel. It's best known for its sherry.

Mamá Inés (Map p753; ☎ 91 523 23 33; www.mamaines.com in Spanish; Calle de Hortaleza 22; Ⓜ Gran Vía or Chueca) Popular with gay men, this is a meeting point and a great spot for coffee.

Tupperware (Map pp750-1; Corredera Alta de San Pablo 26; 🕒 8pm-3.30am Sun-Wed, 9pm-3.30am Thu-Sat; Ⓜ Tribunal) Unbelievably kitschy, with plastic dolls and pictures of old TV stars as decor, this fun bar plays danceable pop and '80s music every night of the week.

Stop Madrid (Map p753; Calle de Hortaleza 11; Ⓜ Gran Vía) This terrific old *taberna* is friendly, invariably packed and serves up a wicked sangria.

> **MADRID'S FAVOURITE POST-CLUBBING MUNCHIES**
>
> **Chocolatería de San Ginés** (Map p753; Pasadizo San Ginés 5; 🕒 9am-7am Wed-Sun, 6pm-7am Mon & Tue; Ⓜ Sol) Join the sugar-searching throngs who end the night at this mythic bar (it doesn't close until 7am), famous for its freshly fried *churros* (fried sticks of dough) and syrupy hot chocolate.

ENTERTAINMENT

The *Guía del Ocio* (€1), is the city's classic weekly listings magazine. Better are **Metropoli** (www.elmundo.es) and **On Madrid** (www.elpais.com), respectively *El Mundo*'s and *El País'* Friday listings supplements. **La Netro** (http://madrid.lanetro.com) is a comprehensive online guide.

Nightclubs

No *barrio* is without a decent club or disco, but the most popular dance spots are in the centre. For intimate dancing or quirky decor, head to Chueca or Malasaña. Don't expect dance clubs or *discotecas* (nightclubs) to get going until after 1am at the earliest. Standard entry fee is €10, which usually includes the first drink, although megaclubs and swankier places charge a few euros more.

Palacio Gaviria (Map p753; Calle del Arenal 9; Ⓜ Sol) Special international student nights and other theme nights bring the big crowds to this converted mansion near the Puerta del Sol.

Teatro Joy Eslava (Map p753; www.joy-eslava.com in Spanish; Calle del Arenal 11; Ⓜ Sol) Housed in a 19th-century neoclassical theatre, Joy hosts lots of theme parties and student nights. It's a megaclub, but can still be a good place to meet people.

Siroco (Map pp750-1; www.siroco.es in Spanish; Calle de San Dimas 3; 🕒 10pm-6am Thu-Sat; Ⓜ Noviciado) One of the most eclectic nightclubs in Madrid, Siroco does everything from Reggae to acid jazz, from 1970s to funk, house and hip-hop. It's a good place to hear local music too.

Kapital (Map pp750-1; www.grupo-kapital.com in Spanish; Calle de Atocha 125; Ⓜ Atocha) This massive seven-storey nightclub has something for everyone: from cocktail bars and dance music to karaoke, salsa, hip-hop and more chilled spaces for R&B and soul.

Cinemas

Several movie theatres are huddled around Gran Vía and Calle de la Princesa.

Cine Doré (Map pp750-1; ☎ 91 369 11 25; Calle de Santa Isabel 3; ⌚ Tue-Sun; Ⓜ Antón Martín) The National Film Library offers fantastic classic and vanguard films for just €2.

For a selection of original-version (international films shown with subtitles) flicks in this area, head to **Princesa** (Map p753; ☎ 91 541 41 00; Calle de la Princesa 3; Ⓜ Plaza de España) or **Renoir** (Map p753; ☎ 91 541 41 00; Calle de Martín de los Heros 12; Ⓜ Plaza de España).

Gay & Lesbian Venues

Chueca is Madrid's lively, gay-friendly neighbourhood, and you'll find lots of gay and lesbian bars and clubs in the area.

Café Acuarela (Map p753; ☎ 91 522 21 43; Calle de Gravina 10; ⌚ 2pm-3am; Ⓜ Chueca) For something low-key, head to this quiet bar.

Why Not? (Map p753; Calle de San Bartolomé 7; ⌚ 10.30pm-6am; Ⓜ Chueca) This is a hetero-friendly place where nothing's left to the imagination (things get pretty amorous here). Pop and top-40s music are the standard.

Two of the more outrageous gay nightspots in Madrid are **Sunrise** (Map p753; Calle de Barbieri 7; ⌚ midnight-6am Thu-Sat; Ⓜ Chueca) and **La Fulanita de Tal** (Map p753; www.fulanitadetal.com in Spanish; Calle del Conde de Xiquena 2; ⌚ 10pm-3am Sun-Wed, 10pm-4am Thu-Sat; Ⓜ Chueca).

SPAIN

Theatre

Madrid has a lively cultural scene, with concerts and shows taking place throughout the city.

Teatro Albéniz (Map p753; ☎ 91 531 83 11; Calle de la Paz 11; Ⓜ Sol) Staging both commercial and vanguard drama, this is just one of Madrid's quality theatres. For more listings, check out *Guía del Ocio* or local newspapers.

Teatro Real (Map p753; ☎ 902 244848; www.teatro-real.com in Spanish; Plaza de Oriente; Ⓜ Ópera) The Teatro Real is the city's grandest stage for elaborate operas and ballets. You'll pay as little as €15 for a spot so far away you will need a telescope, although the sound quality is consistent throughout.

Teatro de la Zarzuela (Map p753; ☎ 91 524 54 00; http://teatrodelazarzuela.mcu.es; Calle de Jovellanos 4; Ⓜ Banco de España) Come here for *zarzuela*, a very Spanish mixture of dance, music and theatre.

Live Music

FLAMENCO

Many of flamenco's top names perform in Madrid, making it an excellent place to see interpretations of this Andalucian art. The more 'serious' shows are usually set up in a dinner/theatre style and are aimed at tourists. But many smaller bars also host once-weekly flamenco concerts or shows.

Casa Patas (Map p753; ☎ 91 369 04 96; www.casapatas.com; Calle de Cañizares 10; admission about €35; Ⓜ Antón Martín) One of the best *tablaos* in the city, this is a great place to see passionate dancing, although it's one of the pricier options. It puts on shows at various times.

Las Tablas (Map p753; ☎ 91 542 05 20; www.lastablasmadrid.com in Spanish; Plaza de España 9; admission €10-30; ⌚ show 10.30pm; Ⓜ Plaza de España) Las Tablas has quickly earned a reputation for quality flamenco. Most nights you'll see a classic flamenco show, with plenty of throaty singing and soul-baring dancing.

Cardamomo (Map p753; ☎ 91 369 07 57; www.cardamomo.es in Spanish; Calle de Echegaray 15; admission €10; ⌚ 9pm-3.30am, live shows 10.30pm Tue & Wed; Ⓜ Sevilla) This is a place for those of you who believe that flamenco is best enjoyed in a smoky bar where the crowd is predominantly local and where you can clap, shout '*Olé!*' and sing along.

JAZZ

Café Central (Map p753; ☎ 91 369 41 43; www.cafecentralmadrid.com in Spanish; Plaza del Angel 10; admission €9-15; ⌚ 1pm-2.30am Sun-Thu, 1pm-4am Fri & Sat; Ⓜ Antón Martín or Sol) This art deco bar is worth a visit on its own, but the live shows, which range from classic jazz to Latin, fusion or tango-style, are what has made it one of the most popular bars in the city.

Populart (Map p753; ☎ 91 429 84 07; www.populart.es; Calle de las Huertas 22; admission free; ⌚ show 11pm; Ⓜ Antón Martín or Sol) Get here early if you want a seat because this smoky, atmospheric bar is always packed with fans yearning for some soothing live jazz, blues or flamenco.

ROCK & OTHER

Café La Palma (Map pp750-1; www.cafelapalma.com in Spanish; Calle de la Palma 62; Ⓜ Noviciado) Live shows featuring hot local bands are held at the back, while DJs mix up the front. You might find live music other nights, but there are always two shows at 10pm and midnight from Thursday to Saturday.

Clamores (Map pp750-1; www.clamores.es, in Spanish; Calle de Alburquerque 14; admission €5-20; Ⓜ Bilbao) Clamores is one of the most diverse live music stages in Madrid. Jazz is a staple here, but world music, flamenco, soul fusion, singer-songwriter, pop and rock also make regular appearances.

Honky Tonk (Map pp750-1; www.clubhonky.com in Spanish; Calle de Covarrubias 24; Ⓜ Alonso Martínez) Despite the name, this is a great place to see local rock 'n' roll, though many acts have a little country or some blues thrown into the mix too.

Kabokla (Map pp750-1; www.kabokla.es in Spanish; Calle de San Vicente Ferrer 55; admission free; 9pm-3am Tue-Thu, 9pm-5am Fri & Sat, 2.30pm-midnight Sun; Ⓜ Noviciado) Dedicated to all things Brazilian, Kabokla is terrific. Live Brazilian groups play most nights from around 10pm (from percussion to samba and cover bands playing Chico Buarque).

Sport

Get tickets to football matches and bullfights from box offices or through agents such as **Localidades Galicia** (Map p753; ☎ 91 531 27 32; www.eol.es/lgalicia; Plaza del Carmen 1; 9.30am-1pm & 4.30-7pm Tue-Sat; Ⓜ Sol).

FOOTBALL

Madrid's major football clubs and accompanying delirious fans are a guarantee that football fever runs high in the city.

Estadio Santiago Bernabéu (off Map pp750-1; ☎ 91 398 43 00; www.realmadrid.com; Avenida de Concha Espina 1; tour adult/child under 14 €10/8; 10am-7pm Mon-Sat, 10.30am-6.30pm Sun, closed day of game; Ⓜ Santiago Bernabéu) The mythic Real Madrid plays at this stadium. Fans can visit the stadium and take an interesting tour through the presidential box, dressing room and field.

Estadio Vicente Calderón (Map pp750-1; ☎ 91 366 47 07; www.at-madrid.com; Paseo de la Virgin del Puerto) This is home to Atlético de Madrid, whose fans are famed as being some of the country's most devoted.

BULLFIGHTING

Plaza de Toros Las Ventas (off Map pp750-1; ☎ 91 356 22 00; www.las-ventas.com in Spanish; Calle de Alcalá 237; Ⓜ Las Ventas) Some of Spain's top *toreros* swing their capes in Plaza de Toros Las Ventas. Fights are held every Sunday afternoon from mid-May through October. Get tickets (from €5 standing in the sun) at the plaza box office, Localidades Galicia (left), or from official ticket agents on Calle Victoria.

SHOPPING

The key to shopping Madrid-style is knowing where to look. Salamanca is the home of upmarket fashions, with chic boutiques lining up to showcase the best that Spanish and international designers have to offer. Some of it spills over into Chueca, but Malasaña is Salamanca's true alter ego, home to fashion that's as funky as it is offbeat and ideal for that studied underground look that will fit right in with Madrid's hedonistic after-dark crowd. Central Madrid – Sol, Huertas or La Latina – offers plenty of individual surprises.

During *las rebajas*, the annual winter and summer sales, prices are slashed on just about everything. The winter sales begin around January 7 and last well into February. Summer sales begin in early July and last into August.

All shops may (and most usually do) open on the first Sunday of every month and throughout December.

SPAIN

MARKET WATCH

Madrid's street markets are great places to browse and, sometimes, to find a bargain. The most famous market is El Rastro, but others specialising in books, stamps or art are fun too.

El Rastro (Map pp750-1; Calle Ribera Curtidores; 8am-2pm Sun; Ⓜ La Latina) A bustling flea market, the chaotic El Rastro sells a bit of everything. The madness begins at Plaza Cascorro and worms its way downhill. Watch your wallet.

La Cuesta de Moyano (Map pp750-1; Paseo del Prado or Cuesta de Moyano; 9.30am-dusk Mon-Fri, 9.30am-2pm Sat & Sun; Ⓜ Atocha) A treasure trove of old books.

Mercadillo de Filatelia y Numismática (Stamp & Coin Market; Map p753; Plaza Mayor; 8am-2pm Sun; Ⓜ Sol) This classic stamp and coin market draws hobbyists from all over the city.

Mercado de Pintura (Art Market; Map p753; Plaza del Conde de Barajas; 8am-2pm Sun; Ⓜ Sol) Browse the original works at this small art market near Plaza Mayor.

Mantequería Bravo (Map pp750-1; ☎ 91 576 76 41; Calle de Ayala 24; Ⓜ Serrano) Behind the attractive old facade lies a connoisseur's paradise, filled with local cheeses, sausages, wines and coffees.

Agatha Ruiz de la Prada (Map pp750-1; ☎ 91 319 05 01; Calle de Serrano 27; 10am-8.30pm Mon-Sat; Ⓜ Serrano) This boutique has to be seen to be believed, with pinks, yellows and oranges everywhere you turn. It's fun and highly original fashion.

José Ramírez (Map p753; ☎ 91 531 42 29; www.guitarrasramirez.com; Calle de la Paz 8; Ⓜ Sol) Find handmade guitars at this family-run shop. There's a small museum of old guitars out the back.

Gil (Map p753; ☎ 91 521 25 49; Carrera de San Jerónimo 2; Ⓜ Sevilla) Spanish shawls and veils are the speciality at this historic shop.

Mercado de Fuencarral (Map p753; ☎ 91 521 41 52; www.mdf.es; Calle de Fuencarral 45; Ⓜ Chueca) With shops such as Ugly Shop and Black Kiss, this reverse snobs' mall is funky, grungy and filled to the rafters with torn T-shirts and more black leather and silver studs than you'll ever need. There has been talk of relocation to Valencia. Check the web for details.

El Corte Inglés (Map p753; ☎ 90 222 44 11; www.elcorteingles.es; Calle de Preciados 1, 2, 3 & 9; Ⓜ Sol) Spain's enormous department store has branches all over the city and sells everything from food and furniture to clothes, appliances and toiletries. It's truly one-stop shopping.

SPAIN

GETTING THERE & AWAY

Air

Madrid's international Barajas airport (MAD), 16km northeast of the city, is a busy place, with flights coming in from all over Europe and beyond. See p848 for more information.

Bus

Estación Sur de Autobuses (off Map pp750-1; ☎ 91 468 42 00; www.estaciondeautobuses.com in Spanish; Calle de Méndez Álvaro 83; Ⓜ Méndez Álvaro), just south of the M-30 ring road, is the city's principal bus station. It serves most destinations to the south and many in other parts of the country. ALSA has buses to Barcelona (€28 to €39, 7½ to 8½ hours, 27 daily), Zaragoza (€15 to €20, four hours, 28 daily) and many other destinations.

Car & Motorcycle

If you arrive by car, be prepared to face gridlock traffic. The city is surrounded by three ring roads: the M30, M40 and M50 (still not 100% completed). You'll probably be herded onto one of these, which in turn give access to the city centre.

Car rental companies abound in Madrid; most have offices both at the airport and in town. **Pepecar** (www.pepecar.com) has several locations.

Train

Renfe (www.renfe.es) trains connect Madrid with destinations throughout Spain. There are two main train stations: Atocha, southeast of the city centre, and Chamartín, to the north. Long-distance and *cercanías* (local area trains) trains pass through these two stations.

High-speed AVE trains run to Barcelona (€105 to €124, three hours, up to 18 daily) and Seville (€67 to €74, 2½ hours, up to 20 daily).

GETTING AROUND

To/From the Airport

Metro line 8 zips you into the city from the airport's T2 and T4 terminals. The 12-minute trip to the Nuevos Ministerios station costs €1; from there, you can easily connect to all other stations.

A taxi ride to the centre should cost about €25 (€35 from Terminal 4) and the trip takes around 20 to 30 minutes.

Car & Motorcycle

Public transport in Madrid is excellent, so having a car or motorcycle is not necessary (and is usually a big headache!). If you do have a car, be prepared to face plenty of traffic and complicated parking (virtually all meter parking in the streets as well as private parking stations).

Driving around Plaza Mayor and the centre is especially challenging, as several roads dive underground and following them can be tricky.

Public Transport

Madrid's 284km of **metro** (www.metromadrid.es) is Europe's second-largest metro system, after London. A single-ride costs €1 and a 10-ride ticket is €6.70. You can also get a one-, two-, three-, five- or seven-day travel pass. The metro is quick, clean, relatively safe and runs from 6am until 2am.

The bus system is also good, but working out the maze of bus lines can be a challenge.

Contact **EMT** (www.emtmadrid.es) for more information. Twenty-six night-bus *búhos* (owls) routes operate from midnight to 6am, with all routes originating in Plaza de la Cibeles.

Taxi

Madrid's taxis are inexpensive by European standards. Flag fall is €1.95 from 6am to 10pm daily, €2.15 from 10pm to 6am Sunday to Friday and €2.95 from 10pm Saturday to 6am Sunday.

Among the 24-hour taxi services are **Radio-Taxi** (☎ 91 405 55 00), **Tele-Taxi** (☎ 91 371 21 31) and **Radio-Teléfono Taxi** (☎ 91 547 82 00; www.radiotelefono-taxi.com); the latter runs taxis for people with a disability.

AROUND MADRID

Get out of the city buzz and explore Comunidad de Madrid, the province surrounding the capital. Home to some of Spain's finest royal palaces and gardens, the Comunidad offers several easy day trips.

Places worth exploring include the royal palace complex at **San Lorenzo de El Escorial** (☎ 91 890 78 18; www.patrimonionacional.es; admission €8, EU citizens Wed free; ⏲ 10am-6pm Apr-Sep, 10am-5pm Oct-Mar, closed Mon). Check also www.sanlorenzoturismo.org.

Other worthwhile excursions include **Aranjuez** (☎ 91 891 04 27; www.aranjuez.es in Spanish), with its **royal palace** (☎ 91 891 07 40; www.patrimonionacional.es; adult/child, senior & student €5/2.50, EU citizens Wed free, gardens free; ⏲ palace 10am-5.15pm Tue-Sun Oct-Mar, 10am-6.15pm Tue-Sun Apr-Sep, gardens 8am-6.30pm Tue-Sun Oct-Mar, 8am-8.30pm Tue-Sun Apr-Sep), the traditional village of **Chinchón** (www.ciudad-chinchon.com), and the university town (and birthplace of Miguel de Cervantes), **Alcalá de Henares** (www.turismoalcala.com). Also interesting is the **Valle de los Caídos** (www.patrimonionacional.es; Carretera de Guadarrama/El Escorial M-600; admission €8; ⏲ 10am-6pm Tue-Sun Apr-Sep, to 5pm Oct-Mar), Franco's ostentatious civil war memorial. The basilica and monument are just 9km north of San Lorenzo de El Escorial.

CASTILLA Y LEÓN

The true heart of Spain, Castilla y León is littered with hilltop towns sporting magnificent Gothic cathedrals, monumental city walls and mouth-watering restaurants.

ÁVILA

pop 53,800 / elev 1130m

Its pretty Old Town huddled behind impressively intact medieval walls, Ávila has a picture-postcard look and an open-museum feel. It's a perfect place to spend a day strolling narrow laneways and soaking up history. The city is known as the birthplace of Santa Teresa, a mystical writer and reformer of the Carmelite order.

There's a **tourist office** (☎ 920 21 13 87; www.turismocastillayleon.com; Plaza de Pedro Dávila 4; ⏲ 9am-2pm & 5-8pm mid-Sep–Jun, 9am-8pm Sun-Thu, 9am-9pm Fri & Sat Jul–mid-Sep) near the Puerta del Rastro. Try also the **Centro de Recepción de Visitantes** (Tourist Office; ☎ 902 10 21 21; www.avilaturismo.com; Avenida de Madrid 39; ⏲ 10am-6pm Nov-Mar, 9am-8pm Apr-Oct).

Sights

Don't even *think* of leaving town without enjoying the walk along the top of Ávila's 12th-century **murallas** (walls; ☎ 920 21 13 87; adult/child €4/2.50; ⏲ 11am-6pm Tue-Sun Sep-Jun, 10am-8pm Jul & Aug). The two access points are at **Puerta del Alcázar** (⏲ 11am-6pm Tue-Sun Oct-Apr, 11am-8pm Tue-Sun May-Sep) and **Puerta de los Leales** (Casa de las Carnicerias; ⏲ 10am-6pm Tue-Sun Oct-Apr, 10am-8pm Tue-Sun May-Sep), which allow walks of 300m and 800m respectively.

Embedded into the eastern city walls, the splendid 12th-century **cathedral** (☎ 920 21 16 41; Plaza de la Catedral; admission €4; ⏲ 10am-7pm Mon-Fri, 10am-8pm Sat, noon-6pm Sun Jun-Sep, shorter hours Oct-May) was the first Gothic-style church built in Spain. It boasts rich walnut choir stalls and a long, narrow central nave that makes the soaring ceilings seem all the more majestic.

The **Convento de Santa Teresa** (☎ 920 21 10 30; admission free; ⏲ 8.45am-1.30pm & 3.30-9pm Tue-Sun) was built in 1636 at the birthplace of 16th-century mystic and ascetic, Santa Teresa. It's home to relics, including a piece of the saint's ring finger, as well as a small museum about her life.

Sleeping

Hostal San Juan (☎ 920 25 14 75; www.hostalsanjuan.es; Calle de los Comuneros de Castilla 3; s/d Nov-May from €24/38, Jun-Oct €30/48) With warm tones throughout, Hostal San Juan is pleasant, friendly and close to everything in Ávila. The rooms don't have a lot of character, but they're terrific value.

Hostal Arco San Vicente (☎ 920 22 24 98; www.arcosanvicente.com; Calle de López Núñez 6; s €45-50, d €60-70) Another terrific option, this engaging *hostal* has lovely, brightly painted rooms and friendly owners. The rooms at the back are quieter and have a private terrace.

Hospedería La Sinagoga (☎ 920 35 23 21; lasingoga@vodafone.es; Calle de los Reyes Católicos 22; s/d/tr from €53/74/106) Hidden down a quiet lane, this delightful spot incorporates details from Ávila's main 15th-century synagogue with bright, spacious rooms. Rates for doubles can drop as low as €42 on winter weekdays.

Eating & Drinking

Posada de la Fruta (☎ 920 22 09 84; www.posadadelafruta.com in Spanish; Plaza de Pedro Dávila 8; meals €10-18) Informal meals can be had here at the cafe-bar in a light-filled, covered courtyard, while the traditional *comedor* (dining room) serves *menús* (fixed-price meals) and à la carte dishes.

Restaurante Reyes Católicos (☎ 920 25 56 27; www.restaurante-reyescatolicos.com in Spanish; Calle de los Reyes Católicos 6; meals €25-35, menú del día €16.90) Most *asadores* (restaurants serving roasted meats) in Ávila are old-school with dark, wood-panelled dining areas. This slick, modern restaurant is a refreshing change. The cuisine offers a mix of traditional and fusion dishes with a range of set menus (€16.90 to €48).

Mesón del Rastro (☎ 920 21 12 19; Plaza del Rastro 1; menú del día €20; lunch & dinner Thur-Sat, lunch Sun-Wed) The dining room at Mesón del Rastro, with its dark-wood beams, is a bastion of Castilian cooking. Expect hearty, delicious mainstays such as *chuletón de avileño* (a huge lamb chop; €13) and *cordero asado* (roast lamb; €15).

There are several good bars just outside the Puerta de los Leales, the best of which is the noisy, smoky and welcoming **Bodeguito de San Segundo** (☎ 920 22 59 17; www.vinoavila.com in Spanish; Calle de San Segundo 19; 11am-midnight Thu-Tue). This gem of a wine and tapas bar is standing-room only most nights and more tranquil in the quieter afternoon hours.

Getting There & Away

The **bus station** (☎ 920 22 01 54; Avenida de Madrid 2) is a five-minute walk northeast from the cathedral. Up to nine buses (€7.10, one hour 20 minutes) connect with Madrid's Estación Sur. **Avanza** has buses to Segovia (€4.30, 55 minutes, five daily Monday to Friday, one to two on weekends) and Salamanca (€5.60, 1½ hours, four daily Monday to Friday, one to three on weekends).

From the **train station** (Paseo de la Estación), more than 30 trains run daily to Madrid (from €6.50, 1¼ to two hours) and a handful to Salamanca (€8.40, one to 1½ hours).

SALAMANCA

pop 156,000

This is a city of rare architectural splendour, awash with sandstone overlaid with Latin inscriptions in ochre and an extraordinary virtuosity of plateresque and Renaissance styles. The monumental highlights are many, especially the Catedral Nueva and grand Plaza Mayor. King Alfonso XI founded what was long Spain's greatest university in 1218 and this is still a university town. A favourite with young foreigners who come to learn Spanish, it can be quite a party town.

Information

Cyberplace (Plaza Mayor 10; per hr €1; 11am-midnight Mon-Fri, noon-midnight Sat & Sun) Internet access.

Municipal tourist office (☎ 923 21 83 42; www.salamanca.es; Plaza Mayor 14; 9am-2pm & 4.30-8pm Mon-Fri, 10am-8pm Sat, 10am-2pm Sun)

Regional tourist office (Casa de las Conchas; ☎ 923 26 85 71; www.turismocastillayleon.com; Rúa Mayor; 9am-2pm & 5-8pm daily Sep-Jun, 9am-8pm Sun-Thu, to 9pm Fri & Sat Jul-Aug)

Sights & Activities

The harmonious **Plaza Mayor** was completed in 1755 to a design by Alberto Churriguera, one of the clan behind, at times, an overblown variant of the baroque style that bears their name.

Curiously, Salamanca is home to two cathedrals: the newer and larger cathedral was built beside the old Romanesque one instead of on top of it, as was the norm. The **Catedral Nueva** (New Cathedral; ☎ 923 21 74 76; Plaza de Anaya; admission free; 9am-8pm), completed in 1733, is a late Gothic masterpiece that took 220 years to

FIND THE FROG

The university's facade (see right) is an ornate mass of sculptures and carvings, and hidden among this 16th-century plateresque creation is a tiny stone frog. Legend says that those who find the frog will have good luck in studies, life and love. A hint: it's sitting on a skull on the pillar that runs up the right-hand side of the facade.

SPAIN

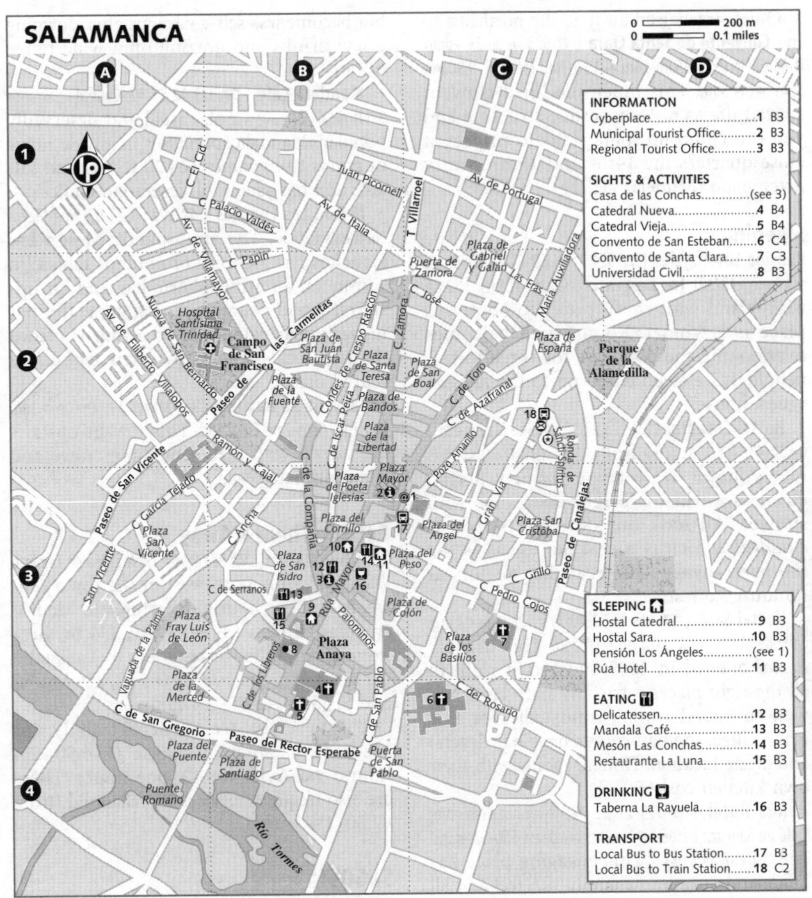

build. Its magnificent Renaissance doorways, particularly the Puerta del Nacimiento, stand out. For fine views over Salamanca, head to the southwestern corner of the cathedral facade and the **Puerta de la Torre** (Ieronimus; Plaza de Juan XXIII; admission €3.25; 10am-7.15pm), from where stairs lead up through the tower. Once inside the cathedral, make your way to the largely Romanesque **Catedral Vieja** (Old Cathedral; admission €3.50; 10am-12.30pm & 4-5.30pm Oct-Mar, 10am-1.30pm & 4-7.30pm Apr-Sep), a 12th-century temple with a stunning 15th-century altarpiece whose 53 panels depict scenes from the life of Christ and Mary, topped by a representation of the Final Judgement.

The **Universidad Civil** (university; ☎ 923 29 44 00; Calle de los Libreros; adult/student €4/2, Mon morning free; 9.30am-1pm & 4-7pm Mon-Fri, 9.30am-1pm & 4-6.30pm Sat, 10am-1pm Sun) is a tapestry in sandstone, bursting with images of mythical heroes, religious scenes and coats of arms. It's dominated in the centre by busts of Fernando and Isabel. You can visit the old classrooms and library.

Among the other stand-out buildings are the glorious **Casa de las Conchas** (House of Shells; ☎ 923 26 93 17; Calle de la Compañia 2; admission free; 9am-9pm Mon-Fri, 9am-2pm & 4-7pm Sat & Sun), a city symbol since it was built in the 15th century, and the **Convento de San Esteban**, whose **church** (☎ 923 21 50 00; adult/concession €3/2; 10am-2pm & 4-8pm) has an extraordinary altarlike facade with the stoning of San Esteban (St Stephen) as its central motif.

Quiet streets lead away to the northeast to the **Convento de Santa Clara** (☎ 923 26 96 23; adult/child €2/1; 9.35am-2pm & 4.20-7pm Mon-Fri, 9.30am-3pm Sat & Sun). This much-modified convent started life as a Romanesque structure and you can climb up some stairs to inspect at close quarters the 14th- and 15th-century *artesonado* (Mudéjar ceiling).

Sleeping

Pensión Los Ángeles (☎ 923 21 81 66; Plaza Mayor 10; s/d from €18/30) In a prime location on Plaza Mayor and with cheap prices to boot, this place is a winner. Rooms with balconies overlooking the plaza are for three to five people. It's a steep climb up to the *pensión* (guest house).

Hostal Catedral (☎ 923 27 06 14; Rúa Mayor 46; s/d €30/48) Just across from the *catedrales*, this lovely *hostal* has a few extremely pretty, clean-as-a-whistle, bright bedrooms with shower. All look out onto the street or *catedral*, which is a real bonus, as is the motherly owner who treats her visitors as honoured guests.

Hostal Sara (☎ 923 28 11 40; www.hostalsara.org; Calle de Meléndez 11; s/d from €45/50) This friendly *hostal* opened in 2005 and gets it right in all the right places – friendly staff, large and well-equipped rooms (unusually for this price range, the bathrooms have hairdryers) and a fine location. Double rooms with their own kitchen cost €58.

Rúa Hotel (☎ 923 27 22 72; www.hotelrua.com; Calle de Sánchez Barbero 11; s incl breakfast €50-57, d incl breakfast €67-115;) This engaging place has modern decoration, a family-run feel and all rooms are apartments/suites (with kitchen) of around 30 sq metres. The best rooms are those facing north with terrific views. The breakfast room in the basement includes a 13th-century stone arch.

Eating & Drinking

Restaurante La Luna (☎ 923 21 28 87; Calle de los Libreros 4; set menu €11; lunch & dinner Tue-Sun, lunch Mon) We like this place almost as much as Mandala (see below). Downstairs is crowded and intimate, upstairs is bright and modern, and the food is a good mix of hearty meat staples and fresh lighter meals.

Delicatessen (☎ 923 28 03 09; Calle de Meléndez 25; menú del día €14.50, meals €20-25; 9am-late) The youngish patrons tend to start out striking poses while lolling on the sleek furniture, but become less self-conscious after downing a few drinks and grazing on a wide range of tapas.

Mandala Café (☎ 923 12 33 42; Calle de Serranos 9-11; meals €15-20) Cool, casual and deservedly popular, Mandala specialises in a wide range of *platos combinados* (€4.20 to €9) and salads, and has plenty of vegetarian choices.

Mesón Las Conchas (☎ 923 21 21 67; Rúa Mayor 16; meals €20-30) The atmospheric Mesón Las Conchas has a choice of outdoor tables (in summer), an atmospheric bar and an upstairs, wood-beamed dining area; the bar in particular caters less to a tourist crowd than to locals who know their *embutidos* (cured meats).

Taberna La Rayuela (Rúa Mayor 19; 6pm-1am Sun-Thu, 6pm-2am Fri & Sat) This low-lit upstairs bar buzzes with a 20-something crowd and is an intimate place.

Getting There & Away

The **bus station** (☎ 923 23 67 17; Avenida de Filiberto Villalobos 71-85) is northwest of the town centre. **Avanza** has hourly departures to Madrid (regular/express €11.90/17.40, 2½ to three hours) with other buses going to Valladolid (€7.40, 1½ hours), Ávila (€5.58, 1½ hours) and Segovia (€9.90, 2¾ hours).

Up to eight trains depart daily for Madrid's Chamartín station (€16.50, 2½ hours) via Ávila (€8.40, one hour). There are also frequent services to Valladolid (from €7.50, 1½ hours).

SEGOVIA

pop 56,100 / elev 1002m

This high and, in winter, chilly city, warms the traveller's heart with such extraordinary sights as the grand Roman aqueduct and fairytale Alcázar (castle), not to mention steaming serves of hearty suckling pig in many an Old Town restaurant.

Information

Centro de Recepción de Visitantes (☎ 921 46 67 20; www.turismodesegovia.com; Plaza del Azoguejo 1; 10am-7pm Sun-Fri, 10am-8pm Sat) Tourist office.

InternetCaf (☎ 921 42 51 58; Calle de Teodosio el Grande 10; per hr €2; 9am-11pm)

Regional tourist office (☎ 921 46 03 34, 902 20 30 30; www.segoviaturismo.es; Plaza Mayor 10; 9am-2pm & 5-8pm mid-Sep–Jun, 9am-8pm Sun-Thu & 9am-9pm Fri & Sat Jul–mid-Sep)

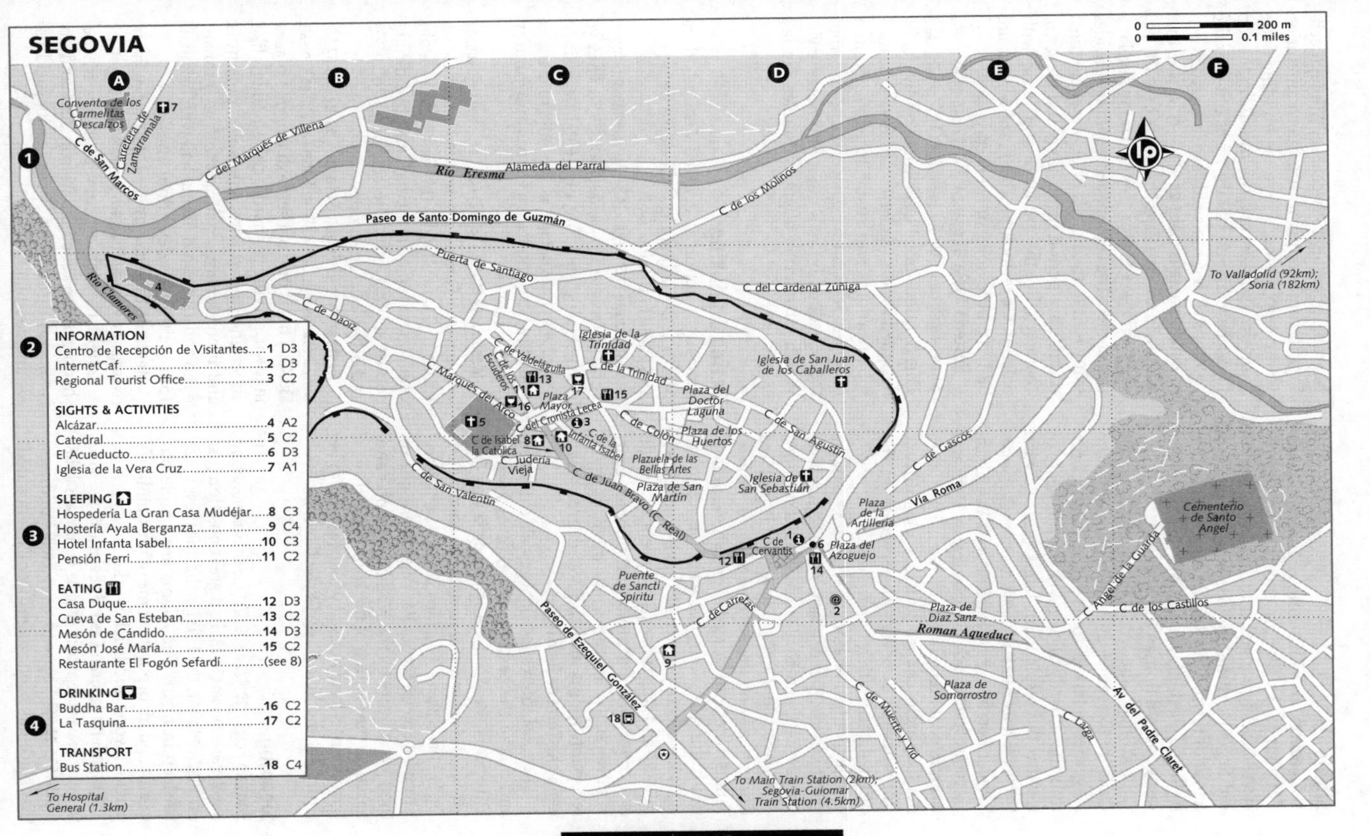
SEGOVIA
0 200 m
0 0.1 miles
INFORMATION
Centre de Recepción de Visitantes.....1 D3
InternetCaf.....2 D3
Regional Tourist Office.....3 C2
SIGHTS & ACTIVITIES
Alcázar.....4 A2
Catedral.....5 C2
El Acueducto.....6 D3
Iglesia de la Vera Cruz.....7 A1
SLEEPING
Hospedería La Gran Casa Mudéjar.....8 C3
Hostería Ayala Berganza.....9 C4
Hotel Infanta Isabel.....10 C3
Pensión Ferri.....11 C2
EATING
Casa Duque.....12 D3
Cueva de San Esteban.....13 C2
Mesón de Cándido.....14 D3
Mesón José María.....15 C2
Restaurante El Fogón Sefardí.....(see 8)
DRINKING
Buddha Bar.....16 C2
La Tasquina.....17 C2
TRANSPORT
Bus Station.....18 C4
Convento de los Carmelitas Descalzos
Carretera de Zamarramala
C de San Marcos
C del Marqués de Villena
Río Eresma
Alameda del Parral
Paseo de Santo Domingo de Guzmán
Río Clamores
Puerta de Santiago
C de los Molinos
C del Cardenal Zúñiga
To Valladolid (92km); Soria (182km)
Cementerio de Santo Angel
C Ángel de la Guarda
C de los Castillos
Av del Padre Claret
C Larga
Vía Roma
C de Gascos
Plaza de la Artillería
Plaza del Azoguejo
Plaza de Díaz Sanz
Roman Aqueduct
Plaza de Somorrostro
C de Muerte y Vid
To Main Train Station (2km); Segovia-Guiomar Train Station (4.5km)
Iglesia de San Juan de los Caballeros
C de San Agustín
Iglesia de San Sebastián
C de Cervantes
C de Carretas
Plaza del Doctor Laguna
Plaza de los Huertos
C de Colón
Plazuela de las Bellas Artes
Plaza de San Martín
C de Juan Bravo (C Real)
Puente de Sancti Spiritu
Paseo de Ezequiel González
Iglesia de la Trinidad
C de la Trinidad
C de Valdeláguila
C de los Escuderos
Plaza Mayor
C del Cronista Lecea
C de la Infanta Isabel
C de Isabel la Católica
C Judería Vieja
C Marqués del Arco
C de San Valentín
C de Daoíz
To Hospital General (1.3km)

SPAIN

Sights

El Acueducto, an 894m-long engineering wonder that looks like an enormous comb of stone blocks plunged into the lower end of old Segovia, is the obvious starting point of a tour of town. This Roman aqueduct is 28m high and was built without a drop of mortar – just good old Roman know-how.

From here, the lively commercial streets Calle de Cervantes and Calle de Juan Bravo (together referred to as Calle Real) climb into the innards of Segovia. In the heart of town is the resplendent late-Gothic **Catedral** (☎ 921 46 22 05; Plaza Mayor; adult/concession €3/2, Sunday 9.30am-1.15pm free; ⏰ 9.30am-5.30pm Oct-Mar, 9.30am-6.30pm Apr-Sep), which was started in 1525 and completed a mere 200 years later. The Cristo del Consuelo chapel houses a magnificent Romanesque doorway preserved from the original church that burned down.

The fortified **Alcázar** (☎ 921 46 07 59; www.alcazardesegovia.com; Plaza de la Reina Victoria Eugenia; adult/concession €4/3, tower €2, EU citizens 3rd Tue of month free; ⏰ 10am-6pm Oct-Mar, 10am-7pm Apr-Sep) is perched dramatically on the edge of Segovia. Roman foundations are buried somewhere underneath the splendour, but what we see today is a 13th-century structure that burned down in 1862 and was subsequently rebuilt. Inside is a collection of armour and military gear, but even better are the ornate interiors of the reception rooms and the 360-degree views from the **Torre de Juan II**.

The most interesting of Segovia's churches, and one of the best preserved of its kind in Europe, is the 12-sided **Iglesia de la Vera Cruz** (☎ 921 43 14 75; Carretera de Zamarramala; admission €1.75; ⏰ 10.30am-1.30pm & 4-7pm Tue-Sun Apr-Aug, 10.30am-1.30pm & 4-6pm Tue-Sun Sep-Mar, closed Nov). Built in the 13th century by the Knights Templar and based on the Church of the Holy Sepulchre in Jerusalem, it long housed what was said to be a piece of the Vera Cruz (True Cross).

Sleeping

Pensión Ferri (☎ 921 46 09 57; Calle de Escuderos 10; s/d with shared bathroom €18/28) In a great position just off Plaza Mayor, the Ferri is the cheapest place to sleep in town. The rooms are simple but quaint and incorporate some of the building's original wood and brick work.

Hospedería La Gran Casa Mudéjar (☎ 921 46 62 50; www.lacasamudejar.com; Calle de la Infanta Isabel 8; d €60-160; ❄ 💻) Spread over two buildings, this place has been magnificently renovated, blending genuine, 15th-century Mudéjar ceilings in some rooms with modern amenities. In the newer wing, where the building dates from the 19th century, the rooms on the top floors have fine mountain views out over the rooftops of Segovia's old Jewish quarter.

Hotel Infanta Isabel (☎ 921 46 13 00; www.hotelinfantaisabel.com; Plaza Mayor 12; s €64-128, d €83-128; ❄) Right on Plaza Mayor, this charming hotel is a fine choice. The colonnaded building provides some hint to the hotel's interior, where most rooms have period furnishings and plenty of character. Rooms are large and those with balconies overlooking the Plaza Mayor are best, if a little noisy on weekends.

Hostería Ayala Berganza (☎ 921 46 04 48; www.partner-hotels.com; Calle de Carretas 5; d €115-150; ❄ 💻) This boutique hotel has elegant, individually designed rooms (all have tiled floors, beautiful bathrooms and rustic accents) within a restored 15th-century palace. It's not far from the aqueduct, but it's quiet and oozes style. Watch for internet offers as doubles can fall as low as €60.

Eating & Drinking

Late-night action is centred around Plaza Mayor (especially along Calle de los Escuderos and Calle la Infanta Isabel).

Casa Duque (☎ 921 46 24 87; www.restauranteduque.es; Calle de Cervantes 12; menú del día €21-39.50) They've been serving suckling pig (€19) here since the 1890s. Downstairs is the informal *cueva* (cave), where you can get tapas and yummy *cazuelas* (stews).

Mesón José María (☎ 921 46 11 11; www.rtejosemaria.com in Spanish; Calle del Cronista Lecea 11; meals €30-40) Close to Plaza Mayor, this respected *mesón* offers great tapas in the bar, and five dining rooms serving exquisite *cochinillo* (€21.35) and other local specialties.

Restaurante El Fogón Sefardí (☎ 921 46 62 50; www.lacasamudejar.com; Calle de Isabel La Católica 8; meals €30-40) This is one of the most original places in town, serving Sephardic cuisine (items like aubergine stuffed with vegetables, pine nuts and almonds) in a restaurant with an intimate patio and a splendid dining hall with original, 15th-century Mudéjar flourishes.

Mesón de Cándido (☎ 921 42 59 11; www.mesondecandido.es; Plaza del Azoguejo 5; meals €30-40) Set in a delightful 18th-century building in the shadow of the aqueduct, Mesón del Cándido is famous throughout Spain for its suckling pig and roast lamb.

Cueva de San Esteban (☎ 921 46 09 82; www.lacuevadesanesteban.com in Spanish; Calle Valdeláguila 15; meals €35; ⏲ 11am-midnight) One of the only restaurants in Segovia not devoted to suckling pig, this popular spot focuses on seasonal dishes, with a few seafood treats from Galicia.

La Tasquina (☎ 921 46 19 54; Calle de Valdeláguila 3; ⏲ 9pm-late) This wine bar draws crowds large enough to spill out onto the pavement nursing their good wines, *cavas* (sparkling wines) and cheeses.

Buddha Bar (Calle de los Escuderos 3; ⏲ 9pm-late) This bar has lounge music that can turn more towards house as the night wears on.

Getting There & Away

The **bus station** (☎ 92 142 77 07; Paseo Ezequiel González 12) is a 15-minute walk from the aqueduct. **La Sepulvedana** buses leave half-hourly from Madrid's Paseo de la Florida bus stop (€5.87, 1½ hours). There are also regular buses between Segovia and Ávila, Salamanca and Valladolid.

Up to nine normal trains run daily from Madrid to Segovia (two hours, one-way €5.90), leaving you at the main train station 2.5km from the aqueduct. The high-speed AVE (€9, 35 minutes) deposits you at the Segovia-Guiomar station, 5km from the aqueduct.

LEÓN

pop 135,100 / elev 527m

León's stand-out attraction is the cathedral, one of the most beautiful in Spain. By day, this pretty city rewards long exploratory strolls. By night, the city's large student population floods into the narrow streets and plazas of the city's picturesque old quarter, the Barrio Húmedo.

The **tourist office** (☎ 987 23 70 82; Plaza de la Regla; ⏲ 9am-2pm & 5-8pm Mon-Fri, 10am-2pm & 5-8pm Sat & Sun Oct-Jun, 9am-8pm daily Jul-Sep) is opposite the cathedral. For internet access, try **Locutorio La Rua** (☎ 987 21 99 94; Calle de Varillas 3; per 1/5 hr €2/5; ⏲ 9.30am-9.30pm Mon-Fri, 10.30am-2.30pm & 5.30-9.30pm Sat).

Sights

León's 13th-century **cathedral** (☎ 987 87 57 70; www.catedraldeleon.org in Spanish; admission free; ⏲ 8.30am-1.30pm & 4-7pm Mon-Sat, 8.30am-2.30pm & 5-7pm Sun Oct-Jun, 8.30am-1.30pm & 4-8pm Mon-Sat, 8.30am-2.30pm & 5-8pm Sun Jul-Sep) is a marvel of Gothic architecture. Beyond the lovely facade lies an extraordinary gallery of stained-glass windows. The kaleidoscope of coloured light is offset by the otherwise gloomy interior. There seems to be more glass than brick – 128 windows with a surface of 1800 sq metres in all. Inside, there's a **museum** (admission incl cloister €3.50; ⏲ 9.30am-1.30pm & 4-7pm Mon-Fri, 9.30am-1.30pm Sat Oct-Jun, 9.30am-1.30pm & 4-7.30pm Mon-Fri, to 7pm Sat Jul-Sep), entered through the church's charming **cloister** (admission €1).

Nearby, the **Real Basílica de San Isidoro** provides a stunning Romanesque counterpoint to the cathedral. Behind its magnificent **Puerta del Perdón** (the entrance door on the right), lies the **Panteón Real** (☎ 987 87 61 61; admission €4, Thu afternoon free; ⏲ 10am-1.30pm & 4-6.30pm Mon-Sat, 10am-1.30pm Sun Sep-Jun, 9am-8pm Mon-Sat, 9am-2pm Sun Jul & Aug) or royal burial place. Old Leónese royalty lies buried beneath a canopy of fine Romanesque frescoes.

Across town is the impressive **Hostal de San Marcos**, a former pilgrims' hospital that now houses a *parador* (luxurious state-owned hotel). The **Museo de León** (☎ 987 24 50 61; adult/student €0.60/free, Thu free; ⏲ 10am-2pm & 4-7pm Tue-Sat Oct-Jun, 10am-2pm & 5-8pm Tue-Sat Jul-Sep, 10am-2pm Sun all year) allows access to some parts of the building.

On a contemporary note, the **Museo de Arte Contemporáneo** (Musac; ☎ 987 09 00 00; www.musac.org.es; Avenida de los Reyes Leóneses 24; admission free; ⏲ 11am-8pm Tue-Thu, 11am-9pm Fri, 10am-9pm Sat & Sun) belongs to the new wave of innovative Spanish architecture. Some 37 shades of coloured glass adorn the facade. Although the museum has a growing permanent collection, it mostly houses temporary displays of cutting-edge Spanish and international art, photography, video installations and so on.

Sleeping & Eating

Hostal Bayón (☎ 987 23 14 46; Calle del Alcázar de Toledo 6; s/d with washbasin €15/28, with shower €25/35) The laid-back owner presides over cheerful, brightly-painted rooms with pine floors. You're surrounded by modern León, but just a five-minute walk from the Old Town.

Hostal Albany (☎ 987 26 46 00; www.albanyleon.com; Calle de la Paloma 13; s/d €35/50; 💻) The sort of place you'd expect to find in Barcelona or Madrid, Hostal Albany is a high-class *hostal* with a designer touch. Clean lines, plasma TVs, great bathrooms and cheerful colour schemes abound. Some rooms have partial cathedral views.

La Posada Regia (☎ 987 21 31 73; www.regialeon.com in Spanish; Calle de Regidores 9-11; s €55-65, d €90-120) A

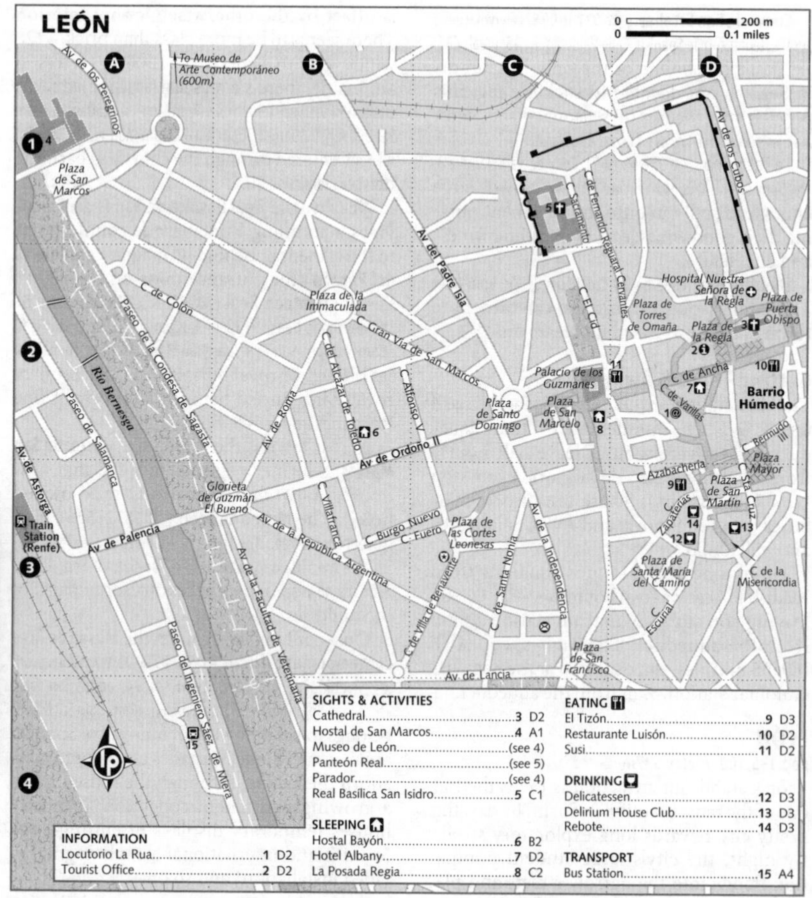

magnificently restored 14th-century building (wooden beams, exposed brick and understated antique furniture) offers individually-styled rooms, supremely comfortable beds and bathrooms and loads of character.

Restaurante Luisón (☎ 987 25 40 29; Plaza Puerta Obispo 16; menú del día €8, meals €15-20) Offhand waiters sling out hearty food that keeps the locals fortified during cold winters. You'll need to book ahead, especially at lunchtime when locals can't get enough of the local *botillo berciano*, a succulent pork dish, or *cocido leónes* (León-style chickpea stew).

Susi (☎ 987 27 39 96; Calle de López Castrillón 1; menú del día €12, meals €25-30; ⌚ closed dinner Sun) The service is attentive, the wine list long, and the menu in this gourmet haven has some dishes that will live in the memory – the *solomillo relleno con foie y datiles* (sirloin filled with foie gras and dates) stands out.

El Tizón (☎ 987 25 60 49; Plaza de San Martín 1; menú del día €13, meals €25-30; ⌚ lunch & dinner Mon-Wed, Fri & Sat, lunch Sun) The tapas are good here, but the small sit-down restaurant, with an abundant set lunch, is even better. House specialities include the local *embutidos*.

Drinking

The Barrio Húmedo's night-time epicentre is Plaza de San Martín and surrounding streets (especially Calle de Juan de Arfe and Calle de la Misericordia). A good night could begin at **Rebote** (Plaza de San Martín 9; ⌚ 8pm-1am), then move on to funky **Delicatessen** (Calle de Juan de

Arfe 10; 10pm-3am Wed-Sat) before ending up at the **Delirium House Club** (Calle de la Misericordia 9; 11pm-5am Thu-Sat).

Getting There & Away

ALSA has numerous daily buses from the bus station on Paseo del Ingeniero Sáez de Miera to Madrid (€20.80, 3½ hours) and Burgos, Oviedo (€8.10, 1½ hours) and Valladolid (€8.50, two hours).

Regular daily trains travel to Valladolid (from €9.60, two hours), Burgos (from €17.90, two hours), Oviedo (from €7.15, two hours), Madrid (from €22.40, 4¼ hours) and Barcelona (from €43.20, 10 hours).

BURGOS

pop 174,100 / elev 861m

The legendary warrior El Cid was born just outside Burgos and is buried in its magnificent cathedral. Perhaps this is where the city's noble atmosphere comes from. The city's extraordinary Gothic cathedral is one of Spain's glittering jewels. The grey-stone architecture, fortifying cuisine and a climate of extremes can lend Burgos a chilly edge, but below the Spartan surface lies vibrant nightlife, good restaurants and, when the sun's shining, pretty streetscapes.

Information

Ciber-Café Cabaret (Calle de la Puebla 21; per hr from €2.50; noon-1am Sun-Thu, 7pm-4am Fri & Sat)

Municipal tourist office (947 28 88 74; www.aytoburgos.es in Spanish; Plaza del Rey Fernando 2; 10am-2pm & 4.30-7.30pm Mon-Fri, 10am-1.30pm & 4-7.30pm Sat & Sun mid-Sep–Jun, 10am-8pm daily Jul–mid-Sep)

Regional tourist office (947 20 31 25; www.turismocastillayleon.com; Plaza Alonso Martínez 7; 9am-2pm & 5-8pm daily mid-Sep–Jun, 9am-8pm Sun-Thu, 9am-9pm Fri & Sat Jul–mid-Sep)

Sights

The World Heritage–listed **Catedral** (947 20 47 12; Plaza del Rey Fernando; adult/senior/pilgrim & student/child €4/3/2.50/1; 9.30am-7.30pm 19 Mar-Oct, 10am-7pm Nov-18 Mar) is a masterpiece. Largely completed in 40 years from 1221, bits and pieces were added over the following centuries. The main altar is an overwhelming piece of gold-encrusted extravagance, while directly beneath the star-vaulted central dome lies the **tomb of El Cid**. Another highlight is the **Escalera Dorada** (Gilded Stairway; 1520) on the cathedral's northwestern flank, the handiwork of Diego de Siloé.

The **Monasterio de las Huelgas** (947 20 16 30; guided tours adult/student €5/4, Wed free; 10am-1pm & 3.45-5.30pm Tue-Sat, 10.30am-2pm Sun) was founded in 1187 by Eleanor of Aquitaine and is still home to Cistercian nuns. Guided tours (in Spanish) are compulsory and leave the ticket office every 50 minutes or so. From the cathedral, it's a pleasant 30-minute walk west along the southern bank of the Río Arlanzón.

Sleeping & Eating

Pensión Peña (/fax 947 20 63 23; Calle de la Puebla 18; s/d with shared bathroom from €20/26) This impeccable place with a motherly owner has rooms with delightful individual touches, such as hand-painted washbasins. The central location is a plus.

Hotel Norte y Londres (947 26 41 25; www.hotelnorteylondres.com; Plaza de Alonso Martínez 10; s €46-75, d €55-120;) Set in a former 16th-century palace and with understated period charm, this fine hotel promises spacious rooms with antique furnishings, polished wooden floors and pretty balconies.

Cervecería Morito (947 26 75 55; Calle de la Sombrerería; 1-3.30pm & 7.30pm-midnight) This place is the king of Burgos tapas bars and its two floors are usually full. A typical order is *alpargata* (lashings of cured ham with bread, tomato and olive oil; €2.70).

La Cabaña Arandino (Calle de la Sombrerería; 1-3.30pm & 7-11pm) Opposite Cervecería Morito, this place also does good tapas; locals love the *tigres* (mussels with spicy sauce).

La Fabula (947 26 30 92; www.lafavorita-taberna.com; Calle de la Puebla 18; meals €25-30) A good place for nouveau Castilian cuisine, La Fabula offers slimmed-down rice and fish dishes in a light, modern dining room filled with classical music. Rice, fish and seafood dominate the menu.

Casa Ojeda (947 20 90 52; www.grupojeda.com in Spanish; Calle de Vitoria 5; meals €30-40; lunch & dinner Mon-Sat, lunch Sun) This Burgos institution, sheathed in dark wood, is one of the best places to try *cordero asado* (€20.55).

Getting There & Away

From Burgos' **bus station** (Calle de Miranda 4), **ALSA** runs regular buses to Madrid (€15.70, 2¾ hours), Vitoria (€7.40, 1½ hours), Bilbao (€11.20, two hours), San Sebastián (€14.90,

3½ hours), León (€13.40, 3¼ hours) and Valladolid (€8.20, two hours).

Burgos is connected by train with Madrid (from €23.10, four hours, up to seven daily), Bilbao (from €16.60, three hours, five daily), León (from €17.90, two hours, four daily), Valladolid (from €8.20, 1¼ hours, up to 13 daily) and Salamanca (from €20.10, 2½ hours, three daily).

CASTILLA-LA MANCHA

Known as the stomping ground of Don Quijote and Sancho Panza, Castilla-La Mancha conjures up images of lonely windmills, medieval castles and bleak, treeless plains. The characters of Miguel de Cervantes provide the literary context, but the richly historic cities of Toledo and Cuenca are the most compelling reasons to visit.

TOLEDO

pop 55,100 / elev 655m

Toledo is a corker of a city. Commanding a hill rising above the Tajo River, it's crammed with monuments that attest to the waves of conquerors and communities – Roman, Visigoth, Jewish, Muslim and Christian – who have called the city home during its turbulent history. It's one of the country's major tourist attractions.

Information

Locutorio Santo Tomé (☎ 925 21 65 38; Calle de Santo Tomé 1; per hr €2; 🕒 11am-10.30pm) Internet access.
Main tourist office (☎ 925 25 40 30; www.toledo-turismo.com; Plaza del Ayuntamiento s/n; 🕒 10.30am-2.30pm Mon, 10.30am-2.30pm & 4.30-7pm Tue-Sun)
Tourist office (☎ 925 22 08 43; fax 925 25 26 48; Puerta Nueva de Bisagra s/n; 🕒 9am-6pm Mon-Fri, 9am-7pm Sat, 9am-3pm Sun)

Sights

The **Catedral** (adult/under 12yr €7/free; 🕒 10.30am-6.30pm Mon-Sat, 2-6.30pm Sun) is Toledo's major landmark. There's loads to see within its hefty stone walls, including stained-glass windows, tombs of kings and art in the sacristy by the likes of El Greco, Zurbarán, Crespi, Titian, Rubens and Velázquez. Behind the main altar lies a mesmerising piece of 18th-century Churrigueresque baroque, the **Transparente** which also provides welcome light. Look out for the **Custodia de Arfe**, by the celebrated 16th-century goldsmith Enrique de Arfe. With 18kg of pure gold and 183kg of silver, this 16th-century conceit bristles with some 260 statuettes.

The **Museo de Santa Cruz** (☎ 925 22 10 36; Calle de Cervantes 3; admission free; 🕒 10am-6pm Mon-Sat, 10am-2pm Sun) contains a large collection of furniture, faded tapestries and paintings. Upstairs is an impressive collection of El Greco's works, including the masterpiece *La Asunción de la Virgen* (Assumption of the Virgin).

In the southwestern part of the old city, the queues outside an otherwise unremarkable church, the **Iglesia de Santo Tomé** (☎ 925 25 60 98; www.santotome.org; Plaza del Conde; admission €1.90; 🕒 10am-6pm), betray the presence of El Greco's masterpiece *El Entierro del Conde de Orgaz* (The Burial of the Count of Orgaz).

The **Museo Sefardi** (☎ 925 22 36 65; www.museosefardi.net in Spanish; Calle Samuel Leví s/n; adult/under 12yr/12-25yr €2.40/free/1.20, audioguide €3; 🕒 10am-6pm Tue-Sat, 10am-2pm Sun) is housed in the beautiful 14th-century **Sinagoga del Tránsito**. Toledo's other synagogue, the nearby **Santa María La Blanca** (☎ 925 22 72 57; Calle de los Reyes Católicos 4; admission €2.30; 🕒 10am-6pm), dates back to the beginning of the 13th century. It's characterised by the horseshoe arches that delineate the five naves – classic Almohad architecture.

A little further northwest is **San Juan de los Reyes** (☎ 925 22 38 02; Calle San Juan de los Reyes 2; admission €1.90; 🕒 10am-6pm), a Franciscan monastery and church founded by Fernando and Isabel. Throughout the church and cloister, their coat of arms dominates, and the chains of Christian prisoners liberated in Granada in 1492 dangle from the walls. The late Flemish Gothic style is enhanced with lavish Isabelline ornament and counterbalanced by unmistakable Mudéjar decoration, especially in the cloister.

The **Alcázar** fort, largely destroyed by Republican forces in 1936 and rebuilt under Franco, is closed for renovation; it should be open by the time you read this.

Sleeping

Accommodation is often full, especially from Easter to September.

HI Albergue Juvenil en San Servando (☎ 925 22 45 54; ralberguesto@jccm.es; dm under/over 26yr €9.50/12) This youth hostel has a grand setting in a castle, no less, with fine views, plus an attractive interior with beamed ceilings in the communal room and modern sleeping quarters.

La Posada de Zocodover (☎ 925 25 58 14; Calle Cordonerías 6; r €40) There are just seven clean

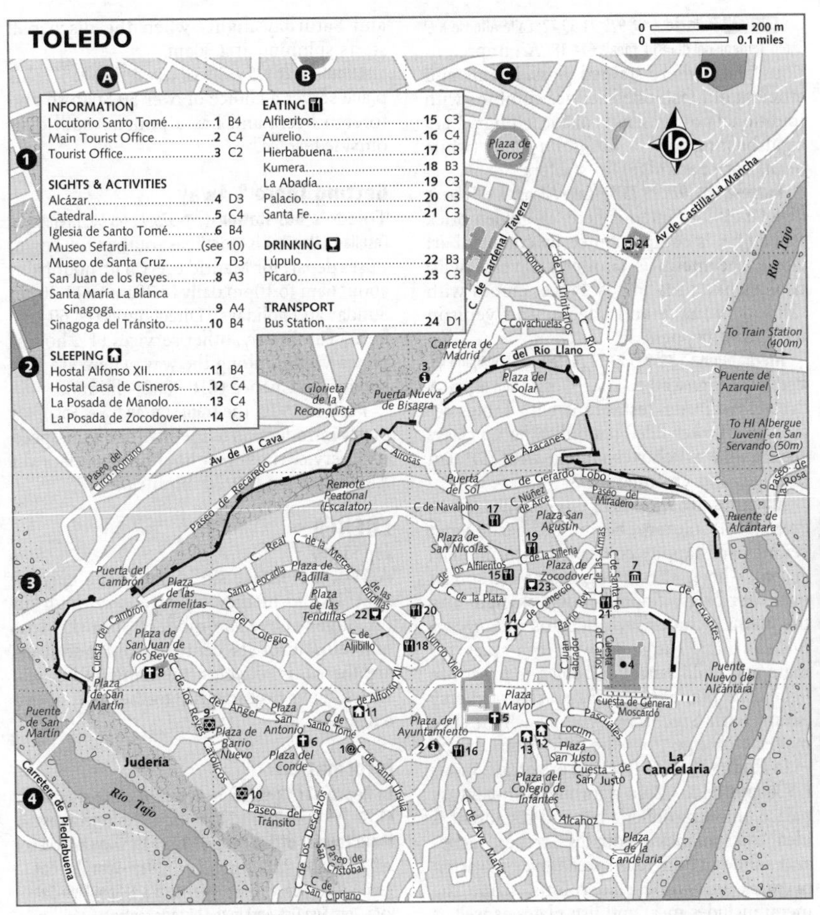

and acceptable rooms at this superbly located place near the city's main square – which can equal earplugs at weekends.

La Posada de Manolo (☎ 925 28 22 50; www.laposadademanolo.com; Calle de Sixto Ramón Parro 8; s/d incl breakfast from €42/66) This boutique-style hotel has themed each floor with furnishings and decor reflecting one of the three cultures of Toledo. There are stunning views of the Old Town from the terrace.

our pick Hostal Casa de Cisneros (☎ 925 22 88 28; www.hostal-casa-de-cisneros.com; Calle Cardenal Cisneros; s/d €50/80; ❄) Across from the cathedral, this seductive *hostal* is built on the site of an 11th-century Muslim palace, parts of which can be spied via a glass porthole in the lobby floor. In comparison, this building is a 16th-century youngster with pretty stone-and-wood-beamed rooms.

Hostal Alfonso XII (☎ 925 25 25 09; www.hostal-alfonso12.com; Calle de Alfonso XII; r €65; ❄) A gingerbread cottage of a place with original beams, terracotta tiles and stylish, albeit small, rooms decorated with impeccable taste.

Eating

Santa Fe (☎ 670 65 42 16; Calle Santa Fe 6; menú del día €8, tapas €2) You can eat here better and for half the price than the restaurants on nearby Zocodover. Sit down in the half-tiled dining room to enjoy tapas, tortilla with green pepper, homemade paella and *pollo al ajillo* (chicken in tomato and garlic sauce).

our pick Palacio (☎ 925 21 59 72; Calle Alfonso X el Sabio 3; menú del día €14, meals €14-18) An unpretentious place where stained glass, beams and efficient old-fashioned service combine with traditional no-nonsense cuisine. Hungry? Try a gut-busting bowl of *judias con perdiz* (white beans with partridge) for starters.

Kumera (☎ 925 25 75 53; Calle Alfonso X el Sabio 2; meals €18-25) The interior here, all golden brick and stone, is complimented by colourful art work; the menu is similarly diverse with choices like tuna in soy sauce, crepes with salmon, spinach and cheese, and venison with roast peppers.

Hierbabuena (☎ 925 22 39 24; Calle de Navalpino 45; meals €18-25, menú del día €35; closed Sun night) A dress-for-dinner restaurant with tables set around a flower-filled patio dishing up classy cuisine like artichokes stuffed with Catalan sausages and creamed leeks.

Alfileritos (☎ 925 23 96 25; Calle de los Alfileritos 24; meals €18-25) Columns, beams and barrel vault ceilings are happily combined with modern art work here. The dining rooms are spread over four bright floors below a skylight and the menu includes such delights as *langostinos con mojo* (large prawns in a spicy tomato and chilli sauce) and *sopa de fresas con helado de pimiento de Sichuan* (strawberry 'soup' with Szechuan pepper) which sure makes a change from the ubiquitous flan.

La Abadía (☎ 925 25 11 40; Plaza de San Nicolás 3; meals €25-30, menú del día €28) In a former 16th-century palace, this atmospheric bar and restaurant is ideal for romancing couples. Arches, niches and subtle lighting are spread over a warren of brick-and-stone clad rooms, while the menu includes meat and fish plates as well as lightweight dishes such as goat's cheese salad with pumpkin and sunflower seeds – perfect for small (distracted) appetites.

Casa Aurelio (☎ 925 22 13 92; Plaza del Ayuntamiento 4; meals from €35; closed Sun night) The three restaurants under this name are among the best of Toledo's expensive restaurants (the other locations are Calle de la Sinagoga 1 and 6). Game, fresh produce and traditional Toledan dishes are prepared with panache.

Drinking

Pícaro (☎ 925 22 13 01; Calle de las Cadenas 6) A popular cafe-*teatro* (theatre) serving an eclectic range of *copas* (drinks). From Monday to Thursday it's perfect for a quiet beverage, while the weekend ups the pace on Friday and Saturday nights when the disco ball starts spinning at 2.30am.

Lúpulo (☎ 925 25 71 36; Calle de Aljibillo 5) This place serves a choice of over 50 Spanish and foreign beers and has a popular spill-over outside terrace.

Getting There & Away

Toledo's **bus station** (☎ 925 21 58 50; Avenida de Castilla-La Mancha) is northeast of the Old Town. Buses depart for Madrid every half-hour from about 6am to 10pm daily (8.30am to 11.30pm Sunday and holidays). Direct buses (€4.60, one hour) run hourly; other services (1½ hours) go via villages along the way. There are also services to Cuenca (€10.90, 2¼ hours).

Built in 1920, the **train station** (Paseo Rosa) is a pretty introduction to the city. The high-speed AVE service runs every hour or so to Madrid's Atocha station (€9, 30 minutes).

CUENCA

pop 53,000

A World Heritage site, Cuenca is a curious spot. Its old medieval centre is set high up on ridges above the modern sprawl. Most emblematic of its centuries-old buildings are the *casas colgadas*, the hanging houses, which cling precariously to the cliffs above a deep gorge.

Information

La Repro 11 (☎ 969 23 14 40; Fray Luis de León 16; per hr €1.20; 10am-2pm & 5-8pm Mon-Sat) Internet access.

Main tourist office (☎ 969 32 31 19; www.aytocuenca.org in Spanish; Plaza Mayor s/n; 9am-9pm Mon-Sat, 9am-2.30pm Sun May-Sep, 9am-2pm & 5-8pm Mon-Sat, 9am-2pm Sun Oct-Apr) In the historic centre.

Tourist office (☎ 969 23 58 15; Plaza Hispanidad; 10am-2pm & 5-8pm Mon-Thu, 10am-8pm Fri-Sun) In the new town.

Sights & Activities

Cuenca's 16th-century **casas colgadas** seem to tumble over a clifftop, their balconies projecting out over the gorge. To view them properly, walk over the **Puente San Pablo** (1902), an iron footbridge that crosses the ravine, or walk to the northernmost tip of the Old Town where a *mirador* offers unparalleled views. Within one is the **Museo de Arte Abstracto Español** (Museum of Abstract Art; ☎ 969 21 29 83; www.march.es; adult/under 12yr/12-25yr €3/free/1.50; 11am-2pm & 4-6pm Tue-Fri, 11am-2pm & 4-8pm Sat, 11am-2.30pm Sun), whose constantly evolving displays include works by Eduardo Chillida, Manuel Millares, Pablo Palazuelo, Eusebio Sempere and Antoni Tápies. Don't miss Sempere's extraordinary landscapes of Castilla-La Mancha.

Another innovative museum is the **Museo de Las Ciencias** (Science Museum; ☎ 969 24 03 20; Plaza de la Merced; adult/child €1.20/free, weekends free; 10am-2pm & 4-8pm Tue-Sat, 10am-2pm Sun), where displays range from a time machine to plenty of interactive gadgets to keep the kiddies happy, as well as a **planetarium** (admission €1.20).

The **Museo de Cuenca** (☎ 969 21 30 69; Calle del Obispo Valero 6; adult/under 12yr/12-25yr €1.20/free/0.60; 10am-2pm & 4-7pm Tue-Sat, 11am-2pm Sun) has exceptionally well laid-out and documented (in Spanish) exhibits, ranging from the Bronze Age to the 18th century.

The **Catedral** (☎ 96 922 46 26; Plaza Mayor; admission €2; 10am-2pm & 4-6pm Mon-Fri, 10am-7pm Sat, 10am-6.30pm Sun) is an odd pastiche of 16th-century Gothic experimentation and 20th-century restoration. The stained-glass windows look like they would be more at home in the abstract-art museum. Look out for the Chapter House and Deep Chapel.

Sleeping & Eating

Pensión Central (☎ 969 21 15 11; Calle de Alonso Chirino 7; s/d/tr with shared bathroom €14/24/31) This is a cheap sleep in a clean and tidy place in the new town. Rooms are adequate and clean with TV and washbasin.

Pensión La Tabanqueta (☎ 969 21 12 90; Calle de Trabuco 13; s/d with shared bathroom €15/30) Room prices in this listed building are the best you'll find in the historic centre and some rooms have five-star views of Río Júcar. This place is plain but charming, and there's a popular bar-restaurant attached.

Posada de San José (☎ 969 21 13 00; www.posadasanjose.com; Ronda de Julián Romero 4; s/d with shared bathroom from €25/38) A 17th-century former choir school, this place retains an extraordinary monastic charm with its crumbling portal, uneven floors and original tiles. Enjoy spectacular views and fresh flowers in the room. Their restaurant is recommended. Rooms with a view cost from €55 to €86.

Posada Huécar (☎ 969 21 42 01; www.posadahuecar.com; Paseo del Huécar 3; s/d €29/49;) Feel luxurious on a tight budget; located squarely between the old and new towns, this upbeat place has large rooms with terracotta tiles, rustic furnishings, river views and bicycles for rent.

Leonor de Aquitania Hotel (☎ 969 23 10 00; www.hotelleonordeaquitania.com; Calle de San Pedro 60; s/d incl breakfast €77/99;) In an 18th-century house, this is a well-aged classic although the floral theme in the rooms may be a touch fussy for some of the chaps. Ask for rooms 105 or 106 with unequalled views of the gorge. The restaurant is excellent.

our pick **La Bodeguilla de Basilio** (☎ 969 23 52 74; Calle Fray Luis de León 3; raciones €10-13) Arrive here with an appetite as you are presented with a complimentary plate of tapas when you order a drink – typical freebies are a combo of quail eggs, ham, fried potatoes, lettuce hearts and courgettes. The restaurant out back has more good tucker.

Restaurante San Nicolás (☎ 969 24 05 19; Calle de San Pedro 15; menú del día €16, meals €25-35) Another fine establishment for solid Castilian-Manchegan food, although the service can be sniffy. The braised wild boar in a fennel and thyme sauce (€21.75) is particularly good.

Getting There & Away

Up to nine buses daily serve Madrid (€10.50, two hours). Other bus services include Valencia (€11.95, 2½ hours, up to three daily) and Toledo (€10.90, 2¼ hours, one or two daily).

Cuenca lies on the train line connecting Madrid and Valencia. Trains to Madrid's Atocha station depart six times on weekdays and four times on weekends (€10.65, 2½ hours). Trains to Valencia leave four times daily (€11.75, 3¼ hours).

CATALONIA

Home to stylish Barcelona, ancient Tarragona, romantic Girona, and countless alluring destinations along the coast, in the Pyrenees and in the rural interior, Catalonia (Catalunya in Catalan, Cataluña in Castilian) is a treasure box waiting to be opened. A proud, triangular piece of territory in the northeast corner of the peninsula, Catalonia is a distinct region rich with possibilities.

BARCELONA

pop 1.59 million

Barcelona has two millennia of history but is a forward-thinking place, always on the cutting edge of art, design and cuisine. Whether you explore its medieval palaces and plazas,

BARCELONA IN TWO DAYS

Be sure to see Gaudí's masterpieces: **La Sagrada Família** (p784), **La Pedrera** (p784) and **Casa Batlló** (p784) in L'Eixample. Stroll down **Passeig de Gràcia** (p789) to reach Plaça de Catalunya and the old quarter. Head down **La Rambla** (opposite) and duck into the **Barri Gòtic** (opposite) for a glimpse of the cathedral and a wander of the city's ancient, twisting lanes.

On day two, visit **Museu Picasso** (opposite) and the **Església de Santa Maria del Mar** (p783) in El Born. Stop off for tapas and wine at **La Vinya del Senyor** (p788) before heading to the **waterfront** (p783). End the day with a meal in **La Barceloneta** (p787).

gawk at the Modernista masterpieces, shop for designer duds along its bustling boulevards, sample its exciting nightlife, or just soak up the sun on the beaches, you'll find it hard not to fall in love with this vibrant city.

Barcelona is a master at reinventing itself. It has morphed from a wannabe Roman town into a prosperous medieval centre, to Republican capital during the civil war, and finally to its modern cosmopolitan self. The effects of so many changes can be seen on the streets. Vivid splashes of Romanesque, Gothic, Modernista and contemporary works pop up in the most unexpected corners of the city.

As much as the city is a visual feast, it will also lead you into culinary temptation. Anything from traditional Catalan cooking through the latest in avant-garde new Spanish cuisine will have your appetite in overdrive. Digestion comes easily in the phalanxes of bars and clubs.

Orientation

Central Plaça de Catalunya marks the divide between historic and modern Barcelona. From here, the long pedestrian boulevard La Rambla shoots southeast to the sea, with the busy Old Town Barri Gòtic (Gothic Quarter) and El Raval districts hugging it on either side. To the northwest of the plaza spreads L'Eixample, the vast gridlike district, laced with Modernista marvels, endless shopping options and plenty of restaurants and bars mixed in with turn-of-the-century apartment and office blocks.

Information

BOOKSHOPS

Altaïr (Map p782; ☎ 93 342 71 71; www.altair.es; Gran Via de les Corts Catalanes 616; Ⓜ Universitat) All travel books.

Casa del Llibre (Map pp780-1; ☎ 902 026407; www.casadellibro.com; Passeig de Gràcia 62; Ⓜ Passeig de Gràcia) Good English section.

EMERGENCY

Guardia Urbana (City Police; Map p782; ☎ 092; La Rambla 43; Ⓜ Liceu)

Mossos d'Esquadra (Catalan police; Map pp780-1; ☎ 088; Carrer Nou de la Rambla 80; Ⓜ Liceu)

INTERNET ACCESS

Bornet (Map p782; ☎ 93 268 15 07; www.bornet-bcn.com; Carrer de Barra de Ferro 3; per 1/10hr €2.80/20; 🕑 10am-11pm Mon-Fri, noon-11pm Sat & Sun & holidays) A cool little internet centre-cum-art gallery.

easyInternetcafé (Map p782; www.easyeverything.com; La Rambla 31; per hr €2.50; 🕑 8am-2.30am)

LAUNDRY

Lavaxpress (Map p782; www.lavaxpres.com; Carrer de Ferlandina 34; 🕑 8am-11pm) An 8kg wash costs €3.50, drying is €3.50 for 30 minutes. It has other branches around town.

MEDICAL SERVICES

24-hour Pharmacy La Rambla 98 (Map p782; Ⓜ Liceu); Passeig de Gràcia 26 (Map pp780-1; Ⓜ Passeig de Gràcia). These are two of several 24-hour pharmacies in the city.

Hospital Clínic (Map pp780-1; ☎ 93 227 54 00; www.hospitalclinic.org; Carrer Villarroel 170; Ⓜ Hospital Clínic) Modern hospital with good services.

MONEY

Banks abounds in Barcelona, many with ATMs, including several around Plaça de Catalunya, on La Rambla and on Plaça de Sant Jaume in the Barri Gòtic.

The foreign-exchange offices that you see along La Rambla and elsewhere are open for longer hours than banks but generally offer poorer rates. **Interchange** (Amex; Map p782; ☎ 93 342 73 11; La Rambla dels Caputxins 74; 🕑 9am-10.30pm) represents American Express.

POST

Main post office (Map p782; Plaça d'Antoni López; 🕑 8.30am-10pm Mon-Sat, noon-10pm Sun; Ⓜ Barceloneta)

SPAIN

TOURIST INFORMATION

Main tourist office (Map p782; ☎ 93 285 38 32; www.barcelonaturisme.com; Plaça de Catalunya 17-S underground; 9am-9pm; M Catalunya)

Dangers & Annoyances

Purse snatching and pickpocketing are major problems, especially around Plaça de Catalunya, La Rambla and Plaça Reial. See p845 for common scams.

Sights & Activities

LA RAMBLA

Spain's most famous boulevard, the part-pedestrianised **La Rambla**, explodes with life. Stretching from **Plaça de Catalunya** to the waterfront, it's lined with street artists, news stands and vendors selling everything from mice to magnolias.

The colourful **Mercat de la Boquería** (Map p782; La Rambla; 8am-8pm Mon-Sat; M Liceu), a fresh food market with a Modernista entrance, is one of La Rambla's highlights. Nearby, stop for a tour of the **Gran Teatre del Liceu** (Map p782; ☎ 93 485 99 00; www.liceubarcelona.com; La Rambla dels Caputxins 51-59; admission with/without guide €8.50/4; guided tour 10am, unguided visits 11.30am, noon, 12.30pm & 1pm; M Liceu), the city's fabulous opera house.

Also stop at the **Plaça Reial**, a grand 19th-century square surrounded by arcades lined with restaurants and bars. At the waterfront end of La Rambla stands the **Monument a Colom** (Map pp780-1; ☎ 93 302 52 24; Plaça del Portal de la Pau; lift adult/under 4yr/senior & 4-12yr €2.50/free/1.50; 9am-8.30pm Jun-Sep, 10am-6.30pm Oct-May; M Drassanes), a statue of Columbus atop a tall pedestal. A small lift will take you to the top for panoramic views.

Just west of La Rambla is the **Museu Marítim** (Map pp780-1; ☎ 93 342 99 20; www.museumaritimbarcelona.org; Avinguda de les Drassanes; adult/senior & student €6.50/3.25; 10am-8pm; M Drassanes). Housed in the city's once mighty medieval shipyards, a gorgeous Gothic creation, the museum takes an in-depth look at Catalonia's seafaring past. The full-scale replica of Don Juan of Austria's royal galley from the Battle of Lepanto is the highlight.

BARRI GÒTIC

Barcelona's Gothic **Catedral** (Map p782; ☎ 93 342 82 60; Plaça de la Seu; admission free, special visit €5; 8am-12.45pm & 5.15-8pm, special visit 1-5pm Mon-Sat, 2-5pm Sun & holidays; M Jaume I) was built on top of the ruins of an 11th-century Romanesque church. The facade is a neo-Gothic addition tacked on in the 19th century. Highlights include the cool cloister, the crypt tomb of martyr Santa Eulàlia (one of Barcelona's two patron saints), the choir stalls (€2.20), the lift to the rooftop (€2.20) and the modest art collection in the **Sala Capitular** (chapterhouse; admission €2). You only pay the individual prices if you visit outside the special visiting hours.

Not far from the cathedral is pretty **Plaça del Rei** and the fascinating **Museu d'Història de la Ciutat** (Map p782; ☎ 93 256 21 00; www.museuhistoria.bcn.cat; Carrer del Veguer; adult/senior & student €6/4; 10am-2pm & 4-7pm Tue-Sat, 10am-3pm Sun; M Jaume I), where you can visit a 4000-sq-metre excavated site of Roman Barcelona under the plaza. The museum encompasses historic buildings including the **Palau Reial Major** (Main Royal Palace), once a residence of the kings of Catalonia and Aragón, and its **Saló del Tinell** (Great Hall). In summer, outdoor concerts are often held in Plaça del Rei.

EL RAVAL

To the west of La Rambla is El Raval district, a once-seedy, now-funky area overflowing with cool bars and shops. Visit the **Museu d'Art Contemporani de Barcelona** (Macba; Map p782; ☎ 93 412 08 10; www.macba.es; Plaça dels Àngels 1; adult/concession €7.50/6, Wed €3.50; 11am-8pm Mon & Wed, 11am-midnight Thu & Fri, 10am-8pm Sat, 10am-3pm Sun & holidays late Jun–late-Sep, 11am-7.30pm Mon & Wed-Fri, 10am-8pm Sat, 10am-3pm Sun & holidays late Sep-May; M Universitat), which has an impressive collection of international contemporary art.

LA RIBERA

In medieval days La Ribera was a stone's throw from the Mediterranean and the heart of Barcelona's foreign trade. Down the years, land was later filled in and the city expanded out into the sea. Home to Barcelona's bustling textile industry and to its wealthy merchants, La Ribera was the city's most prosperous quarter. Now it's a trendy district full of boutiques, restaurants and bars.

A series of palaces where some of those wealthy merchants lived now house the **Museu Picasso** (Map p782; ☎ 93 256 30 00; www.museupicasso.bcn.es; Carrer de Montcada 15-23; adult/senior & child under 16/student €9/free/3, temporary exhibitions adult €5.80, 1st Sun of month free; 10am-8pm Tue-Sun & holidays; M Jaume I), home to more than 3000 Picassos, most from early in the artist's career. This

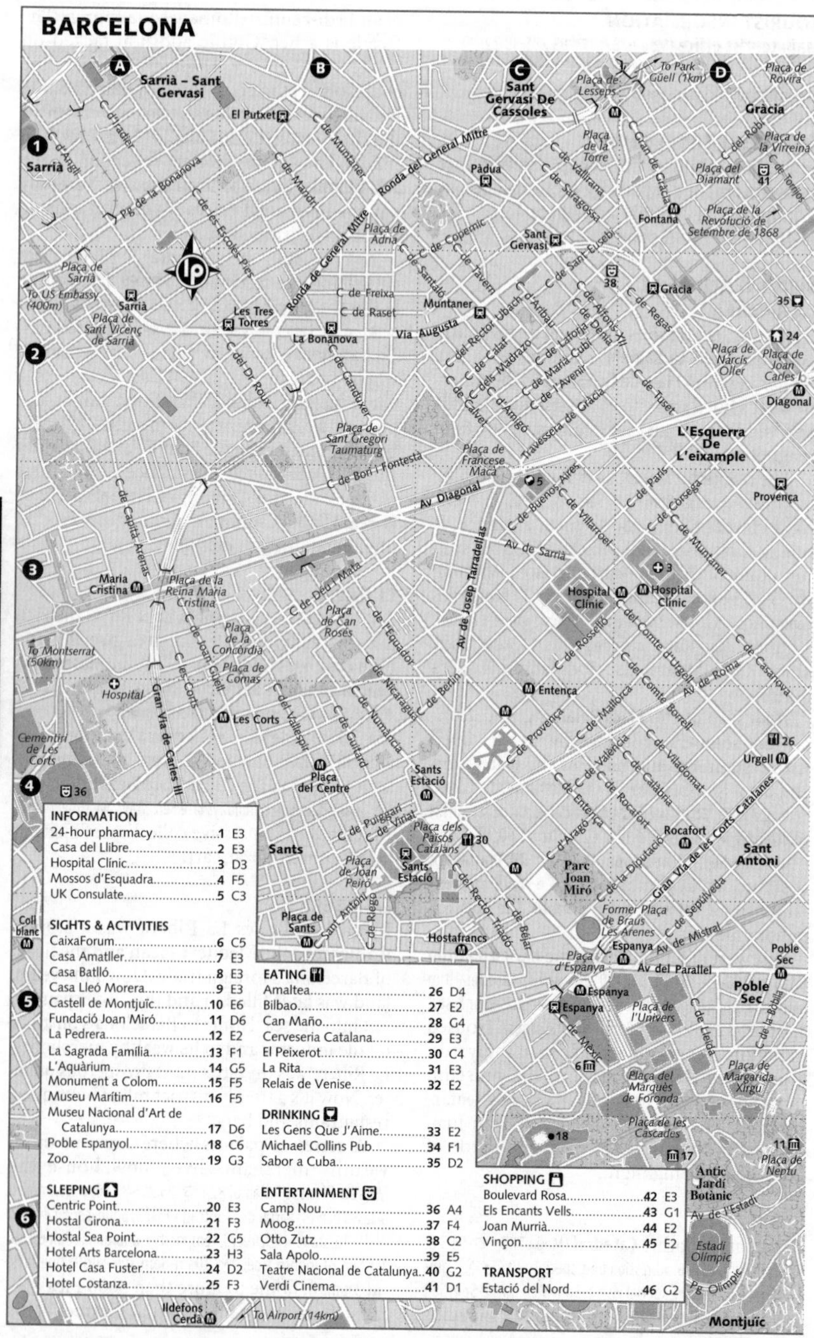
BARCELONA
Sarrià – Sant Gervasi
Sant Gervasi De Cassoles
Gràcia
Sarrià
El Putxet
Pàdua
Plaça de Lesseps
To Park Güell (1km)
Plaça de Rovira
Plaça de la Torre
Plaça del Diamant
Plaça de la Virreina
Fontana
Plaça de la Revolució de Setembre de 1868
Sant Gervasi
Ronda del General Mitre
Ronda de General Mitre
Plaça de Adrià
Pg de la Bonanova
C de les Escoles Pies
C d'Iradier
C d'Anglí
C de Muntaner
C de Mandri
C de Copèrnic
C de Santaló
C de Tavern
C de Vallirana
C de Saragossa
C de Sant Eusebi
Gran de Gràcia
C del Robí
C de Torrijos
Plaça de Sarrià
To US Embassy (400m)
Plaça de Sant Vicenç de Sarrià
Les Tres Torres
La Bonanova
C de Freixa
C de Raset
Muntaner
Via Augusta
Gràcia
Plaça de Narcís Oller
Plaça de Joan Carles I
Diagonal
C del Dr Roux
C de Ganduxer
C del Rector Ubach
C de Calaf
C dels Madrazo
C de Calvet
C d'Amigó
C d'Aribau
C de Laforja
C de Maria Cubí
C de l'Avenir
C de Dènia
C d'Alfons XII
C de Regàs
C de Tuset
Travessera de Gràcia
Plaça de Sant Gregori Taumaturg
Plaça de Francesc Macià
L'Esquerra De L'eixample
C de Bori i Fontestà
Av Diagonal
C de Buenos Aires
C de Villarroel
C de París
C de Còrsega
C de Muntaner
Provença
C de Capità Arenas
Av de Sarrià
Av de Josep Tarradellas
Maria Cristina
Plaça de la Reina Maria Cristina
C de Déu i Mata
Plaça de Can Rosés
Hospital Clínic
C del Comte d'Urgell
C de Rosselló
C de Casanova
C de Joan Güell
Plaça de la Concòrdia
Plaça de Comas
C de l'Equador
C de Nicaragua
C de Berlín
Av de Roma
C del Comte Borrell
To Montserrat (50km)
Hospital
Gran Via de Carles III
C les Corts
Les Corts
C del Vallespir
C de Guitard
C de Numància
Entença
C de Provença
C de Mallorca
C de Viladomat
Cementiri de Les Corts
Plaça del Centre
Sants Estació
C de València
C de Calàbria
Urgell
C d'Entença
C de Rocafort
Gran Via de les Corts Catalanes
C de Puiggarí
C de Viriat
Plaça dels Països Catalans
Sants
Plaça de Joan Peiró
C d'Aragó
Parc Joan Miró
C de la Diputació
Rocafort
Sant Antoni
C del Rector Triadó
C de Béjar
C de Sepúlveda
Former Plaça de Braus Les Arenes
Coll blanc
Plaça de Sants
C de Sant Antoni
C de Riego
Hostafrancs
Espanya
Av de Mistral
Poble Sec
Plaça d'Espanya
Av del Paral·lel
Plaça de l'Univers
C de Mèxic
C de Lleida
C de la Bobila
Plaça del Marquès de Foronda
Plaça de Margarida Xirgu
Plaça de les Cascades
Plaça de Neptú
Antic Jardí Botànic
Av de l'Estadi
Estadi Olímpic
Pg Olímpic
Montjuïc
Ildefons Cerdà
To Airport (14km)
INFORMATION
24-hour pharmacy 1 E3
Casa del Llibre 2 E3
Hospital Clínic 3 D3
Mossos d'Esquadra 4 F5
UK Consulate 5 C3
SIGHTS & ACTIVITIES
CaixaForum 6 C5
Casa Amatller 7 E3
Casa Batlló 8 E3
Casa Lleó Morera 9 E3
Castell de Montjuïc 10 E6
Fundació Joan Miró 11 D6
La Pedrera 12 E2
La Sagrada Família 13 F1
L'Aquàrium 14 G5
Monument a Colom 15 F5
Museu Marítim 16 F5
Museu Nacional d'Art de Catalunya 17 D6
Poble Espanyol 18 C6
Zoo 19 G3
SLEEPING
Centric Point 20 E3
Hostal Girona 21 F3
Hostal Sea Point 22 G5
Hotel Arts Barcelona 23 H3
Hotel Casa Fuster 24 D2
Hotel Costanza 25 F3
EATING
Amaltea 26 D4
Bilbao 27 E2
Can Maño 28 G4
Cerveseria Catalana 29 E3
El Peixerot 30 C4
La Rita 31 E3
Relais de Venise 32 E2
DRINKING
Les Gens Que J'Aime 33 E2
Michael Collins Pub 34 F1
Sabor a Cuba 35 D2
ENTERTAINMENT
Camp Nou 36 A4
Moog 37 F4
Otto Zutz 38 C2
Sala Apolo 39 E5
Teatre Nacional de Catalunya 40 G2
Verdi Cinema 41 D1
SHOPPING
Boulevard Rosa 42 E3
Els Encants Vells 43 G1
Joan Murrià 44 E2
Vinçon 45 E2
TRANSPORT
Estació del Nord 46 G2

SPAIN

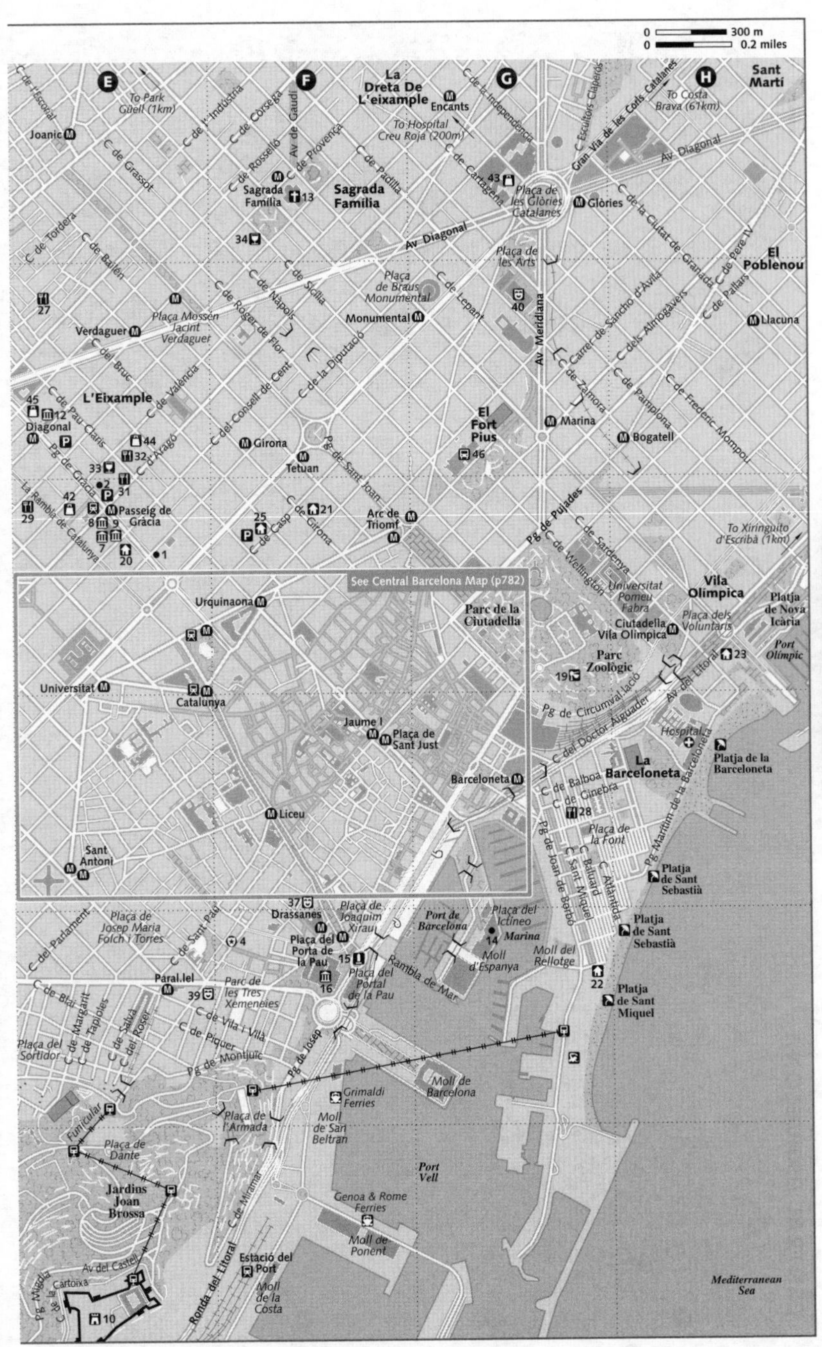

La Dreta De L'eixample
Sagrada Família
L'Eixample
El Fort Pius
El Poblenou
Sant Martí
Vila Olímpica
La Barceloneta
Parc de la Ciutadella
Parc Zoològic
Jardins Joan Brossa
See Central Barcelona Map (p782)
To Park Güell (1km)
To Hospital Creu Roja (200m)
To Costa Brava (61km)
To Xiringuito d'Escribà (1km)
Platja de Nova Icària
Port Olímpic
Platja de la Barceloneta
Platja de Sant Sebastià
Platja de Sant Miquel
Port de Barcelona
Port Vell
Mediterranean Sea
Moll d'Espanya
Moll del Rellotge
Moll de Barcelona
Moll de Sant Beltran
Moll de Ponent
Moll de la Costa
Grimaldi Ferries
Genoa & Rome Ferries
Estació del Port
Av Diagonal
Gran Via de les Corts Catalanes
Av Meridiana
Pg de Gràcia
La Rambla de Catalunya
Ronda del Litoral
Pg de Pujades
Pg de Circumval·lació
Pg Marítim de la Barceloneta
Rambla de Mar
Plaça de les Glòries Catalanes
Plaça de les Arts
Plaça de Braus Monumental
Plaça Mossèn Jacint Verdaguer
Plaça dels Voluntaris
Plaça de Josep Maria Folch i Torres
Plaça del Portal de la Pau
Plaça de l'Armada
Plaça de Dante
Plaça de Joaquim Xirau
Plaça del Ictineo
Plaça de la Font
Parc de les Tres Xemeneies
Joanic
Verdaguer
Diagonal
Passeig de Gràcia
Girona
Tetuan
Monumental
Encants
Glòries
Llacuna
Marina
Bogatell
Arc de Triomf
Urquinaona
Universitat
Catalunya
Jaume I
Plaça de Sant Just
Barceloneta
Liceu
Sant Antoni
Drassanes
Plaça del Porta de la Pau
Paral.lel
Ciutadella Vila Olímpica
Universitat Pompeu Fabra
Hospital
Funicular
Av del Castell
0 300 m
0 0.2 miles

SPAIN

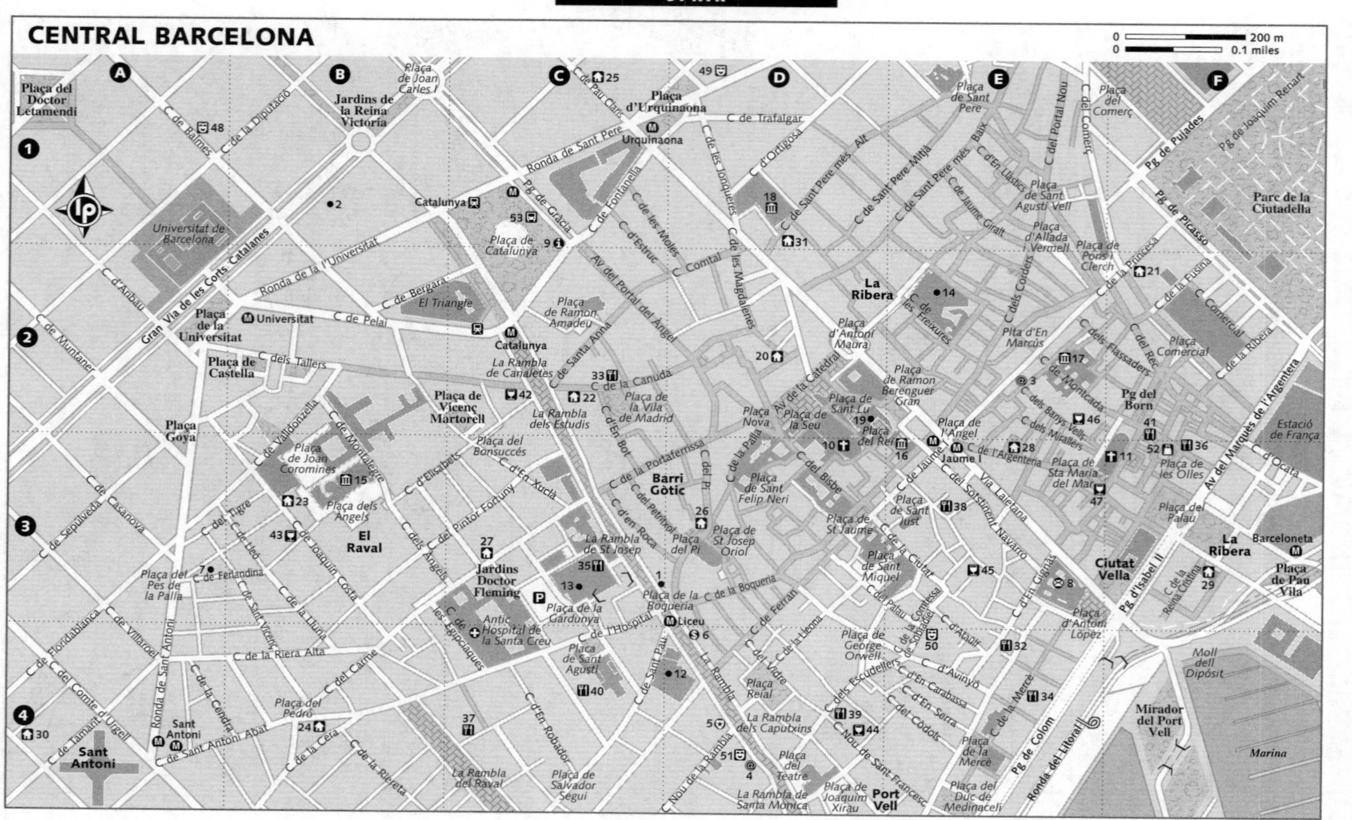
CENTRAL BARCELONA
0 200 m
0 0.1 miles
Plaça del Doctor Letamendi
Jardins de la Reina Victòria
Plaça de Joan Carles I
Plaça d'Urquinaona
Urquinaona
Universitat de Barcelona
Plaça de la Universitat
Universitat
Plaça de Castella
Plaça Goya
Catalunya
Plaça de Catalunya
El Triangle
Plaça de Ramon Amadeu
La Rambla de Canaletes
La Rambla dels Estudis
Plaça de Vicenç Martorell
Plaça del Bonsuccés
Plaça de la Vila de Madrid
Plaça de Joan Coromines
Plaça dels Àngels
El Raval
Jardins Doctor Fleming
Antic Hospital de la Santa Creu
Plaça de la Gardunya
La Rambla de St Josep
Plaça de Sant Agustí
Plaça del Pes de la Palla
Plaça del Pedró
Sant Antoni
La Rambla del Raval
Plaça de Salvador Seguí
Barri Gòtic
Plaça del Pi
Plaça de St Josep Oriol
Plaça de la Boqueria
Liceu
La Rambla
Plaça Reial
La Rambla dels Caputxins
Plaça del Teatre
La Rambla de Santa Mònica
Plaça de Joaquim Xirau
Port Vell
Plaça Nova
Plaça de la Seu
Plaça de Sant Felip Neri
Plaça de Sant Lu
Plaça del Rei
Plaça de St Jaume
Plaça de Sant Miquel
Plaça de Sant Just
Plaça de George Orwell
Plaça d'Antoni Maura
Plaça de Ramon Berenguer Gran
Plaça de l'Àngel
Jaume I
La Ribera
Plaça de Sant Pere
Plaça de Sant Agustí Vell
Plaça d'Allada i Vermell
Plaça de Pons i Clerch
Plta d'En Marcús
Plaça Comercial
Pg del Born
Plaça de Sta Maria del Mar
Plaça de les Olles
Plaça del Palau
Plaça del Comerç
Ciutat Vella
Plaça d'Antoni López
Plaça de la Mercè
Plaça del Duc de Medinaceli
Parc de la Ciutadella
Estació de França
Barceloneta
Plaça de Pau Vila
Moll del Dipòsit
Mirador del Port Vell
Marina
Ronda de Sant Pere
Pg de Gràcia
Av del Portal de l'Àngel
Gran Via de les Corts Catalanes
Ronda de la Universitat
Ronda de Sant Antoni
Via Laietana
Pg de Pujades
Pg de Joaquim Renart
Pg de Picasso
Av del Marquès de l'Argentera
Pg d'Isabel II
Pg de Colom
Ronda del Litoral
C de Balmes
C de la Diputació
C d'Aribau
C de Muntaner
C de Casanova
C de Sepúlveda
C de Floridablanca
C del Comte d'Urgell
C de Tamarit
C de Villarroel
C de Pelai
C de Bergara
C dels Tallers
C de Valldonzella
C de Montalegre
C del Tigre
C de Lleó
C de Ferlandina
C de Sant Vicenç
C de la Riera Alta
C de Joaquín Costa
C de la Lluna
C de la Cendra
C de Sant Antoni Abat
C de la Cera
C de la Riereta
C del Carme
C dels Àngels
C d'Elisabets
C del Pintor Fortuny
C d'En Xuclà
C d'En Robador
C de l'Hospital
C de Sant Pau
C de Santa Anna
C de la Canuda
C d'En Bot
C de la Portaferrissa
C del Petritxol
C d'en Roca
C de la Boqueria
C de Ferran
C de la Lleona
C del Vidre
C Nou de la Rambla
C de Pau Claris
C de Fontanella
C de les Moles
C d'Estruc
C Comtal
C de les Jonqueres
C de les Magdalenes
C de Trafalgar
C d'Ortigosa
C de Sant Pere més Alt
C de Sant Pere Mitjà
C de Sant Pere més Baix
C d'En Llàstics
C de Jaume Giralt
C del Portal Nou
C del Comerç
C dels Corders
C de les Freixures
C de la Princesa
C de la Fusina
C Comercial
C de la Ribera
C dels Flassaders
C del Rec
C de Montcada
C dels Banys Vells
C dels Mirallers
C de l'Argenteria
C de Jaume I
C del Sotstinent Navarro
C de la Palla
Av de la Catedral
C del Bisbe
C de la Ciutat
C del Palau
C de la Comtessa de Sobradiel
C d'Ataülf
C d'En Gignàs
C d'Avinyó
C dels Escudellers
C d'En Carabassa
C d'En Serra
C del Còdols
C de la Mercè
C Nou de Sant Francesc
C de la Reina Cristina
C d'Ocata

INFORMATION
24-hour Pharmacy....1 C3
Altäir....2 B1
Bornet....3 E2
easyInternetcafé....4 D4
Guàrdia Urbana (Local Police)..5 D4
Interchange....6 D4
Lavaxpress....7 A3
Main Post Office....8 E3
Main Tourist Office....9 C1

SIGHTS & ACTIVITIES
Catedral....10 D3
Església de Santa Maria del Mar....11 F3
Gran Teatre del Liceu....12 D4
Mercat de la Boquería....13 C3
Mercat de Santa Caterina....14 E2
Museu d'Art Contemporàni de Barcelona....15 B3
Museu d'Història de la Ciutat..16 E3
Museu Picasso....17 E2
Palau de la Música Catalana..18 D1
Palau Reial Major....(see 19)
Saló del Tinell....19 D2

SLEEPING
Alberg Hostal Itaca....20 D2
Chic & Basic....21 F2
Hostal Campi....22 C2
Hostal Gat Raval....23 B3
Hostal Gat Xino....24 B4
Hostal Goya....25 C1
Hostal Jardí....26 D3
Hotel Aneto....27 C3
Hotel Banys Orientals....28 E3
Hotel del Mar....29 F3
Market Hotel....30 A4
Pensió 2000....31 D1

EATING
Agut....32 E4
Bagel Shop....33 C2
Bar Celta....34 E4
Bar Pinotxo....35 C3
Cal Pep....36 F3
Casa Leopoldo....37 C4
El Café de l'Académia....38 E3
Los Caracoles....39 D4
Organic....40 C4
Orígen 99.9%....41 F2

DRINKING
Boadas....42 C2
Casa Almirall....43 B3
Club Soul....44 D4
La Clandestina....45 E3
La Fianna....46 E2
La Vinya del Senyor....47 E3

ENTERTAINMENT
Arena Madre....48 A1
DBoy....49 D1
Harlem Jazz Club....50 E4
Tablao Cordobés....51 D4

SHOPPING
Custo Barcelona....52 F3

TRANSPORT
Aerobús Bus Stop....53 C1
Bus Turístic Bus Stop....(see 53)

is one of the most visited museums in the country, so expect queues.

The heart of the neighbourhood is the elegant **Església de Santa Maria del Mar** (Map p782; Plaça de Santa Maria del Mar; admission free; 9am-1.30pm & 4.30-8pm; M Jaume I), a stunning example of Catalan Gothic and arguably the city's most elegant church.

The opulent **Palau de la Música Catalana** (Map p782; ☎ 902 47 54 85; www.palaumusica.org; Carrer de Sant Francesc de Paula 2; adult/child/student incl guided tour €10/free/9; 50min tours every 30min 10am-6pm Easter & Aug, 10am-3.30pm Sep-Jul; M Urquinaona) is one of the city's most delightful Modernista works. Designed by Lluís Domènech i Montaner in 1905, it hosts concerts regularly. It is well worth joining the guided tours to get a look inside if you don't make a concert.

Nearby, the **Mercat de Santa Caterina** (Map p782; www.mercatsantacaterina.net; Avinguda de Francesc Cambó 16; 8am-2pm Mon, 8am-3.30pm Tue, Wed & Sat, 8am-8.30pm Thu & Fri; M Jaume I), with its loopily pastel-coloured wavy roof, is a temple to fine foods designed by the adventurous Catalan architect Enric Miralles.

La Ribera is bordered to the northeast by the sprawling **Parc de la Ciutadella** (8am-6pm Nov-Feb, 8am-8pm Oct & Mar, 8am-9pm Apr-Sep; M Barceloneta), a park ideal for strolling or picnics. It's home to a small, kid-friendly **zoo** (Map pp780-1; ☎ 93 225 67 80; www.zoobarcelona.com; Passeig de Picasso & Carrer de Wellington; adult/under 4yr/senior/4-12yr €15.50/free/8.50/9.50; 10am-7pm Jun-Sep, 10am-6pm mid-Mar–May & Oct, 10am-5pm Nov–mid-Mar; M Barceloneta), which holds about 7500 living thingies, from gorillas to insects.

WATERFRONT

Barcelona has two major ports, **Port Vell** (Old Port) at the base of La Rambla, and **Port Olímpic** (Olympic Port) 1.5km up the coast. Shops, restaurants and nightlife options are plentiful around both marinas, particularly Port Olímpic. Between the two ports sits the onetime factory workers and fishermen's quarter, **La Barceloneta**. It preserves a delightfully scruffy edge and abounds with crowded seafood eateries.

At the end of Moll d'Espanya in Port Vell is **L'Aquàrium** (Map pp780-1; ☎ 93 221 74 74; www.aquariumbcn.com; Moll d'Espanya; adult/under 4yr/4-12yr/over 60yr €16/free/11/12.50; 9.30am-11pm Jul & Aug, 9.30am-9.30pm Jun & Sep, 9.30am-9pm Mon-Fri & 9.30am-9.30pm Sat & Sun Oct-May; M Drassanes), with its 80m-long shark tunnel. Short of diving among them (which can be arranged here too) this is as close as you can get to a set of shark teeth without being bitten.

Barcelona boasts 4km of city *platjas* (beaches), beginning with the gritty **Platja de la Barceloneta** and continuing northeast, beyond Port Olímpic, with a series of cleaner, more attractive strands. All get packed in summer. From Easter to October, a series of beach bars (*chiringuitos*) operate from about 10am until as late as 1am. Snack food, cocktails and funky music are more or less the standard diet.

L'EIXAMPLE

Modernisme, the Catalan version of art nouveau, transformed Barcelona's cityscape in the early 20th century. Most Modernista works were built in L'Eixample, the grid-plan district that was developed from the 1870s on.

Modernisme's star architect was the eccentric Antoni Gaudí (1852–1926), a devout Catholic whose work is full of references to nature and Christianity. His masterpiece, **La Sagrada Família** (Map pp780-1; ☎ 93 207 30 31; www.sagradafamilia.org; Carrer de Mallorca 401; adult/senior & student €10/8; ⏰ 9am-8pm Apr-Sep, 9am-6pm Oct-Mar; Ⓜ Sagrada Família), is a work in progress and Barcelona's most famous building. Construction began in 1882 and could be completed in 2020.

Gaudí spent 40 years working on the church, though he only saw the crypt, the apse and the nativity facade completed. Eventually there'll be 18 towers, all more than 100m high, representing the 12 apostles, four evangelists and Mary, Mother of God, plus the tallest tower (170m) standing for Jesus Christ. Climb high inside some of the towers (or take the elevator, €2) for a new perspective.

Gaudí's **La Pedrera** (Map pp780-1; ☎ 902 40 09 73; www.fundaciocaixacatalunya.es; Carrer de Provença 261-265; adult/student & EU senior €8/4.50; ⏰ 9am-8pm Mar-Oct, 9am-6.30pm Nov-Feb; Ⓜ Diagonal) is his best-known secular creation. Formally called the Casa Milà, after the businessman who commissioned it, it's better known as La Pedrera (The Quarry) because of its uneven grey-stone facade, which ripples around the corner of Carrer de Provença. The wave effect is emphasised by elaborate wrought-iron balconies. Inside, you can visit a museum about Gaudí and his work, a Modernista apartment and the surreal rooftop with its bizarre chimneys.

Just down the street is the unique facade of the **Casa Batlló** (Map pp780-1; ☎ 93 216 03 66; www.casabatllo.es; Passeig de Gràcia 43; adult/student & senior €16.50/13.20; ⏰ 9am-8pm, on occasion these hr can be shortened; Ⓜ Passeig de Gràcia), an allegory for the legend of St George (Sant Jordi in Catalan) the dragon-slayer. On the same block are two other Modernista gems, **Casa Amatller** (Passeig de Gràcia 41) by Josep Puig i Cadafalch and the **Casa Lleó Morera** (Passeig de Gràcia 35) by Lluís Domènech i Montaner. This mishmash of architectural styles gave the block its nickname, the *Manzana de Discordia* (Block/Apple of Discord, a play of words on an ancient Greek myth – *manzana* means both apple and block).

High up in the Gràcia district sits Gaudí's enchanting **Park Güell** (☎ 93 413 24 00; Carrer d'Olot 7; admission free; ⏰ 10am-9pm Jun-Sep, 10am-8pm Apr, May & Oct, 10am-7pm Mar & Nov, 10am-6pm Dec-Feb; Ⓜ Lesseps or Vallcarca, 🚌 24), originally designed to be a self-contained community with houses, schools and shops. The project flopped, but we're left with a Dr Seuss–style playground filled with colourful mosaics and Gaudí-designed paths and plazas.

The website www.rutadelmodernisme.com is a great resource on Modernisme in Barcelona.

MONTJUÏC

Southwest of the city centre and with views out to sea and over the city, Montjuïc serves as a Central Park of sorts and is a great place for a jog or stroll. It is dominated by the **Castell de Montjuïc** (Map pp780–1), a one-time fortress with great views. Buses 50, 55 and 61 all head up here. A local bus, the PM (Parc de Montjuïc) line, does a circle trip from Plaça d'Espanya to the *castell*. **Bus Montjuïc Turístic** (adult/child €3/2) operates two hop-on, hop-off circuits (red and blue) in single-deck, open-top buses around the park. Cable cars and a funicular line also access the area.

Apart from the many fine gardens and parks, there are several museums and attractions.

Museu Nacional d'Art de Catalunya (Map pp780-1; ☎ 93 622 03 76; www.mnac.es; Mirador del Palau Nacional; adult/senior & child under 15/student €8.50/free/6; ⏰ 10am-7pm Tue-Sat, 10am-2.30pm Sun & holidays) is a broad panoply of Catalan and European art. The Romanesque frescoes are second to none and truly stunning.

Fundació Joan Miró (Map pp780-1; ☎ 93 443 94 70; www.bcn.fjmiro.es; Plaça de Neptu; adult/senior & child €8/6; ⏰ 10am-7pm Tue-Wed, Fri & Sat, 10am-9.30pm Thu, 10am-2.30pm Sun & holidays) is the definitive museum showcasing Joan Miró's works.

A showcase of typical Spanish architecture from around the country, **Poble Espanyol** (Map pp780-1; ☎ 93 508 63 30; www.poble-espanyol.com; Avinguda del Marquès de Comillas; adult/child/senior & student €8/5/6; ⏰ 9am-8pm Mon, 9am-2am Tue-Thu, 9am-4am Fri & Sat, 9am-midnight Sun) has craft shops, restaurants and nightlife.

CaixaForum (Map pp780-1; ☎ 93 476 86 00; www.fundacio.lacaixa.es in Spanish; Avinguda del Marquès de Comillas 6-8; admission free; ⏰ 10am-8pm Tue-Fri & Sun, 10am-10pm Sat; Ⓜ Espanya) is housed in a remarkable former Modernista factory designed by Puig i Cadafalch and puts on major art exhibitions.

Tours

The three routes of the **Bus Turístic** (one day adult/child aged four to 12 €19/11, two consecutive days €23/15; 9am-7.45pm) link all the major tourist sights. Buy tickets on the bus or at the tourist office (p778).

The main tourist office also offers various **walking tours** (tours €11-15) in English, Spanish or Catalan.

Festivals & Events

The **Festes de la Mercè** (around 24 September; www.bcn.cat/merce) is the city's biggest party, with four days of concerts, dancing, *castellers* (human castle-builders), fireworks and *correfocs* – a parade of firework-spitting dragons and devils. The evening before the **Dia de Sant Joan** (24 June) is a colourful midsummer celebration with bonfires and fireworks. The beaches are crowded with revellers to the wee hours.

Sleeping

There is no shortage of hotels (with new ones opening seemingly every five minutes) in Barcelona.

Those looking for cheaper accommodation close to the action should check out the Barri Gòtic and El Raval. Some good lower-end *pensiones* are scattered about L'Eixample, as well as a broad range of midrange and top-end places, most in easy striking distance of the Old Town. A growing range of options now makes it easier to stay in La Ribera and near the beaches at La Barceloneta.

Numerous private apartment-rental companies operate in Barcelona. These can often be a better deal than staying in a hotel. Start your search at **Apartment Barcelona** (www.apartmentbarcelona.com), **Barcelona Apartments** (www.barcelonapartments.com) and **Barcelona On Line** (www.barcelona-on-line.es).

LA RAMBLA & BARRI GÒTIC

The Ciutat Vella (Old City) is packed with budget *hostales* and *pensiones*. This selection of especially charming, and good-value-for-money options merely scratches the surface.

Alberg Hostel Itaca (Map p782; ☎ 93 301 97 51; www.jo-oh.com/itaca; Carrer de Ripoll 21; dm €18, d €50-55; Ⓜ Jaume I;) A bright option near La Catedral, Itaca has spacious dorms with parquet floors, pleasant spring colours and a couple of doubles with private bathroom. Whip up a storm in the kitchen.

Hostal Campi (Map p782; ☎ 93 301 35 45; hcampi@terra.es; Carrer de la Canuda 4; s/d with shared bathroom €31/54, d with private bathroom €62; Ⓜ Catalunya) An excellent bottom-end deal. The best rooms are the doubles with their own loo and shower. Although basic, they are extremely roomy and bright.

Hotel Jardí (Map p782; ☎ 93 301 59 00; www.hoteljardi-barcelona.com; Plaça de Sant Josep Oriol 1; d €79-106; Ⓜ Liceu;) The best rooms in this attractively located spot are the doubles with a balcony over one of the prettiest squares in the city.

EL RAVAL

Hostal Gat Raval (Map p782; ☎ 93 481 66 70; www.gataccommodation.com; Carrer de Joaquín Costa 44; s/d with shared bathroom €50/70, d with private bathroom €80; Ⓜ Universitat;) A pea green and lemon-lime colour scheme has been adopted in this hip young 2nd-floor *hostal*, deep in El Raval. Rooms are pleasant, secure and each behind a green door.

Hotel Aneto (Map p782; ☎ 93 301 99 89; www.hotelaneto.com; Carrer del Carme 38; s/d €55/75; Ⓜ Liceu;) Nestled in a lively street, in one of the nicer parts of El Raval, the Aneto is a good-value, simple midrange base to range out from. The best rooms are the doubles with the shuttered street-side balconies.

Hostal Gat Xino (Map p782; ☎ 93 324 88 33; www.gataccommodation.com; Carrer de l'Hospital 149-155; s/d/suite with terrace €66/84/130; Ⓜ Sant Antoni;) Better still than Gat Raval is this newer version. The lime-green decor theme continues but rooms are more spacious and all have bathroom. The suite has views to Montjuïc.

LA RIBERA & LA BARCELONETA

Hostal Sea Point (Map pp780-1; ☎ 93 231 20 45; www.seapointhostel.com; Plaça del Mar 1-4; dm €21.50; Ⓜ Barceloneta;) What this youth hostel lacks in charm it makes up for in position. Set in an ugly high-rise and with rather tight dorms, it is right on the beach.

Pensió 2000 (Map p782; ☎ 93 310 74 66; www.pensio2000.com; Carrer de Sant Pere més Alt 6; s/d with shared bathroom €54/67, with private bathroom €66/86; ; Ⓜ Urquinaona) Opposite the Palau de la Música Catalana (p783), this cheerful *pensión*, with its seven canary yellow rooms, is a conveniently placed option.

our pick **Hotel Banys Orientals** (Map p782; ☎ 93 268 84 60; www.hotelbanysorientals.com; Carrer de l'Argenteria 37; s/d €89/107; M Jaume I;) Cool blues and aquamarines combine with dark-hued parquet floors to lend this boutique beauty an understated charm.

Chic & Basic (Map p782; ☎ 93 295 46 52; www.chicandbasic.com; Carrer de la Princesa 50; d €96-171; M Arc de Triomf;) The 31 spotlessly white rooms here have high ceilings, enormous beds (room types are classed as M, L and XL!) and lots of detailed touches (LED lighting, TFT TV screens) and the retention of many beautiful old features of the original building.

Hotel del Mar (Map p782; ☎ 93 319 33 02; www.gargallohotels.es; Plaça de Palau 19; s/d €102/118; M Barceloneta;) The 'Sea Hotel' is neatly placed between Port Vell and El Born. Some of the rooms in this classified building have balconies with waterfront views.

Hotel Arts Barcelona (Map pp780-1; ☎ 93 221 10 00; www.ritzcarlton.com; Carrer de la Marina 19-21; r €425; M Ciutadella-Vila Olímpica;) In one of the two sky-high towers that dominate Port Olímpic, these are Barcelona's most fashionable digs, frequented by VIPs from all over the planet. The rooms have unbeatable views.

SPAIN

L'EIXAMPLE

Centric Point (Map pp780-1; ☎ 93 215 65 38; www.centricpointhostel.com; Passeig de Gràcia 33; dm €21-27, d €50; M Passeig de Gràcia;) Stay on Barcelona's snootiest boulevard without paying the commensurate rent! One of four hostels run by the same people, this one offers 400 beds in a Modernista building close to Plaça de Catalunya.

Hostal Girona (Map pp780-1; ☎ 93 265 02 59; www.hostalgirona.com; Carrer de Girona 24; r up to €66; M Arc de Triomf) A 2nd-floor, family-run *hostal*, the Girona is a basic but clean and friendly spot. The atmosphere is Catalan and somewhat frozen in time but good value.

Hostal Goya (Map p782; ☎ 93 302 25 65; www.hostalgoya.com; Carrer de Pau Claris 74; s €70, d €96-113; M Urquinaona;) The Goya is a gem of a spot on the chichi side of L'Eixample and a short stroll from Plaça de Catalunya. Rooms have parquet floors and a light colour scheme.

Market Hotel (Map p782; ☎ 93 325 12 05; www.markethotel.com.es; Passatge de Sant Antoni Abad 10; s/d/ste €80/93/112; M Sant Antoni;) Attractively located in a renovated building along a narrow lane just north of the grand old Sant Antoni market, this place has an air of simple chic. Room decor is a pleasing combination of white, dark nut browns, light timber and reds.

Hotel Constanza (Map pp780-1; ☎ 93 270 19 10; www.hotelconstanza.com; Carrer del Bruc 33; s/d €90/120; M Urqinaona;) Constanza is a boutique belle that has stolen the heart of many a visitor to Barcelona. Even smaller single rooms are made to feel special, with broad mirrors and strong colours (reds and yellows, with black furniture).

Hotel Casa Fuster (Map pp780-1; ☎ 93 255 30 00; www.hotelcasafuster.com; Passeig de Gràcia 132; d from €407; M Diagonal;) A Modernista mansion totally refurbished to house this luscious five-star hotel, the Casa Fuster is the ultimate splurge. Even if you don't stay in one of the opulent rooms, come by for a coffee in the beautiful Café Vienés.

Eating

Barcelona is foodie heaven. The city has firmly established itself as one of Europe's gourmet capitals, and innovative, cutting-edge restaurants abound. Some of the most creative chefs are one-time students of Ferran Adrià (see p792), whose influence on the city's cuisine is strong.

Although Barcelona has a reputation as a hot spot of 'new Spanish cuisine', you'll still find local eateries serving up time-honoured local grub, from squid-ink *fideuà* (a satisfying paella-like noodle dish) through pigs' trotters, rabbit with snails, and *butifarra* (a tasty local sausage).

LA RAMBLA & BARRI GÒTIC

Skip the over-priced traps along La Rambla and get into the winding lanes of the Barri Gòtic. Self-caterers should explore the Mercat de la Boquería (p779).

Bagel Shop (Map p782; ☎ 93 302 41 61; Carrer de la Canuda 25; meals €10; 9.30am-9.30pm Mon-Sat, 11am-4pm Sun; M Liceu) Top your bagel with anything from turkey and cheese to Mallorcan *sobrassada* (soft, tangy sausage) or *butifarra* at this informal cafe.

Bar Celta (Map p782; ☎ 93 315 00 06; Carrer de la Mercè 16; meals €20; noon-midnight; M Drassanes) Specialists in *pulpo* (octopus) and other seaside delights from Galicia, the waiters waste no time in serving up bottles of crisp white Ribeiro wine to wash down the *raciones* (large tapas servings).

Agut (Map p782; ☎ 93 315 17 09; Carrer d'En Gignàs 16; meals €35; ⏲ lunch & dinner Tue-Sat, lunch Sun; Ⓜ Liceu or Jaume I) Contemporary paintings set a contrast with the fine traditional Catalan dishes offered in this timeless restaurant. You might start with something like the *bouillabaisse con cigalitas de playa* (little seawater crayfish) and follow with an oak-grilled meat dish.

Los Caracoles (Map p782; ☎ 93 302 31 85; Carrer dels Escudellers 14; meals €30-35; Ⓜ Drassanes or Liceu;) A city institution, 'The Snails' is a maze of tile-laden dining rooms, all decorated with photos of the famous faces who've eaten here. Specialities include snails, roasted chicken, and *suquet*, a Catalan seafood stew.

El Café de l'Acadèmia (Map p782; ☎ 93 319 82 53; Carrer de Lledó 1; meals €30-35; ⏲ Mon-Fri; Ⓜ Jaume I) This fine restaurant serves strictly Catalan dishes in a romantic atmosphere. If you're with a group, ask to sit in the downstairs *bodega* (cellar).

EL RAVAL

Organic (Map p782; ☎ 93 301 09 02; www.antonia organickitchen.com; Carrer de la Junta de Comerç 11; meals €14-20; ⏲ noon-midnight; Ⓜ Liceu) A long sprawl of a vegetarian diner, Organic is always full. Choose from a limited range of options that change from day to day, and tuck into the all-you-can-eat salad bar in the middle of the restaurant.

Bar Pinotxo (Map p782; ☎ 93 317 17 31; Mercat de la Boquería; meals €15-20; ⏲ 6am-5pm Mon-Sat Sep-Jul; Ⓜ Liceu) Of the half-dozen or so tapas bars and informal eateries scattered about the market, this one near the Rambla entrance is the most popular. Dig into tapas and *raciones* of hearty market food.

ourpick Casa Leopoldo (Map p782; ☎ 93 441 30 14; www.casaleopoldo.com; Carrer de Sant Rafael 24; meals €50; ⏲ lunch & dinner Tue-Sat, lunch Sun Sep-Jul; Ⓜ Liceu) Rambling dining areas with magnificent tiled walls and exposed timber-beam ceilings make this a fine option. The seafood menu is extensive and the local wine list strong.

LA RIBERA & WATERFRONT

La Barceloneta is the place to go for seafood; Passeig Joan de Borbó is lined with eateries but locals head for the back lanes.

Orígen 99.9% (Map p782; ☎ 93 310 75 31; www .origen99.com; Carrer de la Vidrieria 6-8; meals €15-20; ⏲ 12.30pm-1am; Ⓜ Jaume I) A shop-restaurant combo, Origins boasts that 99.9% of everything it sells is from Catalonia. The ever changing daily *menú* features local specialities such as *escalivada* (roasted veggies on bread) and Catalan sausages.

Can Maño (Map pp780-1; ☎ 93 319 30 82; Carrer del Baluard 12; meals €15-20; ⏲ Mon-Sat; Ⓜ Barceloneta) You'll need to be prepared to wait, before being squeezed in at a packed table for a raucous night of *raciones* (posted on a board at the back) over a bottle of *turbio* – a cloudy white and pleasing plonk.

Xiringuito d'Escribà (off Map pp780-1; ☎ 93 221 07 29; www.escriba.es; Platja de Bogatell, Ronda Litoral 42; meals €40-50; ⏲ lunch only daily; Ⓜ Ciutadella-Vila Olímpica) The Barcelona pastry family serves up top quality seafood at this popular waterfront eatery. This is one of the few places where one person can order from their selection of paella and *fideuà* (normally served to a minimum of two people).

Cal Pep (Map p782; ☎ 93 310 79 61; www.calpep .com; Plaça de les Olles 8; meals €45; ⏲ lunch & dinner Tue-Fri, dinner Mon, lunch Sat Sep-Jul; Ⓜ Barceloneta) This gourmet tapas bar is one of the most popular in town and difficult to snaffle a spot in. Pep recommends *cloïsses amb pernil* (clams and ham – seriously!) or the *trifàsic*, a combo of calamari, whitebait and prawns (€12).

L'EIXAMPLE & GRÀCIA

Amaltea (Map pp780-1; ☎ 93 454 86 13; www.res taurantamaltea.com; Carrer de la Diputació 164; meals €10-15; ⏲ lunch Mon-Thu, lunch & dinner Fri & Sat; Ⓜ Urgell) The weekday set lunch (€10) offers a series of dishes that change frequently with the seasons. Savour the *empanadillas* (pastry pockets stuffed with spinach or hiziki algae and tofu).

La Rita (Map pp780-1; ☎ 93 487 23 76; Carrer d'Aragó 279; meals €20; Ⓜ Passeig de Gràcia) For a bit of style, this popular restaurant does the trick. Be prepared to wait in line for its pasta, seafood and traditional dishes.

Cerveseria Catalana (Map pp780-1; ☎ 93 216 03 68; Carrer de Mallorca 236; meals €25; FGC Provença) Arrive early to try the delicious tapas and *flautas* (long skinny sandwiches) at this busy tavern off Rambla de Catalunya.

Relais de Venise (Map pp780-1; ☎ 93 467 21 62; Carrer de Pau Claris 142; meals €30; ⏲ Sep-Jul; Ⓜ Passeig de Gràcia) There's just one dish, a succulent beef entrecote with a secret 'sauce Porte-Maillot' (named after the location of the original restaurant in Paris), chips and salad. It is served in slices and in two waves so that it doesn't go cold.

Bilbao (Map pp780-1; ☎ 93 458 96 24; Carrer del Perill 33; meals €40; Mon-Sat; M Diagonal) The back dining room, with bottle-lined walls stout timber tables and a yellowing light evocative of distant country taverns, will appeal to carnivores especially.

El Peixerot (Map pp780-1; ☎ 93 424 69 69; Carrer de Tarragona 177; meals €40-50; M Tarragona) With its sea-blue decor and long-standing fame for fresh seafood (sold by weight) and rice dishes (€17 to €29), this is a quality stop in the rather unlikely train-station area.

Drinking

The city abounds with day-time cafes, laid-back lounges and lively night-time bars. Closing time is generally 2am Sunday to Thursday and 3am on Friday and Saturday.

BARRI GÒTIC

Club Soul (Map p782; Carrer Nou de Sant Francesc 7; M Drassanes) One of the hippest club-style hangouts in this part of town. Each night the DJs change the musical theme, ranging from deep funk to deeper house.

La Clandestina (Map p782; Baixada de Viladecols 2bis; 10am-10pm Sun-Thu, 9am-midnight Fri & Sat; M Jaume I) Opt for tea, a beer or a Middle Eastern *narghile* (the most elaborate way to smoke). You can even get a head massage or eat cake in this chilled tea shop.

SPAIN

EL RAVAL

Boadas (Map p782; Carrer dels Tallers 1; M Catalunya) One of the city's oldest cocktail bars, Boadas is famed for its daiquiris. The bow-tied waiters have been serving up their poison since 1933.

Casa Almirall (Map p782; Carrer de Joaquín Costa 33; M Universitat) In business since the 1860s, this corner drinkery is dark and intriguing, with Modernista decor and a mixed clientele.

LA RIBERA

La Fianna (Map p782; Carrer dels Banys Vells 15; M Jaume I) There is something rather medieval Oriental in the style of this bar, with its bare stone walls, forged iron candelabras and cushion-covered lounges. As the night wears on, it's elbow room only.

La Vinya Del Senyor (Map p782; Plaça de Santa Maria del Mar 5; noon-1am Tue-Sun; M Jaume I) The wine list here is as long as *War & Peace*, and the terrace lies in the shadow of Santa Maria del Mar.

L'EIXAMPLE & GRÀCIA

Les Gens Que J'Aime (Map pp780-1; Carrer de València 286; M Passeig de Gràcia) This intimate relic of the 1960s offers jazz music in the background and a cosy scattering of velvet-backed lounges around tiny dark tables.

Michael Collins Pub (Map pp780-1; Plaça de la Sagrada Família 4; M Sagrada Família) To be sure of a little Catalan-Irish craic, this barn-sized and storming pub is just the ticket.

Sabor a Cuba (Map pp780-1; Carrer de Francisco Giner 32; M Fontana) A mixed crowd of Cubans and fans of the Caribbean island come to drink mojitos and shake their stuff in this home of *ron y son* (rum and sound).

Entertainment

NIGHTCLUBS

Barcelona clubs are spread a little more thinly than bars across the city. They tend to open from around midnight until 6am. Entry can cost from nothing to €20 (one drink usually included).

Sala Apolo (Map pp780-1; www.sala-apolo.com; Carrer Nou de la Rambla 113; M Parallel) In this old theatre, the Nitsaclub team provides house, techno and break-beat sounds from Thursday to Sunday nights. Earlier in the evening, concerts generally take place.

Moog (Map pp780-1; www.masimas.com/moog; Carrer de l'Arc del Teatre 3; M Drassanes) This fun, minuscule club is a downtown hit. In the main downstairs dance area, DJs dish out house, techno and electro, while upstairs you can groove to indie and occasional classic pop.

Otto Zutz (Map pp780-1; www.ottozutz.es; Carrer de Lincoln 15; M Fontana) Beautiful people only need apply for entry into this three-floor dance den. Head downstairs for house or upstairs for funk and soul.

CINEMA

A popular cinema for subtitled foreign films is **Verdi** (Map pp780-1; ☎ 93 238 79 90; www.cines-verdi.com; Carrer Verdi 32; M Fontana). There's plenty of places to kick on after the film here.

GAY & LESBIAN VENUES

The gay and lesbian scene is concentrated in the blocks around Carrers de Muntaner and Consell de Cent (dubbed Gayxample). Here you'll find ambience every night of the week in the bars, discos and drag clubs.

Party hard at classic gay discos such as **Arena Madre** (Map p782; www.arenadisco.com; Carrer de Balmes 32; Ⓜ Universitat) and **Dboy** (Map p782; www.dboyclub.com; Ronda de Sant Pere 19-21; ⏲ Fri-Sun; Ⓜ Urquinaona).

THEATRE

Most theatre in the city is in Catalan.

There are quite a few venues that stage vanguard drama and dance, including **Teatre Nacional de Catalunya** (Map pp780-1; ☎ 93 306 57 00; www.tnc.es; Plaça de les Arts 1; Ⓜ Glòries).

SPORT

Football fans can see FC Barcelona play at **Camp Nou** (Map pp780-1; ☎ 902 18 99 00, from overseas 34 93 496 36 00; www.fcbarcelona.com; Carrer Arístides Maillol; Ⓜ Collblanc). Even if you can't score tickets, stop by for a peek at the **museum** (adult/senior & child €8.50/6.80; ⏲ 10am-8pm Mon-Sat, 10am-2.30pm Sun & holidays mid-Apr–mid-Oct, 10am-6.30pm Mon-Sat, 10am-2.30pm Sun & holidays mid-Oct–mid-Apr).

LIVE MUSIC

Harlem Jazz Club (Map p782; ☎ 93 310 07 55; Carrer Comtessa de Sobradiel 8; Ⓜ Liceu) Here you'll find a guaranteed dose of quality jazz and enough smoke to cook a sausage.

Tablao Cordobés (Map p782; ☎ 93 317 57 11; www.tablaocordobes.com; La Rambla 35; show only €35, with dinner €68; Ⓜ Liceu) Although Barcelona is not the best place to see flamenco, you can catch a reasonable show here.

Shopping

Most mainstream fashion stores are along a shopping 'axis' that runs from Plaça de Catalunya along Passeig de Gràcia, then left (west) along Avinguda Diagonal.

The El Born area in La Ribera is awash with tiny boutiques, especially those purveying young, fun fashion. There are plenty of shops scattered throughout the Barri Gòtic (stroll Carrer d'Avinyò and Carrer de Portaferrissa). For secondhand stuff, head for El Raval, especially Carrer de la Riera Baixa.

Boulevard Rosa (Map pp780-1; Passeig de Gràcia 53-57; Ⓜ Passeig de Gràcia). In L'Eixample this mall is good, and links Passeig de Gràcia with another elegant shopping boulevard, Rambla de Catalunya.

Els Encants Vells (Map pp780-1; ☎ 93 246 30 30; Carrer Dos de Maig 186; ⏲ 8.30am-6pm Mon, Wed, Fri & Sat; Ⓜ Glòries) Bargain hunters love this free-for-all flea market.

Vinçon (Map pp780-1; ☎ 93 215 60 50; www.vincon.com; Passeig de Gràcia 96; Ⓜ Diagonal) This is a design emporium where home decorators and gadget-lovers should head.

Custo Barcelona (Map p782; ☎ 93 268 78 93; www.custo-barcelona.com; Plaça de les Olles 7) Custo bewitches people the world over with a youthful, psychedelic panoply of women's and men's fashion.

Joan Murrià (Map pp780-1; ☎ 93 215 57 89; Carrer de Roger de Llúria 85) The century-old Modernista shop-front ads will draw you into this delicious delicatessen, where the shelves groan under the weight of speciality food from around Catalonia and beyond.

Getting There & Away

AIR

Barcelona's airport, **El Prat de Llobregat** (BCN), is 12km southwest of the city centre and Spain's second airport after Madrid. See p848 for contact details.

BUS

The main terminal for most domestic and international buses is the **Estació del Nord** (Map pp780-1; ☎ 902 30 32 22; www.barcelonanord.com; Carrer d'Ali Bei 80; Ⓜ Arc de Triomf). ALSA goes to Madrid (€27, eight hours, 16 daily), Valencia (€24.50, 4½ to 6½ hours, 14 daily) and many other destinations.

CAR & MOTORCYCLE

The AP-7 motorway comes in from the French border, and the AP-2 motorway heads towards Zaragoza. Both are toll roads. The N-II is a nontoll alternative, but it can get choked with traffic at peak times.

TRAIN

Virtually all trains travelling to and from destinations within Spain stop at **Estació Sants** (Map pp780-1; Ⓜ Sants-Estació). High-speed trains to Madrid via Lleida and Zaragoza take as little as two hours 40 minutes (€40 to €163 depending on conditions). Other trains run to Valencia (€32.50 to €38, three to 3½ hours, 15 daily) and Burgos (€38.50, eight to nine hours, four daily).

Getting Around

Information about Barcelona's public transport is available online at www.tmb.net and on ☎ 010.

TO/FROM THE AIRPORT

Renfe's *rodalies* line 10 runs between the airport and Estació de França in Barcelona (about 35 minutes), stopping at Estació Sants and Passeig de Gràcia. Tickets cost €2.60, unless you have a T-10 multitrip public transport ticket.

The **A1 Aerobús** (Map p782; ☎ 93 415 60 20) runs from the airport to Plaça de Catalunya (€4.05, 30 to 40 minutes), via Plaça d'Espanya, every six to 15 minutes (depending on the time of day) from 6am to 1am.

CAR & MOTORCYCLE

Parking can be a hassle but it's better than driving around town. Street parking in blue and green zones costs €2.35 to €2.85 an hour (generally 8am to 8pm Monday to Saturday). Garages can be more convenient.

PUBLIC TRANSPORT

Barcelona's metro system spreads its tentacles around the city in such a way that most places of interest are within a 10-minute walk of a station. Buses and suburban trains are needed only for a few destinations. A single metro, bus or suburban train ride costs €1.30, but a T-1 ticket, valid for 10 rides, costs €7.20.

TAXI

Barcelona's black-and-yellow taxis are plentiful and reasonably priced. The flag fall is €1.75 weekdays, and €1.85 for nights and weekends. If you can't find a street taxi, call ☎ 93 303 30 33.

MONESTIR DE MONTSERRAT

The monks who built the Monestir de Montserrat (Monastery of the Serrated Mountain), 50km northwest of Barcelona, chose a spectacular spot. The Benedictine **monastery** sits on the side of a 1236m mountain of weird, bulbous peaks. The monastery was founded in 1025 and pilgrims still come from all over Christendom to kiss the Black Virgin (La Moreneta), the 12th-century wooden sculpture of the Virgin Mary.

Mass is held several times daily; at the 1pm Monday to Saturday mass the monastery's boys' choir sings.

The **information office** (☎ 93 877 77 01; www.abadiamontserrat.net; 🕑 9am-6pm) has information on the complex and panoramic walking trails.

The **Museu de Montserrat** (☎ 93 877 77 77; Plaça de Santa Maria; adult/student €6.50/5.50; 🕑 10am-6pm) has an excellent collection, ranging from an Egyptian mummy to art by El Greco, Monet, Degas and Picasso.

If you're around the basilica at the right time, you'll catch a brief performance by the **Montserrat Boys' Choir** (Escolania; www.escolania.net; admission free; 🕑 performances 1pm & 6.45pm Mon-Fri, 11am & 6.45pm Sun Sep-Jun).

Montserrat is an easy day trip from Barcelona but there are a couple of sleeping options and eateries.

The FGC R5 train runs from Plaça d'Espanya station in Barcelona to Monistrol de Montserrat, where it connects with the rack-and-pinion train, or **cremallera** (☎ 902 31 20 20; www.cremallerademontserrat.com; one way/return €4.10/6.50), which takes 17 minutes to make the upwards journey.

HUMAN CASTLES

Catalans love a *festa* (traditional feast day) and some celebrate it by making *castells* (human castles). Teams of *castellers* create complex human structures as many as nine storeys tall. The best teams come from Vilafranca del Penedès and Valls, both southwest of Barcelona. Displays can be seen at most town *festes* throughout the year, including Barcelona. Every two years a huge *casteller* competition is held in early October in Tarragona's bullring – well worth the trip.

GIRONA

pop 92,200

Medieval Girona, built along the banks of the Onyar River, is an easy daytrip from Barcelona or a pleasant base in itself. The old city sits along the river's eastern bank. Get information at the **tourist office** (☎ 972 22 65 75; www.ajuntament.gi/turisme; Rambla de la Llibertat 1).

Sights & Activities

The **Catedral** (☎ 972 21 44 26; www.lacatedraldegirona.com; admission €4; 🕑 10am-2pm & 4-7pm Tue-Sat Mar-Jun, 10am-8pm Tue-Sat Jul-Sep, 10am-2pm & 4-6pm Tue-Sat Oct-Feb, 10am-2pm Sun & holidays) boasts Europe's widest Gothic nave (23m), a lovely Romanesque cloister, and a blustering baroque facade.

Wander the narrow streets of the nearby **Call** (one time medieval Jewish quarter) and visit the **Museu d'Història dels Jueus de Girona**

(Jewish History Museum, aka the Centre Bonastruc Ça Porta; ☎ 972 21 67 61; Carrer de la Força 8; adult/under 16yr/senior & student €2/free/1.50; ⌚ 10am-8pm Mon-Sat Jun-Oct, 10am-6pm Mon-Sat Nov-May, 10am-3pm Sun & holidays). Named after Jewish Girona's most illustrious figure, a 13th-century cabbalist philosopher and mystic, the centre – a warren of rooms and stairways around a courtyard – hosts temporary exhibitions and is a focal point for studies of Jewish Spain.

Walk along the medieval **walls** (⌚ dawn-dusk) that surround the edge of the old quarter.

Sleeping & Eating

Bed & Breakfast Bells Oficis (☎ 972 22 81 70; www.bellsoficis.com; Carrer dels Germans Busquets 2; r €35-85; ❄ 💻) With just five rooms, this family-run option is perfectly placed just off Rambla de la Llibertat. The rooms are all very different. The two best ones have balconies overlooking the Rambla.

Residència Bellmirall (☎ 972 20 40 09; www.grn.es/bellmirall; Carrer de Bellmirall 3; s/d €40/75; ⌚ closed Jan & Feb; ❄) Carved out of a 14th-century building in the heart of the old city, this 'residence' oozes character. Rooms with shared bathroom are marginally cheaper.

König (☎ 972 22 57 82; Carrer dels Calderers 16; meals €8-15) For a quick sandwich or simple hot dishes, 'King' boasts a broad outdoor terrace shaded by thick foliage.

Mimolet (☎ 972 20 21 24; Carrer del Pou Rodó 12; meals €35-40; ⌚ Tue-Sat) A stylish, designer spot just inside the Old Town walls, Mimolet offers an excellent wine list to accompany the seasonally varied menu.

> **DIVING ON THE COSTA BRAVA**
>
> The Costa Brava is one of the best places to dive in the Mediterranean, thanks to its interesting underwater rock formations and relatively healthy environment. The **Illes Medes** (www.visitestartit.com), seven small islets a kilometre off the coast from L'Estartit, constitute a marine reserve. This means they are packed with marine life… but also divers. Many companies lead dives. If you're a qualified diver, a two-hour trip usually costs around €30 per person. Full gear rental can cost more than €45 a day. Night dives are possible (usually about €30 to €35).

Getting There & Away

Note, Girona airport is a budget hub.

Girona is on the railway line between Barcelona, Figueres and Portbou on the French border. There are more than 20 trains per day to Figueres (€2.60 to €2.90, 30 to 40 minutes) and Barcelona (€5.90 to €6.70, 1½ hours).

FIGUERES

A short train ride north of Girona, Figueres is home to the zany **Teatre-Museu Dalí** (☎ 972 67 75 00; www.salvador-dali.org; Plaça de Gala i Salvador Dalí 5; adult/student €11/8; ⌚ 9am-8pm Jul-Sep, 10.30am-6pm Tue-Sun Oct-Jun), housed in a 19th-century theatre converted by Salvador Dalí (who was born here), it has a fascinating collection of his strange creations and is the site of his crypt.

Dalí fans will want to travel south to visit the equally kooky **Castell de Púbol** (☎ 972 48 86 55; www.salvador-dali.org; La Pera; adult/student & senior €7/5; ⌚ 10.30am-7.15pm mid-Jun–mid-Sep, 10.30am-5.15pm Tue-Sun mid-Mar–mid-Jun & mid-Sep–Oct, 10.30am-4.15pm Tue-Sat Nov-Dec) at La Pera, 22km northwest of Palafrugell, and his summer getaway at Port Lligat (1.25km from Cadaqués, see p792), the **Casa Museu Dalí** (☎ 972 25 10 15; www.salvador-dali.org; Port Lligat; adult/student & senior €10/8; ⌚ 10.30am-9pm mid-Jun–mid-Sep, 10.30am-6pm Tue-Sun mid-Sep–mid-Jan & mid-Mar–mid-Jun).

There are plenty of sleeping options in Figueres and Cadaqués.

THE COSTA BRAVA

The Costa Brava (Rugged Coast) was Catalonia's first tourist centre, and after you visit its rocky coastline, romantic coves, turquoise waters and onetime fishing villages, you'll see why. Overdevelopment has ruined some stretches but much of the coast retains its spectacular beauty.

There are tourist offices in **Palafrugell** (☎ 972 30 02 28; www.turismepalafrugell.org; Carrer del Carrilet 2) and other towns on the coast and inland.

Sights & Activities

The Costa Brava is all about picturesque inlets and coves – and there are many. Although buses run along much of the coast, the best way to uncover some of these gems is with your own wheels.

The first truly pretty stop on the Costa Brava when heading northeast from Barcelona is **Tossa de Mar**, with its golden beach, ochre medieval village core and nearby coves. The coast road on to **Sant Feliu de Guíxols** is spectacular.

Further north are three gorgeous beach towns near Palafrugell: **Tamariu** (the smallest, least crowded and most exclusive), **Llafranc** (the biggest and busiest), and **Calella de Palafrugell**. There are further fine beaches and coves on the coast near Begur, a little further north.

North of the Costa Brava's main dive centre, **L'Estartit**, are the ruins of the Greek and Roman town of **Empúries** (☎ 972 77 02 08; http://ftp.mac.es/empuries; adult/senior & child/student €3/free/2.50; 🕑 10am-8pm Jun-Sep, 10am-6pm Oct-May), 2km outside **L'Escala**.

Cadaqués, at the end of an agonising series of hairpin bends one hour from Figueres, is postcard perfect. Beaches are of the pebbly variety, so people spend a lot of time sitting at waterfront cafes or strolling. Some 10km northeast of Cadaqués is **Cap de Creus**, an impressive cape that is Spain's easternmost point. There are several pleasant, low-key coastal resorts on the road north to the French border.

It's a pleasant 2km walk from central Cadaqués to Port Lligat, where you'll find Dalí's summer residence.

Of the many historic towns inland from the Costa Brava, the pretty walled town of **Pals** (www.pals.es), 6km inland from Begur, and the nearby impeccably preserved medieval hamlet of **Peratallada** (www.peratallada.info) are the most charming.

SPAIN

Sleeping & Eating

TOSSA DE MAR

Five camping grounds are spread out around the town. The nearest is **Camping Can Martí** (☎ 972 34 08 51; www.canmarti.org; Rambla Pau Casals; camp sites per 2-person tent & car €32; 🕑 late May–mid-Sep;), 1km back from the beach and well equipped.

Hostal Cap d'Or (☎ 972 34 00 81; Passeig de la Vila Vella 1; s/d incl breakfast €49/93) Rub up against the town's history in this spot right in front of the walls. Rooms are comfortable and the best look straight onto the beach.

CADAQUÉS

Fonda Vehí (☎ 972 25 84 70; Carrer de l'Església 5; s with shared bathroom €30, d with shared/private bathroom €55/65;) Near the church in the heart of the Old Town, this simple but engaging *pensión* tends to be booked up for July and August. Easily the cheapest deal in town, it remains a popular choice because of its unbeatable position and very good restaurant (meals cost from €25 to €30; open daily from June to September, and Thursday to Tuesday from October through to May), where seafood, fresh fish and *suquets* are the order of the day.

PALS & PERATALLADA

There are several camping grounds on the coast near Pals. Both towns also have several small hotels and rural stays.

Ca l'Aliu (☎ 972 63 40 61; www.calaliu.com; Carrer de la Roca 6, Peratallada; d €64-86) This place is an 18th-century village home, where the old stone-and-timber frame has been teamed with modern comforts to create an atmospheric place with seven smallish but welcoming rooms.

KING OF THE KITCHENS

Once a simple bar and grill clutching on to a rocky perch high above the bare Mediterranean beach of Cala Montjoi and accessible only by dirt track from Roses, 6km to the west, **El Bulli** (☎ 972 15 04 57; www.elbulli.com; Cala Montjoi; meals €200 plus; 🕑 Apr-Sep) is one of the world's most sought-after dining experiences (usually fully booked a year or more in advance), thanks to star chef Ferran Adrià, considered by some to be the greatest creative mind in the planet's kitchens today.

Getting There & Away

Sarfa (☎ 902 30 20 25; www.sarfa.com) runs buses from Barcelona, Girona and Figueres to most towns along the Costa Brava.

TARRAGONA

pop 134,200

Barcelona's senior in Roman times and a lesser medieval city, Tarragona is a provincial sort of place with some outstanding attractions: Catalonia's finest Roman ruins, a magnificent medieval cathedral in a pretty Old Town and some decent beaches.

Get more information at the **tourist office** (☎ 977 25 07 95; www.tarragonaturisme.cat; Carrer Major 39; 🕑 9am-9pm Mon-Sat, 10am-3pm Sun Jul-Sep, 10am-2pm & 4-7pm Mon-Sat Oct-Jun, 10am-2pm Sun & holidays year-round).

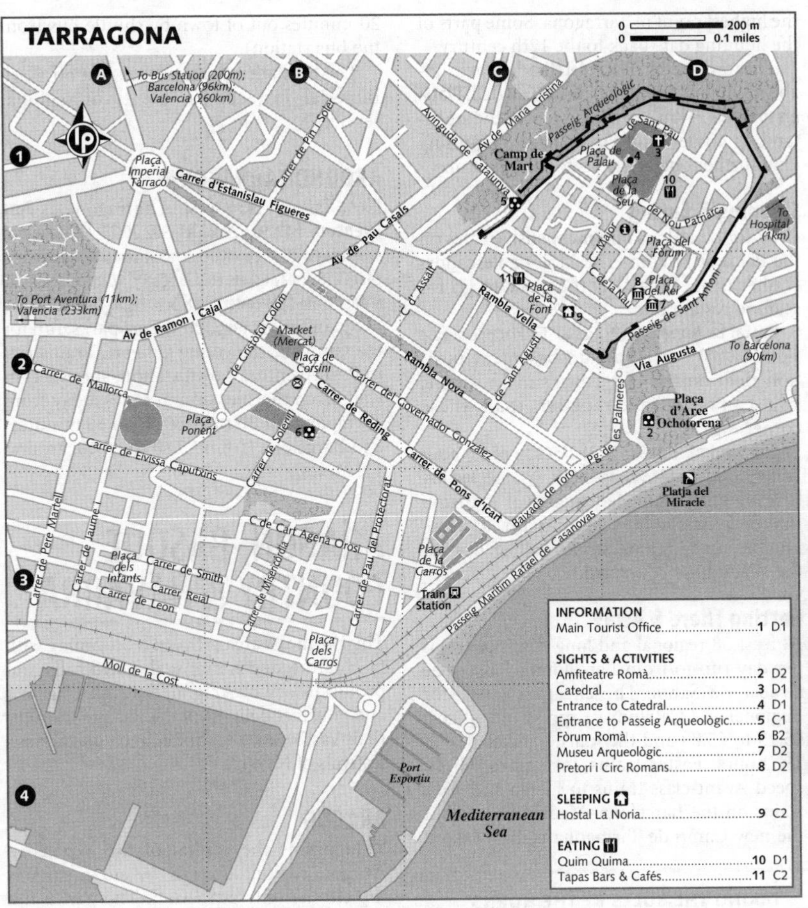

Sights & Activities

Start at the fascinating **Museu Arqueològic** (☎ 977 23 62 09; www.mnat.es; Plaça del Rei 5; adult/senior & under 18yr/student €2.40/free/1.20; 9.30am-8.30pm Tue-Sat, 10am-2pm Sun & holidays Jun-Sep, 9.30am-1.30pm & 3.30-7pm Tue-Sat, 10am-2pm Sun & holidays Oct-May), where you'll get an excellent understanding of Roman Spain.

Four major Roman sites around town, plus a 14th-century mansion, make up the **Museu d'Historia de Tarragona** (www.museutgn.com; adult/concession per site €2.45/1.25, ticket to all sites €9.25/4.60; 9am-9pm Mon-Sat, 9am-3pm Sun Easter-Sep, 9am-7pm Mon-Sat, 10am-3pm Sun & holidays Oct-Easter). The **Pretori i Circ Romans** (Pretorium & Roman Circus; ☎ 977 23 01 71; Plaça del Rei) includes part of the vaults of the Roman circus, where chariot races were held. Near the beach is the well-preserved **Amfiteatre Romà** (Roman Amphitheatre; ☎ 977 24 25 79; Plaça d'Arce Ochotorena), where gladiators battled each other, or wild animals, to the death. Southeast of Carrer de Lleida are remains of the **Fòrum Romà** (Roman Forum; ☎ 977 24 25 01; Carrer del Cardenal Cervantes), dominated by several imposing columns. The **Passeig Arqueològic** is a peaceful walk around part of the perimeter of the Old Town between two lines of city walls; the inner ones are mainly Roman, while the outer ones were put up by the British during the War of the Spanish Succession.

The **Catedral** (☎ 977 23 86 85; Plaça de la Seu; admission €3.50; 10am-1pm & 4-7pm Mon-Sat mid-Mar–May, 10am-7pm Mon-Sat Jun–mid-Oct, 10am-5pm Mon-Sat mid-Oct–mid-Nov, 10am-2pm Mon-Sat mid-Nov–mid-Mar) sits at the highest point of Tarragona. Some parts of the building date back to the 12th century.

The town beach, **Platja del Miracle**, is reasonably clean but can get terribly crowded. **Platja Arrabassada**, 1km northeast across the headland, is longer, and **Platja Llarga**, beginning 2km further out, stretches for about 3km.

Sleeping & Eating

Look for tapas bars and inexpensive cafes on the Plaça de la Font. The Moll de Pescadors (Fishermens' Wharf) is the place to go for seafood restaurants.

Hostal La Noria (☎ 977 23 87 17; Plaça de la Font 53; s/d €30/48) For a bargain basement position right on the Old Town's main square, you can't do much better than these corner digs.

Quim Quima (☎ 977 25 21 21; Carrer de les Coques 1bis; menú del día €14.90, meals €35; lunch Tue-Thu, Fri & Sat) This renovated medieval mansion makes a marvellous setting for a meal. Huddle up to a bare stone wall or opt for the shady little courtyard.

Getting There & Away

At least 38 regional and long-distance trains per day run to/from Barcelona's Passeig de Gràcia via Sants. The cheapest fares (for Regional and Catalunya Express trains) cost €5.15 to €5.80 and the journey takes one to 1½ hours. Faster trains cost more. High-speed Avant-class trains to Lleida and AVE trains on the Barcelona–Madrid line call at the new Camp de Tarragona station (about 20 minutes out of town by shuttle bus from the bus station).

The **bus station** (Avinguda Roma), just off Plaça Imperial Tarraco, has plenty of regional services.

TAKING THE BULLS BY THE HORNS

Many Catalans advertise their loathing of bullfighting but some may not be aware that in the southern corner of their region, locals have indulged in their own summer bovine torment. In Amposta and neighbouring towns, people celebrate *bous capllaçats* and *bous embolats,* the former a kind of tug-of-war between a bull with ropes tied to its horns and townsfolk, the latter involving bulls running around with flaming torches attached to their horns. Denounced by animal rights groups, they are allowed by the Catalan government, which recognises the right to hold these *festas* because of their long history and the fact that the bulls are not killed.

AROUND TARRAGONA

Near Salou, 11km west of Tarragona, is **Port Aventura** (☎ 902 20 20 41, 902 20 22 20; www.portaventura.es; mid-Sep–mid-Jun adult/senior & child 5-12yr €42/33.50, 2-day tickets €63/50.50; 10am-midnight Jul & Aug, 10am-8pm Easter-Jun & Sep, 10am-7pm Oct), one of Spain's most popular theme parks, fun for the family or the young at heart. Trains run to Port Aventura's own station, about a 1km walk from the site, several times a day from Tarragona (€1.30 to €1.60, 10 to 15 minutes) and Barcelona (from €5.80 to €6.40, around 1½ hours).

ARAGÓN, BASQUE COUNTRY & NAVARRA

This northeast area of Spain is brimming with fascinating destinations: the arid hills and proud history of Aragón; the lush coastline and gourmet delights of the Basque Country (País Vasco); and the wine country and famous festivals of Navarra.

ARAGÓN

Zaragoza is the capital of the expansive Aragón region, though by no means is the city its only attraction. The parks and pretty towns of the Pyrenees are well worth exploring too.

Zaragoza

pop 624,700 / elev 200m

Sitting on the banks of the mighty Ebro River, Zaragoza (a contraction of Caesaraugusta, the name the Romans gave to this city when they founded it in 14 BC) is a busy regional capital with a seemingly voracious appetite for eating out and late-night revelry. The historic old centre, crowned by the majestic Basílica del Pilar, throws up echoes of its Roman and Muslim past. The Old Town is also home to El Tubo (The Tube), a maze of streets with countless tapas bars and cafes.

SPAIN

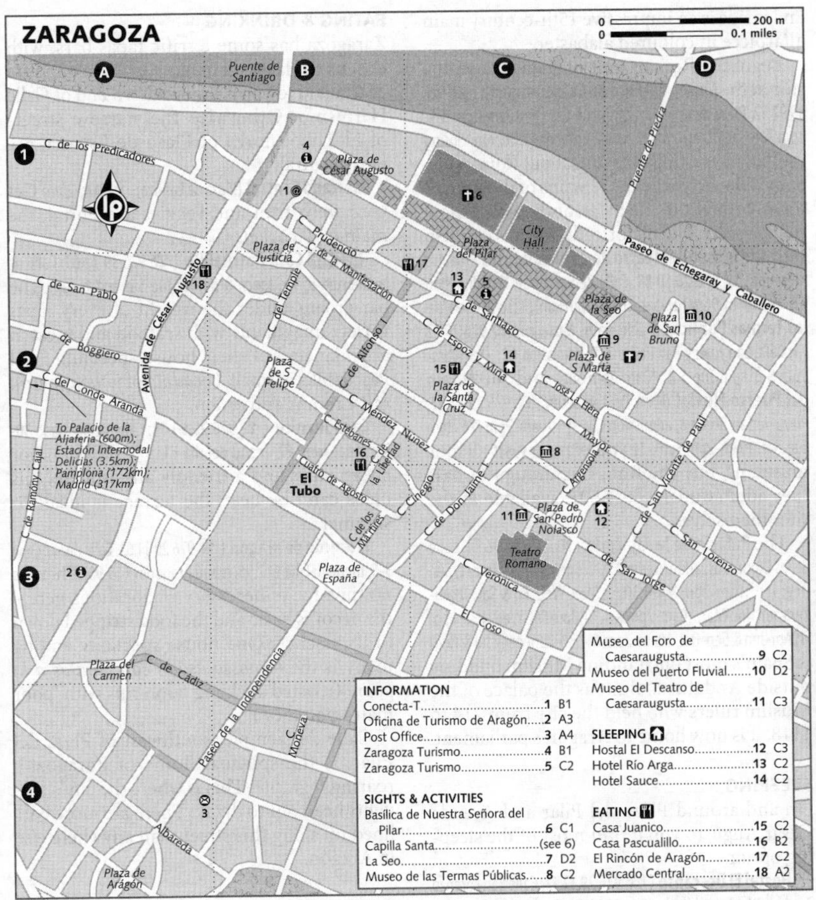

INFORMATION

Conecta-T (☎ 976 20 59 79; Murallas Romanas 4; per hr €1.60; 🕑 10am-11pm Mon-Fri, 11am-11pm Sat & Sun) Internet access.

Post office (Paseo de la Independencia 33)

Oficina de Turismo de Aragón (☎ 976 28 21 81; www.turismodearagon.com; Avenida de César Augusto 25; 🕑 9am-2pm & 5-8pm Mon-Fri, from 10am Sat & Sun)

Zaragoza Turismo (☎ 902 142008; www.zaragoza.es/ciudad/turismo) Plaza del Pilar (🕑 9am-9pm Easter-Oct, 10am-8pm Nov-Easter); Glorieta de Pío (Torreón de la Zuda, Glorieta de Pío XII; 🕑 10am-2pm & 4.30-8pm Nov-Easter, 9am-9pm Easter-Oct)

SIGHTS

Follow the Roman route through the city, visit the many Mudéjar-styled buildings and churches, or simply soak up Zaragoza's easy-going atmosphere.

The baroque **Basílica de Nuestra Señora del Pilar** (☎ 976 39 74 97; admission free; 🕑 6.45am-9.30pm) towers over Zaragoza literally and figuratively. The spiritual heart of Aragón, this has long been a place of pilgrimage. The faithful flock to the **Capilla Santa** to kiss a piece of marble *pilar* (pillar). The faithful believe the Virgin Mary appeared to St James atop this pillar in AD 40.

At Plaza del Pilar's southeastern end is Zaragoza's brooding 12th- to 17th-century cathedral, **La Seo** (☎ 976 29 12 38; Plaza de la Seo; admission €2.50; 🕑 10am-6pm Tue-Fri, 10am-2pm & 3-6pm Sat, 10-11.30am & 2.30-6pm Sun Jun-Sep, shorter hr rest of year). Its northwest façade is a Mudéjar masterpiece, and inside is an impressive 15th-century main altarpiece in coloured alabaster.

Begin the Roman tour of Zaragoza with a stop at the **Museo del Foro de Caesaraugusta** (☎ 976 39 97 52; Plaza de la Seo 2; admission €2; ⏰ 10am-2pm & 5-8pm Tue-Sat, 10am-2pm Sun, last entry one hr before closing time), an interesting museum about Roman life. Some 70m below lie the remains of the Roman town, brought to life by an audiovisual show (in Spanish). The historically curious can also visit the **Museo del Teatro de Caesaraugusta** (Theatre Museum; ☎ 976 20 50 88; Calle de San Jorge 12; admission €3; ⏰ 10am-9pm Tue-Sat, 10am-2pm Sun), the **Museo de las Termas Públicas** (Public Baths Museum; ☎ 976 29 72 79; Calle San Juan y San Pedro 3-7; admission €2; ⏰ 10am-2pm & 5-8pm Tue-Sat, 10am-2pm Sun) and the **Museo del Puerto Fluvial** (River Port Museum; ☎ 976 39 31 57; Plaza de San Bruno 8; admission €2; ⏰ 10am-2pm & 5-8pm Tue-Sat, 10am-2pm Sun). If you plan to visit all four museums, buy the Ruta Caesaraugusta pass (per adult/student €6/4.50), available at the sites themselves.

The **Palacio de la Aljafería** (☎ 976 28 96 84; Calle de los Diputados; adult/under 12yr/concession €3/free/1, Sun free; ⏰ 10am-2pm & 4-6.30pm Mon-Wed, Fri & Sat, 10am-2pm Sun Nov-Mar, 10am-2pm & 4.30-8pm Sat-Wed, 4.30-8pm Fri Apr-Jun & Sep-Oct, 10am-2pm & 4.30-8pm daily Jul & Aug) is Spain's most outstanding Muslim building outside Andalucía. Built as the palace of the Muslim rulers who held the city from 714 to 1118, it is now home to Aragón's parliament.

SPAIN

SLEEPING

On and around Plaza del Pilar and Avenda César Augusto you'll find most of the sleeping options.

Hostal El Descanso (☎ 976 29 17 41; Calle San Lorenzo 2; s/d with shared bathroom €20/30) Simple, bright rooms, a family-run atmosphere and a central location overlooking a pretty plaza near the Roman theatre add up to a good budget deal.

Hotel Rio Arga (☎ 976 39 90 65; www.hotelrioarga.es; Contamina 20; s/d €43/60; ❄ 💻) In a quiet location, yet ideal for all central needs, there are comfy rooms here. Most of the rooms have been renovated with flat-screen TVs and a modern look; those with recently overhauled bathrooms are the best.

Hotel Sauce (☎ 976 20 50 50; www.hotelsauce.com; Calle de Espoz y Mina 33; s/d €59/75; ❄ 💻) This small hotel has good rooms with a mix of styles from traditional and cosy to pastel tones and a modern, classy look. Bookings are advisable whichever night you're planning on staying. Breakfast costs €7.50.

EATING & DRINKING

Zaragoza has some terrific tapas bars, with dozens of places on or close to Plaza de Santa Marta and towards the southern end of Calle Heroísmo. Otherwise the narrow streets of El Tubo, north of Plaza de España, are tapas central.

Mercado Central (Plaza de Lanuza; ⏰ 8am-2pm) Get your fresh fruit and veggies at Central, the main city market.

our pick **Casa Pascualillo** (☎ 976 39 72 03; Calle de la Libertad 5; ⏰ lunch & dinner Tue-Sat, lunch Sun) The bar groans under the weight of every tapas variety imaginable with seafood and meat in abundance, but their house speciality is El Pascualillo, a 'small' *bocadillo* of *jamón* (ham), mushrooms and onion.

Casa Juanico (☎ 976 29 50 88; Calle de Santiago 30-32; tapas from €2, menú del día €11; ⏰ closed Tue) For cheap tapas and a friendly atmosphere, this place can't be beat; the terrace is ideal for summer.

El Rincón de Aragón (☎ 976 20 11 63; Calle de Santiago 3-5; menú del día €12.95, menú Aragonés €19.90) There is no time for unnecessary elaborations here – the decor is basic and the food stripped down to its essence. One house speciality among many is the *ternasco asado con patatas a la pobre* (roasted suckling lamb ribs with 'poor man's potatoes').

Calle del Temple, southwest of Plaza del Pilar, is the spiritual home of Zaragoza's roaring nightlife. This is where the city's students head out to drink. There are more bars lined up along this street than anywhere else in Aragón.

GETTING THERE & AWAY

High-speed AVE trains leave Zaragoza's futuristic **Estación Intermodal Delicias** (Calle Rioja 33) for Madrid (€51, 1½ hours, 17 daily) and Barcelona (€59, one hour). There are also services to Valencia (€23.20, 4½ hours, two daily) and to main towns across Aragón.

Dozens of bus lines fan out across Spain from the bus station attached to the train station.

Around Aragón

Aragón is a land of stark contrast. The centre is largely barren, stretching south to the cold, wintry but greener territory around **Teruel**, and north to Huesca and on to the pretty Pyrenees. Little visited Teruel is home to some stunning Mudéjar architecture, and a **tourist office** (☎ 978 60 22 79; Calle Tomás Nogués 1).

In the north, the **Parque Nacional de Ordesa y Monte Perdido** (www.ordesa.net) and the **Parque Natural Posets-Maladeta** (www.cerler.es), are excellent for hiking. The village of **Torla** is the gateway to the Parque Nacional de Ordesa y Monte Perdido, while **Benasque** is a popular base for the Parque Natural Posets-Maladeta. Another enchanting base for exploration in the region is **Aínsa**, a valley town of stone houses an hour's bus ride from Torla.

South of the hamlet of **La Besurta** is the great Maladeta massif, a superb challenge for experienced climbers. This forbidding line of icy peaks, with glaciers suspended from the higher crests, culminates in **Aneto** (3404m), the highest peak in the Pyrenees. There are plenty of hiking and climbing options for all levels in these mountain parks bordering France.

BASQUE COUNTRY

The Basques, whose language is believed to be among the world's oldest, claim two of Spain's most interesting cities – San Sebastián and Bilbao – as their own. Stately San Sebastián offers a slick seaside position and some of the best food Spain has to offer. The extraordinary Guggenheim Bilbao museum is that city's centrepiece.

San Sebastián

pop 183,400

Stylish San Sebastián (Donostia in Basque) has the air of an upscale resort, complete with an idyllic location on the shell-shaped Bahía de la Concha. The natural setting – crystalline waters, a flawless beach, green hills on all sides – is captivating, but the city itself has plenty to offer. Head to the buzzing Parte Vieja (Old Quarter) for tempting tapas bars and restaurants showing off the best of Basque cuisine.

INFORMATION

Street signs are in Basque and Spanish and can be confusing. If navigation is proving tough, try picking up tourist office maps in each language.

Donosti-Net (☎ 943 42 94 97; Calle de Narrica 3; per 10min/1hr €0.90/3.30; 🕑 9am-11pm) This is a one-stop travellers' service, with email, office services, travel info and even a spot to leave your luggage.

Centro de Atracción y Turismo (☎ 943 48 11 66; www.sansebastianturismo.com; Blvd Reina Regente 3; 🕑 8.30am-8pm Mon-Sat, 10am-7pm Sun Jun-Sep, 9am-2pm & 3.30-7pm Mon-Sat, 10am-2pm Sun Oct-May)

Post office (Calle de Urdaneta 7)

SIGHTS & ACTIVITIES

San Sebastián's beautiful city beaches, **Playa de la Concha** and **Playa de Ondarreta**, are popular spots year-round. East of the Urumea River is the somewhat less crowded **Playa de la Zurriola**, popular with surfers. To escape the crowds, take the small **boat** (🕑 10am-8pm Jun-Sep) to the **Isla de Santa Clara**, an island in the middle of the bay. From here you can enjoy pretty views of the seafront.

For more good views, take the 30-minute walk up to **Monte Urgull**, a hill topped by low castle walls and a statue of Christ. The walk begins at a stairway in Plaza de Zuloaga.

The best vista in San Sebastián is from **Monte Igueldo**. Drive up or catch the **funicular** (return adult/child €2.30/1.70; 🕑 10am-10pm Jul & Aug, 10am or 11am-6pm or 9pm Sep-Jun) from the western end of the seafront *paseo*. At the top, visit the **Parque de Atracciones** (☎ 943 21 02 11; 🕑 11am-6pm Mon-Tue & Thu-Fri, 11am-8pm Sat & Sun), an old-time funfair.

San Sebastián's best museum is the **Museo Chillida Leku** (☎ 943 33 60 06; www.museochillidaleku.com; adult/child/student €8.50/free/6.50; 🕑 10.30am-3pm Wed-Mon Sep-Jun, 10.30am-8pm Mon-Sat, 10.30am-3pm Sun Jul & Aug), 10km outside the city centre. An outdoor sculpture garden featuring 40 large-scale works by the famed Basque artist Eduardo Chillida, this is a peaceful place ideal for picnics. To get here, take the G2 bus (€1.25) for Hernani from Calle de Okendo in San Sebastián and get off at Zabalaga.

Kids and adults alike will have fun at San Sebastián's **aquarium** (☎ 943 44 00 99; www.aquariumss.com; Paseo del Muelle 34; adult/under 3yr/child/student €10/free/6/8; 🕑 10am-9pm Jul & Aug, 10am-8pm Apr-Jun & Sep, 10am-7pm Mon-Fri & 10am-8pm Sat & Sun Oct-Mar), which is home to more than 5000 tropical fish, morays, sharks and a variety of other finned creatures.

SLEEPING

our pick **Urban House** (☎ 943 42 81 54; www.enjoyeu.com; Alameda del Boulevard 24; dm/r €27/50; 💻) Loud and colourful rooms set the tone for this superb party house where summer fun rules supreme. It's smack in the centre of the action and the young, beautiful, multilingual staff will ensure you have a good time. During the high season it only offers beds in four-person dorms.

SPAIN

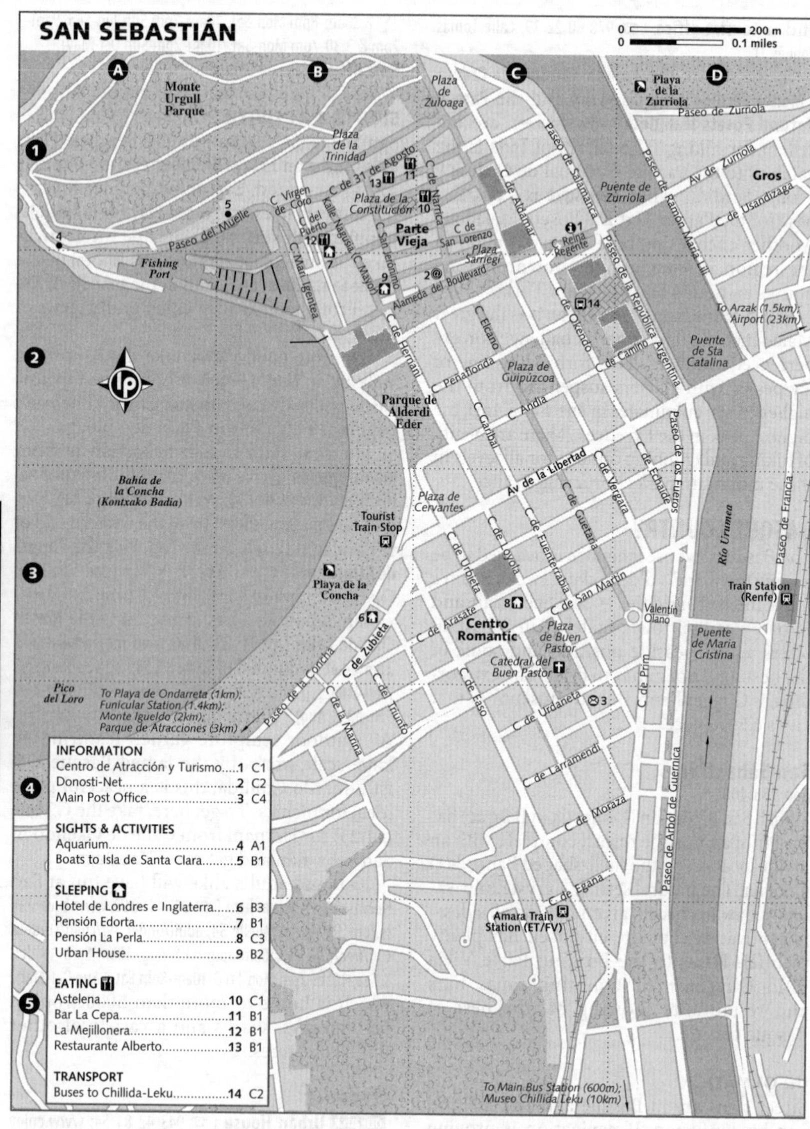

Pensión La Perla (☎ 943 42 81 23; www.pensionlaperla.com; Calle de Loyola 10; s/d/tr €35/55/70) Brisk, old-fashioned service and clean, fairly plain rooms, keep this well-located central digs busy. The no-nonsense woman who runs it is very helpful.

Pensión Edorta (☎ 943 42 37 73; www.pensionedorta.com; Calle del Puerto 15; r with shared/private bathroom €60/80; 💻) A fine spot with rooms that are all tarted up in brash modern colours but with a salute to the past in the stone walls and ceilings. Most rooms share bathrooms.

Hotel de Londres e Inglaterra (☎ 943 44 07 70; www.hlondres.com; Calle de Zubieta 2; s/d from €175/225; ❄ 💻) Queen Isabel II set the tone for this hotel well over a century ago and things have stayed pretty regal ever since. It oozes class and some rooms have stunning views over Playa de la Concha.

EATING

San Sebastián is paradise for food lovers. Considered the birthplace of *nueva cocina española,* this area is home to some of the country's top chefs. Yet not all the good food is pricey. Head to the Parte Vieja for San Sebastián's *pintxos,* Basque-style tapas.

Pintxos

Do what the locals do – crawls of the city centre's bars. *Pintxo* etiquette is simple. Ask for a plate and point out what *pintxos* (bar snacks – more like tasty mounds of food on little slices of baguette) you want. Keep the toothpicks and go back for as many as you want. Accompany with *txakoli,* a cloudy white wine poured like cider to create a little fizz. When you're ready to pay, hand over the plate with all the toothpicks and tell bar staff how many drinks you've had. It's an honour system that has stood the test of time. Expect to pay €2.50 to €3.50 for a *pintxo* and *txakoli.*

Bar La Cepa (Calle de 31 de Agosto 7) The best *jamón jabugo* does not disappoint here and you eat beneath the blank eyes of a very large bull's head. The kitchens here also produce decent no-frills menus for €13.50.

La Mejillonera (Calle del Puerto) If you thought mussels came only with garlic sauce come here and discover mussels (from €3) by the thousand in all their glorious forms.

our pick Astelena (Plaza de la Constitució/Calle Iñigo 1) The *pintxos* draped across the counter in this bar, tucked into the corner of the plaza, stand out as some of the best in the city. Many of them are a fusion of Basque and Asian inspirations, but maybe the king of them all are the foie gras–based treats.

Restaurants

Restaurante Alberto (☎ 943 42 88 84; Calle de 31 de Agosto 19; mains from €15; 🕑 closed Tue) A charming old seafood restaurant with a fish monger-style window display of the day's catch. Small, dark and friendly, but much of the fish is sold by the kilo so bring a friend.

Arzak (☎ 943 27 84 65; Avenida Alcalde Jose Elosegui 273; meals €150-160) Three-star Michelin star chef Juan Mari Arzak is a national institution. Arzak is now assisted by his daughter Elena and they never cease to innovate. The restaurant is about 1.5km east of San Sebastián. Reservations, well in advance, are obligatory.

DRINKING

The Parte Vieja is a fun place any night of the week. Around 8pm the tapas bars start hopping as people enjoy a pre-dinner round of *pintxos.* The revelry lasts until midnight midweek, and until the cock crows on weekends. Another hot spot is the area around Calle de los Reyes Católicos, behind the Catedral del Buen Pastor.

GETTING THERE & AWAY

From San Sebastián airport (EAS), catch the Interbus that runs regularly to the Plaza de Gipuzkoa in town (€1.55, times vary).

The main **Renfe train station** (Paseo de Francia) is just across Río Urumea, on a line linking Paris to Madrid. There are several services daily to Madrid (from €37.20, six hours) and two to Barcelona (from €38.20, eight hours). ET/FV trains run from Amara train station west to Bilbao (€6.50, 2½ hours, hourly) via Zarautz, Zumaia and Durango.

The **bus station** (Plaza Pío XII) is a 20-minute walk south of Parte Vieja. City bus 28 makes the run to and from the centre. PESA has frequent services to Bilbao (€9.20, one hour). La Roncalesa has up to 10 buses daily to Pamplona (€6.50, one hour).

Bilbao

pop 354,200

The commercial hub of the Basque Country, Bilbao (Bilbo in Basque) is best known for the magnificent Guggenheim Museum. An architectural masterpiece by Frank Gehry, the museum was the catalyst of a turn-around that saw Bilbao transformed from an industrial port city into a vibrant cultural centre. After visiting this must-see temple to modern art, spend time exploring Bilbao's Casco Viejo (Old Quarter), a grid of elegant streets dotted with shops, cafes, *pintxos* bars and several small but worthy museums.

INFORMATION

L@zar (☎ 944 45 35 09; Sendeja 5; per min €0.06; 🕑 10.30am-1.30am Mon-Fri, 11am-1.30am Sat & Sun) Internet access.

Local Police (Calle Luis Briñas 14)

Main post office (☎ 944 22 05 48; Alameda de Urquijo 19)

SPAIN

Tourist office (☎ 944 79 57 60; www.bilbao.net/bilbaoturismo; Plaza del Ensanche 11; ⌚ 9am-2pm & 4-7.30pm Mon-Fri) Has other branches at the Teatro Arriaga, Museo Guggenheim and airport.

SIGHTS

Designed by Frank Gehry, the spectacular **Museo Guggenheim** (☎ 944 35 90 80; www.guggenheim-bilbao.es; Avenida Abandoibarra 2; adult/under 12yr/student €12.50/free/7.50; ⌚ 10am-8pm Tue-Sun Sep-Jun, daily Jul & Aug) is an experience to remember. For many, the building is much more interesting than the exhibitions inside. With its undulating forms covered in titanium scales, the structure was inspired by the shapes of ships and fish. Inside, the guts of the building are exposed, with few columns, support beams or, for that matter, floors and walls obstructing the view. Many credit this creation with revitalising modern architecture and creating a new standard in vanguard design.

Five minutes from the Museo Guggenheim, the **Museo de Bellas Artes** (Fine Arts Museum; ☎ 944 39 60 60; www.museobilbao.com; Plaza del Museo 2; adult/student €5.50/4, Wed free; ⌚ 10am-8pm Tue-Sun) often seems to exceed its more famous cousin for content.

The **Casco Viejo**, Bilbao's old quarter, is a compact coin of charming streets, boisterous bars and plenty of quirky and independent shops. At its heart are Bilbao's original 'seven streets', Las Siete Calles, which date from the 1400s. The Gothic 14th-century **Catedral de Santiago** (⌚ 10am-1pm & 4-7pm Tue-Sat, 10.30am-1.30pm Sun) has a splendid Renaissance portico and pretty little cloister, and the 19th-century arcaded **Plaza Nueva**, a rewarding *pintxo* haunt.

The **Euskal Museoa** (Museum of Basque Archaeology, Ethnography & History ☎ 944 15 54 23; www.euskal-museoa.org; Plaza Miguel Unamuno 4; adult/under 10yr/student €3/free/1.50, Thu free; ⌚ 11am-5pm Tue-Sat, 11am-2pm Sun) is a complete and well-executed lesson in Basque history.

Take the metro to the **Puente Colgante** (Hanging Bridge; www.puente-colgante.com; Calle Barria 3, Las Arenas Getxo; ⌚ 10am-sunset) to walk or, better yet, ride across on the gondola (€0.30 each way) that hangs from the world's oldest 'transporter bridge'. The walkers' view from the top is great.

SLEEPING

The Bilbao tourism authority has a useful **reservations department** (☎ 902 87 72 98; www.bilbaoreservas.com) for accommodation.

Pensión Mardones (☎ 944 15 31 05; www.pensionmardones.com; Calle Jardines 4; s/d €34/48; 💻) This well kept number has nice carved wooden wardrobes in the rooms and lots of exposed wooden roof beams. The cheerful owner is very helpful and all up it offers great value.

Pensión Gurea (☎ 944 16 32 99; hostalgurea@yahoo.es; Calle de Bidebarrieta 14; s/d €45/65; 💻) It's a family affair at this bright and breezy *pensión* where husband and wife run around trying to please you, and the kids just run around. It's well-organised with large rooms.

Pensión Iturrienea Ostatua (☎ 944 16 15 00; www.iturrieneaostatua.com; Calle de Santa María 14; d/tr €70/96) Easily the most eccentric hotel in Bilbao, this part farmyard/part old fashioned toyshop is a work of art in its own right. Try to get a room on the first floor as they have so much character you'll have trouble fitting in yourself.

Xukeia (☎ 944 15 97 72; Calle el Perro; pintxos €1-1.50) One of the more character-infused places in the Old Town. It has something of the look of a small-town French bistro overlaid with raucous Spanish soul. The drool-inducing *pintxos* have won awards and are cheaper than elsewhere.

El Globo (☎ 944 15 42 21; Calle de Diputación 8) One of the best *pintxos* options in the more modern Ensanche part of town, this popular bar has a terrific range of *pintxos modernos,* including favourites such as *txangurro gratinado* (spider crab) and *morcilla rebozada* (blood sausage in light batter).

Abaroa (☎ 944 13 20 51; Campo Volantin 13; mains €7-12) This brightly furnished restaurant is a big name with locals and specialises in hearty countryside fare with a twist of today. Black pudding and a bowl of beans never tasted so good!

DRINKING

Las Siete Calles are transformed into one big street party at night. Bars and discos line the streets, especially rowdy Calle Barrenkale. For something a bit more low-key, take your pick of the cafes on Plaza Nueva.

GETTING THERE & AWAY

Bilbao's airport (BIO) is near Sondika, 12km northeast of the city. **Easyjet** (www.easyjet.com) has cheap flights between London and Bilbao. The airport bus Bizkaibus A3247 (€1.25, 30 minutes) runs to/from Termibus (bus station), where there is a tram stop and a metro station.

Two Renfe trains runs daily to Madrid (from €39.80, six hours) and Barcelona (€39.80, nine hours) from the Abando train station. Slow **FEVE** (www.feve.es) trains run from Concordia station next door west into Cantabria and Asturias.

Bilbao's main bus station (Termibus) is southwest of town. Regular services operate to/from Madrid (€26.20, 4¾ hours), Barcelona (€40.60, seven hours), Pamplona (€12.85, 1¾ hours) and Santander (€9.30, 1½ hours).

NAVARRA

Navarra, historically and culturally linked to the Basque Country, is known for its fine wines and for the Sanfermines festival in Pamplona.

Pamplona

pop 195,800 / elev 456m

Immortalised by Ernest Hemingway in *The Sun Also Rises*, the pre-Pyrenean city of Pamplona (Iruña in Basque) is home of the wild Sanfermines (aka Encierro or Running of the Bulls) festival, but is also an extremely walkable city that's managed to mix the charm of old plazas and buildings with modern shops and a lively nightlife.

INFORMATION

Kuria.Net (☎ 948 22 30 77; Calle Curia 15; per hr €2.50; ⏰ 10am-10pm Mon-Fri, 10am-2pm & 3-10pm Sat) A more stylish internet cafe it would be hard to find.

Tourist office (☎ 848 42 04 20; www.navarra.es; Calle de Esclava 1; ⏰ 10am-2pm & 4-7pm Mon-Sat, 10am-2pm Sun) This well-organised office has English-speaking staff and plenty of city info.

SIGHTS

The **Catedral** (☎ 948 22 29 90; Calle Dormitalería; guided tours admission €4.40; ⏰ 10am-7pm Mon-Fri, 10am-2.30pm Sat mid-Jul–mid-Sep, 10am-2pm & 4-7pm Mon-Fri, 10am-2pm Sat mid-Sep–mid-Jul) stands on a rise just inside the city ramparts. It is a late-medieval Gothic gem spoiled by a dull neoclassical facade. The vast interior reveals some fine artefacts, including a silver-plated Virgin and the splendid 15th-century tomb of Carlos III of Navarra and his wife Doña Leonor. The real joy is the Gothic cloister.

The walls and bulwarks of the grand fortified citadel, the star-shaped **Ciudadela** (Avenida del Ejército; admission free; ⏰ 7.30am-9.30pm Mon-Sat, 9am-9.30pm Sun), lurk amid the greenery in what is now a charming park, the portal to three more parks that unfold to the north and lend the city a green escape.

Around 9km northeast of Pamplona in Alzuza, the impressive **Museo Oteiza** (☎ 948 33 20 74; www.museooteiza.org; Calle de la Cuesta 7; adult/child/student €4/free/2, Fri free; ⏰ 11am-7pm Tue-Sun Jun-Sep, 10am-3pm Tue-Fri, 11am-7pm Sat & Sun Oct-May) contains almost 3000 pieces by the renowned Navarran sculptor, Jorge Oteiza. **Río Irati** (☎ 948 22 14 70) has at least one bus a day to Alzuza from Pamplona's bus station.

> **SURVIVING SANFERMINES**
>
> The Sanfermines festival is held on 6 to 14 July, when Pamplona is overrun with thrill-seekers, curious onlookers and, oh yeah, bulls. The Encierro (Running of the Bulls) begins at 8am daily, when bulls are let loose from the Coralillos Santo Domingo. The 825m race lasts just three minutes, so don't be late. The safest place to watch the Encierro is on TV. If that's too tame for you, try to sweet-talk your way onto a balcony or book a room in a hotel with views.

SLEEPING

Accommodation is hard to come by during Sanfermines – book months in advance. Prices below don't reflect the huge (up to fivefold) mark-up you'll find in mid-July.

Habitaciones Mendi (☎ 948 22 52 97; Calle de las Navas de Tolosa 9; r €40) This charming guest house is a find. Creaky, wobbly, wooden staircases and equally creaky, chintzy rooms make it just like being at your gran's, and the woman running it will cluck over you as if she were your gran.

Hostal Arriazu (☎ 948 21 02 02; www.hostalarriazu.com; Calle Comedias 14; s/d incl breakfast €55/65; 💻) Falling somewhere between a budget *pensión* and a midrange hotel there is superb value in this former theatre. The rooms are plain but the bathrooms as good as you'll find.

Hotel Europa (☎ 948 22 18 00; www.hreuropa.com; Calle de Espoz y Mina 11; s/d €87/96; 💻) Wow! What a bizarre concoction of fake marble, equally fake gold-framed portraits of historical figures, and photographs of the famous and not-so famous visitors to the hotel.

EATING & DRINKING

Central streets such as Calle San Nicolás and Calle Estafeta are lined with tapas

SPAIN

bars, many of which morph into nightspots on weekends.

Sarasate (☎ 948 22 57 27; Calle de San Nicolás 21; menú del día Mon-Fri/Sat & Sun €10.50/16.50) This bright, uncluttered vegetarian restaurant on the 1st floor offers excellent veggie dishes and gluten-free options.

our pick Baserri (☎ 948 22 20 21; Calle de San Nicolás 32; menú del día €14) This place has won tons of food awards. As you'd expect from such a certificate-studded bar, the meals and the *pintxos* are superb. A *menú de degustación*, a sampler of *pintxos*, costs €24. There are also gluten-free options.

Café Iruña (☎ 948 22 20 64; Plaza del Castillo 44) This old Hemingway haunt was mentioned 14 times in *The Sun Also Rises*. It's a popular spot for breakfast, coffee, a light meal or some early evening tipples.

Cool (☎ 948 22 46 22; www.coolounge.com; Calle de Navas de Tolosa 11) As the name suggests this clean steel bar on the edge of the old city is a place to lounge around seeing and being seen.

SPAIN

GETTING THERE & AWAY

Renfe trains run to/from Madrid (€52, three hours, three daily) and San Sebastián (from €14.70, two hours, three daily). Bus 9 connects the station with the centre.

From the **main bus station** (☎ 948 22 38 54; Calle Conde Oliveto 8) buses leave for most towns throughout Navarra, although service is restricted on Sunday. Regular bus services travel to Bilbao (€12.50, 1¾ hours) and San Sebastián (€6.50, one hour).

CANTABRIA, ASTURIAS & GALICIA

With a landscape reminiscent of parts of the British Isles, 'Green Spain' offers great walks in national parks, seafood feasts in sophisticated towns and oodles of opportunities to plunge into the ice-cold waters of the Bay of Biscay. Oh, and there's loads of rain, too. Even in summer, you can strike four seasons in a day, so be prepared for anything!

SANTANDER

pop 181,800

Most of modern Santander stands in drab contrast to its pretty beaches, particularly the old-world elegance of El Sardinero. A huge fire raged through the city in 1941, but what's left of the 'old' centre is a lively source of entertainment for the palate and liver.

Information

Ciberlope (www.ciberlope.com; Calle de Lope de Vega 14; per 30min from €1.20; ⌚ 10.30am-midnight Mon-Fri, 11.30am-midnight Sat, 5pm-midnight Sun) Internet access.

Municipal tourist office (☎ 942 20 30 00; www.ayto-santander.es in Spanish; Jardines de Pereda; ⌚ 9am-9pm daily mid-Jun–mid-Sep, 8.30am-1.30pm & 4-7pm Mon-Fri, 10am-2pm Sat mid-Sep–Easter & 10am-7pm Sat Easter–mid-Jun)

Regional tourist office (☎ 942 31 07 08; www.turismodecantabria.com in Spanish; Calle de Hernán Cortés 4; ⌚ 9am-9pm Jul-Sep, 9.30am-1.30pm & 4-7pm Oct-Jun) In the Mercado del Este.

Sights & Activities

The **Catedral** (☎ 942 22 60 24; Plaza del Obispo José Eguino y Trecu s/n; ⌚ 10am-1pm & 4-8pm Mon-Fri, 10am-1pm & 4.30-8pm Sat, 10am-1.30pm & 5-9pm Sun & holidays) is composed of two 13th-century Gothic churches, one above the other. Several other museums are dotted about town.

The beaches on the **Bahía de Santander** are more protected than **Playa del Sardinero**. The latter is a hike from the city centre, so catch bus 1, 2 or 3 from outside the post office. **Playa del Puntal**, a finger of sand jutting out from the eastern side of the bay, is idyllic on calm days (but beware the currents). Boats sail there every 30 minutes between 10am and 8pm from June to late September, from the Estación Marítima Los Reginas (€3.90 return).

Sleeping

Hospedaje Botín (☎ 942 21 00 94; www.hospedajebotin.com; Calle de Isabel II No 1; s/d €38/54.50) The homey Botín has some spacious rooms with showers and *galerías* (glassed-in balconies).

Pensión La Corza (☎ 942 21 29 50; Calle de Hernán Cortés 25; r with washbasin/bathroom €42/55) The best deal around, La Corza is on pleasant Plaza de Pombo, with high-ceilings and handsomely furnished rooms up on the 3rd floor, some with balconies overlooking the square.

Eating & Drinking

La Conveniente (☎ 942 21 28 87; Calle de Gómez Oreña 9; meals €15-20; ⌚ dinner Mon-Sat) This cavernous bodega (wine cellar) has high stone walls, wooden pillars and beams, and more wine bottles than you may ever have seen in one place. You

WORTH THE TRIP: PICOS DE EUROPA

These jagged mountains straddling Asturias, Cantabria and northeast Castilla y León amount to some of the finest walking country in Spain.

They comprise three limestone massifs (whose highest peak rises 2648m). The 647-sq-km **Parque Nacional de los Picos de Europa** covers all three massifs and is Spain's second-biggest national park. Check out www.turismopicosdeeuropa.com (in Spanish), www.liebanaypicosdeeuropa.com and also www.picosdeeuropa.com (in Spanish).

There are numerous places to stay and eat all over the mountains. Getting here and around by bus can be slow going but the Picos are accessible from Santander and Oviedo (the latter is easier) by bus.

If you fancy exploring dramatic mountain country that few foreigners know, consider the 300-sq-km **Parque Natural de Somiedo** (www.somiedo.es), southwest of Oviedo, the capital of Asturias. You really need your own vehicle to get around here, but one or two daily buses (weekends) run to/from Oviedo to Pola de Somiedo (€6.85, 1¼ to two hours), the main town in the area.

might go for a cheese *tabla* (platter) or other classic *raciones*. Servings are generous.

Bodega Cigaleña (☎ 942 21 30 62; Calle de Daoiz y Velarde 19; tapas from €2; 🕑 Mon-Sat) A classic bar for tapas, wine and laughter, this is one of the most popular of its ilk in the Old Town.

Café de Pombo (☎ 942 22 32 24; Calle de Hernán Cortés 21) On the square of the same name, Pombo is an elegant spot for lingering breakfasts. A hot chocolate on the square comes in at €1.75.

Plaza de Cañadío is home to several *bares de copas*, where you can enjoy an outdoor beer in the evening. Calle de Santa Lucía, along with Calle del Río de la Pila and its immediate neighbourhood, also teem with bars of all descriptions. Most stay open until between 3am and 4am.

Getting There & Away

From Plymouth in the UK, **Brittany Ferries** (☎ UK 0870 9076103, Spain 942 36 06 11; www.brittany-ferries.co.uk) runs a twice-weekly car ferry to Santander (20½ hours) from mid-March to mid-November.

From the **bus station** (☎ 942 21 19 95; www.santandereabus.com), ALSA runs at least six buses daily to/from Madrid (€26.50 to €39, 5¼ to 6½ hours).

Renfe has three trains daily to/from Madrid (€44, 4½ to 5¼ hours). FEVE, next door, operates two trains daily to Oviedo (Asturias) and three to/from Bilbao (Basque Country).

AROUND SANTANDER

Some 34km west of Santander, **Santillana del Mar** (www.santillanadelmar.com) is a bijou medieval village and the obvious overnight base for visiting the nearby Cueva de Altamira.

The country's finest prehistoric art, in the Cueva de Altamira, 2km southwest of Santillana del Mar, is off-limits to all but the scientific community. Since 2001, however, the **Museo Altamira** (☎ 942 81 80 05; http://museodealtamira.mcu.es; adult/senior & under 18yr/student €2.40/free/1.20; 🕑 9.30am-8pm Tue-Sat, 9.30am-3pm Sun & holidays May-Oct, shorter hr Nov-Apr) has allowed all comers to view the inspired, 14,500-year-old depictions of bison, horses and other beasts (or rather, their replicas) in this full-size, dazzling re-creation of the cave's most interesting chamber, the Sala de Polícromos (Polychrome Hall).

Buses run three to four times a day from Santander to Santilla del Mar.

OVIEDO

pop 216,700 / elev 232m

The elegant parks and modern shopping streets of Asturias' capital are agreeably offset by what remains of the *casco antiguo* (old town).

Information

Oficina Municipal de Turismo (☎ 985 22 75 86; http://turismo.ayto-oviedo.es; Calle Marqués de Santa Cruz 1; 🕑 9.30am-2pm & 4.30-8pm mid-Jun–mid-Sep, 10am-2pm & 4.30-7pm mid-Sep–mid-Jun)

Regional tourist office (☎ 985 21 33 85; www.infoasturias.com; Calle de Cimadevilla 4; 🕑 10am-8pm mid-Jun–mid-Sep, 10am-7pm mid-Sep–mid-Jun) Check out the website for inspiration on beautiful stretches of coast and deep green hill country.

Sights

The mainly Gothic **Catedral de San Salvador** is home to the Cámara Santa, a chapel built by

SPAIN

Alfonso II to house holy relics. The **Cámara Santa** (☎ 985 22 10 33; admission incl Museo Diocesano adult/under 10yr/10-15yr €2.50/free/1, Thu afternoon free; 10am-1pm & 4-6pm or 7pm Mon-Sat) contains some key symbols of medieval Spanish Christianity. Alfonso II presented the Cruz de los Ángeles (Cross of the Angels) to Oviedo in 808, and it's still the city's emblem. A century later Alfonso III donated the Cruz de la Victoria (Cross of Victory), which in turn became the sign of Asturias.

Explore the Old Town's nooks and crannies. **Plaza de la Constitución** is capped at one end by the **Iglesia de San Isidoro** and fronted by an eclectic collection of old shops, cafes and the 17th-century *ayuntamiento* (city hall). To the south, past the **Mercado El Fontán** food market, arcaded **Plaza Fontán** is equipped with a couple of *sidrerías* (cider houses). Other little squares include **Plaza de Trascorrales**, **Plaza de Riego** and **Plaza del Paraguas**.

Just outside the city (within 3km) is a scattering of 9th-century, pre-Romanesque buildings, including the **Iglesia de San Julián de los Prados**, **Palacio de Santa María del Naranco** and the **Iglesia de San Miguel de Lillo**. Get information from the tourist offices in town.

SPAIN

Sleeping & Eating

Oviedo's *sidrería* rules include getting good grub at reasonable prices. Most of those on Calle de la Gascona serve *raciones* from €8 to €18.

Hostal Arcos (☎ 985 21 47 73; Calle de Magdalena 3; s/d €35/50) The only lodging in the Old Town is a modern brick building with nine simple, clean rooms (with TV and heating) that is ideally located within stumbling distance of some of Oviedo's best watering holes.

Hostal Belmonte (☎ 985 24 10 20; calogon@teleline.es; Calle de Uría 31; s/d €38.50/49) A quick stroll from the train station, this charming 3rd-floor (there's a lift) lodging offers cosy rooms with timber floors and an at-home feel. Cheaper rooms with shared bathroom are also available.

Tierra Astur (☎ 985 20 25 02; Calle de la Gascona 1; meals €20-25) A particularly atmospheric *sidrería*/restaurant, Tierra Astur is famed for its grilled meats and prize-winning cider.

Getting There & Away

The **Aeropuerto de Asturias** is at Santiago del Monte, 47km northwest of Oviedo and 40km west of Gijón. There are flights to London and Geneva (easyJet), destinations in Germany (Air Berlin), and Paris and Brussels with Iberia.

From the **ALSA bus station** (Calle de Pepe Cosmen), direct services head up the motorway to Gijón (€1.99, 25 to 30 minutes) every 10 or 15 minutes from 6.30am to 10.45pm. Other daily buses head to/from Galicia, Cantabria and elsewhere.

One train station serves both rail companies, Renfe and FEVE, the latter located on the upper level. For Gijón, it's best to use the Renfe *cercanías* (local trains that serve large cities; €2.45, 35 minutes).

AROUND OVIEDO

If you have kids in tow, a short hop to **Gijón** on the coast could be in order for a visit to the new **Acuario** (☎ 958 18 52 20; www.acuariodegijon.com; adult/child €12/6; 10am-10pm Jul-Aug, 10am-7pm Mon-Fri, 10am-8pm Sat, Sun & holidays Sep-Jun), with 4000 specimens (from Cantabrian otters to grey sharks) in 50 tanks.

LA CORUÑA

pop 252,000

A lively port city adorned with 19th-century houses with distinctive *galerías* (glassed-in balconies), La Coruña (A Coruña in Gallego) has an insouciant and welcoming air. It is also a fabulous place to sample seafood.

Information

Municipal tourist office (☎ 618 79 06 65; www.turismocoruna.com; Plaza de María Pita; 9am-8.30pm Mon-Fri Feb-Oct, 9am-2.30pm & 4-8.30pm Mon-Fri Nov-Jan, 10am-2pm & 4-8pm Sat, 10am-3pm Sun year-round)

Regional tourist office (☎ 981 22 18 22; Dársena de la Marina; 10am-2pm & 4-7pm Mon-Fri, 11am-2pm & 4-7pm Sat, 11am-2pm Sun)

Sights

La Coruña's city **beach** is a glorious protected sweep of sand 1.4km long. Named Playa del Orzán at its east end and Playa de Riazor at the west, it gets busy in summer.

The city's best-known and best-loved monument is the **Torre de Hércules** (☎ 981 22 37 30; admission €2; 10am-5.45pm Oct-Mar, 10am-6.45pm Apr-Jun & Sep, 10am-8.45pm Sun-Thu, to 11.45pm Fri & Sat Jul & Aug), which locals claim is the oldest functioning lighthouse in the world.

The Old Town is worth an amble.

Sleeping & Eating

Hostal La Provinciana (☎ 981 22 04 00; www.laprovinciana.net in Spanish; Rúa Nueva 9; s/d/tr €37/49/67) The 20, all-exterior rooms here are bright and squeaky clean, with generous-sized bathrooms and hardwood floors.

Hostal Linar (☎ 981 22 78 37; Calle General Mola 7; d/tr/q €45/65/85) Sophisticated little rooms with hardwood furniture and a rich gold-and-garnet colour scheme, this side-street *hostal* is surprisingly elegant.

Restaurante Bania (☎ 981 22 13 01; Calle de Cordelería 7; mains €4-15, menú del día €9.25; closed Mon night & Sun) Interesting salads, tofu dishes and vegetable ensembles are the heart of this classy all-vegetarian eatery a short walk from the main drag.

Mesón do Pulpo (☎ 981 20 24 44; Calle de la Franja 9; raciones €4-12; closed Sun) Here it's all about octopus; as the name suggests. Eat it classically prepared with paprika, rock salt and olive oil.

Popular seafood eateries line the Plaza de María Pita. For tapas, *raciones* and cheap lunch *menús,* hit the narrow lanes west of the plaza, especially Calle de la Franja. **Pablo Gallego Restaurante** (☎ 981 20 88 88; Plaza de María Pita 11; mains €10-29; closed Sun) is the classiest choice on the plaza. This serene, stone-walled dining room prepares 21st-century updates on traditional Galician ingredients. Try lobster croquettes, braised sea bass, or grilled eel.

Getting There & Away

From the **bus station** (☎ 981 18 43 35; Calle Caballeros 21), **Monbus-Castromil** (☎ 902 29 29 00; www.monbus.es) operates regular services to southern cities including Santiago de Compostela (€5.75 to 6.70, one to 1½ hours).

Trains also make that run. Long-distance train routes include Madrid (from €48, 10 hours, three daily) and Barcelona (from €51, 16 to 17 hours, two daily).

> **PIPERS & FIDDLERS**
>
> Much of Galician folk music has Celtic roots, and the sounds of the *gaita* (bagpipe), *bombo* (big drum) and *zanfona* (accordion-like instrument) provide the soundtrack to many festivals and cultural events. Several summer folk music festivals liven up the summer months. The biggest and best – the **Ortigueira International Celtic Music Festival** (www.festivaldeortigueira.com) – is held in July.

SANTIAGO DE COMPOSTELA

pop 88,000 / elev 260m

The supposed burial place of St James (Santiago), Santiago de Compostela is a bewitching city. Christian pilgrims journeying along the Camino de Santiago often end up mute with wonder on entering its medieval centre. Fortunately, they usually regain their verbal capacities over a celebratory late-night foray into the city's lively bar scene.

Information

Cyber Nova 50 (☎ 981 56 41 33; Rúa Nova 50; per hr €1.20; 9am-midnight Mon-Fri, 10am-11pm Sat & Sun)

Oficina de Acogida de Peregrinos (Pilgrims' Reception Office; ☎ 981 56 88 46; www.archicompostela.org/peregrinos; Rúa do Vilar 1; 9am-9pm) For pilgrims on the Camino de Santiago.

Municipal tourist office (☎ 981 55 51 29; www.santiagoturismo.com; Rúa do Vilar 63; 9am-9pm Jun-Sep, 9am-2pm & 4-7pm Oct-May)

Sights

The **Catedral del Apóstol** (www.catedraldesantiago.es; Praza do Obradoiro; 7am-9pm), a superb Romanesque creation of the 11th to 13th centuries, is the heart and soul of Santiago. It's said that St James' remains were buried here in the 1st century AD and rediscovered in 813. Today, visitors line up to kiss his statue, which sits behind the main altar. The **Museo da Catedral** (☎ 981 56 05 27; Praza do Obradoiro; adult/child €5/1; 10am-2pm & 4-8pm Jun-Sep, 10am-1.30pm & 4-6.30pm Oct-May, closed Sun afternoon) includes the cathedral's cloisters, treasury and crypt. Stroll around the grand **Praza do Obradoiro** (Worker's Plaza), which earned its name because it was under construction for a full century while the grand palaces on it were constructed. On the northern end, the Renaissance **Hostal dos Reis Católicos** (now a luxury hotel) was built in the early 16th century by Isabel and Ferdinand.

To get a grasp on local culture, visit the **Museo do Pobo Galego** (Galician Folk Museum; ☎ 981 58 36 20; Rúa San Domingos de Bonaval; admission free; 10am-2pm & 4-8pm Tue-Sat, 11am-2pm Sun), housed in the attractive former Convento de San Domingos de Bonaval.

The **Museo das Peregrinacións** (☎ 981 58 15 58; Rúa de San Miguel 4; admission €2.40; 10am-8pm Tue-Fri, 10.30am-1.30pm & 5-8pm Sat, 10.30am-1.30pm Sun) explores the pilgrim culture that has so shaped

Santiago. Look out for the fascinating illuminated map showing pilgrimage destinations across the world.

Sleeping

Hostal Suso (☎ 981 58 66 11; Rúa do Vilar 65; s/d €20/40) Stacked above a bar, this family-run *hostal* represents the best deal in town. Immaculate rooms with spic-n-span bathrooms have firm beds and modern wood furniture. Light sleepers, request an interior room.

Hostal Seminario Mayor (☎ 981 58 30 09; www.viajesatlantico.com/pinario; Praza da Inmaculada 5; s/d/tr incl breakfast €30/47/60; Jul-Sep) Rooms are basic, but this *hostal* offers the rare experience of staying inside a Benedictine monastery. With 126 rooms, it's a good bet when everywhere else is full.

our pick Casa-Hotel As Artes (☎ 981 55 52 54; www.asartes.com; Travesía de Dos Puertas 2; r €88-98;) On a quiet street near the Cathedral, these lovely stone-walled rooms exude a romantic rustic air. Breakfast (€9) is served in a homey dining room overlooking the street.

San Francisco Hotel Monumento (☎ 981 58 16 34; www.sanfranciscohm.com; Campillo San Francisco 3; s/d €130/170;) The stone hallways, with their low lights and stone doorframes, recall the hotel's former life as a 16th-century monastery. The rooms, minimalist and modern, are all about contemporary comfort.

Eating

O Gato Negro (☎ 981 58 31 05; Rúa da Raíña; raciones €3-9) Marked only with a green door and a black cat, this old-town haunt serves plates of seafood, ham, cheese or peppers on five sought-after tables.

Carretas (☎ 981 56 31 11; Rúa das Carretas 21; mains €10-18, menú del día €18) On the edge of the Old Town, this classic *marisquería* is known for its shellfish platters (€48 per person) and excellent fish fresh from the *rías* (Galicia's fjordlike inlets).

O Beiro (☎ 981 58 13 70; Rúa da Raíña 3; mains €11-24) The house speciality are *tablas* (trays) of delectable cheeses and sausages, but you can also get tapas and *raciones* at this friendly two-storey tavern and *viñoteca* (wine bar).

Restaurante Ó Dezaseis (☎ 981 56 48 80; Rúa de San Pedro 16; mains €11-13, menú del día €11.50) Wood-beam ceilings and exposed stone walls give an invitingly rustic air to this popular tavern just beyond the touristy buzz. The mixed crowd tucks into specialities like *caldo Gallego* (Galician soup).

Drinking

If you're after tapas and wine, graze along Rúa do Franco and Rúa da Raíña. For people watching, hit the cafe's along Praza da Quinatana and Rúa do Vilar. The liveliest area lies east of Praza da Quintana, especially along Rúa de San Paio de Antealtares, known as a hotspot for live music.

Getting There & Around

Flights from various Spanish and European destinations (including Dublin, Frankfurt and London) land at **Lavacolla airport** (SCQ). Some 21 **Empresa Freire** (☎ 981 58 81 11) buses run daily between Lavacolla airport and the bus station (€1.70). About half continue to/depart from Rúa do Doutor Teixeiro, southwest of Praza de Galicia.

Services fan out from the **bus station** (☎ 981 54 24 16; Rúa San Caetano) to destinations all over Galicia and the rest of Spain.

From the **train station** (Avenida de Lugo), trains travel to/from Madrid (€45) on a daytime Talgo (seven hours) or an overnight Trenhotel (nine hours). Regional trains operate to La Coruña (€3.90 to €5.25, 45 to 70 minutes) and other destinations.

VALENCIA & MURCIA

A warm climate, an abundance of seaside resorts, and interesting cities make this area of Spain a popular destination. The beaches of the Costa Blanca (White Coast) draw most of the visitors, but venture beyond the shore to get a real feel for the region.

VALENCIA

pop 805,300

Valencia is where paella first simmered over a wood fire. It's a vibrant, friendly, slightly chaotic place with two outstanding fine-arts museums, an accessible old quarter, Europe's newest cultural and scientific complex – and one of Spain's most exciting nightlife scenes. It has been radically overhauled in recent years (partly to host the 2007 America's Cup and the city's first Formula One Grand Prix race in 2008.

Head to the Barrio del Carmen, Valencia's oldest quarter, for quirky shops and the best nightlife. Other key areas are the Plaza del Ayuntamiento, the Plaza de la Reina and the Plaza de la Virgen.

Information

Main post office (Plaza del Ayuntamiento 24)
Ono (☎ 96 328 19 02; Calle San Vicente Mártir 22; per hr €3.50; 🕑 10am-10pm)
Regional tourist office (☎ 96 398 64 22; Calle Paz 48; 🕑 9am-2.30pm & 4.30-8pm Mon-Fri)
Turismo Valencia (VLC) tourist office (☎ 96 315 39 31; www.turisvalencia.es; Plaza de la Reina 19; 🕑 9am-7pm Mon-Sat, 10am-2pm Sun) There's also a branch at the train Station.

Sights & Activities

You'll see Valencia's best face by simply wandering around the **Barrio del Carmen**, strolling the **Jardines del Turia** (in what was once the city's river) or people watching in one of the city's many plazas.

Valencia's Romanesque-Gothic-baroque-Renaissance **catedral** (adult/under 3yr/3-12yr incl audioguide €4/free/2.70; 🕑 10am-5.30pm/6.30pm Mon-Sat, 2-5.30pm Sun) is a compendium of centuries of architectural history and home to the Capilla del Santo Cáliz, a chapel said to contain the Holy Grail, that is the chalice Christ supposedly used in the last supper. Climb the 207 stairs of the **Micalet (or Miguelete) bell tower** (adult/under 14yr €2/1; 🕑 10am-7.30pm) for sweeping city views.

Valencia's other architectural pride and joy, the state-of-the-art **Ciudad de las Artes y las Ciencias** (City of Arts & Sciences; ☎ reservations 902 10 00 31; www.cac.es; Autovía a El Saler; combined ticket for all three attractions adult/child €30.60/23.30) is a complex of museums including the **L'Oceanográfic aquarium** (adult/child €23.30/17.60; 🕑 10am-6pm or 8pm Sep–mid-Jul, 10am-midnight mid-Jul–Aug); the **Museo de las Ciencias Príncipe Felipe** (adult/child €7.50/5.80; 🕑 10am-7pm or 9pm) interactive science museum; and **L'Hemisfèric** (adult/child €7.50/5.80) planetarium, IMAX theatre and L'Umbracle covered garden. Also here is the shimmering, beetle-like **Palau de les Arts Reina Sofía** performing arts centre (☎ 902 20 23 83; www.lesarts.com; Autovía a El Saler). Bus 35 goes from Plaza del Ayuntamiento.

Check out the latest exhibitions of contemporary art and the permanent collection of 20th-century paintings at the **Instituto Valenciano de Arte Moderno** (IVAM; ☎ 96 386 30 00; www.ivam.es; Calle Guillem de Castro 118; adult/student €2/1, Sun free; 🕑 10am-8pm or 10pm Tue-Sun).

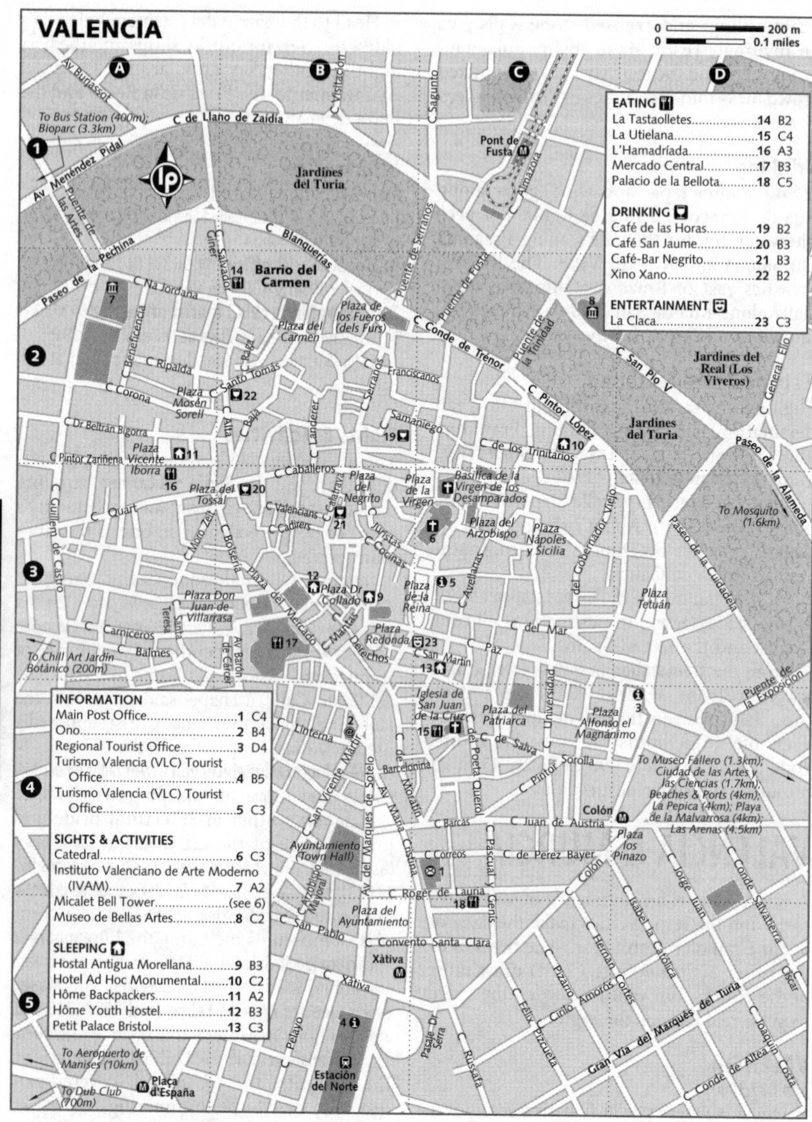

The **Museo de Bellas Artes** (Fine Arts Museum; ☎ 96 378 03 00; Calle San Pío V 9; admission free; 10am-8pm Tue-Sun) ranks among Spain's best. Highlights include the grandiose Roman *Mosaic of the Nine Muses*, a collection of late medieval altarpieces and works by El Greco, Goya, Velázquez and Murillo, plus artists such as Sorolla and Pinazo of the Valencian Impressionist school.

Stretch your towel on broad **Playa de la Malvarrosa**, which runs into **Playa de las Arenas**, each bordered by the Paseo Marítimo promenade and a string of restaurants. One block back, lively bars and discos thump out the beat in summer. Take bus 1, 2 or 19, or the high-speed tram from Pont de Fusta or the Benimaclet Metro junction.

Bioparc (☎ 902 25 03 40; www.bioparcvalencia.es; Avenida Pio Baroja 3; adult/child €20/15; 10am-dusk) is Valencia's latest attraction, an ecofriendly hyper-modern zoo opened in 2008. Take bus 3, 81 or 95 or get off at the Nou d'Octubre metro stop.

Sleeping

Hôme Backpackers (☎ 96 391 37 97; www.likeathome.net; Calle Santa Cristina s/n; dm €17.80;) This, the simplest of the Hôme team's three excellent budget hostels, each with self-catering facilities, has 170 beds and a large roof terrace for chilling out or soaking in the sun. The owners also run Hôme Youth Hostel (www.homeyouthhostel.com) and rental flats.

Hostal Antigua Morellana (☎ 96 391 57 73; www.hostalam.com; Calle En Bou 2; s €45-55, d €55-65;) In an elegant renovated 18th-century building, this helpful hotel has cosy, good-sized rooms with satellite TV and balconies.

Hotel Ad Hoc Monumental (☎ 963 91 91 40; www.adhochoteles.com; Calle Boix 4; s €76-101, d €89-125;) This charming boutique hotel has stencilled ceilings, pretty balconies and fabulous colour schemes.

Petit Palace Bristol (☎ 96 394 51 00; www.hthoteles.com; Calle Abadía San Martín 3; s €80-120, d €90-140;) Hip, minimalist and friendly, this boutique belle retains the best of its 19th century past and does a particularly scrumptious buffet breakfast.

Chill Art Jardín Botánico (☎ 96 315 40 12; www.hoteljardinbotanico.com; Calle Doctor Peset Cervera 6; s €94-133, d €94-149;) Welcoming and megacool, this intimate hotel is furnished with flair.

> **BURN BABY BURN**
>
> In mid-March, Valencia hosts one of Europe's wildest street parties: **Las Fallas de San José** (www.fallas.es in Spanish). For one week (12 to 19 March), the city is engulfed by an anarchic swirl of fireworks, music, festive bonfires and all-night partying. On the final night, giant *ninots* (effigies), many of political and social personages, are torched in the main plaza.
>
> If you're not in Valencia then, see the *ninots* saved from the flames by popular vote at the **Museo Fallero** (Plaza Monteolivete 4; adult/child €2/1, Sat & Sun free; 10am-2pm & 4.30-8.30pm Tue-Sat, 10am-3pm Sun).

Candles flicker in the lounge and each bedroom has original art.

Eating

At weekends, locals in their hundreds head for Las Arenas, just north of the port, where a long line of restaurants overlooking the beach all serve up authentic paella in a three-course meal costing around €15. Sprawling beachside **La Pepica** (☎ 96 371 03 66; Playa de Levante 6; mains €8-20) is one of the locals' favourites.

La Tastaolletes (☎ 96 392 18 62; Calle Salvador Giner 6; tapas €5-9, mains €8-10; lunch & dinner Tue-Sat, dinner Mon) This tiny place does a creative range of vegetarian tapas using quality prime ingredients. Salads are frondy and the cheesecake with stewed fruits, a dream.

L'Hamadríada (☎ 96 326 08 91; www.hamadriada.com; Plaza Vicente Iborra 3; midday menú del día €10; lunch daily, dinner Wed-Sat) Down a blind alley, this slim white rectangle of a place does an innovative midday *menú*, perfectly simmered rice dishes that change daily and great meat grills.

La Utielana (☎ 96 352 94 14; Plaza Picadero dos Aguas 3; meals around €15; lunch & dinner Mon-Fri & lunch Sat) Tucked away off Calle Prócida, La Utielana is ultra-Valencian. It packs in the crowds, drawn by the wholesome fare and exceptional value for money.

Palacio de la Bellota (☎ 96 351 53 61; Calle Mosén Femades 7; Mon-Sat) The cured ham that hangs from the ceilings here is absolutely divine, but this place is also famous for its Valencian *all i pebre* (eel and pepper stew).

Mercado Central (Plaza del Mercado; 7.30am-2.30pm Mon-Sat) This is a feast of colours and smells, with nearly 1000 stallholders crammed under the market's modernist glass domes.

Drinking

The Barrio del Carmen, the university area (around Avenidas de Aragón and Blasco Ibáñez), the area around the Mercado de Abastos and, in summer, the new port area and Malvarrosa, are all jumping with bars and clubs.

Café San Jaume (☎ 96 391 24 01; Calle Caballeros 51) This is a stalwart of Carmen's bar scene, with lots of room upstairs and a particularly fine terrace.

Cafe-Bar Negrito (Plaza del Negrito) At this bar, which traditionally attracts a more left-wing, intellectual clientele, the crowd spills out onto the square.

Xino Xano (Calle Alta 28) The genial owner, a well-known DJ in his own right, picks from his collection of dub, reggae and funk.

Café de las Horas (Calle Conde de Almodóvar 1) This place offers high baroque, tapestries, music of all genres, candelabras and a long list of exotic cocktails.

Entertainment

Head to these clubs after midnight for drinks and dancing.

La Claca (☎ 669 32 50 79; www.laclaca.com in Spanish; Calle San Vicente Mártir 3; 🕑 7pm-3.30am) La Claca, central and popular with overseas visitors, has nightly DJs playing funk, hip hop and indie. Earmark Sunday evening for some of the best live flamenco in town.

Dub Club (www.dubclubvalencia.com in Spanish; Calle Jesús 91; 🕑 Thu-Sun) With the slogan 'We play music not noise', this is a bar that has great music: reggae (Thursday), dub, drum 'n' bass, funk and more.

Mosquito (Polo y Peyrelon 11) DJs at this tiny box of a place dispense classic soul, R&B and a leavening of hip-hop. However many shots you knock back, you'll know you're in the right place by the giant papier maché mosquito hovering above its circular bar.

Getting There & Away

Valencia's airport, Aeropuerto de Manises (VLC), is 10km west of the centre.

Valencia's **bus station** (☎ 96 346 62 66) is beside the riverbed on Avenida Menéndez Pidal. There are regular services to/from Madrid (€23 to €29, four hours), Barcelona (€25.15 to €38.50, four to 5½ hours) and Alicante (€17.60 to €20, 2½ hours).

From Valencia's **Estación del Norte** (Calle Jativa), trains also go to/from Madrid, Barcelona and Alicante, among other destinations.

Regular car and passenger ferries go to the Balearic Islands (see p814).

Getting Around

Metro line 5 connects the airport, downtown and port.

Valencia has an integrated bus, tram and metro network. EMT buses ply town routes, while MetroBus serves outlying towns and villages. Tourist offices stock maps for both services.

The high-speed tram leaves from the FGV tram station, 500m north of the cathedral, at the Pont de Fusta. This is a pleasant way to get to the beach, the paella restaurants of Las Arenas and the port. Metro lines primarily serve the outer suburbs.

ALICANTE

pop 322,700

With its elegant, palm-lined boulevards, lively nightlife scene, and easy-to-access beaches, Alicante (Alacant in Valenciano) is an all-in-one Spanish city. The city is at its most charming at night, when tapas bars and taverns in El Barrio (Old Quarter) come alive.

Information

Main post office (Calle de Alemania)

Municipal tourist office (www.alicanteturismo.com) Branches at bus station and train station.

Xplorer Cyber Café (Calle San Vicente 46; per hr €1.20; 🕑 9am-midnight) Internet access.

Sights & Activities

From the 16th-century **Castillo de Santa Bárbara** (admission free; 🕑 10am-9.30pm May-Sep, 9am-6.30pm Nov-Mar) there are sweeping views. Inside is a permanent display of contemporary Spanish sculpture. A lift/elevator (€2.40 return; closed for renovation at the time of writing), reached by a footbridge opposite Playa del Postiguet, rises through the bowels of the mountain. Otherwise, it's a pleasant walk through Parque de la Ereta via Calle San Rafael to Plaza del Carmen.

Immediately north of the port is the sandy beach of **Playa del Postiguet**. Larger and less crowded beaches are at **Playa de San Juan**, easily reached by the tram.

From the harbour, **Kon Tiki** (☎ 96 521 63 96) makes the 45-minute boat trip (€16 return) to the popular island of **Tabarca**.

To learn about Alicante's ancient history, visit **Museo Arqueológico** (MARQ; ☎ 96 514 90 00; Plaza Doctor Gómez Ulla s/n; adult/child €3/1.50; 🕑 11am-2pm & 6pm-midnight Tue-Sun Jul & Aug, 10am-7pm Tue-Sat, 10am-2pm Sun Sep-Jun). The **MUBAG** (Museo de Bellas Artes Gravina; ☎ 96 514 67 80; Calle Gravina 13-15; admission free; 🕑 10am-2pm & 4-8pm or 5-9pm Mon-Sat, 10am-2pm Sun), Alicante's stimulating fine arts museum, is within an 18th-century mansion. **Museu de Fogueres** (☎ 96 514 68 28; Rambla de Méndez Núñez 29; admission free; 🕑 10am-2pm & 5-7.45pm or 6-9pm Tue-Sat, 10am-1.45pm Sun) focuses on the **Fiesta de Sant Joan**. Spread either side of 24 June, the longest day, this is the city's version of Las Fallas (see the boxed text, p809).

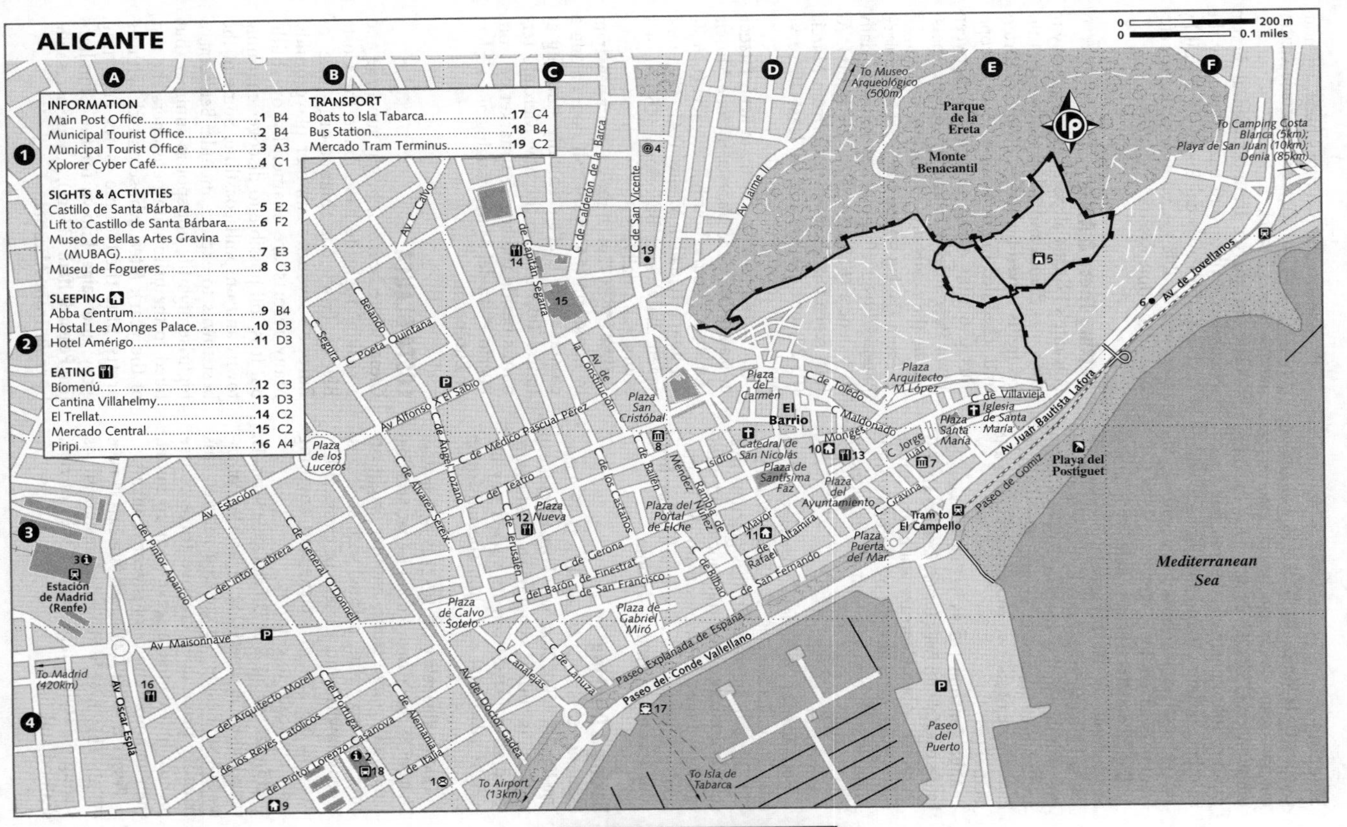
ALICANTE
INFORMATION
Main Post Office 1 B4
Municipal Tourist Office 2 B4
Municipal Tourist Office 3 A3
Xplorer Cyber Café 4 C1
SIGHTS & ACTIVITIES
Castillo de Santa Bárbara 5 E2
Lift to Castillo de Santa Bárbara 6 F2
Museo de Bellas Artes Gravina (MUBAG) 7 E3
Museu de Fogueres 8 C3
SLEEPING
Abba Centrum 9 B4
Hostal Les Monges Palace 10 D3
Hotel Amérigo 11 D3
EATING
Bíomenú 12 C3
Cantina Villahelmy 13 D3
El Trellat 14 C2
Mercado Central 15 C2
Piripi 16 A4
TRANSPORT
Boats to Isla Tabarca 17 C4
Bus Station 18 B4
Mercado Tram Terminus 19 C2
Mediterranean Sea
Parque de la Ereta
Monte Benacantil
El Barrio
Playa del Postiguet
To Museo Arqueológico (500m)
To Camping Costa Blanca (5km); Playa de San Juan (10km); Denia (85km)
Tram to El Campello
Estación de Madrid (Renfe)
To Madrid (420km)
To Airport (13km)
To Isla de Tabarca
Paseo del Puerto
Av de Jovellanos
Av Juan Bautista Lafora
Paseo de Gomiz
Paseo del Conde Vallellano
Paseo Explanada de España
Rambla de Méndez Núñez
Av de la Constitución
Av Alfonso X El Sabio
Av Maisonnave
Av Oscar Esplá
Av del Doctor Gadea
Av Jaime II
Av Estación
Plaza de los Luceros
Plaza de Calvo Sotelo
Plaza de Gabriel Miró
Plaza Nueva
Plaza San Cristóbal
Plaza del Carmen
Plaza del Portal de Elche
Plaza Puerta del Mar
Plaza del Ayuntamiento
Plaza de Santísima Faz
Plaza Santa María
Plaza Arquitecto M López
Iglesia de Santa María
Catedral de San Nicolás
200 m
0.1 miles

SPAIN

Sleeping

Camping Costa Blanca (☎ 96 563 06 70; www.campingcostablanca.com; Calle Convento, Campello; camp sites per person/tent/car €5.65/8.25/5.65;) This camping ground, 10km north of Alicante, has a poolside bar, restaurant and minilibrary, where you can exchange your holiday reading. The tram passes right by.

our pick **Hostal Les Monges Palace** (☎ 96 521 50 46; www.lesmonges.net; Calle San Agustín 4; s €30-44, d €45-56;) This agreeably quirky place is a treasure with its winding corridors, tiles, mosaics and antique furniture. To pamper yourself, choose one of the two rooms with sauna and jacuzzi (€97).

Abba Centrum (☎ 96 513 04 40; www.abbahoteles.com; Calle del Pintor Lorenzo Casanova 31; r €83-125;) Abba Centrum is a hugely attractive option, located right by the bus station. Popular with business visitors, its weekend rates (August too) drop to a bargain €65 per room.

Hotel Amérigo (☎ 96 514 65 70; www.hospes.es; Calle Rafael Altamira 7; r from €140;) Within an old Dominican convent, this glorious five-star choice blends the traditional and ultramodern. Enjoy the views from the rooftop pool – if you can tear yourself away from your stunningly designed room.

Eating & Drinking

Bíomenú (☎ 96 521 31 44; Calle Navas 17; 9.30am-7pm Mon-Sat, 9.30-11.30pm Sun) This ultracheap option is both vegetarian restaurant (load your plate from its varied pay-by-weight salad bar) and shop specialising in organic produce.

Cantina Villahelmy (☎ 965 21 25 29; Calle Mayor 37; mains €8-16; lunch & dinner Tue-Sat, lunch Sun) One wall's rough stone, another bright orange and navy blue, painted with skeletons, creepycrawlies and a frieze of classical figures. It has lots of snacks and anything from couscous to octopus.

El Trellat (☎ 965 20 62 75; Calle Capitán Segarra 19; menús lunch €11.50, dinner €17.50; lunch Mon-Sat, dinner Fri & Sat) Beside the covered market, this friendly place does creative three-course *menús:* first course a serve-yourself buffet, then an ample choice of inventive mains.

Piripi (☎ 96 522 79 40; Avenida Oscar Esplá 30; mains €13-23) This highly regarded restaurant is strong on stylish tapas and dishes of rice, seafood and fish.

Browse around Alicante's huge, art nouveau twin-storey covered **Mercado Central** (Avenida Alfonso X El Sabio).

The old quarter around Catedral de San Nicolás is wall-to-wall bars. Down by the harbour, the Paseo del Puerto, tranquil by day, is a double-decker line of bars, cafes and night-time discos.

Getting There & Away

Alicante's El Altet airport (ALC), gateway to the Costa Blanca and 12km southwest of the centre, is served by budget airlines, charters and scheduled flights from all over Europe. Bus C-6 runs every 40 minutes between Plaza Puerta del Mar and the airport, passing by the north side of the bus station.

From the **bus station** (☎ 96 513 07 00; Calle del Portugal 17) over 10 motorway buses go daily to Valencia (€17.60 to €20, 2½ hours). At least seven fast services run to/from Murcia (€5.20, one hour), and at least 10 serve Madrid (€26.30, 5¼ hours).

Destinations from the main **Renfe Estación de Madrid** (Avenida de Salamanca) include Murcia (€4.30, 1¼ hours, hourly), Valencia (€26.30, 1¾ hours, 10 daily), Madrid (€41, 3¾ hours, seven daily) and Barcelona (€50.70, 4¾ hours, eight daily).

TRAM (☎ 900 72 04 72) runs a smart new tram to Benidorm (€4, every half hour) along a coastal route that's scenically stunning at times. Take it from the new Mercado terminus beside the covered market or from Puerto Plaza del Mar, changing at La Isleta or Lucentum.

COSTA BLANCA

Clean white beaches, bright sunshine and a rockin' nightlife have made the Costa Blanca (www.costablanca.org) one of Europe's favourite summer playgrounds. Many resorts are shamefully overbuilt, but it is still possible to discover charming towns and unspoilt coastline. Some of the best towns to explore include: **Benidorm**, a highrise nightlife hot spot in summer (but filled to the brim with pensioners the rest of the year); **Altea**, whose church with its pretty blue-tiled dome is its crowning glory; and **Calpe**, known for the Gibraltar-like **Peñon de Ifach** (332m). All are accessible by train from Alicante.

MURCIA & THE COSTA CALÍDA

With its rural interior, small coastal resorts and lively capital city, **Murcia** (www.murciaturistica.es) is as authentically Spanish as it gets. A conservative province, Murcia is known for its fabulous local produce, rich tapas and unusually warm coast.

Murcia

pop 417,000

Murcia City was founded in AD 825 as an Islamic settlement and suffered much destruction in the civil war. Today it's a pleasant, laid-back provincial capital. Get more information at the **tourist office** (☎ 968 35 87 49; www.murciaciudad.com; Plaza del Cardenal Belluga; 🕑 10am-2pm & 5-9pm Mon-Sat, 10am-2pm Sun Jun-Sep, 10am-2pm & 4.30-8.30pm Mon-Sat, 10am-2pm Sun Oct-May).

SIGHTS & ACTIVITIES

Head straight to the **Catedral de Santa María** (Plaza Cardinal Belluga; 🕑 7am-1pm & 5-8pm) to marvel at its opulent baroque facade. The cathedral took four centuries to build and is a hotchpotch of architectural styles. Highlights include the 92m-tall tower and the Capilla de los Veléz, a Gothic jewel. There's a handful of minor museums around town.

SLEEPING & EATING

Pensión Murcia (☎ 968 21 99 63; Calle Vinadel 6; s/d with shared bathroom €43/25, with private bathroom €50/40; ❄) Tucked into a quiet elbow near bars and shops, this 16-room *pensión* has tidy rooms with floral bedspreads, modern bathrooms and more space than most cheap sleeps in the city.

our pick Hotel Casa Emilio (☎ 968 22 06 31; www.hotelcasaemilio.com; Alameda de Colón n 9; s/d €45/55; ❄) Across from the leafy Floridablanca gardens and near the river, this is a well-designed and maintained hotel with spacious, brightly lit rooms, large bathrooms and good firm mattresses.

El Churra (☎ 968 23 84 00; www.elchurra.net; Avenida Marqués de los Vélez 12; s €54, d Mon-Thu €75, d Fri-Sun €54; ❄ 💻) Take a look at the photos in the lobby when Churra was a rough-and-ready snack bar surrounded by fields and orchards. Fifty years on, this slickly-run hotel has small, stylish rooms.

Figón de Alfaro (☎ 968 21 68 62; Calle Alfaro 7; meals €12-15; 🕑 lunch & dinner Mon-Sat, lunch Sun) Choose between the chaotic bar area or more sedate interconnecting dining room. Have a full meal or snack on juicy *montaditos* (minirolls) or innovative one-offs like *pastel de berejena con salsa de calabacín* (aubergine pie with a courgette sauce).

Los Arroces del Romea (☎ 968 21 84 99; Plaza Romea s/n; meals €20-25) Watch the speciality paella-style rice dishes being prepared in cartwheel-size pans over the flames while you munch on circular *murciano* bread drizzled with olive oil. Los Arroces has five rice dishes to choose from, including a vegetarian option.

Las Cadenas (☎ 968 22 09 24; Calle de los Apóstoles 10; meals €20-28; 🕑 Mon-Sat) Las Cadenas has leaded windows and an elegant feel. The menu should suit the fussiest of families with dishes including pasta, *pulpo a la Gallega* (Galician-style octopus) and *tortilla española* (potato omelette).

DRINKING

La Muralla (☎ 968 21 22 39; Calle Apóstoles 34; 🕑 10.30pm-late Thu) For sophisticated jazz nights head to this cocktail bar snuggled up against the original city walls.

Fitzpatrick (☎ 968 21 47 70; Plaza Cetina) This spot has all the predictable ales on tap and has a suitably blarney atmosphere.

Most through-the-night life buzzes around the university with vibrant bars, including **Che Che** (Calle del Doctor Fleming 16) and **El Sentío** (Calle Trinidad 14).

GETTING THERE & AWAY

Various low cost airlines fly from UK cities to **San Javier airport**, beside the Mar Menor and closer to Cartagena. A taxi between the airport and Murcia city costs around €40.

There are up to five trains daily that connect Murcia with Madrid (€41.30, 4¼ hours). Hourly trains operate to/from Lorca (€14.50, one hour).

ALSA has buses to Granada (€18.75, 3½ hours, seven daily), Valencia (€14.50, 3¾ hours, four to six daily) and Madrid (€24, five hours, 10 daily).

Costa Calída

You'll find plenty of attractive spots on Murcia's Costa Calída (Warm Coast). Most popular is the **Mar Menor**, a vast saltwater lagoon separated from the sea by a hideously overdeveloped 22km sliver of land known as **La Manga**. You can swim year-round.

BALEARIC ISLANDS

pop 1.07 million

The Balearic Islands (Illes Balears in Catalan) adorn the glittering Mediterranean waters off Spain's eastern coastline. Beach tourism destinations *par excellence*, each of the four islands has a quite distinct identity and have managed to retain much of their individual character and beauty. All boast beaches second to none in the Med but each offers reasons for exploring inland too. From mysterious ancient archaeological sites to intriguing country towns, from pine-clad cliffs to almond stands that blossom bright in late winter, these islands reward those with the curiosity to drag themselves away from the undeniably pretty waterfront.

Check out websites like www.illesbalears.es, www.baleares.com, http://abc-mallorca.com and www.newsmallorca.com.

Getting There & Away

AIR

If your main goal in Spain is to visit the Balearic Islands, there are plenty of direct flights from European cities to Mallorca and, to a lesser extent, Ibiza and Menorca. Your flight may be routed via the mainland but it generally makes no sense to take a flight to the mainland and then organise a separate local flight unless you specifically want to visit the mainland.

If already in Spain, scheduled flights from major cities are operated by Iberia, Air Europa, Clickair, Spanair and Vueling.

Inter-island flights are expensive (given a flying time of less than 30 minutes), with a trip from Palma de Mallorca to Maó or Ibiza easily costing up to €140. There are no flights to Formentera.

BOAT

The main company, **Acciona Trasmediterránea** (www.trasmediterranea.es), runs ferry services between Barcelona and Valencia on the mainland, and Ibiza City, Maó and Palma de Mallorca. Tickets can be purchased from any travel agency or online. Timetables and fares vary constantly.

From Barcelona, two daily services run to Palma de Mallorca from about Easter to late October. A high-speed catamaran leaves at 4pm (€90 for standard seat, €180 for small car, four hours), while an overnight ferry leaves at 11pm (€47 for standard seat, €154 for small car, 7¼ hours). The return trips from Palma are at 10am or 11.30am (catamaran) and 1pm (ferry). Between late October and Easter, only the overnight ferry continues to run most days. All these ferries continue to Ibiza. You pay the same price as for Mallorca but add three hours to the journey time.

From Valencia, a high-speed catamaran leaves for Palma (six hours) via Ibiza (3½ hours) at 4pm, and a direct overnight ferry at 11pm (7½ hours). The fast ferry operates Thursday to Tuesday and the overnight Monday to Saturday. The return catamaran trip from Palma leaves at 7.30am, while the ferry departs at 11.45am (seven hours) or midnight (eight hours). Prices are similar to those from Barcelona. In August, a direct Valencia–Mallorca catamaran service is usually added.

In the peak summer period a daily overnight ferry does the Barcelona–Maó run (€46 per person in standard seat, €176 per small vehicle, 9½ hours).

The company adds a cheeky extra ticket fee of €11 per person and €13 per vehicle on all tickets. You can get discounts by booking early.

Acciona Trasmediterránea runs two fast ferries or catamarans a day between Palma and Ibiza City (generally leaving Ibiza at 7am and 7.45pm, and Palma at 7.30am and 8.45pm) from Easter to the end of October (€61 for standard seat, €116 for small car, 2¼ hours).

Baleària (☎ 902 160180; www.balearia.com) operates ferries to Palma de Mallorca from Barcelona, Valencia and Denia (via Ibiza). Check fares and departure times online.

Iscomar (☎ 902 11 91 28; www.iscomar.com) has a ferry service from Barcelona to Palma (€48 per person, €140 per small car, 7½ hours, daily in summer). There are sometimes services to Ibiza and Maó too. From Valencia (nine hours, six days a week in summer) the prices are similar.

Cala Ratjada Tours (☎ 902 10 04 44; www.calaratjadatours.es) operates summer ferries between Cala Ratjada, in Mallorca, and Ciutadella, in Menorca.

MALLORCA

pop 814,300

The sunny, ochre hues of the medieval heart of Palma de Mallorca (pop 383,110), the archipelago's capital, make a great introduction to the islands. The northwest coast, dominated by the Serra de Tramuntana mountain range, is a beautiful region of olive groves, pine forests and ochre villages, with a spectacularly rugged coastline. Most of Mallorca's best beaches are on the north and east coasts and, although many have been swallowed up by tourist developments, you can still find the occasional exception. There is also a scattering of fine beaches along parts of the south coast.

GETTING AROUND

Sant Joan airport (PMI) is approximately 10km east of Palma. Bus 1 runs every 15 minutes between Sant Joan airport and Plaça d'Espanya in central Palma (€1.85, 15 minutes) and on to the ferry terminal. Alternatively, a taxi will charge you around €15 to €18 for the trip.

Most of the island is accessible by bus from Palma. All buses depart from (or near) the **bus station** (Estació d'Autobusos; Carrer d'Eusebi Estada). For information contact **Transport de les Illes Balears** (TIB; ☎ 971 17 77 77; http://tib.caib.es). One-way fares from Palma include Cala Ratjada (€9.50), Ca'n Picafort (€4.65), Port de Pollença (€4.90) and Port d'Andratx (€3.80).

The popular, old train run to **Sóller** (☎ 971 75 20 51, 902 36 47 11; http//:trendesoller.com; one way/return €9/14, child 3-6 yrs half price, under 3 yrs free) is a very pretty ride.

Palma de Mallorca

INFORMATION

Azul Cybercafé (☎ 971 71 29 27; www.azulgroup.com; Carrer de la Soledat 4; per hr €2.90; ⌚ 8.30am-8pm Mon-Fri, noon-6pm Sat)

Consell de Mallorca tourist office (☎ 971 71 22 16; www.infomallorca.net; Plaça de la Reina 2; ⌚ 9am-8pm Mon-Fri, 9am-2pm Sat) Covers the whole island.

Main post office (Carrer de la Constitució 6; ⌚ 8.30am-8.30pm Mon-Fri, 9.30am-2pm Sat)

Municipal tourist office (☎ 902 10 23 65; www.palmademallorca.es; ⌚ 9am-8pm) main office (Casal Solleric, Passeig d'es Born 27); branch office (Parc de les Estacions)

SIGHTS & ACTIVITIES

An awesome mass of sandstone walls and flying buttresses, Palma's landmark Gothic **cathedral** (La Seu; ☎ 977 72 31 30; www.catedraldemallorca.org; Carrer del Palau Reial 9; adult/under 10yr/student €4/free/3; ⌚ 10am-6.30pm Mon-Fri, 10am-2.30pm Sat Jun-Sep, 10am-5.30pm Mon-Fri, 10am-2.30pm Sat Apr-May & Oct, 10am-2.30pm Mon-Sat Nov-Mar) overlooks the city and its port. It is also home to some interesting Modernista touches by Antoni Gaudí and the spectacular modern remake by local artist Miquel Barceló of the Capella del Santíssim i Sant Pere chapel.

Opposite the cathedral is the **Palau de l'Almudaina** (☎ 971 21 41 34; www.patrimonionacional.es; Carrer del Palau Reial s/n; adult/student €3.20/2.30; ⌚ 10am-6pm Mon-Fri, 10am-2pm Sat Apr-Sep, 10am-2pm & 4-6pm Mon-Fri, 10am-2pm Sat Oct-Mar), a one-time Muslim fort turned into the residence of the Mallorcan monarchs.

Es Baluard (Museu d'Art Modern i Contemporani; ☎ 971 90 82 00; www.esbaluard.org; Porta de Santa Catalina 10; adult/student & senior €6/4.50, temporary exhibitions €4/3; ⌚ 10am-10pm Tue-Sun mid-Jun–Sep, 10am-8pm Tue-Sun Oct–mid-Jun), set among Renaissance-era seawalls, is Palma's striking museum dedicated to modern and contemporary works of art – anything from Joan Miró to Oskar Kokoschka.

Those wanting to see even more of Miró's work should visit the **Fundació Pilar i Joan Miró** (☎ 971 70 14 20; http://miro.palmademallorca.es; Carrer de Joan de Saridakis 29; adult/under 17yr/student & senior €6/free/3; ⌚ 10am-7pm Tue-Sat, 10am-3pm Sun & holidays mid-May–mid-Sep, 10am-6pm Tue-Sat, 10am-3pm Sun & holidays mid-Sep–mid-May), west of the city in Cala Major. Take bus 3 or 46 from Plaça d'Espanya.

Museu d'Art Espanyol Contemporani (☎ 971 71 35 15; www.march.es/arte/palma; Carrer de Sant Miquel 11; admission free; ⌚ 10am-6.30pm Mon-Fri, 10.30am-2pm Sat) makes a good introduction to Spanish modern art, with some 70 pieces of mostly 20th century artists, including Picasso, Miró, Juan Gris (of Cubism fame), the sculptor Julio González and Salvador Dalí.

Museu Diocesà (☎ 971 21 31 00; Carrer del Mirador 5; admission €3; ⌚ 10am-2pm Tue-Fri) is a fascinating excursion for those interested in Mallorca's Christian art history.

Museu de Mallorca (☎ 971 71 75 40; www.museudemallorca.es; Carrer de la Portella 5; admission free; ⌚ 10am-7pm Tue-Sat, 10am-2pm Sun) houses archaeological finds (including an outstanding collection of 4th century BC bronze statuettes), as well as paintings and furniture from the 19th and 20th centuries. Nearby, the atmospheric **Banys Àrabs** (Arab Baths; ☎ 971 72 15 49; Carrer de Serra 7; adult/child €1.50/free; ⌚ 9am-7.30pm Apr-Nov, 9am-6pm Dec-Mar), are the only remaining monument to early medieval Mallorca's Muslim overlords.

SLEEPING

Hostal Pons (☎ 971 72 26 58; Carrer del Vi 8; s/d with shared bathroom €25/45) This *hostal* seems unchanged since the 1880s. The downstairs chambers are cluttered with antiques and artworks, and the

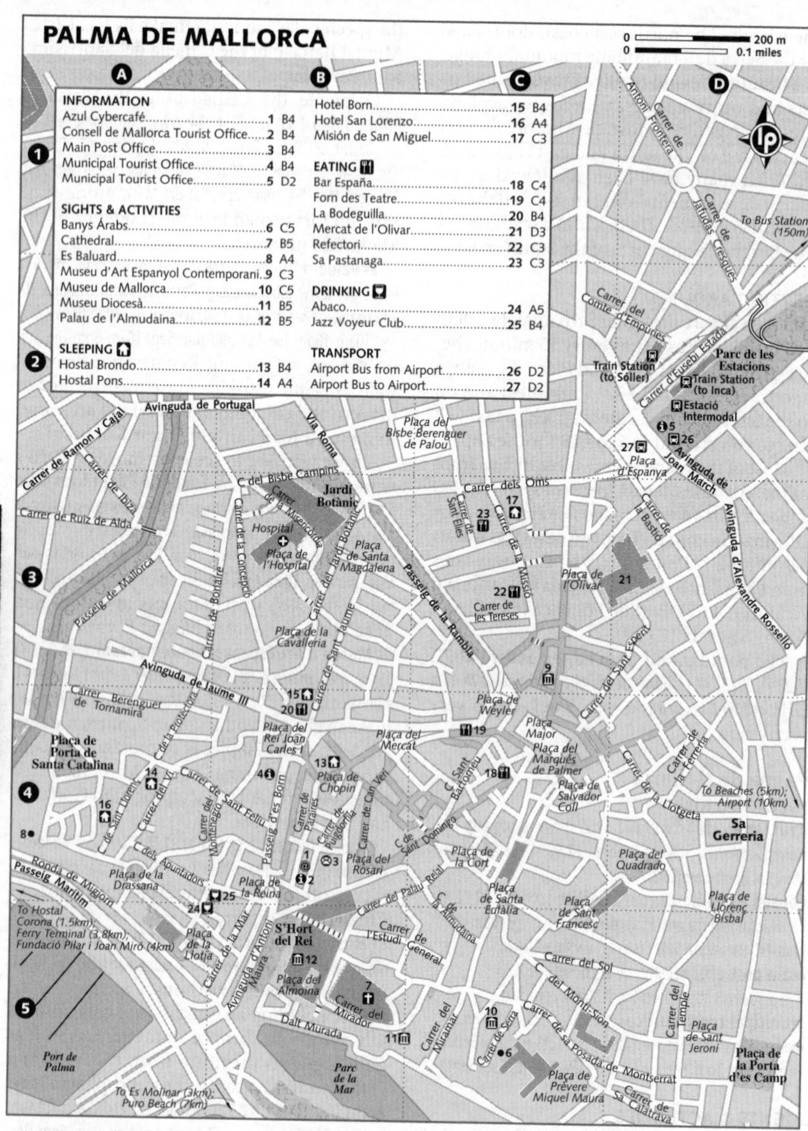

quaint bedrooms all have timber bedsteads and rickety tiled floors.

Hostal Corona (☎ 971 73 19 35; www.hostal-corona.com; Carrer de Josep Villalonga 22; s €30, d €45-55) With its palm trees and cornucopia of plants, the generous courtyard garden of this little hotel has a far-away feel. The rooms are simple, with timber furnishings and old tiled floors. In the evening, the courtyard turns into a chilled out bar (open 6pm to 1am Tuesday to Sunday). The nearest bus stop is at Avinguda de Joan Miró 24 (take bus 3 or 46 from Plaça d'Espanya).

Hostal Brondo (☎ 971 71 90 43; www.hostalbrondo.net; Carrer de Ca'n Brondo 1; s/d with shared bathroom €40/55, d €70) Climb the courtyard stairs to arrive in a homey sitting room overlooking the narrow lane. High-ceilinged rooms (No 3 with a glassed-in gallery) furnished in varying styles (from Mallorcan to vaguely Moroccan) are atmospheric.

Hotel Born (☎ 971 71 29 42; www.hotelborn.com; Carrer de Sant Jaume 3; s €55, d €80-100) A superb place in the heart of the city, this hotel is in an 18th-century palace. The rooms combine elegance and history, with all the mod-cons. The best rooms have a view on to the courtyard.

Hotel San Lorenzo (☎ 971 72 82 00; www.hotelsanlorenzo.com; Carrer de Sant Llorenç 14; s/d from €118/140;) Tucked away inside the old quarter, this hotel is in a beautifully restored 17th-century building, and has a marvellous Mallorcan courtyard, its own bar, dining room and rooftop terrace with swimming pool.

our pick **Misión de San Miguel** (☎ 971 21 48 48; www.hotelmisiondesanmiguel.com; Carrer de Can Maçanet 1; r €125-130;) The hotel is on a side alley off Carrer Oms and its spacious rooms are quiet, with free wi-fi, firm mattresses and rain showers. Their restaurant serves a fabulous made-to-order breakfast and the patio area is romantic and relaxing.

EATING & DRINKING

Sa Pastanaga (☎ 971 72 41 94; Carrer de Sant Elies 6b; meals €12.20; lunch Mon-Fri) Locals queue here for vegetarian set lunches. Yellow walls and exposed beams lend a huggy feel to the place. Starters (juice or salad) could be followed by a main course of *burritos de verdura amb salsa de formatge* (vegetable burritos in cheese sauce).

Bar España (☎ 971 72 42 34; Carrer de Ca'n Escurrac 12; meals €15-20; 6pm-midnight Mon, 10am-midnight Tue-Sat) Pick your *pintxos* at the bar (where you can't smoke) and sample with house wine. Or take them to a table (smoker-friendly).

La Bodeguilla (☎ 971 71 82 74; Carrer de Sant Jaume 1-3; meals €35-45; 1-11.30pm Mon-Sat) This gourmet eatery does lightly creative interpretations of dishes from across Spain, such as *cochinillo* from Segovia, and *lechazo* (young lamb, baked Córdoba-style in rosemary).

Refectori (☎ 971 22 73 47; Carrer de la Missió 7a; meals €70-80; lunch & dinner Mon-Fri, dinner Sat) Lovingly prepared Mediterranean grub with a special touch is the order of the day. The restaurant has a modern air, with angular high-back chairs, and a rigorously white, black and timber decor.

If you're putting together a picnic, go to the **Mercat de l'Olivar** (Plaça del Olivar; 7am-2pm Mon-Sat), the city's central produce market, and then stop in at **Forn des Teatre** (☎ 97 171 52 54; Plaça de Weyler 9; 8am-8pm Mon-Sat) for some of the island's signature *ensaimadas* (yeast-based pastries).

The old quarter is the city's most vibrant nightlife zone – particularly along the narrow streets between Plaça de la Reina and Plaça de la Drassana. Look around the Santa Catalina (especially Carrer de Sant Magí) and Es Molinar districts too.

Abaco (☎ 971 71 59 47; Carrer de Sant Joan 1) Behind a set of ancient timber doors is the bar of your wildest dreams. Inside, a Mallorcan *pati* and candlelit courtyard are crammed with elaborate floral arrangements, cascading towers of fresh fruit and bizarre artworks.

Jazz Voyeur Club (☎ 971 90 52 92; www.jazzvoyeur.com; Carrer dels Apuntadors 5) A tiny club no bigger than most people's living room, Voyeur hosts live jazz bands nightly, starting at 10pm.

Puro Beach (☎ 971 74 47 44; www.purobeach.com; 11am-2am) This uber-laid-back sunset chill lounge is perfect for sunset cocktails, DJ sessions and fusion food escapes.

Palma's clubs are largely concentrated west of the city centre along Passeig Marítim, Avinguda de Joan Miró and Plaça de Gomila.

Around Mallorca

Mallorca's northwestern coast is a world away from the high-rise tourism on the other side of the island. Dominated by the Serra de Tramuntana, it's a beautiful region of olive groves, pine forests and small villages with shuttered stone buildings; it also has a breathtaking rugged and rocky coastline offering plenty of options for hikers and cyclists. There are a couple of highlights for drivers: the hair-raising road down to the small port of **Sa Calobra**, and the amazing trip along the peninsula leading to the island's northern tip, **Cap Formentor**.

Sóller is a good place to base yourself for hiking and the nearby village of **Fornalutx** is one of the prettiest on Mallorca.

From Sóller, it is a 10km walk to the beautiful hilltop village of **Deià** (www.deia.info), where Robert Graves, poet and author of *I Claudius*, lived for most of his life. From the village, you can scramble down to the small shingle beach of **Cala de Deià**. Boasting a fine monastery and pretty streets, **Valldemossa** (www.valldemossa.com) is further southwest down the coast.

Further east, **Pollença** and **Artà** are attractive inland towns. Nice beaches include those at **Cala Sant Vicenç**, **Cala Mondragó** and around **Cala Llombards**.

SLEEPING & EATING

The Consell de Mallorca tourist office in Palma (p815) can supply information on rural and other accommodation around the island.

Deià

Hostal Miramar (☎ 971 63 90 84; www.pensionmiramar.com; Carrer de Can Oliver s/n; d €84) Hidden up in what could almost be described as the jungle above the main road, this 19th-century stone house with gardens is a shady retreat.

El Barrigón de Xelini (☎ 971 63 91 39; Avinguda del Arxiduc Lluís Salvador 19; meals €20; 12.30pm-12.30am Tue-Sun) You never quite know what to expect here, but tapas is at the core. It has a penchant for mains of lamb too. In the evenings, you may encounter a bit of live jazz.

Sóller

Hotel El Guía (☎ 971 63 02 27; www.sollernet.com/elguia; Carrer del Castañer 2; s/d €51/80) Handily located beside the train station, this is a good place to meet fellow walkers. Its bright rooms feature timber trims and modern bathrooms.

Ca's Carreter (☎ 971 63 51 33; Carrer del Cetre 9; meals €25-30; lunch & dinner Tue-Sat, lunch Sun) Set in a leafy cart workshop (founded in 1914), this is a cool and welcoming spot for modest local cooking, with fresh fish and meat options.

Cala de Sant Vicenç

Hostal los Pinos (☎ 971 53 12 10; www.hostal-lospinos.com; s/d €44/72;) This place is set on a leafy hillside back off the road between Cala Molins and Cala Carbo. The best of the simple rooms have partial sea views with balconies to hang up your beach towel.

East Coast

Hostal Playa Mondragó (☎ 971 65 77 52; www.playamondrago.com; Cala Mondragó; s/d €59/88;) Barely 50m back from one of the beaches, it's a tranquil option, and the better rooms have balconies and fine sea views.

IBIZA

pop 117,700

Ibiza (Eivissa in Catalan) is an island of extremes. Its formidable party reputation is completely justified, with some of the world's greatest clubs attracting hedonists from the world over. The interior and northeast of the island, however, are another world. Peaceful country drives, hilly green territory, a sprinkling of mostly laidback beaches and coves, and some wonderful inland accommodation and eateries, are light years from the ecstasy-fuelled madness of the clubs that dominate the west. And the old centre of Ibiza City itself is a gem that should on no account be missed.

GETTING AROUND

Four bus companies operate around the island and fares don't exceed €3 for the longest journey. Buses between the airport (7km west of Ibiza City) and the central port area of Ibiza City via Platja d'En Bossa operate hourly between 6.30am and 11.30pm (€1.50, 20 to 25 minutes).

Most other buses leave from the series of bus stops along Avinguda d'Isidoro Macabich.

Plenty of ferries make the 25 to 35 minute trip between Ibiza City and the neighbouring island of Formentera each day. Tickets cost at least €21.50 each way.

Ibiza City

INFORMATION

Surf@Net (☎ 971 19 49 20; Carrer de Riambau 8; per hr €2.40; 11am-11pm Mon-Fri, 3-11pm Sat)

Tourist office Main office (☎ 971 30 19 00; www.ibiza.travel; Passeig de Vara de Rei 1; 9am-8pm Mon-Fri, 9am-7pm Sat, 9am-3pm Sun); D'Alt Vila office (☎ 971 39 92 32; Carrer Major 2; 10am-2pm & 6-8pm Mon-Sat)

SIGHTS & ACTIVITIES

Ibiza City's port area of **Sa Penya** is crammed with funky and trashy clothing boutiques and arty-crafty market stalls. From here, you can wander up into **D'Alt Vila**, the atmospheric old walled town. You can walk along the length of the walls – a stiff climb in parts but great for views. Along the perimeter walk, the **Museu d'Art Contemporani** (☎ 971 30 27 23; Ronda de Narcís Puget s/n; admission free; 10am-1.30pm & 5-8pm Tue-Fri, 10am-1.30pm Sat & Sun May-Sep, 10am-1.30pm & 4-6pm Tue-Fri, 10am-1.30pm Sat & Sun Oct-Apr) is in an 18th-century powder store and armoury that hosts contemporary art exhibitions. High up in the town is the 14th-century **cathedral** and adjoining **Museu Arqueològic** (☎ 971 30 17 71; Plaça de la Catedral 3; adult/child & senior/student €2.40/free/1.20; 9am-3pm Tue-Sat, 10am-2pm Sun Oct-Mar, 10am-2pm

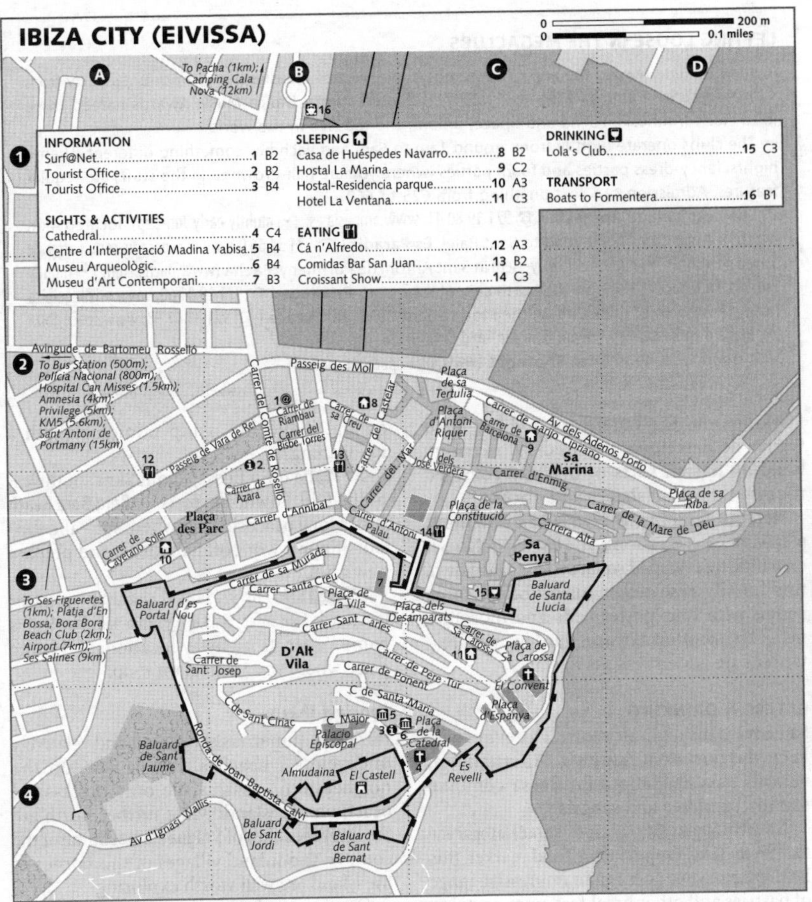

& 6-8pm Tue-Sat, 10am-2pm Sun Apr-Sep). A few steps down Carrer Major, the **Centre d'Interpretació Madina Yasiba** (☎ 971 39 92 32; Carrer Major 2; admission free; ⏲ 10am-1.30pm & 5-8pm Tue-Fri, 9.30am-1.30pm Sat & Sun May-Sep, 10am-1.30pm & 4-6pm Tue-Fri, 9.30am-1.30pm Sat & Sun Oct-Apr) takes us into the medieval Muslim city of Madina Yasiba (Ibiza City), as it was prior to Christian conquest in 1235.

The heavily developed **Platja de ses Figueretes** is a 20-minute walk southwest of Sa Penya, but you're better off heading south to the beaches at **Ses Salines**, a half-hour ride on bus 11 (€1.50).

SLEEPING

Many of Ibiza City's hotels and *hostales* are closed in the low season and heavily booked between April and October. Make sure you book ahead.

Casa de Huéspedes Navarro (☎ 971 31 07 71; Carrer de sa Creu 20; s/d €30/55) Right in the thick of things, this simple place has 10 rooms at the top of a long flight of stairs. The front rooms have harbour views, the interior rooms are quite dark (but cool in summer) and there's a sunny rooftop terrace.

Hostal-Residencia Parque (☎ 971 30 13 58; www.hostalparque.com; Carrer de Vicent Cuervo 3; s with shared bathroom €60, d with private bathroom €110-170) The best doubles overlook pleasant Plaça del Parc from above the eponymous cafe. Doubles are comfortable but singles are predictably pokey.

Hostal La Marina (☎ 971 31 01 72; www.hostal-lamarina.com; Carrer de Barcelona 7; s €68, d €85-175; ❄)

SPAIN

LETTING LOOSE IN THE MEGACLUBS

In summer (late May to the end of September), the west of the island is a continuous party from sunset to sunrise and back again. In 2007, the International Dance Music Awards named three Ibiza clubs (Amnesia, Pacha and Space) among the top five in the world.

The clubs operate nightly from around 1am to 6am and each has something different. Theme nights, fancy-dress parties and foam parties (where you are half-drowned in the stuff) are regular features. Admission can cost anything from €25 to €60.

The best include **Amnesia** (☎ 971 19 80 41; www.amnesia.es; nightly early Jun-Sep), located 4km north of Ibiza City on the road to Sant Rafel; **Es Paradis** (☎ 971 34 66 00; www.esparadis.com; Carrer de Salvador Espriu 2; nightly mid-May–Sep) in Sant Antoni de Portmany; **Pacha** (www.pacha.com; nightly Jun-Sep, Fri & Sat Oct-May), on the north side of Ibiza port; **Privilege** (☎ 971 19 81 60; www.privilegeibiza.com), 5km north of Ibiza City on the road to Sant Rafel; and **Space** (☎ 971 39 67 93; www.space-ibiza.es; Platja d'en Bossa; 4.30pm-6am Jun–mid-Oct).

A good website is **Ibiza Spotlight** (www.ibiza-spotlight.com).

Looking onto the waterfront and bar-lined Carrer de Barcelona, this mid-19th-century building has all sorts of brightly coloured rooms in different shapes and prices.

Hotel La Ventana (☎ 971 39 08 57; www.laventanaibiza.com; Carrer de sa Carossa 13; d from €177;) Set on a little tree-shaded square in the Old Town, this funkily restored mansion offers some rooms with four-poster beds and mosquito nets. The rooftop terrace, gardens and restaurant are added reasons to stay.

SPAIN

EATING & DRINKING

Sa Penya is the nightlife centre. Dozens of bars keep the port area jumping. Alternatively, various bars at Platja d'En Bossa combine sounds, sand, sea and sangria.

Croissant Show (☎ 971 31 76 65; Plaça de la Constitució s/n; 6am-11pm) Opposite the food market, this is where *everyone* goes for an impressive range of pastries and other breakfast, post-partying goodies. It is quite a scene all on its own.

our pick **Comidas Bar San Juan** (☎ 971 31 16 03; Carrer de Guillem de Montgri 8; meals €15-20; Mon-Sat) A family-run operation with two small dining rooms, this simple eatery offers outstanding value, with fish dishes for around €10 and many small mains for €6 or less.

Ca' n'Alfredo (☎ 971 31 12 74; Passeig de Vara de Rei 16; meals €40-45; lunch & dinner Tue-Sat, lunch Sun) Locals love Alfredo's place for the freshest of seafood and other island cuisine that's so good it's essential to book. Try the *filetes de gallo de San Pedro en salsa de almendras* (fillets of fine local white fish in almond sauce).

Lola's Club (Via de Alfonso XII 10) Anyone who remembers Ibiza in the '80s will have fond memories of Lola's Club, one of the first on the island. It's a hip miniclub (with a gay leaning).

At Platja d'En Bossa, about 2km southwest of the Old Town, *the* place is **Bora Bora Beach Club**, a long beachside bar where sun- and fun-worshippers work off hangovers and prepare new ones.

our pick **KM5** (☎ 971 39 63 49; www.km5-lounge.com; Carretera de Sant Josep, Km5.6; 8pm-4am May-Sep) is named after its highway location, and is the place where you go to glam it up.

Around Ibiza

Ibiza has numerous unspoiled and relatively undeveloped beaches. **Cala de Boix**, on the northeastern coast, is the only black-sand beach on the island, while further north are the lovely beaches of **S'Aigua Blanca**. Some of the country and inland villages of this corner of the island are well worth exploring.

On the north coast near Portinatx, **Cala Xarraca** is in a picturesque, secluded bay, and near Port de Sant Miquel is the attractive **Cala Benirrás**.

In the southwest, **Cala d'Hort** has a spectacular setting overlooking two rugged rock islets, Es Verda and Es Verdranell.

The best thing about rowdy **Sant Antoni**, the island's second biggest town and north of Ibiza City, is heading to the small rock-and-sand strip on the north shore to join hundreds of others for sunset drinks at a string of chilled bars. The best known remains **Café del Mar** (☎ 971 34 25 16; www.cafedelmar.es; 5pm-4am), our favourite, but it's further north along the pedestrian walkway. Places such as **Coastline Café**, **Sun Beach Bar** and **Kanya** have pools and attract plenty of punters. After the sun goes down all turn up the rhythmic heat and pound on until 4am, from about June to October.

Local **buses** (www.ibizabus.com) run to most destinations between May and October.

SLEEPING & EATING

Check out rural accommodation at www.ibizaruralvillas.com and www.casasruralesibiza.com (in Spanish). For more standard accommodation, start at www.ibizahotelsguide.com.

Camping Cala Nova (☎ 971 33 17 74; www.campingcalanova.com; camp sites per 2 people, tent & car €26.15) Close to a good beach and 12km northeast of Ibiza City, this is one of Ibiza's best camping grounds.

Hostal Es Alocs (☎ 971 33 50 79; www.hostalalocs.com; s/d €35/55; May-Oct) Right on the beach at Platja Es Figueral. Rooms are simple, with their own bathroom and are over a couple of floors. Downstairs it has a bar-restaurant with shady terrace.

our pick **Hostal Cala Boix** (☎ 971 33 52 24; www.hostalcalaboix.com; d incl breakfast €68;) Set uphill and back from the beach, this solitary place has big, cheap rooms and a hearty restaurant. On the beach you'll find a daytime bar in summer.

Bar Anita (☎ 971 33 50 90; Sant Carles de Peralta; meals €20-25) A timeless tavern opposite the village church in inland Sant Carles, this place offers anything from pizza to slabs of *entrecote con salsa de pimiento* (entrecote in a pepper sauce; €15).

FORMENTERA

pop 8450

The 20km-long island of Formentera is a legend for some. The coast is alternately fringed with jagged cliffs and beaches backed by low dunes. Much of the tough inland farming land has been abandoned. Except when the island is filled to capacity from mid-July to late August, it is a wonderful place to escape to. There is little to do but enjoy the crystal sea, zip around on a scooter, eat and then start all over again.

Ferries from Ibiza City arrive at La Savina (where you'll find plenty of outlets to hire motorbikes, scooters and bicycles). Three kilometres south is the island's administrative capital, Sant Francesc Xavier, and another 5km southwest is windswept Cap de Barbaria, the southernmost point. Es Pujols, the main tourist resort (and possibly least interesting part of the island!), is 3km east of La Savina.

Formentera's **tourist office** (☎ 971 32 20 57; www.turismoformentera.com; 9am-7pm Mon-Fri, 9am-3pm Sat & Sun May-Sep) is in La Savina.

Among the island's best beaches are **Platja de Llevant** and **Platja de ses Illetes** – beautiful strips of white sand that line the eastern and western sides, respectively, of the narrow promontory stretching north towards Ibiza.

East of Sant Ferran de ses Roques, towards Es Caló, a series of bumpy roads leads to the south coast beaches, known collectively as **Platja de Migjorn**. The best are at the eastern end around **Es Arenals**.

Hostal Pepe (☎ 971 32 80 33; Carrer Major 68, Sant Ferran de ses Roques; s/d incl breakfast €46/60), located on the pleasant (and on summer nights lively) main street near the village's old sandstone church, is a whitewashed place with flashes of blue and has 45 simple and breezy rooms with bathroom.

our pick **Fonda Rafalet** (☎ 971 32 70 16; Es Caló; s/d €64/107), overlooking a small rocky harbour in a diminutive fishing hamlet, has spacious rooms (many with sea views). The guest house also incorporates a bar and popular seafood restaurant.

our pick **S'Eufabi** (☎ 971 32 70 56; Carretera La Mola, Km 12.5; meals €25-30; lunch & dinner Wed-Mon, dinner Tue) has some of the best paella and *fideuá* on Formentera. The shady eatery is located about 1km east of Es Caló on the left as you begin the gentle ascent towards Es Pilar de la Mola.

There are plenty of bars in Es Pujols.

our pick **Blue Bar** (☎ 971 18 70 11; www.bluebarformentera.com; Km 8; noon-4am Apr-Oct) is perfect for a sundowner. It is the south's chill-out bar par excellence, and everything is blue – the seats, the sunshades, the tables, lounges, loos and walls.

MENORCA

pop 90,300

Renowned for its pristine beaches and archaeological sites, tranquil Menorca was declared a Biosphere Reserve by Unesco in 1993. The capital, Maó, is known as Mahón in Castilian.

Information

Tourist office airport (☎ 971 15 71 15; 8am-10pm daily Jul-Aug, 8am-10pm Mon-Fri, 8am-2pm Sat May, Jun, Sep & Oct); Ciutadella (☎ 971 38 26 93; Plaça de la Catedral 5; 9am-2pm & 4-9pm Mon-Fri, 9am-2pm Sat May-Sep, 9am-1pm & 5-7pm Mon-Fri Oct-Apr)

SPAIN

Sights & Activities

Maó and Ciutadella are both harbour towns, and from either place you'll have to commute to the beaches. **Maó** absorbs most of the tourist traffic. While you're here, you can take a boat cruise around the impressive harbour.

North of Maó, a drive across a lunar landscape leads to the lighthouse at **Cap de Favàritx**. South of the cape stretch some fine sandy bays and beaches, including **Cala Presili** and **Platja d'en Tortuga**, reachable on foot.

Ciutadella, with its smaller harbour and historic buildings, has a more distinctly Spanish feel to it and is the more attractive of the two. A narrow country road leads south of Ciutadella (follow the 'Platges' sign from the *ronda*, or ringroad) and then forks twice to reach some of the island's loveliest beaches: (from west to east) **Arenal de Son Saura**, **Cala en Turqueta**, **Es Talaier**, **Cala Macarelleta** and **Cala Macarella**. As with most beaches, you'll need your own transport.

In the centre of the island, the 357m-high **Monte Toro** has great views; on a clear day you can see Mallorca.

On the northern coast, the picturesque town of **Fornells** is on a large bay popular with windsurfers.

Scattered across the island (some are visible from or signposted off the main road linking Maò and Ciutadella) are some remarkable ancient sites dating as far back as 2000 BC. In the east of the island are several major forts dating to the 18th and 19th centuries. The tourist offices can provide more information.

Sleeping

Many accommodation options on the island are closed between November and April.

MAÓ

Posada Orsi (☎ 971 36 47 51; Carrer de la Infanta 19; s/d with washbasin €30/49, d €60) Pastel colours are all the go here, and you may pick up the scent of incense. Rooms are equally bright (with lots of pink, hot orange and sky blue) and have mosquito nets (handy).

CIUTADELLA

Hostal-Residencia Oasis (☎ 971 38 21 97; Carrer de Sant Isidre 33; s/d €40/55) Set around a spacious garden courtyard, this quiet place close to the heart of the old quarter has pleasant rooms.

OTHER AREAS

Camping S'Atalaia (☎ 971 37 42 32; www.campingsatalaia.com; camp sites per 2 people, tent & car €23.50;) This pleasant place, shaded by pine trees, is two-thirds of the way down the Ferreries-Santa Galdana road.

Hostal La Palma (☎ 971 37 66 34; Plaça S'Algaret 3, Fornells; s/d €48/84;) Out the back of this bar-restaurant are cheerful rooms with bathrooms, balconies and views of the surrounding countryside. Singles aren't available in summer.

Eating & Drinking

The ports in both Maó and Ciutadella are lined with bars and restaurants.

MAÓ

Ses Forquilles (☎ 971 35 27 11; Carrer de Rovellada de Dalt 20; meals €30-35; lunch & dinner Thu-Sat, lunch Mon-Wed) This self-proclaimed 'gastronomic space' offers tasty snacks and a handful of dishes ranging from steak tartar to *fideuá de sépia negra* (a noodle and cuttlefish dish). It offers a good gourmet set lunch for €16.

Akelarre (☎ 971 36 85 20; www.akelarrejazz.es; Moll de Ponent 41-43; 3pm-4am daily Jun-Sep, 7pm-4am Thu-Sat, 7pm-3am Sun-Wed Oct-May) Ambient and jazz dance music dominate the wee hours in this place, made welcoming by the warm stone interior. Live music frequently enlivens proceedings earlier in the evening (starting around 11pm, and costing €10).

CIUTADELLA

Café Balear (☎ 971 38 00 05; Placa de Sant Joan 15; meals €25-30; Mon-Sat) This long-standing favourite offers attractive outdoor seating and an excellent seafood-dominated menu.

Café des Museu (Carreró d'es Palau 4; 10pm-3.30am) A charming old-town cocktail bar tucked away down a tight lane. It's an occasional host to live gigs, anything from acid jazz to bossa nova.

FORNELLS

Es Port (☎ 971 37 64 03; Passeig Marítim 10; meals €30-35; Sat-Thu) This place does some fine, fresh fish and seafood here. Try the tender white meat of the *gall de Sant Pere*, a popular Balearic catch (€20.50). The speciality in most places here is *caldereta de langosta* (spiny lobster stew) – reckon on at least €60 per person.

Getting Around

Menorca's airport (MAH) is served by buses to the bus station in Maó (€1.55, 15 minutes) every half-hour from 5.55am to 10.25pm and then (June to September only) hourly to 12.25am.

You can catch **TMSA** (☎ 971 36 04 75; www.tmsa.es) buses from the bus station. In summer (May to October), at least eight go to Ciutadella (€4.40, one hour). Other destinations are served less regularly.

ANDALUCÍA

The tapping feet and clapping hands of a passionate flamenco performance is an Andalucian signature that's as distinctive as the sweet aroma of orange blossom or the voluptuous flavour offered by a glass of chilled summer *gazpacho*.

In years past, armies of Christians and Muslims fought over this sun-drenched part of Spain; these days, tourists are the only visitors to arrive in battalions, lured here by Andalucía's beaches, incomparable Islamic monuments and full-blooded culture. Have a look at www.andalucia.org.

SEVILLE

pop 699,200

A completely sexy, gutsy and gorgeous city, Seville is home to two of Spain's most colourful festivals, fascinating and distinctive *barrios* and a local population that lives life to the fullest. A fiery place (as you'll soon see in its packed and noisy tapas bars), it is also hot climatewise – try to avoid July and August!

Information

Internetia (Avenida Menéndez Pelayo 45; per hr €2; 11am-11pm)

Municipal tourist office (☎ 954 22 17 14; Calle de Arjona 28; 9am-7.30pm Mon-Fri, 9am-2pm Sat & Sun)

Regional tourist offices Avenida de la Constitución 21 (☎ 954 22 14 04; otsevilla@andalucia.org; 9am-7pm Mon-Fri, 10am-2pm & 3-7pm Sat, 10am-2pm Sun, closed holidays); Estación Santa Justa (☎ 954 53 76 26; 9am-8pm Mon-Fri, 10am-2pm Sat & Sun, closed holidays).

Turismo Sevilla (☎ 954 21 00 05; www.turismosevilla.org; Plaza del Triunfo 1; 10.30am-7pm Mon-Fri)

Sights & Activities

CATEDRAL & LA GIRALDA

Seville's **Catedral** (☎ 954 21 49 71; adult/under 12yr/student & senior €7.50/free/1.50, admission free Sun; 11am-6pm Mon-Sat, 2.30-7pm Sun Sep-Jun, 9.30am-4.30pm Mon-Sat, 2.30-7pm Sun Jul & Aug) was built on the site of Muslim Seville's main mosque between 1401 and 1507. The structure is primarily Gothic, although most internal decoration is in later styles. One highlight of the cathedral's lavish interior is Christopher Columbus' supposed tomb, although research indicates he was probably laid to rest in the Caribbean. The four sepulchre-bearers represent the four kingdoms of Spain at the time Columbus sailed to the Americas. The adjoining tower, **La Giralda**, was the mosque's minaret and dates from the 12th century. Climb to the top for the city views.

ALCÁZAR

Seville's **Alcázar** (☎ 954 50 23 23; adult/under 16yr, senior & student €7/free; 9.30am-8pm Tue-Sat, to 6pm Sun & holidays Apr-Sep, to 6pm Tue-Sat, to 2.30pm Sun & holidays Oct-Mar), a royal residence for many centuries, was founded in 913 as a Muslim fortress. The Alcázar has been expanded and rebuilt many times in its 11 centuries of existence. The Catholic Monarchs, Fernando and Isabel, set up court here in the 1480s as they prepared for the conquest of Granada. Later rulers created the Alcázar's lovely gardens.

WALKS & PARKS

Seville's medieval *judería* (Jewish quarter), the **Barrio de Santa Cruz**, east of the cathedral and Alcázar, is a tangle of quaint, winding streets and lovely plant-decked plazas perfumed with orange blossom. Its most characteristic plaza is **Plaza de Santa Cruz**.

A more straightforward walk is along the **river bank** and past Seville's famous bullring, the **Plaza de Toros de la Real Maestranza** (☎ 954 22 45 77; www.realmaestranza.es; Paseo de Cristóbal Colón 12; tours adult/over-65 €5/4; 9.30am-7pm Nov-Apr, 9.30am-8pm, May-Oct, 9.30am-3pm bullfighting days), one of the oldest in Spain. The tour departs half-hourly, and is in English and Spanish.

South of the centre is **Parque de María Luisa**, with its maze of paths, tall trees, flowers, fountains and shaded lawns. Be sure to seek out the magnificent **Plaza de España** with its fountains, canal and a simply dazzling semicircle of *azulejo-* (ceramic tile) clad buildings.

SPAIN

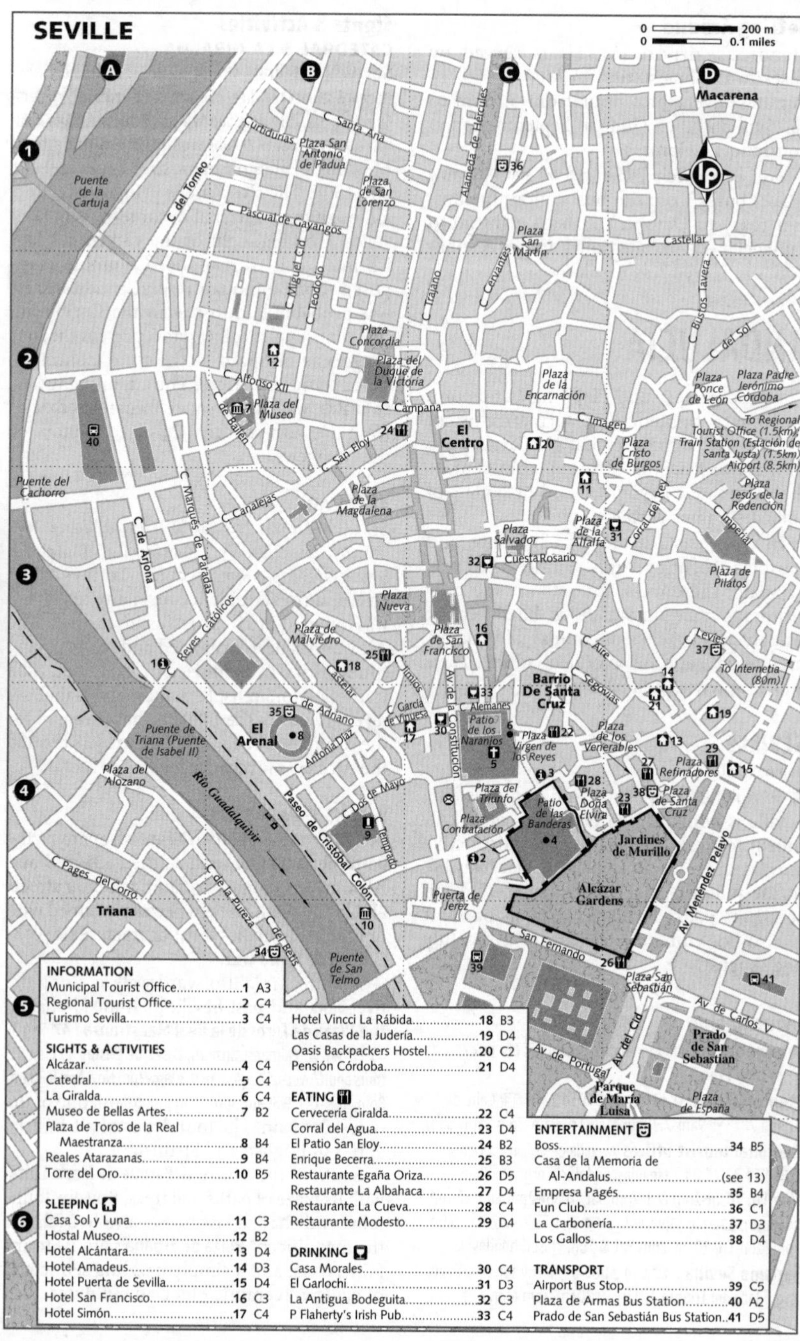
SEVILLE
0 200 m
0 0.1 miles
A
B
C
D
1
2
3
4
5
6
Macarena
C Santa Ana
Curtidurías
Plaza San Antonio de Padua
Plaza de San Lorenzo
Alameda de Hércules
36
Puente de la Cartuja
C del Torneo
C Pascual de Gayangos
Plaza San Martín
C Castellar
Miguel Cid
Teodosio
Trajano
Cervantes
Bustos Tavera
C del Sol
Plaza Concordia
12
Plaza del Duque de la Victoria
Plaza de la Encarnación
Plaza Ponce de León
Plaza Padre Jerónimo Córdoba
C Alfonso XII
C de Bailén
7
Plaza del Museo
C Campana
C Imagen
To Regional Tourist Office (1.5km); Train Station (Estación de Santa Justa) (1.5km); Airport (8.5km)
24
El Centro
20
Plaza Cristo de Burgos
40
C San Eloy
Puente del Cachorro
C Marqués de Paradas
11
Plaza de la Magdalena
Plaza Jesús de la Redención
C Canalejas
Corral del Rey
C Imperial
C de Arjona
Plaza Salvador
Plaza de la Alfalfa
31
32
Cuesta Rosario
Plaza de Pilatos
Plaza Nueva
Reyes Católicos
Plaza de Malviedro
Plaza de San Francisco
16
C Aire
C Levíes
37
1
25
18
C Castelar
Jimios
Av de la Constitución
Barrio De Santa Cruz
C Segovias
14
To Internetia (80m)
33
Alemanes
21
C de Adriano
García de Vinuesa
35
19
Puente de Triana (Puente de Isabel II)
El Arenal
8
17
30
Patio de los Naranjos
6
Plaza Virgen de los Reyes
22
Plaza de los Venerables
13
5
29
C Antonia Díaz
Plaza del Alozano
3
27
Plaza Refinadores
15
Río Guadalquivir
Paseo de Cristóbal Colón
C Dos de Mayo
Plaza del Triunfo
28
Plaza Doña Elvira
38
Plaza de Santa Cruz
23
Patio de las Banderas
9
Plaza Contratación
4
Jardines de Murillo
C Temprado
2
C Pages del Corro
C de la Pureza
Alcázar Gardens
Av Menéndez Pelayo
Puerta de Jerez
Triana
10
C del Betis
C San Fernando
34
Puente de San Telmo
26
39
Plaza San Sebastián
41
Av de Carlos V
Prado de San Sebastian
Av de Portugal
Av del Cid
Parque de María Luisa
Plaza de España
INFORMATION
Municipal Tourist Office 1 A3
Regional Tourist Office 2 C4
Turismo Sevilla 3 C4
SIGHTS & ACTIVITIES
Alcázar 4 C4
Catedral 5 C4
La Giralda 6 C4
Museo de Bellas Artes 7 B2
Plaza de Toros de la Real Maestranza 8 B4
Reales Atarazanas 9 B4
Torre del Oro 10 B5
SLEEPING
Casa Sol y Luna 11 C3
Hostal Museo 12 B2
Hotel Alcántara 13 D4
Hotel Amadeus 14 D3
Hotel Puerta de Sevilla 15 D4
Hotel San Francisco 16 C3
Hotel Simón 17 C4
Hotel Vincci La Rábida 18 B3
Las Casas de la Judería 19 D4
Oasis Backpackers Hostel 20 C2
Pensión Córdoba 21 D4
EATING
Cervecería Giralda 22 C4
Corral del Agua 23 D4
El Patio San Eloy 24 B2
Enrique Becerra 25 B3
Restaurante Egaña Oriza 26 D5
Restaurante La Albahaca 27 D4
Restaurante La Cueva 28 C4
Restaurante Modesto 29 D4
DRINKING
Casa Morales 30 C4
El Garlochi 31 D3
La Antigua Bodeguita 32 C3
P Flaherty's Irish Pub 33 C4
ENTERTAINMENT
Boss 34 B5
Casa de la Memoria de Al-Andalus (see 13)
Empresa Pagés 35 B4
Fun Club 36 C1
La Carbonería 37 D3
Los Gallos 38 D4
TRANSPORT
Airport Bus Stop 39 C5
Plaza de Armas Bus Station 40 A2
Prado de San Sebastián Bus Station 41 D5

Turismo Sevilla publishes an excellent booklet with self-guided walks.

MUSEUMS & MONUMENTS

Museo de Bellas Artes (☎ 954 78 65 00; Plaza del Museo 9; adult/EU citizen, senior & student €1.50/free; 🕑 2.30-8.30pm Tue, 9am-8.30pm Wed-Sat, to 2.30pm Sun, closed Mon) has an outstanding collection of Spanish art, focusing on local artists such as Bartolomé Esteban Murillo and Francisco Zurbarán.

The **Torre del Oro** (Golden Tower), a 13th-century river-bank Islamic watchtower, supposedly had a dome covered in golden tiles. Inside is a small **maritime museum** (☎ 954 22 24 19; adult/student & senior, €2/1; 🕑 10am-2pm Tue-Fri, 11am-2pm Sat & Sun Sep-Jul, closed holidays).

The maritime museum will one day find a spectacular new home in the former **Reales Atarazanas** (Royal Shipyards; ☎ 954 21 66 72; Calle Temprado 1; admission free; 🕑 10am-6pm Mon-Sat, to 2pm Sun & holidays). In all, 17 *naves* or bays were built in the 13th century on what were then the sandy banks of the Guadalquivir. They are being restored.

Festivals & Events

The first of Seville's two great festivals is **Semana Santa**, the week leading up to Easter Sunday. Throughout the week, thousands of members of religious brotherhoods parade in penitents' garb with tall, pointed *capirotes* (hoods) accompanying sacred images through the city, while huge crowds look on.

The **Feria de Abril**, a week in late April, is a welcome release after this solemnity: the festivities involve six days of music, dancing, horse-riding and traditional dress, plus daily bullfights.

The city also stages Spain's largest flamenco festival, the month-long **Bienal de Flamenco**. It's held in September in even-numbered years.

Sleeping

There's plenty of accommodation in the Barrio de Santa Cruz (close to the Alcázar), El Arenal and El Centro.

Prices over Semana Santa and the Feria de Abril can be up to double the high-season prices cited here. The city's accommodation is often full on weekends and is always booked solid during festivals, so book well ahead then.

DEATH IN THE AFTERNOON

Seville's bullfight season runs from Easter to October, with fights about 7pm most Sundays, and every day during the Feria de Abril and the preceding week. Tickets cost between €32.50 and €110. *Sol* (sun) seats are cheaper than *sombra* (shade) seats. Bullfighting can be gory and isn't for everyone; but if it is your thing, and you get a skilled matador, the atmosphere in the ring can be electrifying. Tickets can be purchased in advance from **Empresa Pagés** (☎ 954 50 13 82; Calle de Adriano 37) and from 4.30pm on fight days at the bullring.

BUDGET

Oasis Backpackers' Hostel (☎ 954 29 37 77; www.oasissevilla.com; Plaza de la Encarnación 29; 1-2 dm/d incl breakfast €20/46; ❄ 💻 🏊) Offbeat, buzzing backpacker central in a narrow street behind the church of the Anunciación. Each dorm bed has a personal safe and there is a small rooftop pool.

Casa Sol y Luna (☎ 954 21 06 82; www.casasolyluna1.com; Calle Pérez Galdós 1A; s/d/tr with shared bathroom €22/38/60, d with private bathroom €45) A first-rate *hostal* in a beautifully decorated house dating from 1911, with embroidered linen that makes you feel like you're at your grandma's.

Pensión Córdoba (☎ 954 22 74 98; Calle Farnesio 12; s/d with shared bathroom €40/60, with private bathroom €55/75; ❄) Run for the past 30 years by a friendly older couple, on a quiet pedestrian street. Rooms are basic but spotless.

Hostal Museo (☎ 954 91 55 26; www.hostalmuseo.com; Calle Abad Gordillo 17; s/d €48/60; ❄ 💻) The immaculate rooms here are endowed with solid wooden furniture and comfortable beds.

MIDRANGE & TOP END

Hotel San Francisco (☎/fax 954 50 15 41; www.sanfranciscoh.com; Calle Álvarez Quintero 38; s/d €55/68; 🕑 closed Aug; ❄ 💻) This good-value hotel on a pedestrianised street occupies an 18th-century home.

Hotel Simón (☎ 954 22 66 60; www.hotelsimonsevilla.com; Calle García de Vinuesa 19; s €60-70, d €95-110; ❄) A charming small hotel in a grand old 18th-century house, with spotless and comfortable rooms. Even the light filtering into the antique patio seems dipped in tea.

Hotel Puerta de Sevilla (☎ 954 98 72 70; www.hotelpuertadesevilla.com; Calle Puerta de la Carne 2; s/d €66/86; ❄ 💻) A small, shiny hotel in a great location, the Puerta de Sevilla is all flower-pattern textiles and wrought-iron beds.

Hotel Alcántara (☎ 954 50 05 95; www.hotelalcantara.net; Calle Ximénez de Enciso 28; s/d €68/89;) This small, friendly hotel on a pedestrian street punches above its weight with sparkling modern bathrooms, windows on to the hotel's patio and pretty floral curtains.

Hotel Amadeus (☎ 954 50 14 43; www.hotelamadeussevilla.com; Calle Farnesio 6; s/d €80/90;) This musician family converted their 18th-century mansion into a stylish hotel with 14 elegant rooms. Five new rooms have been added, one or two soundproofed for piano or violin practice.

Las Casas de la Judería (☎ 954 41 51 50; www.casasypalacios.com; Callejón Dos Hermanas 7; s/d from €140/175;) This charming five-star hotel is in fact a series of luxuriously restored houses and mansions.

Hotel Vincci La Rábida (☎ 954 50 12 80; www.vinccihoteles.com; Calle Castelar 24; s/d €159/195;) A beautiful four-storey columned atrium-lounge greets you in this converted 18th-century palace.

SPAIN

Eating

El Patio San Eloy (Calle San Eloy 9; tapas €1.50-3) Patches of old tiling remain at the always busy Patio San Eloy, where you can sit on the tiled steps at the back and feast on a fine array of *burguillos* (small filled rolls).

Cervecería Giralda (☎ 954 22 82 50; Calle Mateos Gago 1; tapas €3.50-5) Exotic variations are merged with traditional dishes in this one-time Muslim bathhouse.

Restaurante La Cueva (☎ 954 21 31 43; Calle Rodrigo Caro 18; mains €11-24, menú del día €16) This popular bull's head–festooned eatery cooks up a storming fish *zarzuela* (casserole; €30 for two people) and a hearty *caldereta* (lamb stew; €14.90).

Restaurante Modesto (☎ 954 41 68 11; Calle Cano y Cueto 5; mains €11-34) This bustling place is famed for its lobster and monkfish stew.

Corral del Agua (☎ 954 22 48 41; Callejón del Agua 6; mains €16.50-22; Mon-Sat) Inventive Al-Andalus and traditional dishes served in a semitropical courtyard under a twining canopy of vines and jacaranda.

Enrique Becerra (☎ 954 21 30 49; Calle Gamazo 2; mains €16.50-24; Mon-Fri) Adding a smart touch to El Arenal, Enrique Becerra cooks up hearty Andalucian dishes. The lamb drenched in honey sauce and stuffed with spinach and pine nuts is delectable.

Restaurante La Albahaca (☎ 954 22 07 14; Plaza de Santa Cruz 12; mains €20-30) Gastronomic invention is the mainstay of this elegant, gilded restaurant with its azure blue interior. Try the leg of duck confit in a sauce of bitter orange and rosemary honey.

Restaurante Egaña Oriza (☎ 954 22 72 11; Calle San Fernando 41; mains €22-32; lunch & dinner Mon-Fri, dinner Sat) Regarded as one of the city's best restaurants, Egaña Oriza cooks up superb Andalucian-Basque cuisine, including lasagne with seafood, lobster and truffles.

Drinking

Bars usually open until 2am weekdays and 3am at the weekend. Drinking and partying really get going around midnight on Friday and Saturday. In summer, dozens of open-air late-night bars *(terrazas de verano)* spring up along the river.

P Flaherty's Irish Pub (☎ 954 21 04 17; Calle Alemanes 7; 11am-late) Sports fans tend to gravitate towards Flaherty's, which occupies a premium position opposite the cathedral.

Casa Morales (☎ 954 22 12 42; Garcia de Vinuesa 11) Founded in 1850, not much has changed in this defiantly old-world bar, with charming anachronisms wherever you look. Towering clay *tinajas* (wine storage jars) carry the chalked-up tapas choices of the day. Locals sweat it out on summer nights like true Sevillanos.

El Garlochi (Calle Boteros 4) Named after the *gitano* (Roma) word for 'heart', this deeply camp bar hits you with clouds of incense, Jesus and Virgin images displayed on scarlet walls, and potent cocktails with names like Sangre de Cristo (Blood of Christ).

Plaza del Salvador is brimful of drinkers from mid-evening to 1am. Grab a drink from **La Antigua Bodeguita** (☎ 954 56 18 33) and sit on the steps of the Parroquia del Salvador. Calle Pérez Galdós, off Plaza de la Alfalfa, also has a handful of busy bars.

Entertainment

Seville is arguably Spain's flamenco capital and you're most likely to catch a spontaneous atmosphere (of unpredictable quality) in one of the bars staging regular nights of flamenco with no admission fee.

The Alameda de Hércules area, a former red-light district north of the city centre, is a buzzing place with lots of offbeat bars. Some have live music.

La Carbonería (☎ 954 21 44 60; Calle Levíes 18; admission free; ⏲ about 8pm-4am) The sprawling converted coal yard throngs every night of the week with tourists and locals who come to mingle and enjoy live flamenco.

Casa de la Memoria Al-Andalus (☎ 954 56 06 70; Calle Ximénez de Enciso 28; adult/child €14/8; ⏲ 9pm & 10.30pm) Book a ticket here for nightly shows with a focus on medieval and Sephardic Al-Andalus styles of music, in a room of shifting shadows.

Fun Club (☎ 958 25 02 49; Alameda de Hércules 86; live-band nights €3-6, other nights free; ⏲ 11.30pm-late Thu-Sun, from 9.30pm live-band nights) Try this place, with funk, Latino, hip-hop and jazz bands taking the stage – it's not surprising that this little dance warehouse is a music-lovers' favourite.

For flamenco, hotels and tourist offices tend to steer you towards *tablaos* (expensive, tourist-oriented flamenco venues). Of these, **Los Gallos** (☎ 954 21 69 81; www.tablaolosgallos.com; Plaza de Santa Cruz 11; admission incl 1 drink €30; ⏲ 2hr shows 8-10pm & 10.30-12.30pm) is a cut above the average. On Calle del Betis, on the far bank of the Guadalquivir, you'll find some good dance bars/discos, including **Boss** (Calle del Betis 67; admission with flyer free; ⏲ 8pm-7am Tue-Sun), one of Seville's top dance spots.

Getting There & Away

AIR

A range of domestic and international flights lands in Seville's San Pablo airport (SVQ), 8.5km from the city centre.

BUS

Regular services run from the **Plaza de Armas bus station** (☎ 954 90 80 40; Avenida del Cristo de la Expiración). Destinations include Madrid (€18.65, six hours, 14 daily), Mérida (€11, three hours, 12 daily), Cáceres (€15, four hours, six daily) and northwestern Spain. This is also the station for buses to Portugal. **ALSA** (www.alsa.es) runs two daily buses to Lisbon (€41, seven hours).

Buses to other parts of Andalucía use **Prado de San Sebastián bus station** (☎ 954 41 71 11; Plaza San Sebastián). Twelve or more buses run daily to/from Córdoba (€9.43, two hours) and Granada (€18.57, 3½ hours), and five to Ronda (€10.50, 2½ hours) and Málaga (€14.75, 2¾ hours). This is also the station for other towns in Cádiz province, the east of Sevilla province, and destinations along the Mediterranean coast from the Costa del Sol to Barcelona.

TRAIN

From Seville's **Estación de Santa Justa** (Avenida Kansas City), 1.5km northeast of the centre, there are superfast AVE trains as well as regular trains to Madrid (€59 to €75.10, 2½ to 3½ hours, hourly). Other destinations include Barcelona (€57.50 to €88, 10½ to 13 hours, three daily), Cádiz (€9.80, 1¾ hours, 13 daily), Córdoba (€8.20 to €28.30, 40 minutes to 1½ hours, 21 or more daily) and Granada (€21.65, three hours, four daily).

Getting Around

Amarillos Tours (☎ 902 21 03 17) runs buses between the airport and Puerta de Jerez (€2.20 to €2.50, 30 to 40 minutes, at least 15 daily). A taxi costs about €18.

Buses are run by Seville's urban transport authority, **Tussam** (☎ 902 45 99 54; www.tussam.es). The C1, C2, C3 and C4 buses link the main transport terminals and the city centre. Two new tram lines operate between Plaza Nueva (near the Ayuntamiento) and along Avenida de la Constitución to the Archivo de Indias and Puerta de Jerez, then down San Fernando to the bus station at Prado de San Sebastian. Tickets cost €1.10. A metro line is under construction.

SeVici (☎ 902 01 10 32; www.sevici.es; ⏲ 7am-9pm) is a cycle hire network comprising almost 200 fully automated pickup/drop off points across the city. A one-week subscription costs €5. Your first 30 minutes cycling is free, the next hour costs €1, second and subsequent hours are €2 per hour.

CÓRDOBA

pop 323,600

Córdoba pays graceful testament to its Moorish past. Its magnificent Mezquita (Mosque) has been described as the greatest visual representation of homesickness ever constructed, and is one of the highlights of any visit to Spain.

Information

Ch@t (Calle Claudio Marcelo 15; per hr €1.80; ⏲ 9am-1.30pm & 4.30-8.30pm Mon-Fri Nov-Mar, 9.30am-1.30pm & 5.30-8.30pm April-Oct, 10am-1.30pm Sat year-round) Internet access.

Policía Nacional (☎ 95 747 75 00; Avenida Doctor Fleming 2)

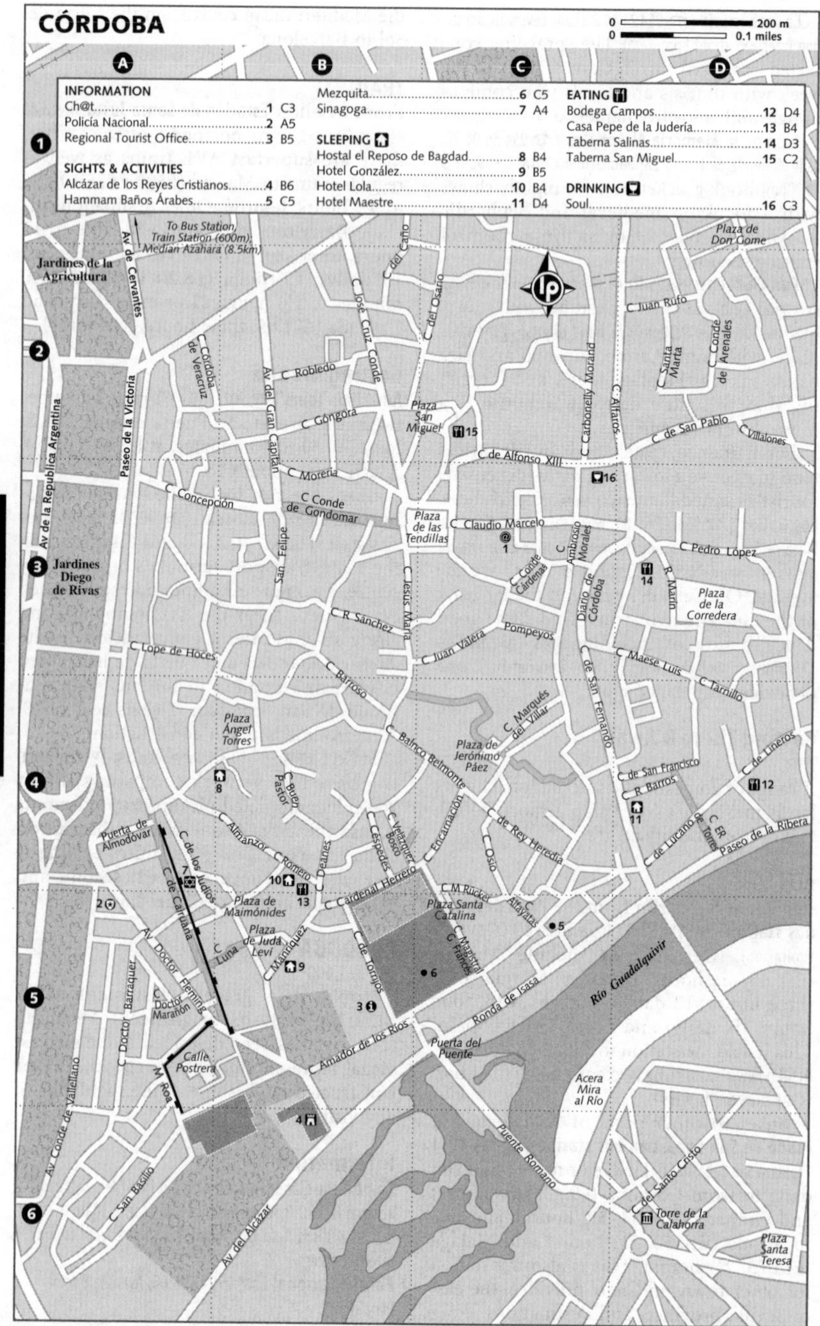
CÓRDOBA
0 200 m
0 0.1 miles
INFORMATION
Ch@t 1 C3
Policía Nacional 2 A5
Regional Tourist Office 3 B5
SIGHTS & ACTIVITIES
Alcázar de los Reyes Cristianos 4 B6
Hammam Baños Árabes 5 C5
Mezquita 6 C5
Sinagoga 7 A4
SLEEPING
Hostal el Reposo de Bagdad 8 B4
Hotel González 9 B5
Hotel Lola 10 B4
Hotel Maestre 11 D4
EATING
Bodega Campos 12 D4
Casa Pepe de la Judería 13 B4
Taberna Salinas 14 D3
Taberna San Miguel 15 C2
DRINKING
Soul 16 C3
To Bus Station, Train Station (600m); Median Azahara (8.5km)
Jardines de la Agricultura
Jardines Diego de Rivas
Av de Cervantes
Paseo de la Victoria
Av de la República Argentina
Plaza San Miguel
Plaza de las Tendillas
Plaza de la Corredera
Plaza de Don Gome
Plaza Ángel Torres
Plaza de Jerónimo Páez
Plaza de Maimónides
Plaza de Judá Leví
Plaza Santa Catalina
Puerta de Almodóvar
Puerta del Puente
Calle Postrera
Río Guadalquivir
Acera Mira al Río
Puente Romano
Torre de la Calahorra
Plaza Santa Teresa
Paseo de la Ribera
Ronda de Isasa
Amador de los Ríos
Av del Alcázar
Av Conde de Vallellano
Av Doctor Fleming
SPAIN

Regional tourist office (☎ 957 35 51 79; Calle de Torrijos 10; 9am-7.30pm Mon-Fri, 9.30am-3pm Sat, Sun & holidays) Facing the western side of the Mezquita, this helpful office offers information on the city and the surrounding countryside.

Sights & Activities

The inside of the famous **Mezquita** (☎ 957 47 05 12; adult/child €8/4; 10am-7pm Mon-Sat Apr-Oct, to 6pm Mon-Sat Nov-Mar, 9-10.45am & 1.30-6.30pm Sun year-round), which was begun by emir Abd ar-Rahman I in 785 and enlarged by subsequent generations, is a mesmerising sequence of two-tier arches amid a thicket of columns. From 1236, the mosque was used as a church and in the 16th century a cathedral was built right in its centre – somewhat wrecking the effect of the original Muslim building.

The **Judería**, Córdoba's medieval Jewish quarter northwest of the Mezquita, is an intriguing maze of narrow streets, small plazas and traditional houses with flower-filled patios. Don't miss the beautiful little **Sinagoga** (Calle de los Judíos 20; adult/EU citizen €0.30/free; 9.30am-2pm & 3.30-5.30pm Tue-Sat, to 1.30pm Sun & holidays).

Southwest of the Mezquita stands the **Alcázar de los Reyes Cristianos** (Fortress of the Christian Monarchs; ☎ 957 42 01 51; Campo Santo de Los Mártires s/n; adults/concession €4/2, free Fri; 10am-2pm & 4.30-6.30pm Tue-Sat mid-Oct–Apr, 10am-2pm & 5.30-7.30pm Tue-Sat May-Jun & Sep–mid-Oct, 8.30am-2.30pm Tue-Sat Jul-Aug, 9.30am-2.30pm Sun & holidays year-round), with its large and lovely gardens.

Indulge your senses at the renovated **Hammam Baños Árabes** (Arab Baths; ☎ 957 48 47 46; www.hammamspain.com/cordoba; Calle Corregidor Luis de la Cerda 51; bath/bath & massage €12/16; 2hr sessions at 10am, noon, 2pm, 4pm, 6pm, 8pm & 10pm) where you can enjoy an aromatherapy massage, with tea, hookah and Arabic sweets.

It's well worth the 8km trip west of Córdoba to the intriguing **Medina Azahara** (Madinat al-Zahra; ☎ 957 32 91 30; Carretera Palma del Río, Km 5.5; adult/EU citizen €1.50/free; 10am-6.30pm Tue-Sat, to 8.30pm May–mid-Sep, to 2pm Sun), a mighty Muslim city-palace from the 10th century. A taxi costs €37 for the return trip, with one hour to view the site, or you can book a three-hour coach tour for €6.50 to €10 through many Córdoba hotels. Guided visits can also be arranged for around €15.

Sleeping

Hostal El Reposo de Bagdad (☎ 957 20 28 54; Calle Fernández Ruano 11; s/d €30/45) Hidden in a tiny street in the Judería, this 200-year-old house feels thrillingly Moorish. The rooms are simple but clean.

Hotel González (☎ 957 47 98 19; hotelgonzalez@wanadoo.es; Calle Manríquez 3; s €35-37, d €49-66;) Rich baroque decor lends a graciousness to this well-priced hotel. The restaurant is set in the pretty flower-filled patio.

Hotel Maestre (☎ 957 47 24 10; Calle Romero Barros 4; s/d €38/52, apt €58;) This place has comfortably furnished rooms with all the mod cons, although bathrooms are grudging of both space and supplies.

Hotel Lola (☎ 957 20 03 05; www.hotelconencantolola.com; Calle Romero 3; d incl breakfast €114;) A quirky hotel with large antique beds and full of smaller items that you just wish you could take home. You can eat your breakfast on the roof terrace overlooking the Mezquita bell tower.

Eating & Drinking

Córdoba's liveliest bars are mostly scattered around the newer parts of town and come alive at about 11pm or midnight on weekends. Most bars in the medieval centre close around midnight.

Taberna San Miguel (☎ 957 47 01 66; Plaza San Miguel 1; tapas €2-5, media raciones €5.50-10; closed Sun & Aug) Known locally as *El Pisto* (Barrel), this busy place has been serving rustic food and cheap jugs of Moriles wine since 1880.

Taberna Salinas (☎ 957 48 01 35; Calle Tundidores 3; tapas 2.50, raciones €8; closed Sun & Aug) Dating back to 1879, this large patio restaurant fills up fast. Try the delicious aubergines with honey or potatoes with garlic.

Casa Pepe de la Judería (☎ 957 20 07 44; Calle Romero 1; tapas €2.50, media raciones €9.50, mains €11-18, menu €27.82) A great roof-terrace with views of the Mezquita and a labyrinth of busy dining rooms. Down a complimentary glass of Montilla before launching into the house specials, including venison fillets.

Bodega Campos (☎ 957 49 75 00; Calle de Lineros 32; tapas €6.50, raciones €16, mains €17.50-29; closed Sun evenings) This atmospheric vineyard-cum-restaurant offers the peak dining experience in Córdoba. Corridors and rooms are lined with oak barrels. The establishment offers its own house Montilla.

Soul (☎ 957 49 15 80; Calle de Alfonso XIII 3; 9am-3am Mon-Fri, 10am-4am Sat & Sun, closed Aug) Sparsely furnished, student-filled DJ bar that gets hot and busy on weekends.

Getting There & Away

The **bus station** (☎ 957 40 40 40; Glorieta de las Tres Culturas) is located 1km northwest of Plaza de las Tendillas, behind the train station. Destinations include Seville (€10, 1¾ hours, six daily), Granada (€12 to €16.60, 2½ hours, seven daily), Madrid (€14.40, 4½ hours, six daily) and Málaga (€12.20, 2¾ hours, five daily).

The **train station** (Avenida de América) is on the high-speed AVE line between Madrid and Seville. Destinations include Seville (€27.80, 90 minutes, 23 or more daily), Madrid (€49 to €62, 1¾ to 6¼ hours, 23 or more daily), Málaga (€19 to €23, 2½ hours, nine daily) and Barcelona (€56 to €125, 10½ hours, four daily).

GRANADA

pop 300,000 / elev 685m

Granada's eight centuries as a Muslim capital are symbolised in its keynote emblem, the remarkable Alhambra, one of the most graceful architectural achievements in the Muslim world. Islam was never completely expunged here and today it seems more present than ever in the shops, restaurants, tearooms and mosque of a growing North African community in and around the maze of the Albayzín. The city's lively nightlife scene is undiminished. The tapas bars fill to bursting with hungry and thirsty revellers, flamenco dives resound to the heart-wrenching tones of the south and contemporary clubs keep hedonists dancing until dawn.

ALHAMBRA TICKETS

Theoretically you can buy tickets on the day from the ticket window but it's advisable to book in advance (€1 extra per ticket). You can book in two ways: **Alhambra Advance Booking** (☎ 902 88 80 01, from overseas 34 93 492 37 50; 🕑 8am-9pm); and **Servicaixa** (www.servicaixa.com), online booking in Spanish and English. You can also buy tickets in advance from **Servicaixa cash machines** (🕑 8am-7pm Mar-Oct, 8am-5pm Nov-Feb), but only in the Alhambra grounds.

Alhambra tickets are only valid for half a day, so specify whether you wish to visit in the morning or afternoon.

Information

Cyberlocutorio Alhambra (Calle Joaquin Costa 40; per hr €1.50; 🕑 10.30am-midnight)

Provincial tourist office (☎ 958 24 71 28; www.turismodegranada.org; Plaza de Mariana Pineda 10; 🕑 9am-8pm Mon-Fri, 10am-7pm Sat, 10am-3pm Sun Mar-Oct, 9am-7pm Mon-Fri, 10am-7pm Sat, 10am-3pm Sun Nov-Feb) Information on Granada province.

Regional tourist office Plaza Nueva (☎ 958 22 10 22; Calle Santa Ana 1; 🕑 9am-7.30pm Mon-Sat, 9.30am-3pm Sun & holidays); Alhambra (☎ 958 22 95 75; ticket-office bldg, Avenida del Generalife s/n; 🕑 8am-7.30pm Mon-Fri, 8am-2pm & 4-7.30pm Sat & Sun Mar-Oct, 8am-7.30pm Mon-Fri, 8am-2pm & 4-6pm Sat & Sun Nov-Feb, 9am-1pm holidays) Information on all of Andalucía.

Sights & Activities

ALHAMBRA

The mighty **Alhambra** (☎ 902 44 12 21; www.alhambra.org; adult/under 12yr/student & EU senior €12/free/9, Generalife only €6; 🕑 8.30am-8pm Mar-Oct, to 6pm Nov-Feb, closed 25 Dec & 1 Jan) is breathtaking. Much has been written about its fortress, palace, patios and gardens, but nothing can really prepare you for seeing the real thing.

The **Alcazaba**, the Alhambra's fortress, dates from the 11th to the 13th centuries. There are spectacular views from the tops of its towers. The **Palacio Nazaríes** (Nasrid Palace), built for Granada's Muslim rulers in their 13th- to 15th-century heyday, is the centrepiece of the Alhambra. The beauty of its patios and intricacy of its stuccoes and woodwork, epitomised by the *Patio de los Leones* (Patio of the Lions) and *Sala de las Dos Hermanas* (Hall of the Two Sisters), are stunning. The **Generalife** (Palace Gardens) is a great spot to relax and contemplate the complex from a little distance.

The Palacio Nazaríes is also open for **night visits** (🕑 10pm-11.30pm Tue-Sat Mar-Oct, 8pm-9.30pm Fri & Sat Nov-Feb). Tickets cost the same as daytime tickets: the ticket office opens 30 minutes before the palace's opening time, closing 30 minutes after it. Book for night visits the same way as for day visits (see the boxed text, left).

OTHER ATTRACTIONS

Exploring the narrow, hilly streets of the **Albayzín**, the old Moorish quarter across the river from the Alhambra, is highly enjoyable. When doing this, make sure you keep your wits about you, as muggings sometimes occur around here. After heading uphill to reach the **Mirador de San Nicolás** – a viewpoint with breathtaking vistas and a relaxed scene – you

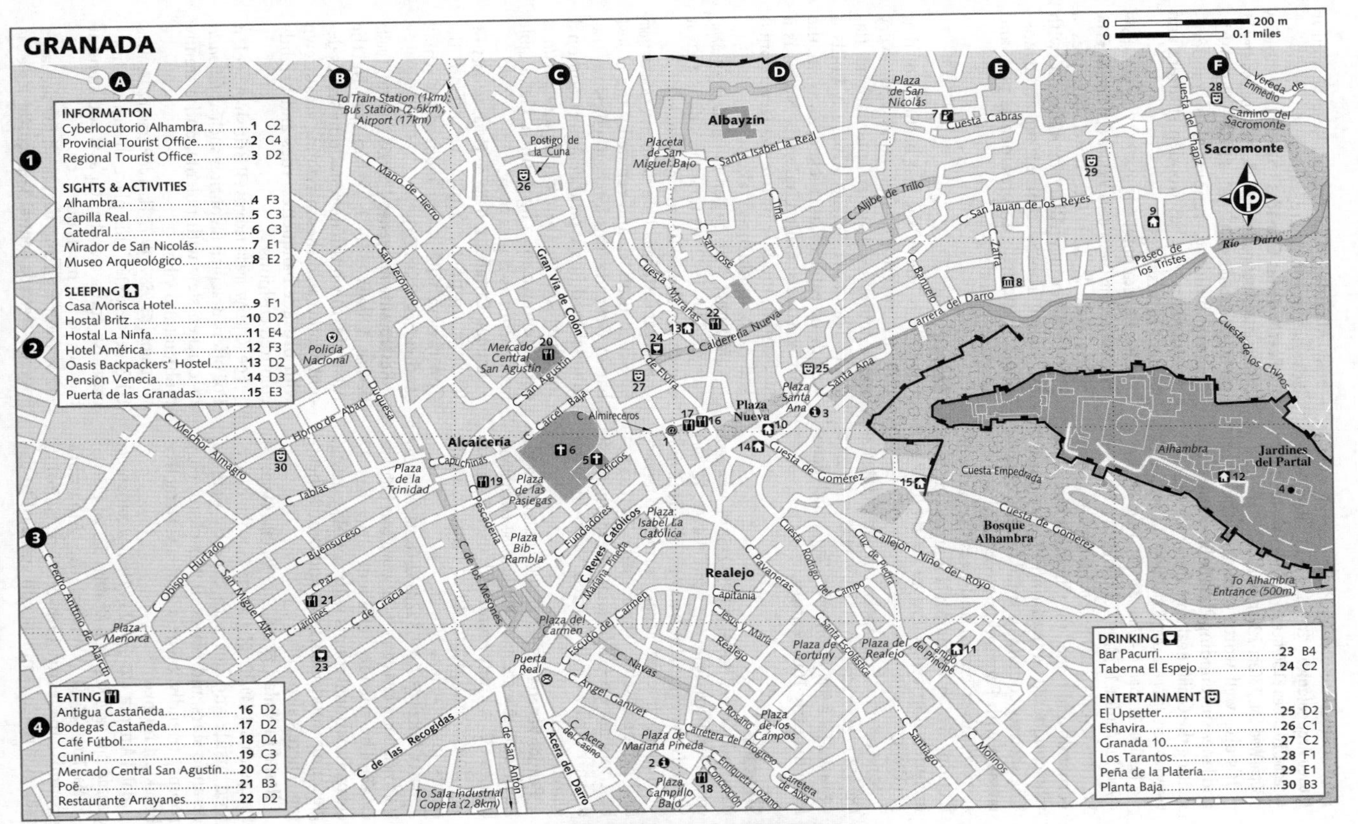
GRANADA
INFORMATION
Cyberlocutorio Alhambra.....1 C2
Provincial Tourist Office.....2 C4
Regional Tourist Office.....3 D2
SIGHTS & ACTIVITIES
Alhambra.....4 F3
Capilla Real.....5 C3
Catedral.....6 C3
Mirador de San Nicolás.....7 E1
Museo Arqueológico.....8 E2
SLEEPING
Casa Morisca Hotel.....9 F1
Hostal Britz.....10 D2
Hostal La Ninfa.....11 E4
Hotel América.....12 F3
Oasis Backpackers' Hostel.....13 D2
Pension Venecia.....14 D3
Puerta de las Granadas.....15 E3
EATING
Antigua Castañeda.....16 D2
Bodegas Castañeda.....17 D2
Café Fútbol.....18 D4
Cunini.....19 C3
Mercado Central San Agustín.....20 C2
Poë.....21 B3
Restaurante Arrayanes.....22 D2
DRINKING
Bar Pacurri.....23 B4
Taberna El Espejo.....24 C2
ENTERTAINMENT
El Upsetter.....25 D2
Eshavira.....26 C1
Granada 10.....27 C2
Los Tarantos.....28 F1
Peña de la Platería.....29 E1
Planta Baja.....30 B3
Albayzín
Sacromonte
Alhambra
Jardines del Partal
Bosque Alhambra
Realejo
Alcaicería
Plaza Nueva
Gran Vía de Colón
C Reyes Católicos
C Acera del Darro
Río Darro
Carrera del Darro
Cuesta de Gomérez
To Alhambra Entrance (500m)
To Train Station (1km); Bus Station (2.5km); Airport (17km)
To Sala Industrial Copera (2.8km)
200 m
0.1 miles

SPAIN

may wish to return to Plaza Nueva via the **Museo Arqueológico** (☎ 958 22 56 03; Carrera del Darro 43; adult/EU citizen €1.50/free; ⌚ 2.30-8.30pm Tue, 9.30am-8.30pm Wed-Sat, 9.30am-2.30pm Sun).

It's also well worth exploring the streets and lanes surrounding **Plaza de Bib-Rambla**, and visiting the **Capilla Real** (Royal Chapel; ☎ 958 22 92 39; www.capillarealgranada.com; Calle Oficios; admission €3.50; ⌚ 10.30am-12.45pm & 4-7pm Mon-Sat, 11am-12.45pm & 4-7pm Sun Apr-Oct, 10.30am-12.45pm & 3.30-6.15pm Mon-Sat, 11am-12.45pm & 3.30-6.15pm Sun Nov-Mar), where Fernando and Isabel, the Christian monarchs who conquered Granada in 1492, are buried. The sacristy contains a small but impressive **museum** with Fernando's sword and Isabel's sceptre, silver crown and personal art collection, which is mainly Flemish but also includes Botticelli's *Prayer in the Garden of Olives*.

Next door to the chapel is Granada's **Catedral** (☎ 958 22 29 59; admission €3.50; ⌚ 10.45am-1.30pm & 4-8pm Mon-Sat, 4-8pm Sun, to 7pm Nov-Mar), which dates from the early 16th century.

SPAIN

Sleeping

Oasis Backpackers' Hostel (☎ 958 21 58 48; www.oasisgranada.com; Placeta Correo Viejo 3; dm €18, d €40; ❄ 💻) Seconds away from the bars on Calle de Elvira. There's free internet access, a rooftop terrace and personal safes. The location is tricky – best to walk up Caldereria Nueva, then left down narrow Calle Correo Viejo into the *placeta* itself.

Pension Venecia (☎ 958 22 39 87; Cuesta de Gomérez 2; s/d/tr/q with shared bathroom €19/30/53/60, r with private bathroom €32) A lovely *hostal* with friendly hosts and flower-and-picture-filled turquoise corridors, just off Plaza Nueva.

Hostal Britz (☎ /fax 958 22 36 52; Cuesta de Gomérez 1; s/d with shared bathroom €26/36, with private bathroom €36/48) The friendly, efficient Britz has 22 clean, functional rooms with double glazing, gleaming wooden surfaces and central heating. There's also a lift.

Hostal La Ninfa (☎ 958 22 79 85; Calle Campo del Príncipe s/n; s/d €46/70; ❄) A rustic place covered inside and out with brightly painted ceramic stars and plates. It has clean, cosy rooms, friendly owners and an attractive breakfast room.

Hotel América (☎ 958 22 74 71; www.hotelamericagranada.com; Calle Real de la Alhambra 53; s/d €70/115; ⌚ Mar-Nov; ❄ 💻) Within the Alhambra grounds, the early 19th-century building creates a restful ambience in contrast to the busy Alhambra foot traffic. Reserve well in advance, as rooms are limited.

Puerta de las Granadas (☎ 958 21 62 30; www.hotelpuertadelasgranadas.com; Calle Cuesta de Gomérez 14; s/d €77/99, superior r €107-180; ❄ 💻) This 19th-century building, renovated in modern-minimalist style, has wooden shutters and elegant furnishings.

Casa Morisca Hotel (☎ 958 22 11 00; www.hotelcasamorisca.com; Cuesta de la Victoria 9; d interior €118, exterior €148; ❄ 💻) The hotel occupies a late-15th-century Albayzín mansion, with 14 stylish rooms centred on an atmospheric patio with an ornamental pool and wooden galleries.

Eating

Granada is one of the last bastions of that fantastic practice of free tapas with every drink, and some have an international flavour. The labyrinthine Albayzín holds a wealth of eateries all tucked away in the narrow streets. Calle Caldereria Nueva is a fascinating muddle of *teterías* (tea rooms) and Arabic-influenced takeaways.

Café Fútbol (Plaza de Mariana Pineda 6; ⌚ 6am-midnight) This 1922 art nouveau cafe is a great choice for chocolate and *churros*.

Bodegas Castañeda (Calle Almireceros; raciones from €6) An institution, and reputedly the oldest bar in Granada, this kitchen whips up traditional food in a typical *bodega* (traditional wine bar) setting. Their free tapa of *paella* is almost enough for a light lunch. Get a table before 2pm as it gets busy.

Antigua Castañeda (Calle de Elvira; raciones €8-16) Soak up potent 'Costa' wine from the Contraviesa with a few *montaditos* (small sandwiches; €5 to €6).

Restaurante Arrayanes (☎ 958 22 84 01; Cuesta Marañas 4; mains €8.50-19; ⌚ from 8pm) In the Albayzín, this intimate restaurant serves decent Moroccan dishes in a dining area strewn with brocade banquettes, rugs and brightly coloured cushions.

Poë (Calle Paz; media raciones €3) British-Angolan Poë offers Brazilian favourites such as *feijoada* or chicken stew with polenta, and a trendy multicultural vibe.

Cunini (☎ 958 25 07 77; Plaza de Pescadería 14; mains €11-23, set menu €19) This place dishes up first-class fish and seafood as tapas if you stand at the bar, or full meals out back.

For fresh fruit and veg, head for the large covered **Mercado Central San Agustín** (Calle San

Agustín; 8am-2pm Mon-Sat), a block west of the cathedral.

Drinking

The best street for drinking is rather scruffy Calle Elvira (try above-average Taberna El Espejo at number 40) but other chilled bars line Río Darro at the base of the Albayzín, and Campo del Príncipe attracts a sophisticated bunch.

Bodegas Castañeda (opposite) and Antigua Castañeda (opposite) are the most inviting and atmospheric bars, with their out-of-the-barrel wine and generous tapas to keep proceedings going.

Bar Pacurri (☎ 958 25 27 75; Calle de Gracia 21; tapas €2.50-5; 1pm-1am) At this small, arty bar munch on above-average tapas with well-chosen wines.

Entertainment

The excellent monthly *Guía de Granada* (€1), available from kiosks, lists entertainment venues.

NIGHTCLUBS

Sala Industrial Copera (☎ 958 25 84 49; www.industrialcopera.net; warehouse 7, Carretera Armilla, Calle la Paz; admission varies; midnight-late Fri & Sat) This warehouse club is where Granada's serious clubbers go for all-nighters, with a constantly changing schedule of live acts. You can count on lots of techno and hip-hop, and DJs from Ibiza, Madrid and Barcelona. Get a cab.

FLAMENCO FUSION

Once exclusively the music of the Gitanos (Roma people), flamenco has also morphed since the 1970s into a modern fusion of different rhythms and styles. Bands have experimented with blues, rock, Latin, jazz and even punk to create cool new sounds as well as a new fan base of young Spaniards.

Bands that first broke ground in this new wave include the bluesy-style Pata Negra, Ketama (African, Cuban and Brazilian rhythms) and Radio Tarifa (North African and medieval mix). In recent years, Chambao has hit the mark with its flamenco chill and Ojos de Brujo mix it up with reggae, Asian and even club dance rhythms. Mala Rodríguez put flamenco zip into hip-hop.

Granada 10 (Calle Cárcel Baja; admission €6; from midnight, closed mid-Jul–Aug) A glittery converted cinema is now Granada's top club for the glam crowd, who recline on the gold sofas and go crazy to cheesy Spanish pop tunes.

Planta Baja (☎ 630 95 08 24; www.plantabaja.net; Calle Horno de Abad 11; admission €5; 12.30am-6am Tue-Sat) Planta Baja's popularity never seems to wane, and it's no wonder since it caters to a diverse crowd *and* has top DJs.

FLAMENCO

El Eshavira (☎ 958 29 08 29; Postigo de la Cuna 2; from 10pm) Duck down a spooky alley to this shadowy haunt of flamenco and jazz. It is jam-packed on Thursdays and Sundays, the performance nights.

El Upsetter (☎ 958 22 72 96; Carrera del Darro 7; admission for flamenco show €12; 11pm-late) The Upsetter has a decent nightly flamenco show from 10pm to midnight only, and doubles as a dreadlock-swinging reggae bar for the rest of the week.

Peña de la Platería (☎ 958 21 06 50; Placeta de Toqueros 7) Buried deep in the Albayzín warren, this is a genuine aficionados' club with a large outdoor patio. Catch a 9.30pm performance on Thursday or Saturday.

The Sacromonte caves harbour touristy flamenco haunts for which you can pre-book through hotels and travel agencies, some of whom offer free transport. Try the Friday or Saturday midnight shows at **Los Tarantos** (☎ day 958 22 45 25, night 958 22 24 92; Camino del Sacromonte 9; admission €24) for a lively experience.

Getting There & Away

Autocares J Gonzalez (☎ 95 849 01 64; www.autocaresjosegonzalez.com) runs a bus service between Granada's airport (GRX) and the city centre, 17km distant. A taxi costs €18 to €22.

The **bus station** (Carretera de Jaén) is 3km northwest of the centre. Bus 33 (€1.10) travels between the two. There are buses to Córdoba (€12 to €16.60, 2¾ hours direct, nine daily), Seville (€18.60, three hours direct, eight daily), Málaga (€9, 1½ hours direct, 16 daily) and Madrid (€15.66, five to six hours, 10 to 13 daily).

The **train station** (Avenida de Andaluces) is 1.5km northwest of the centre. Four trains run daily to/from Seville (€21.65, three hours), three to/from Ronda (€12.25, three hours) and Algeciras (€18.35, 4½ hours). One or two trains go to Madrid (€62.20, four to five hours) and Valencia (€46 to €73, 7½ to eight hours).

To reach the city centre from the train station, walk to Avenida de la Constitución and pick up bus 4, 6, 7, 9 or 11 going to the right (east). From the centre (Gran Vía de Colón) to the train station, take bus 3, 4, 6, 9 or 11.

COSTA DE ALMERÍA

The coast east of Almería in eastern Andalucía is perhaps the last section of Spain's Mediterranean coast where you can have a beach to yourself. This is Spain's sunniest region – even in late March it can be warm enough to strip off and take in the rays. For information, visit the **regional tourist office** (☎ 950 27 43 55; Parque de Nicolás Salmerón s/n; 9am-7pm Mon-Fri, 10am-2pm Sat & Sun) in Almería City.

Sights & Activities

The **Alcazaba** (☎ 950 17 55 00; Calle Almanzor s/n; adult/EU citizen €1.50/free; 9am-8.30pm Apr-Oct & 9am-6.30pm Nov-Mar), an enormous 10th-century Muslim fortress, is the highlight of Almería City.

The best thing about the region is the wonderful coastline and semidesert scenery of the **Cabo de Gata** promontory. All along the 50km coast from El Cabo de Gata village to Agua Amarga, some of the most beautiful and empty beaches on the Mediterranean alternate with precipitous cliffs and scattered villages. Roads or paths run along or close to this whole coastline, which is a protected area. The main village is laid-back **San José**, with excellent beaches nearby, such as **Playa de los Genoveses** and **Playa de Mónsul**.

SPAIN

Sleeping & Eating

ALMERÍA CITY

Hostal Sevilla (☎ 950 23 00 09; Calle de Granada 23; s/d €38/54;) This best budget bet is a cheerful and efficient place that offers clean rooms and a good central location. Bathrooms are miniscule but modern.

Hotel Torreluz (☎ 950 23 43 99; www.torreluz.com; Plaza de las Flores 2 & 3; s/d 2-star €39/64, 3-star €56/74;) Burnt plum walls, comfortable beds and good prices make this one of Almería's best value places to stay.

Comidas Sol de Almería (Calle Circunvalación, Mercado Central; menú del día €10.50; 12.30pm-4pm, closed Sun) A jolly restaurant, opposite the busy covered market, with a large sunlit yet sheltered patio behind it. Hungry shoppers stream in for the extensive and hearty lunch *menú*.

CABO DE GATA

Hostal Sol Bahía (☎ 950 38 03 07; fax 950 38 03 06; Avenida de San José, San José; d €40-70;) The Sol Bahía and its sister establishment, Hostal Bahía Plaza, across the street, are in the centre of San José and have functional, clean rooms in bright, modern buildings.

MOJÁCAR

Hostal Arco Plaza (☎ 950 47 27 77; fax 950 47 27 17; Calle Aire Bajo 1, Plaza Nueva; s/d €36/52;) Bang in the centre of the village, the Arco Plaza has rooms in pretty pastel shades with spacious bathrooms and crisp, white linen. Management and staff seem incredibly friendly and efficient.

Pensión El Torreón (☎ 950 47 52 59; Calle Jazmín 4; d with shared bathroom €60;) This beautiful *hostal*, with its five quaint rooms and stained-glass windows, is timeless. It was allegedly the birthplace of Walt Disney, who locals maintain was the love child of a village girl and a wealthy landowner.

La Taberna (☎ 647 72 43 67; Plaza del Cano 1; tapas & platos combinados from €4) This thriving little eatery, inside a warren of cavelike rooms, serves extremely well-prepared meals with plenty of tasty vegetarian options.

Restaurante El Viento del Desierto (Plaza Frontón; mains from €7.50; closed Sunday & January) Good value, long-established Moroccan-cum-Spanish eatery just by the church.

Getting There & Away

From Almería's **bus station** (☎ 95 026 20 98; Plaza de Barcelona), Alsina Graells travels to Granada (€10.10 to €12.25, 2½ to four hours, five daily), Málaga (€14.55, 3¼ hours, nine daily) and Seville (€27.70 to €28.60, 7½ to nine hours, three daily).

From the **train station** (Plaza de la Estación) there are services to Madrid (€33.90 to €38, seven hours, one daily), Granada (€13.40, 2¼ hours, four daily) and Seville (€32.10, 5½ hours, four daily).

MÁLAGA

pop 720,000

The exuberant port city of Málaga may be uncomfortably close to the overdeveloped Costa del Sol, but it is a wonderful amalgam of old Andalucian town and modern metropole. The centre presents the visitor with narrow old streets and wide, leafy boulevards, beautiful gardens and impressive monuments, fashionable shops and a burgeoning cultural life. The historic centre is being restored and much of it is pedestrianised; the port is being developed as a leisure zone. The city's terrific bars and nightlife, the last word in Málaga joie de vivre, stay open very late.

Information

Meeting Point (Plaza de la Merced 20; per min €0.20, per hr €1-2; 10am-11pm Mon-Sat, 1.30-11pm Sun) A big, bright centre with 25 internet stations and video game stations in front of the store.

Municipal tourist office (www.malagaturismo.com in Spanish; 9am-7pm Mon-Fri, 10am-7pm Sat & Sun Apr-Oct, to 6pm Mon-Fri, 10am-6pm Sat & Sun Nov-Mar) Casita del Jardinero (952 13 47 31; Avenida de Cervantes 1); Plaza de la Marina (952 12 20 20)

Regional tourist office (951 30 89 11; www.andalucia.org; Pasaje de Chinitas 4; 9am-7.30pm Mon-Fri, 10am-7pm Sat, 10am-2pm Sun)

Sights & Activities

The fabulous **Museo Picasso Málaga** (902 44 33 77; www.museopicassomalaga.org; Palacio de Buenavista, Calle San Agustín 8; permanent collection €6, temporary exhibition €4.50, combined ticket €8, seniors & under-26 students half price; 10am-8pm Tue-Thu & Sun, to 9pm Fri & Sat) is set in the lovely 16th-century Palacio de Buenavista. The museum is stacked with more than 200 works covering the length of Picasso's astonishing career.

Málaga's **catedral** (952 21 59 17; www.3planalfa.es/catedralmalaga; Calle Molina Lario; admission €3.50; 10am-5.30pm Mon-Fri, to 5pm Sat, closed Sun & holidays) has a peculiar lopsided look (the south tower was never completed) and a magnificent 18th-century baroque facade. The entrance is on Calle Cister.

The **Alcazaba** (952 22 51 06; Calle Alcazabilla; admission €2, incl Castillo de Gibralfaro €3.20; 9.30am-8pm Tue-Sun Apr-Oct, 8.30am-7pm Tue-Sun Nov-Mar, closed Mon & major holidays) fortress and palace dates from the 8th century. Above the Alcazaba rises the older **Castillo de Gibralfaro** (952 22 72 30; admission €2, incl Alcazaba €3.20; 9am-9pm Apr-Sep, to 6pm Oct-Mar), built by Abd ar-Rahman I, the 8th-century Cordoban emir, and rebuilt in the 14th and 15th centuries. Nothing much remains of the interior of the castle, but the walkway around the ramparts affords exhilarating views and there's a tiny museum with a military focus. Below the Alcazaba is a **Roman theatre**.

Casa Natal de Picasso (952 06 02 15; Plaza de la Merced 15; admission free; 9.30am-7.45pm, closed major holidays), Picasso's birthplace, is a centre for exhibitions and academic research on contemporary art.

Sandy city beaches stretch several kilometres in each direction from the port. **Playa de la Malagueta**, handy to the city centre, has some excellent bars and restaurants close by. **Playa de Pedregalejo** and **Playa del Palo**, about 4km east of the centre, are popular and reachable by bus 11 from Paseo del Parque.

Sleeping

Hostal Derby (952 22 13 01; 4th fl, Calle San Juan de Dios 1; s/d €36/49;) A good-value *hostal* with spacious rooms and big windows, some overlooking the harbour.

Hostal Larios (952 22 54 90; www.hostallarios.com; Calle Marqués de Larios 9; s/d with shared bathroom €39/49, s/d/tr with private bathroom €48/58/78;) This central *hostal* outclasses all others in the budget range. The 12 rooms are painted apricot and blue.

El Riad Andaluz (952 21 36 40; www.elriadandaluz.com; Calle Hinestrosa 24; s/d 70/90;) Colourful and exotic, this gorgeous restored monastery offers eight rooms with Moroccan decor set around an atmospheric patio, with tea and coffee on tap all day. Situated in the rapidly gentrifying Centro Historico, it's an easy stroll to all the funkiest bars and restaurants in surrounding plazas. The French owner and his family infuse the Riad with a special magic.

Hotel Don Curro (952 22 72 00; www.hoteldoncurro.com; Calle Sancha de Lara 7; s/d €80/110;) Big, busy Don Curro is efficient, comfortable and central, with well-appointed, spacious rooms, and substantial breakfasts just a few steps away at their own Café Moka.

Eating

La Rebaná (Calle Molina Lario 5; tapas €3, raciones €7-11.50) A great, noisy tapas bar near the Picasso Museum. Dark wood, tall windows and exposed brick walls create a minimal, laid-back space. Try the foie gras with salted nougat for a unique tapa.

Gorki (952 22 14 66; Calle Strachan 6; platos combinados €7.50-16) This popular upmarket tapas bar has pavement tables and a modern interior full of wine-barrel tables and stools.

Comoloco (Calle Denis Belgrano 17; salads €8-10 & pittas €5-6; 1pm-1am) Huge windows look on to the little street – or you can look in at the ravenous crowd inside. The menu features a vegetarian's delight of salads and generously filled pitta wraps amid industrial decor.

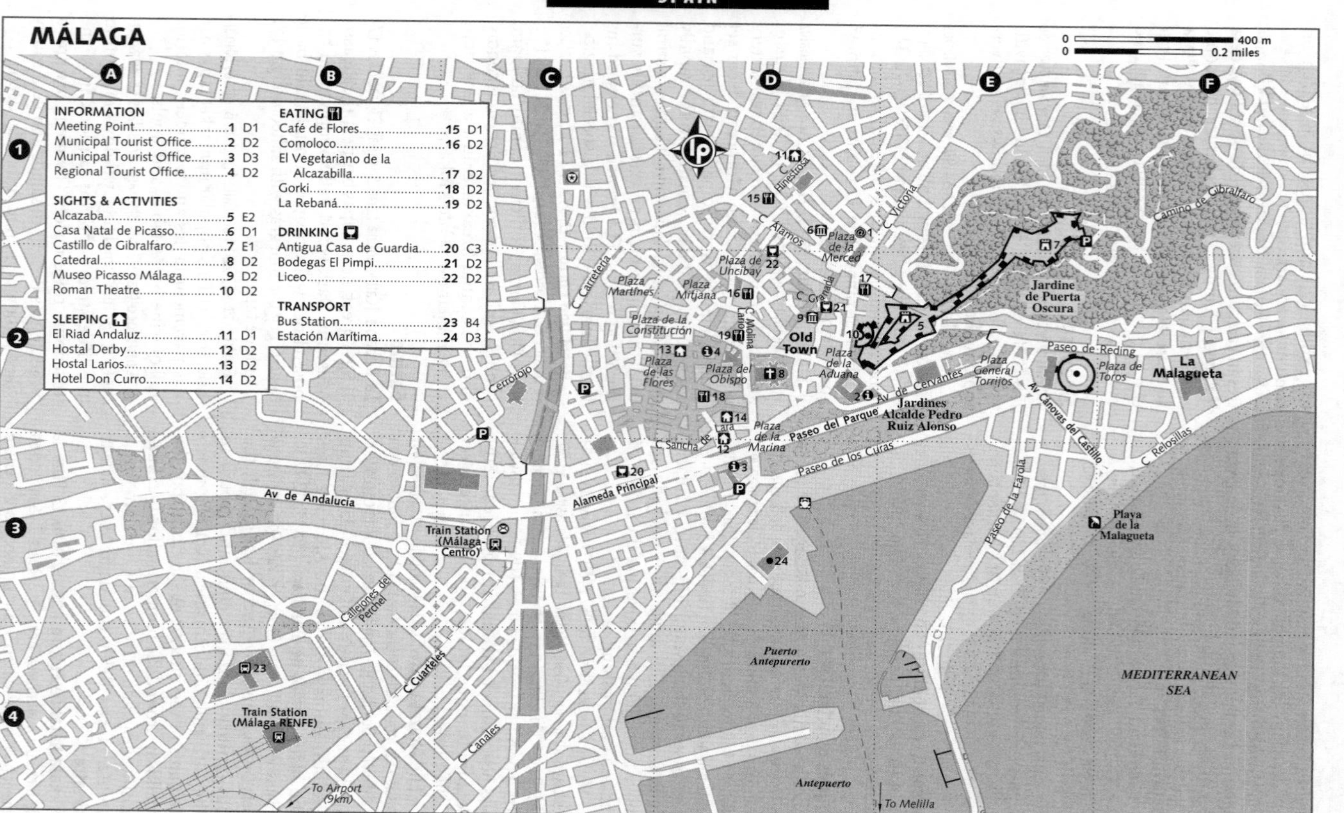
MÁLAGA
INFORMATION
Meeting Point 1 D1
Municipal Tourist Office 2 D2
Municipal Tourist Office 3 D3
Regional Tourist Office 4 D2
SIGHTS & ACTIVITIES
Alcazaba 5 E2
Casa Natal de Picasso 6 D1
Castillo de Gibralfaro 7 E1
Catedral 8 D2
Museo Picasso Málaga 9 D2
Roman Theatre 10 D2
SLEEPING
El Riad Andaluz 11 D1
Hostal Derby 12 D2
Hostal Larios 13 D2
Hotel Don Curro 14 D2
EATING
Café de Flores 15 D1
Comoloco 16 D2
El Vegetariano de la Alcazabilla 17 D2
Gorki 18 D2
La Rebaná 19 D2
DRINKING
Antigua Casa de Guardia 20 C3
Bodegas El Pimpi 21 D2
Liceo 22 D2
TRANSPORT
Bus Station 23 B4
Estación Marítima 24 D3
0 400 m
0 0.2 miles
MEDITERRANEAN SEA
La Malagueta
Playa de la Malagueta
Jardine de Puerta Oscura
Jardines Alcalde Pedro Ruiz Alonso
Old Town
Plaza de Toros
Plaza de la Merced
Plaza de Uncibay
Plaza Mitjana
Plaza Martínes
Plaza de la Constitución
Plaza de las Flores
Plaza del Obispo
Plaza de la Aduana
Plaza de la Marina
Plaza General Torrijos
Paseo de Reding
Av Cánovas del Castillo
Paseo de la Farola
C Relosillas
Camino de Gibralfaro
C Victoria
Av de Cervantes
Paseo del Parque
Paseo de los Curas
Alameda Principal
Av de Andalucía
C Carretería
C Molina Lario
C Granada
C Álamos
C Hinestrosa
C Sancha de Lara
Puerto Antepurerto
Antepuerto
To Melilla
Train Station (Málaga-Centro)
Train Station (Málaga RENFE)
To Airport (9km)
C Cuarteles
Callejones del Perchel
C Canales
C Cerrojo

El Vegetariano de la Alcazabilla (☎ 952 21 48 58; Calle Pozo del Rey 5; mains €9.50-12.50; ⏰ Mon-Sat) Friendly service in this relaxed veggie/vegan restaurant is combined with good food in a shabby-chic setting just a cannonball throw from the Alcazaba walls. Try the seitan 'meatballs'.

Café de Flores (☎ 952 60 85 24; Calle Madre de Dios 29; menu €9.50, mains €14-23; ⏰ 1.30pm-late Tue-Sun) With plexiglass furniture, abstract art and a DJ, this haunt of smart young *malagueños* is a coffee bar and lunch stop by day. At night, good food comes with muted clubbing sounds.

At lunch, locals tend to gravitate towards the excellent fish restaurants at Playas de Pedregalejo and del Palo, a few kilometres east of the centre, which specialise in *fritura malagueña* (fried fish, anchovies and squid).

Drinking & Entertainment

On weekend nights, the web of narrow old streets north of Plaza de la Constitución comes alive. Look for bars around Plaza de la Merced, Plaza Mitjana and Plaza de Uncibay.

Antigua Casa de Guardia (☎ 952 21 46 80; Alameda Principle 18) This venerable old tavern has been serving Málaga's sweet dessert wines since 1840. Try the dark brown, sherry-like *seco* complemented by a simple plate of prawns.

Bodegas El Pimpi (☎ 952 22 89 90; Calle Granada 62; ⏰ 7pm-2am) A Málaga institution with a warren of charming rooms and mini-patios, El Pimpi attracts a fun-loving crowd of all nationalities and generations with its sweet wine and traditional music.

Liceo (Calle Beatas 21; ⏰ 9pm-1am Thu-Sat) A grand old mansion turned young music bar, which buzzes with a student crowd after midnight. Go up the winding staircase and discover more rooms.

Getting There & Away

AIR

Málaga's busy Pablo Ruiz Picasso airport (AGP), the main international gateway to Andalucía, receives flights by dozens of airlines (budget and otherwise) from around Europe.

The Aeropuerto train station on the Málaga–Fuengirola line is a five-minute walk from the airport. Trains run about every half-hour, 6.49am to 11.49pm, to Málaga-Renfe station (€2, 11 minutes) and Málaga-Centro station. Trains depart for the airport between 5.45am and 10.30pm. There are also buses.

BOAT

Acciona-Trasmediterránea (Estación Marítima, Local E1) operates a fast ferry (four hours) and a slower ferry (7½ hours) daily year-round to/from Melilla (passenger/car ferry €33.50/156, fast ferry €55/174).

BUS

Málaga's **bus station** (☎ 952 35 00 61; Paseo de los Tilos) is located 1km southwest of the city centre. Frequent buses travel along the coasts, and others go to Seville (€16, 2½ hours, nine or more daily), Granada (€10, 1½ to two hours, 17 daily), Córdoba (€12.50, 2½ hours, five daily), and Ronda (€9.50, 2½ hours, nine or more daily). Nine buses also run daily to Madrid (€21.50, six hours) and a few go up Spain's Mediterranean coast.

TRAIN

The main station, **Málaga-Renfe** (Explanada de la Estación) is around the corner from the bus station. The superfast AVE service runs to Madrid (€71.20 to €79.20, 2½ hours, six daily).

Trains also head to Córdoba (€19, one hour, 10 daily), Seville (€17.30 to €33, two to 2½ hours, five daily) and Barcelona (€59 to €130, 6½ to 13 hours, two daily). For Granada (€13.50, 2½ hours) and Ronda (€8.90, 1½ hours minimum) you need to change at Bobadilla.

RONDA

pop 37,000 / elev 744m

Perched on an inland plateau riven by the 100m fissure of El Tajo gorge and surrounded by the beautiful Serranía de Ronda, Ronda is the most dramatically sited of Andalucía's *pueblos blancos* (white villages).

The **municipal tourist office** (☎ 952 18 71 19; www.turismoderonda.es; Paseo de Blas Infante; ⏰ 10am-7.30pm Mon-Fri May-Sep, to 6pm Oct-Apr, 10.15am-2pm & 3.30-6.30pm Sat, Sun & holidays) is helpful.

Sights & Activities

The **Plaza de Toros** (built 1785), considered the national home of bullfighting, is a mecca for aficionados; inside is the small but fascinating **Museo Taurino** (Bullfighting Museum; ☎ 952 87 41 32; Calle Virgen de la Paz; admission €6; ⏰ 10am-8pm Apr-Sep, to 6pm Oct-Mar).

The amazing 18th-century **Puente Nuevo** (New Bridge) is an incredible engineering feat crossing the gorge to the originally Muslim Old

Town (La Ciudad). At the **Casa del Rey Moro** (House of the Moorish King; ☎ 952 18 72 00; Calle Santo Domingo 17), you can climb down La Mina, a Muslim-era stairway cut inside the rock, right to the bottom of the gorge. Also well worth a visit are the beautiful 13th-century **Baños Arabes** (Arab Baths; ☎ 656 95 09 37; Calle San Miguel; admission €3; 10am-7pm Mon-Fri, to 3pm Sat & Sun) and **Santa Maía La Mayor** (☎ 952 87 22 46; adult/senior/student €3/2/1.50; 10am-8pm Apr-Oct, to 6pm Nov-Mar), a 13th-century mosque that was converted into a church by Ferdinand the Catholic. Nearby, the amusing **Museo del Bandolero** (☎ 952 87 77 85; Calle de Armiñán 65; admission €3; 10.30am-8pm Apr-Sep, to 6pm Oct-Mar) is dedicated to the banditry for which central Andalucía was renowned in the 19th century.

Sleeping & Eating

Hotel Morales (☎ 952 87 15 38; Calle de Sevilla 51; s/d €25/42;) A small hotel with 18 pleasant rooms and thorough information on the town and nearby parks.

Hotel Alavera de los Baños (☎ 952 87 91 43; www.andalucia.com/alavera; Hoyo San Miguel s/n; s/d incl breakfast €65/85;) A magical hotel with style echoes of the Arab baths next door, this one-time tannery is sumptuously decorated, with a flower-filled patio and pool. The sultan-sized baths are carved from a type of stucco, and their pink tinge is due to natural pigments.

Bar Restaurante Almocábar (☎ 952 87 59 77; Calle Ruedo Alameda 5; tapas €2, mains €12-20; 1.30-5pm & 8pm-1am Wed-Mon, closed August) In the Barrio San Francisco, a little off the tourist path, tiny Almocábar features inspired and exceptional cooking, with a surprising range of vegetarian salads. as well as meaty classics and fish.

Restaurante Pedro Romero (☎ 952 87 11 10; Calle Virgen de la Paz 18; mains €17.50-22; closed dinner Sun Jan, Feb, Jun & Jul) This celebrated eatery, dedicated to bullfighting, turns out classic Ronda dishes – a good place to try the famously man-food bull's tail dish, *rabo de toro*.

Getting There & Away

From the **bus station** (Plaza Concepción García Redondo 2), there are runs to Málaga (€9.10 to €10.20, 1½ to two hours, at least seven daily), Seville (€10.90, 2½ hours, three to six daily) and Cádiz (€13.80, 2½ hours).

The **train station** (Avenida de Andalucía) is on the scenic Granada–Algeciras line. Trains run to/from Algeciras (€6.70 to €17.50, 1¾ hours, six daily), Granada (€12.30, 2½ hours, three daily), Córdoba (€18 to €29.50, 2½ hours, two daily) and Málaga (€8.90, two hours, one daily except Sunday).

ALGECIRAS

pop 111,300

An unattractive industrial and fishing town between Tarifa and Gibraltar, Algeciras is the major port linking Spain with Morocco. Keep your wits about you, and ignore offers from the legions of moneychangers, drug-pushers and ticket-hawkers who hang out here. The **tourist office** (☎ 956 57 32 41; Calle Juan de la Cierva s/n; 9am-7.30pm Mon-Fri, 9.30am-3pm Sat & Sun) is near the port. Hopefully you won't need to seek help from the **Policía Nacional** (☎ 956 66 04 00; Avenida de las Fuerzas Armadas 6).

If you have to stay the night here, then do yourself a favour and stay at **Hostal Marrakech** (☎ 956 57 34 74; Calle Juan de la Cierva 5; s/d with shared bathroom €25/40). The Moroccan family who run this place have a handful of bold and tarty rooms with communal bathrooms only.

Getting There & Away

BOAT

Companies such as **Acciona-Trasmediterránea** (☎ 902 45 46 45; www.trasmediterranea.es) and **EuroFerrys** (☎ 956 65 23 24; www.euroferrys.com) operate frequent ferries to/from Tangier, Morocco (passenger/car and passenger €42/160, 1¼ to 2½ hours) and Ceuta, the Spanish enclave on the Moroccan coast (passenger/car and passenger €39.50/147, 35 minutes). **Buquebus** (☎ 956 65 24 73) operates a similar Ceuta service at least six times daily. From mid-June to September there are ferries almost round the clock to cater for the Moroccan holiday migration. Buy your ticket in the port or at the agencies on Avenida de la Marina.

BUS

The bus station is on Calle San Bernardo. Buses depart for La Línea (€1.86, 30 minutes) every 30 to 45 minutes. Up to 13 buses run to/from Tarifa (€1.86, 30 minutes) and Cádiz (€10.60, 2½ hours), six to/from Seville (€16.60, 2½ hours), and one Monday to Friday to Ronda (€9.40, two to three hours). **Daibus** (☎ 956 58 78 97) runs four daily buses to Madrid (€27.60, eight to nine hours).

TRAIN

From the **station** (☎ 956 63 10 05), adjacent to Calle San Bernardo, trains run to/from Madrid (€39 to €63.50, six or 11 hours, two daily) and Granada (€18.40, four hours, three daily). All go through Ronda (€6.70 to €17.40, 1¾ hours).

CÁDIZ

pop 128,600

Cádiz is crammed onto the head of a promontory like an overcrowded ocean liner. Columbus sailed from here on his second and fourth voyages, and after his success in the Americas, Cádiz grew into Spain's richest and most cosmopolitan city in the 18th century. The best time to visit is during the February *carnaval* (carnival), which rivals Rio in terms of outrageous exuberance.

The **municipal tourist office** (☎ 956 24 10 01; Paseo de Canalejas s/n; 8.30am-6pm Mon-Fri, 9am-5pm Sat & Sun) has helpful staff.

Sights & Activities

The yellow-domed 18th-century **Catedral** (☎ 956 28 61 54; Plaza de la Catedral; adult/student €5/3, free during services; 10am-6.30pm Mon-Fri, 10am-4.30pm Sat, 1-6.30pm Sun, services 7-8pm Tue-Fri, 11am-1pm Sun) is the city's most striking landmark.

Get your bearings by climbing up the baroque **Torre Tavira** (☎ 956 21 29 10; Calle Marqués del Real Tesoro 10; adult/student €4/3.30; 10am-6pm, to 8pm 15 Jun-15 Sep), the highest of Cádiz' old watchtowers, which features sweeping views of the city.

The **Museo de Cádiz** (☎ 956 20 33 68; Plaza de Mina; admission/EU citizen €1.50/free; 2.30-8.30pm Tue, 9am-8.30pm Wed-Sat, 9.30am-2.30pm Sun) has a magnificent collection of archaeological remains, as well as a fine-art collection. The city's lively **central market** (Plaza de las Flores) is on the site of a former Phoenician temple.

The broad, sandy **Playa de la Victoria**, a lovely Atlantic beach, stretches about 4km along the peninsula from its beginning 1.5km beyond the Puertas de Tierra. Bus 1 'Plaza España–Cortadura' from Plaza de España will get you there.

Sleeping & Eating

Casa Caracol (☎ 956 26 11 66; www.caracolcasa.com; Calle Suárez de Salazar 4; hammock/dm incl breakfast €10/16;) Casa Caracol is the only backpacker hostel in the Old Town. Friendly and crowded, it has bunk dorms for four and eight, a communal kitchen, free internet, and a roof terrace with hammocks. It's often full.

Hostal Fantoni (☎ 956 28 27 04; www.hostalfantoni.net; Calle Flamenco 5; s/d €45/70;) The Fantoni offers a dozen attractive and spotless rooms in an attractively modernised 18th-century house. The roof terrace catches a breeze in summer.

Mesón Cumbres Mayores (☎ 956 21 32 70; Calle Zorrilla 4; tapas €1.50-2, mains €9-18) The wood-beamed Cumbres Mayores has an excellent tapas bar in the front and a small restaurant in the back. It's hard to beat the ham and cheese *montaditos*.

La Gorda Te Da De Comer (tapas €2-2.40) Luque (Calle General Luque 1; Mon-Sat); Rosario (cnr Calle Rosario & Calle Marqués de Valdeiñigo; Tue-Sat) Incredibly tasty food at low prices amid trendy pop design. Try the *solomillo* in creamy mushroom sauce or the curried chicken strips with Marie-Rose dip.

El Aljibe (☎ 956 26 66 56; www.pablogrosso.com; Calle Plocia 25; tapas €2-3.50, mains €10-15) *Gaditano* chef Pablo Grosso concocts delicious combinations of the traditional and the adventurous. He stuffs his pheasant breast with dates and his *solomillo ibérico* (Iberian pork sirloin) with Emmental cheese, ham and piquant peppers.

Getting There & Away

From the Cádiz **bus station** (☎ 95 680 70 59; Plaza de la Hispanidad), buses head for Seville (€10.70, 1¾ hours, 10 daily), Tarifa (€7.90, two hours, five daily), Ronda (€12.60, three hours, two daily), Málaga (€19.60, four hours, six daily) and Granada (€28, five hours, four daily).

Secorbus (☎ 956 25 74 15; Avenida José León de Carranza 20) runs three buses daily to Madrid (€22.30, eight hours). The stop is 3.6km southeast of the Puertas de Tierra – to reach it take city bus 1 (€0.93) from Plaza de España to its last stop.

From the **train station** (Plaza Sevilla), up to 15 services run to Seville (€9.80, two hours), three to Córdoba (€34 to €43, three hours) and two to Madrid (€63, five hours).

TARIFA

pop 17,700

Windy, laid-back Tarifa is so close to Africa that you can almost hear the call to prayer issuing from Morocco's minarets. The town is a bohemian haven of cafes and crumbling Moorish ruins. There's also a lively windsurfing and kitesurfing scene.

Stretching west are the long, sandy (and largely deserted) beaches of the Costa de la Luz (Coast of Light), backed by cool pine forests and green hills.

The town's **tourist office** (☎ 956 68 09 93; www.aytotarifa.com in Spanish; Paseo de la Alameda; ⏲ 10am-2pm daily, 4-6pm Mon-Fri Oct-May, 6-8pm Mon-Fri Jun-Sep) has lots of information on the area. For internet, try **Pandora** (Calle Sancho IV El Bravo 13a; per hr €2; ⏲ 10am-2.30pm & 5-9.30pm).

Sights & Activities

When here, explore Tarifa's winding old streets and visit the **Castillo de Guzmán** (Calle Guzmán El Bueno), which dates from the 10th century. Closed for refurbishment at the time of writing, it may reopen in 2010.

On the isthmus leading out to Isla de las Palomas, **Playa Chica** is sheltered but a very small beach indeed. From here the spectacular **Playa de los Lances** stretches northwest to the huge sand dune at **Ensenada de Valdevaqueros**.

Most of the **kite** and **windsurfing** action occurs between Tarifa and Punta Paloma, 11km northwest. The best spots depend on the day's winds and tides: El Porro on Ensenada de Valdevaqueros is one of the most popular. The sports are practised year-round, but the biggest season is from about April to October.

Tarifa has around 30 kitesurf and windsurf schools, many of them with offices or shops along Calle Batalla del Salado or on Calle Mar Adriático. Others are based along the coast. Many rent and sell equipment.

The Strait of Gibraltar is good for **whale-** and **dolphin-watching** from spring to autumn. Various companies organise excursions:

firmm (☎ 956 62 70 08; www.firmm.org; Calle Pedro Cortés 4; ⏲ Mar-Oct) Uses every trip to record data.

Turmares (☎ 956 68 07 41; www.turmares.com; Avenida Alcalde Juan Núñez 3; ⏲ Jan-Nov) Has the largest boats, holding 40 or 60 people (one with a glass bottom).

Whale Watch España (☎ 956 62 70 13; www.whalewatchtarifa.net; Avenida de la Constitución 6; ⏲ Apr-Oct)

Sleeping & Eating

Melting Pot (☎ 956 68 29 06; www.meltingpothostels.com; Calle Turriano Gracil 5; dm €22-25, d incl breakfast €54; 💻) The Melting Pot is a friendly, well-equipped hostel just off the Alameda. A good kitchen adjoins the cosy bar/lounge and all guests get their own keys.

Hostal Africa (☎ 956 68 02 20; hostal_africa@hotmail.com; Calle María Antonia Toledo 12; s/d with shared bathroom €35/50, with private bathrooom €50/65; ⏲ closed 24 Dec-31 Jan) Rooms are attractive and there's an expansive terrace with wonderful views. Short-term storage for boards, bicycles and baggage is available.

La Estrella de Tarifa (☎ 956 68 19 85; www.laestrelladetarifa.com in Spanish; Calle San Rosendo 2; r incl breakfast €75-110, ste incl breakfast €120-145) Full of intriguing nooks and crannies, this comfortable hotel in an old townhouse rambles up and down over four floors with Moroccan decor in soothing blue and white.

Chilimoso (☎ 956 68 50 92; Calle Peso 6; dishes €4-6) This tiny place serves tasty vegan and vegetarian food with oriental leanings. Try the falafel with hummus, tzatziki and salad.

Miramar (☎ 956 68 52 46; Arte Vida Hotel, N340 Km 79.3; mains €8-18) The Miramar's chefs whip up a range of pasta, meat and fish dishes – and the expansive beach and ocean views double your enjoyment.

Bodega La Casa Amarilla (☎ 956 68 19 93; Calle Sancho IV El Bravo 9; mains €14-18) With an attractive, flowery patio, this is a top place in town for local grilled meats and fish, good *revueltos* (scrambled egg dishes), and tapas.

Getting There & Away

Comes runs six or more daily buses to Cádiz (€7.90, 1¾ hours) and Algeciras (€1.90, 30 minutes), four to Seville (€15.30, three hours), two to Málaga (€12.50, two hours), and one to Zahara de los Atunes (€3.25, 40 minutes) on the Costa de la Luz.

FRS (☎ 956 68 18 30; www.frs.es; Estación Marítima) runs fast ferries between Tarifa and Tangier (passenger/car/motorcycle one-way €31/85/31, 35 minutes, eight daily).

GIBRALTAR

pop 28,000

The British colony of Gibraltar is like 1960s Britain on a sunny day, with bobbies, double-decker buses and the fried-egg-and-chip-style eateries. In British hands since 1713, it was the starting point for the Muslim conquest of Iberia a thousand years earlier. Spain has never fully accepted UK control of the island but, for the moment at least, talk of joint sovereignty seems to have gone cold. Inhabitants speak English and Spanish and signs are in English.

INFORMATION

To enter Gibraltar you must have a passport or EU national identity card. Gibraltar is outside the Schengen area, and visitors needing a Schengen-area visa who intend to enter from Spain should ensure that they have a double-entry visa if they wish to return to Spain. Nationals from certain countries require a visa to enter; contact the **Immigration Department** (☎ 46411; rgpimm@gibgibtelecom.net).

The currency is the Gibraltar pound. Change any unspent Gibraltar pounds before you leave. You can also use euros or pounds sterling.

To phone Gibraltar from Spain, the telephone code is ☎ 9567; from other countries dial the international access code, then ☎ 350 and the local number. To phone Spain from Gibraltar, just dial the nine-digit Spanish number.

There's internet access at **General Internet Business Centre** (☎ 44227; 36 Governor's St; per hr £3; 10am-10pm Tue-Sat, noon-9pm Sun & Mon).

There are a couple of **tourist offices** (www.gibraltar.gov.gi; main office ☎ 74950; Duke of Kent House, Cathedral Sq; 9am-5.30pm Mon-Fri; Casemates Sq ☎ 74982; 9am-5.30pm Mon-Fri, 10am-3pm Sat, 10am-1pm Sun).

SIGHTS & ACTIVITIES

The **Gibraltar Museum** (Bomb House Lane; adult/under 12yr £2/1; 10am-6pm Mon-Fri, to 2pm Sat), with its interesting historical collection and Muslim-era bathhouse, is worth a peek. Wander into the **Alameda Botanical Gardens** (Red Sands Rd; 8am-sunset) for some chill-out time.

The large **Upper Rock Nature Reserve** (adult/child incl attractions £8/4, vehicle £1.50, pedestrian excl attractions £1; 9.30am-7pm), covering most of the upper rock, has spectacular views. The rock's most famous inhabitants are its colony of Barbary macaques, the only wild primates in Europe. Some of these hang around the **Apes' Den** near the middle cable-car station; others can often be seen at the top station or Great Siege Tunnels. Other attractions include **St Michael's Cave**, a large natural grotto renowned for its stalagmites and stalactites, and the **Great Siege Tunnels**, a series of galleries hewn from the rock by the British during the Great Siege by the Spaniards (1779–83) to provide new gun emplacements.

Dolphin-watching is an option from April to September. Boats head out to the Bahía de Algeciras from Watergardens Quay or adjacent Marina Bay.

SLEEPING & EATING

Compared with Spain, expect to pay through the nose for accommodation and food.

Cannon Hotel (☎ 51711; www.cannon hotel.gi; 9 Cannon Lane; s/d with shared bathroom £26.50/38.50, d with private bathroom £47, all incl breakfast) This is a small, budget-priced hotel right in the main shopping area.

Caleta Hotel (☎ 76501; www.caletahotel.gi; Sir Herbert Miles Rd; d/ste without/with sea view £110/150;) The Caleta has a wonderful location overlooking Catalan Bay, on the east side of the Rock, five minutes from town. Its cascading terraces have panoramic sea views, and a host of luxurious gym and spa facilities.

Clipper (☎ 79791; 78b Irish Town; mains £3.50-9) Most of Gibraltar's pubs serve British pub meals. The Clipper offers real pub grub and a genuine pub atmosphere, all varnished wood with full-on footy and a cracking Sunday roast. Vegetarians should go for the Greek salad wrap. Full English breakfast is served from 9.30am to 11am.

House of Sacarello (☎ 70625; 57 Irish Town; daily specials £7-11.50; 9am-7.30pm Mon-Fri, 9am-3pm Sat) This chic place in a converted coffee warehouse serves light lunches, including pastas and salads. Linger over afternoon tea (£4) between 3pm and 7.30pm.

GETTING THERE & AWAY

EasyJet (www.easyjet.com), **Iberia** (www.iberia.com) and **Monarch** (www.flymonarch.com) fly daily to/from London Gatwick.

FRS (☎ in Tarifa 956 68 18 30; www.frs.es) operates one ferry a week between Gibraltar and Tangier (Morocco).

There are no regular buses to Gibraltar, but La Línea de la Concepción bus station is only a five-minute walk from the border.

Snaking vehicle queues at the 24-hour border and congested traffic in Gibraltar often make it easier to park in La Línea and walk across the border. To take a car into Gibraltar (free) you need an insurance certificate, registration document, nationality plate and driving licence.

EXTREMADURA

A sparsely populated stretch of vast skies and open plains, Extremadura is far enough from most beaten tourist trails to give you a genuine sense of exploration, something for which Extremeños themselves have always had a flair.

TRUJILLO

pop 9700

Trujillo is a delightful little town that can't be much bigger now than it was in 1529, when its most famous son, Francisco Pizarro, set off with his three brothers and a few buddies for an expedition that culminated in the bloody conquest of the Incan empire.

There's a **tourist office** (☎ 927 32 26 77; www.ayto-trujillo.com in Spanish; Plaza Mayor s/n; 10am-2pm & 4-7pm Oct-May, 10am-2pm & 5-8pm Jun-Sep) in the centre. For internet, try **Ciberalia** (☎ 927 65 90 87; Calle Tiendas 18; per hr €2; 11am-midnight).

Sights

A **statue of Pizarro** dominates the splendid Plaza Mayor. On the plaza's southern side, the **Palacio de la Conquista** (closed to visitors) sports the carved images of Francisco Pizarro and the Inca princess Inés Yupanqui. A couple of other mansions, **Palacio Juan Pizarro de Orellana** (admission free; 10am-1.30pm & 4.30-6.30pm) and the 16th-century **Palacio de los Duques de San Carlos**, (admission €1; 10am-1pm & 4.30-6.30pm), now a convent, can be visited.

Up the hill, the **Iglesia de Santa María la Mayor** (Plaza de Santa María) is an interesting hotchpotch of 13th- to 16th-century styles, with some fine paintings by Fernando Gallego of the Flemish school. At the top of the hill, Trujillo's Moorish **castillo** (☎ 927 32 26 77; Calle Convento de las Jerónimas 12; adult/child €1.30/free; 10am-2pm & 5-8.30pm Jun-Sep, 10am-2pm & 4-8pm Oct-May) is an impressive structure commanding great views.

The **Museo del Queso** (Cheese Museum; ☎ 927 32 30 31; www.quesovino.com; Calle Francisco Pizarro s/n; admission €2.30; 11am-3pm & 6-8pm) is set in a former convent. The admission price includes a tasting of *Torta del Casar*, the local favourite, and some wine too.

Sleeping & Eating

Hostal Orellana (☎ 927 32 07 53; Calle Ruiz de Mendoza 2; s/d €30/45;) The comfortable rooms in this 16th-century house have exposed stone, dark timber and warm decor with terracotta tiles and butter-coloured paintwork. Located a short walk from the centre above a same-name bar and restaurant.

Posada Dos Orillas (☎ 927 65 90 79; www.dosorillas.com; Calle de Cambrones 6; d Sun-Thu €70-90, Fri & Sat €81-107;) This tastefully-renovated 16th-century mansion in the walled town once served as a silk-weaving centre. The rooms replicate Spanish colonial taste. Relax on the sunny patio or dine in its courtyard restaurant.

Restaurante La Troya (☎ 927 32 13 64; Plaza Mayor 10; set meals €15) The *menú* here is absolutely enormous – perfect for patrons who've just spent eight hours labouring in the fields, overwhelming for anyone else. It's quantity over quality but this place is a boisterous and timeless classic.

Mesón Alberca (☎ 927 32 22 09; Calle de Cambrones 8; menú del día €17.50, meals €30-40; Thu-Sun) Dark-timber tables laid with gingham cloths, or a pretty ivy-clad terrace, create a choice of warm atmospheres for sampling classic *extremeño* cooking. The speciality is oven roasts.

Getting There & Away

The **bus station** (Avenida de Miajadas) is 500m south of Plaza Mayor. There are services to/from Madrid (€15.20 to €19, three to 4¼ hours, up to 10 daily), Cáceres (€3.55, 45 minutes, eight daily) and Mérida (€7.35, 1½ hours, three daily).

PLASENCIA

pop 40,100

This pleasant, bustling town is the natural hub of northern Extremadura. It retains long sections of its defensive walls and has an attractive old quarter of narrow streets and stately buildings. Pick up information at the **municipal tourist office** (☎ 927 42 38 43; www.aytoplasencia.es/turismo; Calle Santa Clara 2; 9am-9pm Mon-Fri, 10am-2pm & 4-8pm Sat & Sun).

Plasencia's **cathedral** (Plaza de la Catedral; 9am-1pm & 5-7pm Mon-Sat, 9am-1pm Sun May-Sep, 9am-2pm & 4-6pm Mon-Sat, 9am-1pm Sun Oct-Apr) is actually two in one, a Romanesque original and a Gothic extra.

Hotel Rincón Extremeño (☎ 927 41 11 50; www.hotelrincon.com in Spanish; Calle Vidrieras 6; s/d €35/45;) has simple rooms just off Plaza Mayor and a popular restaurant.

There are regular buses and trains to Cáceres and Madrid.

CÁCERES

pop 89,100

Cáceres' *ciudad monumental* (old town), built in the 15th and 16th centuries, is perfectly preserved. The town's action centres on Plaza Mayor, at the foot of the Old Town, and busy Avenida de España, a short distance south.

SPAIN

Information

Junta de Extremadura tourist office (☎ 927 01 08 34; www.ayto-caceres.es; Plaza Mayor 3; 9am-2pm & 4-6pm or 5-7pm Mon-Fri, 9.45am-2pm Sat & Sun)

Municipal tourist office (☎ 927 24 71 72; Calle Ancha 7; 10am-2pm & 4.30-7.30pm or 5.30-8.30pm Tue-Sun)

Yass (Calle del General Ezponda 12; per hr €1; 10am-10pm) Internet access.

Sights & Activities

Entering the *ciudad monumental* from Plaza Mayor, you'll see ahead of you the fine 15th-century **Concatedral de Santa María** (Plaza de Santa María; 10am-1pm & 5-8pm Mon-Sat, 9.30am-2pm & 5-8pm Sun).

Climb the 12th-century **Torre de Bujaco** (Plaza Mayor; adult/under 12yr €2/free; 10am-2pm & 5.30-8.30pm Mon-Sat, 10am-2pm Sun Apr-Sep, 10am-2pm & 4.30-7.30pm Mon-Sat, 10am-2pm Sun Oct-Mar) for great views.

Many of the old city's churches and imposing medieval mansions can be admired only from the outside, but you can visit the **Museo de Cáceres** (☎ 927 01 08 77; Plaza de las Veletas 1; admission/EU citizens €1.20/free; 9am-2.30pm & 4-7.15pm Tue-Sat, 10.15am-2.30pm Sun), which is housed in a 16th-century mansion built over a 12th-century Moorish *aljibe* (cistern).

Sleeping & Eating

Alameda Palacete (☎ 92 721 12 62; www.alamedapalacete.com; Calle General Margallo 45; s/d incl breakfast €44/60) A restored early-20th-century townhouse with original patterned floor tiles, this boutique option near Plaza Mayor has rooms bathed in light with high ceilings.

Hotel Iberia (☎ 927 24 76 34; www.iberiahotel.com in Spanish; Calle de los Pintores 2; s/d €46/65) Located in an 18th-century former palace, this 36-room hotel has plush, if quirky, public areas and more traditional rooms with parquet floors, cream walls and pale-grey tiled bathrooms.

El Corral de las Cigüeñas (Calle Cuesta de Aldana 6; 8am-1pm Mon-Fri, 7pm-3am Tue-Sat, 5-11pm Sun) The secluded courtyard with its lofty palm trees is perfect for one of the best-value breakfasts around: there are seven versions to choose from!

Mesón El Asador (☎ 927 22 38 37; Calle Moret 34; raciones €6-8, meals €18-25; closed Sun) Enter the dining room and you get the picture right away – one wall is covered with hung hams. You won't taste better roast pork (or lamb) in town.

Getting There & Away

From the **bus station** (☎ 927 23 25 50; Carretera de Sevilla), 1.5km southwest of Plaza Mayor, there are several runs to Trujillo (€3.55, 45 minutes) and Mérida (€4.80, 50 minutes).

Up to five trains per day run to/from Madrid (€17.80 to €24.50, four hours), Plasencia (€4.35, 1½ hours) and Mérida (€5.25, one hour).

MÉRIDA

pop 74,900

Once the biggest city in Roman Spain, Mérida is home to more ruins of that age than anywhere else in the country and is a wonderful spot to spend a few archaeologically inclined days.

Information is available at the **municipal tourist office** (☎ 924 33 07 22; Calle Santa Eulalia 64; 9.30am-2pm & 4-7pm or 5-8pm). For internet access, try **Friends on Line** (Calle Romero Leal 5; per hr €2; 11am-2pm & 4pm-midnight).

Sights

The awesome ruins of Mérida's **Teatro Romano & Anfiteatro** (Calle Alvarez S de Buruaga; adult/under 12yr €7/free; 9.30am-1.45pm & 5-7.15pm Jun-Sep, 9.30am-1.45pm & 4-6.15pm Oct-May) shouldn't be missed. The theatre was built in 15 BC and the gladiators' ring, or Anfiteatro, seven years later. Combined, they could hold 20,000 spectators.

Other monuments of interest are the **Casa del Anfiteatro**, the **Casa del Mitreo**, the **Alcazaba** (Calle Graciano; adult/child €4/free), the **Basílica de Santa Eulalia** (Avenida de Extremadura; adult/child €4/free), remains of the 1st-century **Circo Romano** (Avenida Juan Carlos; adult/child €4/free), the only surviving hippodrome of its kind in Spain (it could accommodate 30,000 spectators), and the **Museo Nacional de Arte Romano** (☎ 924 31 16 90; www.mnar.es; Calle de José Ramón Mélida; adult/under 18yr/senior & 18-25yr €2.40/free/1.20; 10am-2pm & 5-7pm Tue-Sat, 10am-2pm Sun Mar-Nov, 10am-2pm & 4-6pm Tue-Sat, 10am-2pm Sun Dec-Feb).

The opening hours for all sites except the museum are 9.30am to 1.45pm and 4pm to 6.15pm October to May, and 9.30am to 1.45pm and 5pm to 7.15pm June to September. A combined ticket for admission to all sites except the museum is €10/free per adult/child under 10 years.

Other reminders of imperial days are scattered about town, including the **Puente**

Romano. At 792m, it's one of the longest bridges the Romans ever built.

Sleeping & Eating

Hotel Cervantes (☎ 924 31 49 61; www.hotelcervantes.com; Calle Camilo José Cela 8; s €40-50, d €60-70; ❄) The best deal in this price bracket, Cervantes has attractive half-panelled rooms with marble floors, full baths and dark wood furniture. The bar-restaurant serves a bacon-and-egg breakfast.

Hotel Velada (☎ 924 31 51 10; www.veladahoteles.com; Avda. Reina Sofia s/n; r €60-85; 💻 ❄) The city's newest hotel is just 600 metres from the Teatro Romano and has a faux-temple exterior complete with columns. The rooms are modern, carpeted and comfortable with gleaming marble bathrooms.

Casa Benito (☎ 924 33 07 69; Calle San Francisco 3; tapas €2.60) Squeeze onto a tiny stool in the wood-panelled dining room, prop up the bar or relax on the sunny terrace for tapas at this bullfight enthusiasts' hang-out. The adjacent *asador* specialises in roasts including *rabo de toro* (bull's tail).

Restaurante Nicolás (☎ 924 31 96 10; Calle Felix Valverde Lillo 15; meals €20-25; 🕑 lunch & dinner Mon-Sat, lunch Sun) Long admired as a local favourite, this is one of the classier city dining options. Its relaxing ground-floor bar serves *raciones* while upstairs the food is decidedly more exciting than the rather drab decor.

Getting There & Away

The **bus station** (Avenida de la Libertad) is across the river. Destinations include Seville (€12, 2½ hours), Cáceres (€4.80, 50 minutes), Trujillo (€7.35, 1¼ hours) and Madrid (€21 to €27, four to five hours).

From the **train station** (Calle Cardero), there are four trains to Madrid (€28.80 to €31.80, 4½ to 5½ hours) and two to Seville (€12.20, five hours). Up to six trains run to/from Cáceres (€5.25, one hour).

SPAIN DIRECTORY

ACCOMMODATION

In this chapter, budget options (doubles €60 and under) include everything from dorm-style youth hostels to family-style *pensiones* and slightly better heeled *hostales*. At the upper end of this category you'll find rooms with air-conditioning and private bathrooms. Midrange *hostales* and hotels (€61 to €180) are more comfortable and most offer standard hotel services. Business hotels, trendy boutique hotels, and luxury hotels are in the top-end category (€181 and up). All prices quoted are for rooms with private bathroom unless otherwise specified. Be aware that hotels in the big cities and popular tourist areas can cost much more than in less visited parts of the country.

Some hotels have nonsmoking rooms or floors but this is far from common practice.

Always check room charges before putting down your bags and remember that prices can and do change. The price of any type of accommodation varies with the season and accommodation prices listed in this book are a guide only. As a rule, we've given high-season prices.

Virtually all accommodation prices are subject to IVA *(impuesto sobre el valor añadido)*, the Spanish version of value-added tax, which is 7%. This may or may not be included in the price. To check, ask: *Está incluido el IVA?* (Is IVA included?).

Camping

The country's camping grounds vary greatly in service, cleanliness and style. They're rated from first to third class and priced accordingly. Camping grounds usually charge per person, per tent and per vehicle – typically €4 to €8.50 for each. There are lots of helpful online guides, including www.campingsonline.com/espana and www.campinguia.com.

Some camping grounds close from around October to Easter. With few exceptions, camping outside camping grounds is illegal, as is building fires. You'll need permission to camp on private land.

Hotels, Hostales & Pensiones

Most options fall into the categories of hotels (one to five stars, full amenities), *hostales* (high-end guest houses with private bathroom; one to three stars) or *pensiones* (guest houses, usually with shared bathroom; one to three stars). Expect a double room at a *pensión* or *hostal* to cost €40 to €60 per night. A three-star hotel will generally cost from €80 up. Often, you can get great hotel deals online.

Youth Hostels

Albergues juveniles (youth hostels) are cheap places to stay, especially for lone travellers. Expect to pay from €12 to €27 per night, depending on location, age and season. Spain's Hostelling International (HI) organisation, **Red Española de Albergues Juveniles** (REAJ; www.reaj.com), has more than 200 youth hostels throughout Spain. Official hostels require HI membership (buy a membership card at virtually all hostels) and most have curfews.

ACTIVITIES

Cycling

The Vuelta de España is one of Europe's great bike races (after the Tour de France and Giro d'Italia) and the country has produced many fine cyclists. They are confronted by all sorts of terrain, from vast plains to tough mountains. It is especially popular among locals and tourists on the Balearic Islands. Mountain biking is popular; areas such as Andalucía and Catalonia have many good tracks. Mountain chains like the Pyrenees offer plenty of opportunities for cyclists to inflict pain on themselves!

Skiing

Skiing is cheaper but less varied than in much of the rest of Europe. The season runs from December to mid-April. The best resorts are in the Pyrenees, especially in northwest Catalonia. The Sierra Nevada in Andalucía offers the most southerly skiing in Western Europe.

Surfing, Windsurfing & Kitesurfing

The Basque Country has good surf spots, including San Sebastián, Zarautz and the legendary left at Mundaka. Tarifa (p840), with its long beaches and ceaseless wind, is generally considered to be the windsurfing capital of Europe. It is also a top spot for kitesurfing.

Walking

Spain is a trekker's paradise. Read about some of the best treks in the country in Lonely Planet's *Walking in Spain*. Useful for hiking, especially in the Pyrenees, are maps by Editorial Alpina. The series combines information booklets with detailed maps. Buy them at bookshops, sports shops and sometimes at petrol stations near hiking areas.

Some of Spain's best walking is in its parks. Throughout Spain, you'll find GR (*Grandes Recorridos*, or long distance) trails. These are indicated with red-and-white markers. The Camino de Santiago (St James' Way, with several branches) is perhaps Spain's best-known long-distance walk.

BUSINESS HOURS

Generally, people work Monday to Friday from 9am to 2pm and then again from 4.30pm or 5pm to about 8pm. Some people still follow the tradition of heading home for lunch and a siesta. Shops and travel agencies are usually open regular business hours on Saturday too – some skip the evening session. Many supermarkets open from 9am until 9pm, but many smaller grocers close for lunch from 2pm until 5pm. Department stores tend to open from 10am to 10pm, Monday to Saturday.

Museums have their own unique opening hours; major ones tend to open for something like normal business hours (with or without the afternoon break), but often have their weekly closing day on Monday.

Banks are open from 8.30am until 2pm, Monday to Friday. Savings banks also open from 4pm to 7pm on Saturday, while regular banks open on Saturday mornings.

Main post offices in provincial capitals are usually open from either 8.30am to 2pm or 8.30am to 8.30pm Monday to Friday, and from about 9am to 1.30pm Saturday.

Restaurants in Spain are open from 1.30pm until 4pm and from 8.30pm until 11pm; bars are open in the early evenings and continue serving until at least around 2am, usually until 3am on Fridays and Saturdays. Most clubs open until 6am. Times can vary enormously, depending on the establishment and location.

COURSES

There are hundreds of private language colleges throughout the country. The **Instituto Cervantes** (www.cervantes.es) has branches around the world and can send you lists of schools and universities running language courses. Also check out www.spanish-in-spain.biz for information.

DANGERS & ANNOYANCES

Stay alert and you can avoid most thievery techniques. Algeciras, Barcelona, Madrid and Seville are the worst offenders, as are many popular beaches in summer (never leave belongings unattended). Common scams include the following:

- Kids crowding around you asking for directions or help. They may be helping themselves to your wallet.
- A person pointing out bird droppings on your shoulder (some substance their friend has sprinkled on you) – as they help clean it off they are probably emptying your pockets.
- The guys who tell you that you have a flat tyre. This if often a ruse. While your new friend and you check the tyre, his pal is emptying the interior of the car.
- The classic snatch-and-run. Never leave your purse, bag, wallet, mobile phone etc unattended or alone on a table.

EMBASSIES & CONSULATES

Some 70 countries have their embassies in Madrid. Most embassies' office hours are around 9am to 2pm Monday to Friday.

Australia (off Map pp750-1; ☎ 91 353 66 00; www.spain.embassy.gov.au; Plaza del Descubridor Diego de Ordás 3)
Canada (Map pp750-1; ☎ 91 423 32 50; www.canada-es.org; Calle de Núñez de Balboa 35)
France (Map pp750-1; ☎ 91 423 89 00; www.ambafrance-es.org; Calle de Salustiano Olózaga 9)
Germany (Map pp750-1; ☎ 91 557 90 00; www.madrid.diplo.de; Calle de Fortuny 8)
Ireland (Map pp750-1; ☎ 91 436 40 93; Paseo de la Castellana 46)
Netherlands (off Map pp750-1; ☎ 91 353 75 00; www.embajadapaisesbajos.es; Avenida del Comandante Franco 32)
New Zealand (off Map pp750-1; ☎ 91 523 02 26; www.nzembassy.com; Calle del Pinar 7)
Portugal (off Map pp750-1; ☎ 91 782 49 60; www.embajadaportugal-madrid.org; Calle del Pinar 1)
UK Madrid (Map pp750-1; ☎ 91 700 82 00; www.ukinspain.com; Calle de Fernando el Santo 16); Barcelona (Map pp780-1; ☎ 93 366 62 00; Avinguda Diagonal 477)
USA Madrid (Map pp750-1; ☎ 91 587 22 00; www.embusa.es; Calle de Serrano 75); Barcelona (☎ 93 280 22 27; Passeig de la Reina Elisenda de Montcada 23-25)

FESTIVALS & EVENTS

Spaniards indulge their love of colour, noise, crowds and partying at innumerable local festivals, fiestas and *ferias* (fairs). Many are based on religion. Most local tourist offices can supply detailed information. Following is a partial list of important festivals.

January

Festividad de San Sebastián Held in San Sebastián (p797) on 20 January; the whole town dresses up and goes berserk.

February & March

Carnaval A time of fancy-dress parades and merrymaking celebrated around the country on the eve of the Christian Lent season (40 days before Easter). Among the wildest parties are those in Cádiz (p839) and Sitges, near Barcelona.
Las Fallas (www.fallas.com) Valencia's week-long mid-March party, with all-night dancing and drinking, mammoth bonfires, first-class fireworks and processions. See the boxed text, p809.

April

Semana Santa Parades of holy images and huge crowds, notably in Seville (p825), during Easter week.
Feria de Abril (http://feriadesevilla.andalunet.com) A week-long party held in Seville (p825) in late April, a kind of counterbalance to the religious peak of Easter.

July

Sanfermines (www.sanfermin.com) The highlight of this originally religious festival is the running of the bulls, in Pamplona (p801). It's held in early July.

August

Semana Grande A week of heavy drinking and hangovers all along the northern coast during the first half of August.

September

Festes de la Mercè (www.bcn.cat/merce) Barcelona's big annual party, held around 24 September. See p785 for more info.

HOLIDAYS

Spain has at least 14 official holidays a year, some observed nationwide, some very local. When a holiday falls close to a weekend, Spaniards like to make a *puente* (bridge), taking the intervening day off, too. The holidays listed are observed virtually everywhere.

New Year's Day 1 January
Three Kings' Day 6 January
Good Friday before Easter Sunday
Labour Day 1 May
Feast of the Assumption 15 August
National Day 12 October
All Saints' Day 1 November
Feast of the Immaculate Conception 8 December
Christmas 25 December

The two main periods when Spaniards go on holiday are Semana Santa (the week leading up to Easter Sunday) and the month of August. At these times accommodation in beachside resorts can be scarce and transport heavily booked.

LANGUAGE

Spanish, or Castilian *(Castellano)* as it is more precisely called, is spoken throughout Spain, but there are also three other important regional languages: Catalan *(Català)* – another Romance language with close ties to French – is spoken in Catalonia, and dialects of it are spoken in the Balearic Islands and in Valencia; Galician (*Galego*), similar to Portuguese, is spoken in Galicia; and Basque (*Euskera*; of obscure, non-Latin origin) is spoken in the Basque Country and in Navarra.

LEGAL MATTERS

Spaniards no longer enjoy liberal drug laws. No matter what anyone tells you, it is not legal to smoke dope in public bars. There is a reasonable degree of tolerance when it comes to people having a smoke in their own home, but not in hotel rooms or guest houses.

If you are arrested in Spain, you have the right to an attorney and to know the reason you are being held. You are also entitled to make a phone call.

MAPS

If you're driving around Spain, consider investing in a road atlas with detailed road maps as well as maps of all the main towns and cities. Most travel shops stock them.

Good city and road maps are widely available in bookshops and petrol stations. Michelin maps, which come in many scales and formats, are among the most reliable.

MEDIA

Newspapers

The major daily newspapers in Spain are the solidly liberal *El País*, the very conservative *ABC*, the more populist *El Mundo*, and the Catalonia-focused *La Vanguardia*. There's also a welter of regional news and sports dailies.

International press, such as the *International Herald Tribune*, and daily papers from Western European countries reach major cities and tourist areas on the day of or day after publication.

Radio

You'll hear a lot of talk radio and a substantial proportion of music in English. The national pop/rock station, RNE 3, has varied programming.

Television

Gossip shows, talent shows and *Big Brother*–style reality shows make up the bulk of programming. Most TVs receive at least seven or eight channels: two state-run (TVE1 and La2), five privately run (Antena 3, Tele 5, Cuatro, La Sexta and Canal Plus) and one regional channel.

MONEY

Spain's currency is the euro (€). Banks tend to give better exchange rates than do the currency-exchange offices. Travellers' cheques attract a slightly better rate than cash. It's easy to withdraw money – ATMs are ubiquitous.

In Spain, VAT (value-added tax) is known as *impuesto sobre el valor añadido* (IVA). On accommodation and restaurant prices it's 7%, but it's not always included in quoted prices. On retail goods and car hire, IVA is 16%. Non-EU visitors, if they spend €90.16 or more in one store (services don't count), are eligible for a tax refund. Request the appropriate form, fill it out and present it to a customs officer on leaving the European Union. They will stamp it and you can then cash it in or mail it for a refund to your credit card. Find more information at www.spainrefund.com.

In restaurants, tipping is a matter of personal choice – most people leave some small change; 5% is plenty, 10% is generous. It's common to leave small change in bars and cafes. Bargaining in Spain is not common, although you could ask for a discount for long-term room rental and the like.

POST

Stamps are sold at post offices and *estancos* (tobacco shops with the Tabacos sign in yellow letters on a maroon background). A postcard or letter weighing up to 20g costs €0.60 from Spain to other European countries, and €0.78 to the rest of the world.

Mail to/from Europe normally takes up to a week, and to North America, Australia or New Zealand around 10 days.

EMERGENCY NUMBERS

- Ambulance ☎ 061
- Fire ☎ 080
- Police ☎ 091

Poste-restante mail can be addressed to you at either poste restante or *lista de correos*, the Spanish name for it, at the city in question. It's a fairly reliable system.

TELEPHONE

Blue public payphones are common and fairly easy to use. They accept coins, phonecards and, in some cases, credit cards. Phonecards come in €6 and €12 denominations and, like postage stamps, are sold at post offices and tobacconists.

International reverse-charge (collect) calls are simple to make: dial ☎ 900 followed by the appropriate code. For example: ☎ 99 00 61 for Australia, ☎ 99 00 44 for the UK, ☎ 99 00 64 for New Zealand, ☎ 99 00 15 for Canada, and ☎ 99 00 11 (AT&T) for the USA.

Fax

Most main post offices have a fax service, but you'll often find cheaper rates at internet cafes or copy shops.

Mobile Phones

Mobile phone numbers in Spain start with the number 6. Call prices to mobiles vary.

Phone Codes

Telephone codes in Spain are an integral part of the phone number. All numbers are nine digits and you just dial that nine-digit number. All numbers prefixed with ☎ 900 are toll-free numbers.

TOURIST INFORMATION

Most towns and large villages of any interest have a helpful *oficina de turismo* (tourist office) where you can get maps and brochures. **Turespaña** (www.spain.info, www.tourspain.es), the country's national tourism body, presents a variety of general information and links on the entire country in its web pages.

VISAS

Citizens of EU countries can enter Spain freely with their national identity card or passport. Non-EU nationals must take their passport.

Spain is one of the Schengen countries; see p955.

Nationals of Australia, Canada, Israel, Japan, New Zealand and the USA do not need visa for stays of up to 90 days, but must have a passport valid for the whole visit.

Norwegian, Swiss, Icelandic and EU nationals planning to stay in Spain more than 90 days are supposed to register with the police and obtain a resident's number during their first month in the country.

South Africans are among the nationalities that do need a visa. You must obtain the visa in your country of residence. Multiple-entry visas will save you trouble if you plan to leave Spain for Gibraltar and/or Morocco, then re-enter it. Visas are not renewable.

WORK

Norwegian, Swiss, Icelandic and EU nationals may work in Spain without a visa. Everyone else is supposed to obtain (from a Spanish consulate in their country of residence) a work permit and, if they plan to stay more than 90 days, a residence visa. These procedures can be complex.

Teaching English is an obvious option; a TEFL (Teaching English as a Foreign Language) certificate will be a big help. Other possibilities include summer bar and restaurant work, as well as getting work on yachts in major ports.

TRANSPORT IN SPAIN

GETTING THERE & AWAY

Air

Flights from all over Europe, including budget airlines, serve main Spanish **airports** (☎ 902 404704; www.aena.es), including Alicante (ALC), Almería (LEI), Barcelona (BCN), Bilbao (BIO), Girona (GRO), Ibiza (IBZ), Madrid (MAD), Málaga (AGP), Menorca (MAH), Palma de Mallorca (PMI), Reus (REU), Santiago de Compostela (SCQ), Seville (SVQ), Valencia (VLC) and Zaragoza (ZAZ).

You'll find a list of major airlines operating throughout Europe on p957. The website www.flycheapo.com tells you which budget airlines fly where. For information on the main budget airlines operating across Europe, see p962.

Some of the airlines, including budget carriers, operating to/from and within Spain include:

Aer Lingus (EI; ☎ 902 50 27 37; www.aerlingus.com)
Air Berlin (AB; ☎ 902 32 07 37; www.airberlin.com)
Air Europa (UX; ☎ 902 40 15 01; www.aireuropa.com)
Air Nostrum (IB; ☎ 902 40 05 00; www.airnostrum.es)
Alpi Eagles (E8; ☎ in Italy 899 500058; www.alpieagles.com)
BMI (BD; ☎ 912 75 46 29; www.flybmi.com)
British Airways (BA; ☎ 902 11 13 33; www.britishairways.com)
Brussels Airlines (SN; ☎ 807 22 00 03; www.flysn.com)
Clickair (XG; ☎ 902 25 42 52; www.clickair.com)
Continental (CO; ☎ 900 96 12 66; www.continental.com)
Delta (DL; ☎ 901 11 69 46; www.delta.com)
easyJet (U2; ☎ 807 260026; www.easyjet.com)
Germanwings (4U; ☎ 916 25 97 04; www15.germanwings.com)
Iberia (IB; ☎ 902 40 05 00; www.iberia.es)
Jet2 (LS; ☎ 902 88 12 69; www.jet2.com)
Lufthansa (LX; ☎ 902 22 01 01; www.lufthansa.com)
Monarch (ZB; ☎ 800 099260; www.flymonarch.com)
Ryanair (FR; ☎ 807 220032; www.ryanair.com)
Sky Europe (NE; ☎ 807 001204; www.skyeurope.com)
Spanair (JK; ☎ 902 13 14 15; www.spanair.com)
Swiss (LX; ☎ 901 11 67 12; www.swiss.com)
Transavia (HV; ☎ 807 075022; www.transavia.com)
Vueling (VY; ☎ 902 33 39 33; www.vueling.com)
Windjet (IV; ☎ 900 99 69 33; w2.volawindjet.it)
Wizz (W6; ☎ 807 450010; http://wizzair.com)

Land

BUS

There are regular international bus services to Spain from European cities such as Lisbon, London and Paris. From London, the popular megacompany **Eurolines** (www.nationalexpress.com/eurolines) offers regular services to Barcelona (24 to 26 hours), Madrid (25 to 30 hours) and other cities. Advance bookings and student ID cards can get you large discounts.

CAR & MOTORCYCLE

If you're driving or riding to Spain from England, you'll have to choose between going through France or taking a direct ferry from England to Spain (see p850).

TRAIN

Unless you're simply hopping over the border from France or you already have a rail pass, travelling to Spain by train will usually be more expensive than by air. That said, rail travel for slow travellers can be a pleasant (and ecologically friendlier) alternative.

For details on long-distance rail travel, contact the **Rail Europe Travel Centre** (☎ in UK 08448 484064; www.raileurope.co.uk) in London. See p969 for more on train travel through Europe.

From France, sleeper trains run from Paris Austerlitz daily to Madrid or Barcelona. The Barcelona service stops at Orléans, Limoges, Perpignan, Figueres, Girona and Barcelona Sants; the Madrid equivalent stops at Orléans, Blois, Poitiers, Vitoria, Burgos and Valladolid. There are several other less-expensive (and less-luxurious) possibilities. Two or three TGV trains leave from Paris Montparnasse for Irún, where you change to a normal train for the Basque Country and carry on towards Madrid. Up to three TGVs also put you on the road to Barcelona (leaving from Paris Gare de Lyon), with a change of train at Montpellier or Narbonne. One or two daily direct services connect Montpellier with Barcelona in 4½ hours (and on to Murcia). A slow overnight train runs from Paris to Latour-de-Carol, where you change for a local regional train to Barcelona.

From Portugal, an overnight sleeper train runs daily from Lisbon to Madrid and another train connects the Portuguese capital with Irún. See **Renfe** (www.renfe.es) for details.

Sea

MOROCCO

Several companies offer regular ferry services between Spain and Morocco. **Acciona Trasmediterránea** (☎ 902 45 46 45; www.trasmediterranea.es) offers routes including Algeciras–Tangier (€42, up to 2½ hours) and Almería–Nador (€40, six hours). Other possible routes include Algeciras–Ceuta, Gibraltar–Tangier, Tarifa–Tangier, Málaga–Melilla and Almería–Melilla. Fast jetfoil service (at nearly double the price) is available for most of these routes. Taking a car will cost €100 and up.

Don't buy Moroccan currency until you reach Morocco, as you will get ripped off in Algeciras.

Grandi Navi Veloci (Grimaldi) runs a weekly ferry service (24 hours) between Barcelona and Tangier.

UK

If you drive your own car, a ferry is your best bet. **Brittany Ferries** (☎ in UK 0870 907 6103; www.brittany-ferries.co.uk) runs Plymouth–Santander ferries (24 hours) twice-weekly from mid-March to mid-November. Fares vary enormously depending on when you book and travel. Two people travelling with a car in August might pay UK£454 one-way for a standard interior cabin if they book in May.

P&O Ferries (☎ in UK 0871 664 5645; www.poferries.com) runs Portsmouth-Bilbao ferries (35 hours) two or three times weekly year-round. Tickets prices vary due to special offers, but a guide is €190 per passenger with cabin, and €400 per car (with two passengers).

ITALY

The Grimaldi group's **Grandi Navi Veloci** (☎ 902 41 02 00, in Italy 010 209 4591; www1.gnv.it; Moll de San Beltran) runs a daily ferry service from Genoa to Barcelona (18 hours). An economy-class airline-style seat can cost as little as €16 in winter. A single cabin suite in high season can cost €199. **Grimaldi Ferries** (☎ 902 53 13 33, in Italy 081 496444; www.grimaldi-ferries.com) has a similar service between Barcelona and Civitavecchia (for Rome, 20 hours) and Livorno (Tuscany, 19½ hours) up to six days a week. An economy-class airline-style seat costs from €29 in low season to €72 in high season on both routes.

ALGERIA

Acciona Trasmediterránea (www.trasmediterranea.es) runs daily ferries from Alicante to Oran (nine hours, leaving at 11pm or noon, late June to early September). Check the website for fare details.

GETTING AROUND

Students and seniors are eligible for discounts of 30% to 50% on almost all types of transport within Spain.

Air

Iberia has an extensive network covering all of Spain. Competing with Iberia are Spanair and Air Europa, as well as the low-cost companies Clickair (an Iberia subsidiary) and Vueling. Between them, they cover a host of Spanish destinations. The busiest route by far, in spite of strong competition from the high-speed AVE train, is the Barcelona–Madrid *puente* ('bridge'). EasyJet has a hub in Madrid and offers domestic flights to Oviedo, Ibiza and La Coruña. Ireland's Ryanair also runs a handful of domestic Spanish flights.

Bicycle

Finding bikes to rent in Spain is a hit-and-miss affair, so it's best to bring your own. However, the Spanish do enjoy recreational cycling, so getting hold of spare parts shouldn't be a problem.

All regional trains have space where you can simply load your bike. Bikes are also permitted on most *cercanías* (local area trains around big cities such as Madrid and Barcelona). On long-distance trains there are more restrictions. As a rule, you have to be travelling overnight in a sleeper or couchette to have the (dismantled) bike accepted as normal luggage.

Boat

Regular ferries connect the Spanish mainland with the Balearic Islands. For more details see p814. The main companies:

Acciona Trasmediterránea (☎ 902 45 46 45; www.trasmediterranea.es)
Baleària (☎ 902 16 01 80; www.balearia.com)
Iscomar (☎ 902 11 91 28; www.iscomar.com)

Bus

Spain's bus network is operated by countless independent companies, and reaches into the most remote towns and villages. Many towns and cities have one main bus station where most buses arrive and depart, and these will usually have an information desk giving details on all services. Tourist offices can also help with information on buses. The best-known national company, under whose umbrella many smaller companies operate, is **ALSA** (☎ 902 42 22 42; www.alsa.es).

Bus tickets vary, depending on the popularity of the route and the comfort and speed of the service. Generally, fares are cheaper than on the faster, long-distance trains. The trip from Madrid to Barcelona costs around €27 one way. From Barcelona to Seville, one of the longest trips you could do (15 to 16 hours), you pay around €74.

It is not necessary, and often not possible, to make advance reservations for local bus journeys. It is, however, a good idea to turn up at least 30 minutes before the bus leaves

SPAIN

to guarantee a seat. For longer trips, you can and should buy your ticket in advance.

Other bus companies include the following:

Avanza (☎ 902 02 00 52; www.avanzabus.com)
Comes (☎ 902 19 92 08; www.tgcomes.es)
La Roncalesa (☎ 943 46 10 64)
Larrea/La Sepulvedana (☎ 902 22 22 82; www.lasepulvedana.es)
Los Amarillos (☎ 902 21 03 17; www.losamarillos.es)
PESA (☎ 902 10 12 10; www.pesa.net)
Portillo (☎ 902 14 31 44; www.ctsa-portillo.com)
Socibus/Secorbus (www.socibus.es)

Car & Motorcycle

Spain's roads vary enormously but are generally good. Fastest are the *autopistas;* on some, you have to pay hefty tolls (from Zaragoza to Barcelona, for example, it's €22.60). Minor routes can be slow going but are usually more scenic. Trying to find a parking spot in larger towns and cities can be a nightmare. *Grúas* (tow trucks) can and will tow your car. The cost of bailing out a car can be €200 or more.

Spanish cities do not have US-style parking meters at every spot. Instead, if you park in a blue zone (frequently from 8am to 2pm or from 4pm to 8pm), you have to obtain a ticket from a street-side meter, which may be a block away. Display the ticket on the dash. If you bring your own vehicle into Spain, remember to always carry the vehicle registration document.

Petrol stations are easy to find along highways and *autopistas.*

AUTOMOBILE ASSOCIATIONS

The Spanish automobile club **Real Automovil Club de España** (RACE; ☎ 902 40 45 45; www.race.es) offers a 24-hour, nationwide, on-road emergency service. You will pay for this, so you should use the service that comes with your own insurance if possible.

DRIVING LICENCE

All EU member states' driving licences are recognised. Other foreign licences should be accompanied by an International Driving Permit. These are available from automobile clubs in your country and valid for 12 months.

HIRE

Rates vary widely from place to place. The best deals tend to be in major tourist areas, including airports. Prices are especially competitive in the Balearic Islands. Expect a compact car to cost around €30 and up per day. See p966 for information on major car-hire companies.

INSURANCE

Third party motor insurance is a minimum requirement and it is compulsory to have a Green Card, an internationally recognised proof of insurance, which can be obtained from your insurer.

ROAD RULES

Driving in the cities can be a little hair-raising at times but, otherwise, Spain doesn't present any special driving difficulties. Speed limits are 120km/h on the *autopistas,* 80km/h or 100km/h on other country roads and 50km/h (sometimes 30km/h) in built-up areas. The blood-alcohol limit is 0.05%. Seat belts must be worn and motorcyclists must always wear a helmet and keep headlights on day and night.

Train

Trains are mostly modern and comfortable, and late arrivals are the exception rather than the rule. The high-speed network is in constant expansion.

Renfe (☎ 902 24 02 02; www.renfe.es), the national railway company, runs numerous types of trains. Travel times and fares vary greatly depending on the speed and comfort of the service, and in some cases on the day of travel.

Regionales are all-stops trains (think cheap and slow). *Cercanías* provide regular services from major cities to the surrounding suburbs and hinterland, sometimes even crossing regional boundaries. High-speed AVE trains link Madrid with Barcelona (via Zaragoza, Lleida and Tarragona), Burgos, Huesca (via Zaragoza), Málaga, Seville (via Córdoba), Valladolid (via Segovia) – and in coming years Madrid with Valencia (via Cuenca) and Madrid with Bilbao).

Similar trains used on conventional Spanish tracks (which differs from the standard European gauge) connect Barcelona with Valencia and Alicante in the Euromed service.

A host of modern intermediate services (Alaris, Altaria, Alvia, Arco and Avant) offer speedy and comfortable service around the country on shorter distance runs like Madrid–Toledo and Barcelona–Lleida.

Some slow overnight services offer bed and couchette options.

You can buy tickets and make reservations online, at stations, at travel agencies displaying the Renfe logo and in Renfe offices in many city centres.

Rail passes are valid for all long-distance Renfe trains, but Inter-Rail users have to pay supplements on Talgo, InterCity and AVE trains. All pass-holders making reservations pay a small fee.

Turkey

Hoş geldiniz (welcome) to the Med's own slice of the Middle East. While many Turks see their country as European, the nation packs in as many towering mosques and spice-trading bazaars as neighbouring Iran, Iraq and Syria. This bridge between continents has absorbed Europe's modernism and sophistication, and Asia's culture and tradition. Travellers can enjoy historical hot spots, mountain outposts, expansive steppe and caravanserai-loads of the exotic, without having to forego comfy beds and buses.

Turkey's charms range from sun-splashed Mediterranean and Aegean beaches to İstanbul's minarets. While these gems fit its reputation as a continental meeting point, the country can't be easily pigeonholed. Cappadocia is a dreamscape dotted with fairy chimneys, completely unlike anywhere else on the planet. The ethereal beauty of Mt Nemrut, littered with giant stone heads, and Olympos, where Lycian ruins peek from the undergrowth, is quintessentially Turkish.

Such potent mixtures of natural splendour and ancient remains result from millennia of eventful history, which saw empires including the Byzantines and the Ottomans establish capitals here. So many Turkish names are familiar from history lessons and Hollywood blockbusters that travelling the beaches and plains is like turning the pages of a historical thriller.

When it's time to close the book and seek worldly pleasures, Turkey still shines as brightly as its red-and-white flag, being the land that introduced the world to the *kebap* (kebab). Vegetarians can tuck into meze, ideally consumed on a panoramic terrace with *rakı* (aniseed spirit) or *çay* (tea). And that's before you lace up your hiking boots or pull on a dive mask…

FAST FACTS

- **Area** 779,452 sq km
- **Capital** Ankara
- **Currency** Turkish lira (TL); €1=TL2.08; UK£1=TL2.35; US$1=TL1.53; A$1=TL1.17; ¥100=TL1.59; NZ$1=TL0.91
- **Famous for** Turkish delight, *hammams* (Turkish baths), carpets, moustaches, ruins
- **Official language** Turkish
- **Phrases** *merhaba* (hello); *tamam* (OK); *teşekkürler* (thank you); *bu akşam olmaz* (not tonight, thanks)
- **Population** 71.9 million
- **Telephone codes** country code ☎ 90; international access code ☎ 00
- **Visas** available on entry (US$20 to US$60); see p933

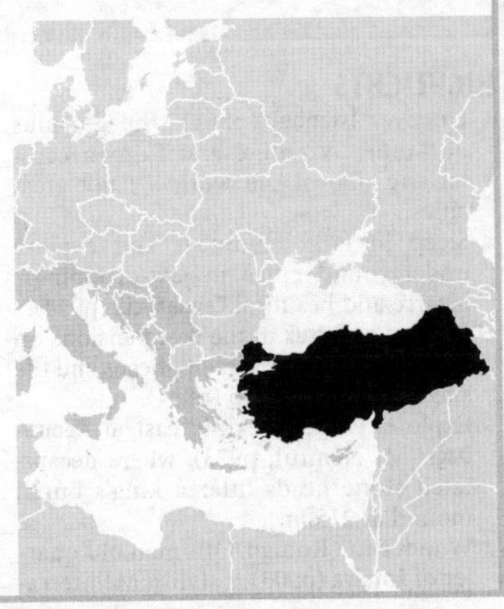

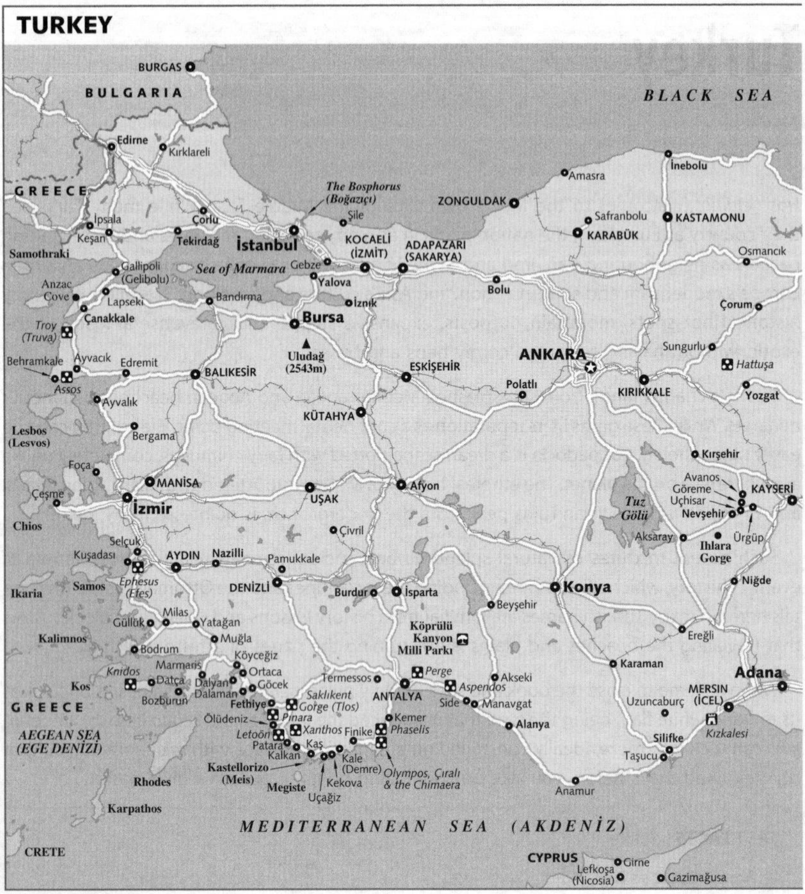

HIGHLIGHTS

- Uncover **İstanbul** (p861), the glorious one-time Byzantine and Roman capital and one of the world's truly great cities.
- Sleep in fairy chimneys and explore underground cities in jaw-droppingly bizarre and beautiful **Cappadocia** (p914).
- Pit stop at **Selçuk** in the best pensions on the coast, near awesome Ephesus and the site of St John's tomb (p884).
- Explore Turkey's exotic east at **Nemrut Dağı** (Mt Nemrut; p923), where decapitated stone heads litter a king's burial mound at 2150m.
- Wander the Roman-Ottoman old quarter of **Antalya** (p903), a stylish Mediterranean hub located on both the 'Turquoise Coast' and the 'Turkish Riviera'.

ITINERARIES

- **One week** Devote two or three days to magical İstanbul, then head down the Aegean coast, via the Gallipoli battlefields and Troy, to marvel at the ruins of Ephesus. Squeeze in a side trip to Pamukkale's shiny travertine formations from Selçuk.
- **Two weeks** From Pamukkale, head to another sea – the Mediterranean – and travel eastward to Roman-Ottoman Antalya, stopping in laid-back Kaş and checking out Olympos' tree-houses along the way. Return to İstanbul via

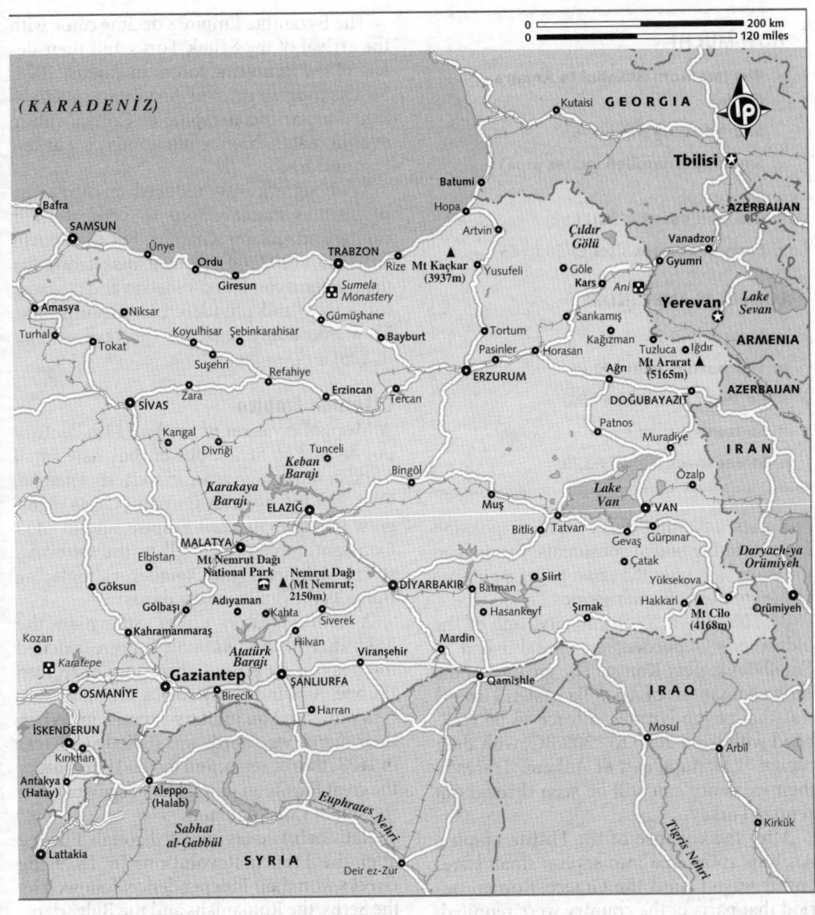

Cappadocia – it's a little out of the way, but you won't regret making the effort when you clap eyes on the fairy chimneys.

CLIMATE & WHEN TO GO

In general, spring (April to May) and autumn (September to October) are the best times of year to visit. The heat and crowds of July and August can be unbearable, especially in İstanbul.

The Aegean and Mediterranean coasts have mild, rainy winters and hot, dry summers. In İstanbul, summer is stinking hot, and winters are chilly with rain and, occasionally, snow. The Anatolian plateau can be boiling hot (although less humid than the coast) in summer and freezing in winter.

Many accommodation options along the Aegean and Mediterranean, and in some parts of Cappadocia, close from mid-October until late April.

For more details, see Climate Charts, p944.

HISTORY

The sheer weight and depth of history in Turkey is overwhelming – the Anatolian plateau features in various guises in both Homer's *Iliad* and the Bible; it has produced some of the world's longest-lasting empires, been instrumental in maintaining control in much of Europe and the Middle East for

HOW MUCH?

- **Bus fare from İstanbul to Ankara** €17.50
- **Short dolmuş trip** €0.75
- **Smoking a nargileh (water pipe)** €2.50
- **Old man's şapka (hat)** €5
- **Entry to ancient sites** €1.50 to €5

LONELY PLANET INDEX

- **1L petrol** €1.75
- **1.5L bottled water** €1.25
- **Bottle of Efes beer** €2.50
- **Souvenir T-shirt** €5
- **Street snack (simit)** €0.25

centuries, and still holds a strategic position at the meeting of two continents. Just look at the ruins that litter the coast to get a glimpse of the country's former glories.

By 7000 BC a Neolithic city, one of the oldest ever recorded, was established at Çatalhöyük, near Konya. The greatest of the early civilisations of Anatolia (Asian Turkey) was that of the Hittites, a force to be reckoned with from 2000 to 1200 BC, with their capital at Hattuşa, east of Ankara. Traces of their existence can still be seen throughout central Turkey.

After the collapse of the Hittite empire, Anatolia splintered into several small states and it wasn't until the Graeco-Roman period that parts of the country were reunited. Later, Christianity spread through Anatolia, carried by the apostle Paul, a native of Tarsus (near Adana).

Byzantine Empire & The Crusades

In AD 330, the Roman emperor Constantine founded a new imperial city at Byzantium (modern İstanbul). Renamed Constantinople, this strategic city became the capital of the Eastern Roman Empire and was the centre of the Byzantine Empire for 1000 years. During the European Dark Ages, the Byzantine Empire kept alive the flame of Western culture, although it was occasionally threatened by the empires of the East (Persians, Arabs and Turks) and West (the Christian powers of Europe).

The Byzantine Empire's decline came with the arrival of the Seljuk Turks and their defeat of the Byzantine forces in August 1071. Seljuks overran most of Anatolia, and established a provincial capital at Konya, ruling over domains that included today's Turkey, Iran and Iraq.

With significantly reduced territory, the Byzantines endeavoured to protect their capital and reclaim Anatolia, but the Fourth Crusade (1202–04) proved disastrous for them when a combined Venetian and crusader force took and plundered Constantinople. They eventually regained the ravaged city in 1261.

Ottoman Empire

A Mongol invasion of the late 13th century put an end to Seljuk power, but new small Turkish states soon arose in western Anatolia. One, headed by Gazi Osman (1258–1326), grew into the Ottoman Empire, and in 1453 Constantinople finally fell to the Ottoman sultan Mehmet II (the Conqueror), replacing Bursa as the capital of the dynasty.

A century later, under Süleyman the Magnificent, the Ottoman Empire reached the peak of its power, spreading deep into Europe, Asia and North Africa. Ottoman success was based on military expansion. When their march westwards was stalled at Vienna in 1683, the rot set in, and by the 19th century the great European powers had begun to covet the sultan's vast domains.

Nationalist ideas swept through Europe after the French Revolution. In 1829 the Greeks won their independence, followed by the Serbs, the Romanians and the Bulgarians. In the ensuing territorial scrambles, Italy took Tripolitania (now Libya) in North Africa from Turkey, and in 1913 the Ottomans lost both Albania and Macedonia.

Having sided with the Axis powers in 1914, the Turks emerged from WWI stripped of their last non-Turkish provinces: Syria, Palestine, Mesopotamia (Iraq) and the Arabian peninsula. Most of Anatolia itself was to be parcelled out to the victorious Europeans, leaving the Turks with virtually nothing.

Mustafa Kemal Atatürk

At this low point (around 1920), Mustafa Kemal, the father of modern Turkey, took over. Atatürk, as he was later called, had made his name by repelling the Anzacs in their heroic but futile attempt to capture the strategic Dardanelles strait at Gallipoli during WWI.

Rallying the remnants of the Turkish army during the Turkish War of Independence that followed WWI, Kemal pushed the last of the Ottoman rulers aside and out-manoeuvred the Allied forces. The Turks finally won in 1922 by repelling the invading Greeks at Smyrna (present-day İzmir). In the ensuing population exchange, whole communities were uprooted as Greek-speaking people from Anatolia were shipped to Greece, while Muslim residents of Greece were transferred to Turkey. These exchanges brought great disruption and the creation of 'ghost villages' that were vacated but never reoccupied.

After the renegotiation of the WWI treaties, a new Turkish republic, reduced to Anatolia and part of Thrace, was born. Atatürk then embarked on a rapid modernisation program, establishing a secular democracy, introducing the Latin script and European dress, and adopting equal rights for women (at least in theory). The capital was also moved from İstanbul to Ankara. Such sweeping changes did not come easily, and some of the disputes from that period have never been fully resolved.

Relations with Greece improved in the 1930s (the Greek president even nominated Atatürk for the Nobel Peace Prize in 1934), but soured again after WWII due to the conflict over Cyprus, particularly after the Greek-led anti-Makarios coup and the subsequent Turkish invasion in 1974. For more, see p177.

Modern Turkey

After Atatürk's death on 10 November 1938, Turkey experienced three military coups and a lot of political turbulence – no fewer than 60 different governments have held office since independence. During the 1980s and '90s the country was also wracked by the conflict with the PKK (Kurdistan Workers' Party), led by Abdullah Öcalan, who wanted the creation of a Kurdish state in Turkey's southeastern corner. This conflict led to an estimated 35,000 deaths and huge population shifts inside the country. In 1999 Öcalan was captured and a ceasefire called.

In 2001 the Turkish economy collapsed in spectacular fashion. More than a million people lost their jobs, and the value of the Turkish lira slumped from TRL650,000 for US$1 to TRL1.6 million.

In 2002 the newly formed AKP (Islamic Justice and Development Party), a religious party dominated by one-time İstanbul mayor Recep Tayyip Erdoğan, won an unprecedented victory, becoming the first noncoalition government in 15 years and ousting 90% of the existing members of parliament. Only one other party won any seats at all.

With concerns over Erdoğan's controversial past (he was once jailed for inciting religious hatred, and was still banned from sitting in parliament at the time his party came to power), many people feared the AKP would bring a rush of hardline Islam to national politics. So far, the new regime has proved reassuringly moderate, concentrating on stabilising the economy and strengthening the country's bid to join the EU, but many Turks remain uneasy about the government's pro-Islamic leanings.

Current Events

Terrorism and the increasing polarisation of the Eastern and Western worlds have reinforced Turkey's position as a United States ally and

CONNECTIONS: MOVING ON FROM TURKEY

İstanbul is well connected to Europe. Buses leave the *otogar* (bus station) for countries including Austria, Bulgaria, Germany, Greece, Italy, Macedonia and Romania, but trains and ferries are more romantic.

The most useful daily trains are the *Bosphorus Express* to Chişinău (Moldova) or Budapest (Hungary) via Bucharest (Romania), or to Belgrade (Serbia) via Bulgaria (Dimitrovgrad and Sofia); and the *Filia-Dostluk Express* to Thessaloniki (Greece). A suggested train route from London to İstanbul is via Paris, Munich and Zagreb (Croatia), where you can catch trains to Belgrade to join the *Bosphorus Express*. For some train-related inspiration, visit www.seat61.com/Turkey.htm.

Ferries connect Turkey's Aegean and Mediterranean coasts with Greek islands, Northern Cyprus and Italy; İstanbul with Ukraine; and Trabzon on the Black Sea coast with Russia. See p934 for more information.

NATO member, and joining Europe remains a key priority for the country. The death penalty has been abolished to meet EU criteria (incidentally reprieving PKK leader Öcalan) and the Kurdish minority have been granted greater rights and freedoms. Accession talks began in October 2005. The ongoing issue of Turkish-held North Cyprus, however, continues to drive a wedge between it and EU member states Greece and Cyprus, whose support it will need if Turkey's bid is to succeed.

In addition to this, the negative press generated when Turkey's best-known author Orhan Pamuk was tried for 'insulting Turkishness', has put the spotlight on the government's declared commitment to freedom of expression. With accession talks offering no guarantee of acceptance into the EU anyway, it seems that Turkey may remain teetering on the edge of Europe for some time.

Following the AKP's re-election in mid-2007, the tussle between 'secularists' and 'Islamists' grew more heated. A legal case to close the AKP for pursuing an antisecular agenda brought tensions to boiling point. In mid-2008, police arrested scores of people associated with the ultranationalist Ergenekon movement, alleging they were fomenting a coup against the government, and a series of terrorist bombs exploded in İstanbul. Political meltdown was averted when the Constitutional Court voted not to close the AKP.

More positively, relations are improving with Armenia, which has long pressured its western neighbour to acknowledge that Ottoman troops carried out genocide against Armenians in 1915. In September 2008 president Abdullah Gul became the first Turkish leader to visit Armenia, in a day trip that coincided with the countries' soccer World Cup qualifying match.

In January 2009 the Turkish lira ditched the *yeni* (new) prefix introduced in 2005, signalling a stronger currency. Later that month, flamboyant Erdoğan returned home to a hero's welcome after he stormed out of a World Economic Forum debate about Israel's assault on the Gaza Strip – claiming the moderator was not allowing him to challenge Israeli president Shimon Peres.

PEOPLE

Turkey's population (71.9 million) is predominantly made up of Turks, with a big Kurdish minority (perhaps 14 million) and much smaller groups of Laz, Hemşin, Arabs, Jews, Greeks and Armenians. The Laz and Hemsin people are natives of the northeastern corner of Turkey on the Black Sea coast, while Arab influence is strongest in the Antakya (Hatay) area abutting Syria. Southeastern Turkey is pretty solidly Kurdish, although the problems of the last 20 years have led many to head west in search of a better life.

As a result of Atatürk's reforms, republican Turkey has largely adapted to a modern Westernised lifestyle, at least on the surface. In the big cities and coastal resorts you will not feel much need to adapt to fit in. In smaller towns and villages, however, particularly in the east, you may find people warier and more conservative.

The Turks have an acute sense of pride and honour. They are fiercely proud of their history and heroes, especially Atatürk, whose portrait and statues are ubiquitous. The extended family still plays a key role and formality and politeness are important; if asked 'how is Turkey?', answer '*çok güzel*' (excellent).

Technology- and communication-loving Turks make the country the world's third-highest user of MSN Messenger, with a third of the population chatting.

RELIGION

Turkey is 98% Muslim, overwhelmingly Sunni, with Shiites and Alevis mainly in the east. The religious practices of Sunnis and Alevis (who make up an estimated 20% of the population) differ markedly, with the latter incorporating aspects of Anatolian folklore and less strict segregation of the sexes.

The country espouses a more relaxed version of Islam than many Middle Eastern nations. Many men drink alcohol (although almost no one touches pork) and many women uncover their heads.

The small Jewish community includes some 25,000 Jews in İstanbul. There's also a declining community of Nestorian and Assyrian Orthodox Christians in the southeast.

ARTS

As with everything else, Atatürk changed Turkey's cultural picture, encouraging painting, sculpture, Western music (he loved opera), dance and drama. Today's arts scene is a vibrant, if at times discordant, mix of the traditional, the innovative and the painfully modern.

Carpets

Turkey is famous for its beautiful carpets and *kilims* (woven rugs). It's thought that the Seljuks introduced hand-woven carpet-making techniques to Anatolia in the 12th century. Traditionally, village women wove carpets for their family's use, or for their dowry; today, the dictates of the market rule, but carpets still incorporate traditional symbols and patterns. The Ministry of Culture has sponsored projects to revive aged weaving and dyeing methods in western Turkey; some shops stock these 'project carpets'.

Architecture

Turkey's architectural history encompasses everything from Hittite stonework and Graeco-Roman temples to modern tower-blocks, but perhaps the most distinctively Turkish styles are Seljuk and Ottoman. The Seljuks left magnificent mosques and *medreses* (Islamic schools), distinguished by their elaborate entrances. The Ottomans also built grand religious structures, and fine wood-and-stone houses in towns such as Safranbolu and Amasya (see the boxed text, p912).

Literature

The most famous Turkish novelists are Yaşar Kemal, nominated for the Nobel prize for literature on numerous occasions, and Orhan Pamuk, the Nobel Prize Laureate in 2006. Kemal's novels, which include *The Wind from the Plains, Salman the Solitary* and *Memed, My Hawk,* chronicle the desperate lives of villagers battling land-grabbing lords.

An inventive prose stylist, Pamuk's books include the Kars-set *Snow,* and the existential İstanbul whodunit *Black Book,* told through a series of newspaper columns. Other well-known writers include Elif Şafak *(Flea Palace),* Latife Tekin *(Dear Shameless Death)* and Buket Uzuner *(Long White Cloud, Gallipoli).*

Cinema

Several Turkish directors have won worldwide recognition, most notably the late Yılmaz Güney, director of *Yol* (The Road), *Duvar* (The Wall) and *Sürü* (The Herd). Cannes favourite Nuri Bilge Ceylan probes the lives of village migrants in the big city in *Uzak* (Distant), and looks at male-female relationships in *İklimler* (Climates).

Ferzan Özpetek's *Hamam* addresses the hitherto hidden issue of homosexuality in Turkish society. The current name to watch is Fatih Akin, who ponders the Turkish experience in Germany in *Duvara Karsi* (Head On) and *Edge of Heaven.*

Music

Turkey's successful home-grown pop industry managed to gain European approval faster than the country's politicians, when Sertab Erener won the Eurovision Song Contest with 'Every Way that I Can' in 2003.

The big pop stars include pretty-boy Tarkan, whom Holly Valance covered, and chanteuse Sezen Aksu. Burhan Öçal is one of Turkey's finest percussionists; his seminal *New Dream* is a funky take on classical Turkish music. Ceza is the king of İstanbul's thriving hip hop scene.

With an Arabic spin, Arabesk is also popular. The genre's stars are Orhan Gencebay and the Kurdish former construction worker, Ibrahim Tatlıses.

Two Kurdish folk singers to listen out for are Aynur Doğan and Ferhat Tunç.

For an excellent overview of Turkish music, watch Fatih Akin's documentary *Crossing the Bridge: the Sound of İstanbul,* which covers styles from rock and hip hop to *fasıl* (Romani music).

SPORT

Turks are fanatical lovers of football (soccer), and if you can get to a match involving one of the big İstanbul three – Galatasaray, Fenerbahçe and Beşiktaş – you're guaranteed to have a good time. Try to make sure you're cheering for the right side!

The other main spectator sport here is *yağı güreş* (oil wrestling), where burly men in leather shorts grease themselves up with olive oil and go at it – be in Edirne (p875) in June for oily action. Another unusual sporting highlight is the main camel-wrestling bout, which takes place near Selçuk on the third Sunday in January.

ENVIRONMENT

The Land

The Dardanelles, the Sea of Marmara and the Bosphorus divide Turkey into Asian and European parts. Eastern Thrace (European Turkey) comprises only 3% of the country's 779,452-sq-km land area; the remaining 97% is Anatolia, a vast plateau rising eastward towards the Caucasus mountains.

With more than 8300km of coastline, snow-capped mountains, rolling steppes, vast lakes and broad rivers, Turkey is geographically diverse. Turkey's 33 national parks include Uludağ National Park (p877) near Bursa, Cappadocia's Ala Dağlar National Park (p914) and Mt Nemrut National Park (p923) north-east of Gaziantep.

Wildlife

Turkey's location at the junction between Asia and Europe and its varied geology has made it one of the most biodiverse temperate-zone countries in the world, blessed with an exceptionally rich flora of more than 9000 species, 1200 of them endemic. In addition, some 400 species of bird are found in Turkey, with about 250 of these passing through on migration from Africa to Europe.

In theory, you could see bears, deer, jackals, caracal, wild boars and wolves in Turkey. In practice you're unlikely to see any wild animals at all unless you're hiking. Instead you can look out for Kangal dogs, originally bred to protect sheep flocks from wolves and bears on mountain pastures. People wandering off the beaten track, especially in eastern Turkey, are often alarmed at the sight of these huge, yellow-coated, black-headed animals, especially as they often wear ferocious spiked collars to protect them against wolves. They are generally harmless, but if you feel the need to stroke one, proceed with caution as attacks have occurred!

Environmental Issues

Turkey's embryonic environmental movement is making slow progress; discarded litter and ugly concrete buildings (some half-finished) disfigure the west in particular.

While desertification is a long-term threat in Turkey, big dam projects have caused environmental ding-dongs. The 22-dam Güneydoğu Anadolu Projesi (GAP) project is changing southeastern Anatolia's landscape as it generates hydroelectricity for industry. Parched valleys have become fish-filled lakes, causing an explosion of diseases such as Malaria. GAP has also generated problems with Syria and Iraq, the countries downriver.

In 2008 dam-builders' plans to drown Hasankeyf saw the historic southeastern town named on the World Monuments Watch list (alongside four other Turkish sites).

Another major environmental challenge facing the country is the threat from maritime traffic along the Bosphorus. A noted *cause célèbre* is the loggerhead turtle *(caretta caretta)*, whose beach nesting grounds such as İztuzu Beach at Dalyan (p895), the Göksu Delta and Patara Beach (p898) have long been endangered by tourism and development. Various national and international schemes are underway to protect these areas during the breeding season – look out for signs telling you when to avoid which stretches.

On the plus side, Turkey is slowly reclaiming its architectural heritage; Central Anatolia's Ottoman towns Safranbolu and Amasya are masterpieces of restoration (see the boxed text, p912). The country is doing well when it comes to beach cleanliness, with 250-plus beaches qualifying for Blue Flag status (which recognises success in areas such as water quality, environmental education and information, environmental management and safety); go to www.blueflag.org for the complete list.

İstanbul has a branch of **Greenpeace Mediterranean** (☎ 0212-292 7619; fax 0212-292 7622; www.greenpeace.org/mediterranean; Kallavi Sokak 1/2, Beyoğlu).

FOOD & DRINK

Afiyet olsun (good appetite)! Not without reason is Turkish food regarded as one of the world's greatest cuisines. *Kebaps* (kebabs) are, of course, the mainstay of restaurant meals; you'll find *lokantas* (restaurants) that sell a wide range of *kebaps* everywhere. Try the ubiquitous *dürüm döner kebap* – compressed meat (usually lamb) cooked on a revolving upright skewer over coals, then thinly sliced. When laid on pide bread, topped with tomato sauce and browned butter and with yoghurt on the side, *döner kebap* becomes İskender *kebap*, primarily a lunchtime delicacy. Equally ubiquitous are *köfte* (meatballs).

For a quick, cheap fill you could hardly do better than a Turkish pizza, a freshly cooked pide topped with cheese, egg or meat. Alternatively, *lahmacun* is a paper-thin Arabic pizza topped with chopped onion, lamb and tomato sauce. Other favourites are *gözleme* (thin savoury crepes) and *simit*, a small ring of bread decorated with sesame seeds. *Mantı*, the Turkish version of ravioli, is also a good bet.

Fish dishes, although excellent, are often expensive – always check the price before ordering.

For vegetarians, a meal made up of meze can be an excellent way to ensure a varied diet. Most restaurants will be able to rustle up at least *beyaz peynir* (ewe- or goat's-milk cheese), *sebze çorbası* (vegetable soup), *börek* (flaky pastry stuffed with white cheese and parsley), *dolma* (stuffed vegetables), *kuru fasulye* (beans) and *patlıcan tava* (fried aubergine).

For dessert, try *fırın sütlaç* (rice pudding), *aşure* ('Noah's Ark' pudding, made from up to 40 different ingredients), baklava (honey-soaked flaky pastry stuffed with walnuts or pistachios), *kadayıf* (dough soaked in syrup, often topped with cream) and *dondurma* (ice cream). The famously chewy sweet called *lokum* (Turkish delight) has been made here since the 18th century; there's not a bus station in the country that doesn't sell it.

The national hot drink, *çay* (tea), is served in tiny tulip-shaped glasses with copious quantities of sugar. The wholly chemical *elma çay* (apple tea) is caffeine-free and only for tourists – locals wouldn't be seen dead drinking the stuff. If you're offered a tiny cup of traditional Turkish *kahve* (coffee), you will be asked how sweet you like it – *çok şekerli* means 'very sweet', *orta şekerli* 'middling', *az şekerli* 'slightly sweet' and *sade* 'not at all'. But these days Nescafé is fast replacing *kahve*. In tourist areas it usually comes *sütlü* (with milk).

The Turkish liquor of choice is *rakı*, a fiery aniseed drink like the Greek *ouzo* or Arab *arak*; do as the Turks do and cut it by half with water if you don't want to suffer ill effects. Turkish *şarap* (wine), both *kırmızı* (red) and *beyaz* (white), is improving in quality and is well worth the occasional splurge. You can buy Tuborg or Efes Pilsen beers everywhere, although outside the resorts you may need to find a Tekel store (the state-owned alcoholic-beverage and tobacco company) to buy wine.

Ayran is a yoghurt drink that's made by whipping up yoghurt with water and salt. Bottled water is sold everywhere, as are all sorts of packaged fruit juices and canned soft drinks.

Restaurants in Turkey are open roughly from 8am to 10pm, depending on the venue's size and clientele. Bars usually start serving between 5pm and 8pm, although in tourist areas they might be open all day as well.

If smoking were a sport, this country would be unbeatable. Antismoking laws are gradually being introduced but it's still a common sight to see people lighting up at breakfast tables in hotels.

İSTANBUL

☎ 0212 / pop 16 million

İstanbul's populous neighbourhoods, dating from the Byzantine era, from the golden age of the Ottoman sultans and from recent, less affluent times, form a dilapidated but ultimately cohesive mosaic. Here you can retrace the steps of the Byzantine emperors when visiting Sultanahmet's monuments and museums; marvel at the magnificent Ottoman mosques on the city's seven hills; and wander the cobbled streets of ancient Jewish, Greek and Armenian neighbourhoods. Centuries of urban sprawl unfurl before your eyes on ferry trips up the Bosphorus.

The feeling of *hüzün* (melancholy) that the city once had is being replaced with a sense of energy, innovation and optimism not seen since the days of Süleyman the Magnificent. Stunning contemporary art galleries are opening around the city, and the possibility of a European-flavoured future is being embraced in the rooftop bars of Beyoğlu and the boardrooms of Levent. There has never been a better time to visit.

HISTORY

Late in the 2nd century AD, the Roman Empire conquered the small city-state of Byzantium, which was renamed Constantinople in AD 330 after Emperor Constantine moved his capital there. The city walls kept out barbarians for centuries while the western part of the Roman Empire collapsed. When Constantinople fell for the first time in 1204, it was ransacked by the loot-hungry Europeans of the Fourth Crusade.

İstanbul only regained its former glory after 1453, when it was captured by Mehmet the Conqueror and made capital of the Ottoman Empire. During the glittering reign of Süleyman the Magnificent (1520–66), the city was graced with many beautiful new buildings, and retained much of its charm even during the empire's long decline.

Occupied by Allied forces after WWI, the city came to be thought of as the decadent playpen of the sultans, notorious for its

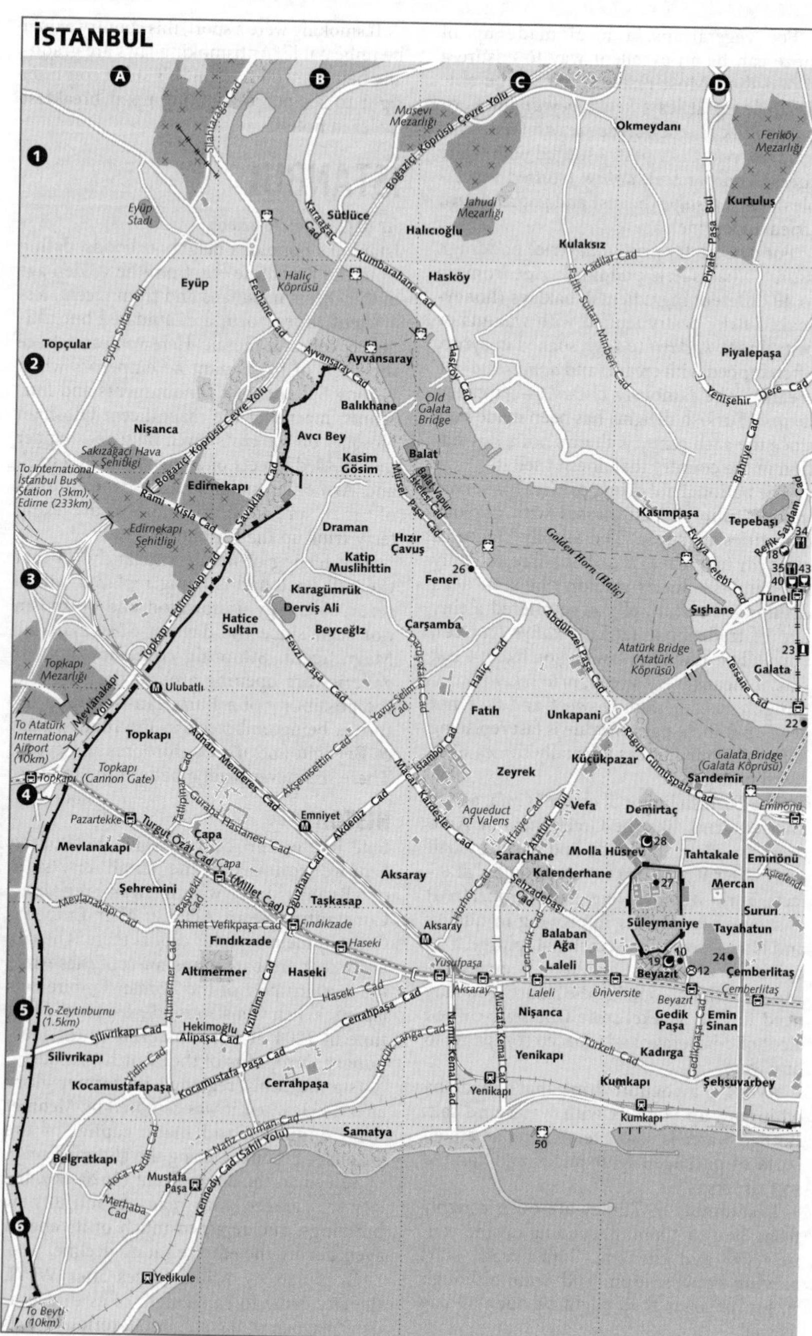
İSTANBUL
Musevi Mezarlığı
Okmeydanı
Feriköy Mezarlığı
Silahtarağa Cad
Boğaziçi Köprüsü Çevre Yolu
Eyüp Stadı
Sütlüce
Jahudi Mezarlığı
Kurtuluş
Karaağaç Cad
Halıcıoğlu
Kulaksız
Kadılar Cad
Piyale Paşa Bul
Eyüp
Haliç Köprüsü
Kumbarahane Cad
Hasköy
Fatih Sultan Minber Cad
Eyüp Sultan Bul
Feshane Cad
Topçular
Ayvansaray
Hasköy Cad
Piyalepaşa
Ayvansaray Cad
Yenişehir
Dere Cad
Balıkhane
Old Galata Bridge
Nişanca
Avcı Bey
Sakızağacı Hava Şehitliği
Balat
Bahriye Cad
To International İstanbul Bus Station (3km); Edirne (233km)
Kasim Gösim
Balat Vapur İskelesi Cad
Mürsel Paşa Cad
Edirnekapı
Savaklar Cad
Rami Kışla Cad
Kasımpaşa
Tepebaşı
Refik Saydam Cad
Draman
Edirnekapı Şehitliği
Hızır Çavuş
Golden Horn (Haliç)
Evliya Çelebi Cad
Katip Muslihittin
Fener
Tünel
Karagümrük
Derviş Ali
Topkapı - Edirnekapı Cad
Şişhane
Hatice Sultan
Beyceğiz
Çarşamba
Abdülezel Paşa Cad
Topkapı Mezarlığı
Fevzi Paşa Cad
Haliç Cad
Atatürk Bridge (Atatürk Köprüsü)
Galata
Ulubatlı
Darüşşafaka Cad
Tersane Cad
Yavuz Selim Cad
Mevlanakapı Yolu
Fatıh
Unkapani
To Atatürk International Airport (10km)
Topkapı
Adnan Menderes Cad
Akşemsettin Cad
İstanbol Cad
Ragıp Gümüşpala Cad
Galata Bridge (Galata Köprüsü)
Topkapı (Cannon Gate)
Zeyrek
Küçükpazar
Sandemir
Tatlıpınar Cad
Guraba Hastanesi Cad
Macar Kardeşler Cad
Vefa
Eminönü
Pazartekke
Turgut Özal Cad
Emniyet
Akdeniz Cad
Aqueduct of Valens
İtfaiye Cad
Atatürk Bul
Demirtaç
Çapa
Molla Hüsrev
Mevlanakapı
Saraçhane
Tahtakale
(Millet Cad)
Oğuzhan Cad
Aksaray
Kalenderhane
Aşirefendi
Şehremini
Şehzadebaşı Cad
Mercan
Başvekil Cad
Taşkasap
Horhor Cad
Mevlanakapı Cad
Süleymaniye
Sururi
Tayahatun
Ahmet Vefikpaşa Cad
Fındıkzade
Gençtürk Cad
Balaban Ağa
Haseki
Laleli
Beyazıt
Çemberlitaş
Altımermer
Altımermer Cad
Kızılelma Cad
Yusufpaşa
Üniversite
Haseki Cad
Mustafa Kemal Cad
Nişanca
Gedik Paşa
Emin Sinan
To Zeytinburnu (1.5km)
Cerrahpaşa Cad
Gedikpaşa Cad
Silivrikapı Cad
Hekimoğlu Alipaşa Cad
Namık Kemal Cad
Küçük Langa Cad
Türkeli Cad
Silivrikapı
Yenikapı
Kadırga
Vidin Cad
Kocamustafa Paşa Cad
Kocamustafapaşa
Cerrahpaşa
Kumkapı
Şehsuvarbey
A Nafiz Gürman Cad
Samatya
Belgratkapı
Hoca Kadın Cad
Kennedy Cad (Sahil Yolu)
Mustafa Paşa
Merhaba Cad
Yedikule
To Beyti (10km)

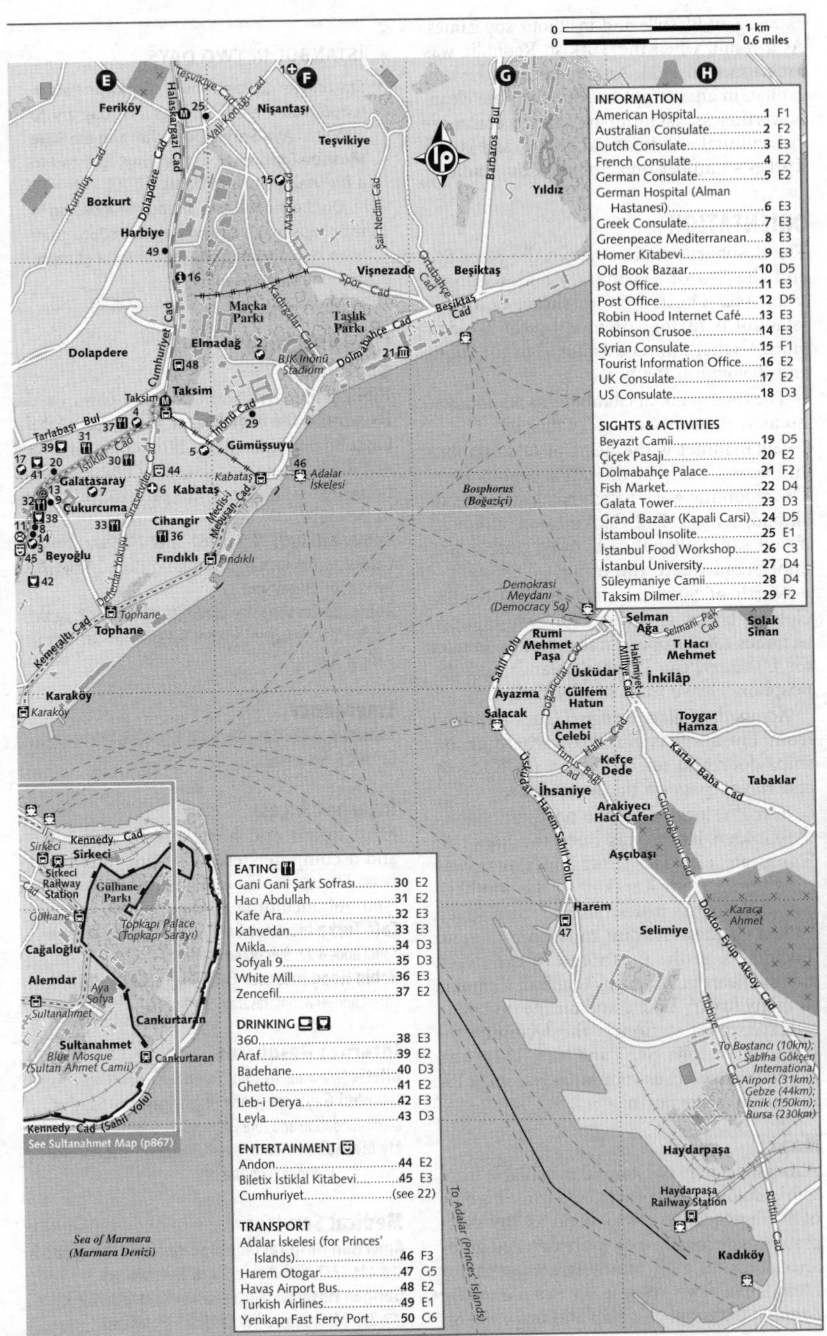
0 1 km
0 0.6 miles
E
F
G
H
INFORMATION
American Hospital....1 F1
Australian Consulate....2 F2
Dutch Consulate....3 E3
French Consulate....4 E2
German Consulate....5 E2
German Hospital (Alman Hastanesi)....6 E3
Greek Consulate....7 E3
Greenpeace Mediterranean....8 E3
Homer Kitabevi....9 E3
Old Book Bazaar....10 D5
Post Office....11 E3
Post Office....12 D5
Robin Hood Internet Café....13 E3
Robinson Crusoe....14 E3
Syrian Consulate....15 F1
Tourist Information Office....16 E2
UK Consulate....17 E2
US Consulate....18 D3
SIGHTS & ACTIVITIES
Beyazıt Camii....19 D5
Çiçek Pasajı....20 E2
Dolmabahçe Palace....21 F2
Fish Market....22 D4
Galata Tower....23 D3
Grand Bazaar (Kapali Carsi)....24 D5
İstamboul Insolite....25 E1
İstanbul Food Workshop....26 C3
İstanbul University....27 D4
Süleymaniye Camii....28 D4
Taksim Dilmer....29 F2
EATING
Gani Gani Şark Sofrası....30 E2
Hacı Abdullah....31 E2
Kafe Ara....32 E3
Kahvedan....33 E3
Mikla....34 D3
Sofyalı 9....35 D3
White Mill....36 E3
Zencefil....37 E2
DRINKING
360....38 E3
Araf....39 E2
Badehane....40 D3
Ghetto....41 E2
Leb-i Derya....42 E3
Leyla....43 D3
ENTERTAINMENT
Andon....44 E2
Biletix İstiklal Kitabevi....45 E3
Cumhuriyet....(see 22)
TRANSPORT
Adalar İskelesi (for Princes' Islands)....46 F3
Harem Otogar....47 G5
Havaş Airport Bus....48 E2
Turkish Airlines....49 E1
Yenikapı Fast Ferry Port....50 C6
Feriköy
Nişantaşı
Teşvikiye
Bozkurt
Harbiye
Yıldız
Vişnezade
Beşiktaş
Maçka Parkı
Taşlık Parkı
Elmadağ
BJK İnönü Stadium
Dolapdere
Taksim
Gümüşsuyu
Galatasaray
Kabataş
Çukurcuma
Cihangir
Beyoğlu
Fındıklı
Tophane
Karaköy
Bosphorus (Boğaziçi)
Adalar İskelesi
Demokrasi Meydanı (Democracy Sq)
Selman Ağa
Solak Sinan
Rumi Mehmet Paşa
T Hacı Mehmet
Üsküdar
İnkilâp
Ayazma
Gülfem Hatun
Salacak
Ahmet Çelebi
Toygar Hamza
Kefçe Dede
Tabaklar
İhsaniye
Arakiyeci Haci Cafer
Aşçıbaşı
Harem
Selimiye
Karaca Ahmet
Haydarpaşa
Haydarpaşa Railway Station
Kadıköy
To Bostancı (10km); Sabiha Gökçen International Airport (31km); Gebze (44km); İznik (150km); Bursa (230km)
To Adalar (Princes' Islands)
Sirkeci
Sirkeci Railway Station
Gülhane Parkı
Topkapı Palace (Topkapı Sarayı)
Cağaloğlu
Alemdar
Aya Sofya
Sultanahmet
Cankurtaran
Blue Mosque (Sultan Ahmet Camii)
Kennedy Cad (Sahil Yolu)
See Sultanahmet Map (p867)
Sea of Marmara (Marmara Denizi)
TURKEY

extravagant lifestyle and insidious spy games. As a result, when the Turkish Republic was proclaimed in 1923, Ankara became the new capital, in an attempt to wipe the slate clean. Nevertheless, İstanbul remains a commercial, cultural and financial centre, and is still Turkey's number-one city in all but name.

ORIENTATION

The Bosphorus strait, between the Black Sea and the Sea of Marmara, divides Europe from Asia. On its western shore, European İstanbul is further divided by the Golden Horn (Haliç) into Old İstanbul in the south and Beyoğlu in the north.

The International İstanbul Bus Station is at Esenler, about 10km west of the city.

Sultanahmet is the heart of Old İstanbul and boasts many of the city's famous sites. The adjoining area, which has hotels to suit all budgets, is called Cankurtaran, although if you say 'Sultanahmet' most people will understand where you mean.

North of Sultanahmet, situated on the Golden Horn, is Sirkeci Railway Station, terminus for European train services. Ferries for Üsküdar, the Princes' Islands and the Bosphorus leave from nearby Eminönü.

Across the Galata Bridge (Galata Köprüsü) from Eminönü is Karaköy, where cruise ships dock and ferries depart for Kadıköy and Haydarpaşa on the Asian shore.

Beyoğlu, located on the northern side of the Golden Horn, was once the 'new', or 'European', city. The Tünel funicular railway runs uphill from Karaköy to the southern end of Beyoğlu's pedestrianised main street, İstiklal Caddesi. A tram runs from there to Taksim Sq, at the north end of the street, and the heart of 'modern' İstanbul; it's home to many luxury hotels and airline offices.

Haydarpaşa station is the terminus for trains to Anatolia, Syria and Iran. There's an intercity *otogar* (bus station) at Harem, a 10-minute taxi ride north.

Maps

A free sheet map of İstanbul is available from tourist information offices, and while it's only of average quality, it's as good as any sheet map on sale locally. For more detailed guidance, including all minor streets, look for MepMedya's two-volume *İlçe İlçe A'dan Z'ye İstanbul* (İstanbul city plan and map; TL75).

İSTANBUL IN TWO DAYS

Starting in Sultanahmet, **Topkapı Palace** (p866) could easily fill your first day; try to also fit in **Aya Sofya** (opposite) and the **Blue Mosque** (opposite). In the evening, head to a *hammam* (Turkish bath).

On the second day, spend the morning in the chaos of the **Grand Bazaar** (p866), then head over to **Beyoğlu** (p869) for a glimpse of modern İstanbul.

INFORMATION

Bookshops

Bibliophiles will want to head towards the Byzantine **Old Book Bazaar** (Map pp862-3; Sahaflar Çarşısı, Beyazıt), in a shady little courtyard west of the Grand Bazaar; İstanbul's best range of bookshops is along or just off İstiklal Caddesi in Beyoğlu.

Homer Kitabevi (Map pp862-3; ☎ 249 5902; Yeni Çarşı Caddesi 28, Galatasaray, Beyoğlu; ⏰ 10am-7.30pm Mon-Sat, 12.30-7.30pm Sun)

Robinson Crusoe (Map pp862-3; ☎ 293 6968; İstiklal Caddesi 389, Beyoğlu; ⏰ 9am-9.30pm Mon-Sat, 10am-9.30pm Sun)

Emergency

Tourist police (Map p867; ☎ 527 4503; Yerebatan Caddesi 6, Sultanahmet)

Internet Access

Most hotels and hostels have wi-fi access and a computer terminal with internet access. There are also internet cafes throughout İstanbul, including the following:

Café Turka Internet Café (Map p867; 2nd fl, Divan Yolu Caddesi 22, Sultanahmet; per hr TL2)

Robin Hood Internet Café (Map pp862-3; 4th fl, Yeni Çarşı Caddesi 8, Galatasaray; per hr TL2)

Internet Resources

Biletix (www.biletix.com) Entertainment listings.

Istanbul Gay.com (www.istanbulgay.com) Gay chat, accommodation and tours.

My Merhaba (www.mymerhaba.com) Expat resource giving the low-down on the city.

Medical Services

American Hospital (Amerikan Hastanesi; Map pp862-3; ☎ 444 3777; Güzelbahçe Sokak 20, Nişantaşı)

German Hospital (Alman Hastanesi; Map pp862-3; ☎ 293 2150; Sıraselviler Caddesi 119, Taksim)

Money

Banks, ATMs and exchange offices are widespread, including in Sultanahmet's Aya Sofya Meydanı (Map p867) and along İstiklal Caddesi in Beyoğlu. The exchange rates offered at the airport are usually as good as those offered in town.

Post

İstanbul's central **post office** (Map pp862–3) is a few blocks southwest of Sirkeci Railway Station. There are branch post, telephone and telegraph offices (PTTs) in the Grand Bazaar, in Beyoğlu (Map pp862–3) near the Galata Bridge and near Galatasaray Sq, and at both airports.

Telephone

İstanbul has two area codes: ☎ 0212 for the European side, ☎ 0216 for the Asian zone. All numbers here use the ☎ 0212 code unless otherwise indicated.

Tourist Information

Tourist offices can be found at several locations:

Atatürk International Airport (🕑 24hr) Booth in international arrivals area.

Elmadağ (Map pp862-3; ☎ 233 0592; 🕑 9am-5pm Mon-Sat) In the arcade in front of the İstanbul Hilton Hotel, just off Cumhuriyet Caddesi. About a 10-minute walk north of Taksim Sq.

Sultanahmet (Map p867; ☎ 518 8754; 🕑 9am-5pm) At the northeast end of the Hippodrome.

Travel Agencies

Fez Travel (Map p867; ☎ 516 9024; www.feztravel.com; Akbıyık Caddesi 15, Sultanahmet)

Senkron Travel (Map p867; ☎ 638 8340; www.senkrontours.com; Arasta Bazaar 51, Sultanahmet)

DANGERS & ANNOYANCES

İstanbul is no more nor less safe a city than any large metropolis, but are there some dangers worth highlighting. Some İstanbullus drive like rally drivers, and there is no such thing as right of way for pedestrians, despite the little green man. As a pedestrian, give way to cars and trucks in all situations, even if you have to jump out of the way. Bag-snatching is also a slight problem, especially on Galipdede Sokak in Tünel and on İstiklal Caddesi's side streets. Lastly, and probably most importantly, you should be aware of the long-standing scam involving men, bars and women. See p929 for the low-down. The PKK (Kurdistan Workers Party) separatist group sporadically targets İstanbul with bombings, normally aimed at affluent, touristy neighbourhoods; the most recent was a double bomb attack in July 2008.

SIGHTS & ACTIVITIES

Old İstanbul

The Sultanahmet area is 'Old İstanbul', a Unesco-designated World Heritage site packed with so many wonderful sights you could spend several weeks here and still only scratch the surface.

AYA SOFYA (CHURCH OF HOLY WISDOM)

No doubt you will gasp at the overblown splendour of **Aya Sofya** (Map p867; ☎ 522 0989; Aya Sofya Meydanı, Sultanahmet; adult/child under 6 TL20/free; 🕑 9am-7.30pm Tue-Sun, upper gallery closes 15-30 mins earlier), one of the world's most glorious buildings. Built as part of Emperor Justinian's (527–65) effort to restore the greatness of the Roman Empire, it was completed in AD 537 and reigned as the grandest church in Christendom until the Conquest in 1453. The exterior does impress, but the interior, with its sublime domed ceiling soaring heavenward, is truly over-the-top.

Supported by 40 massive ribs, the dome was constructed of special hollow bricks made in Rhodes from a unique light, porous clay. These rest on huge pillars concealed in the interior walls, which creates an impression that the dome hovers unsupported. An official guide costs TL50 for 45 minutes.

BLUE MOSQUE

Another striking monument, the **Blue Mosque** (Sultan Ahmet Camii; Map p867; Hippodrome, Sultanahmet; 🕑 closed during prayer times), just south of Aya Sofya, is a voluptuous architectural feat. It was built between 1606 and 1616, and is light and delicate compared with its squat neighbour, Aya Sofya. The graceful exterior is notable for its six slender minarets and a cascade of domes and half domes; the inside is a luminous blue, created by the tiled walls and painted dome.

Rents from the *arasta* (row of shops) to the east provide support for the Blue Mosque's upkeep, and it's also a great hassle-free spot to shop. Nearby the *arasta* is the entrance to the **Great Palace Mosaic Museum** (Büyüksaray Mozaik Müzesi; Map p867; ☎ 518 1205; Torun Sokak; admission

WI-FI ACCESS

There's wi-fi access at Atatürk International and Sabiha Gökçen International airports, at **Java Studio** (Map p867; ☎ 0212-517 2378; Dalbastı Sokak 13) in Sultanahmet, at Kahvedan (p872) in Cihangir and at branches of Kahve Dünyası, Starbucks, Ozsüt and Gloria Jeans.

TL8; 9am-6.30pm Tue-Sun), a spectacular stretch of ancient Byzantine pavement featuring hunting scenes.

TOPKAPI SARAYI

Possibly İstanbul's most iconic monument, opulent **Topkapı Sarayı** (Topkapı Palace; Map p867; ☎ 512 0480; Babıhümayun Caddesi; palace TL20, harem TL15; 9am-7pm Wed-Mon summer) is a highlight of any trip. The palace was begun by Mehmet shortly after the Conquest in 1453, and Ottoman sultans lived in this impressive environment until the 19th century. It consists of four massive courtyards and a series of imperial buildings, including pavilions, barracks, audience chambers and sleeping quarters. Make sure you visit the mind-blowing **harem**, the palace's most famous sight, and the **treasury**, which features an incredible collection of precious objects.

GRAND BAZAAR

Hone your haggling skills before dipping into the mind-boggling **Grand Bazaar** (Kapalı Çarşı; Map pp862-3; 9am-7pm Mon-Sat) covered market. Just north of Divan Yolu, this labyrinthine medieval shopping mall consists of some 4000 shops selling everything from carpets to clothing, including silverware, jewellery, antiques and belly-dancing costumes. Starting from a small masonry *bedesten* (market enclosure) built during the time of Mehmet the Conqueror, the bazaar has grown to cover a vast area. It's probably the most discombobulating and manic shopping precinct you could hope to experience. Sure, the touts are ubiquitous, but come in the right frame of mind and you'll realise it's part of the fun. With several kilometres of lanes, it's also a great place to ramble and get lost – which you will certainly do at least once.

BASILICA CISTERN

Across the tram lines from Aya Sofya is the entrance to the majestic Byzantine **Basilica Cistern** (Yerebatan Sarnıçı; Map p867; ☎ 522 1259; Yerebatan Caddesi 13, Sultanahmet; admission TL10; 9am-6.30pm Apr-Sep), built by Justinian in AD 532. This vast, atmospheric, column-filled cistern stored up to 80,000 cubic metres of water for regular summer use in the Great Palace, as well as for times of siege.

İSTANBUL ARCHAEOLOGY MUSEUM

Downhill from the Topkapı Palace, this superb **museum complex** (Arkeoloji Müzeleri; Map p867; ☎ 520 7740; Osman Hamdi Bey Yokuşu, Gülhane; admission TL10; 9am-5pm Tue-Sun) is a must-see for anyone interested in the Middle East's ancient past. The main building houses an outstanding collection of Greek and Roman statuary, including the magnificent sarcophagi from the royal necropolis at Sidon in Lebanon.

In a separate building, the **Museum of the Ancient Orient** houses Hittite and other older archaeological finds. Also on the grounds is the **Tiled Pavilion** (Çinili Köşk), one of İstanbul's oldest Ottoman buildings.

DIVAN YOLU CADDESI

Walk or take a tram westward along Divan Yolu from Sultanahmet, looking out on your right for a complex of **tombs** (Map p867) that was constructed for some 19th-century sultans, including Mahmut II (1808–39), Abdülaziz (1861–76) and Abdülhamid II (1876–1909).

A bit further along, on the right, you can't miss the **Çemberlitaş**, also known as the Banded Stone or Burnt Column. Constantine the Great erected the monumental column in 330 to celebrate the dedication of Constantinople as capital of the Roman Empire; it has been covered with hoardings and awaiting renovation for years.

HIPPODROME

In front of the Blue Mosque is the **Hippodrome** (Atmeydanı; Map p867), where chariot races once took place. It was also the scene of a series of riots during Justinian's rule. While construction started in AD 203, the Hippodrome was later added to and enlarged by Constantine.

The **Obelisk of Theodosius** (Map p867) is an Egyptian column from the temple of Karnak. It features 3500-year-old hieroglyphics and rests on a Byzantine base. The 10m-high **Obelisk of Constantine Porphyrogenitus** (Map p867) was once covered in bronze, subsequently stolen by the Crusaders. The base

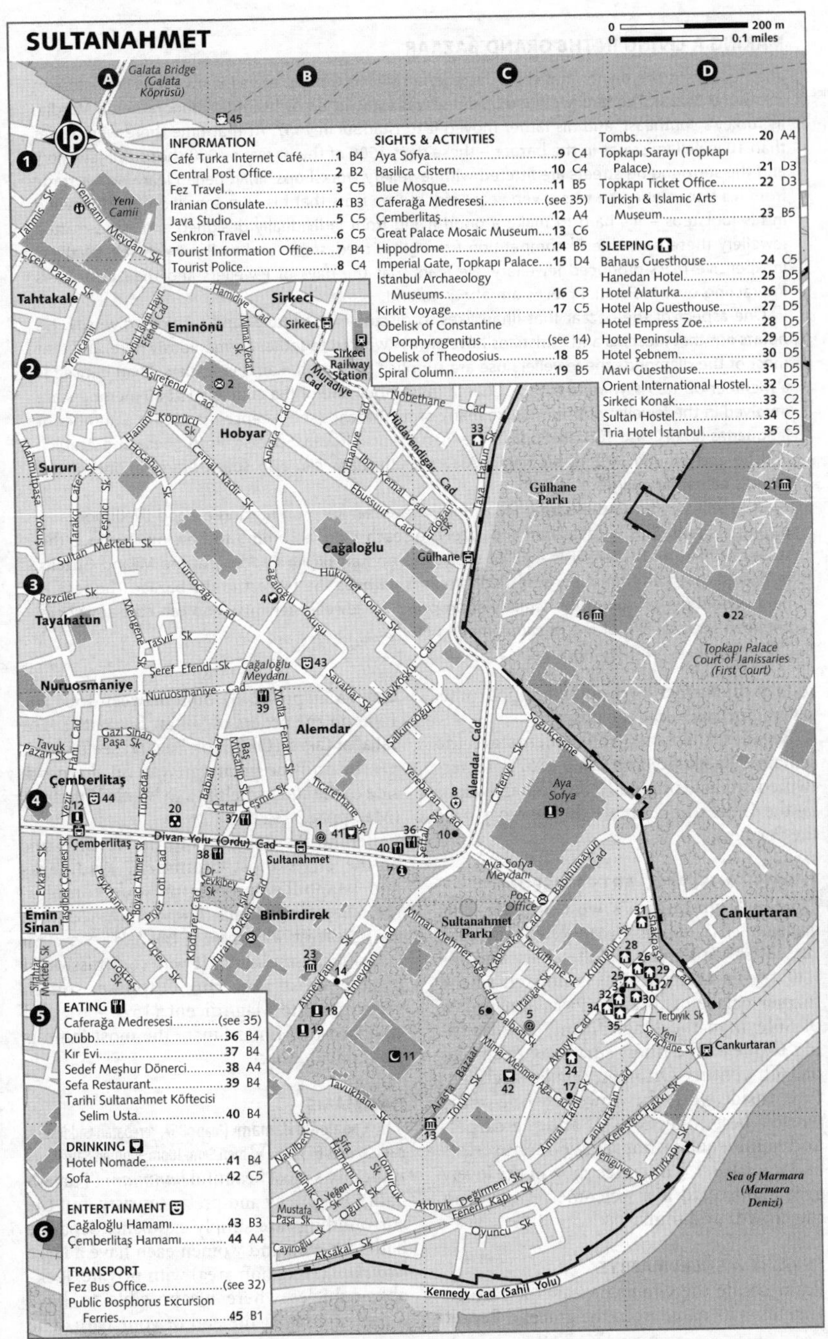
SULTANAHMET
0 200 m
0 0.1 miles
INFORMATION
Café Turka Internet Café.........1 B4
Central Post Office.........2 B2
Fez Travel.........3 C5
Iranian Consulate.........4 B3
Java Studio.........5 C5
Senkron Travel.........6 C5
Tourist Information Office.........7 B4
Tourist Police.........8 C4
SIGHTS & ACTIVITIES
Aya Sofya.........9 C4
Basilica Cistern.........10 C4
Blue Mosque.........11 B5
Caferağa Medresesi.........(see 35)
Çemberlitaş.........12 A4
Great Palace Mosaic Museum.........13 C6
Hippodrome.........14 B5
Imperial Gate, Topkapı Palace.........15 D4
İstanbul Archaeology Museums.........16 C3
Kirkit Voyage.........17 C5
Obelisk of Constantine Porphyrogenitus.........(see 14)
Obelisk of Theodosius.........18 B5
Spiral Column.........19 B5
Tombs.........20 A4
Topkapı Sarayı (Topkapı Palace).........21 D3
Topkapı Ticket Office.........22 D3
Turkish & Islamic Arts Museum.........23 B5
SLEEPING
Bahaus Guesthouse.........24 C5
Hanedan Hotel.........25 D5
Hotel Alaturka.........26 D5
Hotel Alp Guesthouse.........27 D5
Hotel Empress Zoe.........28 D5
Hotel Peninsula.........29 D5
Hotel Şebnem.........30 D5
Mavi Guesthouse.........31 D5
Orient International Hostel.........32 C5
Sirkeci Konak.........33 C2
Sultan Hostel.........34 C5
Tria Hotel İstanbul.........35 C5
EATING
Caferağa Medresesi.........(see 35)
Dubb.........36 B4
Kır Evi.........37 B4
Sedef Meşhur Dönerci.........38 A4
Sefa Restaurant.........39 B4
Tarihi Sultanahmet Köftecisi Selim Usta.........40 B4
DRINKING
Hotel Nomade.........41 B4
Sofa.........42 C5
ENTERTAINMENT
Cağaloğlu Hamamı.........43 B3
Çemberlitaş Hamamı.........44 A4
TRANSPORT
Fez Bus Office.........(see 32)
Public Bosphorus Excursion Ferries.........45 B1
Galata Bridge (Galata Köprüsü)
Sea of Marmara (Marmara Denizi)
Topkapı Palace Court of Janissaries (First Court)
Gülhane Parkı
Sultanahmet Parkı
Aya Sofya Meydanı
Sirkeci Railway Station
Eminönü
Sirkeci
Tahtakale
Hobyar
Cağaloğlu
Alemdar
Çemberlitaş
Binbirdirek
Cankurtaran
Nuruosmaniye
Tayahatun
Sururi
Emin Sinan
Divan Yolu (Ordu) Cad
Kennedy Cad (Sahil Yolu)

MAKING A LIVING IN THE GRAND BAZAAR

İlhan Güzeliş is the owner and chief designer at Milano Güzeliş, a well-known jewellery store in the Grand Bazaar. The family-owned business was established by his great-grandfather in Mardin, in Turkey's southeast, and his father moved it to İstanbul in 1957. At that time there were fewer than 10 jewellery stores in the bazaar – these days 1500 of the bazaar's 4000 shops sell jewellery and the surrounding streets are littered with jewellery workshops. İlhan began learning his trade from his father when he was seven years old, but he fears that his own sons won't be following in his footsteps – it's hard to make a good living from individually designed and hand-crafted jewellery these days due to competition from glitzy megastores and malls, which sell relatively inexpensive mass-produced jewellery. He fears that the days of jewellers and their customers interacting over individual pieces are about to end.

One aspect of the bazaar that İlhan likes to discuss is its cultural and religious diversity. He points out that Muslims and Christians have always worked together harmoniously here, and that most of the diamonds the jewellers use are supplied by Jewish diamond traders. İlhan himself is a member of the Assyrian Orthodox Church in İstanbul; half of the church's 15,000 members are involved in the jewellery business. Like many of the bazaar's shopkeepers he speaks a number of languages (in his case Turkish, English, German, French, Italian, Spanish, Portuguese and Arabic), and he and around 50% of his fellow Assyrian Christians can also speak Aramaic, one of the world's oldest languages.

İlhan will stay on in the bazaar for as long as he can keep on making a good livelihood and paying his rent. This is calculated separately for each store according to how much space the store occupies and where it is – all of the stores on Kalpakçılar Caddesi, where Milano Güzeliş is located, pay hefty rents because their street is perhaps the busiest in the bazaar. The rent is paid in gold (which seems particularly appropriate for jeweller tenants), and can cost anywhere between 500g to 8kg of the precious metal per year.

rests at the former level of the Hippodrome, several metres below the ground.

Between these two monuments are the remains of a **spiral column** (Map p867) of intertwined snakes, originally erected at Delphi by the Greeks to celebrate their victory over the Persians.

TURKEY

TURKISH & ISLAMIC ARTS MUSEUM

On the Hippodrome's western side, this **museum** (Türk ve İslam Eserleri Müzesi; Map p867; ☎ 518 1805; At Meydanı 46, Sultanahmet; admission TL10; 🕑 9am-4.30pm Tue-Sun) is housed in the former palace of İbrahim Paşa, son-in-law of Süleyman the Magnificent. The building is one of the finest surviving examples of 16th-century Ottoman secular architecture. Inside, you'll be wowed by one of the world's best collections of antique carpets and some equally impressive manuscripts and miniatures. The coffee shop in the lovely green courtyard is a welcome refuge from the crowds and touts.

BEYAZIT & SÜLEYMANIYE

Right beside the Grand Bazaar, the Beyazıt area takes its name from the graceful **Beyazıt Camii** (Map pp862–3), built between 1501 and 1506 on the orders of Sultan Beyazıt II. The **Sahaflar Çarşısı** (Old Book Bazaar; see p864) is nearby and the great gateway on the north side of the square belongs to **İstanbul University** (Map pp862–3).

Behind the university to the north is one of the city's most prominent landmarks and İstanbul's grandest mosque complex, the **Süleymaniye Camii** (Mosque of Sultan Süleyman the Magnificent; Map pp862-3; Prof Sıddık Sami Onar Caddesi; donation requested). It was commissioned by the most powerful Ottoman sultan, Süleyman the Magnificent (1520–66), and designed by Mimar Sinan, the most famous Imperial architect.

HAMMAMS

The **Cağaloğlu Hamamı** (Map p867; Yerebatan Caddesi 34; bath services €15-50; 🕑 men 8am-10pm, women 8am-8pm) is the city's most beautiful *hammam* (Turkish bath). It's pricey and pretty touristy, but the surroundings are simply exquisite. Separate baths for men and women each have a large *camekan* (reception area) with private, lockable cubicles where it's possible to have a nap or a tea at the end of your bath. The

Çemberlitaş Hamamı (Map p867; Vezir Hanı Caddesi 8, Çemberlitaş; bath services €14.50-39.50; 6am-midnight) was designed by the great Ottoman architect Mimar Sinan in 1584, and is one of İstanbul's most atmospheric *hammams.*

Dolmabahçe Palace

Cross the Galata Bridge and follow the shore road along the Bosphorus from Karaköy towards Ortaköy and you'll come to the grandiose **Dolmabahçe Palace** (Dolmabahçe Sarayı; Map pp862-3; ☎ 236 9000; Dolmabahçe Caddesi, Beşiktaş; selamlık TL15, harem-cariyeler TL10, selamlık & harem-cariyeler TL20, crystal palace & clock museum TL4; 9am-4pm Tue-Wed & Fri-Sun), right on the waterfront. The palace was built between 1843 and 1856 as a home for some of the last Ottoman sultans. It was guaranteed a place in the history books when Atatürk died here on 10 November 1938 and all the palace clocks stopped.

Visitors are taken on guided tours of the two main buildings: the over-the-top **selamlık** (men's apartments) and the slightly more restrained **harem-cariyeler** (harem and concubines' quarters).

Buses heading out of Karaköy along the Bosphorus shore road stop at Dolmabahçe.

Beyoğlu

Beyoğlu is the heart of modern İstanbul and *the* hot spot for galleries, cafes and boutiques, with hip new restaurants opening almost nightly, and more bars then a bar-hopper could hope to prop up in a lifetime. The neighbourhood is a showcase of cosmopolitan Turkey at its best – miss Beyoğlu and you haven't seen İstanbul.

Stretching from Tünel Sq to Taksim Sq, **İstiklal Caddesi** (Independence Ave; Map pp862–3) was known as the Grande Rue de Péra in the late 19th century, and now it carries the life of the modern city up and down its lively promenade. It's indisputably Turkey's most famous thoroughfare, and a stroll along its length is a must – or ride on the picturesque restored tram that trundles up and down the pedestrianised boulevard.

There's a plethora of sights, but the **fish market** (*balık pazar*; Map pp862–3) and, in the Cité de Pera building, the **Çiçek Pasajı** (Flower Passage; Map pp862–3) are absolute must-sees; both are near the Galatasaray Lisesi (a prestigious public school). These days locals bypass the touts and the mediocre food on offer at Çiçek Pasjı and make their way behind the passage to one of İstanbul's most colourful and popular eating and drinking precincts, Nevizade Sokak.

Uphill from Karaköy, the cylindrical **Galata Tower** (Galata Kulesi; Map pp862-3; Galata Meydanı, Karaköy; admission €5; 9am-8pm) dates from 1348, when Galata was a Genoese trading colony. It has survived several earthquakes, as well as the demolition of the rest of the Genoese walls in the mid-19th century. There are spectacular views from its vertiginous panoramic balcony, but the entry fee is a little inflated, so you may prefer the terrace of the Anemon Galata Hotel opposite.

THE PLEASURES OF THE BATH

After a long day's sightseeing, few things could be better than relaxing in a *hammam* (Turkish bath). The ritual is invariably the same. First, you'll be shown to a cubicle where you can undress, store your clothes and wrap the provided *peştamal* (cloth) around you. Then an attendant will lead you through to the hot room, where you sit and sweat for a while.

Next you'll have to make a choice. It's cheapest to wash yourself with the soap, shampoo and towel you brought with you. The hot room will be ringed with individual basins that you fill from the taps above, before sluicing the water over yourself with a plastic scoop. But it's far more enjoyable to let an attendant do it for you, dousing you with warm water and then scrubbing you with a coarse cloth mitten. Afterwards you'll be lathered with a sudsy swab, rinsed off and shampooed.

When all this is complete, you're likely to be offered a massage, an experience worth having at least once during your trip.

Bath etiquette dictates that men should keep the *peştamal* on at all times.

Traditional *hammams* have separate sections for men and women or admit men and women at separate times. In tourist areas, most *hammams* are happy for foreign men and women to bathe together.

FREE THRILLS

İstanbul is such a richly cultural city that just wandering its streets and markets, marvelling at the mosques and smelling the *kebaps* (kebabs), is a great way to a get a taste of the place. At these six spots you can amble for free:

- **İstiklal Caddesi** (p869)
- **Grand Bazaar** (p866)
- **Sahaflar Çarşısı** (Old Book Bazaar; p868)
- **Divan Yolu Caddesi** (p866)
- **Blue Mosque** (p865)
- **Hippodrome** (p866)

Bosphorus Cruise

Don't leave the city without exploring the Bosphorus. Most day trippers take the much-loved **Public Bosphorus Excursion Ferry** (Map p867; one way/return TL10/17; 10.35am, noon & 1.35pm) trip up its entire length (90 minutes one way). These depart from Eminönü and stop at various points before turning around at Anadolu Kavağı. The shores are sprinkled with monuments and various sights, including the monumental Dolmabahçe Palace (p869), the majestic Bosphorus Bridge, the waterside suburbs of Arnavutköy, Bebek, Kanlıca, Emirgan and Sarıyer, as well as lavish *yalıs* (waterfront wooden summer residences) and numerous mosques.

Princes' Islands (Adalar)

With good beaches, open woodland, a couple of monasteries, Victorian villas and transport by horse-drawn carriages, this string of nine spotless islands, especially **Büyükada** (the biggest), make an ideal escape from the noise and hustle of İstanbul. Ferries (TL2.60) to the islands leave from the Adalar İskelesi dock at Kabataş (Map pp862–3), opposite the tram stop. Try to go midweek to avoid the crowds.

COURSES

Caferağa Medresesi (Map p867; ☎ 513 3601; www.tkhv.org; Caferiye Sokak, Sultanahmet) The Turkish Cultural Services Foundation runs courses in techniques such as calligraphy, miniature painting, *ebru* (traditional Turkish marbling), binding and glass painting.

İstanbul Food Workshop (Map pp862-3; ☎ 534 4788; www.istanbulfoodworkshop.com; Yıldırım Caddesi 111, Fener) A well-respected outfit running foodie walking tours as well as Turkish and Ottoman cooking classes.

Taksim Dilmer (Map pp862-3; ☎ 292 9696; www.dilmer.com; Tarık Zafer Tunaya Sokak 18, Taksim) This is probably the best known of the city's Turkish language schools, with courses lasting from four to 12 weeks.

TOURS

İstamboul Insolite (Map pp862-3; ☎ 241 2846; www.istanbulguide.net/insolite; Bahtiyar Sokak 6, Nışantaşı; full-day tours per person €50-150) This small agency runs a variety of offbeat tours.

Kirkit Voyage (Map p867; ☎ 518 2282; www.kirkit.com; Amiral Tafdil Sokak 12, Sultanahmet; half- & full-day tours €23-50) Kirkit specialises in small-group walking tours of the must-see sights.

FESTIVALS & EVENTS

The **İstanbul International Music Festival** (www.iksv.org/muzik), from early June to early July, attracts big-name artists from around the world, who perform in venues that are not always open to the public (such as Aya İrini Kilisesi).

SLEEPING

İstanbul's accommodation is becoming quite pricey. For the time being, the best area to stay remains Cankurtaran, where the quiet streets have moderate hotels with stunning views from their roof terraces, as well as some more luxurious options. Unless otherwise stated, rates include breakfast and private bathrooms; the exception is hostel dorms, which have shared bathrooms.

Budget

Private rooms are overpriced at some of these options.

Mavı Guesthouse (Map p867; ☎ 517 7287; www.maviguesthouse.com; Kutlugün Sokak 3, Sultanahmet; rooftop mattress/dm/d €8/12/36;) Tiny Mavi's management is very friendly, which is just as well since some of its rooms are cramped and windowless, with uncomfortable beds. Diehard backpackers might want to claim one of the 24 mattresses on the decrepit rooftop.

Bahaus Guesthouse (Map p867; ☎ 638 6534; www.travelinistanbul.com; Akbıyık Caddesi, Bayramfırını Sokak 11-13; dm €15, d with shared/private bathroom €40/50;) Generating great word of mouth, Bahaus' friendly and knowledgeable staff run a professional operation that avoids the institutional feel of some of its nearby competitors. Top marks go to the rooftop terrace bar.

Sultan Hostel (Map p867; ☎ 516 9260; www.sultanhostel.com; Akbıyık Caddesi 21, Cankurtaran; dm €14, d with shared/private bathroom €38/44;) The Sultan offers freshly painted dorms with new bunk beds and good mattresses, and a 10% discount for HI cardholders.

Orient International Hostel (Map p867; ☎ 518 0789; www.orienthostel.com; Akbıyık Caddesi 13, Cankurtaran; dm €14, s with shared bathroom €30, d with private bathroom €70; 🖳) Bursting with backpackers, the Orient should only be considered if you're young, don't care about creature comforts and are ready to party. There's a shower for every 12 guests and an array of dorms – from light and quiet to dark and uncomfortable.

our pick Hotel Peninsula (Map p867; ☎ 458 6850; www.hotelpeninsula.com; Adliye Sokak 6, Cankurtaran; s/d €35/45; ❄) This unassuming, superfriendly hotel has 12 comfortable rooms with private bathrooms, plus a lovely terrace with sea views and comfortable hammocks.

Midrange & Top End

Sultanahmet and Cankurtaran harbour a veritable smorgasbord of high-quality midrange options.

Hanedan Hotel (Map p867; ☎ 516 4869; www.hanedanhotel.com; Adliye Sokak 3, Cankurtaran; s €40, d €60-65; ❄) Pale lemon walls and polished wooden floors give the Hanedan's rooms an elegant feel, and the roof terrace offers views of the sea and Aya Sofya.

Hotel Alp Guesthouse (Map p867; ☎ 517 7067; www.alpguesthouse.com; Adliye Sokak 4, Cankurtaran; s/d €45/65; ❄) The Alp lives up to its location in Sultanahmet's premier small-hotel enclave, offering attractive, well-equipped rooms with four-poster beds at reasonable prices.

Hotel Alaturka (Map p867; ☎ 458 7900; www.hotelalaturka.com; Akbıyık Caddesi 5, Cankurtaran; s €70, d €85-105; ❄) Large rooms with mod-cons such as minibars and satellite TVs are the hallmarks of this immaculately maintained hotel. The decor is conservative, but pleasantly so, and the roof terrace has one of the area's best views.

Hotel Şebnem (Map p867; ☎ 517 6623; www.sebnemhotel.net; Adliye Sokak 1, Cankurtaran; s €70, d €90-100; ❄ 🖳) The Şebnem's pleasantly simple rooms have wooden floors, recently renovated bathrooms and comfortable beds. Framed Ottoman prints provide a touch of class.

Hotel Empress Zoe (Map p867; ☎ 518 2504; www.emzoe.com; Adliye Sokak 10, Cankurtaran; s €75, d €110-135, ste €120-240; ❄ 🖳) This American-owned boutique hotel has individually and charmingly decorated rooms and suites. Breakfast is served in a flower-filled garden, and there's a rooftop lounge-terrace with excellent views.

Tria Hotel İstanbul (Map p867; ☎ 518 4518; www.triahotelistanbul.com; Terbıyık Sokak 7, Cankurtaran; s €180, d €218-280; ❄ 🖳) Extremely comfortable and quiet rooms offer tea- and coffee-making equipment, flat-screen TVs, work desks and large beds; all are attractively decorated with polished floorboards, silk curtains, embroidered bedspreads and objets d'art. There's a comfortable lounge and a roof terrace with great views.

Sirkeci Konak (Map p867; ☎ 528 4344; Taya Hatun Sokak 5, Sirkeci; r €190-320; ❄ 🖳) Sirkeci's owners know what keeps guests happy: large, well-equipped rooms, with extras such as tea- and coffee-making equipment, satellite TV, quality toiletries and luxe linen. There's also a wellness centre with pool, gym and *hammam*, as well as complimentary afternoon teas and Anatolian cooking lessons.

EATING

Teeming with affordable fast-food joints, cafes and restaurants, İstanbul is a food-lover's paradise. Unfortunately, Sultanahmet has the least impressive range of eating options in the city, so we recommend crossing the Galata Bridge to join the locals.

Sultanahmet & Around

Nominating Sultanahmet's best take-away *döner kebap* is a hard ask, but many locals are keen on the *döner* (TL4 to TL9) at **Sedef Meşhur Dönerci** (Map p867; Divan Yolu), only open during the day.

Caferağa Medresesi (Map p867; ☎ 513 3601; Cafariye Sokak; soup TL3, köfte TL10; 🕑 8.30am-6pm) This teensy *lokanta* in the gorgeous courtyard of a Sinan-designed *medrese* near Topkapı Palace is a rare treat in Sultanahmet, allowing you to nosh in stylish surrounds without paying through the nose.

Tarihi Sultanahmet Köftecisi Selim Usta (Map p867; ☎ 520 0566; Divan Yolu Caddesi 12; 🕑 11am-11pm) Beware the other *köfte* places along this strip purporting to be the *meşhur* (famous) *köfte* restaurant – No 12 is the real McCoy.

Sefa Restaurant (Map p867; ☎ 520 0670; Nuruosmaniye Caddesi 17, Cağaloğlu; mains TL6.50-16; 🕑 7am-5pm) Locals favour this place on the way to the Grand Bazaar. You can order from an English-language menu or choose from the bain-marie. Try to arrive earlyish for lunch; many dishes run out by 1.30pm.

Kir Evi (Map p867; ☎ 512 6942; Hoca Rüstem Sokak 9; mains TL16.50-21; 🕑 10.30am-2.30am) Meals score for their size and price rather than their quality, but the biggest draw is the entertainment. Waiters serenade guests with everything from disco anthems to Arabesk numbers, and everyone joins in.

Dubb (Map p867; ☎ 513 7308; İncili Çavuş Sokak, Alemdar; TL12-24; ⌚ noon-3pm & 6-10.30pm) One of İstanbul's few Indian restaurants, Dubb specialises in mild tandoori dishes, but serves a range of fragrant curries, including vegetarian options. Its 4th-floor terrace offers views of Aya Sofya.

Beyoğlu & Around

Gani Gani Şark Sofrası (Map pp862-3; ☎ 244 8401; www.naumpasakonagi.com; Taksim Kuyu Sokak 11, Taksim; kebaps TL7.50-10; ⌚ 10am-11pm) Young Turkish couples love lolling on the traditional Anatolian seating at this cheap and friendly eatery. Tables and chairs are also available to enjoy the *kebaps, mantı* and pide.

Hacı Abdullah (Map pp862-3; ☎ 293 8561; www.haciadbullah.com.tr; Sakızağacı Caddesi 9a; mains TL9-18; ⌚ 11am-11pm) Just thinking about this İstanbul institution's *imam bayıldı* (eggplant stuffed with tomatoes, onions and garlic and cooked in olive oil) makes our taste buds go into overdrive.

Zencefil (Map pp862-3; ☎ 243 8234; Kurabiye Sokak 8, Taksim; mains TL10-12; ⌚ 11am-11pm Tue-Sun) Comfortable and quietly stylish, this popular vegetarian cafe offers crunchy-fresh organic produce, homemade bread and guilt-free desserts.

our pick **Sofyalı 9** (Map pp862-3; ☎ 245 0362; Sofyalı Sokak 9, Tünel; mains TL10-16; ⌚ 11am-1am Mon-Sat) Tables at this gem are hot property at weekends. It serves some of the city's best *meyhane* (tavern) food – notably the *Arnavut ciğeri* (Albanian fried liver), fried fish and meze – in surroundings as welcoming as they are attractive.

Kafe Ara (Map pp862-3; ☎ 245 4104; Tosbağ Sokak 8a, Galatasaray; mains TL13-18; ⌚ 8am-midnight) A converted garage with tables and chairs spilling into a wide laneway, Ara's a funky setting to enjoy paninis, salads and pastas.

Kahvedan (Map pp862-3; ☎ 292 4030; www.kahvedan.com; Akarsu Caddesi 50, Cihangir; mains TL13-21; ⌚ 9am-2am Mon-Fri, 9am-4am Sat & Sun) This expat haven serves dishes such as bacon and eggs, French toast and falafel wraps.

White Mill (Map pp862-3; ☎ 292 2895; www.whitemillcafe.com; Susam Sokak 13, Cihangir; mains TL15-23; ⌚ 9.30am-1.30am) This industrial-chic bar-restaurant serves tasty, organic food and, in fine weather, its rear garden is a wonderful spot to enjoy a leisurely breakfast.

> **SPLURGE**
>
> **Mikla** (Map pp862-3; ☎ 0212-293 5656; Marmara Pera Hotel, Meşrutiyet Caddesi 15, Tepebaşı; mains TL36-46.25; ⌚ noon-3pm & 7pm-1am Mon-Fri, 7pm-1am Sat) is the city's best restaurant – bar none. Local celebrity chef Mehmet Gürs is a master of perfectly executed Mediterranean cuisine, and the Turkish accents he employs make his food truly memorable. Extraordinary views, luxe surrounds and exemplary service complete the experience.

DRINKING

There's a thriving bar scene in Beyoğlu, which is almost permanently crowded with locals who patronise the atmosphere-laden *meyhaneler* (taverns) lining the side streets. There's nothing better than swigging a few glasses of *rakı* around Balo Sokak and Sofyalı Sokak, or in the sleek rooftop bars on both sides of İstiklal Caddesi.

Sultanahmet isn't as happening but it has a few decent watering holes, particularly on Akbıyık Caddesi in summer. The area's alcohol-free, atmosphere-rich *çay bahçesis* (tea gardens) or *kahvehanes* (coffee houses) are great for relaxing and sampling that great Turkish institution, the *nargileh* (water pipe), along with a cup of *Türk kahvesi* (Turkish coffee) or *çay*.

Sofa (Map p867; Mimar Mehmet Ağa Caddesi 32, Cankurtaran; ⌚ 11am-11pm) Candlelit tables beckon patrons into this friendly cafe-bar just off Akbıyık Caddesi, with a daily happy hour between 5pm and 6.30pm.

Hotel Nomade (Map p867; Ticarethane Sokak 15, Alemdar; ⌚ noon-11pm) This boutique hotel's terrace bar overlooks Aya Sofya and the Blue Mosque. Settle down in a comfortable chair to enjoy a glass of wine, beer or freshly squeezed fruit juice.

Badehane (Map pp862-3; ☎ 249 0550; General Yazgan Sokak 5, Tünel; ⌚ 9am-2am) This tiny unsigned watering hole is a favourite with locals for its cheap beer. On balmy evenings the laneway is crammed with chattering, chain-smoking artsy types.

Leyla (Map pp862-3; Tünel Sq 186a, Tünel; ⌚ 7am-2am) With a great location opposite the

Tünel entrance, trendy Leyla is a popular meeting place.

our pick **360** (Map pp862-3; 8th fl, İstiklal Caddesi 311, Galatasaray; ⌚ noon-2am Mon-Thu & Sun, 3pm-4am Fri & Sat) İstanbul's most famous bar, and deservedly so. If you can score one of the bar stools on the terrace you'll be happy indeed – the view is truly extraordinary.

Leb-i Derya (Map pp862-3; 7th fl, Kumbaracı Yokuşu 115, Tünel; ⌚ 11am-2am Mon-Fri, 8.30am-3am Sat & Sun) This unpretentious place, on the top floor of a dishevelled building off İstiklal Caddesi, is an İstanbul favourite for its Bosphorus and Old City views.

Beyoğlu's nightclubs include **Araf** (Map pp862-3; 5th fl, Balo Sokak 32; ⌚ 5pm-4am), popular among English teachers and Turkish-language students for its in-house Roma band and cheap beer; and, behind Çiçek Pasajı, **Ghetto** (Map pp862-3; Kalyoncu Kulluk Caddesi 10; ⌚ 8pm-4am), with bold postmodern decor and an interesting musical program featuring local and international acts.

ENTERTAINMENT

Check the newspaper booths in Sultanahmet for a copy of *Time Out Istanbul* (TL4), which carries monthly listings on every aspect of the city's cultural scene. **Biletix** (☎ 0216-556 9800; www.biletix.com) has booths throughout the city, including at **İstiklal Kitabevi** (Map pp862-3; İstiklal Caddesi 55, Beyoğlu), or you can buy tickets on its website using a credit card.

A classic İstanbul night out involves carousing to live *fasıl*, a raucous local form of Romani music. Two good *meyhaneler* for indulging in this time-honoured activity are **Cumhuriyet** (Map pp862-3; Sahne Sokak 4; ⌚ music 8.30pm-midnight most nights) in Beyoğlu's Balık Pazar; and **Andon** (Map pp862-3; Sıraselviler Caddesi 51, Taksim; ⌚ music 9pm-2am most nights) just off Taksim Sq.

GETTING THERE & AWAY

Air

Many people fly into İstanbul's **Atatürk International Airport** (off Map pp862-3; Atatürk Hava Limanı; ☎ 465 5555), 23km west of Sultanahmet. **Sabiha Gökçen International Airport** (off Map pp862-3; ☎ 0216-585 5000), some 50km east of Sultanahmet, on the Asian side of the city, is increasingly popular for cheap flights from Europe.

Many foreign airlines have their offices north of Taksim, along Cumhuriyet Caddesi in Elmadağ. Travel agencies can also sell tickets and make reservations. **Turkish Airlines** (Map pp862-3; ☎ 252 1106; www.thy.com; Cumhuriyet Caddesi 7) is the main domestic carrier, and Onur Air, Atlasjet and Fly Air also operate domestic flights from İstanbul.

For more details on flying to/from and within Turkey, see p934.

Boat

Yenikapı (Map pp862–3), south of Aksaray Sq, is the dock for fast ferries across the Sea of Marmara to Yalova, Bursa and Bandırma (from where you can catch a train to İzmir). These carry both passengers and cars.

Bus

The huge **International İstanbul Bus Station** (Uluslararası İstanbul Otogarı; off Map pp862-3; ☎ 658 0505) is the city's main *otogar* for intercity and international routes. It's in Esenler, about 10km northwest of Sultanahmet. The Light Rail Transit (LRT) service stops here en route to/from the airport. If you're coming from Taksim Sq, bus 83O (one hour, TL1.30) leaves about every 20 minutes from around 6.30am to 8.40pm. A taxi from Sultanahmet to the *otogar* costs around TL22 (20 minutes); from Taksim Sq around TL30 (30 minutes). Many bus companies offer a free *servis* (shuttle bus) to or from the *otogar*.

Buses leave from here for virtually anywhere in Turkey and for international destinations including Azerbaijan, Armenia, Bulgaria, Georgia, Greece, Iran, Romania and Syria.

If you're heading east to Anatolia, you might want to board at the smaller **Harem Otogar** (Map pp862-3; ☎ 0216-333 3763), north of Haydarpaşa Railway Station on the Asian shore, but the choice of services here is more limited. Arriving in İstanbul, it's considerably quicker to get out at Harem and take the car ferry to Sirkeci/Eminönü (TL1.40), which runs between 7am and 9.30pm daily.

Train

For services to Edirne and Europe go to **Sirkeci Railway Station** (Map p867; ☎ 527 0051). Daily international services from Sirkeci include the *Bosfor/Balakan Ekspresi* service, stopping in Sofia (Bulgaria), Bucharest (Romania) and Belgrade (Serbia) for TL92.40 to TL252.60, and the *Dostlu/Filia Ekspresi* service to Thessaloniki (Greece; TL101 to TL178). European trains will terminate at Yenikapı after the completion

THREE CHEERS FOR MARMARAY

Marmaray (www.tcdd.gov.tr/tcdding/marmaray_ing.htm), an ambitious public transport project aiming to relieve İstanbul's woeful traffic congestion, takes its name from the Sea of Marmara and *ray* (Turkish for rail). Plans show the Sirkeci–Halkali rail line, which presently follows the coast to Yeşilköy near the airport, going underground at Yedikule and travelling to underground stations at Yenikapı and Sirkeci. From Sirkeci it will travel some 5km in a new tunnel being built under the Bosphorus to Üsküdar, on the Asian side. From there it will come to ground level at Sögütluçeşme, 2km east of Kadıköy, where it will connect with the Gebze Anatolian rail line.

The project's deadline has been extended to 2012, and it may take even longer. No sooner had workmen commenced digging than they found an ancient port and bazaar in Üsküdar, and a 4th-century Byzantine harbour in Yenikapı. The resulting archaeological works are documented in the 'Light of Day' exhibition at the İstanbul Archaeology Museum (p866).

of Marmaray, an ambitious public transport project aimed at relieving İstanbul's woeful traffic congestion, but this will not come about until 2012 at the earliest (see above).

Trains from Anatolia and from countries to the east and south terminate at **Haydarpaşa Railway Station** (Map pp862-3; ☎ 0216-336 4470), on the Asian shore of the Bosphorus. International services from Haydarpaşa include the *Trans-Asya Ekspresi* to Tabriz, Iran and the *Toros Ekspresi* to Aleppo, Syria.

GETTING AROUND

Tickets on public transport in İstanbul generally cost TL1.40.

To/From the Airport

There is a quick, cheap and efficient LRT service from Atatürk International Airport to Zeytinburnu, from where you connect with the tram that takes you directly to Sultanahmet; the whole trip takes about 50 minutes and costs TL2.80 in total.

If you are staying near Taksim Sq, the **Havaş airport bus** (Map pp862-3; ☎ 244 0487) is your best bet. Buses leave Atatürk (TL9) every 15 to 30 minutes from 4am until 1am, and Sabiha Gökçen (TL10) 25 minutes after planes land. From the Havaş office at Taksim, buses depart every 15 to 30 minutes from 4am to 1am (less frequently to Sabiha Gökçen).

Hostels and some of the smaller hotels in Sultanahmet can book minibus transport from the hostel to the airport for around TL10 per person. Unfortunately, this option only works going *from* town to the airport and not vice versa, and there are only six or so services per day.

A taxi to Atatürk from Sultanahmet costs from TL35; to Sabiha Gökçen, at least TL80.

Boat

The cheapest and most scenic way to travel any distance in İstanbul is by ferry. The main ferry docks are at the mouth of the Golden Horn (Eminönü, Sirkeci and Karaköy) and at Beşiktaş, a few kilometres northeast of the Galata Bridge, south of Dolmabahçe Palace.

Bus

İstanbul's efficient bus system has major bus stations at Taksim Sq, Beşiktaş, Aksaray, Rüstempaşa-Eminönü, Kadıköy and Üsküdar. Most services run between 6.30am and 11.30pm. You must have a ticket before boarding; buy tickets from the white booths near major stops or, for a small mark-up, from some nearby shops (look for 'İETT *otobüs bileti satılır*' signs).

Funicular Railway

There is a one-stop Tünel funicular system between Karaköy and İstiklal Caddesi (every 10 or 15 minutes from 7.30am to 9pm). A newer funicular railway runs through a tunnel from the Bosphorus shore at Kabataş (where it connects with the tram) up to the metro station at Taksim Sq.

Light Rail Transit (LRT)

An LRT service connects Aksaray with the airport, stopping at 15 stations, including the *otogar*, along the way. It operates from 5.40am until 1.40am.

Taxi

İstanbul is full of yellow taxis, all of them with meters – even if not every driver wants to use them. From Sultanahmet to Taksim costs around TL10.

Train

Every 30 minutes, suburban trains from Sirkeci Railway Station run along the southern walls of Old İstanbul and west along the Marmara shore. There's a handy station in Cankurtaran for Sultanahmet.

Tram

A tramway (*tramvay*) service runs from Zeytinburnu (where it connects with the airport LRT) to Kabataş (connecting with the funicular to Taksim Sq) via Sultanahmet, Eminönü and Karaköy (connecting with the funicular to Tünel). Trams run every five minutes or so from 6am to midnight.

A quaint antique tram rattles up and down İstiklal Caddesi in Beyoğlu, from the Tünel station to Taksim Sq via the Galatasaray Lisesi.

AROUND İSTANBUL

Since İstanbul is such a vast city, few places are within easy reach on a day trip. If you make an early start, however, it's just possible to see the sights of Edirne in Thrace (Trakya), the only bit of Turkey that is geographically within Europe. The fast ferry link means that you can also just make it to Bursa and back in a day, although it's much better to overnight there. Another must-see is İznik, a historic walled town on the shores of a peaceful lake, easily accessible from İstanbul.

EDIRNE

☎ 0284 / pop 136,000

European Turkey's largest settlement outside İstanbul, Edirne is disregarded by all but a handful of travellers, who come to enjoy the stunning architecture. It was briefly the capital of the Ottoman Empire, and many of its key buildings are in excellent shape. You'll find none of the razzamatazz or crowds of the Aegean or Mediterranean coasts here, but Edirne is hardly a backwater. With the Greek and Bulgarian frontiers a half-hour's drive away, the streets are crowded with foreigners, locals and off-duty soldiers. At the end of June is the oily Kırpınar Wrestling Festival.

Sights

Dominating Edirne's skyline like a massive battleship is the **Selimiye Mosque** (1569–75), the finest work of the great Ottoman architect Mimar Sinan. Its lofty dome and four tall (71m), slender minarets create a dramatic perspective. In the southeast corner of the complex is the 15-room **Turkish & Islamic Arts Museum** (Türk İslam Eserleri Müzesi; ☎ 225 1120; admission TL2; 🕑 8am-5pm Tue-Sun), which features displays on oil wrestling and dervishes. Smack-bang in the centre of town, you can't miss the 15th-century **Eski Cami** (Old Mosque), which has rows of arches and pillars supporting a series of small domes. Another example of architectural magnificence is the **Üçşerefeli Cami** (Three-Balcony Mosque), which has four strikingly different minarets, all built at different times. The great imperial mosque built by the Ottoman architect Hayreddin, **Beyazıt II complex** (1484–1512), stands in splendid isolation to the north of town.

Festivals

One of the world's oldest and most bizarre sporting events takes place annually in late June/early July at Sarayiçi in northern Edirne. At the 650-year-old **Tarihi Kırkpınar Yağlı Güreş Festivali** (Historic Kırpınar Oil Wrestling Festival), muscular men, naked except for a pair of heavy leather shorts, coat themselves with olive oil and throw each other around. For more information, visit the **Kırpınar Evi** (Kırpınar House; ☎ 212 8622; www.kirkpinar.com; 🕑 10am-noon & 2-6pm) in Edirne or check out www.turkishwrestling.com.

Sleeping & Eating

Hotel Aksaray (☎ 212 6035; fax 225 6806; Alipaşa Ortakapı Caddesi; s/d/tr/q TL35/65/80/100; ❄) This cheapie has basic rooms in a charmingly decrepit old building, with bathrooms rammed into small spaces.

Tuna Hotel (☎ 214 3340; fax 214 3323; Maarif Caddesi 17; s/d/tr/q TL50/70/90/100; ❄ 💻) An excellent choice for the price, the Tuna is at the quieter southern end of Maarif Caddesi.

Efe Hotel (☎ 213 6166; www.efehotel.com; Maarif Caddesi 13; s/d TL85/125; ❄ 💻) The Efe is a stylish place, especially the lobby, which is filled with antiques and curios. The rooms, particularly the 2nd-floor doubles, are big and bright, with fridges and electric kettles.

There's an assortment of eateries along Saraçlar Caddesi. The riverside restaurants south of the centre are more atmospheric, but most open only in summer and are booked solid at weekends.

Getting There & Away

The *otogar* is 9km east of the city centre. There are regular bus services for İstanbul (TL20, 2½ hours, 235km) and Çanakkale (TL25, four hours, 230km). If you're heading for the Bulgarian border crossing at Kapıkule, catch a *dolmuş* (minibus that follows a prescribed route; TL5, 25 minutes) from opposite the tourist office on Talat Paşa Caddesi.

İZNIK

☎ 0224 / pop 20,000

A historic walled town on the shores of a peaceful lake, İznik is popular with weekending İstanbullus but largely ignored by tourists, which has helped preserve its Turkish character. Stroll along the lake-front or mosey around the city centre, admiring the ruins of **Aya Sofya** (Church of the Divine Wisdom; admission TL5; 9am-noon & 1-6pm Tue-Sun) and the Seljuk-style **Yeşil Cami** (Green Mosque), built between 1378 and 1387. The minaret, decorated with green- and blue-glazed zigzag tiles, is a wonder. The town was famous during the Ottoman era for making these tin-glazed earthenware tiles that were incorporated into the finest buildings of the period. It's also worth sparing an hour to visit the **İznik Museum** (İznik Müzesi; ☎ 757 1027; Müze Sokak; admission TL2; 8am-noon & 1-5pm Tue-Sun), which contains examples of İznik tiles. More active types can follow a 5km circuit around most of İznik's **walls**, which were first erected in Roman times. Four main **gates** pierce the walls; the Lefke and İstanbul Gates are most impressive.

TURKEY

Sleeping & Eating

Kaynarca Pansiyon (☎ 757 1753; www.kaynarca.s5.com; cnr Kılıçaslan Caddesi & Gündem Sokak 1; dm/s/d/tr TL20/30/50/75;) This cheerful and central pension is a budget traveller's dream. It's pathologically clean, with BBC World on the telly and a spacious rooftop terrace for leisurely breakfasts (TL5).

Hotel Aydın (☎ 757 7650; www.iznikhotelaydin.com; Kılıçaslan Caddesi 64; s/d/tr TL50/80/100) Known locally for its on-site *pastanesi* (patisserie/bakery), the Aydın's smallish rooms come with TV, phone, balcony and chintzy bedspreads.

Çamlık Motel (☎ 757 1631; www.iznik-camlikmotel.com; Göl Sahil Yolu; s/d TL60/100;) At the southern end of the lakefront, this modern motel has spacious rooms and a restaurant with water views. It's a favourite with tour groups, so book ahead on summer weekends. The restaurant is recommended by locals as İznik's best spot to enjoy fish.

Köfteci Yusuf (☎ 757 3597; Atatürk Caddesi 75; mains from TL5) A favourite lunchtime spot for juicy *köfte* and other grills with chunky bread and hot green peppers. Leave room for the gorgeous desserts.

On the lakefront the Köşk Café, Sedef Aile Café Salonu and Lambada Café are all good for (nonalcoholic) drinks and snacks.

Getting There & Away

There are hourly buses from the *otogar* to Bursa (TL7.50, 1½ hours) and frequent buses to Yalova (TL7.50, one hour), where you can catch fast ferries to İstanbul.

BURSA

☎ 0224 / pop one million

Sprawling at the base of Uludağ, Bursa was the first capital of the Ottoman Empire. Today, Turkey's biggest winter-sports centre is a modern, prosperous city with lots of vitality and personality. Allow at least a day to take in the ancient mosques, *medreses* and *hammams* and their enthralling designs. If you feel in need of some pampering, the thermal springs in the village-like suburb of Çekirge are the perfect salve after exploring the city or Uludağ's tree-clad slopes.

Orientation & Information

The city centre, with its banks and shops, is along Atatürk Caddesi, between the Ulu Cami (Grand Mosque) to the west and the main square, Cumhuriyet Alanı, commonly called Heykel (Statue), to the east.

Çekirge is a 10-minute bus or *dolmuş* ride from Heykel via Atatürk Caddesi. Bursa's *otogar* is an inconvenient 10km north of the centre; take bus 38 or a taxi (around TL20).

The **tourist office** (☎ 220 1848; 8am-12.30pm & 1.30-5.30pm Mon-Fri, 9am-12.30pm & 1.30-6pm Sat & Sun) is beneath Atatürk Caddesi, in the row of shops at the northern entrance to Orhan Gazi Alt Geçidi. For internet access, try **Discover Internet Centre** (Taşkapı Caddesi; per hr TL1.25).

Sights & Activities

About 1km east of Heykel is the supremely beautiful **Yeşil Cami** (Green Mosque; 1424) and its stunningly tiled **Yeşil Türbe** (Green Tomb;

admission free; 8am-noon & 1-5pm). Right in the city centre, the largest of Bursa's mosques is the Seljuk **Ulu Cami** (Grand Mosque; Atatürk Caddesi), built in 1396. Behind the Ulu Cami, Bursa's sprawling **covered market** *(kapalı çarşı)* is proudly local, especially if you find İstanbul's Grand Bazaar too touristy.

Uphill and west of the Ulu Cami, on the way to Çekirge, don't miss the 14th-century **tombs of Osman and Orhan**, the first Ottoman sultans. A kilometre beyond lies the delightful **Muradiye Complex**, with a mosque and 12 decorated tombs dating from the 15th and 16th centuries. With a shady park in front, it's a peaceful oasis in a busy city.

Whether it's winter or summer, it's worth taking a cable-car ride up the 2543m-high **Uludağ** (Great Mountain) to take advantage of the views and the cool, clear air of **Uludağ National Park**. As well as containing Turkey's most popular ski resort (the season runs from December to early April), the park offers pine forests and the occasional snowy peak. Hiking to the summit of Uludağ takes three hours. To get to the **teleferik** (cable car; TL8 return) from Bursa, take a city bus from stop 1 or a *dolmuş* from behind the City Museum (Kent Müzesi). Bear in mind that the skiing facilities, while some of Turkey's best, are not up to the best European ski resorts.

Sleeping

There are a couple of decent sleeping options in Bursa, but also consider Çekirge, which has better, quieter options. Çekirge's hotels are generally more expensive, but prices include the use of the mineral baths. To get there, take a 'Çekirge' bus or *dolmuş* from Heykel or along Atatürk Caddesi.

Hotel Güneş (222 1404; İnebey Caddesi 75, Bursa; s/d/tr/q with shared bathroom TL26/46/54/68) The family-run Güneş is Bursa's best budget pension, with small, neat rooms in a restored Ottoman house.

Mutlu Hotel (233 2829; mutluhotel@mynet.com; Murat Caddesi 19, Çekirge; s/d/tr TL50/78/90;) A reliable choice, the Mutlu combines a rustic wooden exterior with spacious marble thermal baths. The decor sometimes struggles to get past 1973, but the cafe outside is more modern.

Termal Hotel Gold 2 (235 6030; www.hotelgold.com.tr; I Murat Camii Aralığı, Çekirge; s/d TL60/90;) This restored 1878 house next to the I Murat Camii has wooden interiors and deep-red drapery. Baths and parking are included, and the roof terrace is a bonus.

Hotel Artıç (224 5505; www.artichotel.com; Ulu Cami Karşısı 95, Bursa; s/d/tr TL60/90/100;) This is a decent option towards the western end of Atatürk Caddesi, with light, spacious rooms and good views of Ulu Cami from the breakfast salon. Ask for a discount on the posted rates.

Eating & Drinking

Sakli Bahçe (Çekirge Caddesi 2, Çekirge; mains TL4-8; 11am-11pm) The perfect place to watch the sunset, this chilled-out hilltop garden is the preferred meeting point for Bursa's bright young things, lured by excellent pizza and *kebaps*.

Yusuf (Culture Park; meze TL4-10; 11am-11pm) 'Joe's Place' features a meze- and grill-laden terrace set among shady trees. The service is so good that we saw middle-aged waiters break into a brisk trot.

Çiçek Izgara (221 6526; Belediye Caddesi 15; mains TL9-12; 11am-9.30pm) One block from Koza Parkı, behind the half-timbered *belediye* (town hall), this modern grillhouse is good for lone women and has a 1st-floor salon to watch the flower market below.

Make sure you spend an evening at one of the fish restaurants on Sakarya Caddesi, Bursa's most atmospheric eating precinct.

After eating there, you'll find a few bars nearby, including **Barantico** (Sakarya Caddesi), **Gedikli Meyhane** (Sakarya Caddesi) and **Müsadenızle** (Altıparmak Caddesi).

If you're after a cafe, **Mehfel Mado** (Namazgah Caddesi) is the city's oldest, with live music on its riverside terrace and a basement art gallery. Across the stream, the multiterraced **Set Café** (Köprü Üstü) also offers live music.

Getting There & Away

The fastest way to get to İstanbul (TL20, 2½ to three hours) is to take a bus to Yalova, then a catamaran to İstanbul's Yenikapı docks. Get a bus that departs Bursa's *otogar* at least 90 minutes before the scheduled boat departure.

Karayolu ile (by road) buses to İstanbul take four to five hours and drag you around the Bay of İzmit. Those designated *feribot ile* (by ferry) go to Topçular, east of Yalova, and take the ferry to the Eskihisar terminal, a much quicker and more pleasant way to go.

THE AEGEAN COAST

Turkey's Aegean coast can convincingly claim more ancient ruins per square kilometre than any other region in the world. Since time immemorial, conquerors, traders and travellers have beaten a path to the mighty monuments, and few leave disappointed. Here you'll see the famous ruins of Troy, Ephesus and Pergamum (Bergama), and you can contemplate the devastation of war at the battlefield sites of Gallipoli.

GALLIPOLI (GELIBOLU) PENINSULA

☎ 0286

Antipodeans and many Britons won't need an introduction to Gallipoli; it is the backbone of the 'Anzac legend', in which an Allied campaign in 1915 to knock Turkey out of WWI and open a relief route to Russia turned into one of the war's greatest fiascos. Some 130,000 men died, a third from Allied forces and the rest Turkish.

Today the Gallipoli battlefields are peaceful places, covered in brush and pine forests. But the battles fought here nearly a century ago are still alive in many memories, both Turkish and foreign, especially Australians and New Zealanders, who view the peninsula as a place of pilgrimage. The Turkish officer responsible for the defence of Gallipoli was Mustafa Kemal (the future Atatürk); his victory is commemorated in Turkey on 18 March. On Anzac Day (25 April), a dawn service marks the anniversary of the Allied landings.

The easiest way to see the battlefields is with your own transport or on a minibus tour from Çanakkale (opposite) or Eceabat (Maydos; below) with **Hassle Free Tours** (☎ 213 5969; www.hasslefreetour.com; Anzac House Hostel, Çanakkale; TL45-55), **Trooper Tours** (☎ 217 3343; www.troopertours.com; Yellow Rose Pension, Çanakkale; TL55) or **TJs Tours** (☎ 814 3121; www.anzacgallipollitours.com; TJs Hotel, Eceabat; TL45). With a tour you get the benefit of a guide who can explain the battles as you go along.

Most people use Çanakkale (opposite) or, on the Thracian (European) side of the strait, Eceabat (Maydos; below) as a base for exploring Gallipoli. Car ferries frequently cross the straits between Çanakkale and Eceabat (from TL2). From Eceabat, take a *dolmuş* or a taxi to the Kabatepe Information Centre & Museum on the western shore of the peninsula. See opposite for information on getting to Eceabat and Çanakkale.

Some travellers prefer to join an organised tour from İstanbul (p861).

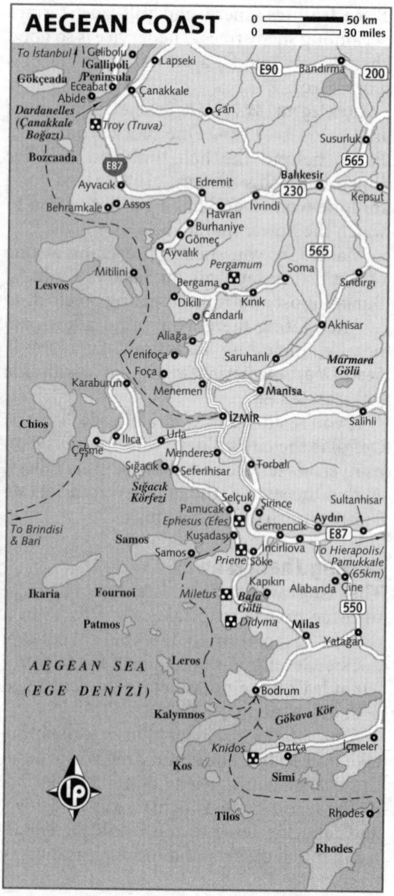

ECEABAT (MAYDOS)

☎ 0286 / pop 5500

Eceabat (Maydos) is a small, easy-going waterfront town with the best access to the main Gallipoli battlefields of any main centre.

Ferries dock next to the main square, Cumhuriyet Meydanı, which has hotels, restaurants, ATMs, a post office, bus company offices, and *dolmuş* and taxi stands. Like most of the peninsula, Eceabat is swamped with students and tour groups at weekends from April to mid-June and in late September.

Sleeping & Eating

Hotel Boss I (☎ 814 1464; www.heyboss.com; Cumhuriyet Meydanı 14; s/d/tr TL20/40/60;) Behind its clapboard facade, this small, narrow place is as cheap and basic as you'll find here. Opt for a corner room or one facing the water (eg No 1) to get more space. It's no surprise that the same management run Hotel Boss II (Mehmet Akif Sokak), which charges the same rates, as well as the pricier Aqua Boss Hotel (İstiklal Caddesi).

Hotel Crowded House (☎ 814 1565; www.crowdedhousegallipoli.com; Huseyin Avni Sokak 4; dm/s/d TL20/35/50;) Eceabat's newest backpacker caravanserai, named after the Antipodean band rather than the state of the accommodation, is housed in a four-storey building near the dock.

TJs Hotel (☎ 814 2458; www.anzacgallipolitours.com; Cumhuriyet Meydanı 2/A; dm/s/d TL15/50/70;) With a commanding central position, the former Eceabat Hotel has rooms to suit every budget, from basic hostel bunk rooms upwards. The Ottoman-style roof bar has regular live events. TJs Tours (opposite), which offers tours of Gallipoli and Troy, is based here.

Liman Restaurant (☎ 814 2755; İstiklal Caddesi 67; mains TL6-15; 10am-12.30am) At the southern end of the waterfront, this is generally considered to be Eceabat's best fish restaurant; its covered terrace is a delight in all weather.

Getting There & Away

Long-distance buses pass through Eceabat to İstanbul (TL30, five hours) on the way from Çanakkale. There are frequent ferry services to Çanakkale (from TL2).

ÇANAKKALE

☎ 0286 / pop 86,600

The liveliest settlement on the Dardanelles, this sprawling harbour town would be worth a visit for its sights, nightlife and overall vibe even if it didn't lie opposite the Gallipoli Peninsula. Its sweeping waterfront promenade heaves during the summer months.

A good base for visiting Troy, Çanakkale has become a popular destination for weekending Turks; if possible plan your visit for midweek. The **tourist office** (☎ 217 1187; Cumhuriyet Meydanı; 8am-noon & 1-7pm Jun-Sep, to 5pm Oct-May) is 150m from the ferry pier, and you can access the internet at **Maxi Internet** (Fetvane Sokak 51; per hr TL1.50).

Sights

Built by Sultan Mehmet the Conqueror in 1452, the **Ottoman castle** at the southern end of the waterfront now houses the **Military Museum** (Askeri Müze; admission TL3; 9am-noon & 1.30-5pm Tue, Wed & Fri-Sun). About 1.5km south of the *otogar*, on the road to Troy, the **Archaeological Museum** (Arkeoloji Müzesi; admission TL2; 8am-5pm) holds artefacts found at Troy (p880) and Assos (p880).

Sleeping

Rooms are expensive around Anzac Day and are usually booked solid months before 25 April arrives.

Anzac House Hostel (☎ 213 5969; www.anzachouse.com; Cumhuriyet Meydanı 59-61; dm/s/d/tr with shared bathroom TL16/28/40/54;) Not to be confused with the three-star Anzac Hotel, central, cheap Anzac House is the main backpacker haunt.

Efes Hotel (☎ 217 3256; www.efeshotelcanakkale.com; Aralık Sokak 5; s/d TL30/50;) An excellent budget choice, with cheery decor and a welcoming owner. The best rooms have open showers and orthopaedic mattresses. The breakfasts are great, and there's a little garden with a fountain.

Yellow Rose Pension (☎ 217 3343; www.yellowrose.4mg.com; Aslan Abla Sokak 5; dm/s/d/tr TL17/30/55/60;) This bright, attractive guest house has a central but quiet location and extras including a laundry service and fully equipped kitchen.

our pick **Kervansaray Hotel** (☎ 217 8192; www.otelkervansaray.com; Fetvane Sokak 13; s/d/tr €35/50/60;) Çanakkale's only boutique hotel is as lovely as you could hope for, laying on Ottoman touches in keeping with the restored house it occupies. The 19 rooms (including eight in a sympathetic new annexe) have a dash of character without being overdone.

Çanak Hotel (☎ 214 1582; www.canakhotel.com; Dibek Sokak 1; s/d €35/60;) This excellent midrange option, just off Cumhuriyet Meydanı, has a stunning roof bar, games room and sky-lit atrium.

Eating & Drinking

To eat on the hoof, browse the stalls along the waterfront, which offer corn on the cob, mussels and other simple items. A local speciality is *peynir helvaş*, made with soft white village cheese, flour, butter and sugar.

Köy Evi (☎ 213 4687; Yalı Caddesi 13; menu TL5) Proper home cooking rules in this tiny eatery, where local women make *mantı, börek* and *gözleme* (TL1.50).

Doyum (☎ 217 1866; Cumhuriyet Meydanı 13; dishes TL4.50-10) Generally acknowledged to be the best *kebap* and pide joint in town, a visit to Doyum is worth it for the good cheer alone.

Benzin (☎ 212 2237; Eski Balıkhane Sokak 11; pizzas TL8-12.50) This 1960s-style waterfront cafe-bar is a relaxing spot for a drink and a bite, but gets packed at weekends.

Hayal Kahvesi (☎ 217 0470; Saat Kulesi Meydanı 6) Facing the clock tower, this cafe-bar (also called TNT Bar) with courtyard seating is Çanakkale's most popular live-music venue.

Getting There & Away

There are regular buses to Ayvalık (TL20, 3½ hours), İstanbul (TL30, six hours) and İzmir (TL30, 5½ hours), and frequent ferry services to Eceabat (from TL2, 25 minutes).

TROY (TRUVA)

☎ 0286

Of all the ancient sites in Turkey, the remains of the great city of Troy are in fact among the least impressive; you'll have to use your imagination. It's an important stop for history buffs, however, and if you have read Homer's *Iliad*, the ruins have a romance few places on Earth can match

The ticket booth for the ruins of **Troy** (☎ 283 0536; per person/car TL10/3; 8.30am-7pm May-15 Sep, to 5pm 16 Sep-Apr) is 500m before the site. The site is rather confusing for nonexpert eyes (guides are available), but the most conspicuous features, apart from the reconstruction of the Trojan Horse, include the **walls** from various periods; the Graeco-Roman **Temple of Athena**, of which traces of the altar remain; the Roman **Odeon**, where concerts were held; and the **Bouleuterion** (Council Chamber), built around Homer's time (c 800 BC).

From Çanakkale, *dolmuşes* to Troy (TL2, 35 minutes, 30km) leave every hour on the half-hour from 9.30am to 5.30pm from a station under the bridge over the Sarı River and drop you by the ticket booth. *Dolmuşes* run back to Çanakkale on the hour, until 5pm in high season and 3pm in low season.

The travel agencies offering tours to the Gallipoli battlefields (p878) also offer tours to Troy (around €25 per person).

BEHRAMKALE & ASSOS

☎ 0286

Behramkale, southwest of Ayvacık, is an old hilltop Greek village spread out around the ruins of a 6th-century temple. The Ionic **Temple of Athena** (admission TL5; 8am-dusk) has spectacular views of Lesvos and the dazzling Aegean – well worth the admission fee. Beside the entrance to the ruins, the 14th-century **Hüdavendigar Camii** is a simple early Ottoman mosque.

Just before the entrance to the village, a road winds 2km down to Assos harbour. It's a cluster of half-a-dozen old stone houses-turned-hotels overlooking a picture-perfect harbour, and is the ideal place to unwind over a cup of tea.

Behramkale and Assos make a fine combination, but are no longer sleeping beauties and get overcrowded. Over summer weekends and public holidays, İstanbullus and İzmirlis pour in by the bus load.

Sleeping

You can either stay in Behramkale village or in the hotels around Assos harbour.

BEHRAMKALE

Dolunay Pansiyon (☎ 721 7172; s/d TL25/50) In the centre of the village by the *dolmuş* stop, the homely Dolunay has six spotless, simple rooms set around a courtyard.

Old Bridge House (☎ 721 7426; www.assos.de/obh; camp sites/dm/d TL10/20/100; Mar-Nov;) Near the Ottoman bridge at the entrance to town, this long-time travellers' favourite offers large double rooms, a six-bed dorm and garden cabins.

Eris Pansiyon (☎ 721 7080; erispansiyon.com; Behramkale Köyü 6; s/d TL90/130; Apr-Nov) Set in a stone house with gardens at the far end of the village, this has ordinary (for the price) but peaceful rooms. Afternoon tea is served on a terrace with views over the hills.

ASSOS

In high season virtually all of the pricey hotels by Assos harbour insist on *yarım pansiyon* (half-board).

Çakır Pansiyon (☎ 721 7048; www.assoscakirpansiyon.com; s/d TL40/60;) Around 100m east of the town entrance, this seafront pension has simple bungalows and a small camp site (per person TL8). Breakfast is served on a floating platform; dinner is in a lantern-lit restaurant.

Yıldız Saray Hotel (☎ 721 7025; www.yildizsaray-hotels.com; r TL180;) The small rooms are traditionally furnished, attractive and good value, with views across the harbour and three with

TURKEY

access to a small terrace. The brassiere-style restaurant has a good reputation.

Biber Evi (☎ 721 7410, www.biberevi.com; s/d TL150/200; ❄) A real delight, this old stone house boasts a peaceful garden, a small terrace with lovely views and a gourmet restaurant. Rooms are Ottoman-rustic in style, complete with *gusulhane* – washing facilities hidden in a cupboard!

Eating

In contravention of the way these things usually work, the settlement at the bottom of the hill is actually the 'posh' part of town where prices, if not standards, are higher than at the top. Be sure to check the cost of fish and bottles of wine before ordering. You can eat for less than TL10 in Behramkale.

Getting There & Away

To get to Behramkale during the summer, catch the regular shuttle (TL1) from Assos. In winter, workers shuttle to and fro and you can normally jump on one of their buses.

Regular buses run from Çanakkale (TL7.50, 1½ hours) to Ayvacık, where you can pick up a *dolmuş* (which leaves when full) to Behramkale (TL3, 20 minutes). Some *dolmuşes* make a second stop down in Assos.

AYVALIK

☎ **0266 / pop 34,650**

Back from the palm trees and touristy restaurants on Ayvalık's waterfront, the tumbledown old Greek village provides, in the words of local hotelier Annette, a 'wonderful outdoor museum'. Horses and carts clatter down narrow streets, past headscarf-wearing women holding court outside picturesque shuttered houses.

Olive-oil production is the traditional business here, although the town is now better known as a gateway to local islands and the Greek isle of Lesvos.

The *otogar* is 1.5km north of the town centre and the tourist office is 1.5km south; in summer there's an information kiosk on the waterfront south of the main square, Cumhuriyet Alanı. Offshore is **Alibey Island** (Alibey Adası; known locally as Cunda), which is lined with open-air fish restaurants and linked by ferries and a causeway to the mainland. In summer, it is included in **cruises** (TL10 to TL12 per person including meal) around the bay's islands, leaving Ayvalık at about 11am and stopping here and there for sunbathing and swimming.

Sleeping & Eating

Taksiyarhis Pension (☎ 312 1494; www.taksiyarhispension.com; r with shared bathroom per person TL28) These 120-year-old Greek houses have exposed wooded beams and a jumble of cushions, rugs and handicrafts. Facilities include a communal kitchen, book exchange and bicycles for hire. Breakfast costs TL7.

Annette's House (☎ 312 5971; www.annetteshouse.com; Neşe Sokak 12; s/d €21/42) On a square that hosts a Thursday market, Annette's is an oasis of calm and comfort. Nothing is too much trouble for the eponymous German owner, who presides over a charming collection of large, clean, well-decorated rooms.

Şehir Kulübü (☎ 312 1088; Yat Limanı; fish TL15 per 500g) Jutting over the water, the 'city club' is the top choice for reasonably priced fish. You choose your fish from the giant freezer, and mezes (TL4 to TL7) from the counter.

Martı Restaurant (☎ 312 6899; Gazinolar Caddesi 9; mains TL14-22) Another excellent choice, Martı specialises in Ayvalık and regional specialities as well as fish.

Getting There & Away

There are frequent direct buses from İzmir (TL7.50, three hours) and Bergama (TL6, 1¾ hours) to Ayvalık. Coming from Çanakkale (TL12, 3¼ hours), some buses drop you on the main highway to hitch to the centre.

For Alibey Island, take a *dolmuş* taxi (white with red stripes) from the main square (TL1.50) or a boat (TL2; June to August) from behind the nearby tourist kiosk.

Daily boats operate to Lesvos (Greece) between June and September (€40/50 one way/return). There are two boats a week from October to May. For information and tickets, contact **Jale Tours** (☎ 312 2740; Gümrük Caddesi 24).

BERGAMA (PERGAMUM)

☎ **0232 / pop 58,200**

As Selçuk is to Ephesus, so Bergama is to Pergamum: a workaday market town that's become a major stop on the tourist trail because of its proximity to the remarkable ruins of Pergamum, site of the pre-eminent medical centre of Ancient Rome. During Pergamum's heyday (between Alexander the Great and the Roman domination of Asia

Minor) it was one of the Middle East's richest and most powerful small kingdoms.

İzmir Caddesi (the main street) is where you'll find banks with ATMs and the PTT. There is a basic **tourist office** (☎ 631 2851; İzmir Caddesi 54; 8.30am-noon & 1-5.30pm), just north of the museum, and most pensions and hotels offer free internet access.

Sights

One of the highlights of the Aegean coast, the well-proportioned **Asclepion** (Temple of Asclepios; admission/parking TL10/3; 8.30am-5.30pm), about 3km from the city centre, was a famous medical school with a library rivalling that of Alexandria in Egypt. The ruins of the **Acropolis** (admission TL10; 8.30am-5.30pm), 6km from the city, are equally striking. The hilltop setting is absolutely magical, and the well-preserved ruins are magnificent, especially the vertigo-inducing 10,000-seat **theatre** and the marble-columned **Temple of Trajan**, built during the reigns of Emperors Trajan and Hadrian and used to worship them as well as Zeus.

The excellent **Archaeology Museum** (Arkeoloji Müzesi; İzmir Caddesi; admission TL2; 8.30am-5.30pm Tue-Sun) has a small but substantial collection of artefacts from both of these sites, including a collection of 4th-century statues from the so-called 'Pergamum School'.

Sleeping

Odyssey Guesthouse (☎ 653 9189; www.odysseyguesthouse.com; Abacihan Sokak 13; dm TL10, s/d with shared bathroom TL20/35) This 180-year-old house has clean (but sparse) rooms, furnished with copies of Homer's *Odyssey*. There's a trading library and breakfast is served on the rooftop terrace.

Gobi Pension (☎ 633 2518; www.gobipension.com; Atatürk Bulvarı 18; s/d €20/32;) On the main road behind a greenery-draped terrace, this is a great family-run place with bright, cheery rooms, most with new private bathrooms.

our pick **Akropolis Guest House** (☎ 631 2621; www.akropolisguesthouse.com; Kayalik Caddesi 5; s/d €20/49;) This 150-year-old stone house is the closest Bergama gets to boutique, with eight attractively decorated rooms surrounding a pool and garden, a restaurant set in a barn and a terrace with acropolis views.

Eating

Pala Kebap Salonu (☎ 633 1559; Kasapoğlu Caddesi 4; kebap €2.20) Though small and simple, this place is terrifically popular and the food's delicious. Try the spicy Bergama *köfte* (TL6).

Bergama Ticaret Odası Sosyal Tesisleri (☎ 632 9641; Ulucamii Mahallesi; meze TL5, mains TL6-8 10.30am-11pm) Run by Bergama municipality, this restaurant occupies a beautifully restored 200-year-old Greek house.

Sağlam Restaurant (☎ 632 8897; Cumhuriyet Meydanı 47; mains TL6-11) This large, simple place is well known in town for its high-quality home cooking. It does a good selection of meze, which change daily, and delicious *kebaps*.

Getting There & Around

There are frequent buses to/from İzmir (TL10, two hours) and Ayvalık (TL7.50, 1¼ hours). Bergama's new *otogar* lies 7km from the centre at the junction of the highway and the main road into town. From here a *dolmuş* service shuttles into town (TL2); a taxi should cost around TL15 during the day.

There's no public transport to the archaeological sites. A taxi tour of sites including the Acropolis, the Asclepion and the museum costs from TL40 to TL60, depending on the time of year.

İZMIR

☎ 0232 / pop 2.6 million

Though you may eventually fall for its hectic nightlife, great shopping and top-notch museums, İzmir can take some getting used to. Certainly nowhere else in the region can prepare you for the sheer size, sprawl and intensity of the place.

At the water's edge, İzmir's traffic has been beaten back and the city really comes into its own. The seafront is one of its main attractions; the wide, pleasant esplanade of Birinci Kordon provides eating, drinking and sunset-watching opportunities. Inland things are more hectic, but you'll find a buzzing bazaar, plenty of interesting ruins and a newly restored Jewish quarter.

Orientation & Information

İzmir's two main avenues run parallel to the waterfront. Atatürk Caddesi (Birinci Kordon or First Cordon), known locally as the Kordon, is on the waterfront; a block inland is Cumhuriyet Bulvarı (the İkinci Kordon or Second Cordon). Main squares Konak Meydanı (Government House Sq) and Cumhuriyet Meydanı are on these avenues.

Konak opens onto the bazaar and Anafartalar Caddesi, the bazaar's main street, leads to the train station (Basmane Garı). The Basmane–Çankaya area, near the station, has medium-priced hotels, restaurants and bus ticket offices.

İzmir's shopping, restaurant and nightclub district of Alsancak is to the north, while the *otogar* is 6.5km northeast of the centre.

There is a **tourist office** (☎ 483 5117; fax 483 4270; Akdeniz Mahallesi 1344 Sokak 2) on the seafront, and web access at **Internet Café** (1369 Sokak 9; per hr TL1.70).

Sights

Since most of old İzmir was destroyed after WWI by a Greek invasion and a fire, there's little to see here compared to other Turkish cities. It does boast the remains of an extensive 2nd-century-AD Roman **agora** (marketplace; admission TL2; 8am-5pm), however, just southeast of the sprawling, atmospheric modern **bazaar**. It's also worth taking bus 33 to the hilltop **Kadifekale** (*kale* means fortress), where women still weave *kilims* (pileless woven rugs) on horizontal looms and the views are breathtaking.

Sleeping

İzmir's waterfront is dominated by high-end business hotels, which fill up quickly during the summer; inland there are cheap and mid-priced places, particularly around the train station. On 1296 Sokak, southwest of the station, a number of hotels occupy restored Ottoman houses, but their interiors can be grungy.

Otel Hikmet (☎ 484 2672; 945 Sokak 26; s/d TL20/45) The sign outside says 'Hotel very good' and it's not wrong. Tucked away on cobbled streets off a cafe-lined square, this family-run house is full of character.

Imperial Hotel (☎ 425 6883; fax 489 4688; 1294 Sokak 54; s/d TL20/45) Past the grandiose entrance columns, marble floors and carpets, the rooms are more modest, but they're still a decent size and terrific value.

Hotel Alican 2 (☎ 425 2912; alicanotel@hotmail.com; 1367 Sokak; s/d €19/35) One of the safer choices in the station area (there's a 24-hour reception), this hotel has well-maintained rooms with modern bathrooms.

Konak Saray Hotel (☎ 483 7755; www.konaksaray hotel.com; Anafartalar Caddesi 635; s/d €35/50) This beautiful Ottoman house has been transformed into a superior boutique hotel. Rooms are a touch small, but stylish and modern, and soundproofed to keep bazaar noise out.

Eating

For fresh fruit, vegetables, freshly baked bread and delicious savoury pastries, head for the canopied market, just off Anafartalar Caddesi. *The* place to be seen on a romantic summer's evening is the sea-facing Kordon, though you pay for the location. In Alsancak, you lose the sunset views but gain on atmosphere; try 1453 Sokak (Gazi Kadinlar Sokağı).

Sakız (☎ 484 1103; Şehıt Nevresbey Bulvarı 9/A; mains TL8-12; 11am-midnight) It was a bold move opening a vegetarian cafe in carnivorous İzmir, but it has paid off. The food is traditional Turkish, just removed of its meat and fish elements, and made with fresh local ingredients. Good wine list.

Kefi (☎ 422 6045; 1453 Sokak 17; mains TL14; 11am-midnight) Kefi has stood the test of time with its superb cooking and elegant dining room in a restored Ottoman house. Fish and seafood dominate the menu, but they also do some mean meats; try the lamb with fennel.

Getting There & Away

AIR

Turkish Airlines offers nonstop flights from İzmir to İstanbul (from TL109) and Ankara (from TL59), with connections to other destinations. Onur Air, Atlasjet, Fly Air, Sun Express Airlines and **Izair** (www.izair.com.tr) also fly to İzmir. Flights to the city from European destinations have greatly increased in recent years.

BUS

İzmir is a major transport hub. From the *otogar*, frequent buses leave for Bergama (TL10, two hours), Kuşadası (TL10.5, 1¼ hours), Selçuk (TL6, one hour), and other destinations nationwide. Buses to Çeşme (TL10, 1½ hours) leave from a local bus terminal in Üçkuyular, 6.5km southwest of Konak.

TRAIN

The daily *Alti Eylül Ekspresi* and, between April and October, the *Onyedi Eylül Ekspresi* go to Bandırma (TL16, 6½ hours), where you can catch a ferry to İstanbul. Express trains also run to Ankara (sleeper TL26.50, 13 to 15 hours), Selçuk (for Ephesus; TL3.50, 1½ hours) and Denizli (for Pamukkale; TL11, five hours).

Getting Around

Frequent Havaş airport buses (TL10, 30 minutes) leave from Gaziosmanpaşa Bulvarı, north of the Hilton, and from the airport (where they meet flights). Intercity bus companies run *servis* shuttles to the *otogar; dolmuşes* run there from Basmane and Bornova.

The most pleasant way to get around İzmir is by **ferry** (6.30am-1am). Frequent timetabled services link the piers at Konak, Pasaport, Alsancak and Karşiyaka. *Jetons* (travel tokens) cost TL4 each.

ÇEŞME

☎0232 / pop 21,300

The Çeşme Peninsula is İzmir's summer playground, which means it can get busy with Turkish tourists at weekends and during the school holidays. Çeşme itself is a family-orientated resort and transit point for the Greek island of Chios, 8km west. It has a tangle of narrow backstreets and a dramatic Genoese fortress, and makes a good base for visiting Alaçatı's old Greek stone houses and windsurfing beach.

The **tourist office** (☎/fax 712 6653; İskele Meydanı 6; 8.30am-noon & 1-5.30pm Mon-Fri), ferry and bus ticket offices, banks with ATMs, restaurants and hotels are all within two blocks of the main square.

Sleeping

There's a wealth of good-value, homely pensions in Çeşme, usually open from May to October. Bookings are essential in summer and at weekends.

Uz Pansiyon (☎712 6579; uzpansiyon@gmail.com; Sokak 3010 7; s/d TL35/55) Near the bus station and 450m from the centre, this is one of Çeşme's cheapest pensions, but it's spotless and terrific value, with a communal kitchen.

Otel Sesli (☎712 8845; www.otelsesli.com; 3025 Sokak 35; s/d €20/40) On a hill above the waterfront, a 10-minute walk from the centre, the Sesli has bare rooms around a pool and potted plants.

Sahil Pansiyon (☎712 6934; www.cesmesahilpansiyon.com; 3265 Sokak 3; d from €40) This peaceful place is up some stairs in a rambling house and garden. The immaculate rooms have small balconies, some with sea views (ask for room 9).

Ertan Oteli (☎712 6795; www.ertanotel.com.tr.tc; Hurriyet Caddesi 12; d €55) In the same block as the Rıdvan (also recommended), the Ertan has a better location on the seafront. Though by no means a good-looking hotel, the restaurant is reasonable, the staff helpful and the rooms have balconies.

Eating

On the waterfront are touristy restaurants specialising in seafood – and multilingual menus. For cheaper, more locally orientated places, head to İnkilap Caddesi.

Tokmak Hasan'in Yeri (☎712 0519; Çarsı Caddesi 11; mains TL4-8) Rather hidden away, this simple place serves terrific home cooking at low prices.

Patika Restaurant Café & Bar (☎712 6357; Cumhuriyet Meydanı; mains TL10-16; 3pm-midnight) This is the place for fish at affordable prices. Between 9pm and 1am there's live Turkish music and sometimes belly dancing.

Pasifik Otel Restaurant (☎712 7465; 3264 Sokak; mains TL10-16; noon-9pm) If you fancy a walk and some fish, head to the Pasifik, at the northern end of the seafront, where you can enjoy a great fish casserole.

Getting There & Away

Buses from the *otogar* run every 45 minutes to İzmir's main *otogar* (TL8, two hours) and its smaller, western Üçkuyular terminal (TL7.5, 1¼ hours).

In summer there are five weekly ferries to the Greek island of Chios, and two in winter. Buy your ticket (passenger one way/return €40/65, car return €140-180) at the harbour; you don't need to do so in advance unless you have a car.

There are also weekly ferry services to Brindisi and Ancona (Italy). See p934 for more information.

SELÇUK

☎0232 / pop 27,300

Selçuk boasts one of the Seven Wonders of the Ancient World, an excellent museum, a fine basilica and mosque, a stork nest-studded aqueduct and, right on the town's doorstep, Ephesus. Compared to the vast tourism factory of nearby Kuşadası, however, Selçuk's tourism industry is a small-scale, workshop-sized affair.

TURKEY

Orientation & Information

Selçuk's *otogar* lies just east of the İzmir–Aydın road (Atatürk Caddesi), with the town centre and some pensions immediately north of it. Pedestrianised shopping streets Namık Kemal, Cengiz Topel and Siegburg Caddesis run east from the main road to the train station.

On the western side of the main road a park spreads out in front of one wing of the Ephesus Museum. Many pensions can be found in the quiet, hilly streets between the museum and Ayasuluk Hill, northwest of the centre.

The **tourist office** (☎ 892 6945; www.selcuk.gov.tr; Agora Caddesi 35; 8am-noon & 1-5pm Mon-Fri winter, daily in summer) is opposite the museum.

Sights

Selçuk is not only close to Ephesus, it is also blessed with superb monuments scattered around the centre. Don't miss the conspicuous **Basilica of St John** (St Jean Caddesi; admission TL2; 8am-5pm Oct-Apr, to 7pm May-Sep), atop Ayasuluk Hill. It was built in the 6th century on the site where it was believed St John the Evangelist had been buried. The less-impressive **Temple of Artemis** (admission free; 8am-5pm Oct-Apr, to 7pm May-Sep), between Ephesus and Selçuk, was once one of the Seven Wonders of the Ancient World. In its prime, it was larger than the Parthenon in Athens. Unfortunately, little more than one pillar now remains.

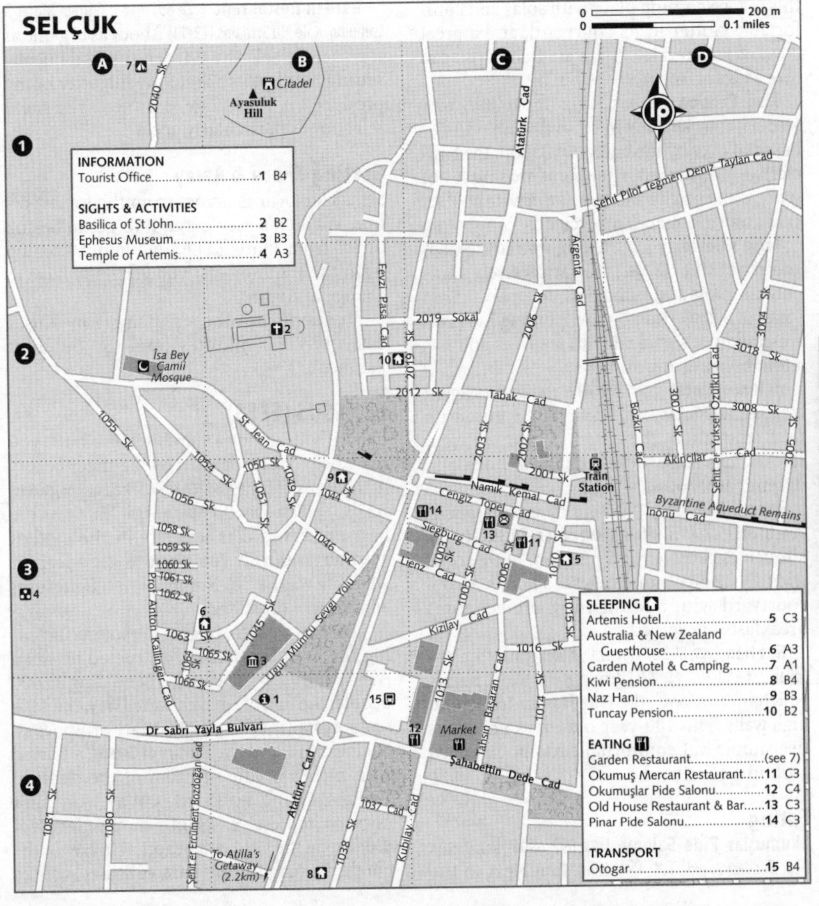

TURKEY

The **Ephesus Museum** (☎ 892 6010; Uğur Mumcu Sevgi Yolu Caddesi; admission €2.50; ⌚ 8am-5pm Oct-Apr, to 7pm May-Sep) houses a striking collection of artefacts, including the effigy of Priapus, the Phallic God, which pops up in postcard racks throughout Turkey.

Sleeping

Garden Motel & Camping (☎ 892 6165; info@galleriaselciukidi.com; Kale Altı 5; per person/tent/car/campervan TL10/5/5/10, tent hire TL12; 💻 🏊) Located 200m north of the mosque, this grassy camping ground is large and well designed, with facilities including a good restaurant and children's amusements.

Australia & New Zealand Guesthouse (☎ 892 6050; www.anzguesthouse.com; 1064 Sokak 12; dm/d TL12.5/45; ❄ 💻) Despite the rules posted in the rooms, this is a welcoming place with sofas and comfortable clutter in its courtyard, and a great covered roof terrace. Bikes are free or you can hire a motor-scooter.

Kiwi Pension (Alison's Place; ☎ 892 4892; www.kiwipension.com; 1038 Sokak 26; dm/s/d TL12/25/40; 💻 🏊) Presided over by the energetic Alison, the Kiwi receives glowing reports. Rooms are simple but spotless and bright, and there's a private pool set 1km away in a mandarin orchard.

Atilla's Getaway (☎ 892 3847; www.atillasgetaway.com; dm/r €8/16; 💻 🏊) An attractively laid-out camping and bungalow complex 2.5km south of Selçuk. Run by a welcoming Turkish-Australian, it's packed with facilities and has a fun, buzzing atmosphere.

Artemis Hotel (☎ 892 6191; www.artemisguesthouse.net; 1012 Sokak 2; s/d €25/40; ❄) Spruced up by a renovation, the Artemis, near the train station, has large, new beds, fresh linen and decent bathrooms.

Tuncay Pension (☎ 892 6260; www.tuncaypension.com.tr; 2019 Sokak 1; d with/without air-con €50/35; ❄) It's a touch expensive for a pension, but a good, friendly choice nonetheless. There's a cool courtyard with a fountain where generous breakfasts are served.

Naz Han (☎ 892 8731; nazhanhotel@gmail.com; 1044 Sokak 2; r €50-70; ❄ 💻) Living up to its name, which means 'coy', the Naz Han hides behind high walls. This 100-year-old Greek house has five simple but comfortable rooms arranged around a courtyard.

Eating

Okumuşlar Pide Salonu (☎ 892 6906; Şahabettin Dede Caddesi 2; pide TL4; ⌚ 10am-11pm) Next to the bus station, this busy branch of the pide chain does fabulous pides (including veggie options).

Pinar Pide Salonu (☎ 892 9913; Siegburg Caddesi 3; pide TL4) Some travellers claim that this little place serves the best pide anywhere. It also does some good *kebaps* and salads.

Old House Restaurant & Bar (Eski Ev; ☎ 892 9357; 1005 Sokak 1/A; mains TL6-9) Set in a courtyard among fruit trees, this cool, intimate place serves tasty Turkish dishes. Try the Old House Kebap.

Okumuş Mercan Restaurant (☎ 892 6196; 1006 Sokak 44; mains TL7-9) This place is loved locally for its traditional home fare, served in a courtyard beside a fountain in the shade of a mulberry tree.

Garden Restaurant (☎ 892 6165; Garden Motel & Camping, Kale Altı 5; mains TL7-11) About as organic as it gets in Selçuk, the Garden enjoys a bucolic setting amid plots where the majority of the produce on your plate is grown. The meze selection is particularly good.

Getting There & Away

Selçuk's *otogar* is across from the tourist office. While it's easy enough to get to Selçuk direct from İzmir (TL6, one hour), coming from the south or east you generally have to change at Aydın.

Frequent minibuses head for Kuşadası (TL4, 30 minutes) and the beach at Pamucak.

EPHESUS (EFES)

Even if you're not an architecture buff, you can't help but be dazzled by the sheer beauty of the ruins of **Ephesus** (☎ 892 6010; admission/parking TL15/3; ⌚ 8am-5pm Oct-Apr, to 7pm May-Sep), the best-preserved classical city in the eastern Mediterranean. If you want to get a feel for what life was like in Roman times, Ephesus is an absolute must-see.

There's a wealth of sights to explore, including the **Great Theatre**, reconstructed between AD 41 and 117, and capable of holding 25,000 people; the marble-paved **Sacred Way**; the 110-sq-m **agora** (marketplace), heart of Ephesus' business life; and the **Library of Celsus**, adorned with niches holding statues of the classical Virtues. Going up Curetes Way, you can't miss the impressive Corinthian-style **Temple of Hadrian**, on the left, with beautiful friezes in the porch; the magnificent **Terraced Houses** (admission

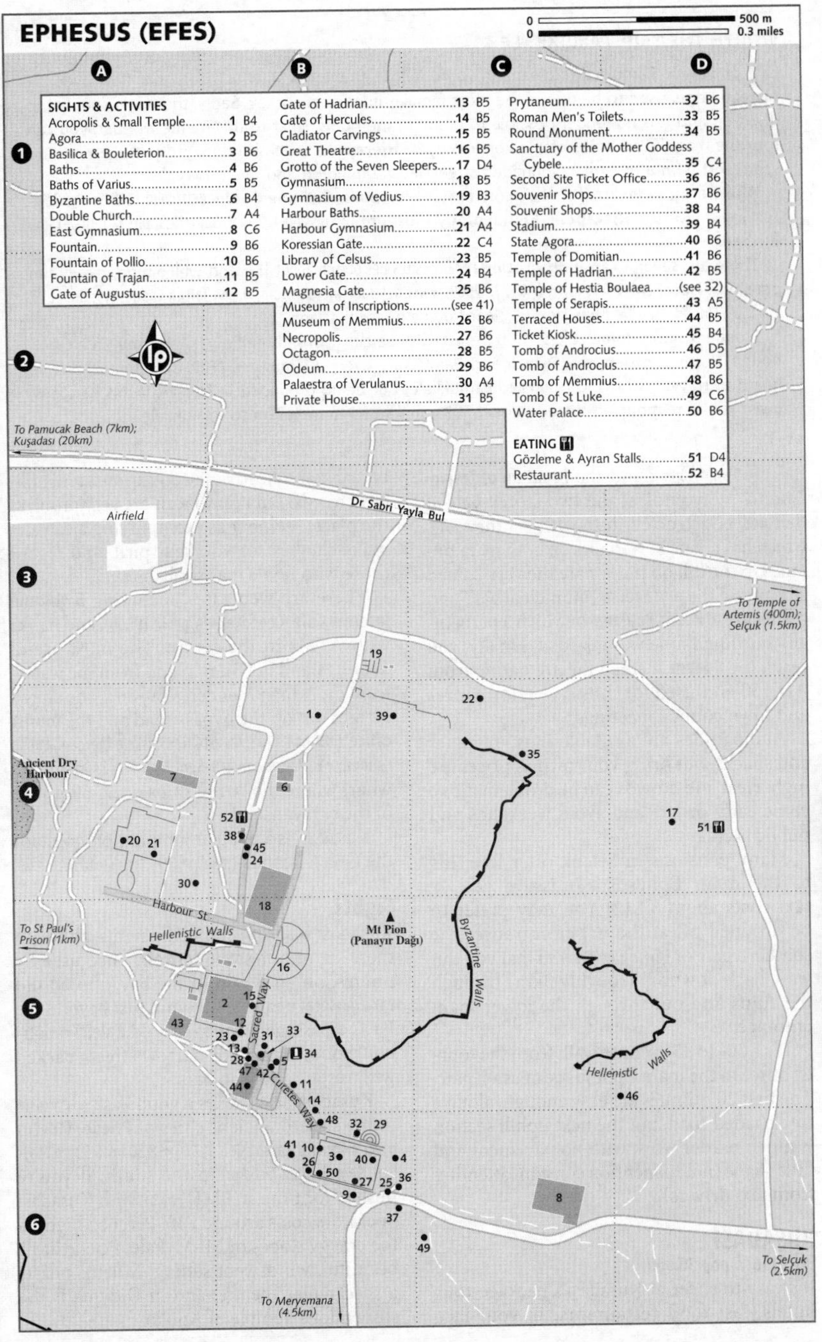
EPHESUS (EFES)
0 500 m
0 0.3 miles
A
B
C
D
1
2
3
4
5
6
SIGHTS & ACTIVITIES
Acropolis & Small Temple....1 B4
Agora....2 B5
Basilica & Bouleterion....3 B6
Baths....4 B6
Baths of Varius....5 B5
Byzantine Baths....6 B4
Double Church....7 A4
East Gymnasium....8 C6
Fountain....9 B6
Fountain of Pollio....10 B6
Fountain of Trajan....11 B5
Gate of Augustus....12 B5
Gate of Hadrian....13 B5
Gate of Hercules....14 B5
Gladiator Carvings....15 B5
Great Theatre....16 B5
Grotto of the Seven Sleepers....17 D4
Gymnasium....18 B5
Gymnasium of Vedius....19 B3
Harbour Baths....20 A4
Harbour Gymnasium....21 A4
Koressian Gate....22 C4
Library of Celsus....23 B5
Lower Gate....24 B4
Magnesia Gate....25 B6
Museum of Inscriptions....(see 41)
Museum of Memmius....26 B6
Necropolis....27 B6
Octagon....28 B5
Odeum....29 B6
Palaestra of Verulanus....30 A4
Private House....31 B5
Prytaneum....32 B6
Roman Men's Toilets....33 B5
Round Monument....34 B5
Sanctuary of the Mother Goddess Cybele....35 C4
Second Site Ticket Office....36 B6
Souvenir Shops....37 B6
Souvenir Shops....38 B4
Stadium....39 B4
State Agora....40 B6
Temple of Domitian....41 B6
Temple of Hadrian....42 B5
Temple of Hestia Boulaea....(see 32)
Temple of Serapis....43 A5
Terraced Houses....44 B5
Ticket Kiosk....45 B4
Tomb of Androcius....46 D5
Tomb of Androclus....47 B5
Tomb of Memmius....48 B6
Tomb of St Luke....49 C6
Water Palace....50 B6
EATING
Gözleme & Ayran Stalls....51 D4
Restaurant....52 B4
To Pamucak Beach (7km); Kuşadası (20km)
Dr Sabri Yayla Bul
Airfield
To Temple of Artemis (400m); Selçuk (1.5km)
Ancient Dry Harbour
Harbour St
To St Paul's Prison (1km)
Hellenistic Walls
Mt Pion (Panayır Dağı)
Byzantine Walls
Sacred Way
Curetes Way
Hellenistic Walls
To Selçuk (2.5km)
To Meryemana (4.5km)

TURKEY

WORTH THE TRIP: PAMUKKALE

East of Selçuk, Pamukkale's gleaming white ledges (travertines), with pools that flow over the plateau edge, used to be one of the most familiar images of Turkey. Sadly, the water supply has dried up and it is no longer possible to bathe in the pools. Next to this fragile wonder, you can tour the magnificent ruins of the Roman city of **Hierapolis** (admission TL5; daylight), an ancient spa resort with a theatre, colonnaded street, latrine building and necropolis.

Afterwards, swim amid sunken columns at Hierapolis' **Antique Pool** (adult/child TL18/9; 9am-7pm), and visit the **Hierapolis Archaeology Museum** (admission TL3; 9am-12.30pm & 1.30-7.15pm Tue-Sun).

There are several **camping grounds** (camp sites per person about TL7) and welcoming, family-run pensions. **Hotel Dört Mevsim** (272 2009; www.hoteldortmevsim.com; Hasan Tahsin Caddesi 19; dm TL10, s/d TL20/35;) has simple, clean rooms in a quiet lane.

Frequent buses connect local hub Denizli with Selçuk (TL18, three hours) and İzmir (TL20, four hours). Buses run between Denizli and Pamukkale every 15 minutes (TL2, 30 minutes). We've heard of travellers buying tickets to Pamukkale, but being offloaded in Denizli. If this happens, insist you're reimbursed the additional TL2 you'll need to travel on to Pamukkale.

TL15; 9am-4.30pm); and the **Fountain of Trajan**. Curetes Way ends at the two-storey **Gate of Hercules**, constructed in the 4th century AD, which has reliefs of Hercules on both main pillars. Up the hill on the left are the very ruined remains of the **prytaneum** (municipal hall) and the **Temple of Hestia Boulaea**, in which a perpetually burning flame was guarded. Finally, you reach the **Odeum**, a small theatre dating from AD 150 and used for musical performances and town council meetings.

Audioguides are available – as are water and snacks, but bring your own as prices are high. Heat and crowds can be problematic so come early or late and avoid weekends and public holidays.

Many pensions in Selçuk offer free lifts to the main Ephesus admission gate; a taxi costs about TL12. You may prefer to be dropped off at the upper entrance (the southern gate or *güney kapısı*) so that you can walk back downhill (roughly 3km) through the ruins and out through the lower main entrance.

It's a 30- to 45-minute walk from the tourist office to the main Ephesus admission gate. The first 20 minutes are easy enough, along a tree-shaded road, but the next uphill section is much harder work with no pavement and little shade (not to mention constant attention from taxi drivers).

KUŞADASI

0256 / pop 50,000

It's easy to sneer at Kuşadası's package-tour hotels, fast-food restaurants, in-your-face bazaar, karaoke bars, tattoo parlours and holiday crowds. But many locals are very proud of the place, seeing it as exemplifying a can-do, make-the-best-of-yourself spirit, and regard those who revile it as snobs.

There are web cafes, including **B@h@ane Internet Café** (Öge Sokak 4/A; per hr TL1.50), and banks with ATMs in the centre. The most useful *dolmuş* stand is 1.5km inland from the waterfront on Adnan Menderes Bulvarı. The *otogar* is right out on the bypass road and the **tourist office** (614 1103; fax 614 6295; İskele Meydanı, Liman Caddesi; 8am-noon & 1-5pm Mon-Fri) is near the wharf where the cruise ships dock, 60m west of the caravanserai.

Kuşadası is a popular jumping-off point for the Greek Islands (see p889) for details.

Sights

Kuşadası is short on specific sights, although there's a minor stone **fortress**, once used by pirates, on an island in the bay, and an old **caravanserai** near the harbour. Just beyond the PTT, a passage leads to the old **Kaleiçi** neighbourhood, which has narrow streets packed with restaurants and bars.

Kuşadası also makes a good base for visits to the superb ancient cities of **Priene**, **Miletus** and **Didyma** (admission TL2; 8.30am-6.30pm May-Sep, 9am-5.30pm Oct-Apr) to the south; if you're pushed for time, a 'PMD' tour with Kuşadası operators costs around €30. Perched high on the craggy slopes of Mt Mykale, Priene has a beautiful, windswept setting; Miletus boasts a spectacular theatre; and in Didyma is the stupendous Temple of Apollo.

Kuşadası's most famous beach is **Kadınlar Denizi** (Ladies Beach), 2.5km south of town and served by *dolmuşes* running along the coastal road.

Sleeping

Beware the touts at the *otogar* and harbour; decide where you're heading before arrival and stand your ground.

Sezgin's Guesthouse (☎ 614 4225; www.sezginhotel.com; Aslanlar Caddesi 68; s/d €20/24;) Perhaps the top budget choice, with large, almost Swiss-style wood-panelled rooms, comfortable beds, armchairs, TVs, fridges and balconies overlooking a garden.

Panorama (☎ 614 6619; www.otelpanorama.com; Kıbrıs Caddesi 14; s/d €20/28;) A few steps from the bazaar, this used to be Sammy's Palace, a long-standing backpacker favourite. The rooms are Spartan and dog-eared, but there's a roof terrace for breakfasts and optional dinners.

Villa Konak (☎ 612 2170; www.villakonakhotel.com; Yıldırım Caddesi 55; s/d €40/50;) Hidden in the old quarter of town is this restored 140-year-old stone house. The rooms, attractively updated with the odd Orientalist flourish, are arranged around a rambling courtyard-garden. It's peaceful and cool and there's a bar, restaurant and library.

Eating & Drinking

There's an abundance of eateries to suit every wallet. As ever, check the cost before ordering fish.

Köfteci Ali (Aslanlar Caddesi 14; 24 hr) Situated near Bar St, ready to satisfy the postclub traffic, this street booth does some terrific spicy wrapped pide *kebaps* (TL5).

Avlu (☎ 614 7995; Cephane Sokak 15; mains TL5-8; 8am-midnight) In the Old Town, Avlu offers first-class home cooking in a clean and cheerful environment. A long-standing local fave, it has a great pick-and-point counter, some great veggie options and delectable Turkish puds.

Saray (☎ 612 0528; Bozkurt Sokak 25; mains TL10-18; 9am-2am) Enjoying a following among both locals and expats, the Saray has a refined courtyard and, inside, an unpretentious dining room that often rocks with happy-hour sing-a-longs. The menu, a typical Kuşadası calling-all-ports affair, includes some decent Turkish and vegetarian choices.

Barlar Sokak (Bar St) is chock-a-block with Irish-theme pubs. It's a scruffy-round-the-edges kind of street, but after a few drinks it can be lots of fun.

Getting There & Away

BOAT

All Kuşadası travel agencies sell tickets to the Greek island of Samos. There's at least one daily boat to/from Samos (one way/same-day return €30/35) between April and October, but ferries do not operate in the winter.

BUS

From the *otogar*, direct buses depart for several far-flung parts of the country, or you can change at İzmir. In summer, three buses run daily to Bodrum (TL20, 2½ hours); in winter, take a *dolmuş* to Söke (TL4, every 30 minutes) for onward connections. For Selçuk (TL4, 25 minutes), pick up a minibus on Adnan Menderes Bulvarı.

BODRUM

☎ 0252 / pop 28,600

Some people will tell you Bodrum is an unsophisticated, low-end resort town; they obviously haven't been to Kuşadası. In fact, Bodrum manages to welcome the summer hordes without diluting its character and charm. With laws in place restricting the height of buildings, the town has nice architectural uniformity. Out of season, the whitewashed houses and subtropical gardens can appear almost idyllic.

Orientation & Information

The *otogar* is on Cevat Şakir Caddesi, 500m inland from the Adliye (Yeni) Camii, a small mosque in the centre of the town. The PTT and several banks with ATMs are on the same thoroughfare. There are internet cafes on Üçkuyular Caddesi, all charging about TL2 per hour – including **Cybernet Internet Café** (☎ 316 3167; Üçkuyular Caddesi 7; 24hr). The **tourist office** (☎ 316 1091; Kale Meydanı; 9am-6pm) is beside the Castle of St Peter, and there is an information booth at the *otogar* entrance.

Eastern Bay, a good area to hunt for sleeping, eating and drinking options, stretches away to the east of the tourist office.

Sights & Activities

Bodrum's star attraction is the conspicuous **Castle of St Peter**. Built in 1437 by the Crusaders, the castle houses the **Museum of Underwater Archaeology** (☎ 316 2516; admission TL10;

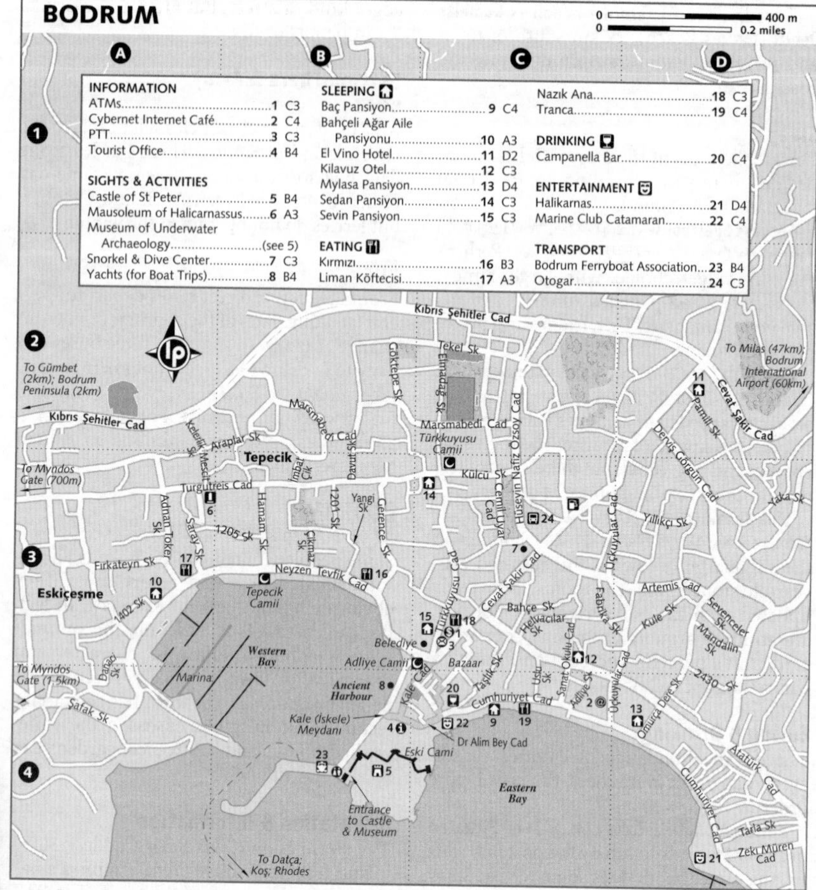

TURKEY

(9am-noon & 1-7pm Tue-Sun), containing finds from shipwrecks dating back to AD 1025; and a model of a Carian princess's tomb, inside the **French Tower** (admission €2.75; 10am-noon & 2-4pm Tue-Fri). Sadly there's little left of the **Mausoleum of Halicarnassus** (admission TL5; 8.30am-5.30pm Tue-Sun), the monumental tomb of King Mausolus, which was once among the Seven Wonders of the Ancient World.

Bodrum is famous for its **scuba-diving**. Look for the dive centres on the boats moored near the tourist office; companies include **Snorkel & Dive Center** (313 6017; Cevat Şakir Caddesi 5). Numerous yachts moored along Neyzen Tevfik Caddesi on the Western Bay run **day trips** (around €12) around the bay.

Sleeping

There are plenty of budget hotels and pensions in the centre and along Eastern Bay, although be aware that the closer you are to the front, the less chance you'll have of getting a good night's sleep. A number of upmarket boutique hotels line the coast just east of the Eastern Bay.

Sedan Pansiyon (316 0355; off Türkkuyusu Caddesi 121; s/d €12/24) At the basic end of the spectrum, with rooms of varying sizes and states of repair arranged around a ramshackle but peaceful courtyard.

Sevin Pension (316 7682; www.sevinpension.com; Türkkuyusu Caddesi 5; dm/s/d from €13/18/25;) Sevin may be basic, but for the price it offers a lot: a prime (albeit noisy) location,

TV, free wi-fi, good breakfasts and helpful staff.

Bahçeli Ağar Aile Pansiyonu (☎ 316 1648; 1402 Sokak 4; s/d €20/36) This endearing little pension is located in a passageway off Neyzen Tevik Caddesi, opposite the marina. With a little courtyard overhung by vines, it has an intimate feel, and guests can use the kitchen.

Mylasa Pansiyon (☎ 316 1846; www.mylasapansiyon.com; cnr Cumhuriyet Caddesi & Dere Sokak 2; s/d €25/35; ❄) This is the archetypal Bodrum pension, back from the beach but very much at the heart of the party scene. Rooms are small with TVs, but none too modern-looking. The cafe-restaurant is lively and there are great panoramic views from the terrace.

Baç Pansiyon (☎ 316 2497; bacpansiyon@turk.net; Cumhuriyet Caddesi 14; s/d from €28/45; ❄) Small but stylish and decked out in marble, wood and wrought iron, this central hotel also boasts about the best views in Bodrum. It sits right above the water and four of its 10 comfortable room have delightful balconies over the waves.

Kilavuz Otel (☎ 316 3892; www.kilavuzotel.com; cnr Atatürk Caddesi & Adliye Sokak 17; s/d €35/40; ❄ 🏊) Striking a good balance between proximity to the waterfront and the need for peace and quiet, this family-run place offers 15 simply furnished, clean rooms.

El Vino Hotel (313 8770; www.elvinobodrum.com; Pamili Sokak; s/d €80/120; ❄ 🏊) The dark backstreet location doesn't look that promising, but behind the stone wall is one of the town's loveliest hotels. Rooms are large and well appointed with wooden floors, large beds, TVs and writing desks.

Eating & Drinking

Bodrum's finest, and most expensive, restaurants are all located along the Western Bay; it's worse on the Eastern Bay. In between, on Cevat Şakir Caddesi and in the bazaar, are the best value options. Here you'll find a collection of Turkish restaurants and *büfes* (snack bars), where you can pick up a doner wrapped in pide for TL4. As elsewhere, check prices before ordering fish.

For drinking follow the normal rule of thumb: for cheap and cheerful head to the Eastern Bay; for expensive and classy, think Western Bay.

Nazik Ana (☎ 313 1891; Eski Hukumet Sokak 7; mains TL2-5) Hidden away down a narrow alley and definitely worth hunting out, this simple but atmospheric place is a huge hit locally. With its point-and-pick counter, it's a great place to sample different Turkish dishes.

Liman Köftecisi (☎ 316 5060; Neyzen Tevfik Caddesi 172; mains TL7-12.50) The famous Liman serves delicious food at decent prices. *Köfte* is the speciality; of the six types, the *Liman köfte* (with yoghurt, tomato sauce and butter) is the house speciality.

Kırmızı (☎ 316 4918; Neyzen Tevik Caddesi 44; mains TL10-14; 🕑 11.30am-midnight) Serving Mediterranean food made from fresh local ingredients, the Kırmızı is a characterful place with three floors and a garden terrace. The walls are used to exhibit local artwork.

Tranca (☎ 316 6610; Cumhuriyet Caddesi 36; mains TL12-24; 🕑 11am-midnight) Jutting out into the bay, the family-run Tranca boasts some of the best views of anywhere in Bodrum. Its specialities are *tuzda balık* (fish baked in salt) and *testi kebabı* (casserole served in a clay pot); both cost TL40 to TL50 with a minimum of two people.

Campanella Bar (☎ 316 5302; Cumhuriyet Caddesi) Though small, this Orientalist-style bar, adorned with flower boxes and set above a shop on a small alley, is full of atmosphere and usually has live music playing.

Entertainment

Nightclubs such as **Halıkarnas** (The Club; ☎ 316 8000; www.halikarnas.com.tr; Cumhuriyet Caddesi; admission weekday/weekend YTL30/35, beer & spirits from YTL10; 🕑 10pm-5am mid-May–Oct) and the floating **Marine Club Catamaran** (☎ 313 3600; www.clubbodrum.com; Hilmi Uran Meydanı 14; admission weekday/weekend YTL30/35, beer YTL10; 🕑 10pm-5am mid-May–Sep) are famous party hot spots, but there are quieter hang-outs, too. As with drinking spots, entertainment venues at the Eastern Bay are cheaper than Western Bay.

Getting There & Away

Airlines including Turkish Airlines fly from İstanbul and elsewhere to Bodrum International Airport, which is 60km away and connected to Bodrum by Havaş shuttle bus.

By bus, there are services to more or less anywhere you could wish to go. Useful services include those to İstanbul (TL70, 12 hours), Kuşadası (TL20, 2½ hours) and Marmaris (TL20, three hours).

Daily ferries (same-day return €25) link Bodrum with Kos (Greece); hydrofoils (same-day return €35) operate from Monday to Saturday between May and October. In summer there are also two weekly hydrofoils to Rhodes (Rhodos; one way €50, same-day return €60); check with the **Bodrum Ferryboat Association** (☎ 316 0882; www.bodrumferryboat.com; Kale Caddesi Cümrük Alanı 22), on the dock past the western entrance to the castle.

There are boats between Rhodes and Marmaris in Turkey (one way/return €50/70; 1¼ hours); see www.marmari sinfo.com.

THE MEDITERRANEAN COAST

The Western Mediterranean, known as the 'Turquoise Coast', is a glistening stretch of clear blue sea where Gods once played in sublime pebble coves, and where spectacular ruins abound. In villages too pretty to postcard, sun-kissed locals yawn and smile at travellers' never-ending quest for the 'Med Life'.

The region's seamless mix of history and holiday inspires and enchants. At places such as Patara and Olympos, your hand-packed sandcastles are humbled by vine-covered Corinthian temples and Lycian tombs. If you prefer to interact with your surroundings, plunge into activities such as scuba-diving at Kaş and kayaking atop the underwater city in Kekova.

The Eastern Mediterranean, meanwhile, has long lived in its more fashionable western neighbour's shadow. But the Arab-spiced area has at least as many pristine beaches as the Turquoise Coast.

MARMARIS

☎ 0252 / pop 35,200

An unashamedly brash harbour town that swells to over 200,000 people during summer, Marmaris is heaven or hell depending which way your boat floats. It sports one of Turkey's swankiest marinas, and a stunning natural harbour where Lord Nelson organised his fleet for the attack on the French at Abukir in 1798. Not far away, the deeply indented Reşadiye and Hisarönü Peninsulas hide azure bays backed by pine-covered mountains and gorgeous fishing villages.

Orientation & Information

İskele Meydanı (the main square) and the **tourist office** (☎ 412 1035; İskele Meydanı 2; 8am-noon & 1-5pm) are by the harbour, north of the castle. The **post office** (PTT; 51 Sokak; 8.30am-midnight) has phones accessible 24 hours a day, and there's web access at **CED Internet C@fé** (☎ 413 0193; 28 Sokak 63b; per hr TL3). Hacı Mustafa Sokak, also called Bar St, runs inland from the bazaar; action here keeps going until the early hours.

The *otogar* is 3km north of town, near the turn-off to Fethiye.

Sights & Activities

The small **castle** (admission TL2; 8am-noon & 1-5pm Tue-Sun) houses a modest museum and offers lovely views of Marmaris.

Numerous yachts along the waterfront offer day tours of Marmaris Bay and its beaches and islands. A day's outing usually costs between TL50 and TL80 per person, but you'll have to negotiate. You'll usually visit Paradise Island, Aquarium, Phosphoros Cave, Kumlubuku, Amos, Turunç, Green Sea and İçmeler. Two- and three-day trips often travel to Dalyan (p895) and Kaunos (p895).

Marmaris is also a popular place to scuba-dive, and there are several dive centres on the waterfront. **Deep Blue Dive Center** (☎ 412 4438; Yeni Kordon Caddesi) charges €340 for a PADI Open Water course over two to four days. Day excursions cost €35, and include two dives, all equipment, a dive master and lunch. Excursions and courses run from April to October.

Sleeping

Marmaris has hundreds of good-value sleeping options, especially for self-caterers; in the off season, expect serious discounts.

Interyouth Hostel (☎ 412 3687; interyouth@turk.net; 42 Sokak 45; dm/s/d with shared bathroom TL15/15/30; 💻)

TOP FIVE R&R SPOTS

- In a **tree-house hammock** (p902), Olympos.
- Steaming in **Çemberlitaş Hamamı** (p868), İstanbul.
- Wetting the toes at **Patara beach** (p898).
- Doing blissfully nothing on a **Blue Cruise** (p897), Fethiye.
- Tramping and camping in the **Ihlara Valley** (p920), Cappadocia.

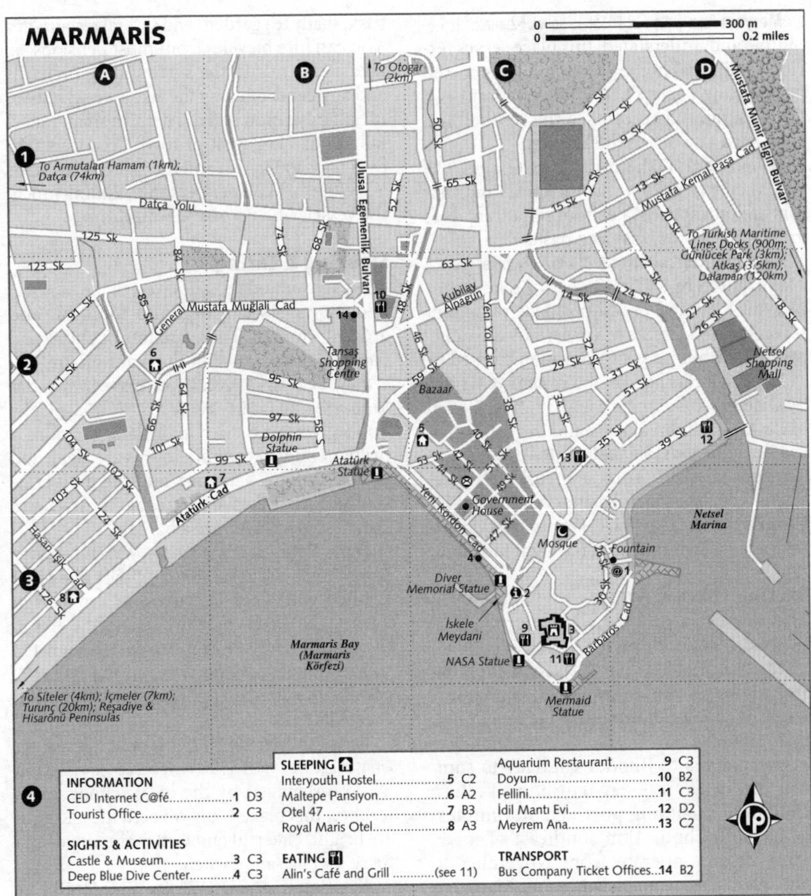

Located inside the covered bazaar, this hostel is efficiently run and a great source of travel information. Rooms, though smallish and rather spartan, are spotless and well maintained. There are bags of extras, even free pasta nights on the rooftop between June and September.

Maltepe Pansiyon (☎ 412 1629; 66 Sokak 9; s/d TL30/50;) The shady garden is the main attraction of this long-standing budget choice. Rooms are small but spotless, and internet access is free.

Otel 47 (☎ 412 4747; www.hotel47.com; Atatürk Caddesi 10; s/d TL60/90;) Amid the bright lights and swaying palm trees of Atatürk Caddesi, there's a Miami Beach vibe at 47. Regulars return for the prime location and white terrace.

Royal Maris Otel (☎ 412 8383; www.royalmarisotel.com; Atatürk Caddesi 34; s/d TL100/150;) With two pools, a private beach, a *hammam* and fitness centre, and spacious balconies with stunning views, the Royal Maris is remarkably affordable.

Eating & Drinking

For something cheap and cheerful, try the bazaar area between the post office and the mosque, or the Old Town area around the castle, where there's a host of small Turkish restaurants.

Marmaris is a party town and hedonists should stagger straight to the aptly named Bar St (39 Sokak), where stalls also cater to ravenous late-night revellers.

Meryem Ana (☎ 412 7855; 35 Sokak 62; mains TL5-6) Simple and understated, this place serves terrific traditional home cooking; a large mixed veggie plate costs TL10. The restaurant is a family affair – you can see the mother and aunt hard at work in the kitchen.

Fellini (☎ 413 0826; Barboras Caddesi 61; meals TL20) Perennially popular with both locals and visitors, this attractive waterfront restaurant does great thin-crust pizzas and pasta.

Aquarium Restaurant (☎ 413 1522; Barboras Caddesi; meals TL20) Run by a Turkish–New Zealand couple, this loud and proud port-side restaurant serves grills and steaks to a jovial crowd. Slightly overpriced, but it's got the location covered.

For quick eats head to the **Doyum** (☎ 413 4977; Ulusal Egemenlik Bulvarı 17; mains TL4-5; 24 hr), a good place for early breakfasts and veggie dishes; chicken joint **Alin's Café and Grill** (☎ 413 0826; Barboras Caddesi 61; meals TL12), full of young Turkish families feasting on healthy grills and *kebaps;* and **İdil Mantı Evi** (☎ 413 9771; 39 Sokak 140; mains TL8-20; 4pm-4am), a great spot on Bar St for night nibbles.

Getting There & Away

The nearest airports to Marmaris are at Dalaman and Bodrum (p889).

The *otogar* in Marmaris has frequent buses and minibuses to Bodrum (TL18, four hours), İzmir (TL30, 4½ hours) and Fethiye (TL14, three hours).

Catamarans to Rhodes sail daily in summer (one way/same-day return/open return €50/50/75 including port tax, 50 minutes) from the harbour 1km southeast of town. They do not operate from November to mid-April. Buy your ticket in any Marmaris travel agency.

KÖYCEĞIZ

☎ 0252 / pop 7520

The star attraction here is the beautiful and serene Lake Köyceğız. As it's so tough to rival the Med, this farming town attracts only modest tourism, and still depends mostly on citrus fruits, olives, honey and cotton for its livelihood. The region is also famous for its liquidambar trees, source of precious amber gum. The surrounding **Köyceğiz-Dalyan Nature Reserve** has a growing reputation among outdoor types for its excellent hiking and cycling.

Sights & Activities

This is a town for strolling. Hit the lakeshore promenade and walk past the pleasant town park, shady tea gardens and several restaurants. You can hire bicycles from most pensions, so take a ride out to the surrounding orchards and farmland; or along the lake's western shore to Sultaniye mud baths. There's a small waterfall about 7km west of town. You can take boat trips to Dalyan and the Kaunos ruins for YTL20 to YTL30 per person including lunch; the vessels line up on the waterfront.

Sleeping & Eating

Most accommodation lies west of the mosque, and managers can organise tours on and around the lake. There are lots of cheap and cheerful restaurants off the main square.

Fulya Pension (☎ 262 2301; fulyapension@mynet.com; Ali İhsan Kalamaz Caddesi 100; s/d TL20/40;) The bubbly young owner maintains Fulya as a brilliant budget option. Rooms are clean and cheap, all have balconies and there's a large roof terrace. Bikes are available for free, and the TL15 boat trips are a bargain.

Flora Hotel (☎ 262 4976; www.florahotel.info; Kordon Boyu 96; s/d/apt TL20/40/60;) The foyer is filled with flags in tribute to the foreign guests who often come for arranged walks in the nearby Gölgeli Mountains. Though the rooms only have side views of the lake, the good-value apartments sleep two adults and two children.

Tango Pansiyon (☎ 262 2501; www.tangopension.com; Ali İhsan Kalmaz Caddesi 112; dm/s/d per person TL15/30/50;) Managed by the local school sports teacher, this place is big on activities. Rooms are bright, cheerful and well maintained, and there's a pleasant garden.

Alila Hotel (☎ 262 1150; Emeksiz Caddesi 13; s/d TL40/70;) This spot is by far the most character-filled hotel in town, and 12 of its rooms boast direct views of the water. Friendly owner Ömar attends to every detail (right down to the towels folded to look like swans).

Mutlu Kardeşler (☎ 262 2480; Tören Alanı 52; mains TL5-6; 7am-1am) Funky in a rural kind of way, this simple place is much loved locally and has tables on a little terrace out the back.

Colıba (☎ 262 2987; Cengiz Topel Caddesi 64; köfte TL6; 10am-1am) Cool-headed staff serve meze, grills and the house speciality *alabalık* (trout) to young couples and businesspeople. Whitewashed and wooden, Colıba has a shaded terrace with views of the lake front.

Next to Colıba, the pink-and-purple **Pembe Restaurant** (☎ 262 2983; Cengiz Topel Caddesi 70; meals TL8-10) does cheap seafood and meat dishes.

Getting There & Away

There are frequent buses and *dolmuşes* to Fethiye (TL8, 1¾ hours), Marmaris (TL5, one hour) and Dalyan (TL4, 30 minutes). Köyceğiz can also be reached by an easy boat trip across the lake from Dalyan.

DALYAN

☎ 0252

Dalyan is a laid-back river-mouth community with a strong farming pedigree and a growing penchant for tourism. It makes an entertaining base for exploring the surrounding fertile waterways, in particular the popular turtle-nesting grounds of İztuzu Beach and Lake Köyceğiz.

In summer excursion boats go out to explore the river and the lake. You can save yourself a lot of money, and ensure your lira is spread evenly around town, by taking boats run by the **Dalyan Kooperatifi** (☎ 284 7843), located near the turtle statue. The cooperative's cruises cost about TL20 and take in the **Sultaniye hot springs** and **mud baths** on the shores of Lake Köyceğiz, the ruined city of **Kaunos** (admission TL5; 8.30am-5.30pm) and unspoilt **İztuzu Beach** on the Mediterranean coast.

Sleeping & Eating

Dalyan's restaurant scene swings between high quality and lousy value, so be selective. For a drink, keep your ears pricked along Maraş Caddesi.

Dalyan Camping (☎/fax 284 4157; Maraş Caddesi 144; camp sites per tent/caravan TL15/25, 2-/3-/4-person bungalows TL20/40/60; Apr-Oct) This compact, well-shaded site is centrally located by the river. The eight pinewood bungalows are simple, clean and quite attractive.

Kilim Hotel (☎ 284 2253; www.kilimhotel.com; Kaunos Sokak 7; s/d TL35/70; Apr-Nov;) The active English owner, Becky, presides over this buzzing midrange hotel, which has a pool and palm-shaded seating area, and spacious rooms containing king-sized beds. There's a ramp for wheelchair access, complimentary use of bicycles, and daily yoga and aerobic workouts.

Midas Pension (☎ 284 Kaunos Sokak 30; www.midasdalyan.com; Kaunos Sokak 32; s/d TL50/60;) Selçuk and Saadet Nur are wonderful hosts of this riverside pension raised on stilts. The 10 rooms are smartly decked out, with private bathrooms attached.

Caretta Caretta (☎ 284 3039; Maraş Caddesi 124; mains TL10-20; Mar-Nov) Wagons and wooden platforms adorn this signature riverbank restaurant, which is also a great place for a beer. The *bonfile ve tavuk cığerli börek* (beef fillet with chicken livers baked in puff pastry) leads the impressive menu.

Getting There & Away

There are some direct *dolmuşes* to Dalyan from Köyceğiz (TL4, 30 minutes), but getting here normally involves changing at Ortaca (TL1.50). To get to Dalaman from Dalyan you must change in Ortaca and Köyceğiz. Dalyan's minibuses leave from the stop behind the mosque.

FETHIYE

☎ 0252 / pop 50,700

In 1958 an earthquake levelled the old harbour city of Fethiye, sparing only the ancient remains of Telmessos (400 BC) from its wrath. Fifty years on and Fethiye is once again a prosperous and proud hub of the Western Mediterranean. Its natural harbour, tucked away in the southern reaches of a broad bay scattered with pretty islands, is perhaps the region's finest.

Orientation & Information

Fethiye's *otogar* is 2.5km east of the centre. Atatürk Caddesi, the main street, has banks with ATMs. Most pensions are either up the hill or west of marina; the **tourist office** (☎ 614 1527; Iskele Meydanı; 10am-noon & 1-5.30pm) is opposite the marina, just past the Roman theatre.

Sights & Activities

In central Fethiye, little remains of the original town of Telmessos other than a **Roman theatre** and several **Lycian sarcophagi**. The cliffs hold several rock-cut tombs, including the Ionic **Tomb of Amyntas** (admission TL5; 8am-7pm). **Fethiye Museum** (505 Sokak; admission TL5; 8.30am-5pm Tue-Sun) has some small statues and votive stones.

Most people enjoy the well-promoted 12-island boat tour (TL25 per person), the Butterfly Valley tour (TL20) via Ölüdeniz, the Saklıkent Gorge tour (TL40) and the Dalyan tour (TL40).

Dolmuşes run to the nearby evocative Ottoman Greek 'ghost town' of **Kayaköy** (admission TL5; 9am-7pm), abandoned after the population exchange of 1923.

Fethiye is the starting (or finishing) point for the **Lycian Way** (p928), a superb scenic walking trail along the coast. The town

FETHİYE

INFORMATION
Tourist Office....1 C2

SIGHTS & ACTIVITIES
Fethiye Museum....2 E1
Lycian Sarcophagi....3 D1
Roman Theatre....4 C2
Tomb of Amyntas....5 E2

SLEEPING
Ideal Pension....6 B2
Tan Pansiyon....7 C2
Villa Daffodil....8 A2
Yacht Plaza Hotel....9 B2

EATING
Café Oley....10 C2
Hilmi et Balık Restaurant....11 D2
Meğri Lokantasi....12 D2
Paşa Kebab....13 D2

DRINKING
Club Bananas....14 C2
Val's Bar....15 D1

TRANSPORT
Minibus Station....16 E2
Minibuses to Ölüdeniz....17 D2

also makes a good base for day trips to the beautiful **Saklıkent Gorge**, an 18km-long crack in the Akdaglar mountains too narrow for even sunlight to squeeze through; and to the ruins at **Tlos** (admission TL8; 8am-6pm) and **Pınara** (admission TL3).

Sleeping

Fethiye has some good-value midrange digs, but not much at the deluxe end.

Ideal Pension (614 1981; www.idealpension.net; 26 Sokak 1; dm/s/d from TL20/35/40;) For the past two decades Ideal Pension has provided high quality and cheap beds to weary travellers. Aside from the clean (albeit small) rooms, there's a large terrace with bay views and generous breakfasts.

Tan Pansiyon (614 1584; fax 614 1676; 30 Sokak 43; s/d TL30/50) When the backpacker grind wears thin, try this traditional Turkish pension run by a charming elderly couple. Rooms are small (the bathrooms smaller), but it's sparkling-clean and quiet.

Villa Daffodil (614 9595; www.villadaffodil.com; Fevzi Çakmak Caddesi 115; s/d TL50/90;) This large Ottoman-designed guest house is one of the few surviving older buildings in town. The rooms have slanted ceilings and a homely feel; the best have sea views and anterooms. Hussein, a retired colonel, is a genial manager.

Eating & Drinking

One way to taste Fethiye's fabulous fish without losing too many lira is to bring your own! Follow fishy smells to the market, browse what's on offer and check the day's prices chalked up on the boards. Next, ferry the fish to one of the restaurants surrounding the market (pick the most popular) and ask them to cook it. For just TL5.50, they will cook your flipper and throw in a sauce, green salad, garlic bread, fruit and coffee.

Fethiye's bars and nightclubs are mostly cheek by jowl on one little street, Hamam Sokak, just off İskele Meydanı.

Paşa Kebab (614 9807; Çarşı Caddesi 42; mains TL8-10) Considered locally to offer the best *kebaps* in town, this honest and unpretentious place has a well-priced menu. Try the Paşa special, an oven-baked beef, tomato and cheese concoction.

Café Oley (612 9532; 38 Sokak 4; meals TL8-10;) Famed for her smoothies, Vegemite and pancakes, superchef Atilla also does good salads and sandwiches.

Meğri Lokantasi (614 4047; Çarşı Caddesi 26; mains TL14-25) Packed with locals who spill onto the streets, the Meğri does excellent and hearty home-style cooking. The *güveç* (casseroles) are a speciality.

Hilmi et Balık Restaurant (612 6242; Hal ve Pazar Yeri 53; 400g fish TL15-20; 10am-midnight) Set inside the fish market building, this place does meat dishes as well as fish (which is its speciality) and is a firm favourite locally. You can also bring your own fish.

Val's Bar (Müge Sokak) Englishwoman Val's cute little bar, near the new Cultural Centre, stocks a mean selection of poison and strong coffee.

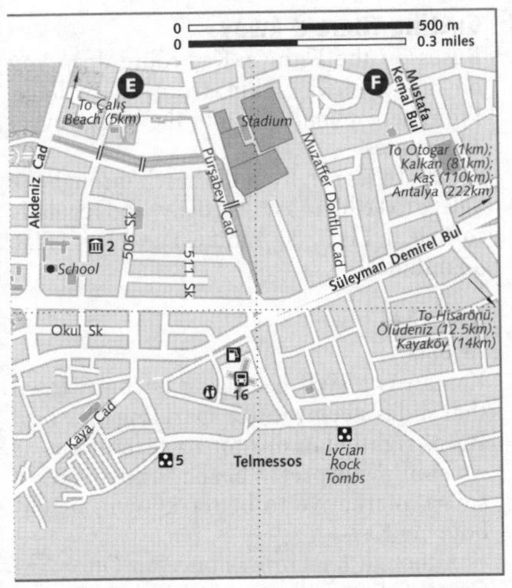

Club Bananas (off Hamam Sokak) Any venue where staff set fire to the bar then dance on it is going to be hard to overlook on a big night out.

Getting There & Away

For northbound buses, you must change at Antalya or Muğla. Buses from the *otogar* to Antalya (TL20, 7½ hours) head east along the coast (*sahil*) via Kalkan (TL7, 1½ hours), Kaş (TL8, 2½ hours) and Olympos (TL15, five hours). The inland (*yayla*) road to Antalya (TL16, four hours) is quicker but less scenic. *Dolmuşes* to more-local destinations, including Ölüdeniz (TL3, 25 minutes), leave from behind the big white mosque (Yeni Cami) in the town centre.

ÖLÜDENIZ

☎ 0252

Over the mountains to the south of Fethiye, lovely Ölüdeniz's sheltered blueish lagoon, lush national park and long spit of sandy beach have been a curse as much as a blessing. Ölüdeniz (Dead Sea) is now one of the Mediterranean's most famous beach spots, with far too many package-holiday hotels backed up behind the sands. Still, the **lagoon** (admission TL2; 8am-8pm) itself remains tranquillity incarnate and is a gorgeous place to sun yourself. Ölüdeniz is also a hot spot for **paragliding** (and less-cool parasailing). Companies here offer tandem paragliding flights off 1960m-high Baba Dağ (Mt Baba) for TL150 to TL200.

You may prefer to catch a boat from Ölüdeniz to the beautiful **Butterfly Valley** (TL12.50 return), where there is a handful of laid-back accommodation options.

Sleeping & Eating

Despite all the package-tour colonies, camping grounds are the only budget options for independent travellers. Some offer bungalows or cabins.

Sugar Beach Club (☎ 617 0048; www.thesugarbeachclub.com; Ölüdeniz Caddesi 20; camp site/bungalow per person TL10/70; Apr-Oct;) About 600m to the right of the main drag, this well-run theme park for beach-party backpackers has a private strip of beach and palms, shaded lounging areas, a beach cafe-bar and spotless bungalows. Bikes can be hired and small shops are on-site.

Oba Restaurant (☎ 617 0158; Mimar Sınan Caddesi; mains TL15-25) Built like a log cabin, the Oba

BLUE CRUISE

Fethiye is the hub of Turkey's cruising scene, dispatching dozens of yachts on a daily basis in summer. The most popular voyage is the 'Blue Cruise' to Kale (Demre), 1¼ hours by bus from Olympos – a four-day, three-night journey on a *gület* (traditional wooden yacht) that attracts young party animals. You call in at bays along the way for swimming, sunbathing and variable amounts of boozing. A less common route is between Marmaris and Fethiye, also taking four days and three nights. Aficionados say this is a much prettier route but for some reason it's not as popular.

Depending on the season the price is €100 to €180 per person (food and water should be included). Make sure you shop around for a service that suits – there are many shoddy operators working the waters (and your wallet). Recommended operators include **Almila Boat Cruise** (☎ 0535-636 0076; www.beforelunch.com), **Big Backpackers** (☎ 0252-614 9312; www.bluecruisefethiye.com) and **Olympos Yachting** (☎ 0242-892 1145; www.olymposyachting.com).

For more-ambitious trips you can charter the whole boat yourself, with or without crew, and set off wherever the fancy takes you. Fethiye (p895) and Marmarıs (p892) are both good starting points.

Hostel's restaurant has a great reputation for home-style food at a palatable price. It also does great Turkish/European breakfasts including homemade muesli with mountain yoghurt and local pine honey.

Getting There & Away

Frequent minibuses run between Ölüdeniz and Fethiye (TL3, 25 minutes).

PATARA

☎ 0242

Scruffy little Patara (Gelemiş) is the perfect spot to mix your ruin-rambling with some dedicated sand-shuffling on 20-odd kilometres of wide, golden **beach** (admission incl ruins TL2). With its rural setting and unhurried pace of life, it's a great place to chill out for a few days. The extensive **ruins** include a triple-arched triumphal gate at the entrance to the site, with a necropolis containing several Lycian tombs nearby. All in all, it's a good combination of nature and culture.

Sleeping & Eating

All the places to stay and most of the places to eat are in Gelemiş village, 1.5km inland from the ruins and 2.5km from the beach.

Rose Pension (☎ 843 5165; www.rosepensionpatara.com; s/d TL20/35;) This large, sand-coloured pension is favoured by shrewd travellers who appreciate genuine hospitality. Extra efforts such as garden-fresh produce and a stylish lounge make this an alluring place to stay.

Akay Pension (☎ 843 5055; www.pataraakaypension.com; s/d/t TL25/35/45;) Run by super-keen-to-please Kazım and family, the pension has well-maintained little rooms and comfortable beds with balconies overlooking orange trees.

Sema Hotel (☎ 843 5114; www.semahotel.com; s/d TL25/40;) The Sema is not a luxurious hotel, but it's ideal for those who prefer to share their travel experience with warm locals. Perched 60 steep steps above town, the rooms are basic but spotless, cool and pretty much mosquito-free.

Golden Pension (☎ 843 5162; www.goldenpension.com; s/d TL30/40;) With homely rooms with balconies, a pretty shaded terrace and a friendly family that's not overeager to please, this pension is peaceful and private. There are plans for a pool and the restaurant (mains TL10 to TL20) enjoys good foot traffic thanks to a comprehensive menu of meat, fish and vegetarian dishes.

Getting There & Away

Buses on the Fethiye–Kaş route drop you on the highway 4km from the village. From here *dolmuşes* run to the village every 45 minutes.

Minibuses run from the beach through the village to Fethiye (TL6, six daily) and regularly to Kalkan (TL5, 20 minutes) and Kaş (TL8, 45 minutes).

KALKAN

☎ 0242

Kalkan is a stylish hillside harbour town that slides steeply into a sparkling blue bay. It's as rightly famous for its restaurants as its sublimely pretty beach, and makes a smart alternative to better-known, neighbouring Kaş.

Although Kalkan was once an Ottoman-Greek fishing village called Kalamaki, the town is now devoted to upscale tourism. Development continues unchecked on the outskirts of town, but thankfully Kalkan's charms are found right in the middle. Spend a night or two in one of many great-value pensions, and you'll quickly see why foreign investors have driven up property prices.

Sleeping

Çelik Pansiyon (☎ 844 2126; Süleyman Yılmaz Caddesi 9; s/d TL30/40;) One of the few cheap guest houses open year-round, the Çelik has rather spartan rooms, though they're quite spacious and spotless, and a roof terrace.

Holiday Pension (☎ 844 3777; Süleyman Yılmaz Caddesi; d TL50) The rooms are simple but charming, some with old wooden beams, antique lace curtains and delightful balconies with good views.

Türk Evi (☎ 844 3129; www.kalkanturkevi.com; Hasan Altan Caddesi; d TL60-80;) Multilingual and multitalented Önder and Selma Elitez run one of the more endearing places to stay on the Western Mediterranean. The beautifully restored stone house has eight rooms filled with rare antique furniture, some with original bathtubs.

Elixir (☎ 843 5032; Kalamar Yolu 8; d €100-120;) It's always exciting to see a hotel attempt something new, especially when they pull it off. Part body-focused retreat, part designer hotel, the Elixir features two handsome pools (one on the roof) and a smooth-edged Turkish bath.

Eating & Drinking

İstanbul Restaurant (☎ 844 2282; Süleyman Yılmaz Caddesi; mains TL10-20) This understated eatery's few white-clothed tables are usually filled with knowing diners enjoying dishes such as *ali nazik* (aubergine, pepper and beef purée) and *ahtapot güveç* (octopus casserole).

Belgin's (☎ 844 3614; Hasan Altan Caddesi; mains TL12-20; 10am-midnight Apr-Oct) In a 150-year-old former olive-oil press, Belgin's serves traditional Turkish food at tempting prices. The speciality is *mantı*. There's usually live Turkish music from 8pm.

Daphne Restaurant (☎ 844 3547; Kocakaya Caddesi; mains TL15-30; May-Oct) Owned by the same crowd as the heralded Aubergine, big things were expected of the former Daphne Hotel. It certainly delivers, with an emphasis on wok-style dishes and seafood. Live music is played on most nights.

Korsan Kebap (☎ 844 2116; Atatürk Caddesi; meals TL20) With tables on a terrace by the harbour, Korsan does delicious, upmarket *kebaps* and pide. Try the speciality, the *dürüm kebap* with spicy tender steak.

Aubergine (☎ 844 3332; İskele Sokak; meals €13) With tables right on the yacht marina, as well as cosy seats inside, this restaurant is famous for its slow-roasted wild boar, and its swordfish fillet served in a creamy vegetable sauce.

Moonlight Bar (Süleyman Yılmaz Caddesi 17) Kalkan's oldest bar is still its most 'happening', though 95% of people at the outside tables, or on the small dance floor, are tourists.

Getting There & Away

In high season minibuses connect Kalkan with Fethiye (TL7, 1½ hours) and Kaş (TL2.50, 35 minutes). Around eight minibuses also run daily to Patara (TL3, 25 minutes).

KAŞ

☎ 0242 / pop 7700

The 500m-high mountain known as 'Sleeping Man' (Yatan Adam) has watched Kaş evolve from a beautiful place of exile for political dissidents, to a funky boutique shopping and cafe strip, to a seaside adventure playground. While Kaş proper may not sport the finest beach culture in the region, it's a yachties' haven, and the atmosphere of the town is wonderfully mellow. The surrounding areas are ideal for day trips by sea or scooter, and a plethora of adventure sports are on offer, in particular some world-class diving.

The **tourist office** (☎ 836 1238; 8am-noon & 1-7pm Mon-Fri May-Oct, to 5pm Nov-Apr) is on the main square; log on at **Net-C@fé** (☎ 836 4505; İbrahim Serin Caddesi 16/B; per hr TL2).

Sights & Activities

Apart from enjoying the town's mellow atmosphere and small pebble **beaches**, you can walk west a few hundred metres to the well-preserved **Roman theatre**. You also can walk to the **Lycian rock tombs** in the cliffs above the town. The walk is strenuous so go at a cool time of day. It's well worth walking up the hill on the street to the east of the tourist office to reach the **Monument Tomb**, a Lycian sarcophagus mounted on a high base.

The most popular **boat trip** (TL25 to TL30) is to Kekova Island and Üçağız, a three-hour excursion that includes time to see several interesting ruins as well as stops for swimming. Other standard excursions go to the Mavi Mağara (Blue Cave), Patara and Kalkan, or to Liman Ağzı, Longos and several nearby islands. There are also overland excursions to the wonderful 18km-long Saklıkent Gorge.

If you want to do anything active while you are in Kaş, contact **Bougainville Travel** (☎ 836 3737; www.bougainville-turkey.com; İbrahim Selin Caddesi 10). This long-established English-Turkish tour operator offers scuba-diving, hiking, mountain biking and canyoning trips in the area. The sea-kayaking day trips over the Kekova sunken city (TL50), suitable for all fitness levels, will be the highlight of your stay in Kaş.

Sleeping

Cheap pensions are mostly west of Atatürk Bulvarı, and more-expensive hotels and restaurants to the east.

Santosa Pension (☎ 836 1714; Recep Bilgin Sokak 4; s/d TL20/40;) Clean, quiet and cheap is how best to describe this backpacker hang-out. The rooms are bare and simple, but excellent for the price.

Ateş Pension (☎ 836 1393; www.atespension.com; Amfi Tiyatro Sokak 3; s/d TL30/50;) Well run by Ahmed and family, this is a friendly place with a pleasant roof terrace where BBQs are held. Guests have free use of the kitchen and internet.

Hilal Pansiyon (☎ 836 1207; www.korsan-kas.com; Süleyman Çavuş Caddesi; dm/s/d TL15/30/50;) The friendly Hilal has a plant-potted terrace where BBQs take place. The travel agency below the

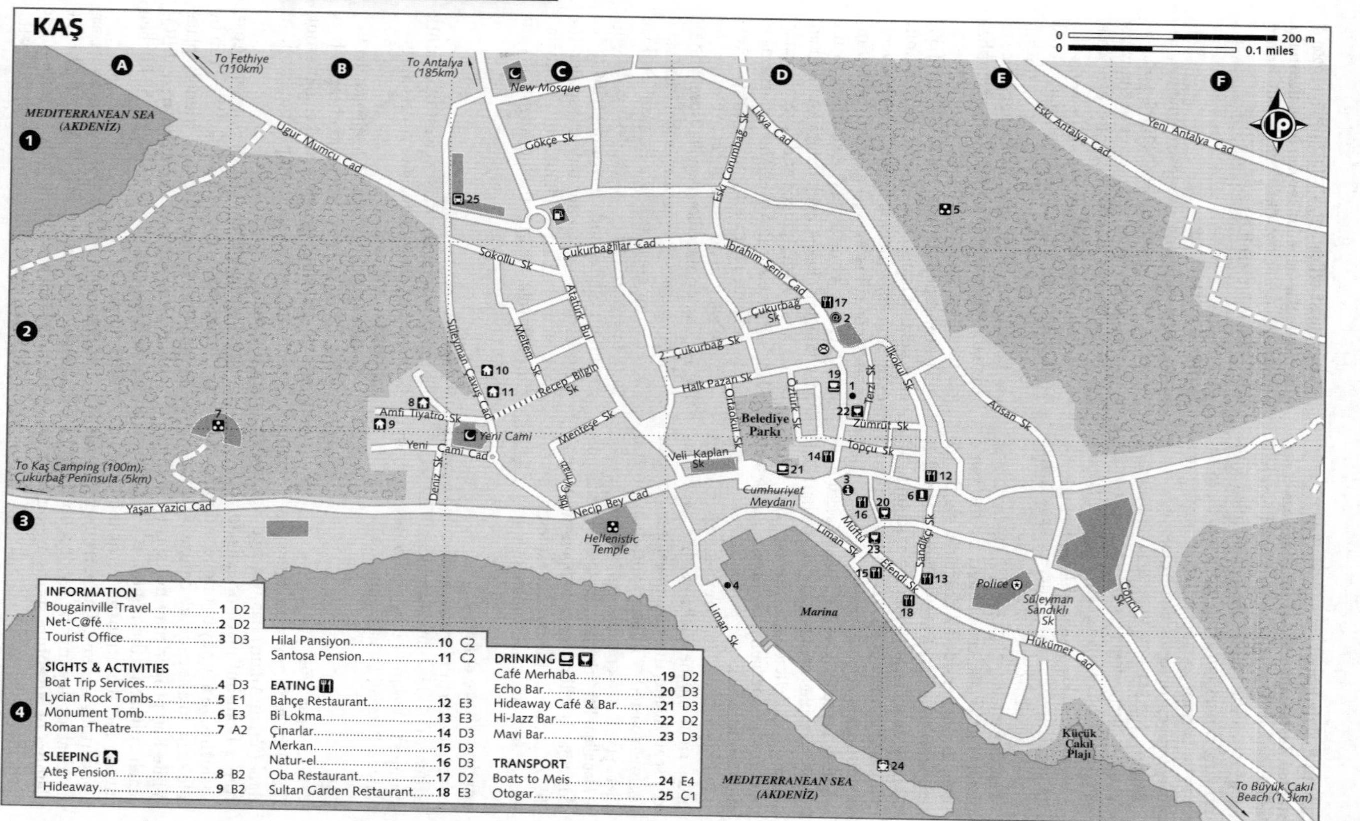
KAŞ
0 200 m
0 0.1 miles
INFORMATION
Bougainville Travel 1 D2
Net-C@fé 2 D2
Tourist Office 3 D3
SIGHTS & ACTIVITIES
Boat Trip Services 4 D3
Lycian Rock Tombs 5 E1
Monument Tomb 6 E3
Roman Theatre 7 A2
SLEEPING
Ateş Pension 8 B2
Hideaway 9 B2
Hilal Pansiyon 10 C2
Santosa Pension 11 C2
EATING
Bahçe Restaurant 12 E3
Bi Lokma 13 E3
Çınarlar 14 D3
Merkan 15 D3
Natur-el 16 D3
Oba Restaurant 17 D2
Sultan Garden Restaurant 18 E3
DRINKING
Café Merhaba 19 D2
Echo Bar 20 D3
Hideaway Café & Bar 21 D3
Hi-Jazz Bar 22 D2
Mavi Bar 23 D3
TRANSPORT
Boats to Meis 24 E4
Otogar 25 C1
MEDITERRANEAN SEA (AKDENİZ)
To Fethiye (110km)
To Antalya (185km)
To Kaş Camping (100m); Çukurbağ Peninsula (5km)
To Büyük Çakıl Beach (1.3km)
Uğur Mumcu Cad
Yaşar Yazıcı Cad
Süleyman Çavuş Cad
Yeni Cami
Yeni Cami Cad
Amfi Tiyatro Sk
Deniz Sk
New Mosque
Gökçe Sk
Sokollu Sk
Meltem Sk
Recep Bilgin Sk
Menteşe Sk
İbs Çıkmazı
Atatürk Bul
Çukurbağlılar Cad
Necip Bey Cad
Hellenistic Temple
Veli Kaplan Sk
1. Çukurbağ Sk
2. Çukurbağ Sk
Halk Pazarı Sk
Ortaokul Sk
Belediye Parkı
Cumhuriyet Meydanı
İbrahim Serin Cad
Eski Çorumbağ Sk
Likya Cad
Öztürk Sk
Topçu Sk
Zümrüt Sk
Terzi Sk
İlkokul Sk
Arısan Sk
Liman Sk
Marina
Mutfu Sk
Efendi Sk
Sandıkçı Sk
Police
Süleyman Sandıklı Sk
Hükümet Cad
Göncü Sk
Küçük Çakıl Plajı
Eski Antalya Cad
Yeni Antalya Cad
MEDITERRANEAN SEA (AKDENİZ)

TURKEY

pension offers guests 10% discounts on activities including kayaking, diving and trips to Saklıkent.

Hideaway (☎ 836 1887; www.kasturkey.com; Amfi Tiyatro Sokak; s TL50, d TL70-80;) Aptly named, the quiet Hideaway is located at the far end of town. Rooms are simple but in good order and all have a balcony. There's a roof terrace with sea views over the water and amphitheatre.

Eating

Oba Restaurant (☎ 836 1687; İbrahim Serin Caddesi 26; meze TL4) With a pleasant walled terrace under orange trees, the Oba offers tasty Turkish dishes cooked daily by Nuran, the owner's mother. Hearty, tasty and great value, it's simple Turkish home cooking at its best.

Bi Lokma (☎ 836 3942; Hukumet Caddesi 2; mains TL8-12) The Bi Lokama has tables meandering around a terraced garden overlooking the harbour. Sabo (Mama) turns out great traditional dishes including famous *mantı* and pastries. The wine list is also reasonably priced.

Çinarlar (☎ 836 2860; Mütfü Efendi Sokak 4; pizza TL8-15) Perennially popular among Kaş' young, who come for the affordable pide and pop music, Çinarlar also has a pleasant courtyard tucked away off the street.

Natur-el (☎ 836 2834; Gürsöy Sokak 6; meals TL15-20) With its dishes cooked to old Ottoman recipes passed down from generation to generation, Natur-el provides a chance to sample Turkish cuisine at its brilliant best. If you haven't yet tried *mantı,* then choose between three varieties here.

Sultan Garden Restaurant (☎ 836 3762; Hükümet Caddesi; mains TL15-25; 10am-midnight) This is a very pretty place complete with original Lycian tombs and a functional cistern. The veggie burger is awesome, and the *hünkar beğendı* (spiced lamb pieces on aubergine puree) is soft and flavoursome.

Bahçe Restaurant (☎ 836 2370; Likya Caddesi 31; meals TL25; dinner) Up behind the Lycian sarcophagus, Bahçe has a pretty garden and serves excellent dishes at decent prices, including a terrific range of meze. The fish in paper receives rave reviews.

Mercan (☎ 836 1209; Balıkçı Barınağı 2; mains TL15-30) Since 1956, when the owner's father was working his magic, the Mercan has been satisfying customers with fish and meat creations and confident, disarming service. The swordfish *kebap* should win awards.

Drinking

Rejoice! There are a couple of buzzing bars in Kaş. Not the kind of boisterous places you would find in Marmaris (p892) or Kuşadası (p887), but more civilised venues heavy on atmosphere. Check out **Echo Bar** (Gürsoy Sokak), **Mavi Bar** (Mütfü Efendi Sokak) or, run by a retired New York taxi driver with a few stories to tell, **Hi-Jazz Bar** (Zümrüt Sokak 3). For caffienated concoctions, make for **Café Merhaba** (Ibrahim Serin Caddesi 19) or **Hideaway Café & Bar** (Cumhuriyet Caddesi 16/A).

Getting There & Away

There are half-hourly *dolmuşes* to Kalkan (TL2.50, 30 minutes), Olympos (TL8, 2½ hours) and Patara (TL5, 45 minutes), and daily buses to İstanbul (TL65, 15 hours), Ankara (TL50, 11 hours) and İzmir (TL25, 8½ hours). For other destinations, connect at Fethiye (TL7, three hours) or Antalya (TL9, 3½ hours).

Ferries from Kaş sail daily throughout the year for the Greek island of Meis (Kastellorizo) – though, as it consists of little more than a tiny fishing village and a sprinkle of restaurants, it's an expensive mission (per person return TL70) just to get your passport stamped. Note also that you can't stay overnight in Meis, nor enter Greece there. Bizarrely you can enter Turkey through Kaş if coming from Meis.

OLYMPOS & ÇIRALI

☎ 0242

Olympos has long had an ethereal hold over its visitors. It was an important Lycian city in the 2nd century BC, when the Olympians devoutly worshipped Hephaestus (Vulcan), the god of fire. No doubt this veneration sprang from reverence for the mysterious Chimaera, an eternal flame that still springs from the earth nearby. Along with the other Lycian coastal cities, Olympos went into decline in the 1st century BC, before its fortunes twisted and turned through Roman rule, 3rd-century AD pirate attacks, and fortress building during the Middle Ages and by the Venetians, Genoese and Rhodians (you can still see remains hanging from the cliffs). By the 15th century the site had been abandoned.

Neighbouring Çiralı, 1km to the east, is another gem of a place. While Olympos has a well-established party reputation (though it has gentrified considerably during the last decade), Çiralı is the perfect place to experience the fine art of *keyif* (quiet relaxation).

The drive here is also a treat, strewn with mountain views all the way from Kaş.

Sights

Don't miss the fascinating ruins of **ancient Olympos** (admission TL2). A skip away from the beach, it's a wild, abandoned place where ruins peek out from forested coppices, rocky outcrops and riverbanks.

If you just want to spend a lazy day, nothing beats the **beach** in Olympos. Çiralı also boasts a fine stretch of clear sand.

Most pensions in Olympos and Çiralı run tours (TL10) to **Chimaera**, a cluster of flames that blaze from crevices on the rocky slopes of Mt Olympos. It's located about 7km from Olympos.

Sleeping & Eating

OLYMPOS

Staying in an Olympos tree house has long been the stuff of travel legend – it offers fabulous value, community-minded accommodation in a stunning natural setting. The tree-house dream is fading in the face of modern conveniences, but all camps include breakfast and dinner in the price, although drinks are extra. Bathrooms are generally shared, but many bungalows have private bathrooms and some have air-conditioning.

Not all tree houses have reliable locks, so store valuables at reception. It's also worth being extra attentive with personal hygiene while staying here – every year some travellers get ill. The huge influx of visitors, over the summer in particular, can overwhelm the camps' capacity for waste disposal. Be vigilant when it comes to eating, and don't swim around the point area.

Kadir's Yörük Top Treehouse (☎ 892 1250; www.kadirstreehouses.com; dm/bungalow TL20/40; ❄ 💻) Kadir's started the tree-living trend. For the first time in many years, the quirky place has grown smaller due to a fire damaging a large section of the property. But the fun has not gone away: there are three bars (including the time-honoured Bull Bar) and a rock-climbing wall. A range of other activities are also on offer.

Şaban (☎ 892 1265; www.sabanpansion.com; dm/tree house TL20/30, bungalow TL35-40; ❄ 💻) The sight of travellers laid out in hammocks snoozing in the shade soon confirms the local lore: that you come here to chill. Şaban is not a party place, and instead sells itself on tranquillity, space, a family feel, and great home cooking. It's a good choice for single women.

Orange Pension (☎ 892 1317; www.olympos orangepension.com; bungalow TL40; ❄) A longstanding favourite that's especially big with Turkish university students and Japanese guests, the Orange has grown in recent years, but Yusuf and friends still run a good show. The wooden rooms upstairs have a futuristic Swiss Family Robinson feel, while the concrete rooms downstairs are perhaps the future of Olympos. It's got a great communal dining area, and the same guys run a nightclub hidden in the valley.

Bayram's (☎ 892 1243; www.bayrams.com; tree house TL30, bungalow from TL40; ❄ 💻) Here chilled-out 20-somethings sit on cushioned benches in postparty states. Backgammon, books and the odd swim in the sea are Bayram's activities of choice.

Varuna (☎ 892 1347; mains TL10-15) Next to Bayram's, this popular restaurant serves snacks and mains including fresh trout, *gözleme* and *şiş kebaps* (roast skewered meat) in attractive open cabins.

ÇIRALI

Çıralı, to put it crudely, is just two dirt roads lined with pensions. To put it another way, it's a delightful beach community for nature lovers and postbackpackers. There are about 60 pensions here, some near the path up to the Chimaera and others close to the beach and the Olympos ruins.

Olympia Treehouse & Camping (☎ 825 7311; camp site/tree house per person TL10/20) Offering a tree-house experience outside Olympos (and sans party atmosphere), this is a pleasant, peaceful place set by the beach amid fruit trees. Boat and snorkelling excursions can be organised.

Orange Motel (☎ 825 7327; www.orangemotel.net; s/d TL50/90; ❄ 💻) Another smart and affordable choice right on the beach. The garden is hung with hammocks, and the stairs leading to the agreeable rooms are wrought in iron design. The evening meal is about as wild as it gets in Çıralı; nonguests often drop by for a taste of what's cooking.

Hotel Canada (☎ 825 7233; www.hotelcanada.com; s/d TL80/100; ❄ 💻 🚭) This is a beautiful place to stay, offering pretty much the quintessential Çıralı experience: warmth, friendliness, and steady relaxation among hammocks and citrus trees. It's ideal for families and children. Carrie and Saban are impeccable hosts.

Arcadia Hotel (☎ 825 7340; www.arcadiaholiday.com; d with half-board TL200;) The Canadian-Turkish owners of these four luxury bungalows have established a lovely escape amid verdant gardens at the northern end of the beach, across the road from Myland Nature (also recommended). The place is well laid out and well managed, and the restaurant is of a high standard.

Getting There & Away

Buses and minibuses plying the Fethiye–Antalya road will drop you at a roadside restaurant from where hourly minibuses go on to Çiralı and Olympos (TL2.75, 20 minutes). From October to April they wait until enough passengers arrive, which can sometimes take a while.

The most pleasant way to get from Fethiye to Olympos is on a cruise (see p897).

ANTALYA

☎ 0242 / pop 603,200

Once seen by travellers as the gateway to the 'Turkish Riviera', Antalya is generating a buzz among culture vultures. Situated directly on the Gulf of Antalya (Antalya Körfezi), the largest Turkish city on the Mediterranean is both stylishly modern and classically beautiful. It boasts the creatively preserved Roman-Ottoman quarter of Kaleiçi, a pristine Roman harbour, plus stirring ruins in the surrounding Beydağları (Bey Mountains). The city's restaurants and boutique hotels rival those throughout the country, the archaeological museum is world class, and there is a smattering of chic Med-carpet clubs. The opera and ballet season at the Aspendos amphitheatre continues to draw attention.

Orientation & Information

The *otogar* is 4km north of the centre on the D650 highway to Burdur. The city centre is at Kale Kapısı, a major intersection marked by a clock tower. To get into Kaleiçi, head south down the hill from the clock tower or cut in from Hadrian's Gate (Hadriyanüs Kapisi), just off Atatürk Caddesi.

There are several post offices within walking distance of Kaleiçi, and a **tourist information booth** (☎/fax 241 1747; Yavuz Ozcan Parkı; 8am-7pm). **Natural Internet Cafe** (Kaleiçi, 8am-11pm) is the city's most atmospheric internet den, located within the maze of eateries down the steps behind the Atatürk statue; and **Owl Bookshop** (☎ 243 2944; Barbaros Mahallesi, Hesapçi Sokak 21) is the best secondhand bookshop on the Turkish Mediterranean.

Sights & Activities

Around the harbour is the lovely historic district called **Kaleiçi**, whose walls once repelled raiders. It's a charming area full of twisting alleys, atmosphere-laden courtyards, souvenir shops and lavishly restored mansions, while cliffside vantage points on either side of the harbour provide stunning views over a beautiful marina and the soaring Bey Mountains (Beydağları).

Heading down from the **clock tower** you will pass the **Yivli Minare** (Grooved Minaret), which rises above an old church that was converted into a mosque. In the southern reaches of Kaleiçi, the quirky **Kesik Minare** (Cut Minaret) is built on the site of a ruined Roman temple.

Just off Atatürk Caddesi, the monumental **Hadrian's Gate** was erected during the Roman emperor Hadrian's reign (AD 117–38).

Don't miss the excellent **Suna & İnan Kıraç Kaleiçi Museum** (Kocatepe Sokak 25; admission TL1.70; 9am-noon & 1-6pm Thu-Tue), in the heart of Kaleiçi. It houses a fine collection of Turkish ceramics, together with rooms set up to show important events in Ottoman family life.

Need some hush and a cool place to rest your sightseeing-abused feet? Nothing beats **Karaalioğlu Parkı**, a large, attractive and flower-filled park that's good for a stroll. Alternatively, do some yoga at the ambitiously named **Association for the Unity of Mankind** (☎ 244 5807; Hesapçı Sokak 7).

Excursion yachts tie up in the Roman Harbour in Kaleiçi, offering **boat trips** that visit the Gulf of Antalya islands and some beaches for a swim (TL20 to TL80).

Sleeping

There are pensions aplenty in Kaleiçi, and most are housed in renovated historic buildings.

White Garden Pansiyon (☎ 248 9115; www.xhost.co.uk/whitegarden; Hesapçı Geçidi 9; s/d TL30/40;) The White Garden combines tidiness, discretion and class beyond its price, not to mention impeccable service from Metin and co. The building and courtyard have been beguilingly restored.

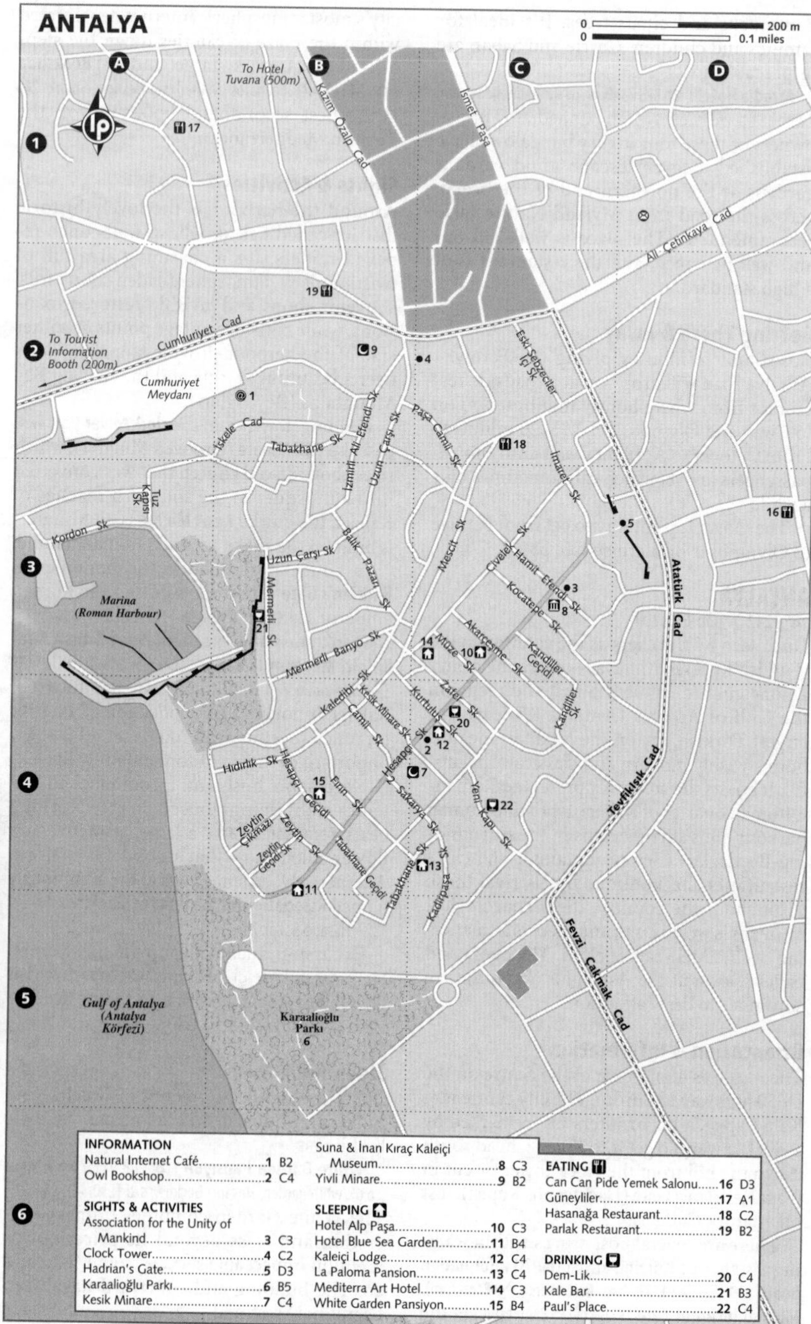
ANTALYA
0 200 m
0 0.1 miles
A
B
C
D
1
2
3
4
5
6
To Hotel Tuvana (500m)
Kazım Özalp Cad
İsmet Paşa
Ali Çetinkaya Cad
Cumhuriyet Cad
To Tourist Information Booth (200m)
Cumhuriyet Meydanı
Eski Sebzeciler İçi Sk
İskele Cad
Tabakhane Sk
İzmirli Ali Efendi Sk
Uzun Çarşı Sk
Paşa Camii Sk
İmaret Sk
Tuz Kapısı Sk
Kordon Sk
Uzun Çarşı Sk
Balık Pazarı Sk
Mescit Sk
Civelek Sk
Hamit Efendi Sk
Kocatepe Sk
Marina (Roman Harbour)
Mermerli Sk
Mermerli Banyo Sk
Akarçeşme Sk
Müze Sk
Kandiller Geçidi
Kandiller Sk
Atatürk Cad
Kaledibi Sk
Kesik Minare Sk
Camii Sk
Kurtuluş Sk
Zafer Sk
Hıdırlık Sk
Hesapçı Sk
Hesapçı Geçidi
Fırın Sk
Sakarya Sk
Yeni Kapı Sk
Tevfikiye Cad
Zeytin Çıkmazı
Zeytin Sk
Zeytin Geçidi Sk
Tabakhane Geçidi
Tabakhane Sk
Kadirpaşa Sk
Fevzi Çakmak Cad
Gulf of Antalya (Antalya Körfezi)
Karaalioğlu Parkı
INFORMATION
Natural Internet Café 1 B2
Owl Bookshop 2 C4
SIGHTS & ACTIVITIES
Association for the Unity of Mankind 3 C3
Clock Tower 4 C2
Hadrian's Gate 5 D3
Karaalioğlu Parkı 6 B5
Kesik Minare 7 C4
Suna & İnan Kıraç Kaleiçi Museum 8 C3
Yivli Minare 9 B2
SLEEPING
Hotel Alp Paşa 10 C3
Hotel Blue Sea Garden 11 B4
Kaleiçi Lodge 12 C4
La Paloma Pansion 13 C4
Mediterra Art Hotel 14 C3
White Garden Pansiyon 15 B4
EATING
Can Can Pide Yemek Salonu 16 D3
Güneyliler 17 A1
Hasanağa Restaurant 18 C2
Parlak Restaurant 19 B2
DRINKING
Dem-Lik 20 C4
Kale Bar 21 B3
Paul's Place 22 C4

Hotel Blue Sea Garden (☎ 248 8213; www.bluesea garden.com; Hesapçı Sokak 65; s/d with half-board TL40/60;) The two pluses here are the extra-large swimming pool area and the go-getting management team. The rooms are nothing special (the elevated ones are more peaceful) but the restaurant prepares excellent meals.

Kaleiçi Lodge (☎ 243 2270; www.kaleicilodge.com; Hesapçi Sokak 37; s/d TL50/80;) This stylish, small hotel is sparklingly new and very affordable. The stark white lobby and hallways lead to red-draped, sharp-lined rooms.

La Paloma Pansion (☎ 244 8497; www.lapaloma pansion.com; Tabakhane Sokak 3; s/d TL80/100;) Housed in an Ottoman building, La Paloma has surprisingly large rooms, some with jacuzzi. The best rooms face inwards to the figure-eight-shaped swimming pool.

Tuvana (☎ 247 6015; www.tuvanahotel.com; Karanlýk Sokak 7; s/d TL100/150;) This hidden, once-royal compound of Ottoman houses has been converted into a fine old city inn. Rooms are suitably plush, with *kilims*, linen and light fittings emitting soft oranges and yellows.

Hotel Alp Paşa (☎ 247 5676; www.alppaşa.com; Hesapçı Sokak 30-32; s/d from €65/190;) The most effectively signposted hotel in the Kaleiçi labyrinth has 60 individually designed rooms, fitted out with tasteful Ottoman detail. The outdoor courtyard displays Roman columns and other artefacts unearthed during the hotel's construction. There's an on-site *hammam* and an atmospheric stone-walled restaurant.

Mediterra Art Hotel (☎ 244 8624; www.mediterraart .com; Zafer Sokak 5; d/ste TL160/200;) The sign of things to come in Antalya, perhaps, is this brand-new upscale masterpiece of wood and stone, offering sanctuary by a cutting-edge pool, and a marvellous winter dining room. The small though modestly luxurious rooms have LCD TVs.

Eating & Drinking

A nearly endless assortment of cafes and eateries are tucked in and around the harbour area; those perched over the bay command the highest prices. For cheap eating, cross Atatürk Caddesi and poke around deep in the commercial district.

Can Can Pide Yemek Salonu (☎ 243 2548; Hasim Iscan Mahallesi, Arik Caddesi 4a; kebap TL6) Looking for something cheap and cheerful? The Can Can most certainly can, offering fantastic *çorba* (soup), pide and Adana *dürüm*. It's elbow room only, so nudge right in.

Hasanağa Restaurant (☎ 242 8105; Mescit Sokak 15; meals TL10-20) Expect to find the garden here absolutely packed on Friday and Saturday nights, when traditional Turkish musicians and folk dancers entertain. Entrées are predictable, but the chefs have some wonders up their aprons.

Güneyliler (☎ 241 1117; Elmali Mahallesi 4 No 12; meals TL12) With its spare, cafeteria-style interior, this *very* reasonably priced locals-only joint isn't much to look at. But the wood-fired *lahmacun* and grilled *kebaps* are served with so many complimentary extras, you'll likely return again and again.

Parlak Restaurant (☎ 241 6553; Kazım Özlap Qvenue Zincirlihan 7; meals TL12-25) This sprawling, open-air patio is a local legend for its slow-roasted chicken. The service is theatrical and exact, as waiters shuffle meze and seafood off white tablecloths. A good choice if you're looking to relax for a while, and just steps from Kale Kapısı.

There are innumerable bars in Kaleiçi and around the yacht harbour. It's well worth seeking out the atmospheric **Kale Bar** (Mermerli Sokak 2), attached to the Tütav Turk Evi Hotel and artfully constructed around the old city wall; the lively **Dem-Lik** (☎ 247 1930; Zafer Sokak 16), filled with Turkish students; and the religiously inclined **Paul's Place** (Yeni Kapı Sokak 24). The good word comes in coffee cups at this informal expat 'club' on 2nd floor of St Paul Cultural Center.

Getting There & Away

Antalya's airport is 10km east of the city centre on the Alanya highway. Turkish Airlines offers frequent flights to/from İstanbul and Ankara. Atlasjet also has flights to/from İstanbul.

From the *otogar*, buses head to Göreme (TL38, 10 hours), Konya (TL18, six hours), Olympos (TL8, 1½ hours) and Manavgat/Side (TL8, 1½ hours).

AROUND ANTALYA

Between Antalya and Alanya there are several magnificent Graeco-Roman ruins to explore. You can't help but be dazzled by the sheer beauty of the ruins at **Perge** (admission TL10; 9am-7.30pm), 15km east of Antalya and 2km north of Aksu. The site has a 12,000-seat stadium and a 15,000-seat theatre. Another stunning place is **Aspendos** (admission TL10, parking TL4; 8am-7pm), 47km east of Antalya. Here you'll see the world's best-preserved Roman theatre, dating from the 2nd century AD and still used for performances during the Aspendos Festival every June/July.

The former capital of the fierce Termessians, who fought off Alexander the Great, **Termessos** (admission TL10; 8am-5.30pm) is high in the mountains, 34km inland from Antalya. The ruins have a spectacular setting but demand some vigorous walking and climbing. Unless a coach party turns up, these places are all eerily deserted.

The only gripe is that it's not convenient to get to these sights by public transport. The easiest way to see them is with your own transport or on a tour from Antalya. A full-day tour to Perge and Aspendos, with side trips to spots such as Side (below), costs TL80 per carload; a half-day tour taking in Termessos costs TL60. Ask at your pension or hotel in Antalya. There are plenty of agencies in Antalya hiring out cars for TL50 to TL70 per day.

The **Köprülü Kanyon**, located 96km north-east of Antalya, is a deservedly popular spot for white-water rafting. Agencies in Antalya offer rafting trips – including **Medraft Outdoor Camp** (☎ 312 6296; www.medraft.com), which charges TL80 for a lesson and a four-hour trip. Other operators charge less, but be wary of compromise.

SIDE

☎ 0242 / pop 18,000

The seasonal village of Side (*see*-duh) is the Turkish version of a carnival by the sea. With its souvenir-sellers, quaint beaches, family friendliness and peculiar slapstick charm, this once-docile fishing town is now a firmly established playground. It's almost like a film set; glorious Roman and Hellenistic ruins mark out the road, and the evening performance at the ancient amphitheatre is spectacular showbiz. The touts are a tedious downside, but visitors to Side often return, happy to get fleeced now and then by the same 2000-year-old tricks, happy to swim in the sea, happy to bask on the rocks, happy to unwind in Side.

You'll find ATMs on the main drag.

Sights

Side's impressive ancient structures include a huge **theatre** (admission TL10; 8am-7pm) with 15,000 seats, one of the largest in Anatolia; a Roman bath, now a **museum** (admission TL5; 9am-7pm), with an excellent small collection of statues and sarcophagi; and seaside **temples** to Apollo and Athena, dating from the 2nd century AD. It's also blessed with sandy **beaches**.

Sleeping & Eating

While the number of restaurants here increases every season, the menus tend to repeat. Fresh fish (TL15 to TL25) is usually the way forward – check what's included in the price.

Beach House Hotel (☎ 753 1607; www.beachhouse-hotel.com; Barbaros Caddesi; s/d TL35/70;) Run by a long-term Australian expat, this justifiably popular choice manages to be relaxing as well as boasting a prime beachside locale. Most rooms face the sea, and all have spacious balconies. The neighbouring Soundwaves Restaurant, run by the same crew, is also recommended.

Chillout Side (☎ 753 2041; www.chilloutside.com; Zambak Sokak 32; dm/s/d TL25/40/60;) The backpacker scene is set to return to Side with the opening of these keenly run new premises. Set around a pretty garden of mulberry trees, palms and roses, the hostel features a smart little bar and a genuine travel vibe.

Moonlight Restaurant (☎ 753 1400; Barbaros Caddesi 49; meals around TL25) Probably the classiest joint in town, with an extensive Turkish wine list and unfussy service. The mostly seafood offerings are well presented and very fresh. The biggest drawcard, however, is the romantic back patio.

Getting There & Away

In summer, Side has direct bus services to Ankara, İzmir and İstanbul. Otherwise, frequent minibuses connect Side with Manavgat *otogar*, 4km away, from where buses go to Antalya (TL8, 1¼ hours), Alanya (TL8, 1¼ hours) and Konya (TL25, 5½ hours).

ALANYA

☎ 0242 / pop 110,100

Alanya has mushroomed from a sparsely populated highway town on a silky sand beach to a densely populated tourist haven. Aside from the odd boat cruise or beach stroll, many visitors to Alanya shuffle between the airport shuttle and the hotel pool, perhaps venturing to a restaurant and banging nightclub after dark. But Alanya has something special up its dusty sleeve. Looming high above the modern centre is a brilliant fortress district, with a fine Seljuk castle, a wonderful mess of ruins, active remnants of village life and a touch of revamped 'Ottomania'.

The *otogar* is on the coastal highway (Atatürk Caddesi), 3km west of the centre. You'll find numerous banks with ATMs in the centre and, opposite the Alanya Museum, the **tourist office** (☎ 513 1240; Kalearkası Caddesi; 8.30am-5.30pm). **C@fé Pruva Internet** (☎ 519 2306; 8am-midnight) is off Müftüler Caddesi, just south of Atatürk Caddesi.

Sights & Activities

Alanya's crowning glory is the Seljuk **fortress** on top of the promontory, overlooking the city as well as the Pamphylian plain and the Cilician mountains. The octagonal **Kızıl Kule** (Red Tower; admission TL2; 9am-7.30pm Tue-Sun), down by the harbour, was also built in 1226.

Every day at around 10.30am **boats** (per person incl lunch TL35) leave from near Gazipaşa Caddesi for a six-hour voyage around the promontory, visiting several caves and **Cleopatra's Beach**.

Many local operators also organise tours for landlubbers. A typical tour to sights including Aspendos and Side costs around TL55 per person, while a village-visiting 4WD safari into the Taurus Mountains costs about TL40.

Sleeping

Sadly, Alanya is low on affordable accommodation, as pensions have been superseded by faceless concrete lumps. There are, however, two recommended options close to the main drag.

Baba Hotel (☎ 513 1032; İskele Caddesi 6; s/d TL35/45) Baba is about the cheapest pad in town, but you pay for what you get (which is not much). The front entrance is located on the left side of a cement stairway just off the street.

Otel Temiz (☎ 513 1016; fax 519 1560; İskele Caddesi 12; s/d TL50/100;) Hotel 'Clean' is just that. Plus the rooms are spacious, and the balconies offer a bird's eye view of the thumping club and bar action below.

Eating & Drinking

The cheap restaurant scene is being swallowed by rising rents, so if you're tired of tourist traps, look for a *köfte* joint, or any *lokanta* popular with workers.

Köfte D' Köfte (☎ 512 1270; Kale Caddesi; meals TL12) A flashy yellow-and-red sign greets diners at this new 'boutique' fast-food joint. Attentive service and generous meat, rice and salad combinations are all part of the deal.

Gaziantep Sofrası Restaurant (☎ 513 4570; İzzet Azakoğlu Caddesi; meals TL15) For something more adventurous than standard grills and seafood, this is one of central Alanya's best options. Traditional food from Gaziantep is on offer.

Mahperi Restaurant (☎ 512 5491; www.mahperi.com; Rıhtım Caddesi; meals €15-25) A much-loved fish and steak restaurant that's been in operation since 1947 (an astonishing feat in Alanya), this place is a class act, offering an escape from the tourism glitz.

Red Tower Brewery Restaurant (☎ 513 6664; İskele Caddesi 80) If EU membership were dependent on a good brewpub, the Red Tower would be Turkey's star delegate. Not only is this place rare, it also makes staggeringly good Pilsen.

Cuba (☎ 511 8745; İskele Caddesi) The newest addition to the Alanya party junket, this stylish and relatively small club is a (slightly) less manic alternative to its cohorts. Girls dressed in white get a free mojito.

Getting There & Away

There are frequent buses to Antalya (TL10, two hours) and to Adana (TL25, 10 hours), stopping in a number of towns (including Anamur) en route.

Fergün Denizcilik (☎ 511 5565; www.fergun.net) runs ferries to Girne (Northern Cyprus) twice a week (TL148 return, including taxes).

ANAMUR

☎ 0324 / pop 50,000

There's nothing special about the service town of Anamur, but it's well worth making a stop here on your way through for the ruined Byzantine city of **Anamurium** (admission TL2; 8am-8pm), 8.5km west of the town. A number of buildings are still identifiable and the occasional fragmented mosaic pokes through the topsoil. About 7km on the other side of town, **Mamure Castle** (Mamure Kalesi; admission TL2; 8am-6pm) is the biggest and best-preserved castle on both the eastern and western Mediterranean coasts. The roadside monolith retains all its original 36 towers.

If you get stuck overnight, good options are **Eser Pansiyon** (☎ 814 2322; www.eserpansiyon.com; İnönü Caddesi 6; s/d/tr TL25/40/50;) and, operated by the same owner, **Hotel Bella** (☎ 816 4751; www.mybellahotel.com; Kursat Caddesi 5; s/d/tr TL35/60/75;).

A bus from Alanya (three hours) will cost you TL15.

SILIFKE

☎ 0324 / pop 85,100

Silifke is a lush country town of historic significance and contemporary charm, with a handsome park alongside the gushing Göksu River. Stop here to visit the medieval **fortress** (admission free), with its gateless walls and ancient rock-carved cistern, and the ruined Roman **Temple of Jupiter** (admission free). The 1st-century stone **bridge** over the Göksu River holds an interesting place in local folklore, worth investigating for fans of the bizarre.

Hourly buses depart for Adana along the highway east of Silıfke (TL15, two hours) throughout the day, and will stop to pick up ruin ramblers.

From **Taşucu**, 11km southwest, boats and hydrofoils depart for Girne (Kyrenia) in Northern Cyprus (see p934).

KIZKALESI

☎ 0324

'Maiden's Castle' is a growing holiday resort, named after the astounding **Byzantine castle** offshore, which looks from a distance as if it's suspended on top of the water. Unless you're up to swimming 200m, you'll need to take a boat (TL5) to get out and see it. The ruins of **Korykos Castle** (admission TL2) are on the shore itself; the two were once linked by a causeway, a very unusual defensive ploy.

If you are staying, **Yaka Hotel** (☎ 523 2444; yakahotel@yakahotel.com; s/d TL60/90; ❄) is an excellent choice. There are frequent buses to Silifke (TL2, 30 minutes).

TARSUS

☎ 0324 / pop 216,000

The birthplace of St Paul doesn't offer much for budding pilgrims, though everything from churches to bars is named after him. You may find other features nearby more interesting: the stretch of Roman road in the **Old City**, the medieval **Eski Cami** (Old Mosque), and the lovely **waterfall** on the Cydnus River (accessible by *dolmuş* from the Eski Cami).

ADANA

☎ 0322 / pop 1.13 million

Turkey's fourth-largest city is not the kind of place you visit for fun. Lacking the mystique of İstanbul and the sophistication of İzmır, it's main use is as a transport hub. If you end up with some time to kill, it's worth having a look at the extravagant **Sabancı Merkez Cami**, built by legendary tycoon Sakip Sabancı, and the two city **museums**.

If you get stuck overnight, some budget options are fairly sleazy. Your best bet is **Otel Mercan** (☎ 351 2603; Ocak Meydanı; s/d TL35/70; ❄) or **Akdeniz Oteli** (☎ 363 1510; İnönü Caddesi 14/1; s/d TL60/100; ❄).

Şakirpaşa airport is just 4km from the centre; a taxi will cost TL10. Adana's *otogar*, 2km beyond the airport, serves destinations throughout Turkey, including Antakya (TL18, 3½ hours), Konya (TL35, 6½ hours), Ankara (TL35, 10 hours) and İstanbul (TL50, 16 hours).

ANTAKYA (HATAY)

☎ 0326 / pop 141,000

Part of Syria until 1938, you might recognise Antakya from its biblical name, Antioch – the city was vilified as the Roman Empire's most depraved outpost, a claim that the local tourist board keeps strangely quiet about. Sadly, present-day Antakya isn't nearly that exciting, though it's a thoroughly amenable modern town with distinct Arabic influences, and worth a wander even if you're not heading for the border.

Ferah Kırtasiye ve Kitabevi (Hürriyet Caddesi 17/D) has books, newspapers and magazines. Behind the bookshop is the ultrastylish **Oasis Internet Cafe** (☎ 216 5697; off Hürriyet Caddesi). The **tourist office** (☎ 216 6098; 🕒 8am-noon & 1-5pm) is on a roundabout on Atatürk Caddesi, a good 10-minute walk from town.

Sights

The magnificent Roman and Byzantine mosaics in the **Archaeology Museum** (Gündüz Caddesi; admission TL5; 🕒 8.30am-noon & 1.30-5pm Tue-Sun) more than justify a trip here, with some extraordinary examples from nearby Daphne (Harbiye) and Tarsus. You can also visit the ancient **Cave-Church of St Peter** (St Pierre Kilisesi; admission TL5; 🕒 8.30am-noon & 1.30-4.30pm Tue-Sun), 3km northeast of town, where Peter and Paul dropped by to do their bit in the war on debauchery.

Sleeping & Eating

You'll find just about everything you need on the main street, İstiklal Caddesi, though it's more fun to wander off into the extensive bazaar area.

Divan Oteli (☎ 215 1518; İstiklal Caddesi 62; s/d TL20/40; ❄) Certainly the best of Antakya's budget options, some rooms here have balconies and small desks.

Mozaik Otel (☎ 215 5020; www.mosaikotel.com; Istiklal Caddesi 18; s/d TL50/80) Rooms are decorated with multicoloured bedspreads and pretty mosaics at this excellent midrange choice, and the restaurant is excellent.

Syrian influences permeate Antakya's cuisine. Handfuls of mint and wedges of lemon accompany many *kebaps*. For dessert, try the local speciality, *künefe*, a cake of fine shredded wheat laid over a dollop of fresh, mild cheese, on a layer of sugar syrup, topped with chopped walnuts and baked. Try and get it hot, straight from the oven. Kral Künefe near the Ulu Cami makes a mean one.

Next to the Mosaic Hotel, **Sultan Sofrası** (☎ 213 8759; İstiklal Caddesi 20; meals around TL12) is spotless and turns over the food at a rapid pace. The articulate manager loves to guide diners through the menu; try the *İskender* doner or the veggie soup.

Getting There & Away

Regular buses heading west into Turkey go via Adana (TL10, 3½ hours). The Jet bus company at the *otogar* has direct buses to Aleppo (TL6, four hours) at 9am and noon daily, and to Damascus (TL11, eight hours) at noon daily.

CENTRAL ANATOLIA

On central Turkey's hazy plains, the sense of history is so pervasive that the average *kebap* chef can remind you that the Romans preceded the Seljuks. This is, after all, the region where the Whirling Dervishes first swirled, Atatürk began his revolution, Alexander the Great cut the Gordion Knot and King Midas turned everything to gold. Julius Caesar came here to utter his famous line, *'Veni, vidi, vici'* ('I came, I saw, I conquered').

In Safranbolu and Amasya, drinking in the history involves sipping *çay* and gazing at the half-timbered Ottoman houses. While these are two of Turkey's most beautiful towns, offering Ottoman digs with cupboard-bathrooms, other spots are so little visited that foreigners may find themselves entered as just *turist* (tourist) in hotel guest books. This offers the opportunity to get to grips with everyday Anatolian life in a coach-party-free environment – where historical heavyweights from the Hittites to Atatürk established major capitals.

ANKARA

☎ 0312 / pop 4.5 million

İstanbullus may quip that the best view in Ankara is the train home, but the Turkish capital has more substance than its reputation as a staid administrative centre suggests. The capital established by Atatürk offers a mellower, more manageable vignette of urban Turkey than İstanbul, and claims two of the country's most important sights: the Anıt Kabir, Atatürk's hilltop mausoleum; and the Museum of Anatolian Civilisations, which will help you solve clues at sites left on the Anatolian plateau by Hittites, Phrygians and other ancient folk. Ankara can be a disjointed place, but two or three neighbourhoods have some charm: the historic streets in the hilltop citadel; the chic Kavaklıdere district; and Kızılay, one of Turkey's hippest urban quarters.

Orientation & Information

Ankara's *hisar* (citadel) crowns a hill 1km east of Ulus Meydanı (Ulus Sq), the heart of Old Ankara and near most of the inexpensive hotels. The newer Ankara lies further south, with better hotels, restaurants and nightlife in Kızılay and Kavaklıdere.

Atatürk Bulvarı is the main north–south axis. Ankara's mammoth *otogar* is 5.5km southwest of Ulus and 4.5km west of Kızılay. The train station is just over 1km southwest of Ulus Meydanı along Cumhuriyet Bulvarı.

The **tourist office** (☎ 310 8789/231 5572; Anafartalar Caddesi 67, Ulus; 🕑 9am-5pm Mon-Fri, 10am-5pm Sat), southeast of Ulus Meydanı, plans to move to a new office at the train station. The **main post office** (Atatürk Bulvarı) is just south of Ulus Meydanı. There are internet cafes and banks with ATMs around Ulus Meydanı, and Karanfil Sokak in Kızılay. Bookshops cluster at the north end of Konur Sokak in Kızılay.

Sights

With the world's richest collection of Hittite artefacts, the state-of-the-art **Museum of Anatolian Civilisations** (Anadolu Medeniyetleri Müzesi; ☎ 324 3160; admission TL15; 🕑 8.30am-5pm), housed in a beautifully restored 15th-century *bedesten*, is Turkey's best museum outside İstanbul. Just up the hill, it's also well worth exploring

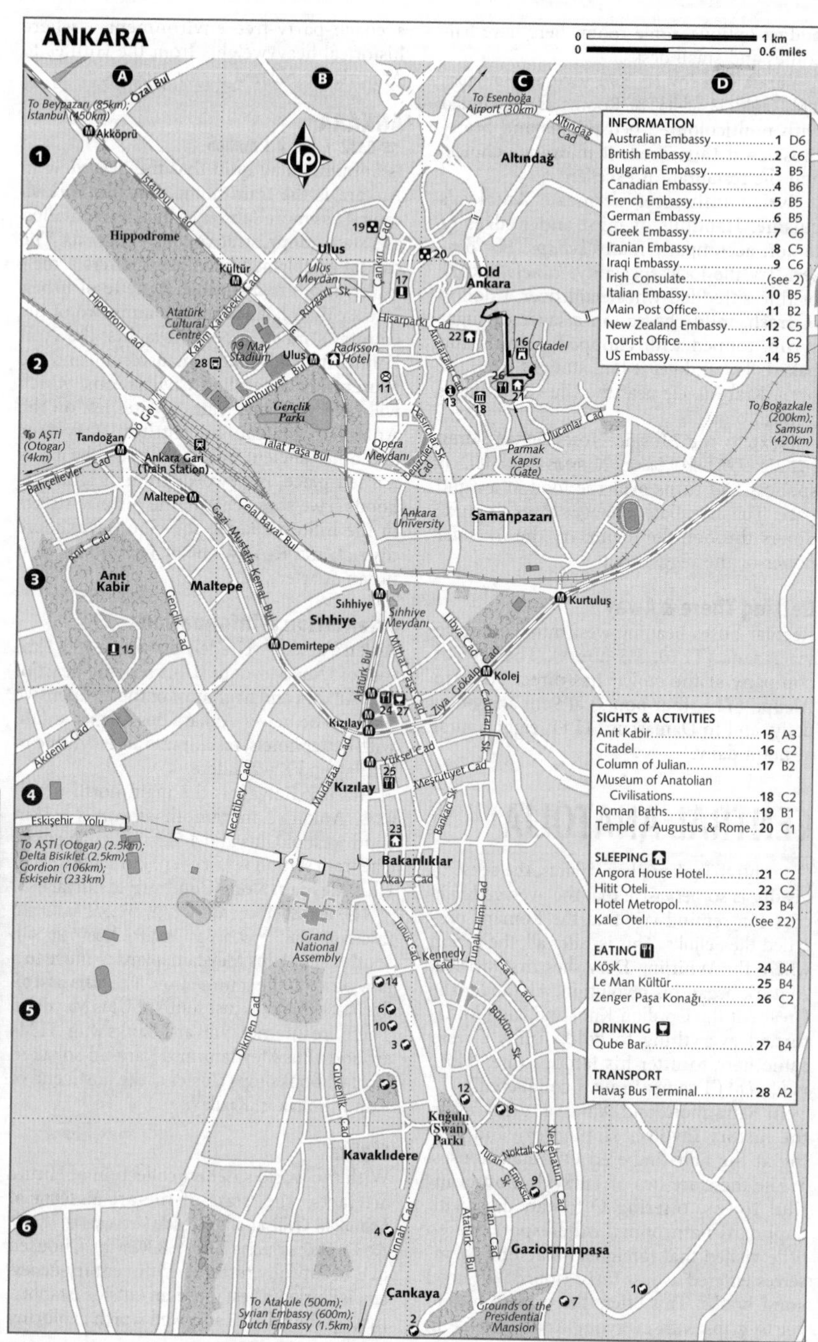
ANKARA
0 1 km
0 0.6 miles
INFORMATION
Australian Embassy 1 D6
British Embassy 2 C6
Bulgarian Embassy 3 B5
Canadian Embassy 4 B6
French Embassy 5 B5
German Embassy 6 B5
Greek Embassy 7 C6
Iranian Embassy 8 C5
Iraqi Embassy 9 C6
Irish Consulate (see 2)
Italian Embassy 10 B5
Main Post Office 11 B2
New Zealand Embassy 12 C5
Tourist Office 13 C2
US Embassy 14 B5
SIGHTS & ACTIVITIES
Anıt Kabir 15 A3
Citadel 16 C2
Column of Julian 17 B2
Museum of Anatolian Civilisations 18 C2
Roman Baths 19 B1
Temple of Augustus & Rome 20 C1
SLEEPING
Angora House Hotel 21 C2
Hitit Oteli 22 C2
Hotel Metropol 23 B4
Kale Otel (see 22)
EATING
Köşk 24 B4
Le Man Kültür 25 B4
Zenger Paşa Konağı 26 C2
DRINKING
Qube Bar 27 B4
TRANSPORT
Havaş Bus Terminal 28 A2
To Beypazarı (85km); İstanbul (450km)
To Esenboğa Airport (30km)
To Boğazkale (200km); Samsun (420km)
To AŞTİ (Otogar) (4km)
To AŞTİ (Otogar) (2.5km); Delta Bisiklet (2.5km); Gordion (106km); Eskişehir (233km)
To Atakule (500m); Syrian Embassy (600m); Dutch Embassy (1.5km)
Özal Bul
Akköprü
İstanbul Cad
Hippodrome
Kültür
Ulus
Ulus Meydanı
Rüzgarlı Sk
Çankırı Cad
Altındağ Cad
Altındağ
Old Ankara
Hisarparkı Cad
Anafartalar Cad
Citadel
Atatürk Cultural Centre
Kazım Karabekir Cad
Hipodrom Cad
19 May Stadium
Radisson Hotel
Cumhuriyet Bul
Gençlik Parkı
Hasırcılar Sk
Ulucanlar Cad
Parmak Kapısı (Gate)
Tandoğan
Dö Gol
Ankara Garı (Train Station)
Talat Paşa Bul
Opera Meydanı
Denizciler Cad
Bahçelievler Cad
Maltepe
Celal Bayar Bul
Gazi Mustafa Kemal Bul
Ankara University
Samanpazarı
Anıt Cad
Anıt Kabir
Maltepe
Gençlik Cad
Sıhhiye
Sıhhiye Meydanı
Kurtuluş
Libya Cad
Demirtepe
Atatürk Bul
Mithat Paşa Cad
Ziya Gökalp Cad
Kolej
Çaldıran Sk
Kızılay
Akdeniz Cad
Yüksel Cad
Meşrutiyet Cad
Necatibey Cad
Mudafaa Cad
Bankacı Sk
Eskişehir Yolu
Bakanlıklar
Akay Cad
Tunalı Hilmi Cad
Grand National Assembly
Tunus Cad
Kennedy Cad
Esat Cad
Büklüm Sk
Dikmen Cad
Güvenlik Cad
Kuğulu (Swan) Parkı
Kavaklıdere
Turan Sk
Noktalı Sk
Emeksiz
Nenehatun Cad
Cinnah Cad
Atatürk Bul
İran Cad
Gaziosmanpaşa
Çankaya
Grounds of the Presidential Mansion

TURKEY

the side streets of the **citadel**, the most scenic part of Ankara. Inside it, local people still live as if in a traditional Turkish village.

About 400m north of Ulus Meydanı, it's worth taking a look at the surprisingly well preserved remains of the **Roman baths** (Roma Hamaları; admission TL3; 8.30am-12.30pm & 1.30-5.30pm), dating back to the 3rd century. Southeast of the baths, you'll find more Roman ruins, including the **Column of Julian** (AD 363) in a square ringed by government buildings, and the **Temple of Augustus & Rome**.

Pay your respects to the founder of modern Turkey and observe the Turks' enduring reverence for Atatürk at his mausoleum, the **Anıt Kabir** (admission free; 9am-5pm mid-May–Oct, to 4pm Nov-Jan, to 4.30pm Feb–mid-May), 2km northwest of Kızılay Meydanı.

Sleeping

The first three listings are in the citadel or on the hill leading to it from Ulus Meydanı. Locals advise against wandering Ulus' streets after about 9pm, however, so you may prefer to stay in Kızılay, which is pricier but has better restaurants and bars. Book ahead to beat the businesspeople and bureaucrats to a room.

Kale Otel (☎ 311 3393; Şan Sokak 13, Ulus; s/d TL30/50) One of the closest hotels to the museum, the Kale's yellow-and-red facade is rather off-putting but its pink-and-red interior is more palatable. It's one of Ulus' pleasanter budget options. Wi-fi is available.

Hitit Oteli (☎ 310 8617; www.otelhitit.com; Hisarparkı Caddesi 12, Ulus; s/d TL75/100) This place is a noticeable step up in quality from the nearby budget places. The rooms are not as smart as the reception, with its fish tank and budgie, but this is a reasonable option near the museum.

our pick **Angora House Hotel** (☎ 309 8380; angora house@gmail.com; Kalekapısı Sokak 16-18, Ulus; s/d/tr €45/60/75; Mar-Oct;) Ankara's original boutique hotel is in a great location inside the citadel and offers beautiful, individually decorated rooms in a restored house, benefiting from some fine half-timbering and a walled courtyard.

Hotel Metropol (☎ 417 3060; www.hotelmetropol.com.tr; Olgunlar Sokak 5, Kızılay; s/d TL70/100;) Quite a snip at these prices, the three-star Metropol provides quality and character across the board. The breakfast is excellent, but laundry rates are high.

Eating & Drinking

Head to Ulus Meydanı for cheap eats.

Le Man Kültür (☎ 310 8617; Konur Sokak 8a-b, Kızılay; mains TL6-11; 10am-11pm) One of Kızılay's coolest hang-outs, this restaurant packs in the ripped denim and beehives (of the Amy Winehouse variety) between walls decorated with subversive cartoons. The menu ranges from *kebaps* to Mexican and even Argentinian dishes.

Zenger Paşa Konağı (☎ 311 7070; www.zengerpasa.com; Doyran Sokak 13, Ulus; mains TL12-17; noon-12.30am;) Built in 1721 for governor Mehmet Fuat Paşa, the Zenger Paşa is crammed with Ottoman ephemera. It looks at first like a deserted ethnographic museum, but the pide, meze and grills, cooked in the original oven, and the perfect citadel views attract wealthy Ankaralıs.

Köşk (☎ 432 1300; İnkılap Sokak 2, Kızılay; mains TL15-30) Ankara's best fish restaurant has a glass-fronted dining room with views of the pedestrianised boulevards, and a chanteuse warbling away. Meze such as fresh calamari with peppers, and simple but effective grills and fish mains, are just as alluring.

Slightly more sophisticated than the neighbouring pubs, **Qube Bar** (Bayındır Sokak 16b, Kızılay) has a removable glass roof. Food is available.

Getting There & Away

AIR

Ankara's Esenboğa airport, 33km north of the city centre, is the hub for Turkish Airlines' domestic flight network; there are daily nonstop flights to most Turkish cities with Turkish Airlines or Atlasjet. International flights to İstanbul are generally cheaper.

BUS

Ankara's huge *otogar* (Ankara Şehirlerarası Terminali İşletmesi; AŞTİ), 5.5km southwest of Ulus and 4.5km west of Kizilay, is the vehicular heart of the nation, with coaches going everywhere all day and night. They depart for İstanbul (TL25 to TL33, six hours) at least every 30 minutes.

TRAIN

Train services between İstanbul and Ankara are the best in the country, with eight departures daily from TL23. There are also services to Adana, Kayseri, Sivas and a few other cities, but the long-haul services can be excruciatingly slow.

WORTH THE TRIP: SAFRANBOLU & AMASYA

Safranbolu and Amasya, respectively 145km north and 270km northeast of Ankara, are slightly off the beaten track, but beckon savvy travellers with their ethereal settings and historic atmosphere. Both retain many of their original Ottoman buildings.

Safranbolu is such an enchanting city that was declared a Unesco World Heritage site in 1994. It boasts a wonderful old Ottoman quarter bristling with 19th-century half-timbered houses; as part of the ongoing restoration, many have been turned into hotels or museums.

Blissfully located on riverbanks beneath cliffs carved with Pontic tombs, **Amasya** is one of Turkey's best-kept secrets, harbouring historic sites including a lofty citadel, Seljuk buildings and enough picturesque Ottoman piles to satisfy the fussiest sultan.

Both towns boast excellent accommodation, with a profusion of delightful B&Bs set in skilfully restored Ottoman mansions. In Safranbolu, travellers love **Bastoncu Pansiyon** (☎ 0370-712 3411; www.bastoncupension.com; Hıdırlık Yokuşu Sokak, Safranbolu; dm TL20, s/d/tr TL35/50/70; 💻). In Amasya, **Grand Pasha Hotel** (☎ 0358-212 4158; www.grandpashahotel.com; Tevfık Hafız Çıkmazı 5, Amasya; s/d TL50/100) is a good deal. There are a few direct buses from Ankara to both Safranbolu (TL20, three hours) and Amasya (TL30, five hours); the latter is closer to Sivas.

Getting Around

TO/FROM THE AIRPORT

Havaş buses depart from Gate B at 19 May Stadium every half-hour between 4.30am and midnight daily (TL10, 45 minutes). They may leave sooner if they fill up, so get there early to claim your seat. Don't pay more than TL50 for a taxi.

PUBLIC TRANSPORT

Buses marked 'Ulus' and 'Çankaya' run the length of Atatürk Bulvarı. Those marked 'Gar' go to the train station; those marked 'AŞTİ' go to the *otogar*. You can buy tokens (TL3), valid for 45 minutes of travel on most buses and the subway, from subway stations and major bus stops or anywhere displaying an EGO Bilet sign.

Ankara's underground train network currently has two lines: the Ankaray line running between AŞTİ *otogar* in the west through Kızılay to Dikimevi in the east; and the Metro line running from Kızılay northwest via Sıhhiye and Ulus to Batıkent. The two lines interconnect at Kızılay.

A taxi costs about TL15 from AŞTİ to the city centre.

TURKEY

SIVAS

☎ 0346 / pop 294,000

Sivas lies at the heart of Turkey politically as well as geographically, thanks to its role in the run-up to the War of Independence. The Congress building resounded with plans, strategies and principles as Atatürk and his adherents discussed their great goal of liberation. With a colourful, sometimes tragic, history and some of the finest Seljuk buildings ever erected, Sivas is a good stopover en route to the wild east.

The **tourist office** (☎ 222 2252; 🕑 9am-5pm Mon-Fri) is in the *valılık* (provincial government headquarters) building on the main square. Don't miss the buildings in the adjoining park: the **Çifte Minare Medrese** (Seminary of the Twin Minarets) with a grand Seljuk-style gateway; the fabulous **Şifaiye Medresesi**, a former medical school that's one of the city's oldest buildings; and the 13th-century **Bürüciye Medresesi**. Southeast of the park are the 1197 **Ulu Cami** (Great Mosque) and the glorious **Gök Medrese** (Blue Seminary); west of it is the **Atatürk Congress & Ethnography Museum** (Atatürk Kongre ve Etnografya Müzesi; Inonü Bulvarı; admission TL2; 🕑 8.30am-noon & 1.30-5pm Tue-Sun), in the imposing Ottoman school building that hosted the Sivas Congress in September 1919.

Hotels line Eski Belediye Sokak, just east of the main square. Among them are **Otel Madımak** (☎ 221 8027; Eski Belediye Sokak 2; s/d/tr TL60/90/115), although be aware that the site has sad resonances as a hate crime took place here in 1993, and **Sultan Otel** (☎ 221 2986; www.sultanotel.com.tr; Eski Belediye Sokak 18; s/d/tr TL90/140/170).

At the rustic, wood-panelled **Sema Hanımın Yeri** (☎ 223 9496; İstasyon Caddesi Öncü Market; mains TL2.50-5), the welcoming Madame Sema serves home-cooked food such as *içli köfte* (meatballs stuffed with spices and nuts). Friendly cafe-restaurant **Yeşil Café** (☎ 222 2638; Selçuklu Sokak; mains TL4-8) has a tiny balcony upstairs with the best views of spotlit twin minarets, like, ever.

Buses go to destinations including Amasya (TL20, 3½ hours) and Erzurum (TL30, seven hours). Services are not that frequent, so you may want to book ahead at one of the ticket offices in town

Sivas is a main rail junction. The *Doğu Ekspresi* and *Erzurum Ekspresi* go through Sivas to Erzurum and Kars daily; the *Güney Ekspresi* (from İstanbul to Kurtalan) runs four times a week in either direction.

KONYA

☎ 0332 / pop 762,000

Turkey's equivalent of the 'Bible Belt', conservative Konya treads a delicate path between its historical significance as the home town of the Whirling Dervish orders and a bastion of Seljuk culture on the one hand, and its modern importance as an economic boom town on the other. The city derives considerable charm from this juxtaposition of old and new, and boasts one of Turkey's finest and most characteristic sights, the Mevlâna shrine.

Orientation & Information

The town centre stretches from Alaaddin Tepesi, the hill topped by the Alaaddin Camii mosque (1221), along Mevlâna Caddesi to the tomb of Mevlâna, now called Mevlâna Museum. The *otogar* is 7km north of the centre; free *servis* minibuses take half an hour for the trip into town.

The **tourist office** (☎ 353 4020; Mevlâna Caddesi 21; 8.30am-5.30pm Mon-Sat) is across the square from the Mevlâna Müzesi. You'll find numerous banks with ATMs and web cafes, including **Elma Net** (Çinili Sokak 14; per hr TL1), around Alaaddin Tepesi; the PTT is just south of Mevlâna Caddesi, near Hükümet Meydanı.

Sights

Join the pilgrims and head straight to the wonderful **Mevlâna Museum** (☎ 351 1215; admission TL2; 9am-6.30pm Tue-Sun, 10am-6pm Mon), at the eastern end of Mevlâna Caddesi. The former lodge of the Whirling Dervishes, it is topped by a brilliant turquoise-tiled dome – one of the most inspiring images of Turkey. Although it's virtually under siege from devout crowds, there's a palpable mystique here.

It's also well worth visiting two outstanding Seljuk buildings near Alaaddin Tepesi. **Karatay Müzesi** (☎ 351 1914; Alaaddin Meydanı; admission TL3; 9am-noon & 1.30-5.30pm), once a Muslim theological seminary, is now a museum housing a superb collection of ceramics (although it was closed for renovations when we visited). **İnceminare Medresesi** (Seminary of the Slender Minaret; ☎ 351 3204; Adliye Bulvarı; admission TL3; 9am-12pm & 1.30-5.30pm), now the Museum of Wooden Artefacts and Stone Carving, has an extraordinarily elaborate doorway.

Sleeping

Otel Mevlâna (☎ 352 0029; Cengaver Sokak 2; s/d/tr from TL40/60/85) Across Mevlâna Caddesi from Otel Bera Mevlâna, this friendly central option is a good choice for backpackers of both sexes. The rooms have firm beds, fridges and private bathrooms.

Otel Derya (☎ 352 0154; Ayanbey Sokak 18; s/d/tr TL50/80/100;) Quiet and spotless, the four-year-old Derya is a good choice for families and female travellers. The rooms, although slightly bland, have TVs and minibars, and the management is friendly and efficient.

Hotel Rumi (☎ 353 1121; www.rumihotel.com; Durakfakih Sokak 5; s/d/tr €50/75/100;) Boasting a killer position near the Mevlâna Museum, the stylish Hotel Rumi has 33 rooms and suites with curvy chairs, slender lamps and mirrors. There's a *hammam* in the basement.

Hotel Balıkçılar (☎ 350 9470; www.balikcilar.com; Mevlâna Karşısı 2; s/d/tr €89/120/140;) Easily the best reception area in town, styled as a cobbled Ottoman street. Facilities include a large lobby bar, restaurant, sauna, *hammam* and there are occasional *sema* (Whirling Dervish) performances. Breakfast costs extra.

Eating & Drinking

Gülbahçesı Konya Mutfağı (☎ 351 0768; Gülbahçe Sokak 3; mains TL4-8) One of Konya's best restaurants, mostly because of its upstairs terrace with views of the Mevlâna Museum's gardens. Dishes include *yaprak sarma* (stuffed grape leaves), spicy Adana *kebap* and *etli ekmek* (pide-style bread with meat); no beer is served.

Osmanlı Çarşısı (☎ 353 3257; İnce Minare Sokak) Looking like an apple-smoke-spewing pirate ship, this early-20th-century house near Alaaddin Tepesi has terraces and seats on the street. *Nargilehs* are being lit or bubbling away everywhere you look.

Getting There & Away

There are three daily flights to and from İstanbul with Turkish Airlines.

From the *otogar*, accessible from Alaaddin Tepesi by tram, there are frequent buses to all major destinations, including Ankara (TL20, four hours), İstanbul (TL45, 11½ hours), Kayseri (TL25, four hours) and Sivas (TL30, seven hours). There are ticket offices in the centre.

Two express trains link Konya with İstanbul via Afyon. A new direct, high-speed rail link between Konya and Ankara, scheduled to open in 2010, will trim the journey time from 10½ hours to 1¼ hours.

CAPPADOCIA (KAPADOKYA)

Between Kayseri and Nevşehir, Central Anatolia's mountain-fringed plains give way to a land of fairy chimneys and underground cities. The fairy chimneys – rock columns, pyramids, mushrooms and even a few shaped like camels – were formed, alongside the valleys of cascading white cliffs, when Erciyes Daği (Mt Erciyes) erupted. The intervening millennia added to the remarkable Cappadocian canvas, with Byzantines carving out cave churches and subterranean complexes to house thousands of people.

You could spend days touring the rock-cut churches and admiring their frescos (technically seccos; one of many factoids visitors learn on a hike through the canyons). Alternatively, view the troglodyte architecture from far above on a dawn hot-air balloon ride or from a panoramic hotel terrace. Whether it's a pension or a boutique hideaway with as few rooms as it has fairy chimneys, Cappadocia's accommodation rates as some of Turkey's best and allows guests to experience cave dwelling first hand.

Between your lingering looks at the rocky remains of Cappadocia's unique history, it's worth checking out some further-flung spots such as the seemingly lost valley of Ihlara and former Greek settlements such as Mustafapşa. Two hours' drive south of Göreme, Ala Dağlar National Park protects the rugged middle range of the Taurus Mountains. It's famous throughout the country for its extraordinary trekking routes, which make their way through craggy limestone ranges dotted with waterfalls.

Tours

The following Göreme-based agencies offer good daily tours (costing around TL60) of local highlights. There are also agencies in nearby Avanos, Urgup and Nevsehir, but be aware that Nevsehir has a reputation for unscrupulous operators.

Heritage Travel (☎ 0384-271 2687; www.turkishheritagetravel.com; Yavuz Sokak 31, Göreme)

Middle Earth Travel (☎ 0384-271 2559; www.middleearthtravel.com; Cevizler Sokak 20, Göreme) Intrepid outfit offering walking tours and activities such as abseiling.

Neşe Tour (☎ 0384-271 2525; www.nesetour.com; Avanos Yolu 54, Göreme)

Nomad Travel (☎ 0384-271 2767; www.nomadtravel.com.tr; Müze Caddesi 35, Göreme)

Yama Tours (☎ 0384-271 2508; www.yamatours.com; Müze Caddesi 2, Göreme)

Tours usually start at a lookout point with a view across the valleys, then continue to locations such as Ihlara Valley, a pottery workshop in Avanos, the rock formations in Devrent Valley, Uçhisar's rock citadel and one of the fascinating underground cities at **Kaymaklı** or **Derinkuyu** (admission €7.50; ⏲ 8am-5pm, last admission 4.30pm). Many companies also offer trips further afield, for example to eastern Turkish locations such as Nemrut Dağı (Mt Nemrut; see p923).

Getting There & Away

Central Cappadocia has two airports: Kayseri (for daily Turkish Airlines and Onur Air flights to/from İstanbul, and weekly Sun Express flights to/from İzmir) and Nevşehır (for flights to/from İstanbul four times a week). Transfer buses operate between Kayseri airport and accommodation in central Cappadocia for passengers leaving or arriving on flights between the mid-morning and evening. The buses pick up from and drop off at hotels and pensions in Ürgüp (TL15), Göreme, Uçhisar, Avanos and Nevşehir (all TL17). Prebook the buses by phone or email with **Argeus Tours** (☎ 0384-341 4688; www.argeus.com.tr, www.cappadociaexclusive.com; İstiklal Caddesi 7, Ürgüp) if you fly Turkish Airlines; or with **Peerless Travel Services** (☎ 0384-341 6970; www.peerlessexcursions.com; İstiklal Caddesi 59a, Ürgüp) if you fly Onur Air or Sun Express. Alternatively, you can easily request your hotel or pension in Cappadocia to book a seat for you.

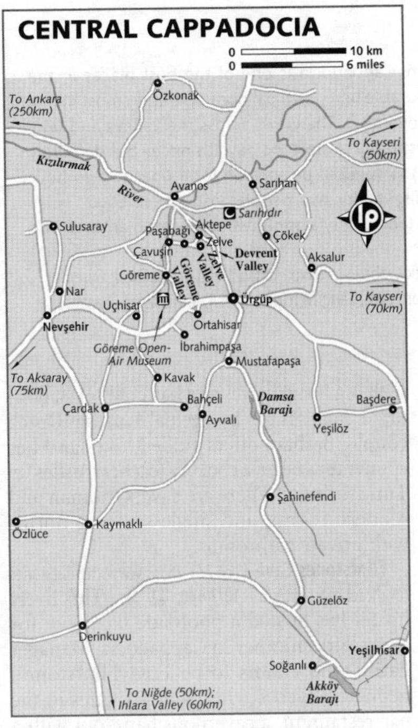

It's very easy to get to Cappadocia by bus from elsewhere in Turkey. Most long-haul buses will bring you to Nevşehır, the provincial capital. When you purchase your bus ticket, make sure it clearly states that it is for Göreme (or Ürgüp or wherever), as many readers have complained that although they purchased tickets to Göreme, they found themselves deposited at Nevşehır *otogar* or even on the highway outside Avanos! Good bus companies (including Göreme, Metro, Nevşehir, Öncü and Kapadokya) always transfer their passengers from Nevşehır to the surrounding villages on free *servis* buses. A taxi from Nevşehır to Göreme should cost no more than TL25.

Departing Cappadocia, the best places to pick up long-distance buses are Nevşehir, Kayseri, Ürgüp and Göreme. The bus from Göreme to Ankara costs TL25 (4½ hours), Konya TL20 (three hours), İstanbul TL40 (11 hours) and Antalya TL35 (nine hours).

Getting Around

The most convenient bases for exploring central Cappadocia are Göreme, Ürgüp and Avanos. Bus and *dolmuş* services are frequent in high summer, apart from on Sundays, and much less so in winter.

Belediye Bus Corp *dolmuşes* (TL2) travel between Ürgüp and Avanos via Ortahisar, the Göreme Open-Air Museum, Göreme village, Çavuşin and (on request) Paşabaği and Zelve. The services leave Ürgüp every two hours between 8am and 4pm (6pm in the summer) and Avanos between 9am and 5pm (7pm in the summer). You can hop on and off anywhere around the loop.

There's also an hourly *belediye* (municipal council) bus running from Avanos to Nevşehir (TL3) via Çavuşin (10 minutes), Göreme (15 minutes) and Uçhisar (30 minutes). It leaves Avanos from 7am to 6pm.

GÖREME

☎ 0384 / pop 2250

Göreme is the archetypal travellers' utopia: a beatific village where the surreal surroundings spread a fat smile on everyone's face. Beneath the honeycomb cliffs, the locals live in fairy chimneys – or increasingly, run hotels in them. The wavy white valleys in the distance, with their hiking trails, panoramic viewpoints and rock-cut churches, look like giant tubs of vanilla ice cream. Rose Valley, meanwhile, lives up to its name; watching its pink rock slowly change colour at sunset is best accompanied by meze in one of the excellent eateries.

Tourism is having an impact on this village, where you can start the day in a hot-air balloon (see p916), before touring a valley of rock-cut Byzantine churches at Göreme Open-Air Museum. Nonetheless, you can still see rural life continuing in a place where, once upon a time, if a man couldn't lay claim to one of the rock-hewn pigeon houses, he would struggle to woo a wife.

All the services useful to travellers are in the centre, including the *otogar*, where there are four ATMs and a **tourist information booth** (☎ 271 2558; www.goreme.org); the **PTT** (off Bilal Eroğlu Caddesi), **Flintstones Internet Center** (Belediye Caddesi; per hr TL2); and **1001 Books** (Müze Caddesi 35), one of Turkey's best bookshops for English reads.

Sights & Activities

Cappadocia's number one attraction, **Göreme Open-Air Museum** (Göreme Açık Hava Müzesi; admission TL10; 🕑 8am-5pm), may be pricey but it's worth every lira. Medieval frescos can be seen in the

TURKEY

SPLURGE: BALLOONS AT DAWN

If you've never taken a flight in a hot-air balloon, Cappadocia is one of the best places in the world to do it. Flight conditions are especially favourable here, with balloons operating most mornings from the beginning of April to the end of November. The views across the valleys and fairy chimneys are simply unforgettable and it's a magical way to start the day. It's pricey but definitely worth blowing your budget on, costing about €155 to €250 per person for a one- to two-hour flight in an eight- to 20-passenger balloon. 'VIP flights' for two people cost a mere €600.

The various operators offer different packages (and safety standards), so do shop around. The following have good credentials:

Kapadokya Balloons (☎ 0384-271 2442; www.kapadokyaballoons.com; Adnan Menderes Caddesi, Göreme)

Sultan Balloons (☎ 0384-353 5249; www.sultanballoons.com; Sarıgüvercinlik Mevkii, Mustafapaşa Kasabası, Ürgüp)

rock-hewn monastic settlement where some 20 monks lived. The best-preserved churches are from the 10th to 13th centuries, although some are even older than that. The stunning **Karanlık Kilise** (Dark Church) is one of the most famous and fresco-filled of the churches, and it is worth paying the extra TL5 admission fee to enter. Across the road from the main entrance, the **Tokalı Kilise** (Buckle Church) is also impressive, with an underground chapel and fabulous frescos.

There are a number of **hiking** options around Göreme village. It's surrounded by a handful of gorgeous valleys that are easily explored on foot, allowing about one to three hours for each of them. The valleys are remote in places and there have been attacks in them, so walk with a companion if possible. Most pension owners will be happy to guide you on the trails for a minimal fee.

Sleeping

With about 100 hostels, pensions and hotels in Göreme, competition keeps prices low. If you're visiting between October and May, pack warm clothes as it gets very cold at night.

Köse Pension (☎ 271 2294; www.kosepension.com; dm/d/tw/tr TL12/60/60/75; 🏊) Köse Pension has some rough edges, but unlike most hostels, it has a swimming pool in the garden and a terrace where communal meals are served. Run by Edinburgh-born Dawn Köse and family, the backpacker institution is cheerily painted with grinning spiders and winding creepers. On the roof are wooden huts and a 20-bed dorm.

Kemal's Guest House (☎ 271 2234; www.kemalsguesthouse.com; Karşıbucak Sokak; dm/s/d/tr/q €6/24/30/42/52) Entered via a flowery garden and a reception with big bookshelves and battered sofas, popular Kemal's is run by a genial Turkish–Dutch couple. Barbara offers guided hikes and her eponymous beau, a cookery teacher, rustles up Turkish feasts. There are cave, Ottoman and modern rooms, and single-sex cave dorms with private bathrooms.

Flintstones Cave (☎ 271 2555; www.theflintstonescavehotel.com; dm/s/d TL10/20/40; 💻 🏊) This lively hostel has hosted a pool-side barbecue for every fairy chimney in Cappadocia. Manager Fatih, who claims to be Fred Flintstone's nephew, advertises heaps of activities in the bar-restaurant, a cavernous hang-out with a pool table. Ask to see a few rooms because there is a range of choices.

Kookaburra Pension (☎ 271 2549; kookagoreme@hotmail.com; Konak Sokak 10; dm/s/d TL10/20/40; 💻) This small pension, with agricultural tools and pot plants decorating its stone passages, has tidy, spacious rooms. The roof terrace is a knockout and there's internet access in the bar-restaurant up top.

Kelebek Hotel & Cave Pension (☎ 271 2531; www.kelebekhotel.com; Yavuz Sokak 31; s/d from €28/35; 💻 🏊) Pioneering Ali Yavuz converted his family home into Göreme's first boutique hotel, which boasts the village's best terrace for surveying the Cappadocian dreamscape. Divided into the modestly named Kelebek Pension and the newer Kelebek Suites, the 32-room complex ranges across stone houses and two fairy chimneys. More than the *hammam*, garden and small swimming pool, it's the helpful staff and Yavuz's passion for village life that make this a magical spot.

Fairy Chimney Inn (☎ 271 2655; www.fairychimney.com; Güvercinlik Sokak 5/7; s/d/tr from €44/55/66; 💻) This fairy chimney high on Aydınlı Hill has been wonderfully converted by its owner, a German

TURKEY

anthropologist. Rooms are beautifully decorated, with simple furniture, cushions and carpets everywhere, and a refreshing lack of TVs and jacuzzis. Other treats include the cave *hammam*, communal lounge, home-cooked meals and glorious garden terrace.

Kismet Cave House (☎ 271 2416; www.kismetcavehouse.com; Kağnı Yolu 9; d standard/deluxe €60/80) Opened in 2007, this eight-room guest house has quickly built a strong reputation. The arched rooms up top have the edge on the chimney chambers, but Afghani bedspreads, jacuzzis and views of Rose Valley feature throughout. Owner Faruk encourages communal Anatolian living at long dining tables.

Eating

Most of Göreme's pensions provide good, cheap meals, but you could also take advantage of some fine eateries in town.

Nazar Börek (☎ 271 2441; Müze Caddesi; mains TL5) If you're after a cheap and filling meal, sample the *börek*, *gözleme* and *sosyete böregi* (stuffed spiral pastries with yoghurt and tomato sauce) at this simple place. Friendly staff and a pleasant outdoor eating area on the canal make it a perennially popular option.

Fırın Express (☎ 271 2266; Eski Belediye Yanı Sokak; pide & pizza TL4-8, mains TL8-13; 11am-11pm) Set slightly back from the main strip, this wood-cabin-like eatery is praised by carnivores and vegetarians alike for its pide and pizza. More-substantial clay-pot dishes are also available.

Cappadocia Pide Salonu (☎ 271 2858; Hakki Paşa Meydanı; pide TL5-9) Göreme's pide hotspot has a more local feel than most of the village's eateries. Sitting under the canal-side umbrellas, you can tuck into 12 types of pide, as well as spaghetti, grills, pottery *kebaps*, beer and *rakı*.

Point Café (Müze Caddesi; mains TL10) Missing your favourite comfort foods? A Turkish–South African couple dishes up curries, burgers, fruit smoothies, filter coffee and home-baked cakes.

our pick **Dibek** (☎ 271 2209; Hakkı Paşa Meydanı 1; mains TL10-15; 9am-11pm) Dibek is one of Göreme's most original restaurants, and the best place to try a *testi kebap* (kebab cooked in a terracotta pot, broken at the table to serve). You must give three hours' notice before eating, so the dish can be slow-cooked in an oven in the stone floor.

Local Restaurant (☎ 271 2629; Müze Caddesi 38; mains TL11) At the start of the road to the Open-Air Museum, the Local is one of Göreme's best eateries, with an outdoor terrace and an elegant stone-walled dining room. The service is attentive, ingredients are fresh, and prices are reasonable for the scrumptious dishes.

EKREM ILHAN

During Persia's 300-year occupation of Turkey (beginning in the mid-6th century BC), Katpatuka (Cappadocia) was famous throughout the empire for its beautiful horses. In Iran's Persepolis palace, among the reliefs depicting delegates from Persia's subject states, visitors from Katpatuka are pictured with equine offerings.

It seems appropriate, then, that present-day Göreme has a horse whisperer. Ekrem Ilhan brings wild horses to Göreme from Erciyes Daği (Mt Erciyes), where a tribe of 400 has grown as local farmers have replaced them with machinery.

'They are in shock when they arrive here, but when their eyes open they see me, talking and giving them sweet things,' he says. 'People teach animals to bite and kick, because they are angry with them. But when you're friends, and you talk to them and give them some carrot and cucumber, you don't have any problems.'

Looking like a Cappadocian Clint Eastwood in a hat brought from America by a carpet-dealing friend, Ilhan tells a story about two pregnant mares he returned to Mt Erciyes to give birth. 'One year later, I went into the mountains, among the 400 horses, and called their names and they came directly to me.'

Ilhan treats the 11 horses in his cave stable using homemade remedies, such as grape water to extract parasites and olive oil, mint and egg for indigestion. He is starting a trekking company, called **Dalton Brothers** (☎ 05322-756 869; two hours TL50) at the suggestion of a Canadian traveller and *Lucky Luke* fan. 'People like wild horses because it's difficult riding in the mountains, it's rocky, and the horses are used to it,' he says.

Göreme-born Ekrem Ilhan and Dalton Brothers are based at the stables behind the Anatolian Balloons office.

Manzara Restaurant (☎ 271 2712; Harim Sokak 14; mains TL12) With its bird's eye view of Göreme's flat roofs and less-flat rock formations, Manzara is a prime spot to spend a meze-and-*rakı* evening. Choose between two terraces and an indoor dining room with a fireplace.

A'laturca (☎ 271 2882; Müze Caddesi; mains TL10-25) Style meets substance at this elegant eatery. The menu here has been thoughtfully and creatively designed and the food is exceptionally well prepared and tasty to boot.

UÇHISAR

☎ 0384 / pop 6350

Between Göreme and Nevşehir is picturesque, laid-back yet stylish Uçhisar, built around a **rock citadel** (admission TL3; 8am-8.15pm) that offers panoramic views from its summit. The local 'kilometre zero' for Gallic gallivanters since Club Med revived the village's fortunes in the 1960s, Uçhisar is quieter than Göreme and worth considering as an alternative base.

There are some excellent places to stay; the following, all located in the same area, are brilliant value and have formidable views of Pigeon Valley, Rose Valley and the rest of the rocky gang.

Blue-and-white bedspreads give the clean, simple rooms at **Uçhisar Pension** (☎ 219 2662; www.uchisarpension.com; Kale Yani 5; s/d TL30/60) the feel of a breezy country escape.

French-owned **Les Terrasses d'Uçhisar** (☎ 219 2792; www.terrassespension.com; Eski Göreme Yolu; s & d/tr/ste €38/46/80) has simple but stylish cave and arch rooms, a great terrace and a well-regarded restaurant.

Inspiring love hearts in the guest book, **Lale Saray** (☎ 219 2333; www.lalesaray.com; Göreme Caddesi; s €45-80, d €50-85, tr €60-95) has sweet-smelling cave and arch rooms, a large restaurant and a terrace splashed with cushions.

ZELVE VALLEY

Be sure to visit the excellent **Zelve Open-Air Museum** (admission TL5, parking TL2; 8am-5pm, last admission 4.15pm), off the road from Göreme to Avanos. It's less visited than the Göreme Valley (though the monastic seclusion once offered here is certainly long gone) and has rock-cut churches, a rock-cut mosque and some opportunities for serious scrambling. In the same area, some of the finest fairy chimneys can be seen at **Devrent Valley**, also known as 'Imagination Valley' for its chimneys' anthropomorphic forms; and **Paşabağı**, where you can climb inside one formation to a monk's quarters, decorated with Hellenic crosses.

AVANOS

☎ 0384 / pop 11,800

Avanos is famous for pottery made with red clay from the Kızılırmak (Red River), which runs through its centre, and white clay from the mountains. Its Old Town is run down and its riverside setting does not match the other Cappadocian centres. It boasts some superb views of Zelve, however, and when the pottery-purchasing tour groups have moved on, it's an appealingly mellow country town.

The **tourist office** (☎ 511 4360; Atatürk Caddesi; 8.30am-5pm) is on the main street. To check your emails head to the **Hemi Internet Café** (Uğur Mumcu Caddesi; per hr TL1); there are banks with ATMs on and around the main square.

As well as the usual guided tours, **Kirkit Voyage** (☎ 511 3148; www.kirkit.com; Atatürk Caddesi 50) can arrange walking, biking, canoeing, horse-riding and snowshoe trips.

Set in converted old stone houses, the long-running **Kirkit Pension** (☎ 511 3148; www.kirkit.com; Atatürk Caddesi; s/d/tr €30/40/55) is known throughout Cappadocia for its congenial, laid-back atmosphere. The simple rooms are decorated with *kilims*, historical photographs of the region and Uzbek bedspreads.

Lots of Cappadocian cave establishments have their idiosyncrasies, but **Sofa Hotel** (☎ 511 5186; www.sofa-hotel.com; Orta Mahallesi Baklacı Sokak 13; s/d TL60/100) is downright bonkers. Staircases, bridges and terraces lead you up the hill, past eyes that stare out from a mosaic fragment or a pottery face, to 33 rooms crammed with knick-knacks.

A basic but welcoming eatery on the main square **Sanço-Panço Restaurant** (☎ 511 4184; Çarşi Sokak; mains TL6-7) is a great people-watching spot. Given Avanos' pottery trade, it's hardly surprising that the speciality is *güveç (*beef stew baked in a clay pot).

The shiny, modern **Dayının Yeri** (☎ 511 6840; Atatürk Caddesi 23; mains TL10) is one of Cappadocia's best *ocakbaşıs* (grill restaurants) and is an essential stop on any visit to Avanos. The *kebaps* and pide are equally sensational.

ÜRGÜP

☎ 0384 / pop 15,500

If you have a soft spot for upmarket hotels and fine dining, look no further. The ever-growing battalion of boutique hotels in Ürgüp's honey-coloured stone buildings (left over from the pre-1923 days when the town had a large Greek population) win over discerning travellers. With a spectacular natural setting and a wonderful location at the very heart of central Cappadocia, this is one of the most seductive holiday spots in the whole of Turkey.

Around Cumhuriyet Meydanı, the main square, you'll find banks with ATMs, restaurants, and internet cafes including **Teras Internet Café** (3rd fl, Suat Hayri Caddesi 40; per hr TL1.25), adorned with pot plants and *nargilehs.* The **tourist office** (☎ 0384 341 4059; Kayseri Caddesi 37; 🕑 8am-5pm Mon-Fri Oct-Apr, to 5.30pm Mon-Fri May-Sep) gives out a walking map and has a list of hotels. Many of the boutique hotels are on Esbelli Hill.

Local travel agencies Argeus Tours and Peerless Travel Services (see p914) can arrange tours and transfers.

Sleeping

Hotel Elvan (☎ 341 4191; www.hotelelvan.com; Barbaros Hayrettin Sokak 11; s/d/tr TL35/60/80; 💻) A friendly welcome and homely atmosphere await you at this unpretentious but immaculate guest house. There's a small roof terrace and comfortable dining room. Excellent value.

Cappadocia Palace (☎ 341 2510; www.hotel-cappadocia.com; Duayeri Mahallesi Mektep Sokak 2; s/d/tr from TL35/70/85; 💻) This large, comfortable hotel is housed in a converted Greek mansion near Cumhuriyet Meydanı. There's a lovely arched restaurant-lounge and an attractive foyer area. Book ahead.

Razziya Evi (☎ 341 5089; www.razziyaevi.com; Cingilli Sokak 24; s/d/tr TL70/80/120) This lovingly restored *evi* (house) has seven cheerful rooms (some in slightly musty caves). There's a *hammam,* a salon with satellite TV, a pretty courtyard and a kitchen that guests can use.

Kemerli Evi (☎ 341 5445; www.kemerliev.com; Dutlu Camii Mahallesi Çıkmaz Sokak 12; s/d €60/80; 💻 🏊) This converted 13th-century house is lost up backstreets inhabited by friendly locals. The eight rooms have antique chairs and carpets, there are nooks and crannies everywhere, and an air of calm hangs between the thick stone walls. The elevated terrace has a beautiful swimming pool and panoramic views.

Esbelli Evi (☎ 341 3395; www.esbelli.com; Esbelli Mahallesi Sokak 8; s/d/ste €80/90/200; ❄ 💻) Having bought surrounding properties to preserve Esbelli's atmosphere of hilltop serenity, consummate host Süha Ersöz's complex now has 10 rooms and five suites in nine houses. Cappadocia's first boutique hotel still feels small and intimate, though, thanks to the welcoming atmosphere and the communal areas where guests are encouraged to congregate.

Melekler Evi (☎ 341 7131; www.meleklerevi.com.tr; Dereler Mahallesi Dere Sokak 59; d €90-145) This seven-room hotel's name, House of Angels, could refer to its lofty position at the top of the old town, eye to eye with pigeon houses. Restored by an architect and an interior designer, the cave and arch rooms are tastefully decorated in subtle shades.

Eating & Drinking

The main square is best place to grab an alcoholic or caffeinated beverage at an outside table and watch Cappadocia cruise by. *Pastanes* (patisseries) and cafes such as Şükrüoğlu and Café Naturel vie for attention with their sweet eats and shiny window displays.

Şömine Cafe & Restaurant (☎ 341 8442; Cumhuriyet Meydanı; mains TL9-15) This popular restaurant on the main square has a roof terrace and an attractive indoor dining room. Start with a salad or a meze choice such as *sosyete mantısı* (one large ravioli), then attack a *kiremit* (clay-baked meat or vegetable dish).

Dimrit (☎ 341 8585; Yunak Mahallesi, Teyfik Fikret Caddesi 40; mains TL10-21) With meze served in curvy dishes and three types of *rakı,* Dimrit's hillside terraces are top spots to spend a sunset. The extensive menu features salads, fish, classic grills and house specials.

Micro Café & Restaurant (☎ 5341 5110; Cumhuriyet Meydanı; mains TL11) Micro's diverse menu, ranging across Ottoman chicken, spinach crepe and peppered T-bone steak, attracts tourists and locals alike.

Ehlikeyf (☎ 341 6110; Cumhuriyet Meydanı; mains TL12-25) Competing with nearby Şömine in the sophistication stakes, Ehlikeyf occupies a sleek dining room with a wavy ceiling. Dishes such as the fabulous *Ehlikeyf kebap* (steak served on slivered fried potatoes, garlic yoghurt and a demi-glace sauce) arrive on glass plates.

Ziggy's (☎ 341 7107; Yunak Mahallesi, Teyfik Fikret Caddesi 24; mains TL13-16) Cool Ziggy's, named after a David Bowie song, has a series of terraces. Whether you opt for a cocktail or the 12-course set menu (TL30), which features 10 meze plates such as the distinctive smoked aubergine, hosts Selim and Nuray add some İstanbul sophistication to the Cappadocian views.

Local institution **Han Çirağan Restaurant** (Cumhuriyet Meydanı) has a good terrace for a beer (though we wouldn't recommend eating here, as the service is lacklustre and the food is bog-standard).

MUSTAFAPAŞA

☎ 0384 / pop 1600

Mustafapaşa is the sleeping beauty of Cappadocia – a peaceful village with pretty old stone-carved houses, some minor rock-cut churches and a few good places to stay. If you want to get away from it all, this is the place to base yourself. Until WWI it was called Sinasos and was a predominantly Ottoman-Greek settlement.

At **Hotel Pacha** (☎ 353 5331; www.pachahotel.com; Sinasos Meydanı; s/d €20/30) you'll find the real deal: a family-run business that offers a warm welcome and home cooking by the lady of the house, Demra. The restored Ottoman-Greek pile has a great feel about it from the moment you enter its pretty vine-trellised courtyard.

Ukabeyn Pansiyon (☎ 353 5533; www.ukabeyn.com; d/tr €55/75;), a boutique hotel high on the hill overlooking the town, has six arched and cave rooms furnished in an attractive modern style. There's a swimming pool, a series of terraces and a fully equipped apartment (from €75). From Cumhuriyet Meydanı, it's a stiff 1km up the hill.

our pick **Old Greek House** (☎ 353 5306; www.oldgreekhouse.com; Şahin Caddesi; mains TL6-20, menu TL22-30) has been inhabited by the same family since 1938, and is about the best place to try Ottoman cuisine in Cappadocia. Prepared by half-a-dozen village women, the dishes include unusual choices and some of the best baklava we've tasted. The hotel (singles/doubles from TL60/80) is an excellent place to stay thanks to its historic aura.

Nine buses per day (three on Sundays) travel between Mustafapaşa and Ürgüp's Mustafapaşa *otogar* (TL1, 10 minutes), next to the main bus station.

IHLARA VALLEY

☎ 0382

A beautiful canyon full of greenery and rock-cut churches dating back to Byzantine times, **Ihlara Valley** (Ihlara Vadısı; admission TL5; 8am-6.30pm) is a definite must-see. Footpaths follow the course of the river, Melendiz Suyu, which flows for 13km between the narrow gorge at Ihlara village and the wide valley around **Selime Monastery** (dawn-dusk).

In the words of one Slovakian traveller: 'The deep canyon with lots of churches and trees opens up as you approach Selime. After that you're in a sleepy valley with the river flowing, big mountains typical of Cappadocia in the distance, and a gorgeous monastery in Selime.'

The easiest way to see the valley is on a day tour from Göreme (p914), which allows a few hours to walk through the central part of the gorge. To get there by bus, you must change in Nevşehir and Aksaray, making it tricky to get there and back from Göreme and walk the valley in a day.

If you want to walk the whole way – and it's definitely worth the effort – there are modest pensions in both Ihlara village and Selime. You can also break your journey into two parts with an overnight stay in Belisırma's camping grounds or lone pension. Note that all accommodation is closed out of season (December to March).

Ten *dolmuşes* a day travel down the valley from Aksaray, stopping in Selime, Belisırma and Ihlara village. In Belisırma, *dolmuşes* stop up on the plateau, and you have to hike a few hundred metres down into the valley.

To travel in the opposite direction, you have to catch a taxi (about TL70 to Aksaray from Ihlara village; TL45 from Selime).

KAYSERI

☎ 0352 / pop 1.2 million

Mixing Seljuk tombs, mosques and modern developments, Kayseri is both Turkey's most devoutly Islamic city after Konya and one of the economic powerhouses nicknamed the 'Anatolian tigers'. Colourful silk headscarfs are piled in the bazaar, one of the country's biggest, and businesses shut down at noon on Friday for prayer, but Kayseri's religious leanings are less prominent than its economic prowess. Its inhabitants are often less approachable than folk in Göreme et al, and this can be frustrating and jarring if you arrive fresh from the fairy chimneys. Nevertheless, if you are passing through this transport hub, it's worth taking a look at a Turkish boom town with a strong sense of its own history.

Orientation & Information

The basalt-walled citadel at the centre of the Old Town, just south of Cumhuriyet Meydanı (the huge main square) is a good landmark. The train station is at the northern end of Atatürk Bulvarı, 500m north of the Old Town. The futuristic *otogar* is about 3km northwest of the centre.

You'll find banks with ATMs and a helpful **tourist office** (☎ 222 3903; Cumhuriyet Meydanı; 8am-5pm Mon-Fri) in the centre. To check your emails, head to **Soner Internet Café** (Düvenönü Meydanı; per hr TL1.50), west of the Old Town.

Sights

The fabulous **citadel** was constructed in the early 13th century, during the Seljuk sultan Alaattin Keykubat's reign, then restored over the years (twice in the 15th century). Just southeast of the citadel is the wonderful **Güpgüpoğlu Konağı** (admission TL2; 8am-5pm Tue-Sun), a fine stone mansion dating from the 18th century, which now houses an interesting ethnographic museum.

Among Kayseri's distinctive features are important building complexes founded by Seljuk queens and princesses, such as the impressive **Mahperi Hunat Hatun Complex**, east of the citadel. The *kapalı çarşı*, one of the largest built by the Ottomans, remains the heart of the city and is well worth a wander. On the other side of the bazaar is the **Ulu Cami** (Great Mosque), a good example of early Seljuk style. Another striking monument is the **Çifte Medrese** (Twin Seminaries). These adjoining religious schools, in Mimar Sinan Parkı north of Park Caddesi, date back to the 12th century.

Scattered about Kayseri are several conical **Seljuk tombs**.

Sleeping & Eating

Elif Hotel (☎ 336 1826; elifotelkayseri@elifotelkayseri.com; Osman Kavuncu Caddesi 2; s/d/tr TL40/70/90) Despite their slightly worn bathrooms, rooms are a bargain, with satellite TV and minibars. Ask for a spot at the rear of the building, which is quieter.

Hotel Çapari (☎ 222 5278; www.hotelcapari.com; Gevher Nesibe Mahellesi Donanma Caddesi 12; s/d/tr/ste TL60/90/110/120;) With thick red carpets and friendly staff, this three-star hotel on a quiet street off Atatürk Bulvarı is one of the best deals in town.

Bent Hotel (☎ 221 2400; www.benthotel.com; Atatürk Bulvarı 40; s/d/tr TL75/100/120) Its name may not inspire confidence, but the Bent is a good midrange choice overlooking the pedal boats in Mimar Sinan Parkı.

Hotel Almer (☎ 320 7970; www.almer.com.tr; Osman Kavuncu Caddesi 15; s/d/tr TL75/120/150;) Kayseri's top sub-Hilton establishment is smoothly professional from the moment you reel through the revolving door. The relaxing reception has a backlit bar and little alcoves for working your way through the magazine rack.

The western end of Sivas Caddesi has a strip of fast-food joints that still seem to be pumping when everything else in town is quiet, including the fish-loving **İstanbul Balık Pazarı** (Sivas Caddesi; mains TL3).

Kayseri's best restaurants are **Tuana** (☎ 222 0565; 2nd fl, Sivas Caddesi; mains TL7), with views of the citadel and Erciyes Dağı (Mt Erciyes) and a roll-call of classic dishes such as *kebaps* and Kayseri *mantı;* and **Elmacioğlu İskender et Lokantası** (☎ 222 6965; 1st & 2nd fl, Millet Caddesi 5; mains TL8-13), where *İskender kebaps* are the house speciality, available with *köfte* or in 'double' form. Mmmm…

Getting There & Away

Situated at an important north–south and east–west crossroads, Kayseri has lots of bus services. Destinations include Sivas (TL18, three hours), Ürgüp (TL6, 1¼ hours) and Göreme (TL10, 1½ hours).

There are useful train services to Adana, Ankara, Diyarbakır, Kars and Sivas, most of which are daily.

EASTERN TURKEY

Like a challenge? Eastern Turkey – vast, remote and culturally very Middle Eastern – is the toughest part of Turkey to travel in but definitely the most exotic, and certainly the least affected by mass tourism. Winter here can be bitterly cold and snowy.

It's worth checking with your embassy for the latest information on the area before you head out, but the conflict between the Turkish army and the PKK (Kurdistan Workers Party) separatist group has simmered down in recent years (see the boxed text, p925).

GAZIANTEP (ANTEP)

☎ 0342 / pop 1.1 million

Antep is a greatly underrated city with a modern, laissez-faire attitude that thumbs its nose at nearby Şanlıurfa's piety. It's one of the most desirable places to live in eastern

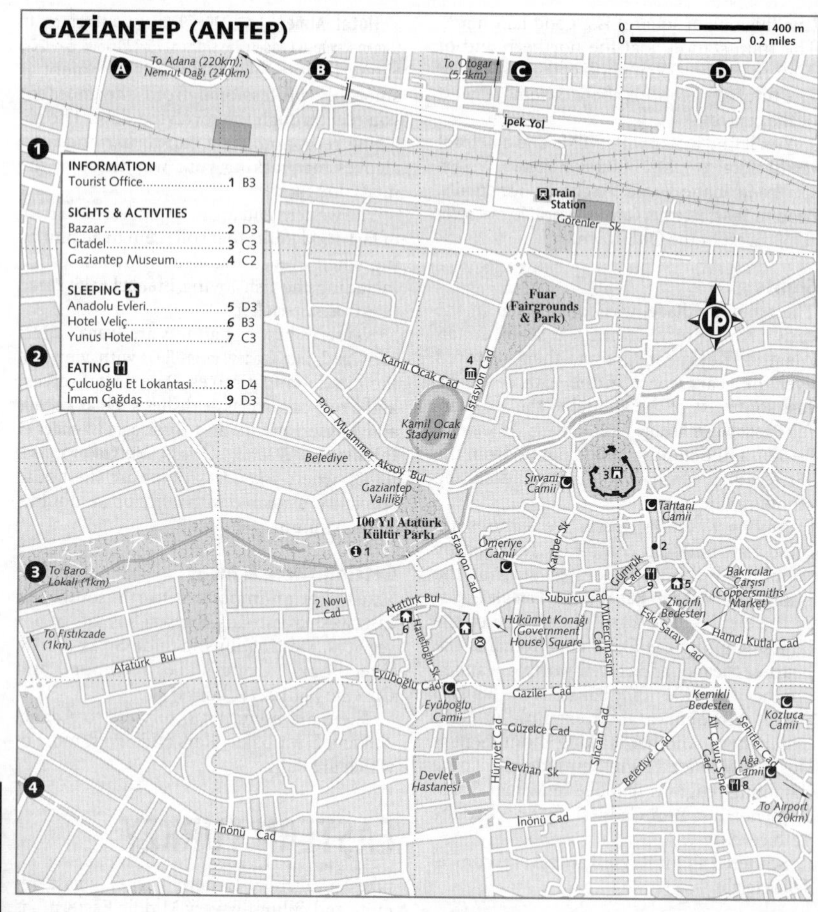

Anatolia, with the biggest city park this side of the Euphrates and a buzzing cafe culture. Its Mosaic Museum also makes the trip across Turkey well worth the fare.

Orientation & Information

Antep's throbbing heart is the intersection of Atatürk Bulvarı/Suburcu Caddesi and Hürriyet/İstasyon Caddesis, marked by a large Atatürk statue. Most hotels, banks with ATMs, and sights are within walking distance of this intersection. The *otogar* is about 6km north of the centre; the train station is 800m north.

The **tourist office** (☎ 230 5969; 100 Yıl Atatürk Kültür Parkı İçi; 🕑 8am-noon & 1-5pm Mon-Fri) is in the city park.

Sights

The unmissable **citadel** (admission free; 🕑 8.30am-4.30pm Tue-Sun) offers superb vistas over the city, and nearby is a buzzing, recently restored **bazaar**. Scattered in the centre are numerous old **stone houses** and **caravanserai**, also being restored as part of Antep's ongoing regeneration.

Gaziantep Museum (☎ 324 8809; İstasyon Caddesi; admission TL2; 🕑 8.30am-noon & 1-5pm Tue-Sun) is also known as the Mosaic Museum for its display of fabulous mosaics unearthed at the rich Roman site of Belkıs-Zeugma.

Sleeping & Eating

Antep is rolling in accommodation, much of it on or near Suburcu, Hürriyet and Atatürk Caddesis.

Antep is reckoned to harbour 180-plus pastry shops, producing arguably the best *fıstık* (pistachio) baklava in the world.

Yunus Hotel (☎ 221 1722; hotelyunus@hotel.com; Kayacık Sokak; s/d TL30/50; ❄) As far as physical beauty goes, this is a real plain Jane, but it's a secure spot to hang your rucksack, the rates are good and it's handily set in the centre of town.

Hotel Veliç (☎ 221 2212; www.velicotel.com; Atatürk Bulvarı; s/d TL35/55; ❄) A recent lick of paint (yellow and lilac) has elevated this concrete lump on the main drag a couple of notches up the comfort ladder. The rooms are on the small side, but top marks go to the bright top-floor breakfast area.

our pick **Anadolu Evleri** (☎ 220 9525, 0533 558 7996; www.anadoluevleri.com; Köroğlu Sokak; s/d TL105/135; ❄ 💻) A tastefully restored old stone house in a lovely position, just out of earshot of the bazaar, this oasis celebrates local tradition, with flourishes such as mosaic floors and secret passageways.

İmam Çağdaş (☎ 231 2678; Kale Civarı Uzun Çarşı; mains TL4-10) This pastry shop and restaurant is run by culinary wizard Imam Çağdaş, whose pistachio baklava are delivered throughout Turkey. And if there were a *kebap* Oscar, this place would also be a serious contender.

Çulcuoğlu Et Lokantasi (☎ 231 0241; Kalender Sokak; mains TL5-10; ⏰ 11.30am-10pm Mon-Sat) Surrender to your inner carnivore at this local institution. The yummy *kebaps* are the way to go, but grilled chicken also puts in menu appearances. Don't be discouraged by the unremarkable entrance.

Getting There & Away

Gaziantep's Oğuzeli airport is 20km from the centre. An airport bus departs from outside each airline office 1½ hours before flights (TL5).

Turkish Airlines has daily flights to/from Ankara and İstanbul. Onur Air and Pegasus also serve İstanbul; Sun Express serves İzmir; and Cyprus Turkish Airlines has a weekly flight to London Stansted.

From the *otogar* you can reach many destinations in Turkey, including Şanlıurfa (TL12, 2½ hours) and Antakya (TL12, four hours).

MT NEMRUT NATIONAL PARK

Nemrut Dağı (Mt Nemrut; 2150m) is one of the country's most awe-inspiring sights. Two thousand years ago, right on top of the mountain and pretty much in the middle of nowhere, an obscure Commagene king chose to erect fabulous temples and a funerary mound. The fallen heads of the gigantic decorative statues of gods and kings, toppled by earthquakes, form one of the country's most enduring images.

Access to Nemrut Dağı Milli Parkı (Mt Nemrut National Park) costs TL5. There are a few possible bases for visiting Mt Nemrut. To the north is Malatya, where the **tourist office** (☎ 0422-323 2942; malatyakt@gmail.com; Atatürk Caddesi; ⏰ 9am-5pm Mon-Fri) organises all-inclusive daily minibus tours (TL80, early May to late September/early October), with a sunset visit to the heads, a night at the Güneş Hotel below the summit and a second visit at dawn.

Alternatively, visit the mountain from the south via Kahta, where eight-hour sunrise and sunset trips are available, as well as the three-hour 'small tour'. This route is more scenic, but note that Kahta has a reputation as a rip-off town so you need to be wary of what's on offer. When you book a tour, always check exactly what you will be seeing, and how long you'll be away. One of the better operators is **Nemrut Tours** (☎ 0416-725 6881; Mustafa Kemal Caddesi, Kahta), based in Hotel Nemrut p924).

The two-day tours (TL120, minimum four people) and sunset/sunrise tours (TL80, minimum four people) from Şanlıurfa (Urfa), run by **Harran-Nemrut Tours** (☎ 0414-215 1575; ozcan_aslan_teacher@hotmail.com; Köprübaşı Caddesi), are relatively good value. They usually take you to the Atatürk Dam along the way.

Some people take a two-day tour (about TL250) from Cappadocia, but it's a tedious drive. If you have enough time, it's better to opt for a three-day tour, which should also include a few stops, such as Harran, Şanlıurfa and Gaziantep.

Sleeping

MALATYA

Malatya Büyük Otel (☎ 0422-325 2828; fax 0422-323 2828; Halep Caddesi, Yeni Cami Karşısı; s/d TL35/60; ❄) This sharp-edged monolith wins no awards for character but sports serviceable (if small) rooms with salubrious bathrooms and dashing views of a huge mosque. The location is handy – the bazaar is one block behind – and the staff are obliging.

Yeni Hotel (☎ 0422-323 1423; yenihotel@turk.net; Yeni Cami Karşısı Zafer İşhanı; s/d TL35/60; ❄) Quite transparently intended to rival the neighbouring

Malatya Büyük, this well-run establishment has rooms in pastel hues, with electric-blue bedspreads.

Grand Akkoza Hotel (☎ 0422-326 2727; www.grandakkozahotel.com; Çevre Yolu Üzeri Adliye Kavşağı; s/d TL75/110; ❄ 💻) This glass-fronted three-star establishment provides a good level of comfort and service, with a *hammam*, sauna and gym. It's awkwardly placed (if you're not driving) on the busy ring road, but within easy access of the city centre.

KAHTA

Hotel Nemrut (☎ 0416-725 6881; www.hotelnemrut.net; Mustafa Kemal Caddesi; s/d TL45/70; ❄) Your run-of-the-mill motel, with uninspiring yet well-maintained rooms and tour groups passing through en route to Nemrut. A few smiles in reception would sweeten the deal.

Zeus Hotel (☎ 0416-725 5694; www.zeushotel.com.tr; Mustafa Kemal Caddesi; camp sites per person TL20, s/d TL80/100; ❄ 🏊) Another group-friendly stalwart, this solid three-star option gets an A+ for its swimming pool in the manicured garden. Angle for one of the renovated rooms, which feature top-notch bathrooms and flat-screen tellies.

In high summer the most pleasant places to stay, especially if you have your own transport, are not in Kahta itself but on the slopes of the mountain. At the northern end of Karadut village, pension-cum-hostel **Karadut Pension** (☎ 0416-737 2169; www.karadutpansiyon.net; camp sites per person TL5, d per person TL20; ❄ 💻) has 11 neat rooms (some with air-con), cleanish bathrooms and a kitchen you can use.

ŞANLIURFA

Hotel Bakay (☎ 0414-215 8975; fax 0414-215 4007; Asfalt Yol Caddesi; s/d TL30/50; ❄ 💻) The hip-pocket-friendly Bakay is remarkably clean, but be prepared to trip over your backpack in the tiny rooms. Some rooms are brighter than others, so ask to ogle a few. It's popular with Turkish families – a good sign for female travellers.

Hotel Rabis (☎ 0414-216 9595; www.hotelrabis.com, in Turkish; Sarayönu Caddesi; s/d TL60/80; ❄) Urfa's latest arrival is a model of shiny midrange quality, with thick carpets, flat-screen TVs, double glazing and good views from the rooftop terrace. One of the best deals in town.

Hotel Arte (☎ 0414-314 7060; www.otel-arte.com.tr; Atatürk Bulvarı; s/d TL60/90; ❄) The Arte's design-led interior, with Barbie-esque plastic chairs in the lobby, laminate floors and contemporary furniture in the rooms, is appealing, and the floor-to-ceiling windows afford superb views of the main drag.

Getting There & Away

Malatya, Kahta and Şanlıurfa are well connected, with buses running to/from locations including Ankara, İstanbul and Kayseri. Malatya and Şanlıurfa's airports both have daily Turkish Airlines flights to/from Ankara and İstanbul, and Malatya is also served by Onur Air and Sun Express.

MARDIN

☎ 0482 / pop 55,000

What a beauty! Pretty as a picture, Mardin is a highly addictive, unmissable spot with a fabulous setting, a breathtaking layout and a wealth of architectural treasures. With its minarets poking out of a labyrinth of brown lanes, its castle dominating the Old City and the honey-coloured stone houses that trip down the hillside, it emerges like a phoenix from the roasted Mesopotamian plains.

Another draw is the mosaic of people. With Kurdish, Yezidi, Christian and Syrian cultures, among others, it has a fascinating social mix.

Mardin has started to become popular with Turkish travellers. Get here before it becomes too touristy!

Sights

Strolling through the rambling **bazaar**, keep your eyes open for the ornate **Ulu Cami**, a 12th-century Iraqi Seljuk structure.

Mardin Museum (Mardin Müzesi; admission TL2; 🕒 8am-5pm), prominently positioned on Cumhuriyet Meydanı, is housed in a superbly restored mansion dating from the late 19th century. Back on Cumhuriyet Caddesi, head east and keep your eyes peeled for the three-arched facade of an ornately carved **house**, a fabulous example of Mardin's domestic architecture.

Continue east, looking for steps on the left (north) that lead to the **Sultan İsa Medresesi** (🕒 daylight), which dates from 1385 and is the town's prime architectural attraction.

Opposite the **post office**, housed in a 17th-century caravanserai, you can't miss the minaret of the 14th-century **Şehidiye Camii**. It's superbly carved, with colonnades all around and three small domes superimposed on the summit.

Also worth visiting is the 15th-century **Forty Martyrs Church** (Kırklar Kilisesi; Sağlık Sokak); the martyrs are depicted above the doorway of the church as you enter. If it's closed, bang on the door to alert the caretaker.

The **Kasımiye Medresesi** (1469), 800m south of Yeni Yol, sports a sublime courtyard walled in by arched colonnades, as well as a magnificent carved doorway.

Sleeping & Eating

Otel Bilem (☎ 213 0315; fax 212 2575; Yenişehir; s/d TL60/120; ❄) A safe, albeit unsexy choice in the new part of Mardin (Yenişehir), 2km northwest of Cumhuriyet Meydanı. Despite a renovation, the Bilem is no architectural beauty queen, but it's often full to the brim with tour groups.

Artuklu Kervansarayı (☎ 213 7353; www.artuklu.com; Cumhuriyet Caddesi; s/d TL90/140; ❄) Dark floorboards and furniture, stone walls, sturdy wooden doors: you'll feel like you're in a castle. We're not sure how to take this self-proclaimed boutique hotel, but the 'medieval' interior certainly breaks the mould.

our pick **Cercis Murat Konağı** (☎ 213 6841; Cumhuriyet Caddesi; mains TL10-18) The Cercis occupies a traditional Syrian Christian home with a terrace affording stunning views. There's a TV screen where you can watch local women at work in the kitchen, conjuring up dainty dishes including *mekbuss* (eggplant pickles with walnut), *kitel raha* (Syrian-style meatballs) and *dobo* (piece of lamb with garlic, spices and black pepper).

Getting There & Away

Mardin airport is 20km south of Mardin. There's no airport shuttle, but any minibus to Kızıltepe can drop you at the entrance (TL2). Turkish Airlines has a daily flight to/from İstanbul and Pegasus Airlines has weekly flights to/from İzmir. There are frequent minibuses to Diyarbakır (TL7, 1¼ hours) and Şanlıurfa (Urfa, TL15, three hours).

VAN

☎ 0432 / pop 391,000

Young couples walking hand in hand on the main drag, students flirting in the pastry shops, live bands knocking out Kurdish tunes in pubs, unscarved girls sampling ice cream and daring to make eye contact with foreigners…frontier towns never looked so liberal! Van is different in spirit from the rest of southeastern Anatolia – more urban, more casual – and boasts a brilliant location, near the eponymous lake.

> **SAFETY IN THE EAST**
>
> The security situation in southeastern Turkey has improved considerably since it was the epicentre of the Kurdish rebellion during the 1980s and '90s. Although it's always wise to keep your ear to the ground, there is currently little reason to think travellers would suffer anything worse than delays at checkpoints along their way. If there is any trouble, the military will simply not let you get anywhere near it. The only road that was closed at the time of research was the long stretch from Şırnak to Hakkari, on the Iraqi border.

Everything you'll need (hotels, restaurants, banks, internet cafes, bus company offices and the PTT) lies on or around Cumhuriyet Caddesi, the main commercial street, including the **tourist office** (☎ 216 2530; Cumhuriyet Caddesi; 🕒 8.30am-noon & 1-5.30pm Mon-Fri).

Sights

Van's main claim to fame is its **castle** (admission TL2; 🕒 9am-dusk), about 3km west of the city centre, where you'll also find the foundations of **Eski Van** (the Old City). The small **Van Museum** (Van Müzesi; Kışla Caddesi; admission TL2; 🕒 8am-noon & 1-5pm Tue-Sun) boasts an outstanding collection of Urartian exhibits, with gold jewellery, bronze belts, helmets, horse armour and terracotta figures.

Around the city, Van's 8th-century Armenian rulers took refuge on **Akdamar Island** in Van Gölü (Lake Van) when the Arab armies flooded through from the south. The recently restored **Akdamar Kiliseli** (Church of the Holy Cross) is one of the wonders of Armenian architecture. The island is a day trip from Van by minibus or the occasional boat.

A slightly longer excursion to the southeast takes you to the spectacular **Hoşap Castle** (admission TL2), a Kurdish castle perched on top of a rocky outcrop. To get there, catch a Başkale- or Yüksekova-bound minibus on Cumhuriyet Caddesi, and say you want to get out at Hoşap (TL5). After seeing the castle, flag down a bus to Çavuştepe, where you can pick up a bus to Van. Frequent minibuses and buses ply the route.

Büyük Asur Oteli organises tours to Hoşap Castle, Akdamar Island and other local attractions.

Sleeping

Otel Aslan (☎ 216 2469; Özel İdare İş Merkezi Karşısı; s/d from TL15/20) The great central location and budget rates keep this hotel-cum-hostel popular with thrifty backpackers. Cheaper rooms share bathrooms (pray you're not the last in line to shower) and no breakfast is served. Don't leave valuables in your room.

Büyük Asur Oteli (☎ 216 8792; asur_asur2008@hotmail.com; Cumhuriyet Caddesi, Turizm Sokak; s/d TL45/75) At this reliable midrange venture, the rooms come complete with fresh linen, back-friendly beds, TVs and well-scrubbed bathrooms. It has an ultracentral location and a vast lobby where you can unwind over a beer.

Hotel Yakut (☎ 214 2832; fax 216 6351; PTT Caddesi; s/d TL45/80) The Yakut's interior and exterior aren't going to inflame many architects' or interior designers' passions, but the renovated rooms, laminate floors, pristine (yet pokey) bathrooms and attentive service make this one of central Van's more solid midrange options.

Eating & Drinking

Van is famed for its tasty *kahvaltı* (breakfast), best tried on pedestrianised Eski Sümerbank Sokak, also called 'Kahvaltı Sokak' (Breakfast St). Here, a row of eateries offers complete Turkish breakfasts for around TL8. Sample *otlu peynir* (cheese mixed with a tangy herb, Van's speciality), *beyaz peynir* (a mild yellow cheese), honey from the highlands, olives, *kayma* (clotted cream), tomatoes, cucumbers, and *sucuklu yumurta* (omelette with sausage).

Safa 3, Çorba 1 Paça Salonu (☎ 215 8121; Kazım Karabekir Caddesi; soups TL2) Gastronomic adventurers, head to this quirky little restaurant, where regulars swear by the *kelle* (sheep's head). The spicy lentil soup takes you into more-traditional culinary territory.

Ayça Pastaneleri (☎ 216 0081; Kazım Karabekir Caddesi; snacks TL2-4) With its see-and-be-seen glass front and modern furnishings, this patisserie lures students in search of a pleasant spot to flirt and relax over toothsome baklava and decent snacks.

Akdeniz Tantuni (☎ 216 9010; Cumhuriyet Caddesi; sandwiches TL3) Make a beeline for this delightful little den on the main drag, which prepares devilish chicken sandwiches at paupers' prices.

Halil İbrahim Sofrası (☎ 210 0070; Cumhuriyet Caddesi; mains TL6-12) One word describes this downtown hot spot: yum. The eclectic food is well presented and of high quality, with service and sleek surrounds to match. Ahh, the *İskender kebap:* so rich, so tender.

Barabar Türk Evi (☎ 214 9866; Sanat Sokak) The closest thing Van has to a pub, the Barabar is a rare breed in eastern Turkey. There is a fever-pitch energy to its mainly student crowd of both sexes gulping down frothy pints of draught beer.

Getting There & Away

The airport is 6km from the centre; a taxi there costs about TL20. There are daily flights to/from Ankara and İstanbul with Turkish Airlines and Pegasus Airlines. Sun Express operates weekly flights to/from İzmir and Antalya.

Daily buses connect Van with destinations including Ankara (TL40, 22 hours), Malatya (TL35, 10 hours) and Şanlıurfa (TL30, nine hours).

A ferry crosses Lake Van between Tatvan and Van on a twice-daily basis (there's no fixed schedule). The trip costs TL6 per passenger and takes about four hours.

The twice-weekly *Vangölü Ekspresi* train from İstanbul and Ankara meets the ferry in Tatvan. The weekly *Trans Asya Ekspresi* connects İstanbul to Tehran (Iran) via Van.

KARS

☎ 0474 / pop 78,500

What a quirky city. 'Where am I?' is probably what you'll find yourself wondering on arrival. With its stately, pastel-coloured stone buildings dating from the Russian occupation and its grid layout, Kars looks like a slice of Russia teleported to northeastern Anatolia. And the mix of influences – Azeri, Turkmen, Kurdish, Turkish and Russian – adds to the feeling of surprise.

It won't be love at first sight (especially on a rainy day), but Kars is high on personality and atmosphere. No wonder it provided the setting for Orhan Pamuk's award-winning novel *Kar* (Snow).

Information

Most banks (and ATMs), internet cafes, hotels and restaurants are on or close to Atatürk Caddesi, the main street. The **tourist office** (☎ 212 6817; Lise Caddesi; ⌚ 8am-noon & 1-5pm Mon-

Fri) can help you organise a taxi to the ruins of Ani (below), but your best bet is to contact **Celil Ersoğlu** (☎ 212 6543), who acts as a private guide and speaks good English.

Sights

The most prominent point of interest is **Kars Castle** (admission free; 8am-5pm), which has smashing views over the town and the steppe. Most people come to Kars to visit the dramatic ruins of **Ani** (admission TL5; 8.30am-5pm), 45km east of town. Set amid spectacular scenery, the site exudes an eerie ambience. Ani was completely deserted in 1239 after a Mongol invasion, but before that it was the stately Armenian capital, rivalling Constantinople in power and glory. Fronted by a hefty wall, the ghost city now lies in fields overlooking the Arpaçay River, which forms the border with Armenia. The ruins include several notable churches and a cathedral built between AD 987 and 1010.

To get to Ani, take the taxi *dolmuşes* organised by Kars tourist office or Celil Ersoğlu. It costs about TL30 per person, provided there's a minimum of six people. If there are no other tourists around, you'll have to pay the full fare of TL100 return plus waiting time. You can hire a taxi from TL70, but make sure the driver understands you want a few hours at the site.

Sleeping & Eating

Kars is noted for its excellent honey. It's on sale in several shops, which also sell the local *kaşar peyniri* (mild yellow cheese) and *kuruyemiş* (dried fruits) – perfect ingredients for a picnic on the steppe.

Kent Otel (☎ 223 1929; Hapan Mevkii; s/d with shared bathroom TL15/30) The beds are lumpy and the decor is plain; the facilities are a little outdated and the shared bathrooms have seen their fair share of bodies and odours. But it's well taken care of and secure, and the great central location and economical rates keep Kent Otel popular with thrifty backpackers.

Güngören Hotel (☎ 212 5630; fax 223 4821; Millet Sokak; s/d TL30/50) This fine pile has attentive staff, good-sized rooms with modern furniture, and a handy location. Perks include a satisfying breakfast, a restaurant and a men-only *hammam*. It's popular with savings-minded European groups, and is a good choice for solo women travellers.

Hotel Temel (☎ 223 1376; fax 223 1323; Yenipazar Caddesi; s/d TL30/45) Unlike the Güngören, the Termel offers a lift, as well as neat rooms with immaculate sheets and a soothing blue-and-yellow colour scheme. The management gets mixed reviews.

Kar's Otel (☎ 212 1616; www.karsotel.com; Halit Paşa Caddesi; s/d TL190/260;) Seeking a luxurious cocoon with homely qualities, efficient hosts and a big dollop of atmosphere? Look no further than this savvy boutique hotel, housed in an old Russian mansion. It breathes an air of repose, though some might find the white colour scheme a bit too clinical, and its Ani Restaurant (mains TL6 to TL15) is also recommended.

Antep Lahmacun Salonu (☎ 223 0741; Atatürk Caddesi; mains TL2-4) Pide and *lahmacun* aficionados head straight to this humble joint to gobble a flavoursome local-style pizza at paupers' prices.

Ocakbaşı Restoran (☎ 212 0056; Atatürk Caddesi; mains TL5-8) This well-established restaurant is the pinnacle of Kars' eating scene. Sample its signature dishes, *ali nazık* (eggplant puree with yoghurt and meat) and *Anteplim pide* (sesame bread stuffed with meat, cheese, parsley, nuts and eggs), and you'll understand why. It has two rooms, including a mock troglodytic one (wow!), but it's not licensed (boo!).

Getting There & Away

Turkish Airlines has daily flights to/from Ankara and İstanbul; Sun Express has two weekly flights to/from İzmir. From the *otogar,* 2km southeast of the centre, daily buses run to destinations including Ankara (TL50, 16 hours) and Van (TL30, six hours, mornings only).

TURKEY DIRECTORY

ACCOMMODATION

Hotels quote tariffs in Turkish lira or euros, sometimes both, so we've used the currency quoted by the business being reviewed. In general, you will find more-Westernised spots such as İstanbul quote in euros, while less-touristy locations use lira; most hotels happily accept either currency.

Be prepared to find other guests smoking in accommodation. Top-end hotels, and accommodation in tourist-orientated areas, sometimes offer nonsmoking rooms.

Camping

Camping facilities are dotted about Turkey, although not perhaps as frequently as you might hope. Some hotels and pensions will also let you camp in their grounds for a small fee (TL5 to TL15), and they sometimes have facilities especially for campers.

Hostels

Given that pensions are so cheap, Turkey has no real hostel network. The best place to find hostels are backpacker hang-outs such as Göreme (p916), where many establishments offer dormitories and hostel-style facilities.

Pensions & Hotels

Most tourist areas offer simple, family-run pensions where you can get a good, clean single room from around TL20 a night (and a dorm bed from around TL10). Pensions are often cosy and represent better value than full-blown hotels. These places usually offer a choice of simple meals (including breakfast), laundry services, international TV services and so on, and it's these facilities that really distinguish them from traditional small, cheap hotels. Many pensions also have staff who speak English.

In most cities there is a variety of old and new hotels, which range from heart-sinkingly basic to full-on luxurious. The cheapest nonresort hotels (around TL30 per person per night) are mostly used by working Turkish men travelling on business and are not always suitable for lone women, who may face stares whenever they enter the lobby. Moving up a price bracket, one- and two-star hotels vary from TL70 to TL120 for a double room with shower, but these hotels are less oppressively masculine in atmosphere, even when the clientele remains mainly male.

If you fancy top-notch accommodation at reasonable prices, Turkey is the place to find it. Boutique hotels are all the rage in the country. Increasingly, old Ottoman mansions and other historic buildings are being refurbished, or completely rebuilt, as hotels equipped with all the mod cons and bags of character. The best boutique hotels are located in İstanbul (p861) and Cappadocia (p914), but almost every city boasts some character-filled establishments.

We have quoted high-season rates in this chapter. In tourist-dependent areas, such as the coast and Cappadocia, many hotels close from November to April. More stay open than in the past, but your choice will still be diminished; one consolation is that rates fall during the winter.

Unless otherwise stated, breakfast and private bathrooms are included in the rates quoted in this chapter. Dorms in İstanbul often have shared bathrooms.

Note that virtually nowhere in Turkey is far from a mosque – light sleepers might want to bring earplugs for the early morning call to prayer.

Tree Houses

Olympos (p901), on the coast southwest of Antalya, is famous for its 'tree houses', wooden shacks of minimal comfort in forested settings near the beach. Increasingly, these basic shelters are being converted into chalets with more comfort.

ACTIVITIES

Popular activities include hiking and trekking in the Uludağ National Park near Bursa (p877) and southern Cappadocia's Ala Dağlar National Park. Another popular stroll is the Lycian Way, a 30-day, 509km walk around the coast and mountains of Lycia, starting at Fethiye (p895) and finishing near Antalya (p903). The country's other way-marked national route is St Paul's Trail (Perge/Aspendos to Lake Egirdir), which is a similar length. The spectacular valleys of central Cappadocia are also excellent for hiking. If you're a serious hiker, you could consider conquering Turkey's highest mountain, the 5137m-high Mt Ararat, near Doğubayazıt, but you need a permit. Middle Earth Travel (see p914) is a good contact.

All sorts of water sports, including diving, waterskiing, rafting and kayaking, are available on the Aegean and Mediterranean coasts. The best diving is offered off Kaş (p899), Bodrum (p889) and Marmaris (p892). You can also try tandem paragliding at Ölüdeniz (p897).

Skiing is becoming more popular, with the best facilities at Palandöken, near Erzurum, and the most scenic runs at conifer-studded Sarıkamış, near Kars. Note their facilities do not meet the standards of the better European resorts.

Those of a lazier disposition may want to take a *gület* (wooden yacht) trip along the coast, stopping off to swim in bays along the way (see p897). The laziest 'activity' of all consists of paying a visit to a *hammam*, where

> **RESIST THE TOUTS!**
>
> In smaller tourist towns such as Fethiye (p895), Pamukkale (p887) and Selçuk (p884), touts for pensions may accost you as you step from your bus and string you whatever line they think will win you over. Of course they are after commission from the owner. Taxi drivers often like to play this game, too. Avoid letting these faux friends make your choices for you by deciding where you want to stay and sticking to your guns.

you can get yourself scrubbed and massaged for a fraction of what it would cost in most Western countries.

BUSINESS HOURS

Opening hours in Turkey are never set in stone, but most banks, businesses and offices are open from 8.30am to noon and from 1.30pm to 5pm Monday to Friday. Shops are open from 9am to 6pm Monday to Friday, but in tourist areas food and souvenir shops are often open virtually around the clock.

Markets often get going early and shopkeepers generally don't close for lunch, even if it means munching on a *kebap* behind their counter. During the hot summer months the working day in some cities begins at 7am or 8am and finishes at 2pm.

As a rule, restaurants are open roughly 8am to 10pm, depending on size and clientele. Bars usually start serving between 5pm and 8pm, though in tourist areas they might be open all day as well.

Many museums close on Mondays. Internet cafes usually open from around 9am until late at night, or until the last customer has left.

Main post offices in large cities are open every day. Smaller post offices may be closed on Saturday afternoons and all day Sunday.

The working day gets shortened during the holy month of Ramazan, and devoutly Islamic cities such as Konya (p913) and Kayseri (p920) virtually shut down during noon prayers on Friday (the Muslim Sabbah). Apart from that, Friday is a normal working day in Turkey. The day of rest, a secular one, is Sunday.

COURSES

The best Turkish language courses include Taksim Dilmer (see p870) in İstanbul and the Ankara University–affiliated **Tömer** (☎ 0212-230 7083; www.tomer.com.tr), which has branches throughout the country.

Courses are also available in craftwork and cooking (see p870) and, at the **Gökpinar Retreat** (☎ 0252-313 1896; www.caravanturkey.com) near Bodrum or with **Les Arts Turcs** (☎ 0212-458 1318; www.lesartsturcs.com; 3rd fl, İncili Çavuş Sokak 37, Sultanahmet) in İstanbul, belly dancing.

CUSTOMS REGULATIONS

Two hundred cigarettes and 50 cigars or 200g of tobacco, and five 1L or seven 700ml bottles of alcohol can be imported duty-free.

It's strictly illegal to export antiquities. Customs officers spot-check luggage and will want proof that you have permission from a museum before letting you leave with an antique carpet.

DANGERS & ANNOYANCES

Although Turkey is in no way a dangerous country to visit, it's always wise to be a little cautious, especially if you're travelling alone. Conceal your money in a safe place (such as a discreet money belt, or in a zippable shirt pocket) and be wary of pickpockets on buses, in markets and in other crowded places. Keep an eye out for anyone suspicious lurking near ATMs.

As a pedestrian, note that there is no such thing as right of way, despite the little green man. Give way to cars and trucks in all situations. Things are changing slowly, but parents of young children in particular will need to be on their guard at all times.

In İstanbul, single men are sometimes approached in areas such as Sultanahmet and Taksim and lured to a bar by new 'friends'. The scammers may be accompanied by a fig leaf of a woman. The victim is then made to pay an outrageous bill, regardless of what he drank. Drugging is also a risk, especially for lone men. Again, it most commonly happens in İstanbul, and involves so-called friends, a bar, and perhaps a willowy temptress. Sometimes on the bus, the person in the seat next to you offers you a drink, slips a drug into it and then makes off with your luggage. So be a little cautious about who you befriend, especially when you're new to the country.

More commonly, the hard-sell tactics of carpet sellers can drive you to distraction. Despite their idyllic appearances, tourist hot spots are driven by foreign spenders and there is often no such thing as a free *kebap*. 'Free' lifts and other suspiciously cheap services often lead to near-compulsory visits to carpet showrooms or hotel commission for touts.

At the time of writing, travelling in the southeast is safe. The Kurdish issue remains unresolved, however, so check the situation before setting out. Visitors should also note that sporadic bombings, often linked to the PKK Kurdish separatists, target affluent areas frequented by tourists, including a double-bomb attack in İstanbul in 2008. Again, check advisories for the latest information.

EMBASSIES & CONSULATES

Foreign embassies are in Ankara but many countries also have consulates in İstanbul. In general they are open from 9am to noon Monday to Friday, and some open in the afternoon. For more information, visit http://tinyurl.com/6ywt8a.

Australia Ankara (Map p910; ☎ 0312-459 9521; www.embaustralia.org.tr; Uğur Mumcu Caddesi 88/7, Gaziosmanpaşa); İstanbul (Map pp862-3; ☎ 0212-243 1333; 2nd fl, Suzer Plaza, Asker Ocağı Caddesi 15, Elmadağ, Şişli)

Bulgaria (Map p910; ☎ 0312-467 2071; Atatürk Bulvarı 124, Kavaklıdere, Ankara)

Canada (Map p910; ☎ 0312-409 2700; Cinnah Caddesi 58, Çankaya, Ankara)

France Ankara (Map p910; ☎ 0312-455 4545; Paris Caddesi 70, Kavaklıdere); İstanbul (Map pp862-3; ☎ 0212-334 8730; İstiklal Caddesi 8, Taksim)

Germany Ankara (Map p910; ☎ 0312-455 5100; Atatürk Bulvarı 114, Kavaklıdere); İstanbul (Map pp862-3; ☎ 0212-334 6100; İnönü Caddesi 16-18, Taksim)

Greece Ankara (Map p910; ☎ 0312-448 0873; greekemb@superonline.com; Zia Ur Rahman Caddesi 9-11, Gaziosmanpaşa); Edirne (☎ 0284-235 5804; Nolu Caddesi 2); İstanbul (Map pp862-3; ☎ 0212-245 0596; Turnacıbaşı Sokak 32, Galatasaray)

Iran Ankara (Map p910; ☎ 0312-427 4320; Tahran Caddesi 10, Kavaklıdere); Erzurum (☎ 0442-316 2285; fax 0442-316 1182; Atatürk Bulvarı); İstanbul (Map p867; ☎ 0212-513 8230; Ankara Caddesi 1/2, Cağaloğlu)

Iraq (Map p910; ☎ 0312-468 7421; fax 0312-468 4832; Turan Emeksiz Sokak 11, Gaziosmanpaşa, Ankara)

Ireland Ankara (☎ 0312-446 6172; fax 0312-446 8061; Uğur Mumcu Caddesi, MNG Binasi B-Bl 88/3, Gaziosmanpaşa); İstanbul (☎ 0212-482 2434; fax 0212-482 0943; Ali Riza Gurcan Caddesi 2/13, Merter)

Italy Ankara (Map p910; ☏ 0312-457 4200; ambasciata.ankara@esteri.it; Atatürk Bulvarı 118, Kavaklıdere 06680 Çankaya); İstanbul (☏ 0212-243 1024; consolatogenerale.istanbul@esteri.it; Boğazkesen Caddesi Tom Tom Kaptan Sokak 15, 80073 Tophane, Beyoğlu); İzmir (☏ 0232-463 6676; consolato.izmir@esteri.it; Cumhuriyet Meydanı Cumhuriyet Apartmanı 12/3, 35212 Alsancak)

Netherlands Ankara (off Map p910; ☎ 0312-409 1800; fax 0312-409 1898; Hollanda Caddesi 3, Yıldız); İstanbul (Map pp862-3; ☎ 0212-393 2121; fax 0212-292 5031; İstiklal Caddesi 393, Beyoğlu)

New Zealand Ankara (Map p910; ☎ 0312-467 9054; www.nzembassy.com/turkey; İran Caddesi 13/4, Kavaklıdere); İstanbul (☎ 0212-244 0272; nzhonconist@hatem-law.com.tr; İnönü Caddesi 48/3, Taksim)

Syria Ankara (off Map p910; ☎ 0312-440 9657; fax 0312-438 5609; Abdulhahcevdet Sokak 7, Çankaya); İstanbul (Map pp862-3; ☎ 212-232 6721; Maçka Caddesi 59, Ralli Apt 3, Nişantaşı)

UK Ankara (Map p910; ☎ 0312-455 3344; fax 0312-455 3320; Şehit Ersan Caddesi 46/A, Çankaya); İstanbul (Map pp862-3; ☎ 0212-334 6400; fax 0212-334 6401; Meşrutiyet Caddesi 34, Tepebaşı, Beyoğlu)

USA Ankara (Map p910; ☎ 0312-455 5555; fax 0312-467 0019; Atatürk Bulvarı 110, Kavaklıdere); İstanbul (Map pp862-3; ☎ 0212-335 9000; fax 0212-335 9019; Kaplıcalar Mevkii 2, İstiniye)

FESTIVALS & EVENTS

Following are some of the major annual festivals and events in Turkey:

Camel Wrestling Hoof it to Selçuk (p884) on the last Sunday in January.

Nevruz Kurds and Alevis celebrate the ancient Middle Eastern spring festival on 21 March. Banned until recent years, Nevruz is now an official holiday.

Anzac Day The WWI battles at Gallipoli (p878) are commemorated with dawn services on 25 April.

International İstanbul Music Festival (www.iksv.org/muzik) Every June to July, İstanbul (p861) hosts world-class classical concerts.

Aspendos Festival Opera and ballet in the Roman theatre (p906), near Antalya, from mid-June to early July.

Kırkpınar Oil Wrestling Championship Huge crowds watch oil-covered men wrestling in a field near Edirne (p875) in late June or early July.

Mevlâna Festival The dervishes whirl in Konya (p913) from 10 to 17 December.

GAY & LESBIAN TRAVELLERS

Although not uncommon in a culture that traditionally separates men and women, overt homosexuality is not socially acceptable, except in a few small pockets in İstanbul, Bodrum and some resorts. In İstanbul there is an increasing number of openly gay bars and nightclubs, mainly around the Taksim Sq end of İstiklal Caddesi. Some *hammams* are known to be gay meeting places.

For more information, contact Turkey's gay and lesbian support group, **LAMBDA İstanbul** (www.lambdaistanbul.org), and Ankara-based **Kaos GL** (www.kaosgl.com), which publishes the country's only gay and lesbian magazine of the same name (in Turkish only). Gay-friendly travel agents include **Pride Travel** (www.turkey-gay-travel.com) and **Absolute Sultans** (www.absolutesultans.com).

HOLIDAYS

Public holidays in Turkey:

New Year's Day 1 January
Nevruz 21 March
Children's Day 23 April
Youth & Sports Day 19 May
Victory Day 30 August
Republic Day 29 October
Anniversary of Atatürk's Death 10 November

Turkey also celebrates all of the main Islamic holidays, the most important of which are the month-long **Ramazan** (September/October) and, about two months later, **Kurban Bayramı**. Due to the fact that these holidays are celebrated according to the Muslim lunar calendar, the exact dates change from year to year.

INTERNET ACCESS

Wherever you go, you'll never be far from an internet cafe. Fees are generally TL1 to TL2 per hour. Throughout the country, hotels of all standards often offer free wi-fi access, as do many restaurants and cafes.

INTERNET RESOURCES

My Merhaba (www.mymerhaba.com) Information site aimed at expats.
Turkey Travel Planner (www.turkeytravelplanner.com) Regularly updated travel information.
Tourism Turkey (www.tourismturkey.org) Government website with grab-bag of info.
Turkish Daily News (www.turkishdailynews.com) Newspaper home page.

MONEY

Turkey's currency, the Türk Lirası (Turkish Lira; TL), replaced the Yeni Türk Lirası (New Turkish Lira; YTL) in January 2009. Lira come in notes of five, 10, 20, 50 and 100, and one lira coins. One Turkish lira is worth 100 *kuruş,* which is available in one, five, 10, 25 and 50 coins.

After 31 December 2009, YTL notes and the associated *kuruş* coins will no longer be accepted for payment, but can be exchanged for the new currency at branches of Türkiye Ziraat Bankasi.

Inflation is an ongoing problem in Turkey and many businesses quote prices in the more-stable euro. We have used both lira and euros in listings, according to the currency quoted by the business in question.

ATMs

ATMs readily dispense Turkish lira to Visa, MasterCard, Cirrus, Maestro and Eurocard holders; there's hardly a town without a machine. Some tellers also dispense euros and dollars. Provided that your home banking card only requires a four-digit personal identification number (PIN), it's possible to get around Turkey with nothing else but plastic. But remember to draw out money in the towns to tide you through the villages, and keep some cash in reserve for the inevitable day when the ATM decides to throw a wobbly.

Note that some overseas banks levy high charges for the conversion and/or the withdrawal, so check your bank's fees before you leave home.

Cash

US dollars and euros are the easiest currencies to change, although many banks and exchange offices will change other major currencies such as UK pounds and Japanese yen. You may find it difficult to exchange Australian or Canadian currency, except at banks and money-change offices in major cities.

Credit Cards

Visa and MasterCard are widely accepted by hotels, restaurants, carpet shops and so on, although many pensions and local restaurants outside the main tourist areas do not accept them. You can also get cash advances on these cards. Amex cards are not accepted as often.

Moneychangers

It's easy to change major currencies in most exchange offices, some PTTs, shops and hotels, although banks may make heavy weather of it. Places that don't charge a commission usually offer a worse exchange rate instead.

Foreign currencies are readily accepted in shops, hotels and restaurants in main tourist areas. Taxi drivers accept foreign currencies for big journeys, which may drive down the price if the exchange rate is working in your favour.

Tipping & Bargaining

Turkey is fairly European in its approach to tipping and you won't be pestered by demands for baksheesh. Leave waiters and bath attendants around 10% of the bill; in restaurants, check a tip hasn't been automatically added to the bill. It's usual to round up metered taxi fares.

Hotel and transport prices are sometimes negotiable, and you should always bargain for souvenirs, even if prices are 'fixed'.

Travellers Cheques

Banks, shops and hotels often see it as a burden to change travellers cheques, and will probably try to get you to go elsewhere or charge you a premium. In case you do have to change them, try Akbank.

POST

The Turkish postal service is known as the PTT. *Postanes* (post offices) are indicated by black-on-yellow 'PTT' signs.

The base rate for sending postcards and letters to Europe is TL0.85, and TL0.90 to Australia, New Zealand and the USA. Parcels sent by surface mail to Europe cost around TL40 for the first 1kg, then TL12 per kg thereon; to North America, Australia and New Zealand, TL58 for the first 1kg, then TL17 per kg thereon.

RESPONSIBLE TRAVEL

Respecting Muslim sensibilities should be a point of principle, even when you're surrounded by half-naked sun-seekers. Women should keep their legs, upper arms and neckline covered, except on the beach. When entering a mosque, women should cover their heads, shoulders and arms, while everyone should cover their legs and remove their shoes.

Equally, though, there's no need to go overboard: obvious non-Muslims wearing headscarves and the like will probably attract just as much curious attention as those without!

There are a number of low-emission ways to get to and around Turkey, notably by ferry (see p934) and the train (p937). You can travel by train from London to İstanbul, then tackle an 'express' journey such as the 1900km, two-day journey from İstanbul to Lake Van! See the boxed text, p857, for a few ideas.

TELEPHONE

Türk Telekom (www.telekom.gov.tr) has a monopoly on phone services, and service is efficient if costly. Payphones can be found in many major public buildings and facilities, public squares and transport termini. International calls can be made from payphones; to call the international operator, dial ☎ 115.

Mobile Phones

The Turks just love *cep* (mobile) phones, but calling a mobile costs roughly three times the cost of calling a landline, no matter where you are. Mobile phone numbers start with a four-figure code beginning with ☎ 05. If you set up a roaming facility with your home network, most mobiles can connect to the Turkcell, Vodafone and Avea networks.

If you buy a Turkcell SIM card (the most comprehensive network) and use it in your home mobile, the network detects and bars foreign phones within a fortnight. Removing your phone from the blacklist requires a convoluted bureaucratic process. You can pick up a basic mobile phone for about TL50, or get one thrown in with the SIM card for a little extra. New Turkcell credit is readily available at shops displaying the company's blue-and-yellow logo, found on every street corner.

Phone Codes

The country code for Turkey is ☎ 90, followed by the local area code (minus the zero), then the seven-digit subscriber number. We have listed local area codes at the start of each city or town section. Note that İstanbul has two codes: ☎ 0212 for the European side and ☎ 0216 for the Asian side. The international access code (to call abroad from Turkey) is ☎ 00. Telephone numbers that start with ☎ 444 are national, so they don't require an area code.

Phonecards

Türk Telekom's public telephones mostly require telephone cards, which can be bought at telephone centres or, for a small mark-

EMERGENCY NUMBERS

Most emergency services have only Turkish-speaking operators, so your best bet is to find an English-speaking local to help.

- Ambulance ☎ 112
- Fire ☎ 110
- Police ☎ 155

up, from some shops and street vendors. If you're only going to make one quick call, it's easier to look for a booth with a sign saying '*köntörlü telefon*', where the cost of your call will be metered. The cheapest option for international calls is with phonecards such as Bigalo.

TOURIST INFORMATION

Local tourist offices can rarely do more than hand out glossy brochures and sketch maps. That said, some staff have a genuine interest in their region and make a real effort to help you with any specific queries.

TRAVELLERS WITH DISABILITIES

Turkey is a nightmare for travellers with physical disabilities, not just because of a lack of facilities. Obstacles lurk everywhere, properly equipped toilets are almost unheard of, and crossing the road is tough even for the fully mobile. Plan your trip very carefully and budget to patronise mostly luxury hotels, restaurants and transport.

Utilising the Joelette system, **Mephisto Voyage** (www.mephistovoyage.com) offers special tours of Cappadocia for mobility-impaired people.

VISAS

Nationals of the following countries don't need a visa to visit Turkey for up to three months: Denmark, Finland, France, Germany, Ireland, Israel, Italy, Japan, New Zealand, Sweden and Switzerland. Although nationals of Australia, Austria, Belgium, Canada, the Netherlands, Norway (one month only), Portugal, Spain, the UK and the USA need a visa, this is just a stamp in the passport that you buy on arrival at the airport or at an overland border.

Make sure you join the queue to buy your visa before joining the one for immigration. How much you pay depends on your nationality; at the time of writing, Australians and Americans paid US$20 (or €15), Canadians US$60 (or €45), and British citizens UK£10 (or €15 or US$20). Customs officers expect to be paid in one of these currencies, in hard cash, and may not accept Turkish lira. They also don't give any change.

The standard visa is valid for three months and, depending on your nationality, usually allows for multiple entries. Your passport must be valid for at least six months from the date you enter the country.

In theory a Turkish visa can be renewed once after three months, but the bureaucracy and costs involved mean that it's much easier to leave the country (usually to a Greek island) and then come back in again on a fresh visa.

See the **Ministry of Foreign Affairs** (www.mfa.gov.tr) for the latest information.

WOMEN TRAVELLERS

Things may be changing, but Turkish society is still basically sexually segregated, especially once you get away from the big cities and tourist resorts. Although younger Turks are questioning the old ways and women do hold positions of authority (there's even been a female prime minister), foreign women can find themselves being harassed. It's mostly just catcalls and dubious remarks, but serious assaults do occasionally occur.

Travelling with companions usually improves matters, and it's worth remembering that Turkish women ignore men who speak to them in the street. Dressing appropriately (see opposite) will also reduce unwanted attention. Follow these sartorial recommendations, and most men will treat you with kindness and generosity. Wearing a wedding ring and carrying a photo of your 'husband' and 'child' can help, as can wearing dark glasses to avoid eye contact.

Men and unrelated women are not expected to sit beside each other in long-distance buses, and lone women are often assigned seats at the front of the bus near the driver.

Women can sit where they like in eateries in tourist areas. Elsewhere, restaurants that aim to attract women often set aside a section for families. Look for the term *aile salonu* (family dining room). The same applies to *çay bahçesi* (tea gardens).

WORK

One of the most lucrative nonspecialist jobs available to foreigners involves nannying for the wealthy city elite, work mainly restricted to English-speaking women who must be prepared for long hours and demanding employers. Payment ranges from €300 to €650 per week, including accommodation with the family. **Anglo Nannies** (☎ 0212-287 6898; www.anglonannies.com; Bebek Yolu Sokak, Ebru Apt 25/2 Etiler, İstanbul, 80630) is the main agency dealing with placements.

Otherwise there is some work available for qualified teachers of English (whose employers should be able to arrange a work permit). Payment varies from €1000 to €2000 per month, often with accommodation, flights home and a work permit thrown in. Two useful resources are www.tefl.com and www.eslcafe.com.

If you don't have any teaching qualifications, you can usually still find a job, though it'll be private tuition (which pays €17 to €30 per hour) or at a private language school (where you can expect around €11 per hour).

Most travellers who want casual work end up grafting illegally for subsistence wages in pensions, bars and carpet shops, leaving the country every three months to renew their visas. Job hunters may have luck with the *Turkish Daily News* and the expat websites www.mymerhaba.com, www.expatinturkey.com and http://istanbul.craigslist.org.

There is a slowly growing number of volunteering opportunities in Turkey, offering everything from working on an organic farm to helping out on an archaeological dig. Handy websites are www.volunteerabroad.com, www.alternativecamp.org, www.genctur.com and www.bugday.org/tatuta.

TRANSPORT IN TURKEY

GETTING THERE & AWAY

Air

TURKEY

The cheapest fares for Turkey are usually to İstanbul's **Atatürk International Airport** (IST; ☎ 0212-465 5555; www.ataturkairport.com), 25km west of the city centre and, increasingly, **Sabiha Gökçen International Airport** (SAW; ☎ 0216-585 5000; www.sgairport.com), some 50km east of Sultanahmet on the Asian side of the city. To reach other Turkish airports, even Ankara, you often have to transit in İstanbul. Other international airports are at Adana, Ankara, Antalya, Bodrum, Dalaman and İzmir.

Turkey's national carrier, **Turkish Airlines** (Türk Hava Yolları, THY; ☎ İstanbul 0212-252 1106; www.thy.com), and European carriers fly to İstanbul from most major European cities. If you're planning a two- or three-week stay, it's also worth inquiring about charter flights.

The following are a few of the airlines flying to/from Turkey:

Air France (AF; ☎ 0212-310 1919; www.airfrance.com)
American Airlines (AA; ☎ 0212-237 2003; www.aa.com)
British Airways (BA; ☎ 0212-317 6600; www.britishairways.com)
Corendon Airlines (CAI; ☎ 0216-467 6710; www.corendon.com)
Cyprus Turkish Airlines (YK; ☎ 0216-444 5849; www.kthy.net)
easyJet (U2; www.easyjet.com)
germanwings (4U; www.germanwings.com)
Emirates (EK; ☎ 0212-315 4545; www.emirates.com)
KLM (KL; ☎ 0212-230 0311; www.klm.com)
Lufthansa (LH; ☎ 0212-315 3400; www.lufthansa.com)
Olympic Airlines (OA; ☎ 0212-296 7575; www.olympicairlines.com)
Qantas (QF; ☎ 0212-325 5536; www.qantas.com)
Singapore Airlines (SQ; ☎ 0212-463 1800; www.singaporeair.com)

Also see opposite for details of more Turkish airlines, many of which run international flights.

Land

Turkey shares borders with Armenia, Azerbaijan, Bulgaria, Georgia, Greece, Iran, Iraq and Syria. There are plenty of ways to get into and out of the country by rail or bus.

Austria, Bulgaria, Germany, Greece, Italy, Macedonia and Romania have the most direct buses to İstanbul; if you're travelling from other European countries, you'll likely have to catch a connecting bus. Two of the best Turkish companies, **Ulusoy** (www.ulusoy.com.tr) and **Varan** (www.varan.com.tr), operate big Mercedes buses on these routes. Sample one-way fares to/from İstanbul include Athens €68 (20 hours) and Vienna €110 (27 hours).

At the time of writing there were no direct trains to/from Western Europe, other than the comfy overnight *Filia-Dostluk Express* between Thessaloniki (Greece) and İstanbul. For more information, contact **Turkish State Railways** (www.tcdd.gov.tr) or the **Hellenic Railways Organisation** (www.ose.gr). The *Bosphorus Express* (see the boxed text, p857) runs between İstanbul and Eastern Europe.

Sea

Ferrylines (www.ferrylines.com) is a good starting point for information about ferry travel in the region.

Marmara Lines (www.marmaralines.com) ferries connect Brindisi and Ancona in Italy with Çeşme. There is also a handful of routes over the Black Sea.

FERRIES BETWEEN TURKEY & GREECE

Route	Cost (one way/return)	Frequency	More details
Ayvalık-Lesvos	€40/50	daily Jun-Sep; twice a week Oct-May	(p881)
Bodrum-Kos	hydrofoil €30/35, open return €60; ferry €25/25, open return €50	daily	(p891)
Bodrum-Rhodes	€50/60, open return €100	twice weekly Jun-Sep	(p891)
Çeşme-Chios	€40/65	5 times a week Jun-Sep; twice a week in winter	(p884)
Datça-Rhodes	TL90/180	Sat May-Sep	(p894)
Datça-Simi	hydrofoil TL60/120, *gület* TL120	hydrofoil Sat May-Sep, *gület* on demand	(p894)
Kaş-Kastellorizo (Meis)	TL70 return	daily	(p901)

Private ferries link Turkey's Aegean and Mediterranean coasts and the Greek islands, which are in turn linked by air or boat to Athens. In summer boats run roughly daily on a variety of routes: Lesvos–Ayvalık, Chios–Çeşme, Kos–Bodrum, Samos–Kuşadası, Rhodes–Marmaris, Rhodes–Bodrum, Rhodes–Simi-Datça, and Kastellorizo (Meis)–Kaş. See the individual destinations for information about the services.

Services are generally daily in summer, and are operating with increasing frequency at other times of year, but bad sailing conditions mean they often run on a weekly basis during winter. The table, above, summarises the services between Turkey and the Greek islands.

The main crossing point between Turkey and Northern Cyprus is between Taşucu (near Silifke) and Girne (Kyrenia) on the island's north coast, operated by **Akgünler Denizcilik** (www.akgunler.com.tr). **Fergün Denizcilik** (www.fergun.net) travels between Alanya and Girne, and **Turkish Maritime Lines** (www.tdi.com.tr, in Turkish) links Mersin and Gazimağusa (Famagusta) on the east coast of Northern Cyprus.

GETTING AROUND

Air

Turkish Airlines (Türk Hava Yolları, THY; ☎ İstanbul 0212-252 1106; www.thy.com) connects all the country's major cities and resorts, often via one of its two main hubs, İstanbul and Ankara.

The most useful destinations for travellers include Ankara, Antalya, Bodrum, Dalaman (for Marmaris), Gaziantep, İstanbul, İzmir, Kars, Kayseri, Konya, Mardin, Şanlıurfa and Van.

A one-way fare usually costs between €75 and €200. You can buy tickets through travel agencies or directly through the airlines; domestic flights can fill up rapidly so try to book in advance.

Cheaper domestic flights are also available:

Atlasjet (KK; www.atlasjet.com) Flies from İzmir to Ankara, Antalya, İstanbul, Siirt (for Van) and Tokat (for Amasya and Sivas), and from İstanbul to these locations and others, including Bodrum and İzmir.

Fly Air (www.flyair.com.tr) Ceased operations in 2007 but was restructuring at the time of research, set to serve domestic destinations.

Onur Air (8Q; www.onurair.com.tr) Flies from İstanbul to Antalya, Bodrum, Dalaman, Diyarbakır, Erzurum, Gaziantep, İzmir, Kayseri and Trabzon, among others.

Pegasus Airlines (H9; www.pegasusairlines.com) Flies between İstanbul and locations from Antalya to Van.

Sun Express Airlines (XQ; www.sunexpress.com.tr) A Turkish Airlines subsidiary.

Bicycle

Riding a bike can be a good way of exploring, especially in backpacker areas, where many pensions lend them out for free. Road surfaces are acceptable, if a bit rough, though many Turkish drivers regard cyclists as a curiosity and/or a nuisance. In touristy areas, bikes are often available for hire from pensions or rental outfits, costing about TL5 an hour or TL15 for a day.

Bus

The Turkish bus network is a very pleasant surprise: coaches go just about everywhere, they're cheap and comfortable, smoking isn't permitted, drinks and snacks are often provided, regular toilet stops are built into longer routes, and drivers even use the stops to wash down their vehicles!

The premium companies have nationwide networks offering greater speed and comfort for slightly higher fares. They also have the best safety records. Departures on popular routes can be as frequent as every 15 minutes, with hourly services the norm from major cities. Costs vary according to distance and popularity of the route; typically, a ticket from İstanbul to Çanakkale costs TL30 to TL35, from İstanbul to Ankara TL25 to TL44, and from İstanbul to Göreme (Cappadocia) TL40.

Although you can usually walk into an *otogar* and buy a ticket for the next bus, it's wise to plan ahead for public holidays, at weekends and during the school-holiday period from mid-June to early September. You can reserve seats over the web with the better companies.

A town's *otogar* is often on the outskirts, but most bus companies provide free *servis* minibuses to ferry you into the centre and back again. Besides intercity buses, *otogars* often handle *dolmuşes* (see opposite) to outlying districts or villages. Larger bus stations have an *emanetçi* (left luggage) room, which you can use for a nominal fee.

An easy option, geared towards backpackers (don't expect to meet many Turks on it), is the **Fez Bus** (Map p867; ☎ 0212-516 9024; www.feztravel.com; Akbıyık Caddesi 15, Sultanahmet, İstanbul). The hop-on, hop-off bus service links the main resorts of the Aegean and the Mediterranean with İstanbul, Cappadocia and Nemrut Dağı.

The best bus companies, with extensive route networks:

Boss Turizm (☎ 444 0880; www.bossturizm.com in Turkish) Specialises in superdeluxe İstanbul–Ankara services.

Kamil Koç (☎ 444 0562; www.kamilkoc.com.tr, in Turkish)

Ulusoy (☎ 444 1888; www.ulusoy.com.tr)

Varan (☎ 444 8999; www.varan.com.tr)

Car & Motorcycle

In the major cities, plan to leave your car in a parking lot and walk – traffic is terrible. **Türkiye Turing ve Otomobil Kurumu** (Turkish Touring & Automobile Association; ☎ 0212-282 8140; www.turing.org.tr) can help with questions and problems.

BRING YOUR OWN VEHICLE

Carnets (permits to import cars) are not required for stays of less than six months, but details of your car are stamped in your passport to ensure it leaves the country with you.

DRIVING LICENCE

An international driving permit (IDP) is not required, but may be handy if your driving licence is from a country likely to seem obscure to a Turkish police officer.

FUEL & SPARE PARTS

There are plenty of modern petrol stations in the west, many open 24/7. In the east they are a bit less abundant but you won't have trouble finding one. Be warned: petrol prices are high, and not showing any signs of going down.

Yedek parçaları (spare parts) are readily available in the big cities, especially for European models such as Renaults, Fiats and Mercedes-Benz, and repairs are usually quick and cheap.

HIRE

Hiring a car is quite expensive (often around TL70 to TL120 per day with unlimited mileage, less for a longer period). All the main car-hire companies are represented in the main towns and resorts. It's better to stick to the well-established companies (such as Avis, Budget, Europcar, Hertz and Thrifty) as they have bigger fleets and better emergency backup. You can get great discounts through **Economy Car Rentals** (www.economycarrentals.com), which covers most of the country, but you need to book at least 24 hours in advance.

INSURANCE

You *must* have third-party insurance, valid for the entire country. If you don't have it, you can buy it at the border.

ROAD RULES

Drink-driving is a complete no-no. Maximum speed limits, unless otherwise posted, are 50km/h in towns, 90km/h on highways and 120km/h on an *otoyol* (motorway). Driving is hair-raising during the day because of fast, inappropriate driving and overladen trucks, and dangerous at night, when some drivers see fit to speed along with their headlights off.

Hitching

Hitching (*otostop*) is possible but not common in Turkey, and works better over short distances. Commercial vehicles are most likely to pick you up, but the driver will often expect payment. Women should never hitchhike alone. Instead of sticking out your thumb for a lift you should face the traffic, hold your arm out towards the road, and wave it up and down as if bouncing a basketball.

Local Transport

Short-distance and local routes are usually served by medium-sized 'midibuses' or smaller *dolmuşes* (minibuses that follow prescribed routes), run by private operators. A few cities, including Bursa and İzmir, have old-fashioned shared-taxi *dolmuşes*. Most towns have an internal bus network funded by the council; this may be supplemented by underground, tram, train and even ferry services in the largest cities. Taxis are plentiful; they have meters – just make sure they're switched on.

Tours

Areas where an organised tour makes sense, particularly with limited time, include Troy (p880) and the Gallipoli battlefields (p878), and Cappadocia (p914).

Train

Turkish State Railways (☎ 444 8233; www.tcdd.gov.tr) runs services throughout the country. Although most people still opt to travel by bus, as train journey times are notoriously long and the system is being overhauled, several fast lines, such as the one between İstanbul and Ankara, are now in service. The train network covers central and eastern Turkey fairly well, but doesn't travel along the coastlines at all, apart from a short stretch between İzmır and Selçuk. If you wanted to travel the Aegean and Mediterranean coasts you could travel by train to either İzmır or Konya, and take the bus from there. The sleeper trains linking İstanbul, İzmır and Ankara are well worth considering.

Turkish train travel has a growing legion of fans; the trick is not to attempt a trans-Turkey trip in one go, as the country is large and the trains slow. For example, the *Vangölü Ekspresi* from İstanbul to Lake Van (Tatvan), a 1900km trip, takes almost two days. See http://tinyurl.com/6fxmml and www.seat61.com/Turkey2.htm for more information.

Regional Directory

CONTENTS

This chapter provides information on Mediterranean Europe as a whole. It complements both the Getting Started chapter (p23) at the beginning of the book and the individual country directories. So if you're planning to visit more than one country, refer first to this Regional Directory for the big picture and then to individual country chapters for specific details.

ACCOMMODATION

Whatever your budget, you'll have no trouble finding accommodation in Mediterranean Europe. There's a vast choice, ranging from world-famous five-star hotels to modest family rooms. As with the rest of Europe, the cheapest places to stay are camping grounds, followed by hostels and student dormitories. Guest houses, pensions and private rooms often offer good value, as do rooms in religious institutes. Self-catering flats and cottages are also worth considering for group stays, especially for longer sojourns. You can also bunk down in a B&B or stay on a farm. Or you can crash out on a local's couch – through one of the online hospitality clubs, such as **Couch Surfing** (www.couchsurfing.com), **Global Freeloaders** (www.globalfreeloaders.com) or **Hospitality Club** (www.hospitalityclub.org), you can contact 'members' across the world who'll let you sleep on their sofa or in their spare room for free. Another cheap alternative is house swapping, whereby you sign up to an online agency such as **Home Exchange** (www.homexchange.com/co.uk) or **Global Home Exchange** (www.4homex.com) and arrange to swap houses with a fellow member.

Mediterranean Europe is a hugely popular holiday destination, and although there's plenty of accommodation available, it can be hard to find in the peak holiday periods of Easter, summer and Christmas. Cheap hotels in big destinations such as Paris, Rome and Madrid are busy year-round, and beach resorts swarm in July and August. The solution is to book ahead wherever possible. It's a good idea to make reservations as many weeks ahead as possible – at least for the first night or two. Most hotels and hostels accept online reservations, although you might have to provide a credit-card number in lieu of a deposit.

In the low season, it's often worth bargaining a little, as many places reduce their rates without necessarily advertising the fact.

Most airports and many large train stations have accommodation-booking desks, although they rarely cover budget hotels. Tourist offices can generally supply accommodation lists and the more helpful ones will even help you find a hotel. There's usually a small fee for this service, but if accommodation is tight it can save you hassle. Agencies offering private rooms are also worth considering.

In some destinations locals wait at train stations or ferry terminals, touting rented rooms. Don't necessarily reject these out of hand, as in some places they're genuine offers.

However, before accepting, make sure the accommodation isn't in a far-flung suburb or an outlying village that requires you to make a difficult journey to get to it. Also confirm the price beforehand. As always, be careful when someone offers to carry your luggage: they might carry it off altogether.

Unless otherwise stated, prices in this book are for rooms with private bathrooms and are quoted at high-season rates. And in all chapters prices are quoted in the currency in which they're advertised on the ground, whether that's local currencies, euros, US dollars or British pounds. For an overview of local accommodation options, see the directories in the individual country chapters.

B&Bs

B&B accommodation is widely available across the region and usually provides excellent value. There's a huge selection of places, ranging from traditional B&B set-ups (private homes offering a room or two to paying guests) to smart boutique-style outfits that offer quality accommodation at midrange and top-end prices. Prices vary accordingly, but as a general rule a B&B room will be cheaper than a hotel room of corresponding comfort.

Most B&Bs will give you a key, allowing you to come and go as you like, although some places might insist that you're back by a certain time. Most smarter B&Bs will have private bathrooms; in others you might have to share with other guests or the host family.

When booking, make sure you're happy with the location of the B&B. City B&Bs are often not central, so check local transport connections; if it's in a remote rural spot, work out in advance how it fits in with your plans.

Contact tourist offices or check on the internet for lists of local B&Bs. Useful resources include **International Bed and Breakfast Pages** (www.ibbp.com), **Bed & Breakfast in Europe** (www.bedandbreakfastineurope.com) and **Europe and Relax** (www.europeandrelax.com).

Camping

Camping is very popular in Mediterranean Europe, and there are thousands of grounds dotted around the region. These range from large, resort-style sites with swimming pools and supermarkets to more simple affairs in isolated countryside locations. If you really want to get back to nature, there are nudist camping grounds in Croatia. National tourist offices and local camping organisations can provide lists of camping grounds. At designated grounds, there are often charges per tent or site, per person and per vehicle. Many places also have bungalows or cottages accommodating two to eight people.

Cheap as it is, camping is not without its drawbacks. For one thing, many sites close over winter, typically between October and April. Then there's the difficulty of carting your kit around with you – not a problem if you've got a car, but a real pain if you haven't. If you're relying on public transport, note that most city camping grounds are some distance from city centres, so the money you save on accommodation can quickly be eaten up in bus and train fares.

Free camping is often difficult as it can be hard to find a suitably private spot. It's also often illegal without permission from the local authorities (the police or local council) or from the owner of the land (don't be shy about asking, however – you may be pleasantly surprised by the response). In some countries (eg France and Spain) free camping is illegal on all but private land, and in Greece, Croatia and Slovenia it's illegal altogether. This doesn't prevent hikers from occasionally pitching their tent for the night, and you'll usually get away with it if you have only a small tent, stay only one or two nights, take the tent down during the day and don't light a campfire or leave rubbish. At worst, you'll be woken up by the police and asked to move on.

If you're intent on camping around the region, consider the **Camping Card International** (CCI; www.campingcardinternational.com), an ID-style card that can be used instead of a passport when checking into a camping ground. It provides third-party insurance and entitles you to discounts of up to 25% at more than 1100 camping grounds across Europe. Note, however, that in some cases discounts are

BOOK YOUR STAY ONLINE

For more accommodation reviews and recommendations by Lonely Planet authors, check out the online booking service at www.lonelyplanet.com/hotels. You'll find the true, insider low-down on the best places to stay. Reviews are thorough and independent. Best of all, you can book online.

not available if you use a credit card to pay for your stay.

CCIs are issued by automobile associations, camping federations and, sometimes, on the spot at camping grounds. In the UK, you can get them from the **Camping and Caravanning Club** (☎ 0845 130 7701; www.campingandcaravanningclub.co.uk) for UK£4.95. In the USA, **Family Campers and RVers** (☎ 1-716-668-6242; www.fcrv.org) sells them to members for US$20.

Farmstays

Farmstays are an excellent way of escaping the crowds and experiencing the local countryside. They are particularly popular in Italy, where an *agriturismo* (plural *agriturismi*) can be anything from a working farm to a luxurious rural resort in a converted castle. Room rates are usually much less than in hotels of comparable comfort. Many farmstays offer activities such as horse riding, hiking and cycling, and often serve delicious food. Their country locations mean that most have plenty of space for kids to run round in, making them a good family choice. On the downside, you'll almost certainly need a car to get to them.

Italian tourist offices have lists of farmhouses for specific areas. Online information is available at **Agriturist** (www.agriturist.it).

In Portugal, accommodation is available in farmhouses and country homes as part of **Turihab** (www.turihab.pt), a major project to promote rural tourism.

Always book ahead, as in the high season (May to September) places fill quickly, while in the low season (October to April) many only open on request.

Guest Houses & Pensions

The distinction between a guest house and a hotel is fairly blurred. Although most guest houses are simple family affairs offering basic rooms and shared bathrooms, there are more expensive ones with rooms on a par with those in hotels.

Widespread throughout the region, pensions are basically small, modest hotels. In cities, they are often housed in converted flats that occupy one or two floors of a large apartment block. Rooms tend to be simple, often with just a basin and bidet.

Homestays & Private Rooms

Renting a room in a local home is generally a good, cheap option, especially for longer stays. It's not so good for solo travellers (most rooms are set up as doubles or triples) or for quick stopovers (many places levy hefty surcharges, typically 30% to 40%, for stays of under three or four days).

Room quality and price vary considerably – some rooms come with private bathrooms, some have cooking facilities, some might even have both. When you book, make sure you check if the price is per room or per person, and whether or not breakfast is included. Also make sure you're happy with the location.

You can book rooms either privately or through an agency (to whom you'll have to pay a fee). Once you've booked a room, it's always worth phoning ahead to say when you're arriving as, in many cases, the owners will pick you up at the station or port.

Room rentals are particularly widespread in Bosnia and Hercegovina (BiH), Croatia, Greece and Montenegro.

Hostels

Hostels are widespread across the region and offer the cheapest (secure) roof over your head. Hostels referred to as 'official' are affiliated with **Hostelling International** (HI; www.hihostels.com), while independent hostels are just that and operate independently of HI.

To stay at an official hostel you'll need to be an HI member, although in practice you can usually stay by buying a 'welcome stamp' (generally about €3; buy six and you qualify for full HI membership) directly at the hostel. HI membership is available at affiliated hostels or through your national hostelling association – there's a full list on the HI website.

Hostel accommodation is a lot slicker than it once was. Alongside dorms of varying sizes – small ones typically for four or five people, larger ones for up to 12 people – many also offer hotel-standard private rooms with en suite bathrooms. Dorms might or might not be single sex. Typical facilities include a communal kitchen, a TV room, laundry facilities and internet access.

Generally speaking, independent hostels are a lot less rule bound than HI hostels, many of which impose a maximum length of stay, a daytime lockout and a curfew. But with the rules come standards, and affiliated hostels have to comply with HI safety and cleanliness standards.

These days few hostels impose age limits, although some may give priority to younger, student-age travellers in peak periods. Many hostels offer a complimentary breakfast and some serve an evening meal (about €9).

It's a good idea to book ahead whenever possible, especially in summer, when popular hostels are packed to the gills. The easiest way is to book online, either through individual hostel websites or through the HI website. Many hostels also accept reservations over the phone or by fax, but during peak periods you will probably have to call in person to bag a bed. If you are heading on to another hostel, most places will book the next place for you for a small fee.

Two useful websites, both with booking engines, are **Hostelworld.com** (www.hostelworld.com) and **HostelPlanet.com** (www.hostelplanet.com).

Hotels

Hotels in the region range from dodgy fleapits with rooms to rent by the hour to some of the world's grandest five-star palaces. Each country operates its own hotel-classification system, so a three-star hotel in İstanbul, say, might not correspond exactly to a three-star hotel in Barcelona. As a rule, the hotels recommended in this book range from one to three stars.

You'll often find inexpensive hotels clustered around bus and train stations. These can be useful for late-night/early-morning arrivals or departures, but are rarely much more than convenient, and the streets around major transport hubs are rarely enticing. As a general rule, you'll do better looking in a more interesting part of town.

If you're undecided about a place, check your room and bathroom before you agree to take it. Always make sure you know exactly what it's going to cost. If there's aircon, check that it's included in the price. Similarly, ask about breakfast; sometimes it's included, sometimes it costs extra. If you have the choice, bear in mind that you could easily find yourself paying about €5 for something that might cost €2 in the cafe across the road.

Rates fluctuate enormously from season to season. Discounts are often available for groups or for longer stays, particularly in the slower winter months. In slack periods, hoteliers may even be open to a little bargaining – it's worth trying. It's also worth checking hotel websites for weekend discounts, as many business hotels (usually three stars and upwards) slash their rates by up to 40% on Friday and Saturday nights.

Well-known hotels in major destinations fill quickly in high season, so always make sure you phone ahead to check room availability. Some hotels insist on a faxed confirmation of your reservation, as well as a credit-card number in place of a deposit. If you don't have a credit card you might be asked to send a money order to cover the first night's stay. Booking over the internet will usually spare you the bother.

To avoid embarrassing scenes at reception, always check that your hotel accepts credit cards. Most do, but it's dangerous to assume that a request for a credit-card number with your booking means that the hotel accepts payment by plastic.

SWEAT IT OUT IN A HAMMAM

Pampering yourself in a steaming *hammam* (Turkish bath) is a time-honoured tradition in Turkey and Morocco. Public *hammams* are widespread, offering hot rooms, washing facilities and massages. For information on *hammam* etiquette, see the boxed text, p869.

University Accommodation

Student accommodation is sometimes opened to travellers in the holidays – particularly in France, where you should ask about *foyers d'étudiant* – and provide an alternative to sleeping in a hostel. In Slovenia dorms in student residence halls are open to travellers in July and August.

Accommodation will sometimes be in single rooms but is more commonly in doubles or triples. There might also be cooking facilities available. Enquire at the university, at student information services or at local tourist offices.

ACTIVITIES

Beautiful beaches, tempting seas, mountains, lakes and rivers – Mediterranean Europe is a magnificent outdoor playground. Whether you're an afternoon ambler or a hard-core adrenalin junkie, you'll find something to suit your style. Activities run the whole gamut, from gentle strolls to tough mountain treks, and from windsurfing and scuba diving to mountain-biking, paragliding and white-water rafting. You might even like to explore the Sahara on a camel in Morocco (p653).

What follows is a general overview of some of the many activities on offer. For more-detailed information, see the individual country directories.

Cycling

Cycling is a popular sport in southern Europe. The great cycling races, such as the Tour de France and Giro d'Italia, are followed by millions of fans, while thousands of enthusiasts take to the roads at the weekend.

Popular cycling destinations include Andalucía and Catalonia in Spain, Tuscany and Umbria in Italy (p542), France's Dordogne and Loire Valley (p268), and Portugal's Parque Nacional da Peneda-Gerês (p697). Cycling is also a good, environmentally friendly way of getting round the Med's islands, including Spain's Balearic Islands and Sardinia. For teeth-rattling mountain biking, head to the summer resorts in the Alps, Dolomites and Pyrenees.

On a health note, never underestimate the effects of the heat. Always cover your head (helmets are mandatory in the region anyway) and make sure you drink plenty of fluid. Sunburn can be highly unpleasant and heatstroke very serious. See p973 for tips on dealing with heat-induced problems.

See p963 for information about transporting and hiring bikes.

Diving

The Med's azure waters are ideal for diving. Throughout the region there are hundreds of diving centres offering everything from beginners' courses to trips exploring sunken wrecks. Cave diving is a speciality in Croatia (p170), one of the region's top diving destinations. You'll also find excellent diving in the waters off Greece (p418), Malta (p570), Montenegro (p598) and Italy (p545).

Extreme Sports

The region's eastern countries provide rich pickings for thrill seekers. Slovenia, in particular, is well set up for adventure sports. At Bovec (p724) you can try paragliding, caving, canyoning, hydrospeed (boogie-boarding down a river), as well as a host of more traditional activities. To the east, Bled (p719) is another adventure-sports centre. Southeast of Slovenia, you'll find canyoning (p106), rafting (p101) and climbing (p107) in BiH, and a range of activities in Montenegro, including paragliding at Budva (p586).

France offers superb flying opportunities, with paragliding and hang-gliding (p334) available in the Pyrenees, Brittany and Languedoc-Roussillon. Climbing (p334) is also popular, particularly in the Alps, where the icy slopes attract mountaineers, rock climbers and ice climbers.

Hiking

Keen hikers could spend a lifetime exploring Mediterranean Europe's many trails. In the summer season (June to September), the region's mountain chains offer stunning hiking. The Italian Dolomites (p496) are a top destination, with the well-marked trails covering everything from tough high-altitude routes to gentle afternoon strolls. Mountain refuges provide summer accommodation on many of the longer hikes in the region. In Morocco, the High Atlas mountains (p647) are a prime hiking area; you can even summit the Atlas' highest peak, Jebel Toubkal (4167m). The Spanish Pyrenees (p796) also provide plenty of challenges.

The Mediterranean's national parks encompass some spectacular scenery, and hiking opportunities abound. Hot spots include Albania's Mt Dajti National Park (p53), Triglav National Park (p719) in Slovenia, and Durmitor National Park (p595) in Montenegro. Elsewhere, you'll find good hiking in Croatia (p170), Cyprus (p198) and Turkey (p928).

It's worth noting that, although most high-level mountain paths are only open in the summer, there are possibilities for hiking in the winter snow. Contact tourist offices for information on routes and local guides.

Kayaking & Rafting

The region's lakes, rivers and reservoirs offer ample sport for water lovers. In mountainous areas, kayaking and white-water rafting provide thrills and possibly the odd spill. Both sports are well catered to in the Massif Central in France and in the Julian Alps (p719) in Slovenia. BiH (p108) also has some excellent white-water rafting for all levels. Sea kayaking is widely available in Croatia (p170).

Skiing & Snowboarding

Winter sports are big business in southern Europe, and each year thousands take to the

WINTER & SUMMER HOURS

Throughout this book we have quoted summer opening hours. In winter, hours are often reduced, typically by bringing forward evening closing times. In coastal areas, many seasonal businesses (hotels, souvenir shops, bars etc) close over winter, generally from November to March.

pistes to ski (downhill or cross-country), snowboard and snowshoe hike. These activities are rarely cheap, however. For a ski holiday you'll need to budget for ski lifts, accommodation and the inevitable après-ski entertainment. You'll save a bit by bringing your own equipment, but often not enough to compensate for the hassle of lugging it around with you. As a general rule, cross-country skiing costs less than downhill.

The region's swishest and most expensive resorts are in the French and Italian Alps, although there are plenty of opportunities elsewhere in Mediterranean Europe. Some of the cheapest skiing is to be found in BiH – Jahorina (p91), Bjelašnica (p91) and Vlašić (p103) are the main centres – and in Durmitor National Park (p595) in Montenegro. There's also good-value skiing in the Sierra Nevada in the south of Spain, in Greece (p418) and in Turkey (p928).

The skiing season traditionally lasts from early December to late March, though at higher altitudes in the French and Italian Alps it may extend an extra month either way. Snow conditions vary greatly from one year to the next and from region to region, but January and February tend to be the best, busiest and most expensive months.

Surfing, Windsurfing & Kitesurfing

Windsurfing is one the most popular of the region's water sports. It's easy to rent sailboards in many tourist centres, and courses are usually available for beginners. Hot destinations include Tarifa (p839) in Spain, generally considered the Med's windsurfing capital; Lefkada (p415) in Greece; and the Atlantic beaches at Essaouira (p627) in Morocco.

Surfers can strut their stuff too, with excellent waves on the coast around Biarritz (p301) in France, along the north and southwest coasts of Spain (p845) and off Sagres (p682) in Portugal.

Kitesurfing is taking off in a big way – pun intended – and is readily available across the region. A good place to test your nerve is windy Tarifa (p839).

BUSINESS HOURS

Although there are no hard and fast rules respected by all the countries in this guide (or even by all the businesses in any one country), the Mediterranean countries do share some habits. It's not unusual, especially outside the main cities, for small shops to close for a long lunch. Typically a shop might open from 8am or 9am until 1.30pm, and then from about 4pm to 8pm or so. Larger department stores tend to stay open all day.

Banks generally open early and either close for the day at around 1.30pm or reopen for a brief two-hour window in the early afternoon, perhaps from 2.30pm to 4.30pm.

Businesses usually operate from Monday to Friday and possibly Saturday morning; Sunday opening is not unheard of, but it's not widespread. It's also worth noting that many museums are closed on Mondays.

See individual country directories for specific hours.

CHILDREN

Despite a dearth of child-friendly sights and activities, the Mediterranean is a great place to travel with children. Kids are universally adored, and are welcome just about everywhere.

You will, however, have to plan your time carefully. A common cause of strife is trying to do too much – high summer temperatures and crowded streets can fray the nerves of even the most patient of kids (and parents!). Always allow free time for play and make sure you balance those heavy days at the museum with a day at the beach or a visit to the local park. Where possible, include children in the trip planning – if they've helped to work out where you're going, they'll be much more interested when they get there. Making a scrapbook of things to see or of what you've seen is a good way of keeping their attention. Picnics are another sure-fire winner.

You should have no problems finding baby food, formulas, soy and cows' milk, disposable nappies etc. But remember that shop opening hours might be different from those at home, so if you run out of nappies on Saturday afternoon you could be in for a messy weekend.

Most car-rental firms have safety seats for hire at a nominal cost, but it's essential you book them in advance. The same goes for high chairs and cots – they're available in most restaurants and hotels, but numbers will be limited.

For more information, see Lonely Planet's *Travel with Children*, or check out **TravelWithYourKids.com** (www.travelwithyourkids.com) or **Family Travel Network** (www.familytravelnetwork.com).

CLIMATE CHARTS

The typical Mediterranean climate consists of long hot summers and mild winters. Which isn't to say that it doesn't get cold in winter – it does, especially in mountainous areas, where winter snow is an annual fixture. Summer sunshine is virtually guaranteed between June and September, with temperatures regularly topping 40°C in some parts. Early October can also be pleasantly warm

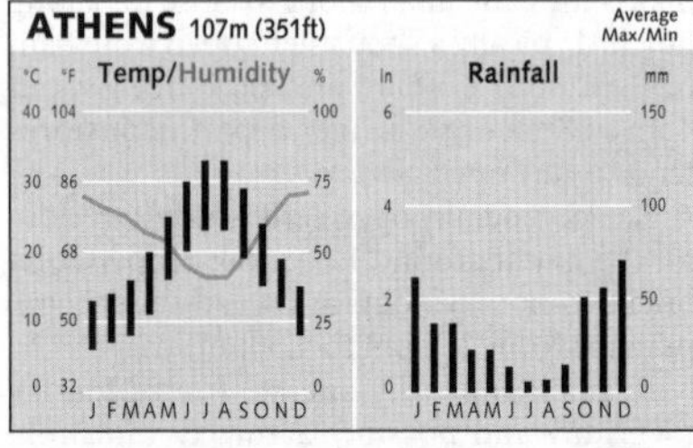

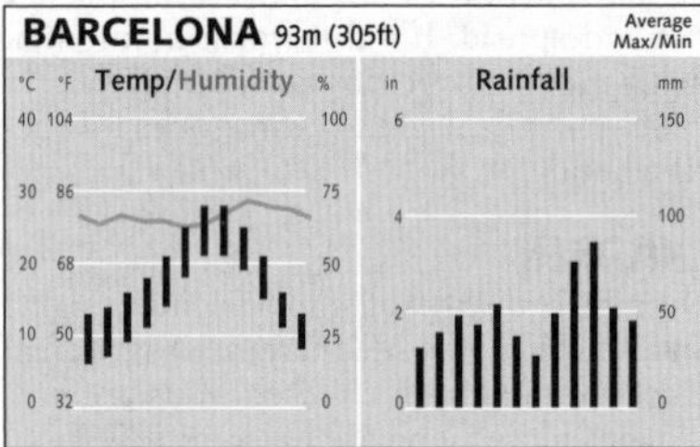

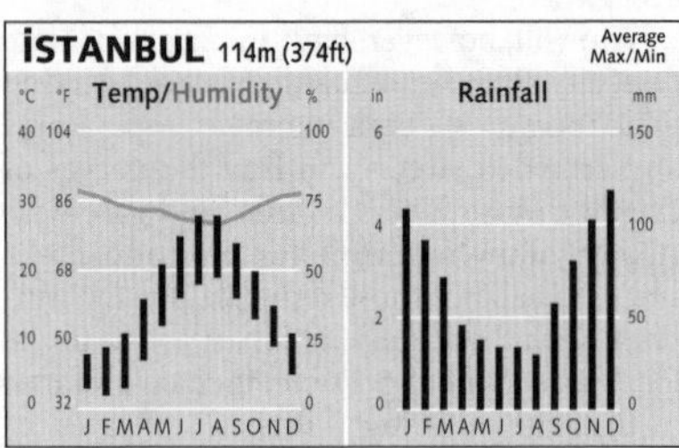

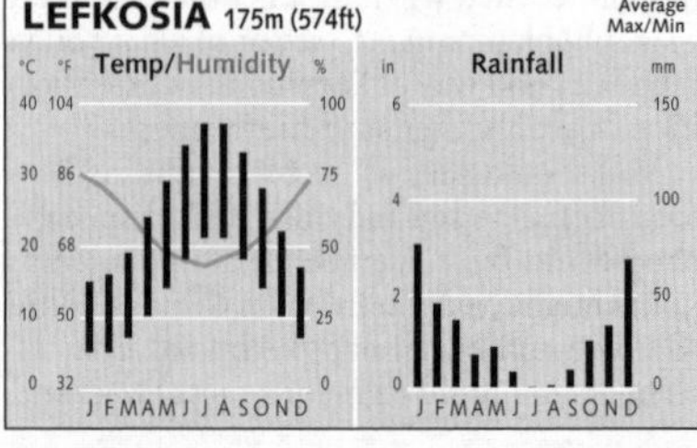

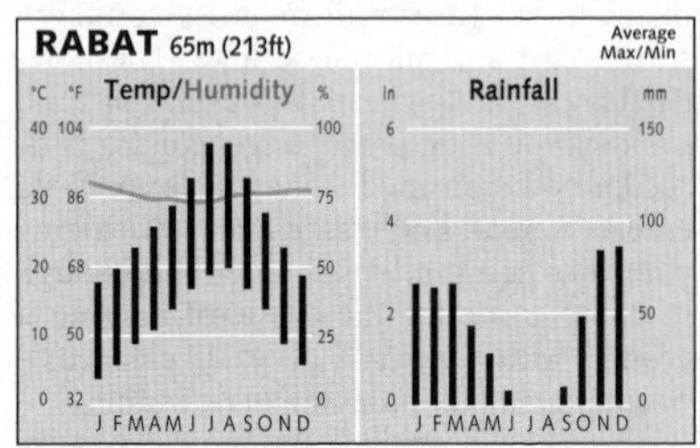

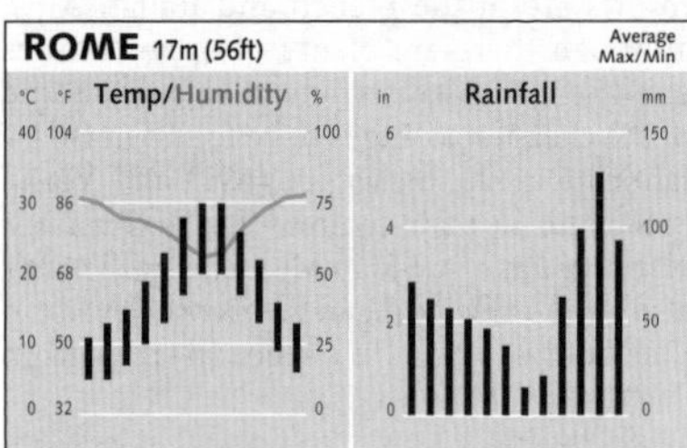

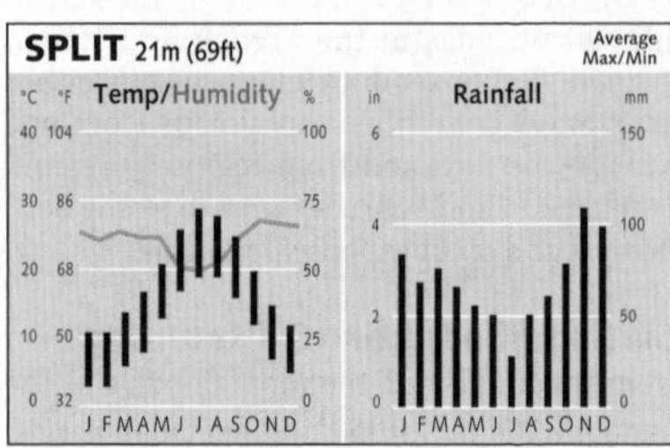

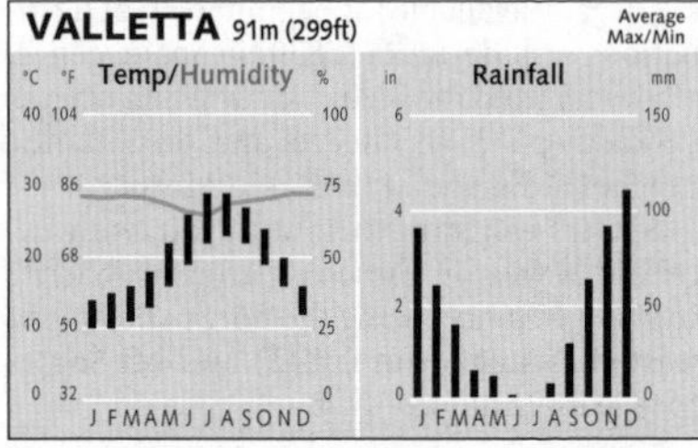

as summer gives way to autumn, the wettest period of the Mediterranean year. And if you were thinking that it doesn't rain much in the Med, think again – Paris and Rome regularly receive a greater annual rainfall than London. Summer storms are distinct possibilities in many places, but they are usually short violent affairs that blow over quickly.

For general advice on when to travel to Mediterranean Europe, see p23.

The climate charts, opposite, provide a snapshot of the Mediterranean's weather patterns.

COURSES

A holiday course is a great way of tapping into the local culture. Whether you want to learn Arabic in Morocco, painting in Italy or cooking in France, there's a school ready to teach you how. Language and cooking are the most popular choices but the list of subjects is endless, and include art, literature, architecture, drama, music, fashion and photography.

In Italy, the Università per Stranieri (p511) in Perugia is a popular place to study, with hundreds of courses available to non-Italians. Elsewhere, language courses are widely available at universities and in private language schools – see the country chapters for specific details.

Information about courses is available from the cultural institutes maintained by many European countries around the world, such as Italy's Istituto Italiano di Cultura and the Spanish **Istituto Cervantes** (www.cervantes.es). National tourist authorities, student-exchange organisations and student travel agencies should also be able to help. Ask about special holiday packages that include a course.

CUSTOMS REGULATIONS

If you're travelling from one EU country to another you're allowed to carry 800 cigarettes, 200 cigars or 1kg of loose tobacco; 10L of spirits (more than 22% alcohol by volume), 20L of fortified wine or aperitif, 90L of wine or 110L of beer; and – ooh la la! – unlimited quantities of perfume.

Entering or leaving the EU, you can carry the following duty-free: 200 cigarettes, 50 cigars or 250g of tobacco; and 1L of spirits (more than 22% alcohol), 2L of fortified wine or aperitif, 4L of still wine, or 16L of beer. On top of this you can also carry goods, including perfume and electronic devices, up to a value of €430 for air and sea travellers, and €300 for land travellers. On leaving the EU, non-EU residents can reclaim value-added tax (VAT) on expensive purchases (see boxed text, p951).

Non-EU countries each have their own regulations, although most forbid the exportation of antiquities and cultural treasures.

DANGERS & ANNOYANCES

Travelling in Mediterranean Europe is pretty safe. Violent crime is rare and there are no special security risks – tensions have cooled in the Balkans, and terrorist activity is now the exception rather than the norm.

The main threats facing travellers are bag snatchers, pickpockets and scam artists.

Drugs

Drugs are easy to come by in Mediterranean Europe, but you'd do well to avoid them. Local attitudes vary, but drug busts are not unheard of, particularly in Morocco, where authorities are keen to rid the country of its reputation as a hippy hang-out. In many places a smidgen of hash might be overlooked if you can persuade the police that it's for personal use, but if they decide you've got enough to deal you could find yourself in big trouble. In some countries the police can hold you for as long as it takes to analyse your case. Hard drugs are rarely overlooked anywhere.

If you do decide to dabble, beware of new 'friends'. A classic scam involves your just-acquired mate selling you a lump of hash and then threatening to call the cops unless you pay up.

Pollution

Air pollution is a problem in many of the region's larger cities. Relentless traffic fumes and heat make unpleasant bedfellows, and after a day walking the streets of Athens or Rome, you could well find your head thumping from the effects of carbon monoxide and lead. Some cities are experimenting with traffic restrictions but much still needs to be done. Dog crap is another urban blight to watch out for – Parisian dogs apparently produce 16 tonnes of the stuff every day.

The Mediterranean Sea also suffers from pollution, although the waters in the main resorts should be clean enough. For details of the region's cleanest beaches consult **Blue Flag** (www.blueflag.org).

GOVERNMENT TRAVEL ADVICE

For up-to-date travel advice consult the following:

Australian Department of Foreign Affairs and Trade (DFAT; www.smartraveller.gov.au)

British Foreign and Commonwealth Office (FCO; www.fco.gov.uk)

US State Department (http://travel.state.gov)

Scams

Mediterranean con artists are good at what they do and you should be on your guard against scams. Typical scenarios include the following:

Bar scam Typically worked on solo male travellers. You're approached by a bloke who claims to be a lone out-of-towner like you but who's heard of a great bar. You go to the bar and enjoy a boozy evening with a crowd of new friends. At the end of the evening you're presented with an outrageous bill.

Druggings These are unlikely but do happen, especially on trains. A new 'friend' slips something into your drink or food and then fleeces you of your valuables as you sleep off the effects.

Flat-tyre ruse While driving you stop to help someone with a flat tyre (or someone stops to help you change your tyre which they've just punctured). As you change the tyre, an accomplice empties the interior of your car.

Phoney cops These often appear as the end-play in cons involving moneychangers or arguments about money. If approached by someone claiming to be a police officer, offer to go with them to the nearest police station.

Swapping banknotes You pay for a taxi fare or a train ticket with a €20 note. The taxi driver or ticket seller deftly palms the note and produces a €5 note, claiming that you paid with this. In your confusion you're not sure what you did and accept their word.

Touts and unofficial guides Be wary of people directing you to hotels or shops (they'll usually be collecting a commission) and people offering to show you around tourist sites (they'll demand hefty payment afterwards).

Theft

Theft is the biggest problem facing travellers in Mediterranean Europe. There's no need for paranoia but be aware that pickpockets and bag snatchers are out there. As always, common sense is the key. Don't store valuables in train-station lockers or at luggage-storage counters, and be careful about people who offer to help you operate a locker. Also, be vigilant if someone offers to carry your luggage: they just might carry it away. Carry your own padlock for hostel lockers.

Be careful even in hotels; don't leave any valuables lying around in your room.

When going out, spread your valuables, cash and cards around your body or in different bags. A money belt with your essentials (passport, cash, credit cards, airline tickets) is usually a good idea. However, to avoid delving into it in public, carry a wallet with a day's cash. Don't flaunt watches, cameras and other expensive goods. Cameras and shoulder bags are an open invitation for snatch thieves, many of whom work from motorcycles or scooters. A small day pack is better, but watch your rear. Also be very careful at cafes and bars – always loop your bag's strap around your leg while seated.

Pickpockets are particularly active in dense crowds, especially in busy train stations and on public transport. A common ploy is for one person to distract you while another whips through your pockets. Beware of gangs of dishevelled-looking kids waving newspapers and demanding attention. In the blink of an eye, a wallet or camera can go missing. Remember also that some of the best pickpockets are well dressed.

Parked cars, especially those with foreign number plates or rental-agency stickers, are prime targets for petty criminals. While driving through cities, beware of thieves at traffic lights. Keep your doors locked and the windows rolled up. A favourite tactic of scooter snatchers is for a first rider to brush past your car, knocking the side mirror out of position; then, as you reach out to re-adjust the mirror, an accomplice on a second scooter will race past, snatching the watch off your wrist as he goes.

In case of theft or loss, always report the incident to the police and ask for a statement. Without one, your travel-insurance company will probably not pay up.

DISCOUNT CARDS

Many major cities now offer cards that provide discounts on public transport and entry to selected sights. See individual city entries in the country chapters. Alternatively, **European Cities Marketing** (www.europeancitycards.com) sells cards for cities in Croatia, France, Italy, Portugal and Spain.

Senior Cards

EU citizens over 65 are often entitled to free or discounted entry to museums and tourist sites, provided proof of age can be shown. A passport or ID card is usually sufficient.

There are a growing number of tour operators specialising in senior travel, all of which can provide information about special packages and discounts.

For information about senior rail passes see p971.

Student & Youth Cards

The **International Student Travel Confederation** (ISTC; www.istc.org) issues three types of cards: the International Student Identity Card (ISIC), available to full-time students and gappers who have a confirmed place at uni or college; the ITIC (International Teacher Identity Card); and the IYTC (International Youth Travel Card) for nonstudents under 26. All three offer worldwide discounts on transport, museum entry, youth hostels and even some restaurants. They also provide access to a 24-hour emergency telephone help line. The price varies from country to country but in the UK the cards cost UK£9, in Australia A$25 and in the USA US$22. See the ISTC website for details of worldwide issuing offices.

For people aged under 26 (or under 30 in Croatia, Greece, Italy, Malta and Slovenia), there's the **Euro<26 card** (www.euro26.org), which offers a similar array of benefits and discounts.

Another option is the **International Student Exchange Card** (www.isecards.com), available to full-time students, teachers and under-26s.

See p939 for information on the Camping Card International.

Note also that membership of Hostelling International (p940) also guarantees discounts and benefits.

ELECTRICITY

Most of the countries listed in this book run off 230V, 50Hz AC. An exception is Morocco, which uses 220V. Most appliances set up for 230V will handle 220V or 240V without modifications (and vice versa), but if you want to run an American 110V to 120V appliance, you'll need a power converter (transformer). When using a transformer, always check that its power rating (in watts) exceeds that of all the appliances you're plugging in.

You'll also need a plug adaptor. Apart from Cyprus and Malta, which use UK-style plugs (three flat pins), the rest of Mediterranean Europe uses the 'europlug', which has two round pins. In Greece and Italy, you'll still find plugs with three pins (two for current and one for earth), but the standard two-pin plug should still work. Always get an adaptor before you leave, as the adaptors available in Europe usually work the other way round. If you find yourself without one, a specialist electrical-supply shop should be able to help.

Several countries outside Europe (such as the USA and Canada) use 60Hz AC, which will affect the speed of electric motors even after the voltage has been adjusted to European values. This will affect CD players, as motor speed is all important, but things such as electric razors, hair dryers, irons and radios will be fine.

EMBASSIES & CONSULATES

See individual country directories for contact details of embassies and consulates.

As a traveller, it's important to realise what your embassy can and can't do for you. Generally speaking, it won't be much help in emergencies if the trouble you're in is even remotely your own fault. Remember, you're bound by the laws of the country you're in. Your embassy will not be sympathetic if you end up in jail after committing a crime locally, even if such actions are legal in your own country.

In genuine emergencies, however, you might get some assistance, but only if other channels have been exhausted. Most importantly, your consulate can (a) issue an emergency passport; (b) help get a message to friends or family; and (c) offer advice on money transfers. A loan to buy a ticket for onward travel is almost always out of the question.

GAY & LESBIAN TRAVELLERS

Discretion is the key. Although homosexuality is acknowledged and in the large part tacitly accepted in Mediterranean Europe, attitudes remain conservative, especially outside the major cities. In terms of legislation, Spain has legalised same-sex marriages, and same-sex relationships are recognised in Croatia, Slovenia and France. Homosexuality is officially illegal in Morocco.

Of the big cities, Paris, Madrid, Barcelona, Lisbon and Athens have thriving gay scenes.

Off the mainland, the Greek islands of Mykonos (p381) and Lesvos (p409) are popular gay destinations.

Contact addresses, and gay and lesbian venues are listed in individual country directories. Useful resources include the following:

Damron (www.damron.com) Publishes the *Damron Men's Travel Guide* (US$21.95); for the ladies there's the *Damron Women's Traveller* (US$18.95).

Gay Journey (www.gayjourney.com) Travel services (package deals, accommodation, insurance etc), gay-friendly listings and loads of links.

Spartacus International (www.spartacusworld.com) Gay publisher famous for the *Spartacus International Gay Guide* (US$32.95, UK£19.99), a male-only directory of worldwide gay venues.

HOLIDAYS

Public Holidays

Most holidays in the southern European countries are based on the Christian calendar. In the countries with a Muslim majority (Morocco and Turkey), the month-long holiday of Ramadan is celebrated, usually around September and October. Its exact timing depends on lunar sightings. See country directories for specific information.

School Holidays

August is the peak holiday period for Mediterranean dwellers. The major school holidays run from about June to September, and many businesses simply shut up shop for much of August. Schools also pause for breaks over Easter and Christmas.

For details of the school calendar, check out **Organisation of School Time in Europe** (http://eacea.ec.europa.eu/portal/page/portal/Eurydice/showPresentation?pubid=092EN), a European Commission website that lists holiday dates for many European countries.

INSURANCE

Travel insurance to cover theft, loss and medical problems is highly recommended. There is a whole range of policies available so make sure you get one tailored to your needs – if you're going skiing you'll need one policy, if you're planning a beach holiday you'll need another – and always check the small print. The policies handled by STA Travel and other student travel agencies are usually good value. A good resource is the price comparison website **Money Supermarket** (www.moneysupermarket.com), which compares 450 policies and comes up with the best for your needs. It also has a useful FAQ section and some good general information regarding travel insurance.

When choosing a policy, you'll need to consider a number of factors, including the following:

- Does the policy have lower and higher medical-expense options?
- Are 'dangerous activities' (scuba diving, motorcycling and, for some policies, trekking) covered? Some policies might not cover you if you're riding a motorbike with a locally acquired motorcycle licence.
- Does the policy cover every country you're planning to visit? Some policies don't cover certain countries, such as Montenegro or BiH.
- Does it cover ambulance service or an emergency flight home?

Some policies pay doctors or hospitals directly, although most require you to pay up front and claim later. In this case make sure you keep all your documentation. (Similarly, if you have to claim for a theft, make sure you've got a statement from the local police.) Some policies ask you to call back (reverse charges) to a centre in your home country, where an assessment of your problem is made.

EU nationals can obtain free emergency treatment in EU countries on the presentation of a European Health Insurance Card, available in their home country.

For more information on health insurance see p972; for car insurance refer to p966.

Worldwide travel insurance is available through **Lonely Planet** (www.lonelyplanet.com/bookings/insurance.do).

INTERNET ACCESS

The easiest way to access the internet on the road is at an internet cafe, of which there are thousands across the region – see individual country chapters for details. Many hotels and hostels also provide access, and you might even be able to log on at banks, department stores, post offices, libraries and universities. Costs average about €3 to €5 per hour.

Wi-fi (sometimes free, usually not) is increasingly available in hotels, airports and internet cafes, although you shouldn't rely on finding it wherever you go. To find regional hot spots, try **JiWire** (www.jiwire.com).

If you're travelling with your own laptop, you can connect through a telephone line or through a mobile phone. Alternatively, if you have a wi-fi-enabled device, simply open it and see what providers are out there. To connect through the telephone line, you'll need a local ISP or a provider that has local dial-up numbers, such as **AOL** (www.aol.com), **AT&T** (www.att.com) or **Earthlink** (www.earthlink.net). If your computer and mobile phone support Bluetooth, you can connect your computer to the phone, which then acts as a modem.

Remember also that if you have to plug your computer into a power socket you might need a power transformer (to convert from 110V to 220V if your computer isn't set up for dual voltage), an RJ-11 telephone jack that works with your modem, and a plug adaptor.

Throughout this book the internet icon (💻) is used to denote accommodation with a computer for guest use.

LEGAL MATTERS

The most likely reason for a brush with the law is to report a theft. If you do have something stolen and you want to claim it on insurance, you must make a statement to the police, as insurance companies won't pay up without official proof of a crime.

However, the region's laid-back atmosphere shouldn't be mistaken for a laissez-faire free-for-all. You are, for example, required by law to prove your identity if asked by police, so always carry your passport, or your ID card if you're an EU citizen. Road checks are also common in some parts so, if driving, make sure (a) you're sober and (b) you have the correct documents at hand; see p965 for further driving information.

For specifics on smoking bans around Mediterranean Europe, see individual country chapters' Food & Drink and Accommodation sections.

MAPS

Good maps are easy to find in bookshops throughout the region. The maps in this book will help you get an idea of where you might want to go and will be a useful first reference when you arrive. Proper road maps are essential if you're driving or cycling. Quality European map publishers include **Michelin** (www.michelin.com), **Freytag & Berndt** (www.freytagberndt.com) and **Kümmerly+Frey** (www.kuemmerly-frey.ch).

As a rule, maps published by automobile associations (for example ACI in Italy or ELPA in Greece) are excellent, and are sometimes free if membership of your local association gives you reciprocal rights. Tourist offices are a good source for free, basic maps.

MONEY

Of the countries covered in this book, Cyprus, France, Greece, Italy, Malta, Montenegro, Portugal, Slovenia and Spain use the euro. The euro is also widely accepted in BiH and Croatia.

There are seven euro notes (€5, €10, €20, €50, €100, €200 and €500) and eight euro coins (€1 and €2, then 1, 2, 5, 10, 20 and 50 cents); one euro is equivalent to 100 cents.

While travelling in the region, the best way to carry your money is to bring a mix of ATM cards, credit cards and cash, and one or two travellers cheques as backup. Before you leave home you could also set up an internet banking account, so you can track your spending.

If you have to have money sent to you, international bank transfers are good for secure one-off movements of large amounts of money, but they might take three to five days and there will be a fee. Be sure to specify the name of the bank, plus the sort code and the address of the branch where you'd like to pick up your money.

It's quicker and easier (although more expensive) to have money wired via **American Express** (www.americanexpress.com), **Western Union** (www.westernunion.com) or **MoneyGram** (www.moneygram.com).

A cheaper option is **Moneybookers** (www.moneybookers.com), a British money-transfer website that allows you to send and receive money via email.

ATMs

Every country listed in this book has ATMs that allow you withdraw cash. They're widely available and easy to use (many have instructions in English). It's always prudent, though, to have a backup option in case something goes wrong with your card or you can't find a working ATM – in some remote villages, for example, they might be scarce).

There are four types of card you can use in an ATM: an ATM card, a debit card, a credit card and a prepaid cash card (sometimes called a stored-value card; see below). ATM cards, which you use to withdraw money from your home bank account, can be used in ATMs linked to international networks such as Cirrus and Maestro. Ditto for debit cards, which can also be used to make purchases over the counter. Credit cards and prepaid cash cards can be used in ATMs displaying the appropriate logos; for further information, see right.

Note that you'll need a four-digit PIN (in numbers rather than letters) for most European ATMs and might have difficulties if your card doesn't have a metallic chip; check with your bank. Sometimes you might also have problems using your card if it's very early in the morning back in your home country, when banks sometimes back up their systems. If your card is rejected, try again in a few hours' time. Make sure you bring your bank's phone number, and call them if your card fails again.

When you withdraw money from an ATM, the amounts are converted and dispensed in local currency. However, you will be charged various fees. Typically, you'll be charged a transaction fee (usually around 3% with a minimum fee of €3 or more), as well as a 1% to 3% conversion charge. If you're using a credit card, you'll also be hit by interest on the cash withdrawn. Fees vary from company to company: in the UK, the Nationwide charges no fees for withdrawals and foreign currency purchases; the US bank Capital One applies a US$1.50 transaction fee but no conversion charges. For further investigation of transaction fees and other card-related costs check out the British website **Money Supermarket** (www.moneysupermarket.com/travel-money).

As a security measure, be wary of people who offer to help you use an ATM or, at ports or stations, people who claim that there are no ATMs at your destination.

Black Market

Black-market money exchange is relatively rare in Mediterranean Europe, although it's not totally absent. If you do encounter it, stay well clear. The rates rarely outweigh the risk of being caught, and by dealing with unofficial moneychangers you greatly increase your chances of being conned – many people offering illegal exchanges are professional thieves.

EUROS WILL BE FINE, THANK YOU

Something to look out for when making payments with a credit card is what's known as 'dynamic currency conversion'. This is used when a vendor offers to convert your bill into your home currency rather than charging you in the local currency. The catch here is that the exchange rate used to convert your bill will usually be highly disadvantageous to you, and the vendor might well add his or her own commission fee. Always ask to be billed in the local currency.

Cash

Nothing beats cash for convenience, or risk. If you lose it, it's gone forever and very few travel insurers will come to your rescue. Those that will insure you limit the amount to somewhere around US$300. For tips on carrying your money safely, see p946. As a general rule of thumb, carry no more than 10% to 15% of your total trip money in cash.

It's still a good idea, though, to bring some local currency in cash, if only to tide you over until you find an ATM.

Credit Cards

Credit cards are good for major purchases such as airline tickets or car hire, as well as for providing emergency cover. They also make life a lot easier if you need to book hotels while on the road – many places request a credit-card number when you reserve a room. However, don't assume that they are accepted everywhere. In Albania and Montenegro, for example, many restaurants, shops and small hotels won't take them; indeed, outside of the main cities very few places at all will accept them.

As a general rule, Visa and MasterCard are more widely accepted in the region than American Express and Diners Club.

Using your credit card in ATMs can be costly. On every transaction there's a fee, which with some credit-card issuers can reach US$10, as well as interest per withdrawal. Check the charges with your issuer before leaving home. Remember also that there'll probably be a daily limit on what you can withdraw.

As a backup to your debit or credit card, consider a prepaid cash card, such as the

Travelex Cash Passport. Before you leave home, load the card with as much money as you want to spend and then use it as an ATM card – the money you withdraw comes off the card and not out of your account. If necessary, you can then reload it via telephone or online. Note, however, that you'll still be stung by ATM and conversion fees, as well as loading fees.

If you want to rely heavily on plastic, go for two different cards – an American Express or Diners Club, for instance, plus a Visa or MasterCard. Better still is a combination of a credit or ATM card, cash and travellers cheques, so you have something to fall back on if an ATM swallows your card or the banks in the area are closed.

Make sure you can always see your card when making transactions and, if possible, let your credit-card company know of your travel plans – it'll lessen the risk of fraud, or of your bank cutting off the card when it sees (your) unusual spending.

Moneychangers

US dollars, pounds sterling and the euro are the easiest currencies to exchange in Europe. You might have trouble exchanging Canadian, Australian and New Zealand dollars.

Most airports, central train stations, big hotels and many border posts have banking facilities outside working hours, sometimes on a 24-hour basis. Post offices in Europe often perform banking tasks, and they tend to have longer opening hours and outnumber banks in remote places. However, while they'll always exchange cash, they might not change travellers cheques unless the cheques are in the local currency.

The best exchange rates are generally offered by banks. *Bureaux de changes* usually, but not always, offer worse rates or charge higher commissions. Hotels are almost always the worst places to change money. American Express and Travelex offices don't usually charge for changing their own travellers cheques, but don't always offer great rates.

Travellers Cheques

Although they're the dinosaurs of the travel world, travellers cheques are not quite extinct. While they're largely outmoded by ATM cards, they are still useful as emergency backup, especially as you can claim a refund if they're stolen (providing, of course, you've kept a separate record of their numbers).

Note, however, that it's becoming increasingly hard to find places to cash them, and you might have difficulties outside of the main centres (in Albania, for example, it's difficult to cash them outside of Tirana). American Express, Visa and Travelex cheques are the most widely accepted, particularly in US dollars, British pounds or euros. When changing, ask about fees and commissions, as well as the exchange rate. There may be a

GET YOUR MONEY BACK

You don't have to be an accountant to save yourself a few euros while travelling in Mediterranean Europe. Tax-free shopping is available across the region – look for signs in shop windows – and while it won't save you a fortune, it won't cost you anything extra.

Value-added tax (VAT) is a sales tax imposed on most goods and services sold in Europe; it varies from country to country but is typically around 20%. In most countries visitors who spend more than a certain amount can claim VAT back on purchases they're taking out of the country, provided they don't use the purchase prior to leaving. EU residents, however, are not entitled to a refund on goods bought in another EU country. Thus an American citizen who is a resident in Madrid is not entitled to a VAT rebate on items bought in Paris, while an EU-passport holder living in New York is.

The procedure is straightforward. When you make your purchase ask the shop assistant for a tax-refund voucher (sometimes called a tax-free shopping cheque), which is filled in with the date of your purchase and its value. When you leave the EU, get this voucher stamped at customs – the customs agent might want to check the item so try to ensure you have it ready to hand – and take it to the nearest tax-refund counter. Here you can get an immediate refund, either in cash or charged onto your credit card. If there's no refund counter at the airport or you're travelling by sea or overland, you'll need to get the voucher stamped at the port or border crossing and mail it back for your refund.

BLU MOVIES (& DVDS)

When buying a DVD or Blu-ray disc in Europe, you'll need to check two things: its regional code and its format. All discs are encoded with a regional code: for US and Canadian DVDs this is code 1; European, Japanese and South African discs are code 2; Australian and New Zealand discs are code 4. Blu-ray discs are coded slightly differently, with European, Australian and New Zealand discs coded B, and American discs coded A.

Always check that the code of the disc you're buying corresponds with that of your player at home – a DVD player coded 1 or 4 will not play a disc coded 2. A way around this is to look for all-region players and discs. Some players can also be 'chipped' to enable them to play discs from all regions. Note that regional codes don't apply to blank, recordable discs.

European discs and players are formatted for the PAL/SECAM TV system rather than the NTSC system used in the USA and Japan. As a general rule, a DVD player bought in a PAL country (including Australia) will play NTSC- and PAL-formatted discs. On the other hand, most NTSC players can't play PAL discs.

service fee charged per cheque; a flat transaction fee; or a fee that's a percentage of the total amount, irrespective of the number of cheques. Some banks charge exorbitant fees to cash cheques, but not to change cash; others do the reverse.

PHOTOGRAPHY

Film and camera equipment is available everywhere in the region. If you're shooting digitally, make sure that you have enough memory to store your snaps – a 256MB card will probably be enough, although if you're shooting high-resolution photos you might consider a 516MB card. If you do run out of memory your best bet is to burn your photos onto a CD, something which many internet cafes will do for you.

To download your pics at an internet cafe, you'll need a USB cable and a card reader. Some places provide a USB cable on request, but be warned that many of the chain cafes don't let you plug your gear into their computers. If you have a photo-enabled MP3 player or iPod you can store photos on these, although to download direct from your camera you might need an additional connector.

Remember also that you might need a plug adaptor and transformer (to ensure the correct voltage) for your battery charger.

As a general rule, early morning and evening are the best times to take photos, as the light lacks the harsh glare of the afternoon. For further tips, Lonely Planet publishes a series of photo guides, including *Travel Photography, Landscape Photography, People Photography* and *Urban Travel Photography*.

POST

From major European centres, airmail typically takes about five days to North America and a week to Australasian destinations. Postage costs vary from country to country, as does post-office efficiency.

Most central post offices offer poste restante services, which allow people to write to you care of the post office, but email has rendered these largely obsolete. Ask people writing to you to print your name clearly and underline your surname. When collecting mail, you'll need your passport and you may have to pay a small fee. If an expected letter has not arrived, ask the staff to check under your first name; letters commonly get misfiled. Post offices usually hold mail for about a month, but sometimes less.

You can also have mail (but not parcels) sent to you at American Express offices if you have an Amex card or travellers cheques. Courier services such as **DHL** (www.dhl.com) are best for essential deliveries.

SOLO TRAVELLERS

Lone travellers should face no major problems in Mediterranean Europe as it's a relatively safe place with plenty of accommodation and an efficient transport network. That said, in some parts your presence as a solo traveller will arouse curiosity and even incredulity. In Turkey, for example, solo travel is something usually only undertaken for business, and the idea that someone would choose to travel alone is not readily comprehended. Don't worry though – this rarely translates into anything more than curious stares and a grilling as to why you're on your own and why you haven't got any companions.

Security for solo travellers is mainly a matter of common sense – watch your possessions, don't go wandering down dark alleys at night and be wary of overly friendly people you've just met. For more on possible dangers, see p946; specific advice for female travellers is included on p955.

If you're thinking about travelling alone, bear in mind that single rooms in hotels are often more expensive (relatively speaking) than doubles or triples, and that crowded restaurants might be reluctant to give you a table for one. Seasoned solo travellers advise staying in hostels as much as possible, not only to save money but also as a means of meeting people.

TELEPHONE & FAX

Telephoning into, or out of, Mediterranean Europe is not difficult. Public payphones are widespread and you'll find many private call centres across the region. Some internet cafes have started offering Skype. As a general rule, phoning from a post office or a public payphone is cheaper than calling from a private phone office or a hotel.

To call abroad simply dial the international access code (IAC) of the country you're calling *from* (most commonly ☎ 00), the country code (CC) of the country you're calling *to*, the local area code (usually, but not always dropping the leading zero if there is one) and then the number.

Area codes for individual cities are provided in the country chapters; for information on country codes, see right.

To have someone else pay for your call, you can, from many countries, dial directly to your home-country operator and then reverse the charges. Alternatively, you can use the Home Direct (or Country Direct) system, which lets you phone home by billing the long-distance carrier you use at home. Home Direct numbers, which can often be dialled from public phones without even inserting a phonecard, vary from country to country.

> **EMERGENCY NUMBERS**
>
> The EU-wide general emergency number is ☎ 112. This can be dialled for emergencies in Cyprus, France, Greece, Italy, Malta, Portugal, Slovenia and Spain. See the individual country directories for country-specific emergency numbers.

Fax

Largely outmoded by email, faxes are sometimes required by hotels as confirmation of a reservation. You can generally send faxes and telexes from major post offices and large hotels.

Mobile Phones

Most European mobile phones operate on the GSM 900/1800 system, which also covers Australia and New Zealand, but is not compatible with the North American GSM 1900 system. Some American GSM 1900/900 phones, however, do work in Europe, although high roaming charges make it an expensive business.

If you have a GSM tri- or quad-band phone that you can unlock (check with your service provider), the easiest way of using it is to buy a prepaid SIM card in each country you visit. SIM prices vary from country to country – see country chapters for details – but you can usually pick one up pretty cheaply. You can then top up the account as you go along. Remember, though, that each time you change your SIM card you change your telephone number, and that most SIMs expire if not used within a certain time. Most country-specific SIMs can only be used in the country of origin.

Phone Codes

For individual country and city area codes see the Fast Facts box at the start of each country chapter or the inside front cover.

Toll-free numbers in Mediterranean Europe often have an ☎ 0800 or ☎ 800 prefix (also ☎ 900 in Spain). You'll find toll-free emergency numbers under Telephone in the country directories.

Phonecards

To call from a public payphone, you'll need a phonecard, available from post offices, telephone centres, news-stands and retail outlets.

There's a wide range of local and international phonecards. Most international cards come with a toll-free number and a PIN code, which gives access to your prepaid credit. However, for local calls you're usually better off with a local phonecard. Note also that (a) many cards have an expiry date and (b) those sold at airports and train stations are rarely good value for money.

If you've got an International Student Identity Card (see p947), consider paying an extra US$20 to activate the ISIConnect service. This allows you to use your ISIC card as a PIN-protected prepaid phonecard. See **ISIConnect** (www.isiconnect.ekit.com) for further details.

If you don't have a phonecard, you can often telephone from a booth inside a post office or telephone centre and settle your bill at the counter.

TIME

Most of the countries covered in this book are on Central European Time (GMT/UTC plus one hour) except for Portugal, which runs on Western European Time (GMT/UTC); Morocco, which follows GMT/UTC, but does not observe daylight savings; and Cyprus, Greece and Turkey, which are on Eastern European Time (GMT/UTC plus two hours).

In most European countries, clocks are put forward one hour for daylight-saving time on the last Sunday in March and turned back again on the last Sunday in October. Thus, during daylight-saving time, Western European Time is GMT/UTC plus one hour, Central European Time GMT/UTC plus two hours and Eastern European Time GMT/UTC plus three hours.

TOILETS

Public toilets are pretty thin on the ground in much of the region. The best advice if you're caught short is to nip into a train station, fast-food outlet, bar or cafe and use their facilities. A small fee (typically €0.20 to €0.70) is often charged in public loos, so try to keep some small change handy.

Most loos in the region are of the sit-down Western variety, but don't be surprised to find the occasional squat loo. And don't ever assume that public loos will have paper – they almost certainly won't.

TOURIST INFORMATION

Tourist information is widely available throughout the region. Most towns, big or small, have a tourist office of some description, which at the very least will be able to provide a rudimentary map and give information on accommodation. Some even provide a hotel-reservation service, which might or might not be free. In the absence of a tourist office, useful sources of information include travel agencies and hotel receptionists.

Tourist-office staff will often speak some English in the main centres, but don't bank on it away from the tourist hot spots.

For country-specific tourist information, see the country chapters.

TRAVELLERS WITH DISABILITIES

With the notable exception of Croatia, which has improved wheelchair access due to the large number of wounded war veterans, the region does not cater well to disabled travellers. Steep cobbled streets, ancient lifts and anarchic traffic all make life difficult for wheelchair-using visitors. Wheelchair access is often limited to the more expensive hotels and major airports; public transport is usually woefully ill equipped; and tourist sites rarely cater well to those with disabilities.

However, it's not impossible to travel the region, even independently. If you're going it alone, pretrip research is essential – find out about facilities on public transport; work out how to get to your hotel or hostel; and check if there are care agencies available and how much they cost. Experts also recommend that you give your wheelchair a thorough service before departing, and that you prepare a basic tool kit, as punctures can be a problem.

National support organisations can help. They often have libraries devoted to travel, and can put you in touch with travel agents who specialise in tours for the disabled. The following are also useful resources:

Access-able (www.access-able.com) Practical advice, including country-by-country information and contact details.

Accessible Travel (www.accessible.travel) An online booking engine for people with disabilities. Book hotels in Athens and Barcelona, and check out the useful blog.

Flying with Disability (www.flying-with-disability) Comprehensive and easy-to-use site covering all aspects of air travel – pretrip planning, navigating the airport, boarding the flight, on the plane etc.

Lonely Planet (www.lonelyplanet.com) The Thorn Tree forum has a section dedicated to travellers with disabilities.

Mobility International USA (www.miusa.org) Publishes guides and advises travellers with disabilities or mobility issues.

Society for Accessible Travel and Hospitality (www.sath.org) Has loads of useful information, including a need-to-know section and travel tips.

VISAS

Citizens of the USA, Australia, New Zealand, Canada and the UK need only a valid passport to enter most of the countries in this guide for up to three months, provided they have some sort of onward or return ticket and/or 'sufficient means of support' (ie money).

France, Greece, Italy, Malta, Portugal, Slovenia and Spain have all signed the Schengen Agreement, which abolishes customs checks between signatory states. Cyprus has also signed the agreement, but has yet to implement the provisions. For the purposes of visa requirements, the Schengen area should be considered a single unit, as all member states operate the same entry requirements. These include the following:

- Legal residents of one Schengen country do not need a visa for another Schengen country.
- Nationals of Australia, Canada, Israel, Japan, New Zealand and the USA do not need a visa for tourist visits of up to 90 days.
- The UK and Ireland are not part of the Schengen area but their citizens can stay indefinitely in other EU countries, and only need to fill in paperwork if they want to work long term or take up residency.

If you do require a Schengen visa for a tourist visit, you'll need the category C short-stay visa. This is divided into single-entry and multiple-entry models, and allows for either an uninterrupted stay of 90 days in the Schengen area or several stays for a total of 90 days in any 180-day period. Remember, though, the clock starts ticking from the moment you enter the Schengen area.

It's obligatory to apply for a Schengen visa in your country of residence at the embassy of your main destination country or, if you have no principal destination, of the first Schengen country you'll be entering. A visa issued by one Schengen country is generally valid for travel in other Schengen countries, but individual countries may impose restrictions on certain nationalities. You can only apply for two Schengen visas in any 12-month period. Note also that you can not work in a Schengen country without a specific work permit.

Always check which documents you'll need. You'll almost certainly require a passport valid for three months beyond the end of your proposed visit; a return air or train ticket; proof of a hotel reservation or similar accommodation arrangement; proof of your ability to support yourself financially; and medical insurance.

Apart from the Schengen visas, it's generally easier to get your visas as you go along, rather than arranging them all beforehand. Carry spare passport photos (you may need from one to four every time you apply for a visa).

Of the non-Schengen countries in this book, only Turkey requires visas from Australian, Canadian, British and US nationals. They can be bought at any point of entry into the country. See p933 for details.

Visa requirements change, and you should always check with the embassy of your destination country or a reputable travel agent before travelling.

For more information about work visas and permits see p956.

WOMEN TRAVELLERS

It's sad to report, but machismo is alive and well in Mediterranean Europe, a region in which gender roles are still largely based on age-old social norms. But even if attitudes are not always very enlightened, a deep sense of hospitality runs through many Mediterranean societies, and travellers (of both sexes) are usually welcomed with warmth and genuine kindness. That said, women travellers continue to face more challenging situations than men do, most often in the form of unwanted harassment. Staring is much more overt in Mediterranean countries than in the more reticent northern parts of Europe, and although it is almost always harmless, it can become annoying. If you find yourself being pestered by local men and ignoring them isn't working, tell them you're waiting for your husband (marriage is highly respected in the area) and walk away. If they continue, call the police.

Gropers, particularly on crowded public transport, can also be a problem. If you do feel someone start to touch you inappropriately, make a fuss – molesters are no more admired in Mediterranean Europe than they are anywhere else.

In Muslim countries, where women's roles are clearly defined and unmarried men have little contact with women outside of their family unit, women travelling alone or with other women will attract attention. This is rarely dangerous, but you'll need to exercise common sense. Dress conservatively, avoid eye contact and, if possible, don't walk alone at night.

Of the numerous guides available, Beth Whitman's *Wanderlust & Lipstick: The Essential Guide for Women Travelling Solo* is particularly good for nervous first-timers. Other resources include the following:

Journeywoman (www.journeywoman.com) An online women's travel magazine.

Lonely Planet (www.lonelyplanet.com) Exchange thoughts and ideas on the Women Travellers branch of the Thorn Tree forum.

Women's Travel Tips (www.womentraveltips.com) Experienced female travellers provide plenty of on-the-road tips.

For further information, see the individual country directories.

WORK

Working in Mediterranean Europe is not always easy. Unemployment in the region is high, and the ever growing immigrant population provides local employers with a ready pool of cheap labour, particularly for unskilled, seasonal agricultural work. However, it's not all gloom and doom, and with a bit of planning and determination you should be able to find something.

On a bureaucratic level, life is much easier for EU citizens, as they can work in any other EU country without a visa or specific permit. Paperwork, which can be complicated, only really becomes necessary for long-term employment or if you want to apply for residency. Non-EU nationals require work permits, which can be difficult to arrange, especially for temporary work.

There are ways around this, though. If, for example, one of your parents or a grandparent was born in an EU country, you may have certain rights you never knew about. Get in touch with that country's embassy and ask about dual citizenship and work permits – if you go for citizenship, ask about any obligations, such as military service and residency. Be aware that your home country may not recognise dual citizenship.

Much of the temporary work offered in the region is seasonal – ski resorts provide winter opportunities, while beach bars, clubs, restaurants and hotels are a rich source of summer employment. Remember, though, that if you find a temporary job, the pay might be less than that offered to locals (little more than pocket money in some cases), although you might get board and lodging thrown in. Au pairing is a good way of ensuring accommodation for your stay.

Teaching English is a favourite option, although many schools now ask for a degree and a TEFL (Teaching English as a Foreign Language) certificate. There are no such requirements to give private lessons. For information on TEFL courses and jobs, try **TEFL International** (www.teflinternational.org.uk) or the **British Council** (www.britishcouncil.org). Alternatively, the *Guardian* newspaper has a useful online TEFL section (www.guardian.co.uk/education/tefl) and the *Times Educational Supplement* (www.tes.co.uk) has a comprehensive job database. Big international schools include **Berlitz** (www.berlitz.com), **Inlingua** (www.inlingua.com) or **Wall Street Institute International** (www.wallstreet institute.com).

If you can afford it, a volunteer work placement is a great way to gain an insight into local culture. Typical volunteer jobs include working on conservation projects, participating in research programs, or helping out at animal-welfare centres. In some cases volunteers are paid a living allowance; sometimes they work for their keep; and times volunteers are required to pay for the experience, typically from about US$300 per week.

There are hundreds of guides dedicated to working abroad, but Susan Griffith's *Work Your Way Around the World* is usually considered the classic of the genre. Lonely Planet's *The Gap Year Book* also has information about work and volunteering across the world. Useful websites include the following:

Gap Work (www.gapwork.com) Comprehensive website aimed at gappers. Has good advice, job searches and hundreds of useful links.

Go Abroad (www.goabroad.com) Huge site with information on hundreds of jobs and volunteer opportunities.

International Willing Workers on Organic Farms Association (WWOOF; www.wwoof.org) International organisation that puts volunteers in contact with organic farms across the world. In exchange for your labour, you'll receive free lodging and food.

Transitions Abroad (www.transitionsabroad.com) Publishes the comprehensive guide *Work Abroad: The Complete Guide to Finding a Job Overseas.*

Working Abroad (www.workingabroad.com) Has good job and volunteer information. For UK£29 you can get a personal report advising on the best jobs to suit your requirements and travel preferences.

Working Overseas (www.workingoverseas.com) The 1800-page *BIG Guide to Living and Working Overseas* provides advice for US and Canadian readers.

Transport in Mediterranean Europe

CONTENTS

This chapter provides a general overview of transport in Mediterranean Europe. For more-detailed country-specific information, see the Transport sections in individual country chapters; check out p955 for visa information.

Unless otherwise specified, all telephone numbers are local numbers and do not include international dialling codes.

Flights, tours and rail tickets can be booked at www.lonelyplanet.com/travel_services.

GETTING THERE & AWAY

AIR

It's not difficult to find a flight to the Med. Most major airlines fly into the region, and there are upt to 42 low-cost carriers in Europe, which operate more than 4400 routes. In summer, charter flights add to the congestion.

Major gateways include the two Paris airports, Orly and Roissy Charles de Gaulle; Rome's Leonardo da Vinci airport (better known as Fiumicino); Madrid's Barajas airport; and Atatürk International Airport in İstanbul. Many no-frills airlines use secondary provincial airports – see individual country chapters for details.

Expect to pay high-season prices between June and September; the two months either side of this period are the shoulder seasons. Low season is November to March.

Airlines

The main airlines serving Mediterranean countries:

Adria Airways (JP; www.adria-airways.com)
Air Canada (AC; www.aircanada.ca)
Air China (CA; www.airchina.com.cn)
Air France (AF; www.airfrance.com)
Air Malta (KM; www.airmalta.com)
Air New Zealand (NZ; www.airnewzealand.com)
Alitalia (AZ; www.alitalia.com)
American Airlines (AA; www.aa.com)
British Airways (BA; www.britishairways.com)
Cathay Pacific (CX; www.cathaypacific.com)
Croatia Airlines (OU; www.croatiaairlines.hr)
Cyprus Airways (CY; www.cyprusairways.com)
Delta Air Lines (DL; www.delta.com)
Emirates (EK; www.emirates.com)
Iberia (IBE; www.iberia.com)
Japan Airlines (JL; www.jal.co.jp)
KLM (KL; www.klm.com)
Lufthansa (LH; www.lufthansa.com)
Malaysia Airlines (MH; www.malaysiaairlines.com)
Olympic Airlines (OA; www.olympicairlines.com)
Qantas (QF; www.qantas.com.au)
Royal Air Maroc (AT; www.royalairmaroc.com)
Singapore Airlines (SQ; www.singaporeair.com)
South African Airways (SA; www.flysaa.com)
TAP (TAP; www.flytap.com)

THINGS CHANGE...

The information in this chapter is particularly vulnerable to change. Check directly with the airline or a travel agent to make sure you understand how a fare (and ticket you may buy) works and be aware of the security requirements for international travel. Shop carefully. The details given in this chapter should be regarded as pointers and are not a substitute for your own careful, up-to-date research.

CLIMATE CHANGE & TRAVEL

Climate change is a serious threat to the ecosystems that humans rely upon, and air travel is the fastest-growing contributor to the problem. Lonely Planet regards travel, overall, as a global benefit, but believes we all have a responsibility to limit our personal impact on global warming.

Flying & Climate Change

Pretty much every form of motor travel generates CO_2 (the main cause of human-induced climate change) but planes are far and away the worst offenders, not just because of the sheer distances they allow us to travel, but because they release greenhouse gases high into the atmosphere. The statistics are frightening: two people taking a return flight between Europe and the US will contribute as much to climate change as an average household's gas and electricity consumption over a whole year.

Carbon Offset Schemes

Climatecare.org and other websites use 'carbon calculators' that allow jetsetters to offset the greenhouse gases they are responsible for with contributions to energy-saving projects and other climate-friendly initiatives in the developing world – including projects in India, Honduras, Kazakhstan and Uganda.

Lonely Planet, together with Rough Guides and other concerned partners in the travel industry, supports the carbon offset scheme run by climatecare.org. Lonely Planet offsets all of its staff and author travel.

For more information check out our website: lonelyplanet.com.

Thai Airways International (TG; www.thaiair.com)
Turkish Airlines (TK; www.thy.com)

Budget airlines operating in Mediterranean Europe:
Air Berlin (AB; www.airberlin.com)
bmibaby (WW; www.bmibaby.com)
easyJet (U2; www.easyjet.com)
germanwings (4U; www.germanwings.com)
Jet2 (LS; www.jet2.com)
Ryanair (FR; www.ryanair.com)
Thomsonfly (BY; www.thomsonfly.com)
TUIfly (X3; www.hlx.com)
Vueling (VY; www.vueling.com)

Tickets

The best place to find and book tickets is the internet. Airline websites often have excellent online fares and most low-cost carriers operate solely on the web. To help you find the best fare, there is a whole host of price comparison websites, which scan airline and agency sites and find the most competitive fares. Useful sites include the following:
Air Treks (www.airtreks.com) Specialists in multistop, round-the-world (RTW) tickets.
Cheap Tickets (www.cheaptickets.com)
Expedia (www.expedia.com)
Flightbookers (www.ebookers.com)
Kayak (www.kayak.com)
Opodo (www.opodo.com)
Orbitz (www.orbitz.com)
Priceline (www.priceline.com)
Skyscanner (www.skyscanner.net)
Travelocity (www.travelocity.com)

Note, however, that some low-cost airlines, most notably Ryanair, only accept bookings made on their own website.

Note also that paper tickets have almost entirely been replaced by electronic tickets (e-tickets). In effect, these are not tickets at all, just printouts of your booking details. When you book online, you'll be given a ticket/booking number, a payment-confirmation receipt and an itinerary – print these out and you've got your e-ticket. This printout, along with your passport and, if necessary, your visa, is usually all you'll need to show at check-in, although some airlines insist that you also show the credit card you used to pay for your ticket. If you'd prefer a paper ticket, most airlines will supply one at extra cost.

For advice on booking online, check out **How to Buy Cheap Flights Online** (www.stanfords.co.uk/articles/how-to/how-to-buy-cheap-flights-online,264,AR.html), which has some excellent tips.

The internet has not, however, completely done away with travel agents, and if you're planning a more complex itinerary you're probably better off talking to a competent agent who can find you the best fares, advise on connections and sell travel insurance. There are plenty of agencies specialising in cheap flights. Most are honest but it pays to be cautious. Paying by credit card offers some protection, as most card issuers provide refunds if you can prove you didn't get what you paid for. After you've made a booking or paid your deposit, call the airline and confirm that the booking has been made.

If you purchase a ticket and later want to change it or get a refund, you'll need to contact the original travel agency. Airlines issue refunds only to the purchaser of a ticket – usually the travel agency that bought the ticket on your behalf.

Full-time students and people aged under 26 (under 30 in some countries) have access to discounted fares. You'll have to show a document proving your date of birth, such as a valid International Student Identity Card (ISIC) or an International Youth Travel Card (IYTC) when buying your ticket. See **International Student Travel Confederation** (www.istc.org) for more information.

Africa

STA Travel (www.statravel.co.za) and **Flight Centre** (www.flightcentre.co.za) have offices throughout southern Africa. Check their websites for branch locations.

If you're heading to Morocco, consider getting a cheap ticket to Paris, London or Amsterdam and catching a connecting flight from there.

Asia

STA Travel proliferates in Asia:

Bangkok (☎ 662 236 0262; www.statravel.co.th)
Hong Kong (☎ 2730 2800; www.hkst.com, in Chinese)
Japan (☎ 03 5391 2922; www.statravel.co.jp)
Singapore (☎ 6737 7188; www.statravel.com.sg)

In Hong Kong you could also try **Four Seas Tours** (wwwfourseastravel.com), while in Japan **No 1 Travel** (☎ 03 3205 6073; www.no1-travel.com) has offices in Tokyo and Yokohama.

A website worth checking out is **Zuji** (www.zuji.com), an online agency serving the Asia-Pacific region.

Australia

Europe-bound flights from Australia generally travel via Southeast Asian capitals such as Kuala Lumpur, Singapore or Bangkok, or via the Middle East, typically Dubai.

Flight Centre (☎ 133 133; www.flightcentre.com.au) and **STA Travel** (☎ 134782; www.statravel.com.au) both have offices across the country; you'll also find STA on many university campuses. For online bookings, try **Travel.com.au** (www.travel.com.au).

Canada

Canada's main student travel organisation, **Travel Cuts** (☎ 866 246 9762; www.travelcuts.com) has offices in all major cities. For online bookings try **Expedia** (www.expedia.ca) and **Travelocity** (www.travelocity.ca).

Germany & the Netherlands

With 42 low-cost carriers operating across Europe, it's always worth scanning airline websites for cheap fares. You'll find a list of airlines and the routes they serve at **flycheapo.com** (www.flycheapo.com). **Expedia** (☎ 01805 007 146; www.expedia.de) and **Lastminute** (☎ 01805 284 366; www.lastminute.de) have offices in Germany, as does **STA Travel** (☎ 069 743 032 92; www.statravel.de), which caters to travellers under 26. In the Netherlands a reliable operator is **Airfair** (☎ 0900 7 717 717; www.airfair.nl).

New Zealand

Both **Flight Centre** (☎ 0800 24 35 44; www.flightcentre.co.nz) and **STA Travel** (☎ 0800 474 400; www.statravel.co.nz) have branches throughout the country.

UK & Ireland

Discount air travel is big business in London. Recommended agencies include the following:

Flight Centre (☎ 0870 499 0040; www.flightcentre.co.uk)
Flightbookers (☎ 0871 223 5000; www.ebookers.com)
North-South Travel (☎ 01245-608 291; www.northsouthtravel.co.uk) North-South Travel donates some of its profits to projects in the developing world.
Quest Travel (☎ 0845 263 6963; www.questtravel.com)
STA Travel (☎ 0871 2 300 040; www.statravel.co.uk) For travellers under 26.
Trailfinders (☎ 0845 058 5858; www.trailfinders.co.uk)
Travel Bag (☎ 0800 804 8911; www.travelbag.co.uk)

USA

Discount travel agents in the USA are known as consolidators (although you won't see a sign on the door saying 'Consolidator'). San Francisco is heralded as the ticket-consolidator capital of America, although some good deals can be found in Los Angeles, New York and other big cities. Consolidator tickets rarely allow for any changes, so make sure you've got your itinerary sorted out before buying one.

The following agencies are recommended for online bookings:

American Express (www134.americanexpress.com/consumertravel/travel.do)
Cheap Tickets (www.cheaptickets.com)
Expedia (www.expedia.com)
Lowest Fare (www.lowestfare.com)
Orbitz (www.orbitz.com)
STA Travel (www.sta.com) For travellers under 26.
Travelocity (www.travelocity.com)

See also the list of websites, p958.

LAND

The main overland routes into Mediterranean Europe enter the region from the north and east. Countries bordering the region to the north include Switzerland, Austria and Hungary; to the east they include Serbia, Kosovo and Macedonia. France is bordered on the east by Switzerland, Germany, Luxembourg and Belgium. To the east of Turkey lies Iran, and to the south Syria and Iraq. Morocco is bordered by Algeria and the disputed Western Sahara territories.

For details of overland transport into individual countries, refer to the Transport sections in the country chapters.

Asia

The overland trail from Asia enters the region via Turkey, passing through Iran, Pakistan and India. At the time of research, the **British Foreign and Commonwealth Office** (www.fco.gov.uk) was advising against all rail transport in Pakistan and the **Australian Department of Foreign Affairs and Trade** (www.smartraveller.gov.au) was advising travellers to avoid areas in Pakistan bordering Afghanistan. If you're determined to try the route, make sure to check on the latest security situation.

Allow at least eight days to get to Mediterranean Europe from central and eastern Asia by train.

Continental Europe

Bus and train links between Mediterranean Europe and the rest of Continental Europe are comprehensive. A good resource for train planning is the **German Deutsch Bahn journey planner** (http://reiseauskunft.bahn.de/bin/query.exe/en?datesel=custom). For more information, see individual country Transport sections.

Eurolines (www.eurolines.com) is a consortium of coach companies that operates across Europe and Morocco. The website, through which you can book tickets, has timetable information and details of ticket offices in each country.

UK

Underwater rather than overland, the Channel Tunnel provides a rail link between Britain and France. If you're travelling without a car, you'll need the Eurostar; with wheels you'll want the Eurotunnel vehicle service.

Eurostar (☎ in the UK 08705 186 186, in France 0892 35 35 39; www.eurostar.com) operates direct trains from London, Ebbsfleet and Ashford in the UK (the last two are in Kent) to Paris' Gare du Nord station, Lille, Calais and Avignon in France. There are also services to Paris Disneyland, several Alpine ski resorts and Brussels. In London, trains depart from St Pancras International Station. Current journey times are approximately 2½ hours to Paris, 1½ hours to Lille, and 6¾ hours to Avignon.

There are 15 ticket types available (child, youth, senior, minimum one-night stay, Saturday night stay etc), with a corresponding range of fares and restrictions – the cheapest are generally nonrefundable returns with restrictions on departure times and the length of stay. For some bizarre reason, one-way tickets generally cost more than returns, so if you're only going one way it still pays to look for a cheap return. There are often special deals on offer, so always check out the website. A standard 2nd-class return ticket from London to Paris with a minimum one-night stay costs between UK£59 and UK£159. Tickets are available direct from Eurostar; from travel agencies; at St Pancras, Ebbsfleet and Ashford; from other UK mainline stations; and from **Rail Europe** (☎ in the UK 08448 484 064; www.raileurope.co.uk), which also sells other European rail tickets.

You can take a bike on Eurostar as part of your luggage only if it's in a bike bag. Otherwise it must go as registered baggage, for which there's a UK£20 fee.

The **Eurotunnel vehicle service** (☎ UK 08705 35 35 35, France 0810 63 03 04; www.eurotunnel.com) operates between Folkestone and Calais. Trains run 24 hours a day, every day of the year, with up to three departures an hour.

To save money it makes sense to book in advance, although it is possible to drive into the terminal, buy a ticket and get on the next train. Fares range from UK£49 to UK£199 one way for a car, including all passengers, unlimited luggage and taxes. Note that both terminals are directly linked to motorways (the M20 in the UK and the A16 in France) and both have petrol stations.

Bicycles can be taken on only two trains per day and they must be booked 24 hours in advance. The standard fares for cyclists are UK£16/32 for a single/return.

SEA

Not surprisingly, the Mediterranean has an extensive ferry network. Whether you're travelling south from the UK or north from North Africa, ferry options are available. For information on timetables, routes, ports and prices, check out **aferry** (www.aferry.to).

Africa

To enter Europe from North Africa there are regular ferries from Morocco to Spain and France, and from Tunisia to Italy and France. Of Morocco's Mediterranean ports, the busiest is Tangier, from where ferries sail for the Spanish ports of Algeciras and Tarifa, and the French port of Sète. Ferries are often filled to capacity in summer, so book well in advance if you're taking a vehicle across.

Ferry companies operating to/from North Africa include the following:

Acciona Trasmediterránea (☎ in Spain 902 454645; www.trasmediterranea.es) Services from Morocco to Spain, including Tangier to Algeciras; Ceuta to Algeciras; Nador to Almería; and Melilla to Almería and Málaga. There are also services from Ghazaouet (Algeria) to Almería.

SNCM (☎ in France 08 36 672 100; www.sncm.fr) Services from Tunisia (Tunis) and Algeria (Algiers, Oran, Béjaia, Skikda and Annaba) to France (Marseille).

See country chapters for more information.

UK

In recent years competition from budget airlines and Channel Tunnel rail links has hit the cross-Channel ferry business hard, forcing operators to cut routes and reduce fares.

There are several UK–France ferry routes. The quickest, busiest and most expensive is Dover to Calais (75 to 90 minutes), but Newhaven to Dieppe (four hours), Poole to Cherbourg (4½ to 6½ hours) and Portsmouth to Cherbourg (5½ hours) are also popular. See p850 and p339 for more information on ferries between the UK and Spain, and the UK and France, respectively.

Fares depend on the usual mix of factors – the time of day/year, the flexibility of the ticket and, if you're driving, the length of your vehicle. Vehicle tickets include the driver and often up to five passengers free. There are also plenty of reductions on off-peak crossings and advance-purchase tickets. On most routes there is generally little price advantage in buying a return ticket rather than two singles. To compare fares check out the website of **Ferry Savers** (www.ferrysavers.com).

Rail-pass-holders are entitled to discounts or free travel on some lines, and most ferry companies give discounts to drivers with disabilities.

Major ferry companies include the following:

Brittany Ferries (☎ 0871 244 0744; www.brittany-ferries.com) Services from Portsmouth to Caen, Cherbourg and St Malo (all France), and Santander (Spain); from Poole to Cherbourg (France); and from Plymouth to Roscoff (France) and Santander (Spain).

Condor Ferries (☎ 0845 609 1024; www.condorferries.co.uk) Services to France, including Portsmouth to Cherbourg; Poole to St-Malo; and Weymouth to St-Malo.

Norfolk Line (☎ 0844 847 50 42; www.norfolkline.com) Ferries from Dover to Dunkirk (France).

P&O Ferries (☎ 08716 645 645; www.poferries.com) Ferries from Dover to Calais (France); and Portsmouth to Bilbao (Spain).

SeaFrance (☎ France 03 21 17 70 33; www.seafrance.net) From Dover to Calais (France).

Transmanche Ferries (☎ 0800 917 12 01; www.transmancheferries.com) Services to France, including Dover to Dieppe and Boulogne; Newhaven to Dieppe; and Portsmouth to Le Havre.

USA

Unless you've got a real desire to see the Atlantic close up or hate flying, then sailing from the USA doesn't make much sense. It's slow (typically between seven and 13 days) and not especially cheap. If you're determined to test your sea legs, however, you've got two choices: you can either sign up for an expensive passage on a cruise ship, or you can hop on a freighter as a paying passenger. Freighters are cheaper, more frequent and offer more routes.

Freighters usually carry up to 12 passengers (more than 12 would require a doctor to be on board), with passage typically costing between US$80 and US$140 per day. Vehicles can often

BORDER CROSSINGS

Passage between the region's Schengen countries (France, Greece, Italy, Malta, Portugal, Slovenia and Spain) involves no border controls, and it's quite possible to pass from one country to another without even stopping. That said, spot checks are not unusual, particularly on trains, and individual countries are within their rights to reinstate controls if they feel the security situation warrants it.

Elsewhere in the region there are no special problems. Individual country chapters list border crossings, including those between Albania and Montenegro; between Montenegro, Bosnia and Hercegovina (BiH) and Croatia; and between Croatia and Slovenia.

be included for an additional fee. If you're not travelling with a car, you'll need to organise transport from the port to the centre of town – ask the port agent (who'll be on board when the vessel docks) to arrange a taxi for you. Note also that you'll need to be flexible, as shipping schedules can change at very short notice due to weather conditions, delays in cargo loading, port congestion etc. Sea sickness pills are probably a good idea, as many cargo ships are not fitted with stabilisers.

If you're still interested, **Strand Travel** (☎ in the UK 020-7010 9290; www.strandtravel.co.uk) is a good source of information, as is **A la Carte Freighter Travel** (www.freighter-travel.com).

GETTING AROUND

Getting around Mediterranean Europe poses no great difficulties. There's a comprehensive transport network, and relations between countries are generally good. Ensure that you have a valid passport and check any visa requirements before travelling – see p955 and individual country directories.

AIR

Flying around Mediterranean Europe is definitely an option. The effect that the global recession will have on low-cost flying is unclear, although lower fares are a possibility as airlines attempt to induce people back on to their planes. There are currently 42 budget European airlines operating out of 336 airports, and with a credit card, access to the internet and a little patience, you've a pretty good chance of finding a cheap flight. But while budget airlines offer fares that the bigger airlines struggle to compete with (even if economic necessity has forced many to try), they rarely provide much in the way of comfort or service. On-flight food, hold baggage, airport check-in, priority boarding – these are all things you might be charged extra for. When booking online, always ensure that you untick any add-on options you don't want, as the default page settings of many airline websites have them automatically ticked.

Another consideration when flying low cost is that many budget carriers use provincial airports that might be some way from your destination city. For example, Ryanair's Venice flights actually land at Treviso, which is some 30km from the lagoon city. If you're arriving late at night, make sure you have checked up on transport options into town, otherwise you could end up forking out for an expensive taxi ride. On the whole, though, the region's main airports are well connected to city centres via dedicated shuttle services or public transport links.

For tips on finding tickets, see p958; for details about fares and routes to specific countries, see the Transport sections in the individual country chapters.

If you're planning to do a lot of flying in the region and prefer to sort out your transport before you leave, check out the European air passes that many major airlines offer. They are generally only available to non-Europeans, who must purchase them in conjunction with a long-haul international return ticket. Typically, they involve the purchase of flight coupons (usually around US$60 to US$200 each) for travel between a number of European destinations.

The following are the main European passes:

Europe by Air Pass (www.europebyair.com) Valid for one-way travel between 150 European cities, the non-refundable coupons cost US$99 to US$129 per flight. They are only available to US and Canadian residents, but are valid for 120 days and are very flexible – you can decide where and when to use them as you go along. Airport taxes are not included.

Oneworld Visit Europe Pass (www.oneworld.com) Available to non-Europeans who buy an intercontinental ticket with a Oneworld member airline. There's a minimum of two coupons (€55 to €240), although you must only confirm the first flight when you buy. Valid on routes between 160 cities.

Skyteam Europe Pass (www.skyteam.com) Flight coupons (US$60 to US$205) are valid for flights in 44 countries. There's a minimum of three coupons but no maximum. The pass is available with purchase of an intercontinental flight with any of SkyTeam's 11 member carriers or three associate airlines.

Star Alliance European Air Pass (www.staralliance.com) When you buy a round-trip international ticket with a Star Alliance operator you can buy a minimum of three and a maximum of 10 coupons (from US$85) for one-way flights between 44 European countries. Coupons, the first of which you must reserve when you buy the pass, are valid for three months.

BICYCLE

Although cycling is a popular sport in France, Spain, and Italy, as a means of everyday transport it is not particularly common in Mediterranean Europe. Outside certain areas there are very few dedicated cycle lanes, and drivers tend to regard cyclists as an oddity. Poor road conditions, particularly in the Eastern European countries, and mountainous terrain provide further obstacles.

There are no special road rules for cyclists, although it's advisable to carry a helmet, lights and a basic repair kit. This might contain spare brake and gear cables, spanners, Allen keys, spare spokes and some strong adhesive tape. Take a good lock and make sure you use it when you leave your bike unattended.

Transporting your bike to the region poses no great problems. Different airlines apply different rules – some insist that you pack it in a bike bag, others simply require you to remove the pedals and deflate the tyres, some even sell specially designed bike boxes. Remember that the bike's weight will be included in your luggage allowance.

Bikes can generally be carried on slower trains, subject to a small supplementary fee. On fast trains they might need to be sent as registered luggage and will probably end up on a different train from the one you take.

In the UK, **European Bike Express** (☎ 01430 422 111; www.bike-express.co.uk) is a coach service on which cyclists can travel with their bikes. It runs in the summer from Stokesley in north-east England to France and northern Spain, with pick-up and drop-off points en route. Return fares range from UK£214 to UK£234; singles cost UK£129. Members of the **Cyclists' Touring Club** (CTC; ☎ 0844 736 8450; www.ctc.org.uk; membership adult/student/senior UK£36/12/22.50) qualify for a discount of UK£10 on return fares. The CTC can also offer advice and organise tours for you.

Bike hire is available throughout the region – tourist offices can usually direct you to rental outlets. See the country chapters for details.

There are plenty of shops selling new and secondhand bikes, although you'll need a specialist outlet for a touring bike. European prices are quite high; expect to pay from €100 for a new bike.

For more information on cycling, see p942, p968, and individual country chapters.

BOAT

Ships have been ferrying people around the Mediterranean for thousands of years. Not surprisingly, the region's modern ferry network is comprehensive, covering all corners of the region. There are routes between Morocco, Spain and France; between Italy, Spain, Greece, Croatia, Turkey and Malta; and between the hundreds of Mediterranean islands. See the relevant country chapters for further details. Popular routes get very busy in summer, so try to book ahead.

The following are the major Mediterranean companies and the main routes they serve:

Acciona Trasmediterránea (☎ in Spain 902 454645; www.trasmediterranea.es) Spanish company with services from Barcelona to Ibiza, Maó and Palma de Mallorca, and Civitavecchia and Livorno (both Italy); from Valencia to Palma de Mallorca, Maó and Ibiza; and from Algeciras to Ceuta and Tangier (both Morocco).

Agoudimos (☎ in Greece 210 414 1300, in Italy 0831 52 90 91; www.agoudimos-lines.com) Services from Bari (Italy) to Igoumenitsa, Patra and Corfu (all Greece).

Corsica Ferries (☎ in Corsica 04 95 32 95 95, in Italy 199 400 500; http://corsica-ferries.it) Services from Bastia (Corsica) to Toulon (France), Nice (France), Savona (Italy) and Livorno (Italy); and from Golfo Aranci (Sardinia) to Civitavecchia and Livorno (both Italy).

Grandi Navi Veloci (☎ in Italy 010 209 45 91; www.gnv.it) Services from Genoa (Italy) to Barcelona (Spain), Porto Torres (Sardinia), Olbia (Sardinia) and Palermo (Sicily); and from Palermo to Malta.

Grimaldi Ferries (☎ in Italy 081 496 444, in Spain 902 531 333; www.grimaldi-ferries.com) Services from Barcelona (Spain) to Civitavecchia (Italy), Livorno (Italy), and Porto Torres (Sardinia); and from Toulon (France) to Civitavecchia (Italy).

HML Ferries/Endeavor Lines (☎ in Italy 0831 52 85 31; www.hml.it) Ferry services from Brindisi (Italy) to

Igoumenitsa, Patra, Corfu, Kefallonia and the Ionian Islands (all Greece).

Jadrolinija (☎ in Croatia 051-666 111; www.jadrolinija.hr) Services from Ancona (Italy) to Split (Croatia); and from Bari (Italy) to Dubrovnik (Croatia).

Marmara Lines (☎ in Italy 071 207 61 65, in Turkey 0232-712 22 23; www.marmaralines.com) Links Çeşme (Turkey) with Brindisi and Ancona (both Italy).

Minoan Lines (☎ in Italy 041 504 12 01, in Greece 210 4145700; www.minoan.gr) Ferries from Ancona (Italy) to Igoumenitsa and Patra (both Greece); and from Venice (Italy) to Corfu, Igoumenitsa and Patra (all Greece).

SNAV (☎ in Italy 081 428 55 55; www.snav.it) Italian company with services from Ancona to Split (Croatia); Brindisi to Corfu (Greece); and Naples to Olbia (Sardinia), and Palermo and the Aeolian Islands (all Sicily).

Superfast Ferries (☎ in Italy 071 207 02 40; www.superfast.com) Services from Ancona (Italy) to Igoumenitsa and Patra (both Greece); and from Bari (Italy) to Igoumenitsa, Patra and Corfu (all Greece).

Tirrenia (☎ in Italy 892 123; www.tirrenia.it) Italian company with services from Genoa to Porto Torres and Olbia (both Sardinia); Civitavecchia to Olbia, Arbatax and Cagliari (all Sardinia); Bari to Durrës (Albania); and Naples to Palermo (Sicily) and Cagliari.

BUS

Travelling by bus is generally the cheapest way of getting around the region, although it's neither comfortable nor particularly quick. In some of the eastern countries, including Bosnia and Hercegovina (BiH), Croatia and Montenegro, the rail networks are limited and buses tend to be quicker than trains, if more expensive. Buses also cover more routes, especially away from the main coastal areas; in mountainous countries (eg Albania and Greece) they are sometimes the only option.

Eurolines (www.eurolines.com) consists of 32 European coach operators serving 500 destinations throughout Europe and Morocco. Country contact details are as follows:

Bosnia & Hercegovina (☎ 033-21 12 82)
Croatia (☎ 051-66 03 22)
France (☎ 0892 8990 91)
Italy (☎ 055 35 70 59)
Morocco (☎ 022 43 82 82)
Spain (☎ 934 904 000)
Turkey (☎ 444 18 88)

In conjunction with Eurolines, the Moroccan national bus line, **Compagnie des Transports Marocains** (CTM; www.ctm.co.ma), operates buses from Spain, France and northern Italy to most large Moroccan towns.

London-based **Busabout** (www.busabout.com) runs buses that complete three loops (northern, southern and western) around Europe, stopping off at the major cities. The western and southern loops include cities in Italy, France, Spain. Note, however, that you don't simply buy a ticket from A to B; rather, you pay for unlimited travel within a specified loop, allowing you to hop off at any scheduled stop, then resume with a later bus. See below for ticket information.

Busabout buses are often oversubscribed, so book each sector to avoid being stranded. Departures are every two days from May to October.

See the individual country chapters for further information about long-distance buses.

Bus Passes

Bus passes make sense if you want to cover a lot of ground as cheaply as possible. However, they're not always as extensive or flexible as rail passes, and to get your money's worth you'll be spending a lot of time crammed into a bus seat.

The **Eurolines Pass** (www.eurolines-pass.com) covers 40 European cities. Most of the trips must be international, although a few internal journeys are possible between major cities. There are two passes: one valid for 15 days (low/high season adult €199/329, under 26 €169/279) and one valid for 30 days (low/high season adult €299/439, under 26 €229/359).

Busabout (www.busabout.com) offer various tickets. A pass for a single loop costs UK£329/315 per adult/student; two loops costs UK£569/545. The Flexitrip Pass allows you to choose where you want to go and buy tickets (flexistops) for those destinations; you can then add extra flexistops as you go along. The pass is valid for the entire operating season (May to October) and costs UK£289/279 per adult/student for six flexistops. Discounts are available for early booking.

For more information on Busabout tours, see p968.

Costs & Reservations

Booking a seat in advance is not usually obligatory, but if you know when you want to travel it makes sense to do so. In summer it's always advisable to book on popular routes.

As a rough guide, a one-way bus ticket from Paris to Rome costs €90, and from Madrid to Lisbon costs €48.

CAR & MOTORCYCLE

Driving brings its own pleasures and pains. Once you've got used to driving on the right and mastered the local driving habits, you'll begin to enjoy the increased flexibility that a car or motorcycle offers. On the other hand, you'll often have to deal with congestion, one-way systems, traffic-free zones and nonexistent city parking. In winter, ice and fog can prove hazardous, particularly in mountainous areas such as Albania and BiH, where roads are badly signposted and often in poor condition.

Tolls are charged on motorways (*autoroutes, autostrade* etc) in many Mediterranean countries, including Croatia, France, Greece, Italy, Portugal, Slovenia, Spain and Turkey. You can generally pay by cash or credit card, and in some cases you can avoid the queues altogether by buying a prepaid card. See individual chapters for details.

Mediterranean Europe is well suited to motorcycle touring, as it has an active motorcycling scene and plenty of panoramic roads. On ferries, motorcyclists can sometimes be squeezed in without a reservation, although booking ahead is advisable in peak travelling periods. Take note of local customs about parking on pavements.

Useful motoring resources:

British Motorcyclists Federation (☎ in the UK 0116-279 5112; www.bmf.co.uk) Click on the Touring link for information on all aspects of European touring, including specialist tour operators, recommended maps and updated European fuel prices.

Idea Merge (www.ideamerge.com/motoeuropa) An extensive US guide to motoring in Europe, with information on renting, leasing and purchasing, and specific country-by-country details.

International Motorcyclists Tour Club (www.imtc.org.uk) Provides practical touring advice (what bike to use, what gear to take, how to carry it etc) and loads of links to other motorbike sites.

Bringing Your Own Vehicle

Bringing your own vehicle into the region is fairly straightforward if you're approaching it from elsewhere in mainland Europe. In addition to your vehicle registration document you'll need a valid driving licence and proof of third-party (liability) insurance (p966). Shipping a vehicle from the US or Canada, however, is an expensive and time-consuming business that will generally cost from US$3000 return for a car and from US$350 for a motorbike. For further information consult **Idea Merge** (www.ideamerge.com/motoeuropa/car_leasing_europe_car_leases_france.html).

Some countries require you to carry certain pieces of equipment. For example, you'll need a first-aid kit in Croatia, Greece and Slovenia; a warning triangle in Cyprus, Greece, Italy, Portugal and Slovenia; a fire extinguisher in Greece and Turkey; and a spare bulb kit in Croatia and Spain.

Note that there's sometimes a maximum time limit (typically six or 12 months) for keeping your car in a foreign country.

For more information contact the **RAC** (www.rac.co.uk) or **AA** (www.theaa.com) in the UK, or the **AAA** (www.aaa.com) in the USA.

Driving Licence

A European Union driving licence is valid for driving throughout Europe. However, if you've got an old-style green UK licence or a licence issued by a non-EU country you will need an International Driving Permit (IDP). Valid for 12 months, these are inexpensive (about US$15 or UK£5.50) and are available from your national automobile association – take along a passport photo and your home driving licence. When driving in Europe, you should always carry the your home licence with the IDP, as the IDP is not valid on its own.

An IDP is required in Albania and recommended in Montenegro, Morocco and Turkey.

Fuel & Spare Parts

Surges in international oil prices saw fuel prices go through the roof in 2008. Since then things have calmed down a bit and prices have returned to a more normal level. As a rough guide, reckon on anything from €0.83 in Greece to €1.13 in France for 1L of unleaded fuel; and from €0.88 in Spain to €1.13 in Italy for diesel. You can get updated petrol prices for France, Greece, Italy, Portugal, Slovenia and Spain at **AA Roadwatch** (www.aaroadwatch.ie/eupetrolprices).

Prices tend to be higher at motorway service stations and lowest at supermarket petrol stations. You'll also save by filling up in the cheapest countries (for example, Spain rather than France) and in the cool of the morning or evening, when fuel is more dense.

You should have no great problems getting spare parts.

Hire

You shouldn't have many problems finding a car-hire agency. **Avis** (www.avis.com), **Budget** (www.budget.com), **Europcar** (www.europcar.com) and **Hertz** (www.hertz.com) have offices throughout the region, and there are any number of local firms. The international agencies are generally more expensive, but guarantee reliable service and a good standard of vehicle. Usually you'll have the option of returning the car to a different outlet at the end of the rental period.

Regulations vary but there's often a minimum hire age (typically 21 or 23) and sometimes a maximum age (usually about 65 or 70). The hire company might also insist that you've held your licence for at least a year. You'll almost certainly need a credit card.

If you know in advance that you want a car, you'll get a better deal arranging it at home. Walking into a hire office, particularly one at an airport, and asking for a car on the spot means you'll pay over the odds, even allowing for special weekend deals. Fly-drive packages and other programs are also worth considering. A useful online resource is **TravelJungle** (www.traveljungle.co.uk), which finds the best rates available for your destination.

Hiring through a broker can cut costs. Reliable operators include the following:

Autos Abroad (☎ UK 0845 029 1945; www.autosabroad.com)
Holiday Autos (☎ USA 866 392 9288 24; www.holidayautos.com)
Kemwel Holiday Autos (☎ USA 877 820 0668; www.kemwel.com)

As an approximate guide, expect to pay about €40 per day for a small car and from €210 per week. Americans should note that there are very few automatic cars in Mediterranean Europe and that they cost a lot more to hire. Check individual chapters for country-specific prices.

You can combine train and car travel with a rail-and-drive pass. The Eurail Drive Pass is a typical option, allowing four or 10 days of 1st-class train travel and two days of Avis or Hertz car hire. Available to non-European residents, it's valid for travel in 21 European countries over a two-month period. Prices for two adults start at US$992/1554 for four/10 days.

No matter where or what you hire, it's imperative that you understand exactly what's included in your rental agreement (collision waiver, unlimited mileage etc). Most agreements provide basic insurance that you can supplement by buying additional coverage. This supplemental insurance is often expensive if bought directly from the hire agency. As an alternative, check if your home car insurance covers foreign hire or if your credit-card company offers insurance. If you're going to be crossing national borders, make sure your insurance policy is valid from one country to the next.

For longer stays, leasing can work out cheaper. The **Renault Eurodrive** (www.renault-eurodrive.com) scheme provides new cars for non-EU residents for a period of between 17 and 170 days. Under this arrangement, a Renault Clio Campus for a month in France costs about €850, including comprehensive insurance and roadside assistance. In the US, **Kemwel Holiday Autos** (www.kemwel.com) arranges similar deals.

Motorcycle and moped hire is common in Italy, Spain, Greece and the south of France. See the Transport section in individual country chapters for further details.

Insurance

To drive your own vehicle in Europe you'll need third-party insurance – most UK motor insurance policies automatically provide this for EU countries – and an International Insurance Certificate, commonly called a Green Card. When you get this, check with your insurance company that it covers all the countries you intend to visit, and if you're driving in Turkey, make sure that it covers both the European and Asian parts.

In the event of an accident a European Accident Statement form is a useful document to have. Available from your insurance company, it allows each party at an accident to record identical information for insurance purposes. The **Association of British Insurers** (☎ 020 7600 3333; www.abi.org.uk) can give more information. Never sign statements that you don't understand – insist on a translation and only sign it if it's acceptable.

Taking out a European motoring assistance policy to cover roadside assistance and emergency repair is a good idea. In the UK, both the AA and the RAC offer such services. The price varies depending on the area where you'll be travelling, the age of your car and the number of passengers, but is typically between UK£40 and UK£55 per week. Non-Europeans might find it cheaper to arrange international coverage with their national motoring organisation. Also ask about free services offered by affiliated organisations around Mediterranean Europe. See individual country Transport sections for information on automobile associations.

Purchase

Buying a car in Mediterranean Europe is generally not worth the hassle. The biggest challenge is to get round the law that bans non-EU residents from registering a car in the EU. Without registering you cannot get insurance, and without proof of insurance you cannot buy a car. The only practical way round this is to convince a resident or relative to buy the car for you.

If you want a left-hand-drive vehicle (as is the norm in most of Continental Europe), prices are usually best in Greece and France. Paperwork can be tricky wherever you buy, and many countries have compulsory roadworthiness checks on older vehicles.

Road Conditions

Road conditions vary enormously across the region. At best, you'll find well-maintained four- or six-lane dual carriageways or motorways. At worst, you'll be driving on rough, badly signposted single-lane tracks. You will, for example, encounter some pretty dodgy roads in Albania and BiH, although things are improving all the time. Minor roads might also be less than smooth in Morocco, Malta and Greece.

Many of the region's motorways are toll roads, requiring payment on exit.

Road Rules

Motoring organisations can supply members with country-by-country information on road rules. Online, Idea Merge has details on driving in Croatia, France, Greece, Italy, Portugal, Slovenia, Spain and Turkey.

With the exceptions of Malta and Cyprus, driving in Mediterranean Europe is on the right, and cars are set up with the steering wheel on the left. If you're bringing over a UK or Irish right-hand-drive vehicle you should adjust its headlights (which are angled differently to those in Mediterranean Europe) to avoid blinding oncoming traffic at night (a simple solution on older headlights is to cover up a triangular section of the lens with tape). Note that some countries require you to have your headlights on even when driving during the day.

In countries where you drive on the right, unless otherwise indicated you should always give way to cars entering a junction from the left.

Take care with speed limits, as they vary from country to country. You may be surprised at the apparent disregard for speed limits (and traffic regulations in general) in some places, but as a visitor it's always best to be cautious. Random police checks are common in some countries and many driving infringements are subject to on-the-spot fines. If you're clobbered with a fine, always ask for a receipt.

Drink-driving laws are strict, with the blood-alcohol concentration (BAC) limit generally between 0.05% and 0.08%.

On two-wheel vehicles, the wearing of helmets is compulsory everywhere in Mediterranean Europe. It's also recommended that motorcyclists use their headlights during the day.

HITCHING

Hitching is more common in northern Europe than in Mediterranean countries, and although it is possible, you'll need to be patient. It's never entirely safe, however, and we don't recommend it. If you do decide to go for it, there are a few, simple steps you can take to minimise the risks.

- Travel around in pairs – ideally a man and a woman together. A woman hitching on her own is taking a big risk.
- Let someone know where you're going and when you'll be on the road. If possible, carry a mobile phone.
- When a driver stops, ask where they're going before getting in. This gives you the time to size up the driver and, if you don't like the look of them, to politely decline the ride.
- Don't let the driver put your backpack in the boot; if possible, keep it with you in the car.

Don't try to hitch from city centres – take public transport to suburban exit routes. Hitching is often illegal on motorways, so stand on the slip roads or approach drivers at petrol stations and truck stops. Look presentable and cheerful, and make a cardboard sign indicating the road you want to take. A sign will also mean you're less likely to use the wrong gesture – the thumbs-up sign, for example, means 'up yours' in Sardinia. Never hitch where traffic passes too quickly (drivers will want to check you out before stopping, so don't wear sunglasses) or where drivers can't stop without causing an obstruction.

If your itinerary includes a ferry crossing, try to score a ride before the ferry rather than after, as vehicle tickets sometimes include all passengers free of charge.

It is sometimes possible to arrange a lift in advance: scan student notice boards in colleges, or contact car-sharing agencies such as **Allostop Provoya** (☎ France 01 53 20 42 42; www.allostop.net, in French) in Paris.

Online resources include **BUG** (www.bugeurope.com), which has some useful tips; **Hitchhikers** (www.hitchhikers.org), which helps organise ride-share options; and **Digihitch** (www.digihitch.com), a comprehensive site with hitchers' forums, links and country-specific information.

LOCAL TRANSPORT

The region's local transport network is comprehensive and efficient. Clearly, services may be irregular in remote rural regions, but wait long enough and sooner or later a bus will pass.

In many places you have to buy your ticket before you get on the bus/boat/train. Once onboard you then have to validate it if the driver hasn't already checked it. It's often tempting not to do this – many locals don't appear to – but if you're caught with an unvalidated ticket you risk a fine.

If you're going to use public transport a lot, check out the daily, weekly and monthly passes available.

Boat

In some parts of the region, jumping on a ferry is as common as taking a bus. In Venice, *vaporetti* (small passenger ferries) ply the city's canals, ferrying tourists and locals alike, while in İstanbul ferries are the cheapest way of getting around the city.

Bus

On city buses you usually buy your ticket in advance from a kiosk or machine, and then validate it upon boarding. See the country chapters and individual city sections for more details on local bus routes.

Metro

All the region's major capitals (Athens, Paris, Madrid and Rome) have metro systems, as do several other large cities (Milan, Barcelona, İstanbul). It's often quicker to travel underground, but it can get unpleasantly hot and crowded, especially in summer rush hours.

Taxi

Taxis are generally metered and rates are uniformly high. There are also add-on charges for things such as luggage, time of day, pick-up location and extra passengers. As a rule, always insist on a metered fare rather than an agreed price, as it minimises the risk of unpleasant disagreements on arrival.

To catch a cab you'll usually have to phone for one or queue at a taxi rank, which are often found outside train stations and big hotels.

TOURS

Tours exist for all ages, interests and budgets. Specialist operators offer everything from tours of the region's gardens to island-hopping cruises, walking holidays and adventure-sports packages.

Established outfits include the following:

Busabout (www.busabout.com) Best known for its European bus tours (see p964), London-based Busabout also offers tours to Italy (UK£159), Spain (UK£439) and Morocco (from UK£339), and cruises in Greece (from UK£199) and Croatia (from UK£389).

CBT Tours (☎ in the USA 800 736 24 53; www.cbttours.com) A US operator specialising in walking and cycling holidays, including a six-day bike ride through Tuscany.

Contiki (www.contiki.com) Contiki runs a range of European tours for 18 to 35-year olds, including city breaks, camping trips and island-hopping journeys. Also has its own resort on Mykonos.

Ramblers Holidays (☎ UK 01707 33 11 33; www.ramblers holidays.co.uk) A British-based outfit that offers hiking holidays, ski packages and much more.

Saga Holidays (☎ in the UK 0800 096 00 74; www.saga.co.uk) Serving people aged over 50, Saga sells everything from travel insurance to bus tours, river cruises and special-interest holidays.

Top Deck (☎ in the UK 020 8987 3300; www.topdeck travel.co.uk) A youth specialist, this London-based outfit offers everything from Croatian coastal cruises to festival weekends and tapas trails.

Many national tourist offices offer organised trips. These range from one-hour city tours to circular excursions taking several days. They often work out more expensive than going it alone, but are sometimes worth it if you are pressed for time. A short city tour will give you a quick overview of the place and can be a good way to begin your visit.

TRAIN

There's never been a better time to jump on a train. Environmental concerns surrounding flying and its contribution to climate change have led to a revival in long-distance train travel. Mediterranean Europe's rail network is comprehensive, and trains are comfortable, frequent and generally punctual. You'll have no trouble travelling between the region's main cities, although if you want to get off the beaten track, particularly in the eastern Balkan countries, you'll probably find the bus a better option.

To check train schedules in any European country get hold of the **Thomas Cook European Timetable** (www.thomascooktimetables.com), which lists train, bus and ferry times. Updated monthly, the timetable (UK£13.99) can be ordered online or bought from Thomas Cook outlets in the UK. Another useful publication is the *European Planning & Rail Guide,* available to US residents from **Budget Europe Travel** (☎ in the USA 800 441 9413; www.budgeteuropetravel.com).

The speed and cost of your journey depends on the type of train you take. Fast trains include the TGV in France, the AVE in Spain and the Eurostar Italia Alta Velocità in Italy. Extra charges usually apply on fast trains, and it's often obligatory to make seat reservations. See individual country chapters for details.

Overnight trains – which save you a night's accommodation bill – usually offer a choice of couchettes or sleepers. Couchettes are mixed sex, and are fitted with four or six bunks, for which pillows, sheets and blankets are supplied. Sleepers are for between one and four passengers, and are more expensive. They are generally single sex, come with towels and toiletries, and have a washbasin in the compartment. On some routes, you can now get a private room with an en suite shower and toilet.

Most long-distance trains have a dining car or an attendant with a snack trolley. If possible, buy your food before travelling, as on-board prices tend to be high.

You should be quite safe travelling on most trains in Mediterranean Europe, but it pays to be security-conscious nonetheless. Keep an eye on your luggage at all times (especially when stopping at stations) and lock the compartment doors at night.

Note that European trains sometimes split en route in order to service two destinations, so even if you're on the right train, make sure you're also in the correct carriage.

You'll find as much train info as you can digest at **The Man in Seat 61** (www.seat61.com).

Classes

On most trains there are 1st- and 2nd-class carriages. As a rough guide, a 1st-class ticket generally costs about double the price of a 2nd-class ticket. In 1st-class carriages there are fewer seats and more luggage space. On overnight trains, your comfort depends less on which class you're travelling than on whether you've booked a regular seat, couchette or sleeper. See left for information on the differences between a couchette and a sleeper.

Costs

Rail travel throughout the region is pretty economical, especially if you're used to expensive British trains. How much you pay depends on the type of train you take (high-speed trains are more expensive), whether you travel 1st or 2nd class, the time of year (or even the time of day) when you travel, and whether or not you have a seat, a couchette or a sleeper. As a rough guide, a ticket from Barcelona to Madrid costs €110 to €30 (€41 overnight); from Paris to Marseille costs €55 to €80; and from Rome to Florence costs €27.50 to €36.

Reservations

On many local services it's not possible to reserve a seat – just jump on and sit where you like. On faster, long-distance trains it's sometimes obligatory to make a reservation; regardless of whether it's necessary, it's often a good idea to do so, especially on popular routes in peak periods. Most international trains require a seat reservation, and you'll also need to book sleeping accommodation on overnight trains. Bookings can be made for a small, nonrefundable fee (usually about €3) when you buy your ticket.

Supplements and reservation costs are not covered by most rail passes.

Train Passes

Your first consideration when considering a rail pass should be 'do I really need one?' Unless you're planning to cover a lot of ground in a short space of time, you'd probably do as well buying regular train tickets, especially given all the advance-purchase deals, one-off promotions and special circular-route tickets available. Also, normal international tickets are valid for two months and allow you to stop as often as you like en route. However, rail passes do provide a degree of flexibility that many discount tickets do not.

Which pass you choose depends on a number of factors – how many countries you want to see, how flexible you want to be, and whether you want to go 1st or 2nd class – but the most important factor is where you hold residency. Non-European residents can buy Eurail passes; for European residents, there are the Inter-Rail passes.

Available online or at travel agents, passes vary in price, so shop around before committing yourself. Once you've purchased a pass, take care of it, as it cannot be replaced or refunded if it is lost or stolen. Passholders must always carry their passport for identification purposes.

Comprehensive information and online bookings are available at **Rail Europe** (www.raileurope.com, www.raileurope.co.uk) and **Rail Pass** (www.railpass.com).

EURAIL

Passes that are sold by **Eurail** (www.eurail.com) are available to non-European residents only, and are best bought before you leave home. You can buy them in Europe – provided you can prove you've been on the continent for less than six months – but sales outlets are limited and you'll pay up to 20% more than you would at home.

There are four types of pass – the Global Pass, Select Pass, Regional Pass and One Country Pass – which come in adult (over 26), 'saver' and youth (under 26) forms. Prices quoted here are for the adult and youth versions; savers, available for two to five people travelling together, cost about 15% less than adult passes. With adult passes, children aged three and under travel free, and kids aged between four and 11 travel for half price. Adult and saver passes provide 1st-class travel; the youth version is for 2nd class.

Global Pass (15 days/3 months adult US$686/1935, youth US$449/1259) This provides unlimited rail travel in 21 countries – including Croatia, France, Greece, Italy, Portugal, Slovenia and Spain – for five validity periods, which range from 15 days to three months. Alternatively, you can opt for 10 or 15 days' travel within a two-month period (10/15 days adult US$815/1069, youth US$529/695). The pass is valid on some ferries between Italy and Greece. Before using the pass for the first time, you'll need to have it validated at a ticket counter (for which you'll need your passport).

Select Pass (4 countries 5/6/8/10 days adult US$489/535/625/715, youth US$319/349/405/459) This allows travel between three, four or five bordering countries for five, six, eight or 10 days within a two-month period (the five-country pass also has a 15-day option). Countries covered include Croatia, France, Greece, Italy, Portugal, Montenegro, Slovenia and Spain.

For details of Eurail's Regional and One Country Passes, see below.

INTER-RAIL

Passes that are sold by **Inter-Rail** (www.interrail.net) are only available to European residents of at least six months' standing (passport identification is required). There are two types of pass: the Global Pass and the One Country Pass. Adult passes are available in 1st and 2nd class, while the youth passes (under 26) are for 2nd class only. Child fares are available for One Country Passes for kids between four and 11; kids aged under three travel free.

The Global Pass is valid for travel in 30 countries, including BiH, Croatia, France, Greece, Italy, Montenegro, Portugal, Slovenia, Spain and Turkey. You can opt for five days of travel in a 10-day period (adult/youth €249/159); 10 days in a 22-day period (adult/youth €359/239); 22 days of continuous travel (adult/youth €469/309); or one month of continuous travel (adult/youth €599/399). Before you start each trip, fill in the journey details on the provided form.

For details of Inter-Rail's One Country Passes, see below.

ONE COUNTRY & REGIONAL PASSES

If you're going to stay in one country or plan on concentrating on a particular area it makes sense to go for a One Country or Regional Pass, rather than the more expensive Global Passes. Both Eurail and Inter-Rail offer a variety of One Country Passes.

For non-Europeans, Eurail has 25 Regional Passes for Austria, Hungary, Slovenia and Croatia; France and Italy; France and Spain; Greece and Italy; and Spain and Portugal. Prices and conditions vary but, as an example, the France and Italy pass provides between four and 10 days' unlimited travel within a two-month period. It costs €399/519 per adult/youth for 10 days' travel.

The Balkan Flexipass gives five/10/15 days of 1st-class travel in a one-month period in Bulgaria, Greece, Macedonia, Montenegro, Romania, Serbia and Turkey. Reckon on US$539/324 per adult/youth for 15 days.

Eurail One Country passes are available for 17 countries, including Croatia, Greece, Italy, Portugal, Slovenia and Spain. The most popular pass, the Italy Pass, offers between three and 10 days of travel within a two-month period. Ten days costs €299/365 per adult/youth.

Most of these passes can only be purchased prior to arrival in the country concerned.

European residents are served by Inter-Rail, which has One Country Passes for 29 European countries. These provide between three and eight days of travel within a one-month period, with prices based on a geographic grouping system. As a rough guide, a pass for a Group 2 country, such as Italy, Spain costs €229/149 per adult/youth for eight days of travel.

SENIOR PASSES

Senior discounts are available on many routes, although they don't necessarily represent a saving over advance-purchase deals. Rail Europe sells a France Senior Pass (US$268) that allows for three days of 1st-class travel.

Health

CONTENTS

BEFORE YOU GO

Prevention is the key to staying healthy while abroad. Some predeparture planning will save trouble later. See your dentist before a long trip, carry a spare pair of contact lenses and glasses, and take your optical prescription with you. Bring medications in their original, clearly labelled containers. A signed and dated letter from your physician describing your medical conditions and medications, including generic names, is also a good idea. If you're carrying syringes or needles, be sure to have a physician's letter documenting their medical necessity.

INSURANCE

If you're an EU citizen, a **European Health Insurance Card** (EHIC; ☎ in the UK 0845 606 2030; www.ehic.org.uk) entitles you to cheaper, sometimes free, medical care in EU countries. It does not, however, cover you for nonemergencies or emergency repatriation. It's available from health centres or, in the UK, post offices; you can also apply by visiting the website. Citizens from other countries should find out if there is a reciprocal arrangement for free medical care between their country and the country visited. If you do need health insurance, consider a policy that covers you for the worst possible scenario, such as an accident requiring an emergency flight home. Find out in advance if your insurance plan will make payments directly to providers, or will reimburse you later for overseas health expenditures. The former option is generally preferable, as it doesn't require you to be out of pocket in a foreign country.

RECOMMENDED VACCINATIONS

No jabs are necessary for Mediterranean Europe. However, the World Health Organization (WHO) recommends that all travellers, regardless of their destination, should be covered for diphtheria, tetanus, measles, mumps, rubella and polio. Since most vaccines don't produce immunity until at least two weeks after they're given, visit a physician at least six weeks before departure.

INTERNET RESOURCES

The WHO's publication *International Travel and Health* (www.who.int/ith) is revised annually. Other useful websites include **MDtravelheath.com** (www.mdtravelhealth.com), which has travel-health recommendations for every country and is updated daily; **Fit for Travel** (www.fitfortravel.scot.nhs.uk), which provides general travel advice, **Age Concern** (www.ageconcern.org.uk), which has advice on travel for the elderly; and **Marie Stopes International** (www.mariestopes.org.uk), which has information on women's health and contraception.

FURTHER READING

Health Advice for Travellers (known also as the *T7.1* leaflet) is a leaflet by the Department of Health in the UK, available free from post offices. It contains some general information, legally required and recommended vaccines

WARNING

Codeine, which is commonly found in headache preparations, is banned in Greece; check labels carefully or risk prosecution. There are strict rules applying to the importation of medicines into Greece, so obtain a certificate from your doctor that outlines any medication you may have to carry into the country with you.

for different countries, reciprocal health agreements and an EHIC application form. Lonely Planet's *Travel with Children* includes advice on travel health for younger children.

IN TRANSIT

DEEP VEIN THROMBOSIS (DVT)

Blood clots may form in the legs during plane flights, chiefly because of prolonged immobility. The chief symptom of DVT is swelling or pain of the foot, ankle or calf, usually but not always on just one side. When a blood clot travels to the lungs, it may cause chest pain and breathing difficulties. Travellers with any of these symptoms should immediately seek medical attention.

To prevent the development of DVT on long flights you should walk about the cabin, contract the leg muscles while sitting, drink plenty of fluids and avoid alcohol and tobacco.

IN MEDITERRANEAN EUROPE

AVAILABILITY OF HEALTH CARE

Good health care is readily available, and for minor illnesses pharmacists can give valuable advice and sell over-the-counter medication. They can also advise when more specialised help is required and point you in the right direction. The standard of dental care is usually good; however, it is sensible to have a dental check-up before a long trip.

TRAVELLER'S DIARRHOEA

If you develop diarrhoea, be sure to drink plenty of fluids, preferably an oral rehydration solution such as Dioralyte. You should seek medical attention if diarrhoea is bloody, persists for more than 72 hours, or is accompanied by a fever, shaking, chills or severe abdominal pain.

ENVIRONMENTAL HAZARDS

Altitude Sickness

Experiencing a lack of oxygen at high altitudes (over 2500m) affects most people to some extent. Symptoms of acute mountain sickness (AMS) usually develop during the first 24 hours at altitude but may be delayed up to three weeks. Mild symptoms include headache, lethargy, dizziness, difficulty sleeping and loss of appetite. AMS may become more severe without warning and can be fatal. Severe symptoms include breathlessness, a dry cough (which may progress to the production of pink, frothy sputum), severe headache, lack of coordination and balance, confusion, irrational behaviour, vomiting, drowsiness and unconsciousness. There is no hard-and-fast rule as to what is too high: AMS has been fatal at 3000m, although 3500m to 4500m is the usual range.

Treat mild symptoms by resting at the same altitude until recovery, usually a day or two. Paracetamol or aspirin can be taken for headaches. If symptoms persist or become worse, however, *immediate descent is necessary;* even 500m can help. Drug treatments should never be used to avoid descent or to enable further ascent.

Diamox (acetazolamide) reduces the headache of AMS and helps the body acclimatise to the lack of oxygen. It is only available on prescription, and those who are allergic to the sulphonamide antibiotics may also be allergic to Diamox.

In the UK, fact sheets are available from **British Mountaineering Council** (177-79 Burton Rd, Manchester, M20 2BB).

Heat Exhaustion & Heatstroke

Heat exhaustion occurs when excessive fluid loss is combined with inadequate replacement of fluids and salt. Symptoms include headache, dizziness and tiredness. Dehydration is already happening by the time you feel thirsty – aim to drink sufficient water to produce pale, diluted urine. Replace lost fluids by drinking water and/or fruit juice, and cool the body with cold water and fans. Treat salt loss with salty fluids such as soup, or add a little more table salt to foods than usual.

Heatstroke is much more serious, resulting in irrational and hyperactive behaviour, and eventually loss of consciousness and death. Rapid cooling by spraying the body with water and fanning is ideal. Emergency fluid and electrolyte replacement by intravenous drip is recommended.

Insect Bites & Stings

Mosquitoes are found in most parts of Mediterranean Europe. They may not carry malaria, but they can cause irritation and infected bites. Use a DEET-based insect repellent.

Sandflies are found around the Mediterranean beaches. They usually cause only a nasty, itchy bite, but can carry a rare skin disorder called cutaneous leishmaniasis.

Water

Tap water is generally safe to drink, but in Eastern European countries it's best to stick to bottled water or purified water. Don't drink water from rivers or lakes, as it may contain bacteria or viruses that can cause diarrhoea or vomiting.

TRAVELLING WITH CHILDREN

Travellers with children should know how to treat minor ailments and when to seek medical treatment. Ensure the children are up to date with routine vaccinations, and discuss travel vaccines well before departure, as some are not suitable for children under one year.

WOMEN'S HEALTH

Travelling during pregnancy is usually possible, but always seek a medical check-up before planning your trip. The most risky times for travel are during the first 12 weeks of pregnancy and after 30 weeks.

SEXUAL HEALTH

Condoms are widely available in Mediterranean Europe; however, emergency contraception may not be, so take the necessary precautions. The **International Planned Parent Federation** (www.ippf.org) can advise about the availability of contraception in different countries.

When buying condoms, look for a European CE mark, which means they have been rigorously tested. Remember also to keep them in a cool, dry place so that they don't crack and perish.

Language

CONTENTS

This chapter has basic vocabulary and pronunciation tips to help you get around Mediterranean Europe. For more coverage of the languages included here, see Lonely Planet's *Mediterranean Europe* phrasebook, or one of the single-language phrasebooks.

ALBANIAN

PRONUNCIATION

Written Albanian is phonetically consistent and pronunciation shouldn't pose too many problems for English speakers. The **r** is trilled and each vowel in a diphthong is pronounced. Some Albanian letters differ from English:

ë often silent; at the beginning of a word it's as the 'a' in 'ago'
c as the 'ts' in 'bits'
ç as the 'ch' in 'church'
dh as the 'th' in 'this'
gj as the 'gy' in 'hogyard'
j as the 'y' in 'yellow'
q between 'ch' and 'ky', similar to the 'cu' in 'cure'
th as in 'thistle'
x as the 'dz' in 'adze'
xh as the 'j' in 'jewel'
zh as the 's' in 'pleasure'

ACCOMMODATION

camping ground *kamp pushimi*
hotel *hotel*
Do you have any rooms available? *A keni ndonjë dhomë të lirë?*
How much is it per night/person? *Sa kushton për një natë/ njeri?*
Does it include breakfast? *A e përfshin edhe mëngjesin?*

a single room *një dhomë më një krevat*
a double room *një dhomë më dy krevat*
one night *një natë*
two nights *dy natë*

CONVERSATION & ESSENTIALS

Hello. *Tungjatjeta./Allo.*
Goodbye. *Lamtumirë.* (polite)
Mirupafshim. (informal)
Yes. *Po.*
No. *Jo.*
Please. *Ju lutem.*
Thank you. *Ju falem nderit.*
That's fine. *Eshtë e mirë.*
You're welcome. *S'ka përse.*
Excuse me. *Me falni.*
Sorry. *Më vjen keq.*
Do you speak English? *A flisni anglisht?*
How much is it? *Sa kushton?*
What's your name? *Si quheni ju lutem?*
My name is ... *Unë quhem .../ Mua më quajnë ...*

EMERGENCIES – ALBANIAN

Help! *Ndihmë!*
Call a doctor! *Thirrni doktorin!*
Call the police! *Thirrni policinë!*
Go away! *Zhduku!/Largohuni!*
I'm lost. *Kam humbur rrugë.*

DIRECTIONS

Where is ...? *Ku është ...?*
Go straight ahead. *Shko drejt.*
Turn left. *Kthehu majtas.*
Turn right. *Kthehu djathtas.*
near *afër*
far *larg*

SHOPPING & SERVICES

a bank *një bankë*
a chemist/pharmacy *një farmaci*

SIGNS – ALBANIAN

Hyrje	Entrance
Dalje	Exit
Informim	Information
Hapur	Open
Mbyllur	Closed
Policia	Police
Stacioni i Policisë	Police Station
E Ndaluar	Prohibited
Nevojtorja	Toilets
Burra	Men
Gra	Women

the … embassy	*… ambasadën*
the market	*pazarin*
newsagency	*agjensia e lajmeve*
the post office	*postën*
the public toilet	*banja publike*
the stationers	*kartoleri*
the telephone centre	*centralin telefonik*
the tourist office	*zyrën e informimeve turistike*

What time does it open/close?	*Në ç'ore hapet/mbyllet*

TIME, DAYS & NUMBERS

What time is it?	*Sa është ora?*
today	*sot*
tomorrow	*nesër*
yesterday	*dje*
in the morning	*në mëngjes*
in the afternoon	*pas dreke*

Monday	*e hënë*
Tuesday	*e martë*
Wednesday	*e mërkurë*
Thursday	*e ënjte*
Friday	*e premte*
Saturday	*e shtunë*
Sunday	*e diel*

1	*një*
2	*dy*
3	*tre*
4	*katër*
5	*pesë*
6	*gjashtë*
7	*shtatë*
8	*tetë*
9	*nëntë*
10	*dhjetë*
100	*njëqind*
1000	*njëmijë*

TRANSPORT

What time does the … leave/arrive?	*Në ç'orë niset/arrin …?*
boat	*barka/lundra*
bus	*autobusi*
tram	*tramvaji*
train	*treni*

I'd like …	*Dëshiroj …*
a one-way ticket	*një biletë vajtje*
a return ticket	*një biletë kthimi*

1st class	*klas i parë*
2nd class	*klas i dytë*
timetable	*orar*
bus stop	*stacion autobusi*

CROATIAN & SERBIAN

PRONUNCIATION

The writing systems of Croatian and Serbian are phonetically consistent: letters are pronounced consistently from word to word. With regard to the position of stress, only one rule can be given: the last syllable of a word is never stressed. In most cases the accent falls on the first vowel in the word.

Serbian uses both the Cyrillic and Roman alphabets, so it's worth familiarising yourself with the former (see the boxed text, p977). Croatian uses the Roman alphabet.

The principal difference between Serbian and Croatian is in the pronunciation of the vowel 'e' in certain words. A long **e** in Serbian becomes **ije** in Croatian (eg *reka*, *rijeka* (river), and a short **e** in Serbian becomes **je** in Croatian, eg *pesma*, *pjesma* (song). Sometimes, however, the vowel 'e' is pronounced **e** in both languages, as in *selo* (village). There are also a number of variations in vocabulary between the two languages. Where significant differences occur, we've included both, with Croatian marked (C) and Serbian marked (S).

ACCOMMODATION

camping ground	*kamping*	кампинг
hotel	*hotel*	хотел
guest house	*privatno prenočište*	приватно преноћиште
youth hostel	*omladinsko prenočište*	омладинско преноћиште

LANGUAGE

SERBIAN & CROATIAN ALPHABETS

Cyrillic	Roman	English Pronunciation
А а	A a	as in 'rather'
Б б	B b	as in 'be'
В в	V v	as in 'vodka'
Г г	G g	as in 'go'
Д д	D d	as in 'do'
Ђ ђ	Đ đ	as the 'du' in British 'duty'
Е е	E e	as in 'there'
Ж ж	Ž ž	as the 's' in 'pleasure'
З з	Z z	as in 'zero'
И и	I i	as in 'machine'
Ј ј	J j	as the 'y' in 'young'
К к	K k	as in 'keg'
Л л	L l	as in 'let'
Љ љ	Lj lj	as the 'lli' in 'million'
М м	M m	as in 'map'
Н н	N n	as in 'no'
Њ њ	Nj nj	as the 'ny' in 'canyon'
О о	O o	as the 'aw' in 'shawl'
П п	P p	as in 'pop'
Р р	R r	as in 'rock'
С с	S s	as in 'safe'
Т т	T t	as in 'to'
Ћ ћ	Ć ć	as the 'tu' in 'future'
У у	U u	as in 'plume'
Ф ф	F f	as in 'fat'
Х х	H h	as in 'hot'
Ц ц	C c	as the 'ts' in 'cats'
Ч ч	Č č	as the 'ch' in 'chop'
Џ џ	Dž dž	as the 'j' in 'judge'
Ш ш	Š š	as the 'sh' in 'shoe'

Do you have any rooms available?
Imate li slobodne sobe?
Имате ли слободне собе?
How much is it per night/person?
Koliko košta za jednu noć/po osobi?
Колико кошта за једну ноћ/по особи?
Does it include breakfast?
Da li je u cijenu uključen i doručak?
Да ли је у цену укључен и доручак?

I'd like …	*Želim …*	Желим …
a single room	*sobu sa jednim krevetom*	собу са једним креветом
a twin room	*sobu sa duplim krevetom*	собу са дуплим креветом

CONVERSATION & ESSENTIALS

Hello.	*Zdravo.*	Здраво.
Goodbye.	*Doviđenja.*	Довиђења.
Yes.	*Da.*	Да.
No.	*Ne.*	Не.
Please.	*Molim.*	Молим.

EMERGENCIES – CROATIAN & SERBIAN

Help!	*Upomoć!*	Упомоћ!
Go away!	*Idite!*	Идите!

Call a doctor!
Pozovite lekara (S)/*liječnika!* (C) — Позовите лекара!
Call the police!
Pozovite miliciju (S)/*policiju* (C)! — Позовите милицију!
I'm lost.
Izgubljen/Izgubljena sam se. (m/f) — Изгубио/Изгубила сам се. (m/f)

Thank you.	*Hvala.*	Хвала.
You're welcome.	*Nema na četi.*	Нема на чему.
Excuse me.	*Oprostite.*	Опростите.
Sorry.	*Pardon.*	Пардон.

Do you speak English?
Govorite li engleski? Говорите ли енглески?
How much is it …?
Koliko košta …? Колико кошта …?
What's your name?
Kako se zovete? Како се зовете?
My name is …
Zovem se … Зовем се …

DIRECTIONS

Where is the bus/tram stop?
Gdje je autobuska/tramvajska stanica (S)/*postaja* (C)?
Где је аутобуска/трамвајска станица?
Can you show me (on the map)?
Možete li mi pokazati (na karti)?
Можете ли ми показати (на карти)?
Go straight ahead.
Idite pravo naprijed.
Идите право напред.

Turn left.	*Skrenite lijevo.*	Скрените лево.
Turn right.	*Skrenite desno.*	Скрените десно.
near	*blizu*	близу
far	*daleko*	далеко

SHOPPING & SERVICES

I'm looking for …	*Tražim …*	Тражим …
a bank	*banku*	банку
the … embassy	*… ambasadu*	… амбасаду
the market	*pijacu*	пијацу
the post office	*poštu*	пошту
the tourist office	*turistički biro*	туристички биро

SIGNS – CROATIAN & SERBIAN

Ulaz/Izlaz **Улаз/Излаз**	Entrance/Exit
Informacije **Информације**	Information
Otvoreno/Zatvoreno **Отворено/Затворено**	Open/Closed
Slobodne Sobe **Слободне Собе**	Rooms Available
Nema Slobodne Sobe **Нема Слободне Собе**	Full/No Vacancies
Milicija (S)/**Policija** (C) **Милиција**	Police
Stanica Milicije (S)/ **Policije** (C) **Станица Милиције**	Police Station
Zabranjeno **Забрањено**	Prohibited
Toaleti (S)/**Zahodi** (C) **Тоалети**	Toilets

TIME, DAYS & NUMBERS

What time is it?	*Koliko je sati?*	Колико је сати?
today	*danas*	данас
tomorrow	*sutra*	сутра
yesterday	*jučer*	јуче
in the morning	*ujutro*	ујутро
in the afternoon	*popodne*	поподне
Monday	*ponedjeljak*	понедељак
Tuesday	*utorak*	уторак
Wednesday	*srijeda*	среда
Thursday	*četvrtak*	четвртак
Friday	*petak*	петак
Saturday	*subota*	субота
Sunday	*nedjelja*	недеља
1	*jedan*	један
2	*dva*	два
3	*tri*	три
4	*četiri*	четири
5	*pet*	пет
6	*šest*	шест
7	*sedam*	седам
8	*osam*	осам
9	*devet*	девет
10	*deset*	десет
100	*sto*	сто
1000	*hiljadu* (S) *tisuću* (C)	хиљаду

TRANSPORT

one-way ticket	*kartu u jednom pravcu*	карту у једном правцу
return ticket	*povratnu kartu*	повратну карту
1st class	*prvu klasu*	прву класу
2nd class	*drugu klasu*	другу класу
What time does the ... leave/arrive?	*Kada ... polazi/dolazi?*	Када ... полази/долази?
boat	*brod*	брод
bus (city/intercity)	*autobus (gradski/međugradski)*	аутобус (градски/међуградски)
train	*voz* (S)/*vlak* (C)	воз
tram	*tramvaj*	трамвај

FRENCH

PRONUNCIATION

Most letters in French are pronounced more or less the same as their English counterparts. Here are a few that may cause some confusion:

c	before **e** and **i**, as the 's' in 'sit'; before **a**, **o** and **u** it's pronounced as English 'k'. With a cedilla attached (**ç**), it's always pronounced as the 's' in 'sit'.
j	as the 's' in 'leisure'
m, n	where a syllable ends in a single **n** or **m**, these letters aren't pronounced, but the preceding vowel is given a nasal pronunciation
r	pronounced from the back of the throat while constricting the muscles to restrict the flow of air

ACCOMMODATION

a hotel	*un hôtel*
a guest house	*une pension (de famille)*
a youth hostel	*une auberge de jeunesse*
Do you have any rooms available?	*Est-ce que vous avez des chambres libres?*
for one person	*pour une personne*
for two people	*pour deux personnes*
How much is it per night/person?	*Quel est le prix par nuit/personne?*
Is breakfast included?	*Est-ce que le petit déjeuner est compris?*

CONVERSATION & ESSENTIALS

Hello.	*Bonjour.*
Goodbye.	*Au revoir.*
Yes.	*Oui.*
No.	*Non.*
Please.	*S'il vous plaît.*
Thank you.	*Merci.*

You're welcome.	*Je vous en prie.*
Excuse me.	*Excusez-moi.*
Sorry.	*Pardon.*
Do you speak English?	*Parlez-vous anglais?*
How much is it?	*C'est combien?*
What's your name?	*Comment vous appelez-vous?*
My name is ...	*Je m'appelle ...*

DIRECTIONS

Where is ...?	*Où est ...?*
Go straight ahead.	*Continuez tout droit.*
Turn left.	*Tournez à gauche.*
Turn right.	*Tournez à droite.*
near	*proche*
far	*loin*

EMERGENCIES – FRENCH

Help!	*Au secours!*
Call a doctor!	*Appelez un médecin!*
Call the police!	*Appelez la police!*
Leave me alone!	*Fichez-moi la paix!*
I'm lost.	*Je me suis égaré(e). (m/f)*

SHOPPING & SERVICES

I'm looking for ...	*Je cherche ...*
a bank	*une banque*
a chemist/pharmacy	*une pharmacie*
the ... embassy	*l'ambassade de ...*
the market	*le marché*
a newsagency	*un agence de presse*
the post office	*le bureau de poste*
a public telephone	*une cabine téléphonique*
a stationers	*une papeterie*
the tourist office	*l'office de tourisme/ le syndicat d'initiative*

What time does it open/close?	*Quelle est l'heure de ouverture/fermeture?*

TIME, DAYS & NUMBERS

What time is it?	*Quelle heure est-il?*
today	*aujourd'hui*
tomorrow	*demain*
yesterday	*hier*
in the morning	*du matin*
in the afternoon	*de l'après-midi*

Monday	*lundi*
Tuesday	*mardi*
Wednesday	*mercredi*
Thursday	*jeudi*
Friday	*vendredi*
Saturday	*samedi*
Sunday	*dimanche*

SIGNS – FRENCH

Entrée	Entrance
Sortie	Exit
Renseignements	Information
Ouvert	Open
Fermé	Closed
Chambres Libres	Rooms Available
Complet	Full/No Vacancies
(Commissariat de) Police	Police Station
Interdit	Prohibited
Toilettes/WC	Toilets
Hommes	Men
Femmes	Women

1	*un*
2	*deux*
3	*trois*
4	*quatre*
5	*cinq*
6	*six*
7	*sept*
8	*huit*
9	*neuf*
10	*dix*
100	*cent*
1000	*mille*

TRANSPORT

When does (the next) ... leave/arrive?	*À quelle heure part/arrive (le prochain) ...?*
boat	*bateau*
bus (city)	*bus*
bus (intercity)	*car*
tram	*tramway*
train	*train*

the bus stop	*l'arrêt d'autobus*
the ferry terminal	*la gare maritime*
the left luggage office	*la consigne*
a timetable	*un horaire*
the train station	*la gare*
the tram stop	*l'arrêt de tramway*

I'd like a ... ticket.	*Je voudrais un billet ...*
one-way	*aller simple*
return	*aller retour*
1st-class	*de première classe*
2nd-class	*de deuxième classe*

I'd like to hire a car/ bicycle.	*Je voudrais louer une voiture/ un vélo.*

GREEK

PRONUNCIATION

Pronunciation of Greek letters is shown in the Greek alphabet table (right). The pronunciation guides use the closest-sounding English letter to represent the Greek.

ACCOMMODATION

a camping ground	*ena kamping*
a hotel	*ena xenothohio*
a youth hostel	*enas xenonas neoitos*
for one night	*ya mia nichta*
for two nights	*ya dhio nichtes*
Is breakfast included?	*Simberilamvanete to proiono?*

I'd like a … room.	*Thelo ena dhomatio …*
single	*ya ena atomo*
double	*ya dhio atoma*

How much is it …?	*Poso kostizi …?*
per person	*ya ena atomo*
per night	*ya ena vradhi*

CONVERSATION & ESSENTIALS

Hello.	*Yasu./Yasas.* (inf/pol)
Goodbye.	*Andio.*
Yes.	*Ne.*
No.	*Okhi.*
Please.	*Sas parakalo.*
Thank you.	*Sas efharisto.*
You're welcome.	*Ine endaksi/parakalo.*
I'm sorry.	*Signomi*
Do you speak English?	*Milate anglika?*
How much is it?	*Poso kani?*
What's your name?	*Pos sas lene/pos legeste?*
My name is …	*Me lene …*

DIRECTIONS

Go straight ahead.	*Pighenete efthia.*
Turn left.	*Stripste aristera.*
Turn right.	*Stripste dheksya.*
near	*Konda*
far	*Makria*

SHOPPING & SERVICES

Where is a /the …?	*Pu ine …?*
bank	*mia trapeza*
… embassy	*i … presvia*
market	*i aghora*
newsagency	*to efimeridhon*
pharmacy	*to farmakio*
post office	*to takhidhromio*
telephone centre	*to tilefoniko kentro*
tourist office	*to ghrafio turistikon pliroforion*

THE GREEK ALPHABET

Greek	English	Pronunciation
Α α	a	as in 'father'
Β β	v	as in 'vine'
Γ γ	gh, y	like a rough 'g', or as the 'y' in 'yes'
Δ δ	dh	as the 'th' in 'then'
Ε ε	e	as in 'egg'
Ζ ζ	z	as in 'zoo'
Η η	i	as in 'marine'
Θ θ	th	as in 'throw'
Ι ι	i	as in 'marine'
Κ κ	k	as in 'kite'
Λ λ	l	as in 'leg'
Μ μ	m	as in 'man'
Ν ν	n	as in 'net'
Ξ ξ	x	as the 'ks' in 'looks'
Ο ο	o	as in 'hot'
Π π	p	as in 'pup'
Ρ ρ	r	a slightly trilled 'r'
Σ σ	s	as in 'sand' (written as ς at the end of a word)
Τ τ	t	as in 'to'
Υ υ	i	as in 'marine'
Φ φ	f	as in 'fit'
Χ χ	kh, h	as the 'ch' in Scottish *loch*, or as a rough 'h'
Ψ ψ	ps	as the 'ps' in 'lapse'
Ω ω	o	as in 'lot'

What time does it open/close?	*Ti ora aniyi/klini?*

TIME, DAYS & NUMBERS

What time is it?	*Ti ora ine?*
today	*simera*
tomorrow	*avrio*
in the morning	*to proi*
in the afternoon	*to apoyevma*

Monday	*dheftera*
Tuesday	*triti*
Wednesday	*tetarti*
Thursday	*pempti*
Friday	*paraskevi*
Saturday	*savato*
Sunday	*kiryaki*

EMERGENCIES – GREEK

Help!	*Voithia!*
Call a doctor!	*Fonakste ena yatro!*
Call the police!	*Tilefoniste tin astinomia!*
Go away!	*Fighe!/Dhromo!*
I'm lost.	*Eho hathi.*

1	*ena*
2	*dhio*
3	*tria*
4	*tesera*
5	*pende*
6	*eksi*
7	*epta*
8	*okhto*
9	*enea*
10	*dheka*
100	*ekato*
1000	*khilya*

TRANSPORT

What time does the … leave/arrive?	*Ti ora fevyi/ftani …?*
boat	*to plio*
bus (city)	*to leoforio (ya tin poli)*
bus (intercity)	*to leoforio (ya ta proastia)*
train	*to treno*

I'd like a … ticket.	*Tha ithela isitirio …*
one-way	*horis epistrofi*
return	*me epistrofi*
1st-class	*proti thesi*
2nd-class	*dhefteri thesi*

left luggage	*horos aposkevon*
timetable	*dhromologhio*
bus stop	*i stasi tu leoforiu*

SIGNS – GREEK

Εισοδος	Entrance
Εξοδος	Exit
Πληροφοριες	Information
Ανοικτο	Open
Κλειστο	Closed
Αστυνομικο Τμημα	Police Station
Απαγορευεται	Prohibited
Τουαλετες	Toilets
Ανδρων	Men
Γυναικων	Women

ITALIAN

PRONUNCIATION

Vowels

a as in 'art', eg *caro* (dear); sometimes short, eg *amico/a* (friend)

e short, as in 'let', eg *mettere* (to put); long, as in 'there', eg *mela* (apple)

i short, as in 'it', eg *inizio* (start); long, as in 'marine', eg *vino* (wine)

o short, as in 'dot', eg *donna* (woman); long, as in 'port', eg *ora* (hour)

u as the 'oo' in 'book', eg *puro* (pure)

Consonants

c as the 'k' in 'kit' before **a**, **o**, **u** and **h**; as the 'ch' in 'choose' before **e** and **i**

g as the 'g' in 'get' before **a**, **o**, **u** and **h**; as the 'j' in 'jet' before **e** and **i**

gli as the 'lli' in 'million'

gn as the 'ny' in 'canyon'

h always silent

r a rolled 'r' sound

sc as the 'sh' in 'sheep' before **e** and **i**; as 'sk' before **a**, **o**, **u** and **h**

z as the 'ts' in 'lights', except at the beginning of a word, when it's as the 'ds' in 'suds'

Note that when **ci**, **gi** and **sci** are followed by **a**, **o** or **u**, the 'i' is not pronounced unless the accent falls on the 'i'. Thus the name 'Giovanni' is pronounced jo-*van*-nee.

A double consonant has a longer, more forceful sound than a single consonant.

Word Stress

Word stress generally falls on the second-last syllable, as in spa-*ghet*-ti, but when a word has an accent, the stress falls on that syllable, as in cit-*tà* (city).

ACCOMMODATION

camping ground	*campeggio*
hotel	*albergo*
guest house	*pensione*
youth hostel	*ostello per la gioventù*

Do you have any rooms available?	*Ha delle camere libere?*
How much is it per night/person?	*Quanto costa per notte/persona?*
Is breakfast included?	*È compresa la colazione?*

a single room	*una camera singola*
a twin room	*una camera doppia*
a double room	*una camera matrimoniale*
for one night	*per una notte*
for two nights	*per due notti*

CONVERSATION & ESSENTIALS

Hello.	*Buongiorno.* (pol)
	Ciao. (inf)
Goodbye.	*Arrivederci.* (pol)
	Ciao. (inf)

EMERGENCIES – ITALIAN

Help!	*Aiuto!*
Call a doctor!	*Chiama un dottore!*
Call the police!	*Chiama la polizia!*
Go away!	*Vai via!*
I'm lost.	*Mi sono perso/a.* (m/f)

Yes.	*Sì.*
No.	*No.*
Please.	*Per favore./Per piacere.*
Thank you.	*Grazie.*
You're welcome.	*Prego.*
Excuse me.	*Mi scusi.*
I'm sorry.	*Mi perdoni.*
Do you speak English?	*Parla inglese?*
How much is it?	*Quanto costa?*
What's your name?	*Come si chiama?*
My name is …	*Mi chiamo …*

DIRECTIONS

Where is …?	*Dov'è …?*
Go straight ahead.	*Si va sempre diritto.*
Turn left.	*Giri a sinistra.*
Turn right.	*Giri a destra.*
near	*vicino*
far	*lontano*

SHOPPING & SERVICES

a bank	*una banca*
a chemist/pharmacy	*una farmacia*
the … embassy	*l'ambasciata di …*
the market	*il mercato*
a newsagency	*un'edicola*
post office	*la posta*
a stationers	*un cartolaio*
the tourist office	*l'ufficio di turismo*
What time does it open/close?	*A che ora (si) apre/chiude?*

TIME, DAYS & NUMBERS

What time is it?	*Che ora è?/Che ore sono?*
today	*oggi*
tomorrow	*domani*
morning	*mattina*
afternoon	*pomeriggio*

Monday	*lunedì*
Tuesday	*martedì*
Wednesday	*mercoledì*
Thursday	*giovedì*
Friday	*venerdì*
Saturday	*sabato*
Sunday	*domenica*

SIGNS – ITALIAN

Ingresso/Entrata	Entrance
Uscita	Exit
Informazione	Information
Aperto	Open
Chiuso	Closed
Polizia/Carabinieri	Police
Questura	Police Station
Proibito/Vietato	Prohibited
Gabinetti/Bagni	Toilets
Uomini	Men
Donne	Women

1	*uno*
2	*due*
3	*tre*
4	*quattro*
5	*cinque*
6	*sei*
7	*sette*
8	*otto*
9	*nove*
10	*dieci*
100	*cento*
1000	*mille*

TRANSPORT

When does the … leave/arrive?	*A che ora parte/arriva …?*
boat	*la barca*
bus	*l'autobus*
ferry	*il traghetto*
train	*il treno*
tram	*il tram*

bus stop	*fermata d'autobus*
train station	*stazione*
ferry terminal	*stazione marittima*
1st class	*prima classe*
2nd class	*seconda classe*
left luggage	*deposito bagagli*
timetable	*orario*

I'd like a (one-way/return) ticket.	*Vorrei un biglietto (di solo andata/di andata e ritorno).*
I'd like to hire a car/bicycle.	*Vorrei noleggiare una macchina/bicicletta.*

MALTESE

You'll have no problems getting around Malta using English, but if you know a few words in Maltese, it'll always be welcomed.

PRONUNCIATION

ċ	as the 'ch' in child
g	as in good
ġ	as the 'j' in job
għ	silent; lengthens the preceding or following vowel
h	silent, as in 'hour'
ħ	as the 'h' in 'hand'
j	as the 'y' in 'yellow'
ij	as the 'igh' in 'high'
ej	as the 'ay' in 'day'
q	a glottal stop; like the missing 't' in the Cockney pronunciation of 'bottle'
x	as the 'sh' in shop
z	as the 'ts' in 'bits'
ż	as in 'buzz'

ACCOMMODATION

Do you have a room available?	*Għandek kamra jekk jogħoġbok?*
Is breakfast included?	*Il-breakfast inkluż?*
Do you have a room for ...?	*Għandek kamra għal ...?*
one person	*wieħed*
two people	*tnejn*
one night	*lejl iljieli*
two nights	*zewgt iljieli*

CONVERSATION & ESSENTIALS

Hello.	*Merħba.*
Good morning./Good day.	*Bonġu.*
Goodbye.	*Saħħa.*
Yes.	*Iva.*
No.	*Le.*
Please.	*Jekk jogħoġbok.*
Thank you.	*Grazzi.*
Excuse me.	*Skużani.*
Do you speak English?	*Titkellem bl-ingliż?*

EMERGENCIES – MALTESE

Help!	*Ajjut!*
Call a doctor!	*Qibgħad ghat-tabib!*
Police!	*Pulizija!*
I'm lost.	*Ninsab mitluf.*

How much is it?	*Kemm?*
What's your name?	*X'ismek?*
My name is ...	*Jisimni ...*

SIGNS – MALTESE

Dhul	Entrance
Hrug	Exit
Informazjoni	Information
Miftuh	Open
Maghluq	Closed
Tidholx	No Entry
Pulizija	Police
Toilets	Toilets
Rgiel	Men
Nisa	Women

DIRECTIONS

Where is ...?	*Fejn hu ...?*
Go straight ahead.	*Mur dritt.*
Turn left.	*Dur fuq il-lemin.*
Turn right.	*Dur fuq il-ix-xellug.*
near	*il-viċin*
far	*il-bogħod*

SHOPPING & SERVICES

the bank	*il-bank*
chemist/pharmacy	*l-ispiżerija*
the ... embassy	*l'ambaxxata ...*
the hotel	*hotel/il-lakanda*
the market	*is-suq*
the post office	*il-posta*
a public telephone	*telefon pubbliku*
shop	*ħanut*
stamp	*timbru*
What time does it open/close?	*Fix'ħin jiftaħ/jagħlaq?*

TIME, DAYS & NUMBERS

What's the time?	*X'ħin hu?*
today	*illum*
tomorrow	*għada*
yesterday	*il-bieraħ*
morning	*fil-għodu*
afternoon	*nofs in-nhar*
Monday	*it-tnejn*
Tuesday	*it-tlieta*
Wednesday	*l-erbgħa*
Thursday	*il-ħamis*
Friday	*il-gimgħa*
Saturday	*is-sibt*
Sunday	*il-ħadd*
0	*xejn*
1	*wieħed*
2	*tnejn*

3	*tlieta*
4	*erbgħa*
5	*ħamsa*
6	*sitta*
7	*sebgħa*
8	*tmienja*
9	*disgħa*
10	*għaxra*
100	*mija*
1000	*elf*

TRANSPORT

When does the boat leave/arrive?	*Meta jitlaq/jasal il-vapur?*
When does the bus leave/arrive?	*Meta titlaq/jasal il-karozza?*
I'd like a ... ticket.	*Nixtieq biljett ...*
one-way	*one-way*
return	*return*
1st-class	*1st-class*
2nd-class	*2nd-class*
left luggage	*hallejt il-bagalji*
bus/trolleybus stop	*xarabank/coach*
I'd like to hire a car/ bicycle.	*Nixtieq nikri karozza/rota.*

MOROCCAN ARABIC

PRONUNCIATION

Arabic is a difficult language to learn, but even knowing a few words can win you a friendly smile from the locals.

Vowels

a	as in 'had'
aa	as in 'far'
e	as in 'bet'
i	as in 'hit'
ee	as the 'e' in 'here'
o	as in 'hot'; sometimes as in 'for'
u	as the 'oo' in 'book'
oo	as the 'oo' in 'food'

Vowel Combinations

aw	as the 'ow' in 'how'
ai	as the 'i' in 'high'
ei, ay	as the 'a' in 'cake'

CONSONANTS

Many consonants are the same as in English, but there are some tricky ones:

j	as in 'John'
H	a strongly whispered 'h', almost like a sigh of relief
q	a strong guttural 'k' sound
kh	a slightly gurgling sound, like the 'ch' in Scottish *loch*
r	a rolled 'r' sound
sh	as in 'she'
z	as the 's' in pleasure
gh	similar to the French 'r', but more guttural

GLOTTAL STOP (')

The glottal stop is the sound you hear between the vowels in the expression 'uh-oh!'. In Arabic it can occur anywhere in a word – at the beginning, middle or end. When the glottal stop occurs before a vowel (eg 'ayn), the vowel is 'growled' from the back of the throat. If it is before a consonant or at the end of a word, it's as in 'uh-oh!'.

ACCOMMODATION

Where is a ...?	*Feen kayn ...?*
camping ground	*shee mukheyyem*
hotel	*shee ootayl*
youth hostel	*daar shshabab*
Is there a room available?	*Wash kayn shee beet khaweeya?*
How much is a room for one day?	*Bash hal kayn gbayt l wahed nhar?*
Is breakfast included?	*Wash lftur mhsoob m'a lbeet?*
air-conditioning	*kleemateezaseeyun*
bed	*namooseeya*
blanket	*bttaaneeya*
hot water	*lma skhoon*
room	*beet*
sheet	*eezar*
shower	*doosh*
toilet	*beet lma*

CONVERSATION & ESSENTIALS

Hello.	*Ssalamu 'lekum.*
Goodbye.	*M'a ssalama.*
Yes.	*Eeyeh.*
No.	*La.*
Please.	*'Afak.*
Thank you (very much).	*Shukran (jazilan).*
You're welcome.	*La shukran 'la wezhb.*
Excuse me.	*Smeh leeya.*
Do you speak English?	*Wash kat'ref negleezeeya?*
What's your name?	*Asmeetek?*
My name is ...	*Smeetee ...*

LANGUAGE

I understand.	*Fhemt.*
I don't understand.	*Mafhemtsh.*
How much (is it)?	*Bish-hal?*

DIRECTIONS

Where is (the) ...?	*Feen ...?*
I'm looking for ...	*Kanqellab 'la ...*
Go straight ahead.	*Seer neeshan.*
Turn right.	*Dor 'al leemen.*
Turn left.	*Dor 'al leeser.*

SHOPPING & SERVICES

the bank	*al-banka*
the ... embassy	*as-seefara dyal ...*
the market	*as-sooq*
the police station	*al-koomeesareeya*
the post office	*al-boosta*
a toilet	*beet lma*

TIME, DATES & NUMBERS

What time is it?	*Shal fessa'a?*
today	*al-yoom*
tomorrow	*ghaddan*
yesterday	*al-bareh*
in the morning	*fis-sabaH*
in the evening	*fil-masa'*

Monday	*(nhar) letneen*
Tuesday	*(nhar) ttlat*
Wednesday	*(nhar) larb'*
Thursday	*(nhar) lekhmees*
Friday	*(nhar) zhzhem'a'*
Saturday	*(nhar) ssebt*
Sunday	*(nhar) lhedd*

Arabic numerals are simple enough to learn and, unlike the written language, run from left to right. In Morocco, European numerals are also often used.

1	*wahed*
2	*zhoozh*
3	*tlata*
4	*reb'a*
5	*khamsa*
6	*setta*
7	*seba'a*
8	*tmenya*
9	*tes'ood'*
10	*'ashra*
100	*mya*
1000	*alf*

EMERGENCIES – MOROCCAN ARABIC

Help!	*Teqnee!*
Call a doctor!	*'Ayyet 'la shee tbeeb!*
Call the police!	*'Ayyet 'la lboolees!*
Go away!	*Seer fhalek!*

TRANSPORT

What time does the ... leave/arrive?	*Wufooqash katwsul/keiwsul ...?*
boat	*flooka*
bus (city)	*ttubees*
bus (intercity)	*lkar*
train	*tran*

bus stop	*blasa dyal tobeesat*
train station	*lagaar*
1st class	*ddarazha lloola*
2nd class	*ddarazha ttaneeya*

Where can I hire a car/bicycle?	*Feen yimken li nkri tumubil/bshklit?*

PORTUGUESE

Portuguese uses masculine and feminine word endings, usually '-o' and '-a' respectively. To say 'thank you', a man will therefore use *obrigado;* a woman, *obrigada.*

PRONUNCIATION

Vowels

a	short, as the 'u' in 'cut'; long, as in 'father'
e	short, as in 'bet'; long, as in 'there'
é	short, as in 'bet'
ê	long, as the 'a' in 'gate'
i	short, as in 'it'; long, as the 'ee' in 'see'
o	short, as in 'pot'; long as in 'note' or as the 'oo' in 'good'
ô	long, as in 'note'
u	as the 'oo' in 'good'

Nasal Vowels

Nasalisation is represented by an 'n' or an 'm' after the vowel, or by a tilde over it, eg **ã**. You can practise by trying to pronounce vowels while holding your nose, as if you have a cold.

Diphthongs

au	as the 'ow' in 'now'
ai	as the 'ie' in 'pie'

LANGUAGE

ei as the 'ay' in 'day'
eu as 'e' followed by 'w'
oi similar to the 'oy' in 'boy'

Nasal Diphthongs

Try the same technique as for nasal vowels. To say *não*, pronounce 'now' through your nose.

ão nasal 'ow' (owng)
ãe nasal 'ay' (eing)
õe nasal 'oy' (oing)
ũi similar to the 'uing' in 'ensuing'

Consonants

c as in 'cat' before **a**, **o** or **u**; as the 's' in 'sin' before **e** or **i**
ç as the 'c' in 'celery'
g as in 'go' before **a**, **o** or **u**; as the 's' in 'treasure' before **e** or **i**
gu as in 'guest' before **e** or **i**
h never pronounced when word initial
nh as the 'ni' in 'onion'
lh as the 'lli' in 'million'
j as the 's' in 'treasure'
m not pronounced when word final – it simply nasalises the previous vowel, eg *um* (oong), *bom* (bong)
qu as 'k' before **e** or **i**; elsewhere as in 'queen'
r when word initial, or when doubled (**rr**) within a word it's a harsh, guttural sound similar to the 'ch' in Scottish *loch*; in the middle or at the end of a word it's a rolled 'r' sound. In some areas of Portugal it's always strongly rolled.
s as in 'so' when word initial and when doubled (**ss**) within a word; as the 'z' in 'zeal' when between vowels; as 'sh' when it precedes a consonant, or at the end of a word
x as the 'sh' in 'ship', as the 'z' in 'zeal', or as the 'x' in 'taxi'
z as the 's' in 'treasure' before a consonant or at the end of a word

Word Stress

Word stress is important in Portuguese, as it can affect meaning. It generally occurs on the second-to-last syllable of a word, though there are exceptions. In words with a written accent, the stress always falls on that syllable.

ACCOMMODATION

camping ground *parque de campismo*
hotel *hotel*
guest house *pensão*
youth hostel *pousada da juventude*

Do you have any rooms available? *Tem quartos livres?*
How much is it per night/person? *Quanto é por noite/pessoa?*
Is breakfast included? *O pequeno almoço está incluído?*

a single room *um quarto individual*
a twin room *um quarto duplo*
a double room *um quarto de casal*
for one night *para uma noite*
for two nights *para duas noites*

CONVERSATION & ESSENTIALS

Hello. *Bom dia.*
Goodbye. *Adeus.*
Yes. *Sim.*
No. *Não.*
Please. *Se faz favor.*
Thank you. *Obrigado/a.* (m/f)
You're welcome. *De nada.*
Excuse me. *Com licença.*
I'm sorry. *Desculpe.*
Do you speak English? *Fala Inglês?*
How much is it? *Quanto custa?*
What's your name? *Como se chama?*
My name is ... *Chamo-me ...*

DIRECTIONS

Where is ...? *Onde é ...?*
Go straight ahead. *Siga sempre (a direito/em frente).*
Turn left. *Vire à esquerda.*
Turn right. *Vire à direita.*
near *perto*
far *longe*

SHOPPING & SERVICES

a bank *um banco*
a chemist/pharmacy *uma farmácia*
the ... embassy *a embaixada de ...*

EMERGENCIES – PORTUGUESE

Help! *Socorro!*
Call a doctor! *Chame um médico!*
Call the police! *Chame a polícia!*
Go away! *Deixe-me em paz!* (pol)/ *Vai-te embora!* (inf)
I'm lost. *Estou perdido/a.* (m/f)

SIGNS – PORTUGUESE

Entrada	Entrance
Saída	Exit
Informações	Information
Aberto	Open
Fechado	Closed
Posto Da Polícia	Police Station
Proíbido	Prohibited
Lavabos/WC	Toilets
Homens	Men
Senhoras	Women

the market	*o mercado*
the newsagents	*a papelaria*
the post office	*os correios*
the stationers	*a tabacaria*
the tourist office	*o (posto de) turismo*
What time does it open/close?	*A que horas abre/fecha?*

TIME, DAYS & NUMBERS

What time is it?	*Que horas são?*
today	*hoje*
tomorrow	*amanhã*
yesterday	*ontem*
morning	*manhã*
afternoon	*tarde*

Monday	*segunda-feira*
Tuesday	*terça-feira*
Wednesday	*quarta-feira*
Thursday	*quinta-feira*
Friday	*sexta-feira*
Saturday	*sábado*
Sunday	*domingo*

1	*um/uma* (m/f)
2	*dois/duas* (m/f)
3	*três*
4	*quatro*
5	*cinco*
6	*seis*
7	*sete*
8	*oito*
9	*nove*
10	*dez*
100	*cem*
1000	*mil*

TRANSPORT

bus stop	*paragem de autocarro*
train station	*estação ferroviária*
timetable	*horário*

What time does the … leave/arrive?	*A que horas parte/chega …?*
boat	*o barco*
bus (city/intercity)	*o autocarro/a camioneta*
tram	*o eléctrico*
train	*o combóio*

I'd like a … ticket.	*Queria um bilhete …*
one-way	*simples/de ida*
return	*de ida e volta*
1st-class	*de primeira classe*
2nd-class	*de segunda classe*

I'd like to hire …	*Queria alugar …*
a car	*um carro*
a bicycle	*uma bicicleta*

SLOVENE

PRONUNCIATION

Slovene pronunciation isn't difficult. The alphabet consists of 25 letters, most of which are very similar to English. It doesn't have the letters 'q', 'w', 'x' and 'y', but it does include the following letters: **ê**, **é**, **ó**, **ò**, **č**, **š** and **ž**. Each letter represents only one sound, with very few exceptions. The letters **l** and **v** are both pronounced like the English 'w' when they occur at the end of syllables and before vowels.

Though words like *trn* (thorn) look unpronounceable, most Slovenes add a short vowel like an 'a' or the German 'ö' (depending on dialect) in front of the 'r' to give a Scot's pronunciation of 'tern' or 'tarn'.

c	as the 'ts' in 'its'
č	as the 'ch' in 'church'
ê	as the 'a' in 'apple'
e	as the 'a' in 'ago' (when unstressed)
é	as the 'ay' in 'day'
j	as the 'y' in 'yellow'
ó	as the 'o' in 'more'
ò	as the 'o' in 'soft'
r	a rolled 'r' sound
š	as the 'sh' in 'ship'
u	as the 'oo' in 'good'
ž	as the 's' in 'treasure'

ACCOMMODATION

camping ground	*kamping*
hotel	*hotel*
guest house	*gostišče*
youth hostel	*počitniški dom*

SIGNS – SLOVENE

Vhod	Entrance
Izhod	Exit
Informacije	Information
Odprto	Open
Zaprto	Closed
Prepovedano	Prohibited
Stranišče	Toilets

Do you have a ...? *Ali imate prosto ...?*
bed *posteljo*
cheap room *poceni sobo*
single room *enoposteljno sobo*
double room *dvoposteljno sobo*

for one night *za eno noč*
for two nights *za dve noči*
How much is it per night/person? *Koliko stane za eno noč/osebo?*
Is breakfast included? *Ali je zajtrk vključen?*

CONVERSATION & ESSENTIALS

Hello. *Pozdravljeni.* (pol)
Zdravo./Živio. (inf)
Good day. *Dober dan!*
Goodbye. *Nasvidenje!*
Yes. *Da.* (pol)
Ja. (inf)
No. *Ne.*
Please. *Prosim.*
Thank you (very much). *Hvala (lepa).*
You're welcome. *Prosim./Ni za kaj.*
Excuse me. *Oprostite.*
What's your name? *Kako vam je ime?*
My name is ... *Jaz sem ...*
Where are you from? *Od kod ste?*
I'm from ... *Sem iz ...*

DIRECTIONS

Where is ...? *Kje je ...?*
Go straight ahead. *Pojdite naravnost naprej.*
Turn left. *Obrnite levo.*
Turn right. *Obrnite desno.*
near *blizu*
far *daleč*

SHOPPING & SERVICES

Where is the/a ...? *Kje je ...?*
bank *banka*
consulate *konzulat*
embassy *ambasada*
exchange *menjalnica*
post office *pošta*
tourist office *turistični informacijski urad*

TIME, DAYS & NUMBERS

today *danes*
tonight *nocoj*
tomorrow *jutri*
yesterday *včeraj*
in the morning *zjutraj*
in the evening *zvečer*

Monday *ponedeljek*
Tuesday *torek*
Wednesday *sreda*
Thursday *četrtek*
Friday *petek*
Saturday *sobota*
Sunday *nedelja*

1 *ena*
2 *dve*
3 *tri*
4 *štiri*
5 *pet*
6 *šest*
7 *sedem*
8 *osem*
9 *devet*
10 *eset*
100 *sto*
1000 *tisoč*

TRANSPORT

What time does ... leave/arrive? *Kdaj odpelje/pripelje ...?*
boat/ferry *ladja/trajekt*
bus *avtobus*
train *vlak*

one-way (ticket) *enosmerna (vozovnica)*
return (ticket) *povratna (vozovnica)*
bus stop *avtobusno postajališče*
train station *železniska postaja*

EMERGENCIES – SLOVENE

Help!	*Na pomoč!*
Call a doctor!	*Pokličite zdravnika!*
Call the police!	*Pokličite policijo!*
Go away!	*Pojdite stran!*
I'm lost.	*Izgubil/Izgubila sem se.* (m/f)

SPANISH

PRONUNCIATION

Vowels

An acute accent (as in *días*) generally indicates a stressed syllable and doesn't change the sound of the vowel.

e as in 'met'
i as in 'marine'
o as in 'or' (without the 'r' sound)
u as in 'rule'; the 'u' is not pronounced after **q** and in the letter combinations **gue** and **gui**, unless it's marked with a dieresis (eg *argüir*), in which case it's pronounced as English 'w'

Consonants

b a cross between English 'b' and 'v'
c a hard 'c' as in 'cat' when followed by **a**, **o**, **u** or a consonant; as the 'th' in 'thin' before **e** and **i**
ch as in 'church'
g as in 'get' when word initial and before **a**, **o** and **u**. Before **e** or **i** it's a harsh, breathy sound, similar to the 'h' in 'hit'
h silent
j a harsh, guttural sound similar to the 'ch' in Scottish *loch*
ll as the 'lli' in 'million'; some pronounce it more like the 'y' in 'yellow'
ñ as the 'ni' in 'onion'
q as the 'k' in 'kick'; **q** is always followed by a silent **u** and combines only with **e** (as in *que*) and **i** (as in *qui*)
r a rolled 'r' sound; longer and stronger when initial or doubled
v the same sound as **b**
x as the 'ks' sound in 'taxi' when between vowels; as the 's' in 'see' when it precedes a consonant
y at the end of a word or when standing alone (meaning 'and') it's pronounced like the Spanish **i**; as a consonant, it's somewhere between the 'y' in 'yonder' and the 'g' in 'beige', depending on the region.
z as the 'th' in 'thin'

ACCOMMODATION

camping ground *camping*
hotel *hotel*
guest house *pensión/casa de huéspedes*
youth hostel *albergue juvenil*

Do you have any rooms available? *¿Tiene habitaciones libres?*
How much is it per night/person? *¿Cuánto cuesta por noche/persona?*
Is breakfast included? *¿Incluye el desayuno?*
a single room *una habitación individual*
a double room *una habitación doble*
a room with a double bed *una habitación con cama de matrimonio*
for one night *para una noche*
for two nights *para dos noches*

CONVERSATION & ESSENTIALS

Hello. *Hola.*
Goodbye. *Adiós.*
Yes. *Sí.*
No. *No.*
Please. *Por favor.*
Thank you. *Gracias.*
You're welcome. *De nada.*
I'm sorry. *Lo siento./Discúlpeme.*
Excuse me. *Perdón./Perdóneme.*
Do you speak English? *¿Habla inglés?*
How much is it? *¿Cuánto cuesta?/¿Cuánto vale?*
What's your name? *¿Cómo se llama?*
My name is ... *Me llamo ...*

DIRECTIONS

Where is ...? *¿Dónde está ...?*
Go straight ahead. *Siga/Vaya todo derecho.*
Turn left. *Gire a la izquierda.*
Turn right. *Gire a la derecha/recto.*
near *cerca*
far *lejos*

SHOPPING & SERVICES

a bank *un banco*
chemist/pharmacy *la farmacia*
the ... embassy *la embajada ...*
the market *el mercado*
newsagents *el quiosco*
stationers *la papelería*

EMERGENCIES – SPANISH

Help! *¡Socorro!/¡Auxilio!*
Call a doctor! *¡Llame a un doctor!*
Call the police! *¡Llame a la policía!*
Go away! *¡Váyase!*
I'm lost. *Estoy perdido/a.* (m/f)

the post office *los correos*
the tourist office *la oficina de turismo*
What time does it open/close? *¿A qué hora abren/cierran?*

TIME, DAYS & NUMBERS

What time is it? *¿Qué hora es?*
today *hoy*
tomorrow *mañana*
yesterday *ayer*

SIGNS – SPANISH

Entrada	Entrance
Salida	Exit
Información	Information
Abierto	Open
Cerrado	Closed
Comisaría	Police Station
Prohibido	Prohibited
Servicios/Aseos	Toilets
Hombres	Men
Mujeres	Women

morning *mañana*
afternoon *tarde*

Monday *lunes*
Tuesday *martes*
Wednesday *miércoles*
Thursday *jueves*
Friday *viernes*
Saturday *sábado*
Sunday *domingo*

1 *uno/una (m/f)*
2 *dos*
3 *tres*
4 *cuatro*
5 *cinco*
6 *seis*
7 *siete*
8 *ocho*
9 *nueve*
10 *diez*
100 *cien/ciento*
1000 *mil*

TRANSPORT

What time does the next … leave/arrive? *¿A qué hora sale/llega el próximo …?*
boat *barco*
bus (city) *autobús/bus*
bus (intercity) *autocar*
train *tranvía*

I'd like a … ticket. *Quisiera un billete …*
one-way *sencillo/de sólo ida*
return *de ida y vuelta*
1st-class *de primera clase*
2nd-class *de segunda clase*

left luggage *consigna*
timetable *horario*
bus stop *parada de autobus*
train station *estación de ferrocarril*

I'd like to hire … *Quisiera alquilar …*
a car *un coche*
a bicycle *una bicicleta*

TURKISH

PRONUNCIATION

The Turkish alphabet is phonetic and thus reasonably easy to pronounce once you've learned a few basic rules. Each Turkish letter is pronounced, there are no diphthongs, and the only silent letter is **ğ**.

Vowels

Turkish vowels are pronounced as follows:

A a as the 'a' in 'art' or 'bar'
E e as in 'fell'
İ i as 'ee'
I ı as the 'a' in 'ago'
O o as in 'hot'
U u as the 'oo' in 'moo'
Ö ö as the 'ur' in 'fur'
Ü ü as the 'ew' in 'few'

Note that both **ö** and **ü** are pronounced with pursed lips.

Consonants

Most consonants are pronounced as they are in English, with a few exceptions:

Ç ç as the 'ch' in 'church'
C c as English 'j'
Ğ ğ not pronounced; draws out the preceding vowel a bit
H h as in 'half'
J j as the 's' in 'treasure'
Ş ş as the 'sh' in 'shoe'
V v as the 'w' in 'weather'

ACCOMMODATION

camping ground *kampink*
hotel *otel(i)*
guest house *pansiyon*
youth hostel *öğrenci yurdu*

Do you have any rooms available? *Boş oda var mı?*

a single room *tek kişilik oda*
a double room *iki kişilik oda*
one night *bir gece*
two nights *iki gece*

How much is it per night/person?	*Bir gecelik/Kişibaşına kaç para?*
Is breakfast included?	*Kahvaltı dahil mi?*

CONVERSATION & ESSENTIALS

Hello.	*Merhaba.*
Goodbye.	*Allahaısmarladık./Güle güle.*
Yes.	*Evet.*
No.	*Hayır.*
Please.	*Lütfen.*
Thank you.	*Teşekkür ederim.*
You're welcome.	*Bir şey değil.*
Excuse me.	*Affedersiniz.*
Sorry.	*Pardon.*
Do you speak English?	*İngilizce biliyor musunuz?*
How much is it?	*Ne kadar?*
What's your name?	*Adınız ne?*
My name is …	*Adım …*

DIRECTIONS

Where is a/the …?	*… nerede?*
Go straight ahead.	*Doğru gidin.*
Turn left.	*Sola dönün.*
Turn right.	*Sağa dönün.*
near	*yakın*
far	*uzak*

SHOPPING & SERVICES

a bank	*bir banka*
a chemist/pharmacy	*bir eczane*
the … embassy	*… büyükelçiliği*

EMERGENCIES – TURKISH

Help!/Emergency!	*İmdat!*
Call a doctor!	*Doktor çağırın!*
Call the police!	*Polis çağırın!*
Go away!	*Gidin/Git!/Defol!*
I'm lost.	*Kayboldum.*

the market	*çarşı*
the newsagency	*haber agensı*
the post office	*postane*
the stationers	*kırtasiyeci*
the telephone centre	*telefon merkezi*
the tourist office	*turizm danışma bürosu*
What time does it open/close?	*Ne zamam açılır/kapanır?*

TIME, DAYS & NUMBERS

What time is it?	*Saat kaç?*
today	*bugün*
tomorrow	*yarın*
yesterday	*dün*
morning	*sabah*
afternoon	*öğleden sonra*
Monday	*pazartesi*
Tuesday	*salı*
Wednesday	*çarşamba*
Thursday	*perşembe*
Friday	*cuma*
Saturday	*cumartesi*
Sunday	*pazar*
January	*ocak*
February	*şubat*
March	*mart*
April	*nisan*
May	*mayıs*
June	*haziran*
July	*temmuz*
August	*ağustos*
September	*eylül*
October	*ekim*
November	*kasım*
December	*aralık*
1	*bir*
2	*iki*
3	*üç*
4	*dört*
5	*beş*
6	*altı*
7	*yedi*
8	*sekiz*
9	*dokuz*
10	*on*
100	*yüz*
1000	*bin*
1,000,000	*bir milyon*

SIGNS – TURKISH

Giriş	Entrance
Çikiş	Exit
Danişma	Information
Açik	Open
Kapali	Closed
Polis/Emniyet	Police
Polis Karakolu/ Emniyet Müdürlüğü	Police Station
Yasak(tir)	Prohibited
Tuvalet	Toilets

TRANSPORT

What time does the next ... leave/arrive?	*Gelecek ... ne zaman kalkar/gelir?*
ferry/boat	*feribot/vapur*
bus (city)	*şehir otobüsü*
bus (intercity)	*otobüs*
train	*tren*

left luggage	*emanetçi*
timetable	*tarife*
bus stop	*otobüs durağı*
tram stop	*tramvay durağı*
train station	*gar/istasyon*
ferry/ship dock	*iskele*

I'd like ...	*... istiyorum.*
a one-way ticket	*gidiş bileti*
a return ticket	*gidiş-dönüş bileti*
1st-class	*birinci mevkii*
2nd-class	*ikinci mevkii*

I'd like to hire a car/bicycle.	*Araba/bisiklet kirala mak istiyorum.*

LANGUAGE

The Authors

DUNCAN GARWOOD — Coordinating Author, Italy

Ever since backpacking around the Greek Islands as a student, Duncan has been fascinated by the Mediterranean and its apparently idyllic lifestyle. In an attempt to live it himself, he gave up a stuttering career in corporate journalism and moved to southern Italy in 1997. Two years later he transferred north to Rome, where he lives with his Italian wife and two young kids. These days Duncan spends much of his time running up and down the Italian peninsula, writing for Lonely Planet, but he's still drawn to the south, and heads to the Ionian Coast every summer to test the beaches and enjoy the superb Puglian food. Duncan also wrote Destination Mediterranean Europe, Getting Started, Events Calendar, Itineraries, Mediterranean Treasures, Regional Directory and Transport.

ALEXIS AVERBUCK — Greece

Alexis Averbuck lives in Hydra, Greece and makes any excuse she can to travel the isolated back roads of her adopted land. She is committed to dispelling the stereotype that Greece is simply a string of sandy beaches. A California native and a travel writer for two decades, Alexis has lived in Antarctica for a year, crossed the Pacific by sailboat and written books on her journeys through Asia and the Americas. Each trip inspires new work, both written and visual – see her paintings at www.alexisaverbuck.com.

JAMES BAINBRIDGE — Turkey

James first visited Turkey as a student, at the end of an Inter-Railing trip through Eastern Europe, and subsisted on cheese triangles for a week in İstanbul and the Princes' Islands. His most recent Turkish trip was more successful: wandering Anatolia and making up for student starvation by spending his entire fee on *kebaps*. When he's not charging around with a notebook in one hand, James lives in London – right on Green Lanes, the city's 'little Turkey'. He has contributed to a dozen Lonely Planet books and media worldwide.

LONELY PLANET AUTHORS

Why is our travel information the best in the world? It's simple: our authors are passionate, dedicated travellers. They don't take freebies in exchange for positive coverage so you can be sure the advice you're given is impartial. They travel widely to all the popular spots, and off the beaten track. They don't research using just the internet or phone. They discover new places not included in any other guidebook. They personally visit thousands of hotels, restaurants, palaces, trails, galleries, temples and more. They speak with dozens of locals every day to make sure you get the kind of insider knowledge only a local could tell you. They take pride in getting all the details right, and in telling it how it is. Think you can do it? Find out how at **lonelyplanet.com**.

OLIVER BERRY

France

Oliver graduated with a degree in English from University College London and spent the next few years seeing what the rest of the world had to offer (quite a lot as it turned out). He now lives and works in Cornwall as a writer and photographer. His travels for Lonely Planet have carried him everywhere from the snowy mountains of Canada to the sunny beaches of the Cook Islands, but he always finds the best adventures have a French flavour. He has worked on several editions of Lonely Planet's *France*, and can often be found wandering around the more remote corners of L'Hexagone.

PAUL CLAMMER

Morocco

As a student, Paul had his first solo backpacking experience when he took a bus from his Cambridgeshire home all the way to Casablanca. Morocco instantly enchanted him. After an interlude when he trained and worked as a molecular biologist, he eventually returned to work as a tour guide, trekking in the Atlas and trying not to lose passengers in the Fez medina. He returns on a regular basis both as coordinating author for Lonely Planet's *Morocco* and for recreation, and is currently fighting the temptation to buy an old medina townhouse to restore into a more permanent bolt-hole.

JAYNE D'ARCY

Albania

Ever since she watched Celtic Tigers eat up and commercialise Irish culture in the mid-'90s, Jayne's been attracted to countries with more character and lower GDPs. Albania hit her radar in 2006, when she joined her first-ever package tour; although she complained about her fellow travellers, she was pretty stoked to get a new passport stamp and see some amazing ruins in relative peace. The changes in Albania since then are astonishing, but while the similarities to the 'old Ireland' are huge (homemade spirits, dodgy roads), the Albanian Tiger is yet to emerge. As well as writing about travel, Jayne produces features on design, people and the environment.

PETER DRAGICEVICH

Montenegro

After a dozen years working for newspapers and magazines in both his native New Zealand and Australia, Peter finally gave into Kiwi wanderlust, giving up staff jobs to chase his diverse ancestral roots around much of Europe. While it was family ties that first drew him to the Balkans, it's the history, natural beauty, convoluted politics, cheap *rakija* (fruit brandy) and, most importantly, the intriguing people that keep bringing him back. He's contributed to 12 Lonely Planet titles, including writing the Macedonia and Albania chapters for the previous edition of the *Eastern Europe* guide. He's just completed Lonely Planet's first guidebook to *Montenegro*.

MARK ELLIOTT

Bosnia & Hercegovina

British-born travel writer Mark Elliott was only 11 when his family first dragged him to Sarajevo and stood him in the now defunct concrete footsteps of Gavrilo Princip. Fortunately no Austro-Hungarian emperors were passing at the time. He has since visited virtually every corner of BiH, supping fine Hercegovinian wines with master vintners, talking philosophy with Serb monks and Sufi mystics, and drinking more Bosnian coffee than any healthy stomach should be subjected to. When not travel writing he lives a blissfully quiet life in suburban Belgium with the lovely Danielle, who he met while jamming blues harmonica in a Turkmenistan club.

STEVE FALLON

Slovenia

Steve has been travelling to Slovenia since the early 1990s, when a travel-publishing company initially refused his proposal to write a guidebook to the country because of 'the war going on' (it had ended two years before) and a US newspaper of record told him that their readers weren't interested in 'Slovakia'. Never mind, it was his own private Idaho for over a decade. Though he *still* hasn't reached the top of Mt Triglav (next time – *domen*, promise!), Steve considers at least part of his soul Slovenian and returns to the country as often as he can for a glimpse of the Julian Alps, a dribble of *bučno olje* (pumpkin-seed oil) and a dose of the dual.

VESNA MARIC

Croatia, Cyprus

Vesna was born in Bosnia and Hercegovina while it was still a part of Yugoslavia and, as a result, she has never been able to see Croatia as a foreign country. A lifelong lover of Dalmatia's beaches, pine trees, food and wine, she expanded her knowledge during this book by exploring Zadar and Zagreb, two cities she discovered anew. Researching Croatia was a true delight.

Visiting Cyprus is a different experience each time, as the country's changes are so rapid, and Vesna's curiosity about the island has never ceased. She has always felt an affinity with the Cypriots from both sides of the Green Line. The landscape, beaches, fresh figs and halloumi all lure her back for more.

TOM MASTERS

Malta

Tom jumped at the chance to research sunny Malta for this guidebook. With childhood summers spent all over the Mediterranean and a love for the region's cuisine and architecture, he has a blast discovering Malta's culinary scene, the secluded beaches of Gozo and the gorgeous architecture and dramatic history of Valletta. Tom is a freelance writer living and working in Berlin. You can see more of his work at www.mastersmafia.com.

VIRGINIA MAXWELL

Italy

After working for many years as a publishing manager at Lonely Planet's Melbourne headquarters, Virginia decided that she'd be happier writing guidebooks rather than commissioning them. Since making this decision she's written or contributed to Lonely Planet books about nine countries, eight of which are on the Mediterranean. Virginia has covered Rome and ventured to the north of Italy for Lonely Planet's *Italy*.

CRAIG MCLACHLAN

Greece

A Kiwi with a bad case of wanderlust, Craig enjoys nothing more than visiting the Greek Isles to down Mythos beer, retsina and to consume countless gyros. He regularly leads hiking tours to Greece and has even taken a group of Japanese doctors to Kos to see where Hippocrates came from. Describing himself as a 'freelance anything', Craig runs an outdoor activity company in Queenstown, New Zealand in the southern hemisphere summer, then heads north for the winter. Other jobs have included author, pilot, hiking guide, interpreter and karate instructor. Check out his website at www.craigmclachlan.com.

DAMIEN SIMONIS

Spain

The spark was lit on a short trip over the Pyrenees to Barcelona during a summer jaunt in southern France. It was Damien's first taste of Spain and he found something irresistible about the place – the way the people moved, talked and enjoyed themselves. Damien came back years later, living in medieval Toledo, frenetic Madrid and, finally, settling in Barcelona. He has ranged across the country, from the Picos de Europa to the Sierra Nevada, from Córdoba to Cáceres, and slurped cider in Asturias and gin in the Balearic Islands. Apart from *Spain,* Damien wrote *Barcelona, Madrid, Mallorca,* the *Canary Islands* and the now-defunct *Catalunya & the Costa Brava* for Lonely Planet.

REGIS ST LOUIS

Portugal

A lover of wine, rugged coastlines and a bit of *bacalhau* (dried cod) now and again, Regis was destined for a romance with small, irresistible Portugal when he first began exploring the country some years back. Favourite memories of his most recent trip include delving into the bohemian side of Porto, sampling fine vintages from wineries along the Douro and visiting remote corners of the north. Regis was the coordinating author of Lonely Planet's *Portugal*, and he has covered numerous other destinations for Lonely Planet. His travel essays have appeared in the *Los Angeles Times* and the *San Francisco Chronicle*, among other publications. He lives in New York City.

Behind the Scenes

THIS BOOK

Mediterranean Europe is part of Lonely Planet's Europe series, which includes *Western Europe, Eastern Europe, Central Europe, Scandinavian Europe* and *Europe on a Shoestring*.

Mediterranean Europe 9 was commissioned in Lonely Planet's London office, and produced by the following:

Commissioning Editors Fiona Buchan, Lucy Monie
Coordinating Editors Susan Paterson, Laura Stansfeld
Coordinating Cartographer Valentina Kremenchutskaya
Coordinating Layout Designer Cara Smith
Managing Editor Imogen Bannister
Managing Cartographers Mark Griffiths, Herman So
Managing Layout Designer Laura Jane
Assisting Editors Penelope Goodes, Carly Hall, Kim Hutchins, Amy Karafin, Helen Koehne, Alan Murphy, Sally O'Brien, Simon Williamson, Helen Yeates
Assisting Cartographers Fatima Basic, Barbara Benson, Csanad Csutoros, Tony Fankhauser, Alex Leung, Joanne Luke, Khanh Luu, Peter Shields, Tom Webster
Assisting Layout Designer Paul Iacono
Cover Designer Naomi Parker
Project Manager Glenn van der Knijff

Thanks to Lucy Birchley, Katrina Browning, Sally Darmody, Ryan Evans, Mark Germanchis, Indra Kilfoyle, Robyn Loughnane, Katie Lynch, John Mazzocchi, Anna Metcalfe, Wayne Murphy, Trent Paton, Sally Schafer, Sarah Sloane, Lyahna Spencer, Gina Tsarouhas

THANKS

DUNCAN GARWOOD

At Lonely Planet, I'd like to thank Lucy Monie in London for her calm and assured advice, to Glenn van der Knijff and Herman So out in Melbourne, and to Fiona Buchan and Korina Miller for commissioning me in the first place. Thanks also to authors Tom Masters, Vesna Maric, Paul Clammer and James Bainbridge for putting up with so many of my tedious requests, and to all the other Lonely Planet scribes who worked on this big project. As usual I owe a huge hug to Lidia and the boys. *Grazie.*

ALEXIS AVERBUCK

Many thanks to Alexandra Stamopoulou for all of her invaluable tips, to Marijke Verstrepen for her marvellous insights into the Ionian Islands, to Margarita Kontzia for exceptional Athens advice, to Dimitris Foussekis for showing me the many faces of modern Athens, and to Anthy and Costas for their infinite hospitality and matchless insider knowledge of Athens. Special thanks to Craig McLachlan for seamlessly pulling the chapter together.

THE LONELY PLANET STORY

Fresh from an epic journey across Europe, Asia and Australia in 1972, Tony and Maureen Wheeler sat at their kitchen table stapling together notes. The first Lonely Planet guidebook, *Across Asia on the Cheap*, was born.

Travellers snapped up the guides. Inspired by their success, the Wheelers began publishing books to Southeast Asia, India and beyond. Demand was prodigious, and the Wheelers expanded the business rapidly to keep up. Over the years, Lonely Planet extended its coverage to every country and into the virtual world via lonelyplanet.com and the Thorn Tree message board.

As Lonely Planet became a globally loved brand, Tony and Maureen received several offers for the company. But it wasn't until 2007 that they found a partner whom they trusted to remain true to the company's principles of travelling widely, treading lightly and giving sustainably. In October of that year, BBC Worldwide acquired a 75% share in the company, pledging to uphold Lonely Planet's commitment to independent travel, trustworthy advice and editorial independence.

Today, Lonely Planet has offices in Melbourne, London and Oakland, with over 500 staff members and 300 authors. Tony and Maureen are still actively involved with Lonely Planet. They're travelling more often than ever, and they're devoting their spare time to charitable projects. And the company is still driven by the philosophy of *Across Asia on the Cheap*: 'All you've got to do is decide to go and the hardest part is over. So go!'

JAMES BAINBRIDGE

Teşekkür ederim (thank you) to Padi and Hülya for the bed in İstanbul, and to Jahid, Aziz and the Hemi posse for the paragliding demo in Sivas; to Pat, Süha, Ali, Mustafa, Maggie, Kaili and everyone who brought Cappadocia to life, and to Crazy Ali for giving a poem to the Queen of Spain; to Mustafa in Boğazkale and Nazlı in Konya/Ibiza; to Ollagh for the whisky and Reuters anecdotes in Kayseri, and to the Kurds in Çorum for the beers and manly companionship. Finally, *şerefe* (cheers) to Lucy Monie, Duncan Garwood and all my *Mediterranean Europe* cohorts.

PAUL CLAMMER

At Lonely Planet thanks to Lucy Monie, who is always a delight to work with, and to my coauthors on the *Morocco* guide: Anthony Sattin, Alison Bing and Paul Stiles. Special thanks also to Fez resident and fellow Lonely Planet author Helen Ranger, who smoothed several crooked medina pathways. Also in Fez, thanks to Mike, Max, Jess and the rest of the Café Clock crew, and again to Jen and Sebastian. *Mulţumesc* to Alexa Radulea. And of course, thanks and love to Jo, for looking after the home front.

JAYNE D'ARCY

Thanks to Sharik Billington for taking on Albania with me and my three year old; to Miles for coping with all the cheek pinching; to Will Gourlay for sending me up the Accursed Mountains in the first place; and to Orieta Gliozheni in Korça, Stavri Cifligu in Tirana, Marius Qytyku in Berat, Yolanda Kebo in Saranda and Edward Shehi and his Italian tourists in Voskopoja. Thanks to Dr Shannon Woodcock at La Trobe University, Australia; Mada at Sunrock, Corfu; and everyone else along the way who had the keys and let us in.

PETER DRAGICEVICH

A huge thanks to all the wonderful people who helped me along the way, especially my beloved Dragičević cousins, Hayley and Jack Delf, Goran and Jadranka Marković, Dragana Ostojić, Slavko Marjanović, Danica Ćeranić, Kirsi Hyvaerinen and David Mills. Extra special thanks to Milomir Jukanović and to Will Gourlay.

MARK ELLIOTT

Many thanks to Will Gourlay and the Lonely Planet team, and to Edis Hodžić, Guillaume Martin, Olivier Janoschka, Snezhan in Trebinje, Vlaren at Tvrdoš Monastery, Semir in Blagaj, Narmina in Mostar, Branislav Andrić in Višegrad and so many more, including the mysterious 'angel' who provided me with such insights to the Bjelašnica highland villages then disappeared without my ever knowing his name. As ever my greatest thanks go to my endlessly inspiring wife Dani Systermans and to my unbeatable parents who, three decades ago, had the crazy idea of driving me to Bosnia in the first place.

STEVE FALLON

A number of people assisted in the research and writing of the Slovenia chapter, in particular my dear friends and fonts of all knowledge at the Ljubljana Tourist Board: Verica Leskovar, Tatjana Radovič and Petra Stušek. Others to whom I'd like to say *najlepša hvala* for assistance, inspiration, sustenance and/or a few laughs along the way include the boys (Miha Anzelc, Luka Esenko and Tomaž Marič) of Židana Marela in Ljubljana; Brina Čehovin and Tina Križnar of the Slovenian Tourist Board, Ljubljana; Marino Fakin of Slovenian Railways, Ljubljana; Aleš and Tanja Hvala of the Hotel Hvala and Restavracija Topli Val, Kobarid; Lado Leskovar of Unicef, based in Ljubljana; Tomaž Škofic of Adria Airways in Ljubljana; Robert Stan of Adventure Rafting Bled; and the staff at the Tourist Information Centre Ptuj for assistance (way beyond the call of duty) in helping me find an industrial-strength *klopotec* (wind rattle) on short notice as I whizzed in on a rainy morning from southwest Hungary. Goodbye pigeons! As always, my efforts here are dedicated to my partner, Michael Rothschild, who is way overdue a visit to God's own country.

VESNA MARIC

Hvala to Maja Gilja, my mother, Toni and Marina Ćavar, Ružica, Stipe, Ante, Dana and Loreta Barać. Also *hvala* to Kristina Hajduka, and Janica and Matej. Thanks to Gabriel and all the travellers I chatted to along the way. Thanks also to Anja Mutić and William Gourlay.

TOM MASTERS

Thanks to James Bridle for keeping me company on Gozo and thanks to the great staff at the British and Castille Hotels in Valletta for looking after me so well. Big shout out to Marco, Silvia and Caroline in Sliema for being so helpful, and to the staff at Malta's various tourist offices for their tireless help.

VIRGINIA MAXWELL

Greatest thanks and much love go to Max, who once again accompanied me on a Europe jaunt. Boldly taste-testing gelato after gelato, putting up

SEND US YOUR FEEDBACK

We love to hear from travellers – your comments keep us on our toes and help make our books better. Our well-travelled team reads every word on what you loved or loathed about this book. Although we cannot reply individually to postal submissions, we always guarantee that your feedback goes straight to the appropriate authors, in time for the next edition. Each person who sends us information is thanked in the next edition – and the most useful submissions are rewarded with a free book.

To send us your updates – and find out about Lonely Planet events, newsletters and travel news – visit our award-winning website: **lonelyplanet.com/contact**.

Note: we may edit, reproduce and incorporate your comments in Lonely Planet products such as guidebooks, websites and digital products, so let us know if you don't want your comments reproduced or your name acknowledged. For a copy of our privacy policy visit lonelyplanet.com/privacy.

with cathedral after cathedral and racing to catch innumerable trains – what a star you are, Maxie! Thanks and love to Peter for looking after things at home and to Liz and Matthew for the stopovers en route and back. Thanks also to my coauthor Duncan for his expert advice; to my coauthors on the *Italy* book, whose excellent work I extensively road-tested for this project and to Mark Griffiths for steering the mapping.

CRAIG MCLACHLAN

A hearty thanks to all those who helped me out on the road, but most of all to my exceptionally beautiful wife Yuriko and our boys Riki and Ben.

DAMIEN SIMONIS

In Barcelona, countless folks keep me on my toes and make rediscovering the city as fun as it is challenging (they all know who they are!). In Cantabria and Asturias, *gracias a* Ricardo, Begoña, Esperanza and Juan for a memorable last night of cider and *baile vaquiero,* and to the friendly people of Somiedo. In Mallorca, especial thanks go to Roberto Fortea, Verónica García, Carlos García, Felipe Amorós, Miquel Àngel Part, Antonio Bauzá, Alessandra Natale and Verónica Carretero. In Ibiza, *mille mercis* to the multicultural Daraspe family.

REGIS ST LOUIS

Thanks to all the helpful locals and travellers who helped along the way. *Muito obrigado* to my fellow *Portugal* 7 colleagues, whose fine research contributed immeasurably to this title. Thanks to all the Lonely Planet staff whose hard work made this book shine. I also want to thank everyone who voted for Barack Obama. You've helped make travelling as an American fun again. *Beijos* to Cassandra and Magdalena, who joined me in the journey across the north.

OUR READERS

Many thanks to the travellers who used the last edition and wrote to us with helpful hints, useful advice and interesting anecdotes:

Diana Brown, Caroline Fradin, Hanno Haes, Claire Howat, Claire Keith, Andrew Medley, Jessica Ordman, Dawn Pillsbury, Kate Scarth, Mem Smith, Ombretta Zanetti

ACKNOWLEDGMENTS

Many thanks to the following for the use of their content:

Globe on title page ©Mountain High Maps 1993 Digital Wisdom, Inc.

Internal photographs p436 (#2) by David Gregs/Alamy. All other photographs by Lonely Planet Images, and by John Banagan p435 (#3); Alan Benson p433 (#4); Bethune Carmichael p431 (#3); Chris Christo p430 (#1); Olivier Cirendini p429; Greg Elms p433 (#3); Rick Gerharter p434 (#2); Richard I'Anson p434 (#1); Diego Lezama p436 (#3); Witold Skrypczak p436 (31); Oliver Strewe p432 (#1 & 2); Dallas Stribley p431 (#2); David Tomlinson p435 (#4).

Index

INDEX

INDEX

INDEX

000 Map pages
000 Photograph pages

INDEX

000 Map pages
000 Photograph pages